The Dictionary of Art · volume twenty-one

The Dictionary of Art

CONSULTING EDITOR Hugh Brigstocke

EDITOR Jane Turner

21

Medallion

TO

Montalbani

GROVE

An imprint of Oxford University Press

Oxford University Press

Oxford   New York
Auckland   Bangkok   Buenos Aires   Cape Town   Chennai
Dar es Salaam   Delhi   Hong Kong   Istanbul   Karachi   Kolkata
Kuala Lumpur   Madrid   Melbourne   Mexico City   Mumbai   Nairobi
São Paulo   Shanghai   Taipei   Tokyo   Toronto

ISBN 0-19-517068-7

The Dictionary of Art, edited by JANE TURNER, was published in thirty-four volumes
in 1996 by Macmillan Publishers Limited

Text keyboarded by Wearset Limited, Sunderland, England
Database management by Pindar plc, York, England
Imagesetting by William Clowes Limited, Suffolk, England
Printed and bound by China Translation and Printing Services Ltd. , Hong Kong

Contents

List of Colour Illustrations

PLATE I. **Metal**

1. Brass pencase, inlaid with gold and silver, l. 197 mm, from Iran, 1281–2 (London, British Museum/Photo: Trustees of the British Museum)

2. Silver *Neptune* dish, diam. 605 mm, Romano-British, part of the Mildenhall Treasure from Suffolk, 4th century AD (London, British Museum/Photo: Trustees of the British Museum)

3. Copper teapot with niello and brass mounts, h. 225 mm, ?Austrian, *c.* 1900 (Prague, Museum of Decorative Arts/Photo: Museum of Decorative Arts)

4. Bronze *hu* (ritual wine vessel), h. 406 mm, from China, 12th–11th centuries BC (Kansas City, MO, Nelson–Atkins Museum of Art/Photo: Nelson–Atkins Museum of Art, Purchase, Nelson Trust; no. 55–52; photographer: E. G. Schempf)

PLATE II. **Metal**

1. Gold vessel ending in the forepart of a lion, h. 178 mm, diam. of rim 137 mm, from Iran, Achaemenid period, *c.* 6th–5th centuries BC (New York, Metropolitan Museum of Art/Photo: Metropolitan Museum of Art, Fletcher Fund, 1954; no. 54.3.3)

2. Pewter broad-rimmed dish with wrigglework decoration and inscription, diam. 405 mm, from England, *c.* 1650–60 (London, British Museum/Photo: Trustees of the British Museum)

3. Cut-steel shoe buckle, *Bourbonnais Shepherd*, set with a jasper cameo after a design by Lady Elizabeth Templetown, h. 61 mm, probably by Boulton & Fothergill with the factory of Wedgwood, near Burslem, Staffordshire, *c.* 1785 (Barlaston, Wedgwood Museum/Photo: Trustees of the Wedgwood Museum)

4. Bronze bust of *Mary, Queen of Hungary* by Leone Leoni, h. 675 mm, 1549–53 (Vienna, Kunsthistorisches Museum/Photo: Kunsthistorisches Museum)

PLATE III. **Mosaic**

1. Mosaic of the *Nine Muses*, from the Imperial Palace at Trier, early 3rd century AD (Trier, Rheinisches Landesmuseum/Photo: Rheinisches Landesmuseum)

2. Mosaic of *Christ* (detail), from the *Deësis* (*c.* 1260–61), south gallery, Hagia Sophia, Istanbul (Photo: AKG Ltd, London/Eric Lessing)

PLATE IV. **Mosaic**

1. Mosaic mask of Quetzalcóatl, wood, turquoise and shell, 165 × 152 mm, from Mexico, AD 1400–1500 (London, British Museum/Photo: Trustees of the British Museum)

2. Mosaic fountain (1900–14) in the form of a dragon by Antoni Gaudí, Parc Güell, Barcelona (Photo: Ancient Art and Architecture Collection, London)

General Abbreviations

The abbreviations employed throughout this dictionary, most of which are listed below, do not vary, except for capitalization, regardless of the context in which they are used, including bibliographical citations and for locations of works of art. The principle used to arrive at these abbreviations is that their full form should be easily deducible, and for this reason acronyms have generally been avoided (e.g. Los Angeles Co. Mus. A. instead of LACMA). The same abbreviation is adopted for cognate forms in foreign languages and in most cases for plural and adjectival forms (e.g. A.= Art, Arts, Arte, Arti etc). Not all related forms are listed below. Occasionally, if a name, for instance of an artists' group or exhibiting society, is repeated within the text of one article, it is cited in an abbreviated form after its first mention in full (e.g. The Pre-Raphaelite Brotherhood (PRB) was founded...); the same is true of archaeological periods and eras, which are abbreviated to initial letters in small capitals (e.g. In the Early Minoan (EM) period...). Such abbreviations do not appear in this list. For the reader's convenience, separate full lists of abbreviations for locations, periodical titles and standard reference books and series are included as Appendices A–C in vol. 33.

A.	Art, Arts	Anthropol.	Anthropology	Azerbaij.	Azerbaijani
A.C.	Arts Council	Antiqua.	Antiquarian, Antiquaries	B.	Bartsch [catalogue of Old Master prints]
Acad.	Academy	app.	appendix		
AD	Anno Domini	approx.	approximately	*b*	born
Add.	Additional, Addendum	AR	Arkansas (USA)	BA	Bachelor of Arts
addn	addition	ARA	Associate of the Royal Academy	Balt.	Baltic
Admin.	Administration			*bapt*	baptized
Adv.	Advances, Advanced	Arab.	Arabic	BArch	Bachelor of Architecture
Aesth.	Aesthetic(s)	Archaeol.	Archaeology	Bart	Baronet
Afr.	African	Archit.	Architecture, Architectural	Bask.	Basketry
Afrik.	Afrikaans, Afrikaner	Archv, Archvs	Archive(s)	BBC	British Broadcasting Corporation
A.G.	Art Gallery				
Agrar.	Agrarian	Arg.	Argentine	BC	Before Christ
Agric.	Agriculture	ARHA	Associate of the Royal Hibernian Academy	BC	British Columbia (Canada)
Agron.	Agronomy			BE	Buddhist era
Agy	Agency	ARIBA	Associate of the Royal Institute of British Architects	Beds	Bedfordshire (GB)
AH	Anno Hegirae			Behav.	Behavioural
A. Inst.	Art Institute	Armen.	Armenian	Belarus.	Belarusian
AK	Alaska (USA)	ARSA	Associate of the Royal Scottish Academy	Belg.	Belgian
AL	Alabama (USA)			Berks	Berkshire (GB)
Alb.	Albanian	Asiat.	Asiatic	Berwicks	Berwickshire (GB; old)
Alg.	Algerian	Assist.	Assistance	BFA	Bachelor of Fine Arts
Alta	Alberta (Canada)	Assoc.	Association	Bibl.	Bible, Biblical
Altern.	Alternative	Astron.	Astronomy	Bibliog.	Bibliography, Bibliographical
a.m.	ante meridiem [before noon]	AT&T	American Telephone & Telegraph Company	Biblioph.	Bibliophile
Amat.	Amateur	attrib.	attribution, attributed to	Biog.	Biography, Biographical
Amer.	American	Aug	August	Biol.	Biology, Biological
An.	Annals	Aust.	Austrian	bk, bks	book(s)
Anatol.	Anatolian	Austral.	Australian	Bkbinder	Bookbinder
Anc.	Ancient	Auth.	Author(s)	Bklore	Booklore
Annu.	Annual	Auton.	Autonomous	Bkshop	Bookshop
Anon.	Anonymous(ly)	Aux.	Auxiliary	BL	British Library
Ant.	Antique	Ave.	Avenue	Bld	Build
Anthol.	Anthology	AZ	Arizona (USA)	Bldg	Building

Bldr	Builder	Chin.	Chinese	Cur.	Curator, Curatorial, Curatorship
BLitt	Bachelor of Letters/Literature	Christ.	Christian, Christianity		
BM	British Museum	Chron.	Chronicle	Curr.	Current(s)
Boh.	Bohemian	Cie	Compagnie [French]	CVO	Commander of the [Royal] Victorian Order
Boliv.	Bolivian	Cinema.	Cinematography		
Botan.	Botany, Botanical	Circ.	Circle	Cyclad.	Cycladic
BP	Before present (1950)	Civ.	Civil, Civic	Cyp.	Cypriot
Braz.	Brazilian	Civiliz.	Civilization(s)	Czech.	Czechoslovak
BRD	Bundesrepublik Deutschland [Federal Republic of Germany (West Germany)]	Class.	Classic, Classical	$	dollars
		Clin.	Clinical	_d_	died
		CO	Colorado (USA)	d.	denarius, denarii [penny, pence]
Brecons	Breconshire (GB; old)	Co.	Company; County		
Brez.	Brezonek [lang. of Brittany]	Cod.	Codex, Codices	Dalmat.	Dalmatian
Brit.	British	Col., Cols	Collection(s); Column(s)	Dan.	Danish
Bros	Brothers	Coll.	College	DBE	Dame Commander of the Order of the British Empire
BSc	Bachelor of Science	collab.	in collaboration with, collaborated, collaborative		
Bucks	Buckinghamshire (GB)			DC	District of Columbia (USA)
Bulg.	Bulgarian	Collct.	Collecting	DDR	Deutsche Demokratische Republik [German Democratic Republic (East Germany)]
Bull.	Bulletin	Colloq.	Colloquies		
bur	buried	Colomb.	Colombian		
Burm.	Burmese	Colon.	Colonies, Colonial	DE	Delaware (USA)
Byz.	Byzantine	Colr	Collector	Dec	December
C	Celsius	Comm.	Commission; Community	Dec.	Decorative
C.	Century	Commerc.	Commercial	ded.	dedication, dedicated to
_c._	_circa_ [about]	Communic.	Communications	Democ.	Democracy, Democratic
CA	California	Comp.	Comparative; compiled by, compiler	Demog.	Demography, Demographic
Cab.	Cabinet			Denbs	Denbighshire (GB; old)
Caerns	Caernarvonshire (GB; old)	Concent.	Concentration	dep.	deposited at
C.A.G.	City Art Gallery	Concr.	Concrete	Dept	Department
Cal.	Calendar	Confed.	Confederation	Dept.	Departmental, Departments
Callig.	Calligraphy	Confer.	Conference	Derbys	Derbyshire (GB)
Cam.	Camera	Congol.	Congolese	Des.	Design
Cambs	Cambridgeshire (GB)	Congr.	Congress	destr.	destroyed
can	canonized	Conserv.	Conservation; Conservatory	Dev.	Development
Can.	Canadian	Constr.	Construction(al)	Devon	Devonshire (GB)
Cant.	Canton(s), Cantonal	cont.	continued	Dial.	Dialogue
Capt.	Captain	Contemp.	Contemporary	diam.	diameter
Cards	Cardiganshire (GB; old)	Contrib.	Contributions, Contributor(s)	Diff.	Diffusion
Carib.	Caribbean	Convalesc.	Convalescence	Dig.	Digest
Carms	Carmarthenshire (GB; old)	Convent.	Convention	Dip. Eng.	Diploma in Engineering
Cartog.	Cartography	Coop.	Cooperation	Dir.	Direction, Directed
Cat.	Catalan	Coord.	Coordination	Directrt	Directorate
cat.	catalogue	Copt.	Coptic	Disc.	Discussion
Cath.	Catholic	Corp.	Corporation, Corpus	diss.	dissertation
CBE	Commander of the Order of the British Empire	Corr.	Correspondence	Distr.	District
		Cors.	Corsican	Div.	Division
Celeb.	Celebration	Cost.	Costume	DLitt	Doctor of Letters/Literature
Celt.	Celtic	Cret.	Cretan	DM	Deutsche Mark
Cent.	Centre, Central	Crim.	Criminal	Doc.	Document(s)
Centen.	Centennial	Crit.	Critical, Criticism	Doss.	Dossier
Cer.	Ceramic	Croat.	Croatian	DPhil	Doctor of Philosophy
cf.	_confer_ [compare]	CT	Connecticut (USA)	Dr	Doctor
Chap., Chaps	Chapter(s)	Cttee	Committee	Drg, Drgs	Drawing(s)
		Cub.	Cuban	DSc	Doctor of Science/Historical Sciences
Chem.	Chemistry	Cult.	Cultural, Culture		
Ches	Cheshire (GB)	Cumb.	Cumberland (GB; old)	Dut.	Dutch
Chil.	Chilean			Dwell.	Dwelling
				E.	East(ern)

EC	European (Economic) Community	figs	figures	Heb.	Hebrew
Eccles.	Ecclesiastical	Filip.	Filipina(s), Filipino(s)	Hell.	Hellenic
Econ.	Economic, Economies	Fin.	Finnish	Her.	Heritage
Ecuad.	Ecuadorean	FL	Florida (USA)	Herald.	Heraldry, Heraldic
ed.	editor, edited (by)	*fl*	*floruit* [he/she flourished]	Hereford & Worcs	Hereford & Worcester (GB)
edn	edition	Flem.	Flemish		
eds	editors	Flints	Flintshire (GB; old)	Herts	Hertfordshire (GB)
Educ.	Education	Flk	Folk	HI	Hawaii (USA)
e.g.	*exempli gratia* [for example]	Flklore	Folklore	Hib.	Hibernia
Egyp.	Egyptian	fol., fols	folio(s)	Hisp.	Hispanic
Elem.	Element(s), Elementary	Found.	Foundation	Hist.	History, Historical
Emp.	Empirical	Fr.	French	HMS	His/Her Majesty's Ship
Emul.	Emulation	frag.	fragment	Hon.	Honorary, Honourable
Enc.	Encyclopedia	Fri.	Friday	Horiz.	Horizon
Encour.	Encouragement	FRIBA	Fellow of the Royal Institute of British Architects	Hort.	Horticulture
Eng.	English			Hosp.	Hospital(s)
Engin.	Engineer, Engineering	FRS	Fellow of the Royal Society, London	HRH	His/Her Royal Highness
Engr., Engrs	Engraving(s)			Human.	Humanities, Humanism
		ft	foot, feet	Hung.	Hungarian
Envmt	Environment	Furn.	Furniture	Hunts	Huntingdonshire (GB; old)
Epig.	Epigraphy	Futur.	Futurist, Futurism	IA	Iowa
Episc.	Episcopal	g	gram(s)	ibid.	*ibidem* [in the same place]
Esp.	Especially	GA	Georgia (USA)	ICA	Institute of Contemporary Arts
Ess.	Essays	Gael.	Gaelic		
est.	established	Gal., Gals	Gallery, Galleries	Ice.	Icelandic
etc	*etcetera* [and so on]	Gaz.	Gazette	Iconog.	Iconography
Ethnog.	Ethnography	GB	Great Britain	Iconol.	Iconology
Ethnol.	Ethnology	Gdn, Gdns	Garden(s)	ID	Idaho (USA)
Etrus.	Etruscan	Gdnr(s)	Gardener(s)	i.e.	*id est* [that is]
Eur.	European	Gen.	General	IL	Illinois (USA)
Evangel.	Evangelical	Geneal.	Genealogy, Genealogist	Illum.	Illumination
Exam.	Examination	Gent.	Gentleman, Gentlemen	illus.	illustrated, illustration
Excav.	Excavation, Excavated	Geog.	Geography	Imp.	Imperial
Exch.	Exchange	Geol.	Geology	IN	Indiana (USA)
Excurs.	Excursion	Geom.	Geometry	in., ins	inch(es)
exh.	exhibition	Georg.	Georgian	Inc.	Incorporated
Exp.	Exposition	Geosci.	Geoscience	inc.	incomplete
Expermntl	Experimental	Ger.	German, Germanic	incl.	includes, including, inclusive
Explor.	Exploration	G.I.	Government/General Issue (USA)	Incorp.	Incorporation
Expn	Expansion			Ind.	Indian
Ext.	External	Glams	Glamorganshire (GB; old)	Indep.	Independent
Extn	Extension	Glos	Gloucestershire (GB)	Indig.	Indigenous
f, ff	following page, following pages	Govt	Government	Indol.	Indology
		Gr.	Greek	Indon.	Indonesian
F.A.	Fine Art(s)	Grad.	Graduate	Indust.	Industrial
Fac.	Faculty	Graph.	Graphic	Inf.	Information
facs.	facsimile	Green.	Greenlandic	Inq.	Inquiry
Fam.	Family	Gr.-Roman	Greco-Roman	Inscr.	Inscribed, Inscription
fasc.	fascicle	Gt	Great	Inst.	Institute(s)
fd	feastday (of a saint)	Gtr	Greater	Inst. A.	Institute of Art
Feb	February	Guat.	Guatemalan	Instr.	Instrument, Instrumental
Fed.	Federation, Federal	Gym.	Gymnasium	Int.	International
Fem.	Feminist	h.	height	Intell.	Intelligence
Fest.	Festival	ha	hectare	Inter.	Interior(s), Internal
fig.	figure (illustration)	Hait.	Haitian	Interdiscip.	Interdisciplinary
Fig.	Figurative	Hants	Hampshire (GB)	intro.	introduced by, introduction
		Hb.	Handbook	inv.	inventory

Inven.	Invention	m	metre(s)	Moldov.	Moldovan
Invest.	Investigation(s)	m.	married	MOMA	Museum of Modern Art
Iran.	Iranian	M.	Monsieur	Mon.	Monday
irreg.	irregular(ly)	MA	Master of Arts; Massachusetts (USA)	Mongol.	Mongolian
Islam.	Islamic			Mons	Monmouthshire (GB; old)
Isr.	Israeli	Mag.	Magazine	Montgoms	Montgomeryshire (GB; old)
It.	Italian	Maint.	Maintenance	Mor.	Moral
J.	Journal	Malay.	Malaysian	Morav.	Moravian
Jam.	Jamaican	Man.	Manitoba (Canada); Manual	Moroc.	Moroccan
Jan	January	Manuf.	Manufactures	Movt	Movement
Jap.	Japanese	Mar.	Marine, Maritime	MP	Member of Parliament
Jav.	Javanese	Mason.	Masonic	MPhil	Master of Philosophy
Jew.	Jewish	Mat.	Material(s)	MS	Mississippi (USA)
Jewel.	Jewellery	Math.	Mathematic	MS., MSS	manuscript(s)
Jord.	Jordanian	MBE	Member of the Order of the British Empire	MSc	Master of Science
jr	junior			MT	Montana (USA)
Juris.	Jurisdiction	MD	Doctor of Medicine; Maryland (USA)	Mt	Mount
KBE	Knight Commander of the Order of the British Empire	ME	Maine (USA)	Mthly	Monthly
		Mech.	Mechanical	Mun.	Municipal
KCVO	Knight Commander of the Royal Victorian Order	Med.	Medieval; Medium, Media	Mus.	Museum(s)
		Medic.	Medical, Medicine	Mus. A.	Museum of Art
kg	kilogram(s)	Medit.	Mediterranean	Mus. F.A.	Museum of Fine Art(s)
kHz	kilohertz	Mem.	Memorial(s); Memoir(s)	Music.	Musicology
km	kilometre(s)	Merions	Merionethshire (GB; old)	N.	North(ern); National
Knowl.	Knowledge	Meso-Amer.	Meso-American	*n*	refractive index of a medium
Kor.	Korean			n.	note
KS	Kansas (USA)	Mesop.	Mesopotamian	N.A.G.	National Art Gallery
KY	Kentucky (USA)	Met.	Metropolitan	Nat.	Natural, Nature
Kyrgyz.	Kyrgyzstani	Metal.	Metallurgy	Naut.	Nautical
£	libra, librae [pound, pounds sterling]	Mex.	Mexican	NB	New Brunswick (Canada)
		MFA	Master of Fine Arts	NC	North Carolina (USA)
l.	length	mg	milligram(s)	ND	North Dakota (USA)
LA	Louisiana (USA)	Mgmt	Management	n.d.	no date
Lab.	Laboratory	Mgr	Monsignor	NE	Nebraska; Northeast(ern)
Lancs	Lancashire (GB)	MI	Michigan	Neth.	Netherlandish
Lang.	Language(s)	Micrones.	Micronesian	Newslett.	Newsletter
Lat.	Latin	Mid. Amer.	Middle American	Nfld	Newfoundland (Canada)
Latv.	Latvian	Middx	Middlesex (GB; old)	N.G.	National Gallery
lb, lbs	pound(s) weight	Mid. E.	Middle Eastern	N.G.A.	National Gallery of Art
Leb.	Lebanese	Mid. Eng.	Middle English	NH	New Hampshire (USA)
Lect.	Lecture	Mid Glam.	Mid Glamorgan (GB)	Niger.	Nigerian
Legis.	Legislative	Mil.	Military	NJ	New Jersey (USA)
Leics	Leicestershire (GB)	Mill.	Millennium	NM	New Mexico (USA)
Lex.	Lexicon	Min.	Ministry; Minutes	nm	nanometre (10^{-9} metre)
Lg.	Large	Misc.	Miscellaneous	nn.	notes
Lib., Libs	Library, Libraries	Miss.	Mission(s)	no., nos	number(s)
Liber.	Liberian	Mlle	Mademoiselle	Nord.	Nordic
Libsp	Librarianship	mm	millimetre(s)	Norm.	Normal
Lincs	Lincolnshire (GB)	Mme	Madame	Northants	Northamptonshire (GB)
Lit.	Literature	MN	Minnesota	Northumb.	Northumberland (GB)
Lith.	Lithuanian	Mnmt, Mnmts	Monument(s)	Norw.	Norwegian
Liturg.	Liturgical			Notts	Nottinghamshire (GB)
LLB	Bachelor of Laws	Mnmtl	Monumental	Nov	November
LLD	Doctor of Laws	MO	Missouri (USA)	n.p.	no place (of publication)
Lt	Lieutenant	Mod.	Modern, Modernist	N.P.G.	National Portrait Gallery
Lt-Col.	Lieutenant-Colonel	Moldav.	Moldavian	nr	near
Ltd	Limited				

Nr E.	Near Eastern	Per.	Period	Ptg(s)	Painting(s)
NS	New Style; Nova Scotia (Canada)	Percep.	Perceptions	Pub.	Public
		Perf.	Performance, Performing, Performed	pubd	published
n. s.	new series			Publ.	Publicity
NSW	New South Wales (Australia)	Period.	Periodical(s)	pubn(s)	publication(s)
NT	National Trust	Pers.	Persian	PVA	polyvinyl acetate
Ntbk	Notebook	Persp.	Perspectives	PVC	polyvinyl chloride
Numi.	Numismatic(s)	Peru.	Peruvian	Q.	quarterly
NV	Nevada (USA)	PhD	Doctor of Philosophy	4to	quarto
NW	Northwest(ern)	Philol.	Philology	Qué.	Québec (Canada)
NWT	Northwest Territories (Canada)	Philos.	Philosophy	*R*	reprint
		Phoen.	Phoenician	*r*	*recto*
NY	New York (USA)	Phot.	Photograph, Photography, Photographic	RA	Royal Academician
NZ	New Zealand			Radnors	Radnorshire (GB; old)
OBE	Officer of the Order of the British Empire	Phys.	Physician(s), Physics, Physique, Physical	RAF	Royal Air Force
				Rec.	Record(s)
Obj.	Object(s), Objective	Physiog.	Physiognomy	red.	reduction, reduced for
Occas.	Occasional	Physiol.	Physiology	Ref.	Reference
Occident.	Occidental	Pict.	Picture(s), Pictorial	Refurb.	Refurbishment
Ocean.	Oceania	pl.	plate; plural	*reg*	*regit* [ruled]
Oct	October	Plan.	Planning	Reg.	Regional
8vo	octavo	Planet.	Planetarium	Relig.	Religion, Religious
OFM	Order of Friars Minor	Plast.	Plastic	remod.	remodelled
OH	Ohio (USA)	pls	plates	Ren.	Renaissance
OK	Oklahoma (USA)	p.m.	post meridiem [after noon]	Rep.	Report(s)
Olymp.	Olympic	Polit.	Political	repr.	reprint(ed); reproduced, reproduction
OM	Order of Merit	Poly.	Polytechnic		
Ont.	Ontario (Canada)	Polynes.	Polynesian	Represent.	Representation, Representative
op.	opus	Pop.	Popular	Res.	Research
opp.	opposite; opera [pl. of opus]	Port.	Portuguese	rest.	restored, restoration
OR	Oregon (USA)	Port.	Portfolio	Retro.	Retrospective
Org.	Organization	Posth.	Posthumous(ly)	rev.	revision, revised (by/for)
Orient.	Oriental	Pott.	Pottery	Rev.	Reverend; Review
Orthdx	Orthodox	POW	prisoner of war	RHA	Royal Hibernian Academician
OSB	Order of St Benedict	PRA	President of the Royal Academy	RI	Rhode Island (USA)
Ott.	Ottoman			RIBA	Royal Institute of British Architects
Oxon	Oxfordshire (GB)	Pract.	Practical		
oz.	ounce(s)	Prefect.	Prefecture, Prefectural	RJ	Rio de Janeiro State
p	pence	Preserv.	Preservation	Rlwy	Railway
p., pp.	page(s)	prev.	previous(ly)	RSA	Royal Scottish Academy
PA	Pennsylvania (USA)	priv.	private	RSFSR	Russian Soviet Federated Socialist Republic
p.a.	per annum	PRO	Public Record Office		
Pak.	Pakistani	Prob.	Problem(s)	Rt Hon.	Right Honourable
Palaeontol.	Palaeontology, Palaeontological	Proc.	Proceedings	Rur.	Rural
		Prod.	Production	Rus.	Russian
Palest.	Palestinian	Prog.	Progress	S	San, Santa, Santo, Sant', São [Saint]
Pap.	Paper(s)	Proj.	Project(s)		
para.	paragraph	Promot.	Promotion	S.	South(ern)
Parag.	Paraguayan	Prop.	Property, Properties	s.	solidus, solidi [shilling(s)]
Parl.	Parliament	Prov.	Province(s), Provincial	Sask.	Saskatchewan (Canada)
Paroch.	Parochial	Proven.	Provenance	Sat.	Saturday
Patriarch.	Patriarchate	Prt, Prts	Print(s)	SC	South Carolina (USA)
Patriot.	Patriotic	Prtg	Printing	Scand.	Scandinavian
Patrm.	Patrimony	pseud.	pseudonym	Sch.	School
Pav.	Pavilion	Psych.	Psychiatry, Psychiatric	Sci.	Science(s), Scientific
PEI	Prince Edward Island (Canada)	Psychol.	Psychology, Psychological	Scot.	Scottish
Pembs	Pembrokeshire (GB; old)	pt	part	Sculp.	Sculpture

SD	South Dakota (USA)	suppl., suppls	supplement(s), supplementary	Urb.	Urban
SE	Southeast(ern)	Surv.	Survey	Urug.	Uruguayan
Sect.	Section	SW	Southwest(ern)	US	United States
Sel.	Selected	Swed.	Swedish	USA	United States of America
Semin.	Seminar(s), Seminary	Swi.	Swiss	USSR	Union of Soviet Socialist Republics
Semiot.	Semiotic	Symp.	Symposium		
Semit.	Semitic	Syr.	Syrian	UT	Utah
Sept	September	Tap.	Tapestry	*v*	*verso*
Ser.	Series	Tas.	Tasmanian	VA	Virginia (USA)
Serb.	Serbian	Tech.	Technical, Technique	V&A	Victoria and Albert Museum
Serv.	Service(s)	Technol.	Technology	Var.	Various
Sess.	Session, Sessional	Territ.	Territory	Venez.	Venezuelan
Settmt(s)	Settlement(s)	Theat.	Theatre	Vern.	Vernacular
S. Glam.	South Glamorgan (GB)	Theol.	Theology, Theological	Vict.	Victorian
Siber.	Siberian	Theor.	Theory, Theoretical	Vid.	Video
Sig.	Signature	Thurs.	Thursday	Viet.	Vietnamese
Sil.	Silesian	Tib.	Tibetan	viz.	*videlicet* [namely]
Sin.	Singhala	TN	Tennessee (USA)	vol., vols	volume(s)
sing.	singular	Top.	Topography	vs.	versus
SJ	Societas Jesu [Society of Jesus]	Trad.	Tradition(s), Traditional	VT	Vermont (USA)
Skt	Sanskrit	trans.	translation, translated by; transactions	Vulg.	Vulgarisation
Slav.	Slavic, Slavonic			W.	West(ern)
Slov.	Slovene, Slovenian	Transafr.	Transafrican	w.	width
Soc.	Society	Transatlant.	Transatlantic	WA	Washington (USA)
Social.	Socialism, Socialist	Transcarpath.	Transcarpathian	Warwicks	Warwickshire (GB)
Sociol.	Sociology	transcr.	transcribed by/for	Wed.	Wednesday
Sov.	Soviet	Triq.	Triquarterly	W. Glam.	West Glamorgan (GB)
SP	São Paulo State	Tropic.	Tropical	WI	Wisconsin (USA)
Sp.	Spanish	Tues.	Tuesday	Wilts	Wiltshire (GB)
sq.	square	Turk.	Turkish	Wkly	Weekly
sr	senior	Turkmen.	Turkmenistani	W. Midlands	West Midlands (GB)
Sri L.	Sri Lankan	TV	Television		
SS	Saints, Santi, Santissima, Santissimo, Santissimi; Steam ship	TX	Texas (USA)	Worcs	Worcestershire (GB; old)
		U.	University	Wtrcol.	Watercolour
SSR	Soviet Socialist Republic	UK	United Kingdom of Great Britain and Northern Ireland	WV	West Virginia (USA)
St	Saint, Sankt, Sint, Szent			WY	Wyoming (USA)
Staffs	Staffordshire (GB)	Ukrain.	Ukrainian	Yb., Y.-b.	Yearbook, Year-book
Ste	Sainte	Un.	Union	Yem.	Yemeni
Stud.	Study, Studies	Underwtr	Underwater	Yorks	Yorkshire (GB; old)
Subalp.	Subalpine	UNESCO	United Nations Educational, Scientific and Cultural Organization	Yug.	Yugoslavian
Sum.	Sumerian			Zamb.	Zambian
Sun.	Sunday	Univl	Universal	Zimb.	Zimbabwean
Sup.	Superior	unpubd	unpublished		

A Note on the Use of the Dictionary

This note is intended as a short guide to the basic editorial conventions adopted in this dictionary. For a fuller explanation, please refer to the Introduction, vol. 1, pp. xiii–xx.

Abbreviations in general use in the dictionary are listed on pp. vii–xii; those used in bibliographies and for locations of works of art or exhibition venues are listed in the Appendices in vol. 33.

Alphabetization of headings, which are distinguished in bold typeface, is letter by letter up to the first comma (ignoring spaces, hyphens, accents and any parenthesized or bracketed matter); the same principle applies thereafter. Abbreviations of 'Saint' and its foreign equivalents are alphabetized as if spelt out, and headings with the prefix 'Mc' appear under 'Mac'.

Authors' signatures appear at the end of the article or sequence of articles that the authors have contributed; in multipartite articles, any section that is unsigned is by the author of the next signed section. Where the article was compiled by the editors or in the few cases where an author has wished to remain anonymous, this is indicated by a square box (□) instead of a signature.

Bibliographies are arranged chronologically (within a section, where divided) by order of year of first publication and, within years, alphabetically by authors' names. Abbreviations have been used for some standard reference books; these are cited in full in Appendix C in vol. 33, as are abbreviations of periodical titles (Appendix B). Abbreviated references to alphabetically arranged dictionaries and encyclopedias appear at the beginning of the bibliography (or section).

Biographical dates when cited in parentheses in running text at the first mention of a personal name indicate that the individual does not have an entry in the dictionary. The presence of parenthesized regnal dates for rulers and popes, however, does not necessarily indicate the lack of a biography of that person. Where no dates are provided for an artist or patron, the reader may assume that there is a biography of that individual in the dictionary (or, more rarely, that the person is so obscure that dates are not readily available).

Cross-references are distinguished by the use of small capital letters, with a large capital to indicate the initial letter of the entry to which the reader is directed; for example, 'He commissioned LEONARDO DA VINCI . . .' means that the entry is alphabetized under 'L'.

M

[continued]

Medallion. Large medal struck normally in commemoration of an event or as a reward of merit and used here to refer to Roman pieces; for Renaissance and later periods *see* MEDAL.

In the standard study of Roman medallions, J. M. C. Toynbee struggled to distinguish them from coins on the one hand and medals on the other, while admitting that medallions share features of each. She defined medallions as monetiform (coinlike) pieces that do not correspond completely to a denomination in regular use; they were 'struck by the Emperor for special or solemn commemoration' and were intended as 'individual, personal gifts, any idea of their circulation as currency being either wholly absent or, at the most, quite secondary and subordinate'. This functional definition omits mention of the high level of artistry that characterizes the pieces and constitutes the internal evidence for their status as presentation pieces. For while medallions were produced at imperial mints using the same techniques as those employed for regular coinage, they uniformly display a higher level of artistry; their larger format invited more ambitious and original compositions even when they commemorated events otherwise noted in contemporary coinage.

The first true Roman medallions stand outside the currency system, and it is this that distinguishes them from magnificent Greek coins, notable for their size and artistry, that have sometimes been called medallions. The Damareteion, the Syracusan dekadrachms made during the closing years of the 5th century BC, the dekadrachms of Alexander the Great (356–323 BC) and other heavy Greek coins all share types and weight standards with the mainstream coinage, and while a higher level of artistic expression is arguable for some of them, the principal distinction from regular coins is nothing more than their size.

Multiples of gold and silver denominations (some of dubious authenticity) exist for Augustus (*reg* 27 BC–AD 14) and Domitian (*reg* AD 81–96), and 1st-century AD coins of high style struck on unusually large flans have been called 'proto-medallions', but the continuous series of Roman medallions, in bronze or other copper-based alloys, begins with the emperor Hadrian (*reg* AD 117–38), and the objects in question are clearly not coins. Not only do they lack the letters S C, which characterize virtually all Roman base-metal coinage, but they are far less regular, in both size

and weight, than the *sestertius* (around 27 grams or one Roman ounce), otherwise the heaviest coin in the Roman system.

The motifs employed were highly varied. Toynbee argued convincingly that many of them have to do with the new year and reflect the presentation of medallions as *strenae* (new year's presents); but just as commonly the themes are variations of those encountered in coinage: imperial consulships, triumphs and marriages; the birth of an heir; building or restoration of monuments at Rome; aspects of religious ritual. The urban nobility and foreign dignitaries were the principal recipients of medallions. The evidence of the surviving corpus is sufficient to show that the circulation of medallions was limited. Seldom are individual obverse/reverse combinations known in more than a few specimens, and often dies were carried over from year to year, even when this required elaborate recutting. This practice, almost unknown in Roman coinage, attests to the value placed on the work of highly skilled die-engravers, whose efforts can seldom be detected in the coinage.

Bronze medallions—what Toynbee called 'medallions proper'—continued to be produced into the 4th century AD, but even in the late 3rd century medallions began to be produced more commonly in precious metals, mainly gold. Toynbee used the term 'money medallions' to describe these objects, generally multiples of standard precious-metal denominations such as the gold *aureus* ($\frac{1}{60}$ of the Roman pound, or 5.45 grams) or *solidus* ($\frac{1}{72}$ pound, 4.5 grams) or the silver *siliqua* (2.6 grams). Their easy compatibility with the existing monetary system led to the inclusion of 'money medallions' in hoards, and several large hoards have included substantial numbers of medallions. The most famous of these is the 'Arras' hoard (Arras, Mus. B.-A.), discovered at Beaurains, France, in 1922, in which the medallions, like the *aurei*, correspond to imperial donatives (see fig. 1). It is likely that medallions were included among coins distributed to high-ranking military officials on the occasions of donatives. They continued to serve as presentation pieces for foreign dignitaries and are frequently found outside the empire. There are also large numbers of imitation 4th-century medallions, mainly framed for use as jewellery, attesting to their popularity. In the 4th century the focus of medallions narrowed to

1. Roman medallion of Constantius I (top, obverse; bottom, reverse), gold, diam. 33 mm, part of the 'Arras' hoard, *c.* AD 250–306 (London, British Museum)

the great 50-*solidus* medallion of Justinian I (*reg* 527–65) found at Caesarea, Cappadocia, in Turkey in 1751 (ex-Bib. N., Paris). This piece may have been the one referred to by George Cedrenus, writing in the 12th century. But the occasions for striking were fewer and fewer, and most Byzantine 'medallions' are no more than one and a half- or two-*solidus* pieces with types similar to those of the coinage.

Despite their quiet demise, Roman medallions may be considered the progenitors of Renaissance medallions, which adopt similar size, format and idiom. The combination of an obverse portrait accompanied by identifying legend with a pictorial reverse is generally thought to derive from Roman coins in general, but the high plane of artistic achievement, the limited audience and the non-monetary origin all point more directly to continuity with the tradition of Roman medallions.

See also ROME, ANCIENT, §X, 2(i).

BIBLIOGRAPHY

G. Cedrenus: *Synopsis historiou*; ed. I. Becker (Bonn, 1838–9) [Gr. text]

F. Gnecchi: *I medaglioni romani* (Milan, 1912)

J. M. C. Toynbee: *Roman Medallions*, American Numismatic Studies (New York, 1944/*R* with corrections and intro. by W. E. Metcalf, New York, 1986)

L. Michelini Tocci: *I medaglioni romani e i contorniati del medagliere vaticano* (Vatican City, 1965)

H. Dressel: *Die römische Medaillone des Münzkabinetts der Staatlichen Museen zu Berlin* (Dublin and Zurich, 1972)

C. L. Clay: 'Roman Imperial Medallions: The Date and Purpose of their Issue', *Actes du 8ème congrès international de numismatique: New York and Washington, DC, 1973*, pp. 253–65

C. C. Vermeule: *Roman Medallions*, Boston, MA, Mus. F.A. cat. (Boston, 1975)

A. Alföldi and E. Alföldi: *Die Kontorniat-Medaillons*, 2 vols (Berlin, 1976/*R* 1989)

WILLIAM E. METCALF

Medd, Henry (Alexander Nesbitt) (*b* North Cerney, Glos, 21 Sept 1892; *d* 26 Oct 1977). English architect, active in India. He was the son of Peter Goldsmith Medd, an Anglican clergyman and one of the founders of Keble College, Oxford. In 1911 he was articled to F. C. Eden (1884–1944), a designer of churches and ecclesiastical fittings, from whom he acquired a love of the Italian Renaissance. In 1915 Medd worked in Edwin Lutyens's London office on the designs for New Delhi before starting war work as a turner. In 1919 he applied to be Herbert Baker's second representative at New Delhi, where, until 1931, he supervised the construction of the secretariats and other public buildings to Baker's designs.

In 1925 and 1927 he won competitions to design the Anglican Church of the Redemption and the Roman Catholic Church of the Sacred Heart (both now cathedrals in New Delhi). The Anglican Cathedral (1934–5), strongly influenced by Edwin Lutyens's Free Church (1908–10), Hampstead Garden Suburb, and by Andrea Palladio's Il Redentore in Venice, as well as the work of Christopher Wren, is a sophisticated architectural essay, well adapted to the Indian climate. The nearby Roman Catholic Cathedral (1930–34) was altered during construction to accommodate a large cartouche of St Francis and two Italianate towers, which interfered with the austere simplicity of Medd's original concept, of a single open tower.

Following the inauguration of the capital of New Delhi, Medd went back to England, but he returned to India in

the emperor and the Empire, and the typology is assimilated to that of the coinage. Common motifs include the emperor as conqueror, and gradually the Christianization of the Empire emerges as a theme: the *labarum*, for example, is decorated with a chi-rho or Christogram (see fig. 2), and the legend TRIVMFATOR GENTIVM BARBARVM thus refers not only to the Roman conqueror of the barbarian foe but to the Christian victor over a pagan enemy.

The tradition of medallions lived on into the Eastern Roman Empire; one of the most spectacular examples is

2. Roman medallion of Theodosius I (left, obverse; right, reverse), decorated with a Christogram, *c.* AD 394–5 (Washington, DC, Freer Gallery of Art)

1935 as Consulting Architect to the Government of the Central Provinces, for whom he built the High Court, Nagpur (1937–42) to designs consciously influenced by Lutyens's Viceroy's House (1912–31; now Rashtrapati Bhavan). In 1939 he became Chief Architect to the Government of India, but apart from war work and restoration projects in Lahore and Agra, his only other significant building was the New Mint, Calcutta, completed in 1947 after he had left India. After his return to England, he became Master of the Art Workers' Guild in 1959.

See also INDIA, Republic of, §III, 8(i) and DELHI, §I, 8.

BIBLIOGRAPHY
G. Stamp: 'Indian Summer', *Archit. Rev.* [London] no. 952 (1976), pp. 365–72
Obituary, *Ind. Architect*, xix (1977), p. 178; *The Times* (31 Oct 1977), p. 14
R. G. Irving: *Indian Summer: Lutyens, Baker and Imperial Delhi* (New Haven, 1981)
G. Stamp: 'British Architecture in India, 1857–1947', *J. Royal Soc. A.*, cxxix (1981), pp. 358–79
P. Davies: *Splendours of the Raj: British Architecture in India, 1660–1947* (London, 1985)

PHILIP DAVIES

Medeiros (Anaya), Gustavo (*b* Cochabamba, Bolivia, 16 Dec 1939). Bolivian architect and painter. He graduated from the Facultad de Arquitectura, Universidad Nacional de Córdoba, Argentina, in 1964 and taught in the architectural departments of the Universidad de Cochabamba (1964–9) and the Universidad de La Paz (1974–8). The most widely known architect of the 1970s and 1980s in Bolivia, Medeiros came to notice with his own late Modernist house, on 21st Street in the Calacoto zone of La Paz, in 1970. In the same year he began his major work, the Ciudad Universitaria de Oruro, in collaboration with Franklin Anaya (*b* 1924). On the highland to the northwest of Potosí and Sucre on an open site in view of the town of Oruro, he began to work out his ideas for an architecture that is authentic in its cultural and physical context. The buildings are mainly in exposed board-marked concrete and brickwork, and the design relies largely on standard single-storey units, square in plan, with tiled pitched roofs. One of the later buildings, the Escuela de Metallurgia (1981), however, is contained in two linked, single-storey buildings, with pitched roofs spanning the long dimension of their rectangular plan forms. High and deep concrete-framed window embrasures, whose forms suggest Pre-Columbian inspiration, alternate with slender brick panels, the whole contributing to a rather unusual late Brutalist expression. His work in La Paz includes an urban development plan (1975–7), in collaboration with Teresa Gisbert, which proposes preservation and rehabilitation of the historic centre of the city, and private houses such as the Casa Buitrago (1982), a unique Post-modernist solution closely in context with its setting against the mountainside (*see* BOLIVIA, fig. 4). He regarded painting as parenthetic to his architecture but exhibited in America, Europe and Asia. He drew his initial inspiration from Pre-Columbian textiles, and, at a later stage, portrayed rural groups, represented in the form of indigenous amulets.

WRITINGS
'Inovación y adaptación', *Summa*, 232 (1986), p. 34
BIBLIOGRAPHY
'Université Technique d'Oruro, Bolivie', *Archit. Aujourd'hui*, 173 (1974), pp. lv–lvii
'Casa en La Paz', *Summa*, 230 (1986), pp. 66–8
'Ciudad Universitaria de Oruro: Facultad de Ingenieria, Bolivia', *Summa*, 232 (1986), pp. 34–9

TERESA GISBERT

Medellín. City located in a mountainous area in the northwest of Colombia, with a population in the late 20th century of *c.* 1.6 million. It grew from the hamlet of San Lorenzo de Aburrá (founded in 1616), in the mining province of Antioquia, and was a small town by 1674, with a merchant class that controlled the growing gold production. The only significant remaining colonial building is the church of the Veracruz (1791–1802) by José Ortiz (1761–1837), with a typical ornamented Baroque façade and triple bell-chamber (*espadaña*). After independence (1819), new industries emerged, and there was increased construction, with the traditional brick continuing to be a popular material. New buildings included the Metropolitan cathedral of Villanueva (1889–1931), a vast brick edifice by the French architect Charles Carré (1863–1923), who was responsible for the first stage of construction, and the Italian Giovanni Buscaglione (1874–1941), who was responsible for the second stage of construction and designed altars and pulpits (1919–31). Notable 20th-century buildings include the Art Nouveau Teatro Junín–Europa Hotel complex (1924; destr. 1967), Villanueva, by the Belgian architect Agustin Goovaertz, one of the most innovative and advanced buildings of its time in Colombia. The Facultad de Minas (1940–44) by PEDRO NEL GÓMEZ had nationalist murals (also by Nel Gómez) inspired by Mexican muralism. Although skyscrapers such as the Torres Coltejar (1968–70) by the firm of Esguerra, Sáenz, Urdaneta and Samper (Rafael Esguerra García (*b* 1931), Alvaro Sáenz Camacho (*b* 1925), Rafael Urdaneta Holguín (*b* 1928) and Germán Samper Genneco (*b* 1924)) began to appear, brick was still used in such buildings as the imposing Teatro Metropolitano (1985–7) by Oscar Mesa Rodríguez (*b* 1950). The city's museums include the Museo de Antioquia, with works by Fernando Botero, the Museo de Arte Moderno and the Museo Etnológico Miguel Angel Builes.

BIBLIOGRAPHY

A. Rueda Meléndez: *Medellín, Patrimonio Representativo* (Medellín, 1978)
N. Tobón Botero: *Arquitectura de la colonización antioqueña*, 3 vols (Bogotá, 1985–7)
G. Vires Mejía: *Inventario del Patrimonio Cultural de Antioquia* (Medellín, 1988)

FERNANDO CARRASCO ZALDÚA

Medes. Ancient people in Iran, whose empire flourished from the 8th century BC to the mid-6th century BC. The Indo-European speaking Medes entered Iran during the 2nd millennium BC and are first mentioned in Assyrian records from 835 BC. They captured Nineveh in 612 BC, but were overthrown by the Achaemenids in 550 BC. The most important Median site to have been excavated is at TEPE NUSH-I JAN. *See also* IRAN, ANCIENT, §I, 2(ii)(b).

BIBLIOGRAPHY

R. Ghirshman: *Perse: Proto-Iraniens, Mèdes, Achéménides*, A. Mankind (Paris, 1963); Eng. trans. as *The Art of Ancient Iran from its Origins to the Time of Alexander the Great* (London, 1964)

Medgyaszay [Benkó], **István** (*b* Budapest, 23 Aug 1877; *d* Budapest, 29 April 1959). Hungarian architect and illustrator. He studied (1900–03) with Otto Wagner at the Akademie der Bildenden Künste, Vienna, producing a notable design (1902; unexecuted) for a department store. He also studied at the Technische Hochschule in Vienna, and the Hungarian Palatine Joseph Technical University, Budapest, where he graduated in 1904. Influenced by such contemporaries as Károly Kós and Béla Jánszky (1884–1945), he studied the architecture of Hungarian villages and produced illustrations to the multi-volume *A magyar nép művészete* ('The art of the Hungarian people'), by

Dezső Malonyai (1866–1916) and published from 1907. His two villas incorporating studios (1904–6) at GÖDÖLLŐ, for Leó Belmonte (*b* 1870) and Sándor Nagy, are outstanding examples of the domestic architecture of the period, containing suggestions of a functional approach. In 1906–7, working with François Hennebique in Paris, Medgyaszay discovered the structural potential of reinforced concrete, which he developed for the Petőfi Theatre (1908), Veszprém, and the reconstruction (1908) of the theatre in Sopron. In both cases the problem of spanning the auditorium was solved by employing a double-layered vault consisting of an inner, softly moulded suspended ceiling under an outer barrel vault of reinforced concrete. In his theatre buildings he also achieved some of the earliest European examples of a specific modern language of reinforced concrete architecture. (In the same year, at the 8th International Congress of Architects in Vienna, he lectured on the theory underlying these experiments.) He used the same technique for the church (1908–10) in Rárosmulyad (now Mul'a, Slovak Republic), where the cupola is made from prefabricated segments of reinforced concrete secured by a visible external steel hoop. Medgyaszay's travels in Egypt (1911) and India (1931–2), searching for the origins of Hungarian forms, influenced the four-storey Sports Hotel (1927), Mátraháza (near Gyöngyös, Hungary), with its pagoda-like roof, while his residential blocks are characterized by façades clad with stone slabs, or imitation-stone plaster, and reinforced concrete banisters inspired by the forms of traditional wooden architecture, as in the office and tenement block, built in 1938–9 for the TÉBE Pension Fund, Budapest.

BIBLIOGRAPHY

I. Kathy: *Medgyaszay István* (Budapest, 1979)
Á. Moravánszky: *Die Architektur der Jahrhundertwende in Ungarn und ihre Beziehungen zu der Wiener Architektur der Zeit* (Vienna, 1983)

ÁKOS MORAVÁNSZKY,
KATALIN MORAVÁNSZKY-GYÖNGY

Medgyessy, Ferenc (*b* Debrecen, 10 Jan 1881; *d* Budapest, 19 July 1958). Hungarian sculptor. He graduated from the Medical University in Budapest, where as a trainee he drew corpses. Between 1905 and 1907 he studied drawing, painting and modelling in Paris, at the Académie Julian, the Académie Colarossi and the Académie des Beaux-Arts. He also made regular visits to the Louvre and travelled in Italy in 1908–9, examining Etruscan sculpture and that of Michelangelo. He was always particularly attracted to solid, pronounced shapes; as a result his sculpture can best be characterized by its striving for simplicity, its massiveness and its thick-set forms. His works have an indestructible vigour and a wholesome eroticism, while conveying a sense of gaiety and optimism. Excessive movement, exaggerated gestures or intense emotions are almost completely absent. He continually reworked his sculptures in different sizes. A work that couples the worldly with the sublime, and scorching carnality with the rapture of oblivion, is *Fat Thinker* (bronze, 1911; Budapest, N.G.), according to Medgyessy 'a hymn to the flesh'. His *Charwoman* (bronze, 1913; Budapest, N.G.), on the other hand, reflects a more grotesque conception of the flesh.

Most of Medgyessy's figurines were bronzes, while the majority of his larger statues, including his tombstones, were executed in stone (e.g. *Polish Memorial*, 1943; Budapest, N.G.). Notable exceptions are the four allegorical bronze statues *Science, Archaeology, Ethnography* and *Art* (1930; Debrecen, Déri Mus.). His humanist perspective is reflected in one of his most popular statues, *Nursing Mother* (stone, 1932; Budapest, N.G.). Medgyessy strove to establish a characteristically Hungarian art form by adopting national themes, such as *Turan Rider* (bronze, 1930; Budapest, N.G.). Although he never taught formally, an informal school developed around him. An exhibition of his entire oeuvre was held in 1956 in the Art Hall of Budapest. In 1982 the Medgyessy Memorial Museum in Debrecen was inaugurated.

WRITINGS
Életemről, művészetemről [On my life and art] (Budapest, 1960)

BIBLIOGRAPHY
Z. Farkas: *Medgyessy Ferenc* (Budapest, 1934)
Medgyessy Ferenc: 100 rajz [Ferenc Medgyessy: 100 drawings] (Budapest, 1956)
Medgyessy, Ferenc (exh. cat., preface K. Lyka; Budapest, A. Hall, 1956)
G. László: *Medgyessy Ferenc* (Budapest, 1956)
——: *Medgyessy Ferenc* (Budapest, 1968)
Medgyessy Ferenc (exh. cat. by K. S. Kürti, Debrecen, Déri Mus., 1980)
K. S. Kürti, ed.: *Medgyessy Ferenc emlékezete* [Recollections of Ferenc Medgyessy] (Debrecen, 1981)

S. KONTHA

Medical illustrated books. Books in which the primary aim of the illustration is the conveyance of factual medical information. Medical book illustration, however, still deserves consideration in an art-historical context. Distinguished artists have worked in the field, and medical illustrated books can be works of art in their own right. This article is concerned primarily with the Western tradition; for information on other traditions, *see under* the relevant geographical and civilization survey articles.

See also ANATOMICAL STUDIES.

1. MANUSCRIPT. From antiquity to *c.*1550, several types of medical texts were written and illustrated (*see also* ANATOMICAL STUDIES). Some treated medicine as a branch of learning (Aristotle's *Physica*, for example, was closely allied to cosmology, meteorology and natural philosophy); others, as a practical science, involving diagnosis, animal and herbal remedies (*see also* HERBAL, §1), and surgery; and others, as a mixture of theory and practice. Their illustrations reflect these different functions and are equally varied.

The most finely illustrated medical manuscripts are of the works of such ancient medical authors as Hippocrates (5th–4th century BC), Galen (AD 129–*c.* 200) and Dioskurides (1st century AD). These manuscripts contain sophisticated decorative and didactic paintings as a tribute to the authors' ancient wisdom. Many were created not for use in medical or surgical practice but for persons of high estate, who would treasure them as they would manuscripts of ancient verse or history. Examples include the Hippocrates manuscript produced in Constantinople *c.* 1340–45 for Grand Duke Alexis Apocaucus (Paris, Bib. N., MS. gr. 2144), which has his portrait facing that of the author; a now partly destroyed Galen manuscript (Dresden, Sächs. Landesbib., MSS Db. 92–3); and a text drawn from Dioskurides' *De materia medica*, on medicinal plants and animals, written for the princess Juliana Anicia in Constantinople *c.* AD 512 (Vienna, Österreich. Nbib., Cod. med. gr. 1; *see* EARLY CHRISTIAN AND BYZANTINE ART, §V, 2).

Much ancient medical learning was lost in the West after the 5th century but continued to be studied in Arabic and Persian territories (*see* ISLAMIC ART, §III, 4(ii)(a)). From the 11th century, Latin translations of Arabic translations of lost Greek texts were disseminated in the West under the Latinized names of Arabic authors such as Avicenna (980–1037) and Rhazes (*c.* 854–925) and were often finely illustrated (e.g. Avicenna: Rome, Bib. Lanci* siana, Cod. LXXV. 1). Notable paintings of medicinal substances and of the pharmacies in which they were dispensed are found later in the medieval period in manuscripts of the *Tacuinum sanitatis* (e.g. *c.* 1400; Vienna, Österreich. Nbib., Cod. s. n. 2644), a text derived from the Arabic of Ibn Butlan (11th century).

One of the greatest centres for the study of medicine was the school of Salerno, where, among others, Arabic texts were studied. The works of scholars from this university include the anonymous *Regimen sanitatis*, a verse guide to health, and the *De chirurgia* of the 12th-century surgical author Roger of Salerno (e.g. 14th century; London, BL, Sloane MS. 1977). These manuscripts were lavishly illustrated both with fine decoration, as found, for example, in the *Regimen sanitatis* written for the royal secretary Jean Budé (*c.* 1486; Paris, Bib. N., MS. lat. 6931), and with paintings of surgeons performing such operations as cutting out bladder-stones and restoring dislocations (e.g. Rome, Bib. Casanatense, MS. 1382). Other surgical authors whose works received luxurious illustration include Guy de Chauliac (*c.* 1298–1368), for example in the manuscripts made for Charles, Duke of Orléans (1461; Paris, Bib. N., MS. lat. 6966), John of Arderne (1307–?1390) (e.g. Stockholm, Kun. Bib., MS. Holm. X. 118) and Charaf ed Din (1404–68) (e.g. Paris, Bib. N., MS. or., suppl. turc. 693).

Other medically related texts that were illustrated include the encyclopedias of Thomas of Cantimpré (*c.* 1201–70) and Bartholomaeus Anglicus (13th century), the illustrations of which show the curiosities of the physical world (*see* ENCYCLOPEDIA, MANUSCRIPT). A standard cycle of anatomical illustrations, known as the 'five-picture series' (often with more than five pictures), show human figures with, respectively, the arteries, veins, bones, nerves, muscles and viscera (e.g. late 13th century; Oxford, Bodleian Lib., MS. Ashmole 399). Possibly of ancient Greek origin, they survived into the age of printing, for example in Johannes de Ketham's work (*see* §2 below), and are often found pasted into Persian and Urdu medical manuscripts. They sometimes include the *Zodiac Man*, in which a human figure is surrounded by signs of the zodiac keyed to parts of the body, the *Wound Man* (see fig.), which illustrates a range of military and civil injuries, and the *Disease Man*, in which names of diseases are written over pertinent organs of the body. The *Zodiac Man* was of use to the practitioner in choosing the best dates for letting blood, and it is therefore found in folding manuscripts that could be carried from the belts of medieval surgeons (e.g. London, Wellcome Inst. Hist. Medic. Lib., W. MS. 40). Also for ready reference were diagrams showing different colours of urine corresponding to

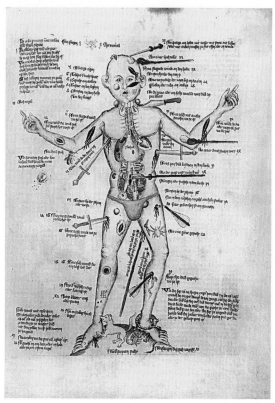

Medical book illustration of the *Wound Man*, diagrammatic drawing on parchment, 320×240 mm; from the Wellcome *Apocalypse*, Germany, *c*. 1425 (London, Wellcome Institute for the History of Medicine Library, Western MS. 49, fol. 35*r*)

different conditions of the humours and elements (e.g. London, Wellcome Inst. Hist. Medic. Lib., W. MS. 49, fol. 42*r*).

After *c*. 1550 manuscripts were largely replaced by printed books, but they remained in use as presentation copies, occult texts and drafts for the press; they were collected by such physicians as Sir Hans Sloane, Richard Mead and William Hunter.

BIBLIOGRAPHY

K. Sudhoff, ed.: *Studien zur Geschichte der Medizin*, i, iv, x–xii (Leipzig, 1907–)
L. C. MacKinney: *Medical Illustrations in Medieval Manuscripts* (London, 1965)
M.-J. Imbault-Huart: *La Médecine au moyen âge à travers les manuscrits de la Bibliothèque Nationale* (Paris, 1983)
P. M. Jones: *Medieval Medical Miniatures* (London, 1983)

WILLIAM SCHUPBACH

2. PRINTED. The illustrations in medical printed books reflect changes in printing techniques and advances in scientific knowledge. The woodcut, at first a crude medium, had by the mid-16th century attained considerable sophistication, and the engraved copperplate, with its greater potential for detail, was well suited to illustrate the researches of the 17th and 18th centuries into the functioning of the internal organs and nerves. Scope for the display of artistic skill was provided by the convention, which continued well into the 18th century, of showing didactic images in a naturalistic setting: military surgery, perhaps, in the foreground of a battle scene or skeletons and *Muscle Men* in lifelike postures in a landscape. Further potential for accuracy was provided in the 19th century by lithography and by improved methods of colour printing. Earlier efforts at colour printing in medical books include the polychrome woodcuts of the lacteal vessels by Gaspare Aselli (1581–1626) and the anatomical mezzotints of Jacques-Fabien Gautier-Dagoty, for example in his *Exposition anatomique de la structure du corps humain* (Marseille, 1759). In the late 19th century and the 20th, photography opened up new possibilities while line drawing came to be used diagrammatically.

The earliest 15th-century woodcuts of medical interest continue the medieval manuscript tradition in depicting skeletons, zodiacal men and uroscopy and bloodletting charts. Sickroom and birth scenes are found, often in religious contexts, while representations of bubonic plague and syphilis tend to be more symbolic than realistic. Also of relevance are such early herbals and compendia as the *Hortus sanitatis* (Mainz, 1491).

The first significant medical illustrations are the dissection scenes in the *Fasciculus medicinae* (Venice, 1491) ascribed to Joannes de Ketham, and anatomy long remained the most popular subject for illustration. A development of the early 16th century was the use of superimposed flaps to reveal the various layers of the anatomy, particularly in the so-called *Anatomical Fugitive Sheets* (first published Augsburg and Strasbourg, *c*. 1538), which were broadsheets aimed at a lay audience.

The anatomical landmark of the 16th century is the *De humani corporis fabrica* (Basle, 1543) by Andreas Vesalius (*see* BOOK ILLUSTRATION, fig. 2), which set a new standard of accuracy with its woodcuts after drawings from dissections. The Vesalian woodcuts were reproduced as engravings by Thomas Geminus (*d* 1562) in his *Compendiosa totius anatomie delineatio aere exarata* (London, 1545). The fashion for folio anatomical atlases was continued by, among others, Charles Estienne (1504–64), Giulio Casserio (?1561–1616), Govert Bidloo (1649–1713), William Cheselden (1688–1752), Bernhard Siegfried Albinus (1697–1770), Albrecht von Haller (1708–77), Paolo Mascagni (1752–1815), Sir Charles Bell (1774–1842), Jones Quain (1796–1865) and Richard Quain (1800–97). This tradition perhaps culminated in the *Traité complet de l'anatomie de l'homme* (16 vols; Paris, 1831–54) of Jean Baptiste Marc Bourgery (1797–1849) and Nicolas Henry Jacob (1781–1871). All these were expensive items, of limited circulation.

Surgery and obstetrics were also popular subjects for illustration from the 16th century. Early illustrated surgical works include the *Cirurgia* (Strasbourg, 1497) by Hieronymus von Brunschwig (*c*. 1450–*c*. 1512), the work of Hans von Gersdorff (*c*. 1455–1529) and Ambroise Paré (1510–90), the latter notable for their illustrations of instruments and artificial limbs, the *Chirurgia e Graeco in Latinum conversa* (Paris, 1544) by Guido Guidi (1508–69), which contains striking woodcuts of the treatment of fractures and dislocations, and the work of Gaspare Tagliacozzi (1545–99), an early practitioner of plastic surgery. Examples of later works are those by Joannes Scultetus (1595–1645), Lorenz Heister (1683–1758) and

Sir Charles Bell. Among obstetrical works, *The Byrth of Mankynde* (London, 1540), originally written in German by Eucharius Roesslin (*d* 1526), is the earliest medical work illustrated with copperplates.

Medical artists have generally been overshadowed by the authors of their texts or are better known for other kinds of work. Jan van Rymsdyk (*d c.* 1789) is important as the illustrator of the obstetric works of William Smellie (e.g. *A Sett of Anatomical Tables*, London, 1754), William Hunter (*The Anatomy of the Human Gravid Uterus*, Birmingham, 1774) and Thomas Denman. George Stubbs illustrated an obstetric text by John Burton (1710–71) but is better known for his work on equine and comparative anatomy. Christopher Wren provided some of the illustrations for the *Cerebri anatome* (London, 1664) of Thomas Willis (1621–75).

Advances in illustrative techniques in the 19th century made possible the depiction of new topics. Skin diseases were illustrated by Robert Willan (1757–1812), Thomas Bateman (1778–1821), Ferdinand von Hebra (1816–80) and Moritz Kaposi (1837–1902). The study of physiognomy was applied to mental patients by Jean Etienne Dominique Esquirol (1772–1840) and Sir Alexander Morison (1779–1866), and in the photographs of Hugh Welch Diamond. Under the influence of Jean Martin Charcot (1825–93), two journals were devoted to the subject: *Iconographie photographique de la Salpêtrière* (3 vols; Paris, 1877–80) and *Nouvelle iconographie de la Salpêtrière* (28 vols; Paris, 1888–1918).

BIBLIOGRAPHY
J. L. Choulant: *Geschichte und Bibliographie der anatomischen Abbildung* (Dresden, 1852; Eng. trans. by M. Frank, Chicago, 1920; rev. New York, 1945/*R* 1962)
R. Herrlinger and M. Putscher: *Geschichte der medizinischen Abbildung*, 2 vols (Munich, 1967–72; Eng. trans. of vol. 1, London, 1970)
J. L. Thornton and C. Reeves: *Medical Book Illustration: A Short History* (Cambridge, 1970)
W. Schupbach: *The Iconographic Collections of the Wellcome Institute for the History of Medicine* (London, 1989)
G. D. R. Bridson and J. J. White: *Plant, Animal and Anatomical Illustration in Art and Science: A Bibliographical Guide* (Winchester, 1990)
                                                    JOHN SYMONS

Medici, de'. Italian family of merchants, bankers, rulers, patrons and collectors. They dominated the political and cultural life of Florence from the 15th century to the mid-18th. Their name and their coat-of-arms showing five to nine spheres were not derived from medical ancestors, since the family had always been merchants. However, they appropriated this interpretation, making the physicians Cosmas and Damian their patron saints. International trade in wool, silk, metals and spices made them one of the wealthiest and most influential families in Italy. The family seat was in Cafaggiolo in the Mugello region, 25 km north of Florence, but by 1201 several towers belonging to them are mentioned in notarial records in Florence. In 1240 the Medici appear among the financiers of Conte Guido Guerra and of the abbey of Camaldoli and on several occasions thereafter in the list of the ruling council of Florence. They extended their trade by setting up branches in Genoa, Treviso, Nîmes and Gascony and were one of the few Florentine houses that survived the economic crisis of the first half of the 14th century. In 1348 Vieri de' Medici was enrolled in the Arte del Cambio,

the guild of bankers and changers. The banking business flourished, the Medici becoming suppliers of credit to the most important Italian courts. Through their financial situation they already belonged to the wealthy class of the *popolo grasso* but continued to support the *popolo minuto* in their political outlook. The rise of the Medici began its final stage with (1) Giovanni di Averardo and his son (2) Cosimo (see fig.). This main line of the Medici family, to which (5) Lorenzo the Magnificent, (7) Leo X, (8) Clement VII and Catherine, Queen of France (*see* VALOIS, (16)), belonged, was especially zealous in patronizing the arts and sciences, making Florence the cultural centre of the Italian Renaissance. Although the Medici were twice expelled from Florence (1494–1512; 1527–30), they were always able to regain their political power and their cultural prestige. After the murder of (13) Alessandro, who was named Duke of Florence in 1532 and was regarded as a tyrant, power passed to a secondary line of the family. With (14) Cosimo I the Medici became Grand Dukes of Tuscany. His successors, (16) Francesco I and (17) Ferdinando I, attempted to maintain the family's role as patrons, but the decline of the once most important Florentine family began in the following generations. The last Grand Duke, (30) Gian Gastone, was outlived by his sister, (29) Anna Maria Luisa, who bequeathed the entire Medici collection to the city of Florence.

BIBLIOGRAPHY
R. Clayton: *Memoirs of the House of Medici* (London, 1797)
G. F. Young: *The Medici*, 2 vols (London, 1910)
G. Pieraccini: *La stirpe de' Medici di Cafaggiolo*, 3 vols (Florence, 1924–5)
Y. Maguire: *The Women of the Medici* (London, 1927)
R. de Roover: *The Rise and Decline of the Medici Bank, 1397–1494* (Cambridge, MA, 1963)
S. Camerani: *Bibliografia medicea* (Florence, 1964)
N. Rubinstein: *The Government of Florence under the Medici, 1434–1494* (Oxford, 1966)
M. Biron: *Le Siècle des Médicis* (Paris, 1969); Eng. trans. as *The Medici: A Great Florentine Family* (London, 1980)
E. Cochrane: *Florence in the Forgotten Centuries, 1527–1800: A History of Florence and the Florentines in the Age of the Grand Dukes* (Chicago and London, 1973)
C. Hibbert: *The Rise and Fall of the House of Medici* (London, 1974)
J. Cleugh: *The Medici: A Tale of Fifteen Generations* (New York, 1975)
J. R. Hale: *Florence and the Medici: The Pattern of Control* (London, 1977)
G. Pottinger: *The Court of the Medici* (London, 1977)
R. Brogan: *A Signature of Power and Patronage: The Medici Coat of Arms, 1299–1492* (diss., Tallahassee, FL State U., 1978)
Le arti del principato mediceo (exh. cat., Florence, Pal. Vecchio, 1980)
D. J. B. Ritchie: *Florence and the Medici: Book Lists* (St Andrews, 1981) [bibliog.]
K. Langedijk: *The Portraits of the Medici, 15th–18th Centuries*, 3 vols (Florence, 1981–7)
E. L. Goldberg: *Patterns in Late Medici Art Patronage* (Princeton, 1983)
Firenze e la Toscana dei Medici nell'Europa del '500, 3 vols (exh. cat., Florence, Pal. Vecchio, 1983)
J. Cox-Rearick: *Dynasty and Destiny in Medici Art: Pontormo, Leo X and the Two Cosimos* (Princeton, 1984)

(1) Giovanni di Averardo de' Medici [Giovanni di Bicci] (*b* Florence, 1360; *d* Florence, 20 Feb 1429). He established the financial and political power of the Medici in Florence and was one of the richest bankers in Italy when he turned to public life in 1400. In 1402, 1406 and 1422 he was appointed prior of his guild, the Arte del Cambio, and in 1421 was made gonfaloniere or chief magistrate. His views were democratic, and he sided with the *popolo minuto* against the oligarchical regime of Rainaldo degli Albizzi (1370–1442) and Niccolò da Uzzano

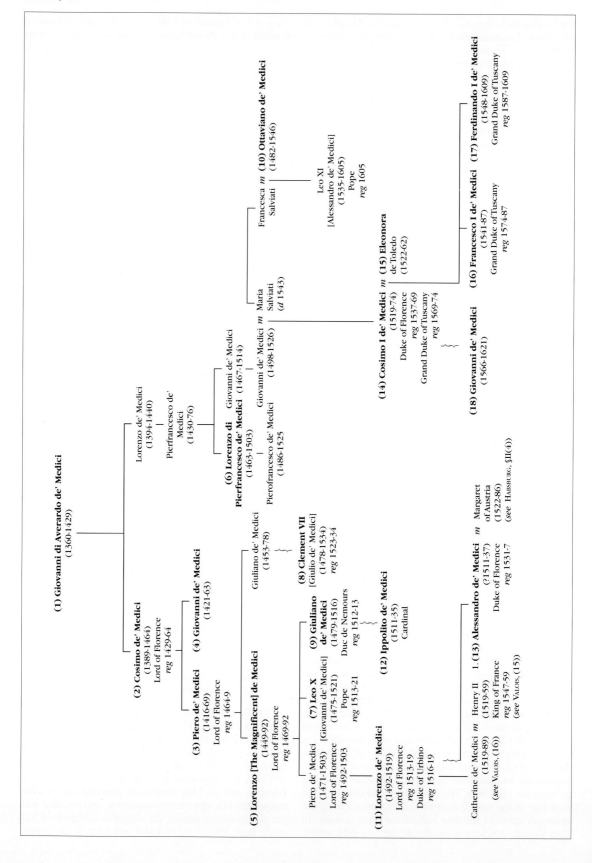

(1) Giovanni di Averardo de' Medici
(1360-1429)

Lorenzo de' Medici
(1394-1440)

Pierfrancesco de'
Medici
(1430-76)

(2) Cosimo de' Medici
(1389-1464)
Lord of Florence
reg 1429-64

(4) Giovanni de' Medici
(1421-63)

(6) Lorenzo di
Pierfrancesco de' Medici
(1463-1503)

Pierofrancesco de' Medici
(1486-1525)

Giovanni de' Medici
(1467-1514)

Giovanni de' Medici *m*   Maria
(1498-1526)   Salviati
                          (*d* 1543)

Francesca *m*   **(10) Ottaviano de' Medici**
Salviati   (1482-1546)

Leo XI
[Alessandro de' Medici]
(1535-1605)
Pope
reg 1605

(14) Cosimo I de' Medici *m* **(15) Eleonora**
(1519-74)   de' Toledo
Duke of Florence   (1522-62)
reg 1537-69
Grand Duke of Tuscany
reg 1569-74

(16) Francesco I de' Medici **(17) Ferdinando I de' Medici**
(1541-87)   (1548-1609)
Grand Duke of Tuscany   Grand Duke of Tuscany
reg 1574-87   *reg* 1587-1609

(18) Giovanni de' Medici
(1566-1621)

(3) Piero de' Medici
(1416-69)
Lord of Florence
reg 1464-9

Giuliano de' Medici
(1453-78)

(5) Lorenzo [The Magnificent] de' Medici
(1449-92)
Lord of Florence
reg 1469-92

(8) Clement VII
[Giulio de' Medici]
(1478-1534)
reg 1523-34

Piero de' Medici   **(7) Leo X**
(1471-1503)   [Giovanni de' Medici]
Lord of Florence   (1475-1521)
reg 1492-1503   Pope
                    reg 1513-21

(9) Giuliano
de' Medici
(1479-1516)
Duc de Nemours
reg 1512-13

(12) Ippolito de' Medici
(1511-35)
Cardinal

(11) Lorenzo de' Medici
(1492-1519)
Lord of Florence
reg 1513-19
Duke of Urbino
reg 1516-19

Catherine de' Medici *m*   Henry II   1. **(13) Alessandro de' Medici** *m* Margaret
(1519-89)   (1519-59)   (?1511-37)   of Austria
(*see* VALOIS, (16))   King of France Duke of Florence   (1522-86)
                           reg 1547-59   *reg* 1531-7   (*see* HABSBURG, §II(4))
                           (*see* VALOIS, (15))

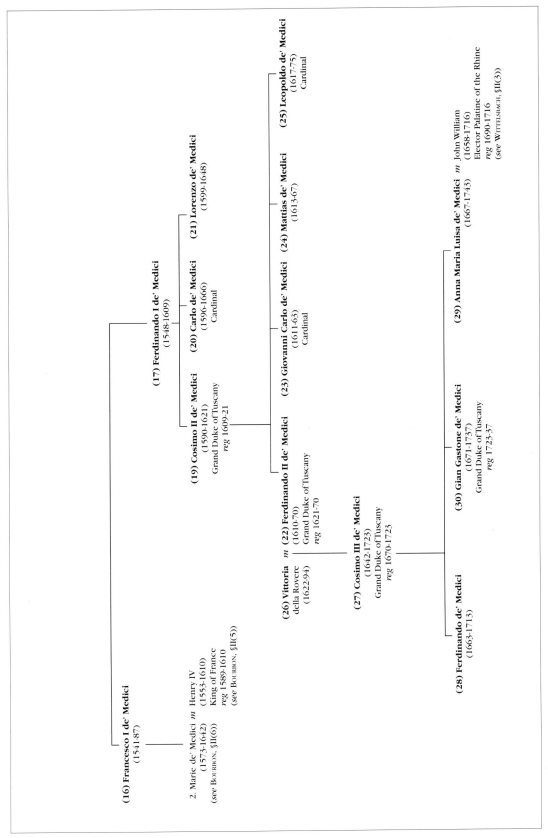

(16) Francesco I de' Medici
(1541-87)

2. Marie de' Medici *m* Henry IV
(1573-1642)   (1553-1610)
(*see* BOURBON, §II(6))   King of France
                           reg 1589-1610
                           (*see* BOURBON, §II(5))

(17) Ferdinando I de' Medici
(1548-1609)

(19) Cosimo II de' Medici
(1590-1621)
Grand Duke of Tuscany
reg 1609-21

(20) Carlo de' Medici
(1596-1666)
Cardinal

(21) Lorenzo de' Medici
(1599-1648)

(26) Vittoria *m* **(22) Ferdinando II de' Medici**
della Rovere   (1610-70)
(1622-94)   Grand Duke of Tuscany
            reg 1621-70

(23) Giovanni Carlo de' Medici
(1611-63)
Cardinal

(24) Mattias de' Medici
(1613-67)

(25) Leopoldo de' Medici
(1617-75)
Cardinal

(27) Cosimo III de' Medici
(1642-1723)
Grand Duke of Tuscany
reg 1670-1723

(28) Ferdinando de' Medici
(1663-1713)

(29) Anna Maria Luisa de' Medici *m* John William
(1667-1743)   (1658-1716)
               Elector Palatine of the Rhine
               reg 1690-1716
               (*see* WITTELSBACH, §II(3))

(30) Gian Gastone de' Medici
(1671-1737)
Grand Duke of Tuscany
reg 1723-37

Family tree of the Medici family, 1360–1743

(1359–1431). Giovanni was the first Medici to surround himself with and support art. He was one of the few Florentines who had the walls of his house frescoed, and he commissioned Dello Delli to paint the furnishings (untraced) of an entire room. He was on the panel of advisers for the celebrated competition (1401) for the commission to execute the bronze doors for the Baptistery, and as gonfaloniere he was involved in the government's decision to promote the Ospedale degli Innocenti and supported its building financially. In 1418 the rebuilding of S Lorenzo was planned, and Giovanni undertook to finance a chapel and the Old Sacristy, designed by Filippo Brunelleschi (*see* BRUNELLESCHI, FILIPPO, §I, 1(iv)). Finally, he supervised the erection of the tomb (*c.* 1424; Florence, Baptistery) of *Baldassare Coscia, Anti-Pope John XXIII* (*d* 1419) by Donatello and Michelozzo di Bartolomeo. Giovanni had secured Coscia's release from prison during the Council of Constance and later sheltered him in his house. He left a large fortune to his sons, (2) Cosimo and Lorenzo (1394–1440), and was buried with his wife Piccarda de' Bueri in a marble sarcophagus by Buggiano at the centre of the Old Sacristy in S Lorenzo.

BIBLIOGRAPHY
B. Dami: *Giovanni Bicci dei Medici nella vita politica, 1400–1429* (Florence, 1899)
G. F. Young: *The Medici* (London, 1910), i, pp. 19–59
G. Pieraccini: *La stirpe de' Medici di Cafaggiolo* (Florence, 1924), i, pp. 7–13

(2) Cosimo [*il vecchio*] **de' Medici**, Lord of Florence (*b* Florence, 27 Sept 1389; *d* Careggi, 1 Aug 1464). Son of (1) Giovanni di Averardo de' Medici. He was the greatest private patron of his time, who, motivated through ambition for his family, and perhaps through a desire to expiate the sin of usury, introduced a new conception of patronage; a humanist, he fully appreciated the propaganda value of architecture and sculpture, and his ambitions rivalled those of the Comune. Primarily an architectural patron, Cosimo favoured MICHELOZZO DI BARTOLOMEO, but he also gave generous support to DONATELLO and others. Cosimo increased his father's trading and banking business and became one of the wealthiest men of his time. He dominated Florence from 1434; yet he himself valued his burgher status and constantly emphasized it, and the artistic tradition associated with him is simple and restrained. He was prior of his guild in 1415 and 1417, accompanied the antipope John XXIII to the Council of Constance and then travelled in Germany and France. He was Florentine ambassador to Milan (1420), Lucca (1423), Bologna (1424) and the court of Pope Martin V in Rome. His long association with Michelozzo began in this period: in the 1420s Michelozzo remodelled Cosimo's austere villa at Trebbio and the monastery of S Francesco at Bosco ai Frati, both of which were situated in his patron's native region of the Mugello. Cosimo had mastered the French and German languages on his travels in Europe and had been introduced to Latin and Arabic in the monastery of Camáldoli, and an inventory of his library made in 1418 indicates that from early on he owned an extensive collection of contemporary and Classical literature.

In 1433 Cosimo's support of the people led to his banishment by the dominant Albizzi family, but in Padua and Venice he was received like an honoured visitor rather than a fugitive, and his business interests flourished. He was accompanied by Michelozzo, whom he commissioned to design the library (destr.) of the Benedictine monastery of S Giorgio in gratitude for Venetian hospitality. He then endowed the library with precious manuscripts. In 1434 he was recalled from exile and became the unofficial ruler of Florence until his death. The republican form of government was maintained, but Pius II commented that Cosimo lacked only the title and pomp of royalty. One of Cosimo's great achievements for his native city was the transfer of the Council of Ferrara, a meeting of the Eastern and Western churches, to Florence in February 1439; many contemporary Florentine paintings were enriched by the portrayal of exotic Eastern figures, lavishly clad in gold-embroidered silk garments and elaborate headgear. The Council was attended by such scholars as Gemistos Pletho (1355–1452), who stimulated a profound interest in Platonic philosophy. Cosimo later founded the Platonic Academy, which, under the guidance of Marsilio Ficino, whom Cosimo encouraged to produce Latin translations of Plato, became the centre of humanist thought.

Much of Cosimo's patronage was for churches and monasteries, and in 1436 he initiated the rebuilding of the Dominican monastery of S Marco, whose sole patron he remained until his death. He awarded the commission to Michelozzo. The interior was decorated by Fra Angelico, who executed the high altar, known as the S Marco Altarpiece (Florence, Mus. S Marco), which unites Dominican and Medicean themes, and directed the frescoed decoration of the interior (*see* ANGELICO, FRA, figs 4–5), where two double cells were reserved for Cosimo's private use. For the library, the monastery's most innovative feature (*see* MICHELOZZO DI BARTOLOMEO, fig. 2), Cosimo had 200 books copied from other collections within two years, according to Vespasiano da Bisticci, his contemporary biographer; he also assembled precious manuscripts from all parts of the world and, in repayment of a loan, acquired the collection of the humanist Niccolò Niccoli, donated to the library on the condition that it was made accessible to the public.

Cosimo also supported the continuation of Brunelleschi's work on the Old Sacristy of S Lorenzo (*see* FLORENCE, §IV, 5 and BRUNELLESCHI, FILIPPO, fig. 2), where he initially acted as joint patron with his brother, Lorenzo de' Medici (1394–1440), and for which Donatello produced the twin pairs of bronze doors, the lunettes above them and eight roundels on the walls and pendentives showing the *Four Evangelists* and scenes from the *Life of St John the Evangelist* (1435–43). From 1442 Cosimo was the dominant patron of the church (see fig.), and from this year, apart from the family chapels, the building was financed by Cosimo alone. Donatello's two pulpits, decorated with bronze panels, date from the 1460s. Cosimo also initiated the building of a dormitory for the novices of Santa Croce and was involved in the alterations to the church of SS Annunziata.

Cosimo's largest building project of the 1440s, however, was the new Palazzo Medici in the Via Larga, Florence. Tradition relates that the first plans were by Brunelleschi, but Cosimo rejected these as too monumental and presumptuous. Nonetheless, the subsequent design by Michelozzo (1444) produced a palazzo of unprecedented

Cosimo de' Medici is Presented with a Model of S Lorenzo by Brunelleschi and Ghiberti (*c.* 1555–72), fresco by Marchetti Marco da Faenza after a design by Giorgio Vasari, Palazzo Vecchio, Florence

grandeur and became the model for many subsequent town palazzi (*see* MICHELOZZO DI BARTOLOMEO, fig. 3). Cosimo commissioned Donatello to make two large-scale bronzes, *Judith Slaying Holofernes* (Florence, Pal. Vecchio) and *David* (Florence, Bargello), for this palazzo (for the latter *see* STATUE, fig. 1), and he was probably responsible for the commission to Paolo Uccello for a series of decorative paintings of the *Rout of San Romano* (London, N.G., *see* UCCELLO, PAOLO, fig. 3; Paris, Louvre; Florence, Uffizi). In this period Cosimo also had the country villa at Careggi remodelled by Michelozzo, and here, influenced by the classical ideal of villa life (*see* VILLA, §I, 2), he sought spiritual refreshment in the beauty of the countryside.

Vespasiano emphasized that Cosimo 'had a good knowledge of architecture … and all those who were about to build came to him for advice'. Thus it seems likely that he played a significant role in the planning of his palazzo and probably an even larger part in designing the Badia of Fiesole (from 1456). The ample documentation on the latter never mentions the name of an architect, but only that of Cosimo, who inspected the work daily. He is said to have spent 70,000 gold florins on the architecture of this monastery and a further 14,000 florins on the embellishment of its interior; he endowed the library with precious manuscripts. Yet, despite the scale of his involvement, he regretted having started his activity as patron so late in life.

Cosimo was also involved in commissions to Desiderio da Settignano, Andrea del Castagno and Fra Filippo Lippi; he and his brother, Lorenzo, commissioned from Lorenzo Ghiberti the reliquary chest of *SS Protus, Hyacinthus and Nemesius* (*c.* 1425–8; Florence, S Maria degli Angeli). A number of other cities benefited from Cosimo's interest in art. In Milan he had the courtyard of the Medici bank, a palazzo previously owned by the Sforza family, extended by Michelozzo and commissioned frescoes (mid-1460s; mainly destr.) from Vincenzo Foppa. In Paris he restored the Collegio degl'Italiani (destr.) and in Jerusalem built a hostel for pilgrims. He died on his country estate at Careggi and was carried in state to S Lorenzo and buried in the crypt there. A porphyry ledger by Andrea del Verrocchio before the altar bears the inscription posthumously awarded to him by the Signoria of Florence on 20 March 1465: 'Pater Patriae'. His role as patron was later celebrated in the frescoes designed by Giorgio Vasari in the Sala di Cosimo il Vecchio in the Palazzo Vecchio (*see also* VASARI, (1), fig. 4).

BIBLIOGRAPHY

A. Fabronius: *Magni Cosmi Medicei vita*, 2 vols (Pisa, 1789)
G. Cavalcanti: *Della carcere, dell'ingiusto esilio e del trionfale ritorno di Cosimo padre della patria* (Florence, 1821)
A. Gelli: 'L'esilio di Cosimo de' Medici', *Archv Stor. Ital.*, 4th ser., x (1892), pp. 52–96, 149–69
Vespasiano da Bisticci: 'Cosimo de' Medici', *Vite di uomini illustri del secolo XV* (Bologna, 1893), iii, pp. 37–75
K. D. Ewart: *Cosimo de' Medici* (London, 1899)
C. Gutkind: *Cosimo de' Medici 'pater patriae'* (Oxford, 1938)
E. H. Gombrich: 'The Early Medici as Patrons of Art: A Survey of Primary Sources', *Italian Renaissance Studies*, ed. E. F. Jacob (London, 1960), pp. 279–311 (282–97); repr. in E. H. Gombrich: *Norm and Form* (London, 1966), pp. 35–57
A. M. Brown: 'The Humanist Portrait of Cosimo de' Medici, pater patriae', *J. Warb. & Court. Inst.*, xxiv (1961), pp. 186–221
I. Hyman: *The Palazzo Medici and a Ledger for the Church of S Lorenzo* (diss., U. New York, 1968)
U. Procacci: 'Cosimo de' Medici e la costruzione della Badia Fiesolana', *Commentari*, xix (1968), pp. 80–97
D. Kent: *The Rise of the Medici Faction in Florence, 1426–34* (Oxford, 1978)
G. A. dell'Acqua: 'Le teste all'antica del banco mediceo a Milano', *Paragone*, xxxiv/401–3 (1983), pp. 48–55
B. A. Bennett and D. G. Wilkins: *Donatello* (Oxford, 1984)
D. Kent: 'The Dynamic of Power in Cosimo de' Medici's Florence', *Patronage, Art and Society in Renaissance Italy*, ed. F. W. Kent, P. Simons and J. C. Eade (Oxford, 1987), pp. 63–77
I. Lavin: 'Donatellos Kanzeln in S Lorenzo und das Wiederaufleben frühchristlicher Gebräuche', *Donatello-Studien* (Munich, 1989), pp. 155–69
F. Ames-Lewis, ed.: *Vecchio de' Medici, 1389–1464* (Oxford, 1992) [with bibliog.]

MARLIS VON HESSERT

(3) Piero (di Cosimo) [the Gouty] **de' Medici**, Lord of Florence (*b* Florence, 1416; *reg* 1464–9; *d* Florence, 3 Dec 1469). Son of (2) Cosimo de' Medici. Raised in early humanist Florence, he was trained to assume his father's civic and cultural leadership. His artistic tastes were apparently stimulated less by the aesthetic ideals of Republican Florence, however, than by those manifested in such north Italian centres of patronage as Ferrara and Venice, where the Medici lived in exile in 1433–4. Piero watched over family interests at the Council of Ferrara (1437–9) and responded positively to the style of Este court patronage, which he may have sought to emulate (with the wealth of the Medici bank behind him) in the decorations he commissioned for the new Palazzo Medici in Florence. His aesthetic preferences may be deduced from such commissions, which contrast with the large-scale ecclesiastical projects that his father sponsored: typically they show precise, often minute detailing (as in a bust of Piero by Mino da Fiesole; *see* BUST, fig. 2), brilliant and resonating colour and rich surface finish.

The best-documented works commissioned by Piero are two small, precious tabernacles built to the designs of MICHELOZZO DI BARTOLOMEO to house miracle-working images: the chapel of the Crucifixion, S Miniato al Monte, Florence (begun 1447; *see also* MASO DI BARTOLOMMEO), and the chapel of the Annunciation, SS Annunziata,

Florence (1448–52). In both, high-quality architectural sculpture was carved with intricate richness and variety of detail in the finest marble. Piero's preoccupation with heraldry is evident in the inclusion of his personal device (a falcon holding a diamond ring) on the S Miniato tabernacle and in the glazed terracotta tiles in the white, green and mauve of his livery that Luca della Robbia provided for its roof.

The barrel vault of Piero's study (destr.) in the Palazzo Medici, probably completed by 1456, was also decorated by Luca della Robbia: the 12 enamelled terracotta roundels, the *Labours of the Months* (London, V&A), were set once more against the background of Piero's livery colours. The architect Filarete wrote of this vault that 'it causes greatest admiration in anyone who enters'; early records also emphasize the richness of the study's glazed terracotta floor and of the elaborate intarsia work on the furnishings. The superbly produced books that lined the shelves had bindings coloured according to subject classification: red for books on history, for example, and green for rhetoric. Filarete described how Piero, crippled by gout, was carried into his study to feast his eyes on his books or to rejoice in his collections of Classical gems, coins and other small, highly valued objects.

The two inventories of Piero's possessions, drawn up in 1456–8 and after Cosimo de' Medici's death in 1464, list numerous domestic furnishings, now lost or unidentifiable, including French or Flemish tapestries, silverware, jewellery, tournament apparel and weapons, musical instruments and also the treasures that Piero kept in his study. Among the wide-ranging and valuable collection of Classical gems and cameos was the *Daedalus and Icarus* (Naples, Capodimonte), which provided the source for one of the medallions decorating the courtyard of the Medici palace. The closely written listings of books show the importance of Piero's manuscript commissions, often placed through the agency of the major *cartolaio* and biographer of Quattrocento Florence, Vespasiano da Bisticci. The descriptions indicate special concern for the binding of each manuscript and for the type of script in which it was written. Most of the books commissioned by Piero survive in the Biblioteca Medicea–Laurenziana, Florence, and the quality of their production and illuminated decoration warrants the high values recorded in the inventories. His patronage stimulated the development of a new type of green-tendril border decoration, evident, for example, in the two-volume Plutarch (Florence, Bib. Medicea–Laurenziana, MSS. Plut. 65.26–7), which from the early 1460s dominated Florentine manuscript illumination for the rest of the 15th century.

Letters written by Benozzo Gozzoli indicate that Piero was also responsible for the decoration of the chapel of the Palazzo Medici, probably completed in 1461. Michelozzo's architectural articulation of this small space is again rich in decorative detail and colour, and the floor and intarsiated seating are emblazoned with Medici heraldic devices. Gozzoli's *Procession of the Magi* frescoes convincingly blend finely executed surface details (highly individualized portraits and figure-types, splendid costumes and pattern-book bird and animal motifs) with deep recession into beautifully observed, atmospheric landscape vistas. The goal of the Magi's journey, Fra Filippo Lippi's

Adoration of the Magi altarpiece (Berlin, Gemäldegal.), shows similar aesthetic emphases. Jewel-like colours, brilliant refinement of surface finish—noticeable in the spray of golden dots that link together the persons of the Trinity—and a delicate, expressive sentiment are brought together in this exquisite altarpiece which perhaps quintessentially reflects Piero's artistic sensibilities.

BIBLIOGRAPHY
E. H. Gombrich: 'The Early Medici as Patrons of Art: A Survey of Primary Sources', *Italian Renaissance Studies*, ed. E. F. Jacob (London, 1960), pp. 279–311; repr. in E. H. Gombrich: *Norm and Form* (London, 1966), pp. 35–57
R. Hatfield: 'Some Unknown Descriptions of the Medici Palace in 1459', *A. Bull.*, lii (1970), pp. 232–49
F. Ames-Lewis: *The Library and Manuscripts of Piero di Cosimo de' Medici* (New York, 1984)
A. Beyer and B. Boucher, eds: *Piero de' Medici 'il bottoso' (1416–1464): Kunst in Dienste der Mediceer* (Berlin, 1993)

FRANCIS AMES-LEWIS

(4) Giovanni (di Cosimo) de' Medici (*b* Florence, 1421; *d* Florence, 1463). Son of (2) Cosimo de' Medici. Although less well-known to posterity than his older brother (3) Piero, he may actually have been Cosimo's preferred successor in finance and politics. He was enrolled at a young age in the Florentine Arte del Cambio (1426) and the Arte della Lana (1435). In 1438 he served an apprenticeship in the Ferrara branch of the Medici bank and in 1455 became the manager of the entire bank. In the political sphere, in addition to holding important guild memberships, he was elected to the Florentine priorate in 1454, and he was one of the Florentine ambassadors sent to Rome in 1455 to congratulate Calixtus III on his elevation to the papacy. Throughout the 1450s Giovanni often spoke in Florentine political councils on behalf of the Medici. He received a humanist education and in 1447 served as an official at the Studio Fiorentino, the university of Florence.

Like Piero, Giovanni was a collector of ancient and contemporary art as well as a patron of art and architecture. His penchant for ancient art may have been a logical result of his humanist education; it must also have been nurtured by his father, himself a collector of antiquities. Giovanni became an avid collector of ancient coins, statues and manuscripts; he also commissioned copies of Classical texts. Giovanni's interest in Classical culture was recognized in a letter of 1443 in which the writer, Alberto Averadi, informed him of the ruined state and contemporary destruction of ancient monuments in Rome and of the unsatisfactory nature of their modern replacements. As a patron of art and architecture, Giovanni may have sought a reconciliation between the Roman past and the Florentine present. In the 1450s he had Michelozzo di Bartolomeo construct the Medici villa at Fiesole and remodel the nearby church and cloister of S Girolamo. The villa, later celebrated in Angelo Poliziano's writings, is located in a position overlooking Florence (*see* GARDEN, fig. 39) that calls to mind Pliny the younger's description of his Tuscan villa. The Classical and the modern were also wedded in the ornamentation of Giovanni's apartments in the Palazzo Medici in Florence: in the portrait bust (*c.* 1456–61) by Mino da Fiesole, Giovanni is shown in a suit of pseudo-antique armour; for his study Giovanni

commissioned DESIDERIO DA SETTIGNANO to make reliefs of the heads of the 12 Caesars, most probably modelled after ancient coins.

Giovanni may also have commissioned the paintings by Domenico Veneziano and Pesellino that appear in an inventory of his apartments. Documents of 1454 and 1455 indicate that he commissioned works from Donatello. His artistic interests extended beyond the works of the ancients or his Florentine contemporaries; letters of 1448 and 1460 addressed to him by Medici agents in Bruges indicate his interest in the tapestries and paintings of northern Europe. The Medicean banking establishments in Bruges undoubtedly played a role in his acquisition of these products, just as the family's political commitments explain certain of his transactions with Florentine artists and with other rulers of the Italian peninsula. In 1449 Sigismondo Malatesta of Rimini contacted him for recommendations of painters who might supply works for the church of S Francesco, the so-called Tempio Malatestiano. Giovanni may have recommended either or both Piero della Francesco and Fra Filippo Lippi. It is known that in the late 1450s he arranged for an altarpiece by Lippi to be sent as a diplomatic gift to Alfonso I, King of Naples and Sicily. Giovanni was buried together with Piero di Cosimo, in an elaborate double tomb by Verrocchio (1472; Florence, S Lorenzo, Old Sacristy; *see* VERROCCHIO, ANDREA DEL, fig. 2).

BIBLIOGRAPHY
R. de Roover: *The Rise and Decline of the Medici Bank, 1397–1494* (Cambridge, MA, 1963)
N. Rubinstein: *The Government of Florence under the Medici, 1434–1494* (Oxford, 1966)
C. Bargellini and P. de la Ruffinière du Prey: 'Sources for a Reconstruction of the Villa Medici, Fiesole', *Burl. Mag.*, cxi (1969), pp. 597–605
E. Grasselini and A. Fracassini: *Profili medicei* (Florence, 1982)
K. Langedijk: *The Portraits of the Medici, 15th–18th Centuries*, ii (Florence, 1983)
W. A. Bulst: 'Uso e trasformazione del Palazzo Mediceo fino ai Riccardi', *Il Palazzo Medici Riccardi di Firenze*, ed. G. Cherubini and G. Fanelli (Florence, 1990), pp. 98–129

ROGER J. CRUM

(5) Lorenzo the Magnificent [Lorenzo de' Medici; Lorenzo il Magnifico], Lord of Florence (*b* Florence, Jan 1449; *reg* 1469; *d* Florence, 8 April 1492). Son of (3) Piero de' Medici. In 1469 Piero organized a joust to celebrate Lorenzo's marriage to Clarice Orsini, and in the same year the succession passed, without discord, to Lorenzo. The Pazzi conspiracy (1478) and the following war challenged Medici predominance, yet Lorenzo's leadership was consolidated by constitutional changes and by his securing peace with the papacy in 1480. Traditionally Lorenzo has been regarded as one of the great patrons of the Renaissance, under whom the arts flourished in a golden age. This view has since been rejected by modern writers, on the grounds that to accept it would be to perpetuate a myth created by the Medici themselves. Instead, Lorenzo began to be portrayed as primarily a collector of antiquities, who, unable to afford to commission art on a grand scale, had to satisfy himself with offering amateur advice to others. This view is now, in its turn, being challenged as an oversimplification that underestimates and misunderstands Lorenzo's role as a patron: his patronage was more than a mere matter of political expediency, and his advice was sought by both rulers and civic bodies because he was considered an expert.

Lorenzo was both ruler and scholar. A distinguished vernacular poet, he was also passionately interested in Classical antiquity and became the centre of a humanist circle of poets, artists and philosophers, which included Marsilio Ficino, Pico della Mirandola, Angelo Poliziano, Botticelli, Bertoldo di Giovanni and Michelangelo. His taste in architecture was formed by Leon Battista Alberti, with whom he had studied antiques in Rome in 1465 and whose treatise he read repeatedly. He showed great interest in the architectural projects of his day; this has stimulated a debate on whether he may have been an amateur architect. Even if Lorenzo was not a practising architect, there is no doubt that Giuliano da Sangallo, whom he saw as able to revive the glories of antiquity, worked in close collaboration with him.

Lorenzo continued the Medici patronage of ecclesiastical institutions. He enriched the family church of S Lorenzo, where the tomb of Piero and Giovanni de' Medici was completed by Verrocchio between 1469 and 1472, and had Sangallo build the Augustine Observant Monastery at San Gallo in 1488 (destr.). Lorenzo's position as *de facto* ruler of Florence gave him an added importance as a patron, since little was done by public or semi-public authorities without his approval. He planned to build houses and roads to beautify his quarter of S Giovanni, although only four houses on the newly proposed Via Laura were erected. His choice of Giuliano da Sangallo for the building of the sacristy of Santo Spirito was accepted in 1489, and he was involved in two decisions concerning the cathedral: to delay the selection of a design to complete the façade and to decorate with mosaic two vaults in the chapel of S Zenobius, a project later abandoned. Even the building boom of the late 1480s was in part due to Lorenzo, as he encouraged the legislation that promoted it. Other patrons were influenced by him, and in this period the Palazzo Strozzi and the house of Bartolommeo Scala were built.

Lorenzo's influence on the patronage of others extended outside Florence. Pistoia's choice of Verrocchio for the cenotaph for *Niccolò Forteguerri* in Pistoia Cathedral in 1476 was the result of his intervention, as was Prato's decision, in 1485, to employ Giuliano da Sangallo to build the church of S Maria delle Carceri (*see* SANGALLO, (1) fig. 1). He also gave artists introductions to foreign courts, both through letters of recommendation and gifts of work, recommending Filippino Lippi to Cardinal Oliviero Carafa in 1488, resulting in Lippi's decoration of the Carafa Chapel in S Maria sopra Minerva, Rome, and Giuliano da Maiano to the Duke of Calabria in 1484, which led to the building of the hugely influential villa of Poggio Reale (begun 1497; destr.). Among Lorenzo's gifts was a palazzo design by Giuliano da Sangallo sent to the King of Naples and two marble reliefs of *Darius* and *Alexander* by Verrocchio sent to the King of Hungary. Lorenzo's manoeuvring in the world of patronage must in part be understood in a political context. At home the results it produced and the work it provided could increase his popularity and his network of clients, on both of which he depended to maintain political control. Outside Florence it could help in his dealings with foreign rulers. His

patronage increased in scale in the 1480s, after Florence had made peace with the papacy and the Kingdom of Naples.

Lorenzo's more private interests are best represented by his country retreats, where he indulged a taste for rural life modelled on Classical ideals, and in the collections that he built up at the Palazzo Medici in Florence. His major architectural commission was the Villa Medici at Poggio a Caiano (*c.* 1480; *see* VILLA, fig. 3 and POGGIO A CAIANO, VILLA MEDICI), where Sangallo created a villa *all'antica*, deeply influenced by Lorenzo's ideals. He also commissioned *c.* 1487 an illustrious team of artists—Botticelli, Perugino, Filippino Lippi and Domenico Ghirlandaio—to decorate his villa of Spedaletto (destr.), near Volterra, and ordered two works from Verrocchio, thought to be the *Putto with a Fish* (Florence, Pal. Vecchio) and the *David* (Florence, Bargello; *see* VERROCCHIO, ANDREA DEL, fig. 3) for his villa at Careggi. Both Verrocchio and Botticelli were employed to make ceremonial decorations for jousts.

Lorenzo's interest in antiquity is further underlined by the keenness with which he built up an expensive collection of antiquities, including sculptures, gems, cameos, vases and large-scale marble sculpture (for illustration of Giorgio Vasari's posthumous portrait *see* VASARI, (1), fig. 1); among the most celebrated items were the Farnese Cup (2nd or 1st century BC; Naples, Mus. Archeol. N.), the *Apollo and Marsyas* gem (Naples, Mus. Archeol. N.) and a red jasper two-handled vase with cover (Florence, Pitti). It has been claimed that this collection was made at the expense of the patronage of contemporary artists, but Lorenzo's role as a collector cannot be wholly divorced from his activities as a patron. He encouraged the revival of the ancient arts of mosaic and gem-engraving, and he consciously used antiquities to inspire modern artists. His collection was cared for by Bertoldo di Giovanni, from whom he commissioned a relief, *The Battle* (Florence, Bargello), inspired by an ancient Roman relief in Pisa, and he possessed Antonio Pollaiuolo's antique-inspired bronze of *Hercules and Antaeus* (*c.* 1475–80; Florence, Bargello; *see* POLLAIUOLO, (1), fig. 2). Moreover, he established a sculpture garden at S Marco (*see* FLORENCE, §V, 2), where he encouraged Michelangelo to study from the Antique, and before 1492 Michelangelo had carved his *Virgin of the Steps* and the *Battle of the Centaurs* (both Florence, Casa Buonarroti). Both Bertoldo and Michelangelo formed part of Lorenzo's household, and this treatment of artists as the equals of humanist scholars and poets was unprecedented in Republican Florence. It introduced a new type of patronage and was associated with an increasing emphasis on the production of collector's pieces.

BIBLIOGRAPHY

G. Vasari: *Vite* (1550, rev. 2/1568); ed. G. Milanesi (1878–85)
W. Roscoe: *The Life of Lorenzo de' Medici* (London, 1796, rev. Heidelberg, 2/1825–6)
A. Chastel: 'Vasari et la légende médicéenne', *Studi Vasariani: Atti del convegno internazionale per il IV centenario della prima edizione delle Vite di Vasari: Florence, 1952*
C. Ady: *Lorenzo de' Medici and Renaissance Italy* (London, 1955)
E. H. Gombrich: 'The Early Medici as Patrons of Art: A Survey of Primary Sources', *Italian Renaissance Studies*, ed. E. F. Jacob (London, 1960), pp. 279–311; repr. in E. H. Gombrich: *Norm and Form* (London, 1966), pp. 35–57

E. Barfucci: *Lorenzo de' Medici e la società artistica del suo tempo* (Florence, 2/1964)

M. Martelli: 'I pensieri architettonici del Magnifico', *Commentari*, xvii (1966), pp. 107–11

J. R. Hale: *Florence and the Medici: The Pattern of Control* (London, 1977)

C. Elam: 'Lorenzo de' Medici and the Urban Development of Renaissance Florence', *A. Hist.*, i (1978), pp. 43–66

F. W. Kent: 'Lorenzo de' Medici's Acquisition of Poggio a Caiano and the Early Reference to his Architectural Expertise', *J. Warb. & Court. Inst.*, xlii (1979), pp. 250–56

P. Foster: 'Lorenzo de' Medici and the Florence Cathedral Façade', *A. Bull.*, lxiii (1981), pp. 495–500

F. W. Kent: 'New Light on Lorenzo de' Medici's Convent at Porta San Gallo', *Burl. Mag.*, cxxiv (1982), pp. 292–4

P. Morselli and G. Corti: *La chiesa di Santa Maria delle Carceri in Prato* (Florence, 1982)

L'architettura di Lorenzo il Magnifico (exh. cat., ed. G. Morolli; Florence, Spedale degli Innocenti, 1992)

Il disegno fiorentino del tempo di Lorenzo il Magnifico (exh. cat., ed. A. P. Tofani; Florence, Uffizi, 1992)

Il giardino di San Marco (exh. cat., ed. P. Barocchi; Florence, Casa Buonarroti, 1992)

MARY BONN

(6) Lorenzo di Pierfrancesco de' Medici (*b* 1463; *d* 20 May 1503). Great-grandson of (1) Giovanni di Averardo de' Medici. His father was Pierfrancesco de' Medici (1430–76). Lorenzo di Pierfrancesco was head of the junior line of the Medici. At the age of 13 he was orphaned, and he and his brother Giovanni (1467–1514) were brought up under the guardianship of their second cousin (5) Lorenzo the Magnificent, who chose as their tutors 'men of excellence in character and letters'. Among them were the poet Naldo Naldi (*d c.* 1470) and the humanist Giorgio Antonio Vespucci (*b* 1435), one of a family closely associated with Sandro Botticelli. Lorenzo also received letters of guidance and instruction in early and later life from the Neo-Platonic philosopher Marsilio Ficino and was a friend and patron of Angelo Poliziano. After attaining his majority, Lorenzo di Pierfrancesco became hostile to his guardian when he discovered that he had taken 53,643 florins from his and his brother's joint patrimony to counter a threatened bankruptcy of the Medici bank. The two brothers obtained the villa of Cafaggiolo and other properties in compensation, but their lurking hostility broke out in 1494, when they sided with the French to expel Piero de' Medici (1471–1503), Lorenzo the Magnificent's son, from Florence. Their taking of the popular side in this conflict won them the surname of Popolano. After a brief period of self-imposed exile (1498–9), Lorenzo di Pierfrancesco returned to Florence. Like all his family, he engaged in commerce and banking. He was also a poet, writing in the vernacular, and a patron of poets. He and his brother inherited a palazzo in Florence adjoining the Palazzo Medici, the family villa of Trebbio in Mugello and in 1477 acquired the villa of Castello. Inventories of the Florentine palazzo from 1498, 1503 and 1516 survive and have been published (Shearman, 1975).

In art history Lorenzo is important as Botticelli's most significant and constant patron. Botticelli made drawings to illustrate Cristoforo Landino's edition of Dante's *Divine Comedy* published in Florence (1481) at Lorenzo's expense; he also made for Lorenzo an illuminated manuscript of the work (untraced). He painted for him the *Primavera* (see BOTTICELLI, SANDRO, fig. 2) and *Pallas and the Centaur* (both Florence, Uffizi) as decorations for a

room in the town palazzo and was still working for Lorenzo at Cafaggiolo in 1495. In the villa of Trebbio there were works from Botticelli's workshop: an altarpiece (Florence, Accad. B.A. & Liceo A.) and a *Madonna* (untraced). Lorenzo was also one of Michelangelo's first patrons: Vasari recorded that Michelangelo carved for him *c.* 1495 a young *St John the Baptist* in marble (untraced). It was Lorenzo who in 1495 gave Michelangelo the famous advice to bury his *Sleeping Cupid* and then pass it off as an antique in Rome, where he would get a much higher price for it, and then gave him commendatory letters for the Cardinal di S Giorgio and others in Rome. Lorenzo is also said to have founded the ceramics factory that was later transferred by him or by his son Pierfrancesco (1486–1525) to Cafaggiolo.

BIBLIOGRAPHY

D. Guasti: *Cafaggiolo e altre fabbriche di ceramiche in Toscana* (Florence, 1902), p. 76

G. Pieraccini: *La stirpe de' Medici di Cafaggiolo*, i (Florence, 1924), pp. 383–7 [fullest account]

R. de Roover: *The Rise and Decline of the Medici Bank, 1397–1494* (Cambridge, MA, 1963)

J. Shearman: 'The Collections of the Younger Branch of the Medici', *Burl. Mag.*, cxvii (1975), pp. 12–27

W. Smith: 'On the Original Location of the *Primavera*', *A. Bull.*, lvii (1975), pp. 31–9

R. W. Lightbown: *Sandro Botticelli* (London, 1978), *passim*

R. W. LIGHTBOWN

(7) Pope Leo X [Giovanni de' Medici] (*b* Florence, 11 Dec 1475; *reg* 1513–21; *d* Rome, 1 Dec 1521). Son of (5) Lorenzo the Magnificent. His mother was Clarice Orsini. His teachers included the humanists who frequented the Palazzo Medici in Florence, such as Angelo Poliziano, Pico della Mirandola (1463–94) and Marsilio Ficino. By the age of eight he was admitted into minor orders, and by 1486 he was Abbot of Montecassino and Morimondo. He spent three years at the University of Pisa, where he was introduced to the study of theology and canon law by Filippo Decio (1454–1535) among others. In 1492 he was made a cardinal by Pope Innocent VIII. When his brother Piero de' Medici (1471–1503) was expelled from Florence in 1494, Giovanni also went into exile, which he spent mainly in Città di Castello, Perugia, Urbino and Milan; in 1499 he travelled to Germany, the Netherlands and France. In 1500 he went to Rome, occupying the Palazzo di S Eustachio, later the Palazzo Madama, where he gathered around him many of the leading personalities in Rome, including the writers Tommaso Inghirami (1470–1516) and Jacopo Sadoleto (1477–1547) and the artist Baldassare Peruzzi. During his years as cardinal he commissioned the rebuilding of S Maria in Domenica and the façade of S Cristina in Bolsena, Rome. He was appointed papal legate in Bologna by Pope Julius II, and in 1512, with the support of the Pope, he secured the return of the Medici to Florence. When Julius II died in 1513, the 37-year-old Giovanni was elected pope as Leo X.

Like his father, Leo X devoted much of his time to the arts and sciences. He attracted Paolo Giovio to the Roman university, set up Greek colleges in Rome and Florence, promoted the study of Hebrew and Arabic writings and, not least, gave strong support to printing. By 1508 he had brought the remains of his father's library from Florence and set up a private library in Rome, which, like the

Vatican library, he enriched with rare manuscripts and books from Europe and the East. He also supported scholars and poets, including Pietro Bembo, Francesco Guicciardini (1483–1540), Baldassare Castiglione, Giangiorgio Trissino, Jacopo Sannazaro (1456–1530) and Marco Girolamo Vida (1490–1566). Under his aegis, Bernardo Bibbiena's *La Calandria* was performed, and Ludovico Ariosto staged his *Suppositi* in 1519, with décor by Peruzzi and Raphael. He had a large collection of musical instruments and maintained a private orchestra as well as the official papal musicians.

Although his patronage of art did not match that of his predecessor, Leo continued most of the buildings begun under Julius II and their decoration, notably the decoration of the Vatican staterooms, the Stanze, begun by Raphael in 1508. The frescoes in the Stanza della Segnatura were completed before Leo X's election, and those in the two adjoining rooms were painted during his pontificate. In the Stanza di Eliodoro, Leo is depicted on the white horse he rode in the battle of Ravenna. The frescoes in the Stanza dell'Incendio (*see* RAPHAEL, fig. 4) are also designed to demonstrate Leo X's power, as the scenes from the lives of the earlier popes Leo III and IV allude to his own political activities. Another important commission for Raphael was the design of a set of ten tapestries illustrating the *Acts of the Apostles Peter and Paul*, intended for the lower walls of the Sistine Chapel in the Vatican. The tapestries, which were executed in the workshop of Pieter van Aelst in Brussels, are in Rome (Pin. Vaticana); the seven surviving cartoons by Raphael are in London (V&A; *see* RAPHAEL, fig. 5). Although the main fields are devoted to the Apostles, the border scenes glorify Leo X, portraying events from his time as cardinal. From 1513 Leo had open galleries, Logge, built on the east side of the Vatican palace, overlooking the Cortile di S Damaso. In 1518–19 the walls were decorated with frescoes designed by Raphael, 52 biblical scenes and grotesque figures based on antique models. Leo also commissioned several paintings from Raphael, including his portrait, *Leo X with Cardinals Giulio de' Medici and Luigi de' Rossi* (1517–19; Florence, Uffizi; see fig.). He gave no significant commissions to other artists who came to Rome, including Leonardo da Vinci and Sodoma.

Leo's main area of patronage was architecture. To continue the rebuilding of St Peter's, begun by Donato Bramante, he employed Fra Giovanni Giocondo, Giuliano da Sangallo, Raphael, Antonio da Sangallo (ii) and Peruzzi, but the work made little progress. He commissioned a new church in Rome, for his fellow Florentines, S Giovanni dei Fiorentini, begun by Jacopo Sansovino. He had chapels built in the Cortile di Onore of the Castel Sant'Angelo and restored several churches in Rome, including S Maria Maggiore, S Maria sopra Minerva, the baptistery of S Giovanni in Laterano, as well as the monastery of S Cosimato. He also had the streets of Rome widened and improved, commissioned Giuliano da Sangallo to extend the Via Alessandrina and laid out three streets leading to the Piazza del Popolo. To stop the destruction of the remains of ancient Rome, in 1515 he appointed Raphael Romanarum Antiquitatum Praes, a post that entailed the conservation of antiquities in Rome and its environs and the supervision of excavations. One of the most important

Leo X with Cardinals Giulio de' Medici and Luigi de' Rossi by Raphael, oil on panel, 1.55×1.19 m, 1517–19 (Florence, Galleria degli Uffizi)

archaeological discoveries during Leo's pontificate was the excavation of the monumental antique statue of the river-god *Nile* (Rome, Vatican, Braccio Nuo.).

Leo's patronage also extended outside Rome. In 1513 he commissioned the marble-carving on the Santa Casa in the Basilica of Loreto from Andrea Sansovino, assisted by Baccio Bandinelli, Niccolò Tribolo, Francesco da Sangallo and Raffaello da Montelupo. In Florence in 1516 he commissioned Michelangelo to design a façade for S Lorenzo, which was never built. In 1519 he entrusted Michelangelo with another project, the building and decoration of the New Sacristy of S Lorenzo, including Medici family tombs (*see* FLORENCE, §IV, 5 and MICHELANGELO, fig. 5). His relations with Michelangelo were often strained, and on several occasions Leo withdrew commissions already granted, notably the statue of *Hercules* intended as a pendant for Michelangelo's *David* (*see* ITALY, fig. 54), which was transferred to Baccio Bandinelli. Leo had the Medici Villa at Poggio a Caiano rebuilt and decorated in 1520–21 with frescoes by Andrea del Sarto, Pontormo and Franciabigio. Leo also collected small *objets d'art*, gems, cameos and medals. He had his papal seal made by Pietro Maria Serbaldi da Pescia and employed other important medallists such as Vittore Gambello, Caradosso and Valerio Belli. The period of Leo X's pontificate was a minor golden age, though as a result of his generous patronage he left not only numerous works of art but debts amounting to 600,000 ducats.

See also POLYCHROMY, colour pl. V, fig. 1.

BIBLIOGRAPHY

P. Giovio: *Pauli Iovii de vita Leonis decimi pont. max. libri quatuor* (Florence, 1551)

A. Fabroni: *Leonis X pontificis maximi vita* (Paris, 1797)

W. Roscoe: *The Life and Pontifical of Leo the Tenth*, 4 vols (London, 1806)

M. Audin: *Histoire de Léon X* (Paris, 1844)

Paride De Grassi: *Diario di Leone X*, ed. M. Armellini (Rome, 1884)

F. Nitti: *Leone X e la sua politica secondo documenti e carteggi inediti* (Florence, 1892)

H. M. Vougham: *The Medici Popes: Leo X and Clement VII* (London, 1908)

L. Pastor: *Geschichte der Päpste seit dem Ausgang des Mittelalters*, IV/i (Freiburg im Breisgau, 1923)

G. B. Picotti: *La giovinezza di Leone X* (Milan, 1927)

E. Rodocanachi: *Histoire de Rome: Le Pontificat de Léon X, 1513–1521* (Paris, 1931)

D. Gnoli: *La Roma di Leone X* (Milan, 1938)

G. Truch: *Léon X et son siècle* (Paris, 1941)

R. Steiner: 'Von Leo X. bis Clemens VII', *Festschrift Arnold Geering zum 70. Geburtstag* (Berne and Stuttgart, 1972), pp. 136–54

J.-M. Kliemann: *Politische und humanistische Ideen der Medici in der Villa Poggio a Caiano*, (diss., U. Berlin, 1976)

J. F. d'Amico: 'Papal History and Curial Reform in the Renaissance: Raffaele Maffei's *Brevis Historia* for Julius II and Leo X', *Archv Hist. Pont.*, xviii (1980), pp. 157–210

A. Boldorini: 'Una stupefacente pinacoteca di Leone X', *Renovatio*, xxxviii (1982), pp. 221–34

V. de Caprio: *Il ruolo della corte di Leone X* (Rome, 1984) [anthol. & ess., 1846–1919]

C. Falconi: *Leone X, Giovanni de' Medici* (Milan, 1987)

MARLIS VON HESSERT

(8) Pope Clement VII [Giulio de' Medici] (*b* Florence, 26 May 1478; *reg* 1523–34; *d* Rome, 25 Sept 1534). Nephew of (5) Lorenzo the Magnificent. He was the illegitimate son of Giuliano de' Medici (1453–78) and Fioretta Gorini. An intellectual and a renowned musician, he was a highly discriminating patron whose circle included Baldassare Castiglione and Paolo Giovio. Educated at Padua University, he travelled extensively in Europe during the Medici exile from Florence (1494–1512). When the Medici were restored to power, Giulio was created Archbishop of Florence and cardinal by his cousin Pope Leo X. He travelled to Rome in 1513 and became Papal Vice-Chancellor in 1517. He is depicted on the left in Raphael's *Leo X with Cardinals Giulio de' Medici and Luigi de' Rossi* (1517–19; Florence, Uffizi; for illustration *see* (7) above). In late 1516 he commissioned Sebastiano del Piombo and Raphael to execute altarpieces for his archiepiscopal church, the cathedral of Narbonne, France: Sebastiano's *Resurrection of Lazarus* (1517–19; London, N.G.; *see* SEBASTIANO DEL PIOMBO, fig. 3) and Raphael's *Transfiguration* (1518–20; Rome, Pin. Vaticana). He continued the Medici patronage of Raphael and requested him to design a villa (later known as Villa Madama) outside Rome (*see* RAPHAEL, fig. 9 and VILLA, fig. 4). Work began *c.* 1518, with the assistance of Giulio Romano and Antonio da Sangallo (ii). Fresco decorations were painted by Giulio Romano, Giovanni da Udine and Giovanni Francesco Penni, and Baccio Bandinelli produced a pair of stucco Herculean *Giants* (destr.) for the gardens. Only part of the villa was completed, and it was largely destroyed in 1527, in the Sack of Rome. Giulio governed Florence from 1519 onwards, and the marble sculpture of *Orpheus* (Florence, Pal. Medici–Riccardi; *in situ*) he ordered from Bandinelli dates from that year. In 1520 he was involved with commissioning Pontormo's lunette fresco of *Vertumnus and Pomona* for the *salone* of the Medici villa at Poggio a Caiano (*in situ*; *see* PONTORMO, JACOPO DA, fig. 1).

Giulio was elected Pope, at the age of 45, on 19 November 1523 and took the title Clement VII: the decorations for his coronation were produced by Bandinelli. Clement continued the decoration by Giulio Romano and Penni of the Sala di Costantino (Rome, Vatican), in which they incorporated a portrait of Clement as Pope Leo I. On 10 December 1523 Clement confirmed the commission given by Leo X to Michelangelo to design a chapel at S Lorenzo in Florence for Medici family tombs. In January 1524 he asked Michelangelo to design a library at S Lorenzo to display the Medici book collection to the public (*see* FLORENCE, §IV, 5 and MICHELANGELO, fig. 10). Numerous drawings exist for these two projects (e.g. Florence, Casa Buonarotti; London, BM), and the surviving correspondence reveals Clement's high degree of involvement: he requested an unusual design with small figures for the ceiling and asked Paolo Giovio to devise an inscription for the entrance to the reading-room; he even specified the type of wood to be used for the desks and ceiling of the library (Barocchi, 1973). By 1525 Sebastiano had produced two further works for Clement; a head of Christ (untraced) and a Holy Family; the latter is identified with the *Holy Family with St John the Baptist* (Prague, N.G., Šternberk Pal.). In 1525 Clement commissioned Bandinelli to produce a statue of *Hercules and Cacus* for the Piazza della Signoria, Florence (*in situ*; *see* BANDINELLI, BACCIO, fig. 2) as a pendant to Michelangelo's *David* (Florence, Accad.; *see* ITALY, fig. 54).

During the Sack of Rome on 6 May 1527 Clement took refuge in Castel Sant'Angelo; he then fled to Orvieto and Viterbo, where he remained in exile. After his return to Rome in October 1528, he vowed, according to Vasari, to order bronze statues of the Deadly Sins for the gate-tower of Castel Sant'Angelo to commemorate this traumatic event. The commission was given to Bandinelli but never executed. Sebastiano's magnificent portrait of *Clement VII* (Naples, Capodimonte) dates from this period. Benvenuto Cellini, who was master of the Papal Mint from 1529 to 1534, produced seals, medals and finely wrought coins bearing the Pope's portrait with the highly personal iconography of the obverses chosen by Clement himself (e.g. 1534; Florence, Bargello; *see* CELLINI, BENVENUTO, fig. 1). Cellini also produced *c.* 1529 a renowned papal morse (destr.; watercolour by Francesco Bartoli, London, BM). After 1529 Clement concentrated his resources on completing the Medici chapel and library at S Lorenzo. From November 1529 to March 1530 Clement was in Bologna to crown Charles V as Holy Roman Emperor, and Sebastiano drew a double portrait of them (London, BM). In 1531 Clement rewarded Sebastiano for his loyalty by appointing him keeper of the papal seal, the *Piombo*. For the marriage of Henry II of France to Clement's niece Catherine de' Medici in 1533, Clement commissioned a jewelled unicorn's horn (untraced) as a gift. In August 1533 Clement commissioned Michelangelo to fresco the *Last Judgement* on the altar wall of the Sistine Chapel (Rome, Vatican; *see* ROME, fig. 43). Work was started only after Clement's death. His tomb (Rome, S Maria Sopra

Minerva) was begun by Bandinelli but completed by assistants after 1540.

BIBLIOGRAPHY

DBI

E. Müntz: 'L'oreficeria sotto Clemente VII, documenti' and 'Gli allievi di Raffaello durante il pontificato di Clemente VII', *Archv Stor. A.*, i (1888), pp. 68ff, pp. 447ff

G. F. Young: *The Medici*, 2 vols (London, 1910), pp. 436–55, 464–92

J. S. Ackerman: *The Architecture of Michelangelo*, 2 vols (London, 1961/R 1964), pp. 28–9, 31–43

P. Barocchi, ed.: *Il carteggio di Michelangelo* (Florence, 1973)

M. Hirst: *Sebastiano del Piombo* (Oxford, 1981), pp. 106–8, 110–12, 115–16, 123

K. Langedijk: *The Portraits of the Medici, 15th–18th Centuries*, i (Florence, 1981), pp. 52–5

J. Pope-Hennessy: *Cellini* (London, 1985), pp. 47–54, pls 18, 22–34

(9) Giuliano de' Medici, Duc de Nemours (*b* 1479; *reg* 1512–13; *d* Florence, 17 March 1516). Son of (5) Lorenzo the Magnificent. He was the brother of (7) Giovanni de' Medici, who became Pope Leo X, and Piero de' Medici (1471–1503). Domenico Ghirlandaio portrayed Giuliano as a boy (1485; Florence, Santa Trìnita, Sassetti Chapel), standing next to his tutor, Angelo Poliziano. After the Medici were expelled from Florence in 1494, he spent some time in exile in Urbino. He returned to Florence with his brother Giovanni in 1512 and assumed the title of head of state, a position he held without great effect for only one year before handing it over to his nephew (11) Lorenzo. Giuliano was represented as cultured and of a literary bent by Baldassare Castiglione in *The Courtier*, although subsequent descriptions referred to him as feckless and weak. He was awarded the title Duc de Nemours by the French king, Francis I. His marble tomb in the New Sacristy of S Lorenzo, Florence, was sculpted by Michelangelo, who portrayed Giuliano above the figures of Night and Day, in an 'active' pose, wearing fanciful antique armour and holding coins, perhaps to suggest his liberality.

BIBLIOGRAPHY

G. Fatini, ed.: *Giuliano de' Medici: Poesie* (Florence, 1939)

G. Taborelli: *I Medici a Firenze* (Milan, 1981)

H. Butters: *Governors and Government in Early 16th-century Florence, 1502–1519* (Oxford, 1985)

ANABEL THOMAS

(10) Ottaviano de' Medici (*b* Florence, 14 July 1482; *d* Florence, 28 May 1546). The son of Lorenzo di Bernardetto, he belonged to a cadet branch of the family and assisted the ruling Medici as adviser and artistic administrator. Guardian of the young (12) Ippolito de' Medici and (13) Alessandro de' Medici and a member of the Florentine government, on the accession of (14) Cosimo I de' Medici in 1537 as Duke of Florence he became one of the Duke's most trusted counsellors. He married Francesca Salviati, the sister of Cosimo's mother Maria, and their son Alessandro (1535–1605) had a brief reign as Leo XI in 1605. Heartily disliked by Benvenuto Cellini for his influence, or interference, in artistic affairs, Ottaviano was nevertheless appreciated by other artists, and by the poet and writer on art Pietro Aretino in Venice, for his generous support, and his palazzo by S Marco, Florence, near the Medici sculpture garden, was looked on as home by Giorgio Vasari, whose studies and first visit to Rome had been assisted by Ottaviano. A friend of Michelangelo, Ottaviano was the patron of Titian (from whom he was awaiting, in July 1539, paintings promised by Aretino) and Sebastiano del Piombo and the owner, according to Vasari, of a collection that included a tapestry cartoon by Leonardo da Vinci. In the 1520s he was the supervisor of the decoration of the Villa Medici at Poggio a Caiano, commissioning the painters Franciabigio, Pontormo and Andrea del Sarto. As custodian of Medici property, when Federico I Gonzaga requested Raphael's portrait of *Leo X with Cardinals Giulio de' Medici and Luigi de' Rossi* (1517–19; Florence, Uffizi; for illustration *see* (7) above) Ottaviano ordered a copy from Andrea del Sarto and sent the copy, not the original, to Mantua. Vasari later made a copy of Raphael's picture for Ottaviano's collection of Medici portraits, which included *Cosimo il Vecchio* (1519; Florence, Uffizi) by Pontormo and *Lorenzo the Magnificent* (Florence, Uffizi) by Vasari and constituted a form of archive of the House.

BIBLIOGRAPHY

G. Vasari: *Vite* (1550, rev. 2/1568); ed. G. Milanesi (1878–85)

B. Cellini: *Vita*, ed. A. Cocchi (Cologne, 1728); Eng. trans. by J. A. Symonds, 2 vols (London, 1887, abridged Oxford, 1983)

A. M. Bracciante: *Ottaviano de' Medici e gli artisti* (Florence, 1984)

J. Cox-Rearick: *Dynasty and Destiny in Medici Art: Pontormo, Leo X and the two Cosimos* (Princeton, 1984)

JANET SOUTHORN

(11) Lorenzo de' Medici, Lord of Florence and Duke of Urbino (*b* Florence, 12 Sept 1492; *reg* 1513–19; *d* Florence, 4 May 1519). Grandson of (5) Lorenzo the Magnificent. He was the son of Piero 'lo Sfortunato' de' Medici (1471–1503) and Alfonsina Orsina. He was reared in Rome during the Medici exile and accepted the government of Florence unwillingly from his uncle, (7) Leo X, in August 1513, taking over from his uncle, (9) Giuliano de' Medici. His rule was frequently clouded by his lack of interest in Florentine affairs and an obvious preference for Rome. He was made Captain General of the Florentine Republic on 6 June 1515, and in the following year the Pope made him Duke of Urbino. Niccolò Machiavelli (1469–1527) dedicated *Il principe* (1513) to Lorenzo in the hope that Italy might be unified under Florentine rule. Lorenzo's tomb was designed by Michelangelo; it stands in the New Sacristy of S Lorenzo, Florence, embellished by a figure of the Duke in a melancholy pose (*see* MICHELANGELO, fig. 5) that contrasts with the vigorous stance of Giuliano de' Medici, whose tomb is opposite. Hopes for a Medici dynasty ended when Lorenzo died without a son; however, his daughter, Catherine de' Medici (*see* VALOIS, (16)), became Queen of France on her marriage to Henry II in 1533.

BIBLIOGRAPHY

A. Giorgetti: 'Lorenzo de' Medici, capitano general della Repubblica fiorentino', *Archv. Stor. It.*, iv–xi (1883), pp. 194–215

J. N. Stephens: *The Fall of the Florentine Republic, 1512–1530* (Oxford, 1983)

H. Butters: *Governors and Government in Early 16th-century Florence, 1502–1519* (Oxford, 1985)

ANABEL THOMAS

(12) Cardinal **Ippolito de' Medici** (*b* Urbino, 19 April 1511; *d* Itri, 10 Aug 1535). Illegitimate son of (9) Giuliano de' Medici. He was considered by the Medici popes (7) Leo X and (8) Clement VII as the possible future head of the family. In the event he was passed over in favour of

(13) Alessandro de' Medici and was created a cardinal in January 1529, in which capacity he travelled to Hungary in 1532 as papal legate to Emperor Charles V, who was then at war with the Turks. Believing himself unfairly treated in the succession, he worked to displace Alessandro as Duke of Florence, dying in southern Italy on the way to present his case to the Emperor on campaign in north Africa. Unsuited by nature to the cardinalate (his friendship with the Venetian courtesan Angela Zaffetta and passion for Giulia Gonzaga were public knowledge), he nevertheless entered readily into the lavish style of living of his peers, to the extent that Clement VII once tried to sack members of his household, which Ippolito resisted on the grounds that while he probably did not need them, they needed him. He was a generous patron of Michelangelo (to whom he gave a horse) and of the poet and art enthusiast Pietro Aretino, with whose help he summoned Titian from Venice to Bologna in 1530 to work for Charles V. When Titian returned to Bologna for the Emperor's second visit in 1533, he painted the portrait of *Ippolito de' Medici in Hungarian Costume* (Florence, Pitti). Other artists enjoying Ippolito's patronage included Benvenuto Cellini, the gem-engraver GIOVANNI BERNARDI, Sebastiano del Piombo (who painted the portrait of *Giulia Gonzaga*; untraced, but known from copies) and the sculptors ALFONSO LOMBARDI and Giovanni Angelo Montorsoli, who on the recommendation of Michelangelo was sent by Ippolito to France in response to a request from Francis I. Giorgio Vasari acknowledged Ippolito as his first patron and repaid him with the many references in the *Vite* to his generous patronage of the arts.

BIBLIOGRAPHY
G. Vasari: *Vite* (1550, rev. 2/1568); ed. G. Milanesi (1878–85)
B. Cellini: *Vita*, ed. A. Cocchi (Cologne, 1728); Eng. trans. by J. A. Symonds, 2 vols (London, 1887, abridged Oxford, 1983)
G. Moretti: 'Il Cardinale Ippolito dei Medici dal trattato di Barcellona alla morte, 1529–1535', *Archv Stor. It.*, xcviii (1940), pp. 137–78
JANET SOUTHORN

(13) Alessandro de' Medici, Duke of Florence (*b* Florence, ?1511; *reg* 1531–7; *d* Florence, 5–6 Jan 1537). Illegitimate son of (8) Clement VII but officially the illegitimate son of (11) Lorenzo de' Medici. He was not a liberal patron and commissioned little, his patronage guided purely by political motives. The most outstanding sculpture created during his reign, Baccio Bandinelli's colossal marble group of *Hercules and Cacus* (1533–4; Florence, Piazza della Signoria; *see* BANDINELLI, BACCIO, fig. 2), was in fact commissioned by Clement VII. In 1531, the year of his election as head of the Florentine Republic, Alessandro commissioned Pontormo to continue with the decoration of the *gran salone* in the Medici villa of Poggio a Caiano (Vasari), a project that Pontormo had started in 1520 but was never to complete. In 1532 Alessandro was appointed Duke of Florence; emphasizing his absolute power, he had the council bell removed from the Palazzo della Signoria and reduced to coins and weapons. Other small-scale commissions were for gems and medals, the most famous of the latter made in 1534 by Domenico di Polo (1480–1547) and in (?)1535 by Francesco dal Prato, glorifying Alessandro as a peace-maker. In 1534 the Duke had his portrait painted by Giorgio Vasari (Florence, Uffizi), who depicted him as the defender and protector

of Florence and a resurgent offshoot of the Medici family. Other portraits were painted by Pontormo (1534; Philadelphia, PA, Mus. A.) and Giulio Romano (Madrid, Mus. Thyssen-Bornemisza). The commission that was most characteristic of Alessandro was the Fortezza Alessandra (1533–6; now Fortezza da Basso), which was designed by Antonio da Sangallo (ii) (*see* SANGALLO, (4)). An absolute ruler's citadel against the city, it is architecturally important for its technical and formal achievements. In 1536 Alessandro married Margaret of Parma, the natural daughter of Charles V. He was murdered on the night of 5–6 January 1537 on the order of Lorenzino de' Medici (1514–48).

BIBLIOGRAPHY
M. Rastrelli: *Storia d'Alessandro de Medici, Primo Duca di Firenze* (Florence, 1781)
J. Pope-Hennessy: *Italian High Renaissance and Baroque Sculpture* (London, 1963, 3/1985), pp. 362–4, 457, pl. 64
J. R. Hale: *Florence and the Medici: The Pattern of Control* (London, 1977)
K. Langedijk: *The Portraits of the Medici, 15th–18th Centuries*, i (Florence, 1981), pp. 70–77, 221–42
K. Weil-Garris: 'On Pedestals: Michelangelo's *David*, Bandinelli's *Hercules and Cacus* and the Sculpture of the Piazza della Signoria', *Rom. Jb. Kstgesch.*, xx (1983), pp. 393–403
J. Cox-Rearick: *Dynasty and Destiny in Medici Art: Pontormo, Leo X and the Two Cosimos* (Princeton, 1984), pp. 234–5
THOMAS HIRTHE

(14) Cosimo I de' Medici, Grand Duke of Tuscany (*b* Florence, 11 June 1519; *reg* 1569–74; *d* Castello, 21 April 1574). Nephew of (10) Ottaviano de' Medici. His mother, Maria Salviati (*d* 1543), was a granddaughter of (5) Lorenzo the Magnificent; his father, the professional soldier Giovanni delle Bande Nere (1498–1526), was killed when Cosimo was seven. When, in 1537, Lorenzino de' Medici murdered (13) Alessandro de' Medici, the tyrannical Duke of Florence, Cosimo was the only available successor. Initially his power was limited, but he became Duke of Florence in 1537, after his victory at the Battle of Montemurlo, and Grand Duke of Tuscany in 1569.

Cosimo, more powerful than any earlier Medici, strove to create a court whose splendour should rival the proudest European courts and to express the triumphs and ambitions of his dynasty through the architectural magnificence of his palazzi and public works (*see* FLORENCE, §I, 5). He cultivated the myth of the great tradition of Medici art patronage, restoring the plundered Palazzo Medici, and reassembling and enriching the Biblioteca Laurenziana, founded by Cosimo *il vecchio*. He commissioned from Giorgio Vasari a portrait of *Lorenzo the Magnificent* (Florence, Uffizi; *see* VASARI, (1), fig. 1) as an act of homage to his ancestors, and the desire for a noble lineage led to his claiming descent from the first Etruscan settlers in Tuscany and the title Ducatus Etruriae. Cosimo supported archaeological excavations at Etruscan sites, where the *Chimaera of Arezzo* was found in 1553 and the *Arringatore* in 1566 (both Florence, Mus. Archeol.). Humanists and poets, such as Vincenzo Borghini, and artists, such as Agnolo Bronzino, Benvenuto Cellini, Pierino da Vinci and Giorgio Vasari, gathered around him and enhanced his glory and power. In 1554 he established the Arazzeria Medicea (*see* FLORENCE, §III, 3), and he was joint head, with Michelangelo, of the Accademia del Disegno (founded 1563; *see* FLORENCE, §V, 1). Florence

Cosimo I de' Medici among the Artists of his Court (1563), fresco ceiling painting by Giorgio Vasari, Sala dei Cinquecento, Palazzo Vecchio, Florence

again became an important centre for gems and medals (*see* GEM-ENGRAVING, §I, 10).

AGNOLO BRONZINO was court artist from 1539, and his many state portraits of Cosimo and his family (e.g. *Cosimo in Armour*, 1543; Florence, Uffizi; *see* FLORENCE, fig. 9) are propagandistic images of power and authority. In 1545 a bust of *Cosimo I* was commissioned from BENVENUTO CELLINI, but this dramatic work was replaced by a more conservative image by BACCIO BANDINELLI (both Florence, Bargello).

The first Medici residence to receive embellishment was the Villa di Castello, where in 1538 Cosimo commissioned Niccolò Tribolo to realize a grandiose garden, adorned with allegorical sculptures glorifying the Medici, that contrasted with the relative modesty of earlier Medici villa gardens. In 1540 the Duke moved from the Palazzo Medici to the Palazzo della Signoria (which from this time began to be known as the Palazzo Vecchio) and began extending the latter, having the Salone del Cinquecento remodelled by Bandinelli; the Sala dell'Udienza was frescoed (1542–5) by Francesco Salviati (*see* SALVIATI, FRANCESCO, fig. 2). In 1549 he moved to the former Palazzo Pitti on the other side of the River Arno, which had been bought by his wife, (15) Eleonora of Toledo. Cosimo had this new family palace enlarged and altered by Bartolomeo Ammanati from 1560 to 1568 (although according to Vasari it was Eleonora who made the arrangements for this). Especially noteworthy is the Mannerist treatment of the courtyard, which opens on to the Boboli Gardens (*see* FLORENCE, §IV, 9(iii) and fig. 24), laid out by Tribolo in 1549–50.

The Palazzo Vecchio was now used exclusively for government business. In 1554 Giorgio Vasari (*see* VASARI, (1)) replaced Bronzino as the favoured court artist, and he became artistic superintendent (1555–72) of an ambitious project to transform its interior. A series of rooms, with frescoes designed by Vasari, was dedicated to the glorification of the Medici. The sequence opened with a room extolling Cosimo *il vecchio* (for illustration *see* (2) above) and culminated in the Sala dei Cinquecento, where the ceiling decoration (1563), whose programme was devised by Borghini, glorifies Cosimo's rule (*see* VASARI, (1), fig. 5); Cosimo is shown dominating the artists of his court (see fig.). In several rooms frescoed decorations were accompanied by sets of tapestries, most of which were designed for the Arazzeria Medicea by Joannes Stradanus. Cosimo also kept his magnificent collection of bronzes, marble statuettes, curios, medals and miniatures in a small room in the palace, called the Scrittoio di Calliope, which was the first Medici museum of this kind. Ancient works were added to Lorenzo the Magnificent's 15th-century collection of small bronzes and medals, and Cosimo searched for rare Roman, Greek and Egyptian works. In 1562 a show-case (destr.) of medals was presented to him by Conte Orsini di Pitigliano. Cosimo also had medals made with his own image, a series by Domenico Poggini from *c.* 1560 and one by Pietro Paolo Galeotti from *c.* 1569.

Cosimo was also concerned that Florence itself should reflect the triumph of his dynasty, and he enriched the city with buildings and with sculpture. The building of the Uffizi, begun in 1559 by Vasari (*see* FLORENCE, fig. 4 and §IV, 10, and VASARI, (1), fig. 6), expressed order and harmony. It was an administrative structure, in the ground-floor of which Cosimo housed the offices (*gli uffici*) of the Florentine state; on the first floor he accommodated the art treasures assembled by the Medici, laying the foundation of one of the most important art collections in Italy. In 1564, to secure a safe passage from the palace of government to his private palace at all times, the Duke commissioned Vasari to construct a long corridor, running from the Palazzo Vecchio, through the Uffizi, to the Ponte Vecchio and thence to the Palazzo Pitti. Cellini's bronze *Perseus with the Head of Medusa* (1543–53; Florence, Loggia Lanzi), perhaps symbolizing Cosimo's leadership (*see* CELLINI, BENVENUTO, §I, 4 and fig. 6), and Ammanati's Fountain of Neptune (*c.* 1560–75; *see* AMMANATI, BARTOLOMEO, fig. 1) were commissioned for the Piazza della Signoria; columns commemorating the Medici were erected in the piazzas of S Marco, Santa Trìnita and S Felice.

Cosimo had a special relationship with Pisa, reinforcing its naval power and founding the Order of the Knights of S Stefano in 1526; he also supported the reopening of the University of Pisa. In place of the earlier republican city centre, he commissioned Vasari to build the church of S Stefano and the Palazzo dei Cavalieri. His interest is commemorated in Pierino da Vinci's marble relief *Pisa Restaurata* (1552–3; Rome, Pin. Vaticana; for illustration *see* PIERINO DA VINCI). In 1564 Cosimo, in poor health, decided to withdraw from political life in favour of his son (16) Francesco I de' Medici.

For a posthumous equestrian monument of Cosimo I *see* GIAMBO-LOGNA, fig. 5.

BIBLIOGRAPHY

A. Mannucci: *Vita di Cosimo de' Medici, primo gran duca di Toscana* (Bologna, 1586)
L. A. Ferrai: *Cosimo de' Medici, duca di Firenze* (Bologna, 1882)
P. E. Giambullari: *Personificazione delle città, paesi e fiumi della Toscana, festeggianti le nozze di Cosimo I ed Eleonora di Toledo*, ed. U. Angeli (Prato, 1898)
V. Maffei: *Dal titolo di Duca di Firenze e di Siena a Granduca di Toscana* (Florence, 1905)
E. Borsook: 'Art and Politics at the Medici Court: The Funeral of Cosimo I de' Medici', *Mitt. Ksthist. Inst. Florenz*, xii (1965–6), pp. 31–54
A. C. Minor and B. Mitchell: *A Renaissance Entertainment: Festivities for the Marriage of Cosimo I, Duke of Florence, in 1539* (Columbia, MO, 1968)
K. W. Forster: 'Metaphors of Rule: Political Ideology and History in the Portraits of Cosimo I de' Medici', *Mitt. Ksthist. Inst. Florenz*, xv (1971), pp. 65–104
P. W. Richelson: *Studies in the Personal Imagery of Cosimo I de' Medici, Duke of Florence* (diss., Princeton U., 1973)
D. R. Wright: *The Medici Villa at Olmo a Castello: Its History and Iconography* (diss., Princeton U., 1976)
Le arti del principato mediceo (exh. cat., Florence, Pal. Vecchio, 1980), pp. 31–45 [article on ant. sculp. col. of Cosimo I de' Medici]
R. Cantagalli: *Cosimo I de' Medici, Granduca di Toscana* (Milan, 1985)
T. Hirthe: 'Die Perseus-und-Medusa-Gruppe des Benvenuto Cellini in Florenz', *Jb. Berlin. Mus.*, xxix–xxx (1987–8), pp. 197–216

MARLIS VON HESSERT

(15) Eleonora de' Medici [Eleanora of Toledo], Grand Duchess of Tuscany (*b* Naples, 1522; *d* Pisa, 1562). First wife of (14) Cosimo I de' Medici. She was the second daughter of the Viceroy of Naples, Don Pedro di Toledo, Marquis of Francavilla, the Emperor Charles V's senior lieutenant. In 1539 Cosimo I married her as part of his policy to strengthen his connections with the Emperor. The union appears to have been happy and resulted in 11 children, two of whom eventually succeeded to the Grand Duchy of Tuscany: (16) Francesco I de' Medici, on Cosimo's death in 1574, and (17) Ferdinando I de' Medici in 1587. Spanish by birth, and notably pious, Eleonora retained the influences—and language—of her upbringing throughout her life. Her physical beauty is attested to by a considerable number of portraits by Agnolo Bronzino (e.g. 1546, Florence, Uffizi; 1560, Berlin, Gemäldegal.; for a portrait of her with her son Giovanni *see* BRONZINO, AGNOLO, fig. 3).

An imperious woman of considerable intelligence, Eleonora was passionately interested in gambling, despite her deeply religious nature. Once settled in Florence, she demonstrated great business acumen and was instrumental in enlarging the Medici fortune by astute dealings in land and property. In 1550, for example, she bought the Palazzo Pitti, which then became the official Medici residence in Florence. According to Vasari, it was Eleonora who arranged for it to be enlarged and for the redesigning of the land attached to it (now the Boboli Gardens; *see* FLORENCE, §IV, 9(iii) and fig. 25).

As a patron, Eleonora embraced both charitable causes and the arts, although, according to Benvenuto Cellini, she was as autocratic and capricious in this respect as she was in most other matters. She was closely associated with many of the major Florentine artists of the period, including Niccolò Tribolo, Bronzino, Pierino da Vinci, Cellini himself and Baccio Bandinelli. Cellini discussed Eleonora's pleasure both in acquiring and wearing jewellery—an interest evident in the Bronzino portraits, in all of which she is extremely richly dressed in heavy brocade robes liberally embroidered with pearls, for which she had a particular passion. The project with which the Duchess is most closely associated is the chapel bearing her name in the Palazzo Vecchio, Florence, which Cosimo commissioned Bronzino to decorate. The small private chapel, frescoed with scenes from the *Life of Moses* (1540–45), is a major work of Florentine Mannerism, and perhaps the most complete extant indication of Eleonora's own taste. Bronzino's altarpiece, a *Lamentation* (1545; Besançon, Mus. B.-A. & Archéol.; *see* BRONZINO, AGNOLO, fig. 1), includes an idealized portrait of Eleonora in a prominent position within the narrative. She was also involved in the 'Elevati', a literary academy founded by her husband in 1547. The poet Laura Battiferri (1525–89), who, in common with Eleonora, was influenced by Jesuit thought, dedicated the first publication of her poetry to Eleonora in 1560.

BIBLIOGRAPHY

G. Vasari: *Vite* (1550, rev. 2/1568); ed. G. Milanesi (1878–85)
B. Cellini: *Vita*, ed. A. Cocchi (Cologne, 1728); Eng. trans. by J. A. Symonds, 2 vols (London, 1887; abridged Oxford, 1983)
A. Baia: *Leonora di Toledo: Duchessa di Firenze e Siena* (Todi, 1907)
C. McCorquodale: *Bronzino* (London, 1981)

WARREN HEARNDEN

(16) Francesco I de' Medici, Grand Duke of Tuscany (*b* Florence, 25 March 1541; *reg* 1574–87; *d* Poggio a Caiano, 19 Oct 1587). Son of (14) Cosimo I de' Medici and (15) Eleonora de' Medici. His education included instruction in science and the decorative arts, and these were to remain his abiding interests. Bronzino painted a portrait of *Eleonora with Francesco* (1549–50; workshop versions, Pisa, Mus. N. S. Matteo; Cincinnati, OH, A. Mus.). He was again painted in 1551 (Florence, Uffizi), the first of a series of *quadretti* of Cosimo's children at the same age. The last image of his youth was the idealized portrait by Bronzino's pupil Alessandro Allori (*c.* 1559; replica in Chicago, IL, A. Inst.) of Francesco with a miniature of his sister Lucrezia (*d* 1561).

In the 1550s Francesco became interested in the art of GIAMBOLOGNA and from 1561 paid him a monthly salary. The Prince's first major commission to the sculptor was for *Samson Slaying a Philistine* (1560–62; London, V&A; *see* ITALY, fig. 55); it marked the beginning of a long patronage. In 1564 Francesco was made Prince Regent, and celebratory medals were struck, the first of many by Pastorino de Pastorini and Domenico Poggini. At about the same time Poggini carved a marble portrait bust of *Francesco de' Medici* (Florence, Uffizi), which, in contrast to Benvenuto Cellini's tensely realistic portrayal of *Cosimo de' Medici* (1548; Florence, Bargello), presents a generic and romanticized image, the forerunner of the idealized rulers of the Baroque.

In 1565 Francesco travelled to Vienna and Innsbruck and returned with the promise of an imperial bride. One result of this trip was a full-length portrait, probably by Allori, showing Francesco standing in armour in the Habsburg manner (studio versions, e.g. Antwerp, Mus. Mayer van den Bergh). The other was the ceremonial arrival in Florence in December 1565 of Joanna of Austria (1547–78), daughter of the Holy Roman Emperor Ferdinand I; the wedding, celebrated over several weeks, was intended to mark the full grandeur of the new Tuscan state. Some of its lavish features still survive, such as Giorgio Vasari's redecoration of the courtyard of the Palazzo Vecchio, Francesco's residence, with gilded stuccoes on the columns and frescoes of Austrian cities on the inner walls (1565; *in situ*). Also associated with these celebrations is Giambologna's marble group *Florence Triumphant over Pisa* (Florence, Bargello; for red wax modello *see* MODELLO, fig. 5). In the Palazzo Vecchio, Vasari also built Francesco a private apartment, consisting of a bedchamber, a secret closet and a small, richly decorated treasure-room, connected by a hidden stairway to his famous *studiolo* (*see* STUDIOLO, fig. 2 and BANDINI, GIOVANNI). The decoration of the *studiolo* (1570–75; *in situ*) displays, in an arcane programme devised by Vincenzo Borghini, the range of Francesco's interests, expressed in terms of man's dominance of nature through art and science and illustrated by scenes and figures symbolic of the Four Elements and the Seasons and their presiding gods. The scheme, under Vasari's direction, combined frescoes, oil paintings, mosaics and bronze statuettes in an elaborately varied exhibition, on a tiny scale, of the finest examples of Florentine Late Mannerism, employing, besides Vasari himself (*see* VASARI, (1), fig. 8), the talents of Giambologna, Bartolommeo Ammannati, Francesco Poppi, Giovan Battista Naldini (for illustration *see* NALDINI, GIOVAN BATTISTA) and others. Francesco appears as a spectator in such scenes (all *in situ*) as Giovanni Maria Butteri's *Glassblower's Workshop* (1570–71) and Alessandro Fei's *Goldsmith's Workshop* (*c.* 1570), and, more remarkably, as the protagonist in Joannes Stradanus's *Alchemist's Laboratory* (*see* STRADANUS, JOHANNES, fig. 1). There was indeed a private laboratory in the Palazzo Vecchio, built earlier by Vasari for Cosimo I, in which Francesco was reputed to experiment in alchemy and chemistry, metalwork and crystal-cutting, and developments in the manufacture of fireworks, paste jewellery and porcelain. He certainly encouraged his favoured artist (who was also his art tutor), BERNARDO BUONTALENTI, in the last, and in 1572 he brought Ambrogio and Stefano Caroni from Milan to Florence, followed in 1575 by Giorgio Gaffurri, to set up a workshop specializing in hardstone products (*see* FLORENCE, §III, 1 and 2(i)).

These un-princely activities were unpopular with the Florentines, who were only too aware that Francesco's ten-year apprenticeship had failed to remake him in Cosimo's heroic self-image. His accession in 1574 was marked by disparaging assessments by diplomatic observers, describing his short stature, melancholy mien, graceless bearing and taciturn circumspection. His preference for his various private pursuits over public duties was also noted; these included his notorious affair with the Venetian beauty Bianca Capello, who had become his mistress in 1568. It was for Bianca that Buontalenti created the second masterpiece of Francesco's patronage, the Villa

Medici at Pratolino, near Florence. The main building (1569–75; destr.) was on the traditional lines of the Villa Medici at Poggio a Caiano. Buontalenti's inventive artistry was concentrated on the amazing gardens, with their terraces, grottoes, fountains, set-pieces and automata. (For Buontalenti's façade of the Boboli Gardens, carried out for Francesco from 1583, see BUONTALENTI, BERNARDO, fig. 1.) Most of these were completed by 1581, when Montaigne visited and described them in his *Journal de voyage en Italie par la Suisse et l'Allemagne*, and were still functioning a century later. Virtually all that remains is the gigantic fountain-figure of the *Appennines* (1580), created by Giambologna. Francesco appointed Buontalenti as his court artist after Vasari's death in the year of his accession. One of his earliest duties was to arrange the celebrations of the birth of Francesco's heir, Filippo, in 1577. Also being celebrated was the Emperor's belated approval of the title of Grand Duke of Tuscany, originally granted to Cosimo I by Pope Pius V in 1570. In 1578 the death of Joanna of Austria was commemorated in elaborate obsequies; less than two months later Francesco secretly married Bianca. Their union was officially celebrated the following year with the most lavish festivities yet seen in Florence (again designed by Buontalenti). Bianca's new status was recorded in a number of portraits by Allori (all destr.), depicting her with both the Grand Prince Filippo and her own older, illegitimate son Antonio. After Filippo's death in 1582, Antonio was legitimized. Perhaps to emphasize the continuity of his line Francesco commissioned in 1584–5 a series of paintings of his ancestors, known as the *Serie Aulica*, from various minor artists; a hieratic double portrait of his late wife and son (Florence, Uffizi) by Giovanni Bizzelli (1556–1612) was added to it in 1586. He himself was portrayed with rather more effective dignity by Hans von Aachen (Florence, Pitti), wearing the Order of the Golden Fleece conferred on him in 1585.

Francesco's extravagance, and his second wife and son, were deeply resented by his subjects; however, he did much to improve the cultural life of Florence. In 1583 he founded the Accademia della Crusca ('chaff') for the purification of the Italian language and the promotion of Tuscan literature. He had already (from 1572) encouraged those decorative arts he loved by grouping craft workshops, particularly those producing jewellery, glass and porcelain, in Buontalenti's Casino de' Medici in Piazza S Marco; he even moved his own laboratory there. In 1581 he ordered the transformation of the upper storey of the Uffizi, newly completed by Buontalenti and Alfonso Parigi, into an art gallery to display his collections, with the choicest pieces grouped in Buontalenti's octagonal, domed Tribuna (*see* DISPLAY OF ART, fig. 3). In the centre of the latter was placed a tempietto decorated with gold reliefs by Giambologna (Florence, Pitti), five of which showed Francesco supervising building projects: the fortifications of Livorno and of Portoferraio, the villa at Pratolino, the Forte di Belvedere and the façade of Florence Cathedral. In fact, Pratolino was the only one completed by Francesco and, of the others, only the work at Livorno was begun by him. The competition for the façade of the cathedral was held in 1587, and the various models for it (including Buontalenti's) survive (Florence, Mus. Opera Duomo). But this, like the other projects, was interrupted

by the sudden death from malaria, one day apart, of both Francesco and his wife.

BIBLIOGRAPHY
G. Vasari: *Ragionamenti sopra le inventioni da lui dipinte in Firenze . . .* (Florence, 1588); ed. G. Milanesi (1882)
J. Shearman: *Mannerism* (Harmondsworth, 1967)
E. Pucci: *Palazzo Vecchio* (Florence, 1968)
M. Levey: *Painting at Court* (London, 1971)
C. Hibbert: *The Rise and Fall of the House of Medici* (London, 1974)
J. R. Hale: *Florence and the Medici: The Pattern of Control* (London, 1977)
S. J. Schaefer: *The Studiolo of Francesco de' Medici in the Palazzo Vecchio in Florence* (microfilm, Ann Arbor, 1980)
K. Langedijk: *The Portraits of the Medici, 15th–18th Centuries*, 3 vols (Florence, 1981–7)
M. L. Mariotti Masi: *Bianca Capello: Una Veneziana alla corte dei Medici* (Milan, 1986)

(17) Ferdinando I de' Medici, Grand Duke of Tuscany (*b* Florence, 30 July 1548; *reg* 1587–1609; *d* Florence, 7 Feb 1609). Son of (14) Cosimo I de' Medici and (15) Eleanora de' Medici. His future career seemed uncertain until, in 1562, two of his brothers and his mother suddenly died (he was the fourth son). The older of the two, Giovanni, had been a cardinal; Cosimo arranged with Pius IV that Ferdinando should inherit Giovanni's title and benefices (1563). The investiture took place in Rome the following year. For the next decade Ferdinando spent increasingly long periods in Rome, lodging frequently with the Tuscan cardinal Giovanni Ricci, and made numerous influential contacts and alliances. He also began, from 1569, to collect antique sculptures, housing them in a small villa (destr.) outside the Porta del Popolo. In 1572 Cosimo commissioned Bartolomeo Ammannati to remodel and enlarge considerably the Palazzo di Firenze in Campo Marzio, Rome, as Ferdinando's main residence, but little work was done before Cosimo's death (1574) put paid to the scheme. Nevertheless Ferdinando was determined to move permanently to Rome. (His relations with his elder brother (16) Francesco I de' Medici were strained.) In 1576 he completed the purchase of Cardinal Ricci's magnificent villa on the Pincio, which is still known as the Villa Medici. Over the next decade it was rendered even more splendid, with the approaches and entrances regularized and embellished, the gardens enlarged and beautified, and the main building remodelled and redecorated. Two of the new architectural features were especially influential on subsequent Roman villas and palazzi: the crowning of the doubled turrets with decorative belvederes, and the encrustation of the garden front, above a deep loggia, with antique fragments framed in rich stuccowork. The other main new feature was an immense gallery below a raised terrace, built to house Ferdinando's by then superb collection of Classical sculpture, which eventually included the *Venus de' Medici* (see ANTIQUE, THE, fig. 3), the *Wrestlers*, the *Niobids* (all Florence, Uffizi) and the *Spinario* (Rome, Mus. Conserv.; *see* STATUE, fig. 2).

Ferdinando's fine physical presence, good humour and liberality made him popular both in Florence and Rome; but it was clear from the decisive influence of his intervention in the papal conclaves of 1572 and 1585 that his fellow cardinals recognized more solid qualities beneath his affable exterior. The Florentines too were to discover that he could be both decisive and ruthless. In 1582 Francesco's only legitimate son had died; the son of

Francesco's second wife, Bianca Capello, was then legitimized. When both Francesco and Bianca died suddenly in 1587, Ferdinando quickly found witnesses to swear that the boy was not, in fact, Francesco's son (and soon entered him, for good measure, in the celibate Order of the Knights of S Stefano). Ferdinando himself had never taken priestly vows and was thus able, with Pope Sixtus V's permission, to doff his cardinalate (which was conferred on Francesco Maria del Monte) and become Grand Duke of Tuscany.

Ferdinando's coup was popular with his new subjects, who had come increasingly to detest his brother. He proved an able administrator and with firmness and efficiency secured for Tuscany stability and prosperity at home and independence and respect abroad. He spent as lavishly as Francesco had, but was less resented for it, perhaps because his projects tended to be of a more public and lasting nature, and many more of them were brought to completion. In fact, several were based on his brother's initiatives. He regularized the haphazard grouping of craft workshops in the Casino de' Medici by transferring them, together with painters' studios, to the newly completed Uffizi, under the supervision of a single Soprintendente. In 1588 he founded a workshop, later known as the Opificio di Pietre Dure (see FLORENCE, §III, 2(i)), for the control and encouragement of workers in hardstones. He had Bernardo Buontalenti execute the planned Forte di Belvedere (1590–95) above the Boboli Gardens, and in 1596 he held a second competition for the façade of Florence Cathedral. (This was won by his half-brother (18) Giovanni de' Medici; work was eventually begun to the latter's design, but soon abandoned.) Above all, Ferdinando continued his predecessor's development of the port of LIVORNO from virtually nothing into an international trading centre. Even more important was the city's internal rearrangement: in 1594 Francesco had begun the rebuilding of the cathedral by Alessandro Pieroni (1550–1607) to Buontalenti's design; but it was under Ferdinando that the symmetrical Piazza Grande (in the centre of town) in front of it was laid out, with mixed commercial and residential properties encased in a consistent architectural configuration. This was soon imitated by Ferdinando's nephew-in-law, Henry IV, King of France, in the Place Royale (1605; now Place des Vosges), Paris, and subsequently by Inigo Jones at Covent Garden, London (1631), both with dramatic effect on European urban planning.

Livorno also contained another influential feature, an over life-size marble statue (1595–9) of Ferdinando by Giovanni Bandini in the Piazza Micheli, overlooking the port. Inspired by his love of the Antique and knowledge of Roman monuments, Ferdinando replaced painting with sculpture as the dynastic image-maker. Two other large statues of himself, by Pietro Francavilla to Giambologna's designs, had been set up in Arezzo (1590–95; Piazza del Duomo) and Pisa (1594–5; Piazza Carrara). The latter accompanied a similar figure of *Cosimo I* by the same artists, surmounting a fountain before the Palazzo dei Cavalieri (1593–6). Cosimo had been even more influentially immortalized by his son in Giambologna's superb bronze equestrian statue in Florence (1587–95; Piazza della Signoria; see GIAMBOLOGNA, fig. 5). Ferdinando was

portrayed in similar guise, the metal supposedly from Turkish arms captured by his victorious fleet (1601–8; Florence, Piazza SS Annunziata). While Giambologna was working on the latter (completed by Pietro Tacca), he was commissioned to produce comparable statues of *Henry IV* (destr. 1792) and *Philip III* (1606–17; Madrid, Plaza Mayor). These conquering images were to become a staple of Baroque portraiture.

Ferdinando sat for only one official portrait painting, by Scipione Pulzone, a pair with that of his wife (1590; Florence, Uffizi). He had married Christine of Lorraine (Catherine de' Medici's granddaughter) in 1589, with festivities more lavish than any before, including processions, masques, theatrical intermezzi and a mock sea battle in the flooded courtyard of Palazzo Pitti. Equally lavish, though more sober, ceremonies marked the obsequies of Philip II (1598) and the marriage of Marie de' Medici and Henry IV (1600). Most splendid of all were those celebrating the wedding (1608) of Ferdinando's son (19) Cosimo II de' Medici to Maria Maddalena of Austria, which culminated in a mock battle on the Arno between numerous fancifully decorated ships. The true splendour of the Medici, however, was expressed in the Cappella dei Principi at S Lorenzo (begun 1604), a huge octagonal mausoleum in which the tombs of the Grand Dukes were to be preserved in the gloomy opulence of imperishable pietre dure.

BIBLIOGRAPHY
C. Hibbert: *The Rise and Fall of the House of Medici* (London, 1974)
G. M. Andres: *The Villa Medici in Rome*, 2 vols (New York, 1976)
J. R. Hale: *Florence and the Medici: The Pattern of Control* (London, 1977)
Theater Art of the Medici, (exh. cat., Hanover, NH, Dartmouth Coll., Hood Mus. A., 1980)
K. Langedijk: *The Portraits of the Medici, 15th to 18th Centuries*, 3 vols (Florence, 1981–7)
E. L. Goldberg: *Patterns in Late Medici Art Patronage* (Princeton, 1983)

□

(18) Giovanni de' Medici (*b* Florence, 1566; *d* Murano, 1621). Illegitimate son of (14) Cosimo I de' Medici. His mother was Leonora degli Albizzi. Although legitimized, he played no role in Florentine politics and instead embarked on a military and diplomatic career outside Tuscany. His activities as an amateur architect, however, all fell within Tuscany. He studied at the Accademia del Disegno in Florence. In 1590 he designed the Fortezza Nuova at the port of Livorno, his only contribution to military architecture, and in 1593 he designed the façade of S Stefano, Pisa. In 1596 he won the competition for the façade of Florence Cathedral over entries submitted by Bernardo Buontalenti, Giovanni Antonio Dosio, Lodovico Cigoli and Giovanni da Bologna (1524–1608); work began but was abandoned. In 1602 Giovanni was invited to redesign the cupola and piazza of S Maria di Provenzano, Siena. His major architectural achievement was the monumental Cappella dei Principi at S Lorenzo, Florence, which was built by MATTEO NIGETTI from 1604 to a revision of Giovanni's design (1597; Florence, Bib. N. Cent.) as a mausoleum to the Medici Grand Dukes (see FLORENCE, §IV, 5). Excepting the lavish marble revetment of the Cappella dei Principi and the utilitarian nature of the Fortezza, the richly decorative and sculptural quality of Giovanni's works have their origins in the architecture of Michelangelo, Vasari and such later 16th-century architects as Buontalenti and Giovanni da Bologna.

BIBLIOGRAPHY

A. Venturi: *Storia* (1901–40), xi, pp. 587–94

K. Langedijk: *The Portraits of the Medici, 15th to 18th centuries*, ii (Florence, 1983), pp. 1020–26

ROGER J. CRUM

(19) Cosimo II de' Medici, Grand Duke of Tuscany (*b* Florence, 12 May 1590; *reg* 1609–21; *d* Florence, 28 Feb 1621). Son of (17) Ferdinando I de' Medici. His comparatively brief reign was a period of peace and prosperity for Tuscany, thanks largely to the political and economic policies adopted by his father and to the guidance of his mother, Christine of Lorraine. Although the family's own banking activities ceased, Tuscan commercial interests were served by peace between France and Spain and a foreign policy that sought friendly relations with trading centres in the Levant. Cosimo's marriage, celebrated in Florence on 19 October 1608, to the Archduchess Maria Maddalena of Austria (1587–1633), sister of Emperor Ferdinand II, allied the family with the Habsburg dynasty.

Cosimo upheld the reputation of the Medici as patrons of learning by his protection of Galileo Galilei, whom he appointed Professor of Philosophy and Mathematics at the University of Pisa and for whom he later had a telescope set up at Arcetri. In return Galileo christened the four satellites of Jupiter, discovered in 1610, the *Medicea Sidera*. Cosimo also inherited his family's interest in art patronage both for the glorification of the dynasty and for pleasure. During his reign, work on the Medici funerary chapel, the Cappella dei Principi, in S Lorenzo continued under Matteo Nigetti, and Pietro Tacca completed the bronze monument to *Ferdinando I* (1601–8; Florence, Piazza della Signoria) begun by Giambologna. Decorations for court festivals and official celebrations were commissioned from Giulio Parigi, who, together with the painter Lodovico Cigoli, had organized the festivities that accompanied Cosimo's marriage. Parigi also remodelled the villa that was acquired for the Archduchess Maria Maddalena in 1619 and known thereafter as Poggio Imperiale. In 1611 Cosimo appointed the Flemish artist Jacques Bijlivert designer to the Medici pietre dure workshops and in 1620 made the Fleming Giusto Suttermans his court painter (for his portrait of Maria Maddalena *see* SUTTERMANS, GIUSTO, fig. 1). In these appointments, as in his patronage at large, Cosimo revealed the breadth of his interest in contemporary painting. He was a patron of the Florentine artists Agostino Tassi and the young Giovanni da San Giovanni, and of Neapolitan painters, including Giovanni Battista Caracciolo and Filippo Napoletano, both of whom he summoned to court in 1617. His acquisition of paintings by Gerrit van Honthorst indicated an interest in the north European followers of Caravaggio, while his patronage of Cornelis van Poelenburch showed also a taste for northern landscape painting. From 1611 or 1612 the graphic artist Jacques Callot was working at Cosimo's court and dedicated his etching of the *Fair at Impruneta* (1620; e.g. Washington, DC, N.G.A.) to the Grand Duke, for which Cosimo rewarded him with a medal. After Cosimo's early death in 1621, the economizing measures introduced by his wife and mother, who acted as co-regents during the minority of his son (22) Ferdinando de' Medici, clouded the animated cultural life at court and obliged many of his artists to leave Florence.

BIBLIOGRAPHY

H. Acton: *The Last Medici* (London, 1932, rev. 3/1980)

A. Banti: *Giovanni da San Giovanni* (Florence, 1977)

P. Bigongiari: *Il Seicento fiorentino* (Florence, 1982)

E. Goldberg: *Patterns in Late Medici Art Patronage* (Princeton, 1983)

R. Contini: *Bilivert* (Florence, 1985)

E. Galasso Calderara: *La Granduchessa Maria Maddalena d'Austria* (Genoa, 1985)

JANET SOUTHORN

(20) Cardinal **Carlo de' Medici** (*b* Florence, 19 March 1596; *d* Florence, 17 June 1666). Son of (17) Ferdinando I de' Medici. His mother was Christine of Lorraine. He was created cardinal in 1615. While in Rome, he lived at the Villa Medici or the Palazzo Madama, both inherited from his father. In Florence he resided in the Casino di S Marco, which he bought in 1621. In the following years he had this building decorated with frescoes by Florentine artists, including Fabrizio Boschi (1570–1642), Matteo Rosselli, Anastagio Fontebuoni (1580–1626), Ottavio Vannini and Michelangelo Cinganelli (*c.* 1580–1635). Here he kept his rich library and his collection of more than 300 paintings, most of which are now in public galleries in Florence. Among contemporary artists Cardinal Carlo showed an interest in Florentine and Emilian painters (especially Guido Reni); he also had a passion for the Florentine painting of the first half of the 16th century, especially that of Andrea del Sarto, several of whose works he possessed. In addition to paintings of sacred and secular subjects, the collection contained various portraits of members of the Medici family, an unusual number of landscape paintings of medium and large size and some small landscapes on copper. In Rome, Cardinal Carlo employed the architect Paolo Maruscelli to enlarge the Palazzo Madama (1636–42; for illustration *see* MARUSCELLI, PAOLO). Between 1638 and 1641 he had the *piano nobile* decorated with fresco paintings by Giovanni Antonio Lelli (?1591–1640), Pietro Paolo Baldini, Raffaelle Vanni and Giovanni Antonio Galli.

BIBLIOGRAPHY

G. Pieraccini: *La stirpe de' Medici di Cafaggiolo* (Florence, 1924–5), ii, pp. 411–33

A. R. Masetti: 'Il Casino Mediceo e la pittura fiorentina del seicento', *Crit. A.*, ix/50 (1962), pp. 1–27; ix/53–4 (1962), pp. 77–109

M. Chiarini: 'Filippo Napoletano e il Cardinale Carlo de' Medici', *Paragone*, cccxiii (1976), pp. 61–7

E. Fumagalli: 'Affreschi dello Spadarino in Palazzo Madama', *Paragone*, cdxxxv (1986), pp. 28–39

—: *La 'fabbrica' di Palazzo Medici in Piazza Madama a Roma* (diss., Florence, U. Studi, 1986)

—: 'Pittori senesi del seicento e committenza medicea: Nuove date per Francesco Rustici', *Paragone*, 479–81 (1990), pp. 69–82

—: 'La Villa Médicis au XVIIe siècle', *La Villa Médicis*, ii: *Etudes* (Rome, 1991), pp. 568–86

—: 'Guido Reni e il cardinale Carlo de' Medici', *Paragone*, 527–31 (1994)

ELENA FUMAGALLI

(21) Lorenzo de' Medici (*b* Florence, 1 Aug 1599; *d* Florence, 15 Nov 1648). Son of (17) Ferdinando I de' Medici. In 1609, aged ten, he inherited from his father the beautiful Villa della Petraia, near Florence, which he made his country home. His private residence in Florence was the present Palazzo Corsini in the Via del Parione. Unfortunately, there is no known inventory for this house covering the period when it belonged to Lorenzo; it is known, however, that he used it as the meeting-place for a theatrical academy. Always a bachelor, despite matrimonial negotiations (1624–8) with the Princess of Stigliano, he showed no interest in politics but devoted his energies to sports, hunting and patronage of art and the theatre, becoming renowned as an organizer of festivities and entertainments. Most of the important information on his activities as an art patron comes from analysing the collection he kept at the Villa della Petraia. Among his favourite artists, almost all contemporary Florentines, were Giovanni da San Giovanni, Carlo Dolci, Francesco Furini, Cesare Dandini, Baldassarre Franceschini and Stefano della Bella, who was among the artists maintained by Lorenzo's court from 1629. He also showed a certain interest in Flemish artists, especially after 1626, when he escorted his sister Claudia to her betrothed, the Archduke Leopold of Austria. His most important artistic commission was of the fresco cycle in the courtyard of the Villa della Petraia, depicting *Splendours of the House of Medici* (1636–46) by Franceschini.

BIBLIOGRAPHY

E. Borea: 'Dipinti alla Petraia per Don Lorenzo de' Medici: Stefano della Bella, Vincenzo Mannozzi, i Dandini e altri', *Prospettiva*, ii (1975), pp. 24–38

La quadreria di Don Lorenzo de' Medici (exh. cat. by E. Borea, A. M. Petrioli Tofani and K. Kangedijk, Poggio a Caiano, Mus. Villa Medicea, 1977)

SILVA MASCALCHI

(22) Ferdinando II de' Medici, Grand Duke of Tuscany (*b* Florence, 14 July 1610; *reg* 1621–70; *d* Pisa, 24 May 1670). Son of (19) Cosimo II de' Medici. His father's death marked the start of a long regency that extended beyond Ferdinando's majority (1628). The regency was conservative in all aspects of governance and continued to patronize Tuscan artists who had been supported by Cosimo II. From 1621 to 1630 there was little artistic activity at the court apart from theatre spectacles, for which scenery was designed by Giulio Parigi and his son Alfonso the younger. Successive plague epidemics (1631–3) and economic depression in the linen and wool industries provoked a vigorous response from the young Grand Duke: a dole and a government-supported public works programme were established, the latter including construction of the Monte Reggi aqueduct and the installation of new public fountains. In addition the Palazzo Pitti (*see* FLORENCE, §IV, 9 and fig. 23) was expanded from a 7- to a 23-bay façade, the Boboli Gardens were reorganized and an amphitheatre built. Most of this programme (largely completed in the 1640s) was stylistically conservative. The enlargement of the palazzo, under the Parigi family, repeated the original Quattrocento façade design; the amphitheatre has frequently been mistaken for a Cinquecento construction. The Moses Grotto in the Palazzo Pitti courtyard received sculpture by Antonio Novelli, Giovanni Battista Pieratti (*d* 1662), Domenico Pieratti, Raffaello Curradi (1570–1661) and Cosimo Salvestrini (*fl* 1650). Above the grotto the Artichoke Fountain, in the traditional candelabrum form, by Francesco Susini was installed. Two monumental sculptures originally commissioned from Giambologna were adapted (the *Dovizia*, which was recut by Pietro Tacca) and repositioned (the Ocean Fountain) in the garden (1637). New fountains in the city included two sea monster fountains originally planned for Livorno by Tacca but installed in the Piazza SS Annunziata (1639–41); Tacca's *Porcellino*, modelled from an antique sculpture and installed in the Mercato Nuovo (1639); and an antique sculpture group of *Menelaus and Patroclus* used to mark a fountain head at the Ponte Vecchio. Tacca also made two monumental statues of Grand Dukes *Cosimo II* and *Ferdinando I* for the Cappella dei Principi, begun in 1626 but not completed until 1644, under Pietro's son, Ferdinando Tacca.

In painting a conservative patronage pattern obtained until the late 1630s. At the Palazzo Pitti, Matteo Rosselli worked with Giovanni da San Giovanni, who was commissioned to fresco the public rooms of the summer apartments in his highly informal style. However, on Giovanni's death (1636), the room he had partially completed was programmatically revised and turned over to younger Florentine artists: Francesco Furini, Cecco Bravo and Ottavio Vannini. Thereafter Florentine artists were employed in secondary areas of the palace, and the completion of the summer apartment decorations was assigned to the internationally fashionable Bolognese *quadratura* specialists Angelo Michele Colonna and Agostino Stanzani Mitelli. The decoration of the public rooms on the *piano nobile* was given to the Rome-based Tuscan artist Pietro da Cortona and subsequently completed by his pupil Ciro Ferri (*see* CORTONA, PIETRO DA, fig. 2). The work of these artists (1637–65) brought the Roman High Baroque to Florence and had a profound influence on Florentine art, notably that of Stefano della Bella and Baldassare Franceschini, both patronized by Ferdinando II; but several artists were unaffected by the intrusion of the Roman Baroque, notably the Grand Duke's portrait painter, Giusto Suttermans, whose style was Rubensian, and Carlo Dolci, who continued to produce portraits and religious paintings in his painstakingly brilliant manner.

During Ferdinando's reign the efforts of Florentine architects and sculptors were heavily invested in the Cappella dei Principi at S Lorenzo, a project initiated in 1604. The public works projects of 1630–40 and the War of Castro (1641–4) exhausted the grand-ducal treasury and curtailed other large-scale projects.

BIBLIOGRAPHY

R. Galluzzi: *Istoria del granducato di Toscana sotto il governo della Casa Medici* (Florence, 1781, 2/1823)

M. Campbell: 'Medici Patronage and the Baroque: A Reappraisal', *A. Bull.*, xlviii (1966), pp. 133–46

Artisti alla corte granducale (exh. cat., ed. M. Chiarini; Florence, Pitti, 1969), pp. 23–5

E. Cochrane: *Florence in the Forgotten Centuries, 1527–1800: A History of Florence and the Florentines in the Age of the Grand Dukes* (Chicago and London, 1973)

M. Campbell: *Pietro da Cortona at the Pitti Palace* (Princeton, 1977)

E. Goldberg: *Patterns in Late Medici Art Patronage* (Princeton, 1983)

MALCOLM CAMPBELL

(23) Cardinal **Giovanni Carlo de' Medici** (*b* Florence, 13 April 1611; *d* Florence, 23 Jan 1663). Son of (19) Cosimo II de' Medici. He became a cardinal in 1644, yet his main interests were in collecting paintings, books and furnishings and in the art of the theatre. In 1629 he bought the Villa di Mezzomonte, which Francesco Albani, Giovanni da San Giovanni and Angelo Michele Colonna decorated with mythological frescoes, and around this time began to collect pictures. He housed the most precious works in the Casino in Via della Scala, Florence, acquired in 1640, where Pietro da Cortona frescoed an *Allegory of Tranquillity* (1643). A huge statue of *Polyphemus* by Antonio Novelli adorns the garden. In 1645 Pietro da Cortona decorated an apartment for the Prince in the Palazzo Pitti, Florence; the lunette frescoes have been attributed to Salvator Rosa. Giovanni Carlo's collection of more than 560 paintings, which, unusually, did not become part of the family patrimony but was auctioned on his death, included Raphael's *Madonna with a Goldfinch* (Florence, Uffizi), Nicolas Poussin's *Adoration of the Shepherds* (London, N.G.) and works by Correggio, Parmigianino, Veronese and Rubens. Salvator Rosa painted a series of works for Giovanni Carlo between 1641 and 1645, among them *Alexander and Diogenes* and *Cincinnatus Called from the Plough* (both Althorp House, Northants). Guido Reni's *Sibyl* (London, D. Mahon priv. col.; see Mascalchi, fig. 5) appears to have been commissioned from the artist. In 1654 he and his brother (25) Leopoldo de' Medici purchased the collection of Paolo del Sera. The opening of the Teatro della Pergola (1658) in Florence, designed by Ferdinando Tacca, was due to Giovanni Carlo.

BIBLIOGRAPHY
G. Pieraccini: *La stirpe de' Medici di Cafaggiolo*, 3 vols (Florence, 1924–5), ii, pp. 553–77
M. Chiarini and K. Noehles: 'Pietro da Cortona a Palazzo Pitti: Un episodio ritrovato', *Boll. A.*, iii (1967), pp. 233–9
S. Mascalchi: 'Giovan Carlo de' Medici: An Outstanding but Neglected Collector in Seventeenth Century Florence', *Apollo*, cxx (1984), pp. 268–72

(24) Mattias de' Medici (*b* Florence, 9 May 1613; *d* Siena, 11 Oct 1667). Son of (19) Cosimo II de' Medici. In 1630 he became Governor of Siena, where he lived for most of his life. Fascinated by engraving, he collected works by Stefano della Bella, Giulio Parigi and Giuliano Periccioli and was himself an amateur engraver. He encouraged artistic interchange between Florence and Siena and collected ivory objects of vertu and glassware. Between 1632 and 1639 Mattias was in Germany, where he fought in the crucial battles of the Thirty Years War (1618–48). In 1644, as a reward for military victories in the War of Castro (1641–4), his brother (22) Ferdinando II de' Medici presented him with the villa of Lappeggi, near Florence. His interest turned to painting, and he paid for the training of Livio Mehus, many works by whom are listed in the inventory of Mattias's possessions made in 1669. A soldier, he was particularly interested in battle painting, and Jacques Courtois, who, like Mattias, had experienced military combat, was employed by him in the 1650s. Baldinucci stated that Mattias delighted in the vivid naturalism of Courtois's four paintings of battles in which the Prince had fought. Two sets of such paintings have been identified (Rudolph, 1972), four pictures on canvas (Florence, Uffizi) and four frescoed battle scenes in a room in the villa of Lappeggi. This room also contains a damaged fresco, which may be identified as *Victory and Fame* by Baldassare Franceschini, described by Baldinucci. In his country residence Mattias gathered a collection of pictures that included, among many landscape and battle paintings, works by Astolfo Petrazzi, Raffaelle Vanni, Giovanni Domenico Cerrini and Giacinto Gimignani.

UNPUBLISHED SOURCE
Florence, Archv Stato, MS. Guardaroba 703 [*Inventario della Guardaroba del Principe Don Mattia*, 1669]

BIBLIOGRAPHY
F. Baldinucci: *Notizie* (1681–1728); ed. F. Ranalli (1845–7), v, pp. 204–19
A. Solerti: *Musica, ballo e drammatica alla corte medicea dal 1600 al 1637* (Florence, 1905)
G. Pieraccini: *La stirpe de' Medici di Cafaggiolo* (Florence, 1924–5), ii
S. Rudolph: 'A Medici General, Prince Mattias, and his Battle-Painter, il Borgognone', *Stud. Seicent.*, xiii (1972), pp. 183–92

SILVA MASCALCHI

(25) Cardinal **Leopoldo de' Medici** (*b* Florence, 6 Nov 1617; *d* Florence, 10 Dec 1675). Son of (19) Cosimo II de' Medici. His education was unusually wide-ranging, including instruction in painting by Sigismondo Coccapani and in the natural sciences by disciples of Galileo Galilei. He served his eldest brother (22) Ferdinando II de' Medici as Governor of Siena in 1637 and 1644 and made official visits to Modena in 1639, Innsbruck in 1646, and an informal visit to Rome in 1650. He was created a cardinal in 1667 (though he did not take priestly orders until 1674) and achieved much influence in the Curia during his visits to Rome in 1668 and 1669–70.

Leopoldo was an energetic patron of literature, the natural sciences and the fine arts. He wrote poetry himself and long served as the Medici representative in the Accademia della Crusca, the academy of Tuscan language and literature. He and Ferdinando shared a keen interest in natural philosophy, and Leopoldo presided over the Accademia del Cimento (active 1657–67), Europe's first academy of experimental science. He was an amateur artist of some talent, as can be seen from his one known painting, the portrait of the singer *Martelli* (Florence, Uffizi). Many of his papers (Florence, Archv Stato and Accad. Crusca) contain casual drawings, caricatures, landscape drawings and designs for scientific instruments. His celebrated collections, housed primarily in his apartment in the Palazzo Pitti, included Classical antiquities, paintings, drawings, ivories, ceramics and a noted library of books. His most sustained interest was in Classical antiquities, mostly coins and engraved gems, although he owned notable sculptures, including the Ludovisi *Hermaphrodite* and the *Venus* of the Casa Palmieri-Bolognini (Florence, Uffizi). From 1651 to 1656 Father Peter Fytton supervised his acquisition of antiquities; he later relied on the antiquarians Francesco Gottifredi, Ottavio Falconieri, Leonardo Agostini, Pietro Andrea Andreini and Francesco Camelli. The last catalogued the collection of coins and gems (many examples, Florence, Mus. Archeol. and Bargello), which in 1671 were arranged in two specially designed cabinets (untraced).

Leopoldo began purchasing significant paintings in 1639, when he commissioned Guido Reni's *Cleopatra* (Florence, Pitti). At his death he owned 700 pictures, including distinguished 16th-century Venetian works acquired in the 1640s and 1650s through Paolo del Sera, a Medici agent in Venice. In 1654 he and his brother (23) Giovanni Carlo de' Medici bought del Sera's famous collection, including Titian's *Concert* (1508–11; Florence, Pitti), Giovanni Girolamo Savoldo's *Transfiguration* (1525–8) and Paolo Veronese's *Annunciation* (*c*. 1555; both Florence, Uffizi). Though Leopoldo owned contemporary Florentine paintings, his patronage of living artists was relatively modest. Balthasar Stockamer, however, carved many ivories for him in the late 1660s, including a large *Crucifixion* (Florence, Pitti), designed by Ciro Ferri.

The collection of drawings, a comprehensive one organized in accordance with Giorgio Vasari's principles of historical progress, was begun in 1658 and grew rapidly with the help of agents throughout Italy and in the Netherlands, to whom, in 1662, Leopoldo circulated lists of the works collected to date so that they could attempt to fill in the gaps. By 1663 he owned drawings attributed to 308 artists; by 1673 he had 8143 drawings attributed to 535 artists; and in 1675 he had 11,247 drawings attributed to 654 artists. They were organized, after his death, into 105 volumes by Filippo Baldinucci and Lorenzo Gualtieri and now form the core of the Uffizi collection, though the volumes were dismantled in the 19th century. The most highly valued were the Venetian, Florentine and Emilian drawings, mainly figure drawings and compositional studies from the 16th and 17th centuries. There were many 17th-century Florentine drawings by such artists as Lodovico Cigoli, Cristofano Allori and Bernardino Poccetti. Among the non-Italian drawings were some outstanding examples of Jacques Callot and Claude Lorrain.

In 1664 Leopoldo set out to form a gallery of self-portraits by all noteworthy artists, past and some present, which should reflect their creators' essential style. Again the main strength of the collection was 16th- and 17th-century Italian, with Tuscan and Emilian artists being most prominent and including specially commissioned portraits of Guercino and Pietro da Cortona (1664; Florence, Uffizi; the Guercino is possibly a copy). Self-portraits by foreign artists included those of Rembrandt, Jusepe de Ribera and Robert Nanteuil. The gallery, finally numbering 130 examples arranged in chronological sequence, was celebrated for its rarity, originality of conception and scholarly significance. After Leopoldo's death, the whole collection was moved to the Uffizi and greatly augmented. From the mid-1660s, too, he collected painted portrait miniatures (Florence, Uffizi), which by 1673 numbered *c.* 700 and were mostly installed in a specially designed cabinet (untraced).

Leopoldo's collecting demonstrated an exceptional historical consciousness and methodological rigour, reflecting his scientific and antiquarian experience. He is often cited as a pioneer of modern connoisseurship and museum practice. A feature of his practice was the extensive use of a network of Medici dependants (Ferdinando Cospi, Annibale Ranuzzi and Carlo Malvasia in Bologna; Paolo Falconieri in Rome; Paolo del Sera and Marco Boschini in Venice), co-ordinated from the early 1670s by Baldinucci, his curator and agent in Florence. Committees met throughout Italy to share art-historical information and to attribute available drawings and portraits. It was through this kind of involvement with his patron's interests that Baldinucci came to produce his *Notizie de' professori del disegno* (Florence, 1681–1728), which represented a successful outcome to Leopoldo's efforts to promote a publication that would update Vasari's *Vite* (Florence, 1550). The systematic organization of Leopoldo's collections, albeit motivated by a desire to suggest the perfection of the arts under Medici patronage, influenced the subsequent development of Florentine art historiography. Leopoldo was depicted posthumously by Giovanni Battista Foggini (1897; Florence, Uffizi; *see* FLORENCE, fig. 9).

BIBLIOGRAPHY

W. E. K. Middleton: 'A Cardinalate for Prince Leopoldo de' Medici', *Studi Seicent.*, xi (1970), pp. 167–80
——: *The Experimenters: A Study of the Accademia del Cimento* (Baltimore, 1971)
S. Parodi: *Accademia della Crusca: Inventario delle carte Leopoldiane* (Florence, 1975)
Omaggio a Leopoldo de' Medici (exh. cat., ed. A. Forlani Tempesti, A. M. Petrioli Tofani and S. Meloni Trkulja; Florence, Uffizi, 1975) [Leopoldo's drgs and portrait miniatures]
E. L. Goldberg: *Patterns in Late Medici Art Patronage* (Princeton, 1983)
L. Giovanni, ed.: *Lettere di Ottavio Falconieri a Leopoldo de' Medici*, Carteggio d'artisti dell'Archivio di Stato di Firenze, x (Florence, 1984) [important introductory ess.]
E. L. Goldberg: *After Vasari: History, Art and Patronage in Late Medici Florence* (Princeton, 1988)

EDWARD L. GOLDBERG

(26) Vittoria della Rovere, Grand Duchess of Tuscany (*b* Urbino, 7 Feb 1622; *d* Pisa, 5 March 1694). Wife of (22) Ferdinando II de' Medici. She was the daughter of Federigo-Ubaldo della Rovere (1604–48) and Claudia de' Medici. She is best known as the last heir of the art collection assembled by her family in Urbino and as the person who, through marriage, passed them on to the Grand Duchy of Tuscany. Always interested in worldly and cultural affairs, she spoke Spanish and French, knew Latin and sponsored a variety of *literati*, becoming patroness in 1654 of a literary academy in Siena called Le Assicurate, devoted exclusively to women. As a patron she commissioned various decorations: for example, Baldassare Franceschini worked on a series of commissions for her, including painting the ceiling (*c.* 1657–8) of the Sala delle Allegorie in the Palazzo Pitti, Florence. Between 1681 and 1683 she commissioned the decoration of certain rooms in the villa at Poggio Imperiale near Florence, including the ground-floor *salone*, which was frescoed by the Roman artist Francesco Coralli. Vittoria was also protectress of the Conservatorio della Quiete, near Florence, and sponsored the building of the church, begun in 1686 under Pierfrancesco Silvani. Many portraits of her have survived. Among the most famous likenesses are those by Francesco Furini (1645; Florence, Uffizi), Carlo Dolci (*c.* 1642; Vienna, Ksthist. Mus.; *c.* 1674; Florence, Pitti) and Giusto Suttermans, who portrayed her several times (e.g. *c.* 1640–42; Florence, Uffizi) from childhood onwards. There are also portrait sculptures by Giovanni Battista Foggini (*c.* 1681; Florence, Uffizi) and one in pietre dure (Florence, Conserv. Quiete) created posthumously by Giuseppe Antonio Torricelli, who also portrayed the Grand Duchess, in her later years, on a cameo.

BIBLIOGRAPHY

G. Menichetti: *Firenze e Urbino: Gli ultimi rovereschi e la corte medicea* (Fabriano, 1927)
O. Panichi: 'Due stanze della Villa del Poggio Imperiale', *Ant. Viva*, v (1973), pp. 32–43
K. Langedijk: 'Giovanni Battista Foggini: The Monument to Vittoria della Rovere at the Villa La Quiete and the Busts from Poggio Imperiale', *Mitt. Ksthist. Inst. Florenz*, xxiii (1979), pp. 347–56
——: *The Portraits of the Medici, 15th–18th Centuries*, ii (Florence, 1983)

SILVA MASCALCHI

(27) Cosimo III de' Medici, Grand Duke of Tuscany (*b* Florence, 14 Aug 1642; *reg* 1670–1723; *d* Florence, 31 Oct 1723). Son of (22) Ferdinando II de' Medici and (26) Vittoria della Rovere. He was a vigorous patron of the arts, concerned to uphold the splendour of his court and the prestige of Medici patronage. The considerable breadth of his interests in learning and the arts was influenced by the example of his uncle, (25) Cardinal Leopoldo de' Medici, and by a brilliant entourage, which included his secretary (from 1662) Apollonio Bassetti (1631–99) and the Florentine dilettante architect Paolo Falconieri (*see under* FALCONIERI). The bibliophile Antonio Magliabechi was his librarian, and the archivist and biographer of artists Filippo Baldinucci worked at his court. His interests were also stimulated by his youthful travels; in 1656, at the age of 14, he visited Rome in the company of the artists Stefano della Bella and Livio Mehus. On 20 June 1661 his marriage to Marguerite-Louise d'Orléans was celebrated in Florence; the splendour of the accompanying festivities is preserved in Stefano della Bella's etchings, *Il mondo festeggiante*. The marriage had been arranged by his father in the interests of an alliance with France, but the incompatibility of the couple was soon evident, and as a means of easing tensions Ferdinando sent Cosimo on further travels. In 1664 he travelled in northern Italy; between October 1667 and May 1668 he travelled in Germany, where he met Queen Christina of Sweden in Hamburg, and in the Low Countries; from September 1668 to November 1669 he travelled in Spain, Portugal, England (where Samuel Pepys saw him in London and noted in his diary for 5/15 April 1669 that he seemed 'a very jolly and good comely man'), France and the Netherlands. In England he acquired topographical paintings and sat to Samuel Cooper for his portrait in miniature (Florence, Uffizi); in Leiden, on 22 June 1669, he met Frans van Mieris (i).

Cosimo acquired a lasting interest in northern European art and returned to Florence one of the most widely travelled princes in Europe. Through his agent, Francesco Terriesi, he ordered English books and paintings, including portraits by Sir Peter Lely (Florence, Pitti) and the portrait of the *Duchess of Portsmouth* (Florence, Uffizi) by the miniaturist Richard Gibson. He subsequently commissioned many pictures from van Mieris, including the *Sleeping Courtesan* (1669; Florence, Uffizi), though on one occasion the painter disappointed him by refusing, as uncongenial, a commission to paint an episode from the life of the Jesuit St Francis Xavier. In 1667 van Mieris complied with Cosimo's request for a *Self-portrait*, which, together with those of Gerrit Dou and Gerard ter Borch (ii), was added to the collection of artists' self-portraits begun by Cardinal Leopoldo (all Florence, Uffizi).

Cosimo's interest in the careers of Florentine artists is reflected by his establishment of the Accademia Fiorentina (1673–86) in the Palazzo Madama in Rome, where Florentine painters and sculptors trained under the direction of Ciro Ferri and Ercole Ferrata. This was crucial to the development of the Baroque in Florence, and the style of Cosimo's court, the *Stile Cosimo terzo*, blends the grandeur and seriousness of the Roman Baroque with the Mannerist elegance of Florentine court art. Ciro Ferri was himself the most distinguished artist patronized by Cosimo and in

1675 began the renovation of the choir chapel in S Maria Maddalena dei Pazzi, Florence. Cosimo also commissioned from him 14 tondi of the *Stations of the Cross* (three, Montelupo, SS Quirico e Lucia all'Ambrogiana; one, London, V&A) for the garden of the convent church of S Pietro d'Alcantra, near the Villa d'Ambrogiana, Montelupo, which were executed to his designs by students at the Accademia, among them Giuseppe Piamontini and Giovanni Camillo Cateni. Cosimo sent both Giovanni Battista Foggini and Massimiliano Soldani to study in Rome; Foggini succeeded Pietro Tacca as court sculptor, and also directed the Galleria dei Lavori, creating those elegant works in hardstone with which the *Stile Cosimo terzo* is particularly associated. Soldani was trained for the mint, in Rome and Paris (1682), and created outstanding medals, coins and elegant small bronzes for the Medici court. The architect Alessandro Galilei, who served as Superintendent of Buildings, also enjoyed Cosimo's patronage.

Among Florentine painters, Cosimo's tastes ranged from Carlo Dolci, whose religious paintings presumably appealed to his extreme piety, and Anton Domenico Gabbiani to the specialist in still-life painting Bartolommeo Bimbi. Bimbi's paintings of specimens of flowers and fruits, painted to adorn the casino, La Topaia, at the Medici Villa di Castello, reflect the scientific interests that Cosimo shared with other members of his family and with his physician, Francesco Redi (1626–98), and which are also present in Bimbi's portraits of natural curiosities (Florence, Mus. Botan.), such as animals born with two heads. A similar interest, or a taste for the bizarre, attracted Cosimo to the work of GAETANO ZUMBO, as represented in his wax relief of the *Plague* (Florence, Mus. Zool. La Specola), presented to Ferdinando II. Cosimo commissioned two similar works from the artist.

As a collector Cosimo continued Cardinal Leopoldo's work of systematizing the family collections, seeking to enlarge them wherever possible. The sculpture collection was reorganized, and in 1677 three Classical statues, the *Wrestlers*, the *Knife Sharpeners* and the *Venus de' Medici* (*see* ANTIQUE, THE, fig. 3) were transferred to Florence (all Florence, Uffizi) from the Villa Medici in Rome. In 1681 Falconieri, acting as art agent, was urged to redouble his efforts to find more artists' self-portraits, and a request to the painter Anton Domenico Gabbiani to inspect a picture by Veronese in Rome in 1718 shows that Cosimo's desire to enrich the family collections continued into his declining years.

Cosimo was formally separated from his wife in 1674, and thereafter the public image of the increasingly corpulent Grand Duke was that of a deeply religious man whose piety became more pronounced. In Florence he introduced ever stricter legislation to impose his standards of morality on his subjects. In 1713 his son and heir (28) Ferdinando de' Medici died without issue, as a result of which it was foreseen that the male line of the Medici would terminate with his dissolute second son, (30) Gian Gastone de' Medici. Cosimo negotiated an agreement that the succession should pass to the House of Bourbon, though in the event it passed to the House of Lorraine.

BIBLIOGRAPHY

H. Acton: *The Last Medici* (London, 1932, rev. 3/1980)
L. Lankheit: *Florentinische Barockplastik: Die Kunst am Hofe der letzten Medici, 1670–1743* (Munich, 1962)
S. Rudolph: 'Mecenati a Firenze tra Sei e Settecento', *A. Illus.*, xlix (1971), pp. 228–39; liv (1972), pp. 213–28
E. Cochrane: *Florence in the Forgotten Centuries, 1527–1800: A History of Florence and the Florentines in the Age of the Grand Dukes* (Chicago and London, 1973)
The Twilight of the Medici: Late Baroque Art in Florence, 1670–1743 (exh. cat., ed. S. F. Rossen; Detroit, MI, Inst. A.; Florence, Pitti; 1974)
P. Bigongiari: *Il seicento fiorentino* (Florence, 1982)
E. L. Goldberg: *Patterns in Late Medici Art Patronage* (Princeton, 1983)

JANET SOUTHORN

(28) Ferdinando de' Medici, Grand Prince of Tuscany (*b* Florence, 9 Aug 1663; *d* Florence, 30 Oct 1713). Son of (27) Cosimo III de' Medici. He was the last great personality of the Medici family and inherited the taste and spirit of his great-uncle (25) Cardinal Leopoldo de' Medici. His enlightened patronage made Florence once again an artistic centre and encouraged the development of the lighter, more vivid and painterly style of the 18th century.

Ferdinando's only journeys outside Tuscany were in 1688 and 1696 to Venice, where he developed a lasting enthusiasm for Venetian painting. In Florence, and in his country villas, he indulged his passion for collecting paintings and antique furnishings and for the patronage of contemporary artists and musicians. The theatre at his villa (destr.) at Pratolino, where the sets were designed by Francesco and Ferdinando Galli-Bibiena, was celebrated, and here he entertained scholars, painters and musicians, among them Alessandro Scarlatti.

Ferdinando enriched his picture collection by removing works from the churches and convents, which were compensated by copies or economic benefits. Outstanding works acquired in this way between 1690 and 1704 included Fra Bartolommeo's *St Mark*, Andrea del Sarto's *Madonna of the Harpies*, Lodovico Cigoli's *Deposition* (all Florence, Pitti), Parmigianino's *Madonna of the Long Neck* (see PARMIGIANINO, fig. 3) and Carlo Maratti's *Virgin with St Philip Neri* (both Florence, Uffizi). These works were displayed in his apartment in the Palazzo Pitti, Florence, in a symmetrical pattern devised by Giacinto Maria Marmi (*fl c.* 1650–1700), which involved enlarging and cutting down some of the pictures and creating special frames. Self-portraits by Giovanni Lanfranco, Mattia Preti, Sebastiano Ricci and Rosalba Carriera were among his additions to the self-portrait collection in the Uffizi.

In the villa at Poggio a Caiano Ferdinando assembled some 174 small pictures, densely patterned on the walls, in a small room (6×6 m): his 'gabinetto d'opere in piccolo'. This collection (now dispersed), for which he was indebted to the generosity of his brother-in-law, the Elector Palatine John William and the advice of NICCOLÒ CASSANA, included works of various schools (mainly Flemish, Dutch, Venetian and Bolognese) and periods; among them were Raphael's *La muta* (Urbino, Pal. Ducale), Dürer's *Virgin with the Pear* (Florence, Uffizi) and Titian's *Knight of Malta* (Madrid, Prado). His letters to Cassana and Sebastiano Ricci (Fogolari, 1937), who bought paintings for him in Venice, give a lively picture of his taste and learning. He discussed 16th-century Venetian paintings with Cassana, and his collection included many works attributed to Titian; his letters to Ricci, mostly from 1704 to 1708, discuss possible purchases and contain penetrating observations on the work of Giovanni Battista Moroni, Tintoretto, Johann Liss, Livio Mehus, Simon Vouet and other artists.

Ferdinando's patronage of contemporary artists revealed an increasing preference for freedom of handling and sumptuous colour. He nevertheless remained loyal to Anton Domenico Gabbiani, who, at Pratolino, painted five canvases of *Musicians* (1685–7; Florence, Pitti); these show instruments made for the Prince that now belong to the Florence Conservatory. Gabbiani, encouraged by Ferdinando, visited Venice in 1699 to improve his handling of colour. The year before he had frescoed the *Apotheosis of Cosimo il vecchio* for the Prince at the villa Poggio a Caiano (for illustration *see* GABBIANI, ANTON DOMENICO). Antonio Ferri (*d* 1716) and Giovanni Battista Foggini sculpturally enriched the 16th-century fountains at Pratolino, while Crescenzio Onofri, who had arrived at the Tuscan court in 1689, collaborated with Antonio Giusti, Francesco Petrucci (1660–1719) and Pietro Dandini on the decoration of the villa with landscape frescoes (destr.) and a series of vast canvases (Massa & Carrara, Ammin. Prov.). Cassana painted copies, portraits and history paintings for Ferdinando, among them the spirited *Portrait of a Cook* (1707; Florence, Pitti). The Prince's love of Venetian art is suggested by his purchase of pictures by Johann Carl Loth, whom he had met in Venice in 1688, including the *Flaying of Marsyas* (Florence, Pitti), and a number of Venetianizing works by Mehus. Alessandro Magnasco collaborated with Antonio Francesco Peruzzini on works for the Tuscan court in 1703, Magnasco painting a *Hunting Scene* (Hartford, CT, Wadsworth Atheneum) in which he portrayed himself, Sebastiano Ricci and Ferdinando. Ferdinando's greatest success, however, was his patronage of Sebastiano Ricci (*see* RICCI (i), (1)) and Giuseppe Maria Crespi (*see* CRESPI, (ii) (1)). Ricci decorated his small gallery at Poggio a Caiano with an *Allegory of the Arts* (destr.); his ceiling painting in the Palazzo Pitti, *Venus and Adonis* (1704–7), is one of the most elegant Rococo decorations in Tuscany. Crespi arrived at Pratolino in 1708, bearing as a gift his *Massacre of the Innocents* (1706; Florence, Uffizi; *see* CRESPI (ii), (1), fig. 2); during this visit he painted two compositions entitled *Still Life with Fish and Birds* (both untraced). Ferdinando admired his intimate and lively art, and Crespi sent further works from Bologna, returning by invitation to stay at Pratolino for eight months in 1709, on which visit he painted the *Fair at Poggio a Caiano* (Florence, Uffizi).

Ferdinando planned to have a large part of his collection engraved, under the direction of Foggini, and about 150 engravings were completed. Francesco Petrucci and Carlo Sacconi (*fl* 1697–1747) made most of the drawings; the engravers were Giovanni Antonio Lorenzini (1665–1740), Cosimo Mogalli, Giovanni Domenico Picchianti and Theodor Verkruys (*d* 1739). The inventory of Ferdinando's estate (Chiarini, 1975) includes more than a thousand paintings and drawings, sculptures, decorative objects and furnishings. Ferdinando's marriage was without issue, and the succession passed to his brother (30) Gian Gastone de' Medici.

BIBLIOGRAPHY

G. Pieraccini: *La stirpe de' Medici di Cafaggiolo* (Florence, 1924–5), ii, pp. 717–35

H. Acton: *The Last Medici* (London, 1932, rev. 3/1980)

G. Fogolari: 'Lettere pittoriche del Gran Principe Ferdinando di Toscana a Niccolò Cassana (1698–1709)', *Riv. Reale Ist. Archeol. & Stor. A.*, vi (1937), pp. 145–86

F. Haskell: *Patrons and Painters: A Study in the Relations between Italian Art and Society in the Age of the Baroque* (London, 1963, rev. New Haven and London, 1980)

Artisti alla corte granducale (exh. cat., ed. M. Chiarini; Florence, Pitti, 1969)

The Twilight of the Medici: Late Baroque Art in Florence, 1670–1743 (exh. cat., ed. S. F. Rossen; Detroit, MI, Inst. A.; Florence, Pitti; 1974)

M. Chiarini: 'I quadri della collezione del Gran Principe Ferdinando di Toscana', *Paragone*, xxvi/301 (1975), pp. 57–98; 303, pp. 73–108; 305, pp. 53–88

M. L. Strocchi: 'Il gabinetto d' "opere in piccolo" del Gran Principe Ferdinando di Toscana a Poggio a Caiano', *Paragone*, xxvi/309 (1975), pp. 115–26; xxvi/311 (1976), pp. 83–116

——: 'Pratolino alla fine del seicento e Ferdinando di Cosimo III', *Paradigma*, ii (1978), pp. 419–38

F. Borroni Salvadori: 'Riprodurre in incisione per far conoscere dipinti e disegni: Il settecento a Firenze', *Nouv. Répub. Lett.*, i (1982), pp. 7–69

F. Petrucci: 'La "ragione trionfante" alla corte medicea: Il Gran Principe Ferdinando e Giuseppe Maria Crespi', *Artibus & Hist.*, iii/5 (1982), pp. 109–23

M. L. Strocchi: 'Il Gran Principe Ferdinando collezionista e l'acquisizione delle pale d'altare', *La Galleria Palatina: Storia della quadreria granducale di Palazzo Pitti* (exh. cat., ed. M. Mosco; Florence, Pitti, 1983), pp. 42–9

MARIA LETIZIA STROCCHI

(29) Anna Maria Luisa de' Medici, Electress Palatine (*b* Florence, 11 Aug 1667; *d* Florence, 18 Feb 1743). Daughter of (27) Cosimo III de' Medici. She married John William, Elector Palatine of the Rhine (*see* WITTELSBACH, §II(3)), in Düsseldorf in 1691 but returned to Florence in 1717 after his death. She survived her brother (30) Gian Gastone de' Medici, the last Grand Duke, and remained the only Medici after Tuscany passed to the Duchy of Lorraine in 1737. In the tradition of her family, she took an active interest in the arts. As Electress Palatine she encouraged artistic exchange between Florence and Düsseldorf: works by Raphael, Andrea del Sarto, Domenichino and Federico Barocci were sent to the German city, while the Medici collections were enriched by Dutch and Flemish paintings. In Germany she collected mainly jewellery, forming one of the richest collections of the time (Florence, Pitti). In Florence she patronized many Tuscan artists: a series of bronzes on religious subjects was commissioned between 1722 and 1731 from Giovanni Battista Foggini, Massimiliano Soldani, Giuseppe Piamontini and others (now dispersed in museums throughout Europe and America). She ordered religious paintings from Matteo Bonechi, Ranieri del Pace, Giovanni Sagrestani, Giovanni Domenico Ferretti, Francesco Conti and others for the Conservatorio della Quiete, near Florence, which she arranged to have completely renovated (1721–8). Other commissions included studies of animals, vegetables and plants painted from life by Bartolomeo Bimbi and Gaspare Lopez (*d* 1732); self-portraits; and miniatures. Under Anna Maria Luisa's patronage various important works were undertaken in S Lorenzo, Florence, between 1738 and 1743: Vincenzo Meucci (1699–1766) frescoed the cupola, and Federico Ruggieri rebuilt the campanile (1740) and supervised various works in the Cappella dei Principi. Her name is associated with the family pact of 1737 that was made with the Lorraine, stipulating that the Medici art collections were to remain in Florence.

BIBLIOGRAPHY

H. Acton: *The Last Medici* (London, 1932, rev. 3/1980)

H. Kühn Steinhausen: *Eine deutsche Kurfürstin: Die letzte Medicäerin Anna Maria Luisa von der Pfalz, 1667–1743* (Düsseldorf and Linz, 1939)

K. Lankheit: 'Florentiner Bronzearbeiten für Kurfürsten Johann Wilhelm von der Pfalz: Zu den künstlerischen Beziehungen der Häuser Medici und Pfalz-Neuburg im Spät-Barock', *Münchn. Jb. Bild. Kst*, vii (1956), pp. 185–210

K. Aschengreen Piacenti: 'The Jewels of the Electress Palatine', *Apollo*, c (1974), pp. 230–33

J. Montagu: 'The Bronze Groups made for the Electress Palatine', *Kunst des Barock in der Toskana*, ed. H. Keutner (Munich, 1976), pp. 128–36

S. Meloni Trkulja: 'Anna Maria Luisa', *The Portraits of the Medici, 15th–18th Centuries*, ed. K. Langedijk, i (Florence, 1981), pp. 256–300

S. Casciu: 'Due episodi della scultura fiorentina del settecento nel mecenatismo di Anna Maria Luisa de' Medici', *Paragone*, xxxvii/435 (1986), pp. 83–100 [deals with her commission of a ser. of bronzes; doc.]

E. Ciletti: 'Cosimo III and the Electress Palatine's Objectives at S Lorenzo', *Paragone*, xxxvii/435 (1986), pp. 52–67

C. Vossen: *Anna Maria: Die letzte Medici Kurfürstin zu Düsseldorf* (Düsseldorf, 1987)

S. Casciu: *Anna Maria Luisa de' Medici: Elettrice Palantine (1667–1743)* (Florence, 1993) [with new bibliog.]

STEFANO CASCIU

(30) Gian Gastone de' Medici, Grand Duke of Tuscany (*b* Florence, 24 May 1671; *reg* 1723–37; *d* Florence, 9 July 1737). Son of (27) Cosimo III de' Medici. He showed promise as a youth, gaining a reputation for learning that ranged from antiquarian studies to an interest in the work of the mathematician Leibniz (1646–1716). At the same time, however, he was prone to bouts of hypochondria and gradually declined into a life of dissolution and drunkenness. To some extent this appears to have been due to his unhappy marriage, celebrated in Düsseldorf on 2 July 1697, to the unprepossessing Anna Maria of Saxe-Lauenburg, which necessitated his enforced absence from Florence and residence in remote Reichstadt and then in Prague. He returned to Florence in 1708 and on the death of his brother Ferdinando in 1713 was required to prepare himself for the succession ten years later. As Grand Duke, Gian Gastone repealed much of the legislation imposed by his father to control popular morality and relaxed literary censorship, while his political appointments were directed towards reducing church influence in his state. Measures were also taken by him to reduce the national debt, though the economies in court expenditure he introduced resulted in the departure from Florence of many artists and especially architects, including Alessandro Galilei and Ferdinando Fuga. His own artistic tastes are difficult to define, but he appears to have shared his brother's interest in the work of the Genoese painter Alessandro Magnasco and was a patron of the sculptor Giuseppe Piamontini. In 1729 he retired from public life and spent the last eight years of his reign in bed, entertained by the companies of young debauchees he had gathered about him and who were known as the *ruspanti* (from *ruspare*: 'to scratch about'). On his death the title passed to Francis Stephen, Duke of Lorraine (1708–65), husband of Maria-Theresa of Austria.

BIBLIOGRAPHY

H. Acton: *The Last Medici* (London, 1932, rev. 3/1980)

K. Lankheit: *Florentinische Barockplastik: Die Kunst am Hofe der letzten Medici, 1670–1743* (Munich, 1962)

E. Cochrane: *Florence in the Forgotten Centuries, 1527–1800: A History of Florence and the Florentines in the Age of the Grand Dukes* (Chicago and London, 1973)

JANET SOUTHORN

Medici, Catherine de', Queen of France. *See* VALOIS, (16).

Médici, Eduardo (*b* Buenos Aires, 15 Dec 1949). Argentine painter. He studied drawing and painting under Anselmo Piccoli (1915–93) and obtained a degree in psychology. His work occupies a transitional position between Neo-Expressionism and painting with a more symbolic emphasis and is characterized by an abstraction full of semiotic nuances. The lyricism of such works as *Buenos Aires Is a Fiesta* (1984; see Glusberg, 1985, p. 525) has a rhythmic measured structure. It depicts coloured areas that revolve around a more densely coloured nucleus, the expanding universe, as it were. Portrayal of movement is constant in the works of the 1980s, some of which also depict bodies whose contours merge into the harmonic fabric of the painting. In subsequent works Médici used a more clearly semiotic approach, combining anthropomorphic figures with numbers, letters, lines, crosses, spirals and various designs suggestive of animals or other forms.

BIBLIOGRAPHY
J. Glusberg: *Arte en Argentina: Del Pop art a la nueva imagen* (Buenos Aires, 1985); Eng. trans., abridged as *Art in Argentina* (Milan, 1986), pp. 121, 130–31

JORGE GLUSBERG

Medici, Gian Angelo de'. *See* PIUS IV.

Medici, Jacopo Filippo de'. *See* JACOPO FILIPPO D'ARGENTA.

Medici Society. English commercial enterprise, founded in 1908. The Society was established by Philip Lee Warner and his cousin by marriage, Eustace Gurney, with the purpose of publishing photographic reproductions of Old Master prints. The first 'Medici' prints had been commissioned in 1906 by Lee Warner from the offices of the publishers Chatto & Windus, London. These were reproduced by Hoesch of Milan using the COLLOTYPE process, which had recently been improved, permitting editions of several thousand to be run off and the introduction of full-colour prints of exceptional quality. Initially, colour separations were made directly from the paintings with the aid of huge cameras, and artists' copies of the paintings were used as colour guides for later retouching. Subscribers to the scheme received copies of Old Master prints as they were produced. The *Burlington Magazine* was quoted on the first prospectus: 'Nothing of the kind so good and so cheap has ever been issued before'. The membership scheme was later abandoned because of insufficient support, and the prints were then sold in shops and galleries. In 1909 Herbert Horne designed the Riccardi typeface for the Society. Subsequent book publications in this hand-set type included the Medici edition of Vasari's *Lives of the Artists* (1911–14). The Modern Art Society, a subsidiary company, was founded in 1917 in order to publish paintings by modern artists and subjects for children by such artists as Margaret Tarrant (1888–1959). The Modern Art Society was incorporated with the Medici Society in 1928, and the company continued to produce prints and a wide range of greetings cards.

BIBLIOGRAPHY
J. Gurney: *Margaret Tarrant and her Pictures* (London, 1982)
The Image Multiplied: Five Centuries of Printed Reproductions of Paintings and Drawings (exh. cat. by S. Lambert, London, V&A, 1987), pp. 29, 42, 110, 115, 158, 186, 191, 197

SOPHIE DICKENS

Medina [al-Madīna; al-Madīnat al-Munawwara (Arab.: 'The radiant city')]. City in Saudi Arabia and the second holiest city in Islam. It lies on the eastern edge of the Hijaz Mountains, and it was an agricultural oasis where the first Islamic society was established. In AD 622 the Prophet Muhammad emigrated there from Mecca with the nascent Muslim community, and the town, which had previously been known as Yathrib, was known thereafter as al Madinah ('City [of the Prophet]'). Its most esteemed building, the house and mosque of the Prophet, became the archetype for all subsequent mosques (*see* MOSQUE). It was an enclosure 100 cubits (*c.* 56 m) on a side, built of mud-brick with palm trunks to support a flat roof. Originally the building had a roofed area on the north to shade those praying towards Jerusalem, the first qibla, but after a Koranic revelation in 624 the qibla was redirected to Mecca to the south, and colonnades on the southern side of the courtyard became the prayer-hall. Rooms for the Prophet and his wives were built against the east side of the mosque (*see* ISLAMIC ART, §II, 2 and fig. 16). At some time between 628 and 631 the Prophet began to use a wooden chair with two steps as a MINBAR, or pulpit. When he died in 632, he was buried in one of the chambers on the east.

The caliph 'Umar (*reg* 634–44) enlarged the mosque in 638, and his successor 'Uthman (*reg* 644–56) rebuilt it entirely in 649, using stone for the walls and imported teak for the roof. The new qibla wall remains the southern limit of the mosque, although the original qibla wall is still clearly marked and the site of the Prophet's minbar is still used for the Friday sermon (Arab. *khuṭba*). Under the Umayyad caliph al-Walid (*reg* 705–15), the chambers of the Prophet's wives, where the first caliphs had also been buried, were demolished and the area incorporated into the mosque. The first curved MIHRAB recess in Islam was introduced in the qibla wall at this time, and a MINARET was added at each of the four corners of the building. The walls were lavishly decorated with marble panelling and mosaics; according to Ibn Jubayr (1184), they showed inscriptions and trees, and they were probably comparable to the contemporaraneous wall mosaics at the Dome of the Rock (*see* JERUSALEM, §II, 1(iii)) and the mosque of Damascus (*see* DAMASCUS, §3). Ibn Jubayr also said that the tomb of the Prophet was marked by a wooden screen and that it was designed to ensure that no one could face it when praying.

The mosque was enlarged again under the Abbasid caliphs al-Mahdi (*reg* 775–85) and al-Mutawwakkil (*reg* 847–61), but most of it was destroyed in a catastrophic fire in 1256. In the subsequent restoration, a domed structure was first built over the Prophet's tomb, but another fire in 1481 led the Mamluk sultan Qa'itbay (*reg* 1468–96) to reconstruct the mosque and domed tomb

Medina, mosque of the Prophet, founded 622; from a photograph by Rifa'at Pasha, 1909

in 1487. The minaret at the south-east corner dates from this restoration. The renovations in the 16th century under the Ottoman sultans Süleyman (*reg* 1520–66) and Selim II (*reg* 1566–74) gave the building the form it maintained into the 19th century, when a ground-plan was drawn by J.-L. Burckhardt. Further rebuilding under the Ottoman sultan Abdülmecid I (*reg* 1839–61) was recorded in another ground-plan and photographs by Rifa'at Pasha, who visited Medina in 1909 (see fig.). In 1951, under Saudi authority, the mosque was extended to accommodate the large numbers of pilgrims who include a visit to the Prophet's mosque in their pilgrimage to Mecca. A new courtyard and arcades were constructed to the north of the original mosque, which was left intact. The prayer area and roof were subsequently extended to the west, and, starting in 1986, new extensions were added so that by the late 1990s the mosque covered an area of 40 ha. The large curved mihrab recess in 'Uthman's qibla wall is still in use, while a 19th-century mihrab marks the spot were the Prophet led prayers. His tomb and those of the caliphs lie behind an ornate grille in the south-east corner of the mosque. It is considered meritworthy for the visitor to 'greet' the Prophet and his companions, but this is the limit of permissible honour at these graves.

Other mosques in Medina associated with the Prophet include the mosque of Quba', where the Prophet prayed before he actually entered the city on his emigration from Mecca. The mosque was initially orientated towards Jerusalem before the change of qibla and was enlarged under 'Uthman and al-Walid. It essentially retains its Umayyad form, with a roofed prayer-hall and arcades around the court. Both the mosque of the Two Qiblas (Arab. *masjid al-qiblatayn*), where the Prophet received the revelation about the change in the direction of prayer, and the 'Ajaba Mosque have been rebuilt. The five mosques of al-Fath mark sites where the Prophet prayed, while the Ghamama Mosque marks the site where he twice prayed the 'Id (festival) prayer. It has been repeatedly restored and has a minaret and a prayer-hall vaulted with six domes. It is unusual among the mosques of the Hijaz, although it has parallels with mosques in south-west Arabia and Egypt.

Other old buildings of the city include the ruins of the palace (Arab. *qasr*) of Sa'id ibn al-'As, apparently of Umayyad date, which is built in stone with traces of plaster covering. The Qasr 'Asim, consisting of a walled enclosure and groups of chambers with a dam near by, probably dates from the caliphate of 'Uthman. Early photographs show that the older houses of the city (destr.) had affinities with the houses of Jiddah, Mecca and Ta'if.

See also SAUDI ARABIA, including bibliography.

BIBLIOGRAPHY
Enc. Islam/2: 'Madīna' [Medina]
Ibn Jubayr: *Riḥla* [Travels] (1183–5); Eng. trans. by R. J. C. Broadhurst as *The Travels of Ibn Jubayr* (London, 1952)
J.-L. Burckhardt: *Travels in Arabia* (London, 1829/*R* 1968)

R. F. Burton: *Personal Narrative of a Pilgrimage to al-Madinah & Meccah*, ed. I. Burton (London, 1893/*R* New York, 1964)

I. Rifa'at Pasha: *Mir'at al-ḥaramayn* [Mirror of the two sanctuaries] (Cairo, AH 1344/1925)

K. A. C. Creswell: *Early Muslim Architecture*, i, pt 1 (Oxford, 1932/*R* and enlarged 1969)

A. al-Ansari: *Āthār al-madīnat al-munawwara* [Monuments of Medina] (Damascus, 1935/*R* Medina, AH 1393/1973)

J. Sauvaget: *La Mosquée omeyyade de Médine* (Paris, 1947)

al-Samhudi (*d* 1506): *Wafā' al-wafā'* [A history of Medina], ed. M. M. 'Abd al-Hamid (Cairo, AH 1373/1954)

A. H. al-Khayari: *Ta'rīkh masājid al-madīnat al-munawwara qadīman wa-ḥadīthan* [History of the mosques of Medina, ancient and modern], *Al-Manhal*, xx (AH 1379/1960), pp. 622–4; xxi (AH 1380/1960), pp. 69–71

E. Esin: *Mecca the Blessed, Madinah the Radiant* (London, 1963)

I. A. al-'Ayyashi: *al-Madīna bayn al-māḍī wa'l-ḥāḍir* [Medina past and present] (Medina, AH 1392/1972)

M. Hamidullah: *The Battlefields of the Prophet Muḥammad*, rev. edn (Hyderabad, 1973)

G. R. D. King: *The Historical Mosques of Saudi Arabia* (London, 1986)

G. R. D. KING

Medina, Deir el-. *See* THEBES (i), §XI.

Medina, Sir **John (Baptiste de)** (*b* Brussels, 1659; *d* Edinburgh, 5 Oct 1710). Painter of Flemish-Spanish origin, active in Scotland. He was the son of a Spanish army officer who had settled in Brussels; there Medina began his training under the French painter François Duchatel (1625–94). In 1686 he moved to London and appears immediately to have specialized in portraying Scottish nobles. Through the offices of one of them, David Melville, 3rd Earl of Leven, he was persuaded to move to Scotland *c.* 1693 where a subscription of £500 was collected to enable him to set up practice in Edinburgh. Success for Medina came quickly: he was well prepared with a repertory of poses that he could use time and again (*see* PORTRAITURE), his prices were moderate, and the sober Baroque portrait style in which he worked seems to have suited his patrons well. He undertook several portrait commissions for the Earl of Leven, including one of the Earl himself (*c.* 1691; Edinburgh, N.P.G.); other portraits of Scottish nobles include *Archibald Campbell, 1st Duke of Argyll* (Inverary Castle, Strathclyde) and *John Murray, 1st Marquess of Atholl* (Blair Castle, Tayside). A number of his male sitters were portrayed wearing full armour, for example *Thomas Hamilton, 6th Earl of Haddington* (1694; Edinburgh, N.P.G.).

Between *c.* 1697 and 1708 Medina produced a remarkable set of about 30 oval portraits of members of the Surgeons' Company for their Royal College in Edinburgh (*in situ*); the set, which includes a self-portrait of *c.* 1708, are not unlike the kit-cat series (London, N.P.G.) undertaken during the same period by Godfrey Kneller in London. Indeed, in style and posture much of Medina's work compares well with that by his London-based contemporary, although Medina's sitters appear more stiffly posed. Medina particularly liked to use red and blue draperies, and his portraits of women, for example *Agnes Mackenzie, Lady Stuart* (*c.* 1703; Mt Stuart, Bute), are in a similar vein, if less sensuous, to Peter Lely's slightly earlier sequence of 'Windsor Beauties' (London, Hampton Court Pal.). When occasionally Medina made less formal portraits, such as *The Artist's Children* (Gosford House,

Lothian) or that of the butler *Aytoun* (Wemyss Castle, Fife), he worked in a much freer style.

Medina enjoyed great success in Scotland, and in 1707 he was knighted. His principal student was WILLIAM AIKMAN, who became the leading Scottish portrait painter of the first quarter of the 18th century. According to George Vertue, Medina would have made a good history painter 'had he lived where suitable encouragement was to be had' ('Note-books', *Walpole Soc.*, xviii, 1930, p. 49). Among his few attempts in this genre still to be found in country houses in Lothian are an *Apelles and Pancaspe* ('*Campaspe*'; Gosford House) and a *Prometheus* (Penicuik House), the latter made for the Clerk family; he also made a copy (Yester House) of Domenichino's *Hercules in the Garden of the Hesperides*. A rare example of his ventures into book illustration are the designs he made for the fourth edition of John Milton's *Paradise Lost* (London, 1688); the plates for this, the first illustrated edition, were engraved by M. Burgess. In addition to the Royal College picture, three other self-portraits by Medina are known (Edinburgh, N.P.G.; Florence, Uffizi; and Providence, RI, Sch. Des., Mus. A.). After his death one son, John Medina the younger (*d* 1764), carried on the practice in Edinburgh, if with less success.

BIBLIOGRAPHY

J. Fleming: 'Sir John Medina and his "Postures"', *Connoisseur*, cxlviii (1961), pp. 23–5

D. Irwin and F. Irwin: *Scottish Painters at Home and Abroad, 1700–1900* (London, 1975), pp. 39–41

D. Mannings: 'Sir John Medina's Portraits of the Surgeons of Edinburgh', *Medic. Hist.*, xxiii (1979), pp. 176–90

R. K. Marshall: *John de Medina, 1659–1710*, Scottish Masters (Edinburgh, 1988)

J. Holloway: *Patrons and Painters: Art in Scotland, 1650–1760* (Edinburgh, 1989), pp. 33–42

DAVID CAST

Medina Azzahra. *See* MADÎNAT AL-ZAHRĀ'.

Medina Barba, Diego González de. *See* GONZÁLEZ DE MEDINA BARBA, DIEGO.

Medinaceli, Duques de. Spanish family of collectors, active in Italy.

(1) 9th Duque de **Medinaceli** [Luís de la Cerda Fernández de Córdoba Folch de Cardona y Aragón] (*b* Puerto de Santa Maria, 2 Aug 1660; *d* Pamplona, 26 Jan 1711). As heir to one of the oldest and wealthiest families in Spain, he was appointed at an early age to high office: in 1682 Commander General of the Galleys of Andalucia and then of Naples in 1684. In 1687 he was made Ambassador to Rome and in 1692 Viceroy of Naples, where he remained until 1706. Back in Spain in 1709 he became Prime Minister, dying two years later in prison, probably murdered on the orders of Philip V, who it was rumoured believed Don Luís guilty of high treason.

Don Luís must have inherited many works of art from his father, the 8th Duque (1637–91), whose palace and furnishings were described by Madame d'Aulnoy (1691) as 'de la dernière magnificence'; but it was in Rome and in Naples that Don Luís amassed a superb collection of paintings, recorded in an inventory of 1711 (V. Lleó Cañal, 1989). It lists 388 paintings, among which 195 are identified, often with remarkable accuracy. It also includes a few works that belonged to the heir of the 9th Duque, his nephew, Don Nicolas Maria Fernández.

The relative scarcity of religious paintings (103, slightly over 26%) is striking. Landscapes form the most numerous group (107), including 37 views by Gaspar van Wittel. The paucity of Spanish paintings is also remarkable, although there may have been more among the unattributed works. Only three Spanish painters are identified, Diego Velázquez, Jusepe de Ribera and Matías de Torres. Velázquez is represented by two works, one described as 'a portrait of a man' (untraced) and the other as 'women working on tapestry', which must be the *Fable of Arachne*, or the *Hilanderas* (or *Weavers*; *c.* 1656; Madrid, Prado; *see* VELÁZQUEZ, DIEGO, fig. 9). This hypothesis is supported both by an annotation in the inventory recording that 'it was sent to the Palace when my Master died' and by the fact that the painting entered the Prado from the royal collections with an unknown provenance. The gift may have been an act of appeasement by the heir of the disgraced Duque. Ribera is represented by six paintings, including the famous *Bearded Woman* (1631; Toledo, Hosp. Tavera), which Medinaceli had inherited from his ancestor the (3rd) Duque de Alcalá who had commissioned it, and which had previously hung in his Seville palace.

There is a small group of 36 paintings dating from the 16th century, mainly Italian and of the Venetian school, including seven works by Domenico Tintoretto, six by Veronese, three by Titian and three by Jacopo Bassano. The remainder from other Italian schools were six paintings by Federico Zuccaro, three by Raphael and one each by Perino del Vaga and Parmigianino (all untraced), Federico Barocci (*Nativity*; 1593; Madrid, Prado) and Sebastiano del Piombo (untraced).

The main body of the collection was formed of 17th-century Italian paintings. In Naples, Don Luís acquired exclusive rights to all the *vedute* painted by Gaspar van Wittel, of which 37 are recorded. Two of the series are *Views of the Bay of Naples* (*c.* 1700; Seville, Casa Pilatos). There were 14 works by Guido Reni (one a copy; all untraced), including a copy (untraced) after *Judith with the Head of Holofernes* (Geneva, Sedlmayer, priv. col.) and 10 by Carlo Maratti's workshop, all unidentified, except 2 canvases thought to be *Nymphs with Flower Baskets* (Madrid, Prado, on dep. Brussels, Sp. Embassy, and Barcelona, Ajuntament) and 5 by Michelangelo di Campidoglio (1610–*c.* 1670; untraced). Many of the classicist masters are represented, and this group includes one work each by Andrea Sacchi (*Birth of St John the Baptist*; 1628–9; Madrid, Prado), Pier Francesco Mola (untraced) and Domenichino (untraced). In Naples, Don Luís must also have bought the six paintings by Luca Giordano, all unidentified except for *Rubens Painting the 'Allegory of Peace'* (*c.* 1687; Madrid, Prado), three by Salvator Rosa, two of which show landscapes with figures (all untraced) and one by Francesco Solimena (untraced).

A number of these paintings entered royal collections in unknown circumstances (later Prado), for example Giordano's *Rubens Painting the 'Allegory of Peace'* (purchased from the estate after 1711 by the Marqués de Ensenada; 1702–81). Others, such as *Venus and Adonis* by Carlo Cignani (London, Apsley House), must have entered the Spanish royal collection (first recorded 1772), from which it was taken by Joseph Bonaparte and subsequently given by Ferdinand VII to the Duke of Wellington.

(2) 13th Duque de **Medinaceli** [Luís de la Soledad Fernández de Córdoba y Figueroa de la Cerda] (*b* Medinaceli, 17 April 1749; *d* Madrid, 12 Nov 1806). In 1764 he married the 3rd Duquesa de Santisteban. She was descended from the Conde de Santisteban (*d* 1716), who had been Viceroy of Naples from 1687 to 1695, where he was very active as a collector. The inventory of the Santisteban paintings (*c.* 1764), which were united with the Medinaceli collection in 1764 at the Medinaceli Palace in Madrid, includes 251 works, of which 145 are attributed. The Santisteban collection is particularly strong in Italian 17th-century painting and is dominated by 82 works by Luca Giordano together with a book of 24 drawings (untraced). These works, which included 13 based on Torquato Tasso's *Gerusalemme liberata* (first draft written 1563) were noted by Palomino (1715–24), and it is probable that admiration in Spain for the paintings of Giordano led to his appointment at the Court as *pintor de cámara* (1692). There was a marked emphasis on the Italian schools of the 17th century, one of the most interesting of which is the drawing by Gianlorenzo Bernini of *Constantine on Horseback* (1654–68; Madrid, Real Acad. S Fernando, Mus.).

Both inventories include revealing valuations. In the inventory (1711) of the 9th Duque de Medinaceli the most highly valued item is a painting by Guido Reni, described as a 'School of Children', which may be a version of *Combat of Cupids and Putti* (Rome, Pal. Doria-Pamphili), priced at 20,000 reales, followed by *Rubens Painting the 'Allegory of Peace'* by Giordano (Madrid, Prado), valued at 15,000 reales. By comparison Velázquez's *Weavers* is priced at a low 3000 reales. In the inventory of the 13th Duque de Medinaceli the most valuable items are three paintings by Giordano based on *Gerusalemme Liberata* (two in Seville, Casa Pilatos), each valued at 15,000 reales.

A large part of the combined collection has been dispersed, but part of it remains in the possession of descendants, principally the Duquesas de Medinaceli y Lerma, and their step-sister, the Duquesa de Cardona in Córdoba. This last collection, distributed among several residences in Spain and Switzerland, has not been available for study and may include works recorded above as untraced.

UNPUBLISHED SOURCES

Seville, Archivo Ducal de Medinaceli, Documentos sin clasificar, legajo 'inventarios' *Razón de las pinturas vinculadas: Agregación de los antecesores al Sr D. Franco*, n. d. [*c.* 1764]

BIBLIOGRAPHY

Comtesse d'Aulnoy: *Mémoires de la cour d'Espagne* (Paris, 1691), p. 185
A. A. Palomino de Castro y Velasco: *Museo pictórico* (1715–24)
Storia di Napoli, vii (1972), p. 105
V. Lleó Cañal: 'The Art Collection of the Ninth Duke of Medinaceli', *Burl. Mag.*, cxxxi (1989), pp. 108–15

VICENTE LLEÓ CAÑAL

Medina de las Torres, Duque de [Guzmán, Ramiro Nuñez de] (*d* Madrid, 1668). Spanish statesman, collector and patron. Son-in-law of the powerful Gaspar de Guzmán y Pimentel, Conde-Duque de OLIVARES, he served as Viceroy of Naples from 1637 to 1644. He collected Italian and northern European paintings, as well as several by Jusepe de Ribera that were almost certainly commissioned in Naples. These included the *Martyrdom of St Philip*, a gift to Philip IV; the *Liberation of St Peter*; and the *Dream of Jacob* (the last two signed and dated 1639; all Madrid, Prado). Medina de las Torres was also involved in the furnishing of the Palacio del Buen Retiro (*see* MADRID, §IV, 1) and in providing equipment for its park (in 1639, for example, he sent 12 elaborate gondolas from Naples for the canals) and for the festivals celebrated there. Among the paintings he donated to the redecoration of the Escorial were Correggio's *Noli me tangere* (*c.* 1525) and possibly Giorgione's *Virgin and Child with SS Anthony and Roch* (*c.* 1510; both Madrid, Prado).

UNPUBLISHED SOURCES

Madrid, Archv Hist. Protocolos, MS. 8181, fols 39–44 [doc. dated 26 Nov 1668]

BIBLIOGRAPHY

V. Carducho: *Diálogos de la pintura* (Madrid, 1633); repr. in F. J. Sánchez Cantón: *Fuentes literarias para la historia del arte español*, ii (Madrid, 1933), p. 110

J. Brown and J. Elliott: *A Palace for a King* (New Haven, 1980), pp. 22, 117, 216–19

M. Burke: *Private Collections of Italian Art in 17th-century Spain* (diss., New York U., 1984; microfilm, Ann Arbor, 1986), pp. 84–5; docs 2.8a–c

MARCUS BURKE

Medina del Campo. Town in Valladolid province, Spain, notable for the 15th-century LA MOTA CASTLE.

Medina de Rioseco, Duquesa de. *See under* CASTILLA (ii).

Medina y Peñas, Sabino de (*b* Madrid, 31 Dec 1812; *d* Madrid, 10 May 1888). Spanish sculptor. He studied at the Real Academia de Bellas Artes de S Fernando, Madrid, and was a pupil of Valeriano Salvatierra y Barriales. He was awarded a prize by the Academia in 1832 and continued his studies in Rome for six years as a pupil of Giuseppe Tenerani. The classicism that had dominated his training is evident in the marble statue of *Eurydice Bitten by an Asp* (1836; Madrid, Prado). In 1838, on his return to Madrid, Medina y Peñas was made a member of the Real Academia de Bellas Artes de S Fernando. He became a teacher at the Escuela Superior in 1845 and in 1866 was named honorary sculptor (*escultor honorario*) to the Municipality of Madrid; he was also Escultor de Cámara to Isabella II. His work consisted of allegorical figures, portraits and monuments. The most important of the figures include that of *Virtue* on the monument of Dos de Mayo, the allegorical caryatids for the chamber of the Congreso de los Diputados and the impressive representation of *Río Lozoya* (Canal de Isabel II), all in Madrid. In addition to the religious sculptures, such as *Immaculate Conception* (Madrid, Las Calatravas) and those at Riotinto and Huelva, Medina y Peñas also executed portraits of contemporary politicians, such as those of *Agustín Argüelles* (Madrid, Pal. de las Cortes), *Diego de León* (Madrid, Mus. Romántico) and *Antonio Gil y Zárate* (1853; Madrid, Real Acad. S Fernando Mus.). These show that his style was already changing towards a greater realism, which is also reflected in his monument to the painter *Bartolomé Esteban Murillo* (1862; versions in Seville, Plaza del Museo, and Madrid, Plaza de Murillo).

BIBLIOGRAPHY

E. Martín: 'Don Sabino de Medina y Peñas', *Bol. Real Acad. B. A.*, x (1890), pp. 178–80

E. Pardo Canalís: 'El escultor Sabino de Medina', *Rev. Archvs, Bib. & Mus.* (1978), p. 51

F. Portela Sandoval: *La escultura madrileña durante el reinado de Isabel II* (Madrid, 1993)

FRANCISCO PORTELA SANDOVAL

Medinet Habu. *See* THEBES (i), §VII.

Méditateurs, Les. *See* PRIMITIFS, LES.

Medium. Term used to refer to the actual physical material chosen as a vehicle of expression for any work of art. In painting it is used more specifically for the liquid in which the PIGMENT is suspended. By diluting the vehicle (the liquid binding agent in which the pigment particles are dispersed), the paint is made thinner and easier to apply.

RUPERT FEATHERSTONE

Medley, Robert (*b* London, 19 Dec 1905; *d* 20 Oct 1994). English painter, illustrator and designer. He studied at the Byam Shaw School of Art (1921–3) and at the Slade School of Art (1923–4) followed by two years in Paris (1926–8). During the 1930s he was involved with the progressive Group Theatre Project, mounting new and experimental work often with political themes. He designed masks for T. S. Eliot's *Sweeney Agonistes* (1934–5) and costumes and sets for works including Auden and Isherwood's *The Dog beneath the Skin* (1935–6) and *The Ascent of F.6* (1937). Medley was a founder-member of the anti-fascist Artists International Association. In his paintings he explored social and humanist themes, depicting the daily life of ordinary people, and also experimented with Surrealism. During World War II he served as a camouflage officer. On his return to England he produced figurative works on a variety of subjects, ranging from a series about cyclists to mythological scenes. Following a representative approach his delicate, almost feather-like brushstrokes created work of great sensitivity. For a time he experimented successfully with an abstract style, as in *Figuration in White* (1963; London, Tate), always with a sure sense of composition but with little of the autobiographical import that informed his best work. In later work Medley dwelt upon the autobiographic content of his earlier pictures to create images that analysed relationships between people and his attitude towards himself. He held the positions of Head of Theatre Design, Slade School of Art, London (1949–58), and of Fine Art at Camberwell School of Arts & Crafts, London (1958–65). In 1994 an exhibition of his work was held at the Coram Gallery, London, and he won the Charles Woolaston Prize, awarded for *Preparation for the Execution*, the most distinguished work in the Royal Academy Summer Exhibition 1994.

WRITINGS

Drawn from Life: A Memoir (London, 1983)

BIBLIOGRAPHY

Robert Medley, 1928–1963 (exh. cat., London, Whitechapel A.G., 1963)

Robert Medley Paintings, 1928–1984 (exh. cat., Oxford, MOMA; Colchester, Minories, 1984)

EMMANUEL COOPER

Mednyánszky, László, Baron (*b* Beczkó [now Beckov, Slovakia], 23 April 1852; *d* Vienna, 17 April 1919). Hungarian painter. Although an aristocratic landowner, he led a wandering and secluded life. He attended the Akademie der Bildenden Künste in Munich, and from 1873 he studied under Isidore-Alexandre Augustin Pils in Paris, where he stayed until 1877. After a few months in Barbizon and a longer trip in Italy he returned to his birthplace in 1879. From 1880 he lived alternately in Vienna and Hungary, and in 1889–92 he was once more in France. His only one-man exhibition was held in Paris at the Galerie Georges Petit in 1897. Mednyánszky never gave up his itinerant lifestyle and lived alternately in Budapest, Vienna and Beczkó. During World War I he roamed the front lines using his drawing skills as a war correspondent. Mednyánszky's earliest known pictures were inspired by the Great Hungarian Plains. His desire to bridge the 'finite and the infinite' and his emerging pantheism are already apparent in the transparent nacreous greys or glowing reds of these marshlands and hazy shores. The search became more profound in his later landscapes of the Tatra Mountains, especially in the intimacy and sublimity of their snow-capped ridges, waterfalls and mountain lakes. In the 1890s he made clear, impressionistic portrayals of increasingly congenial landscapes.

As an itinerant artist Mednyánszky had direct experience of landscape, and most of the pictures exhibited in Budapest were landscapes. In his exhibition in Paris, however, up to two-thirds of the paintings portrayed subjects from the lower social strata with which he associated ('tramp paintings'), and these came to predominate in his oeuvre from the end of the 1890s. *Down-and-out* (*c*. 1898; Budapest, N.G.) depicts a tramp in tattered clothes sitting on the ground with his mouth open and an empty gaze; his reddish-brown face is surrounded by almost luminous, gradually deepening blues. Mednyánszky painted wild and terrified heads with primitive expressions; types living by instinct, incapable of independent judgement or self-defence (e.g. *After Fighting*; Budapest, N.G.). His studies of heads of his younger friends are simpler, even laconic in their structure and colour, with immobile faces staring at the spectator. Around 1910 his portrayals became more subtle: individuals conscious of their fate, or even determined, intrepid criminals. The hues became lighter while the use of line became more expressionist. His landscapes of this period are intimately drawn depictions of snowy countryside and courtyards, or solemn scenes, and his works of this time also reveal his interest in the effects of light.

From 1914 to 1918 Mednyánszky painted mainly frontal scenes. Even his landscapes are populated by advancing carts, and white crosses fill the tranquil fringes of the forest. In *Serbia* (1914; Budapest, N.G.) two wounded soldiers lie down to rest in a snowy landscape, and the soldier on the left has the same conscious expression depicted in the later tramp pictures. The discursive brushwork of *The Dead* (Budapest, N.G.) conveys his increased expressiveness. In its sequel, *Decay* (Budapest, N.G.), the figures are nearly dissolved into the ground by the lyrically tame colour-scheme of greyish-brown, yellow, green and blue. In his last series Mednyánszky painted urban ruins

and made novel use of tensions of light with dark, and pure blue with yellow.

Throughout his career Mednyánszky made numerous sketches for each painting. He rendered nature and man with an almost philosophical application, and he is known to have been attracted to Buddhist philosophy. Because of his itinerant lifestyle it is impossible to catalogue his oeuvre, as hundreds of his works are now untraced.

WRITINGS
I. P. Brestyánszky, ed.: *Mednyánszky naplója* [Mednyánszky's diary] (Budapest, 1960)

BIBLIOGRAPHY
D. Malonyai: *Mednyánszky* (Budapest, 1905)
E. Kállai: *Mednyánszky* (Budapest, 1943)
I. P. Brestyánszky: *Mednyánszky* (Budapest, 1963) [also in Eng.]
M. Egri: *Mednyánszky* (Budapest, 1975)
Ladislaw Mednyánsky: Súborné dielo [László Mednyánszky: collected works] (exh. cat., foreword K. Vaculik; Bratislava, Slovak N.G., 1979)
M. Sarkantyú: *Mednyánszky* (Budapest, 1981)
N. Aradi: *Mednyánszky* (Budapest, 1983) [also in Eng.]
NÓRA ARADI

Medoro, Angelino (*b* Italy, *c*. 1567; *d* Spain, *c*. 1631). Italian painter and draughtsman, active in South America. After a brief stay in Seville, he arrived in South America in 1587, working particularly in Tunja and Bogotá (Colombia), Quito (Ecuador) and Lima (Peru). He returned to Spain some time after 1624. Medoro worked in the Mannerist style of Vasari and Francesco Salviati, and he was an important influence on the developing South American schools. His known work comprises a series dedicated to the *Passion* in the chapel of los Mancipe, Tunja Cathedral, a *Virgin of Antigua* in the Dominican church and a *Flagellatio* in the Franciscan monastery, both in Tunja. Other works include a *Virgin of the Rosary* (with four saints) in the convent of S Clara, Quito; *St Bonaventura* and the *Entry into Jerusalem* in the monastery of S Francisco, Lima; two paintings of the *Crucifixion*, one of *St Diego of Alcalá* and one of *St Anthony of Padua* (all Lima, church of los Descalzos); *St Rose of Lima*; in the sanctuary of S Rosa, Lima; a painting of *Christ with Franciscan Saints* in S Marcelo, Lima; and a *Crucifixion* in the Franciscan monastery of Potosí. There are two drawings dating from his time in Spain in the Alcubierre collection in Madrid.

BIBLIOGRAPHY
M. S. Soria: *La pintura del siglo XVI en Sudamérica* (Buenos Aires, 1956)
J. Mesa and T. Gisbert: 'El pintor Angelino Medoro y su obra en Sudamérica', *An. Inst. A. Amer. & Invest. Estét.*, xviii (1967), pp. 23–47
——: 'Dos dibujos inéditos de Medoro en Madrid', *A. & Arqueol.* (1969)
Salazar: 'Nueva obra de Angelino Medoro en Lima', *A. & Arqueol.* (1969)
J. Mesa and T. Gisbert: *La pintura cuzqueña* (Lima, 1983)
MARIA CONCEPCIÓN GARCÍA SÁIZ

Medović, Celestin Mato (*b* Kuna, Pelješac, 17 Nov 1857; *d* Sarajevo, 20 Jan 1920). Croatian painter. He left home as a young boy and lived in a monastery in Dubrovnik, where he was ordained in 1880. Between 1880 and 1886 he studied irregularly in Italy and in 1888–93 he studied at the Munich Akademie der Bildenden Künste under Gabriel von Hackl (*b* 1843), Ludwig von Löfftz (1845–1910) and Alexander Wagner (1826–94). Although Medović painted religious subjects, his creative potential was most fully realized in large compositions such as *Bacchanalia* (1893; Zagreb, Gal. Mod. A.), highly praised among academic circles in Europe. On his return to Dubrovnik he painted altarpieces and psychologically sophisticated portraits. Between 1895 and 1907 he lived in Zagreb, where he joined Vlaho Bukovac's group of artists, adopting the aesthetic programme of the Zagreb 'colourful school' through a poetic approach to natural light and an enriched palette. He then painted a series of large historical wall paintings such as *Split Church Assembly* (1897) and *Arrival of the Croats* (1903) in the Golden Hall of the former College for the Priesthood and Theological Studies, Opatička Street 10, in Zagreb. At the same time he executed genre paintings, many portraits, religious paintings, landscapes and still-lifes. In 1907 he left Zagreb and lived a solitary life on the Pelješac peninsula. In the landscapes painted between 1908 and 1912, he reached the peak of colourfulness with his characteristic divisionistic technique, as in *Heather* (1911; Zagreb, Gal. Mod. A.). He then abandoned analytical observation and experimented with small-scale, freer impressions of nature.

BIBLIOGRAPHY
V. Kružić Uchytil: *Medović* (Zagreb, 1978)

ZDENKO RUS

Medrano, Sebastián Fernández de. *See* FERNÁNDEZ DE MEDRANO, SEBASTIÁN.

Medrea, Cornel (*b* Mercurea, 8 March 1888; *d* Bucharest, 25 July 1964). Romanian sculptor and teacher. He studied at the School of Arts and Crafts, Zlatna, Transylvania, and at the High School of Decorative Arts, Budapest (1905–10). In 1912 he travelled to Vienna, Dresden, Leipzig and Munich, and in 1914 settled in Bucharest where he was introduced to the literary and artistic world by the poet George Coșbuc, of whom he made a portrait bust (1914; Sibiu). Unlike other Romanian sculptors he was influenced less by French art than by the Central European artistic environment. Instead of following Rodin, he was attracted towards a sculpture that did not sacrifice the integrity of volume to strongly accentuated modelling. Following the classical tradition Medrea cared above all for the harmony and balance of the whole, to which those details that contributed to the overall expression were subordinated. He made many portrait busts of Romanian writers and cultural personalities, including *Barba Delavrancea* (1920; Bucharest), and statues of national heroes, such as *Avram Iancu* (1927; Cimpeni) and *Anrei Mureșanu* (bronze, h. 3.2 m, 1935; Bistrita-Năsăud, Union Sq.). As a monumental sculptor his full potential was realized in the monument to *Vasile Lucaciu* (bronze, h. 4.5 m, 1936; Satu Mare), whose massive figure radiates the energy and tension of a man of action. He also sculpted female nudes, in the round or in bas-relief, whose heavy contours were sensitively modelled. He was a founder-member in 1918 of the association Arta Română, and from 1933 he was a professor at the Fine Arts School in Bucharest.

BIBLIOGRAPHY
G. Oprescu: *Sculptura românească* (Bucharest, 1965), pp. 104–8
M. Mihalache: *Cornel Medrea* (Bucharest, 2/1986)
N. Lăptoiu: *Incursiuni in plastica românească* (Cluj-Napoca, 1987), pp. 157–64

V. Florea and I. Vlasiu: 'Cornel Medrea: Prezenta sculpturii' [Cornel Medrea: presence of sculpture], *Arta*, iii (1988), pp. 6–9

IOANA VLASIU

Medulić, Andrija. *See* SCHIAVONE, ANDREA.

Medunetsky, Konstantin [Kazimir] **(Konstantinovich)** (*b* Moscow, 1899; *d c.* 1935). Russian sculptor and stage designer. He studied at the Stroganov School in Moscow from 1914 to 1918, specializing in stage design, and then at the State Free Art Studios (Svomas). He was involved in decorating Moscow for May Day 1918 and for the first anniversary of the October Revolution and became a founder-member of the Society of Young Artists (Obmokhu) in 1919. His contributions to the group's exhibitions included a series of abstract constructions at the third show of May 1921.

Medunetsky was one of the original members of the First Working Group of Constructivists, founded in March 1921, which inaugurated Constructivism in Russia. The following January he displayed six sculptural works entitled *Construction of a Spatial Structure* in a joint exhibition with Georgy and Vladimir Stenberg. The artists' declaration in the catalogue was the first publication of the principles of CONSTRUCTIVISM and was elaborated in their paper to the Institute of Artistic Culture (Inkhuk), in February. The only extant example of Medunetsky's sculpture, *Spatial Construction* (1920/21; New Haven, CT, Yale U.A.G.), exploits the colour of metals, juxtaposing brass and zinc with an iron rod painted red. The forms thread through each other with a minimum of contact, producing a sensation of weightlessness and dynamism. In 1923 Medunetsky and the Stenberg brothers began designing sets, costumes and posters for the Kamerny Theatre of Alexander Tairov (1885–1950) in Moscow. In the same year they visited Paris with the company and exhibited their work at the Galerie Paul Guillaume. In 1925 Medunetsky devised kiosks for the Soviet section at the Exposition Internationale des Arts Décoratifs et Industriels Modernes and later worked on his own as a stage designer.

UNPUBLISHED SOURCES
Moscow, priv. col. [with G. Stenberg and V. Stenberg: *Tezisy po dokladu 'Konstruktivizm'* (Theses from the paper 'Constructivism'), 1922]

BIBLIOGRAPHY
Katalog vystavki: Konstruktivisty K. K. Medunetskii, V. A. Stenberg, G. A. Stenberg [Catalogue of the exhibition: the Constructivists K. K. Medunetsky, V. A. Stenberg, G. A. Stenberg] (exh. cat., Moscow, Kafe Poetov, 1922)
A. Nakov: *2 Stenberg 2* (exh. cat., London, Annely Juda F.A., 1975)
C. Lodder: *Russian Constructivism* (New Haven, 1983)

CHRISTINA LODDER

Meegeren, Han [Henricus Antonius] **van** (*b* Deventer, 1889; *d* Amsterdam, 30 Dec 1947). Dutch painter and forger. He studied art at The Hague Academie and obtained his degree in 1914. He became a painter of mediocre talent, though a respected one. It is said that he developed a grievance against the critics who had slighted his work and began to manufacture forgeries of 17th-century Dutch masters, perhaps as early as 1923, in order to avenge himself. In 1932 van Meegeren left the Netherlands and retired to the south of France, where he began experimenting and producing fakes in earnest. His most successful forgery, and perhaps the most famous forgery of modern times, was his *Supper at Emmaus* (*c.* 1936; Rotterdam, Mus. Boymans–van Beuningen; *see* FORGERY, fig. 1), painted in imitation of JOHANNES VERMEER. The brilliance of the forgery lay in van Meegeren's decision to represent a work of the least documented early period of Vermeer's career. Knowing that experts were alert to Italian influences on Vermeer's work, van Meegeren based his composition on a Caravaggio painting of the same title (London, N.G.). He used canvas and pigments of the 17th century and employed clever techniques of aging so that the picture appeared genuine even under X-ray. The art world, including Abraham Bredius, was thoroughly deceived, and the painting was bought by the Dutch collector F. J. O. Boymans. There followed a succession of forgeries of Dutch Old Masters, although none was as brilliant as the *Supper at Emmaus*. In total van Meegeren painted eleven fake Vermeers, two Pieter de Hoochs, two Gerard ter Borchs (ii), three Frans Halses and one Dirck Baburen. After World War II a Vermeer painting, *Christ and the Adultress*, was found in the private collection of the Nazi leader Hermann Goering and traced to van Meegeren, the supposed owner. He was brought to trial, accused of financial collaboration with the Nazis, but confessed to the forgery and demonstrated this by painting another 'Vermeer' in the court. Van Meegeren was found guilty of forgery in 1947 and died of a heart attack in the same year.

BIBLIOGRAPHY
J. Kilbracken: *Van Meegeren: A Case History* (London, 1967)
R. Breek and W. Froentjes: 'Application of Pyrolysis Gas Chromatography on some of Van Meegeren's faked Vermeers and Peter de Hooghs', *Stud. Conserv.*, xx/4 (1975), pp. 183–9
M. Roskill: *What is Art History?* (London, 1976), pp. 155–67
M. van den Brandhof: *Een vroege Vermeer uit 1937: Achtergronden van leven en werken van de schilder/vervalser Han van Meegeren* [An early Vermeer of 1937: life and work of the painter/forger Han van Meegeren] (Utrecht, 1979)

Meerman. Dutch family of government officials and collectors. The family, originally from Delft, branched out across Delft, Leiden and Amsterdam in the course of the 17th century. The Leiden branch included (1) Gerard Meerman and (2) Johan Meerman, who assembled an important library and whose name is perpetuated in the Rijksmuseum Meermanno–Westreenianum in The Hague, which still contains a small part of their collections.

(1) Gerard Meerman (*b* Leiden, 6 Dec 1722; *d* Aachen, 15 Dec 1771). He worked first as a lawyer in The Hague (1741) and later became a city official in Rotterdam (1748). He started to accumulate his library of books in the early 1740s, of which his handwritten catalogue begins in 1745. The books he collected were determined by his interests in law and history, early printed books and medieval manuscripts. In the course of over 25 years, Meerman amassed an extensive collection of incunabula, including many important examples of 15th-century printing. His collection of medieval manuscripts was of international importance; some 970 medieval codices came from the library of the Collège de Clermont in Paris, which he bought *en bloc* in 1764 when this Jesuit establishment was dissolved. He also bought at auction, particularly in the Netherlands and in France. He published a study of early printed books in 1765. After his retirement in 1767,

Gerard Meerman moved to The Hague; he died while taking a cure in Germany.

WRITINGS
Origines typographicae (The Hague, 1765)

(2) Johan Meerman (*b* The Hague, 1 Nov 1753; *d* The Hague, 19 Aug 1815). Son of (1) Gerard Meerman. He studied at the universities of Leipzig, Göttingen and Leiden and at the age of 18 inherited his father's library, which remained, however, in The Hague, where his mother was still living. Family wealth enabled Johan to devote himself exclusively to travel and to the study of history and literature; his publications include historical works, accounts of his travels and translations of works of literature into Dutch. He also corresponded widely with scholars and artists.

From 1787 Meerman occupied the occasional political post, but it was only in 1806, after the accession of Louis Bonaparte to the throne of the Netherlands as Louis Napoleon, that Meerman became Director-General of Sciences and, soon thereafter (1807), of Arts as well. He played a decisive role in the cultural policy of the King and helped to found the Koninklijk Museum in Amsterdam (later the Rijksmuseum) in 1808. He was also active in the promotion of artistic education in the Netherlands. After annexation of the Netherlands by the French, he became a senator in Paris from 1811 to 1814.

Johan Meerman added considerably to the library that he inherited from his father, particularly in the areas of historical and literary manuscripts and printed books. He was also an occasional collector of antiquities and contemporary works of art. Meerman and his wife bequeathed their entire collection to the city of The Hague, but in 1821 the city refused the bequest. The bulk of the library was dispersed in 1824 at an auction; the sale, accompanied by a four-volume catalogue, fetched the sum of 131,000 guilders, a very high figure at this time. The most important buyers were Sir Thomas Phillipps, whose purchases included the major portion of the manuscripts from the Collège de Clermont, and Meerman's great-nephew, WILLEM HENDRIK JACOB VAN WESTREENEN VAN TIELLANDT, the founder of the Rijksmuseum Meermanno–Westreenianum in The Hague, which he named as a tribute to his great-uncle.

BIBLIOGRAPHY
J. H. Kernkamp: *Inventaris der familiepapieren Meerman, van Westreenen, Dierkens en van Damme aanwezig in het Museum Meermanno–Westreenianum* (The Hague, 1948)
R. Ekkart: 'The Dutch Museum of the Book', *A. Libs J.*, xii (1987), pp. 25–8

RUDOLF EKKART

Meer van Haarlem, van der. *See* VERMEER VAN HAARLEM.

Megalithic architecture. Term describing structures composed of massive stones (anc. Gr. *megas lithos*; 'large stone'); it is applied by extension to monuments of undressed stone, especially those constructed in Neolithic Europe (*see* PREHISTORIC EUROPE, §IV, 2). Construction using massive dressed-stone blocks is usually termed cyclopean (*see* MASONRY, §II). Megalithic structures occur in many places throughout the world; most are of local stone, the particular characteristics of which are reflected in both the construction methods and the form of the monuments.

1. Introduction. 2. Regional survey.

1. INTRODUCTION. True megalithic architecture is that in which the stones form the primary structural elements of the monument. In the case of megalithic tombs (*see* fig. 1; *see also* DOLMEN), these elements are generally the walls and roof, while in the henges (*see* HENGE) and standing stones (*see* MENHIR), the slabs are exclusively the construction elements. Owing to their visibility, megaliths were among the earliest monuments of western Europe to attract the attention of antiquarians: in the 17th century JOHN AUBREY documented AVEBURY and STONEHENGE in southern England and argued that they were Druid temples. By the end of the 18th century, many megalithic tombs in England, France and Denmark had been opened, a practice that continued during the following century, as antiquarian attention shifted from the monuments themselves to the artefacts they contained. At the beginning of the 20th century various ideas were developed to explain the origins and development of megaliths.

One idea that gained popularity was that they were the monuments of an ancient religion that originated in the eastern Mediterranean and spread through Spain and France to the British Isles and eventually to northern continental Europe. However, developments in radiocarbon dating had, by the late 1960s, led to the abandonment of this diffusionist view and resulted in a revised model that emphasized indigenous development. The clear connection between megalithic architecture and prehistoric social, ritual and symbolic behaviour continues to keep it in the focus of archaeological inquiry.

(i) Construction methods. (ii) Interpretation.

(i) Construction methods. A question that frequently perplexes students of megalithic architecture is how prehistoric societies were able to construct such monumental structures. In fact, the technology of megalithic construction is no more complex than the knowledge of joinery required to build a timber longhouse: the massiveness of the stones simply required the builders to solve the problems of raw material acquisition, transport and erection.

Materials for the megaliths were generally of local origin. For instance, the tabular blocks used for the alignments of standing stones at CARNAC in France were of local

1. Megalithic dolmen, known as Arthur's Quoit, Trethevy, Cornwall, England, *c.* 3000–*c.* 2500 BC

2. Megalithic trilithons at Stonehenge, Wiltshire, England, *c.* 2000 BC

granite, while the uprights and capstones of the megalithic tombs of northern Germany and southern Scandinavia were taken from the morainic residue of the Pleistocene glaciations that covered this region. While a number of such blocks would have been needed for a single structure, the area from which they were drawn was probably within a relatively small radius of the site. Elsewhere some quarrying was required; this was especially true in the few cases in which megalithic monuments were built from limestone. Transport was the next task; moving an 80-tonne capstone even a few metres would have been a challenge for a prehistoric community. Ropes, levers, rollers made from tree trunks and human and animal traction are the most likely combinations of power and tools to have been used, although the possibility of the deliberate icing of tracks in winter for sliding the blocks has also been raised. Experiments have shown that, although the movement of a large monolith was a difficult task, it was possible for a communal labour force to accomplish it with teamwork and ingenuity. In one such experiment, directed by J.-P. Mohen (Bougon, France, July 1979), 200 people succeeded in moving a replica megalithic slab 40 m using oak rollers, ropes and levers and raising it to capstone height by the technique suggested below for raising lintels at Stonehenge.

The final task for the megalithic builders was the erection of the stones. For uprights in megalithic tombs and for standing stones, a combination of levers and scaffolding was probably employed to raise the stone and tip it on end into a prepared pit. It is more difficult to reconstruct the method used in the placement of capstones on dolmens and gallery graves and the lintels on the Stonehenge trilithons (see fig. 2). Two possibilities have been suggested. The first involves the construction of ramps of earth once the uprights were in place. The capstone or lintel would have been dragged, pulled, rolled or levered up the inclined ramp, positioned over the uprights and finally settled into place. For megalithic tombs, which in any event were eventually covered by an earthen mound, this procedure makes sense. At Stonehenge, however, there is no trace of earthen mounds, although the society that built this monument was capable of massive earth-moving, as the huge volume of soil and chalk moved at Avebury, for example, attests. For Stonehenge, a different technique of raising lintels has been suggested, involving levering the lintel up one end at a time and placing scaffolding underneath, until it reached the top of the uprights, whereupon the lintel would be slid across and lowered into place, enabling the mortices carved into the undersides of the lintels to fit into the tenons shaped on top of the uprights.

In the 1950s Alexander Thom examined the diameters of 46 British stone circles and noticed that these measurements fell into a consistent pattern of peaks in a frequency distribution that suggested the use of a consistent unit of measurement. Further study led him to propose the 'megalithic yard' (*c.* 0.829 m). Thom's hypothesis has since been viewed sceptically: although it has some statistical support, critics have argued that the precision of the data is such that a more plausible explanation is that the use of a generalized human dimension, such as the pace, would produce similar results. Nonetheless, even if a common unit of measurement did not exist, it seems clear that the placement of stones in circles and henges was not haphazard but the result of a conscious design by their prehistoric builders.

(ii) Interpretation. It is not known what purpose megalithic monuments served in prehistoric societies. Clearly, they were not functional necessities to permit simple human survival: other Neolithic cultures in Europe found straightforward interment in grave pits or under simple mounds to be quite adequate without expending energy on the transport and erection of huge blocks of stone. The standing stones are clearly associated with social, ideological or intellectual processes apart from daily necessity. The meaning of the European megalithic monuments has been sought in a variety of explanations. During the 20th century, four major, often interrelated, factors have emerged: ideology and religion; territoriality; astronomy; and symbolism in the landscape.

(a) Ideology and religion. During the first half of the 20th century, the prevailing view of European megaliths was that they represented a cultural trait that had diffused from the eastern Mediterranean. The beehive tombs (*tholoi*) of Crete and Greece (*see* THOLOS TOMB) were assumed to be earlier than similar tombs in Italy and Sicily and the rock-cut tombs of Malta. These were presumed to have inspired the megaliths of the Iberian peninsula, whence the technique and tradition of megalithic building supposedly spread to France, Britain and northern Europe. The prevailing model was one of *ex oriente lux*, in which the 'Tower' cultures of north-west Europe could not have built the megaliths except under influence from the 'higher' cultures of the Ancient Near East and the Mediterranean region. This diffusionist model led to megaliths being seen as part of a 'megalithic religion', in which the ideology of monumental, communal tombs was spread by colonists or 'missionaries' from the Mediterranean. The existence of megalithic monuments outside Europe in places as distant as Korea and Japan (*see* §2(iv) below) fed hyperdiffusionist models of megalithic dispersal.

While the idea of a megalithic religion has lost favour, it is nonetheless plausible that the megalithic tombs held considerable importance in the collective ideology of Neolithic communities. As such, they served not only as chambers in which to dispose of the dead but also as focal points for ritual and ceremony. While elaborate grave offerings are rarely found in megalithic tombs, their occupants were commonly subject to defleshing elsewhere, perhaps at ceremonial sites, such as Hambledon Hill in England. Although there was clearly ritual significance to the construction of alignments and of stone circles and henge monuments, this does not have to be attributed to ideas from elsewhere, as developments in dating techniques have shown.

(b) Territorial markers. The application of radiocarbon dating to many megalithic structures in western Europe proved revolutionary in that it demolished the developmental theory that sought to derive them from Eastern and Mediterranean precursors. Instead, it was possible to demonstrate an indigenous development of megalithic architecture, subject at best to short-distance influences. In particular, it emerged that the tombs of Brittany, northwest France (*see* BARNENEZ and GAVRINIS) were among the earliest known, dating before *c.* 4000 BC, with local evolution of megalithic structures occurring in other regions shortly thereafter. Colin Renfrew, who suggested several independent local centres of megalithic development in the Iberian peninsula, Brittany, southern England, Ireland and Denmark, has argued that megalithic tombs served as territorial markers in Neolithic society. Clearly the communal burials in the tombs were accumulated over years, decades or even centuries, and these structures were central elements of the landscape. Renfrew proposed that as the populations of Neolithic societies grew, they would have found it increasingly necessary to maintain their territorial rights, and that they did so by erecting monumental and permanent symbols that contained the bones of generations of ancestors. Thus these structures would not simply be places to dispose of the dead but were also visible public social focuses, perhaps also serving as meeting-places and ritual locations.

(c) Astronomy. Many megalithic monuments have prominent features or axes that are aligned to celestial events, leading to the hypothesis that they functioned as observational tools. Indeed, the hypothesis that Stonehenge was an astronomical observatory has been so widely espoused as to have been accepted uncritically outside the field of archaeology. The hypothesis of megalithic astronomy is based largely on studies by Gerald Hawkins (1965) and Alexander Thom (1971) and elaborated by others, but it remains difficult to prove, given the imprecise data and the incremental, and sometimes incomplete, construction sequences of the monuments. What is clear is that some megalithic monuments were positioned in ways that had some basis in celestial observation. For instance, it had already been noticed in the 18th century that Stonehenge had been constructed along the axis of the summer solstice. Similarly, at the passage grave of NEWGRANGE in Ireland, the rising sun at the summer solstice shines directly down the passage to the central chamber. The stone circle and alignments at Callanish, Scotland, also have an astronomical orientation, as do many other Scottish stone circles. Yet the orientation of these monuments with reference to celestial phenomena does not necessarily mean that they functioned as active devices in a purposeful system of knowledge and prediction.

(d) Inscribed landscape. Most of the theories that have been put forward to explain megalithic architecture have focused on the monuments themselves. However, Julian Thomas attempted to reorientate the discussion towards a consideration of the entire prehistoric landscape, in which megalithic monuments would have been prominent elements. He pointed out that the monumental Neolithic landscapes of north-western Europe were quite different

from those that both preceded and followed them. Megalithic monuments in such a landscape would have been artificial landmarks that controlled the 'reading' of the terrain by its inhabitants, imposing a structure that in a sense determined the human encounter with the surroundings. Thus, rather than simply serving as 'temples', 'territorial markers' or 'observatories', the megalithic monuments were part of a massive human reorganization of the landscape. Moreover, the relationship between this 'inscribed landscape' and human society would not have been static but continually changing, and thus monuments were redefined and reinterpreted as patterns of power and human relationships shifted. Clearly many megalithic monuments were sited to take advantage of natural features, and the way in which they impose structure and definition on a landscape is often very striking: the alignments of standing stones at Carnac completely transformed the character of a large tract of Brittany. Moreover, the view of megalithic monuments as part of an overall landscape accords well with the fact that they must be seen as part of a coherent architectural vocabulary in which the various forms of megalithic and non-megalithic architecture are interrelated.

BIBLIOGRAPHY

G. Hawkins: *Stonehenge Decoded* (London, 1965)
A. Thom: *Megalithic Sites in Britain* (Oxford, 1967)
——: *Megalithic Lunar Observatories* (Oxford, 1971)
C. Renfrew: *Before Civilization* (London, 1973)
C. Chippindale: *Stonehenge Complete* (London, 1983)
R. Joussaume: *Dolmens for the Dead: Megalith-building throughout the World* (London, 1988)
J.-P. Mohen: *The World of Megaliths* (New York, 1989)
G. Wainwright: *The Henge Monuments: Ceremony and Society in Prehistoric Britain* (London, 1989)
E. S. Twohig: *Irish Megalithic Tombs* (Princes Risborough, 1990)
J. Thomas: *Rethinking the Neolithic* (Cambridge, 1991)
M. S. Midgley: *TRB Culture: The First Farmers of the North European Plain* (Edinburgh, 1992)
A. Burl: *From Carnac to Callanish* (New Haven, 1994)
P. Rahtz: *Glastonbury* (London, 1994)
C. Thomas: *Tintagel* (London, 1994)

PETER BOGUCKI

2. REGIONAL SURVEY.

(i) Europe. The megalithic architectural tradition of Europe began *c.* 4500 BC and flourished until *c.* 1500 BC, after which it gradually died out. It comprises the most numerous and diverse group of megalithic monuments, and includes some of the earliest known stone architecture in the world. The monuments are clustered along the Atlantic seaboard from southern Scandinavia through France and Britain to the tip of the Iberian Peninsula (*see* PREHISTORIC EUROPE, §§IV, 2, and V, 3). There were also important megalithic traditions on certain Mediterranean islands, especially Malta (*see* MALTA, §II), Sardinia and the BALEARIC ISLANDS. European megalithic structures can be loosely divided into two morphological groups: in the first, the earliest and largest group, the monuments served primarily as tombs, while in the second group the megaliths defined a ceremonial area. The funerary monuments normally enclose an internal space, while the megaliths of the ceremonial monuments are usually free-standing. It was believed that the megalithic traditions derived from Near Eastern and Mediterranean cultures until the 1970s when the recalibration of radiocarbon dating (*see* PREHISTORIC EUROPE, §I) proved that western European megalithic monuments were an independent development.

(ii) Africa, Near East and Central Asia. Megalithic structures are particularly densely scattered across North and Central Africa. While the Moroccan, Algerian and Tunisian chamber tombs—the earliest of which date from the late 3rd millennium BC—could conceivably be related to megalithic structures across the Mediterranean, such influence is much less plausible in the case of the simple chamber tombs of the Harar region of Ethiopia (possibly built during the 2nd millennium BC), and irrelevant when considering the multi-period anthropomorphic and uncarved stelae distributed across the rest of that country. In the Bouar group of tombs in the Central African Republic (*c.* 1st millennium BC) the dead were placed in cists under mounds surmounted by standing stones. Simple standing stones and carved stelae are scattered throughout West Africa, along with stone circles apparently dating from *c.* 200 BC to *c.* AD 1000. At Sine-Ngayene in Senegal multiple circles of megaliths mark the collective graves of up to 60 individuals. However, these monuments certainly have no connection with their European counterparts, or with the free-standing circles of the Arabian Peninsula.

The Madagascan tradition of erecting standing stones and chamber tombs is particularly interesting in that it survived into the 19th century and continues in a limited form. The tombs were ancestral and collective, although certain people (such as smallpox victims) were excluded. Standing stones continue to be erected for reasons varying from the political to the personal. Hundreds of people might be involved in the erection of a large stone, the accompanying ceremony often involving elaborate ritual, sacrifices and feasting.

There is a large number of structures in the Near East that might be termed megalithic, most notably in the cemeteries of the Jordan Valley. At Ala-Safat there are over 160 tombs, most consisting of a simple four-sided chamber and an antechamber with a perforated entrance stone with a rectangular opening. Twelve stone circles, where the corpses may have been cremated before deposition, are associated with the tombs. Perforated entrance stones (in this case with a circular aperture) also characterize the chamber tombs of the 3rd millennium BC onwards found in the western Caucasus. The sides and roofs of the chambers are usually formed of single slabs, but occasionally a megalith was hollowed out to form a compartment.

(iii) India. The ancient megaliths of India are scattered over the Deccan peninsula, with smaller groups to the north and in Pakistan. By contrast, the living megalith tradition is largely confined to the north-east of the subcontinent, where standing stones continue to be erected occasionally. However, this minor current tradition does not seem to be linked to ancient megalith construction, which appears to have begun during the later 2nd millennium BC and persisted into the early centuries AD.

Setting aside rock-cut tombs and burials simply covered by a large slab, the most interesting and common types of Indian megalithic structure are the slab cist and the dolmenoid cist. Slab cists consist of large, flat, dressed

3. Indian megalitic structure, slab cist with 'porthole'; watercolour by Philip Meadows-Taylor, 1850 (London, British Library)

slabs arranged either in a pit of variable depth or on the ground to form a square or rectangular funerary chamber capped by one or more large slabs. They are commonly embellished by the addition of enclosing cairns and/or surrounding circles of slabs or blocks, and some may be partly formed or enclosed by dry-stone masonry. Slab cists often have an artificial 'porthole' in one of the slabs (if the cist is partitioned each partition may have an aperture) and commonly feature entrance passages formed by one or more pairs of slabs (see fig. 3). The portholes vary in size from those large enough to admit a man to small holes less than 100 mm in diameter; underground examples generally have a closing slab. Simpler slab cists without portholes or entrance passages also exist; these tend to be set in pits and are rectangular in form, some having multiple capstones.

Dolmenoid cists are similar in plan to the slab cists, except that they have an entrance gap rather than a porthole; however, their appearance is quite distinct because their chambers consist of unhewn or roughly dressed boulders rather than slabs. Certain massive examples in north Karnataka are sometimes referred to as 'chamber tombs' because of their similarity to European types.

Cairn circles, comprising simple stone cairns enclosed by circles of large boulders, are common in peninsular India. A cairn circle may cover either a cist of one of the types described above or a non-megalithic feature, such

as a pit burial, an urn burial or a terracotta sarcophagus. Simple low circles of megaliths are also common in southern India and parts of the north. Generally representing the only visible components of a cist, pit, urn or sarcophagus burial monument, they are effectively a variant of cist and cairn burials. Alignments of boulders and orthostats are also found in certain regions, notably south of Hyderabad in Andhra Pradesh. The more complex examples can contain hundreds of stones set in squares. There is an impressive, if enigmatic, series of long lines of large low rounded boulders at Vibhutihalli in north Karnataka. Some of the most distinctive Indian megaliths are peculiar to Kerala. In the simpler version one or more hemispherical 'hoodstones' (*kodakal*) lie directly on the ground covering urn burials, while in the more elaborate *topikal* version a wide hemispherical capstone is supported by the tips of four carefully set uprights.

(iv) South-east Asia, China and Japan. Megalithic remains in these regions are particularly difficult to date, partly because very few have been radiocarbon dated. Furthermore, in some regions megaliths continue to be erected, while in many others ancient monuments continue to be the focus of religious rites. Stone-constructed tombs are relatively scarce in central China, but some megalithic structures are found in such peripheral and adjacent regions as the Shandong peninsula, Zhejiang, Tibet and Taiwan. However, the best-documented concentrations

of megaliths are in Korea and Japan. Formerly the North Korean monuments were characterized as having simple (though occasionally massive) megalithic chambers covered by a large capstone, while those in South Korea and a closely related series on the island of Kyushu, Japan, were typified as having non-megalithic chambers set into the ground and covered by a megalith either set directly over them or supported by low slabs or dry-stone masonry. However, this scheme is over-simplified, as tombs with unsupported capstones are known to be widely distributed in North Korea. Both types probably date from the 1st millennium BC; the Japanese monuments are associated with the final Jōmon and the early Yayoi cultural stages. Some of the tombs of the early Japanese emperors and aristocracy of the 3rd to 7th centuries AD were constructed in an essentially megalithic style. Japan also has a limited number of small-scale prehistoric stone circles and related monuments, chiefly in the mountainous regions of Hokkaido. However, most of these monuments in fact comprise circular cairns of small stones with occasional pillars rather than rings of free-standing orthostats.

Indonesia and Malaysia are rich in megalithic structures of many types, dating from the prehistoric period to the present. Indonesian examples include the tombs on Sumba: strikingly regular table-shaped structures with flat tops supported by four legs that cover burial pits. In central Java, funerary enclosures are ringed by large megaliths, and in Toraja, Central Sulawesi, standing stones up to 5 m high are often arranged in groups. The monumental stone sculptures of Indonesia also represent a rich tradition. Malaysia has some notable examples of stone alignments, including one in the state of Negri Sembilan that consists of three megaliths decorated with vegetal and animal motifs. Negri Sembilan, Sarawak and Malacca possess many other examples of undecorated alignments, while Sabah has some particularly impressive examples of standing stones.

BIBLIOGRAPHY

B. K. Gururajarao: *The Megalithic Culture in South India* (Mysore, 1972)

A. Sundara: *The Early Chamber Tombs of South India* (Delhi, 1975)

V. N. Misra and P. Bellwood, eds: *Recent Advances in Indo-Pacific Prehistory* (Pune, 1978), pp. 447–501

B. Narasimhaiah: *Neolithic and Mesolithic Cultures in Tamil Nadu* (Delhi, 1980)

A. Thom, A. S. Thom and A. Burl: *Megalithic Rings*, Brit. Archaeol. Rep., Brit. Ser., lxxxi (Oxford, 1980)

S. Heggie: *Megalithic Science* (London, 1981)

C. Renfrew, ed.: *The Megalithic Monuments of Western Europe* (London, 1981)

B. Allchin and A. Allchin: *The Rise of Civilization in India and Pakistan* (Cambridge, 1982), pp. 330–45

Byung-mo Kim, ed.: *Megalithic Cultures in Asia* (Seoul, 1982)

R. Bradley: *The Social Foundations of Prehistoric Britain* (London, 1984)

C. L. N. Ruggles: *Megalithic Astronomy*, Brit. Archaeol. Rep., Brit. Ser., cxxiii (Oxford, 1984)

D. V. Clarke and others: *Symbols of Power at the Time of Stonehenge* (Edinburgh, 1985)

R. Joussaume: *Dolmens for the Dead: Megalith-building throughout the World* (London, 1988)

A. Ghosh, ed.: *An Encyclopaedia of Indian Archaeology*, 2 vols (Delhi, 1989)

ROB JAMESON

Megalopolis. City in Arcadia, southern Greece, which flourished from *c.* 368 BC to the 2nd century BC. Several small and previously separate communities in south-western Arcadia united *c.* 368 BC to form a state based on a new urban centre, both of which were called Megalopolis ('Great City'). This city rapidly became a major power in the Peloponnese, and remained so despite its partial destruction by Kleomenes of Sparta (223 BC, followed by rebuilding). Under Roman rule it declined in prosperity, although it was still inhabited until the 6th or 7th century AD. Its name is now borne by a small modern town to the south. The ancient city occupied a large walled area crossed by the River Helisson. Its architecture is known chiefly from the description by Pausanias (*Guide to Greece* VIII.xxx–xxxii), who visited it around AD 170, and from the British excavations of 1890–93. Bury suggested that the public buildings of the city itself were situated north of the Helisson, while those of the Arcadian Federation lay to its south, but the location of the Thersilion constitutes the only evidence for this view.

The city's most notable remains belong to the Thersilion and the theatre. The Thersilion (4th century BC; named after its dedicator) served as a meeting place for the Arcadian Federation. It was a rectangular building (66.65×52.43 m) with its main entrance on the south side, fronted by a portico of 14 Doric columns. The single large chamber inside had a timber roof supported by an ingeniously designed grid of columns, which radiated from the speaker's platform in a way that obscured the audience's view as little as possible. The floor also rose from the speaker's platform to the outside walls, since the furthest surviving column bases are *c.* 2.5 m above those beside the platform. The Thersilion was probably destroyed in the sack of 223 BC.

Immediately to the south was the theatre, built into a hillock adapted for the purpose. Though of the Greek standard form, with semicircular rows of seats rising around the orchestra, it has three notable features. First, according to Pausanias it was the largest in Greece; the *orchestra* has a diameter of 30.2 m and the auditorium (diam. 129.5 m) may have seated 17,000 to 21,000 spectators. Second, when the theatre was built no stage was provided, its place being occupied by the porch of the Thersilion, although by the Roman period a stone stage had been added. Finally, perhaps in the 3rd century BC, the western parodos was filled by a building for props.

The other excavated public buildings, which include the great Stoa of Philip (*c.* 340–*c.* 330 BC) with its three aisles and projecting wings, are heavily overgrown. However, in the south-east of the city there are well-preserved mosaics from a Roman house of the 6th century AD, depicting three Graces, animals, cupids, birds and fishes in geometric settings, although they are not first-rate works.

Some of the older settlements in the territory of Megalopolis that coexisted with the new city have been excavated. Gortys had two sanctuaries of Asklepios (one 5th–4th century BC, the other 4th century BC), and a rare example of a Greek bathhouse (4th century BC), while at Alipheira temples of Athena (late 6th century BC to early 5th) and Asklepios (*c.* 300 BC) have been found; but the most interesting of these sites is Lykosoura, where there was a Sanctuary of Despoina ('the Mistress') and a Temple of Artemis. The prostyle Doric Temple of Despoina measuring (ultimately) 21.5×12.5 m was originally built in the 4th century BC; the history of subsequent changes is not wholly clear. The colossal cult group was by the sculptor DAMOPHON of Messene (the heads in Athens, N. Archaeol. Mus.). An unusual feature of this temple is a door in the south side of the cella (similar to the side door of the Temple of Apollo at Bassai). This opened on to a flight of 10 steps nearly 29 m long that led nowhere but formed a retaining wall for the slope and may have accommodated worshippers watching ritual at the temple door.

BIBLIOGRAPHY

E. A. Gardner and others: *Excavations at Megalopolis, 1890–1891* (London, 1892)

J. B. Bury: 'The Double City of Megalopolis', *J. Hell. Stud.*, xviii (1898), pp. 15–22

A. Petronotes: *E Megale Polis tes Arkadias* [Megale Polis in Arcadia] (Athens, 1973)

D. Leekley and R. Noyes: *Archaeological Excavations in Southern Greece* (Park Ridge, NJ, 1976)

M. Jost: *Sanctuaires et cultes d'Arcadie* (Paris, 1985)

J. ROY

Megaron. Term used in Homeric epic for the great hall of a house or palace, and sometimes for the whole building. (In this article relative dates for the Bronze Age are being used; for discussion of chronology *see* HELLADIC, §I, 3.) The first excavators of TIRYNS and MYCENAE applied it to the main apartments of the palaces and houses there. Since then it has become the generally accepted archaeological term for an oblong structure (see fig.) entered at its narrow end and consisting of an almost square main room (*domos* (a)) with one or two vestibules (*aithousa* and *prodomos* (b)), the outer one (*aithousa* (c)) being a porch *in antis*. It is generally assumed that the megaron originated north or east of the Greek peninsula, though not from central Europe, and that it was brought south by immigrants whose ethnic identity and time of arrival remain a matter for conjecture. The Middle Neolithic square huts at Otzaki Magoula in Thessaly with their short partition walls projecting from the sides and one or two wooden columns at their entrances, which were claimed to be the archetypes, hardly qualify as such. The earliest megaron forms, however primitive, are the Late Neolithic structures at Sesklo and Dimini near Volos. The few known Early and Middle Helladic buildings are either insufficiently preserved or clearly different in plan. The first genuine Late Helladic (LH) megaron is the middle wing (LH II A–B) of Mansion I at the Menelaion, Sparta.

In the LH palaces the megaron was the stateroom, the structure dominating the whole complex. Special materials (e.g. coloured stone, gypsum) were used in its construction, and its lime-plastered walls and floors were decorated with sculptured or painted dados and frescoes. The *domos* had a central hearth, also painted, which was surrounded by four wooden columns, fluted or sheathed in bronze. At Tiryns and PYLOS, and presumably at Mycenae, a throne stood against its side wall. Smaller megara were less elaborately constructed. Walls were coated with a lime and clay stucco, column and doorjamb bases were roughly shaped, floors were plastered but unpainted. Such megara had single (e.g. Agios Kosmas, Attica) or columnless vestibules (e.g. Korakou, Corinthia, Houses H and O; Mouriatada, Arcadia; Tiryns; Mycenae, West House and Tsountas's House; Menelaion, Sparta) or even closed vestibules, accessible from the sides (e.g. Mycenae, House

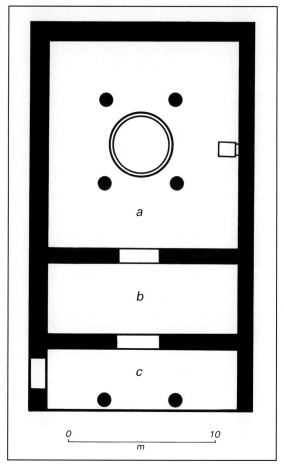

Megaron from the palace at Mycenae, LH III B, plan: (a) *domos* with hearth; (b) *prodomos*; (c) *aithousa*

of the Warrior Vase and House M; GLA, Boiotia) with no internal supports, no hearth and no throne in the *domos*.

Megara were originally isolated structures, but by the 15th century BC they were already being incorporated into larger complexes, fronting courtyards and linked by passages or party walls to other rooms. As an architectural from they occurred only in prehistoric Greece, the Aegean (e.g. Phylakopi, Melos; Poliochni, Lemnos) and Troy I, II and VI, being unknown even in contemporary Crete. But, although distinctively Helladic, the megaron is far from being ubiquitous, or even frequent, especially in Pre-Palatial Helladic settlements, where megara are not necessarily the largest structures either. The term is often used indiscriminately: true megara have been found at less than a tenth of the prehistoric sites with architectural remains, and there are about as many megaron-like buildings with some but not all the appropriate features. In historical times the term was used for sacrificial pits or caves dedicated to chthonic deities (e.g. Demeter and Persephone) and for the inner sanctums of certain temples in Greece (e.g. the Temple of Apollo, Delphi, 7th century BC; Hekatompedon, Athens, mid-6th century BC) and Egypt. The form survived, somewhat modified, in the plans of the Greek temple (*see* TEMPLE, §IV).

BIBLIOGRAPHY

Enc. A. Ant.; Pauly–Wissowa

E. B. Smith: 'The Megaron and its Roof', *Amer. J. Archaeol.*, xlvi (1942), pp. 99–118

V. Müller: 'Development of the "Megaron" in Prehistoric Greece', *Amer. J. Archaeol.*, xlviii (1944), pp. 342–8

B. Schweitzer: 'Megaron und Hofhaus in der Ägäis des 3–2 Jahrtausends v.Chr.', *Annu. Brit. Sch. Athens*, xlvi (1951), pp. 160–67

☐

Megiddo [now Tell el-Mutesellim]. Site in Israel of a Canaanite and Israelite town *c.* 35 km south-east of Haifa. It is mentioned both in the Bible (e.g. as Armageddon, the site of the eschatological battle between the forces of Good and Evil; Revelation 16:16) and in other ancient sources. Excavations at the site by G. Schumacher (1903–5), C. S. Fisher, P. L. O. Guy and G. Loud (1925–39) and Y. Yadin (1960–72) have established its almost continuous occupation between *c.* 5000 and *c.* 300 BC and its pre-eminent position among the cities of Palestine.

1. URBAN DEVELOPMENT AND ARCHITECTURE. Only slight traces of the earliest, Late Neolithic (Yarmukian) occupation (*c.* 5500 BC) have been found, but in the later Chalcolithic period (*c.* 3500–*c.* 3100 BC) a village existed in the south-east of the site, with a rectangular temple surrounded by a courtyard. The pottery attests contact with settlements in southern Palestine. In the Early Bronze Age, probably *c.* 2700 BC, substantial building operations made Megiddo into one of the large towns of Palestine, with complex buildings, terrace walls, a drainage system and a large circular altar (diam. 8 m) within its own enclosure. Towards the end of the 3rd millennium BC three broad-room temples of identical plan were constructed around this altar. These and other buildings show that Megiddo continued to be occupied during the transition period (Early Bronze IV, *c.* 2300–*c.* 2000 BC), when many sites in Palestine were deserted.

Megiddo shared in the revival of urban culture in Palestine *c.* 2000 BC and was one of the first towns to be refortified. At this time burials were made generally within the town, and technological advances can be seen in the manufacture of wheelmade pottery (*see* SYRIA-PALESTINE, fig. 9b) and the introduction of bronze for tools and weapons. The latter development presupposes wider trading relations with areas of tin production, and imported pottery types (e.g. from Cyprus) were also increasingly common. Palatial buildings appeared in the centre, the east and eventually in the north of the town, which was defended by strong walls with a succession of gates. Eventually (the date is disputed) a larger temple with 3 m-thick walls and twin towers was constructed: in its ruins bronze figurines, clay liver-models, pendants and miniature cymbals were found (examples U. Chicago, IL, Orient. Inst. Mus.), providing some indication of its rituals. By the early 15th century BC Megiddo was a centre of power in Palestine, but after the siege and capture of the town *c.* 1457 BC by Pharaoh Tuthmosis III (*reg c.* 1479–*c.* 1426 BC) it became a vassal of Egypt and flourished under Egyptian control until *c.* 1150 BC.

In the mid-12th century BC the long period of continuity in town plan and culture, which had lasted through the Middle and Late Bronze Age, finally came to an end. For some 50 years there was a return to a village-type of settlement, similar to many others in the hills of Palestine at this time. Around 1100 BC, however, large public buildings were again constructed, with the use of distinctive reddish, partially baked bricks on stone foundations, and there was a flourishing metal industry in the southern part of the town. New pottery styles appeared, including Philistine types, and Megiddo possibly came under Philistine control at this time. The destruction of the town *c.* 1000 BC, attested by a thick layer of ash, can plausibly be attributed to King David (*reg c.* 1010–970 BC). The town was at first rebuilt on a modest scale, but later in the 10th century BC, probably under Solomon (*reg c.* 970–931 BC; cf. 1 Kings 9:15), four large public buildings and a fortified town gate were constructed with ashlar masonry and proto-Aeolic capitals (*see also* JEWISH ART, §II, 2(i)). Following the division of the Israelite kingdom and the Egyptian capture of Megiddo by Sheshonq I (*reg c.* 945–924 BC), commemorated on a stele erected at the site, the town became a major military base in the times of Omri and Ahab (*c.* 885–853 BC). It was surrounded by a town wall 3.6 m thick, and extensive stables (or possibly storehouses) and a protected underground access to the water supply were constructed. Megiddo fell to the Assyrians under Tiglath-pileser III (*reg* 745–727 BC) in the late 730s BC, and it became the centre of an Assyrian province. Most of the city was rebuilt on a grid plan, with some typically Assyrian open-court buildings in the north near the gate. With the transition to Babylonian rule in 605 BC, the site seems to have been abandoned, but under the Persians (538–332 BC) it was occupied again, probably by garrison troops.

2. ARTEFACTS. The earliest art at Megiddo is from the Chalcolithic period. On some paving-stones of the temple courtyard there are incised drawings, for example of a harpist and a horned animal (Loud, 1948, pls 271–82). Some potsherds of this period bear similar designs. Much fine gold and faience jewellery was found in the tombs of the Middle and Late Bronze Age, including headbands, ornate earrings and bracelets, as well as beads from polychrome necklaces and bone inlays of animals and geometric designs (Loud, 1948, pls 192–5, 208–15, 224–7; examples U. Chicago, IL, Orient. Inst. Mus.). Among the decorated pottery the Bichrome ware (Cypriot and local imitation, *c.* 1550–*c.* 1400 BC), which combines geometric panels with lifelike paintings of birds, fish and other animals in red and black, is especially fine (Loud, 1948, pls 39, 48–9, 53, 56, 58).

A remarkable collection of carved ivories (382 pieces) was found in a cellar beneath the ruins of the 12th-century BC town (Loud, 1939). Various techniques are represented: incised designs, high and low relief, and openwork. Many pieces were from cosmetic objects, such as combs and bowls; others were for the decoration of furniture or for game-playing. The motifs are geometrical, natural and sometimes mythological. Comparative study has distinguished several different styles, including Mycenaean Greek and Syrian, as well as native Canaanite. One exceptional piece, of Hittite origin, shows two kings standing under winged sun-discs with the pantheon and four bulls beneath. Many of these ivories are exhibited in the Oriental Institute Museum at the University of Chicago; they provide an unparalleled insight into the culture and luxury goods of the time. A Philistine jug of the 11th century BC has a frieze showing a lyre-player surrounded by animals, recalling the Orpheus legend (Loud, 1948, pl. 76.1). From the same period is a tripod stand discovered by Schumacher, the upper part of which had been cast as a naked female figure playing a double flute. There are fewer objects of artistic interest from the Israelite period, but three inscribed seals from the 8th century BC are worthy of note: one of 'Shema, servant of [King] Jeroboam' (untraced) shows a roaring lion, while two others, of 'Asaph' (now in Istanbul) and 'Haman' (now in Jerusalem) feature winged griffins in Egyptian style, probably a sign of Phoenician influence on the northern kingdom of Israel.

For general discussion of the ancient art and architecture of the region *see* SYRIA-PALESTINE.

BIBLIOGRAPHY
P. L. O. Guy and R. M. Engberg: *Megiddo Tombs*, Oriental Institute Publications (Chicago, 1938)
R. S. Lamon and G. M. Shipton: *Megiddo I*, Oriental Institute Publications (Chicago, 1939)
G. Loud: *The Megiddo Ivories*, Oriental Institute Publications (Chicago, 1939)
——: *Megiddo II*, 2 vols, Oriental Institute Publications (Chicago, 1948)
R. D. Barnett: *Ancient Ivories of the Middle East*, Qedem Monographs (Jerusalem, 1982)
G. I. Davies: *Megiddo*, Cities of the Biblical World (Cambridge, 1986)

G. I. DAVIES

Megillah. Parchment scroll containing the text of the Old Testament Book of Esther, which recounts the deliverance of the Jews from persecution in the Persian empire and which was probably written during the reign of the Hasmonean Jewish king John Hyrcanus (*reg c.* 135–105 BC). The Book of Esther has since then traditionally been read in the synagogue on the festival of Purim, for which purpose it was copied separately in the form of a scroll (Megillah; *see also* JEWISH ART, §VI, 3).

Those scrolls intended for use in the synagogue had no ornament, but every well-off family had an elegantly decorated scroll for its own use, kept in a costly silver case (*see* JEWISH ART, §VI, 3). It is not possible to trace the history of the decorated Megillah (pl. Megillat); a few exceptional and relatively old pieces served as models and were frequently copied. A 14th-century manuscript (Rome, Vatican, Bib. Apostolica, MS. hébr. 324, fol. 180) has the earliest description of a scroll of Esther, showing a cantor holding an undecorated Megillah. The illustrations of the Castilian Bible of the Duke of Alba, which were executed in 1422–30, depicted scenes from the Book of Esther that were later to become part of the customary repertory of Megillah illustrations. The earliest illustrated Megillat come from 16th-century Italy, and the golden age of the decorated Megillah spanned the 17th and 18th centuries, flourishing especially in Italy and the Low Countries.

Two types of Megillah were distinguished in Italy. The first is decorated exclusively with floral ornaments arranged between the columns of writing. Subsequently, small pictures, depicting scenes from the Book of Esther, were placed at the head and foot of the columns (e.g.

Paris, Mus. Cluny, Strauss-Rothschild collection, No. Inv. Cl. 18305). The second type is linked with the name of Griselini, a 17th-century Christian engraver: the scrolls of Esther signed by or attributed to him for stylistic reasons are decorated with arches surrounding the columns of text and supporting floral motifs, amphorae and birds. Under the columns of writing, between the pillars supporting the arches, are small pictures showing episodes from the story. There is often a final frame reserved for the blessings recited before and after the reading. In some cases the small pictures at the foot of the page are paired with a second series, placed at the head of the columns, showing allegorical scenes whose relation to the Book of Esther is not always clear. The Megillat with architectural and biblical decorations were enormously successful, being produced in increasingly large numbers in Italy during the 18th century; numerous examples of varying technical quality exist.

Another group of Megillat, with engraved decorations, appears also to have originated in Italy in the 18th century (see fig.). The columns of text, arranged in rectangular frames, are extended above and below by bands of floral decorations, interrupted at the top by medallions containing the portraits of the counsellors of Ahasuerus, and at the bottom by miniatures depicting episodes from the story. Between the columns, against a sepia background, are the figures of the principal characters. Despite the deliberately archaicizing style of the decorations and the human figures, this series of Megillat dates only from the 18th century. It was probably inspired by the work of Shalom Italia (*c.* 1619–*c.* 1655), who made a great number of scrolls. In one such Megillah, executed in 1640 in Amsterdam (Jerusalem, Israel Mus.), the text is placed between the Corinthian columns of a classicizing arcade. The tympana have amphorae of flowers, and the keystones of the arches are replaced by scallops, on which landscapes are depicted. The spandrels of the arches are decorated with female allegorical figures. The characters of the story are represented between the columns; at their feet, small framed pictures depict the principal episodes of the book.

Shalom Italia's work was widely imitated in versions that did not always equal its quality. This type of scroll also spread through the Low Countries and Germany. From the end of the 18th century engravings gave way to painted decorations, and the traditional themes were enriched by folk elements. Genre scenes were added, and the scenes from the Bible were sometimes updated by references to contemporary events: thus, in one scroll, made in Alsace towards the end of the 18th century, Queen Vashti, with the features of Queen Marie-Antoinette, is shown being executed on the guillotine.

The practice of decorating the Megillah flourished also among some Jewish communities in Islamic lands. Preserved examples date mostly from the 19th century and early 20th. Unlike in the West, human figures and illustrations of the narrative are strictly avoided. Instead, floral and geometric patterns in bright colours profusely decorate these scrolls. Iraqi Megillat produced in 19th-century Baghdad are characterized, in addition, by the traditional genealogies of Mordecai and Haman. These lists are written in monumental square letters, coloured red and green, along the upper and lower margins of the scroll

Megillah (esther scroll) from Italy, mid-18th century (Paris, Musée de Cluny, Inv. Cl. 12296e)

(e.g. parchment rolled on wood, *c.* 1860s–1870s; Jerusalem, Wolfson Mus.). In Morocco architectural decoration was common: in the coastal town of Mogador (now Essaouira), where Sephardi immigrants settled early on, examples show a typical Moorish arcade framing the columns of the text. Pairs of loving birds are found at times in the Megillat of Tétouan (Morocco).

In the 1920s the art of the illuminated Megillah was revived by the artists of the Bezalel Academy of Arts and Design in Jerusalem. A typical example, in a silver case, illuminated in 1927 by the Bezalel artist Ze'ev Raban (1890–1970), is preserved at the B'nai B'rith Klutznick Museum, Washington, DC.

For further discussion of Jewish illuminated manuscripts *see* JEWISH ART, §V, 1.

RDK
BIBLIOGRAPHY
R. Wischnitzer: 'The Esther Story in Art', *The Purim Anthology*, ed. P. Goodman (Philadelphia, 1949), pp. 222–49, 519–21
M. Metzger: 'The John Rylands Megillah and Some Other Illustrated Megilloth of the XVth to XVIIth Centuries', *Bull. John Rylands Lib.*, xlv (1962–3), pp. 148–84
——: 'A Study of Some Unknown Hand-painted Megilloth of the Seventeenth and Eighteenth Centuries', *Bull. John Rylands Lib.*, xlvi (1963–4), pp. 84–126
——: 'The Earliest Engraved Italian Megilloth', *Bull. John Rylands Lib.*, xlviii (1965–6), pp. 381–432
——: 'La megillàh illustrata della comunità israelitica di Padova', *Rass. Mens. Israel*, xxxii (1966), pp. 88–98
The Stieglitz Collection: Masterpieces of Jewish Art (exh. cat. by C. Benjamin, Jerusalem, Israel Mus., 1987)
S. Sabar: 'Sephardi Elements in North African Hebrew Manuscript Decoration', *Jew. A.*, xviii (1992), pp. 168–91

GABRIELLE SED-RAJNA, with SHALOM SABAR

Megilp [magilp]. Oil painting medium composed of mastic resin dissolved in turpentine and linseed oil to give a gelatinous consistency. It was used in the 18th and 19th centuries to produce an enamel-like finish, but it becomes brittle and yellow with age and is vulnerable to some cleaning solvents.

RUPERT FEATHERSTONE

Megisba, Qasr el-. *See under* BAHARIYA OASIS.

Meglio, Jacopo del. *See* COPPI, GIACOMO.

Megyeri, Barna (*b* Oradea, Romania, 12 July 1920; *d* Budapest, 14 March 1966). Hungarian sculptor. He moved from Transylvania to Hungary when he was 17 and studied at the College of Fine Arts, Budapest (1937–42), under Zsigmond Kisfaludi Strobl, although he considered Ferenc Medgyessy, in whose studio he also worked for a while, to have been his real tutor. Megyeri began his career considering Easter Island heads, Etruscan, Hindu and Inca art as ideal models. As an artist he was of a searching, contemplative disposition. In April 1944 he exhibited a number of works (e.g. *Grenade Thrower*, *Woman with a Balalaika*, etc.) along with other young artists at the National Salon in Budapest. His own style was consolidated only in the latter part of his life. *Spartacus* (erected 1958; Budapest, Kerepesi Ave.) portrays the naked warrior falling to his knees with his body and limbs moving in opposite directions; it is a varied and exciting play on forms that creates a strong sense of space.

Megyeri received many public commissions, for which he usually fashioned smooth-surfaced, slender and elegant statues. His large public sculptures are characterized by their formal variation and professional execution (e.g. the *Rape of Europa*, 1966; Debrecen U. Agrar. Sci.), and he often collaborated successfully with architects. From the late 1940s he experimented with systems art, and his paper and metal sheet foldings, drawings and constructions, prepared using various techniques, can be related to later trends in Pop art. The foyer of the Hotel Metropol in Budapest is decorated with his folded metal sheets, and the ceiling sculptures of the National Theatre, Budapest, were created to his designs.

BIBLIOGRAPHY

I. Rozgonyi: 'Beszélgetés Megyeri Barnával' [Conversation with Barna Megyeri], *Művészet* (March 1964), pp. 31–4
J. Frank: 'Megyeri Barna (1920–1966)', *Élet & Irodalom* (19 March 1966)
C. Sík: 'Ellentétek szorításában: Megyeri Barna szobrairól' [In the grip of contradictions: on Barna Megyeri's sculptures], *Tükör* (2 Nov 1971)

S. KONTHA

Mehmed II. *See* OTTOMAN, §II(1).

Mehmed Ağa [Sedefkâr: 'mother-of-pearl worker'] (*b* Kalkandelen, western Macedonia or Ilbasan, Albania, *c.* 1550; *d* Istanbul, 1622). Ottoman architect and worker in mother-of-pearl. He followed the typical career path of architects at the Ottoman court: recruited as a janissary (*c.* 1562), from 1569 to 1588 he studied architecture in the imperial palace under Sinan (*see* SINAN (ii)) and mother-of-pearl inlay under Usta Muhammed. He was appointed superintendent of the water supply, the second ranking official in the corps of imperial architects, in 1597 or 1598, and finally replaced AHMED DALGIÇ as chief court architect on 11 October 1606. Mehmed Ağa travelled extensively: appointed court gate-keeper in 1589–90, he went to Egypt on official business and returned via Syria and Anatolia, visiting the holy shrines along his route, and as inspector of fortresses and garrisons he was sent to the Balkans, Hungary and the Crimea. From 1593 to 1597 he also worked in the provincial administration of Diyarbakır, Damascus and Hawran.

According to his biographer Ca'fer Efendi in the *Risāle-i Mi'māriyye* (1614–15), Mehmed Ağa was the architect of numerous mosques, madrasas, baths, palaces, pavilions, bridges and fountains. His attested works in Istanbul include the complex of Ahmed I (1609–16; *see* ISTANBUL, §III, 11), the Mimar Ağa Mosque, the Istavroz Mosque (destr.) and the fountain of Ahmed I at Tophane (destr.). He is also said to have built 40 fountains in Ilbasan, Albania. He supervised repairs to the Ka'ba and the great mosques in Mecca and Medina and carried out restorations on the Ibrahim Pasha and Topkapı palaces in Istanbul. He was probably also responsible for the completion of Sinan's complex for Murad III in Manisa (1586) and the tomb of Mehmed III in Istanbul. His work is largely derivative; size and splendour do not compensate for the lack of inspiration. Works in mother-of-pearl attributed to him include an ornamental wooden ceiling (1587–92) in the mosque of Murad III at Manisa, which is signed 'Mehmed Halife, one of the decorators of the imperial court', the 'Arife Tahtı (1607–8), a throne for Ahmed I in the treasury of Topkapı Palace (*see* THRONE, §III) and a Koran box dated 1616 formerly in the tomb of Ahmed I. The doors and shutters for the mosque of Ahmed I in Istanbul, if not Mehmed Ağa's own work, were surely created under his supervision.

BIBLIOGRAPHY

Ca'fer Efendi (*d* 1623): *Risāle-i Mi'māriyye: An Early Seventeenth-century Ottoman Treatise on Architecture*, ed. and trans. H. Crane (Leiden, 1987)
L. A. Mayer: *Islamic Architects and their Works* (Geneva, 1956)
G. Goodwin: *A History of Ottoman Architecture* (Baltimore and London, 1971), pp. 342–50

Z. Nayır: *Osmanlı mimarlığında Sultan Ahmet külliyesi ve Sonrası, 1609–1690* [The Sultan Ahmed complex and its successors in Ottoman architecture, 1609–1690] (Istanbul, 1975), pp. 35–153

HOWARD CRANE

Mehmed Çelebi, Kara. *See* KARA MEMI.

Mehmed Esad Yesari. *See* ESAD YESARI.

Mehmed-i Siyah. *See* KARA MEMI.

Mehmed of Bosnia [Mehmed-i Bosna] (*fl* Istanbul, 1588–1605). Ottoman Turkish goldsmith. As one of the craftsmen attached to the Ottoman court, he produced a number of elaborate pieces that are either signed by him or can be attributed to him on stylistic grounds. The latter group includes the crown presented by Sultan Ahmed I to his vassal Stephen Bocskay of Transylvania in 1605 (Vienna, Ksthist. Mus.).

See also ISLAMIC ART, §IV, 4(i).

BIBLIOGRAPHY

E. Atıl: *The Age of Sultan Süleyman the Magnificent* (Washington and New York, 1987), pp. 61, 63

Mehmed Pasha. *See* SOKOLLU MEHMED PASHA.

Mehmed Rasim [Eğrikapılı Hoca Mehmed] (*b* 1687; *d* 1755). Ottoman calligrapher. He studied with his father, Yusuf Efendi, and with the court calligrapher Sayyid Abdallah of Yediküle (*d* 1731). Achieving some reputation at an early age, Mehmed Rasim became a major court calligrapher in the Tulip period during the reign of Ahmed III (*reg* 1703–30; *see* OTTOMAN, §II(5)). In addition to copying over 60 manuscripts of the Koran (e.g. Istanbul, Topkapı Pal Mus.), he was skilled at marbling (*see* ISLAMIC ART, §III, 5) and was also responsible for the lovely inscriptions on the fountain of Saliha Sultan at Azap Kapı in Istanbul.

BIBLIOGRAPHY

Ş. Rado: *Türk hattatları* [Turkish calligraphers] (Istanbul, n.d.), pp. 155–6
A. Schimmel: *Calligraphy and Islamic Culture* (New York, 1984)

WALTER B. DENNY

Mehmed Şefik [Şefik Bey; Muḥammad Shafīq] (*b* Istanbul, 1819; *d* Istanbul, 1880). Ottoman calligrapher. He first studied calligraphy with Ali Vasfi and then with MUSTAFA İZZET. In 1845 he was appointed teacher of calligraphy to the Muzika-i Hümayun, the imperial brass band. Together with the calligrapher Abdülfettah (1814–96), he was sent by Sultan Abdülmecid (*reg* 1839–61) to Bursa to repair the inscriptions in the Ulu Cami (congregational mosque), which had been severely damaged in the earthquake of 1855. His inscriptions there are reckoned among his finest works. During the three years he spent on this project he also wrote inscriptions in other mosques. His work includes beautiful compositions in *thuluth*, *jalī*, *naskh* and *dīvānī* scripts.

BIBLIOGRAPHY

K. Baykal: *Bursa'da Ulu Câmi* [The Ulu Cami of Bursa] (Istanbul, 1950)
A. S. Ünver: *Hattat Şefik Bey (1819–1880): Hayatı ve eserleri* [The calligrapher Şefik Bey (1819–1880): his life and works] (Istanbul, 1956)
Ş. Rado: *Türk hattatları* [Turkish calligraphers] (Istanbul, n.d.), pp. 220–21

Mehmed Şevki [Şevki Efendi; Muḥammad Shawqī] (*b* Kastamonu, 1829; *d* Istanbul, 1887). Ottoman calligrapher. He was brought to Istanbul at a young age and learned *thuluth* and *naskh* scripts from his maternal uncle Mehmed Hulusi (*d* 1874), receiving his diploma (Turk. *icazet*) at the age of 14. Despite the insistence of his teacher, he refused to study with any other master and directed his attention towards an examination of the calligraphic models prepared by MUSTAFA İZZET. He taught penmanship in the Ministry of War and in several schools. In *naskh* script he adopted the style of HAFIZ OSMAN and Isma'il Zühdü (*d* 1806), while in *thuluth* he followed MUSTAFA RAQIM. Among his work are several complex calligraphic compositions.

BIBLIOGRAPHY

A. S. Ünver: *Hilyei saadet hattat-ı Mehmed Şevki* [Calligraphic compositions of the calligrapher Mehmed Şevki] (Istanbul, 1953)

Mehoffer, Józef (*b* Ropczyce, nr Rzeszów, 19 March 1869; *d* Wadowice, nr Kraków, 8 July 1946). Polish painter, printmaker and decorative artist. From 1887 he studied at the School of Fine Arts in Kraków under Władysław Łuszczkiewicz (1828–1900) and Jan Matejko. In 1889 Mehoffer and Stanisław Wyspiański, as the two most talented pupils of the School, were engaged to assist Matejko in his decorative wall paintings for the Gothic Church of St Mary in Kraków. This work aroused Mehoffer's interest in both fresco and stained glass. In 1889–90 he studied at the Kunstakademie, Vienna, and in 1891 he travelled through Salzburg, Innsbruck and Basle (where the work of Arnold Böcklin caught his imagination), eventually going to Paris. There he studied at the Académie Colarossi, at the Ecole Nationale des Arts Décoratifs and, from 1892, in the atelier of Léon Bonnat at the Ecole Nationale des Beaux-Arts. During his stay in Paris (1891–6) he devoted much time to studying works by the Old Masters in the Louvre; he also studied architecture, making a tour of medieval cathedrals in France in 1893. He took an interest in current history painting and exhibitions of contemporary art, especially the paintings of Pierre Puvis de Chavannes and James Abbott McNeill Whistler. Mehoffer's early works, such as *Maternity* (1894), *Objects on a Mantelpiece* (1895; both Poznań, N. Mus.) and *Dance Naive* (1898; Kraków, N. Mus.), inspired by a theme from Paul Verlaine's poem *Les Ingénues*, reveal the extent to which he had absorbed the characteristics of the Nabi artists, to whom he was drawn for their tendencies towards decorative synthesis, refined stylization and tasteful tonality. Mehoffer employed an expressionistic variant of Symbolism to create an atmosphere suggestive of unease and impending disaster, as in the painting *The Ravine (La Gorge de Reusse*, 1897; Poznań, N. Mus.), as well as in the several versions from this period of *The Muse* (e.g. Warsaw, N. Mus.).

In Paris, Mehoffer continued to work on projects involving both fresco and stained glass, attempting to unite tradition with new stylistic currents. Projects from this period include stained-glass windows for the Mariacki Church in Kraków, carried out jointly with Wyspiański (1890–91; *in situ*), wall paintings for the Rudolfinum in Prague (1891; unexecuted) and stained glass for the Roman Catholic cathedral in Lemberg (now L'viv,

Ukraine, 1893; *in situ*). In 1895 Mehoffer won the international competition for a stained-glass design for the collegiate church (later cathedral) of St Nicolas in Fribourg, for which 47 designs had been submitted by well-known European artists. This success enabled him to embark on a large cycle of monumental compositions in stained glass, work that lasted 40 years. Mehoffer regarded these windows as a product of his own age, which could not be allowed to come into conflict with the ideal of the medieval building. While employing a *Jugendstil* stylization in the ornament to strengthen the expressive quality of the main motifs, he nonetheless eschewed the extreme expressive freedom more characteristic of *Jugendstil*. Colouristic exuberance and richness of decorative design were linked with an individual sense of harmony and an elegance of composition and line. European critics recognized the richness of Mehoffer's invention, the originality and innovative nature of his style, but also the typically Polish character of his work.

After 1900 Mehoffer designed numerous stained-glass windows in Poland. Alongside those in Fribourg, these ensure him a place among the finest designers of modern European stained glass and also among the most significant Polish decorative artists. Subsequently completed projects include the windows for Wawel Cathedral in Kraków (1904–24). At the same time Mehoffer worked in the field of wall painting, decorating, for example, the Treasury (1901–3) and the Szafraniec Chapel (1906–7) in Wawel Cathedral. Among the more important unrealized decorative projects are those for the cathedral in Płock (1903) and for the Armenian cathedral in Lemberg (now L'viv, Ukraine; 1906–8; sketches, Kraków, N. Mus.).

As a painter, Mehoffer produced his most important works during the last years of the 19th century, and he has been recognized as one of the leading exponents of new trends in Polish art at this period. Closely allied to the prevailing stylistic tendencies of the turn of the century and drawing on both Symbolism and *Jugendstil*, his work nonetheless retains its individual character, in particular because he felt little need to respond in his paintings to the conflicts and disturbances of the period, or to adopt the fatalistic and apocalyptic tendencies of the work of many of his contemporaries. The most characteristic feature of his work was, as he himself described it, a search for a style adequate to the beauty of the natural world as an affirmation of its loveliness; the *May Sun* (1911; Warsaw, N. Mus.) typifies this approach. His most renowned painting, *Strange Garden* (1903; Warsaw, N. Mus.; see fig.), is an expression of praise for happiness and, from its first showing, the painting excited a variety of interpretations of its symbolic content. In this large composition, with its curiously glowing colours, Mehoffer united reality with decorative fiction, placing his own wife, his small son and his son's nursemaid against a background of a garden filled with garlands of flowers and guarded by a vast golden dragonfly, here intended by Mehoffer as a symbol of the sun. His love of richly decorative effects and unusual colouring and his individual form of *Jugendstil* stylization also found expression in numerous female portraits such as *The Singer* (1896; L'viv, Pict. Gal.), as well as an extensive series of portraits of his wife, including the *Artist's Wife against a Yellow Background* (1907; Warsaw,

Józef Mehoffer: *Strange Garden*, oil on canvas, 2.23×2.09 m, 1903 (Warsaw, National Museum)

interior decoration of the church of Lubień, nr Piotrków Trybunalski, at the age of 73.

WRITINGS

Uwagi o sztuce i jej stosunku do natury [Remarks on art and its relationship with nature] (Kraków, 1897)
J. Puciata-Pawłowka, ed.:*Dziennik* [Diary] (Kraków, 1975)

BIBLIOGRAPHY

R. Bazin: 'Notes d'un amateur de couleurs' *J. Débats* (29 Dec 1908)
W. Ritter: 'Etudes d'art étranger: Un Peintre polonais, Joseph Mehoffer', *Mercure France* (1906), p. 123
J. Berthier: *Les Vitraux de Mehoffer à Fribourg* (Lausanne, 1918)
Józef Mehoffer (exh. cat., Kraków, N. Mus., 1964)
J. Puciata-Pawłowska: *Józef Mehoffer* (Wrocław, 1969)
A. Radajewski: *Józef Mehoffer* (Warsaw, 1976)
Het Symbolisme in Europa (exh. cat., ed. J. E. Ebbinge-Wubben and R. Hammacher van den Brande; Rotterdam, Boymans–van Beuningen; Brussels, Mus. Royaux B.-A.; Baden-Baden, Staatl. Ksthalle; Paris, Grand Pal.; 1976)
Ein seltsamer Garten: Polnische Malerei des XIX. Jahrhunderts: Romantik, Realismus, Symbolismus (exh. cat., ed. M. Kunz and A. Morawińska; Lucerne, Kstmus., 1980)
A. Morawińska: 'Hortus deliciarum Józefa Mehoffera' [The *garden of delights of Jø1zef Mehoffer*], *Ars Auro Prior: Studia Ioanni Białostocki sexagenario dicata* [Art [is] better when gold: studies in honour of Ioanni Białostocki on his 60th birthday] (Warsaw, 1981), pp. 713–18
T. Adamowicz: *Witraże frybuskie Józefa Mehoffera* [The Fribourg stained-glass windows of Józef Mehoffer] (Wrocław, 1982)
Symbolism in Polish Painting, 1890–1914 (exh. cat., ed. A. Morawińska; Detroit, MI, Inst. A., 1984)
A. Zenczak: 'Józefa Mehoffera *Dziwny Ogród*' [Józef Mehoffer's *Strange Garden*], *Fol. Hist. A.*, iii (1986), pp. 93–109

LIJA SKALSKA-MIECIK

Mehrenan. *See* ELYMAIS, §10.

Mehta, Tyeb (*b* Kapadvanj, Gujarat, 26 July 1925). Indian painter, sculptor and film maker. He studied painting from 1947 to 1952 at the Sir Jamshetjee Jeejebhoy School of Art, Bombay, where he became acquainted with AKBAR PADAMSEE and was a close associate of the painters in the Progressive Artists' Group. In 1954 he visited London and Paris for four months, then returned to India to devote himself to painting and sculpture. He took part in several group exhibitions and held his first solo exhibition of drawings, paintings and sculptures at the Jehangir Art Gallery, Bombay, in 1959. From 1959 to 1965 he lived and worked in London, exhibiting his paintings at the Bear Lane Gallery, Oxford (1962), among other locations. From 1965 to 1968 he lived in Delhi and in 1968 visited New York on a fellowship from the J. D. Rockefeller III Fund. By that time he was an acknowledged figure in contemporary Indian art. His paintings of the 1970s include *Diagonal* (oil on canvas, 1.75×1.75 m, 1973; New Delhi, N.G. Mod. A.) and *The Gesture No. 3* (oil on canvas, 1.15×0.90 m, 1977; New Delhi, N.G. Mod. A.). He worked in an expressionist manner with some recurring motifs such as the falling figure. In the 1980s he taught at the Vishua-Bharati University, Shantiniketan, West Bengal. With regard to his primary influences, he commented: 'In my case what happened was that I came into contact with minimal paintings and also Barnett Newman, whose work influenced me a lot' (Bickelmann and Ezekiel, 1987).

In addition to holding numerous solo and group exhibitions he received such national and international awards as the National Award from the Lalit Kala Akademi, New Delhi (1965), the Gold Medal at the first International Triennale India in Delhi (1968) and the Prix National at

N. Mus.) and the *Artist's Wife with Pegasus* (1913; Łódź, Mus. A.).

Mehoffer also worked in a variety of printmaking techniques (e.g. the cycle of etchings *The Dancer Guerrero*, 1905) and produced designs for books and magazines, for example vignettes and initials for the Polish avant-garde periodical *Chimera*. He also designed interiors and furniture. From 1897 he was active in the association of Polish artists, Sztuka ('Art'), of which he was a founder-member, making intensive efforts to develop it after the restoration of Polish independence in 1918. From 1900 he taught at the Academy of Fine Arts in Kraków, from 1902 as a professor, and he was rector of the Academy in 1914–15, 1917–18 and 1932–3. After World War I Mehoffer's painting gradually evolved away from linear *Jugendstil* stylization and his pure, saturated hues gave way to brighter, more heterogeneous colouring. Losing its decorative quality, his painting inclined more to the traditional and the conventional. The most significant work of his later years was in the field of large-scale decorative painting and stained-glass design. In the 1920s and 1930s he designed and executed numerous decorative schemes and windows for important public buildings in Poland, and in 1934 he completed his work on the stained-glass windows in Fribourg. The most important project of this period was the decoration of the church in Turko, nr Kalisz (1933–9), which included windows, wall paintings, framed paintings and designs for the altars and liturgical objects; this work occupies an important place in the history of Polish religious art. Following his liberation from the camp at Aš, to which he had been taken by the Germans in 1939, Mehoffer carried out his last decorative project, the

the Festival International de la Peinture at Cagnes-sur-Mer in France (1974). His experimental film *Koodal* won the Filmfare Critics Award for 1969–70. His works are to be found in major private and public collections in India (e.g. New Delhi, N.G. Mod. A.; Bhopal, Bharat Bhavan) and abroad.

BIBLIOGRAPHY
Tyeb Mehta: Catalogue of Paintings and Drawings (exh. cat., foreword G. M. Butcher; Oxford, Bear Lane Gal., 1962)
Modern Indian Paintings: From the Collection of the National Gallery of Modern Art, New Delhi (exh. cat., New Delhi, N.G. Mod. A., 1982)
Contemporary Indian Art: From the Chester and Davida Herwitz Family Collection (exh. cat., essays G. Patel, T. W. Sokolowski and D. A. Herwitz; New York, Grey Gal. & Stud. Cent., 1985)
U. Bickelmann and N. Ezekiel, eds: *Artists Today – East West Visual Arts Encounter* (Bombay, 1987), p. 94

ANIS FAROOQI

Mehus, Livio [Lieven] (*b* Oudenaarde, *c.* 1630; *d* Florence, 7 Aug 1691). Flemish painter and draughtsman, active in Italy. He painted allegorical and mythological scenes, landscapes and religious works. He was an eclectic artist, drawing on a wide variety of sources to create a highly individual and innovative style. His art united Venetian colour with elements of the proto-romanticism of Salvator Rosa, Pier Francesco Mola and Pietro Testa, and he was also inspired by Genoese, Bolognese and Flemish sources.

At the age of about ten Mehus moved with his family to Milan, where he changed his first name to Livio. After early studies with a Flemish battle-painter named Carlo Fiammingo, Mehus set out at the age of 14 for Rome. On the journey, at Pistoia, his landscape drawings attracted the attention of Prince Mattias de' Medici, who offered him the opportunity to assist Pietro da Cortona in his decorations in the Palazzo Pitti, Florence, in 1645. Mehus had a restless personality (Baldinucci) and moved on to Lucca and the area around Genoa, and then spent three years in Piedmont and Lombardy. He met Prince Mattias again, in Milan, re-entered his service and returned to Florence. In 1650 Mehus was in Rome with Stefano della Bella and then made a journey to northern Italy with Raffaello Vanni. From 13 May to 13 August 1652 he contributed, with Borgognone and other painters, to the decoration of the Medici villa at Lappeggi. He was again in Rome in 1655 and in 1660–61 in order to study with Pietro da Cortona, and during this period he also spent 18 months in Venice (Baldinucci) with Federico Panza (*d* 1703).

There are no documented works by Mehus from before 1665, and his chronology remains uncertain. A date in the mid-1650s has been proposed for the *Genius of Sculpture* (Florence, Pitti), which shows a half-length figure of a youth before an array of the most celebrated antique sculptures, and for the *Triumph of Ignorance* (Florence, Pitti) and the *Blind Man of Gambassi* (priv. col., see 1986 exh. cat., p. 471). These are sombre works, combining an interest in allegory and iconographical novelty indebted to Rosa and Mola with a robust Flemish realism.

On 19 April 1665 Mehus contracted to fresco the dome of S Maria della Pace, Florence, on which he worked for part of 1666. In 1667 he is mentioned as supervising the restoration of paintings in the Medici collection, and in

1670 his first payments, albeit irregular, were registered at the Accademia del Disegno (1986 exh. cat.). The *Triumph of Neptune and Amphitrite* (Massa, Pal. Cybo Malaspina) may date from the 1660s. It is more decorative in style than the works previously mentioned and is indebted to the Roman Baroque of Cortona and Ciro Ferri. The signed and dated *Holy Family with SS John the Baptist and John the Evangelist* (Prato, S Bartolomeo) is from 1670 and shows the influence of such Genoese artists as Domenico Maria Canuti and Gregorio de' Ferrari. On 12 September 1673 Mehus is recorded at Parma with the Farnese family. Other datable works are the *Gathering of Manna* (1676; untraced), painted for Alessandro Strozzi, and *St Peter of Alcantara Administering Communion to St Teresa* (1683; Prato, Mus. Opera Duomo; see fig.). These pictures, which are indebted to the late, ecstatic art of Giovanni Battista Castiglione, are visionary works, in which the expressive gestures and flickering light anticipate the art of the late 18th century.

In 1684 Mehus taught at the Florentine Accademia, with Baldassare Franceschini, Pietro Dandini and Giovanni Battista Fuggini. Baldinucci mentioned landscapes painted for Paolo Falconieri and the Cavaliere Ambra in Rome, and a small group of landscapes have been attributed to Mehus, among them *Four Landscapes* (?1675–85; Holkham Hall, Norfolk) that anticipate the romanticism

Livio Mehus: *St Peter of Alcantara Administering Communion to St Teresa*, oil on canvas, 2.60×1.60 m, 1683 (Prato, Museo dell'Opera del Duomo)

of Marco Ricci and Alessandro Magnasco (Chiarini, 1978).
In his last years Mehus was patronized by Prince Ferdinando de' Medici, who, as well as paying for the artist's
funeral expenses, acquired the works—mainly drawings
and *bozzetti* (see Chiarini (1975))—that remained in his
studio at his death. The Prince continued to be an
enthusiastic collector, and finally owned 45 works by
Mehus, at least half of which are still in the Palazzo Pitti,
Florence.

BIBLIOGRAPHY

F. Baldinucci: *Notizie* (1681–1728); ed. F. Ranalli (1845–7), v, pp. 526–38
M. Chiarini: 'I quadri della collezione del Principe Ferdinando II', *Paragone*,
    xxvi/301 (1975), pp. 57–98
P. Bigongiari: 'Livio Mehus dalla macchia al tocco e la coeva scultura
    tardobarocca fiorentina', *Paradigma*, ii (1978), pp. 145–69
M. Chiarini: 'Nuove schede per Livio Mehus', *Paradigma*, ii (1978),
    pp. 171–2
M. Gregori: 'Livio Mehus o la sconfitta del dissenso', *Paradigma*, ii (1978),
    pp. 177–226
G. Cantelli: *Repertorio della pittura fiorentina del seicento* (Florence, 1983),
    pp. 111–13, pls 571–84
Il seicento fiorentino: Arte a Firenze da Ferdinando I a Cosimo III (exh. cat.,
    ed. G. Guidi and D. Marcucci; Florence, Pal. Strozzi, 1986), i, pp. 468–
    76; ii, pp. 364–6; iii, pp. 121–3
Il seicento: Le Siècle de Caravage dans les collections françaises (exh. cat.,
    Paris, Grand Pal.; Milan, Pal. Reale; 1988–9)
M. Chiarini: 'Due quadri fiorentini del seicento al Poldi Pezzoli', *A. Crist.*,
    lxxx (1992), pp. 45–8

FRANCO MORO

Mei, Bernardino (*b* Siena, 1612; *d* Rome, 1676). Italian
painter, draughtsman and printmaker. His early art drew
on a variety of sources, which included the naturalism of
Rutilio Manetti and Francesco Rustici, the descriptive
realism of the engraver Giuliano Periccioli (*d* 1646) and
the Baroque of Raffaelle Vanni. Mei's interests even
embraced 16th-century Sienese art. This stylistic variety is
evident in his first known works, such as a bier (Casole
d'Elsa, Collegiata), three signed miniatures in the *Libro dei
leoni* (1634; Siena, Pal. Piccolomini, Archv Stato) and
frescoes of scenes from the *Life of St Bernard* (1639; Siena,
oratory of S Bernardino). His experimental approach is
also displayed in such works as the *Annunciation* (Siena,
Mus. Semin. Montarioso), which may be dated between
the mid-1630s and the early 1640s. Mei's early maturity is
marked by a conscious return to the naturalism of Manetti,
enriched with a Baroque pathos and soft, fluid brushwork,
as in the *St Peter in Prison Awoken by the Angel* and *St
Peter Freed by the Angel* (both Siena; Conservatori Fem-
minili Riuniti). His interest in both naturalism and the
Baroque made him responsive to the art of Mattia Preti,
possibly seen in Rome, as in the *Beheading of St John the
Baptist* (1647; Siena, oratory of S Giovannino in Panta-
neto) and the frescoes of scenes from the *Life of St Roch*
and *Life of St Job* (1648; Siena, S Rocco), which also reveal
the influence of Pier Francesco Mola.

Mei reached maturity in the 1650s, when, rejecting
Preti's influence, he created a series of outstanding works,
distinguished by complex rhythms and forms and great
expressive power, inspired by Roman painting and the
sculpture of Bernini. Most of these portray allegorical
subjects or scenes from Classical history and include *Love
Healed by Time with Water from the River Lethe* (1653) and
its companion *Fortune between Virtue and Necessity* (1654);
Orestes Killing Aegisthus and Clytemnestra (1654) and its
companion *Artemisia Drinking the Ashes of King Mausolus*

Mixed with her own Tears; *The Charlatan* (1656; all Siena,
Monte Paschi); and *Faith* (1656) and *Hope* (both Siena,
Col. Chigi–Saraceni). Also mainly from the same period
are a group of drawings (Siena, Col. Chigi–Saraceni;
Florence, Uffizi) and a group of signed and dated engrav-
ings (e.g. *Atlas and Hercules Supporting the Universe*, 1656;
Siena, Bib. Com. Intronati). The subject of the painting of
Alexander the Great and the Fates (Cincinnati, OH, A.
Mus.) alludes to Pope Alexander VII, suggesting a date
after his election in 1655.

In 1657 Mei was summoned by Alexander VII to Rome,
where in the same year he was elected to the Accademia
di S Luca. In Rome he executed a number of paintings for
the Pope, including a *Rest on the Flight into Egypt* (1659;
Rome, S Maria del Popolo) and two scenes from the *Life
of St John the Baptist* (both 1659; Rome, S Maria della
Pace). In its lighter palette and more monumental and
sculptural forms, the former shows Mei's response to the
new classicism of Carlo Maratti. The latter two paintings,
however, return to the naturalism of Preti, as does Mei's
Winter (Ariccia, Pal. Chigi), painted for Cardinal Flavio
Chigi in collaboration with Mario dei Fiori. Mei executed
many works for this patron for his palazzo in Ariccia and
for that in the Piazza SS Apostoli, Rome. Among those
that have been identified are *St Augustine Meditating on the
Trinity* (1665; *in situ*), completed for the collegiate church
at Ariccia, and *Fortune Donated by Virtue* (Rome, Min.
Grazia & Giustizia). These late works are less sculptural,
while such pictures as the *Mary Magdalene* (Siena, Monte
Paschi) attain a new psychological depth.

BIBLIOGRAPHY

Bernardino Mei e la pittura barocca a Siena (exh. cat. by F. Bisogni and
    M. Ciampolini, Siena, Pal. Chigi–Saraceni, 1987), pp. 189–99 [with
    earlier bibliog.]
Bernardino Mei: Sette dipinti nella collezione dei Monte dei Paschi di Siena
    (exh. cat. by F. Bisogni, Siena, Monte Paschi, 1987)
Pitture senesi del seicento (exh. cat. by G. Pagliarulo and R. Spinelli, Florence,
    Pal. Ridolfi, 1989)

FABIO BISOGNI

Mei Ch'ing. *See* MEI QING.

Meidias Painter. *See* VASE PAINTERS, §II.

Meidner, Ludwig (Baruch) (*b* Bernstadt, Prussia [now
Germany], 18 April 1884; *d* Darmstadt, 14 May 1966).
German painter, draughtsman, graphic artist, writer and
teacher. He was born into a middle-class Jewish family
during the late Wilhelmine period, and his parents wanted
him to pursue a profession more practical than an artistic
one. Nonetheless, while apprenticed to a bricklayer in
1901, Meidner produced highly accomplished pen-and-
ink drawings. Their imagery reveals his attempts to align
his Jewish heritage with that of modern-day Christianity
and Socialism, an intellectual preoccupation that was to
remain consistent throughout his career (e.g. *Ibn Esra*,
1901; Darmstadt, Stadtmus. & Städt. Kstsamml.). In 1903
he studied at the Königliche Akademie in Breslau (now
Wrocław, Poland) and in 1905 moved to Berlin where, to
earn a living, he designed advertisements for furriers. A
stipend from an aunt enabled him to visit Paris between
1905 and 1907. There he met Modigliani, briefly attended
the Académie Julian and Académie Cormon and generally
broadened his experience of city life. Nonetheless, his

correspondence at that time reveals his preference for Berlin, the 'struggling, earnest burgeoning city...the world's intellectual and moral capital' (letter to Franz Landsberger, 3 Jan 1907; see 1991 exh.cat., ii, p.16).

Meidner's return to Berlin in June 1907 for a compulsory military examination coincided with a renewed, yet unprolific, interest in themes of modernity. Such paintings as *Subway Construction in Berlin* (1910; Cologne, Mus. Ludwig) depict, in a broadly applied, *plein-air* style, the rapid transformations that overtook the urban landscape. By 1911, however, he had made contact with avant-garde groups who frequented the Café des Westens, and this signalled his vigorous engagement with literary and artistic Expressionism well into the period of the Weimar Republic. In emulation of the Neopathetische Cabaret that attracted such well-known poets as Georg Heym and Jakob van Hoddis, he adopted the title *Die Pathetiker* for a major group exhibition held in November 1912 at the Sturm-Galerie. The exhibition included work by Richard Janthur (1883–1950) and Jacob Steinhardt, with whom he formed the group Die Pathetiker (*see* EXPRESSIONISM, §1); they committed themselves to the notion of 'pathos', a vitalist and Dionysian concept adapted from the writings of Friedrich Nietzsche. The urban landscape was invested with elements of the primal and the cosmic as Meidner responded to the theoretical and formal inspiration of the Italian Futurists and Robert Delaunay, featured in exhibitions at the Sturm-Galerie in spring 1912. Scholarship (Charles Haxthausen, 1990 exh. cat.) has demonstrated that a tendency to view all Meidner's urban paintings of 1912–16 as 'apocalyptic' is misleading. Indeed, of the 15 paintings exhibited, only one as yet unidentified example was labelled as such, and it is possible that titles were retrospectively applied by Meidner after 1915. In fact, many works of this period relate to specific locations in Berlin. In the painting *Halensee Station* (1913; Los Angeles, CA, Co. Mus. A.) Meidner activated the local colour and impastoed surface of the street with scurrying pedestrians and angular lines of force, surmounting the destabilized urban landscape with light-filled cloud formations. Rather than portraying the alienation of the metropolis, works such as these celebrate the dynamism and tumultuousness of contemporary life, a view confirmed in Meidner's theoretical text 'Anleitung zum Malen von Grossstadtbildern', written in 1914 for the periodical *Kunst und Künstler*. Nevertheless, many works by Meidner are unquestionably apocalyptic, for example the painting *Apocalyptic City* (1913; Münster, Westfäl. Landesmus.), which shows burning buildings, fleeing crowds and comets, evoking Heym's poem *Umbra vitae* (1911) or van Hoddis's *Weltende* (1911; both pubd in *Modern German Poetry*, ed. M. Hamburger and C. Middleton (New York, 1964)). It is not surprising that Meidner envied the skills of poets, a view formulated in his essay 'Gruss des Malers an die Dichter' included in *Im Nacken das Sternemeer* (Leipzig, 1918), an anthology of his own literary endeavours.

Well before his conscription into military service (1916) Meidner voiced his protest against the psychological and physical devastation of modern warfare in *Krieg* (Berlin-Wilmersdorf, 1914), a portfolio of eight lithographs reproduced from his drawings. The content fervently displayed his political affinities: his membership of the Sozialistische Partei Deutschlands and his links with the radical left-wing journal *Die Aktion*, edited by Franz Pfemfert, to which Meidner contributed many anti-war images (e.g. *Battlefield*; pen and ink; reproduced as title page, iv/48–9 (1914); Marbach, Schiller-Nmus & Dt. Litarchv). In the wake of the Revolution of November 1918 in Berlin, he was at the forefront of the ARBEITSRAT FÜR KUNST and the NOVEMBERGRUPPE, both of which aspired to democratize artistic life in the capital. He also achieved a measure of stability by being appointed a lecturer (1919–35) at the Studien-Atelier für Malerei und Plastik, Charlottenburg, and by marrying the artist Else Meyer (1901–77) in 1927.

Meidner's works include a number of introspective self-portraits (e.g. *I and the City*, 1913; priv. col., see 1989 exh. cat., fig. 72) and highly acclaimed drawings, prints and paintings of literati (e.g. *Max Herrmann-Neisse*, 1920; Darmstadt, Stadtmus. & Städt. Kstsamml.; see fig.). During the Weimar Republic he remained a consistent devotee of Expressionism while sustaining a firm link with traditional figural representation. The illustrations for his prose work *Septemberschrei: Hymnen, Gebete, Lästerungen* (Berlin, 1920) and drawings on religious themes (e.g. *Prophet with Scroll*, charcoal, *c.* 1920; Darmstadt, estate of Ludwig Meidner) focus on the contortions of the monumental figure within a highly reduced pictorial space in a manner reminiscent of the work of the 17th-century German painter Michael Willmann, often cited by him as a source of inspiration.

Ludwig Meidner: *Max Herrmann-Neisse*, tempera on board, 1.01×0.72 m, 1920 (Darmstadt, Stadtmuseum und Städtische Kunstsammlung)

Political events had a substantial impact on Meidner's career. Shortly after the advent of the Third Reich (1933), he was forced, as a Jew, to accept alternative employment at a Jewish secondary school in Cologne. Moreover, a *Self-portrait* of 1912 (Darmstadt, Hess. Landesmus.) was included in the notorious exhibition of ENTARTETE KUNST held in Munich in 1937. He and his family sought asylum in Britain in 1939, but, after a short sojourn in London, he was interned until 1942 in camps near Liverpool and on the Isle of Man. During his exile he produced character portraits to earn a living (e.g. portrait of *Mrs Aronsfeld*, charcoal and crayon, 1943; Darmstadt, estate of Ludwig Meidner) and he resumed his interest in portraying Jewish religious rituals (e.g. *In the Synagogue*, charcoal, 1944–5; Darmstadt, estate of Ludwig Meidner). Most chilling, however, were his apocalyptic renderings honouring the fate of Jews of Poland (1942–3; Darmstadt, estate of Ludwig Meidner; see 1991 exh. cat., figs 6 and 7, p. 178). His artistic isolation continued even after World War II, and in 1953 he accepted an invitation from the Federal Republic to return to Germany, where he remained until his death. His later landscapes, self-portraits (e.g. litho-graph, 1966; Milwaukee, WI, A. Mus.) and still-lifes vigorously retain an engagement with expressive realism and serve as a fitting testimony to his lasting perseverance.

WRITINGS
'Anleitung zum Malen von Grossstadtbildern', *Kst & Kstler*, xii (1914), pp. 312–14
Im Nacken das Sternemeer (Leipzig, 1918)
Septemberschrei: Hymnen, Gebete, Lästerungen (Berlin, 1920)
'The Young Modigliani', *Burl. Mag.*, lxxxii (1943), pp. 87–91

PRINTS
Krieg (Berlin, 1914)

BIBLIOGRAPHY
T. Grochowiak: *Ludwig Meidner* (Recklinghausen, 1966)
V. Miesel, ed.: *Voices of German Expressionism* (Englewood Cliffs, 1970)
R. Allen: *Literary Life in German Expressionism and the Berlin Circles* (Ann Arbor, 1983)
The Apocalyptic Landscapes of Ludwig Meidner (exh. cat., ed. C. Eliel; Los Angeles, CA, Co. Mus. A., 1989)
R. Heller: *Art in Germany, 1909–1936: From Expressionism to Resistance (The Marvin and Janet Fishman Collection)* (Munich, 1990)
J. Weinstein: *The End of Expressionism: Art and the November Revolution in Germany, 1918–1919* (Chicago and London, 1990)
Art in Berlin, 1815–1989 (exh. cat., ed. K. Morris and A. Woods; Atlanta, GA, High Mus. A., 1990)
Ludwig Meidner: Zeichner, Maler, Literat, 1884–1966, 2 vols (exh. cat., ed. G. Breuer and I. Wagemann; Darmstadt, Ausstellhallen Mathilden-höhe, 1991)

SHULAMITH BEHR

Meier, Jeremias. *See* MEYER, JEREMIAH.

Meier, Melchior (*fl c.* 1572–82). German engraver and draughtsman, active in Italy. He worked for a time in the circle of the engraver Martino Rota but was later influenced by the engraving technique of Cornelis Cort, which he subsequently combined with that of Giorgio Ghisi. From 1573 Meier is thought to have been in Florence. His works confirm that he was attached to the Medici court: he engraved a portrait of *Cosimo I de' Medici* (*c.* 1573; Vienna, Albertina) and one of *Francesco I de' Medici* (*c.* 1574–5; Vienna, Albertina), to whom he dedicated the engraving of *Apollo with the Flayed Marsyas and with Midas* (1581; Florence, Uffizi). Stylistically, he was in later years close to the Florentine school, influenced by Vasari and Agnolo

Bronzino, but Dürer also affected his work on occasion. His drawings, insofar as they are signed, carry the mono-gram MM or the combination MF for 'Meier Fecit' or MS for 'Meier Sculpsit'.

BIBLIOGRAPHY
Hollstein: *Ger.*
J. Rapp: 'Ein Meisterstich der Florentiner Spätrenaissance', *Pantheon*, xliii (1985), pp. 61–70

VERONIKA BRAUNFELS

Meier, Richard (Alan) (*b* Newark, NJ, 12 Oct 1934). American architect and teacher. He received his architec-tural education at Cornell University, Ithaca, NY (BArch 1957), and then worked in New York with Davis, Brody and Wisniewski (1958–9), Skidmore, Owings and Merrill (1959–60) and Marcel Breuer and Associates (1960–63). In 1963 he established his own office in New York and began a long teaching career at Cooper Union, New York (1963–73), and several other American universities includ-ing Princeton, NJ, Yale, New Haven, CT, and Harvard, Cambridge, MA. Meier's work was dominated by explo-rations of the modernist theme of counterpointing space, form and structure, with particularly strong references to Le Corbusier's designs of the 1920s and 1930s. He first attracted critical attention with distinctive designs for private houses such as the Jerome Meier House (1963–5), Essex Falls, NJ; the Dotson House (1964–6), Ithaca; the Smith House (1965–7), Darien, CT; the Saltzman House (1967–9), East Hampton, NY; the Maidman House (1971–6), Sands Point, NY; and the Douglas House (1971–3), Harbor Springs, MI.

In these houses Meier stressed the artificial and abstract characteristics of architecture. His buildings, while de-signed in relation to their natural settings, are pristine structures that stand in contrast to nature. Spaces are defined and penetrated by horizontal and vertical planes, clearly emphasized by intensity of surface treatment such as white tiled walls and wood flooring; there is also a domination of the vertical dimension of space over the horizontal. For example, the Douglas House (see fig.), built on a steep, heavily wooded hillside above a river, stands out among the trees as a geometric white box composed of horizontal and vertical elements and win-dows, dominated by a pair of tall, elongated chimney stacks.

Meier was a member of the NEW YORK FIVE, a group of architects whose work, representing a return to the formalism of early modern rationalist architecture, was exhibited at MOMA in 1969. It was a loose association that disintegrated in due course as members of the group later pursued different formal directions. In contrast to Michael Graves's adoption of painterly solutions to archi-tectural problems, Meier, who was the most prolific builder of the group, continued the constructional approach that has its origins in the work of Frank Lloyd Wright and De Stijl and was later transformed by the plastic expressions of Le Corbusier and Aalto.

The rapid development of Meier's reputation led to larger commissions including the Athenaeum (1975–9), New Harmony, IN; the Hartford Seminary (1978–81), Hartford, CT; the Museum für Kunsthandwerk (1979–85), Frankfurt am Main; the High Museum of Art (1980–83), Atlanta, GA (for illustration *see* ATLANTA); and the

Richard Meier: Douglas House, Harbor Springs, Michigan, 1971–3

J. Paul Getty Arts Center, Brentwood, CA, begun in 1985 (due for completion in 1997). In these buildings, as well as in the houses, he clearly articulated public and private zones in an attempt to clarify and redefine a sense of order, and this articulation is expressed again in the structure. For example, the High Museum of Art is a complex composition of structural forms, cylindrical and rectilinear, with the entrance and public areas defined by large expanses of windows while the gallery walls are solid, white surfaces. The relationships of solid and void are emphasized by the whiteness and by the play of sunlight and shadow on the interlocking geometric volumes. In the uncertain climate of American Post-modernism, Meier's buildings exhibited a strong continuity of the formal concerns of modernism. His approach centred upon a dialogue between spatial configurations and structure, and he achieved a freedom of relationships that expressed the modernist reconstruction of architectural space and form. This offered a modern experience rather than a collage of historical references. Meier's work was widely exhibited in

the USA and Europe, and he received several awards for his work including the prestigious Pritzker Prize (1984).

WRITINGS

Richard Meier: Architect, 1964–1984, intro. J. Rykwert (New York, 1984)
Richard Meier: Buildings and Projects, 1979–1989 (London, 1990)

BIBLIOGRAPHY

K. Frampton and C. Rowe: *Five Architects: Eisenman/Graves/ Gwathmey/Hejduk/Meier* (New York, 1972, rev. 1975)
C. Hoyt: 'Richard Meier: Public Space and Private Space', *Archit. Rec.*, cliv/7 (1973), pp. 89–98
'Spatial Structure of Richard Meier', *A & U*, 64 (1976), pp. 45–120 [special feature]
'White Existence: Richard Meier, 1961–1977', *Space Des.*, 160 (1978), pp. 3–158 [special feature]
V. Vaudou: *Richard Meier* (Paris, 1986)
K. Frampton and J. Rykwert: *Richard Meier: Architect 2* (New York, 1992)

MALCOLM QUANTRILL

Meier-Denninghoff, Brigitte. *See* MATSCHINSKY-DENNINGHOFF.

Meier-Graefe, Julius (*b* Pesitza, Austria–Hungary, 10 June 1867; *d* Vevey, Switzerland, 5 June 1935). German art historian. He studied engineering in Munich, Zurich and Liège, before moving to Berlin in 1890, where he attended the university and became involved in artistic circles. In 1894 he co-founded the periodical *Pan*, becoming its art editor and financial manager, though he was dismissed in April 1895 by wealthy and conservative patrons unhappy with the emphasis given to French art, after publication of the first issue. He moved in 1895 to Paris, where he had already met avant-garde artists, and in 1898 founded the periodical *Dekorative Kunst*, in which he championed Art Nouveau; he opened an Art Nouveau gallery, La Maison Moderne, in Paris in 1899, which closed in 1903. Returning to Berlin in 1904, he published his most significant contribution to art history, *Die Entwicklungsgeschichte der modernen Kunst*, in which he was concerned to define the specifically artistic ('das Bildhafte') in isolation from socio-economic or historical factors, to trace its development in the 19th century, and to offer a basis for a new aesthetic: 19th-century painting from Delacroix to the Post-Impressionists was presented as a series of solutions to formal problems. In further controversial essays on Arnold Böcklin and Adolf Friedrich Erdmann Menzel, Meier-Graefe questioned prevailing academic and nationalistic judgements. Subsequently he published studies devoted to Jean-Baptiste-Camille Corot and Courbet, and to the French Impressionists. His *Spanische Reise* (1910) offered a startling reappraisal of El Greco, whose work he was deemed to have rediscovered, describing him as a kind of prototype of the Expressionist artist. Confronted with Expressionism, he retreated to a conservative position. His biography of van Gogh, *Vincent* (1922), presents the painter as the tragic victim of modern social alienation. In 1930 Meier-Graefe moved to France; after 1933 he remained in exile, reviled by the Nazis as an apologist of 'degenerate' art.

WRITINGS

Die Entwicklungsgeschichte der modernen Kunst, 3 vols (Stuttgart, 1904); *Entstehung der Malerei*, i (rev. Munich, 1914), *Traum und Wirklichkeit*, ii (rev. Munich, 1915), *Kunst unserer Tage*, iii (rev. Munich, 1924); all 3 vols repr. (Munich, 1966)
Impressionisten (Munich, 1907)
Hans von Marées, 2 vols (Munich, 1909–10)

Paul Cézanne (Munich, 1910/*R* 1932)
Spanische Reise (Berlin, 1910)
Vincent van Gogh (Munich, 1910/*R* 1929)
Vincent: Der Roman eines Gottsuchers (Munich, 1922/*R* 1959)

BIBLIOGRAPHY

B. Reiffenberg: 'Julius Meier-Graefe', *Neue Rundschau*, lxii (1963), pp. 735–56
K. Moffett: *Julius Meier-Graefe as Art Critic*, Studien zur Kunst des 19. Jahrhunderts, xix (Munich, 1973)

RHYS W. WILLIAMS

Meiger von Werde, Hans. *See* HAMMER, HANS.

Meigs, Montgomery (Cunningham) (*b* Augusta, GA, 3 May 1816; *d* Washington, DC, 2 Jan 1892). American engineer and architect. He was educated at the University of Pennsylvania and the US Military Academy. He achieved distinction in the construction of government buildings and public works as an officer in the Corps of Engineers, US Army, and as Quartermaster-General of the Union Armies during the American Civil War. He was superintendent of construction for a number of federal projects in Washington, DC, most important of which were the aqueduct of the city water supply system (1852–60) and the wings and dome of the US Capitol (1857–61). The aqueduct included two unusual works of structural engineering: the aqueduct over Cabin John Creek near Washington, an elegant masonry arch bridge with what was then the longest unsupported span in the USA; and the Pennsylvania Avenue Bridge over Rock Creek, a fixed-arch span in which the cast-iron tubular arch ribs functioned also as the water mains of the aqueduct system. For the building of the Capitol, Meigs designed and made extensive use of mechanized construction equipment, of which the most notable examples were the travelling cranes for the wings and the huge radial crane for the dome. Among federal buildings erected in Washington under his authority, the most important were the additions to the General Post Office (1855–9), the War Department (1866–7), the National Museum (1876) and the Hall of Records (1878), all of which are classical in style but structurally innovative.

DAB   BIBLIOGRAPHY

C. W. Condit: *American Building Art: The Nineteenth Century* (New York, 1960)
M. E. Campioli: 'Building the Capitol', *Building Early America*, ed. C. Peterson (Radnor, PA, 1976), pp. 202–31
R. M. Vogel: 'Building in the Age of Steam', *Building Early America*, ed. C. Peterson (Radnor, PA, 1976), pp. 119–34

CARL W. CONDIT

Meij [Mey], J(ohann) M(elchior) van der (*b* Delfshaven, 19 Aug 1878; *d* Geulle, 24 June 1949). Dutch architect. After attending technical school he worked in several architectural offices. In 1897 he joined the office of Eduard Cuypers in Amsterdam, where Michel de Klerk and P. L. Kramer were already working. In 1906 he won the Prix de Rome, which enabled him to travel in Europe. Between 1911 and 1919 he was aesthetics adviser to the Board of Works and Public Buildings of Amsterdam. In 1912 he commenced his major work, the Scheepvaarthuis, the head offices in Amsterdam of six Dutch shipping companies (*see* AMSTERDAM, fig. 3). This building was the earliest realization of the aims of the AMSTERDAM SCHOOL

to integrate architecture and decoration. A reinforced concrete structure designed by A. D. N. van Gendt and J. G. van Gendt, it is clothed in a skin of terracotta and ornamental brickwork. The extravagant decoration marks an important change in the thinking of Dutch architects, since this was a clear attempt to solve the duality of loadbearing and non-loadbearing elements, with the structure hidden behind the ornamental façade. Van der Meij was assisted by de Klerk and Kramer, whose creative influence was considerable. The first stage was undertaken between 1912 and 1916, and the building was completed in 1926–8. In 1919 van der Meij designed a hotel in Amsterdam that resembled the Scheepvaarthuis; this, however, was not built. He was responsible for many bridges in Amsterdam, including one over the Waalseilandgracht (1914), the Bantammer Bridge (1914) and one at the Muntplein (1914). He also designed a number of housing blocks for the city, only a few of which were built, for example the block (1928–30) on Titianstraat.

BIBLIOGRAPHY

G. Fanelli: *Architettura moderna* (1968), pp. 91–5
H. Boterenbrood: *Het Scheepvaarthuis* (Amsterdam, 1988)

HELEN BOTERENBROOD

Meijer, (Johan Hendrik) Louis (*b* Amsterdam, 9 March 1809; *d* Utrecht, 31 March 1866). Dutch painter. He received his training at the Akademie voor Beeldende Kunsten in Amsterdam, where he was a pupil of Pieter George Westenberg (1791–1873) and Jan Willem Pieneman (1779–1853). In his youth he worked with the landscape painter Joseph Jodocus Moerenhout (1801–74). From 1827 to 1830 Meijer studied in Paris; thereafter he spent a further three years in Amsterdam. From 1833 to 1839 he worked in Deventer. In his early years he was particularly fond of painting mountainous landscapes, woods and ice scenes. From 1839 to 1841 he was again in Amsterdam, where a change occurred in his work and he began to paint seascapes, sometimes with a historical setting (e.g. the *Conquest of Palembang*, 1857; Amsterdam, Rijksmus.). With such paintings he established an international reputation. In 1842 in Paris, where he had by then settled, he received a gold medal at the Salon with *Fire on the Ship 'The India'* and *Fisherman on the Coast of Normandy* (both untraced). He also attracted attention at many exhibitions in the Netherlands between 1826 and 1863.

In 1864 Meijer travelled along the coast of the Mediterranean. Subsequently he lived in The Hague, where the sea became the dominant subject of his work. He finally settled in Utrecht in 1865. He had many pupils, of whom Jacob Maris was the most famous.

Scheen   BIBLIOGRAPHY

Op zoek naar de gouden eeuw [In search of the golden age] (exh. cat., ed. G. Jansen and L. van Tilborgh; Haarlem, Frans Halsmus., 1986)

G. JANSEN

Meiji period. Term given to a Japanese era (*nengō*) corresponding to the reign of Emperor Mutsuhito (*reg* 1868–1912), posthumously known as Emperor Meiji. Internal economic pressure on the Japanese feudal system and external pressure from the Western powers for Japan to emerge from its two and a half centuries of self-imposed isolation (*see* EDO PERIOD) led to the overthrow of the

Tokugawa shogunate (*bakufu*) in the Meiji Restoration (*Meiji isshin*; 1868). The members of the first Meiji government, though initially pledged to restore a system of imperial rule, unknown since the Heian period (794–1185), and expel Westerners from the country, quickly changed their policy and promoted a programme of rapid modernization and industrialization under the slogan *bunmei kaika* ('civilization and enlightenment'). The imperial capital was moved from Kyoto to Edo, which was renamed Tokyo ('Eastern capital'; 1869).

The arts were accorded a significant role in the government's blueprint for modernization. The Technical Fine Arts School (Kōbu Bijutsu Gakkō), opened in 1876, was Japan's first officially sponsored art school (*see* JAPAN, §XVIII). Its twofold purpose was to introduce Western techniques at every level of Japanese industry and to modernize Japan's traditional arts. The school's first teachers of oil painting, sculpture and architecture were Italians: ANTONIO FONTANESI, Vincenzo Ragusa (1841–1927) and Giovanni Cappelletti.

The Japanese government also provided stipends for artists to study abroad. Japanese painters progressed rapidly from mere technical competence to the production of works acceptable to the French Academy as early as 1881. The accomplishments of such artists as SEIKI KURODA, TAKEJI FUJISHIMA, Keiichirō Kume (1866–1943) and Saburōsuke Ōkada (1869–1939) are all the more remarkable considering that they arrived in Paris at just the moment French artists were renouncing the classical tradition that the Japanese had come to absorb.

Sculpture, which had reached its last creative peak in Japan during the 12th and 13th centuries, was revived and redirected by MORIE OGIWARA and KŌTARŌ TAKAMURA, who were both deeply influenced by the works of Auguste Rodin. A tremendous revolution occurred in architecture, not only in materials, building techniques and design but also in the classification of architects as creative artists, where in Japanese tradition they had been placed among craftsmen. The face of Tokyo was transformed as Western-style public buildings—Tokyo Station (Tokyoeki), various banks and the Akasaka Detached Palace (Akasaka Rikyū)—replaced traditional wooden buildings. By the 1880s a wave of reaction against rapid Westernization swept the country. In the arts, a movement was begun both to preserve interest in pre-Edo period arts, and to adapt the traditional painting styles and techniques to the new age. The movement was led by Kakuzō Okakura (1862–1913) and ERNEST FRANCISCO FENOLLOSA, through the Tokyo School of Fine Arts (Tokyo Geijutsu Gakkō; now Tokyo University of Fine Arts and Music) founded in 1887. The result was *Nihonga* (Japanese-style painting; *see* JAPAN, §VI, 5(iii)), the major proponent of which, TAIKAN YOKOYAMA, lived and worked through much of the century of modernization.

The fine tradition of woodblock printmaking (*ukiyoe*, 'pictures of the floating world'; *see* JAPAN, §IX, 3(ii)) suffered a drop in quality at first, but recovered as artists found new themes and patrons. Photography entered Japan at this time as another medium to document change.

BIBLIOGRAPHY

M. Harada: *Meiji no yōga*, Nihon no bijutsu [Arts of Japan], xxx (Tokyo, 1968); Eng. trans. as *Meiji Western Painting*, Arts of Japan, vi (New York and Tokyo, 1974)

M. Kawakita: *Modern Currents in Japanese Art* (Tokyo, 1974)
C. Yamada, ed.: *Dialogue in Art: Japan and West* (Tokyo, 1976)
H. Munsterberg: *The Arts of Modern Japan: From the Meiji Restoration to the Meiji Centennial, 1868–1968* (New York, 1978)
H. Varley: *Japanese Culture* (Honolulu, 1984)
Paris in Tokyo: The Japanese Encounter with Western Painting (exh. cat., ed. S. Takashina; Tokyo and St Louis, MO, 1987)

BONNIE ABIKO

Meikaku. See KUSAKABE MEIKAKU.

Meil, Johann Wilhelm (*b* Altenburg, 23 Oct 1733; *d* Berlin, 2 Feb 1805). German engraver and designer. He is regarded as one of the most important 18th-century German engravers. His father, Johann Christoph Meil, who died young, had been court sculptor in Altenburg. His stepfather, also a sculptor, directed Meil towards a career in science. At the university of Leipzig, however, Meil trained as an engraver and attended lectures on art history, art theory and philosophy. In 1752 he went to Berlin, where he met the brothers Johann Christian Hoppenhaupt and Johann Michael Hoppenhaupt II (*see* HOPPENHAUPT), who engaged him primarily as an engraver for their designs. Between 1752 and 1755 Meil produced a number of engravings of tables, clock-cases, chandeliers and other items in the Rococo style, based on drawings by the Hoppenhaupt brothers. Meil also designed furniture, jewellery and motifs for porcelain painting and the 12 vases that stand in front of the picture gallery in Schloss Sanssouci, Potsdam. His major field of work, however, was book illustration. He joined the circle of the poet Gotthold Ephraim Lessing and in 1756 became a member of the Montagsclub in Berlin for renowned figures of the German Enlightenment, which provided contacts with writers, poets and publishers. He illustrated not only works by Moses Mendelssohn, Karl Wilhelm Ramler, J. G. Sulzer and Lessing but also editions of Alexander Pope and Denis Diderot, several natural science books and even the frontispiece and headpieces to Frederick the Great's *Poésies diverses* (1760). Meil was careful to illustrate the text with allegorical or symbolical representations that, until the late 1760s, reflected the light playfulness of the Rococo period in both form and content. Meil's illustrations later took a more severe form, often with oval or circular frames, developing into the so-called *Zopfstil* and moving some way towards Neo-classicism. Under the influence of new literary forms and changing fashions, Meil later took up scenic illustration in the style of his contemporary Daniel Nikolaus Chodowiecki. In 1766 Meil became a member of the Akademie der Künste in Berlin, where in 1787 he became Professor of composition and expression. He was appointed Rector in 1788 and in 1801 succeeded Chodowiecki as Director of the Akademie. Meil's work as a costume designer for the theatre and opera in Berlin from 1774 is also noteworthy. His designs for the production of Goethe's *Götz von Berlichingen* (1774) were the first attempts towards historical dress in theatre costume. A large collection of Meil's work is in the Staatliche Museen, Berlin. Another 650 drawings also survive.

BIBLIOGRAPHY

F. L. Hopffer: *Verzeichnis sämtlicher Titelkupfer und Vignettenabdrücke von Johann Wilhelm Meil* (Berlin, 1808)

E. Bock: *Die deutschen Meister: Beschreibendes Verzeichnis sämtlicher Zeich- nungen Staatliche Museen zu Berlin* (Berlin, 1921)

W. Dorn: *Meil Bibliographie: Verzeichnis der von dem Radierer Johann Wilhelm Meil illustrierten Bücher und Almanache* (Berlin, 1928)

W. Klara: *Schauspielkostüm und Schauspieldarstellung: Entwicklung des deutschen Theaters im 18. Jahrhundert* (Berlin, 1931)

H. S. Altcappenberg: 'Graphik', *Panorama der friderizianischen Zeit: Fried- rich der Grosse und seine Epoche*, ed. J. Ziechmann (Bremen, 1985), ii, pp. 177–86

P. Dehnert: 'J. W. Meil als Klassiker des Buchschmucks', *Philobiblon*, 29 (1985), pp. 221–8

Deutsche Zeichnungen des 18. Jahrhunderts: Zwischen Tradition und Aufklä- rung (exh. cat., ed. T. W. Gaethgens and others; W. Berlin, Kupferstich- kab., 1987)

FREYA PROBST

Mei Qing [Mei Ch'ing; *zi* Yuangong; *hao* Qushan, Xuelu, Meichi] (*b* Xuancheng, Anhui Province, 1623; *d* 1697). Chinese painter and poet. He came from a family with a history of distinguished scholarship, but himself failed the examinations for an official career. His father died when he was young and his elder brothers saw to his education. In 1642 the family left Xuancheng to escape Manchu troops, and in 1649 they moved again. Some of Mei Qing's poems reflect these experiences. He travelled widely to places such as Mt Tai, Shandong Province, in 1670 and to Mt Huang, Anhui Province, in 1671 and 1690, but returned to his birthplace where he spent the rest of his life, probably making his living as a scholar, poet and painter and helping to compile a local history in 1673.

He seems to have known various members of the ANHUI SCHOOL of landscape painting, notably Cheng Sui (?1605–?1691), Zha Shibiao and Dai Benxiao, but much of his reputation derives from his association with the great Individualist monk–painter DAOJI. Although Mei was 18 years the elder, the two artists became friends and painting partners, directing a large part of their artistic endeavour to the production of hanging scrolls and album leaves depicting the scenery of Mt Huang. Most of Mei Qing's surviving paintings date from between 1690 and 1695; works of this late period, such as *Mountain Stream, Large Pines and Projecting Cliff* (1691; Detroit, MI, Inst. A.) reveal the influence of Daoji. *Mountain Stream* is a tall, narrow hanging scroll depicting bizarre rock formations and contorted pine trees; the landscape is depicted using a wide variety of brush techniques, including washes of light ink and colour, long texture strokes and stippling. The loose organization of this work contrasts with Mei's meticulous album paintings, exemplified by *Nineteen Views of Mt Huang* (1693; Shanghai Mus.). In this smaller format the idiosyncrasies of his landscape manner—his light, dry brushwork and use of pale blue and green colours—were more appealing. Mei Qing's relatives Mei Chong (probably a nephew, *fl c.* 1690) and Mei Geng (1640–*c.* 1716; perhaps a younger brother) were also painters of the Anhui school.

BIBLIOGRAPHY

DMB: 'Mei Ch'ing'

O. Sirén: *Chinese Painting: Leading Masters and Principles* (London and New York, 1956–8), v, pp. 118–21

Chu-tsing Li: *A Thousand Peaks and Myriad Ravines* (Ascona, 1974), pp. 186–99

J. DeBevoise: 'Mei Qing, Mei Chong, and Shitao', *Shadows of Mt Huang: Chinese Painting and Printing of the Anhui School*, ed. J. Cahill (Berkeley, 1981), pp. 127–32

VYVYAN BRUNST, with JAMES CAHILL

Meir [anc. Mer-wer; Gr. Cusae]. Site of the western necropolis of the ancient city Cusae, capital of the 14th nome of Upper Egypt. In the desert west of the modern village of Al-Quṣiyyah, some 50 km north of modern Asyut, the nomarchs of Cusae in the Old and Middle Kingdoms (*c.* 2575–*c.* 1630 BC) were buried in chamber tombs halfway up the cliff leading to the high desert plateau, while their retainers were interred in shaft tombs. Irregularly located, the nobles' tombs have been divided into groups labelled A–E. Nine of the decorated chapels are of nomarchs of the 6th Dynasty (*c.* 2325–*c.* 2150 BC)

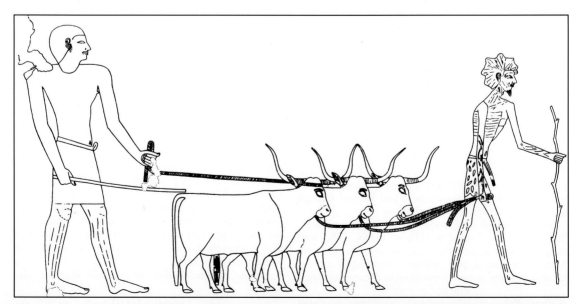

Meir, tomb chapel of Ukhhotpe, relief of a herdsman tending cattle, 12th Dynasty, *c.* 1938–*c.* 1756 BC; from A. Blackman: *The Rock Tombs of Meir*, ii (London, 1915), pl. xxx (1)

in a continuous family sequence, father to son and elder to younger brother. All show the influence of the Memphite school of sculpture. That of Pepyankh (labelled A2) contains scenes reminiscent of those in the TOMB OF MERERUKA at Saqqara: scenes from daily life on his estate, including craftsmen, farmers and herdsmen at work; the owner in a carrying chair; and the owner seated on a bed while his wife plays the harp.

The six 12th Dynasty decorated tombs have unimpressive façades, but the artists of the local school who carved and painted the chapels were outstandingly gifted and original: familiar themes were treated in a realistic and often humorous way. The tomb of Senbi (B1) includes a lively depiction of the owner hunting with his dogs in the desert; that of Ukhhotpe (B2) contains the celebrated figures of the emaciated herdsman tending fat cattle (see fig.) and the old man chatting to boat-builders, as well as a scene of papyrus gathering (for illustration *see* PAPYRUS). The latest tomb (*c*. 1880 BC), that of another Ukhhotpe (C1), though sadly mutilated, contains some of the finest painting of the Middle Kingdom. Jewellery, statuettes and funerary models found in tombs at Meir are now in the Metropolitan Museum of Art, New York. The reliefs and paintings copied by Aylward Blackman in 1911–14 (completed 1949–50) are reproduced in his study of the rock tombs.

LÄ

BIBLIOGRAPHY

A. M. Blackman: *The Rock Tombs of Meir*, 6 vols (London, 1914–53)

M. S. DROWER

Meirelles de Lima, Victor (*b* Desterro [now Florianópolis], 18 Aug 1832; *d* Rio de Janeiro, 22 Feb 1903). Brazilian painter. He entered the Academia Imperial das Belas Artes in Rio de Janeiro in 1847 as a student of history painting. In 1852 he was awarded a trip to Europe, which took him in 1853 to Rome, where he studied with Tommaso Minardi and Nicolao Couronni. He settled in Florence, where his hard work persuaded the Brazilian government to extend his stay. Some of his major works, such as the *First Mass in Brazil* (1860; Rio de Janeiro, Mus. N. B.A.), were painted during this period. On his return to Brazil in 1861 he was made Professor of History painting at the Academia Imperial. Together with Pedro Américo he is considered the greatest exponent of history painting in Brazil, combining a Neo-classical precision with an intense Romantic atmosphere in works such as the *Oath of Princess Isabel* (1875; Petrópolis, Mus. Imp.), the *Battle of Guararapes* (1879; Rio de Janeiro, Mus. N. B.A.) and the *Naval Combat at Riachuelo* (1882; Rio de Janeiro, Mus. Hist. N.). He also painted portraits and some indigenous subjects, as in *Moema* (1866; São Paulo, Mus. A.). Among his rare landscapes was a very detailed circular view of Rio de Janeiro (115 m, destr.), which he first exhibited in Brussels in 1888 on a rotating cylinder that permitted the viewer to stand still as the images went by in front of him. Only six preparatory studies of this work are extant (Rio de Janeiro, Mus. N. B.A.), although he also published *Panorama de la ville de Rio de Janeiro* (Brussels, 1888).

Pontual

BIBLIOGRAPHY

J. M. dos Reis Júnior: *História da pintura no Brasil* (São Paulo, 1944)

E. R. Peixoto: *Victor Meirelles no Museu Nacional de Belas Artes* (Rio de Janeiro, 1970)

A. P. Rosa and others: *Victor Meirelles de Lima* (Rio de Janeiro, 1982)

ROBERTO PONTUAL

Meiselas, Susan (*b* Baltimore, MD, 21 June 1948). American photographer. She studied at Sarah Lawrence College, Bronxville, NY, graduated from Harvard University, Cambridge, MA, in 1971 and taught in public schools until she joined the photographic agency Magnum in 1976 on the strength of a black-and-white photographic essay on *Carnival Strippers*. A self-taught photojournalist, Meiselas did most of her photography in troubled locations or among developing nations. She went to Chad and Cuba before travelling to Nicaragua in 1978; she was there when the Sandinista revolution erupted and later published her chronicle of the uprising in uncompromising colour photographs in *Nicaragua* (1981). She subsequently continued to work as a photojournalist.

PHOTOGRAPHIC PUBLICATIONS

Nicaragua (New York, 1981)

El Salvador (New York, 1984)

Chile: From within (New York, 1990)

BIBLIOGRAPHY

D. Snyder: 'Mixing Media', *Photo Communique* (Spring 1987), pp. 28–36

SHERYL CONKELTON

Meiss, Millard (*b* Cincinnati, 25 March 1904; *d* Princeton, 12 June 1975). American art historian. He was educated at the universities of Princeton (BA) and New York (MA, PhD), lecturing at the latter from 1931 to 1933. He subsequently became Lecturer and finally Professor of Fine Arts and Archaeology at Columbia University (1934–53); Professor as well as Curator of Paintings at the Fogg Museum, Harvard University (1954–8); Professor at the Institute for Advanced Study, Princeton, from 1958 to 1975. He was editor of the *Art Bulletin* from 1940 to 1942, an honorary trustee of the Metropolitan Museum of Art in New York and a member of the American Academy of Arts and Sciences, the American Philosophical Society and the Medieval Academy of America, receiving the Haskins Medal in 1953; he was also a corresponding member of a number of foreign societies, including the British Academy, the Société des Antiquaires de France and the Accademia delle Arti del Disegno, Florence. A student of Richard Offner, Meiss specialized in late medieval and early Renaissance painting of Italy, France, the Netherlands and Spain. His work combined rigorous connoisseurship with socio-historical approaches. *Painting in Florence and Siena after the Black Death* (1951) is one of the earliest attempts at establishing a tangible and demonstrable connection between a change of style (previously dismissed as a mere 'decline') and antecedent developments in social, economic, literary and religious life. While focused on illuminated manuscripts, *French Painting in the Time of Jean de Berry* (1967–74) is also a comprehensive survey of the interaction between Italian and north European art in the 14th and 15th centuries.

WRITINGS

Painting in Florence and Siena after the Black Death (Princeton, 1951)

with L. Tintori: *The Painting of the Life of St Francis in Assisi* (New York, 1962)

Giovanni Bellini's St Francis in the Frick Collection (Princeton, 1964)

Giotto and Assisi (New York, 1967)

French Painting in the Time of Jean de Berry, 5 vols (New York and London, 1967–74)
The Great Age of Fresco (New York, 1970)
The Painter's Choice (New York, 1976) [a selection of earlier pubns]

BIBLIOGRAPHY

H. B. J. Maginnis, ed.: *Francesco Traini* (Washington, DC, 1983) [contains articles first pubd in 1933, 1960, 1965 and 1971]
I. Lavin and J. Plummer, eds: *Studies in Late Medieval and Renaissance Painting in Honor of Millard Meiss*, i (New York, 1977), pp. xiii–xx [complete bibliog.]

EDITH W. KIRSCH

Meissen. German city at the confluence of the rivers Triebisch and Elbe, on the northern edge of the Elbe basin, *c.* 25 km north-west of Dresden. It has a population of *c.* 45,000 and is the site of the oldest porcelain factory in Europe, founded 1710.

1. History and urban development. 2. Cathedral. 3. Porcelain Factory.

1. HISTORY AND URBAN DEVELOPMENT. In AD 928 Henry the Fowler, Duke of Saxony (*reg* 912–36), founded a castle (Misni) to protect the Elbe line against the Slavs, as part of his policy of eastward expansion. A bishopric under the archdiocese of Magdeburg was established in 968 by Emperor Otto I, and a margrave of Meissen is mentioned in the same year. In 1125 Conrad von Wettin became margrave, and the city remained a Wettin possession, although it became a free city in 1423 when the first Elector of Saxony, Frederick I (*reg* 1423–8), received the Duchy of Saxe-Wittenberg. The sons of Frederick II (*reg* 1428–64)—Ernest and Albert V—ruled jointly from 1464 but partitioned the Wettin lands in 1485, and Meissen remained a possession of the Albertine line. Conquered and burnt by the Swedes in 1637, Meissen experienced an economic revival after the foundation of the porcelain factory.

The development of the town reflected the powers of the margraves, the bishops and the burgrave, an office added in 1068. The margraves' castle and the cathedral (*see* §2 below) dominate the town from the Burgberg, the cliff on the left bank of the Elbe, with the burgrave's castle originally to the west. The margraves' castle, known as the Albrechtsburg since 1676, was built by ARNOLD VON WESTFALEN for Ernest and Albert (*see* WETTIN, (1)) from 1471: it is one of the earliest buildings to show the transition from fortified stronghold to residential palace and is noted for Arnold's use of cell vaults and curtain arches. The bishop's palace was completed after 1518, and there were also residences for the canons.

The second main area of the city, the Afraberg, was populated in the 10th century to protect the castle hill; a roadside chapel is mentioned in 983. The settlement was independent and free of taxes. In 1205 the Augustinian monastery of St Afra was founded: the core of the basilical church dates from a rebuilding of *c.* 1300, with the Schleinitz chapel added in 1408 and the Taubenheimische chapel in 1454. Surviving conventual buildings include the cloister, St Barbara's Chapel, the kitchens and the residence of the Provost. The convent was suppressed in 1539 at the Reformation, and the Fürstenschule (royal school) was established there in 1543. The oldest surviving building in the parish of St Afra is a sturdy house with a fortified tower, but stables and open courtyards also survive,

together with the Pönitenzturm, the remains of the fortifications that protected the area. The Wasserburg, to the east by the Elbe, is marked by the Jakobskirche, dating from the late 15th century. An unfortified settlement with an annual market was established under the protection of the castle and the Wasserburg in the 10th century and was documented in 1002. Its existence can still be traced in the long Theaterplatz (the theatre, originally a warehouse, was built in 1545–7 by Ambrosius Ottenbach).

From the late 12th century the margraves established a planned town, first mentioned in 1295, between the castle, the Afraberg and the market. The main craft was cloth-weaving. Four arterial roads radiated from the central market, on the north side of which stands the town hall, built *c.* 1472 with the aid of Arnold von Westfalen on the foundations of an earlier fortification. At the south-west corner the church square adjoins the Frauenkirche, first mentioned in 1205 when it was subordinate to St Afra. After a fire in 1447 it was rebuilt (1455–7) as the town parish church. Originally a three-aisled hall church, it was altered in the 16th and 17th centuries and was restored in 1884 and 1928. A Franciscan friary originally built at the south-east corner of the town *c.* 1285 was also rebuilt after the 1447 fire. The chancel was demolished in 1823 and the conventual buildings in 1855.

A stone bridge over the Elbe is documented from the 13th century, and the town fortifications were completed in 1220; the six gates were demolished between 1832 and 1843. Since the 15th century the city has expanded outside the walls; the Neugasse was built *c.* 1420. Later buildings include Bahrmann's Brauerei an der Frauenkirche (1569–71), a tall, narrow town house with bevelled window-jambs decorated with hemispherical ornament. The portal, set asymmetrically in the façade, has Corinthian detailing and a relief of *Samson and the Lion*.

BIBLIOGRAPHY

C. Gurtlitt, ed.: *Beschreibende Darstellung der alteren Bau- und Kunstdenkmäler in Sachsen*, xl and xli (Dresden, 1919 and 1923)
W. Hentschel: *Dom und Schloss Meissen* (Berlin, 1944)
H.-J. Mrusek: *Meissen* (Dresden, 1957)
E. Lehmann, ed.: *Die Bezirke Dresden, Karl-Marx-Stadt, Leipzig*, Hb. Dt. Kstdkml. ed. G. Dehio (Berlin, 1965)
H.-J. Mrusek, ed.: *Die Albrechtsburg zu Meissen* (Leipzig, 1972)

ERNST ULLMANN

2. CATHEDRAL. Dedicated to SS John the Baptist and Donatus, the cathedral is on the Burgberg between the Albrechtsburg and the bishop's palace. The Romanesque building (1006–73), known from excavations, was a cruciform aisled basilica with three apses to the east and a façade with two towers to the west. The Gothic cathedral that replaced it was planned under Bishop Albert II (*reg* 1259–66). Bishop Withego I (*reg* 1266–93) replaced the old plan with a more grandiose one, the construction beginning in the east with the chancel. During the 14th century the nave, originally planned as a basilica, was built as a seven-bay aisled hall church based on the Elisabethkirche, Marburg. The first two storeys of the west towers were begun in 1315 under the influence of Magdeburg Cathedral, and the large portal between them was built *c.* 1400. The tympanum depicts the *Nativity*, the *Adoration of the Magi* and the *Coronation of the Virgin* and is surmounted by a gable with a series of smaller figures.

The margraves' burial chapel (Fürstenkapelle) was built after 1423, and the first to be buried there was Frederick I; most of the later bronze slabs come from the Vischer workshop (*see* GOTHIC, §V, 4). The vault was constructed in 1443–6, probably by Moyses of Altenburg. After 1479 Arnold von Westfalen added two further storeys to the towers and filled in the space between them. They were altered between 1903 and 1909 to designs by Carl Schäfer after a competition *c*. 1900.

The elongated chancel is formed by a square bay with a sexpartite rib vault and closed walls combined with a rectangular bay with sail vault and high windows, terminating in a $\frac{5}{8}$ polygonal apse, each wall of which is entirely filled by a window. On the walls of the square bay are standing figures (*c*. 1268–80) of *Otto I* and his wife *Adelheid* (*d* 999) on the north side and *St John the Baptist* and *St Donatus* on the south side, from the workshop of the Naumburg Master. The back rests of the choir-stalls, with their blind ornaments and canopies, are reminiscent of those at Naumburg. In the chancel are clustered responds of circular cross-section, which support Corinthian capitals. A two-storey ambulatory runs around the chancel, connecting the towers that are in the corners between the chancel and the transept and that house the sacristy to the north and the treasury, enlarged to a chapel, to the south. A rood screen separates the chancel from the transept, which is formed by three rib-vaulted squares. The screen and details of the chancel were based on Naumburg Cathedral and French Cistercian architecture. Adjoining the transept to the south-west is a decorative octagonal structure with three open sides, which serves as an entrance to the bishop's palace and has a chapel (ded. 1291) above. Inside the structure are figures (*c*. 1268–80) of the *Virgin and Child*, *St John the Baptist* and a deacon, which were originally intended for the west portal and are also from the Naumburg Master's workshop. Together with the figures in the chancel, they form the last of the grand cycles of 13th-century cathedral sculpture that started with Bamberg.

The articulation of the west piers of the crossing resembles that of the piers in the chancel, although the continuation of the responds into the vaulting shows inconsistencies. The rectangular nave bays are matched by square ones in the side aisles. Between the west towers is a large portal with figures, and before it is the Fürstenkapelle, resembling a west chancel, with a rich net vault with quatrefoils. To the south is the Georgskapelle. The large open arches of the tower stages added by Arnold von Westfalen reveal staircases inside, creating a magnificent effect; the linking of the towers by arches and a parapet indicates the possibility that Arnold planned a central tower to complete the west part of the building.

BIBLIOGRAPHY
E. Lehmann, ed.: *Die Bezirke Dresden, Karl-Marx-Stadt, Leipzig*, Hb. Dt. Kstdkml., ed. G. Dehio (Berlin, 1965)
E. Lehmann and E. Schubert: *Der Dom zu Meissen* (Berlin, 1975)
H.-J. Mrusek: *Drei sächsische Kathedralen: Merseburg–Naumburg–Meissen* (Dresden, 1976)
E. Lemper: *Der Dom zu Meissen* (Berlin and Munich, 1990)
BETTINA GEORGI, ERNST ULLMANN

3. PORCELAIN FACTORY. It was the first European ceramics factory to produce 'true' or hard-paste porcelain and was the most influential European ceramics factory during the first half of the 18th century. Production included tablewares, ornamental wares and figures. The factory continued to operate in the late 20th century as the Staatliche Porzellan-Manufaktur Meissen.

(i) Before 1800. (ii) 1800 and after.

(i) Before 1800. The introduction to Europe of such beverages as tea, coffee and cocoa by the East India Companies changed many social mores and stimulated the desire to imbibe these pleasurable drinks from such delicate vessels as porcelain cups. Throughout Europe there was a feverish quest for 'true' porcelain, and experiments aimed at producing it were carried on at almost all the courts. Its successful invention and production in Saxony were directly dependent on the mining and smelting industries, centred on Freiberg in the Erz Mountains, which provided the necessary technical and intellectual basis for a systematic scientific search for the secret of producing the coveted East Asian porcelain. In addition, the absolutist court and government of Frederick-Augustus I, Elector of Saxony (also Augustus II, King of Poland; known as Augustus the Strong), modelled on the court of Louis XIV, was an important force in the development of technology, science and the arts in Saxony.

The invention of the first European hard-paste porcelain was the outcome of the collaboration of JOHANN FRIEDRICH BÖTTGER, the Freiberg mining official Gottfried Pabst von Ohain (1656–1729), the natural scientist Ehrenfried Walther von Tschirnhaus (1651–1708) and a small number of highly qualified mining and smelting experts from Freiberg. Böttger, who is often regarded as the sole inventor of European hard-paste porcelain, came to the notice of princes in both Prussia and Saxony through his spectacular claims and experiments concerned with making gold by artificial means. After his attempts to produce gold at the Saxon court failed, his genuine alchemistic talents were guided into more scientific channels by von Tschirnhaus. Between *c*. 1702 and 1706 the collaboration yielded important information concerning the vitrifying processes of clay mixtures during firing; the basic formula for producing porcelain was available *c*. 1706–7. At first a brown, water-impermeable stoneware made of high-firing clays containing iron-oxide and various fluxes was produced. Böttger called this material *Jaspisporzellan* in view of its hardness and colour. Wares included tea- and coffeepots, flasks, bowls, teacups, vases and teajars (e.g. teajar, *c*. 1715; Meissen, Porzellanmus.; see fig. 1).

At the beginning of 1708 Böttger and his collaborators fired a mixture of kaolin (china-clay), clay and alabaster at a high temperature to create what was later called *Böttgerporzellan*. At first the mixture contained lime and was therefore also called 'lime' porcelain. From *c*. 1725 the alabaster was increasingly replaced by feldspar, so that from *c*. 1735 a feldspathic porcelain was produced. On 28 March 1709 Böttger notified Augustus in a 'memorial' (a type of patent) that, in addition to other discoveries, he had invented white porcelain that was similar or even superior to the East Asian variety. On 23 January 1710 an edict was issued from the court chancellery in Dresden to

1. Meissen *Jaspisporzellan* teajar (without lid) with six relief panels of *indianische Blumen* and bird motifs, h. 113 mm, *c.* 1715 (Meissen, Porzellanmuseum)

the effect that Augustus intended to establish a porcelain factory.

The factory was opened on 6 June 1710 in the Albrechtsburg, a Late Gothic palace in Meissen. This location, outside the residency of Dresden, was chosen for a variety of reasons: the spacious castle was not used for residential purposes at the time; the secret process could easily be guarded at this site; and the wood needed for the kilns could be transported on the River Elbe. The first director, Michael Nehmitz (1670–1739), was appointed in 1710, and on 29 December of the same year Böttger became the first manager. The first artists to be involved in the modelling of *Jaspisporzellan* and *Böttgerporzellan* included the court goldsmith Johann Jacob Irminger (1635–1724), the sculptor and wood-carver Johann Benjamin Thomae (1682–1751) from the workshop of Balthasar Permoser, and the sculptor Paul Heermann (1673–1732). At first they used the existing designs made for such other materials as gold and silver, but special designs and decorations for porcelain were progressively developed. With the appointment in 1720 of the painter and colour chemist JOHANN GREGORIUS HÖROLDT, and with the increasing availability of various special enamel colours, porcelain decoration at Meissen began to faithfully copy East Asian decoration and adapt it to European taste. A distinct European style developed: flower paintings based on various graphic models and copied from nature; decoration after Antoine Watteau, Johann Elias Ridinger, François Boucher and Philips Wouwerman; harbour

scenes and urban and landscape views. Höroldt favoured flat surfaces without relief to allow his decorative paintings to have their full effect. His graceful and imaginative scenes of Chinese and Japanese life, so-called 'Höroldt chinoiseries' (e.g. vase, 1726; Dresden, Porzellansamml.), and his versions of 'Indian' designs (*indianische Blumen*) had a decisive influence on European porcelain painting. By 1739 cobalt-blue underglaze painting had been fairly securely mastered so that the coveted blue-and-white decoration (later known as the 'blue onion' pattern) could be executed.

Important stimuli during the early development of the factory were Augustus's obsessive, almost pathological craving for porcelain and his plan to display his collection in an appropriate setting. In 1717 he acquired the Holländisches Palais in Dresden and had it converted by the architect Matthäus Daniel Pöppelmann into a small porcelain palace. In 1719, on the occasion of the marriage of his son Frederick-Augustus II (later Augustus III, King of Poland) to Maria Josepha of Austria, the tasteful display of East Asian and early Meissen porcelain in the palace, based on the porcelain cabinets in the Prussian palaces of Charlottenburg and Oranienburg, attracted widespread attention (*see* CABINET (i), §4(i)). In 1727 work began to convert the Holländisches Palais into what was called the Japanisches Palais; under the direction of the architects Pöppelmann, Johann Christoph Knöffel, Zacharias Longuelune and Jean de Bodt, a four-winged building intended solely to accommodate Augustus's porcelain collection was constructed. Large commissions for the decoration of the palace were awarded to the Meissen factory. Although Augustus died before the exterior of the Japanisches Palais was completed, the designs for it gave an important impetus to the Meissen factory.

In 1731 the 24-year-old court sculptor JOHANN JOACHIM KÄNDLER, who had assisted with the decoration of the Grünes Gewölbe in the palace of Dresden, began work at the factory; his success as a modeller may have been due to his training. At first he worked with the sculptor JOHANN GOTTLOB KIRCHNER executing a commission for 910 figures, mainly animals (e.g. pelican, 1732; Dresden, Porzellansamml.). He was gradually entrusted with the production of models for all kinds of vessels and was the first to translate the style of the French Rococo into porcelain. His output is characterized by a selective use of existing images and idioms, which were specifically adapted to porcelain, and by his ability to assemble and unify different forms into complete services of various sizes. The apogee of his creative work is undoubtedly the 'Swan' service (1737–41; Meissen, Porzellanmus.; see fig. 2) made for Heinrich, Graf von Brühl, on which he collaborated with such artists as JOHANN FRIEDRICH EBERLEIN and Johann Gottlieb Ehder (1717–50). The service comprised between 1400 and 2000 items and was the largest contemporary porcelain service. Engravings of designs for a table centrepiece composed of shell shapes by Juste-Aurèle Meissonnier probably served as the pattern. In his work record of July 1738 Kändler referred to the groups on the tureens as figures from the story of Galatea. Francesco Albani's painting *Galatea in the Shell Carriage* (1722; Dresden, Gemäldegal. Alte Meister) inspired Kändler to produce a sculptural version on a tureen

2. Meissen porcelain pieces, including coffeepot, h. 250 mm, from the 'Swan' service, made for Heinrich, Graf von Brühl, from the workshop of Johann Joachim Kändler, with *indianische Blumen* decoration by Johann Gregorius Höroldt, 1737–41 (Meissen, Porzellanmuseum)

lid. The countless porcelain figures (*see* CERAMICS, colour pl. I, fig. 2) produced in addition by Kändler and his assistants were partly cabinet figures and partly table-decorations.

The primary sources for porcelain figures were such emblematic and iconographical works as *Iconologica* (Rome, 1593; Ger. trans., Frankfurt am Main, 1669–70) by Cesare Ripa. Since porcelain was in the first place an imitative art—especially when used for sculptural pieces—these writings were an important source of inspiration for porcelain makers. The early Meissen porcelain 'sculptures', with their simple, primitive modelling and painting, clearly show their origin in tragacanth-sugar art, a method used by pastry cooks to model elaborate table-decorations from a compound of tragacanth (astragalus gum) and sugar. Kändler is particularly well known for his figure production, which included street-vendors, artisans, mythological characters, figures from the court or the country (e.g. shepherd group, 1750; Dresden, Porzellansamml.) and his characters from the *commedia dell'arte*.

During Kändler's lifetime there was not only a shift towards the Louis XVI style but also the beginning of an emancipation of the middle classes. In the ensuing changes the exclusivity of porcelain, and particularly its use in court festivities, was irretrievably lost. Small porcelain sculptures took on a primarily educative and moralizing function. Table-services became more sober and functional and more in keeping with bourgeois aspirations.

From 1764 to 1780 the French sculptor Michel Victor Acier (1736–99) worked at the factory under the direction of Camillo, Graf von Marcolini (1739–1814). Between 1772 and 1775 Acier worked with Kändler on the 'Large Russian' order (Lomonosov, Oranienbaum Castle), a table-service stylistically based on late Baroque traditions comprising a total of 40 groups and individual figures for Catherine II, Empress of Russia. Acier's figures differ from Kändler's through their strict, sculptural quality and usually by a didactic moral intention. Nevertheless, these figures give specific expression to the ideals of the time, the quest for education, rational behaviour and irreproachable family life (e.g. the *Good Mother*, 1774; Dresden, Porzellansamml.).

Many drawings for figures, vases and candelabra in the 'ancient' style were submitted to the Meissen factory by Johann Eleazar Schenau (or Schönau; identified as Johann Elias Zeissig; 1737–1806) and then translated into porcelain by Acier, Johann Gottlieb Matthaei (1753–1832), Christian Gottlieb Jüchtzer (1752–1812), Johann Carl Schönheit (1730–1805) and Johann Daniel Schöne (1767–1805). A particularly popular material of the period was biscuit porcelain because it was reminiscent of alabaster and marble; it was used at the factory from *c.* 1780. The inspiration for the use of this material came from the factories of Sèvres and Wedgwood. For vessels, cylindrical, smooth-walled and amphora-like shapes were preferred, and the decoration was often mythological or classical (e.g. *Ganymede and Hebe* candlestick, 1790; Hamburg, Mus. Kst & Gew.).

(ii) 1800 and after. The years *c.* 1800 were marked by the effects of the French Revolution (1789–95), by problems arising from increasing competition from other factories, by a reduction in the number of employees, by fundamental changes in style and public taste and by the onset of the Industrial Revolution. Heinrich Gottlob Kühn (1788–1870) was the most influential innovator and technical reorganizer during the early 19th century. The installation of beehive and double-deck kilns, the use of coal rather than wood as fuel and the introduction of steam-powered

machines were among the important innovations. During his period as director (1833–70) the factory moved from the Albrechtsburg to a new building in the Triebisch Valley near Meissen, where the foundation stone of the new factory was laid in 1861.

During the 19th century Romantic, Biedermeier and historicist tendencies dominated, and, in conjunction with the technical modernization, the factory flourished once again. Such painters as Georg Friedrich Kersting and Ludwig Richter were employed by the factory, the latter as a drawing instructor (1828–35). Kersting contributed an innovative style of flower painting that combined botanical accuracy with a highly sensitive response to nature. The decorative motif *Voller grüner Weinkranz* (vine-leaf decoration) was developed in 1817 by the Meissen flower painter Johann Samuel Arnhold (1766–1828) as a green chrome-oxide underglaze decoration (e.g. plate, 1820; Meissen, Porzellanmus.), although the first designs had been produced in 1790. Such decorations as 'strewn flowers' and the 'purple rose' became well known during the Biedermeier period (*c.* 1818–48). During the historicist phase the Rococo Revival style was particularly popular, although the Gothic and Renaissance styles were also adapted with a sophisticated eclecticism. Lithophanes (for lampshades and windows) were produced at Meissen as early as *c.* 1828. About 1830 a bright gold was invented at Meissen, and porcelain was decorated with lustres from 1837 (e.g. vase, 1861; Meissen, Porzellanmus.; see fig. 3). *Pâte-sur-pâte* decoration, a form of slip painting first introduced at the factory at Sèvres, was introduced *c.* 1880 (e.g. Renaissance-style display vase, 1875; Meissen, Porzellanmus.). Influenced by Impressionist painting, a special, extremely subtle variation of flower painting was introduced under the direction of Julius Eduard Braunsdorf (1841–1922), who developed this pastel style to a high pitch of refinement.

The sculptor Erich Hösel (1869–1953), a pupil of Johannes Schilling and Robert Diez (1844–1922), was probably the first to make a critical study of the factory's stock of models; he revived some of the old forms from archive documents and freed many of them from historicist accretions. His own output—mainly animal sculptures and folk groups—was, however, quite small.

Between 1903 and 1905, during the *Jugendstil* period, Henry Van de Velde and Richard Riemerschmid submitted designs for table-services decorated with underglaze-blue decoration; they were, however, produced only in relatively small numbers, as they showed little regard for the characteristic manufacturing possibilities and exclusive qualities of Meissen porcelain. *Jugendstil* designs that made better use of the manufacturing processes were produced by the brothers Julius Konrad Hentschel (1872–1907) and Johannes Rudolf Hentschel (1869–1951), who designed services (e.g. plate with vetch decoration, 1910; Meissen, Porzellanmus.), vases, candlesticks, decorative motifs and sculptures. Other *Jugendstil* artists included Otto Friedrich Theodor Grust (1857–1919), Philipp Lange (*b* 1879), Hans Meid (1883–1957), Willi Münch-Khe (1885–1961), Karl Ludwig Achtenhagen (1865–1938), Otto Eduard Gottfried Voigt (1870–1949), Eugen Albert William Baring (1881–1961) and Julius Arthur Barth (1878–1926).

3. Meissen porcelain vase decorated with royal-blue ground and gold lustre, h. 360 mm, made by Ernst August Lenteritz, 1861 (Meissen, Porzellanmuseum)

In 1919 *Jaspisporzellan* was re-created using a new formula (since the original 18th-century composition was lost). This new, fine-grained stoneware was called *Böttgersteinzeug*. Animal sculpture was given a new impetus in both expressive power and artistic originality by the sculptor Paul Walther (1876–1933), who worked at Meissen before and after World War I (e.g. toucan, 1919; Meissen, Porzellanmus.). The sculptor Max Esser (1885–1943), a pupil of August Gaul, was given a studio at the factory in 1920, which allowed him, as a freelance artist, the opportunity to work in both porcelain and *Böttgersteinzeug*. He produced impressive animal figures, including the *Fish Otter* (e.g. of 1926; Meissen, Porzellanmus.) for which he was awarded the Grand Prix at the Exposition Internationale des Arts et Techniques dans la Vie Moderne of 1937 in Paris, a table-service design and an imposing centrepiece (vessels and figures, 1921–7) in which he made use of the fables about Reynard the Fox. Another freelance artist, Paul Scheurich (1883–1945), worked for the factory between 1913 and 1933. With over 100 works, he is regarded as the most creative, individual, sensitive and original porcelain sculptor of the period. His figures are a synthesis of the Rococo Revival and Art Deco styles and produce an effect that is erotic, theatrical and striking, while being at the same time naive, reserved and serene (e.g. *Spanish Lady*, 1930; Meissen, Porzellanmus.).

The sculptor and printmaker Gerhard Marcks produced works for the factory including *Funerary Angel for B. Harkort*, which was produced in *Böttgersteinzeug* from 1919 (e.g. Meissen, Porzellanmus.), and the *Sleepwalking Woman*, which was produced from 1919 in both porcelain and *Böttgersteinzeug*. Two works by the sculptor and printmaker ERNST BARLACH continued to be produced in the late 20th century: *Sleeping Vagrants*, also called *Sleeping Peasants*, was produced in porcelain from 1922 and in *Böttgersteinzeug* from 1923; and the *Hovering God the Father* was produced from 1923 exclusively in *Böttgersteinzeug*. Various bronze casts by the animal sculptor August Gaul were used for reproduction, predominantly in *Böttgersteinzeug*. The manager of the factory, Max Adolf Pfeiffer (1875–1957), was attempting to use these and other works to achieve an acceptable representation in the field of modern, small sculptures, in which he was assisted by his connections with the well-known publisher and dealer Paul Cassirer. An independent and highly productive artist working at Meissen from the 1920s was Emil Paul Börner (1888–1970), who designed table-sets, sculptures, vases, candlesticks and medals in which he sought to combine proven manufacturing traditions with modern industrial techniques. He also produced the first tunable porcelain bells for the bell-tower of the Frauenkirche in Meissen for the millennial celebrations of the town (1929; *in situ*).

During World War II the factory was not damaged. In 1946 it exhibited at the first post-war Frühjahrsmesse at Leipzig, and on 19 July of the same year it became a subsidiary of the Soviet company Zement. After the establishment of East Germany (7 October 1949), it was returned as a nationalized company. It was styled the VEB Staatliche Porzellan-Manufaktur Meissen on 23 June 1950. During the 1950s, in addition to the traditional lines, very simple forms with restrained, heavily stylized decoration were produced, such as the cylindrical vase (1958; Meissen, Porzellanmus.) by Hans Merz (1921–87).

During the early 1960s, with the foundation of the artistic group Kollektiv Künstlerische Entwicklung/1960, a critical and productive exploration of the Meissen wares began. The group included the designer Ludwig Zepner (*b* 1931), the sculptor Peter Strang (*b* 1936) and the painters Heinz Werner (*b* 1928), Rudi Stolle (*b* 1919) and Volkmar Breitschneider (*b* 1930). Their goal was to revive exclusive tablewares, and one of their first successes was the design of the 'Münchhausen' table-service (1964), the form of which was influenced by industrial design, while the decoration respected the typical style and techniques of the factory. This development was continued in the 'grid-relief' service (1964), which combined overglaze and underglaze decoration representing tales from the *Thousand and One Nights*, and in the 'floral relief/floral dance' design (1969), inspired by Shakespeare's *A Midsummer Night's Dream*. In 1973 the 'Grosser Ausschnitt' service complex designed by Zepner was produced, comprising a dining-, coffee-, tea- and mocha-service decorated in over- and underglaze colours with such designs as the 'Hunting scene', 'Waterfowl hunt', 'Forest foliage' and 'Tall stories

about the hunt'. Other decorative schemes were added until 1978.

Peter Strang increasingly broke away from the factory tradition of producing serial figures and instead created designs for small porcelain figures, often of a humorous nature (e.g. *Oberon*, 1969; Meissen, Porzellanmus.). In the late 20th century the artists produced almost exclusively individual works. A special area of modern Meissen porcelain is the design of murals or wall panels. A group of younger artists including Sabine Wachs (*b* 1960), Silvia Klöde (*b* 1956), Güdrün Gaübe (*b* 1961) and Jörg Danielzyck (*b* 1952) were increasingly influential on late 20th-century designs, which considered both international trends and innovative uses of manufacturing traditions.

The Staatliche Porzellan-Manufaktur Meissen has a public museum, with an adjoining demonstration workshop. The exhibits trace the development of Meissen porcelain from its inception to the present.

BIBLIOGRAPHY

K. Berling: *Das Meissner Porzellan und seine Geschichte* (Leipzig, 1900)
E. Zimmermann: *Meissner Porzellan* (Leipzig, 1926)
F. H. Hofmann: *Das Porzellan der europäischen Manufakturen im XVIII. Jahrhundert* (Berlin, 1932)
A. Schönberger and H. Soehner: *Die Welt des Rokoko: Kunst und Kultur des 18. Jahrhunderts*, 2 vols (Munich, 1963)
H. J. Hansen, ed.: *Kunstgeschichte des Backwerks* (Oldenburg and Hamburg, 1968)
J. Just: *Der künstlerische Erneuerungsprozess der Porzellan-Manufaktur Meissen um 1900* (diss., Halle, Martin Luther-U., 1972)
M. Shono: *Japanisches Aritaporzellan im sogenannten 'Kakiemonstil' als Vorbild für die Meissner Porzellanmanufaktur* (Munich, 1973)
O. Walcha: *Meissner Porzellan* (Dresden, 1973, rev. 7/1984)
S. Bursche: *Tafelzier des Barock* (Munich, 1974)
J. Schärer, ed.: *Meissen '75: Informationen über das gegenwärtige Wirken der ersten europäischen Porzellanmanufaktur* (Meissen, 1975)
R. Rückert and J. Willisberger: *Meissen Porzellan des 18. Jahrhunderts* (Dortmund, 1977)
H. Jedding: *Meissner Porzellan des 18. Jahrhunderts* (Munich, 1979)
W. Neuwirth: *Meissener Marken: Original, Imitation, Verfälschung, Fälschung* (Vienna, 1980)
H. Jedding: *Meissner Porzellan des 19. und 20. Jahrhunderts* (Munich, 1981)
H. Kürth: *Die Kunst der Model* (Leipzig, 1981)
Johann Friedrich Böttger: Die Erfindung des europäischen Porzellans (Leipzig, 1982)
W. Goder and others: *Johann Friedrich Böttger zum 300. Geburtstag* (exh. cat., Dresden, Staatl. Kstsammlungen, 1982)
K. Hoffmann: *Johann Friedrich Böttger: Vom Alchemistengold zum weissen Porzellan: Biografie* (Berlin, 1985)
Meissen heute: Atelierkunst (Meissen and Konstanz, 1987)
G. Sterba: *Gebrauchsporzellan aus Meissen* (Leipzig, 1988)
I. Menzhausen: *Alt-Meissner Porzellan in Dresden* (Berlin, 1989)
G. Reinheckel: *Prachtvolle Service aus Meissner Porzellan* (Leipzig, 1989)
Bergbau und Kunst in Sachsen: Führer durch die Ausstellung (exh. cat., Dresden, Staatl. Kstsammlungen, 1989)
Meissener Blaumalerei aus drei Jahrhunderten (exh. cat., ed. K.-P. Arnold and V. Diefenbach; Dresden, Staatl. Kstsammlungen; Hamburg, Mus. Kst & Gew.; 1989)
D. Nadolski: *Wahre Geschichten um das Meissener Porzellan* (Leipzig, 1990)
H. Sonntag and B. Schuster: *Meissen & Meissen* (Munich, 1990)
K. -D. Arnold: *'Ey! wie schmeckt der Coffee süsse': Meissener Porzellan und Graphik* (Dresden, 1991)
G. Meier: *Porzellan der Meissener Manufaktur* (Berlin, 1991)
J. Schärer, ed.: *Meissener Konturen: Porzellane von Zepner, Werner, Strang, Stolle und Bretschneider aus den Jahren 1960–1990* (Leipzig, 1991)
H. Sonntag: *Meissener Porzellan—Schönheit im Detail* (Berlin, 1991)
K. -P. Arnold: *Porzellan im Dresdner Zwinger: Führer durch die Porzellansammlung* (Dresden, 1992)
L. Danckert: *Handbuch des europäischen Porzellans* (Munich, 1992)

HANS SONNTAG

Meissner, Johann Heinrich (*b* Königsberg [now Kaliningrad], 1700; *bur* Danzig [now Gdańsk], 8 May 1777). German sculptor. Although his large sculptural work, such as the monuments to *Frederick William I, King of Prussia* (1730–36; ex-Schloss Königsberg) and *Augustus III, King of Poland* (1752–5; destr. 1945), and his church decoration, for example the pulpit (1762–4) in the church of St Mary, Gdańsk, have been held to be of inferior quality, his small sculptures earned him the reputation of being one of the most important carvers working in the Rococo style in north-east Germany in the first half of the 18th century. Among these works are statues of children, mythological scenes and female nudes. His female figures are either delicate and slim, for example in the lively *Hercules and Venus* (?1750; Stockholm, Hallwylska Mus.), one of his best works, in which the lightness of the Rococo is evident, or stocky and heavy (e.g. *Hercules and Omphale*, 1740; Berlin, Staatl. Museen Preuss. Kultbes.), so that they are reminiscent of 17th-century small Flemish sculptures: the body is only slightly articulated; the relationship between surfaces and space is not completely defined. This inspiration from earlier examples was typical of Meissner, who had studied these works in local collections and had a tendency to be eclectic; this also makes it more difficult to establish the chronology of his small sculptures. The modelling of his figures is soft and palpable, and the erotic, almost lascivious, details are emphasized. Meissner's exceptionally beautiful daughters were allegedly his models.

BIBLIOGRAPHY

H. F. Secker: 'Der Danziger Bildhauer Johann Heinrich Meissner', *Z. Bild. Kst*, lv (1920), pp. 133–44

R. Verres: 'Zur Kleinplastik Johann Heinrich Meissners', *Pantheon*, viii (1931), pp. 467–70

I. Koska: *Johann Heinrich Meissner: Ein Danziger Bildhauer des 18. Jahrhunderts* (diss., U. Danzig, 1936)

Barockplastik in Norddeutschland (exh. cat., ed. J. Rasmussen; Hamburg, Mus. Kst & Gew., 1977), pp. 599–607

A. GERHARDT

Meissonier, (Jean-Louis-)Ernest (*b* Lyon, 21 Feb 1815; *d* Paris, 31 Jan 1891). French painter, sculptor and illustrator. Although he was briefly a student of Jules Potier (1796–1865) and Léon Cogniet, Meissonier was mainly self-taught and gained experience by designing wood-engravings for book illustrations. These included Léon Curmer's celebrated edition of J.-H. Bernardin de Saint-Pierre's *Paul et Virginie* (Paris, 1838), the series *Les Français peints par eux-mêmes* (Paris, 1840–42) and Louis de Chevigné's *Les Contes rémois* (Paris, 1858). Such images, typically measuring 60×90 mm and composed of still-life motifs (books or drapery cascading from a chest, intricately arranged and exhaustively detailed), helped form the style for which Meissonier became famous as a painter.

Meissonier's first painting was the *Flemish Burghers* (190×250 mm, 1834; London, Wallace), exhibited at the Salon of 1834; thereafter he specialized in very small-scale genre scenes featuring costumes and accessories exquisitely rendered with meticulous detail. He was inspired in part by the work of Dutch and Flemish masters such as Gabriel Metsu and Gerard ter Borch (ii) and French painters and engravers such as Chardin, Gravelot and Greuze, as well as by contemporary romantic theatre and costume design. His subjects include tranquil 17th- and 18th-century artists and musicians (e.g. *Painter Showing his Drawings*, *c.* 1850; London, Wallace; see fig.), gentlemen reading, playing chess and smoking (e.g. *Young Man Writing*, 1852; Paris, Louvre; and *Smoker in Black*, 1854; London, N.G.) and rowdy cavaliers (e.g. *A Guardroom*, 1857; London, Wallace; and *Jovial Trooper*, 1865; Baltimore, MD, Walters A.G.). Even the artist's eye-witness view of a demolished barricade and its fallen defenders (*Remembrance of Civil War*, 290×220 mm, 1848; Paris, Louvre) reflects his habit of making a close study of stationary objects and then combining details into more elaborate, but still diminutive compositions. For simpler works Meissonier often began work directly on a small panel or page, expanding the support if he required more space.

Meissonier also developed a range of military subjects in his paintings. Although he depicted the reigning emperor in *Napoleon III at the Battle of Solférino* (1863; Paris, Louvre), he otherwise devoted himself to re-creating the past, chiefly of the Revolutionary and Empire periods. He executed both small panels of individual guards and cavalrymen and more elaborate canvases, such as *Information: Gen. Desaix and the Peasant* (1867; Dallas, TX, Mus. A.) and *Moreau and Dessoles before Hohenlinden* (1876; Dublin, N.G.). His most ambitious project was a series of moments in Napoleon I's military career, including *1814, the Campaign of France* (1864; Paris, Louvre), *1807, Friedland* (1875; New York, Met.) and *1805, the Cuirassiers before the Battle* (1876; Chantilly, Mus. Condé). Though some are on a larger scale with more, active figures, these paintings are still distinguished by painstaking research, close work from the model and virtuoso attention to detail.

Extending his ambition to be a history painter and impelled by his own experiences, Meissonier sketched an allegorical response to the Franco-Prussian War (*Siege of Paris, 1870–1871*, begun 1870; Paris, Louvre) and in 1874 obtained a commission (never realized) for a mural in the Pantheon. In 1871 he painted his more monumental *Ruins of the Tuileries* (1.36×0.96 m; Compiègne, Château), fusing personal observation and objective description with larger meaning conveyed in the details. Above a pile of rubble the shell of the great Palace, burnt during the Commune, frames the distant sculpture of *Peace* on top of Napoleon I's Arc de Triomphe at the Carrousel; with her back turned, she seems to depart from a France recently defeated by the Prussians and then ravaged by civil war. Yet a Latin inscription affirms that the glory of the past survives the flames, and still intact are architectural reliefs commemorating Napoleon's victories at Marengo and Austerlitz.

By 1862, perhaps as early as 1848, Meissonier began to construct sculptures of figures and especially horses. Modelled of wax over an internal skeleton, with cloth, leather and metal for clothing and harnesses, these works served largely as an aid in composing paintings involving more figures or varied movement. Only after Meissonier's death were the sculptures exhibited and two groups of the waxes cast in bronze multiples. These include *Napoleon I in 1814* (wax, 1862; France, priv. col.; Siot-Decauville bronzes, 1894; Shreveport, LA, Norton A.G., and Bordeaux, Mus. B.-A.) done for *1814, the Campaign of France*;

Wounded Horse (wax, *c.*1881–4; Lyon, Mus. B.-A.; bronzes, *c.* 1893–5; Bayonne, Mus. Bonnat, Dijon, Mus. B.-A. and Grenoble, Mus. Peint. & Sculp.) for the *Siège of Paris*; and *The Voyager* (wax, 1878; Paris, Mus. d'Orsay; Siot-Decauville bronzes, 1894; Lille, Mus. B.-A., and Washington, DC, Hirshhorn) used for several paintings.

From 1840 Meissonier's paintings prompted effusive reviews by critics such as Théophile Gautier, who stressed their affinity with 17th-century Dutch and Flemish masters and exclaimed at the 'microscopic' perfection of the artist's 'Lilliputian' gallery. The disproportionate expense of these diminutive panels became well known, with members of the financial and social élites of the July Monarchy (1830–48) and Second Empire (1852–70) vying for works, both directly from the artist and at resales by auction. Early collectors include members of the Rothschild and Pereire families; Richard Seymour-Conway, 4th Marquis of Hertford, and his son Sir Richard Wallace; Auguste, Duc de Morny; and Napoleon III, who presented *The Brawl* (London, Buckingham Pal., Royal Col.) to Prince Albert at the 1855 Exposition Universelle in Paris. In the 1870s and 1880s Meissonier's work (represented by the fashionable dealer Georges Petit) was sought out by wealthy Americans such as A. T. Stewart, William Vanderbilt and William T. Walters, who were travelling in Europe.

For such authors as Charles Baudelaire, Honoré de Balzac, the de Goncourts and Emile Zola, who wrote both exhibition criticism and fiction, Meissonier's paintings epitomized the taste of the *nouveaux-riches*. His success after the 1850s increasingly made him a target for critics and younger artists in the Realist tradition, among them Degas, Manet and Toulouse-Lautrec; attitudes hardened when Meissonier led the jury to exclude Courbet from the Salon of 1872 because of his political activities during the Commune of 1871. Meissonier gradually withdrew from the public forum of the Salon, preferring to exhibit at less frequent and more selective international exhibitions for which he often served as juror. In the 1880s, he also exhibited in shows organized by dealers and small clubs of amateurs. In 1890 he came back into public life, leading a secession from the established salon of the Société des Artistes Français (then identified with Bouguereau) and, with Puvis de Chavannes, founding the more innovative Société Nationale des Beaux-Arts.

Meissonier was much honoured during his lifetime: he was elected to the Académie des Beaux-Arts (1861), of which he was President twice (1876 and 1891), President of the jury of the Exposition Universelle Internationale in Paris (1889) and the first artist to receive the Grand-croix in the Légion d'honneur (1889). He had only a few pupils, notably his son Charles Meissonier (1844–1917) and the military painter Edouard Detaille, but his success encouraged many derivative artists to specialize in historical genre pieces. Two years after his death his studio was sold, and his reputation declined rapidly, but since the 1970s there has been renewed appreciation of his historical importance.

BIBLIOGRAPHY

V. C. O. Gréard: *Meissonier: Ses souvenirs — ses entretiens* (Paris, 1897)
L. Bénédite: *Meissonier* (Paris, 1910)
C. Hungerford: *The Art of Jean-Louis-Ernest Meissonier: A Study of the Critical Years 1834 to 1855* (diss., U. CA, 1976)

Ernest Meissonier: *Painter Showing his Drawings*, oil on panel, 375×291 mm, *c.* 1850 (London, Wallace Collection)

——: 'Meissonier's *Souvenir de Guerre Civile*', *A. Bull.* [New York], lxi (1979), pp. 277–88
P. Guilloux: *Meissonier: Trois siècles d'histoire* (Paris, 1980)
C. Hungerford: 'Meissonier's First Military Paintings: *The Emperor Napoleon III at the Battle of Solférino* and *1814, The Campaign of France*', *A. Mag.*, liv (1980), pp. 89–107
A. Le Normand-Romain: '*Le Voyageur* de Meissonier', *Rev. Louvre*, xxxv (1985), pp. 129–35

CONSTANCE CAIN HUNGERFORD

Meissonnier, Juste-Aurèle (*b* Turin, 1695; *d* Paris, 31 July 1750). French designer, architect and goldsmith. He was apprenticed to his father Etienne Meissonnier, a sculptor and silversmith of some importance, before making his way to Paris, arriving in 1714. He worked there as a die-cutter and medallist, progressing through the ranks of the metalworkers' guild. He was variously described as a chaser, a designer and, in 1723, as a maker of watchcases; he worked for ten years at the royal furnishings factory of Gobelins, Paris. In September 1724 Louis XV appointed him by *brevet* a master of the Corporation des Marchands-Orfèvres Joailliers. It would appear, however, that his main occupation was as a chaser. His mark, a crowned fleur-de-lis, J O M and two *grains de remède*, has been found on only one piece, a gold and lapis lazuli snuff-box (1728; Geneva, J. Ortiz Patino priv. col., see Snowman, pl. 146). In spite of this scarcity of signed pieces, it is reasonable to

Juste-Aurèle Meissonnier: silver tureen, 305×354×388 mm, *c.* 1734–40 (Madrid, Museo Thyssen-Bornemisza)

assume that he closely supervised the work that he contracted to other goldsmiths. In 1735 Evelyn Pierrepont, 2nd Duke of Kingston (1711–73), commissioned a pair of silver tureens (Madrid, Mus. Thyssen-Bornemisza; see fig.; Cleveland, OH, Mus. A.) that bear the marks of the silversmiths Henry Adnet (1683–1745) and Pierre-François Bonnestrenne (1685–after 1737/8) and inscriptions that identify Meissonnier as the designer. Silver pieces with the mark of Claude Duvivier (1688–1747), made after designs by Meissonnier, show an extremely close relationship between the executed object and the engraved design.

In 1726 Meissonnier was appointed Dessinateur de la Chambre et du Cabinet du Roi in succession to Jean Berain the younger (1678–1726). The duties involved the designing of all court festivities, an activity Meissonnier apparently enjoyed; he had already in 1725 created a fireworks display near the Orangerie at Versailles to celebrate the King's recovery from illness. Another festivity that Meissonnier orchestrated, to celebrate the birth of the Dauphin, took place at Versailles in 1729.

Surviving autograph drawings by Meissonnier are not numerous; however, his designs have been recorded in engravings that were published by the widow Chereau in small groups during his lifetime; one series of 50 was announced in 1734 in the *Mercure de France.* After Meissonnier's death, the plates were acquired by Gabriel Huquier, who published, between 1742 and 1751, a complete set of the engravings entitled *Oeuvre de Juste-Aurèle Meissonnier.* The volume includes 74 engravings of his architectural works: exteriors, interiors and plans; structures for fireworks and altars; and books of ornament, including designs for cartouches, candlesticks (*see* RO-COCO), mouldings, frames, desk accessories, cane handles, clocks, small boxes and all manner of tableware from salts to centrepieces. Some furniture is also depicted; many of the sheets show more than one design.

Of particular interest among the architectural plates is Meissonnier's design (dated 1733) for a house in Bayonne for Léon de Brethous. The triangular shape of the site inspired Meissonnier to design an irregularly shaped house; along with rooms that were regular in form, he designed octagonal rooms, as well as several with rounded corners and concave, curved, walls. Another notable architectural project was that for Count Franciszek Bieliński, Grand Marshal of the court in Dresden of Augustus III, King of Poland. Meissonnier designed for Bieliński a cabinet with an elaborately painted ceiling and walls with swirling panelling and mouldings. The *Oeuvre* also contained engravings of Meissonnier's projects for St Sulpice, Paris, presented to the priest of the church in 1726 and 1727. The four bays of the façade recall Francesco Borromini's S Carlo alle Quattro Fontane, Rome. The positioning of each bay, forward at the sides and recessed in the centre, creates an illusion of movement and allows for the play of light and shadow. The curving roof-line and undulating silhouette of the lantern are typical of Meissonnier's innovative approach and the free-flowing, fluid movement of his designs. He also submitted designs for the altar and a chapel; none of these architectural designs were, however, executed.

It was in the ideal compositions depicted in the engravings that Meissonnier's fullest originality was exploited. His designs, developed from the basic form of the cartouche, stretched the bounds of fantasy and caprice. Diagonal perspective, asymmetry and elastically curved and spiralling lines are combined with such characteristic elements of the Rococo as shell forms, rocks, cascades, fountains and broken scrolls, to create an elegant and graceful world. As the first to incorporate irregularity of a picturesque nature into his designs, Meissonnier bore the brunt of attack from those critics who preferred straight lines and perpendicularity. For them, ornament was subordinate to structure, and Meissonnier's asymmetry and spiralling lines were objectionable. He is now considered, however, to be the most versatile and brilliant practitioner of the *genre pittoresque.*

BIBLIOGRAPHY
G. Huquier: *Oeuvre de Juste-Aurèle Meissonnier* (Paris, 1742–51/R New York, 1969) [intro. by D. Nyberg]
M. I. Bataille: 'Meissonnier: 1695 à 1750', *Les Peintres français du XVIIIe siècle,* ed. L. Dimier, ii (Paris and Brussels, 1930)
F. Kimball: *The Creation of the Rococo* (Philidelphia, 1943/R New York 1980)
W. Kalnein and M. Levey: *Art and Architecture of the Eighteenth Century in France,* Pelican Hist. A. (Harmondsworth, 1972), pp. 293–4
Rococo: Art and Design in Hogarth's England (exh. cat., ed. M. Snodin and E. Moncrieff; London, V&A, 1984), pp. 43–4
A. K. Snowman: *Eighteenth-century Gold Boxes of Europe* (London, 1990)
P. Fuhring: *Un Génie du Rococo: Juste-Aurèle Meissonnier, 1695-1750, orfèvre, dessinateur et architecte* (diss., Leiden U., 1994)

ELAINE EVANS DEE

Meister Hartman. *See* HARTMANN MEISTER..

Meister Loedewich. *See* JUPAN, LUDWIG.

Meistermann, Georg (*b* Solingen, 16 June 1911; *d* Cologne, 12 June 1990). German painter, stained-glass artist and teacher. He left school a year before the *Abitur* to train as a painter. From 1928 to 1933 he studied at the Kunstakademie, Düsseldorf, with Heinrich Nauen and

Ewald Mataré. In 1933 he was banned from studying and exhibiting and was consequently forced to work in secret. Nevertheless, during this period he managed to lay the foundations for his later work, which after World War II included painting and the design of stained-glass windows. Many of his early works were, however, lost in a bombing raid in 1944. The first windows he designed (see 1977 exh. cat.), for St Engelbertkirche in Solingen in 1938, were also destroyed in the war. He was exempted from military service and worked intermittently as a drawing teacher at his old school. Through journeys to Paris and Chartres between 1937 and 1939 he became familiar with contemporary French art, the influence of which was reflected in his work in the later 1940s.

After the war Meistermann soon became one of the best-known representatives of contemporary German art, concentrating mainly on painting during the 1940s. In 1945 an exhibition of his work took place in the studio of the Städtisches Museum Wuppertal. In the same year he painted *The Dowser* (priv. col., see 1981 exh. cat., p. 34), a disguised self-portrait, which depicts a male figure against a background of apparent ruins. A tension exists in the work between objectivity and abstractions, which remained in Meistermann's work. Pictures painted in the following years are marked by a dynamic ornamentalization of the subjects depicted, although the objective world with garden views, landscapes and still-lifes could still be recognized. The jagged, black outlines used to describe this world form a lattice across the surface of the picture. In 1948 he painted the *New Adam* (untraced, see 1981 exh. cat., p. 110), which is reminiscent of the right-hand figure in Picasso's *Guernica*. For this picture Meistermann was awarded the Blevin–Davis prize, endowed by the Americans to foster art by young Germans. In 1949 the forms became freer and biomorphic. From 1950 the subjects became distanced from specifically identifiable objects, yet retained a clear differentiation between figure and background, which can be interpreted as world and cosmos.

In the mid-1950s Meistermann's compositions became simpler. Clearly structured geometric configurations appeared to float on a surface. Brushstrokes layered one on top of another meant that what lay behind the surface could not be clearly discerned. Despite these reductionist techniques his pictures never become purely artistic inventions, seeking rather to be understood as allegories of this world, sometimes with a religious content too, indicated by such titles as *Lenten Veil* (1958; version, priv. col., see 1981 exh. cat., p. 46). In the late 1960s and 1970s he concentrated on portraits, including those of the painter *Hans Purrmann* (1966; priv. col., see 1981 exh. cat., p. 41), the Federal Chancellor *Willy Brandt* (1969–73; Bonn, Friedrich-Ebert-Stift.) and the Federal President *Walter Scheel* (1976–7; Nuremberg, German. Nmus.).

Meistermann received regular commissions for stained-glass windows and murals in churches, public buildings and private houses from the 1950s. The mural of the *Revelation of St John* (c. 19×10 m, 1954) at St Alfons in Würzburg is the largest and most important of that decade. At first it aroused controversy and dispute but later it won general recognition. Darting, splintered shapes represent lightning, thunder and the seven torches before the throne of God, the wings of the angels and the sea of glass, although colour is used to make this recede into the background. In later murals and stained-glass windows, while using an increasingly abstracted visual language, Meistermann also tried to make a statement specific to each case with some reference to the particular place; for example when the Hearing-Saal of the Federal Parliament in Bonn was created in 1970, the names of famous men and women who were important to the development of democracy were inscribed in a free sequence on the glass windows, or in the gigantic tripartite mural for the administrative building of the ZdF television company in Mainz, the motifs in the picture play on the technology of broadcasting. Meistermann's belief in the artist's socio-political mission is also revealed in his work with the Deutscher Künstlerbund, of which he was President from 1967 to 1972, and in his wide-ranging work as a teacher at the Städelschule, Frankfurt am Main (1953), the Kunstakademie, Düsseldorf (1955), the Kunstakademie, Karlsruhe (1960–76) and the Akademie der Bildenden Künste, Munich (1964–7).

BIBLIOGRAPHY
Georg Meistermann (exh. cat., Bonn, Gal. Hennemann, 1977)
Georg Meistermann: Werke und Dokumente (exh. cat., Nuremberg, German. Nmus.; Munich, Kath. Akad.; Solingen, Dt. Klingenmus.; Leverkusen, Schloss Morsbroich; 1981)
Georg Meistermann: Gemälde, 1958–1984 (exh. cat., Aachen, Suermondt-Ludwig-Mus.; Koblenz, Mittelrhein-Mus.; 1984)
Georg Meistermann: Die Fenster in Profanbauten (Bonn, 1985)
ANGELA SCHNEIDER

Meit [Meijt; Meyt], **Conrat** [Konrad] (*fl c.* 1506–50; *d* Antwerp, 1550–51). German sculptor, active in the Netherlands. In 1511 Christoph Scheurl, professor of law at the University of Wittenberg, described a lavish carving by Meit of the *Virgin and Child with 40 Angels* (destr.) in the castle chapel of Frederick the Wise, Elector of Saxony, at Wittenberg. Scheurl stated that Meit came from Worms and was a member of the workshop of Lucas Cranach the elder.

At the time of his marriage in 1514, Meit was in the service of Margaret of Austria, Regent of the Netherlands, in Mechelen. He may have been the German sculptor, previously employed by Admiral Philip of Burgundy, whose services Margaret wanted to borrow from an unidentified cousin in 1512 in order to have a portrait made of her deceased husband Philibert of Savoy. Meit received a court salary from 1515 and remained in Margaret's service until her death in 1530.

Several works by Meit, none of which can be identified with certainty, are mentioned in Margaret's accounts and inventories between 1516 and 1526: a *Self-portrait* and a model of a horse, both of wood (1516); two bronzes of *Hercules* (one of which was presented to Hendrik III, Count of Nassau-Breda), a wooden *Hercules*, two wooden portraits of *Margaret*, a wooden tower and a stag's head to decorate the chimney-piece of the library (1518); a *Pietà* for a convent in Bruges that Margaret supported and a bronze *Adam and Eve* (1519); many other works, including two pairs of portrait busts of *Margaret* and her late husband *Philibert* (one of marble and the other of wood), a small wooden *Lucretia* and a small nude man holding a dog and a baton (1523–4); and a polychromed wooden *Noli me tangere* and a wooden portrait of *Philibert* (1526).

Many of these works appear to have been small-scale collectors' items kept in Margaret's library. The lost marble portrait busts listed in the inventory of 1523–4 were probably those described by Antonio de' Beatis in a visit to Margaret's palace in 1517. It is possible that the pair of miniature boxwood busts in the British Museum, London, representing the young *Margaret* (h. 94 mm) and *Philibert* (h. 116 mm) served as models for the marble portraits. These portraits are remarkable not only for their characterization but also for the technical virtuosity, the subtle undulation of the facial surfaces, which produces detailed effects of light and shade, and the variety of surface textures and the fragile detail in such passages as Margaret's headdress. The almost identical bust of *Philibert* (h. 116 mm; Berlin, Gemäldegal.) and a second, rather different portrait of *Margaret* (h. 83 mm; Munich, Bayer. Nmus.) probably do not form a pair.

Meit's major surviving documented works for Margaret are the effigies of *Philibert of Savoy*, his mother *Margaret of Bourbon* and of *Margaret* herself for their tombs in the church of St Nicholas of Tolentino in Brou on the outskirts of Bourg-en-Bresse. Jean Perréal, Michel Colombe and Jan van Roome were responsible for the design of the tombs, the construction of which was already advanced when Meit arrived in Brou. Following a preliminary visit in 1524, Meit was commissioned in 1526 to carve the faces and hands of all the figures and the 'living images'; three assistants, including Meit's brother, were assigned to help him with the figures and the fourteen attendant angels.

The recessed wall tomb of *Margaret of Bourbon* comprises the alabaster effigy, a greyhound at the foot, with four of the original six nude putti behind and to either end. Only the putto to the left on the back wall may be attributed to Meit himself. The tombs of both *Philibert* and *Margaret of Austria* comprise two images; above, the official stately marble representation and, below, a less formal and more youthful effigy of each in death. The upper image of Philibert is attended by six putti, that of Margaret by four; several different carvers appear to have been responsible but not Meit himself.

Margaret died in 1530, and in January 1531 Meit signed a contract for the tomb of the late Philibert of Chalon, Prince of Orange, in Lons-le-Saunier. Commissioned by Philibert's mother Philiberte, the tomb was to incorporate figures of both her and her deceased husband Jean de Chalon, a kneeling representation and an effigy of Philibert and subsidiary statues within a chapel-like structure. The decorative sculpture, which was to be carved after the Antique, was entrusted to the Florentine Giambattista Mariotto (*fl* 1526–31). Philiberte died, and the church was destroyed by fire; the many figures that were delivered have since disappeared, and it seems that the tomb was neither installed nor completed.

In 1532 Margaret's former chaplain Antoine de Montcut arranged in his will that a *Pietà*, which had been ordered from Meit, should be placed in the chapel of St Vincent in Besançon. On the destruction of the chapel, the group was moved to the cathedral, where it remains. The dead Christ seated on a step supported by the Virgin and an angel follows the design of the lost Puccini *Pietà* by Andrea

del Sarto, which Meit could have known, if not in the original, at least from the engraving by Agostino Veneziano.

In 1534 Meit purchased a house in Antwerp, and in 1536 he entered the Guild of St Luke as a wood-carver. He seems to have lived in Antwerp until his death. His last documented works are three sibyls of 1536 (destr.), carved for the sacramental tabernacle of the abbey of Tongerlo, and a large complex involving an *Entombment* (destr.) for the same abbey, for which he received payment in 1542.

Meit's only other authenticated work is the alabaster *Judith with the Head of Holofernes* (*c.* 1512–14; see fig.), signed *Conrat Meit von Worms*. Some of Meit's extant carvings in marble, alabaster and boxwood, for instance the *Judith*, have touches of polychromy in the facial

Conrat Meit: *Judith with the Head of Holofernes*, alabaster, h. 295 mm, *c.* 1512–14 (Munich, Bayerisches Nationalmuseum)

features. Bronzes such as the *Mars and Venus* (*c*. 1520; Nuremberg, German. Nmus.) appear to have been cast after models by Meit.

Certain features of the Brou tombs and the alabaster *Judith*, for example the nudity of Judith and the Brou putti and the facial types of the formal effigies of *Margaret of Austria* and *Philibert*, appear to have been inspired by the Antique; but Meit's idiosyncratic approach to anatomy and proportions shows the influence not of the Antique, but rather of Dürer, whom he might have known in Wittenberg; the two certainly met during Dürer's visit to the Netherlands in 1520–21. Although Meit's carvings possess the dignity of Classical art, their delicacy of detail, for example the elaborate coiffure of the *Judith*, is more Netherlandish in character.

BIBLIOGRAPHY

G. Troescher: *Conrat Meit von Worms: Ein rheinischer Bildhauer der Renaissance* (Freiburg im Breisgau, 1927)

J. Duverger: 'Conrat Meijt', *Bull. Cl. B.-A., Acad. Royale Sci., Lett. & B.-A. Belgique*, n. s. 4, v (1934)

J. Borchgrave d'Altena: 'A propos d'une madonne de Conrat Meijt', *Rev. Belge Archéol. & Hist. A.*, xxiii (1954), pp. 225–8

C. von der Osten and H. Vey: *Painting and Sculpture in Germany and the Netherlands, 1500–1600*, Pelican Hist. A. (Harmondsworth, 1969)

C. Lowenthal: 'Conrat Meit's Judith and a Putto at Brou', *Marsyas*, xvi (1972–3), pp. 89–96

——: *Conrat Meit* (diss., New York U., 1976; microfilm, Ann Arbor, 1980) [most comprehensive survey]

KIM W. WOODS

Mejorada, Marqués de [Fernández del Campo, Pedro] (*b* Bilbao; *d* Madrid, 3 March 1680). Spanish statesman and collector. He came from a family from Bilbao, whose wealth derived from agriculture and commerce, and settled in Madrid, where he worked in the royal administration. He joined the Order of Santiago and held state offices, including that of Secretary of State for Italy, and was a member of the Junto de Gobierno during the minority of Charles II (1665–76). In 1673 he was granted the title of Marqués de Mejorada. He owned many works of art: tapestries, mirrors, clocks and escritoires of papier-mâché decorated with coral and silver leaf. Sculpture was represented by 16 valuable pieces on religious subjects, mostly from Naples, although some were produced in Seville and Málaga. The 164 paintings and engravings in his collection were mainly on religious themes, but there were also mythological paintings, landscapes, still-lifes and portraits of Spanish and foreign kings and leading Spanish aristocrats and political figures of the 16th century. The inventory of his collection records few artists' names: a *St Dominic* and a *St Francis* were attributed to El Greco; other items included an engraving of *St Jerome* by Francisco Collantes; a *Christ on the Cross* by Eugenio Cajés; a copy of an *Ecce homo* by Tintoretto; a copy of a *Deposition* by Raphael; and a *Virgin and Child* by Massimo Stanzione. Funerary effigies by Eugenio Guerra (*c*. 1680; Madrid, Mus. Arqueol. N.) were placed on his tomb in the convent of the Agustinos Recoletos in Madrid (destr.).

BIBLIOGRAPHY

V. Pollero: *Estatuas tumulares de personajes españoles de los siglos XIII al XVIII* (Madrid, 1903)

J. A. Escudero: *Los secretarios de estado y del despacho (1474–1724)*, iii (Madrid, 1976)

J. L. Barrio Moya: 'Las colecciones de escultura y pintura del primer Marqués de Mejorada', *Hidalguía*, clxxv (1982), pp. 839–55

NATIVIDAD SÁNCHEZ ESTEBAN

Mekeren, Jan van (*b* Tiel, ?15 Jan 1658; *d* Amsterdam, 18 Feb 1733). Dutch cabinetmaker. He is particularly associated with spectacular floral-marquetry cabinets. His Amsterdam workshops also produced such other furniture in the Baroque style as tables and *guéridons* en suite with the cabinets. The marquetry designs, derived from Dutch still-life paintings, achieved brilliant *trompe l'oeil* effects through the use of various coloured veneers. His work ranks among the most illustrious of the period; compared with that of his contemporary André Charles Boulle, however, van Mekeren's style is freer and less disciplined. The marquetry decoration, for example, often extends down the legs and over the cornices. The value of his estate indicates that commercially his business was highly successful. Nine cabinets can be attributed to him, the most impressive of which is in the Rijksmuseum, Amsterdam (*see* MARQUETRY, fig. 1).

BIBLIOGRAPHY

C. H. de Jonge and W. Vogelsang: *Höllandische Möbel und Raumkunst von 1650–1780* (The Hague, 1922)

C. Boyce, ed.: *Dictionary of Furniture* (New York, 1985)

JOHN MAWER

Meknès [Miknās; Mequinez]. City in Morocco. Meknès takes its name from the Miknasa, a tribe of Zanata Berbers who, in the 10th century, settled in the fertile region around the Boufekrane River between the Zerhoun massif on the north and the Middle Atlas on the south. Their group of unwalled villages was called *miknāsat al-zaytūn* (Meknès of the olive trees). In the 11th century the Almoravids (*reg* 1056–1147) founded a fortified village south of these dispersed rural habitations. The Almohads (*reg* 1130–1269) took the village in the middle of the 12th century after a long siege (seven years, according to one 15th-century source). In the following years of peace and prosperity the congregational mosque was reconstructed (early 13th century) and new quarters with mosques and baths created. In 1244 Meknès submitted to the Marinids (*reg* 1196–1465), who constructed a citadel (destr.) south of the town. Within the town they built the Bu 'Inaniyya (*c*. 1345; rest. 1917–22) and Filala madrasas and a hospice (Arab. *zāwiya*) for Jazuli Sufis. The Bu 'Inaniyya Madrasa, a two-storey building around a central court, has fine decoration in glazed tile, carved wood and plaster. It is a smaller version of the Bu 'Inaniyya Madrasa in FEZ. The Marinids also repaired the minaret of the congregational mosque, the ramparts and the water supply (*see* ISLAMIC ART, §II, 6(iv)(b)). These years of calm prosperity were followed in the 15th and 16th centuries by a period of general anarchy throughout Morocco, during which Meknès was only a modest agricultural centre.

Meknès achieved its greatest glory under the 'Alawi ruler Mawlay Isma'il (*reg* 1672–1727), who made it his capital (*see* ISLAMIC ART, §II, 7(v)). Alongside the medina, he created an extended and complex royal city containing palaces, mosques, military and commercial quarters and vast gardens, all surrounded by over 7 km of ramparts. He had the walls of the medina rebuilt and embellished with monumental gates, such as the impressive Bab Barda'in, spanned by a pointed horseshoe arch with a masonry frame decorated with tiles. Meknès suffered during the succession crisis following his death, and one-quarter of the royal city was entirely razed, although the decoration of some monumental façades, such as that of the Bab Mansur (1732), was completed. The grandest gate of the city, the Bab Mansur has flanking towers raised on arcades and extensive lattice decoration in green tile. Meknès was then abandoned as the capital, although Muhammad III ibn 'Abdallah (*reg* 1757–90) constructed the al-Barda'in and Barrima mosques and the mausolea of Sidi Bu 'Uthman and Sidi Muhammad ibn 'Isa in the medina as well as the Dar al-Bayda' Palace and al-Rwa (Roua) Mosque in the royal city. Under French colonial rule Meknès became an important centre of viniculture, and a new quarter was built north-east of the old centre. The Dar Jamaï, the late 19th-century palace of a vizier, was transformed in 1926 into a museum of Moroccan art; its collection includes specialities of the Meknès region, such as painted wood, ceramics and woollen textiles (*see* MOROCCO).

BIBLIOGRAPHY

O. Houdas: 'Monographie de Méquinez', *J. Asiat.* (1885)
H. Saladin: 'Les Portes de Meknès (d'après les documents envoyés par M. le Capitaine Emonet du Service des Renseignements à Meknès', *Bull. Archéol. Maroc* (1915), pp. 242–68
M. Barrucand: *L'Architecture de la qasba de Moulay Ismaïl à Meknès*, 2 vols (Casablanca, 1976)
——: *Urbanisme princier en Islam: Meknès et les villes royales islamiques post-médiévales* (Paris, 1985)
——: 'Die Palastarchitektur Mulāy Ismā'īls: Die Qaṣaba von Meknes', *Madrid. Mitt.*, xxx (1989), pp. 506–23

MARIANNE BARRUCAND

Melaka. *See* MALACCA.

Melamid, Aleksandr. *See under* KOMAR AND MELAMID.

Melanes. *See under* NAXOS, §2(ii).

Melanesia. Conventional geographic and cultural division of the South Pacific Ocean, comprising a group of islands with a total land area of 966,975 sq. km, lying north-east of Australia, including the large island of New Guinea. It has a population of around 6 million. Culturally, Melanesia is especially famous for its rich traditions of communal architecture, sculpture in a vast range of media and body arts. For discussion of these and other Melanesian arts *see under* PACIFIC ISLANDS. *See also* FIJI; IRIAN JAYA; NEW CALEDONIA; PAPUA NEW GUINEA; SANTA CRUZ ISLANDS; SOLOMON ISLANDS; and VANUATU.

Melani, Alfredo (*b* Pistoia, 23 Jan 1860; *d* Milan, 29 Dec 1928). Italian architect, architectural historian, designer and writer. After attending the Accademia in Florence, in 1881 he settled in Milan, where two years later he became professor in the Scuola Superiore d'Arte Applicata all'Industria. He was a supporter of the avant-garde, but, as an architectural historian, was also interested in the Renaissance and the Baroque. A lecture by him on modern art in Turin in 1890 aroused a great deal of criticism and opposition. In 1902 he was a member of the Scottish jury at the first Esposizione Internazionale d'Arte Decorativa Moderna in Turin. Regarded as a typical representative of 19th-century eclecticism, Melani was, in fact, one of the greatest exponents in the early avant-garde of the future Modernist movement in Milan, supporting the concept of artistic independence as a means of furthering the establishment of modern art. Finding himself in the same theoretical position as Raimondo D'Aronco, he denounced the paralysing effect of antiquated and academic styles of teaching. He proposed a complete liberalization of the profession and teaching of architecture and conducted a lifelong campaign to raise the general level of architects' learning, not only from a scientific, but also a humanist, literary and philosophical point of view. He also worked on a number of journals and reviews, both Italian and foreign, and published many manuals on various art forms such as the *Manuale della pittura antica e moderna* and the *Manuale dell'ornatista* (both undated).

As an architect his main works include a plan (unexecuted) for the restoration of the Palazzo Municipale at Pistoia (1881). He also planned the Cappella Merli Maggi (undated) in the Cimeterio Monumentale, Milan, and the Villa Rosa (undated) at Corlanzone near Lonigo. Melani also designed furniture, glass, lace, embroidery and jewellery.

WRITINGS

Jules Gailhabaud ed il Palazzo Communale di Pistoia (Pistoia, 1880)
Manuale d'architettura italiana antica e moderna (Milan, 1883)
Raccolta di 150 tavole di modelli architettonici, figurativi e ornamentali di diverso stile, che si debbono a artisti eminenti . . . scelti dall'architetto Alfredo Melani (Milan, 1888)
L'ornamento nell'architettura (Milan, 1927)
Dizionario dell'arte e delle industrie artistiche (Milan, 1930)

BIBLIOGRAPHY

Portoghesi; Thieme–Becker
E. Bairati, R. Bossaglia and M. Rosci: *L'Italia Liberty: Arredamento e arte decorativa* (Milan, 1973)
E. Bairati: 'Raimondo D'Aronco e il dibattito sulla cultura architettonica alla svolta del secolo', *Atti del congresso internazionale di studi su 'Raimondo D'Aronco e il suo tempo': Udine, 1981*, pp. 227–33

PETER BOUTOURLINE YOUNG

Melano, Ernesto (*b* Pinerolo, nr Turin, 11 March 1792; *d* Turin, 18 April 1867). Italian architect. He was one of the few architects in Italy to work in the Gothic Revival style in the early 19th century. He studied architecture at the University of Turin, graduating in 1812, and was licensed to practise in 1816. He worked first as a military engineer, mainly on the construction of bridges and roads. In 1824 Charles-Felix, King of Sardinia, appointed Melano to take responsibility for the restoration of the abbey of Hautecombe, Savoie, France; he was commissioned to build new works at Hautecombe in 1828, which continued until 1843. Also in Savoie, Melano worked on the internal decoration (1833) of the cathedral at Chambéry; on the church of St Pierre-de-Marché (consecrated 1836), in a classical style; and on the decoration of the cathedral at St Jean-de-Maurienne.

Melano was summoned to Turin in 1833 and in the same year was appointed Royal Architect, with responsibility for the Ufficio d'Arte from 1836. Several of the commissions he received, however, were in collaboration with Pelagio Palagi, who had initially been in charge only of the decoration of the Palazzo Real, and their contributions to the renovations of the Palazzo Real, Castello Racconigi and Castello Pollenzo, the restoration of the

Teatro Regio, and the decoration of Turin Cathedral for the funeral (1849) of Charles Albert, King of Sardinia, are not easy to distinguish. To the main body of the Castello Racconigi, a resolutely Baroque building (begun 1677) by Guarino Guarini (ii), Melano added two stylistically sympathetic wings ending in pavilions (1834–42), while the hunting-lodge and garden pavilion 'Le Margherie' were in an English Gothic Revival style, which was much favoured by Charles Albert. The alterations to the Castello Pollenzo (1843) were also in a Gothic Revival style.

Other works by Melano included the church of S Carlo (1828) at San Martino Alfieri, near Asti, built in a Neoclassical style; the chapel of S Vicenzo de Paoli (1838) at the monastery of the Visitation; the design (1839) for the new parish church at Torre Péllice, near Pinerolo; the church of S Vittore (1843) at Pollenzo near Bra; and the unexecuted designs for the renovation (1847) and extension (1855), in a Gothic Revival style, of the Palazzo Madama, Turin, built (1718–21) in the Baroque style by Filippo Juvarra. In 1853, due to poor health, Melano left the Ufficio d'Arte and instead served as adviser and inspector to several official bodies. In this capacity he criticized (1856) the structure of two buildings by Alessandro Antonelli: the churches of S Gaudenzio, Novara, and S Luca, Turin.

BIBLIOGRAPHY
A. Griseri: 'L'architettura del neoclassico a Torino', *Boll. Cent. Int. Stud. Archit. Andrea Palladio*, xiii (1971), pp. 195–207
A. Giseri and R. Gabetti: *Architettura dell'eclettismo*, Saggi 519 (Turin, 1973)
Cultura figurativa e architettonica negli Stati del Re di Sardegna, 1773–1861, 3 vols (Turin, 1980)
L. Tamberini: *L'architettura dalle origini al 1936*, iv of *Storia del Teatro Regio di Torino* (Turin, 1983)

Melanthios (*fl* later 4th century BC). Greek painter. He was a pupil of Pamphilos, a master who was said to charge extravagant fees. Apelles was a fellow pupil, and the more famous painter conceded to Melanthios superiority in composition. Pliny (*Natural History*, XXXV.50) listed him among the four-colour painters who restricted their palettes to white, yellow, red and black, but it is unlikely that Melanthios used such a limited palette in all his paintings. None of his works survives. His fame rested in part on the theoretical emphasis he placed on painting. He wrote about *symmetria* (proportion) and, in his book *On Painting*, he recommended stamping a certain wilfulness of character on works of art. When Quintilian wrote that both Pamphilos and Melanthios were renowned for *ratio* (*Principles of Oratory* XII.x.6), he was no doubt referring to the intellectual aspect of their work. One of Melanthios' most renowned paintings, a collaboration perhaps with Apelles, was a portrait of the tyrant *Aristratos*. The tyrant was depicted standing beside a chariot driven by Victory. When Aratos of Sikyon (271–213 BC), a connoisseur who collected paintings by Melanthios, freed Sikyon from a tyrant's rule, he decreed that all portraits of tyrants should be destroyed, reluctantly including that of Aristratos. A compromise was reached when the artist Nealkes painted a palm tree over the tyrant, although the tyrant's feet remained visible below the chariot.

BIBLIOGRAPHY
J. Overbeck: *Die antiken Schriftquellen zur Geschichte der bildenden Künste bei den Griechen* (Leipzig, 1868/*R* Hildesheim, 1959), nos 1748–50, 1754–9, 1895

C. HOBEY-HAMSHER

Melbourne. Australian city and capital of the state of Victoria. It is Australia's second largest city (metropolitan population *c*. 3,200,000) and is situated on the flat coastal plain of the Yarra River at the head of Port Phillip Bay in the south-eastern corner of the continent. European settlement of the area, then part of the colony of New South Wales, began in 1835 when two separate groups of entrepreneurial settlers or 'squatters' led by John Batman and John Pascoe Fawkner arrived from Tasmania (formerly Van Diemen's Land) in search of grazing land. Crown ownership of the unauthorized settlement was reasserted in 1836 and Robert Hoddle (1794–1881) defined a rectangular town reserve based on a grid related to the river bank, its principal streets designed as broad boulevards backed with a network of 'little' streets or service lanes. In 1844 the town reserve was extended, allowing for generous areas of parkland (e.g. the Domain and the gardens created by Baron Sir Ferdinand von Mueller; later the Royal Botanic Gardens) and parkland boulevards, notably St Kilda Road, Flemington Road, Victoria Parade and Royal Parade. Despite successive construction cycles, much of the original parkland system has been retained.

Melbourne grew extremely rapidly; by 1839 many wealthy speculators had arrived, land prices had soared and a thriving town with busy port facilities had been constructed. Early prosperity was based on the wool industry, but the discovery of gold (1851) in the hills north-west of the city, at Clunes, Ballarat and Bendigo, brought a huge boom in migration, trade and development. The independent colony of Victoria was created (1851), with Melbourne as its capital and, for a time, the largest city in Australia. Boom conditions lasted, with interruptions, for nearly 40 years and during that time Victorian Melbourne acquired its distinctive form and character, with opulent mansions, churches, banks and ambitious public buildings built in the latest styles from Europe, often using the local blue-black basalt ('bluestone'). Gothic Revival buildings include St Patrick's Cathedral (begun 1858; for illustration see WARDELL, WILLIAM WILKINSON) and several ornamental polychrome commercial buildings by WILLIAM PITT. The prevailing taste, however, was for classical styles, seen in Italianate mansions (e.g. Government House, 1873, St Kilda Road, by Wardell), Renaissance Revival government buildings (e.g. the Treasury Building, 1862, Spring Street, by J. J. Clark) and the work of such architects as JOSEPH REED (e.g. Exhibition Building, 1879; see AUSTRALIA, fig. 3) and JOHN A. B. KOCH. This tendency culminated in the BOOM STYLE of the 1880s. Inner suburbs (e.g. East Melbourne, Carlton and Fitzroy) were also given character by the construction of streets of terraced houses with elaborate plasterwork, wrought-iron lacework balcony railings and polychrome brickwork.

With the growing popularity of the motor car and the easy availability of land, the most popular form of housing in Melbourne, as elsewhere in Australia throughout the

20th century, was the single-storey, free-standing house, typically on a site of about 600 sq. m. The evolution of this house type, coupled with large-scale European migration to Melbourne after World War II, led to widespread suburban land subdivisions and a lively progression of styles echoing European and American fashions and philosophies. In the 1950s house design became more experimental, notably in the work of such architects as ROY GROUNDS and Robin Boyd (see BOYD, (1)), although 30 high-rise towers encircle the city as evidence of public housing policy of the 1960s. By the 1990s the conurbation of Melbourne embraced 58 cities, towns and shires spreading east and south for 50 km along the shores of Port Phillip Bay. The city centre remained the commercial and financial focus, however, and a development boom in the 1980s resulted in the construction of some of Australia's most striking skyscrapers (e.g. the Rialto Building, Collins Street, 1986, by Gerard de Preu, and the Post-modern 101 Collins Street, 1992, by the Denton Corker Marshal partnership).

Melbourne was the first city in Australia to establish a museum of art (1861), which became the National Gallery of Victoria in 1875; at the beginning of the 20th century it was the richest gallery in the British Empire. It was also the only art museum in Australia with its own art school, which had a considerable impact on art education and the development of the Australian art profession (see AUSTRALIA, §§XI, XII and XIII). TOM ROBERTS, ARTHUR STREETON, FREDERICK McCUBBIN and CHARLES CONDER, who became members of the influential Melbourne-based HEIDELBERG SCHOOL in the 1880s, introducing plein-air Impressionism to Australia, all studied at the school. New buildings for Melbourne's art institutions were subsequently provided on the south bank of the Yarra in the Victorian Arts Centre (1959–84; see fig.) by Roy Grounds

and others, incorporating the National Gallery of Victoria, Melbourne Concert Hall, State Theatre and College of the Arts, which is surmounted by a flared, open-frame metal spire.

See also AUSTRALIA, §§II, III and IV.

BIBLIOGRAPHY
R. Boyd: *Victorian Modern* (Melbourne, 1947)
M. Casey and others, eds: *Early Melbourne Architecture, 1840 to 1888: A Photographic Record* (Melbourne, 1953, rev. 2/1975)
D. Saunders, ed.: *Historic Buildings of Victoria* (Brisbane, 1966)
G. Davison: *The Rise and Fall of Marvellous Melbourne* (Melbourne, 1978)
D. Dunstan: *Governing the Metropolis* (Melbourne, 1978)
M. Fraser and others: *Heritage of Australia* (South Melbourne, 1981)
M. Lewis, ed.: *Victorian Churches* (Melbourne, 1991)
Historic Buildings Council: Register, 1993 (Melbourne, 1993)

NEIL CLEREHAN

Melbye, (Daniel Herman) Anton (*b* Copenhagen, 13 Feb 1818; *d* Paris, 10 Jan 1875). Danish painter. He had originally wanted to be a sailor, but abandoned this ambition because of bad eyesight. Similarly, he later gave up training as a shipbuilder, deciding instead to become a marine painter. In 1838 he entered the Akademi for de Skonne Kunster in Copenhagen. He received private tuition from C. W. Eckersberg, and was one of several of his pupils who devoted themselves to marine painting. He exhibited for the first time in 1840, provoking an immediate response from the public. His early pictures followed the style of Eckersberg's marine paintings, which are characterized by a heightened calm and clear colour, but Melbye soon moved towards a more international, Romantic style.

Melbye went on several voyages in order to study the sea at close range; one of his major works, *Eddystone Lighthouse* (1846; Copenhagen, Stat. Mus. Kst), resulted from a voyage to Morocco. In the painting an evocative atmosphere is created by the interplay between dramatic waves and a threatening sky. The lighthouse is a fixed point in the troubled seas. His studies of the sea, together with his thorough knowledge of shipbuilding, enabled him to produce a large number of paintings, many of them on a large scale. Melbye's dramatic compositions and choice of colours were close to the genre style of painters of the Düsseldorf school, such as Johann Peter Hasenclever and Ludwig Knaus. From 1858 he lived in Copenhagen, Hamburg and Paris, where he achieved considerable international success.

BIBLIOGRAPHY
H. Bramsen: *Danske Marine malere* [Danish marine painters] (Copenhagen, 1962)

ELISABETH CEDERSTRØM

Melchers, (Julius) Gari(baldi) (*b* Detroit, MI, 11 Aug 1860; *d* Falmouth, VA, 30 Nov 1932). American painter. Son of a Westphalian sculptor, Julius Theodore Melchers (1829–1909), he studied at the Königliche Kunstakademie in Düsseldorf with Eduard von Gebhardt (1838–1925) and Peter Janssen (1844–1908) between 1877 and 1881. He then moved to Paris where he attended the Académie Julian and the Ecole des Beaux-Arts under the instruction of Gustave Boulanger and Jules Lefebvre.

In 1884 Melchers established himself in the small Dutch town of Egmond-aan-den-Hoef and shared a studio in nearby Egmond-aan-Zee with the American painter

Melbourne, Victorian Arts Centre (1959–84) by Roy Grounds and others

George Hitchcock. His most important large-scale early works, such as *The Sermon* (1886; Washington, DC, N. Mus. Amer. A.) and *The Communion* (1888; Ithaca, NY, Cornell U., Johnson Mus. A.), depict the peasants of this region at prayer and work. They also show the influence of Max Liebermann and Fritz von Uhde in their use of bright natural light and sympathetic portrayal of the worker.

During the 1890s Melchers began painting murals and works with biblical themes. His *Arts of Peace* and *Arts of War* (both 1893; Ann Arbor, U. MI Mus. A.) are two large-scale lunettes painted for the Manufacturers and Liberal Arts Building at the World's Columbian Exposition, Chicago, in 1893. These works show the influence of his friend Pierre Puvis de Chavannes. His *Last Supper (Lamplight)* (Richmond, VA Mus. F.A.) is perhaps the finest example of his Symbolist inspired religious works. The influence of Impressionism is increasingly evident in the artist's domestic interiors of the early 1900s such as the *Open Door* (Falmouth, VA, Melchers Mem. Gal.). In 1915 Melchers returned to America where he purchased the Belmont estate in Falmouth, VA, which contains an important collection of his work. He also maintained a studio on 40th Street in New York.

BIBLIOGRAPHY

D. B. Burke: *American Painters in the Metropolitan Museum of Art*, iii (New York, 1980), pp. 378–83 [full bibliog.]

J. G. Dreiss: *Gari Melchers: His Works in the Belmont Collection* (Charlottesville, 1984)

JOSEPH G. DREISS

Melchett, 1st Baron. *See* MOND, (2).

Meldahl, Ferdinand (*b* Frederiksberg, Copenhagen, 16 March 1827; *d* Copenhagen, 3 Feb 1908). Danish architect, architectural historian and teacher. After being apprenticed as a moulder in his father's iron foundry, he trained as a bricklayer (1842–4). He then studied architecture at the Kongelige Danske Kunstakademi, Copenhagen, graduating in 1853. During the early 1850s he travelled extensively in Spain, Italy and the Near East, gaining an exceptionally wide knowledge of architecture. In his early years of private practice, Meldahl studied and designed agricultural buildings, playing an important role in the reorganization of the Danish dairy industry, and during this period functional considerations determined the severe shapes of his own designs. He soon began, however, to use his knowledge of European styles. For the brick town halls of Ålborg (1857–61) and Fredericia (1859–60) he took features from Italian medieval architecture: moulded bricks formed patterned borders, blind niches and crenellated gables. The Venetian Renaissance inspired the style of the Institute for the Blind (1857–8) in Copenhagen, with its characteristic shaped gables, while for the Navigation School (1863–5) at Havnegade 23, Copenhagen, he used a particular early Renaissance model: the Palazzo Vendramin-Calergi in Venice. He also designed other institutional buildings, such as the Home for the Mentally Handicapped (1859–60) at Rahbeksallé 21 in Copenhagen and the Anchor Smithy (1860–62) at the Naval Dockyard on Holmen, Copenhagen, but these are in a more restrained style.

These early buildings established Meldahl's reputation as an internationalist and the leader of the school known as 'the Europeans', which opposed 'the Nationals' led first by Daniel Herholdt (1818–1902) and later by MARTIN NYROP. Meldahl also undertook numerous rebuilding projects, and here again the breadth of his historical knowledge is clear. When the Frederiksberg Castle was burnt in 1859 (*see* HILLERØD, FREDERIKSBERG CASTLE), Meldahl was put in charge of its reconstruction. While his work there was conscientious and sober, his conversions of older manor houses, such as Pederstrup on Lolland (1858), Bonderupgård on Zealand (1859) and Trolleholm in Scania (1886–9), were harsher. In these modernizations he combined mansard roofs with medieval towers and brickwork. Meldahl was always interested in roof shapes and helped introduce the revival of French classicism into Danish architecture.

Meldahl was professor at the Kunstakademi in Copenhagen from 1864 and held other important teaching and administrative posts. From 1865 to 1902 he was Royal Surveyor, supervising numerous projects in which it is difficult to detect an individual artistic idiom. From 1866 to 1892 he was a member of the Municipal Council in Copenhagen. In this capacity he made an important contribution to the planning of the rapidly expanding capital: in 1864 he had presented his first plan to develop the former ramparts to form a green belt around the town centre, as in Vienna (*see* COPENHAGEN, §1). This met with opposition from civil servants, which was finally overcome when, 15 years later, the plan was sanctioned by the Municipal Council. From 1872 to 1905 Meldahl was adviser to, then Director of, the Copenhagen Building Society. In this role he supervised the layout of a group of blocks of flats (1873–6) on Søtorv, a square facing one of Copenhagen's lakes. These were crowned with towers and French-style roofs and narrow domes, and their façades were decorated with the stucco always associated with Meldahl's work. One of his greatest achievements, however, was the completion of Frederikskirke, begun by Nicolas-Henri Jardin and upon which other architects (notably C. F. Harsdorff) had unsuccessfully exercised their ingenuity. The ruined church was purchased from the State in 1874 by the financial magnate C. F. Tietgen. Meldahl finally completed it in 1894, in an Italian Renaissance style with a dome considered to be his most successful design.

WRITINGS

Venedig: Dets historie og dets mindesmaerker [Venice: its history and its monuments] (Copenhagen, 1903)

Venedigs kirken [The churches of Venice] (Copenhagen, 1903)

BIBLIOGRAPHY

H. H. Madsen: *Meldahls rædselsprogram: F. Meldahl arkitekt og politiker 1827–1908* [Meldahl's programme of horror: F. Meldahl architect and politician] (Copenhagen, 1983)

WIVAN MUNK-JØRGENSEN

Meldolla, Andrea. *See* SCHIAVONE, ANDREA.

Meldrum, (Duncan) Max (*b* Edinburgh, 3 Dec 1875; *d* Melbourne, 6 June 1955). Australian painter and teacher. He moved with his family in 1889 to Melbourne, where he studied art at the National Gallery of Victoria Art School under Frederick McCubbin and L. Bernard Hall

(1859–1935), winning the triennial Travelling Scholarship in 1899 which enabled him to further his studies in Paris at the Académie Julian and the Académie Colarossi. However, he grew to dislike what he called the 'ineptitude and academic conventions' of the Paris schools and left them in order to study in 'the school of nature'. Living at Pacé in Brittany, he exhibited with the Société des Artistes Français and was elected an associate of the Société Nationale des Beaux-Arts. The *Bell Tower, Pacé* (c. 1908; Castlemaine, A.G. & Hist. Mus.) is characteristic of his work in this period. He returned to Melbourne in 1911 and held his first solo exhibition there in 1913 at the Athenaeum Art Gallery, receiving considerable praise for his work. In 1916 he founded the Meldrum School of Painting, in which he taught the theory that painting 'is a pure science—the science of optical analysis'. He maintained that it is the business of the artist to translate optical impressions within the limitations of a medium and in the scientific order in which they are perceived. He emphasized the importance of tonal quality in painting to the exclusion of all but the barest elements of drawing and colour. Meldrum's large following of students included Archibald Colquhoun (1894–1983) and Justus Jorgensen (1893–1975), and his influence on Australian art between the two World Wars was considerable. He became, and remained, a figure of controversy for he was uncompromising in the advocacy of his opinions. An original member (1912) of the Australian Art Association, he was also President of the Victorian Artists' Society in 1916–17. He exhibited in London with the Royal Society of Portrait Painters (1933) and returned to France in 1926. He lectured on painting in the USA, before returning to Melbourne (1931). Meldrum's ability as a painter was widely recognized; his best-known works include *Portrait of the Artist's Mother* (1913; Melbourne, N.G. Victoria) and *Picherit's Farm*. After 1920 his painting technique became broader. Many of his portraits and still-lifes, for example *Interior* (1936; Sydney, A.G. NSW), show a simplified tonal range and less individual style. He admired and was indirectly influenced by the work of Velázquez, Rembrandt, Corot, Whistler and other Western Realist painters.

WRITINGS
The Science of Appearances (Sydney, 1950)

BIBLIOGRAPHY
C. Colahan, ed.: *Max Meldrum: His Art and Views* (Melbourne, 1919)
W. Moore: *The Story of Australian Art* (Sydney, 1934)

PETER W. PERRY

Mele, Pandi (b Hoçisht, Korçë, 18 Aug 1939). Albanian printmaker, painter and critic. He studied graphic arts at the Higher Academy of Arts, Leningrad (now St Petersburg; 1959–61), and at the Higher Institute of Arts in Tiranë (1964). He first achieved recognition with the series of 12 linocuts *Migjeni Motifs* (1964; Tiranë, A.G.; see fig.). In later works, such as *Friends* (series of four linocuts, 1972; Tiranë, A.G.), Mele attempted to reflect advanced social developments in Albanian society. His work is distinguished for its skilful composition and his use of an economical and laconic means of expression. His expressive lines and balance of tones are permeated by an epic spirit with a tendency for the monumental. He also worked as a painter (e.g. *This is Radio Tirana*, 1976; Tiranë, A.G.)

Pandi Mele: linocut from the series *Migjeni Motifs*, 1964 (Tiranë, Art Gallery)

and designed posters and postage stamps. Mele published numerous articles as an art critic.

WRITINGS
'Monumenti i Skënderbeut në krujë', *Drita* (24 March 1985), p. 12

BIBLIOGRAPHY
K. Buza: 'Rinia entuziste në grafikën e P. Meles' [Enthusiastic youth in the graphic art of P. Mele], *Zëri i Rinisë* (5 Jan 1966), p. 3
B. Tula: 'Nga krijimtaria e piktorit Pandi Mele' [Works by the painter Pandi Mele], *Pioneri*, 24 (1976), pp. 26–8

SULEJMAN DASHI

Mele [Melo] da Stigliano (fl first half of the 13th century). Italian sculptor. His name appears with another on one of the capitals in the loggia of the courtyard in the Castello Svevo, Bari. The capital, datable to c. 1240 and decorated with eagles among stylized foliage, is the only documented work by Mele; the inscription MINERRVS DE CANVSIA ME FECIT and MELIS DE STELLIANO ME FECIT was recorded by Petroni, a 19th-century historian of Bari. The stylistic vocabulary of this and the adjacent capital, combining vegetal and animal forms, is characteristic of Pugliese Romanesque sculpture and resembles the capitals in the nave and the pulpit of Bitonto Cathedral. Two columns with carved capitals in the entrance hall of the castle at Gioia del Colle are also attributed to Mele da Stigliano and Minarro da Canosa. A controversial attribution was made by Iusco who suggested that Mele was responsible for the sculpture on the stairs of the pulpit in Bitonto Cathedral.

BIBLIOGRAPHY
G. Petroni: *Della storia di Bari dagli antichi tempi sino all'anno 1856* (Naples, 1857–8), i, p. 607
S. Iusco: 'Mele da Stigliano', *Studi lucani e meridionali*, ed. P. Borraro (Galatina, 1978), pp. 227–33

☐

Meleghino, Jacopo (*b* Ferrara, *c.* 1480; *d* Rome, 17 Nov 1549). Italian administrator and architect. He was the son of a notary and chancellor of the episcopal curia in Ferrara and was educated in law and languages. Around 1520 he entered the service of Cardinal Alessandro Farnese in Parma as treasurer, a position of trust that made him indispensable to Farnese as a general organizer and expert in architectural and antiquarian matters. Once Farnese had ascended the papal throne as Paul III in 1534, Meleghino became supervisor of the Belvedere and its antiquities in the Vatican. He organized and oversaw the restoration of the Belvedere corridor and the extension of the gardens by Baldassare Peruzzi, who bequeathed him some of his drawings and papers on architectural theory. Paul III appointed Meleghino his chief accountant and, later, the architect for the construction of St Peter's, Rome, as well as general administrator of papal buildings. As such, in 1538–40, together with the architect Antonio da Sangallo (ii), he directed the rebuilding and extension of the state rooms of the Vatican Palace (Scala Regia and Sala Regia, Sala Ducale and Capella Paolina; *see also* ROME, §V, 14(iii)(a)).

Meleghino was employed chiefly as a fortifications engineer, notably at the Rocca, or fortress, in Perugia, and in Parma, Castro and Frascati, where in the latter in 1538–45 he had districts of the newly erected town built to his own plans. In 1546 he finally became chief architect for the fortifications of Rome. He was also expert both in the layout of gardens and in the interior decoration of villas and palaces. From 1535 to 1544 he erected in Rome, to his own designs, Paul III's villa near Aracoeli, and its connecting corridor to the Palazzo S Marco (now Palazzo di Venezia), and the garden and palace of Orazio Farnese near San Rocco; he restored the Vigna Carafa on the Quirinal, helped in the furnishing of the Vigna del Monte, and in 1548–9 designed for his superior, Cardinal Guido Ascanio Sforza, the summer palace in Proceno, Viterbo.

The few surviving drawings by Meleghino's hand are of a technical nature, giving no information about his architectural style. His villa palaces near Aracoeli and in Proceno are in the tradition of the Roman High Renaissance, adapting details from the Palazzo Farnese. The palace in Proceno reveals an individualistic combination of stylistic motifs from Tuscany, Emilia-Romagna and, predominantly, Rome. Although he was self-taught and had only modest gifts, he was competent in adapting and combining existing styles.

BIBLIOGRAPHY
A. Ronchini: 'Jacopo Meleghino', *Atti & Mem. RR. Deput. Stor. Patria Prov. Moden. & Parm.*, iv (1868), pp. 125–35
J. S. Ackerman: *The Cortile del Belvedere* (Rome, 1954)
F.-E. Keller: 'Der Palast des Guido Ascanio Sforza in Proceno', *Jahrbuch der Max-Planck-Gesellschaft, 1983* (Göttingen, 1983), pp. 758–60

FRITZ-EUGEN KELLER

Melehi, Mohammed (*b* Asilah, 22 Nov 1936). Moroccan painter and graphic artist. He studied art in Morocco at the Escuela Preparatoria de Bellas Artes in Tétouan between 1953 and 1955, then in Seville and Madrid, as well as at the Accademia di Belle Arti in Rome, at the Ecole des Beaux-Arts in Paris and at Columbia University, NY. After the independence of Morocco in 1956 its painters began to search for a national and cultural identity, and Melehi was among the leaders of this movement. He taught at the Ecole des Beaux-Arts in Casablanca from 1964 to 1969, along with fellow Moroccan artists Farid Belkahia (*b* 1935) and Mohamed Chebaa (*b* 1935).

As one of the 'Casablanca Group' Melehi objected to the foreign monopoly of artistic thought in Morocco, and organized the first exhibition of this group in 1965. He also organized the *Exposition manifeste* in the Jama' al-Fna Square in Marrakesh in 1969. Along with 39 other Moroccan painters, such as Belkahia, Chebaa, Moustapha Hafid (*b* 1942) and Mohamed Hamidi (*b* 1941), he formed the Moroccan Association of Plastic Arts (AMAP) in 1972. Between 1971 and 1977 he was editor of the art magazine *Intégral*, published in Casablanca, which reflected the search for an indigenous language in Moroccan art. From 1976 to 1982 he was president of the Moroccan Association of Plastic Arts, later becoming Director of Arts at the Ministry of Culture, Rabat. With Mohamed Benaïssa, the Minister of Culture, he helped to create the annual Asilah Festival of Culture (from 1978) and the Musée d'Art Contemporain in Tangier (1990).

He held one-man exhibitions in Italy, Kuwait, Mexico, Morocco and the USA, and designed posters and murals in Morocco, Mexico and Chicago. He employed silkscreen and cellulose lacquer or shellac techniques, and his work incorporated Arabic calligraphy, large geometric shapes of solid colour, wave motifs and optical illusions (for illustration *see* MOROCCO).

BIBLIOGRAPHY
T. Maraini: *Ecrits sur l'art: Choix de textes Maroc, 1967–1989* (Rabat, 1989)
M. Sijelmassi: *L'Art contemporain au Maroc* (Paris, 1989), pp. 206–9

S. J. VERNOIT

Meleiha. *See under* ARABIA, PRE-ISLAMIC, §§II–IV.

Meléndez. Spanish family of painters.

(1) Miguel Jacinto Meléndez (*b* Oviedo, 1679; *d* Madrid, 1734). He studied in Madrid, where he was influenced by the late 17th-century Baroque school of that city and in particular by the works of Jean Carreño de Miranda. Meléndez was a sensitive portrait artist. In 1712 he was appointed Pintor del Rey and painted portraits of *Philip V* in 1712 (Madrid, Mus. Cerralbo) and *c.* 1727 (Madrid, Bib. N.); two portraits of the King's first wife, *María Gabriela de Saboya* (both 1712; Madrid, Mus. Cerralbo and Mus. Galdiano); one of his second wife, *Elizabeth Farnese* (1727; Madrid, Bib. N.); and portraits of his four children (all 1727; Madrid, Bib. N.). He also worked for private individuals, painting such portraits as that of the *Marqués de Vadillo* (*c.* 1729–30; Madrid, Mus. Mun.). His art fluctuated between the traditional Baroque and the traits introduced into portraiture by the French artists Michel-Ange Houasse and Jean Ranc, and by van

Dyck. Carreño de Miranda's influence is clear in Melén-dez's religious compositions, especially in the *Immaculate Conception* (1731), which he painted for the church of S Diego in Bogotá in Colombia, and in other paintings of the same subject, which are also close to works by Palomino de Castro y Velasco. Preparatory sketches for his paintings, such as the sketch on canvas (Madrid, Prado) depicting the *Burial of the Señor de Orgaz*, show both imagination and interpretative skill but nevertheless contain old-fashioned traits that betray his lack of development beyond his training. Meléndez built up a large collection of religious paintings and engravings, which further influenced his religious compositions, particularly the more complex ones. His own work affected that of several young painters in the 18th-century Baroque school of Madrid, such as Andrés de la Calleja.

BIBLIOGRAPHY

E. Santiago Paez: 'El pintor Miguel Jacinto Meléndez', *Rev. Archvs Bib. & Mus.*, lxxiii (1966), pp. 205–24
——: *Miguel Jacinto Meléndez: Pintor de Felipe V* (Oviedo, 1986)

(2) Francisco Antonio Meléndez (*b* Oviedo, 1682; *d* Madrid, 1752). Brother of (1) Miguel Jacinto Meléndez. He was sent by his parents to Madrid at an early age to begin training alongside his brother. He went to Italy in 1699 and, alternating his artistic apprenticeship with military service, joined the Spanish troops there. He lived in several cities, mainly Rome and Naples, married and returned to Spain in 1717. He devoted himself to painting portrait miniatures and soon became Philip V's court specialist in this field. He produced numerous portraits of the royal family that, along with jewellery and other art objects, were used as gifts to ministers, ambassadors and friends. However, he never obtained a permanent court post and had to work for private patrons. His most important miniature is the *Votive Offering to the Virgin of Atocha* (1728; Madrid, priv. col.), in which he portrays himself and his family. He was also interested in the teaching of art, and he wrote a text in 1726 demonstrating the need for founding an academy of fine arts. When the Junta Preparatoria was established in 1744 to prepare for the foundation of the Academia de Bellas Artes de S Fernando in Madrid, Meléndez took an active part and was appointed honorary director of painting. In 1746 he had a disagreement with several members of the Junta, which resulted in his eventual expulsion, and he died before the inauguration of the Academia in 1752.

Ceán Bermúdez

BIBLIOGRAPHY

C. Bedat: *L'Académie des beaux-arts de Madrid, 1744–1808* (Toulouse, 1974)

JUAN J. LUNA

(3) Luis Meléndez (*b* Naples, 1716; *d* Madrid, 11 July 1780). Son of (2) Francisco Antonio Meléndez. He was taken to Madrid as a child when his parents returned from Naples. His first teacher was his father, whom he assisted in the painting of miniature portraits. He moved to larger-scale oil portraiture when he became an assistant to Louis Michel van Loo, court painter to Philip V. Luis was one of the first students accepted in the new, provisional Academia de Bellas Artes de S Fernando in Madrid, and his *Self-portrait* (1746; Paris, Louvre) was painted while he was a student there. In 1748 he travelled to Italy and

settled in Naples, where he remained until his father recalled him to Madrid to assist on a large commission to paint choir-books for the new Royal Chapel, a project on which he worked for five and a half years. Luis was responsible for 12 full-page miniatures painted in resplendent colours and featuring strongly modelled figures in substantial architectural or landscape settings. These already show a tendency to use powerful geometric forms, evident in the solid passages of celestial light. His interest in still-life is seen in the decorated borders of the miniatures and in the initial letters.

During the 1760s Meléndez became a specialist in painting still-lifes, of which about a hundred survive. Forty-five (Madrid, Prado and Pal. Real; Valladolid, Sección Pint.), apparently commissioned by Charles III, formerly decorated the walls of the Palacio Real at Aránjuez, the royal summer residence outside Madrid. His works in this genre are specifically of food and dishes on bare wooden tables, as in the *Still-life: Cherries, Plums, Cheese and a Pitcher* (*c.* 1760; Madrid, Prado; see fig.) or the *Still-life* (*c.* 1765; Madrid, Prado, cat. no. 924) of burst figs with a spherical piece of bread and a small cylindrical barrel. In a style recalling that of such 17th-century painters as Juan Sánchez Cótan and Zurbarán, he managed to convey the solidity and precise texture of his chosen objects, which were always placed in different arrangements and defined in sharp light against a neutral background. All varieties of fruits were depicted, the objects creating depth in the compositions. In a letter of 1772 to

Luis Meléndez: *Still-life: Cherries, Plums, Cheese and a Pitcher*, oil on canvas, 470×340 mm, *c.* 1760 (Madrid, Museo del Prado)

Charles III requesting a post as court painter, he described the subject-matter of his oils: 'Its representation consists of the four seasons of the year or more properly the four elements, in order to decorate a sitting room with all the species of comestibles that the Spanish climate produces' (Tufts, p. 22). Typical of the Enlightenment, Meléndez's systematic presentation of the fruits of Spain reflected the scientific interest stimulated by Carolus Linnaeus's plant studies, recently translated into Spanish. A slight evolution in Meléndez's style occurred between the compact compositions of his early kitchen still-lifes and his more airy later scenes, such as that of a still-life with a piece of salmon, or the four larger paintings that display contrasting fruits in a landscape (all, Madrid, Prado).

BIBLIOGRAPHY

Luis Meléndez, bodegonista español del siglo XVIII (exh. cat. by J. J. Luna, Madrid, Prado, 1983)

E. Tufts: *Luis Meléndez: 18th-century Master of the Spanish Still-life, with a Catalogue Raisonné* (Columbia, MO, 1985)

Luis Meléndez: Spanish Still-life Painter of the 18th Century (exh. cat. by J. J. Luna and E. Tufts, Dallas, TX, S. Methodist U., Meadows Mus. & Gal., 1985)

ELEANOR TUFTS

Meleto, Evangelista di Pian di. *See* EVANGELISTA DI PIAN DI MELETO.

Meletos Painter. *See under* VASE PAINTERS, §II: ACHILLES PAINTER.

Mélida y Alinari. Spanish family of artists. Three of the sons of Nicolás Mélida Lizana, a lawyer, achieved artistic prominence: (1) Enrique Mélida y Alinari, (2) Arturo Mélida y Alinari and (3) José Ramón Mélida y Alinari.

(1) Enrique Mélida y Alinari (*b* Madrid, 6 April 1838; *d* Paris, 28 April 1892). Painter, illustrator and critic. He graduated in law at Madrid University in 1860. He studied with J. Méndez and later with Ernest Meissonier in Paris. There he became known for his paintings of Spanish scenes, such as the *Procession of Spanish Penitents in the 18th Century* (Sydney, N.A.G. NSW). In 1882 he married Marie Bonnat, the sister of the painter Léon Bonnat, and settled in Paris from the following year. He frequently exhibited his genre paintings and portraits, with their refined technique, for example at Bayonne (1864), the Nacionales in Madrid (1866, 1871 and 1876) and the Exposition Universelle (1878) in Paris, where he was awarded several mentions and medals. He made numerous drawings for engravings, including illustrations for the 46-volume *Episodios nacionales* (Madrid, 1873) by Benito Pérez Galdós (1843–1920). He also published many works of literary criticism, writing notably for the journal *Arte in España*, which he helped found.

WRITINGS

Regular contributions to *A. España* (1862–73)

(2) Arturo Mélida y Alinari (*b* Madrid, 24 July 1849; *d* Madrid, 15 Dec 1902). Architect, sculptor and painter, brother of (1) Enrique Mélida y Alinari. He embarked on a military career in 1866 but abandoned it two years later to study architecture, in which he graduated from the Escuela de Arquitectura, Madrid, in 1873 and which was to remain his prime concern. He worked on architectural decoration for the archives and library of the Congreso de los Diputados, the assembly room (Salón de Actos, 1884) of the Ateneo, and the lunettes at S María, Alcoy. He also provided mural and ceiling paintings for various aristocratic mansions in Madrid, including the houses of Zuburu, Veragua, Urquijo and that of the banker Bäuer, the latter in collaboration with the sculptor Mariano Benlliure. In addition he restored the paintings of the façade of the Casa de la Panadería, Madrid. He provided illustrations for several books, including the *Leyendas* (Madrid, 1901) of José Zorrilla y Moral (1817–93); an unpublished set for the complete works of Gaspar Núñez de Arce (1834–1903); and the frontispiece to *La hija del Rey de Egipto* by J. Ebers (1885). He also designed furniture, grilles and carpets, and decorated such luxury items as fans for the royal family. He was therefore an architect–craftsman, close in spirit to the Arts and Crafts Movement in late 19th-century Spain. He believed that such practical activity was part of a historic tradition: when he applied for the chair of modelling at the Escuela de Arquitectura, where he also taught drawing, he stated that, as in the 16th century, an architect should also produce designs for furniture or for gold- and silverwork. In a lecture (1886) given at the Ateneo Madrileño and in his acceptance speech (1889) at the Academia de Bellas Artes he was one of the first to defend Baroque art.

In 1877 Mélida y Alinari won the competition to design the supporting pedestal for the monument to *Christopher Columbus* (Madrid, Plaza de Colón). Three earlier unexecuted designs show a decreasing architectural and an increasing sculpturesque quality (Madrid, Casón Buen Retiro; Santa-Ana). The pedestal contains reliefs by the architect alluding to the discovery of America, and the slender column is surmounted by a statue of *Columbus* (1885) by Jerónimo Suñol. The decorative inscription, characteristic of Mélida y Alinari's style, is derived from Isabelline art. This interest in early Spanish styles is also evident in the Mudéjar revival Escuela de Industrias Artísticas (1882), Toledo, in which he also employed modern materials, including iron and glass. The Pabellón de la Exposición de Ganados (1882; destr.), Madrid, shared these qualities, but an even better example was the Spanish Pavilion (destr.) that he designed for the Exposition Universelle (1889) in Paris, adding elements taken from Plateresque art and fine glazed chinaware. This work brought him international fame and access to the Institut de France. He also designed the Gothic Revival mausoleum of the Marquis de Amboage in the cemetery of S Isidro, Madrid, which is topped with a cast-iron obelisk.

In 1891 Mélida y Alinari designed his most important work, a Gothic Revival monument to *Christopher Columbus* for Havana Cathedral; this was moved to the south transept of Seville Cathedral in 1899. It is reminiscent of the tomb of *Philippe Pot* (*c*. 1480; Paris, Louvre), comprising a sarcophagus carried by four heralds, representing the kingdoms of Castile, León, Aragon and Navarre, cast in metal and decorated in coloured enamels. This monument in particular has given him the reputation of a sculptor dependent on archaeology, while his work on the restoration (1881–2) of the monastery of S Juan de los Reyes (begun 1477), Toledo, originally built by Juan Guas, shows the influence of the ideas of Viollet-le-Duc. Mélida y Alinari also provided statues and ceiling paintings for the Palacio Toki Eder, Castro Urdiales, which was designed by Eladio Laredo and completed in 1900.

WRITINGS

El monumento a Colón erigido en Madrid por suscripción de los Títulos del Reino (Madrid, 1886)
'Rodríguez Villanueva: La arquitectura y las artes decorativas', *19a Conferencia en la España del siglo XIX: Madrid, 1886*

BIBLIOGRAPHY

J. Moya: 'En el centenario de D. Arturo Mélida y Alinari', *Academia: Bol. Real Acad. B.A. San Fernando*, i (1951), pp. 57–62
P. Navascués Palacio: 'Arturo Mélida y Alinari, 1849–1902', *Goya*, 106 (1972), pp. 234–41
—: *Arquitectura y arquitectos madrileños del siglo XIX* (Madrid, 1973)
P. Navascués Palacio and others: *Del neoclasicismo al modernismo* (Madrid, 1979)
F. de Santa-Ana y Alvarez-Ossorio: 'Los proyectos de Arturo Mélida para el monumento de Cristóbal Colón en Madrid', *Miscelanea de arte* (Madrid, 1982), pp. 259–63
Guía de arquitectura y urbanismo de Madrid (Madrid, 1982–3)
I. Ordiers: *Eladio Laredo, el historicismo nacionalista en la arquitectura*, Ayuntamiento de Castro Urdiales (Cadiz, 1992)

J. R. NIETO GONZALEZ,
with ALBERTO VILLAR MOVELLÁN

(3) José Ramón Mélida y Alinari (*b* Madrid, 26 Oct 1856; *d* Madrid, 30 Dec 1933). Archaeologist, art historian and writer, brother of (1) Enrique Mélida y Alinari and (2) Arturo Mélida y Alinari. He studied in Madrid, and in 1881 he became an assistant in the department of Archiveros, Bibliotecarios y Arqueólogos at the Museo Arqueológico Nacional, Madrid. In 1884 he was appointed head of the department of Prehistoria y Edad Antigua at the museum. There he began his work on the inventory and cataloguing of items that resulted in the organization and establishment of the Sala de Antigüedades Ibéricas. In the same year he was appointed Director of the Museo de Reproducciones Artísticas, Madrid. In 1899 he became a member of the Real Academia de Bellas Artes de S Fernando and in 1906 was elected a member of the Real Academia de la Historia. His two areas of specialization were those of Classical art and ancient Spain, and in 1906 he was in charge of excavations at Numancia in Soria. As Chairman of the Department of Archaeology at the Universidad Complutense de Madrid, he excavated in 1916 the Roman theatre, amphitheatre and circus at Mérida in Cáceres. From 1916 to 1930 he was Director of the Museo Arqueológico Nacional and subsequently was appointed Honorary Director of the museum. In 1931 he became President of the Council created by the government of the Second Spanish Republic. His duties were to supervise the maintenance of the museum and its equipment, to make acquisitions and to promote museum publications. He also gave courses and lectures at the Ateneo in Madrid and wrote several novels, including *El Sortilegio de Karnak* (Madrid, 1880).

WRITINGS

Regular contributions to *Bol. Real Acad. Hist.*, *Bol. Soc. Esp. Excurs.*, *España Mod.*, *Ilus. Esp. & Amer.* and *Rev. Archvs, Bib. & Mus.*
Vasos griegos, etruscos e italo-griegos del Museo Arqueológico Nacional (Madrid, 1882)
Esculturas de barro cocido griegas, etruscas y romanas del Museo Arqueológico Nacional (Madrid, 1884)
Historia del arte egipcio (Madrid, 1897)
Historia del arte griego (Madrid, 1897)
'Excavaciones de Numancia', *Rev. Archvs, Bib. & Mus.*, xi (1907), nos 7–8, pp. 26–40; nos 9–10, pp. 196–208; xii (1908), nos 1–2, pp. 118–41; nos 5–6, pp. 460–68; nos 7–8, pp. 79–86

El teatro romano de Mérida (Madrid, 1915)
Arqueología española (Barcelona and Buenos Aires, 1929)

BIBLIOGRAPHY

Homenaje que tributan el patronato y funcionarios facultativos del Museo Arqueológico Nacional a D. José Ramón Mélida y Alinari (Madrid, 1934)
J. A. Gaya Nuño: *Historia de la crítica de arte en España* (Madrid, 1975)

CONCHA VELA

Meliore (*fl* Florence, *c.* 1260–80). Italian painter. The signature *Melior* appears on a dossal dated 1271 depicting *Christ with the Virgin and Saints* (Florence, Uffizi), and it can be identified as that of *Meliore dipintore, populi Sancti Jacobi tra le fosse* ('Meliore the Painter, of the Parish of St Jacob between the Ditches') mentioned among the combatants in the Battle of Montaperti in 1260. Richter's suggestion that the artist was the Megliore di Jacopo documented at Pistoia from 1239 to 1253 is less certain. There is also evidence of a panel (untraced) signed and dated 1270 that existed in the 17th century in the church of S Francesco, Barberino di Val d'Elsa. On the basis of stylistic similarities, a dossal depicting the *Virgin and Child with SS Peter and Paul and Four Scenes from the Saints' Lives* (Panzano, Greve, S Leolino) is also attributed to Meliore and is regarded as the most important work of his early period. The influence of contemporary Pisan painting is evident in this work, but the deliberate placing of the characters in a narrative context recalls the style of the Bigallo Master.

These stylistic features also occur in the Uffizi dossal but with a heightened sense of plasticism, probably due to the influence of Coppo di Marcovaldo and his technique of enriching the modelling of the clothing of his figures with copious gold striations. Meliore's later works are characterized by an increased similarity with Coppo's methods, as can be seen in the *Virgin and Child with Two Angels* (Bossolo, Tavarnelle Val di Pesa, S Pietro). Longhi's suggestion that the group of paintings attributed to the so-called Bagnano Master by Garrison ought to be re-attributed to Meliore has met with some agreement and should be emphasized.

BIBLIOGRAPHY

G. M. Richter: 'Megliore di Jacopo and the Magdalen Master', *Burl. Mag.*, lvii (1930), pp. 223–36
R. Offner: 'The Mostra del Tesoro di Firenze Sacra—I', *Burl. Mag.*, lxiii (1933), p. 79
R. Longhi: 'Guidizio sul duecento', *Proporzioni*, ii (1948), p. 43
E. B. Garrison: *Italian Romanesque Panel Painting: An Illustrated Index* (Florence, 1949), pp. 12, 23
C. L. Ragghianti: *Pittura del dugento a Firenze* (Florence, 1955), pp. 79–100
M. Boskovits: *Cimabue e i precursori di Giotto: Affreschi, mosaici e tavole* (Florence, 1976)
A. Tartuferi: 'Pittura fiorentina del duecento', *La pittura in Italia: Le origini*, ed. E. Castelnuovo (Milan, 1986), p. 275

ANGELO TARTUFERI

Melisende Psalter. Richly decorated Latin Psalter (London, BL, Egerton MS. 1139), probably commissioned for but not by Queen Melisende, wife of Fulk V of Anjou, King of Jerusalem (*reg* 1131–43), in the scriptorium of the church of the Holy Sepulchre in Jerusalem (*c.* 1135). When it was bought by the British Museum in 1845, it was said to have come from the Grande Chartreuse, the mother house of the Carthusian Order, in Grenoble. There are 24 prefatory New Testament illustrations (fols 1*r*–12*v*) by an artist who signed one of the folios, 12*v*, in Latin *Basilius me fecit*. Although Basilius was apparently of Western origin, he had a Greek name and was thoroughly steeped in the Byzantine painting tradition (for illustration of fol. 9*v*, *see* JERUSALEM, LATIN KINGDOM OF, fig. 2). The 12 roundels with *Signs of the Zodiac* in the calendar (fols 13*v*–19*r*) are, however, painted in a fluent Romanesque style by a different illuminator. Yet another technique and style can be seen in the eight exquisite historiated and illuminated initials at the Psalter divisions (fols 23*v*–177*r*). These are reminiscent of earlier work from Montecassino Abbey and combine English, Italian and Islamic motifs. A fourth illuminator, who imitated the Byzantine style of Basilius but in a Romanesque idiom, painted the portraits of the saints accompanying the prayers composed for a lay woman at the end of the codex (fols 177*v*–218*r*). The remarkable ivory covers, with scenes from the *Life of King David* and from the *Psychomachia* carved on one side and a *King Performing Acts of Mercy* on the other, reflect the royal patronage of the manuscript. Byzantine royal iconography is combined with the Western imagery of the Virtues and Vices and the theme of the acts of mercy in a Byzantine–Islamic style. A purely Byzantine silk embroidered with a *polystavrion* design of equal-armed crosses in red, green and blue completes the binding on the spine of the book. This rich *mélange* of East and West is characteristic of Crusader art, of which this manuscript is the finest 12th-century example.

BIBLIOGRAPHY

H. Buchthal: *Miniature Painting in the Latin Kingdom of Jerusalem* (Oxford, 1957, R/1986), pp. 1–14, 122–8, 132–5, 139–40, pls 1–19
F. Steenbock: *Der kirchliche Prachteinband im frühen Mittelalter* (Berlin, 1965), pp. 186–8, pls 124–5
T. S. R. Boase: 'Ecclesiastical Art in the Crusader States in Palestine and Syria', *A History of the Crusades*, ed. K. M. Setton, iv of *The Art and Architecture of the Crusader States*, ed. H. W. Hazard (Madison, WI, and London, 1977), pp. 125–31, 138–9, 327
B. Kühnel: 'The Kingly Statement of the Bookcovers of Queen Melisande's Psalter', *Jb. Ant. & Christ.*, xviii (1991), pp. 340–57

JAROSLAV FOLDA

Melito and Eboli, Princes of. *See under* MENDOZA.

Melk Abbey. Benedictine abbey situated on a rocky ledge overlooking the River Danube in Lower Austria, halfway between Linz and Vienna. The Baroque pomp of the building is dramatically heightened by its romantic and picturesque setting. The abbey is the outcome of a creative partnership between the architect JAKOB PRANDTAUER and the client Berthold Dietmayr, who was Abbot from 1700 to 1739 and had to overcome his Order's aversion to worldly show to enable the scheme to proceed. The work was completed by Joseph Munggenast to Prandtauer's plans.

1. Introduction. 2. Abbey church. 3. Conventual buildings.

1. INTRODUCTION. The Babenberg Markgraf Leopold I (*reg* AD 976–94) conquered the original castle in 976 and made the site his principal residence. The earliest evidence of a collegiate church dates from 1014, when the remains of St Colman were taken to Melk. Monks of the Benedictine Order were moved there from Lambach in 1089 by Leopold II (*reg* 1075–96), whose son Leopold III (*reg* 1096–1136) aided the monastery by making donations and

Melk Abbey by Jakob Prandtauer, from 1702; view from the River Danube

by handing over the castle itself. The remains of St Colman were buried (1170) in the newly built church of SS Peter and Paul, the first church to have been built within the fortified monastery. In 1297 a fire ended this period of prosperity; rebuilding and refortification were not possible until the 14th century, when the monastery won the favour of the Habsburg Rudolf IV (*reg* 1358–65) and became the recipient of various treasures including the *Melk Cross* (1363), produced in Vienna as a reliquary for fragments of the True Cross. In 1418 Melk became the centre for Benedictine monastic observance reform in Austria and Bavaria. After becoming somewhat dilapidated during the Reformation, Melk subsequently experienced a period of economic consolidation. The southern bastion (1652) and the guests' quarters (1676–80) were restored in Early Baroque style.

All previous ecclesiastical structures, including a Gothic church with a high altar featuring panel paintings by Jörg Breu (i), were swept away in the 18th century at the instigation of Abbot Dietmayr, who determined on a scheme of total reconstruction. He evolved a plan by choosing the features of existing buildings and designs that appealed to him, for example St Florian Abbey (from 1686) by Carlo Antonio Carlone, which were then worked up by Prandtauer into a brilliantly effective group that seems to rise naturally from a tongue of rock above an arm of the Danube (see fig.). This group is dominated by the abbey church, and in particular by its towers and dome, in a cumulative build-up that commands the view down the Danube to the west, while the horizontal thrust of the austere 59-bay conventual range ties the composition back into the forested landscape. The converse view, from the west door of the church, is projected through a Palladian arch opening in the centre of low semicircular wings that complete the enclosure of the parvis (St Colman's Court), flanked to the rear by two prestige buildings, the Marble Hall (*Marmorsaal*) and the library; these jut forward and slightly inwards in front of the church as continuations of the long conventual ranges.

2. ABBEY CHURCH. Prandtauer's church (1702–14) is a pioneering work of the Austrian Baroque. At the west front, clustered pilasters in three diminishing heights of two storeys with angle towers evoke a powerful upward thrust that is countered by the horizontal drive of the cornices, layered to reflect the profiles of the vertical articulation. The plan is of the wall pillar type, with a three-bay nave (two-storey externally but with a third storey in the corner towers) and a slightly projecting transept bay capped by a drummed dome over the crossing, with beyond it a two-storey apsidal choir. The most striking feature of the design is the effect produced by the concavity of the nave-bay entablatures when set off by the forward thrust of the gallery arches beneath them, an impact that has been weakened by the conversion of the galleries into a series of loggias. The wall piers are faced by a giant order of pilasters in reddish-brown marble against a background of lighter red. These are the work of Antonio Beduzzi, who also designed the summer sacristy adjoining the church on the south-east side (from 1701) and made sketches for the frescoes, which were created by Johann Michael Rottmayr with *quadratura* painting (1718–22) by Ippolito Sconzani (*fl c.* 1711–24). The dome frescoes (1716–17) depict the heavens full of rejoicing saints, while the choir frescoes depict the *ecclesia militans* and *ecclesia triumphans* and those in the three-bay nave the *Apotheosis of St Benedict* (1718–22). Beduzzi's work was completed (from 1725) by his successor Giuseppe Galli-Bibiena, who designed the marble high altar, the altars of SS Colman and Benedict in the transept chapels, and the pulpit (1725–36). Peter Widerin (1684–1761) executed the sculptures, the gilt statues of the high altar (*St Peter* and *St Paul* with prophets on either side) being created after *bozzetti* by Lorenzo Mattielli. With its unique harmony of colour and light, architecture, painting and sculpture, the abbey church ranks among the supreme spatial achievements of European Baroque.

3. CONVENTUAL BUILDINGS. Access to the complex is from the little town of Melk on the east side. The entrance block (*Torbau*), which houses a domed octagonal entrance hall, has a façade articulated with Ionic pilasters in the form of a triumphal arch, its delicate details in striking contrast to the massive bastions on either side. The gateway is adorned by fine statues of the abbey's patron saints, *Colman* and *Leopold*, on high bases (1716) by Widerin after Lorenzo Mattielli. Beyond the *Torbau* is a forecourt, dominated at the far side by the entrance front (1723–4) of the conventual buildings in an imposing style that recalls Johann Bernhard Fischer von Erlach's Palais Trautson (*c.* 1710–16), Vienna. The plinth is surmounted by an order of giant pilasters that articulate the two upper storeys. The slightly raised central range is capped by a pediment that encloses a reproduction of the *Melk Cross*. The entrance, flanked by free-standing obelisks, displays statues of *St Peter* and *St Paul* at an upper level. It gives on to St Benedict's Hall, surrounded by galleries supported on four columns and vaulted by segmental arches. Beyond this hall, in the centre of the east wing of the conventual buildings, lies the prelates' court (*Prälatenhof*), the largest courtyard (84×42 m) of the abbey, surrounded by the uniform façades of the conventual buildings. From this

courtyard, which was decorated in 1988–9 by Peter Bischof and Helmut Krumpel with frescoes depicting the four cardinal virtues, in celebration of the 900th anniversary of the Benedictines' arrival at Melk, the dome of the church is visible beyond the abbot's residence (*Prälatur*) at the far end. The Festsaal of the abbot's residence contains 140 small oil paintings, including a *Virgin in the Vine Arbour* (1520) by Lucas Cranach (i). The ceiling fresco (1739) is by Paul Troger and Gaetano Fanti (1687–1759) and depicts the *Triumph of St Benedict.*

At the south-west corner of the prelates' court a gateway gives on to a two-storey stair-hall, housed in part of the central projection of the 59-bay south elevation of the complex. The central flight of the imperial staircase (*see* STAIRCASE, §I) turns and rises from its landing into two side flights with newel blocks surmounted by putti. The flights give access to the abbot's residence, and to a suite of prestigious rooms known as the *Kaiserzimmer*, some of which have been adapted as the abbey museum. Alongside these rooms runs the Imperial Gallery, hung with portraits of the rulers of Austria. This leads, via an antechamber, to the light-filled Marble Hall, a reception room for state occasions, which juts forward beyond the west front of the abbey church, on the south flank of the parvis. The hall rises through two storeys, and three of its internal walls, pierced by windows, are articulated by giant pilasters with red shafts and gold composite capitals, or with copper-coloured half-length atlantids, which contrast with their grey background. Above, Fanti's *quadratura* painting leads into Troger's fresco of the *Triumph of Moderation* (1731) on the shallow-vaulted ceiling. The Marble Hall is balanced on the other side of the parvis by a library (completed 1735) of the same size, again with *quadratura* painting by Fanti and a fresco by Troger, of *Divine Wisdom and the Virtues* (both 1731–2). The two buildings are joined by a low link-block, opened up in the centre by the Palladian arch that affords a view down the Danube Valley.

BIBLIOGRAPHY

R. Schachinger: *Die Wiegendrucke der Stiftsbibliothek in Melk* (Melk, 1901)
E. Katschthaler: 'Melk', *Topographie von Niederösterreich*, vi (Vienna, 1909), pp. 370–508, 954–7
T. Gottlieb, ed.: *Mittelalterliche Bibliothekskataloge Österreichs*, i (Vienna, 1915/*R* 1974), pp. 137–261
H. Hantsch: *Jakob Prandtauer: Der Klosterarchitekt des österreichischen Barock* (Vienna, 1926)
Jakob Prandtauer und sein Kunstkreis: Ausstellung zum 300. Geburtstag des grossen österreichischen Baumeisters im Stift Melk (exh. cat., ed. R. Feuchtmüller; Melk, Stiftsmus., 1960)
G. Flossmann, W. Hilger and H. Fasching: *Stift Melk und seine Kunstschätze* (St Pölten, 1976, rev. 2/1980, 3/1985)
E. Hubala: 'Beduzzi und Rottmayr in Melk', *Festschrift für W. Messerer* (Cologne, 1980), pp. 297–307
W. Kowarik, ed.: *Stift Melk: Geschichte und Gegenwart*, 4 vols (St Pölten, 1980–85)
'Die Restaurierung von Stift und Stiftskirche Melk', *Österreich. Z. Kst & Dkmlpf.*, xxxiv (1980), pp. 69–129 [studies on restoration campaign, 1976–80]
Österreich zur Zeit Kaiser Josephs II (exh. cat., ed. K. Gutkas; Melk, Stiftsmus., 1980)
G. Brucher: *Barockarchitektur in Österreich* (Cologne, 1983), pp. 217–24
M. Bruck: 'Codex Mellicensis 391', *NÖLA: Mitt. Niederösterreich. Landesarchv*, viii (1984), pp. 31–44
H. Engelhart: *Die Würzburger Buchmalerei im hohen Mittelalter: Untersuchungen zu einer Gruppe illuminierter Handschriften aus der Werkstatt der Würzburger Dominikanerbibel von 1246*, Quellen und Forschungen zur Geschichte des Bistums und Hochstifts Würzburg, xxxiv (Würzburg, 1987), pp. 242–60

H. Fillitz and M. Pippal: *Schatzkunst: Die Goldschmiede- und Elfenbeinar-beiten aus österreichischen Schatzkammern des Hochmittelalters*, viii (Salzburg, 1987)
900 Jahre Benediktiner in Melk (exh. cat., ed. E. Bruckmüller; Melk, Stiftsmus., 1989)
Stift Melk: Alte Ansichten und Schrifttum (exh. cat., Vienna, Niederöster-reich. Landesbib., 1989)
G. Glassner: 'Kostbarkeiten aus der Bibliothek des Stiftes Melk', *Imagi-nation*, v/3 (1990), pp. 7–10
W. Hilger and others: *Die vier Kardinaltugenden im Prälatenhof des Stiftes Melk* (Melk, 1991)

GOTTFRIED GLASSNER

Mellan, Claude (*b* Abbeville, May 1598; *d* Paris, 9 Sept 1688). French draughtsman, engraver and painter. He moved to Paris at a young age, his first print, produced for a theological thesis presented at the Mathurins College (Préaud, no. 288) indicating that he was in the capital from 1619 onwards. Anatole de Courde de Montaiglon catalogued 400 engravings by him, and about 100 of his drawings are known. Mellan was also active as a painter; a number of lost paintings are recorded in his own engravings (e.g. *Samson and Delilah*, P 5; and *St John the Baptist in the Desert*, P 84). Several paintings have been attributed to him since *c.* the 1970s, but none has support generally (see Ficacci in 1989–90 exh. cat.).

Mellan's masters are not recorded, but his first engravings seem much influenced by Léonard Gaultier. In 1624 Mellan left for Rome, and after a brief spell in the studio of the engraver Francesco Villamena, who died that same year, he found a new master in Simon Vouet, already in Rome since 1614. Vouet guided Mellan towards drawing, judging it indispensable for both engraving and painting. Mellan engraved Vouet's works (for illustration *see* SAVOY, (3)) and turned towards portraiture, specializing in small detailed portraits done from life, such as that of the painter *Maddalena Corvina* (Stockholm, Nmus.), in black and red chalk. Unlike his later portraits, these were never engraved. For such drawings there were many examples in Rome, such as the work of Taddeo Zuccaro, Federico Zuccaro and Ottavio Leoni. While in Rome, Mellan adopted a simplicity and naturalness that were to mark his work throughout his career. Many of his prints in Italy were reproductive engravings, from compositions by Vouet, Pietro da Cortona and Gianlorenzo Bernini; the handful of his engravings after his own designs, such as *St Francis de Paul* (P 77) and the *Penitent Magdalene* (P 113), show that his inspiration came from many sources.

Back in Paris in 1637 after a stay in Aix-en-Provence with Nicolas-Claude Fabri de Peiresc, Mellan was again much in demand as a portrait artist. He drew his models from life and engraved the portraits. He was widely sought after, and his models, among whom were members of the Bourbon royal family, came from influential circles in Paris during the years 1640–60. In his drawings of this period Mellan abandoned red chalk and used only black chalk or pastel, and his portraits were larger and more ambitious than those of his Italian period (see fig.). His drawings, showing concern for the effects of light, reveal more variety of style and execution than he showed in the engravings. Examples include two portrait drawings (both Stockholm, Nmus.; both engraved), one of *Marie-Louise de Gonzague-Nevers* (P 167) and the other of *Henri de Savoie, Duc de Nemours* (P 182).

Claude Mellan: *Charles de Condren*, black chalk, 173×134 mm, *c.* 1640 (Besançon, Musée des Beaux-Arts et d'Archéologie)

By the mid-century Mellan's engraving style had reached maturity and achieved an extraordinary technical virtuosity. His most famous print, the *Face of Christ* (1649; P 21), was executed with a single continuous line, and his other engravings also had a simpler cutting style. His portraits, simple and yet full of life, give evidence of a restrained technique, and he produced large religious works with a geometric approach to form and pose, emphasizing the contrast between black and white, with the single line giving an abstract effect. Mellan engraved his own compositions during his Paris years, except for frontispieces to devotional works after designs by Nicolas Poussin (P 294) and Jacques Stella (P 296) in 1640 and 1641. As an engraver he proved sensitive to the classical ideal developed by Poussin, Stella and others in Paris in the middle of the 17th century.

Other examples of Mellan's stylized and refined art include the *Rest on the Flight into Egypt* (P 12), *Virgin and Child in a Landscape* (P 11), *St Augustine* (1660; P 57), *St Claudius* (1664; P 69) and *St Genevieve* (1680; P 108). Most of his drawings are preserved in the Stockholm National-museum (having come from the collection of Carl Gustav Tessin) and in the Hermitage, St Petersburg (with a provenance from the Cobenzl collection, bought by Catherine II).

BIBLIOGRAPHY
A. de Montaiglon: *Catalogue raisonné de l'oeuvre de Claude Mellan d'Abbe-ville* (Abbeville, 1856)
J. Thuillier: 'Poussin et ses premiers compagnons français à Rome', *Actes du colloque. Nicolas Poussin: Paris, 1958*, i, pp. 71–116
B. Brejon de Lavergnée: *Catalogue des dessins de Claude Mellan* (diss., U. Paris IV, 1979)
——: 'Portraits dessinés de Claude Mellan conservés au Musée de l'Ermitage', *Gaz. B.-A.*, cv (Jan 1985), pp. 15–28

——: *Claude Mellan*, Cahiers du dessin français, iii (Paris, 1987)

M. Préaud: 'Claude Mellan', *Inventaire du fonds français: Graveurs du XVIIe siècle*, xvii (Paris, 1988) [P]

L'Oeil d'or. Claude Mellan (exh. cat. by M. Préaud, Paris, Bib. N., 1988)

Claude Mellan, gli anni romani—un incisore tra Vouet e Bernini (exh. cat. by L. Ficacci, Rome, Pal. Barberini, 1989–90)

BARBARA BREJON DE LAVERGNÉE

Mellerio, André (*b* 1862; *d* 1943). French critic. He was greatly interested in SYMBOLISM, and in *Le Mouvement idéaliste en peinture* (Paris, 1896) he charted the rise of 'idealist art', claiming that the idealist movement had first publicly emerged at the Exposition des Peintres du Groupe Impressionniste et Synthétiste, organized by the Pont-Aven group at the Café Volpini, Paris, in 1889. This exhibition had included work by artists of several theoretical persuasions (Chromo-Luminarists, Neo-Impressionists, Synthetists, Mystics). According to Mellerio, the progenitors of 'idealist' painting were Gustave Moreau, Paul Gauguin, Pierre Puvis de Chavannes and Odilon Redon. He first met Redon in 1889 and soon became one of his closest friends and supporters, writing the preface to the catalogue for the Redon exhibition at the Durand Ruel galleries in 1894, in which he stated that Redon occupied a distinctive position in contemporary art as he belonged to no group. He compiled a catalogue of Redon's graphic work (1913), referring to him as a 'mystic' whose aim was to reveal the 'vague unknown that we sense beneath contingent appearances' (pp. 45–6), and using the term 'corrective parallelism' (p. 9) to describe the relationship between the artist's literary sources and his lithographic images. His *Odilon Redon: Peintre, dessinateur et graveur* (Paris, 1923) is a comprehensive survey of Redon's work and contains valuable biographical details. Mellerio appears in two paintings by Maurice Denis: the *Mellerio Family* (1897) and *Homage to Cézanne* (1900; both Paris, Mus. d'Orsay; for illustration of the latter *see* DENIS, MAURICE).

See also LITHOGRAPHY, §II, 1(iii).

WRITINGS
Le Mouvement idéaliste en peinture (Paris, 1896)

La Lithographie originale en couleurs (Paris, 1898)

Odilon Redon (Paris, 1913/*R* New York, 1968)

Odilon Redon: Peintre, dessinateur et graveur (Paris, 1923)

BIBLIOGRAPHY
K. Berger: *Odilon Redon: Fantasy and Colour* (London, 1965)

P. Jullian: *The Symbolists* (London, 1973)

R. Hobbs: *Odilon Redon* (New York, 1977)

☐

Mellery, Xavier (*b* Laeken, nr Brussels, 9 Aug 1845; *d* Laeken, 4 Feb 1921). Belgian painter, decorative artist and draughtsman. A gardener's son, he was brought up in a quiet suburb of Brussels, bordering the Parc Royal. He studied under the decorative artist Charles Albert (1821–89) and then, between 1860 and 1867, took a course in decorative design at the Brussels Académie. In 1864 he joined the studio of Jean-François Portaels to learn the techniques of modelling, painting from life and history painting. Having won the Belgian Prix de Rome in 1870, he travelled to Italy, where he was inspired by the work of Mantegna. His early work treated the working lives of the Belgian poor in a social realist manner influenced by

Charles de Groux: for example *The Peasants* (Antwerp, Kon. Mus. S. Kst.).

From 1878 to 1879 Mellery stayed on the island of Marken, in the Netherlands, in order to illustrate a book by Charles De Coster, but the writer's death in 1879 brought a halt to the project. He produced paintings and drawings depicting the way of life of the inhabitants of Marken, such as the profoundly dramatic *Burial on the Island of Marken* (drawing; Brussels, Mus. Royaux B.-A.), which anticipates the expressionism of van Gogh's Nuenen period. In 1878 he again travelled to Italy, where he painted very sombre views of Venice and copied Carpaccio. In 1882 he produced 48 drawings representing the ancient guilds and corporations of Brussels, which served as models for the statuettes in the Petit Sablon, Brussels. From 1885 he was several times invited to exhibit with Les XX in Brussels, and from 1894 he showed with La Libre Esthétique.

Mellery's ambition was to emulate the decorative achievements of Puvis de Chavannes. In 1887 he travelled in Germany and what are now the Czech and Slovak Republics, passing through the Tyrol and Switzerland, in order to study the sgraffito technique. He devised a series of monumental schemes to decorate the public buildings of Brussels, including the Palais des Beaux-Arts, the Palais de Justice, the Palais des Académies and the Salle de Mariage in the Hôtel de Ville, but they all proved abortive. However, his designs for these projects survive—allegorical subjects in watercolour, black chalk and India ink on a gold background: *Inspiration* (Antwerp, Kon. Mus. S. Kst.), *Terpsichore* (*c.* 1894), and *Immortality, Gentleness is the Daughter of Strength* (*c.* 1894) and the *Fall of the Last Leaves of Autumn* (all Brussels, Mus. Royaux B.-A.). His feeling for balance and harmony is expressed through a chain of nude or clothed figures, floating between heaven and earth against an abstract golden background, their draperies billowing with 'a motionless undulation' (C. Lemonnier). These works, idealist in style and arranged by Mellery under the title *Modern Synthesis*, express his faith in a hidden harmony underlying the universe. They were meticulously executed, using a *sotto in su* viewpoint, and were generally signed with the artist's monogram. Mellery exhibited them from 1888 onwards.

During the same period Mellery produced *intimiste* drawings in conté crayon of stairs, studio corners and bedrooms, such as *The Staircase* (see fig.), with chiaroscuro light effects that recall the drawings of Georges Seurat. They are pervaded by a poetic feeling for the quiet mystery inherent in everyday things. According to Mellery, 'All life around us is a subject for study, everything is living, even if it does not move: a chair, a door, a wall are as so many organs, making up the true, ordinary life of men and things'. He gave these drawings, along with several very sombre paintings, the general title the *Soul of Things* and exhibited them in 1889 with the Société des Aquarellistes Belges and with Les XX from 1890.

At the end of his career Mellery became interested in the Béguine order of nuns and in the monastic life with its vows of silence and contemplation, which he depicted, usually at night, in works like *After Evening Prayers* (*c.* 1900; Brussels, Mus. Ixelles). The same spirit of meditation pervades such snowscapes as *Garden in Winter*

Xavier Mellery: *The Staircase*, conté crayon and sanguine on paper, 570×450mm, *c.* 1889 (Antwerp, Koninklijk Museum voor Schone Kunsten)

under Snow (Otterlo, Kröller-Müller) and some bleak landscapes of the Ardennes. His faith in the didactic power of art led him to design posters for worthy causes, as well as commemorative plaques and medals. He was elected a member of the Académie Royale des Beaux-Arts de Belgique in 1903 and spent his last years living in isolation on the outskirts of Brussels. The spirituality of his work foreshadowed Symbolism and particularly inspired Fernand Khnopff, who was his pupil at the Brussels Académie (1876–9).

BIBLIOGRAPHY
J. Potvin: *Xavier Mellery, 1845–1921* (Brussels, 1925)
F. Hellens: *Xavier Mellery* (Brussels, 1932)
S. Houbart-Wilkin: 'La Maison du peintre Xavier Mellery', *Mus. Royaux B.-A. Belgique Bull.*, 1/2 (1964)
N. Walch: 'Carnets de voyage de Xavier Mellery', *Rev. U. Libre Bruxelles* (1981–3), pp. 75–86
Académie royale des beaux-arts de Bruxelles (exh. cat., Brussels, Acad. Royale B.-A., 1987)

FRANCINE-CLAIRE LEGRAND

Melli, Roberto (*b* Ferrara, 21 March 1885; *d* Rome, 4 Jan 1958). Italian painter, sculptor and writer. He began painting and sculpting at a very young age in his native city. In 1902 he was apprenticed to a wood-carver in Genoa and in the following year he took part in the activities of the artistic and literary publication *Ebe*. In 1910 he moved to Rome, where he lived for the rest of his life. Melli rapidly established himself as a prominent figure in Roman artistic circles. In 1914 he became a member of the steering committee of the Rome Secession, at which he showed *Woman with Hat (Zoe Lampronti)* (bronze, h. 375 mm, *c.* 1913; Rome, G.N.A. Mod.), and,

with Vincenzo Constantini, Garzia Fioresi and Cipriano Efisio Oppo, founded the 'Gruppo Moderno Italiano'. In 1918, together with Mario Broglio (1891–1948) and others, he founded the journal VALORI PLASTICI. He showed his paintings in the exhibitions that it promoted: a travelling exhibition in Germany in 1921 and one in Florence in 1922.

Shortly after *Valori plastici* ceased publication in 1921 Melli underwent a profound crisis that prevented him from painting for at least six years. By the beginning of the 1930s, however, he was back in avant-garde circles, both as a painter and as a critic for *Quadrivio* (1933–6). His representational style of carefully constructed flat areas of unmodelled colour, as in *Still-life with Vases* (1928; Rome, Pal. Braschi), show a debt not only to the most lively years of *Valori plastici* but also to Pittura Metafisica and to the work of Giorgio Morandi. Such works were instrumental in the development of Tonalismo, a painting tendency that, after 1930, gathered together the youngest and most interesting painters of the SCUOLA ROMANA, including among others Mario Mafai, Giuseppe Capogrossi, Corrado Cagli and Alberto Ziveri (1908–90). Melli, with an authority deriving from his wider experience, lent his critical support to this development in *Quadrivio*.

During these years Melli's only one-man show was held at the Galleria della Cometa in Rome in 1936. In 1938 his artistic activity was abruptly halted by the racial laws (he was of Jewish origin) that denied him the possibility of exhibiting his work in public. The situation provoked another deep personal crisis. After World War II Melli recommenced work, holding a one-man show at the Galleria del Secolo in Rome in 1947, and later in Florence, Milan and at the Venice Biennale of 1950. From 1945 he taught at the Accademia di Belle Arti in Rome and resumed his work as a critic, contributing to *Fiera letteraria*.

BIBLIOGRAPHY
M. Calvesi: *Roberto Melli* (Rome, 1954)
Roberto Melli (exh. cat., ed. R. Bossaglia; Ferrara, Gal. Civ. A. Mod., 1975) [incl. anthol. of writings]
Roberto Melli (exh. cat., ed. G. Apella and M. Calvesi; Macurata, Palazzo Ricci, 1992)

VALERIO RIVOSECCHI

Mellifont Abbey. Former Cistercian abbey in Co. Louth, Ireland. It was the first Cistercian foundation in Ireland and was colonized from Clairvaux in 1142. Its buildings exerted a profound impact on the course of Irish architecture, helping to introduce to the country European concepts of planning and design. The abbey was founded on the initiative of Malachy, Archbishop of Armagh, following visits to Clairvaux in 1139 and 1140, and the chief benefactor was the local king of Uriel, Donough O'Carroll. The founding community included a group of French monks, among them a certain Robert, one of whose tasks was to advise on building operations. The monastery achieved success very rapidly, and by 1148 six daughter houses had been established, the start of an affiliation that eventually numbered twenty-one. As the head of a group of monasteries, Mellifont occupied an influential position, helping to disseminate architectural methods from abroad. It also became one of the richest houses in the country. At the Reformation its property was valued at £352 3s. 10d. When the community was dissolved in 1539, the abbey passed into secular ownership, and a fortified house (destr.) was erected amidst the ancient buildings.

The ruins of the abbey (see fig.) lie beside the River Mattock approximately 8 km north-west of Drogheda. The best-preserved buildings are the chapter house of *c.* 1210–30 and an octagonal lavabo of *c.* 1200, the latter a finely detailed structure in the Transitional style. The foundations of the buildings around the cloister garth were recovered in a series of excavations, the first undertaken soon after the monument was taken into state care in 1882. More comprehensive excavation took place in 1954–5. Although only fragments of the domestic buildings survive, the history and design of the church can be followed in some detail.

The first stone church on the site was substantially complete by 1157, when an elaborate consecration ceremony took place. This church was planned with a typically short Cistercian chancel, transepts, each with three eastern chapels, and an aisled nave of eight bays. In two respects the layout was unusual: the design of the transept chapels with alternating square and semicircular apses was a departure from the normal scheme found in the affiliation of Clairvaux, and so too was the crypt, covered by a wooden ceiling, installed at the west end of the nave to counter a fall in the ground. Little is known about the elevation of the church, but the presence in daughter houses of such Burgundian features as pointed arches and pointed barrel vaults (in the presbytery and chapels) lends support to the view that these features were also employed at Mellifont. Although not large by European standards (external length 57.34m), the scale of the building was a dramatic contrast to the simple oratories of earlier Celtic monasteries, a point underlined by the abbey's colloquial name, An Mainistear Mór ('The Great Monastery').

The 12th-century church was altered or remodelled on at least three subsequent occasions. Following the establishment of English rule in Ireland, the presbytery and north transept were rebuilt *c.* 1240 in an English Gothic manner; the presbytery was extended to the east, and the north transept was provided with east and west aisles. Early English characteristics include crisply cut moulding profiles, stepped lancet windows, moulded capitals and dogtooth decoration. About 1325 the south transept, together with the two eastern bays of the nave, was reconstructed in the Decorated style. The use of sophisticated mouldings and elaborate compound piers indicates a design well abreast of contemporary English fashion. In the 15th century a more general remodelling of the nave occurred, though few details of this remain. It was at this time that a substantial tower was erected over the crossing, following a fashion widespread in late medieval Ireland. The excavations of 1954–5 brought to light traces of a serious fire in the early 14th century, but how this related to the building sequence is a matter of debate.

The cloister was rectangular rather than square in plan, having been extended southwards *c.* 1200. Fragments of a late 12th-century cloister arcade, supported on twin colonnettes, were discovered in the 1954–5 excavation, and these have since been reconstructed on the site. The presence of an enclosed cloister garth surrounded by

Mellifont Abbey (founded 1142), looking south across the ruins of the transepts and crossing to the lavabo (*c.* 1200)

covered walkways was a novelty in mid-12th-century Ireland; so too was the ordered sequence of buildings along regular axes, in striking contrast to the scattered layout of early Irish monasteries.

BIBLIOGRAPHY

H. G. Leask: 'Mellifont Abbey', *J. Co. Louth Archaeol. Soc.*, xi (1945), pp. 29–33
C. Conway: *The Story of Mellifont* (Dublin, 1958)
L. de Paor: 'Excavations at Mellifont Abbey, Co. Louth', *Proc. Royal Irish Acad.*, lxviii (1969), pp. 109–64
R. A. Stalley: 'Mellifont Abbey: A Study of its Architectural History', *Proc. Royal Irish Acad.*, lxxx (1980), pp. 263–354
——: *The Cistercian Monasteries of Ireland* (New Haven, 1987)

ROGER STALLEY

Mellin [le Lorrain], Charles (*b* Nancy, *c.* 1600; *d* Rome, 21 Sept 1649). French painter and draughtsman, active in Italy. He came from a Liégeois family recently settled in Nancy, then the capital of the independent duchy of Lorraine. He trained in that city at a time when the leading artist was Jacques Bellange. He must have left for Italy, perhaps with the help of Duke Henry II (*reg* 1608–24), around 1618–20, since he was in Rome from 1620 onwards. He built his career principally in Rome but spent two lengthy periods in Naples. In Rome he remained in contact with other artists from his native duchy, including Claude Lorrain who witnessed his will.

Mellin was a member of the Roman Accademia di S Luca from at least 1626, when Simon Vouet was at its head. The classicizing female type in Mellin's painting *Roman Charity* (Geneva, Mus. A. & Hist.; see fig.) suggests the influence of Vouet, as perhaps does the intense colour scheme. The luminosity of the blues and yellows in *St Francis de Paul at Prayer* (*c.* 1630; Nancy, Mus. Hist. Lorrain) gives the same impression, suggesting the attraction exercised by Venetian painting in certain parts of the Roman milieu in the 1620s. (Mellin's later works were more sombre in colour.)

In the years 1627–31 Mellin is recorded as living in the house of the Marchese Vincenzo Muti, where he executed decorations now difficult to identify. The success of his career was established from 1630, when, in competition with Giovanni Lanfranco and Nicolas Poussin (the second important and perhaps reciprocal influence on his art), he won the commission to decorate the chapel of the Virgin in S Luigi dei Francesi, Rome. A *Visitation* on the vault survives, as does a badly damaged *Annunciation* on one of the walls. The rest was almost entirely repainted by a 19th-century restorer and now preserves only Mellin's compositions. Also at this time he began to work for the French convent of Trinità dei Monti, Rome, for which the *St Francis de Paul at Prayer* was one of his first works. It was subsequently engraved by Charles Audran. Shortly afterwards Mellin painted for the cloister of the same convent *St Francis de Paul at the Feet of Pope Sixtus IV* (*in situ*). It was during this time of promise that Joachim von Sandrart met him.

In 1636–7 Mellin executed decorations for the choir of the church at the abbey of Montecassino in the kingdom of Naples. The paintings were all destroyed in 1944, but a canvas of the *Sacrifice of Abel* intended for the abbey survived (Nancy, Mus. Hist. Lorrain). Mellin was recorded in Rome in 1638–9 and in Naples again in 1643, although

Charles Mellin: *Roman Charity*, oil on canvas, 1.02×0.82 m, 1629 (Geneva, Musée d'Art et d'Histoire)

it is not clear when he arrived there. He was commissioned in Naples to paint a *Purification of the Virgin* (1644–5; destr. 1757) for the church of SS Annunziata, and an *Annunciation* and an *Immaculate Conception* for the church of S Maria Donnaregina (both still *in situ*). He left Naples in July 1647, following popular disturbances.

Mellin's working method sometimes involved the production of oil sketches, such as that (Tours, Mus. B.-A.) for *St Francis de Paul at the Feet of Pope Sixtus IV*, but he was also a prolific draughtsman. Many of his numerous lively and nervously handled pen and wash compositional drawings appear unfinished: the outlines of heads are marked, but often the features are not indicated, and the extremities of the limbs of the figures are unformed. The swiftness of execution is evident from the numerous reworkings of the pen and the way in which the washes go beyond pen outlines. Mellin made many drawings for each work; nine drawings have been associated with a painting of the *Assumption* (Ponce, Mus. A.), and eight (Vienna, Albertina, and Paris, Louvre) are linked with the S Luigi dei Francesi *Annunciation*. In this practice Mellin was closer to Poussin than to Vouet, who used the more traditional technique of careful finished studies of individual figures and parts of figures. For a long time many of the drawings that now constitute Mellin's oeuvre were more or less plausibly attributed to Poussin; however, since the articles by Wild of 1966 and 1967, around 20 paintings have been reattributed to Mellin, although specialist opinion is not unanimous. The points of difference between the work of the two artists lie in Mellin's lack of rational compositional structure, his preference for strong contrasts of light and dark and his liking for relatively more demonstrative gesticulation by his figures. Also indicative of his hand is the generally awkward sense of design and the comparatively poor quality of execution.

BIBLIOGRAPHY

J. Bousquet: 'Un Rival inconnu de Poussin: Charles Mellin, dit "le Lorrain", 1597–1649', *An. E.*, i (1955), pp. 3–35

B. Lossky: 'Le Peintre Charles Mellin dit le Lorrain et les Musées de Tours', *Bull. Soc. Hist. A. Fr.* (1956), pp. 50–58

J. Thuillier: 'Poussin et ses premiers compagnons français à Rome', *Actes du colloque international Nicolas Poussin: Paris, 1958*, i, pp. 80–83

D. Wild: 'Charles Mellin ou Nicolas Poussin, I', *Gaz. B.-A.*, n. s. 5, lxviii (1966), pp. 177–214

——: 'Charles Mellin ou Nicolas Poussin, II', *Gaz. B.-A.*, n. s. 5, lxix (1967), pp. 3–44

E. Schleier: 'Charles Mellin and the Marchese Muti', *Burl. Mag.*, cxviii (1976), pp. 69–74

J. Thuillier: 'Charles Mellin "Très excellent peintre"', *Les Fondations nationales dans la Rome pontificale*, Col. Ecole Fr. Rome, 52 (Rome, 1981), pp. 583–684 [numerous illus.]

——: 'Charles Mellin', *Claude Lorrain e i pittori lorenesi in Italia nel XVII secolo* (exh. cat., Rome, Acad. France; Nancy, Mus. Hist. Lorrain; 1982), pp. 207–74

P. Choné: 'A propos du peintre Charles Mellin: Un Essai d'industrialisation à Nancy au début du XVIIe siècle', *Pays Lorrain*, 1 (1983), pp. 35–50

MICHEL SYLVESTRE

Mello, Heitor de (*b* Rio de Janeiro, 1876; *d* Rio de Janeiro, 15 Aug 1920). Brazilian architect. He trained as an architect at the Escola Nacional de Belas Artes, Rio de Janeiro, and in 1898 he founded an office that became Rio de Janeiro's first large planning and construction organization. This was a period of large-scale building in Rio: Mello built several warehouses (1902) in the new port; a commercial building (1905) in Swiss-German style, on the Avenida Central (now the Rio Branco); and the Renaissance-style Eduardo Teiler residence (1905) on Avenida Beira-Mar. Following the successful Exposition Universelle in Paris (1900), Rio de Janeiro adopted the Beaux-Arts style for its own national exhibition in 1908; Mello won the grand prize for his pavilion designs, but he was not asked to direct the building works. Thereafter he adopted versions of Beaux-Arts styles for all his large-scale public and private commissions in Rio, including the police station and barracks, the Jockey Club (1912) and Municipal Council, the central hospital and the Derby Club (1914); also the post office in Belo Horizonte, Minas Gerais. In Niterói he built the State Government Legislative Assembly, the Palace of Justice and a teacher training college, all in Greek Revival style. His plans for private houses, of which there are about 50, include some in the Vienna Secession style, some Tudor- and Swiss-style bungalows, and mansions in various classical styles. He was also one of the first to adopt the neo-colonial style, favoured by the Traditionalist Movement, that was introduced during the mid-1910s in an attempt to express a national cultural identity; he designed some houses, school buildings and two hotels (unexecuted) in this new style. Following his death, his office continued to operate under his name, directed by Archimedes Memória (1893–1960) and Francisque Cuchet, and some later works were built to Mello's design, for example the Chamber of Deputies (1921). Memória also took over the Chair of Architectural Composition in the Escola Nacional de Belas Artes, which Mello had held since 1912.

BIBLIOGRAPHY

'Homenagem a Heitor de Mello', *Arquit. Brasil*, i/1 (1921), pp. 29–30

P. F. Santos: *Quatro séculos de arquitetura* (Barra do Piraí, 1977)

SYLVIA FICHER

Mellon. American family of financiers, collectors and benefactors.

(1) Andrew W(illiam) Mellon (*b* Pittsburgh, PA, 24 March 1855; *d* Southampton, NY, 26 Aug 1937). His father worked his way up from poverty to prominence as a lawyer, judge and the founder and director of a major bank. Mellon was put in charge of the bank, and over 35 years he built a powerful industrial and financial empire. From 1921 to 1932 he served three presidents as Secretary of the Treasury, and in 1933 he was US Ambassador to Britain.

Following a four-month trial for tax-fraud in 1933, Mellon devoted himself to collecting. Although neither brought up with nor trained in art, he became part of the USA's first generation of serious collectors, including such industrialists as Charles Lang Freer, J. Pierpont Morgan and Henry Clay Frick, a close friend. Mellon made most of his acquisitions through Knoedler's, the prestigious New York firm, and through the art dealer Joseph, 1st Baron Duveen, with advice from Frick and (after Frick's death in 1919) David Finlay, a lawyer and Mellon speechwriter with a strong knowledge of European art. Never a risk-taker, Mellon restricted himself to buying Old Master paintings, excluding nudes and 'unpleasant' subjects. His initial acquisitions were serene landscapes by Constant Troyon, Aelbert Cuyp and J. M. W. Turner (e.g. *Approach to Venice*, *c.* 1843), and portraits by Frans Hals, Johannes Vermeer (e.g. *The Lacemaker*, early 1660s) and Joshua Reynolds. Mellon achieved his greatest collecting coup in 1931, when he acquired 21 paintings (including Raphael's *Alba Madonna*, Sandro Botticelli's *Adoration of the Magi* and works by Pietro Perugino, Jan van Eyck and Matthias Grünewald) from the Hermitage Museum, St Petersburg. (All pictures mentioned are in Washington, DC, N.G.A.)

Embarrassed that the USA lacked a national art gallery, in December 1936 Mellon offered to give the American people some 125 paintings, plus £16 million for a building in which to house them and another £5 million to pay for future acquisitions and salaries. President Franklin D. Roosevelt accepted the gift and Mellon's conditions that it be named the National Gallery of Art and that it be run by a board of directors. The Gallery's Neo-classical building, designed by John Russell Pope, opened in Washington, DC, in 1941, four years after Mellon's death, with David Finlay as the first Director.

BIBLIOGRAPHY

B. Hersh: *The Mellon Family: A Fortune in History* (New York, 1978)

NANCY G. HELLER

(2) Paul Mellon (*b* Pittsburgh, PA, 11 June 1907). Son of (1) Andrew W. Mellon. (Unless otherwise mentioned, all works are in New Haven, CT, Yale Cent. Brit. A.) He studied at Yale University, New Haven, CT (1925–9) and Clare College, Cambridge University, England, and later became Director of the family bank. His first art purchases were made in England during the early 1930s, and they included two animal pictures by Ben Marshall and *Pumpkin with Stable Lad up* by George Stubbs, his favourite artist. These works reflect the love of English life and country pursuits that characterize his collection. After meeting Basil Taylor, an enthusiast for British art and for Stubbs in particular, in 1959, Mellon acquired the core of his own collection during the next four years. He bought for pleasure, selecting from among Taylor's suggestions on the basis of his own preference for small-scale scenes of everyday life and his intuitive appreciation of painterly qualities. Particularly well represented in the collection is 18th-century British art: sporting painting by Francis Sartorius sr, James Seymour and Jacques-Laurent Agasse, as well as Stubbs; topographical views and landscapes from Peter Tillemans to Richard Wilson and John Constable; seascapes by Charles Brooking and Dominic and John Thomas Serres; portraits and conversation pieces by Joseph Highmore, Arthur Devis and Francis Hayman; watercolours by Thomas Rowlandson; and a number of works by William Hogarth.

Mellon's collection was first exhibited publicly in 1963 at the Virginia Museum of Fine Arts, Richmond, VA, and next in 1964 at the Royal Academy in London. In 1966 he announced his intention to donate his collection to Yale University, and in 1977 the Yale Center for British Art opened in New Haven, CT. For the building in which the collection is displayed Mellon specified room-like spaces and natural lighting from the architect Louis Kahn. Mellon's further acquisitions of British art were determined by the public function the collection was to perform, and he sought greater quality and diversity. In addition to the first acquisition of a Reynolds, *Mrs. Abingdon*, Mellon enhanced the collection with a group of Tudor portraits, van Dyck's *Earl of Newport* and examples of 17th-century topographical painting. After the opening of the centre, Mellon was closely involved with an acquisitions policy to make the collection more representative of British art, strengthening the holdings of 19th- and 20th-century painting. At the same time he continued to develop the aspects of the original collection that remained his primary interest and secured, for example, an important work by Stubbs, *Turf, with Jockey up at Newmarket*. From 1964 the Paul Mellon Centre for Studies in British Art in London and subsequently the Yale Center have promoted research and publications that have made valuable contributions to the understanding of British art.

Largely due to his second wife's enthusiasm for Impressionist painting, Mellon made important acquisitions at the sale of Jakob Goldschmidt's collection (London, Sotheby's, 15 Oct 1958), to which he continued to add. He donated a number of 19th-century French paintings to the Virginia Museum of Fine Arts and to the National Gallery of Art in Washington, DC (including Monet's *Woman with a Parasol*), where he was elected President of the Founding Committee in 1938, serving as a trustee and becoming the first Honorary Trustee in 1985.

BIBLIOGRAPHY

Painting in England, 1700–1850 (exh. cat., Richmond, VA, Mus. F.A., 1963)

Selected Paintings, Drawings and Books (exh. cat., New Haven, CT, Yale Cent. Brit. A., 1977)

J. Wilmerding, ed.: *Essays in Honour of Paul Mellon* (Washington, DC, 1986)

P. Mellon and J. Baskett: *Reflections in a Silver Spoon: A Memoir* (New York, 1992)

CLAIRE BRISBY

Mellor, David (*b* Sheffield, 5 Oct 1930). English silversmith and industrial designer. He trained as a silversmith at Sheffield College of Art (1946–8) and the Royal College of Art (1950–54). In 1954 he established a silversmithing workshop and studio in Sheffield and became a design consultant to the firm of Walker & Hall. It manufactured his earliest designs, including the 'Pride' range of silver cutlery (1954), the simple and elegant forms of which were inspired by 18th-century English cutlery. This was the first in a series of cutlery designs, for which he is best known (examples London, V&A; Goldsmiths' Co.) and which received numerous Design Centre awards. In 1962 he became a Royal Designer for Industry. In 1963 the Ministry of Public Buildings and Works commissioned from him a range of silver cutlery and tableware for use in British embassies and in 1965 the minimalist 'Thrift' range of stainless steel cutlery, to be manufactured at low cost and used in government institutions. In 1975 he began to manufacture his own cutlery at Broom Hall, Sheffield, using innovative, highly mechanized methods; in 1988 production was transferred to a purpose-built factory, designed by Michael Hopkins (*b* 1935), at Hathersage, Derbys. Although Mellor concentrated on industrial design, including bus shelters (1960) and road traffic signals (1965–70) as well as cutlery, he continued to execute private commissions for the Worshipful Company of Goldsmiths, London, and commercial organizations.

BIBLIOGRAPHY

Contemp. Designers

G. Hughes: *Modern Silver throughout the World, 1880–1967* (London, 1967)

Eye for Industry: Royal Designers for Industry, 1936–1986 (exh. cat. by F. MacCarthy and P. Nuttgens, London, V&A, 1986–7)

20th Century Silver (exh. cat., London, Crafts Council Gal., 1993)

SARAH YATES

Mel'nikov, Avraam (Ivanovich) (*b* Oraniyenbaum [now Lomonosov], nr St Petersburg, 30 July 1784; *d* St Petersburg, 1 Jan 1854). Russian architect. He studied (1795–1808) under Andreyan Zakharov at the St Petersburg Academy of Arts before winning a scholarship to travel abroad (1808–11). In Italy he stayed in Rome, measuring the ancient monuments, and also visited Verona, Mantua, Florence and Siena, and, further south, Pompeii, Herculaneum and Paestum. After returning to Russia he taught at the St Petersburg Academy of Arts, where he was elected an academician (1812) and was later appointed Rector (1833–54). His plans for public buildings are closely linked to the classical tradition of the late 18th century. The most important of his early works, the Demidov Lyceum (planned 1812; built 1818–66) in Yaroslavl' is a monumental building with a dodecastyle portico of the Composite order on a high, arched basement. His commercial and civic projects included laying out a semicircular square and the town governor's house in Odessa (1826; destr.) and bazaars in Rostov (1829) Izmailo and Simbirsk (both 1830s). Mel'nikov's preference for the Greek Revival style, in particular the Paestum Doric, is most apparent in his ecclesiastical work. With occasional exceptions, such as the Mozolovskiy Monastery of the Transfiguration (1827) in Mstislavl', which is built on the lines of a parish church, with church, refectory and bell-tower in one east–west axis, his churches are compact square or cruciform buildings crowned by cupolas, the façades identical and with Doric porticos. The best and most original example of this type is the church of St Nicholas (designed 1818; built 1820–27), St Petersburg, which has unusual two-tiered colonnades connecting the square domed corner belfries. These combine with the central dome to form the traditional five cupolas. Many of the houses built by Mel'nikov in St Petersburg in the 1820s and 1830s are of the type of multi-apartment building that had developed in the early 18th century, with flat, sparely decorated, astylar façades and an even rhythm of windows. Examples include the Yakovlev house (1823–6) on Tuchkov (now Admiral Makarov) Embankment and the Kukanova house (1831–2) on the Fontanka Embankment. The dachas that he designed on the outskirts of the city, for example the Shishmarev dacha (1824–5; extant) on the Bol'shaya Nevka Embankment in Novaya Derevnya, were single-storey buildings with an attic and a central portico, reminiscent of the contemporary building type around Moscow popularized by Afanasy Grigor'yev.

BIBLIOGRAPHY

N. Y. Leyboshits: 'Materialy k tvorcheskoy biografii A. I. Mel'nikova' [Material for a creative biography of A. I. Mel'nikov], *Arkhit. Nasledstvo*, ix (1959)

M. P. Tubli: *Avraam Mel'nikov* (Leningrad, 1980)

YE. I. KIRICHENKO

Mel'nikov, Konstantin (Stepanovich) (*b* Petrovsko-Razumovsky, nr Moscow, 22 July 1890; *d* Moscow, 28 Nov 1974). Russian architect and teacher. He was a leading Modernist in Moscow in the 1920s, and his built works are exceptional for their quantity and for their empirical inventiveness. Mel'nikov rejected theory and any suggestion of a design 'method', such as the Constructivists espoused. By contrast he insisted on the necessity for a single generating formal idea to materialize the social and symbolic 'essence' of a building, and on the primacy of intuition. He was, therefore, equally opposed to the scientific investigation of perception conducted by the Rationalist group under Nikolay Ladovsky and Vladimir Krinsky. His characteristic individualism left him with few professional friends after the mid-1930s during a 30-year period of expulsion from the profession.

Mel'nikov's family was of peasant origin. After some primary schooling he was apprenticed to a firm of heating engineers, whose director recognized his talents and put him through the painting faculty (1905–11) and then the architectural faculty (1912–17) of the College of Painting, Sculpture and Architecture, Moscow. His teachers included Illarion Ivanov-Shits and Ivan Zholtovsky, and he gained early professional experience under A. V. Kuznetsov (1874–1954) and the engineer L. A. Loleit. In 1918, Zholtovsky and Aleksey Shchusev included him in their Mossoviet studio, working on a New Moscow Plan, where he undertook his last ventures in classicism. In 1921–3 he returned to his former school, by then transformed into the VKHUTEMAS, to run a studio with Ilya Golosov.

Entitled the New Academy, its programme was a polemical middle way between Zholtovsky's classical studio and Ladovsky's experimental approach.

Mel'nikov's first built works were of timber: the Makhorka Tobacco pavilion at the All-Russian Agricultural Exhibition (1923), the New Sukharev market (1924), Moscow, and the Soviet pavilion (1924–5) at the Exposition Internationale des Arts Décoratifs et Industriels Modernes, Paris. All were dramatic compositions, and they put Mel'nikov in the forefront of Soviet and European critical attention. The buildings that principally consolidated his reputation were the six workers' clubs built over three years in and around Moscow: the Rusakov (see fig.), Frunze and Kauchuk (1927–8), the Svoboda and Pravda (1928), and the Burevestnik (1929). Where Constructivist projects tended to separate functionally different parts of a club into separate linked volumes, Mel'nikov tended to link them all into a single synthetic and unique form. All were characterized by rich and flexible spatial organization achieved by simple structural means. The same principle inspired his own house (1927–9), Krivoarbatskiy Lane, Moscow, formed of two interlocking cylinders. As a one-family house of pre-Revolutionary scale and pretensions this was unique among new Moscow buildings of the 1920s. It particularly demonstrated Mel'nikov's conviction that the 'rationalization of construction' could proceed better through the imaginative rethinking of Russian artisan traditions than through the importation of new Western technologies. He also built three bus and lorry garages: the Bakhmetevskaya (1926), Novo-Ryazan'skaya (1929) and Gosplan (1929), all in Moscow. During the 1920s he also entered several major competitions with equally innovative and inventive schemes, including the Palace of Labour (1923; unexecuted) and the Arcos Building (1924; unexecuted), Moscow.

From 1930 Mel'nikov's architectural and urban planning concepts became increasingly theatrical and grandiose, for example the competition schemes for 'Green City' (1930), the Palace of Soviets (1931–2) and the Palace of Culture (1932–3), Tashkent. In the reorganization (1933) of Soviet architecture following the formation (1932) of the Union of Soviet Architects, he became head of Studio No. 7 in Mossoviet, Moscow, where he designed a bus garage for Intourist (1934), Moscow, but this was his last significant construction. In the Commissariat for Heavy Industry scheme (1934) he responded to official demands for explicit historicism with obscure formal symbolism and exaggerated monumentality. The fierce criticism this attracted, which by 1936 had extended to his whole studio, led to his dismissal from his teaching post at the Moscow school. Criticism heightened in 1937 during the anti-Modernist First Congress of Soviet Architects, which affirmed the conservative principles of Socialist Realism as the official 'method' of Soviet architecture, and in 1938 his right to practise professionally was removed. After a period of personal isolation he was partially readmitted in 1944 to the Union of Architects and to some teaching work, but without professional title until 1953. Only in 1960 through an invitation from the All-Union Distance Learning Institute for Engineering and Construction did he return to significant employment. During his years of official rejection Mel'nikov continued to design and wrote

Konstantin Mel'nikov: Rusakov Workers' Club for employees of Moscow Municipality, Moscow, 1927–8; photographed shortly after completion

extensively on his philosophy. Rehabilitation came eventually in 1965, following efforts by colleagues and his own initiatives. He was accorded recognition in the form of a short-lived personal exhibition and in an article in the official journal *Arkhitektura SSSR* (1966). By the time of his internationally celebrated centenary in 1990, a more balanced critical appraisal had begun to reassess the aesthetic qualities of his work and the characteristically Russian mystical philosophy that underpinned it.

WRITINGS
'Oformlenie proekta' [Delineation of a design], *Arkhit. SSSR*, v (1933), p. 35
'Arkhitekture pervoe mesto' [First place to architecture], *Stroitel'stvo Moskvy*, i (1934), pp. 9–13

BIBLIOGRAPHY
N. Lukhmanov: *Arkhitektura kluba* [Architecture of the workers' club] (Moscow, 1930)
Yu. Gerchuk: 'Arkhitektor Konstantin Mel'nikov', *Arkhit. SSSR*, viii (1966), pp. 51–5
S. F. Starr: 'Konstantin Melnikov', *Archit. Des.*, vii (1969), pp. 367–73
A. Kopp: *Town and Revolution* (London and New York, 1970)
S. F. Starr: *Melnikov: Solo Architect in a Mass Society* (Princeton, 1978)
——: *K. Melnikov: Le Pavillon soviétique* (Paris, 1981), pp. 60–61
A. A. Strigalev and I. V. Kokkinaki, eds: *Konstantin Stepanovich Melnikov* (Moscow, 1985) [incl. writings by Mel'nikov and his contemporaries]
S. O. Chan-Magomedov: *Pioniere der sowjetischen Architektur* (Dresden, 1983); Eng. trans. as S. O. Khan-Magomedov: *Pioneers of Soviet Architecture* (London, 1987)
——: *Konstantin Mel'nikov* (Moscow, 1990)
A. Wortmann, ed.: *Melnikov: The Muscles of Invention* (Rotterdam, 1990)
C. Cooke: 'Professional Diversity and its Origins', *The Avant-garde: Russian Architecture in the Twenties*, eds C. Cooke and J. Ageros (London, 1991), pp. 8–21, 30–31
C. Cooke and I. Kazus: *Soviet Architectural Competitions, 1924–1936* (London and The Hague, 1992)

CATHERINE COOKE

Melo, de. *See* CADAVAL, Duques de.

Melo, João de Almada e. *See* ALMADA, (1).

Melo, Pedro Américo de. *See* AMÉRICO DE MELO, PEDRO.

Melo, Sebastião José de Carvalho e. *See* POMBAL, 1st Marquês de.

Melone, Altobello (da) (*b* Cremona, *c.* 1490; *d* before 3 May 1543). Italian painter. With Gian Francesco Bembo, he reacted against the classicism of such Cremonese painters of the preceding generation as Boccaccio Boccaccino and Tommaso Aleni (*fl* 1505–15). His first work, the *Virgin and Child with the Infant St John the Baptist* (Philadelphia, PA, Mus. A.), is similar to compositions by Aleni, with carefully constructed perspective in the manner of Donato Bramante. From 1500 to 1507 the Venetian painter Marco Marziale lived in Cremona; Melone was only superficially affected by him but seems to have been attracted to Marziale's sources: northern European painting, particularly that of Dürer, and the work of Giorgione and Titian, as can be seen in his *Virgin and Child with the Infant St John the Baptist* (Bergamo, Gal. Accad. Carrara).

Melone's *Adoration of the Christ Child with Saints* (U. London, Courtauld Inst. Gals, 39674A) shows the influence of GEROLAMO ROMANINO, and Marcantonio Michiel, who saw a full-length painting of *Lucretia* (untraced) by Melone in the house of the Prior of S Antonio in Cremona, described Melone as 'a young man with a good talent and instinct for painting, and a pupil of Armanin [Romanino]'. For almost a decade from *c.* 1508 Melone

Altobello Melone: *Journey to Emmaus*, oil on panel, 1.46×1.44 m, *c.* 1518 (London, National Gallery)

was closely associated with Romanino, which has, with some works, led to difficulties of attribution. Melone's *Lamentation over the Dead Christ* (Milan, Brera) is a reworking of Romanino's painting of the same subject (1510; Venice, Accad.), painted for S Lorenzo in Brescia. The *Portrait of a Man*, traditionally identified as Cesare Borgia, is influenced equally by Venetian and northern portraiture. Melone was influenced by Romanino's Titian-esque style, as is evident in such works as *The Lovers* (Dresden, Gemäldegal.); *St Prosper* (London, priv. col., see exh. cat., p. 92) and *St Jerome* (Verona, Castelvecchio), the wings of a triptych originally in the former church of S Prospero, Cremona.

In December 1516 Melone was commissioned to work on the series of frescoes in Cremona Cathedral begun by Boccaccio Boccaccino and continued by Bembo: the *Flight into Egypt* and the *Massacre of the Innocents* were executed before 15 August 1517. They are some of Melone's finest works, in which he combined German and Venetian traits with those of Romanino to produce dramatic and dynamic scenes by means of a remarkably expressive use of light and colour. The *Resurrection* (Rome, priv. col.) is extremely close to the work of Albrecht Altdorfer and belongs to the same period. A second group of frescoes in the cathedral was commissioned on 13 March 1518; the cycle consists of the *Last Supper*, *Christ Washing the Disciples' Feet*, the *Agony in the Garden*, *Christ Taken by the Soldiers* and *Christ before Caiaphas*. They differ considerably from the first frescoes and are more conservative in character. Melone borrowed motifs from northern engravings and employed colder tones, perhaps influenced by the work of Lorenzo Lotto, then living in Bergamo. He returned to using perspectival devices derived from Bramante, took care in the depiction of character and, in *Christ Taken by the Soldiers*, was less adventurous with his light effects. The

Journey to Emmaus (*c.* 1518; London, N.G.; see fig.) is of the same date. The triptych from Torre dei Picenardi (dismembered; wings, Oxford, Ashmolean; central panel, Columbia, U. MO, Mus. A. & Archaeol.; predella, Algiers, Mus. N. B.-A.) has a 15th-century format, but the still figures and the delicacy with which their expressions are conveyed, create a contemplative and subtle mood. The *Nativity with St Dominic* (Lurago d'Erba, Sormani Andreani Verri priv. col.) is a mature work in which Melone continued his experiments in the use of dramatic light effects started in the frescoes in Cremona Cathedral to the point where he anticipated the proto-Caravaggism of the Campi family. In the late 1520s, however, his allegiance to Romanino was shaken by the arrival of Giulio Romano in Mantua, which resulted in such paintings as the *Annunciation* at Isola Dovarese, Cremona, the *Virgin and Child with SS John the Baptist and Nicholas* (Cremona, Mus. Civ. Ala Ponzone) and *Christ in Limbo* (Cremona Cathedral), in which he attempted to emulate Giulio's Mannerist elegance, unfortunately a style that did not come naturally to him.

BIBLIOGRAPHY
Thieme–Becker
G. Vasari: *Vite* (1550, rev. 2/1568); ed. G. Milanesi (1878–85), iv, p. 583; vi, pp. 459, 492
M. A. Michiel: *Notizie d'opere di disegno* (MS. before 1552); as *Der Anonimo Morelliano*, ed. T. Frimmel (Vienna, 1888), pp. 44–5, 50
L. Grassi: 'Ingegno di Altobello Meloni', *Proporzioni*, iii (1950), pp. 143–63
F. Zeri: 'Altobello Melone: Quattro tavole', *Paragone*, iv (1953), pp. 40–44
F. Bologna: 'Altobello Melone', *Burl. Mag.*, xcvii (1955), pp. 240–50
M. Gregori: 'Altobello, il Romanino e il cinquecento cremonese', *Paragone*, vi (1955), pp. 3–28
——: 'Altobello e G. Francesco Bembo', *Paragone*, viii (1957), pp. 16–40
M. L. Ferrari: 'Un recupero per Altobello', *Paragone*, ix (1958), pp. 48–53
M. Tanzi: 'Novità e revisioni per Altobello Melone e Gianfrancesco Bembo', *Ric. Stor. A.*, xvii (1982), pp. 49–56
——: 'Appunti sulla fortuna visiva degli "eccentrici" cremonesi', *Prospettiva*, 39 (1984), pp. 53–60
I Campi e la cultura artistica cremonese del cinquecento (exh. cat., ed. M. Gregori; Cremona, Mus. Civ. Ala Ponzone, 1985), pp. 85–98
M. Tanzi: 'Riflessioni sull'attività di Altobello Melone dopo il 1520', *Stud. & Bibliog. An. Bib. Stat. & Lib. Civ. Cremona*, xxxvii (1987), pp. 97–107
M. Gregori, ed.: *Pittura a Cremona dal romanico al settecento* (Milan, 1990), pp. 26–39

MARCO TANZI

Melos [Milos]. Greek island at the south-western extremity of the Aegean Cyclades. Its importance in the Bronze Age is evident from the finds at the main prehistoric settlement of Phylakopi, which suggest that Melian culture was influential throughout the Cyclades and beyond. This influence was probably derived from the fact that Melos was the main Aegean source of obsidian—an opaque glassy stone of volcanic origin, which was used, like flint, to provide cutting edges for tools and weapons and is found on all prehistoric sites in the Aegean, as well as farther afield. Two obsidian quarries have been located, as well as the debris of a workshop at Phylakopi. Although it is sometimes suggested that raw obsidian was collected by visitors to Melos and taken away to be worked elsewhere, it seems most unlikely that the indigenous people did not attempt to exploit this important commercial asset. The Melos Museum at Plaka contains finds excavated in 1911, a cast of the *Venus de Milo* (see below) and various Classical antiquities from the island.

Phylakopi, on the north coast of Melos, was the first major Cycladic settlement site to be excavated (British School at Athens, 1896–9, 1911, 1974–7). It was settled during Early Cycladic (EC) I (*c.* 3500–*c.* 2800/2600 BC). The earliest buildings may have been scattered and some of them flimsy. The most substantial remains of the 'First City' belong to later EC III (*c.* 2300–*c.* 2000 BC), when it seems to have grown and to have had stone-built structures. The site was then destroyed and rebuilt soon after. In the 'Second City' (Middle Cycladic (MC); *c.* 2000–*c.* 1600 BC), the houses were larger and were laid out on a rough grid plan. There may have been a fortification wall across the neck of the promontory. This phase of the settlement also ended with destruction and rebuilding. The 'Third City' is the best known. Again, it was laid out on a grid plan, the blocks separated by streets, sometimes stepped, with drains running beneath them. In its earliest stage (Late Cycladic (LC) I–II; *c.* 1600–*c.* 1390 BC) the material culture was heavily influenced by that of Crete, and there was a large administrative building with which were associated some fragments of a tablet inscribed in a Cretan script (Melos Mus.). In LC III (*c.* 1390–*c.* 1050 BC) this was replaced by a Mycenaean-style megaron (palace)—an architectural symbol of the change in dominant power in the Aegean. Also built in the Mycenaean period was a sanctuary that has yielded many ritual objects, mostly of characteristic Mycenaean type. There was much fortification building in the time of the 'Third City'—indeed all the defences may belong to this period. The final system consisted of a thick wall with towers and casemates, though the sequence of its construction is not entirely clear. The site continued to be occupied until it was deserted in the early 12th century BC (*see also* CYCLADIC, §II, 3).

The importance of Phylakopi in the origination and dissemination of art styles was considerable. In late EC III the 'Geometric' style of pottery decoration apparently began there, subsequently spreading to other Cycladic islands and radically influencing the character of the Middle Helladic Matt-painted class of the Greek mainland (*see* CYCLADIC, §III, 1). Scientific clay analysis has supported the stylistic arguments for a Melian origin of the attractive 'Cycladic White' class of pottery of the MC period, which has many original elements and is found widely on other islands. Melian too is the fine 'Black-and-red' style. In the LC period the pottery, like the architecture, became dependent on inspiration first from Crete and then from the Greek mainland. The site has also yielded some wall paintings, including a scene of *Flying Fish* (LC I–II; Athens, N. Archaeol. Mus.; *see* CYCLADIC, §VI, 2). A number of interesting minor objects, mostly of Mycenaean type, were found in the sanctuary: human and animal terracotta and bronze figures, pottery, sealstones and a gold mask (Melos Mus.).

Most of the other prehistoric sites on the island are known from surface finds, though an EC I cemetry at Pelos was excavated by the British School at Athens in 1896–7. In common with other Cycladic islands, a wide spread of settlement in the Early Bronze Age seems to have contracted sharply in the MC period. In LC I–II there

was once again some expansion. The site of the later town of Melos, which flourished particularly from the Archaic to the Roman periods, lies between the present island capital of Plaka and the coastal village of Klima (the ancient harbour); little excavation has taken place. There are substantial remains of fortifications. The sites of the gymnasium, where the *Venus de Milo* (Paris, Louvre) was found, and the agora (below the hill of Ayios Ilias) have been located. There is also a Roman theatre. In the same area are impressive early Christian catacombs and a baptistery. Here and elsewhere (e.g. Provatás), Roman houses have been found with mosaic floors. Above Plaka the Venetian *kastro* is ruinous but contains the attractive ?13th-century church of Thalassitra, with a Frankish chapel added.

BIBLIOGRAPHY

H. M. Fletcher and S. D. Kitson: 'The Churches of Melos', *Annu. Brit. Sch. Athens*, ii (1986), pp. 155–68

T. D. Atkinson and others: *Excavations at Phylakopi in Melos*, Society for the Promotion of Hellenic Studies Supplementary Paper 4 (London, 1904)

R. M. Dawkins and J. P. Droop: 'The Excavations at Phylakopi in Melos', *Annu. Brit. Sch. Athens*, xvii (1911), pp. 1–22

I. Khatzidhakis: *Istoria tes Melou* [History of Melos], 1927

A. Furumark: 'The Settlement at Ialyssos and Aegean History, *c.* 1500–*c.* 1400 BC', *Opuscula Archaeol.*, vi (1950), pp. 150–271

Z. A. Baos: *Naoi kai naydria tes Melou* [Shrines and temples of Melos], 1964

R. L. N. Barber: 'Phylakopi 1911 and the History of the Later Cycladic Bronze Age', *Annu. Brit. Sch. Athens*, lxix (1974), pp. 1–53

C. Renfrew: 'The Mycenaean Sanctuary at Phylakopi', *Antiquity*, lii (1978), pp. 7–15

——: 'Phylakopi and the Late Bronze I Period in the Cyclades', *Thera and the Aegean World*, ed. C. Doumas, i (London, 1978), pp. 403–21

C. Renfrew and J. M. Wagstaff, eds: *An Island Polity: The Archaeology of Exploitation on Melos* (Cambridge, 1982)

C. Renfrew: *The Archaeology of Cult: The Sanctuary at Phylakopi*, British School at Athens Supplementary Volume xviii (London, 1985)

R. L. N. BARBER

Melotti, Fausto (*b* Rovereto, 8 June 1901; *d* Milan, 22 June 1986). Italian sculptor. He trained at the Accademia di Brera in Milan under Adolfo Wildt, but his works of the early 1930s, such as *Sculpture 17* (1935; Milan, Civ. Mus. A. Contemp.), were very different from those of his teacher: abstract and shunning any display of volume or monumental bulk, they consist of thin, vibrating rods and delicately curving surfaces, which in addition to their visual and tactile qualities seem to possess an acoustic dimension, as though they were musical instruments. Beyond their appeal to the physical senses, they suggest metaphysical and meditative qualities. Only in a few cases, such as a group of allegorical bas-reliefs in marble (1937–9) for the portals of the Palazzo della Giustizia in Milan, did he produce figurative sculpture.

As a student at the Brera, Melotti met Lucio Fontana, who became a lifelong friend and whose career ran more or less parallel to his own. Like Fontana, Melotti combined a conceptual clarity with a strong visual element, to which he imparted a sense of vibrancy and restlessness. In the years immediately after World War II, however, he did not include any abrupt or decisive elements in his works, such as the holes and incisions employed by Fontana. He worked at this time mainly in ceramics, a medium he had taken up after the poor reception accorded to his first exhibition of abstract sculptures at the Galleria Il Milione,

Milan, in 1935. The decorativeness of his ceramic works, together with his move towards *Art informel*, led to the temporary eclipse of his reputation. At the end of the 1960s, however, with the advent of conceptual art, the more advanced critical circles were once again prepared to give proper appreciation to Melotti's light, almost disembodied creations, skilfully balanced between the physical and the metaphysical. By this time he was producing works made of cloth and wire mesh, whose patterns produced an illusion of vibration. Melotti's work began at this time to be re-evaluated and met with growing success on an international level.

WRITINGS
Lo spazio inquieto (Turin, 1971)

BIBLIOGRAPHY
M. Fagiolo: *Progetti di Melotti* (Turin, 1971)
A. M. Hammacher: *Melotti* (Milan, 1975)
Fausto Melotti (exh. cat. by M. Calvesi, U. Parma, Cent. Studi & Archv Communic., 1976)
Fausto Melotti: L'acrobata invisibile (exh. cat., Milan, Padiglione A. Contemp., 1987)

RENATO BARILLI

Melozzo da Forlì [Melozzo degli Ambrogi] (*b* Forlì, 8 June 1438; *d* Forlì, 8 Nov 1494). Italian painter. Melozzo occupied a transitional position between the early and High Renaissance. His contact with Piero della Francesca at the court of Urbino was fundamental to his stylistic development. He rose to prominence in Rome during the papacy of Sixtus IV (*reg* 1471–84) and later worked for the Pope's family. Many of his works have been lost or

1. Melozzo da Forlì: *Sixtus IV Founding the Vatican Library*, fresco transferred to canvas, 3.75×3.25 m, *c.* 1476–7 (Rome, Pinacoteca Vaticana)

damaged, but he enjoyed a long and illustrious career and was famed for his skill in the use of illusionistic perspective.

1. LIFE AND WORK. Melozzo was probably trained near Forlì in the Romagna, and it is likely that he was first active in his native town. The fresco known as the '*Pepper Pestle*' (*c.* 1460–65; Forlì, Pin. Civ.), formerly located over the entrance to an apothecary's shop, is traditionally attributed to him. It shows a man energetically pounding pepper. Piero della Francesca is regarded as the major influence on Melozzo during this period and may have introduced him to Rome as early as 1460. Presumably during that visit Melozzo executed two processional banners on canvas. The frontally viewed, enthroned *St Mark, Pope* and a three-quarter view of *St Mark, the Evangelist* (*c.* 1460; both Rome, S Marco) are obviously early works. Despite the constricted banner format, both figures are strongly modelled and seem to project into the viewer's space, evidence that Melozzo had begun to experiment with the foreshortening that later became his hallmark. An anonymous epigram of *c.* 1461 says that Melozzo made a replica (untraced) of the *Madonna of St Luke*, the icon in S Maria del Popolo, Rome, for Lord Alessandro Sforza of Pesaro. The painting is sometimes mistakenly identified as the *Madonna of St Luke* (*c.* 1469–70; Montefalco, Pin.-Mus. Com.).

From *c.* 1465 to *c.* 1475 Melozzo is believed to have been resident at Urbino, painting at the court of Federico da Montefeltro, Duke of Urbino. This period is undocumented, but Melozzo is praised for his skill in perspective by Giovanni Santi in a poem of 1488, and Luca Pacioli, a resident at the court, noted Melozzo's skill and that of his pupil Marco Palmezzano at measuring proportion. At Urbino, Melozzo could have strengthened his ties with Piero della Francesca. A series of paintings of the *Liberal Arts* (*c.* 1475; Berlin, Kaiser-Friedrich Mus., destr.; London, N.G.), a series of *Famous Men* (1476–7; Paris, Louvre; Urbino, Pal. Ducale) and a portrait of *Federico Montefeltro with his Son* (*c.* 1475; Urbino, Pal. Ducale) have in the past been associated with Melozzo, but current opinion favours as the artist the Fleming Justus of Ghent, who was also employed by the Duke, as was possibly the Spaniard Pedro Berruguete.

Melozzo probably returned to Rome *c.* 1475 and must have immediately entered the service of Pope Sixtus IV. His fresco of *Sixtus IV Founding the Vatican Library* (*c.* 1476–7; Rome, Pin. Vaticana; see fig. 1) was originally located on the north wall of the Vatican Library facing the entrance to the Biblioteca Latina. The scene depicts the Pope surrounded by four nephews: Raffaele Riario, Cardinal Giuliano della Rovere (later Julius II), Giovanni della Rovere and Girolamo Riario. The librarian Platina kneels and points to an inscription praising the Pope's urban renovations. The figures are arranged in the foreground of a deep architectural setting, with grand proportions and classicizing ornament, the space articulated by imposing marble piers and a coffered ceiling. The modelling of form, calculated juxtaposition of individuals, careful delineation of character and use of a low viewpoint recall Mantegna's group portrait of the Gonzaga family in the Camera degli Sposi (*c.* 1471–4; Mantua, Pal. Ducale) which must have been familiar to Melozzo. The artist also demonstrated his debt to Piero della Francesca by emphasizing the harmony between space and the human figure. Melozzo began the work after 15 July 1475 and had finished it by 15 January 1477. He received payments for further work (destr.) on the library with Antoniazzo Romano from June 1480 to April 1481.

In 1478 Melozzo signed the statutes of the Compagnia di S Luca, Rome, by designating himself painter of the pope. Around 1479–80 he was occupied with the decoration of the apse of SS Apostoli, Rome, commissioned by Cardinal Giuliano della Rovere (later Pope Julius II) for his titular church. Only fragments of the fresco of the *Ascension*, which originally occupied the vault, survive; they include *Christ Blessing* (Rome, Pal. Quirinale; see fig. 2) and musical angels (Rome, Pin. Vaticana). The authenticity of one angel (Madrid, Prado) has been questioned (Tumidei). Melozzo's expert handling of spatial effects made the fresco of SS Apostoli his most influential work. He represented numerous figures of apostles and angels in steeply foreshortened poses circling the figure of Christ, who was illumined by radiant seraphim and cherubim. The composition was dynamic, conveying the idea of revolving figures ascending towards heaven. Vasari praised its illusionism and provided a description of the work *in situ*.

The frescoes of the vault of the sacristy of the Treasury at the Santa Casa, Loreto, are undocumented. There is general agreement that Melozzo devised the decorative scheme (1477–8) but left its execution to assistants *c.* 1480–84, probably to his leading pupil, Marco Palmezzano, and possibly also to Giovanni Santi. The painted figures of prophets, angels and cherubs ring the interior of the octagonal dome, resting on, or floating before, a simulated architectural framework. The illusion of a heavenly chorus occupying real space demonstrates Melozzo's mastery of foreshortening. However, the stiffness of the figures and their uniformity of expression confirm the intervention of his assistants.

Although Melozzo seems to have been the preferred artist of Sixtus IV and his court, he worked in Rome only until 1481 and was not involved in the decoration of the most important project of the Pope's later years, the Sistine Chapel. Instead, he was engaged in projects in Loreto and Forlì at the behest of Cardinal Girolamo Basso della Rovere, Captain General of the Church and Lord of Forlì. Presumably, he secured Melozzo the title of Painter to the Pope and the patronage of Caterina Sforza of Forlì.

In his later life Melozzo increasingly relied on assistance from his pupils. It is unknown if he received any commissions in Rome during these years. By 1493 he had departed for the north where he painted in the Palazzo degli Anziani in Ancona. He left in May for Forlì and began work on the fresco decoration of the Feo Chapel, S Biagio (destr. 1944). The narrative scenes in the lunettes, representing miracles from the lives of saints, incorporated portraits of the donors, Giacomo Feo and Caterina Sforza. The vault was painted with prophets and cherubs against a background of illusionistic coffering. The somewhat weak execution of the powerful design is given to Palmezzano who completed the work after his master's death. The architecture of the oratory of S Sebastiano, Forlì, exhibits the classical forms and proportions found in

2. Melozzo da Forlì: *Christ Blessing* (1479–80), fresco, Palazzo del Quirinale, Rome

Melozzo's paintings. He probably designed it and left its execution to the local architect and textile artist Pace di Maso, called Bambase (*d* 1500).

2. WORKING METHODS AND TECHNIQUE. Melozzo's fresco technique conformed to established practice. Examination of the fragments from SS Apostoli has revealed that he used cartoons to transfer his designs. The portions relating to faces and hands were pounced and then dusted with charcoal while other lines were incised. Melozzo's acknowledged ability as a draughtsman has resulted in the attribution of several figural studies associated with large-scale projects, although the attributions are unproven (see Ruhmer, 1968). No large working drawings or cartoons have survived. Melozzo may also have worked in mosaic, directing the design of the Chapel of S Elena in Santa Croce in Gerusalemme, Rome *c.* 1489–92. Melozzo was aware of historical prototypes; he reinterpreted medieval images, and some paintings from his circle were modelled on icons. He also borrowed motifs from early Christian iconography: for the fresco in SS Apostoli, he placed a row of standing apostles at the base and the heavenly apparition in the curvature of the apse above in imitation of a scheme typical of early medieval chapels and basilicas. The seated prophets decorating the dome at Loreto hold plaques with biblical passages; the prominence of inscriptions in Melozzo's work recalls the practice of incorporating dedicatory texts in medieval church decoration. During his years in Rome, he presumably studied Antique works because ancient Roman reliefs, architecture and epigraphy

were essential to his development as an artist. It is tempting to see Melozzo as a learned artist, familiar with the theories of Leon Battista Alberti and conversant with the ideas of Piero della Francesca.

3. STUDIO AND INFLUENCE. Melozzo influenced artists of his native Romagna, Urbino and the local school of Rome. His principal pupil was Marco Palmezzano, who imitated the sculptural forms and dramatic devices developed by his master; he may also have worked as an architect. In Urbino, Giovanni Santi perpetuated the discoveries of Melozzo, perhaps transmitting a knowledge of perspective to his own son, Raphael. Antoniazzo Romano worked closely with Melozzo in Rome. Many works formerly attributed to Melozzo should be credited to Antoniazzo or his workshop: the frescoes in S Giovanni Evangelista, Tivoli (c. 1480), long associated with Melozzo on the basis of a dubious inscription, should be attributed to Antoniazzo. Melozzo's work also had an impact on painters of diverse regional schools such as Lorenzo da Viterbo (c. 1437–70) and Donato Bramante in Milan and Bergamo. There is an obvious relationship between Melozzo's perspective and proportion studies and his dynamic style and other branches of the arts, particularly architectural design, sculpture and decorative objects, including maiolica wares from Pesaro and Faenza. Melozzo's earliest biographer, Leone Cobelli of Forlì, refers to 'la sua brigada', most likely members of his studio who remained active after his death. They included Pace di Maso, Cristoforo Bezzi, an architect, and Bernardino Guiritti (d 1511) of Ravenna, an architect, sculptor and decorator. A document cited in the early 19th century refers to Melozzo as the architect of the Cathedral at Forlì. High Renaissance painters were influenced by Melozzo's apse decoration in particular; Raphael drew inspiration from the papal portrait of Sixtus IV and the apse of SS Apostoli. Later 16th-century painters, particularly in northern Italy, studied Melozzo's illusionistic cupola paintings which opened the way for Baroque effects.

4. CRITICAL RECEPTION AND POSTHUMOUS REPUTATION. Although Melozzo was praised by Giovanni Santi (1488) and Luca Pacioli (1492), Vasari omitted him from the first edition of the *Vite* (1550), but in the second edition he corrected the oversight by praising the frescoes in SS Apostoli. Sebastiano Serlio (*Trattato dell'architettura*, 1540) lauded Melozzo for his mastery of perspective and foreshortening. A resurgence of interest in Melozzo's career took place when the history of Forlì (the birthplace of Mussolini) attracted attention. A major exhibition of Melozzo's work was organized in 1938 on the occasion of the fifth centenary of his birth.

Thieme–Becker

BIBLIOGRAPHY

G. Santi: *La vita e le geste di Federico da Montefeltro duca d'Urbino* (MS., 1488); ed. L. Michelini Tocci, ii (Rome, 1985), pp. 674–5
L. Pacioli: *Summa de arithmetica geometria proportioni et proportionalità* (Venice, 1492), col. 2r
L. Cobelli: *Cronache forlivesi dalla fondazione della città sino all'anno 1498* (1498); ed. G. Carducci and E. Frati (Bologna, 1887), p. 533
G. Vasari: *Vite* (1550, rev. 2/1568); ed. G. Milanesi (1878–85), iii, pp. 51–2, 63–8; vi, p. 82
E. Muntz: *Les Arts à la cour des papes*, iii (Paris, 1882), pp. 95–134
A. Schmarsow: *Melozzo da Forlì: Ein Beitrag zur Kunst und Kulturgeschichte Italiens im 15. Jahrhundert* (Berlin, 1886)

O. Okkonen: *Melozzo da Forlì und seine Schule* (Helsinki, 1910)
A. Schmarsow: *Joos von Ghent und Melozzo da Forlì in Rom und Urbino* (Leipzig, 1912)
R. Buscaroli: *Melozzo da Forlì nei documenti, nelle testimonianze dei contemporanei e nella bibliografia* (Rome, 1938)
A. Pasini: 'Melozzo nei documenti di archivio', *Atti & Mem. Reale Deput. Stor. Patria Emilia & Romagna*, n.s. 5, iii (1938), pp. 121–36
Mostra di Melozzo e del quattrocento romagnolo (exh. cat. by C. Gnudi and L. Becherucci, Forlì, Pal. Mus., 1938)
R. Buscaroli: *Melozzo e il melozzismo* (Bologna, 1955)
E. Ruhmer: 'Melozzo als Zeichner', *Festschrift Ulrich Middeldorf*, i (Berlin, 1968), pp. 201–5
A. Schiavo: 'Melozzo a Roma', *Presenza Romagnola*, ii (1977), pp. 89–110
R. di Paolo: 'L'oratorio di San Sebastiano in Forlì e Pace di Maso, architetto', *Boll. A.*, n. s. 4, lxvii/15 (1982), pp. 1–26
B. Montuschi Simboli: 'Bernardino Guiritti, architetto e decoratore', *Faenza*, lxx/3–4 (1984), pp. 168–77
S. Tumidei: 'Un falso Melozzo: L'angelo musicante del Prado', *Prospettiva* [Florence], 53 (1988), pp. 64–7
N. Clark: *Melozzo da Forlì* (London, 1990)
J. Ruysschaert: 'La Fresque de Melozzo de l'ancienne Bibliothèque Vaticane: Réexamen', *Miscellanea bibliotecae apostolicae vaticanae*, iv (Rome, 1990), pp. 328–41

EUNICE D. HOWE

Mel'tser, Roman (Fyodorovich) [Meltzer, Robert Friedrich] (*b* 1860; *d* 1929). Russian architect. He worked as court architect for Alexander III (*reg* 1881–94) and Nicholas II (*reg* 1894–1917) and was known as an outstanding draughtsman. Among his first commissions in St Petersburg were designs for grilles for the gates of the Winter Palace (1885–8; with Nikolay Gornostayev). Later he created a notable example of Art Nouveau in the railings (1898–1901) for the private garden along the west side of the Winter Palace (later the 9 January Children's Park, Stachek Prospect). The flowing plant motifs harmonized well with Bartolomeo Francesco Rastrelli's Baroque façade. Mel'tser also worked on the interiors of imperial residences: the Winter Palace and the Aleksandrovsky Palace in Tsarskoye Selo (now Pushkin), as well as the library of the Polovtsev Mansion (1911–13; by Ivan Fomin) on Stone Island (Kamenny ostrov). Space in his interiors is organized on a human scale, and the wood he used for the furniture creates a sense of comfort.

In several early 20th-century buildings, Mel'tser created an inimitable kind of façade, with a fine graphic approach to the tiniest details on the walls, which were usually faced with white ceramic tiles, as at the V. S. Kochubey Mansion (1908–10) at Furshtadts Street 24 and the V. E. Brandt Mansion (1909) at Dvoryanskaya Street 4. Along with other architects, such as Aleksandr Gogen, he was inspired by the version of the urban mansion developed in St Petersburg by Viktor Shreter. On Stone Island, traditionally the site of country residences for the emperor, aristocracy and bourgeoisie, Mel'tser built his own house (1900) and the E. G. Follenveyder Mansion (1904). Both buildings are set into an existing architectural environment on small green plots, while Mel'tser's house is surrounded on three sides by water. The three-storey, rectangular building has steeply pitched roofs and façades that combine various materials, ashlar, brick and wood, enabling Mel'tser to make an organic link between house and environment. The powerful vertical of the timber beams, the line of the sloping roofs, the varied windows and the projecting entrance create an unusual effect. The Follenveyder Mansion is more restrained: it has two storeys, pitched roofs, a main entrance on the central axis and tall rounded windows. Mel'tser's experiments in the design of individual mansions culminated in the construction of a palace for Grand Duke Mikhail Aleksandrovich at English (Angliyskaya) Embankment 54. The decoration of the façade is simple, with a restrained colour scheme, using granite and white stone tiles. The composition is built along three axes: the two wings have oriel windows with balconies while the central block has a Venetian window.

Mel'tser's Orthopaedic Institute (1904) in the Aleksandrovsky Park at Tsarskoye Selo is an example of the artistic and constructional merits found in late 19th- and early 20th-century hospital buildings and provides a high level of comfort for patients. The Institute's church is decorated with a mosaic, *Mother of God* (1904), by Kuz'ma Petrov-Vodkin, who was 'discovered' by Mel'tser in Khvalynsk. Mel'tser demonstrated a historicist approach in using Louis XVI motifs to decorate the façade of the residence (1913) at Moyka Embankment 58, which fits in well with the surrounding aristocratic palaces.

BIBLIOGRAPHY

W. C. Bromfield: *The Origins of Modernism in Russian Architecture* (Berkeley, 1991), pp. 206–10

SERGEY KUZNETSOV

Meltwitz [Melthewitz; von Torgau], **Hans** (*fl* 1481; *d* Torgau, between 18 Nov 1520 and 7 Jan 1521). German architect. He worked as a journeyman under Arnold von Westfalen on Albrechtsburg castle at Meissen, and in 1481 he appears in the Meissen Türkensteuerregister (register of tax payments to fund defences against the Turks). He seems, however, to have been resident at Torgau all his life and took part in important building works there: the castle (1484), the parish church of St Mary (choir vault *c.* 1485; addition to sacristy *c.* 1510) and the Franciscan church (remodelling of chancel *c.* 1495; new hall nave before 1517). Outside Torgau, Meltwitz worked mainly for the electors of Saxony. In 1493/4 he was involved with building the residence at Wittenberg, to which he was summoned in 1504, 1508 and 1514. From 1504 to 1507 he did extensive work at the hunting castle of Frederick the Wise at Lochau (destr. 1572). In 1515 he was Master of the Works of the Vorschloss at Wittenberg (destr.), and in 1516 he was in charge of building the second church of St Wolfgang at Schneeberg (burnt 1945; rest.). He became one of the leading Saxon masters of works and took a leading part in the masons' congress at Annaberg in 1518. In 1519, with Benedikt Ried and Hans Schickendantz (*fl* 1493–1528), he was an assessor for the continuation of work on St Anne's, Annaberg. In 1520 he was in charge of a fundamental renovation of the Schlosskirche at Weimar (destr. 1618).

Meltwitz's forms are similar to Arnold's style at Meissen, but he aimed at greater simplification and regularization. The high point of this development is St Wolfgang's, Schneeberg. Its more standardized forms and severe vaulting patterns make it the opposite of Annaberg, the other major Late Gothic work in Upper Saxony.

UNPUBLISHED SOURCES

Dresden, Staatsarchv, and Weimar, Staatsarchv [doc.]

BIBLIOGRAPHY

Thieme–Becker

R. Mielsch: 'Der Baumeister von St Wolfgang in Schneeberg', *Wiss. Beil. Dresdner Anz.*, v (1928), p. 104

S. Harksen: *Hallenkirchen in Torgau* (diss., U. Halle-Wittenberg, 1958)

——: 'Schloss und Schlosskirche in Wittenberg', *450 Jahre Reformation*, ed. L. Stern and M. Steinmetz (Berlin, 1967), pp. 341–65

K. Kratzsch: *Bergstädte des Erzgebirges, Städtebau und Kunst zur Zeit der Reformation*, Münchner kunsthistorische Abhandlungen, iv (Munich, 1972)

P. Findeisen and H. Magirius: *Die Denkmale der Stadt Torgau* (Leipzig, 1976)

N. Nussbaum: *Deutsche Kirchenbaukunst der Gotik: Entwicklung und Bauformen* (Cologne, 1985)

HANS-JOACHIM KRAUSE

Meluel, Jean. *See* MALOUEL, JEAN.

Melville, Arthur (*b* Loanhead of Guthrie, Angus, Tayside, 10 April 1858; *d* Redlands, nr Witley, Surrey, 28 Aug 1904). Scottish painter. He was trained in Edinburgh under James Campbell Noble (1846–1913) and at the Royal Scottish Academy Schools. His early works are peasant subjects in a subdued tonal style. While at the Académie Julian in Paris and at Grez-sur-Loing (1878–81) he developed a colouristic watercolour style with strong chiaroscuro. This was consolidated during his journey in 1881 to Egypt and Constantinople, and on trips between 1890 and 1893 to Spain (with Frank Brangwyn) and North Africa. Contrasts of strong sunlight and coloured shadows were created in his 'blottesque' technique of colour droplets on paper saturated with Chinese white: sponge and brushwork were used to clarify form, as in *Little Bullfight: 'Bravo Toro'* (*c.* 1888–9; London, V&A). He was associated with the Glasgow Boys and influenced their development of colour and design. His closest contact with them came during outdoor sketching trips in Scotland between 1882 and 1889, and in Paris in 1886 and 1889. In 1886 he became an Associate of the Royal Scottish Academy and developed a strongly decorative oil style, seen in *Audrey and her Goats* (1884–9; London, Tate). In 1889 he moved to London, and his subsequent work includes a Whistlerian phase, exemplified by *White Piano* (1897; Preston, Harris Mus. & A.G.) and the Venice 'nocturnes'. His series of watercolours depicting scenes at Spanish bullfights, such as *Bullring Crowd* (Kirkcaldy, Fife, Mus. & A.G.), shows his developing interest in crowd movement and spatial contrast. Watercolour remained his principal medium, and he was elected to the Royal Scottish Water Colour Society in 1900.

BIBLIOGRAPHY

A. E. Mackay: *Arthur Melville, Scottish Impressionist (1854–1904)* (Leigh-on-Sea, 1951)

W. Hardie: *Scottish Painting, 1837 to the Present*, 3 vols (London, 1976–90)

Arthur Melville (1855–1904) (exh. cat. by G. Deslandes, Dundee, Cent. Mus. & A.G., 1977)

J. Halsby: *Scottish Watercolours, 1740–1940* (Braintree, 1986)

For further bibliography *see* GLASGOW BOYS.

CLARE A. P. WILLSDON

Melvin, James. *See under* GOLLINS, MELVIN, WARD.

Melzi, Francesco (*b* Milan, 1491–3; *d* Vaprio d'Adda, *c.* 1570). Italian painter and draughtsman. Belonging to a noble Lombard family, he began to attend the workshop of Leonardo da Vinci around 1508, during Leonardo's second visit to Milan. From that time on he was always associated with Leonardo, whose favourite pupil he became: he followed Leonardo to Rome in 1513 and moved with him to France in 1515, staying with him until his death in 1519. In his will Leonardo entrusted Melzi with all the works he had with him at Cloux—mainly drawings and manuscripts—which Melzi brought back to Italy in 1520 and guarded jealously in his villa at Vaprio, where Leonardo had stayed as a guest in 1512. Vasari visited Melzi at Vaprio during his tour of Lombardy in 1566 and described him as 'a beautiful and kind old man'. Melzi played a crucial role in conserving Leonardo's manuscripts and in ensuring that his theories on painting survived as the *Trattato della pittura*, which Melzi took great pains to organize, using Leonardo's notes as a basis.

Melzi's career as a painter is problematic, given that it is based on only two works, chronologically far apart, and on the unverifiable statement of Lomazzo and Morigia that Melzi was an expert illuminator. The first work is a signed and dated drawing of a *Head of an Old Man* (1510; Milan, Bib. Ambrosiana) obviously inspired by Leonardo. On the drawing Melzi gave his age as 17 on one line and 19 on another; his approximate birthdate is based on this inscription. The second work is a painted panel of a *Youth with a Parrot* (Milan, Gallarati Scotti priv. col.) inscribed OPUSF/MELTIUS/1525, which scholars, with the exception of Salmi, have accepted as being autograph. The picture is, however, devoid of Leonardesque traits, which suggests a later date of execution; Marani has proposed this to be 1555.

Other paintings attributed to Melzi include the *Vertumnus and Pomona* (Berlin, Bodemus.), for which a preparatory drawing of Pomona's foot exists (Milan, Bib. Ambrosiana, fol. Resta; inscribed with autograph writing by Leonardo), the *Holy Family* (Prague, N.G., Šternberk Pal.) and the *Flora* or *Colombina* (untraced; copy, St Petersburg, Hermitage); doubts have been expressed about the *Leda and the Swan* (Rome, Gal. Borghese), previously attributed to Melzi. The list of attributed paintings is still largely that of Suida. However, Pedretti has recognized Melzi's hand on many of Leonardo's autograph drawings, reinforcing outlines and annotating the studies; he has also attributed some copies of lost drawings by Leonardo to Melzi.

BIBLIOGRAPHY

Thieme-Becker

G. Vasari: *Vite* (1550, rev. 2/1568); ed. G. Milanesi (1878–85), iv, p. 39
G. P. Lomazzo: *Trattato dell'arte della pittura* (Milan, 1584); also in *Scritti sulle arti*, ed. R. P. Ciardi, ii (Florence, 1974), p. 96
P. Morigia: *La nobiltà di Milano*, with suppl. by G. Borsieri (Milan, 1619), p. 469
I. Lermolieff [G. Morelli]: *Kunstkritische Studien über italienische Malerei: Die Galerie zu Berlin* (Leipzig, 1893), pp. 141–5
A. Venturi: *Storia* (1901–40), VII/iv, pp. 1061–3
C. J. Ffoulkes: 'Una mezza figura di donna di scuola leonardesca in una collezione privata a Londra', *Ant. Viva*, x (1910), pp. 27–9
E. Möller: 'Leonardo da Vincis *Brustbild eines Engels* und seine Kompositionen des St Johannes-Baptista', *Mhft. Kstwiss.*, iv (1911), pp. 541–5
P. Parente: 'Una vivace polemica su Francesco Melzi e Francesco Neapolitano discepoli del divino Leonardo', *A. & Stor.*, xxxvii (1918), pp. 195–200, 213–19
M. Salmi: 'Una mostra di antica pittura lombarda', *Arte*, xxvi (1923), p. 158
P. D'Ancona: 'Antichi pittori lombardi', *Dedalo*, iv (1923–4), pp. 375–6
W. Suida: *Leonardo und sein Kreis* (Munich, 1929)
A. De Hevesy: 'Un compagno di Leonardo: Francesco Melzi', *Emporium*, cxvi (1952), pp. 243–54
Leonardo da Vinci on Painting: A Lost Book (Libro A), ed. C. Pedretti (Berkeley and Los Angeles, 1964)
K. Clark: 'Francesco Melzi as Preserver of Leonardo da Vinci's Drawings', *Studies in Renaissance and Baroque Art Presented to Anthony Blunt on his 60th Birthday* (London, 1967), pp. 24–5
C. Pedretti: *Leonardo e la lettura del territorio* (1981), i of *Lombardia: Il territorio, l'ambiente, il paesaggio*, ed. C. Pirovano (Milan, 1981–5), pp. 250–51
Leonardo da Vinci: Nature Studies from the Royal Library, Windsor Castle (exh. cat., intro. K. Clark; ed. C. Pedretti; London, RA, 1981; It. trans., Florence, 1982), pp. 7, 9, 11, 40, 45
M. T. Fiorio: *Leonardeschi in Lombardia* (Milan, 1982), pp. 34–6
C. Pedretti: *Landscapes, Plants and Water Studies* (1982), i of *Leonardo da Vinci: Drawings and Miscellaneous Papers at Windsor Castle* (London, 1982–)
Leonardo all'Ambrosiana (exh. cat., ed. A. Marinoni and L. Cogliati Arano, Milan, Ambrosiana, 1982), pp. 136, 155–6
C. Pedretti, ed.: *Leonardo: Studi per il 'Cenacolo' dalla Biblioteca Reale nel Castello di Windsor* (Milan, 1983), pp. 110, 128
Leonardo e il leonardismo a Napoli e a Roma (exh. cat., Naples, Capodimonte; Rome, Pal. Venezia; 1983), pp. 97, 103
Renaissance Drawings from the Ambrosiana (exh. cat., ed. R. Coleman; Washington, DC, N.G.A., and elsewhere; 1984), pp. 58–9
P. C. Marani: 'A New Date for Francesco Melzi's *Young Man with a Parrot*', *Burl. Mag.*, cxxxi (1989), pp. 479–81

MARIA TERESA FIORIO

Memento mori [Lat.: 'Remember that you must die']. Any VANITAS symbol, such as a skull, candle or hourglass, or even an insect, employed to remind the viewer of the transitoriness of human existence.

☐

Memi, Kara. *See* KARA MEMI.

Memling [Memlinc], **Hans** (*b* Seligenstadt, 1430–40; *d* Bruges, 11 Aug 1494). South Netherlandish painter of German origin. Together with Dieric Bouts I and Hugo van der Goes, he was one of the most important exponents of the new artistic developments that flourished in the southern Netherlands in the 15th century in the wake of Jan van Eyck, the Master of Flémalle and Rogier van der Weyden. Their principal innovation was to apply optic realism to devotional or mystical subjects. Although Memling lived in the turbulent period of transition from the Burgundian ruling house to that of the Habsburgs, little of this is evident in his work. His commissions were almost exclusively from rich burghers in Bruges (bankers, merchants and politicians) or churchmen and the occasional aristocrat. Often they were foreigners, especially Italians, who had political or financial connections with the town, whose central economic position was to last only a few decades longer. They had Memling paint their portraits, bust or full length, in devotional paintings or on altarpieces for their chapel in Bruges or back home. He seems not to have received official commissions (from the town council or court). An exceptional proportion of this oeuvre has survived. Besides about 20 altarpieces, often in several panels and of considerable size, there are about 15 individual paintings of the *Virgin and Child*, for which the side panels with figures or donor portraits are missing, another 20 paintings depicting saints or various themes from the Gospels and more than 30 portraits (some in the form of a diptych with a *Virgin and Child*).

1. Life and work. 2. Style and technique. 3. Critical reception and posthumous reputation.

1. LIFE AND WORK.

(i) Training and early works, to 1475. (ii) The productive years, 1475–80. (iii) Late years, after 1480.

(i) Training and early works, to 1475. The earliest record of Hans Memling is his registration on 30 January 1465 as a citizen of Bruges, under the name of Jan van Mimnelinghe. His parents, Hammann Momilingen and Luca Styrn, are mentioned repeatedly in the archives of Seligenstadt (a small town on the Main, near Aschaffenburg), and his ancestors may have come from the village of Mömlingen, near Obenburg am Main. His German origin is confirmed by Romboudt de Doppere, a beneficiary of the cathedral of St Donation, Bruges, and apostolic registrar, who names him in his diary (1491–8) as coming from the Mainz area.

The close similarity between Memling's style and that of Rogier van der Weyden suggests that he probably completed his training in the latter's studio in Brussels, where he may have worked for a while as a journeyman. Memling arrived in Bruges shortly after van der Weyden's death (18 June 1464). Vasari (1550) also described Memling as a pupil of van der Weyden. A triptych with a *Pietà* in the collection of Margaret of Austria was described in an inventory of 1516 as having a central panel by 'Rogier' and side panels by 'Master Hans', which supports the theory that the two artists worked together.

Memling was not registered in the painters' guild in Bruges and held no public office there, which might indicate that he held a protected and privileged position in the town. Nevertheless there is nothing to suggest that he held a position at court, which would have freed him from obligations to the guild. In 1466 he was living in a large stone house in the Sint-Jorisstraat, a property he later owned. It must have been immediately following his arrival in Bruges that the Florentine Angelo Tani, chief agent of the Medici bank in Bruges between 1455 and 1465, commissioned him to paint the large triptych with the *Last Judgement* (Gdańsk, N. Mus.; see fig. 1). If the incomplete date on a tombstone on the central panel is read as 1467, this is the earliest painting attributable to Memling; it is also the most impressive. Angelo Tani and Catarina Tanagli, whom he married in 1466, are depicted on the outside of the side panels. The altarpiece was shipped abroad in 1473, but captured by Hanseatic pirates who took it to the church of St Mary in Gdańsk. The ship was owned by TOMMASO PORTINARI, successor to Angelo Tani as the Medici banker in Bruges and an adviser to Charles the Bold. It was presumably to mark Portinari's marriage in 1470 to Maria Maddalena Baroncelli that Memling painted the miniature-like *Panorama with Scenes from the Passion* (Turin, Gal. Sabauda), in which the couple are depicted as onlookers. This was installed in the Portinari Chapel in the hospital of S Maria Nuova in Florence. About the same time Memling also painted their portraits (New York, Met.). In 1472 he painted the portrait

1. Hans Memling: triptych with the *Last Judgement*, oil on panel, central panel 2.22×1.60 m, each wing 2.22×0.72 m, ?1467 (Gdańsk, National Museum)

of *Gilles Joye* (Williamstown, MA, Clark A. Inst.), a well-known musician who served Philip the Good and also canon of St Donatian, Bruges. The *Virgin and Child with Donor and St Anthony* (Ottawa, N.G.) dates from the same year. In 1473–4 Memling was admitted to the Confraternity of Our Lady in the Snow, based at the church of Onze Lieve Vrouw in Bruges. The brethren were all members of the aristocracy, the wealthy middle classes and the church. Among his fellow members were Lodewijk de Valkenaere, who was later made guardian of his children, and Willem Moreel, from whom he was to receive important commissions.

(ii) The productive years, 1475–80. With the exception of a *Pietà* (*Man of Sorrows in the Arms of the Virgin*) from 1475 (Melbourne, N.G. Victoria; see fig. 2), there is no dated work before the productive years 1479–80. However, in 1478 Memling was commissioned to paint the portraits of the Bruges illuminator Willem Vrelant and his wife on the side panels of an altarpiece for the chapel of the guild of book illuminators in Eekhout Abbey (installed 1480; untraced). It is not known what was depicted on the central panel (authors claim, wrongly, that it was a *Passion*). In 1479 Memling completed two triptychs intended for the hospital of St Jan in Bruges. That with the *Adoration of the Magi* (Bruges, Memlingmus.) was commissioned by Jan Floreins, who became a brother at the hospital in 1472 and was master of the congregation from 1488 to 1497.

2. Hans Memling: *Pietà* (*Man of Sorrows in the Arms of the Virgin*), oil on panel, 274×199 mm, 1475 (Melbourne, National Gallery of Victoria)

He was 36 years old at the time his portrait was painted on the central panel. The original frame bears the artist's name and the date, thus making it the only genuinely authenticated work by Memling. The composition is a reduced version of a large triptych (Madrid, Prado), presumably painted in the period in which Memling was strongly influenced by Rogier van der Weyden (e.g. the latter's Columba Triptych, Munich, Alte Pin.; *see* WEYDEN, VAN DER, (1), fig. 3). Perhaps the most famous work by Memling is the triptych of *St John the Baptist and St John the Evangelist* also known as the *Mystic Marriage of St Catherine* (Bruges, Memlingmus.); it was also completed in 1479, according to the original inscription formerly on the frame. The largest triptych he apparently ever painted, it was intended for the high altar of the hospital's church and was paid for jointly by two brethren and two sisters of the hospital: Jacob de Ceuninc, Antheunis Seghers, Agnes Casembrood and Clara van Hulsen, each of whom is painted with his or her patron saint on the outer wings. The commission must have been given before 1475, the year Seghers died. The central panel depicts the *Virgin and Child Enthroned* flanked by the two St Johns, patron saints of the hospital, and SS Catherine and Barbara. Represented on the left panel is the *Beheading of St John the Baptist*, while the right wing shows *St John the Evangelist on the Island of Patmos* and his vision of the apocalypse.

Close in style and composition to the St John Altarpiece is the *Virgin and Child with Saints and Donors* (the *John Donne* triptych; *c.* 1479–80; London, N.G.; see fig. 3), painted for Sir John Donne of Kidwelly (*c.* 1430–1503) and his wife Elisabeth Hastings. The donor was a knight in the service of Richard, Duke of York and was in northern France, Bruges and elsewhere in Flanders on several occasions between 1470 and 1483 as a lieutenant of Edward IV. In 1480 Memling painted a small triptych showing the *Lamentation* (Bruges, Memlingmus.) for Adriaan Reins, another brother at the hospital of St Jan. His *Portrait of a Young Woman* (Bruges, Memlingmus.) dates from the same year, as does the *Panorama with Scenes from the Life of the Virgin* (Munich, Alte Pin.). The latter was intended for the altar of the chapel of the tanners' guild in the church of Onze Lieve Vrouw, Bruges, and was donated by Pieter Bultinc and Katelijne van Ryebeke, according to an inscription on the old frame that was still in place at the end of the 18th century. In this period (1480–81) Memling was one of the 247 citizens of Bruges who were repaid the money they had lent to support Maximilian of Austria in the war against Louis IX of France. He was not among the richest group but was one of the 107 wealthy citizens who each lent 20 'large schillings'. On 8 May 1480 a certain Annekin Verhanneman was registered at the painters' guild as his apprentice.

(iii) Late years, after 1480. In 1482 Memling painted a large *Annunciation* (New York, Met.), the only Annunciation in his oeuvre that was not conceived as a grisaille on exterior wings. Apparently the date used to be on the frame. In 1483 or 1484, the year in which Gerard David became a member of the painters' guild, Memling took on another apprentice, called Passcier van der Mersch (*see* MASTERS, ANONYMOUS, AND MONOGRAMMISTS, §I: MASTER OF HOOGSTRATEN). No work is known by either

3. Hans Memling: *Virgin and Child with Saints and Donors* (the *John Donne* triptych), oil on panel, central panel 708×705 mm, each wing 711×305 mm, *c.* 1479–80 (London, National Gallery)

pupil. In 1484 Memling completed the Moreel Triptych (w. 3.5 m; Bruges, Groeningemus.), for the altar dedicated to SS Maurus and Egidius built that year in the church of St Jacob at Bruges by Willem Moreel, an important politician in the town, and his wife Barbara van Vlaenderbergh, alias van Hertsvelde. The date was inscribed at the bottom on the original frame. The central figure is St Christopher, who seems to have no relevance to the chapel foundation, but he is flanked by the two patron saints. On the side panels are the kneeling donors, protected by the saints after whom they were named and surrounded by their children. Separate bust-length portraits of both donors have also survived (Brussels, Mus. A. Anc.), apparently the wing panels to a lost triptych. Judging from their younger features, these portraits date from before the Moreel Triptych.

In 1487 Memling's wife Tanne (Anna) died. As was customary, his children, Hannekin (Jan), Neelkin (Cornelis) and Claykin (Nicolaas), who were all minors, received half of his possessions in trust, which consisted principally of his houses and land on the Sint-Jorisstraat and the Jan Miraelstraat. Two similar devotional portraits painted that year have been preserved: the diptych of *Maarten van Nieuwenhove* (Bruges, Memlingmus.; see fig. 4), depicting the future mayor of Bruges at the age of 23, worshipping the *Virgin and Child*, and the so-called triptych of *Benedetto Portinari* (central panel, Berlin, Gemäldegal.; side panels, Florence, Uffizi). This scene of contemplation in the diptych is set in a civic room with Gothic architecture, which is not the case with the triptych, where it takes place in an open gallery. Portinari's name saint, *St Benedict*, is depicted on the left-hand panel. The side panels certainly came from the hospital of S Maria Nuova, Florence, founded by the Portinari family, but the

identification of the sitter as Benedetto, a cousin of Tommaso Portinari, cannot be proved.

Memling's most popular work, the shrine of *St Ursula* (Bruges, Memlingmus.) was completed at the latest by 21 October 1489 (the feast day of St Ursula), when the saint's relics, which were kept in the hospital of St Jan, were placed in the new shrine by Bishop Gillis de Bardemakere. Among the brothers present were Jan Floreins and Jacob de Ceuninc, respectively master and bursar, both of whom are known from earlier paintings by Memling, and sister Jossine van Dudzeele, at that time mistress of the community and presumably one of the two sisters portrayed as donors. The shrine is conceived as a Gothic chapel in gilded wood, decorated with tracery and carved ornament. Six arcades on the sides are painted with scenes from the *Life of St Ursula* as though they were stained-glass windows. On the narrow gable ends are depicted *St Ursula Protecting her 11,000 Virgin Attendants* and the *Virgin and Child Worshipped by Two Sisters*. The roof is decorated in Memling's style by another hand, with medallions containing saints and angels playing musical instruments. The minute attention paid to the buildings in the scenes, which take place in Cologne, indicates Memling's familiarity with the German town.

Towards the end of Memling's life the recognition he gained as a master resulted in an important German commission, the last recorded. The triptych with the *Passion* (1491; Lübeck, St Annen-Mus.) was painted for Heinrich Greverade or his brother Adolf (or both) for their chapel in the cathedral at Lübeck, although, due to unforeseen circumstances, the chapel was not furnished until 1504. Heinrich was a merchant and represented the Hanseatic interests in the Oosterlingenhuis in Bruges. His brother was canon of Lübeck Cathedral after 1494. One of Memling's most extensive works, it is a triptych with

4. Hans Memling: diptych with the *Virgin and Child* and *Maarten van Nieuwenhove*, oil on panel, each panel 440×330 mm, 1487 (Bruges, Memlingmuseum)

double outer wings. When fully open, the central panel shows the *Crucifixion* with the *Road to Calvary* and a donor portrait (presumably of Adolf), between wings with the *Resurrection* and the *Entombment*. When the first pair of wings is closed, panels with the four saints to whom the altar was dedicated occupy the entire breadth of the triptych. Only after closing the outer wings is the real exterior visible, with the *Annunciation* in grisaille. This type of altarpiece, uncommon in the Low Countries, was presumably inspired by German examples, particularly ones in Lübeck. Around 1492 Memling finished a commission from Spain for a monumental altarpiece with nine fixed panels in three storeys for the church of the abbey at Nájera. The central panel (untraced) depicted the *Assumption of the Virgin*; only the upper tier with *Christ and Music-making Angels* (Antwerp, Kon. Mus. S. Kst.) has survived. It was presumably completed with the help of an assistant.

Memling was buried in the churchyard of St Gillis, Bruges, and around four months later, on 10 December 1495, his estate was registered for his children, who were still under the age of 25. Attempts have been made to identify Memling's self-portrait among figures in the backgrounds of his pictures, especially in the central panel of the St John Altarpiece, in the *Donne* triptych and, more recently (Evers, 1972), in the *Passion* triptych in Lübeck (in the company of the German painters Wolgemut and the young Dürer). In 1521 the Italian historian Marcantonio Michiel saw a *Self-portrait* of Memling, which he described as 'puffy and red', in the house of Cardinal Grimani in Venice (untraced).

2. STYLE AND TECHNIQUE. Memling's style is static and spacious, his aesthetics idealizing and rational, his message narrative. The analytic realism peculiar to Netherlandish painting is certainly present, even to a smooth perfection, but it gives the impression of having been applied, not to reality, but rather to an artificial world of forms modelled and coloured in unvarying light and set in a definitive arrangement. His paintings are open constructions, with a clearly articulated space in which the figures are placed like sculptures or figurines. The landscape and architectural elements serve only as theatrical props. Compositions are based on a carefully considered symmetry, preferably constructed from verticals, and the different elements of the subject-matter, or episodes in the narrative, are united within a continuous setting, usually a landscape. The story is presented as a series of 'tableaux vivants', which, as in theatre, take place in different locations or in separate buildings or interiors. These are ordered according to their respective chronological and symbolic context in space and composition to form a total visual spectacle.

The colouring is bright, almost Mediterranean, and promotes the effect of space. Objects appear coloured, rather than possessing their own natural hue, thus creating a sort of artificial and evenly spread balance of colour that encompasses the entire surface of the painting and makes it glow. In Memling's work colour replaces the archaic use of gold and silver. The human figures, which dominate his work, are of a standard type: they are tall, with empty, emotionless expressions, and are placed like living columns that support the composition. Their faces are oval, with long, narrow noses and high foreheads, softly modelled, as though chiselled in marble. The individuality of the sitters in portraits is based only on the precise description of physiognomy and not on character or expression. Neither do they convey any impression of real age. By approaching the face as a sculpture, Memling created an idealized fusion between the observed portraits of Jan van Eyck and the stylized portraits of Rogier van der Weyden.

Another characteristic aspect of Memling's style is the prominent position allotted to such decorative features as heraldic shields or emblematic devices associated with the name of the donor or the subject of the portrait. All these elements are ingeniously integrated into the work, either on the reverse side of the portrait, or on the side panel, sumptuously and realistically elaborated with the knowledge and skill of a specialist decorative artist. The dates too are often worked into the scene in the manner of van Eyck, as if in relief or chiselled in stone. Much of Memling's work is dated (see above).

There is little sign of stylistic evolution in his oeuvre. The only difference between the earliest dated works, the *Last Judgement* (?1467) and the *Panorama with Scenes from the Passion* (*c.* 1470), and his last, the Greverade Triptych (1491) is the initially pronounced influence of van der Weyden, recognizable in the sharp, characterful depiction of faces and hands, and in a certain angularity and asceticism in the figures. This more archaic style can be found in a number of other works, including the triptych with the *Crucifixion* (interior wings, New York, Pierpont Morgan Lib.; outer wings, Bruges, Groeningemus.; central panel, Vicenza, Mus. Civ.), and the *Martyrdom of St Sebastian* (Brussels, Mus. A. Anc.). The fact that Memling translated van der Weyden's language of form into something more graceful and paradisal is sometimes—perhaps rightly—attributed to his German origins and to his early training in the Rhine area. Stefan Lochner's delightful figure style and some of his compositions are similar to Memling's work: Lochner's *Last Judgement* (Cologne, Wallraf-Richartz Mus.) certainly seems to have been a source of inspiration for Memling's own version of the subject. In his later works too there is evidence of German influence. The theatrical representation of Calvary with many figures, as in the Greverade Triptych, was unknown in the Netherlands at that time, but had been common in Westphalia for quite some time.

The notably classical character of his work, on the other hand, presupposes a knowledge of Italian models. In his later works this is particularly evident in his use of Renaissance ornament, such as garlands of fruit and putti (e.g. the *Virgin and Child Enthroned*, New York, Met.). Memling is the first known south Netherlandish artist to set a portrait against a landscape background. This type of portrait appears in his dated work only after 1480, but may have developed earlier. It was probably inspired by such Italian painters as Piero della Francesca and Filippo Lippi, although from about this time, especially in Florence, Memling's portraits and Virgins were eagerly imitated, often because of their landscape backgrounds.

Memling's painting technique did not differ in essence from that customary in the southern Netherlands in the 15th century, but it was simplified in his work. He used considerably fewer layers of paint than van Eyck. Detailing and modelling were often completed in one application of paint, using small brushstrokes. Moreover, light and shade are no longer always optically fused in the layer of pigment, but are applied as fine strokes of lead-white and neutral dark tones on top of the surface of the paint. The particularly thin paint layer, especially in areas of flesh-tones and madder-lake, has, over the course of time, caused the preliminary underdrawing to show through. These underdrawings, compared to those of other contemporary painters, are peculiarly muddled and sketchy, with many repetitions and alterations. This is no doubt the result of Memling's predilection for composing his compositions directly on to the panel rather than planning them first on paper. The entire creative process is therefore visible under infra-red light. In the case of the portrait of *Maarten van Nieuwenhove* (Bruges, Memlingmus.), there is a precise perspective construction, which is the earliest known example of this in a Netherlandish preparatory drawing.

3. CRITICAL RECEPTION AND POSTHUMOUS REPUTATION. Memling was singled out by the Romantics during the Gothic Revival at the beginning of the 19th century as being the symbol of mystic Christian medieval art. This sentimental approach led, during the first decades of the 20th century, when aesthetics promoted the virtues of abstraction and expression, to a partial revilement of his work in art criticism. It has since become increasingly apparent that Memling created his own ideal representational world, which gave form for the last time to the religious lamentations of prosperous and rational citizens on the eve of the age of humanism. Memling was the artist who introduced to Bruges the tall, stylized designs of Rogier van der Weyden, thus initiating the style that subsequently became typical of the city. Among the many anonymous masters who developed this style, which continued until the beginning of the 16th century, are the Master of 1473, the Master of the Legend of St Ursula, the Master of the Legend of St Lucy and the Master of the Baroncelli Portraits (for all of whom *see* MASTERS, ANONYMOUS, AND MONOGRAMMISTS). Gerard David, who knew Memling for ten years in Bruges, adapted his strongly north Netherlandish style under the latter's influence. The young Michel Sittow, who lived in Bruges between *c.* 1484 and 1491, and Juan de Flandes, both of whom later emigrated to Spain, were also strongly affected by him.

See also STILL-LIFE, fig. 2.

BIBLIOGRAPHY

EARLY SOURCES

G. Vasari: *Vite* (1550, rev. 2/1568); ed. G. Milanesi (1878–85), i, pp. 184–5; ii, p. 566; vii, p. 580

W. H. J. Weale: 'Documents authentiques concernant la vie, la famille et position sociale de Jean Memlinc, découverts à Bruges', *J. B.-A. & Litt.*, iii (1861), pp. 20–28, 34–6, 45–9, 53–5

——: 'Documents inédits sur les enlumineurs de Bruges', *Beffroi*, iv (1872–3), pp. 299, 301, 303–4, 321, 336

H. Dussart: *Fragments inédits de Romboudt de Doppere, découverts dans un manuscrit de Jacques de Meyere, chronique brugeoise de 1491–1498* (Bruges, 1892)

C. Vanden Haute: *La Corporation des peintres de Bruges* (Bruges [1913]), pp. 28, 35, 198

R. A. Parmentier: *Indices op de Brugsche poorterboeken*, ii (Bruges, 1938), pp. 630–31

A. Schouteet: 'Nieuwe teksten betreffende Hans Memling' [New texts concerning Hans Memling], *Belg. Tijdschr. Oudhdknd. & Kstgesch.*, xxiv (1955), pp. 81–4

H. W. Strasser: 'Hans Memling te Seligenstadt', *Hand. Genoot. Gesch. 'Soc. Emul.' Brugge*, xcviii (1961), pp. 97–100

M. G[oetinck] and M. R[yckaert]: 'Hans Memling: Brugse archivalia betreffende Hans Memling', *Sint-Janshospitaal, 1188–1976* (exh. cat., Bruges, Memlingmus., 1976), pp. 495–501

GENERAL WORKS

M. J. Friedländer: *Die altniederländische Malerei* (Berlin, 1924–37), vi, pp. 9–56; Eng. trans. as *Early Netherlandish Painting* (Leiden, 1967–76), vi

C. Aru and E. de Geradon: *La Galerie Sabauda de Turin* (1952), ii of *Les Primitifs flamands, I: Corpus* (Antwerp, 1951–), pp. 14–20

A. Janssens de Bisthoven: *Musée communal des Beaux-arts (Musée Groeninge) Bruges* (1951, rev. 2/1959), i of *Les Primitifs flamands, I: Corpus* (Antwerp, 1951–), pp. 90–107

E. Panofsky: *Early Netherlandish Painting* (Cambridge, MA, 1953), pp. 347–50

M. Davies: *The National Gallery London* (1954), iii of *Les Primitifs flamands, I: Corpus* (Antwerp, 1951–), pp. 157–72

H.-W. von Löhneysen: *Die ältere niederländische Malerei: Künstler und Kritiker* (Eisenach, 1956), pp. 336–60

C. T. Eisler: *New England Museums* (1961), iv of *Les Primitifs flamands, I: Corpus* (Antwerp, 1951–), pp. 62–70

R. Van Schoute: *La Chapelle royale de Grenade* (1963), vi of *Les Primitifs flamands, I: Corpus* (Antwerp, 1951–), pp. 58–86

J. Białostocki: *Les Musées de Pologne* (1966), ix of *Les Primitifs flamands, I: Corpus* (Antwerp, 1951–), pp. 55–123

M. Sonkes: 'Le Dessin sous-jacent chez les primitifs flamands', *Bull. Inst. Royal Patrm. A.*, xii (1970), pp. 212–17

A. Viaene: 'Vijf eeuwen ontmoeting met het Sint-Janshospitaal' [Five centuries of the St John's Hospital], *Sint-Janshospitaal, 1188–1976*, 2 vols (exh. cat., Bruges, Memlingmus., 1976), pp. 225–46

H. Lobelle-Caluwe: *Memling Museum* (Bruges, 1985)

E. J. Mundy: *Painting in Bruges, 1470–1550: An Annotated Bibliography* (Boston, 1985), pp. 39–74

D. de Vos: 'The Middle Ages: Painting', *Flemish Art from the Beginning till Now* (Antwerp, 1985), pp. 125–32

MONOGRAPHS

W. H. J. Weale: *Hans Memlinc, zijn leven en zijne schilderwerken: Eene schets* [Hans Memling, his life and paintings: a sketch] (Bruges, 1871/R Roeselare, 1976)

L. Kämmerer: *Memling* (Bielefeld, 1899)

W. H. J. Weale: *Hans Memling* (London, 1901)

——: *Hans Memlinc: Biographie, tableaux conservés à Bruges* (Bruges, 1901)

K. Voll: *Memling: Des Meisters Gemälde*, Klass. Kst, xiv (Stuttgart, 1909)

Memling (exh. cat., Bruges, Groeningemus., 1939) [non-academic]

G. Bazin: *Memling* (Paris, 1939)

J. Lavalleye: *Hans Memling* (Bruges, 1939)

L. von Baldass: *Hans Memling* (Vienna, 1942)

M. J. Friedländer: *Hans Memling* (Amsterdam, 1949)

G. T. Faggin: *Hans Memlinc*, Maestri Colore (Milan, 1966)

M. Corti and G. T. Faggin: *L'opera completa di Memling*, Class. A., xxvii (Milan, 1969) [complete short monograph]

K. B. McFarlane: *Hans Memling* (Oxford, 1971)

W. Jahn: *Der Maler Hans Memling aus Seligenstadt: Burger zu Pruck in Flandern gewest* (Michelstadt, 1980)

A. Zöller: *Hans Memling: Seligenstadt um 1430–Brugge 1494* (Seligenstadt, 1983)

D. de Vos: *Hans Memling: The Complete Works* (London, 1994)

SPECIALIST STUDIES

E. Tormo y Monzó: 'Las tablas memlingianos de Nájera, del Museo de Amberes: Su primitivo destino, fecha y autor', *Mélanges Bertaux* (Paris, 1924)

G. Hulin de Loo: 'Hans Memling in Rogier van der Weyden's Studio', *Burl. Mag.*, lii (1928), pp. 160–77

M. J. Friedländer: 'Noch etwas über das Verhältnis Roger van der Weyden zu Memling', *Oud-Holland*, lxi (1946), pp. 11–19

——: 'Van der Goes und Memling', *Oud-Holland*, lxv (1950), pp. 167–71

P. Coremans, R. Sneyers and J. Thissen: 'Memling's *Mystiek huwelijk van de H. Catharina*' [Memling's *Mystic Marriage of St Catherine*], *Bull. Inst. Royal Patrm. A.*, ii (1959), pp. 83–96

F. Van Molle: *Identification d'un portrait de Gilles Joye attribué à Memlinc* (1960), iii of *Les Primitifs flamands, III*

M. Hasse: *Hans Memlings Lübecker Altarschrein*, Lübecker Museumshefte, vi (Lübeck, 1967)

J. K. Steppe: 'Hans Memling en zijn atelier: Christus en de musiceerende engelen' [Hans Memling and his workshop: Christ and the angel musicians], *Jb. Kon. Vl. Acad. Wetsch. Lett. & S. Kst.*, xxix (1967), p. 169

H. G. Evers: *Dürer bei Memling* (Munich, 1972)

N. Schneider: 'Zur Iconographie von Memlings "Die sieben Freuden Mariens"', *Münchn. Jb. Bild. Kst*, xxiv (1973), pp. 21–32

E. Kluckert: 'Die Simultanbilder Memlings, ihre Wurzeln und Wirkungen', *Münster*, xxvii (1974), pp. 284–95

N. Reynaud: 'Reconstitution d'un triptyque de Memling', *Rev. Louvre*, xxiv (1974), pp. 79–90

L. Campbell: 'A Double Portrait by Memlinc', *Connoisseur*, cxciv/781 (1977), pp. 187–9

D. Hollanders-Favart: 'Le Dessin sous-jacent chez Memling: La *Châsse de Sainte Ursule*', *Hand. Genoot. Gesch. 'Soc. Emul.' Brugge*, cxv (1978), pp. 174–86

V. J. Hull: *Hans Memling's Paintings for the Hospital of St John in Bruges* (New York, 1981)

L. Campbell: 'Memlinc and the Followers of Verrocchio', *Burl. Mag.*, ccxv (1983), pp. 675–6

P. Philippot: 'Icône et narration chez Memling', *An. Hist. A. & Archéol.*, v (1983), pp. 33–45

D. de Vos: 'De constructie van Memlings Van Nieuwenhoveportret: Een probleem van interpretatie van de voorbereidende tekening' [The construction of Memling's portrait of van Nieuwenhove: the problems of interpreting the preparatory drawing], *Oud-Holland*, c (1986), pp. 165–71 [Eng. summary]

DIRK DE VOS

Memmi, Lippo. *See* LIPPO MEMMI.

Memmo, Andrea (*b* Venice, 1729; *d* Venice, 27 Jan 1793). Italian politician, patron and theorist. He came from a noble family and received a traditional and formal education from his uncle Andrea Memmo (1670–1754), which was later augmented by encounters with major intellectual figures of the age. Memmo was particularly influenced by the teaching of the monk CARLO LODOLI, from whom he acquired his passion for architecture. As governor of Padua (1775–6), Memmo initiated a series of projects for the urban reorganization of the city and for the functional and spatial redesign of its public buildings. This also affected the private building sector: as well as promoting repairs and reconstruction of roads and bridges and the repainting of porticos, façades, windows and balconies, he sponsored the new Civic Hospital (1776–98), which was designed by DOMENICO CERATO. Most importantly, he was responsible for the creation of the great Prato della Valle, a new monumental centre for fairs and commerce, which was also built by Cerato. This involved draining a vast uncultivated marshy area by digging an elliptical ditch crossed by four bridges, and adorned with 88 statues of famous men, including one of *Giovanni Poleni* (limestone, 1779–80; Padua, Mus. Civ.) by Antonio Canova. As Venetian ambassador to Constantinople (now Istanbul) from 1778 to 1782, Memmo arranged for the restoration and embellishment of the Embassy. It was given a Palladian porch with Ionic columns and a tympanum, and windows similar to those created by Lodoli in 1743 for S Francesco della Vigna in Venice (for illustration *see* LODOLI, CARLO).

In 1784, while ambassador to Rome, Memmo began his *Elementi d'architettura lodoliana* in an effort to preserve what he could remember of Lodoli's architectural theories. The first of Memmo's two planned volumes was published anonymously in 1786. It was intended to lead the reader towards an understanding of the theoretical principles and conclusions that were to be contained in the second volume. The latter, however, did not appear until 1834. In

1786 a short work on the Prato della Valle was published by Vincenzo Radicchio. In 1787, on the occasion of Memmo's installation as Procurator of S Marco, he edited and published Lodoli's *Apologhi*, as well as *Luna d'agosto*, an instructive fable modelled on those of Lodoli. In 1788 Memmo's refutation of the criticisms levelled against Lodoli's theories by Pietro Zaguri (1733–1804) was published in Padua, and he was supported by Lodoli's former pupils. Memmo was interested in theatre architecture, especially during the competition (1792) for the reconstruction of the Fenice theatre in Venice. He also produced a *Progetto di accademia* (now lost), an unpublished work on the fine arts.

WRITINGS

with M. Cesarotti: *La luna d'agosto: Apologo postumo del P. Lodoli. Dagli Elisj, l'anno dell'Era di Prosperina 9999 M.V.* (Bassano, 1787)
Semplici lumi tendenti a render cauti i soli interessati nel teatro da erigersi nella Parrocchia di S Fantino in Venezia (Venice, 1792)
Elementi d'architettura lodoliana, 2 vols (Zara, 1834)

BIBLIOGRAPHY

G. Memmo: *Raccolta di opere, documenti e manoscritti riguardanti la storia di casa Memmo* (Turin, 1928)
T. Bertele: *Il Palazzo degli Ambasciatori di Venezia a Costantinopoli e le sue antiche memorie* (Bologna, 1932), pp. 193–311, 331–2
G. Memmo: *Bibliografia Memmo* (Rome, 1949)
G. Torcellan: *Una figura della Venezia settecentesca: Andrea Memmo* (Venice and Rome, 1963)
E. Kaufmann: 'Memmo's Lodoli', *A. Bull.*, xlvi (1964), pp. 159–75
S. P. Caligaris: 'Fra Carlo Lodoli, Andrea Memmo, un tricentenario, un bicentenario', *A. Crist.* (1981), pp. 89–92
V. Farinati: 'Andrea Memmo: elementi dell'architetture lodoliana', *I Querini Stampalia: Un ritratto di famiglia nel settecento* (exh. cat., Venice, Fond. Querini-Stampalia, 1987), p. 213

VALERIA FARINATI

Memmo di Filippuccio (*fl* 1288–1324). Italian painter and illuminator. He was the son of the goldsmith Filippuccio (*fl* 1273–93). In 1948 Longhi attributed a fresco of the *Virgin and Child Enthroned with SS James and John the Evangelist* in the church of S Jacopo, San Gimignano, and others in the tower of the Palazzo del Popolo there (see fig.) to Memmo, who is documented as having lived and worked in the town from 1303 to 1317. A document of 1303 also records him as having worked in the upper church of S Francesco, Assisi, and Longhi suggested this might have been on the frescoes of the *St Francis* cycle, which would account for the Giottesque influence he had noted in the frescoes in San Gimignano. Previtali (1962) further attributed to Memmo the frescoes of *Carlo d'Angio Administering Justice* (1292; San Gimignano, Pal. Pop., Sala dell'Udienza), an altarpiece of the *Virgin and Child Enthroned with Saints* (Oristano, Pal. Arcisp.), which also shows the influence of Giotto's work at Assisi, a *Virgin and Child* (Pisa, S Francesco) and a polyptych of the *Virgin and Child Enthroned with Saints*, formerly in the convent of S Chiara, San Gimignano (San Gimignano, Pin. Civ.). Memmo is also documented in 1305 as having worked in the Collegiata Pieve, San Gimignano, and it has been suggested that the lunette of the *Virgin with Saints* on the inside of the entrance wall and frescoes of the *Annunciation* and the *Virgin and Child Enthroned with SS Catherine of Alexandria and Mary Magdalene* in S Pietro, San Gimignano, should also be attributed to him; and that given their fluid, gentle style these should be dated before 1321, when Memmo was recorded in Siena (Carli, 1963).

The document of 1303 also mentions Memmo's activity as an illuminator, and Previtali (1964, 1967) suggested the following chronology of his works: the *Entry into Jerusalem*, *Ascension* and *Pentecost* in a Gradual (Siena, Mus. Opera Duomo, MS. 46–2) are datable to 1285–90, as are illuminations of the four Evangelists (Siena, Bib. Com. Intronati, MS. F.iii.6), *St Paul* and *St Andrew* (Siena, Bib. Com. Intronati, MS. F.v.26) and the *Ascension* and the *Adoration of the Magi* (Venice, Fond. Cini, MSS L.vii and ix); the frescoes in the upper church at Assisi, including the *Doctors of the Church* in the

Memmo di Filippuccio: *Story of the Dissolute Young Man*, detail from the frescoed wall (*c.*1303–5) of the Stanza della Torre, Palazzo del Popolo, San Gimignano

vault, the *Brothers before Joseph*, the *Trial by Fire before the Sultan* and the *Deposition* and *Pentecost*, were executed between 1290 and *c.* 1300, and the frescoes in the Sala dell'Udienza in 1292. From 1300 Memmo worked on the Oristano altarpiece, the S Chiara polyptych, the Choirbooks M, N, O and P in Pisa (Mus. N. & Civ. S Matteo) and the figures of saints painted on the front of a cupboard in S Lucchese, Poggibonsi. The frescoes in S Jacopo, and others in the Collegiata, San Gimignano, would have followed. Other critics (Boskovits and De Benedictis) have added further manuscript illuminations and paintings to this list of attributions. In 1981 Carli suggested that a fresco of the *Surrender of a Castle* discovered in 1980 in the Palazzo del Popolo, Siena, should also be attributed to Memmo, and should therefore be dated to *c.* 1320. The reconstruction of Memmo's career is, however, still the subject of debate. It has been suggested that the frescoes in the Sala dell'Udienza are by two different artists (Bologna) while Boskovits noted distinct differences in quality between the illuminations and the panel paintings and frescoes, which led him to suggest that these may also represent the work of two different artists. Whether or not the illuminations are by Memmo, he remains an original and prolific artist, who strove to create a personal synthesis between the more sinuous, Gothic style of his early pieces (closely associated with Duccio and Simone Martini) and the volumetric, spacious and rational images of Giotto's work at Assisi. His sons LIPPO MEMMI and Tederigho Memmi were also painters.

BIBLIOGRAPHY

R. Longhi: 'Giudizio sul duecento', *Proporzioni*, i (1948), p. 50

G. Cecchini and E. Carli: *San Gimignano* (Milan, 1962)

G. Previtali: 'Il possibile Memmo di Filippuccio', *Paragone*, xiii/155 (1962), pp. 3–11 [with list of documents]

E. Carli: 'Ancora dei Memmi a San Gimignano', *Paragone*, xiv/159 (1963), pp. 27–44

G. Previtali: 'Miniature di Memmo di Filippuccio', *Paragone*, xv/169 (1964), pp. 3–11

——: *Giotto e la sua bottega* (Milan, 1967, 2/1974)

F. Bologna: *I pittori alla corte angioina di Napoli, 1266–1414* (Rome, 1969)

E. Carli: *La pittura senese del trecento* (Milan, 1981)

M. Boskovits: 'Il gotico senese rivisitato: Proposte e commenti su una mostra', *A. Crist.*, lxxi (1983), p. 260

C. De Benedictis: 'Memmo di Filippuccio tra Assisi e Siena', *Roma anno 1300: Atti della IV sentimana di studi di storia dell'arte medievale dell'Università di Roma 'La Sapienza': Roma, 1983*, pp. 211–16 [full bibliog. and notes]

——: 'Pittura e miniatura del duecento e del trecento in terra di Siena', *La pittura in Italia: Le origini*, ed. E. Castelnuovo (Milan, 1985, 2/1986), pp. 333–4

CRISTINA DE BENEDICTIS

Memnon, Colossi of. *See* THEBES (i), §V.

Memphis. Egyptian site *c.* 20 km south of Cairo on the west bank of the Nile. Memphis was founded at the beginning of the 1st Dynasty (*c.* 2925 BC), traditionally by King Menes or possibly by King Narmer, and served as the national capital during the Early Dynastic Period and the Old Kingdom (*c.* 2925–*c.* 2150 BC). Thereafter it retained its political, economic, strategic, religious and artistic pre-eminence over three millennia, into the Roman period (30 BC–AD 395). A systematic survey of the site is being conducted by the Egypt Exploration Society under the direction of Harry Smith and David Jeffreys.

The city's Greek name 'Memphis' is derived from the Egyptian Men-nefer ('Stable of beauty'), an abbreviation of the name for the pyramid complex of Pepy I at Saqqara. Memphis was also known by other names in different periods; these included Ineb-hedj (anc. Egyp.: 'White Wall'), which was also the title of the nome of Memphis, and Ankh-tawy ('Life of the Two Lands') and Mekhet-tawy ('Balance of the Two Lands'), titles that reflected the importance of its situation at the junction of the Nile Valley and the Delta. The city consisted of a vast agglomeration of structures that grew over time and must have appeared as a haphazard network of urban sites, large estates and almost rural stretches of land (see fig. 1). A number of mounds correspond to the remains of certain parts of the town including its centre, but the modern village of Mit Rahina and the small town of el-Badrashein largely cover the site. Additional difficulties, such as the destruction and pillage of monuments, quarrying and the rising of the water table also partly explain the unspectacular character of the site and the fact that Memphis has not been explored and excavated as extensively as the great southern city of Thebes. However, it would be unjust to compare the ruins of Memphis with those at Thebes without also taking into account the Memphite cemeteries. An enormous necropolis, over 30 km in length, stretches into the desert to the west of the town from ABU RAWASH in the north to DAHSHUR in the south, passing through GIZA, ABUSIR and SAQQARA (the last being the cemetery closest to the city). This considerable area, with its royal pyramids and mastabas, sanctuaries, sacred animal necropoleis and private tombs of all periods, must be considered as part of Memphis in terms of urban planning, religion and art.

Memphis was certainly densely populated. In the course of centuries, and particularly at the end of the New Kingdom (*c.* 1075 BC), an increasing number of Near Eastern and Mediterranean settlers was attracted to the area. This cosmopolitanism, one of the characteristics of

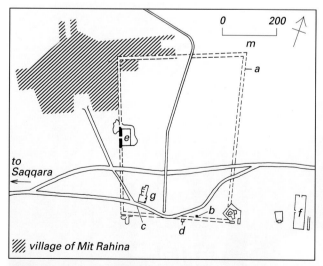

1. Memphis, plan: (a) enclosure of the Temple of Ptah; (b) calcite alabaster sphinx; (c) shrine of Sethos I; (d) colossus of Ramesses II; (e) hypostyle hall of the Temple of Ptah; (f) palace of Merneptah; (g) embalming house of the Apis bulls

Memphis at the close of the 2nd millennium BC, was partly the cause of the introduction of oriental cults and divinities alongside the traditional Egyptian cults of the Memphite 'triad' (Ptah, Sekhmet and Nefertum), Bastet, Sokar, the Apis bull and (one millennium later) the Ptolemaic deity Sarapis. This cosmopolitanism must also have influenced artistic styles and techniques.

The chief priest of Ptah at Memphis was traditionally given the title 'Chief of Craftsmen', a reference to the creative aspect of Ptah and an indication of the importance to Memphis of crafts: craftsmen, including goldsmiths, had quarters both in the town of the living and in the necropolis. The city's reputation as an artistic centre was widespread. Since the borderline between craftsmanship and art was not always clearly defined in ancient Egypt, this reputation must have influenced artistic practices both in Memphis and in the rest of the country: it is probable that some of the funerary furniture of Theban royal tombs of the New Kingdom (c. 1540–c. 1075 BC) was made in Memphis. The ruinous state of the town, however, and the fact that it has scarcely been excavated, explain the relative lack of direct evidence for artistic activity in the city itself, although the necropoleis include striking and characteristic examples of Memphite art from throughout the Dynastic Period (for a discussion of Memphite sculpture see EGYPT, ANCIENT, §IX, 3(iii)(a)). There is some evidence from the city itself of its buildings and architectural decoration. Most dates from the New Kingdom and Late Period (750–332 BC). Spectacular pieces include a calcite alabaster sphinx of the 18th Dynasty (in situ; see figs 1b and 2); a shrine of Sethos I (reg c. 1290–c. 1279 BC), with statues (1c); a pair of colossal statues of Ramesses II (reg c. 1279–c. 1213 BC), one fallen in situ (1d), the other in Ramses Square, beside Cairo's main railway station; the ruins of a hypostyle hall of the Temple of Ptah (1e), and a small temple to the goddess Hathor, both also dating to the reign of Ramesses II; parts of the palace of Merneptah (reg c. 1213–c. 1204 BC; fig. 1f); and the embalming house

2. Memphis, calcite alabaster sphinx, l. 8 m; New Kingdom, 18th Dynasty, c. 1540–c. 1292 BC

of the Apis bulls (Third Intermediate Period, c. 1075– c. 750 BC; fig. 1g).

BIBLIOGRAPHY
LÄ
W. M. F. Petrie and others: *Memphis*, 5 vols (London, 1909–13)
B. Porter and R. Moss: *Topographical Bibliography* (1927–), III/ii, pp. 830–75
A. Badawy: *Memphis als zweite Landeshauptstadt im neuen Reich* (Cairo, 1948)
R. Anthes: *Mit Rahineh 1955* (Philadelphia, 1959)
——: *Mit Rahineh 1956* (Philadelphia, 1965)
H. S. Smith: *A Visit to Ancient Egypt: Life at Memphis and Saqqara, c. 500–30 B.C.* (Warminster, 1974)
D. G. Jeffreys: *The Archaeological Report*, i of *The Survey of Memphis* (London, 1985)
D. J. Thompson: *Memphis under the Ptolemies* (Princeton, 1988)

ALAIN ZIVIE

Men. *See under* BEK.

Mena, de. Spanish family of sculptors.

(1) Alonso de Mena (y Escalante) (*b* Granada, 20 Jan 1587; *d* Granada, 4 Sept 1646). A cultivated man from a family of printers, Alonso de Mena maintained the most active sculpture workshop in Granada from the 1620s until his death. He worked in clay, stone and wood. In 1604 he began a four-year apprenticeship with the Sevillian sculptor Andrés de Ocampo, but his works display little of his master's influence. By 1610 Mena was back in Granada. His early works, such as *St Lucy* (c. 1615; Granada Cathedral) and the *Virgin of Mercy* (1615; Granada, S Cecilio), derive from the style of Pablo de Rojas. Many of Mena's notable Virgins show types later cultivated by both his son (2) Pedro de Mena and Alonso Cano. His *Immaculate Conception* (before 1630; Granada, S José) shows the influence of Gregorio Fernández. Mena's mature period began about 1630. The most impressive of his numerous crucifixes is the *Forsaken Christ* (1635; Madrid, S José), which depicts the moment of Christ's death. The warrior figure of *St James on Horseback* (1640; Granada Cathedral) is associated with the idea of a victorious Philip IV. Mena emphasized the spiritual life of the saint—he wears a peasant's hat rather than a helmet. Deeply religious, Mena prepared himself spiritually before beginning a work by confessing and taking communion. His most notable pupils were his son Pedro, and Pedro Roldán.

BIBLIOGRAPHY
A. Gallego Burín: *Un contemporáneo de Montañés: El escultor Alonso de Mena* (Seville, 1952)
J. Hernández Díaz, J. J. Martín González and J. M. Pita Andrade: *La escultura y la arquitectura españolas del siglo XVII*, Summa Artis, xxvi (Madrid, 1982), pp. 149–55
J. J. Martín González: *Escultura barroca en España, 1600–1770* (Madrid, 1983), pp. 190–3

A. S. ARBURY

(2) Pedro de Mena (y Medrano) (*bapt* Granada, 20 Aug 1628; *d* Málaga, 13 Oct 1688). Son of (1) Alonso de Mena. He studied with his father and followed his style in the early part of his career. After the death of his father, he worked with Bernardo de Mora (ii), who had moved to Granada in 1650. The arrival of Alonso Cano in 1652, however, caused a change in Mena's artistic direction; he and Mora began to collaborate directly with Cano, and this close working relationship left a permanent mark on both of the younger artists' styles. Mena's first important works are based on figures by Cano, who had been commissioned to produce four sculptures for the convent of the Angel Custodio: *St Anthony of Padua*, *St Diego of Alcalá*, *St Peter of Alcántara* and *St Joseph* (all 1656–7; Granada, Alhambra). These were executed by Mena, who managed to gain Cano's trust and to earn a significant place for himself among Granada's makers of religious images. He remained a sought-after sculptor in the city until 1658, when he was commissioned by Bishop Diego Martínez de Zarzosa and the Málaga chapter of the cathedral to complete the choir-stalls there that had been begun in the 1630s by Luis Ortiz de Vargas (*fl* 1629–47). The contract required that Mena live in the city for two years and called for 40 panels to be carved with reliefs of saints, and for carving to be done on the edges of the stalls. He therefore left Granada and moved permanently to Málaga. As he worked on the figures of the saints, which were essentially relief sculptures attached to the panels, he made a notable effort to introduce the greatest possible variety in their treatment by emphasizing their characteristic attributes while allowing the background to remain flat.

The fame that Mena achieved with this work enabled him to travel to Madrid in 1662. This visit was significant in that it put him in contact with the vigorous sculptural life of the city and with a new and influential clientèle, both in the Spanish court and at Toledo. For Toledo Cathedral he created one of his best-known works, *St Francis of Assisi* (1663; Toledo, Mus. Catedralicio), a small sculpture in polychromed wood representing the figure of the dead saint standing upright in the position in which he was found, according to legend. The undoubted quality of this piece led to Mena's nomination in 1663 as Escultor de la Catedral. As a result of his stay at the court in Madrid, he received other commissions, all executed in Málaga. The most important of these is a *Magdalene* (1664; Valladolid, Mus. N. Escul.) for the Casa Profesa de los Jesuitas in Madrid. The saint is depicted standing, as was usual with Mena's figures, and she contemplates a crucifix with an expression of penitence that refers more to spiritual exercise than to physical effort. The virtuosity of the wood-carving is apparent in the contrast between the naked feminine arms and the coarseness of the dress of plaited rushes. *Christ of Light* (destr.), executed for the convent of S Domingo in Málaga, is another significant work. It is Mena's only crucifix, as he tended to avoid themes of extreme pain. The *Virgin of Bethlehem* (c. 1666), of which only the head remains, was also originally at this convent. Mena sculpted the polychromed marble figures of *Ferdinand the Catholic* and *Queen Isabella* (1675–7; Granada Cathedral), who are shown in an attitude of prayer, and he repeated the figures for Málaga Cathedral, where they flank the altarpiece of Nuestra Señora de los Reyes. Although he never created actual funerary monuments, these representations of Ferdinand and Isabella are the closest he came in that regard.

The presence of replicas and copies of Mena's work is a testimony to his wide acclaim. He tended to repeat his most popular figures, producing them almost as series; this accounts for their widespread diffusion, particularly in religious orders. The numerous replicas could easily be turned out, due to the skill of his workshop assistants, and images most particularly in demand were those of St

Francis of Assisi, St Anthony of Padua, St Peter of Alcántara, the Virgin and Child with St Joseph and the Immaculate Conception, all of which could be rendered in a variety of poses. The busts of saints, and especially those of the Mater dolorosa and the Ecce homo, are also very common. The two latter types, characterized by a mood of veiled pain and by melancholic faces shedding tears of glass, were produced both as short busts and as longer ones also showing the arms. A *Mater dolorosa* (1673) for the monastery of the Descalzas Reales in Madrid (*in situ*) and one for the convent of the Carmelitas Descalzas in Alba de Tormes (Salamanca) are two of the finest examples of the longer bust. Mena's accomplished technique owed much to Cano but was nevertheless typical of sculptors from Granada. However, he was able to improve on this tradition as he avidly searched for a wide range of images and for a new repertory of poses. This attempt at a new means of expression, coupled with the devotional nature of his art and the fact that the individual statues and busts were fundamentally intended for close contemplation, ensured that his images achieved remarkable popularity. One of the most important members of his workshop was Miguel de Zayas (*fl* c. 1693–5), a faithful adherent to his style.

BIBLIOGRAPHY

R. de Orueta: *La vida y la obra de Pedro de Mena y Medrano* (Madrid, 1914/*R* 1989)

A. Gallego Burín: 'Tres familias de escultores: Los Menas, los Moras y los Roldanes', *Archv Esp. A. & Arqueol.*, i (1925), pp. 323–31

Pedro de Mena, escultor: Homenaje en su tercer centenario, intro. by R. de Orueta y Duarte (Málaga, 1928)

M. E. Gómez Moreno: *Escultura del siglo XVII*, A. Hisp., xvi (Madrid, 1963), pp. 227–60

D. Sánchez-Mesa: 'Algunas noticias sobre la obra de Pedro de Mena', *Archv Esp. A.*, xl (1967), pp. 245–62

J. J. Martín González: *Escultura barroca en España, 1600–1700*, Manuales Arte Cátedra (Madrid, 1986/*R* 1991), pp. 207–19

Pedro de Mena: III centenario de su muerte, 1688–1988 (exh. cat., Málaga Cathedral, 1989)

NATIVIDAD SÁNCHEZ ESTEBAN

Mena, Juan Pascual de (*b* Villaseca de la Sagra, Toledo, 1707; *d* Madrid, 16 April 1784). Spanish sculptor. His early training involved work on the extensive sculpture programmes at the royal palaces of Aranjuez and La Granja and at the Palacio Real in Madrid. These works were mainly being directed by foreign artists, who were a considerable influence on Mena. He was appointed Assistant Director for Sculpture at the Real Academia de Bellas Artes de S Fernando in 1752, Director of Sculpture in 1762 and Director General in 1771, which position he held until his death. His teaching was important, as was his restoration on pieces that came as models for his students. In 1768 he was made Individuo de Mérito at the Academia de S Carlos, Valencia.

In 1749 Mena was commissioned to contribute to the sculpture programme on the façade of the Palacio Real, Madrid, and he carved the statues of the kings *Gesaleico* (untraced), *Liuva I* (Vitoria, gardens of La Florida), *Dona Urraca* and *Charles II* (both Madrid, Buen Retiro), and *Motecuhzuma* (*in situ*), who is shown wearing native dress. He also carved for the façade the statue of *Charles II* (*in situ*). In collaboration with his pupil José Arias, Mena carved the Fountain of Neptune (c. 1777–86), Plaza de Cánovas del Castillo, Paseo del Prado, Madrid. This impressive and dramatic work shows the sea-god Neptune standing majestically on a sea-shell; it combines an academic classicism with a highly effective realism. The design of the fountain was by Ventura Rodríguez (c. 1777; Madrid, Mus. Mun.).

Mena carved the magnificent marble bust of *Charles III* (1764) for the Sala de Juntas, Real Academia de Bellas Artes de S Fernando (*in situ*), in which he successfully conveyed the monarch's good-natured temperament while at the same time faithfully depicting his less-than-attractive features. In 1768 Charles III invited Mena, together with four other sculptors, to submit models for an equestrian statue of Philip V. This project was not realized, but Mena's model (Madrid, Real Acad. S Fernando Mus.) shows his abandonment of the Baroque and a representation of the monarch that has the aesthetic gravity of a Roman emperor.

Mena made many religious images in painted wood following the traditional Spanish material and technique. These tend to have a rather idealized and stereotyped Baroque character and therefore stand slightly apart from the more realistic and immediate quality of contemporary Spanish sculpture. Mena's style can be seen in such works as the statue of *St Mark* and *St Benedict* and *St Scholastica* (all c. 1753) in the side aisles of the church of S Marcos, Madrid. He carved the *Crucifixion* (date unknown) in S Jerónimo el Real, Madrid; the statue of *St Eloi* (date unknown), in S José, Madrid; the statue of *St Mariana of Jesus* (date unknown; Madrid, church of Santiago); and those in stone of *St Isidore the Farmer* and *St María de la Cabeza* (date unknown) on the façade of the cathedral of S Isidro, Madrid.

BIBLIOGRAPHY

Ceán Bermúdez

J. Nicolau Castro: 'Dos posibles obras desconocidas de Juan Pascual de Mena', *Archv Esp. A.*, 45 (1972), pp. 63–6

C. Bedat: *L'Académie de Beaux-arts de Madrid, 1744–1808* (Toulouse, 1974), pp. 283–6

F. J. de la Plaza Santiago: *Investigaciones sobre el Palacio Real nuevo de Madrid* (Valladolid, 1975), pp. 184–5, 197–9, 209, 216, 218

J. J. Martín González: *Escultura barroca en España, 1600–1770* (Madrid, 1983), pp. 390–93

G. RAMALLO ASENSIO

Menabuoi, Giusto (di Giovanni) de' (*fl* 1349–*c.* 1390). Italian painter. He was a native of Florence, but all records of his activity and all surviving works are in or from northern Italy. Together with the Veronese painter Altichiero, and following in the wake of the native Guariento, Giusto helped establish Padua as a major centre for the development of late 14th-century painting. His work illustrates the widening stylistic gulf in the years following the Black Death between the activities of Florentine painters working in Florence and those of artists either born there or exposed to the influence of Florentine art before the mid-century, but working further north, where, after *c.* 1350, the most significant developments of the Giottesque legacy took place. Beyond a shared Florentine tendency to monumental form, his art increasingly diverged from the style of Orcagna and his school, and Giusto's expansion of the pictorial possibilities suggested by Giotto, Maso di Banco and Taddeo Gaddi in the early decades of the century is bolder than anything attempted by the painters of late 14th-century Florence. His career

may be divided into two phases: work in Lombardy, 1350s and 1360s; and from *c.* 1370 in Padua, where he enjoyed the patronage of the Carrara court.

1. LOMBARDY, BEFORE *c.* 1370. No surviving documents record Giusto's early life in Florence or his Lombard activity; the earliest work that can justifiably be attributed to him is a fresco of the *Virgin and Child with Four Saints and a Donor* (1349) above the high altar of S Pietro abbey at Viboldone near Milan. Elsewhere in the building, frescoes of the *Last Judgement* and *Four Doctors of the Church*, long attributed to Giusto, are probably to be dated rather later, given the evident reflections of Nardo di Cione's *Last Judgement* (*c.* 1354–7; Florence, S Maria Novella). These frescoes indicate the decisive influences on Giusto's early style, and, although elements drawn from Bernardo Daddi's work can be detected, it is to the weighty figure groups of Giotto and Maso di Banco that the *Last Judgement*, compositionally a reinterpretation of Giotto's Arena Chapel rendering of the subject, clearly points. Some of the seated figures in Giusto's *Last Judgement* exhibit a monumentality hardly equalled in the 14th century.

In 1363 Giusto signed the central panel (Rome, Schiff-Giorgini priv. col.) of a now dispersed polyptych of the *Virgin and Child with Saints*. This was painted, as the inscription on the throne base records, for Isotta de Terzaga of Milan. Other evidence suggests Milan as the base for Giusto's activities at this period. A number of fragmentary frescoes from the former S Maria di Brera have clear affinities with the Viboldone frescoes and can be safely regarded as Giusto's. Furthermore, the inscription on a signed and dated triptych of the *Coronation of the Virgin* and the *Life of the Virgin*, the *Nativity* and the *Crucifixion* (1367; London, N.G. (see fig. 1)) specifies that it was painted in Milan. This small work is of a common Florentine type and elements of the narrative scenes are again borrowed from the equivalent scenes in the Arena Chapel. Even on this restricted scale the salient features of Giusto's mature style can be seen: the figures have great bulk, and in the *Coronation of the Virgin* (central panel) there is a concern for showing deeply receding space. Giusto must have revisited Florence not long before 1367, given the clear references in his *Birth of the Virgin* (exterior of the right wing) to the same scene in Giovanni da Milano's fresco cycle (1365) in the Rinuccini Chapel, Santa Croce, Florence. Giovanni's influence is strong in Giusto's later work; Giusto's stock facial type, with a long, conspicuously illuminated nose, puffy eyes and a short upper lip, can be ascribed to it, as can the smoky chromatic range of his flesh tones, which is very close to Giovanni's, though often less refined in execution.

2. PADUA, *c.* 1370–90. The first series of documentary records of Giusto's presence in Padua is dated September 1373, but substantial fragments of a fresco cycle in the church of the Eremitani in Padua can be dated to 1370. These frescoes, uncovered after the bombing of the church in 1944, were commissioned by Tebaldo de' Cortellieri for his newly built chapel on the south side of the nave. They comprise enthroned figures of the *Liberal Arts*, *Philosophers* and *Virtues* in fictive niches on the side walls and

1. Giusto de' Menabuoi: triptych of the *Coronation of the Virgin*, with scenes from the *Life of the Virgin*, the *Nativity* and the *Crucifixion*, tempera on panel, central panel 438×248 mm, side panels 483×134 mm, 1367 (London, National Gallery)

half-length *Saints* on the soffit of the entrance arch. The whole cycle, which is of the greatest iconographic interest, was described while still intact in the *Memorialenbuch* of the 15th-century Nuremberg humanist Hartmann Schedel. A document of 1373 records a payment to Giusto by the heirs of Enrico Spisser for painting in another chapel in the Eremitani. This can be identified with the present Sanguinacci Chapel to the north of the sanctuary, in which a fresco of the *Virgin and Child with Saints*, attributable to Giusto, survives. Two smaller frescoes of the *Virgin and Child* in the choir at the nearby Arena Chapel may have been done at this time.

By April 1375 Giusto had become a Paduan citizen, and his major work in Padua, the decoration of the Romanesque baptistery, cannot have been begun long after this. The frescoes there are associated with the patronage of Fina Buzzacarina, wife of the ruler of Padua, Francesco I da Carrara, and with the evident intention to transform the building into a Carrarese mausoleum. Fina

and Francesco were buried in the baptistery in 1378 and 1393 respectively. Giusto's frescoes and Fina's tomb, of which only the arch and votive fresco survives, were probably finished by the latter date. The iconography of the cycle is wide-ranging and complex. At the centre of the cupola is the *Pantokrator*, surrounded by the *Blessed*, with Old Testament scenes beginning with the *Creation* in the supporting drum. The four pendentives contain seated *Evangelists*, and the four main walls below have scenes from the *Life of St John the Baptist*, and the *Life and Passion of Christ*. There is a large *Crucifixion* (see fig. 2) above the entrance to the small sanctuary, where Giusto's polyptych with the *Virgin and Child*, the *Life of St John the Baptist* and *Saints* stands on the altar. Frescoes of the *Apocalypse* decorate the walls, with the *Pentecost* painted on the small cupola above.

The full range of Giusto's skills as well as his limitations can be seen in the baptistery frescoes. Everywhere the bulky figure style is put to impressive use, for example in the columnar grandeur of the *Presentation in the Temple* and in the powerfully twisting figure of Abraham in the *Sacrifice of Isaac*. Such scenes as the *Annunciation*, the *Marriage at Cana* and the *Calling of St Matthew* show Giusto's exceptionally advanced use of architectural settings for narrative, elaborated in many instances by such devices as glimpses through half-open doors. Nowhere else in the late 14th century, except in Altichiero's Paduan frescoes, are the possibilities of deep pictorial space so fully realized. Giusto is less impressive in scenes involving crowds. The bystanders in the *Miracles of Christ* coalesce into monotonous files, and the *Crucifixion* appears congested. The expressive range of individual figures is narrow, and the emotional lives of the participants in the narratives are more effectively suggested by a lively and varied vocabulary of gesture than by facial expression. Colours are mostly subdued, with the grey of the architectural backdrops predominating, but with accents of warm green and pink, some fine examples of shot colour, and the ice-blues of Christ's and the Virgin's robes. Giusto's sharp eye for detail is seen, for example in the casually open cupboards in *Joseph's Dream*, the desks of the *Evangelists*, the interior of the boat in the *Miraculous Draught of Fishes* and above all in the meticulously observed and delineated architectural detail of the distant cities of the Old Testament scenes and the containing structures of the lower-wall frescoes.

Between January 1376 and January 1377 Giusto moved into a house near Padua Cathedral, where he lived for the rest of his life. His last major works are the fresco

2. Giusto de' Menabuoi: *Crucifixion*, detail from the frescoed wall (completed ?1393) of the baptistery, Padua

decoration of the tomb of *Nicolò and Bonzanello da Vigonza* in the cloister passage of Il Santo and a fresco cycle in the Belludi Chapel in the same church. The Vigonza tomb frescoes—the *Coronation of the Virgin*, *Annunciation* and a set of imposing and vigorous *Prophets* on the arch soffits—can be dated to *c.* 1380. The Belludi Chapel was built in 1382 by Naimero and Manfredino de' Conti to house the tomb of *Beato Luca Belludi*, a Franciscan opponent of the despotic rule of Ezzelino III da Romano in the 13th century. Giusto's fresco cycle comprises a votive *Virgin and Child with Saints* over the tomb, and scenes from the *Life of Beato Luca Belludi* and the *Lives of SS Philip and James*, the chapel's dedicatees. The fresco of *Beato Luca's Vision of St Anthony* contains a remarkable and topographically accurate bird's-eye view of Padua from the south. The architectural backdrops of the narratives, with the orthogonals plunging into the far distance and the perspective controlled with absolute clarity, are even more adventurous and fantastic than those of the baptistery frescoes. Giusto died between 1387 and 1391; if the evidence of a reading of his long-buried tomb inscription in Padua Baptistery is correct, the precise date is 28 September 1390.

BIBLIOGRAPHY

S. Bettini: *Giusto de' Menabuoi e l'arte del trecento* (Padua, 1944)

——: *Le pitture di Giusto de' Menabuoi nel Battistero del duomo di Padova* (Venice, 1960)

G. A. Dell'Acqua and S. Matalon: *Affreschi lombardi del trecento* (Milan, 1964)

B. J. Delaney: 'Giusto de' Menabuoi in Lombardy', *A. Bull.*, lviii/1 (1976), pp. 19–35

A. Sartori: *Documenti per la storia dell'arte a Padova* (Vicenza, 1976), pp. 116–18

JOHN RICHARDS

Ménageot, François-Guillaume (*b* London, 9 July 1744; *d* Paris, 4 Oct 1816). French painter. He was the son of Augustin Ménageot (*d* 1784), an art dealer and adviser to Denis Diderot, and he studied with Jean-Baptiste-Henri Deshays and with François Boucher, whose bravura style and use of light, warm colours he adopted in his early works. He won the Prix de Rome in 1766 with *Tomyris Plunging the Head of Cyrus into a Bowl of Blood* (Paris, Ecole N. Sup. B.-A.). From 1769 to 1774 he was at the Académie de France in Rome. Having been approved (*agréé*) as a history painter by the Académie Royale in Paris in 1777, he exhibited at the Salon the *Farewells of Polyxena to Hecuba* (Chartres, Mus. B.-A.), a vast already Neoclassical work that was warmly received. His *morceau de réception* was a powerfully classicizing work entitled *Learning Resisting the Passage of Time* (1780; Paris, Ecole N. Sup. B.-A.). A year later he triumphed at the Salon with the *Death of Leonardo da Vinci in the Arms of Francis I* (Amboise, Hôtel de Ville). Ménageot was one of the painters who was involved in the return to the Grand Style: his compositions became more horizontal, the architecture more monumental, the drapery sculptural and the colouring increasingly cold. Works that bear witness to this development include *Astyanax Torn from the Arms of Andromache* (1783), *Cleopatra Paying her Last Respects to Anthony* (1785; both Angers, Mus. B.-A.), the *Continence of Scipio* (1787; Židlochovice Mus.) and *Meleager Implored by his Family* (1789; Paris, Louvre), the last being one of his most resolutely Neo-classical works.

Ménageot, however, had a predilection for gentle subjects (e.g. the *Adoration of the Shepherds* (versions in Paris, St Eustache; Villeneuve-sur-Yonne, church of the Assumption); for happy episodes from mythology or antiquity; for intimate scenes (e.g. the *Young Mother*, priv. col., see Willk-Brocard, fig. 41); and for caricature (examples in Montpellier, Mus. Atger). In 1787 he was appointed Director of the Académie de France in Rome, but with the upheavals of the French Revolution (1789–94), he resigned in 1792 and moved to Vicenza. Two *Self-portraits* of 1797 (Florence, Uffizi; Montpellier, Mus. Fabre) reveal a serious, sad-looking man. Ménageot painted portraits, probably out of necessity (e.g. *Family Portrait*, 1801; Ferrara, Pin. N.). His few known works from this period show a change of mood, already seen in the *Virgin Commending St Teresa to the Protection of St Joseph* (1787; Quebec, Hôtel-Dieu) Such works as the *Virgin with Angels* (1797; Vicenza, Madonna del Monte), in which line was emphasised and which are reminiscent of Raphael, with an archaizing purism, heralded the 19th century. Returning to Paris in 1801, he was named a Chevalier of the Légion d'honneur in 1804 and was elected to the Institut de France in 1809. Paintings that he exhibited at the Salon of 1806 had little success, however (e.g. the *Deception of Venus* (untraced; known from an engraving by Charles P. J. Normand, see Willk-Brocard, fig. 57b); his *Marriage of Prince Eugène de Beauharnais and Princess Augusta of Bavaria* (1808; Versailles, Château) failed to please Napoleon. From 1809 to 1813 he designed costumes for the Opéra (drawings, Paris, Bib.–Mus. Opéra). Having been away from developments in Paris, he was unable to adapt to the new styles and devoted himself to his academic posts. An exquisite *Holy Family* (1804; St Petersburg, Hermitage) shows his true talent: Ménageot contributed to the development of Neo-classicism, imbuing his works with grace and an individual sensitivity that maintained the spirit of the 18th century; but he was overtaken by the movement that he had helped to establish. Having been forgotten, his importance should now be reconsidered.

BIBLIOGRAPHY

N. Willk-Brocard: *François-Guillaume Ménageot (1744–1816)* (Paris, 1978) [with extensive bibliog.]
A.-C. Venturini: 'Ritratto di famiglia: Un dipinto inedito di François-Guillaume Ménageot, 1744–1816', *Mus. Ferrar.: Boll. Annu.*, 9/10 (1982), pp. 207–11

NICOLE WILLK-BROCARD

Ménard, (Marie Auguste Emile) René (*b* Paris, 15 April 1862; *d* Paris, 13 Jan 1930). French painter. He was the son of the landscape painter René-Joseph Ménard (1827–87) and nephew of the philosopher and writer Louis Ménard. He spent his youth with the Barbizon school of painters. He trained in the studios of William-Adolphe Bouguereau and other artists, but his period at the Académie Julian (from 1880) influenced him to choose a Symbolist style of landscape painting. He combined the French classical tradition of Pierre Henri de Valenciennes and Jean-Victor Bertin with the rural poetry of Jean-François Millet and Jean-Baptiste-Camille Corot. In his frescoes he looked to the monumental classicism of Puvis de Chavannes.

Around 1898 Ménard travelled to the Classical sites of the Mediterranean, which inspired him to paint a visionary

arcadia, silent and grand in its pantheistic solitude. These landscapes are peopled with gods and goddesses, naked nymphs and shepherds, drawn from life but worked into the texture of their rural background. He also used *plein-air* sketches to build up his studio paintings. In 1909 he painted frescoes for the Library of the Ecole des Hautes Etudes at the Sorbonne, and in the same year he took themes from Theocritus to decorate the Ecole de Droits (now Paris, Mus. d'Orsay). Finished pastel and oil paintings based on these decorations were exhibited at Buffalo in 1920. In 1911 he abandoned his studio in the Place du Panthéon in favour of a house on the cliffs at Varengeville near Dieppe. During most of his career he worked in gentle and muted colours, for example in his pastel *Antique Vision* (1911; Paris, Petit Pal.), but towards the end of his life he adopted a new intensity of colour. For health reasons he spent many of his last years at Les Lecques in Provence, where he created vivid twilight visions of the luxuriant Mediterranean shorescapes, transposed into Grecian pastoral scenes of an almost tragic intensity, for example *Classical Shepherds* and *Pastoral Idyll* (1929; both priv. col.; illus. U. London, Courtauld Inst. Gals).

BIBLIOGRAPHY

E. R. Ménard (exh. cat., preface L. Hourticq; Paris, Gal. Petit, 1928)
René Ménard, 1862–1930 (exh. cat., preface P. Bazin; Dieppe, Château-Mus., 1969)
E. R. Ménard, 1862–1930 (exh. cat., Paris, Gal. Tanagra, 1975)

SIMON REYNOLDS

Menars, Marquis de. *See* POISSON, (2).

Mende. Mande-speaking agricultural people, numbering *c.* one million, occupying the southern part of Sierra Leone and adjacent areas of Liberia. The Mende are art historically most famous for their wooden masks and rich masking traditions, although they also have traditions of figure sculpture and textile production. Wood-carving is done by men, traditionally in isolation from the community. The ability to carve is said to be the gift of nature spirits, and possession of special talents is said to be potentially dangerous. The carver is thus simultaneously distrusted and admired for his extraordinary achievements. Carvers' names are well-known and remembered. Carvers themselves often adopt a boastful rhetoric when talking about their work, publicly denying the apprenticeship they served with an established carver and stressing their virtuosity in being able to reproduce perfectly traditional forms and to invent new variations. In the 20th century most carvers have been semi-itinerant, travelling widely in response to commissions. When working in a village they are supported by their patrons. In the 1980s carvers also produced ready-made masks for sale, and the system of 'copying' had largely broken down.

Mende art has been collected by outsiders since the 1890s. There are, as a result, a number of important museum collections, for example in Britain (London, BM; Brighton, Royal Pav.; Liverpool Mus.; U. Glasgow, Hunterian Mus.), in Switzerland (e.g. Berne, Hist. Mus.; Basle, Mus. Vlkerknd.) and in the USA (Philadelphia, U. PA, Mus.; Cambridge, MA, Harvard U., Peabody Mus.). Apart from the Pörö society masks, Mende art has also been widely illustrated (see bibliography).

1. Geography and cultural history. 2. Masks and masquerades. 3. Figure sculpture. 4. Textiles.

1. GEOGRAPHY AND CULTURAL HISTORY. The modern Mende population is descended from Mande-speaking invaders who probably began to enter modern Mende territory during the 16th century and intermarried with the aboriginal population. During the 20th century the dominance of the Mende language and artistic traditions over the neighbouring groups of Vai, Gola, Krim and Sherbro–Bullom has steadily increased, blurring distinctions in artistic styles and genres that were more marked at the beginning of the colonial period. Some Mende artistic traditions have also spread to the Temne living along their northern border. Most Mende are nominally Muslim, although they continue to engage in traditional non-Islamic ritual activity.

Two secret societies, the Pörö and the Sande, perform major political, economic and educational functions in Mende society. All boys and girls are initiated at puberty and remain members for life. Other secret societies perform more specialized functions. Each of these societies performs its functions through possession of a powerful medicine, or *hale*, the term also used for maskers. During the 20th century stricter Islamic groups have periodically suppressed masking and other traditional practices in individual villages.

2. MASKS AND MASQUERADES. Masquerades are the major genre of Mende visual artistic expression. The Mende conceive of their masquerades as an aesthetically balanced set. Each has a distinctive personality expressed through drama, mime, dance and costume. The audience's perception of each masker is heightened by contrasts and parallelisms with other maskers. Perceived contrasts include such visual elements as lightness versus darkness, male versus female, beauty versus ugliness and such aspects of performance as silence versus speech, slowness versus quickness, seriousness versus parody. The set of maskers also reflects Mende social and family structure. The Pörö Gbini and Sande Sowei, for example, symbolize the corporate power of men and women and are likened to 'husband' and 'wife'. The most sacred maskers appear in public at key moments during the initiation of new members to the secret societies, at inauguration and at funeral ceremonies for chiefs, and on other solemn and important public occasions. More secular maskers perform in the wake of the major secret society maskers as well as at such festivals as the end of Ramadan, Christmas and on major holidays.

(i) Sande society masks. The mask of the Sande society spirit is known as Sowei and is the only documented wooden African mask worn by women. Although for Mende, Sowei is second in importance to the Pörö society masker (*see* §ii below), outside Mendeland it is the best-known example of Mende art. It is also the most numerous of Mende masks and wood-carvings; every village has one or more. The Sowei headpiece is also the most iconographically and stylistically varied of the Mende carver's products and the genre most subject to general critical evaluation. Two-faced masks are known, especially among the western Mende. Sowei wears a helmet-shaped carved wooden headpiece (h. *c.* 400 mm), a knee-length black raffia cape and a black cloth costume. She personifies the river spirit that lends its power to the Sande society. Her black colour is unique among Mende maskers and refers to water, coolness, and—because black is the colour of people—to the human, civilized world.

Sowei is always represented with semi-closed eyes, a closed or pursed mouth, an elaborate coiffure and a ringed neck (see fig. 1). The basic attributes of the mask communicate multiple references to beauty, high status and wealth (Phillips, 1980). The self-contained expression and elaborate coiffure of the mask are generally recognized as marks of beauty in women as is the ringed neck—a stylized representation of neck lines. Neck rings may also refer to the concentric ripples of river water out of which the Sande spirit emerges (Lamp, 1985). The full, rounded volumes of the face and neck and the luminous polished black surface of the masks are associated with the healthy, attractive plumpness of young girls in their prime, as they are at the completion of their Sande initiation (Boone). As such they contribute to the idealized portrayal of female beauty. Elaborate coiffures are a sign of wealth because they have been worn traditionally by women of high status. The intricate patterns of braiding and parallel hair partings

1. Sande society, Sowei mask, wood, h. 440 mm, eastern Mende, collected before 1901 (London, British Museum)

may also refer to the role of women as planters and, more broadly, as cultivators and civilizers in the village world (Lamp, 1985). A number of older hairstyles, no longer worn by women, have become conventional aspects of the mask, most notably a style consisting of parallel, graduated ridges running from the front to the back of the head.

Two types of protective amulet are attached to the masks: horns filled with medicine and magical Arabic inscriptions folded into a rectangular piece of cloth or leather-encased packet. Carved representations of these amulets are important iconographic features of the masks and are signs of both wealth and power. On masks belonging to prominent families they may be covered with beaten silver. Individual Sowei masks may also display carved motifs of birds, snakes, animals, pots, crowns, human figures, combs, miniature guns or cannons, or of *kololewengoi*, a ring of semi-circular or rectangular medallions worn by dancers and medicine specialists. It is difficult to interpret these motifs with assurance as the secrecy imposed on Sande members has prevented researchers from observing and investigating the society's meetings and rituals. Educated guesses can, however, be made about the meaning of many of them. The role of birds in Mende folk-tales and proverbs suggests that they think of them as messengers between the human and spiritual worlds; snakes, too, may signify transition between the physical world and the spiritual realm beneath the water (Lamp, 1985).

The personal names given to Sowei masks are a source of further information about their general symbolism. The names most often commemorate prominent male warrior ancestors of the owners. Unlike some neighbouring groups, the Mende identify the Sande spirit as female, but these male names together with the trousers the masker wears and other male traits she sometimes exhibits invest her with a degree of sexual ambiguity and male aggressive power. Such iconographic motifs as carved crowns and guns underline these associations. The many names stressing the dancing ability of the Sowei are reflected in the motif of the *kololewengoi*, while the combs, cowrie shells and other ornaments added to the coiffure parallel other names expressing the magnetic power of her refinement and beauty. The money she receives from the crowd is important proof of this power, and it is expressed by another common type of personal mask name meaning 'money'.

There are regional styles of carving of Sowei masks, although a mixture of styles is present in any area because of the itineracy of the carvers. Individual hands may also be distinguished, as well as 'workshop' or family styles. The western or Kpa–Mende style is characterized by an elongated diamond-shaped face, a triangular facial concavity between the brow and mouth, and the placement of the mouth at the point of the chin. The eastern or Ko–Mende style emphasizes the width rather than the length of the face, and the head is conceived as a single volume whose continuous rounded surface is broken by the horizontal crease at the eyes. The facial features are carved in low relief. In the central, or Sewa Mende, region modified influences from both east and west are evident. Some masks display extreme flatness of relief while others show a subtle concavity of the face reminiscent of Kpa–Mende pieces.

Great importance is also given to the uniqueness of each Sowei mask, and carvers strive to differentiate masks through the invention of surprising new motifs. The Mende often explain unusual or unique motifs as demonstrations of a carver's virtuosity. Traditionally, Sowei masks were commissioned secretly by society officials. Old or damaged masks were brought to a carver to copy, and in such circumstances the substitution of a new piece was not openly recognized. Sowei masks are, however, also said to be acquired supernaturally, through dreams in which the Sande spirit reveals the location in a river of a mask that the dreamer must go to retrieve. Unusual-looking masks are often said to have been acquired in this way.

From the 1950s there was an increasing tendency towards naturalism, together with a tendency on the part of some carvers towards greater inventiveness and elaboration of the superstructure of the mask. An overall decrease in the carefulness and quality of carving also occurred, though with some notable exceptions.

In addition to Sowei, Sande women also perform a satiric masquerade featuring Gonde, often referred to as the 'sister' of Sowei, a forceful, humorous presence at Sande dances. She wears either a broken, discarded Sowei headpiece with a marred surface and sparse straggling raffia, or a black helmet mask carved as a grotesque version of a Sowei.

(ii) Pörö society masks. The Gbini and Goboi masks of the Pörö society are the most powerful of Mende masks. They are both closely identified with the paramount chief and are nearly identical in appearance. (Researchers disagree on the precise relationship between them.) The power of Gbini is supreme and potentially dangerous, and it rarely appears in public. It is possible that Goboi, referred to as Gbini's 'speaker', acts as a substitute on all but the most important occasions.

The costumes of both consist of a cape of undyed raffia and a flat cylindrical headpiece of leather, appliquéd cloth and mirrors. Wooden plaques with Arabic inscriptions on them are attached to the back. Projecting below the headpiece is a trunklike form suggestive of a monstrous zoomorphic being of the 'legendary ancestor' type widespread in the region of Western Sudan. Gbini also wears a leopard skin. The masker embodies the Pörö society spirit, who ritually swallows and 'kills' new initiates before giving them new life as adults. It is associated with the uncultivated bush, and the whiteness of its body costume connects it to the spirit world. The Nafali masker acts as a messenger for Gbini and Goboi and is renowned for its quick dancing. It wears an articulated body costume of raffia and cloth and a cloth headpiece in the shape of a bishop's mitre, ornamented with mirrors and cowrie shells.

Three further minor masquerades, Falui, Jobai and Yayi, are also widespread throughout Mendeland. They are performed by men and thus come under the general control of the Pörö society, although they represent minor bush spirits rather than Pörö spirits as such. They entertain on festive occasions by doing conjuring tricks and dancing. The body costume of Falui consists of a cloth suit with a

2. Pörö society, Gongoli mask, wood (Glasgow, Art Gallery and Museum)

long natural-coloured raffia cape. Its headpiece is tall and conical, topped with feathers and covered with red or black cloth, mirrors and cowries. Falui talks in an incomprehensible language and performs conjuring tricks. Jobai wears a voluminous full-length natural raffia cape and a square headpiece covered with coloured wool and mirrors. It moves slowly, swirling and making objects 'disappear' under its cape. Yayi's headpiece is nearly identical to that of Jobai, but its body costume consists of ruffs of natural raffia that follow the articulation of the limbs. It is known primarily as a dancer. Each of these masks has a group of entrepreneurial attendants who own and 'control' it and profit from the fees it collects. Humorous Gongoli is the least sacred but most frequently encountered of the men's masks. It wears an oversize wooden face mask grotesquely carved in the image of an ugly old man (see fig. 2). The costume consists of sparse raffia that reverses normal masquerade decorum by clearly revealing the body. Gongoli clowns, parodying the serious maskers and satirizing members of the community in a deep, growling voice.

(iii) Other secret society masks. The Njayei and Humoi societies possess medicines effective against madness and

illnesses caused by infractions of incest laws. Their masks are relatively rare and poorly documented. The Njayei spirit, like Sowei, is associated with water, and the headpiece worn by the masker is also a carved, black-stained wooden helmet displaying female traits, although the specific form can vary greatly. It is worn with a full-length natural raffia cape. All Njayei masks are daubed with spots of white, brown, yellow, or black paint. Little is known about the Humoi society masker. One example wears a headpiece closely resembling a Sowei mask, but smaller, with a natural raffia cape and leg coverings (for illustration see Migeod, 1926).

3. FIGURE SCULPTURE. In western Mendeland the Njayei society uses paired male and female guardian figures called *kambeisia* (sing. *kambei*). Guardian figures are probably used by the other societies. In the past the Sande society used a palette for mixing the white clay worn by initiates and other officials, the handles of which were often carved as a female head and neck. Most Mende carved figures, however, belong to the category of decorative, prestige carvings known as *gewe haka* (idle things). Other decoratively carved objects include staffs carried traditionally by chiefs and senior secret society officials, often with a rattle and a female head at the top. Hammock bars, spoons, game boards and other objects with similar carved female heads are also known. Many wood-carvers also carve in ivory. The most notable ivory objects of the Mende are the large horns used to herald the approach of a paramount chief. These were previously used by warriors and have been made since at least the 18th century. They sometimes have human and animal heads carved in low relief as well as non-representational ornamental elements.

Small (*c.* 150–200 mm) anthropomorphic steatite figurines called *nomoli* are sometimes found by Mende farmers when digging their fields. These figures have disproportionately large heads and rounded, bulging features and body forms. Mende claim that *nomoli* were not made by their own ancestors. They are regarded as agricultural deities and used as medicines. (For an account of similar figures among another people of this region, *see* KISSI.)

4. TEXTILES. The Mende weave cloth on a double-heddle, narrow-strip loom of a tripod type that is moved along the warp as the weaving progresses. Narrow strips (*c.* 800 to 1600 mm wide) are made from native cotton yarn and left undyed or dyed with indigo and brown vegetable dye. Imported thread is also used. The strips are edge-sewn to produce vertically striped 'country cloths' or the more intricate patterns of rarer *kpokpoi* and *njaye* cloths. Woven cloth is used for bedding, hangings, hammocks and men's gowns. Tie-dyed and resist-dyed cloth called *gara* is made by women using both vegetable and commercial dyes and imported damask cloth in a wide variety of patterns.

BIBLIOGRAPHY
T. J. Alldridge: *The Sherbro and its Hinterland* (London, 1901)
W. Volz: 'Eine Reise an die Flüsse Kittam und Bum in der Sierra Leone', *Jber. Geog. Ges. Bern*, xx (1905–6), pp. 231–49
T. J. Alldridge: *A Transformed Colony: Sierra Leone as it Was, and as it Is, its Progress, Peoples, Native Customs and Undeveloped Wealth* (London, 1910)

W. Volz: 'Reise durch das Hinterland von Liberia, im Winter 1906–7, nach seinen Tagebüchern bearbeitet von Dr. Rud. Zeller', *Jber. Geog. Ges. Bern*, xxii (1911) [whole issue]

R. Zeller: 'Die Bundu Gesellschaft: Ein Geheimbund der Sierra Leone', *Jber. Hist. Mus. Bern* (1912), pp. 103–44

F. W. Migeod: *A View of Sierra Leone* (London, 1926)

J. Staub: 'Beiträge zur Kenntnis der materiellen Kultur der Mendi in der Sierra Leone', *Jb. Bern. Hist. Mus.*, xv (1935) [whole issue]

R. Eberl-Elber: *Westafrikas letztes Rätsel: Erlebnisbericht über die Forschungsreise 1935 durch Sierra Leone* (Salzburg, 1936)

S. Brown: 'The Nomoli of Mende Country', *Africa*, xviii/1 (1948), pp. 18–20

J. B. O. Richards: 'The Sande Mask', *Afr. A.*, vii/2 (1974), pp. 48–51

Art of the Mende (exh. cat., ed. W. Hommel; College Park, U. MD A.G., 1974)

L. R. Reinhardt: *Mende Carvers* (diss., Edwardsville, S. IL U., 1975)

W. Siegmann and J. Perani: 'Men's Masquerades of Sierra Leone and Liberia', *Afr. A.*, ix/3 (1976), pp. 42–7, 92

R. B. Phillips: 'Masking in Mende Sande Society Initiation Rituals', *Africa*, xlviii/3 (1978), pp. 265–77

——: *The Sande Society Masks of the Mende of Sierra Leone* (diss., U. London, 1979)

——: 'The Iconography of the Mende *Sowei* Mask', *Ethnol. Z. Zürich*, i (1980), pp. 113–32

J. Henggeler: 'Ivory Trumpets of the Mende', *Afr. A.*, xiv/2 (1981), pp. 59–63

F. Lamp: 'Cosmos, Cosmetics, and the Spirit of Bondo', *Afr. A.*, xviii/3 (1985), pp. 28–43, 98

S. A. Boone: *Radiance from the Waters: Ideals of Feminine Beauty in Mende Art* (New Haven, CT, and London, 1986) [well illus.]; review by F. Lamp in *Afr. A.*, xx/3 (1987), pp. 17–26, 72–4

J. P. Edwards: 'The Sociological Significance and Uses of Mende Country Cloth', *History, Design, and Craft in West African Strip-woven Cloth: Papers Presented at a Symposium Organized by the National Museum of African Art, Smithsonian Institution, February 18–19, 1988*, pp. 133–68

R. B. Phillips: *Representing Woman: Sande Masquerades of the Mende of Sierra Leone*, (Los Angeles, 1995)

RUTH B. PHILLIPS

Mende, Valér (*b* Pinkóc [now Pinkafeld, Austria], 4 Sept 1886; *d* Vienna, 7 Jan 1918). Hungarian architect. He studied at the Hungarian Palatine Joseph Technical University, Budapest, under Samu Pecz, between 1904 and 1908. One of his chief works is the collection of buildings (1909–12) in the main square at Kecskemét. The building housing the Reform Theological College and High School, with its lively proportions and high roof, shows the influence of Eliel Saarinen and of English work, but Mende also used medieval elements, including natural stone and plaster, raw brick and ceramic decoration. Facing the square, the Evangelical Church residential block, in addition to medieval elements, shows vernacular influences associated with the Fiatalok (Hung.: 'The young') group. The bank building (1911–12) in the main square at Gyöngyös is a small building, partly in Viennese style but revealing Mende's distinctively English orientation, for which he was notable among his contemporaries, while the interior of his Komló Hotel (1911), Gyula, reveals Wiener Werkstätte elements. Mende also built numerous residential blocks and villas in Budapest and Nagyvárad.

BIBLIOGRAPHY
J. Gerle: 'Mende Valér', *Magyar Építőművészet*, lxxviii/4–5 (1987), pp. 43–8

F. BOR

Mendelsohn, Erich (*b* Allenstein [now Olsztyn, Poland], 21 March 1887; *d* San Francisco, 15 Sept 1953). German architect, teacher and writer, active also in England, Palestine and the USA. He was one of the most influential exponents of architectural Expressionism, his sketches of fluid organic building forms and his Einstein Tower, Potsdam, being among the best-known products of the movement. Although his later work abandoned three-dimensional forms in favour of more conventional, geometric designs, these often incorporated curvilinear plans and retained an innovative dynamism.

1. Early work and career in Germany, before 1933. 2. England, Palestine and the USA, 1933 and after.

1. EARLY WORK AND CAREER IN GERMANY, BEFORE 1933. He grew up as one of six children of a Jewish business family in the small East Prussian town of Allenstein. Following his father's wishes, in 1907 he began to study economics at the University of Munich but in 1908 followed his own inclinations and enrolled as an architecture student at the Technische Hochschule, Berlin. In 1910 he returned to Munich to complete his architectural studies under Theodor Fischer, one of the most progressive teachers at the Technische Hochschule, and as a student he met several Expressionist artists, including Paul Klee, Franz Marc, Vasily Kandinsky and Hugo Ball. After graduating in 1912 Mendelsohn began to work independently as a designer, decorating shop-windows and producing drawings for costumes for a masked ball in Munich (1912). For a time he considered becoming a stage designer and became involved with his Expressionist artist friends and their efforts to revitalize Munich's avant-garde theatre.

On the outbreak of World War I Mendelsohn was drafted into the army and served as an engineer until 1918, first on the Russian front and then on the French. Most of his famous visionary architectural sketches (Berlin, Kstbib. & Mus.) were drawn during this period, some of them while serving in the trenches. They were first exhibited at the Galerie Paul Cassirer in Berlin in 1919, and some were published by Mendelsohn in his *Das Gesamtschaffen des Architekten* (1930). Several are no larger than a postage stamp; all are free, often bold, perspective sketches of organic building forms with such names as Machine Factory (1914), Central Railway Station (1915) and Sanctuaries in Reinforced Concrete (1917). Although misunderstood by most contemporary critics as 'nice vignettes', they represented Mendelsohn's faith in the potential of reinforced concrete as a monolithic building material that would open the way to a new architecture of dynamic sculptural forms, freely moulded in three dimensions and unconstrained by the morphological disciplines of column-and-beam construction. Stylistically, he was influenced by the new formal freedoms emerging from the innovations of Art Nouveau architecture in Vienna, Barcelona and elsewhere. He admired the work of the Secession, particularly that of Joseph Maria Olbrich, as well as that of Henry Van de Velde, who, with Bruno Taut, had led the Expressionist bid for freedom from the machine aesthetic at the Deutscher Werkbund exhibition (1914) at Cologne with his model theatre (destr.). At the end of 1918 Mendelsohn joined the radical Arbeitsrat für Kunst and the avant-garde Novembergruppe.

Before the war Mendelsohn had become acquainted with the astronomer Erwin Freundlich, who worked in Potsdam and was involved in the experimental proof of

Albert Einstein's General Theory of Relativity. Mendelsohn had sent sketches for an observatory (1917) to Freundlich from the Russian front, and when he opened his office in Berlin in 1919 he was commissioned to build a combined observatory and astrophysical laboratory. The resulting design of the Einstein Tower (Einsteinturm; 1920–24; see fig. 1), although symmetrical about its long axis, is highly original in form. Erected in Potsdam, it appears to have been cast rather than built, and it reflects with remarkable accuracy the character of the multi-layered buildings of the wartime sketches; this is even more remarkable perhaps because much of the building was in fact constructed of brick, cement-rendered to give the monolithic appearance of concrete, as it proved too difficult to construct shuttering for the curved surfaces. The Einstein Tower achieved immediate international acclaim and remains the symbol of architectural Expressionism.

Mendelsohn visited Rotterdam and Amsterdam in 1920 at a critical time in his development. He contrasted the rational, rectilinear architecture of De Stijl with the dynamism of the Amsterdam school and thought it conceivable that they could be combined. His Steinberg, Hermann & Co. hat factory (1921–3; destr.), Luckenwalde, was as angular as the Einstein Tower is fluid, its direct expression of purpose conveyed by innovative portal-frame construction in concrete. The buildings that immediately followed included a double villa (1922) on the Karolinger Platz, Berlin; extensions to the Tageblatt Building (1921–3), Jerusalemstrasse, Berlin, for Rudolf Mosse; and, in 1923, the Weichmann store at Gleiwitz, Upper Silesia (now Gliwice, Poland) and the Sternefeld Villa, Heerstrasse, Berlin. Of these, only the Tageblatt Building relied on a curved-corner plan profile for its expressive dynamism. In all of them, however, Mendelsohn began to introduce dynamic forms into rectilinear façades through a characteristic horizontality, expressed in projected, sometimes grooved or lined, slabs above and below windows and spandrel walls.

By 1923 Expressionism was no longer central to the development of the Modern Movement in architecture, and about this time Der Ring was founded in Berlin to support the concepts of *Neues Bauen*; Mendelsohn became a member in 1925. He also undertook trips to Palestine (now Israel) in 1923, having won a competition for a business centre in Haifa, but this and two other projects in Haifa—the Ruthenberg Power Station and a garden city on Mt Carmel (both 1923)—were not realized. In 1924 he met Frank Lloyd Wright on a visit to the USA, where he wrote a series of articles with photographs that was later published as a book (1928), and in 1925 he went to Russia, where he designed a hosiery factory (1925–7) at Leningrad (now St Petersburg); another book (1929) followed this trip. Back in Germany, his next important client was Salman Schocken, a publisher and businessman for whom Mendelsohn designed three large department stores over the next few years, at Nuremberg and Stuttgart (1926–7; the latter destr. 1960) and at Chemnitz (1928–9; see fig. 2). In these stores he was able to retain some reminiscences of his visionary sketches by means of sweeping plan forms, creating a linear, horizontal dynamism in the contrasting effects of repeated continuous bands of windows and

1. Erich Mendelsohn: Einstein Tower, Potsdam, 1920–24

smooth, light-coloured spandrel walls; this was especially effective when linking intersecting streets with curving façades, as at Chemnitz, or in contrasting curved projections with straight wall surfaces, as at Stuttgart, with its projecting cylindrical stairwell. His stores are also remarkable for the integration of their signage with the architecture. Other commercial urban buildings designed in the second half of the 1920s included the Cohen & Epstein store (1926), Duisburg; Deukon Haus (1927–8), Markgrafenstrasse, Berlin; Rudolf Petersdorff store (1927–8), Breslau (now Wrocław, Poland); and the WOGA-Komplex (1927–31) flanking the Kurfürstendamm in Berlin, a mixed development of shops, housing, a hotel, theatre and the well-known Universum cinema, a prototype for urban cinemas of the 1930s. In smaller buildings of the same period, such as the Bejach House, Neue Babelsberg, near Potsdam, and the Jewish cemetery buildings at Königsberg (now Kaliningrad, Russia; both 1927; the latter destr.), Mendelsohn achieved his dynamic horizontality by means of rustication, contrasting wider bands of brickwork with narrow, lighter bands of stucco.

At the end of the 1920s Mendelsohn's office was one of the largest and most successful in Europe, with 40 employees. He usually designed while listening to music, particularly that of Bach, and he continued to work with spontaneous perspective sketches, often combining pen and pencil with coloured crayons and often with suggestions of strong Futurist influence. His own house (1929–30) at Rupenhorn, Berlin, with large windows and a garden terrace overlooking the Havelsee, is simple, stuccoed, rectilinear, technically sophisticated and more in the spirit of *Neue Sachlichkeit* than Expressionism. For a brief period it became the centre of intellectual society in Berlin, with Albert Einstein, André Gide, Albert Kahn and Henry Morgenthau among Mendelsohn's guests. His work was widely exhibited at this time, for example in New York (1929), London (1931) and Milan (1932). His last major building in Germany, the Columbushaus (1931–2; destr.), Berlin, was a ten-storey shop and office building with a graceful convex façade to the street. With its continuous bands of windows with narrowly spaced mullions made

2. Erich Mendelsohn: Schocken Department Store, Chemnitz, 1928–9

possible by a steel frame set back from the outer wall, and a top storey recessed under a boldly cantilevered roof, it provided a prototype for office buildings all over Europe. A few months after its completion, however, and immediately following Hitler's rise to power in 1933, Mendelsohn left Germany.

2. ENGLAND, PALESTINE AND THE USA, 1933 AND AFTER. Following an invitation from the RIBA, Mendelsohn went to London where he formed a partnership with SERGE CHERMAYEFF. The partnership was short-lived (1933–6), and their executed work together consisted of only three buildings: the De La Warr Pavilion (1934–5), Bexhill-on-Sea, won in open competition, and two white Modern Movement houses: the Nimmo House (1935), Chalfont St Giles, and the Cohen House (1936), Chelsea, London. At the De La Warr Pavilion, a seaside entertainment complex, the cylindrical, three-storey drum of the south staircase, with open galleries at each of the higher levels, is in dynamic contrast to the rectilinear entertainment and restaurant wings. The transparency of the seaward elevation is made more striking by the innovative cantilevered floors, carried on one of the first all-welded steel frames in Britain.

At the end of 1934 Mendelsohn was invited to Palestine by the chemist and Zionist leader, Chaim Weizmann (later the first President of Israel), who commissioned him to design a villa (completed 1936) at Rehovot, south of Tel Aviv, which was built around an internal courtyard. This commission marked the start of Mendelsohn's career in Palestine, and in 1935 he opened a branch of his practice in Jerusalem, ultimately moving his office there altogether in 1939. During this period, as well as a stone house (1936) in Jerusalem for his old German client Salman Schocken, he designed and built several large-scale works in Palestine, including a government hospital (1937–8) facing the sea at Haifa; the Hadassah University Medical Centre (1937–9; rest. 1976), Mt Scopus, Jerusalem, which dominated the Dead Sea and Jordan Valley; the Anglo-Palestinian Bank (1938–9; now the National Bank of Israel), Jerusalem; and the Agricultural University and the Daniel Wolf Research Laboratories (both 1939–41) at Rehovot. The three-storey rectilinear buildings of the Hadassah Centre are enlivened by cupolas and retain Mendelsohn's innovative spirit, but like all his buildings in Palestine they reflect a responsible attitude to the physical, climatic and cultural context, far removed from the radical, extrovert Expressionism of his German work in the 1920s: here a more contemplative aesthetic is closely related to traditional local building forms. Mendelsohn himself felt that in his bank building he had at last found the ideal balance between the static and the dynamic. By 1941, however, the outbreak of World War II and increasing local political problems resulted in a lack of commissions, and he accepted an offer of teaching work in the USA.

Mendelsohn went to New York in 1941, and an exhibition of his work was held there at MOMA in 1942, but for the first five years his activities were largely confined to teaching at different colleges and universities. He was able to practise only after becoming naturalized, and he subsequently set up an office in 1945 in San Francisco, where he was commissioned to design the seven-storey Maimonides Hospital (1946–50; remod. 1953), Sutter Street. After building a Jewish community centre (1946–50) at St Louis, MO, consisting of a synagogue and assembly room, he began to receive similar commissions in which he developed a new plan arrangement, allowing more flexible use of the main spaces. Four of these were built, including the Park Synagogue (1946–52; *see* JEWISH ART, fig. 11) at Cleveland, OH; the Emanu-El Center (1948–52) at Grand Rapids, MI; and the Mount Zion Center (1950–54; completed after his death) at St Paul, MN. He also built a house for Leon B. Russell (1950–51) at Pacific Heights, San Francisco, which was reminiscent of his own house in Berlin. There were flashes of his earlier creativity in the balcony plans of the Maimonides Hospital and also in the synagogues, seen in the great dome over a windowed drum at Cleveland. His wish to use the more advanced structural techniques then available in order to re-create the dynamic forms of his early sketches in his projects of this period, which included the American Monument to the Jewish War Dead in New York, remained unfulfilled, however, at his death.

WRITINGS

Bauten und Skizzen (Berlin, 1924)
Amerika: Bilderbuch eines Architekten (Berlin, 1928)
Russland, Europa, Amerika: Ein architektonischer Querschnitt (Berlin, 1929)
Das Gesamtschaffen des Architekten (Berlin, 1930/*R* Brunswick, 1988; Eng. trans., 1992)
Neues Haus, Neue Welt (Berlin, 1931)
Palestine and the World of Tomorrow (Jerusalem, 1940)
O. Beyer, ed.: *Erich Mendelsohn: Briefe eines Architekten* (Munich, 1961; Eng. trans., London, 1967)

BIBLIOGRAPHY

A. Whittick: *Eric Mendelsohn* (London, 1940, rev. New York, 2/1965)
M. F. Roggero: *Il contributo di Mendelsohn all'evoluzione dell'architettura moderna* (Milan, 1952)
P. R. Banham: 'Mendelsohn', *Archit. Rev.* [London], cxvi/692 (1954), pp. 84–93
W. von Eckardt: *Erich Mendelsohn* (Ravensburg, 1962)
Erich Mendelsohn (exh. cat., W. Berlin, Akad. Kst., 1968)
J. Posener: 'Erich Mendelsohn (1969)', *Aufsätze und Vorträge, 1931–1980* (Brunswick, 1981), pp. 175–87
B. Zevi: *Erich Mendelsohn: Opera completa* (Milan, 1970)
J. Posener: 'Erich Mendelsohn', *Archit. Plus*, 48 (1979), pp. 8–13
Eric Mendelsohn: Drawings of an Architect (exh. cat., ed. N. Guralnik; Tel Aviv, Tel Aviv Mus. A., 1979)
B. Zevi: *Erich Mendelsohn* (Bologna, 1982; Eng. trans., 1985)
I. Heinze-Mühleib: *Erich Mendelsohn: Bauten und Projekte in Palästina, 1934–1941* (Munich, 1986)
J. Brook and others, eds: *Erich Mendelsohn, 1887–1953* (London, 1987)
I. Heinze-Greenberg: 'Erich Mendelsohn', *Berliner Lebensbilder* (Berlin, 1987)
Erich Mendelsohn (exh. cat., ed. S. Achenbach; Berlin, Kstbib. & Mus., 1987)
Erich Mendelsohn in Palestine (exh. cat., ed. I. Heinze-Greenberg and G. Herbert; Haifa, Technion, 1987)
J. Glancey: 'Mendelsohn in England', *30s Soc. J.*, vii (1991), pp. 40–45

ITA HEINZE-GREENBERG

Mendelssohn, Moses (*b* Dessau, 26 Sept 1729; *d* Berlin, 4 Jan 1786). German philosopher. He overcame ill-health, the restrictions placed on Jews and his family's straitened circumstances to become one of the most influential philosophers of the German Enlightenment. He was largely self-taught, and in his own writing he discussed a wide range of metaphysical and aesthetic problems in a lively and approachable manner. The framework of his thought was provided by the work of Gottfried Wilhelm von Leibniz and Christian Wolff, but he was an eclectic philosopher and through his reading of J. G. Sulzer, the Earl of Shaftesbury and later Johann Joachim Winckelmann and Edmund Burke, and by his close association with Gotthold Ephraim Lessing, he moved beyond defining the beautiful purely in terms of either logic or ethics. In his early writings Mendelssohn explained the nature of the beautiful by referring to the concept of perfection, whether the perfection of the object perceived or the perfection of the perceiving subject. He later focused attention on the effects of the beautiful and on the process of perception, contributing to the psychological understanding of aesthetic perception and arguing for the importance of mixed emotions. He thus contributed towards a notion of aesthetic autonomy and towards the process by which art came to include subjects that were neither beautiful nor desirable.

WRITINGS

Gesammelte Schriften, 7 vols (Berlin and Breslau, 1929–38); rev. 22 vols (Stuttgart, 1971–)

BIBLIOGRAPHY

J. H. Schoeps: *Moses Mendelssohn* (Königstein im Taunus, 1979)
K. W. Segreff: *Moses Mendelssohn und die Aufklärungsästhetik im 18 Jh.*, Abhandlungen zur Philosophie, Psychologie und Pädagogik, 187 (Bonn, 1984)

DAVID HILL

Mendes [now Tall al-Rub'a and Tall Timay; Tell el-Rub'a and Tell Timay]. Egyptian city in the Nile Delta, which flourished from at least the Old Kingdom (2575–*c.* 2150 BC) to the Christian era (*c.* AD 800). The site, which was first excavated by François Mariette in 1860, consists of two contiguous mounds. To the north is Tall al-Rub'a, the site of the capital of Egypt in the 29th Dynasty (399–380 BC), and to the south Tall Timay (Gr. Thmuis), the site of an ancient settlement, which superseded that of Tall al-Rub'a during the Roman period (30 BC–AD 395). The principal deity of Mendes was Banebdjed, usually represented as a ram or a ram-headed man. Numerous stone sarcophagi of the sacred ram abound in the north-western part of Tall al-Rub'a. Banebdjed, Hatmehyt the dolphin-goddess (worshipped at Mendes in Predynastic times) and their child, Harpocrates, formed a group of deities known as the Mendesian triad.

The earliest monuments at Tall al-Rub'a are late Old Kingdom mastabas. The principal owner of one mastaba was, unusually, a woman. Her funerary equipment included a bronze mirror and pieces of galena as well as fragments of thin gold leaf, which covered the body here and there. In the 26th Dynasty, Amasis (*reg* 570–526 BC) embellished the sanctuary of Banebdjed. All that remains of this is a colossal red granite naos, which stands on a platform of limestone. This monolithic naos, which dominates the site, was one of four originally erected in a court before the temple. Each was associated with one of the incarnations of Banebdjed. The massive mud-brick enclosure wall of the temple has been dated to the 29th Dynasty, and the discovery of a stone sarcophagus probably belonging to Nepherites I (*reg* 399–393 BC) suggests that the kings of the 29th Dynasty were interred at Mendes, their capital. A cache of pharaonic sculpture was found in the vicinity of the sarcophagus, including a representation of the Roman emperor Caracalla (*reg* AD 211–217) in Egyptian style (Cairo, Egyp. Mus.).

The site has also yielded many Classical works, including a hoard of silver objects and a cache of Greek marble sculptures (e.g. Cairo, Egyp. Mus.; Alexandria, Gr.-Rom. Mus.). One of the marbles may represent Ptolemy III Euergetes I (*reg* 246–221 BC) as Dionysos, while another may depict Arsinoe III, the sister and consort of Ptolemy IV (*reg* 221–205 BC). There are also several mosaics, including one signed by SOPHILOS, the subject of which is perhaps a personification of Alexandria. From the Roman Imperial period there is a series of libation tables, provisionally dated to the 2nd and 3rd centuries and now in several museum collections (e.g. Cairo, Egyp. Mus.; New York, Met.; Paris, Louvre).

BIBLIOGRAPHY

C. C. Edgar: 'A Terracotta from Mendes', *Bull. Soc. Royale Archéol., Alexandrie*, n. s. 8, i/3 (1905), pp. 7–10
H. de Meulenaere and P. MacKay: *Mendes*, ii (Warminster, 1976)
P. Holz, D. Stieglitz, D. P. Hansen and E. Ochenschlager: *Mendes*, i (Warminster, 1980)
K. L. Wilson: *Mendes: A Preliminary Report of the 1979 and 1980 Seasons*, ii of *Cities of the Delta* (Malibu, 1981)
W. A. Daszewski: *Corpus of Mosaics from Roman Egypt*, i (Mainz, 1985)
V. A. Hibbs: *The Mendes Maze: A Libation Table for the Inundation of the Nile (II–III A.D.)* (New York, 1985)

ROBERT S. BIANCHI

Mendes da Costa, Joseph [Jozef] (*b* Amsterdam, 4 Nov 1863; *d* Amsterdam, 20 July 1939). Dutch sculptor and ceramicist. His first training was in the stone-carving workshop of his father. He also attended the Quellinus School (1879–81) and the Rijksschool voor Kunstnijverheid (1882–5) in Amsterdam. With some of his fellow students, including Lambertus Zijl, Gerrit Willem Dijsselhof and T. W. Nieuwenhuis, he formed the artists' group Labor et Ars in 1885. Their principal concern was the design of utensils, in which they aimed to produce an individual style and to react against the styles of the past; in this they belonged to the group of artists who initiated a revival of the Dutch applied arts. Between 1885 and 1888 Mendes da Costa formed a partnership with Zijl for the creation of sculptures and applied-art products. From 1888 until 1902 he was a teacher of modelling at the Industrieschool of the Society for the Working Classes in Amsterdam.

From 1880 Mendes da Costa made such utensils as vases and dishes in clay, which he glazed himself and had fired in a pottery. His first sculptural works, including a number of groups inspired by scenes observed in the Jewish quarter of Amsterdam, also date from this time. As the results of the glazed earthenware pieces were not always to his satisfaction, he built his own kiln in 1898 and then began to work in stoneware with salt-glaze, producing objects in series as well as single items. He used the medium to make figures, animals and utensils with stricter and more stylized forms, a tendency that he continued in

ceramic and bronze biblical figures and animals made between 1907 and 1912. In his bronze statues of *Vincent van Gogh* (h. 380 mm, *c.* 1908) and the philosopher *Benedict Spinoza* (h. 330 mm, 1909; both Otterlo, Rijksmus. Kröller-Müller) and other portraits, his first consideration was to represent the essence of the person portrayed, likeness being of secondary importance. His animal figurines were highly praised and led to his receiving an honorary doctorate in biology in 1914 from the University of Groningen. Further recognition for his work came in the form of the Grand Prix at the Exposition Internationale des Arts Décoratifs et Industriels Modernes in Paris in 1925.

Although Mendes da Costa became particularly known for his small sculptures, he also sculpted on and in several buildings, thus realizing his ideals of the unity of architecture and sculpture. He obtained his first large commission in 1900: two stone threshold guards, winged lions, for an office block by H. P. Berlage in Surabaya, Java; he had recourse here to Egyptian and Assyrian art, which he had studied with his brother-in-law, the graphic artist S. Jessurun de Mesquita (1868–1944), in the Rijksmuseum van Oudheden, Leiden. He also worked on another building by Berlage, the Koopmansbeurs in Amsterdam (1898–1903), with, among others, Zijl, Richard Roland Holst, Antoon Derkinderen and Jan Toorop. Mendes da Costa made two chimney-pieces and the wood-carvings on desks and cupboards. In addition he worked with the architects A. J. Kropholler and J. F. Staal on the offices of the life insurance firm Utrecht, for their branches in Amsterdam (1904–6) and Utrecht (1909), and made sculptures on the building of the Nederlandsche Handel Maatschappij (Dutch Trading Company; 1925), Amsterdam, designed by K. P. C. de Bazel.

Mendes da Costa also made some free-standing monuments, including two commissioned by Hélène Kröller-Müller, one to the South African general *Rudolph Christiaan de Wet* (stone, h. *c.* 13 m, 1915–17) and the other, *The Counsellor* (stone, h. 2.5 m, 1920–24; both Otterlo, Hoge Veluwe N. Park), to the South African President Marthinus Theunis Steijn. During the work for the latter he became convinced that he should abandon the idea of making an ordinary portrait and that he must express the essence of statesmanship. He devoted the last years of his life, between 1927 and 1939, to the monument the *Course of Life*, in which the main motif is the life of a man from birth to adulthood and old age. The work, however, was never completed. With Zijl, he was considered to be important in his role of reviving sculpture in the Netherlands, and with Willem Brouwer and the ceramicist Christiaan Johannes Lanooy (1881–1948), he was influential in his technical mastery as a ceramicist.

BIBLIOGRAPHY

Scheen
F. M. Huebner: *Niederländische Plastik der Gegenwart* (Dresden, n.d.), pp. 19–21
Wendingen, n. s. 4, 5–6 (1923) [issue devoted to Mendes da Costa]
T. B. Roorda: *Dr. J. Mendes da Costa* (Amsterdam, 1929)
A. M. Hammacher: *Mendes da Costa: De geestelijke boodschap der beeldhouwkunst* [Mendes da Costa: the spiritual message of sculpture] (Rotterdam, 1941)
T. van Reijn: *Nederlandse beeldhouwers van deze tijd* [Dutch sculptors of this time] (Amsterdam, 1949), pp. 25–9

A. M. Hammacher: *Beeldhouwkunst van deze eeuw* [Sculpture of this century] (Amsterdam, 1955), pp. 18–20, 22–33

Dr. Joseph Mendes da Costa, 1863–1939—beeldhouwer (exh. cat. by A. Pieters, Amsterdam, Joods Hist. Mus., 1976)

M. G. Spruit-Ledeboer: *Nederlandse keramiek, 1900–1975* (Amsterdam, 1977), pp. 240–43, 358–9

F. de Miranda: *Mendes da Costa, Jessurun de Mesquita: Nederlandse beeldende kunstenaars—joden in de verstrooiing* [Mendes da Costa, Jessurun de Mesquita: Dutch artists—Jews of the Diaspora] (Wassenaar, 1978)

MIEKE VAN DER WAL

Mendes da Rocha, Paulo (Archias) (*b* Vitória, Espirito Santo, 25 Oct 1928). Brazilian architect. He graduated in architecture in 1954 from Mackenzie University, São Paulo, one of a new generation of professionals from the newly created, autonomous architecture faculties that replaced the specialist courses in engineering schools. He entered private practice in São Paulo in 1955, and in 1957 he won a competition for the Paulistano Athletics Club, São Paulo. His design incorporated an ingenious structural system and a dramatic trussed roof; it also won a prize at the 1961 Biennale in São Paulo. In 1961 he was invited by João B. Vilanova Artigas, one of the runners-up in the competition for the athletics club, to lecture at the Faculty of Architecture and Urbanism at the University of São Paulo; he was later dismissed by the military government because of his political views (1969). His architecture was increasingly influenced by Brutalism; the influence of Artigas was particularly evident in his early designs, although he also admired Oscar Niemeyer and Affonso Eduardo Reidy. His affinity with Artigas can be seen in his ability to create imaginative and unexpected spatial solutions from architectural briefs. Other buildings resulting from prizewinning competition entries include the Jockey Club (1963), Goiânia, and the Brazilian Pavilion (1970; with Flavio Motta, Julio Katinsky and Ruy Ohtake) at Expo' 70 in Osaka, Japan, and in 1971 he was placed in the international competition for the design of the Centre Georges Pompidou, Paris. During the 1960s and 1970s, frequently working with others, he completed several schools and housing estates, office buildings such as the Municipal Insurance Headquarters (1975) in the new administrative centre of São Paulo, cultural buildings such as the Museu de Arte Contemporânea (1975; with Jorge Wilheim) at the University of São Paulo, and university buildings such as those (1977) at Rondonôpolis, Mato Grosso.

BIBLIOGRAPHY

F. Motta, ed.: 'Obra do arquiteto Paulo A. Mendes da Rocha'. *Acrópole*, 343 (Aug–Sept 1967), p. 17 [special issue]

'Museu de Arte Contemporânea, Universidade de São Paulo', *Módulo*, 42 (1976), pp. 60–67

Y. Bruand: *Arquitetura contemporânea no Brasil* (São Paulo, 1981)

CARLOS A. C. LEMOS

Méndez, Leopoldo (*b* Mexico City, 30 June 1902; *d* Mexico City, 8 Feb 1969). Mexican painter, printmaker, illustrator and draughtsman. He studied in Mexico City at the Academia de San Carlos (1917–19) and at the Escuela de Pintura al Aire Libre de Chimalistac (1920–22). During the 1920s he was associated with ESTRIDENTISMO, and from 1925 to 1928 he worked as an illustrator for magazines such as *Horizonte* and *Norte de Veracruz*. After exhibiting his work for the first time in the USA in 1930 he held several exhibitions abroad, and in 1939 he received a grant from the Guggenheim Foundation in New York.

Méndez was co-founder in 1934 of the Liga de Escritores y Artistas Revolucionarios, which operated until 1937. On its dissolution he and two other printmakers from the group founded the TALLER DE GRÁFICA POPULAR, whose plastic arts section he headed and which he directed until 1952. As an ideologically committed member of the Mexican Communist Party, he produced outstanding prints in a social realist style, which reflect the problems of social struggle and reveal him as the heir to José Guadalupe Posada. Some of his prints were woodcuts and linocuts, made for films during the 'golden age' of Mexican cinema, such as *Río escondido* (1947), *Pueblerina* (1948), *El rebozo de Soledad* (1949) and *Memorias de un mexicano* (1950). He also had various books published, winning a prize for the best illustrated book with *Incidentes melódicos del mundo irracional* (Mexico City, 1946) by Juan de la Cabada. In addition he produced mural and other large-scale works, sometimes in collaboration with other artists, such as *Playing with Lights* (12 sq. m, 1949), engraved on 12 sheets of transparent plastic and housed in the former Nacional Financiera building in Mexico City. Méndez taught drawing and printmaking, and in 1946 he received the Primer Premio de Grabado de México.

BIBLIOGRAPHY

Leopoldo Méndez (1902–1969) (exh. cat., ed. Inba; Mexico City, Pal. B.A., 1970)

Leopoldo Méndez: Artista de un pueblo en lucha (exh. cat., ed. Ceestem; Mexico City, Cent. Estud. Econ. & Soc. Tercer Mundo, 1981)

LEONOR MORALES

Méndez de Haro y Guzmán, Luis. *See* CARPIO, (2).

Mendieta, Ana (*b* Havana, 18 Nov 1948; *d* New York, 8 Sept 1985). American sculptor, performance artist, video artist and painter of Cuban birth. From the age of 13, when she was sent to the USA from Cuba by her parents, she lived in orphanages and foster homes in Iowa. Her sense of exile and the separation from her family proved strong motivating forces on her later work. After completing an MA in painting at the University of Iowa in 1972 she entered the university's new Multimedia and Video Art programme, in which she was free to experiment and develop a unique formal language, gaining an MFA in 1977.

In the 1970s Mendieta began to create 'earth-body sculptures' outdoors in Iowa, using the primal materials of blood, earth, fire and water, having first executed performances that she documented in photographs or black-and-white films. In the *Silueta* series she traced or sculpted the image of her body on the ground, using ignited gunpowder, leaves, grass, mud, stones, other natural elements or cloth. She visited Mexico in 1971 (and again in 1973, 1974, 1976 and 1978) and Cuba in 1980 and 1981, thus re-establishing her connections with Latin America and stimulating her interest in the Afro-Caribbean Santería religion. Her *Rupestrian Sculptures*, carved in the rocks at the Escaleras de Jaruco in Cuba, refer to primitive goddess images.

Mendieta married Carl André in 1975 and lived from 1978 in New York. In 1983 she moved to Rome on an American Academy Fellowship. There she created her first permanent objects in a studio setting. She extended and refined the principles of her early work in floor sculptures representing generalized female shapes, delicate and elegant drawings on leaves and bark paper, and large-scale sculptures in which her characteristic abstracted female silhouettes were burnt into tree trunks. Her feelings of alienation, which resulted not only from her exile but from her sense of being marginalized as a Latin American woman, were channelled into powerful, magical and poetic work. André was charged with her murder but acquitted.

BIBLIOGRAPHY

Ana Mendieta: A Retrospective (exh. cat., ed. P. Barreras del Rio and J. Perreault; New York, New Mus. Contemp. A., 1987)

J. Tully: 'André Acquitted', *New A. Examiner*, 15 (April 1988), pp. 22–4

A. S. Wooster: 'Ana Mendieta: Themes of Death and Resurrection', *High Performance*, 11 (Spring/Summer 1988), pp. 80–83

SUSAN S. WEININGER

Mendívil, Luis Aladrén y. *See* ALADRÉN Y MENDÍVIL, LUIS.

Mendonça, Francisco de Almada e. *See* ALMADA, (2).

Mendoza. Spanish family of collectors and patrons. The family settled in Guadalajara in the 14th century. Pedro González de Mendoza (*d* 1385) became Chief Steward to King Juan I, and his grandson, Iñigo López de Mendoza I, became Marqués de Santillana. The family, who assumed the title of the Duques del Infantado, played a prominent role in the political and cultural life of Spain from the 15th to the 17th centuries, when it was united by marriage with the de Silva family, Duques de Pastrana, in 1657. Successive members of the family assumed both ducal titles. Both families included a number of notable female patrons—both titles often passed to female heirs—although by the end of the 16th century the role of the duquesas as patrons and collectors seems to have diminished, and they concentrated on the acquisition of religious works of art.

The impact of the patronage of the Mendoza family on the history of Renaissance architecture in Spain is enormous, especially in the late 15th century and early 16th. (1) Cardinal Pedro González de Mendoza, brother of the 1st Duque del Infantado, Diego Hurtado de Mendoza II, was Archbishop of Seville and Toledo and chief counsellor to Ferdinand and Isabella, and he was one of the most powerful men of his time; his commission for the Colegio Mayor de S Cruz, Valladolid (1486–94), by Lorenzo Vázquez and others, resulted in the construction of one of the earliest buildings in the Renaissance style in Spain. Renaissance elements are also evident in the PALACIO DEL INFANTADO GUADALAJARA, commissioned by the 2nd Duque, Iñigo López de Mendoza II (1442–1515), including a Plateresque façade and patio (1480–83) designed by Juan Guas (for illustration *see* GUAS, JUAN), and the Capilla del Condestable (1482–94) by Simón de Colonia in Burgos Cathedral, commissioned by the 2nd Duque's aunt and sister of Cardinal Pedro González de Mendoza, Doña Mencia de Mendoza, Condesa de Haro, and her husband, PEDRO FERNÁNDEZ DE VELASCO, Conde de Haro and Condestable of Castile. Another of the 1st Duque's and Cardinal Pedro's sisters, Doña Leonor de Mendoza, passed the interest of the Mendoza family in Renaissance architecture to the Medinaceli family; the Palacio Medinaceli

(1492–5) at Cogolludo, commissioned by her son Luis de la Cerda y Mendoza, Conde de Medinaceli, was the first palace in Spain with a Florentine Renaissance façade. In the early 16th century Rodrigo Díaz de Vivar y de Mendoza, 1st Marqués del Zenete [Cenete] (*c.* 1464–1523), son of Cardinal Pedro González de Mendoza, constructed one of the last fortified castles in Spain at LA CALAHORRA, near Granada (1509–12), designed by Vázquez. The Italian Renaissance patio was designed by the Genoese Michele Carlone using carved marble imported from Italy. The inscriptions on the patio walls, however, suggest that Don Rodrigo's wife, Doña Maria de Fonseca, commissioned the interior decoration of this building.

The Mendozas were also noted patrons and collectors during the reigns of the Emperor Charles V and Philip II, King of Spain. In 1559–60 the 4th Duque del Infantado, Don Iñigo López de Mendoza III (1493–1566), escorted and entertained the entourage of Philip II's future third wife, Isabel de Valois (1546–68), until the marriage, which was celebrated on 31 January 1560 at the Palacio del Infantado, Guadalajara. The wedding celebrations were particularly lavish, in spite of the withdrawal from the festivities of the Duquesa del Infantado, Doña Isabel de Aragón, and her attendants in a dispute over precedence. Contemporary accounts describe a large, immensely rich collection of tapestries in the palace. The Mendozas also became important patrons in the Low Countries. The daughter of Don Rodrigo and Doña Maria, Doña Mencia de Mendoza, Marquesa del Zenete (1508–54), became the third wife of Hendrik III, Count of Nassau (*d* 1538), and from 1530, when she moved with her husband to the Netherlands, was a patron of Jan Gossart, Bernard van Orley and other Flemish artists. Her patronage also facilitated the dissemination of Spanish art in the Low Countries, as well as introducing Flemish influences to Spain.

Under Philip II the artistic interests of the Mendoza family expanded, and they favoured Italian art. In 1601 the estate of the 5th Duque del Infantado, Don Iñigo López de Mendoza IV (*b* 1536; *d* Guadalajara, 29 Aug 1601), included many relatively avant-garde secular works, and by the 1620s the collection comprised nearly 500 pictures, numerous tapestries and many sculptures and objects of vertu. The inventory of the 6th Duque del Infantado, Juan Hurtado de Mendoza (*d* 1 Aug 1624), records the thematic arrangement of the picture collection, including a gallery of 250 portraits.

In the mid-17th century the Mendoza family were closely linked to the de Silva family, Duques de Pastrana and Princes of Melito and Eboli, whose members were prominent statesmen from the 16th century. The collections and titles of the two families were eventually combined. From 1623 to 1626 the 3rd Duque de Pastrana, Ruy Gómez de Silva de Mendoza y de la Cerda, served as Ambassador to Rome, and his official diaries, which record his commissions for applied arts, also provide information concerning his patronage of many northern European artists. In addition to the important collections of pictures assembled by the Mendoza and de Silva families, there were also significant collections of arms and armour, sculpture, objects of vertu and series of tapestries, including the *Taking of Tangier and Arzila by the Portuguese* (15th

Don Gregorio María de Silva Mendoza y Sandoval, Duque del Infantado y Pastrana, by Juan Carreño de Miranda, oil on canvas, 2.17×1.55 m, after 1666 (Madrid, Museo del Prado)

century; Pastrana, Colegiata). These were given to the Colegiata, Pastrana, in 1667 by Don Rodrigo de Silva, 4th Duque de Pastrana and Duque del Infantado by marriage (*d* 25 Dec 1675) and the son of the 3rd Duque de Pastrana. Don Gregorio María de Silva Mendoza y Sandoval, Duque del Infantado y Pastrana, Prince of Melito and Eboli and Conde de Saldaña (*b* Pastrana, 22 March 1649; *d* Madrid, 10 Nov 1693), was a leading statesman, ambassador, collector and patron of Juan Carreño de Miranda, who painted his portrait (after 1666; Madrid, Prado; see fig.), and other Spanish artists at the end of the 17th century. The collections of the conjoint families of the Duques del Infantado and the Duques de Pastrana are largely dispersed. Some of the works passed into the family of the Duques de OSUNA, but these were sold in 1896. Others remain in the ducal collections in Madrid.

BIBLIOGRAPHY
A. A. Palomino de Castro y Velasco: *Museo pictórico* (1715–24), p. 868
C. de Arteaga y Falguera: *La casa del Infantado*, i, (Madrid, 1940)
F. Layna Serrano: *Historia de Guadalajara y sus Mendozas en los siglos XV y XVI* (Madrid, 1942)
M. Burke: *Private Collections of Italian Art in 17th-century Spain* (diss., New York U., 1984; microfilm, Ann Arbor, 1986), i, pp. 95–8; ii, docs 2.14–2.20 [further bibliog.]
S. Schroth: 'Early Collectors of Still-life Painting in Castile', *Spanish Still-life in the Golden Age* (exh. cat., ed. W. B. Jordan; Fort Worth, TX, Kimbell A. Mus., 1985), pp. 31–4
J. K. Steppe: 'Mécénat espagnol et art flamand au XVIe siècle', *Splendeurs d'Espagne et les villes belges, 1500–1700* (exh. cat., Brussels, Musées Royaux B.-A., 1985), i, pp. 247–82

MARCUS BURKE

(1) Cardinal **Pedro González de Mendoza** (*b* Guadalajara, 3 May 1428; *d* Guadalajara, 11 Jan 1495). He was the son of Iñigo López de Mendoza, 1st Marqués de Santillana, and was a firm supporter of the development in Spain of Late Gothic architecture, although he was also responsible for introducing early Italian Renaissance elements. He was trained at Salamanca University, chose an ecclesiastical career and in his youth translated some Classical Greek and Latin texts. He was a courtier during the reigns of John II and Henry IV and was named Bishop of Calahorra (1453) and of Sigüenza (1467) and Archbishop of Seville (1473) and of Toledo (1483). In 1473 he became a cardinal and in 1478 was appointed Cardinal of Santa Cruz in Jerusalem. He took an active part in the War of Granada (1482–92) and became known as the 'Cardenal de España' and 'Tercer Rey de España'. He owned an important library, which was inherited by his son, the 1st Marqués del Zenete, and an exceptional collection of coins and medals, cameos, jewels (examples in Toledo Cathedral Treasury), small statues and exotica that were sold after his death. He was primarily interested in architecture (*see also* SPAIN, §II, 2). However, he commissioned an altarpiece, with scenes from the *Life of Christ* (*c.* 1483–5), which has been attributed to the Master of the Luna (Juan de Segovia, *fl* 1483–8), that contains his own portrait as donor, for the church of S Francisco de Guadalajara (now S Ginés, Guadalajara). Documents suggest that as Archbishop of Toledo he instigated the fresco paintings in the Sagrarium (1483–8; destr.) and those in the cathedral cloister, showing biblical scenes that were executed by Master Antonio (*fl* 1482–8) and Pedro Berruguete (*see* BERRUGUETE, (1)). He would also have initiated the carving of the lower choir-stalls (1485–95) by RODRIGO ALEMÁN and of the area behind the altar (1483–91), which was the work of Martín Sánchez Bonifacio (*fl* 1448–93), Pedro Guas (*fl* 1459–85) and JUAN GUAS and Egas Cueman (*see* EGAS, (1)). In Rome the Cardinal commissioned, through Bishop Bernardino López de Carvajal (1456–1523), the decoration by Antoniazzo Romano, depicting the *Legend of the True Cross* (after 1491; *in situ*) of Santa Croce in Gerusalemme. He had already sent money for the repair and adornment of the building in 1486 through his nephew, Iñigo López de Mendoza, Conde de Tendilla (1442/4–1515), and he left a further bequest for such work in his will of 1494.

González de Mendoza's activity as patron of architecture began in the 1470s, when as Archbishop of Seville he commissioned the reconstruction of the church of Santa Cruz de Sevilla (destr.); as Archbishop of Toledo he continued the work on the Archbishop's Palace in Alcalá de Henares (1491–3) and erected the main chapel (*c.* 1485) of the church of S Catalina in Puente de Arzobispo, Toledo, although the extent of his influence on these projects is not known. He also carried out work at the castles of LA CALAHORRA (begun 1492), Granada, and Puebla de la Almenara (Cuenca, 1492) as well as the construction of his palace in Guadalajara (1486; destr.), although on these projects of a private nature it is probable that he was interested only in introducing a new and more Italian style of decoration. His contribution to various religious buildings in Guadalajara are of indeterminate date: cloisters for the monasteries of La Merced and S

Francisco (where the director of works was Antonio Vázquez), a portico for the parish church of S María de la Fuente and the hermitage of Nuestra Señora de Fuera, as well as the monastery of Nuestra Señora de Sopetrán (near Hita, Guadalajara). The principal work carried out under his patronage was the Colegio Mayor de Santa Cruz (1486–94), Valladolid (see fig.). Although a building in the Gothic style, its façade portal is the first example of the use of decorative elements from the Italian Renaissance in Spain: pilasters paired at the buttress, rusticated treatment and grotesques. The altarpiece (before June 1494) of the chapel was designed by LORENZO VÁZQUEZ, who was also involved in the main building, and the contract for the altarpiece states that entablatures *a la antigua* should be used. Pedro Gumiel executed the paintings (1492; destr.) for the Cardinal's private library in the Colegio. González de Mendoza's interest in Renaissance forms was reflected after his death in his tomb (1494–1504; *in situ*), of Italian design, in Toledo Cathedral, and in the Hospital de Santa Cruz (1504–24), Toledo, both erected by his nephew Diego Hurtado de Mendoza, Archbishop of Seville, and by his executors.

Façade of the Colegio Mayor de Santa Cruz, Valladolid, 1486–94

WRITINGS
Cronica de El Gran Cardinal de España, Don Pedro Gonçalez de Mendoza (Toledo, 1625)

BIBLIOGRAPHY
M. Gómez-Moreno: 'Sobre el renacimiento en Castilla: Notas para un discurso preliminar I: Hacia Lorenzo Vázquez', *Archv. Esp. A. & Arqueol.*, i (1925), pp. 1–40
F. de B. San Román: 'Las obras y los arquitectos de Cardenal Mendoza', *Arch. Esp. A. & Arqueol.*, v (1931), pp. 153–61
J. M. de Azcárate: 'El Cardenal Mendoza y la introducción del renacimiento', *Santa Cruz*, xvii, 22 (1962), pp. 7–16
R. Díez del Corral Garnica: *Arquitectura y mecenazgo: La imagen de Toledo en el renacimiento* (Madrid, 1987)

FERNANDO MARÍAS

Mendoza, Pedro Salazar de. *See* SALAZAR DE MENDOZA, PEDRO.

Mendoza y Moreno, Francisco de Paula (*b* Madrid, 1812; *d* Madrid, 1885). Spanish painter and writer. He studied literature at the University of Madrid and painting at the Academia de Bellas Artes de S Fernando in Madrid and was later a pupil of the painter José Aparicio Inglada whom he helped in some of his work. He then went to the Museo del Prado where he studied the works of the Venetian and Spanish schools, copying Velázquez and Murillo. In 1832 he was appointed professor of drawing at the Real Seminario de Nobles and in 1835 at the S Fernando academy and at the Liceo Artístico y Literario. He showed genre paintings at the academy exhibitions in 1834 and 1846, when he was decorated with the Cross of the American Order of Isabel la Católica. In 1849 he was appointed an honorary royal painter to Queen Isabella II and in the following year her secretary. He continued teaching—in 1858 as professor in the Escuela de Pintura, Escultura y Grabado, a department of the S Fernando academy—and exhibiting. In Madrid in 1850 he showed *Diana Caressing her Hounds on Returning from the Chase* and in Paris in 1855, *Isabella the Catholic with Christopher Columbus*. As an artist he produced mainly history paintings and portraits, and among the latter is *Isabella II*, a work remarkable for its correctness of composition and use of colour. In 1870 he published his *Manual del pintor de historia*, a compilation of the chief rules, maxims and precepts for would-be painters and especially for those who aimed at history painting, which was the vogue in 19th-century Spain.

WRITINGS
Manuel del pintor de historia (Madrid, 1870)

BIBLIOGRAPHY
M. Ossorio y Bernard: *Galería biográfica de artistas españoles del siglo XIX*, 2 vols (Madrid, 1868–9/*R* 1883–4)
A. Beruete y Moret: *Historia de la pintura española del siglo XIX* (Madrid, 1926)

PILAR BENITO

Mène, Pierre-Jules (*b* Paris, 25 March 1810; *d* Paris, 21 May 1879). French sculptor. Having learnt to cast and chase bronze from his father, who was a metal-turner, he began his career by executing models for porcelain manufacturers and making small-scale sculptures for the commercial market. He received his first professional lessons from the sculptor René Compaire and augmented these with anatomical studies and life drawings of animals in the Jardin des Plantes, Paris. From 1838 he regularly exhibited animal sculptures at the Salon. His statuettes and groups, such as *Flemish Cow and her Calf* (wax, 1845; Paris, Mus. d'Orsay), depicted the animal world with great physical precision. He even made sculptures of horses, such as *Ibrahim, an Arab Horse Brought from Egypt* (exh. Salon 1843), *Djinn, Barb Stallion* (exh. Salon 1849) and the *Winner of the Derby* (exh. Salon 1863). Mène was distinguished from other animal sculptors by his well-developed sense of business. He established his own foundry, where he formed a partnership with his son-in-law Auguste-Nicolas Cain, also an animal sculptor; they published a catalogue of their works, which could be ordered directly from the studio. The wide dissemination of reproductions of Mène's works ensured his popularity in France and abroad, especially in England.

BIBLIOGRAPHY

Lami

J. Cooper: *Nineteenth-century Romantic Bronzes: French, English and American Bronzes, 1830–1915* (London, 1975)

LAURE DE MARGERIE

Menelas [Menelaws], **Adam (Adamovich)** (*b* ?Edinburgh, 1753; *d* St Petersburg, 1831). Russian architect of Scottish birth. He moved to Russia in 1784 at the invitation of Charles Cameron and first worked as an assistant to Nikolay L'vov on the construction of the cathedral in Mogilev (1780–98) and a monastery in Torzhok (1785–96). He was a member of the Construction Committee (formed 1812) of the Ministry of Internal Affairs. His independent works are associated with the development in Russia of large landscape parks, whether private urban estates, such as the park (1818) behind the Mikhaylovsky Palace in St Petersburg, or urban public parks, which became popular in Russia in the 1820s, for example the Peter (Petrovsky) Park (1826; destr.; now a sports stadium) on the Peterburgskoye Shosse (later Leningrad Prospect), near Moscow. Most important are his parks for the imperial residences near St Petersburg, which represent a new development in the Romantic synthesis of park and palace. On the site of the former Menagerie at Tsarskoye Selo (now Pushkin) he created the picturesque Alexander (Aleksandrovsky) Park (begun 1817), in collaboration with the artist Ivan Alexeyevich Ivanov (1779–1848). The Romantic spirit was intensified by the Gothic park pavilions, utilitarian buildings and gates, including the White Tower, the Ruin, the Guardroom and the Llama House, the Indian-style Elephant House and the Egyptian gates. Menelas's masterpiece was the palace and park ensemble of Alexandria (Aleksandriya), laid out in 1826–31 and remarkable for the consistency of its picturesque planning, both of the landscape and its buildings. The Cottage, a small palace for Emperor Nicholas I (*reg* 1825–55), the farm, Guardroom, Telegraph House and lesser buildings, such as the iron summer-house, were all in the Gothic Revival style, as were the interiors, furniture and household articles of the Cottage. Menelas's final project, undertaken in collaboration with I. Charlemagne, was the Aleksandrinsky Park (1832–6) at Peterhof which was constructed posthumously. At the centre of the composition lies an artificial pond with meandering banks and three islets.

BIBLIOGRAPHY

D. O. Schvidkovsky: 'Architect to Three Emperors: Adam Menelas in Russia', *Apollo*, cxxxv (1992), pp. 36–41

YE. I. KIRICHENKO

Meneller, Caspar (*b* Kaufbeuren, Swabia, *c.* 1575; *d* Augsburg, between 14 June and 10 Dec 1630). German sculptor. He came from a family of sculptors in Kaufbeuren, where he probably served his apprenticeship, in his father's or uncle's workshop. He must have subsequently worked for a sculptor in Munich, as from 1593 there exist numerous signed and dated drawings by him based on works of art in Munich (Copenhagen, Stat. Mus. Kst). He remained there until 1595 and was there again in October 1597; the subject-matter of his drawings indicates that in 1596 he must have travelled to Regensburg and Prague. In 1601 he qualified as a master in Augsburg, and in 1608 he took on Jeremias Geisselbrunn as his second apprentice.

Meneller's earliest known work was a lavish marble epitaph for *Graf Nikolas Palffy* (*d* 1600) in Pressburg (now Bratislava) Cathedral: all that remains of it is the signed, rather conventional full-length statue of the deceased. According to archives, in 1608 Meneller made figures for an *Agony in the Garden* in Ehingen bei Wertingen in Swabia. These figures and the statue in Bratislava are the only known works by Meneller to have survived World War II; but the sculptor Christoph Murmann the younger (1564–1630) also used the signature CM, and it is not certain whether the two artists' work has always been correctly attributed. In 1611 Meneller collaborated on the famous Pomeranian 'Kunstschrank', an elaborately decorated cabinet (destr. World War II), which Philipp Hainhofer had made for Duke Philip of Pomerania-Stettin, employing Augsburg artists. Working from Johann Mathias Kager's designs, Meneller carved the models used for casting in silver the crowning *Parnassus* group of the seated figures of the Muses and also the reliefs of the *Liberal Arts* (*see* HAINHOFER, PHILIPP).

In 1621 Meneller was paid 50 florins for carving in wood two pedimental sculptures, designed by Kager, for the Goldene Saal of the Augsburg Rathaus (destr. World War II). This prestigious commission shows that *c.* 1620 he was one of the most highly regarded sculptors in Augsburg. However, his few surviving works do not provide an adequate basis for assessing his style as a sculptor. The copies that he made of designs for sculptures and pictures show that, particularly in his earlier years of journeying, he was building up a collection of models; this collection throws an interesting light on the part played by travel around 1600 in the education of artists in southern Germany.

BIBLIOGRAPHY

Thieme–Becker

K. Feuchtmayr: 'Studien zur Augsburger Plastik der Spätrenaissance II', *Schwäb. Mus.*, iii (1927), pp. 91–123

H. Geissler: 'Die Zeichnungen des Augsburger Bildhauers Caspar Meneller: Überlegungen zum Kopierwesen in Deutschland um 1600', *Münchn. Jb. Bild. Kst*, n. s. 2, xxxiv (1983), pp. 59–100

Augsburg und sein Rathaus, 1985: Die Sanierung des Rathauses und des Perlachturmes. Die Rekonstruktion des Goldenen Saales und eines Fürstenzimmers (Augsburg, 1985)

DOROTHEA DIEMER

Menéndez y Pelayo, Marcelino (*b* Santander, 3 Nov 1856; *d* Santander, 19 May 1912). Spanish writer. He read humanities at the Universitat de Barcelona, where one of his professors was Manuel Milá i Fontanals (1818–84), the author of *Manual de estética* (Barcelona, 1884). Milá i Fontanals had a powerful influence on his intellectual formation, orientating him to the Realist aesthetic that he later developed in his own work, in which he gave special attention to the role of literature in artistic production. In 1877 he travelled throughout Europe, studying in the libraries of Rome, Naples, Florence, Bologna, Venice, Milan, Paris, Brussels, Antwerp and Amsterdam to compile documentation for his future publications. From 1878 he held the chair in literature at the Universidad Central in Madrid. In 1880 he published one of his best-known books, *Historia de los heterodoxos españoles*, which kindled a great enthusiasm for historical-philosophical research and offered copious source material on Spanish history.

Menéndez y Pelayo's second great work, *Historia de las ideas estéticas en España*, on which he had been working since 1876, appeared from 1883 to 1891. Largely comprised of a study of European literature in order to discover origins and influences, this work constitutes a philosophic, aesthetic and literary history of the whole of Europe. It has no antecedents in Europe other than Robert Zimmermann's *Aesthetik* (2 vols, Vienna, 1858–65). However, Menéndez y Pelayo was not able to consult this at the time as he was not familiar with German, and for the same reason he was unacquainted with Max Schasler's *Ästhetik als Philosophie des Schönen und der Kunst* (Berlin, 1872). Reissued on numerous occasions, *Las ideas estéticas* is a monumental work of compilation and literary criticism and displays an immense amount of bibliographic information and an abundance of solid general criteria. Chronologically, the book ended in 1800, and the author's declared plan to extend it into the 19th century was ultimately never carried out, for which reason the work is sometimes considered unfinished. One of its great contributions is the idea that aesthetic criticism should never be separated from historical criticism; that is to say, in order to judge a work of art it is necessary to have knowledge of the life of its author and of the social and cultural milieu in which he developed. Menéndez y Pelayo was primarily a critical historian of Spanish literature and philosophy, and his work greatly influenced 20th-century Spanish culture in the fields of literary criticism, historical and sociological research, poetry and so on. He was a member of the Academia de la Lengua, Academia de la Historia and Academia de Bellas Artes, director of the Biblioteca Nacional and he also held the political posts of Senator and Member of Parliament in the conservative party.

WRITINGS

Humanistas españoles del siglo XVI (Madrid, 1878)
Historia de los heterodoxos españoles, 3 vols (Madrid, 1880–82)
Historia de las ideas estéticas en España, 5 vols (Madrid, 1883–91)
Estudios de crítica literaria, 5 vols (Madrid, 1884–1908)
Ensayos de crítica filosófica (Madrid, 1892)
R. Blanco y Sánchez, ed.: *Obras completas* (Santander, 1940–)

BIBLIOGRAPHY

A. Gonzalez Blanco: *Marcelino Menéndez y Pelayo* (Madrid, 1912)
A. Rubió y Lluch: 'Algunas indicaciones sobre los educadores intelectuales y las ideas filosóficas de Menéndez y Pelayo', *Rev. Archvs, Bib. & Mus.*, xxvii (1912), pp. 22–59
A. Bonilla y San Martín: *Marcelino Menéndez y Pelayo* (Madrid, 1914)
M. P. Laín Entralgo: *Menéndez y Pelayo* (Madrid, 1944)
M. Olguín: *Marcelino Menéndez Pelayo's Theory of Art, Aesthetics and Criticism* (Berkeley and Los Angeles, 1950)
A. Alonso Muñoz: *Las ideas filosóficas en Menéndez Pelayo* (Madrid, 1956)
E. Sánchez Reyes: *Biografía crítica y documental de Marcelino Menéndez Pelayo* (Santander, 1974)

M. DOLORES JIMÉNEZ-BLANCO

Meneses, Antonio Luis de. *See* MARIALVA, 1st Marquês de.

Meneses, Luís Pereira, Visconde de (*b* Oporto, 4 April 1817; *d* Lisbon, 5 May 1878). Portuguese painter. He was of English origin on his mother's side and belonged to a traditionally Liberal middle-class family. He fought with the Liberal army during the siege of Oporto (1832–3). In 1834 he settled in Lisbon, where he had painting lessons with António Manuel da Fonseca and in 1836 entered the newly founded Academia de Belas-Artes. With Tomás José da Anunciação, Cristino da Silva and Francisco Metrass he began his career during the rise of the Portuguese Romantic movement. In 1843 he exhibited at the Academia de Belas-Artes. Although advised by his friend Atanazy Raczynski to study in Munich, he chose to go to Rome, where in 1844 he was appointed honorary attaché at the Portuguese Embassy. There he frequented the studio of Friedrich Overbeck, and the influence of the Nazarenes is seen in his religious pictures, such as *Supper at Emmaus* (1845; Lisbon, Mus. N. A. Contemp.).

During 1847 Meneses travelled in Italy and after a brief stay in Belgium and Holland settled in Paris. There he copied works by Anthony van Dyck and Hyacinthe Rigaud in the Louvre, but it was his discovery of Franz Xaver Winterhalter that proved decisive in his choice of career as a portrait painter. Between 1847 and 1849 he visited London, where he admired the work of Thomas Lawrence. One of his finest portraits, painted in England, is that of the Cambridge academic *Charles William King* (1847; Lisbon, Mus. N. A. Contemp.), which was probably exhibited in 1848 at the Royal Academy.

In 1851 Meneses returned to Lisbon, where he exhibited with Metrass and at the Academia de Belas-Artes in 1852. In 1862 and 1867 his work was shown at the Sociedade Promotora de Belas-Artes, of which he became vice-president. In 1867 he sent a stately, full-length portrait of his wife, *Carlota Emilia Mac-Mahon Pereira Guimaraés, Viscondessa de Meneses* (1862; Lisbon, Mus. N. A. Contemp.), to the Exposition Universelle, Paris. Displaying an English influence and a Second Empire taste (absorbed through the art of Winterhalter), it shows her wearing a luxurious white silk crinoline; her aristocratic bearing reflects a world of social elegance and Romantic splendour. It is a fine example both of the Portuguese Romantic movement and of Meneses's painting; his religious and sentimental works, influenced by his apprenticeship under the Nazarene painters, are of lesser quality.

Meneses became increasingly involved with official and social functions. He was created Visconde in 1853; among his several other titles was that of Noble Knight of the Royal House. In 1861 he was elected president of the Junta do Crédito Público.

BIBLIOGRAPHY

D. de Macedo: *Quatro pintores românticos* (Lisbon, 1949), pp. 3–12
——: *Visconde de Meneses* (Lisbon, 1951)
J.-A. França: *A arte em Portugal no século XIX*, i (Lisbon, 1966), pp. 280–84
Soleil et ombres: L'Art portugais du XIX siècle (exh. cat. by J.-A. França and L. V. da Costa, Paris, Petit Pal., 1987–8), pp. 63ff, p. 143, pls 130–31

LUCÍLIA VERDELHO DA COSTA

Meneses, Rodrigo Aires de Sá e. *See* FONTES E ABRANTES, Marquês de.

Meneses Osorio, Francisco (*b* ?Seville, *c.* 1640; *d* Seville, *bur* 20 Jan 1721). Spanish painter. The single documentary reference to the artist describes him as a pupil of Murillo. He probably began his career *c.* 1660, since he is recorded as a member of the Academia de Sevilla from 1666, and there are dated paintings by him from 1668. He is best known for completing the paintings for the high altar of the Capuchin convent church in Cádiz, works that had been left unfinished by Murillo at his death in 1682. Meneses Osorio used his master's preparatory studies and sketches, carefully following them to complete the principal canvas, the *Mystic Marriage of St Catherine.* He executed this and the remaining paintings, *St Joseph, St Francis, St Michael* and the *Guardian Angel,* soon after Murillo's death. For the convent itself he painted the *Stigmatization of St Francis* (all now Cádiz, Mus. Pint.). In his other work Meneses Osorio reveals himself to be a faithful follower of Murillo, working in his style and using similar colouring, though lacking his master's technical ability. Characteristic of his painting are *St Joseph and the Holy Child* (1684; Seville, Casa Murillo) and *St Cyril at the Council of Ephesus* (1701; Seville, Mus. B.A.). Other works signed but not dated include *St Joseph and the Holy Child* (Baltimore, MD, Mus. A.). The *Apparition of the Virgin to St Peter Nolasco* (Seville, Mus. B.A.) is an impressive work that was formerly attributed to Murillo but assigned to Meneses Osorio in 1982.

BIBLIOGRAPHY

D. Angulo Iñiguez: *Pintura del siglo XVII*, A. Hisp., xv (Madrid, 1958), p. 364
——: *Murillo y su escuela* (Seville, 1978), p. 3
E. Valdivieso: *Historia de la pintura sevillana* (Seville, 1986), p. 250
S. Serra: *Francisco Meneses Osorio, discípulo de Murillo* (Seville, 1990)
A. E. Pérez Sánchez: *Pintura barroca española* (Madrid, 1992), p. 363

ENRIQUE VALDIVIESO

Menez [Maria Inês Carmona Ribeiro da Fonseca] (*b* Lisbon, 6 Sept 1926). Portuguese painter. Her early paintings are atmospheric and luminous lyrical abstractions that demonstrate a taste for Bonnard. By 1954, in works evoking views of the city seen through a window, the reference to the visible is accompanied by a more rigorous structure. She spent 1960 in Paris and was in London in 1964–5. Shortly after her return she painted *Henry VIII* (1966; Lisbon, Mus. Gulbenkian). Her frequent use of watercolours is reflected in the fluid oil washes that permit great luminosity in the larger works. After a brief period of experimentation with painted ceramics and the depiction of imaginary figures using a more strident palette in the 1960s, Menez's works consistently dealt with intimist and landscape themes, flirting on the boundaries between figuration and abstraction and allowing for the play of colour and light which is perhaps her real subject.

BIBLIOGRAPHY
S. Tavares: *Menez* (Vila da Maia, 1983)

RUTH ROSENGARTEN

Mengelberg, (Friedrich) Wilhelm (*b* Cologne, 10 Oct 1837; *d* Utrecht, 6 Feb 1919). German sculptor, painter and architect. He was the grandson of the painter Egidius Mengelberg (1770–1849) and received his training in the art school founded by the latter in Cologne, where his tutors included the architect Friedrich von Schmidt and the sculptor Christoph Stefan (1797–1864). Mengelberg then established a studio in Cologne, which from about 1860 was led in his absence by his brother Heinrich Otto Mengelberg (1841–91). From this period Mengelberg produced several altars with reliefs, statues and plaques, for example the high altar (1867) for St Paul in Aachen and the side altar (1882–3) for St Mariae Rosenkranz in Mönchengladbach. He also provided oil paintings and furniture for Cologne Cathedral, as well as designs for decorations and frescoes.

From 1869 onwards Mengelberg worked mainly for the Dutch bishopric of Utrecht. He was a leading member of the Guild of St Barnulphus, which took a great interest in medieval art, and, with the help of a large workshop, he created the archiepiscopal throne, the ciborium altars and the rood screen for the cathedral of St Catharina (now Utrecht, Catharijneconvent). He also provided the decoration for St Willibrordus (*c.* 1876) in Utrecht, an important example of neo-Gothic architecture in the city. After completing a design for St Willibrordus (1869) in Olbruggen, Mengelberg produced works in stone and wood in the style of the Guild of St Barnulphus for many churches, for example those in Groningen and Haarlem, as well as in Utrecht.

Apart from north Netherlands models of *c.* 1500, the south Netherlands, Burgundian and Italian variants of the International Style of *c.* 1400 were also vital sources of inspiration. The figurative and ornamental bronze reliefs on the north portal of Cologne Cathedral (1887–91) intensified the elegance of Mengelberg's models—Lorenzo Ghiberti's reliefs for the Baptistery in Florence—into a restrained expression of half-elegiac, half-insistent feeling that prefigured Jugendstil. In Mengelberg's late works, the *Stations of the Cross with a Group of Mourners* (1893–8), which Mengelberg produced for the aisles of Cologne Cathedral in a style reminiscent of Jacques de Baerze, the fall of drapery of the coloured figures became a dominant, schematically solid structural medium. Mengelberg was the last significant exponent of neo-Gothic sculpture in Germany, but after the turn of the century this style, lacking the potential for further development, lost its momentum.

BIBLIOGRAPHY
H. P. R. Rosenberg: *De 19de-eeuwse kerklijke bouwkunst in Nederland* (The Hague, 1972)
P. Bloch: *Skulpturen des 19. Jahrhunderts im Rheinland* (Düsseldorf, 1975)
Der Kölner Dom im Jahrhundert seiner Vollendung, 2 vols (exh. cat., Cologne, Josef-Haubrich-Ksthalle, 1980)
E. Trier and W. Weyres, eds: *Kunst des 19. Jahrhunderts*, iv and v (Düsseldorf, 1980 and 1981)

M. PULS

Mengoni, Giuseppe (*b* Fontanelice, 23 Nov 1829; *d* Milan, 30 Dec 1877). Italian architect. He graduated in engineering from the Università di Fisica e Matematica, Bologna, in 1854. While there, he also studied pictorial perspective at the Accademia di Belle Arti. After working for two years for the railway industry, during which time he also built a theatre (1861) at Magione (Umbria), Mengoni moved to Milan. The city was then enjoying a period of lively and dynamic renewal in the wake of its freedom in 1859 from Austrian domination. The new city council had on its agenda, among other things, the reorganization of the city centre, in particular the streets around Piazza del Duomo, following plans that had been conceived as early as the Napoleonic period. In 1861 Mengoni presented a project in the competition for the Piazza del Duomo, which envisaged a new street linking the Piazza and the Teatro alla Scala. This won the jury's approval, and he was invited to participate in a second limited competition (1863) between Mengoni, Giuseppe Pestagalli (*fl*1840–72) from Milan and the Florentine Niccola Matas. Amid fierce controversy, Mengoni was declared the winner, above all because of his plan for the link between the cathedral and La Scala and despite the fact that his project was bitterly criticized in Milanese professional circles for the excessive pomp and grandeur it imparted to the Piazza. His plan envisaged a covered walkway for commercial use (like a wide bazaar), initially articulated along a single axis and later refined to form four avenues converging on a central octagon topped by a dome of iron and glass.

The actual construction, which involved major demolition of the existing fine medieval fabric, was undertaken by an English firm (the City of Milan Improvement Co. Ltd) under contract to the city council. Within just two years, the new Galleria (see fig.) was officially opened, except for the entrance arch from the Piazza del Duomo. It was an immediate success with the public, who were attracted by the rich decorative scheme that articulated the building, emphasized by the play of light produced by

Giuseppe Mengoni: Galleria Vittorio Emanuele II, Milan, begun 1863; from a photograph, looking west, of 1867 (Milan, Castello Sforzesco, Raccolte delle Stampe Achille Bertarelli)

the iron and glass roof. The latter, built with prefabricated sections made by the Paris firm of Henry Joret, was something of a technological coup for Milan, which, while it had another covered arcade (the Galleria De Cristoforis of 1831 by Andrea Pizzala, inspired by the Parisian arcades), had never had iron and glass brought to such technical and expressive perfection. The later stages of the Galleria were drawn out for another ten years, during which time the construction company went bankrupt and the city council itself took over the work. Meanwhile, Mengoni also executed three iron-and-glass covered markets (1870–75) in Florence (at S Lorenzo, la Mattonaia and Porta S Frediano) and continued his work in the Piazza del Duomo, adopting a Renaissance Revival style for the arcaded palaces flanking the cathedral. In the same style, he built the Palazzo della Cassa di Risparmio (1868–76; interior modernized) for a bank in Bologna and directed architectural and urban planning schemes (1873–7) in Rome, Rimini and Cesena. During the 1870s he continued to work on the entrance arch to the Galleria from the Piazza del Duomo, which was in fact the least successful part of the entire scheme, due to its pronounced mixture of styles and its excessive and much criticized monumentality. This work marked the culmination, not just of the Galleria, but also of the architect's life, since he died from a fall from some scaffolding a few days before the Galleria's official opening.

WRITINGS
Progetto della nuova piazza del Duomo di Milano e della via Vittorio Emanuele (Milan, 1863)

BIBLIOGRAPHY
A. Betocchi: *Dell'architetto Giuseppe Mengoni* (Rome, 1878)
G. Chizzolini and F. Poggi: 'Piazza del Duomo e Galleria Vittorio Emanuele', *Milano tecnica dal 1859 al 1884* (Milan, 1885), pp. 193–220
A. Annoni: 'Nel cinquantesimo anniversario della morte di Giuseppe Mengoni', *Milano: Riv. Mens. Com.*, vi/1 (1928), pp. 3–9
G. Ricci: *La vita e le opere di Giuseppe Mengoni* (Fontanelice, 1930)
A. Rondello: *La Galleria Vittorio Emanuele II, Milano* (Milan, 1967)
J. F. Geist: *Passagen: Ein Bautyp des 19. Jahrhunderts* (Munich, 1979), pp. 102–3, 223–31
O. Selvafolta: 'La Galleria Vittorio Emanuele II', *Costruire in Lombardia. Aspetti e problemi di storia edilizia*, ed. A. Castellano and O. Selvafolta (Milan, 1983), pp. 221–65
V. Fontana and N. Pirazzoli: *Giuseppe Mengoni 1829–1877: Un architetto di successo* (Ravenna, 1987)

ORNELLA SELVAFOLTA

Mengs. German family of artists, one of whom was also a writer. Ismael Israel Mengs (*b* Copenhagen, 1688; *d* Dresden, 26 Dec 1764) was court painter at Dresden to Frederick-Augustus II, Elector of Saxony. Three of Mengs's children became painters: (1) Theresia Concordia Mengs, (2) Anton Raphael Mengs and Juliane Charlotte Mengs (*b* Ústi nad Labem [Ger. Aussig], Bohemia [now the Czech Republic], after 1728; *d* after 1789). They received a rigorous early training in art from their ambitious and strict father, who expected all his children to become artists. Theresia Concordia was primarily a miniature painter who worked for the court in Dresden, but she lived most of her life in Rome. Juliane Charlotte was also a court painter but entered the Belvedere Convent in Marca d'Ancona, Italy, in 1765. No works have been attributed to her with certainty. Their more famous brother Anton Raphael worked in Rome, Naples and Madrid and became one of the most significant Neo-classical painters and theorists. His daughter Anna Maria Mengs (*b* Dresden, 1751; *d* Madrid, 29 Oct 1793) lived in Spain and painted miniatures and pastel portraits (e.g. Madrid, Bib. N.).

(1) Theresia [Teresa] **Concordia Mengs** (*b* Ústi nad Labem [Ger. Aussig], Bohemia [now the Czech Republic], *bapt* 1 Nov 1725; *d* Rome, 1806 or 1808). Painter and teacher. From 1741 she worked in Rome and in 1765 married Anton von Maron, a pupil of her brother (2) Anton Raphael Mengs. In the same year she was elected a member of the Accademia di S Luca in Rome. She also worked in Dresden, where she was court painter to the Electors of Saxony. She specialized in miniature portraits in pastels and in painting on enamel. The pastel of the *Artist's Sister Juliane Mengs* (*c.* 1750; Dresden, Gemäldegal. Alte Meister) depicts the sitter wearing a frilled cap that frames her face, the plain background concentrating attention on her alert expression. A counterpart to this work is the artist's *Self-portrait* (*c.* 1750; Dresden, Gemäldegal. Alte Meister). Theresia Concordia also produced miniature copies after Raphael and Correggio (e.g. *Night*, after Correggio, 1530; Dresden, Gemäldegal. Alte Meister). In Rome she taught a number of students, among whom was Apollonie Seydelmann (1767–1846), who became a member of the Akademie der Bildenden Künste, Dresden, in 1792.

BIBLIOGRAPHY
Women Artists, 1550–1950 (exh. cat. by A. S. Harris and L. Nochlin, Los Angeles, CA, Co. Mus. A.; Austin, U. TX A. Mus.; Pittsburgh, PA, Carnegie Inst.; New York, Brooklyn Mus.; 1976–7), pp. 39–40

□

(2) Anton Raphael Mengs (*b* Ústi nad Labem [Ger. Aussig], Bohemia (now in Czech Republic), 12 March 1728; *d* Rome, 29 June 1779). Painter and writer, brother of (1) Theresia Concordia Mengs. His early career was at the Dresden court; thereafter he worked principally in Rome and Madrid, notably on the frescoes at the Villa Albani and the Palacio Real respectively. As an early exponent of Neo-classicism he produced some impressive classical and religious scenes, though he was most accomplished as a portrait painter. Under the influence of Johann Joachim Winckelmann he also wrote some theoretical works, of which the most important is the *Gedanken über die Schönheit und über den Geschmack in der Malerey* (1762). Although acclaimed during his lifetime, he was later regarded as an unimaginative eclectic, a view that continues to be widely held.

1. Life and work. 2. Writings.

1. LIFE AND WORK.

(i) Dresden and Italy, to 1755. In the autumn of 1740 Mengs accompanied his father to Rome, where he remained until the summer of 1744. Drawings from this period reveal serious study of the works of antiquity, the Renaissance and the Baroque, for example a red chalk drawing (Vienna, Albertina) after the Farnese *Hercules*, three drawings in black chalk (Frankfurt am Main, Städel. Kstinst.) after Michelangelo's *Last Judgement* in the Sistine Chapel and a drawing (London, BM) after Carlo Maratti's engraving *Lament of the Arts around the Genius of Raphael* of 1675. From 1742 Mengs attended the studio of the painter Marco Benefial in Rome in order to study the nude.

On the family's return to Dresden, Mengs soon established himself as a master of the pastel portrait. Among several pictures of sitters from the artistic circle of Dresden, that of *Herr von Hofmann* (1744; Dresden, Gemäldegal. Neue Meister) encouraged Frederick-Augustus II, Elector of Saxony to commission from Mengs his own portrait in pastel (1745; Dresden, Gemäldegal. Neue Meister), a warmly affectionate rendering of the sitter, made imposing, however, by his suggested superior position. This result was derived from a combination of the two main influences on Mengs's portraits from this time: the intimate head-and-shoulders portraits by the Venetian Rosalba Carriera, whose work was especially popular in Dresden; and the rather formal, pompous tradition of French court portraiture seen at Dresden in the work of Louis de Silvestre (i), whom Mengs portrayed in pastel (1745; destr., see Honisch, pl. 3). Mengs also began a long series of self-portraits, of which the *Self-portrait in a Blue Coat* (*c.* 1744; destr., see Honisch, pl. 4) is notable for its allusions to Raphael in the pose, with a cloak thrown over the left shoulder and the head turned to look across it at the spectator.

A larger and much more complex form of portrait composition, including a landscape background, is evident in the portrait of *Frederick-Christian of Saxony* (1745; Munich, Residenzmus.), which was also Mengs's first attempt at work in oils. A more significant advance occurred during a second stay in Rome (1746–9), where Mengs painted an oil portrait of his father *Ismael Mengs* (1747–8; Chicago, IL, A. Inst.). This work, touching in its simplicity and humanity, suggests a rather different approach to portraiture, less akin to the courtly than to the bourgeois tradition represented by such contemporary painters as Anton Graff. The second stay in Italy was important to Mengs not only for the renewed chance to copy and study works in Rome but also for the opportunity to look at the work of Titian in Venice, Correggio in Parma, and that of Annibale and Agostino Carracci and their school in Bologna. At the end of this stay Mengs converted to Roman Catholicism and married a young Roman woman, Margherita Guazzi.

Having returned to Dresden, Mengs devoted himself to portraiture in oils, carrying out a large series of commissions for the court, for example the portrait of the *Electress Maria Antonia* (*c.* 1750; Dresden, Gemäldegal. Neue Meister), in the rather grand style derived from the 17th-century French court tradition. Sitters from other circles, however, encouraged Mengs to greater invention in the treatment of pose, accessories and setting: his portrait of the singer *Domenico Annibali* (*c.* 1751; Milan, Brera), for example, is especially notable for the sense of texture in the costume—the lace jabot, the brocade waistcoat and the fur trim on the cloak—while the presence of a piano renders the pictorial space one in which the sitter acts as well as merely poses. In 1750 Mengs was commissioned to produce three altarpieces for the Dresden Hofkirche. The commission for the *Ascension* (installed 1766; *in situ*) for the main altar provided Mengs with a reason to request permission for a third journey to Rome, in order to be able to profit from further study of the work of Raphael. Having been appointed Hofmaler in March 1751, he left Dresden the following September, eventually spending the next ten years in Italy and never returning to Dresden again.

The influence of Venetian art, imbibed during an initial five-month stay in Venice on the way to Rome, is suggested not only in the finished Dresden altarpiece but also in Mengs's reception piece for the Accademia di S Luca in Rome, *St Mary Magdalene* (Dresden, Gemäldegal. Neue Meister), submitted in the spring of 1752; it depicts the figure of the Magdalene reclining in a landscape setting and is strongly reminiscent of works by Titian. The esteem with which Mengs was already regarded in Rome is suggested by his appointment to a post on the teaching staff of the Accademia del Nudo on the Capitoline, founded in 1754 by Pope Benedict XIV. He had also become known abroad and was commissioned by Hugh Smithson Percy, 1st Duke of Northumberland, to make a full-size copy (1752–5; London, V&A) of Raphael's *School of Athens* (Rome, Vatican, Stanza della Segnatura). It was, however, Mengs's meeting with Johann Joachim Winckelmann towards the end of 1755 that set the tone of this stay in Rome and, indeed, conditioned Mengs's approach to the history, theory and practice of art for the rest of his career.

(ii) Rome and Naples, 1756–61. A break with the Dresden court occurred in 1756, when the agreed payments to Mengs ceased. Preferring to remain in Rome, Mengs now took on a greater number of portrait commissions than before, being especially in demand among aristocratic English visitors, with whom he also acted as a dealer in art and antiquities; he also painted a portrait of his mentor *Johann Joachim Winckelmann* (1761–2; New York, Met.).

Mengs accepted two important commissions in Rome for fresco decoration: the first in 1757 from the Celestine monks of Sant' Eusebio for a *Glory of St Eusebius* (1757–8; *in situ*), on which he worked with his pupil and future brother-in-law Anton von Maron and which was extremely well received; and the second in 1759 from Cardinal Alessandro Albani for frescoes of *Parnassus with Apollo and the Muses* to decorate the ballroom of his villa (now Villa Torlonia) on the Via Salaria (1760–61; *in situ*). In both of these the example of Carlo Maratti, valued by Mengs as a representative of the classical strain in the Baroque tradition, was important, especially so in the light of Mengs's view of himself (influenced by Winckelmann) as instrumental in the revival of art by referring back to instances of its earlier development.

Before embarking on the Villa Albani frescoes, Mengs spent eight months in Naples where, as had been agreed in 1755, he carried out portraits of the royal family (related by marriage to that of Elector Frederick-Augustus II), for example *Ferdinand IV, King of Naples* (two versions, 1760; Madrid, Prado; Naples, Capodimonte). In Naples, Mengs also made a collection of antique vases and took a great interest in the examples of antique painting recently unearthed at Herculaneum. In connection with the discovery that the painting technique used here was not tempera but a form of fresco, Mengs painted a *Jupiter and Ganymede* (1760; Rome, Pal. Corsini) in imitation of antique work,

successfully convincing Winckelmann that it was an authentic work of antiquity.

Mengs's strong antiquarian interest and his continuing capacity for drawing on a wide range of sources are both evident in the two versions of the *Meeting of Octavian and Cleopatra* (1760–61; Stourhead, Wilts, NT; Vienna, Cernin priv. col.). In the first (see fig. 1), which has a rather severe setting with strictly balanced horizontals and verticals, Mengs used Poussin as his model. The second version, more sentimental in the presentation of the figures, is based on Guercino's treatment of the same subject (Rome, Pin. Capitolina). In both versions, but especially the second, with its concern with 'Egyptian' décor, the character of the setting seems as important as the action taking place within it.

On his return from Naples, Mengs approached the Villa Albani *Parnassus* commission very much in the spirit of one seeking to reform art via the inspiration of antiquity. This is clear in the distinct treatment of the two tondi and the central rectangular scene. The tondi are treated illusionistically in the traditional manner of Roman ceiling frescoes, suggesting a continuation of the space occupied by the spectator, but the central scene is presented as nothing more or less than a painted record of an ideal realm distinct in every way from that inhabited by the spectator. While some sense of depth is conveyed in the landscape setting, and the figures are separated into various groups (such as the two dancing Muses at the left), the

1. Anton Raphael Mengs: *Meeting of Octavian and Cleopatra*, oil on canvas, 3.00×2.11 m, 1760–61 (Stourhead, Wilts, NT)

formal integrity of each figure is subordinated to the overall decorative scheme.

(iii) Madrid and Rome, 1761–79. In his next major fresco commission, Mengs was forced to bend the consciously reformist approach seen in the *Parnassus* to the exigencies of a fresco scheme entirely conceived in the Baroque decorative tradition. Both Giambattista Tiepolo and Mengs had been summoned to Madrid by Charles III; Mengs undertook to produce for the Palacio Real a ceiling fresco of the *Triumph of Aurora* (1762–4; *in situ*) for the quarters of the Queen Mother Isabella Farnese, now part of the state dining-room, and an *Apotheosis of Hercules* (1762–9 and 1775; *in situ*) for the Antecámara de Gasparini. The second of these, especially, shows the degree to which Mengs consciously resisted the need to think in terms of continuous decorative pattern—tending, for example, to isolate groups of figures at the centre and edges of the field, and to insist on the earth-bound dynamics of balance and support rather than attempting to convey an ethereal floating state. Mengs's series of oil paintings on religious themes executed at this time are rather more successful of their type; the pathos of the *Flagellation* (1765–8; Madrid, Pal. Real), for instance, is strongly conveyed in the manner of Correggio.

During his first years in Madrid Mengs took on no portrait commissions, but he went on to produce some of his most successful records of royal sitters, sufficiently imposing yet relaxed, and also formally well integrated into their setting, as in the charming series of the four children of Charles III and Maria Amalia: *Gabriel*, *Antonio Pascual*, *Francisco Xavier* and *Maria Carolina* (all 1767; Madrid, Pal. Real). From 1763 Mengs was also concerned with the reform of the Academia de S Fernando in Madrid and in 1766 produced two theoretical texts in this connection: the *Discorso sopra i mezzi per far fiorire le belle arti in Spagna* and the *Ragionamento su l'Accademia delle Belle Arti di Madrid*. It was not, however, until 1773 that his recommendations found acceptance.

In 1769, his health suffering from overwork and the debilitating Madrid climate, Mengs requested a break in his service to the Spanish court (he had been officially appointed Primer Pintor in the autumn of 1766, after the death of Corrado Giaquinto, whose duties at court he had gradually assumed). He was granted leave for three years but eventually spent the next five years in Italy. He travelled via Florence to Rome where, in 1771, he was commissioned (probably through the intervention of Cardinal Albani) to decorate the Camera dei Papiri in the Biblioteca Vaticana. The frescoes, including an *Allegory of History* on the ceiling (1772–3; *in situ*), are the only example of a complete decorative and symbolic scheme designed according to Mengs's concept of interior architecture, itself based on his understanding of the antique tradition. His rather eclectic approach also relied on such examples of Roman ceiling painting as the work of the Carracci brothers at the Palazzo Farnese (1597–1604). In the realm of portraiture this particular stay in Italy engendered both an increasingly rebellious attitude to the constraints of courtly commissions, for example in the unusually casual depiction of *Ferdinand I, King of Naples, and his Consort* (1772; Madrid, Pal. Real), and a boldness in more intimate

2. Anton Raphael Mengs: *Self-portrait*, oil on canvas, 970×726 mm, 1773–4 (Florence, Galleria degli Uffizi)

portraiture, most notably in the simple but eloquent depiction of a Spanish diplomat (and later Ambassador) at the Roman court, *José Nicolas de Azara* (1773–4; Saragossa, Mus. Prov. B.A.), and in the fervent *Self-portrait* of 1773–4 (Florence, Uffizi; see fig. 2).

Mengs returned to Madrid in the summer of 1774 to complete his frescoes at the Palacio Real, producing in the *Apotheosis of Trajan* (1774–5; *in situ*) in the Saleta de Gasparini the most insistently 'architectural' of his Madrid frescoes. The ceiling paintings for the Aranjuez court theatre (*c.* 1776, unfinished) include *Time Kidnapping Pleasure* (*in situ*), an unconventional compromise between realism and traditional Baroque illusionism in which the two main figures cut across the edge of the circular frame through which they are supposedly soaring, thus giving an uncomfortable impression of falling towards the spectator. Following these commissions, however, Mengs was in such poor health that he was relieved of his duties and allowed to return to Italy on a pension. His last years were overshadowed by illness and (especially after the death of his wife in 1778) by depression: states all too clearly reflected in the tragically strained look of his last *Self-portrait* (1776–9; Berlin, Gemäldegal.). He continued to accept commissions; the most important of these was in 1777 for the *Delivery of the Keys to St Peter* for an altarpiece for St Peter's in Rome, but only a *bozzetto* was completed (*c.* 1777–9; ex-Incisa della Rocchetta priv. col., Rome).

2. WRITINGS. Mengs wrote down his ideas on art during the last two decades of his life but it was not until

these were edited and published by G. N. d'Azara (José Nicolas de Azara) in 1780, and translated into several languages during the next ten years, that Mengs became widely known as a theorist. His handbook for painters *Gedanken über die Schönheit und über den Geschmack in der Malerey* (Zurich, 1762) shows that he derived many of his ideas from theorists of the Baroque period, chiefly Giovanni Paolo Lomazzo and Giovanni Pietro Bellori. He was, however, able to make useful additions to such borrowings, in the case of the *Gedanken* by developing a conceptual system for stylistic criticism through analogy with rhetorical categories, in which he defined style as elevated, beautiful, charming, significant or natural and saw it as deriving essentially from the artist's inherent talent and inclination.

Mengs relied to a large extent on insights derived from his own experience as a painter: this approach enabled him, for example, to establish that the progress of work on the Sistine Chapel ceiling had not followed the narrative sequence from east to west. A significant degree of connoisseurship is also revealed in his emphasis on perfect execution in his discussion of works from antiquity and the Renaissance in his *Riflessioni sopra i tre gran pittori Raffaello, Correggio, Tiziano e sopra gli antichi*. Often Mengs proved least acceptable to his readers where he was most original in his insights: in his *Lettere a Fabroni*, written towards the end of his life, he argued that many of the best-known antique sculptures were not in fact Greek originals but Roman copies. Mengs's claim, which seemed to many quite heretical, was based on the argument that the Greeks had striven for a degree of realism that the Roman copyists had not preserved.

WRITINGS

Gedanken über die Schönheit und über den Geschmack in der Malerey (Zurich, 1762, 3/1771; Eng. trans., London, 1796)
Discorso sopra i mezzi per far fiorire le belle arti in Spagna (Madrid, 1766)
Ragionamento su l'Accademia delle Belle Arti di Madrid (Madrid, 1766)
G. N. d'Azara, ed.: *Opere di Antonio Raffaelo Mengs, primo pittore della Maestà di Carlo III, Re di Spagna*, 2 vols (Parma, 1780, rev., 4 vols, Rome, 3/1787); Eng., Fr., Ger., Sp. trans., see Lüdecke (1917)
H. von Einem, ed.: *Briefe an Raimondo Ghelli und Anton Maron* (Göttingen, 1973)

BIBLIOGRAPHY

G. L. Bianconi: *Elogio storico del Cavaliere Antonio Raffaello Mengs* (Milan, 1780)
K. Woermann: 'Ismael und Anton Raphael Mengs', *Z. Bild. Kst*, n.s., v (1894), pp. 7–14, 82–91, 168–76, 208–15, 285–93
W. Lüdecke: 'Mengs-Bibliographie', *Repert. Kstwiss.*, xl (1917), pp. 255–60 [incl. list of all editions of Mengs's writings]
W. Waetzold: 'Mengs als Kunsthistoriker', *Z. Bild. Kst*, n.s., xxx (1919), pp. 121–6
D. Honisch: *Anton Raphael Mengs und die Bildform des Frühklassizismus* (Recklinghausen, 1965)
M. Sutter: *Die kunsttheoretischen Begriffe des Malerphilosophen Anton Raphael Mengs* (Munich, 1968)
T. Pelzel: 'Winckelmann, Mengs and Casanova: A Reappraisal of a Famous Eighteenth-century Forgery', *A. Bull.*, liv (1972), pp. 300–15
S. Röttgen: 'Mengs, Alessandro Albani und Winckelmann: Idee und Gestalt des Parnass in der Villa Albani', *Stor. A.*, 30–31 (1977), pp. 88–156
T. Pelzel: *Anton Raphael Mengs and Neoclassicism* (New York, 1979)
A. D. Potts: 'Greek Sculpture and Roman Copies: I. Anton Raphael Mengs and the Eighteenth Century', *J. Warb. & Court. Inst.*, xliii (1980), pp. 150–73
S. Röttgen: 'Das Papyruskabinett von Mengs in der Biblioteca Vaticana: Ein Beitrag zur Idee und Geschichte des Museo Pio Clementino', *Münchn. Jb. Bild. Kst*, n.s. 2, xxxi (1980), pp. 189–246
R. Cioffi Martinelli: *La ragione dell'arte: Teoria e critica in Anton Raphael Mengs e Johann Joachim Winckelmann* (Naples, 1981)
S. Röttgen: 'Zum Antikenbesitz des Anton Raphael Mengs und zur Geschichte und Wirkung seiner Abguss- und Formensammlung', *Antikensammlungen im 18. Jahrhundert* (Berlin, 1981), pp. 129–48
——: 'Hofkunst, Akademie, Kunstschule, Werkstatt: Texte und Kommentare zur Kunstpflege von August III von Polen und Sachsen bis zu Ludwig I von Bayern', *Münchn. Jb. Bild. Kst*, n.s. 2, xxxvi (1985), pp. 131–81
——: 'Winckelmann, Mengs und die deutsche Kunst', *Johann Joachim Winckelmann, 1717–1768* (Hamburg, 1986), pp. 161–78

BARBARA STEINDL

Menhir. Standing stone. The term derives from Celtic words for stone (*men*) and long (*hir*), and it is generally applied to individual standing stones (monoliths) in Europe and, to a lesser extent, elsewhere in the world. While menhirs characteristically occur singly, some scholars have used the term rather loosely, for example when referring to individual stones within a row, circle or other configuration. The date and function of a menhir is seldom clear, for they are not often associated with datable archaeological finds such as burials, and their sites are rarely excavated. A range of megalithic stone-built monuments (*see* MEGALITHIC ARCHITECTURE, §1) is known to belong to the Neolithic period (*c.* 6500–*c.* 2300 BC) and the Bronze Age (*c.* 2300–*c.* 750 BC), and these single stones are usually placed in the same time bracket, namely between *c.* 3500 and *c.* 1500 BC. A further use of the term is in the context of 'statue menhirs' of the Neolithic period and Bronze Age (*see* PREHISTORIC EUROPE, §§IV, 2(iv)(a) and V, 2(ii)).

SARA CHAMPION

Menil, de. American collectors, of French birth. John de Menil (1904–73) and his wife Dominique de Menil [née Schlumberger] (*b* 1908) were forced by World War II to emigrate from France in 1941, relocating the headquarters of Dominique de Menil's family's business, Schlumberger Ltd, to Houston, TX, where they settled. They soon began acquiring art, under the guidance of Father Marie-Alain Couturier (1897–1954), a French Dominican who advocated a new sacred art within the Roman Catholic Church; the dealer Alexandre Iolas (*d* 1987), who introduced them to Surrealist art and artists; and Dr Jermayne MacAgy (1914–64), a former director of the California Palace of the Legion of Honor in San Francisco, CA. After MacAgy's death, the de Menils' formal art education ended, and they relied increasingly on their own judgement. They also played a more active role in the local art community: in the 1960s John de Menil sat on the board of the Museum of Fine Arts, Houston, and on the boards of the Museum of Primitive Art and of MOMA, both in New York.

In 1959 the de Menils created a 'teaching collection' in the art department of the University of St Thomas, Houston, where they mounted innovative exhibitions drawn from their own collection that brought the disparate arts and artefacts of different cultures together. The collection was housed in a building designed in 1957 by Philip Johnson, and there students were able to attend lectures by such art historians as Meyer Schapiro and Leo Steinberg (*b* 1920), and to meet the many visiting artists, who included Max Ernst and René Magritte. The de Menils left St Thomas in 1969 to found the Institute for the Arts at Rice University, also in Houston, which had an academic art history programme, a media centre under the stewardship of Roberto Rossellini, and an exhibition hall at the Rice Museum that operated until 1986. In 1964 the de Menils commissioned Mark Rothko and Johnson to create a chapel in Houston dedicated to spiritual ecumenism and human rights. The site came to include Barnett Newman's *Broken Obelisk* (1963–7; *in situ*; version, New York, MOMA), dedicated to Martin Luther King jr. Consecrated in 1971, the octagonal Rothko Chapel houses 14 abstract works painted by Rothko in 1964 and 1965.

The success of the commission encouraged the de Menils in the early 1970s to plan a museum, with Louis Kahn as architect. These plans were abandoned after the death of John de Menil and of Kahn shortly afterwards. However, in 1980 Dominique de Menil commissioned Renzo Piano to design a museum on land adjacent to the Rothko Chapel and its park. The museum, constructed between 1981 and 1986 and opened as the Menil Collection in June 1987, contains *c.* 13,000 objects dating from the Palaeolithic period to the 20th century. In a general sense the collection is linked by religious, political and social customs. The art of ancient cultures from the Palaeolithic to the pre-Christian era concentrates on the Mediterranean tradition; the collection of Byzantine icons and Western medieval art embodies the spirituality of the de Menils' vision. They were among the first collectors of the tribal arts of Africa, Oceania and the Native Americans of the north-west coast. The 20th-century collection centres on work from the Ecole de Paris, Cubism and Neo-plasticism. Surrealist art also forms an important part of the collection, with paintings and sculpture by Ernst, Magritte, de Chirico, Picabia and Man Ray. In addition there are major works by Abstract Expressionists (Newman, Rothko, Jackson Pollock, and the European exponents Wols and Jean Fautrier), Post-painterly abstractionists (Rauschenberg, Jasper Johns and Cy Twombly), Pop artists (especially Warhol, Yves Klein, Jean Tinguely and Niki de Saint Phalle) and Minimalists such as Brice Marden. The curators of the Menil Collection arrange temporary exhibitions and changing presentations of its permanent collection, as well as publishing scholarly studies.

The Menil Foundation, also based in Houston, is responsible for a major research project, *Image of the Black*, which studies the images and iconography of blacks in Western art. Beyond archival documentation and publications, the project has stimulated a collection of important objects and paintings depicting blacks from antiquity to the present.

WRITINGS
W. Hopps and D. de Menil, eds: *The Menil Collection: A Selection from the Palaeolithic to the Modern Era* (New York, 1987)

BIBLIOGRAPHY
A. Holmes: 'Dominique de Menil: From Jeune Fille to Renaissance Woman', *ARTnews*, lxxxii/1 (1983), pp. 80–85
The First Show: Painting and Sculpture from Eight Collections, 1940–1980 (exh. cat., ed. J. Brown and B. Johnson; Los Angeles, Mus. Contemp. A., 1983) [incl. interview with D. de Menil by P. Hultén]
La Rime et la raison: Les Collections Ménil (Houston–New York) (exh. cat. by W. Hopps and others, Paris, Grand Pal., 1984)
J. Glancy: 'A Homely Gallery', *The Architect*, xciv/9 (1987), pp. 38–41
SUSAN E. DAVIDSON

Menkheperre. *See* TUTHMOSIS III.

Menn, Barthélemy (*b* Geneva, 20 May 1815; *d* Geneva, 11 Oct 1893). Swiss painter and teacher. He began his career with drawing lessons from W. A. Töpffer but *c.* 1831 began painting under Léonard Lugardon (1801–84), who had studied with Ingres and Antoine-Jean Gros. In 1833 Menn went to Paris to study with Ingres; when Ingres became Director of the Académie de France in Rome in 1835 Menn followed him to Italy, where he met such artists as Léopold Robert, Alexandre-Gabriel Decamps, the Flandrin brothers, Xavier Sigalon, Bertel Thorvaldsen and Dominique Papety (with whom he later shared a studio). In 1838 he returned to Paris, where he was attracted to the works of the landscape painters François-Louis Français, Charles-François Daubigny, Théodore Rousseau and Jean-Baptiste-Camille Corot, whom he especially admired for his control of tonal values. In Paris Menn was also introduced to George Sand, whose son Maurice Dudevant became his pupil; he attended her salon and met Chopin, who bought some of his works, as well as Delacroix, who later asked him to assist in the decoration of the Palais Bourbon, an invitation that Menn declined.

Menn returned to Geneva in 1843 to apply for a teaching post, but, despite letters of recommendation from Ingres, he was turned down. During the following years, Menn travelled in central Switzerland and France painting landscapes, most of which were harshly criticized. In 1850 he was finally appointed to the Ecole des Beaux-Arts in Geneva. He devoted 42 years to teaching two generations of Swiss painters, including Ferdinand Hodler in 1871. Menn continued to associate with important French landscape painters, particularly Corot, with whom he had worked in Gruyère in the 1850s. He also organized several significant exhibitions in Geneva of the works of Corot, Daubigny, Rousseau, Delacroix and Courbet, but these received neither critical nor public approval. Discouraged, Menn refused to exhibit his own works after 1859 and four years later even declined to sell his paintings to a public that he believed to be hostile.

Menn's works may be divided into two distinct periods. The first is essentially figurative, with an emphasis on historical subjects, such as *Solomon Presented to Wisdom by his Parents* (1836; Geneva, Mus. A. & Hist.; see fig.). This painting shows the influence of Lugardon and Ingres, who were equally important sources for the portraits of the 1830s and 1840s. The landscapes executed during this period are more idealized than based on direct observation (e.g. *Italian Landscape*, 1842; Geneva, Mus. A. & Hist.). The second period (from 1843) reveals a freer approach to painting from nature, in which observation of the subject becomes central. Menn's painting trips to central Switzerland, France and Italy, as well as his contacts with Corot and the Barbizon painters, were crucial. The paintings finished in Gruyère in the late 1850s combine vibrant lighting with diffuse shadows and a freer use of paint. Even the Italian landscapes lose qualities inspired by the work of Poussin in favour of atmosphere and spontaneity. This is equally true of Menn's later portraits, for example his *Self-portrait* (1867; Geneva, Mus. A. & Hist.), which conform to a more direct, personal approach quite unlike the precision of his earlier works.

Barthélemy Menn: *Solomon Presented to Wisdom by his Parents*, oil on canvas, 385×460 mm, 1836 (Geneva, Musée d'Art et d'Histoire)

BIBLIOGRAPHY
B. Bodmer: 'Barthélemy Menn, peintre', *Nos Anciens et leur ouvrages* (Geneva, 1902), pp. 67–102
D. Baud-Bovy: *Barthélemy Menn, dessinateur* (Geneva, 1943)
J. Brüschwiler: *Barthélemy Menn, 1815–1893* (Zurich, 1960)

WILLIAM HAUPTMAN

Menna, tomb of. Small painted Egyptian tomb chapel (TT 69) in the Theban necropolis (now Luxor). The chapel of Menna (*fl c.* 1400 BC), an 18th Dynasty official, comprises a transverse hall and a passage terminating in a statue-niche. The well-preserved wall paintings on mud plaster are among the finest surviving examples of their kind, and outstanding artistic skill is apparent in the carefully balanced scenes and the many interesting details of daily life. The hall contains standard funerary scenes and depictions of Menna at his official duties; he appears overseeing various agricultural operations and supervising the collection of taxes. The paintings provide an unusually complete record of these activities and include rarely depicted episodes, such as scribes measuring the fields with a knotted rope. Among the numerous incidental details of these scenes are a woman carrying her child in a pouch, two girls quarrelling, a labourer drinking and a girl removing a thorn from another's foot. In the passageway are depicted Menna's funeral procession and the posthumous judgement, in which his heart is weighed in a balance against an image of the goddess of truth, Maat. On the opposite wall are shown other religious rituals and a particularly fine scene of Menna and his family fishing and fowling in the papyrus marshes. The fish, birds and butterflies are painted with striking realism, and a cat and an ichneumon are seen stalking their prey among the reeds. A noteworthy feature of this chapel is the selective obliteration of parts of the decoration (notably Menna's eyes), an attempt by some enemy to deny to Menna the benefit he expected to derive from the things depicted; this is a revealing illustration of the ancient Egyptians' belief in the magical efficacy of the painted image.

BIBLIOGRAPHY
A. Mekhitarian: *Egyptian Painting* (Geneva, Paris and New York, 1954), pp. 72–95

J. H. TAYLOR

Mennecy Porcelain Factory. French porcelain factory. In 1734 François Barbin (?1689–1765), the son of a Parisian *menuisier* of the same name, was documented in the parish records of Mennecy (Seine-et-Oise) as a 'fabriquant de faillance et de porcelaine', a 'maître manufacturier de porselaine demeurent' at the château of Villeroy, which was near Mennecy, and as a 'marchant fayencier porselainier' on the Rue de Charonne in Paris. He is known to have produced porcelain in the grounds of the château of François-Louis de Neufville, Marquis de Villeroy (1695–?1765), near Mennecy, between 1737 and 1748, although it does seem probable that production was established prior to 1737. In 1748 Barbin was denied permission to build a kiln in Paris, a refusal probably ordered to protect the factory at Vincennes, for in 1749 Charles Adam (*fl*1745–52) complained that the products made at the château of Villeroy, which were possibly decorated in Paris, were too similar to those of Vincennes. Therefore in 1749 Barbin bought a house in the village of Mennecy and leased another for the porcelain factory. In 1750 Barbin went into partnership with his son-in-law, Louis Evrard des Pitons (*d*1754). In 1755 Barbin's son, Jean-Baptiste Barbin (*d*1765), was also taken into the partnership; in 1762 Jean-Baptiste bought out his father and in 1764 also bought out his brother-in-law. In 1765 Jean-Baptiste's widow leased the factory to the sculptor Charles-Symphorien Jacques (*d*1798) and the painter Joseph Jullien (*d*1774), entrepreneurs who set up the factory at Sceaux (Hauts-de-Seine). In 1773 the factory was sold to Jacques and Jullien, who transferred it to Bourg-la-Reine (Seine).

The first wares produced by François Barbin were covered in a tin glaze similar to that of Chantilly porcelain, although Mennecy tin-glazed porcelain does not have the greenish tinge of Chantilly wares. Later, a lead, glossy, milky-white glaze was employed. Until *c.* 1750 decoration was inspired by Chinese and Kakiemon designs (e.g. tin-glazed bowl decorated in a polychrome Chinese style, *c.* 1740; Sèvres, Mus. N. Cér.). Decoration was subsequently European in inspiration and similar to that of Vincennes, with naturalistic flower and bird painting (e.g. covered jug, Paris, Mus. A. Déc.; *see also* FRANCE, fig. 69) and figures in landscapes. Birds and animals are modelled after Vincennes or Meissen examples, as seen in the pair of seated monkeys mounted in gilt bronze (*c.* 1740; New York, Met.) and a potpourri modelled as a parrot on a rocky base with vase (*c.* 1760; Paris, Louvre). The order prohibiting factories other than Vincennes to use gilding was respected at Mennecy, for borders and Rococo scrollwork are usually painted in a characteristic pink or, less frequently, blue.

Mennecy produced a great number of figures: fantastical grotesques after Jacques Callot's dwarfs (examples in Paris, Mus. A. Déc.), *cris de Paris*, figures from the *commedia dell'arte*, and exotic, rustic and mythological figures (e.g. the *Four Seasons*; Paris, Mus. A. Déc.). Among the figures produced is a *River God* (*c.* 1755; London, V&A) after a model by Nicolas-François Gauron (*fl*1753–70), who was employed at the factory in 1753 and who later worked in the factories at Vincennes, Tournai in the southern Netherlands and Derby in England. Mennecy also produced a fountain (Paris, Mus. A. Déc.) with boldly modelled relief decoration of flowers, foliage and dolphins. Spiral reeding was typical of Mennecy tablewares, and the factory produced numerous pots, jars, boxes, knife-handles, cane pommels and 'toys'.

BIBLIOGRAPHY

A. Darblay: 'La Porcelaine de Villeroy', *Bull. Soc. Hist. & Archéol. Corbeil Est. & Hurepoix* (1897)

——: *Villeroy, son passé, sa fabrique de porcelaine, son état actuel* (Corbeil, 1901)

H.-P. Fourest: 'Les Boîtes en porcelaine tendre au Musée Adrien-Dubouche', *Cah. Cér. Verre & A. Feu*, xiii (1959), pp. 44–51

G. Le Duc: 'La Porcelaine de Villeroy', *Fr. Porc. Soc.*, iii (1987)

N. Duchon: *La Manufacture de porcelaine de Mennecy Villeroy* (Le Mée-sur-Seine, 1988)

□

Mennicken, Jan Emens (*b* ?Raeren, *fl* 1568–94; *d* ?Raeren). Belgian potter. He was the most important potter and producer of stoneware at RAEREN during the period 1568 to 1594. Mennicken manufactured *schnellen* (tall, tapering tankards) influenced by the stoneware of Sieburg, large *bartmannkrugen* (jugs with a bearded mask in relief below the neck), which resemble stoneware from Cologne, or wares decorated with biblical, secular and mythological scenes, ornamental motifs, grotesques and armorial bearings (*see* BELGIUM, fig. 35). Initially Mennicken produced golden-brown stonewares, but *c.* 1580 he was the first to apply a cobalt-blue glaze to his wares that was later to typify production at the Westerwald potteries in Germany.

BIBLIOGRAPHY

M. Kohnemann: *Auflagen auf Raerener Steinzeug: Ein Bildwerk* (Raeren, 1982)

CLAIRE DUMORTIER

Menniti, Mario. *See* MINNITI, MARIO.

Men of the Year 1909. *See under* YOUNG ONES.

Menologion of Basil II. Byzantine illuminated calendar manuscript (Rome, Vatican, Bib. Apostolica, MS. Vat. gr. 1613) of 439 pages (363×287 mm). It covers the first half of the administrative year (1 Sept–28 Feb) and contains up to eight commemorations for each day. It is presumed to be the surviving first volume of a two-volume set and, according to the dedicatory poem on p. XIII, was made for Emperor Basil II (*reg* 976–1025). It is organized as a picture book, with each page divided horizontally in half for a miniature and its accompanying 16-line text. The 430 miniatures alternate between the upper and lower halves of the page, and include scenes from the *Life of Christ* (e.g. *Nativity, Baptism*), as well as standing saints, numerous scenes of martyrdom (see fig.), and more unusual events, such as the discovery of relics.

There are some peculiar features about the book. On 15 pages the illuminations lack any accompanying text, indicating that, contrary to normal practice, the illustrations were supplied first. Eight different names (e.g. PANTOLEON) are found beside the illuminations. On the first occurrence each name is qualified as '[A work] by the painter...'. I. Ševčenko has shown that the puzzling distribution of names corresponds to the principle of one artist per sheet of parchment. Though not signatures, for all were written by the same scribe, the names could record, or at least were intended to suggest, that several hands were at work. Yet such is the manuscript's overall homogeneity that its artists (if the 'signatures' are to be believed) were supremely skilful in reproducing a common style.

Menologion of Basil II, miniature of the *Martyrdom of SS Menas, Victor, Vincent and Stephanie*, 120×180 mm, AD 976–1025 (Rome, Vatican, Biblioteca Apostolica, MS. Vat. gr. 1613, p. 174)

The Menologion contains the largest body of visual material for the study of the Byzantine religious calendar. It is also important for its relation to the ten-volume sets of illustrated saints' lives known as the *Metaphrastian Menologion* (or Menologion of Symeon Metaphrastes). This vast work was first assembled in the mid-10th century and was produced in surprisingly large numbers, notably in the second half of the 11th century. These manuscripts have many fewer commemorations than the Menologion of Basil II, and much longer texts, but some of the images are closely related.

BIBLIOGRAPHY

Menologion of Basil II (late 10th century; Rome, Vatican, Bib. Apostolica, MS. Vat. gr. 1613); facs., Codices e Vaticanis selecti phototypice expressi, vii (Turin, 1907)

I. Ševčenko: 'The Illuminators of the Menologium of Basil II', *Dumbarton Oaks Pap.*, xvi (1962), pp. 244–70

N. P. Ševčenko: *Illustrated Manuscripts of the Metaphrastian Menologion* (Chicago, 1990)

JOHN LOWDEN

Menon Painter. *See under* VASE PAINTERS, §II, PSIAX.

Menorca. *See under* BALEARIC ISLANDS.

Menpes, Mortimer (*b* Port Adelaide, Australia, 22 Feb 1855; *d* Pangbourne, England, 1 April 1938). British painter and etcher of Australian birth. He studied at the Adelaide School of Design with John Hood. In 1875 his family moved to London and he married. Three years later he enrolled at the South Kensington School of Design, studying with Edward John Poynter. In 1880 Menpes went on a sketching tour of Brittany and later that year met Whistler. He left art school to study informally with Whistler, learning much from him about composition and etching technique. Menpes's reputation was soon established. He regularly exhibited at the Royal Academy, was elected to the Royal Society of Painters and Etchers in 1881 and became a member of the Society of British Artists in 1885. In 1887 he began an extended journey to Japan. When he returned, his Japanese paintings formed the first of many successful one-man exhibitions; the exhibition was hold at Dowdeswell, London.

In 1900 Menpes worked as a war artist in South Africa for the *Black and White*. From about 1902 until 1917 he travelled extensively, producing numerous books illustrating people and places around the world, such as *Venice* (1904). He was equally skilled in watercolour, oil (e.g. *Flower of the Tea*, 1887–8; London, Tate) and etching. His subject-matter was influenced in part by 19th-century realism. Typically, his compositions are sparse, and his love of Japanese art prompted clear brilliant colour. A strong luminosity pervades both his paintings and prints.

WRITINGS

Whistler as I Knew him (London, 1904/*R* Ann Arbor, 1980)

India (London, 1905/*R* New Delhi, 1982)

BIBLIOGRAPHY

C. Roberts: 'Mortimer Menpes: The Man and his Methods', *Harper's New Mthly Mag.*, ci (1900), pp. 703–11

ROSEMARY T. SMITH

Mente, Giovan de. *See* MONT, HANS.

Mentessi, Giuseppe (*b* Ferrara, 29 Sept 1857; *d* Milan, 14 June 1931). Italian painter, engraver and teacher. He was born into a peasant family and lost his father when he was five. His mother managed to send him to drawing classes at the Civico Ateneo in Ferrara, where Gaetano Previati was his classmate, and then to the Accademia di Belle Arti in Parma, where he studied decoration and stage design. Between 1877 and 1881 he attended the Accademia di Brera in Milan and was introduced by Previati into the circle of Gli Scapigliati. His friendships with Emilio Longoni (1859–1932), Cesare Tallone, Leonardo Bistolfi and the socialist lawyer Luigi Majno date from this time. In 1880 Mentessi won a prize at the Scuola di Architettura and became assistant to Luca Beltrami at the Brera, beginning a lifelong career as a teacher of architectural drawing and geometry. In 1887 he was appointed Professor of Landscape Painting at the Brera and in the early years of the 20th century he also gave courses at the Società Umanitaria in Milan. Due to his friendship with the Swiss painter Luigi Rossi (1853–1923), he acted as a consultant in the commission for the teaching of drawing in the canton of Ticino. He was also active in organizing exhibitions. In the 1890s Mentessi painted landscapes and pictures dealing with social issues, among them *Our Daily Bread* (1894; Ferrara, Gal. Civ. A. Mod.), which was shown at the first Venice Biennale in 1895. The theme of the painting is pellagra, a disease caused by malnutrition that was widespread in the Ferrarese countryside. Gradually he developed his own manner of depicting poverty and suffering, central to which is the theme of motherhood, in either a secular or a religious context. Apart from imaginative compositions, he worked on engravings from the beginning of the 20th century. With *Sad Vision* (1899; Venice, Ca' Pesaro), a large pastel exhibited in Paris in 1900, Mentessi began a series of works on religious subjects in the Symbolist vein. With *Gloria* (1901; Rome, G.N.A. Mod.), which was much acclaimed when it was exhibited in Venice in 1901, the artist took up the theme of antimilitarism. This he repeated in various minor works during World War I. The triptych *Passion Week* (1914; Ferrara, Gal. Civ. A. Mod.) has, in the scene of a massacre, intense passages of raw realism.

BIBLIOGRAPHY

Thieme–Becker

E. Majno: *Giuseppe Mentessi* (Milan, 1932)

Giuseppe Mentessi, 1857–1931: Mostra antologica (exh. cat. by Z. Birolli, Ferrara, Gal. Civ. A. Mod., 1972)

G. Ginex: 'Giuseppe Mentessi', *La pittura in Italia: L'ottocento*, ii (Milan, 1991), pp. 915–16

GIOVANNA GINEX

Mentuemhet (*fl* mid-7th century BC; *d* before 647 BC). Egyptian priest, administrator and patron. First documented in Thebes under the Kushite king Taharqa, Mentuemhet survived the subsequent Assyrian invasion and sack of Thebes, and he continued to control most of Upper Egypt even after the reunification of the country in 656 BC under the 26th (Saite) Dynasty. He is mentioned in an oracle papyrus dated to 651 BC.

During the 26th Dynasty, numerous aspects of ancient Egyptian culture were revived, including artistic, religious and linguistic traditions; motifs and styles of earlier periods were deliberately copied, creating a consciously archaic style. This is somewhat misleadingly called the 'Saite Renaissance'.

Mentuemhet possessed the status and wealth to wield a powerful influence on his age both politically and artistically. Over a dozen statues reflect a wide range of earlier tastes and styles (e.g. Cairo, Egyp. Mus., CG 42236, and London, BM, 1643). These constitute some of the most successful examples of Late Period portrait sculpture. Mentuemhet's massive Theban tomb, one of the largest ever constructed in Egypt, exemplifies the archaizing and yet synthetic style expanded to new horizons. The ancient motif of bound papyrus plants, for example, was enlarged to previously unattested towering proportions in the tomb's open court. Some of the carved scenes of daily life hark back to Old Kingdom models, while others actually seem to borrow from themes found in the New Kingdom tombs in the surrounding Theban necropolis.

BIBLIOGRAPHY

J. Leclant: *Montouemhat, quatrième prophète d'Amon* (Cairo, 1961)

I. Nagy: 'Remarques sur le souci d'archaïsme en Egypte à l'époque saïte', *Acta Ant. Acad. Sci. Hung.*, xxi (1973), pp. 53–64

D. Eigner: *Die monumentalen Grabbauten der Spätzeit in der thebanischen Nekropole* (Vienna, 1984)

P. D. Manuelian: *Living in the Past: Studies in Archaism of the Egyptian Twenty-sixth Dynasty*, Stud. Egyptol. (London, 1994)

PETER DER MANUELIAN

Menuisier. French joiner or carpenter. Unlike *ébénistes* (cabinetmakers), *menuisiers* specialize in small objects, such as chairs carved of plain wood.

□

Menus Plaisirs du Roi. *See* MAISON DU ROI, §III.

Menzel, Adolph (Friedrich Erdmann von) (*b* Breslau, Silesia [now Wrocław, Poland], 8 Dec 1815; *d* Berlin, 9 Feb 1905). German painter, draughtsman, illustrator, printmaker and teacher. He was the most important artist working in Berlin in the second half of the 19th century and in his later years was one of the most successful and respected artists in Germany. Living virtually all his life in Berlin, he executed numerous paintings and illustrations relating to events in Prussia's recent history and was the foremost chronicler of the life of Frederick the Great (*reg* 1740–86). Through his portraits and industrial scenes and his more intimate studies of interiors and local religious events he became one of the greatest German proponents of Realism (*see* REALISM, §3 and BERLIN, fig. 7).

1. Life and work. 2. A pioneer of Realism. 3. Personality and character.

1. LIFE AND WORK. He was the son of Carl Erdmann Menzel (*d* 1832), the head of an educational institute in Breslau, who abandoned his profession in 1818 to establish a lithographic printing works. In 1827, at age 12, Adolph Menzel exhibited a drawing and in 1829 contributed eight lithographs to an illustrated *Geschichte des preussischen Staates* (Breslau) printed in his father's workshop. In 1830 Carl Erdmann Menzel moved his family to Berlin, where he hoped for more commissions for his printing works, and Adolph Menzel became an apprentice in his father's shop. After his father's death, Menzel took over operation of the shop and had to support his mother and his younger sister and brother. In 1833 he studied in the plaster of

1. Adolph Menzel: *Funeral of the Martyrs of the Berlin Revolution, 1848*, oil on canvas, 1848 (Berlin, Alte Nationalgalerie)

Paris class at the Königliche Akademie der Künste. His first major commission was for 11 illustrations for Goethe's *Künstlers Erdenwallen* (Berlin, 1834), which made his name known. At this time he also became friendly with Carl Heinrich Arnold, a factory-owner, and he began to make contact with artists in Berlin, becoming a member of the VEREIN BERLINER KÜNSTLER. From 1834 to 1836 he produced 12 lithographs for *Denkwürdigkeiten aus der brandenburgisch-preussischen Geschichte* and in 1837 first began to paint in oils. His 400 drawings for woodcut illustrations to Franz Kugler's *Geschichte Friedrichs des Grossen* (Leipzig, 1840) had as their prototype Laurent de l'Ardèche's life of Napoleon (*Histoire de Napoléon*, 8 vols, Paris, 1852), with illustrations by Horace Vernet. This publication immediately made Menzel well known as an artist who specialized in depicting events from Frederick the Great's reign. In 1839 he produced 16 woodcuts illustrating Adelbert von Chamisso's *Peter Schlemihls wundersame Geschichte* and the following year went on a study trip to Leipzig and Dresden. A series of 200 woodcuts for *Die Werke Friedrichs des Grossen*, on which he worked from 1843 to 1849, and one of 436 lithographs for *Die Armee Friedrichs des Grossen in ihrer Uniformierung* (Berlin, 1851–7), which occupied him from 1842 to 1857, were two of his most important projects in the 1840s and 1850s. *Radierversuche*, a smaller project consisting of seven etchings of landscapes, was done in 1844.

By the mid-1840s Menzel was producing his first important paintings: *Room with a Balcony* (1845) and the *Berlin–Potsdam Railway* (1847; Berlin, Alte N.G.) are two of the earliest. In 1847 he visited Kassel, where he drew the cartoon (ex-Kaiser-Friedrich-Mus., Magdeburg) for a large-scale historical picture (unexecuted) depicting events in the history of Hesse. In response to the revolutions of 1848 he painted the *Funeral of the Martyrs of the Berlin Revolution, 1848* (see fig. 1), which remained unfinished, and the following year began a series of major oil paintings dealing with episodes from Frederick the Great's reign, the first of which was *Frederick II with his Guests in Sanssouci* (1849–50; destr. 1945). Further works in the series include *Frederick the Great's Flute Concert in Sanssouci* (1852; see fig. 2), *Frederick the Great on his Travels* (1854), the *Diet of Silesia Paying Tribute in Breslau, 1741* (1855), *Frederick and his Family near Hochkirch, 1758* (1856; destr. 1945), *Meeting with the Emperor Joseph II in Neisse, 1769* (1857), *'Bonsoir, messieurs'* (1858) and *Frederick the Great Addressing his Generals before the Battle of Leuthen* (begun 1858; unfinished). During the 1850s he also travelled, visiting Vienna and Prague (1852) and Dresden (1857). A trip to Paris in 1855 to attend the Exposition Universelle was, however, more significant for his development. In 1852 he became part of the Tunnel über der Spree, a literary association in Berlin, meeting the writers Paul Heyse, Franz Kugler and Theodor Fontane and establishing friendships with them, and in 1853 he became a member of the Königliche Akademie der Künste in Berlin. His gouache illustrations for *Fest der weissen Rose am 13 Juli 1829*, a commemorative album for the Russian empress Alexandra, was an important commission of the 1850s. In 1856 he became a professor at the Akademie der Künste, a position he retained for life.

In 1859 Menzel's sister Emilie married Hermann Krigar, the Königliche Musikdirektor, and from that time the artist lived with them. His major painting of the 1860s is the *Coronation of King William I in Königsberg* (1861–5), a work more than 3 m high and 4 m wide (*see* §2(ii) below). In 1862 he painted *In the Opera House* (Hamburg, Ksthalle), after which he began work on his *Kinderalbum* (completed 1883; pubd. Leipzig, 1912) with illustrations in gouache. In 1866 he visited the area of conflict of the Seven Weeks War (Austro-Prussian War), where he drew dead and wounded soldiers. He visited Paris in 1867 to attend the Exposition Universelle, where he saw Courbet's work, although he was not impressed by it. However, Menzel met Ernest Meissonier, who painted similar historical scenes in a Naturalist vein. Back in Berlin he rendered views of Paris (e.g. *Afternoon in the Tuileries Gardens* and *In the American Restaurant*; both 1867). A year later he returned to Paris to have the *Coronation of King William I* shown at the annual Salon. Renewing his friendship with Meissonier, he painted *Meissonier in his Studio* (1869; San Francisco, CA Pal. Legion of Honor).

From 1869 on, Menzel spent each summer away from Berlin, usually at such spas as Bad Hofgastein in Austria or Bad Kissingen in Bavaria, where he painted such works as *Procession in Gastein* (1880; Munich, Neue Pin.), *Grinding Shop at the Smithy in Hofgastein* (1881; Hamburg, Ksthalle) and the gouaches *A Promenade by the Fountain in Kissingen* (1890) and *Beer Garden in Kissingen* (1891). In the 1870s he continued to paint scenes of Prussian history, among them *King William I's Departure for the Army, 31 July 1870* (1871), *Supper at the Ball* (1878) and *Circle at the Court of William I* (1879; Schweinfurt, Samml. Schäfer). He paid a lengthy visit to the ironworks at Königshütte, Upper Silesia, in 1872 in order to study the subject more carefully for his oil painting the *Iron-rolling Mill* (1872–5; Berlin, Alte N.G.). In 1876 he visited the Netherlands and also completed 30 woodcuts for Heinrich von Kleist's *Der zerbrochene Krug*.

By the 1880s Menzel had achieved an international reputation. In 1884 the Nationalgalerie in Berlin held the first major retrospective of his works to celebrate the 50th anniversary of his career as an artist and in the late 1880s began to acquire many of his paintings for their collection, eventually obtaining his entire estate. An exhibition of his works was also held in Paris in 1885 at the Pavillon de la Ville. He was made an honorary citizen of Breslau, the city of his birth, and Fontane wrote a dedicatory poem for his 75th birthday. Despite Chancellor Bismarck's prohibition, Menzel exhibited in the Exposition Universelle in Paris in 1889. *In the White Room* (1888) and *After the Celebration at Court* (1889) are two important paintings of the 1880s. He received further honours in the 1890s,

2. Adolph Menzel: *Frederick the Great's Flute Concert in Sanssouci*, oil on canvas, 1.42×2.05 m, 1852 (Berlin, Alte Nationalgalerie)

becoming an honorary citizen of Berlin (1895) and a Knight of the Order of the Black Eagle (1898) and being made an honorary member of the nobility. He remained productive in his last years; a gouache, *Visit to the Iron-rolling Mill* (1900), shows his continuing interest in industrial themes and the *End of the Festival of Reconciliation* (1901) his fascination with ceremonies and social occasions. He was given a retrospective exhibition in London in 1903, and on his death in 1905 received a state funeral.

2. A PIONEER OF REALISM.

(i) Graphic work. Menzel was one of the first German artists to lead the way in the development of Realism. This is especially true of his graphic work, which set new standards not just in the field of illustration but in German art as a whole. In its vitality, historical accuracy and brilliant grasp of situations worth pictorial treatment, his work can be favourably compared to that of the French illustrators J. J. Grandville and Gustave Doré. Moreover, he made greater use of the illustrative techniques then coming into prominence, and developed them further, than any other German artist of his time. Mostly as a result of his illustrations of episodes from the life of Frederick the Great, he became, after the foundation of the German Empire in 1871, the most popular artist in Germany. As one of the most skilled and prolific draughtsmen of the 19th century, his motto *nulla die sine linea* (not a day without drawing) characterizes his almost fanatical will to appropriate the visible world. His preferred medium was the pencil, which he often used in combination with erasers or sponges, and from about 1850 on he used a broad carpenter's pencil (*see* DRAWING, fig. 8). In his more than 10,000 drawings there is evidence that he was easily able to deal with complicated subject-matter, awkward compositions and unusual viewpoints. He was one of the few artists who successfully competed against the increasingly popular art of photography, desiring that his work be even more exact, true-to-life and precise than the camera's eye. In the process, however, his drawings developed from a linear treatment of form to a more dense, full-bodied rendition in which chiaroscuro is important. In their approach, his late drawings are strikingly similar to those of Seurat.

(ii) Painting. As a painter, Menzel was one of the most significant and progressive in Germany. His small-scale oil studies of the mid-1840s, such as *Room with a Balcony* (1845), the *Artist's Bedroom, Living-room with Menzel's Sister* (both 1847) and the *Artist's Sister, Sleeping* (*c.* 1848; Hamburg, Ksthalle) were developed exclusively out of colour and have the freedom of execution of Delacroix's oil studies of the same period. Menzel's landscapes (e.g. the *Berlin–Potsdam Railway*) reveal his preoccupation with Constable's paintings. Most of these smaller studies became well known only towards the end of Menzel's life or after his death, his fame resting chiefly on his large, carefully researched historical pictures. He had hoped that the eight large oil paintings (1849–58) of Frederick II's life would bring him recognition as a painter of historical subjects (*see* §1 above). These brought together all his skills as a painter and his knowledge as a historical chronicler. As with his illustrations, he valued accuracy of

the period; not only did he search out and draw the architectural features and landscape settings appropriate to the locations but, after exhaustive studies in arsenals in Berlin and Dresden, he became an undisputed authority on 18th-century Prussian uniforms and weapons. Like a positivist historian, he disclosed his sources: every object in a painting had to be correct for its time, including buttons on uniforms, hilts of swords, horses' harnesses and style of wigs. In addition, his figures had to be authentically depicted, and for this he relied on earlier engraved or painted portraits or profiles on coins. He was also concerned with a realistic representation of light. In *Frederick the Great's Flute Concert in Sanssouci*, for example, the light from a chandelier pervades the whole room (see fig. 2). The *Coronation of King William I in Königsberg* (1861–5), his most ambitious historical painting, has a contemporary setting of great authenticity. Menzel travelled to Königsberg (now Kaliningrad, Russia) with his pupil Fritz Werner (1827–1908) to attend the coronation and to familiarize himself with the Schlosskirche, its setting. During the four years he worked on the painting, he completed 268 pencil or watercolour studies to be used as preliminary drawings for the 132 portraits included in the work.

Although still concerned with historical subjects, from 1865 Menzel became increasingly interested in the way of life led by many residents of Berlin, a city that in the mid-19th century was developing a prosperous and well-to-do middle class. His subject-matter now often concerned bourgeois society, and he himself, because of his fame and wealth, also lived the life of a *grand bourgeois*. He became interested in painting scenes set in areas where people of society ostentatiously paraded. *Afternoon in the Tuileries Gardens* (1867) and *Weekday in Paris* (1869; Düsseldorf, Kstmus.), for example, are reworkings of impressions gained on previous visits to Paris. His portrayals of court society at the King's entertainments in Berlin or gouaches of city people enjoying the rural environment of the spas (e.g. *Confectioner's Shop in Kissingen*, 1893) show the self-confidence of imperial German society but are not without an edge of caricature. Even in such a political painting as *King William I's Departure for the Army, 31 July 1870*, Menzel placed the monarch well in the background, luxuriating instead in a highly detailed portrayal of thronging citizens. His last important picture, *Market in Piazza d'Erbe, Verona* (1884; Dresden, Gemäldegal. Neue Meister) also has as its theme the bustling turmoil of bourgeois society and the life of ordinary folk.

Menzel also revealed an interest in social display through the highly individual and original manner in which he depicted church interiors and religious customs. As early as 1847, in *Sermon in the Old Monastery Church in Berlin* (Dresden, Gemäldegal. Neue Meister), he focused not only on the architecture but also on the Protestant service. In *Morning Mass* (1853) he depicted the faithful attending the Catholic Mass, while in *Interior of the Old Synagogue, Prague*, Jews in prayer-shawls study holy scriptures. Such paintings as *Missionary Service in the Buchenhalle near Kösen* and *Procession in Hofgastein* and smaller gouaches of sermons, High Mass, confessions and celebrations of liturgical rites also reflect his keen eye for depicting religious customs. In these works, Menzel observed and, in an almost detached way, recorded a wealth of detail in faces, poses, clothing and objects. Being a religious sceptic and a follower of Schopenhauer, he probably saw these activities more as fascinating curiosities of human interaction than as events of truly religious significance.

Menzel's greatness, however, rests primarily on two works. The earlier painting, *Funeral of the Martyrs of the Berlin Revolution, 1848* (see fig. 1 above), remained uncompleted, because the failure of the revolution made him lose all confidence in the subject. Even so, this picture is an incunabulum of politically committed art in Germany. The later work, the *Iron-rolling Mill* (1872–5), is on a grander scale and shows his capabilities: the painting, shown at the Exposition Universelle in Paris in 1878, was the first artistically valid representation of an industrial scene in European art.

3. PERSONALITY AND CHARACTER. Menzel, a mostly self-taught artist of great talent, found himself caught up in a society that forced him to create his own place as an artist by straining all his abilities to the utmost; he had little time to travel or to cultivate his own interests until he was past 50. His ethos of unremitting hard work and the unconditional performance of his duties, which enabled him to complete such artistically intractable commissions as his extensive series of lithographs for *Die Armee Friedrichs des Grossen in ihrer Uniformierung*, made it impossible for him to be easy-going in the ordinary sense or uncompromising as an artist. Thus, as a person and as an artist, he was contradictory. On the one hand he was a committed citizen of the Prussian State, which was responsible for bringing about the unification of the other German states, while on the other hand he was an outsider by virtue of his short stature of 1.4 m. Although honoured and fêted by the Hohenzollerns as the eulogist of Frederick the Great and his army, he nevertheless remained a remorselessly observant artist, scrutinizing the world around him with its technological progress and its social pressures. He was a revolutionary artist who laid the foundations of Impressionism and, by depicting scenes of labour and social customs, explored a new range of subject-matter for art. Yet at the same time he tended to squander his talent by often overcrowding his pictures with a multitude of detailed observations. He was a great lover of music, an admirer of Brahms as well as his antithesis Wagner. Although a close friend of Theodor Fontane, the leading writer of the Wilhelmine period, he was in only a few of his own works as critical and enlightened as Fontane. The neutrality of observation into which Menzel, on principle, retreated was, among other things, a reflection of the unpolitical attitude of German bourgeois society, which saw its desires fulfilled by the Empire under Bismarck. In spite of portraying the working classes, Menzel did not recognize them as a dynamic political and social force. Notwithstanding, his immense oeuvre is of great significance in 19th-century German art.

WRITINGS

H. Wolff, ed.: *Adolph von Menzel: Briefe* (Berlin, 1914)

PRINTS

J. W. von Goethe: *Künstlers Erdenwallen* (Berlin, 1834)
Denkwürdigkeiten aus der brandenburgisch-preussischen Geschichte (Berlin, 1836)

A. von Chamisso: *Peter Schlemihls wundersame Geschichte* (1839; Berlin, 1928)
Radierversuche (Berlin, 1844)
Die Werke Friedrichs des Grossen (Berlin, 1849)
Die Armee Friedrichs des Grossen in ihrer Uniformierung, 3 vols (Berlin, 1851–7)
H. von Kleist: *Der zerbrochene Krug* (Berlin, 1877)

BIBLIOGRAPHY

M. Jordan and R. Dohme: *Das Werk Adolph Menzels: Vom Künstler autorisierte Ausgabe*, 5 vols (Munich, 1890–1905)
J. Meier-Graefe: *Der junge Menzel: Ein Problem der Kunstökonomie Deutschlands* (Leipzig, 1906)
E. Bock: *Adolph Menzel: Verzeichnis seines graphischen Werkes* (Berlin, 1923) [cat. rais.]
K. Kaiser: *Menzel: Das Eisenwalzwerk* (Leipzig, 1959)
I. Wirth: *Mit Adolph Menzel in Berlin* (Munich, 1965)
——: *Adolph Menzel, der Maler* (Stuttgart, 1966)
H. Ebertshäuser: *Adolph von Menzel: Das graphische Werk*, intro. by J. C. Jensen and essay by M. Liebermann, 2 vols (Munich, 1976)
F. Forster-Hahn: 'Adolph Menzel's "Daguerreotypical" Image of Frederick the Great: A Liberal Bourgeois Interpretation of German History', *A. Bull.*, lix (1977), pp. 242–61
——: 'Authenticity into Ambivalence: The Evolution of Menzel's Drawings', *Master Drgs*, xvi (1978), pp. 255–83
Adolph Menzel: Gemälde, Zeichnungen (exh. cat., ed. V. M. Ruthenberg; Berlin, Staatl. Museen Preuss. Kultbes., 1980)
W. Hütt: *Adolph Menzel* (Munich, Wiesbaden and Leipzig, 1981)
Adolph Menzel: Realist-Historist-Maler des Hofes: Gemälde, Gouachen, Aquarelle, Zeichnungen und Druckgraphik aus der Sammlung Georg Schäfers, Schweinfurt, und aus der Kunsthalle Bremen, ergänzt durch die Bestände der Kunsthalle zu Kiel und des Museums für Kunst und Kulturgeschichte in Lübeck (exh. cat., ed. J. C. Jensen; Kiel, Christian-Albrechts U., Ksthalle; Bremen, Ksthalle; Lübeck, Mus. Kst & Kultgesch.; and others; 1981–2)
J. C. Jensen: *Adolph Menzel* (Cologne, 1982)
Menzel: Der Beobachter (exh. cat., ed. W. Hofmann; Hamburg, Ksthalle, 1982)
Adolph Menzel: Zeichnungen, Druckgraphik und illustrierte Bücher: Ein Bestandskatalog der Nationalgalerie, des Kupferstichkabinetts und der Kunstbibliothek, Berlin, Staatl. Museen Preuss. Kultbes. cat. (Berlin, 1984)
Prints and Drawings by Adolph Menzel (exh. cat., ed. L. Griesbach; Cambridge, Fitzwilliam, 1984)

JENS CHRISTIAN JENSEN

Meo da Caprino [Amedeo di Francesco; Meo da Settignano; Meo Fiorentino] (*b* Settignano, nr Florence, 1430; *d* 1501). Italian architect. One of the earliest Florentine architects to work in Rome in the Renaissance manner, he is first recorded there in 1462, when he became one of Giuliano da Sangallo's assistants working for Pope Paul II at the Palazzo S Marco (now Palazzo Venezia). The original architect of the palace is not certain, although Alberti and Benedetto da Maiano have been suggested; it is essentially a transitional work, the product of many architects over some decades, and Meo's individual contribution cannot be identified. He is also associated with Giuliano at the Vatican Palace, where he may have assisted on the Benediction Loggia, adjacent to the façade of St Peter's.

Meo's most important work is the rebuilt cathedral of S Giovanni in Turin, which shows the influence of the façade (*c.* 1477) of S Maria del Popolo, Rome, by Baccio Pontelli and Andrea Bregno Alberti's façade (1456–70) of S Maria Novella in Florence. The cathedral was rebuilt on the instructions of Cardinal Bishop Domenico della Rovere, and it replaced three smaller, much earlier adjacent basilicas. Meo worked with eight other Florentine masons and sculptors; the first stone was laid in July 1491 and the whole church completed with great rapidity by 1497.

Its plan is a Latin cross, with a seven-bay nave and aisles, which are lined with shallow niches forming side chapels. Above the crossing is a tall, octagonal drum, with a cupola supported by eight Doric columns. The nave and aisles are separated by piers with marble half columns and Doric capitals. On the nave side, these extend vertically, becoming flat pilasters at clerestory level, where they meet the simple barrel vault. The overall appearance of the interior is attractive and well proportioned; the church is not particularly large, and all the detailing is simple to the point of austerity. It is this extreme simplicity that makes the interior imposing. It is significant that at the time of the cathedral's construction Turin was still very small, with a population of only about 5000; the church's scale was thus appropriate to such a settlement.

The exterior is dominated by the white marble west façade, which, however, is less successful than the interior, its proportions being rather squat and the carving shallow and timid. The façade has three vertical sections corresponding to the ground-plan. The central part is capped by a triangular pediment and is connected to the much lower aisles by large simple volutes rather in the manner of Alberti. The central portal is well proportioned and in the form of a triumphal arch; smaller-scale versions lead to the aisles, which, with their chapels, are nearly as wide as the nave and thus contribute to the squat proportions of the whole façade. The two windows above the main portal are still Gothic in detail, and their design is repeated in the tall drum of the dome above the crossing. The dome itself is too small to successfully dominate the exterior.

The cathedral interior is Meo's best work; the east end, however, which was almost certainly originally built with a semicircular apse, was destroyed when work began (1668) on the construction of Guarino Guarini's extraordinary chapel of S Sindone, built to house the Holy Shroud. This elaborate structure stands immediately to the east of Meo's crossing, and its impressive dome (completed 1680) now dominates the exterior of the church, dwarfing Meo's modest cupola.

BIBLIOGRAPHY
Thieme–Becker
F. Rondolino: *Il Duomo di Torino* (Turin, 1898)
A. Venturi: *Storia* (1901–40)
S. Solero: *Il Duomo di Torino* (Turin, 1956)
L. Tamburini: *Le chiese di Torino dal rinascimento al barocco* (Turin, 1968)

□

Meo (di Guido) da Siena (*fl* 1319; *d* before 1334). Italian painter. He was active chiefly in Perugia, where he was documented as a citizen in 1319. A number of Sienese painters, such as Duccio and later Taddeo di Bartolo, worked temporarily in Perugia, but Meo da Siena was unusual in that he settled in the city and established a prolific workshop there. He successfully integrated the decorative elegance of Sienese painting with the cruder, more provincial style of Umbrian art and became one of the most influential painters in Umbria in the first half of the 14th century. Meo and his followers dominated painting in Perugia during this period and monopolized local patronage, producing a large number of altarpieces and, mostly votive, frescoes.

Meo da Siena's only signed work, a large polyptych of the *Virgin and Child with Saints* (Perugia, G.N. Umbria; see fig.), painted for the Benedictine abbey of Santa Maria di Valdiponte ('Montelabate') near Perugia, is generally dated *c.* 1318–20, since the Virgin and Child are identical in pose to the same figures in the polyptych painted *c.* 1319 by Segna di Bonaventura (New York, Met.). Other works generally accepted as by Meo include a triptych of the *Virgin and Child with Saints* (Perugia, Mus. Opera Duomo), painted for S Lorenzo, Perugia; an altarpiece with the *Virgin and Child with Saints* said to have come from S Domenico, Perugia (although it contains no Dominican saints); a ruined dossal of the *Virgin and Child with Saints* from S Maria della Misericordia, Perugia, and what is perhaps his most exquisite work, the *Virgin and Child* from Montelabate (all Perugia, G.N. Umbria). All of these works were greatly influenced by Duccio, in particular by his altarpiece painted for S Domenico, of which only the centre panel, showing the *Virgin and Child*, remains (Perugia, G.N. Umbria). The only dated work attributed to Meo da Siena is probably one of his latest, a dossal of a traditional Umbrian long, low, double-sided design. On the front it shows a small *Maestà* (Virgin and Child enthroned) with a kneeling Benedictine donor and six standing figures, including St Peter as pope; and on the reverse *Christ Enthroned with the Twelve Apostles* (Frankfurt am Main, Städel. Kstinst.). The date, 1333, is given in an inscription that also names the donor, Ugolino di Montevibiano, Abbot of S Pietro, Perugia (1331–*c.* 1360), where the altarpiece originated. It seems possible that the comparatively rare iconography of Christ enthroned may derive from an altarpiece by the St Francis Master, possibly painted for S Francesco al Prato, Perugia, of which only fragments showing standing saints remain, rather than from Giotto's Stefaneschi altarpiece (Rome, Pin. Vaticana). The quality of execution of the figure of St Peter on both sides is outstanding, and it seems likely that Meo da Siena designed the altarpiece but painted only this small part of it before his death. He was certainly dead by 1334 when a document refers to him as 'olim Mey de Senis'.

Meo da Siena's followers apparently continued to work in his style and in the late 1330s or early 1340s moved their workshop south to Subiaco where they executed a number of works for San Benedetto Abbey (Sacro Speco). They painted a long, low, rectangular, double-sided dossal, similar in design to the S Pietro dossal, for the high altar of the church, where it remains, although not in its original position. On the front is the figure of *Christ Enthroned* with two Benedictine supplicants, flanked by standing saints under a cusped arcade; on the back is a small *Maestà* similarly flanked by standing saints. In the nave they executed a fresco cycle of the *Passion* with a narrative *Crucifixion* over the central arch and in the lower church painted a small chapel with frescoes showing scenes from the *Life of the Virgin*, while the staircase leading to the cemetery bears rare scenes of the *Three Living and the Three Dead*.

BIBLIOGRAPHY
P. Egidi and others: *I monasteri di Subiaco* (Rome, 1904)
M. Salmi: 'Quando morì Meo da Siena?', *Rass. A. Sen.*, xvi (1924), pp. 76–7
E. Ricci: *La chiesa di S Prospero e i pittori del duecento in Perugia* (Perugia, 1929)

Meo da Siena: *Virgin and Child with Saints*, tempera on panel, *c.* 1318–20 (Perugia, Galleria Nazionale dell'Umbria)

F. Santi: *Dipinti, sculture e oggetti d'arte di età romanica e gotica*, Perugia, G.N. Umbria cat. (Rome, 1969)

M. Boskovits: *Pittura umbra e marchigiana fra medioevo e rinascimento* (Florence, 1973)

F. Todini: *La pittura umbra dal duecento al primo cinquecento* (Milan, 1989), i, p. 222; ii, pp. 107–9

DILLIAN GORDON

Mequinez. *See* MEKNÈS.

Merano, Giovanni Battista (*b* Genoa, 1632; *d* Piacenza, 1698). Italian painter. He was a pupil in Genoa of Giovanni Andrea de' Ferrari and perhaps also of Giulio Benso, from whom he acquired an inclination towards narrative and naturalism. Later he entered the workshop of Valerio Castello. About 1651 Merano went to Parma to study the works of Correggio and Parmigianino. Here he painted two oval frescoes of *St Lucy* and *St Apollonia* (both Parma, Santa Croce). These first works, stylistically still immature,

were strongly influenced by 16th-century Emilian painters, especially Girolamo Bedoli Mazzola, as well as by Castello.

Probably in 1658 Merano returned to Genoa. Shortly afterwards he received the prestigious commission to paint a large lunette of the *Massacre of the Innocents* in the Church of Il Gesù, Genoa. Here his style is freer and more personal, revealing a close study of the works of Giovanni Benedetto Castiglione and of Rubens, whose sumptuous theatricality in particular he absorbed.

Little is known of Merano's subsequent movements. He was definitely in Genoa in 1663 and probably also in the early 1670s, when Mulinaretto (1660–1745) frequented his workshop. In 1673 he completed an altarpiece of the *Crucifixion* (Piacenza, Ospizi Civili), which indicates a knowledge of the works (in Genoa) of Veronese and Vouet. In 1678 he executed frescoes of *St Nicholas in Glory* and the *Coronation of the Virgin* for S Giovanni

Battista in Finale Marina. From 1683 he received several commissions for the church of S Giovanni Evangelista, Parma, from the abbot, Angelo Maria Arcioni. Among these are the frescoes in the chapels of S Giacomo (1684) and S Nicola di Bari (1685), with scenes from the lives of these saints. These frescoes are perhaps Merano's most poetic works, painted in a free and elegant manner with a colourful play of refined and delicate tonalities. The success of this commission led to Merano's employment by Ranuccio II Farnese, Duke of Parma, for whom he produced numerous paintings and designs for tapestries, as well as fresco decorations in the Palazzo Ducale, Colorno, and the Palazzo del Giardino in Parma (all dispersed or destr.).

In 1687 Merano painted the enormous *Vision of St John the Evangelist* (Parma, S Giovanni Evangelista). The following year he executed the important fresco of the *Coronation of the Virgin with Saints* on the façade of the Palazzo del Governatore, Parma, in collaboration with Francesco Galli-Bibiena, who provided the *quadratura* framework. It was destroyed in 1760, but a *bozzetto* has been identified (Parma, G. N.) that gives an idea of the compositional complexity and formal elegance of the original fresco. Towards the end of his life, the artist returned to Genoa. In San Remo, in 1695, he painted his last, rather weak fresco decorations, in the Palazzo Borea dell'Olmo, and the *Apotheosis of St Ignatius* in Il Gesù, Genoa (*in situ*).

BIBLIOGRAPHY

R. Soprani: *Vite* (1674); enlarged, ed. C. G. Ratti (1768–9), i, pp. 270, 285, 348; ii, pp. 61–8
Genoese Baroque Drawings (exh. cat. by M. Newcome, Binghamton, SUNY; Worcester, MA, A. Mus.; 1972), nos 102–4
V. Belloni: *Pittura genovese del seicento* (Genoa, 1974), ii, pp. 124–36
G. Godi: 'Ritrovata la Madonna di Piazza', *Gaz. Parma* (14 Dec 1979), p. 3
C. Cirillo and G. Godi: 'Un modelletto di G. B. Merano per la sua attività nel ducato parmense', *Boll. Mus. Civ. Genov.*, ii/4–6 (1980), pp. 71–81
J. P. Marandel: 'Giovanni Battista Merano in Parma', *Paragone*, xxxii/377 (1981), pp. 3–11
C. Cirillo and G. Godi: 'Inediti piacentini di Giovanbattista Merano e Gianlorenzo Bertolotto', *Boll. Stor. Piacent.* (Jan–June 1982)
M. Newcome: 'Giovanni Battista Merano in Liguria', *Paragone*, xxxiii/389 (1982), pp. 19–32

FEDERICA LAMERA

Mérard, Pierre (*b* ?Paris, *c*. ?1740; *d* Paris, 6 May 1800). French sculptor. A student of Edme Bouchardon, this little-known portrait sculptor was never a member of the Académie Royale de Peinture et de Sculpture, although in 1763 he was received (*reçu*) into the rival Académie de St Luc. He exhibited there in 1774 and later became one of its professors. After the French Revolution (1789–95) Mérard showed sculptures in the Salons of 1795, 1796 and 1799. His earliest known production is a wax medallion portrait of *Louis XV*, signed and dated 1771 (ex-Marquis de Menars sale, Paris, 1782). Mérard's materials were terracotta, plaster, marble and wax. The few works by Mérard that are known today include a marble bust of *Louis-François de Bourbon, Prince de Conti* (1777; ex-Edouard Kann priv. col., Paris) and a terracotta *Bust of an Unknown Man* (1786; London, V&A). Another terracotta *Bust of an Unknown Man* (Lawrence, U. KS, Spencer Mus. A.), signed 'P.M.', is attributed to him and may be the portrait of the writer Jacob-Nicolas Moreau that

Mérard exhibited at the Académie de St Luc in 1774. In addition to portraits he executed the tomb of *Louis-François de Bourbon* (marble, 1777–9; L'Isle-Adam, Val-d'Oise, St Martin). Mérard's works exemplify the late 18th-century taste for delicate, realistic portraiture, in contrast to Bouchardon's more classicizing and monumental style.

BIBLIOGRAPHY

Lami
'Notes critiques sur les oeuvres de peinture et de sculpture réunies à l'exposition de cent pastels du XVIIIe siècle', *Bull. Soc. Hist. A. Fr.* (1908), pp. 176–7
P. Vitry: 'Exposition de cent pastels et des bustes du XVIIIe siècle', *Les Arts* [Paris], 82 (1908), p. 9
J. Maxon: 'A Bust Attributed to Pierre Mérard', *A.Q.* [Detroit], xv (1952), p. 337
F. H. Dowley: 'Toward an Attribution to Pierre Mérard', *Register* [Lawrence, U. KS], 4 (1954), pp. 17–18
T. Hodgkinson: 'French Eighteenth-century Portrait Sculptures in the Victoria and Albert Museum', *V&A Mus. Yb.*, 3 (1972), pp. 100–15

MICHAEL PRESTON WORLEY

Mercadal, Fernando García. *See* GARCÍA MERCADAL, FERNANDO.

Mercadante, Lorenzo (*fl* 1453–67). French sculptor, active in Spain. He came from Brittany, but his style is related to that of the Burgundian school of Claus Sluter, in which he must have been trained. Between 1453 and 1458 Mercadante made the magnificent alabaster tomb of Cardinal *Juan de Cervantes* (*d* 1453) for the chapel of S Hermengildo founded by the Cardinal in Seville Cathedral. The tomb, which is signed LORENZO MERCADANTE DE BRETANA, was a work that introduced the Netherlandish-Burgundian style into Andalusian sculpture through the technical perfection of its execution and through its naturalism (particularly the physiognomy of the effigy). On the sides of the sepulchral bed (1.26×2.63 m) are statues of the Apostles under small canopies and pairs of angels holding the Archbishop's shield. The recumbent effigy of the deceased (l. 2.7 m) is dressed in pontificals and rests on cushions and drapery imitating brocade; a hind lies at his feet. The rich chasuble and mitre bear imitation embroideries of the *Apostles* and the *Annunciation*; both are enriched with precious stones and cameos.

A document of 1454 records a payment of 15,000 *maravides* for the tomb of another, unidentified archbishop and a statue of the Virgin, which may perhaps be identified with the *Virgen del Madroño* or the *Virgen de la Cinta*, both in Seville Cathedral. Between 1464 and 1467 Mercadante worked on the sculptures for the lateral portals of the west façade of Seville Cathedral; they were executed in terracotta, a medium that was to become widely adopted in Seville. The Puerta del Nacimiento bears statues of the four Evangelists, SS Laurence and Hermengild on the embrasures, with exquisitely modelled draperies. The fine tympanum relief of the *Nativity* is closely related to Netherlandish examples and is notable for its anecdotal detail (the dancing shepherds), happy expressions (especially St Joseph and the smiling figure who approaches with an offering) and the townscape in the background. The Puerta del Bautismo bears terracotta jamb statues of local saints (SS Florence, Justa, Rufina, Isidore, Leander and Fulgentius); the fine quality of execution and the naturalism (especially the splendid head of St Isidore) are particularly notable. The tympanum relief of the *Baptism of Christ* may have been carved by pupils.

A *Virgin and Child* in the convent of S Clara at Fregenal de la Sierra, Badajoz, is attributed to Mercadante, as is a *St Michael* (Barcelona, Mus. A. Catalunya) that also came from this convent. Other works thought to be by Mercadante's school are a terracotta *St Simeon* in S Andrés, Seville; a *Virgin and Child* in S Isidoro del Campo, Santiponce, nr Seville; the *Virgin* in the Hermitage-Sanctuary of La Fuensanta, Córdoba, and the recumbent glazed terracotta figure of *Prior Vázquez* in the church of Aracena Castle, Huelva. The sculptor PEDRO MILLÁN was a follower of Mercadante.

BIBLIOGRAPHY
J. Gestoso Pérez: *Sevilla monumental y artistica* (Seville, 1890)
D. Angulo: *La escultura en Andalucia* (Seville, 1927–8)
A. Durán Sanpere and A. Ainaud de Lasarte: *Escultura gótica*, A. Hisp., v (Madrid, 1956)
La catedral de Sevilla (Seville, 1986)
JOSÉ MARIA AZCARATE RISTORI

Mercado, Antonio Rivas. *See* RIVAS MERCADO, ANTONIO.

Mercado, Melchor María (*b* La Plata [now Sucre], 1816; *d* Sucre, 1871). Bolivian painter, photographer, museum founder, scientist and soldier. He was self-taught as a painter and established a reputation through his work in various techniques. His major work was an album (1841–60; Sucre, Bib. & Archv N.) composed of 116 watercolours of ordinary people, native and mestizo, fauna, flora, landscapes and nature scenes of various regions of Bolivia. His work is spontaneous and naive, painted with an almost dry brush. The importance of his work lies principally in his realistic approach to his country and its natural environment. He also painted academic portraits, such as *Casimiro Olañeta* (1857; La Paz, priv. col.), and he established (*c.* 1845) the first Bolivian museum of cultural, mineral, plant and animal specimens (dispersed after 1871). He took up photography towards the end of his life.

BIBLIOGRAPHY
M. Chacón Torres: *Pintores del siglo XIX*, Bib. A. & Cult. Boliv.: A. & Artistas (La Paz, 1963)
L. Castedo: *Siglo XIX, siglo XX* (Madrid, 1988), ii of *Historia del arte ibero-americano*
P. Querejazu: *La pintura boliviana del siglo XX* (Milan, 1989)
G. Mendoza: *Vocación de arte y drama histórico nacional en Bolivia: El pintor Melchor María Mercado (1816–1871): Un precursor* (La Paz, 1991)
PEDRO QUEREJAZU

Mercié, (Marius-Jean-)Antonin [Antoine] (*b* Toulouse, 30 Oct 1845; *d* Paris, 13 Dec 1916). French sculptor and painter. Principally a sculptor, he studied at the Ecole des Beaux-Arts in Paris under François Jouffroy and Alexandre Falguière. In 1868 he won the Prix de Rome with the marble statue *Theseus, Vanquisher of the Minotaur* (Paris, Ecole N. Sup. B.-A.) and completed his studies at the Académie de France in Rome. There he was awarded a first-class medal and the cross of the Légion d'honneur for his elegant neo-Florentine bronze statue *David Victorious* (Paris, Mus. d'Orsay). Further success came with the bronze group *Gloria victis* (exh. Salon 1874; Paris, Petit Pal.), composed of a young warrior borne heavenwards

by a flying figure, combining the formal elegance of Renaissance sculpture with a powerful Baroque composition. Replicas of it were used on monuments to the dead of the Franco-Prussian War of 1870 in many French towns, including Niort, Deux-Sèvres (1881), Agen, Lot-et-Garonne (1883) and Bordeaux (1884).

Mercié's later output of monumental sculpture tended towards the academic, and, though prolific, he produced little that lived up to the promise of his early works. Among his principal pieces are the statue of *François Arago* (bronze, 1879; Perpignan, Place Arago), the equestrian monument to *William II, King of the Netherlands and Grand Duke of Luxembourg* (bronze, 1884; Luxembourg, Place Guillaume), the patriotic group *Quand même!* (bronze, 1884; Belfort, Place d'Armes) and the funerary effigies of *Louis-Philippe* and *Queen Marie-Amélie* (marble, 1886; Dreux, Eure-et-Loire, Orléans Chapel), as well as numerous funerary monuments in Père Lachaise Cemetery, Paris. Many of his sculptural works were reproduced in reduced-scale bronze editions by Ferdinand Barbedienne (1810–92) and Gustave Leblanc and in biscuit porcelain by the Sèvres manufactory.

One of the most successful French sculptors of his generation, Mercié accrued numerous honours. From 1900 he was a professor at the Ecole des Beaux-Arts and from 1913 he was President of the Société des Artistes Français. From 1880 he exhibited paintings (e.g. *Galathé*, 1909; Paris, Petit Pal.), several of which were acquired by the State.

BIBLIOGRAPHY
Lami
The Romantics to Rodin: French Nineteenth-century Sculpture from North American Collections (exh. cat., ed. P. Fusco and H. W. Janson; Los Angeles, Co. Mus. A.; Minneapolis, Inst. A.; Detroit, Inst. A.; Indianapolis, Mus. A.; 1980–81)
Rodin Rediscovered (exh. cat., Washington, DC, N.G.A., 1981–2)
De Carpeaux à Matisse: La Sculpture française de 1850 à 1914 dans les musées et les collections publiques du nord de la France (exh. cat., Paris, Mus. Rodin, 1982–3)
C. Vogt: 'Un Artiste oublié: Antonin Mercié', *La Sculpture du XIXe siècle: Une Mémoire retrouvée. Les Fonds de sculpture* Paris, 1986)
La Sculpture française au XIXe siècle (exh. cat. ed. A. Pingeot; Paris, Grand Pal., 1986)
CHRISTIANE VOGT

Mercier, Philip [Philippe; Pierre-Philippe] (*b* Berlin, 1689 or 1691; *d* London, 18 July 1760). French painter and etcher, active in England. George Vertue records that he was born in Berlin of French extraction and Horace Walpole gave the painter's age on his death as 71, which suggests he may be the Pierre-Philippe, son of a Huguenot tapestry-worker Pierre Mercier (*d* Dresden, 1729), who was born in 1689; however, a Philippe Mercier, also the son of a Huguenot tapestry-worker in Berlin, was born there in 1691. According to Vertue, Mercier studied painting at the Berlin Akademie and under Antoine Pesne, who had arrived in Berlin in 1710, and afterwards he travelled in Italy and France before arriving in London—'recommended by the Court at Hannover'—probably in 1716 (Vertue's MS may be read as 1716, though it is printed as 1711). He married in London in 1719 and lived in Leicester Fields, whence he sold some pictures in 1724 which he had 'collected abroad'.

Between *c.* 1720 and *c.* 1725 Mercier etched 17 plates after paintings by himself, David Teniers (ii) and Antoine

Watteau, with whose work he was obviously familiar (there is no firm evidence to support the assertion that he looked after Antoine Watteau during the latter's trip to London in 1719–20). By 1726 Mercier had painted two remarkable group portraits which may be seen as introducing the conversation piece to English art—*Party on a Terrace* (The Schutz Family, 1725; London, Tate) and *Viscount Tyrconnel with his Family* (1725–6; priv. col., see 1969 exh. cat., no. 12). For each of these pictures a drawing for a single figure survives (ex-Sotheby's, Paris, 1989; see Raines and Ingamells, no. 279). His paintings at this time were otherwise somewhat clumsy essays in Watteau's manner. In 1729 he was made Principal Painter to Frederick, Prince of Wales (who had arrived from Hannover in December 1728), and in 1730 the Keeper of his library. His set of four state full-length portraits of Frederick and his three sisters (all 1728–9; Hertford, Shire Hall) contrast with the *Music Party* (1733; see fig.), showing the Prince and his sisters ostensibly in concert with the 'Dutch House', or Kew Palace, in the background (versions London, N.P.G.; Cliveden, Bucks, NT, and Windsor Castle, Berks, Royal Col.); Mercier's talent was far more suited to the informal occasion. He taught the princesses to draw, and one drawing of a *Shepherd and Shepherdess* (priv. col.), formerly given to Mercier, bears an inscription showing it to be by Princess Caroline. A *Self-portrait* was engraved by John

Faber (1684–1756) in 1735 with the title *Scutarius, primarius pictor et bibliothecarius . . . Walliae Principis*, but Mercier was replaced as the Prince's Painter in 1736 and as Librarian in 1738. He had remarried as a widower in 1735, and in 1736–7 he retired, in Vertue's words, into the country, where he painted a number of portraits for the Samwell family of Upton, Northants, and the Hesilriges of Noseley, Warwicks.

In 1739 Mercier moved to York, where he was based for the next eight years, extensively patronized as a portrait painter by the Yorkshire gentry. During this period he developed his 'fancy' subjects, derived from Jean-Siméon Chardin (whose work he knew through engravings) and 17th-century Dutch genre paintings, but also including theatrical scenes. Such fancy pictures were frequently engraved in London—by Faber, Richard Houston and James McArdell in particular—suggesting a successful commercial purpose. A visit to Ireland in 1747, recorded by Vertue, is attested by dated portraits of Irish sitters, and a visit to Edinburgh in 1750 is similarly proven. Mercier returned to London in 1751. The following year Vertue says he went to Oporto, to paint portraits for the English merchants there, but nothing is otherwise known of such a visit. Of his last works in London there is the *Burton Family* (1775–60; Paris, Louvre) and a number of single figure genre scenes, many of which were engraved

Philip Mercier: *Music Party*, oil on canvas, 451×578 mm, 1733 (London, National Portrait Gallery)

by Richard Purcell (*d* 1766) and Johann Simon Negges (1726–92). In 1760 he exhibited a *Girl Washing* and a *Girl Sewing* at the Society of Arts.

Mercier's influence on English painting was out of all proportion to his rather uneven talent; he introduced Watteau and the French taste, he pioneered the CONVERSATION PIECE and the FANCY PICTURE, while his pretty and ingenuous female portraits evidently affected, for example, the young Joshua Reynolds. Mercier's second wife, Dorothy (née Plante), practised as a miniaturist and in watercolour and maintained a printselling business in Great Windmill Street, London, from *c.* 1761 to 1768 (for a portrait in oil by her, see 1969 exh. cat., no. 69). His daughter Charlotte (1738–62) was a pastellist of some ability, to judge by a signed pair of portraits, dated 1757 (ex-Sotheby Parke Bernet, New York, 1980; for another, dated 1757, see 1969 exh. cat., no. 70). Since Charlotte died in St James's Workhouse, it seems likely that her father had died in somewhat straitened circumstances.

BIBLIOGRAPHY

H. Walpole: *Anecdotes of Painting in England* (1762–71); ed. R. N. Wornum (1849)

'The Note-books of George Vertue—III', *Walpole Soc.*, xxii (1934), pp. 37, 40, 64, 72, 82, 122, 135, 158–9, 161

Philip Mercier (exh. cat. by R. Raines and J. Ingamells, York, C.A.G.; London, Kenwood House; 1969)

M. Eidelberg: 'Watteau's *La Boudeuse*', *Burl. Mag.* (1969), pp. 275–8

—: 'Watteau Paintings in England in the Early Eighteenth Century', *Burl. Mag.*, cxvii (1975), pp. 576–82

R. Raines and J. Ingamells: 'A Catalogue of the Paintings, Drawings and Etchings of Philip Mercier', *Walpole Soc.*, xlvi (1978), pp. 1–70

J. Ingamells: 'La Scène d'intérieur à l'écureuil par Philippe Mercier', *Rev. Louvre.*, iv (1983), pp. 282–4

JOHN INGAMELLS

Mercx [Mercks], Peter Paul [Petrus Paulus] (*b* ?Brussels; *d* Brussels, 15 March 1685). Flemish engineer and architect. As an apprentice of Jacques Francart, he worked as an architectural engineer from about 1640, when he designed the lively Baroque gable of the Sack on the Grote Markt in Brussels. He was involved with the plans to improve the harbour at Ostend, and in 1642 and 1658 he opposed plans to alter the course of the Zenne to avoid flooding in Brussels. In 1661 he built the stone lantern tower of the church of Our Lady in Rupelmonde, East Flanders. Attributions of other Baroque churches in Brussels to Mercx cannot be confirmed through archival sources. When the army commander, the Count de Monterey, had the fortifications of Brussels reinforced against the armies of Louis XIV in 1671–5, Mercx assisted in the supervision of the work. He was appointed architect and engineer to the king of Spain on 16 October 1674, and in 1680 was made city architect to Brussels.

BIBLIOGRAPHY

BNB

St Leurs: *De Groote Markt van Brussel* (Antwerp, 1942)

A. Demey: *Het land van waas: Tien eeuwen bouwkunst* (St-Niklaas, 1983)

J.-P. ESTHER

Mercy [Mersy]. *See* MARSY.

Meredith [née Twamley], Louisa Ann (*b* Hamstead, nr Birmingham, 12 July 1812; *d* Melbourne, 21 Oct 1895). English illustrator, draughtsman, writer and painter, active in Australia. She was educated at home and was taught by Thomas Lawrence to paint portrait miniatures on ivory. In 1832, at the age of 20, she earned the respect of Henry Parkes (later Premier of New South Wales, Australia) for her writings in support of the Chartist movement, begun in Birmingham in that year. In 1835 she published her first book, *Poems: With Original Illustrations Drawn and Etched by the Authoress* (London, 1835), and the following year wrote and illustrated *The Romance of Nature or The Flower Seasons*, containing 26 coloured plates engraved after her original drawings. She married her cousin Charles in 1839 and moved to Sydney, Australia, and then to Tasmania. Having attributed her botanical knowledge to a study of the works of the draughtsman and engraver James Sowerby (1757–1822), she described and illustrated the plant and animal life of Tasmania and painted landscapes and miniatures. Some of her writings are in the form of picturesque travel books accompanied by her illustrations, for example *Notes and Sketches of New South Wales* (1846) and *My Home in Tasmania during a Residence of Nine Years* (1852). She also published *Some of my Bush Friends in Tasmania* (1860), dedicated to Queen Victoria, and *Tasmanian Friends and Foes, Feathered, Furred and Finned* (1880), a moralistic account written for children and relating the adventures of a Tasmanian family; original illustrations for the latter are in the Royal Society of Tasmania, Hobart. In 1866 she exhibited her botanical paintings in Melbourne and from 1862 to 1884 sent works back to England, where they were awarded medals in several London exhibitions. Her paintings, drawn from nature, are chiefly arrangements of wildflowers and fruit, often accompanied by butterflies, as in *Mountain Fruits* (Hobart, Tasman. Mus. & A.G.). Unlike the work of Marian Ellis Rowan (1847–1922), also an Australian botanical artist, her paintings are rather two-dimensional. They are, however, drawn with scientific accuracy and are invaluable documents of plant and animal life in 19th-century Tasmania. She also published seven books of poems, some of which were written for children.

PRINTS

Poems: With Original Illustrations Drawn and Etched by the Authoress (London, 1835)

The Romance of Nature or The Flower Seasons (London, 1836)

Notes and Sketches of New South Wales (London, 1846)

My Home in Tasmania during a Residence of Nine Years, 2 vols (London, 1852)

Some of my Bush Friends in Tasmania (London, 1860)

Tasmanian Friends and Foes, Feathered, Furred and Finned (London and Hobart Town, 1880, London, 2/1881)

Last Series: Bush Friends in Tasmania (London and New York, 1891)

BIBLIOGRAPHY

M. Swann: 'Mrs Meredith and Miss Atkinson, Writers and Naturalists', *J. Proc. Royal Austral. Hist. Soc.*, xv (1929), pp. 1–29

V. R. Ellis: *Louisa Ann Meredith: A Tigress in Exile* (Sandy Bay, Tasmania, 1979)

DENIS J. CARR

Meremetçi. *See* MUSTAFA AĞA.

Mereruka, tomb of. Stone-built tomb in the Saqqara necropolis, built for Mereruka (*fl c.* 2307 BC), chief justice and vizier of Egypt. Mereruka was granted permission by Teti (*reg c.* 2325–*c.* 2291 BC) to construct his tomb not far from the King's own pyramid at Saqqara. By Old Kingdom standards, the superstructure of this tomb is unusually large, for it contains thirty-two rooms forming three connecting chapels. The principal chapel was owned by Mereruka himself, while the smaller ones belonged to his wife, Watetkhethor, and son, Meryteti. There is evidence that late 6th Dynasty artists visited these chapels in order to copy reliefs for their own compositions; therefore the tomb must have been accessible until the end of the Old Kingdom. However, encroaching sand eventually buried the lower half of the superstructure, leaving the upper wall courses of the decorated interior exposed to ruin and theft until 1893.

The tomb of Mereruka represents an important phase in the decoration of large multi-roomed chapels dating to the Old Kingdom. Compared with earlier tomb reliefs, the sculptures are noticeably bold in scale, yet the subject-matter does not extend beyond the themes created in preceding dynasties. This was a period of consolidation rather than one of artistic change. Equally important is the varying quality of the sculpture, ranging from expert and mediocre carving in the chapels of Mereruka and Watetkhethor to the poorly executed reliefs in the chapel of Meryteti. Collectively, the three chapels are a striking illustration of the work of several teams of artists and reflect a gradual decline in the quality of two-dimensional sculpture during the 6th Dynasty.

BIBLIOGRAPHY

B. Porter and R. L. B. Moss: *Topographical Bibliography* (1927–), iii, pp. 525–37
W. Wreszinski: *Atlas zur altägyptischen Kulturgeschichte*, iii (Leipzig, 1936)
P. Duell: *The Mastaba of Mereruka*, 2 vols (Chicago, 1938)
J.-P. Lauer: *Saqqara, the Royal Cemetery of Memphis: Excavations and Discoveries since 1950* (London, 1976)

YVONNE HARPUR

Meretta, Gustav (*b* Brünn [now Brno], 26 June 1832; *d* Olmütz [now Olomouc], 4 Aug 1888). Moravian architect. He studied (1847–52) at the Polytechnic in Brünn under E. Ringhoffer and was subsequently employed (until 1857) on the Lobkowitz estate in Bohemia. He completed his education (1857–8) in Vienna. From 1858 until his death he worked in the projects section of the office of works of the archdiocese of Olmütz, becoming director of the department in 1882. In this post he became one of the leading contemporary architects of ecclesiastical buildings in Moravia, most of them designed in the Gothic Revival style, although he also produced designs that reflected an appreciation of Early Christian basilica architecture. His first period of creative activity in the 1860s and 1870s was marked by a free interpretation of the past. His work in Silesia, now part of Moravia, included the churches of the Assumption (1865–70) at Liebenthal (now Liptaň), St Andrew (1869–71) at Deutsch-Pauwlowitz (now Slezské Pavlovice), in the Gothic Revival style, and the church of St Catherine (1869–73) at Rosswald (now Slezské Rudoltice), in the Romanesque Revival style. In central Moravia he designed the Gothic Revival churches of St Florian (1872–5) at Bochorz (now Bochoř) and the Virgin Mary (1873–9) at Altendorf (now Stará Ves). Linked to these designs is his grand project for the convent church of St Carlo Borromeo (1871–2) at Friedland (now Frýdlant), designed in a manner that combined the *Rundbogenstil* and the Gothic Revival, and the secondary school (1875–7) at Kremsier (now Kroměříž), in the Italian Renaissance Revival style. Meretta's activity as a restorer distinguished

the second phase of his creative work as his projects moved towards a stricter interpretation of the Gothic Revival. Projects in this style include his designs for the restoration (1878–85) of the parish church of St Maurice at Olmütz, SS Peter and Paul (1881–4) at Rataj (now Rataje) and particularly the restoration (1883–93) of Olmütz Cathedral, which marked the culmination of Meretta's work. He continued, however, to work occasionally in a much earlier style, evident in the church of the Most Sacred Saviour (1883–9) at Mährisch Ostrau (now Ostrava), built as an Early Christian basilica with a façade in the Renaissance Revival style.

BIBLIOGRAPHY

A. Prokop: *Die Markgrafschaft Mähren in kunstgeschichtlicher Beziehung*, iv (Vienna, 1904), pp. 1348–9, 1358–63
P. Zatloukal: 'Gustav Meretta', *Výroční Zpráva Okresní Archiv Olomouci* (1987), pp. 83–97

PAVEL ZATLOUKAL

Méréville. French Picturesque garden near Etampes, Essonne. The garden was laid out for Jean-Joseph de Laborde (1724–94) between 1784 and 1794, initially by François-Joseph Bélanger but from 1786 by the landscape painter Hubert Robert. Laborde, an immensely wealthy financier and banker to the courts of Louis XV and Louis XVI, acquired Méréville in 1784. At that time its garden consisted of regularized parterres, and he spent almost 10,000 livres, an enormous sum even at that time, on transforming it into a fashionable *jardin anglais*. The varied terrain of the site was enhanced by the diversion of its small river, La Juine, from its natural course to traverse the park in a serpentine manner until it reached a manmade lake. Four bridges, including one deliberately built so as to appear ruinous, were carefully placed to create the best views and further emphasize the picturesque effects of the river. In addition to the standard vocabulary of *fabriques* for a *jardin anglais* (these included a Chinoiserie pavilion, a Gothick and a ruined tower, a dairy, windmill and cascade), which reflected the intellectual interests and taste of the later 18th century, Laborde added a more personal item to the garden iconography: a rostral column commemorating the drowning of his two sons off the coast of California, and a monument to Captain James Cook.

At the end of the 19th century Arthur Dufresne de Saint-Léon transported the rostral column, the Temple of Filial Piety (based on the Temple of the Sibyl at Tivoli), the monument to Cook and the façade of the dairy to the estate of Jeurre, approximately 20 km from Méréville, where they remain; Méréville itself has fallen into deplorable decay.

See also GARDEN, §VIII, 4(ii).

BIBLIOGRAPHY

E. de Ganay: *Jardins de la France et leur décor* (Paris, 1949), pp. 237–8
J. de Cayeux: 'Hubert Robert dessinateur des jardins et sa collaboration au Parc de Méréville', *Bull. Soc. Hist. A. Fr.* (1968), pp. 127–33
O. Choppin de Janvry: 'Méréville', *L'Oeil*, clxxx (1969), pp. 39–40, 83, 96
S. de Lassus: 'Les Fabriques de Méréville et de Jeurre', *Bull. Inf. Inst. N. Hist. A.* (Jan–Feb 1975), pp. 32–6
——: 'Quelques détails inédits sur Méréville', *Bull. Soc. Hist. A. Fr.* (1976), pp. 273–87

SUSAN B. TAYLOR

Mergem, Jan van. *See* JEAN DE MARVILLE.

Merian. Family of artists and publishers of Swiss origin, active in Germany and Holland. The engraver (1) Matthäus Merian (i), whose forebears were sawyers and timber-merchants in Basle, married Maria Magdalena de Bry (*d* 1645), the daughter of the publisher Johann Theodor de Bry, in 1617. Taking control of his father-in-law's business in 1626, at its base in Frankfurt am Main, he established it as one of Europe's leading producers of topographical and historical work. Matthäus Merian (i)'s elder son (2) Matthäus Merian (ii) became a successful portrait painter before taking over the publishing house on his father's death in 1650; his younger son Caspar Merian (1627–86) concentrated on engraving. Matthäus Merian (i)'s two daughters by his marriage to Maria Magdalena married the engravers Christoph Le Blon II and Melchior Küsel I. From the second marriage of Matthäus Merian (i) in 1646 to Johanna Sibylla Heimy, a further daughter, (3) Maria Sibylla Merian, was born; she became an outstanding painter of plants and insects, working in Holland and Surinam. She had two daughters by her marriage to the painter Johann Andreas Graff (1637–1701), Johanna Helena (*b* 1688) and Dorothea Henrica (1678–1745): the latter married the painter Georg Gsell. The Frankfurt publishing house remained under the family's control until 1727.

BIBLIOGRAPHY
Hollstein, *Ger.*; *SKL*; Thieme–Becker
J. von Sandrart: *Teutsche Academie* (1675–9); ed. A. R. Peltzer (1925), pp. 200–02, 245–6
P. F. Gwinner: *Kunst und Künstler in Frankfurt am Main* (Frankfurt am Main, 1862), pp. 145–74; app. and suppl. (Munich, 1867), pp. 45–54
K. W. Zülch: *Frankfurter Künstler 1223–1700* (Frankfurt am Main, 1935), pp. 500–02, 548, 568–9

(1) Matthäus Merian (i) (*bapt* Basle, 25 Sept 1593; *d* Bad Schwalbach, 19 June 1650). He was first trained as a glass-engraver in Basle, then learnt etching under Dietrich Meyer I (1572–1658) in Zurich in 1609–10. His earliest works are thus sketches for glass-engravings (1607; Basle, Kstmus. and Munich, Staatl. Graph. Samml.). Thirty-three early etchings from Zurich survive, mainly hunting and calendar pictures with definite topographical backgrounds. In 1611 Merian began to travel, first to Strasbourg—probably to work in Friedrich Brentel's workshop—then to Nancy, where he contributed to the engravings of the *Funeral of Charles III, Duke of Lorraine* (Wüthrich 1966, i, nos 32–45), working under Claude de La Ruelle. In Paris (1612–4), working for Nicolas de Mathonière (*fl* 1st quarter of 17th century) among others, he engraved scenes from the court life of Maria de' Medici and Louis XIII, emblems and a plan of the city (W 1966, 46–79; 244–6). In 1615 he returned to Basle, where he drew a major plan of the city (London, BM and Basle, Hist. Mus.) and copied engravings by Jacques Bellange (W 1966, 85–95) and hunting scenes by Antonio Tempesta (W 1966, 478–94). In Stuttgart in 1616 he illustrated a royal baptism of the house of Württemberg (Repraesentativ der Fürstlichen Aufzug und Ritterspil... bey Ihr Fl. G. Neügebornen Sohn, Fridrich Hertzog zu Württemberg etc. Fürstlicher Kindtauffen (10–17 März, 1616)) for E. van Hulsen. He then travelled via Augsburg to Oppenheim.

Here Merian entered, as an engraver, the publishing house of Johann Theodor de Bry, whose daughter Maria Magdalena he married on 11 February 1617. This marriage was to be of decisive importance for his later career. His most important work in Oppenheim was the continuation

Matthäus Merian (i): *Münchenstein*, a village near Basle, etching, 168×267 mm, *c.* 1624 (Zurich, Schweizerisches Landesmuseum)

of de Bry's travel books and the illustration (Wüthrich, 1972, ii, nos 62–6) of Robert Fludd's cosmological works and of Julius Wilhelm Zincgref's *Emblemata* (Frankfurt, 1619; w 1972, 108). He was already beginning to work for himself, engraving his 1615 plan of Basle and hunting pictures in the style of Gillis van Coninxloo. Until 1620 he also worked partly in Frankfurt, Cologne and Heidelberg, where he engraved large views of the town (w 1966, 617) and the Hortus Palatinus (1620; w 1966, 618) after Jacques Fouquier. The War of the League of Augsburg caused him to return to Basle, where from 1620 he was very profitably occupied in etching small landscapes, mainly of the city's immediate surroundings (w 1966, 473–89; see fig.); these are artistically his finest work. Some studies for these etchings are extant; they show him to be a skilful draughtsman in the style of Paul Bril, Jan Breughel and Antoine Mirou.

The death of Merian's father-in-law in 1623 led to his final departure for Frankfurt in 1624. His mother-in-law asked him to help her with the management of the great publishing house, which had moved from Oppenheim to Frankfurt. Though his brother-in-law William Fitzer and de Bry's widow carried on the business together for a year as the 'Officina Bryana', from mid-1626 Merian ran the publishing business alone. He rapidly built up the house to become one of the most important in Europe. Until *c.* 1645 he etched most of the plates himself or had them done in his own style by an increasing staff of assistants and pupils—among them Wenceslaus Hollar, Rudolf Meyer and Conrad Meyer of Zurich, and his sons-in-law Christoph Le Blon and Melchior Küsel: Merian also had close relations with Sebastian Furck, with whom he worked on the *Thesaurus philopoliticus* between 1623 and 1625.

Merian's first large-scale independent works are his *Icones biblicae* (233 plates, 4 vols; 1625–7) and the illustrations to Johann Ludwig Gottfried's *Historische chronica* (329 plates, 8 vols; 1629–34). In 1626–7 he produced copperplates for *Argenis* by John Barclay (pubd Schleich, Frankfurt, 1630) and in 1628–30 he brought out an illustrated German edition of Philip Sidney's *Arcadia*. In 1633 Merian began his greatest work, the *Theatrum Europaeum*, a contemporary history written by various authors, which is a valuable source on the Thirty Years War. Five volumes appeared in his lifetime; in the years to 1738 a further 16 were published. Gottfried's *Archontologia cosmica*, a lavishly illustrated combination of world geography and history, appeared in 1638. The *Topographia Germaniae* appeared from 1642 onwards, beginning with the volume on Switzerland, Merian's homeland. It was completed by his heirs in 1654 with the 16th volume, on the Netherlands and Burgundy. This topographical encyclopedia contains a text by Martin Zeiller and *c.* 1800 views and sketches. Companion volumes for all the European countries were planned, but the project was discontinued in 1688 after the appearance of volumes with more than 500 views of France, Rome and Italy. The total 21 volumes (including index) provided indispensable illustrative material for the German-speaking nations from the 17th century to the early 19th: Goethe and Jacob Burckhardt learnt from them. The picture that we have of European cities as they were in the Late Gothic and early Baroque periods is largely based on Merian engravings (*see*

for instance BERLIN, fig. 1, INNSBRUCK, fig. 3 and MUNICH, fig. 1).

In the prefaces to his illustrated topographical, historical and theological publications (to which, in a wider sense, the Emblem books also belong), Merian testified to his strict Reformist beliefs and his considered conviction of the imminent end of the world. After 1645, Merian's son Caspar largely took over the work of etching for the publishing house, which was run from 1650 by his brother (2) Matthäus Merian (ii). The house produced altogether over 8000 copperplates, the majority being town views, often bird's-eye, of considerable topographical accuracy and documentary value.

BIBLIOGRAPHY

C. Schuchhard: 'Die Zeiller-Merianschen Topographien bibliographisch beschrieben', *Centbl. Bibwsn*, xiii/5, 6 (1896), pp. 193–232; as booklet (Hamburg, 1960)

D. Burckhardt-Werthemann: 'Matthäus Merians Jugendjahre', 'Matthäus Merians Frankfurter Aufenthalt 1625–1650', 'Des alten Merian Kinder und Enkel', *Basl. Kstver.: Berstatt.* (Basle, 1907–09)

H. Bingel: *Das Theatrum Europaeum* (diss., U. Munich, 1909/*R* Wiesbaden, by M. Sändig, 1969)

J. P. Zwicky von Gauen: *Schweizerisches Geschlechterbuch*, x (Zurich, 1935), pp. 281–6

F. Bachmann: *Die alten Städtebilder* (Leipzig, 1939; 2nd edn, Stuttgart, 1965), pp. 23–41, 269–80

L. H. Wüthrich: *Die Handzeichnungen von Matthaeus Merian d.Ae.* (Basle, 1963) [W]

——: 'Matthaeus Merians Oppenheimer Zeit', *1200 Jahre Oppenheim am Rhein* (Oppenheim, 1965), pp. 129–46

——: 'Matthaeus Merians Jugendjahre in Basel', *Basl. Stadtb.* (1966), pp. 34–49

——: *Das druckgraphische Werk von Matthaeus Merian d.Ae.*, 4 vols (Basle, 1966–95)

——: *Register zu Merians 'Topographia Germaniae'* (Kassel and Basle, 1967)

Matthaeus Merian der Aeltere (exh. cat., Frankfurt am Main, Mus. Ksthandwk, and Basle, Kstmus., 1993–4)

(2) Matthäus Merian (ii) (*bapt* Basle, 25 March 1621; *bur* Frankfurt am Main, 15 Feb 1687). Son of (1) Matthäus Merian (i). The chief sources for his life are a short autobiography and a large collection of correspondence in the Nationalmuseets Archiv, Stockholm. He first learnt etching with his father, then in 1635 studied painting with Joachim von Sandrart. In 1637 he travelled with Sandrart to Amsterdam, where he ended his apprenticeship. He then went to England, working under Anthony van Dyck. After the latter's death in 1641 he went via Paris (where he came under the influence of Simon Vouet) back to Frankfurt. From 1643–5 he lived in Italy, first in Venice and then in Rome and Naples, where he studied the work of Jusepe de Ribera. He spent the years from 1648–50 mainly in the service of the Swedish field-marshal Carl Gustav Wrangel (1613–76), achieving much success in painting portraits of him and his officers. After his father's death in 1650 Merian the younger took over the management of the Merian publishing house in Frankfurt. He promoted the publication of the *Theatrum Europaeum*, to which he added many engravings after his portraits. In the meantime he travelled in Germany from court to court, painting many portraits, and also history pictures and church paintings: for example for the Tucher family altarpiece an *Ecce homo* (1659; now Nuremberg, St Sebald, Kirchenverwalt.). His virtuosity in portrait-painting—he became a competitor of his teacher Sandrart—brought

Matthäus Merian (ii): *Family of Matthäus Merian the Elder*, oil on canvas, 1.17×1.93 m, 1641 (Basle, Kunstmuseum)

commissions from Emperor Leopold I to mark his coronation in Frankfurt in 1658 (e.g. equestrian portrait, 1659; Vienna, Ksthist. Mus.), the Duke of Brunswick-Lüneburg, the Margrave of Baden-Baden and Baden-Durlach and also from Elector Frederick William of Brandenburg. These oil-paintings, sometimes rather hastily executed, and sketches are to be found in great numbers in museums (e.g. Basle, Kstmus. and Hist. Mus.) and collections such as the castles of Skokloster and Gripsholm in Sweden. The portrait of the Merian family (1641; Basle, Kstmus.; see fig.) with the artist, his parents and five brothers and sisters is a notable example. Also extant are numerous portrait sketches (e.g. Basle, Kstmus.; Karlsruhe, Staatl. Ksthalle; and Munich, Staatl. Graph. Samml.) in black and white chalk on blue paper. His liberal, eclectic style led the secretary of the French Ambassador to dub him in 1663 'the best artist in Germany'. From his papers Merian emerges as a likable, self-confident man of the world and a talented businessman.

BIBLIOGRAPHY
R. Wackernagel, ed.: 'Selbstbiographie des jüngeren Matthäus Merian', *Basl. Jb.* (1895), pp. 227–44

LUCAS WÜTHRICH

(3) Maria Sibylla Merian (*b* Frankfurt am Main, 2 April 1647; *d* Amsterdam, 13 Jan 1717). Daughter of (1) Matthäus Merian (i). After her father's death, her mother married in 1651 the flower still-life painter Jacob Marell, who also became Maria Sibylla's teacher. On 16 May 1665 she married Johann Andreas Graff, a pupil of her stepfather. She thenceforth specialized in illustrations of flowers, fruit and, especially, grubs, flies, gnats and spiders. In 1670 the family moved to Nuremberg. In 1675 Sandrart referred to her in the *Teutsche Academie*, reporting that she painted on cloth (i.e. silk, satin). With Graff, she produced a book of flowers, the first part appearing in 1675; a second edition, enlarged by parts 2 and 3 came out in 1680, entitled *Florum fasciculi tres.* It included 36 engravings intended to serve as patterns for embroidery. Only five copies of this book have survived, including a single first edition in the Stadt– und Universitätsbibliothek, Berne (others, Dresden, Sächs. Landesbib., and Inst. Dkmlpf.; Mainz, Stadt-& Ubib.; London, V&A). This was followed by *Der Raupen wunderbare Verwandlung und sonderbare Blumennahrung* (i, Nuremburg, 1679; ii, Frankfurt, 1683), 'in which, by a new invention, the origins, food and metamorphoses of caterpillars, grubs, butterflies, moths, flies and other such creatures ... are diligently examined, briefly described and painted from life, engraved in copper and published by the author'. The work went into five editions, including those of 1713 and 1714 in Dutch; a third volume was posthumously published (with vols 1 and 2), *c.* 1718, by her daughter Dorothea. Each of its 50 engravings is minutely rendered by Maria Sibylla from her own observations.

In 1681 Maria Sibylla's stepfather Marell died, and after separating from her husband she returned to her mother in Frankfurt. In 1685 she moved with her mother and daughters to Waltha in West Friesland, where she joined a Labadist community. In 1686 Graff tried to persuade his wife to return; when she did not comply he sought legal divorce. In 1690, after her mother's death, Maria Sibylla took her two daughters to Amsterdam, where she soon achieved success as a flower and animal painter. In 1699 she travelled with her younger daughter, Johanna Helena, to Surinam. After a time she fell seriously ill, returning home early (1701) with copious notes, paintings on parchment, dried plants and animals preserved in alcohol. In 1705, after lengthy preparation, her work on Surinamese insects, *Metamorphosis insectorum Surinamensium*, was published in Amsterdam (later edns; *see* SURI-NAM, fig. 3). Most of the copies are hand-coloured. This is the first scientific work to be produced on Surinam. Despite a few biological errors, the illustrations (see fig.) are convincing, especially in their rendering of the full brilliance of the tropical colours. Apart from tranquil studies of nature, there are pictures showing its ferocity,

such as the sheet depicting a spider eating a hummingbird.

For her flower paintings Maria Sibylla favoured watercolours applied to parchment, which brought out the natural and fresh qualities of her subjects (examples in Basle, Kstmus.; Berlin, Kupferstichkab.; Darmstadt, Hess. Landesmus.; London, BM; Nuremberg, Ger. Nmus.; Vienna, Albertina; Windsor Castle, Berks, Royal Col.). She engraved her copperplates herself, using a line-and-point technique as well as a crayon style. The sheets coming from the press were run through again with a second plate, producing transfer prints that were lighter and more delicate, and then hand-coloured. Merian's illustrations of flora and fauna not only demonstrate her mastery as a painter and engraver, but express a concern for botany uncommon in a woman of the late 17th century. In Amsterdam she was in close touch with scientists; this intrepid scholar and artist, who paid scant heed to the conventions of her time, is also recognized as a founder of entomology.

BIBLIOGRAPHY
Maria Sibylla Merian: Leben und Werk, 1647–1717 (exh. cat., ed. M. Phister Burkhalter; Basle, 1980)
Das verborgene Museum (exh. cat., Berlin, Akad. Kst., 1987), i, pp. 91–3
For further bibliography *see* §(1) above

C. HÖPER

Merice [Merige], **Petrus a** [Merecinus, Merecynus, Petrus]. *See* HEYDEN, PIETER VAN DER.

Mérida (i). *See* AUGUSTA EMERITA.

Mérida (ii). Mexican city, capital of the state of Yucatán, at the north-western tip of the Yucatán peninsula, with a population of *c.* 700,000. The city's situation on a limestone platform in the 'sisal region' has favoured its rapid development. Mérida was founded in 1542 by Francisco de Montejo II on the site of the earlier Mayan city of T'Ho, which was demolished by colonizing Spaniards to make way for Spanish constructions. The cathedral of S Ildefonso, begun in 1562 when Fray Diego del Toral was bishop, is the earliest cathedral in Mexico; it was completed in 1598 by Juan Miguel de Agüero (*fl* 1574–1613), who travelled from Spain specially for the purpose. The Renaissance façade is composed of five sections, surmounted by slender towers (*see* YUCATECO). Little of the original interior survives, as the church was burnt down in 1915 during the Mexican Revolution (1910–20). Nevertheless, it contains the statue known as *Christ of the Blisters*, formerly in the church of Ichmul, where another fire produced the blistering on the figure of Christ. The Convento de Monjas Concepcionistas, founded in 1589 for the daughters of conquistadors, retains the church of Nuestra Señora de la Consolación, with its magnificent low choir and, on the exterior, a belvedere that offers a splendid view of the city. The 17th-century conventual church of La Mejorada has one of the finest façades in the city. Among other notable churches is that of S Cristóbal (18th century), with its unusual flared portal.

One of the most significant examples of secular architecture in Mérida is the Casa Montejo, the house of the city's founder. Built in the mid-16th century, only the façade of the original building survives; but it is one of

Maria Sibylla Merian: *Pomegranate*, 730×503 mm, hand-coloured engraving; from her *Metamorphosis insectorum Surinamensium* (Amsterdam, 1705), pl. 9 (Nuremberg, Germanisches Nationalmuseum)

the most important Plateresque secular works in Mexico: it has an abundance of low relief and, in the centre, the coat of arms of the Montejo family, flanked by two halberdiers stepping on the heads of indigenous people. The Palacio de Gobierno (1892) was built on the site of the old Casas Reales; on the walls of the staircase are three murals (completed 1978) by Fernando Castro Pacheco, representing Mayan cosmology, the symbolism of the four cardinal points and the creation of Man. In the Salón de la Historia other works by Castro Pacheco illustrate the evolution of Yucatán. Paseo Montejo, a bustling avenue shaded by tamarind trees, is the commercial zone of Mérida and the location of the Museo de Antropología in the Italianate Palacio Cantón; the museum contains Mayan and other archaeological artefacts. There is an active craft industry in Mérida, producing artefacts made from wood and sisal as well as textiles.

BIBLIOGRAPHY

G. Ferrer de Mendiolea: *Nuestra ciudad Mérida de Yucatán* (Mérida, 1938)
J. Fernández: *Catálogo de construcciones religiosas, Yucatán*, 2 vols (Mexico City, 1945)
R. Aguilar and J. Stella: *Mérida colonial: Su historia y sus monumentos* (Mexico City, 1971)

S. LETICIA TALAVERA, P. MARITANO MONTERROSA

Mérida, Carlos (*b* Guatemala City, 2 Dec 1891; *d* Mexico City, 21 Dec 1985). Guatemalan painter and printmaker. He came to painting through music, when incipient deafness made him exchange his piano for paintbrushes. His attendance at meetings organized by the Spanish Catalan painter Jaime Sabartés (1881–1968) proved decisive, for they brought him into contact with the paintings of Picasso; in 1912 he travelled to Paris, armed with a letter of introduction from Sabartés to Picasso. In Paris he frequented the studios of Amedeo Modigliani, Kees van Dongen and Hermengildo Anglada Camarassa and learnt about the artistic avant-garde. He also visited other European cultural centres.

On his return to Guatemala, Mérida, together with Rafael Yela Gunther, began to revalue indigenous art not for its folkloric aspects but for its essential local values prior to the Spanish conquest. At exhibitions held in Guatemala in 1919 and in Mexico in 1920 Mérida showed works such as *Profile* (1920; priv. col., see Nelken, illus. 2) in which he began to establish the distinctive characteristics of his later work: a search for geometric abstraction based implicitly on Mayan plastic arts; the use of intense flat colour, precisely delineated and clearly influenced by autochthonous art; static designs deriving from his European apprenticeship; elegance and good taste; and an emphasis on the human figure.

In the early 1920s Mérida settled permanently in Mexico, although he always retained his Guatemalan nationality. The Mexican muralist movement was just beginning when he arrived, and he collaborated with Diego Rivera on his first mural work. His withdrawal from political concerns and from official art, however, distanced him from the movement, and in the 1940s he emerged instead as a member of the avant-garde in conscious opposition to Mexican muralism. On his return to Mexico after another stay in Paris in 1927, during which he had got to know Picasso, Vasily Kandinsky, Joan Miró, Paul Klee and Joaquín Torres García, he explored Surrealism, geometric abstraction and Constructivism. His work oscillated thereafter between Surrealism and abstraction, emphasizing his qualities as a draughtsman and colourist and making use of innovative materials and techniques. The influence of Surrealism is particularly evident in a portfolio of screenprints, *Estampas del Popol-Vuh* (Mexico City, 1943), and in oil paintings such as *Ubiquitous Fascination* (1940; New Haven, CT, Yale U. A.G.) and *Self-portrait* (1948; Luna Arroyo priv. col., see Luján, p. 245).

Little by little abstraction and especially geometric abstraction began to predominate in Mérida's work, particularly after 1950, and it was to this style, with variations, that he remained committed until his death. In these pure geometric works straight lines cross each other and precisely delineate areas illuminated with clear vibrant colours, with a sense of rhythm and proportion that convey the artist's close affinities with music, dance and architecture. The subjects that inspired him were of local origin, in particular pre-Hispanic texts and codices. There are many fine examples from this period of both his prints and paintings. Many of them make use of diverse materials and techniques, including bark and parchment, sometimes painted with vinyl (e.g. *Architectures*, 1956; Houston, TX, Mus. F.A.), casein or even screenprinted.

Having reached maturity as an artist and found his own style, Mérida returned during this period to mural painting, but in his own way and as part of a movement concerned with the integration of the plastic arts. Like others aligned with this movement, he collaborated closely with architects in placing and carrying out his murals. His abstract style was suited to contemporary architecture because of the simplicity of its lines and because of his use of such architectural materials as stone, concrete and mosaic. The best of the considerable number of murals he carried out using a great variety of techniques, about 20 in Mexico and 10 in Guatemala, are those on which he collaborated with Mario Pani, because of the harmonious coordination of the mural with its architectural context. In his most successful work, the *Unidad Habitacional Benito Juárez* (1952; Mexico City, destr. 1985 earthquake), Mérida used polychrome concrete as his basic material for the panels and outside staircases, taking his inspiration from pre-Hispanic codices. Although many of his murals were later destroyed, they nevertheless account for much of Mérida's high reputation in Latin America.

WRITINGS

Modern Mexican Artists (Mexico City, 1937)

BIBLIOGRAPHY

L. Cardoza y Aragón: *Carlos Mérida* (Madrid, 1927)
M. Nelken: *Carlos Mérida* (Mexico City, 1961)
El diseño, la composición y la integración plástica de Carlos Mérida (exh. cat., Mexico City, U.N. Autónoma, 1962)
X. Moyssén: 'Los mayores: Mérida, Gerszo, Goeritz', *El geometrismo mexicano* (Mexico City, 1977), pp. 51–75
M. de la Torre, ed.: *Carlos Mérida en sus 90 años* (Mexico City, 1981)
L. Luján: *Carlos Mérida* (Guatemala City, 1985)
L. Noelle: 'Los murales de Carlos Mérida', *An. Inst. Invest. Estét.*, xv (1987), pp. 125–43

LOUISE NOELLE

Merigliano, Giovanni. *See* MARIGLIANO, GIOVANNI.

Merinid. *See* MARINID.

Merino, Francisco (*b* Jaén, *c.* 1530; *d* Toledo, 1611). Spanish silversmith. He may have trained under Juan Ruiz, el Vandalino (*fl* 1533–50), and he is recorded working in Jaén in 1557 as a painter's assistant, but he moved to Toledo shortly afterwards. In 1569 he made the silver reliquary urn of St Eugenius (Toledo Cathedral), after a design by Nicolás de Vergara (i) replete with Renaissance figuration. Ten years later he moved to Seville in an attempt to secure the contract for the large stationary monstrance in the cathedral, a commission that was given to Juan de Arfe in 1580. Merino then went to Córdoba in 1581, where he made two crosses (untraced) for Montoro and the convent of S Jerónimo near Medina Azahara. From 1585 to 1588 he was recorded working in Jaén where he executed another cross (destr.). In 1587, however, he was employed in Seville Cathedral to work on the small monstrance in front of de Arfe's monstrance and on the metropolitan cross. The latter inspired numerous 17th-century Spanish silversmiths; it is flat and geometrical with engraved ornamentation and figuration on the ends of the arms and along the sides. Merino returned to Toledo in 1589 and executed the crosses in Colmenar Viejo and La Mata, which have similar characteristics. He was commissioned to execute the reliquary urn (1590–93; *in situ*) of St Leocadia in Toledo Cathedral. Its structure and ornamentation correspond to Merino's new geometrical style. His last known work is the reliquary cross showing St Helen in adoration (1595–1601; Toledo Cathedral), which has small figures of Adam and Eve similar to the work of Cellini.

For bibliography *see* SPAIN, §IX, 1.

JOSÉ MANUEL CRUZ VALDOVINOS

Merino, Ignacio (*b* Piura, 30 Jan 1817; *d* Paris, 17 Feb 1876). Peruvian painter. He had a cosmopolitan existence as a child, living first in Paris, where he worked in the studios of Raymond Monvoisin (1794–1870) and Paul Delaroche after completing his schooling, and later in Italy and Spain. He returned to Peru at the age of 21, later becoming a drawing teacher at the Convictorio de San Carlos and the assistant director (and eventually director) of the Academia de Dibujo y Pintura, both in Lima. During his second trip to Europe, he visited Spain, the Netherlands, Italy and France, finally settling in Paris.

In his paintings Merino demonstrated a taste for literary and historical subjects, fed by his knowledge of Spanish, English and French literature, which he combined in his early works with the influence of Ingres and later with that of Velázquez, Ribera and Rembrandt. Later in his career he also executed numerous portraits and self-portraits. His more important works include *Columbus before the University of Salamanca* (Lima, Mun. Lima Met.), the *Hand of Carlos V*, *Hamlet*, *Lima Woman in Doorway* and *Reading 'Don Quixote'*, all in collections in Lima.

BIBLIOGRAPHY

T. Núñez Ureta: *Pintura peruana contemporánea: Primera parte, 1820–1920* (Lima, 1975)
L. E. Tord: 'Historia de las artes plásticas en el Perú', *Historia del Perú*, ix (Lima, 1980)

LUIS ENRIQUE TORD

Merisi, Michelangelo. *See* CARAVAGGIO, MICHELANGELO MERISI DA.

Merkelbach, Ben(jamin) (*b* Amsterdam, 10 Oct 1901; *d* Amsterdam, 19 Oct 1961). Dutch architect. He trained at the Kunstnijverheidsschool in Haarlem. In 1924–5 he worked in Belgium, and in 1927 he worked for nine months in the office of Mart Stam in Frankfurt am Main. Also in 1927, with five other former students of the school in Haarlem, he founded ARCHITECTENGROEP DE 8; Merkelbach helped draw up the manifesto and later became editor of the periodical *De 8 en Opbouw* (The 8 and construction).

Merkelbach was also active internationally within CIAM. Together with Johannes Duiker (1890–1935) and Cornelis van Eesteren he formulated nine conditions for modern architecture for the CIAM congress held in Brussels in 1930 and was directly involved in organizing the CIAM congress of 1932 and the accompanying exhibition material about the rational city.

In 1929 Merkelbach formed a partnership with Charles Karsten (1904–79), another founder of de 8, and during the 1930s their work included two commissions that were much published and discussed as examples of the issues the group had raised. The first was for Landlust, a housing development in west Amsterdam. This had been shown in preliminary area plans as a series of closed-perimeter blocks as was the usual practice. Merkelbach & Karsten began detailed designs in 1932, and the blocks, when built in 1936–7, were the first completed examples in the Netherlands of *strokenbouw* ('strip buildings'), the open-ended parallel rows that had become common in Germany, and that such Netherlandish modernists as J. J. P. Oud had been proposing since the beginning of the decade. The AVRO Radio Studio building (1934–6) in Hilversum was designed on strictly functionalist lines, although some purists saw the irregular plan layout as an example of incipient formalism. Both projects were executed in brick with standard window and roof details. They are prime examples of de 8's concept of 'a-aesthetic' architecture.

Merkelbach spent the years of World War II as a member of the Post-war Housing Committee formed by the architects' professional associations in the Netherlands. In 1949 Pieter Elling (1897–1962) replaced Karsten, and the practice continued until Merkelbach's appointment as municipal architect in Amsterdam in 1956; Elling continued as co-architect on subsequent projects. Merkelbach's post-war work included two small office buildings for the Tetterode Type Foundry (1950; with Elling) and for the Illustrated Press Company (1959; with Mart Stam), and a larger municipal office block (1960; with Elling), all in Amsterdam. They are notable for the way in which their standard office construction is enlivened and refined by careful detailing of the window walls.

WRITINGS

'Schrijven en bouwen' [Writing and building], *De 8 & Opbouw*, iii (1935), pp. 39–44

BIBLIOGRAPHY

R. Blijstra: *B. Merkelbach* (Amsterdam, 1968)
G. Fanelli: *Architettura moderna* (1968)
H. J. F. de Roy van Zuyderwijn: *Amsterdamse bouwkunst, 1815–1900* [Amsterdam architecture, 1815–1900] (Amsterdam, 1970), pp. 200–01
B. Rebel: *Het Nieuwe Bouwen* [The new architecture] (Utrecht, 1980)

FRANK VAN DEN HOEK, DIANNE TIMMERMAN

Merklin [Märklin; Merckell], **Konrad** (*fl* Ulm, 1495; *d* 1518). German painter. Although there is documentary evidence of his existence, his work is a matter of hypothesis. In 1495 he was named in a register of members of the painters' brotherhood based in the Wengenkloster at Ulm; the register also gives the year of his death. As it names him 'pictor noster', Late Gothic works from the Wengenkloster have been attributed to him (Leitschuh), notably the former high-altarpiece, depicting scenes from the *Childhood of Christ* and *Passion* (1490s; now in sixteen parts: one, Dublin, N.G.; two, Karlsruhe, Staatl. Ksthalle; two, Lübeck, St Annen-Mus.; six, Ulm Cathedral; three, Stuttgart, Staatsgal.; two, ex-art market, London, see Stange, no. 636, f, n). However, the hypothesis has been disputed, and the altarpiece continues to be attributed to an artist from the circle of Bartholomäus Zeitblom. As Albrecht Dürer called Merklin his 'dear friend' in a draft letter, there have been attempts to assemble an oeuvre of higher quality than the Wengen altarpiece. Thus Merklin has been named by Buchner as the Master of the Hutz Portrait (*c.* 1510; Dessau, Staatl. Gal.) and by Stange as the Master of the Decapitation of St John (1493–4; Blaubeuren, former Klosterkirche). Although he has been attributed with a *Lamentation* (*c.* 1510–13; ex-Ulm, Wengenkloster; Nuremberg, Ger. Nmus.) by Leitschuh and Stange, it is still labelled as a work by Bartholomäus Zeitblom with the collaboration of Martin Schaffner.

BIBLIOGRAPHY
F. Leitschuh: 'Das Wengenkloster in Ulm und sein Maler Konrad Märklin', *Studien und Quellen zur deutschen Kunstgeschichte, Collct. Friburg.*, n. s., xiv (1912), pp. 185–97
E. Buchner: *Das deutsche Bildnis der Spätgotik und der frühen Dürerzeit* (Berlin, 1953), pp. 197–8
H. Rupprich: *Dürers schriftlicher Nachlass*, i (Berlin, 1956), p. 132
A. Stange: *Die deutschen Tafelbilder vor Dürer*, ii (Munich, 1970), pp. 142–3

BRIGITTE HERRBACH

Merkurov, Sergey (Dmitriyevich) (*b* Aleksandropol' [now Kumairi], Armenia, 7 Nov 1881; *d* Moscow, 8 June 1952). Russian sculptor of Armenian birth. He came from a merchant's family, and he studied in Zurich at the studio of the sculptor Adolf Meyer and in Munich at the Akademie der Bildenden Künste (1902–5). Until 1909 he worked in Paris. He was a member of the Association of Artists of Revolutionary Russia (AKhRR) from 1925. He frequently made death-masks of eminent politicians, writers and artists. His works are based on a late Art Nouveau style, but the emphasis on the weight of the stone and the clear edges of the blocks (Merkurov's favourite medium was granite) give the works an archaic heaviness of shape, which suggests a close study of ancient Egyptian and Assyrian sculpture and lends them a solemn grandeur.

The statue of the writer *Fyodor Dostoeyevsky* (1911–13; erected in 1918 in the courtyard of the Dostoeyevsky Hospital, formerly the Mariya Hospital, Moscow) and the statue of the botanist *K. A. Timiryazev* (1922–3; Nikitskiye Gates, Moscow) are among Merkurov's finest monuments. He also sculpted the mourning group *Death of the Leader* (1927; Gorki Leninskiye, Lenin House-Mus.), other statues of *V. I. Lenin* (1937; Moscow Canal; and 1939; Meeting Hall, Great Kremlin Palace, Moscow) and also the most renowned monuments to *Joseph Stalin*. The largest of these (beaten copper, h. 16 m on 33 m base) was erected in Yerevan in 1950, but all of them were dismantled in the years immediately following the exposure of Stalin's personality cult at the 20th Communist Party Congress in 1956. In spite of the pompously apologetic intention behind these official commissions, Merkurov managed to convey in them the cruel, despotic character of Stalin's rule.

WRITINGS
Zapiski skul'ptora [Notes of a sculptor] (Moscow, 1953)

BIBLIOGRAPHY
Monument I. V. Stalina v Yerevane [Monument to I. V. Stalin in Yerevan], (Moscow, 1952)
G. S. Merkurov, ed.: *Sergey Merkurov* (Moscow, 1988) [with Eng. summary]

M. N. SOKOLOV

Merleau-Ponty, Maurice (*b* Rochefort-sur-Mer, 14 March 1908; *d* Paris, 5 May 1961). French philosopher. He followed Edmund Husserl's call for a phenomenological philosophy to investigate the objects and structures of consciousness at a pre-cognitive and pre-reflective level, but developed this programme in distinctive, existentialist directions (*see* PHENOMENOLOGY and EXISTENTIALISM). In the course of a close critical examination of psychological theories, Merleau-Ponty sought in *Phénoménologie de la perception* (1945), his main work, to elaborate a conception of the unique and original perceptual relationship to the world enjoyed by the human subject, a relationship that is said to be presupposed by natural science and immune to retroactive explanation in scientific terms, since it cannot even be described with the aid of categories formed by objective thought. The wholly unanalysable nature of the point of perception at which the subject encounters the external world led Merleau-Ponty to claim further that phenomenology had finally resolved the metaphysical dispute of realism with idealism.

By virtue of his identification of the body as the primary locus of subjectivity, and his insistence on the limitations of pure consciousness, as displayed in the presence of indeterminacy and ambiguity in perceptual experience, Merleau-Ponty stood in sharp opposition to Jean-Paul Sartre's dualism and libertarianism. On account of his rejection of the autonomy of the subject Merleau-Ponty may be argued to have anticipated some of the central tenets of STRUCTURALISM.

Merleau-Ponty's writings subsequent to the *Phénoménologie* focused on the study of expression and aimed to show how the field of perception is transposed into a world of signs and cultural objects with a history and public meaning. In painting he found a convergence of all his central philosophical themes. In 'Le Doute de Cézanne' (1948) Merleau-Ponty undertook to show, following an interpretative method that he explicitly contrasted with that of art history, that Cézanne's representation of nature was directed at revealing the spontaneous self-organization of things in the 'primordial world' and that this artistic project manifested the particular 'possibility of existence' constituted by Cézanne's personal being.

In 'Le Langage indirect et les voix du silence' (1952) Merleau-Ponty explored the analogy of painting with language, claiming for each a dimension that is fundamentally tacit and creative. Merleau-Ponty's outlook led him to contest André Malraux's claim that the modern age has witnessed a transformation in painting that divides the art's history into two discrete parts. Denying that factors such as classical perspective suffice to mark off one class of works as non-subjective, Merleau-Ponty argued instead that the history of painting derives its unity from the fact that all painting recapitulates and attempts to re-express the artist's metaphysical condition of bodily insertion into the world, with the result that all paintings function in some sense as universal emanations of the perceiving human body. Artistic individuality is achieved through style, a term that Merleau-Ponty extended beyond its normal signification, regarding style as immanent in perception.

'L'Oeil et l'esprit' (1961), the last work he saw published, returned to the theme of painting's basis in perception, a relation that Merleau-Ponty now conceived in reverse, declaring that painting answers to being's demand to receive expression: the specific task of painting is defined as that of 'rendering visible the phenomenon of visibility'.

WRITINGS

Phénoménologie de la perception (Paris, 1945; Eng. trans., London and New York, 1962)
'Le Doute de Cézanne', *Sens et non-sens* (Paris, 1948), pp. 15–44; Eng. trans. in *Sense and Non-sense* (Evanston, 1964), pp. 9–25
'Le Langage indirect et les voix du silence', *Temps Mod.*, vii (June 1952), pp. 2113–44; viii (July 1952), pp. 70–94 (*R* in *Signes*, Paris, 1960, pp. 49–104); Eng. trans. in *Signes* (Evanston, 1964), pp. 39–83
'L'Oeil et l'esprit', *A. France*, i/1 (1961), pp. 187–208; as book (Paris, 1964; Eng. trans., 1964)

BIBLIOGRAPHY

E. F. Kaelin: *An Existentialist Aesthetic* (Madison, 1960)
D. Rey: *La Perception du peintre et le problème de l'être: Essai sur l'esthétique et l'ontologie de Maurice Merleau-Ponty* (diss., U. Fribourg, 1978)
G. B. Madison: *The Phenomenology of Merleau-Ponty: A Search for the Limits of Consciousness* (Athens, OH, 1981)

SEBASTIAN GARDNER

Merlini, Domenico [Dominik] (*b* Castello di Vasoldo, Lake Lugano, 22 Feb 1730; *d* Warsaw, 20 Feb 1797). Italian architect, active in Poland. He probably trained in Warsaw under Jakub Fontana (*d* 1773), to whom he was related on his mother's side. He moved to Poland before 1760 and was appointed architect to the court of Augustus III, King of Saxony and Poland, in 1761. In 1768 he was conferred with Polish nobility, and five years later he succeeded Fontana as first architect to Stanisław II Augustus Poniatowski, King of Poland, and the Polish state. In 1775–6 he converted Tylman van Gameren's Bath House (Łazienka) at Ujazdów into a two-storey miniature palace for the King (*see* WARSAW, §V, 2). A new wing was added (1779–82) to house the royal library. From 1773 Merlini was engaged on the Royal Castle (*see* WARSAW, §V, 1). He completed the bedchamber (1773–5), which had been designed by Fontana, decorated and furnished the Canaletto Hall and remodelled the Old Audience Chamber in a simple and restrained style. He fitted a small chapel in the south tower with a nave measuring 9 sq. m and a tiny chancel capped with a dome and embellished by eight columns. Assisted by Jan Chrystian Kamsetzer, he also remodelled the Ballroom (or Great Hall; *see* WARSAW, fig. 8) in the centre of the Castle, and between 1781 and 1786, with Kamsetzer and others, he decorated the magnificent interiors of the Throne Room and the

Knights' Hall. In 1784 work on the Łazienki Palace was resumed with the erection of a south façade that featured a recessed portico framing four columns of a giant composite order. The same order was used four years later on a north front in 13 bays (by Kamsetzer; *see* WARSAW, fig. 9). Merlini's private commissions include a palace (1775) at Jabłonowa, outside Warsaw, for Michał Poniatowski, featuring a large circular salon in a two-storey octagon, and the Palladian Królikarnia Palace (destr. 1944; rebuilt 1959–64), Warsaw. His architecture is characterized by its delicacy of form (e.g. the south front of the Łazienki Palace) and his interiors by their contrasting colour schemes (red, green, yellow), with painted ceilings and walls covered with pictures. In his own compositions he simplified the Baroque style and embellished it with Neoclassical decoration. These features place him as a typical representative of the early phase of European Neoclassicism. His work shows the influence of the compositional and decorative designs of VICTOR LOUIS, with whom he had personal contact in Warsaw in 1765.

BIBLIOGRAPHY

W. Tatarkiewicz: 'Wiadomości o życiu i pracach Dominika Merliniego' [Information on the life and work of Domenico Merlini], *Roc. Hist. Sztuki*, i (1956), pp. 369–423
M. Kwiatkowski: *Stanisław August Król-Architekt* [Stanislas Augustus, king–architect] (Wrocław, 1983)

ANDRZEJ ROTTERMUND

Merlini, Lorenzo (*b* Florence, 13 May 1666; *d* Rome, after 1739). Italian sculptor, medallist, miniaturist and architect. He came from a family of craftsmen (his brother Cosimo Merlini (*fl* 1692–1736) was a silversmith of some repute) and, like his father, trained in the grand ducal workshops in Florence. He then worked for the Medici court. His emergence as a sculptor dates to *c.* 1692, with his two marble *Angels* for the Ferroni Chapel (Florence, SS Annunziata). In November 1694 he moved to Rome, where for about a year he was active as a medallist and miniaturist. For the altar in the chapel of St Ignatius in the church of Il Gesù, Rome, Merlini executed a bronze relief of *St Peter Appearing to St Ignatius* (1695–6), based on a drawing by Andrea Pozzo, and *Two Putti Flanking a Cartouche* (1697). His monument to the *Marchesa Riccardi* (*c.* 1700; Rome, S Giovanni dei Fiorentini), which demonstrates his fine abilities as a portrait artist in the manner of Lorenzo Ottoni, is the most significant work of his first stay in Rome. Returning to Florence in 1702, Merlini was active as an architect at the Villa Orlandini at Poggio Torselli and at the Villa Acciaioli at Monte Grufoni. He also designed the extension to the Palazzo Dati and the reconstruction of the Palazzo Bagnano, both in Florence. For the Orlandini Chapel in S Maria Maggiore, Florence, he sculpted *Purity* and *Innocence* (both *in situ*). In 1715 he was recalled to Rome by Cardinal Pietro Ottoboni. During this last period he worked as a gold- and silversmith, providing furnishings for S Agnese in Agone. John V, King of Portugal, commissioned Merlini to produce various ornaments for the chapel of St John the Baptist in S Roch, Lisbon, and after Cardinal Neri Corsini became Protector of Portugal (1739), there were many Portuguese commissions for artists based in Rome. Various liturgical furnishings and sacred ornaments in the Vatican and Lateran basilicas were copied, such as the six *Angels with* *the Symbols of the Passion*, based on those on the papal altar in St Peter's.

BIBLIOGRAPHY
K. Lankheit: *Florentinische Barockplastik: Die Kunst am Hofe der letzten Medici, 1670–1743* (Munich, 1962)
R. Enggass: *Early Eighteenth-century Sculpture in Rome* (University Park, PA, and London, 1976), pp. 120–23
A. Nava Cellini: *La scultura del settecento* (Turin, 1982), pp. 22, 137
——: 'Nota per alcune sculture romane di Lorenzo Merlini', *Imagination und Imago: Festschrift Kurt Rossacher* (Salzburg, 1983), pp. 229–34

DONATELLA GERMANÒ SIRACUSA

Merlo [Merli; Merula], **Carlo Giuseppe** (*b* Milan, 5 Nov 1690; *d* Milan, 8 Nov 1761). Italian architect, engineer, mathematician and writer. He worked in the local Lombard architectural tradition but incorporated late Baroque elements, reflecting architectural trends throughout Europe. His early works included the completion of the parish church at Desio (1726–36) and the Villa Perego (*c.* 1740) at Cremnago, both near Milan, but his most important work was at the cathedral in Milan. Following the rejection of plans by Luigi Vanvitelli, the cathedral chapter entrusted Merlo and Francesco Croce (*fl* 1738–65) with the task of carrying out the new façade (plans; Milan, Bib. Ambrosiana). Merlo's plans, prepared in 1745, proposed Gothic pilasters similar to those of the interior, replacing the twisted columns proposed by Vanvitelli. Work did not begin until 1765 but was completed under Croce's supervision by 1769. Merlo also made proposals in 1759 for the great spire of the cathedral. During his years of association with the cathedral Merlo also designed the façade of S Andrea (1745) at Pioltello, which incorporated vegetable motifs on the volutes connecting the upper and lower storeys, and the elaborate patterned marble high altar (1759) of S Sebastiano. He was a member of the Accademia dei Trasformati, Milan, and left two printed works on hydraulics as well as several manuscript studies, one of which was on curves. This interest in curvilinear form derived from Guarino Guarini and was reflected in his elliptical ground-plan for S Giuliana at Caponago (1742), where the interior is planned as a series of free-flowing lines articulated with free-standing Ionic columns and Ionic pilasters.

BIBLIOGRAPHY
M. L. Gatti Perer: 'Filippo Cagnola, Maria Quarantini, Gioacchino Besozzi, Carlo Giuseppe Merlo e la loro opera per la Visitazione di Milano', *A. Lombarda*, viii (1963), pp. 161–83
——: *Carlo Giuseppe Merlo architetto* (Milan, 1966), pp. 465–502
——: 'Cultura e socialità dell'altare barocco nell'antica diocesi di Milano', *A. Lombarda* (1985), pp. 11–66

PETER BOUTOURLINE YOUNG

Merlo, Giraldo de (*b* ?Toledo, *c.* 1574; *d* 1620). Spanish sculptor. He lived in Toledo but in 1603 was associated in Madrid with Antón de Morales (*fl* 1586–1625) who was a member of the circle of Pompeo Leoni. Merlo followed the classical style of Juan Bautista Monegro. He executed the sculptures for the principal retable in the monastery of S Pedro Mártir, Toledo, in collaboration with Jorge Manuel Theotocopoulos. Merlo's marble group of *St Joseph and Child* (1608; Ávila, Convent of S José, façade) was commissioned by the royal architect, Francisco de Mora, architect and benefactor of this Carmelite foundation. In 1609 Merlo was commissioned to carve the choir-stalls of S Pedro Mártir, Toledo, which incorporate a complete series of Dominican saints. In 1610 he was in Sigüenza, where he executed the important principal retable in the cathedral. This work, with pilasters, statues and pictorial reliefs flanking the large central *Assumption* and *Calvary*, shows the high quality of his carving. The retable of 1611 for the church of the Virgen del Prado, Ciudad Real, is also composed of numerous reliefs. In 1615 Jorge Manuel and Merlo were contracted by royal commission to carve the sculpture for the principal retable designed by Juan Gómez de Mora, of the royal foundation of Guadalupe (Caceres), but almost all the carving is by Merlo, including the great relief dedicated to *St Jerome*. In the same church he also carved in stone the kneeling funerary statues of *Henry IV of Castile and León* (*reg* 1454–74) and *Mary of Aragón*. In 1619 Merlo and Jorge Manuel collaborated again to complete the principal retable in the Hospital de Tavera in Toledo (hospital de S Juan Bautista or de Afuera), originally commissioned in 1608 from El Greco, but unrealized. Merlo did not complete the carving before his death, but it is possible that he used El Greco's designs.

BIBLIOGRAPHY
R. Ramírez de Arellano: 'Giraldo de Merlo', *A. Esp.*, ii (1914–15), pp. 251–63
J. María de Azcárate: 'Algunos juicios sobre Giraldo de Merlo', *Archv Esp. A.*, x (1948), p. 308
F. Marías: 'Giraldo de Merlo: Precisiones documentales', *Archv Esp. A.*, liv (1981), pp. 163–84

J. J. MARTÍN GONZÁLEZ

Merlo, Tomás de (*b* Santiago de Guatemala [now Antigua], 15 July 1694; *d* Santiago de Guatemala, 15 Dec 1739). Guatemalan painter. A son of the master painter Tomás de la Vega Merlo (*b c.* 1659; *d* 26 April 1749), he was the most important Guatemalan painter of his generation and the one by whom there are the most identified works. In 1730 he married Lucía de Gálvez, daughter of the master craftsman Antonio Joseph de Gálvez. In 1737 he began a series of eleven paintings of the *Passion* for the church of the Calvario (six, *in situ*; five, Antigua, Mus. Colon.). Two were finished by an unnamed pupil in 1740, and the general quality of the series is not high, perhaps because of poor retouching. In his painting of *St Ignatius of Loyola* (Antigua, Mus. Colon.), which is probably based on an engraving, the saint is depicted preaching, against a graceful background of angels in the upper part. In the Capuchin church in Guatemala City is his *Virgen del Pilar* (1736–8), popularly known as *Nuestra Señora de las Monjitas*, which depicts the six founder nuns of the church kneeling in the lower part of the work. Executed in a style typical of the Baroque, the more skilful upper part shows the Virgin being carried by angels. There are two known works by Merlo's brother, Pedro Francisco de Merlo (1698–1780), a less celebrated painter, in S Pedro Almolonga, Quetzaltenago, each depicting four scenes from the *Life of the Apostle St Peter*.

BIBLIOGRAPHY
H. Berlin: 'El pintor Tomás de Merlo', *Antropol. & Hist. Guatemala*, v/1 (1953), pp. 53–8
E. Núñez: 'Pintura del período colonial, Pedro Francisco de Merlo', *Antropol. & Hist. Guatemala*, 2nd ser., v (1983), pp. 89–99

JORGE LUJÁN-MUÑOZ

Meroë [now Kabushiya and Begarawiya]. Site of one of the capitals of the ancient kingdom of Kush, situated on the east bank of the Nile, in the Butana region of Sudan. The city of Meroë, which gave its name to the Meroitic period (*c.* 300 BC–*c.* AD 360; *see* NUBIA, §IV, 1 and 4), flourished from the early 7th century BC until *c.* AD 360. J. Garstang excavated a palace complex and several temples (1909–14), George Andrew Reisner worked in the royal necropolis (1920–23) and P. L. Shinnie, A. M. Ali Hakem and R. J. Bradley excavated in the residential areas (1965–76). The site consists of the town and, about 4 km to the east, a necropolis of small royal pyramids (at Begarawiya).

Members of the Kushite royal family were buried at Meroë during the Napatan period (*c.* 657–*c.* 250 BC), but it was only after the mid-3rd century BC that the Kushite kings themselves were buried at Meroë, in southern Begarawiya. Later, between *c.* 200 BC and *c.* AD 360 (with only a few interruptions *c.* 100 BC), the Kushite kings were buried in northern Begarawiya. Like their Napatan predecessors, whose cemeteries were at el-Kurru and Nuri, the rulers of the Meroitic period were buried under small, steep-sided pyramids (each originally surmounted by a flagstaff). The surface of each pyramid was cased with white mortar and occasionally adorned with miniature false windows and red painted decoration. At the east side of the pyramid was a small pyloned mortuary temple with a roofless portico (mid-2nd century AD onwards).

The town consisted of a complex of royal palaces and an adjacent temple of Amun, separated from the northern and southern residential areas by two branches of the Nile. The palaces were two-storey buildings with rooms arranged around courtyards (3rd century BC onwards). Several later palaces (*c.* 1st century AD) were arranged around pillared peristyle courts. From the 3rd century BC until the 2nd or 3rd century AD the palace complex was surrounded by a stone temenos wall (with Greek masons' marks indicating the work of Ptolemaic craftsmen). In the south-western part of this royal enclosure was a 'water sanctuary', consisting of a covered channel and a square basin surrounded by columns with capitals in a Ptolemaic style. The water sanctuary (*c.* 100 BC) was decorated with sandstone statues, covered in stucco and paint, copying Hellenistic, Napatan and perhaps Egyptian pharaonic originals (*see* NUBIA, §IV, 4). Most of these sculptures were of poor quality but some, such as the head of a reclining man (Copenhagen, Ny Carlsberg Glyp.), were of higher quality. When the sanctuary was rebuilt (late 1st or 2nd century AD), new sculptures, copying Egyptian types of the Roman period, were added.

The Temple of Amun (*c.* 1st century BC; enlarged late 1st century AD) had a conventional Egyptian ground-plan, like the 25th Dynasty (*c.* 750–*c.* 657 BC) temples at KAWA, Sanam and Tabo. In the 1st century AD, when the branches of the Nile surrounding the centre of Meroë silted up, a processional way was built, leading up to the temple and flanked on both sides by small temples of Egyptian plan (KC 100–101, KC 104 and M 720) containing wall paintings in an Egyptianizing style. Chapel M 292, located within the royal enclosure, was decorated in the 1st century AD with wall paintings in the same style. The decoration of chapel M 292 was perhaps connected with the head of a bronze statue of Augustus (London, BM) found buried

under its threshold and originating probably from a statue erected in the fortress of Qasr Ibrim between 25 BC and 21/20 BC. About 500 m north of the Temple of Amun was a temple built in the 1st century BC, probably dedicated to the Egyptian goddess Isis, with an identical orientation and a similar layout.

In the 3rd to 2nd century BC a temple of the Kushite lion-god Apedemak, consisting of a pyloned cella within temenos walls, was erected immediately to the east of the town. A schist votive tablet of King Tanyidamani (*c.* 100 BC; Baltimore, MD, Walters A.G.; see fig.) was found in this temple. A fourth temple (M 250) was constructed by King Aspelta (*c.* 6th century BC) about one km east of the Amun temple. It was rebuilt by Prince Akinidad (*c.* 1st century BC) in the form of a chapel with pylons, standing on an artificial terrace and surrounded by a columned peristyle court; this later lay-out is a combination of Meroitic and Ptolemaic architectural traditions.

The similarities between the reliefs in the mortuary chapels of the pyramids at Meroë and reliefs in other parts of Meroitic Kush suggest that Meroë played a leading role

Meroë, Temple of Apedemak, votive tablet of King Tanyidamani, schist, h. 178 mm, *c.* 100 BC (Baltimore, MD, Walters Art Gallery)

in transmitting influences from Egypt and spreading iconographic and stylistic innovations. Meroë was also a centre of the production of bronze and iron artefacts, and the manufacture of fine decorated pottery, from the Napatan period onwards.

LÄ

BIBLIOGRAPHY

F. Caillaud: *Voyage à Meroe* (Paris, 1823)
J. Garstang, A. H. Sayce and F. Ll. Griffith: *Meroe: City of the Ethiopians* (Oxford, 1911)
Liverpool An. Archaeol. & Anthropol., iii–iv (1911–14) [annual preliminary reports on the excavations at Meroe, published by J. Garstang and others]
S. Chapman and D. Dunham: *Decorated Chapels of the Meroitic Pyramids at Meroe and Barkal* (Boston, 1952)
D. Dunham: *Royal Tombs at Meroe and Barkal* (Boston, 1957)
——: *The West and South Cemeteries at Meroe* (Boston, 1963)
P. L. Shinnie: *Meroe: A Civilization of the Sudan* (London, 1967)
S. Wenig: *Africa in Antiquity: The Arts of Ancient Nubia and Sudan, II. The Catalogue* (Brooklyn, 1978)
P. L. Shinnie and R. J. Bradley: *The Capital of Kush*, Meroitica, iv (E. Berlin, 1980)
R. J. Bradley: *Varia from the City of Meroe*, Meroitica, vi (E. Berlin, 1982), pp. 163–70
——: *Wall-paintings from Meroe Townsite*, Meroitica, vii (E. Berlin, 1984), pp. 421–3
P. L. Shinnie: *Excavations at Meroe, 1974–76*, Meroitica, vii (E. Berlin, 1984), pp. 498–504
L. Török: *Kush and the External World*, Meroitica, x (E. Berlin, 1988)
——: *Meroe City, an Ancient African Capital: John Garstang's Excavations in the Sudan* (London, 1996)

L. TÖRÖK

Merovingian art. Art of the Frankish kingdom of north-west Europe between the 5th century AD and the 8th, named after Merovech (*d c.* 457), the founder of the dynasty.

1. Introduction. 2. Metalwork and industry. 3. Architecture. 4. Sculpture. 5. Manuscripts.

1. INTRODUCTION. The Merovingian kingdom was founded in the 5th century AD from a loose confederation of Germanic tribes known as the Franks who had settled on the north and west boundaries of the Roman Empire in the 3rd and 4th centuries as part of the general migratory movements of barbarian peoples (*see* MIGRATION PERIOD). The Franks came from east of the River Rhine; by the 4th century they were occupying parts of Belgium, the Rhine Valley and northern France. They were recognized as 'federated' tribes by the Romans and allowed to settle peacefully within the frontiers of the Empire in return for military service; they fought for the Romans against the various invaders of the collapsing Empire in the mid-5th century but gradually became the masters themselves.

Merovech, who fought victoriously against the Huns, founded the dynasty that was to be named after him. His son Childeric (*d* 481), another successful warrior, halted the advance of the Visigoths. His spectacular burial at Tournai contained jewellery and weapons appropriate to an important leader who was already calling himself king. His son Clovis I (466–511) made the Franks masters of central and eastern Gaul, unified the Frankish kingdom and gained the support of the surviving Gallo-Roman population by adopting Christianity; he was said to have been buried in the dress of a Roman consul. There was further expansion under his sons and grandsons; the vigour of the new Germanic rulers combined with the

administrative and religious structures of the old empire to produce a powerful state extending over the whole of modern France, Belgium and western Germany, the art of which reflected this mingling of barbarian and Classical traditions. During the 7th century and early 8th there was further consolidation, culminating in the establishment of the Carolingian dynasty under Pépin, King of the Franks, in 751.

The evidence for the beginnings of Merovingian art comes from cemeteries. From as early as the 4th century, Frankish settlers within the imperial frontiers were beginning to adopt the later Roman rite of inhumation rather than the Germanic custom of cremation; the rows of burials contained jewellery and weapons whose decoration and manufacture showed the strong influence of provincial Roman styles, although combined with the Nordic tendency towards abstraction. Cemeteries remain an important source of evidence throughout the period: many thousands of graves have been excavated, and their contents illustrate the blending of Frankish and native Gallo-Roman elements. While jewellery and weapon types continue to belong to a broad Germanic range, there are many specifically Frankish objects corresponding to the other regional variants of barbarian material culture. The royal graves of the 5th and 6th centuries, however, contained a different range of possessions of great luxury and new artistic styles, exhibiting a confident growth from the imitation of late Roman art to a distinctively Merovingian type of ornament, which was to influence other areas of Europe.

The presence of the native late Roman culture and the adoption of Christianity were also significant to the development of Merovingian art. There were continuing links with the Mediterranean world where the first Christian art had developed; objects of Christian ritual and worship needed to be manufactured, and artists could draw on Christian iconography. The first churches and monasteries were built using Classical forms, while Roman industrial and manufacturing techniques continued to be used.

2. METALWORK AND INDUSTRY. Merovingian art is best represented by the wide range of metalwork that survives from the many cemeteries and tombs. Personal jewellery included brooches of various forms: discs, S-shapes, birds and fish, radiate- and square-headed types (see fig. 1). These were made of gold, silver or bronze and decorated in the polychrome manner common to the Germanic peoples, learnt by them from the Gothic tribes of south Russia. The multi-coloured effects were achieved by the use of cloisonné inlay (the setting of hardstones such as garnets within frames of gold), which was particularly elaborated by Frankish craftsmen, and by the studding of coloured stones on the surface.

Other jewellery in burials included necklaces of glass beads, earrings, bracelets, pins for hair and garments and different types of buckles, fastenings and strap ends designed to be attached to leather and textiles. These were decorated by techniques learnt from the local Roman workshops, such as chip-carving (a way of faceting metal to provide a glittering surface), filigree (gold or silver wire made from droplets of the metal), and engraving and chasing the surfaces to provide a richer texture. Roman coins were also reused as ornaments, set in the centre of brooches or hanging from a necklace. The patterns used on jewellery developed from the geometric or simple animal forms of late Roman art of the 5th century to the more complex interlacing animal designs of the 6th and 7th centuries, which were seen not only in Merovingian art but also in all areas of Germanic occupation, with particularly rich variants in England and Scandinavia. The vigour of the Frankish metalworking industry played an important role in the distribution of this distinctive style.

A series of princely burials provides useful dating evidence for the development of the art styles seen in the jewellery. The tomb of Childeric, the first king of the Franks, was discovered at Tournai in 1653. It contained a gold signet ring (lost 1831) with his portrait in the manner of a Roman emperor, inscribed *Childerici Regis*. There was a sword hilt (Paris, Bib. N., Cab. Médailles) and fittings ornamented with the cloisonné garnets that were to become characteristic of Frankish jewellery, and 300 gold and garnet cicadas, symbols of immortality, which had been sewn on to his cloak. Other items included gold buckles and mounts, gold and silver coins, his spear and battle-axe and his horse's head, with decorated harness.

The contents of two royal burials at Cologne (Cologne, Röm.-German.-Mus.), which can be dated to the 6th century, show the maturing Merovingian style in a Christian context. A princess buried before the mid-6th century in a chapel beneath Cologne Cathedral was wearing a gold headband, a pair of linked garnet cloisonné disc brooches in the shape of rosettes, a necklace of Roman coins, filigree and garnet pendants and a belt with a silver buckle; her shoe fastenings were ornamented with garnet cicadas. She

1. Merovingian disc fibula, gold leaf on bronze with filigree, inlaid with garnets, pearls, enamels and a Roman cameo, diam. 90 mm, from Molsheim, Germany, 7th century AD (Darmstadt, Hessisches Landesmuseum)

was dressed in a red silk gown with gold embroidery on the cuffs. There were also gold and silver coins and many grave goods. A second Cologne burial was that of a young boy wearing a gold ring, accompanied by a small wooden sceptre as a mark of rank, a miniature helmet, adult-sized sword, spears, bow and shield, as well as glass and bronze vessels and a bed and chair (*see* §4 below). Another rich burial (finds in Saint-Denis, Trésor Cathedral), excavated in 1958 from beneath the crypt of Saint-Denis Abbey, near Paris, was that of a woman, identified from her inscribed ring as Queen Arnegunde (*d c.* 570), second wife of King Chlotar I (*reg* 511–61). Her clothes were fastened by pins, buckles and strap ends, whose ornament of animal interlace proves that this type of decoration was already well established in Merovingian court circles (previously it had been thought to be a 7th-century development). She wore gold filigree earrings and cloisonné garnet brooches, and a man's heavy garnet and niello belt buckle had been laid across her body.

The contents of these burials show that a confident and sophisticated Germanic-based style was being used by the aristocracy. There were further rich burials in the 7th century. A burial chamber within the Frankish church of Morken, near Cologne, held a coffin with the body of a warrior accompanied by his weapons, personal possessions and glassware (Bonn, Rhein. Landesmus.); his gilt-bronze helmet has panels with engraved patterns, and its headband shows human masks, monsters and vine scrolls of Mediterranean origin. Another early 7th-century burial is that from Krefeld-Gellep (Krefeld, Mus. Burg Linn), a cemetery of around 2000 burials; the most lavish contained weapons, gold and garnet jewellery and a silver spoon from the east Mediterranean area. Similar developments can be traced on the equipment from ordinary graves as well as those with luxury metalwork. Mediterranean figural art, previously unfamiliar to the Germanic tradition of abstract and animal ornament, was now being copied, and figures of both Classical and Early Christian origin were used as decorative plaques and buckles, such as horse and rider, griffin and *Daniel in the Lions' Den*.

Elaborate jewellery techniques of ultimately pagan origin were also being applied to purely Christian metalwork. Two early examples, the paten and chalice from Gourdon (Paris, Bib. N., Cab. Médailles; see fig. 2), date from the reign of Clovis. The paten has cloisonné garnet inlay in the step-patterns familiar from brooches and buckles, while the chalice combines a late Roman form with Germanic beasts for handles. The reliquary caskets of the 7th and 8th centuries were made in the form of small sarcophagi to house the precious relics of saints; they were treated as jewels, being made out of gold or copper gilt and decorated with cloisonné, inlaid stones or cameos, their ornament combining interlaced animals, foliage and scrollwork of east Mediterranean type and figural designs as on the stone models (e.g. the reliquary casket of Teuderigus, ?7th century; St Maurice, Abbey Treasury).

The Franks developed various late Roman industries, including another aspect of metalworking: gold coinage. Coins survive from burials, where they can be used for dating evidence, and from merchants' hoards. They have inscribed portraits of Frankish kings dressed as Roman emperors. More than 2000 mints are known to have been

2. Merovingian gold paten (left) and chalice (right), gold with filigree and cloisonné enamel, h. paten 119.5 mm and chalice 75 mm, from Gourdon, France, *c.* AD 500 (Paris, Bibliothèque Nationale, Cabinet des Médailles)

established, most of which provided careful and fine minting of a high standard. The Franks also developed the late Roman glass industry, especially in the Rhineland. Although many Roman forms continued to be made, there were also new shapes such as drinking horns and the striking mould-blown claw beakers (e.g. London, BM), which were widely distributed both inside and beyond the Frankish territories.

3. ARCHITECTURE. Owing to the collapse of the Roman Empire there was an inevitable decline in the urban life of the Gallo-Romans, and there are few traces of Merovingian secular architecture. The Germanic peoples built in wood, which has not survived; most of the Frankish population lived in hamlets or small villages, the plans of whose timber huts have been revealed in excavations. The main standing remains are those of churches and monasteries, and there appear to be some regional variations: in the south influence can be traced from the neighbouring Visigothic tradition (*see* VISIGOTHIC ART), while further north Classical architectural styles prevailed. There are traces of evidence for 5th-century architecture from the baptisteries at Fréjus, which had a square plan with a central dome, and possibly the earliest phase at Poitiers (*see* POITIERS, §2(ii) and fig. 3), using Roman brick, with cornices and pediments of Roman type. The 6th-century baptistery of Venasque (Vaucluse) is in the same tradition, with dome and arcades. Modifications were made at Poitiers in the 7th century, when it became a cruciform building with square apses and distinctive external decoration. Crypts were an important feature, with examples surviving at Poitiers (*see* POITIERS, §2(v)), Grenoble (*see* GRENOBLE, §2) and JOUARRE ABBEY. The monastic expansion also contributed to the building tradition, with the foundation of more than 400 monasteries by the end of the 7th century. Frankish masons were by then held in great respect and were brought to Northumbria to build the first stone Anglo-Saxon churches. Features of Merovingian architecture that were to survive into

the Carolingian period include the popularity of towers and the development of sculptural decoration and ornamental masonry, employing the emphasis on pattern that was always characteristic of Germanic taste.

For further discussion *see* GREGORY, Bishop of Tours.

4. SCULPTURE. The technique of stone-carving was totally unfamiliar to the Franks until after their settlement in Roman territories and conversion to Christianity. Architectural sculpture was learnt from existing Classical buildings; the earliest examples are the carved capitals from La Daurade, Toulouse (Toulouse, Mus. Augustins), dating from the 5th century, and the 6th-century capitals of the basilica at Selles-sur-Cher (reset in Romanesque times), which are still of late Roman type. By the 7th century, however, more Germanic styles and subjects came to be used, such as the entwined snakes from the steps to the Hypogée des Dunes at Poitiers, shown in symbolic combination with fish and vine scrolls. One of the closure slabs from the basilica at Saint-Denis has carved geometric patterns of the type seen on inlaid jewellery, while the fragments from the mid-7th-century choir-screen from St Pierre-aux-Nonnains at Metz (now in Metz, Mus. A. & Hist.) show the combination of interlace and animal heads with east Christian monastic themes, derived from Coptic Egypt. Local schools of sculptors grew up, including a group in Aquitaine whose marble capitals have been recognized in the Baptistère St Jean at Poitiers, Jouarre and as far away as Paris (e.g. St Pierre, Montmartre) in the 6th and 7th centuries.

The sarcophagi again demonstrate the advance from the copying of late Roman art to an assured 7th- and 8th-century manner. These marble or stone coffins were originally decorated with geometric or foliage patterns inspired by east Mediterranean art, as in an example from Poitou dating from the 6th century (Poitiers, Mus. Baptistère St Jean), but they were subsequently carved in relief, with biblical scenes or standing figures under pediments;

the formerly well-proportioned Classical figures were reinterpreted with Merovingian vigour and other ornament from different sources, including Byzantine, Coptic and LOMBARD ART. There are three coffins in the crypt at JOUARRE ABBEY; that of Bishop Agilbert in Notre-Dame de Vic (Vaucluse) is carved with the *Last Judgement* and *Christ in Majesty* with Evangelist symbols of possibly Coptic iconography. Sarcophagi could be carved in deep or shallow relief, and many are simply engraved with biblical motifs such as *Daniel in the Lions' Den* (Bourges, Mus. Berry) or Early Christian symbols such as peacocks (Vienne, St Pierre) or griffins.

Frankish memorial grave slabs or tombstones show the same developments, combining figural art of late Classical type with Germanic and Mediterranean ornament. The deceased warrior may be shown mounted, a motif also popular on metalwork and jewellery, or, as in the example from Niederdollendorf (Bonn, Rhein. Landesmus.; see fig. 3), standing, holding his sword, his Christianity indicated by the accompanying pilgrim flask as well as the haloed Christ holding a spear on the reverse of the slab. A 7th-century tombstone from Gondorf (Bonn, Rhein. Landesmus.) in the Rhineland shows a bearded saint between two doves, framed by Germanic-looking beasts and a patterned border of Late Antique type; that of Bishop Boethius of Carpentras (Venasque, Church of Notre-Dame de Vic) has a Classical pediment, a cross, rosette patterns and the Alpha and Omega symbols, but shown with the Greek letters reversed, as if the sculptor had misunderstood his model. Other slabs have engraved figures from the Old or New Testament. Another type of sculpture was the base for a monumental cross now in the Hypogée des Dunes, Poitiers, carved with the figures of the two thieves of the Crucifixion.

There were also religious carvings in bone and ivory. The Werden Casket (Essen-Werden, St Lindger) has figures of Christ crucified and two angels carved in very low relief, set in rectangular frames surrounded by geometric borders. Ivory book covers and diptychs are strongly influenced by 6th-century Byzantine models but reinterpreted with over-large heads and stiff folds of garments. Remains of wood-carving are rare but show much skill, as in the bed and chair from the 6th-century boy's grave at Cologne as well as his lathe-turned wooden sceptre (*see* §2 above). The reading-desk associated with St Radegund (518–87) and preserved at St Croix Abbey near Poitiers shows the Lamb surrounded by Evangelist symbols; it may be an east Christian import.

5. MANUSCRIPTS. The development of manuscript art in the late 7th century and the 8th can be associated with the expansion of monasticism, and there were several regional centres. The polychrome style of the earlier Frankish jewellers was completely reworked into a Christian art inspired by eastern models. The manuscripts are characterized by simple, lively patterns of animals, architectural features, foliage ornament and geometric forms in tones of red, green and yellow; the human figure is comparatively rare. The most distinctive feature is the combination of the sophisticated frames of arches, columns and arcades with an exotic vocabulary of fish, birds, lions and other more fantastic beasts. These, however, do not come from the Germanic repertory, although they are patterned like inlaid jewellery, but are quite new. Another new element is the way in which the bodies of the animals are sometimes used to make actual letters; they are treated not just as ornament but as an integral part of the design. The mid-8th-century Sacramentary of Gelasianum (Rome, Vatican, Bib. Apostolica, MS. Vat. Reg. lat. 316), written near Paris, has whole pages filled with geometric details, animals and plants; an initial letter of the Gellone Sacramentary (Paris, Bib. N., MS. lat. 12048), written at Meaux Abbey in the later 8th century, has the figure of the Virgin, patterned with angular forms, while other pages show exuberant animal designs. A manuscript from Laon (*c.* 770; Paris, Bib. N., MS. lat. 12168) uses two lions to support an arch, a feature derived from Lombardic Italy. The manuscripts also show some awareness of contemporary Anglo-Saxon illumination in forms of interlace and some

3. Merovingian carved sandstone gravestone depicting (obverse) Frankish warrior with comb, sword and pilgrim flask, attacked by snakes, h. 475 mm, from Niederdollendorf, Germany, late 7th century AD (Bonn, Rheinisches Landesmuseum)

of the animal features. Although the manuscript art of the subsequent Carolingian renaissance was quite different, some of the ornamental details produced by the creative Merovingian scribes were to survive within it.

Merovingian art is a major step in the development of early medieval art. From the tentative copying of the existing Gallo-Roman models in the 5th century and the early 6th, there was a rapid advance in confidence and quality from the second half of the 6th century to the late 8th, in which Germanic styles and techniques were deliberately blended with elements of late Roman, Italian, Byzantine and Coptic art. This process of fusion led directly to the Carolingian renaissance, which would not have been possible without the firm foundations laid by the Frankish craftsmen.

BIBLIOGRAPHY

L. Coutil: *L'Art mérovingien et carolingien* (Paris, 1930)

J. Baum: *La Sculpture figurale en Europe à l'époque mérovingienne* (Paris, 1937)

N. Åberg: *The Merovingian Empire* (1947), iii of *The Occident and the Orient in the Art of the Seventh Century* (Stockholm, 1947)

E. Salin: *La Civilisation mérovingienne*, 4 vols (Paris, 1949–59)

J. Werner: 'Frankish Royal Tombs in the Cathedrals of Cologne and Saint-Denis', *Antiquity*, xxxviii (1964), pp. 201–16

H. Busch and B. Lohse, eds: *Pre-Romanesque Art* (London, 1966)

M. Backes and R. Dölling: *Art of the Dark Ages* (New York, 1969)

J. Hubert, J. Porcher and W. F. Volbach: *Europe in the Dark Ages* (London, 1969)

P. Lasko: *The Kingdom of the Franks* (London, 1971)

P. Dixon: *Barbarian Europe*, The Making of the Past (London, 1976)

M. Durliat: *Des Barbares à l'an mil* (Paris, 1985)

M. Vieillard-Troïekouroff: 'La Sculpture en Neustrie', *Colloque historique international. La Neustrie: Les Pays au nord de la Loire de 650 à 850: Paris, 1985*, pp. 225–57

CAROLA HICKS

Merrifield [née Watkins], **Mary Philadelphia** (*b* ?1804–5; *d* 1889). English writer and editor. She was the editor of the first English translation of Cennino Cennini's *Libro dell'arte* (1844), which appeared concurrently with the exhibition of cartoons for frescoes in Westminster Palace and was seen as valuable for the practical instruction of contemporary artists. In 1845 she was commissioned by the British government to collect artists' manuscripts, which she published in *The Art of Fresco Painting*, a volume of extensively annotated texts dating from antiquity to the 17th century. In *Original Treatises, Dating from the XIIth to XVIIIth Centuries on the Arts of Painting* (1849) she gave more weight to texts as historical documents than as practical guides; indeed, the main importance of her work lies in her development of the historical study of documents, although it did affect practice, especially among the Pre-Raphaelites: her emphasis on the historical and aesthetic value of white grounds to colour purity was probably strategic for their rejection of tonal painting and adoption of the 'wet ground' technique. Mrs Merrifield also wrote manuals for amateur artists, and in *Dress as a Fine Art* (1854) she advocated the application of Michel-Eugène Chevreul's principles of colour harmony to counter servile conventionality in women's fashions. She was granted a government pension in 1857 for her services to art.

WRITINGS

ed.: *A Treatise on Painting, Written by Cennino Cennini* (London, 1844)

ed.: *The Art of Fresco Painting, as Practised by the Old Italian and Spanish Masters, with a Preliminary Inquiry into the Nature of the Colours Used in Fresco Painting* (Brighton, 1846/*R* 1952)

ed.: *Original Treatises, Dating from the XIIth to XVIIIth Centuries on the Arts of Painting, in Oil, Miniature, Mosaic, and on Glass*, 2 vols (London, 1849)

Practical Directions for Portrait Painting in Watercolours (London, 1851)

Dress as a Fine Art (London, 1854)

Handbook of Light and Shade, with Especial Reference to Model Drawing (London, 1855)

BIBLIOGRAPHY

F. Boase: *Modern English Biography*, 6 vols (London, 1892–1921/*R* 1965)

C. R. Sherman and A. M. Holcomb, eds: *Women as Interpreters of the Visual Arts, 1820–1979* (Westport, CT, and London, 1981)

ADELE M. ERNSTROM

Merrill, John O(gden). *See under* SKIDMORE, OWINGS & MERRILL.

Merritt [née Lea], **Anna Lea** (*b* Philadelphia, PA, 13 Sept 1844; *d* Hurstbourne Tarrant, Hants, 7 April 1930). English painter, muralist and printmaker of American birth. She is best known for her Victorian portraits, allegorical and religious paintings, landscapes and floral scenes and was successful in spite of the difficulties that she encountered as a professional woman artist working in Victorian England. After brief artistic tours to Florence, Dresden and Paris, where she studied in Léon Cogniet's atelier, she began intensive instruction in 1870 from Henry Merritt (1822–77), an Englishman who restored works of art from important collections and wrote on art, exhibitions and conservation. Anna Lea and Henry Merritt were married in July 1877; three months later he died. *Love Locked out* (1889; London, Tate), depicting love at the door of a tomb, was painted as a memorial to her husband. This was the first painting by a woman to be purchased by the Chantrey Bequest. In order to illustrate her publication of Merritt's writings, she learnt to etch and became recognized as a leading woman etcher.

As a portrait painter, Merritt was commissioned in the USA and England. Her work included *James Russell Lowell* (1882; Cambridge, MA, Harvard U., Portrait Col.), *Dorothea Beale* (1893; Cheltenham, Ladies' Coll.) and *Horace Howard Furness* (1895; Philadelphia, U. PA, Furness Lib.). As a muralist she worked on religious subjects in St Martin's, Chilworth, Hants, and on depictions of women at work for the Women's Building at the Columbian Exposition, Chicago (1893). In 1891 she moved to Hurstbourne Tarrant, where she wrote and illustrated two garden books, *A Hamlet in Old Hampshire* (London, 1902) and *An Artist's Garden* (London, 1908).

WRITINGS

Henry Merritt: Art Criticism and Romance (London, 1879)

'A Letter to Artists: Especially Women Artists', *Lippincott's Mthly Mag.*, lxv (1900), pp. 463–9

BIBLIOGRAPHY

M. van Rensselaer: 'American Etchers', *C. Mag.*, xxv (1883), pp. 483–99

G. Gorokhoff, ed.: *Love Locked out: The Memoirs of Anna Lea Merritt* (Boston, 1982)

GALINA GOROKHOFF

Mersch, Passcier van der. *See under* MASTERS, ANONYMOUS, AND MONOGRAMMISTS, §I: MASTER OF HOOGSTRATEN.

Merse, Pál Szinyei. *See* SZINYEI MERSE, PÁL.

Mersin. Site in Turkey with notable settlements from the Neolithic, Chalcolithic and Early Bronze Age periods (*c.* 6200–*c.* 2200 BC). The modern seaport of Mersin is situated at the western corner of the great crescent-shaped plain surrounding Adana, where the foothills of the Taurus Mountains almost reach the sea. On the outskirts of Mersin, a mound called Yümük Tepe, on the left bank of a fast-flowing stream, seems likely to have marked the crossing of an important ancient highway leading west towards Silifke (ancient Seleucia) and the Calycadnus Valley. The site was excavated by John Garstang in 1937–8 and 1946. The stratified 'Cilician' material from Garstang's excavations covered occupation from a primitive Neolithic settlement (*c.* 7th or 6th millennium BC) up to Byzantine times.

It seems that the earliest settlement at Mersin, from level XXXIII up to XXII (*c.* 5000 BC), was comparatively impoverished. The only exceptional aspect of this period, from Neolithic to early Chalcolithic, was the advanced flint industry, in which implements and weapons were predominantly of fine obsidian from an Anatolian source. The long, leaf-shaped javelin heads are particularly elegant. The houses, however, were constructed with undressed stone from the river-bed and are almost indistinguishable from the adjoining sheepfolds. The combined material from Mersin and Gözlüküle (an ancient suburb of nearby Tarsus, excavated by Hetty Goldman) constitutes a source of chronological connections between prehistoric finds in western Anatolia and the Levant, extending more remotely to Mesopotamia and Egypt.

The unpainted Neolithic pottery at Mersin was followed by a series of Chalcolithic occupations, characterized by painted ware, continuing until level XII (almost 15 m above the present-day stream). The Chalcolithic period included ceramics similar to those familiar from Mesopotamian and Syrian prehistory, recognized by cross-dating, as well as less well-known local wares. The conspicuous craftsmanship of the local pottery involved unusual refinement and ability in ceramic ornament. The unique designs, often painted with a multiple brush in dark paint on a cream slip (or even in white on burnished black), were variously adapted to the forms of the vessels themselves.

In level XVI (late 5th millennium BC) the settlement was ingeniously fortified, giving an impression of unusually sophisticated planning for its time. The architecture and general appointments were those of a quasi-military establishment, with towered gateway, garrison quarters and other accommodation. Built against the inner face of the defensive wall was a row of identical apartments, each entered through an enclosed yard, with small piles of sling ammunition in evidence. The rooms themselves were equipped with hearths, grindstones and grain bins. They were lit by ground-level slit windows that overlooked the approaches to the mound. A building with larger rooms, adjoining the gateway, could have been a guard-house.

The Early Bronze Age levels (*c.* 2400 BC) were conveniently dated by the intrusion of recognizably Syrian pot-shapes and by other foreign imports. Garstang excavated a segment of the mound measuring 25 m wide, exposing the heavy foundations of a Bronze Age chambered fortress wall, which he controversially dated to the time of the Hittite empire (1400–1200 BC).

BIBLIOGRAPHY

J. Garstang: 'Explorations in Cilicia', *Liverpool An. Archaeol. & Anthrop.*, xxiv (1937), pp. 52–68; xxv (1938), pp. 12–23, 71–110; xxvi (1939), pp. 38–50, 89–158

——: *Prehistoric Mersin: Yümük Tepe in Southern Turkey* (Oxford, 1953)

SETON LLOYD

Merson, Luc Olivier (*b* Paris, 21 May 1846; *d* Paris, 14 Nov 1920). French painter and illustrator. He was the son of the painter and art critic Charles-Olivier Merson (1822–1902) and trained initially at the Ecole de Dessin in Paris under Gustave Adolphe Chassevent (1818–1901) and then at the Ecole des Beaux-Arts under Isidore-Alexandre-Augustin Pils. He made his début at the Salon in 1867 and won the Grand Prix de Rome in 1869 with the melodramatic work, the *Soldier of Marathon* (1869; Paris, Ecole N. Sup. B.-A.). As a prizewinner he then spent five years in Italy, where he was impressed and influenced by the works of the Italian Primitives, as is apparent in such works as *St Edmund, King and Martyr* (1871; Troyes, Mus. B.-A. & Archéol.), with its muted colours and rigid composition. In the Salon of 1875 he exhibited *Sacrifice for the Country, St Michael*, which had been commissioned as a design for a Gobelins tapestry for the Salle des Evêques in the Panthéon, Paris. Soon afterwards he was chosen to decorate the Galerie de St Louis in the Palais de Justice, Paris, with scenes from the life of Louis IX. This resulted in two large works, *Louis Opening the Doors of the Gaols on his Accession* and *Louis Condemning Sire Enguerrand de Coucy* (both 1877). He also used historical, often religious, subjects for his smaller-scale works, as in *St Francis of Assisi Preaching to the Fish* (1880; Nantes, Mus. B.-A.). Some, such as *Rest on the Flight into Egypt* (1880; Nice, Mus. B.-A.), resemble Symbolist art in their sense of mystery and use of diffuse light effects.

Merson received numerous further commissions for public buildings, for example he painted the altarpiece *St Louis* (1888) for the church of St Thomas d'Aquin in Paris and *Music in the Middle Ages* (1898) for the Théâtre National de L'Opéra-Comique, Paris, which demonstrated his continuing delight in distant historical subjects. He also produced tapestry cartoons for the Vredespaleis, The Hague, the Musée Municipal, Limoges, and the Ecole des Beaux-Arts, Paris. Commissions for stained-glass window designs came not only from French but also from some American and Russian churches. In 1901 he produced a series of three large works for the Hôtel Watel-Dehaynin in Paris, entitled *Family*, *Truth* and *Fortune* (Paris, Mus. d'Orsay).

Merson also had a successful career as an illustrator. In addition to the work he did for such magazines as *Harper's Magazine* and *Revue illustrée*, he illustrated books, including Victor Hugo's *Notre-Dame de Paris* (Paris, 1895), Gustave Flaubert's *La Légende de Saint-Julien l'Hospitalier* (Paris, 1895) and Léon Gautier's *La Chevalerie* (Paris, 1884). His drawings (Paris, Mus. d'Orsay) for an illustrated edition of Shakespeare's *Macbeth*, executed sometime between 1880 and 1890, were never published. In 1892 Merson was elected a member of the Académie des Beaux-Arts and in 1894 was made professor at the Ecole des Beaux-Arts, of which he became Director in 1906. He resigned the post in 1911 in protest at the lack of emphasis placed on drawing and preparatory studies for paintings, an act that admirably demonstrates his position as one of the last representatives and supporters of 19th-century academic art.

Edouard-Joseph

BIBLIOGRAPHY

J. Martin: *Nos peintres et sculpteurs* (Paris, 1898), p. 279
A. Soubies: *Les Membres de l'Académie des beaux-arts depuis la fondation de l'institut*, 4 vols (Paris, 1904–17), iv, pp. 70–75
H. Loyrette: 'Dessins de Luc Olivier Merson pour Macbeth', *Rev. Louvre*, iii (1982), pp. 199–207

□

Mertens, Charles (*b* Antwerp, 14 April 1865; *d* Calverley, Yorks, 20 Feb 1919). Belgian painter. A pupil of Charles Verlat at the Antwerp Academie, he initially painted genre scenes in the tradition of Henri De Braekeleer; his style, however, was more spirited. In 1883 he became a member of the Als Ik Kan group, and in 1886 he was appointed Professor at the Antwerp Academie. From 1887 his concern for capturing the material nature of things developed in tandem with a growing interest in the effects of natural and changing light. His painting grew more expansive, the handling freer and the detail more blurred. He exhibited in Brussels (1893) and Antwerp (1897) and won medals at the Expositions Universelles of 1889 and 1892 in Paris.

Mertens's favourite subjects were popular genre scenes and small interiors; for example, *Singing Children in Flanders*, *The Waffle Seller* (both Antwerp, Kon. Mus. S. Kst) and *In the Studio* (1885; Brussels, Mus. A. Mod.). He was particularly fond of visiting Zeeland, where he was inspired to produce such powerful compositions as *The Couple from Zeeland* (pastel; Antwerp, Kon. Mus. S. Kst). In 1891 he was the co-founder of Les XIII group and in 1905 of Kunst van Heden. In 1907 he embarked on a programme of decorative schemes, including the ceiling of the Antwerp Opera house. During World War I, Mertens went to England, where he produced boldly painted landscapes that are nevertheless acutely aware of the precise motif. Mertens was also one of the best portrait painters of the 19th-century Antwerp school, and in several respects he anticipated the Flemish Expressionist school of the 20th century.

Bénézit

BIBLIOGRAPHY

P. Colin: *La Peinture belge depuis 1830* (Brussels, 1930), pp. 105–6
W. Koninckx: 'Trois Peintres anversois: Charles Verlat, Piet Verhaert, Charles Mertens', *Conférences des Musées Royaux des Beaux-Arts: Brussels, 1943–4*

ALAIN JACOBS

Mertens [Janssone; van Dornicke], **Jan**, the younger [Master of the Abbey of Dilighem; Master of 1518] (*b* Antwerp, *c*. 1470; *d* Antwerp, *c*. 1527). South Netherlandish painter. His father was the sculptor Jan Mertens the elder (*fl c*. 1473–1509), whose family is thought to have originated in Tournai; he was a respected member of the Antwerp Guild of St Luke, serving as regent in 1478, 1481 and 1487. Mertens the younger was apprenticed to the painter Jan Gossart in 1505, and he became a master of the Antwerp guild in 1509. He was the father-in-law and

perhaps teacher of Pieter Coecke van Aelst, who married Mertens's daughter Anna before 1526 and whose work has been used as the basis for the identification of Mertens with the Master of 1518, an Antwerp painter named after the date inscribed on the painted wings of a carved wooden altarpiece of the *Life of the Virgin* in the Marienkirche, Lübeck. The sharp focus, lively narrative and exaggerated poses evident in the painted wings in Lübeck are characteristic of ANTWERP MANNERISM, but Mertens's work is distinguished by its brilliant colour, sense of structure, thoughtful composition and delicacy of style. Mertens formed an important link in the artistic dynasties of Antwerp, for his second daughter married first Jan van Amstel, now usually identified with the Brunswick Monogrammist, and subsequently Gillis van Coninxloo III.

BIBLIOGRAPHY

M. J. Friedländer: *Die altniederländische Malerei* (Berlin, 1924–37); Eng. trans. as *Early Netherlandish Painting* (Leiden, 1967–76), xiii, pp. 29–33
S. Bergmans: 'Jan van Amstel dit Jean de Hollande', *Rev. Belge Archéol. & Hist. A.*, xxvi (1957), pp. 25–36 [geneal. of the van Dornicke fam.]
G. Marlier: *La Renaissance flamande: Pierre Coeck d'Alost* (Brussels, 1966), pp. 40–41, 112–15
S. Bergmans: 'Une Résurrection du premier quart du XVIe siècle anversois, attribuable à Jan van Dornicke alias le Maître de 1518', *Rev. Belge Archéol. & Hist. A.*, xl (1971), pp. 61–79
J. van Laarhoven: 'Twee Antwerpse schilderijen uit de 16de eeuw', *Tableau*, i (1978–9), pp. 16–20
E. Starcky: 'A propos d'un dessin maniériste anversois', *Rev. Louvre* (1981), pp. 96–102
R. Szmydki: 'Une Sainte Famille à Gdansk attribuable à Jean Mertens Janssone, dit "Van Dornicke"', *Archivum artis Lovaniense: Bijdragen tot de geschiedenis van de kunst der Nederlanden, opgedragen aan professor-emeritus Dr J. K. Steppe* (Leuven, 1981), pp. 215–24
M. W. Ainsworth and M. Faries: 'Northern Renaissance Paintings: The Discovery of Invention', *Bull. St Louis A. Mus.*, xviii (1986), pp. 31–7 [drgs by the Master of 1518]

KIM W. WOODS

Merv [Marv; Marw; Mary]. City in the delta of the Murgh (Murghab) River in Turkmenistan. The ruins of Old Merv include five settlements known as Erk-kala, Gyaur-kala, Sultan-kala, Abdallahkhan-kala and Bairamalikhan-kala. More is known about the history and urban development of Old Merv than about any other city in Iran or western Central Asia. The name Mary is applied to New Merv, the administrative centre founded in 1883 several km east of Old Merv, which lies near the village of Bayram-Ali.

1. History and urban development. 2. Mausoleum of Sultan Sanjar.

1. HISTORY AND URBAN DEVELOPMENT.

(i) Before AD *651.* Archaeological evidence reveals that the Merv Oasis was a centre of civilization by the beginning of the 1st millennium BC. The Mouru region, which takes its name from the old Persian word for a thicket or overgrown river pond, is mentioned in the *Avesta*, and the country Marguš is cited in the inscription of Darius I (*reg* 521–486 BC) at Bisitun as one of the satrapies that rose against the Achaemenids of Iran. Although settlements had appeared on the site in the pre-Achaemenid period, the enclosure wall and the first monumental buildings on the Erk-kala (the oval citadel; see fig. 1) were erected in the early Achaemenid period (Yaz III period, 6th–5th century BC). Residential buildings were constructed to the south and east of the citadel and a system of irrigation canals was developed. By the end of the 5th

1. Merv, aerial view of the site of Erk-kala, 6th–5th centuries BC

century BC Merv had become the urban centre of the oasis. From the end of the 4th century BC the region, known as Margiana, was part of the Seleucid empire. Under Antiochos I (*reg* 281–261 BC) the town that had grown up to the south of Erk-kala (known as Gyaur-kala) was refounded as Antiochia Margiana and surrounded by a mud-brick wall in the form of a square (400 ha) with its north-west corner bevelled by a canal to serve as a moat. The regular plan of Antiochia Margiana, quartered by roads connecting gates, copied Hellenistic models. The area within the walls was gradually filled, the north-west and south-west corners given to parks and gardens.

The region was incorporated into the Parthian state at the beginning of the 2nd century BC, for Parthian coins were minted at Merv beginning with the reign of Phraates II (*c.* 138–?128 BC). Construction was particularly intensive during the early Parthian period, when the walls of the town and citadel were rebuilt. The new wall was 10 m thick and had a sloping socle, rectangular towers and powerful corner forts. During the first centuries AD almost the entire territory within the walls was filled, and copper-smelting workshops and residential buildings have been identified. Remains of a free-standing monumental building, probably a temple, have been found in the north-east corner of the town. The suburbs developed apace.

After Merv was included into the Sasanian empire in the first half of the 3rd century AD, the fortifications were rebuilt again so that the wall measured 20 m in height and was up to 30 m thick at the base. The towers of the citadel and the keep over the gates were rebuilt, and such new buildings as the 'arsenal' were constructed within the citadel. Urban construction was again uneven: the centre and north-west parts of the town were artisans' quarters. In the mid-4th century a Buddhist sanctuary (stupa or

sangha) was constructed in the south-east corner of the town; it functioned until the end of the 6th century. One of the architectural complexes in the north-east corner has been linked with a heterodox Christian community. The town reached its apogee during the 3rd and 4th centuries, for it was a military outpost on the north-east border of Iran and an entrepôt on the trade routes linking Iran, Central Asia and India.

The damage wrought by the wars between the Sasanians and the nomads, however, led to a partial decline in urban life at the end of the 4th century and in the 5th, a decline seen at other settlements and fortresses in the oasis. The restabilization of urban life under Kavadh I (*reg* 488–531) can be seen in the resumption of minting of silver coins, which had ceased early in the reign of Yazdagird II (*reg* 438–57). In the 6th century the walls were repaired and construction resumed, although at a lower level than in earlier times. On the central platform of the citadel at Erk-kala a new administrative building was erected. A new Buddhist stupa was erected in the eastern suburb during the reign of Khusraw I (*reg* 531–79). Late Sasanian urban temples in Merv, decorated with paintings and sculptures, are described in Arab sources. In the suburbs and throughout the oasis, numerous castles (Pers. *keshk*) were erected as the central structures on fortified rural estates. A cemetery (3rd–7th century) was discovered south-west of the town.

(ii) AD *651–1883*. In 651 Merv was taken by the Arabs, and for the rest of the century the local governors of the town and region were dependent on the Arab governors of Khurasan. Merv was an important centre under the Umayyad (*reg* 661–750) and Abbasid (*reg* 749–1258) dynasties, and under the early Abbasids Merv was the capital city of the eastern Islamic lands, although this role was transferred to Nishapur under the Tahirids (*reg* 821–73). It was known as Marw al-Shahijan ('royal Merv') to distinguish it from Marw al-Rudh ('riparian Merv'), a town five or six stages up the Murgh. Merv had a Friday mosque in the citadel (the mosque of the Bani Mahan) and behind it the governor's palace (Arab. *dār al-imāra*). Under the governor Abu Muslim (748–55), whose revolt helped bring the Abbasids to power, the palace is reported to have had a brick dome measuring 55 cubits (27 m) which projected above the flat roof. Four doors led to four iwans opening on to four square courts. From 808 to 817 the caliph al-Ma'mun (*reg* 813–33) resided in a palace outside the north-east gate. Gyaur-kala, corresponding to the Sasanian settlement, remained the nucleus of the town, with commercial and artisanal quarters; its prosperity was based on sericulture and the raising and weaving of cotton, which was facilitated by the torrid climate. Shaim-kala, an empty square with pisé ramparts to the east of Gyaur-kala, is thought to have been a cantonment for the Arab troops.

After the transfer of the capital to Nishapur, some of the inhabitants left Merv, and many houses were abandoned, according to the Arab geographer al-Maqdisi (985). The neglect of Gyaur-kala in the 10th century is confirmed by archaeological evidence, as inhabitants moved to the unfortified suburbs; these became a new town (Sultan-kala), which flourished in the mid-11th century. Covering 401 ha, Sultan-kala was enclosed by defensive walls under the Saljuq ruler Malikshah (*reg* 1072–92). In the 12th century the city became the eastern capital of the Saljuq sultan Sanjar (*reg* 1118–57), for whom a mausoleum was erected (*see* §2 below), and territories to the north (120 ha) and south (110 ha) were included within the walls, defended by semicylindrical towers 10–12 m high and spaced 25–30 m apart. Including the suburbs, the town covered some 1500–1800 ha. A fortified citadel in the north-east corner, Shahriyar-Ark (23 ha) was separated from the town by a defensive system. Sultan-kala had four gates linked by two main roads. The Manjan Canal, which bisected the town from north to south, was faced with fired brick, and the canals leading from it were sometimes covered. Fired brick and terracotta were used for many civic, religious and residential structures in the city, and Sultan-kala reached its greatest size. A house excavated there in 1967–9 has a court (40×40 m) surrounded by rooms of varying sizes and functions. The walls were decorated with a dado (h. 1.5 m) of carved plaster, and the upper walls and ceilings were of white plaster painted in polychrome. The architectural masterpiece of the period, however, was the mausoleum of Sultan Sanjar and its surrounding complex (*see* §2 below). After Sanjar's death the city was annexed by the Khwarazmshahs (1193): crafts flourished, and the town was famous for its fabrics and ceramics.

In 1221 Merv was taken and destroyed by the Mongols under Genghiz Khan and lay in ruins for over 200 years. During the reign of the Timurid Shahrukh (*reg* 1405–47), the irrigation system of the oasis was rebuilt, and the town itself moved 1 km south of the pre-Mongol settlement. Shahrukh intended to make Merv his capital: he sent for craftsmen, who were given great privileges, and mosques, madrasas, *khānaqāh*s, bazaars, bathhouses, caravanserais and bridges were built. Construction slowed once Shahrukh transferred his residence to Samarkand in 1420, and the city passed through a period of strife after his death.

Under the Shaybanids (*reg* 1500–98) major construction in Merv began again. A fortified enclosure (630×695 m) with towers, known as Abdallahkhan-kala, encompassed the city of Shahrukh and was bisected by a road running north-east to south-west. An ensemble comprising a mosque, madrasa and reservoir stood in the centre of the northern half, and the citadel comprising the palace, baths and other buildings stood in the north corner. In the 17th century the Safavid rulers of Iran began to send Qajar tribes to Merv, who fortified a rectangular area adjacent to the wall of Abdallahkhan-kala. It is known as Bairama-likhan-kala, taking its name from the last Qajar ruler of Merv, Bayram 'Ali Khan (*d* 1785). In this period, however, the city fell into a long decline, functioning mainly as a fortress in the Turkoman tribal wars. Most of its buildings were destroyed during the second half of the 19th century, when the fired bricks were robbed for use in new construction. In 1883 Merv was incorporated into the Russian empire.

BIBLIOGRAPHY

Enc. Islam/2: 'Marw al-Shāhijān'
V. A. Zhukovsky: *Razvaliny starogo Merva* [The ruins of Old Merv] (St Petersburg, 1894)
V. V. Bartol'd: *Istoriko-geograficheskii obzor Irana* (St Petersburg, 1903); Eng. trans. by S. Soucek as *An Historical Geography of Iran* (Princeton, 1984), pp. 35–46

——: *K istorii Merva* [On the history of Merv] (St Petersburg, 1909)
M. Ye. Masson: 'Narody i oblasti yuzhnoy chasti Turkmenistana v sostave Parfyanskogo gosudarstva' [Peoples and regions of southern Turkmenistan within the Parthian state], *Trudy Yuzhno-Turkmen. Arkheol. Kompleksnoy Eksped.*, v (1955), pp. 7–70
G. A. Pugachenkova: *Puti razvitiya arkhitektury yuzhnogo Turkmenistana pory rabovladeniya i feodalizma* [The development of architecture in southern Turkmenistan in the period of slave-ownership and feudalism] (Moscow, 1958)
S. B. Lunina: 'Goncharnoye proizvodstvo v Merve, X-nachala XIII vv' [Pottery in Merv in the 10th century to the early 13th], *Trudy Yuzhno-Turkmen. Arkheol. Kompleksnoy Eksped.*, xi (1962), pp. 217–418
M. I. Filanovich: 'Istoriko-kul'turnyye arkheologischeskiye tablitsy po gorodishchu Gyaur-kala v Starom Merve' [Historico-cultural archaeological tables on the settlement of Gyaur-kala in Old Merv], *Trudy Yuzhno-Turkmen. Arkheol. Kompleksnoy Eksped.*, xix (1989), pp. 62–121
Merv v drevney i srednevekovoy istorii Vostoka: Tezisy dokladov [Merv in the ancient and medieval history of the East: outlines of papers] (Ashkhabad, 1990)
Z. I. Usmanova: 'New Material on Ancient Merv', *Iran*, xxx (1992), pp. 55–64

A. B. NIKITIN, YE. V. ZEYMAL'

2. MAUSOLEUM OF SULTAN SANJAR. Situated in the middle of Sultan-kala (see fig. 2), it is a domed cube (exterior dimensions 27×27 m; h. 38 m) erected probably in the 1140s by Muhammad ibn Atsiz al-Sarakhsi, whose name appears on a decorative medallion beneath the dome. Built of fired bricks of two sizes (*c.* 275×275×65–70 mm in the socle and walls, and 250×250×50 mm used in halves or multiples in the squinches, galleries and upper parts), the building has foundations 4.2 m deep. The walls were lightened with galleries and a system of hidden grooved vaults. Squinches in an octagonal zone of transition, concealed on the exterior by a gallery, supported a sixteen-sided zone and the dome, made of two thin brick shells. The outer walls were covered with carved plaster and gilding, the gallery arcade faced with carved brick and the dome covered with blue glazed tiles. The interior walls were painted with geometric, vegetal and epigraphic motifs

2. Merv, mausoleum of Sultan Sanjar, probably 1140s; from a photograph by Nadar, late 19th century

in red and blue on a white ground with gold highlights. The mausoleum formed the centrepiece of an ensemble comprising a mosque and palace, parts of which have been excavated. In addition to being one of the most important buildings of the Saljuq dynasty, it is one of the architectural masterpieces of Iran and western Central Asia, and it became a model for such structures as the mausoleum of the Ilkhanid ruler Uljaytu at Sultaniyya in Iran. After the 17th and 18th centuries the site became a place of pilgrimage for local Turkoman tribesmen.

BIBLIOGRAPHY

G. A. Pugachenkova: *Puti razvitiya arkhitektury yuzhnogo Turkmenistana pory rabovladeniya i feodalizma* [The development of architecture in southern Turkmenistan in the period of slave-ownership and feudalism] (Moscow, 1958), pp. 315–28

YE. V. ZEYMAL'

Mervile, Jehan de. *See* JEAN DE MARVILLE.

Merville, Karl Georg (*b* Plieningen am Neckar [now in Stuttgart], 1751; *d* Pressburg [Bratislava], 10 March 1798). Austrian sculptor. It is not known where he trained before his arrival in Vienna in 1779, accompanied by his brother Friedrich Merville, a metal-caster. In the same year he married Maria Anna Torricella, the daughter of an art dealer from Como and herself a sculptor. Merville's largest and most important work was the central stucco relief of the *Fall of the Angels*, with nine pewter reliefs covering the *Life of the Virgin*, for the high altar of the Michaelerkirche in Vienna (1780–82; *in situ*). From the same period came a portrait of an *Unknown Man* (metal, 1780; Prague, N.G.) and metal statuettes representing figures from classical mythology. Merville must also have conceived an unexecuted monument to *Catherine II* (lead casting, Vienna, Belvedere) during the 1780s, although its history remains unclear.

Merville consistently maintained a somewhat arid, early classical style, showing the influence of 15th-century Florentine sculpture besides a predilection for Roman antiquity. He remained a loner in Vienna, both artistically and socially. To escape creditors he fled to Pressburg in 1792. One of the works he left behind in Vienna was a bust of *Emperor Leopold II* (bronze, 1792; Vienna, Belvedere). He was little more successful in his new base. A few tombs and several lead statuettes date from this period; four of the statuettes treat erotic subjects in an antique style (Bratislava, Mun. Gal.), two more are of bathing nymphs (Hamburg, Kst- & Gewsch.). These works draw on Mannerism, both in style and typology.

BIBLIOGRAPHY

R. Guby: 'Der Hochaltar der Michaelerkirche in Wien', *Mitt. Ver. Gesch. Stadt Wien*, i (1919–20), pp. 45–66

V. Luxová: 'Sochaři A. Marschall a K. G. Mervill v Bratislavě' [The sculptors Marschall and Merville in Bratislava], *Umění*, xviii (1970), pp. 540–42

E. Baum: *Katalog des österreichischen Barockmuseums*, i (Vienna and Munich, 1980), pp. 360–67

M. Malíková: 'Neznámé diela K. J. Mervilla v Galérii mesta Bratislavy' [An unknown work by K. G. Merville in the City Gallery in Bratislava], *Ars* (1987)

MARIA PÖTZL-MALÍKOVÁ

Meryon, Charles (*b* Paris, 23 Nov 1821; *d* Charenton, 14 Feb 1868). French printmaker. He was the illegitimate son of Lady Hester Stanhope's companion and chronicler, Dr Charles Lewis Meryon, and Narcisse Chaspoux, a dancer at the Paris Opéra. He was acknowledged in 1824, but initial separation from his father and the stigma of illegitimacy oppressed him throughout his life. After private schooling at Passy, he entered the French Naval Academy at Brest in 1837 and travelled with his parents in western Europe and on voyages to North Africa and the eastern Mediterranean. A precocious draughtsman, Meryon took some drawing lessons on his return to Toulon in 1840 from Vincent Courdouan (1810–93), from whom he learnt to value the elegant precision of line he was later to develop to a supreme degree. He served as midshipman on the corvette *Le Rhin* during its mission to the French possessions in Oceania (1842–6). Meryon drew small but lively sketches of shipboard life, minor ethnographic studies and more laboured topographical views. Signs of incipient mental instability occurred as he resigned from the navy in 1848. Having travelled in northern France, Belgium and to London, he settled in Paris to study painting with the minor David pupil, Charles-François Phélippes (*d* 1867), when he was diagnosed as colour-blind. Despite his unusual visual acuity, Meryon suffered from a common form of Daltonism, or red–green confusion, as is poignantly attested in the pastel *Fishing Boat* (Paris, Louvre).

The Revolution of 1848 stimulated only verbal plans for an allegorical painting, but an elaborately finished, if somewhat conventional, monochrome cartoon for the *Assassination of Marion Dufrêsne in 1772* (Wellington, NZ, Turnbull Lib.) was exhibited at the Salon of 1848. In the same year Meryon encountered Eugène Bléry, with whom he resided temporarily, and studied etching (1849–50). He began by copying prints by Philippe Jacques de Loutherbourg, Salvator Rosa, Karel Dujardin, Adriaen van de Velde and, most enthusiastically, eight by Reinier Nooms, the Dutch sailor–artist whom he venerated as 'another self' and whose Paris views clearly prompted his own series, *Etchings of Paris*. The first great original print of this series, the haunting *Petit Pont* (1850), was shown at the Salon of that year and was followed by the spectacular sequence of master prints on which his consistent reputation as a major etcher rests: the *Clock Tower Turret, Rue de la Tixéranderies, Saint-Etienne-du-Mont* and the *Notre-Dame Pump* (1852), *The Chimera*, the *Arch of the Pont Notre-Dame*, the *Notre-Dame Gallery* and *The Pont-Neuf* (1853), and, climactically, the *Rue des Mauvais-Garçons*, *The Morgue* and the *Apse of Notre-Dame* (1854; see fig.). A projected suite devoted to the early architecture of Bourges was not realized, but three subjects, most importantly the compelling *Rue des Toiles at Bourges* (1853), preceded by the extremely rare *Gate of an Old Convent* (1851), were produced. Prior to the commercially published editions, principally for the *Artiste*, most subjects were proofed through numerous states by the artist himself, who was unprecedentedly sensitive to the effect of printing variation in wiping, ink tint and paper tone and texture, and inscribed presentation impressions of great brilliance and subtlety exist. From the outset a few enthusiasts realized that for all the precise clarity and ostensible objectivity of his views of the old buildings of Paris, the plates project a mysterious aura and a dream-like, somewhat sinister atmosphere.

Charles Meryon: *Apse of Notre-Dame*, etching, 4th state, 160×300 mm, 1854 (London, British Museum)

From 1855 Meryon's physical and mental health deteriorated and the concentration of his incisive style and geometrically crisp composition weakened, although he began to receive increasing recognition—select, but important—from Baudelaire, Gautier, Hugo, Mantz, Bürger and Burty. His precarious and inadequate livelihood became based on reproductive hack-work, book titles and illustrations, many portraits and ephemera, although the privately commissioned panoramic views of San Francisco of 1856 (based on photographs) is more ambitious. The connoisseur Duc d'Arenberg invited him to Enghien to work, but the visit from the summer of 1857 to March 1858 was unproductive. Beset by melancholia and bizarre and complex delusions, Meryon was confined to the asylum at Charenton from 12 May 1858 to 25 August 1859.

When he resumed printmaking, Meryon reworked and modified in hallucinatory manner the earlier Paris views and elaborated several new subjects, but both conception and execution had deteriorated in intensity and images of arcane and more obvious allegory intrude on the architectural compositions. Always apprehensive of drawing publicly from life, Meryon appended reproductive etchings from Paris drawings by earlier artists to the initial group, and a sequence of his youthful drawings made in Oceania was etched, together with a frontispiece, between 1860 and 1866 in a loose and more casually diffuse manner. Friends and admirers attempted to obtain sales and minor commissions for Meryon. The *Ministère de la Marine* (1865), the sky replete with Polynesian and marine phantasmagoria, was published by the Société des Aquafortistes in 1866. In the same year his sole plate for the Louvre Chalcographie, the *Old Louvre*, after a painting by Reinier Nooms, was finished.

Although Meryon was represented in the Salon from 1863 to 1866, serious paranoid delusions, semi-starvation and religious mania necessitated re-admission to Charenton on 12 October 1866. He died there insane in February 1868 and was buried in Père Lachaise Cemetery in Paris, with a copper tomb plaque by Félix Bracquemond, who had etched the two most important portraits of the artist.

BIBLIOGRAPHY
P. Burty: 'L'Oeuvre de Charles Meryon', *Gaz. B.-A.*, xiv (1863), pp. 519–33; xv (1863), pp. 75–88; Eng. trans. as *Charles Méryon, Sailor, Engraver and Etcher: A Memoir* (London, 1879)
A. Bouvenne: *Notes et souvenirs sur Charles Meryon* (Paris, 1883)
L. Delteil and H. J. L. Wright: *A Catalogue Raisonné of the Etchings of Charles Meryon* (New York, 1924, rev. with addenda and errata, London, 1925)
G. Geffroy: *Charles Meryon* (Paris, 1926)
Charles Meryon: Officier de marine, peintre-graveur, 1821–1868 (exh. cat. by J. Ducros, Paris, Mus. Mar., 1968)
R. D. J. Collins: *Charles Meryon: A Bibliography* (Dunedin, 1986)

HARLEY PRESTON

Merz (i). Term applied to a flat or relief collage of collected junk. It is associated with KURT SCHWITTERS, who apparently invented the word when cutting out the word 'Commerzbank' from a newspaper for a collage he was making. *Merz* is also the title of a Dada magazine that he edited from 1923.

□

Merz (ii). Italian artists. (1) Mario Merz and his wife, (2) Marisa Merz met while studying in Turin in the 1950s. Both are associated with the development of Arte povera, and at times they collaborated on works.

(1) Mario Merz (*b* Milan, 1 Jan 1925). Sculptor and painter. He began work as a painter in Turin during the 1950s in the then dominant style of *Art informel*. Analysing, on a macroscopic scale, certain natural phenomena such as the leaves of plants, he aimed to expose their essential structure and in so doing created paintings containing spirals and parabolic lines within a 'picturesque' network, for example *Seed in the Wind* (1953; priv. col., see 1983 exh. cat., p. 27). He also addressed himself to the human image, as in *The Welder* (1956; Turin, Gal. Civ. A. Mod.). After experiencing a crisis in his work during the early 1960s, from 1966 (probably under the influence of Neo Dada and Nouveau Réalisme) Merz rejected the reproduction of images by means of paint on canvas, replacing such traditional methods with the direct use of objects such as bottles or raincoats. Merz did not content himself, however, with the mere presentation of ready-made objects; it was not that he turned his back on the informal, organic inspiration of his work, but that he now entrusted it to a medium derived from the technical world, from human intervention. In works such as *Pierced Glass, Pierced Bottle* (1967; priv. col., see 1983 exh. cat., p. 40) this took the form of the neon tube, which acts as a shaft of cosmic, yet 'cold' and concentrated energy, that penetrates objects and prevents them from becoming enclosed in static isolation. NEON had already been used by other artists including Dan Flavin, but in ways still linked to the old Constructivist ideal. Merz's ideas were closer to those of Bruce Nauman, who also used neon in an organic way, as though it were a capillary vein, a thin irrigation canal.

With the emergence of ARTE POVERA in Turin in 1967–8, closely paralleled in other parts of the world by movements such as process art, land art and conceptual art, Merz rejected the use of ready-made objects and began to make his own objects, which would be better suited to his needs. A typical example of this was his use of the igloo (for illustration *see* ARTE POVERA), a primary unit of 'poor' dwelling with roots in man's origins, but full of tensions and with the same curvilinear quality possessed by electric energy. One of the first of these, *Giap's Igloo* (1.2×2.0×2.0 m, 1968; Paris, Pompidou), consists of an iron armature covered in plastic bags filled with dirt; on top of this is a quotation in Italian from General Giap, spelt out in neon letters in a spiralling form: 'Se il nemico si concentra perde terreno, se si disperde perde forza' (If the enemy masses his forces he loses ground, if he scatters he loses strength). Echoing ideas already proposed in the writings of Marshall McLuhan, for example concerning the notion of a 'global village', he suggested that the future of electronic progress lay in the revival of primeval nomadic civilizations and their implements. An ambiguous suspension between past and future was proposed by Merz in his juxtaposition of 'poor' materials, such as earth, sticks and wax, with materials suggestive of modern progress and sophistication, such as neon or glass panels.

In 1969 and 1970 Merz made his most important discovery, a sort of cosmic law extrapolated from the numerous natural phenomena he had thus far examined. In works such as *Crocodilus Fibonacci* (1972; Paris, Pompidou) he made particular reference to the Fibonacci sequence, named after the 13th-century Italian mathematician Leonardo Fibonacci, which consists of an infinite succession of numbers, each calculated as the sum of the two preceding ones. When graphically interpreted, it results in elliptical or parabolic schemes that in effect regulate a large number of organic schemes in vegetable and animal life, such as the spiral arrangements of certain petals or branches. It could be said that in basing works

on this principle Merz arrived at a conceptual or 'dematerialized' art, in which the mental element (the phrase, the number) counts for more than its physical support. Even though in reality there is always an opportune correlation between these two aspects in Merz's work, the role accorded to the concept of the Fibonacci sequence prevents the physical data from imposing a picturesque element, as it had in *Art informel*; on the other hand, the physical element gives a solidity and bite to the excessive abstraction of the pure concept.

During the early 1970s Merz gave pride of place to the concept, with the physical elements appearing solely in an exemplary role. In this way he demonstrated that the Fibonacci sequence is capable of explaining, with no distinction, the structure of the scales on a crocodile, the branches on a tree, the curvature of the Mole Antonelliana (a late 19th-century high-domed building in Turin, originally designed as a synagogue by Alessandro Antonelli), or the rhythm at which people enter a room. Such phenomena represent a thin veil, beneath which the relentless flow of a mathematical principle (brought into prominence by neon tubes in the shape of numbers) is immediately perceptible. In the 1980s Merz demonstrated a renewed interest in colour, image and manual values, through which he relaunched aspects of the picturesque that he had favoured at the beginning of his career, now enlivened by more abstract conceptual schemes and by the continued use of neon.

BIBLIOGRAPHY

Mario Merz (exh. cat., London, Whitechapel A.G., 1980)
Mario Merz (exh. cat., Paris, Mus. A. Mod. Ville Paris, 1981)
Mario Merz (exh. cat. by G. Celant, San Marino, Pal. Congressi, 1983)
Mario Merz (exh. cat. by D. Zacharopoulos and M. Grüterich, Zurich, Ksthaus, 1985)
Mario Merz (exh. cat. by G. Celant, New York, Guggenheim, 1989)

For further bibliography *see* ARTE POVERA and NEON.

RENATO BARILLI

(2) Marisa Merz (*b* Turin, 1931). Sculptor, wife of (1) Mario Merz. She made a folded aluminium foil installation for her first one-person show (1967; Turin, Gal. Sperone), and she was included in the important *Arte Povera + Azione Povera* exhibition (1968; Amalfi, Arsenale). The importance of her baby daughter Bea was evident in such pieces as the suspended plane of *Bea's Swing* (priv. col., see 1994 exh. cat., p. 24) and in Merz's characteristic open-work structures made of knitted copper wire. Their process related to a view of the historical condition of women, while their formal effect hovered between the current polarities of geometry and automatism. A second one-person show (1970; Rome, Gal. Attico) included knitted-copper elements in an installation, entitled *Ad occhi chiusi gli occhi sono straordinariamente aperti* ('To closed eyes, the eyes are extraordinarily open'; see 1994 exh. cat., p. 48). She exhibited rarely in the 1970s, although she collaborated with her husband and continued to make pieces in copper, waxed paper and paraffin wax, which reflected her home environment. In the 1980s these emerged in site-specific installations, in which amorphous and coloured wax heads became new components at the Venice Biennale of 1988.

BIBLIOGRAPHY

Marisa Merz: Bilderstreit, Widerspruch, Einheit, und Fragment in der Kunst seit 1960 (exh. cat. by C. Meyer-Thoss, Cologne, Rheinhallen Köln. Messe, 1989)

Marisa Merz (exh. cat. by G. Celant, R. Fuchs and C. Grenier, Paris, Pompidou, 1994)

MATTHEW GALE

Mesa, Juan de (*b* Córdoba, *bapt* 26 June 1583; *d* Seville, 26 Nov 1627). Spanish sculptor. He was one of the most forceful personalities to emerge among 17th-century Spanish sculptors of carved and painted statues. He specialized in processional images and was Seville's leading interpreter of the popular concept of the life of Christ depicted in the most profound and tragic moments of the Passion. In 1606 Mesa joined the workshop of Juan Martínez Montañés in Seville as an *oficial*, remaining there for four years. His first commission, contracted in 1615, is untraced. At his death, 12 years later, he left a complete series of processional images that are associated with the Seville Holy Week ceremonies.

Mesa's style was characteristic of the Counter-Reformation, and his skill lay in bringing a degree of naturalism to the classicism in which he was trained. His studies from life included drawing corpses and the dying in order to achieve authenticity in the anatomy and in the expressions of his crucified and recumbent figures of Christ. He was also able to capture the required sense of divinity, the primary aim of all Spanish holy images, so as to arouse devotion among the faithful. The polished and brilliant execution of his figures, which were immediately comprehensible, together with their strong emotional force, led to his becoming the image maker most sought after by the confraternities of Seville. His charges were low, and at his own expense he created the standard processional models of the Crucified Christ, Christ the Nazarene, and the Pietà, which the Church and other artists of Seville adopted, creating types that are still reproduced. His representations of Christ are distinguished by highly realistic details, such as thorns piercing the lobe of the ear and the brow of the Crucified Christ and Christ the Nazarene and the deformation and calluses of the feet.

The series of images of the Crucified Christ by Mesa began with the '*Crucifix of Love*' (Seville, El Salvador), commissioned in 1618 by the Sevillian Cofradía del Amor and completed in 1620. Also in 1620 he completed his processional '*Christ of the Conversion of the Good Thief*' (Seville, Montserrat Chapel) for the Sevillian confraternity of the Buen Ladrón. In the same year he carved the '*Christ of the Good Death*' for the Jesuit Casa Profesa of Seville (U. Seville, Chapel; see fig.). The impact of this work led to its adoption as a model by Mesa's contemporaries, and when in 1621 he was commissioned to execute the '*Crucifixion of the Good Death*' (Madrid Cathedral) the condition was made that it should be like the one that he had made for the Jesuits of the Casa Profesa in Seville. Mesa continued to create new iconographical types. The most personal and most poignant of Mesa's images is his larger-than-life *Christ in Agony* (1622; Vergara, Guipúzcoa, S Pedro), commissioned by the Basque Juan Pérez de Irazábal, which is still deeply revered. Mesa also worked for the South American market, and in 1624 the Jesuit Nicolás de Villanueva embarked for Lima with a *Crucified Christ* intended for the Jesuit college there (*in situ*).

In 1620 Mesa undertook his most celebrated devotional image, the powerful *Christ the Almighty* (Seville, Basilica

Juan de Mesa: *Christ of the Good Death* (detail), wood, h. 1.76 m, 1620 (Universidad de Sevilla, Chapel)

del Grand Poder), a figure designed to be dressed in a tunic, in which, bearing the cross on his shoulder, Christ is depicted in the act of striding forwards. Mesa also carved figures of saints and of the Virgin; his last work before his death was the *Mater dolorosa* (Córdoba, S Pablo) for the confraternity of the Angustias of Córdoba. This was also an image designed to be dressed, and it shows the Virgin holding in her arms the recumbent figure of Christ.

BIBLIOGRAPHY

J. Hernández Díaz: *Juan de Mesa* (Seville, 1972, 2/1983)
J. M. Palomero Páramo: *La imaginería procesional sevillana: Misterios, nazarenos y cristos* (Seville, 1981, 2/1987)

JESÚS M. PALOMERO PÁRAMO

Mesara. Region in southern central Crete that flourished in the Bronze Age. One of the most fertile parts of Crete, this flat alluvial plain is about 50 km east–west, but never more than 10 km north–south, and it is surrounded on the north, east and south by foothills and mountains. It was in and around the Mesara plain in the Early Bronze Age (for discussion of Bronze Age absolute dates *see* MINOAN, §I, 4) that a distinctive culture developed, characterized by small village communities, perhaps composed of extended family groups, who buried their dead in circular communal tombs known as the Mesara type. The wealth of attractively painted pottery, finely carved sealstones and stone bowls, well-made bronze weapons and gold jewellery from these tombs suggest that the Mesara was a prosperous area and that its people were inventive and skilled. Early in the 2nd millennium BC the whole area was presumably dominated by the Minoan palace at PHAISTOS, and much later a major Greco-Roman city was built near by at GORTYN, which flourished until AD 670.

BIBLIOGRAPHY
S. Xanthoudides: *The Vaulted Tombs of Mesará* (Liverpool, 1924)
K. Branigan: *The Tombs of Mesara* (London, 1970)

KEITH BRANIGAN

Mesastris, Pierantonio. *See* MEZZASTRIS, PIERANTONIO.

Mesa Verde. Archaeological zone of Pre-Columbian sites in the USA, in south-west Colorado, the heartland of the Anasazi culture. Deep, steep-sided canyons here were formed by streams cutting into the plateau (mesa: 'table-shaped hill'). Between *c.* 200 BC and *c.* AD 1350 some 800 sites were established and abandoned on Wetherill Mesa and over 1000 on Chapin Mesa. The earliest sites comprised groups of pit houses with central entrances in the roofs. By *c.* AD 700 these were being replaced by surface dwellings of apartment-like blocks of adobe or stone construction, while many pit houses were retained as *kivas* (ceremonial rooms for men; *see* KIVA). Society was matrilineal, and the houses were owned by women. Between *c.* 950 and *c.* 1150, conflict increased between groups, and mesa-top sites were abandoned for defensible dwellings built on shelves beneath overhanging cliffs in the canyons. These blocks of multi-storey, terraced apartment-like structures of adobe bricks and stone blocks include those named Cliff Palace (see fig.), Cedar Tree Tower, Spruce Tree House, Sun Temple and Balcony House. The earliest rooms often became storage rooms as later dwellings were built above and in front of them. Wooden ladders gave access between terraces; floors between storeys were made with log rafters. Walls had key-hole and trapezoidal doorways and in some cases square windows. Open spaces in front were levelled as ceremonial areas, and circular, semi-subterranean *kivas* were dug out. Cliff Palace (99 m wide×30 m deep) had over 200 rooms and 23 *kivas*, an unusually high number per apartment; it may have served as a central town for the entire mesa. Crop failure and possibly invasion by Navajo and Apache groups may have caused the abandonment of the cliff-dwellings by *c.* 1350.

For further discussion of the indigenous arts and architecture of the Southwest region of the USA *see* NATIVE NORTH AMERICAN ART.

BIBLIOGRAPHY
P. S. Martin and F. Plog: *The Archaeology of Arizona: A Study of the Southwest Region* (New York, 1973)

Mesa Verde, view of Cliff Palace site, occupied *c.* AD 950–1350

H. W. Mesdag: *Return of the Lifeboat*, oil on canvas, 0.95×1.56 m, 1876 (Rotterdam, Museum Boymans-van Beuningen)

A. Ortiz, ed.: *Southwest*, Hb. N. Amer. Ind., ix (1979); x (1983) [whole vols]

L. S. Cordell: *Prehistory of the Southwest* (New York, 1984)

——: 'Southwest Archaeology', *Annu. Rev. Anthropol.*, xiii (1984), pp. 301–32

M. Coe, D. Snow and E. Benson: *Atlas of Ancient America* (Oxford, 1986), pp. 68–79

DAVID M. JONES

Mesdag, H(endrik) W(illem) (*b* Groningen, 23 Feb 1831; *d* The Hague, 10 July 1915). Dutch painter and collector. As a child and while he worked as a clerk in his father's bank, he took lessons in drawing and painting, first with C. B. Buijs (1808–72) and later with J. H. Egenberger (1822–97), Director of the Academie Minerva in Groningen. It was not until 1866 that Mesdag made painting his profession. That summer he and his wife, Sientje van Houten (1834–1909), worked *en plein air* near Oosterbeek with the landscape painter J. W. Bilders (1811–90). From the autumn of 1866 to 1869 they lived in Brussels, where Mesdag trained with Willem Roelofs, the first Dutch artist to pay regular visits to Barbizon, and where he came into contact with young Belgian Realist painters, such as Alfred Verwée, Louis Artan and Louis Dubois. In this period Mesdag learnt to render his impressions from nature accurately and directly.

In the summer of 1868 Mesdag discovered the theme that was to remain his major source of inspiration: the sea. In May 1869 he moved to The Hague, where many artists were then gathered and where he could conveniently study the sea at Scheveningen. At the Salon of 1870 in Paris, Mesdag was awarded a gold medal for *Breakers in the North Sea* (Wassenaar, Mesdag Doc. Found.), which brought him international fame. The Belgian critic Camille

Lemonnier was among the first to praise Mesdag's paintings, impressed by their truthfulness to life. The marine pictures that Mesdag painted between 1870 and 1890 (e.g. *Return of the Lifeboat*, 1876; Rotterdam, Mus. Boymans-van Beuningen; see fig.), based on his detailed studies of Scheveningen, became increasingly direct. *Scheveningen Fishing Boats at Sea* (Groningen, Groninger Mus.) shows the recurring motif of a group of boats on the open sea with their numbers clearly discernible on the sails. Virtually identical subjects and compositions appear in Mesdag's sketchbooks dating from the 1880s (The Hague, Rijksdienst Beeld. Kst). Several of the smaller canvases appear to have been painted directly from nature, for example the freely painted canvas *Waves Battering a Lighthouse* (Amsterdam, Rijksmus.).

In 1881, over a period of four months, Mesdag painted his most important work: a panorama of 120×14 m of the view from the Seinpostduin ('Signal box dune') in Scheveningen. Similar in style to his marine panels, the *Panorama Mesdag* was painted in the Zeestraat in The Hague, where it is still housed (*see* THE HAGUE, fig. 4). Mesdag was helped not only by his wife, but also by B. J. Blommers, Théophile de Bock and G. H. Breitner. In rendering and mood Mesdag's work is similar to that of other HAGUE SCHOOL painters, such as Jacob Maris and Jan Hendrik Weissenbruch, although his paintings were mostly of lesser quality. After 1885 Mesdag lapsed into repetition of the same theme in a consistent style.

Mesdag was an active participant in The Hague's artistic life. From 1874 to 1892 he was chairman of the Pulchri Studio painting society, and as such he may be regarded as a key figure of the Hague school. Mesdag was one of the first governors, together with Willem Maris and Anton Mauve, of the Hollandsche Teeken-Maatschappij ('Dutch drawing society'), founded in The Hague in 1876 to promote drawing as an independent medium.

Mesdag's collection of contemporary French and Dutch pictures included a large number of works by the Barbizon painters: for example, Charles-François Daubigny's *Villerville-sur-mer* (1872; The Hague, Rijksmus. Mesdag). For many Dutch artists the collection provided their first major exposure to this movement. In 1903 Mesdag gave the Dutch nation his collection and house in The Hague, subsequently opened as the Rijksmuseum Hendrik Willem Mesdag.

BIBLIOGRAPHY

A. C. Croiset van der Kop: 'Hendrik Willem Mesdag', *Elsevier's Geïllus. Mdschr.*, i (1891), pp. 429–44
P. Zilcken: *Verzameling 'H. W. Mesdag'* (Amsterdam, 1895)
E. van Schendel: *Museum Mesdag* (The Hague, 1975)
S. de Bodt: 'Hendrik Willem Mesdag en Brussel', *Oud-Holland*, xcv (1981), pp. 59–87
S. de Bodt and M. van Delft: 'Het Panorama Mesdag', *Antiek*, xvi (1981), pp. 145–57
J. Poort: *Hendrik Willem Mesdag: 'Artiste peintre à La Haye'* (Wassenaar, 1981)
The Hague School: Dutch Masters of the Nineteenth Century (exh. cat., ed. R. de Leeuw, J. Sillevis and C. Dumas; Paris, Grand Pal.; London, RA; The Hague, Gemeentemus.; 1983), pp. 256–61
J. M. Eikelenboom: 'De schilder H. W. Mesdag en zijn verzameling Franse schilderijen' [The painter H. W. Mesdag and his collection of French paintings], *Tableau*, vi/4 (1984), pp. 60–68
S. de Bodt: 'Schetsboeken van H. W. Mesdag', *Jong Holland*, i (1985), pp. 36–45
J. Poort: *Hendrik Willem Mesdag: Oeuvrecatalogus* (Wassenaar, 1989)
——: *H. W. Mesdag: Life and Work* (Wassenaar, 1992)
——: *H. W. Mesdag (1831–1915): Schetsboek 3* (Wassenaar, 1995)
——: *De schetsen van H. W. Mesdag en S. M. Houten* (Wassenaar,1996)
——: *De brieven van H. W. Mesdag* (in preparation)

SASKIA DE BODT

Mesembria. *See* NESEBĂR.

Mesens, E(douard-)L(éon-)T(héodore) (*b* Brussels, 27 Nov 1903; *d* Brussels, 13 May 1971). Belgian writer, exhibition organizer, collagist and composer. As a young composer he was influenced by Erik Satie. He collaborated on Dadaist-inspired journals and published, with René Magritte, *Œsophage* (1925), the only issue of which, containing the poems of Hans Arp, Tristan Tzara and Georges Ribemont-Dessaignes, remained faithful to the Dada spirit. In 1926 *Marie*, a 'journal bi-mensuel pour la belle jeunesse', published under his direction, pursued the same vein; it only had two issues. Mesens was involved in the establishment of a Surrealist movement (*see* SURREALISM), which was strongly permeated with Dadaism in Belgium. In 1927 he became Director of the Galerie L'Epoque and in 1931 of the Galerie Mesens, both in Brussels. Miró, Magritte and Max Ernst all exhibited with him. He founded the Editions Nicolas Flamel, which published the Surrealists' collective homage to a parricide, *Violette Nozières* (Brussels, 1933), André Breton's lecture 'Qu'est-ce que le surréalisme', held on the occasion of the first international Surrealist exhibition organized in Brussels by Mesens under the auspices of *Minotaure*, and a special issue, 'Intervention surréaliste', of the journal *Documents 34*. His *Alphabet sourd aveugle* (Brussels, 1933), made up of 26 poems, in which all the words of each poem begin with the same letter of the alphabet, experimented with sense and language. He went to London during World War II, where he had organized the International Surrealist Exhibition at the New Burlington Galleries (1936), and established and ran the London Gallery. He also published the *London Gallery Bulletin* (later the *London Bulletin*; 20 issues, 1938–42) and initiated the exhibitions *Surrealism Today* (London, Zwemmer Gal., 1940) and *Surrealism Diversity* (London, Arcade Gal., 1945). Having also worked as an announcer of French broadcasts for the BBC he returned to Belgium after the War and devoted himself to poetry and to making collages, such as *Cult Object* (1961; see Pierre, p. 278).

WRITINGS
Poèmes 1923–1958 (Paris, 1959)

BIBLIOGRAPHY
J. Vovelle: *Le Surréalisme en Belgique* (Brussels, 1965)
S. Otlet-Moutoy: 'Les Etapes de l'activité créatrice chez E. L. T. Mesens et l'esprit du collage comme aboutissement d'une pensée', *Mus. Royaux B.-A. Belgique: Bull.* (1973)
M. Marien: *L'Activité surréaliste en Belgique* (Brussels, 1979)
J. Pierre: *L'Univers surréaliste* (Paris, 1983)

For further bibliography *see* SURREALISM.

HENRI BÉHAR

Meshal ha-Kadmoni [Heb.: 'The fable of the ancients']. Collection of Jewish fables and tales completed in 1281. It was the greatest work of the poet, cabbalist and physician Isaac ben Solomon ibn Sahula (*b* 1244), who studied in Burgos and lived in Guadalajara (Castile). He wrote in Hebrew and drew his inspiration from Jewish culture, conceiving his work as a substitute for the Hebrew translations of *Kalilah and Dimnah* (a collection of fables of Indian origin; transmitted via the Arabic *c.* AD 750) and the *Voyages of Sindbad the Sailor*. The protagonists are both animal and human, and each fable or tale is preceded by an illustration, with a caption written by the author identifying the figures and explaining the action. The original illustrations included five astronomical diagrams and *c.* 76 images with figures.

The earliest extant manuscripts of the book date from the mid-15th century. All five surviving manuscripts come from Ashkenazi circles in southern Germany (1450, Oxford, Bodleian Lib., MS. Opp. 154; *c.* 1450, Munich, Bayer., Staatsbib., fols 1*r*–94*v*) or northern Italy (1450–70, Oxford, Bodleian Lib., MS. Can. Or. 59; 1460–70, Jerusalem, Israel Mus. MS. 180/51, fols 298*v*–371*r*; 1483, Milan, Bib. Ambrosiana, MS. X. 112. Sup.). The *editio princeps* of the *Meshal ha-Kadmoni* was also printed in northern Italy, in Brescia, in 1490–91 by Gershom Soncino (*see* SONCINO) and was illustrated with a cycle of engravings, the scheme and style of which can be related to none of the illuminated cycles but which show some affinity with Manfredus de Bonellis's Aesop's *Fables* printed in 1481 in Venice. The second edition, also printed by Gershom Soncino, is believed to date from 1496–7. The second edition used the same woodcuts as the first, but, because it had a more compact layout, it was possible to reduce the original 86 folios to only 66. Meïr Parenzo published another edition of the *Meshal c.* 1547–50 in Venice. It used a completely new series of woodcuts, consistent neither in style nor in quality, the best of which are notable for their beautiful animals and the elegant Mannerist outlines of their human figures, much finer than in Soncino's editions. The second Venetian edition was printed by Di Gara in 1610. In 1693 the first German and Yiddish editions were published in Frankfurt an der Oder, both illustrated with a complete cycle of woodcuts, all new. No new images have been created in modern times for this enduringly attractive text; the 1953 Israeli edition reproduces the pictures from the first Venetian edition. A facsimile of the *editio princeps* was published in 1977.

BIBLIOGRAPHY

Enc. Jud.: 'Sahula, Isaac ben Salomon Abi'

M. L. Gengaro, F. Leoni and G. Villa: *Codici decorati e miniati dell' Ambrosiana, ebraici e greci*, Fontes Ambrosiana, xxxiii–A (Milan, 1958), pt. 1, pp. 47–50 and pls XXXI–XLVIII [MS. X. 112. Sup.]

H. M. Z. Meyer: 'Incunabula', *Encyclopaedia Judaica*, viii (Jerusalem, 1972), columns 1319–44

A. M. Haberman: *Izhaq ben Shlomo ibn Sahula Meshal ha-qadmoni [Isaac ben Solomon ibn Sahula's Meshal ha-qadmoni]: Facsimile of the First Edition: Brescia, 1490–1* (Jerusalem, 1977), intro., pp. 5–12 [in Heb.]

H. Striedl: 'Hebräische Literatur', *Das Buch im Orient, Handschriften und kostbare Drucke aus zwei Jahrtausenden* (exh. cat., eds. K. Dachs and E. Klemm; Munich, Bayer. Staatsbib., 1982), pp. 31–66 [60(one reprod. with incorrect caption)–61], no. 20 [Cod. hebr. 107]

B. Narkiss and G. Sed-Rajna: *The Rothschild Miscellany, Jerusalem, Israel Museum, MS. 180/51*, Index of Jewish Art (Jerusalem, 1983), cards 88–176 [original Heb. captions and Eng. trans.]

U. Bauer-Eberhardt: 'Die Rothschild-Miscellanea in Jerusalem; Hauptwerk des Leonardo Bellini', *Pantheon*, xlii (1984), pp. 229–37 [on Jerusalem, Israel Mus., MS. 180/51 illuminator]

The Rothschild Miscellany (London, 1989), fols 298*v*–369*r* [facs. edn]

T. Metzger: 'The Iconography of the Hebrew Psalter from the Thirteenth to the Fifteenth Century', *The Visual Dimension: Aspects of Jewish Art* (Boulder, San Francisco and Oxford, 1993) pp. 47–81 [77, n. 41, on Jerusalem, Israel Mus., MS. 180/51 style and illuminator]

THÉRÈSE METZGER, MENDEL METZGER

Meshed. *See* MASHHAD.

Mesius, Quintinus. *See* METSYS, (1).

Mesken [Meskene]. *See* MASKANA.

Mesmakher [Messmacher], **Maksimilian (Yegorovich)** (*b* St Petersburg, 1 April 1842; *d* Dresden, 1 Sept 1906). Russian architect of German descent. He studied at the St Petersburg Academy of Arts and made a detailed study of Old Russian architecture. He also carried out excavations (with V. Kossov) at the Roman theatre in Taormina, Sicily. From the 1870s onwards he proved himself to be an outstanding draughtsman, his best-known works being his so-called Italian and Spanish series of architectural watercolours (St Petersburg, Hermitage). He took part in restoring several St Petersburg interiors, including those of the Stroganov Palace and of the palace of Grand Duke Vladimir Aleksandrovich (1847–1909) on Palace Embankment, among others, and he also worked for Alexander III (*reg* 1881–94) at the Anichkov Palace, St Petersburg, and at Massandr (Crimea). He used wood in the decoration of interiors, which distinguished him from other architects of the time, and he gave the interiors an unusually sumptuous appearance by using expensive materials, as in the bronze hall at the residence of A. Polovtsev on Bolshaya Morskaya Street (1892). Mesmakher's palace (1882–5) for Grand Duke Aleksey Aleksandrovich (1850–1908) on the Moyka River Embankment is built on an irregular plan, with structures of different heights, and is set in an English garden. The rooms are decorated in various styles, using painting, stucco, marble and maiolica: the Flemish Room, for example, is in 17th-century Dutch

style. The latest technology (gas, plumbing, sewerage) was used in the construction of the palace of Grand Duke Mikhail Mikhaylovich (1861–1929) on Admiralty Embankment (end of 1880s–1900). In 1885–95 Mesmakher designed and supervised the construction of the museum attached to the Baron Stieglitz School of Technical Drawing, of which he had been principal from 1879. He retired to Dresden in 1896.

BIBLIOGRAPHY

T. Ye. Tyzhnenko: *Maksimilian Mesmakher* (Leningrad, 1984)

SERGEY KUZNETSOV

Mesoamerica, Pre-Columbian. Term used to designate the Pre-Columbian region comprising present-day central and central-southern Mexico, the Yucatán Peninsula, Guatemala, Belize and El Salvador, and parts of Honduras, Nicaragua and Costa Rica. Culturally it was one of two New World areas where civilization developed (the other being the central Andes, home of the Incas; *see* SOUTH AMERICA, PRE-COLUMBIAN, §III). In Mesoamerica a set of technological, social, economic, religious and political traits was shared by several different cultures, including the AZTEC, HUASTEC, MAYA, MIXTEC, TARASCAN, TEOTIHUACÁN, TOLTEC, Totonac, West Mexican and ZAPOTEC. This set of cultural traits is recognizable as early as 1500 BC and continued, with additions, up to the Spanish Conquest in 1519. There was considerable regional diversity in details—some linger even today—but the presence of this elaborate cultural pattern set Mesoamerica apart from its neighbours to the north and south.

The northern boundary of Mesoamerica corresponded approximately to the northern limit of sufficient rainfall for reliable agriculture, and this was always the most clearly defined of its frontiers (see fig. 1). Thus excluded was the northern third of Mexico, which was more strongly tied culturally to the south-western USA. Mesoamericans who lived near the northern frontier looked down on those who lived outside it and characterized them as uncivilized; these peoples, known as the Chichimecs, were primarily hunter-gatherers, although during a few periods of increased rainfall they did practise farming. The southern boundary had no such distinct environmental feature and undoubtedly varied over time. The peoples who lived beyond it followed a settled agricultural way of life generally similar to that of Mesoamerica. Nevertheless, Mesoamerican cultural patterns, with large cities and distinctive art and architectural styles, were not present south and east throughout Central America. (The southern boundary is placed in a conservative position on the map in fig. 1, including only westernmost Honduras and a very small part of Nicaragua; some scholars are more inclusive, incorporating almost all of Honduras and about half of Nicaragua into Mesoamerica.)

BIBLIOGRAPHY

M. D. Coe: *Mexico* (London, 1962, rev. 3/1984)

R. Wauchope, ed.: *Handbook of Middle American Indians*, 11 vols (Austin, 1964–71)

M. D. Coe: *The Maya* (London, 1966, rev. 4/1987)

W. T. Sanders and B. J. Price: *Mesoamerica: The Evolution of a Civilization* (New York, 1968)

M. Porter-Weaver: *The Aztecs, Maya and their Predecessors: Archaeology of Mesoamerica* (New York, 1972, rev. 2/1981)

R. E. W. Adams: *Prehistoric Mesoamerica* (Boston, 1977)

R. E. Blanton and others: *Ancient Mesoamerica: A Comparison of Change in Three Regions* (Cambridge, 1981)

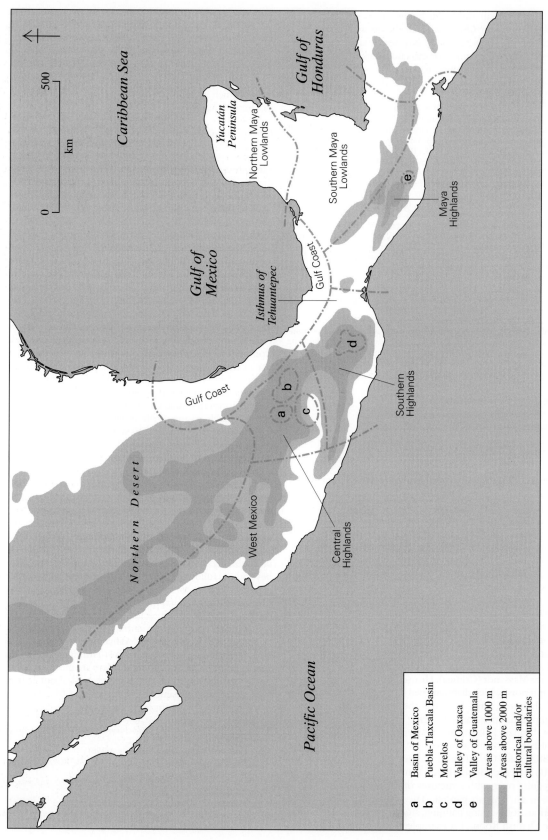

Caribbean Sea

Gulf of Honduras

Yucatán Peninsula

Northern Maya Lowlands

Southern Maya Lowlands

Gulf of Mexico

Maya Highlands

e

Isthmus of Tehuantepec

Gulf Coast

d

Gulf Coast

a b

c

Southern Highlands

Northern Desert

West Mexico

Central Highlands

Pacific Ocean

500

km

0

a	Basin of Mexico
b	Puebla-Tlaxcala Basin
c	Morelos
d	Valley of Oaxaca
e	Valley of Guatemala
	Areas above 1000 m
	Areas above 2000 m
–··–··–	Historical and/or cultural boundaries

1. Map of Mesoamerica; those areas with separate entries in this dictionary are distinguished by CROSS-REFERENCE TYPE

V. R. Bricker, ed.: *Supplement to the Handbook of Middle American Indians*, 4 vols (Austin, 1981–6)

I. Introduction. II. Chronology and cultural traditions. III. Architecture. IV. Monumental stone sculpture. V. Wall painting. VI. Manuscripts. VII. Pottery and clay sculpture. VIII. Lapidary arts. IX. Other arts. X. Rediscovery and collecting.

DETAILED TABLE OF CONTENTS

I. Introduction.

1. Geography and climate. 2. Ethnic and language groups. 3. Resources, trade and economy. 4. Religion and iconography. 5. Craftspeople, artists and their patrons.

1. GEOGRAPHY AND CLIMATE. Mesoamerica's primary geographical subdivision is between highland and lowland zones. These are defined by mountain chains and by more or less humid tropical jungles, grasslands and marshes. The highland zones, c. 1000 to over 5000 m above sea-level, comprise parts of West Mexico; the Central and the Southern Highlands, including central and southern Mexico west of the Isthmus of Tehuantepec; and the Maya Highlands of south-eastern Mexico and Guatemala. The lowland zones comprise the peripheries of the highlands: the narrow Pacific coastal strip, the Gulf Coast tropical lowlands and the Maya Lowlands of northern Yucatán. Within these zones there is wide diversity in vegetation and rainfall.

Tropical Mesoamerica includes both warm, wet lowlands and cool, dry highlands. The *tierra caliente* (low hot country below 1000 m in elevation) is level along the coasts, then slopes steeply inland towards the mountains.

As there are no frosts, the growing season is potentially year-round. The *tierra caliente*, most of which lies along the Gulf of Mexico and the Caribbean Sea, is well-watered by rainfall in a band extending eastwards from the coast of the southernmost part of the Gulf of Mexico across Guatemala and Belize to the Caribbean coast. Here the natural vegetation is tropical forest, and massive rivers wind slowly toward the sea through seasonally flooded marshlands. Conditions are much drier further north along the Gulf Coast and especially in the Maya Lowlands of Yucatán.

The *tierra templada* (temperate country between 1000 and 2000 m above sea-level) is subject to winter frosts, although only on the coldest nights, and agriculture is focused on the summer months. Most of the land lying in the *tierra templada* comprises steep slopes, making transport and agriculture difficult. For the last few thousand years, therefore, settlement has been concentrated in mountain valleys that provide level land for farming, including the Valley of Oaxaca, Morelos and other areas in the headwaters of the Río Balsas, the Puebla Basin, the Central Depression of Chiapas and the Valley of Guatemala. But the rainfall shadow effects of surrounding high mountains create water shortages in most of these highland valleys, often posing a serious obstacle to large-scale agricultural production and requiring artificial irrigation. The land has been so intensively exploited for so many centuries that little remains of the original vegetation, though oak and mixed oak and pine forests are common on the steeper slopes, giving way to mesquite, cactus and thorn scrub in the driest areas.

The *tierra fría* (cold country above 2000 m including snow-capped volcanic peaks over 5000 m) has a long season of winter frosts. Land here is also steeply sloped except in a few large mountain valleys, of which the most important is the Basin of Mexico. Permanent occupation in Mesoamerica above 3000 m has always been very limited.

At all altitudes rainfall is seasonal. The rainy season begins in late May or early June, tapers off a little in July or early August and reaches its heaviest in September just before the dry season begins again. The unpredictable nature of the rainfall has made the timing of planting critical in the *tierra templada* and *tierra fría*, where short, heavy downpours, falling erratically, provide some fields with a good water supply while leaving others dry. Much the same sequence characterizes the drier parts of the *tierra caliente*. It is small wonder that maintaining the goodwill of Tlaloc, god of water, loomed so large in Pre-Columbian ritual. The major staple crop was maize, which was domesticated in Mesoamerica by 5000 BC. Several varieties of beans, pumpkins, squashes and chillies provided important nutritional supplements, as did tomatoes, avocadoes and other fruits and vegetables. Especially in warmer, more humid parts of the area, manioc and sweet potatoes were important crops. An important luxury food was chocolate, made from the cacao beans that could only be grown in wet lowland regions. The principal source of fibre for fine cordage and textiles was cotton, which was cultivated extensively in the lower, wetter regions. Maguey, which thrived in the drier highlands, provided tougher fibre for rope, sandals and coarser textiles.

2. ETHNIC AND LANGUAGE GROUPS. Linguistically and culturally the principal division within Mesoamerica falls near the Isthmus of Tehuantepec: to the east was the Maya region, inhabited almost exclusively by speakers of a single language family; to the west there was much greater cultural diversity. This division had developed by at least 500 BC and is roughly still true today. The Pre-Columbian Maya area was characterized by remarkable cultural continuity in the ensuing 20 centuries until the Spanish Conquest, recognizable throughout the Yucatán Peninsula, the tropical forests and highlands of Guatemala and Chiapas, and the hot, rainy Pacific coastal plain. It formed the southern bulwark of Mesoamerican culture. Although it was once fashionable to describe the Maya as peaceful and the peoples of Central Mexico as warlike and bloodthirsty, archaeological and iconographic evidence amply document Maya participation in all of the typical Mesoamerican activities.

Languages spoken west of the Isthmus of Tehuantepec do not belong to the Mayan language family, with the single exception of Huastec, an isolated relative spoken along the northern Gulf Coast. The Totonac and Mixe-Zoque groups dominated the central and southern Gulf Coast, with Mixtec and Zapotec the most widely spoken in the Southern Highlands. Nahuatl, the language of the Aztecs, dominated the Central Highlands, but this probably only dates from the last few centuries before the Spanish Conquest. To the north and west were Otomí, Tarascan and Uto-Aztecan speakers. Literally dozens more languages are known, some defying classification into any of the major families. Linguistically, ethnographically, archaeologically and artistically this non-Maya part of Mesoamerica displayed far less cultural continuity and overall identity. The Pre-Columbian sequence of these regions was one of continued interaction between culturally distinct, often hostile peoples involving considerable long-term movement of populations. While the same was true of the Maya region, it retained a basic linguistic unity.

3. RESOURCES, TRADE AND ECONOMY. Local resources, which differed from region to region, were fully exploited by Mesoamericans throughout the Pre-Columbian period. Those raw materials not available locally were explored for, fought for and transported over long distances from diverse sources. Natural Mesoamerican resources included metals (copper, gold, silver, tin); ores (haematite, ilmenite, magnetite, pyrite), rock and hardstones (amethyst, andasite, basalt, bitumen, chalcedony, chert, cinnabar, jade and jadeite, mica, obsidian, onyx, rock crystal, serpentine, slate, turquoise); and a variety of other materials (amber, cacao, copal resin, colourful feathers, lime, mahogany, mother-of-pearl, pearls, rubber, salt, shells).

Local and long-distance trade of both raw materials and finished works was vital in Pre-Columbian Mesoamerica from at least the 2nd millennium BC. Lacking draught animals and faced with difficult terrain for road-building, Mesoamericans made no use of wheeled vehicles, although small ceramic pieces with wheels were produced. Transport was on human backs, except along the coasts and on lowland rivers where dugout canoes were used, sometimes large enough to hold 20 or 30 people in addition to cargo.

Obsidian, a vitreous volcanic rock that was highly prized and widely traded for its fine cutting edge, has been of incomparable importance as a tool for the study of trade patterns because of its restricted availability and the ease of identifying its point of origin through the chemical fingerprinting of sources. Complicated exchange networks for trading obsidian covered large areas before 1000 BC, but the small quantities of obsidian involved make it impossible to think in terms of an obsidian 'industry' at such an early stage. Moreover, the extent to which most Mesoamericans went to obtain obsidian from multiple sources and often at far greater distances than was necessary suggests that the acquisition of obsidian was a reflection more of extensive networks of relationships between élites of different regions than of the underlying economic rationale of those networks.

By the Classic period (c. AD 250–c. 900) there is more evidence of large-scale production of obsidian for export, for example at Teotihuacán. Artefacts from all over Mesoamerica have been found to have been made of obsidian from distant sources. Scholars disagree as to whether production for export represented a major underpinning factor in the Teotihuacán economy, an exchange of presents on a peripheral basis between distant élites or a combination of these two. Organized markets for the local exchange of food and craft products apparently did not develop until the 1st century AD or later, although craft specialization in the manufacture of goods such as flaked and ground stone tools, pottery and ornamental items existed earlier.

The long-range distribution of precious and elaborately worked craft items has also attracted scholarly attention. For Aztec times immediately preceding the Spanish Conquest, documents such as the *Matrícula de tributos* (Mexico City, Mus. N. Antropol.) record details of tribute received regularly by the Aztec ruler from his various provinces. Tribute from provinces on the frontiers of Mesoamerica consisted largely of luxury goods such as gold, copper, copal incense, turquoise, brightly coloured feathers, richly worked cotton mantles and cacao. Most of these items were not available in or around the Basin of Mexico and could be obtained only by importing them. The large 16th-century population of the Basin of Mexico and its sizeable élite required such goods in substantial amounts. The production of such items in regions with significantly smaller populations could form a major component of the local economy. Aztec rulers obtained such goods not only through tribute but also through the long-distance trading efforts of a professional merchant class, or *pochteca* (Nahuatl), who frequently travelled beyond the imperial frontiers. The acquisition of luxury goods was critical to the maintenance of the Aztec political system since the ruler distributed them to his subordinates, helping to ensure their loyalty and in turn providing them with a means of maintaining their own retinues of subordinates.

Textiles, both fine ones of cotton and coarser ones of maguey, were also imported to the Basin of Mexico from near by and distant regions. These also played a critical role in the Aztec economy because they represented one of the few practical ways—given the limitations of transporting goods overland—that large amounts of human labour could be transferred from one place to another.

Since textile production was labour-intensive and since the product weighed little, it was possible for a human bearer to carry the result of much human labour a substantial distance profitably. Tribute alone brought enough textiles into the Basin of Mexico from outside to provide every man, woman and child there with several garments annually; more textiles arrived as a result of trade. The limitations of transport and the bulkiness of food staples made it impossible to sustain the extremely large population by importing food on a large scale, but the importation of textiles and other laboriously produced craft goods freed human energy from such production and allowed the Aztecs to concentrate on intensive local agriculture.

In addition, within the Basin of Mexico, Aztec rulers collected taxes in labour and goods from the local population. Their households and political activities were also underwritten by the products of their estates. Large, regular, well-ordered markets are described in Spanish Colonial sources, and it was in such markets that farmers and craftsmen sold their surplus and bought items they needed but did not produce. Because of the system of shallow lakes that occupied much of the floor of the basin, transport of goods to and from these markets was facilitated by the use of canoes, as was the practice along the coasts and lowland rivers. In other parts of Mesoamerica economic systems at the time of the Spanish Conquest may have been less intensively developed than that of the Basin of Mexico, but similar principles of organization seem to have applied.

BIBLIOGRAPHY

B. de Sahagún: *Historia general de las cosas de Nueva España* (MS., untraced, 1569; Spanish/Nahuatl illus. copy, *Florentine Codex*, Florence, Bib. Medicea-Laurenziana, MS. Palat. 218–20, n.d.); facs. *Códice Florentino: El manuscrito 218–20 de la colección Palatina de la Biblioteca Medicea Laurenziana*, 3 vols (Mexico City and Florence, 1979); Eng. trans., Nahuatl text and ed. C. E. Dibble and A. J. O. Anderson as *Florentine Codex: General History of the Things of New Spain*, 13 vols (Santa Fe, 1950–69)
R. H. Barlow: 'The Extent of the Empire of the Culhua Mexica', *Ibero-Americana*, xxviii (1949) [whole issue]
J. W. Pires-Ferreira: *Formative Mesoamerican Exchange Networks with Special Reference to the Valley of Oaxaca*, Mem. Mus. Anthropol.: U. MI, 7 (Ann Arbor, 1975)
E. M. Brumfiel: 'Specialization, Market Exchange, and the Aztec State: A View from Huexotla', *Current Anthropol.*, xxi (1980), pp. 459–78
R. D. Drennan: 'Long-distance Movement of Goods in the Mesoamerican Formative and Classic', *Amer. Ant.*, xlix (1984), pp. 27–43
——: 'Long-distance Transport Costs in Pre-Hispanic Mesoamerica', *Amer. Anthropologist*, lxxxvi (1984), pp. 105–12

ROBERT D. DRENNAN

4. RELIGION AND ICONOGRAPHY. The imagery of Pre-Columbian Mesoamerican art relates above all to the beliefs and rituals that played such a pervasive role in the cultures of the region. To understand the Mesoamerican artistic achievement it is, therefore, of crucial importance to consider the available information concerning its religious content. This section discusses the types of imagery associated with several prominent aspects of Mesoamerican religion.

The development in Mesoamerica of a sophisticated level of aesthetic expression enabled religious concepts and themes to be conveyed through rich and elaborate iconographies with remarkable effectiveness. Although the imagery of each leading Mesoamerican cultural tradition encoded its religious ideologies somewhat differently, as the result of a long history of contacts and diffusions they all shared many basic features. Complex religious iconographies were undoubtedly created by religious specialists cooperating closely with artisans, primarily to serve the purposes of cult and ritual. However, the ruling élites effectively adapted and manipulated the sacred symbols to proclaim and legitimize their political power and privileged status, particularly in monumental art intended for public display.

(i) Cosmogonies. (ii) Cosmologies. (iii) Deities and their attributes. (iv) Ritual. (v) Death imagery. (vi) Hallucinogenic drugs.

(i) Cosmogonies. All well-developed religions include some account of the origins of the universe and the forms of life in it, including mankind. Certain cosmogonical themes were particularly characteristic of Mesoamerica. One was the concept of a fundamental creative force, personified in a primordial bisexual supernatural entity or male–female deity pair, that initiated, structured and maintained the universe. Their abode was in the highest celestial level. The male member of the pair was often merged with the sun, the female with the moon. Their images occur in Aztec, Mixteca–Puebla and Lowland Maya pictorial manuscripts (*see* §VI below) but rarely in other Mesoamerican traditions.

Another fundamental theme was that of a succession of cosmogonical eras, each characterized by different phenomena. All terminated in cataclysmic destruction, and the last in the series, current when the European conquistadores arrived, was also doomed to perish in a universal holocaust. The number of ages varied (usually from three to five), as did their durations, which typically comprised long timespans. The overall pattern is best documented for the Central Highlands, but cognate versions occur elsewhere, especially in the Highland and Lowland Maya regions. Even Central Highland schemes differed considerably in specifics. The best-attested version was that of the capital of the Triple Alliance or Aztec empire, Mexico-Tenochtitlan. Here the eras, known as 'suns', numbered five (four previous and one current). Each was designated by a particular name, reflecting the nature of the catastrophe that terminated it, and also by the day in the 260-day divinatory cycle, the *tonalpohualli*, on which it commenced and ended (*see* §II below). Each age was assigned to a different element and directional colour and was presided over by a particular deity.

The First Sun was 4 Ocelotl (Jaguar), assigned to the earth, with the supreme god Tezcatlipoca presiding. Giants, subsisting on acorns, flourished in this age, which terminated with their destruction by ferocious jaguars. The Second Sun, 4 Ehecatl (Wind), was assigned to the air and wind and presided over by the wind and fertility deity Ehecatl–Quetzalcóatl. It was destroyed by hurricanes, following which the human population, which had subsisted on piñon nuts, was transformed into monkeys. The Third Sun, 4 Quiahuitl (Rain), was assigned to the element fire and presided over by the rain god Tlaloc. It ended in a fiery rain, and its humans, who had subsisted on a wild seed-bearing aquatic plant, were transformed into turkeys, butterflies and dogs. The Fourth Sun, 4 Atl (Water), was assigned to water and presided over by the goddess of that element, Chalchiuhtlicue. The era terminated in a great flood, whereupon the population, which had subsisted on another wild seed-bearing plant, turned into fish. The Fifth, and current, Sun, 4 Ollin (Movement), presided over by the solar deity Tonatiuh, would be destroyed by great earthquakes.

The imagery of this 'canonical' Mexica version of Mesoamerica's cosmogonical myth must have been striking and powerful, but, unfortunately, no genuine depictions of it survive. Four stone monuments (Mexico City, Mus. N. Antropol.; see fig. 24 below; Chicago, IL, A. Inst.; New Haven, CT, Yale U., Peabody Mus. Nat. Hist.), three of them found in Mexico City, and a shell pectoral (untraced), depict the dates that designated them, but no additional relevant imagery. However, the Codex Vaticanus A (Rome, Vatican, Bib. Apostolica)—a mid-16th-century illustrated account of native Central Highland religious, ritual and calendric divinatory systems, cosmogony, history and customs—does include a somewhat Europeanized pictorialization of the myth. It is quite aberrant, showing only four suns in a different sequence—water, wind, fire, ?—with the final era, rather than being terminated by a holocaust, grading into Toltec history.

A number of significant cosmogonical events were believed to have occurred at the beginning of the Mexica Fifth Sun, including the creation of the final heaven and earth, of fire, of the new generation of mankind and his sustenance (above all, maize), of the current sun and moon and associated sacrificial practices (the auto-sacrifice of the gods and the institution of terrestrial war and sacrifice to provide the sun with sustenance—human hearts and blood). At this juncture, cosmogony merges with legendary history, involving the primordial ancestors of the dominant peoples at the time of the Spanish Conquest. In the Central Highlands a widespread theme was mankind's emergence from underground, particularly from caves, usually a sacred point of origin known as 'The Seven Caves' or Chicomoztoc. In the Southern Highlands Mixtec ancestral emergence from trees was a prominent motif. Again, the imagery must have been rich and colourful, but almost nothing has survived except several depictions of Chicomoztoc and of tree emergence in various Mixtec pictorial manuscripts.

In the Maya region various cycles of mythological tales narrate the adventures of humans, often brother and sister or sometimes twin brothers, on earth before they were transformed into the celestial orbs. The best-known example is the cosmogonical saga of the Quiché Maya of highland Guatemala, the *Popol Vuh* (16th century; Chicago, IL, Newberry Lib.), featuring the colourful deeds of the Hero Twins, Hunahpú and Xbalanqué, in overcoming the Lords of the Underworld (Xibalba). Scenes that possibly illustrate the Hero Twins and episodes in the myth have been identified on Late Classic (*c.* AD 600– *c.* 900) painted ceramics in the Southern Maya lowlands, implying that versions of the myth were ancient and widespread throughout the Maya region. Certain Classic period Lowland Maya deities depicted on stone sculptures and ceramics, especially two of the gods of the 'Palenque Triad', denominated GI and GIII, have also been identified with the Hero Twins (GI with Hunahpú; GIII with

Xbalanqué). In the *Popol Vuh* the Twins, after their terrestrial and sub-terrestrial adventures, became the sun and the moon (or ?Venus).

(ii) Cosmologies. The basic scheme of the Mesoamerican universe is well-established. Although its fundamental features were probably ancient (this is supported by archaeological evidence), most information concerning Pre-Columbian Mesoamerican cosmology is derived from ethnohistorical and pictorial evidence from the Late Post-Classic Central and Southern Highlands (*c.* 1200–1521).

The earth's land mass was conceived as a great rectangular central space with trapezoidal extensions reaching out to the four cardinal directions, the overall pattern resembling a Maltese cross. It was surrounded by the cosmic ocean, which curved up at its edge to provide a wall-like support for the lowest celestial level. A different colour was assigned to each direction, including the centre. The directional colour assignments apparently varied considerably throughout Mesoamerica, and perhaps even in the same area within different ritual and ideological contexts, but the colours of the Lowland Maya region seem to have been standardized throughout the Classic and Post-Classic periods (*c.* AD 250–1521): in the usual Mesoamerican counter-clockwise ritual circuit, east=red, north=white, west=black, south=yellow and centre= ?green. In the Late Post-Classic Central Highlands the four pre-eminent directional colours were yellow, red, blue-green and white, respectively, and in his *Historia general* (written *c.* 1569) Fray Bernardino de Sahagún assigned these colours, in that order, to the four houses in Tollan of the legendary Toltec ruler, Topiltzin Quetzalcóatl. Such chromatic directional symbolism is well represented in the ritual–divinatory Aztec and Mixteca–Puebla pictorial manuscripts (codices). In codices from the Lowland Maya region the colour assignments were more frequently indicated by the hieroglyphs for the appropriate colours than by the actual application of the colours. Sacred, botanically distinct, trees were also assigned to the cardinal directions and centre, and each frequently featured a different sacred bird perched on top. Finally, different deities, often in pairs, supernatural sky- and earth-bearers, and the day and year signs of the native calendar were also assigned to the directions.

Two famous pictorial examples of cruciform cosmograms are extant, one from the Lowland Maya region— Codex Madrid (Madrid, Mus. América; see fig. 2), and one from the Mixteca–Puebla area—Codex Fejéváry-Mayer (Liverpool Mus.). The latter belongs to the Codex Borgia group, two other members of which, the Codex Borgia itself and the Codex Vaticanus B (both Rome, Vatican, Bib. Apostolica), provide extensive directional layouts that include most of the features described, plus a number of additional elements in the Codex Borgia. The four directional cosmic trees, without birds, are also pictured in the mid-16th-century Aztec-style Codex Tudela (Madrid, Mus. América), together with sets of deity pairs.

The concept of the directionally oriented cosmogram may have occurred as early as the Middle Pre-Classic period (*c.* 1000–*c.* 300 BC) in the Olmec culture of the Gulf Coast. The Humboldt Celt depicts a symbolic ensemble,

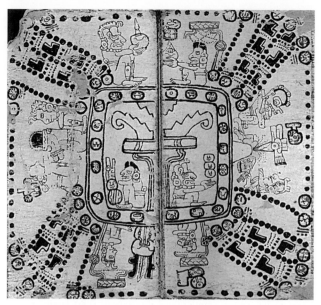

2. Cosmogram of the Lowland Maya universe, showing 260 day signs of the divinatory cycle and deity pairs assigned to the four cardinal directions and the centre, 16th century (Madrid, Museo de América, Codex Madrid, 75/76)

Few images of the vertical cross-section of the universe have survived. For the Central Highlands there is only a rather poorly drawn, somewhat Europeanized scheme in the Codex Vaticanus A, which provides the Nahuatl names for each celestial and sub-terrestrial level. For the Southern Highlands there is a simpler version of the celestial tiers, with only nine levels, in the Selden Roll (Oxford, Bodleian Lib.), an early colonial pictorial from north-west Oaxaca. Both Vaticanus A and the Selden Roll depict the primordial creator male–female deity pair in the highest celestial tier. Other images of this duo, depicting only the uppermost tier, occur in the two best-known Mixtec pictorials, the Vienna Codex (Vindobonensis) (Vienna, Österreich. Nbib.) and the Codex Nuttall (London, BM). In the Lowland Maya region a few images of the celestial tiers, nine in number, occur at Classic period archaeological sites.

Both the earth and the sky were also conceived of mystically and metaphorically as monsters, essentially reptilian but incorporating features of other creatures. The Izapan, Classic Maya, Mixteca–Puebla and Aztec traditions provide particularly vivid depictions of such fantastic polymorphs. Best known are the variegated, often bicephalic celestial and terrestrial monsters of the Lowland Maya (variously referred to as 'Two-Headed Dragon', 'Bearded Dragon', 'Cauac Monster' or 'Celestial Monster') and the different versions of the grotesque crouching 'Earth Lord', Tlaltecuhtli, frequently carved on the undersides of Aztec stone sculptures.

(iii) Deities and their attributes. One of the most striking features of Mesoamerican religion was the development of extensive pantheons of individualized deities, who personified the principal spheres and forces of the natural world. Most were conceived anthropomorphically, but they often incorporated zoomorphic features. An extraordinarily rich imagery evolved to depict them; each deity was characterized by particular combinations of costume and insignia. This pattern is already evident in the iconography of the Olmec (see fig. 3) in the Pre-Classic period. A small array of ostensibly individualized deities, including versions of the so-called 'jaguar baby', were depicted with relatively standardized features and characteristics. It has been suggested that some were prototypes for later deities, including some that were prominent at the time of the Spanish Conquest. Another typical Mesoamerican iconographic configuration, also of Olmec origin, fused feline, saurian, ophidian, cervine, avian and other zoomorphic features in a single supernatural creature. The most important was the 'Long-lipped Dragon' that evolved into one of the most prominent and ubiquitous images in later Mesoamerican iconographic traditions, particularly in Izapan and Lowland Maya cultures.

The pantheonic imagery of the Late Pre-Classic Izapan tradition, forming a link between Olmec and Classic Lowland Maya traditions, was somewhat more amorphous, with fewer discernible discrete deities. Nevertheless, Izapan iconography, largely confined to low-relief carving on stone monuments, was rich and complex. Many of its images were directly prototypical to Classic Lowland Maya iconography. Some elements, in particular variations on the Long-lipped Dragon, spread widely during the Late

albeit somewhat different from the Maltese cross layout, and a simpler, linear diagram is depicted on a celt found at La Venta. Cosmic trees, possibly with directional associations, appear in the Izapan tradition of the Late Pre-Classic period (*c.* 300 BC–*c.* AD 250) of the coast and piedmont region of Chiapas–Guatemala. Some probable examples also appear on Late Classic Lowland Maya painted ceramic vessels and in two of the surviving ritual and divinatory pictorials, the Codex Dresden (Dresden, Sächs. Landesbib.) and Codex Madrid, from that region. The most noteworthy examples, however, are three famous relief carvings at Classic period PALENQUE on wall panels in the 'Temple of the Cross' and the 'Temple of the Foliated Cross', and on the sarcophagus lid in the tomb of Pacal in the 'Temple of the Inscriptions' (see fig. 20 below). These include the perched serpent-birds and, in the case of the sarcophagus lid, a semi-recumbent figure at the base of the tree analogous to those in the Mixteca–Puebla Codices Borgia and Vaticanus B.

Vertically, the universe was believed to comprise a series of celestial and sub-terrestrial tiers. Different phenomena were assigned to these tiers, including, in the celestial sphere, heavenly bodies, certain meteorological phenomena and different deities and colours. A scheme of nine heavens, which survived up to the Spanish Conquest in some areas, may have predated the 13-layer scheme that predominated in the Late Post-Classic Central Highlands and perhaps also in other parts of Mesoamerica. The number of sub-terrestrial layers was almost invariably nine. In the Central Highlands at least, the underworld levels also served as hazard stations to be surmounted by the souls of the deceased on their post-mortem journey to the lowest tier, the final resting place of most of those who died from natural causes.

Pre-Classic period to form a kind of Izapanoid iconographic universe throughout isthmian Mesoamerica and to the north in the Maya Lowlands.

During the Classic period the Maya developed perhaps the most sophisticated, imaginative and complex iconographic system in Mesoamerican cultural history, including numerous distinct deities depicted in relatively standardized formats. The most prominent Late Pre-Classic Maya images of supernaturals, including versions of the Long-lipped Dragon, consisted of enormous stucco masks flanking the stairways of temple pyramid-platforms. A more variegated pantheonic imagery, principally in relief sculpture and painting, later flourished throughout the Classic period. Most Maya deities continued to be depicted, sometimes with modifications, in the Post-Classic period, both in relief sculpture and painting and in ritual and divinatory codices (see §VI below). The deity images featured in them are usually labelled with their Maya hieroglyphic names, and many attempts have been made to identify them with those deities mentioned by Diego de Landa in his *Relación de las cosas de Yucatán* (1566) and in other ethnohistorical sources. An alphabetic classification was devised by Schellhas (1904) and refined and enhanced by Thompson (1950), Zimmermann (1956), Anders (1963) and others; it has the advantage of scholarly clarity, but Yucatec names have become widely accepted in general use.

In the post-Olmec Gulf Coast region, the Classic Veracruz tradition flowered, especially in the period *c.* AD 550–*c.* 1000 at TAJÍN. In Classic Veracruz stone sculpture and monumental ceramic sculpture various deities have been identified; some of these apparently evolved into important Post-Classic deities, in particular a major fertility goddess.

In the neighbouring Classic period Southern Highlands, Zapotec civilization based at MONTE ALBÁN and in the Oaxaca Valley developed a varied pantheonic imagery displaying various Olmecoid and Izapanoid features. Gods were depicted most strikingly on ceramic funerary urns, and many were named after the days of the 260-day divinatory cycle. Attempts have been made, with only partial success, to link these Classic period images with various supernaturals named in Zapotec ethnohistorical sources at the time of the Spanish Conquest.

In the Pre-Classic Central Highlands discrete deities are difficult to identify, although Middle and Late Pre-Classic traditions featured small solid and large hollow anthropomorphic clay figurines, mostly female. One exception, dating near the end of the Late Pre-Classic period, is the effigy image that appears to represent the 'Old Fire god', with a brazier for burning incense on his head. Such effigy figures were prototypical to similar figures, usually of stone, at Classic TEOTIHUACÁN. During the Classic period the pantheon developed at Teotihuacán came to dominate the Central Highlands and was spread through trade and political contact to other parts of Mesoamerica. Deities were depicted in stone and ceramic sculpture, and painted on ceramic vessels and stuccoed walls. An important icon, the 'Feathered Serpent', made its first unequivocal appearance at Teotihuacán in the Late Pre-Classic–Early Classic period, and continued to be important until the Spanish Conquest, when it was known as Quetzalcóatl (Nahuatl:

'quetzal-feather snake'). Many classifications and interpretations of the Teotihuacán pantheon have been made, including attempts to identify some of its gods as those recorded at the time of the Conquest. Apart from the Old Fire god and the probable creativity–fertility deity symbolized by the Feathered Serpent, prototypes of the Aztec rain god, Tlaloc, and of a putative fertility and earth goddess have been identified. At the end of the Classic period, following the demise of Teotihuacán, the two new Central Highland centres of XOCHICALCO and CACAXTLA developed sophisticated iconographic imageries that both preserved aspects of Teotihuacán tradition and anticipated features of Post-Classic Toltec and Mixteca–Puebla traditions. The Feathered Serpent icon was prominent, but other discernible deities are few. At Cacaxtla there are also many Lowland Maya themes and stylistic influences on its painted walls.

In West Mexico the identification of deities in the images depicted in the distinctive ceramic tradition is the subject of considerable debate. Although various rituals,

3. Olmec seated figure holding a 'jaguar baby', greenstone, h. 550 mm, *c.* 1000–*c.* 300 BC; engraved heads on shoulders and knees of principal figure may represent Olmec deities (Las Limas, Veracruz, Museo de Antropología de Jalapa)

including the rubber ball-game and one akin to the *volador* or 'flying pole ceremony', are represented in the ceramic effigies, there are no images similar to prototypical Pre-Classic or Classic period deities depicted elsewhere in Mesoamerica (*see* §II, 2(ii) and 3(v) below).

In the Early Post-Classic period (*c.* AD 900–*c.* 1200) the focus of power in the Central Highlands shifted north of the Basin of Mexico to Toltec Tollan (TULA). Toltec style and iconography was somewhat eclectic, inheriting much from earlier Mesoamerican traditions. Although the Feathered Serpent icon was ubiquitous, other distinct deities are rare at Tula itself. However, various identifiable gods and goddesses—all included in the Late Post-Classic Aztec pantheon—are depicted on Toltec-style cliff paintings at Ixtapantongo, south-west of the Basin of Mexico, including a pulque god and goddess; Xipe Totec, the 'flayed god'; the sun god; the Venus god; and the fire god. Other deities, including the rain god Tlaloc, were depicted on flattish Toltec Mazapan ceramic figurines. A closely related style and iconography flourished briefly at CHICHÉN ITZÁ in northern Yucatán, mixed with Maya features. The exact nature of the relationship between Tula and Chichén Itzá, however, is still little understood.

At the same time a major new stylistic and iconographic synthesis called MIXTECA-PUEBLA emerged to the southeast of the Basin of Mexico. During the Late Post-Classic period its influence spread widely throughout Mesoamerica. Its iconographic style is particularly well exemplified by the ritual and divinatory pictorials of the Codex Borgia group and by Cholultec and Mixtec polychrome ceramics. Mixteca–Puebla iconography inherited numerous elements and patterns from earlier traditions and used them to standardize the images of the gods, most of whom are identifiable as those recorded by Spanish chroniclers shortly after the Conquest. Most information comes from the Mixtec codices in the Southern Highlands and from Aztec ethnohistory and stone and ceramic sculpture of the Central Highlands. Compared to Mixteca–Puebla imagery, Aztec imagery was less conventionalized and more literally depictive of symbolic and anthropomorphic or zoomorphic representation.

Aztec pantheonic imagery was particularly rich. Examples survive of almost every deity mentioned in ethnohistorical documents. They were portrayed in codices, stone, wood and ceramic sculpture, ornamental metallurgy, cotton textiles, feather and hardstone mosaics, and in wall paintings. A distinctive feature of Aztec religious art is the frequency with which the deities are represented by three-dimensional images, or 'idols', of stone and wood, much more than in any other Mesoamerican tradition.

(iv) Ritual. Mesoamerican ceremonial, which was principally directed towards the promotion of fertility, was clearly one of the most theatrical in world history. Many ritual activities were depicted in its religious art. Early examples are known in Izapan and Classic Lowland Maya sculpture and painting, providing depictions of a wide range of ceremonial activities. These include: players in the ceremonial ball-game; pre- and post-battle rituals; sacrificial scenes, both auto-sacrifice and immolation of captives; rituals of rulership, including coronations and investitures; and numerous miscellaneous ceremonies.

Similar scenes are known from tomb and palace murals, on ballcourt and pyramid-platform stone panelling and on plastered and carved benches at Monte Albán, Teotihuacán, Tajín, Xochicalco, Cacaxtla, Tula and Chichén Itzá. However, it is in the Mixteca–Puebla and Aztec ritual and divinatory codices that the most complex depictions occur, including, in the Aztec pictorials, the 18 principal annual ceremonies. They provide an intimate link to the pantheonic imagery, as the principal performers were deity impersonators wearing diagnostic costume and insignia.

BIBLIOGRAPHY

P. Schellhas: *Representations of Deities of the Maya Manuscripts*, Pap. Peabody Mus. Archaeol. & Ethnol. (Cambridge, MA, 1904)
H. J. Spinden: 'A Study of Maya Art: Its Subject Matter and Historical Development', *Mem. Peabody Mus. Archaeol. & Ethnol.*, vi (1913) [whole issue]
J. E. Thompson: *Sky Bearers, Colors and Directions in Maya and Mexican Religion*, Carnegie Inst. Washington, Contrib. Amer. Archaeol. (Washington, DC, 1934)
J. Soustelle: *La Pensée cosmologique des anciens Mexicains: Représentations du monde et de l'espace* (Paris, 1940)
T. Proskouriakoff: *A Study of Classic Maya Sculpture* (Washington, DC, 1950)
J. E. Thompson: *Maya Hieroglyphic Writing: Introduction* (Washington, DC, 1950)
A. Caso and I. Bernal: *Urnas de Oaxaca* (Mexico City, 1952)
T. Proskouriakoff: *Varieties of Classic Central Veracruz Sculpture*, Carnegie Inst. Washington, Contrib. Amer. Anthropol. & Hist. (Washington, DC, 1954)
G. Zimmermann: *Die Hieroglyphen der Maya-Handschriften* (Hamburg, 1956)
F. Anders: *Des Pantheon der Maya* (Graz, 1963)
A. Caso: 'Dioses y signos Teotihuacanos', *Teotihuacan: Onceava Mesa Redonda, Sociedad Mexicana de Antropología* (Mexico City, 1966), pp. 249–75
G. Kubler: *The Iconography of the Art of Teotihuacan*, Studies in Precolumbian Art and Archaeology (Washington, DC, 1967)
——: *Studies in Classic Maya Iconography*, Memoirs of the Connecticut Academy of Arts and Sciences (New Haven, 1969)
J. E. Thompson: *Maya History and Religion* (Norman, 1970)
P. D. Joralemon: *A Study of Olmec Iconography*, Studies in Precolumbian Art and Archaeology (Washington, DC, 1971)
H. B. Nicholson: 'The Iconography of Classic Central Veracruz Ceramic Sculptures', *Ancient Art of Veracruz* (exh. cat., Los Angeles, CA, Nat. Hist. Mus., 1971), pp. 13–17
——: 'Religion in Pre-Hispanic Central Mexico', *Hb. Mid. Amer. Ind.*, x (1971), pp. 395–446
M. E. Kampen: *The Sculptures of El Tajín, Veracruz* (Gainesville, 1972)
M. Coe: *The Maya Scribe and his World* (New York, 1973)
M. León-Portilla: *Time and Reality in the Thought of the Maya* (Boston, 1973)
H. B. Nicholson: 'The Late Pre-Hispanic Central Mexican (Aztec) Iconographic System', *The Iconography of Middle American Sculpture* (New York, 1973), pp. 72–97
G. V. Norman: *Izapa Sculpture*, Papers of the New World Archaeological Foundation (Provo, 1973, 1976)
J. Quirarte: *Izapan-Style Art: A Study of its Form and Meaning*, Studies in Precolumbian Art and Archaeology (Washington, DC, 1973)
H. von Winning: *The Shaft Tomb Figures of West Mexico*, Southwest Museum Papers (Los Angeles, 1974)
V. G. Smith: *Izapa Relief Carving: Form, Content, Rules for Design and Role in Mesoamerican Art History and Archaeology*, Studies in Precolumbian Art and Archaeology (Washington, DC, 1984)
L. A. Parsons: *The Origins of Maya Art: Monumental Stone Sculpture of Kaminaljuyu, Guatemala, and the Southern Pacific Coast*, Studies in Precolumbian Art and Archaeology (Washington, DC, 1986)
L. Schele and M. E. Miller: *The Blood of Kings: Dynasty and Ritual in Maya Art* (Fort Worth, 1986)
E. Matos Moctezuma: *Cacaxtla* (Mexico City, 1987)
H. B. Nicholson: 'Mesoamerican Iconography', *The Encyclopedia of Religion*, vii, ed. M. Eliade (New York, 1987), pp. 21–7

H. von Winning: *La iconografía de Teotihuacan: Los dioses y los signos*, Universidad Nacional Autónoma de México, Instituto de Investigaciones Estéticas, Estudios y Fuentes del Arte en México (Mexico City, 1987)

E. P. Benson and G. G. Griffin, eds: *Maya Iconography* (Princeton, 1988)

D. Carrasco: *Religions of Mesoamerica: Cosmovision and Ceremonial Centers* (New York, 1990)

L. Schele and D. Freidel: *A Forest of Kings: The Untold Story of the Ancient Maya* (New York, 1990)

M. Miller and K. Taube: *The Gods and Symbols of Ancient Mexico and the Maya: An Illustrated Dictionary of Mesoamerican Religion* (London, 1993)

H. B. NICHOLSON

(v) Death imagery. Mesoamerican images of death and symbols associated with death were used to express a wide range of political, mythological, religious and economic purposes. By the Post-Classic period (*c.* AD 900–1521) death and death imagery had become prominent indicators of a unified and consistent cosmological system. Such images are depicted in all media—sculpture, architecture, ceramics, mural and manuscript painting, jewellery and textiles—and in both colossal and small-scale works.

Scholars recognize two types of imagery: motifs universally recognized as representing death, and abstract symbols that allude to death within certain contexts. Thus, death was expressed most frequently as crossed bones, skulls, severed heads and dismembered limbs, but there are also depictions of sacrificial victims, skeletons and flayed humans and of animals that were considered to bring about death, such as bats, owls, spiders and centipedes, as well as such indirect indications of death as hearts, symbols for blood, black spots on the body in Maya art and closed eyes, usually accompanied by an open mouth.

(a) Myth and divination. Death was pivotal in creation myths, especially in the Central Highlands. One of the best documented Pre-Columbian creation myths is that of the succession of five ages of creation and destruction (*see* §(i) above). In one version—the anonymous *Leyenda de los Soles* written down in 1558—several images of death play a prominent part, including the ultimate place of death, the underworld. After the destruction of the Fourth Sun by flood and the creation of the Fifth (current) Sun, the god Quetzalcóatl was entrusted with creating mankind. He descended to the underworld to obtain from the Lord of the Underworld, Mictlantecuhtli, the bones and ashes from the previous human generation. Mictlantecuhtli gave him these materials, but Quetzalcóatl dropped the bones, breaking them into pieces. Nevertheless, he took the pieces to the assembly of gods at Tamoanchán (a mythical place), where one of the deities ground the bone fragments into a mass, which was placed in a precious vessel. The gods then performed self-sacrifice, allowing their blood to fall on the mass, which, when kneaded together, formed the raw material for the creation of mankind.

Death, represented by a skull glyph, was also one of the 20 day-names of the Mesoamerican divinatory calendar, each of which had a number from 1 to 13 attached to it (*see* §II below). Each day-name and number combination was of special importance at birth, and the strongest such combination for the Aztecs was the day 'One Death'. This birth date was especially good for rulers and leaders, and the skull glyph came to stand for fame and glory.

(b) In relation to the ball-game. The Mesoamerican ball-game was played from *c.* 1200 BC to the Spanish Conquest and was closely associated with death imagery. Its purpose was mainly ritual, and it frequently led to the sacrifice of the defeated team. Pottery figurines depict players grasping knives and trophy heads, and decapitated ball-players (e.g. Leiden, Rijksmus. Vlkenknd). Some examples feature a decapitated player with six serpents and a central device spurting from the neck. At Vega de Alatorre and Aparicio in Veracruz there are stone relief panels showing decapitated players, and at Aparicio one stele depicts a decapitated player from whose head issue seven intertwined serpents. Similar scenes of ball-players holding severed heads with sprouting serpents are depicted on Teotihuacán-style tripod vases found at Escuintla in Guatemala.

Several ballcourts incorporate relief panels along their playing field walls or 'benches' depicting sacrificial and death scenes. Six such bench panels at the Great Ballcourt at Chichén Itzá depict processions of fully accoutred ball-players. Directly facing the ball at the centre of each scene, with a skull motif, is a half-kneeling, decapitated player with six serpents and a flowering vine emerging from his neck. On the other side of the ball the captain of the opposing team holds the severed head and a stone knife. One of the six carved stone panels of the principal ballcourt at TAJÍN in the Gulf Coast depicts the moment of execution of a losing ball-player. An eagle-masked player holds his arm aloft over the stretched-out sacrificial victim, while a skeleton floats above the scene. Other skeletal figures feature in the remaining panels.

The elaborate and highly patterned symbolism used on much Maya pictorial pottery has been interpreted by Michael Coe in terms of the adventures of the Hero Twins of the mid-16th-century Quiché Maya sacred book, the *Popul Vuh* (Chicago, IL, Newberry Lib.). Both the pottery scenes and the book portray death imagery and decapitation associated with the ball-game and regeneration associated with skulls. The story goes that two brothers, the 'first fathers', called 1 Hunahpú and 7 Hunahpú, were the best ball-players on earth. But the noise of their tireless practising disturbed the Lords of Xibalba (the Maya underworld), who summoned them to a ball-game there. The gods won the game by deception and the two brothers were sacrificed. The body of 7 Hunahpú was buried in the ballcourt and the head of 1 Hunahpú was hung as a trophy in a calabash tree. One day the daughter of an underworld lord walked past the tree and spoke to the skull, whereupon it spat into her hand, miraculously making her pregnant. Her outraged father ordered that she be sacrificed, but she fled to the middleworld, where she sought refuge in the house of 1 Hunahpú and 7 Hunahpú. She gave birth to the twins Hunahpú and Xbalanque, who discovered the ball-game and again annoyed the Lord of Xibalba with the noise of the bouncing ball. Again the gods challenged the twins in a ball-game, but this time they were defeated and the Hero Twins Hunahpú and Xbalanque became the heavenly bodies of the sun and moon. The myth is interpreted as the re-enactment of the combat between the forces of darkness and light.

(c) Chronological development. There is less information on the role of death imagery for the Pre-Classic

(*c.* 2000 BC–*c.* AD 250) and Classic (*c.* AD 250–*c.* 900) periods than for the Post-Classic period (*c.* AD 900–1521). Nevertheless, it is possible to speculate on the meanings of Pre-Classic and Classic period imagery on the basis of archaeological and ethnohistorical information on Post-Classic cultures, particularly the Aztec culture.

Death imagery occurs in Mesoamerica as early as *c.* 1000 BC at TLATILCO in the Basin of Mexico, where a clay mask was excavated sculptured with one half as a skull and the other half as a face (Mexico City, Mus. N. Antropol.). Bones and skulls were probably conceived as a source of life and regeneration in the Late Pre-Classic period (*c.* 300 BC–*c.* AD 250). For example, Stele 50 at IZAPA on the coastal plains of Chiapas is sculpted with a skeletal figure, to whom a small being is attached by a rope or umbilical cord. Another stele at Izapa depicts a man with a stone knife in his right hand standing over a decapitated body. In his left hand he holds the severed head, from the neck of which blood pours. Two other figures approach him from behind, carrying a stretcher.

In the Classic period the site of ZAPOTAL in the Gulf Coast region was the focus of a cult of the dead between *c.* AD 400 and 700. There is a shrine to the god of death, Mictlantecuhtli. On the god's sides are modelled skulls. There are also clay figures of Cihuateteos, patron deities of women who died in childbirth (see fig. 4). Much of Classic Maya religion was also concerned with the world of the dead, manifested in painted ceramics and in monumental sculpture on their architecture. The greatest funerary monument of the Classic period is the stone sarcophagus lid of the Maya ruler, Lord Pacal, buried in the Temple of the Inscriptions at PALENQUE (see fig. 20 below). It is carved with a scene showing the moment of death as a fall into the maw of the underworld, and it is indicative of the Maya élite's concern with death that the sarcophagus was begun before Pacal died. The symbolic representation of death as a fall into the underworld is also depicted on a carved bone of Early Classic date (New York, Amer. Mus. Nat. Hist.).

During the Post-Classic period the representation of death became a much more important subject than in earlier periods. The warfare and militarism of this time are associated with many representations of death, and the concept of life coming out of death was commonplace. In the Early Post-Classic period (*c.* AD 900–*c.* 1200) the HUASTEC of the northern Gulf Coast region were the first to produce limestone sculptures depicting skulls and visible hearts. One such figure (Mexico City, Mus. N. Antropol.), from the site of El Naranjo, depicts a man with the typical Huastec conical hat and a skull mask over the headdress. His heart is shown in the lower part of his stomach. At both CHICHÉN ITZÁ in the Maya region and TULA in the Central Highlands scenes of jaguars eating human hearts are carved in relief on platform panels, walls and benches. The jaguar and the eagle became the symbols for élite warrior knights (see §IX, 1 below). Decapitation became another common subject, manifested in particular as carved stone TZOMPANTLIS (skull racks), such as those at Chichén Itzá, Uxmal and the Great Temple of Tenochtitlan (with 240 carved skulls) (see MEXICO CITY, §I).

The Late Post-Classic (*c.* AD 1200–1521) MIXTEC maintained a strong cult of the dead. Some, if not all, skeletal

4. Cihuateotl with a crown of skulls, basalt with remains of white paint, h. 770 mm, *c.* 1300–1519 (Mexico City, Museo Nacional de Antropología)

figures were deities with generative and life-sustaining functions. At Zaachila a terracotta vessel was excavated that depicts the god of the underworld holding a sacrificial knife (Mexico City, Mus. N. Antropol.). Mixtec death imagery in the codices (*see* §VI below) depicts numerous deities with skeletal jaws or skulls, associated with maize growing and with the gods' need for blood offerings.

The Aztecs produced the largest surviving corpus of death imagery. There are depictions of death in every available medium and in all dimensions. The Aztecs are particularly notable for their stone sculptures. The colossal stone statues of the goddesses Coatlicue and Yollotlicue, and smaller examples such as that of Cihuateotl (see fig. 4), incorporate multiple death symbols in their necklaces of hearts, hands and skulls, skirts decorated with hearts and crowns of skulls. The *cuauhxicalli* (eagle vessel; Mexico City, Mus. N. Antropol.) of Motecuhzoma I (*reg* 1440–68) has 11 cartouches with the repeated figure of the 'divine warrior', Huitzilopochtli (the Mexica Aztec tribal god), capturing prisoners of war. Above and below the scenes are relief panels depicting several hands, human hearts, skulls and crossed bones, sacrificial knives, year bundle symbols and other motifs. The stone was probably used for gladiatorial combats in which victims were immolated to feed the earth and sun deities, once again associating death imagery with regeneration and life-sustenance.

The image of the 'flayed one', Xipe Totec, in the Late Post-Classic period, is represented in dozens of stone and pottery figurines wearing masks of flayed skins dating from the Pre-Classic period to the Late Post-Classic period (e.g. Basle, Mus. Vlkerknd). The central ritual act of the Xipe cult was the sacrifice of human victims, followed by the wearing of their skins by votive penitents as a form of political intimidation and, symbolically, to signal the arrival of spring and regeneration of life.

BIBLIOGRAPHY

H. B. Nicholson: 'Religion in Pre-Hispanic Central Mexico', *Hb. Mid. Amer. Ind.*, x (1971), pp. 395–446

——: 'The Cult of Xipe Totec in Mesoamerica', *Religion in Mesoamerica*, ed. J. Litvak King and N. Castillo Tejero (Mexico City, 1972), pp. 213–22

M. D. Coe: *The Maya Scribe and his World* (New York, 1973)

——: 'Death and the Ancient Maya', *Death and the Afterlife in Pre-Columbian America*, ed. E. P. Benson (Washington, DC, 1975), pp. 87–104

F. Robicsek: *The Maya Book of the Dead: The Ceramic Codex: The Corpus of Codex Style Ceramics of the Late Classic Period* (Charlottesville, 1981)

E. G. Umberger: *Aztec Sculptures, Hieroglyphics and History* (diss., New York, Columbia U., 1981)

J. L. Furst: 'Skeletonization in Mixtec Art: A Re-evaluation', *The Art and Iconography of Late Post-Classic Central Mexico*, ed. E. H. Boone (Washington, DC, 1982), pp. 207–25

D. Tedlock, ed.: *Popol Vuh: The Definitive Edition of the Mayan Book of the Dawn of Life and the Glories of the Gods and Kings* (New York, 1985)

The Blood of Kings: Dynasty and Ritual in Maya Art (exh. cat. by L. Schele and M. E. Miller, Fort Worth, TX, Kimbell A. Mus., 1986)

M. Graulich: *Mythes et rituels du Mexique ancien préhispanique* (Brussels, 1987)

E. Baquedano: 'Iconographic Symbols in Aztec Elite Sculptures', *Recent Studies in Pre-Columbian Archaeology*, ed. N. J. Saunders and O. de Montmollin (Oxford, 1988), pp. 191–204

E. Matos Moctezuma: *The Mask of Death* (Mexico City, 1988)

E. Baquedano: *Aztec Death Sculpture* (diss., U. London, 1989)

ELIZABETH BAQUEDANO

(vi) Hallucinogenic drugs. Ecstatic communion with the spirit world was a cornerstone of the shamanic-based religions in Pre-Columbian Mesoamerica. It was achieved primarily through the skilful manipulation of psychoactive compounds. According to early Spanish reports, such compounds were venerated or deified by Mesoamericans, and the first missionaries strove diligently to end their use. Most substances were botanically derived, although other sources were also known. Botanical, ethnographical and archaeological discoveries underscore the central importance of hallucinogens to native Mesoamerican religion, and there are many related representations in art.

Various types of sacred mushroom were used to induce altered perception of time and both auditory and visual hallucination (through the active ingredients psilocybine and psilocine). Historically identified as the Aztec *teonanacatl* (Nahuatl: 'divine flesh') and Maya *xibalbaj okox* (Maya: 'hell mushroom') or *muxan okox* (Maya: 'crazy mushroom'), such mushrooms appear to have had a long tradition of use. Stone representations of mushrooms may extend back to the Early Pre-Classic period (*c*. 2000–*c*. 1000 BC) in Guatemala, and they are found throughout Mesoamerica up to the end of the Classic period (*c*. AD 250–*c*. 900). Mushrooms are depicted on pottery, as ceramic effigies and in the codices (*see* §VI below), often in association with anthropomorphic and zoomorphic figures (especially toads, jaguars and birds). For example, stylized sculptured representations of the mushroom *Psilocybe aztecorum* adorn the base of the Late Post-Classic (*c*. AD 1200–1521) Aztec statue of Xochipilli ('God of Flowers') in the Museo Nacional de Antropología, Mexico City.

Cacti such as the 'divine' *peyotl* (*Lophophora williamsii*), and numerous false peyotes, were exploited by the Aztecs and other Pre-Columbian peoples. Peyote effigies appear on Late Pre-Classic (*c*. 300 BC–*c*. AD 250) ceramic vessels and figurines of West Mexico (Colima, Mus. Reg.; Guadalajara, Mus. Reg. Antropol. & Hist.), and a Middle Pre-Classic (*c*. 1000–*c*. 300 BC) snuffing pipe from MONTE ALBÁN depicts a deer with the cactus in its mouth. Peyote is usually orally administered, but enema scenes, showing syringes through which many psychoactive compounds could have been used, are depicted on Late Classic (*c*. AD 600–*c*. 900) Maya vases, occasionally in association with zoomorphs, such as jaguars. The deified Aztec *ololiuqui* (Nahuatl: 'round thing') is identified as the morning glory, *Rivea corymbosa*. The related *Ipomoea violacea* may have been the Aztec *tlitliltzin*. Naturalistic depictions of *ololiuqui* are identified on the statue of Xochipilli described above, and are common in the terminal Pre-Classic and Classic period art of TEOTIHUACÁN, often in association with gods and drinking ceremonies. Historic accounts describe its addition to fermented brews and to *teotlacualli* (Nahuatl: 'divine food'), which was smeared on ritual participants and consumed before human sacrificial ceremonies. Tobacco was the ritual plant *par excellence*. Clay effigy snuffing pipes occur as early as the Middle Pre-Classic period in West Mexico (e.g. Mexico City, Mus. N. Antropol.), but these could also have been for *ololiuqui* or for a member of the genus *Justica*. The depiction of *Nicotiana tabacum* was an important symbol in monumental stone art throughout Mesoamerica.

Toad symbolism is a prevalent feature of Mesoamerican art. Toads appear on monumental carvings and sculptures, stone mortars, pottery vessels and stone *yugos* (see §II, 3(i) below), often in association with jaguars and serpents. Recurrent and distinguishing features in such representations are the parotid glands of the neotropical toad *Bufo marinus*, a natural source of the indole alkaloid bufotenine. The Aztec *guetzalaxochiacatl* (Nahuatl: 'precious water flower') may be the water lily *Nymphaea ampla*, which contains the morphine-like aporphine. Representations abound in Classic-period Maya art, often in association with depictions of mythic beings, sensory areas of the body and toads.

Other native Mesoamerican hallucinogens depicted in art include *sinucuichi*, an auditory hallucinogen obtained from *Heima salicifolia*, which has been identified on the statue of Xochipilli, and the divinatory *tsite*, illustrated in the Maya book, the *Popol Vuh*, which may be a member of the genus *Erythrina*.

Hallucinations need not necessarily have been induced exclusively through the use of chemical hallucinogens of plant or animal derivation. Ecstatic states may also have been attained through combinations of fasting, rhythmic exercise, repetitive auditory stimulation, autohypnosis and deliberately inflicted pain. The early Spanish chronicler

Diego de Landa stated that Maya artists consulted visions brought about through fasting and smoking. Mesoamerican Pre-Columbian art in general, and especially Maya monumental and figurine art, contain frequent depictions of self-inflicted pain and bloodletting, but association of these scenes with quests for ecstatic visions must remain speculative.

BIBLIOGRAPHY

R. E. Schultes and A. Hofmann: *The Botany and Chemistry of Hallucinogens* (Springfield, 1973, rev. 1980)

P. T. Furst: 'Hallucinogens in Precolumbian Art', *Art and Environment in Native America*, ed. M. E. King and I. R. Traylor (Lubbock, 1974), pp. 55–101

——: *Hallucinogens and Culture* (Novato, CA, 1976, rev. San Francisco, 2/1985)

M. Dobkin de Ríos: *Hallucinogens: Cross-cultural Perspectives* (Albuquerque, 1984)

PETER W. STAHL

5. CRAFTSPEOPLE, ARTISTS AND THEIR PATRONS. The extraordinary results achieved by Mesoamerican craftspeople and artists are remarkable given that they usually worked within prescribed formats with simple tools and technology. Craftspeople used mostly stone tools, obsidian and flint blades and bone drills to work even the hardest surfaces. The wheel was known but was not employed for practical purposes. Metallurgy, not introduced into Mesoamerica until c. AD 800, was used chiefly for ornamental items, although metal tools played a role. The use of metals (*see* §X, 5 below) increased in the Late Post-Classic period (c. 1200–1521), and metal artefacts included axes, chisels, awls and punches, such small objects as tweezers, needles and pins, as well as the occasional beaten metal disc (several of which were recovered from the Sacred Cenote at Chichén Itzá, Yucatán). Raw materials were frequently imported over long distances with great effort, and production was often slow and painstaking, particularly for such ambitious work as monumental architecture and sculpture (*see* §§III and IV below).

Superbly made works from the Pre-Classic period (c. 2000 BC–c. AD 250) to the Post-Classic period (c. AD 900–1521) indicate that craft specialization was early and enduring. Only the most competent artists could carve stone monuments or figures in the hard jade used by the Olmec in the Middle Pre-Classic period (c. 1000–c. 300 BC), or produce large-scale ceramic figures or mural paintings in the Classic period (c. AD 250–c. 900; *see* §§V, VII and VIII below). The range of quality in surviving works demonstrates varying degrees of skill, suggesting hierarchies among the various craftspeople. Artists whose works demanded knowledge of esoteric religious iconography, complex symbolism, calendrical systems or hieroglyphic writing were highly educated and perhaps priests themselves, or possibly worked in conjunction with sacerdotal advisers. At the other end of the spectrum, the craftspeople who mass-produced common household or ceremonial items required less specialized education.

Archaeological excavation of lithic and ceramic remains has provided abundant evidence of craft workshops at various sites, some of them devoted not only to particular crafts but even to specialities within them. The recent identification of 'schools' of Maya vase painting suggests similar artistic workshops within recognized regional or metropolitan traditions. And major, long-term projects, such as the series of stone ballcourt reliefs at Tajín (in Veracruz state), Chichén Itzá and the hieroglyphic staircase at Copán (Honduras), required teams of workers, possibly grouped in workshops. The coherence of such organized work suggests that planning and supervision took place under master artists, as well as through cooperation between different groups of specialized craftspeople. Later, among the Aztecs, training within workshops was by apprenticeship, as illustrated in the Codex Mendoza (c. 1540s; Oxford, Bodleian Lib., MS. 3134, Arch. Selden A.1), providing a company of workers whose varying skills could be matched to suitable tasks. Other crafts, particularly those associated with women, such as weaving and embroidery, were probably products of household instruction and manufacture in all periods.

The artist's skill and ingenuity were highly esteemed, as was the quality of his or her work. As in most traditional societies, however, Mesoamerican art primarily emphasized mastery of the accepted forms, and social and cultural conventions, rather than self-expression. The interplay between imagination and tradition is evident in the varied articulations of inherited art forms throughout the lifespan of a culture and from culture to culture. Ceramic vessels and figurines, for example, were produced by virtually all Mesoamerican cultures in all regions during all periods. Yet the stylistic features of different cultures were highly distinctive, and within each tradition handmade items were remarkably diverse. Rather than degenerating into static and repetitive renderings over time, these works rank among the most inventive of Mesoamerican art forms. Although Mesoamerican artists and craftspeople have long been thought to be anonymous, advances in Maya hieroglyphic decipherment have revealed the signatures of Maya vase painters and sculptors. Other artists whose names are

5. Aztec craftspeople and artists: (a) goldworker; (b) lapidary; (c) featherworker; (d) painter; redrawn images from the Codex Mendoza, compiled c. 1540s (Oxford, Bodleian Library)

still unknown, but whose works reveal distinctive personal traits, have been tentatively identified as 'Masters'.

In Book IX of the Florentine Codex (Florence, Bib. Medicea-Laurenziana, MS. Palat. 218–220) the Franciscan missionary and early ethnographer Bernardino de Sahagún, with the aid of indigenous informants and assistants, described and illustrated three Aztec crafts in Central Mexico at the time of Spanish contact. Although Sahagún gathered his information in the mid-16th century, his texts and images record late pre-Hispanic artistic traditions, some of which were still being practised during the early colonial period. While selective, the data provides rare documentation on the role of the Mesoamerican artist and craftsperson in general. Sahagún focused his inquiry on three groups of artists: goldsmiths and casters, lapidaries who worked precious stones and featherworkers who were attached to the palace of the Aztec ruler (see fig. 5). Although concentrating on these élite master craftspeople, he also mentions other artisans who made and sold their uncommissioned works in the market-place. Distinctions existed between different specialist goldworkers, who were classed according to their workmanship and the tasks they performed. Honour was paid to the patron deities of the different crafts, and their feast days were celebrated. A close relationship existed between palace artisans and merchants who imported raw materials, such as the brightly coloured feathers of tropical birds. Passages in Book X extol the professional and personal qualities of good craftspeople; thus a good featherworker was not only 'accomplished' and 'ingenious' but 'diligent' and 'trustworthy'. The bad featherworker not only wasted feathers but was a sluggish and uncouth 'hypocrite'.

The artists Sahagún described represented an esteemed professional group within Aztec society, whose work was used for important public ceremonies. The 'featherworkers of the palace' created brilliant arrays for Motecuhzuma II to wear, as well as to place on a statue of the Aztec patron god Huitzilopochtli during ritual events or to be presented as gifts to foreign diplomats and rulers. In addition to commissions from rulers, the large number of surviving deity images and ritual items attests to regular religious patronage throughout Mesoamerica. Rich funerary furnishings in earlier periods show patronage by the noble classes, including luxury items commissioned during the patron's lifetime or expressly for his burial, such as personal adornments, expertly decorated vessels, intricate gold ornaments and finely carved stone, jade (*see* JADE, colour pl. II, fig. 1), shell and bone objects. Even lesser burials contained numerous ably made, decorated household and offertory items, which may have been privately commissioned from artisans or purchased from market sellers. The interment of such works in tombs and ceremonial caches, along with items made for commercial exchange, supplied Mesoamerican artists and craftspeople with a steady demand for their products.

BIBLIOGRAPHY

B. de Sahagún: *Historia general de las cosas de Nueva España* (MS., untraced, 1569; Spanish/Nahuatl illus. copy, *Florentine Codex*, Florence, Bib. Medicea-Laurenziana, MS. Palat. 218–20, n.d.); facs. *Códice Florentino: El manuscrito 218–20 de la colección Palatina de la Biblioteca Medicea Laurenziana*, 3 vols (Mexico City and Florence, 1979); Eng. trans. Nahuatl text and ed. C. E. Dibble and A. J. O. Anderson as *Florentine Codex: General History of the Things of New Spain*, 13 vols (Santa Fe, 1950–69)

M. Coe: *Mexico* (New York, 1994)

ELOISE QUIÑONES KEBER

II. Chronology and cultural traditions.

The Mesoamericans themselves developed several calendrical systems for time reckoning. Throughout most of Mesoamerica peoples used a sacred period count of 260-day cycles (20 weeks of 13 days each), an approximate solar year of 365 days (18 months of 20 days each and a 19th week of 5 days) and a Venus year of 584 days. A permutation of the 260- and 365-day calendars, known as the Calendar Round, coincided every 18,980 days or 52 years. All three cycles coincided every 104 years, or two 52-year cycles.

A second major system, known as the Long Count, was invented in the southern Gulf Coast region and further elaborated by the Maya. This was a running count of days, grouped into units of increasing magnitude, from a fixed point perhaps thought to be the beginning of time. Since this system had fallen into disuse before the Spanish arrival, considerable research has been necessary to establish its correlation with the Christian calendar. The 'Goodman–Martinez–Thompson' correlation, or some slight variation of it, has been generally accepted, which places the Maya Long Count date 11.16.0.0.0 on 13 November 1539. The units are *kin* ('day'; pl. *kinob*), *uinal* (20 *kinob*), *tun* (18 *uinlob* or 360 *kinob*), *katun* (20 *tunob* or 7200 *kinob*) and *baktun* (20 *katunob* or 144,000 *kinob*). Thus the Maya date 11.16.0.0.0 displays 11 *baktunob*, 16 *katunob*,

Arrival of man in the Americas	*c.* 20,000 BC
Archaic period	before *c.* 2000 BC
Pre-Classic period	*c.* 2000 BC–*c.* AD 250
Early	*c.* 2000–*c.* 1000 BC
Middle	*c.* 1000–*c.* 300 BC
Late	*c.* 300 BC–*c.* AD 250
Classic period	*c.* AD 250–*c.* 900
Early	*c.* AD 250–*c.* 600
Late	*c.* AD 600–*c.* 900
Post-Classic period	*c.* AD 900–1521
Early	*c.* AD 900–*c.* 1200
Late	*c.* 1200–1521
Spanish Conquest	1519–21

6. Chronological chart of Mesoamerican prehistory

0 *tunob*, 0 *uinob* and 0 *kinob*, or 1,699,200 days, and corresponds to a starting-date in August 3114 BC.

Mesoamerican prehistory is subdivided by modern scholars into Archaic, Pre-Classic, Classic and Post-Classic periods (see fig. 6), a scheme first applied by scholars working in the Maya region east of the Isthmus of Tehuantepec (see fig. 7). The scheme initially worked less well when applied to the more diverse cultures west of the Isthmus, and it works even less well for the cultures of West Mexico. Scholars thus vary the dates of the periods as appropriate for the pace of development in different regions with which they are concerned.

When the scheme was proposed the Classic period was seen as the apogee of Maya civilization, originally defined as the period during which the Maya carved stone inscriptions with dates in their Long Count calendar system. The Pre-Classic was perceived as a period of relatively little achievement and the Post-Classic as a protracted, decadent period following a spectacular collapse of the Classic Maya cities. Subsequent scholarship has shown that the Pre-Classic was in all regions a period of vigorous cultural development that laid the foundations of Mesoamerican culture and of Classic period civilization. All those cultural elements characteristic of Mesoamerica were in place by the end of the Pre-Classic period, which is therefore sometimes called the Formative period. As well as the rise of important ceremonial centres in the Gulf Coast region in the Middle Pre-Classic period, there was the development in the Late Pre-Classic of Zapotec civilization in the Valley of Oaxaca, Southern Highlands, and the beginning of Teotihuacán civilization in the Basin of Mexico, Central Highlands. Research has also shown that the Post-Classic, far from being a period of cultural decline, was one of social and cultural reorganization and development in its own right. This newly understood complexity in Meso-american culture led to proposals of several alternative chronological schemes, all of which become cumbersome in use. Most scholars thus continue to use the three-part scheme for its advantage of enabling them to relate events to each other throughout Mesoamerica while recognizing its rich cultural diversity.

ROBERT D. DRENNAN

1. Palaeoindian and Archaic periods. 2. Pre-Classic period (*c*. 200 BC–*c*. AD 250). 3. Classic period (*c*. AD 250–*c*. 900). 4. Post-Classic period (*c*. 900–1521).

1. PALAEOINDIAN AND ARCHAIC PERIODS.

(i) Palaeoindian period. The date of the entry of human inhabitants into the New World is uncertain, being variously fixed between *c*. 40,000 BP and *c*. 15,000 BP. In the area that became the Mesoamerican culture region, the Palaeoindian period, corresponding to the late Pleistocene period, can be divided into two broad chronological subdivisions.

The first period, from *c*. 30,000 to *c*. 15,000 BP, referred to by some authors as 'pre-projectile points stage' is characterized by the dominance of unifacially retouched lithic tools and the use and reworking of large mammal bones. In some cases, evidence is limited to the presence of hearths. This period includes sites in Nicaragua (El Bosque), and in Mexico such as El Cedral (San Luis Potosí), Valsequillo (Puebla), Tlapacoya and Tequixquiac

(Basin of Mexico). At Tlapacoya, hearths dated to *c*. 22,000 BP have yielded bone tools and unifacially retouched lithic artefacts associated with bones of American bear and of a fossil cervidae (*Odocoileus hallii*). Tequixquiac's area represents a formidably rich fossiliferous deposit of late Pleistocene date, potentially also important in anthropological data. Although the site has not been systematically excavated, manmade bone and stone artefacts have been found in association with remains of now extinct proboscidians, equines, camelids, ancient bisons, glyptodonts and ground sloths. Reported from this site was the sacrum of a fossil camelid bearing careful manmade cuts, perforations and groovings, giving it the appearance of a dog or a coyote's head (Mexico City, Mus. N. Antropol). This sacrum has been the centre of numerous debates, but for the prehistorian Aveleyra de Anda (1964, p. 387), the Tequixquiac sacrum 'would be American prehistory's first unquestionable example of Paleo-Indian true *art mobilier*'.

During the following period (*c*. 15,000–*c*. 9000 BP), hunter–gatherer cultures developed new lithic and bone technologies for hunting, gathering and food-processing. The lithic industry includes cores from which flakes were retouched to make side-scrapers, end-scrapers, burins and bifacial artefacts. Among the diagnostic features of this period is the fine bifacially retouched projectile point of obsidian, chert or chalcedony called 'Lerma' type—a laurel-leaf shaped, bi-pointed arrowhead—and 'Clovis' type—named after the eponymous site in New Mexico where it was first found. On each side of the base the 'Clovis' projectile point has diagnostic flutes or channels, made to facilitate its insertion on a wooden spear. Lerma and Clovis fluted points, with their fine parallel flaking scars, offer a clear testimony to the development of a remarkable skill in stone working at the end of Pleistocene times.

Numerous sites have been reported from Los Tapiales (Guatemala) to the Basin of Mexico, and in the Mexican states of Puebla, Chiapas, Oaxaca, Durango, Nuevo León, Tamaulipas, Coahuila and Sonora. In the Cueva Blanca site, Oaxaca, burnt and man-fractured bones of Pleistocene fauna were found. In the Tehuacán Valley, Puebla, 20 small sites have been reported. In the Basin of Mexico, several mammoth kill-sites have been excavated, for example Los Reyes Acozac, Santa Isabel Iztapán and San Bartolo Atepehuacán. San Bartolo Atepehuacán, with obsidian and basalt waste products of butchering tools, yielded a radiocarbon dating of 9661±400 BP. During the following millennium, the fluted point tradition disappeared, and large Pleistocene mammals faced total extinction.

Middle America is rich in undated rupestrian paintings, some probably from the Palaeoindian period. Rock shelter and cliff paintings of negative or positive hands, geometric motifs, man and animal silhouettes reflect traditions extending over millennia, even extending into the Spanish colonial period in northern Mexico.

(ii) Archaic period. The Archaic period between *c*. 9000 BP and the beginning of early 'Mesoamerican' village life represented a period of significant changes in food procurement systems and settlement patterns. Technology was marked by an impressive development of food-grinding implements and a greater variety of bone and

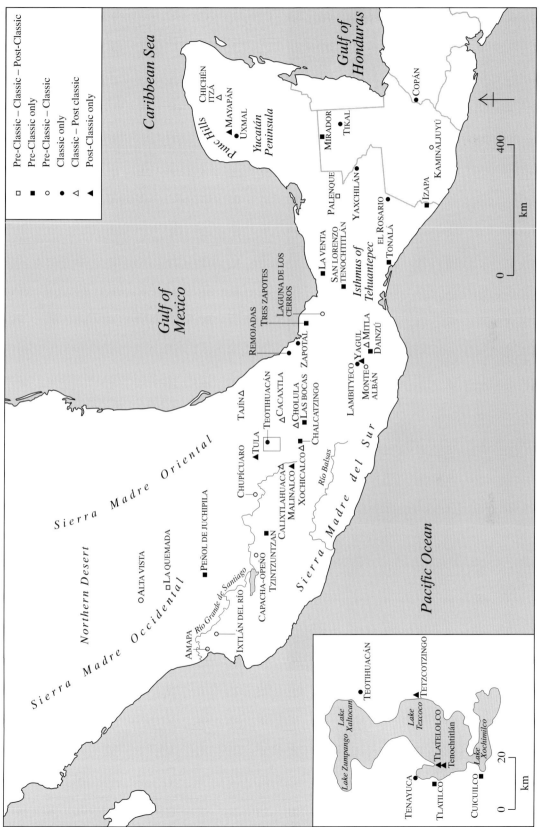

7. Map of Mesoamerica showing Pre-Classic, Classic and Post-Classic sites, all of which have separate entries in this dictionary

8. Anthropomorphic figurine of a pregnant female (other perspectives show a hermaphrodite or phallic image), fired clay, h. 54 mm, from the lake site of Tlapacoya-Zohapilco (Basin of Mexico), *c.* 4250 ± 110 BP (uncalibrated)

lithic tools. Middle America is considered one of the major centres of plant domestication in the world. During the Archaic period, and as a consequence of close man/plant relationships, such important food crops as maize, but also amaranth, squash, bean, chilli pepper, avocado and tomato, were gradually brought into cultivation. Although

semi-arid zones such as the valley of Tehaucán have yielded the best corpus of well-preserved botanical remains and early cultivated plants, it is probable that these regions had only a marginal role in putting in motion not only agrarian practices but also the whole integrated set of phenomena that characterized a 'neolithic' way of life. Within the contrasted environments of Middle America, coastal estuary zones as well as Highlands lake basins, highly favourable to early settlement, played a significant role. Early settlement led to demographic growth, new economic strategies, a more complex socio-political organization and changes in plastic expression. At the lake site of Tlapacoya-Zohapilco (Basin of Mexico), where a permanent site is attested since *c.* 7500 BP, diversified lithic tools and well-made standardized grinding mortars and mullers have been found, together with the earliest known specimen of a baked clay figurine with four eyes and no mouth, radiocarbon dated to 4250 ± 110 BP (uncalibrated) (see fig. 8).

By the eve of the Pre-Classic period (*c.* 2000 BC), fully agrarian villages and pottery-making communities had developed throughout the southern regions of Middle America, setting the economic and socio-cultural bases for the emergence of Mesoamerican civilization.

BIBLIOGRAPHY

R. S. MacNeish: 'Preliminary Archaeological Investigations in the Sierra de Tamaulipas, Mexico', *Trans. Amer. Philos. Soc.*, xlviii (1958) [whole issue]

L. Aveleyra Arroyo de Anda: 'The Primitive Hunters', *Hb. Mid. Amer. Ind.*, i (1964), pp. 348–412

C. Irwin-Williams: 'A Summary of Archaeological Evidence from the Valsequillo Region, Puebla, Mexico', *Proceedings of the 9th International Congress of Anthropological and Ethnological Sciences: La Haye, Mouton, 1967*, pp. 7–22

D. S. Byers and R. S. MacNeish, eds: *The Prehistory of the Tehuacán Valley*, 5 vols (Austin, 1967–77)

J. Lorenzo: 'Los primeros pobladores', *Del nomadismo a los centros ceremoniales*, ed. R. Piña Chan (Mexico City, 1975), pp. 15–59

K. V. Flannery, ed.: *The Early Mesoamerican Village* (New York, 1976)

R. Gruhn and A. L. Bryan: 'Los Tapiales: A Paleo-Indian Campsite in the Guatemala Highlands', *Proc. Amer. Philos. Soc.*, cxxi (1977), pp. 235–73

C. Niederberger: 'Early Sedentary Economy in the Basin of Mexico', *Science*, 203 (1979), pp. 131–41

K. V. Flannery, J. Marcus and S. A. Kowalewski: 'The Preceramic and Formative of the Valley of Oaxaca', *Hb. Mid. Amer. Ind.*, suppl., i (1981), pp. 48–93

R. S. MacNeish: 'Mesoamerica', *Early Man in the New World*, ed. R. Shutler (Beverly Hills, 1983), pp. 125–35

M. Coe, D. Snow and E. Benson: *Atlas of Ancient America* (Oxford, 1986), pp. 28–34, 89–91

K. Flannery, ed.: *Guilá Naquitz: Early Foraging and Early Agriculture in Oaxaca, Mexico*, Studies in Archaeology (New York, 1986)

J. L. Lorenzo and L. Mirambell: 'Preliminary Report on Archaeological and Paleoenvironmental Studies in the Area of El Cedral, San Luis Potosí, Mexico, 1977–1980', *New Evidence for the Pleistocene Peopling of the Americas*, ed. A. L. Bryan (Orono, 1986), pp. 107–13

J. L. Lorenzo and L. Mirambell, eds: *Tlapacoya: 35,000 años de historia del Lago de Chalco* (Mexico, 1986)

CHRISTINE NIEDERBERGER

2. PRE-CLASSIC PERIOD (*c.* 2000 BC–*c.* AD 250). The Pre-Classic period may be dated from the establishment of permanent village life based on subsistence agriculture, a simple definition that has been surprisingly difficult to put into practice. The transition to village life was not swift, but spread over several thousand years as different plants were domesticated in various parts of Mesoamerica from *c.* 7000 BC. The earliest known domesticated maize

appeared in the Tehuacán Valley, Puebla, about 5000 BC, but at this point it made up no more than a minor supplement of the diet. During this time Mesoamerica's inhabitants continued to live as hunter–gatherers in small mobile groups while cultivating plants on a scale which eventually produced true domesticates.

(i) Central and southern regions. (ii) West Mexico.

(i) Central and southern regions. From at least 1500 BC the first permanent villages appeared in the Basin of Mexico; the Puebla–Tlaxcala Basin; the Tehuacán Valley, Puebla; the Valley of Oaxaca; and on the Gulf Coast and the coasts of Guatemala, Belize and Chiapas. The villagers relied on plant cultivation for the bulk of their diet and made and used pottery in substantial quantities, although this was not the earliest pottery in Mesoamerica (*see* §VII, 2 below).

Most villages comprised no more than a dozen small pole-and-thatch houses scattered through an area of 1 to 3 ha. Each house probably corresponded to a single nuclear family whose members carried out daily activities in the area around the house structure. Burials were placed beneath the house floor or in the area around it. The evidence suggests that these earliest villages were economically self-sufficient. Although some materials were acquired from far away, such as sea shells and obsidian (volcanic glass), none of these can be considered necessities. Ceramics were used primarily for cooking and serving food, but they were well made and often elegantly decorated using a variety of techniques, including painting, incising and stamping. Forms included hemispherical and flat-bottomed bowls, and globular jars of all sizes with and without necks. The appearance of occasional pottery figurines of humans and animals began a long Mesoamerican tradition of figurine-making. Differences of status or wealth were apparently minimal. Regional population levels were low: the Valley of Oaxaca had less than 1000 inhabitants and the Basin of Mexico still fewer. All the villages in a region shared a well-defined pottery style, indicating close communication between the villages in a region, but although styles shared a number of general features they varied from region to region.

Once a pattern of autonomous egalitarian farming villages (in which decision-making was evidently communal) was established, it began to change. By *c.* 1200 BC the village at San José Mogote in the Valley of Oaxaca had grown to a population of hundreds, and that at SAN LORENZO TENOCHTITLÁN in the southern Gulf Coast to as much as 2000 inhabitants, reflecting a pattern of population growth that characterized most regions throughout the Pre-Classic period, although rates of growth varied. The majority of village populations, however, split up to found new villages, usually colonizing the unsettled parts of regions. OLMEC and ZAPOTEC civilizations began to take on recognizable form. New forms of architecture at Olmec San Lorenzo Tenochtitlan and at Zapotec San José Mogote imply the introduction of a more organized society. At San José Mogote stone and adobe platforms were constructed to support what were probably public buildings and two carved stone monuments were placed on a terraced hillside. At San Lorenzo

Tenochtitlán several sizeable earthen mounds were constructed to support buildings made of perishable materials. Open plazas were left between the mounds, creating an architectural complex similar to the pyramid temples and plazas described by the Spanish conquistadores nearly 3000 years later. A large number of monumental stone sculptures were originally located in the temple complex at San Lorenzo Tenochtitlán. Thus there developed, immediately after the establishment of a sedentary agricultural way of life, the kind of large-scale, centralized society that was to produce the art of Pre-Columbian Mesoamerica.

At San José Mogote there was evidence for the emergence of hereditary status distinctions and of the presence of specialist craftsmen who made ornaments for the new upper class. Ornaments were made of local materials, such as mica and bone, and from materials imported from outside the Valley of Oaxaca, such as shells from the Gulf Coast and the Pacific, and feathers of colourful lowland birds. Magnetite was brought from the mountains around the Valley of Oaxaca and laboriously polished into concave mirrors of thumbnail size, many of which were exported as luxury items to the surrounding regions. Chemical analysis of these objects demonstrates that at least one mirror from San Lorenzo Tenochtitlán was made of material that came from Oaxaca. The inhabitants of the valley of Oaxaca also began to make flaked stone-cutting tools from obsidian, which had to be brought from outside the valley, initiating a complex network of exchange that brought obsidian from sources all over Mesoamerica.

San José Mogote became a centre for the surrounding villages but probably did not exercise any rigorous territorial control. People from these villages would have come to the centre for the activities conducted in the public buildings and to help build them. Craftsmen were concentrated at San José Mogote near the largest number of high-status individuals, but many smaller villages also show evidence of status differentiation, albeit on a more modest scale.

Much less is known about the organization of San Lorenzo Tenochtitlán's inhabitants and surrounding region, although it is clear that a large labour force was mobilized to build the large earth-filled platforms and other public works; and that specialist craftsmen produced a large amount of monumental art. Massive blocks of basalt for carving were brought to the site from considerable distances, and areas of the natural landscape were altered to accommodate the settlement. Its population of 2000 to 2500 seems disproportionately small to support such architectural and artistic endeavours, and it is assumed that the surrounding region was dotted with small villages whose inhabitants provided much of the labour it required and shared in the social, cultural, religious and economic benefits generated by the centre. It is uncertain whether the monumental scale of public art and architecture at San Lorenzo Tenochtitlán constitutes evidence of a society ruled by powerful lords who could order the populace to undertake hard labour, or of a populace willing to participate in a communal effort to glorify the gods. In either case the society certainly integrated thousands of inhabitants in numerous settlements and included an élite group that was strongly differentiated from the commoners and provided leaders of considerable authority, if not power. It was from this social matrix that the Olmec art style developed and spread to distant parts of Mesoamerica.

The Middle Pre-Classic (*c.* 1000–*c.* 300 BC) was a period of rapid social development elsewhere in Mesoamerica, similar to that at San Lorenzo Tenochtitlán and San José Mogote. The most spectacular centre of development remained the southern Gulf Coast, where San Lorenzo Tenochtitlán was all but abandoned after *c.* 900 BC, to be replaced by the site of LA VENTA from *c.* 800–*c.* 400 BC. La Venta also comprised a large complex of public architecture with many public sculptures carved from massive stone blocks. Numerous smaller works of art were carved from serpentine, jadeite or other stone or fashioned in ceramics. There was considerable stylistic continuity between San Lorenzo Tenochtitlán and La Venta and possibly political and social continuity as well, although it seems unlikely that either centre directly dominated an area extending more than a few dozen square km.

In the Valley of Oaxaca, San José Mogote increased in scale and complexity, and similar or larger centres emerged in several other highland valleys, including TLATILCO and others in the Basin of Mexico, CHALCATZINGO in Morelos, KAMINALJUYÚ in the Valley of Guatemala, and others. Pottery and portable stone sculpture in many regions show strong stylistic affinities to Olmec art, but it is uncertain whether all examples were manufactured at one place— presumably in the Gulf Coast 'Olmec Heartland', although other regions have been suggested—and traded to distant centres, or were locally made imitations in many regions. Public architecture at centres outside the Gulf Coast increased in size during the Middle Pre-Classic period, and truly monumental sculpture was also produced elsewhere, notably in the series of relief-carvings at Chalcatzingo and at several sites near the Pacific coast of Chiapas and Guatemala. The parallel social development in a number of regions, as new communities adopted stylistic forms from their neighbours, was undoubtedly responsible for the widespread similarities in Middle Pre-Classic period art.

The beginning of the Late Pre-Classic period (*c.* 300 BC–*c.* AD 250) brought more fundamental change throughout Mesoamerica than had the transition from Early to Middle Pre-Classic. The Olmec art style disappeared, and there was greater emphasis on regional economic development. A ceremonial centre founded at MONTE ALBÁN *c.* 450 BC expanded to become larger than any previous settlement in the Valley of Oaxaca. Major Late Pre-Classic settlements in the Maya lowlands included MIRADOR, Cerros and Komchén, while other centres such as TIKAL, which were to become important in the Early Classic period, had already begun to develop.

BIBLIOGRAPHY

P. Drucker: 'La Venta, Tabasco: A Study of Olmec Ceramics and Art', *Bureau Amer. Ethnol. Bull.*, cliii (Washington, DC, 1952)
P. Drucker, R. F. Heizer and R. J. Squier: 'Excavations at La Venta, Tabasco, 1955', *Bureau Amer. Ethnol. Bull.*, clxx (Washington, DC, 1959)
D. S. Byers and R. S. MacNeish, eds: *The Prehistory of the Tehuacán Valley*, 5 vols (Austin, 1967–77)
Dumbarton Oaks Conference on the Olmec: Dumbarton Oaks, 1967
I. Marquina, ed.: *Proyecto Cholula* (Mexico City, 1970)
K. V. Flannery: 'Origins of Agriculture: A Review', *Annu. Rev. Anthropol.*, ii (1973), pp. 271–310
R. Millon: *Urbanization at Teotihuacán, Mexico*, 2 vols (Austin, 1973)
K. V. Flannery, ed.: *The Early Mesoamerican Village* (New York, 1976)
R. E. Blanton: *Monte Albán: Settlement Patterns at the Ancient Zapotec Capital* (New York, 1978)
C. Niederberger: 'Early Sedentary Economy in the Basin of Mexico', *Science*, 203 (1979), pp. 131–41
W. T. Sanders, J. R. Parsons and R. S. Santley: *The Basin of Mexico: Ecological Processes in the Evolution of a Civilization* (New York, 1979)
M. D. Coe and R. A. Diehl: *In the Land of the Olmec: The Archaeology of San Lorenzo Tenochtitlán*, 2 vols (Austin, 1980)
E. P. Benson, ed.: *The Olmec and their Neighbors: Essays in Memory of Matthew W. Stirling* (Washington, DC, 1981)
R. E. Blanton and others: *The Prehispanic Settlement Patterns of the Central and Southern Parts of the Valley of Oaxaca, Mexico*, i of *Monte Albán's Hinterland*, Mem. Mus. Anthropol.: U. MI, no. 15 (Ann Arbor, 1982)
D. C. Grove: *Chalcatzingo: Excavations on the Olmec Frontier* (London, 1984)
B. L. Stark: 'Origins of Food Production in the New World', *American Archaeology, Past, and Future: A Celebration of the Society for American Archaeology, 1935–1985*, ed. D. J. Meltzer, D. D. Fowler and J. A. Sabloff (Washington, DC, 1986), pp. 277–321

ROBERT D. DRENNAN

(ii) West Mexico. The prehistory of West Mexico does not fit easily into the Pre-Classic–Classic–Post-Classic chronological scheme applied to the rest of Mesoamerica. The term West Mexican refers to peoples and cultures of the Mexican states of Michoacán, Jalisco, Colima, Nayarit, Sinaloa and parts of Guerrero and Guanajuato, bordering the Pacific coastline. Two major river systems, the Lerma–Santiago and the Balsas, traverse the region, and two mountain ranges, the Sierra Madre Occidental and the Sierra Madre del Sur, merge in Guerrero, creating a topography of cool highlands, moderate temperate zones, hot tropics and a varied coastline of mangrove swamps in the south and rocky shores in the north. In this region cultures developed within the general framework of Mesoamerica but with distinctive local styles and traits and without the practice of recording dates and records in hieroglyphic texts. The archaeology of the area is known from sporadic and uncoordinated excavations carried out by various institutions and individuals since the 1930s, often stimulated by the wealth of looted pottery vessels and figurines that appeared for sale on the open market.

The fine hollow ceramic figurines of people and animals, executed in a lively naturalistic style and often of highly polished red or brown clay, are the best-known objects from West Mexico. Nevertheless they represent only a small fragment of West Mexico's past. They often accompanied the deceased into shaft-and-chamber tombs (*see* §III, 2(iii)(a) below) and are believed to date from between *c.* 1500 BC and AD 400. The 'Chinesco' figures from Nayarit, with an oriental cast to their features, may be the oldest. Figurines of all dates, ranging in height from 270 mm to 500 mm, depict animals and people carrying out a variety of daily activities including fishing, carrying jars, playing musical instruments (such as drums, rattles and flutes), dancing or doing acrobatics. Among the most charming are small village groups depicting houses, temples and people, or even ball games complete with players and spectators according to some 16th-century descriptions. Some of the human figures may represent shamans, and red dogs from Colima were manufactured to 'carry' the soul of the deceased across a river, one of the obstacles to overcome in order to reach a paradise.

Early occupation of West Mexico dates from *c.* 2000 BC. At Matanchén Bay on the coast of Nayarit a hunter–gatherer 'food extraction station' has been excavated, where chopper tools, cobble hammerstones and obsidian flakes used to open shells were found. Fibre-tempered sherds known as 'Pox' pottery dating to *c.* 2300 BC have been found in coastal Guerrero at Puerto Marqués near Acapulco and constitute some of the earliest pottery known in Mesoamerica.

Contemporary with the middle and later Pre-Classic period are numerous coastal midden sites in Colima and Nayarit and hundreds of shaft-and-chamber tombs in the highland area from Nayarit through Jalisco to Colima. Dating from 1500 BC to AD 400, the latter consist of a shaft 4–6 m deep leading to one or more side chambers containing skeletons accompanied by lavish offerings. Many of the tombs were reused in antiquity and also, unfortunately, looted more recently. Such tombs are well known in north-west South America (*see* SOUTH AMERICA, PRE-COLUMBIAN, §II, 2). Similarities in pottery also indicate contact between the two areas. Peoples in the highland lake basin of Jalisco and along the Río Grande de Santiago developed a distinctive architectural style comprising circular pyramids surrounded by round patios and platforms, including sites such as Teuchitlán (near Ahualulco), which gave its name to a distinctive architectural tradition (*see* §III, 2(iii)(b) below).

BIBLIOGRAPHY

B. Bell: 'Archaeology of Nayarit, Jalisco and Colima', *Hb. Mid. Amer. Ind.*, xi (1971), pp. 694–753

R. Chadwick: 'Archaeological Synthesis of Michoacan and Adjacent Regions', *Hb. Mid. Amer. Ind.*, xi (1971), pp. 657–93

C. W. Meighan: 'Archaeology of Sinaloa', *Hb. Mid. Amer. Ind.*, xi (1971), pp. 754–67

M. Porter-Weaver: *The Aztecs, Maya and their Predecessors: Archaeology of Mesoamerica* (New York, 1972, rev. 3/1993), pp. 112–20, 220–23, 469–75

M. E. Smith and C. M. Heath-Smith: 'Waves of Influence in Postclassic Mesoamerica? A Critique of the Mixteca–Puebla Concept', *Anthropology*, iv/2 (1980), pp. 15–50

M. S. Foster and P. C. Weigand: *The Archaeology of West and Northwest Mesoamerica* (Boulder and London, 1985)

D. Hosler: 'Ancient West Mexican Metallurgy: South and Central American Origins and Mexican Transformations', *Amer. Anthropologist*, xl (1988), pp. 832–55

P. C. Weigand: 'The Teuchitlán Tradition of Western Mesoamerica', *La época clásica: Nuevos hallazgos, nuevas ideas*, ed. A. Cardos de Méndez (Mexico City, 1990), pp. 25–54

H. P. Pollard: 'The Construction of Ideology in the Emergence of the Prehispanic Tarascan State', *Anc. Mesoamerica*, ii (1991), pp. 167–79

P. C. Weigand: *Evolución de una civilización prehispanica: Arqueología de Jalisco, Nayarit y Zacatecas* (Michoacán, 1993)

MURIEL PORTER-WEAVER

3. CLASSIC PERIOD (*c.* AD 250–*c.* 900). Classic-period Mesoamerica was marked by the widespread development of numerous cities and ceremonial centres and by the rise of large-scale states in three regions: the Basin of Mexico in the Central Highlands, the Valley of Oaxaca in the Southern Highlands and the Maya lowlands. Although there was substantial cultural change, each region developed a consistent pattern and style. In the Gulf Coast and Maya lowland regions several city-states vied for political and economic power, while the Central Highlands were dominated by Teotihuacán and the Southern Highlands by the Zapotec capital at Monte Albán. Political upheavals between *c.* AD 700 and 900 brought an end to Teotihuacán,

Monte Albán and the Classic Maya cities, together with population decline and migration. Reasons for these upheavals were many and varied from region to region. Principal among them were overpopulation, environmental degradation, disruption of long-distance trade patterns and increased competition from centres in other regions.

(i) Gulf Coast. (ii) Central Highlands. (iii) Southern Highlands. (iv) Maya region. (v) West Mexico.

(i) *Gulf Coast.* In the final centuries of the Pre-Classic period all traces of Olmec culture were transformed beyond recognition. At the long-occupied site of TRES ZAPOTES, which succeeded La Venta as an important Olmec ceremonial centre, aspects of Olmec sculptural traditions remained, but artistic links were otherwise stronger with the site of IZAPA in the Maya highlands. In the final century BC the Long Count calendar was developed, only to be abandoned six centuries later.

In the central Gulf Coast the sites of Cerro de las Mesas and REMOJADAS, both occupied from the Middle Pre-Classic period to the Post-Classic, developed distinctive artistic styles that influenced their immediate regions during the Classic period and were exported elsewhere. The heyday of Cerro de las Mesas was between *c.* AD 300 and 600, when its inhabitants built ceremonial mounds and other structures, mostly of earth and clay, and erected numerous stone stelae bearing Long Count dates between AD 468 and 533. Relief-carvings on the stelae depict individuals straddling male figures, presumably as a record of historical events. Ceramics featured large, hollow figures of deities. Beneath the clay stairway of one mound a large cache of jade and serpentine objects was found, including a treasure trove of jade items: a La Venta-style Olmec canoe incised with jaguar faces, celts from Central America, and early Classic Maya plaques and earspools (all Jalapa, U. Veracruzana, Mus. Antropol.). At Remojadas the ceramic tradition featured figures decorated with bitumen paint, huge, hollow figures of gods and goddesses, and 'laughing figures' of grinning boys and girls with upraised arms.

The dominant Classic north Gulf Coast site was TAJÍN of the Totonac people. There they built a vast ceremonial centre of stone pyramidal platforms and other structures, including the Pyramid of the Niches and a ballcourt with six relief panels depicting scenes of myth, ritual and sacrifice.

Distinctive artefacts of the Classic-period Gulf Coast include *yugos, hachas* and *palmas*, each associated with the ball-game. The Mesoamerican ball-game, probably invented by the Olmec, was further developed and ritualistically formalized in the Classic period. The *yugo* was a U-shaped stone object, often richly carved with characteristic Totonac interlace, raised-edge scrolls and mythological themes. Wooden and leather *yugos* were worn about the hips by ball-players. *Hachas*, thin, stone slabs reminiscent of hatchet blades, and *palmas*, narrow, spade-shaped stones, were similarly carved and may have been placed on the fronts of *yugos* during post-game rituals.

Totonac scroll motifs occur in murals at Teotihuacán (*see* §(ii) below), but there is less evidence of reciprocal influence at Tajín or Cerro de las Mesas. However, in the southern Gulf Coast the site of Matacapan appears to have been a Teotihuacán trading station, featuring typical Central Highlands TALUD-TABLERO architecture.

BIBLIOGRAPHY

T. Proskouriakoff: *Varieties of Classic Central Veracruz Sculpture*, Carnegie Inst. Washington, Contrib. Amer. Anthropol. & Hist., 606/58 (Washington, DC, 1954), pp. 61–121 [stylistic classification of *yugos*, *hachas* and *palmas*]

M. Porter-Weaver: *The Aztecs, Maya and their Predecessors: Archaeology of Mesoamerica* (New York, 1972, rev. 2/1981), pp. 243–56

M. Coe, D. Snow and E. Benson: *Atlas of Ancient America* (Oxford, 1986), pp. 108–13

M. E. Miller: *The Art of Mesoamerica from Olmec to Aztec* (London, 1986), pp. 92–102

DAVID M. JONES

(ii) Central Highlands. In the Late Pre-Classic Basin of Mexico the two ceremonial centres of TEOTIHUACÁN and CUICUILCO began to dominate the northern and southern halves respectively. Little is known about Cuicuilco other than its distinctive four-tiered round pyramid. It was surrounded by agricultural land that probably supported a population larger than that at Teotihuacán. In the early 1st century AD a volcanic eruption deposited a thick layer of lava and ash over Cuicuilco, effectively ending its rivalry with Teotihuacán, although it is uncertain whether this destruction was the primary reason for Cuicuilco's decline.

Teotihuacán grew dramatically during the first few centuries AD, reaching a peak of perhaps as many as 200,000 inhabitants by *c.* AD 500. It was not only the largest city in Mesoamerica, but among the half-dozen largest cities in the world. The inhabitants lived in crowded multi-family apartment compounds lining a uniform grid-plan of streets that had been established early in the city's development. The grid plan extended beyond the city limits to determine the location and orientation of outlying settlements as well. The ideological, social, political and economic forces that drew people into the city were so strong that from the Early Classic period (*c.* AD 250–*c.* 600) more than 80% of the population of the Basin of Mexico lived in this one centre. Settlements of intermediate size, domination of which had formerly been contested between Teotihuacán and Cuicuilco, were abandoned, and even the towns and villages of the once populous southern Basin around Cuicuilco vanished.

The concentration of the population and the regularity of the city's plan suggest considerable centralized political control. Whether this situation was due to forced settlement by powerful rulers or to the drawing power of the city's thriving economy is uncertain. Economic factors seem to have dominated Teotihuacán more than any other Classic period city. There is evidence of specialized craftsmen working together in compounds to produce figurines, pottery, ground and flaked stone tools and, apparently most important, sharp cutting blades of obsidian collected from nearby sources. Some evidence suggests that the working of obsidian was a state-controlled enterprise that supplied not just the residents of Teotihuacán and the Basin of Mexico but also much more distant markets throughout Mesoamerica. A large open area near the centre of the city may have served as a market-place for the exchange of craft goods and foodstuffs.

By the middle of the Classic period there were once again some mid-sized towns, but all were dominated by Teotihuacán, and the distinction between city and countryside remained strong. Small-scale canal systems were essential to reliable agriculture in the north-east Basin, and springs near Teotihuacán were one of a number of sources of water that were exploited. The boundaries of the city and of smaller towns are relatively easy to recognize and with the population concentrated in the city the farmers living there must have had to travel substantial distances to reach their fields.

Teotihuacán, in keeping with Mesoamerican cultural patterns, was also a ceremonial centre. Religious buildings dominated the city along the broad north–south avenue now called the 'Street of the Dead', including the 'Pyramid of the Sun', the single largest pyramid-temple of the Classic period, and scores of smaller ones. Sculpture was less common than in other areas of Mesoamerica, but interiors and exteriors of important buildings were often decorated with painted murals, a small portion of which survive. Hieroglyphic texts, in contrast to the Southern Highlands and the Maya region, are rare and of limited value for understanding the culture of Teotihuacán.

The size of Teotihuacán and the wide distribution of Teotihuacán-made objects and architectural style throughout Mesoamerica have led some scholars to argue that Teotihuacán had created a vast empire maintained by military force. Although Teotihuacán is not fortified, abundant wall paintings show warriors carrying shields and spears. Contemporary evidence of political organization in the southern Maya Lowlands and in the Valley of Oaxaca, however, does not indicate subjugation to Teotihuacán. Nevertheless, the inhabitants of both regions acquired goods from Teotihuacán, including unworked obsidian, and borrowed Teotihuacán architectural and sculptural styles. Other scholars interpret the evidence to show the scope of Teotihuacán's commercial empire, but there is disagreement as to whether the extent of control included luxury and prestige items only, or basic necessities as well. At Monte Albán, Teotihuacán goods and styles were considerably less common than in the more distant southern Maya Lowlands. On the other hand, several carved stone reliefs and glyphic texts at Monte Albán refer to Teotihuacán in contexts that suggest peaceful and regular political relationships between rulers at the two cities.

(iii) Southern Highlands. The most important centre of development in the Classic Southern Highlands was in the Valley of Oaxaca, where the Zapotec settlement at Monte Albán was founded *c.* 450 BC. There was strong cultural continuity with the Pre-Classic period. Monte Albán was the largest community in the valley, with a population of about 5000, and immediately replaced San José Mogote as the region's principal town (*see* §1(i) above). At the same time the population of the valley surged from fewer than 2000 to about 15,000. The entire valley population was dominated politically by Monte Albán, and politics provided much of the content for public art. The *'danzante'* relief-carvings in the main plaza, once thought to represent dancers, are now known to depict captives and corpses, some of which are individually identified with glyphs representing either their personal names or the names of their towns. Whether they were slain in battle, captured

and executed, or captured and sacrificed in religious ritual, their deaths were undoubtedly part of Monte Albán's conquest of the region. At San José Mogote the earliest and only known *danzante* found outside Monte Albán shows that the Monte Albán *danzantes* were part of an earlier practice. The San José Mogote *danzante* was placed horizontally on the ground between two temple platforms so that people entering the town plaza walked across the figure, perpetuating after death the public humiliation of the individual depicted and of his town. The more than 300 *danzantes* at Monte Albán formed an impressive display in the south-west quarter of the main plaza, surrounded by the city's most important buildings.

Monte Albán grew in size and political power during the Classic period, adding and improving temples and palaces around the main plaza. Smaller complexes of temples and élite residences were scattered within a large residential zone covering the tops of a ridge and several associated hills. At its peak, Monte Albán's population exceeded 20,000 inhabitants, divided into 14 clearly identifiable neighbourhoods. The *danzantes* were carved during the first few centuries of the city's existence and by the 1st century AD public sculpture depicted primarily glyphs in relief commemorating conquests. Each brief text comprises three elements: a 'place sign', an inverted head and a third element that varies from one carving to another, naming the place conquered. Some of the places have been tentatively identified by comparing them to glyphic place-names in use at the time of the Spanish Conquest. All are outside the Valley of Oaxaca, indicating that Monte Albán extended its empire by conquest over much of the Southern Highlands. After *c.* AD 100, relief-carvings became less common at Monte Albán and probably portray elaborately costumed rulers performing political activities sufficiently important to merit commemoration.

Monte Albán was a religious centre as well as a political capital. Its territory was evidently administered by a bureaucracy headed by Monte Albán's ruler. Tribute was collected, by military force when necessary, and garrisons of soldiers were maintained in some conquered provinces. Agricultural development within the valley was planned and directed by the state, and canal systems were used to ensure sufficient production. Residents of the city included artists and craftsmen, but Monte Albán does not seem to have been a regional economic centre as Teotihuacán was, redistributing goods throughout the region. Goods produced at and brought to Monte Albán were primarily for the use of its inhabitants, rather than for trade, and the mechanisms for provisioning the rest of the region were apparently diffused through several valley towns.

(iv) Maya region. Maya architectural and sculptural styles were firmly established in the Late Pre-Classic period. In the Classic period they were influenced by social and political systems. From the Late Pre-Classic onwards large stone palaces and temples were constructed at ceremonial centres such as KAMINALJUYÚ, TIKAL, COPÁN, PALENQUE, UXMAL, YAXCHILÁN and others. Here also were the carved stone monuments whose scenes and glyphic texts have provided important information about the Classic Maya, particularly regarding their methods of recording political and historical events—the Long Count—and their mathematics.

Maya mathematics and the Long Count used the vigesimal number system, in which each unit is 20 of the next smaller unit, except for the *tun* of only 18 *uinalob*, a deviation probably used to provide a rough correspondence between the *tun* and the solar year. Numerals were combinations of bars and dots and included the zero as a place value. Each dot represented one and each bar five, combined in a fashion reminiscent of Roman numerals up to nineteen. Twenty was represented by a one (dot) in the '20s column' and a zero in the 'units column'. Precise astronomical observations were made and confirmed over very long periods of time, including the accurate computation of lunar and solar cycles, and of several planets, most prominently Venus. Records of these observations were carved on stone monuments and provide important evidence in establishing the correlation between the Long Count and the Christian calendar.

Since the late 1950s it has become clear that the subjects of Classic Maya glyphic texts and the figures that accompany them describe not only religious affairs, as was once thought, but also political events. The monuments depict and were mostly erected by rulers and their wives to commemorate the dates of births, marriages and accessions, making it clear that the Maya were ruled by a hereditary aristocracy, with ruling houses competing between cities. Warfare was endemic, but it does not seem that any one centre ever dominated the entire southern Maya Lowlands, although marriage alliances between ruling houses were made. A few centres, such as Tikal, have evidence of fortifications, and painted murals and sculptures amply document the public humiliation, mutilation and execution of war captives.

Maya centres were once thought to have been 'vacant ceremonial centres', occupied only by priests and their retainers to maintain the temples and perform religious rituals. But the realization that the elaborately dressed figures carved on stelae depict hereditary rulers showed that the centres were also the capitals of defined territories. Mesoamerican politics and religion were always closely intertwined. Political monuments were placed in front of temples, and rulers undoubtedly took part in rituals and sacrifices to appease the gods. The populations of Maya cities numbered into the tens of thousands and were widely distributed around ceremonial cores. The exact locations of the homes of artists and craftsmen, whether in the cores or surrounding 'suburbs', is uncertain, but Classic Maya cities seem to have functioned less as economic centres than did their Central and Southern Highlands counterparts. Maya economy seems to have been more decentralized and unspecialized.

In similar contrast to the Central and Southern Highlands, the Maya region included a substantial 'rural' population, particularly in the Late Classic period (*c.* AD 600–*c.* 900), and the distinction between city and countryside was not as clearly marked. Agriculture comprised elaborate and labour-intensive systems, including terraced hillsides and artificial, 'ridged' fields in low, swampy areas.

BIBLIOGRAPHY
S. G. Morley, G. W. Brainerd and R. J. Sharer: *The Ancient Maya* (Stanford, 1946, rev. Palo, Alto, 4/1983)

I. Marquina, ed.: *Proyecto Cholula* (Mexico City, 1970)

T. P. Culbert, ed.: *The Classic Maya Collapse* (Albuquerque, 1973)

R. Millon: *Urbanization at Teotihuacán, Mexico*, 2 vols (Austin, 1973)

E. R. Wolf, ed.: *The Valley of Mexico: Studies in Pre-Hispanic Ecology and Society* (Albuquerque, 1976)

R. E. W. Adams, ed.: *The Origins of Maya Civilization* (Albuquerque, 1977)

R. E. Blanton: *Monte Albán: Settlement Patterns at the Ancient Zapotec Capital* (New York, 1978)

P. D. Harrison and B. L. Turner II, eds: *Pre-Hispanic Maya Agriculture* (Albuquerque, 1978)

W. Ashmore, ed.: *Lowland Maya Settlement Patterns* (Albuquerque, 1981)

R. E. Blanton and others: *The Prehispanic Settlement Patterns of the Central and Southern Parts of the Valley of Oaxaca, Mexico*, i of *Monte Albán's Hinterland*, Mem. Mus. Anthropol.: U. MI, no. 15 (Ann Arbor, 1982)

K. V. Flannery, ed.: *Maya Subsistence: Studies in Memory of Dennis E. Puleston* (New York, 1982)

N. Hammond: *Ancient Maya Civilization* (New Brunswick, NJ, 1982)

G. R. Willey: 'Maya Archaeology', *Science*, 215 (1982), pp. 260–67

K. V. Flannery and J. Marcus, eds: *The Cloud People: Divergent Evolution of the Zapotec and Mixtec Civilizations* (New York, 1983)

J. A. Sabloff and E. W. Andrews V, eds: *Late Lowland Maya Civilization: Classic to Postclassic* (Albuquerque, 1986)

ROBERT D. DRENNAN

(v) West Mexico. During the Classic period there was increased contact with the peoples of the Central Highlands, especially with the city of TEOTIHUACÁN. Teotihuacán explorers and merchants ventured north and west in search of sources of special obsidian, turquoise and various ores. Some Teotihuacán-type artefacts are found sporadically in the west of the region—stone masks, frescoed vessels, pyrite mirrors, turquoise—and local workers imitated the Teotihuacán TALUD-TABLERO style. However, a unique and important architectural complex of concentric circular construction (called the Teuchitlán tradition) is found in the highland lake districts of Jalisco and Nayarit (see §III, 2(iii)(b) below). By *c.* AD 900 or a little earlier the first metallurgy in Mesoamerica appeared at sites on the coast of Guerrero and at Amapa, Nayarit, thought to be further evidence of contact with north-west South America.

For bibliography *see* §2(ii) above.

MURIEL PORTER-WEAVER

4. POST-CLASSIC PERIOD (*c.* 900–1521). Simultaneous with the Late Classic demise of Teotihuacán, Monte Albán and various Maya southern lowlands cities was the rise or revival of numerous cities throughout Mesoamerica, both in rivalry to the dominance of the former and in response to the power vacuum created by their disappearance. In the Gulf Coast the florescence of TAJÍN spans the Late Classic–Early Post-Classic periods; several cities in the Central Highlands ringed the Basin of Mexico— TULA, CHOLULA and XOCHICALCO. In the Southern Highlands, Zapotec Monte Albán was all but abandoned by *c.* AD 1000 and succeeded by Zapotec–Mixtec valley sites such as MITLA and YAGUL; in the Maya region the emphasis shifted north into the northern lowlands of the Yucatán Peninsula, to sites such as CHICHÉN ITZÁ and later MAYAPÁN. The chronological overlap between the Classic-period powers and their Early Post-Classic rivals varied considerably.

With the rise of the TOLTEC state in the Early Post-Classic period and the subsequent rise of the AZTEC empire in the Late Post-Classic, central Mesoamerica became increasingly politically unified. In contrast, the large MAYA states of the Early Post-Classic period finally broke up into smaller states during the final years of the Late Post-Classic.

(i) Gulf Coast. (ii) Central Highlands. (iii) Southern Highlands. (iv) Maya region. (v) West Mexico.

(i) Gulf Coast. The site of Tajín continued to be occupied into the Early Post-Classic period (*c.* AD 900–*c.* 1200), exercising considerable regional influence until *c.* 1200, when it was virtually abandoned. Its place in the Gulf Coast region was taken up by the foundation at Cempoala (or Zempoala), also *c.* 1200, shifting Totonac interests to the south. North of Totonac territory the HUASTEC peoples came to greater notice from *c.* AD 900, possibly through direct conquest from the west by the Toltecs, who built the fortified site of Castillo de Teayo in Huastec territory, and partly in the general movement of northern peoples at the time. The Huastecs are known particularly for their construction of round platforms and other structures at sites such as Las Flores and Tancol, otherwise rare in Mesoamerica, and for their use of bitumen as paint and glue.

Both the Huastecs and Totonacs maintained considerable trade and cultural contacts with their Maya neighbours to the south as well as with the Central Highlands. In the late 15th century their territories were incorporated by trade and conquest into the Aztec empire and they were made to pay tribute.

BIBLIOGRAPHY

M. Porter-Weaver: *The Aztecs, Maya and their Predecessors: Archaeology of Mesoamerica* (New York, 1972, rev. 2/1981), pp. 243–50, 375, 385–7, 404, 425

J. Kelly: *The Complete Visitor's Guide to Mesoamerican Ruins* (Norman, 1982), pp. 145–58

DAVID M. JONES

(ii) Central Highlands. Many of the centres that emerged in the Early Post-Classic Central Highlands had probably been part of the Teotihuacán economic 'empire' as providers of important goods. Other cities, although they must have had contact with Teotihuacán, were otherwise outside its control: Xochicalco was beyond the western limits of Teotihuacán power; Tula was further north than any previous large centre; and cities in the Valley of Oaxaca, the Gulf Coast and the Maya region were outside the Central Highlands altogether. None of these cities and their regional sustaining populations was as large as Teotihuacán. Tula's peak population was 30,000 to 40,000 inhabitants and its sustaining rural population was not dramatically larger; estimates for Xochicalco and Cholula are similar or smaller. General patterns of social, political and economic organization followed the outlines established in the Classic period.

For the Post-Classic period, oral tradition and legendary history can be added to archaeological data. At the heart of Early Post-Classic history is Tula, identified as the legendary Toltec capital Tollán. Information about the Toltecs and Tollán comes largely through a filter of later Aztec myth and legend written down after the Spanish Conquest and must therefore be used cautiously. But it is clear that for the Aztecs 'Toltec' and 'Tollán' were labels for a vaguely defined ancient 'Golden Age', which at the time of the Spanish Conquest represented the skills and wisdom of traditional Mesoamerican civilization as opposed to 'Chichimec', referring to the uncivilized barbarians of the northern frontier. The Aztecs regarded all Central Highland Classic cities as 'Toltec' and were enormously concerned with claiming the entire heritage of Mesoamerican civilization as their own direct ancestry. Careful collation of the documentary sources reveals a fabric of historical truth under this Aztec embroidery, especially concerning the people who built Tula and their history.

Sources differ on the chronology of Toltec history. One account attributes the founding of Tollán to the ruler Ce Acatl Topiltzin and places the event in AD 968, approximately the period when archaeological evidence shows Tula growing into a major city. Ce Acatl Topiltzin is much confused in the sources with the feathered serpent god Quetzalcóatl, in whose name he ruled. His reign is traditionally depicted as one of wisdom, peace and lavish patronage of the arts. Quetzalcóatl's arch rival, Tezcatlipoca, is said to have constantly sought to undermine this order through a cult dedicated to the blood sacrifices he required. Ce Acatl Topiltzin was eventually tricked into incestuous relations with his sister, after which he left Tollán in disgrace in 987. According to different versions, he travelled to the Gulf Coast, where he either burnt himself and became the Morning Star or boarded a raft and sailed off to the east promising to return one day. Despite his absence, Tollán went on to its period of greatest glory in the 11th century, which also accords with the archaeological evidence. Another account gives a different version of the departure of Topiltzin–Quetzalcóatl and places the events after 1100, or towards the end of Tollán's peak.

In general terms, the legendary vanquishing of Quetzalcóatl by Tezcatlipoca at Tollán was once taken to symbolize the end of fundamentally peaceful and theocratic political organization in the Classic period and the beginning of militarism in the Post-Classic. But it is now known from archaeological, epigraphic and iconographic evidence that militarism, exploitation and human sacrifice were aspects of the Post-Classic period inherited from the Classic.

The exact nature of the Toltec 'empire' is uncertain. Militarism was a hallmark of the Toltecs but so too was their vast long-distance trading network. Their power lasted only a little more than 200 years and came to an abrupt end at Tula when the city was attacked and ruined c. 1179. Despite this, Toltec culture left a lasting mark on both the Central Highlands and on the Maya of the Yucatán Peninsula (see §(iv) below).

After the fall of Tula, the focus of power in the Central Highlands returned to the Basin of Mexico. The population was increasing again, and the small centres left in the wake of Teotihuacán had grown into city states almost continuously at war with each other. There were frequent incursions of Chichimec barbarians from the north, one or more of which included the Aztecs, or Mexica, from Aztlán far to the north-west. According to Mexica legend, their long migration began in 1111, and they were guided, protected and chastised by the god Huitzilopochtli, who in consequence became their principal deity. They had arrived at the city of Chapultepec in the Basin of Mexico

by 1300 but were driven out repeatedly. Taking refuge in the city of Culhuacán, they helped their hosts win a battle against nearby Xochimilco. In gratitude, the ruler of Culhuacán gave them his daughter as a ruler and wife to Huitzilopochtli. In one version she was promptly sacrificed and flayed, and her father invited to a feast at which a priest appeared wearing her skin. Forced to flee from Culhuacán into the swamps and shallow lakes that occupied much of the centre of the Basin of Mexico, they discovered on an island the spot where an eagle had made its home in the top of a giant cactus, precisely where Huitzilopochtli had told them they should end their migration and found their city. The traditional date of this founding of Tenochtitlán is 1325.

The Mexica continued to fight wars for others, serving especially as mercenaries and allies of Azcapotzalco as it extended its conquests beyond the Basin of Mexico, but they also campaigned increasingly on their own behalf. By 1411 a coalition of towns, including Azcapotzalco, was arrayed against Tenochtitlán, which by 1430, in alliance with Tetzcoco, had conquered and destroyed Azcapotzalco. Tenochtitlán and Tetzcoco were joined by Tlacopan to form the Triple Alliance, which began a new programme of conquest in the mid-15th century. By 1460 Tenochtitlán was clearly the senior partner of the Alliance and none of the 50 or so 'independent' city states of the Basin of Mexico was able to challenge it. Conquests outside the Basin of Mexico were made by Motecuhzoma I (reg 1440–68) and by Ahuitzotl (reg 1486–1502), but the Aztec empire involved only limited control of territory, emphasizing tribute collection instead, and many areas near the Basin of Mexico, such as Tlaxcala to the east or the Tarascan kingdom to the north-west, were never conquered. Revolts against Aztec rule were frequent and repeated.

Tenochtitlán had a population of c. 200,000 inhabitants when Cortés arrived in 1519, and the entire Basin of Mexico more than a million. In less than 200 years since its traditional founding date, the Mexica had undertaken public works on a phenomenal scale. Houses were arranged on a regular grid of wide streets and canals that gave direct access to the lake by canoe. Pyramid temples and plazas were scattered throughout the city, but the largest and most impressive plaza was in the centre, flanked by the main temples to Huitzilopochtli (god of war) and Tlaloc (god of water), the ruler's palace and other pyramid platforms and palaces. The island was connected to the shore in several directions by raised causeways; long dikes were constructed to prevent the salt water of Lake Texcoco from invading Lake Xochimilco's intensively cultivated *chinampas* (Sp. from Nahuatl *chinamitl*: artificial fields anchored to the lakebed and extending out from the shore); and an aqueduct brought fresh water from Chapultepec on the mainland.

The basic unit of social organization, known as the *calpulli* (Nahuatl), was a corporate group of patrilineages that owned land and largely regulated its own internal affairs. There were 60 or 70 such units in 1519. The ruling class or *pipiltin* (Nahuatl), who tended to marry only within their class, owned private estates worked by landless peasants, known as *mayeque* (Nahuatl), or 'slaves' (*mayeque* were forced by economic circumstances to enslave themselves until they could repurchase their freedom). Human sacrifice, especially of war captives, was practised on a large scale.

Markets supplied the city with food and other basic goods. Tribute collection from distant provinces brought exotic items such as cacao, cotton, bright bird feathers, gold and hardstones. These materials were worked by Aztec craftsmen, by craftsmen imported to Tenochtitlan from provincial cities and in the provinces. Regions beyond the imperial frontiers were penetrated by special merchants known as *pochteca* (Nahuatl), who traded and reconnoitred for possible future military expeditions.

BIBLIOGRAPHY

B. Díaz del Castillo: *Historia verdadera de la conquista de la Nueva España* (Madrid, 1576); Eng. trans., abridged by J. M. Cohen, as *The Conquest of New Spain* (London, 1963)
J. Soustelle: *La Vie quotidienne des Aztèques à la veille de la conquête espagnole* (Paris, 1955; Eng. trans., London, 1961)
M. León-Portilla: *Aztec Thought and Culture: A Study of the Ancient Nahuatl Mind* (Norman, 1963)
I. Marquina, ed.: *Proyecto Cholula* (Mexico City, 1970)
N. Davies: *The Aztecs: A History* (Norman, 1973)
E. R. Wolf, ed.: *The Valley of Mexico: Studies in Pre-Hispanic Ecology and Society* (Albuquerque, 1976)
N. Davies: *The Toltecs until the Fall of Tula* (Norman, 1977)
F. F. Berdan: *The Aztecs of Central Mexico: An Imperial Society* (New York, 1982)
R. A. Diehl: *Tula: The Toltec Capital of Ancient Mexico* (London, 1983)
K. Hirth: 'Xochicalco: Urban Growth and State Formation in Central Mexico', *Science*, 225 (1984), pp. 579–86

ROBERT D. DRENNAN

(iii) Southern Highlands. The Zapotec hilltop capital of Monte Albán declined in the Late Classic period simultaneously with Teotihuacán, and political power devolved to several cities in the Valley of Oaxaca such as LAMBITYECO, Zaachila, MITLA and YAGUL. To the north-west of the Zapotec the Mixtec, like the Gulf Coast Huastec, came into prominence as the Post-Classic period progressed. A group of pre-Conquest texts known as the Mixtec Codices, written on deerskin, chronicle the histories of Mixtec mountain fortress cities, under Toltec domination in the Early Post-Classic period, then independent after the fall of Tula (Aubin Manuscript 20, Paris, Bib. N.; Codex Becker 1, Vienna, Mus. Vlkerknd.; Codex Bodley and Codex Laud, both Oxford, Bodleian Lib.; Codex Borgia and Codex Vaticanus B, both Rome, Vatican, Bib. Apostolica; Codex Colombino, Mexico City, Bib. N. Antropol. & Hist.; Codex Cospi, Bologna, Bib. U.; Codex Fejérváry–Mayer, Liverpool Mus.; Codex Nuttall, London, BM; and Vienna Codex, Vienna, Österreich. Nbib.; *see* §VI below).

From *c.* 1200, in close contact with their neighbours in the Puebla Basin to the north-west, the Mixtec developed a distinct polychrome style of pottery painting and stone sculpture known as MIXTECA-PUEBLA. Production was originally centred on the city of Cholula, then later at Mixtec cities such as Tilantongo, Coixtlahuaca and Tutupec, from which items were widely distributed throughout Mesoamerica. The style comprised a synthesis of elements from Teotihuacán, Xochicalco, Cholula and the southern and central Gulf Coast. Pottery vessels were decorated with painted panels similar in subject-matter to the codices or with perforated geometric friezes.

By *c.* 1350 the Mixtec were beginning to expand southeast into Zapotec territory down the Valley of Oaxaca,

using a combination of conquest and carefully considered marriage alliances. They reused many Zapotec tombs at the now silent city of Monte Albán, and much Mixteca–Puebla pottery and other artefacts have been found in Post-Classic Zapotec sites.

At the eastern end of the Valley of Oaxaca the new Zapotec capital of Mitla was built in a combination of Zapotec and Mixtec styles, each influenced by elements from their more distant Maya and Central Highlands neighbours. Five palace complexes were built with distinctive stepped-fret mosaics made up with small blocks of cut stone. The numerous geometric motifs used show influences from the Puuc Maya (*see* §(iv) below) and Mixteca–Puebla styles. The nearby hilltop fortress site of Yagul exemplifies Late Post-Classic Mixtec and Zapotec towns in their response to intermittent rivalry.

Aztec incursions into Mixtec and Zapotec territory began in the second quarter of the 15th century and continued into the 16th. Resistance was stiff, sometimes independent and sometimes as a Mixtec–Zapotec alliance; but in the end an Aztec garrison was established in the Valley of Oaxaca. The Mixtec were renowned and exploited (by the Aztecs) as artisans, particularly for their gold, jade and turquoise work.

BIBLIOGRAPHY

G. Kubler: *The Art and Architecture of Ancient America*, Pelican Hist. A. (Harmondsworth, 1962, rev. 3/1984), pp. 168–87
M. Porter-Weaver: *The Aztecs, Maya and their Predecessors: Archaeology of Mesoamerica* (New York, 1972, rev. 2/1981), pp. 390–91, 462–9
J. W. Whitecotton: *The Zapotecs: Princes, Priests and Peasants* (Norman, 1977), pp. 81–172
R. Spores: *The Mixtecs in Ancient and Colonial Times* (Norman, 1984), pp. 10–96
M. Coe, D. Snow and E. Benson: *Atlas of Ancient America* (Oxford, 1986), pp. 113, 141–3

DAVID M. JONES

(iv) Maya region. The transition from the Classic to the Post-Classic period in the Maya region, as in the Central Highlands, involved shifts in centres of power and influence. As the Classic period cities of the Maya Southern Lowlands were abandoned in the Late Classic, the rulers of cities in the northern lowlands—the Puuc Hills and plains of the Yucatán Peninsula—began to assert themselves. Many of the cities had been founded during the Classic period, or even earlier, and their inhabitants had built impressive complexes of limestone temples and palaces in the distinctive Puuc style, as at CHICHÉN ITZÁ, UXMAL and many other sites. But because of incessant warfare none of these cities was to remain powerful for as long as the Classic period cities had.

Despite changes in sculptural and architectural styles, there was much cultural continuity between the Maya Southern and Northern Lowlands. Commemorative monuments with glyphic texts and Long Count dates were rare in Puuc cities, but texts with dates continued to be carved on stone. In contrast, the legendary history of the departure of Ce Acatl Topiltzin–Quetzalcóatl from Tula suggests a connection to one of the most striking facts of Early Post-Classic Mesoamerica: a direct artistic and architectural link between the Toltecs and the Maya northern lowland cities, particularly at Chichén Itzá, where the link was specifically with Tula.

The dramatic intrusion of a distinctly foreign sculptural and architectural style suggests sharp cultural change, but recent research shows that Puuc and Toltec styles were used side by side for a considerable period of time. In many examples at Chichén Itzá there was a combination of Maya and Toltec styles, but at other Maya cities Toltec influence was rather attenuated, while at others there was no Toltec influence.

As with the Central Highlands, historical records of the Maya begin in the Early Post-Classic period, although increasingly detailed information about specific rulers and events can be gleaned from Classic period inscriptions. Maya history encourages the connection of the intrusion of Toltec style to what is known of Toltec history, for Maya tradition records the arrival in Yucatán of Quetzal-cóatl or Kukulcán at a date arguably in the late 10th century. Legend describes the wandering Itzá, who founded their capital city at the existing site of Chichén Itzá somewhat earlier. The convergence of Itzá traditions with the Central Highlands account of Ce Acatl Topiltzin–Quetzalcóatl's eastern departure as in 987, and their general correspondence to the date when Toltec architectural and sculptural features appeared at Chichén Itzá, is too strong to be simple coincidence.

But reading the legends as literal history, recounting how a ruler-god, bested in Tula politics by a rival, led a group of supporters to Yucatán where he was able to rebuild an existing city in the style of his homeland, may also strain credulity. Some Mesoamericanists interpret the evidence as Toltec military conquest, establishing Chichén Itzá as a colonial capital. However, the logistical difficulty of establishing and maintaining a colony at such a distance, given the transportation impediments of Pre-Columbian Mesoamerica, cannot be overlooked. Not even the Aztecs were able to extend their military conquest to such a distance from Tenochtitlán, a much more populous and powerful capital than Tula. Thus the striking stylistic links between Tula and Chichén Itzá, and the general absence of these stylistic features from the intervening territory, seem to argue for some special relationship between the two cities rather than a pan-Mesoamerican empire centred at Tula. The links may have been more commercial than military. Trade over long distances, especially in luxury goods, is well documented in Mesoamerican prehistory; and Aztec traders did reach such distant areas. Yet it remains true that cultural influence as powerful as that of the Toltecs to cause the rebuilding of Chichén Itzá was something the Aztecs had not accomplished at such distances by the time of the Spanish arrival.

Although scholarly attention has focused heavily on the relationship between Tula and Chichén Itzá, it was not the only such phenomenon of the transition period of the Classic to the Post-Classic. Maya stylistic elements also appeared in the Central Highlands at Xochicalco and Cacaxtla in the Puebla Basin, both of which flourished slightly earlier than the 'Toltec intrusion' at Chichén Itzá. These phenomena may have been simply part of the development of a more complex and multilateral network of 'foreign relations' between a larger number of cities of more nearly equal power after the breakup of the Classic period dominance of Teotihuacán, Monte Albán and a small number of southern Maya Lowlands cities.

The power of Tula was short-lived (see §3(ii) above). By AD 1250 Chichén Itzá had also declined rapidly as a major city of the Maya region and was superseded by the growing centre of MAYAPÁN. Mayapán was different from earlier centres in either the northern or southern Maya Lowlands. It was physically larger than any contemporary city in the Yucatán Peninsula, but its population (no more than 12,000) was much smaller than Classic-period Maya cities. Its citizens directed much less energy toward the construction of temples and palaces. Their pyramids were smaller and less numerous, and their palaces less elaborate.

The art and architecture of Mayapán and elsewhere in Yucatán during the Late Post-Classic period have been called decadent; but it has also been argued that Mesoamerican culture and society underwent much more fundamental changes in the Late Post-Classic period than in the Classic–Early Post-Classic transition. Some scholars have suggested that there was a rising mercantilism that de-emphasized traditional religious beliefs and their role in political affairs, including strong links between rulers and gods. The rulers of Mayapán did, however, forge political unity over most of the Yucatán Peninsula, and the formerly independent aristocracy of the 16 provinces of this 'League' were forced to live in Mayapán under direct supervision of the ruling family. The captives' descendants conspired to break up the League, resulting in the destruction and abandonment of Mayapán c. 1450 and the fragmentation of the Maya region into the 16 'states' that existed when the Spanish explorer Córdoba sighted Yucatán in 1517.

BIBLIOGRAPHY

S. G. Morley, G. W. Brainerd and R. J. Sharer: *The Ancient Maya* (Stanford, 1946, rev. Palo Alto, 4/1983)

H. E. D. Pollock and others: *Mayapán, Yucatán, Mexico*, Carnegie Institution Publication, 619 (Washington, DC, 1962) [whole issue]

N. Davies: *The Toltecs until the Fall of Tula* (Norman, 1977)

P. D. Harrison and B. L. Turner II, eds: *Pre-Hispanic Maya Agriculture* (Albuquerque, 1978)

W. Ashmore, ed.: *Lowland Maya Settlement Patterns* (Albuquerque, 1981)

K. V. Flannery, ed.: *Maya Subsistence: Studies in Memory of Dennis E. Puleston* (New York, 1982)

N. Hammond: *Ancient Maya Civilization* (New Brunswick, 1982)

R. A. Diehl: *Tula: The Toltec Capital of Ancient Mexico* (London, 1983)

J. A. Sabloff and E. W. Andrews V, eds: *Late Lowland Maya Civilization: Classic to Postclassic* (Albuquerque, 1986)

ROBERT D. DRENNAN

(v) West Mexico. In the Early Post-Classic period contact with the Central Highlands continued along routes through the Lerma River drainage. Toltec Mazapan pottery and Tula-type figurines are scattered through Michoacán, Jalisco and Nayarit. Crude, locally made copies of stone reclining figures (chacmool) were made in the Lake Pátzcuaro region. There does not, however, seem to have been any effort at colonization from central Mexico.

The Aztatlan complex developed to the north-west in Sinaloa. Its earliest manifestations were at the site of Chametla, but richer, later remains are known from Guasave where iron pyrite beads, onyx and alabaster vases, and paint cloisonné (polychrome decoration in which surface colour is excised and the hollow filled with another colour, then smoothed down to the original surface) and turquoise mosaics were found. An art style similar to that of Mixteca–Puebla spread up the west coast between c. 1200 and c. 1350, possibly by way of Central America.

During the Late Post-Classic period there was a resurgence of local cultural and political elements, which distanced themselves from central Mesoamerica. The TARASCAN state in Michoacán, with a capital at TZINTZUNTZAN on Lake Pátzcuaro, created an efficient and powerful government with a state religion and a professional full-time army that was able to maintain a firm eastern frontier against the Aztecs.

For bibliography *see* §2(ii) above.

MURIEL PORTER-WEAVER

III. Architecture.

For more than a thousand years in Mesomerica, during the Early Pre-Classic period (*c.* 2000–*c.* 1000 BC) and later, simple huts served for domestic, communal and religious purposes. During the Middle Pre-Classic period (*c.* 1000–*c.* 300 BC) more lasting and elaborate structures began to be built, and in the Late Pre-Classic period (*c.* 300 BC–*c.* AD 250) most of the basic components of Mesoamerican monumental architecture were developed.

1. Forms and functions. 2. Regional developments.

1. FORMS AND FUNCTIONS.

(i) Monumental structures. (ii) Other structures.

(i) Monumental structures. Large-scale Mesoamerican buildings can be analysed in terms of primary and complementary architectural elements, layout and variation in form and function, although it is not always possible to deter-

mine the purposes for which specific buildings were used. While particular traits make some structures easy to identify, for example ballcourts, steam baths, monumental platforms or tombs, determining the function of most other buildings is difficult. Thus the residential functions of range-type buildings, usually termed 'palaces', can be deduced, though only in a few regions, by the presence of large integrated masonry benches in the interiors of many rooms. Few other features, however, provide a clear distinction between the residential buildings of élites or of priestly orders, houses of a 'monastic' nature or used for spiritual retreat, or houses for the education of the young, for servants or other members of society. Sometimes a clear distinction cannot be made between a temple and a palace (e.g. the Hall of Columns at MITLA), and sometimes the two functions appear to be combined in the same structure, as in the Palace of Five Floors at EDZNÁ (see fig. 9). The position of a structure within a site is often the primary clue to its function.

(a) Primary elements. (b) Complementary elements. (c) Layout.

(a) Primary elements. Sizeable quantities of earth were moved to make fillings of compacted earth or adobe and to provide the cores of terraces, platforms, causeways, esplanades and stairways. The borders of such works frequently had an inclined plane, which matched the natural angle of settlement of the filling material and gave rise to the 'talus' (*talud*) silhouette so characteristic of Mesoamerican architecture. Retaining walls, ranging from dry-stone, via mud and stone, to masonry walls set in lime

9. Palace of Five Floors, Edzná, Maya region, 7th–8th centuries AD

10. Arch at Labná, h. *c.* 5 m, w. at base *c.* 2.9 m, Maya region, early 10th century AD

mortar, were used both to protect the edges of terraced works and in some cases to contain steeper inclines of fill. Complexity increased as more advanced construction techniques were developed. The use of lime for mortar and for plastering was usually confined to works for public functions. The upper surfaces were carefully compacted, covered with one or two layers of plaster, burnished and often painted in bright colours. The relative importance of a structure was reflected by the care taken in its construction and by the elaboration and treatment of its plaster covering.

Free-standing masonry walls began to be made at the end of the 1st century BC. They were complemented, or sometimes replaced, by masonry columns and pillars or were reinforced by pilasters of masonry or, as at Teotihuacán, of timber. Construction techniques varied from dry-stone or stones set in mud mortar to protect fills of earth or rubble, to elaborate veneers of stone slabs. For example, in the Late Classic period (*c.* AD 600–*c.* 900) the carefully adjusted stones on the inner and outer faces of Puuc Maya walls functioned both as a finish and as the encasement of the core made from the roughest rubble. In areas with a scarcity of stone, walls were made of narrow, flat bricks (e.g. Comalcalco; *see* BRICK, §II, 9) or of adobe bricks and mud.

By the end of the Pre-Classic period, in the principal regions of Mesoamerica, the roofs of ceremonial buildings were predominantly solid coverings, either flat or vaulted. Flat roofs predominated in the Central Highlands, the Southern Highlands and the Gulf Coast region and were supported by wooden beams resting on walls, and later on columns or pilasters, especially after the Toltecs arrived in Tula. In the Maya Lowlands a roofing system based on corbel vaulting was used extensively, generating different versions of the false arch. Despite the limitations of this system on the amplitude of spaces and the flexibility of solutions, it has proved its durability by its survival, in many cases, for twelve or more centuries since abandonment. Corbel vaulting was frequently limited to the roofing of interior spaces and was more widely used in the northern Maya region, where it was also used to cover passageways (generally below stairways backing on to the façade of a building) or to create monumental arches at the ends of causeways, within and between cities (e.g. KABÁH, LABNÁ, UXMAL and other late Puuc sites; see fig. 10).

(b) Complementary elements. To platforms, walls, supports and roofs were added such complementary elements as stairs, niches, integrated benches, *talud–tablero* and other architectural profiles, roof-combs and borders, and sculptural embellishments. In the context of general Mesoamerican architectural structural unity and coherence, such complementary elements add the distinctive stamp of local or regional styles.

Talud–tablero. This feature creates a characteristic profile element of Mesoamerican stepped pyramids, in which sloping (*talud*) and vertical panel (*tablero*) elements combine (for illustration *see* TALUD–TABLERO). The *tablero* is supported in cantilever by the inclined plane of the *talud* and the associated architectural decoration consists of sets of mouldings, panels and other carved elements arranged in formal patterns. The form originated after *c.* 300 BC at such sites as Tlalancaleca and Tetla in the Puebla–Tlaxcala Valley. It was adopted at TEOTIHUACÁN, in the north-east Basin of Mexico, and became the most widely diffused form from the Early Classic period onwards. The *tablero* panel was decorated with paintings or, in exceptional cases, such as the Pyramid–Temple of Quetzalcóatl at Teotihuacán, with high-relief sculptures (see fig. 11), and framed by projecting borders. Usually constructed on religious

11. Pyramid–Temple of Quetzalcóatl, Teotihuacán, detail showing relief-decorated *tablero*, 3rd century AD

architecture, this model was either repeated on each tier of a stepped pyramid or used to crown extended platforms. It was eventually adapted, with surprising flexibility, to all kinds of structures, from modest domestic altars to the fronts of imposing pyramid-platforms.

Many regional styles were also developed. For example, at TAJÍN, in the Gulf Coast region, the *tablero* is frequently perforated by deep-set quadrangular niches or decorated with stepped frets in high relief; and it is invariably crowned by a bevelled, 'flying' cornice cantilevered to balance inversely the slope of the *talud*. The *talud–tablero* was also used at Tajín to decorate the central walls of stairways to form the border of the flat ramps that flank them. Another important variation, known as the 'Oaxaca *tablero*', comprises three planes: the main plane is cut at intervals into panels joined to each other by a thin upper border; the secondary plane is constructed in the manner of a continuous band on the lower part and repeats the peculiar cuttings of the main plane, powerfully emphasizing the effects of light and shadow produced by the latter; and the third plane, which is even deeper, extends laterally and occasionally has relief decorations, as at Lambityeco. The three planes are sometimes complemented by a chamfered cornice, separated by a thin, recessed moulding from a short *talud*, although when the *tablero* crowns the lintel of

a tomb chamber, the short *talud* is less often present. A third variation, somewhat distinct from the *talud–tablero* form proper, is characteristic of the Maya Petén region. It was developed over more than a thousand years and consists of an apron moulding formed by inclined planes, subdivided by recessed moulding set in deep cantilevered moulding, which itself stands out above a short plinth. In each of these variants, the form of the *tablero* creates elements capable of breaking the continuity of the *talud*, using lateral lines of shade that contribute to the definition and animation of the main architectural elements.

Stairways. The stairway (*see* STAIRCASE, §III) was one of the first elements in Mesoamerican architecture to be constructed in stone. During the earliest periods, it was incorporated into the general mass of the platform or pyramid it ascended; later stairways were constructed to stand as a separate element of the pyramidal mass. In ceremonial architecture the stairway is frequently bordered by flat ramps at each side, usually inaccurately referred to as balustrades. Stairways were embellished by mouldings, *tableros*, masks and other sculptures but ranged in style from the imposing bareness of the stairs at TIKAL to the opulence of those at COPÁN. Monumental stairways were generally designed in proportion to and in sympathy with the angle of the slope of the pyramids or platforms they ascend, without necessarily taking into consideration the convenience afforded by the height or depth of the steps. For example, at MONTE ALBÁN the central stairway that ascends from the Great Square to the North Platform is built in proportion to match the overall volumes of the platform and square, with unusual 12-foot wide flat ramps. Similarly, the angles of the stairways ascending the great temples at Tikal equal the slope of the sides of the pyramids. Few internal stairways have survived, other than those that lead to antechambers of tombs or subterranean corridors at Monte Albán, or at PALENQUE and a few other Maya cities. The evidence suggests that their use was infrequent.

Other façade elements. In addition to stairways, and to the horizontal emphasis of *talud–tablero* mouldings, other mouldings and pilasters were used to emphasize the vertical aspects of façades, and to frame the main entrances. In the Maya Lowlands recessed vertical mouldings were used quite frequently to differentiate two sections of a façade. On the sides of the temples at Tikal, for example, a clear distinction is established in this manner between the front and rear parts of the sanctuary. Recessed mouldings on the façades of many range-type buildings in the Río Bec and Chenes styles (*see* §2(ii) below) were used to divide the façades according to the so-called tripartite rule. The divisions are frequently complemented by subtle changes in panelling and/or emphasized by engaged columns at the corners of the differentiated parts (e.g. Chicanná, Xpuhil, Santa Rosa Xtampak and Xkichmook).

Roof decoration. In the Central Highlands, at Teotihuacán, the parapets on the roofs of palaces and temples are described as crenellated, not because of their defensive character but because of their superficial resemblance to battlements. The roof of the main court in the Palace of Quetzalpapalotl provides a particularly good example (see fig. 12); and in general the diversity and quality of roof borders at Teotihuacán are especially excellent: some are made of baked clay set in moulds; others are made of opaque limestone or of translucent onyx. Forms included stepped mouldings, variants of mythological animals and, especially abundant, Tlaloc (the rain god) masks. By contrast, during the Aztec period (Late Post-Classic; *c.* AD 1200–1521) imitations of transverse sections of seashells and crossed arrows predominated, and longitudinal sections of shells and stylized butterflies were also abundant.

Another type of finial, greater in volume and developed among the Maya, is known as the roof-comb. It seems to have originated in the Petén region as a monumental appendage of the temple. Gradually narrowing towards the top, it formally extends upwards the rear of the sanctuary. Roof-combs are imposing in the Petén region, where their mass dominates the temples (e.g. Temple II at Tikal), but are of lighter construction in western sites, such as YAXCHILÁN and, especially, Palenque. At Palenque the roof-comb was converted into a double wall with much open fretwork and rests directly on the central longitudinal axis of the building (rather than the rear), thus allowing for greater size in internal spaces. Simple roof-combs were favoured in the northern Maya area, made from a single wall with rhythmically placed openings, and also resting on the central wall or, in the case of flying roof-combs, acting as an extension of the main façade. A few Puuc constructions dating from the end of the Classic period incorporate large panels decorated with masks whose tops extend above the level of the roof while the bases rest in the middle moulding (e.g. the northern building of the Nunnery at Uxmal).

(c) Layout. It has been suggested by George Andrews (1975) that the basis of Mesoamerican architectural organization is the temple–pyramid–square unit, an assertion repeatedly upheld by analysis of the large spaces used for worship at Teotihuacán: for example the square at the foot of the Pyramid of the Moon; the inner square at the Citadel; the square at the foot of the Pyramid of the Sun; and numerous smaller examples of this tripartite unit. In each case a main pyramid on a central axis is aligned with a platform–altar, which, in many cases, marks the junction with a transverse axis, along which secondary pyramids were constructed. Together with platforms and stairways, these secondary pyramids comprise an internal square. The symmetry that prevails with particular complexity and rigour in the main sides of the square of the Pyramid of the Moon was frequently also applied to groups of buildings probably of administrative and governmental function (e.g. those flanking the Pyramid of Quetzalcóatl in the interior of the Citadel); and to civilian buildings, such as a suburban house (e.g. Yayahuala), a house for spiritual retreat (e.g. Tetitla) or an élite residence (e.g. Zacuala). In general there is a markedly clear distribution of the principal architectural units around patios, in which there are nearly always openings in the corners leading to smaller cells via secondary patios and/or passageways. There are no windows, both illumination and ventilation being provided by porticos opening on to patios or occasionally by open skylights in flat roofs.

12. Palace of Quetzalpapalotl, Teotihuacán, main court, 7th century AD

Maya architects exercised much greater flexibility in the handling of open spaces and in the placement of the principal buildings and spaces in relation to each other. Even when buildings are not aligned along a symmetrical axis, they nearly always serve as the visual end point for a square or a causeway. Maya architects seem to have been concerned less with symmetry than with visual relationships and, in many cases, with astrological considerations. For example, several groups of buildings at Maya sites served as indicators of solstices and equinoxes (e.g. Group E at UAXACTÚN). Nevertheless, flexibility in the disposition and intercommunication of interior spaces in civilian architecture was limited by the near exclusive use of corbel vaulting. Such limitations gave rise to schemes of a stereotypical nature, such as corridors or rows of rooms that are usually double, with little intercommunication between the rows, applied indiscriminately to the architecture of élite residences (e.g. the Governor's Palace at Uxmal, or palaces at Santa Rosa Xtampak and Palenque (see fig. 13)) or administrative buildings (e.g. Building I at Becán). The Palace at Palenque thus combines diverse functions within one outer structure. Although the galleries that open to the exterior on at least three sides give the Palace the aspect of a public building, the interior is subdivided into more or less private units serving different functions, including a 'patio of honour', a throne room, subterranean corridors, secondary patios that may have functioned as storage spaces, steam baths and—a rarity in Mesoamerica—toilet facilities.

(ii) Other structures.

(a) Domestic. Residential housing developed in Mesoamerica as one of the basic elements associated with a

13. Palace at Palenque, main court, showing House C, Maya region, AD 692

sedentary way of life. It is undoubtedly one of the oldest and most traditional forms, although there is little evidence concerning its initial development. A stucco floor found at Cuello in Belize is one of the earliest examples, laid *c.* 2200 BC. It served as the base for a hut of wood, palm and other perishable materials, probably of a type similar to the apsidal-plan huts still used by present-day Maya. These have a main door and a back door on the transverse axis, but no windows, and can be used in a number of ways as a family space according to the time of day. Alternatively, when divided by a longitudinal wall, the front part may be used as a more formal space (for reception) and the rear section as a more private area. The front part may extend to the outside as an area of contact with the rest of the community, and the rear part may contain areas for cooking, washing, grain storage and other domestic functions. It may be complemented by a vegetable garden and by an irrigated area.

In Pre-Columbian Maya cities dwellings other than élite residences tended to be loosely scattered in clusters of houses on low platform mounds, covering a large area around the ceremonial cores of sites. In contrast, at Teotihuacán—where the evidence is most clear—the civilian population was packed into closely knit, apartment-like compounds around small squares and patios. Residents commuted daily to fields outside the city. Elite residences were larger, more elaborately decorated and tended to be closer to the central ceremonial precincts. At Monte Albán, in the Southern Highlands, dwellings were ranged along terraces on the hills around the two principal hills levelled for the ceremonial plaza. At Tula, in the Early Post-Classic period (*c.* AD 900–*c.* 1200), blocks consisting of apartment-like housing have been excavated. In Aztec cities of the Late Post-Classic period (*c.* 1200–1521) around the lakes of the Basin of Mexico, commoners lived in huts on their individual *chinampa* plots (artificial fields anchored to the lake beds and extending out from the shores) around the ceremonial precincts.

(b) Fortifications. Mesoamerican fortifications are known primarily from the Post-Classic period, when there

was greater political instability, although a few defensive structures appeared at the end of the Pre-Classic period (*see also* MILITARY ARCHITECTURE AND FORTIFICATION, §X). One of the oldest examples is the dry moat surrounding the small site of Becán in Campeche, Mexico, with only seven entrances. It is 10 m wide at its narrowest point, 4 m deep and has a parapet made of the compacted excavated earth that is another 4 m in places. One of the best-known Post-Classic examples is at Huexotla, a dependency of Tetzcoco, which has an elaborate moat around the ceremonial core. Several restored sections of the ramparts have large indentations in the upper part, one of which has been enlarged and includes a parapet to provide shelter for several warriors, and what may have been a watch path. Other Post-Classic cities were in defensive positions on hilltops (e.g. XOCHICALCO, YAGUL and Quiengola), and the enclosed nature of many ceremonial precincts may also have been put to defensive use when necessary.

(c) Rock-cut structures. Architecture built into cliff faces was developed in the Central Highlands less than a century before the Spanish Conquest. There are two outstanding examples. The first was built under the poet-king Nezahualcóyotl (1402–72) on the hill of TETZCOTZINGO, where a series of elements were carved directly into the rock face: stairs, benches, parapets, the principal water basin and anthropomorphic relief sculptures, possibly effigies of princes or deities. The second example is a ceremonial site established by the Aztecs on artificial terraces at MALINALCO in the Toluca Valley. Known as the Eagles' Nest, it was built for the exaltation of the two highest-ranking military orders, the Eagles and the Jaguars. It comprises a small sanctuary and other buildings partially or totally carved out of the craggy escarpments. The façade of the principal temple, which includes a series of terraced sections and a stairway and its sculptures, is rock-cut. Its exquisite inner chamber comprises a circular ground plan and contains three attached sculptures of eagles and one of a jaguar in high-relief on the floor and on its horseshoe-shaped bench.

(d) Water systems. The distribution and use of water was vital to the urban structure of Mesoamerican society. The two most ancient manifestations of structures for capturing, conveying and storing water are a system of channels and ponds dating from *c.* 1200 BC at Olmec SAN LORENZO TENOCHTITLÁN and the later system found at Teopantecuanitlán, Guerrero. In the Central Highlands there are dispersed remains of structures used for the collection and drainage of rainwater, and for its storage and distribution on a public and a domestic scale at Teotihuacán and other sites through the Classic and Post-Classic periods. Aztec Tenochtitlán, on an island in Lake Texcoco, was supplied with fresh water by an aqueduct with two channels coming from Chapultepec on the mainland.

(e) Cuezcomates. The *cuezcomate* (Nahuatl) was a storage building for maize corn cobs. Such structures are still used in several regions of central Mexico; the common shape resembles an enormous pot resting on a narrow base.

Access to the upper part is gained through a hole protected by a palm roof.

BIBLIOGRAPHY

I. Marquina: *Arquitectura prehispánica* (Mexico City, 1950, 2/1964/R 1981)
L. Séjourné: *Arquitectura y pintura en Teotihuacán* (Mexico City, 1966)
G. F. Andrews: *Maya Cities: Placemaking and Urbanization* (Norman, 1975)
D. Heyden and P. Gendrop: *Pre-Columbian Architecture of Mesoamerica* (New York, 1975)

PAUL GENDROP

2. REGIONAL DEVELOPMENTS. Hundreds of large and small ritual places and urban centres were built throughout Mesoamerica between the early 1st millennium BC and 1521. Three fairly distinct regions of architectural development can be distinguished: central Mesoamerica, including the Gulf Coast region; the Maya zone; and West Mexico.

(i) Central Mesoamerica. (ii) Maya region. (iii) West Mexico.

(i) Central Mesoamerica. For over 2000 years in this metropolitan region, ritual centres and cities were created by rulers who sought to validate the concerns of a series of different complex societies. On one level, their architecture referred to historical circumstances—places, times and peoples—creating an extended present and representing the synchronic aspect of political and cultural events. On another level, it related to cosmological imagery—reaching back in time and referring to a fundamental self-image among highland peoples and to their relation to earth, sky and the forces of natural phenomena (*see also* §I, 4 above). This diachronic imagery reaffirmed perceived basic principles and truths and represented a sense of order in the highland way of life. It legitimized the social order, and new state organizations, diverse regional cults and immigrant populations were all required to acknowledge its unifying force.

Ritual monuments represented a process of transmission whereby cosmological geometry and topographic imagery were adapted by a succession of state-like societies, in a pattern widely shared by different peoples who maintained a basic frame of reference in times of political collapse and cultural change. Cosmological geometry and the imagery of landscape assumed diverse forms according to the individual styles and historical backgrounds of different populations, but they were not totally different symbolic systems. Unlike the changes in Western Europe between Late Antiquity and medieval times, Mesoamerican architecture displays a pattern of synthesis, dissolution and resynthesis of a basic inventory of cosmic themes. A few key examples will serve to characterize the interplay between cosmology, monumental architecture and the activities and interests of state-like organizations.

(a) Chalcatzingo. (b) Cuicuilco. (c) Teotihuacán. (d) Xochicalco. (e) Tula. (f) Tenochtitlán.

(a) Chalcatzingo. The first important ritual places of the Central Highlands were affiliated with the powerful OLMEC civilization of the southern Gulf Coast region. Colossal stone sculpture and earthwork architecture at the Olmec capitals of SAN LORENZO TENOCHTITLÁN (*c.* 900 BC) and LA VENTA (*c.* 700 BC) influenced the construction of monuments at distant seats of power on the Mexican plateau. At CHALCATZINGO and related sites in the states of Morelos and Guerrero, local chiefs with Olmec connections developed trading, religious and administrative centres between *c.* 900 and *c.* 500 BC. The central feature at Chalcatzingo is a huge rock formation jutting from the level of the plain. On the western side a settlement was organized in a hierarchy of levels: the lower residential area led to an élite residential and administrative section, with commemorative stone stelae and earthen ritual platforms on the talus slope above; a series of ritual stations, marked by petroglyphic relief carvings from the upper zone, completed a spatial progression that linked the community to the sacred rock.

Sited with a view across the plain to the snow-capped volcano of Popocatépetl, the Chalcatzingo rock formation was a symbolic microcosm of the great rain-producing mountains that were the sources of life in the highland region. Based on an old and widespread system of beliefs concerning sacred geography, the monuments at Chalcatzingo invested the land with new symbols of a powerful state-like society. The site was an important trading centre, but it was also a place of religious authority and a centre for the communication of unifying ideas that played a pivotal role in propagating a fundamental pattern of belief and symbolism for the development of complex urban societies in the Central Highlands.

(b) Cuicuilco. By the 2nd and 1st centuries BC the Basin of Mexico had become a major centre of urban development. The lakes that formerly covered the basin afforded a rich and varied economy for numerous communities. At CUICUILCO, in the south of the basin, a circular pyramid–platform was built in four tiers, with access ramps to the east and west, and became the ritual focus of a densely populated urban–agricultural district. The plan of the structure—a circle traversed by an east–west line—has cosmological implications, suggesting a central omphalos, the outer rim of the created world, the vertical axis of the earth and the celestial path of the sun. The processional ramps also lead the eye towards rain mountains to the east of the basin. The platform was crowned by a dual altar, one of which may have been associated with the cult of fire. The architectural setting at Cuicuilco almost certainly formed a symbolic stage for the ritual re-enactment of mythical cosmogonic events and for the establishment of their relationship to the world of historical, human time.

(c) Teotihuacán. During the 1st century BC TEOTIHUACÁN, in the north-east of the basin, was a rival ritual centre. When Cuicuilco was devastated by the nearby volcano Xitle, the population of the basin apparently shifted to a dense agglomeration of agricultural villages at Teotihuacán. During the 1st century AD Teotihuacán's rulers began a programme of construction that gave the developing urban district a coherent regular plan and monumental definition (see fig. 14). The principles of design incorporated cosmological geometry, open-volume composition and topographic references that became fundamental to urban planning in the Central Highlands long after Teotihuacán collapsed during the 7th or 8th century AD.

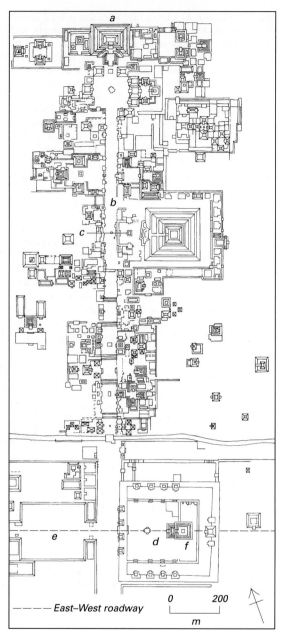

14. Teotihuacán, plan of urban centre, c. AD 400: (a) Pyramid of the Moon; (b) processional avenue; (c) Pyramid of the Sun; (d) Ciudadela administrative quadrangle; (e) market plaza; (f) Pyramid–Temple of Quetzalcóatl

The tiered levels of the Pyramid of the Moon (14a) were framed against the looming mass of Cerro Gordo, the sacred mountain to the north. A processional avenue (14b) led south from the plaza of the Pyramid of the Moon, past the huge Pyramid of the Sun (14c), which was orientated on an east–west axis conforming to the solstice transit of the sun. The ritual way continued through a building complex thought to be the ruler's residence, between the vast open Ciudadela administrative quadrangle (14d) and opposing rectangular market plaza (14e), to

arrive at the agricultural zone in the southern section of the city. Conceived on an almost geological scale, the composition extends 4 km in a ritual line linking rain mountain, city and cultivated fields. An east–west roadway, crossing the north–south ritual way at the Ciudadela and the market plaza, completed the quadripartite plan of the city.

The Pyramid of the Moon was probably dedicated to a cult of the mountain, rain and flowing water. The Pyramid of the Sun, as well as being aligned with the solstice path, was built above a long, natural cave ending in a lobed chamber. Such a subterranean feature was associated with water, but perhaps more importantly was connected with origin myths of tribal emergence from the womb of 'mother earth' in creation time. At the pivot of the four quarters, the Ciudadela was the ceremonial seat of government and religious authority. The quadrangle was commanded by the stepped Pyramid–Temple of Quetzalcóatl (14f), ornamented with repeated sculptural motifs of a plumed serpent-dragon bearing on its tail a mask-like headdress with earth and rain emblems. Such symbolism refers to the seasonal rise of powerful electric rainstorms from the earth and alludes to the cult responsibilities and military power of the city's rulers.

The immense structures at Teotihuacán were religious focal points for a city of c. 100,000 people, inhabiting apartment compounds arranged in a compact, grid-like system conforming to the cardinal axes of the two principal avenues. One or two doors led into the quadrangular walled compounds, within which open, porched rooms faced small patios. The interior dimensions of rooms were limited by the length of wooden beams. Walls were covered with repetitive polychromatic frescoes (see §V below). Repetitive wall paintings, dominated by red, also covered the talud–tablero faces of major public buildings. Portraits are absent, and there are no unequivocal glyphic references to individuals. This was an art of corporate identity and communal ritual endeavour.

Teotihuacán's initial programme of construction and its subsequent additions reflected the use of art and architecture as a vital part of a larger political, economic and religious strategy. It was the responsibility of the city's rulers ritually to coordinate the organization and activities of a complex society with the structure of the land and the cycle of the seasons, to show the links between myth, history and sacred geography. As a cosmological diagram this urban configuration gave the social order a unifying framework.

(d) Xochicalco. Connections with foreign peoples were important throughout Mesoamerican history. At CHOLULA, south of the Basin of Mexico, an immense pyramid even larger than those at Teotihuacán was built overlooking a city with ties to Gulf Coast capitals at TAJÍN and elsewhere. Similarly, trading and political relations were maintained throughout the Classic period (c. AD 250– c. 900) between Teotihuacán, the ZAPOTEC capital at MONTE ALBÁN and Maya capitals to the south and east (see TIKAL; KAMINALJUYÚ). Maya connections and influence in the Central Highlands survived the disintegration and collapse of Teotihuacán and of Classic Maya civilization in the 8th and 9th centuries, to find expression at

XOCHICALCO and CACAXTLA in the Late Classic period (*c*. AD 600–*c*. 900). At these 'epiclassic' sites, old cultural and artistic traditions were maintained and partly rephrased to express the new circumstances of a dramatically changing period.

Topographic considerations were a primary consideration in the selection of the hilltop site of Xochicalco. The hill forms part of a low mountain chain separating the northern Morelos basin from agricultural bottomlands to the south. The Tembembe River emerges from a deep canyon immediately below the site and flows out to cultivated areas some 10 km away. To support residential structures, wide terraces were built along the irregular contours of the mountain-sides. Such sophisticated use of complex topography recalls construction at such Classic-period Maya capitals as PIEDRAS NEGRAS. At the same time, the north–south processional way leading straight from the base of the hill to a broad plaza in the upper ceremonial zone suggests a plan derived from Teotihuacán.

The plaza is dominated by a tiered pyramid façade that encloses a protruding section of the mountain-side, an architectural envelope indicating the sacred character of the underlying topographic feature. To the west, a promontory overlooking the river was levelled to accommodate a Maya-like ballcourt (*see* BALLCOURT, §1) and an agricultural temple at the end of the promontory. On the north side of the site, a cave leading into the mountain was modified by the addition of a small shaft to admit light into the inner chamber through the ceiling. The shaft is orientated to receive direct sunlight on the zenith of the solstice day.

On the partly excavated upper area of Xochicalco sits the celebrated Pyramid of the Serpent, a platform and structure overlooking a plaza that served as the seat of authority, recalling the Pyramid of Quetzalcóatl and Ciudadela at Teotihuacán. The stone *talud–tablero* of the platform is covered with finely carved reliefs in repetitive segments, the dominant motif of which is a plumed serpent whose undulating form encloses hieroglyphs and seated human figures (*see also* §IV, 3(ii)(b) below). In general, Xochicalco's architecture and sculpture incorporate selected elements of a foreign (Maya) vocabulary in a formal plan deriving from Teotihuacán.

The eclectic art of Xochicalco and the related capital at Cacaxtla reflects cultural changes in a period that has often been compared to the time following the Roman collapse in Western Europe. By historical analogy Xochicalco's architecture and sculpture have been described in terms of a 'synchronic' pattern, whereby familiar forms were selected from recent symbolic systems and invested with new meaning to replace older ideas and institutions that had decayed. From this point of view the monuments record pivotal changes that separate Classic- and Post-Classic-period civilization in Mesoamerica.

(e) Tula. The TOLTEC capital at TULA succeeded Xochicalco as a dominant Central Highland urban centre. Its architecture is more distantly related to Teotihuacán's but shows a close relationship with that at Maya–Toltec CHICHÉN ITZÁ in the Yucatán Peninsula. At Tula both

15. Tula, Temple B and columned hall, 12th century AD

the artistic vocabulary and the craftsmanship were diminished: architecture and other arts have a harsh and simplified appearance.

The principal excavated building at Tula, known as Temple B (also called the Temple of Quetzalcóatl; see fig. 15), and the adjacent columned palace closely resemble the Temple of the Warriors complex at Chichén Itzá. They are also distantly related to the Pyramid of Quetzalcóatl and Ciudadela complex at Teotihuacán. Temple B's tiered surfaces were covered with panels depicting eagles, felines and coyotes, as emblems of military societies. Colossal, atlantean warriors and plumed serpent columns (only the round body sections of which were found at Tula) rose as supports for the roof of the vanished platform chamber. Other buildings of central Tula include two ballcourts and what may be a headquarters with two large halls confronting a colonnaded patio. Although the capital was orientated to the cardinal points, thus preserving a required cosmological significance, the architecture and sculpture were orchestrated primarily to serve the stern requirements of a warrior aristocracy.

(f) Tenochtitlán. The rise of Tenochtitlán (*see* MEXICO CITY, §1) and TETZCOTZINGO (Tetzcoco) in the 15th century brought a revival of complex urban symbolism not seen on a major scale in the Basin of Mexico since the demise of Teotihuacán. With the aid of abundant descriptions by Spanish friars, soldiers and historians of the early 16th century, as well as of Aztec documents and pictorial manuscripts, it is possible to interpret Aztec archaeological remains in a verifiable historical and cultural context. The rulers of Tenochtitlán and Tetzcotzingo employed monuments as an integral part of imperial strategy. Their programmes of construction called for the revival of ancient themes, both Toltec and Teotihuacano, and for the incorporation of religious cults and imagery from many conquered regions.

The Mexica Aztec capital, Tenochtitlán, was built upon an island by the western shore of Lake Texcoco. Four avenues led to the cardinal points from the central ritual enclosure. Palaces of the emperors surrounded this sacred precinct and were ringed in turn by the houses of élite citizens, wealthy merchants and the outer residential districts, ordered by a regular grid of canals and walkways, all in a pattern resembling ancient Teotihuacán.

The central ritual enclosure was dominated by a dual pyramid–platform for two temples. The excavation of its successive foundations has provided conclusive information on the orchestration of landscape imagery, mythology and the agricultural and military economy of the imperial city. The pyramid was orientated east–west and aligned with a rain-cult temple on the summit of Mt Tlaloc, c. 25 km to the east. Enlarged by successive emperors during the 15th century, the pyramid and temples were dedicated to the ancient cult of Tlaloc (rain, earth, fertility) and to the cult of Huitzilopochtli (ancestral hero and demigod of the Mexica Aztec people). The body of the pyramid represented the conflation of two symbolic mountains: an agricultural mountain of sustenance and the legendary *coatepetl* (Nahuatl: 'snake mountain'), birthplace of Huitzilopochtli and mythic scene of his first victorious battle. Other temples within the enclosure and the four city wards were dedicated to an array of deities from the different parts of the empire. Encompassed within their variety were the basic ancient cults: earth, moisture, plants, fire, wind and sun. Architectural caves, symbolic springs and similar features completed the landscape theme. The imagery of Tenochtitlán's ritual centre illustrates the Nahuatl word *atl-tepetl* ('water mountain'), meaning city or community. The habitat of humankind was thus defined in terms of the traditional, natural elements that made life possible in highland Mesoamerica.

BIBLIOGRAPHY

GENERAL

W. Krickeberg: *Felsplastik und Felsbilder beiden Kulturvolken Altamerikas* (Berlin, 1949)
I. Marquina: *Arquitectura prehispánica* (Mexico City, 1950, 2/1964/R 1981)
G. Kubler: *The Art and Architecture of Ancient America*, Pelican Hist. A. (Harmondsworth, 1962, rev. 3/1984)
G. R. Willey: 'The Early Great Styles and the Rise of the Pre-Columbian Civilizations', *Amer. Anthropologist*, lxiv (1962), pp. 1–14
G. Kubler: 'Period, Style and Meaning in Ancient Art', *New Lit. Hist.*, i/2 (1970), pp. 127–44
G. R. Willey: 'Mesoamerican Art and Iconography and the Integrity of the Middle American Ideological System', *The Iconography of Middle American Sculpture: New York, 1970*
P. Carrasco: 'Social Organization of Ancient Mexico', *Hb. Mid. Amer. Ind.*, xi (1971), pp. 349–75
D. Heyden and P. Gendrop: *Pre-Columbian Architecture of Mesoamerica* (New York, 1975)
A. Aveni and S. Gibbs: 'On the Orientation of Pre-Columbian Buildings in Central Mexico', *Amer. Ant.*, xli (1976), pp. 510–17
M. D. Coe: 'Religion and the Rise of Mesoamerican States', *The Transition to Statehood in the New World*, ed. G. D. Jones and R. R. Kautz (London, 1981), pp. 157–71

CHALCATZINGO AND OLMEC

P. Drucker, R. Heizer and R. Squier: 'Excavations at La Venta, Tabasco, 1955', *Bureau Amer. Ethnol. Bull.*, clxx (1959) [whole issue]
S. Milbraith: *A Study of Olmec Sculptural Chronology* (Washington, DC, 1979)
M. D. Coe and R. A. Diehl: *In the Land of the Olmec: The Archaeology of San Lorenzo Tenochtitlán*, 2 vols (Austin, 1980)

D. C. Grove: *Chalcatzingo: Excavations on the Olmec Frontier* (London, 1984)

CUICUILCO

D. Schávelzon: *La Pirámide de Cuicuilco: Album fotográfico* (Mexico City, 1983)

TEOTIHUACÁN

R. Millon: *The Teotihuacan Map*, 2 vols (Austin, 1973)
——: 'Teotihuacan: City, State and Civilization', *Hb. Mid. Amer. Ind.*, suppl. i (1981), pp. 198–243

XOCHICALCO AND CACAXTLA

J. Litvak King: 'Xochicalco en la caída del clásico: Una hipótesis', *Anales Antropol.*, vii (1970), pp. 131–44
G. Kubler: 'Eclecticism in Cacaxtla', *The Third Palenque Round Table*, V/ii (Austin, 1980), pp. 163–73
K. Hirth: 'Xochicalco: Urban Growth and State Formation in Central Mexico', *Science*, 225 (1984), pp. 579–86
D. McVicker: 'The "Mayanized" Mexicans', *Amer. Ant.*, l (1985), pp. 82–101

TULA AND CHICHÉN ITZÁ

E. H. Morris, J. Charlot and A. A. Morris: *The Temple of the Warriors at Chichén Itzá, Yucatán*, 2 vols (Washington, DC, 1931)
W. Jiménez Moreno: 'Tula y los Toltecas según fuentes históricas', *Rev. Mex. Estud. Antropol.*, v (1941), pp. 79–83
K. Ruppert: *Chichén Itzá: Architectural Notes and Plans* (Washington, DC, 1952)
R. Rands: 'Artistic Connections between the Chichén Itzá Toltec and the Classic Maya', *Amer. Ant.*, xix (1954), pp. 281–2
R. A. Diehl and R. A. Benfer: 'Tollan, the Toltec Capital', *Archaeology*, xxviii/2 (1975), pp. 112–24
N. Davies: *The Toltecs until the Fall of Tula* (Norman, 1977)
E. Matos Moctezuma: 'The Tula Chronology: A Revision', *Middle Classic Mesoamerica*, ed. E. Pasztory (New York, 1978), pp. 172–7
G. Kubler: 'Serpent and Atlantean Columns: Symbols of Maya–Toltec Polity', *J. Soc. Arch. Historians*, xli (1982), pp. 93–115
R. A. Diehl: *Tula: The Toltec Capital of Ancient Mexico* (London, 1983)

TENOCHTITLÁN

B. de Sahagún: *Historia general de las cosas de Nueva España* (MS., untraced, 1569; Spanish/Nahuatl illus. copy, *Florentine Codex*, Florence, Bib. Medicea-Laurenziana, MS. Palat. 218–220, n.d.); facs. *Códice Florentino: El manuscrito 218–20 de la colección Palatina de la Biblioteca Medicea Laurenziana*, 3 vols (Mexico City and Florence, 1979); Eng. trans. Nahuatl text and ed. C. E. Dibble and A. J. O. Anderson as *Florentine Codex: General History of the Things of New Spain*, 13 vols (Santa Fe, 1950–69)
B. Díaz del Castillo: *Historia verdadera de la conquista de la Nueva España* (Madrid, 1576); Eng. trans., abridged J. M. Cohen, as *The Conquest of New Spain* (London, 1963)
D. Durán: *Historia de las Indias de Nueva España y Islas de Tierra Firme* (MS, Madrid, Bib. N., c. 1581); 2 vols and *Atlas*, ed. J. F. Ramírez (Mexico City, 1967–80); Eng. trans., ed. F. Horcasitas and D. Heyden as *Book of the Gods and Rites* and *The Ancient Calendar* (Norman, 1971, 3/1977)
C. Gibson: 'The Structure of the Aztec Empire', *Hb. Mid. Amer. Ind.*, x (1971), pp. 376–93
W. Bray: 'The City State in Central Mexico at the Time of the Spanish Conquest', *J. Latin Amer. Stud.*, iv/2 (1972), pp. 161–85
E. E. Calnek: 'The Internal Structure of Tenochtitlán', *The Valley of Mexico*, ed. E. R. Wolf (Albuquerque, 1976), pp. 278–302
E. Matos Moctezuma, ed.: *Trabajos arqueológicos en el centro de la Ciudad de México* (Mexico City, 1979)
R. F. Townsend: *State and Cosmos in the Art of Tenochtitlán* (Washington, DC, 1979)
E. Matos Moctezuma: *El Templo Mayor: Excavaciones y estudios* (Mexico City, 1980)
——: 'New Finds in the Great Temple', *N. Geog.*, clviii (1980), pp. 767–75
E. H. Boone, ed.: *The Aztec Templo Mayor* (Washington, DC, 1987)
E. Matos Moctezuma: *The Great Temple of the Aztecs: Treasures of Tenochtitlan* (London, 1988)

RICHARD F. TOWNSEND

(ii) Maya region. MAYA architectural form and meaning have their roots in the Pre-Classic period (c. 2000 BC–c. AD 250). It was, however, during the Classic period

(c. AD 250–c. 900) that Maya architecture reached its apogee, exemplified by the construction of pyramid-temples throughout the region. At this time, the Maya region supported a large population living in urban communities. Imposing pyramid-temples dominated nearly every settlement: the total number of such structures built must have been in the thousands; but, although most survive in some form, fewer than a hundred have been sufficiently well preserved or excavated to provide detailed architectural information. In general, Maya architecture conformed to wider Mesoamerican practice in the use of space (see §1(i)(c) above), with quadrangular plazas, colonnaded ranges of palace-like buildings (see fig. 13), and pyramid-platforms for the support of temples. In addition, the Maya also built monumental archways (see fig. 10 above), sub-pyramidal tombs (see also TOMB, §V) and causeways (termed sacbé, pl. sacbeob; see CAUSEWAY) within and between sites. It is, however, in pyramid-temple design that the regional identity of Maya architecture is best illustrated, and this is the subject of the discussion below.

(a) Construction techniques. (b) Form. (c) Interpretation.

(a) Construction techniques. Most Maya pyramid-temples were built of limestone, cemented together with lime mortar, and sealed by a coating of lime plaster. Finished surfaces were often painted bright red, and sculptural details were emphasized in blue, green, black and yellow. Inner core masonry was often of rubble or boulders bedded in mortar of varying quality or sometimes dry laid. In some cases, for example the pyramid known as 'Str 5D-33, 1st' at TIKAL (c. AD 650), the inner core masonry was built up in terrace levels, each as a series of nested wall-like units entirely composed of bedded rubble masonry in high quality lime mortar. Outer facings were of cut stone, and, particularly in the Late Classic period (c. AD 600–c. 900), were sometimes dressed to a smooth finish after they had been set in place. Although outer facings are often referred to as 'retaining walls', this is usually not quite accurate. Facings, particularly on substructure components, established the precise shapes of terraces, but did not actually hold back the inner core material, except in low structures where the loose inner core material did not exert a great deal of outer thrust. The term 'fill', implying a non-structural capacity of core masonry, is generally not appropriate in pyramidal structures of any significant height. (See also §1(i)(a) above.)

(b) Form. There is no generally accepted definition of the pyramid-temple as an architectural type. Pyramid-temples are here defined as those with at least one pyramidal component, consisting of at least three terraces. This is enough to produce a distinct pyramidal effect, even when the absolute height is minimal. Most frequently the pyramidal part is a substructure that supports a building, either directly, or with other components intervening. A number of Maya pyramidal temples did not support buildings, and some have the building at the front of the pyramid rather than on top of it.

Maya pyramid-temples usually comprise a number of distinct components that make up the complete form in an additive manner. For example, at Tikal, Guatemala, one of the primary sites for architectural studies, these components occur as a standard set consisting of a basal platform, pyramid, supplementary platform, building platform (a component that directly supports the building and has the same plan outline), building and roof-comb (a tall, vertical stone extension of the roof, usually carved). The Tikal temples are assemblages of these components, stacked vertically. Only Temple IV (c. AD 750) has the complete set, however; Temples I, II, III and V (Late Classic period, c. AD 600–c. 900) each include only the pyramid, building platform, temple and roof-comb, and this is probably the most common combination at all Maya sites. There are many temples without roof-combs, but few, if any, without building platforms. Basal platforms, too, are relatively infrequent.

Most pyramid-temples are rectangular in plan, with a single staircase (see STAIRCASE, §III). The angle of slope at the front and rear is usually steeper than at the two sides. The ground plan is often elaborated by inset corners and projections at the centre of the rear and sometimes at the sides (e.g. as at Temple I, Tikal; c. AD 700). Projected elements frequently border the staircase and often contain panels of masks representing deities. The terraces themselves most frequently have an upper part that projects over an inset lower element, together known as an 'apron' profile. Projecting elements often have distinct profiles, with upper and lower mouldings, or may have differently proportioned aprons, either higher or lower than the terrace aprons. Early Classic period (c. AD 250–c. 600) aprons frequently have a convex curvature, as in Temple 5D-22, 1st, at Tikal (c. AD 550). Late Classic aprons generally have straight-line profiles with the apron inset reduced to a narrow, horizontal slot.

A few temples have stairways arranged radially, with a central staircase on each of the four sides. An early example is Temple E-VII sub, UAXACTÚN (c. 400 BC); other examples include the Temple of the Seven Dolls at DZIBILCHALTÚN (c. AD 500), Structure A-3 at SEIBAL (c. AD 830) and the Castillo at CHICHÉN ITZÁ (c. AD 900). The twin pyramid temples erected as calendric monuments at Tikal and Yaxhá during the Late Classic period also have this form, and apparently did not support buildings. These structures are square in plan, and, although the pyramidal component may exhibit radial symmetry, other parts usually do not. Temples with staircases on all four sides were obviously meant to face in one particular direction.

The component of the structure usually described as the 'building' is generally rather small, with a limited amount of roofed interior space. Although some temple buildings had thatched roofs (e.g. as at several major Classic period structures at PIEDRAS NEGRAS), most Classic period examples were vaulted. In the Post-Classic period (c. AD 900–1521), temples with flat, beam and mortar roofs began to be built, particularly in the Maya Highlands of Guatemala, for example Temple I at ZACULEU (c. AD 1200).

The temple buildings of Tikal have a distinctive form that produces the appearance of two 'house' images, one in front of the other, separated by a narrow vertical slot. Within, the rooms are arranged on axis, one behind the other, each one step higher; and temple buildings of the same exterior form may contain one, two or three rooms.

16. Temple of the Magician, Uxmal, 10th century AD

Such combinations began at Tikal in the Early Classic period and persisted until the end of the Classic period (*c.* AD 900). The form appears only at Piedras Negras, Tikal, Uaxactún (Structure XVIII) and Holmul (Building B, Group II). Temple buildings formed as two 'house' images *not* separated by a vertical slot were built at Uaxactún, Piedras Negras and other sites such as Río Bec. The site of PALENQUE presents a different building type, again site-specific, with three rooms; here, though, the exterior appearance is of a single 'house', and the third room has the form of an interior shrine, entirely within the inner room (e.g. the Temple of the Sun, the Temple of the Cross and the Temple of the Foliated Cross).

Pyramid-temples with relatively long, palace-like buildings were erected at several sites. The Temple of the Inscriptions at Palenque (*c.* AD 683) is of this type, with five frontal doorways, as are Structure A-5 (single frontal doorway; 5th century AD) and Structure A-6 (thirteen frontal doorways; also 5th century) at ALTUN HA, and Structure 33 at YAXCHILÁN (Late Classic period). Structure B-4, 2nd, at Altun Ha (*c.* AD 600) and Structure N10-43 at LAMANAI (*c.* 200 BC) are examples of temples with long building components (nine and eleven frontal doorways, respectively), placed not on the tops of the pyramids but near their bases, at the fronts.

The combination of temple and palace architecture is represented most dramatically in the Palace of the Five Floors at EDZNÁ (7th–8th centuries AD; see fig. 9 above). Each of the four terraces of the pyramid supports vaulted buildings, and the top level supports a smaller building with an unusual double-fronted plan and a towering roof-comb. A somewhat similar theme, relating temple and palace, is exemplified by Late Classic period Structure IV at Becán, in which a quadrangular set of rooms surmounts a steep pyramidal substructure.

At other sites, groups of buildings, rather than single units, were more characteristic. Structure N10-43 at Lamanai had four building components, all facing the central axis. Temple N at Late Classic period Nakum has three buildings, two of which are placed forward and face inward; they occupy the top of a very steep pyramid. The Danta and El Tigre temples at MIRADOR (*c.* 200 BC) each have three buildings on pyramidal components supported on lower pyramidal platforms. These are the largest known Maya pyramidal temples. The most spacious building units built as components of pyramid-temples are those of the 9th–10th century Temple of the Warriors and the Temple of the Chacmool at Chichén Itzá. These had masonry vaults supported on columns, such that the interior space, more commonly comprising separate rooms, here merges into a single large space.

The 10th-century Temple of the Magician at UXMAL (see fig. 16) presents the most extraordinary treatment of building components in all Maya pyramidal temples. Its summit is occupied by a building that had no evident means of access. On its east side a large staircase ascends to a blank wall. On the west is another building component with a doorway in the form of a monster mouth (*see* DOOR, §VIII), making it evident that a symbolic intent lies behind the arrangement.

(c) Interpretation. While there is no doubt that pyramid-temples were used as settings for ritual activities, incense burning, offerings and sacrificial ceremonies of an essentially religious nature, it seems equally certain that their meaning also involved kingship, the political authority of the ruling élite and the legitimacy of dynastic lineages. A consensus on the meaning that pyramidal temples had for the ancient Maya has not been reached, and will probably remain highly speculative, but research seems to be converging towards interpretations that involve cosmic imagery and dynastic identity. The temples may have been models of both the visible and invisible supernatural aspects of the Maya world. It is possible that the Maya understood the temples as not merely symbolic references to the supernatural but as direct manifestations of supernatural will and purpose in the same way that such solar events as the solstices and eclipses were seen. From this point of view the temples could be understood as supernatural landscapes—in a sense, the actual supernatural realm—and, as such, the visible proof of the claims made by the élite. (For a discussion of Mesoamerican religion, *see also* §I, 4 above.)

The Temple of the Inscriptions at Palenque (see fig. 17) has been linked to the winter solstice sunset and to the death of the Lord Pacal in AD 683. Seen from the Palace building, the solstice sun appears to set into the temple on the angle of the stair that leads down to the tomb of Pacal, beneath the pyramidal substructure. Pacal and the sun could thus be considered to enter the Underworld together. Temple I at Tikal is associated with Ruler A, whose death must have taken place at about the time it was built: AD 711. Ruler A may be portrayed on the roof-comb and on Lintel 3 inside the building, and his body may lie in the tomb beneath the pyramid. His son, Ruler B (inaugurated AD 734), is portrayed on the lintel of Temple IV, built *c.* 750, a date that must have been close to his death. A ruler named Akbal Lord was entombed in Structure B-4 2nd A at Altun Ha on his death (*c.* AD 600), and placed over his pelvis was a spectacular jade carving of the sun god.

Such examples seem to be unequivocal evidence that pyramid-temples were related to rulership, but whether they were simply commemorative monuments is less clear. The meaning of the temples, and the motivation for their construction, may have been more concerned with the claim to a special kind of relationship between the élite and the supernatural powers—the claim on which the right to rulership would have been based. The temples could therefore have been built as demonstrations of this relationship more than as funerary monuments.

The same concern may lie behind the astronomical alignments that many temples embody. Temple E-VII sub

17. Temple of the Inscriptions, Palenque, *c.* AD 683

at Uaxactún faces west towards three other structures that are set in alignments to the winter and summer solstice sunsets. The Temple of the Magician (fig. 16 above) at Uxmal is orientated towards a sunset position exactly two Maya months (*uinals*) before the day of the passage of the solar zenith, a key day in the ancient Maya year, and at the centre of the main agricultural season. Equinox sunsets at Chichén Itzá cast a shadow from the pyramid terraces on to the side of the serpent stair in a pattern that undulates like a serpent entering the earth. Thus, although only a few astronomical orientations have been recognized and determined for pyramidal temples, it seems likely that most temples did have such alignments. Nevertheless, it is unlikely that these were set up for the purpose of making astronomical observations: they probably served to establish a visible, tangible, demonstrable relationship between the manmade structure and the celestial object, to reinforce the idea that both reflected the same supernatural influences and associations.

BIBLIOGRAPHY

T. Proskouriakoff: *An Album of Maya Architecture* (Washington, DC, 1946, Norman, 2/1963)
I. Marquina: *Arquitectura prehispánica* (Mexico City, 1950, 2/1964/R 1981)
G. Kubler: *The Art and Architecture of Ancient America*, Pelican Hist. A. (Harmondsworth, 1962, rev. 3/1984)
H. E. D. Pollock: 'Architecture of the Maya Lowlands', *Hb. Mid. Amer. Ind.*, ii (1965), pp. 378–440
A. L. Smith: 'Architecture of the Guatemalan Highlands', *Hb. Mid. Amer. Ind.*, ii (1965), pp. 76–145
G. F. Andrews: *Maya Cities: Placemaking and Urbanization* (Norman, 1975)
D. Heyden and P. Gendrop: *Pre-Columbian Architecture of Mesoamerica* (New York, 1975)

H. STANLEY LOTEN

(iii) West Mexico. In the Pre-Classic period (*c.* 2000 BC–*c.* AD 250) the architecture of this region (*see* WEST MEXICAN ART, PRE-COLUMBIAN) was largely independent of the mainstream developments in central Mesoamerica. During the Classic period (*c.* AD 250–*c.* 900), however, as the influence of TEOTIHUACÁN became increasingly dominant, many Teotihuacán-derived architectural practices spread to West Mexico. Nevertheless, in both the Pre-Classic and Classic periods West Mexican builders produced distinct traditions of their own, as well as regional versions of Central Highland styles in the Classic period.

(a) Pre-Classic period (c. *2000* BC–c. AD *250*): *shaft tombs.* The term shaft tomb has been extended by some scholars to include graves in the form of bell-shaped pits; strictly speaking, however, it describes only those tombs that have vertical shaft entrances and chambered anterooms at the bases of the shafts. Many have been described without reference to their surface architecture, although such features invariably accompany the burial tomb. Variations in the quality, size and contents of shaft tombs imply social ranking, and the nature of their contents and decoration suggests ancestor veneration. The most elaborate shaft tombs date from the Late Pre-Classic period (*c.* 300 BC–*c.* AD 250) and were built throughout the highland lake districts of Jalisco and adjoining regions of Nayarit. Within this area the Teuchitlán–Etzatlán zone is especially notable for its shaft tombs of the El Arenal phase (up to *c.* AD 200). The Late Pre-Classic shaft tombs

were preceded in the Early Pre-Classic period (*c.* 2000–*c.* 1000 BC) by more modest, but still elaborately built shaft tombs in the Jalisco–Nayarit lakeland region and at the site of El Opeño in north-western Michoacán; and in the Middle Pre-Classic period (*c.* 1000–*c.* 300 BC; known locally as the San Felipe phase) by burial mounds. None are protected, and most have been looted.

The Early Pre-Classic tombs at El Opeño have modest shafts, seldom more than 2 m deep, some with adits, and stairways at their bases. The tombs have oval-shaped chambers used as crypts over extended periods. The offerings were elegant: figurines, obsidian eccentrics (pressure-flaked obsidian objects of curious shapes, sometimes of animals or humans), painted ceramic vessels and other valued items. Late Pre-Classic tombs are usually entered by square or rectangular shafts and have square or rectangular burial chambers. The deepest known shaft is at El Arenal, Jalisco, beneath a circular banquette that surrounds a circular patio and small pyramid. The tomb, called 'El Frijolar', is 17 m deep and has three large chambers at the base. One chamber is reached through another, rather than directly from the shaft. Another tomb at El Arenal has an 8 m shaft. In the Teuchitlán–Etzatlán zone of Jalisco, where shaft tombs reached their fullest expression, tombs have been classified into three categories: Category I tombs have two or more chambers and shafts of 12 m or more; Category II tombs are 6–8 m deep, and usually have only one chamber, sometimes two; Category III tombs are 2–4 m deep and have one chamber. Each category represents a distinct cluster of the 120 recorded shaft tombs in this zone. The evidence of such categorization has been used to postulate a ranked or stratified social order in Late Pre-Classic West Mexico, but it is important to note that all three categories constituted only a small percentage of the total number of burials. The economic and labour investments necessary for the deeper tombs, many cut into rock, also imply social ranking.

A second classification of shaft tombs, into six types, is based on details of shape and contents. The contents of shaft tombs vary according to the status of the lineages using the crypts and by region. Almost all tombs contain offerings of hollow clay figurines; beads, pendants and other jewellery; obsidian artefacts, usually eccentrics or prismatic blades; *manos* (grinders) and *metates* (grinding stones); ceramic vessels; shell objects, including trumpets; and pyrite mosaic mirrors (*see* MIRROR, §V). Several late tombs have polychrome wall paintings with motifs similar to those found on pseudo-cloisonné decorated pottery vessels.

(b) Classic period (c. AD *250*–c. *900*): *Teuchitlán tradition.* Teuchitlán is the name applied to the architecture both of the site of this name and of sites throughout the highland lake region of Jalisco during the Classic period. The tradition had its roots in the burial-mound and shaft-tomb traditions of the Pre-Classic period (*see* §(a) above) in the immediate area, but reached its peak in the middle of the Classic period between *c.* AD 400 and 700, when the region developed closer contacts with the Central Highlands (*see* §II, 3(v) above).

Characteristic Teuchitlán architecture was composed of concentric circles and was used for both monumental and everyday structures. The circles comprised five basic formal elements. Constant features were: a flat-topped, terraced, circular pyramid supporting a structure; a surrounding, elevated, circular patio; a circular banquette; between four and sixteen evenly spaced and rectangular pyramid-platforms on top of the banquette; and burial crypts beneath the platforms and banquette. Ballcourts and rectangular patios composed of at least four pyramid-platforms were frequently associated with the circular structures.

The greatest concentration of circular platforms occurs near the modern village of Teuchitlán, where there are monumental, interconnected circles, two with a shared ballcourt, and five other circles near by. The largest circle is 128 m in diameter. The circular structures are made from rubble and stacked rock, or on rare occasions of earth with rock facings, plastered over and painted, usually red. Staircases ascended both pyramid-platforms and central pyramids. These buildings are the products of formal architectural design and are highly sophisticated; they are replicated with precision throughout the zone, and show the use of set proportions in their construction.

The distribution of Teuchitlán architecture coincides with, and was perhaps unified by, the availability of several highland resources, including rich obsidian deposits (six of which were mined, two intensively), quartz, copper, malachite, azurite, haematite and opal. The opal and obsidian mines at Llano Grande were protected by a ditch-and-wall fortification. In addition, the rich soils and plentiful water supplies of the lake valleys permitted extensive marshland gardens (or *chinampas*), collection dams and terracing.

Within the lake zone, settlement sizes differed dramatically. Some sites, such as Ahualulco and Huitzilapa, were semi-nucleated habitation zones and fields, and measured 3000 to 5000 ha. Their ceremonial complexes were between 300 and 500 ha. The Teuchitlán–El Refugio habitation zone, however, was *c.* 30,000 ha, with a 3000 ha ceremonial core. Away from the habitation zones are smaller sites with simple circular platforms and usually no ballcourt. These were frequently scattered around the major sites, forming a settlement hierarchy of at least four tiers. Governing the hierarchy was the accessibility of obsidian. Population estimates are 20,000 to 25,000 for the Teuchitlán–El Refugio habitation zone and 3000 to 5000 for other sites. In Early Classic period Teuchitlán it has been suggested that urbanization was initiated by a concentration of the population around the ceremonial core.

Teuchitlán family crypts were not as elaborate in the Classic period as they were in the Pre-Classic period. It appears that labour resources were invested in monumental buildings and agricultural features rather than in funerary ritual. Nonetheless, some chambers were painted, and their offerings fully reflect the area's richness in resources and trade materials. Prestige burials were usually accompanied by a set of figurines; blue-green stone beads and pendants; rare pieces of chemical turquoise from the south-western USA; occasional copper artefacts; mosaic mirrors; a range of obsidian artefacts, including prismatic blades; and elegant ceramics. Cloisonné painted ceramic vessels were the most elaborate; the iconography of these vessels and of a few surviving crypt paintings, which depict dancing priests with pointed noses, in elegant clothes and plumed headdresses, strongly suggests aspects of Quetzalcóatl–Ehecatl (the plumed serpent as god of the winds) in association with the circular architecture.

BIBLIOGRAPHY

S. Long: *Archaeology of the Municipio of Etzatlán, Jalisco* (diss., Los Angeles, UCLA, 1966)
A. Oliveros: 'Nuevas exploraciones en El Opeño, Michoacán', *The Archaeology of West Mexico*, ed. B. Bell (Ajijíc, Mexico, 1974), pp. 182–201
H. von Winning: *The Shaft Tomb Figures of West Mexico*, Southwest Museum Papers, xxiv (Los Angeles, 1974)
L. J. Galván: *Rescate arqueológico en el fraccionamiento Tabachines, Zapopan, Jalisco* (Mexico City, 1976)
D. Soto de Arechavaleta: *Análisis de la tecnología de producción del taller de obsidiana de Guachimontón, Teuchitlán, Jalisco* (diss., Mexico City, Escuela N. Antropol. & Hist., 1982)
P. Weigand and M. Spence: 'The Obsidian Mining Complex at La Joya, Jalisco', *Anthropology*, vi (1982), pp. 175–88
T. Cabreros: *Civilización en el norte de México: Arqueología en el Río Bolaños* (diss., Mexico City, Escuela N. Antropol. & Hist., 1984)
P. Weigand: 'Evidence for Complex Societies during the Western Mesoamerican Classic Period', *The Archaeology of West and Northwest Mesoamerica*, ed. M. Foster and P. Weigand (New York, 1985), pp. 47–91
——: *Evolución de una civilización prehispánica: Arqueología de Jalisco, Nayarit y Zacatecas* (Zamora, Mexico, 1993)

PHIL C. WEIGAND

IV. Monumental stone sculpture.

Stone-carving first appeared in Mesoamerica during the Pre-Classic period (*c.* 2000 BC–*c.* AD 250) with the freestanding sculpture of the Olmecs of the Gulf Coast. During the Classic period (*c.* AD 250–*c.* 900), when two-dimensional art and architectural decoration predominated, the finest sculptors were Maya relief-carvers in modern southern Mexico and the central lowlands of Guatemala and Honduras. Monumental figural sculpture in the round was reintroduced during the Post-Classic period (*c.* AD 900–1521), by the Toltecs in the Central Highlands and the northern Maya region and by the Huastecs in the northern Gulf Coast. In the 15th century and early 16th the Aztecs in central Mexico created fine images in the round as well as relief-covered sculpture, some of colossal size. Other distinctive sculptural styles were created by the Classic-period inhabitants of the central Gulf Coast, by the Zapotecs in the Southern Highlands and by the Post-Classic Tarascans of West Mexico in Michoacán.

1. Introduction. 2. Pre-Classic period (*c.* 2000 BC–*c.* AD 250). 3. Classic period (*c.* AD 250–*c.* 900). 4. Post-Classic period (*c.* 900–1521).

1. INTRODUCTION. Knowledge of the context and function of Mesoamerican sculpture varies. For example Olmec sculpture is least understood because of the Olmecs' own systematic destruction and burial of monuments. Some were also reused when sites were reoccupied by later peoples. Teotihuacán and the Toltec city of Tula also show signs of massive destruction, and later inhabitants of these sites moved most sculptures from their original positions. In the case of the Aztecs and other Late Post-Classic peoples, modern cities and towns cover most major sites, and only rarely have sculptures been found *in*

situ. In contrast, many monuments at Maya sites were architectural, and even free-standing sculptures were not greatly disturbed by later peoples until modern times.

Iconographic interpretations of Mesoamerican sculpture are generally based on written sources from the early Colonial period (most of them on the Aztecs and Maya), on analogies with other Pre-Columbian peoples and on modern ethnographic studies. Until the 1960s studies of Mesoamerican sculpture dealt mostly with cosmology, mythology, religion and the representation of supernatural figures. Since then significant advances have been made, beginning with Tatania Proskouriakoff's pioneering studies of Maya sculpture, involving the decipherment of hieroglyphic texts and the discovery of their historical content.

Mesoamerican artists usually used local stone for their work, although the Olmecs and later the Aztecs sometimes quarried stone many kilometres from the intended setting. The cultures of the Central and Southern Highlands favoured basalt, andesite and other volcanic rocks; in the central Gulf Coast sandstone and limestone were used in the north, while basalt and other volcanic rocks were used in the south; and in the northern and central Maya region limestone and lime stucco were used. Hardstones, such as jade and other green-coloured stones, and *tecali* (Mexican onyx), were traded across greater distances because of their rarity and value; they were usually reserved for small sculptured items (*see* §VIII below), although some greenstone objects, such as the head of Coyolxauhqui found at Tenochtitlán (Mexico City, Mus. N. Antropol.), are of monumental size.

Sculptures were worked with blades, chisels and hammers of stone, saws made of stone, wood or fibre, and drills of reed, wood or bone. Sand or powdered obsidian served as an abrasive, and reeds, animal skins and stones were used for polishing. Most Mesoamerican sculpture was painted, either directly on the stone or over a red or white undercoat, and many still have traces of paint on them. Sculpture in wood was probably also common, but only a few examples have survived.

2. PRE-CLASSIC PERIOD (*c.* 2000 BC–*c.* AD 250). The earliest Pre-Columbian monumental stone sculpture was produced by the Olmecs of the Gulf Coast and was associated with the earliest ceremonial architecture. Olmec sculptural traditions spread into the Central Highlands, and independent traditions were developed in the Southern Highlands by the Zapotecs and later in the Maya region at such sites as Izapa.

(*i*) *Gulf Coast (Olmec)*. About 1200 BC the Olmecs began to produce finely carved, large-scale stone sculpture. Smaller Olmec-style works are found throughout much of Mesoamerica, but, with few exceptions, monumental sculpture is confined to the Olmec heartland of the southern Gulf Coast. The two major excavated sites, SAN LORENZO TENOCHTITLÁN and LA VENTA, probably dominated the area, or at least functioned as major ceremonial centres, during the Early (*c.* 2000–*c.* 1000 BC) and Middle (*c.* 1000–*c.* 300 BC) Pre-Classic periods, respectively. However, sculpture has also been found at unexcavated sites.

Most Olmec sculptures are single three-dimensional figures, some human and individualized and others unnatural beings, treated with the same organic realism. Surfaces are sensitively carved, sometimes with fine patterns incised on modelled forms (a combination that continued into Classic-period Veracruz and Huastec sculpture). Facial expressions and bodies are active, and the positions of limbs, hands and feet are often asymmetrical.

Olmec basalt figural sculptures and jade portrait masks are among the most naturalistic human images created by Mesoamerican sculptors. One common type has heavy features and sometimes a slightly snarling, jaguar-like expression. Another type is bearded and entirely human (see fig. 18). Naturalistic representations of animals are, by contrast, relatively rare, while 'jaguar–men', combining feline and human features and ranging in age from infants to adults, are common. Figures of 'jaguar–human' babies carried by adult men with less animal-like faces—such as a large greenstone sculpture found near Las Limas (Veracruz, Mus. Reg.)—may represent 'heirs to the throne' or the first 'jaguar–men' from whom the Olmecs believed themselves to be descended.

At San Lorenzo Tenochtitlán colossal basalt portrait heads (the largest is 2.85 m tall), figures of humans and 'jaguar–men' and basalt platforms (sometimes called 'thrones' or 'altars') were found. The stone was quarried in the Tuxtla Mountains 70 km to the north-west. These pieces must have been distributed about the ceremonial centre for various ritual functions. By *c.* 900 BC the occupation of the site ended soon after the ritual and deliberate

18. Olmec figure of an acrobat, basalt, h. 660 mm, from Uxpanapan, Veracruz, Early to Middle Pre-Classic period, *c.* 1200–*c.*300 BC (Mexico City, Museo Nacional de Antropología)

mutilation and burial of a number of sculptures. Subsequently, La Venta seems to have become the primary ceremonial centre of Olmec culture. In addition to colossal heads, platforms and other sculptures resembling those at San Lorenzo Tenochtitlán, the finds at La Venta included both fine and crude relief sculptures; stelae, a form that became important in the Classic period, appeared here for the first time. Non-basaltic stones were used, and jade, serpentine and other greenstones were imported for carving figurines, celts and other smaller sculptures. Although monumental earthen architecture, such as platform mounds around plazas, occurred at both San Lorenzo Tenochtitlán and La Venta, the stone sculpture appears to have been non-architectural.

At least fifteen colossal heads wearing close-fitting headgear have been found in the Olmec heartland: nine certain examples at San Lorenzo Tenochtitlán (for illustration see OLMEC), four at La Venta, one at Tres Zapotes, one at nearby Cerro Nestepe and one in the Tuxtla Mountains, plus a further disputed example from San Lorenzo Tenochtitlán. Each head portrays a distinctive face and, according to some scholars, depicts a ruler. At San Lorenzo Tenochtitlán and La Venta one type of platform 'throne' or altar also depicts a dynastic image in the form of a ruler or ancestor emerging from a niche under the tabletop. The art of wood-carving is represented by 11 rare figural sculptures at El Mantí, Veracruz.

As Olmec influence and trade connections declined, new styles were developed in the Gulf Coast in the Late Pre-Classic period (c. 300 BC–c. AD 250). Narrative reliefs (often incorporating several figures) predominated, but forms became increasingly abstract and were often crudely carved. Stelae feature single figures of important personages and some include Long Count dates (see §II above). Stele C at TRES ZAPOTES depicts a figure seated on a large jaguar face (probably a throne) and a Long Count date corresponding to 31 BC. This is one of the earliest dated monuments in Mesoamerica (Stele 2 at Chiapa de Corzo is badly damaged, but dates to 36 BC, assuming a *baktun* 7 reading). A finely carved stele (h. 2.34 m) of a ruler from La Mojarra, Veracruz, but in the Izapan style of the southern Maya area, bears Long Count dates corresponding to AD 143 and 156 and one of the lengthiest hieroglyphic texts on a Mesoamerican sculpture, seemingly detailing events of his reign.

(ii) Central Highlands. Locally produced small stone sculptures in the Olmec style have been found at several sites in the Central Highlands, but monumental stone sculpture occurs only at CHALCATZINGO, a trading centre with strong ties to the Gulf Coast. On the hillside overlooking Chalcatzingo's ceremonial plaza there are numerous whole and fragmentary Olmec-style reliefs on rock faces. They incorporate more narrative features than contemporary Gulf Coast sculpture, although their iconography is clearly Olmec. Monument 1 (for illustration see CHALCATZINGO), a relief-carving showing a seated figure in a large jaguar mouth or cave, recalls the stone platforms with emerging rulers at La Venta.

At the site of Teopantecuanitlán, in the state of Guerrero, the architecture of the ceremonial plaza was decorated with 'jaguar–man' faces, and a mutilated colossal head was also found, proving contact with the Olmec heartland. Other stone sculpture from Guerrero includes small-scale jade and greenstone figures and masks and miniature carvings of temples (several of which are in Mexico City, Mus. N. Antropol.) made for burial in graves. These feature a variety of abstract and geometric styles (the best known being from the Mezcala area), but they are difficult to date precisely and may have been made at any time from the Pre-Classic period until the Spanish Conquest.

(iii) Southern Highlands (Zapotec). Relief-carving was important from the Middle Pre-Classic period (c. 1000–c. 300 BC) in the Valley of Oaxaca. At Monte Albán, founded in the mid-5th century BC, 320 reliefs or fragments of reliefs on stone slabs known as *danzantes* were incorporated into the wall and stair risers of Monte Albán Building L to form a gallery on the south-west side of the main plaza (for illustration see MONTE ALBÁN); and one *danzante*, dated to c. 600 BC, was found at the valley site of San José Mogote (see §II, 3(iii) above). They depict captured and dead enemies, and some bear the earliest hieroglyphic inscriptions in Mesoamerica. Only 42 were found *in situ* at Monte Albán, while others were reused in constructing later buildings. Later Pre-Classic relief panels on Structure J depict conquests emblematically, with upside-down heads hanging from place-name glyphs.

Contemporary slab reliefs at DAINZÚ, facing a terraced mound, depict variously masked and jaguar-headed humans. The masked figures are ball-players, and most are in fallen and reclining postures and are presumed to represent the defeated. Two reliefs represent a standing victor figure; one is set into the platform, and the other is on the hill above the pyramid.

(iv) Maya region (Izapan). At the Middle to Late Pre-Classic site of IZAPA, on the Pacific coast of Guatemala adjacent to the southern Maya highlands, some motifs suggest Olmec ancestry but many others were new developments. Stelae carved in relief were paired with low altars and erected in plazas in front of pyramid-platforms. Reliefs depict ceremonies, hierarchies of important people and mythical scenes with crocodiles and toads (zoomorphic representations of the earth), cosmic trees (for illustration see IZAPA), supernatural humans and animals, flying figures and twins. Some of the scenes are interpreted as early representations of episodes in the Maya hero twins myth. In some reliefs there is a proliferation of scroll patterns, including 'scroll eyes' and 'long lips' on supernatural creatures. Cosmic settings are indicated by bands at the top and bottom; that on the top, known as the 'Izapan signature', is thought to be a stylized jaguar mouth, perhaps evolved from Olmec settings with jaguar features.

Some of the carved stelae elsewhere in the region (but not at Izapa) feature a single important personage, and like Late Pre-Classic Gulf Coast stelae include hieroglyphic inscriptions and dates in the Maya Long Count calendar. Stele 10 from KAMINALJUYÚ (Guatemala City, Mus. N. Arqueol. & Etnol.) represents three figures and columns of hieroglyphs and is a direct antecedent of Classic Maya art. Other Late Pre-Classic indigenous styles in the southern Maya highlands include crude boulder sculptures of fat figures and colossal heads (such as those at El Baúl in

Guatemala), figures on pedestals and small figures seated on benches.

3. CLASSIC PERIOD (*c.* AD 250–*c.* 900). With the rise of large urban complexes and trading 'empires' in Classic-period Mesoamerica, distinctive sculptural styles developed in every major region, each influencing the others. Within the broader regions there was a proliferation of local styles in the Late Classic period (*c.* AD 600–*c.* 900), often centred on particular cities. This was especially true in the Maya region, where several localized, contemporary traditions developed in the southern lowlands and peripheral areas.

(i) Gulf Coast (Classic Veracruz cultures). The Classic-period inhabitants of the Gulf Coast made monumental ceramic figures (*see* §VII, 2 below) and finely carved ceremonial stone sculptures of ball-game paraphernalia: *yugos*, *hachas* and *palmas* (*see* §II, 3(i) above). Monumental stone sculpture is principally represented at TAJíN, where sets of narrative reliefs decorate the walls of its ballcourts and stacked stone columns. The south ballcourt, one of at least eleven in the ceremonial centre, has six panels carved with scenes representing the sacrifice of a ball-player and his journey to the underworld in search of *pulque* (a ritual beverage of fermented agave cactus juice). Reliefs on columns in the Building of the Columns show conquests, sacrifices and other events in the life of the 10th-century ruler '13 Rabbit'. Characteristic of all Classic Veracruz stonework is interlocking scrollwork that frames the scenes or covers surfaces, a feature that spread to the Central Highlands, where it appears at Teotihuacán.

(ii) Central Highlands.

(a) Teotihuacán. In the Classic period the Central Highlands were dominated by the site of TEOTIHUACÁN. The main art form there was mural painting (*see* §V, 2(iii)(a) below), but several important stone sculptures and an important sculptured pyramid were also found at the site. Major sculptures are the two colossal goddesses excavated near the Pyramid of the Moon (one now in Mexico City, Mus. N. Antropol.). These show the same preference for geometric forms as seen in Teotihuacán murals and architecture, the massiveness of the stone preserving its essential bulkiness. At the Temple of Quetzalcóatl, built during Teotihuacán's early period (2nd century AD), the tiers are decorated with tenoned Quetzalcóatl (feathered serpent) heads, which extend from the *tableros* almost as sculptures in the round, alternating with a second head near the tail of the serpent body; there are aquatic symbols (shells) and more feathered serpents on the *talud* sections. Both the heads and the associated symbols were painted, and traces of red and white pigment are still visible.

The most common stone sculptures were stone masks and roughly carved 'Old Fire God' images supporting braziers. The masks represent stereotyped human faces and were probably the focus of ritual ensembles or funerary bundles; the braziers were used in household courtyards. An unusual monument at Teotihuacán is a 'stele' (Mexico City, Mus. N. Antropol.) combining typical Teotihuacán

19. Teotihuacán four-piece stone stele, h. 2.13 m, from the La Ventilla compound, Mexico, Early Classic period, *c.* AD 250–*c.* 600 (Mexico City, Museo Nacional de Antropología)

geometric shapes with interlocking scrollwork characteristic of contemporary Classic Veracruz stone sculpture (see fig. 19).

(b) Xochicalco. The Late Classic-period city of Xochicalco expanded in size and power in the 8th and 9th centuries AD, along with several other Central Mexican cities, at the time of the decline of Teotihuacán. Xochicalco's importance as a regional ceremonial centre, with a proportionately small resident population, is emphasized by the presence of a combination of sculptural influences from diverse parts of Mesoamerica, notably Teotihuacán (*see* §3(ii)(a) above), the Gulf Coast (*see* §3(i) above) and the Maya region (*see* §3(iv) below). Its eclectic style blends

naturalistic characteristics as well as motifs from Maya art with the 'geometric' organization of Teotihuacán and the Central Highlands.

The Pyramid of the Feathered Serpent bears on its platform base monumental reliefs of undulating serpents with Maya-looking figures beneath the loops of the serpents' bodies (for illustration *see* XOCHICALCO). Hieroglyphic inscriptions on this platform and on three stelae excavated from another (Mexico City, Mus. N. Antropol.) are the most extensive on stone in Central Mexico. Although the impulse to carve hieroglyphs on monuments may have come from the Maya area, the forms themselves are Mexican.

(iii) Southern Highlands (Zapotec). In the Classic period Zapotec stone-carving at Monte Albán shifted to stelae. These were carved to a standardized form, depicting a terraced place-name glyph upon which stands a tied captive or high-status figure in human or zoomorphic guise and surrounded by glyphs giving the person's name and the date of the event commemorated. Influence from Teotihuacán is represented by speech scrolls, by reliefs on the narrow edges of stelae that depict Teotihuacán ambassadors or trade representatives (*see* §II, 3(ii) above), and by a large, flat, onyx slab incised with a jaguar–human figure in profile and another richly dressed Teotihuacano behind him.

In the Late Classic and Early Post-Classic periods, after the decline of Monte Albán, slabs were carved at Oaxaca Valley sites such as Etla, Noriega and Zaachila. These show a new concern for genealogy, depicting either a male and female couple seated beneath a sky motif or a single enthroned figure.

(iv) Maya region. The tradition of Maya monumental sculpture began at lowland tropical forest sites (in northern Guatemala and Belize) in the Late Pre-Classic period (*c.* 300 BC–*c.* AD 250), when it took the form of colossal architectural masks flanking pyramid stairways and representing the sun and Venus in various aspects. By the Early Classic period (*c.* AD 250–*c.* 600) ideas from the Southern Highlands were transformed into a new style that focused on the commemoration of ruling dynasties. Important forms include the stele and altar complex; the stele is carved to represent a standing ruler (the 'Classic motif'), with hieroglyphic inscriptions and Long Count dates. At TIKAL, the most important city in this area, stelae with altars lined the plazas between the principal pyramids. The figure on each stele was carved in low relief, in partial or full profile and almost hidden beneath the elaborately carved costume and paraphernalia of rank. Architectural sculpture, carved stucco roof-combs (the vertical stone extensions of temple roofs) and carved wooden lintels, decorated the shrines on the tops of the major pyramids.

In the Late Classic period (*c.* AD 600–*c.* 900) Maya cities in the peripheral areas to the north, west and south-east of Tikal rose to prominence, and distinctive regional sculpture styles developed in the latter two regions. To the south-east, sculptors at Copán varied the classic stele and altar complex by depicting large frontal figures in high relief, covered with dense, extremely elaborate costume detail (for illustration *see* COPÁN). Huge zoomorphic altars

20. Maya lid of Lord Pacal's sarcophagus, line drawing of carving in limestone, 3.72×2.17 m, Temple of the Inscriptions, Palenque, Late Classic period, *c.* AD 683

and other sculptures in the round are also characteristic of Copán sculpture.

In the western region, sites on the Usumacinta River drainage are noted for multifigured carved narrative scenes representing accessions, the taking of important war captives and their presentation at court, bloodletting and other rituals. At PIEDRAS NEGRAS accession stelae, such as Stele 14, depict a young ruler seated frontally in a niche reached by a ladder and surrounded by cosmic symbols. At nearby YAXCHILÁN stone door lintels depict dynastic rituals of the heavy-set ruler Shield Jaguar and his relatives: Lintel 24, for example, depicts Shield Jaguar holding a torch and facing his wife, Lady Xoc, who pulls a bloodletting rope through her tongue. Characteristic of Yaxchilán reliefs are their finely detailed textiles and other costume patterns and the use of two distinct planes in relief-carving.

The most spectacular style of the western area developed at Palenque, in the 7th and 8th centuries AD, beginning in the reign of Lord Pacal (615–83). The stone sarcophagus lid of his tomb beneath the Temple of the Inscriptions is an explicit depiction of a king's cosmic fate: Pacal descends into the maw of the underworld on the

21. Maya portrait head, stucco, h. 280 mm, from Palenque, Late Classic period *c.* AD 700–*c.* 750 (Mexico City, Museo Nacional de Antropología)

head of the dying sun; above him the branches of the cosmic tree form a four-part diagram that symbolizes the cardinal directions, indicating Pacal's position at the centre of the cosmos (see fig. 20). The sides of the sarcophagus are carved with his ancestors growing from the ground as trees. Similar monumental reliefs focusing on cosmic trees and the sun, commemorating the accession of Pacal's son and successor, Chan Bahlúm, were carved in the Temple of the Sun, the Temple of the Cross and the Temple of the Foliated Cross. Reliefs in the palace complex from the reigns of several rulers represent cosmic monsters framing doorways and accession scenes.

The PALENQUE style is distinct in its extensive use of stucco as architectural decoration and in the general absence of the stele (only one example is known). There is a tendency, not seen elsewhere in the Maya region, towards individualization in portraiture, including the faithful depiction of physical deformities in the royal family, probably seen as signs of divine origin (see fig. 21). During the reign of Chan Bahlúm people were portrayed with little idealization. Sculpture production at all these Maya cities ended during the 9th and 10th centuries as the Southern Maya Lowland sites were abandoned and their inhabitants migrated from the area.

4. POST-CLASSIC PERIOD (*c.* 900–1521). Significant changes were introduced in the Early Post-Classic period (*c.* AD 900–*c.* 1200), including the reintroduction of sculpture in the round as a major form, the carving of deity idols—particularly among the Huastecs of the Gulf Coast

and the Aztecs of Central Mexico—and a widespread pictorial vocabulary featuring such motifs as the sun disc with triangular rays. Compared with the Classic period, there were fewer carved inscriptions, and the Maya Long Count system fell into disuse. Nevertheless many features of Post-Classic monumental sculpture had their roots in the Classic period. Archaeology has not yet established the precise chronological relationship among the three areas producing monumental sculptures: the Gulf Coast, the Central Highlands and the Maya region on the Yucatán Peninsula. Thus it is unclear when the Toltec sculptural style was created and whether it began at Tula or Chichén Itzá, the two widely separated sites at which it is found.

(i) Gulf Coast (Huastec). The focus of Gulf Coast stone sculpture shifted north in the Post-Classic period, where the Huastecs developed a new style consisting principally of near life-size, standing figures (for illustration *see* HUASTEC), most of which are considered deity idols. This style seems to have extended into Late Post-Classic times (*c.* AD 1200–1521). The finest examples have softly modelled features and are intricately carved with surface patterns indicating costumes, body paint or tattoos. Notable examples include a youth from Tamuín (Mexico City, Mus. N. Antropol.) and a statue (New York, Brooklyn Mus.) showing a living man on one side (usually interpreted as Quetzalcóatl the deity–hero) and a skeleton on the other. Another common subject, meant to be seen in profile, is the small, hunched figure of an old man leaning on a cane, who probably represents the 'old god Mam' described in ethnohistorical sources.

(ii) Central Highlands.

(a) Toltec. The Toltecs developed and spread a distinct ensemble of monumental stone sculpture that was rooted in Mesoamerican tradition but contained distinctly new elements. It is conventionally dated to the Early Post-Classic period, thus contemporary with early Huastec sculpture, but many of its forms may be earlier. In the course of their movement and conquests, probably from the north-west—during which they established their capital at TULA—the Toltecs' style was mingled with local traditions, resulting in the sculptural style at Tula and also in a Toltec–Maya style at CHICHÉN ITZÁ in the Northern Maya Lowlands (*see* §(iii) below).

Toltec figural and animal sculptures, carved both in relief and in the round, were usually architectural in function (for illustration *see* TOLTEC): they served as roof supports, standard bearers, sacrificial platforms, thrones and benches. On Pyramid B at Tula (as reconstructed), at the north-east corner of the ceremonial plaza, four huge warrior figures (4.6 m tall) known as Atlantes, four low-relief carved square-sectioned pillars and, in theory (only the round, carved body sections and tails remain at the site), two serpent columns supported the roof of the temple (for illustration *see* CAJA-ESPIGA). The Atlantes wear tall, feathered headdresses, rectangular earflaps, breastplates, belts clasped at the back with discs, jewellery and heeled sandals decorated with quetzalcoatls. Each holds an *atlatl* (spear-thrower) in his right hand and a curved blade and bag of incense in his left.

Two other distinctive elements of the Toltec style were the *chacmool* (see fig. 22) and the tzompantli (skull rack;

22. Toltec–Maya *chacmool*, limestone, 1. 1.56 m, from Chichén Itzá, Early Post-Classic-period, *c.* AD 900–*c.* 1200 (Mexico City, Museo Nacional de Antropología)

for illustration *see* TZOMPANTLI). The *chacmool* is a reclining stone human figure with raised knees and upright head turned towards the viewer. A small receptacle rests on the stomach, possibly for offerings. *Chacmools* were placed before seats and altars in temples, and the form was copied by many cultures up to the time of the Spanish Conquest.

Relief-carvings, representing warriors in procession, mythical beings, jaguars, eagles, coyotes, skulls and cross-bones and other death imagery, decorated precinct walls, pyramid-platform walls, piers, altars and benches at Tula. Toltec stone-carving at Tula features simplified shapes, flat and single-curve surfaces and lacks the subtler modelling of details found at Chichén Itzá.

(b) Aztec. The centre of Aztec sculptural production was the Basin of Mexico, where Aztec peoples of several tribal groups had settled during the course of the Post-Classic period, and in particular Tenochtitlán, founded by the Mexica Aztecs in the mid-14th century. Aztec sculptors were probably organized into guild-like groups living in distinct civic districts, some of them working under royal patronage. Aztec rulers took an active part in the creation of monuments, as is known from recorded dialogues between the *Tlatoani* (supreme leader) and his prime minister.

Like the Huastecs, the Aztecs carved anthropomorphic representations of their gods, but none of the principal male images of Tenochtitlán has survived. Examples of male deities all come from elsewhere, such as the sculpture

of Ehecatl (god of wind) from CALIXTLAHUACA (Tenango, Mus. Arqueol. Estado México). The only major female idols known from Tenochtitlan are the andesite statue of Coatlícue ('Serpent-skirt'; 2.56 m; Mexico City, Mus. N. Antropol.) and fragments of companion sculptures. The Aztecs also represented conquered and humiliated deities such as Coyolxauhqui (for illustration *see* AZTEC), the enemy and sister of Huitzilopochtli (god of

23. Aztec colossal conch shell, andesite, 1. 870 mm, from the sacred precinct of Tenochtitlán, late 15th century to early 16th (Brussels, Musées Royaux d'Art et d'Histoire)

24. Aztec Calendar or Sun Stone, line drawing of carving in olivine basalt, diam. 3.6 m, from the sacred precinct of Tenochtitlán, c. 1512 (Mexico City, Museo Nacional de Antropología)

war), who is shown, for example on a relief still *in situ* at the Great Temple of Tenochtitlán, dismembered by her brother for conspiring in the death of their mother. Besides these figure sculptures, the Aztecs were also known for their beautifully simplified plant, animal and shell sculptures (see fig. 23), otherwise unusual in Mesoamerica, as well as for their images in stone of functional objects (such as drums) originally made in other materials.

Relief-carvings were also important and often covered platforms and seats, such as the symbolic throne of Motecuhzoma II (*reg* 1502–20) in the shape of a model pyramid-platform (1.23 m; Mexico City, Mus. N. Antropol.). The most important public monuments in the Aztec city were the large round sacrificial stones, such as the Stone of Tizoc (*reg* 1481–6), the seventh Aztec ruler

(Mexico City, Mus. N. Antropol.), and the Calendar or Sun Stone from Tenochtitlán (diam. 3.6 m; Mexico City, Mus. N. Antropol.; see fig. 24), both of which were set on low platforms. In reliefs as in painting, the Aztecs shared with the MIXTECS a common vocabulary of pictorial symbols, such as the sun disc and date glyphs on the Calendar Stone. The image depicts the sun of the fifth and final era of the Aztec creation myth, at the time of its birth from the Underworld. Glyphs surrounding the central figure refer to the four earlier suns and eras, the Mexica tribal god Huitzilopochtli, Motecuhzoma II and important dates in history, myth and ritual.

Early Aztec sculpture (*c.* 1350– *c.* 1450) was roughly carved, then stuccoed and painted, some examples, such as the *chacmool* of Phase II of the Great Pyramid at

Tenochtitlán, imitating Toltec forms. Later Aztec sculpture (after *c.* 1450) is more refined and characterized by sensitive rendering of details and surfaces and by rounded forms. Fine detailing was applied to hands, feet, ears and costume, contributing to a sense of realism. This style was largely the result of contact with examples both ancient and contemporary and possibly artists of other cultures. Past styles were carefully studied and forms consciously revived. During the Spanish Conquest, barely 70 years after the appearance of this distinctive Aztec tradition, Aztec sculptural production ended and many sculptures were destroyed.

(c) Tarascan. The Tarascans in Michoacan, north-west of the Aztec empire, successfully resisted conquest and created a sculptural style in which some forms were derived from Toltec types, including the *chacmool* (for illustration *see* TARASCAN). The Tarascan style is generally more angular and abstract. Late Post-Classic monumental stone sculptures have been found at TZINTZUNTZAN, the Tarascan capital, and other sites around Lake Pátzcuaro.

(iii) Maya region. At Chichén Itzá, Toltec forms are tempered by Maya craftsmanship. In contrast to that at Tula, Chichén Itzá sculpture is characterized by a more sensitive style of carving. Surfaces are softer and curvilinear, and details are more finely carved and varied. In the Temple of the Warriors small Atlantes, like some at Tula, supported an altar/platform in the temple, warrior piers supported the roof, and serpent columns flanked the entrance. The upright body of the serpent formed the column shaft, while its head rested horizontally on the pyramid-platform and its tail supported the roof structure (for illustration *see* CHICHÉN ITZÁ). As at Tula, reliefs of skulls, jaguars, eagles and warriors decorated platforms, walls, piers and benches; in addition, the walls of Chichén Itzá's great ballcourt were carved with ball-players and sacrifice imagery.

BIBLIOGRAPHY

GENERAL

G. Kubler: *The Art and Architecture of Ancient America*, Pelican Hist. A. (Harmondsworth, 1962, rev. 3/1984), pp. 47–9, 60–64, 68–73, 77, 83–92, 97–110, 117–34, 141–7, 149–53, 160–63, 175–6, 201–7, 247–65, 267–70, 300–315, 325–32
Before Cortés: Sculpture of Middle America (exh. cat. by E. K. Easby and J. F. Scott, New York, Met., 1970)
M. Porter-Weaver: *The Aztecs, Maya and their Predecessors: Archaeology of Mesoamerica* (New York, 1972, rev. 3/1993)
The Iconography of Middle American Sculpture: (New York, 1973)
E. Pasztory: 'Artistic Traditions of the Middle Classic Period', *Middle Classic Mesoamerica: AD 400–700*, ed. E. Pasztory (New York, 1978), pp. 108–42
M. E. Miller: 'A Re-examination of the Mesoamerican Chacmool', *A. Bull.*, lxvii (1985), pp. 7–17
——: *The Art of Mesoamerica from Olmec to Aztec* (London, 1986)

GULF COAST: OLMEC, CLASSIC VERACRUZ AND HUASTEC

M. D. Coe: 'The Olmec Style and its Distribution', *Hb. Mid. Amer. Ind.*, iii (1965), pp. 739–75
M. W. Stirling: 'Monumental Sculpture of Southern Veracruz and Tabasco', *Hb. Mid. Amer. Ind.*, iii (1965), pp. 716–38
T. Proskouriakoff: 'Classic Art of Central Veracruz', *Hb. Mid. Amer. Ind.*, xi (1971), pp. 558–72
M. D. Coe and R. A. Diehl: *In the Land of the Olmec: The Archaeology of San Lorenzo Tenochtitlán*, 2 vols (Austin, 1980)
D. C. Grove: 'Olmec Monuments: Mutilation as a Clue to Meaning', *The Olmec and their Neighbors: Essays in Memory of Matthew W. Stirling*, ed. E. P. Benson (Washington, DC, 1981), pp. 49–68

S. J. K. Wilkerson: 'In Search of the Mountain Foam: Human Sacrifice in Eastern Mesoamerica', *Ritual Human Sacrifice in Mesoamerica: Dumbarton Oaks, 1979* (Washington, DC, 1984), pp. 101–32
F. Winfield Capitaine: 'La estela 1 de la Mojarra, Veracruz, México', *Research Reports on Ancient Maya Writing*, xvi (Washington, DC, 1988)
P. Ortiz, M. del C. Rodríguez and P. Schmidt: 'El Proyecto Manatí, temporada 1988. Informe preliminar', *Arqueología* [Mexico], iii (1990), pp. 141–50
G. E. Stuart: 'New Light on the Olmec', *N. Geog.*, clxxxv/5 (1993), pp. 88–115

CENTRAL HIGHLANDS: PRE-CLASSIC, TEOTIHUACÁN, TOLTEC AND AZTEC

B. Dutton: 'Tula of the Toltecs', *El Palacio*, lxii/7–8 (1955), pp. 195–251
C. T. E. Gay: *Mezcala Stone Sculpture: The Human Figure* (New York, 1967)
H. B. Nicholson: 'Major Sculpture in Pre-Hispanic Central Mexico', *Hb. Mid. Amer. Ind.*, x (1971), pp. 92–134
R. F. Townsend: *State and Cosmos in the Art of Tenochtitlán* (Washington, DC, 1979)
E. T. Baird: 'Naturalistic and Symbolic Color at Tula, Hidalgo', *Painted Architecture and Polychrome Monumental Sculpture in Mesoamerica: Dumbarton Oaks, 1981* (Washington, DC, 1981), pp. 115–44
E. G. Umberger: *Aztec Sculptures, Hieroglyphics, and History* (diss., New York, Columbia U., 1981)
Art of Aztec Mexico: Treasures of Tenochtitlán (exh. cat. by H. B. Nicholson and E. Q. Keber, Washington, DC, N.G.A., 1983)
E. Pasztory: *Aztec Art* (New York, 1983)
G. Martínez Donjuán: 'Teopantecuanitlan', *Primer coloquio de arqueología y etnohistoria del estado de Guerrero: Chilpancingo, 1984* (Chilpancingo, 1984), pp. 55–80
D. C. Grove: *Chalcatzingo: Excavations on the Olmec Frontier* (London, 1984)
E. G. Umberger: 'Antiques, Revivals and References to the Past in Aztec Art', *Res*, xiii (1987), pp. 62–105
S. Sugiyama: 'Iconographic Interpretation of the Temple of Quetzalcóatl at Teotihuacán', *Mexican*, xi (1989), pp. 68–74
——: 'Rulership, Warfare and Human Sacrifice at the Ciudadela: An Iconographic Study of Feathered Serpent Representations', *Art, Ideology and the City of Teotihuacán*, ed. J. C. Berlo (Washington, DC, 1992), pp. 205–30

SOUTHERN HIGHLANDS: ZAPOTEC

A. Caso: *Las estelas zapotecas* (Mexico City, 1928)
I. Bernal: 'Stone Reliefs in the Dainzu Area', *The Iconography of Middle American Sculpture*, I. Bernal and others (New York, 1973), pp. 13–23
J. F. Scott: *The Danzantes of Monte Albán* (Washington, DC, 1978)
J. Marcus: 'Zapotec Writing', *Sci. Amer.*, ccxlii/2 (1980), pp. 51–64

MAYA REGION

T. Proskouriakoff: 'Historical Implications of a Pattern of Dates at Piedras Negras, Guatemala', *Amer. Ant.*, xxv (1960), pp. 454–75
S. W. Miles: 'Sculpture of the Guatemala–Chiapas Highlands and Pacific Slopes, and Associated Hieroglyphs', *Hb. Mid. Amer. Ind.*, ii (1965), pp. 237–75
T. Proskouriakoff: 'Sculpture and Major Arts of the Maya Lowlands', *Hb. Mid. Amer. Ind.*, ii (1965), pp. 469–97
V. G. Norman: *Izapa Sculpture*, Papers of the New World Archaeological Foundation, 30, 2 vols (Provo, 1973–6)
L. Schele: 'Color on Classic Architecture and Monumental Sculpture of the Southern Maya Lowlands', *Painted Architecture and Polychrome Monumental Sculpture in Mesoamerica: Dumbarton Oaks, 1981* (Washington, DC, 1981), pp. 31–49
B. Braun: 'The Serpent at Cotzumalhuapa', *Pre-Columbian Art History: Selected Readings*, ed. A. Cordy-Collins (Palo Alto, 1982), pp. 55–82
M. G. Robertson: *The Sculpture of Palenque*, 3 vols (Princeton, 1983–6)
The Blood of Kings: Dynasty and Ritual in Maya Art (exh. cat. by L. Schele and M. E. Miller, Fort Worth, TX, Kimbell A. Mus., 1986)
C. Cortez: *The Principal Bird Deity in Preclassic and Early Classic Maya Art* (MA thesis, Austin, U. TX, 1986)
L. A. Parsons: *The Origins of Maya Art: Monumental Stone Sculpture of Kaminaljuyú, Guatemala, and the Southern Pacific Coast* (Washington, DC, 1986)
L. Schele and D. Freidel: *A Forest of Kings* (New York, 1990)
C. E. Tate: *Yaxchilan: The Design of a Maya Ceremonial City* (Austin, 1992)
S. D. Houston: *Hieroglyphics and History at Dos Pilas* (Austin, 1993)

EMILY UMBERGER

V. Wall painting.

Although painted decoration was present throughout Pre-Columbian Mesoamerica, adorning artefacts from humble domestic containers to sumptuous palaces or religious edifices, at the beginning of the 20th century only a few examples of wall paintings were known: those described by Stephens (1843) at Maya sites in Yucatán, by Batres (1889) at Teotihuacán and by Seler (1895) at Mitla. Since then many more murals have been found, extending knowledge of the variety of styles and subjects developed by Mesoamerican artists. The oldest known examples of wall painting are the Olmec cave paintings in the caves of Oxtotitlán and Juxtlahuaca, Guerrero, which date from the Middle Pre-Classic period (*c.* 1000–*c.* 300 BC). During the Classic period (*c.* AD 250–*c.* 900), simultaneously with the rise of great cities in the Central and Southern Highlands and the Maya region, wall painting became an established art form throughout Mesoamerica.

1. Materials and techniques. 2. Regional traditions.

1. MATERIALS AND TECHNIQUES. The exterior walls of buildings were generally painted in a single colour; polychrome scenes were reserved for interiors. Throughout Mesoamerica murals were executed in flat colours, without chiaroscuro, and figures were outlined to make them stand out. Colours were toned down in order to reduce contrast in the painting as a whole. Although Mesoamerican painters did not use true perspective, figures were sometimes drawn in different sizes and proportions, and colours blended to give an impression of depth. A feeling of pictorial space was achieved through the use of different planes, so that the lowest appeared closest and the highest furthest away. There are a few exceptional examples of attempts at foreshortening, as in Room 2 at BONAMPAK (*see* §2(iv) below).

The painters of ancient Mesoamerica knew of and developed two basic techniques, namely tempera and fresco. Tempera, as used in some murals at TEOTIHUACÁN, CHICHÉN ITZÁ and Tizatlán, was applied over dry, levelled mud; the pigments were mixed with a binder made from native gums such as *tzautli* or secretions from the prickly pear cactus or from orchids. The fresco technique was used at MONTE ALBÁN, Bonampak, CACAXTLA and Teotihuacán; the wall was first rendered with a thick coat of fine mud mixed with crushed *tezantle* (a red volcanic rock). Then a thin layer of plaster made of lime and pumice sand or obsidian dust was spread in sections. The design was then traced on to this surface in a dilute red paint. The pigments were mixed with lime and water and applied to the wet plaster without shadowing; later the figures were outlined in red or black. Finally, when both the coat of clay and the paint were dry, the surface was thoroughly polished in order to make it more durable.

The pigments used were mainly of mineral origin: orange and red from iron oxide; ochre or yellow from iron hydroxide; green from copper bicarbonate (blue malachite); and blue from sodium silicate and aluminium silicate. The colour known as 'Maya blue'—found at Bonampak (*see* COLOUR, colour pl. I, fig.1) and Cacaxtla—was, however, made up of *atalpujita* and indigo. The pigments were placed in earthenware pots and applied with animal-hair brushes of different thicknesses. Their use was so common that they are known to have been on sale in the large city markets.

2. REGIONAL TRADITIONS.

(i) Gulf Coast. (ii) Central Highlands. (iii) Southern Highlands. (iv) Maya region.

(i) Gulf Coast.

(a) Olmec. Juxtlahuaca and Oxtotitlán caves in the Sierra Madre of southern Guerrero, Mexico, contain the only known examples of Olmec wall paintings, dated to *c.* 900–*c.* 700 BC. Juxtlahuaca (30 km east of Chilpancingo) is a cave of narrow corridors and large chambers. Two large chambers, the 'Hall of Ritual' and the 'Hall of the Serpent', are connected by the 'Gallery of Drawings'. These chambers contain human figures and animals, painted in red, black and yellow and outlined with thick black lines. The principal scene in the 'Hall of Ritual' comprises two schematized figures: one, of monumental proportions, stands upright, and the other is disproportionately small. At Oxtotitlán the cave has two entrances and opens on to a ravine. The first wall painting is on the slope of a gully and shows a seated human wearing an owl mask, a cape of coloured feathers (*máxtlatl*) and a short skirt decorated with the Olmec 'paw-wing' sign. The figure is seated on a kind of altar or throne, represented by a large mask. Colours include green, earth red, yellow and black. Another important wall painting, in the north entrance of the cave, comprises a scene with a human figure and a jaguar. Except for a prominent white face, the human figure is painted entirely in black, with geometric simplicity. The jaguar is shown in movement with the pattern of its fur clearly depicted and its tail appearing to touch the human's pubic area. Other paintings are also outlined, predominantly in black; they include a four-petalled flower, a serpent, the head of a snake-like reptile and another human figure with a serpent mask covering its mouth.

(b) Other peoples. Only a few examples of wall paintings by other Gulf Coast peoples survive, principally at Las Higueras in southern Veracruz and at the northern Veracruz Huastec site of Tamuín, both dating to the Late Classic period (*c.* AD 600–*c.* 900). Las Higueras, near the mouth of the River Colipa, was occupied over a long period during which several layers of wall paintings were applied to one of its temples, demonstrating several styles. The paintings were discovered in 1964, and some are now restored and exhibited in Jalapa (U. Veracruzana, Mus. Antropol.). They are painted in fresco and comprise wide bands or registers of pale yellow, on which small human figures are shown engaged in various everyday and ritualistic activities. Three ethnic groups can be distinguished. Members of the first group have large heads and are depicted in profile, one behind another as if walking in procession. They carry various objects, such as lances, feather fans, standards, snail shells and sea shells. Their bodies, almost naked, are painted dark yellow or dark brown. Members of the second group have elongated figures with brightly coloured clothing. These are also

shown in profile, taking part in ritual practices. One scene appears to be a puberty rite. Another, fragmentary, scene shows three figures, dressed in long skirts, loose smocks and cloaks which trail on the ground, playing a long musical instrument. Their faces, hands and feet are painted burnt red and they carry large, feathered emblems. The third group comprises figures whose iconographical attributes associate them with deities or personifications of deities. One may represent the sun god; others may show a priest seated on a throne and various rituals being carried out in the temple on top of a pyramid. In addition to the human figures there are representations of animals and flowers, outlined in black.

The wall painting at Tamuín in San Luis Potosí is the only known surviving Huastec example. Although poorly preserved, it covers an area 4.6×0.34 m on a conical altar and depicts a procession of 12 deities or priests dressed as deities in a style resembling MIXTECA-PUEBLA.

(ii) Central Highlands. After the Olmec cave paintings of Oxtotitlán and Juxtlahuaca, the oldest known wall paintings in the Central Highlands are the simple red-painted walls of the circular pyramid at Cuicuilco in the southern Basin of Mexico, dating from the final centuries BC.

(a) Teotihuacán. (b) Cholula. (c) Cacaxtla. (d) Tizatlán, Ixtapantongo, Ecatepec, Malinalco, Tenayuca and Tlatelolco. (e) Tenochtitlán.

(a) Teotihuacán. The first wall paintings to be discovered at the ancient city of Teotihuacán, 53 km north-east of Mexico City, were those found in 1889 by Leopoldo Batres. It was not until 1942–4, however, that excavations uncovered numerous wall paintings in palaces around the great ceremonial core of the city. Paintings were exposed, recorded and preserved in the palaces of Tepantitla, Tetitla and Atetelco. During excavations in 1962–4 more paintings were found, including those of the Palace of the Quetzal–Butterfly, a mural of jaguars playing shell trumpets, a frieze of green birds, a jaguar of monumental size on a wall along the main thoroughfare known as the 'Street of the Dead', a quetzal parrot in flight and the work known as the mural of *Mythological Animals*. Although none of the paintings at Teotihuacán can be dated precisely, there is a recognizable trend from more ceremonial and ritualistic themes to warlike themes through the Classic period (*c.* AD 250–*c.* 900).

In the Teotihuacán III period (*c.* AD 300–*c.* 600) painted stucco began to replace architectural reliefs, and shades of red became the most widely used colours. During this period interior and exterior walls of temples and dwellings were covered with scenes in vivid blue-green, yellow ochre and red. After *c.* AD 450 there was less colour variation, and images were copied so perfectly that it is assumed stencils were used.

The use of space and colour in Teotihuacán painting was symbolic. There are scenes with deities and richly attired priests, usually shown performing ritual celebrations. Water gushing from the figures' hands is interpreted as representing rain, while objects painted in green represent jade. Another theme involves a variety of natural and mythical animals. The most frequently depicted is the mythical 'plumed serpent', Quetzalcóatl; but jaguars and quetzal birds are also common. Finally, there are numerous abstract designs involving organic forms and sometimes comprising a plane with crossed rays. Human figures are represented either as ordinary men and women, painted realistically in postures of movement, or as priests, warriors and gods, whose ranks are shown by their costumes and who are represented as rigid figures with geometrical outlines.

There are three groups of paintings in the different rooms of the palace of Tepantitla. One consists of luxuriously dressed priests wearing lizard headdresses and holding bags of resin from which seeds and aquatic motifs fall; they seem to be ritual sowers, and are shown as if walking in procession. A graphic symbol representing speech—known as a 'speech scroll'—emerges from their hands. In another room there are priests painted in various tones of red.

The most important painting at Tepantitla is in a covered patio and is now in very poor condition; there is a replica in the Museo Nacional de Antropología, Mexico City. The two most interesting scenes, on either side of the patio doorway, are divided into two sections. The upper portions are framed on two sides by undulating bands with stars and aquatic fauna. At the top, both scenes are presided over by a deity shown full-face, who is thought to be either the rain god Tlaloc or a goddess of plenty. The deity's face and mouth are masked, and it wears a large quetzal-feather headdress, with two flowering trees rising overhead. Its arms are outstretched, and green drops of liquid fall from its hands. Two priests holding bags of resin stand on either side of this figure, with speech scrolls decorated with flowers, streams of water, seeds and jade beads emerging from their hands. At the edges of the scene there are flowering trees, birds and butterflies.

The lower sections of the two scenes are on sloping walls and are also bordered by interlaced bands. To the right of the entrance is the scene known as *Tlalocán* or *Paradise of Tlaloc*. In the centre of the scene stands a blue mountain from which two courses of a great river flow out in opposite directions. In smaller streams on the mountainside itself human figures swim among fish, plants and animals. Above and to each side of the mountain a mythical garden is peopled by yellow, pink and blue figures depicted in dynamic attitudes—playing, dancing or chasing butterflies (see fig. 25). Only one figure, on the right edge, does not share in the general joy; instead he holds a branch in one arm, has large tears falling from his eyes and seems to be intoning a hymn (five speech scrolls come from his mouth). The rest of the scene is composed of butterflies and dragonflies fluttering among flowering bushes and cacao plants. The scene represents the paradise of those whose deaths have been connected with water. It is a place abundant in food, where the life of humans, animals and plants is renewed.

In the palace of Atetelco the most important wall painting covers the walls of three porticos around a white patio. A similar picture appears on each portico and consists of human figures placed within a lattice, which appears to have been traced with a stencil: the line is uniform, and where the motif comes to the end of the wall it is abruptly cut off and sometimes incomplete. The murals of the eastern portico show images of priests, who, due to the arrangement of the lattice, seem to be framed

25. Wall painting showing detail from *Tlalocán* (or *Paradise of Tlaloc*), fresco on stucco, Palace of Tepantitla, Teotihuacán, Central Highlands, Early Classic period, *c.* AD 250–*c.* 600

within the squares; each holds a bundle of three arrows. Despite a general similarity, each figure has distinct characteristics: those in the south portico wear bird costumes, those in the eastern painting have symbols alluding to Tlaloc, and those in the northern portico wear coyote costumes and masks. The general symbolism of the murals is believed to be related to war and sacrifice.

The palace of Tetitla is an enormous group of rooms with no fewer than 120 painted walls. There are sumptuously dressed gods and priests scattering gifts on the ground, human figures shown amid waves and numerous animals, such as jaguars with feather headdresses, serpents, quetzal birds and owls. In the portico to the east of the main patio there are six large feline figures painted in orange, with blue eyes and wearing feather headdresses. Before their open mouths trilobe motifs with red drops represent bleeding hearts. In the southern portico there are architectural motifs, while to the west there are full-face figures of luxuriously dressed priests wearing jade masks and large round jade earflaps. They each hold a bundle of weapons in their hands and let fall jade gifts and aquatic elements.

In 1985, other murals with images of Tlaloc were discovered to the south-east of the Pyramid of the Moon.

(b) Cholula. CHOLULA was an important trading city and religious centre in Mesoamerica from the end of the Pre-Classic to the Late Post-Classic period (*c.* AD 250–1521). Its main pyramid was decorated with wall paintings, beginning with the first platform built in the 1st century AD. These were discovered and described in 1931 by Ignacio Marquina. They were painted on sloping interior walls and represent the heads of insects (or mythological beasts according to some scholars) seen face-on and placed at regular intervals. They are coloured red and yellow, with blue-black outlines and backgrounds.

During excavations in 1966–70 Ponciano Salazar discovered sections of murals in another of the oldest buildings. These depict a scene known as *The Drinkers* because the figures composing it are shown drinking *pulque* (fermented maguey cactus juice), executed between the 2nd and 3rd centuries AD. The work has an informal yet narrative quality unique among Pre-Columbian wall paintings, and it unfolds its story in three horizontal bands executed in tempera on adobe walls. The lowest band consists of red, yellow ochre, black and blue coloured shapes, while in the middle and upper bands seated and reclining human figures are shown drinking in couples. Heads, arms and bodies show a surprising lack of proportion, and the intoxicating effect of the drink is evident. Two old women, a dog and a bee are also depicted. The almost naked bodies of the drinkers, their loincloths and their complicated cloth headdresses are painted in yellow and white against a blue background. This is an original wall painting, both in the freedom of its subject-matter and in its style, which is markedly different from the more geometric style at Teotihuacán.

(c) *Cacaxtla.* In 1975 looters discovered traces of wall paintings at CACAXTLA, and soon afterwards the archaeologists Daniel Molina and Diana López cleaned extensive surfaces decorated with wall paintings. The main paintings are on two sloping walls of Structure B (the *Battle* mural; *c.* AD 650) and on the walls of Structure A, which has a portico (the *Portico* mural; *c.* AD 750).

Analysis of the pigments and techniques used at Cacaxtla has revealed that the thickness of the painted layer varies between 5 and 50 micrometres, and that the colours were applied to a plaster of almost pure lime, a highly unusual technique in fresco work. The colours used were red, yellow, 'Maya blue' and deep blue, all of which were obtained from clays, as well as black and white.

The *Battle* mural is divided by a small staircase into two sections, one slightly larger than the other (widths 11.74 m and 8.99 m). It depicts a battle between two different ethnic groups. The victors have the features of the inhabitants of the high Mexican plateau and are dressed in jaguar skins; the vanquished have Maya features and wear bird costumes. The warriors are shown standing on a red band, representing the ground, against a background of 'Maya blue'. The artists skilfully captured the cruelty of the struggle, showing the individual combatants' expressions, their hand gestures and the positions of their legs. Some figures are repeated on both sides, for example the two standing leaders of the victors, identified by the 'deer' glyph, whose bodies are painted grey. Two other standing figures appear to be the chiefs of the conquered group: the one on the right displays an enormous headdress with blue feathers and a bird's head and has a bleeding wound on one cheek; the other has a white cape decorated with half-stars and stands in a position resembling figures on the Maya murals at Bonampak (*see* §(iv) below). The jaguar warriors are spearing their victims, who lie dead or dying of bloody wounds on the ground. Some are holding their intestines, painted in yellow, one tries to pull out the spear sticking through him and another lies with body and limbs limp. The artists captured the drama of what was probably a historical battle, and yet gave the scene a symbolic mythological background.

The wall paintings of the *Portico* in Structure A are in red, blue, yellow, black and white. There are four of them— one on the north wall, one on the south wall and two on the doorjambs. On the north wall a large figure appears in jaguar costume; a black human face looks out of the animal's open jaws. The figure holds a thick bundle of spears in its arms, with eight blue drops of water dripping from their tips. The jaguar-man stands on a fantastic reptile with the skin and claws of a jaguar, and a serpent's forked tongue and belly scales. The creature's body lies parallel to and framed by a blue band with aquatic motifs, including shells, crabs, turtles and reptiles. The scene stands out against a red background, and a few hieroglyphs can also be seen. There is a similar picture on the north jamb, showing a figure dressed in a jaguar skin whose face also

26. Wall painting on lime plaster, south wall of portico, Structure A, Cacaxtla, Central Highlands, Classic period, *c.* AD 750; line drawing

appears between the animal's open jaws, wearing a headdress recalling the head of a crocodile. In its right paw the figure holds a vessel decorated with the face of the rain god Tlaloc, from which blue drops of water fall. In its left paw it holds a blue serpent decorated with flowers, and a plant with blue stems and yellow flowers grows out of its stomach. Here too, a few hieroglyphs can be seen on the 'Maya blue' background.

The main figure in the painting on the south wall is a bird-man with a black body (see fig. 26); his face, with Maya features, emerges from an enormous eagle's head. In his arms he holds a large blue bar with serpent's heads at either end and his bird-feet rest on a blue plumed serpent. As with the jaguar-serpent of the north wall painting, the plumed serpent, together with a blue band with aquatic motifs, forms the border framing the scene. Various hieroglyphs and signs can be seen on the red background, including a parrot in flight and a rectangle with half-stars and blue hands. A maize plant faces the bird-man. On the corresponding south jamb is a figure who appears to be dancing. The body is black, has Maya features and holds in its right arm a gigantic green shell, out of which a figure with long red hair emerges.

It has been suggested that the north and south paintings of the Portico Mural are concerned with fertility (because of the representation of Tlaloc) and with war (because of the eagle, an attribute of the war god, Huitzilopochtli).

In 1987 three more painted walls were discovered at Cacaxtla. One represents a plant that, instead of flowers, sprouts human heads with Maya features; another shows a female figure in blue on a red ground; and a third contains a male figure with the segmented yellow tail of a scorpion descending between his spread legs. The tail curls menacingly upwards and ends in a pointed black hook.

(d) *Tizatlán, Ixtapantongo, Ecatepec, Malinalco, Tenayuca and Tlatelolco.* Wall paintings dating to the Late Post-Classic period (*c.* AD 1200–1521) survive at several other Central Highland sites. Those at Tizatlán are on two altars apparently intended for sacrifices. They depict Aztec gods in a style closely related to that of the MIXTECA-PUEBLA screenfold manuscripts (*see also* §VI below). Ixtapantongo and Ecatepec have rock paintings: at Ixtapantongo a 50×15 m rock face is painted with figures of Toltec–Aztec gods and warriors engaged in various ceremonies. The well-proportioned figures are in different scales for gods and humans. Here a new technique was employed, in which a transparent coat was painted on the rock as a base, over which tempera was applied in yellow, green, grey and black. At Ecatepec the rock face was first given a coat of stucco before the paint was applied in the manner of fresco. As its name implies, the painting depicts the wind god Ehecatl–Quetzalcóatl, in typical Aztec style. At MALINALCO, an Aztec warriors' sanctuary perched high up on a cliff-side, the wall paintings depict a procession of three figures dressed and ready for combat. One has attributes identifying him as the god Mixcóatl (Nahuatl: 'cloud serpent'), a deified Toltec–Chichimec leader. At TENAYUCA and TLATELOLCO, two suburbs of the Aztec capital, Tenochtitlán (*see* MEXICO CITY, §I), there are remains of wall paintings in a tomb and altar. Both depict skulls and crossed bones, a typical Aztec theme in all media (*see* §I, 4(v) above). At Tlatelolco the extremely brilliant colours—yellow ochre, dark blue, vermilion and white—stand out against a black background.

(e) Tenochtitlán. The main pyramid platform at Aztec Tenochtitlán had wall paintings in the two temples at its summit, one dedicated to the Aztec tribal deity and war god Huitzilopochtli and the other to the rain god Tlaloc. They were discovered during excavations by Eduardo Matos Moctezuma in 1978–82. Some remains are preserved on the pillars marking the entrance to the Temple of Tlaloc; these comprise black and white circles on a blue background at the front and traces of a figure on the back. The figure has a yellow body, wears red and blue bracelets and armbands and holds a spear in one hand. At the Red Temple, a smaller platform and temple north of the main

pyramid, the surviving murals consist of red circles known as *chalchihuitl*, symbolizing water and preciousness, and white bands, both outlined in black.

(iii) Southern Highlands. The oldest known example of wall painting in the Oaxaca region is an image of a large insect, probably Late Pre-Classic in date (*c.* 300 BC–*c.* AD 250), on natural rock at Caballito Pintado near Tlacolula. ZAPOTEC paintings of the Early Classic period (*c.* AD 250–*c.* 600) are found on the walls of tombs at MONTE ALBÁN (discovered in 1938) and at Huijazoo (discovered in 1987). Stylistically, Zapotec works share several features with other Mesoamerican wall paintings, for example figures in rigid positions symbolizing deities and scenes of religious ritual. Visible reality was not copied. At Monte Albán the subject-matter of tomb wall paintings is, not unnaturally, connected with rites, customs and beliefs concerning life after death. For pink (a diluted red), yellow, yellow ochre and black, fresco technique was used; but green, blue and turquoise were applied using a technique similar to tempera. White was used as a base. In Tomb 104, for example, the painter drew most of the motifs with a pink outline, then filled in each area with colour before outlining again in black.

Tomb 105 and the related Tomb 112 date to Monte Albán period III (*c.* AD 300–*c.* 700). Tomb 105 is cruciform in plan and contains a scene divided into two bands on the north and south walls: the lower band represents the earth, and the upper band, with its motif of symbolic star forms—known as 'stellar eyes'—represents the heavens. Along the earth band walks a procession of nine gods (a number associated with the underworld), each accompanied by his respective female counterpart. The painting in Tomb 112 depicts a similar procession. Tomb 104 is the best preserved and the most sumptuous of the Zapotec tombs (see fig. 27). Inside, the two lateral walls show deities carrying bags of resin; the deity on the north wall wears a serpent headdress, while that on the south wall looks like an old man wearing a conical cap. Each figure

27. Wall painting with procession of Zapotec funerary gods, fresco on stucco, Tomb 104, Monte Albán, Southern Highlands, Classic period, *c.* AD 600

wears a cape fixed by a large brooch, feather ornaments and necklaces. They face the end of the tomb, where a recess contains a large painting of the head of a god, possibly the maize god. Groups of hieroglyphs and 'stellar eyes' decorate the ends of the sides and the recess.

Other Monte Albán tombs with paintings include Tomb 123, the threshold of which is decorated with a procession of jaguars, battlements and interlaced serpents, and the doorjambs with priests and jaguars. Tomb 72, painted only in red, has figures of gods and remains of hieroglyphs.

The Zapotec tomb at Huijazoo, 30 km from Oaxaca City, comprises a portico giving access to two chambers, one of which is a tomb 5 m below ground measuring 4×2 m. In the portico there is a large painted mask of the bird-serpent god, while the funeral chamber itself contains a well-preserved wall painting, covering an area of 40 sq. m, depicting a funeral scene with 60 characters: priests with long cloaks, priestesses wearing *huipiles* (a type of blouse) and carrying bags of resin, warriors, nobles, old chiefs and official mourners. Its style is similar to that of Monte Albán Tomb 104.

The MIXTEC people, who dominated the Zapotecs in the Valley of Oaxaca in the Post-Classic period (*c*. AD 900–1521), produced paintings of religious scenes on the lintels of the Arroyo Group and Church Group palaces and in a tomb at MITLA. These works show a stylistic affinity to the native screenfold books known as the 'Codex Borgia Group' and are thought to be of Late Post-Classic date (*c*. AD 1200–1521; *see* §VI below). The scenes are executed in dark red on an even white background and show mythological figures and symbols among elaborate borders. Those of the Church Group are set between two bands decorated with *chalchihuitl* (in this case symbols for jade or rough Mexican emeralds) and depict buildings, temples and gods, shown in profile, who resemble Central Highland deities such as Tlaloc (water), Mixcóatl ('cloud serpent'), Tezcatlipoca ('smoking mirror', a creator god) and Quetzalcóatl–Ehecatl ('quetzal' or 'plumed serpent', a creator god and brother of Tezcatlipoca, and wind god).

(iv) Maya region.

(a) *Introduction.* Over 60 buildings with wall paintings have been discovered in the Maya region, scattered over 40 archaeological sites. The earliest murals at TIKAL date to the Late Pre-Classic period (*c*. 300 BC–*c*. AD 250). Those in Early Classic (*c*. AD 250–*c*. 600) tombs at RÍO AZUL were executed with red and black lines on white stucco and depict hieroglyphs and 4th-century date glyphs framed by deities, including the Maya sun god with a *k'in* ('sun') glyph on his cheek, presiding over wavy lines and beaded symbols on the side walls, probably representing the watery underworld. Contemporary works at Tikal show hieroglyphic signs and figures outlined with thick black lines on yellowed walls, including a Long Count date (*see* §II above) of 9.1.1.10.10 (19 March AD 457).

Most Maya murals, however, date from the Late Classic period (*c*. AD 600–*c*. 900) and depict elaborate historical, military and ritual scenes, covering the walls, and sometimes even the ceiling vaults, of temples. In this period naturalistically depicted human figures form the central themes, and are frequently placed in everyday urban contexts among pyramids, thrones, staircases and market places, or in landscapes of trees and plants. An increasing desire to represent human physical proportions accurately can be observed, from the earliest Late Classic-period figures at UAXACTÚN, which are small and disproportioned, to the later figures at BONAMPAK and Mul-Chic, which show realistic height and proportions. Similarly, Maya paintings show a progression from figures lacking any individuality to expressive portraits. The scenes unfold along horizontal bands or registers, with human actions shown in the lower registers and deities, observing human events, in the upper registers. The range of colours is extremely rich in different tones and hues, but used primarily for symbolic meanings rather than for realism.

Late Classic-period Maya murals are concentrated in the Yucatán Peninsula. Those at Mul-Chic and those of the central Maya region, particularly at Uaxactún and Bonampak, are outstanding. Other Yucatán sites with murals include Hochob, Santa Rosa Xtampak, Dzibilnocac, Loltun, Chacalal, Olaktún, Sulá and Chacmultún. These are similar in style and their subjects typically include ceremonial processions and offerings to chiefs.

(b) *Uaxactún.* The wall painting at Uaxactún (*c*. AD 600), discovered in 1937, comprises two registers with at least 26 human figures and 72 calendrical daysigns. On a murky pink background the figures are shown in dynamic poses in three different scenes: on the left a conference of standing figures; three people sitting in a house; and on the right figures dancing to the sound of a drum, with a dozen or more spectators. All the figures are Maya except the figure on the extreme left, who has Central Highland dress and weapons and possibly represents a visitor from Teotihuacán.

(c) *Mul-Chic.* The Mul-Chic paintings, originally on the lower parts of all four walls of a small sanctuary, survive on two walls. The wall painting on the west wall shows three pairs of priests, set among smaller figures to give an effect of depth and movement. The other surviving work is markedly different, showing a battle, with hand-to-hand combat in which individual figures are stabbed, crushed beneath huge stones or hanged. Only at Mul-Chic, Cacaxtla (*see* §(ii)(c) above) and Bonampak (*see* (d) below) is such cruelty depicted in battle scenes. Here the scene is accompanied by hieroglyphic signs giving the identity and rank of the characters.

(d) *Bonampak.* Few remains of wall paintings were known from the central Maya region (although decorative borders, stylized flowers and fragments of scenes survived at Tikal, YAXCHILÁN and PALENQUE) until 1946, when Giles Healy discovered the murals at Bonampak. These were painted towards the end of the 8th century AD, and they show considerable mastery of naturalism, colour and line, as well as being of great documentary value. The frescoes fill the interior walls of a three-chambered building, covering an area of 100 sq. m. with hundreds of Maya figures depicted in a unified work showing the celebrations and rituals of Bonampak's last dynastic accession.

On the walls of the first room the central theme is the presentation of the infant heir to the nobility. Individuals in long white cloaks appear to speak together and, on the opposite wall, help to prepare the ceremonial dress of three principal characters. To each side of the doors giving access to the room there are a row of musicians playing tortoise shells with forked antlers, drums and small bells, and dancers wearing aquatic animal masks. The colours used in this festive part of the scene are vigorous (see COLOUR, colour pl. I, fig. 1), including dark blue, earth tones, ochres, whites, pale reds and greens that contrast with the deep 'Maya blue' of the background. The surroundings, with marine flora and fauna, are in shades of green.

Three walls of the second room depict bloody jungle warfare (for illustration see BONAMPAK). The scene is a historical battle with a subtle mythological background shown without conventional features. Compact groups of warriors fight, and masks, various costumes, sun-shades, shields, lances, trumpets, clubs and stones can be seen among the intertwined confusion of bodies. A sense of perspective and volume is achieved by the use of distinct pictorial planes and colour shading, and the scene reveals the warriors' physical vigour and varied, expressive gestures. Framing the doorway of this room is a scene of the surrender of captives—the battle's logical conclusion and the culmination of the painting. In the lower part warriors with weapons in hand guard the captives, who are seated on the steps of a pyramid and look down at their bloody hands. A recumbent, flaccid body, depicted with a kind of foreshortening peculiar to Mesoamerican painting, is particularly noticeable. In the upper part the principal chiefs, wearing jaguar costumes, hand over their prisoners to the supreme leader.

The scenes in the third room depict the victory celebrations, and once again feature musicians, dancers and courtiers. The ruler, his family and retinue enact a ritual of self-sacrifice, piercing their tongues and ears with thorns, as a sign of thanksgiving for victory. The infant prince is present at the scene, held in the arms of a wet-nurse. A dance in front of and on the steps of a pyramid is depicted along three walls.

In all three rooms masks of the Maya gods cover the upper parts of the corbel vaults, and registers of hieroglyphs identify the characters concerned in the various scenes. In the second chamber a Long Count date of 9.18.10.0.0 (2 August AD 792) may commemorate the victory shown in the paintings.

(e) Chichén Itzá. Central Mexican Toltec and Mixtec influences are evident in Maya painting from the end of the 10th century AD to the mid-13th, when a frequent theme is that of Toltec conquerors facing defeated groups of Maya. The best-known scenes include those in the substructures of the Temple of the Warriors and Temple of the Jaguars at CHICHÉN ITZÁ. In the Temple of the Warriors there are two outstanding paintings. One shows scenes of daily life around Maya huts in a series of small images. The village is guarded by Toltec warriors, who keep watch over it while manoeuvring three small boats over the sea. The second scene shows an attack on a Maya village and a procession of victors and captives. In the representation of the buildings, typical Maya vaulted constructions are interspersed with flat-roofed buildings characteristic of the Central Highlands. The most complex

scenes are in the Temple of the Jaguars; they show a multitude of small figures of warriors, armed with lances and shields, rushing out to the attack from a settlement. Discs with solar rays in the Mixtec style are particularly noticeable, as is the image of the god Tlaloc–Quetzalcóatl, known to the Maya as Kukulcán.

(f) Santa Rita Corozal and Tulum. On the eastern coast of Yucatán, Mixtec influence related to the screenfold books of the Codex Borgia Group (see also §(iv) above) can be seen in the wall paintings of SANTA RITA COROZAL in Belize and in those of TULUM in Quintana Roo. The Santa Rita Corozal paintings have been interpreted as allusions to the Maya celebration of the completion of a 21-year calendrical cycle known as *katun*. On one wall two gods dance before a small drum decorated with the mask of the god of death. At Tulum, Toltec and Mixtec styles are combined in paintings showing fragmented images of gods from the Maya pantheon, in superimposed bands, in several buildings: the Castillo, Temple of the Descending God and Temple of the Frescoes. The figures are outlined in black with touches of red on a blue background, recalling the graphic style of the Mixtec codices.

BIBLIOGRAPHY

J. L. Stephens: *Incidents of Travel in Yucatán*, 2 vols (New York, 1843/R 1963)

L. Batres: *Teotihuacán o la ciudad sagrada de los Toltecas* (Mexico City, 1889, rev. 1906)

E. Seler: *Wandmalereien von Mitla: Eine mexicanische Bilderschrift in Fresko, nach eigenen, an Ort und Stelle aufgenommenen Zeichnungen herausgegeben und erläutert* (Berlin, 1895); Eng. trans. as 'The Wall Paintings of Mitla: A Mexican Picture Writing in Fresco', *Bureau Amer. Ethnol. Bull.*, xxviii (1904), pp. 247–324

E. H. Morris, J. Charlot and A. A. Morris: *The Temple of the Warriors at Chichén Itzá, Yucatán*, 2 vols (Washington, DC, 1931)

A. Caso: 'El paraíso terrenal en Teotihuacán', *Cuad. Amer.*, i/6 (1942), pp. 127–36

W. du Solier: 'Primer fresco mural huasteca', *Cuad. Amer.*, v/6 (1946), pp. 151–9

A. Villagra Caleti: 'La pintura mural', *Esplendor del México antiguo*, ed. C. Cook de Leonard, ii (Mexico City, 1959), pp. 651–70

R. Piña Chan: 'Las pinturas de Mul-Chic, Yucatán', *Bol. INAH*, viii (1962) [whole issue]

A. Caso: 'Sculpture and Mural Painting of Oaxaca', *Hb. Mid. Amer. Ind.*, iii (1965), pp. 896–930

C. T. E. Gay: 'Oldest Paintings in the New World', *Nat. Hist.*, lxxvi (1967), pp. 28–35

D. C. Grove: *The Olmec Paintings of Oxtotitlán Cave, Guerrero, Mexico* (Washington, DC, 1970)

P. Gendrop: 'Murales prehispánicos', *A. México*, 144 (1971) [whole issue]

I. Marquina: 'La pintura en Cholula', *A. México*, 140 (1971), pp. 25–40

A. Medellín Zenil: *Exploraciones en Lasigueras, Veracruz* (Mexico City, 1971)

A. Villagra Caleti: 'Mural Painting in Central Mexico', *Hb. Mid. Amer. Ind.*, x (1971), pp. 135–56

A. G. Miller: *The Mural Painting of Teotihuacán* (Washington, DC, 1973)

I. Bernal: 'La pintura en Oaxaca', *Hist. A. Mex.*, iv (1982), pp. 474–7

M. Foncerrada de Molina: 'La pintura mural de Cacaxtla', *Hist. A. Mex.*, iv (1982), pp. 458–73

S. Lombardo de Ruiz: 'La pintura mural Maya', *Hist. A. Mex.*, iv (1982), pp. 484–509

M. E. Miller: *The Murals of Bonampak* (Princeton, 1985)

S. Lombardo de Ruiz and others: *Cacaxtla: El lugar donde muere la lluvia en la tierra* (Tlaxcala, 1986)

M. E. Miller: *The Art of Mesoamerica from Olmec to Aztec* (London, 1986)

E. Matos Moctezuma: *Cacaxtla* (Mexico City, 1987)

BEATRIZ DE LA FUENTE

VI. Manuscripts.

1. Introduction. 2. Materials and techniques. 3. Regional traditions.

1. INTRODUCTION. Writing and a strong tradition of manuscript painting flourished in Pre-Columbian Mesoamerica and continued well into the 16th century, although phonetic writing had not yet evolved when the Spanish arrived. Several graphic systems of record keeping and notation were developed and painted in native books ('codices') to preserve both secular and religious information, generally as a specialized means of communication between rulers, high governmental officials and priests. Secular manuscripts included histories, genealogies, tax and tribute accounts and maps; religious codices included cosmological and mythical histories, manuals for divination and the performance of rituals and records of astronomical and calendrical cycles (see also §I, 4(i) above). Manuscripts were kept in special repositories (Nahuatl *amoxcalli*) by the Aztecs and, among the Maya, were sometimes buried with rulers.

Pictorial writing occurred as early as *c.* 1000 BC, but firm evidence of painted books—codex fragments found in Maya tombs—is dated to only *c.* AD 600. Mesoamerican recording systems range from almost purely representational images ('pictograms') to hieroglyphic texts. The Maya had the most fully developed system, characterized by a structured grammar and a strong phonetic component. However, most other Mesoamerican cultures used largely pictorial systems that combined representational images with pictograms, graphic symbols, ideograms and some phonetically meaningful elements. Some scholars argue that the Maya and Aztecs were on the verge of creating phonetic systems when curtailed by the Spanish Conquest.

When conquest caused the collapse of native cultures in the 16th century, most Pre-Columbian manuscripts were destroyed. Yet, of all the highly developed native artistic traditions, only manuscript painting continued and actually flourished under Spanish domination, for over 500 post-Conquest manuscripts have survived, most from the 16th century.

There are now only 14 known codices of undisputed pre-Conquest date: Aubin Manuscript 20 (Mixtec; Paris, Bib. N., MS. Mexicain 20; also called Le Culte rendu au soleil, Códice del culto a Tonatiuh, Fonds Mexicains 20, Códice de Teozoneas); Codex Becker 1 (Mixtec, Nuttall group; Vienna, Mus. Vlkerknd., MS. 60306; also called Manuscrit du cacique, Codex Saussure, Codex Tzapotèque, Codex Franz Josefino); Codex Bodley (Mixtec, Nuttall group; Oxford, Bodleian Lib., MS. Mex. d.1; also called Codex Bodleianus or Códice Bodleiano; Codex Borgia (Mixtec, Borgia group; Rome, Vatican, Bib. Apostolica, MS. Borg Messicano 1; also called Manuscrit de Veletri); Codex Colombino (Mixtec, Nuttall group; Mexico City, Bib. N. Antropol. & Hist., MS. 35-30; also called Codex Dorenberg); Codex Cospi (Mixtec, Borgia group; Bologna, Bib. U., MS. CC 4093; also called Códice di Bologna, Libro della China); Dresden Codex (Maya; Dresden, Sächs. Landesbib., MS. R.310); Codex Fejérváry-Mayer (Mixtec, Borgia group; Liverpool Mus., M 12014; also called Codex Mayer, Codex Pesth); Codex Laud (Mixtec, Borgia group; Oxford, Bodleian Lib., MS. 54b, Misc. 678; once called Liber hieroglyphicorum aegyptorum); Madrid Codex (Maya; Madrid, Mus. América, Inventory no. 70300; also called Codex Cortesianus, Codex Tro-Cortesianus); Codex Nuttall (Mixtec, Nuttall group; London, BM, MS. 19023-81; also called Codex Zouche); Paris Codex (Maya; Paris, Bib. N., MS. Mexicain 386; also called Codex Peresianus, Codex Pérez—not the same as the post-Conquest Codex Pérez, one book of the Maya Chilam Balam); Codex Vaticanus B (Mixtec, Borgia group; Rome, Vatican, Bib. Apostolica, MS. 3773; also called Códice Vaticano Rituale, Códice Fábrega); Vienna Codex (Mixtec, Nuttall group; Vienna, Nbib., Cod. Mexicanus 1; also called Codex Vindobonensis, Codex hieroglyphicorum Indiae meridionalis, Codex Clementino, Codex Leopoldino, Codex Kriechgauer). Scholars dispute the pre-Conquest date of the Grolier Codex (Toltec–Maya; Mexico City, Bib. N. Antropol. & Hist.).

It is also important to take into account the manuscripts produced in the early decades following the Conquest, since the Spanish found native manuscripts useful in speeding the transition from one cultural and economic system to another and therefore encouraged their production and use. Secular authorities of the viceregal government sponsored the painting of maps, tribute and tax assessments and registers of properties and salaries, the most famous example of which is the Codex Mendoza (Oxford, Bodleian Lib., MS. 3/34, Arch. Selden A.1) commissioned by Viceroy Antonio de Mendoza for Charles V (Charles I of Spain). The native nobility in turn had genealogies, maps and property plans painted to protect their financial interests and holdings. Religious manuscripts, on the other hand, were at first deemed idolatrous by the conquistadors and their priests and destroyed. As friars began to proselytize, however, they began to seek out manuscripts in order to create their own records to help combat native religious practices. Some manuscripts were copied on traditional materials or on European paper, and new forms were created, including Testerian manuscripts (Roman Catholic pictorial catechisms) and encyclopedic compendia of native culture (created for a Spanish ecclesiastical readership). The latter include Codex Magliabechiano (Florence, Bib. N. Cent., Magl. Cl. xiii.3 (B.R. 323)) and Codex Telleriano–Remensis (Paris, Bib. N., MS. Mexicain 385), and their cognates. Nahuatl and other native languages were written for the first time in European script, and annotations and texts in these languages and in Spanish were added to pictorials to explain them to Spanish and mestizo readers; by the early 17th century the native tradition of manuscript painting had completed the transition to European book form.

2. MATERIALS AND TECHNIQUES. Mesoamerican manuscript painters had long apprenticeships to learn the complicated symbolism of calendric and ritual signs and their meanings. Most pigments used were of mineral origin, dissolved in water in a manner similar to European watercolours. The most common form of manuscript was the screenfold of deer hide or native bark paper (Nahuatl *amate*, from the bark of the fig tree), pieced and glued together in a long strip that was then folded into regular panels like a concertina and sized with a white compound

of calcium carbonate. Both sides of the panels were painted, and the end pages were usually attached to wooden boards that were often covered with animal skins. The size and proportions of the screenfolds varied considerably from culture to culture. Maya screenfolds always seem to have been made of *amate* paper, with pages roughly twice as tall as they are wide and measuring about 200×100 mm. In contrast, Aztec, Mixtec and the Borgia Group codices—representing the 'Mexican' tradition—are all roughly square in format. They range in size from the Codex Vaticanus B with pages measuring only *c.* 150×*c.* 130 mm to the post-Conquest Codex Borbonicus (Aztec; Paris, Bib. Assemblée N., Y. 120) with pages measuring *c.* 390×*c.* 385 mm and a total length of *c.* 14 m. Mixtec and Borgia Group manuscripts are all of deer hide, but Aztec screenfolds are of *amate*.

In addition to screenfolds, records were painted on *tiras*, which are long strips of hide or paper that were rolled instead of folded; *lienzos* (large panels of cotton or maguey fibre cloth that may have been folded or rolled— no Pre-Columbian *lienzo* has survived); and *mapas*, a loose term for post-Conquest single sheets of painted paper.

3. REGIONAL TRADITIONS. Maya books represent a distinct tradition distinguished by the tall proportions of their pages and their combinations of hieroglyphic texts and paintings. The texts contain much of the intellectual content, freeing the paintings of a large part of the burden of record keeping. Generally the texts and paintings occupy separate areas on each page, but individual glyphs are incorporated into the illustrations and become fundamental to their meaning. Thus, the paintings do not merely illustrate the text but also offer qualifying or additional

28. Manuscript painting, page illustrating auguries relating to crop fertility (above) and concerning offerings made to deities (below), 175×175 mm; from the Codex Fejérváry–Mayer, l. 4 m, 15th century (Liverpool, Liverpool Museum, M 12014, p. 33)

information. The pages are usually divided into several horizontal registers. When the information is to be read in a particular direction, it proceeds along the registers from left to right, then top to bottom and often across several pages.

The four surviving pre-Conquest Maya manuscripts— the Dresden Codex, the Madrid Codex, the Paris Codex and the Grolier Codex (of disputed date; *see* §1 above)— deal almost entirely with divinatory and prophetic matters, occasionally referring to astronomical ephemera. Most of their texts are devoted to divinatory almanacs of one kind or another, identifying the most propitious days in the 260-day ritual calendar for certain undertakings and events, and sometimes indicating actions or ceremonies necessary to ensure a favourable outcome. They treat such subjects as rain and other celestial phenomena, agriculture, beekeeping, hunting, commerce, warfare, disease, marriage and various other social events. Maya books also contain information on ceremonies and rituals, myths, histories and prophecies of a longer duration, particularly relating to *tuns* (periods of 360 days) and *katuns* (periods of 20×360 days). Histories invariably have both mythical and prophetic qualities and often present genealogical details about the ownership of land and tribute. The Maya also drew maps, but they did not have account books or manuscripts of a purely secular nature.

The 'Mexican' tradition of manuscript painting, represented by Aztec, Mixtec, Borgia Group and other manuscripts, was practised in the Central and Southern Highlands and in the Gulf Coast, from Oaxaca and the Isthmus of Tehuantepec to the northern border of Mesoamerica. Although each group has its own linguistic or ethnic affiliations and can vary in subject and format, the whole is united by a purely pictographic nature, by the treatment of the same kinds of material and by similarities in presentation. Subjects include divinatory and religious matters, histories, genealogies and maps.

Almost all of the religious and divinatory manuscripts are what is known as *tonalamatls* (Nahuatl: 'book of days'), which present the count of a 260-day ritual calendar to foretell fates for given periods of time. In this respect they are both similar to and fundamentally different from the Maya almanacs. Both use the 260-day cycle in many of the same permutations, but the Maya almanacs focus on specific activities or events (planting, harvesting, beekeeping etc) and give prognostications on how these activities are to be carried out on certain days. In contrast the Mexican divinatory books tend to focus on units of time (days and weeks), and show the influence and tendencies associated with the different periods without much regard for the conduct of specific activities. There are exceptions, such as marriage prognostications, but in general the fates given by a *tonalamatl* are more universally applicable than those given in Maya almanacs.

Structurally, the Mexican divinatory codices are much freer than their Maya counterparts. They have no texts to restrict the spatial freedom of the images and calendrical glyphs. Instead their content is organized into sections or chapters that may span several pages and run across one or more registers. They are frequently written to be read from left to right and right to left on alternate lines, but in some cases the material is presented more uniformly and characterized by formal symmetry.

The best examples of Mexican religious manuscripts are the six pre-Conquest codices and one post-Conquest codex collectively known as the Borgia Group: Aubin Manuscript 20, Codex Borgia, Codex Cospi, Codex Fejérváry–Mayer (see fig. 28), Codex Laud, Codex Porfirio Díaz Reverse (post-Conquest) and Codex Vaticanus B. They are grouped together because of their similar style and content, although they come from different regions of Mesoamerica, including the Mixteca (central and southern Oaxaca), Cuicateca (north-central Oaxaca) and probably Veracruz. In addition, there are post-Conquest manuscripts painted in the native tradition and more firmly identified with the Aztec sphere of influence, such as the Tonalamatl Aubin (Paris, Bib. N., MS. Mexicain 18–19), Codex Borbonicus and the *tonalamatl* sections of the Codex Telleriano–Remensis (Paris, Bib. N.) and Codex Ríos (Rome, Vatican, Bib. Apostolica, MS. 3738; also called Codex Vaticanus A). These Aztec manuscripts are far more limited in their divinatory content than the Borgia Group, for they present only one version, although a highly elaborate one, of the 260-day ritual calendar. The Borgia Group codices have much simpler presentations of this version and also give several dozen other arrangements of the cycle.

The Mexican secular histories, dating from both before and after the Spanish Conquest, relate histories of tribes, families and city states. They record births, successions to office and deaths of rulers and their families; conquests, travels, deeds, construction programmes and dedications of important buildings and monuments; and natural and climatic phenomena such as solar eclipses, earthquakes, floods and famines.

There are three types, grouped according to the structure and presentation of the history. The first type is the continuous year-count annals or chronicle, in which time provides the framework for the narrative. Year signs are painted sequentially, often in a continuous line that determines the reading order, and events and people are organized around and linked to them. Examples include the Codex Aubin (London, BM, Add. MSS 31219; not to be confused with Aubin Manuscript 20 or Tonalamatl Aubin), Codex Boturini (Mexico City, Bib. N. Antropol. & Hist., MS. 35–38), Codex Mexicanus (Paris, Bib. N., MS. Mexicain 23–24), Tira de Tepechpan (Paris, Bib. N., MS. Mexicain 13–14) and Anales de Tula (Mexico City, Bib. N. Antropol. & Hist., MS. 35-9).

The second type is the cartographic history, in which a panorama of people, locations and events is depicted on a stylized map. The progression of time is indicated either by a directional line of footprints or by the direction in which the figures face; precise dates are only occasionally given. Examples include many of the Mixtec and West Mexican *lienzos* and *mapas*; the Tetzcocan Mapa Quinatzin, Mapa Tlotzin and Codex Xolotl (all three Paris, Bib. N., MSS Mexicain 11-12, 373, 1-10), and the Aztec Mapa Sigüenza (Mexico City, Bib. N. Antropol. & Hist., MS. 35-14).

The third type is the *res gestae*, in which the deeds of individuals or groups outline the story and where time and place are given lesser importance. Important examples

include the Nuttall Group: Codex Becker 1, Codex Bodley, Codex Colombino, Codex Nuttall and the Vienna Codex. These describe the important deeds and events in the lives of major Mixtec rulers of Tilantongo and other localities, winding pictographically left to right and right to left on alternate lines, with place and time shown conventionally where appropriate.

The Mexican tradition also includes maps and genealogies on large sheets of hide, paper or cloth. Border maps present a principal town in the centre surrounded by a wide ring of place signs designating its boundaries.

BIBLIOGRAPHY

E. Seler: *Codex Borgia: Eine altmexikanische Bilderschrift der Bibliothek der Congregatio de Propaganda Fide*, 3 vols (Berlin, 1904–9; Sp. trans., Mexico City, 1963)
D. Robertson: *Mexican Manuscript Painting of the Early Colonial Period: The Metropolitan Schools* (New Haven, 1959)
K. A. Nowotny: *Tlacuilollo: Die mexikanischen Bilderhandschriften: Stil und Inhalt mit einem Katalog der Codex-Borgia-Gruppe*, Monumenta Americana (Berlin, 1961)
J. E. S. Thompson: *A Commentary on the Dresden Codex: A Maya Hieroglyphic Book* (Philadelphia, 1972)
M. P. Weaver: *The Aztecs, Maya and their Predecessors: Archaeology of Mesoamerica* (New York, 1972, rev. 2/1981), pp. 155–83
M. D. Coe: *The Maya Scribe and his World* (New York, 1973)
M. E. Smith: *Picture Writing from Ancient Southern Mexico: Mixtec Place Signs and Maps* (Norman, 1973)
J. B. Glass: 'A Survey of Native Middle American Pictorial Manuscripts', *Hb. Mid. Amer. Ind.*, xiv (1975), pp. 3–80
J. B. Glass and D. Robertson: 'A Census of Native Middle American Pictorial Manuscripts', *Hb. Mid. Amer. Ind.*, xiv (1975), pp. 81–252
J. B. Glass: 'A Census of Middle American Testerian Manuscripts', *Hb. Mid. Amer. Ind.*, xiv (1975), pp. 281–96
A. Caso: *Reyes y reinos de la Mixteca*, 2 vols (Mexico City, 1977–9)
J. L. Furst: *Codex Vindobonensis Mexicanus I: A Commentary* (Albany, 1978)
N. Troike: 'Fundamental Changes in the Interpretations of the Mixtec Codices', *Amer. Ant.*, xliii (1978), pp. 553–68
M. Jansen: *Huisi Tacu: Estudio interpretativo de un libro mixteco antiguo: Codex Vindobonensis Mexicanus I* (Amsterdam, 1982)
E. H. Boone: *The Codex Magliabechiano and the Lost Prototype of the Magliabechiano Group* (Berkeley, 1983)
J. M. Pohl: *The Earth Lords: Politics and Symbolism of the Mixtec Codices* (diss., Los Angeles, UCLA, 1984)
N. Gutiérrez Solana: *Códices de México* (Mexico City, 1985)

ELIZABETH HILL BOONE,
NELLY GUTIÉRREZ SOLANA

VII. Pottery and clay sculpture.

Ceramics appeared in Mesoamerica as a major craft from the time of the earliest settlements (*c.* 2300 BC) and rapidly developed into a succession of distinctive regional styles. For those Pre-Columbian peoples who did not produce architecture or lithic sculpture, and whose perishable artefacts have not survived, ceramics provide virtually the only material record. Ceramics found in tombs, ceremonial caches and household debris have helped archaeologists to reconstruct Mesoamerican chronology, daily life, artistic conventions, belief systems, ritual practices, social stratification and trade patterns. Many of the aspects of Pre-Columbian ceramic manufacturing techniques have survived in present-day indigenous folk traditions.

1. Introduction and techniques. 2. Chronology and regional traditions.

1. INTRODUCTION AND TECHNIQUES. Clay was a primary material for fashioning both utilitarian and ceremonial artefacts, ranging from common household items to large-scale figural sculptures and masterfully carved and

29. Vessel with figural tripod supports in the form of water carriers, clay with burnished red slip, h. 210 mm, from Colima, West Mexico, Late Pre-Classic or Early Classic period, *c.* 300 BC–*c.* AD 600 (Mexico City, Museo Nacional de Antropología)

painted vessels. Clay objects, some of them finely decorated, had numerous uses, from everyday cooking, eating and drinking vessels to storage containers and utensils such as *comales* (griddles) and ladles. Clay was used for spindle whorls (some with incised figures or abstract designs) and for flat and cylindrical stamps, which may have been used for imprinting fabrics and paper or for decorating pottery (*see* §IX, 8 below). Musical instruments made of clay included rattles, whistles, flutes and drums (*see* §IX, 7 below). Some of these, as well as miniature items and wheeled animal figures, were possibly children's toys.

Complex religious systems and ritual required more elaborate items, such as fertility figurines, deity images, braziers, incense burners and burial offerings. Clay figural sculpture comprised small, solid figurines and larger, hollow figures. Small figurines were variously utilized on a domestic or community level for shrines, curing ceremonies and burial offerings, while larger ceramic representations of deities, like their stone counterparts, functioned as icons in temples and other public religious structures. Other figures were placed in offertory caches and in tombs as companions for the dead in the afterworld. Virtually every major Mesoamerican culture produced figurines, although not all created larger clay sculpture. When both types were made, figurines were not merely replicas of larger figures, but embodied disparate subjects and artistic conventions in their own right. Clay relief sculpture was much less common.

The distinction between ceramic sculpture and utilitarian objects was frequently blurred when the two types were combined (see fig. 29). Clay vessels sometimes convey the effect of sculpture because of their shape and ornamental attachments, including the use of figures as knobs, handles and tripod supports. Effigy vessels in the shapes of humans or animals achieved an equal balance between representation and function.

Despite the absence of the potter's wheel, enclosed kilns or true glazing, Mesoamerican ceramicists achieved remarkable results, less through the mastery of a complex technology than by the skilful use of simple techniques. The construction and firing of monumental clay sculpture represents one of the greatest technical accomplishments of Mesoamerican ceramicists. Although it was long believed that all Pre-Columbian firing was done in open fires or pits, archaeological research has proved that simply constructed open kilns were also used. Since only a closed kiln can attain the higher temperatures required to produce stoneware or porcelain, all Mesoamerican ceramics were porous, low-fired earthenwares.

Forms, decorative techniques and manufacturing methods sometimes coincided within a stylistic tradition, but frequently did not. Clay was obtained from local sources and tempered for plasticity and strength by adding sand, crushed sherds and shells, volcanic ash or organic fibres. Forms were made by three basic methods used singly or in combination: hand-modelling, coiling and moulding. Small vessels and some figurines were hand formed. The walls of larger vessels were built up from a base by joining layers of concentric clay coils. Clay slabs draped on hemispheric convex or concave moulds were used to produce rounded shapes. Clay press-moulds served as a simple means of mass production for entire objects, such as figurines, or for decorative panels and details. Hollow figures and composite forms were individually constructed or assembled from a combination of handbuilt and mould-made sections.

In addition to moulding or construction, decorative details were applied by incising and painting and by adding items made of perishable materials that clothed, adorned or were held by figurines. Surface texturing on vessels was variously effected by clay attachments, or by fluting, incising, carving or stamping the moist clay. Although vitreous glazes were never developed, the colour of the clay could be altered by coating the surface with a coloured slip (liquid clay stained by mineral or vegetal pigments). Bichrome and polychrome effects were achieved by painting designs with tinted slips before firing and by applying pigments before or after firing. Before firing, vessels—particularly slipped ones—were often burnished by polishing the surface with a hard object such as a pebble. The result was both practical and decorative since burnishing rendered the porous surface more impervious to liquids and produced a smooth, lustrous exterior.

Some domestic pottery may have been privately made, but most ceramics appear to have been produced by trained specialists. Elaborate decorative methods and esoteric iconographic features reveal the hands of master craftsmen. Production of standardized wares and trade items indicates the development of local ceramic industries.

2. CHRONOLOGY AND REGIONAL TRADITIONS. The different regions and cultures of Mesoamerica produced distinctive ceramic traditions which archaeologists have organized into a sequence of datable ceramic complexes.

(i) Pre-Classic period (*c.* 2000 BC–*c.* AD 250). (ii) Classic period (*c.* AD 250–*c.* 900). (iii) Post-Classic period (*c.* 900–1521).

*(i) Pre-Classic period (*c. *2000* BC–*c.* AD *250).* Household pottery and figurines were the earliest clay objects in the agricultural villages of the Pre-Classic Central Highlands. The site of TLATILCO on the north-west edge of modern Mexico City contained hundreds of burials accompanied by ceramics and other offerings. Most common were small female figurines, but large, hollow figures, small masks, carved roller stamps, whistles and jewellery were also found. Other ceramics included effigy vessels in the shapes of fish, ducks and other animals; round and flat-bottomed bowls, bulbous long-necked bottles and stirrup-spout bottles, decorated with restrained grooved designs and limited application of slips or pigments in incised areas.

The solid, handmade female figurines were probably fertility images. Some are nude, while others display fancy coiffures or headdresses, flaring skirts and ear and neck ornaments. At Tlatilco there were also solid buff-coloured figurines with traces of slip and paint, depicting acrobats, masked figures, women holding children, deformed individuals and enigmatic creatures with two heads or two faces with shared features. Such variegated figurines probably functioned in distinct religious, ritual or social situations.

During the Pre-Classic period (*c.* 1200–*c.* 300 BC) the Olmecs of the Gulf Coast created Mesoamerica's first great art style. Its influence was widespread and long-lasting, affecting the artistic vocabulary of less advanced contemporaries. Olmec ceramic remains are often fragmentary but include figurines and simple cylinders, bowls and bottles incised with spare geometric designs or boldly excised Olmec motifs, such as the jaguar 'paw-wing'. An exceptional unbroken example is a seated figure depicting a half living/half dead person (Villahermosa, Mexico, Mus. Tabasco). At the site of SAN LORENZO TENOCHTITLÁN a diverse group of solid and hollow figurine fragments, including ball-players, obese individuals, dwarfs and animal figures, were excavated.

The slanted oval eyes and downturned mouths characteristic of figures in the Olmec heartland also recur on finely modelled, hollow ceramic sculptures found at distant sites. One of the outstanding Olmec-related types found in the Central Highlands, notably at the site of Las Bocas, was the fleshy, sexless, 'baby' figure, whose hollow rounded forms are accentuated by cream-slipped, smoothly polished surfaces. Smaller cream-slipped and tan figurines, whose nude or minimally clothed bodies are often rubbed with red pigment, appear in upright, seated and reclining poses.

In the Southern Highlands the Late Pre-Classic (*c.* 300 BC–*c.* AD 250) site of MONTE ALBÁN, Valley of Oaxaca, has yielded Olmec-affiliated plain grey pottery and effigy vessels, as well as finely made hollow zoomorphic and anthropomorphic sculptures, particularly from graves.

In the geographically diverse Maya region the earliest known ceramics (*c.* 2000 BC) come from sites in modern Belize. In the Maya lowlands the earliest use of polychrome slips occurred during the Late Pre-Classic period on tall, fluted vases (known as Usulután ware) with parallel red lines drawn over an orange slip, and on bowls with stylized serpentine forms painted on an exterior rim band from the site of Holmul. Pre-Classic Maya figurines include solid, stocky specimens and somewhat larger, hollow examples.

In the Pre-Classic and Early Classic (*c.* AD 250–*c.* 600) periods the cultures of West Mexico developed their own distinctive ceramic style. Their shaft-chamber tombs and simpler graves have yielded an abundance of ceramics, but most pieces have been looted and therefore lack archaeological contexts. Vessels and figural sculpture, often combined, comprise sleek, rounded shapes in burnished red clay. Surfaces are modelled, rather than carved, emphasizing form rather than decorative effects, and include small attached heads and tripod supports in human and animal forms. An engaging menagerie of animal effigy vessels was produced, particularly plump Mexican hairless dogs depicted asleep, scratching or playing, all well represented in the Museo Nacional de Antropología, Mexico City, and in the Museo de las Culturas de Occidente, Colima.

Craftspeople from the Colima region hand-modelled flat, solid male and female figurines, as well as energetic acrobats, dancers, musicians, masked figures, aggressively posed warriors and small figural groups. Larger, hollow figures characterized by smoothly rounded forms in a burnished red clay also strike dynamic poses. Some are unadorned, but others wear helmets and abbreviated costumes suggested by modelled additions or by incised designs.

Figures from Nayarit are also highly varied. The blocky torsos of reddish and tan coloured figures from the IXTLÁN DEL RÍO area display geometric designs applied in negative resist techniques to represent patterned clothing. Actively engaged in carrying loads, playing instruments and holding clubs or small vessels, they contrast with the more refined male and female 'Chinesco' figures, some quite large, shown in seated, contemplative poses. Typical Nayarit clay compositions show lively figures in architectural settings engaged in village festivals, marriage celebrations, funeral processions, battles, games and dances. Robust, long-headed figures from Jalisco are somewhat less adorned and active. Traditionally considered to be anecdotal expressions of everyday life, some of these West Mexican funerary sculptures are now thought to have deeper religious and ritual meanings, related to the afterworld.

*(ii) Classic period (*c. AD *250–*c. *900).* The rich ceramic tradition of the central Gulf Coast (the modern state of Veracruz) lasted from the Pre-Classic to the Post-Classic period. In the Early Classic period (*c.* AD 250–*c.* 600) a penchant for figural sculpture in this region was expressed in high-relief figures adorning cylindrical jars. A unique feature of Gulf Coast figural sculpture was the use of *chapopote* (black asphalt) to paint the faces and bodies of tan or brown clay figures, many of which are unprovenanced finds.

From the site of REMOJADAS and its environs come superbly modelled, medium- to large-scale hollow figures, including youthful figures with smiling faces displaying a facial animation rare in Mesoamerican ceramics. While some figures are minimally adorned, others wear costumes, headdresses and ornaments formed of modelled clay additions. Large-scale animal sculptures also display an uncommon vivacity.

In the Late Classic period (c. AD 600–c. 900) bowls from the Tierra Blanca region featured mould-made ritual scenes in high relief. Figures from the site of Nopiloa, usually mould-made and coated with a cream-coloured slip, include laughing types and female figures with carved geometric decoration resembling textile patterns. The imposing, life-size ceramic sculptures from ZAPOTAL, which continued to be made into the Post-Classic period, apparently represent deities. Particularly striking are standing and seated female figures with ornate headdresses, beaded necklaces and knotted snake belts (see fig. 30).

Other pottery objects include animals mounted on wheeled platforms and numerous musical instruments. Smaller works include costumed, mould-made figurines, some wearing animal masks, and figural pairs and trios set on swings. Cream-slipped bowls, finely painted with realistic and imaginary animals, characterized both the Late Classic Tuxtla style and Late Classic Cerro Montoso vessels in the MIXTECA-PUEBLA style.

The HUASTEC ceramic tradition of the northern Gulf Coast also spanned the Pre-Classic to Post-Classic periods. Early pottery is mainly monochrome, but later bowls, bulbous vessels with dramatically upturned spouts and effigy pots are painted with simple designs in red or black on a white slip. Clay stamps, whistles, rattles and spindle whorls are also common. Huastec ceramic sculpture is typified by abundantly produced figurines. Nude lifelike figurines, mostly female, with elongated, naturalistically rounded limbs occurred early and continued to be made into the Classic period. More stereotyped, mould-made examples introduced in the Classic period, possibly reflecting influence from the Basin of Mexico, then prevailed into the Post-Classic period.

In the Central Highlands, TEOTIHUACÁN dominated commerce and culture. Clay artefacts from burials and offertory caches included bowls, *floreros* (small, long-necked vases), effigy pots and *candeleros* (rectangular blocks with single or double circular depressions believed to have functioned as incense burners). The most distinctive type of Teotihuacán vessel was a gently concave cylinder, often with a conical lid, mounted on three slab feet, variations of which appeared simultaneously in lowland and highland Maya centres. Surfaces are either plain, or incised, carved, decorated with press-mould designs or painted after firing with emblems or figural motifs on a stucco coating. Stucco-coated vessels share the iconographic motifs of Teotihuacán's longstanding mural painting tradition (*see* §V, 2(ii)(a) above) and often display closely related stylistic forms, suggesting that the same craftsmen were involved in both art forms. Also characteristic of Teotihuacán were large polychrome incense urns topped by towering lids displaying an intricate assemblage of mould-made units surrounding an inset human face. Technically superior thin-walled bowls, jars and effigy vessels known as Thin Orange ware, at one time associated with Teotihuacán, are now known to have been produced in southern Puebla.

Teotihuacán figurines are tan coloured and appear in a variety of types, which became increasingly embellished and mould-made over time. Several finely made figures, whose precise functions are unknown, differ from the usual frontal, static examples. Tiny, animated, sexless figurines were apparently assembled in groups, and miniature figurines filled the chest cavities of larger figures. Specimens with jointed limbs gave a rare active quality to otherwise immobile representations.

In the Southern Highlands, Classic period ceramics from richly furnished ZAPOTEC chamber tombs at Monte Albán comprise grey and brown funerary urns, ranging from modestly sized effigy vessels to large-scale ceramic sculptures. Some tan and grey urns attained a quasi-independent sculptural quality while still bonded to the cylindrical offering containers behind them. In the more ornate versions the seated or standing figure of a lavishly attired deity or mythical animal all but covers the attached vessels. Although similar in their constructed effect to Teotihuacán incense burners, these urns achieve a greater sculptural plasticity by representing the entire figure and using cut clay sections rather than moulds to build form and shape details.

Minimally adorned grey pottery jars, bulbous bottles and open bowls with tripod supports continued to be produced into the Post-Classic period, and the shapes were replicated in later MIXTEC polychrome vessels. Late Classic period tombs contained large-scale, naturalistic human and feline figures.

30. Seated female figure, buff clay, h. 450 mm, from Veracruz, central Gulf Coast, Late Classic period, c. AD 600–c. 900 (Mexico City, Museo Nacional de Antropología)

The Classic Maya, in contrast, produced brilliantly decorated ceramics in various regional styles. Diverse ceramic types, including painted and carved vessels, filled rich burials of Early Classic centres such as the élite tombs at TIKAL. Tripod-based cylinders from Tikal with painted stucco-coated surfaces show a close relationship with Teotihuacán. Lidded, basal-flange containers are monochrome, finely incised or painted with polychrome serpentine scroll designs. Figural incense burners depict animals, humans and deities.

In the Late Classic period, figures and hieroglyphic texts on polychrome plates, bowls and cylindrical vases were drawn with an agile black line against cream, orange or black slip backgrounds. Panels contain narrative scenes, many related to deities and myths of the Maya underworld. The term 'Codex style' has been applied to a singular group of cylindrical vessels, drawn in black on a cream slip, to suggest their affiliation with contemporaneous, now lost, painted manuscripts (see §VI, 1 above). Vigorously carved monochrome wares from highland Guatemala, Yucatán and the eastern Gulf Coast feature figures in high relief, scenes and hieroglyphic inscriptions. Tall, tubular incense stands from Palenque and surrounding sites received dramatic sculptural emphasis from lateral flanges and anterior, vertically stacked deity heads, of which the Jaguar-god of the underworld was most prominent.

Figurines occurred throughout the Maya region during the Classic period, but those of the Late Classic island necropolis of Jaina, off the Yucatán Peninsula, are particularly outstanding. Pieces include fancily dressed males and females, deities, warriors, ball-players (see fig. 31), amorous couples, aged figures, anthropomorphic creatures and animals. The finest of these small, tan clay sculptures are handmade, but others were mould-made or fashioned by both techniques, then painted after firing. Most also functioned as whistles or rattles.

At the site of Largartero in modern Chiapas hundreds of broken Late Classic figurines and clay moulds were discovered along with other ceramics in a refuse heap, rather than in an élite burial ground. Over half of the mould-made figurines depict elegantly garbed females, while modelled examples include sparsely clad males, grotesque creatures and animal forms that generally functioned as whistles.

(iii) Post-Classic period (c. 900–1521). In the Early Post-Classic period (*c.* 900–*c.* 1200) the Central Highlands were dominated by the Toltecs from their centre at Tula. Clay ritual items included braziers, long-handled censers and tobacco pipes. Two rather simple types of buff pottery manufactured during this period were Coyotlatelco ware, with stylized red designs on cream backgrounds, and Mazapán ware, with parallel straight or wavy red lines. Also diagnostic of this period was a pottery type, commonly called 'Plumbate', typified by a metallic grey sheen produced by a highly polished, reduction-fired, iron-rich slip. (These simply grooved and incised globular vessels and effigy pots are thought to have been produced in the Soconusco region of the state of Chiapas and Guatemala and traded throughout Mesoamerica.)

31. Ball-player figurine, buff clay with post-fired paint, h. 120 mm, from Jaina, Maya region, Late Classic period, *c.* AD 600–*c.* 900 (Mexico City, Museo Nacional de Antropología)

Toltec figurines from Tula and contemporary Central Highland sites were mould-made and painted after firing. Flat 'gingerbread' types feature relatively plain female images with high coiffures or headdresses, as well as more elegantly costumed variations. Less common are male warriors wearing armour and carrying shields, and a few recognizable deities.

Post-Classic period, large-scale, clay and stone figures from the Central Highlands were probably inspired by the large ceramic figures of the Gulf Coast. This derivation is specifically suggested by clay sculptures of the fertility god Xipe Totec, which were produced in both areas. The most extraordinary of these pieces are large standing versions, attributed to either the Veracruz or the Puebla area, depicting the deity or his impersonator wearing the flayed human skin of a sacrificial victim.

Southeast of the Basin of Mexico elegantly modelled, brilliant polychrome vessels were produced primarily at Cholula and other sites in modern Puebla, in the Mixtec territory of Oaxaca and in the Gulf Coast region during the Late Post-Classic period (*c.* AD 1200–1521). This Mixteca–Puebla polychrome (sometimes called Cholulteca) shares its repertory of symbolic motifs with several surviving Pre-Columbian pictorial manuscripts. The designs do not appear as narrative scenes, as in Maya ceramics, but as discrete emblems, such as feathers, bird heads, flowers, stepped frets and, occasionally, deity figures, arranged in horizontal registers against an orange background slip (see fig. 32). Prized in their own time as luxury items, these pitchers, plates, bowls, vases and animal effigy vessels were traded widely. The Spanish conquistador Bernal Díaz del Castillo reported that the Aztec ruler Motecuhzoma II (*reg* 1502–20) ate only from such vessels.

Characteristic of the Tehuacán Valley on the border of modern Puebla and Oaxaca was the *xantil*, a large cylindrical censer forming the body of a fertility deity, with

32. Mixtec pedestal bowl with humming-bird on rim, clay with burnished polychrome decoration, h. 170 mm, from Tomb 1 at Zaachila, Oaxaca Valley, Post-Classic period, c. AD 900–1521 (Mexico City, Museo Nacional de Antropología)

costumes and two skeletal figures—during excavations of the Templo Mayor of the Aztec capital of Tenochtitlán (1978–82) provided a glimpse of what became a lost ceramic art form. Their location within the temple precinct identifies them as cult statues. Much better known are abundant, mould-made, tan figurines, chiefly representing female and male fertility gods, who can usually be identified by their standardized headdresses and insignia. Small temple models, sometimes particularized by the figures of deities (to whom they were dedicated) on top of them, probably represented another type of offering. Other common handmade ceramic items include intricately incised spindle whorls and stamps, musical instruments and tobacco pipes.

BIBLIOGRAPHY

A. O. Shepard: *Plumbate: A Mesoamerican Trade Ware* (Washington, DC, 1948)

A. Caso and I. Bernal: *Urnas de Oaxaca* (Mexico City, 1952)

R. E. Smith: 'The Place of Fine Orange Pottery in Mesoamerican Archaeology', *Amer. Ant.*, xxiv (1958), pp. 151–60

Cer. Cult. Maya, i–xv (1961–88)

M. D. Coe: *The Jaguar's Children: Pre-Classic Central Mexico* (New York, 1965)

E. Noguera: *La cerámica arqueológica de Mesoamérica* (Mexico City, 1965, rev. 2/1975)

F. V. Field: *Thoughts on the Meaning and Use of Pre-Hispanic Mexican Sellos*, Studies in Pre-Columbian Art and Archaeology, iii (Washington, DC, 1967)

A. Caso, I. Bernal and J. R. Acosta: *La cerámica de Monte Albán* (Mexico City, 1968)

F. Müller: *La cerámica del centro ceremonial de Teotihuacán* (Mexico City, 1968)

Ancient Art of Veracruz (exh. cat., Los Angeles, CA, Nat. Hist. Mus., 1971)

H. von Winning: *The Shaft Tomb Figures of West Mexico*, Southwest Museum Papers, xxiv (Los Angeles, 1974)

M. D. Coe: *Lords of the Underworld: Masterpieces of Classic Maya Ceramics* (Princeton, 1978)

F. Müller: *La alfavería de Cholula* (Mexico City, 1978)

H. King: *Aztec Pottery Designs* (MA thesis, New York, Columbia U., 1981)

C. C. Kolb: 'Technological and Cultural Aspects of Teotihuacán Period "Thin Orange" Ware', *Pots and Potters*, ed. P. M. Rice (Los Angeles, 1984), pp. 209–20

T. P. Culbert: 'Maya Ceramics', *Maya: Treasures of an Ancient Civilization* (exh. cat., ed. E. Gallenkamp and R. E. Johnson; New York, Amer. Mus. Nat. Hist.; Los Angeles, CA, Nat. Hist. Mus.; Dallas, TX, Mus. A.; and elsewhere; 1985–7), pp. 71–83

P. M. Rice: *Pottery Analysis: A Sourcebook* (Chicago and London, 1987)

M. Kan, C. Meighan and H. B. Nicholson: *Sculpture of Ancient West Mexico*, Los Angeles, CA, Co. Mus. A. cat (Los Angeles, 1989)

J. Kerr: *The Maya Vase Book: A Corpus of Rollout Photographs of Maya Vases*, 4 vols (New York, 1994)

H. B. Nicholson and E. Quiñones Keber: *Mixteca–Puebla: Discoveries and Research in Mesoamerican Art and Archaeology* (Lancaster, CA, 1994)

D. Reents-Budet: *Painting the Maya Universe: Royal Ceramics of the Classic Period* (Durham and London, 1994)

ELOISE QUIÑONES KEBER

VIII. Lapidary arts.

1. Introduction. 2. Stylistic development.

1. INTRODUCTION.

(i) Materials. In the Mesoamerican context lapidary art means essentially the carving of jade and other greenstones. Only two minerals are considered true jade, nephrite and jadeite (*see also* JADE, §1), both of which are valued for hardness, toughness, translucence and beauty when polished. Jadeite, which may have more intense colour, is rarer, being found in only six localities worldwide; the

added modelled heads and limbs. Other examples of this style include long-handled incense burners and capacious polychrome urns attributed to the site of Cempoala in the central Gulf Coast region.

In the Maya region an untempered, well-crafted series of related wares, collectively called Fine Orange ware, was traded widely during the Early Post-Classic period from its sources of manufacture in the eastern Gulf Coast. Typical vessels are pear-shaped with ring bases or cylindrical with spare decoration or mould-pressed panels. At the Late Post-Classic walled city of Mayapán large censers fronted by full-figure representations of deities were brightly painted after firing.

The ceramic wares centred in the Late Post-Classic Basin of Mexico, called Aztec ware, filled a number of practical and ceremonial needs. Several phases of orange ware were typically decorated with black line designs on open tripod bowls. The earliest examples are decorated with thick, loosely drawn parallel lines, dots, circles, spirals and other abstract designs, often encircling a central figural motif. Later types bear smaller-scale abstract and symbolic motifs organized into more tightly structured concentric and radial bands or, occasionally, asymmetrical arrangements. Naturalistically drawn flowers, birds and animals, combined with the abstract designs, represent a late development that continued into the Colonial period.

Burnished red ware bowls, goblets and jugs decorated with black and white geometric and symbolic motifs were rarer. The finest vessels, for holding *pulque* (a fermented drink), were hour-glass-shaped and decorated with black and white symbolic emblems or macabre imagery, including skulls and crossed bones, over a burnished red slip. Polychrome effigy vessels filled with diverse offerings, and hour-glass-shaped urns and braziers featuring figures of fertility deities or their emblems, show continuing links with earlier traditions, particularly with those of the central Gulf Coast.

Post-Classic Aztec ceramics were among the worst casualties of the Spanish Conquest. Thus the unearthing of large-scale ceramic sculptures—two warriors in eagle

Mesoamerican source was rediscovered in 1952 in the Motagua Valley in Guatemala (*see also* SOUTH AMERICA, PRE-COLUMBIAN, §II, 5). Jadeite varies greatly and usually occurs mixed with diopside or albite. Commoner minerals valued for their greenness include chalcedony, prase, jasper and bloodstone (all varieties of quartz); serpentines named bowenite and williamsite (translucent); metadiorite (green-speckled); the amphiboles nephrite, actinolite and amphibolite; and muscovites, especially fuchsite. Chloromelanite (nearly black) is sometimes classed as jade; it was used mainly in tools.

From the earliest times Mesoamerican lapidaries used stones of other colours, including rock crystal, amethyst, various opaque black, brown, reddish and purplish stones, turquoise and amazonite. All were obtainable through the widespread trading network that distributed obsidian and greenstones over long distances, but they were seldom used until shortly before the Spanish Conquest. The preponderance of greenstones, especially at sites where little or no jadeite was found, clearly suggests that it was valued far beyond its inherent superiority in tools, probably for its religious and ritual significance.

(ii) Techniques. Mesoamerican lapidaries did not have the use of iron tools, and even copper tools were not available until the Late Post-Classic period (*c.* AD 1200–1521). Metal tools, however, were never hard enough to cut most of the valued stones, and abrasives are the key to lapidary work. These included emery, fine quartz sand and powdered jadeite. Haematite ('jewellers' rouge'), plants containing silica particles, especially canes or bamboo, and stones, with or without abrasives, were used for polishing.

The real technical disadvantage was the lack of simple rotary mechanisms, such as grinding and polishing wheels, lathes and drills. There is no proof that Pre-Columbian craftsmen used even the bow drill. Similarly, nothing remains of vices or dops for holding small pieces firmly enough to work on. Organic adhesives were used in mosaic work (*see* §IX, 6 below), a technical tradition that made possible larger or more colourful works, such as figurines, masks, shields and mirrors. Some mosaics recovered whole bear evidence of grinding and polishing after the component parts had been mounted on the armature or backing.

Since the lapidary's equipment was largely perishable, little remains to identify workshop sites except finds of raw materials, imported or prepared abrasives, unfinished objects, debris and, more rarely, tools such as flint drills or gravers, stone reamers, saws, hammers, and grinding and polishing stones. Little jadeite was ever wasted: broken pieces were saved for reuse, and the Maya collected even the tiniest bits to sprinkle in offerings.

Valuable stones were often kept in substantially the original form, with most preliminary shaping done economically. Straight saws were the usual tools, some as thin as 1 mm at the cutting edge. Sawing from opposite sides saved time as well as blades and abrasive, as did the practice of stopping before the cuts met and breaking the stone between. Cord saws were sometimes used to cut inward from an edge or enlarge drilled openings.

Drilling was essential for shaping and surface decoration as well as perforating beads and pendants. Holes were commonly drilled from opposite sides or ends, and angular perforations, drilled from adjacent surfaces, were more efficient for a large ornament than a single, much longer transverse drilling. Small-bore solid drill bits were universal until well into the Classic Period (*c.* AD 250–*c.* 900), when a new material or method made tubular drills of small diameter practicable, although large-bore hollow bits made of cane or bone, 15 mm or more in diameter, had been used since *c.* 1000 BC. The use of small-bore hollow bits profoundly changed lapidary production and style.

Pigments were produced by grinding certain minerals: a highly prized blood-red was produced from specular haematite; duller red, browns and black from other iron-ore minerals (magnetite, ilmenite and pyrite). The characteristic metallic lustre of these minerals, when polished, may have led to their use in mirrors and curious small blocks drilled more than one way, both apparently intended for ritual purposes (*see* §(iii) below).

(iii) Forms. Ground stone vessels were made in Mesoamerica as early as *c.* 2500 BC, ranging from roughly made *manos* and *metates* (rubbing and grinding stones) to handsome flat-bottomed bowls. Certain smoothly shallow examples were palettes for grinding pigments, of which some still retain traces. From *c.* 1500 BC small pyrite and ilmenite mirrors, and small drilled blocks were made, particularly in the Gulf Coast and in the Southern Highlands. An imported serpentine pebble dating from before *c.* 1200 BC and a small greenstone pendant from San Lorenzo Tenochtitlán indicate Olmec knowledge of jadeite towards the end of the Early Pre-Classic period (*c.* 2000–*c.* 1000 BC). Both objects lack Mesoamerican antecedents, but primitive stone figurines of various colours from Valdivia, coastal Ecuador, are known from as early as 2400 BC.

The earliest major lapidary forms, vessels and mirrors, were never abandoned. Stone vessels later occur only seldom and sporadically and are not always related closely to current ceramic styles. Most from the Late Pre-Classic period (*c.* 300 BC–*c.* AD 250) onwards are of softer materials, such as fuchsite and aragonite (*tecali* or 'Mexican onyx'). Mirrors gained importance as a symbol worn by Olmec rulers, and this type represents an outstanding achievement of lapidary art. Unlike earlier and later mirrors, they have a concave surface, usually paraboloid, ground with remarkable precision.

In Olmec and later cultures, priests and rulers determined the forms produced by each lapidary school or industry. Some societies apparently required carved pendants of specific kinds as religious or civic insignia or awards; others set more value on unperforated, sometimes large, forms for ritual use. Representational carvings first occur as masks and figurines inspired by Olmec monumental sculpture; they appear in nearly all subsequent styles, but never again were so many made of jadeite. Scarcity of fine materials, and even of substitutes, limited their size, and few hardstone objects exceed 150–200 mm.

Overall, by far the most material and labour went into the production of beads and ear ornaments, either spools or flares (the trumpet-shaped fronts of composite assemblages). These universally prized ornaments played an important role in the trade network; consequently, most

33. Olmec votive axe, light green jadeite, h. 295 mm, from Oaxaca, Middle Pre-Classic period, *c.* 1000–*c.* 300 BC (London, British Museum)

finds cannot be attributed to any style or place of manufacture.

2. STYLISTIC DEVELOPMENT. The rise of the great Mesoamerican lapidary styles began with the Olmec culture *c.* 1200 BC. Before this time the still largely unlocated jadeworking centres of the region produced plain forms, such as beads, ear ornaments, petaloid celts and celt-shaped tablets, and preserved the technical tradition that underlay later achievements. These centres apparently flourished at different times in widely separated places, sometimes unconnected by any stylistic transition. Olmec lapidary art is essentially sculptural and three-dimensional, as are most styles that followed it, with the exception of Maya art and the styles derived from it, which show a two-

dimensional approach derived from writing, painting and relief sculpture.

(i) Olmec. Jade-carving is not well attested in the long archaeological record at San Lorenzo Tenochtitlán, since no burials were found. While lapidary tools occur earlier, evidence of typically Olmec work belongs to the Middle Pre-Classic levels (*c.* 1000–*c.* 300 BC), corresponding apparently to the spectacular jade offerings at LA VENTA. These included a deliberately buried cache of six celts placed upright in a crescent in front of a group of sixteen jade, serpentine and granite figurines (average h. 175 mm) in an arrangement implying a ceremony (Mexico City, Mus. N. Antropol.).

The jade celt was the primary Olmec symbol. Great numbers of beautifully made celts, unusable celts of soft stone and celt blanks were placed in patterned offerings. Jaguar-dragon symbolism was expressed in larger effigy celts or 'votive axes' carved as supernatural figures (see fig. 33) and in seemingly naturalistic sculptures and figurines. Most pendants were ritual objects, typically mirrors, pointed instruments and clam-shell and spoon-like shapes.

Although all raw materials had to be imported, the numbers and wide dispersal of Olmec style objects imply that supplies were relatively plentiful. The most carefully worked material is an almost pure jadeite, often exceptionally translucent and bluish, sometimes with dark emerald-coloured inclusions. The exact source of this distinctive material is not known.

During the Late Pre-Classic period two derivative styles developed near the Pacific Coast in modern Guerrero, Mexico, and Costa Rica (*see also* SOUTH AMERICA, PRE-COLUMBIAN, §II, 5). Neither style is securely dated, but each produced large numbers of distinctive interpretations of the effigy celt. The elegantly simplified, celt-shaped figurines from the Mezcala–Balsas Valley of Guerrero taper from thick heads and shoulders to blade-like feet. Most are carved from greenstones such as local metadiorite, sometimes used by the Olmec. Seated and kneeling figures, animal and cup-like pendants, and large masks with cut-out eyes indicate Olmec prototypes (e.g. Mexico City, Mus. N. Antropol.).

(ii) Teotihuacán. In the lapidary art of Teotihuacán in the Classic period (*c.* AD 250–*c.* 900), the ancient symbolism of celts is no longer evident, but the outstanding forms remain those of the past: small figures and masks. Their uniformly idealized faces (see fig. 34) represent more aristocratic versions of the mould-made heads of thousands of clay figurines and the mask units of composite incense urns. Inlaid eyes and teeth originally enlivened the stone faces, and a few have mosaic or carved patterns. In contrast with this realistic mode, small effigy urns (e.g. Mexico City, Mus. N. Antropol. and Teotihuacán, Mus. Arqueol.) of the rain god Tlaloc relate stylistically more to monumental sculpture (*see* §IV, 3(ii)(a) above). Only a small proportion of work in identifiable Teotihuacán style is jadeite; other hardstones predominate, with *tecali* often used for larger carvings. Large ear flares and plain bead necklaces were common. In mapping the ancient city a lapidary precinct, dating to the Early Classic period (*c.* AD 250–*c.* 600), was identified outside the central ceremonial precinct.

(iii) Tajín. In the Gulf Coast the Late Classic (*c.* AD 600–*c.* 900) Veracruz style of Tajín, in other ways closely related to that of Teotihuacán, is represented by hardly any jade ornaments or small stone objects except for a few relief-decorated slate mirror backs. Instead, Tajín lapidary art concentrated on three forms associated with the sacred ball-game: the *yugo*, *palma* and *hacha* (*see* §II, 3(i) above). Carved in various stones, often very hard and greenish, they include striking examples of minor sculpture, many enriched by low relief in the same interlaced scroll patterns used architecturally at both Tajín and Teotihuacán (e.g. Mexico City, Mus. N. Antropol. and Jalapa, U. Veracruzana, Mus. Antropol.).

(iv) Maya. In the Maya region workshop sites attest to lapidary production throughout the Late Pre-Classic period (*c.* 300 BC–*c.* AD 250), principally in the manufacture of ear ornaments and beads. Rare figures and widely distributed head pendants from unknown sources echo the earlier three-dimensional mode and relatively large size. A characteristic Maya 'bib' and crest make one type recognizable, even when later recut, because of the uncommonly fine stone used. For a time Maya lapidaries worked fuchsite, a soft, translucent stone sparkling with mica flakes.

Maya jade-carving of the Classic period did not evolve directly from the Pre-Classic. The first verifiably Classic jades are plain or reused pieces incised with glyphs and drawings in Lowland Maya style, notably the Leyden Plaque, which bears a Maya ruler's portrait and a dated inscription corresponding to AD 320 (216×80 mm; Leiden, Rijksmus. Vlkenknd.). During the 5th century carved offertory tablets and pendants began to appear, characterized by crowded compositions in soft uniform low relief, generally depicting a figure or head seen full-face as on certain 5th-century stelae in the lowlands. Masks were rare, but the superb death-mask of Lord Pacal from Palenque (*c.* AD 683; ex-Mus. N. Antropol., Mexico City, stolen 1995; *see* JADE, colour pl. II, fig. 1) exemplifies the use of small, flat, shaped jade tablets for mosaic work. In the Maya highlands at least two lapidary centres with access to especially fine jadeite developed distinctive styles. From jade-rich tombs at Nebaj came artefacts that first defined the Early Classic Maya lapidary style (Guatemala City, Mus. N. Arqueol. & Etnol. and Cambridge, MA, Harvard U., Peabody Mus.). The other centre was Kaminaljuyú, where lapidaries developed a style based largely on sawing and vigorous use of tubular drills 10 mm and less in diameter. As knowledge of the new drilling method spread, other jadeworkers refined it in traditional portrait pendants, which followed the current style of stele relief carving. Perfect circles and arcs, unfinished back surfaces, higher relief and less adjustment of design to colour variation in the stone became hallmarks of lapidary work of the Late Classic period. Extraordinarily shaped cobbles were carved into masks or small sculptures, much simplified in comparison to the ornate relief styles.

(v) Southern Highlands. Imported and locally carved objects from the Oaxaca Valley reflect the whole history of Mesoamerican lapidary work, beginning with the reflective iron minerals and mirrors exported in the Early Pre-Classic period. However, in spite of many fine artefacts found

34. Mask, grey-green aragonite, h. 170 mm, from Teotihuacán, Early Classic period, *c.* AD 250–*c.* 650 (Paris, Musée de l'Homme)

there, the next clearly locally made lapidary works are Early Classic figurines in Teotihuacán style. Maya jade pendants inspired increasingly adept local copies that became nearly indistinguishable from Late Classic imports. New copper tubular drills were perhaps literally instrumental in cheapening both styles. In the Post-Classic period (*c.* AD 900–1521) the Mixtecs produced large quantities of blocky-figure pendants, shaped mainly by drills and saws, and mass-produced amulets modelled on larger, finer sculptures of Tlaloc.

Fine lapidary work in Toltec style has come from the 'Sacred Cenote' at Chichén Itzá and other Post-Classic sites, notably large jade pictorial pendants and intricately carved beads. Wherever found, Toltec jades are outnumbered by older pieces, illustrating decreased use of symbolic pendants and, perhaps, an increase in collecting.

By the Late Post-Classic period (*c.* AD 1200–1521) or Aztec–Mixtec era, powerful rulers were gathering other lapidary materials never before used in quantity. The Mixtec burial in Tomb 7 at MONTE ALBÁN contained jade, pearls and *tecali* vessels, but also a footed rock-crystal cup, crystal and obsidian earspools, turquoise, jet, coral and amber ornaments (Oaxaca, Mus. Reg.). Few had any carved decoration.

Ritual ceremonies in Aztec Tenochtitlán required prodigious numbers of plain ornaments from lapidaries. The best works, however, were carved in hardstones: ceremonial vessels might be enhanced by low relief in the style of the codices, but the sporadic tradition of full-round carving also regained favour (see fig. 35). All manner of cult figures, including humans, deities, animals and even plant forms, were carved of jadeite and other greenstones, diorite, chalcedony and rock-crystal, and lapidaries shared

35. Aztec figure of Quetzalcóatl, green porphyry, h. 440 mm, Late Post-Classic period, *c.* AD 1440–1521 (Paris, Musée de l'Homme)

the same vigorous naturalistic style with sculptors who worked on a larger scale in easier materials (*see* §V, 4(ii) above). Turquoise mosaic was also an Aztec speciality (*see* §IX, 4 and 6 below).

BIBLIOGRAPHY

J. McGuire: 'Materials, Apparatus and Processes of the Aboriginal Lapidary', *Amer. Anthropologist*, v (1892), pp. 165–76
A. V. Kidder, J. Jennings and E. M. Shook: *Excavations at Kaminaljuyú, Guatemala* (Washington, DC, 1946)
A. L. Smith and A. V. Kidder: *Excavations at Nebaj, Guatemala* (Washington, DC, 1951)
P. Drucker: 'La Venta, Tabasco: A Study of Olmec Ceramics and Art', *Bureau Amer. Ethnol. Bull.*, cliii (1952) [whole issue]
E. M. Shook and A. V. Kidder: *Mound E-III-3, Kaminaljuyú, Guatemala* (Washington, DC, 1952)
P. Drucker: 'The Cerro de las Mesas Offering of Jade and Other Materials', *Bureau Amer. Ethnol. Bull.*, clvi (1955) [whole issue]
M. Covarrubias: *Indian Art of Mexico and Central America* (New York, 1957)
W. Foshag: 'Mineralogical Studies on Guatemalan Jades', *Smithsonian Inst. Misc. Col.*, cxxxv/5 (1957) [whole issue]
P. Drucker, R. Heizer and R. Squier: 'Excavations at La Venta, Tabasco, 1955', *Bureau Amer. Ethnol. Bull.*, clxx (1959) [whole issue]

M. Stirling: 'The Olmecs, Artists in Jade', *Essays in Pre-Columbian Art and Archaeology*, ed. S. K. Lothrop and others (Cambridge, MA, 1961), pp. 43–59
A. Digby: *Maya Jades* (London, 1964, rev. 1972)
L. Mirambell: 'Técnicas lapidarias prehispánicas', *Invest. INAH*, xiv (1968) [whole issue]
A. Caso: 'El tesoro de Monte Albán', *Mem. INAH*, iii (1969) [whole issue]
T. Lee jr: *The Artifacts of Chiapa de Corzo, Chiapas, Mexico*, Papers of the New World Archaeological Foundation, xxvii (Provo, 1969)
E. Carmichael: *Turquoise Mosaics from Mexico* (London, 1970)
Before Cortés: Sculpture of Middle America (exh. cat. by E. K. Easby and J. F. Scott, New York, Met., 1970)
T. Proskouriakoff: 'Jades from the Cenote of Sacrifice, Chichén Itzá, Yucatán', *Mem. Peabody Mus. Archaeol. & Ethnol.*, x (1974) [whole issue]
Ancient Ecuador: Culture, Clay and Creativity, 3000–300 BC (exh. cat. by D. W. Lathrap, D. Collier and H. Chandra, Chicago, IL, Field Mus. Nat. Hist., 1975)
J. Carlson: 'The Olmec Concave Iron-ore Mirrors: The Aesthetics of a Lithic Technology and the Lord of the Mirror', *The Olmec and their Neighbors: Essays in Memory of Matthew W. Stirling*, ed. E. P. Benson (Washington, DC, 1981), pp. 117–47
M. Thouvenot: 'Chalchihuitl: Le Jade chez les Aztèques', *Mém. Inst. Ethnol.*, xxi (1982) [whole issue]
Cenote of Sacrifice: Maya Treasures from the Sacred Well at Chichén Itzá (exh. cat., ed. C. Coggins and O. Shane; Cambridge, MA, Harvard U., Peabody Mus.; St Paul, MN, Sci. Mus.; 1984)
J. Ceja Tenorio: *Paso de la Amada: An Early Preclassic Site in the Soconusco, Chiapas, Mexico*, Papers of the New World Archaeological Foundation, xlix (Provo, 1985)
L. Gorelick and A. J. Gwinnett: 'Ancient Egyptian Stone-Drilling', *Expedition*, xxix/3 (1987), pp. 40–47
A. J. Gwinnett and L. Gorelick: 'The Change from Stone Drills to Copper Drills in Mesopotamia', *Expedition*, xxix/3 (1987), pp. 15–24
F. Ward: 'Jade: Stone of Heaven', *N. Geog.*, clxxii (1987), pp. 282–315
F. W. Lange and R. Bishop: 'Abstraction and Jade Exchange in Pre-Columbian Southern Mesoamerica and Lower Central America', *Costa Rican Art and Archaeology: Essays in Honor of Frederick R. Mayer*, ed. F. W. Lange (Boulder, 1988), pp. 67–88
R. Sharer and D. Grove, eds: *Regional Perspectives on the Olmec* (Cambridge, 1989)

ELIZABETH K. EASBY

IX. Other arts.

1. Arms and armour. 2. Bone-carving. 3. Featherwork. 4. Masks. 5. Metalwork. 6. Mosaic. 7. Musical instruments. 8. Seals. 9. Shellwork. 10. Textiles and dress.

1. ARMS AND ARMOUR. Warfare played a significant role in Mesoamerican culture. Apart from fighting for political and territorial reasons the cult of the warrior became increasingly important during the Late Classic (*c.* AD 600–*c.* 900) and Post-Classic (*c.* AD 900–1521) periods, when societies of 'knights' were formed, with their own rituals and meeting-places. Warfare was more ritualized in concept than in Western Europe. There were no standing armies. Warriors were led by the élite and were drawn from all able-bodied men. Weapons and armour were kept by individuals, or in central storehouses in the case of the Aztecs. 'Foreign' mercenaries were sometimes used for particular campaigns—for example the Cocom Itzá used Mexican warriors in the conquest of Mayapán in the Late Post-Classic period (*c.* AD 1200–1521). Fighting was hand-to-hand after initial bombardment with arrows, darts and spears. Most 'wars' were decided by a single battle, although continual warfare was the rule, especially in the Late Post-Classic empire-building of the Aztecs.

Information on weapons comes from four main sources: surviving artefacts; representations in wall painting, painted stone and plaster sculpture and pottery;

painted codices; and Spanish accounts. Earlier representations of weapons are often highly stylized, and the precise shapes and materials of weapons and armour are assumed from the surviving examples of Late Post-Classic materials and descriptions.

(i) Types. Weapons and armour remained much the same from the Classic period onwards (see fig. 36). The mainstays in battle were clubs, stone- and (later) copper-bladed hatchets, obsidian-edged wooden swords, thrusting spears, slings of plaited cotton and darts thrown with *atlatls* (Nahuatl: spear-thrower). Bows and arrows were introduced *c.* AD 500 but may not have been used in Yucatán until the 12th century. There were also blow guns, obsidian knives and net-like traps. In the Late Post-Classic period metal weapons were made but played only a minor role. Nevertheless, it has been argued that Tarascan ability to thwart Aztec conquest is attributable to the knowledge, perhaps carefully guarded, of copper weapon-making.

The *atlatl* was a straight stick with a groove to hold the spear or dart shaft. A stub-like hook at the end held the shaft butt and two finger loops provided the grip. Spearheads were either hafted single obsidian tips or comprised a wooden head set with obsidian blades. Darts were shorter, sometimes fletched. Swords were square-ended wooden planks up to 1 m in length, set on both edges with obsidian blades. They either narrowed towards the handle or had parallel sides and a narrower, rounded handle and bulbous pommel. Clubs were long and thin-handled with bulbous ends.

Defensive equipment included wooden or reed wicker shields covered with leather and decorated with feathers (a few examples survive in European museums; *see also* §3 below). Helmets were of wood, skin, paper or, more rarely, copper or bronze, open-faced or, if an animal skull-shape, completely enclosing the head. Some had cheek flaps and tall crests decorated with feathers, beaks, figures of birds and other animals. Body armour included wooden

36. Tlaxcalans and Spaniards in battle against the Tarascans of Michoacan, one of four paintings on cloth from the *Lienzo de Tlaxcala*, 1.05×2.03 m, 1773; copied from the ?16th-century original (Mexico City, Biblioteca Nacional de Antropología e Historia Dr Eusebio Davalos Hurtado)

or bone pectorals, jaguar and coyote skins and cotton-padded tunics soaked in brine. Cotton armour was mostly Late Post-Classic, and even then the amount of body armour allowed to be worn increased with a warrior's experience and expertise.

There were also highly ornate pieces of weaponry and armour: wooden shields decorated with turquoise, red shell and lignite; wooden human-shaped knife handles encrusted with turquoise and coloured shell; and carved *atlatl*s showing scenes with warriors, gods and sacrifices, and covered in gold foil. Whether these special pieces were used in battle is debatable. Most are unprovenanced or classed simply as 'Aztec' and scattered, along with the codices and unembellished weapons, in collections throughout Europe and North America.

(ii) Chronological survey. Sites of hunter–gatherer peoples have yielded *atlatl*s and obsidian and chert projectile points for darts. What manner of fighting these were used for is unknown, although they were certainly also used in hunting. Later, the spread of Olmec influence was marked by increasing conflict between towns: low-relief sculpture at several sites depicts warriors striking or threatening others with war clubs and 'knuckle dusters'. One explicit scene is at the Central Highland site of CHALCATZINGO, and there are battle scenes carved on stone at Las Victorias, El Salvador.

In the Classic period (*c.* AD 250–*c.* 900) warriors and warfare became an increasingly prominent theme in wall painting, reliefs and other sculpture, figurines and pottery. Wall paintings at TEOTIHUACÁN combined ritual subjects with military themes and glorification of the warrior. Armed priests and warriors were depicted with shields, spears and *atlatl*s. The owl became a common emblem of war. A warrior priest in the Tepantitla wall painting at Teotihuacán carries arrows in one hand and a claw in the other. A pot-lid (Mexico City, Mus. N. Antropol.) represents a warrior with shield and *atlatl*. Clay figurines wear helmets and what might be the earliest evidence of padded cotton armour, and they carry round or rectangular shields. Drops associated with weapons depict blood.

One manifestation of Tlaloc, additional to his role as rain god, is associated with a warrior cult. Painted shields from Teotihuacán and elsewhere in the 5th to 7th centuries show him with features of rain, the jaguar—bifurcated tongue and fangs—and a tasselled headdress. In the 7th and 8th centuries another type of warrior-Tlaloc had crocodilian features and a hieroglyphic year-sign on his headdress: examples have been found at Tula, Xochicalco, Tikal, Bonampak, Piedras Negras, Yaxchilán, Uxmal, Copán and elsewhere. Yet, despite Late Classic emphasis on warriors, there are no narrative scenes of battles, sacrifices or lines of captives at Teotihuacán itself. Its spread of artistic, architectural and ceramic influences throughout central Mesoamerica and south into Maya lands was a combination of trade and military persuasion.

Maya military themes show combinations of Teotihuacán, Maya and other local traditions. The *atlatl*, bow and arrow, and possibly cotton armour were introduced from central Mesoamerica, supplementing clubs, blowguns and stone axes. The *atlatl* was portrayed in sculpture for the first time at TIKAL on a stele depicting the ruler 'Curl

Snout' (*reg* AD 378–425). His successor, 'Stormy Sky', was similarly depicted, accompanied by warriors carrying *atlatl*s and shields bearing Tlaloc; the Teotihuacán-style owl appears in the headdress of a mask above his hand.

At other Maya lowland sites battle scenes occur on walls and pottery; they include trophy heads, processions of warriors, bound captives and torture. At Mul-Chic, Northern Lowlands, 7th-century wall paintings depict a fierce battle; many warriors have three trophy skulls and are taking captives or sacrificing them by hanging, stoning and other methods. At BONAMPAK, Southern Lowlands, wall paintings (*c.* AD 790–*c.* 800) and carved and painted lintels in the Temple of Paintings show conference scenes, battles and lines of captives, a leader wearing a jaguar skin, gruesome human sacrifices and victory celebrations. One stele at UAXACTÚN depicts an armed foreigner, while at Becán a large Teotihuacán-style hollow figurine contained ten solid figurines of warriors with *atlatl*s (Mexico City, Mus. N. Antropol.). At YAXCHILÁN lintels depict many battle scenes in low relief, including a portrait of the ruler 'Shield Jaguar' wearing the Teotihuacán Tlaloc mask. At PIEDRAS NEGRAS numerous stelae depict victorious warriors, often standing over a bound prisoner. In the 9th century Itzá Maya moving into the Petén and Yucatán lowlands also brought central Mesoamerican influences: at UXMAL and SEIBAL the warrior-Tlaloc is represented; and at KABÁH warriors with *atlatl*s were carved on doorjambs.

Wall paintings (7th–8th century) at the Central Highland site of CACAXTLA, Tlaxcala, depict a vivid battle scene in which jaguar-men are victorious over bird-men, so called because of their attire. Jaguar-men wear jaguar skins over their shoulders, with the heads and feet dangling over kilt-like garments, sandals, leggings, belts and jewellery, and brandish *atlatl*-held spears or jab them viciously into the bird-men's faces and abdomens, spilling blood and organs. Bird-men wear great bird-beak helmets and jewellery but are otherwise naked. Overlooking the scene is a large Teotihuacán-style owl. These and other figures at Cacaxtla have characteristic facial features and regalia of both central Mesoamerican and Maya peoples. Similarly, at XOCHICALCO monuments show Teotihuacán, Tajín and Maya styles. The upper gallery of the Serpent Pyramid (7th century) depicts a procession of warriors armed with shields and darts.

In the Post-Classic period the rise of the Toltecs in the wake of the collapse of Teotihuacán and the Classic Maya lowland cities brought new military manifestations. At TULA itself warriors are depicted in several media: four great stone atlantean warriors (over 3.5 m high) surmount the Pyramid of Tlahuizcalpantecuhtli, each made of four dowelled sections (*see* CAJA-ESPIGA). Each warrior wears a feathered helmet with rectangular ear pieces, bird-like pectoral, wide belt clasped at the back with a disc shield, necklace, bracelets, anklets and sandals. Each carries an *atlatl* and an obsidian sword. Smaller atlantids and pillars depict similar warriors. Carved and painted plaster-covered benches in the colonnaded courts depict processions of warriors wearing plumed headdresses, kilts and jewellery and carrying shields and darts. Two low-relief stelae depict warriors with the crocodilian Tlaloc on their headdresses.

Contemporary monuments and wall paintings at Maya CHICHÉN ITZÁ depict similar Toltec–Maya warriors and scenes. Frescoes in the Temple of Jaguars above the Great Ballcourt show battle in vivid detail. The attacking group carries round shields and wears elements of Toltec attire. On the Temple of Kukulcán corbel arches carry reliefs of Toltec warriors; and the square columns at the Temple of Warriors are carved with Toltec warriors, while altars inside are supported on small atlantean warriors.

The Aztecs believed themselves chosen to be warriors: each day the young warrior sun god Huitzilopochtli defeated his sister (moon) and brothers (stars), ensuring new life for mankind. Until noon he was borne by warriors killed in battle; after noon by women who died in childbirth (i.e. giving life to a warrior). Post-Classic Maya city states were in continual war against one another. Their weapons and armour were the culmination of earlier styles, and, had it not been for internal strife, rebellions and defections, they might have proved more than a match for Cortés; their stone sculpture, pottery and, above all, codices depict weapons, warriors and combat in abundance.

BIBLIOGRAPHY

Z. Nuttall: *The* atlatl *or Spear-thrower of the Ancient Mexicans*, Pap. Peabody Mus. Amer. Archaeol. & Ethnol., i/3 (1891)
J. Soustelle: *La Vie quotidienne des Aztèques à la veille de la conquête espagnole* (Paris, 1955; Eng. trans. London, 1961)
M. D. Coe: *The Maya* (London, 1966, rev. 4/1987)
W. Bray: *Everyday Life of the Aztecs* (London, 1968)
M. Porter Weaver: *The Aztecs, Maya and their Predecessors: Archaeology of Mesoamerica* (New York, 1972, rev. 3/1983)
W. Du Solier: *Indumentaria antigua mexicana* (Mexico City, 1979)
P. R. Anawalt: *Indian Clothing before Cortés: Mesoamerican Costumes from the Codices* (Norman, 1981)
J. S. Henderson: *The World of the Ancient Maya* (Ithaca, 1981)
B. L. Isaac: 'Aztec Warfare: Goals and Battlefield Comportment', *Ethnology*, xxii (1983), pp. 121–31
E. Pasztory: *Aztec Art* (New York, 1983)
R. Hassig: *Aztec Warfare: Imperial Expansion and Political Control* (Norman, 1988)

DAVID M. JONES

2. BONE-CARVING. The earliest use of bone for tools and as a medium of plastic expression in Mesoamerica dates from *c.* 12,000–*c.* 8000 BC. Bone tools were used to perforate hide, work obsidian and stitch basketry, while notched shoulder-blades, usually from deer, were used as a rasping device and provided one of the earliest forms of musical instrument. A sacrum of an extinct species of camelid, dated to *c.* 12,000–10,000 BC, was carved to resemble the head of a coyote and probably used as a mask (Mexico City, Mus. N. Antropol.); this constitutes the first evidence for the ritual use of bone in this area. Bone was undoubtedly used for ornament, needles, hand-tools and musical instruments throughout Mesoamerican prehistory, but distinct traditions are not usually identified before the 1st–2nd centuries AD in the Maya region and considerably later in areas further north.

(i) Maya region. Bone-carving had a long history in the Maya region. Jaguar, peccary and deer bones were commonly worked (these animals all had important religious significance for the Maya), as well as human bones. Artefacts such as awls used in weaving and basket manufacture, pins, rasps, flutes and perforators and sting-ray spines (used for ritual bloodletting) have been found at many Pre-Classic (*c.* 2000 BC–*c.* AD 250) and Classic (*c.* AD 250–*c.* 900) period Lowland Maya sites, including Copán, Tikal, Uaxactún, Piedras Negras, Altar de Sacrificios, Jaina and Chiapa de Corzo, but sculptured and engraved objects made for adornment or ceremonial use are less common.

Ceremonial and ritual Maya bone-carving can be divided into two categories: three-dimensional sculptures; and incised or engraved bones. In addition, unworked bones taken from defeated enemies sometimes served as trophies or were used as a decorative feature on architectural structures. Among the earliest examples of distinctive Maya bone-carving were two pairs of human femurs found in Tomb 1 at Chiapa de Corzo (*c.* AD 100; Tuxtla Gutiérrez, Mus. Reg. Antropol. & Hist.); these may have been used as receptacles for water during fertility ceremonies. Each pair consists of one carved bone and one polished and cut to similar dimensions but otherwise left unworked. Both the carved bones were decorated with figures of a saurian-like creature (identified as Imix, the Maya earth monster associated with germination) and a feline being, perhaps an underworld deity connected with rain. On the carved bone of the first pair Imix is represented swimming through water, while behind the feline rears backwards. On the example from the second set, the same earth monster is shown from above, as though both it and the feline were surfacing from the water. A third creature with a segmented body, stringy hair and a prominent skeletal jaw is also depicted on the carved bone of the second pair.

An outstanding example of Classic period (*c.* AD 250–*c.* 900) Maya bone sculpture is a standing figure of a jaguar priest (h. 75 mm; Mexico City, Mus. N. Antropol.). The stolid figure, hands resting on hips, wears a jaguar-pelt tunic tied by a belt fashioned into an elaborate knot at the front and a feather headdress with a jaguar mask fastened to its back. The figure may originally have been painted red, and drilled cavities suggest that it was once decorated by stone or shell inlays. Its hollow pedestal may have been attached to a staff and formed part of the regalia of Maya priesthood. Other sculptured human figures have been found in burial 29 at Mirador (Guatemala City, Mus. N. Arqueol. & Etnol.) and in Tomb 23 at Río Azul. The example from Río Azul (made from a deer antler), with one arm slightly upraised to its breast and the other reaching downwards and ending in an outstretched palm, may have represented the tomb's occupant. Both figures were probably used as pendants. Articulated figures with movable limbs were also made, including a small monkey (h. 125 mm), part of a cache of 89 bone objects, 37 of which were carved, found in burial 116 beneath Temple I at Tikal. The same cache also included an exquisitely carved profile of a Maya dignitary, which decorated the head of a tapered awl (both Tikal, Mus. Arqueol.–Sylvanus G. Morley). Sculptured bones sometimes occur in pairs, such as two examples from Río Azul carved from half of a peccary mandible, depicting a human face within a monstrous skeletal jaw.

Maya incised bones, often with carved hieroglyphic inscriptions, are more common than bone sculptures. Examples often occur in pairs made from the matching bones of the same animal and show scenes or designs that are near mirror images. Among the bones excavated at Tikal are two pairs depicting anthropomorphic beings and a human figure making a canoe voyage (Tikal, Mus. Arqueol.–Sylvanus G. Morley). On the first set, the canoe is paddled by the 'Old Jaguar god' and the aged 'Sting-ray god'. Between them are seated iguana, monkey, parrot and dog beings, and amid these one of the city's rulers. On the second pair the canoe is depicted descending at an angle into the water to the underworld. The two carvings in this set differ in that one bone has the 'Sting-ray god' as the paddler while the other shows the 'Jaguar god' in that role; the passengers in each canoe are also arranged differently, and the bones bear dissimilar inscriptions. Another pair of matching femurs, also probably (one is badly damaged) carved in mirror image, was uncovered in burial 16 at Mirador (Guatemala City, Mus. N. Arqueol. & Etnol.). The undamaged femur is carved in light relief and shows a standing man dressed in ceremonial attire holding a trophy head in one hand.

Perhaps the best example of Maya bone-carving is an incised peccary skull from Copán (c. AD 581; Cambridge, MA, Harvard U., Peabody Mus.). It depicts two dignitaries wearing jaguar-skin skirts and seated before an altar framed in a lozenge-shaped space. Surrounding them are three peccaries on their left and, beneath them, a jaguar, monkey, flying bird and a feline-like creature with skeletal details that stands half erect and holds a conch shell. The dignitaries are richly adorned with bracelets, necklaces, ear flares and elaborate headdresses. Partial decipherment of the hieroglyphic inscription suggests that the scene represents the accession of a new ruler at Copán.

Examples of Post-Classic (c. AD 900–1521) Maya bone-carvings, including some in the form of tubes, have been recorded from sites in modern Belize, including Lamanai and Sarteneja. Many have a strong foreign style, distinct from those described from Classic-period cities, which may have been influenced by the Mixteca–Puebla style of central Mesoamerica.

The close association in Mesoamerican religion between the bones of the dead and the regeneration of life (see §I, 4(v) above) may have fostered the widespread practice of collecting the heads of dead enemies and preserving their skulls as trophies. Individual examples were clearly accorded special importance, and the use of the crossed bones and skull motif was widespread in the Post-Classic period. A human skull with intricate carvings of a serpent with head turned sideways to show protruding fangs was found at Kaminaljuyú (Guatemala City, Mus. N. Arqueol. & Etnol.). Another human skull found in the 'Sacred Cenote' at Chichén Itzá had its crown cut away, its eye sockets filled with wooden plugs and still retained on its front the remains of painted plaster, which may have given it a lifelike appearance (Mexico City, Mus. N. Antropol.). The practice may have been similar to that used by the Cocom Maya of Yucatán, who preserved the skulls of high dignitaries by removing the back and replacing the face by a bitumen-like substance modelled to portray their likeness. Evidence in the 'Castillo' and other buildings at Chichén Itzá shows that human skulls and the heads of femurs were embedded in the stucco wall decorations.

(ii) Other areas. Few examples of bonework are known from the northern half of Mesoamerica that date before the 10th century AD, and not until the later period of the Huastec civilization in the northern Gulf Coast does a tradition of bone-carving become clearly discernible. Although distantly related to the Maya (see §(i) above) and sharing with them developed and refined carving techniques, the Huastecs had their own distinct style. Unlike the Maya, their work is lightly carved, with great stylization and exuberance of detail, which fills every available space. Examples include a comb carved with three serpents whose bodies are closely superimposed (London, BM) and small skulls made to be hung around the neck. Toltec artistic styles influenced Huastec bonework in the 12th and 13th centuries AD and contributed to a trend towards the abstraction of peripheral elements and deeper carving techniques.

The largest cache of bonework from the Post-Classic period was recovered from Tomb 7 at Monte Albán, a Zapotec burial chamber reused by the Mixtecs, where 34 jaguar and bird bones were found (Oaxaca, Mus. Reg.). Unlike other Mixtec bones found at Zaachila, many of these pieces were carved in deep relief, and surviving fragments of turquoise still adhered to some pieces, indicating that, as elsewhere in the region, the bones would have been coloured and encrusted with precious stones. Scenes of deities and mythological and historical events are arranged vertically and horizontally and contained in neatly divided cartouches. Some have the first 13 day-signs of the *tonalpohualli* (ritual calendar)—considered particularly propitious—and may have served as amulets. Other ideograms are similar to the pictorial style of the Mixtec codices (see §VI above) and, like them, depict dynastic successions from mythological ancestors and record warfare and conquests.

Huastec, Toltec and Mixtec bone-carving styles greatly influenced Aztec bone-carvers, and there were especially close parallels in symbolism, style and aesthetic criteria between Mixtec and Aztec work, reinforced by the presence of Mixtec craftsmen in the nearby lakeside city of Azcapotzalco and at the Aztec court. The most spectacular Aztec utilization of bone was as a cranial armature for mosaic work. Other uses included ceremonial back ornaments depicting deities, such as Tezcatlipoca ('Smoking Mirror', a creator god), and numerous rattles, rasps and perforators used for ritual bloodletting. The designs on two femurs, from metro excavations in Mexico City and from Culhuacán (both Mexico City, Mus. N. Antropol.), graphically illustrate a central proposition in Post-Classic ideology and indicate the significance of bone objects for the Aztecs. Both pieces illustrate the sun deity Tonatiuh seated in a solar disc receiving offerings of blood, from the sacrifice of enemy warriors or as part of a bloodletting ceremony by his own people. The bone rasp from Culhuacán also shows an earth deity with outstretched claws and open jaws, below the sun, receiving the bones of the sacrificed warriors. The sun is being fed with blood, while bones are consecrated to the earth, and in return the sacrificants were blessed with prosperity and abundant harvests. Other Aztec bone artefacts are decorated with serpents and eagles. Bone was used for perforators in bloodletting and for certain musical instruments to accompany funeral celebrations, both associations with sacrifice and the underworld.

BIBLIOGRAPHY

H. Beyer: *Mexican Bone Rattles*, Tulane University Middle American Publication Series, vii (New Orleans, 1934)

A. Caso: 'Sobre una figurilla de hueso del antiguo imperio Maya', *An. Mus. N. Arqueol., Hist. & Etnog.*, ser. 5, i (1934), pp. 11–16

A. V. Kidder, J. Jennings and E. M. Shook: *Excavations at Kaminaljuyú, Guatemala* (Washington, DC, 1946)

H. von Winning: 'A Decorated Bone Rattle from Culhuacán, Mexico', *Amer. Ant.*, xxv (1959), pp. 86–93

P. Agrinier: *The Carved Human Femurs from Tomb 1, Chiapa de Corzo, Chiapas, Mexico*, Papers of the New World Archaeological Foundation, vi (Orinda, 1960)

A. Trik: 'The Splendid Tomb of Temple 1 at Tikal, Guatemala', *Expedition*, vi (1963), pp. 2–18

A. Caso: 'El Tesoro de Monte Albán', *Mem. INAH*, iii (1969) [whole issue]

D. Heyden: 'Autosacrificios prehispanicos con púas y punzones', *Bol. INAH*, 2nd ser., i (1972), pp. 27–30

P. Agrinier: *Mounds 9 and 10 at Mirador, Chiapas, Mexico*, Papers of the New World Archaeological Foundation, xxxix (Provo, 1975)

N. Gutiérrez Solana: 'Sobre un fémur con grabados perteneciente a la cultura mexica', *An. Inst. Invest. Estét.*, lii (1983), pp. 47–58

M. Boxt and W. Christiansen: 'A Maya Bone Carving from Sarteneja, Belize', *J. New World Archaeol.*, v (1985), pp. 1–12, 52–63

A. Shelton: 'Central and South American Bone-carving', *Ivory: A History and Collectors' Guide*, ed. F. St Aubyn (London, 1987), pp. 314–23, 326–7

ANTHONY ALAN SHELTON

3. FEATHERWORK. The high standard of FEATHER-WORK in Pre-Columbian Mesoamerica was achieved by craft specialization and by skilful use of the wide range of colourful feathers available. Feathers were used to fashion ceremonial items, dress and adornment for the élite, and certain military equipment. Knowledge of the techniques used is based on information and actual specimens collected in 16th-century central New Spain, while the earlier history of Mesoamerican featherwork and its development is mainly derived from native pictorial material.

Two basic techniques were recorded as having been employed by the *amanteca* (Nahuatl: members of the Aztec featherworker guild). In a simple knotting technique feathers—preferably those of the quetzal, but also of other birds—were tied together in rows or shingled layers by strings and nets of maguey fibre, then sewn to a framework of cane. In the second technique, known as *ihuitlacuilolli* (Nahuatl: 'feather painting'), feathers were glued to *amate* (bark paper), cut into shape and glued again to backgrounds of starched cotton or split cane. The feathers in preserved specimens of Central Highland featherwork are attached in shingled layers from top to bottom. Both naturally coloured and dyed feathers of parrots, troupials, quetzals, cotingas, humming-birds, spoonbills, herons, eagles and other birds were used in 'feather painting'. Much attention was paid to matching the colours of the lower layers (or beds) of glue-hardened feathers and the top layers of precious feathers. The vegetal glue used was known as *tzacutli* and was derived from an orchid. Featherworkers' tools included copper knives (formerly obsidian) for cutting the feathers on wooden blocks, bone blades for pressing them to the background and painting equipment for the outline drawings.

The importance of featherwork to the Aztecs can be gleaned from the enormous quantities of feathers in the tributes paid by subject towns, as well as by the high esteem in which the *amanteca* were held. Within the guild, the élite worked as 'palace featherworkers' to make feather garments for the Aztec god Huitzilopochtli and for the Aztec ruler. A second group was known as 'featherworkers of the treasury'. The rank and file were called 'private featherworkers' and specialized in making various feather insignia for the military.

Featherwork in Mesoamerica probably originated in the Late Pre-Classic period (*c.* 300 BC–*c.* AD 250), before the 1st century AD, although the factual evidence is not strong. During the Classic period (*c.* AD 250–*c.* 900), however, feathers figured prominently in dress and adornment in all areas. Southern Mesoamerica, especially the Maya region (then and later the principal source of quetzal feathers), produced elaborate headdresses of quetzal tail feathers, the use of which was restricted to élites. Even during the early historic period such feathers served as a medium of exchange, and the killing of quetzals by commoners was considered a capital offence. Other birds, such as ducks, were bred for their feathers, which were used in the decoration of garments. Downs woven into 20th-century wedding *huipiles* (tunics) by the Tzotzil Maya of Zinacantan, Chiapas, represent the last vestige of a tradition whose decline may have started at the end of the Classic period.

Feather headdresses are also represented in Classic Zapotec pottery urns as the insignia of certain gods (Mexico City, Mus. N. Antropol.), in the contemporaneous relief carvings of Tajín and, most prominently, at Teotihuacán, where murals and figurines depict a great variety of items of clothing and ornament made from exotic feathers. In Teotihuacán iconography, feathers are not only associated with power but also specifically with water. The importance and quality of featherwork seems to have declined in the Central Highlands and in the Maya region during the Early Post-Classic period (*c.* AD 900–*c.* 1200), but was apparently re-invigorated during Aztec times, when trade and conquests once again made quetzal feathers from the south more easily available. According to Aztec tradition, this occurred during the reigns of Ahuitzotl (*reg* 1486–1502) and his successor Motecuhzoma II (*reg* 1502–20). Aztec-type featherwork was probably introduced during the same period to Michoacán which became the centre of early colonial Mexican featherwork, partly due to the efforts of Bishop Vasco de Quiroga. Tarascan (Purhépecha) craftsmen began making bishops' mitres, pictures of saints and a few non-religious works in the *ihuitlacuilolli* technique, using humming-bird feathers and European metal tools to produce work of unrivalled finesse. Feather pictures from Michoacán, made *c.* 1600 (Vienna, Ksthist. Mus., Mus. Vlkerknd), are the earliest examples of signed works by native Mexican artists. Shortly after that, Mesoamerican featherwork quickly lost its former qualities and by the late 18th century had degenerated into a mostly European-inspired form of tourist art.

Only eight items of featherwork in the Pre-Columbian tradition of Mesoamerica (all of them from Mexico) have survived. A feather apron (ex-Mus. Vlkerknd., Berlin) was discovered in a cave in the 19th century, and a feather disc (Mexico City, Mus. N. Antropol.) was found in a wall in the 20th century. The remaining six items entered European 'curiosity cabinet' collections in the 16th century. Of the four shields, the one now at Chapultepec Castle in Mexico City was brought from Austria by Emperor Maximilian of Mexico (*reg* 1864–7). It was formerly in

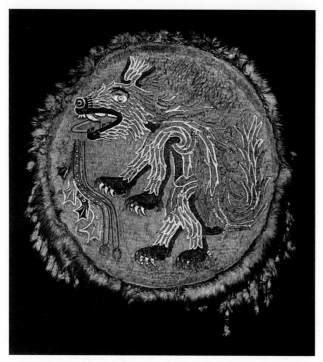

37. Featherwork Aztec shield depicting a singing coyote and the glyph 'water and burnt fields'; seed backing with sheet-gold and cotinga and other feathers glued to bark paper, diam. 700 mm, c. 1522 (Vienna, Museum für Völkerkunde)

Brussels and may have been one of the presents given to Cortés by Motecuhzoma II and sent to Europe in 1519. Two shields now in the Württembergisches Landesmuseum, Stuttgart, show variations of a stepped-fret design and were rediscovered in 1808 in the secularized monastery of Weingarten, near Ravensburg. The Vienna shield (Vienna, Mus. Vlkerknd.; see fig. 37) has a representational design outlined in sheet gold, showing a blue coyote (the patron god of the *amanteca*) singing the Aztec glyph metaphor for 'war'. It was sent from New Spain to Spain in 1522 as a present to the Bishop of Palencia. A quetzal feather headdress (Vienna, Mus. Vlkerknd.), erroneously known as 'Motecuhzoma's headdress', is the only surviving example of a formerly common type and also of the knotted technique. It was apparently not sent to Europe before 1524 at the earliest. The final item (also Vienna, Mus. Vlkerknd.) is a feather mosaic fan made with a combination of Pre-Columbian technique and representational designs of pronounced colonial influence. None of the feather shirts, capes or cloaks, upper-arm bracelets, hand banners, back devices or feather images reported by 16th-century sources and illustrated both in pictorial manuscripts and by pottery figurines has been preserved.

BIBLIOGRAPHY

B. de Sahagún: *Historia general de las cosas de Nueva España* (MS., untraced, 1569; Spanish/Nahuatl illus. copy, *Florentine Codex*, Florence, Bib. Medicea-Laurenziana, MS. Palat. 218-20, n.d.); facs. *Códice Florentino: El manuscrito 218-20 de la colección Palatina de la Biblioteca Medicea Laurenziana*, 3 vols (Mexico City and Florence, 1979); Eng. trans. Nahuatl text and ed. C. E. Dibble and A. J. O. Anderson as *Florentine Codex: General History of the Things of New Spain*, 13 vols (Santa Fe, 1950–69), bk 9

F. Anders: *Tesoros de México: Arte plumario y de mosaico*, Artes de México, cxxxvii (Mexico City, 1971)
——: 'Der altmexikanische Federschild in Wien', *Archv Vlkerknd.*, xxxii (1978), pp. 67–88
P. R. Anawalt: *Indian Clothing before Cortés: Mesoamerican Costumes from the Codices* (Norman, 1981)
C. F. Feest: 'Koloniale Federkunst aus Mexico', *Gold und Macht: Spanien in der neuen Welt* (Vienna, 1986), pp. 173–8

CHRISTIAN F. FEEST

4. MASKS.

(i) Introduction. The role played by masks was important and pervasive throughout Mesoamerican cultural history: they served a variety of functions, have been attributed widely different significance and were constructed from many materials. The transformative powers attributed to masks are indicated by the Yucatec Maya term *koh* ('substitute') and the Nahuatl term *xayacatl* ('face'). This section discusses face masks; but these should perhaps be seen in a wider context that includes the large stucco faces of deities that decorated the walls of Maya temples and palaces, the large mosaic masks buried by the Olmec as part of their architectural complexes, and the Maya and Aztec temple entrances framed by the head or jaws of an animal. All these 'masked' constructions served to mark the boundary between the world of men and spirits.

The antiquity of the masquerade can be inferred from the fossil vertebra of a camelid that was shaped to resemble the head of a coyote, found at Tequixquiac, Mexico, and dated *c.* 12,000–*c.* 10,000 BC (Mexico City, Mus. N. Antropol.). However, face or body painting was probably more widespread at this time. The earliest evidence of a well-defined tradition of masquerade dates from the Middle Pre-Classic period (*c.* 1000–*c.* 300 BC), when clay masks were made; usually circular, these are often grotesque with protruding tongues and seldom made to cover the entire face. Some were buried with the dead, but others were meant to be worn over the lower half of the face. Many examples have survived from such sites as Tlatilco and Tlapacoya in the Basin of Mexico and also further west in Jalisco, Colima and Guanajuato (Mexico City, Mus. N. Antropol.). Outside the Basin of Mexico, isolated regional styles proliferated, although face painting again appears to have been more important than masks (designs used in face painting are preserved on pottery figurines, particularly from Chupícuaro, Guanajuato and the Late Pre-Classic shaft tomb cultures of Nayarit).

(ii) Chronological and regional development. Stone masks were carved by the Olmec of the Gulf Coast and by the Chontal in north-central Guerrero. The highly stylized flattened masks of the Chontal may have been used to cover the faces of mummy bundles entombed in caves, but Olmec masks can be identified with particular beings. Prominent among these is the snarling, fanged jaguar deity associated with rain, often seen as a dominant component of Olmec iconography. A more naturalistic style is evident in the 32 Olmec masks from tombs at Arroyo Pesquero, Veracruz. They are unusual in that their surfaces are incised with patterns outlined in cinnabar, some of which may represent deities (elsewhere the masks themselves were made to resemble deities). To have been included as part of the burial caches of what appear to have been

high-ranking officials, such masks must have been highly prized. Some were purposely mutilated or exposed to fire before burial, suggesting a ritual killing of the object. Only one wooden Olmec mask from this early period has survived (Princeton U., NJ, A. Mus.), preserved in a cave on the cliff face of the Cañón de la Mano, near Iguala, Guerrero. The small pieces of jade attached to it and the hollows on its cheeks, mouth and forehead suggest that the art of mosaic work was mastered as early as *c.* 1150–*c.* 950 BC (*see* §6 below).

Between *c.* AD 300 and *c.* 600 the inhabitants of Teotihuacán made masks similar to those of the Olmec from polished black and green stone, basalt and onyx, closely resembling an inverted triangle in form. Like the Olmec stone masks, many have perforated earlobes, to which accessories can be attached, and perforations around the sides to allow them to be fastened to a support. As with Aztec masks (see below), some specimens were covered with turquoise and coral, with inlaid eyes of obsidian, pyrite or mother-of-pearl and teeth of white shell.

Despite the influence of Olmec, and, to a lesser degree, Classic Teotihuacán art, Maya masks have a unique style. They depict humans and animals, as well as deities which combine features of both. The human masks (see fig. 38) are less stylized and more expressive than those of either the Olmec or Teotihuacán and may even portray actual personages. Maya masks of this type have been recovered from tombs and were sometimes placed over the face of the dead occupant. A jade funerary mask, found in the burial chamber of the Temple of the Inscriptions at PALENQUE, is thought to portray Lord Pacal, the 7th-century ruler of the city (ex-Mus. N. Antropol., Mexico City, stolen 1995; *see also* §VIII above and JADE, colour pl. II, fig. 1). Two similar greenstone masks from Tikal (Guatemala City, Mus. N. Arqueol. & Etnol.) and a jade mask of uncertain provenance from the central Maya Lowlands may also represent deceased nobles. Like Olmec and Teotihuacán masks, they were constructed by fixing jade, shell or obsidian to a wooden template.

Though no example survives, ceremonial masks are represented in frescoes, on lintels and on vases, and modelled in clay as part of figurines. Such masks were made of wood or skin and decorated with perishable materials, and they were widely used during the Classic period (*c.* AD 250–*c.* 900) and worn by musicians, dancers, ball-game players, priests and nobles. Many represented real animals or fabulous beasts and were probably used to manifest their associated deities. After the subjection of the Maya Lowlands by the Itzá peoples, the orders of jaguar and eagle warriors were also established in the Maya region, and their characteristic masks are prominent on relief sculpture at their capital, Chichén Itzá. Eagle and jaguar masks are also shown on wall paintings at Cacaxtla.

The Zapotec made masks in jade and produced outstanding examples of articulated sculptures, such as the bat god found in Burial XIV–10 at Monte Albán (*c.* 200 BC–*c.* AD 100; ex-Mus. N. Antropol., Mexico City). Together with a Maya fuchsite mask of a lowland underworld deity, this shows that it was not only portrait masks that were interred with the dead.

The tradition of making mosaic masks was continued during the Post-Classic period (*c.* AD 900–1521) by the

38. Mask, with Olmec traits, dark green diorite, h. 175 mm, probably early Maya, from ?southern Veracruz, Late Pre-Classic period, *c.* 600 BC–*c.* AD 200 (London, British Museum)

Mixtec in Oaxaca, who also established workshops further north in Azcapotzalco to satisfy demand from the cities around Lake Texcoco. The Codex Mendoza (Oxford, Bodleian Lib., MS. 3134, Arch. Selden A.1) and the Matrícula de Tributos (Mexico City, Mus. N. Antropol.) identify the Mixtec town of Yohualtepec and another five surrounding villages as supplying ten turquoise masks a year to the Aztec court. The importance of the area as a centre of production of turquoise objects is also underlined by a cache of 17 mosaic masks found in a cave in the Mixteca Alta region. Among the Aztecs turquoise seems to have been reserved for the production of masks representing deities (*see* MOSAIC, colour pl. IV, fig. 1). Of some 25 surviving mosaic masks, 6 can be identified as particular deities. The rain god Tlaloc is represented by masks in the British Museum and the Dallas Museum of Art. The sun god Tonatiuh and a priestly deity Texcatlipoca are also represented on masks in the British Museum. A mask with protruding tongue is believed to depict the Maya merchant god, Ekchuah (Rome, Mus. N. Preist. & Etnog.) and another has been identified as Xolotl, twin of Quetzalcóatl (Copenhagen, Nmus). A mosaic mask with a beak-like visage represents another member of the Quetzalcóatl deity complex, the wind god Ehecatl (Washington, DC, Smithsonian Inst., Archvs Amer. A.). It has been suggested that the most common materials used by the Aztecs in the manufacture of masks were bone and flesh. The conquistador Andrés de Tapía claimed that the images of gods housed in shrines wore a 'second face' attached to the back of the head 'like the head of a man without flesh'. Skull masks such as those in the British Museum and Museum für Völkerkunde, Berlin, together with the various examples found in excavations of the Templo Mayor in Mexico City, may have had a similar use. Pedro Mártir de Angleria, the 16th-century historian and Bishop of Jamaica, claimed that mosaic masks were placed on stone deity images when important rulers were sick, as a ritual healing act.

Turquoise, jade and gold all had to be imported by the Aztecs and were imbued with sacred significance. The circulation of objects made from them was restricted and controlled by the ruler and the nobility. The Aztec subordination of conquered states was characteristically accompanied by the removal of their patron deities to Tenochtitlán, where the stewardship of the cult, including rights to the paraphernalia associated with it, titles and revenue, was invested in the conqueror. Once captured, many of the masks made of precious stones and metals and associated with these cults became symbols of political domination and tokens of tribute. On the other hand, threatened states could try to avert conquest by offering their adversaries masks made from precious substances.

Perhaps the most common Aztec masks were those made of the dried and tanned flesh of enemies which their assailants had the right to wear. These were worn during religious ceremonies to represent the god or goddess of growth (Xipe Totec or Toci). They were also used as offerings in shrines and sometimes sent ahead of military expeditions to formerly independent states to indicate the intention to exact tribute. A number of stone masks have survived, including two in the British Museum. These masks, which may have been used as pectorals, show the characteristic stretched skin over the wearer's face, which is believed to represent Xipe Totec.

BIBLIOGRAPHY
M. Saville: *Turquoise Mosaic Art in Ancient Mexico* (New York, 1922)
A. Caso: 'El uso de los máscaras entre los antiguos Mexicanos', *Mex. Flkways*, v (1929), pp. 111–13
S. Borhegyi: 'Pottery Mask Tradition in Mesoamerica', *SW J. Anthropol.*, xi (1955), pp. 205–13
E. Carmichael: *Turquoise Mosaics from Mexico* (London, 1970)
W. von Winning: 'Human Mask Pectorals in Teotihuacan Figurines', *The Masterkey*, lii (1978), pp. 11–16
D. Cordry: *Mexican Masks* (Austin, 1980)
C. Klein: 'Masking Empire: The Material Effects of Masks in Aztec Mexico', *A. Hist.*, ix (1986), pp. 135–67

ANTHONY ALAN SHELTON

5. METALWORK. Metallurgy was unknown in Mesoamerica until introduced from areas further south in the centuries between *c.* AD 500 and *c.* 800. The two main points of entry were the southern frontier of Mesoamerica (the Maya region) and the west coast of Mexico, which was the northern terminus of Pacific trade routes extending to Central and South America. The same basic repertory of manufacturing techniques as those developed in northern South America was also introduced (*see* SOUTH AMERICA, PRE-COLUMBIAN, §VIII, 5). Once Mesoamerican craftsmen had assimilated the new technology, they began to produce objects that reflected the aesthetic canons and belief systems of the Mesoamerican world, with all its regional diversity. Three metallurgical provinces can be defined: the Maya region, the Central and Southern Highlands and West Mexico.

(i) Maya region. The Maya zone lies on the frontier between two distinct metalworking traditions, one centred on Mexico, the other on the Isthmus of Central America, and it is the only region where these two traditions came into direct and continuous contact with one another. Mexico and the Isthmus exported metal items to the Maya zone, and local schools of metalworking had emerged in Maya territory no later than AD 900.

The original impetus came from the south. The oldest dated item on Maya soil is an Isthmian or Colombian trade piece, a jaguar-claw bead of gold alloy from ALTUN HA, Belize, dated *c.* AD 550. There are other Isthmian figurines from a tomb at Tazumal, El Salvador, dated *c.* 750. Craftsmen from this Intermediate area (Isthmian Central America and Colombia) must have taught their skills to the local Maya, for ornaments in native Mesoamerican style were being made at several localities in, or close to, the mountains of Guatemala before *c.* 900. This is not surprising, for the Highland Maya zone has deposits of gold, copper, silver and lead. The Lowland Maya region—the Guatemalan Petén and the Yucatán Peninsula—has no natural sources of metal and had to rely on imported raw materials.

This lack of metals might explain the vigorous trade with Honduras and lower Central America. With the imported metalwork there may have come craftsmen too. In 1502 Columbus encountered a trading canoe off the Bay Islands of Honduras: the cargo included cloth, cacao (chocolate) beans, weapons, copper axes and bells, and 'crucibles for melting the copper' (Bartolome de las Casas). Metalsmiths were almost certainly travelling these same routes hundreds of years before the Spanish Conquest.

A critical site for the study of Lowland Maya metalworking is CHICHÉN ITZÁ, where huge quantities of metal objects were among the offerings dredged from the Sacred Well (*cenote*). Items thrown into the *cenote* included gold alloy human figurines and miniature animals of the 'International Group' current in Panama and Costa Rica between *c.* AD 500 and 900, and also effigy bells, frog pendants and other categories belonging to the more recent styles of the Isthmus (between Mexico City, Mus. N. Antropol. and Cambridge, MA, Harvard U., Peabody Mus.). There were also Honduran copper bells, a necklace bead in the form of a turtle shell (perhaps imported from highland Mexico) and a good deal of material in purely Maya style. The finest Maya pieces are a set of gold discs embossed with scenes of warfare and sacrifice involving Maya warriors and foreigners dressed in TOLTEC costume (Mexico City, Mus. N. Antropol.; see fig. 39). The offerings in the *cenote* are not all of the same age, and they span the period from *c.* AD 650 to the Spanish Conquest; but taken as a whole they illustrate the rich and cosmopolitan cultures of the Maya élite.

Between *c.* AD 900 and 1521 metalworking became common throughout the Maya region, and large quantities of objects were produced in recognizably Maya styles. These included working tools (copper axes, fish hooks, needles etc) but consisted mainly of cast or hammered jewellery: finger-rings, masks (miniature and life-size), ear spools, breastplates, beads and pendants, inlays and overlays for carved wooden regalia, and even gold sandal soles. The rich wore gold or gold alloy ornaments and were buried with these after death; poorer people wore copper jewellery. Early Spanish accounts from Guatemala describe a world in which metal objects were commonplace and were worn by rulers and nobles, extorted as tribute and stored in royal treasuries. In this setting, full-time professional metalsmiths had an honoured place. Much of the technology persists today, but the symbolism and iconography of the native Maya world have been replaced by those of Christian Europe.

(ii) Central and Southern Highlands. By the time that knowledge of metalworking reached Mesoamerica north of the Maya region, sometime after AD 900, the Isthmian stylistic elements had been filtered out. What was transmitted to the Mesoamerican Southern Highlands was a technology, rather than a group of forms, and this imported technology was quickly adapted to serve the aesthetic demands of an internationalized Highland Mesoamerican élite. Almost all the datable material falls within the Post-Classic period (*c.* AD 900–1521). Everyday tools were made of copper and its alloys, but most of the surviving objects consist of personal jewellery, often of the highest technical and artistic quality, made in gold, tumbaga (a gold–copper alloy) or silver.

One of the richest discoveries anywhere in Mesoamerica was made by Alfonso Caso in 1932 at MONTE ALBÁN, Oaxaca. Tomb 7 at this site contained 9 burials (probably of MIXTEC lords) accompanied by 24 silver artefacts, 121 gold items and a range of objects in other precious materials (all Oaxaca, Mus. Reg.). A set of carved jaguar bones had scenes in the style of the Mixtec painted codices (*see* §VI above), and pottery in Mixtec style was plentiful at the site in general.

The jewellery from the tomb comprised ear ornaments, pendants, finger-rings (or perhaps false fingernails), a diadem and a plume in gold sheet, a bracelet, necklace beads in the shape of miniature turtle shells and jaguar molars, a little mask of the god Xipe Totec and a fan handle of cast openwork ending in a serpent head. Technically and stylistically this metalwork forms a coherent group. The finest pieces are cast by the lost-wax process, with great use of false filigree 'wirework' to form elaborate headdresses, beards, bird feathers and ornamental borders. Many objects are composite, made from free-hanging elements joined by loops, often terminating in a row of elongated pear-shaped bells that jingle when the wearer moves. Decorative motifs are drawn from central Mesoamerican iconography and cosmic symbolism. One of the most famous items from Tomb 7 is a large pectoral ornament representing Mictlantecuhtli, Lord of the Dead (see fig. 40), and is unique in bearing dates expressed in terms of the native calendars (which cannot be reliably converted to Christian dates). Another pendant is made from four joined panels representing, in descending order, two deities in a ballcourt, a solar disc, a flint knife with eyes and a wide open mouth and, finally, an earth monster. The design is completed by a row of hanging bells. On

39. Repoussé gold plate, diam. 207 mm, from Chichén Itzá, Yucatán, *c.* AD 800–*c.* 1200; reconstruction drawing of the damaged original by Tatiana Proskouriakoff (both Cambridge, MA, Harvard University, Peabody Museum)

40. Gold pectoral representing Mictlantecuhtli, Lord of the Dead, from Tomb 7, Monte Albán, ? after 1250 (Oaxaca, Museo Regional)

several of the finger-rings and ear ornaments the central figure is an eagle.

A second rich burial, with offerings similar to those of Monte Albán, was discovered at Zaachila, also in Oaxaca, and several individual items are reported from sites in the same general area. Because of the apparent concentration in the State of Oaxaca, the presence of Mixtec pottery at several of the sites and the fact that many of the symbols on the goldwork (and also some of the jewellery categories) are depicted in Mixtec pictorial manuscripts, this style of metalwork has often been labelled 'Mixtec' or 'Mixteca–Puebla'. But this is a misnomer, for objects in identical style have come from more than 50 localities scattered all over south–central Mexico, from Veracruz in the east to Soconusco, near the Guatemalan border on the Pacific side. Distribution ignores ethnic and linguistic boundaries, and the style should not be linked with any one particular ethnic group. In recognition of this situation, the title 'South Mexican International Style' has been proposed for this material. In contrast, little Aztec metalwork has survived, but most of it falls within the South Mexican International tradition. In the present state of knowledge, no separate Aztec style of goldwork can be recognized.

Ethnohistorical documents refer to tribute and trade in raw metal and in finished objects. Trade routes ran from central Mexico to the Maya frontier at Xicalango, on the Gulf of Mexico, and Soconusco on the Pacific coast. At ports of trade in these areas the central Mesoamerican and Maya worlds came into contact, and products from all over Mesoamerica were exchanged by professional merchants. These trade links help to explain the homogeneity of metalwork throughout southern Mexico and show how objects in Mexican style may have made their way to Chichén Itzá.

(iii) West Mexico. The region comprising the modern states of Guerrero, Michoacán, Jalisco, Nayarit and Colima was from earliest times a separate art province on the frontier of Mesoamerica proper (*see* §II, 2(ii), 3(v) and 4(v) above, and WEST MEXICAN ART, PRE-COLUMBIAN). Its metallurgy, too, has a history of its own. The technology of metalworking was introduced to this area *c.* AD 800 as a result of maritime contacts along the Pacific Coast. The Intermediate area contributed an interest in bells cast by the lost-wax process, and a few copper versions of Isthmian gold figurines have been found in Michoacán. The principal stimulus, however, came from coastal Ecuador. Actual Ecuadorian imports are absent, but West Mexico adopted the Ecuadorian repertory of artefacts (depilatory tweezers, open rings, needles, fish-hooks and awls) as well as Ecuadorian techniques for forging and for working sheet metal. A few items of gold and silver belong to this initial period, but the predominant metal is unalloyed copper. Some 60% of all artefacts were bells, sometimes sewn in clusters on textile arm bands or anklets. Sixteenth-century documents indicate that bells were associated with deities and worn by upper-class personages.

In the 12th century, further contacts with the south (including, this time, with Peru as well as Ecuador) brought about changes that greatly expanded the technical range of West Mexican smiths. The main change was the first use of copper alloys, notably copper–tin bronze (with up to 12% tin), copper–arsenic (containing as much as 23% arsenic by weight), copper–silver (for large sheet metal ornaments) and copper–arsenic–tin. These new alloys allowed improved versions of the traditional West Mexican forms and permitted innovations such as thin-walled bells cast by the false filigree technique. The new alloys also allowed jewellers to control colour values; alloys high in tin have a golden hue, while the addition of arsenic gives a silvery colour. A study (1994) by Hosler of more than 3000 objects in the Museo Regional de Antropología e Historia, Guadalajara, suggests that alloys were selected for their colours rather than for their mechanical qualities. All these innovations are well represented in the metalwork of the TARASCAN kingdom in Michoacán during the centuries before the Spanish Conquest.

BIBLIOGRAPHY

S. K. Lothrop: 'Metals from the Sacred Cenote of Sacrifice, Chichén Itzá', *Mem. Peabody Mus. Archaeol. & Ethnol.*, x/2 (1952) [whole issue]
D. M. Pendergast: 'Metal Artifacts in Prehispanic Mesoamerica', *Amer. Ant.*, xxvii (1962), pp. 520–45
A. Caso: 'El tesoro de Monte Albán', *Mem. INAH*, iii (1969) [whole issue]
W. Bray: 'Maya Metalwork and its External Connections', *Social Process in Maya Prehistory*, ed. N. Hammond (London, New York and San Francisco, 1977), pp. 366–403
C. C. Coggins and O. C. Shane III: *Cenote of Sacrifice: Maya Treasures from the Sacred Well at Chichén Itzá* (Austin, 1984)
W. Bray: 'Fine Metal Jewellery from Southern Mexico', *Homenaje a José Luís Lorenzo*, ed. L. Mirambell (Mexico City, 1989), pp. 243–75
D. Hosler: *The Sounds and Colors of Power: The Sacred Metallurgy of Ancient West Mexico* (Cambridge, MA, 1994)

WARWICK BRAY

6. MOSAIC. In the context of Mesoamerica the term mosaic is used for decoration made up of small pieces of hardstones and other materials applied not only to architectural surfaces (as in the Greco-Roman mosaic tradition of Europe) but also to a variety of prized objects, including vessels, shields, masks, human skulls and knife handles.

The earliest supposed Mesoamerican mosaic ornament is a group of turquoise chips found in an Early Pre-Classic (*c.* 2000–*c.* 1000 BC) grave at El Arbolillo, Basin of Mexico. Three large-scale mosaic pavements (each *c.* 4.5×6.0 m) composed of square and rectangular serpentine blocks (*c.* 485 blocks each) depicted stylized jaguar faces at the Olmec site of LA VENTA. Each was an offering, deliberately buried under *c.* 1 m of clay and adobe. A wooden Olmec mask encrusted with jade was found at Cañón de la Mano, Guerrero, dated to *c.* 1150–*c.* 950 BC (Princeton U., NJ, A. Mus.). Jade mosaics were applied to Maya and Teotihuacán stone sculpture in the Classic period (*c.* AD 250–*c.* 900). Numerous carved greenstone, serpentine, onyx and obsidian masks, sometimes with turquoise mosaic and inlaid obsidian or shell eyes, are attributed to Classic Teotihuacán, but none has been found *in situ*. At Classic Maya Palenque, the 'death mask' found in the tomb of Lord Pacal comprised a jade mosaic with inlaid shell and obsidian eyes (AD 683; ex-Mus. N. Antropol., Mexico City, stolen 1995; *see* JADE, colour pl. II, fig. 1). A unique example of portable art from the Classic period is a vessel from central Mexico covered in turquoise mosaic and encrusted with onyx. It was, however, in the Post-Classic period (*c.* AD 900–1521) that mosaic work flourished, particularly under the Mixtecs. Unfortunately, only about 25 Mixtec mosaics have survived, mostly in European collections (e.g. London, Mus. Mankind, and Rome, Mus. N. Preist. & Etnog.).

Most Mixtec mosaics consist primarily of turquoise, but jade, obsidian, malachite, lignite, quartz, beryl, garnet, jet, coral and other shells, as well as gold sheet, are also found. The pieces of mosaic are attached to a foundation material (usually wood) by a vegetal glue. The perishable nature of the foundation materials has contributed to the rarity of this art form, although many of these mosaics must have been dismantled by Europeans after the Spanish Conquest for the intrinsic value of the materials. Despite their scarcity, the surviving specimens demonstrate a rich variety of form, including body ornaments, knives, masks, shields and anthromorphic and zoomorphic shapes.

Most turquoise mosaics were fashioned for religious or ritual purposes. One such example is a mosaic mask, probably of the god Quetzalcóatl (London, Mus. Mankind). It has a cedar-wood foundation completely covered in turquoise mosaic, with teeth and eyes of white shell. The mask is pierced, as if for wearing. The historian Bernadino de Sahagún described how Hernán Cortés was decked out in such a mask by Motecuhzoma II (reg 1502–20). Tezcatlipoca, god of darkness and evil, may be represented on a human skull covered in mosaic pieces (London, BM; see fig. 41); skull ornaments were worn at religious ceremonies, and this example may have been used for that purpose. Another mask with holes for attachment (Rome, Mus. N. Preist. & Etnog.) probably

41. Mosaic mask representing ?Tezcatlipoca, turquoise and lignite on a human skull with iron, leather and shell, h. 203 mm, 15th century–early 16th (London, British Museum)

represents Xiuhcóatl, the fire serpent. At least three turquoise mosaic artefacts served as the handles of sacrificial knives. One (London, Mus. Mankind) still has the chalcedony blade attached. Such knives were used for ritual human sacrifice, a fact confirmed by many sacrificial scenes illustrated in Mesoamerican codices.

Not all mosaics, however, had a religious significance, as demonstrated by the 'monkey head' mirror (London, Mus. Mankind) and other animal designs. The serpent is the most common zoomorphic design on surviving examples. Entwined serpents appear on a serpent mask, a wooden helmet and a pendant ornament (all London, Mus. Mankind), as well as an elaborate turquoise mask (Rome, Mus. N. Preist. & Etnog.).

Shields decorated with pieces of mosaic were originally a common feature of this craft, and numerous shields appear in the inventories of goods dispatched from New Spain to Europe in the 16th century. Cortés sent 16 shields of stone mosaic work with coloured featherwork hanging from the edge of them. A shield was also found in the Great Temple (Templo Mayor) excavations in Mexico City, one of the few examples of turquoise mosaic work in a Mexican collection (Mexico City, Mus. N. Antropol.). The surviving part of another shield (London, Mus. Mankind) has the edges pierced where the featherwork would have been laced. The ornateness of such shields suggests that they had a ceremonial use.

Post-Classic mosaics were mainly of Mixtec origin. They were crafted in western Oaxaca and would have come to the Aztec capital, Tenochtitlan, by way of trade or tribute. Mosaic work was also imported by the Aztecs from as far away as Chichén Itzá in Yucatán. From the tribute list in the Codex Mendoza (Oxford, Bodleian Lib., MS. 3134, Arch. Selden A.1) it is known that Motecuhzoma II received turquoise mosaics both as raw material and as finished art. For example, he received annually from an unidentified town a dish of little mosaic stones, while ten middle-sized turquoise masks, made by Mixtec lapidaries, were sent annually from Oaxaca. The Mixtecs also made large-scale wall mosaics of rectangular stone blocks set in numerous geometric patterns in their palace-like structures at MITLA, YAGUL and other Post-Classic cities in the Oaxaca Valley. Mosaic work was also carried out by groups of Mixtec craftsmen working in Tenochtitlán itself, or in neighbouring towns: Spanish chroniclers describe lapidaries working at nearby Azcapotzalco. There are expansive descriptions in Bernadino de Sahagún's Historia general de las cosas de Nueva España of lapidaries using a special tool (pulidor de turquesas) in the delicate art of mosaic construction. The detail of the finished craft can be appreciated through the fact that a shield discovered at Puebla contained 1400 pieces of mosaic.

Highly prized as they were by their makers, turquoise mosaics were also appreciated by Europeans. Both Albrecht Dürer and Benvenuto Cellini were impressed by their quality, and many examples transported from New Spain passed eventually into Italian ownership. The Medici family of Florence were great collectors, and many of the surviving Mesoamerican mosaics can be traced back to Italian collections. It is tempting to assume that pieces found in European collections must have formed part of

Cortés's booty. Although there are inventories drawn up by Cortés of items sent to the Emperor Charles V, including mosaic work, the descriptions are too unspecific to make definite identifications with existing pieces possible. Moreover, Cortés was not the only conquistador to send items back to Europe (for example, his immediate predecessor, Juan de Grijalva, collected mosaic masks from Yucatán during his expedition of 1518).

BIBLIOGRAPHY

B. de Sahagún: *Historia general de las cosas de Nueva España* (MS., untraced, 1569; Spanish/Nahuatl illus. copy, *Florentine Codex*, Florence, Bib. Medicea-Laurenziana, MS. Palat. 218–20, n.d.); facs. *Códice Florentino: El manuscrito 218–20 de la colección Palatina de la Biblioteca Medicea Laurenziana*, 3 vols (Mexico City and Florence, 1979); Eng. trans. Nahuatl text and ed. C. E. Dibble and A. J. O. Anderson as *Florentine Codex: General History of the Things of New Spain*, 13 vols (Santa Fe, 1950–69)

B. Díaz del Castillo: *Historia verdadera de la conquista de Nueva España* (Mexico City, 1576, rev. 1904); Eng. trans. A. P. Maudslay as *The History of the Conquest of New Spain*, 5 vols (London, 1908–16) [appendix: Motecuhzuma's gifts to Cortés]

L. Pigorini: 'Gli antichi oggetti messicani incrostati di mosaico esistenti nel Museo Preistorico ed Etnografico di Roma', *Atti Accad. N. Lincei; Mem. Cl. Sci. Morali, Stor. & Filol.*, 3rd ser, xii (1885), pp. 336–42

W. Lehmann: 'Altmexicanische Mosaiken und die Geschenke König Motecuzomas an Cortés', *Globus*, xc/20 (1906), pp. 318–22

M. H. Saville: *Turquoise Mosaic Art in Ancient Mexico* (New York, 1922)

G. C. Vaillant: *Aztecs of Mexico: Origin, Rise and Fall of the Aztec Nation* (New York, 1941)

H. R. Wagner: *The Discovery of New Spain in 1518 by Juan de Grijalva: A Translation of the Original Texts with an Introduction and Notes in 'Documents and Narratives concerning the Discovery and Conquest of Latin America'* (Berkeley, CA, 1942)

M. D. Coe: *Mexico* (London, 1962, rev. 3/1984), pp. 74–5, 134, 137–8, 141, 166

G. Kubler: *The Art and Architecture of Ancient America*, Pelican Hist. A. (Harmondsworth, 1962, rev. 3/1984), pp. 185, 488, n. 53

E. Carmichael: *Turquoise Mosaics from Mexico* (London, 1970)

M. P. Weaver: *The Aztecs, Maya and their Predecessors: Archaeology of Mesoamerica* (New York, 1972, rev. 1981), pp. 212, 246

D. Heikamp and F. Anders: *Mexico and the Medici* (Florence, 1977)

Art of Aztec America: Treasures of Tenochtitlan (exh. cat. by H. B. Nicholson and E. Quiñones, Washington, DC, N.G.A., 1983)

KIERAN COSTELLO

7. MUSICAL INSTRUMENTS.

(i) Introduction. Music and musical instruments played a vital role in religious and ceremonial activity in Mesoamerica. Knowledge of the instruments themselves derives not only from surviving examples (frequently inscribed with symbolic designs) but also from their depiction in codices, frescoes, pottery and sculptures. Also important are the descriptions given by 16th-century chroniclers: according to the Spanish conquerors and priests, Mesoamerican music had little in common with European traditions; several early observers found it dismal and horrific.

It was during the Pre-Classic period (*c.* 2000 BC– *c.* AD 250) that the basic forms and shapes of the instruments were developed and Mesoamerican musical patterns and traditions were formed. From the Middle Pre-Classic period (*c.* 1000–*c.* 300 BC) come many fine ceramic figurines and hollow figures; some of these functioned as ocarinas and represented musicians. Unglazed ceramic ocarinas, flutes, whistles and rattles, and conch shells have been found in Pre-Classic tombs. In the Classic period (*c.* AD 250–*c.* 900) new and increasingly elaborate cultures developed rapidly, displaying a greater diversity of musical

instruments. During the Post-Classic period (*c.* AD 900– 1521) instruments became heavily ornamented. The frescoes at Santa Rita Corozal illustrate this type of elaborate decoration, showing the 'Merchant god' playing the rattle and drum.

(ii) Types. The varieties of different instruments were essentially the same throughout Mesoamerica, consisting of percussion instruments, membranophones (instruments producing their sound from lightly stretched membranes) and wind instruments; stringed instruments were unknown.

Mesoamerican percussion instruments consisted of various forms of rattles and drums. There were two main types of rattle: rattling vessels (Nahuatl *ayacachtli*; Maya *zoot*), made of unglazed terracotta or gourds, and rattling sticks of wood (Nahuatl *chicahuaztli*) and bone (*omichicahuaztli*). The *zoot* is depicted in three of the frescoes at Bonampak (*see* COLOUR, colour pl. I, fig. 1) and in the figures next to the 'Reviewing Stand' at Copán. On the fourth page of the Codex Borbonicus (Paris, Bib. Assemblée N., Y. 120), Huehuecoyotl, the god of song, sings, dances and plays a large flowered rattling vessel. One of the musicians depicted in the Maya Codex Dresdensis (Dresden, Sächs. Landesbib., MS. R.310) is shown playing a *zoot*, while the god in front of him holds a larger rattling stick in his left hand. The most spectacular surviving example of a percussion instrument is a whale-rib *omichicahuaztli* (l. 2.11 m; Mexico City, Mus. N. Antropol.) found at Monte Albán. This was carved with four different series of notches. Other types of rattles include bells of pottery or, after the introduction of metal *c.* AD 900, copper. Late Classic Maya figurines incorporating bells have been found at Lubaantún, Belize, and the frescoes at Bonampak include representations of ankle bells.

The turtle carapace (Nahuatl *ayotl*; Maya *kayab*) was struck or scraped with a deer antler. Three musicians are depicted playing the *kayab* in the Bonampak frescoes, and the word *kayab* (meaning 'with what one sings') was also the name of the 17th Maya month, with a glyph showing the head of a sea turtle. The turtle musical instrument depicted on the third page of the Codex Borbonicus was ritually associated with the sun and the moon.

The *teponaztli*, a type of slit-drum, was perhaps the most important Mesoamerican percussion instrument. It consisted of a horizontal hollowed-out cylinder, with an H-shaped incision forming two tongues that produced two different pitches when struck with a drumstick. The *teponaztli* is described in myths as the sacred representation of a god called Teponaztli. Having been thrown out of the sun god's court, Teponaztli brought music to the world so that people could honour the memory of dead gods and mitigate their pains with songs and musical instruments. Many *teponaztli*s were decorated with symbolic carvings, some of them elaborate and of great beauty, as in the fine example in the British Museum, London (see fig. 42). The Tlaxcala *teponaztli*, probably a votive offering, is one of the finest wooden carved objects in the Museo Nacional de Antropología, Mexico City. In the same collection is a Mixtec *teponaztli* carved with an eagle and a jaguar on one side and several gods and warriors on the other, as well as intricate designs inscribed in low relief.

42. Mixtec *teponaztli* (slit-drum), l. *c.* 365 mm, 12th–15th centuries (London, British Museum)

The 'hanging gourd' (*tecomapiloa*), a small *teponaztli* with a hanging gourd resonator, was only played by women during agricultural festivals. There is no evidence of its use in other contexts.

The membranophones included the *pax*, *huehuetl*, the U-shaped drum or *kayum* and the *zacatan*. The membranes were made of deer, monkey or jaguar skin. The *pax* (Maya: 'drum') and the *huehuetl* (Nahuatl: 'the old one') were both hollowed-out horizontal drums of different sizes. They were always played with bare hands. In the Maya region clay drums were extensively used, varying from big kettledrums to small drums in the shape of goblets, lamps and pedestals. Many have been found in tombs. The *kayum*, a U-shaped drum rather like a calabash, appears twice in the Codex Dresdensis in the form of an instrument in front of a squatting player. In the Madrid Codex (Madrid, Mus. América, Inventory no. 70300) a dog sings and plays the *kayum*. There are no surviving examples of the big Maya wooden *zacatan* drum, but it is depicted as the central instrument in the Bonampak frescoes. Macuilxochitl, the Aztec god of music, is shown playing a small *huehuetl* on the fourth page of the Codex Borbonicus, and carvings on the most famous *huehuetl*, from Malinalco (Toluca, Mus. Arqueol.), first described by Seler in 1904, depict dancing jaguars and eagles, the animal manifestations of the warrior cults to which the drum probably belonged. Also carved on the drum is the symbol of the fifth Aztec era.

Wind instruments include conch-shell trumpets and various types of flute. The sea conch shell (*hub*) makes an excellent natural trumpet and the surface of the instrument was often decorated. The Museo Nacional de Arqueología y Etnología in Guatemala City has a splendid conch shell decorated with exquisite Maya calendrical glyphs. Conchshell trumpets with relief decorations depicting deities are especially prevalent in western Mexico. At Teotihuacán the shell is a constant motif on ceramics and architecture; a shell trumpet from this site (Mexico City, Mus. N. Antropol.) is incised with the hieroglyphs for the cycle of time and the numbers nine and twelve. Seashells were possibly signs of birth and generation, and a shell was

therefore a fitting symbol for Quetzalcóatl (the 'plumed serpent'), one of the gods attributed with the creation of mankind. Some trumpets were also made of metal and wood, but none of these has survived. One term for a trumpet is *tepuzquiquiztli*, which derives from the Nahuatl word *tepuztli*, meaning metal. The Bonampak frescoes and polychrome vases from the Maya region include depictions of a large thin trumpet made of wood with a gourd bell.

Flutes in Mesoamerica were made primarily of reeds and wood. There is also documentary evidence for flutes made from pottery, bone, jade and greenstone, but the only surviving examples of these are ceramic flutes. From the Early Pre-Classic period onwards there were ceramic flutes with large bells in the form of flowers. This bell shape had no acoustic advantage but was probably symbolic of music being turned into a flower. The various types of flute included vertical ones with either a fipple or a transverse mouthpiece, as well as transverse and notched open flutes (*quena*s). Double, triple and quadruple flutes, described as the 'crowning jewels of ancient Mexican music', were common. Some multiple flutes were particularly well-crafted, and a few have no holes, being evidently intended as votive offerings rather than for playing music. The ocarina (Nahuatl *huilacapitzli*), the most common member of the Mesoamerican flute family, tends to have the most aesthetically pleasing shapes. Anthropomorphic and zoomorphic whistles and ocarinas have been found in several Mesoamerican sites, especially in the Maya region. The most spectacular ones are from the island of Jaina, off the coast of Campeche; some have remains of 'Maya blue' paint.

BIBLIOGRAPHY

Grove Instr.: 'huehuetl', 'teponaztli'

B. de Sahagún: *Historia general de las cosas de Nueva España* (MS., untraced, 1569; Spanish/Nahuatl illus. copy, *Florentine Codex*, Florence, Bib. Medicea-Laurenziana, MS. Palat. 218-20, n.d.); facs. *Códice Florentino: El manuscrito 218-20 de la colección Palatina de la Biblioteca Medicea Laurenziana*, 3 vols (Mexico City and Florence, 1979); Eng. trans. Nahuatl text and ed. C. E. Dibble and A. J. O. Anderson as *Florentine Codex: General History of the Things of New Spain*, 13 vols (Santa Fe, 1950–69)

D. Durán: *Historia de las Indias de Nueva España y islas de Tierra Firme*, 2 vols (Mexico City, 1867–80); Eng. trans., abridged, by F. Horcasitas and P. Hayden as *Book of the Gods and Rites and the Ancient Calendar* (Norman, 1971)

E. Seler: 'Die holzgeschnitzte Pauke von Malinalco und das Zeichen *atl-tlachinolli*', *Mitt. Antropol. Ges. Wien*, xxxiv (1904), pp. 222–74

D. Castañeda and V. T. Mendoza: *Instrumental Precortesiano* (1933), i of *Instrumentos de percusión* (Mexico City, 1933–)

G. Saldívar: *Historia de la música en México* (Mexico City, 1934)

C. Sachs: *The History of Musical Instruments* (New York, 1940)

R. d'Harcourt: 'Sifflets et ocarinas de Nicaragua et du Mexique', *J. Soc. Amer.*, n. s., xxxiii (1941), pp. 165–72

J. Enciso: *Sellos del antiguo México* (Mexico City, 1947)

R. Stevenson: *Music in Mexico* (New York, 1952)

S. Martí: *Instrumentos musicales precortesianos* (Mexico City, 1955)

D. de Landa: *Relación de las cosas de Yucatán* (Mexico City, 1959)

S. Martí: *Canto, danza y música precortesianos* (Mexico City, 1961)

G. P. Kurath and S. Martí: *Dances of Anahuac* (Chicago, 1964)

R. Stevenson: *Music in Aztec and Inca Territory* (Berkeley, Los Angeles and London, 1968)

N. Hammond: 'Classic Maya Music', *Archaeology*, xxv (1972), pp. 125–31, 222–8

R. Rivera y Rivera: *Los instrumentos musicales de los Mayas* (Mexico City, 1980)

ROBERTO RIVERA Y RIVERA

8. SEALS. Mesoamerican seals (Sp. *pintaderas* or *sellos*) were small and finely formed, with incised or engraved relief patterns, and were used for printing with coloured pigments. Surviving Pre-Columbian examples are made of clay or terracotta and occasionally of stone, but later seals have been found made of wood. There were two basic types: cylinder seals and stamp seals. Cylinder seals were either solid, with small knobs at each end, or hollow, to receive a stick handle. Stamp seals had flat, convex or concave printing surfaces and a straight handle on the uncarved side. The relief patterns were either for a positive or negative image (by contrast, the designs on Ancient Near Eastern seals are always negative, since they were intended to produce positive images on wet clay).

43. Stamp seals, four impressions depicting animal and plant forms: (a) monkey and vulture, Veracruz, Classic period; (b) monkeys, Huastec, Classic period; (c) Toltec design, early Post-Classic period; (d) monkey, Puebla, Late Post-Classic period

Although the seals themselves survive in large numbers, few examples of their printing have survived, and their precise uses are therefore either hypothetical or deduced from other evidence. They may have been used as body stamps or to print on textiles or bark paper, but actual imprints survive only on ceramic vessels and figurines.

The hypothesis that seals were used for body decoration is supported by several sources. Many Pre-Columbian figurines show such stamp-impressed patterns on limbs and torsos, and the general concave curvature of some stamp seals favours such a use on humans. Spanish chroniclers, particularly Diego de Landa, Bishop of Yucatán, record the use of body paint but do not clearly distinguish between seal-impressed and painted decorations. Ethnographic examples of body decoration using wooden stamps are known among Amazonian peoples. Finally, the patterns on many seals are religious symbols, and handles on flat seals were sometimes rattles used in ceremonies; both points support the view that they were used to decorate the bodies of religious leaders for ceremonies. The use of seals to print on textiles or bark paper seems theoretically likely, but no examples survive.

Actual examples of use come from ceramic vessels and figurines (see fig. 43). Concave printing surfaces on stamp seals were used to decorate vessel exteriors; convex printing surfaces for interiors or exteriors. Cylinder seals were used for continuous, rolled designs; stamp seals for single or repetitive but discrete motifs. Designs included figures of humans or animals, often stylized, deity figures and a wide variety of geometric and abstract motifs, often surrounded by repetitive borders. The pigments used were mineral-based.

The use of seals was widespread in Mesoamerica, parts of the Caribbean and in the intermediate areas between Mesoamerica and the central Andes in South America. The prehistoric use of seals in Mediterranean cultures and in the Canary Islands, and certain general similarities in style, have led to the suggestion of trans-Atlantic contact. Use in Mesoamerica began *c.* 1500 BC during the Pre-Classic period, and large numbers of seals have been found at Olmec sites in the Gulf Coast region by *c.* 1500 BC. Seals were used in the Basin of Mexico, where figurines and ceramic vessels from Tlatilco and contemporary sites were stamp-decorated (Mexico City, Mus. N. Antropol.), and as far south as Kaminaljuyú in the Maya highlands in the Middle Pre-Classic (*c.* 1000–*c.* 300 BC) and Late Pre-Classic (*c.* 300 BC–*c.* AD 250) periods.

Seals figured prominently in the Early Classic period (*c.* AD 250–*c.* 600), particularly at Teotihuacán in the Central Highlands; designs from here influenced artists at contemporary sites in the Gulf Coast, Southern Highland and Maya regions, although seals were rarer at Classic Maya sites. West Mexican cultures, particularly around modern Colima, also used seals extensively to decorate pottery. Use diminished in the Late Classic period (*c.* AD 600–*c.* 900), coincidentally with the decline of Teotihuacán. Use increased again among the Toltec in the Early Post-Classic period (*c.* AD 900–*c.* 1200) and appeared among the Huastec in the northern Gulf Coast region, possibly through Toltec influence. The Aztecs and their contemporaries made extensive use of seals throughout the Late Post-Classic period (*c.* AD 1200–1521).

BIBLIOGRAPHY

D. Ripoche y Torrens: 'Les Pintaderas d'Europe, des Canaries, et de l'Amérique', *Actes du XII Congrès International des Américanistes* (Paris, 1902), pp. 99–107

M. Ries: *Stamping: A Man Production Printing Method 2000 Years Old* (New Orleans, 1932)

J. Enciso: *Sellos del antiguo México* (Mexico City, 1947)

——: *Design Motifs of Ancient Mexico* (New York, 1953)

O. Cornaggia Castiglioni: 'Origini e distribuzione delle pintaderas preistoriche euroasiastiche', *Riv. Sci. Preist.*, xi (1956), pp. 109–92

J. Alcina Franch: *Las 'pintaderas' mexicanas y sus relaciones* (Madrid, 1958)

V. E. Estrada: *Arte aborigen del Ecuador: Sellos o pintaderas* (Quito, 1959)

G. Mayagoitia Barragán, G. M. Echaniz and C. Rábago: *Sellos arqueológicos veracruzanos* (Mexico City, 1959)

R. Parducci: 'Representación de casas en los sellos triangulares de Manabí', *Cuad. Hist. & Arqueol.*, x (1961), pp. 231–8

I. Cerezo López: 'Breve estudio de algunas pintaderas-rodillos del Departamento de Antioquia en Colombia', *Bol. Inst. Antropol.*, ii (1962), pp. 104–22

M. D. Coe: *The Jaguar's Children: Pre-Classic Central Mexico* (New York, 1965)

L. Séjourné: *El lenguaje de las formas en Teotihuacán* (Mexico City, 1966)

F. V. Field: *Thoughts on the Meaning and Use of Pre-Hispanic Mexican Sellos*, Studies in Pre-Columbian Art and Archaeology, iii (Washington, DC, 1967)

R. Parducci: 'Sellos antropomorfos de Manabí, Ecuador', *Cuad. Hist. & Arqueol.*, xvii (1967), pp. 143–67

J. Alcina Franch: 'Origen transatlántico de la cultura indígena de América', *Rev. Esp. Antropol. Amer.*, iv (1969), pp. 9–64

——: *Los Orígenes de América* (Madrid, 1985)

A. Chávez Mendoza: 'El simbolismo en los grabados de los sellos precolombinos', *Bol. Antropol.*, iii (1987), pp. 39–41

JOSÉ ALCINA FRANCH

9. SHELLWORK. In Pre-Columbian Mesoamerica shell was cut, drilled, inlaid and polished to produce objects of great religious and ceremonial value and for ornament. Shell was scraped with flint blades, cut and carved with emery and tempered copper tools and polished with water, gravel and sand, with bamboo used to give a final gleam. Its earliest use to make instruments and ornaments for body decoration dates to the Pre-Classic period (*c.* 2000 BC–*c.* AD 250). It is difficult to establish the precise areas where shell was collected and worked, but finds of large quantities of calciferous remains and the provenance of extant examples of the art suggest that it was probably concentrated and most developed in the Huastec region of the northern Gulf Coast, the northern Maya lowlands and in the south-western Central Highlands of Guerrero.

(i) Maya region. Over 190 species of seashell and land molluscs have been found at Maya sites. Most of these were unworked or had a minimum amount of alteration to their structures. Many unworked shells from Pre-Classic contexts have been found deposited around temples and palaces and may simply have been refuse from meals. Later, perhaps because the shells were discarded at the coast once the meat had been scraped out for export, the types of shells found in excavations became increasingly limited to those used for decorative or ceremonial functions. Work at Tikal, for example, shows that by the Late Classic period (*c.* AD 600–*c.* 900) shell objects no longer formed an important part of offerings.

Three distinct patterns of trade in shell can be identified and correlated to specific areas in the Maya region. The inhabitants of cities in northern Yucatán used the malacofauna of the nearby north coast, and the people of the Belize Valley also used local coastal resources. But the inhabitants of the Petén cities and central Yucatán had to import shell from the Pacific coast. At Copán and Piedras Negras, Pacific trade was prominent, but for the Petén as a whole Atlantic species tended to be imported from the Gulf of Mexico rather than from the nearby Caribbean. The Pacific trade may have been regulated by Teotihuacán, via its influence on Kaminaljuyú and sites along the Pacific coastal plain to the south of it. The symbolic significance of shell and its ceremonial use here may also have derived from Teotihuacán, but the only architectural use of shell at a Maya site occurs on a structure on the southern tip of Cozumel Island, off the north-east coast of Yucatán. A miniature temple decorates the roof and is surmounted by a rounded spire into which are embedded four lines of *Strombus* trumpets of various sizes, orientated to the cardinal points to produce distinctive sounds according to the direction of the wind.

Shell motifs occur in other media. At Tikal several large bivalves are depicted on Stele 4 and Stele 31, and Altar 4 illustrates a line of four dwarfs emerging from conch shells, a motif commonly found on Maya polychrome pottery. Sea molluscs are prevalent in the wall paintings decorating the 'Temple of the Chacmool' at Chichén Itzá, and shells appear in various contexts in wall paintings at other sites.

The shell most commonly used for both ceremony and ornament was the *Spondylus*, but larger shells, such as *Strombus*, *Busycon*, *Pinctada*, *Oliva* and various clams were also used to produce ornaments. For example, throughout the Early Classic period (*c.* AD 250–*c.* 600) *Oliva* shells were probably sewn on to textiles after removing the spires and drilling holes in the bases. These 'tinklers' were usually uncarved, but some were drilled and incised to make conical heads with large round goggle-eyes and open mouths showing prominent rows of teeth.

The hinges of the *Spondylus* shell were cut to make small beads that varied in colour from cream-yellow to orange to deep red, and they were often threaded with jade to produce necklaces for élite use. The interior was scraped to reveal its orange or red colour, and sometimes the exterior was also ground. The two valves of the *Spondylus* were often used as caskets for pieces of jade. Examples have been found at lowland sites, including Tikal, Palenque and Pusilha, in élite burials, at Copán, in a stele cache, and at highland Amatitlán, as a lakeside offering. At Bonampak wall paintings on the south wall of Room 1 show two fasteners and a pendant braided together over the white robes of the priests, possibly representing the bivalve caskets found in burials and offerings. Many caskets were found to contain powdered cinnabar, and it has been suggested that the combination of shell, jade and cinnabar compound represents the three realms: the dead, the transcendent and the blood associated with the world of man. This would be an appropriate symbolic configuration for the priesthood, which mediated between these three worlds.

Some of the finest shell carvings, for example shell relief pendants with cloisonné inlaid jade and other hardstones, have been found on Jaina Island, off the north-west coast of Yucatán. A unique work was a pair of large artificial pearls (l. 32 and 36 mm), found in the tomb of the 'Temple of the Inscriptions' at Palenque, which were made from two hollow pieces of mother-of-pearl filled and held together by limestone paste (Mexico City, Mus. N. Antropol.). Other examples include shell mosaics and inlays; splinters shaped into artificial sting-ray spines used for ritual bloodletting; trumpets made from the cut-off apical whorls of large conches; small figurines for bracelets and necklaces; and intricately carved ear spools.

Shells had numerous symbolic meanings for the Maya. Conch shells symbolized the earth, the underworld and the domain of the dead. A carving of a shell in association with the sun glyph symbolized night, and an inverted univalve shell represented the south, associated with the lords of the underworld. Mam, the ancient god of the earth's interior, is often shown emerging from a conch shell, and conventionalized *Oliva* shells and bivalves, sometimes in combination with hands, symbolized completion and zero. 'Completion' may have been synonymous with death. Shells may also have been symbolic of Ixchel, the moon goddess, connected with procreation and fertility and closely associated with water. According to Diego Landa, the 16th-century Bishop of Yucatán, the fertility designations associated with shells were emphasized by the use of *Spondylus* shells to cover the pubes of young unmarried girls. The Maya term for one large conch was *chacpel* (*chac* meaning 'red' and *pel* being the vernacular for the female genitalia).

The ornamental and sacred uses of shell may not have been mutually exclusive. Much decorative work has been found in élite and lower-caste burials, and whether as a casket for priests or as a pubic cover for unmarried girls, shell always remained a potent symbol of the cycle of birth, death and transcendence in Mesoamerican thought.

(ii) Other areas. In the Pre-Classic period large trumpets made of *Pleuroploca gigantea* shells and 'funeral pectorals', both attributed to the Olmecs, are among typical examples from Guerrero. Many examples have small faces carved on the protuberances that encircle the spiral ends of the shells, with stylized human figures and serpents or 'dwarfs' on the smooth, concave surfaces. The style of these early pieces exerted a strong influence on later carving. Sites such as Tlalnextipantli, El Ancón and Xochipala in the Río Balsas region, Guerrero, have yielded particularly fine carvings, dated *c.* AD 200–*c.* 300, incorporating spiral bands decorated with geometric designs and stylized animals. Most examples are pectorals and bracelets made of *Triton tritonis* shell found in the Gulf of Mexico and in the Caribbean. Bead necklaces made from *Oliva* shells, corals and *Spondylus* fragments, sometimes including cut-out animals and birds, jade beads and heads, have also been found in this area. Less elaborate work, of similar date, has been found at sites on the lower reaches of the Río Balsas in Michoacán and Colima.

Guerrero styles may have influenced shell-carvers at Teotihuacán in the 1st to 7th centuries AD; shell was used there to make trumpets and jewellery similar to that already described. Being associated with water and fertility, shells and shell motifs featured prominently in murals and reliefs throughout the metropolis, for example in bands on the *talud–tablero* tiers of the Temple of Quetzalcóatl.

The most accomplished exponents of shell-carving were Huastec craftsmen in the northern Gulf Coast region. In addition to instruments and jewellery, the Huastecs carved

delicate inlaid ear spools and elongated triangular pendant sets, dated *c.* AD 250–*c.* 450, which are often shown in paintings as essential parts of the regalia of Huastec deities. Triangular pendants were closely associated with Tlazoltéotl Ixcuina (an earth–fertility–weaving deity) and with Petacatl (god of pulque), while sections cut to appear as coils, with a serrated outer curve, were the characteristic wind symbol often worn by Quetzalcóatl-Ehecatl.

Pendants were made from *Strombus* or *Fasciolaria* shells, ground to their final shape but retaining part of their natural curve. Holes were drilled in the top for suspension, and the shells were polished on the obverse side. Particularly complex and intricate scenes were then incised on many of the pectorals, and small pieces cut out to enhance the carving. A common scene depicts figures, probably representing deities, astride two intertwined but dissimilar serpents with up-turned jaws. Ear spools often depict central figures surrounded by circular bands of geometric motifs or with alternating concentric bands of human skulls.

In the Post-Classic period (*c.* AD 900–1521) a characteristic Toltec shell ornament was an elliptical, hollowed-out pendant, often with a serrated edge and decorated by concentrically arranged scenes of deities or warriors lightly incised on the polished surface. Its shape suggests sexual significance, and the figure incised on one pendant has been interpreted as the goddess Tlazoltéotl, also found on Huastec pendants. The Aztecs also associated shells and shellwork with water, fertility, sexuality and with various rain and earth deities. At the Great Temple of Tenochtitlán they buried shell and marine animal offerings between the foundations of the superimposed construction phases. Throughout the Post-Classic period shell was carved and incised to make parts of implements and weapons, including finger-grips lashed to *atlatl* (spear-thrower) shafts. These sometimes depicted intertwined serpents with open jaws and eye holes, which may have been inlaid with stones.

BIBLIOGRAPHY

N. Saville: 'A Shell Gorget from the Huasteca, Mexico', *Bull. Amer. Mus. Nat. Hist.*, xiii (1900), pp. 99–103
H. Beyer: *Shell Ornament from the Huasteca, Mexico*, Tulane University Middle American Publication Series, v (New Orleans, 1933)
J. E. S. Thompson: *Maya Hieroglyphic Writing* (Washington, DC, 1950)
G. Ekholm: 'Some Collar-shaped Shell Pendants from Mesoamerica', *Instituto Nacional de Antropología y Historia Homenaje a Pablo Martínez del Río* (Mexico City, 1961), pp. 287–93
G. F. Carrasco: *Arte Pre-Colombiano de México*, i, *Conchas y Caracoles* (Mexico City, 1971)

ANTHONY ALAN SHELTON

10. TEXTILES AND DRESS. Textiles played a fundamental role in the social, aesthetic and economic life of Pre-Columbian Mesoamerica. Unfortunately, in the absence of the combination of burial practices and dry climate that preserved textiles in Egypt and coastal Peru, only fragments have survived, mainly in dry caves or in watery, oxygen-deprived environments, such as the 'Sacred Cenote' at Chichén Itzá. The earliest textile fragments (ex-Mus. Reg., Oaxaca) were found at the cave site of Guilá Naquitz in Oaxaca; they include examples dating to *c.* 8000 BC of materials produced by techniques that did not require looms—knotted netting, cordage, coiled basketry. Similar pieces from Peru and the Great Basin,

Nevada, have comparable dates. King (1973) suggested that certain non-loom techniques may have been brought across the Bering Strait into the Americas by early migrants. However, the earliest piece of Mesoamerican loom-woven cloth, which contains both cotton and yucca threads, dates to *c.* 1500 BC, well after the appearance of cotton textiles in Peru (*see* SOUTH AMERICA, PRE-COLUMBIAN, §III, 6).

Despite the scarcity of textile fragments in archaeological contexts, it is possible to discern increasing diversity and dexterity in Mesoamerican weaving as it developed from the final centuries of the Late Pre-Classic period (*c.* 300 BC–*c.* AD 250) through the Classic period (*c.* AD 250–*c.* 900), up to the arrival of the Spanish in 1519. This understanding is made possible largely by cloth and clothing depictions on painted pottery, sculpture, pictorial manuscripts, monumental carvings on stelae and buildings, and wall paintings such as those at Teotihuacán and Bonampak (*see also* §§IV–VII above). All these representations testify to the splendour of Mesoamerican textiles, and, by using them in conjunction with analysis of surviving fragments, scholars have begun to reconstruct the range of materials, colours and weaving techniques involved in Mesoamerican textile production.

The most valued fibre was cotton, both the cultivated white strain and the wild brown variety (*Gossypium mexicanum*). Although there is early evidence of American cotton (*Gossypium hirsutum L.*), dating to *c.* 5800 BC from Coxcatlán Cave in the Tehuacán Valley in south-east Puebla, by the time of the arrival of the Spanish it was used only for the garments of the upper classes. The bulk of the Mesoamerican population wore clothing made of such bast fibres as yucca, palm and istle, (the thread made from the Mexican agave). The only non-vegetable fibres and materials used were rabbit hair, feathers (*see* §3 above) and animal skins (little used in Mesoamerica). Clothing was sometimes decorated with yarns blended with rabbit fur. This type of thread took a vibrant colour when dyed, and its soft texture, sheen and resistance to fading greatly impressed early Spanish observers.

Dyeing was highly developed in Mesoamerica, and several types of natural dyes were extracted from insects, fish, animals, plants and minerals. The dye was fixed or altered in hue by using mordants, most commonly copperas and alum. There is evidence of resist-dyeing using a batik method, as well as reserved dye techniques, such as cloth tie-dyeing (*plangi*) and probably the stitch-resist (*titik*) method. Yarn tie-dyeing (ikat) may also have been employed.

The ubiquitous weaving implement of Mesoamerica—then and now—was the backstrap loom (*see* TEXTILE, §II, 1(i)). This simple device, which has no rigid encircling framework, consists of two end bars, or sticks, around which the warp is wound in a figure-of-eight to create a cross for the shed. Heddles are attached to the warps to change the weaving configuration and to speed up the weaving process. The shed rod is used to maintain the shed and warp cross, and, while the batten or sword can perform a similar function, its primary use is to press and push the newly inserted weft into place. The weaver can vary the warp tension at will by increasing the pressure on the strap or belt that passes round her back; the other end of the loom is attached to a post or solid object that serves

to anchor it. Surviving textile fragments from *c.* AD 800 to 1521 demonstrate a great diversity of weaving techniques, including plain weave, brocade, slit-tapestry, weft pile, gauze, double cloth warp float patterning, weft-warp openwork, as well as the use of embroidery.

The making of clothes did not involve the concept of tailoring (the cutting and sewing of garments from lengths of fabric was an Old World invention), and Mesoamerican clothing was unfitted. Because the backstrap loom produced webs of cloth that were finished on all four sides, the material could be worn draped on the body without further processing, or several pieces could be joined by simply sewing together the selvages of two or more webs. Thus most Mesoamerican clothing was draped. The predominant male garments were the loincloth (Nahuatl *maxtlatl*), the hip-cloth, a type of vest (*xicolli*) and the principal item of male attire, the cape (*tilmatli*; see fig. 44). The main female garments were the wraparound skirt (*cueitl*), a blouse (Nahuatl *huipilli*) and a triangular shoulder shawl (*quechquemitl*), which is apparently unique to Mesoamerica. Apart from ceremonial or warrior costumes (*see also* §10 below), Mesoamerican apparel was sleeveless.

Clothing reflected the sharply stratified nature of Mesoamerican societies. Although the various classes wore the same basic types of garments, the fabric and degree of ornamentation varied markedly, ranging from the grandeur

44. Clothing worn by Nezahualpilli, ruler of Tetzcoco (*fl* 1472–1516); from the Codex Ixtlilxochitl (Paris, Bibliothèque Nationale); patterns on cape apparently produced by tie-dye and batik techniques

of the Aztec nobles' rich costumes (marvelled at even by European invaders accustomed to the lavish fabrics of Renaissance Spain) to simple bast fibre loincloths and wraparound skirts.

BIBLIOGRAPHY

R. S. MacNeish, A. Nelken-Turner and I. W. Johnson: *Nonceramic Arte-facts* (1967), ii of *The Prehistory of the Tehuacán Valley* (Austin, 1967), pp. 189–226
K. V. Flannery, ed.: *Preliminary Archaeological Investigations in the Valley of Oaxaca, Mexico, 1966–1969* (Ann Arbor, 1970)
I. W. Johnson: 'Basketry and Textiles', *Hb. Mid. Amer. Ind.*, x (1971), pp. 297–321
——: 'Vestido y adorno', *Lo efímero y lo eterno del arte popular mexicano*, ed. R. Carillo Azpeitia (Mexico City, 1971), i, pp. 161–267
M. E. King: 'The Prehistoric Textile Industry of Mesoamerica', *The Junius B. Bird Pre-Columbian Textile Conference: Washington, 1973*, pp. 265–78
P. R. Anawalt: 'The Ramifications of Treddle Loom Introduction in 16th Century Mexico', *Looms and their Products: Irene Emery Roundtable on Museum Textiles: Washington, 1977*, pp. 170–87
J. Bird: 'New World Fabric Production and the Distribution of the Backstrap Loom', ibid., pp. 115–26
P. R. Anawalt: *Indian Clothing Before Cortés: Mesoamerican Costumes from the Codices* (Norman, 1981)

PATRICIA RIEFF ANAWALT

X. Rediscovery and collecting.

1. Exploration and documentation. 2. Museums, exhibitions and collections. 3. Forgeries.

1. EXPLORATION AND DOCUMENTATION. For two hundred years after the Spanish Conquest in 1521, only sporadic writings on Pre-Columbian Mesoamerican civilizations were produced. In the 16th century Fray Diego de Landa, Bishop of Yucatán, recorded many aspects of Maya civilization in his *Relación de las cosas de Yucatán*, and Fray Bernardino de Sahagún wrote about the cultures of central Mexico in his *Historia general de las cosas de Nueva España*. Both works were the result of the deliberate scholarly interests of spiritual conquest, but, in contrast to Sahagún's efforts to preserve, Landa burned his sources, irreplaceable Maya hieroglyphic codices (*see* §VII above), which to him seemed idolatrous. The 12 books comprising Sahagún's work remain the single most valuable source on the Aztecs and discuss all aspects of their culture. The text was written in both Nahuatl (the Aztec language) and Spanish. In the 17th century, the Franciscan Diego López de Cogolludo described the ruins of Uxmal and Chichén Itzá in his *Historia de Yucatán*. In the 18th century Francisco Xavier Clavijero, a Jesuit scholar, wrote the *Historia antigua de México*, rebutting European detractions of indigenous peoples and the flora and fauna of the Americas.

At the end of the 18th century a rebirth of interest in Pre-Columbian Mesoamerica was stimulated by Enlightenment thought. Archaeological sites became the focus of published reports, and archaeological materials were used for interpretation, rather than written and artistic sources alone. One of the pioneers of this approach was the Mexican intellectual Antonio de León y Gama, who provided interpretations of the Aztec 'Calendar Stone' (see fig. 24 above) and of the Coatlicue sculpture (the earth goddess) (both Mexico City, Mus. Antropol.) based on first-hand observation. José Antonio Calderón's documentary report on the Maya site of Palenque, written in 1784, was the first of its kind. Soon afterwards José Antonio

Alzate published a descriptive paper on the Gulf Coast site of Tajín (1785) and on the highland site of Xochicalco (1791). Renewed interest was taken in the ruins of Palenque, and it was explored again in 1787 by Antonio del Río, a military officer under orders from the Governor of Guatemala. His report, published in London in 1822, generated considerable interest in the Maya, which, in turn, led to more extensive exploration of Yucatán, Guatemala and Honduras. Guillaume Dupaix was commissioned by Charles IV of Spain to survey archaeological sites between Mexico City and the region of Tehuantepec from 1805 to 1807, with the Mexican draughtsman Luciano Castañeda. He explored Xochicalco and the sites in the vicinity of Oaxaca, as well as making a study of Palenque, and published an extensive report in 1834.

Through the 19th century the number of North American and European traveller–explorers increased rapidly. Alexander von Humboldt travelled throughout the Americas between 1799 and 1804, and his multi-volume report included geographical, geological, botanical, zoological, meteorological, ethnographical and archaeological treatises. He spent 1803 in Mexico and was the first to study the architecture of Mesoamerica systematically and to propose a chronology and stylistic system for it in his *Voyage aux régions équinoxiales du nouveau continent* (1814–25). In 1838 JOHANN FRIEDRICH WALDECK, traveller and illustrator, published *Voyage pittoresque et archéologique dans la province d'Yucatán pendant les années de 1834 et 1836*. His writings are speculative, and his drawings reflect the influence of the Neo-classical tendencies then predominant in European art. The Irish-born Juan Galindo, Governor of the Department of El Petén, Guatemala, led an official party of exploration to Copán, Honduras, in 1834. He based his documentation on what he observed, avoiding the excessively subjective interpretation so often found in reports of this period.

In 1839 the seasoned North American writer–traveller John Lloyd Stephens and FREDERICK CATHERWOOD, an English illustrator already known for his drawings of ancient ruins in Egypt and the Middle East, explored the Maya sites of Copán, Palenque and Uxmal. In 1841 they returned to Uxmal, as well as exploring Kabáh and Sayil among other sites in Yucatán. Their published works, *Incidents of Travel in Central America, Chiapas and Yucatan* (1841) and *Incidents of Travel in Yucatan* (1843), set a standard of documentary narrative that remained unequalled during the 19th century. Catherwood's drawings of Maya buildings, façades and stelae are outstanding in both their accuracy and aesthetic sense. In the 1850s the French scholar Abbé Charles Etienne Brasseur de Bourbourg travelled extensively in Central America, Guatemala and Mexico, publishing his erudite work *Histoire des nations civilisées du Mexique et de l'Amérique central* in 1857. He recovered Landa's *Relación de las cosas de Yucatán*, long buried in the archives of the Academia de Historia in Madrid, wrote a grammar of the Maya Quiché language and published the sacred Maya book *Popol Vuh* in French and Quiché.

The numbers of historical works on Mexico also increased during the 19th century. The most famous was William H. Prescott's *Conquest of Mexico*, renowned for its thoroughness, vividness and popular appeal. Published in 1834, it was both inspired by, and the inspiration for, much systematic exploration and excavation in the 19th century. Indeed, after the 1860s, more and more archaeological excavations were carried out for the purpose of gaining historical knowledge about Pre-Columbian cultures. Stephens, Catherwood and other travellers had attempted, with limited success, to use the daguerreotype photographic method to document the ruins, but serious photographic documentation began only with the development of the collodion glass-plate negative in the 1850s. DÉSIRÉ CHARNAY made three trips to Mexico (1857–60, 1880–82, 1886), under the auspices of the French Ministry of Public Instruction, and was the first to photograph archaeological sites in Mesoamerica using collodion negatives. He excavated at Teotihuacán, and his books and articles helped to increase popular interest in ancient Mesoamerica. (For a remarkable 17th-century excavation at Teothuacán *see* §2 below.)

The self-styled archaeologist and photographer Augustus Le Plongeon and his wife Alice Dixon, a London-born writer and photographer, lived and travelled in Yucatán and Belize from 1873 to 1884. They carried out a number of excavations, and at Chichén Itzá, Le Plongeon uncovered a reclining statue he named *Chacmool*. Unlike previous explorers, the pair spent months at Chichén Itzá and Uxmal systematically documenting entire buildings, including their architectural details, to create a meticulous photographic record for the purpose of analysis rather than for illustrating travel books. Alice Dixon, one of the first women to investigate contemporary and ancient Maya culture and photograph Maya ruins, wrote about their archaeological investigations and the history and ethnography of the Maya.

After the 1880s, the pioneers in Pre-Columbian studies were gradually replaced by growing numbers of university-trained archaeologists. A few 'amateurs' still made important contributions: the American consul Edward H. Thompson dredged the Sacred Cenote at Chichén Itzá; Alfred Maudslay, an English aristocrat, published extensive written and photographic documentation of Maya archaeological sites in his *Biologia Centrali-Americana*; the Austrian Teobert Maler travelled extensively for the Peabody Museum at Harvard University, documenting Maya sites in Mexico and Guatemala; and at the end of the 19th century the Englishwoman Adela Breton laboriously copied the decaying Maya wall paintings at Chichén Itzá. The archaeologist Leopoldo Batres carried out vast excavations for the Mexican government at Teotihuacán from 1885 to 1910.

Modern archaeology was introduced to Mexico by the Mexican scholar Manuel Gamio when he interpreted the stratigraphy of his excavations at Azcapotzalco in 1911 and proposed a chronological sequence. In the Maya region the North American Sylvanus Morley directed the Carnegie Institution of Washington's archaeological research in Yucatán during the 1920s and 1930s. In the 1930s and 1940s the eminent Mexican intellectual Alfonso Caso established the importance of the cultures of the Valley of Oaxaca to Mesoamerica by his excavations at Monte Albán. Since 1945 hundreds of archaeological field projects in Mexico have been undertaken by scholars and researchers from institutions all over the world. In popularizing and summarizing Mesoamerican archaeology, the National Geographic Society has published numerous books, articles and maps to explain the cultures of the ancient peoples of the region and to illustrate the archaeological sites.

BIBLIOGRAPHY

D. de Landa: *Relación de las cosas de Yucatán* (MS.; 1566; untraced); undated, incomplete copy in Madrid, Real Academia de la Historia (MS. Signatura B. 68), ed. C. E. Brasseur de Bourbourg (Paris, 1864)

B. de Sahagún: *Historia general de las cosas de Nueva España* (MS., untraced, 1569; Spanish/Nahuatl illus. copy, *Florentine Codex*, Florence, Bib. Medicea-Laurenziana, MS. Palat. 218–20, n.d.); facs. *Códice Florentino: El manuscrito 218–20 de la colección Palatina de la Biblioteca Medicea Laurenziana*, 3 vols (Mexico City and Florence, 1979); Eng. trans. Nahuatl text and ed. C. E. Dibble and A. J. O. Anderson as *Florentine Codex: General History of the Things of New Spain*, 13 vols (Santa Fe, 1950–69)

D. López de Cogolludo: *Historia de Yucatán* (Madrid, 1688)

F. X. Clavijero: *Historia antigua de México* (MS.; 1771–8; untraced); ed. G. Biasini as *Storia antica del Messico* (Cesena, 1780–81), ed. S. J. Mariano Cuevas as *Historia antigua de México* (Mexico City, 1945)

J. A. Calderón: 'Informe sobre Palenque' (1784), *Las ruinas de Palenque*, ed. R. Castañeda Paganini (Guatemala City, 1946), pp. 22–9

J. A. Alzate Ramírez: 'Descripción de las antigüedades de Xochicaleo', *Gaceta de literatura* [Mexico City], xxxi (1791)

A. de León y Gama: *Descripción histórica y cronológica de las dos piedras que con ocasión del nuevo empedrado que está formando en la plaza principal de México, se hallaron en ella en 1790* (Mexico City, 1792)

A. von Humboldt: *Voyage aux régions équinoxiales du nouveau continent*, 3 vols (Paris, 1814–25; Eng. trans. by H. M. Williams, 1814–29)

A. del Río: *Description of the Ruins of the Ancient City Discovered near Palenque* (London, 1822) [incl. 17 engrs by Johann Friedrich Waldeck]

G. Dupaix: *Antiquités mexicaines: Relation des trois expéditions pour la recherche des antiquités du pays*, 2 vols (Paris, 1834)

J. Galindo: 'Informe de la Comisión Científica formada para el reconocimiento de las antigüedades de Copán' (Paris, Bib. N., MS. 1834); ed. as 'The Ruins of Copán in Central America', *Archaeol. Amer. Trans.*, ii (1836), pp. 543–50; *R* in S. Morley: *Inscriptions of Copán*, Carnegie Institution of Washington Publication, ccxix (Washington, DC, 1920), pp. 593–604

J. F. Waldeck: *Voyage pittoresque et archéologique dans la province d'Yucatán pendant les années 1834 et 1836* (Paris, 1838)

J. L. Stephens: *Incidents of Travel in Central America, Chiapas and Yucatan*, 2 vols (New York, 1841/*R* 1969)

W. H. Prescott: *The Conquest of Mexico*, 3 vols (New York, 1843)

J. L. Stephens: *Incidents of Travel in Yucatan*, 2 vols (New York, 1843/*R* 1963)

C. E. Brasseur de Bourbourg: *Histoire des nations civilisées du Méxique et d'Amérique Centrale durant les siècles antérieures a Christophe Colomb*, 4 vols (Paris, 1857–9)

D. Charnay: *Les Anciennes Villes du nouveau monde: Voyages d'exploration au Méxique et dans l'Amérique Central, 1857–1882* (Paris, 1885)

A. Dixon le Plongeon: 'The Mayas: Their Customs, Laws and Religion', *Mag. Amer. Hist.*, 17 (1887), pp. 233–8

——: 'Yucatán Since the Conquest', *Mag. Amer. Hist.*, 30 (1893), pp. 158–80

A. P. Maudsley: *Biologia Centrali-Americana*, 6 vols (London, 1889–1902)

A. Le Plongeon: *Queen Moo and the Egyptian Sphinx* (New York, 1896)

L. Batres: *Teotihuacán o la ciudad sagrada de los Toltecas* (Mexico City, 1889, rev. 1906)

A. Breton: 'The Wall Paintings at Chichén Itzá', *Proceedings of the 15th International Congress of Americanists: Quebec, 1907*, pp. 165–7

M. Gamio: 'Arqueología de Atzcapotzalco, D.F., México', *Proceedings of the 18th International Congress of Americanists: London, 1913*, pp. 180–89

A. Caso: 'Exploraciones en Oaxaca: Quinta y sexta temporadas, 1936–1937', *Instituto Panamericano de Geografía y Historia*, 34 (Mexico City, 1938) [whole issue]

S. G. Morley: *The Ancient Maya* (Stanford, 1946)

Archaeological Map of Middle America: Land of the Feathered Serpent, National Geographic Society (Washington, DC, 1968)

G. R. Willey and J. A. Sabloff: *A History of American Archaeology* (London, 1974; London and San Francisco, 2/1980)

G. E. Stuart and G. S. Stuart: *The Mysterious Maya* (Washington, DC, 1977)

I. Bernal: *A History of Mexican Archaeology: The Vanished Civilizations of Middle America* (London, 1980)

Visitor's Guide to the Aztec World, National Geographic Society (Washington, DC, 1980) [map]

G. Daniel: *A Short History of Archaeology* (London, 1981)

G. S. Stuart: *The Mighty Aztecs* (Washington, DC, 1981)

——: *America's Ancient Cities* (Washington, DC, 1988)

Land of the Maya: A Traveler's Map—The Ancient Maya World, National Geographic Society (Washington, DC, 1989)

G. S. Stuart and G. E. Stuart: *Lost Kingdoms of the Maya* (Washington, DC, 1993)

LAWRENCE G. DESMOND

2. MUSEUMS, EXHIBITIONS AND COLLECTIONS. The collection of artefacts and information concerning Pre-Columbian Mesoamerican cultures began in the immediate aftermath of the Spanish Conquest. Much of the plunder and tribute collected by Hernán Cortés and other conquistadores was sent to Europe, some of it finding its way into the *Kunstkammern* of the nobility. Several of the conquistadores also wrote histories of their exploits, incorporating valuable information about the cultures they had conquered; two of the most famous are Cortés's *Cartas de relación* (1519–26), written to Charles I of Spain, and Bernal Díaz's *Historia verdadera de la conquista de la Nueva España* (1568). Descriptions such as those written by Bernardino de Sahagún and Diego de Landa in the 16th century (*see* §1 above) were valuable sources for identifying artefacts when excavations began over a century and a half later. They also provided descriptions of objects analogous to some of those sent to Europe. Dürer saw the objects sent to Charles I of Spain at Brussels in 1520 and wrote in his journals that in 'All the days of my life I have seen nothing that rejoiced my heart so much as these things, for I saw amongst them wonderful works of art, and I marvelled at the subtle *Ingenia* of men in foreign lands.' Few of the pieces sent to Europe have survived, but those that have include many that would not otherwise have been preserved: wooden and feather warriors' shields (London, BM); wooden masks (Princeton U., NJ, A. Mus.); helmets inset with turquoise, shell and black lignite mosaics (London, BM); green quetzal-feather headdresses (Vienna, Mus. Vlkerknd.; Stuttgart, Württemberg. Landesmus.); wooden carved and gilded *atlatl*s or spear throwers (London, BM); several Maya hieroglyphic manuscripts such as the Dresden Codex (Dresden, Sächs. Landesbib., MS. R.310), and Mixtec pictorial codices, for example the Codex Borgia (Rome, Bib. Apostolica, MS. Borg. Messicano 1); and a copy of the Aztec tribute list of Motecuhzuma II (*reg* 1502–20) in the Codex Mendoza (Oxford, Bodleian Lib., MS. 3134, Arch. Selden A.1.).

During the 17th century and early 18th interest in Pre-Columbian Mesoamerica waned as the Spanish concentrated on establishing themselves and administering and exploiting their New World possessions. One remarkable exception was Carlos de Sigüenza y Góngora (1645–1700), who excavated at the site of Teotihuacán, tunnelling into the interior of the main pyramid to determine its construction. He also formed one of the first large collections of books, letters and other manuscripts on Mesoamerica, and was among the first to regard himself as a 'Mexicanist'. In the enlightened scientific spirit of the late 18th century and early 19th Europeans and creoles began to explore ancient Mesoamerica more systematically, and the new Mexican and Central American republics also took an active interest in their heritage. Documents and artefacts were collected, exploration for new sites was undertaken, architecture was studied and the first public displays were mounted.

Earlier collections became the subject of renewed interest. Motecuhzuma II's gift of tributary items to Cortés, kept at the Castle of Ambras, near Innsbruck (by a branch of the House of Habsburg), helped to form the collection of the Museum für Völkerkunde in Vienna, and many items from the collections made in the 16th century by Giulio de' Medici, later Pope Clement VII, and by Duke Cosimo de' Medici I were given to the Museo Nazionale Preistorico ed Etnografico Luigi Pigorini in Rome. Ancient codices had been taken to England during the 17th century; these include the Codex Laud (Oxford, Bodleian Lib., MS. 54b, Misc. 678), brought by Archbishop William Laud before 1636, and the Codex Bodley (Oxford, Bodleian Lib., MS. 54b, Misc. 678), acquired by Sir Thomas Bodley before 1603–5. The Habsburg ruler Rudolf II (*reg* 1576–1608) and the Prussian King Frederick I (*reg* 1701–13) were among the European monarchs who had collections of Mesoamerican antiquities and gave pieces to friends. Philip II (*reg* 1556–98) had begun a collection in Spain in 1572 at the suggestion of the Viceroy Francisco de Toledo of Peru.

The Maya region was of particular interest to 19th-century European and North American travellers and explorers. Among these was Désiré Charnay, commissioned by the French Ministry of Public Instruction to study ancient American civilizations. He photographed sites and made papier-mâché casts of stelae and wall friezes, reporting his work in *Les Anciennes Villes du nouveau monde: Voyages d'exploration au Mexique et dans l'Amérique Centrale* (Paris, 1885). Following his lead, Alfred Percival Maudsley made several trips through the Maya region between 1881 and 1894. He was the first to study Tikal and Yaxchilán, and his casts of Maya inscriptions (London, BM) provided the basis for the first attempts to decipher them.

With the formation of national and public museums in the 19th century came the public display of Mesoamerican antiquities. Alexander von Humboldt's collections were presented to the Museum für Völkerkunde in Berlin, and the British Museum received artefacts from Teotihuacán and Cholula and from excavations on Isla de Sacrificios off the coast of Veracruz (some also went to the Musée de Sèvres, Paris, in 1842). In 1850 the Louvre opened a special gallery for its American antiquities, containing, according to the catalogue by Adrien de Longperier, 657 items from Mexico. By 1878 the Palais du Trocadéro in Paris contained an important collection; and the private collectors William Keating (1799–1840) and Joel Roberts Poinsett (1779–1851) donated a collection of ancient Mexican ceramics to the American Philosophical Society in 1849. In 1850 the English collector Henry Christy travelled in Mexico with the anthropologist Edward B. Tylor, specifically to purchase objects. When he died in 1865 he left his collections, including 602 Mexican pieces, to the British Museum. Similarly the collections of the Museum für Völkerkunde in Berlin were built up by

45. Exhibition of Mesoamerican art at the Egyptian Hall, Piccadilly, London, 1824–5; engraving from W. Bullock: *A Description of the Unique Exhibition Called Ancient Mexico* (London, 1824) (London, British Museum)

additions from Eduard Seler, who travelled throughout Mesoamerica from 1887. Seler was a lifelong scholar of ancient Mesoamerica, who made use of documentary, religious, ethnographic and linguistic as well as archaeological sources.

The earliest well-known public exhibition, however, had been mounted by the pioneer museologist William Bullock (1773–1849). He established his popular Egyptian Hall in Piccadilly, London, in 1815 (see fig. 45). Anticipating Christy, he travelled to Mexico in 1822 to purchase or make casts of Mexican specimens, including casts of a statue, 2.75 m high, of Coatlícue (the earth goddess) and of the Aztec 'Calendar Stone' (see fig. 24 above) (both Mexico City, Mus. N. Antropol.). His exhibition included 52 items and occupied the Egyptian Hall from April 1824 to September 1825; his *Description of the Unique Exhibition Called Ancient Mexico* (London, 1824) was the first such catalogue ever published. Extremely popular, it received accolades in *Ackerman's Repository* and from William Jerdan in the *Literary Gazette*. From his journal Bullock published the 532-page *Six Month's Residence and Travels in Mexico* (London, 1824). Some of his collection was later donated to the British Museum.

The largest collection of Mesoamerican materials, the Museo Nacional de Antropología in Mexico City, began to be assembled in 1771, when Viceroy Bucareli ordered the establishment of a museum for native antiquities at the university in Mexico City. It became an official museum in 1822, under the new Mexican Republic, and in 1825 rooms were found to house it. Its principal proponent was the president, Lucas Alamán, and the collections comprised the statues of Coatlícue and, later, Tizoc (the 7th Aztec ruler), found in the Plaza Mayor excavation of 1790; several small private collections; and half of the collections built up by Guillaume Dupaix while making a survey of Mesoamerican antiquities for Charles IV of Spain. For more than 40 years the museum consisted of two rooms and a patio and was opened and closed according to political vicissitude between 1833 and 1865. In 1865 the Habsburg emperor of Mexico Maximilian (*reg* 1864–7) declared it an independent body and moved the collections to the Palacio Nacional at Calle de Moneda, where they remained and grew until the construction of the purpose-built Museo Nacional de Antropología in Chapultepec Park, opened on 17 September 1964.

Another large collection, now the Museo Nacional in Guatemala City, opened in 1866 and had an equally chequered history; other large collections in Mexico include regional museums in the cities of Tenango del Valle, Veracruz, Jalapa, Mérida, Morelia, Oaxaca, Guadalajara and Colima.

In the USA, one of the largest collections of Mesoamerican artefacts is the Dumbarton Oaks Pre-Columbian Collection (Washington, DC). Other large collections are at the National Museum of Natural History (Washington, DC), the American Museum of Natural History (New York), the Museum of the American Indian, Heye Foundation (New York), and the Princeton University Museum. The Peabody Museum at Harvard University (Cambridge, MA) has a notable Maya collection, and the Peabody Museum of Natural History (Yale University) also has an important Mesoamerican collection.

Europe's largest collections include the British Museum, the Liverpool City Museum, which has important Mesoamerican codices, the University Museum of Archaeology and Anthropology in Cambridge, the Louvre and the Musée de l'Homme in Paris, the Museum für Völkerkunde in Basle, the Museum für Völkerkunde und Vorgeschichte in Hamburg, the Museum für Völkerkunde in Berlin, the Museum für Völkerkunde in Vienna, the Württembergisches Landesmuseum in Stuttgart, which holds jade pieces, feather shields and a *Xolotl* (god) carved in greenstone, the Museo Nazionale Preistorico ed Etnografico Luigi Pigorini in Rome, the Vatican Museum, Rome, and the Real Casa, Patrimonio Nacional, Palacio Real in Madrid.

BIBLIOGRAPHY
R. L. Brunhouse: *In Search of the Maya: The First Archaeologists* (Albuquerque, 1973)

V. von Hagen: *Search for the Maya: The Story of Stephens and Catherwood* (Farnborough, 1973)

G. R. Willey and J. A. Sabloff: *A History of American Archaeology* (London, 1974; London and San Francisco, 2/1980)

R. L. Brunhouse: *Pursuit of the Ancient Maya: Some Archaeologists of Yesterday* (Albuquerque, 1975)

W. M. Bray, E. H. Swanson and I. S. Farrington: *The New World* (Oxford, 1977)

I. Bernal: *A History of Mexican Archaeology: The Vanished Civilizations of Middle America* (London, 1980)

J. L. Lorenzo: 'Notes on the History of Ibero-American Archaeology', *Towards a History of Archaeology*, ed. G. Daniel (London, 1981), pp. 133–45

D. Schávelzon: 'La primera excavación arqueológica de América: Teotihuacán en 1675', *An. Antropol.*, xx (1983), pp. 121–34

E. P. Alexander: 'William Bullock: Little-remembered Museologist and Showman', *Curator*, xxviii/2 (1985), pp. 117–47

DAVID M. JONES

3. FORGERIES. The earliest imitations of Aztec pottery were commissioned in the mid-16th century by Spanish administrators to satisfy increasing demand for such curiosities in their homeland. They are a mixture of native symbols and European designs in grotesque forms, such as jars with whistles around the rim, or clarinet-like flutes in the shape of a crocodile. At Tlatelolco (Mexico City) workshops continued to produce fanciful copies of Pre-Columbian models until the 1860s.

In the later 20th century the production of forgeries of portable art objects mushroomed to satisfy tourist demand. In most cases such forgeries can be recognized on the basis of anomalies in shape, colour and iconographic details, although deceptively sophisticated objects have been produced by skilled commercial fakers, aided by illustrated books and feedback from buyers. A case in point is the application of black spattering (soluble in water or acetone) to ceramic art from West Mexico: authentic figures have black spots resulting from long contact in a tomb with soil containing manganese dioxide, which causes black deposits in characteristic form on the clay surface (these are not removable with ordinary solvents).

Collectors' interest in polychrome Maya vases depicting courtly scenes with hieroglyphs led to high-priced, well-made forgeries, produced in workshops in Yucatán. Iconographically it is possible to detect mistakes in attributes and in the glyphs. More puzzling are genuine vases, the surface decoration of which has flaked off and has been arbitrarily 'restored'. The inside and base retain an antique appearance and would pass a thermoluminescence test. Maya sculptural art—relief panels, stelae, stucco heads—have also been faked. In 1987 a drawing of a monument excavated at Tikal provided the inspiration for a slightly inaccurate copy intended for the art market.

A study in the 1980s of 2000 Zapotec urns, among the estimated 4000 urns in worldwide collections, claims that 400 are forgeries made between 1907 and 1927. These ceramic tomb offerings portray deity impersonators with numerous mould-made ornaments (for which fakers use ancient moulds) (*see also* §VII above). Spurious human masks of polished jade or greenstone usually have exaggerated features but include biconical suspension holes, drilled from both sides in the ancient method. The discovery of a large cache of fine plain jade celts provided

one forger with the opportunity to recarve them to represent spurious but well-made pectorals.

The scarcity of Pre-Columbian and early post-Conquest pictorial manuscripts (*see* §VI above) prompted the faking of dozens of these. Comparison with genuine codices reveals iconographic inconsistencies and the use of improper materials, pigments and format. In the late 19th century a number of forgeries were made by the official draughtsman of a major museum; he etched the designs on copper plates exhibited in connection with the quartercentenary of Columbus's discovery of America, and prints were published in Mexico in 1892, but the plates were not identified as forgeries until much later. The discovery of bundles of ancient bark paper in a dry cave in the Tehuacán Valley gave rise to suspicions that these materials may still be used, as in the 16th century, for making spurious codices.

Although crude forgeries can be readily recognized, the existence of sophisticated forgeries poses difficulties. Thus the authenticity of a number of well-known sculptures in museums is still debated. Among these are stone masks with intricate relief carving on the inside, which were acquired between 1850 and 1870 by the British Museum and other European museums. Although they have frequently been published as masterpieces of Aztec art, and their iconographic details have been found to be correct, some doubt has been cast on their authenticity. The famous Aztec crystal skull (London, BM) may be Italian Renaissance work, as one line of the carving suggests that a jeweller's wheel was used to make the cut.

Detection of forgeries (objects made deliberately to deceive) or fakes (genuine pieces altered to increase their value) by scientific means is not always certain. Radiocarbon tests on organic materials can be misleading when wooden beams, salvaged from ruins, have been recarved as statues. The accuracy of thermoluminescence tests for pottery remains controversial, and there are pitfalls with the process. For example, large Olmec 'baby-face' figures have been pieced together by using authentic fragments in places where test borings are usually performed, such as the underside.

BIBLIOGRAPHY
L. Batres: *Antigüedades mejicanas falsificadas: Falsificación y falsificadores* (Mexico City, 1910)

J. E. S. Thompson: 'The Grolier Codex', *Contributions of the University of California Archaeological Research Facility, Studies in Ancient Mesoamerica II*, xxvii (1975), pp. 1–9

Falsifications and Misreconstructions of Pre-Columbian Art: A Conference: Dumbarton Oaks, Washington, DC, 1978

P. Monge: 'Les "Urnes funéraires" zapotèques: "Collectionnisme" et contrefaçon', *J. Soc. Américanistes*, lxxiii (1987), pp. 7–50

HASSO VON WINNING

Mesopotamia. Region of the ancient world corresponding roughly to modern Iraq, north-east Syria and parts of south-east Turkey. The name Mesopotamia (anc. Gr.: 'between the rivers') was coined by ancient Greek historians and originally applied to the land between the River Euphrates and its tributary the Khabur. It later came to mean the land between two of the great rivers of antiquity, the Tigris and the Euphrates, and by extension includes the surrounding regions (see fig. 1). Modern political boundaries, however, do not reflect the fluctuating cultural

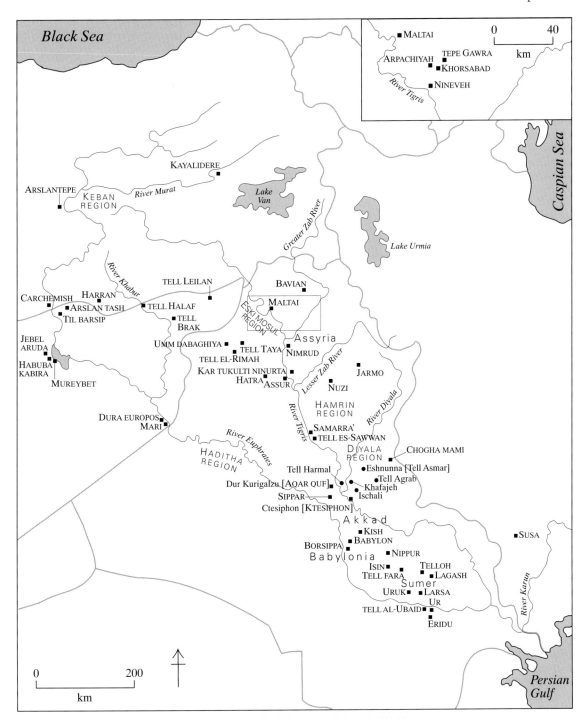

1. Map of Mesopotamia; those areas with separate entries in this dictionary are distinguished by CROSS-REFERENCE TYPE

patterns of antiquity, nor did the ancient inhabitants of the Tigris and Euphrates valleys have one name to describe the area, and the term Mesopotamian is therefore used in this article to define various cultures that grew up in the Land of the Twin Rivers. It was here and in ANCIENT EGYPT that two of the earliest civilizations evolved.

This article covers the major art forms in Mesopotamia before the Islamic conquest (AD 637). Each major bold subsection has cross-references to individual sites of importance. Certain types of object, such as seals or jewellery, the use of some materials (e.g. faience, glass and ivory) and aspects of the cultural history of the region and its rediscovery in modern times by scholars and archaeologists are treated elsewhere in this dictionary in the wider context of the ANCIENT NEAR EAST, where they are discussed in conjunction with ANCIENT ANATOLIA, ANCIENT IRAN and SYRIA-PALESTINE.

GENERAL BIBLIOGRAPHY

H. Frankfort: *The Art and Archaeology of the Ancient Orient*, Pelican Hist. A. (Harmondsworth, 1954, rev. 4/1970)

G. Roux: *Ancient Iraq* (London, 1964/*R* Harmondsworth, 1966, rev. 1980/*R* 1986)

E. Strommenger and M. Hirmer: *The Art of Mesopotamia* (London, 1964)

J.-C. Margueron: *Mesopotamia* (London, 1965)

A. Moortgat: *Die Kunst des alten Mesopotamien* (Cologne, 1967; Eng. trans., London, 1969)

W. Orthmann, ed.: *Der alte Orient*, Propyläen Kstgesch. (Berlin, 1975)

D. Oates and J. Oates: *The Rise of Civilization*, The Making of the Past (Oxford, 1976)

P. Amiet: *L'Art antique du Proche Orient* (Paris, 1977; Eng. trans., New York, 1980)

N. Postgate: *The First Empires*, The Making of the Past (Oxford, 1977)

S. Lloyd: *The Archaeology of Mesopotamia* (London, 1978, rev. 1984)

I. Introduction. II. Architecture. III. Sculpture. IV. Metalwork. V. Pottery. VI. Wall painting. VII. Museums, collections and exhibitions.

I. Introduction.

1. Geography and trade. 2. Chronological survey. 3. Religion and iconography.

1. GEOGRAPHY AND TRADE. Mesopotamia is bounded to the east and north by mountains and to the west by the Syrian desert; to the south-east it includes the Khuzistan Plain and extends to the head of the Persian Gulf. The rivers Tigris and Euphrates both have their sources in eastern Turkey. The Euphrates swings westwards and then runs south-east across Syria. The Tigris crosses the mountains of Kurdistan in the north of Iraq and has a series of left-bank tributaries flowing down from the Zagros Mountains to the east: the Greater and Lesser Zab, the Diyala, the Kerkha and the Karun. Near Baghdad the two rivers come close together, and some of the great cities of the ancient world grew up at this strategic point: Babylon, Agade, Sippar, Ktesiphon, Seleucia-on-the-Tigris and Baghdad itself. This area was known as Akkad and later as Babylonia. Further south the rivers diverge again, and the area between them was the ancient land of Sumer. Still further south the Tigris flows through marshes, which teem with fish and whose reed architecture of cathedral-like *mudhifs* has not altered since it was first depicted on seals of the late 4th millennium BC. Nowadays the rivers join together to form the Shatt al-'Arab, but in antiquity they ran separately into the sea through an area the Sumerians called the Edin, a word meaning 'plain', 'steppe' or 'arable land', which has come down through the Bible as the Garden of Eden. The Sumerian paradise, however, lay well to the south in Dilmun, which from the second half of the 3rd millennium BC can be identified as the island of Bahrain in the Persian Gulf. This was a major staging point on the trade routes to Arabia, the south coast of Iran and the Indus Valley, lands that the inhabitants of ancient Mesopotamia called Magan and Meluhha.

Northern Mesopotamia consists of the area between the rivers Khabur and Tigris, known today as the Jazira or 'island', and the triangle between the Tigris and the Lesser Zab that was the Assyrian heartland where the cities of Assur, Nimrud, Khorsabad and Nineveh were situated. Rainfall in northern Mesopotamia is sufficiently abundant for agriculture to be possible without irrigation, and the whole area is dotted with the ruin mounds of ancient settlement sites, some of which go back to *c.* 10,000 BC. These mounds are known as *tell* (Arab.), *tepe* or *hüyük* (Turk.), words that often occur in the names of ancient sites (*see* ANCIENT NEAR EAST, §I, 2(i)(a)).

In the spring, when the mountain snows melt, the Tigris and Euphrates carry down rich alluvium, which they deposit on the plains of southern Iraq. Sometimes there are disastrous floods, for the Tigris is the only river that can increase its volume 94 times. Memories of some of these floods were incorporated into the *Epic of Gilgamesh* and the biblical story of Noah. A series of dams has been built across the Tigris, the Euphrates and several of their tributaries in attempts to control the flow of water, and the associated rescue excavations have cast light on the cultural development of such areas as the Eski Mosul and Hamrin regions. In antiquity the rich alluvial deposits of the south could be exploited only by means of irrigation, and the earliest settlements do not go back beyond the 6th millennium BC. A network of canals and irrigation channels was built across the land of Sumer, draining from one river into the other. This corporate effort led to the development of an efficient administration, the invention of writing (*see* ANCIENT NEAR EAST, §I, 3) and the gradual development of an urban economy. Clay was used for making tablets on which business transactions and, later, historical and literary compositions were recorded in cuneiform writing.

The dearth in such raw materials as stone, metals and even wood, other than the fibrous date-palm, encouraged trade. Stone and wood were obtained from the mountains to the east and north of Mesopotamia, silver from the Amanus Mountains on the borders of north-west Syria and Turkey, gold may have come from the Caucasus, copper was imported from several sources including Meluhha (possibly the Indus Valley), cedar-wood came from the Lebanon, lapis lazuli and possibly tin from as far afield as Afghanistan. To handle this trade important cities, such as Uruk, Ur, Larsa and Lagash, grew up along the canals leading to the rivers that were Mesopotamia's lifeline, but many smaller settlement mounds are now buried under the alluvium, and the high water table has flooded the early levels of such sites as Babylon.

DOMINIQUE COLLON

2. CHRONOLOGICAL SURVEY. This section discusses developments in Mesopotamia from *c.* 8000 BC to the Islamic conquest (AD 637) in chronological order, outlining the characteristics of the main cultures and civilizations of the region. Major art forms, such as architecture and sculpture, are also treated separately in §§II–VI below. For the methods and evidence used in establishing a chronology *see* ANCIENT NEAR EAST, §I, 2(ii).

(i) Prehistoric period. (ii) Historic period.

(i) Prehistoric period.

(a) Before *c.* 6000 BC. (b) *c.* 6000–*c.* 4000 BC. (c) *c.* 4000–*c.* 2900 BC (Uruk period, including Jemdet Nasr period).

(a) Before c. *6000* BC. The earliest signs of human activity in Mesopotamia, some 100,000 years ago, have

been identified in the western Zagros Mountains. This Middle Palaeolithic (Mousterian) population is best known from the site of Shanidar, where a skeleton found purposefully buried and strewn with flowers provides the world's earliest evidence for such caring treatment of the dead (*c.* 50,000 BC). By *c.* 9000 BC the earliest settlements are found in the foothills of the Zagros and Taurus mountains and at the edge of the northern plain. Of especial significance at this time are the sites of MUREYBET and Abu Hureyra, on the Euphrates in the steppe country of north-west Syria. These are relatively large, apparently permanent village sites, peopled by possibly the earliest farmers so far identified, who also continued to obtain much of their food by hunting, fishing and collecting. The first known pottery is found at Mureybet (*c.* 8000 BC; *see also* §V, 1 below).

In Iraq the aceramic site of Maghzaliyah near Tell Afar is unique in being surrounded by a megalithic stone wall (*c.* 7000 BC). Several other aceramic sites have been identified in this area, significantly altering conventional interpretations of Mesopotamian prehistory. By this time sheep and goats and such plants as cereals and legumes had been domesticated, and by *c.* 6000 BC small farming villages with an economy based on a wide variety of domesticated crops and sheep, goats, cattle and pigs existed throughout Mesopotamia.

The next earliest excavated sites are nearby Kültepe and Tell es-Sotto, together with UMM DABAGHIYA near Hatra in the Jazira, where a 7th-millennium BC culture, characterized by simple, lightly fired buff pottery, often elaborately decorated, has been identified. There is no agreed name for this archaeological assemblage, variously referred to as Sotto, Jazira or simply proto-Hassuna. It is closely related to that at Buqras in Syria and to the succeeding Hassuna culture (6th millennium BC; *see* §(b) below).

(b) c. *6000–c. 4000* BC.

Hassuna culture. The site of Hassuna near Mosul in northern Iraq gave its name to a culture that is found throughout the north Mesopotamian plain in the first half of the 6th millennium BC wherever rain-fed agriculture was possible (roughly north of the 300 mm rainfall isohyet). The distinctive Hassuna pottery is handmade and includes painted, incised, painted-and-incised and simple undecorated types. Pottery kilns capable of reading temperatures of 1000˚C have been found at Yarim Tepe (*see* YARIM TEPE (ii)). Houses are made of *tauf* (packed mud) and are generally multi-roomed rectangular structures. Small hammered copper objects, first attested at Çayönü (*c.* 7200 BC), occur, and at Yarim Tepe I a large lead bracelet was discovered. At the latter site there is evidence for the smelting of both copper and lead (*see* §IV, 1 below).

Zagros culture. Contemporary with the developments on the northern plain are village settlements in the Zagros Mountains, of which the best-known is JARMO. The earliest levels of Zagros sites are often aceramic, but during the 7th millennium BC another early form of painted pottery made its appearance: simple geometric designs are employed, including a distinctive 'tadpole' pattern. At Jarmo over 5000 unbaked clay figurines were found, both animal

and human, the latter normally female and often with stalk-like heads. The relationship between these early Zagros sites and those of the northern plain, namely Maghzaliyah and Tell es-Sotto, is far from clear, though it is hoped that excavations on aceramic sites in the vicinity of the latter will help to resolve this question. However, the distinctive tadpole pottery has not been found at proto-Hassuna sites, while the chipped stone industries of Maghzaliyah and Umm Dabaghiyah display some similarities to those of both the Levant and the Zagros, and a varied ground stone industry, including stone bowls and bracelets, is common to both the Zagros area and the northern plain. Certainly there is no evidence that the culture of the early farmers of Maghzaliyah, Sotto and Umm Dabaghiyah developed directly from that of such sites as Jarmo in the hills. Indeed, in the mountains the Zagros culture persisted well into the 6th millennium BC (e.g. at Tepe Sarab in Iran), by which time the Hassuna culture was flourishing in the northern plain (see above).

Samarra' culture. The SAMARRA' culture (second half of the 6th millennium BC) was at least partially contemporary with the Hassuna culture. The Samarran assemblage is found in central Iraq, from Baghouz on the Euphrates in Syria eastwards to the Zagros foothills, and its farmers appear to have been the first in Mesopotamia to employ irrigation (as at CHOGHA MAMI). The earliest known Mesopotamian use of mud-brick (handmade and usually long 'prismatic' or 'cigar-shaped') is found on Samarran sites (*see also* §II, 2 below). Samarran pottery was remarkably well made, and for the first time humans and animals are common in painted decoration. At TELL ES-SAWWAN exceptional grave goods consisted of ground stone figurines and vessels, often carved with great sensitivity. Samarran sites have also yielded many baked clay figurines, usually female, which vary in style from site to site. Certain shared traits include 'coffee-bean' eyes, elongated headdresses, and appliqué necklaces and other ornament. Some of the figurines from Chogha Mami are unusually naturalistic (for illustration *see* CHOGHA MAMI), and at Yarim Tepe (ii) many of the female figurines wear unusual 'flounced' skirts. The earliest terrestrial iron object comes from a prehistoric Samarran grave at Samarra' itself, while copper objects are not uncommon. The earliest seals and the widespread use of potters' marks suggest an increasing degree of specialization. Samarran pottery is found on sites in the Zagros (Shemshara) and in the later phases of Hassuna occupation in northern Mesopotamia; but whether this extension northwards represented a Samarran incursion or local imitation is unclear. At Chogha Mami the Samarran assemblage is followed by one sometimes termed Chogha Mami Transitional (see fig. 18 below), in which pottery resembling a combination of Samarran and that from the earliest Ubaid settlements in southern Mesopotamia was first identified.

Halaf culture. Contemporary with Hassuna and Samarra', though almost certainly not with their earliest manifestations, is another north Mesopotamian farming society, whose pottery is among the finest ever made in the Near East. It is known as Halaf, after the site of TELL HALAF near the River Khabur in north-east Syria. The Halaf potters, whose sources of clay seem to have differed from those of their Hassuna and Samarra' neighbours, achieved exceptional elaboration and delicacy of design with their fine quality ware (see fig. 17 below). In the latest Halaf phase (*c.* 4500 BC) beautifully painted polychrome ceramics were produced (*see also* §V, 1 below). A great variety of amulets and stamp seals of geometric design occurs on Halaf sites, as well as a variety of largely female terracotta figurines. Although a possible relationship between the Hassuna and Samarra' peoples can be argued, the Halaf assemblage seems to identify a distinct group, whose geographical distribution extends west to the Mediterranean and north-east to the Caucasus. Circular dwellings, built of *tauf*, are characteristic. First identified at Tell Halaf and common on sites in the Khabur region (e.g. TELL BRAK) and the Upper Tigris Valley, this assemblage is best attested at ARPACHIYAH and Yarim Tepe (ii). In the HAMRIN REGION and at Chogha Mami the latest phase of Halaf, characterized by the finest polychrome pottery, is contemporary with Ubaid 3 (see below); in other words, Halaf persists, at least in central Mesopotamia, well into the period occupied by Ubaid. At Yarim Tepe (ii) the evidence for ceramics and material culture is unusually extensive and includes various zoomorphic vessels and a unique example of a hollow female figure, some 250 mm high, with elaborately painted features, apparently part of a ritually broken and burnt cache.

Ubaid culture. In southern Mesopotamia evidence for settlement is not as early as in the north, since village life could only be supported by irrigation, though its use need not have been technologically elaborate. This is not to say that the land was previously empty, since hunters and fishers could have lived well on the resources of the famous marshes. Moreover, in southern Mesopotamia archaeological knowledge is limited by the fact that many early sites are covered by the thick layers of alluvial silt deposited every spring by the flooding rivers.

The Ubaid culture takes its name from TELL AL-UBAID south of the Euphrates near Ur, and its sequence of pottery styles provides the basis for a chronological division into four phases, spanning most of the 5th millennium BC. The earliest site yet identified is Tell el-'Oueili (Tell Awayli), near Larsa, but the nearby site of ERIDU provides the longest sequence for the Ubaid period. Ubaid phase 1, also known as the Eridu phase, is characterized by distinctive and well-made monochrome pottery with a limited distribution in southern Mesopotamia. However, the Ubaid component of Chogha Mami Transitional pottery (see above and fig. 18 below) has now been found at Tell el-'Oueili, in levels that significantly pre-date the earliest levels at Eridu. At both these sites, as well as at related sites in Khuzistan in south-west Iran (e.g. Chogha Mish and Chogha Sefid), cigar-shaped mud-bricks were employed, a tradition that seems to have originated in Samarran Mesopotamia. The precise origin of the 'Oueili ceramic tradition remains to be established, though it seems likely to have been indigenous in the south. The Ubaid phase 2 (also termed Hajji Muhammad after a small site of that name near Uruk) is known as far north as Chogha Mami and the Hamrin region, but the unique presence of a few Ubaid 2 sherds at Tell Brak in Syria identifies an early diffusion up the Euphrates and Khabur

rivers. This distinctive pottery often has all-over paint and 'negative' designs. Ubaid 3 and 4 wares, comprising monochrome pottery with simple geometric designs, are found from the Balkh in Syria to the Eastern Province of Saudi Arabia, a geographical distribution that suggests a pattern of diffusion from southern Mesopotamia northwards and down the Gulf.

During the Ubaid period the farming villages of the south began to develop into towns, with indications of increasingly elaborate social and political institutions. This is demonstrated by the public buildings of the large settlement at Tell 'Uqair, the complex temple architecture at TEPE GAWRA and Eridu (*see also* §II, 2 below) and, at the end of the period, the increasing appearance of stamp seals, used to signify ownership or the receipt of property (e.g. at Tepe Gawra). The site of Tell Abada provides the best illustration of village architecture, the houses being characterized by the use of the cruciform tripartite plan (for illustration of a similar plan at Tell Kheit Qasim III *see* HAMRIN REGION). Unique evidence for the provision of water from a reservoir by means of jointed terracotta pipes was also found there.

Other artefacts from Ubaid Mesopotamia include baked clay figurines, usually though not always female, decorated with painted or appliqué ornament. A distinctive lizard-headed variety has its prototype at Chogha Mami. Model clay shaft-hole axes suggest a development of metallurgy ill-attested in the archaeological record. The earliest cast copper object comes from Arpachiyah, and terrestrial iron is reported from Tell Abada (Ubaid 3). The potter's wheel was in use at least as early as Ubaid 3 (i.e. early in the mid-5th millennium BC), becoming widespread by the beginning of the succeeding Uruk period (*see* §(c) below). At Abada there is unique evidence associating small geometric clay tokens, considered by some scholars to have played a significant role in the origins of writing, with a form of recording system. At contemporary Tepe Gawra similar 'counters' were found in a child's grave, a context which in this case clearly suggests their use as gaming pieces.

BIBLIOGRAPHY
R. W. Ehrich, ed.: *Chronologies in Old World Archaeology*, 2 vols (Chicago, 1965, 3/1992)
D. Oates and J. Oates: *The Rise of Civilization*, The Making of the Past (Oxford, 1976)
S. Lloyd: *The Archaeology of Mesopotamia* (London, 1978, rev. 1984)
J. Oates: 'Ubaid Mesopotamia Reconsidered', *The Hilly Flanks and Beyond: Essays on the Prehistory of Southwestern Asia Presented to Robert J. Braidwood*, ed. T. C. Young, P. E. L. Smith and P. Mortensen (Chicago, 1983), pp. 251–81
S. A. Jasim: *The Ubaid Period in Iraq*, Brit. Archaeol. Rep. (Oxford, 1985)
S. A. Jasim and J. Oates: 'Early Tokens and Tablets in Mesopotamia', *World Archaeol.*, xvii (1985), pp. 348–60
J. Oates: *Prehistoric Mesopotamia* (in preparation)
La Mésopotamie pré- et protohistorique, CNRS colloquium (in preparation)

(c) *c. 4000–c. 2900* BC *(Uruk period, including Jemdet Nasr period).* During this period, which is best known from the excavations at its eponymous site (*see* URUK), the world's first literate, urban civilization developed. The Uruk period is normally divided into four phases: Early, Middle and Late, with a final Jemdet Nasr period, sometimes referred to as Terminal or Latest Uruk. These phases are usually defined in terms of the deep sounding made in 1932 beneath the Eanna precinct at Uruk, though little of its material culture is reliably stratified and the sounding

2. Uruk period: cylinder seal impression, showing figure of 'priest-king' or 'man in the net skirt', h. 54 mm, c. 3300–3000 BC (Berlin, Pergamonmuseum, Vorderasiatisches Museum)

itself is small. NIPPUR also provides stratified material of Middle and Late Uruk date (Inanna sequence), though again from limited contexts. The sequence of levels Eanna (Uruk) VIII–VI, V–IV and III–II is equivalent to Inanna (Nippur) XX–XVII, XVI–XV and XIV–XII (Jemdet Nasr). In northern Mesopotamia TEPE GAWRA provides the best-documented sequence, but the material culture at this site often appears atypical. Extensive Uruk materials are also known from TELL BRAK.

Well-stratified excavated evidence for Early Uruk is lacking in southern Mespotamia, but in general it is characterized by undecorated pottery and the earliest mass-produced types (see §V below). Stamp seals are widespread, displaying a great variety of motifs from naturalistic to geometric (see ANCIENT NEAR EAST, §II, 1(i)).

The ceramic criteria for Middle to Late Uruk remain ill-defined. The material culture of Middle Uruk is best illustrated at south Mesopotamian colonies established at this time on the Upper Euphrates, in particular JEBEL ARUDA and HABUBA KABIRA in north-west Syria. Habuba is surrounded by the earliest example of the type of mud-brick city wall that was to become common in the Early Dynastic period (c. 2900–c. 2340 BC). At both Habuba and Jebel Aruda the pottery is identical with that known from Uruk itself, and crudely made bevelled rim bowls characterize this phase throughout the entire Ancient Near East (these may have been 'ration bowls' or simply containers for some common commodity). The exact dates of the Sumerian colonies on the Upper Euphrates remain to be established, but they can have lasted no later than Eanna IVb (Late Uruk) and are almost certainly partly contemporary with Middle Uruk. The seal impressions from Habuba and Jebel Aruda are identical with those attributed to the Late Uruk and even Jemdet Nasr periods in Sumer, indicating the inapplicability of present classifications. They illustrate the earliest use of the cylinder seal, which was to become such a hallmark of Mesopotamian civilization (see ANCIENT NEAR EAST, §II, 1(ii)). In style the Middle to Late Uruk cylinder seals are among the finest

known from Mesopotamia and include a great variety of motifs; both finely carved and drilled seals are found. Especially notable are beautifully carved animal scenes, including the 'temple herd'; ritual scenes, in which there often appears a bearded, turbanned figure referred to as the 'priest-king' or 'man in the net skirt', probably to be identified with the en (Sum.: 'lord' or local ruler) of later times (see fig. 2); 'heraldic' animals; and scenes depicting naked and bound prisoners. The earliest written documents are found at this time (see ANCIENT NEAR EAST, §I, 3): simple numerical notations on clay tablets are found from the Upper Euphrates sites in Syria as far east as Iran. At the same time hollow spherical clay bullae are found throughout Mesopotamia, Iran and Syria; they contained a limited repertory of small clay counters or tokens, thought to represent an early form of recording system. At Uruk itself (Eanna IVa), Kish and also Tell Brak simple pictographic tablets have been found, largely commercial documents, the precursors of later cuneiform.

Although the invention of writing stands out as the greatest achievement of Uruk Mesopotamia, the architectural innovations of the period are also extraordinary, in both scale and variety (see also §II, 3 below). Especially impressive was the Late Uruk Eanna complex at Uruk itself (see fig. 8 below), with its many elaborately decorated public buildings. Wall paintings were found in the temple at Tell 'Uqair, some depicting leopards and other animals (see also §VI, 1 below), while the façade of the main altar was painted to represent a temple façade with vertical panels of imitation cone mosaic. These paintings were done on a white background in a great variety of colours (the most notable omissions being blue and green), with a deep plum red, like that used on the polychrome pottery of Jemdet Nasr type, especially common. Also from the Eanna precinct are the earliest known stele and the oldest sculptured objects (see §III, 2 below). The former, the Lion Hunt Stele (Baghdad, Iraq Mus.), is of particular importance. The two bearded, turbanned men, carved in relief, almost certainly represent the same figure of authority as the 'man in the net skirt' depicted on contemporary cylinder seals. On the stele he is shown attacking lions, both with a bow and arrow and with a spear, the earliest example of the subject of the 'royal lion hunt'. Also notable are a unique and beautiful alabaster mask (for illustration *see* URUK) and the alabaster Warka Vase (see fig. 12 below), decorated with a ritual procession in relief (Baghdad, Iraq Mus.). Several statues in the round have been found: most portray the turbanned figure, but some represent naked and bound prisoners. The statues are often geometric in style, with heavy legs; simple heavy forms are characteristic.

In the final or Jemdet Nasr phase of the Uruk period the Eanna precinct was converted to a high terrace with a central 'high temple' and adjacent religious or probably administrative buildings. This phase is characterized by more developed pictographic tablets and polychrome pottery, first discovered at the site of Jemdet Nasr itself, and it is often difficult to distinguish in terms of its material culture (especially seals) from the earlier Late Uruk and the succeeding Early Dynastic I periods. At Jemdet Nasr itself are the ruins of a massive administrative building, which together with the largely unexcavated 'Red Temple' at Uruk constitute perhaps the first secular palaces. At Tell Brak in north-east Syria a sequence of temples of Jemdet Nasr date were decorated with precious metals, coloured stone rosettes and cone mosaic in south Mesopotamian fashion. There the mud mortar of an underlying temple platform contained thousands of small stylized alabaster objects known as 'eye idols', presumably reflecting some local cult, and several stylized alabaster masks have also been found. Also from this time are smaller stone vessels decorated with animals carved in high relief and vases, often of chlorite, with coloured inlays. The figure of the bearded naked hero with curly hair, wearing only a girdle, appears first in Jemdet Nasr contexts. Seals with distinctive geometric designs ('Piedmont Jemdet Nasr' or Ninevite 5) occur widely, together with the more usual Uruk types, apparently as late as Early Dynastic I. Finely carved amulet-like stamp seals also occur.

BIBLIOGRAPHY

E. Strommenger and M. Hirmer: *The Art of Mesopotamia* (London, 1964)
D. P. Hansen: 'The Relative Chronology of Mesopotamia, II', *Chronologies in Old World Archaeology*, ed. R. W. Ehrich (Chicago, 1965), pp. 201–13
D. Oates and J. Oates: *The Rise of Civilization*, The Making of the Past (Oxford, 1976)
S. Lloyd: *The Archaeology of Mesopotamia* (London, 1978, rev. 1984)
W. Röllig and U. Finkbeiner: *Ǧamdat Naṣr: Period or Regional Style?* (Wiesbaden, 1986)

JOAN OATES

(ii) Historic period.

(a) Early Dynastic period to Third Dynasty of Ur (*c.* 2900–*c.* 2000 BC). (b) Isin–Larsa period to Middle Assyrian period (*c.* 2000–*c.* 1000 BC). (c) *c.* 1000 BC to Islamic conquest (AD 637).

(a) Early Dynastic period to Third Dynasty of Ur (c. 2900–c. 2000 BC). From the early 3rd millennium BC onwards, written records can increasingly be used to supplement archaeological evidence. Even so, any attempt to reconstruct a historical sequence of events for this period is speculative, and both relative and absolute dates

are the subject of continuing debate (*see also* ANCIENT NEAR EAST, §I, 2(ii)). An important group of later texts, known as the Sumerian King List (?early 2nd millennium BC), purports to give a complete chronological list of the kings who ruled in Sumer after the legendary Deluge: however, many of the dynasties shown in the list as consecutive are known from other sources to have been contemporary, and the regnal years given for each king and the totals for each dynasty also present problems through lacunae, internal contradictions and the fantastical lengths of reign of the earliest kings. Nevertheless, the list remains one of the major sources of information. Perhaps more reliable are the lists of the names given to every year of a king's reign, although before *c.* 2150 BC only occasional year names are known, the earliest being *c.* 2500 BC. The relative dates provided by archaeological and art historical evidence include some useful synchronisms, for example a lapis lazuli bead inscribed with the name of Mesanne-padda, King of Ur, *c.* 2500 BC, which was found in the palace of a king of Mari on the Middle Euphrates. This type of evidence, however, can only provide a crude relative framework: for instance, it is not always possible to distinguish with certainty between early pieces and crude provincial pieces of a later date. Sequences of radiocarbon dates from well-stratified excavations are an urgent need, but enough information is already available to reconstruct a shadowy picture of the major historical events of the 3rd millennium BC.

Early Dynastic period (c. 2900–c. 2340 BC). In the early 3rd millennium BC the south Mesopotamian region of Sumer was apparently divided into a number of small city states based on such major cities as URUK, UR and LAGASH (*see also* SUMERIAN). From time to time an outstanding leader would unite several of these cities under his rule, but at least until the end of the Early Dynastic period (*c.* 2340 BC) such alliances were short-lived. These rulers (known variously as *lugal*, *en* or *ensi*) saw themselves as servants of their city god, and their power, although considerable, seems to have been circumscribed by the economic and political power of the state temple and by an assembly of citizens. This assembly apparently had to ratify major decisions of peace and war. A study of the monumental art of the period (e.g. the Stele of the Vultures; Paris, Louvre; see fig. 3) shows that the ruler was also head of the armed forces and that some sort of small standing army may well date to this time. Long-distance trade is testified to by the presence of lapis lazuli imported from Afghanistan, especially in the Royal Cemetery at Ur, where it was found in large quantities, together with cornelian, agate and metals. At the end of the Early Dynastic period a ruler emerged who seems to have been the first to extend his rule beyond the Sumerian plain. His name was Lugal-zagesi of Uruk, and he claimed to have reached the Mediterranean, though this may have been no more than a successful raiding party. It was, however, a foretaste of the triumphs of the next dynasty, whose founder, Sargon of Akkad, conquered Uruk.

Akkadians, Gutians and the kingdom of Lagash, (c. 2340–c. 2113 BC). The city of Agade was founded, at a still unidentified location not far south of Baghdad, by Sargon (*reg* 2334–2279 BC), a Semite of humble origins and later a hero of many legends (*see* AKKADIAN). Sargon's empire seems to have stretched to the Syrian coast and perhaps even into central Anatolia. In spite of their non-Sumerian origins, the new dynasty displayed strong cultural continuity from the Early Dynastic period, and the idea of a complete break with earlier artistic tradition is no longer tenable. On the other hand, Sargon's grandson, Naram-Sin (*reg* 2254–2218 BC), also a great warrior, introduced one completely new political concept by apparently assuming divine status about halfway through his long reign. He is depicted on a stele (Stele of Naram-Sin; Paris, Louvre; *see* AKKADIAN, fig. 1) wearing the horned headdress that was formerly the exclusive prerogative of the gods. This style was retained by his successor, Shar-Kali-sharri (*reg* 2217–2193 BC), who failed to hold together the empire and was eventually overwhelmed by a coalition of invaders from the south and east led by a tribe called the Gutians.

Some city states seem to have regained a measure of independence, for instance Lagash under the rule of Gudea, sculptures of whom have been found at TELLOH (*see* STONE, colour pl. X, fig. 2). Eventually the Gutians were expelled by a coalition of the old Sumerian city states under Utuhegal of Uruk (*reg c*. 2123–2113 BC) and order was restored.

*Third Dynasty of Ur (*c. 2113–c. 2000 BC*).* Around 2112 BC political power passed to the city of Ur under Ur-Nammu, who founded the Third Dynasty of Ur (also termed the Ur III period) and who seems to have modelled himself on the earlier rulers of Sumer. However, the subsequent kings of the dynasty all assumed divine status. The extent of their domination is unclear, but they certainly controlled the Sumerian plain and perhaps also north Mesopotamia. They presided over a prosperous kingdom, marked by the final flowering of the Sumerian artistic tradition and in particular by an enormously ambitious and successful programme of building in most of the major cities. The great temenos at UR with its ziggurat and other subsidiary buildings largely belongs to this period (see fig. 10 below), as did the first ziggurat at the great religious centre of URUK. In 2004 BC this dynasty was toppled by a combination of weak rule, famine, drought, pressure from the nomadic Amorites (*see* AMORITE) and treachery, with the final blow being administered by Elamites (*see* ELAMITE) from the east.

BIBLIOGRAPHY
T. Jacobsen: *The Sumerian Kinglist* (Chicago, 1939)
W. C. Hayes, M. B. Rowton and F. Stubbings, eds: *Early History of the Middle East*, Cambridge Anc. Hist. (Cambridge, 1962)
W. W. Hallo and W. K. Simpson: *The Ancient Near East: A History* (New York, 1971)
A. B. Knapp: *History and Culture of Ancient Western Asia and Egypt* (Chicago, 1988)
H. Crawford: *Sumer and the Sumerians* (Cambridge, 1991)
J. N. Postgate: *Early Mesopotamia* (London and New York, 1992)

HARRIET CRAWFORD

*(b) Isin–Larsa period to Middle Assyrian period (*c. 2000–c. 1000 BC*).*

Isin–Larsa period. After the fall of the Third Dynasty of Ur, a number of semi-independent city states sprang up. Political power in the south was divided between the rival dynasties of ISIN and LARSA, with first one and then the other in the ascendancy (the Isin–Larsa period). Many

3. Early Dynastic period: detail of Stele of the Vultures, limestone, h. *c*. 1.75 m, from Telloh, *c*. 2450 BC (Paris, Musée du Louvre)

of these rulers have Amorite names, bearing witness to the increasing power of the tribes of Semitic Amorites that were moving into Mesopotamia from the desert to the outskirts of large towns such as SIPPAR, where they gradually became settled and assimilated into the local population.

Old Babylonian period. In the early 19th century BC Sumuabum (*reg* 1894–1881 BC) founded a dynasty in BABYLON, and a century later his descendant Hammurabi (*reg* 1792–1750 BC) set out on a series of conquests that were to make him ruler of a huge kingdom stretching north up the Tigris, and north-west along the Euphrates to Mari. This golden age, exemplified by the large diorite stele known as the Code of Hammurabi (Paris, Louvre; see fig. 14 below), is called the Old Babylonian period, but during the 17th century BC the First Dynasty of Babylon gradually declined, eventually collapsing in 1595 BC, when the Hittites (*see* HITTITE) from Anatolia raided south. This led to a dark age.

Old Assyrian period and kingdom of Mari. Meanwhile, in the north the city of ASSUR on the Tigris had launched a daring trading venture, with merchant colonies operating in Anatolia from the end of the 20th century BC (*see* KÜLTEPE). This brought huge prosperity not only to Assur but to all the city states and kingdoms along the trade routes through Syria and into Anatolia. The exchange of goods and ideas during this Old Assyrian period is best documented in archives of clay tablets written in the cuneiform script and Akkadian language of Mesopotamia, and in the varied iconography and styles of the cylinder seals used to seal them (*see* ANCIENT NEAR EAST, §§I, 3(ii) and II, 1(ii)). Towards the end of the 19th century BC Shamshi-Adad (*reg* 1813–1781 BC) united much of northern Mesopotamia into a kingdom and installed his sons as viceroys in MARI and Ekallatum. The archives of this reign and of that of Zimri-Lim (*reg c.* 1775–*c.* 1760 BC), discovered at Mari and in many other cities, testify to tremendous epistolary activity and paint a vivid picture of life in palaces and temples, such as those excavated at Mari, TELL EL-RIMAH and Tell Asmar and Ischali (*see* DIYALA REGION). During the second half of the 18th century BC trade with Anatolia ceased, and power shifted from northern Mesopotamia to Syria.

Kassites and Mitannians. After the fall of Babylon in 1595 BC, the Kassites (*see* KASSITE) moved into the power vacuum, while in the north a series of small kingdoms, whose population consisted largely of Hurrians (*see* HURRIAN), united under a possibly Indo-European aristocracy to form the kingdom of Mitanni (*see* MITANNIAN). There is, however, a paucity of datable material. A relative chronology can be established for the rich archives at NUZI, sealed with the impressions of several thousand seals over five or six generations, but exact dating within the 15th and 14th centuries remains elusive. The chronology of the second half of the 2nd millennium BC relies heavily on Egyptian synchronisms provided by the EL-AMARNA correspondence between various pharaohs of the 14th century BC and their contemporaries in Babylonia, Assyria and Mitanni. These rulers exchanged lavish gifts and dowries, including gold sculpture, jewellery with a particular emphasis on lapis lazuli, decorated chariots and harnesses and rich textiles, which are described in great detail.

Middle Assyrian period. Dynastic upheavals led to the collapse of Mitanni in the second half of the 14th century BC, and Assyria, under Ashur-uballit I (*reg* 1363–1328 BC), seized the opportunity to increase its boundaries and reestablish itself as an international power in what is known as the Middle Assyrian period. Tukulti-Ninurta I (*reg* 1243–1207 BC) founded a new short-lived capital (*see* KAR TUKULTI-NINURTA) and raided Babylon, but it was the Elamites (*see* ELAMITE) who brought about the end of Kassite rule in 1157 BC and carried off many treasures of earlier periods to Susa. There is little historical evidence for the last 150 years of the 2nd millennium BC. The Kassites were followed by the Second Dynasty of Isin and then by a series of short-lived dynasties. The Middle Assyrian state survived under such powerful kings as Ashur-resh-ishi (*reg* 1132–1115 BC) and Tilgath-pileser I (*reg* 1114–1076 BC). New Semitic tribes, the Chaldaeans in the south and the Aramaeans in the north (*see* §(c) below), were moving into Mesopotamia. These incursions brought about another dark age.

BIBLIOGRAPHY

G. Roux: *Ancient Iraq* (London, 1964/*R* Harmondsworth, 1966, rev. 1980/*R* 1986)

W. C. Hayes, M. B. Rowton and F. Stubbings: 'Chronology', *Cambridge Anc. Hist.*, I/i (Cambridge, 1966), pp. 173–285

DOMINIQUE COLLON

(c) c. 1000 BC *to Islamic conquest (*AD *637).*

Aramaeans. Around the beginning of the 1st millennium BC the Aramaeans (*see* ARAMAEAN) founded a number of petty states in north Syria, increasingly threatening both Assyria and Babylonia and leading to the collapse of central authority in both areas. Their language, Aramaic, a dialect of West Semitic, ultimately replaced Akkadian, becoming the *lingua franca* for the entire Near East. It was the first Mesopotamian language to be written not in cuneiform but in an alphabetic script (*see* ANCIENT NEAR EAST, §I, 3(iv)).

Neo-Assyrian period (883–612 BC*).* Although Babylonia remained politically unstable until a period of Assyrian domination in the 8th century BC, from *c.* 900 BC a new and prosperous state began to develop in Assyria, commonly known as the Late Assyrian empire; the period 883–612 BC is termed Neo-Assyrian. With the reign of Ashurnasirpal II (*reg* 883–859 BC) Assyria emerged as a world power, well symbolized in the palaces and temples of NIMRUD (anc. Calah), NINEVEH and ASSUR (*see also* ASSYRIAN). Ashurnasirpal rebuilt Calah, and the limestone reliefs, statues and stelae from his public buildings and those of his son, Shalmaneser III (*reg* 858–824 BC), are well known (e.g. London, BM): the bronze gates of Balawat (Baghdad, Iraq Mus. and London, BM) also date from their reigns. Shalamaneser's son Shamshi-Adad V (*reg* 823–811 BC) provides the earliest link with Classical tradition in the person of his wife Sammuramat, the Greek Semiramis. In the 8th century BC the empire was further expanded by Tiglath-pileser III (bibl. Pul; *reg* 744–727 BC) and his son Sargon II (*reg* 721–705 BC), who built a new capital at KHORSABAD, another major source of monumental art and architecture. His son Sennacherib (*reg* 704–681 BC) moved the capital to Nineveh, where he, Esarhaddon (*reg* 680–669 BC) and Assurbanipal (*reg* 668–627 BC) undertook the reconstruction of what was then the greatest city of its time. The palaces, temples and city gates of Nineveh, like those at Nimrud and Khorsabad, are the source of a great wealth of stone sculpture (*see* §III, 6(i) below).

Far less is known of Babylonia at this time, but some boundary stones and other objects have been found, especially at SIPPAR (e.g. London, BM). About 780 BC the Chaldaean chief of a wealthy tribe from the 'sea-lands' of southern Babylonia claimed the throne in BABYLON. One of his successors, Nabonassar (*reg* 747–734 BC), was held in both Babylonian and Ptolemaic reckoning as the founder of a new era (26 second month 747), from which time remarkably accurate astronomical observations were kept. In 726 BC, after a brief Assyrian intervention, another Chaldaean, Marduk-apla-iddina II (the first Babylonian mentioned in the Bible, as Merodach-Baladan) seized the throne. The power of Assyria, already overstretched in the 7th century BC by the conquest of Egypt, collapsed within 20 years of the death of Assurbanipal. Nineveh fell to an alliance of Medes and Babylonians in 612 BC, although the last Assyrian king survived at HARRAN until 609 BC.

Neo-Babylonian period (627–539 BC*).* The death of Assurbanipal (627 BC) was followed by civil war in Babylonia from which a Chaldaean general, Nabopolassar, emerged victorious to found a new dynasty in Babylon (known as Chaldaean or Neo-Babylonian). He and his more famous son Nebuchadnezzar II (*reg* 604–562 BC) rebuilt Babylon, which had suffered much destruction in the conflict with Assyria in the 7th century BC. It is this Babylon that can still be seen at the site, in particular the famous palace and the Ishtar Gate, of which the glazed brick decoration has been restored in Berlin (Pergamonmus.). The Neo-Babylonian dynasty came to an end with Nabonidus (*reg* 555–539 BC), noted for his alleged madness and his unexplained sojourn in TAIMA in Arabia.

Achaemenid Mesopotamia (539–331 BC). Nabonidus's Babylon fell in 539 BC to the Indo-European Cyrus the Great (*reg* 559–530 BC), a Persian of the royal line of Achaemenes, the 7th-century BC founder of the dynasty known by his name. The Achaemenid kings ruled in southwest Iran (*see also* IRAN, ANCIENT, §I, 2(ii)(b)): they controlled Mesopotamia, with Babylon as their winter capital, until Alexander the Great defeated Darius III (331 BC). The Persians adopted many Mesopotamian artistic traditions, seen on their palace reliefs at PERSEPOLIS, their use of glazed brick mural ornament in the palace at SUSA and in the iconography of their beautiful cylinder and stamp seals (*see* ANCIENT NEAR EAST, §II, 1). Both Darius I and Xerxes I (of Marathon and Salamis fame respectively) resided in Babylon as crown princes, while the retreat immortalized in Xenophon's *Anabasis* took place in 401 BC, after a battle near Babylon (Cunaxa). Except at Babylon, little architectural material of this date has been identified in Mesopotamia.

Hellenistic period: Seleucid Mesopotamia (311–c. 122 BC). Following earlier tradition, Alexander the Great had made Babylon his eastern capital; indeed he died in the throne-room of Nebuchadnezzar's palace (323 BC). The conflicts among his 'successors' resulted in the creation of two new empires, that of the Ptolemies in Egypt and that of the SELEUCIDS in Syria and Mesopotamia. In 312 BC Seleukos, a former satrap of Babylon, gained control of the city, which remained in the hands of his successors until the late 2nd century BC, while in Syria Seleukos' successors ruled until Pompey made it a Roman province (64 BC). Seleukos' official reign began in the autumn of 312, which marked the advent of the Seleucid era and of a chronological system still employed in some Eastern churches. He founded a new city, Seleucia, on the Tigris *c.* 90 km south of Babylon; its excavation has provided much information about Hellenistic Mesopotamia. Around 275 BC Seleucia became the royal city under Antiochus I, though Babylon continued to be honoured by the Seleucid kings. Hellenistic materials are also known from many Assyrian sites, such as Nineveh, Nimrud and, especially, HATRA.

Parthian Mesopotamia (c. 122 BC–AD 224). In the later 3rd century BC a new dynasty came to power in the east, founded in Turkestan *c.* 257 BC by one Arsaces and eventually based in Parthia, south of the Caspian (*see* PARTHIAN). Between 161 and 122 BC there ensued a struggle for Mesopotamia between its Seleucid rulers and the eastern Parthians, whose king Mithradates II seized Babylon *c.* 122 BC. A large Parthian building with columned halls has been excavated at Babylon, and Assur too has extensive Parthian remains: the restored façade of the Great Palace at Assur can be seen in Berlin (Pergamonmus.). The most famous Parthian site, however, is the desert city of Hatra, a great religious and tribal centre in the Jazira, much of which has now been restored.

With the Parthians in control, Rome now entered the Mesopotamian scene, and over the next few centuries there ensued a bitter power struggle between these two empires. The first serious Roman attack on Parthia was made *c.* 53 BC by Crassus: after the Roman defeat near Harran, Crassus' head was dispatched to the Parthian king, then in Armenia. From the time of Trajan (AD 114), Roman armies marched repeatedly down the River Euphrates towards the new Parthian capital, KTESIPHON. In AD 195 under Septimius Severus northern Mesopotamia briefly became a Roman province, and Ktesiphon was sacked in AD 198, though Hatra resisted the Roman siege. The province was lost under Caracalla (AD 215–17), who committed the sacrilege of looting the Parthian royal tombs at Erbil, and whose assassin and successor, Macrinus, fought the final battle with Artabanus V in AD 217. The only surviving Roman walls in Mesopotamia are those of Sinjar, with round towers probably built in the early 4th century AD. Roman coins and other objects have been recovered from several sites in Assyria, and a recruiting barracks near Sinjar has been excavated.

Sasanian Mesopotamia (AD 224–637). Parthia was seriously weakened by the wars with Rome, and a revolt that began *c.* AD 220 in Persis rapidly brought about its final downfall: Artabanus V was defeated and killed by the Sasanian Ardashir *c.* AD 224 (*see also* SASANIAN). Ardashir chose Ktesiphon as his western capital, and in AD 237 forced the Romans from Assyria and besieged Hatra. Coins bearing the name of Singara (Sinjar) were minted under Gordian III (AD 242), but sometime after AD 250 Shapur I in a great series of campaigns overran Armenia, Mesopotamia and Syria, where he captured the Roman Emperor Valerian. The Emperor Julian the Apostate also campaigned in Mesopotamia, but after his death in AD 363 Rome was finally forced to abandon the frontier fortresses of Nisibis (Nusaybin) and Singara.

Sasanian architecture is perhaps best known from the great palace at Ktesiphon (for illustration *see* KTESIPHON), probably rebuilt by Chosroes I (*reg* AD 531–79), who contested Mesopotamia with Justinian's general Belisarius. The ruins of the great palace banqueting hall are not only one of the architectural wonders of Mesopotamia but also demonstrate the widest single-span vault of unreinforced brickwork in the world. The impressive remains of a monastery at Qasr Serij (*c.* AD 570), west of Mosul, attest the spread of Christianity at this time. Chosroes II (*reg* AD 590–628) moved the capital to Dastagerd in western Iran: despite having a Christian wife he sacked Damascus and Jerusalem, removing the True Cross to Persia, and he then fought the final battle with Rome, being defeated by Heraclius on the ruinfield of Nineveh. It was Chosroes II who was asked to acknowledge Muhammad as the true prophet of God. While Heraclius sacked Dastagerd and returned the True Cross to Jerusalem, the obscure Arabian prophet and his followers fled from Mecca: this was the Hijra or Migration of the Prophet with which the Muslim era begins (AD 622). The victory of an Arab army at Qadisiyya (near al-Hira) in AD 637 marked the final collapse of Persian power in Mesopotamia.

BIBLIOGRAPHY
S. Lloyd: *Twin Rivers* (Oxford, 1943)
D. Oates: *Studies in the Ancient History of Northern Iraq* (Oxford, 1968)
J. Oates: *Babylon* (London, 1979, rev. 1986)
H. F. W. Saggs: *The Might that Was Assyria* (London, 1984)

JOAN OATES

3. RELIGION AND ICONOGRAPHY. Mesopotamian religion developed through the fusion, by assimilation and syncretism, of two different groups of gods, those of the Sumerians (*see* SUMERIAN) and those of the Semitic Akkadians (*see* AKKADIAN). As cities, tribes or nations rose to prominence, so too did their patron deities, and the pantheon and religious myths were altered to accommodate them. There was also a large body of popular belief in demons and monsters, who had to be invoked, propitiated, placated or defeated with elaborate magical rituals often involving their representation as clay figurines.

(i) Interpretation. (ii) Deities, symbols and attributes. (iii) Apotropaic figures and malevolent spirits. (iv) Mythological and ritual scenes.

(i) Interpretation. Much of the art of ancient Mesopotamia was of a religious character, and the visual forms of expression are naturally vast and complex in a land that was a crossroads for many different peoples from the prehistoric period onwards. However, what is striking over the 3000 years from the Early Dynastic period to the Persian conquest is not the diversity but the uniformity of symbols and motifs and so, perhaps also, of some of the underlying beliefs that inspired them. Nevertheless, identification and interpretation are fraught with difficulties because, unlike much Egyptian and Greco-Roman art, correspondences between the iconographic and textual evidence are normally indirect and obscure. It was HENRI FRANKFORT who pioneered the method of interpreting many mythological and ritual scenes, especially on Mesopotamian seals (most notably of the Akkadian period, *c.* 2300–2200 BC) according to later mythological narratives. The validity of specific interpretations is often difficult to assess, although Amiet's dismissal of the practice of identifying deities by their attributes, assuming 'types' of gods rather than 'single divine personalities', is certainly too pessimistic, and there are in turn problems associated with attempts at interpreting the underlying conceptual significances of such scenes (the 'iconology').

Direct 'labelling' of features does occasionally occur. Babylonian *kudurru*s (e.g. London, BM), or copies of 'boundary stones' recording various aspects of land transactions usually involving the crown, are known from the Kassite to Neo-Babylonian periods (14th–7th centuries BC). The top of the stone is usually carved with a series of religious motifs symbolizing different deities. Occasionally, on *kudurru*s found in Elamite Susa (where the meanings may have been less obvious than in Mesopotamia), such symbols are inscribed with the names of the gods they represent in a manner that seems quite unequivocal. Additionally, in Neo-Assyrian and Babylonian art figurines of clay, stone, copper or bronze, depicting demons such as Humbaba (Sum. *Huwawa*), Pazuzu and Lamashtu (e.g. Paris, Louvre; see fig. 4), may be inscribed with omens or incantations giving their names. Some types of Neo-Assyrian and Neo-Babylonian foundation figurines of sun-dried clay also carry inscriptions that suggest reasonably firm identifications, because rituals concerning

the making of such figurines and their placement in a house as a counter to evil spirits prescribed identical legends to be inscribed on examples of named beings. At least one parallel figure from an Assyrian palace relief is inscribed in similar form.

Other correspondences between iconography and texts are more equivocal: cylinder seals (*see* ANCIENT NEAR EAST, §II, 1(ii)) are, for most periods, the main surviving medium for religious art, offering the widest iconographic range; yet the relationship between text and scene on inscribed seals is extremely problematic. The inscriptions often name deities: sometimes these names correspond to the deities depicted, but more usually this is not the case. Possibly the naming of a god might represent an alternative to his depiction, and it is likely that some deities had a readily understood iconographic convention, while others were better known for their deeds or natures than for their form, which may have remained vague.

Commemorative stelae and rock reliefs were carved for Neo-Assyrian and Neo-Babylonian kings (or, exceptionally, for regional governors) especially to mark their visits to cities and parts of the empire or the limits of successful campaigns. On stelae the king is shown beneath the symbols of his gods, while rock carvings show these

4. Assyrian exorcism plaque, depicting the demon Pazuzu overlooking four registers containing (top to bottom) divine symbols, ?apotropaic spirits, a sick man attended by apotropaic figures, and the demoness Lamashtu sailing to the netherworld, bronze, 133×83×25 mm, early 1st millennium BC (Paris, Musée du Louvre)

symbols or the gods themselves. The regular inscriptions commemorating the event also invoke certain important deities: in at least five instances (e.g. on the rock reliefs at Bavian) the correspondence in both number and order is so exact as to suggest clearly a one-to-one relationship. Normally, however, no such correspondence exists; moreover, on *kudurru*s the names of the gods cited in the curse formula of the main text represent an independent invocation and never correspond to the symbols as depicted.

Prescriptions for Neo-Assyrian foundation figurines can allow firm identifications even of types of figures that were not inscribed, as with the *apkallē* ('Sages'), 'furnished with the faces of birds and wings, carrying in their right hands a "purifier", and in their left a "ritual cup", clad in gypsum, cloaked with wings of birds upon their shoulders' (Gurney, p. 65), or another set of *apkallē* 'clad in gypsum, cloaked in fishes' skins'. Similarly, the text on one Kassite *kudurru* clearly refers to some of the divine symbols (though not to the ones carved on it): 'the seat and horned crown of Anu, king of heaven; the walking bird of Enlil, lord of the lands; the ram's head and goat-fish, the sanctuary of great Ea ... the sickle, water-trough [and] wide boat of Sin; the radiant disc of the great judge Shamash; the star-symbol of Ishtar, the mistress of lands; the fierce young bull of Adad, son of Anu'. On the other hand, references to representational art, such as the *Göttertypentext* describing statues of various monsters, or descriptions of gods and creatures in mythological narratives may be either so exotic or, alternatively, so figurative or vague as not easily to correlate with examples of extant art.

(ii) Deities, symbols and attributes. The deities were conceived in anthropomorphic form and can be identified by their distinctive horned headdress (see fig. 5) and often, from the late 3rd millennium BC, by a rod and ring symbolizing divine authority. The Sumerian pantheon in the 3rd millennium BC seems to have consisted of a supreme god An, the sky god, worshipped at Uruk; Enlil, possibly the god of air, in charge of kingship and terrestrial matters, whose seat was at Nippur; and Ea, also known as Enki, the lord of the subterranean waters, crafts, wisdom and magic, who was worshipped at Eridu. There were also fertility deities, such as Inanna, goddess of Uruk, and her consort Dumuzi ('Tammuz'), the shepherd; or the god Ningizzida, patron of Lagash, and a host of deities or aspects of deities worshipped as patrons of the various city states of Sumer. Nergal was a god of the netherworld.

Although astral deities were worshipped by the Sumerians, they seem to have been dominant deities in the Semitic pantheon from about 2300 BC. The moon god Sin (Sum. *Nanna*) was the patron of Ur, Shamash (Sum. *Utu*) was the sun god of Sippar, and Ishtar, the planet Venus and goddess of war, acquired the attributes and titles of Inanna and of other fertility goddesses and was worshipped especially at Uruk and Nippur in the south, and at Assur, Nineveh and Arbela in the north. The Akkadians seem to have attempted to create some order in the pantheon and to have designed an iconography for deities, who, until then, had been depicted relatively rarely, although some were already designated by symbols.

5. Akkadian deities depicted on a cylinder seal impression, *c.* 2250 BC (London, British Museum)

Since representations of deities are rarely identified by accompanying inscriptions, it is usual to identify them, when possible, by their distinctive iconography, most often by the attributes they hold. The symbols and attributes of the gods form a group of images that are remarkably consistent, through different ages and peoples, in the deities they represent. Many, originating in the prehistoric or Akkadian periods, survived with little change in form or meaning until the fall of Assyria (612 BC) and Babylon (539 BC).

Among the most widely represented deities is the sun god Shamash, symbolized by the sun-disc, which, from the late 3rd millennium BC, often has a star inscribed in it and a crescent moon below it. The winged disc, which was adopted in Syria from Egypt in the early 2nd millennium BC and entered Mesopotamian iconography in the 15th century BC, is certainly usually a symbol of Shamash, although the god Assur has also been suggested. The sun god himself is generally depicted with rays issuing from his shoulders, holding his serrated pruning saw (see fig. 5) and resting one foot on a mountain or on a human-headed bull, probably a bison, symbolizing the mountains of the east through which he has cut his way. Sometimes his (subterranean?) journey in a boat is depicted (though it has been suggested that this may sometimes be the moon god). Scorpion-men and bull-men also seem to have been associated with the sun god, particularly in the 3rd millennium BC, and the horse was his attribute animal in some Neo-Assyrian art, including the rock reliefs at MALTAI (*c.* 700 BC; see fig. 6). The moon god Sin was more rarely represented, but his symbol, the crescent, was ubiquitous. On the Maltai reliefs he is depicted with an undulating staff terminating in a lion's head and he stands on a lion-dragon. An eight-pointed star, usually inscribed in a disc, is the symbol of the goddess Ishtar, who, in her warrior aspect, is sometimes winged and has weapons rising from her shoulders (see fig. 5 above) and stands on a lion. In Neo-Assyrian times she was also shown standing in a nimbus of stars. A post with a ring and streamers was the emblem of her Sumerian precursor Inanna, as depicted on the Warka Vase (see fig. 12 below). Ishtar's aspect as goddess of love may have been represented by a frontally portrayed nude female figure, popular on early 2nd-millennium BC seals and terracottas and sometimes shown standing on a plinth as if she were a statue; she never wears the horned headdress of divinity, although occasionally she seems to receive worship.

6. Assyrian deities facing a king (?Sennacherib), rock relief at Maltai, *c.* 700 BC (*in situ*); from F. Thureau-Dangin: 'Les Reliefs rupestres de Maltai', *Revue d'assyriologie*, xxi (1924)

On seals of the Akkadian period (*c.* 2300–*c.* 2200 BC) Ea (Sum. *Enki*), the water god, is depicted seated on a throne in a chamber surrounded by water, with streams, along which swim fish, flowing either from his shoulders (see fig. 5) or from a vessel he holds. He is frequently associated with a long-haired hero and with his double-faced vizier Usmû (Sum. *Isimud*). His symbols are a ram-headed staff, a turtle and a creature with the foreparts of a goat and the body of a fish. The storm god Adad (Sum. *Ishkur*) is represented by a lightning flash or fork. He is depicted brandishing this attribute and generally standing on the back of either a bull or a 'lion-dragon'. Adad's consort, Shala, is associated with an ear of corn and is thought by some to be the nude female figure mentioned above in connection with Ishtar.

Other deities include Gula, a goddess of healing, whose attribute animal was a dog and whose main shrine was at Isin, where her temple and many figurines of dogs have been found. The attributes of the god of the netherworld, Nergal, were probably the scimitar and the double lion-headed sceptre. Ninshubur, messenger of the gods, held a staff, and a lamp was the symbol of Nusku, god of fire. On *kudurru*s, birds in various attitudes represent some little-known deities. Fertility symbols, such as date clusters (see fig. 5), flowing vases, stylized trees or scorpions, were not normally the attribute of any particular deity, although the scorpion was specifically associated with the goddess Ishhara in Kassite times. The plough was probably the attribute of Ningirsu, and an omega-shaped symbol was perhaps that of the goddess of childbirth, Ninhursag. The snake was associated with Ningizzida, while the horned snake and dragon were the attributes of various under-world and fertility deities. Paradoxically, some minor deities are among those most frequently depicted. A suppliant goddess, with both hands raised in entreaty, existed from the late 3rd millennium BC, and can be

identified from inscriptional evidence as the goddess (or type of goddess) Lama, an intermediary between a major deity and a worshipper, and a protector of the king.

Some deities gained importance with the tribe or city of which they were patrons. Amurru was the god of the Amorites (*see* §2(ii)(b) above), who moved into Mesopotamia from *c.* 2000 BC: his emblem was a crook, and his attribute animal was the gazelle. Marduk, the god of Babylon, rose to prominence with his city in the 19th–17th centuries BC (*see* §2(ii)(b) above) and maintained his status as a major deity. His emblem, the triangular-shaped spade, may indicate his origins as an agricultural god. The dragon, previously the attribute of the gods of Eshnunna, may have become his attribute and that of his son Nabû, after Hammurabi of Babylon (*reg* 1792–1759 BC) defeated Eshnunna. Nabû was the god of writing and his emblem was wedge-shaped, either a cuneiform sign or a writing-stylus. The iconography of the national god of Assyria, Assur, is not clear, but in Neo-Assyrian times he seems to have taken over the horned headdress that had previously been the symbol of the sky god Anu. It is possible that his attribute animal was a kid with its legs bunched up as if standing on a peak, but at Maltai he stands on a (snake-) dragon and a 'lion-dragon' and holds an undulating weapon (see fig. 6).

(iii) Apotropaic figures and malevolent spirits. Apotropaic figures, representations of beneficent spirits, were assembled into a definite repertory only in the Neo-Assyrian period (883–612 BC), especially as protectors of buildings, with the types represented in the palace sculpture closely corresponding to the clay images buried as foundation deposits. In origin, however, many of these figures were much more ancient and included some of the former divine attendants. When new types were added, it was considered necessary to model them on existing forms or to give them an artificial 'antiquity', as with the supposedly

antediluvian 'Sages'. Often they were not specifically associated with a deity but were independent agents, whose services might be sought by gods and men alike. Some of the principal apotropaic figures were anthropomorphic in form: a long-haired 'hero' (Akkad. *lahmu*: 'hairy') was originally associated with the water god Ea and was later transferred to Marduk; a human figure in a lion's pelt was perhaps the god Latarāk; *apkallē* were represented as eagle-headed 'griffin-demons', as human figures in fish-skins, and perhaps as male or female genies in helmets; the *sibitti* ('seven') were depicted as armed gods in tall headdresses; a god in smiting posture was possibly Lulal; a deity with a double-axe and mace has been interpreted as the netherworld god Meslamtaea.

A dog (*kalbu*), usually standing, was apotropaic and so were the natural lion (*urgulû*), and the canine-leonine demon Pazuzu (see fig. 4). The human-headed, winged lion is commonly but dubiously identified as the *shedu*; the 'lion-dragon' was possibly the *umu na'iru* ('roaring weather-beast'), a late form of the 'Anzû-bird'; an upright leonine man was probably the *uridimmu* ('mad lion'); a lion-demon was the *ugallu* ('big weather-beast'); and the lion-centaur was the *urmahlullû* ('lion-man'); while the lion-headed eagle was the original Anzû (Sum. perhaps Imdugud), the personification of storms according to Amiet. Bovine apotropaic figures included both the natural bull and the human-headed winged bull (often, though dubiously, identified as *lamassu, shedu* or *aladlammu*), of which the wingless form may sometimes have been a *kusarikku* (bison), although this term was also used for the bull-man originally associated with the sun god Shamash (*see* §3(ii) above). Water creatures included the merman (kulullû: 'fish-man'), which probably influenced Greek and Western art, and the goat-fish (*suhurmashshu*: 'carp-goat'). Other apotropaic creatures were the scorpion-man (*girtablullû*), also associated with the sun god Shamash, the horned snake (*bashmu/ushumgallu*: 'venomous snake') and the (snake-)dragon (*mushhushshu*: 'furious snake').

The numerous malevolent spirits named in the texts are notoriously difficult to equate with artistic representations, because even textual descriptions of their physical forms are rare and extremely vague. The case of the goddess Lamashtu, who appears as a wingless humanoid lion-headed creature with the talons of a bird and possibly ass-ears (see fig. 4), shows that such a being could have a specific and consistent form. Lamashtu was a special case in other respects too: as daughter of the supreme god An she was above the common run of ghouls; she had a clear and developed personality and nature, and she appears, uniquely, to have represented evil for its own sake, acting independently of the will and purpose of the gods. Most other 'evil' spirits were mere agents of the gods; evil as far as their human victims were concerned, but dispensers of justice in the view of heaven. They were possibly not represented visually, at least not in any consistent way.

(iv) Mythological and ritual scenes. The variety of scenes, even for a single period, is large. Some of the more common, long-lived and interesting examples are: ritual banquets in which the human or divine participants were sometimes replaced by animals; scenes with wrestlers, who are traditionally but dubiously identified as Gilgamesh and Enkidu, heroes of the Sumerian *Epic of Gilgamesh*; figures in a boat, who are just as dubiously identified as Gilgamesh and Utnapishtim (the Sumerian Noah) from the same epic; battling gods, animals and hybrids (in what are known as contest scenes) interpreted by Frankfort (*see* §3(i) above) as a cosmic battle between order and chaos; the worship of symbols and deities; the ceremonial attendance on a seated figure; hunting scenes; sexual scenes, possibly sometimes representing the 'Sacred Marriage' or potency rituals. Some mythological scenes are restricted to the Akkadian period. A scene depicting a bird-man brought prisoner before the water god has been interpreted by Frankfort and others as a representation of the judgement of the bird Zû (Anzû), who stole from Enlil (or, in some versions, from the water god Ea) the 'Tablet of Destinies'. Several scenes show a bird carrying a man: this may illustrate the myth of Etana, who was taken on a flight to heaven. Scenes depicting deities and a bull with a winged edifice on its back were thought by Frankfort to show the episode from the *Epic of Gilgamesh* involving Ishtar and the 'bull of heaven', whereas to Amiet they represented a sacrifice and conquest of the skies by a deity. The killing of the 'bull of heaven', and of the monster Humbaba, episodes from the Gilgamesh story, can be recognized in 2nd- and 1st-millennium BC art.

Some scenes, mostly of the 1st millennium BC, show a winged deity with lightning forks attacking a 'lion-dragon': this has variously been interpreted as the storm god Adad in battle, Marduk's victory over Tiāmat in the *Epic of Creation*, or Ninurta defeating Anzû or the Asakku demon in the *Lugale Myth*. The numerous interpretations of a scene involving a stylized tree, usually with a winged disc above, and 'genies' performing a 'cone-smearing' ritual, have included an apotropaic magical rite, a benediction, an anointing of a king, a rite or myth of purification, a literal rendering of fruit picking, a myth of the god Dumuzi, a symbolic reference to fire and water as the elements of life, or a piece of astronomical symbolism.

BIBLIOGRAPHY

H. Frankfort: 'Gods and Myths on Sargonid Seals', *Iraq*, i (1934), pp. 2–29

O. Gurney: 'Babylonian Prophylactic Figures and their Ritual', *Liverpool An. Archaeol. & Anthropol.*, xxii (1935), p. 65

H. Frankfort: *Cylinder Seals: A Documentary Essay on the Art and Religion of the Ancient Near East* (London, 1939)

E. D. van Buren: *Symbols of the Gods in Mesopotamian Art* (Rome, 1945)

F. Köcher: 'Der babylonische Göttertypentext', *Mitt. Inst. Orientforsch.*, i (1953), pp. 57–107

B. L. Goff: *Symbols of Prehistoric Mesopotamia* (New Haven, 1963)

M.-T. Barrelet: *Figurines et reliefs en terre cuite de la Mésopotamie antique*, i (Paris, 1968)

T. Solyman: *Die Entstehung und Entwicklung der Götterwaffen im alten Mesopotamien und ihre Bedeutung* (Beirut, 1968)

P. Amiet: 'The Mythological Repertory in the Cylinder Seals of the Agade Period (*c*. 2335–2155 BC)', *Ancient Art in Seals*, ed. E. Porada (Princeton, 1980)

D. Collon: *First Impressions: Cylinder Seals in the Ancient Near East* (London, 1987)

U. Seidl: *Die babylonischen Kudurru-Reliefs: Symbole mesopotamischer Gottheiten* (Göttingen and Fribourg, 1989)

J. Black and A. Green: *Gods, Demons and Symbols of Ancient Mesopotamia: An Illustrated Dictionary* (London and Austen, 1992)

F. A. M. Wiggermann: *Mesopotamian Protective Spirits: The Ritual Texts* (Groningen, 1992)

F. A. M. Wiggermann and A. Green: 'Mischwesen' [in Eng.], *Reallexikon der Assyriologie*, viii (Berlin and New York, 1994), pp. 222–64

E. A. Braun-Holzinger: *Ikonographie mesopotamischer Götter und ihrer Begleiter* (in preparation)

A. Green: 'Ancient Mesopotamian Religious Iconography', *Civilizations of the Ancient Near East*, ed. J. M. Sasson (in preparation)

——: 'Mythologie. B. In der mesopotamischen Kunst' [in Eng.], *Reallexikon der Assyriologie*, ix (in preparation)

ANTHONY GREEN

II. Architecture.

1. Before *c.* 6000 BC. 2. *c.* 6000–*c.* 4000 BC. 3. *c.* 4000–*c.* 2900 BC (Uruk period, including Jemdet Nasr period). 4. *c.* 2900–*c.* 2000 BC. 5. *c.* 2000–*c.* 1000 BC. 6. *c.* 1000 BC–AD 637.

1. BEFORE *c.* 6000 BC. The earliest structures at such sites as Mureybet and Abu Hureyra in Syria in the 8th millennium BC are circular, semi-subterranean dwellings, while part of a circular wall from the Zagros site of Zawi Chemi Shanidar (*c.* 9th millennium BC) is the earliest recorded architectural feature from eastern Mesopotamia. The first architecture attested in the lowlands of Iraq comes from the aceramic site of Maghzaliyah, near Yarim Tepe in northern Mesopotamia (*c.* 7000 BC), with a megalithic settlement wall and rectangular structures made of *tauf* (packed mud) on stone foundations. The megalithic wall, indeed the site itself, is so far unique in Mesopotamian prehistory, though a number of aceramic sites are known in the Tell Afar and Eski Mosul regions.

Although the earliest dwellings throughout the Near East appear to have been circular, perhaps a reflection of nomadic origins, during the 8th millennium BC rectangular houses made of *tauf*, often on stone foundations, appeared throughout the area. For the early history of architecture the site of Çayönü in southern Anatolia, one of the oldest known farming settlements, is of major importance. Situated midway between the Levant and the Zagros Mountains, the site dates from the 8th–7th millennium BC. Its architecture is already remarkably sophisticated and complex. Various types of plan have been recovered, and some of them must have had special functions. Moreover, their existence, and the obvious standardization of ordinary house plans by *c.* 7000 BC, implies a considerable earlier history of architectural development. At JARMO occurs the type of multi-room courtyard house still built in Iraq, though in the 7th millennium BC construction was of *tauf*.

Connections with Çayönü can be seen in a number of features, including an example of the so-called grill plan, though at Jarmo this perhaps represents only the substructure of a drying platform.

2. *c.* 6000–*c.* 4000 BC. By the 6th millennium BC numerous farming villages are known on the north Mesopotamian plain. Of particular interest are the houses and 'warehouses' of UMM DABAGHIYA. The former consisted of small rooms (1.5×2 m), a common feature of Neolithic houses in Mesopotamia, with low doorways and the earliest well-preserved evidence for heating: exterior ovens and interior hearths with proper chimneys made of gypsum plaster. Toe-holds in the walls gave access to the roof. Traces of wall paintings were also found in these houses, in one case perhaps illustrating an onager hunt. Three unusual building complexes consist of double or triple rows of up to 50 small rooms, which appear to have served for storage and must represent some communal economic activity. A similar building was also found in Hassuna levels at Yarim Tepe (*see* YARIM TEPE (ii)). An interesting feature of village planning at this time is that the central area of a settlement appears deliberately to have been left empty (e.g. Umm Dabaghiyah, Yarim Tepe I).

The next innovations in Mesopotamian architecture are found at 6th-millennium BC Samarran sites in central Mesopotamia, where mud-brick first appears. Mud-bricks are handmade and generally 'cigar-shaped'; in the thicker house walls at CHOGHA MAMI they are laid as headers and stretchers. Such bricks are used also in the post-Samarran Chogha Mami Transitional, and at contemporary and related settlements in Khuzistan (e.g. CHOGHA MISH) and Sumer (Tell el-'Oueili). Also distinctive are the conventionalized house plans: T-shaped at TELL ES-SAWWAN, and regular structures of six to nine rooms in two or three parallel rows at Chogha Mami and in the HAMRIN REGION (Songor A). The use of buttressing, later an ornamental feature, is common to reinforce wall junctions. Of especial interest are the large level I/II structures at Tell es-Sawwan (*c.* 180 sq. m; see fig. 7a), which in plan clearly presage the tripartite houses of the Ubaid period (5th millennium BC). A mud-brick wall and ditch were found at Tell es-Sawwan, though apparently not constructed for defensive purposes,

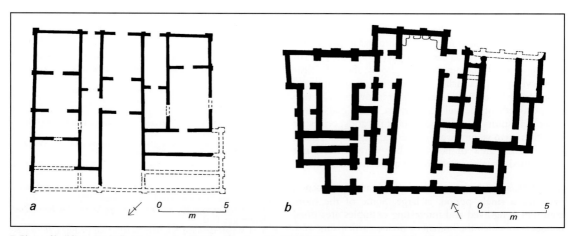

7. Plans of buildings: (a) Tell es Sawwan, level I, 6th millennium BC; (b) Tell Abada, level I/II, mid-5th millennium BC

since they surround only part of the settlement. At Chogha Mami, a less secure settlement at the western edge of the Zagros, a massive guard-tower defended one entrance. An entrance path following round the tower consists of a cobbled pavement with mud-brick and polished stone steps. Defensive structures, however, were not characteristic of Mesopotamian architecture until the Early Dynastic period (*c.* 2900–*c.* 2340 BC).

Halaf architecture differs significantly from that of the Hassuna–Samarra' tradition. Here the houses are single-room, domed, circular structures. One large, unusual circular building was found at Yarim Tepe II: its four rectangular projections comprised some 22 rooms; the inner rooms of the central circular portion were lined with alabaster slabs. At ARPACHIYAH, however, the circular structures, sometimes called 'tholoi', seem to have been isolated within a special precinct: both their unusual situation and their associated graves suggest some ritual function. At Songor B was found an unusual rectangular building with a cruciform central chamber and stepped façades. However, buildings that can certainly be identified as religious are found only from the Ubaid period onwards: of the greatest importance in this context is the excavated sequence of religious buildings beneath the corner of the Ur III ziggurat at ERIDU. In later Mesopotamia there were two types of temple, both of which have their origins in the Ubaid period. One, the 'high temple', was built on a terrace, of which the height increased with successive structures, since the remains of previous temples were enclosed within their foundations. The other, the 'low temple', seems not to have been associated with such a tradition (e.g. TEPE GAWRA and the Eanna precinct at URUK; *see also* §3 below). Eridu provides the earliest and finest example of the former tradition, with a sequence of religious buildings covering a span of some 3500 years. The earliest (Ubaid phase 1) is a simple, single-room shrine, with an altar in a small niche opposite the entrance and a central offering table, a plan precisely paralleled over 2000 years later in the Early Dynastic Inanna Temple at Nippur. By the Ubaid phase 3 period the temple tradition was well-established, with a sequence of tripartite buildings of increasing elaboration. This tripartite plan, especially characteristic of Ubaid and Uruk architecture, consists of a long central chamber with a single row of ancillary chambers on either side and a staircase to the roof in one corner. It is found in both private and ritual structures, the temple being literally conceived as the god's private dwelling. Comparable temples and traditions are known at Uruk in the Anu sequence. At Tepe Gawra, in the north, a simple 'acropolis' has been excavated, perhaps the earliest example of spatial planning.

Excavations in the Hamrin region have provided much evidence of the development of the tripartite plan characteristic of the religious buildings of Eridu and Gawra, in particular at the site of Abada (see fig. 7b), where the ordinary dwelling houses are the earliest known examples of the cruciform tripartite plan (Ubaid phase 3), with its long T-shaped central chamber. This plan was later perfected in the great public buildings of Eanna at Uruk. Similar Ubaid structures have been excavated at Kheit Qasim III (for illustration *see* HAMRIN REGION), Songor

C and Tell Madhur. By the Ubaid period rectangular mud-bricks, presumably moulded, constituted the standard building material.

BIBLIOGRAPHY

D. Oates and J. Oates: *The Rise of Civilization*, The Making of the Past (Oxford, 1976)
J.-D. Forest: 'Aux origines de l'architecture obéidienne: Les Plans de type Samarra', *Akkadica*, xxxiv (1983), pp. 1–47
J. Oates: ''Ubaid Mesopotamia Revisited', *The Hilly Flanks and Beyond: Essays on the Prehistory of Southwestern Asia Presented to Robert J. Braidwood*, ed. T. C. Young, P. E. L. Smith and P. Mortensen (Chicago, 1983), pp. 251–81
R. Bensenval: *Technologie de la voûte dans l'Orient ancien*, 2 vols (Paris, 1984)

3. *c.* 4000–*c.* 2900 BC (URUK PERIOD, INCLUDING JEMDET NASR PERIOD). Few examples of Early Uruk architecture have been discovered: at Tepe Gawra an unusual and apparently heavily fortified Round House dominated the settlement in level XIa, while subsequent Uruk levels revealed a series of tripartite temples with recessed 'porch' entrances (for illustration *see* GAWRA, TEPE), a specifically northern feature probably reflecting no more than the greater incidence of rainfall here. At TELL BRAK traces of an Early Uruk religious building with a niched façade have also been found. The houses of Qalinj Agha near Kirkuk provide further evidence of the widespread tripartite plan (*see* §2 above). Middle Uruk architecture is best attested at two south Mesopotamian colonies on the Upper Euphrates, JEBEL ARUDA and HABUBA KABIRA in north-west Syria. Habuba provides the earliest example of a planned city, unusual in Mesopotamia where most urban centres grew slowly from their ancestral villages. A massive mud-brick wall with square towers surrounded the city. At Jebel Aruda, high on a cliff above the Euphrates, was a religious sanctuary, with adjacent houses for temple personnel. As at Habuba, these were either of tripartite type or large courtyard houses with broad reception suites on either side, the latter themselves often of tripartite plan. A massive wall surrounded an inner precinct, in which were situated an earlier Red Temple and a later Grey Temple, which in plan closely resemble those of the Anu sequence at URUK. At both sites and elsewhere in Late Uruk Mesopotamia a type of small rectangular brick known as Riemchen was employed (usually *c.* 60×60×160 mm).

For the Late Uruk period it is Uruk itself that provides not only the most extensive evidence but also some of the most remarkable architectural remains recovered from the ancient world. Here two precincts existed in the Uruk period, representing two distinct traditions in Mesopotamian religious architecture. Throughout the Uruk period in the area of the later Bit Resh, or Principal Temple, dedicated to Anu, was a high terrace on which was situated a temple of the 'high temple' type (*see* §2 above), of which at least seven rebuildings are attested. To the north-west was an unusual subterranean building, known as the *Steingebäude* or the Cenotaph, with a curious stone trap door on the floor of the central chamber. As at ERIDU the high terrace sequence originated in the Ubaid period (5th millennium BC). At Uruk the best-preserved shrine is the White Temple, which provides a classic example of the tripartite plan, identical to its late Ubaid predecessors. The temple contained a high podium, approached by steps,

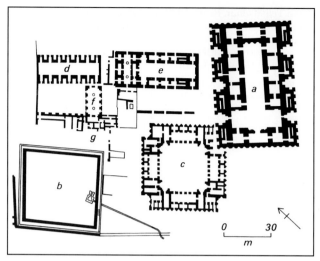

8. Uruk, plan of Eanna precinct, level IVa, before *c.* 3000 BC: (a) Temple D; (b) large arena; (c) Temple E; (d) large hall; (e) Temple C; (f) Stone Cone Mosaic Building; (g) baths

and a second stepped altar in the centre of the long central chamber. Corner staircases gave access to the roof, where evidence from later periods suggests that ritual activities may have taken place. The terrace, built of mud-brick, rose with sloping and recessed walls. The tops of the terrace and stair walls were strengthened as well as ornamented with rows of clay beakers, in a manner comparable with cone mosaic decoration. Only part of the platform was occupied by the temple itself, and the open terrace to the north-east also suggests some outdoor ritual activity. Remains of a fireplace on the external terrace and the large number of very regular installations of this type found elsewhere at Uruk, especially in level III, have been interpreted either as cooking areas or places of sacrificial fires (*Opferstätten*). A comparable high terrace sequence has been excavated at Eridu, while the Painted Temple at 'Uqair, noted for its wall paintings (*see* §VI below), is of the same type. The high terrace was to develop into a true ziggurat in the 3rd millennium BC (*see* §4 below), while its 'high temple' tradition was maintained in Mesopotamia until Persian times.

At Uruk the contrasting 'low temple' tradition can be seen some 50 m to the east in the Eanna precinct, in later times a broad area of courtyards and terraces surrounding a true ziggurat dedicated to Inanna. The Late Uruk complex, of which the excavated area alone occupies some 50,000 sq. m, provides the earliest evidence of architecture on a truly monumental scale. The precinct includes a variety of public buildings, the most common of which are frequently described as temples, since they repeat the usual temple plan, often in extraordinarily elaborate variations, but evidence for cult installations is lacking. Four building phases have been identified in Late Uruk Eanna (V–IVa). The largest building of level V, the Limestone Temple (70×30 m), is unique in its stone construction. Its tripartite plan incorporates the T-shaped central hall (roofed) and ancillary chambers that, again, derive from

Ubaid tradition (*see* §2 above). Not long after the construction of the Limestone Temple, the remarkable Cone Mosaic Court was built. Zigzag and lozenge patterns of clay cones with black, red and white heads covered the walls of the courtyard, perhaps in imitation of matting or textile patterns. Adjacent to this was a gigantic portico comprising a double row of massive cylindrical columns, over 2 m in diameter, which, together with four semi-columns at either end, supported the roof of the hall, one of the rare occurrences of free-standing columns in Mesopotamian architecture. The columns too were decorated with painted clay cones. A number of other public buildings are attested in Eanna IVb, including the remarkable Stone Cone Mosaic Building. This was ornamented with black, red and white limestone and white alabaster cone mosaic. The building itself stood in a rectangular court, surrounded by a curious double-buttressed wall similarly decorated.

The Cone Mosaic Court was subsequently destroyed and filled in, to be replaced by the massive buildings of Eanna IVa (see fig. 8). Of these Temple D (8a) is the largest and most impressive, with its T-shaped cella entered through transepts at one end and its deeply recessed ornamental niches. The earliest pictographic clay tablets (*see* ANCIENT NEAR EAST, §I, 3(i)) were recovered from level IVa, for the most part in unstratified rubbish outside the administrative building known as the Red Temple (to the east of Temple D). At this time the Eanna precinct contained a variety of public structures, including a large arena or gymnasium (8b) with benches around the sides, and a regular building, Temple E (8c), which some interpret as an early palace, since its plan differs significantly from the known temples of the time. Another unusual and isolated building (18×20 m), known as the *Riemchengebäude*, has foundations dug into the Stone Cone Mosaic Building. It had an inner chamber surrounded by a corridor that showed signs of heavy burning and contained a rich collection of objects. The building had no apparent access and had been deliberately filled in, suggesting its interpretation as a ritual structure for the dedication and burial of temple furniture from a superseded shrine.

At the end of Eanna IVa the whole precinct was razed and replaced by a high terrace of the Anu type (Eanna III/Jemdet Nasr period). This was surrounded by various administrative buildings and storerooms, of which the plans are ill-preserved. A monumental gateway gave access to the whole complex. The outer precinct wall, however, remained unchanged from level IVc to level I (Early Dynastic period). Eanna III is the period of the Eye Temple at Tell Brak, notable for the earliest direct association of a temple with ancillary storerooms, later to become a basic feature of major temple plans. Of considerable importance also is the vast administrative complex at Jemdet Nasr itself, perhaps an early palace, though, regrettably, its plan has not been recovered. The earliest shrines at Khafajeh (*see* DIYALA REGION) are also of this date. At 'Uqair a small chapel was excavated, adjacent to the Painted Temple and its terrace, from which an important collection of Jemdet Nasr polychrome pottery and tablets was recovered.

BIBLIOGRAPHY
S. Lloyd and F. Safar: 'Tell Uquair', *J. Nr E. Stud.*, ii (1943), pp. 131–58
E. Strommenger and M. Hirmer: *The Art of Mesopotamia* (London, 1964)
S. Lloyd: *The Archaeology of Mesopotamia* (London, 1978, rev. 1984)
E. Heinrich: *Die Tempel und Heiligtümer im alten Mesopotamien*, Dt. Archäol. Inst., Dkml. Ant. Archit., 2 vols (Berlin, 1982)

JOAN OATES

4. *c.* 2900–*c.* 2000 BC. By the beginning of the 3rd millennium BC builders in Mesopotamia had mastered most of the traditional building techniques. They worked mainly with mud-brick, although stone was also used in the north, where it was more easily available. Mud-bricks were made by puddling together earth and water, tempered with chopped straw. Sometimes they were baked to render them waterproof, but this was an expensive procedure used only sparingly. Mud was used as mortar: bitumen, which occurs naturally in parts of Mesopotamia, is also found, but it was more commonly used as waterproofing in cisterns, bathrooms and courtyards. Walls and floors were finished in mud-plaster or in better-quality gypsum plaster. Floors were more usually just tamped earth.

Flat roofs were constructed by laying reed mats and layers of compressed clay on beams of palm-tree trunks, a technique still widely used. In the north, where the rainfall is heavier, there is circumstantial evidence for pitched roofs made in approximately the same way. Other roofing techniques were also practised, including barrel-vaulting, corbelling and even the dome (in one of the Royal Graves at UR). The true arch already existed, and free-standing pillars, though rare, were well-established in the architect's repertory. This technical expertise made it possible to construct massive, buttressed town walls and a wide variety of buildings, of which the temples are perhaps the best-known. These usually stood in the heart of the town, raised on a platform, which often enclosed the remains of earlier shrines too sacred to destroy. The platform, in some cases approached by monumental stairs, acted as a large walled temenos (anc. Gr. *temenos*, from Sum. *temen*, 'foundation'), supporting a number of religious buildings and towering above the town. At Ur the temenos is surrounded by a massive casemate wall with monumental gateways giving access to the sacred area. At the beginning of the 3rd millennium BC there was a wide variety of temple plans, including a few examples of the tripartite temples typical of the earlier Uruk period (*see* §3 above). Some temples closely resemble private houses in plan, with shrines and offices grouped round a courtyard, while some, for instance at Khafajeh in the DIYALA REGION and at TELL AL-UBAID, are impressive oval enclosures round a raised platform, on which the shrine itself is presumed to have stood. Other temples, such as that at Tell Taya in the north, are simple, single-room shrines. All these buildings have their corners orientated to the points of the compass. The shrines themselves all contain an altar, which probably originally supported a statue of the god. The entrance is usually through a side door on the long wall to give a 'bent-axis' approach to the altar (the '*Langraum*' type), though this changed towards the end of the 3rd millennium BC, when a direct approach to the altar became standard (the '*Breitraum*' type). A hearth or table for offerings and incense is frequently found, as are benches round the walls on which the statues of suppliants could stand. The interior walls were finely plastered, but there is no evidence of the painted decoration found in earlier temples. The exterior walls are usually decorated with alternate buttresses and recesses, and the doorways are often rabbeted.

The most spectacular religious monuments of the second half of the 3rd millennium BC are the great ziggurats

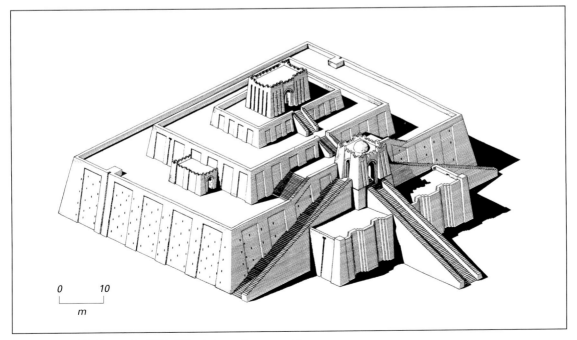

9. Ur, ziggurat of Ur-Nammu (*reg* 2112–2095 BC); isometric reconstruction

or staged towers of which the best surviving example is that of Ur-Nammu at Ur (see fig. 9; *see also* ZIGGURAT). One of these ziggurats is probably the structure referred to in the biblical story of the Tower of Babel (Genesis 11:3–9). The Ur ziggurat has three stages: the lowest measures 50×30 m, and access was by a triple stair; the second is somewhat smaller; and the third, of which only traces remain, is thought to have supported the shrine itself. Other temples clustered at the foot of the stairs, and the whole area was enclosed by a wall and approached through a monumental courtyard. The solid core of the ziggurat is built of unbaked mud-brick, with an outer skin of baked brick and plaster; the vertical sides of the lowest stage are slightly bowed in order to give the illusion of being straight, demonstrating an understanding of the principle of entasis later so important in ancient Greek architecture (*see* ENTASIS). The exterior is decorated with buttresses and recesses to break the monotony of the flat surfaces and to give a play of light and shade.

The earliest monumental secular buildings may date back to the mid-4th millennium BC or even earlier, and by the mid-3rd millennium a number of examples are known from such sites as KISH, ERIDU, Wilaya and Ur. The 'A' palace at Kish is one of the best examples and illustrates several features common to these buildings; typically they divide into a number of self-contained units, often separated by narrow passages in the thickness of the walls. Each unit apparently had a separate function, and all these buildings seem to include domestic, administrative and storage areas. The Kish example also has a fine ceremonial suite with a pillared portico, while the later 'Palace of the Rulers' at Tell Asmar in the Diyala region has its less elaborate audience hall attached to the administrative block. Another late example, the 'Giparu' at Ur, was a somewhat different type of building: it was the home of the high priestess of the Moon god and had an elaborate chapel and a mausoleum attached. It has been suggested that these palaces had upper storeys, but this remains unproven.

Private houses were typically built round a courtyard, facing inwards, with blank walls on to the narrow streets. One larger room served as a reception and living area, and there was sometimes a separate kitchen, which might have a built-in range, ovens and storage bins. The other rooms were used for sleeping and storage, with the flat roof providing extra living space. There is a considerable variation in size and sophistication among the houses excavated, and the plan was often drastically modified to fit the space available. Later in the 3rd millennium BC the wealthier houses sometimes had a private chapel and a paved bathroom with lavatory. Graves and brick-built tombs are found below the floors of rooms and courtyards throughout the period. The houses may also have had an upper storey: Woolley claimed evidence for this on some of the late 3rd-millennium BC houses at Ur, which may have had an internal stair to reach rooms opening out on to a wooden balcony, as can still be seen in traditional Arab town houses.

BIBLIOGRAPHY

C. L. Woolley: *The Ziggurat and its Surroundings* (1939), v of *Ur Excavations* (London, 1939)

H. E. W. Crawford: *The Architecture of Iraq in the Third Millennium* (Copenhagen, 1977)
E. Heinrich: *Tempel und Heiligtümer im alten Mesopotamien*, 2 vols (Berlin, 1982)
J. Margueron: *Les Palais mésopotamiens*, 2 vols (Paris, 1982)
Ö. Tunca: *Recherches sur l'architecture religieuse protodynastique en Mésopotamie*, 2 vols (Leuven, 1984)

HARRIET CRAWFORD

5. *c.* 2000–*c.* 1000 BC.

(i) Introduction. (ii) Temples and palaces. (iii) Ziggurats. (iv) Decoration.

(i) Introduction. The history of architecture in Mesopotamia after the emergence of cities is largely the history of temples, palaces and ziggurats. Much less is known about private houses, but they apparently conformed to a courtyard plan with, on crowded sites, an upper storey. An area of housing of the 20th–19th centuries BC was excavated at UR. By the beginning of the 2nd millennium BC certain architectural traditions were clearly established. The overall organization of palaces and temples followed earlier practice in disposing rows of rooms around interconnecting courtyards that provided communication, light and ventilation and varied in number according to the needs of the establishment for administrative and domestic accommodation and the storage of goods. In the late 3rd millennium BC, however, the major buildings of both types had assumed a more formal aspect, both in plan and in the elevations of their principal façades. This formality was well established by the time of the Third Dynasty of Ur (*c.* 2100–2000 BC), although it may go back to the kings of Agade (*see also* TELL BRAK). Such conscious design certainly suggests the emergence of a school of architects working over a wide area and financed by revenues on an imperial rather than a local scale. The focal point of the larger temple or palace was the reception suite, the shrine or the throne-room. In neither case do written descriptions survive of the routines of approach to the podium or dais, presumably because they were familiar to the participants; however, three different standard plans reflect variant patterns of movement (*see* §(ii) below). Two of these plans are found in both temples and palaces, implying that access to god or king followed the same patterns. The third reception-room plan is confined to temples alone.

Few Mesopotamian buildings of any period have survived to roof height, but TELL EL-RIMAH has provided exceptional examples of two different techniques of vaulting. The first, found in the original temple of *c.* 1800 BC and in a major reconstruction of the cella *c.* 1500 BC, employed radial voussoirs but with a higher pitch than the classical semicircular profile. The spring of the vault was corbelled, and voussoirs were then slanted gradually, supported by their predecessors and the adhesion of the mud mortar until the gap was narrowed to about half the original span, so that wooden centring was needed only to complete the crown. In the second technique, known as 'pitched brick', successive rings of bricks were laid with their edges across the long axis of the vault. Each ring was sloped back to rest on its predecessor and construction started from both ends simultaneously until the rings interlocked; by this method no centring was needed. No earlier examples of radial vaulting on free-standing walls exist, but the technique is not likely to have been invented in a small city and probably originated in Babylonia, whose influence is so clear in the temple plan. The pitched-brick vault seems more likely to represent a local tradition. It was used in a secondary repair in the temple and in 15th- and 14th-century BC houses in Tell el-Rimah, but the earliest and most complete examples occur in a three-tiered structure of late 3rd-millennium BC date that preceded the temple on the central mound.

(ii) Temples and palaces.

(a) Bent-axis plan. The oldest temple or palace plan of the period is the 'bent-axis' type, with the place of honour at one end of a rectangular room and the entrance (or entrances, in the case of some throne-rooms) in one of the long sides. Thus the divine statue or the enthroned ruler was not visible from outside the chamber, and the suppliant or visitor had to turn left or right on entry. As a temple type, the bent-axis plan first occurs in the mid-4th millennium BC at Tell Shaikh Hassan on the Middle Euphrates, but, apart from an early 3rd-millennium BC example in the Inanna temple at NIPPUR, it is unknown in Babylonia. It has, however, a long history at MARI and in the DIYALA REGION, and in the Ishtar Temple, the oldest at ASSUR, where an immutable ritual clearly dictated its retention through many rebuildings until the fall of the city in 614 BC. It was employed in the construction of the Temple of Assur by Shamshi-Adad I (*reg* 1813–1781 BC) *c.* 1800 BC, although here the plan was later changed to the 'long-room' layout standard in the Neo-Assyrian period (1883–612 BC). Bent-axis shrines are also found in the Temple of Ishtar at NUZI, originally constructed as a single sanctuary in the late 3rd millennium BC and extended to include a second similar shrine *c.* 2000 BC; this form was retained until the destruction of the town in the 15th century BC. The type can be seen again on a smaller scale in what appear to be small domestic shrines of the 15th and 14th centuries BC at Tell el-Rimah. It would seem that, apart from the early example at Nippur, this plan and

the associated ritual were characteristic of central and northern Mesopotamia.

The same regional pattern of distribution can be observed in the case of bent-axis throne-rooms. The earliest known example is in the palace of the rulers of Eshnunna, *c.* 2000 BC, and they also occur in the Old Palace at Assur, commonly believed to be of 19th-century BC date and sometimes attributed to Shamshi-Adad I, and in a formal reception room at Tell el-Rimah, which was probably the seat of one of his governors. Unfortunately, the palace of Hammurabi of Babylon, the most famous ruler of this time, is inaccessible beneath the debris of later centuries. The only major palace of this period that has been almost completely excavated is the palace of King Zimri-Lim at Mari (see fig. 10 and MARI, fig. 1). As a result of its destruction by Hammurabi and the absence of major reoccupation of the site, it was found with its walls standing to a considerable height, its fittings and much of the material on its floors in place. In its final form it had at least ten courtyards and provides an excellent illustration of the distribution of functions in a large Mesopotamian royal residence, with administrative, ceremonial and residential quarters, storage areas and a palace-temple of bent-axis form. The ceremonial suite consisted of a bent-axis inner chamber with the principal dais at one end, preceded by a throne-room of the 'broad-room' plan (*see* §(b) below); the outer chamber is evidently a later addition. Opening off the main entrance courtyard is another chamber, with its entrance on the long axis (the 'long-room' plan; *see* §(c) below) and a podium at the far end. This was originally described as an audience hall, but more probably served a religious function. Later examples are sparse.

The palace at Nuzi in the 15th century BC had a bent-axis throne-room, but no late 2nd-millennium BC palaces have yielded detailed plans, because they were cut down to make way for later monumental buildings, particularly

10. Mari, Palace of Zimri-Lim, first half of the 18th century BC; aerial view

at Assur, the only source of information for the Middle Assyrian period (*c.* 1363–1076 BC). The persistence of the bent-axis tradition is, however, attested by its consistent appearance in Neo-Assyrian palaces of the 9th and 8th centuries BC. It is interesting that in the north it has remained the traditional form of the village guest-house to the 20th century.

(*b*) *Broad-room plan.* The second standard plan, employed in both temples and palaces, is known as the 'broad-room' plan. Here the dais or podium is placed in the middle of one long wall, with the entrance immediately opposite. In larger temples of this pattern there was a broad-room antecella preceded by a square or rectangular courtyard, both with their entrances on the axis of the cella doorway. Thus, when some or all the doors were open, the divine statue was visible from the courtyard or even from outside the building. The plan is first attested under the Third Dynasty of Ur in the 'Giparu' at Ur (*see* §4 above), and may be one of the major innovations of this time. It is found in the early 2nd millennium BC at Ischali (Temple of Ishtar–Kititum) and Tell Harmal, both in the Diyala region.

The broad-room plan remained throughout Mesopotamian history a southern architectural tradition, and it is represented in the north on only two sites. The first, Tell el-Rimah, shows a completely symmetrical version; it was founded on the levelled site of an earlier settlement, probably by Shamshi-Adad I, who had lived in Babylonia before his conquest of Assur. The second, KAR TUKULTI NINURTA, was a new capital of Tukulti-Ninurta I (*reg* 1243–1207 BC), who built a broad-room temple of Assur there *c.* 1230 BC. He had himself conquered Babylon, and his reign was a time of strong Babylonian influence in Assyria. As a throne-room plan the broad-room also seems, on the evidence of later periods, to be traditionally southern, although there are no Babylonian examples from the 2nd millennium BC. Indeed, with the exception of the secondary outer reception room at Mari noted above, the only known throne-room of this type is in the 18th-century BC palace at Tell el-Rimah; both sites were within the political orbit of Hammurabi at this time.

(*c*) *Long-room plan.* The third form of Mesopotamian temple plan is the 'long-room', in which again the podium faces the entrance, but on the long axis of the shrine. It first occurs in the Temple of Dagan at Mari *c.* 2100 BC, then in a side chapel of the Ishtar–Kititum complex at Ischali, at Mari, Tell Harmal and *c.* 1800 BC at Tell Leilan. It appears at Assur in the double temples of Anu and Adad, possibly founded by Shamsi-Adad I, and of Sin and Shamash (16th century BC). The only southern example is the Temple of Inanna at URUK, built by the Kassite king Karaindash *c.* 1400 BC. It remained the standard plan in Assyria until the end of the 7th century BC, but was never employed for a royal reception room.

(*d*) *Kassite plan.* Foreign rulers controlled parts of Mesopotamia during much of the second half of the 2nd millennium BC, the Kassites in the south and the Mitanni dynasty across the northern plain. Nothing is known of Mitanni architecture, with the exception of a palace and

nearby broad-room shrine at Tell Brak, both of which show some west Syrian characteristics. The Kassites, who took the title 'King of Babylon', seem to have adopted the cultural and architectural traditions of Babylonia, from which they departed only in a newly founded city, Dur Kurigalzu (*see* AQAR QUF) west of Baghdad. Here the plan of the palace is incomplete and difficult to interpret, but obviously includes major reception rooms with multiple entrances, unknown elsewhere.

(*iii*) *Ziggurats.* Perhaps the most famous feature of Mesopotamian religious architecture is the ZIGGURAT or staged tower. Its origin is unknown, but it may have developed from the 'high terrace' on which some 4th- and early 3rd-millennium BC temples stood. It seems likely that the formalized, symmetrical ziggurat was first conceived by the architects of the Third Dynasty of Ur, who certainly conceived the earliest known version of the famous ziggurat at Ur itself. However, the conventional picture of this ziggurat, complete with a temple on top, is derived from heavily eroded remains that are at best fragmentary outlines above the first stage, and from Herodotus' 5th-century BC description of the ziggurat at Babylon, and does not necessarily apply in all cases. There is again a regional difference in tradition. In Babylonia the ziggurat stood alone in its own precinct, with at most two ancillary temples attached to its base; the Kassite ziggurat at Dur Kurigalzu is unusual in also having a rectangular platform, on which the principal temple probably stood, in front of its central stair. On the middle Euphrates and Assyria the ziggurat was normally attached to a temple and approached from its roof, even when, as at Tell el-Rimah and Kar Tukulti Ninurta, the temple itself was of the Babylonian broad-room plan. A notable exception of 2nd-millennium BC date is the free-standing ziggurat of Enlil/Assur at Assur, perhaps because there was no room on the steep ridge behind the temple. At the same site the twin long-room temples of Anu and Adad had attached ziggurats, probably also built by Shamshi-Adad I. It seems likely, however, that other less symmetrical blocks of brickwork, such as those attached to the Temple of Dagan at Mari and the temple at Tell Leilan, were simple high terraces with no upper stage.

(*iv*) *Decoration.* From the 2nd millennium BC also comes early evidence for architectural decoration and for methods of roofing in mud-brick. Decoration, apart from wall paintings, such as those at Mari and Dur Kurigalzu, was confined to religious buildings. Engaged half-columns appear in the late 19th century BC, and Tell el-Rimah has provided the most elaborate example. The external and courtyard façades of the temple were adorned with 277 columns, set singly or in groups. The 50 large columns were built of carved segmental bricks, laid in complicated sequences to represent spirals or two types of palm trunk, while two, set into the east gate towers, were quatrefoil in plan with two opposed spirals backed by palm trunks. A similar façade occurs at Shubat Enlil (Tel Leilan) in a temple also founded by Shamshi Adad I. Both may have been designed by Babylonian architects, since in the same period palm trunk columns at Ur show an identical technique of construction, and there are spiral columns at Larsa. Engaged columns were used in the Kassite buildings at Ur and components of baked brick spirals, though of simpler shapes than at Rimah, were discovered at Dur Kurigalzu. A more elaborate Kassite baked brick façade, with a row of deities set in niches, adorned the Inanna Temple at Uruk; and a similar composition, in which deities alternate with bull-men holding palm trees, was found in 12th-century BC SUSA.

Similar figures also appear in other positions. At Rimah four limestone impost blocks were found; these had probably supported the lintels of the main east gate of the temple and the antecella door. On their outer faces were high relief carvings of the goddess Lama, who introduced suppliants to the deity, standing between two palm trees, a bull-man flanked by double spiral columns and two masks of the apotropaic demon Humbaba. In the south, terracotta figures of lions flanked the entrances to 19th-century BC temples at Tell Harmal and Mari, and fragments of several figures of the same material have been found at Isin. All these motifs, though decorative, are clearly relevant to the guarding and service of the temple, and there is no doubt that the columned façades also had a symbolic significance.

BIBLIOGRAPHY

E. Heinrich: *Tempel und Heiligtümer im alten Mesopotamien*, 2 vols (Berlin, 1982)
J. Margueron: *Les Palais mésopotamiens*, 2 vols (Paris, 1982)

DAVID OATES

6. *c.* 1000 BC–AD 637.

(i) Neo-Assyrian. (ii) Neo-Babylonian. (iii) Parthian. (iv) Sasanian.

(i) Neo-Assyrian.

(a) Building techniques and plans. (b) Royal building projects.

(a) Building techniques and plans. Neo-Assyrian buildings were constructed almost exclusively of mud-brick. Large structures were usually built on solid mud-brick foundation platforms. Although limestone is plentiful in Assyria, it was used architecturally only for structures exposed to running water, such as river walls and aqueducts, or for defensive purposes, as facing for fortification walls. The walls of monumental buildings, such as palaces and temples, were usually embellished with stone wall-slabs, sometimes carved in relief (*see* §III below), wall paintings (*see* §VI, 2 below) or glazed baked bricks. Major exterior doorways were usually marked by projecting gate-towers. Large doorways were often crowned with arches of mud-brick. Most interior floors were of beaten earth, which in important rooms must have been covered with reed mats and carpets. Floors exposed to the elements, as in courtyards and terraces, or subjected to running water, as in the rooms conventionally called 'bathrooms', were paved with baked bricks or stone slabs. These are sometimes inscribed and provide the most plentiful source of information concerning the identity of royal builders.

Assyrian buildings are occasionally depicted in wall reliefs, sometimes with two storeys. Although upper storeys have not survived, they may be deduced from the presence of unusually thick walls. Stairways and ramps are also found frequently: these may have led either to upper storeys or to a flat roof, which must have been used as a cool place of retreat on summer nights. Roofs were of mud on reed mats supported by wooden beams. The

Assyrian kings recorded that the roofing timbers of exceptionally large rooms were of cedar imported from Lebanon. This wood is very durable. Layard (1853) reports that one cold day, while he was excavating the Ninurta Temple at Nimrud, he smelled burning cedar: his workers had found a well-preserved roof beam and used it to make a fire. One of the finest groups of wall reliefs from Khorsabad shows a great maritime convoy transporting large quantities of roofing timbers for use in the royal palace (Paris, Louvre). Small rooms, such as the underground royal tombs in the North-west Palace at Nimrud, were sometimes roofed with vaults of baked brick.

Neo-Assyrian architecture is conservative and mostly similar to that of the Middle Assyrian period, or indeed any period in Mesopotamia. Buildings were planned around one or more courtyards. Exterior doorways led via gate chambers into a courtyard, and interior rooms opened either from courtyards or other rooms, but rarely from corridors. These usually connected courtyards with other courtyards or with terraces. Perhaps the most distinctive feature of Neo-Assyrian monumental buildings is their great size. The aptly named 'Palace without Rival' of Sennacherib (*reg* 704–681 BC) at Nineveh was the largest single structure then built in the Near East (l. *c.* 500 m).

There are, however, typically Neo-Assyrian room patterns. In residential buildings, the most typical unit was a group of three rooms known as a 'reception suite' (Turner, 1970). A large outer 'reception room' was entered from a courtyard via one or more doors in its long wall. When this served as a throne-room it was usually fitted with a dais at one end, in front of which were stone 'tramlines', apparently for a wheeled brazier. A door in the other long wall led to the smaller 'retiring room'. The third room was a small 'bathroom', often paved and equipped with a floor drain. It was usually entered from the retiring room but sometimes, especially in throne-rooms, from the reception room. There may also have been one or more additional small rooms opening from the larger rooms.

The typical layout of the cult area in Neo-Assyrian temples is the same as that in the Middle Assyrian Sin-Shamash and Anu-Adad temples at Assur. This consisted of a broad antechamber entered from a courtyard through a door in one of its long walls. Another door directly opposite led to a long cult chamber at the far end of which, on a dais usually set in a deep niche or alcove, was the image of the deity. Small temples often lacked the broad antechamber, the long cult room being entered directly from the courtyard via a doorway in either its end or side wall.

(b) Royal building projects.

Assurnasirpal II. The major architectural monuments built by Assurnasirpal II (*reg* 883–859 BC) at his new capital of Nimrud were a city wall, a royal palace and nine temples (*see* NIMRUD, fig. 1). The city wall (l. 7.5 km) was built of mud-brick throughout. The largest building was the so-called North-west Palace on the citadel. A large outer court at the northern end was probably surrounded on three sides by offices and storerooms, while the south side opened on to the throne-room suite, which comprised the throne-room (B) and retiring room (F). There was no bathroom. Beyond this was a smaller inner court, surrounded by large state apartments, to the south of which were smaller undecorated rooms, probably the domestic service area. Vaulted tombs were concealed beneath the floors of at least three rooms in this area.

The plans of three of Assurnasirpal's nine temples at Nimrud are preserved at least in part. The largest, the Ninurta Temple, conforms to the standard Neo-Assyrian type (*see* §(a) above). To the north was a smaller subsidiary shrine entered directly from the courtyard. The temples of Sharrat-niphi and Kidmuru were smaller. Each consisted of a cult room, entered directly from the courtyard via a door in its long wall, with a dais on the short end wall.

Assurnasirpal II was also apparently responsible for rebuilding the Old Palace at ASSUR. Its preserved part measured some 60×60 m, at most only about a third of its original area. The layout seems typically Neo-Assyrian, with a throne-room suite (21–22) and reception suite (1–4) opening off outer and inner courtyards in the western section, and small service rooms surrounding a small courtyard in the eastern wing. Royal tombs were built under the south side of the palace. He also rebuilt the double Temple of Sin and Shamash at Assur. Its plan as reconstructed measured *c.* 65×46 m, with twin shrines of the standard Neo-Assyrian layout. At Nineveh he rebuilt the Ishtar Temple, but its plan has not been reconstructed.

Assurnasirpal II built a temple to Mamu, the god of dreams, and a palace at Imgur-Enlil (now Balawat). The temple, most of which has been excavated, had an outer court with a small shrine opening directly off its northeast side. A gateway in the north-west side led through to the inner court, on the opposite side of which was the doorway to the main shrine, which had wooden doors decorated with bronze bands (London, BM). Only one small room in the palace has been excavated.

Shalmaneser III. The arsenal at Nimrud, called 'Fort Shalmaneser' (*c.* 845 BC; *see* NIMRUD, fig. 2), was the largest complex built by Shalmaneser III (*reg* 858–824 BC). It was planned around four large courtyard areas: the two outer courtyards on the north side were surrounded by storerooms and offices; the south-west inner courtyard was subdivided into smaller courts and long rooms, probably barracks. The throne-room suite was on the south side of the south-east inner court, and beyond was a terrace with an isolated projecting wing; this arrangement was later used by Sargon II (see below) for his palace and arsenal at Khorsabad. West of the throne-room suite was a group of domestic apartments arranged around small courtyards. Also at Nimrud, Shalmaneser built the ziggurat and probably the South-east Palace, the only recorded part of which is a typical Neo-Assyrian reception suite, the Governor's Palace and the 1950 Building.

At Assur, he rebuilt the temple of Anu and Adad. In general it followed the plan of its predecessor and the two shrines conform to the typical Neo-Assyrian pattern. He also rebuilt the outer city wall of Assur and planned to rebuild the inner wall, although the latter may not have been completed. The plan of his new palace beside the Euphrates at Til Barsip in Syria (*see* TIL BARSIP, §2), which includes an entrance court (A), a throne-room court (B),

and an inner court (C) surrounded by typical reception suites, seems to be largely the product of a later restoration by Tiglath-pileser III (see below) or a 7th-century BC king.

Adad-nirari III. At Nimrud, Adad-nirari III (*reg* 810–783 BC) built the Nabu Temple, the palace in 'area PD 5', and probably the Burnt Palace, which included an entrance court (45) and central court (18) with a typical reception suite on its south side. His work on the Nabu Temple survives only in the southern half; the northern half, which was rebuilt by Sargon II or Assurbanipal, had an entrance court and a small inner court from which opened a second smaller pair of twin shrines and a reception suite. He also made additions to the south side of Assurnasirpal II's palace. The plan of the Nabu Temple at NINEVEH is lost and it is uncertain whether the surviving foundations are to be attributed to Adad-nirari or to Sargon II, who rebuilt it. The small Neo-Assyrian Adad Temple at Tell el Rimah is probably to be attributed to the reign of Adad-nirari; in plan it was a long cult chamber opening directly from a courtyard.

Tiglath-pileser III. Tiglath-pileser III (*reg* 744–727 BC) built a new royal palace at Nimrud. He stated that this faced the Tigris, and it may have extended as far as the centre of the citadel, where a number of his wall reliefs were found by Layard stacked in piles awaiting reuse in the palace of Esarhaddon (see below). Layard, however, was unable to locate any palace walls in the vicinity. Meuszyński located fragmentary remains of a monumental late building in this area, but Sobolewski, who published these finds, doubted that they belonged to Tiglath-pileser's palace (*see also* NIMRUD). Tiglath-pileser III was also active at ARSLAN TASH, where he built or restored the west gate, the Ishtar Temple and possibly the palace. The plans of the gate and temple are mostly lost, but that of the palace was well preserved. The palace, measuring at least 150×65 m, consisted of an outer court, a throne-room suite, an inner court that gave access to a typical reception suite and a double-shrine temple, probably dedicated to Nabu and Tashmetum, and a domestic quarter. The layout of the throne-room suite seems to pre-date Khorsabad, and it has been suggested that it was built by Tiglath-pileser III, Shalmaneser V (*reg* 726–722 BC) or Sargon II at the beginning of his reign (Turner, 1970). Tiglath-pileser III probably also restored the palace at Til Barsip.

Sargon II. Sargon II (*reg* 721–705 BC) moved his capital to a new site known as Dur-Sharrukin, where he built a city wall with seven gates, an arsenal and a fortified citadel, on which were a royal palace, four smaller palaces and a Nabu Temple (*see* KHORSABAD). The three major sections of the royal palace, the only late Assyrian palace to be completely excavated, were each built around a large courtyard (see fig. 11). The outer court (XV; 11a) was surrounded by numerous small rooms and courts. Southwest of the throne-room court (VIII; 11b) was the throne-room suite, of typical late Assyrian layout, beyond which was the inner court surrounded by three reception suites. At the east corner of the throne-room court was the entrance to a double temple, probably dedicated to Nabu

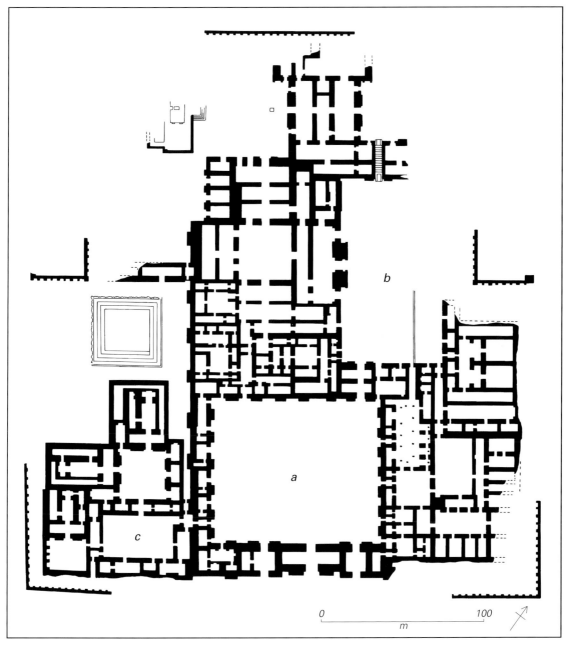

11. Khorsabad, palace of Sargon II, plan, late 8th century BC: (a) outer court; (b) throne-room court; (c) Court XXX

and Tashmetum, and from its north-west side a passage led to a projecting wing that included a secondary throne-room. At the south corner of the palace, around Court XXX (11c), were the palace temples and ziggurat. The larger shrines, dedicated to Sin, Shamash and Ningal, had the typical layout of courtyard, broad antechamber and long cult room. The smaller shrines, dedicated to Ea, Adad, Ninurta and Sebitti (in the lower town), lacked antechambers and were entered directly from the courtyard.

The four smaller palaces on the citadel (residences J, K, L and M) conformed to the same arrangement of an outer court surrounded by service rooms, a principal reception suite, an inner court surrounded by smaller reception suites, and domestic areas. In the Nabu Temple (Building H) the principal shrines were of the usual plan, while a third smaller shrine opened directly off the outer court. The service area, at the south-east side of the temple, included a single large reception room. Palace F near the south corner of the city wall was the arsenal. The excavated part included a throne-room suite facing the central court, a large reception suite facing an outer terrace, and a projecting wing similar to those of the main palace and the Nimrud arsenal.

The Neo-Assyrian Temple at Tell Halaf is of uncertain date, but its layout has been likened to that of the Nabu Temple at Khorsabad (Turner, 1968). There were at least two shrines opening from the courtyard: a main shrine consisting of a broad antechamber and long cult room with a raised alcove at the far end, next to which was a smaller shrine opening directly from the courtyard.

Sennacherib. At his new capital of Nineveh, Sennacherib (*reg* 704–681 BC) built a city wall 12 km in circuit with 18 major gates, a royal palace, an arsenal, temples, roads, bridges and canals (*see* NINEVEH, fig. 2). His royal palace, apparently the largest Assyrian palace, was on a terrace along the south-west side of the mound of Kuyunjik. Only the area that Layard called the South-west Palace has been excavated. It included a throne-room court (H), a throne-room suite (I–VI) of the standard plan, an inner court (VI) surrounded by typical reception suites, a second inner court (XIX), a feature not found in earlier Assyrian palaces, also surrounded by reception suites, and a group of rooms of uncertain plan facing the south-west terrace. In the western part of the excavated area was a group of small domestic rooms and beyond this a reception suite, which an inscription identifies as the residence of Sennacherib's favourite queen. The north-east extremity of the palace is probably to be identified with 'Sennacherib's Eastern Building', which seems to be part of an outer gateway.

On the mound of Nebi Yunus at Nineveh, Sennacherib rebuilt the back palace or arsenal, which was later further expanded by Esarhaddon and Assurbanipal (see below). Excavations by Manhal Jabur have exposed a monumental entrance façade decorated with bull colossi, beyond which is a large room (perhaps a throne-room) panelled with stone slabs. It is unclear which king was responsible for this part of the building, as inscribed slabs of both Esarhaddon and Assurbanipal have been found there. The arsenal's plan is incomplete, but probably incorporated a monumental gateway with a number of inscribed bricks of Sennacherib found at the east end of the mound, while a row of relief slabs at the north-west corner may have lined a passageway leading out of the palace. One of Sennacherib's most spectacular surviving structures near Nineveh is the aqueduct at Jerwan, built entirely of limestone blocks, which carried the canal from Bavian to Nineveh across a small stream on five corbelled, pointed arches.

At Assur, Sennacherib rebuilt and enlarged the Assur Temple. By adding a new court and entrance at the north-east corner, he transformed the shrine's layout into the typical late Assyrian pattern of entrance court, broad antechamber (two in this case) and long cult chamber. Two building phases, both the work of Sennacherib, have been distinguished at a new Temple of the New Year's Festival, just outside the city wall. Both the earlier phase (55×60 m) and later phase (67×60 m) were planned around a large central court with the entrance at one end and a wide cult chamber opposite. The dais was placed centrally

along the long wall of the cult chamber, a layout that is clearly patterned on Babylonian temples.

Sennacherib apparently also rebuilt the Nergal Temple at Tarbiṣu, about 5 km north of Nineveh. Both the inner and outer courtyards in the western part of the temple were surrounded by a single rank of small rooms. At the south side of the inner courtyard were the entrances to two shrines, the one at the east larger than that at the west, both of typical late Assyrian layout.

Esarhaddon. Esarhaddon (*reg* 680–669 BC) restored the arsenal at Nimrud and built a heavily fortified stone postern gate, much of it still well preserved, at the south-west corner. His major new project here, however, was the 'South-west Palace' on the citadel. Only a single group of rooms (*c.* 60×35 m) was fully excavated. Their plan is atypical, consisting of two parallel long rooms with column bases in their side and end doorways, and, beyond and parallel to these, a row of smaller rooms, the central one of which seems to be the focus of the suite (Turner, 1970). The function of this suite is unknown.

Esarhaddon rebuilt the palace at Tarbiṣu as a residence for the crown prince. The known part of this palace combines traditional and novel features. The best-preserved block of rooms consists of a courtyard with reception suites of typical late Assyrian plan on its east and west sides. An unusual feature on its south side, however, was a broad stone staircase that led up to what was apparently a columned porch or vestibule that opened on to a third reception suite, located directly behind the porch. This is the only true *bit hilani* known in Assyria.

Assurbanipal. The most substantial project of Assurbanipal (*reg* 668–627 BC) was a new palace, the 'North Palace', at Nineveh. Only a fraction of the palace has been excavated (*c.* 135×120 m), including an outer court (O), a throne-room suite, an inner court with part of a typical reception suite (F–I) on its north-west side, and some passageways. Unusually, the throne-room suite lacked a bathroom, and there was a shallow alcove at the south-east end of the throne-room (M) in the location traditionally reserved for the throne-base. It is not known whether the throne would have been in this alcove or elsewhere. The throne-room suite of the Town Wall Palace at Nimrud had a similar plan, which seems to support Mallowan's attribution of the structure to the reign of Assurbanipal or one of his successors. Its plan includes an unusual group of three large parallel rooms of uncertain function.

Sin-shar-ishkun. Sin-shar-ishkun (*reg* ?*c.* 627–612 BC), the last king of Assyria, rebuilt the Nabu Temple at Assur. It measured 68.5×55 m and was built around two courts. The twin shrines of Nabu and Tashmetum, both typically Neo-Assyrian in layout, opened from the south court, while from the north court opened a single shrine consisting of an antechamber and a parallel cult chamber entered through a door in the side wall.

BIBLIOGRAPHY

P. E. Botta and E. Flandin: *Monument de Ninive*, 5 vols (Paris, 1849–50)

A. H. Layard: *Discoveries in the Ruins of Nineveh and Babylon* (London, 1853)

V. Place and F. Thomas: *Ninive et l'Assyrie*, 3 vols (Paris, 1867–70)

T. Jacobsen and S. Lloyd: *Sennacherib's Aqueduct at Jerwan*, Orient. Inst. Pubns (Chicago, 1935)

C. Preusser: *Die Paläste in Assur*, Wiss. Veröff. Dt. Orient-Ges. (Berlin, 1955)

A. Haller and W. Andrae: *Die Heiligtümer des Gottes Assur und der Sin-Šamaš-Tempel in Assur*, Wiss. Veröff. Dt. Orient-Ges. (Berlin, 1955)

M. E. L. Mallowan: *Nimrud and its Remains*, 3 vols (London, 1966)

G. Turner: 'The Palace and Bâtiment aux ivoires at Arslan Tash: A Reappraisal', *Iraq*, xxx (1968), pp. 62–8

J. E. Reade: *The Design and Decoration of Neo-Assyrian Public Buildings* (diss., U. Cambridge, 1970)

G. Turner: 'The State Apartments of Late Assyrian Palaces', *Iraq*, xxxii (1970), pp. 177–213

A. Suleiman: 'Excavations at Tarbiṣu', *Adab al-Rafidain*, ii (1971), pp. 15–49 [in Arab.]

D. Oates: 'Balawat (Imgur Enlil): The Site and its Buildings', *Iraq*, xxxvi (1974), pp. 173–8

E. Heinrich: *Die Tempel und Heiligtümer im alten Mesopotamien*, Dt. Archäol. Inst., Dkml. Ant. Archit., 2 vols (Berlin, 1982)

S. Lackenbacher: *Le Roi bâtisseur: Les Récits de construction assyriens des origines à Teglatphalasar III* (Paris, 1982)

R. Sobolewski: 'The Polish Work at Nimrud: Ten Years of Excavation and Study', *Z. Assyriol.*, lxxi (1982), pp. 248–73

E. Heinrich: *Die Paläste im alten Mesopotamien*, Dt. Archäol. Inst., Dkml. Ant. Archit. (Berlin, 1984)

S. Lackenbacher: *Le Palais sans rival: Le Récit de construction en Assyrie* (Paris, 1990)

J. M. Russell: *Sennacherib's 'Palace without Rival' at Nineveh* (Chicago, 1991)

For further bibliography see §III, 6(i) below.

JOHN M. RUSSELL

(ii) Neo-Babylonian. The kings of the Neo-Babylonian dynasty (625–539 BC), principally Nabopolassar (*reg* 625–605 BC) and his son, Nebuchadnezzar II (*reg* 604–562 BC), were great builders, and their main efforts were devoted to the beautification of BABYLON. The city's reputation spread far and wide, and in later times it was famed especially for its city walls and Hanging Gardens (two of the Seven Wonders of the World) and its ziggurat, which inspired the story of the Tower of Babel (Genesis 11:1–9). The city walls and the ziggurat were constructed as early as the Old Babylonian period (first half of 2nd millennium BC) but were rebuilt in the Neo-Babylonian period, and it is the later city which is best known. The location and nature of the Hanging Gardens, however, have not been ascertained, and it has been suggested that the gardens should in fact be identified with those of Sennacherib (*reg* 704–681 BC) at Nineveh.

The principal types of building constructed by the Neo-Babylonian kings were temples, palaces and other public works. Babylonian temples followed the traditional Mesopotamian form of a courtyard, antecella and cella (*see* §(i)(a) above). In the typically Babylonian architectural form the antecella and cella were wide rooms with a direct axis (termed the *Breitraum*). The Babylonian kings also rebuilt the cult centres and ziggurats of other ancient holy places, including those of Eridu, Ur, Uruk, Larsa, Kish, Borsippa and Sippar. The inscriptions of the kings indicate that they carried out archaeological excavations to establish the original plans of the temples, and they often claim to have followed the earlier plan with great precision.

The most famous Babylonian palaces are the three found by the German excavators at Babylon itself: the 'Southern Palace', the 'Northern Palace' and the 'Summer Palace' (*see* BABYLON, figs 1 and 2). The design of these palaces was similar to that of Neo-Assyrian palaces, but instead of the main throne-room separating the outer (*babanu*) courtyard from the inner (*bitanu*) area of the palace, a series of interconnecting courtyards was constructed, each with a reception room on the south side. A

similar design was used for the residences of officials and rich citizens in Babylon and other cities such as Isin and Ur.

Neo-Babylonian buildings were constructed from sun-dried or kiln-fired mud-bricks using a mud-mortar, though in foundations and other places, which were subject to damp, bitumen mortar was used. Arched doorways were normal, and vaults were also used. The orientation of rooms was important, and a characteristic feature of Neo-Babylonian architecture was the use of shallow stepped external buttresses that allowed the internal rooms to be built at an angle to the line of the outer face of the wall. Multicoloured glazed bricks, sometimes moulded, were used to decorate important façades.

Nebuchadnezzar II (*reg* 604–562 BC) constructed two cross-country walls from the Tigris to the Euphrates in order to protect Babylon. One of these ran just north of Babylon and the other, which has been identified on the ground, to the north of Sippar. This wall, perhaps to be identified with the Wall of Media mentioned by Xenophon, was c. 50 km long and 6 m wide, with baked brick outer faces and an earth core.

BIBLIOGRAPHY

E. Heinrich: *Die Paläste im alten Mesopotamien*, Dt. Archäol. Inst., Dkml. Ant. Archit., xv (Berlin, 1982)

——: *Die Tempel und Heiligtümer im alten Mesopotamien*, Dt. Archäol. Inst., Dkml. Ant. Archit., xiv (Berlin, 1982)

J. A. Black, H. Gasche and R. G. Killick: 'Habl as-Sahr, 1983–85: Nebuchadnezzar II's Cross-country Wall North of Sippar', *N. Akkad Proj. Rep.*, i (1987), pp. 3–46

MICHAEL ROAF

(iii) Parthian. Notwithstanding the intermittent lack of systematic dynastic control exercised by the Parthians and Sasanians (141 BC–AD 637), this was a period of great artistic vigour (for Sasanian architecture, *see* §(iv) below). Seleucid buildings had reflected the Hellenistic practices in use elsewhere, though there are examples where architects 'misused' ancient Greek standards of proportions, positioning of features, or even surface treatment. It may be argued, however, that these aberrations were experiments that turned into norms that lasted well into the Islamic period.

A significant innovation was introduced at Seleucia-on-the-Tigris, the Parthian capital, during the mid-1st century AD, when the use of two columns in the portico (*distyle in antis*) of a main hall ceased, and builders presented a completely open-fronted barrel-vaulted room (IWAN) on one or more sides of a courtyard. At Assur in the 1st century AD the same architectural innovation also appeared. There, four iwans faced an inner courtyard. The façade is of stucco laid over baked bricks and composed of three superimposed architectonic registers. The principle of breaking up a façade was inherited from ancient Mesopotamian practices, though the architectonic elements used in the decorative scheme reflect Hellenistic forms. A peristyle court within the palace is a good example of Hellenistic influence on Near Eastern architecture, though, in the same complex, the appearance of a tetrastyle hall in Achaemenid style shows how Parthian architects borrowed indiscriminately from a variety of traditions. Unfortunately there is no archaeological evidence to show how these spaces were used. It is possible that the positioning of the iwans was a response to the climate, providing alternately shade or sun, depending upon the season. The idea of receptions, dining and entertainment all taking place in a common area may be surmised from standard Near Eastern practices.

HATRA helps reinforce the idea that Parthian architecture is an amalgam of disparate elements, though technically Hatra is not Parthian from the political point of view, since it was the capital of an independent principality by the 1st century AD. The use of cut stone and the high rounded arches in the sacred enclosure at the heart of the round walled city give the buildings a markedly non-Near Eastern look, analogous to the impression given by a Roman triumphal gateway. Two free-standing temples in front of the iwan complex reproduce Greco-Roman features, but the free use of mixed orders and unorthodox positioning of columns underline a typical readiness to experiment with western models. However, the long vaulted iwan halls, flanked by corridors and adjoined at the rear by another enclosed, encircled chamber, fit unmistakably with the contemporary ground-plans of 1st- and 2nd-century AD Parthian architecture. Human masks and other relief sculptures applied to the buildings' walls add to their Parthian character. The complex may be clearly identified as a sacred area, since the buildings house over life-size statues of the nobility, hands raised in gestures of worship, and inscriptions refer to the dedications of temples, but the actual activities conducted in these great edifices are not always clearly discernible.

Row housing units, as well as a large ceremonial complex in the 1st- and 2nd-century AD citadel at NIPPUR, which overlies the city's once famous ziggurat enclosure, contain halls that are iwans in ground-plan. In contrast, the architects of the contemporaneous temple deliberately employed an archaic layout, where the use of a sequence of transverse halls leading up to an inner shrine gives a markedly different feeling from that of a longitudinal iwan. The Nippur structures are built almost entirely of huge mud-bricks, with occasionally fired bricks recycled from the older structures. The awkward solutions called for in bonding bricks at the corners reflect experimentation, if not incompetence. Extensive platforming was employed to provide level building surfaces, though often the effort proved counter-productive, since serious subsidence developed from the sheer weight.

Massively buttressed wall systems that preceded the construction of the temple at URUK in the early 2nd century AD were, perhaps as at Nippur, designed more for their imposing presence than for their military potential. The temple itself, built of fired bricks, retains the layout of an ancient Babylonian temple, with a series of transverse halls leading up to the inner shrine. However, the eclectic use of composite orders in a blind façade, with entablatures and arches surmounting the pilasters in between, reflects the free use of Mediterranean-derived forms observed in the small temples at Hatra.

BIBLIOGRAPHY

Enc. Iran.: 'Architecture, ii, Parthian'
W. Andrae and H. Lenzen: *Die Partherstadt Assur*, Wiss. Veröff. Dt. Orient-Ges. (Leipzig, 1933)
E. Heinrich: *Sechster vorläufiger Bericht über die von der deutschen Forschungsgemeinschaft in Uruk-Warka unternommenen Ausgrabungen*, Abhandlungen der Preussischen Akademie der Wissenschaften (Berlin, 1935)
H. J. Lenzen: 'Architektur der Partherzeit in Mesopotamien und ihre Brückenstellung zwischen der Architektur des Westens und des Ostens', *Festschrift Carl Weickert* (Berlin, 1955), pp. 121–36
J. Knudstad: 'A Preliminary Report on the 1966–67 Excavations at Nippur', *Sumer*, xxiv (1968), pp. 96–106
C. Hopkins, ed.: *Topography and Architecture of Seleucia on the Tigris* (Ann Arbor, 1972)
E. J. Keall: 'Some Thoughts on the Early *eyvan*', *Studies in Honor of George C. Miles* (Beirut, 1974), pp. 123–30
F. Safar and M. A. Mustafa: *Al-Ḥaḍr: Madīnat al-shams* [Hatra: the city of the Sun god] (Baghdad, 1974)
M. R. A. Colledge: *Parthian Art* (London, 1977)
G. Hermann: *The Iranian Revival*, The Making of the Past (Oxford, 1977)
D. Schlumberger: 'Parthian Art', *Cambridge History of Iran*, III/ii (Cambridge, 1983), pp. 1027–54
S. B. Downey: *Mesopotamian Religious Architecture: Alexander through the Parthians* (Princeton, 1988)

(iv) Sasanian. The Sasanians (after AD 224) exercised firmer control than the Parthians over most of Mesopotamia, through the use of client kings. This period is known for the entrenchment of architectural innovations begun under the Parthians, and massive barrel-vaulted chambers surrounded by corridors as a buttressing device continue to appear. On the Iranian plateau, round domes in solid masonry over square chambers were erected, but these are rare in Mesopotamia. The increased use of columns opened up the internal space, giving open-fronted halls a basilica-like appearance, which may be due to Roman influence. Numerous engineers and architects are known to have been captured in the wars with Rome and brought back by the Sasanians. There was also a renewed interest in western decorative devices as a result of these contacts, but the indigenous building techniques continued, particularly the use of blind façade decoration.

The Sasanians founded several new cities, often on the occasion of decisive victories abroad. Perhaps because many of them lacked a viable *raison d'être* after the reign of the monarch concerned, few have survived with visible monuments. Excavations at the site of Coche have revealed an urban block of buildings and part of the round city wall of KTESIPHON, the original Sasanian capital. After the Tigris changed course in the 5th century AD, Coche became stranded on the west bank, leaving it rather derelict. In the late 6th century AD Chosroes II moved his capital to Dastagerd, but little survives there except a single massive wall of baked brick. Ktesiphon is otherwise known through a variety of stucco decorations and the Taq-i Kisra, at 35 m high, the largest brick vault in existence (see below).

At KISH, excavations have unearthed structures that reflect the growing pretensions of the nobility. Two palace courts include ornamental pools, while the triple-aisled iwan in one of them, with an apse at the rear, may be interpreted as an audience chamber with throne-hall. The extensive stucco decorations at Kish are similar to those found in 5th- and 6th-century AD Ktesiphon, in a style characterized by extensive use of heraldic figures and symbols, together with human busts.

The archaeological history of the great vaulted Taq-i Kisra, or hall of King Chosroes, at Ktesiphon remains difficult to interpret because of the dispute over the date of its construction, which has been attributed to Shapur I (AD 241–72) and to the two Chosroes (AD 531–79 and AD 590–628). The notoriety that the structures received at the time of the Muslim conquest of AD 637 tends to cloud the issue; generally, great emphasis is placed upon the transfer of captured artisans from Antioch in AD 540. Archaeological work has invariably concentrated on restoration of the monument; one third more of the structure was still standing in 1888 when the flooding Tigris took away the north wing of the main façade. The style of the articulated façade that flanks the great iwan hall is closely linked with that of the Parthian version found at Assur, which makes a 3rd-century AD date feasible; a pre-Islamic literary tradition also attests to this date. Some commentators have found subtle differences between the façades of the two structures, supporting their view that the Ktesiphon version must post-date the 6th century AD with examples from the eastern Mediterranean that they argue must have existed first. Pending more extensive excavations, the question as to the date of its foundation and the significance of the Taq-i Kisra remains open.

BIBLIOGRAPHY
Enc. Iran.: 'Architecture, iii: Sasanian'
J. M. Fiey: 'Topography of al-Madā'in', *Sumer*, xxiii (1967), pp. 41–8
M. M. Negro-Ponzi: 'The Excavations at Coche', *Mesopotamia*, ii (1967), pp. 41–8
B. Finster and J. Schmidt: *Sasanidische und frühislamische Ruinen im Iraq* (Berlin, 1976)
P. R. S. Moorey: *Kish Excavations 1923–1933* (Oxford, 1978)
J. Kröger: *Sasanidischer Stuckdekor* (Mainz, 1982)
D. Shepherd: 'Sasanian Art', *Cambridge History of Iran*, III/ii (Cambridge, 1983), pp. 1055–112
E. J. KEALL

III. Sculpture.

1. Early figurines (before *c.* 4000 BC). 2. Uruk period (*c.* 4000–*c.* 2900 BC). 3. Early Dynastic period (*c.* 2900–*c.* 2340 BC). 4. Akkadians, kingdom of Lagash and Third Dynasty of Ur (*c.* 2340–*c.* 2000 BC). 5. *c.* 2000–*c.* 1000 BC. 6. *c.* 1000–539 BC.

1. EARLY FIGURINES (BEFORE *c.* 4000 BC). At most early Neolithic sites figurines were fashioned in clay in the form of animals and of opulent females; over 5000 (Baghdad, Iraq Mus.; U. Chicago, IL, Orient. Inst. Mus.) were found at the site of JARMO in the Zagros (7th millennium BC). They were probably connected with fertility cults. In the 6th millennium BC at Tell es Sawwan north of Samarra' the villagers carved vases and statuettes in alabaster (Baghdad, Iraq Mus.; for illustration *see* SAWWAN, TELL ES-) and placed them in graves. Standing naked women were depicted with remarkable technical mastery, making full use of the patterning of the stone. The body was soberly treated and the face was deliberately simplified but the eyes were often inlaid with shell set in bitumen and some of the figures were adorned with necklaces of coloured stones. Later, at Choga Mami, at the foot of the Zagros Mountains, painted terracotta female figurines were fashioned with more elaborate, if stylized, features (Baghdad, Iraq Mus.; for illustration *see* CHOGA MAMI). This tendency towards stylization is also apparent during the long period of colonization of southern Mesopotamia during the Ubaid period (5th millennium BC). At Ubaid elongated terracotta figurines were found, predominantly female but also some male; they have reptilian heads and coffee-bean eyes and are decorated with a little paint and pellets of clay on the shoulders (e.g. Baghdad, Iraq Mus.).

2. URUK PERIOD (*c.* 4000–*c.* 2900 BC). During the Middle and Late Uruk period the development of an urban society led to the mastery of new techniques and to greater impetus for artistic creation. Large-scale sculpture in the round and relief carving appeared for the first time, together with metal-casting using the lost-wax process. A new realism is apparent in the treatment of the human form, and figures appear as part of narratives, an innovation particularly clear on the miniature reliefs carved on cylinder seals (*see* ANCIENT NEAR EAST, §II, 1(ii)). A frequent subject is the figure of the priest-king, recognizable by his brow-band and chignon, his beard and his bell-shaped skirt, which is often crosshatched (see fig. 2 above). He is also represented on a basalt stele from Uruk (the Lion Hunt Stele; Baghdad, Iraq Mus.) that depicts two successive moments in a lion hunt: the king is shown spearing a lion and shooting arrows at others. The royal lion hunt became a recurring theme in Mesopotamian art and culminated in the famous Neo-Assyrian lion hunts of the 9th and 7th centuries BC (*see* §6 below). Small figures of animals, cast in the lost-wax technique, sometimes decorated the tops of seals.

During the later 4th millennium BC, stone vessels were carved in both high and low relief. Many bowls have processions of animals, and the heads are often depicted frontally in the round (e.g. London, BM; Baghdad, Iraq Mus.). A cult vessel in Berlin (Pergamonmus.) is supported by a group in the round consisting of a lion attacking bulls, and a ritual trough (London, BM; Berlin, Pergamonmus.) depicts a procession of animals approaching a cattle byre. The most famous stone cult vessel is the Warka Vase from Uruk (Baghdad, Iraq Mus.; see fig. 12): it is over 1 m high, with finely modelled decoration in low relief arranged in several registers. The lowest shows the countryside, where barley and palm trees are growing beside water; above this is a flock of rams and ewes; then comes a line of naked male figures carrying the produce of the land; and, at the top, the damaged figure of the priest-king is recognizable

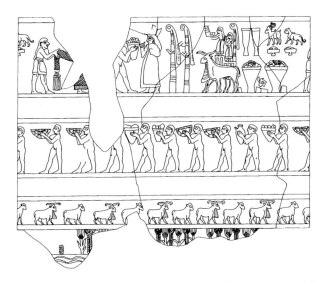

12. Warka Vase, alabaster, h. *c.* 1 m, from Uruk, 4th millennium BC (Baghdad, Iraq Museum); reconstruction drawing

by what remains of his crosshatched skirt. He is preceded and followed by acolytes, and is welcomed by a woman standing at the doorway to a temple that is flanked by reed bundles (these correspond, in pictographic writing, to the name of the great fertility goddess Inanna, personification of the goddess Venus). It is clear from later texts that a priestess played the role of the goddess and welcomed the king, who represented her consort the fertility god Dumuzi (Tammuz); they met to celebrate a sacred marriage. The temple is depicted overflowing with offerings placed beside a dais where two priests pray. Sculpture in the round is represented at Uruk by a fine marble mask, the Warka Head (Baghdad, Iraq Mus.; for illustration *see* URUK), which must originally have formed part of a composite statue: its nose is damaged and its inlaid eyebrows, eyes and hair are missing, but its simple, classic lines still create a remarkable impact. At TELL BRAK, far to the north, alabaster heads from the Eye Temple (London, BM; Aleppo, N. Mus.), with their huge, heavily outlined eyes, still belong to an earlier, more stylized tradition. Indeed the Eye Temple is named after the hundreds of flat, stylized votive figurines found there, on which only the eyes are indicated (e.g. London, BM).

3. EARLY DYNASTIC PERIOD (*c.* 2900–*c.* 2340 BC). Despite architectural innovations, the plastic arts of Early Dynastic I (*c.* 2900–*c.* 2750 BC) are transitional, and, apart from seals, it is difficult to attribute works to this period. From *c.* 2750 BC onwards, ordinary men and women, as well as priests and rulers, became involved in religious ceremonies, and for the next millennium a large number of statues and statuettes of worshippers were set up in the temples. In Early Dynastic II (*c.* 2750–*c.* 2600 BC) statuary, reliefs and seals shared considerable homogeneity; figures were strongly stylized, with no concern for realism or resemblance to a model. The most representative series (Baghdad, Iraq Mus.; U. Chicago, IL, Orient. Inst. Mus.; *see* DIYALA REGION, fig. 1) comes from a deposit at Tell Asmar, where statues from a temple, possibly that of the god Abu, were discovered. They have angular bodies, enormous eyes inlaid with lapis lazuli and white stone, large noses and small mouths. The figures are even more systematically stylized on commemorative stone plaques decorated with reliefs depicting religious banquets. These plaques are approximately 300 mm square and are pierced in the centre for fixing to a wall. The upper register usually shows a couple for whom servants are playing music and serving drink; below this offerings are brought from the countryside; and at the bottom there is an empty chariot, perhaps the supreme royal offering presented to a divinity who is never shown.

During Early Dynastic III (*c.* 2600–*c.* 2340 BC), when the first historical texts occur, Mesopotamia reached a high level of prosperity. Some workshops, notably those of the town of Girsu in the Sumerian state of Lagash, continued to produce archaic and clumsy works, such as a plaque (Paris, Louvre) on which the theme of the banquet is associated with a temple-building ceremony with King Ur-Nanshe (*reg c.* 2520 BC) officiating in both. On a contemporary relief from Ur (London, BM) two libation scenes are depicted with greater elegance. Ur-Nanshe's grandson, Eannatum (*reg c.* 2470 BC), inaugurated a new type of sculpture: a historical event is both narrated and depicted on the two sides of his Stele of the Vultures (Paris, Louvre; *see* fig. 3 above). There is a greater freedom of expression in the way the different episodes of Eannatum's victories have been represented; myth and reality merge, and the god is shown with Eannatum's features, gathering his enemies into an enormous net. This image also appears in the Bible (Ezekiel 12: 13; Luke 21: 35).

There are numerous examples of Early Dynastic III sculpture in the round from northern Sumer (for illustration *see* SUMERIAN), the Diyala region, Susa, Assur and as far as MARI, where a productive workshop produced such masterpieces as the statue of the administrator Ebih-Il (Paris, Louvre). He is bald, bearded, with inlaid bitumen eyebrows, and eyes of shell and lapis lazuli, and he smiles benignly as he sits on a wicker stool, with his hands clasped. His goatskin skirt is realistically rendered, at a time when it was common to depict goatskins with long, stiff tufts, and his bare torso contrasts with the texture of the skirt. A praying female figure from Nippur (Baghdad, Iraq Mus.), carved in translucent green calcite, wears a similar robe; her head is lost, but her enigmatic smile has been preserved in the gold-plating which once covered her face.

4. AKKADIANS, KINGDOM OF LAGASH AND THIRD DYNASTY OF UR (*c.* 2340–*c.* 2000 BC). The advent of Sargon of Akkad *c.* 2340 BC resulted in two important developments: the Sumerians were driven from power and replaced by Semites, who formed the majority in the north, and an imperial state was born that used art to promote its ideology. Almost without exception, the surviving statues are those of kings, and the reliefs depict royal victories. This narrowing of the repertory is counterbalanced by a technical mastery of diorite, a hard stone that was imported by sea, and by the triumph of sculptural realism. Akkadian sculpture displays vigour and sensitivity, the latter seen especially in the treatment of the folded hands of Manishtushu (*c.* 2269–*c.* 2255 BC; Paris, Louvre). Such details as drapery are shown for the first time. The portraits conform to the ideal of a universal monarch: one, badly damaged, is from Telloh (Paris, Louvre) while another in copper, from Nineveh (Baghdad, Iraq Mus.; *see* AKKADIAN, fig. 2), has plaited hair worn like a diadem, a chignon and an exceptionally broad beard. On reliefs the theme of royal victory was developed in monotonous registers (Paris, Louvre; Baghdad, Iraq Mus.). However, under Naram-Sin (*reg* 2254–2218 BC) the registers were discarded, and the royal victory was treated in a single composition of grandiose simplicity (Paris, Louvre; *see* AKKADIAN, fig. 1): the columns of Akkadian warriors climbing the hill lead towards the monumental image of the king, who is wearing horns to indicate divine status and trampling his enemies underfoot.

The fall of the Akkadian empire *c.* 2150 BC led to a Neo-Sumerian revival that combined the artistic and technical achievements of the Akkadians with the humanist traditions developed during the Early Dynastic period (*see* §3 above). This is expressed in the many statues of

Gudea, the *ensi* (ruling prince) of Lagash (e.g. Paris, Louvre; for illustration *see* TELLOH). These statues show Gudea with his hands elegantly folded, either standing or sitting and holding a temple plan on his knees, echoing the earlier 'architect' or temple builder of Lagash, Ur-Nanshe. Gudea's beardless face radiates a new ideal, markedly different from that of the Akkadian kings. Personal characteristics have been attenuated in these 'portraits', and he wears the new royal headdress (a straight-sided fur hat). A statuette of a woman wearing a scarf (Paris, Louvre; fig. 13) may represent a princess of Gudea's family: her face expresses the same idealized serenity, similar to that seen in the Archaic art of ancient Greece. Gudea also set up a series of stelae: at the summit of each he is shown in prayer, guided by his own personal god before the patron god of Lagash. The gods have been given identifying attributes, using the symbolism developed by Akkadian seal cutters: that of Gudea's patron, a vegetation god, is the snake-dragon, while the patron god of Lagash is given the same attributes as the water god Enki of Eridu, and holds vases from which water flows.

The civilization that emerged under Gudea's patronage contributed to that of the Third Dynasty of Ur founded by Ur-Nammu (*reg* 2112–2095 BC) and modelled on the Akkadian empire. Ur-Nammu had a large stele carved

13. Statuette of a woman (?princess of the family of Gudea) wearing a scarf, steatite, h. 170 mm, from Telloh, *c.* 2100 BC (Paris, Musée du Louvre)

(Philadelphia, U. PA, Mus.), on which he is depicted twice in the upper register, honouring the Moon god and his consort. In the scene below he officiates at the ceremonies for the building of the temple.

5. *c.* 2000–*c.* 1000 BC. After the fall of the Third Dynasty of Ur, at the close of the 3rd millennium BC, the Neo-Sumerian tradition of sculpture remained alive, for instance at Isin, Larsa, Eshnunna, Assur and Mari, but the statue of Ishtup-Ilum of Mari (Aleppo, N. Mus.) is a graceless version of Gudea. On the other hand the statue of Puzur-Ishtar (Istanbul, Archaeol. Mus.; Berlin, Pergamonmus.), brought from Mari to Babylon as booty, contrasts the idealized representation of his body with an extremely detailed rendering of his richly fringed dress. His royal headdress is adorned with horns showing that, like the kings of Ur, this prince of Mari was deified in his lifetime. The statue of a minor goddess, found in the palace of the last king of Mari (before 1760 BC), was designed as a fountain (Aleppo, N. Mus.; for illustration *see* MARI, fig. 2). Her gown is engraved with wavy lines and fish, over which water ran from the vase she holds in both hands. Her face is proof of the survival of the humanist tradition seen earlier in the statuette from Telloh of a woman wearing a scarf (see fig. 13 above). The small kingdoms situated at the foot of the Zagros Mountains revived the Akkadian tradition; a rock relief at Darband-i Gaur, for instance, is an imposing transposition of the stele of Naram-Sin. Besides official art, a popular art emerged in the form of terracotta figurines, plaques and ex-votos, both mould-made and modelled, principally depicting nude female figures (e.g. London, BM).

It was Hammurabi (*reg* 1792–1750 BC), the sixth king of the First Dynasty of Babylon, who restored Mesopotamian unity. The relief that decorates the top of his law-code stele (Paris, Louvre; fig. 14) shows the king before the seated Sun god, according to the tradition inherited from the Sumerians. A granite head found at Susa (Paris, Louvre) represents the same king or one of his predecessors, wearing the royal hat: the face expresses a new ideal of kingship, that of the royal legislator. A small bronze, consecrated for the life of Hammurabi, shows a figure kneeling on one knee in prayer, in a remarkably natural posture, again wearing the royal hat (Paris, Louvre). After this date, the Mesopotamian tradition of sculpture in the round died out almost completely and important later works, notably of the Neo-Assyrian period (*see* §6(i) below), are mostly in relief.

In the 16th century BC the First Dynasty of Babylon was replaced by the Kassites, but few Kassite sculptures survive, the principal examples being the 'boundary stones' (*kudurru*s) bearing the texts of royal donations placed under the protection of multiple gods. The gods themselves are rarely shown, but they are symbolized by emblems that correspond to their functions and are set out in rows. These monuments are of great interest to the student of religious iconography, but they reveal a severe decline in the art of composition. However, some realistic terracottas of humans and animals, particularly that of a lioness (Baghdad, Iraq Mus.; for illustration *see* KASSITE), bear witness to a greater sensitivity. On a larger scale, brick reliefs depicting life-size figures of mountain and water

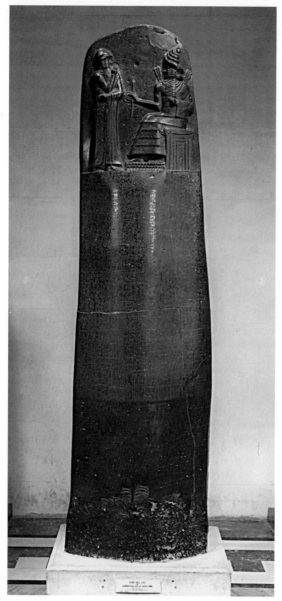

14. Law-code stele of King Hammurabi, basalt, h. 2.25 m, 18th century BC (Paris, Musée du Louvre)

deities (Baghdad, Iraq Mus.) decorated the façade of the Karaindash Temple in Uruk (*c.* 1420 BC). A limestone cult relief from Assur, which depicts two small water deities and a mountain god feeding goats, shows that this theme was also known in north Mesopotamia, where the Assyrians were emerging from a long period of eclipse. An altar from Assur (Berlin, Pergamonmus.) shows King Tukulti-Ninurta I (*reg* 1243–1207 BC) in two moments of worship simultaneously, standing and kneeling before the emblem of the god Nusku. This is more a drawing in relief than true sculpture, but it is executed with careful precision.

BIBLIOGRAPHY

M.-T. Barrelet: *Figurines et reliefs en terre-cuite de la Mésopotamie antique*, i (Paris, 1968)

A. Spycket: *La Statuaire du Proche-Orient ancien*, Handbuch der Orientalistik (Leiden, 1981)

PIERRE AMIET

6. *c.* 1000–539 BC.

(i) Neo-Assyrian. (ii) Neo-Babylonian.

(i) Neo-Assyrian. The art patronized by the kings of Assyria (*see* ASSYRIAN) from the 9th to the 7th century BC consisted largely of architectural decoration in the form of reliefs that were unique in the large surfaces they covered. Such reliefs were almost without exception made for the king, and most are wall reliefs in the form of stone slabs that lined the walls of important rooms in palaces and temples. The slabs bear images and texts recording the activities of the ruler and are carved in low relief, generally in a soft gypsum known as Mosul marble, obtainable in northern Iraq. Figures are shown in the pose commonly used in Mesopotamian sculpture, with the head and legs in profile and the torso generally shown frontally. Door reliefs consisting of strips of bronze decorated with repoussé figures and ornaments were another type of architectural embellishment. Yet another category consists of stelae and obelisks, free-standing monuments to the king, sometimes set up in public locations. Also for public viewing were rock reliefs, carved on natural rock surfaces to mark areas reached during royal campaigns or the location of royal construction projects. The largest groups of Neo-Assyrian reliefs are in the site museums at Nimrud and Nineveh, and the collections of the Iraq Museum, Baghdad, the Pergamonmuseum, Berlin, the Oriental Institute Museum of the University of Chicago, the Museum of the Ancient Orient, Istanbul, the British Museum, London, the Metropolitan Museum of Art and the Brooklyn Museum, both in New York, and the Louvre, Paris. The royal reliefs are discussed below under headings of the kings for whom they were made.

(a) Assurnasirpal II. (b) Shalmaneser III, Shamshi-Adad V and Adadnirari III. (c) Tiglath-pileser III. (d) Sargon II. (e) Sennacherib. (f) Esarhaddon. (g) Assurbanipal and after.

(a) Assurnasirpal II. The earliest group of Neo-Assyrian palace reliefs is from the North-west Palace of Assurnasirpal II (*reg* 883–859 BC) at Nimrud (Budge; Meuszyński, 1981; Paley and Sobolewski; see fig. 15). It is possible that Assurnasirpal was inspired by portal figures and carved orthostats he had seen during his Syrian campaigns. The wall reliefs were confined to the throne-room suite and the large reception suites around the inner court. Most were well preserved, as the destruction of the palace seems not to have been accompanied by extensive burning. The area of the decorated state apartments has been restored as a site museum, with many reliefs in their original context. Another large group of reliefs is in the British Museum.

The throne-room façade and several other major entrances in the palace were decorated with human-headed bull and lion colossi (Baghdad, Iraq Mus.; London, BM; New York, Met.; Nimrud, Iraq, NW Pal. Mus.). Apart from their size (the largest were nearly 6 m in length and height) the most striking feature is the combination in a single figure of two distinct relief images: a static frontal view showing two legs, and a striding side view showing four legs, the result being a five-legged creature. The spaces between the legs and behind the tails were carved with a text that identifies the king and summarizes his accomplishments.

The walls at both ends of the throne-room façade were panelled with slabs bearing images of western foreigners presenting tribute to the king. At the west end these tributaries were shown before an image of the king, while at the east end two processions converged on a doorway, beyond which was the enthroned king himself. Carved across the middle of each slab, and on every other wall slab in the palace, was what is termed the Standard Inscription, giving the king's name, titles and epithets, summarizing his military achievements and describing the appearance of the palace. The throne-room walls were also covered with reliefs. Opposite the central door of the façade and at the east end of the room behind the throne-base were raised niches, each carved with two images of the king and a winged deity symmetrically flanking a stylized palm-tree ('sacred tree'). Variations of this motif, which must represent the role of the king in assuring the prosperity of Assyria, are repeated in the palace decoration of later kings. In the corners of the throne-room and beside doorways are more images of sacred trees and winged deities. The slabs on the long walls were divided into three unequal registers. The wider upper and lower registers displayed a continuous series of images usually termed 'narrative', while on the narrower, central register the 'Standard Inscription' was carved complete on each slab. All but one of the narrative reliefs from the south wall and a few from the mostly destroyed north wall were brought to the British Museum by AUSTEN HENRY LAYARD, although he sawed away the inscribed central register to save weight, thereby altering their proportions and effect as an ensemble. They depict royal hunts and royal

military conquests. Several attempts have been made to identify the cities and regions shown in the latter, but the images carry no written labels and bear no direct relationship to the accompanying Standard Inscription.

Military conquest and hunts were also shown on some of the reliefs in the suite of rooms west of the inner courtyard (Layard was unable to trace these walls because most of the reliefs had been removed for reuse in the South-west Palace of Esarhaddon. In Room G, on the east side of the inner court, the king was shown, accompanied by attendants, sitting or standing holding a bowl, possibly for pouring libations. Here details of jewellery, furniture, weapons and even the embroidered bands decorating the garments are rendered in great detail. The remaining rooms were all decorated with variations of the 'sacred tree' flanked by winged deities with the heads of humans or birds. Most figures are the entire height of the slab, but in Room I the slabs were again divided into registers with the Standard Inscription in the middle.

Assurnasirpal's temples at Nimrud were also decorated with reliefs. The decoration in the Ninurta Temple was confined to major doorways. The main entrance contained two human-headed lion colossi (Mosul Mus.), flanked on the outside by human- and bird-headed protective figures. Both jambs of the subsidiary entrance were lined with reliefs showing a combat between a deity and a monster (London, BM). Human figures flanked this door on the outside and fish-men on the inside. The interior doorway connecting the antechamber and shrine was lined with winged figures carrying maces and flanked inside and out by human figures. The only reliefs in the Temple of Sharrat-niphi were a pair of colossal lions in its main entrance. The façade of the temple in the centre of the Nimrud citadel was decorated with two pairs of addorsed colossi, each pair consisting of a lion on the right and a

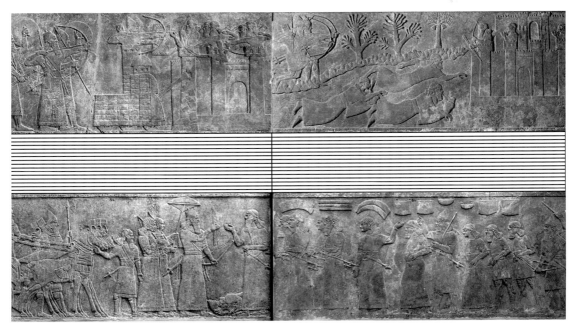

15. Neo-Assyrian relief depicting Assurnasirpal II on campaign, slabs 18–17 from Room B of the North-west Palace, Nimrud, alabaster, each slab *c.* 2.25×2.25 m, *c.* 865 BC (London, British Museum); the 'Standard Inscription' between the two registers has been lost

bull on the left; these were probably human-headed, but the upper parts are now lost. Inside was a doorway lined with a winged figure between rampant lions and flanked on the inside by a human figure and outside by a scorpion-man. Assurnasirpal's Ishtar Temple at Nineveh was also decorated with wall reliefs. Two fragmentary examples survive: one showed a procession of three tributaries before the king; the other had the king hunting lions in the upper register and pouring a libation over a dead lion in the lower.

Assurnasirpal's stelae are of two general types: obelisks, carved with images on all sides, and slabs, sculptured only on the face. The White Obelisk from Nineveh (London, BM) was apparently made for a King Assurnasirpal, but it is unclear whether this was Assurnasirpal I (reg 1049–1031 BC) or his later namesake. The monument is circled by eight relief registers that show the king at war, hunting and making offerings to a deity. The fragmentary Rassam Obelisk (London, BM), found just outside the entrance to Assurnasirpal's temple in the centre of Nimrud citadel, had twenty-eight relief panels, depicting the receipt of tribute, arranged in seven registers. Obelisk fragments probably of Assurnasirpal II were also found in the area of the Ishtar Temple at Nineveh and the Anu-Adad Temple at Assur.

The Banquet Stele (Baghdad, Iraq Mus.), a slab stele, was found in a small room next to the left entrance of the throne-room of Assurnasirpal's palace at Nimrud. The standing king, flanked by symbols of deities and holding a staff in his right hand and a mace in his left, is set in a small rectangular panel at the top centre of the front of the slab, and its remainder is covered with an inscription. Two slab stelae (both London, BM), with a vertical format and arched top, were found near the subsidiary entrance in the courtyard of the Ninurta Temple at Nimrud and at Kurkh on the upper Tigris, c. 20 km south-east of Diyarbakır, Turkey. The standing king is shown facing left in what became the standard pose (i.e. pointing with his raised right hand and holding a mace in his left), with symbols of deities in front of his face. Both carry lengthy inscriptions. A similar fragmentary example with the king facing right (Adana, Archaeol. Mus.) was found at Babil, the source of the ancient River Subnat, c. 25 km south-west of Cizre, Turkey. This is presumably the stele mentioned in the annals of Assurnasirpal II, where he reports that he erected his own stele at the source of the Subnat beside those of a Tiglath-pileser and a Tukulti-Ninurta. Since 'the source of the River Subnat' is frequently referred to in Assurnasirpal's texts as a landmark of the extent of his realm, both this stele and the one from Kurkh were probably erected as territorial markers and as means of establishing Assurnasirpal's place in the line of great Assyrian conquerors. The Ninurta Temple stele, by contrast, had an altar in front of it: unless this was a secondary installation, the stele may have been a locus for the worship of the king or the deities whose symbols were depicted on it.

In 1878 Hormuzd Rassam (1826–1910) found bronze strips that had decorated two pairs of wooden gates in what was probably a palace of Assurnasirpal II at Balawat (anc. Imgur Enlil), c. 28 km south-east of Nineveh on the road to Babylon (London, BM). One had reliefs and inscriptions of Shalmaneser III (see §(b) below) and the other of Assurnasirpal II. The latter comprised sixteen bronze bands, eight on each gate, decorated in repoussé with a single register of relief with a floral border. Four of the bands show the King hunting lions and wild oxen; the rest depict military conquest and tribute. Each image is labelled with a brief cuneiform caption. In 1956, Max Mallowan reinvestigated Balawat and cleared a temple dedicated to Mamu, god of dreams. This contained another Assurnasirpal II bronze gate (Baghdad, Iraq Mus.), also with 16 bands decorated with scenes of conquest and tribute. Neither of the Assurnasirpal gates has been fully published.

(b) Shalmaneser III, Shamshi-Adad V and Adad-nirari III. There were no wall reliefs at the new palace of Shalmaneser III (reg 858–824 BC), the arsenal ('Fort Shalmaneser') at Nimrud, but a large stone throne-base at the east end of the throne-room was decorated with scenes of tribute being brought before the King, each labelled with a brief text describing the origin and type of tribute (Baghdad, Iraq Mus.). Inscribed on top of the throne-base is a lengthy text summarizing the King's first 13 years of rule. There are similar reliefs on the Black Obelisk (London, BM), found in front of the Assurnasirpal II temple in the Nimrud citadel, with its twenty relief panels arranged around four sides in five registers, each labelled and showing the delivery of tribute from a different part of the empire. The upper and lower parts also carry a long inscription summarizing the events of Shalmaneser's first 31 years. At the centre of the Nimrud citadel is a pair of bull colossi, inscribed front and back with a text recounting the King's first 18 years. These probably marked the entrance to a palace or temple, but the building has disappeared. A lion colossus bearing a Shalmaneser inscription was found in the east gate of the Nimrud citadel.

One stele and three rock reliefs of Shalmaneser III are known. The stele is from Kurkh and is very similar to the Assurnasirpal II Kurkh stele (see §(a) above). Two of the rock reliefs are from the tunnel at the source of the Tigris at Birklin, c. 65 km north of Diyarbakır, and the other is from Kenk Boğazı on the Euphrates, c. 60 km north-east of Gaziantep. All these reliefs show the standing figure of the king facing left.

The most extensive group of Shalmaneser III reliefs consists of 16 bronze bands that embellished a pair of wooden doors in the palace at Balawat (mostly in London, BM; see King). Each band was divided into two registers, decorated in repoussé with lively images of royal military campaigns and delivery of tribute. The subjects are drawn from the King's first 11 years, each labelled with a brief epigraph giving the location of the event. A long text summarizing his first 13 years was engraved on two bronze strips, one on the edge of each door. A decorated bronze band, possibly also dating to Shalmaneser III, was found in the Anu-Adad Temple at Assur.

Rassam found a very fine stele of Shamshi-Adad V (reg 823–811 BC) at Nimrud beside the inner door in the gate-chamber (NT1) of the Nabu Temple's sanctuary court (London, BM). The standing king faces left, towards the door, in the usual pose, with deity symbols in front of his face. At least five stelae are known of Adad-nirari III (*reg* 810–783 BC). Four show him facing right in the usual pose: a high-quality stele from Tell el Rimah (Baghdad, Iraq Mus.), and stelae in a rougher provincial style from Saba'a in western Iraq, south of the Jebel Sinjar (London, BM), from Pāra in the north-western part of the Jebel Sinjar (Baghdad, Iraq Mus.) and from Sheikh Hamad on the lower River Habur in western Syria (London, BM). The other, from Pazarçik, near Maraş in Turkey, is carved with a moon standard (Maraş, Archaeol. Mus.). Although the inscriptions on all these stelae mention Adad-nirari, the provincial examples were apparently erected by the powerful provincial governors of this period.

(c) Tiglath-pileser III. Some rooms in the Central Palace of Tiglath-pileser III (*reg* 744–727 BC) were lined with relief slabs, but these were removed by Esarhaddon for reuse in his South-west Palace (Barnett and Falkner; *see* NIMRUD). They were stacked in the Central and South-west palaces, some already on the walls and others on the floor. Since the slabs were not in position, Layard was unable to determine how many rooms might have been decorated. Some reliefs remained stacked in the order in which they had been removed by the Assyrian workers who dismantled the palace. This, together with overlaps in the inscription, enabled Tadmor to reconstruct parts of five or six inscribed relief series and Reade (1979) to identify an additional uninscribed series, each of which may have decorated a different room. Layard shipped some of the reliefs to the British Museum and made drawings of others, but Meuszyński's re-excavation of the Central Palace showed that some slabs had not been recorded.

According to Tiglath-pileser's building account, his palace decoration included bull and lion colossi and apotropaic figures. Layard reported, but did not draw, winged deities and figures holding maces, although only one fragment survives. Three of Tadmor's relief series featured such figures. Two fragments from another series show the king and an attendant. Winged human-headed bulls carved in low relief were also found. Most of the published reliefs, however, depict military subjects drawn from Tiglath-pileser's campaigns, including campaigns to the east and west of Assyria, and to the east, west and north (both Tadmor), while Reade's series showed a southern and probably also a western campaign. These slabs resemble those of Assurnasirpal II in format: two registers of relief separated by a central register of text. In this case, however, the inscription was not a short text repeated on each slab but a long annalistic text that continued from slab to slab, apparently around the entire room. The surviving exemplars of this text, although fragmentary, constitute the most detailed source for the events of Tiglath-pileser's reign. In addition, at least one relief series included brief captions on the images themselves, naming the cities represented.

The only known rock relief of Tiglath-pileser III is at Mila Mergi, *c*. 25 km north-west of Dohuk in northern Iraq. The king faces left in the usual pose, and the area in front of him is covered with an extensive inscription. A fragmentary stele of Tiglath-pileser appeared on the art market in 1967 (Börker-Klähn, no. 171), but its provenance is unknown.

(d) Sargon II. The walls of the two throne-rooms, the major reception suites and the associated courtyard façades of the palace of Sargon II (*reg* 721–705 BC) at Khorsabad were lined with wall reliefs (see Botta and Flandin; Albenda). The published sculptures are mostly from the north-west wing, excavated by Paul Emile Botta, and are known only from drawings by Eugène Flandin, who accompanied him. Victor Place later found more wall reliefs in the area around the principal throne-room. They were not drawn, but many were apparently removed for shipment to Paris, and nearly all were lost when the boats carrying them were sunk in the Shatt al-Arab in southern Iraq. A few sculptures reached the Louvre and the British Museum, and in the 20th century others were removed to the Iraq Museum, Baghdad, and the Oriental Institute Museum of the University of Chicago.

The relief decoration of Sargon's palace was modelled closely on that of Assurnasirpal II at Nimrud (*see* §(a) above). The façade of the principal throne-room ('Court' VII) was decorated with five pairs of human-headed bull colossi: one pair in each of the three doors and two antithetically posed pairs on the buttresses between the doors. A colossal human figure holding a small lion stood between each pair of buttress bulls. The same figural arrangement was used at the main exterior entrance to the palace and (without the figures holding lions) on the façade of the subsidiary throne-room. Several important doorways in the palace and some of the city gates also had pairs of human-headed bull colossi. Like those of Assurnasirpal, these have five legs, between which is an inscription, here devoted mainly to a description of the palace. The colossi were accompanied in some doorways by winged or wingless human figures or by bird-headed human figures; in less important doors these types appeared alone. The 'sacred tree' occurred in some doorways and on the corner slabs in rooms decorated with non-historical subjects.

Tribute processions occupied the space on the courtyard walls not occupied by colossi, the decoration of rooms 6, 10 and 11, and possibly also of the throne-room. With two exceptions, these processions show a single file of figures the full height of the slab, and carry no inscriptions. The exceptions are Room 10, a corridor connecting two courtyards, where two registers of tributaries (westerners above and easterners below) are separated by a band of inscription, and the north corner of the throne-room court, where the transport of timber by water is shown as if viewed from above, with relatively small figures scattered across the surface of the water-patterned slabs, giving an effective approximation of figures in space (Paris, Louvre). Other subjects depicted with large-scale figures in a single register were the punishment of captives (rooms 4 and 8), inscribed with a continuous historical text and captions identifying the malefactors, and processions of courtiers before the king (rooms 9 and 12), which have no inscriptions.

Three other subjects occur: royal military campaigns (rooms 1, 2, 3, 5, 13 and 14), royal hunts (Room 7 and the 'temple' at the west corner) and royal banquets (rooms 2 and 7). Except in the 'temple', the slabs have two registers of relief separated by a band inscribed with a long annalistic text, which provides the most complete record of Sargon's military activities. Some defeated cities shown in the military reliefs are labelled, and some of these are mentioned in the accompanying annals text, so it is usually possible to determine which campaign is depicted: the reliefs in each room apparently show only one or two campaigns, and it has been suggested that the labelled cities mentioned only in the reliefs may be used to augment the annalistic record of Sargon's reign (Reade, 1976). Where two subjects are depicted (rooms 2 and 7), the banquet is in the upper register and the other subject below.

The remains of a stone throne-base, with sides decorated with reliefs, were found at the south-east end of the principal throne-room. The preserved panels depict a royal campaign beside a river (Baghdad, Iraq Mus.) and a campaign in the mountains (U. Chicago, IL, Orient. Inst. Mus.). Nearly all the fragments of embossed bronze bands from doors found in the Adad and Nabu temples at Khorsabad were decorated with processions of mythological figures. Two relief stelae of Sargon II are known, from Najafehabad in western Iran (Tehran, Archaeol. Mus.) and from Larnaca in Cyprus (Berlin, Pergamonmus.). In both the king stands in the usual pose (facing left in the Najafehabad stele and right in that from Larnaca) with deity symbols in front of his face.

(e) Sennacherib. The most extensive known group of Neo-Assyrian reliefs was in the South-west Palace of Sennacherib (*reg* 704–681 BC) at Nineveh (see Paterson; Russell; Bleibtreu, Barnett and Turner). Layard estimated that he uncovered more than 3000 m of wall reliefs (*Discoveries*, 1853), of which a few date to the reign of Assurbanipal and perhaps one of his successors, but most are Sennacherib's. As in the palaces of Assurnasirpal II and Sargon II, only rooms in or around major reception suites were decorated with wall reliefs, but there were many more (nearly 70) such rooms in Sennacherib's palace. This had been thoroughly burnt, and most of the reliefs were badly cracked by the heat. Some of the better-preserved reliefs were drawn by Layard and other 19th-century artists working at Nineveh. A few nearly complete slabs were taken to the British Museum, and fragments are in other collections, but most are *in situ*, deeply buried under later occupation levels. Tariq Madhloom, of the Iraq Department of Antiquities and Heritage, re-excavated the throne-room suite (1965–71); the area has been converted into a site museum where some 100 reliefs are displayed in their original position.

The arrangement of reliefs on the throne-room façade (H) of Sennacherib's palace was the same as that of Sargon II: a pair of human-headed bull colossi in each of the three exterior doors and addorsed pairs of bull colossi (between which were lion-clutching humans) on the two buttresses between the doors (Nineveh, Sennacherib Pal. Mus.). The spaces between the bulls' legs were inscribed with texts, ranging from an extended annalistic text and palace building account on the bulls in the central door (London, BM), to a historical summary and brief palace building account on the façade buttresses bulls, and a detailed description of the size and appearance of the palace on those in the side door. An interesting innovation is that these colossi have only four legs, not five, which

gives them a more naturalistic appearance. A similar arrangement of colossal figures was reported for the poorly recorded west façade, and bull colossi also occurred in other palace doorways, including a well-preserved example in the Nergal Gate on the north stretch of the city wall (Mosul, Nergal Gate Mus.).

The reliefs on the courtyard wall north of the throne-room façade, unlike the tribute processions depicted in this location in the palaces of Assurnasirpal II and Sargon II, showed a military campaign in Babylonia. Tribute processions, the most frequent relief subject in Sargon's palace, were entirely supplanted by scenes of military activity. The reason for this change in subject-matter is unknown. The Babylonian campaign in the throne-room court was subsequently chiselled off by one of Sennacherib's successors and apparently replaced with an Elamite campaign. Some of the reliefs in Room XLIX and all those in Room XLII were similarly erased, possibly as part of a refurbishment in which Court XIX and Rooms XXII and XXVIII were redecorated by Assurbanipal or one of his successors.

Military campaigns formed the theme in all but three of the 38 rooms for which the subject is known, the exceptions showing the procurement of palace building materials, including the quarrying and transportation overland of human-headed bull gateway colossi (London, BM) on two walls in Court VI, and the transportation by water of a huge piece of wood or stone in Room XLIX. Processions of attendants and horses going in and out of the palace were depicted on the walls of Room LI, a corridor that probably led to a postern gate, and deportation of captives was apparently the subject of Room XLIII. Sennacherib began construction of the palace early in his reign, when his artists had only a few campaigns to choose from for the wall reliefs. Consequently, all the military reliefs can be associated with his first three campaigns: to Babylonia, the Zagros Mountains and the Levant. With only one known exception (Court LXIV), each room was decorated with a single campaign.

Sennacherib's wall reliefs differ in format from those of his predecessors. Instead of a band of inscription dividing the slabs into two narrow registers, relief images are carved over the entire surface. On this expanded pictorial area, his artists adopted the spatial conventions of Sargon's timber transport reliefs: a high implied viewpoint with relatively small-scale figures, mostly disposed freely across the slab. The sense of depth is most effective for subjects depicted against a patterned background, such as mountains or water. When the subject does not permit such a setting, as in reliefs showing the Babylonian plain, the slab is divided into registers by multiple groundlines or narrow, uninscribed margins. The only texts are brief captions inscribed next to the King or the cities he encounters.

Sennacherib was also responsible for rock reliefs at BAVIAN, and probably also those at Faida and MALTAI. These are all located in the hills north of Nineveh and show the King standing before one or more gods (see fig. 6 above). Those at Bavian and Faida were definitely associated with aqueducts, and perhaps also the ones at Maltai (Reade, 1978). A fragmentary stele probably from Assur also shows Sennacherib standing before a pair of gods (Istanbul, Mus. Anc. Orient). A group of six rock reliefs of Sennacherib in the Judi Dăg, north of Cizre in Turkey, and one probably attributable to him in the Wadi Bahandawaya near al-Kosh in northern Iraq, together with two slab stelae from Nineveh that apparently marked the course of a royal road (Istanbul, Mus. Anc. Orient; London, BM), all show the king standing in the usual pose with symbols of deities before his face.

Two fragments of a bronze relief from an unidentified object (Baghdad, Iraq Mus.; Paris, Louvre) show a king, almost certainly Sennacherib, and his queen on the left facing at least two courtiers on the right. Finally, one of Sennacherib's texts gives an elaborate description of a bronze door (now lost) for his new Temple of the New Year's Festival at Assur, depicting the battle between the gods, led by Assur, and the forces of chaos, under Tiamat.

(f) Esarhaddon. Layard's excavations at the South-west Palace of Esarhaddon (*reg* 680–669 BC) at Nimrud revealed the intention to reuse wall slabs removed from the North-west and Central palaces (*see* §(c) above), but the project was abandoned before any slabs were recarved. The only recorded Esarhaddon reliefs from the palace were in one of the doorways, where Layard found human-headed bull colossi with protective deities carved on an adjacent slab (Barnett and Falkner). At Nineveh, Esarhaddon's arsenal text states that victories against hostile regions were commemorated in sculpture in that building, presumably in wall reliefs. These sculptures (if they were ever completed) have not been recovered, as the state apartments of the arsenal have not been excavated. Excavations directed from 1989 by Manhal Jabur in a large courtyard of the arsenal have revealed a monumental façade decorated with a pair of addorsed bull colossi with a lion-clutching human between, and several doorways lined with bull colossi. An interesting feature of some of these colossi is that they are built up from small blocks of stone tightly fitted together before carving: some are unfinished. Winged deities were set in the spaces between the bulls. Although the bulls were apparently uninscribed, the backs of some of the other slabs carry an Esarhaddon text.

At least one of the six Assyrian rock reliefs by the Nahr el-Kalb, 12 km north of Beirut, belongs to Esarhaddon, who is depicted in the usual manner, but holding something to his nose in his left hand. The attribution of the other reliefs in the Nahr el-Kalb is uncertain. Two slab stelae from Til Barsip (Aleppo, N. Mus.) and another from Zincirli (Berlin, Pergamonmus.) show a new variant on the traditional pose with images of gods placed before Esarhaddon's face, but his left hand, in addition to the mace, holds ropes attached to rings in the lips of a pair of small kneeling captives. The narrow sides of all three stelae show his heirs: Assurbanipal on the right side and Shamash-shumukin on the left.

(g) Assurbanipal and after. The wall slabs of Room XXXIII in the South-west Palace at Nineveh and the neighbouring Rooms XXIX and XXX were of an attractive fossiliferous limestone imported by Sennacherib from the mountains to the north of Assyria, and he may have left them uncarved. Assurbanipal (*reg* 668–627 BC), however, carved (or recarved) the slabs in Room XXXIII with

scenes of his own successes in battle (Reade, 1979, pp. 52–110). According to the accompanying captions, the slabs to the west of the entrance record Assurbanipal's victory at Til Tuba in Elam, while those to the east show a procession before the king at the city of Arbela (now Erbil) on the upper half, and below a scene of homage outside the moated city of Madaktu in Elam. The compositions are mostly organized by groundlines into registers, but at the right end of the Til Tuba episode, as the battle degenerates into a rout, this organization is replaced by dead and dying enemy soldiers chaotically distributed across the relief. On the basis of the cities labelled by the captions, these reliefs should be dated earlier than Assurbanipal's reliefs in the North Palace.

The largest group of Assurbanipal reliefs was in his North Palace at Nineveh (Barnett, 1976). The excavations of Hormuzd Rassam (1852–4) and William Loftus (1854–5) exposed the central part of the palace, its walls lined with reliefs. Many of the well-preserved slabs were removed to the British Museum, where they form the largest part of the Assyrian collection. Of those consigned to the Louvre, many were lost in the Tigris in the same disaster as the Khorsabad reliefs (*see* §(d) above). No traces of the palace remains are visible.

The throne-room façade (O) was decorated with plain stone slabs, while those on the jambs of its centre door were carved with a group of three deities. The reliefs in the throne-room (M) displayed some of Assurbanipal's military campaigns. The rooms behind the throne-room were also decorated with military subjects, each room apparently depicting a single campaign (rooms F, G, H, I, J and L). A group of passageways that led from the throne-room area to the palace exterior was lined with reliefs featuring hunting scenes: processions to and from a lion hunt (rooms A and R), tame lions (Room E), the king hunting lions (Room C) and lions, gazelles and wild horses (Room S). The finest of these reliefs are beautifully carved in great detail, particularly the richly decorated dress of the King, and the animals are depicted with accuracy and sensitivity. A number of reliefs had fallen from an upper storey. They show lion hunts, military campaigns, and Assurbanipal and his queen dining in a garden, a rare depiction of an Assyrian woman (for illustration *see* ASSYRIAN). The military reliefs are usually arranged in two registers and the hunting reliefs in one; registers are often further subdivided by continuous groundlines. In compositions having multiple registers, these are separated by a narrow uninscribed band of stone. The only inscriptions are captions labelling parts of the image. In most of the North Palace compositions, figures adhere closely to the groundlines, although occasionally they are arranged more freely across the surface, particularly in the hunting scenes.

In the South-west Palace at Nineveh, the wall slabs of Court XIX and Room XXVIII were carved with Babylonian campaign scenes: the King and army campaign beside a wide river that divides the slabs into two registers, with an effect very similar to that of the central text register of Sennacherib's predecessors (Court XIX), and the Assyrian army hunts out enemy refugees in a swamp (Room XXVIII; *see also* MANUSCRIPT, fig. 1). Details indicate that these reliefs post-date Sennacherib: they are similar to the

North Palace reliefs of Assurbanipal. It has been suggested that these sculptures should be attributed to Sin-shar-ishkun (*reg* ?–612 BC) instead of Assurbanipal (Reade, 1979, pp. 52–110), but this remains unproven, since there are no authenticated reliefs of Sin-shar-ishkun. At least some of the reliefs in Room XXII, which show lush scenes of the countryside around Nineveh, also post-date Sennacherib.

On three small stelae, all allegedly from Babylon, Assurbanipal is depicted frontally, holding a basket on his head (London, BM); the accompanying texts record his restoration work in Babylon. A stele from Assur shows Assursharrat, queen of Assurbanipal (Berlin, Pergamonmus.).

BIBLIOGRAPHY

STUDIES

E. A. W. Budge: *Assyrian Sculptures in the British Museum: Reign of Ashur-nasir-pal, 885–860 B.C.* (London, 1914)

C. J. Gadd: *The Stones of Assyria* (London, 1936)

S. Smith: *Assyrian Sculptures in the British Museum from Shalmaneser III to Sennacherib* (London, 1938)

E. F. Weidner and G. Furlani: *Die Reliefs der assyrischen Könige*, Archv Orientforsch., Beihft, iv (Berlin, 1939)

E. Porada and S. Hare: *The Great King, King of Assyria: Assyrian Reliefs in the Metropolitan Museum of Art* (New York, 1945)

H. A. Groenewegen-Frankfort: *Arrest and Movement: An Essay on Space and Time in the Representational Art of the Ancient Near East* (London, 1951)

B. Hrouda: *Die Kulturgeschichte des assyrischen Flachbildes*, Saarbrücker Beiträge zur Altertumskunde (Bonn, 1965)

W. Nagel: *Die neuassyrischen Reliefstile unter Sanherib und Assurbanaplu*, Berliner Beiträge zur Vor- und Frühgeschichte (Berlin, 1967)

T. Madhloom: *The Chronology of Neo-Assyrian Art* (London, 1970)

J. E. Reade: 'The Neo-Assyrian Court and Army: Evidence from the Sculptures', *Iraq*, xxxiv (1972), pp. 87–112

M. Wäfler: *Nicht-Assyrer neuassyrischer Darstellungen*, Alter Orient und Altes Testament, 2 vols (Neukirchen-Vluyn, 1975)

S. M. Paley: *King of the World: Ashur-nasir-pal II of Assyria, 883–859 B.C.* (Brooklyn, 1976)

J. E. Reade: 'Sargon's Campaigns of 720, 716, and 715 B.C.: Evidence from the Sculptures', *J. Nr E. Stud.*, xxxv (1976), pp. 95–104

——: 'Studies in Assyrian Geography: Part I: Sennacherib and the Waters of Nineveh', *Rev. Assyriol.*, lxxii (1978), pp. 47–72, 157–75

——: 'Assyrian Architectural Decoration: Techniques and Subject-matter', *Baghdad. Mitt.*, x (1979), pp. 17–49

——: 'Narrative Composition in Assyrian Sculpture', *Baghdad. Mitt.*, x (1979), pp. 52–110

——: 'The Architectural Context of Assyrian Sculpture', *Baghdad. Mitt.*, xi (1980), pp. 75–87

——: 'Space, Scale, and Significance in Assyrian Art', *Baghdad. Mitt.*, xi (1980), pp. 71–4

I. J. Winter: 'Royal Rhetoric and the Development of Historical Narrative in Neo-Assyrian Reliefs', *Stud. Visual Communic.*, vii/2 (1981), pp. 2–38

J. Börker-Klähn: *Altvorderasiatische Bildstelen und vergleichbare Felsreliefs*, Baghdader Forschungen, 2 vols (Mainz, 1982)

D. Ussishkin: *The Conquest of Lachish by Sennacherib* (Tel Aviv, 1982)

J. E. Reade: *Assyrian Sculpture* (Cambridge, MA, 1983)

M. Marcus: 'Geography as an Organizing Principle in the Imperial Art of Shalmaneser III', *Iraq*, xlix (1987), pp. 77–90

SITES AND SINGLE RELIEFS

A. H. Layard: *Monuments of Nineveh: From Drawings Made on the Spot* (London, 1849)

——: *Nineveh and its Remains*, 2 vols (London, 1849)

P. E. Botta and E. Flandin: *Monuments de Ninive*, 5 vols (Paris, 1849–50)

A. H. Layard: *Discoveries in the Ruins of Nineveh and Babylon* (London, 1853)

——: *A Second Series of the Monuments of Nineveh* (London, 1853)

L. W. King: *The Bronze Reliefs from the Gates of Shalmaneser, King of Assyria, B.C. 860–825* (London, 1915)

A. Paterson: *Assyrian Sculptures: Palace of Sinacherib* (The Hague, 1915)

G. Loud and others: *Khorsabad*, 2 vols (Chicago, 1936–8)

R. D. Barnett and M. Falkner: *The Sculptures of Aššur-naṣir-apli II (883–859 B.C.), Tiglath-pileser III (745–727 B.C.), Esarhaddon (681–669 B.C.) from the Central and South-west Palaces at Nimrud* (London, 1962)

M. E. L. Mallowan: *Nimrud and its Remains*, 3 vols (London, 1966)

H. Tadmor: 'Introductory Remarks to a New Edition of the Annals of Tiglath-Pileser III', *Proc. Israel Acad. Sci. & Human.*, ii/9 (1969), pp. 10–19

R. D. Barnett: 'More Balawat Gates: A Preliminary Report', *Symbolae Biblicae et Mesopotamicae Francisco Maria Theodoro de Liagre Böhl Dedicatae*, ed. M. A. Beek and others (Leiden, 1973), pp. 19–22

E. Sollberger: 'The White Obelisk', *Iraq*, xxxvi (1974), pp. 231–8

J. E. Reade: 'Aššurnaṣirpal I and the White Obelisk', *Iraq*, xxxvii (1975), pp. 129–50

A. A. Agha and M. S. al-Iraqi: *Nimrud* (Baghdad, 1976)

R. D. Barnett: *Sculptures from the North Palace of Ashurbanipal at Nineveh* (London, 1976)

T. Madhloom and A. M. Mahdi: *Nineveh*, Historical Monuments in Iraq, iv (Baghdad, 1976)

J. Meuszyński: 'Neo-Assyrian Reliefs from the Central Area of Nimrud Citadel', *Iraq*, xxxviii (1976), pp. 37–43

J. E. Reade: 'The Rassam Obelisk', *Iraq*, xlii (1980), pp. 1–22

J. Meuszyński: *Die Rekonstruktion der Reliefdarstellungen und ihrer Anordnung im Nordwestpalast von Kalhu (Nimrud)*, Baghdader Forschungen (Mainz, 1981)

P. Albenda: *The Palace of Sargon, King of Assyria: Monumental Wall Reliefs at Dur-Sharrukin, from Original Drawings Made at the Time of their Discovery in 1843–1844 by Botta and Flandin*, Synthèse (Paris, 1986)

S. Paley and R. Sobolewski: *The Reconstruction of the Relief Representations and their Positions in the Northwest-Palace at Kalhu (Nimrud)*, ii, Baghdader Forschungen (Mainz, 1987)

J. M. Russell: *Sennacherib's 'Palace without Rival' at Nineveh* (Chicago, 1991)

E. Bleibtreu, R. D. Barnett and G. Turner: *Sculptures from the Southwest Palace at Nineveh* (in preparation)

JOHN M. RUSSELL

(ii) Neo-Babylonian. In contrast to the Neo-Assyrian reliefs (*see* §(i) above), Neo-Babylonian sculpture remained faithful to the old Mesopotamian traditions. Towards 853 BC, King Nabu-apla-iddina had himself shown, like Gudea, being led by the hand before the sun god Shamash (London, BM); here, however, the god is depicted on a giant scale and is accompanied by other minor gods. Two of these gods appear at the top of the plaque, above the sun god's canopy, and they are using ropes to turn the sun-disc that rests on a stool below. *Kudurrus* continued to be carved, with the donor-king and the beneficiary depicted face to face with a greater feeling for volume than in the 2nd millennium BC. Nabonidus (*reg* 555–539 BC), the last king of Babylon, had himself shown on stelae in an attitude of prayer (e.g. London, BM). The heavy style is a reflection of a decadent monarchy that was about to collapse under the onslaught of the Achaemenid Persians. Thereafter the sculpture and terracottas of Mesopotamia are those of the foreign dynasties that ruled the country: *see* ACHAEMENID, SELEUCID, PARTHIAN and SASANIAN.

PIERRE AMIET

IV. Metalwork.

Despite the fact that Mesopotamia is practically devoid of mineral resources, metalworking there began early and reached high levels of technical and artistic achievement. The sources of the large quantities of metal that had to be imported are not precisely known, and different sources were probably exploited at different periods: the highland areas of Iran and Anatolia were potential suppliers of most metals used in antiquity, and Oman in the Persian Gulf had rich deposits of copper; the origin of the tin that was alloyed with copper to make bronze is still obscure. Metal was thus a valuable commodity and was extensively recycled: this is reflected in the uneven archaeological record, although enough survives to show that Mesopotamia had a flourishing metalworking industry at least on a level with other areas in the Ancient Near East (*see also* ANATOLIA, ANCIENT, §IV and IRAN, ANCIENT, §V). This subsection concentrates largely on the use of copper, bronze and iron; for the working of precious metals in jewellery *see* ANCIENT NEAR EAST, §II, 4.

1. BEFORE c. 2900 BC. The first substantial evidence of Mesopotamian metalworking comes in the 6th millennium BC: there are simple items of jewellery including copper beads from such sites as Yarim Tepe (ii), and gold, silver and lead were also being worked. In the earliest periods objects were worked from native copper (pure copper found in rocks on or near the surface), but the smelting of copper ores such as malachite and azurite was probably soon introduced. However, objects were only cast in simple, open moulds, and the technology was relatively primitive. From the following Ubaid period (5th millennium BC) some more elaborate forms have survived, such as a cast copper celt from Arpachiyah (late 5th millennium BC; London, BM), but the repertory of forms and shapes was still limited. This changed during the Uruk period (4th millennium BC), and by 3000 BC not only were metal objects more plentiful, but lost-wax casting had been introduced, making it possible to cast complex and elaborate shapes in copper and silver.

2. c. 2900–c. 1000 BC. Using the lost-wax technique, some objects of remarkable artistic quality were produced in the Early Dynastic period (c. 2900–c. 2340 BC). There is a copper model of a chariot pulled by four onagers from Tell Agrab, and from nearby Khafajeh a copper group showing a double jar supported by a pair of wrestlers (Baghdad, Iraq Mus.). Also from Khafajeh are three copper statuettes of nude worshippers designed as vessel stands. In Early Dynastic III (c. 2600–2340 BC) two sites in particular have produced extensive evidence of metalworking. The first is Tell al-Ubaid, where the metal fittings of a temple had been taken down in antiquity and stacked at the base of the temple platform (Baghdad, Iraq Mus.; London, BM). They included a hammered copper panel showing the Imdugud bird grasping a pair of stags (London, BM), and free-standing bulls and lions. The latter are of particular interest in that the bodies are fashioned from sheet copper while the massive heads are made from bronze and then filled with bitumen. Possibly a round form was cast and then hammered up into the shape of the heads, but in any event the use of two different alloys would have provided a dramatic colour contrast. It has been said that among the material from the Royal Cemetery at nearby Ur can be found knowledge of virtually every type of metallurgical technique known in antiquity except the working of iron (Baghdad, Iraq Mus.; London, BM; Philadelphia, U. PA, Mus.). Amongst the grave-goods from Ur are weapons and vessels in bronze, gold and silver, and an astonishing amount of elaborate jewellery. There is much use of silver and gold

in such accomplished pieces as the sheet gold helmet of Meskalamdug (Baghdad, Iraq Mus.; cast in London, BM), and other objects, such as the Ram in the Thicket (London, BM; Philadelphia, U. PA, Mus.) show skilful use of gold overlay. At Ur there is also evidence for the use of electrum, as in the beautiful rein-ring surmounted by an onager (London, BM). A fine example of engraving on silver of Early Dynastic date from another Sumerian site, Telloh, is the silver vase made for King Entemena of Lagash and engraved with a scene showing an Imdugud bird pouncing on a pair of lions (Paris, Louvre; see fig. 16).

From the Akkadian period (c. 2340–c. 2100 BC) come two hollow-cast copper objects of outstanding quality. The first is an almost life-size male head from Nineveh (Baghdad, Iraq Mus.; *see* AKKADIAN, fig. 2), probably that of an Akkadian ruler with long beard and elaborate hairstyle held in place by a headband. Although intentionally disfigured in antiquity, this head still retains its original vigour and majesty. The second masterpiece is the lower part of a nude male figure squatting on a large circular drum (Baghdad, Iraq Mus.), found near Dohuk in northeast Iraq. These large copper castings, probably done in multiple piece-moulds, represent a considerable technical achievement. From the succeeding Ur III period (c. 2100–c. 2000 BC) there are a number of copper or copper alloy foundation deposits in the form of figurines mounted on

16. Silver vase, with an engraved scene showing an Imdugud bird pouncing on a pair of lions, made for King Entemena of Lagash, h. 350 mm, from Telloh, c. 2400 BC (Paris, Musée du Louvre)

pegs, as well as tools and weapons from the graves at Ur. At this period metal tools may still have been restricted to the important administrative and religious centres, though by the Old Babylonian period (*c.* 1900–*c.* 1600 BC) there is evidence that metal tools had become widespread. For example, from the comparatively small site of Tell Sifr in southern Iraq comes a hoard of axes, adzes, spades, sickle-blades, chisels and a hammer, together with two sheet-metal cauldrons and an ingot (London, BM). The purpose of these tools seems to have been mainly agricultural. Surprisingly, only three items contained significant amounts of tin, suggesting that at this date tin was still not being widely used in rural areas. In fact, until the mid-2nd millennium BC arsenic rather than tin was often added to copper, or an original ore rich in arsenic was deliberately selected. These arsenical coppers are harder than pure copper, and can be further work-hardened by hammering.

The Middle Assyrian period (*c.* 1350–*c.* 1000 BC) produced fine pieces of gold and silver jewellery, including examples of granulation, cloisonné and filigree from Tomb 45 at Assur (Berlin, Schloss Charlottenburg). This period is also remarkable for the amount of lead used: for example, seven lead blocks weighing between 324 and 532 kg were buried in the foundations of Tukulti-Ninurta I's Ishtar Temple at Assur, and many lead plaques and figurines have been found at Kar-Tukulti-Ninurta (London, BM; Berlin, Pergamonmus.).

3. *c.* 1000–539 BC. The Neo-Assyrian period (9th–7th centuries BC) is notable for a thriving metalworking industry and a rich repertory of objects in bronze, gold and silver. It was probably also during the 9th century BC that the transition took place from an industry dominated by bronzeworking to one where iron was used when appropriate, although there are sporadic earlier occurrences of iron. The reasons for this change are not entirely clear: possibilities include a shortage of bronze, the ability to bring smelting kilns to higher temperatures, the introduction of more sophisticated blacksmiths' tools and an improvement in iron technology. There is some evidence that iron tools and weapons may have been carburized (i.e. the addition of carbon to produce a mild steel). While there is extensive evidence of wrought or hammered iron at this time, the casting of iron did not occur until much later. Objects made of iron were generally tools, such as saws, hoes, sickles, ploughshares and knives, and weapons including arrowheads, swords, daggers, helmets and armour scales. A distinctive group consists of large fish-shaped blocks of iron with a hole in the middle: many were found at Khorsabad (Paris, Louvre), and there are several examples from Nimrud (London, BM; *see* FRIEZE, fig. 2). They are sometimes called ingots. Iron was also occasionally used in combination with bronze in such objects as tripods and maceheads; here, the bronze was skilfully cast on to the iron (e.g. London, BM).

It was in the working of bronze rather than iron, however, that Assyrian smiths excelled. Assyrian historical records reveal that vast quantities of bronze, in the form of both raw material and finished objects, flooded into the Assyrian coffers as booty and tribute from other parts of the Near East. The bronzesmiths had therefore practically unlimited quantities of metal, which they put to good use.

Assyrian texts state that many monumental works were produced in bronze, including some colossal castings. For example, each of the bronze lion colossi of Sennacherib (*reg* 704–681 BC) set up in his palace at Nineveh are said to have weighed 11,400 talents (approx. 42 tonnes). Not surprisingly, such grandiose works have not survived, but enough remains to confirm that the bronzeworking industry was flourishing at this time. There are, for instance, the famous Balawat Gates, strips of bronze with elaborate embossed and chased decoration showing in intricate detail scenes of the Assyrian army on campaign and the Assyrian king hunting (London, BM). These decorative strips were hammered on to large, wooden doors. Elaborate furniture was produced, making plentiful use of bronze for component parts in thrones, chairs and tables. These included bulls' heads, bronze sleeves with embossed volutes, and bronze overlay with mythological scenes featuring winged sphinxes and griffins. Much of this material comes from Nimrud (London, BM; Baghdad, Iraq Mus.), as do many bronze horse trappings including bells, plaques and bosses. Outstanding is a bronze or electrum cheekpiece in the form of a prancing horse (Baghdad, Iraq Mus.). Throne or altar bases were sometimes faced with metal, as for example a large slab of bronze, cast in a piece-mould, showing Esarhaddon (*reg* 680–669 BC) and his mother Naqi'a (Paris, Louvre). A particularly fine example of bronzecasting, found by chance in northern Iraq, represents a bull-man with upstretched arms wearing a horned headdress (Baghdad, Iraq Mus.). Such Atlas figures are seen on Assyrian reliefs, built into pieces of furniture (e.g. London, BM). Last, it is worth recording that in the Neo-Assyrian period even coffins were sometimes made of bronze; they are rounded at one end and squared-off at the other, and occasionally have chased decoration on the vertical strips of bronze on the side showing goats standing on rosettes (e.g. London, BM).

Assyria's southern neighbour, Babylonia, also seems to have had an active bronze industry from the 9th to the 7th century BC. Assyrian reliefs, particularly in the reign of Sennacherib, show a wide range of objects, many of them probably of bronze or even precious metal, being carried from Babylonia as booty, and Assyrian historical sources tell a similar story. After the fall of Assyria in 612 BC and the subsequent rise to pre-eminence of Babylon, the production of bronzes in Babylonia probably continued on a more ambitious scale. For example, Nebuchadnezzar (*reg* 604–562 BC) records that he had monumental bronze figures made in the form of bulls and mushhushshu-dragons to stand in the main city gates of Babylon. Part of a massive bronze door-sill from Borsippa bears an inscription of Nebuchadnezzar (London, BM). Following the Persian conquest of Babylon in 539 BC, Mesopotamia was under the domination of foreign powers, and metalwork of later periods cannot be discussed in purely Mesopotamian terms (for further discussion *see* IRAN, ANCIENT, §V and GREECE, ANCIENT, §VIII, 2(i)(e)).

BIBLIOGRAPHY

J. Deshayes: *Les Outils de bronze de l'Indus au Danube (IVe au IIe millénaire),* 2 vols (Paris, 1960)
A. Spycket: *La Statuaire du Proche-Orient Ancien,* Handbuch der Orientalistik (Leiden and Cologne, 1981)

E. A. Braun-Holzinger: *Figürliche Bronzen aus Mesopotamien* (Munich, 1984)

P. R. S. Moorey: *Materials and Manufacture in Ancient Mesopotamia: The Evidence of Archaeology and Art*, Brit. Archaeol. Rep. (Oxford, 1985)

J. E. Curtis, ed.: *Bronzeworking Centres of Western Asia, c. 1000–539 BC* (London, 1988)

O. W. Muscarella: *Bronze and Iron: Ancient Near Eastern Artefacts in the Metropolitan Museum of Art* (New York, 1988)

JOHN E. CURTIS

V. Pottery.

1. BEFORE *c.* 2900 BC. The earliest known pottery is a lightly, possibly accidentally, fired ware found at Mureybet in north-west Syria *c.* 8000 BC, but even a millennium later many sites around Tell Afar in northern Mesopotamia were still aceramic. Nevertheless, in the same area, at Kültepe and Tell es-Sotto, and at UMM DABAGHIYA near Hatra in the Jazira, a 7th-millennium BC culture has been identified that is characterized by simple, lightly fired, buff pottery, often decorated with applied ornament or with simple geometric patterns in red paint. This culture is variously known as Sotto, Jazira or proto-Hassuna.

The Hassuna culture itself (6th millennium BC; *see also* §I, 2(i)(b) above) is named after the site of Hassuna, south of Mosul. It is found throughout the north Mesopotamian plain and is distinguished by its handmade pottery. Mono-chrome painted wares are decorated with simple geometric patterns; lightly incised herring-bone designs cover the surface of incised pots and some vessels combine painted and incised decoration. Flat-bottomed, oval vessels with heavily ridged or notched interiors may have been used in cereal production and are generally referred to as 'husking trays'. There are also large storage jars with an almost triangular profile. The earliest known two-stage domed pottery kilns (one is reconstructed in Mosul Mus.) date to this period and have been discovered at Yarim Tepe, Iraq (*see* YARIM TEPE (ii)); using them, temperatures of up to 1000°C could have been achieved.

In the Zagros, 7th-millennium BC sites such as JARMO produced painted pottery with simple geometric designs including a distinctive 'tadpole' pattern in red on a buff background, arranged in diagonal lines. This pottery has also been found in 6th-millennium BC contexts at sites in Iran such as Tepe Sarab.

Samarran pottery (second half of the 6th millennium BC), named after the site of Samarra' (*see* SAMARRA', fig. 1), where it was first identified, is found not only in central Iraq but also occurs in the Zagros and in the later levels of Hassuna sites. Samarran pottery, like that of Hassuna with which it was partly contemporary, includes painted, incised, painted-and-incised and plain varieties, but the Samarran ceramic was remarkably well made and the ornament far more elaborate, often consisting of parallel bands of differing and complicated geometric designs. For the first time humans and animals are common as painted decoration, in particular various caprids with elaborate horns, rows of scorpions and centrifugal patterns of women with wavy flowing hair.

Halaf pottery is also contemporary with the later manifestations of Hassuna and Samarran pottery. It is found as far west as the Mediterranean and is best represented at the Mesopotamian sites of Yarim Tepe II and Arpachiyah (for illustration *see* ARPACHIYAH). It must certainly have been made by professional craftsmen, and the Halaf potters, whose sources of clay differed from

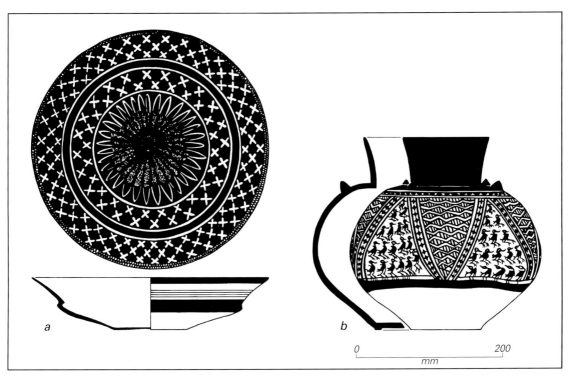

a   *b*

0   200
                mm

17. Halaf pottery, 5th millennium BC: (a) plate from Arpachiyah, diam. 320 mm; (b) pot from Tepe Gawra

those of their Hassuna and Samarra' neighbours, far surpassed their predecessors and successors in the elaboration and delicacy of their design and the fine quality of the ware itself (see fig. 17). In the latest Halaf phase (*c.* 4500 BC) beautifully painted polychrome ceramics were produced, on which a thick white pigment was often applied as a third 'colour'. The background is often a warm buff or peach, with red and black decoration produced on the same pot from the same iron oxide pigment, technically a very advanced achievement. The surface of the finest pottery is highly burnished and a glossy effect is achieved by the use of fluxes, which serve to lower the melting point of the pigments, in some cases accidentally achieving true glazes.

The Ubaid pottery sequence in the south (*see* UBAID, TELL AL-) occupies most of the 5th millennium BC and has been divided into four phases. Ubaid 1 (also known as the ERIDU phase) is characterized by distinctive and well-made monochrome ceramic types, with a relatively limited geographical distribution in southern Mesopotamia. In 1968, at CHOGHA MAMI, a new type of pottery was discovered (now referred to as Chogha Mami Transitional; see fig. 18), which appeared stylistically related to both the preceding Samarra' of central Mesopotamia and the earliest Ubaid of the south. The Ubaid component of this ceramic style has been found at Tell el 'Oueili, in levels that significantly pre-date the earliest levels at Eridu (Ubaid 1). The precise origin of the 'Oueili ceramic tradition has not been established, though it seems likely to have been indigenous in the south.

Ubaid 2 (the Hajji Muhammad phase), first identified at a small site of that name near Uruk, is known as far north as Chogha Mami and the Hamrin region: its most distinctive pottery bears all-over paint and designs in negative. Ubaid 3 and 4 pottery, characterized by distinctive monochrome ware with relatively simple geometric designs, is found from the Balikh Valley in Syria to the Eastern Province of Saudi Arabia. The geographical distribution of the Ubaid assemblage strongly suggests a pattern of diffusion from southern Mesopotamia northwards and down the Persian Gulf. The unique presence of a few Ubaid 2 sherds at TELL BRAK in north-east Syria identifies also an early diffusion up the Euphrates and

Khabur rivers. The use of the potter's wheel is attested at least as early as Ubaid 3 (mid-5th millennium BC).

The succeeding Uruk period (4th millennium BC) is divided into four phases. The Early Uruk phase is characterized by undecorated pottery and the earliest occurrence of mass-produced types. Red-slipped wares appear that, in the north, are sometimes highly burnished ('sealing wax ware') and sometimes decorated with a characteristic branching pattern ('sprig ware'). The latter black-on-red pottery is common at such northern sites as Tell Brak and Tepe Gawra (level XII). The sites of Brak and Tell Hammam et-Turkman (on the River Balikh in north-east Syria) show continuity from Ubaid to Uruk times, with a gradual decrease in painted pottery and an increase, in the earliest Uruk phase, of bowls with scraped exteriors, sometimes referred to as 'Coba bowls', after the site of Sakça Gözü (Coba Hüyük). At Brak and Gawra (level XI) distinctive north Mesopotamian ceramic types occur, including fine stamped and embossed vessels.

Middle to Late Uruk period sites in north-west Syria, such as HABUBA KABIRA and JEBEL ARUDA, have produced pottery that is identical to that from Uruk itself, including such characteristic types as jars with four very long lugs and often incised triangles on the shoulders ('nose-lug jars', a Late Uruk feature at Nippur), and jars with drooping spouts. Coarse, handmade, bevelled-rim bowls characterize this phase throughout the entire Middle East; their purpose remains uncertain, but they may have been ration bowls or perhaps simply containers for some common commodity.

For bibliography *see* §I, 2(i)(b) above.

JOAN OATES

2. *c.* 2900 BC–AD 637. During the Jemdet Nasr period (*c.* 3100–*c.* 2900 BC) the characteristic pot had been broad-shouldered with a rimmed neck, often with ear-lugs on the shoulder. Some were painted in a distinctive, glossy, plum-coloured paint with designs in plum, yellow and black on the shoulder; the designs were generally geometric but were sometimes arranged in panels with figures, animals and vegetation. A later development of this pottery, known as 'Scarlet Ware', is found in the Diyala Region north-east of Baghdad in Early Dynastic I contexts (*c.* 2900–*c.* 2750 BC). The shapes are similar to the earlier ones, but the vessels are taller and often larger, and the designs, which sometimes cover the whole surface, are executed in a brilliant red paint outlined in black on a buff or yellow ground. Some designs are elaborate, and one pot depicts a chariot scene and a banquet accompanied by music on a large, bull-headed lyre (London, BM; see figs 19 and 20). In Central Mesopotamia two distinctive unpainted types of pottery are often found together throughout the Early Dynastic period: upright-handled jars have incised decoration, generally triangles, on the shoulder, and the single, flat handle, which rises vertically from the shoulder but is not attached to the rim, is decorated with eyes and a nose, rarely with a mouth, and sometimes with two pellets to represent breasts; dishes on flaring hollow stems bear incised triangles round the base,

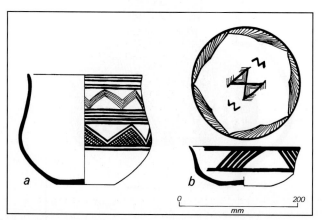

18. Chogha Mami Transitional pottery, 5th millennium BC: (a) deep bowl, h. 180 mm; (b) open bowl, h. 62 mm

separate course from those of the south. The late 3rd-millennium BC pottery of Tell Taya, while sharing some basic forms such as the long-necked cup with the Akkadian/Ur III tradition of Babylonia, includes a highly

19. 'Scarlet Ware' pot, h. 330 mm, from Khafajeh, Diyala Region, c. 2900–2750 BC (London, British Museum)

and vegetation, pubic triangles and combs up the sides. Further south the pottery is generally undecorated, as at Ur and Tell al-Ubaid. In the north, the term Ninevite 5 describes pottery first identified in Level 5 at Nineveh (c. 3000–c. 2500 BC): pedestal jars, pedestal bowls and large hollow-stemmed bowls, painted all over with geometric designs and birds in dark paint, were gradually succeeded by fine, grey-green cups and pedestal bowls bearing incised and excised geometric patterns.

From the start of the Akkadian period (c. 2334 BC) to the Persian conquest (539 BC) the ceramic traditions of southern Mesopotamia emphasize the plain and utilitarian. Vessels are wheel-made, generally buff in colour, and mostly unornamented. The rather dumpy shapes of the late Early Dynastic period gave way to slimmer and more elongated shapes; the previously ubiquitous conical cup soon disappeared, and a beaker form typical of the Akkadian period was introduced. Tall carinated jars with ridged shoulders are characteristic of the Akkadian to Ur III periods (c. 2334–c. 2004 BC). In the succeeding Isin–Larsa period (c. 2004–c. 1792 BC) white inlay was sometimes used to decorate straight-sided grey-ware jars and multiple modelled columns are occasionally found round the necks of high-shouldered jars. Typical forms of the Old Babylonian (c. 1792–c. 1595 BC) and Kassite (c. 1595–c. 1155 BC) periods are elongated jars with short shoulders and plain necks, and chalices and cups with bulbous lower body and button or disc base. Middle and Late Babylonian (c. 1155–539 BC) forms are so little distinctive that it is often difficult to tell them apart: shallow open bowls, often with carinated rims, dominate both assemblages.

Until the end of the 2nd millennium BC the ceramic traditions of northern Mesopotamia followed a largely

20. Painted decoration (showing a chariot and a banquet scene) from the preserved parts of the 'Scarlet Ware' pot, h. 330 mm, from Khafajeh, Diyala Region, c. 2900–2750 BC (London, British Museum); reconstruction drawings

distinctive style of decoration. Painted and, more often, incised patterns are usually geometric, often hatched triangles. Elaborate pedestal vases sometimes have plastic applied snakes crawling over the rim. Both shapes and decoration have links with the Khabur pottery of the early 2nd millennium BC. This includes deep bowls with high carination, sometimes with stripes across the turned-out rim, painted cups, and 'grain-measures' (wide-mouthed waisted jars). Painting was in red or black, often plain horizontal stripes but sometimes including such geometric forms as hatched triangles and occasionally naturalistic designs. The partially contemporary and later Nuzi ware is often associated with the incursions of the Hurrian peoples from Anatolia, and has a wide distribution from Alalakh in the west to the Zagros in the east, and as far south as the Kirkuk region. The most characteristic form is a very fine long, nipple-based beaker with a band of black paint around the rim, overpainted with a repeating white design. The geometric and naturalistic motifs—birds were especially popular—are of exquisitely delicate conception and execution.

The pottery of the Assyrian empire was largely utilitarian, not unlike contemporary southern material, with the exception of the green, eggshell-fine Neo-Assyrian 'palace ware'. Typical palace-ware shapes are a beaker with finger-dimples in the bulbous lower body, and 'istikans' (like modern Iraqi tea-glasses). Other Assyrian forms include lamps, tripod bowls painted red inside and some rhyta.

Mesopotamian pottery during successive Achaemenid, Seleucid, Parthian and Sasanian political domination (538 BC–AD 637) shared the characteristic forms of those widely distributed styles, though often with a degree of regional idiosyncrasy. Stamped designs are common all over the region from Achaemenid times onwards. Red-painted wares are common among Hellenistic pottery, though the typical Greek red and black varnished wares are confined to rare imports. The use of glaze, known from the 2nd millennium BC, becomes much more common during Parthian times. The thick 'Parthian green' glaze effectively limited the possibilities for surface decoration, and perhaps as a result there is a strong feeling for pure shape in Parthian pottery. A variety of bowls, bottles, lamps and jugs is found; handles, especially of the 'twisted rope' variety, are very popular. Amphorae are common, also excessively large storage jars. Glazed 'slipper coffins', with stamped relief decoration, perhaps represent the pinnacle of the Parthian potter's ambitions for size. Sasanian pottery has not received the attention it probably deserves, being largely restricted, even at the capital Ktesiphon, to utility wares. Where luxury pieces do occur, however, they tend to a greater complexity than their Parthian forerunners, with elaborate applied and incised decoration, and begin to foreshadow the early Islamic shapes that gradually succeeded them.

BIBLIOGRAPHY

P. Delougaz: *Pottery from the Diyala Region* (Chicago, 1952)
J. Moon: 'Some New Early Dynastic Pottery from Abu Salabikh', *Iraq*, xliii (1981), pp. 47–75
H. P. Martin: 'The Early Dynastic Cemetery at al-'Ubaid: A Re-evaluation', *Iraq*, xliv (1982), pp. 145–85
J. Moon: 'The Distribution of Upright-handled Jars and Stemmed Dishes in the Early Dynastic Period', *Iraq*, xliv (1982), pp. 39–69
S. Pollock: 'Chronology of the Royal Cemetery of Ur', *Iraq*, xlvii (1985), pp. 129–58
M. Roaf and R. Killick: 'A Mysterious Affair of Styles: The Ninevite 5 Pottery of Northern Mesopotamia', *Iraq*, xlix (1987), pp. 193–8

JANE MOON

VI. Wall painting.

Together with relief sculpture (*see* §III above), glazed faience panels and mosaics (*see* ANCIENT NEAR EAST, §II, 5 and 9), wall paintings were one of the principal media for the decoration of buildings. Such fragments as have survived from ancient Mesopotamia give a static impression, because their elements are outlined in black, filled with unshaded colours and arranged without perspective. They were executed on grounds of clay, lime plaster or gypsum, and apart from black (bitumen, charcoal, soot), colour pigments consisted entirely of minerals: white (calcite), red, ochre red, brown and yellow (ferruginous soils), blue (Egyptian blue, azurite) and green (malachite). The colours were often mixed, and the technique was always *a secco*. Before *c.* 3000 BC wall paintings depicting hunting scenes or geometric designs were not restricted to important buildings (*see also* ANATOLIA, ANCIENT, §VI). Around 3000 BC the persons depicted were narrowed down to an élite, and after *c.* 2000 BC paintings were confined to palaces. In the Neo-Assyrian palaces of the 9th–7th centuries BC there were not only painted murals but paint was also applied to stone reliefs and glazed panels (*see* §2 below). In the Babylonian south, however, painted and glazed faience panels seem to have been the preferred medium.

1. BEFORE *c.* 1000 BC. The oldest representational painting, from a house at UMM DABAGHIYA (*c.* 5500 BC), was painted on gypsum in ochre red on white, black and yellow (Baghdad, Iraq Mus.). It depicts an onager hunt and figures that resemble vultures and spiders. The Late Uruk period is represented by murals from a temple at Tell 'Uqair (*c.* 3000 BC), which were painted on clay in white, black, red, plum red, yellow and orange (Baghdad, Iraq Mus.). They show processions of figures and leopards, depicted for the first time on a base-line within a frame, arranged in space and adapted to the architecture. After *c.* 2000 BC Mesopotamian influence is apparent in the wall paintings from the palace at Mari (*c.* 1800–1760 BC) on the Middle Euphrates in Syria (*see also* SYRIA-PALESTINE, §VI); a little younger are the friezes depicting Hathor heads, bucrania and stylized trees, painted on clay and gypsum in black, ochre red and pink on white or grey, at the height of the doorways in the palace at NUZI (*c.* 1450–1400 BC). At KAR TUKULTI NINURTA (1244–1208 BC), palmettes, bird-headed genii, leaping goats and geometric designs on gypsum in black, red and blue on a white ground are already typically Assyrian. Processions of male figures decorated the doorways of the Kassite palace at AQAR QUF (1173–1161 BC); they are executed on clay in black, red, white, yellow and blue paint (Baghdad, Iraq Mus.).

BIBLIOGRAPHY

R. Koldewey: *Das Ischtar-Tor in Babylon*, Wiss. Veröff. Dt. Orient-Ges., xxxii (Berlin, 1918)
——: *Die Südburg* (1931), i of *Die Königsburgen von Babylon*, Wiss. Veröff. Dt. Orient-Ges., liv (Berlin, 1931–)

R. Starr: *Nuzi*, 2 vols (Cambridge, 1937–9)

S. Lloyd: 'Tell Uqair: Report on the Excavations', *J. Nr E. Stud.*, ii (1943), pp. 135–55

T. Baqir: 'Iraq Government Excavations at 'Aqr Qūf, 1942–3', *Iraq* (1944) [suppl.]

——: 'Iraq Government Excavations at 'Aqr Qūf: Second Interim Report, 1943–4', *Iraq* (1945) [suppl.]

——: 'Iraq Government Excavations at 'Aqr Qūf: Third Interim Report, 1944–5', *Iraq*, viii (1946), pp. 73–93

A. Parrot: *Le Palais: Peintures murales*, II/ii of *Mission archéologique de Mari*, Bibliothèque archéologique et historique, lxix (Paris, 1958)

A. Moortgat: *Alt-vorderasiatische Malerei* (Berlin, 1959)

D. Kirkbride: 'Umm Dabaghiyah: A Fourth Preliminary Report', *Iraq*, xxxvii (1975), pp. 3–10

——: 'Umm Dabaghiyah', *Fifty Years of Mesopotamian Discovery: The Work of the British School of Archaeology in Iraq 1932–1982*, ed. J. Curtis (London, 1982), pp. 11–21

T. Eickhoff: *Kār-Tukulti-Ninurta: Eine mittelassyrische Kult- und Residenzstadt*, Abhandlungen der Deutschen Orient-Gesellschaft, xxi (Berlin, 1985)

A. Nunn: *Die Wandmalerei und der glasierte Wandschmuck im alten Orient*, Handbuch der Orientalistik (Leiden, 1988)

A. NUNN

2. NEO-ASSYRIAN. In Neo-Assyrian public buildings, the use of wall reliefs (*see* §II, 6(i) above) was often complemented or even wholly replaced by paintings. These were done in two different media, probably according to location: on interior walls pigment was applied to the whitewashed mud plaster covering the mud-brick; exterior walls were decorated with painted glazed bricks. Most of these paintings are now lost.

The earliest Assyrian wall paintings are from KAR TUKULTI-NINURTA (*see* §1 above). From ASSUR are fragmentary glazed tiles of Tukulti-Ninurta II (*reg* 890–884 BC) showing military scenes and lion hunts (London, BM); a glazed plaque, possibly of Tiglath-pileser III (*reg* 744–727 BC), decorated with a person before a deity (Berlin, Pergamonmus.); and a section of a glazed brick podium face, also probably from the time of Tiglath-pileser III, showing chariots and horsemen in the mountains (Andrae). At NIMRUD fragments of 9th-century BC painted bricks and wall paintings—mostly depicting stylized arrangements of geometric, floral and animal forms, though narrative subjects also occur—were found in the palaces of Assurnasirpal II (*reg* 883–859 BC), Shalmaneser III (*reg* 858–824 BC), and Adad-nirari III (*reg* 810–783 BC; see Reade, 1979). The best-preserved paintings are on glazed bricks: a large-scale arched panel of Shalmaneser III consisting of over 300 bricks that included symmetrical images of the king flanking a god in a winged disc and bulls flanking a stylized tree (Baghdad, Iraq Mus.) and a single brick (possibly of Assurnasirpal II) showing the king and courtiers (London, BM). Wall paintings from the arsenal showing processions, and bricks painted with battle scenes from the south-west corner of the Nimrud citadel, date to the reign of a later Assyrian king, perhaps Esarhaddon (*reg* 680–669 BC). Geometric wall paintings of uncertain date were also found in the Governor's Palace, the Burnt Palace, and the 1950 Building.

The most complete group of Neo-Assyrian wall paintings was found in the palace at the provincial capital of TIL BARSIP (fragments in Paris, Louvre and Aleppo, N. Mus.; see fig. 21). The great variety of subjects includes protective deities, royal campaigns, audience scenes and lion hunts. Some of these paintings date to the second

21. Neo-Assyrian wall painting, detail showing Assyrian scribes writing on a scroll and on a clay tablet, from Til Barsip, *c.* 725 BC

half of the 8th century BC, while the rest are from the 7th. At the provincial town of ARSLAN TASH, by contrast, the walls of the royal suite of the palace were decorated with a simple geometric frieze. At KHORSABAD, the ceilings of several rooms in the palace of Sargon II (*reg* 721–705 BC) were painted with geometric patterns, and brick fragments decorated with inscriptions and non-narrative subjects were found at unspecified locations. Painted on the wall opposite the main entrance to the great hall of Residence K were friezes of animal, floral, protective and geometric motifs, above which was a single panel showing the king before a god. The curved part of the arches of several of the city gates was faced with a band of bricks decorated with winged genies and rosettes, and the entrances to the palace temples were flanked by glazed brick dados decorated with symbolic animals and objects. No wall paintings have been reported from NINEVEH, but painted bricks that showed military scenes and geometric patterns were found in the area of the Ishtar Temple. At least some of these probably date to the time of Assurnasirpal II. Painted bricks from the 7th century BC have been found in the area of the west façade of Sennacherib's palace and in the Nineveh arsenal (both unpublished).

BIBLIOGRAPHY

W. Andrae: *Coloured Ceramics from Ashur* (London, 1925)

J. Reade: 'A Glazed-brick Panel from Nimrud', *Iraq*, xxv (1963), pp. 38–47

——: 'Assyrian Architectural Decoration: Techniques and Subject-matter', *Baghdad. Mitt.*, x (1979), pp. 18–49

A. Spycket: 'Malerei', *Reallexikon der Assyriologie*, vii (Berlin, 1988), pp. 296–300

JOHN M. RUSSELL

VII. Museums, collections and exhibitions.

In the 19th century the British and the French were the first to undertake excavations in Mesopotamia, and the huge ruin mounds associated by tradition with the Assyrians naturally drew their attention. It is therefore the British Museum in London and the Louvre in Paris that have the largest holdings of Assyrian reliefs outside Iraq. The Germans chose to work at Assur, which was less rich in reliefs, but their excavations at Babylon enabled them to reconstruct in the Pergamonmuseum in Berlin the glazed brick panels from the Ishtar Gate and the throne-room of Nebuchadnezzar.

Mesopotamia in the 19th century was part of the Ottoman empire, and most foreign excavations managed to obtain permits giving them extensive rights to the objects they discovered. After World War I the new state of Iraq came under the British Mandate. The Iraq Museum was founded in 1923, and according to the Antiquities Law of 1924, amended in 1936, all unique objects from excavations were to remain in Iraq together with half the remaining finds; in 1974 the law was changed and now all excavated antiquities must remain in Iraq. The collections of various museums of the world reflect this changing situation.

The largest museum of Mesopotamian antiquities is the Iraq Museum in Baghdad, but, for the reasons outlined above, its collections are not comprehensive. Mosul houses the biggest regional museum, and many Assyrian reliefs and portal figures can be seen *in situ* near by in Nineveh and Nimrud; many other regional museums are being planned and built. Outside Iraq, museums with major holdings of excavated antiquities from Mesopotamia are the following: London (BM; material from Nimrud, Nineveh, Tell el-Rimah, Sippar, Ur, Ubaid), Oxford (Ashmolean; material from Kish, Jemdet Nasr), Paris (Louvre; material from Khorsabad, Nineveh, Telloh, and Sumerian and Babylonian monuments from Susa, where they had been taken as booty), Berlin (Pergamonmus; material held before World War II from Assur, Babylon and Uruk), Philadelphia (U. PA, Mus.; material from Nippur, Ur), and Chicago (U. Chicago, IL, Orient. Inst. Mus.; material from Khorsabad, the Diyala region sites). Antiquities from Mari and Tell Brak, which at times fell within the Mesopotamian cultural sphere, are housed respectively in Paris (Louvre) and Damascus (N. Mus.) in the former case and London (BM), Aleppo (N. Mus.) and Deir ez-Zor Museum in the latter. In addition, these and many other museums and collections, of which the foremost is the Metropolitan Museum of Art in New York, contain antiquities, mostly unprovenanced, obtained by purchase, including large quantities of cylinder seals, which, because of their small size, have become increasingly popular among collectors.

The first exhibitions of Mesopotamian antiquities were put on by the Louvre in Paris and the British Museum in London and contained the Assyrian finds sent back respectively by Paul Emile Botta (1802–70) in 1846 and by AUSTEN HENRY LAYARD in 1848. These caused a sensation: Layard himself wrote that before his excavations 'a case scarcely three feet square enclosed all that remained, not only of the great city, Nineveh, but of Babylon itself' (Layard, 1850, p. xxv), although in fact this was not a fair assessment of the collections brought back by such early travellers as Pietro della Valle and the Abbé de Beauchamp (1752–1801) in the 17th century or of the collection of Claudius James Rich (1787–1821), which had been acquired by the British Museum in 1825. When the inscription on Layard's Black Obelisk of Shalmaneser III was deciphered, and was found to contain the name of 'Jehu son of Omri' mentioned in the Bible, public enthusiasm for Mesopotamia was further stimulated. Assyrian sculpture and artefacts on show during the Great Exhibition in London in 1851 led to the creation of jewellery, figurines and boxes in the Assyrian style (*see* ASSYRIAN REVIVAL), and cartoons in *Punch* depicted Layard in the guise of one of the Assyrian winged bulls he had brought back from Nimrud. Interest was revived when, in the late 1920s and early 1930s, jewellery, gold and silver vessels and musical instruments were brought back by LEONARD WOOLLEY from his excavations in the Royal Cemetery at Ur, and the city was linked by him with the Biblical Flood and with Abraham. All these objects became part of the permanent collections of Mesopotamian antiquities discussed above. There have been few short-term exhibitions specifically devoted to Mesopotamia, with the notable exception of a touring exhibition of some of the masterpieces of the Iraq Museum in Baghdad.

For further discussion of the rediscovery of Mesopotamia *see* ANCIENT NEAR EAST, §III.

BIBLIOGRAPHY
A. H. Layard: *The Monuments of Nineveh*, 2 vols (London, 1849)
P. E. Botta: *Monument de Ninive* (London, 1850)
A. H. Layard: *Nineveh and its Remains* (London, 1853)
C. J. Gadd: *Stones of Assyria* (London, 1936)
S. Smith: *Assyrian Sculpture in the British Museum: From Shalmaneser III to Sennacherib* (London, 1938)
Trésors du musée de Bagdad: 7000 ans d'histoire mésopotamienne (exh. cat., Geneva, Mus. A. & Hist., 1977)
Sumer, Assur, Babylon: 7000 Jahre Kunst und Kultur zwischen Euphrat und Tigris (exh. cat., Hildesheim, Roemer- und Pelizaeus-Mus., 1978)
A Guide to the Oriental Institute Museum, University of Chicago (Chicago, 1982)
'Ancient Near Eastern Art: The Metropolitan Museum of Art', *Bull. Met. Mus. A.*, xli/4 (1984) [whole issue]
La terra tra i due fiumi: Venti anni di archeologia italiana: La Mesopotamia dei tesori (exh. cat., Turin, Centro Ricerche Archeologiche e Scavi di Torino per il Medio Oriente e l'Asia, 1985)

DOMINIQUE COLLON

Messager, Annette (*b* Berck, 30 Nov 1943). French painter, photographer and sculptor. She studied at the Ecole Nationale Supérieure des Arts Décoratifs in Paris (1962–6). Her first one-woman exhibition was at the Städtische Galerie im Lenbachhaus in Munich (1973). During the 1970s her work drew upon everyday life, taking such subjects as toys and needlework. She usually used a range of closely related found-objects (e.g. *Pensioners*, 1972; Paris, Pompidou), as well as creating performance pieces. In her work she questioned accepted perceptions of women. Messager stood out because of the refined cruelty with which she dealt with memories (including those drawn from childhood), obsessions and even minor incursions into the domain of the occult. In conjunction with her exhibitions she produced several artist's books.

BIBLIOGRAPHY
Annette Messager Künstlerin, Annette Messager Sammlerin (exh. cat. by A. Zweite, Munich, Lenbachhaus, 1973)
Annette Messager (exh. cat. by S. Pagé, Paris, Mus. A. Mod. Ville Paris, 1984)
Annette Messager: Comédie tragédie, 1971–1989 (exh. cat., ed. S. Lemoine; Grenoble, Mus. Grenoble; and elsewhere; 1989–90)

VANINA COSTA

Messagier, Jean (*b* Paris, 13 July 1920). French painter and printmaker. He attended the Ecole Nationale Supérieure des Arts Décoratifs and travelled in Italy and Algeria to broaden his artistic education. His first solo exhibition took place in 1943 at the château of Montbéliard. Influenced by Klee's work and by his contact with the art critic Charles Estienne, who as early as 1950 sensed that geometrical abstraction was leading towards a new academicism and pleaded the cause of a freer and more lyrical pictorial expression, Messagier lightened his colours to near transparency and opted for broad, spontaneous brushwork. His landscapes of the Franche-Comté, such as *Après-midi montante* (1958; Eindhoven, Stedel. Van Abbemus.), expressed his sensitivity to nature and the rhythm of the seasons. From 1960 he began to exhibit abroad and took part in some of the major international events as a representative of new trends in French painting. He also transposed his supple brushwork into numerous engravings and from 1968 responded to aspects of American Pop art.

BIBLIOGRAPHY
P. Cabanne: *Jean Messagier: L'Oeil du temps* (Paris, 1969)
Jean Messagier: Das graphische Werk 1944–1970 (exh. cat. by R. Reister, C. Estienne and J. Putman, Freiburg im Breisgau, Stadthalle, 1970; Worpswede, Ksthalle; 1971)
J. Messagier: *Les Estampes et les sculptures, 1945–74* (Paris, 1975) [essay by J. Putman]
D. Vallier: *Repères* (Paris, 1977)
Jean Messagier (exh. cat. by P. Cabanne, Saint-Paul-de-Vence, Fond. Maeght, 1977)
A. Glibota: *'Bourgeons de papier', croquis, 1940–85* (Paris, 1984)

DORA VALLIER

Messel, Alfred (*b* Darmstadt, 22 July 1853; *d* Berlin, 24 March 1909). German architect. In 1873 he entered the Kunstakademie in Kassel with his friend Ludwig Hoffmann, and in the next year they both began a four-year term at the Berlin Bauakademie. From his teacher Johann Heinrich Strack, Messel acquired his love of buildings of the Schinkel period. In 1884 Messel travelled to Italy, France and Spain as part of the Schinkel prize he had won in 1881.

In 1886 Messel established a professional practice and erected numerous large apartment blocks in Berlin, noteworthy for their large courtyards. In his designs for private dwellings he used formal compositions and high style for town houses and informality and vernacular forms for country or suburban residences, a dichotomy that continued throughout his career. His first major commission in the early 1890s was for the Hessisches Landesmuseum, Darmstadt. His design was derived from local 18th-century sources. Inside, he presented the collections chronologically in rooms decorated in period styles, similar to the contemporaneous Nationalmuseum, Munich, designed by Gabriel von Seidl.

In the 1890s Messel began to work as an architect for the department store firm of Wertheim. His second store for Wertheim on the Leipzigerstrasse, Berlin (1896–7; destr.), was the first steel-framed building erected in that city. Messel's stunning design, Gothic in proportion yet classical in detail, united large windows and thin columns into a coherent composition. Messel was praised for his modern design by Henry van de Velde and the Viennese critic Hermann Bahr. Extensions in 1901, 1904 and 1905 complemented the original but with subdued planar surfaces set between deftly articulated piers. The Wertheim store (*see* GERMANY, fig. 11) is Messel's most influential building, and its composition affected the design of J. M. Olbrich's Tietz department store, Düsseldorf (1907), and similar commissions given to Bruno Schmitz, Wilhelm Kreis and Hermann Muthesius.

Although he was invited to join van de Velde and Otto Eckmann in redesigning the Keller and Reiner Gallery, Berlin, in 1898, Messel's praise from the avant-garde was short-lived. His intention had never been to create something new by rejecting the past, but rather to allow the intended purpose of a building to determine its form and style. For the Handelsgesellschaft, Berlin, the architect provided in 1898 a rusticated building in a German Baroque style, expressing established power and tradition. Those who had praised the Wertheim attacked the Handelsgesellschaft as retardataire, failing to see that for Messel both were appropriate symbols of their differing functions.

In his contemporary domestic architecture, Messel employed vernacular forms and such materials as wooden shingles or hung tiles in the suburban villas for Wilhelm Wertheim (in the Grunewald suburb of Berlin, 1899) and Ferdinand Springer (in Wannsee, Berlin, 1901). His Berlin townhouses, including those for Felix Simon (Matthäikirchstrasse 31, 1900) and Eduard Simon (Viktoriastrasse 7, 1902), typically made of stone, or brick and stucco, were classical, with occasional Baroque details.

In the last decade of his career, Messel's overtly Baroque references gradually diminished as the simplicity of the German Neo-classical style became more important to him. Typical of his late style are three structures in Berlin, the AEG office building (1906–7), the National Bank (1907–8) and the Brommy Bridge (1907–9).

Messel's last important design, a royal commission, was for a new edifice to be built on the Museuminsel, Berlin, to house the Near Eastern collections, the Pergamon altar and a collection of Western art. Messel's solution, known as the Pergamonmuseum, is a great C-plan, with the altar placed at the rear and the two subsidiary collections in each wing. A double-screen of Doric columns closed the front court and united the building and its wings with surrounding museums. It was built by Ludwig Hoffmann (1909–30).

BIBLIOGRAPHY
Thieme-Becker
F. Stahl: 'Ein modernes Warenhaus in Berlin', *Dt. Kst & Dek.*, ii (May 1898), pp. 241–59
M. Rapsilber: *Alfred Messel* (Berlin, 1905/R 1911)
F. Wolff: 'Der Neubau des Warenhauses Wertheim in Berlin', *Dt. Kst & Dek.*, xv (Feb 1905), pp. 277–92

V. Zobel: 'Das Landes-Museum in Darmstadt: Erbaut von Professor Alfred Messel', *Dt. Kst & Dek.*, xix (Dec 1906), pp. 186–205
W. C. Behrendt: *Alfred Messel* (Berlin, 1911)

PAUL KRUTY

Messel, Oliver (*b* London, 13 Jan 1904; *d* St James, Barbados, 13 July 1978). English stage designer and painter. He was the grandson of the cartoonist Linley Sambourne (1844–1910) and was educated at Eton College, Berks. After studying at the Slade School of Fine Art, London, he began painting portraits of his friends. An early influence was the English painter Glyn Warren Philpot (1884–1937). Messel's first work for the theatre was to design masks for the production at the Coliseum in London of Serge Diaghilev's ballet *Zéphyr et Flore* (1925), which had sets by Georges Braque. He achieved success with his masks, costumes and décor for C. B. Cochran's revues between 1926 and 1931 (e.g. mask for *This Year of Grace*, painted papier-mâché, 1928; London, Theat. Mus.), and his sets for the production in London of *Helen* (1932) drew accolades from theatre critics. His all-white décor for a bedroom scene inspired the interior decorator Syrie Maugham (1879–1955). Messel became the best-known stage designer in England, his style characteristically combining sophistication and romanticism with elements of Baroque and Rococo fantasy. He designed for the ballet (*see* THEATRE, §III, 4(ii)(b)), opera and theatre in England and the USA, notably for the productions of *The Lady's Not for Burning* (1949) and *Ring Round the Moon* (1950) in London, and *Rashomon* (1959) in New York. He also created many sets for films made in Hollywood, beginning with *Romeo and Juliet* (1936) and including *Caesar and Cleopatra* (1946) and *Suddenly Last Summer* (1960). Carl Toms worked as Messel's assistant from 1952 to 1958, helping on such projects as the decoration of a suite at the Dorchester Hotel (1953; rest. 1981), London. In 1967 Messel moved permanently to his winter home in Barbados.

WRITINGS
Stage Designs and Costumes (London, 1934)
BIBLIOGRAPHY
Oliver Messel (exh. cat. by R. Pinkham and others, London, V&A, 1983)
C. Castle: *Oliver Messel: A Biography* (London, 1986)

□

Messene, walls and tower near the Arcadian gate, *c.* 369–368 BC

Messene. Site on the south side of Mt Ithome in Messenia in southern Greece. The town was founded in 369 BC with the active support of the Boiotians as a permanent stronghold guaranteeing Messenian freedom from Spartan domination following the battle of Leuktra in 371 BC; it flourished into Hellenistic times. The extent of the site is considerable, with a boundary 9 km long, which included the summit of the mountain itself. This boundary was given a strong defensive wall, which, according to Pausanias (*Guide to Greece* IV.xxvii.7), was built immediately after the foundation of the city. Like the contemporary foundation of Megalopolis, which was the chief city of the Arcadians to the north, its purpose was to contain the Spartans within their own district of Lakonia. Military requirements, therefore, came first, and perhaps explain why the fortifications enclosed an area far larger than was ever occupied by the city itself, although there may have been the expectation that it would develop.

The walls (*c.* 2.5 m thick) are built of substantial quarry-faced ashlar blocks on either side of a rubble core. The technique appears identical in many parts to that of contemporary Boiotian fortifications, such as those at Siphai, and Boiotian involvement in the design and construction is virtually certain, although some have argued that they are Hellenistic. The curtain wall was punctuated at intervals by towers, of several distinct types. All have solid, filled bases generally projecting about 6 m from the wall, and about 6 m wide. They are single storey (Hellenistic towers would have been taller). Some are rectangular, others curved to provide a better field of view from their windows. Some sections of the walls—particularly those commanding the approaches from Arcadia and the north—are more substantial than others, as they were more prone to attack. If the walls were really built in haste, it may also imply that different sections were assigned to builders from different parts of the anti-Spartan alliance (it is unlikely that the Messenians themselves had the necessary skills); it is the northern sections that most closely resemble Boiotian work. The best-preserved entrance, the Arcadian gate, is in this northern section, flanked by two rectangular towers (see fig.). It leads into a circular court, surrounded by massive walls of more regular ashlar masonry, with distinctively pointed facing and decorative niches. Another gateway opposite led into the city: both were surmounted by huge lintels. The whole gateway is bonded into the curtain wall and so most unlikely to be Hellenistic, as sometimes suggested.

Few architectural remains have been uncovered within the walls, except for a Sanctuary of Asklepios with a late Hellenistic Doric temple (26.98×12.68 m with 6×12 columns). This stands within a peristyled courtyard with a propylon in its east side flanked by an enclosed (possibly roofed) theatrical structure to its north and a large square room, perhaps a library, to its south. Five smaller rooms are situated behind the western colonnade of the court.

BIBLIOGRAPHY
A. Blouet: *Expédition scientifique de Morée*, 3 vols (Paris, 1831–8)
A. K. Orlandos: 'Anaskaphe en Messene' [Excavation in Messene], *Praktika* (1957), pp. 121–5
——: 'Anaskaphai Messenes', *Praktika* (1958), pp. 177–83
——: 'Anaskaphe Messenes', *Praktika* (1959), pp. 162–73; (1963), pp. 122–9; (1964), pp. 96–101; (1969), pp. 98–120; (1970), pp. 125–41

R. A. TOMLINSON

Messerschmidt, Franz Xaver (*b* Wiesensteig, nr Ulm, 6 Feb 1736; *d* Pressburg [now Bratislava, Slovak Republic], ?19 Aug 1783). Austrian sculptor. He was descended, on his mother's side, from a family of joiners and sculptors called Straub. He was first trained by two of his mother's brothers: from 1746 by Johann Baptist Straub, who was a court sculptor in Munich, then from *c.* 1752 until 1754 by Philipp Jakob Straub in Graz. Messerschmidt then went to Vienna, where he attended the Akademie from the end of 1755. His teachers there were probably Jakob Schletterer (1699–1774) and Balthasar Ferdinand Moll. Messerschmidt was the protégé of Martin van Meytens (1695–1770), the director of the Akademie and a court painter. Van Meytens subsequently helped Messerschmidt to procure his first appointment at the Imperial Arsenal, where he was assigned to decorating canons. Between 1760 and 1763, however, Messerschmidt produced his first known independent works, for the Arsenal state rooms: the gilt-bronze busts of the *Empress Maria Theresa* and her husband *Franz I von Lothringen*, and the bronze reliefs of their son, subsequently Emperor, *Joseph II*, and his first wife, *Maria Isabella von Parma* (all now Vienna, Belvedere, Österreich. Gal.).

With these early works Messerschmidt achieved recognition in Vienna. A number of commissions followed, but little of Messerschmidt's work from this time has survived. Two over life-size statues of *Maria Theresa* and *Franz I von Lothringen* (cast in tin, 1764–6; Vienna, Belvedere, Österreich. Gal.) are official portraits, like those for the Arsenal, and are typical examples of formal court art towards the end of the Rococo period. They were inspired by the work of Moll and van Meytens, exponents of official art at the court of Maria Theresa. Messerschmidt's achievement lay in convincingly breathing life into the traditional style and in reconciling a splendid outward appearance with the sense of a specific personality. As well as carrying out commissions for official portraits, Messerschmidt also sculpted private citizens, although most of these portraits remain untraced (e.g. a relief in lead of *Johann Baptist Straub with his Daughters*; 1768). Messerschmidt also produced a number of religious and allegorical sculptures, but the only ones to have survived are those created, between 1766 and 1770, for Maria Teresa Felicia of Liechtenstein (1694–1772), Comtesse de Soissons (e.g. *St John*; 1768, Vienna, St Stephen's Cathedral). Messerschmidt's familiarity with the work of Georg Raphael Donner is more apparent in such figure sculptures than in his portrait busts.

In 1765 Messerschmidt travelled to Rome in order to study; he remained there for several months. The profit derived from this experience became apparent in the style of works Messerschmidt submitted in support of his application for membership of the Vienna Akademie at the beginning of 1768. One of these, the portrait of the art critic *Franz von Scheyb* (cast in lead; Vienna, Hist. Mus.), is the first known example of Neo-classical portrait sculpture in Vienna; it was soon followed by other similar portrait busts by Messerschmidt, including one of the celebrated doctor *Franz Anton Mesmer* (cast in metal, 1770; Vienna, priv. col.). It is perhaps significant that Messerschmidt's works in this style depict people associated with the Enlightenment, while as late as 1769, in a bust of the doctor *Gerard van Swieten* (gilt-lead; Vienna, Belvedere), commissioned by Maria Theresa, the artist adhered to the traditional late Baroque style. Messerschmidt's first Neo-classical portraits are devoid of any decorative arrangement; the strikingly modelled facial features and the simple, clear composition demonstrate an assimilation of the style of portrait busts of republican Rome, while the strict adherence to a frontal view points to inspiration derived from Roman work influenced by Egyptian art.

During the years 1768–70 Messerschmidt attained full official recognition and greater prosperity: he became a member of the Akademie in 1769 and taught there as Jakob Schletterer's deputy. In 1770 he bought a sizeable house, where he set up his own workshop. Shortly afterwards, however, it appears that there was a remarkable change in his fortunes. Commissions virtually ceased, and there were increasing conflicts with friends and colleagues. There was an open break in 1774 when Schletterer died: Messerschmidt was expected to succeed him, but Johann Baptist Hagenauer was appointed instead. Messerschmidt was dismissed from the Akademie with a small pension, his 'sometimes seemingly deranged behaviour' being given as the reason for this. Messerschmidt left Vienna shortly afterwards, selling everything and moving to his native town of Wiesensteig in 1775. In the same year he accepted an invitation to the court of the Elector in Munich, but the commissions he had been promised were not forthcoming. The only surviving work from his time in Munich is the bust of *Religion* for the tomb of Johann Baptist Straub's wife (marble; Munich, Bayer. Nmus.). This is one of the few surviving works from Messerschmidt's Neo-classical period that is not a portrait.

Messerschmidt left Munich in 1777 and moved to Pressburg, then known usually by its Hungarian name, Pozsony (now Bratislava, Slovak Republic). At first he lived with his brother, Johann Adam Messerschmidt (1738–94), who was active as a sculptor. He then bought himself a house on the outskirts of the town, where he lived and worked until his death, regarded as an eccentric, and the object of many rumours and stories. He devoted his energy mainly to uncommissioned work, in particular a series of remarkable heads (see fig.), some displaying bizarre grimaces, others being blankly staring self-portraits. He had already begun work on these in Vienna, and he continued with them in Wiesensteig and Munich. After his death 69 pieces were found in his studio, 49 of which were exhibited in Vienna in 1793 and itemized in the accompanying brochure as *Charakterköpfe* (character heads). There have been various attempts at interpreting these, following the first superficial assessment of the series based on the ideas of Johann Kaspar Lavater. Among the most significant is the theory proposed by Ernst Kris, in the early 1930s, that Messerschmidt suffered from a psychotic illness and that the 'character heads' were connected with his delusions. According to reports made by several of his contemporaries, Messerschmidt believed he was pursued by spirits and that he could ward these off with the magic properties of the grimacing heads. In Kris's interpretation, the numb self-portraits were certainly engendered by feelings of loss of personality. Forty-three of the original heads are known to have survived, some cast

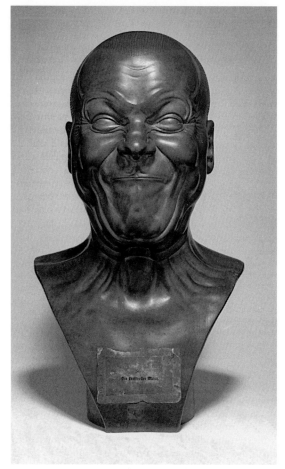

Franz Xaver Messerschmidt: *A Powerful Man*, 'Character Head' no. 7, lead and tin alloy, h. 440 mm, *c.* 1770 (private collection)

E. Kris: 'Die Charakterköpfe des Franz Xaver Messerschmidt', *Jb. Ksthist. Samml. Wien*, n. s., vi (1932), pp. 169–228
——: *Psychoanalytic Explorations in Art* (London, 1953), pp. 128–50
R. Wittkower and M. Wittkower: *Born under Saturn* (London, 1963), pp. 124–32
L. Eitner: 'The Artist Estranged: Messerschmidt and Romako', *The Grand Eccentrics*, ed. T. B. Hess (New York, 1966), pp. 85–95
G. Biedermann: 'Franz Xaver Messerschmidt: Zu den sogenannten Charakterköpfen', *Alte & Mod. Kst*, xxiii (1978), pp. 26–31
E. Baum: *Katalog des Österreichischen Barockmuseums* (Vienna and Munich, 1980), pp. 368–420
M. Pötzl-Malikova: *Franz Xaver Messerschmidt* (Vienna and Munich, 1982)
J. Oberhaidacher: 'Kunstgeschichte oder Psychologie? Zu den Charakterköpfen des Franz Xaver Messerschmidt', *Österreich. Z. Kst & Dkmlpf.*, xxxviii (1984), pp. 25–42
M. Pötzl-Malikova: 'Zur Beziehung Franz Anton Mesmer: Franz Xaver Messerschmidt: Eine wiedergefundene Büste des berühmten Magnetiseurs', *Wien. Jb. Kstgesch.*, xl (1987), pp. 257–67

MARIA PÖTZL-MALIKOVA

Messil, Gabriel (*b* Buenos Aires, 26 Feb 1934; *d* Buenos Aires, 22 Dec 1986). Argentine painter and sculptor. He studied at the Escuela Superior de Bellas Artes in Buenos Aires, leaving in 1963, and in 1967 travelled on a French government scholarship to Paris, where he became associated with the group around Julio Le Parc. He participated in the Paris Biennale in 1970 before returning in 1974 to Buenos Aires. Around the time of his move to France he changed from a figurative style combining expressionist and geometric elements to a more Minimalist style combining painting and sculpture in open, continuous forms made of polychromed wood, canvas and plaster. Shortly afterwards he began to paint again on a conventional canvas support, depicting figures with such ambiguity and dynamism that one's reading shifts constantly from that of the flat surface to the three-dimensional rendering of the image; the psychological and perceptual intensity of these works goes hand-in-hand with the reliance on black and other sombre colours. From the mid-1980s Messil further emphasized the role of irrational elements at the expense of the formal geometric structure of his pictures in order to increase their sensory impact.

BIBLIOGRAPHY
A. Haber: *Arte argentino contemporáneo* (Madrid, 1979), pp. 194–6
F. Fevre: *Gabriel Messil* (Buenos Aires, 1981)

NELLY PERAZZO

Messina, Antonello da. *See* ANTONELLO DA MESSINA.

Messina, Pino da. *See* JACOBELLO D'ANTONIO.

Mestizo [Sp.: 'mixed' or 'hybrid'] **(Baroque).** Term first used by in its art-historical sense Angel Guido (1925) to describe the fusion of Baroque architecture with indigenous art forms in South America and especially the Altiplano or highlands of Bolivia and Peru from the mid-17th century to the late 18th. Mestizo is characterized by massive Baroque structure with finely dressed stone detailing in exuberant flat patterns reminiscent of embroidery or wood-carving. Motifs incorporating indigenous fruits and animals were used on portals, retables and decorative friezes; mythological characters play indigenous musical instruments; and Pre-Columbian decorative details help to fill every available space with dense ornamentation.

in metal, some carved in alabaster. They are in both private and public collections, the largest collection being in Vienna (Belvedere, Österreich, Gal.).

While Messerschmidt's illness left its mark on some of his work, he was able to live in a relatively normal fashion, and he continued to carry out commissions. Even from his final years there are several surviving portraits in the tradition of his earlier Neo-classical work, though with more hardness in the modelling of the features, and specific and detailed treatment of the costume (e.g. *Martin Georg Kovachich*; tin, 1782; Budapest, Mus. F.A.). Messerschmidt also produced small alabaster medallions with finely chiselled relief portraits (e.g. *Unknown Woman* and *Unknown Man*; both *c.* 1780; Bratislava, Mun. Gal.).

BIBLIOGRAPHY
Thieme–Becker
Merkwürdige Lebensgeschichte des Franz Xaver Messerschmidt (Vienna, 1794/*R* 1982)
A. Ilg: *Franz Xaver Messerschmidts Leben und Werke* (Leipzig and Prague, 1885)
E. Tietze-Conrat: *Österreichische Barockplastik* (Vienna, 1920), pp. 27–30, 110–15, 142
G. Weiss: *Franz Xaver Messerschmidt* (diss., U. Vienna, 1924)
A. Feulner: *Skulptur und Malerei des 18. Jahrhunderts in Deutschland* (Potsdam, 1929), pp. 40–44

The most notable examples of the Mestizo style are to be found in the central Andes, at Arequipa in Peru and Potosí in Bolivia. In the region of Arequipa the use of a porous volcanic rock gave rise to a school of plane-surface carving that tended to stress chiaroscuro. The whole façade of the Jesuit church of La Compañia (1698) at Arequipa is carved in a foliated relief that invades the entablatures of the ground- and first-floor orders and fills the tympanum of the pediment (for further discussion and illustration *see* AREQUIPA). The same wealth of surface decoration, but in a finish more akin to wood-carving than embroidery, may be seen at the church of S Lorenzo (1728–44), Potosí (*see* BOLIVIA, fig. 3). Spiral columns flanking the doorway are transformed in the upper portions of their shafts into caryatids with arms akimbo. The whole composition is substantially repeated on a smaller scale in an overdoor feature, where the columns are flanked by two mermaids playing the *charango*, a stringed instrument.

Efforts were made by the monastic orders in Latin America to eradicate pagan religions, but native workmanship was encouraged in church building since it was thought that the use of indigenous techniques and motifs would help spread Christianity. In addition to formal architecture, the Mestizo style also found expression in ephemeral structures such as triumphal arches, crosses, catafalques, street altars, reviewing platforms and other items that reinforced the importance of processional routes through towns. The Mestizo style eventually gave way before the rise of Neo-classicism and the control of the academies, although Mestizo portals and other features continued to appear in otherwise classicizing designs well into the 19th century, and artwork intimately related to Mestizo was still being recreated in indigenous and peasant communities at the end of the 20th century.

BIBLIOGRAPHY
A. Guido: *Fusión hispanoindígena en la arquitectura colonial* (Rosario, 1925)
A. Neumeyer: 'The Indian Contribution to Architectural Decoration in Spanish Colonial America', *A. Bull.*, xxx (1948), pp. 104–21
H. E. Wethey: *Colonial Architecture and Sculpture in Peru* (Cambridge, MA, 1949)
P. Kelemen: *Baroque and Rococo in Latin America* (New York, 1951)
H. E. Wethey: 'Hispanic Colonial Architecture in Bolivia', *Gaz. B.-A.*, n. s., xxxix (1952), pp. 47–60
P. Kelemen: 'El barroco americano y la semántica de importación', *An. Inst. A. Amer. & Invest. Estét.*, xix (1966), pp. 39–44
S. Sitwell: *Southern Baroque Revisited* (London, 1967)
G. Gasparini: 'La arquitectura colonial como producto de la interacción de grupos', *Bol. Cent. Invest. Hist. & Estét. Caracas*, xii (1969), pp. 18–31
R. Gutiérrez: *Arquitectura colonial: Teoría y praxis* (Resistencia, 1979)
——: *Arquitectura y urbanismo en Iberoamérica* (Madrid, 1983)
RAMÓN GUTIÉRREZ

Mestres Esplugas, José Oriol (*b* Barcelona, 1815; *d* Barcelona, 1895). Spanish architect, urban planner and writer. He studied at the Escuela de Arquitectura, Barcelona, as a pupil of its founder, the Neo-classical architect Antonio Cellés y Azcona (1775–1835). Later he studied in Madrid, obtaining his degree in the Real Academia de Bellas Artes de San Fernando in 1841. Despite his Neo-classical training, he distinguished himself as an exponent of Gothic Revival designs, influenced by elements of Romanticism. His best-known work in this style is his design (1864) for the principal façade of Barcelona Cathedral, which was commissioned by the Girona family. After 1882 the design was altered to accommodate that of Augusto Font y Carreras, resulting in a more generalized medieval style. Mestres Esplugas' other decisive work was the Gran Teatro del Liceo (from 1861), Barcelona, which was reconstructed by him from the original building (1844–8; by Miguel Garriga y Roca), which had burnt down. Here he succeeded in building one of the leading opera houses in Spain, with a construction that combines classical splendour with an eclectic use of Baroque decoration. He was the municipal architect of Barcelona, where he won the competition for the Plaza Real, but this was not executed because it contained a proposal to use iron columns. He was also responsible for the restoration of various medieval buildings and wrote numerous articles on monuments and architectural criticism. Among the latter his essay entitled '¿Tenemos en España algun tipo de arquitectura que podamos calificar de arquitectura nacional?' (1876), expressed his long-held concern for the definition of a national style. In 1882 he became a member of the Real Academia de San Jorge in Barcelona.

BIBLIOGRAPHY
J. A. Gaya: *Arte del siglo XIX* (Madrid, 1966)
P. Navascués and others: *Del Neoclasicismo al Modernismo* (Madrid, 1979)
ALBERTO VILLAR MOVELLÁN

Meštrović, Ivan (*b* Vrpolje, 15 Aug 1883; *d* South Bend, IN, 16 Jan 1962). Croatian sculptor. He studied from 1901 to 1905 at the Akademie der Bildenden Künste in Vienna, where he was particularly influenced by Otto Wagner, who was one of his teachers, and more generally by the cultural climate embodied by the Secession. He also became interested in the work of Rodin and in Assyrian and Egyptian sculpture, and he demonstrated his commitment to the Yugoslav patriotic movement in his own art. These influences, particularly that of Rodin, are detectable in the symbolism of his early works, such as the *Fountain of Life* (bronze, 1905; Zagreb, Marshal Tito Square). In the *Kosovo Cycle* (1908–10; Belgrade, N. Mus.) he presented figures cast in bronze or carved in stone as characters from national myths, emphasizing the anatomy of their robust bodies and the dynamic play of light and shadow.

During World War I Meštrović concentrated on figures in bronze or wood and in stylized scenes evoking pathos. In the 1920s, his most prolific period, he turned to a more classical idiom and looked particularly to the example of Michelangelo. At this time he produced mainly sensual and lyrical female figures, most often nudes in marble such as *Daydreaming* (1927; Split, Meštrović Gal.). By contrast he also executed monumental sculptures featuring exaggeratedly athletic figures, such as *Grgur Ninski* (1927; Split, Ivana Lučića–Lavčevića Street; see fig.), in which he sought to transform an individual monument into a universally comprehensible sign.

Although Meštrović remained productive in the 1930s, there was a certain reduction in the quality of his work. From 1923 to 1942 he was rector of the Zagreb Academy. He concentrated mainly on projects combining sculpture with architecture, such as the House of Fine Arts in Zagreb, which later became the Museum of the Revolution

Ivan Meštrović: *Grgur Ninski*, bronze, h. 8 m, 1927 (Split, Ivana Lučića–Lavčevića Street)

Meštrović in Split, the Meštrović Studio in Zagreb and the church of the Holy Redeemer, Otavice.

BIBLIOGRAPHY

M. Čurčin: *Ivan Meštrović* (Zagreb, 1933)
V. Mole: *Ivan Meštrović* (Krakow, 1936)
N. L. Rice, H. H. Hilbery and E. S. Hilbery: *The Sculpture of Ivan Meštrović* (Syracuse, 1948)
L. Schmeckebier: *Ivan Meštrović, Sculptor and Patriot* (Syracuse, 1959)
Z. Grum: *Ivan Meštrović* (Zagreb, 1961)
I. Tupicin: *Ivan Meštrović* (Moscow, 1967)
D. Kečkemet: *Ivan Meštrović* (Belgrade, 1983)
B. Gagro: *Ivan Meštrović* (Zagreb, 1987) [excellent reproductions, chronology and list of works]
Ivan Meštrović: Skulpturen (exh. cat., ed. M. Jura and A. Schneider; W. Berlin, Staatl. Museen Preuss. Kultbes.; Zurich, Ksthaus; Vienna, Mus. 20. Jhts; 1987)

JURE MIKUŽ

of Croatian Peoples, and the *Monument to the Unknown Soldier* (1934–8) in Avala, near Belgrade. Early in World War II he carved *Mother and Child* (1942; Zagreb, Meštrović Studio) from a rough block of wood, conveying great tenderness. He was imprisoned by collaborators for four-and-a-half months in 1941 and afterwards settled in the USA, where he taught at Syracuse, NY, and South Bend, IN, and produced many more sculptures, chiefly on biblical subjects. One of his most poignant sculptures of this period is the figure of *Job* (1946; Split, Meštrović Gal.), in which he again distorted human anatomy for expressive purposes and returned to colourful and dynamic surfaces.

While remaining essentially conservative in his approach, Meštrović became the most internationally renowned Croatian artist in the 20th century. He was influential as a teacher, but his posthumous reputation suffered in spite of attempts to resuscitate it. He was extremely productive, executing nearly 2000 sculptures. His work is displayed widely in Croatia and elsewhere, not only in major museums but also in three specialized collections donated by the artist himself: the Galerija

Mészáros, László (*b* Budapest, 18 Sept 1905; *d* USSR, 10–12 Sept 1945). Hungarian sculptor. On completing his training as a goldsmith (1921–4), he studied ornamental sculpture at the School of Applied Arts, Budapest, for two-and-a-half years. In 1928 he exhibited his first work, a romantic, impressionist *Self-portrait* (bronze, *c.* 1926; Budapest, N.G.). The serene countenance of his second *Self-portrait* (bronze, *c.* 1926–9; Budapest, N.G.) better expresses his fundamental realism, his seriousness and his technical mastery. His early works, created during the Depression, also show his sensitivity to public issues and his social commitment. The working-class models were primarily members of his own family. His figures are generally sculpted in block-like, frontal compositions (e.g. *Peasant Boy Standing* (plaster, 1928–9; Budapest, N.G.).

In 1930 Mészáros became a corresponding member of the Austrian group Sezession Graz. That same year he sculpted his best-known work, the *Prodigal Son* (bronze; Budapest, N.G.); a sensitive work, of great importance for Hungarian sculpture, it employs an archaic standing posture and, although static, it displays an explosive energy. From 1932 to 1934 he lived in Italy, on a scholarship to the Hungarian Academy in Rome. There he modelled life-size figures, a great number of portraits (e.g. *Daughter of the Artist*, plaster, 1934) and several small compositions (e.g. *Old Woman Thinking*, stone, 1933; both Budapest, N.G.). Under the pseudonym P. Ostor (Hung.: 'P. Whip') he made small figurines (e.g. *Rebel*, bronze, h. 203 mm, *c.* 1934; Budapest, N.G.) and plaquettes to be distributed in the underground movement. In his full-size works he abandoned frontal composition and, aided by a better understanding of ancient and Classical sculpture, he developed a much wider range of genres and styles without compromising his individual characteristics and general aims. In 1935 he emigrated to the USSR, and from 1936 until 1938, when he was arrested and subsequently interned, he lived in Frunze (now Bishkek), where he designed a frieze for the Government Palace and executed portraits (Bishkek, Kyrgyz Mus. F.A.).

BIBLIOGRAPHY

Mészáros László (exh. cat. by E. Gádor, Budapest, Adolf Fényes Hall, 1953)
S. Kontha: *Mészáros László* (Budapest, 1961)
——: 'Der ungarische Bildhauer László Mészáros', *Bild. Kst* (1962), no. 6, pp. 309–14

——: 'László Mészáros v Sovetskom Soyuze' [László Mészáros in the Soviet Union], *Acta Hist. A. Acad. Sci. Hung.* (1963), nos 3–4, pp. 343–69
——: *Mészáros László* (Budapest, 1966)

S. KONTHA

Mészöly, Géza (*b* Sárbogárd, nr Dunaújváros, 18 May 1844; *d* Jobbágyi, Nógrád, 1 Nov 1887). Hungarian painter. He began by copying landscapes of Romantic painters and the Old Masters while studying law at university. In 1866 he was admitted to the class of Albert Zimmermann (1808–88) at the Akademie der Bildenden Künste, Vienna. In 1871 he returned to Hungary and settled in Székesfehérvár, where he helped to organize subsidiary exhibitions in the provinces for the Fine Arts Association (Képzőművészeti Társulat).

Between 1872 and 1877 Mészöly worked alternately in Munich and at home. He selected his themes increasingly from the local environment, in particular from the area around Lake Balaton. One of his masterpieces, the large-scale *Fishing on Lake Balaton* (1877; Budapest, N.G.), was commissioned by the Minister for Education. In 1882 he visited Paris and was attracted to the work of Jules Bastien-Lepage; some of his paintings also resemble works by Jean-Baptiste-Camille Corot or Constant Troyon. Mészöly had a successful exhibition in Vienna in 1883. From 1885 he taught at the Budapest Painting Academy for Ladies.

Apart from his early landscapes, Mészöly's still-lifes also confirm his Romantic roots (e.g. *Sheep in Bozsók*, 1871; Budapest, N.G.). With *Szigetvár* (1871; Budapest, N.G.) he began concentrating on specific local scenes, revealing an almost programmatic selection of landscape themes. He was often encouraged in his rendering of minor details to investigate new painting techniques, as in the *Sand-pit* (1871; Budapest, N.G.). In his last period his style is comparable to that of Eugène Boudin. Nearly all Mészöly's paintings contain shores, as in *Lido* (1883) or *Bathers at Lake Balaton* (*c.* 1885; both Budapest, N.G.). He always made good use of size: large scale is never over-used, and his smallest works retain the freshness of his personal experience of the landscape.

BIBLIOGRAPHY
Mészöly Géza emlékkiállítása [Géza Mészöly: commemorative exhibition] (exh. cat., ed. M. Rajnai; Budapest, Met. Gal., 1952)
M. Rajnai: *Mészöly Géza* (Budapest, 1953)
É. Bodnár: *Mészöly Géza* (Budapest, 1985)

NÓRA ARADI

Metabolism. Japanese architectural movement active from 1960 to the early 1970s. It was launched at the World Design Conference in Tokyo (1960), and its initial members were the architects Takashi Asada, KIYONORI KIKUTAKE and KISHŌ KUROKAWA, journalist and critic Noboru Kawazoe, industrial designer Kenji Ekuan and graphic designer Kiyoshi Awazu; they were soon joined by the architects Fumihiko Maki and Masato Otaka. Metabolism was critical of orthodox Modernism as represented by CIAM, advocating instead a more dynamic approach to the problems of architectural design and urban planning (*see* JAPAN, §III, 5). Its manifesto *Metabolism 1960: Proposals for a New Urbanism* was published after the conference. In rejecting CIAM's static and ultimately

classical conception of the city, Metabolism sought rather to emphasize that the city constantly undergoes change like an organism, hence the biological term borrowed for its name. The aim was to give order to such transformations by allowing for the different cycles of growth and decay of urban elements. Elements with longer lifespans were to form an infrastructure to which short-term elements were to be attached in a manner that expedited the

Metabolist building by Kishō Kurokawa: Nakagin Capsule Tower, Tokyo, 1972

latter's periodic replacement, an idea that had been explored earlier by the Groupe d'Etude d'Architecture Mobile of YONA FRIEDMAN.

The Metabolists were also in sympathy with the ideas of mobility and association expounded by Team Ten, and they found inspiration in the works of Louis Kahn, notably the Richards Medical Research Laboratories (1957–61), University of Pennsylvania, Philadelphia, with its clearly distinct 'served' and 'servant' spaces. In the following years Metabolist activity also found parallels in the work of Archigram in England. Among Japanese architects, Kenzō Tange had a particularly close relationship to the Metabolists, having taught a number of them at the University of Tokyo, and his own projects, including the Shizuoka Press and Broadcasting Center (1967) in Tokyo, showed an affinity to Metabolist schemes.

Metabolism never developed a consistent style and each member pursued his own approach, which is why no joint publication, though discussed, ever followed the original manifesto. The manifesto is an exploration into variations and alternative solutions to the megastructure principle advocated by Tange. In it Kikutake presented a proposal for cities built out over water (e.g. Floating City) as a solution to the overcrowding of existing urban environments. A redevelopment scheme for the Shinjuku area of Tokyo by Maki and Otaka was based on the idea of 'group form'. In 1961 Kurokawa presented his Helix City plan, an 'urban unit' with a structure reminiscent of Kahn's city tower project of 1957 and suggestive of the DNA double helix, a fact of questionable relevance but one that sustained, however naively, the biological analogy that was the basic premise of the movement.

Metabolism emerged at a time when Japan was experiencing phenomenal economic growth, and the great expectations raised by the pace of development gave the movement's proposals, despite their ambitious scale and visionary character, an aura of seriousness and possibility. The future society envisioned by Metabolists was technocratic in nature, and for all its criticism of CIAM, Metabolism was as hostile to the existing city as orthodox Modernism. The International Exposition in Osaka in 1970 was the high point of the movement. The Theme Pavilion by Tange was a megastructure with plug-in capsules, and Kurokawa's Toshiba-IHI Pavilion and Takara Beautilion were smaller variations on the same theme. In 1972 Kurokawa completed the Nakagin Capsule Tower in Tokyo, the most complete realization of Metabolist ideas (see fig.). However, a combination of different factors, including the war in Vietnam and the social and ecological imbalances caused by the single-minded postwar drive towards development, had already dampened enthusiasm for futurist proposals, and the energy crises of the early 1970s effectively put an end to the movement.

WRITINGS

N. Kawazoe, K. Kikutake and K. Kurokawa: *Metabolism 1960: Proposals for a New Urbanism* (Tokyo, 1960)
F. Maki: *Metabolism 1960* (Tokyo, 1960)
——: *Investigations in Collective Form* (St Louis, 1964)
K. Kurokawa: *Metabolism in Architecture* (Boulder, 1977)

BIBLIOGRAPHY

H. Watanabe: 'Evaluation: Composition of Cubes in Tokyo', *AIA J.*, lxix (1980), pp. 74–7
B. Bognar: *Contemporary Japanese Architecture: Its Development and Challenge* (New York, 1985)

HIROSHI WATANABE

Metal. Metals can be defined by their properties: they are malleable, so can be shaped by hammering and bending; tough and fairly elastic, so can sustain considerable stress without breaking; and dense and highly reflective, so capable of taking a good polish. They are also good conductors of heat and electricity. With the exception of iron, most common metals have relatively low melting-points (below 1100°C), so they can be easily melted, and on cooling they retain their molten shape. They can, therefore, be shaped by casting. They are also highly reactive, so although abundant in the Earth's crust, they are usually found in combination with other elements.

Many of the distinctive traits of metals, including reactivity, stem from their atomic structures. In any element the electrons move around the atomic nucleus in fixed orbitals or shells, which contain only a certain number of electrons before becoming filled, thus causing the next orbital to be commenced. Metallic elements have just one or two electrons in otherwise unfilled orbitals, and, therefore, these orbitals readily react with other elements, especially those that have an almost filled electron shell. A classic example is sodium chloride: the metal sodium has one spare electron, and it reacts with the non-metal chlorine, which needs just one electron to complete an electron shell. The spare electrons tend to be shared loosely between all the atoms, and they account particularly for the conductivity of metals.

Apart from gold and copper, all metals are called white because of their reflective properties, although zinc is claimed to have a blue tinge. By contrast, metallic salts are often brilliantly coloured, and beautiful effects have been produced through the ages by chemically treating the surfaces of metals (*see* §V, 5 below). Owing to their strength, metals are ideally suited for tools, weapons and machinery; they have also been used throughout history for all kinds of decorative, liturgical and utilitarian objects.

I. Types and properties. II. Extraction and production. III. Shaping. IV. Joining. V. Decorative techniques. VI. Conservation.

I. Types and properties.

1. SINGLE METALS. Like most solids, metals are basically crystalline. When a molten metal sets, the atoms begin to crystallize in regular arrays from the edges and from solid points throughout the melt. These crystals continue to grow until they meet other growing crystals. Thus any solid metal will consist of these interlocked crystals, known as grains (see fig. 1). Their size is determined by the rate of cooling and by the distribution of solid particles in the melt, which act as nuclei for the developing grains and are usually fragments of foreign matter, for example bits of fuel, slag and furnace wall. Small-grained castings tend to be tougher, and thus metalworkers sometimes seed the metal with fine sand to facilitate grain formation. Sometimes the grains are large enough to be visible with the naked eye: the grains of zinc on galvanized items are a familiar example.

Although the chains of atoms in any grain can sustain considerable deformation, at the grain boundaries there is far less cohesion, and these are the points of potential chemical and physical weakness. Corrosion tends to penetrate into the metal along these boundaries, and when metal is worked or bent, cracks tend to develop in these areas. In the 20th century extensive research has gone into this and other areas of potential weakness in basic structure. This, together with new alloys, has resulted in much stronger metals; consequently less metal is now needed in all manner of objects from bridges to typewriters, an important factor behind the light, 'modern' designs of the 20th century.

During working, metals can sustain only a limited amount of deformation before they begin to crack. To overcome this, the metal must be periodically raised to a dull red heat during working in order that the softened grains may rearrange themselves and release the strain that has been generated. This is known as annealing. Under magnification, pairs of parallel lines in the grains indicate that the metal has been extensively worked and annealed (fig. 1). Only pure gold can be worked indefinitely without annealing.

2. ALLOYS. Any mixture of two or more metals is known as an alloy. Some metals, such as gold and silver, dissolve in each other in any proportion to form what are known as solid solutions, but most metals are only partially soluble in each other. Thus, in a typical brass the 30% of zinc will be dissolved in the copper, but if the alloy contained much more zinc, the excess would solidify as a separate phase surrounded by the saturated solid solution. Some metals are virtually insoluble in each other: lead will not dissolve in copper or in its alloys but remains as separate globules of almost pure lead within the copper. In other instances, metals can react together to produce an intermetallic compound with a precise structure and composition. These compounds lose many metallic properties and can be hard and brittle: cast iron is perhaps the most familiar example of a metal made brittle by intermetallics, in this case cementite (Fe_3C), and speculum bronze mirrors contain tin–copper intermetallic compounds and are very fragile.

The properties of alloys are usually intermediate between their constituent metals, thus the colour of gold–silver alloys depends on the relative amounts of gold and silver. There are, however, important exceptions that were discovered and utilized early in the history of metallurgy. The melting-point, in particular, is often depressed so alloys usually melt over a wide temperature range. In casting this allows more time for the metal to fill all extremities of a mould; and with a solder the longer cooling time allows the semi-solidified 'mushy' metal to be worked into the joint (see §III, 3(ii) below). Alloys are also usually harder and stronger than their constituents; thus BRONZE, a mixture of copper and tin (sometimes known as speculum or bell metal if the tin content is over 20%), is much stronger than either tin or copper. Another common alloy is BRASS, a mixture of copper and zinc. PEWTER was traditionally an alloy of tin with a little lead (and/or other metals, such as copper and antimony), although, due to the enormous difference in price between the two metals, the proportion of lead was often much higher. Modern pewter contains no lead and is an alloy of

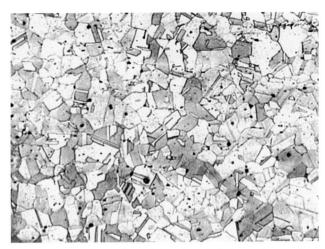

1. Grain structure of cast and annealed metal, detail of a Bronze Age spearhead from Cyprus, magnified × *c.* 270

tin and antimony. SILVER is a rather soft metal, so it is usually alloyed with a little copper. Sterling silver contains 7.5% copper, and the rather uncommon Britannia standard contains 4.2%. There are many artificial silvers, most based on alloys of brass with about 20% nickel. This is the basis of the traditional Chinese *baitong* alloy and of more recent alloys such as German silver. Steel is an alloy of iron with usually up to about 1% carbon, and more rarely up to 2%. Cast iron contains between 2% and 5% carbon plus a little silicon.

II. Extraction and production.

1. NATIVE METALS. Only a few unreactive metals, notably GOLD and the platinum group, regularly occur in their metallic state. A small amount of native COPPER is found in the upper, oxidized levels of many copper deposits and as such was almost certainly the first metal used by man, but it was of little significance after the beginning of the Bronze Age, except in North America, where enormous quantities occur. Meteoric iron (*see* IRON AND STEEL), distinguished by its high nickel content, was also used on a small scale. Terrestrial native iron, known as telluric iron, is very rare but was used, together with meteoric iron, by the Inuit of Greenland. Until the medieval period most gold was obtained from river gravel (placer deposits), brought down from eroding primary deposits. The gold was separated from the waste material (gangue) by agitation in the water, the greater density of the gold making it sink while the lighter gangue was carried off.

2. SMELTED METALS. As most metals are highly reactive, they occur as chemical compounds, notably as oxides or sulphides. They are extracted from these compounds, or ores, by reduction with carbon, traditionally in the form of charcoal, but now usually coke. The furnaces and the principles of smelting changed little over the millennia from the Bronze Age to the Industrial Revolution. The ores were usually roasted or calcined in the presence of air to dehydrate them and make them more

2. Copper-smelting furnace, Khetri, India, 19th century; from Ball: *A Manual of the Geology of India* (Calcutta, 1881)

friable and especially to convert the sulphides (more rarely chlorides) into oxides. The smelting furnace (see fig. 2) was a bowl or a shaft, usually built of clay and sometimes incorporating brick or stone. The furnaces were all small, about 1 m tall with an internal diameter of between 250 and 500 mm. Air was supplied from manually operated bellows through clay tubes (tuyères) near the base of the furnace wall. (The factor that limited the size of the furnace was the amount of air that could be supplied by blowpipe or manually operated bellows.) A small fire was lit in the base of the furnace. Fed with charcoal and supplied with air, it would rapidly reach a temperature of over 1000°C. Then the calcined ore, together with more fuel, was added and the reduction commenced. In the limited air supply, the charcoal burned to produce carbon monoxide, which in turn reduced the metal oxides to metal.

It was then necessary to separate the gangue from the forming metal. Most of the gangue would be either silica (e.g. quartz or sand) or iron minerals, which would react together in the furnace to produce various iron silicates. Melting at about 1200°C, the silicates formed molten slag that could be run out of the furnace. Thus, if the gangue were rich in silica, iron minerals would be added; conversely, if rich in iron then silica would redress the balance. These additions are known as the flux. With high temperatures and the addition of the appropriate flux, all the gangue would be liquefied to form the slag. Periodically the slag would be tapped, allowing the process to continue until a considerable body of metal had built up. The droplets of molten metal drained to the base of the furnace. The metal could also be tapped from the furnace, but it was usually allowed to cool, forming an ingot, and then removed solid from the base of the dismantled furnace. This process was used for all metals except iron, which was usually produced in the solid state in antiquity, and mercury and zinc (*see* BRASS, §II, 1), which were volatile and had to be condensed from a vapour.

In more advanced processes the cycle of roasting and smelting was repeated several times (matte smelting). The resulting metal was highly impure, containing sulphides and oxides, usually of iron. These were removed by melting the raw metal in an open crucible, burning out the sulphur and other substances and skimming impurities from the surface. Finally green twigs (or latterly whole trees) were plunged into the molten metal to generate gases that reduced any residual oxides. This operation, known as poling, continues to be performed, especially in small foundries where alloys are made up.

As production became industrialized, so manually operated bellows were replaced, first, in the medieval period, by water power and then by other sources. From the 17th century coke began to replace charcoal as fuel. It was cheaper and is also much stronger, thus able to support a greater weight of fuel and ore in the furnace. This enables the furnace gases to circulate freely in the combustion zone at the base of the furnace. With the two constraints of air supply and fuel strength removed, furnaces grew rapidly to their present enormous size: modern blast furnaces are capable of producing over 10,000 tonnes of metal per day.

3. ELECTROLYSIS. Many metals are produced from their fused salts by the process of electrolysis from an aqueous solution. The salts are composed of negatively charged anions (such as oxide, chloride or sulphide) and positively charged metal ions, known as cations. When an electrical current is applied, the anions are attracted to the positive electrode (anode), and the cations go to the negative electrode (cathode), where they are deposited as metal. Some metals, such as magnesium and ALUMINIUM, are produced solely by electrolysis. For others, such as ZINC, electrolysis is only one of the methods employed. Electrolysis is also used to produce high-purity metals and is the usual method of refining such metals as copper.

III. Shaping.

1. Casting. 2. Wrought work.

1. CASTING. Perhaps the most direct method of fabrication is to pour the molten metal into a mould of the required shape. The materials of the mould must be capable of withstanding the molten metal without melting or disintegrating. Traditionally the most popular materials have been clay and sand, though others, such as stone and metal itself, have been successfully used. In antiquity most clay moulds were not especially heat-resistant, except in China, where the abundant loess clays were used (*see* BRONZE, §II, 3). Now special heat-resistant ceramics, known as refractories, are made of selected clays to which minerals and sometimes charcoal or graphite are added; true refractories were first made in post-medieval Europe.

(i) Open moulding. The shape to be cast is carved in the flat surface of a suitable material, for example stone, and the metal then poured in. This simple method was used in the earliest stages of metallurgy all over the world and continues to be employed for such uncomplicated shapes as ingots. One surface, however, will be flat, thus severely limiting the range of shapes that can be cast. There is also the danger of oxidization and gas porosity from the exposed surface (*see* §(vii) below), even if a lid is added.

(ii) Two-piece moulding. A better method of casting relatively simple forms is to make a two-piece mould and to

shape it by carving or by pressing a pattern into the wet clay. The two close-fitting halves are then tightly bound together and the metal poured in from the top. In any but the most simple shape, it will be necessary to have small channels, known as risers, through the mould to allow the air displaced by the metal to escape. The metal is poured into the mould through a cup (sprue) at the top. This is kept topped up with metal and acts as a reservoir (or header), which is cut off from the casting afterwards. As the metal cools in the mould, it shrinks, and without replacement from the header cavities will appear in the top of the casting. Solid impurities also tend to float up into the header. The mould can be reused, depending only on the durability of the refractory.

(iii) Piece moulding. For objects of greater complexity, with undercuts and projections that would preclude the use of a simple two-piece mould, a piece mould of many sections can be used. In China this method was employed with great success to cast ritual bronze vessels from the 2nd millennium BC (see colour pl. I, fig. 4). No matter how closely the sections are held together during casting, some metal will penetrate the joints, and these thin fins or 'flashes' of metal are indicative of piece-moulding.

A hollow casting can be made by suspending a core of refractory material in the mould. If the core is to be completely surrounded by metal it must be held in place, without touching the sides, by metal pins (chaplets) set into the mould. After the casting has been made and the mould broken away, the ends of the chaplets sticking out of the casting are cut off and filed down flush with the surface.

(iv) Direct lost-wax casting. Lost-wax casting (*cire perdue*, also known as investment or precision casting) is used where very accurate reproduction of detail is required. The process was developed in the ancient Near East in the 4th millennium BC: initially it was used only for small objects, but by the 6th century BC it was employed in Greece for large-scale statuary (*see* GREECE, ANCIENT, §IV, 1(iv)(c)). The shape to be cast is modelled in a material with a low melting-point, such as wax (see fig. 3a), and the sprue and risers are added in wax. In the 'direct' process the model is dipped in a fine clay slip, the consistency of batter mixture, and allowed to dry. This is repeated until a good coating is built up, and then a stronger, but coarser clay (the investment) is fitted around it for strength (3b). The mould is then heated, which bakes the investment and melts the wax, causing it to run out and leave the mould empty (3c) and ready to receive the metal (3d). The mould is often rotated during casting, and the centrifugal force pushes the molten metal into the details of the mould. When the metal is set the mould is broken away to reveal the casting (3e).

(v) Indirect lost-wax casting. In the direct process the wax model is inevitably destroyed. In reality, however, the wax original is rarely used (hence the survival of many wax models) because the 'indirect' process is used instead. In this process a cast is taken of the original, and from this a piece mould is made. Any number of wax models can then be cast, and the original preserved in case the casting should be spoilt.

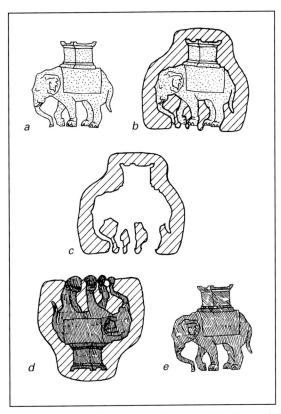

3. Direct lost-wax casting sequence: (a) form is modelled in wax; (b) wax model is covered in clay; (c) clay is baked and wax runs out; (d) clay mould is inverted and hot metal poured in; (e) clay is broken off

A better understanding of the indirect process can be obtained by following the various stages in the production of a life-size statue (for variations and alternatives at each stage see Cellini, 1888 trans.; Mills and Gillespie, 1969; and Choate, 1966). First the statue is modelled in wax or clay. If the piece is to be cast in sections, rather than whole, the model is then cut up into pieces of a size suitable for casting (e.g. head, limbs and torso). Casts are taken of the model or the pieces and cut away in sections so the original can be removed. Traditionally plaster was used for casts, but gelatin and latterly rubber have virtually replaced it. These elastic materials can be easily peeled from the model but then resume the shape of the impression; they are usually backed by a hard case, or mother mould, often made of plaster or resin.

The next stage is to make the core by lining the inside of the mould to the required thickness of the metal with strips of wax or a similar material (Cellini recommended pasta). Clay is then poured in and allowed to set, forming the core. The core is removed, fitted with chaplets and replaced in the mould. Wax is run into the space, giving a wax positive around the core. Sprues and risers of wax are added and the whole invested in clay as described for the direct lost-wax process. After the metal casting has been removed from the mould, the chaplets and sprues are cut off and any defects rectified. The statue is then assembled (if not already whole) and the components welded or soldered together. Finally, cold working with a scraper and chisel adds or sharpens the detail.

For large castings, for example bells, the mould is set in a pit. This makes the pouring of considerable quantities of molten metal much safer, and enables the mould to be supported firmly but evenly by the surrounding soil. Casting pits have survived from antiquity and have been excavated in a number of places, including Olympia and the Athenian Agora. They are usually full of casting debris, including mould fragments, and thus reveal much information on early foundry practice.

(vi) Sand casting. In this process an impression of the original (usually of wood or metal) is taken with a suitable sand–clay mixture in two halves, each contained in a rigid metal frame known as the flask. Air channels and the channel for the sprue are added in the sand. The original is removed and the two halves of the flask brought together to complete the mould. This is a convenient method of producing multiple castings, widely used in industry, but it is not suitable for complex shapes, especially if there are undercuts or fine detail. The method is of uncertain antiquity. Some authors claim it was used in the Classical period, but the earliest certain usage seems to be medieval.

Al-Jazari, writing in northern Mesopotamia in 1206, describes the technique of casting with green sand in connection with the production of lattice work. A particular kind of sand was used for making closed (or open) mould boxes which, unlike the more common clay boxes, contained no surplus moisture and therefore required no heating or drying before the molten metal was poured in. The origin of the technique is somewhat obscure, but it probably came from China, since it is mentioned in Chinese sources slightly earlier than al-Jazari.

(vii) Casting problems. The production of a major casting is a difficult technical operation and is rarely achieved without blemishes. Minor cracks and holes in the mould fill with metal, which then stands proud on the casting. On flat or exposed surfaces these protuberances can be easily filed or chiselled off. When the damage runs over inaccessible areas or complex decoration it can be more difficult to remove. These blemishes, however, provide useful clues as to how the piece was made. If the casting fault runs through a decorated area, the detail must have been part of the mould. Conversely, if a detail runs over and obliterates a casting fault that is otherwise untouched, it suggests that the detail was worked on the metal after casting.

Minor faults can be corrected by judicious working with a scraper and chisel, but more major damage or missing areas can only be repaired by a 'burn in' or by 'casting on'. The damaged area is cut out and replaced by wax. It is then re-cast following the lost-wax procedure. A good repair will fuse or weld perfectly with the rest of the casting. Alternatively the damaged area can be cut out and a patch soldered into place. These are especially prevalent in Classical statuary but due to the excellent workmanship are rarely perceptible.

A common fault is for the metal to set before it has penetrated all the detail or narrow confines of the mould. This is usually because the metal is too cold; a 'cast-on'

repair is the only remedy. Sometimes one pour of metal sets before the next joins it, leaving a distinct line where the metals have met but failed to amalgamate: this is known as a 'cold shut'. It weakens the casting and should be welded or soldered.

If the mould contains material, such as limestone, that is easily decomposed by heat, the molten metal will generate gas and create a potentially dangerous situation. The mould must also be perfectly dry, since even a little dampness will generate enough steam to cause turbulence, leading to gas holes in the casting and to metal droplets spraying over the mould walls. These quickly set and fail to amalgamate with the rest of the metal, remaining as recognizable droplets in the surface of the casting.

It is essential to exclude air from contact with the molten metal either in the crucible or in the mould (hence the drawback in using open moulds). It will cause the metal to absorb oxygen and then oxidize, which will create gas holes in the casting (gas porosity) when the metal cools. Thus the metal in a crucible is always covered with a thick layer of charcoal, and some foundries still pole the metal with green twigs to deoxidize it just before pouring. In addition, various deoxidants can be added.

The rate of cooling of the casting is also important, as considerable strain can be set up within the metal as it solidifies and contracts. In extreme cases this can make the casting crack. The problems resulting from the casting of two famous bells are well known. 'Big Ben', the principal bell in the clock-tower of the Palace of Westminster, London, cracked when the clapper was installed in 1857 due to the strains that had arisen during casting. The 'Tsar's Bell', the largest bell in the world, cracked in the mould when it was cast in Moscow in 1733. It was then left in the bell pit for over 100 years before being taken out and installed.

The rate of cooling also affects the homogeneity of the metal. There are three principal types of segregation of the alloy. In the first, gravity segregation, the denser metal sinks to the bottom of the mould. Heavily leaded alloys are especially prone to this fault. Alloys with a wide cooling range, such as bronze, are prone to the second type, which is known as normal segregation. The first metal to set in the mould—usually that at the extremities—will be rich in the higher-melting-point metals. As cooling proceeds, the metal becomes progressively richer in the lower-melting-point components. These become concentrated in the centre of the casting and at the top near the sprue where the last molten metal remains. Finally, if the rate of cooling of an alloy containing a low-melting-point metal is too swift, there is a danger of 'sweating', the third type of segregation. This is especially prevalent with bronzes. The last metal to remain molten in the casting is that which is rich in the lowest-melting-point metal. As the rest of the metal contracts around it, this is literally squeezed to the surface. In a 'leaded' bronze, in which the metal is rich in tin or lead, this gives a dull grey surface. These segregations can cause noticeable variations in the colour over the surface of a casting, as well as serious internal weaknesses.

2. WROUGHT WORK.

(i) Forging. The simplest, and doubtless the oldest, method of shaping metal is by beating it with a hammer on an

PLATE I   Metal

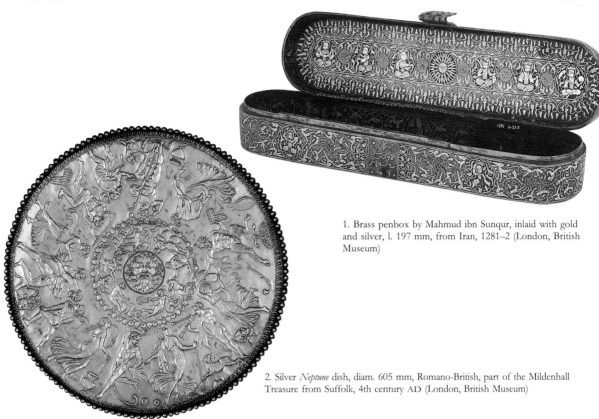

1. Brass penbox by Mahmud ibn Sunqur, inlaid with gold and silver, l. 197 mm, from Iran, 1281–2 (London, British Museum)

2. Silver *Neptune* dish, diam. 605 mm, Romano-British, part of the Mildenhall Treasure from Suffolk, 4th century AD (London, British Museum)

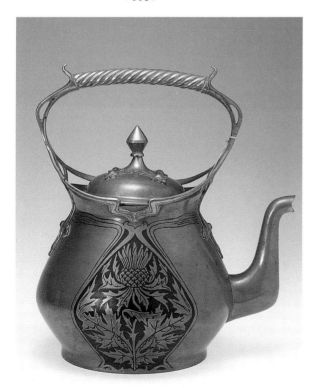

3. Copper teapot with niello and brass mounts, h. 225 mm, probably from Austria, *c.* 1900 (Prague, Museum of Decorative Arts)

4. Bronze *hu* (ritual wine vessel), h. 406 mm, Chinese, 12th–11th centuries BC (Kansas City, MO, Nelson–Atkins Museum of Art)

1. Gold vessel ending in the forepart of a lion, h. 178 mm, diam. of rim 137 mm, from Iran, Achaemenid period, *c.* 6th–5th centuries BC (New York, Metropolitan Museum of Art)

2. Pewter broad-rimmed dish with wrigglework decoration and inscription, diam. 405 mm, from England, *c.*1650–60 (London, British Museum)

3. Cut-steel shoe buckle, *Bourbonnais Shepherd*, set with a jasper cameo after a design by Lady Elizabeth Templetown, h. 61 mm, probably by Boulton & Fothergill with the factory of Wedgwood, near Burslem, Staffordshire, *c.* 1785 (Barlaston, Wedgwood Museum)

4. Bronze bust of *Mary, Queen of Hungary* by Leone Leoni, h. 675 mm, 1549–53 (Vienna, Kunsthistorisches Museum)

PLATE III   Mosaic

1. Mosaic of the *Nine Muses*, from the Imperial Palace at Trier, early 3rd century AD (Trier, Rheinisches Landesmuseum)

2. Mosaic of *Christ* (detail), from the *Deësis* (c. 1260–61), south gallery, Hagia Sophia, Istanbul

1. Mosaic mask of Quetzalcóatl, wood, turquoise and shell, 165×152 mm, from Mexico, AD 1400–1500 (London, British Museum)

2. Mosaic fountain (1900–14) in the form of a dragon by Antoni Gaudí, Park Güell, Barcelona

anvil. This process both shapes and extends the metal. Iron is normally forged hot while held in tongs, but other metals can be more satisfactorily cold forged. The hammering distorts the grain structure, so the metal has to be annealed at frequent intervals to relieve the strain and prevent cracks appearing. Many special processes and tools are used in the forging of iron, including pairs of blunt chisels (sets; see fig. 4a) to cut it. Rods of various diameters can be produced by hammering and rotating a hot iron bar into tools with concave grooves (swages; 4b). Forging tools are often used in pairs, the lower one set into the anvil, and the upper held over the workpiece and hit by the hammer (4d).

(ii) Silversmithing. The production of sheet-metal and its fabrication into various shapes is known as silversmithing. This term applies to all fine metals except iron, in which case the process is known as blacksmithing. Sheet-metal was originally made by hammering down a plate ingot. The practice of rolling metal between steel rollers was introduced in the 16th century (the earliest reference is in Leonardo's notebooks), but sheet-metal was regularly produced by this method only from the 19th century. Sheet-metal is usually cut with snips or shears, and it can be shaped in a number of ways.

(a) Raising, sinking and spinning. Raising is a compressive process where the sheet is beaten against a metal bar anvil (stake) with a round-headed hammer, and periodically annealed. The stake is normally T-shaped, with a projecting shank that is held in a vice or anvil. It has a bar that comes in a wide range of profiles depending on the work to be done (see fig. 5).

Sinking is a stretching process where the disc of metal is hammered into a concave 'former' of leather or wood or into a suitably shaped sandbag. If necessary, the piece can then be raised (see fig. 6). If a tall vessel is required, the edges of the workpiece are hammered (after sinking) on to a specially shaped, grooved stake (see fig. 5) or a wooden form (see fig. 7), until the whole sheet has flutes radiating from the centre: this is known as crimping. The workpiece can then be rapidly raised to the required shape by hammering it from outside against the stake on the inside.

Spinning is a very specific process where a disc of metal is spun on a lathe while pressing the metal back against a wooden former with blunt steel tools. The method is useful when a series of identical shapes is required. Soft metals are more suitable, but mild steel can also be shaped by spinning. The history of the technique is obscure. It requires a powerful continuous-action lathe, which was probably not available in the ancient world, and the earliest certain examples of spun ware seem to be some 13th-century Islamic vessels (Craddock and Lang, 1983). It is difficult to recognize any diagnostic features in spun ware, particularly if the vessel has been carefully finished. Sometimes spun ware can be identified by the broad concentric bands on the inside of vessels that have not been subsequently smoothed out (the presence of concentric marks on the outside of a vessel and of a small pip in the centre, where the vessel was held to the lathe, are not necessarily diagnostic of spinning, but are more likely to

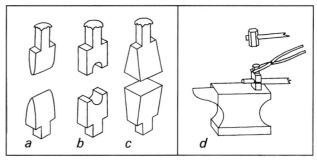

4. Forging tools: (a) sets to cut metal; (b) swages to shape rods; (c) flatters; (d) swages in use on an anvil to draw down a rod of metal

indicate that the piece was finished and polished on a lathe).

Once the basic shape has been formed by the methods above, the rim of the vessel is made by hammering down the thin edge of the workpiece. After this the piece is finished by beating it against an anvil with a highly polished, light hammer. This is known as planishing and produces a series of light facets all over the surface. In the past these facets were usually polished out, but they are often visible on the interior or in inaccessible places. On some craft silverwork produced in Europe and North America from the end of the 19th century the planishing marks have

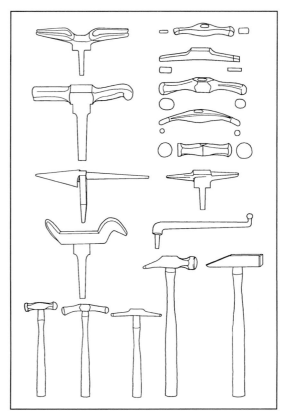

5. Metalworkers' stakes, anvils and raising hammers, including (top left) a crimping or valley stake and (top right) a range of stakes with their profiles

6. Raising a vessel from sheet-silver

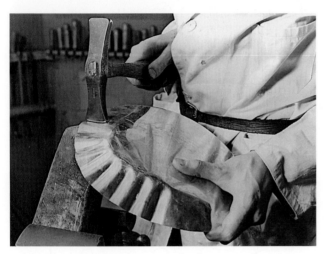

7. Crimping metal by hammering on a wooden form

been retained, not just as part of the design but also to differentiate the work from machine-made pieces; this can be seen in the work of Omar Ramsden, for example. Finally, the piece can be polished and burnished with a steel or stone burnisher. If the piece is circular it can be turned and polished on a lathe—this seems to have been the practice in the Western world for well over 2000 years.

(b) Presswork. Though now the most common method of commercial production, presswork is relatively recent. It involves the use of 'formers' or dies to produce basic shapes pressed into sheet-metal. Simple designs were stamped on to metal with a metal punch or die from early times (*see also* §V, 1(iv) below), and coins were almost always produced by striking between dies until well into the 19th century. From the 18th century small items, such as buttons, lids or spoon-bowls, began to be made from sheet-metal using the fly press, and slowly the practice spread to larger, more complex shapes. However, until the beginning of the 20th century, large brass buckets and bowls were commercially made in Europe by raising, using power-driven trip-hammers, and in the Indian subcontinent and elsewhere vessels continue to be made by hand.

(c) Repoussé. This is a process of great antiquity where deep-relief designs are hammered on to sheet-metal (see colour pls I, fig. 2 and II, fig. 1). The sheet is supported on a bed of firm but soft material, such as pitch mixed with brick dust and linseed oil, and the design is hammered out from behind with tracers, which are like blunt chisels with rounded corners. This pushes the metal into the support. After the main design has been created, the workpiece is removed from the support and annealed. The work is then continued on the front of the piece with smaller tracers and punches, sharpening up the design and adding detail. The punches can carry a variety of designs, ranging from simple grooves for matting the surface to quite intricate patterns.

(d) Wire. For the last 1000 years wire has been made by drawing thin rods through a series of progressively narrowing dies in a steel draw-plate. Now not only wire but a variety of other shapes can be extruded through a suitably-shaped hard steel profile. In earlier times wire was produced by a variety of methods. The two most usual for making gold and silver wires were 'strip twisting' or 'swaging'. In the former process a strip of thin sheet-metal was twisted to give a hollow tube similar to a drinking straw; in the latter a square-section rod was twisted and rolled. The wires produced by both these methods have distinctive helical grooves; these are clearly visible under low magnification and can sometimes be seen with the unaided eye.

IV. Joining.

Metal components have been held together by many means. Sometimes they were just stuck together with resin or other glues, as on the Basse-Yutz Celtic flagons now in the British Museum, London, but this does not give a strong joint, and quite early in the history of metalworking other methods were developed. Pegged dowels were used to hold assemblages of metal parts, for example clock movements, that needed to be easily dismantled. These often worked loose, however, and a more satisfactory solution was the screw. Although occasionally used in Roman times to hold metalwork together, screws only became common in Europe at the end of the medieval period on armour and in clocks.

1. RIVETING. In this technique a pre-formed rivet, of which the head is wider than the body, is pushed through holes drilled in the pieces to be joined. It is then hammered down with a special hollowed punch, causing the head to spread out and grip the metal tightly. Pre-formed bronze rivets with conical heads have been found on sites dating from the Bronze Age, and clearly the technique is of great antiquity. Such items as cauldrons and buckets of riveted bronze were common in Europe from the later prehistoric period. Many rivets were necessary to produce a watertight joint in such articles, and a better join could be made by using hot rivets. As the metal cooled the rivet would contract, pulling the join together even more tightly.

2. SOLDERING. In a soldered joint the metal components are held together by a metal of lower melting-point (the solder). Soldering is the most common method of

3. WELDING. A welded join consists of components that have fused or melted into each other. Most metals can be welded, and many specific techniques, such as 'casting on' (*see* §1(vii) above) or Sheffield plating (*see* §V, 6 below), are technically welding. Welding has always been particularly associated with iron. Traditionally, the iron was heated to white heat and the pieces hammered together to make the weld, but now it is welded with heat alone using an oxy-acetylene torch. The metal has to be clean and free from corrosion, and for this a flux is necessary to protect the surface. Wrought iron traditionally contained a small percentage of slag, which acts as an internal flux and greatly facilitates welding.

V. Decorative techniques.

The methods used to decorate metalwork are numerous and varied in their approach. They will be dealt with by method rather than by material. Some techniques, for example GILDING, are discussed in greater detail elsewhere in this dictionary. The principal general sources for this

8. Afghan silversmith soldering, using a blowpipe to concentrate heat on metal pieces held in tongs

joining non-ferrous metalwork (see colour pl. I, fig. 3) and has been in use from at least Babylonian times. The joint is heated locally, traditionally with a lamp and blowpipe (see fig. 8) or with a hot iron, now with a blowtorch or soldering-iron. The solder should have a wide cooling range and become slushy as it cools, so that it can be worked into the joint with the soldering-iron. The surfaces to be joined must be completely clean and unoxidized, or the solder will not adhere. To protect the surface and to promote the spread of the solder a flux is used—borax has long been the most common.

There are two main classes of solder: 'soft' and 'hard'. 'Soft' solders, such as plumbers' solder that has one part tin to two parts lead, have low melting-points. There is no fusion with the metals to be secured, and the joint is held by capillary action. 'Hard' solders (also known as silver solders) have a much higher melting-point, and the join must be heated to red heat. In these joins there is actual fusion between the solder and the metals, which creates a much stronger bond. A variety of solders were used with a range of melting temperatures sometimes on the same object, so that the craftsman could start with a high-melting-point solder progressing through lower-melting solders without melting the existing joins. The Romans used copper–silver, silver–tin and even mercury as solders on their silver wares. When a copper–zinc alloy is used for hard soldering the process is known as brazing.

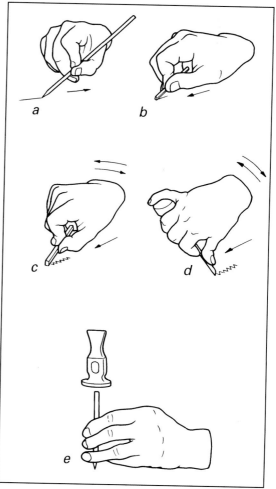

9. Tools and methods used to produce an incised design: (a) scriber; (b) graver; (c) and (d) rocked graver to produce a wriggled line (forward and back); (e) tracer

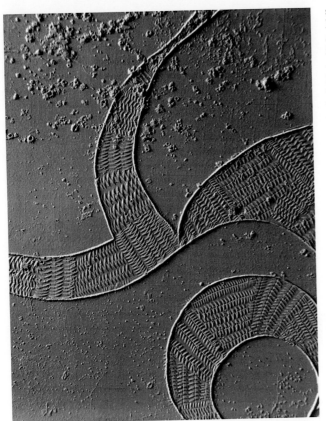

10. Wriggled line produced by a round-nosed graver on an Iron Age mirror, bronze, from Old Warden, Bedfordshire (Bedford, Bedford Museum)

section are Untracht (1968, 1982), Maryon (1971) and Ogden (1982).

1. Worked decoration. 2. Polychromy. 3. Wirework, granulation and filigree. 4. Inlay. 5. Patination. 6. Plating.

1. WORKED DECORATION. This section deals with the execution of a design on the surface of the metal. Repoussé work, though decorative, is a process that actually forms the shape of the metal and thus is discussed in §III, 2(ii)(c) above.

(i) Scribing, engraving and chasing. There are three principal methods of producing an incised design on the surface of metal (Untracht, 1968; Lowery and others, 1976; Formigli, 1985, pp. 83–90; see fig. 9). In scribing a sharp steel point (9a) held like a pencil is used to draw a design on the surface of the metal. This method is widely employed to set out a design, but on some soft metals (e.g. gold) the scribed lines are deep enough to require no further work. In engraving a small gouge, known as the graver (9b), is pushed along to remove a thin sliver of metal. The graver has a 'v' profile and is of hardened steel. In capable hands engraving can give free and flowing lines. By rocking the graver (9c and 9d), usually a broad-bladed type known as a scorper, a wriggled or zigzag line can be produced. This can be used to produce a more decorative line, or with more pronounced rocking, a matted effect over the

surface. Wriggled lines were extensively employed on European pewter from the 17th century (1989 exh. cat.; see PEWTER, fig. 1), though the technique is much earlier in origin, being found on bronzes of the European Iron Age (Lowery and others, 1976; see fig. 10 and colour pl. II, fig. 2). In the 18th century there was a fashion for deeply engraved designs on silver, with steep-sided, faceted channels that reflected light well, hence the name 'bright-cut' to describe such work. The origins of engraving itself are uncertain, but as the graver needs to be of steel to work all but the softest metals, it seems unlikely that the art of engraving preceded the Iron Age. In chasing a straight-edged chisel, known as a tracer (9e), is hammered into the metal to produce a line made up of a continuous chain of individual indentations.

It might be thought that it would be easy to identify the method by which a line has been made, but in fact it can be difficult. All but the most clumsy of chased lines are flowing and continuous with no obvious irregularities. All three methods produce lines of similar section, with raised sides. Engraving tends to pull up the sides and chasing to push them up, though in practice raised sides standing proud of the surface will have been worn or polished level. The problems are exacerbated on antiquities by corrosion and damage, and often the only certain method of identification is the presence of a specific variation, for example the rocked graver technique.

(ii) Carving. In this method the metal is carved with a chisel or a scorper to create the design (see colour pl. II, fig. 3) or make a bed for an inlay (*see* §4 below). Often the carving has been executed not on the metal itself, but on the mould in which the metal was cast (*see* §III, 1 above). For example, much of the so-called 'chip-carved' decoration on Late Roman and Insular metalwork found in western Europe is in fact cast. The problem of identification is compounded where cast carving was subsequently worked over with a chisel to give it a cleaner, brighter appearance. On some types of heavily inlaid metalwork the channels and beds are always carved, thus Indian bidri vessels are cast, but the areas to be inlaid are carved afterwards with tracer and chisel (*see* §§4 and 5(v) below). Similarly, much of the decoration on Islamic sheet brasswork is carved, but on cast metalwork it was often done on the mould.

(iii) Reserving or matting. To provide contrast or to emphasize a design it is often necessary to reserve or matt an area. Sometimes, if the area to be reserved is quite narrow, this can be achieved simply by creating a depression in the surface: the depressed area will inevitably become duller than the more exposed and polished raised areas, as well as retaining dirt. On broad, flat areas, however, other means have to be adopted. The surface can be stippled with a punch or with multi-pointed matting punches. A broad wriggled line can be produced with a rocked graver (*see* §(i) above). Special gravers with three or five channels, known as liners, can be used to create a series of fine parallel lines or, by fine crosshatching, a variety of textured surfaces, known collectively as 'Florentine finishes'. From the late 17th century this could be performed mechanically, and the process, known as engine-turning, produced complex patterns of straight or curved lines over the surface. This technique was described

in manuals, for example that of Charles Plumier (1701). Aside from purely decorative purposes, fine lines have often been scored on to the metal surfaces of scientific and optical instruments where reflections could disrupt measurements (Binnie, 1993).

(iv) Stamping or punching. A design can be built up using decorative punches of varying complexity, from a simple ring to quite elaborate patterns. These reduce repetitive free-hand work and were in use in the Middle East from at least the 3rd millennium BC (Ogden, 1982, p. 36). The punch has to be carefully placed to ensure that the design, when struck, comes out at a uniform depth on the metal. In Pre-Columbian South America sheet-gold was often decorated with quite deep and complex designs, struck with stone dies; in the Classical world metal dies of a hard, high-tin bronze, similar to that used for contemporary coin dies, were preferred. Complete scenes can be struck from an intaglio die on to sheets of soft metal. This technique was used from Hellenistic times, at the latest, for mass-producing small but complex items, for example religious plaques in sheet-metal. It continues to be practised in the Middle East and the Indian subcontinent, where a flat piece of soft metal (gold or silver) is placed over the die with a folded sheet of lead on top. The lead backing is then hammered, forcing the metal into the design. In the 18th century advances in press design, particularly the introduction of the fly press, made it feasible to stamp out complete, decorated pieces from sheet-metal. (See also Untracht, 1968; Ogden, 1982.)

(v) Pierced work. This is done with a punch, a drill or a piercing saw, usually on such soft sheet-metal as gold or silver. The piercing saw is a relatively modern tool, and the superb late Roman and Byzantine *opus interrasile* work, which seems to have begun around the 3rd century AD, was largely executed by setting out the design with a drill and then opening it out with a chisel (Ogden, 1982, p. 43; Deppert-Lippitz, 1993).

2. POLYCHROMY. An obvious and widespread technique for creating polychromy is to juxtapose two metals of a different colour. In parts of Africa bangles have been made by twisting together thin rods of brass and copper to give a pleasing contrast, and in Mexico the *metales casados* (Sp.: 'married metals') are made by soldering silver, copper, brass and other metals (Untracht, 1968, p. 184).

(i) Mokume. This technique was developed and perfected by the Japanese in the late 17th century. Thin plates of various coloured metals, sometimes silver but more usually copper and its alloys, including *shakudo* (*see* §5(iii) below), are soldered together to make a sandwich. This is then drilled or cut with sloping sides to expose the layers beneath. Alternatively, the piece can be deformed with a punch to create raised areas that can then be filed flat, exposing the 'grain' or layers of metal beneath (Maryon, 1971, p. 166; Untracht, 1982, p. 372; see fig. 11). The final appearance depends on the surface treatments, but that of wood grain, from which *mokume* derives its name, or watered effects are especially favoured.

(ii) Pattern welding. Iron and steel can be decoratively contrasted by pattern welding, also known as damascening.

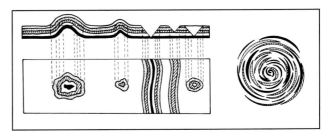

11. *Mokume*, in which a sandwich of variously coloured metals is deformed with a punch and then filed flat to expose the 'grain' beneath

(Damascening can also mean inlaid metalwork; *see* ARMS AND ARMOUR, §II, 1.) In pattern welding (see fig. 12) bundles of iron and steel rods were arranged alternately (or twisted) and welded together. They were then hammered out, twisted and annealed repeatedly to fabricate the basic shape, usually a weapon (Tylecote and Gilmour, 1986; Lang and Ager, 1989), while also building up complex patterns running through the metal. The contrast was revealed by polishing and etching. The technique was probably first used in Late Iron Age Celtic Europe, and became popular in the late Roman period and the early medieval period, when it was used particularly on sword blades but also on spears and knives. There is some debate concerning whether the technique was functional (i.e. to produce a stronger weapon) or decorative; some items were simply inlaid with thin panels of patterned metal, and these must be regarded as purely decorative. The Malayan and Indonesian *kris* blades (Rostoker and Bronson, 1990; Frey, 1990), produced from the medieval period, are made of thin sheets of iron of varying composition forged together and hammered, deformed and filed in a manner similar to *mokume*. They are then welded on to a central plate of steel, and either deep-etched (Malaya and Java) or just patinated (Bali).

The famed damascus blades made by Islamic craftsmen in the Middle East and India relied on the special properties of the *wootz* crucible steel from south India and Sri Lanka. The earliest such blades are medieval, and literary evidence

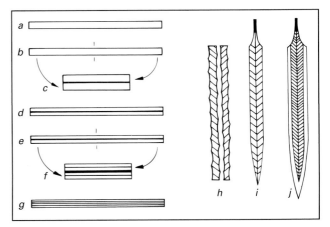

12. Pattern welding: (a) an iron rod is (b) carburized, (c) piled and (d) drawn down; the process is repeated (e), (f) and (g); two such iron and steel rods are (h) twisted and (i) welded to form a core; an edge is welded on (j) and the blade polished and etched to bring out the pattern

would suggest both damascus swords and the use of *wootz* flourished over 1000 years ago (Bronson, 1986).

3. WIREWORK, GRANULATION AND FILIGREE.

(i) Wirework. Many pieces of gold jewellery are built up of wires soldered either together or to a base plate. The basic techniques of wire production are discussed in §III, 2(ii)(d) above, but the wires could be decorated by a variety of techniques (Meryon, 1971, pp. 135–40). Beading was common: this is now done by swaging, i.e. by hammering lengths of wire between two halves of a steel die with a line of conical depressions. In antiquity the wire was rolled under a hard, rounded edge to produce a groove, which, repeated at regular intervals, gave a beaded effect.

The technique of making wires from a twisted ribbon lent itself to decoration, either by incomplete twisting or by flattening and untwisting to produce wavy ribbons. Wires of various sizes and sections could be used together, either laid parallel or twisted: in the Middle East complex chains were interwoven from the 3rd millennium BC. Short lengths of wire could be coiled to form small cones to be used as decorative components, often in conjunction with granulation. (See also Ogden, 1982; Whitfield, 1987, 1989; Untracht, 1982.)

(ii) Granulation. This technique was widely used in antiquity: Etruscan jewellery, for example, was often heavily granulated (*see* GOLD, fig. 3) (Cristofani and Martelli, 1983). The technique was known at Ur in the 3rd millennium BC and was common by the 2nd millennium BC. In this technique small spheres of gold are bonded to gold sheet, either giving total coverage or arranged in patterns. The beads are minute, and even a small design can incorporate thousands, but they are surprisingly easy to make. Small clippings of gold are dispersed in charcoal and carefully heated until the gold just melts, and surface tension pulls each clipping into a sphere. The best ancient work shows no evidence of solder, which has led to much speculation on 'lost' technologies (see Ogden, 1982). The experiments of Littledale suggested that minute granules were stuck to the surface with glue containing finely powdered copper salts. When heated to just below the melting point of gold, the glue would char, reducing the copper mineral to metal, which in turn would dissolve in the gold forming an *in situ* and invisible gold solder. This technique, known as colloidal soldering, was so ingenious and successful that it was assumed that it was universally used in antiquity. In fact, more detailed study from the 1940s showed that a variety of methods were used: the finest Greek and Etruscan work was probably done by colloidal soldering, but another method possibly used in antiquity was to arrange the granules along thin filaments of solder. (See also Walters, 1983; Ogden, 1982, pp. 64–6.)

(iii) Filigree. In filigree work soldered wires are used not just to produce decorative elements but to form the whole object. This 'technique of captured air' has always been especially popular in silver for jewellery and such small items as plaques, frames and glass-lined boxes. After each flat panel has been soldered the wire is normally flattened out by gentle hammering before the work is finally assembled. It is virtually impossible to polish filigree work, and thus it is normally left unpolished after pickling, therefore looking rather white and granular. The technique was widely used in antiquity and continues to be practised as a traditional craft in China and the Indian subcontinent, where it is centred on Cuttack in Orissa. (See also Meryon, 1971, pp. 41–2; Untracht, 1968, pp. 196–200.)

4. INLAY. The craft of inlaying a metal substrate with another metal (see colour pl. I, fig. 1) or material has a long history, and a great variety of methods have been used. In true inlaying the inlay is let into the metal substrate so that it lies flush with the surface. The beds or channels into which the inlay is set can be made in the original casting or chiselled out. The form of the bed is to some degree dictated by the inlay, but it is common for the bottom to be roughened with a chisel to provide a key, and for the sides to be undercut to hold soft or molten inlays. Sometimes the depression is slight, no more than a surface roughening. On most medieval Islamic sheet brasses, for example, the beds, where they exist at all, were made by shallow chisel cuts and the outlines stippled with a punch to give a key on to which silver, or more rarely gold, was hammered. Thus the inlays, or more correctly overlays, stand proud of the surface, and, inevitably after centuries of use, polishing and pilfering, many of them are missing.

Metal inlays can be hammered into place and secured without the need for adhesive, while other materials can be softened by heat and worked in. Clearly this method was not possible with precious gemstones or inlays of *millefiori* glass, as found on Roman or Insular items. Similarly, the shell and coral so prized as an inlay by Iron Age Celtic craftsmen could not be hammered into place. Instead these inlays were sometimes held by adhesives within a raised bronze openwork frame, as on the Basse-Yutz flagons (*c.* early 4th century BC; London, BM; *see* CELTIC ART, fig. 2). A wide variety of adhesives and putties have been identified, usually consisting of an inorganic filler with a drying oil or wax (Arrhenius, 1985).

Metal inlays can be held by burring over the surface of the substrate. This technique can be seen on the copper and silver inlay of the decorative plates made in Thanjavur in Tamil Nadu, India (Saravanavel, 1985; Untracht, 1968, pp. 134–8). A line is scribed around the inlay on to the base plate and opened up with a chisel. The inlay is then laid in this and the outer edge burred. A simpler method, of course, would be to use solder.

A different approach is to build up cells by soldering wires on to the surface. This technique is used when a considerable area of the surface is to be covered with inlay. If the inlay is enamel the technique is known as *cloisonné*; if there is no supporting plate beneath, but just the framework of wires filled with enamel, it is known as *plique à jour*; if the cells that hold the enamel have been cut into the metal beneath, the technique is known as *champlevé*; and if the surface of the metal has been carved to differing depths and covered with translucent enamel to give a three-dimensional effect, it is known as *basse taille* (*see also* ENAMEL, §3).

A variety of other materials can be used as inlays (La Niece, 1988), including virtually all metals: although gold and silver have been especially favoured, copper, pewter and even iron have all been used, the last being quite common on Etruscan and Roman bronzes. Sometimes the contrast is not just in colour but also in texture. Thus the substrate metal can be patinated and inlaid with shiny metal, as in Indian *kuftkäri* and bidri work (*see* §5(iv) and (v) below), or bright metal can be inlaid with a matt or non-metallic material. The carved and engraved areas on some Islamic brasses were picked out with bitumen, and in Europe the designs on some medieval memorial brasses were filled with black wax or bone black.

Another popular inlay was niello, which is a dense, black material formed from single or, latterly, mixed metal sulphides (see colour pl. I, fig. 3). When hot it melts, or at least becomes pasty, and can be pressed into the depressions in the substrate. The early history of the material is rather confused. Laffineur (1974) claimed to have identified it in Mycenaean artefacts, but most of these are untested or have been shown not to be niello. The daggers from the Shaft Graves at Mycenae, for example, were inlaid with patinated metal (*see* §5(iii) below). The strongest claim is made for the black inlay on the silver cup of Mycenaean date found at Enkomi, Cyprus (see fig. 14 below), but no scientific identification was ever published by Plenderleith, who carried out the conservation and examination (see his report in Schaeffer, 1952, p. 381). The material was apparently little used by the ancient Greeks or Etruscans but suddenly became popular in Roman times, especially on silver. The niello used was usually the sulphide of the corresponding body metal. Thus, silver pieces were inlaid with silver sulphide and bronzes with copper sulphides. In one instance a Roman gold ring was found to have been inlaid with a gold sulphide niello, which must have been difficult to make (La Niece, 1983). Pliny described a mixed sulphide niello (*Natural History* XXXIII.xlvi.131), but this did not come into general use until the Byzantine period. By the 12th century AD Theophilus (Hawthorne and Smith, 1963 edn, pp. 104–5) was describing niello made from a mixture of silver, copper and lead sulphides, but this remained a rarity until the Renaissance.

Single sulphide niellos used in the Classical and medieval periods were difficult to use because, when hot enough to be sufficiently soft to work into the inlay bed, they tended to decompose. Mixed sulphide niellos have lower melting-points and are much more fluid, which makes their application easier. The popularity of niello declined in post-medieval Europe, except in Russia, where fine niello inlay continued to be made in the 19th century. Niello was also utilized in East Asia and on traditional Islamic jewellery until the early 20th century, but by the end of the 20th century its use had almost completely dwindled. (See also Meryon, 1971.)

5. PATINATION. The bright, shiny surfaces of metals have usually been one of their most attractive features (Fishlock, 1962; see colour pl. II, fig. 4), but sometimes they have been deliberately patinated, either to provide attractive colours in their own right or to form a contrasting background for metallic inlays. The prevalence of patinated alloys in antiquity is rather uncertain. It is difficult, for example, to assess whether the patinated surface of an ancient bronze represents an original treatment or natural corrosion: in general it would seem that in antiquity most artistic metalwork was kept in a bright and shiny state (see Jones, 1990). Some of the more important patination processes will be discussed below in relation to specific metals. (See also Hiorns, 1892; Field and Bonney, 1925; Hughes and Rowe, 1982; La Niece and Craddock, 1993.)

(i) Silver. Vickers (Vickers, Impey and Allan, 1986) has argued that much ancient Greek silver originally had a black 'oxidized' surface. He suggested that the familiar Greek Red-figure ceramics were imitations of silver originals, with the red figures echoing the gilded figures on the silver. While some pieces of part-gilded Greek silver (e.g. Venedikov and Gerasimov, 1975, pl. 169) look attractive when tarnished and certainly similar to the contemporary Red-figure wares, Vickers's ideas on ancient silver have not found general acceptance (see Boardman, 1987). In the 19th century, however, blackened silver became fashionable in both Europe and North America. Although usually known as 'oxidized' silver, the black patina was in fact sulphidic, produced by reaction with various sulphides. An alternative method was to deposit on the surface a thin layer of another metal, usually platinum, that appeared black.

(ii) Gold. Some gold items, notably those from royal burials from New Kingdom Egypt, have a distinctly rosy appearance, which is almost certainly the result of deliberate treatment (Ogden, 1982; Frantz and Schorsch, 1990). The gold contains small amounts of iron, and with the correct heat treatment a red colour was developed. This effect is not to be confused with *or gris* or *or bleu*, alloys of gold with 10–20% iron, which enjoyed a certain popularity in polychrome jewellery in the early 20th century, mainly in Paris.

(iii) Copper and its alloys. Although most bronzes seem to have been kept in a bright, shiny condition (Craddock, 1992), some were of a specific alloy, treated to produce a purple-black patina and with gold or silver inlay. The earliest of these is the *hesmen kem* or 'black copper' of the Egyptians (Cooney, 1966), shown by surviving inscriptions from the 18th Dynasty (*c.* 1540–*c.* 1292 BC) onwards to be a prestigious material. Analysis of Egyptian statuettes of this distinctive black-patinated, inlaid metal showed that some have a highly unusual composition containing small amounts of gold, silver and arsenic in the alloy, similar to the much later Japanese *shakudo* alloys (Craddock and Giumlia-Mair, 1993; see below). The same type of metal was used for the inlaid daggers from Mycenae (*see* MYCENAE, fig. 3), in which panels of black bronze were inlaid with gold and silver and let into the sides of the blades. Analysis of a panel from a previously unrecorded dagger of this type showed it to contain small amounts of gold and silver (Ogden, 1993).

There are references to black-patinated copper alloys inlaid with gold and silver in the *Iliad*, especially in the description of the shield of Achilles (XVIII), and in other Classical sources. This alloy has also been linked with the mysterious but prestigious 'Corinthian bronze' of the Roman world. From Plutarch (*Moralia* V.395) and Pliny (*Natural History* XXXIV.i, vi–viii) it can be deduced that

'Corinthian bronze' was a patinated alloy of copper with some gold and silver, though there were many imitations; other authors, for example Petronius, lampooned the connoisseurs who claimed to be able to identify the genuine material (e.g. *Satyricon* L) (Heseltine, 1913). Pausanias, writing in the 2nd century AD, mentioned the production of 'Corinthian bronze' in his description of the city of Corinth (*Guide to Greece*, II.iii.3). Unfortunately the description has not survived intact, but it suggests that the hot bronze was plunged into water from the Peirene fountain in order to dye (Gr. *bapto*) or patinate it. The most complete description of the process for making 'Corinthian bronze' is found in the Syriac text by the Alexandrian alchemist Zosimos (VI.2; Berthelot, 1983); it is similar to the Japanese *irogane* method of making *shakudo*. Several examples of Roman copper alloys containing small amounts of gold or silver, patinated black and inlaid with gold or silver, have been identified in the collections of the British Museum, London, either as complete objects or in decorative inlays in bronzework (Craddock and Giumlia-Mair, 1993).

The evidence for the production of Japanese *irogane* alloys (Roberts-Austen, 1888; Gowland, 1915), which continue to be made in Japan, only begins in the 14th century AD, and the vast majority of surviving pieces were made from the late 18th century. The types of *irogane* include *shibuichi*, an alloy of copper with about 30% silver, and *shirome*, a natural alloy of impure copper with small amounts of arsenic and antimony, but the most well-known is *shakudō*, which is composed of copper with small amounts of gold and silver (La Niece, 1990[B]; Notis, 1988)—in modern practice *c.* 0.5–1% imparts a black colour and 5–10% a purple-black. The piece is made, inlaid and then patinated. As in all surface treatments the initial polishing and cleaning are vitally important: first the alloy is carefully polished with the softest of abrasives, often charcoal prepared from deer antler; it is then carefully cleaned and degreased by boiling in solutions containing organic acids derived from such fruit as the bitter cherry plum, though radish juice is now preferred (Murakami, 1993). Finally the prepared metal is boiled in weak, aqueous solutions containing some copper salts. *Shakudō*, inlaid with gold and silver, as well as brass, *shibuichi* and *shirome*, was popular for sword guards and other sword fittings throughout the Edo period and represents the peak of achievement in patinated metal. It has been suggested that the 'purple sheen gold' referred to in many ancient Chinese documents should be equated with the Japanese *shakudō* (Needham, 1974, pp. 257–68). Examples of this have not yet been identified, but black-patinated copper containing small amounts of gold and inlaid with silver continue to be produced under the name of *wu tong* in Yunnan and other remote provinces (Wayman and Craddock, 1993).

(iv) Iron and steel. Damascened or pattern-welded iron relies on surface treatment or etching to bring out the pattern (*see* §2(ii) above), but sometimes the whole surface can be uniformly patinated by careful heat treatment and quenching to produce an attractive blue-black surface that is usually inlaid with gold or silver. Obviously the process has to be carefully controlled to ensure that a stable, firmly adhering magnetite layer is formed rather than the usual flaking iron rust. Islamic blacksmiths produced a black-patinated steel inlaid with gold and silver. This is sometimes known as 'false damascening' or Toledo ware, after the city in Spain where the craft was and continues to be practised. The conquistadors introduced the craft to the Americas, and the small town of Amozoc, near Puebla, in Mexico is well known for the production of saddle and bridle fittings. The steel is inlaid with gold and silver, then oiled and plunged into hot nitre and quenched in water. Finally it is placed in boiling water, followed by a dip in oil to impart a peacock-blue colour to the metal (Untracht, 1968, p. 158).

A similar technique is used in the Indian subcontinent to make *kuftkārī* wares, Kerala and Rajasthan being especially celebrated for this work (Untracht, 1968, pp. 153–8; Bisham Pal, 1984, pp. 27–8). A steel plate is first inlaid with fine silver or gold wire and then patinated by holding it over a charcoal fire until the desired purple-black colour is attained. It is then quenched and treated with vegetable oil to preserve the colour. Methods similar to these were widely used in Renaissance Europe to patinate or 'blue' armour and other steelwork.

(v) Zinc. A patinated alloy of zinc, known as bidri, has been made in India from the 15th century (*see* INDIAN SUBCONTINENT, §VIII, 15(iii) and fig. 348). It takes its name from the city of Bidar in central India, where it continues to be made, though production is centred on Hyderabad. Some production takes place in the Ganga valley, with Lucknow the traditional centre. Bidri is made from an alloy containing *c.* 95% zinc and 5% copper. The objects are sand cast (*see* §III, 1(vi) above) (Stronge and Craddock, 1993) and, after cleaning, inlaid with silver sheet or now usually silver wire. The inlaid casting is then carefully polished and cleaned. The patination is achieved by using an aqueous solution or a poultice of ammonium chloride and mud collected from beneath old walls: as anyone who has been to India will testify, the soil beneath old walls is likely to be rich in minerals deriving from urine, and it is the nitre, salt and ammonium compounds that are the active ingredients. The casting may be heated and then coated in a mud poultice, or the solution may be boiled and the casting placed in it. Within seconds the alloy develops a deep matt black patination, which is permanent. No further treatment is used, other than rubbing with a little coconut oil to enhance the black lustre that contrasts superbly with the silver inlay.

See also PATINA and Stronge, 1985.

6. PLATING. Plating has a history almost as long as that of metallurgy itself (*see also* GILDING, §II, 4), and many ways have been devised to cover one metal with another. The simplest and oldest was to cover the body metal with a foil held in place by adhesive, pins or nails. Several extant Syrian bronze figurines dating from the 2nd millennium BC illustrate this technique well (see fig. 13). A thin foil of the precious metal, usually gold or silver, was stretched over the body metal and burnished into place to ensure a close fit. The edges of the foil overlap at the rear and were held by pins hammered into small troughs of lead let into the back of the figure.

13. Bronze figurine with remains of silver-foil plating, held in place by pins hammered into lead, from Syria-Palestine, 14th–12th centuries BC (London, British Museum)

Foil plating, particularly with silver, continued in the ancient Roman period, when copper-alloy horse trappings and other decorative fittings were often plated with thin foils of silver held by soft solder, and the technique was still widely used to plate minor items in the 18th century and early 19th, when it was known in England as close plating. A much stronger union could be achieved with a hard solder or by diffusion welding, which can be found on ancient metalwork, especially on counterfeit silver coins. In the former process a layer of copper–silver hard solder was introduced between the silver foil and the copper alloy substrate; in the latter the foil and substrate were held together and strongly heated until they fused. Metallographically the joins are usually indistinguishable. Sheffield plating (see SHEFFIELD PLATE) was basically the diffusion welding of silver on to copper. The process is usually thought to date from the 18th century, but claims have been made that it was known in Minoan times (Charles, 1968), though the examples cited to support these arguments could have been hard soldered.

Pure gold can be beaten extremely thin, and the resulting leaves held in place on the carefully cleaned base metal by burnishing (see GILDING, §I, 1(i)). Gold of sufficient purity is not found naturally, and thus true leaf gilding was impossible until the technology of purifying the gold had been perfected; this probably took place in the Middle East in the later 2nd millennium BC (Oddy, 1982). Leaf silvering was also practised to a limited extent, mainly in post-medieval Europe, when it was known in England as French plating and used mainly for clock dials.

Another technique, known as mercury, fire or parcel gilding (see also GILDING, §I, 3), was to make an amalgam with mercury of the metal to be deposited, which was almost invariably gold or silver. This paste was applied to the carefully prepared metal substrate and the mercury driven off by heating. Both mercury gilding and silvering were practised in China by the 4th century BC, but mercury silvering only became popular in Europe in the Middle Ages. Amalgam gilding and silvering were widely used on small fittings, as well as on the dials of scientific instruments and clocks, but were largely replaced by Sheffield plating in the 18th century.

Another technique of plating is to coat the substrate with molten metal. This technique was used to silver copper in Pre-Columbian South America and in early medieval Europe (La Niece, 1990[A]) but is only feasible with low-melting-point plating metals, the two most common being zinc and tin. The process of coating carefully cleaned iron sheet with molten zinc, which is known as galvanizing, was developed in the 19th century. It is used primarily as a method of protecting iron against corrosion, but it was occasionally used decoratively when still novel.

By contrast, the tinning of bronze dates from the Bronze Age, and the Mycenaeans plated some of their ceramic vessels with tin foil. It was not until Roman times, however, that the tinning of bronze became popular (Pliny, *Natural History* XXXIV.xlviii.161–2). By the late 1990s the earliest evidence of tinned iron so far discovered was on the hilt of an Iron Age dagger from Spain (London, BM); the technique remained popular throughout the medieval period (Harrison, 1980). It developed into a considerable industry in Saxony, Bohemia and in Britain at Pontypool. Tin plate was often lacquered or japanned (see LACQUER, §§I, 3 and II, 2), and the trays, teapots and other goods made in Pontypool or nearby Usk were popular throughout Europe in the 18th century and early 19th (Reade, 1968).

Tin melts at a temperature of 232°C, and thus the piece could be coated by dipping the object in molten tin. More usually, however, the piece was heated and a stick of tin wiped across the surface. The tin was then spread evenly with a cloth. These simple techniques continue to be practised across the world by tinkers refurbishing copper cooking pots. Alternatively, if the tinned layer on copper alloy is carefully heated, controlled diffusion takes place, and a high-tin bronze will be formed on the surface (Meeks, 1986, 1993). This will be hard, silvery and corrosion resistant. Perhaps the most familiar examples of this technique are the silvery bronze mirrors of the ancient Romans, though this specialized tinning is common on a wide range of other items, such as the small decorative 'bronzes' that are often described as silvered or silver-plated.

A plating can also be achieved chemically by treating an alloy of base metals and gold or silver to preferentially leach out the base metal, leaving the surface enriched with the precious metal. After treatment the surface appears matt and must be burnished. This technique is of great antiquity, though it continues to be used to enhance the appearance of low-carat gold. Before mineral acids were available, the surface would be heated to oxidize the base metals, which were then removed by the use of certain iron salts or organic acids and vinegars made from fruit juice. The debased Roman silver denarii of the 2nd and 3rd centuries AD are good examples of the technique. In order to make them appear silvery, the base-metal flans were chemically treated to remove copper from the surface. They were then struck, which had the effect of spreading the silver over the surface. In this way coins made of alloys with as little as 10–20% silver could, at least temporarily, have the appearance of silver (Cope, 1972). The technique was also used extensively in Andean and Isthmian South America. An alloy of gold and copper, known as *tumbaga*, was chemically treated to remove the surface copper and burnished. Sometimes part of the surface was protected with a resist and polychrome patterns created (Bray, 1978 exh. cat. and 1993).

Metals can also be deposited on to the surface of more reactive metals from solution. The familiar experiment of plating copper on to an iron blade placed in a copper sulphate solution is a good example of the technique. A thin layer of silver can be deposited from a paste containing silver in solution with a nitrate or ammonium salt. No heat is required, and various patent cold silvering solutions are still quite widely used to repair worn plating (*see* §VI, 3 below). There is less evidence for its use in antiquity, but the thin layers of silver on some South American copper objects of the Mochica culture of 100–600 AD have been postulated as examples of chemical silvering. From the 16th century the technique was quite widely used to silver coffin plates and handles and such other items as clock dials, where the silvering would not be subjected to wear or frequent polishing. In the mid-19th century it was replaced by ELECTROPLATING, as were all the other traditional processes of gilding and silvering metal.

For further information on metalworking techniques *see* AFRICA, §V, 2; CHINA, §XIII, 14; EGYPT, ANCIENT, §VII, 2; and ISLAMIC ART, §IV.

BIBLIOGRAPHY

EARLY SOURCES

Theophilus: *De diversis artibus* (MS.; *c*. 1123); ed. and trans. by J. G. Hawthorne and C. S. Smith (Chicago, 1963)
V. Biringuccio: *De la pirotechnia* (Venice, 1540); ed. C. S. Smith, trans. M. T. Gnudi as *The Pirotechnia of Vannoccio Biringuccio* (New York, 1943, rev. Cambridge, MA, 2/1959)
G. Agricola: *De re metallica* (Basle, 1556); Eng. trans. by H. C. Hoover and L. Hoover (London, 1912/*R* 1950) [contains comprehensive account of metal production in Renaissance Europe]
M. Heseltine: *Petronius*, Loeb Class. Lib. (London, 1913)
B. Cellini: *I trattati dell'oreficeria e della scultura di Benvenuto Cellini*; ed. G. Milanesi (Florence, 1857, rev. 2/1893); Eng. trans. of original by C. R. Ashbee as *The Treatises of Benvenuto Cellini on Goldsmithing and Sculpture* (London, 1888/*R* New York, 1967)

GENERAL

A. R. Bailey: *A Text Book of Metallurgy* (London, 1960)
W. Alexander and A. Street: *Metals in the Service of Man* (London, 1962)
H. Hodges: *Artifacts: An Introduction to Early Materials and Technology* (London, 1964, rev. 2/1989)
O. Untracht: *Metal Techniques for Craftsmen* (New York, 1968)
J. E. Gordon: *The New Science of Strong Materials, or Why you Don't Fall through the Floor* (London, 1976)
J. W. Allan: *Persian Metal Technology, 700–1300 AD* (London, 1979)
J. Ogden: *Jewellery of the Ancient World* (London, 1982)
O. Untracht: *Jewelry: Concepts and Technology* (London, 1982)
E. Formigli: *Tecniche dell'oreficeria etrusca e romana* (Florence, 1985)
R. F. Tylecote: *The Prehistory of Metallurgy* (London, 1986)
——: *A History of Metallurgy* (London, 1992)

NATIVE METALS

R. Maddin, T. S. Wheeler and J. D. Muhly: 'Distinguishing Artifacts of Nature Copper', *J. Archaeol. Sci.*, viii/3 (1980), pp. 211–26
V. F. Buchwald and G. Mosdal: 'Meteoric Iron, Telluric and Wrought Iron in Greenland', *Man & Soc.*, ix (1985) [whole issue]

SHAPING

J. W. Lilco: *Blacksmith's Manual Illustrated* (Oxford, 1930)
S. Choate: *Creative Casting* (London, 1966)
J. W. Mills and M. Gillespie: *Studio Bronze Casting* (London, 1969)
W. A. Oddy: 'The Production of Gold Wire in Antiquity', *Gold Bull.*, x/3 (1977), pp. 79–87
P. T. Craddock and J. Lang: 'Spinning, Turning, Polishing', *J. Hist. Metal. Soc.*, xvii/2 (1983), pp. 79–81
H. Born, ed.: *Archäologische Bronzen, antike Kunst und moderne Technik* (Berlin, 1985)

DECORATIVE TECHNIQUES

P. T. Craddock: 'Gold in Antique Copper Alloys', *Gold Bull.*, xv/2 (n.d.), pp. 69–72
C. Plumier: *L'Art de tourner* (Lyon, 1701)
W. C. Roberts-Austen: 'Cantor Lectures on Alloys: Colours of Metals and Alloys Considered in Relation to their Application to Art', *J. Soc. A.*, xxxvi (1888), pp. 1137–46
A. H. Hiorns: *Metal-colouring and Bronzing* (London, 1892)
M. Berthelot: *La Chimie au Moyen Age*, 3 vols (Paris, 1893)
W. Gowland: 'Metals and Metalworking of Old Japan', *Trans. & Proc. Japan Soc., London*, xiii (1915), pp. 19–100
S. Field and S. R. Bonney: *The Chemical Coloring of Metals* (London, 1925)
C. F. A. Schaeffer: *Enkomi-Alasia: Nouvelles missions en Chypre, 1946–1950* (Paris, 1952), pp. 379–89, figs 116–22, pl. cxvi [includes a technical report by H. J. Plenderleith]
O. Untracht: *Enameling on Metal* (London, 1958)
W. J. Anstee and L. Biek: 'A Study in Pattern-welding', *Med. Archaeol.*, v (1961), pp. 71–93
D. Fishlock: *Metal Colouring* (Teddington, 1962)
J. D. Cooney: 'On the Meaning of *Hesmen Kem*', *Z. Ägyp. Sprache & Altertknd.*, xciii (1966), pp. 43–7
J. A. Charles: 'The First Sheffield Plate', *Antiquity*, xlii (1968), pp. 278–84
B. Reade: *Architectural and Domestic Metalwork*, The *Connoisseur*'s Complete Period Guides (London, 1968), pp. 1163–76
P. R. Lowery, R. D. A. Savage and R. L. Wilkins: 'Scriber, Graver, Scorper, Tracer', *Proc. Prehist. Soc.*, xxxvii/1 (1971), pp. 167–82
H. Maryon: *Metalwork and Enamelling* (New York, 1971)
L. H. Cope: 'Surface-silvered Ancient Coins', *Methods of Chemical and Metallurgical Investigation of Ancient Coinage*, ed. E. T. Hall and D. M. Metcalf (London, 1972), pp. 261–79
R. Laffineur: 'L'Incrustation à l'époque mycénienne', *Ant. Class.*, xliii (1974), pp. 5–31
J. Needham with the collaboration of Lu Gwei-Djen: *Spagyrical Discovery and Invention: Magisteries of Gold and Immortality* (1974), ii of *Chemistry and Chemical Technology*, v of *Science and Civilisation in China* (Cambridge, 1954–)
I. Venedikov and T. D. Gerasimov: *Trakiĭskoto izkustvo/Thracian Art Treasures* (London and Sofia, 1975) [bilingual text]
P. R. Lowery, R. D. A. Savage and R. L. Wilkins: 'A Technical Study of the Designs on the British Mirror Series', *Archaeologia*, cv (1976), pp. 99–126
H. B. Collier: 'X-ray Fluorescence Analysis of Black Copper from Yunnan', *Naturwissenschaften*, lxiv (1977), p. 484
The Gold of Eldorado (exh. cat. by W. Bray, London, RA, 1978)
H. Lechtmann: 'A Precolumbian Technique for Electrochemical Plating of Gold and Silver on Objects of Copper', *J. Metals*, xxxi (1979), pp. 154–60

——: 'New Perspectives on Moche Metallurgy', *Amer. Ant.*, xlvii/1 (1979), pp. 3–30

R. J. Harrison: 'A Tin-plated Dagger of the Early Iron Age from Spain', *Madrid. Mitt.*, xxi (1980), pp. 140–46

R. Hughes and M. Rowe: *The Colouring, Bronzing and Patination of Metals* (London, 1982)

W. A. Oddy: 'Gold in Antiquity', *J. Royal Soc. A.*, cxxx (1982), pp. 730–44

M. Cristofani and M. Martelli: *L'oro degli Etruschi* (Novara, 1983)

J. Lang and M. J. Hughes: 'Soldering Roman Silver Plate', *Oxford J. Archaeol.*, iii (1983), pp. 77–97

S. La Niece: 'Niello', *Antiqua. J.*, lxiii/2 (1983), pp. 279–97

J. Wolters: *Die Granulation* (Munich, 1983)

H. Bhisham Pal: *Handicrafts of Rajasthan* (New Delhi, 1984)

B. Arrhenius: *Merovingian Garnet Jewellery* (Stockholm, 1985)

P. Saravanavel: *A Study on the Thanjavur Art Plate* (Thanjavur, 1985)

S. Stronge: *Bidri Ware* (London, 1985)

B. Bronson: 'The Making and Selling of Wootz', *Archaeomaterials*, i (1986), pp. 13–51

N. D. Meeks: 'Tin-rich Surfaces on Bronze', *Archaeometry*, xxviii/2 (1986), pp. 133–62

R. F. Tylecote and B. J. J. Gilmour: *The Metallography of Early Ferrous Edge Tools and Edged Weapons*, Brit. Archaeol. Rep., Brit. Ser., 155 (Oxford, 1986)

M. Vickers, O. Impey and J. Allan: *From Silver to Ceramic: The Potter's Debt to Metalwork in the Graeco-Roman, Oriental and Islamic Worlds* (Oxford, 1986)

J. Boardman: 'Silver Is White', *Rev. Archéol.*, ii (1987), pp. 279–85

N. Whitefield: 'Motifs and Techniques of Celtic Filigree: Are they Original?', *Ireland and Insular Art*, ed. M. Ryan (Dublin, 1987)

E. Frey: *The Kris* (Singapore, 1988)

S. La Niece: 'White Inlays in Anglo-Saxon Jewellery', *Science and Archaeology: Glasgow 1987*, ed. E. A. Slater and J. A. Tate, Brit. Archaeol. Rep., S 196 (Oxford, 1988), pp. 235–45

R. Murakami, S. Niiyama and M. Kitada: 'Characterisation of the Black Surface on a Copper Alloyed by Traditional Japanese Surface Treatment', *Abstracts of the IIC Congress. The Conservation of Far Eastern Art: Kyoto, 1988*, pp. 13–136

M. R. Notis: 'The Japanese Alloy *Shakudo*: Its History and Its Patination', *The Beginning of the Use of Metals and Alloys*, ed. R. Maddin (Cambridge, MA, 1988), pp. 315–27

J. Lang and B. Ager: 'Swords of the Anglo-Saxon and Viking Period in the British Museum', *Weapons and Warfare in Anglo-Saxon England*, ed. S. Chadwick Hawkes, Oxford University Committee on Archaeology, xxi (Oxford, 1989), pp. 85–123

Pewter: A Celebration of the Craft, 1200–1700 (exh. cat. by P. R. G. Hornsby, R. Weinstein and R. F. Homer, London, Mus. London, 1989)

J. H. Frantz and D. Schorsch: 'Egyptian Red Gold', *Archaeomaterials*, iv (1990), pp. 133–52

S. La Niece: 'Silver Plating on Copper, Bronze and Brass', *Antiqua. J.*, lxx/1 (1990), pp. 102–14 [A]

——: 'Japanese Polychrome Metalwork', *Archaeometry '90*, ed. A. Hauptmann, E. Pernicka and G. Wagner (Basle, 1990), pp. 87–94 [B]

J. V. S. Megaw and M. R. Megaw: *The Basse-Yutz Find*, Soc. Antiqua. London Res. Rep., xlvi (London, 1990)

W. Rostoker and B. Bronson: *Pre-industrial Iron*, Archaeomaterials Monograph, 1 (Philadelphia, 1990)

N. Whitefield: 'Round Wire in the Early Middle Ages', *Jewel. Stud.*, iv (1990), pp. 13–28

P. T. Craddock: 'A Short History of the Patination of Bronze', *Why Fakes Matter*, ed. M. Jones (London, 1992)

L. Binnie: 'Special Finishes on Non-ferrous Metals at the National Maritime Museum', *Metal Plating and Patination*, ed. S. La Niece and P. T. Craddock (London, 1993), pp. 148–54

W. Bray: 'Techniques of Gilding and Surface Enrichment in Pre-Hispanic America', *Metal Plating and Patination*, ed. S. La Niece and P. T. Craddock (London, 1993), pp. 182–91, pl. 16.1

P. T. Craddock and Giumlia-Mair: '*Hsmn Km* Corinthian Bronze and *Shakudo*', *Metal Plating and Patination*, ed. S. La Niece and P. T. Craddock (London, 1993), pp. 101–27

B. Deppert-Lippitz: 'L'Opus interrasile des orfèvres romains', *Outils et ateliers d'orfèvres des temps anciens*, ed. C. Elvère, Antiquités Nationales, ii (Paris, 1993), pp. 69–73

S. La Niece and P. T. Craddock, eds: *Metal Plating and Patination* (London, 1993)

N. D. Meeks: 'Surface Characterization of Tinned Bronze', *Metal Plating and Patination*, ed. S. La Niece and P. T. Craddock (London, 1993), pp. 247–75

R. Murakami: 'Japanese Traditional Alloys', *Metal Plating and Patination*, ed. S. La Niece and P. T. Craddock (London, 1993), pp. 85–94

J. Ogden: 'Aesthetic and Technical Considerations Regarding the Colour and Texture of Ancient Goldwork', *Metal Plating and Patination*, ed. S. La Niece and P. T. Craddock (London, 1993), pp. 39–49

S. Stronge and P. T. Craddock: '*Bidri* Ware of India', *Metal Plating and Patination*, ed. S. La Niece and P. T. Craddock (London, 1993), pp. 135–47

W. Wayman and P. T. Craddock: '*Wu Tong*, a Neglected Chinese Decorative Technology', *Metal Plating and Patination*, ed. S. La Niece and P. T. Craddock (London, 1993), pp. 128–34

VI. Conservation.

With metalwork, as with other art objects, the aim of any conservation treatment must be to enhance the appearance of the object and to arrest its physical or chemical decay, while causing as little irreversible change as possible. The purpose of this section is to give a general outline of the more common conservation treatments, so the principles of these methods can be understood, but not to provide specific instructions for the reader to follow. The conservation of metalwork is a specialized field requiring great skill and long training, so professional advice should be sought in most cases.

When considering the appropriate treatment for a metal object the conservator may have to take into account conflicting priorities. If, for example, damaged metalwork has to be reshaped or badly corroded iron conserved, it may be necessary to anneal the embrittled metal by heating to red heat (*see* §I, 1 above). This, however, will erase much, if not all, of the original metallographic structure, which often provides a unique record of how the metal was fashioned. The nature of the corrosion and its penetration into the metal along the grain boundaries may also provide the only evidence of an object's antiquity, thus its removal will make any future scientific authentication difficult, if not impossible.

There are a number of useful guides for the layman on the care and preservation of antique metalwork, including Plowden and Halahan (1987) and Drayman-Weisser (1992), both books devoted to the general care and maintenance of collectibles and art objects. There are more specific works, such as Browning (1987) on repair, Bradley (1990) on storage and handling and Ashurst and Ashurst (1988) on the conservation and maintenance of architectural metalwork. Some earlier books on the care of antiques that include sections on metalwork should be approached with great caution, as the treatments recommended can be drastic, involving, for example, the total removal of patina by chemical means that is not only irreversible but also potentially ruinous to the whole object. Earlier conservation methods were often intended to restore the original appearance of the object as fully as possible, thus leading to over-restoration. Finally, some of the recommended treatments are dangerous to both the objects and the operators, since they involve procedures and chemicals that should be used only by trained personnel in a fully equipped laboratory. For the specialist the classic textbook on conservation, by Werner and Plenderleith (1971), is now outdated and replaced by more modern texts, such as Cronyn (1990) and articles in *Studies in Conservation*.

Archaeological conservation is covered by Dowman (1970) and by Leigh (1972), both of which contain sections on metals.

1. Cleaning. 2. Repair. 3. Replating. 4. Storage and display.

1. CLEANING. There is considerable difference in approach to the treatment of ancient and more recent metalwork. Even a badly damaged and corroded piece of ancient metalwork is of sufficient art-historical and financial value to justify its conservation, whereas a more recent piece in a similar condition would be worthless. Ancient metalwork may also have been buried or exposed to prolonged environmental attack.

It is common knowledge that metal objects tarnish when their surfaces are attacked by air and moisture.

14. Bull Cup from Enkomi, Cyprus, c. 1400 BC, conserved by the British Museum, London: (top) the cup as excavated, the silver covered with corrosion products; (centre) radiograph disclosing gold and possibly niello inlay under corrosion products; (bottom) the cup after treatment and restoration (Nicosia, Cyprus Museum)

Normally, an oxide is formed initially, and, if it is left for long enough, a more stable mineral may follow: a carbonate, chloride or sulphide, depending on the metal and the environment. This is the process of tarnishing, patination or corrosion. The choice of terminology is to some extent a question of degree but also of desirability: if the mineralization is visually enhancing it is likely to be called a patina, but if disfiguring, tarnish or corrosion; chemically they are similar. Although the corrosion on an ancient piece and the tarnish on a more recent piece are essentially part of the same process, they require quite different conservation treatments.

(i) Removal of corrosion. Often the patinated surface is desirable and should be retained, for example on an ancient Chinese bronze or an antique lead garden trough. Sometimes, however, the corrosion is active and unless treated will lead rapidly to the permanent disfigurement and eventual destruction of the object. During a long period in a specific environment (usually underground) the chemical attack on a metal will have reached an equilibrium, and the corrosion will be reasonably stable. When the object is excavated, however, all the conditions of moisture, temperature and oxygen content will change, destroying this equilibrium. Active corrosion may then recommence, attacking fresh metal and causing the old corrosion to flake off. For example, copper and its alloys, when buried in a salty environment, acquire a patina of copper chlorides that are stable, but the patinated or corroded layer also contains more active chloride minerals that can be activated by a change of environment, causing rapid and potentially serious attack on the metal. This is known as bronze disease because at one time it was believed to be caused by micro-organisms.

In general, modern treatments are much less drastic than previous ones. Only the minimum amount of loose and disfiguring corrosion is removed, preferably mechanically rather than chemically, the only exception being low-value coins from archaeological sites. Before the cleaning begins, the possible existence of hidden decoration or inlays buried deeply in heavy corrosion should be checked by careful examination or by X-radiography (see fig. 14; *see also* TECHNICAL EXAMINATION, §VIII, 4). Loose corrosion is usually removed manually with a needle mounted in a wooden handle or mechanically with a low-powered vibro tool. This will reveal the smooth, firmly adhering patina beneath. Active corrosion, however, has to be treated chemically.

With copper and its alloys it is almost impossible to remove the active chlorides from the corrosion layer. Formerly, the rather drastic solution to this problem was to electrochemically reduce the corrosion back to copper metal. This usually, but not always, eliminated the chlorides but left a granular, coppery surface that was unsightly and bore little resemblance to the original. Alternative chemical treatments, for example repeated washing with sodium sesquicarbonate or treating the affected areas locally with silver oxide, were not always completely successful, and the presence of carbonate minerals or silver on the surface could be confusing to future study. The most common approach now is to treat the active areas selectively with sodium benzotriasole, an organic chelating or molecular binding agent. The powdery, light green, active corrosion is removed mechanically, and the remainder is treated with the benzotriasole, which surrounds and deactivates the chloride ions, thereby preventing further attack. More recently treatment with other chemicals, such as diethylene triamine penta acetic acid, has been reported.

Corroded iron presents serious problems in both its conservation and its storage. Ironwork from archaeological deposits is often so badly corroded as to be unrecognizable, and very difficult to treat. In these cases the best course is to X-ray the pieces. The radiograph will often give a good indication of the object's original state and provide a more permanent and scientifically useful record than the badly corroded original object. The usual treatment for less severely corroded iron is to remove the active salts by washing the corroded iron in a sodium sesquicarbonate solution, but active salts may still be present after many weeks. Before storage the treated iron should be fully dried and impregnated with an organic consolidant such as PVA. It should then be kept in dry conditions and inspected regularly.

An alternative treatment is to reduce the corroded iron to metallic iron by heating the object in a stream of hydrogen at red heat (900–1000°C) in a furnace. This is a drastic treatment that largely destroys any remaining original metallographic structure, but at least the metal is saved from further decay. Research by Archer and Barker (1987) has shown that if the temperature is reduced to 350°C (the minimum temperature at which the reaction will take place), the alteration of the metallographic structure is much reduced. Recently success has been reported in treating iron by plasma reduction (Sjøgren and Buchwald, 1991). This novel approach is still under evaluation but is claimed to be permanent, with very few of the side-effects of more drastic methods.

Active corrosion rarely occurs on silver; the principal corrosion product, silver chloride or horn silver, is usually firm, compact and chemically stable. Thus chemical treatment should not be necessary, and mechanical work can be kept to a minimum. The thin, barely perceptible patina that can often be seen on silver recovered from the ground is probably best left untouched, although the object can be polished if necessary (see §(ii) below). Base silver, which has been adulterated with considerable quantities of copper, is often covered with copper corrosion. This can be removed mechanically, though it may be necessary to loosen it with formic acid.

The corrosion products of lead, tin and pewter are generally stable and not unsightly, thus after the removal of any disfiguring loose corrosion, the remainder can be left. Corrosive agents in lead and its alloys can become active, however, especially in the presence of organic acids, such as those found in wood or cardboard (see §4 below), and can be difficult to control. The best treatment for such small items as coins or tokens is often local electro-chemical reduction.

(ii) Removal of tarnish. When the metalwork is basically in sound condition (tarnished but not heavily corroded), the cleaning can often be undertaken by the non-specialist. It is good practice to experiment on a small, inconspicuous area before proceeding to the whole object. Traditionally,

most metalwork was cleaned with a scouring powder of the appropriate fineness, ranging from fine sand for an iron or brass cooking pot to jewellers' rouge (fine iron oxide) for silverware. Modern proprietary metal polishes usually contain a fine abrasive, a mild, often ammonia-based, chemical to remove grease and the thin oxidized layer and an organic medium to inhibit further tarnishing. On soft metals, for example silver, copper or gold alloys, a soft cloth should be used: a scouring pad, even if made of plastic, or a scouring agent must not be used, as they will remove the tarnish but will leave permanent scratches on the metal.

Before cleaning, it is advisable to check carefully if the metalwork has been previously lacquered to prevent tarnish. If so, the object should be washed in warm, soapy water and then immediately dried with a soft towel or tissues. If the lacquer is peeling or badly cracked it can be removed with an organic solvent, for example white spirit, methylated spirit or acetone. These solvents, especially acetone, should be used with care since they could penetrate any organic binders holding joints or inlays. Organic solvents should only be used outdoors or in a well-ventilated room, away from any exposed flame.

On heavier, more mundane pieces, for example window or door furniture and fireplace fittings, heavy tarnish can be removed more vigorously. First, however, the metal should be carefully inspected for any signs of surface treatment. During the 19th century, for example, many fittings were chemically treated to give a fine patina. Arsenic and antimony salts were commonly used on copper alloys, and these impart a grey colour to the surface of the metal beneath the dirt and tarnish. A small, inconspicuous part of the metal should be tested, and, if the presence of deliberate plating or patination is suspected, professional advice should be sought. Files or sandpaper should never be used on metalwork, in any condition, since the long parallel scratches that result are unsightly and almost impossible to remove.

Cast or wrought iron can be quickly and effectively cleaned with a wire brush or buffing wheel. After cleaning it can be lacquered or blackleaded with a graphite-based polish to give a pleasing appearance and some protection against further rusting. If the iron is heavily tarnished, the rust can be softened with a proprietary paraffin-based rust remover and then brushed off with an old toothbrush or possibly wire wool. The surface beneath the rust will be pitted, but this is unavoidable and irreversible.

Heavily tarnished pieces of copper or copper alloy, for example cast brass door furniture, can be satisfactorily cleaned with the appropriate grade of wire wool or buffing wheel, followed by proprietary polishes. An abrasive powder, for example jewellers' rouge, can also be used. Alternatively, an acceptable soft abrasive can be produced by rubbing together two old, soft, red bricks. All these methods should be tried on a test area to ensure that the metal is not seriously scratched.

The tarnish on silver can be safely and conveniently removed with any of the proprietary cleaners. Heavy tarnish, often caused by long exposure to salt or such sulphur-rich compounds as egg or vinegar, can be removed with Silver Dip. It was a common practice to emphasise the engraved decoration on silver with niello (*see* §IV, 4 above), which is black. This must not be mistaken for dirt. Lead, tin and pewter are generally too soft for abrasive cleaning, but the patina is usually desirable. Old paint, provided it is not original, should be removed with a chemical stripper.

2. REPAIR. The repair of a damaged or deformed piece should only be undertaken by a professional conservator. Apart from the aesthetic implications, extensive repair can seriously damage or even destroy vital metallographic evidence of how and when the object was made, as well as evidence of authenticity. Badly deformed sheet-metal can be hammered back to shape, but it may be necessary to anneal it first by heating it to red heat. Over long periods of time, sheet-metal gradually becomes more brittle, partly as a result of internal corrosion but sometimes through changes in the metallographic structure. This is especially true of silver. Thus, a thin sheet of ancient silver can be as brittle as eggshell and will certainly have to be annealed before reshaping. This would remove all traces of the original metallographic structure, as well as endangering any plating, inlays or soldered joints.

New repairs or additions can be welded or soldered, but original solders or plating can be damaged in the process. It is often better to use a reversible organic adhesive. If the object is badly broken, the fragments can be attached to a clear plastic support. This might seem an unsatisfactory repair, but it is preferable to a badly executed metallurgical join that could destroy the aesthetic, scientific and commercial value of the object.

A new repair or addition may stand out against the rest of the object but can be disguised by the use of sulphur-rich chemicals on the fresh surface or by infilling with suitably coloured waxes or resins. Patinated surfaces, because of their generally variegated nature, can easily be treated to disguise a join, but this is more difficult on clean, polished surfaces. The disguise of a modern repair is a contentious issue, since the boundary between aesthetic 'tidying up' and deceptive, possibly even criminal, concealment is not always clear. Certainly, any new work that is not visible when the object is on display (e.g. the inside of a vessel) should be left untreated, so that even a cursory inspection will reveal the new work.

3. REPLATING. Replating is another contentious subject in the conservation of metalwork, especially when the technique employed is different from that originally used on the object. The electroplating of old Sheffield plate, for example, restores a silver surface but covers the remaining authentic plating and produces a much whiter surface than the original layer of Sterling silver. Simple gilding and silvering kits are also available: the piece is dipped in a plating solution, and a thin layer of gold or silver is deposited on the surface. These treatments are cheap and fairly harmless, but the results are disappointing, since the plating only approximates to the original colour, and the texture is completely wrong. Moreover, the plated layer is very thin and wears off quickly.

4. STORAGE AND DISPLAY. The conditions under which metalwork should be stored and displayed are not as critical as for many other materials, but some precautions are necessary, especially with patinated metalwork, where active corrosion could recommence. Corrosion is promoted by high humidity, and thus metalwork should be stored in dry conditions. Even if sound, metalwork should not be left for long periods in an atmosphere above 55% relative humidity, but where there is evidence of active corrosion the RH should not exceed 45%. As with all materials, a stable environment is desirable but rarely completely attainable, especially in an enclosed space, for example a closed display case. During the day the case will warm up (especially if exposed to sunlight) and the RH drop, but at night the temperature will drop and the RH rise.

Metals are not affected by light, and thus any illumination can be used. In general metals are not at risk at normal temperatures, though tin can decay if left for prolonged periods at a low temperature. This phenomenon, known as 'tin pest', theoretically occurs at 13.2°C, when the metal begins to turn to a grey powder, but in practice tin can survive much lower temperatures for a considerable time before any disintegration takes place.

Since metals are generally reactive they are susceptible to chemical attack. Thus a vulcanized rubber flooring, which gives off volatile sulphur compounds, should not be used in a room in which silver or copper alloys are kept. Lead is susceptible to attack by organic acids: tannic acid from poorly seasoned wood, particularly oak, can have a ruinous effect, especially if the ventilation is poor; lead or pewter medals, for example, stored in an oak cabinet, could quickly suffer irreparable damage. Other woods are not so dangerous, provided they are fully seasoned and sealed and the cabinet kept well ventilated, but it is probably best not to use wooden storage cabinets for lead. Some adhesives used in the manufacture of cardboard also contain volatile organic acids.

All metalwork should be examined periodically for signs of excessive tarnish or fresh corrosion. This is especially important for small items (e.g. coins) that are likely to be stored out of sight in confined spaces, where local environmental changes could cause serious problems. A protective coating greatly reduces the rate of tarnishing, especially in urban environments, and thereby reduces the damage done by frequent polishing. A clear lacquer or silicone wax can be carefully applied to the surface with either a soft brush or an aerosol to avoid unsightly brush-marks and to ensure as complete a coverage as possible. Inevitably, however, some pinholes will remain, and eventually the layer will harden and crack. It is not recommended that corroded metalwork be lacquered, as the corrosion can proceed beneath the lacquer. The shiny appearance thereby given to the corrosion is also unsightly.

See also CONSERVATION AND RESTORATION, §II.

BIBLIOGRAPHY
E. A. Dowman: *Conservation in Field Archaeology* (London, 1970)
H. J. Plenderleith and A. E. A. Werner: *The Conservation of Antiquities and Works of Art* (Oxford, 1971)
D. Leigh and others: *First Aid for Finds: A Practical Guide for Archaeologists* (Southampton, 1972)
R. F. Tylecote and J. W. Black: 'The Effect of Hydrogen Reduction on the Properties of Ferrous Materials', *Stud. Conserv.*, xxv (1980), pp. 87–96

B. D. Barker: 'Conservation of Ferrous Archaeological Artefacts', *Indust. Corrosion*, iii/2 (1985), pp. 9–13

P. J. Archer and B. D. Barker: 'Phase Changes Associated with the Hydrogen Reduction Conservation Process for Ferrous Artifacts', *J. Hist. Metal. Soc.*, xxi/2 (1987), pp. 86–91

C. Browning: *The Care and Repair of Antique Metalware* (London, 1987)

A. Plowden and F. Halahan: *Looking after Antiques* (London, 1987)

J. Ashurst and N. Ashurst: *Metals*, iv of *Practical Buildings Conservation* (London, 1988)

M. Gilberg: 'History of Bronze Disease and its Treatment', *Early Advances in Conservation*, ed. V. Daniels, BM Occas. Pap., lxv (London, 1988), pp. 59–70

S. Bradley, ed.: 'A Guide to the Storage, Exhibition and Handling of Antiquities', *Ethnographia and Pictorial Art*, BM Occas. Pap., lxvi (London, 1990)

J. M. Cronyn: *Elements of Archaeological Conservation* (London, 1990)

A. Sjøgren and V. F. Buchwald: 'Hydrogen Plasma Reactions in a DC Mode for the Conservation of Iron Meteorites and Antiquities', *Stud. Conserv.*, xxxvi (1991), pp. 161–71

T. Drayman-Weisser: 'Metal Objects', *Caring for your Collections*, ed. A. W. Schultz (New York, 1992), pp. 108–21

P. T. CRADDOCK

Metalcut [Fr. *gravure sur métal*; Ger. *Metallschnitt*]. Type of relief print produced by cutting a metal plate rather than a wooden block; the term is also applied to the printmaking process. The technique was favoured for the metal's durability over wood. Copper, brass or lead plates were engraved in relief with a burin or punch, producing a result that often combined black-line engraving, white-line engraving and stipple. Metalcut was superseded by RELIEF ETCHING, and the technique was more or less abandoned after 1500.

1. MATERIALS AND TECHNIQUES. There are two principal methods employed by the metal-engraver to fix an image on the plate and print it: black line and white line. The former, also known as interrasile, derived from goldsmithing practised in the second half of the 15th century. In a black-line metalcut, as in wood-engraving, the motif to be printed in black is not hollowed out but retained, the areas around it being cut away, so forming a relief, across which the ink passes, rather than the incised lines (*see* PRINTS, §III, 1(ii)). White-line metalcut is the opposite of wood-engraving, which gives a black image on a white ground, the black being the strokes that make up the drawing in relief and the white corresponding to the empty spaces in the intervals between lines. In white-line metalcuts a burin is used to cut away the parts that constitute the image and that are to appear white when printed . The whites are the active element of the drawing. The image itself stands out against a black background (the relief), the only part that is inked, and which, when printed, is sometimes set off by a scattering of white dots. This effect, known as *criblé* or dotted, is obtained with various punches. The technique seems to derive from one described by the monk Theophilus in *De diversis artibus* (12th century), when he discussed the work of chasing metal, *opus interrasile*. Such work, which originated with metal chasing and damascening, was subsequently meant to be inlaid with metal. White-line engraving (white stroke on black background) is easier to obtain than black-line (in relief).

The spectacular effect of black–white contrast, looking more decorative than graphic, would seem to suggest that some plates were intended for decoration rather than for printing, a transparent glaze reducing the contrasts between light and shadow. In addition, inscriptions were sometimes engraved on the copper the right way round, appearing in reverse in the print itself. In the vast majority of cases, however, the engraver attempted to get all the elements of the engraving to appear the right way round in the proof, and it would be reasonable to suppose that the plate was therefore meant to be printed. The delicate method of inking required for metalcuts rapidly led to the process being rejected. They were also very limited in the extent to which they could represent depth and different planes. Moreover, the image lacked the luminous white background (of the paper) so precious for any work of graphic art.

2. HISTORY. The history and development of metalcut techniques are very closely related. The term *criblé* is usually applied to the work of all the principal masters and to works combining various methods of engraving. It is practically impossible to distinguish between every individual method and to write a separate history for each. More than 700 metalcuts are extant. Their subject-matter is essentially religious. Their dimensions vary from folio to medium size. Most are duodecimo. Certain series comprise small-scale engravings that have been stuck into prayerbooks as illustrations. Metalcuts are found in the Rhineland, the Netherlands and Basle and around Lake Constance. The first examples appeared in the Upper Rhineland and were stylistically close to contemporary copperplate engravings although distinct from them in their decorative effect. The works may be grouped together (see Schreiber and Hind) by studio, the studio being run by a master distinguished by his style, technique, monogram or stamp. The Monogrammist D (*fl* 1446–65), claimed by France, the Netherlands and Germany, was perhaps an engraver from the region of Bolcholt or perhaps Bernard Milnet de Donai. He was undoubtedly one of the first to use white line. His signature, a Gothic D in a heart and the whole contained in an escutcheon, appears on two engravings, a *Last Judgement* (s. 2407) and a *Resurrection* (s. 2375). On the proofs the letter and image are reversed, which classes them with several other plates attributed to him as works meant for decoration. The same hand is found in the *Annunciation with the Unicorn* (also called the *Mystery of the Incarnation*, s. 2481) without the monogram, in which the lettering and image appear the right way round.

The Master of the Stoeger Passion, active in the Upper Rhineland c. 1455–65, produced a complete series of 20 prints of the *Passion* and seven of the *Joys of the Virgin* (Munich, Kön. Hof- & Staatsbib.; s. 2500), also known as the *Pfister Passion*. These fragments illustrate a little book printed in movable type; there is no indication of date or place of printing, but the work may have been printed by Albert Pfister (*fl* 1454–70) in Bamberg *c.* 1460. Several prints from this series exist elsewhere, and there must have been several editions, as well as some copies. The plates must have been fixed on wood, for the engravings all bear the mark of nail holes. They were made with a stamp and burin. The *Stoeger Passion* may well have been the first typographic book to be illustrated, only five years

Metalcut of the *Annunciation, Visitation* and *Nativity*, attributed to the Master of the Borders Decorated with the Fathers of the Church, 1466: (left) positive impression, 276×193 mm; (right) negative impression, 273×188 mm (Paris, Bibliothèque Nationale)

after the 42-line Bible (Mainz, *c.* 1455) of Johann Gutenberg. These metalcuts are characterized by their backgrounds decorated with arabesques, foliage or tapestry-like motifs. The more prolific Master of the Aix Annunciation, working in the Upper Rhineland *c.* 1460–70, used tapestry backgrounds and secular subject-matter, rare in this type of print, as in the *Battle of the Sexes* (s. 2763). Five engravings have been identified by his stamp, a coat of arms with clubs, but he was undoubtedly the author of several others that do not carry it. The Master of the Reticulated Background, active in the area between Basle and Strasbourg in the last quarter of the 15th century, employed a very decorative fishnet background, with two columns framing its subject and scrolls of foliage ending in an ogival arch.

The Master at Arms (*fl c.* 1470–80) probably worked in Cologne, as indicated by the escutcheon stamped on his work. This city was a major centre for the goldsmith's trade, and numerous books from Cologne are illustrated with *criblé* engravings. Several engravings can be attributed to him. Also active in Cologne, the Master of the Borders Decorated with Fathers of the Church (*fl c.* 1470–80) produced metalcuts surrounded with various types of border, among which are ribboned clouds, stars and medallions with symbols of the Evangelists and the four Fathers of the Church. The Master of Jesus at Bethany (*fl c.* 1465–85), also called the Master of the Anchor, from a stamp interpreted as being from the anchor studio, probably also came from the Cologne region. There is an escutcheon with an anchor, sometimes accompanied by an escutcheon with a compass, on engravings in very different styles and of uneven quality. Several derive their inspiration from the Master of the Berlin Passion. As well as the masters mentioned above, there are the Monogrammist I, the Master of St Catherine (*fl c.* 1460–75), and three copper plates, still preserved, which constitute extremely interesting documents for the study of techniques and the interpretation of metalcuts. One of the plates, of *St John and St Paul* (Paris, Louvre; see A. Blum: *Les Origines du papier, de l'imprimerie, de la gravure* (Paris, 1935), p. 182), is engraved with a burin in relief and bears inscriptions (articles of the creed in Latin) engraved on two banderoles. A date of 1423 (a later addition) appears at the top, as do two holes from pins with which it had been fixed. From its style, the plate may illustrate the work of the Monogrammist D or come from the studio of the Cologne Master at Arms.

The second plate, depicting the *Annunciation, Visitation* and *Nativity* (1466; Paris, Bib. N.; s. 2865; see fig.), is one of the best examples of engraving in relief on metal. It shows the complexity of these techniques, the difficulty of seeing them as a group when studying them individually, and the different interpretations that can be given them. It is copper, engraved mostly in *criblé*, with the burin and the punch, and has been attributed to the Master of the Borders Decorated with Fathers of the Church (Schreiber). The inscription in the banderole appears in reverse on the copper, and the right way round on the proof. The engraver had therefore envisaged an impression on paper, and the plate was not meant mainly for decoration. The plate has been printed in positive and negative, the positive showing the mark of various types of punch used to obtain decorative backgrounds or the effect of clothing in various materials. The punch-work is broken up by strokes cut across it: the white areas are obtained with the burin, and the empty spaces are hollowed out, in the faces particularly. The burin is used in single strokes to trace the folds of the angel's robe or in crosshatching to give half-tones.

The third plate, *St Bathildis* (s. 2564), a French work, has a xylographic text. The copper, with double borderline, is cut like a piece of wood, hollowed out and fixed to a piece of wood of which the lower part bears an inscription of three lines of woodcut; a special technique has been used for the folds, executed by a black line echoed by a white line.

The difficult techniques of metalcut did not last beyond the 15th century, when the punch was laid aside, and metal engraving in relief came close to champlevé. The technique became more simplified, and artists abandoned gold-smiths' techniques for others closer to drawing: copper-plate engraving and etching.

BIBLIOGRAPHY

Theophilus: *De diversis artibus* (12th century); ed. J. G. Hawthorne and C. S. Smith (1963)
W. L. Schreiber: *Manuel de la gravure sur bois et sur métal au XVe siècle*, 5 vols (Berlin, 1891–1910) [s.]
H. Bouchot: *Les Deux Cents Incunables xylographiques du Département des Estampes* (Paris, 1903)
P. Gusman: *La Gravure sur bois et d'épargne sur métal du XIVe au XXe siècle* (Paris, 1916)
——: 'La Gravure en taille d'épargne sur métal', *Byblis*, iii (1922), pp. 118–24
A. Blum: 'Les Débuts de la gravure sur métal', *Gaz. B.-A.*, n. s. 6, vi (1931), pp. 65–77
A. M. Hind: *An Introduction to a History of Woodcut with a Detailed Survey of Work Done in the Fifteenth Century*, 2 vols (London, 1935/R London and New York, 1963)
Fifteenth-century Woodcuts and Metalcuts from the National Gallery of Art (exh. cat. by R. S. Field, Washington, DC, N.G.A., 1966)

GISÈLE LAMBERT

Metalpoint. Drawing instrument (the forerunner of the pencil) made from a small, pointed metal tip, usually of lead, silver, copper or gold, encased in a wooden holder. Metalpoint can be used on various supports, including paper, parchment, wood and ivory, but the surface usually requires a special preparation or ground for the metal to leave a mark. Paper, which is most commonly used, is coated with an opaque white or tinted ground composed of lead-white powdered bone, pigment and gum-water. Several layers are applied. The natural tone for the ground is off-white, but it can be coloured with any pigment. The ground has to be slightly granular for the metalpoint stylus to rub off and must have sufficient 'tooth' to retain the metal particles. The preferred metals are lead and silver. Lead produces a dull, flat grey mark, not unlike that of a pencil. Its popularity was probably due to the fact that the

Silverpoint drawing from a sketchbook by Albrecht Dürer: *Portrait of a Man Aged 24 with a View of St Michael's, Antwerp*, on pinkish prepared paper, 133×194 mm, 1520 (Chantilly, Musée Condé, Château de Chantilly)

paper does not have to be prepared beforehand. If it is not, the leadpoint gives a soft, pleasing line, but on a prepared ground the mark tends to be a little coarse. The soft blue-grey tonality of leadpoint darkens as the lead oxidizes. Another drawback to leadpoint is that the tip blunts quite quickly and needs frequent reshaping. Silver was a more popular medium, perhaps because the point shows no appreciable wear for some time. It produces a delicate silver-grey line, which does not smudge, but this eventually tarnishes, taking on more definition as it gradually oxidizes to a warm brown-black.

1. HISTORY. Although a metal STYLUS had been used to inscribe surfaces since Classical times, metalpoint was employed for drawing only from the medieval period. It was in frequent use from the late 14th century up to the early 17th and was particularly favoured in the Renaissance period in Italy (see BELLINI, (1), fig. 4; DRAWING, fig. 2; and LEONARDO DA VINCI, fig. 7), the Netherlands (see REMBRANDT VAN RIJN, fig. 2) and Germany, where many highly coloured grounds were used. Until the development of the graphite pencil, most sketches and preliminary drawings for paintings were carried out in metalpoint, brush or charcoal. Occasionally metalpoint was used for the whole drawing, but its value was limited because the tonal and textural values were so restricted; for this reason, white lead was often used to highlight silverpoint drawings. Also, the drawn line could not be greatly varied, nor could it be erased without scraping away the ground. However, metalpoint did allow the artist to prepare a meticulous but faint underdrawing, which would be easily obscured by pen and ink, black chalk, graphite or thin layers of paint. It was also used for working drawings on primed panels, which would be scraped down and recoated as necessary. Metalpoint was especially suitable for pocket sketchbooks. The pages could be prepared in advance with tinted grounds, and the metalpoint stylus was a conveniently portable implement before the invention of the lead pencil. On his journey to the Netherlands in 1520–21 Dürer took a sketchbook (dispersed) in which he drew portraits, town- and landscapes and other subjects in silverpoint (see fig.). With the developments in oil painting of the 16th century, preparatory drawing with metalpoint became impractical. Paintings became larger and freer, and chalk was more suitable for the preparatory stages since it could be used on a larger scale and allowed for a greater range of tonality and texture. In the late 19th century, however, there was a brief revival of metalpoint drawing, particularly in England by such artists as Frederic Leighton and William Strang. Its appeal then lay in its ability to emulate the effects of photography and etching and in its association with the Renaissance masters. In the 20th century it was rarely used.

2. CONSERVATION. Metalpoint drawings are easily damaged and should be kept in the best possible environment for their preservation. Atmospheric pollution is dangerous if lead white has been used in the highlights or in the ground. Hydrogen sulphide gas, which is always present in traces in the air, will blacken the lead white, causing disfigurement to the drawing. This oxidization can be reversed by treating the drawing with hydrogen peroxide, a gentle bleach that converts the black lead sulphide to a colourless lead sulphate, allowing the white below the surface to show through. The image is therefore restored to some degree of normality. Excessive light is also hazardous. Visible light can fade many pigments and dyes, and ultraviolet radiation can damage the binding agents within the paper and in the prepared ground. Because paper is a moisture-containing material, it will expand and contract with changes in humidity; the prepared ground of a metalpoint drawing is therefore in danger of cracking if the paper is allowed to flex in an uncontrolled and unmonitored environment. Because of the surface fragility of metalpoint drawings, careful handling, mounting and framing are also important.

For further conservation guidelines see also PAPER, §VI.

BIBLIOGRAPHY

C. Cennini: Il libro dell'arte (c. 1390); Eng. trans. and notes by D. V. Thompson jr as The Craftsman's Handbook: 'Il libro dell'arte' (New Haven, 1933/R New York, 1954)

G. Vasari: Vite (1550, rev. 2/1568); Eng. trans. of the introduction prefixed to the Vite by L. S. Maclehose as Vasari on Technique (London, 1907/R New York, 1960)

J. Meder: Die Handzeichnung (Vienna, 1919); Eng. trans. by W. Ames as The Mastery of Drawing, 2 vols (New York, 1978)

J. Watrous: The Craft of Old-Master Drawings (Madison, 1957/R 1975)

P. Goldman: Looking at Drawings: A Guide to Technical Terms (London, 1979)

Drawing: Technique and Purpose (exh. cat. by S. Lambert, London, V&A, 1981)

C. James and others: Manuale per la conservazione e il restauro di disegni e stampe antichi (Florence, 1991)

SHIRLEY MILLIDGE

Metamorphism. Term applied to the process by which one shape is transformed into another, especially in SURREALISM and other tendencies in 20th-century art. The concept of metamorphosis, encompassing literary sources from Ovid through Dante Alighieri to Johann Wolfgang von Goethe, was revived in the early 19th century. For the ancient Greeks, as outlined by Ovid, it concerned the miraculous process of the transformation from the world of nature to another sphere of existence; in Goethe's reformulation of metamorphosis in terms of the evolution of organic life (1790), however, it means a law of formation. Being based on the principles of 'polarity' and 'enhancement', it rules the transformation of nature and defines art as an enhanced 'second nature'.

Themes relating to such concepts of metamorphosis were dealt with by 19th-century artists in the guise of transformation myths, such as that of Apollo and Daphne, and of Narcissus and Pygmalion, all of which emphasized moments of self-discovery. By the late 19th century, in Symbolism and especially in the representation of organic formative processes in Art Nouveau, such ideas began to be expressed in a more purely visual form. In Cubism different types of objects, and even human figures and inanimate objects, were represented as interchangeable and in that sense as undergoing transformation from one state into another. A more purely psychological interpretation of such processes was proposed in Pittura Metafisica, especially in the use of mannequins as stand-ins for people.

With Surrealism, metamorphism became both a subject and a creative principle allied to other processes and strategies such as biomorphism, automatism, frottage and decalcomania. Their understanding of metamorphosis, spurred by Sigmund Freud's theory of dreams, by Franz Kafka's short story *Die Verwandlung* (1915) and by André Breton's call for a modern mythology, seems also to have been based on models in the ancient Greek philosopher Heraclitus, the North African philosopher Apuleius, the hermetic tradition and Friedrich Nietzsche. It was applied both to the subject-matter and to the overt imagery of a painting such as the *Metamorphosis of Narcissus* (1934; London, Tate) by Salvador Dalí and to the more abstract concerns of artists such as André Masson and Joan Miró. Conceived by the Surrealists as a central aesthetic category, metamorphosis attested to the social power of the individual imagination and to the transcendence of the concept of the marvellous over reason. In the wake of Surrealism, metamorphism was also applied to abstract painting and sculpture, especially by artists working from the 1940s to the early 1960s, such as Fritz Winter, Karl-Otto Götz, Bernhard Schultze and Hann Trier, who created dynamic and even violent images of organic growth as a reaction against realism.

BIBLIOGRAPHY

C. Heselhaus: 'Metamorphose-Dichtungen und Metamorphose-Anschauungen', *Euphorion*, xlvii/2 (1953), pp. 121–46
Metamorphosen: Surrealismus heute (exh. cat., Leverkusen, Schloss Morsbroich, 1965)
Métamorphose de l'objet: Art et anti-art, 1910–1970 (exh. cat., Brussels, Pal. B.-A., 1971)
U. M. Schneede: *Malerei des Surrealismus* (Cologne, 1973)
Natur-Gestalt in der Verwandlung: Baum—Fels—Figur (exh. cat., W. Berlin, N.G.; E. Berlin, Altes Mus.; 1978)
W. Chadwick: *Myth in Surrealist Painting, 1929–1939* (Ann Arbor, 1980)
C. Lichtenstern: *Metamorphose in der Kunst des 19. und 20. Jahrhunderts*, 2 vols (Weinheim, 1990–92)

CHRISTA LICHTENSTERN

Metaphysical painting. *See* PITTURA METAFISICA.

Metapontion [Lat. Metapontum; now Metaponto]. Site of ancient Greek colony in Lucania (now Basilicata), southern Italy, on a flat coastal terrace on the Gulf of Taras. The city was founded in the second half of the 7th century BC by Achaian settlers, and it flourished during the second half of the 6th century BC and the early 5th. In this period most of its public buildings were erected, and in the extensive *chora* (territory) many single-family farmsteads were established. During the later 5th century BC and the 4th Metapontion declined, though there was a revival in the second half of the 4th century BC, and its port still functioned in late Roman times. Metapontion has been the most fully studied of the western Greek colonies in terms of its architecture, owing to the excavations conducted since 1964 by the Archaeological Superintendency and the German Archaeological Institute in Rome, the extensive finds from which are on display in the Museo Archeologico Nazionale, Metaponto.

1. ARCHITECTURE. Many architectural aspects of Metapontion were highly innovative. Its grid plan was among the earliest (*c.* 550 BC), its surviving 4th-century BC pattern of streets following the earlier, Archaic ones. Public and residential areas were divided by one of a series of main thoroughfares (*plateiai*) running north-west to south-east. Only the eastern third of the city has been excavated, but this includes the main sanctuary, agora, theatral/assembly buildings and industrial quarter.

The two largest temples in the urban sanctuary, Temple A (?Apollo) and Temple B (?Hera), both in the Doric order, were begun in the early 6th century BC. Their plans influenced that of the better preserved 'Basilica' at Paestum. However, in their final, elongated form of shortly after 550 BC, they in turn show Sicilian influence, and they have the same orientation as the newly laid out city. Earlier than both temples is the first phase (C1) of an *oikos* (shrine) with terracotta friezes (see fig. below). Terracotta revetments from Metapontion constitute the most complete available record of the evolution of temple entablatures in the 6th and 5th centuries BC, and examples discovered in 1830 (Paris, Bib. N.) provided the first clear knowledge of polychromy in ancient Greek architecture. Outside the city, the Doric Tavole Palatine or Temple of Hera (*c.* 525 BC) has a plan that anticipates, in its system of proportions, the Temple of Athena at Paestum. It is one of the earliest Greek temples with uniform intercolumniation on façade and flank. The Ionic Temple D (*c.* 470 BC) was the last large-scale building in the urban sanctuary. Both its plan and unique decorative elements are well-preserved.

The series of structures that occupied the eastern end of the agora—two stone *ekklesiasteria* (assembly halls; phase I, *c.* 550 BC; II, *c.* 475 BC; these were preceded by a wooden structure of the late 7th century BC) and the theatre (second half of the 4th century BC)—was truly revolutionary. The circular stone wall of the first phase of the *ekklesiasterion* (h. 3.2 m, diam. 62 m) enclosed the earthen fill from which an auditorium of concentric rows was fashioned. No public meeting place of comparable size at such an early date is known elsewhere in the Greek world, and no others stand without reliance on naturally sloping ground. An *orchestra* at the centre was approached by two stone-lined *dromoi* (passageways; w. 7.5 m) aligned east–west along the circle's diameter. In the second phase the slope of the auditorium was increased, and the *orchestra* was enclosed by a rectangular retaining wall with a long axis corresponding to the *dromoi*. The building's capacity of 7500–8000 persons suggests that it was not used exclusively as a meeting-place for citizens; it may also have been used for choral performances. The building that replaced it in the 4th century BC was also free-standing but was indisputably a theatre. Its auditorium was semicircular (diam. *c.* 80 m), as in Roman theatres, and, together with a stage building, it seems to have formed a single unit, again anticipating Roman design. It was also the first theatre designed to be seen from all angles. The exterior façade of the retaining wall was articulated by an engaged Doric colonnade masking the stairs to the top of the auditorium. This is among the earliest Greek examples of purely decorative façade architecture, anticipated only by Macedonian tombs.

Extensive excavations in the *chora* have revealed the plans of farmhouses (6th century BC–4th century AD), which provide the principal evidence for the development of Greek rural domestic architecture. The standard structure from the Archaic period onwards comprises parallel rows of rooms, often on two storeys. Courtyards were introduced in the 4th century BC but were not widely used until Roman times.

2. SCULPTURE. The creativity of Metapontine craftsmen is evident from the long series of terracotta figurines, beginning in the late 7th century BC, and the small bronzes that have been found both within and outside the city. Only the larger-scale sculptures, however, will be considered here; and in this case, despite their outstanding quality, the question of originality is far from clear, not least because of their fragmentary condition.

Before the excavations that began in 1964, only two fragmentary marble sculptures were known: a kouros from the area of the Temple of Apollo, the only one from a southern Italian site (c. 500 BC; Potenza, Mus. Archeol. Prov.), and a draped female torso (?mid-5th century BC; Matera, Mus. N. Ridola) from the Temple of Hera (Tavole Palatine). The kouros has been thought to be by a Greek 'island sculptor', but, like the Grammichele Kouros from Sicily (c. 500 BC; Syracuse, Mus. Reg. Archeol.), which it resembles, it may have been executed in the West. The torso of a terracotta kore (original h. 1.3 m, late 6th century BC; Metaponto, Mus. Archaeol. N.), found near Temple D follows the pattern of works from mainland Greece, but the painted designs on its drapery are more ornate. Herodotus (*Histories* IV. xv) recorded the dedication of a statue of *Aristeas* next to one of *Apollo* in an oracular shrine in the agora and observed that the statues were surrounded by a grove of laurel. Gilded bronze laurel leaves were found in the excavation of this temenos. A few fragments of limestone and marble sculptures come from the main urban sanctuary and are probably architectural. The latter include an ornately coiffed female head (?*Artemis*) of extraordinary beauty and originality, a head of a youth and a male torso. All are in the Early Classical 'Severe Style' (c. 480–c. 450 BC) and resemble contemporary work from Akragas and elsewhere in southern Italy and Sicily. The treatment of surface and the details of eyes and hair indicate the influence of bronze sculpture. The limestone fragments (c. 500–c. 480 BC) are not of the same quality. They include the torso of an *Amazon* and were perhaps attached to previously undecorated metopes of an earlier building. Terracotta architectural sculptures include the friezes from the *oikos* C1 (see fig.) which, with those from the sanctuary at San Biagio (c. 600–c. 575 BC;

Metaponto, Mus. Archaeol. N.) in the *chora*, are among the earliest of their kind and form a link between the art of Asia Minor and that of Etruria. In addition, there are two under life-size horses' heads and male torsos from the roof of a temple of c. 500–c. 475 BC. This must have resembled that of the Portonaccio Temple at Veii (*see* ETRUSCAN, fig. 10). Comparable large terracotta horses from roofs have been found at Gela and Locri. A terracotta torso of an archer (?*Herakles*) was found near Temple D. From the urban sanctuary at Metapontion itself and the rural sanctuaries at San Biagio and Pantanello, there are important marble fragments of acrolithic cult statues, a form long considered characteristic of western Greek sculpture.

BIBLIOGRAPHY

D. Adamesteanu: *La Basilicata antica* (Cava dei Tirreni, 1974)
Metaponto: Atti del tredicesimo convegno di studi sulla Magna Grecia: Napoli, 1974
D. Adamesteanu, D. Mertens and F. d'Andria: *Metaponto*, i (Rome, 1980)
D. Mertens and A. de Siena: 'Metaponto: Il teatro–ekklesiasteron', *Boll. A.*, vi/67 (1982), pp. 1–60
B. Chiartano and others: *Metaponto*, ii (Rome, 1983)
D. Mertens: 'Metaponto: Ein neuer Plan des Stadtzentrums', *Archäol. Anz.* (1985), pp. 645–71
J. C. Carter: 'Metapontum: Land, Wealth and Population', *Greek Colonists and Native Populations* (Oxford, 1990)
—: 'Sanctuaries in the *Chora* of Metaponta', *Placing the Gods: Sanctuaries and Sacred Space in Ancient Greece* (Oxford, 1994)

JOSEPH COLEMAN CARTER

Metcalf, Willard Leroy (*b* Lowell, MA, 1 July 1858; *d* New York, 9 March 1925). American painter and illustrator. His formal education was limited, and at 17 he was apprenticed to the painter George Loring Brown of Boston. He was one of the first scholarship students admitted to the school of art sponsored by the Museum of Fine Arts, Boston, and took classes there in 1877 and 1878. After spending several years illustrating magazine articles on the Zuni Indians of New Mexico, he decided to study abroad and in 1883 left for Paris. There he studied at the Académie Julian under Jules Lefebvre and Gustave Boulanger. During the five years he spent in France he became intimately acquainted with the countryside around the villages of Grez-sur-Loing and Giverny. He returned to America in 1888 and in the following spring exhibited oil studies executed in France, England and Africa at the St Botolph Club in Boston (e.g. *Street Scene, Tunis*, 1887; Worcester, MA, A. Mus.).

In 1890 Metcalf settled in New York, working as an illustrator for *Harper's*, *Century Magazine* and *Scribner's*. He taught at the Cooper Union and the Art Students League. In 1897 he drafted a declaration of independence from the Society of Academic Artists and was thenceforth identified—along with John Twachtman, Childe Hassam and William Merritt Chase—as one of the the TEN AMERICAN PAINTERS. He executed two murals in an academic style, *Justice* and the *Banishment of Discord*, for the Appellate Court of New York in 1899. In the early 1900s Metcalf spent the summers working at the artists' colony in Old Lyme, CT. He was strongly influenced by Impressionism, and his works from this period are characterized by loose brushwork and subtle colours. In 1907 *May Night* (1906; Washington, DC, Corcoran Gal. A.) won the first gold medal awarded by the Corcoran Gallery

Metapontion, terracotta frieze representing a procession of divinities, possibly the marriage of Hera, from the *oikos* (C1), h. 310 mm, second quarter of the 6th century BC (Metaponto, Museo Archeologico Nazionale)

of Art. In 1922 he began a series of ambitious large-scale paintings of the New England landscape, including *The Northcountry* (1923; New York, Met.). He was elected a member of the American Academy of Arts and Letters in 1924.

BIBLIOGRAPHY
C. B. Ely: 'Willard L. Metcalf', *A. America*, xiii (1925), pp. 332–6
Willard Leroy Metcalf: A Retrospective (exh. cat. by F. Murphy, Utica, NY, Munson–Williams–Proctor Inst.; Springfield, MA, Mus. F.A.; Manchester, NH, Currier Gal. A.; Chattanooga, TN, Hunter Mus. A.; 1976–7)
E. de Veer and R. Boyle: *Sunlight and Shadows: The Life and Art of Willard L. Metcalf* (New York, 1988)

FRANCIS MURPHY

Metcalfe, Percy (*b* Leeds, 14 Jan 1895; *d* London, 9 Oct 1970). English medallist. He trained at the Leeds School of Art and at the Royal College of Art, London. His first great success came with the British Empire Exhibition of 1924, when his *Wembley Lion* design won the bronze medal. A similar lion's head in profile, also designed by him, featured on one of the medals struck daily during the exhibition as part of the Royal Mint's exhibit. His handling of the planes and the skilful way in which he stripped complex forms to their basic essentials resulted in almost abstract designs, as in his *Industry Commerce* medal, and the success of these and other medals made by him for the exhibition led to a series of public and private commissions. These included medals for the Wembley Exhibition of 1925 (bronze), for the visit of the Prince of Wales to Cape Town in 1925 (silver and bronze) and for the visit of King Fuad I of Egypt to Britain in 1927 (bronze). In 1935 he designed the official commemorative jubilee medal of *George V* and also the jubilee crown reverse. He won the competition for the coinage of the Irish Free State, issued in 1928, with designs featuring eight different animals. Among his British coins was the final version of the 'Thrift' design, first used in 1937 for the nickel-brass threepenny pieces of George VI.

BIBLIOGRAPHY
Vollmer
C. Eimer: 'Sir Robert Johnson, the Mint and Medal Making in Inter-war Britain', *Brit. Numi. J.*, lv (1985), pp. 169–91
——: 'British Medals and their Makers 1900–1950', *The Medal*, xvi (1990), pp. 58–68

PHILIP ATTWOOD

Met de Bles, Herri. *See* BLES, HERRI MET DE.

Meteora. Series of monastic buildings set high (*c.* 180–280 m) on a cluster of precipitous rocks near the village of Kastraki, *c.* 25 km north-west of Trikala in northern Greece. Still the largest monastic site in Greece after Mt Athos, at its 16th-century apogee it contained 13 monasteries and some 20 smaller settlements, of which 7 monasteries survive: the Transfiguration or Great Meteoron, Varlaam, Roussanos (see fig.), Hagios Nikolaos Anapafsas, St Stephen's, Holy Trinity and the Presentation of Christ in the Temple (Ypapantis).

1. History. 2. Architecture. 3. Wall painting. 4. Other arts.

1. HISTORY. Documentary and literary sources for the Meteora's history include the lives and testaments of the monasteries' founders, the *Syngramma istorikon* [Historical discourse] (1521; ex-Varlaam Monastery, Meteora; from 1858) and the donor inscriptions found in the churches.

Meteora, monastery of Roussanos, before 1545, view from the east

It is not known when the Meteora first became a monastic settlement, but by the 12th century anchorites were probably living in cells served by rudimentary chapels in the area around the Doupiani Rock, and by the second half of the century an idiorrhythmic skete (that is, a monastic 'village' with a central church or kyriakon and refectory for use on Sundays and feasts) of Stagoi or Doupiani is recorded as being under the control of the neighbouring Archbishop of Stagoi (now Kalambaka). Another early indication of the community's existence is the foundation *c.* 1200 of the church of the Mother of God (Theotokos) of Doupiani, which served as the skete's kyriakon. More substantial evidence comes from the 14th century with the establishment at Meteora of great monasteries like those on Mt Athos. Among their founders were monks of noble birth such as the Serbian prince John Uroš Palaiologos (1349–1423), who by 1381 had become the monk Joasaph and second founder of the Great Meteoron; Antonios Kantakouzenos, grandson of Emperor John VI Kantakouzenos (*reg* 1347–54) and founder (*c.* 1400) of St Stephen's; the Apsarades family, founders of Varlaam (early 16th century); and others, who obtained privileges for their monasteries from a succession of rulers during the troubled times that led up to the Turkish occupation (1393–1881).

A number of the monastic katholika date to this first period of expansion. In 1366–7 the monk Neilos built the katholikon of the Ascension at the Monastery of the

Presentation; at the Great Meteoron St Athanasios (1305–c. 1380) built a chapel dedicated to the Virgin for his hermit's cell and at the top of the cliff the katholikon of the Transfiguration (1348; rest. 1388); one of his pupils was St Varlaam, who founded the Varlaam Monastery and built a church of the Three Hierarchs (14th century; the present church dates to 1627). In the 15th century the monastery of the Great Meteoron wrested the primacy from the Skete of Stagoi, which was renamed Skete of Meteora. Katholika were built for St Stephen's (early 15th century) and for Holy Trinity (1476), and in 1483 the katholikon of the Great Meteoron was decorated with wall paintings (*see* §3 below).

In the 16th century the Meteora underwent a second period of expansion, and most of the monasteries acquired their present appearance. Like those on MT ATHOS, each had its katholikon and chapels, refectory, kitchen, cells, library and hospital. In 1510 the katholikon of Hagios Nikolaos Anapafsas was built, and in 1527 it was decorated with wall paintings. In 1517 the brothers Nektarios and Theophanes Apsarades from Ioannina settled in the Varlaam Monastery and constructed a new katholikon of All Saints (1542–4; decoration 1548 and 1566) and a hospital (1566). Following their example, two more brothers from Ioannina, Maximos and Joasaph, built the katholikon of the Transfiguration (before 1545) for Roussanos Monastery and decorated it with wall paintings in 1560. In 1545 the katholikon of St Stephen's was restored by the monk Filotheos; its wall paintings are only slightly later. The katholikon of the Great Meteoron was enlarged (1544–5) and decorated with wall paintings (1552); a refectory (1557) and a hospital (1572) were also built.

In the following centuries the monasteries received their financial support mainly from the rulers of Moldavia and Wallachia, many of whom were of Greek descent. New churches were built and decorated with wall paintings, for example the chapel of the Three Hierarchs at Varlaam Monastery (1627, 1637); at the Holy Trinity Monastery the St John the Baptist Chapel was built in 1682, a skeuophylakeion added in 1684 and a narthex in 1689–92, while the katholikon was decorated with wall paintings in 1741; at the Great Meteoron the St John the Baptist Chapel was restored in 1784 and a chapel dedicated to SS Constantine and Helena built in 1789; the present katholikon of St Stephen's Monastery (St Charalambos) was built in 1798.

2. ARCHITECTURE. Churches of the 12th–15th centuries follow a variety of plans. The first katholikon at Meteora, the Panagia Doupiani, was a small, single-cell church with a barrel-vaulted roof. The katholikon (1366) at the Presentation is of the transverse, vaulted type, while the old katholikon (1388) of the Great Meteoron and that of Holy Trinity (1476) are cross-in-square churches of the two-columned type. The 15th-century katholikon of St Stephen's is a single-cell structure with a pitched wooden roof and a narthex divided from the main body of the church by a triple arcade reminiscent of early Christian basilicas.

In the second period of expansion the Athonite church plan predominated (*see* MT ATHOS). At the Great Meteoron a new katholikon (1545) was built on to the old church, which served as its sanctuary: the katholika at Varlaam (1542–4) and Roussanos (1545) also reflect the Athonite pattern. The katholikon at St Nicholas Anapafsas (1527), on the other hand, is an abbreviated form of the cross-in-square type with a dome supported on pendentives; its *lite* has a wooden roof. Other building types of the period include aisleless vaulted refectories, square kitchens with dome-shaped chimneys and square hospitals with four columns supporting groin vaults. The walling is in limestone blocks faced with cloisonné masonry: sawtooth brick and tile friezes containing crosses and apotropaic inscriptions outline the walls and frame the double-lobed windows. Apses are tripartite and are often decorated with blind conches. The polygonal domes, derivated from forms in Constantinople, are plastered and painted; they are decorated with brick-built colonettes, stepped brickwork arches around the windows and dentil courses.

3. WALL PAINTING. The oldest surviving wall paintings are in the Doupiani kyriakon (*c.* 1200) and are executed in the Komnenian style (*see* EARLY CHRISTIAN AND BYZANTINE ART, §III, 4). During the Meteora's first period of expansion skilful but anonymous artists painted the church of the monastery of the Presentation (1366), the *Second Coming* (1388–93) on the exterior of the north wall of the old katholikon at the Great Meteoron and the same church's interior (the present apse of the katholikon) in 1483. The painting of the interior has been identified as the work of an artist active in and around KASTORIA in the late 15th century who followed the Macedonian school of painting. He is distinguished by his loose modelling of figures and expressive facial features.

The Meteora's most important wall paintings date to its second major period of expansion and feature works by artists of the Creto-Athonite school (*see* POST-BYZANTINE ART, §II, 2) and the school of north-west Greece. In 1527 THEOPHANES THE CRETAN was summoned from Crete to paint the katholikon at Hagios Nikolaos. His work shows a disciplined restraint in which he employed the traditional techniques of icon painting but introduced new subject-matter. In 1552 anonymous artists from the Cretan school painted the new katholikon at the Great Meteoron. The iconographic programme is rich and carefully constructed. In the dome are *Christ Pantokrator*, the angelic host and prophets and evangelists. The barrel vaults and the upper level of the walls depict the Christological cycle together with scenes from the *Life of the Virgin* and *Life of John the Baptist*: the lower level is filled with rows of saints, some depicted half-length and others full-length, portraits of the founders Joasaph and Athanasios and a donor inscription. In the *lite* the groin vaults are covered with scenes of martyrdom taken from the ecclesiastical calendar, and on the walls are representations of the councils of Nicaea (325) and Constantinople (381), a *Deësis*, the *Baptism* and portraits of the founders. Thus the character of the iconographical programme is largely theological and dogmatic, as befits the spirit of the monastic life, and the same programme was followed by the anonymous Cretan painters of the Roussanos katholikon (1560). Although similar in conception, the paintings in Varlaam's katholikon (1548) display a more narrative style with densely populated scenes, new subject-matter and a tendency towards the decorative and the portrayal of emotions, especially in the scenes of the *Passion*. They are the Meteora's principal examples from the school of North-West Greece and were probably painted by the Theban Frangos Katelanos. Acquainted with Italian as well as with Cretan art, he chose Palaiologan models and breathed fresh life into them both thematically and chromatically. The *lite* was painted in 1566 by his less able pupils and the Thebans George Kontaris the priest and his brother Frangos Kontaris. In 1545 or a little later the katholikon of St Stephen's was painted by provincial artists acquainted with the Cretan school; their programme included the Akathist Hymn. A small part of this painting was restored in the 17th century by the painter Nicholas the priest, the Kastrisios, who came from Kalambaka.

After the 16th century wall paintings were executed on a smaller scale by local workshops: examples are the chapel of the Three Hierarchs (1637) at Varlaam by Ioannes, the katholikon of Holy Trinity (1692, 1741) by Antonios the priest and Nikolaos, the Baptist's chapel (1682) and the narthex (1784) of the katholikon at the monastery of the Presentation by Demetrios Zoukes and Georgios.

4. OTHER ARTS. In the 16th and 17th centuries important scriptoria existed in the Great Meteoron, Varlaam, Roussanos and in the now ruined Ypsilotera Monastery (founded 1390). The monasteries also house rich collections of manuscripts and printed books spanning the 6th to 18th centuries: other items of interest include a chrysobull (1336; Meteora, Great Meteoron Mus.) of the emperor Andronikos III Palaiologos (*reg* 1328–41) and a patriarchal seal (1393; Great Meteoron, Varlaam Monastery Mus.) of Antonios IV (*reg* 1389–90; 1391–7).

Among the icons produced by the anonymous group of artists from Ioannina who were active at the Great Meteoron between 1388 and 1393 (*see* §3 above) and still preserved there are those of the *Beneficent Christ*, the *Virgin, St Nicholas* and the *Archangel Michael*, from the katholikon's original iconostasis, and an icon of the *Deësis*. The monastery's other 14th-century works include an icon of the *Baptism*, a diptych showing the *Virgin* and the *Man of Sorrows* and two inscribed icons, one showing the *Virgin* and the other *Doubting Thomas* and the donor Maria Palaiologina, wife of Thomas Preljubovič and sister of St Athanasios's pupil Joasaph, who restored the church in 1388 (all Meteora, Great Meteoron). Some icons from the katholikon's current iconostasis (Meteora, Great Meteoron) are attributed to the workshop responsible for its wall paintings of 1552 (*see* §1 above). Of the many icons of the 17th and 18th centuries, mostly by local artists, two stand out: a *Virgin* (1668) by the Cretan artist and priest Emmanuel Tzanes (1610–90) at Varlaam, and a *Man of Sorrows* at St Stephen's.

A workshop specializing in gold-thread embroidery was also located at Varlaam; among its notable products are three epitaphioi (14th century and 1620; Meteora, Great Meteoron Mus.; 1609; Meteora, Varlaam Monastery Mus.). Notable wood-carving includes the Royal Doors (1388–93) from the original iconostasis of the Great Meteoron's katholikon and the carved wooden abbatial throne (1617; both in Meteora, Great Meteoron). Many other wood-carvings survive from the 17th and 18th

centuries; they are mostly the work of craftsmen from Epiros.

BIBLIOGRAPHY

D. M. Nicol: *Meteora: The Rock Monasteries of Thessaly* (London, 1963/R 1975)

M. Chatzidakis: 'Recherches sur le peintre Théophane le Crétois', *Dumbarton Oaks Pap.*, xxiii–xxiv (1969–70), pp. 311–52

——: *Ellenes zographoi meta ten alose* [Greek painters after the conquest] (Athens, 1987)

N. Nikonaos: *Meteora* (Athens, 1987)

M. Chatzidakis and D. S. Sophianos: *The Great Meteoron: History and Art* (Athens, 1990)

D. S. Sophianos: *Meteora—Odoiporika* [Meteora—an itinerary] (Monastery of the Great Meteoron, 1990)

IOANNA BITHA

Métezeau. French family of architects. The family came originally from Dreux, Eure-et-Loir. Clément Métezeau I (*d c.* 1545) was in charge of construction work on the church of St Pierre and the Belfry in Dreux, during the reign of Francis I. His elder son, Jean Métezeau (*d* April 1600), continued the construction of St Pierre (the Saint-Vincent tower and the south transept). His younger son, Thibaut Métezeau (*b* Dreux, 21 Oct 1533; *d* Paris, before 18 Dec 1586), collaborated with the family before establishing himself in 1569 in Paris, where he worked on the construction of the Tuileries under the direction of Philibert de L'Orme, on the funerary chapel of the Valois family at St Denis (1572–82) and on the Pont Neuf (1578). As architect to the Duc d'Alençon and to Henry III he built the triumphal arch of the Porte Saint-Antoine. He was the father of the architects (1) Louis Métezeau and (2) Clément Métezeau II.

(1) Louis Métezeau. (*b* Dreux, 1559; *d* Paris, 18 Aug 1615). The eldest son of Thibaut Métezeau, he doubtless worked with his father, particularly on the construction of town houses in Paris. The Hôtel d'Angoulême, begun in 1584 for Diane d'Angoulême, Henry II's illegitimate daughter, is attributed to him, and includes the city's first example of a colossal order comprising large Corinthian pilasters, almost certainly inspired by one of Philibert de L'Orme's plates in *Le Premier Tome de l'architecture* (1567; viii, fol. 252v).

Métezeau then entered the service of Henry IV and his sister Catherine of Bourbon (one of Louis's brothers, Jean Métezeau, was the princess's secretary) and during the years of the re-conquest of the kingdom was probably consulted by the King on the major architectural projects to be put into effect immediately after the Pacification. After the resumption of work on the royal houses in September 1594, Métezeau was named Architecte des Bâtiments du Roi to 'occupy himself with the conduct' of work on the châteaux of the Louvre, the Tuileries, Fontainebleau and St Germain-en-Laye. He received 800 écus a year, of which 400 were for work on the Louvre. The King's incumbent architect, Jacques Androuet Du Cerceau (ii), had to yield to authority and work alongside him.

It is impossible to distinguish between the contributions of Métezeau and Du Cerceau at the Louvre or at the Tuileries between 1594 and 1608. Métezeau is mentioned by name as only the interior designer of the King's apartment and Queen's chapel in 1606 and the hall of antiquities in 1608. His primary role can be deduced, however, from the fact that he was named Concierge et Garde des Meubles at the Tuileries in 1605, that he was given a lodging in the Grande Galerie of the Louvre and that he was described on his death as Premier Architecte du Roi.

Métezeau's role in the conception and realization of major urban developments under Henry IV and the Duc de Sully is difficult to define precisely. He may have drawn up designs for the pavilions and houses of the Place Royale (now Place des Vosges), the Place Dauphine, the Place de France and possibly also for the new château of Saint-Germain-en-Laye, or Fontainebleau. In 1609 he built the monuments that were to receive the hearts of Henry IV and Marie de' Medici in the Jesuit chapel at La Flèche, and together with Thomas Francini (d 1648) he was given responsibility for organizing the entry of the Queen into Paris in 1610. The following year the Queen sent Métezeau to Florence to draw the plans of the Pitti Palace, a visit that was to inspire the construction of the Palais du Luxembourg. His talents as a designer must have been recognized, since he drew designs for several carved chimney-pieces in Jean de Fourcy's mansion in the Rue du Jouy and in that of Master Lalanne in the Rue Saint-Honoré.

Métezeau's contribution to the Mannerist style of architecture adopted by Henry IV was a decisive one. His taste for the monumental, the tendency to overload with sculpted decorations, the juxtaposition of elements borrowed from the grammar of Vitruvius (pilasters, columns, pediments, friezes and niches) and the use of the colossal order and vermiculated bossage are all combined into a coherent and individual manner, the roots of which lie in de L'Orme's late style, seen at the Tuileries, and in the work of Jean Bullant and the Du Cerceau family. Two sons, Louis II and Guillaume, became royal architects and engineers.

(2) (Jacques-)Clément Métezeau II (b Dreux, 6 Feb 1581; d Paris, 28 Nov 1652). Brother of (1) Louis Métezeau. He was Thibaut's third son, and was brought up by his brother Louis in the latter's lodgings in the Galeries du Louvre. In 1610 Carlo Gonzaga, Duc de Nevers et de Rethel, employed him as inspector and architect, requesting designs for the new town of Charleville, which he wished to create in the principality of Arches (Ardennes). Clément designed the Place Ducale in the town centre on the model of the Place Royale in Paris. Charleville was laid out on a grid plan and surrounded by fortifications with bastions. Métezeau may also have drawn up the plans for the square that the Duke had built in front of his palace at Nevers. On his brother Louis's death in 1615, Clément succeeded him as Architecte du Roi and also inherited his lodgings in the Louvre. Nothing is left of his numerous domestic works, which included the château of La Meilleraye (Deux-Sèvres), begun in 1620 for Charles de La Porte and continued for the Marshal of La Meilleraye, the château of Chilly (Essonne), which was built from Métezeau's plans for the Marshal of Effiat by Jean Thiriot from 1627 to 1633, and the château of Berny at Fresnes (Val-de-Marne), where he built a chapel and a decorated enclosure in 1623. In Paris he carried out alterations to the Hôtel de Chevreuse in 1624 and to the Hôtel de Mercoeur in 1625. He also built two houses on the Quai Malaquais and the Quai Voltaire for the speculator Louis Le Barbier (1630–34) and worked on the Hôtel de Condé from 1635 to 1637.

Métezeau was the building contractor for Salomon de Brosse's façade of the church of St Gervais (1616–21), Paris, and for the church of the Oratory in Paris, erected (1621) probably on the orders of Jacques Le Mercier. As an engineer, Métezeau shared responsibility with Thiriot for the sea wall (1627–8) at La Rochelle, a bulwark of 1364 m that won him considerable repute. His oeuvre forms a transition between the Mannerism of his brother Louis and the classicism of François Mansart, who succeeded him on the sites of the château of Berny and the Hôtel de Condé. Métezeau owned a collection of antiques and works by French and Italian painters.

BIBLIOGRAPHY

P. Du Colombier: 'Autour des Métezeau', *Bib. Humanisme & Ren.*, iii (1943), pp. 168–89

L. Hautecoeur: *Architecture classique* (1943–57, rev. 1966), i/3, pp. 40–45

E. J. Ciprut: 'Oeuvres inconnues de Clément Métezeau', *Bull Soc. Hist. A. Fr.* (1954), pp. 143–8

E. Baudson: *Un Urbaniste au XVIIe siècle: Clément Métezeau, architecte du roi* (Mézières, 1957)

E. J. Ciprut: 'La Construction du Château de Chilly-Mazarin', *Bull. Soc. Hist. A. Fr.* (1961), pp. 205–9

——: *Nouveaux documents sur le Louvre* (Paris, 1963)

——: 'Documents inédits sur quelques châteaux d'Ile-de-France', *Mém. Soc. Hist. Paris & Ile-de-France*, xvi–xvii (1965–6), pp. 181–5

J.-P. Babelon: 'Les Travaux de Henri IV au Louvre et aux Tuileries', *Mém. Soc. Hist. Paris & Ile-de-France*, xxix (1978), pp. 55–130

D. Thomson: *Renaissance Paris* (London, 1984)

JEAN-PIERRE BABELON

Methodism. Nonconformist Christian denomination. It developed in England in the 18th century from the beliefs and teachings of John Wesley (1703–91) and his brother Charles Wesley (1707–88). After a mystical experience in 1738, John Wesley became particularly important as a preacher, inspired by a vivid sense of the preaching of Christ and emphasizing the personal experience of divine grace and the importance of good works and the avoidance of sin as signs of faith. Although Wesley himself was not hostile to the established Church, some of his doctrines were believed to be unorthodox, and his fervid but unconventional open-air preaching (which disregarded ecclesiastical boundaries) and his support for lay preachers aroused the hostility of the Church of England. This fervour attracted a large following, however: by the time of Wesley's death over 500 itinerant and local preachers and a network of 738 local societies, meeting in hired and purpose-built premises, were under the direction of the Methodist Conference, and the movement had also been introduced into America. In the 19th century differences of emphasis within Methodism precipitated several secessionist churches, but these united in 1932.

In Methodism the arts have been subservient to the purposes of preaching scriptural holiness, personal assurance and spiritual perfection, although in Methodist thought beauty is associated with the divine and ugliness with the demonic. The normal form adopted for the early Methodist churches was rectangular, although the octagon yielded interesting exceptions, as at Yarm (1764), Cleveland, and Arbroath (1772), Tayside. Perhaps the most significant buildings produced by the Methodists in the 18th century, however, were Wesley's Chapel (1777–8; see fig.), City Road, London, built by itinerant preacher Samuel Tooth, which in size, plan, pulpit and gallery echoed Wren's church of St James, Piccadilly, and George Whitefield's Tabernacle (1756; rebuilt 1890–92) in Tottenham Court Road, London. In the early 19th century prosperity and urban immigration engendered some large, rectangular, galleried churches, from Redruth (1826) and Truro (1831), Cornwall, to the fine Renaissance Nicolson Square (1815), Edinburgh. Accommodating about a thousand worshippers, many of these have disappeared, but Carver Street (1804), Sheffield, and Bishop Street (1815), Leicester, have survived. As at Wesley's Chapel, the preference remained for two storeys and five front bays, expressing the gallery and central entrance, and other Nonconformist chapels, such as those of the Baptists, Congregationalists and the Religious Society of Friends, followed much the same pattern (*see* NONCONFORMIST CHAPEL). Until *c.* 1850, Methodist chapels invariably focused on the preacher, with the central pulpit usually at one end but occasionally in the middle of the long side. Backless forms, still evident at the New Room (1739), Bristol, yielded to fixed pews aligned in front of the ordained or local preacher. The communion table was rare until the 19th century, as John Wesley advised attendance at the parish church for this sacrament.

The Gothic Revival, which dominated Anglican architecture in the mid-19th century, had only a limited influence on Methodism. St Paul's (1877), Didsbury, Manchester, and St John's (1888), Ashbrooke, Sunderland, incorporate medieval elements, but others, such as Park Street (1868), Lytham, Lancs, and Saltergate (1870), Chesterfield, Derbys, remained classical. In the late 19th century and early 20th, the evangelical 'Forward Movement' culminated in the building of some 20 central missions, with accommodation for several thousand. Often the ground frontage was reserved for revenue-producing shops to sustain the preaching and social work, and the mission entrance was confined to one bay. Two outstanding and very different examples are the brick-towered Birmingham Mission (1904) in Corporation Street and the domed Baroque Revival Westminster Central Hall (1912), London. Such buildings recalled early Methodist buildings at London, Bristol and Newcastle upon Tyne, where preaching rooms, living accommodation, clinics, classrooms, bookshops and even stables were combined in Christian community centres.

At the turn of the 20th century Art Nouveau briefly influenced Methodist architecture, for example at Boulderclough (1897), Yorks, and Newquay (1904), Cornwall, but church designs generally echoed Neo-classical or occasionally neo-Gothic styles. A more functionalist style dominated from 1930, following architectural fashion and economic restrictions, for example at Punshon Memorial (1930), Bournemouth, Hants. Edward Mill's church (1960) at Mitcham, London, and Gordon Ball's Wagg Street (1968), Congleton, Ches, are sensitively designed, and the octagon has reappeared at Sale (1963), Ches, Woking (1965), Surrey, and Stalybridge (1966), Ches. At

Methodist architecture, Wesley's Chapel, City Road, London, 1777–8

Hazel Grove, Stockport, Ches, the functional church of 1972 links harmoniously with the superbly planned Neo-Georgian Sunday School building of 1914. In the late 20th century Methodist church design in Great Britain was characterized by simplicity of construction, economy of maintenance and flexibility of use, an aesthetic representing a synthesis of the soaring emphasis on personal spirituality and the earthbound community relationships of modern Methodism: steeples and towers symbolize the love of God, but single-storey, multi-purpose compositions express better the love of neighbour.

Methodist church buildings outside Great Britain generally concentrate upon the preaching house, built of locally available materials. In the USA church premises are large and well furnished for the primary purpose of preaching, but with many rooms for ancillary purposes and offices for the full-time ministerial and lay staff. In the 19th century American Methodist architecture tended towards colonial versions of British styles, but later buildings are more frankly functional.

BIBLIOGRAPHY
W. Myles: *Chronological History of the People Called Methodists* (London, 1813)
F. J. Jobson: *Chapel and School Architecture* (London, 1850)
J. Ruskin: *The Stones of Venice* (London, 1851–3)
G. H. Curteis: *Dissent in its Relation to the Church of England* (London, 1872)
G. J. Stevenson: *City Road Chapel, London and its Associations* (London, 1872)
K. Clark: *The Gothic Revival* (London, 1928)
J. Crouch: *The Planning and Designing of a Methodist Church* (Birmingham, 1930)
A. L. Drummond: *The Church Architecture of Protestantism* (Edinburgh, 1934)
M. S. Briggs: *Puritan Architecture and its Future* (London, 1946)
E. B. Perkins and A. Hearn: *The Methodist Church Builds Again* (London, 1946)

E. B. Perkins: *Methodist Preaching Houses and the Law*, Wesley Hist. Soc. Lect. (1952)

E. D. Mills: *The Modern Church* (London, 1956)

E. R. Wickham: *Church and People in an Industrial City* (London, 1957)

G. W. Dolbey: *The Architectural Expression of Methodism* (London, 1963)

A. Bieler: *Architecture in Worship: The Christian Place of Worship* (Edinburgh, 1965)

R. Davies, ed.: *A History of the Methodist Church in Great Britain* (London, 1965)

K. Lindley: *Chapels and Meeting Houses* (London, 1969)

M. Trachtenberg and I. Hyman: *Architecture from Prehistory to Postmodernism* (London, 1986)

GEORGE DOLBEY

Methuen, Sir Paul (*b* 1672; *d* London, 11 April 1757). English diplomat and collector. He was the son of the diplomat John Methuen (1630–1706), who played an important role in concluding the 'Methuen Treaty' with Portugal in 1703. In 1706 Paul Methuen succeeded his father as Ambassador to Portugal, an appointment that he held until 1709, when he returned to London and became a Lord of the Admiralty. Under George I he held a number of important political offices, including that of Ambassador to Spain and Principal Secretary of State. The heir to a considerable fortune, he was also greatly enriched by the emoluments of office and consequently was able to collect on a large scale. The development of his picture collection is documented by accounts at Corsham Court, Wilts, for most of the period 1717–35. He usually spent £200 to £300 a year on pictures, but in both 1722 and 1730 some £900 were spent on these, against an annual household expenditure averaging £1000. (All the following works are at Corsham Court, Wilts, unless otherwise stated.)

Methuen's earliest recorded acquisition was a version of Tintoretto's *Adoration of the Shepherds* (Borenius, no. 88), which he bought with two works *en suite* in Spain in 1715. In London he bought a Caravaggesque *Tobias and the Angel* (Borenius, no. 15) at the sale of the estate of Henry Bentinck, 1st Duke of Portland, in 1722 and a large copy (Borenius, no. 71) of Guido Reni's *Baptism* (Vienna, Ksthist. Mus.) at that of William Cadogan, 1st Earl Cadogan (1675–1726) in 1726. Other acquisitions were made at the sales of the collections of Charles Montagu, 1st Earl of Halifax (1661–1715), in 1723 and the painter Charles Jervas in 1740. Methuen also patronized dealers, including George Bagna, from whom he bought van Dyck's *Betrayal of Christ* (Borenius, no. 119) for £100 in 1747.

Methuen's taste was wide in range. Italian pictures predominated, for example the large *Sacra conversazione* of Bonifazio de' Pitati, Pietro da Cortona's *Tancred and Erminia*, major works by Carlo Dolci and a work by Salvator Rosa, as well as battle scenes and still lifes. Methuen owned a few Spanish pictures, including an early view of Mexico and a copy after Murillo, to whom he attributed Caravaggio's *Boy Bitten by a Lizard* (London, N.G.), which left the collection in the 18th century. Northern European paintings included a *Virgin and Child with Saints* in the style of Mabuse, two outsize works by Gérard de Lairesse and many Dutch and Flemish cabinet pictures.

The collection was kept by Methuen in his house in Grosvenor Street, London. On his death it was bequeathed to his cousin and godson Paul Methuen (1723–94), who,

in 1745, purchased Corsham Court. The house was enlarged by 'Capability' Brown from 1760 specifically to house the collection. Much of the collection was recorded by Dodsley in Grosvenor Street in 1761, but the pictures were progressively transferred to Corsham, where 212 works were listed by Britton in 1806. The collection at Corsham also includes some major works purchased by JOHN SANFORD, whose daughter Anna Horatia Caroline married Frederick Henry Paul Methuen, later 2nd Lord Methuen, in 1844.

BIBLIOGRAPHY

R. Dodsley and J. Dodsley: *London and its Environs Described* (London, 1761), iii, pp. 83–100

J. Britton: *An Historical Account of Corsham House in Wiltshire* (London, 1806)

'The Note-books of George Vertue', *Walpole Soc.*, iii (1934), pp. 10–11

T. Borenius: *A Catalogue of the Pictures at Corsham Court* (London, 1939)

FRANCIS RUSSELL

Methymna. *See under* LESBOS.

Metope. Sunken panel between two triglyphs in a Doric frieze (*see* GREECE, ANCIENT, fig. 9h). Metopes are frequently carved or painted, like those on the Parthenon, Athens (*see* GREECE, ANCIENT, fig. 9h and ORDERS, ARCHITECTURAL, fig. 1xvi; *see also* POLYCHROMY, colour pl. I, fig. 1). □

Metrass, Francisco (*b* Lisbon, 1825; *d* Funchal, Madeira, 1861). Portuguese painter of German origin. In 1836 he entered the Academia de Belas-Artes in Lisbon and was a pupil of António Manuel da Fonseca and Joaquim Rafael. He became interested in historical subjects and first exhibited at the Academia in 1843. In 1844 he went to Rome with Luís Pereira de Meneses; there they frequented the studio of Friedrich Overbeck. Metrass was influenced by the Nazarenes, whose work inspired his early *Jesus Welcoming the Children* (1846; Aveiro, Mus. Reg.). After travelling in Italy he visited Paris before returning to Lisbon in 1847. There he was disillusioned by the failure of an exhibition of his work and went back to Paris, where he remained until 1851. His first history paintings in this period show the influence of French Romanticism, as in *Widow Weeping by her Dead Husband* (*c.* 1849; Lisbon, Mus. N. A. Contemp.). In 1852, after his return to Lisbon in 1851, Ferdinand of Saxe-Coburg-Gotha bought his painting of *Inês de Castro Sensing the Approach of her Assassins* (1852; Lisbon, Mus. N. A. Contemp.).

Metrass was back in Paris in 1853, and here he painted a work on the life of Luis de Camões (1524–80) that is significant in the Portuguese Romantic movement, *Camões in the Grotto at Macau* (1853; Lisbon, Mus. N. A. Contemp., on dep. Lisbon, Tribunal da Relação). Camões, celebrated again in the literature of Almeida Garrett (1799–1854) and last depicted 30 years earlier by Domingos António de Sequeira in the *Death of Camões* (1824; untraced), symbolized to artists and writers the exile longing for home, and in *Camões in the Grotto* the poet is seen in a desolate landscape meditating on his distant country; in it the artist personally identified with the Romantic symbolism. This painting was a turning-point, for Metrass was officially recognized and in 1854 became a teacher of history painting at the Academia de Belas-Artes. In 1855 he was chosen as one of the artists to represent Portugal at the Exposition Universelle, Paris, and in 1856 he exhibited at the Academia *Portrait of a Model* (1855; Lisbon, Mus. N. A. Contemp.), one of the rare nudes in contemporary Portuguese art. Also in 1856 he showed his important *Only God!* (Lisbon, Mus. N. A. Contemp.), a painting that was bought by King Ferdinand II and one of the most powerful images in the Portuguese Romantic movement. It shows the extent of French influence in the artist's work in its depiction of a tragic situation in which only God can intervene to save a woman and her child from drowning in a flood as they cling to a broken tree-trunk that will only briefly delay their fatal end. The woman's half-naked body is shown diagonally; the composition, which follows this movement, is over-dramatic but expresses the artist's Romantic preoccupation with the themes of death and human helplessness before uncontrollable natural forces.

The new generation of artists is depicted in João Cristino da Silva's *Five Artists in Sintra* (1855; Lisbon, Mus. N. A. Contemp.), in which Tomás José da Anunciação and Francisco Metrass, just behind him, are shown as the two leading figures of the new Romantic movement.

BIBLIOGRAPHY

D. de Macedo: *Quatro pintores romanticos* (Lisbon, 1949), pp. 12–20
——: *Francisco Metrass e António José Rodrigues* (Lisbon, 1952)
J.-A. França: *A arte em Portugal no século XIX* (Lisbon, 1966), i, pp. 274–9
Soleil et ombre: L'Art portugais du XIXème siècle (exh. cat. by J.-A. França, Paris, Petit Palais, 1987–8), p. 143, pls 130–31

LUCÍLIA VERDELHO DA COSTA

Metro station. Building serving passengers on urban, mainly underground, railways, comprising entrance, ticket hall, platforms and interchange arrangements. Although some stations are built at ground-level, most are underground in highly congested urban areas. The most noticeable architectural elements are generally therefore the entrances, which range from simple flights of downward steps to buildings resembling Baroque palaces, triumphal arches, classical mansions, vernacular cottages and farmhouses, delicate Art Nouveau kiosks or concrete boxes.

The first metro system was the London Metropolitan Railway, inaugurated on 10 January 1863; its engineer was John Fowler and its architect was John Hargrave Stevens (*d* 1875). The first electric underground railway was opened in London in 1890 and was soon emulated by other industrialized and congested cities, including Budapest (1896), Glasgow (1896–7), Vienna (1898), Paris (1900), Berlin (1902) and Hamburg (1912). In New York the 'subway in the sky', known as the 'El' (elevated railway), was inaugurated in 1868. Chicago's first El opened in 1892; it went underground in 1943. Boston's El dates from 1897, and Philadelphia opened its first line in 1907. The first metro in Latin America opened in Buenos Aires in 1913.

One of the most extravagant early metro stations in London was Blackfriars (1870) on the District line. Flanked by two towers, the main building was four storeys high, its façade ornamented in intricate Moorish style (upper part destr.). A characteristic building type designed for the City and South London Railway (CSLR) is the

Metro station entrance in Paris by Héctor Guimard, Porte Dauphine, *c.* 1905

domed single-storey building with red brick and white stone dressing, as in the stations at Kennington (1890) and Moorgate (1900), both by T. Phillips Figgis (1858–1948). Stations by Harry B. Measures (1862–1940), such as that at Holland Park (1900) with façades of brown stone, were the first to have a canopy over the entrance. Around the beginning of the 20th century Leslie W. Green (1875–1908), who was inspired by the Arts and Crafts Movement, designed over 50 stations with street façades pierced by arched windows and clad in terracotta and glazed red tiles concealing a steel frame, as at South Kensington (1906–7). Meanwhile, in Vienna, Otto Wagner directed the construction of the Stadtbahn in 1894–1901, designing 36 pavilions in *Jugendstil* (for discussion and illustration *see* WAGNER, OTTO and fig. 1). In Paris HÉCTOR GUIMARD designed 141 metro entrances in Art Nouveau style (1900–13; see fig.). Eighty-six survive and are listed. Early 20th-century metro stations in Budapest, Berlin, New York and other cities also embraced what became the common railway language of Art Nouveau.

In the early decades of the 20th century, under Frank Pick (1878–1941), administrator of Underground Electric Railways (later the London Passenger Transport Board), the design of London underground stations was of a consistently high standard. His chosen architect, CHARLES HOLDEN, renovated existing stations and designed new ones, notably on the Piccadilly line, such as the influential Arnos Grove (1932–3). Stylistic consistency in metro stations was also strengthened by Edward Johnston's work (from 1916) on the typography of underground signs. In 1935 the Moscow metro was inaugurated, described at the time by Stalin as 'the most beautiful metro in the world'. Among the architects commissioned to design the stations was ALEKSEY DUSHKIN, whose work influenced the first phase of the system. Particularly notable is the Palace of Soviets metro (Kropotkinskaya station; 1935), designed by Dushkin with Ya. G. Likhtenberg. Moscow metro stations of the 1930s to 1950s are Baroque people-palaces, often of marble, which even such later stations as the Leningrad (now St Petersburg) metro, opened in 1955, found difficult to match, despite its Baroque and luxuriant spirit. Apart from the extravagant stations in Moscow, however, the majority of metro stations of the post-World War II period, designed on functionalist lines, resembled misanthropic concrete shoe-boxes, lit by fluorescent tubes or naked light bulbs suspended from loose wires. None of the earlier appreciation of ornament was apparent; instead stations were covered in plain tiles, as in hospitals or prisons.

The metro expansion of the 1960s derived from the need to alleviate congestion above ground and, to a certain extent, the desire to safeguard the cultural heritage. New tunnelling techniques and new underground construction technology were developed, and the new underground policy inspired daring architectural features with striking artistic components. Once again metro design became the business of architects and artists, most notably in the design of ceilings and vaulting, columns and piers, and lighting. Barrel vaults and flat ceilings sometimes gave way to groin, cloister (Lille, République), star, fan (Mexico City, Candelaria), 'cob-web' (Brussels, Alma) and other vaults; sometimes vaults were pierced to allow daylight to penetrate the station. Supporting piers and columns demonstrate features ranging from slender hexagonal piers (Moscow) to sturdy medieval squat columns (Berlin), while the lighting varied from the most elementary (a bulb fixed to the wall) to the most exquisite (glass chandeliers). 'Grotto-stations' of the early 1970s in Stockholm, for example, with their unevenly excavated granite vaults and walls, were converted into works of art, each station with its own identity, artistically related to its location. Individualized and 'landmark' stations were also built, from Beijing to Rio de Janeiro, regardless of the nature of the station (new, renovated or an extension).

Experiments in concrete, for example in the Montreal metro of the mid-1960s, resulted in a remarkable variety of station design. Metro stations with individual architectural features enhanced with expressive artistic components, often signed by prominent architects and artists, were built in the 1970s (Toronto, San Francisco, Brussels, Amsterdam, Prague), in the 1980s (Baltimore, Lille, Caracas, Cairo, Lisbon) and in the 1990s (Los Angeles, Toulouse). In the 1960s and 1970s renovation became an urgent preoccupation, and numerous *Jugendstil* or Art Nouveau elements, including gates, railings, grids and vaulting, were lost. Some examples have survived, and some are also listed, to testify to this outstanding period in the early history of metro station design.

See also RAILWAY STATION.

BIBLIOGRAPHY

E. Utudjian: *Architecture et urbanisme souterrains* (Paris, 1966)

O. S. Nock: *Underground Railways of the World* (London and New York, 1973)

P. Blake, ed.: *Subways* (New York, 1977)

R. H. Wicker: *The Architectural Development of the Subway Station* (diss., Montreal, McGill U., 1979)

Aesthetics in Transportation, U.S. Department of Transportation (Washington, DC, 1980)

B. Bobrick: *Labyrinths of Iron: A History of the World's Subways* (New York, 1981)

L. Menear: *London's Underground Stations: A Social and Architectural Study* (Tunbridge Wells, 1983)

M. Ström: *Métro-art et Métro-poles/Metro-Art in the Metro-Polis* (Paris, 1994)

MARIANNE STRÖM

Metsu, Gabriel (*b* Leiden, 1629; *d* Amsterdam, *bur* 24 Oct 1669). Dutch painter. He was the son of Jacques Metsue (1587/9–1629), a Flemish painter in Leiden. Gabriel Metsu was one of the leading figures in the founding of the Leiden Guild of St Luke of which he became a member in 1648. According to guild records, Metsu was absent from Leiden *c.* 1650–52; probably some of this time was spent in Utrecht. In 1657 he settled permanently in Amsterdam. The following year he married Isabella de Wolff, a native of Enkhuizen who was a descendant on her mother's side of the Haarlem de Grebber family of painters. There is a *Portrait of the Artist and his Wife* (1661; Dresden, Gemäldegal. Alte Meister), which was clearly inspired by Rembrandt's *Self-portrait with Saskia* (*c.* 1635; Dresden, Gemäldegal. Alte Meister). The Rotterdam painter Michiel van Musscher became one of Metsu's pupils in 1665.

The chronology of Metsu's oeuvre is difficult to establish since most of the *c.* 150 works ascribed to him are undated. He generally painted interiors with figures, although his youthful works consist mainly of street and market scenes and religious subjects. Like most of his contemporaries, he also painted portraits, but these were usually in the form of conversation pieces, the best-known of which is the portrait of the *Geelvinck Family* (*c.* 1662; Berlin, Gemäldegal.). He also produced graphic work, little of which has survived. Some of Metsu's lost works have survived in the form of reproduction mezzotints by Wallerant Vaillant.

1. UTRECHT AND LEIDEN, BEFORE 1657. Metsu's probable sojourn in Utrecht is suggested by several features of his work after *c.* 1650: for example, both the *Justice Protecting the Widows and Orphans* (*c.* 1652; The Hague, Mauritshuis) and the *Exile of Hagar and Ishmael* (*c.* 1653; Leiden, Stedel. Mus. Lakenhal) are painted with a broad, somewhat flat technique, which, like the figures and their flexible poses, is reminiscent of the style of such Utrecht painters as Nicolaus Knüpfer (*c.* 1603–*c.* 1660) and Jan Baptist Weenix. The focal-point of Metsu's *Brothel Scene* (St Petersburg, Hermitage) is significantly like Knüpfer's version of the same subject (Amsterdam, Rijksmus.) from which the motif of the reclining man with his legs spread is taken almost literally. It is not clear whether Metsu's piece was intended primarily as a narrative painting with genre traits (e.g. a scene from the parable of the Prodigal Son) or as a pure genre scene. Metsu also painted several scenes of smithies during the early 1650s (e.g. *The Blacksmith*, London, N.G.), a subject that was popular among Utrecht painters.

During his 'second' Leiden period, Metsu specialized increasingly in the depiction of interiors. Like the paintings of Gerrit Dou, the pacesetting genre painter in Leiden in the 1650s, Metsu's interiors from after 1652 always show a visible source of light—a burning candle or a window. Metsu was also certainly familiar with the work of Jan Steen, also active in Leiden at this time. The dramatic power Steen was able to infuse into his scenes must have appealed to the younger artist. The narrative elements in Metsu's work, as well as his early market and peasant scenes, can also be ascribed to the influence of Steen.

2. AMSTERDAM, 1657 AND AFTER. Later, in Amsterdam, Metsu attempted to achieve a synthesis between the visible light source of Dou and the indirect light source common in the work of Gerard ter Borch the younger. For example, the light in these paintings comes from half-opened shutters or a curtained window. Metsu's tavern scenes are also drawn from ter Borch's repertory. After *c.* 1665 Metsu also painted outdoor scenes, which required yet another type of lighting, as in the *Sleeping Huntsman* (London, Wallace) and the *Woman Selling Herrings* (Amsterdam, Rijksmus.). Other important later influences were Nicolaes Maes and the Delft painters Pieter de Hooch and particularly Vermeer. Around 1660 Metsu's technique became more refined, and details, especially the depiction of drapery, were rendered more successfully. The painter also became more original in his choice of subjects, with works such as the *Sick Child* (see fig. 1) and the *'Cat's Breakfast'* (both *c.* 1662; Amsterdam, Rijksmus.), both of which are unique themes in 17th-century Dutch painting. Though not entirely typical of his style, the *Sick Child* is probably Metsu's best-known work. The composition shows the unmistakable influence of the Delft school, but its unforced simplicity shows Metsu's talent at its best. Here he avoided any distracting details and succeeded in holding the viewer's attention by means of the child's expression, even though the child does not look out from the picture.

The cooler palette and style of the later paintings reveals the influence of Vermeer, whose work clearly inspired the pendant paintings of the *Man Writing a Letter* and the *Woman Reading a Letter* (both ex-Russborough, Co. Wicklow; now Dublin, N.G.). Especially reminiscent of Vermeer are the women, with their high foreheads, dressed in yellow robes bordered with white fur. Nevertheless, the harmony so clearly present in Vermeer's work is often conspicuous by its absence from Metsu's paintings (the *Sick Child* being an exception). There are usually too many details that distract the viewer's attention from the main point of the scene. For instance, in the *Hunter's Gift* (*c.* 1658; City of Amsterdam, on loan to Amsterdam, Rijksmus.; see fig. 2), the hunt is metaphorically interpreted as the chase between man and woman, and to eliminate any possible ambiguity in such an interpretation, a wealth of iconographic and emblematic symbols (Cupid, dog, shoes, weapon, sewing, birds) has been added, emphasizing the work's erotic message. The result is so fragmented that its cumulative effect is lost. In other cases, the figures themselves are not always fully concentrated on what they are doing. They are distracted from their occupations in one way or another, or else they try to make contact with the viewer. The figure in the *Woman Playing the Virginals* (Rotterdam, Boymans–van Beuningen) is disturbed by a little barking dog, those in the *Music Party* (New York, Met.) barely get a chance to make any

1. Gabriel Metsu: *Sick Child*, oil on canvas, 322×272 mm, *c.* 1662 (Amsterdam, Rijksmuseum)

music, and in the scene of the *Woman Reading a Letter* a servant is intrusively present. There is frequently a little dog, either jumping up and barking or demanding attention, resulting in the calm of the actual composition and

2. Gabriel Metsu: *Hunter's Gift*, oil on canvas, 510×480 mm, *c.* 1658 (City of Amsterdam: on loan to Amsterdam, Rijksmuseum)

any repose in the action it portrays being disturbed in different ways.

Several of Metsu's paintings of interiors contain recurring elements. For example, the table in *A Smoker and the Woman Innkeeper* (New York, Met.) is the same as that portrayed in the *Young Couple at Breakfast* (1667; Karlsruhe, Staatl. Ksthalle). According to Metsu's Amsterdam inventory, it was the painter's own table. The chimneypiece in the *Young Woman with Pitcher and Wine Glass* (Paris, Louvre) reappears several times, and the drinking horn in the *Oyster-eaters* (St Petersburg, Hermitage) has been identified as that of the Amsterdam St Sebastian's or Archery Guild. A blonde woman posed frequently for Metsu and appears in several paintings, including the *Apple-peeler* (Paris, Louvre) and *The Lacemaker* (Vienna, Ksthist. Mus.). Another characteristic of Metsu's work is his representation of the paintings of other artists in his own paintings, as in the above-mentioned pendants and the *Man and Woman beside a Virginal* (*c.* 1658; London, N.G.). This is nothing new in the work of 17th-century painters; it can also be found in the work of other artists, including Steen and Vermeer.

BIBLIOGRAPHY

Gabriël Metsu (exh. cat., Leiden, Stedel. Mus. Lakenhal, 1966)
S. J. Gudlaugsson: 'Kanttekeningen bij de ontwikkeling van Metsu', *Oud-Holland*, lxxxiii (1968), pp. 13–44
U. M. Schneede: 'Gabriël Metsu und der holländische Realismus', *Oud-Holland*, lxxxiii (1968), pp. 45–61
F. W. Robinson: *Gabriël Metsu (1629–1667): A Study of his Place in Dutch Genre Painting of the Golden Age* (New York, 1974)
C. Brown: *Niet ledighs of ydels: Nederlandse genreschilders uit de 17e eeuw* (Amsterdam, 1984)
B. Haak: *The Golden Age: Dutch Painters of the Seventeenth Century* (New York, 1984), pp. 431–2, 489–90
Masters of Seventeenth-century Dutch Genre Painting (exh. cat. by P. C. Sutton and others, Philadelphia, PA, Mus. A.; Berlin, Gemäldegal.; London, RA; 1984), pp. XLII–XLIII, 248–53

MARIJKE VAN DER MEIJ-TOLSMA

Metsys [Massys; Matsys]. South Netherlandish family of artists. (1) Quinten Metsys, who spelt his surname variously, was the leading painter of early 16th-century Antwerp. He was the son of a Leuven blacksmith, Joost Massys (*d* 1483), and his wife, Katharina van Kinckem. Joost Massys is known to have executed commissions for the new Leuven Stadhuis (1448–63), one of the most ornate town halls in the Netherlands, as well as other work for the Leuven authorities, and to have been superintendent of the chapel belonging to the Leuven metalsmiths' Guild of St Eligius. There is reason to believe that Joost came originally from Antwerp, where his own father, Hendrik Massys, is documented as early as 1425. About 1492 Quinten married Alyt van Tuylt (*d* 1507), by whom he had three children: Quinten, Pawel and Katelijne. He was by then already living in Antwerp. In 1508 he married Catherina Heyns, with whom he had ten more children: (2) Jan Massys and (3) Cornelis Massys, as well as Quinten II, Maria, Hubrecht, Abraham, Peternella, Katelijne II, Sara and Susannah. Both Jan and Cornelis became artists but were still under the age of majority at the time of their father's death, of the 'sweating sickness' (plague).

(1) Quinten [Quentin] **Metsys** [Quintinus Mesius] (*b* Leuven, between 4 April and 10 Sept 1466; *d* Kiel, nr Antwerp, between 13 July and 16 Sept 1530). Painter.

1. Life. 2. Work. 3. Collaboration and influence.

1. LIFE. Rumours regarding Metsys's early training abound: according to Lampsonius, he was a blacksmith who took up painting in order to woo his sweetheart away from a painter she admired. Van Mander alleged that Metsys was entirely self-taught as a painter, having taken to hand-colouring woodcuts when severe illness prevented his being able to practise the blacksmith's trade. Despite the unlikelihood of a young painter, however gifted, being permitted to ignore guild restrictions controlling the training of apprentices, there may be an element of truth to both rumours. Metsys's elder brother, Joost II, did join the family trade, and it is possible that their father, who died when Quinten was about 17, expected both sons to become partners. A consequent traditional attribution to Metsys is the late 15th-century wrought-iron housing of the so-called Massys Well in the Handschoenmarkt near the west front of Antwerp Cathedral.

Since the Leuven painters' guild kept no membership records before 1494, it is not known if Metsys was apprenticed in his native city, where the leading workshop in the 1480s was that of Dieric and Albrecht Bouts. It has been suggested, in view of his knowledgeable depictions of prayerbooks in later paintings, that Metsys may have been trained as a miniaturist at the priory in the village of Grobbendonk, where his mother's family lived. Hans Memling's studio in Bruges must also be considered a possible source for his style: Metsys's activity as a portrait painter specializing in images of wealthy, rather than noble, clients and his achievement of international renown are comparable with Memling's own success in these areas.

Metsys is first documented on 4 April 1491, when he became a 'free' citizen of Leuven at the request of his widowed mother. Records of the Guild of St Luke in nearby Antwerp show that in the same year he was admitted to membership there as a master painter. On 10 September 1494 he returned to Leuven and appeared belatedly before the magistrates to testify that he was 28 years old (majority was normally declared at 25). He settled in Antwerp, the rapidly expanding commercial capital, rather than in the quieter university environment of Leuven. Between 1495 and 1510, he accepted four apprentices: Ariaen (?van Overbeke), Willem Muelenbroec, Eduart Portugalois (see Reis-Santos) and Hennen Boeckmakere. The fact that one was a Portuguese is of great interest and helps to account for the relatively large number of works by Metsys, as well as works in his style, that are in Portuguese and Spanish museums. Two of Metsys's apprentices presumably were his sons Cornelis and Jan Massys, both of whom became masters in the Guild shortly after their father's death.

In the 1490s Antwerp began to attract large numbers of painters—the Guild of St Luke at this time registered 212 members—due to the city's flourishing markets and the spice trade with Portugal. Painters kept examples of their work on view in the Guild's booth maintained in the courtyard of the Onze Lieve Vrouwekerk (now the cathedral) and were permitted to sell their work from their homes as well as at the Guild Hall. The growing demand for paintings for the open market and the dramatic increase in private wealth in the city is demonstrated by the fact that by the 1520s Metsys owned two luxurious houses, while producing mainly portraits and small panels for private use. The first of his houses, called De Simme (The Ape), was in the Huidenvetterstraat in the heart of Antwerp; it was this house that was visited by Dürer in 1520. After inheriting a substantial sum of money from his wife's family in 1521, Metsys built a new house, St Quinten, around the corner in the Schuttershofstraat, with a polychromed iron statue of his patron saint over the door. At the time of his death, he was living in the Carthusian monastery in Kiel, near Antwerp. By 16 September 1530 his wife is mentioned as a widow.

2. Work.

(i) Religious. (ii) Secular.

(i) Religious. No signed or dated works from Metsys's pre-Antwerp period have survived, and none can be attributed to these years. An early painting of *St Christopher* (*c.* 1491; Antwerp, Kon. Mus. S. Kst.) recalls a compositional type used by Dieric Bouts, yet its exaggerated, brownish chiaroscuro and pink flesh tones are unrelated to the clear, cool palette typical of the Bouts family. Compositional similarities to Memling's works are more numerous, apparently beginning with the early *Virgin and Child Enthroned* (London, N.G.). Metsys's ideal of feminine beauty is closely related to Memling's, as is his occasional use of Renaissance ornament.

Metsys's first major public commission, painted when he was already 41, was the large *St Anne* altarpiece (Brussels, Mus. A. Anc.), a triptych ordered in 1507 by the Confraternity of St Anne for its chapel in the St Pieterskerk, Leuven. It was among the first Antwerp altarpieces not to include a sculpted centre. The subject-matter of the central panel (2.24×2.19 m) is an entire *Holy Kinship*, including the two half-sisters of the Virgin, Mary Cleophae and Mary Salome, with their husbands and children, as well as the nuclear group of St Anne with the Virgin and Christ Child,

and it reflects the immense interest in Christ's earthly family stimulated in the late 15th century by the decree of Pope Sixtus IV authorizing the adoption of the Feast of the Immaculate Conception (1476), and the official endorsement of this dogma by the University of Paris (1497) and by the University of Leuven shortly thereafter. The inscription QUINTE. METSYS SCREEF DIT 1509 ('Quinten Metsys wrote this 1509') on the left outer wing of this triptych is critical for the reconstruction of the painter's chronology. Documents reveal that the confraternity had first offered the commission (before 1503) to two local sculptors, whose prices proved to be too high, and then to an Antwerp sculptor, before finally awarding the contract to Metsys. The altarpiece, apparently painted in tempera glazed with oil, is remarkable for the beauty of its landscape settings, its Italianate cupola and for the sophistication of its colour scheme. The shot-silk draperies in violet and green and the cool, pale combinations of blue and blue-violet represent a significant departure from the heavily symbolic colour conventions of the 15th century, in which red and blue tended to dominate.

Even before the *St Anne* altarpiece was finished, Metsys accepted the commission for the retable that came to be regarded as his masterwork—the enormous *St John* altarpiece (1508–11; Antwerp, Kon. Mus. S. Kst.; see fig. 1) for the chapel of the joiners' guild in Antwerp Cathedral. The centre panel of this monumental triptych depicts the *Lamentation*, which in many ways is a modernization of the great *Descent from the Cross* (*c.* 1442) by Rogier van der Weyden (*see* WEYDEN, VAN DER, (1), fig. 2), a work that Metsys, who was a contemporary of van der Weyden's grandson, Goswijn, would have known well from his youth in Leuven. Metsys, however, stressed the tragic leave-taking of the Virgin from Christ, rather than Rogier's more medieval theme of co-redemption, in which the Virgin is shown falling into a deathlike swoon. The central action of Metsys's composition, in keeping with the

1. Quinten Metsys: *St John* altarpiece, oil on panel, central panel 2.6×2.7 m, 1508–11 (Antwerp, Koninklijk Museum voor Schone Kunsten)

2. Quinten Metsys: *Money-changer and his Wife* ('*Banker and his Wife*'), oil on panel, 740×680 mm, 1514 (Paris, Musée du Louvre)

writings of Ludolphus the Saxon, is placed in time and space between Golgotha, with its empty crosses, and the tomb of Joseph of Arimathea, which is being prepared for the burial. The wings of the triptych depict scenes from the martyrdoms of John the Baptist and John the Evangelist: on the left *Salome before Herod*, on the right the *Martyrdom of St John the Evangelist*.

Metsys's deliberate celebration of native South Netherlandish traditions is also evident in other works. The *Death of St Anne* from the Leuven triptych reflects Hugo van der Goes's *Death of the Virgin* (*c*. 1480; Bruges, Groeningemus.), and Metsys's bust-length diptych of the *Virgin in Prayer* and *Salvator Mundi* (Antwerp, Kon. Mus. S. Kst.) modernizes and refines two of the central images from Hubert and Jan van Eyck's Ghent Altarpiece, the *Virgin in Prayer* and the *Holy Trinity* (*c*. 1423–32; Ghent, St Bavo; for illustration *see* EYCK, VAN, (1)). Moreover, several of Metsys's small-scale depictions of the *Virgin and Child* echo compositions by the Master of Flémalle and Jan van Eyck.

Another striking feature of Metsys's work, coeval with his commitment to local traditions, is his experimentation with Italianate lighting and ornament. While the figures of the Virgin and St John the Evangelist in the *St John* altarpiece have costumes and features reminiscent of those in Rogier van der Weyden's altarpiece, they are not outlined in van der Weyden's crisp and linear style. Instead, the entire altarpiece is pervaded by a remarkable sense of atmosphere, very similar in effect to Leonardo da Vinci's *sfumato*, which softens and modifies forms and colours. The influence of Leonardo is also apparent in Metsys's late *Virgin and Child* (Poznań, N. Mus.), which is an adaptation of Leonardo's *Virgin and Child with St Anne* (Paris, Louvre).

(ii) Secular. In addition to Metsys's use of *sfumato*, or something closely approximating it, Metsys shared several of Leonardo's interests, for instance in the grotesque; his *Grotesque Old Woman* (the '*Ugly Duchess*', *c*. 1513; see fig. 4 below) is based on a famous and much-imitated drawing by Leonardo (Windsor Castle, Royal Lib.), as is the head of the old man in Metsys's *Unequal Lovers* (Washington, DC, N.G.A.). Quinten's portraits too, such as the *Portrait of a Scholar* (*?Cornelius Grapheus*) (1520–22; Frankfurt am Main, Städel. Kstinst. & Städt. Gal.) and the *Portrait of a Canon* (Vaduz, Samml. Liechtenstein) have the fully developed personalities and arbitrary moods of those by Leonardo.

The most remarkable of Metsys's archaizing works, and one of his first known secular paintings, is the signed and dated *Money-changer and his Wife* (the '*Banker and his Wife*', 1514; see fig. 2). This work, which may be the 'portrait of a jeweller by Master Quintinus' cited in Rubens's inventory of 1640, is an interesting example of the iconography of the professions, which probably reflects the influence of the Antwerp rhetoricians (Silver, p. 24). Both the money-changer, or banker, and his wife are shown in outmoded costumes dating from the 1430s and 1440s. The painting recalls certain features of Petrus Christus's half-length *St Eligius* (1449; New York, Met.), which was set in a contemporary goldsmith's shop and painted for the goldsmiths' guild of Bruges. Like the painting by Christus, that by Metsys may have been inspired by a lost work of 1440 by Jan van Eyck (the picture represented 'a gentleman going over accounts with his agent' and was seen in the collection of Camillo Lampognano of Milan by Marcantonio Michiel *c*. 1520–30). Alexander van Fornenbergh, who saw the Metsys painting in what was presumably its original frame in 1658, in the Antwerp collection of Pieter Stevens, reported that it was inscribed *Let the balance be just and the weights equal* (Leviticus 19:35). Jan van Eyck's penchant for extensive inscriptions on picture frames is well known. Equally familiar is the red gown lined with squirrel fur worn by the banker's wife, which is identical to that worn in the portrait of *Margaret van Eyck* (Bruges, Groeningemus.) painted by her husband Jan in 1439.

The still-life objects depicted in the office of Metsys's money-changer have an Eyckian integrity and physical presence as well as, in some cases, an Eyckian symbolic value. The banker's wife is turning the page of her perfectly rendered prayerbook towards its miniature of the Virgin and Child, although she continues to gaze at her husband as he examines the gold content of the coins before him on the table. The convex mirror in the foreground, reminiscent of the one in Jan van Eyck's '*Arnolfini Wedding*' (1434; London, N.G.; *see* EYCK, VAN, (2), fig. 3), can be interpreted as a symbol of the Virgin, as can the crystal carafe and candlestick on the shelf behind. The image reflected in the mirror is that of a church spire and a man reading. The sacramental objects in the picture, including the pokal and paternoster, like the scales themselves, offer a moral warning to the banker to maintain honesty in his business dealings if he is to obtain fair treatment and prosperity in return. Erasmus of Rotterdam, whose portrait Metsys painted (1517; see fig. 3 below) expressed his disapproval of the accumulation of wealth in both the *Praise of Folly* (1511) and the *Adagia* (1515). Nevertheless, Metsys has here displayed the more modern attitude of Antwerp's own businessmen towards financial transactions—and with good reason, since Antwerp was by now the central money market of Europe.

Metsys's dual interests in modern Italian and old Flemish style, like those of many of his contemporaries, reflect the taste of the Habsburg Regent of the Netherlands, Emperor Maximilian I's daughter Margaret of Austria (*see* HABSBURG, §I(4)), whose court was in Mechlin after 1506. She owned an important collection of 15th-century Netherlandish works, including the '*Arnolfini Wedding*'. Metsys's earliest known portrait, the *Portrait of a Man with a Flower* (Chicago, IL, A. Inst.), is pointedly 'old Flemish' in its short-bust format, plain background, presentation of the sitter's hands and betrothal flower and, above all, in its earnest depiction of the face devoid of passing emotion or reference to temperament. A seemingly conscious blend of prototypes by Jan van Eyck and Rogier van der Weyden, it differs dramatically from his later waist-length and animated portraits, such as the *Portrait of a Notary* (Edinburgh, N.G.) or the *Portrait of a Scholar* (?*Cornelius Grapheus*), which have fully developed backgrounds as well as gestures and facial expressions characteristic of the sitters.

Metsys's earliest dated portrait is the *Portrait of a Pilgrim* (1509; Winterthur, Samml. Oskar Reinhart), a half-length and boldly determined figure set against a plain foil with cast shadow, who calls attention to the paper in his hand stating his age (51), the fact that he had been in the Holy Land and the date, which may be either the year of the portrait or that of his pilgrimage or, most probably, both. The diptych (1517) that Metsys painted for Erasmus was a half-length double portrait, a gift from Erasmus to Sir Thomas More, representing *Erasmus of Rotterdam* (London, Hampton Court, Royal Col.; see fig. 3; copy, Rome, Pal. Barberini) and his young friend and proofreader *Pieter Gillis* (or *Petrus Aegidius*, Longford Castle, Wilts; copy, Antwerp, Kon. Mus. S. Kst.), the *stadsgreffier* (secretary to the College of Magistrates) in Antwerp. They are placed in a scholarly setting of desk and bookshelves reminiscent of traditional northern European representations of St Jerome, whose letters Erasmus had edited and published in Basle (1516). The *Hieronymus* edition appears on one of the shelves behind Erasmus, together with the *Praise of Folly*, Erasmus's new Latin translation of the New Testament and the translation of Lucian that he and More had completed together on Erasmus's visit to England in 1506. Erasmus is shown penning the opening lines of his *Paraphrase of St Paul's Epistle to the Romans*. Gillis (1486–1533), who had helped see More's *Utopia* through the press in 1515 during its author's embassy in Flanders, and who is himself one of the *dramatis personae* to whom the *Utopia*'s narrator relates his fictitious adventures, holds in his hand a personal letter from More.

The several replicas of both portraits speak to the popularity of Erasmus and his Ciceronian cult of friendship, as well as to the achievement of Metsys. Although there is no evidence of a continuing relationship between Metsys and Erasmus, who soon transferred his loyalties to Albrecht Dürer and Hans Holbein (ii), Metsys's *Grotesque Old Woman* (see fig. 4) reflects Erasmian thought.

3. Quinten Metsys: *Erasmus of Rotterdam*, panel, 504×450 mm, 1517 (London, Hampton Court, Royal Collection)

This simian creature, a tiny rosebud eclipsed by her decolletage, is a travesty on the traditional engagement portrait, a caricature reminiscent of both Leonardo's grotesques and a dominant theme from Erasmus's *Praise of Folly*, namely that 'no man is ashamed of his own face'. 'The best sport of all', says Folly, 'is to see our old women … daily plastering their faces, scarce ever from the looking-glass, gossiping, dancing and writing love-letters'. The companion profile of a *Grotesque Old Man* (New York, priv. col., see Silver, p. 123) is based on a 15th-century portrait medallion of *Cosimo de' Medici*. (Metsys himself produced at least one portrait medal, of *Erasmus*, 1519, one of the finest examples of the art.) In the *Praise of Folly*, quoting Aristophanes's scorn for old men as 'nasty, crumpled, miserable, shrivelled, bald, toothless and wanting their baubles', who are so delighted with life that they dye their grey hair, acquire false teeth and propose to dowryless young women, Erasmus also touches on a popular rhetorician's theme that Metsys treated with notable success as a genre painting, the half-length pair of *Unequal Lovers*.

3. COLLABORATION AND INFLUENCE. In at least one instance—that of the *Temptation of St Anthony* (before 1522; Madrid, Prado; *see* ANTWERP, fig. 4)—Metsys collaborated with his good friend, the younger landscape painter JOACHIM PATINIR, after whose premature death in 1524 Metsys was named guardian of his young children. While Patinir's panoramic *Weltlandschaften* influenced Metsys's own landscape settings in such late works as the *Crucifixion* (Ottawa, N.G.), Metsys's own rugged landscape backgrounds from such earlier works as the *St Anne*

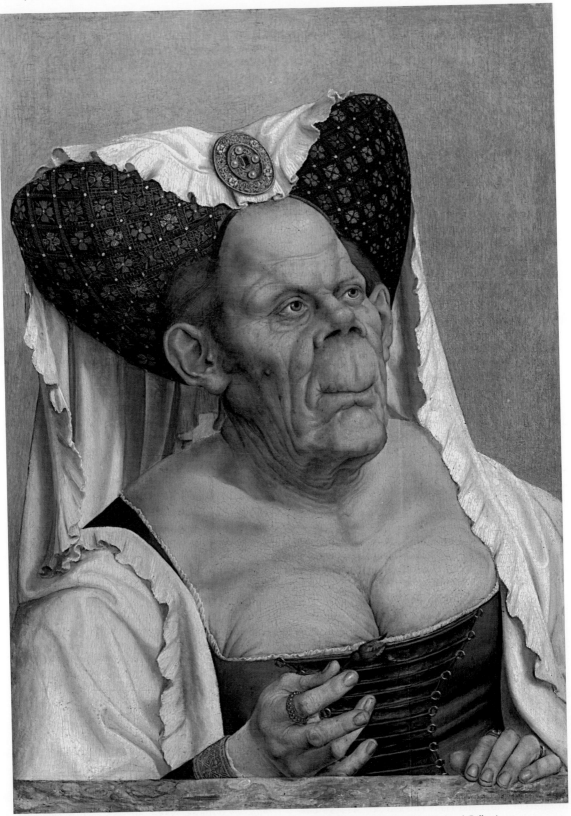

4. Quinten Metsys: *Grotesque Old Woman* ('*Ugly Duchess*'), oil on panel, 641×454 mm, *c.* 1513 (London, National Gallery)

altarpiece and the *Seven Sorrows of the Virgin* altarpiece (*c.* 1509–12; Worcester, MA, A. Mus., and Lisbon, Mus. N. A. Ant.) may have influenced the younger artist.

In addition to the work of his officially acknowledged pupils, Metsys's influence is evident in the work of Joos van Cleve (ii), Marinus van Reymerswaele, Lucas Cranach (i), who travelled to the Netherlands in 1509, and such anonymous painters as the Master of the Holy Blood, the Master of the Mansi Magdalene and the Master of the Morrison Triptych. (For a work from the school of Quinten Metsys *see* OIL PAINTING, fig. 2.)

In his late paintings, all for private clients, Metsys's work became increasingly Italianate. His *Portrait of a Canon* has not only a pyramidal presentation of the figure but also a landscape background highly reminiscent of Raphael, whose tapestry cartoons had been sent to Flanders for weaving. Metsys's image of the Christ Child, in such works as the large *Virgin and Child Enthroned* (*c.* 1523–4; Berlin, Gemäldegal.), became more mature and more complicated in posture, as well as more gossamer-haired. This life-size work, with its luncheon still-life of bread and a monumental butter-mould, was to serve in the 17th century as the altarpiece in Archduchess Isabella's private oratory in the Coudenberg Palace in Brussels, an indication of the esteem in which Metsys was held in Rubens's day.

BIBLIOGRAPHY

D. Lampsonius: *Pictorum aliquot celebrium Germaniae inferioris effigies una cum Dni. Lampsonii elogiis* (Antwerp, 1572)

K. van Mander: *Schilder-boeck* ([1603]–1604)

F. Fickaert: *Metamorphosis, ofte wonderbaere veranderingh' ende leven van den vermaerden Mr. Quinten Matsys, constigh grof-smit, ende schilder binnen Antwerpen* (Antwerp, 1648)

A. van Fornenbergh: *Den Antwerpschen Protheus, ofte cyclopschen Apelles; dat is: Het leven ende konstrijke daden des uyt-nemenden, ende hoogh-beroemden Mr. Quinten Matsys* (Antwerp, 1658)

J. de Bosschere: *Quinten Metsys* (Brussels, 1907)

H. Brising: *Quinten Matsys und der Ursprung des Italianismus in der Kunst der Niederlande* (Leipzig, 1908)

M. J. Friedländer: *Die altniederländische Malerei* (Berlin, 1924–37), vii, pp. 15–79; Eng. trans. as *Early Netherlandish Painting* (Leiden, 1967–76)

K. G. Boon: *Quinten Massys* (Amsterdam, [1942])

F. J. Sánchez-Cantón: 'Notas sobre Quentin Massys en la península', *Archv Esp. A.*, lxv–lxvi (1944), pp. 308–15

G. Marlier: *Erasme et la peinture flamande de son temps* (Damme, 1954)

H.-W. von Lohneysen: *Die ältere niederländische Malerei* (Eisenach and Kassel, 1956)

L. van Puyvelde: 'Eduardo Portugalois', *Pantheon*, xviii (1960), pp. 288–95

H. T. Broadly: *The Mature Style of Quentin Massys* (diss., New York U., 1961)

L. Reis-Santos: 'Eduoardo Portugalois: Disciple et collaborateur de Quentin Metsys', *Pantheon*, xxvi (1968), pp. 185–96

E. Panofsky: 'Erasmus and the Visual Arts', *J. Warb. & Court. Inst.*, xxxii (1969), pp. 200–28

A. de Basque: *Quentin Metsys* (Brussels, 1975)

L. Campbell and others: 'Quentin Metsys, Desiderius Erasmus, Peter Gillis and Thomas More', *Burl. Mag.*, cxx (1978), pp. 716–24

B. L. Dunbar: 'The Question of Cornelis Massys' Landscape Collaboration with Quinten and Jan Massys', *Jb. Kon. Mus. S. Kst* (1979), pp. 125–41

A. Stewart: *Unequal Lovers* (New York, 1979)

L. Silver: *The Paintings of Quinten Massys with Catalogue Raisonné* (Montclair, 1984)

JANE CAMPBELL HUTCHISON

(2) Jan Massys (*b* Antwerp, *c.* 1509; *d* Antwerp, before 8 Oct 1575). Painter, son of (1) Quinten Metsys.

1. Jan Massys: *St Jerome*, oil on panel, 670×960 mm, 1537 (Vienna, Kunsthistorisches Museum)

2. Jan Massys: *Flora*, oil on panel, 1.13×1.13 m, 1559 (Hamburg, Hamburger Kunsthalle)

1. LIFE. More so than his brother (3) Cornelis Massys, who was a less talented artist, Jan worked in the style of his father, whose studio he may have taken over following his death in 1530. Two years later, though still under the age of majority, Jan was admitted as a master in the Guild of St Luke in Antwerp. Like Cornelis, he seems to have left Antwerp immediately after attaining the status of master, for he is not mentioned again in the archives. It has been suggested on stylistic grounds that he worked for a period at Fontainebleau, but this is disputed. He was, in any case, back in Antwerp by 1536, when he took on an apprentice, Frans van Tuylt. In 1538 he married Anna van Tuylt, by whom he had three children. In 1543 Frans de Witte was registered as an apprentice.

In 1544, together with his brother Cornelis and other artists, Jan was sentenced in his absence and exiled from

Brabant because of his heretical sympathies. His wife remained in Antwerp, and he was registered as a fugitive. He may have gone to France, in particular again to Fontainebleau, perhaps also to Germany; he was in Italy around 1549. In 1550 he tried to have his sentence reduced, and before 11 December 1555 (not 1558) he returned to Antwerp. After his return a series of court cases was brought against him by some of his brothers and sisters, because he had defaulted on the distribution of family inheritances. Despite his financial problems, or perhaps because of them, Jan was most productive as an artist during his second Antwerp period (1555–78), when almost all of his dated paintings were executed. Even the town council bought his work; for instance, in 1559–60 he sold them a *Judgement of Solomon* (untraced). Old inventories further reveal that his work enjoyed a certain degree of popularity. In 1569 he took on another apprentice, Olivier de Cuyper.

2. WORK. Only a few works may be attributed with any certainty to the first Antwerp period (1531–43). Jan probably copied a number of his father's works, and they may even have collaborated before the latter's death. Some works designed or left unfinished by Quinten were certainly completed by Jan. The first dated painting generally attributed to Jan is the *St Jerome* (1537; Vienna, Ksthist. Mus.; see fig. 1), which is completely in the style of Quinten. Only one signed and dated painting is known from the artist's period in exile: a *Virgin and Child* (1552; Genoa, Gal. Pal. Bianco).

Throughout his career Jan continued to work in a traditional style. He seems not to have had any contact with his more progressive contemporaries, such as Frans Floris and Jan Sanders van Hemessen. His satirical genre scenes, for example groups of courting couples and unequal lovers, are uninspired variations on themes already treated by his father. Jan stuck mainly to a small number of popular subjects, which he often repeated: the Virgin and Child, St Jerome and Mary Magdalene. However, he is best known as a painter of the female nude. As was often the case in the 16th century, he frequently used Old Testament, allegorical and mythological subjects as a pretext for the depiction of the nude. The sensuality of his figures is reminiscent of the works of the Fontainebleau school, a feature already evident in his early signed *Judith* (1543; Boston, MA, Mus. F.A.). His more mature style, of 1555–75, can be seen in compositions such as *Bathsheba*

Bathing (Paris, Louvre), *Lot and his Daughters* and *Susanna and the Elders* (both Brussels, Mus. A. Anc.). Among his best works are versions of *Flora* (or ? *Venus Cythereia*), one with a view of the harbour at Genoa (Stockholm, Nmus.) and another with the shipping lanes of Antwerp in the background (1559; Hamburg, Ksthalle; see fig. 2). In these works a large-scale, classicizing figure reclines awkwardly in a rhetorical pose in the foreground, with a topographical view in the distance. Jan also painted a number of fine landscapes, for example the signed *Elijah and Elisha* (1572; Antwerp, Kon. Mus. S. Kst.), but he was not as important as a landscape artist as his brother. Two portraits have also been attributed to him.

BIBLIOGRAPHY
A. P. de Mirimonde: 'Jan Massys dans les musées de province français', *Gaz. B.-A.*, civ (1962), pp. 543–64
L. Reis-Santos: 'Jan Quinten Massys: Discipulo e colaborador de seu pai mestre Quinten Metsys', *Belas Artes*, xx (1964), pp. 5–14
M. J. Friedländer: *Early Netherlandish* (1967–76), xiii, pp. 17–20
V. Scaff: 'Ioannes Quintini Masiis pingebat', *Mélanges Jacques Lavalleye* (Leuven, 1970), pp. 259–80
K. Renger: 'Alte Liebe, gleich und ungleich, zu einem satirischen Bildthema bei Jan Massys', *Netherlandish Mannerism: Stockholm, 1984*, pp. 35–46

(3) Cornelis Massys [Matsys] (*b* Antwerp *c.* 1510; *d* between April 1556 and Jan 1557). Painter, draughtsman and engraver, son of (1) Quinten Metsys. Like his elder brother (2) Jan Massys, Cornelis was admitted to the Guild of St Luke in Antwerp in 1532, before reaching the age of majority. It is unlikely that he ever worked with his father or brother. Cornelis signed his works with three different monograms. Only one panel has survived bearing his first

Cornelis Massys: *Mountainous Landscape with Castle in a Village*, pen and brown ink, 156×304 mm, 1541 (Berlin, Kupferstichkabinett)

monogram COR. MET, used from 1537 to 1539: the *Return of the Prodigal Son* (1538; Amsterdam, Rijksmus.). In it Cornelis emerges as a fine painter of imaginary landscapes in the manner of Joachim Patinir, but the figures are less successful and the composition somewhat stiff. No drawings are known from this first period, perhaps because his *View of Brussels* (Berlin, Kupferstichkab.), though bearing a false date, 1522 (added later), was actually produced *c.* 1540. He apparently did, however, learn to engrave during this period, probably *c.* 1537. Initially he copied Italian models such as engravings and etchings by Marcantonio Raimondi and Parmigianino and a tapestry design by Raphael, but he also showed an interest in the prints of the German Little Masters, for instance in his series the *Dancing Cripples* (1538; Hollstein, nos 138–49), although he never copied them.

Cornelis used his second monogram, CME, from 1539 to 1543. Among eight engravings bearing the monogram is the moralizing allegory *Two Couples at the Inn* (*c.* 1539; H 130). His painting the *Arrival of the Holy Family in Bethlehem* (1543; Berlin, Gemäldegal.), with its greater naturalism and more unified composition, marks his first departure from the fantastic landscape compositions painted by Patinir. Five important early landscape sketches by Cornelis, all dated between 1540 and 1542, are among the earliest surviving landscape drawings in the Netherlands. Drawings such as the *Mountainous Landscape with Castle in a Village* (1541; Berlin, Kupferstichkab; see fig.) combine the high viewpoint and formulaic rock formations of Patinir with a realistic treatment of landscape detail that was practically unprecedented in the north at this date. It is on the basis of these drawings that Cornelis is sometimes thought to have been one of the authors of the Errera sketchbook (Brussels, Mus. A. Anc.), which contains some remarkably naturalistic pen-and-wash landscape sketches.

In 1544, after being exiled from Brabant, Cornelis may have fled to England and later to Germany and Italy. The year of his banishment he changed to his third monogram, CMA. Two dated paintings have survived: *St Jerome in a Landscape* (1547; Antwerp, Kon. Mus. S. Kst.) and *Landscape with Singing Figures* (1556; ex-Sticht. de Boer, Amsterdam); two others also bear the CMA monogram: *Landscape with Hunting Scenes* (Dessau, Staatl. Gal.) and *Christ Carrying the Cross* (Prague, N.G., Šternberk Pal.). Only one drawing, *Lot and his Daughters* (1545; Dresden, Kupferstichkab.), is signed CMA. Dating from the same period are engravings portraying the stories of Samson, Tobias, David and John the Baptist, as well as genre themes such as the *Allegory of Adultery* (or the *Farmer's Wife Deceived*). The *Four Blind Men* served as a source of inspiration for Pieter Bruegel the elder's famous painting, the *Parable of the Blind Leading the Blind* (1568; Naples, Capodimonte; see BRUEGEL, (1), fig. 6). Cornelis also drew grotesques and produced a few portraits, among them his engraving of *Henry VIII* (1548; H 170). The importance in Antwerp of his graphic work lay in his wide range of religious and moralizing themes, many of which only later attained widespread popularity.

BIBLIOGRAPHY

Hollstein: *Dut. & Flem.* [H]
A. Zwollo: 'De landschapstekeningen van Cornelis Massys', *Ned. Ksthist. Jb.*, xvi (1965), pp. 43–65
M. J. Friedländer: *Early Netherlandish* (1967-76), xiii, pp. 20–22
B. L. Dunbar: 'Some Observations on the 'Errera Sketchbook' in Brussels, *Mus. Royaux B.-A. Belgique: Bull.*, xxi (1971), pp. 53–82
——: *The Landscape Art of Cornelis Massys* (diss. 'Des Moines' U. IA, 1972)
——: 'The Landscape Paintings of Cornelis Massys', *Mus. Royaux B.-A. Belgique: Bull.*, xxiii–xxix (1974–80), pp. 97–126
——: 'A *View of Brussels* by Cornelis Massys', *Master Drgs*, xvii/4 (1979), pp. 392–401
J. Van der Stock: *Cornelis Matsys fecit (1510/11–1556): Leven en werk met speciale aandacht voor zijn grafisch oeuvre* (diss., Leuven, Katholieke U., 1983)
——: 'Enkele nieuwe gegevens over Cornelis Matsys, 1510/11–April 1556/Januari 1557', *Mus. Royaux B.-A. Belgique: Bull.* (1984), pp. 103–37
Cornelis Matsys (1510/11–1556/7): Grafisch werk (exh. cat. by J. Van der Stock, Brussels, Bib. Royale Albert 1er, 1985)

JAN VAN DER STOCK

Metternich, Franz Wolff, Graf von. *See* WOLFF METTERNICH, FRANZ.

Metz. City in north-eastern France situated on the River Moselle. Originally a Gallic *oppidum* of the Mediomatrices tribe, after the Roman conquest it became Divodurum, one of the principal cities of Belgica Prima. It was fortified in the 3rd century AD and flourished until the barbarian invasions, when, according to tradition, the Huns destroyed the city in 451. After the Frankish conquest Metz was, after Reims, the capital of Merovingian Austrasia from the 6th century to the 8th; in the second half of the 9th century, after the break-up of the Carolingian empire, it was briefly capital of Lotharingia. It was integrated into the Ottonian empire in the 10th century with the Duchy of Lorraine and played no further political role. From the 13th century Mettis, as it was known during the Middle Ages, was a small prosperous republic run by a council of citizens, the *Paraiges*, until it reverted to France in 1552. Of the monuments built before the 12th century, there survives only St Pierre-aux-Nonnains, originally an antique basilican structure (probably the palaestra of a bath complex) that was rebuilt at the end of the 10th century. The main buildings are Gothic, and besides the cathedral (*see* §1 below), the abbey church of St Vincent and the two parish churches of St Martin and St Ségolène, all three of the 13th century, are noteworthy. In the 18th century new squares and public buildings were built, but the city remained enclosed until the end of the 19th. The city wall was then destroyed, and a new city began to develop to the south of the historic centre.

1. CATHEDRAL. The cathedral, dedicated to St Etienne, is situated on the bank of the Moselle. It is an unusual building: the towers are grafted on to the fourth bay of the nave instead of being part of the façade; there is a 20th-century portal in the façade, but the four original portals open into the aisles; and two secondary apses project to the south at 90° to the nave (see fig.). The reasons for these anomalies are principally historical. The cathedral was originally built in a very dense urban area and comprised two separate churches oriented at right angles to one another; the three western bays of the nave

preserving the name of the second, Notre-Dame-la-Ronde (originally Ste Marie), the apse of which extends into the south aisle of the present cathedral.

(i) Architecture.

(a) Early medieval church. According to Gregory of Tours (*Historia francorum*) only the oratory of St Etienne survived the sack of 451. It subsequently became a cathedral and was most likely modified in the 6th century. The *Liber de episcopis mettensibus*, written by Paul the Deacon at the end of the 8th century, records the work of St Chrodegang (*reg* 742–66) on the cathedral and the nearby church of St Pierre-le-Majeur. This consisted primarily in the creation of a *presbyterium* adapted to the use of the Roman liturgy (altar, ciborium, episcopal throne and chancel) and the installation of an 'arcus per girum', the interpretation of which is problematic but suggests the rebuilding of the apse. A group of episcopal chapels was arranged around a cloister, comprising, besides St Etienne and St Pierre-le-Majeur, St Pierre-le-Vieux and St Paul. This complex—which survived until the 18th century, though in an altered form—reflected Chrodegang's desire that his canons should lead a regular life, for which he adapted the Rule of St Benedict.

(b) Ottonian cathedral. The first firmly dated major rebuilding was begun during the episcopate of Thierry I (965-84); Sigebert de Gembloux, author of the *Vita Deoderici I* (*c.* 1050), recorded that the cathedral was completely demolished and rebuilt. The work was probably not finished at Thierry's death, as there was a belated consecration under Bishop Thierry II *c.* 1040. Excavations and documents (a 13th-century copy of an earlier pontifical, which gives incidental details of the architecture, and the Chronicle of Philippe de Vigneulles of *c.* 1500, which refers to the destruction of the Romanesque choir) indicate that the Ottonian building was as wide as the Gothic cathedral, with its façade located in the middle of the fourth bay of the present nave; the transept and choir, excluding the ambulatory, were only slightly narrower than the later Gothic cathedral. The aisled, timber-roofed nave was preceded by a tower-porch with an upper chapel dedicated to St Michael. Excavation has revealed two building campaigns: the massive walls (2 m thick) for the pier footings of the nave and the foundations of the façade wall in herringbone masonry must be attributed to the first, carried out under Thierry I in the second half of the 10th century; to the second, in the first half of the 11th century, belong the transept and east end (a distinct break in the foundations was discovered at the junction of the north transept). Against the monumental transept, which was as high as the nave, stood the 'Rhenish' east end, comprising an apsidal choir flanked by round towers over 40 m high and by apsidal chapels opening on to the ends of the transept arms.

The choir was raised over an aisled, groin-vaulted crypt of three bays, most of which survives, although its eastern termination was destroyed in the late 15th century. Access was provided by two lateral passages leading into the easternmost bay. The style of the crypt is characteristic of Lorraine during the first half of the 11th century: moderately coursed, square piers, imposts decorated by a simple

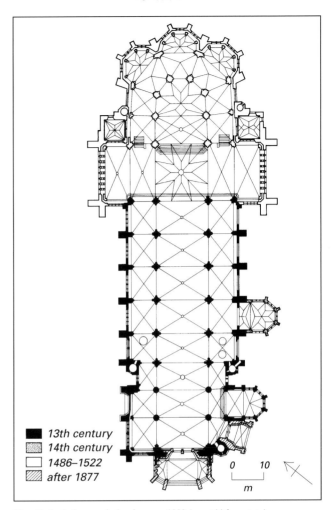

13th century
14th century
1486–1522
after 1877

0   10
m

Metz Cathedral, ground-plan, begun *c.* 1220 (crypt 11th century)

ogee moulding, and small-coursed transverse arches. A cushion capital reused in the early 16th century construction probably came from the earlier choir.

(c) Notre-Dame-la-Ronde. This small sanctuary on the parvis of St Etienne was probably rebuilt in the second half of the 12th century. Described from the early 13th century as *Beata Maria Rotunda*, a name that has survived its integration into the Gothic cathedral, it probably had a centralized plan, which, owing to the oblique setting of the south-west portal of Notre-Dame, may have been dodecagonal, and may possibly never have been completed. Like most churches in Metz, Notre-Dame was orientated towards the south, and this orientation still characterizes the three western bays of the cathedral.

(d) Gothic cathedral. A new building was begun by Bishop Conrad de Scharfeneck (*reg* 1212–24), probably *c.* 1220, when numerous texts mention a series of transactions intended to muster considerable financial resources. The first campaign, not finished until the end of the 14th century, involved only the nave and was based on the old 10th-century layout. Work began with the

erection of two lateral towers over the aisles (present fourth bay) and continued eastwards, up to the base of the clerestory windows. Expansion westwards was prevented by the presence of Notre-Dame-la-Ronde. In the second half of the 13th century Notre-Dame was absorbed into the new building, but it remained autonomous until 1380, when the partition between the two churches was demolished: the five-bay nave of the cathedral was thus extended westwards by three bays. Notre-Dame retained its southern orientation, however, from north portal to southern apse; the triumphal arch that precedes the apse, in the second bay of its nave, was higher than the flanking arcade arches, which necessitated the suppression of the triforium at this point. The relative autonomy of Notre-Dame is also stressed by the use of large round piers, in contrast to the nave piers of St Etienne, which are articulated by shafts. The construction of the upper elevation proceeded throughout the 14th century. Notre-Dame was consecrated in 1347, and the large western windows and the vaults were finished in the last quarter of the 14th century by Pierre Perrat (*fl* 1380–1401), the first documented architect.

Despite the duration of the work and the anomalies at its west end, the Rayonnant nave appears relatively homogeneous. Very high, over 40 m to the keystone of some of the vaults, it incorporates features found also in the cathedrals of Amiens and Beauvais: the design of the arcades, the glazed triforium, large clerestory windows with conventionally arranged tracery (cusped oculi dominating two large lights similarly compartmented). Sculpted decoration is sparse and generally subordinated to the architecture, but there are foliate capitals and cornices and a band of carved drapery along the top of a band of foliate ornament that runs below the clerestory windows. Little remains of the portal sculpture: a heavily restored *Crucifixion* and other fragments from the south portal, and a series of historiated medallions, dating from *c.* 1260–70, from the north portal of Notre-Dame.

The last campaign included the erection of the transepts and choir from 1486 to 1522. The Romanesque foundations served as a guide for the new ground plan, but the choir was extended slightly to the east and an ambulatory with three radiating chapels, opening on to the sites of the former towers, was added. It adopted the same elevation and a style close to that of the nave, with the exception of a few decorative details. Finally, the south tower was completed (the city belfry, named the Tour de la Mutte after its bell): it is 88 m high with a Flamboyant openwork spire. The finished cathedral, which is built of limestone, is 123 m long and 30.8 m wide (internal measurements).

In 1754–5 Jacques-François Blondel demolished the complex of chapels to the south, replacing them with the Place d'Armes, and in 1764 he added a monumental, classicizing portal to the western façade of the cathedral. From 1877 (following a fire that destroyed the roof) to 1903 substantial restorations were carried out, involving the rebuilding of the upper parts and the construction of decorative gables. The Neo-classical portal was destroyed and replaced by an abundantly sculpted Gothic porch.

(ii) Stained glass. From the 13th century there survives only one medallion window, reused in the south transept, depicting *St Paul Preaching*. More important, however, are the large windows of the west façade and the transepts (the absence of portals enabled the windows to fill virtually the entire wall surface). They are strictly compartmentalized: three stages of lights surmounted by a rose on the façade and by three oculi in the transept arms (the west window lost its lower stage when the Neo-classical portal was built), an arrangement suited to the depiction of large figures of saints. The west windows were made in the late 14th century by Hermann of Munster (*d* 1392); Theobald de Lyxheim made the north transept glass in 1504; and the south transept glass was made from 1521 to 1527 by Valentin Bousch of Strasbourg (*d* 1541), who was also responsible for the choir windows. The two transept windows demonstrate the transition from Gothic to Renaissance styles during the first quarter of the 16th century. Among the 20th-century work are windows by Jacques Villon (chapel of Evêques) and especially Marc Chagall (north transept arm and north gallery of the ambulatory).

BIBLIOGRAPHY

A. Prost: 'La Cathédrale de Metz: Etude sur ses édifices actuels et sur ceux qui les ont précédés et accompagnés', *Mém. Soc. Archéol. & Hist. Moselle*, xvi/2 (1885), pp. 217–698

M. Aubert, ed.: *La Cathédrale de Metz* (Paris, 1931)

J. B. Pelt: *Etudes sur la cathédrale de Metz: La Liturgie Ve–XIIIe siècle* (Metz, 1937)

——: *La Cathédrale de Metz* (Metz, 1937) [guidebook]

W. Goetz: 'Senones-Honcourt-Metz, drei verschwundene romanische Zentralbauten', *Aachen. Kstbl.*, xx (1966), pp. 97–105

C. Heitz: 'Le Groupe épiscopal de Metz au temps de saint Chrodegang', *Saint Chrodegang: Actes du colloque: Metz, 1966*, pp. 123–32

F. Heber-Suffrin and D. Courant: 'Dossier sur la cathédrale de Metz aux Xe et XIe siècles', *Eglises de Metz dans le haut moyen âge* (Paris, 1982), pp. 15–69

P. E. Wagner and J. L. Jolin: *15 Siècles d'architectures et d'urbanisme autour de la cathédrale de Metz* (Metz, 1987)

F. HEBER-SUFFRIN

Metz & Co. Dutch retail store and former furniture manufacturing company. Metz & Co. was established by the Metz family in the 18th century, and it originally traded in silk fabrics. In 1902, under the directorship of Joseph de Leeuw (1872–1944), the firm became the sole agents in the Netherlands for Liberty's, supplying the firm's fabrics to a rich, fashion-conscious clientele; later Metz & Co. supplied Liberty furniture equally successfully. In 1918 PAUL BROMBERG joined the firm to design furniture and advise clients on interior furnishings. The firm then launched its own furniture collection, with Liberty's period furniture gradually disappearing from the company range during the 1920s, when the firm also sold work by several other designers. When Bromberg left in 1924, his place was taken by WILLEM PENAAT. From 1930 GERRIT RIETVELD worked with the firm, designing such furniture as the 'Zigzag' chair (see 1983 exh. cat., p. 14) and the so-called 'Crate' furniture (*Kratmeubel*; e.g. Amsterdam, Stedel. Mus.) and drawing up renovation plans for Metz's various establishments. Metz & Co. had good contacts with designers and architects of the De Opbouw and De 8 groups, among them J. J. P. Oud, Mart Stam, Alexander Bodon and Hein Salomonson (1910–94). The company offered them the chance to realize their progressive, ideal interiors on a professional level in collaboration with the master furniture-maker Elmar Berkovich (1897–1968).

Metz & Co. was the first firm in the Netherlands to sell furniture in laminated wood designed by Alvar Aalto and also produced furniture by such French interior designers as Djo Bourgeois (1889–1937) and Jean Burkhalter (1895–1978). After World War II Joseph de Leeuw's policy was carried on by his son Henk de Leeuw (1908–78), and new furniture designers included the Italians Franco Albini and Gio Ponti, the Englishman Robin Day and the American Paul McCobb. Although furniture production ceased at the start of the 1970s, Metz & Co. continued to sell well-known Dutch and international makes of furniture into the 1990s.

BIBLIOGRAPHY

P. Timmer: 'Metz and "Nieuwe Bouwen"', *Het Nieuwe Bouwen: Amsterdam, 1920–1960* (exh. cat., Amsterdam, Stedel. Mus., 1983), pp. 129–41 [bilingual text]

P. Dupuits-Timmer: 'Metz & Co.', *Industry and Design in the Netherlands: 1850–1950* (exh. cat., Amsterdam, Stedel. Mus., 1985), pp. 272–5

PETRA DUPUITS

Metzger, Gustav (*b* Nuremberg, 10 April 1926). German painter, performance artist and writer. He emigrated in 1939 to Britain, where he lived until *c*. 1980, but he regarded himself as stateless from 1948 onwards. He studied at the Cambridge School of Art and in London in 1946, and he was a pupil (1950–53) of David Bomberg. A year after his first exhibition of paintings in 1959 at 14 Monmouth Street, London, he gave his first lecture demonstration of AUTO-DESTRUCTIVE ART at the Temple Gallery, London. In the same year he became a founder-member of the Committee of 100. In 1966 he organized the international Destruction in Art Symposium (DIAS), which brought Viennese followers of Aktionismus and various artists of the FLUXUS movement to London. This attracted much attention in the press but also gave much momentum to the development of kinetic and performance art in Britain. He subsequently participated in many events, publications and exhibitions connected with kinetic, computer and performance art but in the late 1970s began to object profoundly to what he saw as the capitalist-based art world, and he therefore concentrated largely on organizing symposia and exhibitions relating to German Fascist art (e.g. *Art in Germany under Fascism*, London, 1976, and *Artists in Political Exile from Nazi Germany*). After 1980 he spent most of his time in West Germany, Switzerland and Holland, continuing to address these problems.

WRITINGS

'Machine, Auto-creative & Auto-destructive Art', *Ark*, xxxii (1962), pp. 7–8

'Auto-destructive Art', *Granta*, lxxi (1965)

Damaged Nature, Auto-destructive Art (London, 1996) [incl. chronology and bibliog.]

BIBLIOGRAPHY

Documenta 5 (exh. cat., ed. H. Szeemann and others; Kassel, Neue Gal. and Mus. Fridericianum, 1972), pp. 55–7

Art into Society, Society into Art (exh. cat. by C. M. Joachimedes and N. Rosenthal, London, ICA, 1975), pp. 79–86

G. Hoffman: *Destruktionskunst* (Munich, 1995), pp. 43–53, 147–57

NORMAN ROSENTHAL

Metzinger, Jean (*b* Nantes, 24 June 1883; *d* Paris, 3 Nov 1956). French painter, critic and poet. Although he came from a military family, following the early death of his father he pursued his own interests in mathematics, music and painting. By 1900 he was a student at the Académie des Beaux-Arts in Nantes, where he worked under the portrait painter Hippolyte Touront. After sending three pictures to the Salon des Indépendants in 1903, he moved to Paris with the proceeds from their sale. Thus, from the age of 20, Metzinger supported himself as a professional painter, a fact that may account for some of the shifts to which his art submitted in later years. He exhibited regularly in Paris from 1903, taking part in 1904 in a group show with Touront and Raoul Dufy at the gallery run by Berthe Weill and also participating in the Salon d'Automne in that year. By 1906 he had enough prestige to be elected to the hanging committee of the Salon des Indépendants. By the time he began dating his works around 1905 he was an ardent participant in the Neo-Impressionist revival led by Henri Edmond Cross. He also formed a close friendship at this time with Robert Delaunay, with whom he shared an exhibition at Berthe Weill early in 1907. The two of them were singled out by one critic in 1907 as divisionists who used large, mosaic-like 'cubes' to construct small but highly symbolic compositions.

Metzinger soon made contact with other major figures of the avant-garde. Later in 1907 he met the poet Max Jacob and through him Guillaume Apollinaire and then Picasso. It was probably in 1909 that he and Albert Gleizes became acquainted with each other; the two of them, together with Delaunay, Henri Le Fauconnier and Fernand Léger, were identified as a group by 1910, and their separate room at the Salon des Indépendants in 1911 became the first organized presentation of CUBISM. On the strength of the controversy generated by his painting *Tea Time* (1911; Philadelphia, PA, Mus. A.), also known as *Woman with a Teaspoon* or *Mona Lisa with Teaspoon*, Metzinger became known as the 'prince' of Cubism. An article published by him in 1910, moreover, was the first to recognize common concerns in the work of four artists only later grouped together in relation to Cubism: Picasso, Braque, Delaunay and Le Fauconnier. His style developed confidently and independently in the years leading up to World War I, during which he and Gleizes wrote *Du Cubisme* (Paris, 1912), the first substantial text on the new art. His portrait of *Albert Gleizes* (1912; Providence, RI Sch. Des., Mus. A.) dates from the same year. In paintings such as *Dancer in the Café* (1912; Buffalo, NY, Albright–Knox A.G.) he particularly dwelled on the exoticism of modern Parisian life, deliberately conflating visual references to contemporary life (dancing, smoking, drinking) with others drawn either from European traditions or from East Asian or native American cultures. His pictures also reflect his interest in sports, especially bicycle racing (e.g. *The Cyclist*, 1912; Venice, Guggenheim) and sailing, a motif used consistently by him as a metaphor for life. At the same time his paintings obeyed the strictest laws of construction, carefully following the proportions of the golden section with regard not only to orthogonals but also to spiral movement.

In 1912 Metzinger participated in the Salon de la Section d'Or (*see* SECTION D'OR (ii)) and in the second exhibition of the Moderne Kunstkring (Amsterdam, Stedel. Mus.), and he began teaching at the Académie de la Palette in the Montparnasse district, where Le Fauconnier had recently been appointed director. Among his many pupils were Nadezhda Udal'tsova and Lyubov' Popova.

Metzinger had avoided military service in his youth and was resolutely opposed to war. At the outbreak of World War I his friends Gleizes, Léger and Jacques Villon were sent off to join their regiments, while he signed a pacifist manifesto written by the poet Alexander Mercereau, fearful that the momentum of his art and the international thrust of modernism would also be destroyed. In mid-March 1915 the auxiliary service to which he was attached was joined to the fifth section of the military ambulance corps. Metzinger served as a stretcher-bearer for over 18 months and witnessed carnage to which he made only oblique reference in his art. During a period of leave in Paris in 1916, he signed a contract with the dealer Léonce Rosenberg, granting him exclusive rights to his production in return for a monthly stipend. When he was finally discharged in the autumn of 1916, he became friendly with a group of Cubists, almost all of them foreign, that included Maria Blanchard, Juan Gris, Diego Rivera, Jacques Lipchitz and André Lhote, and the poets Pierre Reverdy and Blaise Cendrars. During the bombardment of Paris in the summer of 1918 Metzinger, together with his wife and daughter, joined Gris and Lipchitz at Beaulieu-les-Loches, near Loches. He produced some of the most austere, sombre and haunting paintings of his entire career from 1914 through 1919, his palette heavily weighted towards green and black or towards brown and blue, as in *Woman Knitting* (1919; Paris, Pompidou; see fig.).

In a series of port views painted at Boulogne-sur-Mer in the summer of 1920 Metzinger began to veer towards more readable, less fragmented forms. These pictures were strongly endorsed by Rosenberg, at whose Galerie de l'Effort Moderne in Paris Metzinger showed throughout the 1920s. By 1922 the shift away from Cubism towards PURISM had grown even more pronounced. Metzinger was not an active member of the circle around Le Corbusier and Amédée Ozenfant, but he did contribute to Ozenfant's review *L'Elan*. He also came under the influence of the *rappel à l'ordre*, reviving themes and references, especially harlequins and scenes from the Italian or French comedy, borrowed from Watteau through Corot to Derain, but retaining an underlying solidity residual to his early Cubist convictions. From 1923 he was romantically involved with a young Greek, Suzanne Phocas, whom he married after the death of his first wife in 1929. From 1925, when he adopted much brighter colours, and 1930 he was affected by the example of Léger's work in his preference for urban and still-life subject-matter and for references to science and technology with a firm pictorial construction. Never losing his wry wit, he continued to fill his pictures with visual metaphors, relying during this period on juxtaposition rather than conflation, as in *Roulette* (1926; Iowa City, U. IA Mus. A.), in which a wheel of fortune and croupier's hoe suggest the radically different alternatives imposed on life by fortune.

Elements of Surrealism are apparent in Metzinger's work during the 1930s, for example in the illustrations he produced for the *Poucets* (Paris, 1935) by Fernand Marc and in the large mural *Mystique of Travel*, which he executed for the Salle de Cinéma in the railway pavilion of the

Jean Metzinger: *Woman Knitting*, oil on canvas, 1165×810 mm, 1919 (Paris, Pompidou, Musée National d'Art Moderne)

Exposition Internationale des Arts et Techniques dans la Vie Moderne held in Paris in 1937.

After World War II, however, Metzinger's paintings, rarely dated, were largely pastiches of his earlier Cubist works, combining the iconography that dominated his art during the 1920s with the structural and formal attributes of his pictures of the decade before. At his instigation, he and Gleizes, with whom he had not been in contact since the early 1920s, published a deluxe revised edition of *Du Cubisme* in 1947 with original prints, a new foreword by Gleizes and an afterword by Metzinger. Although the new texts demonstrate each artist's divergence from the goals of 1912, they indicate also that Metzinger retained a practical, commonsense approach, acknowledging the necessity for adapting to changing times.

WRITINGS
with A. Gleizes: *Du Cubisme* (Paris, 1912; Eng. trans., London, 1913; rev. Paris, 1947)
Ecluses, preface H. Charpentier (Paris, 1947) [poems]
Le Cubisme était né: Souvenirs (Chambéry, 1972)
'Cubism as Realism', *Cubism*, 8 (Spring 1985), pp. 1–7

BIBLIOGRAPHY
Metzinger: Pre-Cubist and Cubist Works, 1900–30 (exh. cat. by S. E. Johnson, Chicago, Int. Gals, 1964)
K. Hiscock: *Jean Metzinger: His Role as Painter/Theorist in the Cubist Circle, 1910–15* (diss., Birmingham Poly., 1985)
Jean Metzinger (exh. cat., Nantes, Ecole Rég. B.-A., 1985)
Jean Metzinger in Retrospect (exh. cat., texts D. Robbins and J. Moser; Iowa City, U. IA Mus. A., 1985)

F. Metzinger and D. Robbins: *Die Entstehung des Kubismus: Eine Neubewertung* (Frankfurt am Main, 1990)

For further bibliography *see* CUBISM and SECTION D'OR (ii).

DANIEL ROBBINS

Metzinger, Valentin Janez (*b* Saint-Avold, Lorraine, 19 April 1699; *d* Laibach [now Ljubljana], 12 March 1759). French painter, active in Slovenia. He was first documented in 1727 in Laibach, and his first known painting is dated 1729. He painted *c*. 300 works in oils on religious, historical and mythological themes, still-lifes and portraits, notably that of *Graf von Lamberg* (1746; Ljubljana, N.G.). His style includes characteristics of late European Mannerism and of Italian, especially Venetian, influences. A key figure of 18th-century Baroque art in Slovenia, he influenced Fortunat Wergant, Anton Cebej (1722–74) and other local painters.

BIBLIOGRAPHY
S. Vurnik: 'K Metzingerjevemu življenjepisu' [On the biography of the painter Valentin Metzinger], *Zborn. Umetnostno Zgodovino*, viii (1928), pp. 95–125
——: 'K razvoju in stilu Metzingerjeve umetnosti' [On the style and development of Metzinger's art], *Zborn. Umetnostno Zgodovino*, ix (1929), pp. 65–109
——: 'K razvoju in stilu Metzingerjeve umetnosti' [On the style and development of Metzinger's art] (ed. by M. Marolt), *Zborn. Umetnostno Zgodovino*, xii (1933), pp. 16–63
Natura morta europea dalle collezioni slovene (exh. cat. by F. Zeri and K. Rozman, Ljubljana, N.G., 1989), p. 146

KSENIJA ROZMAN

Metzkes, Harald (*b* Bautzen, 23 Feb 1929). German painter, draughtsman and graphic designer. After his secondary education and a short period of military service he followed a stonemasonry apprenticeship from 1947 to 1949 with the sculptor Max Rothe. He then studied painting at the Hochschule für Bildende Künste in Dresden with Rudolf Bergander, and with Wilhelm Lachnit. In 1953 he left the academy to work on a freelance basis in Bautzen for a short period. From 1957 to 1958 he was a master pupil at the Deutsche Akademie Künste in Berlin with Otto Nagel and painted, among other works, *Transportation of the Six-armed Goddess* (1956; Berlin, Alte N.G.), which, owing to its distinctly symbolic use of the objective or transformation of reality, gave rise to heated public discussions of Metzkes's view of realism. His maxim, 'My programme has only two points. Nature and the eye', clashed with the prevalent requirements of Stalinist propaganda for 'socialist art'. Metzkes evaded these political requirements and began to pursue the symbolic. His work merged reality and symbolism in the contemplation of nature and artistic form. Although influenced by the work of Max Beckmann, Picasso, Carlo Carrá and Giorgio Morandi, his first source of inspiration was the style of his teacher Lachnit, whose clear subjects with accentuated outlines Metzkes sought to develop with various paint tones. In 1956–7 he depicted artistes and circus riders in dark colouring, symbolic of a contemplative distance in the post-war period. Around 1960 the angularity of his early works gave way to a more tonal painting in earthy colours, concerned with the mark of the brush and with light. This reflected the contemporary resurgence of interest in the timelessness achieved by Cézanne. Metzkes soon turned to the pursuit of simpler everyday themes.

On becoming acquainted with the work of Courbet, however, he imbued landscapes and still-lifes, portraits and nudes with moody strength. His large-format group pictures of the 1980s were occasionally narrative or theatrical, but never dramatic.

BIBLIOGRAPHY
Harald Metzkes (exh. cat., E. Berlin, Gal. Arkade, 1975)
H. Schumann: *Ateliergespräche* (Leipzig, 1976)
Harald Metzkes: Bilder aus zwanzig Jahren (exh. cat., E. Berlin, N.G. and Altes Mus., 1977)
Harald Metzkes: Arbeiten von 1957–1986 (exh. cat., W. Berlin, Gal. Neiriz, 1986)

CHRISTOPH TANNERT

Metzner, Franz (*b* Wscherau, nr Pilsen, 18 Nov 1870; *d* Berlin, 24 March 1919). German sculptor. After starting an apprenticeship in stonemasonry in Pilsen in 1886, he worked as an assistant to various sculptors (1890–94). He worked predominantly in Saxony, spending time in Zwickau and Dresden, where he attended an evening class at the Kunstgewerbeschule, as well as in Altenburg and Leipzig. He continued his training on study trips to Paris and Italy. In 1894 he went to Berlin, where he founded his own studio in 1896. He first worked predominantly for the royal porcelain factory. His designs were soon distinguished by a very personal style, which might be broadly defined as a combination of Symbolism and *Jugendstil*. At the Exposition Universelle in Paris in 1900 Metzner achieved artistic recognition with these works. At the same time his sculptures were arousing the interest of the public and critics. Inspired by the work of Georg Minne, he produced sculptures couched in a peculiar idiom with tectonic and *Jugendstil* elements (*Hecker* tomb, *Völkerschlachtdenkmal*, Leipzig, 1902).

With architects and painters Metzner founded the Neue Gruppe Berlin in 1903. In the same year he was appointed to a post at the Kunstgewerbeschule in Vienna. He also joined the Viennese Secession, attaching himself to the circle around Gustav Klimt. In 1904, at the 20th Secession exhibition, he was given a room for his work in which he exhibited *Earth* (erected in Gablonz in 1924; now in Neu-Gablonz). In 1905, as one of the Klimtgruppe, he broke away from the Secession (*see* SECESSION, §3). Metzner returned to Berlin and the years after 1906 were characterized by several important designs in architectural sculpture, such as the Weinhaus Rheingold in Berlin (1906), the tomb of the paper manufacturer M. Krause, also in Berlin (1907), and his work on the *Völkerschlachtdenkmal*, Leipzig (1906–13), the sculptural decoration of which was entrusted to him after the death of Christian Behrens. In all these cases the architectural designer was Bruno Schmitz. The ideas of the two artists complemented each other in a symbiosis of monumentality and symbolism, independent of the official Wilhelmine style and of modernist tendencies. In his own works, particularly in the field of small sculptures, Metzner's style became somewhat ossified. In his late works such as *Pregnant Woman* (1916; Leipzig, Mus. Bild. Kst.) he overcame this rigidity to achieve a more sketchy, mobile style. After his death, Metzner's workshop was kept open for several years as the Metzner Museum. A large memorial exhibition was held there in 1929.

BIBLIOGRAPHY

W. Starke: *Das Völkerschlachtdenkmal* (Leipzig, 1967)

M. Polzl-Malikowa: 'Franz Metzner und die Wiener Sezession', *Alte & Mod. Kst* (1976)

Franz Metzner: Ein Bildhauer der Jahrhundertwende in Berlin–Wien–Prag–Leipzig (Munich, 1977)

P. Bloch and W. Grzimek: *Das klassische Berlin: Die Berliner Bildhauerschule im neunzehnten Jahrhundert* (Berlin and Vienna, 1978), pp. 335–7

S. Einholz: 'Der gezwängte Mensch—Beobachtungen zu Berliner Grabreliefs des frühen 20. Jahrhunderts', *Z. Dt. Ver. Kstwiss.*, xliii (1989), no. 2, pp. 80–93

SIBYLLE EINHOLZ

Meudon, château of. French royal château near Paris. The first château at Meudon (the Vieux Château) was built for Cardinal Sanguin and his niece Anne de Pisselieu, Duchesse d'Etampes (1508–80), mistress of Francis I, between 1520 and 1540. It was of an austere simplicity: two superimposed orders proportioned the façades, and the dormer windows were surmounted by triangular and segmental pediments. On the garden front appeared, probably for the first time, what was to become the classic French façade arrangement. It was divided into five sections with three projecting pavilions, one central and one at each end; each section had a separate roof, those of the pavilions being taller than those of the blocks connecting them. The châteaux of Fontainebleau and Coulommiers, for instance, followed this example. Four small corner towers were built out on corbels like those at Anet.

In 1553 the Duchesse d'Etampes sold Meudon to Charles de Guise, Cardinal of Lorraine, who added a grotto designed by Francesco Primaticcio with decorations by Domenico del Barbieri. In 1654 Abel Servien (1593–1659), Surintendant des Finances to the young Louis XIV, constructed an enormous terrace on the entrance side of the château, and engaged Louis Le Vau (*see* LE VAU, (1)) to work on the interior from 1656. In 1679 the property was bought by the Marquis de Louvois, who employed André Le Nôtre to improve the gardens. He made happy use of the natural contours: to the south the ground falls away steeply and was cut back into two terraces, the lower of which contained an orangery. The main axis of the garden continued south into the distance along the Allée de Trivaux. At the point at which the alley should have been crossed by the park wall, Le Nôtre replaced the wall with a moat from which rose a number of slender jets so closely set as to merit the name of La Grille d'Eau. The grotto dominated a secondary axis that commanded a steep descent into the Jardin Bas and the Grand Parterre de Gazon, beyond which lay the meadows of Fleury. The transition from formal garden to natural landscape was perfectly achieved.

In 1695 Louis XIV bought Meudon for his son, Louis de Bourbon, the Grand Dauphin (*see* BOURBON, §I(9)). In 1706 the latter employed Jules Hardouin Mansart to replace the grotto with a new building, the Château Neuf.

1. Adam Frans van der Meulen: *Louis XIV before Versailles*, oil on canvas, 3.48×5.97 m, *c.* 1669 (Moscow, Pushkin Museum of Fine Arts)

The Vieux Château was burnt down by accident during the French Revolution (1789–95) and demolished in 1795. Napoleon I made the Château Neuf the residence of his son, the King of Rome. In 1870 this too was burnt down, by the Prussians. The central pavilion and the lower storeys of its wings survive as an observatory.

BIBLIOGRAPHY

P. Biver: *Histoire du château de Meudon* (Paris, 1923)
F. H. Hazelhurst; *Gardens of Illusion: The Genius of Le Nôtre* (Nashville, 1980)
I. Dunlop: *Royal Palaces of France* (London, 1985)

IAN DUNLOP

Meulen, Adam Frans van der (*b* Brussels, *bapt* 11 Jan 1632; *d* Paris, 15 Oct 1690). Flemish painter and draughtsman, active also in France. He was the eldest son of the seven children of Pieter van der Meulen and his second wife Marie van Steen Wegen. He went to study with Pieter Snayers, court painter in Brussels, on 18 May 1646, and in 1651 he became a master in the Brussels painters' guild. Probably soon after he married Catherina Huseweel. During the first 15 years of his career, the so-called Brussels period, he painted small-scale genre and history scenes with political and military events in the Baroque style of Sebastiaen Vrancx, Pieter Snayers and Jan Breughel the elder. Typical examples are a *Cavalry Battle* (1653; Geneva, Mus. A. & Hist.), a *Ceremonial Entry into Brussels* (1659; Kassel, Gemäldegal.), a *General on Campaign* (1660; Madrid, Prado) and a *Hunting Scene* (1662; London, N.G.).

His only religious subject, the *Crucifixion* (Besançon, Mus. B.-A.), also dates from these years.

Doubtless partly owing to the worsening economic situation in the Southern Netherlands after the Treaty of Münster (1648), van der Meulen left for Paris, where, from 1 April 1664, he was in the service of Louis XIV. This appointment was due to Charles Le Brun, who was then head of the Gobelins tapestry factory in Paris, with whom van der Meulen collaborated on the project for a series of tapestries on the *History of Louis XIV*. He was mainly responsible for the images of Louis XIV's military campaigns and conquests, themes in which van der Meulen specialized over the years (*see* BATTLE PICTURES AND MILITARY SCENES). The painter usually represented the conclusion of a campaign and worked from topographical studies made on the spot (for illustration *see* ARRAS); the figures were subsequently added in a somewhat arbitrary manner. Using these topographical drawings and watercolours, the finished paintings and tapestry cartoons were worked up in the studio. Between 1665 and 1681 the painter made nine journeys with the royal entourage, mainly to eastern and north-eastern France. Among van der Meulen's numerous depictions of these campaigns are paintings of the *Army of Louis XIV before Doornik* (Brussels, Mus. A. Anc.), *Louis XIV before Versailles* (Moscow, Pushkin Mus. F.A.; see fig. 1), the *View of Dôle*, the *Seizure of Cambrai* and the *Occupation of Valenciennes* (all Versailles, Château). Drawings include the *Army of Louis XIV before Douai* (New York, Met.) and the *View*

2. Adam Frans van der Meulen (after): *Louis XIV before Dunkirk*, Gobelins tapestry from the workshop of Jean-Baptiste Mozin, after 1665 (Versailles, Château)

of Maastricht during the Bombardment (Paris, Fond. Custodia, Inst. Néer.). Tapestries after compositions by van der Meulen include, among many others, the *Siege of Dôle* (Versailles, Château) and *Louis XIV before Dunkirk* (see fig. 2). In 1669 Louis granted van der Meulen a privilege to have engravings made after the campaign scenes. Probably for this he made four paintings (all Versailles, Château) portraying the King in front of Saint-Germain-en-Laye, Versailles, Fontainebleau and Vincennes. The style of all these works is notable for its impressionistic, free technique and rapid sketchy touch, as well as the contrasting use of light, freely moving figures and decorative repoussoirs of foliage and camps in the foreground.

On 13 May 1673 van der Meulen was accepted (*agréé*) into the Académie Royale de Peinture et de Sculpture in Paris, of which he became an adviser in 1681 and principal adviser in 1688. His pupils included François Baudoin, Sauveur Lecomte and Jean Martin, Pierre Scotin and Mathieu Dufresnet. Over the years van der Meulen came to occupy a distinguished position among the painters in the service of the King, who always appreciated his work. The artist also enjoyed the full support of both Le Brun and Jean-Baptiste Colbert, the Surintendant des Bâtiments. In 1682–4 he again collaborated with Le Brun, on four huge painted silk hangings (*c.* 4.0×6.5 m) depicting the *Crossing of the Rhine* (Compiègne, Château). When Louvois Colbert (*d* 6 Sept 1683) succeeded as Surintendant des Bâtiments, Le Brun gradually lost power within the Gobelins. Van der Meulen, however, continued in favour under Louvois, for whom he made various paintings for his château at Meudon, Hauts-de-Seine.

BIBLIOGRAPHY

J. Guiffrey: 'Mémoire des travaux de van der Meulen exécutés pour le roi depuis le 1er avril 1664', *Nouv. Archvs A. Fr.*, n. s. 1, i (1879), pp. 119–45

C. Ma(uricheau-Beaupré: 'Un Peintre de Louis XIV aux armées: Van der Meulen', *Jard. A.*, xxxvii (1957), pp. 1–10

R. A. d'Hulst: 'Tekeningen van A. F. van der Meulen in het Metropolitan Museum te New York', *Mus. Royaux B.-A. Belgique: Bull.*, x (1961), pp. 114–22

W. Schulz: 'Adam François van der Meulen und seine Condé-Ansichten', *Mus. Royaux B.-A. Belgique: Bull.*, xxiii–xxix/1–3 (1974–80), pp. 245–68

Collections de Louis XIV: Dessins, albums, manuscrits (exh. cat., ed. R. Bacou and M.-R. Séguy; Paris, Mus. Orangerie, 1977–8), pp. 256, 333

I. Richefort: *Adam François van der Meulen: L'Homme, l'oeuvre et l'art* (diss., Paris, Ecole Chartes, 1980)

J.-M. Depluvrez: 'Les Victoires d'un règne: Représentations de villes du Hainaut dans l'oeuvre de A.-F. van der Meulen conservée aux Gobelins', *Etud. & Doc. Cerc. Royale Hist. & Archéol. Ath & Rég.*, vii (1986), pp. 321–43

I. Richefort: 'Nouvelles précisions sur la vie d'Adam François van der Meulen, peintre historiographe de Louis XIV', *Bull. Soc. A. Fr.* (1986), pp. 57–80

C. L. Starcky: *Dessins de van der Meulen et de son atelier*, xxxiii of *Inventaire des collections publiques françaises*, Paris, Mobilier N. Cat. (Paris, 1988)

CHRISTINE VAN MULDERS

Meulen, Jan van der. *See* MOLANUS, JOHANNES.

Meulen, Sieuwert van der (*fl* Alkmaar, after 1698; *d* Alkmaar, 18 June 1730). Dutch painter, draughtsman and etcher. Possibly the son of the glass painter Claes Pietersz. van der Meulen (1642–93), he was already drawing and making watercolours, as can be seen from works dated 1698/9 now in Rotterdam (Mus. Boymans–van Beuningen) and Amsterdam (Rijksmus.), before joining the Alkmaar painters' guild in 1700. About then he designed and etched a series of 16 prints, published by Petrus Schenck (1660–1713) in Amsterdam under the title *Navigiorum aedificatio*. This title only partly covers the scope of the images: besides the building of a ship, from the laying of the keel to the heeling over, the illustrations show how a ship is fitted out and launched, how it sustains damage during a sea battle, how it is driven ashore and the final sadness of being towed to a breaker's yard. The series is unique, although a similar plan underlies a series of 17 prints etched by Adolf van der Laan (*c.* 1690–1742) after drawings by van der Meulen, known as the *Groote vissery* (Hollstein, xxv, p. 285). This closely follows the herring industry, from the actual catching of the fish and the repairing of nets to the final moment when the herrings are eaten by the well-to-do. Another series, untitled, engraved by van der Laan after drawings by van der Meulen, represents Dutch and foreign ships. In 1705 van der Meulen etched several battle scenes after his own designs; in 1707 he was working in Haarlem. Other prints after designs by van der Meulen include a series of birds and a title-page (1718).

BIBLIOGRAPHY

Hollstein: *Dut. & Flem.*; Thieme–Becker

I. de Groot and R. Vorstman: *Maritime Prints by the Dutch Masters* (London, 1980), pp. 8, 10; nos 138–53, 157–63

CHRISTIAAN SCHUCKMAN

Meulen, Steven van der (*b* ?Antwerp; *fl* 1543–68). Netherlandish painter active in England. He was a pupil of Willem van Cleve the younger (*c.* 1530–1564) in 1543 and was admitted to the Antwerp Guild of St Luke in 1552; by 1560 he had travelled to London, and he was naturalized in 1562. Van der Meulen brought with him a deep knowledge of the portrait style of Anthonis Mor. This sombre, shadowed style appealed to patrons at the English court who could not travel to Antwerp to sit to the greater artist. Early in 1561 an English merchant, John Dymoch, had visited Sweden in connection with negotiations for a marriage between Queen Elizabeth and Erik XIV, taking with him a Netherlandish painter described as 'Master Staffan', and it seems likely that this was van der Meulen. The King was much pleased with the resulting portrait of himself, for which he paid 100 daler; it was presented to the Queen in June. Its subsequent fate in England is not known, but it has been plausibly identified with a full-length at Gripsholm Castle, Mariefred, near Stockholm.

In England van der Meulen seems to have been extensively patronized by the collector John, 1st Baron Lumley, and his circle and can safely be identified with the 'famous paynter Steven' who appears in the Lumley inventory of 1590; this lists portraits that are presumably the *Lord Lumley aged 30* and his first wife *Jane Fitzalan, Lady Lumley, aged 27* (both dated 8 May 1563; Sandbeck Park, N. Yorks) that were noted in 1735 by George Vertue. Vertue also wrote that William Cavendish, 2nd Duke of Devonshire, 'amongst the old family pictures' had some by 'Stephens'. *Henry Fitzalan, 12th Earl of Arundel*, Lady Lumley's father, is listed in the inventory of 1590 as having been painted twice by 'Steven', and these works are perhaps ones dated 24 December 1562 (Naworth Castle, Cumbria) and 21 December 1565 (ex-N. R. Colville priv. col.; see Strong, 1969, p. 213). Another picture by 'Steven' of the Count of Egmont is also listed. Among other attributions to van der Meulen are portraits of *Elizabeth Fitzgerald, Countess of Lincoln* (1560; J. B. Gold Esq. priv. col.); *Thomas Howard, 4th Duke of Norfolk* (1565; Naworth Castle, Cumbria); *Robert Dudley, Earl of Leicester* (c. 1565; two versions, one New Haven, CT, Yale Cent. Brit. A.); and the Tudor Secretary of State *Sir William Petre aged 61* and his second wife *Anne Browne, Lady Petre, aged 58* (both Lord Petre priv. col., custody of Chelmsford, Essex Co. Rec. Office; other versions of *Sir William*: London, N.P.G.; Oxford, Exeter Coll.; all dated 1567). No work has been identified after 1568, when his dated portrait of *Thomas Wentworth, 2nd Baron Wentworth of Nettlestead* (London, N.P.G.; formerly attributed to Hans Eworth) was painted.

BIBLIOGRAPHY
L. Cust: 'The Lumley Inventories', *Walpole Soc.*, vi (1918), pp. 23–6
G. F. Hill: 'Two Netherlandish Artists in England', *Walpole Soc.*, xi (1923), pp. 29–30
'The Note-books of George Vertue', *Walpole Soc.*, xx (1932), p. 26; xxiv (1936), p. 81
W. G. Constable: 'A New Work by the "Famous Paynter Steven"', *Burl. Mag.*, lxvii (1935), pp. 135–6
R. Strong: *The English Icon: Elizabethan and Jacobean Portraiture* (London, 1969), pp. 10–11, 119–34

MARY EDMOND

Meunier, (Jules-)Arthur. *See* VIERENDEEL, ARTHUR.

Meunier, Constantin (*b* Etterbeek, Brussels, 12 April 1831; *d* Ixelles, Brussels, 4 April 1905). Belgian sculptor, painter and draughtsman. He was directed towards an artistic career by his elder brother, the engraver Jean-Baptiste Meunier (1821–1900). He entered the Académie des Beaux-Arts, Brussels, in September 1845 and studied under the sculptor Louis Jehotte (1804–84) from 1848. In addition, in 1852 he attended the private studio of the sculptor Charles-Auguste Fraikin. Gradually he came to feel that sculpture, at least in the traditional form taught in Brussels, was incapable of providing an adequate vehicle for either exposition or expression. Still at the Academy, he transferred to painting, therefore, in 1853, and followed the courses given by François-Joseph Navez, studying in the evenings at the Saint-Luc studio, with Charles De Groux. He became friends with Louis Dubois, Félicien Rops and other rebellious young artists who were to found the Société Libre des Beaux-Arts in Brussels in 1868. With these, Meunier was part of the realist avant-garde, while seeking out a path of his own in painting. It has been said that De Groux had a decisive influence on Meunier. The latter partly denied this and insisted that he had felt the need very early to practise an art that was more devoted to the masses, to the people. His interest in everyday life, in the experience and condition of man, can already be discerned in the sketches and studies he made during his stays in the Trappist monastery of Westmalle, near Antwerp, between 1857 and 1875. He exhibited some of these works, for example the *Burial of a Trappist* (1860; Kortrijk, Mus. S. Kst.), at the Brussels Salon in the early 1860s. At this time he also carried out a number of commissions for churches, which he accepted in order to support his family.

Between 1875 and 1878 Meunier embarked on history painting, also marked by evident social concern. He chose as his subject episodes from the Peasants' War, drawn from the recent history of Flanders at the end of 1798. In 1878, however, a turning-point in his work occurred when chance led him to the industrial area of Wallonia, in particular to the Régissa rolling-mills. He subsequently visited the Val St-Lambert glassworks and the Seraing Cockerill factories. In 1880, at the triennial exhibition in Ghent, then at the Paris Salon, he showed his first paintings devoted to the world of factories and work, notably *The Brazier (Cockerill Factory)*; and in Brussels he showed *Molten Steel* (Liège, Mus. A. Wallon). It was then that the writer Camille Lemonnier (1845–1913) requested Meunier's collaboration in illustrating his text *La Belgique*. Together with the artist Xavier Mellery, they travelled, in 1881, through the industrial areas of the Borinage, Hainault and Liège. In the same year, in the Brussels Salon, Meunier showed the canvas *Lassitude*, which prefigured his later sculpted work. Meunier was then sent to Spain by the Belgian government to copy a *Descent from the Cross* by a Flemish master. He stayed in Spain from mid-October 1882 to the beginning of April 1883, and this brought a further increase in his self-awareness, in particular his ability to relate to the life around him and to capture it in a quick sketch. He also achieved greater mastery of colour, as can be seen in the *Tobacco Factory in Seville* (1883; Brussels, Mus. Meunier).

Shortly after his return to Brussels, Meunier made his first sculptures, and showed five of them in the 1885 exhibition of the group Les XX in Brussels. Among these was *A Puddler*, a wax version of the work that was to become one of his most famous (bronze version 1886; Brussels, Mus. Meunier). In 1886 Meunier sent *The Hammerer* (*see* BELGIUM, fig. 25) to the Paris Salon where it achieved great success (bronze version 1890; Brussels, Mus. Meunier). Another work of this period was the *Return of the Miners* (see fig.). In March 1887, Meunier was nominated Professor of Painting at the Academy of Leuven where he went to live. There he produced several sculptures in the process of establishing an idea for a *Monument to Labour*. Among these were the *Grisou* group (1889), the *Old Pit Pony* (1890), the *Drinking Man* (1890) and the *Woman of the People* (1893; all Brussels, Mus. Meunier). Although he went on teaching in Leuven until 1896, Meunier returned to Brussels at the end of 1894.

In February 1896, through the mediation of Henry van de Velde, Meunier held a retrospective exhibition of his work in Paris, in the new gallery of Samuel Bing, the Galerie Art Nouveau. This confirmed his international reputation. In 1897 he received a warm welcome in Germany (Dresden and Berlin) and in the spring of 1898 he showed a group of his works at the Vienna Secession exhibition. In 1899 he was elected a Member of the Académie Royale de Belgique and in 1900 he moved into the studio house he had had built at Ixelles, a suburb of Brussels, which now houses the Meunier museum. Gradually his *Monument to Labour* took shape, and its various component parts were purchased by the State, while the artist sought, notably with Victor Horta, to design the best

Constantin Meunier: *Return of the Miners*, oil on canvas, 1.49×2.30 m, late 1880s or early 1890s (Brussels, Musée Constantin Meunier)

architectural setting for it. In 1903, while completely immersed in his great project, he acceded to pressure from the Zola Committee and accepted a commission for a monument dedicated to the writer, a figure group *Fecundity*, alluding to Zola's impressive literary output. Meunier died, however, before being able to complete this work (figure of *Zola*, bronze, 1904; Brussels, Mus. Meunier).

BIBLIOGRAPHY

C. Lemonnier: *Etude sur quelques artistes originaux: Constantin Meunier, sculpteur et peintre* (Paris, 1904)
L'Oeuvre de Constantin Meunier (exh. cat. by A. Thiery and E. Van Dievoet, Leuven, Katholieke U., 1909)
A. Fontaine: *Constantin Meunier* (Paris, 1923)
A. Behets: *Constantin Meunier: L'Homme, l'artiste et l'oeuvre* (Brussels, 1946)
L. Christophe: *Constantin Meunier* (Antwerp, 1947)
P. Baudson: *Les Trois Vies de Constantin Meunier* (Brussels, 1979)
M. Hanotelle: *Paris–Bruxelles: Rodin et Meunier—relations des sculpteurs français et belges à la fin du XIXe siècle* (Paris, 1982)

PIERRE BAUDSON

Meuron, Maximilien de (*b* Corcelles-sur-Concise, 7 Sept 1785; *d* Neuchâtel, 27 Feb 1868). Swiss painter. In 1801 he began studying law in Berlin, but he was also interested in drawing and took lessons with Janus Genelli (1761–1813) at the Akademie der Künste, Berlin. In 1808 he went to Paris, where he was much influenced by the works of Claude Lorrain, and this prompted him to go to Italy two years later. In Rome he allied himself with the German colony and particularly with the Swiss painter Léopold Robert. However, the true direction of de Meuron's art did not become apparent until 1818, when he went on a sketching trip in the Alps of central Switzerland to make studies from nature. Thereafter he mainly painted Swiss mountain landscapes. *The Eiger Seen from the Wengern Alps* (1825; Neuchâtel, Mus. A. & Hist.), generally considered his masterpiece, shows the summit of the mountain piercing the clouds. It is based on direct observation and is painted in a light, airy style devoid of sentimentality. The landscape and the effects of nature are the only focal points of the work, a departure from most previous Swiss painting, in which the landscape acts merely as background. De Meuron's work forms a transition from the traditional Italianate landscape to the later Romantic type that was practised by such Swiss painters as Alexandre Calame and François Diday.

In the late 1840s de Meuron virtually stopped painting in order to teach and to promote cultural life in Neuchâtel. He was responsible for the first important exhibitions of many Swiss painters in the city, as well as a campaign to acquire the works of Léopold Robert through the art society that he had helped to form. His efforts led to the creation of the Musée d'Art et d'Histoire, the first museum of art in Neuchâtel, which today houses his most significant works.

De Meuron's son Albert de Meuron (1823–97) was also a landscape, portrait and genre painter.

See also SWITZERLAND, §III.

BIBLIOGRAPHY

D. Vouga: 'Maximilien de Meuron', *Bib. & Mus. Neuchâtel*, xvii (1967), pp. 63–7
Maximilien de Meuron et les peintres de la Suisse romantique (exh. cat., ed. P. von Allmen; Neuchâtel, Mus B.-A., 1984)

WILLIAM HAUPTMAN

Mewès & Davis. French and English architectural partnership formed in 1900 by Charles Frédéric Mewès (*b* Strasbourg, 1860; *d* Paris, 10 Aug 1914) and Arthur Joseph Davis (*b* Bayswater, London, 21 May 1878; *d* London, 22 July 1951). Mewès studied at the Ecole des Beaux-Arts, Paris (1878–86), in the atelier of Jean-Louis Pascal. He established a large practice, building hôtels particuliers that reinterpreted 18th-century themes for Jules Ferry, W. K. Vanderbilt and Lucien Guitry. In 1900 he built the Ritz Hotel, Paris, skilfully inserting it behind the façades of part of J. H. Mansart's Place Vendôme. In the same year, he was assisted with competition designs for the Grand Palais and Petit Palais by Arthur Davis, a British subject trained at the Ecole des Beaux-Arts in the ateliers of Maximilien Godefroy (1894–7) and of J.-L. Pascal (1897–1900). From 1900 Davis became junior partner to Mewès, designing for César Ritz the interiors of the Carlton Hotel (1902; destr.), Haymarket, London, and the Ritz Hotel (1903–6), Piccadilly, London, the first steel-framed building in the city. Built by the partnership on an ingenious axial plan, the Ritz Hotel has a Parisian exterior with a mansard roof, and light, elegant Louis XVI-style interiors largely carried out by French craftsmen.

Also much admired by contemporaries were Inveresk House (1906–7; altered), Aldwych, London, and the Royal Automobile Club (1908–11), Piccadilly, London, with its fine Pompeian swimming bath. Mewès and Davis designed similar interiors for liners of the Hamburg-Amerika line, and for Cunard (RMS Aquitania, 1914), as well as the Cunard Building (1914–16; with the Liverpool architects Willink & Thicknesse), Pierhead, Liverpool. Their domestic work in England consisted mostly of remodellings in French style for clients associated with King Edward VII, for example Luton Hoo (1903), Beds. The excellence of their work established a fashion for French 18th-century design as interpreted by the Ecole des Beaux-Arts, and led to questioning of English methods of architectural training.

Continuing the practice after the death of Mewès, Davis designed many City of London banks and offices, turning to an Italian Renaissance style. Notable examples are the National Westminster Bank (1925), Threadneedle Street; Morgan Grenfell's Bank (1928–9), Great Winchester Street; and the Hudson's Bay Company Building (1930), Bishopsgate.

BIBLIOGRAPHY

C. H. Reilly: *Representative British Architects of the Present Day* (London, 1931)

A. Service: 'Arthur Davis of Mewès and Davis', *Edwardian Architecture and its Origins*, ed. A. Service (London, 1975)

H. M. Massingberd and D. J. Watkin: *The London Ritz* (London, 1980)

ALAN POWERS

Mexico, United States of [Estados Unidos Mexicanos]. North American country. Situated at the southern tip of the continent between the Gulf of Mexico and the Pacific Ocean, it is bordered by the USA to the north and Guatemala and Belize to the south-east. It is the third largest country in Latin America (area *c.* 1,972,500 sq. km) and is shaped somewhat like a funnel, wide along the USA border and narrowing towards the south-east (see fig. 1); the Isthmus of Tehuantepec, the narrowest point just west of the Yucatán Peninsula, is a low-lying, tropical north–south corridor generally considered to mark the geological division between the continents of North and South America. Physically Mexico is dominated by mountain ranges, which mostly run parallel to the coastline. The northern ranges enclose high central plateaux occupying nearly 50% of Mexico's total area; they comprise arid northern plains and the better irrigated, central Anahuac Plateau, which is the most densely populated region. The Transverse Volcanic Range, which crosses the centre of the country and has several active volcanoes over 4500 m in height, encloses a number of high-altitude valleys and basins originally filled with lakes; these include the Valley of Mexico, site of the capital, Mexico City. Mexico is divided by the Tropic of Cancer; it has a temperate climate in the high plateaux and a hot, tropical climate in the narrow coastal plains and Yucatán Peninsula. Previously the site of several sophisticated indigenous cultures, notably the OLMEC, MAYA, TEOTIHUACÁN, ZAPOTEC, MIXTEC, TOLTEC and AZTEC, the territory of Mexico was colonized by Spain after 1519. It became independent in 1821 and a republic in 1824. The majority of the population is mestizo (of mixed European and Indian descent).

This article covers the art of Mexico after Spanish colonization. For the history and art of Mexico before 1519, *see* individual civilization and site articles; *see also* MESOAMERICA, PRE-COLUMBIAN, especially §§I, II and IV–IX.

I. Introduction. II. Indigenous culture. III. Architecture. IV. Painting, graphic arts and sculpture. V. Interior decoration and furniture. VI. Ceramics and glass. VII. Gold, silver and jewellery. VIII. Textiles. IX. Patronage, collecting and dealing. X. Museums. XI. Art education. XII. Art libraries and photographic collections.

I. Introduction.

The Spanish conquest of Mexico began with a series of conquistador expeditions from Cuba, the first reaching the Yucatán Peninsula in 1517. The Aztecs had extended their domination over most of the region by then, and the third expedition under Hernán Cortés had the help of various disaffected Indian groups in mounting its attack on the Aztec heartland. After founding the settlement of Veracruz (1519), Cortés made for the Aztec capital, Tenochtitlán (now MEXICO CITY), and finally conquered and destroyed the city in 1521. Conquistadors rapidly moved into other areas, founding such towns as PUEBLA (1530), QUERÉTARO (1531), OAXACA (1532) and MÉRIDA (1542), in some cases rebuilding over conquered settlements. The territory thus colonized was quickly consolidated by the Spanish crown as the Viceroyalty of New Spain. The first Viceroy, Antonio de Mendoza, took office in 1535, and the Spanish religious orders, particularly the Franciscans, the Augustinians and the Dominicans, were extremely successful in converting the indigenous Indians to Christianity, with missions and convents dominating the countryside.

As the great wealth of the country, based principally on silver mining, began to be exploited, large ranches were established to support the mining centres and produce such goods as sugar-cane, cotton, silk and indigo. Mining stimulated the development of such towns as Taxco (1524–80), Guanajuato (1557), ZACATECAS (1546–88) and San Luis Potosí (1592); Mexico City, the administrative centre

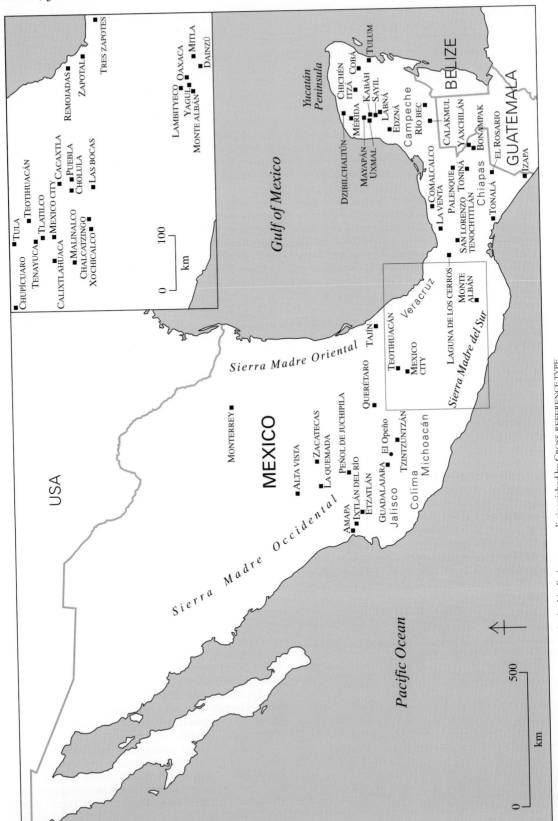

USA

MEXICO

MONTERREY

Sierra Madre Occidental

Sierra Madre Oriental

AMAPA
IXTLÁN DEL RÍO
ETZATLÁN
GUADALAJARA   El Opeño
Jalisco   TZINTZÚNTZAN
Colima   Michoacán

ALTA VISTA
ZACATECAS
LA QUEMADA
PEÑOL DE JUCHIPILA

QUERÉTARO

TEOTIHUACÁN
MEXICO CITY

Veracruz

LAGUNA DE LOS CERROS
MONTE ALBÁN

Sierra Madre del Sur

Pacific Ocean

TAJÍN

Gulf of Mexico

Yucatán
Peninsula

DZIBILCHALTÚN
MÉRIDA
MAYAPÁN
UXMAL

CHICHÉN
ITZÁ   COBÁ
KABÁH   TULUM
SAVIL
LABNÁ
EDZNÁ
Campeche
RÍO BEC

CALAKMUL

BELIZE

GUATEMALA

COMALCALCO
LA VENTA
PALENQUE
SAN LORENZO   TONINÁ
TENOCHTITLÁN
Chiapas
TONALÁ

YAXCHILÁN
BONAMPAK
EL ROSARIO
IZAPA

0   100
km

0   500
km

Inset map sites:

CHUPÍCUARO
TENAYUCA
CALIXTLAHUACA
CHALCATZINGO
XOCHICALCO

TULA
TEOTIHUACÁN
TLATILCO
MEXICO CITY
MALINALCO

REMOJADAS
ZAPOTAL

CACAXTLA
PUEBLA
CHOLULA
LAS BOCAS

TRES ZAPOTES

OAXACA
MITLA
DAINZÚ
LAMBITYECO
YAGUL
MONTE ALBÁN

1. Map of Mexico; those sites with separate entries in this dictionary are distinguished by CROSS-REFERENCE TYPE

rebuilt by the Spanish, had a university (founded 1551), schools, palaces and a royal court (Audiencia). During the 17th century the borders were extended north to California and Texas, and after a period of decline following over-exploitation of the land and the indigenous population, the economy revived in the late 17th century and the 18th. New mining towns were founded, for example Chihuahua (1718). GUADALAJARA, founded in the 1540s, became a centre of wealth and industry; Veracruz dominated European trade, Acapulco was the port through which Spain traded with China via its colony in the Philippines, and Mexico achieved exceptional splendour in the arts and the wealth of the ruling classes, the nobility and the clergy.

At the end of the 18th century the liberal ideas of the European Enlightenment reached the colony, stirring national consciousness and arousing discontent in the mestizos. The Napoleonic invasion of Spain served as the impulse for a series of independence movements. The first (1810–15) was led initially by Miguel Hidalgo and then by José María Morelos, both priests, who called for an independent state with important changes. They were defeated by the Spanish colonial officials, who then entered into a revolt against Spain and, led by Agustín de Iturbide, declared independence in 1821. Iturbide was proclaimed emperor in 1822 but was overthrown in 1824 when a republic was set up. Then began a difficult period in which the country was unable to consolidate a stable government. Its problems were exacerbated by the war with the USA (1846–8), when it lost half its territory to the USA. The war ruined the Mexican economy, and a series of struggles between liberals and conservatives led to armed intervention by France in 1862 and the establishment of the Austrian Archduke Maximilian as emperor in 1864. Three years later the forces of Benito Juárez recovered power and began a series of liberal reforms.

In 1876 General Porfirio Díaz assumed power and held it for nearly 35 years, ushering in a period of order and economic growth supported by foreign investment. However, his long dictatorship and lack of democratic reform resulted in the Mexican Revolution of 1910 and a series of uprisings lasting over ten years. A new constitution (1917) embodied principles of social and land reforms, and after 1921 a series of presidents serving for six-year terms sought to re-establish political order and economic and cultural development; power was retained by the Partido Revolucionario Institucional. In the 1950s and 1960s Mexican governments placed a heavy emphasis on industrial growth, particularly in the central region, Mexico City, MONTERREY (founded 1596) and Guadalajara, which created an imbalance in the distribution of wealth and population as well as environmental and fiscal problems. Economic growth was stimulated by the discovery of large new oil and gas reserves in the mid-1970s.

BIBLIOGRAPHY

D. Angulo Iñiguez, E. Marco Dorta and M. J. Buschiazzo: *Historia del arte hispano-americano*, 3 vols (Barcelona, 1945–56)

P. Rojas, ed.: *Historia general del arte mexicano*, 4 vols (Mexico City, 1964–6)

40 siglos de arte mexicano, 4 vols (Mexico City, 1969)

J. Fernández: *Arte mexicano: De sus orígenes a nuestros días* (Mexico City, 1958; Eng. trans., Chicago, 1969)

——: *Estética del arte mexicano* (Mexico City, 1972)

Historia general de México, 4 vols (Mexico City, 1976)

Historia del arte mexicano, 12 vols (Mexico City, 1982)

México: Splendors of Thirty Centuries (exh. cat., ed. K. Howard; New York, MOMA, 1990)

LOUISE NOELLE

II. Indigenous culture.

The Spanish conquest of Mexico and the introduction of Christianity during the 16th century resulted in profound changes to the economic and social traditions of the indigenous peoples and undermined their entire cultural identity. Most of their architecture, sculpture, paintings and codices were destroyed, and they were forced to adapt to Spanish civilization. There was some initial resistance to this process, especially from the numerous priests of the Pre-Columbian religions who had received a long and rigorous education in traditional Indian *Calmécac* schools; these were responsible not only for propagating the religious doctrines and rites but also for the artistic training of the young, since art was profoundly linked to religion and images were considered sacred. In addition, some of those who had formerly been nobles preserved and communicated a great deal of information about their history and culture, and continued for a time to paint codices. Attempts to resist Christianity met with little success, however, as the Spanish missionaries began to educate the Indian children, who soon became efficient assistants in the spread of Christianity and also undertook artistic work in the convents (*see* §§III, 1(i) and IV, 1(i) below).

The officially promoted evangelization of the Indians resulted in the deepest changes to their culture. In their own communities and in the Spanish urban settlements Indians became members of Christian brotherhoods and participated in civic and religious duties. In the absence of sufficient numbers of Spanish workmen, the missionaries also drew on the Indians' sophisticated building skills—evident in the Pre-Columbian architecture that survived the wars of conquest—to construct their convents. The Franciscans took full advantage of this experience to build their convents in Mexico City, Texcoco, Tlaxcala, Huejotzingo and Cuernavaca—centres that were all chosen because of their great urban and artistic development before the conquest; in many cases stones from Pre-Columbian buildings and even some idols were used as foundation-stones for Christian churches or sometimes used in the construction of external walls. Churches were also frequently built on earlier temple sites, for example the church of S Maria de los Remedios was built on the great pyramid of Cholula in the 16th century.

The Indians adapted quickly to the European style under tutelage from the missionaries (*see* §XI below), but in their techniques and use of materials they gave a particular character to their work that was sometimes later referred to as *tequitqui* or Indo-Christian art and had elements comparable to the Mestizo style in Peru and Bolivia. This can be seen most obviously in the continuing use of Pre-Columbian iconography in sculpture and painting: in the former it occurred as much in ornamental work as it did in religious image-making, for example timid displays of Pre-Columbian symbols were sculpted either in isolation or among other decorative elements on doorways, arches and pilasters. In painting it occurred in the

2. Carved shield on a baptismal font, mid-16th century, Franciscan convent, Acatzingo, Puebla, Mexico

huge wall-painting programmes in the convents that were erected in the second half of the 16th century, although Pre-Columbian symbols are less numerous in painting, either because painter-priests, who alone knew the iconography, intervened only rarely in their execution or because they were eliminated upon their discovery by the monks.

Examples of motifs reminiscent of Pre-Columbian religious ideas that were sculpted in the colonial period include the scrolls that, when placed between the lips of figures, represented speech or song. Coils formed by one or more circles (*chalchihuites*), alone or accompanied by other elements, indicated preciousness or a complex religious concept. Rabbits, lizards, serpents and other creatures, especially eagles, also appear, symbolizing diverse religious ideas; for example the motifs on the carved shield on the baptismal font in the Franciscan convent at Acatzingo (see fig. 2) include eagle and tiger claws, as well as a heart pierced by an arrow and, in the centre, reeds. At other times the eagle motif appears either alone or with other symbols representing the god Huitzilopochtli, or with prickly-pear fruit and leaves as the symbol of Tenochtitlán, the Aztec capital. Vegetal motifs also appear, combined with European flora, making it difficult to determine whether they constitute an indigenous motif. This is the case, for example, with the four-petalled flower, which for the Indians was one of the hieroglyphs representing *Nahui Ollin*, the period in which the Indians lived and in which they believed the earth would be destroyed by earthquakes. The same concept was represented by four dots placed at equal distances from a fifth, central one, although this symbol was also used to represent the four corners of the universe and its centre, the earth (*Tlaltícpac*).

Indian artistic traditions are also evident in the decorative carving of some of the stone 16th-century churchyard crosses, as at the church of Santiago, Atzacoalco, and in silverwork (*see* §VII below). In general, however, indigenous arts and techniques declined in the 16th century. Images of saints were made from a paste of corn stalks similar to papier-mâché, and feather mosaics persisted for a few decades after the conquest, as did the production of traditional codices, but these arts had died out by the early 17th century. As gold and silver were exhausted by the ever-increasing demands by the Spanish rulers for tribute, so the increasingly impoverished Indian artists abandoned making objects from precious metals. The Indians in Azcapotzalco, for example, which had been a major centre for silverwork, began using bronze. In the 17th century indigenous participation in the religious works of the missionaries and church declined as the process of evangelization was completed, and the Indians' artistic production was limited to popular architecture, sculpture and the creation of altarpieces in rural villages. Within the traditional communities that survived, the production of crafts continued, mainly weaving and clothing (*see* §VIII below and fig. 16), furniture, ceramics (of which the major centres were Huitzilopochco, Azcapotzalco, Xochimilco and Cuauhitlan) and items for ceremonial or festive use. By this time the indigenous population had dramatically declined due to exploitation and disease, and, after Mexican independence, their communal property structures were dismantled, and Indians continued to swell the impoverished peasant class. All these factors contributed to the dismembering of the indigenous communities and traditional culture. Despite the loss of some of the traditional artistic techniques, iconography and symbolism, however, certain religious traditions and customs persist in some centres of indigenous population, proving the strength of their ancestral origins.

For the earlier history of indigenous artistic traditions in Mexico, *see* MESOAMERICA, PRE-COLUMBIAN, especially §§II and IV–IX.

BIBLIOGRAPHY

J. Moreno Villa: *La escultura colonial mexicana* (Mexico City, 1942)
G. Kubler: *Mexican Architecture of the Sixteenth Century* (New Haven, CT, and London, 1948)
Métodos y resultados de la política indigenista en México (Mexico City, 1954)
R. Ricard: *La conquista espiritual de México* (Mexico City, 1955)
C. Gibson: *The Aztecs under Spanish Rule: A History of the Indians of the Valley of Mexico, 1519–1810* (Stanford, CA, 1964)
C. Reyes-Valerio: *El arte indocristiano: Escultura del siglo XVI en México* (Mexico City, 1978)
J. Cesar and O. Negrete: *La antropología mexicana* (Mexico City, 1981)
J. Lockhart: *The Nahuas after the Conquest: A Social and Cultural History of the Indians of Central Mexico, Sixteenth through Eighteenth Centuries* (Stanford, CA, 1992)

CONSTANTINO REYES-VALERIO,
CARLOS MARTÍNEZ MARÍN

III. Architecture.

1. 1519–*c*. 1870. 2. After *c*. 1870.

1. 1519–*c*. 1870.

(i) Colonial and Renaissance, 1519–*c*. 1670. (ii) Baroque, Churrigueresque and Neo-classicism, *c*. 1670–*c*. 1870.

(i) Colonial and Renaissance, 1521–c. 1670. During the first part of the colonial period, architecture and urban planning in Mexico were characterized by influences from

all the cultures that met in the region. The first Spanish cities, for example, were based on Mexica- or Tenocha-Aztec urban design, as seen in the capital, Mexico City, rebuilt as the seat of the Viceroyalty of New Spain. There the rectilinear Aztec urban plan of Tenochtitlán, with large open spaces for community activities, was retained for the new colonial city, its principal lines radiating from a vast central square in which the Templo Mayor had stood (see MEXICO CITY, §§I and II). Indigenous traditions were also reflected in the missions and also in the convents built by the mendicant orders, which dominated building activity in the 16th century. These complexes, for which the missionaries relied heavily on Indian labour (see §II above), drew on existing indigenous spatial arrangements for open-air ritual and ceremony: the climate and the size of the congregations determined that the services were conducted from an open chapel facing a spacious walled courtyard or atrium. This was sometimes arcaded to allow for various communal activities, usually with a wide multi-arched entrance portico and often with small, open chapels (capillas posas) at each corner. To these elementary enclosures were added subsidiary chapels, cloisters, a church and school. It is now known that the defensive appearance that characterizes the mid-16th-century convent enclosures did not derive from any military purpose, and that their austere masses, related to determinedly high nave-vaulting, arose from lack of sophistication on the part of the missionary designers, while the almenas (battlemented parapets), in a wide variety of shapes and suggesting Islamic origins, were decorative.

The Franciscan Order was the first to undertake a systematic convent building programme, working from 1524 in the Valley of Mexico and in areas south and west of Mexico City. Among the most prominent of their foundations are those of Huejotzingo (1540s) and Tepeaca (1543–80), both of which have churches with crenellated façades, rib-vaulted, aisleless naves and polygonal apses. The church of S Miguel in Huejotzingo has Plateresque decoration (see PLATERESQUE STYLE) framed in the characteristic Franciscan rope motif later found in a variety of buildings in Latin America. The Franciscans were also active in Yucatán, where the tropical conditions led to an interesting synthesis of colonial and indigenous styles, notably in the ramada chapels, which had no side walls and used branches of trees and foliage to give protection overhead from the sun (see YUCATECO).

The Dominicans, who arrived in Mexico in 1526, were active in Mexico City and to the south-east, in the region of Oaxaca. Their foundations included Oaxaca itself (begun 1575), Tlacolula (1580) and Yanhuitlán, the earliest (1550–80; Kubler, 1948) and probably the finest, which has a massively buttressed, high-waisted church with a single low tower because of the region's susceptibility to earthquakes. In Mexico City the church of S Domingo was already in a state of disrepair by 1552; FRANCISCO BECERRA is associated with its renovation between 1573 and 1575.

The Augustinians, who arrived in the 1530s, were allocated sites to the north and west of Mexico City and constructed a remarkable series of convents, of which more than 20 survive to demonstrate the Order's predilection for Plateresque façades. The most notable Augustinian

convents include those of Acolman (1541–87), in the State of México; Actopan (begun 1546) and Ixmiquilpan (founded 1550), in the region of Hidalgo; others in the more mountainous region to the north-west and Yecapixtla (begun between 1535 and 1540) in Morelos and Cuitzeo (1548–56) in Michoacán. All of these have heavily buttressed 'fortress' churches with almenas and shallow-pitched roofs. The churches of S Miguel, Ixmiquilpan, and S Miguel, Actopan, both by Fray Andrés de Mata (d 1574), who was assisted at Actopan by Fray Martín de Asebeido, have single massive towers. At S Pablo de Yuririapundaro another single massive tower and heavily buttressed chevet give an impression of immense strength that contrasts with the delicate decoration of the Plateresque façade. Designed for Fray Diego de Chávez (c. 1513–72) by Pedro de Toro (fl c. 1560), the church has chapels on either side of the chancel, giving an impression of a cruciform plan.

Only three cathedrals were completed in the 16th century: in Mexico City (1525–32; destr.), Oaxaca (begun 1544; rebuilt 1733) and Mérida (1562–98). The first of these was flat-roofed, with a Mudéjar timber structure, and the windows of the classical portal contained encerados (waxed cloth or paper, later with paintings). Oaxaca and MÉRIDA have hall-church sections. The cathedral of S Ildefonso, Mérida, has an austere Renaissance façade, with a magnificent recessed arch and two elegant towers (one from 1713); its coffered dome (1586–98) is inscribed to its Maestro Mayor Juan Miguel de Agüero (fl 1574–1613). The projected cathedral of S Salvador (1541–68), Pátzcuaro, commissioned by Bishop Vasco de Quiroga (1479–1565), was planned with five separately enclosed naves focusing on a spacious polygonal chancel. Begun by indigenous Tarascan craftsmen, from 1552 the building was under the direction of the Spanish master Hernando Toribio de Alcaraz (b c. 1522; d after 1572), but it was abandoned soon after Quiroga's death, with little completed. The second, Metropolitan, cathedral of Mexico City (see fig. 3), begun in 1563, may have been based on Jaén Cathedral in Spain, although the similarity is not close. The European type of foundations were inadequate and had to be rejected in favour of indigenous technology using friction piles and a continuous layer of masonry. In 1584 CLAUDIO DE ARCINIEGA was appointed to complete the work. He adopted a basilican section, with double clerestory arrangements, and, after his death in 1593, Agüero continued the work. It was dedicated in 1656, but the interior was not completed until 1667 and the towers only in 1813. The cathedral of Puebla (from 1575; for illustration see PUEBLA) is the smaller sister cathedral to the second cathedral in Mexico City. Francisco Becerra claimed to have worked on it as Maestro Mayor from 1575–80. Both buildings show the influence of the classical Renaissance style of the Spanish architect Juan de Herrera, although the cathedral in Mexico City has early Churrigueresque elements (see §(ii) below), while in the 1640s the dome at Puebla was sheathed in luminous local glazed tiles (azulejos) by the Aragonese architect-priest Mosén Pedro García Ferrer (1583–1660). Late decorative additions included star windows, finials and voluted buttresses. In the 17th century the cathedral of GUADALAJARA was also completed (1618), the only one in Mexico with an

3. Mexico City, Plaza de la Constitución: (left) Metropolitan Cathedral by Claudio de Arciniega, Juan Miguel de Agüero and others, 1563–1813; (right) Sagrario Chapel by Lorenzo Rodríguez, 1749–68

interior with Gothic-like elements, and work was begun in 1660 on a new cathedral in Morelia.

Another phase of religious building activity followed the initial period of evangelization: the construction of nunnery chapels in the early 17th century, which was significant in introducing early Baroque features into Mexico, for example at S Clara (begun 1605), Querétaro, and S Jerónimo (1623), Mexico City. That of Jesús María, Mexico City, begun in 1597 by Pedro Briceño and completed in 1621, is characteristic in its flowing decoration, while the nunnery church of La Concepción (1655), Mexico City, directed by Diego de los Santos y Avila (*fl* 1695–1716), has perhaps the earliest example in the country of the polygonal arch.

Few examples of 16th-century secular architecture remain, and the castle–palace of Hernán Cortés in Cuernavaca, the Casa de Montejo, Mérida, and the Casa de Andrés de Tobilla, San Cristobal de las Casas, have all been considerably altered. The two-storey Casa de Montejo in Mérida was built partly of Maya stone by an Indian mason to a Spanish design, and it has a decorated portal of mixed Plateresque, Gothic and *Mudéjar* origin. Schools and colleges were also built by the missionaries, especially the Jesuits, who founded the colleges of SS Pedro y Pablo (1572) and S Ildefonso (1592) in Mexico City, Espíritu Santo (1578) in Puebla, S Nicolás (1578) in Morelia, S Tomás (1591) in Guadalajara and S Martín (1606; now the Museo Nacional del Virreinato) in Tepotzotlán, the church of which has one of the finest Churrigueresque façades (1760–62) in Mexico. Other religious societies devoted to the care of the sick built many hospitals in the main cities.

As the indigenous population declined in the 17th century, so the influence of indigenous traditions in architecture and urban planning declined, and, although cathedrals were established in the traditional open plazas of the cities, important new buildings were built on the perimeter, in European fashion. The use of open chapels and walled atria for communal activities, which were deeply embedded in Central American tradition, lost its importance in the cities and was gradually abandoned, although in more remote areas it persisted. The centres of colonial cities were largely given over to artisans' workshops, grouped together in streets; on the outskirts were the bakeries, abattoirs, tanneries, lime-kilns and other activities proscribed from the centre by regulations governing the diffusion of smells, noise and unpleasant waste materials.

(ii) Baroque, Churrigueresque and Neo-classicism, c. 1670–c. 1870. Towards the end of the 17th century a more homogeneous and prosperous society began to evolve in Mexico, and with it came the development of Mexican Baroque architecture. Generally, however, the tendency towards circular and elliptical plans popular in European Baroque was resisted in favour of straight walls and parallel surfaces. The straight streets and wide squares of the towns lent themselves to the planning of visual focuses and effects of perspective as a logical development, for example in the convent of Las Rosas and the college of S Francisco Xavier (both in Morelia) or the church of S Rosa, Querétaro. Local factors, including a love of ornament, also determined the strong colours and decorated surfaces typical of Mexican Baroque. The bright red *tezontle* stone was used for the main body of many important buildings, while the contrasting yellowish white of *chiluca* stone was used for dressings in Mexico City and in the north and west. In Puebla painted plasterwork (*yeserias*) and ornate red brickwork achieved particular distinction, as did the extensive use of colourful glazed tiles to decorate external surfaces (for description and

illustration *see* POBLANO and POLYCHROMY, colour pl. II, fig. 1).

The prosperity of the period was manifested in the building of several important parish churches and their subsequent elevation to the status of cathedrals. Notable examples include the cathedral of San Luis Potosí (1703–*c.* 1730), an example of the early 'solomonic' style, using carved spiral or 'solomonic' columns, which first appeared in S Teresa la Antigua, Mexico City, and characterized the early Baroque period in Mexico. Carved spiral columns also decorate the façades of the cathedrals of Durango (1695–1765), Aguascalientes (1704–38) and Chihuahua (1725–58), where plain walls contrast sharply with the heavily ornamented portals and upper towers. One of the most representative buildings of the period, however, is the Basilica at Guadalupe, built between 1695 and 1709 to celebrate the miraculous appearance of the Virgin to the Indian Juan Diego. It was built by PEDRO DE ARRIETA to plans by José DURÁN, and it is characteristic in its angularity and use of such forms as polygonal arches, octagonal lunettes and corner towers. Arrieta also collaborated on the Jesuit church of La Profesa (1714–20), Mexico City, which exemplifies the Mexican Baroque urge to cover façades with flowing foliage reliefs; this tendency culminated in the almost totally encrusted upper façade of the cathedral of ZACATECAS (1729–52; see fig. 4), probably by Domingo Ximénez Hernández. Arrieta's contemporary, Miguel Custodio DURÁN, worked in a similar style in Mexico City, using solomonic columns in his best-known building, the church of S Juan de Dios (1729).

The early Baroque in Mexico was followed by a style usually described as CHURRIGUERESQUE, although it is sometimes also called the Ultra Baroque. If the early Baroque was characterized by the use of solomonic columns, the Churrigueresque is largely associated with the *estípite* motif, designed by the Spaniard José Benito de Churriguera, although the style that came to prevail in Mexico had few similarities to his work. A vertical element of square cross-section and tapering downwards, the *estípite* was one of the few motifs to be adopted from the European Baroque, and its introduction is usually attributed to JERÓNIMO DE BALBÁS in his design for the retable (1718–37) of the chapel of the Kings in Mexico City's Metropolitan Cathedral. Its early use has also been noted, however, in the portal (1712–18) of the Jesuit college of S Ildefonso (Kubler, 1948), while its use in the finial elements and main portal of the cathedral in Morelia, by Vicente Barroso de la Escayola (*d* 1695), is cited by Marco Dorta (1973).

By about the middle of the 18th century the use of the *estípite* in civil and religious buildings had achieved not only a richness and variety beyond that achieved in Spain, but also a national aesthetic that overrode regional differences. Notable civil buildings to employ the *estípite* include the Ayuntiamento (1720–24) and Aduana (1731), Mexico City, while the first truly Churrigueresque church was SS Prisca y Sebastián (1748–58), Taxco, by José Cayetano de Sigüenza y Góngora (1714–78). Here twin towers soar two storeys above the retable façade, and balustraded, segmentally arched nave bays reach upwards to a dome of blue and yellow tiles. The outstanding example of the style, however, is the Sagrario Chapel (1749–68; see fig. 3

4. Domingo Ximénez Hernández (attrib.): Zacatecas Cathedral, upper façade, 1729–52

above) of the Metropolitan Cathedral in Mexico City. Designed by LORENZO RODRÍGUEZ on a centralized cruciform plan, the two façades are merged by the masterly use of diagonally arranged planes and the interplay of *estípites*. Other notable Churrigueresque religious buildings are the elegant brick and stucco sanctuary of Ocotlán (*c.* 1750), Tlaxcala, and the church of La Valenciana (1765–88), Guanajuato. The latter, and the church of SS Prisca y Sebastián, are also both further examples of churches financed by prosperous mine-owners.

Houses for the wealthy in Mexico City also incorporated changing architectural styles around the middle of the 18th century: a notable example is Lorenzo Rodríguez's house (1764; with Antonio Rodríguez de Soria (*fl* 1650–86) for the Conde de San Bartolomé de Xala, which introduced new pilaster arrangements. Another house in Mexico City, designed in 1769 by FRANCISCO ANTONIO DE GUERRERO Y TORRES for the Condesa San Mateo Valparaiso (now a branch of the Banco de México), showed an attempt to simplify the existing complexities of style, and Guerrero's principal work, the Pocito Chapel (1779–91), Guadalupe, its centralized plan crowned with tiled domes, has a classicizing façade that heralds the Neo-classical.

Around the end of the 18th century new architectural criteria were being promoted by authorities and scholars, and the founding of the Colegio de Minas (1792) and the

Real Academia de las Nobles Artes de San Carlos (1783; *see* §XI below) led to the emergence of a Neo-classicism based on European models. The style is visible in the ogee tower cupolas (1793) by José Damián Ortiz de Castro (1750–93) in the cathedral in Mexico City, and the church of Carmen de Celaya (1802–7), Guanajuato, by FRANCISCO EDUARDO TRESGUERRAS. Other notable Neo-classical buildings include the Loreto Church (1816) and the residence of the Marqués del Apartado (1810) in Mexico City, by Manuel Tolsá, the Hospicio Cabañas (1805) in Guadalajara, the Alhóndiga de Granaditas (1809) in Guanajuato and the convent of S José (1812) in Orizaba. In addition to Ortiz de Castro and Tresguerras, architects associated with Neo-classicism in Mexico include Miguel Costanzó (1741–1810) in Mexico City and JOSÉ MANZO in Puebla. The most important exponent of the style, however, is MANUEL TOLSÁ, who was head of sculpture at the Academia but who was also active as an architect and whose most notable building was the Palacio de Minería (1797–1813; *see* MEXICO CITY, fig. 3).

Following the struggle for independence, the Academia de San Carlos remained closed, with a consequent interruption not only of the teaching of architecture but also of public building, which virtually ceased. It was not until more settled conditions prevailed in 1843 that the government of Antonio López de Santa Ana reopened the school, although architectural teaching was not resumed until 1856. Foreign teachers began to be hired, the most notable being the Italian Javier Cavallari (1810–79), who reorganized architectural studies at the Academia in 1857, combining artistic and scientific approaches and promoting an eclectic, historicist approach.

Much of the building of the first decades after independence continued, however, to be influenced by Neo-classicism. In Mexico City, for example, LORENZO DE LA HIDALGA, who settled there in 1838, was responsible for the Teatro de Santa Ana (1842–4; later the Teatro Nacional; destr. 1901) and the Mercado El Volador (*c.* 1852). Also active in the capital were Ramón Rodríguez Arangoiti (1830–84) and the brothers Juan Agea (1825–?1896) and Ramón Agea (1828–?1892), who all returned to work in Mexico after completing their training in Europe and were active during the brief reign (1864–7) of the Habsburg Emperor Maximilian. In the provinces a number of master builders were active, for example Juan Sanabria (*fl c.* 1831), who was responsible for the Caja de Agua (1831), San Luis Potosí; though lacking academic training, such builders had a thorough knowledge of construction techniques and were able to draw their inspiration from the increasingly available European treatises and manuals.

BIBLIOGRAPHY
Three Centuries of Mexican Colonial Architecture (New York, 1933)
D. Angulo Iñiguez, E. Marco Dorta and M. J. Buschiazzo: *Historia del arte hispano-americano*, 3 vols (Barcelona, 1945–56), i, pp. 121–478; ii, pp. 2–42, 480–820
G. Kubler: *Mexican Architecture of the 16th Century*, 2 vols (New Haven, CT, 1948)
M. Toussaint: *Arte colonial en México* (Mexico City, 1948)
G. Kubler and M. Soria: *Art and Architecture in Spain and Portugal and their American Dominions, 1500–1800*, Pelican Hist. A. (Harmondsworth, 1959), pp. 69–82
J. McAndrew: *Open Air Churches of Sixteenth Century Mexico* (Cambridge, 1965)
L. Castedo: *A History of Latin American Art and Architecture* (London, 1969), pp. 104–11, 116–32
E. Marco Dorta: *Arte en América y Filipinas*, A. Hisp., xxi (Madrid, 1973), pp. 127–49
S. D. Markman: *Architecture and Urbanisation in Colonial Chiapas* (Philadelphia, 1984)
E. Wilder Weismann and J. Hancock Sandoval: *Art and Time in Mexico: From the Conquest to the Revolution* (New York, 1985)
R. W. Morse: 'Urban Development', *Colonial Spanish America*, ed. L. Bethell (Cambridge, 1987), pp. 165–202
C. Chanfón: *Historia: Temas escogidos* (Mexico City, 1990)
L. Icaza: *Arquitectura civil en la Nueva España* (Mexico City, 1990)
J. Garciá Lascurain, C. Chanfón Olmos and M. Ponce Zavala: *Il barocco del Messico*, i of Corpus Barocco (Milan, 1991–)
M. Sartor: *Arquitectura y urbanismo en Nueva España, siglo XVI* (Mexico, 1992)

CARLOS CHANFÓN OLMOS

2. AFTER *c.* 1870.

(i) Eclecticism, *c.* 1870–*c.* 1910. (ii) Modernism, *c.* 1910–68. (iii) 1968 and after.

(i) Eclecticism, c. *1870–c. 1910.* The accession to the presidency of Porfirio Díaz in 1876 brought a period of national reorganization and economic growth to Mexico, with a significant increase in public building. The railway systems were modernized and enlarged, with new stations being opened, and new factories and manufacturing centres were built. Central and local government buildings and civic amenities appeared in towns. These included markets (such as La Victoria in Puebla or the Hidalgo in Guanajuato), hospitals (such as the Maternidad Tamariz, Puebla) and theatres. In some of these works the influence of Neo-classicism continued to be visible: for example in the Teatro Juárez (1892–1903), Guanajuato, by ANTONIO RIVAS MERCADO, with its classical hexastyle portico and life-size statuary on each pedestal of the balustrade, or the Teatro de la Paz (1889–94), San Luis Potosí, by JOSÉ NORIEGA. The façades of the Penitenciaria, Mexico City, by Antonio Torres Torija (1840–1922) from a modified earlier design by Lorenzo de la Hidalga, are also academic in style, although the building itself has an innovative, functional plan, based on the panoptic theories of Jeremy Bentham. In general, however, Beaux-Arts academicism was predominant, and numerous architects came from Europe to Mexico to work both as professionals and as teachers.

In the early 20th century numerous commercial and residential buildings were constructed in the persisting Beaux-Arts style by such architects as Emilio Dondé (1849–1906), while the brothers Nicolás Mariscal and Federico Mariscal (*see* MARISCAL) built in a variety of styles in Mexico City. Several major projects were also initiated to commemorate the approaching centenary of independence. These included the Teatro Nacional (1904–34; now the Palacio de Bellas Artes; see fig. 5), and the Edificio Central de Correos (1902–7), both in Mexico City, by ADAMO BOARI, and the Secretaría de Comunicaciones (1904–11), also in the capital, by SILVIO CONTRI, which later housed the Museo Nacional de Arte. Both Boari and Contri were Italians who had worked in the USA, and the Correos Central exemplifies the eclecticism of the age: four-storey, stone-faced street elevations deriving from Venetian Gothic are topped with *almenas* (battlemented parapets), and the building is entered by a polygonal-headed portal. The monument to *Independence*

5. Adamo Boari: Palacio de Bellas Artes (formerly Teatro Nacional), Mexico City, 1904–34

(completed 1910), however, was built by the Mexican Rivas Mercado, with sculptures by Enrique Alciati. Similar trends were evident in the provinces; REFUGIO REYES, for example, built some important works in Aguascalientes in eclectic styles, notably his domed church of S Antonio (1908).

(ii) Modernism, c. 1910–68. The Mexican Revolution virtually paralysed the country for ten years, and it was followed by a strong desire for change and modernism, imbued with a profound nationalism. In the field of architecture desire for change had already been expressed in the magazine *El arte y la ciencia*, founded by Nicolás Mariscal and published in Mexico City between 1899 and 1911. The lectures of Jesús T. Acevedo (1882–1918) at the Ateneo de la Juventud also argued for new attitudes to architecture and a reappraisal of the country's cultural heritage. The formation in 1919 of the Sociedad de Arquitectos Mexicanos strengthened the position of those architects arguing for a change of direction away from academic eclecticism and towards a national and more forward-looking architecture. At the same time the revolutionary movement presented the first post-revolution governments with an urgent architectural agenda in the areas of housing, schools and health. The architect most closely associated with this new direction was JOSÉ VIL-LAGRÁN GARCÍA, who by 1925 was building the Instituto de Higiene y Granja Sanitaria at Popotla, Mexico City. Completed in 1927, this is a 'white' building, with similarities to some of the works of the early Modern Movement in Europe. It was followed in 1929–36 by the Hospital para Tuberculosos at Huipulco, a suburb of Mexico City,

which is innovative not only in its pavilion planning, with open patient verandahs carried on exposed concrete frames, but also in its sparse, uncompromising appearance. These buildings, together with his work from 1926 as Professor of Theory at the Escuela Nacional de Arquitectura, in which he advocated the principles of the useful, the logical, the aesthetic and the social, established Villagrán as one of the most significant and influential figures in Mexican Modernism.

Other architects associated with the socially oriented architecture of the decade after the Revolution include ENRIQUE YÁÑEZ, who designed numerous hospitals, and CARLOS OBREGÓN SANTACILIA, among whose most important works is the Secretaría de Salubridad y Assistencia (1929) in Mexico City, built in an Art Deco style; this style remained popular into the 1930s for major public buildings such as the interiors of Boari's Palacio de Bellas Artes, completed by Federico Mariscal in 1930–34, and several significant buildings by JUAN SEGURA and FRANCISCO J. SERRANO. Obregón was also active in the educational field, subscribing to the traditional incremental approach in his neo-colonial Escuela Benito Juárez (1925), also in Mexico City. Probably the most significant contribution in this area was made, however, by JUAN O'GORMAN, whose early works in residential architecture, such as the Casa Diego Rivera (1929–30) or his own house (1931–2), both in San Angel, Mexico City, have undoubted affinities with the work of Le Corbusier. Appointed to design a series of schools in 1933, O'Gorman followed a radical line based on functional criteria to ensure the rapid production of inexpensive, standardized buildings that were later adopted by the Comité Administrador del Programa Federal de Construcción de Escuelas and applied to schools throughout the country. His major work of this period, however, is perhaps the Escuela Técnica (1932–4), Mexico City, which was functionally innovative and had affinities in its expression of structure and movement with the work of the Bauhaus. Another work that helped to lay the basis for a functional response to the demands of education was the Centro Escolar Revolución (1934) by Antonio Muñoz García (1896–1965).

In the 1930s there were also the first serious attempts to address the urgent need for low-cost housing. In this area the work of Juan Legarreta (1902–34), who won a competition in 1932 to design a Worker's House and went on to build several housing complexes, is particularly important and again has similarities with the work of the European Modern Movement. Other architects involved in designing low-cost housing include Enrique Yáñez and ENRIQUE DEL MORAL, as well as Alvaro Aburto (1905–76), who worked in rural housing. With a period of stability following the election in 1946 of Miguel Alemán as president, the first adequate solution was also offered to the urgent need for housing in metropolitan areas with high densities of population. MARIO PANI, who had experience of building private blocks of flats in the mid-1940s, was perhaps the most important architect in this area; he proposed high-rise housing blocks, which were called *multifamiliar* (multi-family) units and which were planned with ample landscape areas and other amenities. The Miguel Alemán housing complex (1947–50) in Mexico City, which consisted of 13-storey blocks providing over 1000 dwellings, is one of Pani's major works and a model of its kind.

The 1940s were also notable for an increasing commitment by Pani and others to the 'plastic integration' movement, in which painters and sculptors collaborated with architects to produce some striking works (*see* §IV, 2(iv)(a) below). Among the first buildings to result from such a collaboration were the Sindicato Mexicano de Electricistas (1940), on which Enrique Yáñez worked with David Alfaro Siqueiros, and the Escuela Nacional de Maestros (1945–7), on which Pani worked with José

Clemente Orozco and Luis Ortiz Monasterio. 'Plastic integration' was also one of the major themes in the design of the Ciudad Universitaria (1948–52). Built on the lava fields of the Pedregal area on what was then the southern edge of Mexico City, the complex was intended to reunite the dispersed parts of the university in a single location and involved more than 60 architects, as well as such artists as Diego Rivera, Siqueiros, Francisco Eppens (*b* 1913), José Chávez Morado and the Columbian-born Rodrigo Arenas Betancourt (*b* 1919). The overall plan was conceived by Pani and Enrique del Moral, who were also responsible, with SALVADOR ORTEGA FLORES, for the 14-storey Rectoría (1951–2) on the highest point of the campus. The exterior of the Rectoría is decorated with murals by Siqueiros, but it is perhaps the stone walls of the 'Frontones' (1952) by ALBERTO T. ARAI, reminiscent of Pre-Columbian pyramid profiles, and Juan O'Gorman's Biblioteca Central (1948–50) that best represent the integration of the plastic arts and architecture with the essence of an indigenous culture: the central block of the latter is decorated with O'Gorman's characteristic reliefs and stone mosaics (for illustration *see* O'GORMAN, JUAN). The structural virtuosity of the cosmic ray laboratory (1951) by FÉLIX CANDELA exhibits an interesting solution, while the Estado Olímpico (1950–52), by AUGUSTO PÉREZ PALACIO, with polychrome stone reliefs by Diego Rivera, reflects the pre-Hispanic theme.

The International Style embraced by AUGUSTO H. ALVÁREZ and JUAN SORDO MADALENO gained numerous disciples, meanwhile, as the mastery of reinforced concrete led, in Mexico as elsewhere, to numerous works characterized by the lightly framed glass membranes of curtain-wall cladding. Notable examples include the strip-windowed Registro Publico de la Propriedad (1950–52) by Federico Mariscal, the L-shaped Secretaría de Trabajo y Prevision Social (1954) by PEDRO RAMÍREZ VÁZQUEZ and Rafael Mijares (*b* 1922), the Edificio Commercial (1956) by Ricardo de Robina (*b* 1919) and the elegant glass-fronted Pasaje Jacaranda store (1956), Calle Londres by TORRES & VELÁZQUEZ, all in Mexico City; the most spectacular work in this genre at the time was the 43-storey, glass-clad Torre Latino Americana (1957) and the Jaysour Building (1962–4) by Alvárez. Other architects producing similar works included Héctor Mestre (*b* 1909), FRANCISCO ARTIGA and Reinaldo Pérez Rayón (*b* 1918), all active in Mexico City. Dramatic structural solutions also continued to interest ENRIQUE DE LA MORA and, in particular, Félix Candela, for example in the latter's shell-vaulted church of the Virgin of the Miraculous Medal (1955; for illustration *see* CANDELA, FÉLIX), Mexico City, and other avant-garde structures that developed a lyrical form of Modernism, avoiding the prismatic rigidity of international architecture through their imagination and creativity. This interest endured into the 1960s in such works as the Museo Nacional de Antropología (1964; see fig. 6), Mexico City, by Ramírez Vázquez, Rafael Mijares and Jorge Campuzano. Here a monumental umbrella, cantilevered from a single support, covers most of a spacious central patio.

A third major strand in the architecture of the post-war period in Mexico was formed by a group of architects anxious to preserve the diverse national heritage. Of these

6. Pedro Ramírez Vázquez, with Rafael Mijares and Jorge Campuzano: Museo Nacional de Antropología, Mexico City, 1964

'regionalists' it is LUIS BARRAGÁN whose work is most significant, and those who worked with him, for example MAX CETTO. Persistently pursuing beauty and the recovery of local traditions, Barragán used such natural materials as wood, clay and textiles, and vibrant colours and textures combined with light and water to achieve an integrated effect. After a period of building influenced by Le Corbusier, he began work in an innovative direction with his own house (1947) in Tacubaya, where the massive walls counterpoint the small asymmetric openings, reminiscent of vernacular examples. The sculptor Mathías Goeritz wrote the manifesto *Arquitectura emocional* on the occasion of the opening in 1953 of the Museo Experimental 'El Eco', and Barragán adopted Goeritz's title to refer to his own work. They worked together on a group of functionless sculptural towers, 30 to 50 m high, at the entrance to the Ciudad Satélite (1957), a residential area planned by Mario Pani to accommodate 200,000 inhabitants 15 km from the centre of Mexico City. Some of Barragán's most notable projects, however, are primarily concerned with the enhancement and definition of the landscape, as in his master-plan and gardens at Jardines del Pedregal de San Angel (1950), next to the university, or the master-plan and fountains at Las Arboledas residential development (1961).

(iii) 1968 and after. Following social unrest in 1968, there was a desire on the part of the government to create a greater number of buildings in response to social needs, but there was also a desire on the part of many architects to contribute a new vision of the role of architecture. This led to three main trends within Mexican architecture, in addition to the more internationalist works that continued to be produced by such architects as Augusto Alvárez and Juan José Díaz Infante (*b* 1936). The first of these is marked by the use of geometric forms to produce bold structural compositions and is sometimes referred to as 'sculptural architecture'. Perhaps the most important representatives of the style are AUGUSTÍN HERNÁNDEZ, who introduced a more complex geometric vision in his own studio (1971) and MANUEL GONZÁLEZ RUL, whose Gymnasium Gustavo Díaz Ordaz (1968), Mexico City, is a spectacularly innovative solution in which roof slabs lean together. Hernández and González Rul collaborated on the design of the Heroico Colegio Militar (1976), Tlapán, which combines geometric innovation with axial planning on a grand scale and building forms reminiscent of Pre-Columbian models. Alejandro Caso (*b* 1920) and Margarita Caso also produced Pre-Columbian-inspired work, such as the impressive Instituto Nacional de Estadistica, Geografía e Informática (1989) in Aguascalientes.

A second, functionalist, approach used exposed concrete as a means of expression while recalling such traditional architectural elements as the portico and the courtyard. The inaugurators of this style were TEODORO GONZÁLEZ DE LEÓN and ABRAHAM ZABLUDOVSKY, who created the Colegio de México (1974–5; see fig. 7) and the Universidad Pedagógica (1983), but others working in a similar vein include DAVID MUÑOZ SUÁREZ, Francisco Serrano, Gustavo Eichermann (*b* 1935), Gonzalo Gómez Palacio (*b* 1944) and ALEJANDRO ZOHN. A third style is represented by RICARDO LEGORRETA, who continued to

7. Abraham Zabludovsky and Teodoro González de León: Colegio de México, Mexico City, 1974–5

produce 'emotional architecture', applying Barragán's premises—originally intended for a domestic scale—to enormous and complex buildings, such as the Hotel Camino Real (1968), Mexico City, and the serene IBM factory (1975) in Guadalajara. Other architects whose work has an affinity with that of Barragán and Legorreta include Antonio Attolini Lack (*b* 1931), Andrés Casillas (*b* 1937) and Carlos Mijares (*b* 1930), who built some exceptional churches. Following the establishment of these three broad stylistic groupings in the late 1960s and 1970s, however, a younger generation of architects began to attract attention.

Many of these styles continued into the 1980s: such architects as Díaz Infante and Alvárez continued to produce standard glass towers, such as the former's Bolsa de Valores (1990) and the latter's Edificio Parque Reforma (1983), Mexico City. Augustín Hernández's geometric approach developed into a more complex virtuosity with such features as the circular cutaways of the Centro de Meditación (1986) at Cuernavaca and the Casa Bosque de las Lomas (1988), Mexico City. Younger architects working in a similar style included Oscar Bulnes Valero (*b* 1944) and the other members of the Grupo 103: Fernando López Martínez (*b* 1960) and Bernardo Lira Gómez (*b* 1949). Among the group's most notable works is the new addition to the Instituto Tecnológico de Monterrey (1988) in Nuevo León. Of those working in a functionalist idiom, Zohn developed an architecture of surface texture in such buildings as the formally thrusting Archivos del Estado de Jalisco (1989) in Guadalajara, its windowless surfaces finished entirely in lined hammered concrete, as Orso Núñez with Arcadio Artiz used it at the Centro Cultural Universitario (1976–80). Serrano and Rafael Mijares, meanwhile, adopted brickwork as the dominant medium in the buildings, galleries and patios (1984–7) of the Universidad Iberoamericana outside Mexico City. The partnership of Abraham Zabludovsky and González de

León was responsible for three banks in Mexico City. González de León also worked with Serrano on a park (1985) in Villahermosa, Tabasco, and the Palacio de Justicia Federal (1992) in Mexico City; and Abraham Zabludovsky on four theatres (1990–92) in the central part of the country.

Ricardo Legorreta's work continued in the 1980s with the screens, patios and pools of another Hotel Camino Real (1981) at Ixtapa, Guerrero, the Museo Marco (1991), Monterrey, and the cathedral of Managua (1993), Nicaragua. Attolini Lack's similar interests are evident in various residences and a factory in Mexico City, where he created an atmosphere of ascetism with spatial richness.   This last tendency has become the more dominant, even fashionable; but certain architects can be considered true exponents of regionalism. One such is Enrique Murillo (*b* 1933), who managed to integrate into the Veracruz environment such works as the Central de Autobuses de Jalapa (1989); Juan Palomar (*b* 1956) worked in a similar way in Guadalajara, as did Ricardo Padilla (*b* 1956) and Jorge Estévez (*b* 1955) with a series of houses in the city of Monterrey inspired by the vernacular architecture of the north-east. Among those who produced holiday homes in the tropical areas are Diego Villaseñor (*b* 1944), José Iturbe (*b* 1946), Javier Sordo (*b* 1956) and Manuel Mestre (*b* 1954), young designers who adapted such local ideas as *palapas* (palm roofs). Finally, in the sphere of urbanism of the type promoted by Luis Barragán, notable figures include FERNANDO GONZÁLEZ GORTÁZAR, with his series of fountains in Guadalajara, and Mario Schjetnan Garduño (*b* 1945), head of the Grupo de Diseño Urbano, who proposed such works as the Parque Tezozómoc (1982) and the Parque Ecológico de Xochimilco (1993).

Notable examples of the formal trend inspired by the Pre-Columbian past include the Universidad de Mayab (1982) in Mérida, Yucatán, planned by Augusto Quijano (*b* 1955) and Alejandro Domínguez (*b* 1956); Eduardo Reyna Medina from Aguascalientes, and the group comprising Jorge Ballina (*b* 1939), José Creixell (*b* 1937) and Fernando Rovalo (*b* 1940), who produced works such as the Universidad Iberoamericana (1988) in Torreón, subscribe to an integral functionalism. Younger generations have been particularly successful in the international avant-garde trends of the late 20th century such as Post-modernism or Deconstruction. Such is the case with the practices of Luis Sánchez (*b* 1944) and Félix Sánchez (*b* 1944) or of Nuño-MacGregor-de Buen, who have offered solutions to housing and transport problems. The workshops TEN and TAX, led by Enrique Norten (*b* 1954) and Alberto Kalach (*b* 1960), have taken a more provocative stance.

The richness and variety of late 20th-century Mexican architecture shows that its practitioners responded to the most important needs of the country and its inhabitants, at the same time searching for suitable technical and aesthetic solutions. In this manner, by using their creativity to maximum effect and by taking into account the cultural and material conditions, they opened the doors to a promising future.

BIBLIOGRAPHY

E. Born: *The New Architecture in Mexico* (New York, 1937)
I. E. Myers: *Mexico's Modern Architecture* (New York, 1952)
C. Obregón Santacilia: *50 años de arquitectura en México* (Mexico City, 1952)
J. Villagrán García: *Panorama de 50 años de arquitectura en México* (Mexico City, 1952)
M. Cetto: *Modern Architecture in Mexico* (New York, 1961)
I. Katzman: *La arquitectura contemporánea mexicana* (Mexico City, 1963)
C. Bamford Smith: *Builders in the Sun: Five Mexican Architects* (New York, 1967)
F. Bullrich: *New Directions in Latin American Architecture* (London, 1969), pp. 13–15, 19–20, 28–32, 59–61
I. Katzman: *La arquitectura del siglo XIX en México* (Mexico City, 1973)
'Modern Mexican Architecture', *Process Archit.*, 39 (1983) [whole issue]
L. Noelle: *Arquitectos contemporáneos de México* (Mexico City, 1989)
A. Toca Fernández, ed.: *Arquitectura contemporánea en México* (Mexico City, 1989)
E. Yáñez: *Del Funcionalismo al Post-Racionalismo: Ensayo sobre la arquitectura contemporánea mexicana* (Mexico City, 1990)
L. Noelle: *Catálogo guía de arquitectura contemporánea mexicana* (Mexico City, 1993)
F. González Gortázar, ed.: *La arquitectura mexicana del siglo XX* (Mexico City, 1994)

LOUISE NOELLE

IV. Painting, graphic arts and sculpture.

1. 1519–*c*. 1830. 2. After *c*. 1830.

1. 1519–*c*. 1830.

(i) Early colonial, Mannerism and Baroque, 1519–*c*. 1780. (ii) Neo-classicism, *c*. 1780–*c*. 1830.

*(i) Early colonial, Mannerism and Baroque, 1519–*c. *1780.* After the arrival of the first Franciscan missionaries in Mexico in the 1520s, there was an immediate demand for painters and sculptors to decorate the churches and convents erected under their prolific building programme. In the absence of a significant number of European artists, indigenous Indian craftsmen, under the tuition of such missionaries as Fray Pedro de Gante (*see* §XI below) proved remarkably skilful at adapting to the new artistic demands, although indigenous motifs continued to appear in their work, giving it a distinctive character known as *tequitqui* (*see* §II above). Until the middle of the 16th century the only alternative to the works of these indigenous artists was the import of works from Europe, but by 1556 sufficient numbers of European artists had arrived in the colony to form the Guild of Painters and Gilders, partly to protect themselves against exploitation from their ecclesiastical patrons and partly to fend off competition from Indian artists. Other craft guilds, including the Guild of Carpenters, Woodcutters, Joiners and Viol-makers, were established soon after, and as these guilds began to train apprentices in their studios they laid the basis of a stylistic identity distinct from European models. In painting and sculpture, however, which both remained predominantly religious in character throughout the colonial period, similar stylistic divisions into Mannerist, Baroque and Neo-classical periods can be made, even if these periods in Mexican art do not follow exactly the same chronology as in European art. Printmaking remained relatively unsophisticated, however, although the name of one 16th-century printmaker, Fray Diego de Valadés (1533–82), is known, as well as those of a few later exponents. Again the subject-matter consisted largely of religious allegories and devotional images, but it also included coats of arms, maps, portraits, or simple vignettes, usually in the form of small prints inserted in books or

more elaborate title-pages and loose prints, engraved on woodblocks or metal sheets.

Although the arrival of the Spanish led to the mutation of traditional indigenous techniques and to such innovations as SUGAR SCULPTURE, probably in the second half of the 16th century, the most significant art form in the colonial period was the retable, on which painters, sculptors, carvers, gilders and joiners collaborated to produce lavish gilded ensembles incorporating paintings on canvas, relief panels and life-size polychrome statues of saints. Most retable workshops were based in Mexico City, at least until the late 18th century, from where completed works would be transported to the provinces, although sometimes a team would be sent out to construct a retable *in situ*. The workshops are relatively well documented, mainly through contracts for work, but as these were signed only by the major artist in the workshop the names of only a few artists are known; examples include Sebastián de Ocampo, responsible for the retable of the King and Queen in the cathedral in Mexico City, Isidoro Vicente de Balbás, who designed the altarpieces in the church of SS Prisca y Sebastián, the parish church of Taxco, and Pedro Requena, who was responsible with the Flemish painter SIMÓN PEREINS for the retable of the church of the Franciscan convent at Huejotzingo (see fig. 8). Pereins, who arrived in New Spain in 1566, was one of the most notable painters in the Mannerist style that dominated until the middle of the 17th century, in which both the elegant, idealistic influence of the Italian tradition and the delight in details of the Flemish school are evident. Outstanding among his known contemporaries are ANDRÉS DE LA CONCHA, Baltasar de Echave Orio (*see* ECHAVE) and Luis JUÁREZ.

During the Baroque period, from about the middle of the 17th century, sculpture continued to be the dominant art form, with retables characterized by their incorporation of carved spiral 'solomonic' columns rather than by the Plateresque decoration that had characterized the Mannerist period. The carvers and joiners who were responsible for the construction of these retables were also responsible for furnishing the chapels of private individuals with free-standing wooden images and for other such works as the carving of choir-stalls. Notable artists of this period include Salvador de Ocampo (*fl* 1696–1722), who executed the choir-stalls in the convent of San Agustín, and Juan de Rojas, who carved those in Mexico City's Metropolitan Cathedral. During this period, although Indian artists continued to be officially excluded from the rank of Master, such sculptors as Salvador de Ocampo were taking on registered Indian apprentices, and at least one eminent 17th-century Indian sculptor is documented: Tómas Juárez, responsible for the retable of the Augustinian church in Mexico City.

The painting of the early Baroque period, covering practically the whole of the second half of the 17th century, is characterized by the incorporation of the austere realism of the Spanish school, reinforced by a taste for contrasts in light and the forceful depiction of volumes and clothing, in the manner of Zurbarán, whose work, with that of Ribera and Rubens, became known through the importation of reproductive engravings. Its most notable exponents were SEBASTIÁN LÓPEZ DE ARTEAGA,

8. Pedro Requena, Simón Pereins and assistants: main retable, gilded wood, *c.* 1586, church of the Franciscan convent, Huejotzingo, Mexico

José JUÁREZ and Pedro Ramirez (*fl* 1633–78). The second phase of the Baroque, covering the transition from the 17th to the 18th centuries, was a brilliant, ostentatious period characterized by paintings that are vibrant in form, with vivid colours and loose brushwork, echoing the splendour and exuberance of the architecture and retables of the period. The outstanding artists of this time, such as CRISTOBAL DE VILLALPANDO and JUAN CORREA, sacrificed correctness of form for a greater expressiveness.

In the 18th century a new form of sculpture was introduced, in which only the heads and the hands were carved and the remainder were simple dummy figures, and, in the quest for greater realism, wigs, glass eyes and natural teeth began to be used in figure sculpture. The Churrigueresque architectural style is also visible in, for example, the construction between 1718 and 1737 of the retable of the chapel of the Kings in the cathedral of Mexico City by Jerónimo de Balbás (*see* §III, 1(ii) above). In painting the late Baroque period was marked by the development of a softer and more sentimental style, which, because of its greater delicacy and emotionalism, has been interpreted as a response to the art of Murillo. This style, whose early exponents included Nicolás Rodríguez Juárez and Juan Rodríguez JUÁREZ, flourished until the last third of the 18th century, when it began to lose ground to the energetic thrust of Neo-classical court painting. The outstanding painters of this period include JOSÉ DE IBARRA, MIGUEL CABRERA, Francisco Antonio Vallejo (*fl* 1752–84) and José de Alcíbar (1730–1810).

Although painting during the late Baroque period remained predominantly religious in character, there are significant examples of portraiture, and although only isolated works or simple references survive, it seems that still-life was practised, for example by Antonio Pérez de Aguilar (e.g. *Still Life*, n.d.; priv. col.), as well as landscape painting and representations of historical, mythological and folk themes. Although such compositional considerations as the use of diagonal axes are visible in Baroque painting, both to articulate the figures or elements that compose the scenes and to endow these with an element of dynamism, nevertheless it is impossible to claim that painting in Mexico at this time shows dynamic movement or broad perspective. In the peaceful postures of the figures there is reserve and elegance but little anatomical exactness and an over-reliance on archetypes.

ROGELIO RUIZ GOMAR

9. Manuel Tolsá: *Charles IV*, bronze, 1796–1803, Plaza Manuel Tolsá, Mexico City

(ii) Neo-classicism, c. 1780–c. 1830. The founding in 1783 of the Academia de las Nobles Artes de S Carlos in Mexico City symbolized the demise of the Baroque in Mexico and its official supersession by Neo-classicism; it also heralded the disappearance of the guilds and a consequent restructuring of the system of artistic production. As the endorsement of an academic training became essential to secure patronage, the Academia became an official arbiter of taste and regulator of artistic production, particularly in Mexico City, although artists trained in the guilds continued for many years to work alongside those who had received an academic education. The works of the former usually appeared more old-fashioned as well as exhibiting 'errors' of draughtsmanship and perspective for which they were later highly esteemed when an anti-academic mood became dominant in the 1920s. The Academia's influence was not confined to Mexico City, however, since the academic community in the capital also set the stylistic parameters that were eventually followed in provincial centres of production, especially those in which local academies were established under the direction of artists trained at the Academia. In Puebla, for example, where the local academy maintained cordial relations with the Academia in Mexico City, the transition from Baroque to Neo-classicism was consolidated by the baldacchino of the cathedral (1797–1819) by MANUEL TOLSÁ, director of sculpture at the Academia de San Carlos. This work is a fine example of the abandonment of the traditional retable, made of gilded wood with statues of decorated, polychromed wood, in favour of an altar of stone, brick and stucco, with statues in bronze, stone or wood that imitated 'refined' materials, in accordance with Neo-classical taste.

Although religious iconography continued to play a leading role due to the dominant influence of the Roman Catholic Church in Mexican life, a secularizing tendency was immediately apparent in the early Neo-classical period. One of the outstanding examples of sculpture in this period, for example, is the monumental bronze equestrian statue of *Charles IV* (1796–1803; see fig. 9) by Tolsá, beside the Museo Nacional de Arte in Mexico City. Mythological themes abounded in academic drawings, while scientific and archaeological drawings were cultivated by such artists as Atanasio Echevarría and José Luciano Castañeda, who had trained at the Academia de S Carlos and also been involved with the expeditions organized by the Spanish Bourbon monarchy to record the natural resources and cultural wealth of Hispanic America. By the end of the 18th century there were also a number of well-known Indian sculptors, including PEDRO PATIÑO IXTOLINQUE and Santiago Cristóbal Sandoval, who worked on the sculptures for the tower of the cathedral of Mexico City. In the graphic arts, among those who trained at the Academia de S Carlos under the Sevillean José Joaquín Fabregat (1748–1807), historical and allegorical topics were also predominant, but popular printmaking continued for many years simply to respond to demands for the representation of devout images. In painting, the outstanding figure of the Neo-classical period was RAFAEL XIMENO Y PLANES, who was Director General of the Academia and who created the prototype of the modern portrait, without identifying inscriptions or heraldic signs and concentrating entirely on re-creating the model, as in his portrait of *Manuel Tolsá* (*c.* 1795; Mexico City, La Profesa). Ximeno's pupils, however, and provincial artists had to submit to tradition and their clients' demands, and the use of inscriptions, which detracted from the illusory effect and bestowed a certain archaic air, continued in their portraits for several decades.

The founding of the Academia de S Carlos and the adoption of Neo-classicism were partly inspired by the same Enlightenment ideas that provided the stimulus for the political emancipation of Mexico in 1821, and for the first few years after independence Neo-classical ideals continued to provide the models for the design of the first allegories of the new nation and the portraits of its first rulers (e.g. the anonymous portrait of the *Liberator Agustín de Iturbide*, 1822; Mexico City, Mus. N. A.).

FAUSTO RAMÍREZ

BIBLIOGRAPHY

J. Morena Villa: *La escultura colonial mexicana* (Mexico City, 1942)
M. Romero de Torreros: *Grabados y grabadores en la Nueva España* (Mexico City, 1948)
M. Toussaint: *Arte colonial en México* (Mexico City, 1949, rev. 1961; Eng. trans., Austin, TX, 1967)
E. Wilder Weismann: *Mexico in Sculpture, 1521–1821* (Cambridge, MA, 1950)
P. Kelemen: *Baroque and Rococo in Latin America* (New York, 1951)
F. Cal'i: *The Art of the Conquistadors* (London, 1961)
M. Toussaint: *Pintura colonial en México* (Mexico City, 1965)
Y. Bottineau: *Ibero-American Baroque* (London, 1971)
G. Tovar de Teresa: *Pintura y escultura del renacimiento en México* (Mexico City, 1979)
E. Wilder Weismann and J. Hancock Sandoval: *Art and Time in Mexico: From the Conquest to the Revolution* (New York, 1985)

ROGELIO RUIZ GOMAR

2. AFTER *c.* 1830.

(i) Romanticism, *c.* 1830–*c.* 1870. (ii) Realism and political art, *c.* 1870–*c.* 1895. (iii) Modernism, *c.* 1895–1920. (iv) Mexican Renaissance, 1920–*c.* 1950. (v) *c.* 1950 and after.

(i) Romanticism, c. *1830*–c. *1870.* Almost immediately after Mexican independence, two versions of romanticism arose. One was a form of nationalist romanticism, which concentrated on the depiction of regional subjects, landscapes and local people and customs in contrast to the universalizing, timeless pretensions of Neo-classicism. A major centre for this regionalist painting was Puebla, where AGUSTÍN ARRIETA, who had trained at the local academy, was active, and in the 1830s paintings of urban scenes by such artists as JOSÉ MANZO and José María Fernández were in great demand in Puebla. Regional themes and character types, as well as urban and rural landscapes, were subjects freely treated in painting and lithography—introduced into Mexico by the Italian Claudio Linati in 1825—by DANIEL THOMAS EGERTON and other 'travelling artists' who, with the opening of the borders after independence, flocked to Mexico between 1820 and 1850. Linati's prints, like those of Karl Nebel (?1800–65) and FREDERICK CATHERWOOD, though directed principally at a European audience, at the same time encouraged local ventures by commercial engravers. In the lithographs printed in workshops set up in the 1830s and 1840s by French and domestic entrepreneurs, there were evident borrowings from the albums of the 'travelling artists'. Mexican lithography reached its maturity with such collections as *Los mexicanos pintados por sí mismos* (1854–5; engravings by HESIQUIO IRIARTE) and

México y sus alrededores (1855; lithographs by CASIMIRO CASTRO and others).

A different form of romanticism developed in the capital, however, where, amid a period of political instability, the Academia de S Carlos was reorganized in 1843. In 1846 PELEGRÍN CLAVÉ and MANUEL VILAR arrived from Europe to take over the teaching of painting and sculpture, respectively. They succeeded in training a substantial group of students who were stylistically affiliated to the Nazarenes and *Purismo*, perhaps the style most suited to the expressive requirements of the conservative Catholic group that dominated the Academia until 1867. Although the iconography of Clavé's school did not avoid mythological and secular subjects, the Old and New Testaments were its principal source of inspiration. Artists used biblical stories of family dissent and the battles of the Jewish people to reflect, with varying degrees of deliberateness, contemporary political and ideological clashes, as in such paintings as the *Hebrews in Babylonian Captivity* (1857; Mexico City, Pal. B.A.) by Joaquin Ramírez (*d* 1886). There was no desire among painters to treat contemporary themes directly, however, or to treat national historical themes. In contrast, in sculpture Vilar portrayed figures of national history and heroes of Pre-Columbian antiquity and national independence (e.g. *Motecuhzuma II*, 1850; Mexico City, Mus. N.A.). Landscape painting was comparatively neglected at the Academia until the arrival in 1856 of the Italian EUGENIO LANDESIO; his most notable pupils included Luis Coto (1830–91) and José María Velasco (*see* §(ii) below).

(ii) Realism and political art, c. *1870*–c. *1895.* The period of peace and prosperity that accompanied the 35-year presidency of Porfirio Díaz acted as an effective force of cohesion for the national consciousness and led to a new interest in archaeology and Mexican history. In the fine arts the secularizing trends of the republican system and positivism ended the primacy of biblical iconography and replaced it with subjects from European or Mexican history. The portrayal of episodes from Pre-Columbian history and from the Spanish conquest became especially popular from *c.* 1870, for example in the work of FÉLIX PARRA (see fig. 10). The idealism of the school of Clavé, which can still be detected in such paintings as the *Discovery of Pulque* (1869; Mexico City, Pal. B.A.) by José María Obregón (1832–1902), gradually gave way to the increasingly realistic portrayal of native types, for example in the *Tlaxcala Senate* (1874; Mexico City, Mus. N.A.) by RODRIGO GUTIÉRREZ; this tendency culminated in a sort of quasi-photographic naturalism exemplified by the *Founding of Mexico City* (1889; Mexico City, Mus. N.A.) by JOSÉ JARA. Landscape painting also developed from the romanticism of Landesio (e.g. the *Valley of Mexico*, n.d.; Mexico City, Mus. N.A.) to the quasi-scientific objectivism demonstrated by José María Velasco in his treatment of the same subject (for illustration *see* VELASCO, JOSÉ MARÍA). Through the influence of realism (encouraged by the popularity of photography), the use of identifying inscriptions was abandoned even in provincial portraits, and the close examination of faces and personalities was intensified, as in the penetrating portraits of HERMENEGILDO BUSTOS (e.g. *Doña Severa Morán de Quintana*, 1894;

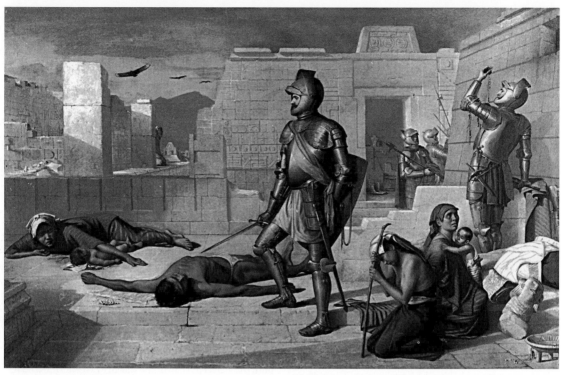

10. Félix Parra: *Episodes of the Conquest*, oil on canvas, 683×1095 mm, 1877 (Mexico City, Museo Nacional de Arte)

Mexico City, Pal. B.A.). Moreover, a new interest in domestic issues led to a greater treatment of regional topics, even within the Academia itself, renamed the Escuela Nacional de Bellas Artes in 1867. Political stability and economic prosperity led also to a flourishing of monumental sculpture. Both in the capital and the provinces statues were erected to the heroes of independence and reform, and even to inspirational native historical figures, as in the monument to *Cuauhtémoc* (1878) by MIGUEL NOREÑA in the Paseo de la Reforma, Mexico City, a balanced synthesis of idealistic conception and realistic detail.

In academic etchings, after 1879 a new importance was attached to original compositions. The most important graphic work in this period, however, was in political etchings and popular prints. Outstanding were the political caricatures in such polemical periodicals as *La orquesta* and *El hijo de Ahuizote*, which contained work by CONSTANTINO ESCALANTE and SANTIAGO HERNÁNDEZ. Opposition to the government of Porfirio Díaz later inspired such caricaturists as Daniel Cabrera (1858–1914) and Jesús Martínez Carrión (1860–1906). At the same time the subject-matter of the popular print broadened considerably: to illustrate posters and pamphlets discussing the most important or sensational events of the day and addressed to a largely uneducated mass audience, such publishers as Antonio Vanegas Arroyo contracted the services of Manuel Manilla (1830–95) and JOSÉ GUADALUPE POSADA, the most notable popular engravers in the 19th century in Mexico.

(iii) Modernism, c. 1895–1920. By the end of the 19th century a growing scepticism towards science and the search for a faith that would replace lost religious beliefs led to the adoption by several artists and intellectuals of many of the attitudes of the Aesthetic Movement in Europe as they struggled to penetrate beneath surface reality in a manner similar to that of the Symbolists. Seeking to achieve a subjective and lyrical art but unable to find adequate models to express their new concept of reality in local tradition, they increasingly turned to European art for models. In Mexico, therefore, the advent of modernism represented a deliberate, violent break with the art of the immediate past.

The first signs of a change in style and attitude became evident *c.* 1895 in sculpture. The allegorical, sensual, female nudes of JESÚS F. CONTRERAS, filled with anguish and suggesting complex states of mind, were treated in an impressionistic manner similar to that of Rodin (e.g. *Malgré tout*, 1898; Mexico City, Mus. N.A.). Other young sculptors followed and continued to work in this style until *c.* 1920. Meanwhile, in painting and the graphic arts JULIO RUELAS, who studied in Germany, popularized the taste for the new stylistic trends among such young artists as ROBERTO MONTENEGRO and Angel Zárraga (1886–1946) through his illustrations (1898–1911) in the *Revista moderna*. Other painters, such as GERMÁN GEDOVIUS, who also studied in Germany, and Alberto Fuster (1870–1922), explored other forms of Symbolism, although in an eclectic manner they also absorbed the chromatic and compositional lessons of Impressionism and Post-Impressionism. The presence of these artists as teachers in the Escuela Nacional de Bellas Artes helped the rapid institutionalization of stylistic change, which was consolidated by the following generation.

Another particularly strong influence on young artists was DR ATL, through both his synthesizing vision of the Mexican landscape and his anarchistic social ideas. Atl's search for new forms of expression in the local landscape and Gedovius's exploration of surviving elements of the culture of the Viceroyalty, together with the insistence of ANTONIO FABRÉS on the portrayal of ordinary people by the students, laid the basis for the start *c*. 1910 of the second phase of modernism. This was an attempt to draw on Symbolism and Post-Impressionism to express what these artists called 'the national soul'. The 'cosmopolitan' iconography of the first phase of modernism, incorporating such elements as the *femme fatale*, the struggle between the sexes and an obsession with death and the macabre, was transformed into recognizably national themes, while retaining their Symbolist, intimist and spiritual significance. It was SATURNINO HERRÁN who most eloquently expressed these aesthetic ideals in such works as *La tehuana* (1914; Aguascalientes, Mus. Aguascalientes). This modernist nationalism, which has affinities with other forms of Symbolist regionalism (such as the work of Ignacio Zuloaga y Zabaleta and other Spanish artists popular in Mexico at that time), reached its climax in the second decade of the 20th century, coinciding with the profound emotional and cultural upheaval caused by the Mexican Revolution. While a few artists sought to go beyond the movement's stylistic horizon, their work had no effect on Mexican art at the time. However, JOSÉ CLEMENTE OROZCO was already starting his experiments in expressionistic deformation, and DIEGO RIVERA and Angel Zárraga (1886–1946), who spent the tumultuous years of the Revolution in Europe, had a substantial Cubist phase between 1913 and 1918, with Rivera producing such works as *Zapatista Landscape (The Guerrilla)* (1915; Mexico City, Mus. N.A.).

(iv) Mexican Renaissance, 1920–c. 1950. Artistic expression after the Mexican Revolution was strongly influenced by political and social revolutionary ideals, including a strong nationalist consciousness. This coincided with the assimilation of the formal lessons propounded by the European avant-garde movements of the preceding decades and resulted in what is known as the Mexican Renaissance. During this period artists were concerned with the restatement of surface in pictorial space, achieved either through the stressing of the decorative or expressive value of line and colour or through the analytical dismantling and geometric reordering of forms, following Cézanne and the Cubists. In very few works was there a desire to suggest mobility and simultaneity in the manner of the Futurists. Another overwhelming influence was the desire to draw inspiration from 'primitive' art (which for the Mexicans often meant Pre-Columbian culture) and from the spontaneity of native and mestizo folk arts and crafts. Possibly as a result of these influences, Mexican art between 1920 and the end of the 1950s remained predominantly figurative, with very few artists experimenting with abstraction.

(a) Mural painting. Another major influence of the post-revolutionary period was the public, socializing role and the need to address a vast but uneducated audience that the most important artists assigned to their work, while on an intellectual level a statement made in the journal *El machete* in December 1923 by the signatories to the Manifesto of the Union of Technical Workers, Painters and Sculptors, who included Rivera, Orozco and DAVID ALFARO SIQUEIROS, rejected the limited private consumption of art. For these artists monumental painting on the walls of public buildings epitomized public art, and they received official support for their artistic beliefs from José Vasconcelos, the Minister for Education in the government (1920–24) of Alvaro Obregón. As part of an ambitious cultural plan, Vasconcelos urged expatriate Mexican artists to return and collaborate on his programme for the mural decoration of public buildings. Although from the outset, then, Mexican muralism was inextricably linked to the official requirements of the post-revolutionary government, the artists involved were eager to express their own ideas. Many of them were highly political (some were affiliated to the incipient Mexican Communist Party) and saw art as an instrument of social and cultural revolution and a means of influencing the public life of the country. Apart from Orozco, Rivera and Siqueiros, other artists of what became known as the Mexican school included FERNANDO LEAL, Fermín Revueltas (*b* 1903), RAMÓN ALVA DE LA CANAL and ROBERTO MONTENEGRO (*see* MURAL, fig. 4).

For as long as these artists maintained a dialectical relationship with officialdom the mural movement remained alive; when it became a submissive mouthpiece of the state, however, it degenerated into neo-academic rhetoric. During Vasconcelos's term as Secretary for Education, there were experiments with various themes and techniques. The greatest activity was concentrated on educational institutions, such as the Escuela Nacional Preparatoria, on which Orozco and Rivera worked, and the former convent of SS Pedro y Pablo, Mexico City, the cradle of Mexican muralism. Historical and allegorical themes, frequently echoing religious iconography, then gave way to the monumental celebration of 'the work and days' of the Mexican people, the theme of Rivera's murals (1923–8) in the Ministry of Public Education. Stylistic influences ranged from Renaissance mosaics and Florentine murals to modern Synthetism and post-Cubist spatial organization, but also included Pre-Columbian and colonial influences. From 1925 to 1933 the muralists met with hostility from the right-wing government of Plutarco Elías Calles and his immediate successors, and only a few remained active. One of these was Rivera, who around this time created some of his greatest works, such as the murals (1926–7) in the former Jesuit chapel and administration building of the Esculea Nacional de Agricultura (now the Universidad Autónoma) at Chapingo (*see* RIVERA, DIEGO, fig. 2) and the central staircase (1930) of the Palácio Nacional. Others, including Orozco, decided to leave the country, while others again, such as Siqueiros, applied themselves completely to trade-union battles.

From the mid-1930s there was a new rapprochement between artists and government in response to the rise of Fascism in Europe, and, during the government (1934–

40) of Lázaro Cardenas, the mural movement was rejuvenated, with commissions for the decoration of markets, union headquarters, state schools and other public spaces. The radical, anti-Fascist, anti-clerical and anti-imperialistic iconography that developed continued to prevail until the end of World War II, when new patrons arose for what was by that time recognized nationally and internationally as an exciting and distinctive form of artistic expression. Commissions followed for the decoration of banks, office buildings, factories, hotels and luxury restaurants, as well as for union buildings (*see* SIQUEIROS, DAVID ALFARO, fig. 2) and for municipal government buildings (*see* OROZCO, JOSÉ CLEMENTE, fig. 2). One of the most interesting later projects was the exterior decoration of some of the buildings of the new university campus in Mexico City built in 1948–52, which posed a double challenge: resistance to the elements and integration with the architecture in accordance with the aims of the 'plastic integration' movement (*see* §III, 2 above). While this led to some interesting works by such artists as JOSÉ CHÁVEZ MORADO and Juan O'Gorman, such as the latter's use of mosaic in his design for the library of the Ciudad Universitaria (1948–50; for illustration *see* O'GORMAN, JUAN), muralism was soon to become a spent force.

(b) Graphic arts. The graphic arts in this period followed a more or less parallel course to that of muralism. In 1921 JEAN CHARLOT arrived in Mexico from France, fully versed in modern wood-engraving techniques. He also admired late medieval woodcuts as well as popular Japanese prints, and he was one of the first to 'rediscover' Posada's graphic work. By 1922 Charlot, Fernando Leal and Gabriel Fernández Ledesma (*b* 1900) were carving with the grain (*bois au fil*) on woodblocks, producing unprepossessing, deliberately coarse figures on backgrounds lined with deeply marked indentations and using brutal contrasts between black and white. This woodcutting technique became widespread in the following years. It was encouraged in open-air schools of painting (*see* ESCUELAS DE PINTURA AL AIRE LIBRE) and in the popular centres of painting that were opened in the mid-1920s in districts of Mexico City to provide art education for young workers, seeking to preserve and cultivate a deliberate simplicity in the works produced there. The same technique was adopted for political illustrations published in opposition newspapers such as *El machete* and in posters and leaflets, such as those published in 1928 by the !30-30¡ group, to which many of the muralists belonged. The search for low-cost materials also led to the use of linocut engraving. Many of the same artists also produced prints in a style influenced by Cubism and Futurism to illustrate books and journals by the ESTRIDENTISMO group of avant-garde artists and poets. Other influences on the graphic arts in the 1920s and 1930s included the posters and typographical compositions of the Soviet Constructivists and, as early as the 1930s, photomontage, which was almost always used for purposes of social criticism. Lithography and metal and wood engraving, which lent themselves to a fine, nuanced treatment of line and colour as opposed to the rustic conciseness of the woodcut, were also given a new lease of life around the mid-1920s by the work of some young graduates of the Escuela Nacional

de Bellas Artes, such as Emilio Amero (*b* 1910) and CARLOS ALVARADO LANG, and by some of the muralists, such as Orozco and Siqueiros.

The intensive politicization of the 1930s and consequent use of graphic art as an ideological weapon, together with the desire to investigate collectively the techniques of graphic arts, led to the founding in 1937 of the TALLER DE GRÁFICA POPULAR by a group of artists led by LEOPOLDO MÉNDEZ and PABLO O'HIGGINS. In the following 20 years they produced an enormous quantity of leaflets, posters, books and portfolios of prints, often of great dramatic force, such as *Song of the Miners' Parade* (linocut, n.d.; U. Austin, TX, Huntington A.G.) by ALBERTO BELTRÁN.

(c) Easel painting. Although easel painting was rejected by the muralists in their manifesto in 1923, many artists continued to use the medium for formal experimentation, for intimist introspection or to depict everyday life, while it enabled the muralists to make copies or small-scale variations of their monumental compositions. In particular, easel painting was a more suitable medium for those artists whose work was essentially lyrical rather than epic and for those who did not share the muralists' radical political ideas, such as MANUEL RODRÍGUEZ LOZANO, JULIO CASTELLANOS, Abraham Angel, AGUSTÍN LAZO, ANTONIO RUIZ, MARÍA IZQUIERDO and RUFINO TAMAYO. For these artists there was no conflict between the desire to express nationalist subjects profoundly and intensely and the assimilation of the most creative developments in European art between the wars. The refined lyricism of these artists constitutes a sort of neo-Symbolism, invested with a renewed formal language derived from the European avant-garde and from a re-evaluation of aspects of Mexico's indigenous art traditions. In this reappraisal the fantastic was an important element. As Fascism advanced, and as the world of the muralists and their associates became more enclosed, many Mexican artists felt drawn to introspection, for example FRIDA KAHLO in such works as *My Grandparents, My Parents and I (Family Tree*; see fig. 11), and this led to some of the clearest expressions of Surrealism in Mexican art. In January 1940 the Exposición Internacional del Surrealismo opened in the Galería de Arte Mexicano, Mexico City, inspired by André Breton, who had visited Mexico in 1938 and met Rivera and Kahlo as well as Leon Trotsky, who had taken refuge in Coyoacán. The exhibition was organized by WOLFGANG PAALEN and the Peruvian César Moro and included, alongside the work of internationally known artists, a number of Mexican paintings and the work of an exceptional photographer, MANUEL ALVAREZ BRAVO. The growth of Surrealism in Mexico was given impetus by the arrival of some European artists connected with the movement, such as Paalen, LEONORA CARRINGTON, Alice Rahon (1916–87) and REMEDIOS VARO, who were fleeing from Fascism and the war. Meanwhile CARLOS MÉRIDA, working in isolation, explored both abstract forms of expression and elementary figurative styles, with occasional suggestions of Surrealist influences, for example in *Plastic Invention on the Theme of Love* (1939; Chicago, IL, A. Inst.).

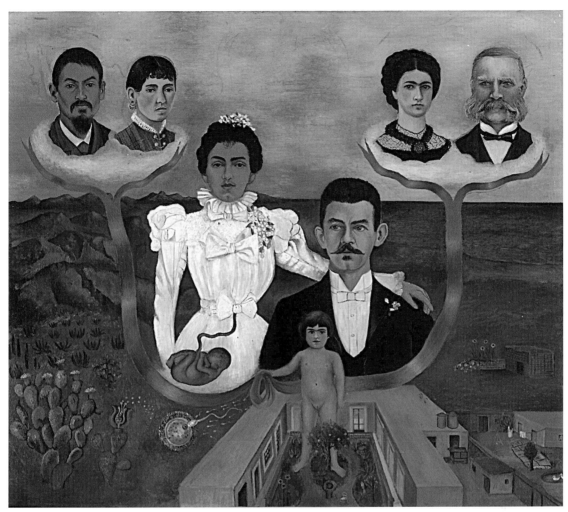

11. Frida Kahlo: *My Grandparents, My Parents and I (Family Tree)*, oil and tempera on metal panel, 307×345 mm, 1936 (New York, Museum of Modern Art)

(d) Sculpture. There was comparatively little significant development in sculpture during this period, despite the patronage offered by the state from the 1920s, beginning with the decoration of the Ministry of Public Education by IGNACIO ASÚNSOLO and Manuel Centurión (1883–1952). One reason for this was the absence of a charismatic leader among sculptors. In the 1920s such French neo-classical sculptors as Aristide Maillol, Charles Despiau and Emile-Antoine Bourdelle began to replace Rodin as the major influence for Mexican sculptors, for example in the works of Asúnsolo, Centurión and Fidias Elizondo (*b* 1909). This led to younger artists, trained in Europe under José de Creeft, realizing the importance of the European reappraisal of direct carving. Such sculptors as Guillermo Ruiz (*b* 1896) and Carlos Bracho (1899–1966) explored Pre-Columbian sculpture and sought to make it the basis on which to create an authentically Mexican style. On his return from Europe, Ruiz founded in 1927 the Escuela de Talla Directa y Escultura in a working-class area of Mexico City, seeking to incorporate into its teaching

the carving techniques of the stonecutters and also to investigate the possibilities of direct carving, in a response to the demotic and the spontaneous. The most representative of the sculptors inspired by tradition and producing work with a strongly artisan flavour was Mardonio Magaña (1866–1947). GERMÁN CUETO was the only Mexican sculptor familiar with the work of Brancusi, Jacques Lipchitz and Julio González and the only sculptor to experiment during this period with abstraction. Given the dominance of different versions of realism, however, the isolation in which he worked is not surprising.

FAUSTO RAMÍREZ

(v) c. 1950 and after. In the 1950s Mexican art changed direction again, as such artists as JOSÉ LUIS CUEVAS, ALBERTO GIRONELLA, Vlady (*b* 1920), MANUEL FELGUÉREZ and Vicente Rojo, who had spent some of their formative years studying in Europe or the USA, became increasingly impatient with the dogmatism of the Taller de Gráfica Popular and with the muralists and the supremacy of their didactic–figurative rhetoric. Seeking to break

with the immediate artistic past and sparing from their disdain only such independently minded figures as Tamayo, Mérida and Orozco, these younger artists applied themselves to experimenting with contemporary aesthetic ideas and with avant-garde developments, such as abstraction, which had been neglected during the 1920s. The value of Germán Cueto's experimental attitude began to be recognized, and MATHÍAS GOERITZ prefigured Minimalism in such sculptures as *Snake* (1953; Mexico City, Mus. A. Mod.). Mexican cultural policy, under the government of Miguel Alemán, without denigrating the achievements of the Mexican Renaissance, gradually began to promote more subjective, existentialist artistic trends, better suited to the government's modernizing, internationalist pretensions. This new direction was epitomized by the official recognition of the value of such artists as Tamayo, who had opposed the politicization of art, and by the transformation of muralism into a straightforward figurative synthesis, close to geometric abstraction, for example in the work of Carlos Mérida, who covered Mario Pani's housing units with concrete mosaics. Although younger artists were obliged to establish their reputations without help from official recognition, they managed, largely through self-promotion (*see* §IX below), gradually to acquire prestige and legitimacy, both nationally and internationally, finally triumphing over the established order in the major exhibition *Confrontation 66.*

In 1968, however, the government of Gustavo Días Ordaz brutally suppressed the expressions of social discontent, to which a new generation of art students had given voice in a short period of anonymous, fiery and sharply political artistic production. This led indirectly to the rise of a number of heterogeneous associations of artists and theoreticians known collectively as 'the groups'. These associations, which included the Suma group and the Pentagon Process, were inspired by social concerns and the rise of international conceptual art, and they produced work that was clearly urban and populist in content and approach, using such innovative forms as installations, performance art and happenings. Their work, which was often ephemeral, sought to involve social groups normally untouched by aesthetic developments through artistic activities intended to arouse people's political consciousness and increase their aesthetic perception of everyday urban life. In the more conventional art forms, many artists in the 1960s and 1970s were interested in geometric art and in Minimalism. These influences extended not only to painting and printmaking but also to monumental urban sculpture, as in such works as *La ruta de la amistad* (the 'Road to friendship'), a collaborative sculptural project in Mexico City of 1968, and the Centro del Espacio Escultórico building (1979–80) at the Universidad Nacional Autónoma de México. In these monumental sculptural works the artists responsible sought to make the urban landscape more human, taking the work of Goeritz as their inspiration.

Around the end of the 1970s and throughout the 1980s there was a revival of painting and sculpture in more traditional formats better suited to a commercial environment. These showed numerous diverse stylistic tendencies, ranging from different types of abstraction to a hyperrealistic figurative style. Although these can be seen to

12. Francisco Toledo: *Four Prints from the Guchachi Portfolio (Iguana)*, etching and aquatint with printed colours, 759×562 mm, 1976 (Austin, TX, University of Texas, Archer M. Huntington Art Gallery)

constitute part of a wider renewal of interest in figurative art, some aspects of conceptual art remained important. One of the most important artists of this period was FRANCISCO TOLEDO, a Zapotec Indian who drew heavily on the fauna and mythology of the Oaxaca region for inspiration, for example in his *Four Prints from the Guchachi Portfolio (Iguana)* (1976; see fig. 12). In the mid-1980s a movement known as Neo-Mexicanism arose, which, in a manner similar to other versions of Post-modernism, delighted in allusion and pastiche, integrating elements of the nationalist, popular iconography of the 1920s into a more personal and less political style. The most notable artist associated with the movement, which enjoyed great commercial and critical success both nationally and internationally, was Nahum B. Zenil (*b* 1947), whose images were highly modern and at the same time deeply rooted in national traditions.

See also LATIN AMERICAN ARTISTS OF THE USA.

FAUSTO RAMÍREZ, with KAREN CORDERO

BIBLIOGRAPHY
J. Fernández: *Arte moderno y contemporáneo de México* (Mexico City, 1952)
Mexican Art (exh. cat., by F. Gamboa and S. Linné, London, Tate, 1953)
B. Myers: *Mexican Painting in our Time* (New York, 1956)
J. Charlot: *Mexican Art and the Academy of San Carlos, 1785–1915* (Austin, TX, 1962)
——: *The Mexican Mural Renaissance* (New Haven and London, 1963)
E. Edwards: *The Painted Walls of Mexico* (Austin, TX, 1966)
A. Rodríguez: *A History of Mexican Mural Painting* (New York and London, 1969)

S. F. Goldman: *Contemporary Mexican Artists in a Time of Change* (Austin, TX, and London, 1977)

H. Covantes: *El grabado mexicano en el siglo XX, 1922–1981* (Mexico City, 1982)

Wand Bild Mexico (exh. cat., ed. H. Kurnitzky and B. Beck; W. Berlin, Staatl. Museen Preuss. Kultbes., 1982)

J. Fernández: *El arte del siglo XIX en México* (Mexico City, 1983)

I. Rodríguez Prampolini: *El surrealismo y el arte fantástico de México* (México City, 1983)

E. Acevedo and others: *Guía de murales del centro histórico de la ciudad de México* (Mexico City, 1984)

F. Ramírez: *La plástica del siglo de la independencia* (Mexico City, 1985)

Surrealistas en México (exh. cat., Mexico City, Mus. N.A., 1986)

E. Uribe and others: *Y todo por una nación: Historia social de la producción plástica de la ciudad de México, 1780–1910* (Mexico City, 1987)

Ruptura, 1952–65 (exh. cat. by F. Ramírez and others, Mexico City, Mus. A. Carrillo Gil, 1988)

Art in Latin America: The Modern Era, 1820–1980 (exh. cat. by D. Ades, London; S. Bank Cent.; and elsewhere; 1989)

La escuela mexicana de escultura: Maestros fundadores (exh. cat., by A. Arteaga and others, Mexico City, Pal. B.A., 1990)

1910: El arte en un año decisivo: La exposición de artistas mexicanos (exh. cat. by F. Ramírez and others, Mexico City, Mus. N.A., 1991)

Modernidad y modernización en el arte mexicano, 1920–1950 (exh. cat. by O. Debroise and others, Mexico City, Mus. N.A., 1991)

FAUSTO RAMÍREZ

V. Interior decoration and furniture.

European-style furniture was introduced into Mexico by the Spanish in the 16th century. Inventories of the period record items that were in common use in the first houses in the colony. These include inlaid, folding, X-frame chairs, 'friary' chairs, trestle tables, beds with carved posts, writing desks, chests, footstools, Flemish tapestries and *guadamecies* (Sp.: 'tooled leather hangings') from Córdoba. In 1568 carpenters' ordinances were established, and in the 17th and 18th centuries Mexican furniture achieved its most distinctive character, marked by massive dimensions and colonial rusticity, combined with vigorous workmanship and exuberant decoration. The furniture trade spread to several centres, each of which developed its own speciality. Michoacán lacquerwork exploited techniques of Pre-Columbian origin; Campeche used tortoiseshell; Puebla was known for wood inlay in the Moorish style; and Oaxaca produced poker-work on trunks and credenzas. Religious furniture was very important and was always in harmony with the architecture of the place of worship for which it was destined. Typical of Mexican Baroque were 'friary' chairs with fantastic carvings on the legs and rails (see fig. 13), monumental vestry cabinets and huge polygonal or circular sacristy tables with profusely carved frames and inlaid tops.

The aristocratic mansions of the colonial period in Mexico consisted of two storeys, with the rooms ranged round a central patio, similar to houses in Andalusia. Inside, the ceilings were usually of cedar beams, the floors were red brick with alternating glazed tiles, and the walls were covered with red damask or hand-painted Chinese wallpaper. The most elegant furniture was to be found in the drawing-room: folding screens decorated on both sides with scenes of the Spanish conquest, allegories or popular festivals, or lacquered in the oriental style; chairs with graceful curves inspired by European designs; corner commodes and console tables with scrolling cabriole legs; mirrors with silvered frames; writing desks inlaid in the

Mudéjar style; and cupboards decorated with floral carvings, chequerboard or polychromatic ornament. In 1783 the Academia de las Nobles Artes de S Carlos was founded in Mexico City, and from then on fashionable furniture conformed to the Neo-classical ideals of elegance, restraint and formality. The proportions were lighter, and the exuberant carvings and Moorish-style inlaid work were replaced by delicate marquetry in tropical woods. The main centre of furniture production at this time was Puebla.

The 19th century was dominated by a sequence of styles derived from European furniture. Neo-classicism was followed by the Empire style and then historical eclecticism. Between 1930 and 1955 functional furniture was in favour, while at the same time elaborately carved neo-colonial furniture enjoyed a revival. At the end of the 20th century a highly purified Mexican style prevailed, related to the monastic spirit of the architecture of Luis Barragán (*see* §III, 2(i) above). This was characterized by large, severe pieces of furniture in white cedar, combined with loom fabrics and popular crafts.

BIBLIOGRAPHY

M. Romero de Terreros: *Las artes industriales en la Nueva España* (Mexico City, 1923)

A. Carrillo y Gariel: *Evolución del mueble en México* (Mexico City, 1957)

T. Castelló Iturbide and M. Martínez del Río de Redo: *Biombos mexicanos* [Mexican folding screens] (Mexico City, 1970)

A. Aguilera, E. Vargas Lugo and others: *El mueble mexicano* (Mexico City, 1985)

13. 'Friary' chair, wood and velvet, w. 770 mm, 18th century (Mexico City, Museo Franz Mayer)

VI. Ceramics and glass.

Although there was a flourishing pottery industry in Pre-Columbian Mexico (*see* MESOAMERICA, PRE-COLUMBIAN, §VII), the potter's wheel and glazes were unknown. These were introduced by Spanish craftsmen from Talavera de la Reina, Seville and Cadiz, who began manufacturing tin-glazed earthenwares in Puebla between 1550 and 1570. Because of the rapid increase in the number of workshops, the first ordinances for potters were passed in 1653, and these regulated the industry until 1820. Pueblan wares—popularly known as Talavera de Puebla—were produced in three classes: fine, common and yellow, for use in convents and by wealthy Mexicans of European descent. The 'fine' pieces are large and thickly made and painted with dark blue foliage, birds and animals. The pigment was applied thickly so that it stands slightly in relief. On early wares decoration adhered closely to the lacey designs and chinoiseries painted on wares from Talavera de la Reina. The most original of later Pueblan wares were those that were inspired by East Asian porcelain imported into Mexico by the Spanish via the Philippines (see fig. 14).

During the 17th century the ceramics industry was so successful that Puebla became the main centre of pottery production in the Americas. Its products were exported to the far corners of Mexico as well as such other South American countries as Cuba, Venezuela and Peru. The production of tin-glazed tiles for decorative, architectural purposes was also very successful (*see* POBLANO). By the end of the 18th century the prominence of blue-and-white

wares had diminished, and rich, polychrome wares became increasingly popular, while Baroque exuberance was replaced by the more measured Neo-classical decorative style.

The War of Independence (1810–21) and the importation of European wares in the 19th century forced many Pueblan potteries to close. Production was thus considerably reduced and wares became more rustic and were decorated with popular motifs. In 1803 Miguel Hidalgo, one of the leaders of the Mexican independence movement, had established the production of tin-glazed earthenware in the town of Dolores Hidalgo, and from about 1850 the manufacture of this type of ware also spread to other areas. In the late 20th century it was still manufactured in Puebla, Guanajuato, Guadalajara, and Dolores Hidalgo using traditional methods. The tin-glazed tiles made in Dolores Hidalgo were particularly well known. In addition to the factories producing tin-glazed wares in the centre and south of the country, families of potters continued to work their kilns using Pre-Columbian craft methods. The glass industry in Mexico was also started in Puebla, in 1542. Useful and decorative objects were supplied to markets throughout Mexico and to the cities of Central and South America. In 1785 the importation of glass from the factory of La Granja de San Ildefonso, near Segovia in Spain, influenced Mexican production and the style known as *pepita*, so called because it employed a decorative method based on almond-shaped designs, was created (e.g. *pepita* work with floral motifs by Frasco de Vidrio; Mexico City, Mus. Franz Mayer). During the 19th century craftsmen from Puebla established workshops for the production of blown glass in Mexico City and Guadalajara, which still continued in the late 20th century, producing a great variety of items in bright, vivid colours. In 1909 the mass production of glass was started in Monterrey. In the late 20th century artistic glass and household items were made for both the export and domestic market.

BIBLIOGRAPHY
E. A. Barber: *The Maiolica of Mexico* (Philadelphia, 1908)
E. A. Cervantes: *Loza blanca y azulejo de Puebla*, 2 vols (Mexico City, 1939)
J. R. Alvárez: *Vidrio soplado* (Mexico City, 1969)
T. Castelló and M. Martínez del Rio: *Cristal de granja en México* (Mexico City, 1971)
L. Cortina, ed.: 'La talavera de Puebla', *A. México*, iii (1989) [whole issue]

LEONOR CORTINA DE PINTADO

VII. Gold, silver and jewellery.

Spanish silversmiths, mostly from Seville, who arrived in Mexico at the beginning of the colonial period, found indigenous craftsmen whose skills in casting, for example, were superior to their own. In the 16th century the building of churches and missions and the increasingly wealthy conquistadors created considerable demand for gold and silver objects. At this time it proved difficult to collect the *quinto* (royal tax of one-fifth), payable when silver was refined, fashioned or exported, and in 1526 a royal decree forbade silversmiths from working in Mexico because some had been defrauding the Crown. Such decrees were, however, largely ignored, and a silversmiths' guild was in existence when, in 1522, the viceregal council appointed assay-masters in Mexico City. In 1554 Bartolomé de

14. Tin-glazed earthenware jar with blue decoration, h. 340 mm, from Puebla, *c.* 1750 (Mexico City, Museo Nacional de Historia, Castillo de Chapultepec)

15. Silver-gilt chalice, rock crystal, boxwood and humming-bird feathers, h. 330 mm, from Mexico City, *c.* 1575 (Los Angeles, CA, County Museum of Art)

Medina arrived in Veracruz; he had developed the process of using mercury to refine silver, first employed at the mines of Pachuca (*see* SILVER).

Surviving 16th-century works, many of them in Spanish churches that received them as votive offerings from successful conquistadors, have vigorous decoration in the Renaissance style, well illustrated by a silver-gilt and rock-crystal crucifix in the church of S Maria in Fregenal de la Sierra, Spain. Other pieces show the successful combination of European features with elements derived from indigenous culture, for example a silver-gilt and rock-crystal reliquary cross (*c.* 1575–8; Mexico City, priv. col., see 1989 exh. cat., no. 16), which has a rock-crystal skull, undoubtedly Aztec in origin, set into the base. Similarly, Indian carved box-wood miniature groups were incorporated into gold and rock-crystal pendants and, in a chalice of *c.* 1575 (Los Angeles, CA, Co. Mus. A.; see fig. 15), are set against multi-coloured feathers and incorporated into the stem. The great reliquary of SS Peter and Paul (*c.* 1580; Tepotzotlán, Mus. N. Virreinato) shows the great creativity of Mexican silversmiths at this date. Although the form has a severely plain outline, the Mannerist decoration includes fruit and foliage interspersed with figures. A few

domestic pieces survive from the 16th century, including a circular brazier (*c.* 1560; Madrid, Inst. Valencia Don Juan) with classical heads amid exotic, Indian-inspired foliage.

Juan de Padilla (*fl* 1622–72) was the most important Mexican exponent of the Mannerist style in the 17th century: the monstrance that he made in 1634 for the church of Castromocho, his birthplace in Spain, has enamel bosses in the *estilo desornamentado* typical of Hispanic silver of the period, but the expressive cherub heads are unmistakably Mexican. By 1671 there were 75 silversmiths' workshops in Mexico City, all employing considerable numbers of Indian craftsmen. In addition, there was a large colony of Chinese goldsmiths in the city, probably selling East Asian work, as well as making jewellery and filigree work. The most important piece of the 18th century was undoubtedly the great architectonic canopy (destr. 19th century), known as the *cipres*, in the cathedral in Mexico City, designed in 1740–41 by Jerónimo de Balbás of Seville (*fl* 1718–41).

Baroque motifs were used in Mexican silver by the second decade of the 18th century, for example in two silver-gilt trays (1712 and 1714) in the church of Comillas, Spain. The magnificent silver-gilt monstrance (1724) attributed to José de Aguilar of Puebla (*fl* 1554–60) in the church of Salvatierra de los Barros, Spain, with a stem in the form of a figure of the Virgin of Guadalupe and an elaborately decorated base, is similar to others attributed to the workshops at Puebla de los Angeles, Spain. The antependium (*c.* 1750), with continuous patterns of exotic foliage, of Saltillo Cathedral, probably made in the town, shows the Mexican Baroque style at its zenith, while a silver-gilt chalice (1760s) in the Basílica de Guadalupe, Mexico City, has a stem formed of an *estípite*, a form of richly ornamented column popular in the Baroque architecture of the period (*see* §III, 1 above). By the mid-18th century domestic silver, especially ewers, basins and candlesticks, had become common. The *mancerina* (holder for a porcelain or glass chocolate-cup) appears to be a Mexican invention and was named after one of the viceroys.

The sudden introduction of Neo-classicism can be seen by comparing the rocaille motifs and asymmetry of the antependium in the church of Nochistlán, Zacatecas, made by Cabrero in 1770 (*fl* 1770–77), with the stark classicism of that made *c.* 1800 for the church of S José Tlaxcala, Tlaxcala. The somewhat ponderous classicism of Mexican silver continued virtually to the end of the 19th century, when increasing mechanization and lack of ecclesiastical commissions resulted in a decline in silversmithing. The craft enjoyed a brief revival, however, in the mid-20th century, largely through the work of William Spratling (*fl* 1931–1967), an American working in Taxco.

From 1522 an assay-master's mark was officially required on silverware, and in 1638 makers' marks were made obligatory, although many unmarked pieces survive. The *quinto* mark for Mexico City was a head above the initial M between the Pillars of Hercules, replaced at the end of the 18th century with a simple crowned M. Variations of the former mark are known, with the M replaced with a Z (possibly for Zacatecas), a D, an IV or an O.

BIBLIOGRAPHY

L. Anderson: *The Art of the Silversmith in Mexico* (New York, 1941, 2/1975)
A. Valle-Arizpe: *Notas de platería* (Mexico City, 1941, 2/1961)
C. Esteras Martín: *Platería hispanoamericana: Siglos XVI–XIX* (Badajoz, 1984)
——: *Orfebrería hispanoamericana: Siglos XVI–XIX* (Madrid, 1986)
E. del Hoyo: *Plateros, plata y alhajas en Zacatecas* (Zacatecas, 1986)
El arte de la platería mexicana: 500 años (exh. cat., ed. L. García-Noriega y Nieto; Mexico City, Cent. Cult. A. Contemp., 1989)
S. Cederwall and others: *Spratling Silver* (San Francisco, 1990)
C. Esteras Martín: *Platería del Museo Franz Meyer* (Mexico City, 1992)
——: *Marcas de platería hispanoamerica, siglos XVI–XX* (Madrid, 1992)

CHRISTOPHER HARTOP

VIII. Textiles.

Cotton continued to be the staple material of rural Mexican textiles after colonization, whereas by the late 20th century agave fibre was used only in bags and sacks. Sheep were introduced from Spain in 1526, and thereafter woollen cloth was used by both those of Spanish descent and the indigenous people. In 1530 flax was brought from Europe, and in 1537 silkworm breeding began, mainly in Oaxaca, where it flourished in the 16th and 17th centuries. In 1676, however, the Spanish Government, fearful of competition, forbade the growth of flax and ordered the eradication of the silk industry's white mulberry trees. Textile production increased after the introduction by the Spanish of the spinning-wheel and the treadle loom. The latter was operated by men, whose output surpassed that of native women using the manually operated backstrap loom. Guilds were established, and in 1577 the first ordinances,

16. *Huipil* tunic, handwoven with gauze technique and a traditional plumed serpent motif embroidered from the back with running stitches, from Ojitlán, Oaxaca, 1958 (private collection)

which controlled textile production in Mexico until independence, were put into force. Commercial textile production increased steadily throughout the 19th and 20th centuries until it became one of the most important industries in Mexico.

In the colonial period a wide variety of vegetable and animal colourants was used, the most popular being indigo, cochineal and shellfish purple (obtained from *Purpura patula pansa*, a species of sea snail). However, chemical dyes became available soon after their first manufacture, and by the late 20th century they had virtually supplanted natural dyes. Similarly, synthetic fibres became widespread in the second half of the 20th century.

Despite the development of extensive industrial production, indigenous textile traditions persist. A wide range of techniques is used: in weaving, brocading and weft-loop patterning; in embroidery, satin, running and cross stitches and draw-thread work. Twining, netting and plangi, a form of tie-dyeing, are also employed. Many of the designs are Pre-Columbian, including the tree of life, the plumed serpent and the jaguar claw, and the richly decorated native dress is still worn, with its fringed belts and embroidered blouses, *huipil* tunics (see fig. 16) and women's *quechquemitl* capes. Two garments in particular have survived from the colonial period: the *rebozo* (Sp.: 'stole') and the serape. The *rebozo*, a narrow rectangular cloth with fringes at both ends, was a woman's garment of mestizo origin. In the 17th and 18th centuries *rebozos* were made of silk interwoven with silver and gold thread and embroidered with traditional and regional motifs. No more than 20 examples survive from that period (e.g. W. Sussex, Parham House). *Rebozos* continue to be woven in many places in Mexico. The most abundant and high-quality production is in Tenancingo, where very fine *rebozos* are produced on treadle looms, and in Santa María del Río, where ikat-dyed silk *rebozos* must pass through a ring as proof of their sheerness. Some weavers employ traditional designs, including the snakeskin or the key or stepped-fret pattern, the giver of life.

The serape is the man's garment common to rural Mexico. It is usually made of wool and consists of two large, rectangular pieces of cloth stitched together with an opening in the middle for the head. The motifs are largely those that the Spaniards borrowed from the Muslims, often various combinations of geometric shapes around a central diamond (e.g. London, V&A). The rural workshops in Texcoco and Chiconcuac, established in the 16th century, are still in existence, and there are factories in Santa Ana Chautempan, Querétaro, Puebla and especially in Saltillo.

BIBLIOGRAPHY

J. Bazant: 'Evolution of the Textile Industry in Puebla, 1544–1845', *Comp. Stud. Soc. & Hist.*, vii/1 (1964), pp. 56–70
T. Castelló Yturbide and C. Mapelli Mozzi: *El traje indígena en México*, 2 vols (Mexico City, 1964, 2/1968)
C. Sayer: *Mexican Costume* (London, 1985); rev. as *Mexican Textiles* (London, 1990)
J. Rivero Quijano: *La revolución industrial en México y la industria textil* (Mexico City, 1990)

CARLOTTA MAPELLI MOZZI

IX. Patronage, collecting and dealing.

The first collectors of Mexican art were the conquistadors themselves, led by Hernán Cortés, and the missionaries who undertook the evangelization of the country. They had little appreciation of the artistic significance of the feathered objects and small pottery figures or pieces of sculpture they encountered, but they recognized the need to preserve them as historical testimony to a civilization so different from their own. In 1519, before the conquest had been completed, Cortés sent the first shipment of artefacts to the Spanish King Charles I. These were exhibited in Spain and Brussels, where Albrecht Dürer saw them, commenting that he had 'never seen anything that so delighted the heart' and that he had been 'amazed by the subtle inventiveness' of the indigenous craftsmen. Particularly attractive to the conquistadors was the work in precious metals, which they were able to acquire by taking advantage of imperial tribute procedures. In addition to such tributes as crops and firewood, some craftsmen were required to pay tributes to their new rulers in the products of their work, or in what they could produce in a given period of time. The historic sense of some of these first Europeans thus led to the collection and preservation of invaluable examples of Pre-Columbian art.

The demise of the tribute system around the middle of the 16th century was partly due to the influence of the missionaries, who also introduced Church patronage. Such humanist-influenced figures as Fray Juan de Zumárraga and Bishop Vasco de Quiroga (1479–1565) were responsible for founding schools, hospitals and a university in Mexico City, as well as religious buildings, most notably convents. The creation of such schools of art as that of S José de los Naturales, Mexico City (*see* §XI below), provided the indigenous population with European models through imported prints, especially wood-engravings in books, and as the missionary–patrons commissioned works from trained artists, the principal collections of early colonial art began to be assembled in the churches and convents of the religious orders.

At the end of the 16th century the first newly rich private patrons appeared, financing the building of churches and convents and their decoration. More sophisticated European prints, for example of works by Rubens and Murillo, began to be imported in the late 17th century, and in the 18th century the first private collectors arose among the descendants of European nobility and the enlightened clergy, many of whom taught at the Real y Pontificia Universidad de México. Private patrons also helped introduce new architectural developments in the 18th century. Notable examples are the churches of SS Prisca y Sebastián (1748–58), Taxco, and La Valenciana (1765–88), Guanajuato. Similarly, many prosperous mine-owners and aristocrats, such as the Conde de San Bartolomé de Xala and the Marqués de San Mateo de Valparaíso, helped consolidate changing architectural styles at about this time in the houses built for them (*see* §III, 1(ii) above).

In the early 19th century wealthy aristocratic families collected European and Mexican paintings, especially depictions of religious themes, portraits, still-lifes and genre paintings, which were highly prized. After independence a few collections changed hands, but a more significant shift in the ownership of works of art came with the disentailment of the property of the clergy in 1856, when the treasures of the churches became nominally part of the cultural property of the nation.

The Mexican Revolution in the early 20th century was followed by the formulation of an official government policy of artistic patronage, for which the Minister of Education, José Vasconcelos, was mainly responsible. This led to the vast programme of mural painting that dominated Mexican art in the 1920s, 1930s and 1940s, although many of the artists involved took the opportunities offered as a chance to criticize government social policy (*see* §IV, 2(iv) above). At the same time some of the most important private collections of modern Mexican art began to be formed, with such collectors as Marte R. Gómez, Alvar Carrillo Gil and Gutiérrez Roldán collecting easel paintings by José Clemente Orozco, Diego Rivera, David Alfaro Siqueiros and other painters of the Mexican Renaissance. Subsequently some of these collections came to form part of the collections of national museums through their acquisition by the Instituto Nacional de Bellas Artes, which was established in 1947 by the government to promote the arts. In the 1950s a number of artists, rebelling against the official system of patronage, began to show their work in private, often transient, galleries. Later, through biennial exhibitions and salons organized by the Instituto and through competitions sponsored by such international bodies as the Organization of American States and such private multinational corporations as Esso, this younger generation acquired international recognition, but collectors continued to concentrate on assembling representative works by particular members of the Mexican school. There was also particular interest in the works of Rufino Tamayo and Francisco Toledo. Some notable modern artists also formed important collections: for example, Diego Rivera collected Pre-Columbian art and in 1942 began to build the pyramid-shaped Museo Diego Rivera de Anahuacalli in Mexico City as a studio and private museum. Pedro Coronel collected works of African art and Japanese prints; these formed the basis of a museum located in the former Jesuit monastery of S Luis Gonzaga in Zacatecas. His brother Rafael Coronel meanwhile assembled a remarkable collection of masks from every region of Mexico (*see* CORONEL).

Many important private collections are located in regional centres such as Oaxaca and Monterrey, where financiers helped establish public museums and formed significant private collections. In Guadalajara the Instituto Nacional de Antropología e Historia formed a collection of works by 20th-century artists, most notably paintings by artists belonging to the 'Círculo Bohemio', while in Puebla José Luis Bello collected mainly 19th-century items but also Pueblan and European furniture and *objets d'art* from all periods as well as paintings by regional artists, most notably Agustín Arrieta. The privately owned Museo Amparo is also situated in Puebla.

One of the most important private collectors of the 20th century in Mexico was Franz Mayer, who was born in Mannheim and moved to Mexico in 1905, where he was successful as a financier during the economic boom of the last years of the government of Porfirio Díaz. While also active as a photographer, Mayer was primarily interested in collecting Mexican paintings and decorative art objects. He was particularly impressed by a visit to the Frick Collection in New York and decided to establish his own collection in a house that was not only equipped to contain the assembled works but was also given the necessary funds to ensure the continued preservation and augmentation of the collection and its research. Each room in the house, which now forms the Museo Franz Mayer in Mexico City, is given over to a particular art form, such as Puebla pottery, silverware or painted screens and tapestries.

There are few notable private collections of late 20th-century art in Mexico, despite its diversity, energy and international critical success. Important exceptions, however, are the collections of S. Autrey, M. Moreno and R. Ovalle in Mexico City, and of D. Sada, N. García, S. Zambrano and L. Zambrano in Monterrey, who have assembled works by many of the artists who sought to break with the nationalist and socialist sentiments of the Mexican school.

BIBLIOGRAPHY

L. Pérez de Salazar: *La pintura mexicana en colecciones particulares* (Mexico City, 1966)
J. A. Manrique: 'El manierismo en Nueva España: Letras y artes', *An. Inst. Invest. Estét.*, 45 (1976)
J. A. Manrique and T. del Conde: *Una mujer en el arte mexicano: Memorias de Inés Amor* (Mexico City, 1987)
'Museo Franz Mayer', *A. México*, iv (1989)
Pintura mexicana y española de los siglos XVI al XVII (Mexico City, 1991)
T. del Conde and others: *La pintura de México contemporáneo en sus museos* (Mexico City, 1991)

TERESA DEL CONDE

X. Museums.

During the first two centuries of Spanish colonization some mendicant priests sought to establish a record of Mexico's cultural heritage in its broadest sense by reproducing manuscripts and establishing a record of the indigenous flora and fauna. However, no representative record of the indigenous Indian cultures was compiled, despite early proposals. For example, Francisco de Toledo, the Viceroy of Peru from 1569 to 1581, suggested that the collection of King Philip II should include items of interest from New Spain for the 'amusement and wonder of any prince who should visit Your Majesty's court'. During the 18th century the European fashion for small private museums containing items of mainly scientific interest rapidly took root in New Spain. For example, between 1779 and 1783 the Catalan military engineer Miguel Constanzó (1741–1810) began negotiations for the enlargement of the Mexico City mint, which included a collection of medals, prints, busts and other items, to accommodate 'eighty drawings of ancient bas-reliefs, twelve plaster heads and busts, six small statues and the complete collection of the sulphur coins of Greece and Rome'. This formed the basis of the collection of the Academia de S Carlos, which was founded in 1783. The first museum of natural history, the predecessor of the modern Museo Nacional, was established at about the same time. Although largely of scientific interest, it did contain some Pre-Columbian artefacts.

After the short-lived rule of Agustín de Iturbide, who ordered the establishment in 1822 of a conservatory of antiques in the university in Mexico City, the first President of the Mexican Republic, José Guadalupe Victoria, issued a decree on 18 March 1825 creating the Museo Nacional.

Provincial museums sprang up throughout the 19th century, some of them becoming celebrated for their perseverance and resilience, such as the Museo Michoacáno. In 1853 Melchor Ocampo tried unsuccessfully to pass a decree providing for the establishment of the museum in Michoacán, but it was not until 1886 that the decree was legally approved and the museum established in the Colegio de S Nicolás de Hidalgo before moving in 1916 to its present site. A similar situation existed in the state of Yucatán, when in 1869 the museum of Yucatán was founded from the collections of the private museum of the Camacho Fathers, set up in the middle of the 19th century in Campeche.

By the end of the 19th century many more museums had been established, including scientific and military museums, and they were followed between 1903 and 1923 by the Museo Regional de Oaxaca (1903); the Museo Arqueológico (before 1910) in Teotihuacán; and the Museo Regional de Antropología e Historia (1918) in Guadalajara. By 1923 others were in operation, though not legally constituted until some time afterwards. These included museums in Guadalupe, Guanajuato, Zacatecas and Veracruz; the Museo Histórico Churubusco; the Museo Colonial de Acolmán (in the convent of S Agustín); the Museo de Arte Colonial in the former Jesuit college of S Martín, Tepotzotlán; the Museo Industrial de Puebla; the Museo Regional de Querétaro (in the monastery of S Francisco) and the Museo Regional de Cuernavaca (in the Palacio de Cortés). In the case of the monasteries, most were converted entirely into art galleries open to the public. This fact, however, points to a shift in emphasis towards the arts. Whereas most of the museums founded between 1869 and 1918 were devoted to the sciences, almost all of those established between 1918 and 1923 concentrated on the arts, in response to a wider need to consolidate a national consciousness. The Museo Nacional de Historia, which moved to the Castillo de Chapultepec, Mexico City, in the 1940s, has a collection on Mexican cultural history.

Following the short-lived Museo Experimental 'El Eco', designed by Luis Barragán and Mathías Goeritz, which opened in 1953, a second important period of museum development began in the early 1960s when the complex of new museums in Chapultepec Park, Mexico City, was built by PEDRO RAMÍREZ VÁZQUEZ; these include the Museo Nacional de Antropología (see fig. 6 above) and the Museo de Arte Moderno (both 1964); the latter houses the most important collection of modern Mexican painting and sculpture. The whole complex, executed between 1963 and 1965, became a landmark in Mexican museum design, while the work of MIGUEL COVARRUBIAS, Fernando Gamboa, Carlos Pellicer (1897–1977), Daniel Rubín de la Borbolla (1907–90) and others gave international prestige to Mexican museum architecture. Another renowned initiative was the creation of the Museo Nacional del Virreinato in the former Jesuit church of S Francisco Xavier in Tepotzotlán. After 1980 numerous important museums were established, both in the capital and in the provinces. These include the Museo Nacional de Arte, Mexico City, which occupies a building constructed between 1904 and 1911 by SILVIO CONTRI for the Secretaría de Communicaciones. Museum design in this period became an increasingly important area for such architects as TEODORO GONZÁLEZ DE LEÓN and ABRAHAM ZABLUDOVSKY, who built the Museo Rufino Tamayo (1981), Mexico City; Fernando Garza Treviño, who was responsible for the Centro Cultural Alfa (1980) in Monterrey; and RICARDO LEGORRETA, who designed the Museo de Arte Contemporáneo in the 1980s, also in Monterrey, one of the most lavish buildings in Mexico. Juan Sordo Madaleno's designs for the Press Centre for the organizing committee of the 1986 Football World Cup in Mexico City included its transformation into the Centro Cultural de Arte Contemporáneo, while in Jalapa, Veracruz, the firm of Edward Durrell built the Museo Arqueológico (1986), one of the museums most celebrated internationally, and in 1988 the Museo de Tuxtla Gutiérrez in Chiapas was built. A particularly important collection is held in the Instituto de Artes Gráficas de Oaxaca, donated by Francisco Toledo, who also founded the Museo de la Gráfica. The continuing interest in contemporary art was also demonstrated by the opening in 1992 of the Museo del Arte Contemporáneo in Oaxaca.

See also §IX above.

BIBLIOGRAPHY
J. Montes de Oca: *Los museos en la república mexicana* (Mexico City, 1923)
L. Castillo Ledón: *El Museo Nacional de Arqueología, Historia y Etnografía, 1825–1925* (Mexico City, 1925)
G. de la Torre and others: *Historia de los museos de la secretaría de educación pública, ciudad de México* (Mexico City, 1980)
Teatros y museos (Mexico City, 1982)
M. A. Fernández: *Historia de los museos en México* (Mexico City, 1988)
Los museos del INBA en la ciudad de México, CD-ROM (1995) [entries on 10,000 objects from the 11 museums that constitute the Ínstituto de Bellas Artes]
AGUSTÍN ARTEAGA

XI. Art education.

In the first decades of the colonial period, when there were very few trained European artists in Mexico, it was the Franciscan missionaries who undertook the task of supervising building works and training the indigenous Indian craftsmen to produce decorative works for churches and convents. The first teaching of Western art was given by Fray Pedro de Gante in the chapel of San José de los Naturales in Mexico City, where European forms of representation and Christian iconography were studied. Although the Indian craftsmen were quick to absorb these lessons, in some cases Pre-Columbian techniques and symbols survived and were applied to the new subject-matter (*see* §II above). From the middle of the 16th century guilds were set up and training took the form of an apprenticeship within the workshop of a master affiliated to one of the various craft guilds. Although guild regulations apparently excluded Indians from becoming masters, many European artists appear to have taken them on as apprentices, and there are instances of Indian and mestizo craftsmen having their own workshops. Until the 18th century most retables were produced in workshops in Mexico City, from where works for provincial churches were transported and installed, and the retable in this way played an important role in the diffusion of new styles and techniques (*see* §IV, 1(i) above). Throughout the colonial period imported reproductive prints of the works of major European artists such as Rubens, and in particular of such

Spanish artists as Zurbarán and Ribera, were also vital in providing models.

Around the middle of the 18th century the first painting academy was founded in Mexico City by a group of artists around MIGUEL CABRERA, with JOSÉ DE IBARRA as its president, but it was very short-lived. In 1783, however, the Academia de las Nobles Artes de S Carlos de la Nueva España was founded in the capital, heralding the demise of the Baroque and its supersession by the new Neoclassical ideas. This was followed by the establishment of local academies in such provincial centres as Guadalajara (1817), where José Manuel Uriarte was the first Director, and Puebla, where the academy developed out of a school of design founded in 1812 and where local guild-trained artists worked as teachers. An academic education gradually became essential to secure commissions, and although guild-trained artists continued for many years to work alongside academically trained artists, their work was seen as antiquated and crude.

Following Mexican independence the Academia de S Carlos was closed until 1843, when it was reorganized after new funding was secured by President Santa Anna, leading to the arrival of such new teachers as Pelegrín Clavé, Manuel Vilar and Eugenio Landesio from Europe (*see* §IV, 2(i) above). Under their influence the Academia became a powerful, essentially conservative, force, but in 1867 it was reorganized and renamed the Escuela Nacional de Bellas Artes. Around the middle of the century it became common for artists trained at the Academia to travel to Europe to complete their studies, first to Rome then, later, to Germany and France, in particular Paris. Julio Ruelas and Germán Gedovius, for example, studied in Germany and later helped to spread new ideas in Mexico. In the first decade of the 20th century Spain joined Paris as the most attractive destinations for the study of the European avant-garde by such Mexican artists as Angel Zárraga (1886–1946), Roberto Montenegro and Diego Rivera, who was strongly influenced by Cubism. Within Mexico, however, the prevailing academicism of the Escuela Nacional de Bellas Artes retained a dominant and stifling influence on the education of aspiring artists until the second decade of the 20th century, when a strike by a group of students including José Clemente Orozco led to the dismissal of its director. After the Revolution the Escuela was again renamed, becoming the Academia Nacional de Bellas Artes. More fundamentally, however, the muralists, led by Orozco, Rivera and David Alfaro Siqueiros, wanted to revolutionize the entire artistic establishment, which they characterized as 'bourgeois', and this aim, allied to a desire to reappraise and reanimate popular art and its links with Pre-Columbian traditions, led to the establishment (with government encouragement) of the ESCUELAS DE PINTURA AL AIRE LIBRE, offshoots of the Academia; this step sought to develop the artistic potential of young, untrained artists in a non-academic manner. The drawing method taught by Adolfo Best Maugard (1891–1965), for example, sought to retain the essential features of Pre-Columbian and folk art. The Escuela de Talla Directa y Escultura, founded in a working-class suburb of Mexico City by Guillermo Ruiz (*b* 1896) in 1927, similarly aimed to encourage a spontaneous popular art. In 1935 the study of art history and art criticism was institutionalized by the establishment within the Universidad Nacional Autónoma de México of the Instituto de Investigaciones Estéticas. After World War II the wide dissemination of educational institutions through Mexico led to a greater and wider understanding of art history, of developments in art outside Mexico and, in particular, to a greater understanding of Mexican art within an international context, but formal academic education continually had to compete with the pursuit of innovative values.

BIBLIOGRAPHY

J. Charlot: *Mexican Art and the Academy of San Carlos, 1785–1915* (Austin, TX, 1962)
R.-J. Clot: *La educación artística* (Barcelona, 1968)
E. Baez Macias: *Fundación e historia de la Academia de San Carlos* (Mexico City, 1974)
Las academias de arte. VII coloquio internacional en Guanajuato: Mexico City, 1985, Estudios de arte y de estética
F. Ramírez: *Crónica de las artes plásticas en los años de López Velarde, 1914–1921*, Cuadernos de historia del arte (Mexico City, 1990)
T. del Conde and others: *La pintura del México contemporáneo en sus museos* (Mexico City, 1991)

ENRIQUE FRANCO CALVO

XII. Art libraries and photographic collections.

Despite the country's long tradition of artistic production and art historical studies, there are few specialist art history archives and libraries in Mexico. The Universidad Nacional Autónoma de México, Mexico City, contains in its various departments the most specialized bibliographical resources. The most important library is that of the Instituto de Investigaciones Estéticas, which holds just over 15,000 volumes on Mexican and international art. This is followed in importance by the libraries of the faculty of architecture and the Escuela Nacional de Artes Plásticas, both specializing in architecture, and by the library of the Academia de San Carlos, which is part of the Escuela Nacional de Artes Plásticas and which holds books from the 18th and 19th centuries and earlier.

The Biblioteca Nacional, the Colegio de México and the Universidad Iberoamericana, all in Mexico City, have general art historical bibliographic material in their libraries. The Biblioteca Nacional has an outstanding collection of documentation belonging to the former convents, among which are thought to be the as yet unclassified treatises on architecture and poetics brought to Mexico during the viceroyalty and in the early years after independence. The Instituto Nacional de Bellas Artes has bibliographical resources in its departments, while the Museo de Arte Moderno and Museo Nacional de Arte both have small libraries containing general works on the history of art (all in Mexico City).

The most important specialized photographical archives again belong to the Universidad Nacional Autónoma de México: the Instituto de Investigaciones Estéticas has a rich holding specializing in colour transparencies and black-and-white negatives of Mexican art of different periods, as well as of international and contemporary Latin American art. It also has black-and-white photographs of colonial art taken by Guillermo Kahlo (1872–1941) and Luis Marquéz during the first half of the 20th century. The second most important collection belongs to the faculty of architecture, the slide library of which specializes in Mexican and international architecture and art. The

Instituto Nacional de Antropología e Historia in Mexico City also has a rich holding of photographs of Mexican art, and its transparencies and black-and-white photographs of such artistic monuments as houses from the old quarter of Mexico City, archaeological sites and colonial churches from all over the country can be consulted at the institute's offices in the former convent of Culhuacán. The institute's regional centre in Pachuca has other photographic records by Guillermo Kahlo of colonial artistic monuments, complementing the holdings of the Instituto de Investigaciones Estéticas. The Hugo Breheme and Felipe Teixidor Collections are also rich in images of destroyed or untraced artistic monuments. The Archivo General de la Nación holds several million images in its audiovisual information department. Outstanding among these are over 3000 photographs taken at the beginning of the century by the Australian Charles B. Waite, including numerous views of plazas, churches, railway stations and other public buildings in the major towns.

BIBLIOGRAPHY

E. Barberena: *Un análisis de la información del arte latinoamericano contemporáneo* (diss., Mexico City, U. Autónoma Met., 1987)
M. Davidson and others: *Picture Collections: Mexico* (London, 1988)

AURELIO DE LOS REYES

Mexico City [Sp. México]. Capital city of Mexico. Located in the high-altitude Valley of Mexico in the central southern part of the country, the city (metropolitan population *c.* 22 million) was originally the site of Tenochtitlán, the capital of the AZTEC empire, which was destroyed by Spanish conquistadors in 1521; large-scale remains of the principal temple at the centre of the Aztec city were excavated only after 1978. Rebuilt by the Spanish as the capital of the Viceroyalty of New Spain, the city flourished as a centre of colonial art and architecture from the 16th century to the early 19th, and it subsequently remained at the forefront of important innovations in the arts, particularly in the 20th century.

I. Tenochtitlán. II. Later history and urban development. III. Art life and organization.

I. Tenochtitlán.

The city was founded *c.* 1325 by the Mexica people—one of several Aztec groups—in the Valley of Mexico, after a wandering period of more than 200 years. Its Náhuatl (Aztec) name, meaning 'place of the fruit of the prickly pear cactus', may refer to its legendary establishment at the place where the wandering Mexica witnessed the scene of an eagle perching on a *nopal* cactus (*tenochtli*) and devouring a serpent; it may also refer to Tenoch, a semilegendary Mexica priest and leader of that time. Inhabitants of the city were referred to as the Tenochca mexicas. Tenochtitlán was built on an island of *c.* 10 sq. km near the western edge of Lake Texcoco in the Valley of Mexico. A rectilinear urban plan was developed, with large open spaces for communal activities; at its centre was a huge ceremonial precinct containing the most important pyramidal temple, the Templo Mayor (Great Temple), dedicated at the time of the city's founding jointly to Huitzilopochtli, the Aztec patron god of war, and to Tlaloc, the god of rain (see fig. 1). The Templo Mayor was the symbolic as well as the physical centre of the Aztec universe, and

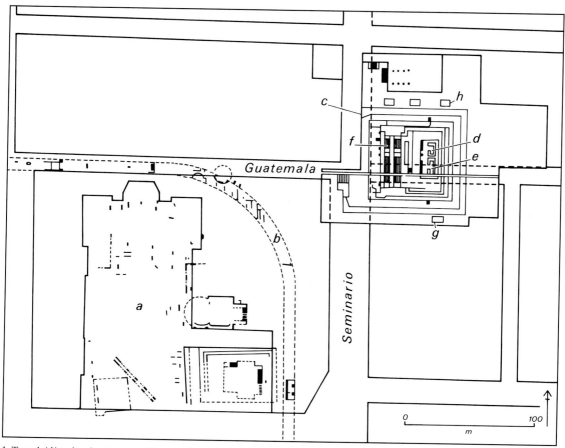

1. Tenochtitlán, plan showing site of Templo Mayor: (a) cathedral; (b) line of subway excavations during the 1960s; (c) Templo Mayor; (d) sanctuary of Tláloc; (e) sanctuary of Huitzilopochtli; (f) Chamber II; (g) Red Temple; (h) Temple C

during the following two centuries of Aztec expansion, when Tenochtitlán became the imperial capital, the structure was enlarged and rebuilt many times (see below).

By 1428 Tenochtitlán was a city of c. 250,000 people living in closely packed, single-storey houses, with brightly coloured pyramid temples, wide streets and canals with timber bridges. TLATELOLCO, a separate community on an island to the north, was physically and politically incorporated by Tenochtitlán in 1473. Canals reached all parts of the city and its suburbs, and three causeways linked it to the mainland. The city's economy was based on a combination of agriculture and warfare, including the tribute brought in by military conquest, particularly between 1440 and 1480, when many southern towns were conquered under Motecuhzoma I Ilhuicamina (reg 1440–68) and by Axayácatl (reg 1468–81). Tenochtitlán flourished for nearly 200 years, its inhabitants increasing to c. 340,000 before 1519, making it one of the most heavily populated cities in the world. In that year, however, the Spanish conquistadors arrived, led by Hernán Cortés; the final battle for the city in 1521 reduced it to ruins, and the stones of its temples and other buildings were used to create a new colonial city.

Early archaeological finds from Tenochtitlán were recorded in 1790, but many years elapsed before systematic

excavation took place in the centre of Mexico City, and until 1978 most knowledge of Aztec architecture came from sites outside the Aztec capital. Limited excavations in the city were undertaken in 1900, 1913–14 (when the south-west corner of the Templo Mayor was discovered), 1933 and 1948, but most finds came to light during the construction of the city's underground subway system in the 1960s (1b). The discovery of the stone sculpture of the moon goddess *Coyolxauhqui* and the subsequent Proyecto Templo Mayor (1978–82; 1c; *see* AZTEC, fig. 2), when the main temple of Tenochtitlán was excavated, transformed archaeological knowledge of the Aztecs by offering an unprecedented view of remains at the very centre of the city.

These excavations, covering a much larger portion (5000–7000 sq. m) of the temple and its ceremonial precinct, revealed the foundations of at least seven construction phases: I, c. 1325; II, c. 1390; III, c. 1431; IV, c. 1454; V, c. 1480; VI, c. 1500; and VII, after 1500. As was customary throughout Pre-Columbian Mesoamerica, the temple pyramid was rebuilt periodically, the previous building and pyramid platform forming the core of each new construction. The earlier six building phases were thus in better condition because they were protected beneath later construction. The second construction phase, for example, was found almost intact; a polychrome painted *chacmool* sculpture (reclining stone figure with flexed legs, holding a small receptacle between its hands on the stomach), was found *in situ* at the entrance of the sanctuary of Tlaloc (1d), and a sacrificial stone stood at the entrance to the sanctuary of Huitzilopochtli (1e). Both shrines were originally decorated inside and out. Two stone pillars were also found at the entrance to the Tlaloc shrine, their external faces each bearing geometric paintings that symbolize the deity: a band of black 'goggle eyes' on a white background and, below this, a horizontal strip of blue, then two red bands. The lower parts of the pillars are painted with black vertical stripes that may represent rain. Huitzilopochtli's shrine was probably similar to the one dedicated to Tlaloc, at least in plan.

Sculpture from Tenochtitlán can be divided into two main groups: élite and folk sculpture. Elite sculptures were those commissioned by Aztec rulers and aristocrats, including several that commemorate rulers' military campaigns, such as the monument of *Motecuhzoma I* (Mexico City, Mus. N. Antropol.), depicting in low relief the cities of his conquests, or the Stone of Tízoc (*reg* 1481–6; Mexico City, Mus. N. Antropol.). More abundant are folk sculptures of cactus plants and eagles (see fig. 2), symbolic of Aztec legend and the founding of their capital. Tenochtitlán's southern conquests are represented in the Templo Mayor by a number of masks and figures from the

Southern Highlands, carved mainly of greenstone, the most revered Mesoamerican material. In the cache known as Chamber II (1f above), on the Tlaloc side of the pyramid-platform (construction phase IV), 56 such human figurines were found, and a total of 162 masks and 220 figurines was excavated by the project (Mexico City, Mus. Templo Mayor). They include some from Guerrero (south-west of Tenochtitlán), carved in a style often referred to as Mezcala after the region that provided much of the raw material; the style is characterized by an angular, geometric treatment of the forms, often extremely simplified and with many variations.

A few specimens from offertory caches are much older, exemplifying major pre-Aztec styles and demonstrating that the Aztecs were, to some extent, aware of the great civilizations that preceded them. The oldest such piece from Tenochtitlán is a small Olmec-style greenstone mask (*c*. 800 BC); other finds included a Teotihuacán-style mask (*c*. AD 500) and a large Teotihuacán-style figure of the fire god (all Mexico City, Mus. Templo Mayor). As well as sculpture, several architectural features at the Templo Mayor demonstrate continuity with past styles. The Red Temple (1g above) and Temple C (1h above), at the south and north sides respectively of the pyramid-platform, were small temples built with typical Teotihuacán TALUD-TABLERO profiles, comprising sloping walls beneath rectangular, vertical panels. Each is also decorated with a series of half-eyes and sectioned conch shells, both of which are motifs frequently employed in Teotihuacán mural paintings.

BIBLIOGRAPHY

J. Soustelle: *La Vie quotidienne des Aztèques à la veille de la conquête espagnole* (Paris, 1955; Eng. trans., London, 1961)
M. León-Portilla: *Mexico-Tenochtitlán: Su espacio y tiempo sagrados* (Mexico City, 1978)
F. F. Berdan: *The Aztecs of Central Mexico: An Imperial Society* (New York, 1982)
E. Matos Moctezuma: 'The Grand Temple of Tenochtitlán', *Sci. Amer.*, ccli/2 (1984), pp. 80–89
J. Broda, D. Carrasco and E. Matos Moctezuma: *The Great Temple of Tenochtitlán: Center and Periphery in the Aztec World* (Berkeley and London, 1987)
E. Matos Moctezuma: *The Great Temple of the Aztecs: Treasures of Tenochtitlán* (London, 1988)
C. Chanfón Olmos: 'Tenochtitlán, la capital Mexica', *Cuad. Urbismo*, 1 (1990), pp. 5–18

ELIZABETH BAQUEDANO,
EDUARDO MATOS MOCTEZUMA

II. Later history and urban development.

1. 1521–1821. 2. 1822–1920. 3. After 1920.

1. 1521–1821. The new city that was built on the ruins of Tenochtitlán became the capital of the Viceroyalty of New Spain, its population greatly reduced to about 30,000. Within a few years the city became known as México-Tenochtitlán, but by the middle of the 16th century it was being called México, in memory of the Mexica people who had founded Tenochtitlán. Although the buildings of the great Aztec capital had been destroyed, this allowed for the combination of indigenous and European elements in the creation of the new city. Numerous authors have commented on the influence of Italian Renaissance urban design on the planning of Mexico City. Later investigations,

2. Tenochtitlán, terracotta figure of an eagle warrior, life-size, from the Eagle House (Mexico City, Museo del Templo Mayor)

however, tend to highlight the value of indigenous Mesoamerican antecedents; these received little attention before the late 20th century, probably because of the lack of information resulting from the systematic destruction of indigenous documents in the 16th century. The peoples of Mesoamerica, owing to the benign climate, had created an outdoor way of life supported by a system of ceremonies that affected all aspects of daily life; this was reflected in the planning of urban spaces with large public squares and wide, straight roads planned in a rectilinear grid. Such qualities were well expressed—albeit with a very medieval conception—in the so-called Plano de Cortés (Nuremberg, 1524), a report made by Hernán Cortés to the King of Spain. The straight roads and many of the large squares of Tenochtitlán were preserved in the new city, for which plans were drawn up by Alonso García Bravo. The reconstruction work used stone from the ruined Aztec monuments in addition to wood, stone and bricks transported from local villages across the lake and through the canals.

Among the earliest buildings of the new city were fortresses based on European models, but architectural activity in the 16th century was dominated by domestic and religious construction. As the seat of viceregal power, Mexico City was also the operational base for the evangelization campaigns; thus the type of mendicant convent that was widely adopted in Mexico by the Franciscans, Augustinians and Dominicans, characterized by walled courtyards or atria and open chapels (*capillas posas*), was first built in the capital. The religious orders, especially the Jesuits, also built schools and colleges, including SS Pedro y Pablo (1572) and S Ildefonso (1592). The first cathedral was built in 1525–32 (destr.); the second, the Metropolitan Cathedral of Mexico City (begun 1563; *see* MEXICO, fig. 3) was built in the Plaza Mayor (now Plaza de la Constitución) in the centre of the city, near the site where the Aztec Templo Mayor was later discovered (see fig. 1 above). It was based on Jaén Cathedral in Spain, and construction was continued under CLAUDIO DE ARCINIEGA and Juan Miguel de Agüero (*fl* 1574–1613); the cathedral was dedicated in 1656, although the towers were completed only in 1813 (see also fig. 4 below). On another side of the square is the National Palace, the original building of which was a gift to Cortés from the King of Spain; it was rebuilt at the end of the 17th century and enlarged in the 1920s. The city's development in the early 17th century was portrayed in a beautiful plan (1628) made by Juan Gómez de Trasmonte, Maestro Mayor at the cathedral.

During the three centuries of the Viceroyalty the Church remained the principal patron of architects working in Mexico City, among whom in the 18th century were PEDRO DE ARRIETA and Miguel Custodio Durán (*see* DURÁN): they introduced the ornate carving and solomonic columns of the Mexican Baroque (e.g the Jesuit church of La Profesa, 1714–20, by Arrieta, and S Juan de Dios, 1729, by Durán). Such changes to the external appearance of the buildings were all that was necessary to turn Mexico City into a Baroque city: the wide, straight streets of its urban layout were inherently suited to the planning of Baroque scenographic perspectives and focus on architectural ornament. At the same time, building activity became more diverse as a result of the economic

3. Mexico City, courtyard of the Real Seminario de Minería (now Palacio de Minería), by Manuel Tolsá, 1797–1813

success of trade and mining. In the centre of the city, around the Plaza Mayor (Plaza de la Constitución; see fig. 4 below), elegant town mansions in the latest styles were built from the last quarter of the 17th century for prosperous merchants and miners, many of whom had bought noble titles from the king and formed the local aristocracy. Examples include the house (1764) for the Conde de San Bartolomé de Xala by LORENZO RODRÍGUEZ and the house (1769) for the Marqués de San Mateo de Valparaíso by FRANCISCO ANTONIO DE GUERRERO Y TORRES. Notable 18th-century civic buildings include the Ayuntamiento (1720–24) and Aduana (1731), which employed the *estípite* (a vertical element tapering downwards), a characteristic feature of the Churrigueresque style, which is more importantly exemplified in Lorenzo Rodríguez's Sagrario Chapel (1749–68) at the Metropolitan Cathedral (*see* MEXICO, fig. 3).

Throughout the 18th century the increasing wealth of the city and patronage of the Church allowed the artisans' workshops to flourish, with silversmiths, engravers, organbuilders, lute-makers, blacksmiths, choral-book illuminators, gilders and embroiderers manufacturing the objects needed for worship. These artisans and artists occupied the area between the aristocratic nucleus of the city and the poorer periphery, where the labourers lived; their workshops, although modest, were well built, while the labourers occupied isolated adobe houses in the indigenous style, generally with open spaces for keeping animals and growing vegetables. A new type of middle-class dwelling also appeared in the 18th century: the *casa de vecindad*, a complex of dwellings giving on to a common patio. The lake on the western side of the city dried up during the 18th century, and Mexico City ceased to be an island. It therefore became necessary to police the access of merchandise arriving by land, and for this purpose gate-houses were built on the Peralvillo, Tlatelolco, Nonoalco, San Cosme, La Piedad, San Antonio Abad and San Lázaro access roads.

In the 1780s the new ideas of the Enlightenment began to arrive in Mexico, and the Academia de las Nobles Artes de S Carlos was founded in Mexico City in 1783 (*see* §III, 1 below). The new ideas gave rise to an awareness of the importance of functionality and order in the city, which can be seen in the work of two viceroys: Antonio María de Bucareli y Urzúa, Viceroy from 1771 to 1779, who created the Paseo Bucareli; and Juan Vicente de Güemes Pacheco, Conde de Revillagigedo, Viceroy from 1791 to 1794, who, despite failing to complete his plan to rejuvenate the city, levelled and paved the streets, numbered the houses, introduced street-lighting and renovated the old aqueducts and drainage systems. Among the principal Neo-classical buildings erected in Mexico City at this time are the Real Seminario de Minería building (1797–1813; now Palacio de Minería; see fig. 3); the church of Nuestra Señora de Loreto (1816); and the palatial residence (1810) of the Marqués del Apartado, all by MANUEL TOLSÁ.

2. 1822–1920. Following independence from Spain in 1821, Mexico City entered a period of change by which it lost its former viceregal appearance. Although the population more than doubled during the 19th century, growing from about 150,000 in 1822 to 350,000 in 1900, its boundaries remained roughly the same until the mid-1860s. The leading architect in the city in the mid-19th century was LORENZO DE LA HIDALGA, who was responsible for the Neo-classical dome (1845–58) of the side chapel of S Teresa la Antigua and the Teatro de S Anna (1844; later the Teatro Nacional), which was destroyed in 1901 to open up the Avenida Cinco de Mayo. The construction of theatres and bars encouraged the extension of street-lighting, which was progressively modernized during the century: the 1200 oil lampposts installed by Viceroy Revillagigedo in the 1790s were replaced by turpentine lanterns in 1835 and by hydrogen lamps in 1869; electric lighting was introduced in 1880. Further modernization of the city's services included new drainage systems and stone pavements in 1851 and the installation of underground lead water-pipes in 1857 instead of the old aqueducts. Urban improvements included the construction in 1847 of the tree-lined Paseo de las Cadenas, an unusually wide promenade in front of the cathedral in the Plaza de la Constitución, which had a spacious, ordered appearance (see fig. 4). The reform laws, which suppressed convents and monasteries from 1857, removed the last traces of the viceregal regime from the city, and of the former religious institutions only the churches were retained, with some exceptions: the Augustinian church, for example, was turned into a library. At the same time, new streets were opened to break up the old estates, which were put up for sale.

Advances in communication and urban transport in Mexico City were made in the mid-19th century, including the first telegraph line (1852), which linked it with the port of Veracruz; the first railway (1857), which linked the city centre with the sanctuary of La Villa de Guadalupe; and the first public omnibus routes (1863). The physical expansion of the city also began in the 1860s. The Habsburg emperor Maximilian ordered the construction of the Avenida del Imperio (now Paseo de la Reforma), a wide boulevard that joined the city centre with the imperial residence at the Castillo de Chapultepec (now housing the

4. Mexico City, view of the Plaza de la Constitución, *c.* 1856; lithograph by Casimiro Castro

Museo Nacional de Historia) on the south-west fringe; this work was carried out by Juan Agea (1825–?1896) and Ramón Agea (1828–?1892), who had trained in Europe. After 1877 elegant houses in eclectic styles were built along the boulevard, which became a popular residential quarter for members of the local governing aristocracy during the long administration (1877–80; 1884–1911) of President Porfirio Díaz. To one side of it lay the new urban district known as the Colonia de los Arquitectos, conceived by the Spanish architect Francisco Somera (?1830–89) and inhabited by teachers and students of architecture; many houses were built there by prominent members of the profession. This began the Mexican custom of referring to new urban subdivisions as *colonias*: several more were built in Mexico City, including the *colonias* Del Rastro (1889), La Candelaria (1891), Peralvillo (1899) and Romero Rubio (1907) for low-cost housing; the *colonias* San Rafael (1881), Morelos (1886) and Del Valle y Escandon (1909) for middle-class housing of one or two storeys with a small patio; and the *colonias* Roma and La Condesa (1902), Juárez (1906) and Cuauhtémoc (1904) for elegant, upper-class housing in Beaux-Arts and eclectic styles, including Swiss chalets and Italian villas.

The new upper-middle class that emerged during the presidency of Porfirio Díaz led to the construction of new commercial and cultural institutions in Mexico City, including such large stores as the Palacio del Hierro, Fábricas Universales, Ciudad de México, Fábricas de Francia and the Gran Sedería. Several historic buildings were occupied by the new institutions and schools, for example the former Palacio de la Inquisición was occupied by the school of medicine; the former convent of the Encarnación by the school of jurisprudence; and the former convent of S Lorenzo by the school of arts and crafts. Several monuments were also raised, especially in the Paseo de la Reforma, including one to *Columbus* (erected 1877), originally conceived in 1865 by Ramón Rodríguez Arangoiti (1830–82), executed in France by Charles Cordier and sent to Mexico for local assembly; the monument to *Cuauhtémoc*, designed (1877) in a style known as 'neo-Aztec eclectic' by Francisco Jiménez (?1845–83) with sculpture by Miguel Noreña and GABRIEL GUERRA; and the Independence Column (1899–1910) by ANTONIO RIVAS MERCADO (sculpture by Enrique Alciati). In the early years of the 20th century several major building projects were initiated with the help of such European architects as SILVIO CONTRI, ADAMO BOARI and Henri-Jean-Emile Bénard (*b* 1844). Contri built the Palacio de Comunicaciones y Obras Públicas (1904–11; later housing the Museo Nacional de Arte), and Boari designed the eclectic Edificio Central de Correos (1902–7) and the new Teatro Nacional (1904–34; later Palacio de Bellas Artes; *see* MEXICO, fig. 5). Bénard was responsible for the Palacio Legislativo (designed 1903–4; begun 1910), work on which was abandoned after the fall of President Díaz in 1912 during the Mexican Revolution (1910–20). The metal structure of its great central dome was converted (1933–8) into a monument dedicated to that conflict in accordance with an idea promoted by Carlos Obregón Santacilia.

3. AFTER 1920. Development in Mexico City was halted during the Revolution, but once peace was restored an increase in population was stimulated by renewed investment and the return of many who had fled the conflict. By 1930 the city's population was more than one million, and it continued to grow rapidly, particularly after 1950. The need for a planning body to regulate growth became evident in 1933, when the first planning and zoning laws for the city were drawn up. Between 1920 and 1940 the social democratic ideals that emerged from the Revolution filled the city with schools, hospitals, sports complexes and low-cost housing projects, and with these buildings the Modern Movement in architecture was introduced by such architects as JOSÉ VILLAGRÁN, ENRIQUE YÁÑEZ, Juan Legorreta (1902–34) and JUAN O'GORMAN, whose Escuela Técnica (1932–4) displayed affinities with the work of contemporary European architects. Many of the new public buildings were painted with murals in a programme initiated by the Education Minister José Vasconcelos (*see* §III, 2 and fig. 5 below). Public works interrupted during the Revolution were also resumed, including the Teatro Nacional, completed in 1934 by Federico Mariscal. In addition, the increase in traffic led to the first scheme (1930; unexecuted) for an underground transport system, proposed by the military engineer Miguel Rebollar (1868–1962).

After 1940, in the aftermath of the Spanish Civil War (1936–9) and with the outbreak of World War II, thousands of foreign refugees arrived in Mexico City, and it began to acquire the image of a great cosmopolitan city. The urgent need for housing was addressed by such architects as MARIO PANI, who built more than 1000 dwellings in one complex of 13-storey housing blocks (1947–50) for the Unidad Habitacional Presidente Alemán. Among the most influential projects of the post-war period was the construction of the Ciudad Universitaria (1948–52) in the south of the city, built on the principles of the 'plastic integration' movement with the collaboration of more than 60 architects led by Pani and ENRIQUE DEL MORAL and such artists as Diego Rivera and David Alfaro Siqueiros (for illustration of the library *see* O'GORMAN, JUAN). The International Style of corporate architecture was also introduced in the 1950s, for example in the Torre Latino Americano (1957) by AUGUSTO H. ALVAREZ, which was made possible only by the new technology of control piles invented by the Mexican engineer Manuel González Flores to resist seismic activity. Elegant new residential districts were developed, including the Jardines del Pedregal, where LUIS BARRAGÁN produced beautiful houses and gardens (1950) reflecting the landscape.

As the population of Mexico City began to increase dramatically, growing from *c.* 3 million in 1950 to more than 9 million in 1970 and *c.* 22 million in the mid-1990s, urban development became less ordered. Several access routes into and around the city were established, including the Tlalpan and Miguel Alemán viaducts (the former comprising the old Mexica road from Iztapalapa to Tenochtitlán), then inner and outer ring roads and axis roads; and an underground railway system was built, the first lines being opened in 1969–70. Public transport, however, continued to be a major problem facing the city in the late 20th century, as well as atmospheric pollution, an endemic housing shortage and inadequate public services. Architectural developments in the city in the last decades of the 20th century included innovative structural designs, as seen in the Museo Nacional de Antropología (1964; *see* MEXICO, fig. 6) by PEDRO RAMÍREZ VÁZQUEZ, one of several museums in Chapultepec Park, and the work of FÉLIX CANDELA, while a more functionalist approach incorporating traditional materials and elements was seen, for example, in the Colegio de México (1974–5; *see* MEXICO, fig. 7) by TEODORO GONZÁLEZ DE LEÓN and ABRAHAM ZABLUDOVSKY.

BIBLIOGRAPHY

M. Rivera Cambas: *México pintoresco, artístico y monumental* (Mexico City, 1883)
J. Galindo y Villa: *Historia sumaria de la ciudad de México* (Mexico City, 1925)
F. de la Maza: *La ciudad de México en el siglo XVII* (Mexico City, 1968)
H. Beacham: *The Architecture of Mexico* (New York, 1969)
A. García Cubas: *El libro de mis recuerdos* (Mexico City, 1969)
L. Unikel, C. R. Crescencsio and G. Garza: *El desarrollo urbano de México* (Mexico City, 1976)
La ciudad de México: Breve evaluación de su crecimiento (Mexico City, 1978)
M. E. Negrete and H. Salazar: 'Zonas metropolitanas en México, 1980', *Estud. Demog. & Urb.*, i/1 (1986)
R. W. Morse: 'Urban Development', *Colonial Spanish America*, ed. L. Bethell (Cambridge, 1987), pp. 165–202
S. Linné: *El valle y la ciudad de México en 1550* (Mexico City, 1988)
Atlas de la ciudad de México (Mexico City, 1988)
Il barocco del Messico, intro. by C. Chanfón Olmos (Milan, 1991)
G. Tovar de Teresa: *La ciudad de los palacios: Crónica de un patrimonio perdido*, 2 vols (Mexico City, 1992)
L. Noelle: *Guía de arquitectura contemporánea de la ciudad de Mexico* (Mexico City, 1993)

CARLOS CHANFÓN OLMOS

III. *Art life and organization.*

1. 1521–1821. In the early years of the colonial period there was a dearth of trained European artists in Mexico, and it was therefore considered important to teach Indian craftsmen the rudiments of European systems of representation, a task largely undertaken by Franciscan missionaries. In the early part of the century most works executed by Indians took the form of tributes exacted by their colonial masters, but in the mid-16th century a guild system was established, and civil or religious patrons subsequently paid workshops for their commissions. Often these patrons were private individuals, who would select the artists that were to participate. The chapel of S José de los Naturales played an important role in the city's art life during this period. It was here that the training of indigenous craftsmen was first undertaken (*see* MEXICO, §XI), and it was here that (from 1552) all works created by them had to be assessed, according to a decree by the Viceroy, Luis de Velasco. Perhaps the most important figures in the city's architectural life in the 16th century were the Maestros Mayores, each with a distinct area of responsibility: one oversaw the general development of the city, for example, while others took care of specific projects, such as the Palacio Real or the Palacio de la Inquisición.

In 1566 SIMÓN PEREINS, the first European-trained painter to settle in Mexico, arrived in the city, and in the last decades of the 16th century he was followed by other artists, who introduced Mannerism and together constituted a circle of refined artists that received the support of viceroys and the ecclesiastical and civil councils. By the early 17th century the art workshops of Mexico City were renowned and highly productive. Artists continued to come from Europe to work in the city, but their numbers diminished, allowing local styles to develop with independence and continuity. The stylistic transition to Baroque, for example, was a natural development from local forms of Mannerism, although European models did provide points of reference. By this time Indians and mulattos were joining the guilds; some even came later to hold important positions within them. JUAN CORREA, for example, had his own workshop, which produced works for churches throughout the whole territory of Nueva España and into North America; some of its works were even imported into Spain.

One of the most celebrated painters in the city in the mid-18th century was Correa's student MIGUEL CABRERA, who with a group of other painters formed Mexico's first academy. Although this was short-lived, it did help to provide the initiative for the foundation in 1783 of the Academia de las Nobles Arts de S Carlos. This was a highly significant event not just for the art life of the city: the academy was the first of its kind to be established in the Americas, and its galleries constituted the first public art museum in the New World. More importantly, perhaps, to the educated élite of Mexican society, the Academia represented a new 'modern' stylistic approach. The dominance of the Baroque was challenged, and, partly through the influence of the Academia, Neo-classicism had been established as the prevailing style by the time the War of Independence ended in 1821.

2. AFTER 1821. After independence and the brief empire (1822–3) of Agustín de Iturbide, Mexico underwent a period of political instability, which was reflected by artistic developments—or the lack of them—in the capital. Whereas the first two decades of the 19th century had been characterized by intense building activity, there was little new construction in the decades that followed. Classes at the Academia were suspended until 1843, and no new works were added to its collection. Church and state had by this time both ceased to be great patrons, and private patrons were cautious about investing in art. There was, however, discussion of artistic subjects in the press, which played a prominent role for the first time: notable reviews of the time included *El pensador mexicano* and the weekly *El iris*. The latter was set up in February 1826 by the Italian CLAUDIO LINATI, who had opened the first lithographic workshop in Mexico City; the political comment implicit in the caricatures printed by Linati led, however, to the swift closure of *El iris* in October of the same year.

Many of the artists active in the city in the period immediately after independence continued to adhere to a Neo-classical approach, but there were also some European artists active in Mexico who depicted the city and its customs in a romantic vein. Artistic links with Europe were strengthened after 1843, when the Academia was reopened and new teachers, such as the Catalans PELEGRÍN CLAVÉ and MANUEL VILAR and the Italian EUGENIO LANDESIO, were brought over. The Academia began holding annual exhibitions, and these helped to foster the first important critical debates between conservatives, such as Clavé, and liberals, who included JUAN CORDERO and Santiago Gutiérrez and who advocated a nationalist and romantic treatment of Mexican history, landscapes and customs. Such artists as the landscape painter JOSÉ MARÍA VELASCO rose to prominence in the mid-19th century, but the city remained the centre of a desultory art market, and it was only at the end of the century, under the dictatorship of Porfirio Díaz, that public and private commissions became plentiful.

At the end of the 19th century new ideas about the arts received the support of such modernist reviews as the periodicals *Savia moderna* and *Revista moderna*. Two schools of thought in particular came to prominence in Mexico City: one advocated a form of internationalism and sought to identify with European movements, while the other supported a 'Mexicanism' that sought to give modern representations of traditional Mexican subjects. The two approaches were not necessarily mutually exclusive: the painter SATURNINO HERRÁN, for example, drew inspiration from European symbolism while incorporating into his works urban Mexican types, customs and landscapes. In the early 20th century avant-garde ideas were also introduced from Europe by such artists as DIEGO RIVERA. The chance to implement these new ideas on a large scale came during the presidency (1921–4) of Alvaro Obregón (the first stable government after the Mexican Revolution). In 1921 the Education Minister José Vascon-

celos invited artists to decorate the walls of public buildings, thus initiating the era of Mexican muralism (*see also* MURAL, §II, 1). Rivera returned from Paris to take part in the project, while other participating artists included DR ATL, RAMÓN ALVA DE LA CANAL, ROBERTO MONTENE-GRO, JEAN CHARLOT, FERNANDO LEAL, JOSÉ CLEMENTE OROZCO and DAVID ALFARO SIQUEIROS. The first mural to be completed, Rivera's *Creation* (1922–3; Mexico City, Escuela N. Prep.), provoked violent controversy and was derided by those who maintained conservative attitudes to art. As the programme continued, there were also disagreements between the muralists themselves, and the debates were eagerly followed in the press by the public. Despite the fact that the artists involved in the scheme were generally further left, politically speaking, than the government that sponsored them, there was a close relationship between the two groups. Indeed the government was eager to continue to be associated with the murals in the light of the warm reception given to them by Mexican and American art critics.

The 1920s was a decade in which many artistic associations and groupings were founded. In 1922, for example, the leading figures in the mural movement formed the Sindicato de Obreros Técnicos, Pintores y Escultores, which published its manifesto, advocating a public mural art, in the journal *El machete* the following year. At the same time the avant-garde literary and artistic group

5. Diego Rivera: *Life in Pre-Columbian Mexico* (1929–32), mural painting on the staircase wall of the Palacio Nacional, Mexico City

ESTRIDENTISMO worked to reject academicism and Symbolism in favour of the more forward-looking European movement Futurism. At the end of the 1920s another intellectual group, Contemporaneos, supported such artists as RUFINO TAMAYO and MANUEL RODRÍGUEZ LOZANO, who did not sympathize with the nationalistic slant of the muralists. More generally, however, there was an interest in a reassessment of Pre-Columbian culture (see fig. 5), to which the government again gave its support through the establishment of such non-academic institutions as the Escuelas de Pintura al Aire Libre (*see* MEXICO, §XI).

In the decades that followed three major institutions were established in Mexico City: the Instituto de Investigaciones Estéticas and the Galería de Arte Mexicano (both 1935) and the Instituto Nacional de Bellas Artes (1947). These reflected to some degree the extent to which the advancement of art had become a government responsibility in the absence of a strong art market; this situation meant that experimentation with new styles was largely left to individual initiatives, however, and received little public financial support. The art life of the city was rejuvenated to some extent in the period after World War II, as many foreign artists and critics settled there, and as the USA replaced Europe as the predominant source of new artistic ideas. In the mid-1950s MANUEL FELGUÉREZ and his wife, Lilia Carrillo, founded Ruptura, a group linked to international movements and opposed to the mural tradition. In 1964 the Museo de Arte Moderno was established in Chapultepec Park, but it was not until 1969 that the Museo began to accept and promote the new artistic approaches adopted by such artists as ALBERTO GIRONELLA, Juan Soriano, PEDRO CORONEL, GUNTHER GERZSO and VICENTE ROJO. Numerous other museums were also founded in Mexico City in the 1960s, but the tendency towards the end of the 20th century was for private, rather than state, promotion of the arts, a trend reflected in the establishment in the 1980s of such institutions as the Museo Rufino Tamayo and the Centro Cultural de Arte Contemporáneo.

See also MEXICO, §§IX and X.

BIBLIOGRAPHY

G. García Maroto: *Acción plástica popular: Educación y aprendizaje a escala nacional* (Mexico City, 1945)
M. Toussaint: *Arte colonial en México* (Mexico City, 1948, 2/1982)
J. Fernández: *Arte moderno y contemporáneo de México* (Mexico City, 1952)
A. Luna Arroyo: *Panorama de las artes plásticas mexicanas, 1910–1960: Una interpretación social* (Mexico City, 1962)
P. Rojas: *Historia general del arte mexicano: Época colonial* (Mexico City, 1962)
D. Rivera: *Arte y política*, ed. R. Tibol (Mexico City, 1979)
J. A. Manrique, ed.: *Arte mexicano* (Mexico City, 1982)
J. A. Manrique and others: *Modernidad y modernización en el arte mexicano, 1920–1960* (Mexico City, 1991)

JORGE ALBERTO MANRIQUE

Mey, J(ohann) M(elchior) van der. *See* MEIJ, J. M. VAN DER.

Meybusch, Anton (*b c.* 1645; *d* Copenhagen, 1 Jan 1702). Danish medallist, die-cutter and wax sculptor of German or Dutch origin. He probably learnt the trade of die-cutting in Copenhagen, where from 1667 onwards he worked for King Frederick III and King Christian V. In 1674 he moved to Stockholm and received a licence to produce medals, among which were several of *Charles XI of Sweden* and *Queen Ulrike Eleonore*. From 1674 to 1684 he was employed as a die-cutter at the Swedish Royal Mint, at the same time working as a goldsmith. In 1681 he accepted an invitation to the Mint in Paris, where he was given the title of Médailleur du Roi de France: he brought with him coining presses of his own invention. Meybusch returned to Stockholm in 1690 but moved back in that same year to Copenhagen, where in 1692 he received a post at the Danish court.

BIBLIOGRAPHY

Forrer; Thieme–Becker
L. O. Lagerquist and E. Nathorst-Böös: *Mynt och medaljer* [Coins and medals] (Stockholm, 1960)
E. Andren and others: *Svenskt silversmide, 1520–1850* [Swedish silversmiths, 1520–1850] (Stockholm, 1963), p. 75
B. Tingström: *Svensk numismatisk uppslagsbok* [Swedish numismatic encyclopedia] (Stockholm, 1963), p. 38

HERMANN MAUÉ

Meyer. Swiss family of artists. Dietrich Theodor Meyer I (1572–1658), a painter and engraver of hunting scenes and peasant dances, myths and allegories, was the initial teacher of his sons (1) Rudolf Meyer, Johannes Meyer I (1614–66) and (2) Conrad Meyer. While Rudolf was most prolific as an etcher and draughtsman, Conrad is best known as a portrait painter; of the work of the painter and etcher Johannes, only two oil paintings (Zurich, Zentbib.) are known. Conrad's sons Dietrich Theodor Meyer II (1651–1733) and Johannes Meyer II (1655–1712) were both engravers; Dietrich was also a goldsmith and Johannes II was also a painter.

BIBLIOGRAPHY

J. R. Rahn: *Die Künstlerfamilie Meyer von Zürich*, 2 vols (Zurich, 1880–82)
F. Deuchler, M. Roethlisberger and H. Lüthy: *La Peinture suisse du moyen âge à l'aube du XXe siècle* (Geneva, 1975)

(1) Rudolf Meyer (*b* Zurich, 12 June 1605; *d* Zurich, 15 Aug 1638). Etcher, draughtsman and painter. He trained first with his father and, in 1629–30, with the topographer Matthäus Merian the elder in Frankfurt am Main. His first large commission came from the theologian Daniel Cramer (*fl* 1595–1620), who ordered 80 illustrations for his *Emblemata moralia nova* (Frankfurt am Main, 1630; e.g. London, BM; Schaffhausen, Ministerialbib.). He is known to have spent some time in Nuremberg in 1630 but returned to Zurich in 1632, probably on account of his health. Most of his work as an etcher and draughtsman was in the field of allegory and moral illustration, but biblical scenes, portraits and erotica also feature. His greatest achievement was a sequence of the *Dance of Death* (Zurich, 1650) completed by his brother Conrad Meyer. In 1636–7 Rudolf Meyer etched 40 illustrations for *Helvetia Sancta* (Zurich, 1637; e.g. Zurich, Eidgenöss. Tech. Hochsch.) by Heinrich Murer (*fl* 1635–8), mainly after designs by Hans Asper. Meyer's surviving work consists of *c.* 550 drawings (mainly Zurich, Ksthaus), 300 etchings and 3 paintings (Zurich, Ksthaus), one of doubtful attribution. His printed graphic work is best represented in the Kunsthaus, Zurich, and in the graphic collection of the Eidgenössische Technische Hochschule, Zurich.

PRINTS

H. Murer: *Helvetia Sancta* (Zurich, 1637/*R* Lucerne, 1648)
Dance of Death (Zurich, 1650, 2/1657/*R* 1978)

BIBLIOGRAPHY
C. Brun: *Schweizerisches Künstlerlexikon*, ii (Frauenfeld, 1908), p. 403
H. von Matt: *Der Radierer Rudolf Meyer von Zürich, 1605–1638* (diss., Freiburg in der Schweiz, Immensee, 1956)
R. Meyer: *Sterbensspiegel: Neudruck der Ausgabe von 1650* [with] R. Zürcher and M. Bircher: *Beitrag im Anhang: Der Zürcher Sterbensspiegel und seine Zeit* (Zurich, 1978)

F. FORTER

(2) Conrad Meyer (*b* Zurich, 1618; *d* Zurich 1689). Painter and engraver, brother of (1) Rudolf Meyer. After studying under his father, Dietrich Theodor Meyer I, his brother Rudolf and Hans Ludwig Stadler I (1605–60), he became a pupil of Matthäus Merian the younger in Frankfurt am Main, where he discovered the works of Abraham of Bloemaert and Joachim von Sandrart. In 1643 he settled in Zurich, where he became the successor to the portrait painter Samuel Hofmann, executing some 200 portraits for the bourgeois families of the city, such as that of *Joseph Orell* (1657; Zurich, Schweiz. Landesmus.). Towards the end of his life Meyer turned more towards drawing and engraving, producing works strongly influenced by Dutch taste. He is believed to have executed some 900 engravings, including those in *Die Kinderspiele* (Zurich, 1657), which exemplify his use of allegorical figures or naked putti backed up by little moral verses. His vignettes for *Des Neuren* [sic] *Testaments Unsers Herren Jesu Christi fornemsste Historien und Offenbarungen*, several of which are evocative of Adam Elsheimer's style, illustrate the influence of the Northern school.

PRINTS
Die Kinderspiele (Zurich, 1657/*R* 1970)

VINCENT LIEBER

Meyer, Adolf (*b* Mechernich, nr Euskirchen, 17 June 1881; *d* Baltrum, East Friesian islands, 24 July 1929). German architect and teacher. He trained as a cabinet-maker and studied at the Kunstgewerbeschule, Düsseldorf, where he was particularly influenced by J. L. M. Lauwerik's theory of proportion. From 1907 to 1908 he worked in Peter Behrens's office, and from 1909 to 1910 he worked in Bruno Paul's office in Berlin. From 1910 until 1925 he worked in close collaboration with Walter Gropius and directed his offices in Berlin and Weimar. In addition he was an outstanding teacher of architecture at the Bauhaus in Weimar (1919–25). When the school moved to Dessau, Ernst May appointed him director of the planning consultancy at the structural engineering office in Frankfurt am Main. He also taught structural engineering at the Kunstgewerbeschule in Frankfurt. In 1919 he signed the manifesto of the Arbeitsrat für Kunst and was a member of the architects' group Der Ring. In 1928 he founded the Frankfurt Oktobergruppe with, among others, Willi Baumeister, Mart Stam and Josef Gantner.

Meyer built bridges and weirs to regulate the Nidda, a coking plant (1927–8) and retail premises for a gas company; his main work was an extensive scheme (1928–9) on the Gutleutstrasse for the city's electricity company, which included administration and test buildings, assembly shop, workshops, cable stores and garages. These buildings, as well as the designs for the planetarium in Jena (1925), the Palais des Nations in Geneva (1927) and the transformer station in Eschersheim (1928), reveal a style of building severe and simple, compact in its plasticity, its material and construction of elemental simplicity. The buildings for the electricity utility have unplastered concrete walls and ceilings, while the roofs of the halls are domed or barrel-vaulted concrete shells. Meyer was a pioneer of the stressed-skin construction discovered in Jena in 1923, using it in many designs, and the assembly shop was covered by the thinnest and flattest shell ever used hitherto. Meyer also designed some interiors, for Fritz Wichert among others, as well as gas appliances and several types of lamps for industrial production.

WRITINGS
Ein Versuchshaus des Bauhauses in Weimar, Bauhausbücher 3 (Munich, 1925)

BIBLIOGRAPHY
Bauten: Walter Gropius mit Adolf Meyer (Berlin, 1920) [illus. only, no text]
E. May and others: Obituary, *Neue Frankfurt*, iii/9 (1929), pp. 165–82
'Elektrizitätswerk Frankfurt am Main: Neue Magazin- und Werkstattsgebäude', *Zentbl. Bauverwalt.*, l (1930), pp. 249–53
A. Jaeggi: 'Due architetture per l'industria a Francoforte di Adolf Meyer', *Casabella*, xlvi (1982), pp. 40–47

KARL-HEINZ HÜTER

Meyer, Baron **Adolf (Gayne) de** (*b* Paris, 1868; *d* Hollywood, CA, 6 Jan 1949). French photographer. He was brought up in Paris and during the 1890s also became established in London as part of a circle of aristocrats and socialites. In 1899 he married Olga Caracciolo, whose godfather was the Prince of Wales (later Edward VII). He soon became noted for his elegant photographic portraits, such as that of his wife *Olga de Meyer* (*c*. 1900; Rochester, NY, Int. Mus. Phot.). He had started exhibiting in London and Paris in 1894 and in 1898 was elected to the LINKED RING. This rapid success was due to the influence of Whistler and the Aesthetic Movement in his works: he used diffuse back-lighting and soft focus to give an air of unreality both to his portraits and to his still-lifes (e.g. *Still-life with Flowers*, Providence, RI Sch. Des., Mus. A.). In 1901 Meyer was made a baron by Frederick-Augustus III, King of Saxony, at the request of his cousin Edward VII.

Having been involved in the Viennese Secession Meyer was, together with its other photographers, invited by Alfred Stieglitz to exhibit at 291 in New York in 1906. He had one-man shows there in 1907 and 1912, and his work appeared in *Craftsman* and, in 1908 and 1912, in *Camera Work*. Meyer followed Serge Diaghilev's Ballets Russes and took numerous photographs while the company was performing in London and Paris: his album *Sur le Prélude à l'après-midi d'un faune* (Paris, 1914) contains photographs of the rehearsals for the London performance of Debussy's ballet in 1912. Accused of being a spy at the outbreak of World War I, he fled Europe for New York, where he became a photographer for *Vogue* and *Vanity Fair*, contributing portraits and still-lifes. In 1916 he took the name 'Gayne' after being told by an astrologer that it would bring him good luck. He returned to Paris after the war and in 1923 was appointed to *Harper's Bazaar*. By this stage his style was becoming outdated. As a result of the Depression he lost his permanent job in 1932, and none of his works was published in *Harper's Bazaar* after 1934. In 1939 war again forced him to move to the USA, where he spent his last decade.

BIBLIOGRAPHY

R. Brandau and P. Jullian: *De Meyer* (London, 1976)

N. Hall-Duncan: *The History of Fashion Photography* (New York, 1979), pp. 32–43

The Art of Photography, 1839–1989 (exh. cat. ed. M. Weaver; Houston, TX, Mus. F.A.; Canberra, N.G.; London, RA; 1989), pp. 416, 462

Meyer, Hannes (*b* Basle, 18 Nov 1889; *d* Savosa, Ticino, 19 July 1954). Swiss architect, theorist and designer. He was born into a family of architects and studied building at the Gewerbeschule, Basle (1905–9). In Berlin he continued his training at the Kunstgewerbeschule and attended classes in urban planning at the Landwirtschafts-Akademie (1909–12). He became increasingly concerned about housing conditions in the modern industrial city and developed a strong interest in urban planning and land reform. In 1912 he went to England where he studied the Co-operative movement and the garden cities of Letchworth, Bourneville and Port Sunlight for a year. After two years' military service in Switzerland (1914–16), he worked for Krupps Housing Welfare Office and became increasingly interested in using standardized components in the construction of housing estates. In 1919 he set up his own practice in Basle, where he designed and supervised the foundation of the Siedlung Freidorf (Freihof) (1919–24) at Muttenz, near Basle, the first full-scale cooperative housing estate in Switzerland. The client (Verband Schweizerische Konsumvereine) rejected the Constructivist approach that Meyer favoured, so he developed a style based on local Jura building types. In 1924 he founded the Theater Co-op and collaborated in a wide range of Co-op activities throughout Europe.

In 1926 Meyer published *Die neue Welt*, a Modernist battle hymn, filled with enthusiasm for all the manifestations of the modern age, from the light bulb to the portable gramophone. The new age demanded standardization and a collective approach. Building, he declared, was a technical not an aesthetic process, and design was a product of the formula 'function multiplied by economics'. By this time such competition projects as the Petersschule in Basle and the General Secretariat and Assembly Hall of the League of Nations in Geneva (1926–7; *see* FUNCTIONALISM, fig. 2) were winning for Meyer and his partner, Hans Wittwer (1894–1952), a reputation for uncompromising Modernism. The design was strenuously Functionalist and was designed to contrast rather than blend in with nature. Meyer was one of the founder–members of CIAM, which arose from the ashes of the mismanagement of the League of Nations competition.

In 1927 Meyer was appointed head of the new architecture department at the Bauhaus in Dessau. His theoretical position on building and society had become even more uncompromising. His manifesto, *Bauen* (1928), is a clear statement of what he called his 'functional-biological' concept of building. The new house was not to be a machine for living in but, rather, a biological apparatus for spiritual and physical needs. He declared that all building was organization: social, technical, economic and psychological; he denied the role of artistic creation in architecture. In 1928, despite opposition among faculty members, Walter Gropius appointed him his successor as Director of the Bauhaus.

Meyer's achievements at the school were considerable. The workshops, always in theory central to the curriculum, were now at the heart of the school's activities; students, organized into work brigades, learned by tackling actual commissions. The theoretical aspect of the curriculum, previously dominated by art theory, was reorientated towards the natural and social sciences. The workshops were extraordinarily productive and fulfilled their aim of providing models for low-cost mass production. The architecture department continued to develop the Törten housing estate (begun 1926) in Dessau, and in 1928 Meyer won a competition for the Allgemeiner Deutscher Gewerkschaftsbund school at Bernau, a Modernist complex of white flat-roofed buildings sensitively grouped around a lake.

Meyer's directorship ended ignominiously, however: in August 1930, amid a tense political situation in Dessau, he was dismissed for allegedly encouraging Communism among the students. Gropius accused Meyer of having dissembled his true political colours and of jeopardizing the future of the school. Meyer departed angrily for the USSR, hoping that there his work would be better received. He became a professor at VASI, the School of Architecture in Moscow, and was also chief architect for Giprovtus, the office responsible for buildings connected with higher education. He worked on urban planning projects throughout the USSR. In 1936 he returned to Switzerland, and in 1939 he was appointed Director of the Instituto del Urbanismo y Planificacion in Mexico City, where he worked until 1949. While living in Mexico City Meyer directed La Estampa Mexicana, the publishing house of the *Taller de Gráfica Popular*.

Meyer remains a controversial figure. His ideas were not always consistent. However, he offered an alternative version of Modernism, in which its principles were used not for the glorification and profit of either the architect or the client/contractor but for the benefit of the end-users, at the expense of the former.

WRITINGS

'Die neue Welt', *Werk*, xiii/7 (1926), pp. 205–24; also in *Hannes Meyer: Bauen und Gesellschaft: Schriften, Briefe, Projekte*, ed. K.-J. Winkler (Dresden, 1980), pp. 27–32

'Bauen', *Bauhaus: Z. Bau & Gestalt.*, 2 (1928), no. 4, pp. 12–13; also in *Hannes Meyer: Bauen und Gesellschaft: Schriften, Briefe, Projekte*, ed. K.-J. Winkler (Dresden, 1980), pp. 47–9

BIBLIOGRAPHY

H. M. Wingler: *Das Bauhaus* (Braunsche, 1962, 2/1975); Eng. trans. by W. Jabs and B. Gilbert

C. Schnaidt: *Hannes Meyer: Bauen, Projekte und Schriften* (Teufen, 1965; Eng. trans., London and New York, 1965)

A. Saint: *The Image of the Architect* (New Haven, 1983), pp. 115–37

ANNA ROWLAND

Meyer, Hans. *See* HAMMER, HANS.

Meyer, (Hans) Heinrich (*b* Stäfa, 16 March 1760; *d* Jena, 11 Oct 1832). Swiss painter and art historian. His first drawing lessons were with Johann Koella (1740–78) in Stäfa, and from 1778 to 1781 he studied with Johann Caspar Füssli in Zurich. Füssli imparted Johann Joachim Winckelmann's theories on 'emulation of the ancients' to him. In 1784 he left for Rome to study Classical works and the art of Raphael. He earned his living from sepia drawings after Roman sculptures and made many drawings from nature; he also worked as a tourist guide. In 1787 he met JOHANN WOLFGANG VON GOETHE, and so impressed him with his extensive knowledge that he was invited to Weimar as Goethe's artistic adviser and associate. Before leaving Rome Meyer made many copies after ancient and more modern work for Goethe, such the Roman fresco *Aldobrandini Wedding* and the compositions *Aurora* (1786; Weimar) influenced by Guido Reni and *Odysseus and Nausica* (1789; Weimar) after Annibale Carraci. Although Goethe greatly admired his artistic output, Meyer's art was less significant than his work as a scholar.

In 1791 Meyer moved to Weimar, where he lived in Goethe's house, and advised him on artistic matters. He painted a portrait of Goethe's companion and the child she bore him, *Christiane Vulpius with August* (1792; Weimar, Goethe-Nmus. Frauenplan), based on a water-colour after Raphael's *Madonna of the Chair*, and also a portrait of *Goethe* (1795; Weimar, Goethe-Nmus. Frauen-plan). He supervised the decoration of Goethe's house in a Roman style, painting various rooms with mythical and allegorical figures. Meyer returned to Rome and Florence between 1795 and 1797, assembling material for Goethe's history of Italian art. He then began working as a drawing tutor at the Freies Zeichen-Institut in Weimar, and became principal there in 1806. He was appointed to supervise the renovation and decoration of the Residenzschloss (1799), and his artistic activity gradually took second place to writing and administration. With Goethe, he founded the art magazine *Propyläen* (1798–1805), and ran the annual exhibitions and competitions associated with it.

Meyer is most important for his art-historical works, such as his article 'Entwurf einer Kunstgeschichte des achtzehnten Jahrhunderts', published in Goethe's *Winck-elmann und sein Jahrhundert* (Weimar, 1805), and for the three-volume *Geschichte der bildenden Künste bei den Griechen* (Weimar, 1824–36). *Neudeutsche religiös-patri-otische Kunst* (Weimar, 1817), which Meyer wrote with Goethe, made Meyer many enemies among German Romantics, and he was abused as Goethe's 'evil genius'.

BIBLIOGRAPHY
Thieme–Becker
M. Hecker, ed.: *Goethes Briefwechsel mit Heinrich Meyer*, 3 vols (Weimar, 1917)
H. Wahl: *Zeichnungen von Johann Heinrich Meyer* (Weimar, 1918)
W. Pfeifer-Belli: *Goethes Kunstmeyer und seine Welt* (Zurich and Stuttgart, 1959)
Goethe und die Kunst (exh. cat., ed. S. Schulze; Frankfurt am Main, Schirn Ksthalle; Weimar, Kstsammlungen; 1994)

INGRID SATTEL BERNARDINI

Meyer [Majer; Meier], **Jeremiah** [Jeremias] (*b* Tübingen, Baden-Württemberg, 18 Jan 1735; *d* Kew, nr London, 20 Jan 1789). German enameller and painter, active in Eng-land. He was the son of a portrait painter at the court of Württemberg. He arrived in England *c.* 1749 and studied in London at St Martin's Lane Academy and then (1757–8) under Christian Friedrich Zincke; as a result of this training, much of Meyer's early work was painted on enamel. He exhibited (1760–67) at the Society of Artists and in 1761 was awarded its gold medal for a profile portrait of *George III*. In 1762 he became a naturalized Englishman. That year he was appointed miniature painter to Queen Charlotte and in 1764 painter in enamel to the

King. Meyer was a founder-member of the Royal Academy and exhibited miniatures, enamels and watercolours there (1769–83). He also painted some portraits in oil.

Meyer's early work bears pronounced similarities to that of Bernard Lens (iii) and Gervase Spencer (*d* 1763). By the early 1770s, when he was painting miniatures in the newly fashionable larger sizes, his own style had evolved. Applying long strokes of watercolour for a soft, luminous effect, he used opaque colour sparingly to accent details of costumes. The National Portrait Gallery, London, has his miniatures on ivory of *Sir William Chambers* (after 1770) and *Gen. Thomas Gage*. His miniature on ivory of *George IV when Prince of Wales* (Baltimore, MD, Walters A.G.) is a fine example of his mature work. Meyer was one of the first artists to refine techniques of miniature painting on ivory and helped to inspire a renaissance of the art in the late 18th century. Among his pupils were the miniature painters Richard Collins (1755–1831) and Diana Dietz (*d* 1844).

BIBLIOGRAPHY
E. E. Simmons: 'Deutsche Einflüsse in der englischen Porträtminiatur-malerei des 18. Jahrhunderts', *Die Weltkunst*, xl (1978), pp. 2686–7
J. Murdoch and others: *The English Miniature* (London, 1981)
D. Foskett: *Miniatures: Dictionary and Guide* (Woodbridge, 1987)

Meyer, Pedro (*b* Madrid, 6 Oct 1935). Mexican photog-rapher of Spanish birth. He became a Mexican citizen in 1942 but was educated in the USA, where he trained as an administrator at the Babson Institute, Boston, MA. He was self-taught as a photographer, and after his return to Mexico in 1956 he enthusiastically promoted photography through the Grupo Arte Fotográfico, which he founded in 1963, and the Consejo Mexicano de Fotografía, which he also founded and whose president he became in 1977. His photography was inspired by a deep humanism, both in his keen observation of social structures and in the reliance on shock and irony in his pictorial documentaries, as is evident in his scenes of Nicaragua. An exhibition of his work, *Los otros y nosotros*, held in Mexico City in 1986, caused an international stir.

PHOTOGRAPHIC PUBLICATIONS
Pedro Meyer (Mexico City, 1986)
BIBLIOGRAPHY
Retrospectiva de Pedro Meyer (exh. cat. by C. Monsivais, Mexico City, 1973)
Los otros y nosotros (exh. cat. by V. Lenero, Mexico City, Mus. A. Mod., 1986)

ERIKA BILLETER

Meyer-Amden, (Friedrich) Otto (*b* Berne, 20 Feb 1885; *d* Zurich, 15 Jan 1933). Swiss painter and draughtsman. After serving an apprenticeship as a lithographer and attending courses at the Kunstgewerbeschule in Zurich he moved to Stuttgart in 1907, where he became a pupil of Adolf Hölzel in 1909. He soon attracted a circle of friends, including Willi Baumeister, Johannes Itten and Oskar Schlemmer. In 1912 he moved to the mountain village of Amden above the Walensee, which was becoming a haven for artists and art enthusiasts. He again became the centre of a group of artists, and the letters he wrote from there to his half-brother Paul Meyer and to Schlemmer are important in charting his artistic and philosophical devel-opment. He had two main themes in his work: the usually naked figure of the young male, as in *Picture of a Gardener* (1911; Zurich, Ksthaus), and the community of youth, as in *Preparation* (*c.* 1930; Basle, Kstmus.). The figures are carefully delineated and psychologically isolated in their surroundings, often placed in a mysterious penumbral setting suggestive of dreams and recalling the symbolism of Ferdinand Hodler. In the later group works the dark but richly coloured compositions are ordered by a strict underlying geometry. In 1928 he took up a teaching appointment at the Kunstgewerbeschule in Zurich, which seemed to him the fulfilment of his life's ambitions.

BIBLIOGRAPHY

O. Schlemmer: *Otto Meyer-Amden, aus Leben, Werk und Briefen* (Zurich, 1934)
C. Huber: *Otto Meyer-Amden* (Berne, 1968)
M. Stettler: *Otto Meyer-Amden* (Lausanne, 1970)

URS-B. FREI

Meyer de Haan, Jacob (Isaac)

Meyer de Haan, Jacob (Isaac) (*b* Amsterdam, 15 April 1852; *d* Amsterdam, 24 Oct 1895). Dutch painter. He was born into a well-to-do manufacturer's family, from whom he inherited a great interest in painting. His earliest known paintings, in the style of David Teniers (ii) and Rembrandt, are somewhat anecdotal in nature and reflect his Jewish background. One of these works, *Uriel Acosta* (1878–88; priv. col.), caused such displeasure in orthodox Jewish circles that Meyer de Haan left for Paris in October 1888 with a monthly allowance from his family. There he stayed with the art dealer Theo van Gogh for some months. In May 1889 he travelled to Brittany, where in Pont-Aven he became friendly with Paul Gauguin. During the winter of 1889–90 Gauguin and Meyer de Haan lived, at the latter's expense, in Marie Henry's inn in Le Pouldu, where Meyer de Haan rented a studio for the two of them and decorated the dining-room with murals; for example *Breton Women Stretching Hemp* (1889; untraced, see J. Rewald, *Post-Impressionism*, London, 1956, rev. 1978, p. 273). The withdrawal of his family allowance and a sudden illness seem to have prevented Meyer de Haan from following Gauguin to Tahiti in early 1891. He probably returned to the Netherlands in 1891 where he continued to suffer from the ill-health that precipitated his early death.

Within Meyer de Haan's comparatively small oeuvre, the few paintings he made in France (1889–90) have a central place. As a devoted pupil of Gauguin he was closely involved in the development of Synthetism in such works as *Self-portrait with Japanese Background* (late 1889; priv. col.) and *Motherhood: Marie Henry and her Child* (autumn 1889; priv. col.). His landscapes were also heavily indebted to Gauguin (e.g. *Le Pouldu*, Otterlo, Kröller-Müller). Gauguin in turn recognized Meyer de Haan's intellect and commemorated their friendship in a series of portraits, which included an imposing polychromed oak bust (1889–90; Ottawa, N.G.) and culminated in his posthumous representation in *Savage Tales* (1902; Essen, Mus. Flkwang; *see* GAUGUIN, PAUL, fig. 4).

BIBLIOGRAPHY

J. Zürcher: *Meijer de Haan's Uriël Acosta* (Amsterdam, 1888)
F. Dauchot: 'Meyer de Haan en Bretagne', *Gaz. B.-A.*, xl (1952), pp. 355–8
W. Jaworska: 'Jacob Meyer de Haan, 1852–1895', *Ned. Ksthist. Jb.*, xviii (1967), pp. 197–221
——: *Paul Gauguin et l'école de Pont-Aven* (Genève, 1971)

Vincent van Gogh and the Birth of Cloisonism (exh. cat. by B. Welsh-Ovcharov, Toronto, A.G. Ont., 1981)

G. JANSEN

Meyerhold, Vsevolod (Emil'yevich)

Meyerhold [Meyerkhol'd]**, Vsevolod (Emil'yevich)** [Karl Theodore Kasimir] (*b* Penza, 9 Feb 1874; *d* Moscow, 2 Feb 1940). Russian theorist, stage director and actor. He was the director of the imperial opera and drama theatres in St Petersburg, but he had established an avant-garde reputation before the appearance of Russian Futurism in late 1912. This was largely due to his innovative and experimental unofficial productions for the House of Interludes cabaret and the Terioki summer theatre of 1912. As early as 1906 Meyerhold had signalled his break with tradition through the production of Aleksandr Blok's *Balaganchik* ('Little fairground booth') at the Kommisarzhevskaya Theatre. Through his use of such 'low' techniques as improvisation, buffoonery, masks, making-up the actors in the auditorium and direct audience involvement, Meyerhold anticipated many features employed in the visual arts by the Russian Neo-primitivists and Futurists.

In August 1918 Meyerhold joined the Bolshevik Party and embarked on a second period of experimentation. By the autumn he had become head of the Petrograd section of TEO, the Theatre department of NARKOMPROS, and simultaneously managed to stage Vladimir Mayakovsky's revolutionary play *Misteriya-Buffa* ('Mystery-Bouffe'). In 1920 Anatoly Lunacharsky appointed Meyerhold as head of TEO in Moscow. In the same year Meyerhold's company, RSFSR Theatre No. 1, performed Emile Verhaeren's *The Dawn*, depicting the international proletarian uprising in the play in a Russian Futurist style. Meyerhold embraced the programmes of 'mass action' and 'theatrical October', proposing that war be declared on the apolitical character of the old stage art and demanding a theatrical revolution in which the theatre would become part of everyday life, accessible to the masses at all times and in all places. This required the continual development of stage design. His most important post-Revolutionary works were Constructivist productions with the designers Lyubov' Popova and Varvara Stepanova (e.g. *The Magnanimous Cuckold* by Fernand Crommelynck and *Smert' Tarelkina* ('The death of Tarelkin') by Sukhovo-Kobylin, both 1922). These revealed his acting system of 'biomechanics', in which theatrical art adopted technological principles: the actor embodied the ideally trained and efficient worker whose Communist soul was externalized in his movements. However, Meyerhold's innovations were increasingly denounced by the authorities and in the 1930s his repertoire and influence were drastically restricted. He was arrested in 1939 as a 'counter-revolutionary' and shot in the following year. In 1955 he was posthumously rehabilitated, but for a long time afterwards conservative critics and the authorities continued to disqualify his work as 'formalist' and 'anti-populist'.

BIBLIOGRAPHY

K. Rudnitsky: *Meyerhold the Director* (Ann Arbor, 1981)

JEREMY HOWARD

Meyeringh [Meyering], **Aelbert** [Albert] (*b* Amsterdam, 1645; *d* Amsterdam, 17 July 1714). Dutch etcher, draughtsman and painter. He trained under his father, the painter and art dealer Frederik Meyeringh (*b* Emden, 1608; *d* Amsterdam, 1669). Aelbert spent the period from 1672 to 1687 away from Amsterdam. In 1675–6 he was in Rome with his artist–friend Johannes Glauber and probably spent a year after that in Padua. He provided the designs for Glauber's series of six etchings with views from the monastery of the Grande Chartreuse (Hollstein, nos 1–6), in which the influence of Gaspard Dughet is evident. His oeuvre includes paintings, drawings, painted wallpaper decorations and etchings of classical Italianate landscapes with mythological and arcadian subjects. The etchings (e.g. the series of 27 landscape etchings after his own designs, 1695) date from after his return to Amsterdam. Gérard de Lairesse's two-volume *Het groot schilderboek* (Amsterdam, 1707) includes two small landscape etchings by Meyeringh (i, p. 335) and one after his drawing (i, p. 350).

BIBLIOGRAPHY
Hollstein: *Dut. & Flem.*; Thieme–Becker; Wurzbach
A. Zwollo: *Hollandse en Vlaamse veduteschilders te Rome, 1675–1725* (Assen, 1973), pp. 19–27

CHRISTIAAN SCHUCKMAN

Meyerowitz, Joel (*b* New York, 3 June 1938). American photographer. He studied at Ohio State University, Columbus (1956–9), and worked in New York as an advertising art director (1959–63). In 1962 he accompanied Robert Frank on a photographic assignment. Deeply impressed by Frank's work, he taught himself photography, becoming a freelance photographer in 1963. He documented New York streets and interiors with great spontaneity; his characteristic subjects were banal, empty rooms, the occupants either absent or caught unawares, for example a photograph of a woman in a room, *Untitled* (1966; New York, MOMA). In the late 1960s and early 1970s he was among the first photographers to work successfully in colour, finding new possibilities for nuance and effect, as in *Madison Avenue and 60th Street* (1976; artist's col., see Turner, ed., p. 235). Meyerowitz taught colour photography at Cooper Union for the Advancement of Science and Art, New York (1971–9), and from 1977 at Princeton University, NJ. In 1976–7, using a vintage field camera, he made a painterly photographic essay of Cape Cod, and in 1980 he took a set of powerful photographic studies of the Gateway Arch, St Louis, MO.

PHOTOGRAPHIC PUBLICATIONS
St Louis and the Arch, text by J. N. Wood (Boston, 1980/*R* 1988)

BIBLIOGRAPHY
J. Szarkowski: *Looking at Photographs* (New York, 1973)
P. Turner, ed.: *American Images: Photography, 1945–1980* (Harmondsworth and New York, 1985)

□

Meyjes, Christian Bernardus Posthumus. *See* POSTHUMUS MEYJES, CHRISTIAN BERNARDUS.

Meynal, Bertrand de. *See* BERTRAND DE MEYNAL.

Meynier, Charles (*b* Paris, 25 Nov 1768; *d* Paris, 6 Sept 1832). French painter and collector. His father intended that he should become a tailor, but he showed an early love for drawing and was allowed to study with the engraver Pierre-Philippe Choffard. He was a proficient student but nevertheless wished to become a painter, so his elder brother Meynier St-Phal, an actor at the Comédie-Française in Paris, paid for him to train from 1785 with François-André Vincent, who then enjoyed a considerable reputation. In 1789 he won the Prix de Rome for *Joseph Recognized by his Brothers* (1789; Paris, Ecole N. Sup. B.-A.), jointly with Anne-Louis Girodet. The events of the French Revolution prevented him spending the usual five years in Rome, but his time there (till 1793) allowed him to make numerous studies of antique sculpture. He returned to Paris during the Reign of Terror and started to produce large Neo-classical works. In 1793 he entered a competition set by the Committee of Public Safety for the best work on a theme from the French Revolution. Taking the competition itself as his subject, he painted *France Encouraging Science and the Arts* (Boulogne-Billancourt, Bib. Marmottan), a classically inspired work in which the generalized features of the figures, with prominent noses and chins, are characteristic of his style. The painting won a prize, though not the first prize, which was won by François Gérard, and thereafter Meynier rapidly established a reputation. He made his début at the Salon in 1795. Under the First Empire he received several public commissions for works celebrating Napoleon's victories. In 1806 he produced a series of drawings (Paris, Louvre) for bas-reliefs and sculptures to ornament the Arc de Triomphe du Carrousel, Paris, the monumental entrance to the Tuileries that was built to celebrate Napoleon's victories of 1805. The arch was designed by Pierre-François Léonard Fontaine and Charles Percier, and Meynier's designs were sculpted by a team that included Pierre Cartellier, Clodion, Louis-Pierre Deseine, Jacques Philippe Le Sueur (1757–1830) and Claude Ramey. In 1808 he painted *Marshal Ney and the Soldiers of the 76th Regiment Retrieving their Flags from the Arsenal of Inspruck* [*sic*] (1808; Versailles, Château), one of 18 works commissioned in 1806 to illustrate Napoleon's German campaign. Other similarly large-scale works were commissioned from such artists as Antoine-Jean Gros, François Gérard and Girodet. The work, which depicts the retrieval in 1805 of three flags that had been lost in the campaign of 1800, was highly praised at the Salon of 1808. In 1807 he was one of 26 artists who entered the competition to paint a scene from the recently fought Battle of Eylau. His *Napoleon on the Battlefield of Eylau* (1807; Versailles, Château; see fig.) won one of the two honourable mentions, though the competition was won by Gros. In the foreground of this bloody battle scene he included numerous nude corpses, in rather slavish accordance with classical ideals.

In 1815 Meynier was elected to the Académie des Beaux-Arts. Following the Bourbon Restoration, he received many decorative commissions, most notably for the Louvre, Paris, where he painted two ceilings, *France Protecting the Arts* (1819) for the Salle Percier and *Triumph of French Painting* (1822) for the Salle Duchâtel (the latter depicting the apotheosis of Nicolas Poussin, Charles Le Brun and Eustache Le Sueur). He returned to the Louvre in 1827 and painted the *Nymphs of Parthenope* for the Salle des Antiquités Egyptiennes. Together with

Charles Meynier: *Napoleon on the Battlefield of Eylau*, oil on canvas, 0.93×1.47 m, 1807 (Versailles, Musée National du Château de Versailles et de Trianon)

Alexandre Abel de Pujol he decorated the Paris Bourse (1826) and in 1829 provided ceiling decorations for the Grand Salon of the Tuileries (Amboise, Mus. Mun.).

Though mainly known for his allegorical and history paintings, Meynier occasionally painted portraits (e.g. *Marshal Ney*; Versailles, Château) and religious works, such as the *Dedication of the Church of St-Denis* (1812) for the sacristy of that church in Paris. One of his last works was the Rubensian *Triumph of St Michael* (1828) for the chapel of the Boulard asylum in Saint-Mandé. Highly linear Neo-classical drawings form a further part of his oeuvre. He ran a painting studio open exclusively to women, his more distinguished pupils including Louise-Marie-Jeanne Hersent (1784–1862). After his death from cholera, a large sale was held of his art collection, comprised mostly of prints but including also paintings by Annibale Carracci, David Teniers (ii), Jacques-Louis David, Anthony van Dyck and Simon Vouet. His prints were largely reproductions of well-known paintings, but there were a few originals, for example some by Albrecht Dürer and Giovanni Battista Piranesi.

BIBLIOGRAPHY

Catalogue des tableaux, dessins et aquarelles, estampes anciennes et modernes. . . . provenant du cabinet et des ateliers de feu M. Meynier (Paris, 1832)

E. B. Garnier: *Funérailles de M. Charles Meynier* (Paris, 1832)

C. Deplace, ed: *Biographie universelle, ancienne et moderne*, 45 vols (Paris, 1843–58), xxviii, p. 173

P. Marmottan: *L'Ecole française de peinture (1789–1830)* (Paris, 1886), pp. 313, 330, 339, 452

French Painting, 1774–1830: The Age of Revolution (exh. cat. by F. J. Cummings, A. Schnapper and R. Rosenblum, Paris, Grand Pal.; Detroit, Inst. A.; New York, Met.; 1975), pp. 544–9

R. Michel: 'Meynier ou la métaphore parlementaire', *Rev. Louvre*, iii (1987), pp. 188–200

Meyr, Johann Ulrich. *See* MAYR, JOHANN ULRICH.

Meyran, Jean-Baptiste-Florentin-Gabriel de. *See* LAGOY.

Meyrick, Sir Samuel Rush (*b* London, 26 Aug 1783; *d* Goodrich Court, Hereford & Worcs, 2 April 1848). English lawyer, collector and historian. He practised as a barrister. In 1815 he published, with Charles Hamilton Smith (1776–1859), *The Costume of the Original Inhabitants of the British Islands*, which brought him into contact with a group of antiquaries and collectors, including Francis Douce, Sir Walter Scott and James Robinson Planché (1796–1880), who devoted themselves to the study of the Middle Ages.

Meyrick collected and studied arms and armour all his life, but it was the publication of *A Critical Inquiry into Antient Armour* (1824) that established his reputation as an authority on the subject. In 1826 he advised on the arrangement of the collection in the Tower of London, which he had criticized severely, and two years later he performed a similar service for the Royal Collection at Windsor Castle. His own collection was regularly available to students in London (Richard Parkes Bonington and Delacroix visited in 1825) or, later, in the armoury at Goodrich Court, Hereford & Worcs, the mock medieval castle designed and built for him between 1828 and 1831 by Edward Blore (destr. 1950). The collection was exhibited at the Manchester Art Treasures Exhibition in 1857 and at the South Kensington Museum, London, in 1868, before being dispersed c. 1871. Many of the pieces were bought by Joseph Noel Paton and Frédéric Spitzer and were later acquired by Sir Richard Wallace (now in the Wallace Collection, London).

WRITINGS

with C. H. Smith: *Costume of the Original Inhabitants of the British Islands, from the Earliest Periods to the Sixth Century; to which Is Added that of the Gothic Nations on the Western Coasts of the Baltic, the Ancestors of the Anglo-Saxons and Anglo-Danes* (London, 1815)

A Critical Inquiry into Antient Armour as it Existed in Europe, but Particularly in England, from the Norman Conquest to the Reign of King Charles II, with a Glossary of Military Terms of the Middle Ages, 3 vols (London, 1824)

ed. J. Carter: *Specimens of the Ancient Sculpture and Painting Now Remaining in England, from the Earliest Period to the Reign of Henry III* (London, 1838, rev. 1844)

ed. L. Dwnn: *Heraldic Visitations of Wales*, Soc. Pubn Anc. Welsh MSS, 2 vols (London, 1846)

Regular contributions to *Archaeologia* (1821–45)

BIBLIOGRAPHY

DNB

J. Skelton: *Engraved Illustrations of Antient Armour, from the Collection at Goodrich Court, from the Drawings and with the Descriptions of Dr. Meyrick* (London, 1830)

[W. Meyrick]: *An Illustrated Catalogue of Weapons and Detached Specimens of Armour from the Collection of William Meyrick, Esq.* (London, 1861)

J. G. Mann: *Wallace Collection Catalogues: European Arms and Armour*, 2 vols (London, 1962); suppl. by A. V. B. Norman (London, 1986)

A. V. B. Norman: 'Amendments and Additions to the Catalogue of Armour in the Wallace Collection, London', *J. Arms & Armour Soc.*, vii (1972), pp. 171–230

M. Girouard: *The Return to Camelot* (London, 1981)

C. Wainwright: *The Romantic Interior* (London, 1989)

SARAH BARTER BAILEY

Meyt, Conrat. *See* MEIT, CONRAT.

Meytens. *See* MIJTENS.

Mézières, Nicolas Le Camus de. *See* LE CAMUS DE MÉZIÈRES, NICOLAS.

Mezyn [Rus. Mezin]. Site in the Ukraine, in the Dnepr Valley. It has yielded a wealth of artefacts and decorated objects dating from the Upper Palaeolithic period (c. 40,000–c. 10,000 BP; *see also* PREHISTORIC EUROPE, §II). Excavations began under P. Efimenko in 1908–14 and continued in 1930–32 and 1954–61 under I. G. Shovkoplias and I. G. Pidoplichko; the material recovered is now held in Kiev (Archaeol. & Zoological Inst.). The cultural level was situated 3–5 m deep in loess (wind-deposited loam), and it contained remains of mammoths, reindeer, horses, musk oxen, foxes and wolves. Five large round concentrations of mammoth bones, some with hearths in the centre, have been interpreted as dwellings, and were probably used in the winter. The numerous artefacts and architectural remains indicate that Mezyn was intensively occupied over a long period by a group of people with a complex social structure. The stone tool assemblage has been assigned to the Mezyn–Mezhirich culture, and is similar to that of the Magdalenian culture, with many burins, perforators and backed pieces. Mammoth tusks were divided by the groove-and-splinter technique, and drop-shaped ivory pendants were manufactured in series. Numerous bone tools, such as projectile points, awls, batons and needles, have also been found.

Many pieces of bone and antler are incised with parallel or oblique line patterns, rhomboids and meander scrolls, while large, rod-like ivory pieces measuring 320–30 mm long and with head-like terminals have been interpreted as anthropomorphic statuettes. A more finely worked type has a tongued end, a triangular vulva engraved on the front and an indication of hips and prominent buttocks, combined with complex ornamentation such as meanders, rows of angles and zigzag lines. Made of ivory, these pieces lack heads and arms, and the shortened, unseparated legs have no feet. Nonetheless, they are now considered to represent schematic statuettes of women, although formerly they were interpreted as phalli or birds. Some of the less elaborate pieces are similar to Late Magdalenian examples from central Europe. Outstanding among the material from the site is a group of large, round ivory bracelets measuring 53 mm deep and engraved with meanders, spirals and herringbone patterns; each end had three holes for fastening. Another type of bracelet was constructed of five narrow ivory bands decorated with a herringbone pattern and pierced at the ends. Painted objects from Mezyn comprise mammoth bones, a scapula with a zigzag motif, two mammoth jaws decorated with parallel lines and some long bones, all painted with red ochre.

BIBLIOGRAPHY

I. G. Shovkoplias: *Mezinskaya stoyanka* [The Mezyn camp] (Kiev, 1965)

Z. A. Abramova: 'Palaeolithic Art in the USSR', *Arctic Anthropol.*, iv/2 (1967), pp. 1–179

R. G. Klein: *Ice-age Hunters of the Ukraine* (Chicago, 1973)

JOACHIM HAHN

Mezzanine. Intermediate floor built between two other levels.   □

Mezzarisa, Francesco di Antonio [Risino] (*fl* Faenza, 1527–81). Italian potter. He directed one of the most famous ceramic workshops in Faenza during the 16th century. Through its production it is possible to follow the stylistic evolution of Renaissance maiolica from the 'severe' style through to the wares known as *bianchi di Faenza*, for the invention of which Mezzarisa is thought to have been largely responsible (*see* FAENZA). He is also noted for a few important *istoriato* (narrative) wares, with skilfully applied decoration, including the large plaque depicting the *Deposition*, signed and dated 1544, and a vase decorated with biblical scenes dated 1558 (both Palermo, Gal. Reg. Sicilia). Mezzarisa was an astute businessman, and from 1540 he was assisted by Pietro di Francesco Zambaldini, a craftsman who specialized in glazes and paints. Among the most important commissions accorded to Mezzarisa was an order (1546) for more than 7000 articles for a Genoese merchant in Palermo. He also worked for the Ferrara court, where he became acquainted with the brothers and court painters Battista Dossi (*d* 1548) and Dosso Dossi (c. 1479–c. 1542). After c. 1550 Mezzarisa discontinued his exuberant narrative designs in favour of the *bianchi di Faenza* decorated with the more sketchy *compendiario* style. Mezzarisa's sons Giovanni Mezzarisa and Antonio Mezzarisa became famous potters, and in 1568 they opened a workshop in Venice.

BIBLIOGRAPHY

G. Ballardini: 'Francesco Mezzarisa alias Risino maiolicaro faentino del cinquecento', *Miscellanea di storia dell'arte in onore di Igino Benvenuto Supino* (Florence, 1933), pp. 519–51

——: 'Giovanni Brame e Francesco Risino', *Faenza*, xxxi (1943–5), pp. 67–9

C. Ravanelli Guidotti: 'Aspetti della cultura maiolicara faentina all'epoca della stesura del trattato piccolpassiano', *Faenza*, lxx (1984), pp. 189–97

LUCIANA ARBACE

Mezzastris [Mesastris], **Pierantonio** (*b* Foligno, *c.* 1430; *d* 1506). Italian painter. A cousin of Bartolomeo di Tommaso, he is first documented in 1458. By 1460 he had a workshop in Foligno. Apart from a banner (Foligno, S Giacomo), he appears to have worked exclusively in fresco. The earliest frescoes attributed to him are those in the Cola delle Casse Chapel in S Maria in Campis, Foligno, executed after 1452 (previously assigned to Niccolò da Foligno). In 1471 Mezzastris frescoed a lunette of the *Virgin and Child with SS Lucy and Clare* (Foligno, Pin. Civ.) in S Lucia, Foligno. In the oratory of the Pellegrini, Assisi, where he is documented in 1477, he painted scenes from the *Lives of SS Anthony Abbot and James* and the *Four Doctors of the Church*. Other frescoes include a *Crucifixion* (1482) in S Damiano, Assisi; the signed *Coronation of the Virgin* (1486; Foligno, Pin. Civ.); those (1487) in S Martin, Trevi; and the *Virgin and Child with SS John and Francis* (1499; Foligno, Pin. Civ.). The principal influence evident in his work is that of Benozzo Gozzoli, in particular Gozzoli's scenes of the *Life of St Francis* (Montefalco, S Francesco), from which Mezzastris's *St Francis* cycle (Narni, S Francesco) is clearly derived. Mezzastris's style is coarser and more expressive than Gozzoli's, however. Mezzastris's son Bernardino was also a painter.

BIBLIOGRAPHY

C. Cenci: *Documentazione di vita assisana, 1300–1530*, ii (Grottaferrata, 1976), pp. 756–7

M. Sensi: 'Nuovi documenti per Niccolò di Liberatore detto l'Alunno', *Paragone*, ccclxxxix (1983), pp. 91–2

La pittura in Italia: Il quattrocento, ii (Milan, 1987), p. 710

F. Todini: *La pittura umbra: Dal duecento al primo cinquecento* (Milan, 1989), i, pp. 226–8; ii, pp. 407–10

Mezzotint. Type of intaglio print or tonal engraving and the technique from which such a print is produced. The plate is grounded (or roughened) so that its surface retains ink according to the degree of burr (or roughness) in any particular area. The earliest mezzotints date from the 17th century.

1. Materials and techniques. 2. History.

1. MATERIALS AND TECHNIQUES. Grounding involves working across the plate in different directions with a rocker, a chisel-like tool with a broad and sharpened fan-shaped end, which has grooves on one side giving it a series of small points along the edge. The ground can be rendered 'coarse' or 'close' depending upon the number of points on the rocker and also upon the number of times the tool is passed across the plate, a tedious process usually given in the past to apprentices. In a totally grounded state the plate prints an intense black; where the engraver wants the light to be, he uses a scraper and a burnisher to produce varying degrees of roughness, hence the name of 'scrapers' popularly attached to British mezzotint-engravers. (For an illustration of the tools used in mezzotint see ENGRAVING, fig. 1e.)

The aesthetic attraction of mezzotint was a rich tonal range much nearer to that of a painting than a line-engraving's. The different textures of flesh or fabric could be reproduced in a sympathetic way, and the best mezzotints have a velvety warmth and internal glow unequalled by other media. Mezzotint has the advantage that the plates are more easily worked than those in line. The line-engraver faced an initial problem in deciding how to translate a picture into a pattern of lines, and the process of engraving involved laborious work. The line-engraver William Sharp, perhaps exaggerating to bolster his own calling, estimated in 1810 that line-engraving took 20 times as long as mezzotint. On the other hand a line plate can produce thousands of good impressions where a mezzotint will yield 100. The deterioration of the roughened surface when it was wiped to remove excess ink before printing meant that sometimes only the first handful of prints were truly brilliant. Hence there was a considerable premium on proofs, the first impressions taken before the plate was fully lettered. In practice plates could be reworked, and if this was done skilfully, preferably by the original engraver, far greater numbers of impressions could be issued than the engravers cared to admit. A great deal depended on the skill of the printing, which was usually done by specialist copperplate printers, who could easily ink the plate wrongly or indeed ruin the plate itself.

Steel plates were first used for mezzotint in the 1820s; these were difficult to work. With steel facing of copper plates (patented in 1857) engravers enjoyed the ease of working on copper with the long life of steel, but this laborious technique, which was by its nature confined largely to the reproduction of paintings, was superseded by the development of photomechanical processes.

2. HISTORY.

(i) 17th century. (ii) 18th century. (iii) 19th and 20th centuries.

(i) 17th century. The earliest engraver in mezzotint was LUDWIG VON SIEGEN, who appears to have made the first of his seven plates, the portrait of the *Landgravine Amelia Elizabeth* (1642), in Amsterdam. He seems to have used a roulette, supplemented with a dotting tool, to build up areas of burr. The first person to obtain his secret was Theodor Caspar von Furstenberg (*c.* 1624–75), a canon of Mainz, who produced his first print in 1656. The other pioneer, working independently of Ludwig von Siegen, was Prince Rupert of the Rhine (1619–82), who used a scraper and, more importantly, can be credited with the invention of the hand rocker. His plates show a progression from reliance on a hand-held roulette, through experimentation with what seems to have been a roulette on a pivoted pole, revealed by the pattern on his masterpiece, the *Great Executioner* (1658; see fig. 1), to the full use of rocker and scraper. The Prince was helped in his work by the painter Wallerant Vaillant, whom he met in Frankfurt am Main in 1658.

The new technique spread through Germany and Austria as a result of the work of von Furstenberg and of Jan

1. Mezzotint by Prince Rupert of the Rhine: *Great Executioner*, after Jusepe de Ribera, 130×160 mm, 1658 (sold London, Christie, Manson & Woods Ltd, 7 Dec 1984, lot 488)

Thomas of Ypres, a painter in the imperial court in Vienna, who executed *c.* 15 plates. More influential was WALLER-ANT VAILLANT, who settled in Amsterdam in 1662 and became the first professional mezzotint-engraver. Most of his *c.* 200 plates have a richness that shows the extent of his use and mastery of both rocker and scraper. Many are after well-known paintings, but there are a number of charming prints said to be from his own studies of his family. His principal pupil was Abraham Blooteling, who learnt mezzotint by *c.* 1671; he produced prints, principally portraits, of great sophistication and power, probably because he rocked the plates in a deeper and more uniform way than earlier engravers. With his brother-in-law and pupil Gerard Valck he was in England from 1672–3, where he produced some outstanding work, notably some large plates, such as *James, Duke of Monmouth* (Hollstein: *Dut. & Flem.*, no. 186) after Peter Lely. Prince Rupert, who had returned to England at the Restoration in 1660, made no further mezzotints of importance himself, although he appears to have helped William Sherwin (*c.* 1645–*c.* 1711), who dedicated his portrait of *Charles II* (1669; Chaloner Smith, no. 10), the first dated English mezzotint, to the

Prince. Another early English mezzotint artist was the versatile Francis Place, but he was not a professional engraver.

Amsterdam became and remained the main centre for mezzotint-engraving for the rest of the century. As well as being used by engravers to reproduce portraits and other types of painting, the technique was employed by a number of painters to translate their own work. Cornelis Dusart of Haarlem produced some lively studies of peasants, and Jan van Huchtenberg (1647–1733), who settled in Amsterdam in 1681, showed in his eight plates how effective mezzotint could be in representing horse-flesh. Such artists were, however, in a minority, and most mezzotints were after contemporary portraits; the engravers of this period included Pieter Schenk, Gerard Valck, Jan van Somer (1641–*c.* 1724) and, most prolific of the engraver–publishers, with over 400 portraits and a number of genre prints in the style of Cornelis Dusart to his name, Jacob Gole (1660–*c.* 1737). In Germany mezzotint became established in a number of cities: in Augsburg Georg Andreas Wolfgang I (1631–1716) and Christoph Weigel (1654–1725) engraved large numbers of mezzotint portraits. Nuremberg was another important centre. In

France, where line-engraving remained the main medium, there were a few mezzotint-engravers at work, notably Isaac Sarrabat (1667–early 18th century) and Jan van der Bruggen (1649–after 1714); both engraved genre pictures as well as portraits.

Following Blooteling's visit to England, attempts were made to take advantage of mezzotint to put prints of newly painted portraits on to the market within a short time. Two publishers, Richard Tompson (d?1693) and Alexander Browne, a drawing-master, whose account of the new technique in his *Ars pictoria* (London, 1669) was the first in English, began publishing portraits. Most were unsigned, and the publishers relied primarily upon various Dutchmen in London, such as Paul van Somer, brother of Jan van Somer, and the painter Jan van der Vaardt. The publishers' success depended upon making arrangements with the painters, and to protect themselves both publishers secured royal privileges.

The first professional mezzotint-engraver to be born in England was ISAAC BECKETT, who began by engraving for publishers but soon set up independently. After Beckett's early death, John Smith (i) showed how successful an independent engraver–publisher could be, retiring a rich man. His many brilliant plates did much to bolster the reputation of Godfrey Kneller, and the best impressions of his prints were eagerly sought by collectors in Britain and on the Continent. Smith also engraved and published smaller subject mezzotints, often based on European prints of paintings, and these were an important part of the output of contemporary engravers. Some interesting small mezzotints, perhaps based on his theatrical and decorative designs, were produced by the painter Robert Robinson. Smith's career coincided with that of the publisher Edward Cooper (d 1725), who employed several of the minor engravers such as the drawing-master Bernard Lens (ii) (1659–1725) who made a few striking mezzotints of fireworks as well as portrait and genre prints.

(ii) 18th century. Largely due to Smith's reputation, the superiority of British mezzotints was recognized to the extent that mezzotint became known as the *manière noire*. In Britain it became the preferred medium for the singly issued portrait. Significantly George White (c. 1671–1732), son of the prominent line-engraver Robert White, became not a line- but a mezzotint-engraver: he produced some powerful plates on which the use of preliminary etching was noticeable. Shortly before George White's death PETER PELHAM moved to Boston in the American colonies and was the first to make mezzotints in North America, where British mezzotints provided a source of poses for portrait painters.

The German engraver Jacob Christoph Le Blon went to London in 1718 in order to publish mezzotints using the three-colour process, which he was the first to apply to printmaking. His venture failed, and in 1734 he moved to Paris, where his example was followed by the family of Gautier-Dagoty, several of whose members engraved large numbers of portraits and also some striking anatomical prints. One, Edouard Gautier-Dagoty (1745–83), settled in Florence, where he had a successful follower, Carlo Lasinio. Mezzotint remained important in various European cities. In Augsburg the painter Georg Philipp Rugendas I produced some striking mezzotints of battle scenes, and his pupil Johann Elias Ridinger engraved animal and battle mezzotints on a smaller scale, often using a good deal of etching. Many portraits and subject prints were produced by the Haid family in Augsburg throughout the century. The importance of Amsterdam was maintained by Nicolaas Verkolje, son of Jan Verkolje I, while Cornelis Troost engraved several mezzotints after his own pictures.

In Britain in the 1730s and 1740s mezzotint went through an undistinguished period, due partly to the uninteresting nature of much of the portraiture. The principal engraver was John Faber the younger (c. 1695–1756), who also engraved many genre pictures, notably after Philip Mercier, who painted several pictures with engraving in mind. Mezzotint provided a quick and inexpensive way of producing decorative or humorous prints, which were often sold in standard sizes. Some were brightly hand-coloured; others were pasted on to glass and painted from behind after the paper had been rubbed away. It was not until the middle of the century, with the arrival of several talented engravers from Dublin, that outstanding work was again produced in London. JAMES MCARDELL and RICHARD HOUSTON both took initiatives in engraving mezzotints of Old Master paintings. At the same time a number of young painters saw the mezzotint as a way of becoming better known, and Joshua Reynolds, Gavin Hamilton and Francis Cotes all published prints engraved by the young Irishmen. Other engravers were encouraged to come from Dublin, including EDWARD FISHER, JOHN DIXON and JAMES WATSON; during the 1760s these men, sometimes referred to as the Dublin group, engraved the most important portraits of the day, and many of their prints were shown at the Society of Artists, which initiated exhibitions in 1760. Among the more unusual mezzotints shown there was *A View of the Inside of the New Prison at Rome* (exh. 1765; Baltimore, MD, Mus. A., see 1984 exh. cat., no. 56) by the Frenchman Georges-François Blondel (c. 1730–c. 1790). The painter whose work became best known through mezzotint was Joshua Reynolds, and most of the mezzotints of his pictures made before 1775 were by members of the Irish group. Another Irishman, who used mezzotint for reproducing his own work, was Thomas Frye, who engraved some remarkable heads after his life-size portrait studies. The work of the Irish engravers was highly regarded by collectors of prints both in Britain and abroad. Some of them were able to publish their own prints rather than work for publishers, and, perhaps because of the difficulty of getting the Irish to work for him, the publisher John Boydell may have invited Johann Gottfried Haid, who had been working in Vienna, to London, where he worked during the mid-1760s.

After 1775 the leading position was taken by younger British engravers, such as Valentine Green, William Dickinson, Richard Earlom, John Raphael Smith, John Dean (*fl* 1776–89) and John Jones, who between them engraved many of the greatest of British mezzotints, many of them after the portraits of Joshua Reynolds's maturity. After 1775 several of them also learnt the tonal process of stipple (*see* STIPPLE (i)), which was better adapted to the increased demand for the decorative prints that were bought not by mezzotint collectors or by those wanting a particular portrait but as 'furniture', that is part of a scheme of interior decoration.

Partly in response to such competition, mezzotint portraits became grander, colour printing was extended to mezzotint and the range of subjects widened, reflecting the progress of British painting. There were the theatrical conversation pieces of Johan Zoffany, several engraved by Johann Gottfried Haid; there were the paintings of Joseph Wright of Derby, the dramatic light effects of which made them particularly suited to mezzotint and which were well engraved by William Pether, Earlom and Green; there were the religious paintings of Benjamin West, many engraved by Green; there were sporting and animal paintings, for example by George Stubbs, who engraved some of his own works in a remarkable series of mixed-method prints; there were scenes from literature, such as those painted by Henry Fuseli, and from *c.* 1780 there were the sentimental genre pictures of William Redmore Bigg and then of George Morland. Many of the latter were engraved by JOHN RAPHAEL SMITH, the outstanding British mezzotint-engraver of the century, who produced remarkably rich prints, more open and bold in treatment than those of his rivals and some based on his own designs.

London remained the recognized centre for mezzotint, and several British engravers went to work abroad; for example James Walker was invited to Russia. Much excellent work was done elsewhere, especially in Vienna, to which Haid returned after his visit to London. The leading engraver after Haid's death in 1776 was Johann Jacobé (1735–97), who worked briefly in London *c.* 1779–80, and, as professor in the Akademie der Künste in Vienna, helped to train a group of brilliant engravers including Johann Peter Pichler (1766–1807), Franz Wrenk (1766–1830), Nicolaus Rhein (1767–1818), Jakob Friedrich Clerck (1769–1834) and Vincenz Georg Kininger (1767–1851), in his turn professor. The Revolutionary Wars with France cut off much of the lucrative British export trade in decorative prints, but publishers continued to sell large numbers of portraits and genre prints. Mezzotint was often chosen in preference to slower and more expensive line-engraving for detailed subject pictures. Engravers generally used preliminary etching for such work, as had been apparent on many of the prints by Earlom, whose prints of Claude Lorrain's *Liber veritatis* (1777; Wenely, nos 149–448) were among the few landscape prints in mezzotint.

(iii) 19th and 20th centuries. Between 1807 and 1819 J. M. W. Turner published a series of landscape etchings by himself, the *Liber studiorum* (e.g. London, BM), for which mezzotint was added by the leading engravers of the day, including S. W. Reynolds, Charles Turner, William Say and Thomas Goff Lupton. The same close attention to prints after his landscapes was paid by John Constable, who worked very closely with the engraver David Lucas (1802–81) on the mezzotint plates of *Various Subjects of Landscape* (1828–32; see fig. 2). The most spectacular of all subject mezzotints of the period were those engraved by JOHN MARTIN after his paintings of subjects drawn from the Bible or Milton; most were on a small scale, but some were impressively large. Martin, who published many of his prints in Paris as well as London, was one of the earliest to employ steel plates, first used for mezzotint by Say and Lupton in 1820–22. These allowed much larger editions to be printed, and, although they often produced hard and glossy prints, this often suited the work of painters such as Thomas Lawrence. The large numbers of prints that could be run off threatened to undermine purchasers' confidence, and in 1847 to restrict the size of

2. Mezzotint by John Constable and David Lucas: *Spring*, 127×245 mm, 1830; from the series *Various Subjects of Landscape*, 1828–32 (London, Tate Gallery)

editions the Printsellers' Association was established . For some detailed subject pictures a form of mixed mezzotint was often used; similar plates were produced in the USA, for example by John Sartain (1808–97), most of whose mezzotints were for periodicals.

Many major Victorian paintings were engraved by SAMUEL COUSINS, whose position as the leading engraver was recognized by his election to full Royal Academician status as an engraver in 1867. His contemporary, John Linnell (ii), engraved a number of remarkably sympathetic mezzotints after his own portraits. Cousins was on the verge of retirement when the revival of interest in Reynolds's paintings renewed the demand for mezzotints of them, and soon many engravers were reproducing 18th-century as well as contemporary portraits. Towards the end of the century a number of artists took an interest in mezzotint for original work after steel facing enabled engravers to work once again on copper plates. Hubert von Herkomer, Alphonse Legros and William Strang all used the technique, while James Tissot engraved four of his paintings, possibly with the guidance of his friend Seymour Haden, who made a few original landscape mezzotints. The professional printmaker who made most use of mezzotint was the influential teacher Frank Short (1857–1945), whose huge output included several large prints after G. F. Watts as well as many landscapes. Among the next generation of original printmakers to make occasional use of mezzotint the landscape work of Christopher Nevinson was notable, but most of the work of British engravers such as Percy Martindale (1869–1943) was reproducing portraiture, generally of the 18th century. The market for these prints was all but destroyed by the Great Depression of the 1930s, although one engraver, Lawrence Josset (*b* 1910), continued to engrave mezzotints of portrait paintings into the 1970s. By the 1990s mezzotint was still practised, unlike other reproductive techniques, and it was rediscovered by a number of printmakers, especially in the USA and Japan, who made imaginative use of its tonal possibilities.

BIBLIOGRAPHY

Hollstein: *Dut. & Flem.*; Hollstein: *Ger.*
A. Browne: *Ars pictoria* (London, 1669)
J. Chaloner Smith: *British Mezzotinto Portraits*, 4 vols (London, 1878–83)
J. E. Wenely: *Verzeichnis seiner Raderungen und Schabkunstblätter* (Hamburg, 1886), pp. 58–82
A. Whitman: *The Masters of Mezzotint* (London, 1898)
A. M. Hind: *A History of Engraving & Etching from the 15th Century to the Year 1914* (London, 1908, rev. 3/1923; *R* New York, 1963)
M. Salaman: *Old English Mezzotints* (London, 1910)
H. C. Levis: *A Descriptive Bibliography of Books in . . . English . . . Relating to . . . Engraving* (London, 1912–13), pp. 96–9 [incl. letter from W. Sharp]
J. Leisching: *Schabkunst* (Vienna, *c.* 1913)
A. J. Finberg: *The History of Turner's 'Liber Studorium', with a New Catalogue Raisonné* (London, 1924)
F. Short: *British Mezzotints: Being a Lecture Delivered to the Print Collectors Club on November 7, 1924* (London, 1925)
C. E. Russell: *English Mezzotint Portraits and their States. A Catalogue of Corrections of and Additions to Chaloner-Smith's 'British Mezzotint Portraits'* (London, 1926)
P. H. Martindale: *Engraving Old and Modern* (London, 1928)
A. Shirley: *Mezzotints by David Lucas after Constable* (London, 1930)
O. C. Pisarro: 'Prince Rupert and the Invention of Mezzotint', *Walpole Soc.*, xxxvi (1956–8), pp. 1–9
W. P. Belknap: *American Colonial Painting* (Cambridge, MA, 1959), pp. 271–329
A. Gross: *Etching, Engraving and Intaglio Printing* (London, 1970), pp. 144–9
Victorian Engravings (exh. cat. by H. Beck, London, V&A, 1973)
The Mezzotint Rediscovered (exh. cat., London, Colnaghi's, 1975)
Darkness into Light: The Early Mezzotint (exh. cat. by J. Bayard and E. D'Oench, New Haven, CT, Yale U. A.G., 1976)
A. Griffiths: 'Prints after Reynolds and Gainsborough', *Gainsborough and Reynolds in the British Museum* (exh. cat., London, BM, 1978)
Painters and Engraving: The Reproductive Print from Hogarth to Wilkie (exh. cat. by D. Alexander and R. T. Godfrey, New Haven, CT, Yale Cent. Brit. A., 1980)
A. Dyson: *Pictures to Print: The Nineteenth-century Engraving Trade* (London, 1984)
Regency to Empire: French Printmaking, 1715–1814 (exh. cat. by V. Carlson and J. W. Ittman, Baltimore, MD, Mus. A., 1984)
C. Wax: *The Mezzotint: History and Technique* (London, 1990)

DAVID ALEXANDER

Mi. Chinese family of calligraphers and painters, active in the 11th and 12th centuries.

(1) Mi Fu [Mi Fei; *zi* Yuanzhang, *hao* Nangong, Lumen Jushi, Xiangyang Manshi, Haiyue Waishi] (*b* Xiangyang, Hubei Province, 1051; *d* Huaiyang, Jiangsu Province, 1107). He was an influential calligrapher whose critical assessments and connoisseurship contributed to Chinese aesthetic scholarship. None of his paintings survive, but authenticated copies display an independence of vision greatly admired and frequently imitated. A dedicated antiquarian, he exemplified the Chinese ideal of integrating scholarship, aesthetics and official life.

Mi came from a family of cultured, landowning aristocrats and grew up familiar with court life. He began his collection of old calligraphy and paintings as a youth and throughout his life sought to upgrade its quality. He was also an individualist and the subject of numerous anecdotes: his reputation for cleanliness was proverbial. He immersed himself in the study of the past and even wore clothes from the Tang period (AD 618–907). He apparently never took official examinations but nonetheless received numerous governmental appointments, perhaps because of his mother's former position as wetnurse to the empress Yongsong (*reg c.* second third of the 11th century). He made use of posts throughout the country to study landscape and art collections. When the emperor Huizong (*reg* 1101–25) founded a college of painting and calligraphy in 1104, Mi was appointed its head (*see* CHINA, §V, 4(i)(c)).

Mi Fu made an extremely thorough study of ancient paintings and calligraphy, and his publications on these subjects are among the most important in the history of Chinese art theory. The *Baozheng daifeng lu* ('Records of searches for precious scrolls'; preface dated 1086) presents astute, though fairly conventional, analyses and assessments of early works and reflects his own poetic ability. The practical advice it gives about the care of scrolls is still commonly accepted. In his *Hua shi* ('History of painting') his commentaries about contemporary works are merciless. He presented no fixed rules or classification for the appreciation of painting but based his judgements on his personal aesthetic response to individual works. He felt that the most important quality in a work of art was its naturalness (Chin. *tianzhen*): not the realism of the image, but rather an artlessness and innocence of content and execution. In keeping with literati theory, his assessments were not confined to form and style but were also concerned with the moral quality of the artist reflected in the work of art (*see* CHINA, §V, 4(ii)). He considered landscapes to be the only subject really worthy of classification as a creative art: landscapes 'possess inexhaustible delights, particularly when they have haze, clouds and mist effects; they are beautiful' (Sirén, p. 34). This description fits his own compositional format.

By the time he was 30 Mi had won recognition both as a critic and as a calligrapher. Indeed, he is listed as a calligrapher rather than a painter in the *Xuanhe huapu* (preface dated 1120), the catalogue of the imperial collection. He is generally classified as one of the Four Great Calligraphers of the Northern Song (960–1127), along with his good friend and mentor, Su Shi, Su's disciple Huang Tingjian and Cai Xiang (*see* CHINA, §IV, 2(iv)).

Mi was proficient in numerous scripts, and many signed examples of his calligraphy still exist. These are much more easily authenticated than his paintings, for he usually signed his calligraphy. Su Shi advised him to study the calligraphy of the Eastern Jin (AD 317–420) masters, such as Wang Xizhi (*see* WANG (i), (1)) in order to attain their 'classical elevation', and he also studied the Tang masters, including YAN ZHENQING, Liu Gongquan (AD 778–865), OUYANG XUN and CHU SUILIANG. His early work was criticized as imitative, but he quickly developed his own cursive interpretations, combining structural discipline with an unprecedented level of technical proficiency in brushwork. His large seal script (*da zhuanshu*) is directly derived from bronze inscriptions but nonetheless emphasizes brushwork over structure. Of the Four Great Calligraphers he was the only one to write in clerical script (*lishu*); he executed it using his customary running stroke technique, however, with the result that it is not considered equal to his other scripts. He had a distinctive manner of executing the grass radical element of a character with alternating horizontal and vertical strokes. Mi's running script (*xingshu*), his best-known style, had a plump brushwork that has been described as making 'one think of a striking tubby figure walking along a road' (1961 exh. cat., p. 82; *see* CHINA, fig. 94). The dashing quality of Mi's other scripts led Su Shi to comment 'like sailing in the wind and riding a horse into battle, his writing is exhilarating'. Huang Tingjian made a similar comparison, 'like a sharp knife in battle, or an arrow in flight, what it touches must be pierced'; and Mi Fu himself described his approach thus, 'other people write with one side [of the brush], I write with four sides' (all 1971 exh. cat., p. 22). In so saying he explained that he used the brush as a painter rather than a

Mi Fu (ascribed): *Auspicious Pine-trees in the Spring Mountains*, hanging scroll, ink and slight colours on paper, 350×441 mm, second half of the 11th century (Taipei, National Palace Museum)

calligrapher, exploiting every possibility of the flexibility of the line as well as the subtle nuances of ink tones. Mi's calligraphy was greatly admired in the Ming period (1368–1644) and was copied by such artists as Wen Zhengming (*see* WEN, (1)), ZHU YUNMING and DONG QICHANG.

Records indicate that Mi Fu did not begin to paint until the last years of his life. He has been said to have painted portraits and figures in the tradition of Li Gonglin, but it was primarily as a landscape painter that he was known and was most influential (*see* CHINA, §V, 3(iv)(a)). His output was modest, and by the Southern Song period (1127–1279) examples were already extremely rare. He was nonetheless considered one of the most important representatives of the SOUTHERN SCHOOL of landscape painting and credited with being one of the first of the literati to paint landscapes. He introduced new ideas into literati painting (*shidaifu hua* or *wenren hua*), emphasizing the character of the artist as revealed in the painting rather than the subject or composition. He developed a distinctive painting technique known as *Mi dian cun* ('Mi's dotting technique'), which was also used by his son, Mi Youren, but has survived only in later imitations. The strokes are formed by laying down the side of the brush approximately parallel to the bottom of the paper. The result is an impressionistic overlaying of ink washes in graded tones that produces a soft and misty effect with a minimum of structured form and draughtsmanship. This style can only be achieved on paper and sometimes requires tools other than the traditional brush. The paintings are small and composed of rhythmically patterned forms that stress rounded, cone-shaped hills rising out of heavily obscuring mists.

Mi's style of painting was influential during the Yuan period (1279–1368); it can be seen in the work of GAO KEGONG, FANG CONGYI and others. While the general characteristics of Mi's innovations can be seen in copies of his works, some of the traits that are re-created in some copies are not present in others. For example, one small scroll generally accepted as representing his principles is *Auspicious Pine-trees in the Spring Mountains* (*Chunshan ruisong tu*; see fig.). The impressionistic quality and use of heavily obscuring mists and patterned conical mountain forms are typical of Mi's style, as are the limited use of linear elements and the rootless trees. The colours also are consistent with those used by Mi and his eldest son, Mi Youren (*see* (2) below), although the particular colour scheme appears to be an innovation of the Yuan period. An accompanying calligraphic inscription by the emperor Gaozong is no criterion of authenticity.

WRITINGS

EWA: 'Mi Fei'; Francke
Baozheng daifang lu [Records of searches for precious scrolls], preface dated 1086
Hua shi [History of painting], *c.* 1103

BIBLIOGRAPHY

Fan Mingtai: *Mi Xiangyang zhilin* [Collected biographical and miscellaneous materials on Mi Fei], 1604
O. Sirén: *Chinese Painting: Leading Masters and Principles*, ii (London, 1956), pp. 26–34
N. Vandier-Nicolas: 'Le Carnet d'un connaisseur d'art sous les Song: Mi Fou (1051–1107) et le "Houa-che"', *Arts Asiatiques*, vii (1960), pp. 121–30
Chinese Art Treasures: A Selected Group of Objects from the Chinese National Palace Museum and the Chinese National Central Museum, Taichung
(exh. cat., Washington, DC, N.G.A.; New York, MOMA; Boston, MA, Mus. F.A.; and elsewhere; 1961–2)
Chinese Calligraphy (exh. cat. by Tseng Yu-ho Ecke, Philadelphia, PA, Mus. A., 1971)
L. Ledderose: 'Mi Fu yu Wang Xianzhi' [Mi Fu and Wang Xianzhi], *N. Pal. Mus. Bull.*, vii, no. 1 (1972), pp. 1–14
Traces of the Brush: Studies in Chinese Calligraphy (exh. cat. by Shen Fu and others, New Haven, CT, Yale U. A.G.; Berkeley, U. CA, A. Mus.; 1977)
M. Loehr: *The Great Painters of China* (New York, 1980), pp. 158–61
Y. Nakata, ed.: *Shoseki*, ii of *Chūgoku no bijutsu* [Calligraphy, ii of The arts of China] (Kyoto, 1982); Eng. trans. by J. Hunter as *Chinese Calligraphy*, A History of the Art of China (New York, Tokyo and Kyoto, 1983)

MARY S. LAWTON

(2) Mi Youren [Mi Yu-jen; original *ming* Yinren; *zi* Yuanhui; *hao* Haiyue Houren, Lanzhou Daoren] (*b* probably in Xiangyang, Hubei Province, 1086; *d* 1165). Son of (1) Mi Fu. He served as Minister of War and Fuwen ge Scholar under the Southern Song emperor Gaozong, authenticating and appraising painting and calligraphy.

The calligrapher Huang Tingjian gave him an ancient seal marked 'Yuanhui' offering him this name as his *zi* (style name), in an allusion to Mi Fu's *zi*, Yuanzhang. This was a reference to the father–son name sequence of 4th-century masters Wang Xizhi and Wang Xianzhi and implied an artistic continuation between the generations. Indeed, in calligraphy Mi Youren did follow Mi Fu's style, though he did not equal him. In painting, Youren did not continue Fu's depiction of figures and objects, but he did develop Fu's famous misty landscape style, attaining such renown that he was overwhelmed by seekers of his paintings, and assistants had to make imitations, which he signed. Youren reinforced literati painting (*wenren hua*) ideals (*see* CHINA, §V, 4(ii)) promulgated by Mi Fu, Su Shi, Wen Tong and others, spawning a genre of private art created by cognoscenti for each other, in which paintings functioned as personal, non-negotiable 'images of the heart' (*xinyin*). Youren called this type of painting 'ink play' (*ximo*). Eschewing linear contours and modelling strokes, he developed an unassertive, amorphous and cursory style of graded wash in wet or dry ink. Extant paintings attributed to Mi Youren include his *White Clouds on the Xiao and Xiang* (*Xiao Xiang baiyun tu*; date uncertain; Shanghai Mus.), *Clearing Clouds over Distant Peaks* (*Yuanxiu qingyun tu*; 1134; Osaka Mun. Mus.) and *Impressions of Cloudy Mountains* (*Yunshan deyi tu*; *c.* 1135; Taipei, N. Pal. Mus.), but these may all be of later date. One reliable Southern Song emanation is the *Dream Journey along Xiao and Xiang* (*Xiao Xiang wayoutu*; Tokyo, N. Mus.), later attached to Li Longmian. It shows the liberal application of dilute inkwash, the minimalist approach to incidents and the perspective of Southern Song vistas. In the Ming period (1368–1644) the Mi style became linearized, with strands of 'Mi dots' (Mi *dian*) arrayed in cascading ranks to cover areas once bathed in graded wash.

BIBLIOGRAPHY

Francke: 'Mi Yu-jen'
Zhou Mi: *Yunyan quoyan lu* [Record of what was seen as clouds and mist], late 13th century, *juan* 2
Deng Chun: *Huaji* [Record of painting], preface dated 1167, *juan* 3
Tuotuo and others: *Song shi* [Standard history of the Song], Yuan period (1279–1368), *juan* 444

Sun Zubo: 'Mi Fu', 'Mi Youren', *Zhongguo huajia congshu* [Compilation of Chinese painters] (Shanghai, 1982)

JOAN STANLEY-BAKER

Miami. North American city and seat of Dade County, located on Biscayne Bay at the mouth of the Miami River in south-eastern Florida. It is a major seaport and tourist resort. Greater Miami (population *c.* 1.6 million) includes Miami Beach, Coral Gables, North Miami and Hialeah, and, together with smaller districts, forms the southern limit of Florida's so-called 'Gold Coast'. In the 16th century Spanish explorers discovered the Tequesta Indian village of Mayaimi on the southern bank of the estuary; in 1567 a Jesuit mission and fort were established on the site, although its fate is unknown. In 1743 the Jesuit mission of S Ignacio was founded on what later became Coconut Grove, and the Spanish crown granted local land to Spanish gentry. In 1821 the US Government purchased the state of Florida from Spain. The landowner Julia D. Tuttle arrived in 1873 and was among the founders of modern Miami, encouraging the oil magnate Henry M. Flagler (1830–1913) to extend his Florida East-Coast Railroad to Miami in return for land. Flagler dredged the harbour and in 1897 opened the six-storey, colonial-style Royal Palm Hotel. From then on tourists came to enjoy the subtropical climate and miles of beaches, and in 1912–13 Miami Beach, a barrier island of 19 sq. km, was dredged and exploited as a holiday resort. The Italianate villa Vizcaya (now Vizcaya Museum of Decorative Arts) was built at Coconut Grove in 1916 by F. B. Hoffmann (1884–1980), and this style became fashionable throughout southern Florida.

Miami's steady expansion was interrupted by World War I, but in the 1920s unprecedented growth drew the affluent from the East Coast and the Midwest, and during this period an eclectic, colonial Spanish–Mediterranean architectural style came to dominate the city's hotels, casinos, marina and country club pavilions, as well as its private homes. Miami also attracted artists from all disciplines, and members of this artistic community were involved with the handful of enterprising architects who built Miami's celebrated Art Deco (or Tropical Deco) district in the 1930s; among its chief designers were L. Murray Dixon (e.g. Royal House, 1939), Henry Hohauser (*b* 1895), Albert Anis and Anton Skislewicz. Dozens of two- and three-storey hotels were erected along Miami Beach, designed in the 'Moderne' style to attract a vast new group of middle-income tourists. Imagination was given full rein in structures that freely adapted Bauhaus, Aztec and Egyptian sources, articulated by such nautical references as porthole windows, curved metal balcony railings and 'conning-tower' finials. Stucco façades were initially painted white, with coloured trims; entire buildings were later painted in pastel shades or tropical colours. Stepped shapes, corner windows beneath 'eyebrow' parapets, quasi-pilasters and the use of glass blocks were also

Miami Beach, Breakwater Hotel, by Anton Skislewicz, 1939

common features, as in Albert Anis's Waldorf Towers (1937). Local artisans executed decorative painting, ornamental plaques and inlaid terrazzo lobby floors; favoured motifs included sunbursts, waves, fountains, seabirds, dolphins, flowers and zigzags, and sanserif signage often running vertically (e.g. Breakwater Hotel, 1939; see fig.). After 1959 thousands of Cuban refugees settled in an area of Miami later known as 'Little Havana', bringing with them their language, arts and culture (*see* LATIN AMERICAN ARTISTS OF THE USA, §4); in 1983 a touring exhibition of their work was held at the Cuban Museum of Arts and Culture, Miami. Following a period of architectural stagnation, in 1979 one square mile (2.58 sq. km) of the city's Art Deco area was saved from destruction and designated a historic district, the first and largest in the world involving 20th-century architecture. During the 1980s the city was revived through a new building programme, which included the classicist Dade County Cultural Center (1980–83) by Philip Johnson, and several buildings by the firm ARQUITECTONICA; and the restoration of such structures as the *Miami Daily News* Tower (1925) and the Fontainebleau Hotel (1950s; now the Fontainebleau-Hilton).

BIBLIOGRAPHY

J. E. Buchanan: *Miami: A Chronological and Documentary History, 1513–1977* (Dobbs Ferry, 1978)
L. Cerwinske: *Tropical Deco: The Architecture and Design of Old Miami Beach* (New York, 1981)
The Miami Generation: Nine Cuban–American Artists (exh. cat., intro. G. V. Blanc; Miami, FL, Cub. Mus. A. & Cult. and others, 1983)
H. Hatton: *Tropical Splendour: An Architectural History of Florida* (New York, 1987)
B. B. Capitman: *Deco Delights* (New York, 1988)

Miaodigou [Miao-ti-kou]. Phase of the Chinese Neolithic Yangshao culture named after Miaodigou village, Shan xian, Henan Province, where the first find was made. Two distinct cultures within the Miaodigou phase have been identified, the first dating from *c.* 4000–*c.* 3300 BC and the second dating from *c.* 3300–*c.* 2600 BC. The cultures extended from Henan Province in the east to Gansu Province in the west.

Miaodigou village settlements were surrounded by ditches and fences and were subdivided into distinct areas for living, production and burial. Their houses, some semi-subterranean, had a round, square or rectangular plan; the walls were of the wattle-and-daub type, and the thatched roofs were supported by wooden pillars and beams. Burials were in single or multiple graves furnished mostly with pottery vessels but sometimes including bone ornaments and stone implements. Most of the pottery is made of a refined red clay, sometimes covered with white or red slip. Typical forms include pointed and flat jars with double lips and small mouths, and bowls with rolled lips or constricted mouths. In Phase I many vessels were painted, mainly with black alone, though occasionally the black was combined with red and a white slip. Decorative motifs are generally geometric, but bird, frog and plant designs were also used. One barrel-shaped jar (Lanzhou, Gansu Prov. Mus.) is topped with a human head; the body of the vessel is painted in black with geometric patterns. On another jar (Lanzhou, Gansu Prov. Mus.) a humorously painted lizard decorates one side. The pottery from Phase II is usually coarse and grey, and there are fewer painted examples than in Phase I. There was a greater use of impressed patterns, such as basket, cord and check marks, and incised or appliqué designs also occur. A few examples of the thin, hard, lustrous pottery typical of the Longshan culture have also been found at Miaodigou sites. In the kilns of the Miaodigou II culture the firing chamber was placed directly on top of the furnace instead of beside it, as in earlier Neolithic kilns such as those at Banpo (*see also* CHINA, §VII, 2(ii)).

BIBLIOGRAPHY

K. C. Chang: *The Archaeology of Ancient China* (New Haven, 1963, rev. New Haven and London, 4/1986), pp. 108–56, 256, 260–64
A. E. Dien, J. K. Riegel and N. T. Price, eds: *Prehistoric to Western Zhou* (1985), ii of *Chinese Archaeological Abstracts* (Los Angeles, 1978–85), pp. 266–70, 283–5

BENT L. PEDERSEN

Miao-ti-kou. *See* MIAODIGOU.

MIAR [Movimento Italiano per l'Architettura Razionale]. Italian architectural movement founded in 1930. Dissolved in 1931, it was a short-lived coalition of the largest group of Italian Rationalist architects assembled between the two world wars. Succeeding two previous associations of Rationalist architects, GRUPPO 7 and the Movimento dell' Architettura Razionale (MAR), it was composed of a range of regional groups: Piero Bottoni (*b* 1903), Luigi Figini, Gino Pollini, Pietro Lingeri and Giuseppe Terragni in Milan, Bruno Lapadula (*b* 1902), Luigi Piccinato (*b* 1899) and Mario Ridolfi in Rome, Gino Levi Montalcini, Giuseppe Pagano and Ettore Sottsass sr (1892–1953) in Turin, as well as a mixed group composed of Alberto Sartoris, Mario Labò and Adalberto Libera, who was the national secretary.

On 30 March 1931 through the initiative of the MIAR, the second Esposizione dell'Architettura Razionale was opened at Pietro Maria Bardi's bookshop and gallery in Rome. It included *la tavola degli orrori*, where reproductions of works by academic architects, such as Marcello Piacentini and Gustavo Giovannoni, were displayed. As well as making joint declarations concerning their fields of research and their aspirations in the *Manifesto per l'Architettura Razionale*, some of the members of MIAR, including Giuseppe Pagano, intended that Rationalism should be recognized officially as an architectural expression of FASCISM. Despite achieving some official recognition, however, MIAR was opposed by the academic front, including Piacentini, and by the Sindicato Fascista degli Architetti, who together formed the RAMI (Raggruppamento degli Architetti Moderni Italiani).

The coherence of MIAR began to break up in the face of this opposition and through internal differences, which were exacerbated by dissent over members' participation in important government projects, such as the building of the new Città Universitaria in Rome. Following the dissolution of the movement, some former members continued to hold their position as Rationalists, and their activity was chiefly focused on competitions and the organization of experimental works for the Triennale exhibitions in Milan.

WRITINGS
Manifesto per l'Architettura Razionale (1931)

BIBLIOGRAPHY
G. Veronesi: *Difficoltà politiche dell'architettura in Italia, 1920–1940* (Milan, 1953)
M. Cennamo, ed.: *Materiali per l'analisi dell'architettura moderna: Il MIAR* (Naples, 1976)
E. Mantero, ed.: *Il Razionalismo italiano* (Bologna, 1984)
MATILDE BAFFA RIVOLTA

Michaelides, Neoptolemos A. (*b* Kyrenia, 1921). Cypriot architect. He graduated from the Pancyprian Gymnasium in Nicosia and in 1939–40 studied architecture in Milan. The outbreak of World War II forced him to return to Cyprus, where, rather than accepting a scholarship from the British Council to study engineering in England, he chose to work (1940–47) with local craftsmen, from whom he learnt the technique of designing with metal, stone and wood. In 1947 he resumed his university studies in Milan, and, while still a student, designed two significant projects. The first was the residence of the artist Theodotos Kanthos, designed in 1949 and built in Nicosia in 1952, which was a highly functional manipulation of materials, structure and space. The second was his submission of a structural frame and panel design (1950) for the Archbishopric Complex in Nicosia. This design, unprecedented for Cyprus, shared first prize with projects by two other groups of designers, but all proposals were ultimately rejected in favour of a local conservative preference for 'traditional Byzantine order'. In 1952, having obtained his doctorate in architecture, he returned to Cyprus and became the first native architect to design and build multi-storey structures there. Two of his major projects were the ten-storey block of offices and flats (1959) in Nicosia and the nine-storey 'Grecian' hotel (1963) near Famagusta. His designs reflect the austere simplicity of the masonry load-bearing wall and flat slab construction or of the reinforced-concrete structural frame, the aesthetics of which were acquired from experiences with Italian design. Built within this structural framework are spaces, surfaces and features executed with the articulate detail of a Cypriot master craftsman.

WRITINGS
'Archiepiskopikou megarou, 1950' [Archbishopric megaron, 1950], *Architekton*, 21 (1993), pp. 22–5

BIBLIOGRAPHY
'Grapheia–Polykatikia' [Offices–flats], 'Oikia Theodotou Kanthou' [Theodotos Kanthos house] and 'Xenodocheion "Gresian"' ['Grecian' hotel], *Architektoniki* (1965), pp. 64–70
P. Georgiades: 'Oikia Theodotou Kanthou' [Theodotos Kanthos house], *Architekton*, 13 (1990), pp. 41–5
KENNETH W. SCHAAR

Michaelis, Adolf (*b* Kiel, 22 June 1835; *d* Strasbourg, 12 Aug 1910). German art historian. Professor of Classical Archaeology at the University of Strasbourg, Michaelis was one of the most perceptive and influential scholars of Greek and Roman sculpture in the 19th century. Both his monograph on the Parthenon (1871) and his catalogue of private collections of ancient sculptures in Great Britain (1882) were pioneering works; by the late 1990s the latter still had not been surpassed. It was the product of three tours around English country houses in 1861, 1873 and 1877, and it furnishes an invaluable record of the contents and display of these sculptural mementos collected by the English aristocracy in their travels around Italy and Greece in the previous two centuries, many of them now dispersed. Its introductory essay, 'The Influx of Antique Sculptures into Great Britain', is still the best account of this curious, extended episode in the history of English collecting. Supplementary work towards a second, better-illustrated edition has been undertaken by Vermeule (1955–9) and others.

WRITINGS
Der Parthenon (Leipzig, 1871)
Ancient Marbles in Great Britain (Cambridge, 1882)
'Ancient Marbles in Great Britain: Supplement i', *J. Hell. Stud.*, v (1884), pp. 143–61
'Ancient Marbles in Great Britain: Supplement ii', *J. Hell. Stud.*, vi (1885), pp. 30–49

BIBLIOGRAPHY
C. C. Vermeule and D. von Bothmer: 'Notes on a New Edition of Michaelis: Ancient Marbles in Great Britain', *Amer. J. Archaeol.*, lix (1955), pp. 129–50; lx (1956), pp. 321–50; lxiii (1959), pp. 139–66, 329–48
H. Oehler: *Foto und Skulptur* (Cologne, 1980)
G. B. Waywell: *The Lever and Hope Sculptures* (Berlin, 1986)
G. B. WAYWELL

Michael of Canterbury (*fl* 1275–1321). English architect. He is first documented at Canterbury in 1275, where he may have remodelled the chapter house and designed the choir-screens at Christ Church: final accounts for these works were rendered in 1304–5, but the chapter house is thought to date from the early 1290s and the screens from 1298–1304. He moved to London to fulfil the royal commission for the Cheapside Eleanor Cross (1291–4; mostly destr., fragments, London, Mus. London), a monument second only to Charing Cross in expense and magnificence (*see* CROSS, §II, 3). Its rich micro-architecture was repeated in the canopied funerary monuments also attributed to him, including the tombs of *Archbishop John Pecham* (*d* 1292) in Canterbury Cathedral and of *Edmund Crouchback, Earl of Lancaster* (*d* 1296) in Westminster Abbey (*see* LONDON, §V, 2(ii)(a)).

Michael was master mason from 1292 at St Stephen's Chapel (partly destr.; *see* LONDON, §V, 3(i)(a)), Palace of Westminster. His design for this innovative building, probably intended to rival Louis IX's Sainte-Chapelle (*see* PARIS, §V, 2(i)), reinterpreted elements of the French Rayonnant style in ways that contributed substantially to the evolution of late Decorated and Perpendicular in England. The lower chapel (survives rest.) featured early examples of ogival tracery and lierne vaults, while the wall arcades of the upper chapel were capped by miniature canopies with panels and gablets. Curtains of vertical linear tracery were applied to the exterior. Fire interrupted work in 1298, and Michael may have returned to Canterbury. From 1306 he undertook a succession of royal commissions at Winchester, London (1312) and Eltham (1315). The accounts at Westminster for 1321 show Michael still in charge when building work resumed on St Stephen's. He probably died shortly after.

BIBLIOGRAPHY
Harvey
H. M. Colvin, ed.: *The Middle Ages* (1963), i and ii of *The History of the King's Works* (London, 1963–82)
F. Woodman: *The Architectural History of Canterbury Cathedral* (London, 1981)
Age of Chivalry: Art in Plantagenet England, 1200–1400 (exh. cat., ed. J. Alexander and P. Binski; London, RA, 1987), cat. nos 325–7, 372, 375–6

C. Wilson: *The Gothic Cathedral: The Architecture of the Great Church, 1130–1530* (London, 1990)

□

Michael of Wiener Neustadt [Chnab, Knab, Michael] (*fl c.* 1380–*c.* 1404). Austrian architect. Documents mention Master Michael without a family name but refer to his origins in Wiener Neustadt. The name Chnab was that of his wife, Margret, and was passed on to their son Martin. Michael is first identified unequivocally by a shield on the tower-like Spinnerin am Kreuz (1382–4; h. 20.5 m) in Wiener Neustadt. This is an equilateral triangle in plan, and it is based ultimately on the Eleanor crosses (1291–4) in England and the *montjoies* (1271–85; destr.) of Louis IX in France. The construction tapers towards the top and is richly decorated with openwork tracery. There are close connections with work at the Stephanskirche, Vienna, especially with the nave buttresses and the lower registers of the south tower. He has therefore been identified with the master appointed to the Stephanskirche in 1359 by Rudolf IV, Duke of Austria, although he may have been too young. He is expressly named in 1395 as architect to Duke Albert III (*reg* 1358–95) at the Altes Schloss, Laxenburg.

In 1394 Michael laid the foundation stone of the nave of Maria am Gestade, Vienna. It is unclear how closely the nave (completed 1414), which has paired windows but no aisles, and the seven-sided tower (completed *c.* 1430) follow his plans (*see* VIENNA, §V, 3). The style of Peter Prachatitz of Prague, architect of the Stephanskirche, can be recognized on the west gable, on the openwork tower with cupola and on the grotesque zoomorphic consoles under the vault responds. The lierne vaults and the construction of the western gallery show English influence. Documentary and stylistic evidence suggests that Michael of Wiener Neustadt was active on the construction of the south tower of the abbey church at Klosterneuburg until 1404. Other buildings have also been attributed to him in Wiener Neustadt, Klosterneuburg, Bad Deutsch Altenburg and Slovakia.

BIBLIOGRAPHY

R. K. Donin: 'Meister Michael Knab', *Zur Kunstgeschichte Österreichs: Gesammelte Aufsätze* (Vienna, 1951), pp. 202–8
M. Zykan: *Der Hochturm von St Stephan in Wien* (diss., U. Vienna, 1967), pp. 69–88
J. Bureš: 'The Castle Church in Kremnica and the Problem of Michael Chnab's Architectural School in Slovakia', *Ars*, i–ii (1970), pp. 109–44
R. Perger: 'Die Baumeister des Wiener Stephansdomes im Spätmittelalter', *Wien. Jb. Kstgesch.*, xxiii (1970), pp. 66–107
M. Zykan: 'Zur Baugeschichte des Hochturmes von St Stephan', *Wien. Jb. Kstgesch.*, xxiii (1970), pp. 28–65
——: 'Zur Identifizierung eines gotischen Gewölberisses in den Wiener Sammlungen', *Mitt. Ges. Vervielfält. Kst*, xxv/3 (Jan 1973), pp. 13–20
P. Crossley: 'Wells, the West Country and Central European Late Gothic', *Medieval Art and Architecture at Wells and Glastonbury* (London, 1981), pp. 97–9
R. Wagner-Rieger: 'Sankt Stephan in Wien', 'Formgelegenheit Turm', *Mittelalterliche Architektur in Österreich*, ed. A. Rosenauer and M. Schwartz (St Pölten and Vienna, 1988), pp. 152–64, 225–6
G. Brucher: *Gotische Baukunst in Österreich* (Salzburg and Vienna, 1990), pp. 124–43

MARLENE STRAUSS-ZYKAN

Michael von Freiburg [Michael von Gmünd]. *See* PARLER, (6).

Michăilescu, Corneliu (*b* Bucharest, 20 Aug 1887; *d* Bucharest, 15 Nov 1965). Romanian painter and sculptor. From 1906 to 1908 he attended the Faculty of Law and the Faculty of Letters and Philosophy at the University of Bucharest. In the autumn of 1908 he transferred to the Fine Arts School, also in Bucharest. On completing his studies in 1912 he visited Florence, attracted by Renaissance art. He returned to Romania in 1915, passing through Zürich, where he met Marcel Janco and Tristan Tzara. In 1919–21 he revisited Florence, attending the engraving courses of Camillo Innocenti (1871–1961) at the Accademia di Belle Arti. In 1922 he returned to Romania and held his first one-man exhibition at the Fine Arts Trade Unions Hall in Bucharest. In 1925 Michăilescu was active in the avant-garde movement centred on the magazine *Integral*, while his paintings of this period evolved from Symbolism with Fauvist elements towards a fragmented geometric style influenced by Futurism and analytical Cubism. After 1930 he experimented with mescaline, under its influence realizing the non-figurative gouache series, *Hour Visions* (Bucharest, N. Mus. A.). Illness prevented him from working consistently and he withdrew into obscurity.

BIBLIOGRAPHY

G. Marinescu: 'Cencetăni asupra acţivnii mescalinei' [Mescaline action research], *Academia Română*, ix/11 (1934), pp. 14–15
P. Oprea: 'Corneliu Michăilescu', *Artişti români* (Bucharest, 1972) [with Fr. summary]
A. Pintilie: 'Elementale pentru o redescoperire a lui Corneliu Michăilescu' [Some elements for rediscovering Corneliu Michăilescu], *Stud. & Cerc. Istor. A.*, xxvi (1979), pp. 89–116

ANDREI PINTILIE

Michallon, Achille (Etna) (*b* Paris, 22 Oct 1796; *d* Paris, 24 Sept 1822). French painter and draughtsman. After the death of his father, the sculptor Claude Michallon (1751–99), and of his mother in 1813, he was brought up by his uncle, the sculptor Guillaume Francin (1741–1830). He drew from life at an early age and studied with Jacques-Louis David, Pierre Henri de Valenciennes and later Jean-Victor Bertin. For four or five years starting in 1808 Michallon may have received financial help from Prince Nicolay Yusupov after the latter had seen some of his works in David's studio. Although no works dating from this period are known, Michallon exhibited a *View of Saint-Cloud, Seen from the Vicinity of Sèvres* and a *Wash-house: Study from Life Executed at Aulnay* at the Salon of 1812. It is possible that two small landscapes, a *View of Sceaux* and a *Site in Ile-de-France* (both Albi, Mus. Toulouse-Lautrec, on loan to Gray, Mus. Martin), date from 1812–15. Their panoramic perspective, spare composition, realistic depiction of weather conditions and the picturesque quality of a figure disappearing into the distance suggest that Michallon was familiar with the work of 17th-century landscape artists.

In 1814 Michallon travelled to Vichy, and in 1815 he drew the fortifications erected around Paris; these views, which follow the 18th-century tradition of topographical landscapes, were published in aquatint in *Les Environs de Paris fortifié*. Three of Michallon's landscapes, representing the *Château of Versailles*, the *Château of Meudon* and the *Château of Vincennes* (all ex-New York, Wildenstein's; see 1982 exh. cat., pp. 30–31), recall the Rationalist tendency in landscape painting, in which an accurate description of architecture is combined with a northern European influence, visible particularly in the realistic treatment of the foreground.

In 1817 Michallon won the Prix de Rome, organized that year for the first time, for the *Woman Struck Down* (Paris, Louvre) and *Democritus and the People of Abdera* (Paris, Ecole N. Sup. B.-A.). Before leaving for Italy, he executed a series of sepia wash drawings (nine in Paris, Bib. N.) in Dieppe, Saint-Valéry-en-Caux and Fécamps for Baron Isidore-Justin-Sévérin Taylor's *Voyage pittoresque de la France*. Michallon left for Rome in 1818 at the same time as Léon Cogniet, whom he befriended. Little is known of the early part of his stay, although there is a drawing of the *Villa Medici* (Paris, Louvre) dated 1818, which is similar to a landscape in the Musée des Beaux-Arts in Orléans. While in Rome Michallon executed the *Death of Roland* (exh. Salon 1819; Paris, Louvre), a commission for the Diana Gallery at Fontainebleau. Two sketches (Strasbourg, Mus. B.-A.; Orléans, Mus. B.-A.) show an idealistic landscape with an air of fiery intensity in the style of Salvator Rosa. Also at the Salon of 1819 he exhibited a *View of Lake Nemi* (ex-Gal. La Scala, Paris), in which the influence of such Italianate painters as Frederik de Moucheron and Nicolaes Berchem can be seen in the light and the arrangement of the foreground. Michallon executed several studies representing Rome and its surroundings, including the *Sabine Hills* (Detroit, MI, Inst. A.) and a *View of the Colosseum* (Paris, Louvre).

In 1819 and 1820 Michallon travelled through southern Italy and Sicily. He made numerous drawings and painted studies of architectural subjects, such as the *Temple of Neptune at Paestum* and the *Forum of Pompeii*, and of picturesque characters, such as *Countrywoman, near Rome* (all Paris, Louvre). He also executed landscapes without figures, such as the *Island of Ischia* (Phoenix, AZ, A. Mus.) and *Eruption of Vesuvius by Night* (Paris, Louvre), in which he displayed his skill at observing atmospheric conditions and the time of day. Some of his drawings were engraved in Gigaud de la Salle's *Le Voyage pittoresque en Sicile* (1822–6) and in *Vues d'Italie et de Sicile* (Paris, 1826).

Michallon returned to France in 1821, travelling through Florence, Bologna, Venice and the Swiss Alps. On his return to Paris he opened a studio that was frequented by Jean-Baptiste-Camille Corot. He executed several pictures based on his memories of Italy; in these he combined the classicism of historical landscape, in which the organization of elements was sometimes artificial, with a study of changing nature. In such dramatic subjects as *Landscape with a Man Frightened by a Snake* (Barnard Castle, Bowes Mus.) and *Philoctetes on the Island of Lemnos* (1822; Montpellier, Mus. Fabre), Michallon suggested the violence of the passions depicted and foreshadowed the new approach to landscape painting that flourished from the 1830s. In his last compositions, such as those executed in the Forest of Fontainebleau (1821–2; untraced), Michallon became more sensitive to nature's melancholy and the dramatization of natural elements, without moving away from Poussinesque models. He died of pneumonia, and his paintings and drawings were sold in Paris in 1822.

BIBLIOGRAPHY

P. Miquel: *L'Ecole de la nature*, ii of *Le Paysage français au XIXe siècle, 1824–1874* (Maurs-la-Jolie, 1975), pp. 76–85

D. G. Cleaver: 'Michallon et la théorie du paysage', *Rev. Louvre*, 5–6 (1981), pp. 359–66

Consulate—Empire—Restoration: Art in Early Nineteenth Century France (exh. cat., New York, Wildenstein's, 1982)

Achille-Etna Michallon (exh. cat. by V. Pomarède, B. Lesage and C. Stefani, Paris, Louvre, 1994)

VALÉRIE M. C. BAJOU

Michałowicz z Urzędowa, Jan (*b* Urzędów, *c.* 1530; *d* Łowicz, *c.* 1583). Polish sculptor and master builder. He trained in Kraków, perhaps at the workshop of Giovanni Maria Mosca Padovano. He directed a building and sculpture workshop in Kraków; although he did not officially become a master in the Kraków guild until 1570, he had been working independently since at the latest 1557, when he executed the tomb of *Bishop Benedykt Izdbieński* (Poznań Cathedral). Michałowicz built two domed chapels in Kraków Cathedral containing the funerary monuments of the Kraków bishops *Andrzej Zebrzydowski* (1562–3) and *Filip Padniewski* (1572–5), and he built a similar chapel and monument in the Łowicz Collegiate Church for the Primate of Poland *Jakub Uchański* (1580–83; epitaph dismantled late 18th century; reassembled in Arkadia, nr Łowicz). He also signed the tomb of *Urszula Leżeńska* (*c.* 1565) in the parish church of Brzeziny. The artist's characteristic style permits the attribution to him of several unsigned tombs, including those of the brothers *Mikołaj and Stanisław Wolski* (1568; Warsaw Cathedral); *Stanisław Tarnowski* (1569; Chroberz); and *Jan Leżeński* (1573; Chełmno). He also executed carved portals for houses at 18 Kanoniczna Street and 3 Floriańska Street, Kraków.

In tomb sculpture Michałowicz repeatedly used the motif of a figure reclining on its side, derived from Andrea Sansovino's Roman funerary monuments. He was the first eminent representative of Mannerism in Poland. His works, artistically unconstrained, did not submit to the rules of classicizing art; he freely combined Italian and Netherlandish architectonic and ornamental forms, deriving motifs from the pattern books of Sebastiano Serlio, Cornelis Floris and Pieter van Aelst, and arranging them into inventive and original compositions. He signed his works with an inscription and the emblem of a burin with a cross and a set square. Michałowicz's epitaph (destr.) in the Łowicz Collegiate Church glorified the artist as 'Praxiteles polonicus'. His many followers include Jan Biały.

BIBLIOGRAPHY

PSB; Thieme–Becker

J. Pagaczewski: 'Jan Michałowicz z Urzędowa', *Roc. Krakow.*, xxviii (1937), pp. 169–81

E. Kozłowska-Tomczyk: *Jan Michałowicz z Urzędowa* (Warsaw, 1967)

H. Kozakiewiczowa: *Rzeźba XVI wieku w Polsce* [16th-century sculpture in Poland] (Warsaw, 1984), pp. 139–52

JERZY KOWALCZYK

Michałowski, Piotr (*b* Kraków, 2 July 1800; *d* Krzyżtoporzyce, nr Kraków, 9 June 1855). Polish painter. Born into a noble family, he studied (*c.* 1815–18) at the Jagiellonian University in Kraków, simultaneously taking drawing and painting with several local teachers. After travelling to Vienna, then Warsaw (1817–18), he continued his studies (1821–3) at Göttingen before entering the service of the Ministry of Finances of the Kingdom of Poland in Warsaw as an unsalaried official. In January 1826 he obtained a permanent position in the ministry, and in June 1827 he was appointed head of the whole of the state's metal industry. In 1828 and 1830 he made official journeys to Germany, France and England and, during the Polish uprising of 1830–31, organized the production of munitions for the Polish army in his factories. In February 1831 he married Julia Ostrowska and, after the failure of the uprising, resigned from his ministry post and left for Kraków, in March 1832 moving on to Paris with the intention of establishing himself as a professional painter.

Until 1832 Michałowski had mainly occupied himself with drawing and watercolours, although he had been familiar with painting in oils since his early childhood. His favourite subjects were genre and military scenes, especially with riders and carriages, and caricatures. His early works show the influence of Aleksandr Orłowski and of Carle and Horace Vernet. In Paris, Michałowski entered the studio of Nicolas-Toussaint Charlet, a painter of military scenes and a fellow Bonapartist. Michałowski also studied the Old Masters, particularly van Dyck, and equestrian anatomy. He was particularly fascinated by the work of Gericault, which he zealously copied and travestied. Michałowski soon attained some success on the Parisian art market. His watercolours fetched high prices, and in 1833 he was able to establish his own studio. He had at least three permanent agents at his disposal: Durand Ruel, Giroux and Mlle Naudet. Michałowski's most commercially successful paintings were equestrian genre scenes. He also painted military subjects, mainly taken from episodes in the Napoleonic wars. In Paris, Michałowski embarked on several series of paintings, which he continued in later years: notable among these were his plans for an ambitious composition, the *Charge in the Somosierra Gorge* (sketch 1832–7; Kraków, N. Mus.). He also made, in plaster, an equestrian statue of *Napoleon* (Kraków, N. Mus.), which was cast in bronze by Debraux d'Anglure in 1841. During his stay in Paris, which lasted nearly five years, Michałowski emerged definitively from his status as a talented amateur and became an artist fully aware of both his strengths and his limitations. He made great progress in technique, particularly in oil painting. Under the influence of Gericault, he started to paint in a sketch-like fashion, applying colour in thick impasto. His colour range, initially dominated by black and brown tones, became broader and increasingly lighter.

In 1835, after a journey to London, Michałowski was summoned to Kraków by his father who was gravely ill. In 1837, following the death of his father, Michałowski inherited the family's country estate at Krzyżtoporzyce, near Kraków, and moved there. In 1840 he moved on to Bolestraszyce, in Galicia, devoting much time to farming and administration but continuing to paint. He drew and painted portraits of his family and friends, as well as of local peasants and Jews, and produced genre and animal paintings, and sometimes also landscapes. He also continued to paint battle scenes. During the 1840s Michałowski embarked on a new series of paintings, which depicted allegorical equestrian portraits of Polish heroes, in which he often used Baroque compositional models (e.g. *Czarniecki on a White Horse*, 1845–55, Kraków, N. Mus.).

Because of his familiarity with the works of Velázquez in the museums of Vienna, Michałowski chose to produce a number of paintings in this style, for example *Cardinal: A Pastiche of Velázquez's 'Portrait of Pope Innocent X'* and *Seńko: Study of a Peasant Dressed as Don Quixote* (both *c.* 1845–8; Kraków, N. Mus., see fig.). In these works, increased fluency in brushwork and an enriched colour range are evident. From 1844, Michałowski travelled annually to France and considered settling in Paris for good and becoming again a professional painter. During the spring of 1848, however, he became more deeply involved in Polish political life. He took an important part in the uprising in Kraków and was subsequently appointed President of the Administrative Council of the Kraków Region and then President of the local Agricultural Society, a post he held until his death. He continued, however, to paint, producing both portraits and genre and military scenes. During the last months of his life, he was embarking on a final version of the subject long prepared in studies and sketches, the *Charge on Somosierra* (1845–55; Kraków, N. Mus.).

A lack of professional constraint combined with his own high standards were the principal reasons why many of Michałowski's works did not progress beyond the stage of drafts and sketches. When dissatisfied he often destroyed his work by painting new compositions over the same canvas. During his lifetime, Michałowski's painting was almost unknown: he had no regular pupils and exhibited very rarely except in Paris. The few critical opinions that were voiced on his work were favourable, although they usually regarded his paintings as mere

Piotr Michałowski: *Seńko: Study of a Peasant Dressed as Don Quixote*, oil on canvas, 620×465 mm, *c.* 1845–8 (Kraków, National Museum)

sketches. His 'rediscovery' occurred in the context of the large exhibition of Polish art held in 1894 in Lwów (now L'viv, Ukraine] when the strong patriotic strain in his work was much appreciated. He is regarded as an important painter in Polish Romanticism. In spite of strong links with Gericault, his work is clearly inspired by Baroque models, with a painterly spontaneity of execution.

BIBLIOGRAPHY

N. N. (C. Michałowska): *Piotr Michałowski* (Kraków, 1911)
M. Sterling: *Piotr Michałowski* (Warsaw, 1932)
J. Sienkiewicz: *Piotr Michałowski* (Warsaw, 1959; Ger. trans., 1964)
J. Zanoziński: *Piotr Michałowski* (Wrocław, 1965)
J. K. Ostrowski: *Piotr Michałowski* (Warsaw, 1985)
——: *Pięć studiów o Piotrze Michałowskim* [Five studies on Piotr Michałowski] (Kraków, 1987)

JAN K. OSTROWSKI

Michals, Duane (Steven) (*b* McKeesport, PA, 18 Feb 1932). American photographer. He had no formal training but recognized his photographic aptitude when he took his first pictures as a tourist in the USSR in 1958. By 1960 he was earning his living through commercial work, including portraiture and fashion photography. In 1964, weary of the demands of photographing people, Michals responded to Eugène Atget's pictures of depopulated Paris with his own views of empty New York shop interiors, which seemed to him like stage sets waiting to be animated. In 1966 he began to produce sequences depicting enigmatic encounters in a static setting as if in the frames of a film (pubd in *Sequences*, New York, 1970). These were inspired by the erotically charged domestic dramas painted by Balthus, whose canvas *The Street* (1933; New York, MOMA) served as the model for Michals's first staged photograph. In order to accommodate the increasing elaboration of his narratives and often metaphysical themes, Michals began to write on the surfaces of such photographs as *Private Acts* (pubd in *Real Dreams*, Danbury, NH, 1977).

Frustrated by the limitations of the single photographic image, Michals experimented with the medium's range, producing extended photo-essays and books such as *The Wonders of Egypt* (Paris, 1978), *The Nature of Desire* (Pasadena, CA, [1986]) and *Eros & Thanatos* (Santa Fe, NM, 1992). In his work of the mid-1980s he paired photographs with drawings of the same subject or complemented the photographic image with hand-painted additions. These technical innovations were widely imitated, but to him they were means of expressing intimate emotions and human relationships not usually considered within the domain of photography. He is distinguished for his inventive extensions of the medium and for the poetry and humanity of his vision.

BIBLIOGRAPHY

Duane Michals: Photographies de 1958 à 1982 (exh. cat. by M. Foucault, Paris, Mus. A. Mod. Ville Paris, 1982)
R. Camus: *Duane Michals* (Paris, 1983)
Duane Michals: Photographs/Sequences/Texts 1958–1984 (exh. cat., ed. M. Livingstone; Oxford, MOMA, 1984)
D. Michals and J. Woody, eds: *The Portraits of Duane Michals* (Pasadena, CA, 1988)
M. Kozloff: *Duane Michals: Now Becoming Then* (Altadena, CA, 1990)

MARCO LIVINGSTONE

Michau, Théobald (*b* Doornik [Tournai], 1676; *d* Antwerp, *bur* 27 Oct 1765). Flemish painter. In 1686 he was a pupil of Lucas Achtschellinck (1626–99) in Brussels, where he became a master in 1698. From 1710 he was an independent master in the Guild of St Luke in Antwerp. Most of his paintings are small-scale cabinet pictures, some on copper. They depict landscapes, river views, scenes of winter, markets and villages, peopled with tiny figures strolling or working, sometimes celebrating or drinking, often dressed in blue or red and accompanied by a few animals. Typical examples include *Landscape with a Group of Farmers* (Valenciennes, Mus. B.-A.), *Landscape* (Brunswick, Herzog Anton Ulrich-Mus.) and *Landscape with Figures* (Antwerp, Kon. Mus. S. Kst.). Michau's anecdotal scenes continue the 17th-century tradition of genre paintings by Jan Breughel the elder, David Teniers the younger and Pieter Bout. His use of colour is indebted to Breughel but lacks the same strength, and the stocky figures seem inspired by Teniers. In comparison with these masters, however, Michau seems a mere 18th-century imitator who did not manage to contribute many original variations. Yet he was successful in his day; engravings of several of his works were made by Jacques-Philippe Lebas and his pupils, and Jacques d'Arthois asked him to paint the figures in some landscapes. Charles, 4th Duke of Lorraine (*d* 1780), then Governor of the southern Netherlands, bought ten of his works.

BIBLIOGRAPHY

Y. Morel-Deckers: *Schilderijen uit de 18de eeuw*, Antwerp, Kon. Mus. S. Kst. cat. (Antwerp, 1988), p. 84 [with extensive bibliog.]

ELS VERMANDERE

Michaux, Henri (*b* Namur, Belgium, 24 May 1899; *d* Paris, 19 Oct 1980). French draughtsman, painter and poet of Belgian birth. From 1911 to 1914 he studied at a Jesuit school in Brussels. In 1919 he started and then abandoned the study of medicine and the following year worked as a seaman. Returning to Brussels in 1921, he started writing in earnest in 1922, soon becoming known in literary circles. He went to Paris in 1924; here he was struck by the paintings of Klee, Max Ernst and de Chirico at a Surrealist exhibition. He started to paint in 1925 and until 1927 worked in a variety of media: India ink, watercolour and oils. The *Alphabet* series in ink, for example *Alphabet* (1925; Paris, Paulhan priv. col., see 1978 exh. cat., p. 10), was based on a series of personal ideograms, and in oils he painted the series of *Blot* works. From 1927 to 1937 he travelled extensively abroad, visiting South America, Turkey, China and India; this experience was a powerful influence on his later work.

On his return Michaux began to paint and draw regularly. From 1937 to 1939 he produced a series of dreamlike gouaches on a black ground, which he called *Phantomisms*. They included such works as *The Prince of the Night* (1937; Paris, Pompidou). In 1937 he had his first one-man show at the Librairie-Galerie de la Pléiade. After the publication of *Entre centre et absence* in 1936, with eight drawings, his *Peintures* was published in 1939 with seven poems and sixteen gouaches. During World War II, while continuing to write and paint, he published several other books with his own illustrations, such as *Exorcismes* (1943). He experimented with *frottage* from 1945 to 1947, and immediately after the accidental death of his wife in 1948 produced several hundred visionary ink and watercolour works.

In 1950 Michaux returned to his earlier use of ideograms in a series of India ink drawings, through which he became closely associated with *Art informel*. This resulted in the poem and 64 drawings that formed the album *Mouvements* (Paris, 1951). He continued this development with the *Mêlées*, *Foules* and *Préhistoire* series of 1952 to 1953 and with the ink paintings of 1954 onwards, such as *Painting in Indian Ink* (1954; Paris, Pompidou). In 1955 he took French citizenship. After experimenting with the drug mescaline, he produced a number of drawings and paintings from 1955 to 1962 executed as meticulous 'all-over' compositions, lacking any real centre, as in *Mescalin Painting* (1956; Paris, Pompidou). During the 1960s he continued to use India ink, watercolour and pastel; some works of this period suggest figurative elements, as in *Untitled* (India ink, 1960; New York, Guggenheim; for illustration *see* ART INFORMEL) or sepia and ink *Untitled* (1962; Paris, Pompidou). He introduced more colour into his work in 1967 by using acrylic, and he later mixed this with watercolour, as in *Untitled* (1970; see 1989 exh. cat., p. 62).

Throughout the 1970s Michaux's style in his ink paintings, oils and acrylics remained spontaneous and abstract. The works of the late 1970s onwards were of a near figurative character, as in *Untitled* (1980; see 1987 exh. cat., p. 13).

WRITINGS
Entre centre et absence (Nice, 1936)
Peintures (Paris, 1939)
Exorcismes (Paris, 1943)

BIBLIOGRAPHY
W. Schmied: *Henri Michaux* (Hannover, 1973)
Henri Michaux (exh. cat. by A. Angliviel and A. Pacquement, Paris, Pompidou, 1978)
Michaux (exh. cat. by J.-C. Bailly, Paris, Gal. Patrice Trigano, 1987)
Henri Michaux (exh. cat., Cologne, Gal. Karsten Greve, 1989)

☐

Michel, Alfonso (*b* Colima, 1906; *d* Mexico City, 1957). Mexican painter. After living for more or less extensive periods in San Francisco, Florence and Paris, he returned in 1930 to Mexico, where he painted at the University of Guadalajara with Jesús Guerrero Galván. Subsequently he settled permanently in Mexico City. Of the Mexican artists working in the 1930s and 1940s he is perhaps the one who most distanced himself from the rigidity imposed by the notion of a Mexican school, his sojourns abroad having undoubtedly introduced him to ideas from the European avant-garde. He was particularly influenced by the Synthetic Cubism of Braque and Picasso in his handling of figures, as in *Horse* and *Still-life with Landscape* (both Colima, Mus. Cult. Occident.), which he enriched with a very personal and sensual use of colour.

BIBLIOGRAPHY
B. Espejo: *Historia de la pintura mexicana*, iii (Mexico City, 1989)
J. A. Manrique: 'Contracorriente pictórica: Una generación intermedia', *El arte mexicano*, xv (Mexico City, 1989)

JORGE ALBERTO MANRIQUE

Michel, André(-Paul-Charles) (*b* Montpellier, 7 Nov 1853; *d* Paris, 12 Oct 1925). French art historian. In 1872 he went to Paris, where he attended Hippolyte Taine's

lectures at the Ecole des Beaux-Arts. Taine's Positivist theories were to influence deeply the development of his ideas on the history of art. In 1880 Michel settled in Paris and in 1884 he joined the *Gazette des beaux-arts*, for which he wrote exhibition reviews. The following year he was entrusted with the review of the annual Paris Salon. Michel's exhibition reviews during the 1880s formed the basis of his published studies on Jean-François Millet (1887), Puvis de Chavannes (1888) and Delacroix (1889). His reviews of the Expositions Universelles of 1889 and 1890 provided the substance for his work on 19th-century French art, *L'Ecole française de David à Delacroix* (1892). In 1893 Michel joined Louis Courajod at the Department of Sculpture in the Louvre, becoming its curator three years later when Courajod died. At the same time he lectured at the Ecole du Louvre on the history of French sculpture from its origins to the 17th century. From 1903 Michel edited the monumental *Histoire de l'art depuis les premiers temps chrétiens jusqu'à nos jours*. Michel's work remains valuable for its historical and disciplined approach to the study of art.

WRITINGS
L'Ecole française de David à Delacroix (Paris, 1892)
ed.: *Histoire de l'art depuis les premiers temps chrétiens jusqu'à nos jours*, 18 vols (Paris, 1905–29)
Sculpture du moyen âge, de la Renaissance et des temps modernes, Paris, Louvre, cat. (Paris, 1923)
Regular contributions to *Gaz. B.-A.* (1884–1922)

BIBLIOGRAPHY
P. Vitry: 'André Michel', *Gaz. B.-A.*, n. s. 4, xvi (1927), p. 317

AMAL ASFOUR

Michel, Claude. *See* CLODION.

Michel, Georges (*b* Paris, 12 Jan 1763; *d* Paris, 7 or 8 June 1843). French painter. He came from a humble background, his father being an employee at the market of Les Halles in Paris. At an early age, a farmer general, M. de Chalue, took an interest in him and found him a place with the curate of Veruts, on the plain of Saint-Denis, north of Paris. It was here that he first developed a love of the countryside. In 1775 he was apprenticed to a mediocre history painter called Leduc, but he preferred to go off and sketch out of doors. In order to assist him, M. de Berchigny, Colonel in the Hussars, engaged him in his regiment garrisoned in Normandy and arranged for him to take lessons in art. He remained there for more than a year and then returned to Paris, where he worked with M. de Grammont-Voulgy, who was Steward to the brother of Louis XVI. In 1789 Grammont-Voulgy took him to Switzerland, and Michel also visited Germany, where he stayed with the Duc de Guiche.

Some time between 1783 and 1789, Michel met the dealer Jean-Baptiste-Pierre Le Brun, who authorized him to copy the 17th-century Dutch paintings that were in his shop. In 1790 he probably met the painter Lazare Bruandet. The two of them became friends, painted at Romainville, north-east of Paris, and in the Bois de Boulogne and shared a dissolute lifestyle. In 1791 he exhibited for the first time at the Salon in Paris, showing two small landscapes and *Horse and Animal Market*. He continued to exhibit regularly there but was ignored by the critics because his style was not yet well defined and his paintings

Georges Michel: *Landscape outside Paris*, oil on canvas, 770×980 mm, after 1830 (Lille, Musée des Beaux-Arts)

were considered too similar to those of the Dutch masters. Around 1800 he was employed by the Musée du Louvre to restore Flemish and Dutch paintings by Rembrandt, Ruisdael and Meindert Hobbema, and it was in this capacity that he developed a true understanding of technique. In 1808 he decided to set up a studio and to give lessons, although he closed it a year later, as he disliked teaching. In 1813 he opened a shop adjacent to his studio in the Rue de Cléry and sold furniture and paintings. Discouraged by numerous refusals, he exhibited for the last time at the Salon of 1814. After the death in 1820 of the last surviving of his eight children, he left Paris to stay for a year at Condé-sur-l'Escaut in Picardy. After his return he began to lead a reclusive life and gradually withdrew from the art world. Because of his self-imposed artistic isolation, he had to rely solely on the patronage of Baron d'Ivry, who purchased almost his entire output. During the July Revolution of 1830, the two men fell out over political differences, and d'Ivry became one of Michel's principal imitators, even pretending that the artist was dead.

Michel always painted within a small area limited to the surroundings of Paris. He commented that 'Whoever cannot paint within an area of four leagues is but an unskilled artist who seeks the mandrake and will only ever

find a void' (Sensier). His preferred locations were Montmartre, where he was inspired by the famous windmills, the plains of Saint-Denis, the villages of Vaugirard, Grenelle, Montsouris, Romainville and Le Pré-Saint-Gervais. He executed small *plein-air* studies: often these were drawings heightened with watercolour wash, which were then used as preliminaries for paintings worked up in the studio. His career may be divided into three phases. The first, until *c.* 1808, includes the period of his collaboration with Jean-Louis Demarne and Jacques-François Swebach, artists who often executed the staffage of his landscapes. These works recall those by the lesser 18th-century masters of northern Europe. Typical of this period is *Animals at the Drinking Trough*, also known as *The Storm* (*c.* 1794–5; Nantes, Mus. B.-A.). From 1808 he developed a more personal vision, in which light and the treatment of the sky and space became his principal concerns. Paintings of this period (e.g. the *Plain of Saint-Denis*, Paris, Carnavalet) are more unified compositionally, with vast expanses of landscape and wide perspectives under stormy skies. The windmills are often the sole accents punctuating the compositions. After 1830 he was at the peak of his talent, his style becoming even more lyrical and visionary. His brushstrokes are broader and his paint thicker. He reinforced the dramatic tension by accentuating the heaviness of the skies and the contrasts of light and dark. The mood is one of unrest, and the inclusion of *Man confronted by the immensity of Nature and its forces* is a theme later used by Romantic painters. Works from this last period include the *Environs of Montmartre* (Paris, Louvre), *The Storm* (*c.* 1830; Strasbourg, Mus. B.-A.) and *Two Windmills* (The Hague, Rijksmus. Mesdag). *Landscape outside Paris* (Lille, Mus. B.-A.; see fig.) is also typical. Various tiny figures, including a horse and rider and two travellers on foot, move through a vast landscape with a sunlit horizon. In the darker mid-ground can be seen a windmill and a thunderstorm.

Michel had little interest in fame, and, with the exception of a few early paintings, his works are unsigned. He said: 'The painting must please without the aid of a name or a label. We should do what our ancestors did: they did not sign [their works], but their talent was their signature' (Sensier, p. 17). He was important as a precursor of the works of the Barbizon school. In 1841, two years before Michel's death, the contents of his studio, consisting of more than 1000 studies and 2000 drawings, were put up at auction, and the Barbizon painter Charles Jacque acquired several of his works, which were of great inspiration to him. Jules Dupré also encountered Michel's art at that time.

An independent artist who never achieved success in his lifetime, Michel's role today is recognized by critics as crucial in the evolution of 19th- and 20th-century landscape painting. However, literature on him remains sparse. The only known facts about his life were collected and published (1873) by Alfred Sensier, his first biographer, and his study is still the principal source of information about the artist.

BIBLIOGRAPHY

A. Sensier: *Etude sur Georges Michel* (Paris, 1873)
J. Bouret: *L'Ecole de Barbizon et le paysage français au XIXe siècle* (Neuchâtel, 1972), pp. 25–32
P. Miquel: *Le Paysage français au XIXe siècle, 1824–1874: L'Ecole de la nature*, ii (Maurs-la-Jolie, 1975), 4–11
C. Parsons and N. McWilliam: '"Le Paysan de Paris": Alfred Sensier and the Myth of Rural France', *Oxford A. J.*, vi/2 (1983), pp. 38–58
H. P. Bühler: 'Der Ruisdael vom Montmartre: Georges Michel, 1763–1843', *Die Weltkunst*, lvi/22 (1986), pp. 3614–18

LAURENCE PAUCHET-WARLOP

Michel, Jorge (*b* Buenos Aires, 24 Dec 1925). Argentine sculptor. He was initially drawn to literature, then worked in advertising before finally turning to sculpture as a form through which he could weave together his life and his work. Self-taught, favouring monumental shapes endowed with internal tension and natural rhythms, he often combined elements carved in wood, marble or granite with other materials such as bronze, wrought iron and stainless steel, for example in *Untitled* (1.2×0.6 m; Buenos Aires, Sheraton Hotel). He chose to remain in Argentina partly because of the importance that he attached to materials, and especially to the granite and hard woods that he was able to obtain there. He usually conceived of his works in homogeneous groupings, sometimes forming a continuity as in *They are Leaning* (white stone from Córdoba, 5×0.5 m, 7 pieces) or a harmony as in *Couple* (bronze on granite base; both Nelly Perazzo priv. col., see Moet, p. 1), sometimes scattering shapes around a central form. At once modern and archaic in their effect, his sculptures

convey ancient truths through an apparently timeless language of tangible forms.

BIBLIOGRAPHY

C. Espartaco: *El estupor del arte* (Buenos Aires, 1984), pp. 133–4
D. G. Moet: 'Entrevista a Jorge Michel', *Rev. Cult.*, iii/15 (1986), pp. 1, 22

NELLY PERAZZO

Michel, Robert (i) (*b* Puy del Velay [Languedoc], 1720; *d* Madrid, 31 Jan 1786). French sculptor, active in Spain. According to Ceán Bermúdez, he trained in France at Lyon, Montpellier and Toulouse. Diverse influences led to the formation of his eclectic style; he was taught by a Franco-Italian (Bonfili), two French sculptors (Perrache and Dupon) and a Fleming (Luquet). In 1740 he went with Luquet to Madrid. There he sculpted in marble, stone, stucco, wood and bronze and was instrumental in the early development of the Real Academia de S Fernando, Madrid, becoming a court sculptor (*Primer Escultor de Cámara*) in 1757, a director of sculpture at the Academia in 1763 and Director General in 1785. From 1749 onwards he executed five stone statues for the new Palacio Real, Madrid (including *Teudis*, *Vermudo III* and *Ferdinand II*; *in situ*), and was responsible for much of the decorative stuccowork in the palace. He also worked at the gardens of the palace of Aranjuez and produced public sculpture in Madrid, such as the lions for the Fountain of Cibeles. His two stone figures of *Virtues* for the façade of S Justo (now S Miguel), Madrid, illustrate his human interpretation of the Antique, as in the figure of *Charity*, clad in swirling draperies and antique-style cross-gartered boots, who turns affectionately towards one child and offers her milk to the other below. Of his many other works for Madrid churches, the *Virgen del Carmen* for the façade of S José (formerly Carmelitas Descalzos) combines Spanish features, such as the cherub heads around the feet, with a Roman restraint in the classically posed, monumental figure of the Virgin. Through his work at the Academia Michel influenced many Spanish sculptors.

BIBLIOGRAPHY

Ceán Bermúdez
E. Serrano Fatigati: *Escultura en Madrid desde mediados del siglo XVI hasta nuestros días* (Madrid, 1912), pp. 156–9
J. J. Martín González: *Escultura barroca en España, 1600–1770* (Madrid, 1983), pp. 405–7

MARJORIE TRUSTED

Michel, Robert (ii) (*b* Vockenhausen, nr Eppstein, 27 Feb 1897; *d* Titisee-Neustadt, 11 June 1983). German painter and architect. As a child he wished to become an engineer. At the outbreak of World War I he became an air pilot, but after a crash in 1917 he was sent to a military hospital in Weimar. That year he enrolled at the Hochschule für Bildende Kunst in Weimar, soon to become part of the Bauhaus, where he met Ella Bergmann, whom he married in 1919, and who adopted the surname Bergmann-Michel. After producing drawings and woodcuts such as *Untitled (Composition)* (1917–18; Hannover, Sprengel Mus.), using circles and other geometrical elements, he turned to collage in 1918. The early works incorporated collage elements into a painted and drawn design, with overtly mechanical images such as cogs, dials and wheels and often words, as in *Mann-Es-Manbild, B127* (1918–19; Hannover, Sprengel Mus.). In 1918 he took a studio of his own in Weimar and in 1919 was in contact with the newly founded Bauhaus. Though the Bauhaus quickly became interested in mechanical images, Michel found Gropius too doctrinaire and so refrained from joining. In 1920 he left Weimar for Vockenhausen, which remained his home until shortly before his death.

In 1921 Michel became a friend of Schwitters and in that year he began using pieced-together, photographic reproductions of technical objects in his collages, together with drawn and spray-painted additions, as in *Anti-Still Life 2 Times 3* (1923; Hannover, Sprengel Mus.). Though many of his works are cool and detached, some have a light-hearted wit characteristic of Dada, such as the wash drawing *Untitled (Bulls and Lorries)* (1923; Hannover, Sprengel Mus.). In the early 1920s he also began to produce commercial posters, such as those for Söhnlein Rheingold champagne of 1921–3. He established an architectural office in Frankfurt in 1927 and from 1928 to 1930 worked with the architect Lucy Hillebrand, producing, for example, petrol stations for Dapolin in Frankfurt and elsewhere. He continued producing mechanical collages and drawings until 1934, when under the Nazi regime he gave up art and devoted himself to agricultural and fishery planning. He resumed his artistic activities in 1955, and until 1969 produced mechanical paintings and collages, some of which included real objects such as cogwheels, as in *Blacky Ornament* (1959; Hannover, Sprengel Mus.).

BIBLIOGRAPHY
Ella Bergmann-Michel, Robert Michel (exh. cat. by A. L. Chanin and H. Wescher, Cologne, Gal. Bargera, 1974)
Robert Michel 1897–1983: Collagen, Malerei, Aquarelle, Zeichnungen, Druckgraphik, Reklame, Typographie, Entwürfe (exh. cat. by C. Reising-Pohl and others, Hannover, Sprengel Mus.; Karlsruhe, Bad. Kstver.; Frankfurt am Main, Kstver.; 1988–9)

Michela, Costanzo (*b* Agliè, nr Ivrea, 1689; *d* Agliè, 1754). Italian architect, foreman and notary. In 1729 his work as foreman on Filippo Juvarra's Palazzina di Caccia at Stupinigi put him in close touch with the Piedmontese architectural establishment. His own work, however, for example at Barone, where in 1729 he built a castle and the parish church, demonstrates the influence of Guarino Guarini, as well as an entirely original interest in pairing contrasts of colour and material, geometrical form and proportion. By the 1740s he was as sought after in the Canavese region near Turin as Bernardo Antonio Vittone, with whom he competed for some of the same commissions. Costanza lost to Vittone the parish church of Borgomasino (1733), despite the sophisticated, curvilinear vigour of his design, but he replaced him in the rebuilding of Santa Trinità (1748), Valperga, where he adopted a composition intended for S Giacomo (1733) at Rivarolo.

Costanzo's most significant design is the church built for the confraternity of S Marta (1739), Agliè. It is a variant on the longitudinal church compositions of Guarini—for example the church of the Immacolata Concezione (begun 1673), Turin—and the only such example built south of the Alps. The church was constructed in two stages and then enlarged in order to accommodate the expanded membership of the confraternity. The plan is divided into three parts: the two-tier choir is circular,

the sanctuary is square and the congregational space is a triangle with concave sides. The extraordinary curvature of the arches that join the bays also emphasizes their independence and separation. The outcurving arches may well be borrowed from Juvarra, while the lens-shaped vaults are similar to those employed by Vittone. The curved walls and cornices of the congregation contain cavernous musicians' balconies. The entrance, through one of the piers, is frescoed in imitation of dark marble, while the interior is painted in lively, unsophisticated hues. Consequently, the initial impact is made by the startling combination of small size and strong colours. The exterior of the church is of unplastered brick. The bell-tower (1785–7) follows the architectural vocabulary of the church so well that its design must be by Costanzo. Its height is masked by vigorous cornices along the concave sides of its triangular form. The main façade is framed by free-standing columns, which guard the numerous pilasters; these compress the central bay, forcing the lines of the central entablature upwards, a theme that is picked up in the upper order. The pediment of the upper storey in turn cleaves the innumerable mouldings crowning the composition. The interior and the façade have no equal in Piedmont, but the churches of the Dientzenhofer brothers, and especially of Balthasar Neumann (for example, the planning of the palace church (1730–43) at the Residenz, Würzburg), have a similar raw energy.

BIBLIOGRAPHY
A. Telluccini: 'Il castello di Rivoli torinese', *Boll. A.*, n. s. 1, x (1930–31), pp. 145–61, 193–216
A. E. Brinckmann: *Theatrum novum Pedemontii* (Düsseldorf, 1931)
C. Celano: 'S Marta ad Agliè', *Architettura*, xii (1967), pp. 750–59
R. Pommer: 'Costanzo Michela and Santa Marta in Agliè: A Guarinesque Rarity', *A. Bull.*, l (1968), pp. 169–82
C. Palmas Devoti: 'Il restauro di Santa Marta di Agliè: Un intervento per il recupero culturale del barocco minore in Piemonte', *Boll. A.*, lxiv/3 (1979), pp. 87–106

MARTHA POLLAK

Michelangelo (Buonarroti) [Michelagnolo di Lodovico Buonarroti Simoni] (*b* Caprese, ?6 March 1475; *d* Rome, 18 Feb 1564). Italian sculptor, painter, draughtsman and architect. The elaborate exequies held in Florence after Michelangelo's death celebrated him as the greatest practitioner of the three visual arts of sculpture, painting and architecture and as a respected poet. He is a central figure in the history of art: one of the chief creators of the Roman High Renaissance, and the supreme representative of the Florentine valuation of *disegno* (see DISEGNO E COLORE). As a poet and a student of anatomy, he is often cited as an example of the 'universal genius' supposedly typical of the period. His professional career lasted over 70 years, during which he participated in, and often stimulated, great stylistic changes. The characteristic most closely associated with him is *terribilità*, a term indicative of heroic and awe-inspiring grandeur. Reproductions of the *Creation of Adam* from the Sistine Chapel Ceiling (Rome, Vatican) or the *Moses* from the tomb of *Julius II* (Rome, S Pietro in Vincoli) have broadcast an image of his art as one almost exclusively expressive of superhuman power. The man himself has been assimilated to this image and represented as the archetype of the brooding, irascible, lonely and tragic figure of the artist. This popular view is drastically oversimplified, except in one respect: the power and originality of his art have guaranteed his prominence as a historical figure for over 400 years since his death, even among those who have not liked the example he gave. For such different artists as Gianlorenzo Bernini, Eugène Delacroix and Henry Moore, he provided a touchstone of integrity and aesthetic value. Although his reputation as a poet has not been so high, his poetry has been praised by such diverse figures as William Wordsworth (1770–1850) and Eugenio Montale (1896–1981).

WRITINGS

G. Milanesi, ed.: *Le lettere di Michelangelo Buonarroti pubblicate coi ricordi ed i contratti artistici* (Florence, 1875)

E. N. Girardi, ed.: *Rime* (Bari, 1960)

P. Barocchi, R. Ristori and G. Poggi, eds: *Il carteggio di Michelangelo*, 5 vols (Florence, 1965–83); Eng. trans. of Michelangelo's letters only in E. H. Ramsden, ed.: *The Letters of Michelangelo*, 2 vols (London, 1963)

P. Barocchi, K. Loach Bramanti and R. Ristori, eds: *Il carteggio indiretto di Michelangelo* (Florence, 1988)

J. M. Saslow, trans.: *The Poetry of Michelangelo: An Annotated Translation* (New Haven and London, 1991)

GENERAL BIBLIOGRAPHY

EARLY SOURCES

A. Condivi: *Vita di Michelagnolo Buonarroti* (Rome, 1553); ed. E. Spina Barelli (Milan, 1964); Eng. trans. by A. S. Wohl as *The Life of Michelangelo* (Oxford and Baton Rouge, 1976)

B. Varchi: *Orazione funerale di M. Benedetto Varchi fatta e recitata da lui pubblicamente nell'esequie di Michelagnolo Buonarroti in Firenze, nella chiesa di San Lorenzo* (Florence, 1564)

Esequie del divino Michelagnolo Buonarroti celebrate in Firenze dall'Accademia de pittori, scultori, & architettori, nella chiesa di San Lorenzo il di 14 luglio MDLXIIII (Florence, 1564), facs. and trans. in R. Wittkower and M. W. Wittkower, eds: *The Divine Michelangelo: The Florentine Academy's Homage on his Death in 1564* (London, 1964)

P. Barocchi, ed.: *G. Vasari: La vita di Michelangelo nelle redazioni del 1550 e del 1568*, Documenti di filologia, v, 5 vols (Milan and Naples, 1962)

G. Corti: 'Una ricordanza di Giovan Battista Figiovanni', *Paragone*, xv/175 (1964), pp. 24–31

L. Bardeschi and P. Barocchi, eds: *I ricordi di Michelangelo* (Florence, 1970)

E. Ristori: 'Una lettera a Michelangelo degli operai di S Maria del Fiore, 31 luglio, 1507', *Rinascimento*, xxiii (1983), pp. 167–72

E. Wallace: 'An Unpublished Michelangelo Document', *Burl. Mag.*, cxxix (1987), pp. 181–4

MODERN WORKS

J. A. Symonds: *The Life of Michelangelo Buonarroti: Based on Studies in the Archives of the Buonarroti Family at Florence*, 2 vols (London, 1893)

H. Thode: *Michelangelo: Kritische Untersuchungen über seine Werke: Verzeichnis der Zeichnungen, Kartons und Modelle*, 3 vols (Berlin, 1913)

E. Steinmann and R. W. Steinmann: *Michelangelo-Bibliographie, 1510–1926* (Leipzig, 1927/*R* Hildesheim, 1967), i of *Römische Forschungen der Bibliotheca Hertziana* (Leipzig, 1927–)

C. de Tolnay: *Michelangelo*, 5 vols (Princeton, 1943–60)

E. N. Girardi: *Studi sulle rime di Michelangelo* (Milan, 1964)

C. de Tolnay: *The Art and Thought of Michelangelo* (New York, 1964)

The Complete Works of Michelangelo, 2 vols (London, 1965)

H. V. Einem: *Michelangelo* (London, 1973)

L. Düssler: *Michelangelo-Bibliographie, 1927–1970* (Weisbaden, 1974)

E. N. Girardi: *Studi su Michelangelo scrittore* (Florence, 1974)

H. Hibbard: *Michelangelo* (London, 1979)

J. Wilde: *Michelangelo: Six Lectures* (Oxford, 1979)

K. Lippincott: 'When Was Michelangelo Born?', *J. Warb. & Court. Inst.*, lii (1989), pp. 282–3

J. K. Cadogan: 'Michelangelo in the Workshop of Domenico Ghirlandaio', *Burl. Mag.*, cxxxv (1993), pp. 30–31

I. Life and work. II. Working methods and technique. III. Character and personality. IV. Critical reception and reputation.

I. Life and work.

Michelangelo frequently practised as a painter, sculptor and architect simultaneously, and, like many of his contemporaries, regarded the three arts as manifestations of the fundamental discipline of *disegno*, itself based on a profound knowledge of the male human form; it is, however, convenient to discuss each art separately.

1. Sculpture. 2. Painting. 3. Drawing. 4. Architecture.

1. SCULPTURE. Michelangelo's reputation as a sculptor was established early and has rarely been questioned. Until the 20th century he was commonly regarded as the most important sculptor of the modern era. His work is idiosyncratic, of exceptional expressive power and of strikingly limited range. It consists in the main of monumental marble statuary. He sometimes worked in media other than marble to oblige friends or especially powerful patrons, but he encouraged the identification of his sculpture with stone.

Michelangelo jokingly told Vasari that he had 'sucked in the chisels and mallet' of his trade with the milk of his wetnurse, a stone-carver's wife from Settignano. Long months spent at the quarries in Carrara in the course of his professional career, choosing pieces of marble, are proof of his care for the materials of the craft. His vision of fashioning colossal figures from the mountains indicates that it was only this aspect of the natural world that could stimulate his art. In his verse, among the conventional metaphors derived from Petrarch, his unconventionally abrasive intellect is signalled by a series of images drawn from the excavation and working of rock.

Attempts have been made to identify a hidden thematic unity in all his work. Notably, it has been argued by Tolnay and others that many projects reflect the ideas of NEO-PLATONISM absorbed by the young artist during his stay in the household of Lorenzo the Magnificent. From this premise the whole oeuvre has been interpreted in the light of Neo-Platonic ideas. While there are loose links between Michelangelo's funerary monuments, there is nothing to warrant the elaborate interpretations that have been proposed. These rely too much on speculation about missing elements, and the analysis of symbols cannot be sustained in detail. Passages in Condivi's biography have been used as evidence that Michelangelo incorporated a private symbolism into his work, but his remarks concern Michelangelo's dramatic interpretation of subjects provided by patrons, not hidden programmes.

(i) Training and early work, to *c.* 1505. (ii) Tomb of *Julius II*: early phases, 1505–19. (iii) New Sacristy, 1519–34. (iv) Late work, 1534–64. (v) Unfinished works.

(i) Training and early work, to c. *1505.* Michelangelo's training as a carver remains mysterious. His family was from the minor bourgeoisie of Florence, and, unlike most artists of his generation, he had formal schooling until the age of 13. In 1488 he was apprenticed as a painter in the workshop of DOMENICO GHIRLANDAIO in Florence. Only during the following year did he join a group of young sculptors in the garden of the Medici casino at S Marco, against the wishes of his father, who believed that sculpture, a manual trade, was beneath the family's standing. At the age of about 17 he simply emerged as the sculptor of a precociously assured relief, the *Battle of the Centaurs* (Florence, Casa Buonarroti).

If formal instruction were offered in the Medici Garden, no information about it has survived. According to Condivi, Michelangelo first taught himself sculpture by borrowing tools from masons working on the S Marco library in order to copy the antique head of a faun. This work supposedly attracted the attention of Lorenzo the Magnificent (see MEDICI, DE', (5)), who made the teenage sculptor a member of his own household and reconciled Lodovico Buonarroti to his son's chosen career. Condivi's account of his master's youth, however, is characterized throughout by a tendency to deny Michelangelo's dependence on any other artist, including Ghirlandaio. Vasari, by contrast, claimed that BERTOLDO DI GIOVANNI was in charge of the young sculptors at S Marco. Although Bertoldo was not a stone-carver but a maker of small bronzes, this version of events seems more plausible than Condivi's because there is a generic relationship between Bertoldo's plaque of a *Battle* (Florence, Bargello) and Michelangelo's *Battle* scene.

It is a superficial resemblance. The *Battle of the Centaurs* is such a confident piece of sculpture that it has been regarded as more 'Michelangelesque' than many works that immediately followed it. To some extent, this impression is due to its suggestively unfinished state, but the relief undoubtedly exhibits two features characteristic of the mature Michelangelo: the expression of narrative or emotional excitement through the male nude, and an extreme economy of means. As in Bertoldo's *Battle*, the device of stacking figures in layers one above the other was derived directly from Roman sarcophagi of the Antonine era, but the types are less elegant than those of the older master. Michelangelo consulted a wider range of antique prototypes than Bertoldo, aiming at creative paraphrase rather than archaeological exactness. There is no attempt to depict antique costume or to give characters identifying attributes. The intertwined bodies were packed into a composition far more condensed than any ancient work or its imitation up to that date. The compression of the relief is emphasized by lateral figures which overlap the thin framing rim. A band of rough-hewn marble running across the top dramatizes the way in which the struggling mass below has been squeezed into an area more confined than that of the already small block.

It is probable that the maturity of the *Battle* relief exemplifies the end of a process of learning rather than its beginning. Earlier work may be represented by an even smaller relief, the *Madonna of the Steps* (Florence, Casa Buonarroti). The dating and authenticity of this work have been questioned unnecessarily. One reason for this is that the figures are represented in uncharacteristic shallow relief against an architectural background. As Vasari noted, in the *Madonna* relief Michelangelo imitated and challenged the example of Donatello. This indicates that even Michelangelo experimented in the work of his early maturity. Throughout his late teens and twenties, he also travelled a great deal and worked for a larger range of clients than at any other time in his life. The variety of works produced before 1505 demonstrate a young man's adaptability.

When Lorenzo the Magnificent died in 1492, Michelangelo returned to his father's house for a time during which he carved a figure of *Hercules* (untraced). He studied anatomy by dissecting corpses at the hospital of Santo Spirito under the protection of the prior, for whom he made a wooden Crucifix. This work has been identified as the Crucifix (Florence, Casa Buonarroti) found at Santo Spirito (Lisner, 1964). Since it is the only recorded wooden sculpture by Michelangelo, it is difficult to compare with his other work. The smooth transitions of the muscular articulation have caused some writers to doubt the attribution, although a comparison with the *Bacchus* (Florence, Bargello) is instructive, and the painting of flesh bears comparison with surviving panel pictures.

For a brief period Michelangelo returned to the Medici household, where he was employed by Piero de' Medici. Before the Medici were expelled by the Republican government in 1494, Michelangelo had left Florence, moving first to Venice, then settling in Bologna in the house of Giovanni Francesco ALDROVANDI, a patron who encouraged his interest in vernacular literature. In Bologna he provided small statues for the shrine of S Domenico, left incomplete by Niccolò dell'Arca: a kneeling *Angel* bearing a candelabrum, and the figures of *St Proculus* and *St Petronius* (Bologna, S Domenico Maggiore). Each of these sculptures displays a different quality, a fact for which various explanations have been offered. For some writers, the *St Petronius* is said to betray the influence of Jacopo della Quercia, although it is difficult to distinguish here between stylistic borrowing and resemblance due to identity of iconographic type. Others have supposed it to represent a figure begun by another sculptor and completed by Michelangelo, a suggestion that has also been made in connection with the *St Proculus*. Scholarly uncertainty reflects Michelangelo's successful accomplishment of a brief to integrate these works into the existing ensemble. The *Angel*, whose authenticity is not in doubt, although more stocky than the counterpart completed by Michelangelo's predecessor, is in finish delicately attuned to Niccolò's example.

Late in 1495 Michelangelo returned to Florence, where he carved a figure of *St John the Baptist* and a *Sleeping Cupid* (both untraced). The *Sleeping Cupid* brought him to the attention of Cardinal RAFFAELE RIARIO, who summoned him to Rome in the summer of 1496 and ordered the figure of *Bacchus* (Florence, Bargello). The statue was initially designed to compliment Riario's collection of antiquities, but for unknown reasons it entered the collection of JACOPO GALLI in 1497 and was exhibited in his garden among a group of antique fragments. Galli commissioned two more sculptures, a *Cupid* and a *St John* (both untraced). The armless figure of a *Cupid* (New York, French Embassy Cult. Bldg), carved in part imitation of the Antique, was attributed to the youthful Michelangelo by Kathleen Weill-Garris Brandt (1996), though so far this must remain a speculative attribution.

The *Bacchus* was undoubtedly conceived as an exercise in the Antique. As a garden statue, it is superficially untypical of Michelangelo, being a free-standing group, designed to be viewed in the round; most of Michelangelo's surviving works were conceived for architectural settings with restricted viewpoints. The 'pictorial' finish of the *Bacchus* has been widely disliked, probably because the dull surface sheen of the god's plump flesh, carefully differentiated from the curling goat-hair of the attendant satyr, is seen as suggestive of an unwholesome sensuality unworthy of the artist. The use of contrasting textures is not unusual in Michelangelo's sculpture, however.

Such contrast certainly is a feature of the Roman *Pietà* (Rome, St Peter's; see fig. 1), the work that marked the turning-point in Michelangelo's fortunes. Commissioned in 1497 by the French Cardinal Jean Villiers de La Grolais (*c.* 1430–99) for his own tomb, it was begun the following year and was finished by 1500. It signals the beginning of Michelangelo's maturity as a sculptor. The style of the group does not differ radically from the practice represented by the *Bacchus*, however. Rather it shows even greater textural richness, a characteristic noted by Vasari in his description of the inert body of Christ. This sensitively carved surface is strongly contrasted with the unpolished textures of rock and tree stump. Although the

1. Michelangelo: *Pietà*, marble, 1.74×1.95 m, 1497–1500 (Rome, St Peter's)

dazzling virtuosity of the carving is less appreciated now than it was in the 16th century, there is general agreement that the *Pietà* is a work of unprecedented elegance. Its grace of contour is most apparent in the drapery: the tight, dampfold loincloth of Christ, the ruches and complex crinkles of Mary's robes and the controlled but generous sweep of the shroud, which both cradles and displays Christ's corpse. Much of the pathos of the group derives from this drapery. The Virgin shows no grief; her features are composed and the gesture of her left hand is designed to draw attention to her dead son.

Following this triumph Michelangelo returned to Florence, where between 1501 and 1504 he executed four out of fifteen small statues he had contracted to provide for the Piccolomini Altar in Siena Cathedral (*in situ*). Simultaneously, he worked on the gigantic *David* (Florence, Accad.; *see* ITALY, fig. 54), and there seems little doubt that he thought of this as the more important commission. The marble block used for the *David* had been roughed out and abandoned by Agostino del Duccio and Michelangelo was thus required to work within predetermined constraints. Some peculiarities of the work, such as the relative shallowness of the lateral views of the figure, may be due to the existing shape of the marble; Vasari claimed that the splayed legs were determined by earlier piercing of the block.

The work's significance does not lie in its technical ingenuity, however. The *David* is the first of Michelangelo's surviving depictions of the heroic male nude in which the entire emotional charge is carried by the articulation and twist of the body and limbs against the head. Stripped of all attributes but the minimal sling, this *David* carries no sword, and not even the head of Goliath distracts from his stark nudity. The figure's authority seems to stem from the swing of the thorax, within which is a dramatic play of intercostal and abdominal muscles, stretched on the left, compressed on the right. But other details—the highly particularized right hand, for example, large, veined, quite unideal—suggest latent power in a figure apparently at rest. In a formal sense, the *David* is a classicizing work recalling the *Dioscuri* (Rome, Quirinale) or nudes found on Roman sarcophagi, perhaps mediated by Nicola Pisano's Herculean figure of *Fortitude* (Pisa, Baptistery, pulpit). Conceptually, however, it was unprecedented. Wölfflin's objection to the representation of David as an adolescent 'hobbledehoy' and to the ugliness of the gap between the figure's legs draws attention to the combination of the heroic with the vulnerable that makes the *David* so foreign to its antique sources.

Work on the marble *David* coincided with an exceptionally busy period of overlapping activity in which, however, Michelangelo left much unfinished or even undone. A second, bronze *David* (untraced), commissioned by the Republican government in 1502 as an ambassadorial gift to the French, was cast only in 1508 in Michelangelo's absence. The scheme initiated in 1503 to provide Florence Cathedral with statues of 12 Apostles resulted in a single unfinished figure of *St Matthew* (Florence, Accad.). A plan to fresco the great hall, the Sala del Gran Consiglio, in the Palazzo Vecchio, Florence, with a depiction of the *Battle of Cascina* certainly interrupted his sculptural activity. A new contract for the remaining

statues for the Piccolomini Altar was signed in 1504, but Michelangelo did nothing further for this project. Failure to fulfil his obligations to the Piccolomini family was the first sign of an increasingly reckless ambition that played havoc with his professional life during the following decade. By the time the second Piccolomini contract had been drawn up, he was probably already at work on the Bruges *Madonna* (Bruges, Onze Lieve Vrouw), a finished statue of the *Virgin and Child* bought by the Flemish merchant Alexander Mouscron and shipped to Bruges in 1506. Two marble roundels of the *Virgin and Child*, the Pitti Tondo (Florence, Bargello) and the Taddei Tondo (London, RA) seem to have been begun between 1504 and 1507, but were left incomplete. It seems quite extraordinary that Michelangelo also completed a panel painting during this period, the *Holy Family* (Doni Tondo; Florence, Uffizi). Around 1504, too, he seems to have made his first experiments as a poet. By this time status, income and force of personality had made him virtual head of the Buonarroti family, though his father survived until 1534.

The Bruges *Madonna* is one of Michelangelo's most accomplished carvings. The apparently simple and compact relationship between Child and Virgin was carefully calculated to take account of its intended position in the church, about which he obviously had reliable information. (Ironically, it was subsequently positioned incorrectly in the niche made for it at Bruges.) The group strikingly contrasts a cool and heiratic figure of the Virgin with an animated Christ Child whose subtly twisting body she encloses and protects as though he were still sheltered within her body. The interplay between infancy and majesty was maintained in the Pitti Tondo while in the Taddei Tondo the contrast between a still Virgin and active child passes over into symbolic narrative, as the infant Christ shrinks from St John's gift, probably a goldfinch signifying the Passion. These two unfinished tondi were the last reliefs Michelangelo carved. The *St Matthew*, which is a relief only by virtue of its incompleteness, often receives more sympathetic attention than Michelangelo's contemporaneous sculpture because, as a figure subjected to powerful torsion, it seems to anticipate later, more famous works.

(ii) Tomb of 'Julius II': early phases, 1505–19. In addition to this remarkable roster of tasks, Michelangelo had other commitments. In 1505 he was called to Rome by Pope Julius II (*see* ROVERE, DELLA (i), (2)) to plan a magnificent tomb for St Peter's. By 1506 he was making drawings preparatory to painting the vault of the Sistine Chapel (Rome, Vatican), also for Julius. This seemingly perfect match between an ambitious pontiff and an ambitious artist was disastrous for Michelangelo's career in one respect: until 1545 his life was dominated by repeated failures to complete the Julian monument, what Condivi called 'the tragedy of the tomb'. In order to discuss the next stage of Michelangelo's development as a sculptor, it is necessary to outline the events that affected work on the monument from 1505 to 1519.

The most valuable source of information on the first plans for the tomb, is Condivi, who gives convincing measurements, although his description is tantalizingly incomplete. What Michelangelo and Julius proposed was a free-standing, three-storey monument, covering an area of over 70 sq. m. The lowest level, housing the papal sarcophagus, was to be decorated with figures of captives symbolizing the Liberal Arts. Above them, on each corner of the cornice, a large figure was to have been seated, one of them a *Moses*. On the upper level was to be an effigy of Julius, flanked by two angels, one weeping to signify that the world had lost a benefactor, one rejoicing at his translation to heaven. It has been calculated that 47 figures would have been required for the tomb. Given the enormous scale of this commission, it is hardly surprising that Michelangelo's attention shifted to Rome in 1505–6. Marble arrived for the gigantic mausoleum, and he was eager to begin work, but Julius unaccountably cooled towards the project. After the first of a series of disputes with the Pope, Michelangelo fled to Florence. When he was recalled to Rome by Julius, it was for a new project. He spent much of 1507 in Bologna preparing a gigantic bronze statue of the Pope. This apparently menacing image of the city's conqueror was set on the façade of S Petronio, Bologna, and subsequently melted down for cannon when the Bentivoglio regained control of the city in 1511.

For four years, between 1508 and October 1512, Michelangelo was occupied by the Sistine Chapel Ceiling. Following the Pope's death in February 1513, he signed a second contract with Julius's executors for a reduced version of the tomb to be completed within seven years. This still massive undertaking, which is recorded in documents and drawings, was for a three-sided structure attached to the wall. There were to be six figures on the cornice, while above the contract specified a 'capelletta', a tabernacle, with a sculpted image of the Virgin and Child. For this scheme he began the *Moses* as well as the figures known as the *Dying Captive* (see fig. 2) and the *Rebellious Captive* (both Paris, Louvre).

The tomb did not occupy Michelangelo's attention exclusively, however. Following the election of Leo X (*see* MEDICI, DE', (7)), he received a commission to refurbish the façade of the papal chapel in Castel Sant'Angelo, Rome. In 1514, moreover, he signed a contract to make the *Risen Christ* (Rome, S Maria sopra Minerva) for Metello Vari, although it was delivered only in 1521. Finally, from 1515 to 1518, he attempted, with some underhand manoeuvres, to obtain the commission to design the façade of S Lorenzo, the Medici church in Florence, and to furnish it with an ambitious number of statues and reliefs. The façade project was cancelled by the patrons in 1519.

A third contract for a still smaller Julian monument had been drawn up in 1516, for which he probably began the four *Slaves* (Florence, Accad.). These commitments did not prevent him from undertaking or allow him to refuse the task of designing windows for Palazzo Medici in 1517. Conflicting demands began to take a heavy toll of his work and of his self-esteem. 'I have become a swindler against my will', he wrote in connection with the *Risen Christ*, but the phrase summed up his general predicament at this time and was marginally more honest than some of his subsequent accounts of this period.

Michelangelo's sculptural manner did not develop in a linear fashion, and the figures prepared for the two versions of the Julian monument present special problems for anyone attempting to characterize his style at any time. One difficulty is that these works do not necessarily represent a unified period in the artist's career. Different schemes for the tomb required Michelangelo to conceive statues in varying ways, and items were worked on over considerable periods of time, with frequent interruptions

2. Michelangelo: *Dying Captive*, figure for the tomb of *Julius II*, marble, h. 2.29 m, *c.* 1514 (Paris, Musée du Louvre)

followed by campaigns of intensive labour. Comparisons with his work in other media may be misleading. It has often been said that Michelangelo realized his impossible dreams for the first version of the Julian tomb in the figures painted on the Sistine Chapel Ceiling. The converse also can be argued: that the inventions of the Sistine Ceiling, which grew in scale and power between its inception in 1508 and its completion in 1512, helped to form a new, more massive ideal perceptible in the sculptured figures. The *Moses* is the statue most obviously related to the Prophets on the Sistine Ceiling (*see* REPRODUCTION OF WORKS OF ART, fig. 7).

Assessment of the *Moses* is further complicated by the fact that it is not in the position for which it was planned. Originally designed to stand some 13 feet above the ground, the statue was incorporated in the central recess of the finished tomb of 1545, only a few feet above floor-level. There are indications that most of the statue had been completed before it was decided to change the intended location. It has been observed that the figure's exaggeratedly long waist and withdrawn left leg would have enabled a viewer below to see the gesture made by the left arm (Wilde, 1954). The resemblance is often noted between this work and Donatello's *St John the Evangelist* (Florence, Mus. Opera Duomo; *see* DONATELLO, fig. 1), the proportions of which were also adapted to be seen from below. Unlike the *St John*, the *Moses* was planned as a corner figure standing free of the architecture and offering a number of subsidiary views. Yet the placement of the statue was Michelangelo's decision. Indeed the effect of confinement was even greater originally, when he set the work further back in the recess. (It was moved forward in 1816 when a cast was taken from it.)

None of these considerations detracts from the magisterial quality of the sculpture. Indeed, by bringing the statue closer to the spectator and squeezing it so uncomfortably within the completed monument, Michelangelo may have enhanced an effect of force and energy that could have been dissipated at longer range. The figure's large size becomes insistent, and the imperious, but strangely indeterminate, facial expression may be discerned clearly, so altering the psychological charge carried by the work. This cannot happen, for example, with the tall, free-standing figure of *David*, whose similar gaze and furrowed brow create less tension.

Almost the opposite change of context has affected the view of the *Dying Captive* (Paris, Louvre; see fig. 2), a figure intended for a niche, but now exhibited as a free-standing pendant to the *Rebellious Captive*. The traditional titles for these statues serve to differentiate their characters, but they should not control the viewer's response: the figures were not created as a pair but as elements in a large sequence, a theme with variations potentially as rich as those provided by the *ignudi* on the Sistine Chapel Ceiling. The *Dying Captive* in particular suggests the quality of work that was lost through Michelangelo's inability to complete the whole tomb satisfactorily: the statue was brought to an unusually high state of resolution and reveals a moving sensuousness unusual in the conception of the male nude in Western sculpture. As a group, the *Captives* were deliberately differentiated from the *Moses* because they served separate functions and had distinct symbolic roles within the scheme of the monument. All three figures, however, show an increased feeling for the three-dimensionality of sculpture. In the *Dying Captive*, a form made to be seen from a relatively restricted series of viewpoints, there is no contour that may be transcribed simply in two dimensions and no surface plane that is not continuously turned into another.

Although planned for a significantly different version of the tomb project, the four *Slaves* (e.g. fig. 3) from the 1516 campaign also exemplify this principle, and they should not be regarded as a totally new departure. While a certain massiveness characterizes all figures devised for the Julian monument, two in particular, the *Bearded Slave* and the *Awakening Slave*, with their grosser proportions, may appear to anticipate the ideal of heroic masculinity that appears in the later frescoes. This view is mistaken. In part the effect is created by Michelangelo's distinctive interpretation of the heavy muscularity that conventionally characterizes older men in antique statuary; in part it

3. Michelangelo: *Atlas Slave*, figure for the tomb of *Julius II*, marble, h. 2.5 m, *c*. 1520 (Florence, Galleria dell'Accademia)

perhaps arises because some sections were only roughed out.

Because of the demands of the tomb project and the fruitless diversion of the S Lorenzo façade, in the three decades after the completion of the Sistine Chapel Ceiling Michelangelo presented to the public only one finished work, the statue of the *Risen Christ* (Rome, S Maria sopra Minerva). This is the second version of the work. While carving the figure, the artist uncovered an unsightly flaw in the area of the face and he began carving a new block. It has been among the least admired of Michelangelo's statues. Pope-Hennessy regarded it as a replica lacking the vibrant surface expected in an authentic marble. It may be, however, that modern critical taste is simply out of sympathy with the whole concept of this naked, Apollo-like Christ languidly supporting the cross and other instruments of the Passion. As a relaxed male nude, it exhibits a refined elegance at variance with those signs of energy, tension and unrest normally associated with Michelangelo's art. Its success as a devotional image, however, suggests that the faithful are more at ease with the notion of a Lord of perfect beauty than scholars have been.

(iii) New Sacristy, 1519–34. When the façade project for S Lorenzo was abruptly dropped in 1519, Michelangelo was ordered to build a Medici funerary chapel at S Lorenzo (the New Sacristy; *see* §4(i) below). Work on this went ahead rapidly until the death of Leo X in 1521. During the brief pontificate of Adrian VI (*reg* 1522–3), when Michelangelo could no longer count on the protection of a powerful patron, the della Rovere heirs of Julius threatened litigation over the tomb. The election of Pope Clement VII (*see* MEDICI, DE', (9)) in 1523 saved him from the worst consequences, but negotiations with the della Rovere family continued. Work resumed on the New Sacristy at this time, and more projects were added to Michelangelo's workload, notably a library over the cloisters adjoining S Lorenzo and a reliquary tribune on the inside of the church façade.

In 1527 the Medicean government of Florence was expelled from the city, and work at S Lorenzo was suspended. Michelangelo probably continued to carve figures for the Julius tomb, but he also agreed to provide the new Republic with a group of *Samson Slaying the Philistines*. Little was done for this, apart perhaps from a small model, since in 1528 he became military engineer to Florence. Disagreement with the military committee caused a temporary flight to Venice but, following a brief visit to Ferrara where he undertook to provide the Duke, Alfonso I d'Este, with a painting of *Leda* (untraced), Michelangelo returned to his post in November 1529.

The Republic fell in 1530, and for some months after Michelangelo hid from possible Medici reprisals. Pardoned by Clement VII, he worked intensively at S Lorenzo and began a statue of *Apollo* (Florence, Bargello) for Baccio Valori. After bitter negotiations with the della Rovere heirs, in 1532 a fourth contract was drawn up for a yet more modest version of the tomb, planned for Julius's former titular church in Rome, S Pietro in Vincoli. That year Michelangelo fell in love with the young Roman nobleman Tommaso de' Cavalieri (*d* 1565). Following the

death of Clement VII in 1534, he settled permanently in Rome.

In terms of sculpture, this period of Michelangelo's life was dominated by the work for the New Sacristy. The ensemble is lamentably incomplete, and many details planned for it remain unknown, but the Medici tombs give a better sense of the plenitude of Michelangelo's inventive powers than the scattered fragments of successive schemes for the Julius monument. The history of the scheme has parallels with that of the project for Julius. Clement's first idea was to construct a free-standing monument beneath the dome of the chapel to house his own sarcophagus. He then decided to exclude himself from the plans and to build two wall tombs for recently deceased members of the family, Giuliano de' Medici, Duc de Nemours, and Lorenzo de' Medici, Duke of Urbino. The two later became known as the *Capitani* because of the Roman military uniforms worn by their effigies. The marble frameworks and the four allegorical figures of the *Times of Day* for these tombs occupy the lateral walls of the chamber (see fig. 4). The ensemble was to have been completed by a splendid double monument on the entrance wall of the chapel to commemorate the *Magnifici*, two 15th-century Medici, also named Giuliano and Lorenzo. As the priest offering masses for the dead officiated from the small tribune behind the altar, looking across to the entrance wall, this double tomb was conceived unusually as a displaced altarpiece, to be surmounted by a

4. Michelangelo: tomb of *Lorenzo de' Medici*, marble, 1519–33, New Sacristy, S Lorenzo, Florence

statue of the *Virgin and Child* (the Medici *Madonna*). No part of this tomb was built, and the only reminder of the original plan is the unfinished *Madonna* flanked by statues of the Medici saints, *Cosmas* and *Damian*. *Cosmas* was carved to Michelangelo's design by Giovanni Angelo Montorsoli (for illustration *see* MONTORSOLI, GIOVANNI ANGELO) and *Damian* by Raffaello da Montelupo. The three figures are mounted on a platform that bears no relation to the original scheme. Additional figures were to have included four river gods beneath the two tombs of the *Capitani*, symbolic figures of a grieving *Earth* and laughing *Heaven* in the niches on either side of Giuliano's effigy and other insecurely identifiable items. According to Condivi, the *Times of Day* symbolized 'the principle of time which consumes everything'. All the autograph carvings for the New Sacristy were executed between 1524 and 1534.

The Medici sculptures represent a distinctly new physical type, also found in Michelangelo's drawings from this period. The aim seems to have been to express great power in the most relaxed and elegant form. The figures have small heads on massive torsos, muscular, tapering thighs and slender ankles, an ideal most clearly articulated in the figure of *Giuliano de' Medici* and that of the youth in a contemporary work, the *Victory* (Florence, Pal. Vecchio). Of the figures prepared for the New Sacristy, only the *Day* departs from this model. Formally, the figures are among the most spatially interesting sculptures in the European tradition. The allegorical figures in particular were designed to be viewed from many different vantage-points within the chapel.

The New Sacristy is also of interest because it contains Michelangelo's only two sculptured female nudes. Unlike comparable figures by other artists, they have been conceived without a trace of eroticism, and it is the absence of obvious sexuality that gives these works their uneasy power. Appropriately, the skin of *Dawn* is sleek and unmarked while the figure of *Night* has a more aged body, marked by greater experience. A similar, less marked contrast is apparent in the two male figures.

The effigies of the *Capitani* partake of these contrasts, the alert figure of Giuliano associated with the positive and negative poles of *Night* and *Day*, Lorenzo with the shadowy allegories of twilight. Michelangelo stated that the *Capitani* figures were not portraits but idealized representations, endowed with the dignity and power that the men should have had. The contrast between the 'melancholic' Lorenzo and the 'sanguine' Giuliano has long been remarked, and Michelangelo seems to have taken great care to place the face of *Lorenzo* in shadow. As a formal invention, this brooding presence is unprecedented. The *Giuliano*, in which sprightliness is mixed with force, remains one of the most original statues of the 16th century.

Of all the unhoused figures carved by Michelangelo, the *Madonna* of the New Sacristy appears the most awkwardly placed in its setting. Perhaps because the still-unpolished surface of the stone blurs much of the definition of the figures, this, Michelangelo's final sculptured *Virgin and Child*, has an especially insubstantial look. As a devotional object, the group also appears puzzling. The tall figure of the Virgin has the regal, expressionless calm

common to all his depictions of this theme, but the infant Christ, dramatically turned to seek his mother's breast, is at once the most actively Herculean and the most withdrawn of Michelangelo's images of the Saviour.

Of the sculptures associated with this period of Michelangelo's life, the *Victory* group poses the greatest difficulty for historians. It has been dated at various times between 1519 and 1530, and its purpose is obscure. The youth kneeling on the body of the bearded old man wears a wreath of oak leaves, and this detail indicates that it is another abandoned work for the Julius tomb. As a model, the *Victory* had a powerful effect in Florence, where younger sculptors including Vincenzio Danti (for illustration *see* DANTI, (1)) and Giambologna (*see* GIAMBOLOGNA, fig. 1) produced variants. Combining helical motion with a pyramidal construction, the group has been regarded as the epitome of the *figura serpentinata* that Lomazzo claimed Michelangelo advocated as a compositional principle. While the *Victory* can indeed be understood in this way, it should be remembered that the words Lomazzo attributed to Michelangelo related to painting, not sculpture.

(iv) Late work, 1534–64. During the 1530s and 1540s the pattern of the aging Michelangelo's life changed drastically. In 1534 Clement VII decided to have him paint the altar wall of the Sistine Chapel, and his successor, Paul III (*see* FARNESE, (1)), proceeded with this plan. In 1535 Pope Paul appointed Michelangelo 'supreme architect, sculptor and painter' to the Apostolic Court, and in the following year he issued a decree freeing him from all obligations to the della Rovere heirs, although plans to complete Julius's monument continued. During 1536 Michelangelo was introduced to VITTORIA COLONNA, and the influence of her commitment to the Catholic Reformation is detectable in the sacred poetry he wrote over the following decade. In the same year he began painting the *Last Judgement* in the Sistine Chapel. On its completion in 1541, the Pope commissioned the frescoes for the Pauline Chapel, also in the Vatican. In 1542 a fifth, and final, contract for the Julius tomb was drawn up, and three years later an unsatisfactory monument was erected in S Pietro in Vincoli. It was the end of the 'tragedy of the tomb'. Only three of the statues, the *Moses*, *Rachel* and *Leah*, were carved by Michelangelo himself. Interrupted by illness, he worked on the Pauline frescoes from 1542 until 1550. During the second half of the 1540s Michelangelo probably began the *Brutus* (Florence, Bargello), his last commissioned sculpture, for Cardinal Niccolò Ridolfi. The Florentine *Pietà* (Florence, Mus. Opera Duomo) and the Rondanini *Pietà* (Milan, Castello Sforzesco) were undertaken on his own initiative. Apart from these works, the final two decades were dominated by an increasingly ramifying architectural practice (*see* §4 below).

The last phase of Michelangelo's sculptural activity comprises the smallest group of works, but the most difficult to assess in conventional terms. These apparently personal sculptures pose the most acute attributional and chronological problems. The figures of *Rachel* and *Leah* are good examples. The final agreement for the Julius tomb specifies that the two statues flanking the *Moses* were to be carved by Raffaello da Montelupo. Condivi and Vasari, however, clearly attributed them to Michelangelo himself, a view that is generally accepted, although it has been suggested that they were conceived at different times. They also show inconsistencies: *Rachel* is noticeably shorter than *Leah* and has a rectangular rather than a rounded base. It is clear, however, that they represent allegories of the Contemplative Life and the Active Life respectively.

Michelangelo gave both the *Brutus* and the Florentine *Pietà* to Tiberio Calcagni (1532–65) for completion. The condition of the *Pietà* is far from ideal. The left leg of Christ is missing and there are obvious repairs to other breaks. Nor is there agreement on the type and scope of Calcagni's intervention. The Palestrina *Pietà* (Florence, Accad.) is of doubtful authenticity. Only the Rondanini *Pietà* is securely authentic and safely datable to the artist's very last years, but it is a shattered fragment. A radical change of plan led Michelangelo to mutilate the group so that the upper parts of the Virgin and Christ were left as shallow, ghostly presences beside a single, substantial right arm, the remnant of a previous more conventional version. A head and part of the torso belonging to the earlier scheme (Florence, Pal. Vecchio) was discovered in 1973. The legs of Christ, which probably date from the earlier composition, also show signs of modification. It is probable that the first carving was begun in the 1550s and the radical cutting back of the two figures took place in the very last years of Michelangelo's life. According to a letter of Daniele da Volterra, he was at work on the group only five days before his death.

The spectral quality of the Rondanini *Pietà* has been used to support the view that at the end of his life Michelangelo inclined towards an aesthetic of renunciation. Allegedly rejecting the full, twisting forms characteristic of his earlier work, he reduced the piece to a pair of stark columnar figures, tensely bent forward. It has been suggested that the compositional scheme shows an affinity with northern, or even with Gothic art. The idea that Michelangelo adopted medieval motifs late in life has become a recurrent theme among writers. The combination of Classical and medieval elements has been noted even in the *Rachel* and *Leah*. But echoes of medieval motifs are not exclusive to work of his last decades. By stressing certain elements in the late figures and linking them with Michelangelo's adherence to the reform movement within the Roman Church, a spurious argument is proposed, falsely associating Gothic with Christian. The private nature of these late uncommissioned works should not be exaggerated, although it is plausible that they reflect Michelangelo's desire for personal redemption and are meditations on salvation akin to his drawings and poems of this period; they also seem to have had a shadowy public purpose. According to Vasari, the Florentine *Pietà*, which includes a self-portrait of the artist as Nicodemus, originally had been intended to surmount Michelangelo's own tomb. The Rondanini *Pietà*, though kept in Michelangelo's studio until his death, seems to have been promised to a client.

(v) Unfinished works. Discussion of abandoned works, the 'non-finito', has been confused by the claim that lack of finish should be regarded as an expressive device essential to Michelangelo's art. This view became especially prominent after Auguste Rodin had established a taste for images only partly emerging from rough stone. The suggestion that Michelangelo's failure to complete works arose from a dissatisfaction with the expressive limitations of craft perfection is an extreme example of the view that great genius manifests impatience with the limitations of any medium. According to one version of this approach, the incomplete state of Michelangelo's carvings was due to an irresolvable tension between pagan and Christian principles. It is far more likely that much of Michelangelo's sculptured oeuvre was abandoned because he committed himself simultaneously to too many projects. Evidence for this comes from his own criticism of the rough surfaces of Donatello's sculpture, as reported in Vasari's biography, and from what is recorded of his fastidious regard for the quality of marble. His abandonment of the first version of the *Risen Christ* on the revelation of a flaw in the stone is a good example of this. Whenever possible, he crisply articulated surface detail and gave his statuary a final polish. In this respect there is no distinction between early and late work. A more accurate idea of Michelangelo's standards of craftmanship may be gained from a study of the *Rachel* and *Leah* than from the Rondanini *Pietà*. Of the apparently 'unfinished' elements in his completed sculptures, most are deliberate textural differentiation. The remainder are parts that were not meant to be seen at close quarters or seen at all, such as the roughly chiselled patch of neck behind the beard of *Moses*, or the back of the *Risen Christ*.

Admiration for Michelangelo's work ensured that much of his statuary was preserved, even when its condition would have been considered unacceptable as the work of other artists. His work was so highly valued that the slightest sketch was coveted, and it is not surprising that even imperfect sculptures were sought after. When there was a delay in delivering the second version of the *Risen Christ*, Metello Vari demanded the unfinished first version (untraced) and installed it in his garden. Michelangelo himself gave the two abandoned *Captives* to Roberto Strozzi as tokens of affection. His contemporaries were therefore forced to come to terms with the incompleteness of the sculpture. This occurred in three ways. First, Michelangelo's inventive power was so much admired that his unfinished works were regarded by other artists as a legitimate quarry for ideas. Raphael, for example, struck by the mere adumbration of the *St Matthew*, copied it in pen and ink (Chatsworth, Derbys). Second, literary strategies were developed for dealing with aborted statues. Vasari was a pioneer, citing the *St Matthew* as a model of decisive carving. He also gave an influential psychological explanation of Michelangelo's abandoned statuary, suggesting that the sculptor did not give final form to his inventions because of his frustration at the gap between conception and execution. Third, in two cases incompleteness was exploited by controlling the conditions of display. The *Brutus*, commissioned by a Medici opponent as a symbol of Republican virtue, was acquired after Michelangelo's death by the Grand Duke of Tuscany, Francesco I (*see* MEDICI, DE', (16)). In the Medici collections it was exhibited accompanied by a Latin verse, which claimed: 'As the sculptor carved the portrait of Brutus from the marble, he remembered his crime, and broke off'. Celebration of the tyrant-slayer was thus subverted, and Michelangelo's failure to complete the work was represented as a praiseworthy moral act. It was also under the Medici that Bernardo Buontalenti incorporated the four *Slaves* from the abandoned Julius tomb into the rough masonry of a grotto in the Boboli Gardens in Florence (replicas *in situ*). Seemingly growing from the rock, the figures served as witty representations of the transformation of nature into artifice.

The predominance of unfinished work in Michelangelo's oeuvre has also contributed to the impression that he was at odds with contemporary aesthetic values. In addition, his incomplete or aborted projects have obscured two aspects of his sculpture that might have modified this picture: relief and the design of ornament. No reliefs appear in Michelangelo's work after 1507, although they were planned for earlier projects for the Julius tomb and for the façade of S Lorenzo, according to drawings (New York, Met.; Florence, Uffizi). In one design for the S Lorenzo façade (Florence, Uffizi), Michelangelo began by adapting a compositional type derived from Lorenzo Ghiberti, a source so unexpected as to bring into question conventional ideas about the limits of his art. Fragmentary survivals give a good idea of Michelangelo's preferences in ornament. The lower storey of the Julius tomb, largely constructed from parts begun between 1513 and 16, shows him to have been a designer of fantastic carving firmly rooted in late 15th-century practice. The New Sacristy, although incomplete, reveals an abundance of invention: the fanciful cuirass of Giuliano's effigy, the bat-headed box on which Lorenzo rests his arm, the poppies and owl of *Night* and the frieze of masks that runs behind (carved by Silvio Cosini). Even what was executed of the decoration for the New Sacristy does not survive intact: stucco figuration for the interior of the dome, designed by Michelangelo and executed by Perino del Vaga, was destroyed by Vasari. Michelangelo's three-dimensional work was fashioned to inhabit a more richly inventive world of ornament than is generally considered appropriate to it. Had these frameworks been completed as he envisaged them, they would have revealed Michelangelo as a less austere sculptor, less isolated from his age, but still dominant of it.

BIBLIOGRAPHY

GENERAL

E. Panofsky: *Tomb Sculpture* (New York, 1964)
C. J. Seymour: *Sculpture in Italy, 1400–1500*, Pelican Hist. A. (Harmondsworth, 1966)
M. Weinberger: *Michelangelo the Sculptor*, 2 vols (London and New York, 1967)
F. Hartt: *Michelangelo: The Complete Sculpture* (London, 1969)
J. Pope-Hennessy: *Italian High Renaissance and Baroque Sculpture* (London, 1970, 3/1985)
J. Poeschke: *Michelangelo und seine Zeit* (1992), ii of *Die Skulptur der Renaissance in Italien* (Munich, 1990–92)

TRAINING AND EARLY WORK

F. Kriegbaum: 'Michelangelos Statuen am Piccolomini-Altar in Dom zu Siena', *Jb. Preuss. Kstsamml.*, lxiii (1942), pp. 57–78
C. Eisler: 'The *Madonna of the Steps*: Problems of Date and Style', *Stil und Überlieferung in der Kunst des Abendlandes: Akten des 21. internationalen Kongresses für Kunstgeschichte: Bonn, 1964*, ii, pp. 115–21
M. Lisner: 'Michelangelos Crucifix aus S Spirito in Florenz', *Münchn. Jb. Bild. Kst*, n. s. 2, xv (1964), pp. 7–37

A. Parronchi: 'Il *Cupido dormiente* di Michelangelo', *Stil und Überlieferung in der Kunst des Abendlandes. Akten des 21. internationalen Kongresses für Kunstgeschichte: Bonn, 1964*, ii, pp. 121–5; repr. in A. Parronchi: *Opere giovanili di Michelangelo, Accademia Toscana di Scienze e Lettere 'La Columbaria': 'Studi'*, x (Florence, 1968)
M. Cali: 'La *Madonna della Scala* di Michelangelo, il Savonarola e la crisi dell'umanesimo', *Boll. A.*, 5th ser., lii (1967), pp. 152–66
C. Seymour: *Michelangelo's 'David': A Search for Identity* (Pittsburgh, 1967)
M. Epton: 'The Taddei Tondi: A Frightened Jesus?', *J. Warb. & Court. Inst.*, xxxii (1969), pp. 391–3
R. Lightbown: 'Michelangelo's Great Tondo: Its Origin and Setting', *Apollo*, lxxxix (1969), pp. 22–31
P. Bargellini: *Michelangelo's 'David': Symbol of Liberty* (Florence, 1971)
H. R. Mancusi-Ungaro: *Michelangelo: The Bruges Madonna and the Piccolomini Altar* (New Haven and London, 1971)
R. de Campos: 'Il restauro della *Pietà* di Michelangelo', *Tutela e conservazione del patrimonio storico e artistico delle chiese in Italia*, xcvii (Rome, 1974), unpaginated insertion
S. Levine: 'The Location of Michelangelo's *David*: The Meeting of January 25, 1504', *A. Bull.*, liv (1974), pp. 31–41
N. R. Park: 'Placement of Michelangelo's *David*: A Review of the Documents', *A. Bull.*, lv (1975), pp. 560–70
D. Ewing: 'Further Observations on the Bruges *Madonna*: Ghiberti as a Source for Michelangelo', *Rev. Belge Archéol. & Hist. A.*, clviii (1979), pp. 77–83
M. Lisner: 'Form und Sinngehalt von Michelangelos *Kentaurenschlacht* mit Notizien zu Bertoldo di Giovanni', *Mitt. Ksthist. Inst. Florenz*, xxiv (1980), pp. 283–344
P. Barocchi: *Il Bacco di Michelangelo* (Florence, 1982)
V. Herzner: 'David Florentinus', *Jb. Berlin. Mus.*, xxiv (1982), pp. 129–34
M. Hirst: 'Michelangelo, Carrara and the Marble for the Cardinal's Pietà', *Burl. Mag.*, cxxvii (1985), pp. 154–9
K. Weil-Garris Brandt: 'Michelangelo's *Pietà* for the Cappella del Re di Francia', *Il se rendit en Italie: Etudes offertes à André Chastel* (Rome, 1987), pp. 77–119
G. Rocchi: 'Tecnica ed espressione nella scultura michelangiolesca con particolare riguardo alla *Pietà* di San Pietro', *Ant. Viva*, xxviii/5–6 (1989), pp. 45–50
J. M. Massing: 'Michelangelo's *Madonna of the Stairs*, Circa 1492: Art in the Age of Exploration*, ed. J. A. Levenson (Washington, 1991), pp. 268–9
C. Elam: 'Lorenzo de' Medici's Sculpture Garden', *Mitt. Ksthist. Inst. Florenz*, xxxvi/1–2 (1992), pp. 41–84
P. Barocchi, ed.: *Il giardino di San Marco: Maestri e compagni del giovane Michelangelo* (Florence, 1992)
K. Weil-Garris Brandt: 'Sculpture Newly Attributed to Michelangelo, *Burl. Mag.* (July 1996; in preparation)

TOMB OF JULIUS II: EARLY PHASES

K. A. Laux: *Michelangelos Juliusmonument* (Berlin, 1943)
J. Wilde: *Michelangelo's 'Victory'*, Charleton Lectures on Art, 36 (Oxford, 1954)
E. Rosenthal: 'Michelangelos *Moses*, dai di sotto in sù', *A. Bull.*, xlvi (1964), pp. 544–50
W. Lotz: 'Zu Michelangelos *Christus* in Santa Maria sopra Minerva', *Festschrift für Herbert von Einem* (Berlin, 1965), pp. 143–50
M. Hirst: 'A Project of Michelangelo's for the Tomb of Julius II', *Master Drgs*, xiv (1976), pp. 375–82
G. S. Panofsky: 'Die Ikonographie von Michelangelos *Christus* in Santa Maria sopra Minerva in Rom', *Münchn. Jb. Bild. Kst*, n. s. 2, xxxix (1988), pp. 89–112
M. Hirst: 'Michelangelo in 1505', *Burl. Mag.*, cxxxiii (1991), pp. 760–66
C. Echinger-Maurach, *Studien zu Michelangelos Juliusgrabmal*, 2 vols (Hildesheim, Zurich and New York, 1991)

NEW SACRISTY

A. E. Popp: *Die Medici-Kappelle Michelangelos* (Munich, 1922)
H. W. Frey: 'Zur Entstehungsgeschichte des Statuenschmuckes der Medici-Kapelle in Florenz', *Z. Kstgesch.*, xiv (1951), pp. 40–96
F. Hartt: 'The Meaning of Michelangelo's Medici Chapel', *Essays in Honour of George Swarzenski* (Chicago, 1951), pp. 145–55
J. Wilde: 'Michelangelo's Designs for the Medici Tombs', *J. War. & Court. Inst.*, xviii (1955), pp. 54–66
W. Goez: 'Annotationen zu Michelangelos Mediceergräbern', *Festschrift für Harald Keller* (Darmstadt, 1963), pp. 235–54
C. Gilbert: 'Texts and Contexts of the Medici Chapel', *A. Q.* [Detroit], xxxiv (1971), pp. 391–407

P. Joannides: 'Michelangelo's Medici Chapel: Some New Suggestions', *Burl. Mag.*, cxiv (1972), pp. 541–51

L. D. Ettlinger: 'The Liturgical Function of Michelangelo's Medici Chapel', *Mitt. Ksthist. Inst. Florenz*, xxii (1978), pp. 285–304

A. Prater: *Michelangelos Medici-Kapelle* (Stiftland, 1979)

G. Neufeld: 'Die Konzeption der Wandgrabmäler der Medici-Kapelle', *Städel-Jb.*, n. s., viii (1981), pp. 247–87

R. C. Trexler and M. E. Lewis: 'Two Captains and Three Kings: New Light on the Medici Chapel', *Stud. Med. & Ren. Hist.*, n. s., iv (1981), pp. 91–177

A. Morrogh: 'The Magnifici Tomb: A Key Project in Michelangelo's Architectural Career', *A. Bull.*, lxxiv/4 (1992), pp. 567–98

W. Wallace: *Michelangelo at San Lorenzo: The Genius as Entrepreneur* (Cambridge, 1994)

LATE WORK

D. J. Gordon: 'Giannotti, Michelangelo and the Cult of Brutus', *Fritz Saxl, 1890–1948* (London, 1957), pp. 281–96

J. Pope-Hennessy: 'The Palestrina *Pietà*, *Stil und Überlieferung in der Kunst des Abendlandes: Akten des 21. internationalen Kongresses für Kunstgeschichte: Bonn, 1964*, ii, pp. 105–14, repr. in J. Pope-Hennessy: *Essays on Italian Sculpture* (London and New York, 1968), pp. 121–31

W. Stechow: 'Joseph of Arimathea or Nicodemus?', *Studien zur toskanischen Kunst: Festschrift für L. H. Heydenreich* (Munich, 1964), pp. 289–302

B. Mantura: 'Il primo Cristo della Pietà Rondanini', *Boll. A.*, lviii (1973), pp. 199–201

F. Hartt: *Michelangelo's Three Pietàs* (London, 1976)

V. Shrimplin-Evangelidis: 'Michelangelo and Nicodemus: The Florentine Pietà', *A. Bull.*, lxxi (1989), pp. 58–66

UNFINISHED WORKS

P. Barocchi: 'Finito e non-finito nella critica vasariana', *A. Ant. & Mod.* (1958), no. 3, pp. 221–35

J. Schulz: 'Michelangelo's Unfinished Works', *A. Bull.*, lvii (1975), pp. 366–73

2. PAINTING. Michelangelo's history of sporadic activity as a painter seems to support his contention that he was primarily a sculptor, despite his training in Ghirlandaio's workshop. He produced few easel pictures. It was in painting, however, that his ambition was realized most completely. His three monumental fresco cycles in the Vatican (the ceiling of the Sistine Chapel; *see* ROME, fig. 42, its altar wall (the *Last Judgement*; *see* ROME, fig. 43) and the two lateral walls of the Pauline Chapel; see fig. 6 below) are among his greatest achievements. Even in the 16th century these works were treated as representing quite distinct phases in Michelangelo's career.

(i) Early work, to *c.* 1507. (ii) Sistine Ceiling, 1508–12. (iii) Late work, 1534–50.

(i) Early work, to c. *1507.* According to documents, Michelangelo was active as a painter in Rome during the early years of the 16th century, when he produced a cartoon for a painting of *St Francis* and worked on, but did not finish, an unspecified altarpiece for S Agostino. This may have been the *Entombment* (London, N.G.), which, alone among the speculative attributions to his early period, seems likely to be authentic. Of the others, the Manchester *Madonna* (*Virgin and Child with St John and Angels*; London, N.G.) looks more convincing (Hirst and Dunkerton, 1994); the *Pietà* (Rome, Pal. Barberini) has no connection with him.

Michelangelo's first commission for a monumental fresco, the *Battle of Cascina* for the Palazzo Vecchio in Florence, was never realized. His cartoon for the *Battle of Cascina* (1504–7) was highly influential, but was dismembered and disappeared in the 16th century. Only an incomplete copy attributed to Bastiano da Sangallo (Holkham Hall, Norfolk) and some autograph preliminary drawings (e.g. London, BM) remain to show why this closely packed composition of muscular nudes had so inspired his contemporaries. These remnants also suggest how important this work was in Michelangelo's development: it gave him an opportunity to refine the composition of the *Battle of the Centaurs* and to develop motifs that he reworked as late as the *Last Judgement*.

It is difficult, then, to follow Michelangelo's earliest development as a painter. This gives a special importance to the Doni Tondo (*Holy Family*; Florence, Uffizi) as his only existing documented panel picture. The survival of the original frame, which may have been designed by Michelangelo, makes the tondo doubly important as the sole intact decorative ensemble in his oeuvre. The frame also provides a clue to the date of commission, since it shows the intertwined devices of AGNOLO DONI and his wife, Maddalena Strozzi. It has been suggested that the painting celebrated their marriage in 1503 or the birth of their first male heir in 1507.

The high colour key and predominantly blond tonality of the Doni Tondo were often contrasted with the apparently more markedly tonal style of the Sistine Ceiling. The cleaning of both the tondo and the Sistine vault, however, has revealed considerable continuity of manner between the two. Because the tondo depicts a conventional subject, it emphasizes Michelangelo's formal independence from contemporaries who were developing motifs and treatments derived from Leonardo da Vinci. In colour, tone and handling, the panel is deeply conservative. Its originality lies in the quite exceptional clarity with which Michelangelo designed the three major figures as a compact, yet coherent, group. The pose of the most prominent figure, the Virgin, is particularly complex. The central group is often cited correctly as an extreme example of what *disegno* came to represent. It has been suggested that the group is essentially sculptural in feeling, but this is true only in the sense that each figure is strongly realized as a turning, three-dimensional form. To dwell excessively on its sculptural properties is to ignore the marked fashion in which Michelangelo emphasized two-dimensional patterning by sharply silhouetting the central mass against the background. Colour plays its part too. The Virgin's rose shift with its brilliant, almost blanched, highlights is the most vibrant element within the pictorial field, and clearly signals her stature as the chief figure of the painting.

Although she is not without tenderness, the Virgin of the Doni Tondo is depicted as muscular, lithe, heroic and unusually authoritative. The relative severity of Michelangelo's conception of the Holy Family has given rise to speculation that this panel had a special significance, a suggestion supported by the puzzling inclusion of a group of naked youths lounging in the background. Similar groups are depicted in tondos by Luca Signorelli (1484–90; Florence, Uffizi; Munich, Alte Pin.), although the meaning of these also remains mysterious. Tolnay's suggestion that the youths represent the epoch before the Law, while the Holy Family stands for the era of Grace and the Baptist an intermediary period, makes sense of the spatial arrangement of the picture in terms of orthodox theology, but it remains speculative. Less credible interpretations include the assertion that two of the youths are homosexual lovers. Whether it commemorates marriage or birth (or both), this exhilarating painting in its magnificent frame is one of the most sumptuous objects to have survived from the Italian Renaissance.

The Doni Tondo was not the last of Michelangelo's panel paintings. Around 1530 he painted a *Leda and the Swan* (untraced) for Alfonso I d'Este, Duke of Ferrara. Alfonso never received the picture, which vanished in France. The power of Michelangelo's conception of the Leda myth is suggested by a number of 16th-century copies (*see* EROTIC ART, fig. 5), of which the most reliable appear to be a painting often attributed to Rosso Fiorentino (London, N. G.) and an engraving by Cornelis Bos (London, BM).

(ii) Sistine Ceiling, 1508–12. It is difficult to exaggerate the importance of the frescoes on the ceiling of the Sistine Chapel (*see* ROME, fig. 42). They mark the arrival of a new type of heroic painting. Through frequent copy, adaptation and parody, they have become the works most commonly associated with Michelangelo's name, and they are central to any discussion of his achievement.

According to his own account, Michelangelo was originally unwilling to paint the Sistine Ceiling, although his statements on the subject are not entirely reliable. The project was already being discussed in 1506, less than a year after the first negotiations for Julius II's monument. At this stage the Pope wished Michelangelo to replace the original ceiling decoration, blue with gold stars, with a scheme of the 12 Apostles in the spandrels and predominantly geometric ornament on the vault. Two drawings (Detroit, MI, Inst. A.; London, BM) give an idea of early plans. In a later account Michelangelo claimed he told the Pope that this was a 'poor' idea and that Julius then allowed him to do what he chose. In view of the importance of the chapel in the life of the papal court, this cannot be literally true. Nevertheless, the transformation of modest schemes into more ambitious projects was a recurrent feature of Michelangelo's career. It is plausible therefore that the Pope accepted his suggestion to decorate the vault more magnificently, but that the biblical themes of the fresco were chosen by an adviser.

In the final scheme the vault was given a fictive stone framework, with a series of nine narratives from the book of Genesis in the centre, each placed at right angles to the long axis of the chapel. The narrative order begins at the altar end with three depictions of the Creation of the Heavens and Earth; there follow scenes representing the creation of Adam, the creation of Eve and a composite narrative of the Fall and the Expulsion from the Garden of Eden. The final trio begins with a scene of sacrifice (identified by Condivi as that of Abel or, more commonly, that of Noah, although this must mean that it is placed out of sequence); it continues with the Flood, and ends with the Drunkenness of Noah. Figures of nude youths (the famous *ignudi*; *see* WALL PAINTING, fig. 5) sit on the simulated architecture framing these narratives. They bear garlands supporting fictive bronze medallions with reliefs depicting other Old Testament stories. In the spandrels at both ends and down the sides of the chapel are colossal enthroned figures, each labelled as a prophet or sibyl. Collectively they represent those who foretold the coming of Christ to the Jews and the Gentiles respectively. Between these, and in the lunettes above the windows beneath, are family groups and paired figures of the Ancestors of Christ. At the four corners, the pendentives are painted with scenes illustrating the salvation of Israel (at the altar end, the *Death of Haman* and the *Brazen Serpent*, at the entrance, *Judith and Holofernes* and *David and Goliath*). Fictive bronze nudes and stone putti add to the wealth of figurative invention.

Michelangelo signed a contract to paint the vault in May 1508. Four years later, in October 1512, the fresco was complete. Considering delays during early stages, when mould developed on the wet plaster, and the interruption of work for almost a year between 1510 and 1511, progress was staggeringly fast. This casts doubt on Condivi's statement that Michelangelo worked without even an assistant to grind colours. The high quality of painting throughout indicates that he exercised the closest supervision, however.

In design, the vault is powerfully articulated by the fictive architecture, which is keyed to that of the chapel itself. This provides a framework for figures and scenes and also distinguishes one part from another, permitting a rational reading of the composition, despite inequalities in scale between the figures. It is this architectural structure that preserves continuity between the first and the last figures Michelangelo painted on the vault. For, in spite of its reputation, the ceiling is not a unified achievement.

While thematically the paintings fall into three contrasting sections, stylistically there are two, the division roughly corresponding to the interruption of work in 1510 and 1511. During the first phase Michelangelo painted everything between the prophet *Zeccharia* and the fifth bay of the vault, representing the *Creation of Eve*. That included Prophets, Sibyls and Ancestors of Christ on either side. The remainder, which took less than a year, comprises the most admired narratives and figures of the ceiling. The break is marked by the discontinuation of gilding on the balusters of the thrones of the Prophets and Sibyls. Later parts of the fresco lack the *a secco* touches that would have given them a rich finish to match the 15th-century paintings below. This is, however, only the most trivial of the distinctions between Michelangelo's two campaigns. More importantly, during the months of interruption, he made major revisions to his designs. All the main figures from the later part of the series are larger and more powerfully presented to the viewer. Prophets and Sibyls were given greater bulk by lowering the base of their thrones, a procedure that may also have suggested changes in the angles from which these platforms ostensibly are seen. The ledges on which the *Persica* and *Jeremiah* are placed tilt forward dramatically in a way quite inconsistent with the projection of the surrounding architecture. The distortion is subtle, although it adds to the sense that these later figures press against a constraining architectural frame, even bearing heavily down upon it. Some, such as the *Daniel*, forcibly burst beyond their confines.

This powerful impression results from Michelangelo's increasing use of illusionism on the vault, culminating in the dramatic figure of *Jonah* placed directly above the altar. This figure was much admired in the 16th century as a *tour de force* of three-dimensional realization, belying the concavity of the surface on which it is painted. Such effects are now taken for granted, but Michelangelo's

5. Michelangelo: *Creation of the Sun and Moon* (1511–12), fresco, 2.8×5.7 m, Sistine Chapel, Vatican, Rome

inventive use of foreshortening to enhance the dramatic interplay between figure and ground is as striking as his related indifference to the use of more conventional illusions of depth within paintings.

As work on the ceiling progressed, these preferences issued in a novel approach to narrative. The first three biblical scenes executed along the centre of the vault, the *Drunkenness of Noah*, the *Flood* and the *Sacrifice*, recognizably conform to the notion of LEON BATTISTA ALBERTI that a history painting should include many figures displaying variety of action and character. By the standards of Michelangelo's later work, they are also the least successful parts of the ceiling. While the scenes contain many fine passages and single inventions, such as the man climbing the blasted tree in the *Flood*, these brilliant bits and pieces are often unhappily put together. This stems from Michelangelo's lack of interest in another requirement stipulated by Alberti: the creation of a convincingly deep space in which to set figures. Recession is either blocked off, as it is by the building and altar in the *Sacrifice*, or flattened, as by the waters in the *Flood*. Landscape is reduced to formulaic elements. In four instances a frontal plane is represented by a featureless wedge at the lower left-hand corner. Within the compressed spaces of these earlier scenes, figures often seem bunched arbitrarily and the narrative unfocused. Only when Michelangelo began to enlarge his figures within the frame and reduce them in number did the narratives become more concentrated. Then conventional spatial indicators grew progressively more ambiguous, and gaps between figures took on a psychological charge, rather than signifying distance.

As Michelangelo's interest in creating plausible settings diminished, his use of foreshortenings became more marked. The most daring examples are in the very last narrative scenes, which show God alone. This is best explained by contrasting them with the three preceding scenes in Eden, at the centre of the ceiling. Although these contain single figures in poses of great complexity, such as the Eve of the *Temptation*, the narratives are conceived as friezes running parallel to the fresco's surface. The most magisterial of the scenes, the *Creation of Adam*, also has the simplest construction. The scene that follows marked an immediate break. In the *Separation of the Waters from the Earth*, a steeply foreshortened figure of God hovers above the waters. The palms of his hands, raised in benediction, appear to press against the surface of the picture. Here it is the figure alone that gives definition to the nebulous setting, a device accentuated in the two following works, the *Creation of the Sun and Moon* (see fig. 5) and the *Division of Light from Darkness*. It has been observed (Hirst, *The Sistine Chapel*, 1986) that the *Division* is the only image on the vault designed to be seen as if from below. It gives the effect of continuous revolving movement, as though the fabric of space itself is being unwound.

What caused the profound differences between the beginning and end of this famous set of paintings? It could be that Michelangelo simply matched style to subject. The biblical scenes were painted in reverse order of the sequence in which they are to be read. It is not difficult to see that some changes in form nicely fit the thematic material of the narratives from Genesis. The stories may have determined the variations in the number of figures depicted between the first and last of the scenes, although the use of simultaneous narrative in the frescoes of the *Fall* and the *Creation of the Sun and Moon* casts doubt on the validity of this argument. It is unlikely, however, that the change was due entirely to the hiatus of 1510.

According to one view, Michelangelo enlarged the size of his figures after the removal of the scaffolding in 1510 when he saw that the biblical scenes were not sufficiently legible from the floor of the chapel. Using the discontinuation of gilding as a guide, however, the first of the newer kind of narrative, the *Fall and Expulsion*, precedes the break between painting campaigns. Moreover, the convincing reconstruction of the scaffolding bridge Michelangelo devised for painting the vault (Mancinelli, 1986) has invalidated the idea that large parts of the fresco remained hidden for lengthy periods. Practical considerations may have played only a small part in these striking transformations.

No single explanation is sufficient. Accounts that stress decorum and legibility alone can apply only to the main series of narratives. As has already been noted, the figures of Prophets and Sibyls also reflect these changes, and there is no logical explanation for this. The increasing grandeur of the section of the ceiling that was painted last demonstrates Michelangelo's increasing confidence as a painter.

The same development may be followed in the figures of the *ignudi*, placed above the thrones of the Prophets and Sibyls. These are among the most admired parts of the ceiling, and admiration has led writers to speculate about their symbolic meaning. It is unlikely that the *ignudi* are symbolic, however. Their function is to support the bronze medallions, and to bear oak leaves and acorns, the heraldic devices of the della Rovere, Julius II's family. Their moods range from grave to playful, although the later ones, painted on a grander scale and more powerfully modelled, perhaps do suggest an emotional complexity that gives them greater significance than their ornamental role would seem to warrant.

A related point could be made about the considerable interpretative literature on the iconology of the Sistine Ceiling as a whole. The greatness of these frescoes and their importance for the subsequent history of the visual arts in Europe are almost inestimable. Their significance is not diminished by the observation that their meaning for the papal retinue was not especially esoteric. The stories at the centre of the ceiling represent the providential history of the world, from Creation through Original Sin to the First Covenant after the Flood. These scenes may be read as the antecedents to the establishment of the Law through Moses and the Redemption of humankind by Christ, depicted in the 15th-century frescoes on the walls beneath. The coming of Christ is celebrated by the Prophets, Sibyls and Ancestors and allegorically foreshadowed by the scenes of Israel's salvation.

Michelangelo's depiction of cosmic mysteries was sufficiently impressive to his contemporaries, but writers have continued to seek a hidden meaning in the work. There have been elaborate attempts to explain the imagery of the ceiling as a coded expression of Michelangelo's adherence to Neo-Platonism (e.g. Hettner, 1879). It has been argued that the ceiling narratives illustrate successively higher states of consciousness, from the forgetfully sensual, signified by Noah's drunkenness, to the direct revelation of divinity in the *Separation of Light from Darkness* (Tolnay). In most Neo-Platonic readings, it is assumed that Michelangelo had sole responsibility for controlling the programme and its subsequent interpretation. This is unlikely, considering his patron. As the ubiquitous della Rovere oak leaves and acorn remind the viewer, the ceiling is also a memorial to its author, not Michelangelo in this context, but Julius II, whose arms were originally placed below the figure of Jonah. Attempts to explain the imagery of the ceiling by reference to Julius or his advisers (Wind, 1944; Hartt, 1951; Sinding-Larsen; Dotson), although in theory more appropriate, have not proved conclusive. It is not implausible, for example, that reflections based on the theology of St Augustine's *City of God* passed through the mind of a cultured 16th-century frequenter of the chapel (Dotson), but biblical exegesis in the early 16th century was so flexible, and allegorical interpretation so easy to manipulate, that writers attempting to identify a hidden key may be in danger of mistaking connotation for denotation. In another approach, the paintings were analysed according to the principles of structuralist anthropology (Leach). It was suggested that the images reflected not the individual temperaments or beliefs of Michelangelo or Julius, but rather contemporary social structures of which its authors were at best semiconscious. These structures manifested themselves as a language of binary oppositions (sacred and secular, light and dark etc). Although this promised a fresh reading of the paintings, it relied almost exclusively on the earlier interpretations of Tolnay. This approach also implied that any reasonably complex 16th-century Roman artefact should yield similar results, and it is not therefore addressed to the peculiarities of the Sistine Ceiling. Although it has not proved persuasive, the article did at least focus attention on Michelangelo's imagery as a form of language that derived its power by radical reformations and sometimes deformations of a contemporary visual grammar. The authority and force of the frescoes are irreducible to any verbal message.

(iii) *Late work, 1534–50.* According to Lomazzo, the frescoes on the Sistine Ceiling were the summit of Michelangelo's achievement as a painter, exemplifying the first and best of his three styles; the *Last Judgement* (see ROME, fig. 43) and the paintings for the Pauline Chapel represented successive stages of decline. While this view is not universally accepted, the preponderance of writing devoted to the ceiling paintings seems to reflect this bias. There are many possible reasons for this. The *Last Judgement* quickly acquired a bad reputation. The dialogues of Gilio da Fabriano contained the most detailed attack on the fresco, but many others found the nudity of the figures unseemly. Consequently parts of the fresco were destroyed and parts overpainted so that in appreciable detail it is not the fresco Michelangelo designed. In addition some plaster above the altar was damaged by the fittings for a canopy. Finally, the surface became coated with centuries of fatty candle smoke owing to Michelangelo's decision to restructure the wall with an overhang to prevent dust settling on the fresco. Critical neglect of the Pauline Chapel frescoes, the *Conversion of Saul* (see fig. 6 below) and the *Crucifixion of St Peter*, could be due to their inaccessibility in the pope's private chapel, although they too attracted Gilio's censure for the licence Michelangelo took with holy stories. These complaints have attracted less attention, presumably because they were not linked to sexual scandal. It is, however, stylistic idiosyncrasies that have made both the *Last Judgement* and the Pauline frescoes difficult to understand.

(a) *Last Judgement.* Michelangelo's commission to decorate the altar wall of the Sistine Chapel dates from 1534, the final year of Clement VII's pontificate. According to Vasari, the project was taken over without alteration by his successor, the Farnese pope Paul III. On the basis of a contemporary letter stating that Michelangelo was preparing to paint a Resurrection in the chapel, it has been suggested that the original scheme was to show Christ rising from the tomb. This proposal would explain a group of drawings of this subject (e.g. London, BM) datable on stylistic grounds to the late 1520s or early 1530s. In other respects, however, the theory does not fit the known facts, and it is probable that the letter referred to a projected Resurrection of the Dead (i.e. a Last Judgement). This is not to imply that the genesis of the fresco was simple. Again, Michelangelo seems to have persuaded his patrons to enlarge the original brief, this time with strange consequences for the decoration of the Sistine Chapel as a whole.

Surviving drawings show that the painting was designed around the existing frescoed altarpiece, Perugino's *Assumption of the Virgin*. The altarpiece frame would have served as a fictive ledge on which angels stood to throw down the damned. This plan was changed when it was decided to destroy the altarpiece and obliterate two lunettes frescoed earlier by Michelangelo. Two windows above the altar were bricked up, depriving the decorative cycles around the lateral walls of their apparent light source.

Damage to the existing decoration was not obviously compensated for by Michelangelo's gigantic fresco, which shouldered its way among the more modest designs of the past. Lacking a framing device like that articulating the vault, the painting has seemed to some observers uncontained, shapeless. It has certainly attracted conflicting compositional analyses. The proposal that the architecture of the chapel determined the organization of the painting (Wilde, 1936) remains the most persuasive. According to this theory, the figure groups in the *Last Judgement* were banded in zones corresponding to the horizontal membering of the lateral walls and the illumination from the lost windows was symbolically replaced by the representation of Christ.

One factor that complicates attempts at compositional analysis is Michelangelo's curious representation of space, which is more unorthodox in this fresco than in any portion of the ceiling. Condivi's seemingly banal statement that 'the whole is divided into sections, left and right, upper and lower, and central' stresses the conventional symbolic orientation observed in most depictions of the *Last Judgement*; the damned fall on Christ's left, the saved rise on his right; Heaven occupies the top and Hell the lower level of the field. Condivi's words, however, also encourage a reading of the fresco as a two-dimensional surface, rather than a window-like projection. While this fits the subject of the Day of Judgement, when time and space will be abolished, it does not account for certain oddities. Each figure is vigorously modelled, and the painting abounds in the bravura demonstrations of foreshortening celebrated by 16th-century writers, yet the characters inhabit individual spaces that cannot be combined consistently. Spiritual importance, not spatial position, determines the size of the figures of Christ and many saints. Moreover, there are boundaries drawn between sections that do not follow *giornate* lines. Such irregular fields mark out the lunettes, and another separates Christ and his mother within a yellow mandorla. This atomization of the pictorial plane makes it difficult to appreciate the overall cohesion to which Wilde drew attention. Vasari concentrated his praise on Michelangelo's impressive representation of individual types and movements. Many 16th-century artists borrowed particular motifs, but only Pontormo appeared interested in its structural principles, and his paintings for the choir of S Lorenzo in Florence were disliked and eventually destroyed. In the best contemporary copy of Michelangelo's fresco, by Marcello Venusti (Naples, Capodimonte), the jarring discrepancies of scale have been subtly toned down, and the intervals between figure groups adjusted to produce a more conventional account of space.

What was admired immediately in the *Last Judgement* was its colour, a feature to which both Vasari and Lomazzo drew attention. Colour in this sense is not the broad, broken brushwork of a Titian, but a high-keyed brilliance that was barely appreciable beneath the surface dirt before the work was cleaned in the late 20th century. Vasari noted a delicacy of effect that he likened to miniature painting. The most obvious hue is the azure ground, striated with parallel white hatchings, which vary the intensity of the blue. In some passages, such as those representing the hosts of the blessed in heaven, Michelangelo employed a fluent and allusive brushwork such as he had used two decades earlier for the Ancestors of Christ in the lunettes of the chapel.

Contemporaries also noted the continued vigour of Michelangelo's powers of invention. Many details have become familiar through photographic reproduction, for example the damned man covering one eye with his hand, or the two blessed creatures soaring heavenward, wrapped in winding sheets, variations on one of the most moving drawings for the Resurrection of Christ (London, BM). For some viewers, however, the painting manifests an awkward development in Michelangelo's representation of the human body. The increased girth of the figures lends weight to Dolce's accusation that men and women, young and old, are hardly distinguishable from one another. The equation of bulk with power is most obvious in the figure of Christ. To take one detail, Michelangelo increased the size of the upper right arm far beyond the line he had traced through from his cartoon. The extravagant attitudes and gestures of many of the figures also caused complaint. The ungainly tumbling of the angels who display the instruments of Christ's Passion seems particularly unwarranted, but it may be a pictorial metaphor for the heaviness of Christ's suffering.

Because of these marked stylistic peculiarities, it is hardly surprising that the painting is sometimes taken as a statement of personal belief. Dolce, writing in the 16th century, seemed to provide evidence for this view when he alleged that Michelangelo had a hidden, although unspecified, allegorical purpose. This was merely a rhetorical ploy, however, to draw attention to the indecency of representing so many nudes in a sacred place. It has been suggested that the painting encodes Michelangelo's secret adherence to Valdesian beliefs, in which the saved are justified by faith alone. Whatever the artist's own views, abstruse points of doctrine would have been difficult to represent in pictorial form. The important question here, as with the ceiling frescoes, is to determine how Michelangelo's patrons would have understood the image within the context of the chapel itself.

For a papal establishment already chastened by the Sack of Rome, it seems likely that the fresco was intended as a powerful reminder of the Four Last Things: Death, Judgement, Heaven and Hell. Two factors contributed to the impact of this message: the fresco's unusual position on the altar wall (representations of the Last Judgement were normally placed on the entrance wall of ecclesiastical buildings) and the removal of Perugino's altarpiece, with its comforting image of the Virgin, as the focal point of the chapel. The painter alone would not have had the power to decide either of these matters, and it is more likely that the attacks on the painting reflected a dramatic swing towards the narrow defence of orthodoxy within the Church. Features acceptable in a devotional image during the 1530s came under more intensive scrutiny during the following two decades, and Michelangelo's art fell victim to the trend.

(b) Pauline Chapel. By contrast to the oppressive appearance of the *Last Judgement*, the Pauline Chapel frescoes (1542–50) seem restrained. They have a lighter tonality and less striking contrasts of colour: violets, greens and blues predominate. Despite this colouristic mildness—which differs from most of Michelangelo's earlier work—these frescoes could not be called serene or lyrical. As scenes of conversion (see fig. 6) and martyrdom they seem unconventional, for reasons it is difficult to specify.

Gilio noted uncanonical illogicalities: Saul is bearded and already aged (which has led to the suggestion that it

6. Michelangelo: *Conversion of Saul* (1542–5), fresco, 6.20×6.66 m, Pauline Chapel, Vatican, Rome

is an idealized portrait of its commissioner, Pope Paul III); Saul's rearing horse has no bit; Peter is unaffected by the pains of martyrdom, and so on. These characteristics typify much of Michelangelo's art, however. Paucity of circumstantial detail and discrepancy between action and facial expression also occur in his earlier painting and sculpture. These traits are merely intensified in the late work. This is also true of his treatment of space. As in the *Last Judgement*, some groups are isolated within map-like patches of ground. Symbolic relation between figure size and narrative importance is also apparent in the *Crucifixion of St Peter*, in which in addition distance is telescoped disconcertingly by the angle of the foreground rock.

Michelangelo's conception of human figures also became more bizarre in these late works, although there was no abrupt departure from the types to be found on the Sistine altar wall. Limb and torso are as gross as before; figures are still conceived in the round; their poses in outline retain all the twisting complexity associated with the earlier painting, but the general effect is insubstantial. Interest has shifted from detailed notation of internal modelling towards forms more generally realized. Bodies have rubbery, tube-like members; enormous eyes stare from broad, flat faces. In late drawings the heavy corporeality of similar figures is disguised by repeated passes of chalk. In the stark clarity demanded by fresco, such shimmering, ambiguous forms are not possible.

Formal asperity is manifested everywhere in these pictures. More than any others in Michelangelo's oeuvre, they upset conventional order. Examples of unorthodox procedure include the many odd repetitions of motif. At the extreme right corner of the *Saul*, a naked angel gestures towards the events beneath. He has a twin in the spectator to the right of the Crucifixion scene. With slight variations, his form is mirrored in turn by a man in a green tunic behind the cross at the upper centre of the *Crucifixion*. By using such repetitions Michelangelo flouted Alberti's requirement of variety in history painting. It is tempting, therefore, to endorse Lomazzo's low opinion and, like him, to see the Pauline frescoes as products of failing powers of invention. This is, however, an unlikely interpretation of their peculiarities, for it was in a letter of 1542, while executing these frescoes, that Michelangelo most forcefully asserted painting to be intellectual rather than manual labour ('you paint by brain, not with your hands'). Besides, during the following decade, he continued to produce powerful drawings. The works' barbarities—if they are that—seem studied. Although 16th-century texts were brief or hostile, visual evidence of borrowing and adaptation shows that the aging Michelangelo's power to impress his artist contemporaries was undiminished. Many 20th-century writers consider the contraventions of rule found in the Pauline Chapel frescoes to be the expressions of a late period of spiritual and formal research. Certainly these last frescoes present the peculiarly modern appearance of powerful, uningratiating works, designed to resist explanation in terms of conventional critical categories.

BIBLIOGRAPHY

GENERAL

F. Hartt: *The Paintings of Michelangelo* (London, 1968)
P. De Vecchi: *Michelangelo pittore* (Milan, 1984)

EARLY WORK

W. Köhler: 'Michelangelos *Schlachtkarton*', *Kstgesch. Jb. Ksr.-Kön. Zent.-Komm. Erforsch. & Erhaltung Kst- & Hist. Dkml.*, i (1907), pp. 115–72
F. Baumgart: 'Contributi a Michelangelo, II: La *Madonna* Doni', *Boll. A.*, 3rd ser., xxviii (1935), pp. 350–53
J. Wilde: 'The Hall of the Great Council in Florence', *J. Warb. & Court. Inst.*, vii (1944), pp. 65–81; repr. in *Renaissance Art* (New York, 1944), pp. 92–132
——: 'Notes on the Genesis of Michelangelo's *Leda*, *Fritz Saxl, 1890–1948*, ed. D. J. Gordon (London, 1957), pp. 270–80
C. Eisler: 'The Athlete of Virtue: The Iconography of Asceticism', *De Artibus Opuscula XL: Essays in Honour of Erwin Panofsky*, ed. M. Meiss (New York, 1961), pp. 82–99
C. Gould: *Michelangelo: 'Battle of Cascina'*, Charlton Lectures on Art (Newcastle-upon-Tyne, 1966)
A. Smart: 'Michelangelo, the Taddei *Madonna* and the National Gallery *Entombment*', *J. Royal Soc. A.*, cxv (1967), pp. 835–62
M. Levi d'Ancona: 'The Doni *Madonna* by Michelangelo: An Iconographic Study', *A. Bull.*, l (1968), pp. 43–50
W. Grohn: 'Michelangelos Darstellung der *Schlacht von Cascina*', *Jb. Hamburg. Kstsamml.*, xvii (1972), pp. 23–42
C. Gould: 'Michelangelo's *Entombment*: A Further Addendum', *Burl. Mag.*, cvi (1974), pp. 31–2
G. Smith: 'A Medici Source for Michelangelo's Doni Tondo', *Z. Kstgesch.*, xxxviii/1 (1975), pp. 84–5
M. Hirst: 'Michelangelo in Rome: An Altarpiece and the *Bacchus*', *Burl. Mag.*, cxxiii (1981), pp. 581–93
Il Tondo Doni di Michelangelo e il suo restauro (Florence, 1985)
M. Hirst: 'I disegni di Michelangelo per la *Battaglia di Cascina*', *Tecnica e stile*, i (Milan, 1986), pp. 43–58
L. Morozzi: 'La *Battaglia di Cascina*: Nuova ipotesi sulla data di commissione', *Prospettiva*, liii (1988–9), pp. 320–24
A. Butterfield: 'A Source for Michelangelo's National Gallery *Entombment*', *Mitt. Ksthist. Inst. Florenz*, xxxiii (1989), pp. 390–93
M. Hirst and J. Dunkerton: *The Young Michelangelo* (London, 1994)

SISTINE CEILING

H. Hettner: 'Michelangelo und die Sixtinische Kapelle', *Italienische Studien zur Geschichte der Renaissance* (Brunswick, 1879), pp. 247–72
E. Steinmann: *Die Sixtinische Kapelle*, 2 vols (Munich, 1905)
E. Wind: 'The *Crucifixion of Haman*', *J. Warb. Inst.*, i (1937–8), pp. 245–8
——: 'Sante Pagnini and Michelangelo: A Study of the Succession of Savonarola', *Gaz. B.-A.*, xxvi (1944), pp. 211–46
F. Hartt: '*Lignum Vitae in Medio Paradisi*: The Stanza d'Eliodoro and the Sistine Ceiling', *A. Bull.*, xxxii (1951), pp. 15–145, 181–218
——: 'Pagnini, Vigerio and the Sistine Ceiling: A Reply', *A. Bull.*, xxxiii (1951), pp. 262–73
J. Wilde: 'The Decoration of the Sistine Chapel', *Proc. Brit. Acad.*, xliv (1958), pp. 61–82
E. Wind: 'Maccabean Histories in the Sistine Ceiling', *Italian Renaissance Studies* (London, 1960), pp. 312–27
S. Sandström: *Levels of Unreality: Studies in Structure and Construction in Italian Mural Painting during the Renaissance* (Stockholm, 1963)
S. Sinding-Larsen: 'A Re-reading of the Sistine Ceiling', *Acta Archaeol. & A. Historiam Pertinentia (Institutum Romanum Norvegiae)*, iv (1969)
C. J. Seymour: *Michelangelo: The Sistine Chapel*, Critical Studies in Art History (London, 1972), pp. 143–58
R. Kuhn: *Michelangelo: Die Sixtinische Decke: Beiträge über ihre Quellen und ihre Auslegung* (Berlin, 1975)
D. Freedberg and C. Hope: 'Structuralism and Michelangelo', *TLS* (22 April 1977), pp. 489–90
E. R. Leach: 'Michelangelo's Genesis: Structuralist Comments on the Paintings on the Sistine Chapel Ceiling', *TLS* (18 March 1977), pp. 311–13
E. G. Dotson: 'An Augustinian Interpretation of Michelangelo's Sistine Ceiling', *A. Bull.*, lxi (1979), pp. 223–56, 405–29
M. Hirst: '*Il modo delle attitudini*: Michelangelo's Oxford Sketchbook for the Ceiling', *The Sistine Chapel: Michelangelo Rediscovered*, ed. A. Chastel (London, 1986), pp. 208–17
F. Mancinelli: 'Michelangelo at Work', *The Sistine Chapel: Michelangelo Rediscovered*, ed. A. Chastel (London, 1986), pp. 218–59
W. E. Wallace: 'Michelangelo's Assistants in the Sistine Chapel', *Gaz. B.-A.*, cx (May–June 1987), pp. 203–16
M. Bull: 'The Iconography of the Sistine Chapel', *Burl. Mag.*, cxxx (1988), pp. 597–605

K. Weil-Garris Brandt: 'The Early Projects for Michelangelo's Sistine Ceiling: Their Practical and Artistic Consequences', *Michelangelo Drawings* (Washington, 1992), pp. 57–87

The Sistine Chapel: A Glorious Restoration (London, 1993)

P. De Vecchi: *The Sistine Chapel: A Glorious Restoration* (New York, 1994)

LAST JUDGEMENT

L. Dolce: *Dialogo della pittura intitolato l'Aretino* (Venice, 1557); repr. in P. Barocchi, ed.: *Trattati d'arte del cinquecento*, i (Bari, 1960); Eng. trans. by M. W. Roskill in *Dolce's 'Aretino' and Venetian Art Theory of the Cinquecento* (New York, 1968)

G. A. Gilio da Fabriano: *Due dialoghi di M. Andrea Gilio da Fabriano* (Camerino, 1564); repr. in P. Barocchi, ed.: *Trattati d'arte del cinquecento*, ii (Bari, 1961)

G. P. Lomazzo: *Idea del tempio della pittura* (Milan, 1590)

F. La Cava: *Il volto di Michelangelo scoperto in 'Giudizio finale': Un dramma psicologico in un ritratto simbolico* (Bologna, 1925)

J. Wilde: 'Der ursprüngliche Plan Michelangelos zum Jüngsten Gericht', *Graph. Kst.*, n. s. 1, i (1936), pp. 7–20

D. Redig de Campos and B. Biagetti: *Il 'Giudizio universale' di Michelangelo*, 2 vols (1943), vii of *Monumenti vaticani di archeologia e d'arte* (Rome)

D. Redig de Campos: *Il 'Giudizio universale' di Michelangelo* (Milan, 1975)

L. Steinberg: 'Michelangelo's *Last Judgement* as Merciful Heresy', *A. America*, lxiii (1975), pp. 48–63

M. Hall: 'Michelangelo's *Last Judgment*: Resurrection of the Body and Predestination', *A. Bull.*, lviii (1976), pp. 85–92

E. Talamo: 'La controriforma interpreta la Sistina di Michelangelo', *Stor. A.*, l (1984), pp. 7–26

B. Barnes: 'A Lost Modello for Michelangelo's *Last Judgement*', *Master Drgs*, xxv (1988), pp. 239–48

J. Greenstein: '"How Glorious the Second Coming of Christ": Michelangelo's *Last Judgment* and the Transfiguration', *Artibus & Hist.*, x/19 (1989), pp. 33–57

PAULINE CHAPEL

D. Redig de Campos: 'La "terza maniera" di Michelangelo nella Cappella Paolina', *Illus. Vatic.*, vii (1936), pp. 212–16

H. van Dam van Isselt: 'Sulla iconografia della *Conversione di Saulo* di Michelangelo', *Boll. A.*, xxxvii (1952), pp. 315–19

L. Steinberg: *Michelangelo's Last Paintings* (Oxford, 1975)

W. E. Wallace: 'Narrative and Religious Expression in Michelangelo's Pauline Chapel', *Artibus & Hist.*, x/19 (1989), pp. 107–12

3. DRAWING. On a sheet of studies containing sketches by his assistant Antonio Mini (*d* 1533), datable to *c.* 1524 (London, BM), Michelangelo wrote, 'Draw Antonio, draw and do not waste time'. This was more than conventional workshop wisdom. Michelangelo himself drew tirelessly, and his draughtsmanship acquired exemplary status for his contemporaries, especially for those who held *disegno* to be the foundational principle of all art. The drawings have become equally important to subsequent critical and historical assessment of the artist because, unlike work in other media, which was often interrupted or left incomplete, they provide a nearly continuous record of Michelangelo's activity.

Initially, as for other artists, drawing was a means of education. In the Ghirlandaio workshop Michelangelo learnt the language of Florentine draughtsmanship. Little survives from the earliest stage of his activity, although two pen drawings after frescoes in Santa Croce, Florence, by Giotto (Paris, Louvre) and in S Maria del Carmine, Florence, by Masaccio (Munich, Staatl. Graph. Samml.) seem to date from the artist's adolescence and demonstrate both how firmly rooted in the Tuscan past Michelangelo's practice was and how quickly he developed an incisive analytical critique of his native tradition.

That process presumably continued well beyond adolescence. Judging by the wealth of adaptation and reference in the artist's mature work, it must have involved drawing from the Antique, although direct trace of this is relatively rare in the surviving record. Vasari testified that Michelangelo burnt a great number of sheets towards the end of his life, because he did not want anyone to know what pains he had taken. Evidence of self-education may have been among these losses. Interesting survivals are various leaves (Florence, Uffizi; London, BM) that show the novice architect copying details of ancient buildings from drawings included in the Codex Coner (London, Soane Mus.). From surviving examples it seems that Michelangelo used drawing almost exclusively in connection with professional needs. Nothing in his output resembles Leonardo's encyclopedic researches. Although, according to Condivi, he planned to illustrate a textbook of anatomy by Realdo Colombo (*c.* 1510–59), the project never materialized, and there is no reason to suppose that Michelangelo's own anatomical dissections concerned anything more than musculature and the articulation of the skeleton. Even by conventional standards his interests as a draughtsman were narrow. He remained incurious about landscape, and only two portraits are recorded, of which perhaps one survives of *Andrea Quaratesi* (London, BM; see fig. 7). The total effect of his drawn work is one of strict dedication.

Strictness does not imply monotony. Within his chosen area, approaches were richly varied. Drawings from almost every stage of the compositional process survive, from slight sketches to cartoons (London, BM; Naples, Capodimonte). Most of them are working sheets; on many he appears to have experimented with ideas for several

7. Michelangelo: *Andrea Quaratesi*, black chalk, 411×292 mm, 1531 (London, British Museum)

projects almost simultaneously (e.g. Oxford, Ashmolean). Words and images are juxtaposed on some sheets, and some have an almost palimpsest-like character inviting, and rewarding, the most painstaking detective work. There is a tendency to exaggerate the degree to which stylistically they are the product of a sculptor's conception of form. Certainly some are textured with vigorous cross-hatchings, resembling marks left by claw chisels on stone (e.g. Berenson, fig. 657). A dramatic example is the powerful study for the *Risen Christ* (*c.* 1514; London, Brinsley Ford priv. col.; see Hirst, 1988, pl. 131). However if this articulation of the figure derived from a carver's need to map each plane and hollow as bone and muscle play beneath skin, the same impulse had surprising consequences elsewhere. The Red chalk study of the *Libyan Sibyl* for the Sistine Chapel Ceiling (New York, Met.; *see* DRAWING, colour pl. I, fig. 1) impresses as much by its luminosity as by its formidable analysis of structure. Part of the effect is due to the relief-like conception of the back, shallowly raked with light. It was achieved, however, by small variations of pressure, clotting or dispersing the red chalk. Saturated colour plays against barely marked areas of paper. Descriptions indicate that the cartoon for the *Battle of Cascina* (destr.) was rich in comparable subtleties of handling observable in some of the surviving preliminary studies for it (London, BM; Oxford, Ashmolean). Such painterly use of chalk may have been stimulated by Leonardo's example. Michelangelo's wash drawings, however, developed from a workshop training shared by Florentine contemporaries. Most of the surviving examples are for architectural projects, but a delicate drapery study for the *Erythrean Sibyl* (London, BM) from the ceiling of the Sistine Chapel may represent a number of lost figurative works. In general, Michelangelo's later drawings are more densely atmospheric. Rubbed black chalk, grey wash and white heightening were often superimposed to blur the sharpness of even measured architectural designs. Function seems to have been forgotten in the drive to make self-sufficient artefacts.

Already during his lifetime Michelangelo's reputation was so great that his slightest sketches became collectors' items. The artist himself often used drawings as a form of diplomatic gift, to seal friendships or to show devotion to social superiors. Discarded preliminary studies or new compositional designs were given to Sebastiano del Piombo, Pontormo, Daniele da Volterra and others to realize as paintings. A design for a salt-cellar (1537; London, BM) was prepared for Francesco Maria I, Duke of Urbino (*see* ROVERE, DELLA (i), (3)), heir of Julius II, a gift designed to signal Michelangelo's intention to finish the tomb of his relative. More characteristic were the 'presentation drawings' made for Tommaso de' Cavalieri (for illustration *see* PRESENTATION DRAWING and GAY AND LESBIAN ART, fig. 1) and VITTORIA COLONNA (e.g. London, BM; Boston, MA, Isabella Stewart-Gardner Mus.). These highly worked sheets were offered, with letters and poems, as tokens of courtly love. Although those addressed to Cavalieri seem today among the most enigmatic examples of Michelangelo's art, they were not essentially private documents and quickly became well known through copies, engravings and gem-carvings.

During the 20th century acceptance or rejection of these presentation drawings as the work of Michelangelo became an indicator of shifting views on his artistic personality. For writers in the early part of the century, who believed such daintiness uncharacteristic of Michelangelo, they were regarded as copies of lost originals. Berenson even removed from the oeuvre preliminary studies that bore formal resemblances to the Cavalieri drawings. Following Wilde, most modern connoisseurs have accepted the status of these sheets, emphasizing the variety and richness of Michelangelo's achievement; only Perrig retains an exceptionally sceptical position.

BIBLIOGRAPHY

B. Berenson: *The Drawings of the Florentine Painters*, 3 vols (London, 1903, Chicago and London, 2/1938)
K. Frey: *Die Handzeichnungen Michelagniolos Buonarroti*, 3 vols (Berlin, 1909–11)
H. Thode: *Michelangelo: Kritische Untersuchungen über seine Werke: Verzeichnis der Zeichnungen, Kartons und Modelle*, 3 vols (Berlin, 1913)
A. E. Popham and J. Wilde: *The Italian Drawings of the XV and XVI Centuries . . . at Windsor Castle* (London, 1949)
J. Wilde: *Italian Drawings in the Department of Prints and Drawings in the British Museum: Michelangelo and his School* (London, 1953)
P. Barocchi: *Michelangelo e la sua scuola: I disegni di Casa Buonarroti e degli Uffizi, Accademia Toscana di Scienza e Lettere, 'La Columbaria'*, Studi, viii, 2 vols (Florence, 1962)
——: *Michelangelo e la sua scuola: I disegni dell'Archivio Buonarroti, Accademia Toscana di Scienza e Lettere, 'La Columbaria'*, Studi, viii (Florence, 1964)
F. Hartt: *The Drawings of Michelangelo* (London, 1971)
Drawings by Michelangelo from English Collections (exh. cat. by J. A. Gere and N. Turner, London, BM, 1975)
C. de Tolnay: *Corpus dei disegni di Michelangelo*, 4 vols (Novara, 1975–80)
P. d. Poggetto: *I disegni murali di Michelangiolo e della sua scuola nella Sagrestia Nuova di San Lorenzo* (Florence, 1978)
C. Elam: 'The Mural Drawings in Michelangelo's New Sacristy', *Burl. Mag.*, cxxiii (1981), pp. 593–602
M. Hirst: *Michelangelo and his Drawings* (New Haven and London, 1988)
J. Roberts: *A Dictionary of Michelangelo's Watermarks* (Milan, 1988)
A. Perrig: *Die Zeichnungen Michelangelos*, Eng. trans. by M. Joyce as *Michelangelo's Drawings* (Princeton, 1992)
C. H. Smyth, ed.: *Michelangelo Drawings*, Stud. Hist. A., 33, Center for Advanced Study in the Visual Arts, Symposium Papers, xvii (Washington, DC, 1992)

ANTHONY HUGHES

4. ARCHITECTURE. The myth of Michelangelo's reluctance to take on architectural commissions was coloured by his retrospective shame at the 'tragedy of the tomb' of Julius II (*see* §1(ii) above). In fact, Michelangelo actively manoeuvred to obtain his first major architectural project—the façade of S Lorenzo, Florence—and from then on the design of buildings played an increasingly dominant role in his career. The originality of his architectural language, at a period when Vitruvianism was hardening into dogma, meant that, while his influence on subsequent architecture was profound, he was also blamed for fostering rule-breaking and licence.

(i) Projects in Rome and Florence for the Medici family, 1516–33. (ii) Work in Rome, 1534–64.

(i) Projects in Rome and Florence for the Medici family, 1516–33. Michelangelo's interest in architecture developed from designing complex monumental sculptural ensembles within a coherent architectonic framework. Indeed, the concept of architecture as a grid intended to set off sculpture, as in the Julius tomb, links all his early architectural designs. His first building, the marble façade (*c.* 1515–16) of Leo X's chapel at Castel Sant'Angelo, Rome, is like

a pedimented wall tomb without sculpture, and it incorporates the niches, lions' heads and Medici devices found in other Leonine buildings. Leo's triumphal entry into Florence in November 1515 sparked off many architectural projects there, including the insertion (*c.* 1516) of pedimented windows designed by Michelangelo into the corner bays of the Palazzo Medici. Their elongated volute brackets supporting both lintel and sill introduced the fashion for 'kneeling windows' in 16th-century Florence.

(a) S Lorenzo façade. (b) New Sacristy. (c) Biblioteca Laurenziana. (d) Fortification designs.

(a) S Lorenzo façade. Leo's entry prompted thoughts of completing the Medici church of S Lorenzo (started 1418) with a marble façade decked in sculpture (*see* FLORENCE, §IV, 5). Many artists hoped for this commission, which in the winter of 1516 was awarded to Michelangelo in collaboration with BACCIO D'AGNOLO. It was initially intended that the lesser sculpture should be contracted out to others, but as Michelangelo gradually shed his collaborators, his ideas for the façade—envisaged as a 'mirror of all Italy for sculpture and architecture'—grew to unworkable proportions, and, although an agreement with Leo was signed (Jan 1518) and marble quarried (1517–20), the project was shelved by March 1520.

Elevation drawings and some plans survive (*Corpus*, 496–510) as evidence of Michelangelo's successive ideas for the façade. An early idea (Florence, Casa Buonarroti, 45A; *Corpus*, 497*r*) envisaged a two-storey central section with recessed bays for the side doors and high tabernacles over the side chapels. A modified version of this modello, known from copies, probably formed the basis for an initial agreement with the Pope in Rome in December 1516, and for a wooden model (destr.) by Baccio d'Agnolo. By mid-January Michelangelo's second thoughts (*Corpus*, 498*r*) led him towards a more regular rhythm; in March he sacked Baccio and started again from scratch, making a terracotta sketch model of a more ambitious design, embodied in the wooden model (Florence, Casa Buonarroti) presented to the Pope in December. The façade had now become an immense two-storey screen with single-bay projections at the sides. Vastly more expensive, it involved over 40 pieces of sculpture. It was not built, however, because the structural problems would have been considerable. The detailed vocabulary of the wooden model (*see* ARCHITECTURAL MODEL) is relatively conventional, but embodies qualities that were to endure in Michelangelo's architecture—respect for vertical and horizontal continuity and the use of overlapping elements and receding planes, producing a complex and enriched silhouette. The orders are laid against plain pilaster strips, at one remove from the wall, an effect that was fundamental to Michelangelo's architectural thinking.

(b) New Sacristy. The New Sacristy (1519–33) of S Lorenzo, Florence, and the Biblioteca Laurenziana (begun *c.* 1524; see fig. 8) were singled out by Vasari as marking a conscious break with ancient and modern tradition in their use of licentious non-Vitruvian detail. Both projects were conceived by Cardinal Giulio de' Medici (later Pope Clement VII) in summer 1519, although the designs for the library were not produced for another five years (*see*

MEDICI, DE', (9)). The New Sacristy was to house the tombs of the recently deceased Medici dukes Lorenzo of Urbino (*d* 1516; see fig. 4) and Giuliano of Nemours (*d* 1519)—the *Capitani*—and their 15th-century forebears Giuliano (*d* 1478) and Lorenzo (*d* 1492) de' Medici—the *Magnifici*. Intermittent plans to introduce additional tombs for the Medici popes were not realized. Again, a large sculptural component was involved. The new chapel was to balance Brunelleschi's Old Sacristy (1421–8) opposite, and its exterior treatment matches the levels and detailing of the 15th-century transept. For the plan and interior elevation, Michelangelo's starting-point was also the Old Sacristy, but he introduced an intermediate level with tabernacle windows, arches and pilasters between the main order and the pendentive zone.

Work began in autumn 1519, and by April 1521 the first interior order was largely in place. The pace of construction slackened after Leo's death that year, but picked up after Clement's election in 1523. In 1525 the exterior was crowned by the innovative marble lantern with its lively broken silhouette and faceted bronze ball, deliberately varied by Michelangelo from the 15th-century example on Florence Cathedral. The marble ornament of the interior was begun in 1524, with the construction of the tombs of the *Capitani* and the doors and tabernacles in the corners. The *Magnifici* tomb opposite the altar was never finished, nor was the sculptural programme, which remained incomplete when Michelangelo moved definitively to Rome in 1534 (*see* §1(iii) above).

The rapid development of Michelangelo's architectural language in these years can be traced in the successive elements of the interior architecture. The *pietra serena* articulation of the first two levels draws on Florentine tradition, but with the layering effect first used on the S Lorenzo façade model. Above the second cornice the more adventurous tabernacle windows with their upwardly converging frames show Michelangelo improvising from an antique motif: the Temple of the Sibyl at Tivoli (2nd century BC; *see* TIVOLI, §1). The wholly unorthodox marble architecture of the tombs and doors seems deliberately contrasted with the sober grey stone pilasters between which it is squeezed. In extending the sacristy upwards to bring in more light (see Elam, 1979) Michelangelo did not entirely succeed in unifying the interior space, which remains rather box-like and planar, but its wealth of invention in detail makes it a pioneering if awkward building (*see also* MANNERISM, §3(iii)).

(c) Biblioteca Laurenziana. When Cardinal Giulio was elected to the papacy in November 1523, he commissioned Michelangelo to design at S Lorenzo a public library, the Biblioteca Laurenziana, to house the library of his uncle Lorenzo the Magnificent (*see also* LIBRARY, §II, 1). The result was one of the most beautiful and coherent interior spaces in Western architecture (the reading room) and a vestibule (*ricetto*) that continues to inspire both controversy and artistic emulation.

After various sites had been considered, it was decided to build the library above the west range of the canons' cloister, with an entrance on the upper level. A system of arches supported by stone piers built up from ground level was inserted to support the new structure; the blind arcading (visible at the rear) does not (*pace* Ackerman) determine the rhythm of the window bays. The reading room, complete with its stone membering, was built in 1525, followed by the lower levels of the entrance vestibule. As at the New Sacristy, building was interrupted by the Medici expulsion from Florence in 1527 and the siege of 1529–30. After a flurry of activity in 1533, Michelangelo departed for Rome, again leaving the work unfinished. Under Grand Duke Cosimo I (*see* MEDICI, DE', (14)), most of the missing pieces were filled in, Niccolò Tribolo and Santi Buglioni (*see* BUGLIONI, (2)) making the floor of the reading room (1549–53), Bartolomeo Ammanati building the staircase (1559–62) in consultation with Michelangelo and Vasari supervising the completion of the desks and ceiling. The exterior windows of the vestibule are an early 20th-century pastiche.

The patron was discriminating, demanding and absent; thus we can follow the library's design through letters and drawings (*Corpus*, 523–62), and see how Clement spurred Michelangelo on to unusually inventive solutions. For the reading room ceiling, Clement wanted 'some new idea', asking Michelangelo to avoid the standard deep coffering found in contemporary Roman interiors. Clement said of Michelangelo's design for the library entrance door that 'he had never seen one more beautiful, neither antique nor

modern'. He rejected, however, Michelangelo's suggestion of lighting the vestibule with round skylights, which, although 'beautiful and novel', would have required incessant cleaning.

The reading room interior is one of Michelangelo's most lucid and rigorous designs. The pilaster articulation of the walls begins just above the level of the desks, which thereby provide visual 'support' for the order. The wide central and narrow outer bays of the short walls are reflected in the tripartite divisions of the ceiling, in turn echoed in Tribolo's pavement. The layering of the walls, whereby the windows and blind tabernacles are set into recessed panels, is matched by the subtle recessions of the ceiling. The detailing is outstandingly crisp and lively.

The Pope's unwillingness to entertain the idea of skylights in the vestibule did not entail a change in the proportions and detail of the main order—for the stone membering was already arriving by that date—but it did mean that an upper order to accommodate windows had to be inserted (begun 1533/4). A series of drawings shows Michelangelo working towards the bizarre articulation, with its embedded columns flanking sections of wall that break forward into the room, themselves hollowed out by empty tabernacles. Giant ornamental volutes hang 'like dewdrops' (Wittkower) below the columns. The tabernacle

8. Michelangelo: vestibule of the Biblioteca Laurenziana, Florence, 1524–62

surrounds take the abstract licence of the New Sacristy door bays one stage further, while the capitals of the recessed columns were described in Michelangelo's lifetime as a composite Doric (see §IV, 2 below)—a reading supported by isolated elements of the Doric order, triglyphs and guttae, which punctuate the herm-like frames.

The vestibule's function was to house the stairs bridging the level between the upper cloister and the reading room (see fig. 8). After experimenting with double-ramp stairs like those of the Villa Medici at Poggio a Caiano, and with combinations of convex and concave as at the Vatican Belvedere, Michelangelo hit on the notion of three flights meeting and fusing into one at a central landing. The central flight is a series of 'overlapping oval boxes' as Michelangelo himself wrote of it, flanked by side 'wings' (for servants when the central flight was being ceremonially used). As built by Ammanati, the stairs diverge slightly from Michelangelo's intentions, but retain the flowing, dream-like invention evident in his description. The vestibule has been seen as the epitome of Michelangelo's Mannerist architectural style. Although Vasari spoke of its 'resolved grace' in the whole and the parts, subsequent commentators have been disturbed by its tall, cavernous proportions, the compressed tension of the paired columns and the apparently arbitrary detail. Wittkower analysed the vestibule's forms in terms of irreconcilable conflict, ambiguity and inversion, although, as Ackerman pointed out, the recessed columns are in fact more functional than many applied orders of the High Renaissance. It is likely that Michelangelo derived the idea of using large monolithic columns from Giuliano da Sangallo's Sacristy vestibule (begun 1492) at Santo Spirito, Florence, and recessed them to reduce the weight on the chapter house below. But no functionalist analysis can explain away the deliberately fantastic qualities of the vestibule.

The rare-books room planned to open off the opposite end of the reading room from the vestibule was never built, but is recorded in two drawings of 1525 (*Corpus*, 559r, 560r). The triangular design is a link between Michelangelo's work on the library and his fortification designs for the Florentine government three years later.

(d) Fortification designs. During the short-lived Republican government of 1527–30, Michelangelo, whose political sympathies were guardedly republican despite his close ties to the Medici pope, was ready to harness his design skills to modernizing the city's medieval defences (see FLORENCE, §I, 3). In April 1529 he was appointed governor general of the city's fortifications, and supervised the construction of bastions and bulwarks (destr.). In late September, despairing of the outcome of the war, he fled to Venice and was declared a rebel. Induced to return in October, he resumed his work in a city now under siege to papal and imperial forces. Michelangelo's fortifications were constructed of earth faced with unbaked bricks, and although the whole circuit of walls was strengthened in this way, more is known of his work at S Miniato and the southern circuit, whereas the magnificent series of surviving drawings in the Casa Buonarroti (*Corpus*, 563r–83v) concentrate mostly on the northern perimeter. The complexity and impracticality of these designs suggests they

were not intended for rapid construction under pressure in 1529, but are proposals drawn up the previous year. They are among the most exciting architectural drawings that Michelangelo ever produced—both in their dynamic response to the needs of modern defence against artillery, and in the extraordinary forms themselves. Making them seems to have aided Michelangelo's development from a planar to a plastic conception of architectural space, from a static to a dynamic architecture. In them he incorporated the curving double volutes and dislocated outlines—which up to now had been applied to the wall as sculptural ornament—into spatial solutions. This more liberated approach to space found its consummation in Michelangelo's last works in Rome.

(ii) Works in Rome, 1534–64. Uncomfortable in the new Medici ducal regime in Florence, Michelangelo moved permanently to Rome in 1534. Here two popes in particular—Paul III and Pius IV—had the imagination to entrust him with architectural projects of the greatest importance.

(a) Piazza del Campidoglio. (b) St Peter's. (c) Palazzo Farnese. (d) S Giovanni dei Fiorentini and the Sforza Chapel. (e) S Maria degli Angeli and the Porta Pia.

(a) Piazza del Campidoglio. Redesigning the Piazza del Campidoglio on the Capitoline Hill was one of Michelangelo's most successful architectural achievements and one of the most perfectly realized examples of Renaissance urban planning (see fig. 9). Although the project was only partially completed in his lifetime, the engravings published by Etienne Dupérac in 1568 and 1569 made it possible in later centuries to follow the general lines of his design.

Initially Michelangelo was asked to design a base for the ancient equestrian statue of the Roman emperor *Marcus Aurelius* (see ROME, ANCIENT, fig. 61), which Paul III had moved from the Lateran to the Capitoline in 1538. His choice of an oval base is echoed in the oval pavement (from 1561), and Ackerman argued that Michelangelo produced the designs for the whole piazza, including the façade of the Palazzo dei Conservatori, at this early date, although the latter was not executed until after 1561. Certainly the triangular, double-ramp staircase in front of the Palazzo Senatorio (rest. 1984) was carried out in 1544–52, but it would have been uncharacteristic for Michelangelo to adhere to fixed overall designs for over 30 years. After the election of Pius IV in 1559, the monumental stairway ramp (*cordonata*) up to the Piazza del Campidoglio was built and the oval steps around the piazza put in place. The year before Michelangelo's death, the façade of the Palazzo dei Conservatori was started according to a new set of drawings produced under his supervision, and the building was completed (1568–84) by GIACOMO DELLA PORTA. The construction of a palazzo of the same design across the square, the Palazzo Nuovo, which established the symmetry of the composition, followed in 1603–60.

The Palazzo dei Conservatori's giant order of Corinthian pilasters on high pedestals gives the façade its immensely powerful character, culminating in a sculpture-crowned balustrade, which dissolves the skyline. A minor order of Ionic columns on the ground floor supports monolithic stone beams, the wide intercolumniations producing effects of dense shadow. The composition is a dramatic opposition of verticals and horizontals, in which

9. Michelangelo: Piazza del Campidoglio, Capitoline Hill, Rome, showing (right) the façade of the Palazzo dei Conservatori (after 1561), with (left) the Palazzo Nuovo (built 1603–60 to the same design) and (centre) the staircase to the Palazzo Senatorio (1544–52); from an early 20th-century photograph

the pilaster order is laid like a grid over wider brick piers that form the structural support. Few Renaissance buildings convey such a powerful sense of structural forces at work.

As completed according to Michelangelo's design, the trapezoidal piazza has strictly symmetrical flanking façades and an oval central space and statue podium, which serve to divert circulation to left and right towards the Palazzo Senatorio staircase. The pattern on the pavement tends to magnify the effect of the statue. It illustrates Michelangelo's firmly held belief in bilateral symmetry around a prominently marked central axis, affirmed in a celebrated letter (untraced), which states that 'the central elements are always free', but that corresponding parts of a plan must be identical, just as 'one hand is obliged to be like the other' in the human body.

(b) St Peter's. Michelangelo's work at St Peter's is unquestionably the crowing achievement of his architectural career. When he was appointed chief architect by Paul III in November 1546, succeeding Antonio da Sangallo (ii), it seemed to Ascanio Condivi that Judgement Day would come sooner than the completion of the basilica. Since Bramante's first designs of 1508, half a dozen architects had worked under five successive popes, all bringing their own revisions with them (*see* ROME, §V, 14(ii)). In the 18 remaining years of his life Michelangelo succeeded in 'uniting into a whole the great body of that machine' (Vasari), ensuring that the crossing and dome would follow his overall design, even though the façade and nave remained unresolved.

Soon after his appointment, Michelangelo outlined in a letter his objections to Sangallo's model, praising Bramante's 'clear, pure and luminous' plan and attacking Sangallo's proposed high ambulatories, which would have deprived the crossing of light. His radical plans for reducing and unifying the building were initially outlined in successive models of terracotta and wood (Millon and Smyth, 1976), then put swiftly into execution. In 1547–8 the north arm walls were constructed; in the following two years the north arm was vaulted and the first and second orders of the south hemicycle erected. The drum was partially built in 1556–7, the southern hemicycle completed in 1557 and the north hemicycle up to the entablature followed in 1558–60 (the vault and attic facing are shown half-finished in an engraving of 1565).

To rationalize Bramante's plan, Michelangelo consolidated the main and subsidiary piers and removed the passages through the latter that had been created for the ambulatories, inserting spiral staircases instead. He demolished the external ambulatory ring and transformed Sangallo's inner transept arms into the external walls, clothing them on the exterior with a system that repeats the internal giant Corinthian order. The rhythm of wide and narrow bays of the exterior elevation is also derived from the interior, but given an added Michelangelesque tension by the multiplication of niches in the narrow bays and the characteristically complex layering of the order. Perhaps most brilliant is the way in which, to make the transition between the rounded apses and the pointed corner chapels, Michelangelo as it were drew between them a diagonal curtain, which both consolidated and unified the plan. Nowhere in his architecture are the expressive results of his habit of squeezing and shaping architectural models out of terracotta to be felt so strongly.

Erection of the present attic facing with its clustered pilaster strips and bizarre detailing began in 1565, the year after Michelangelo's death, and is visible in Dupérac's engraving of 1569 which purports to convey his design (*see* ROME, fig. 36). Behind the attic walls of the transepts are the highly innovative gored vaults of the apses, their three curves swelling out behind the ribs. To Michelangelo's mortification, the foreman on site misunderstood the novel stereometry of the vault, despite the existence of a model, and a great number of stones had to be removed. Michelangelo wrote to Vasari that the error had occurred because his age made frequent visits to the site impossible.

The cupola was probably not included on Michelangelo's 1547 model, and it was not until 1558 that the carpenters began work on the larger-scale model (1:5; Rome, Vatican, Mus. Stor. A. Tesoro S Pietro) for the drum and dome, which Michelangelo justifiably felt to be the last task of his life (he was then 83). Whereas Bramante and Antonio da Sangallo (ii) had favoured an *all'antica* single-shell dome, Michelangelo's was to be composed of two hemispherical shells. His starting-point for the double shell—and the design in general—was Brunelleschi's cupola of Florence Cathedral (he had made an unexecuted project *c.* 1520 for the completion of its drum; Saalman, 1978). Even closer to Brunelleschi's cupola was Giacomo della Porta's dome as built, with its pointed profile, but despite the changes he introduced he retained most of the salient features of Michelangelo's concept. Particularly impressive is the vertical correspondence of the 16-sided lantern and drum, connected by the emphatic ribs of the dome.

Michelangelo's plans for the façade are unclear, and the east arm of the basilica remained untouched during his lifetime. Certainly Carlo Maderno's screen façade (1607–14) and the longitudinal nave behind it have destroyed the unity of Michelangelo's plan. Only from the Vatican gardens is it possible to experience the extraordinary organic power of Michelangelo's design, the massive verticals of the giant order continued up through attic and drum to lantern, the undulating rhythms of the great slow curtain pulled around the apses.

(c) Palazzo Farnese. Michelangelo also took over from Antonio da Sangallo (ii) as architect to Paul III at the Palazzo Farnese, despite the bitter opposition of Sangallo's relatives and supporters (*see* ROME, §V, 25 and PALACE, fig. 1; *see also* SANGALLO, (4), fig. 2). At the Palazzo Farnese, Michelangelo gave the decisive final direction to the exterior cornice and to the upper levels of the courtyard. The design for the cornice was tested in March 1547 in the form of a full-scale wooden model of one corner hoisted into position. It was strongly attacked by Battista da Sangallo for its failure to accord with Vitruvian proportions and ancient practice. With its frieze of Farnese lilies alternating with acanthus, its dentils, egg and dart and thickly set lions' heads, the cornice is indeed neither Doric, Ionic nor Corinthian, but gives a subtly variegated and powerful termination to Sangallo's façade. Above the

10. Michelangelo: top storey window bay of the courtyard (1546), Palazzo Farnese, Rome

central doorway Michelangelo replaced Sangallo's double-arched window with a straight entablature crowned by a gigantic Farnese coat of arms.

In the third order of the courtyard, Michelangelo demonstrated how distant his sensibility was from that of Sangallo. A light order of clustered Corinthian pilasters on high pedestals supports an entablature studded with grinning masks and misplaced triglyphs, while the windows themselves continue the mode of fragmentation and dislocation found in the Medici Chapel: scaly triglyph brackets slip down the frames to be replaced by bucrania, while the pediment floats above brackets detached from the lintel below (see fig. 10).

(d) S Giovanni dei Fiorentini and the Sforza Chapel. In 1559 Michelangelo was asked by the Florentine community in Rome to make fresh designs for their church of S Giovanni dei Fiorentini, begun *c.* 1519 by Jacopo Sansovino and Antonio da Sangallo (ii), but abandoned thereafter. The aging artist agreed, on the condition that he could leave the final drawings and models to others. After one of his five designs had been selected, Antonio Calcagni prepared models in terracotta and wood (the latter destr. 1720; known from engravings), and began to direct the works. In 1562 Michelangelo was replaced, and no further work was done. Michelangelo's designs survive in large pen and wash drawings in the Casa Buonarroti (*Corpus*, 608–12). He seems to have had access to early unexecuted projects by Antonio da Sangallo (ii) and Baldassare Peruzzi, and he returned to the idea of a centralized plan, which was appropriate for a Florentine baptismal church. Perhaps the most original of the surviving designs (*Corpus*, 610) is an octagon or blunted diamond, with semicircular chapels in the corners and diagonally placed piers, which

sets up a dynamic of strongly conflicting axes, emphasized in the drawing by construction lines and by four human eyes drawn in to represent the four principal views.

The chosen design (*Corpus*, 612) is redolent of St Peter's in its use of massive masonry piers of irregular contour and softened exterior transitions. From a central circle spokes of space radiate, terminated by oval and rectangular chapels. In the final version represented by the model, the inner ring of paired columns was pushed out and attached to the eight piers. The exterior was to be simply articulated with pilasters at the lower level, while the drum and dome were apparently to be left bare. Inside, however, the detailing is shown as rich, with the verticals of the superimposed orders continued up into the coffering of the dome. The angled window embrasures are very striking, directing light down into the central space as at the New Sacristy of S Lorenzo. Michelangelo's drawings for S Giovanni dei Fiorentini represent his architectural thinking at its most advanced, providing a starting-point for the radical spatial innovations of Francesco Borromini in the next century.

The same is true of the burial chapel (1561–4) he designed for the Sforza family off the nave of S Maria Maggiore, Rome (*see* ROME, §V, 20). Although Michelangelo was not involved in its execution (and some of the detailing is patently not his), the chapel as built owes everything to his vision. The tombs are placed in niches shaped from gently curving concave arcs, and the vault is supported by four columns pushed diagonally out from the piers into the central space, creating an almost explosive spatial experience in a chapel of modest dimensions.

(e) S Maria degli Angeli and the Porta Pia. As part of his urban improvements to this area of Rome, Pope Pius IV took up the campaign of a Sicilian visionary Antonio del Duca (brother of the architect Giacomo del Duca) that a part of the ancient Baths of Diocletian (AD 298–306; *see* ROME, ANCIENT, fig. 9) should be re-dedicated for Christian use. Michelangelo was called in to convert the *tepidarium* into the Carthusian church of S Maria degli Angeli (built from 1562). He oriented it north-east/south-west, with the main door and high altar on the short axis and long 'transepts' ending in side-entrances. His interventions were minimal. Because the original groin vaulting and the great rose-granite columns that supported it were largely intact, Michelangelo simply walled off the transepts from the rooms beyond, built a long barrel-vaulted choir behind the altar, whitewashed the vault and tiled the roof. The present opulent interior is the result of a major reworking by LUIGI VANVITELLI in the 18th century, which obscures Michelangelo's intentions (for further discussion, *see* DUCA, (1)).

This intensely religious, reforming project went together with Michelangelo's most wilfully eccentric secular design, the Porta Pia (1561–4; *see* ITALY, fig. 13). The function of this city gate was to terminate the vista from the Quirinal to the Aurelian walls down Pius IV's new street the Strada Pia, which was then lined with villas and gardens. In it Michelangelo combined elements of Medieval and Renaissance city-gate tradition with ideas derived from garden and festival architecture, as well as his own rich invention. Thus joky castellation, remnants of rustication and the

Doric order are used as metaphors for strength, while the main portal evolved through a series of extraordinary drawings (*Corpus*, 614–21), superimposing and metamorphosing one solution over and into another. The result is a compendium of all the most fantastic elements of Michelangelo's architectural vocabulary—broken pediments, swags, masks, displaced fragments of the orders, overlapping planes and juxtaposed façades and profiles.

There has been a temptation to see Michelangelo's late architecture as an expression of deepening religious feeling and resignation at the end of his life. The Porta Pia shows that in this last decade a tendency to simplification and spareness (as at S Giovanni dei Fiorentini and S Maria degli Angeli) could go alongside a reaffirmation of the most extremely licentious side of his architectural personality. The same contrasts can be seen at St Peter's.

BIBLIOGRAPHY

R. Wittkower: 'Michelangelo's Biblioteca Laurenziana', *A. Bull.*, xvi (1934), pp. 123–218; also in *Idea and Image* (London, 1978), pp. 11–71; review by P. Joannides in *Burl. Mag.*, cxxiii, pp. 620–22
H. Siebenhühner: *Das Kapitol in Rom: Idee und Gestalt* (Munich, 1954); review by J. Ackerman in *A. Bull.*, xxxviii (1956), pp. 53–7
J. Ackerman: *The Architecture of Michelangelo*, 2 vols (London, 1961, rev. 2/1986)
P. Portoghesi: 'Michelangelo fiorentino', *Quad. Ist. Stor. Archit.*, n. s., ii (1964), pp. 27–60
P. Portoghesi and B. Zevi, eds: *Michelangiolo architetto* (Turin, 1964)
G. de Angelis Ossat and C. Pietrangeli: *Il Campidoglio di Michelangelo* (Milan, 1965)
P. Portoghesi: 'Le strutture della Laurenziana', *Boll. Ingeg.*, 2/3 (1965), pp. 29–35
T. Buddensieg: 'Zum Statuenprogramm in Kapitolsplan Pauls III', *Z. Kstgesch.*, xxx (1969), pp. 177–238
D. Summers: 'Michelangelo on Architecture', *A. Bull.*, liv (1972), pp. 146–57
C. de Tolnay: 'I progetti di Michelangelo per la facciata di S Lorenzo a Firenze: Nuove ricerche', *Commentari*, xxiii/1–2 (1972), pp. 53–71
H. Millon and C. H. Smyth: 'A Design by Michelangelo for a City Gate: Further Notes on the Little Sketch', *Burl. Mag.*, cxvii (1975), pp. 162–6
C. de Tolnay: *Corpus dei disegni di Michelangelo*, 4 vols (Novara, 1975–80)
H. Millon and C. H. Smyth: 'Michelangelo and St Peter's: Observations on the Interior of the Apses, a Model of the Apse Vault and Related Drawings', *Rom. Jb. Kstgesch.*, xvi (1976), pp. 137–206
H. Saalman: 'Michelangelo and St Peter's: The Arborio Correspondence', *A. Bull.*, lx (1978), pp. 483–93
S. Sinding Larsen: 'The Laurenziana and Vestibule as a Functional Solution', *Acta Archaeol. & A. Historiam Pertinentia*, Institutum Romanum Norvegiae, viii (1978), pp. 213–22
C. Elam: 'The Site and Early Building History of Michelangelo's New Sacristy', *Mitt. Ksthist. Inst. Florenz*, xxiii (1979), pp. 155–86
R. Manetti: *Michelangiolo: Fortificazioni per l'assedio di Firenze* (Florence, 1980)
H. Thiess: *Michelangelo: Das Kapitol* (Florence, 1982)
M. Hirst: 'A Note on Michelangelo and the S Lorenzo Façade', *A. Bull.*, lxvii (1986), pp. 323–36
H. Millon and C. H. Smyth: *Michelangelo Architect: The Façade of S Lorenzo and the Cupola of St Peter's* (Washington, DC, 1988)
W. Wallace: 'The Lantern of Michelangelo's Medici Chapel', *Mitt. Ksthist. Inst. Florenz*, xxxiii (1989), pp. 17–36
G. C. Argan and B. Contardi: *Michelangelo architetto* (Milan, 1990); Eng. trans. (in preparation)
C. Elam: 'Drawings as Documents: Michelangelo's Designs for the Façade of S Lorenzo', *Michelangelo Drawings*, ed. C. H. Smyth (Washington, DC, 1992)

CAROLINE ELAM

II. Working methods and technique.

1. SCULPTURE. In sculpture, the expense and physical intractability of marble discourages flexible working methods. Here Michelangelo acted with the care and parsimony

of any craftsman. He first made drawings and small models in wax or clay in order to clarify ideas for figures. Only when the design had been concluded did he send specifications for the block to the quarries. Measurements could be accompanied by diagrams, some indicating the form that was ultimately to be 'revealed' by the process of carving. He also spent several weeks at Carrara to ensure the choice of flawless blocks.

Roughing out was done by masons at the quarry; the extent of this process is debated, however. It has been suggested that only two of the four unfinished *Slaves* (Florence, Accad.) should be regarded as authentic (Kriegbaum, 1940), although most scholars see Michelangelo's work in all of them. The notion that he attacked a cube of stone aided only by inspiration is a romantic fallacy, as is the assertion, elaborated from brief accounts by Vasari and Benvenuto Cellini, that he invariably began carving on the front face of the block, only gradually exposing the flanks of the statue. Examination of surviving unfinished statues reveals that work proceeded according to the nature of the figure. Although the *St Matthew* (Florence, Accad.) does seem to have emerged almost as a relief carved from the front, the *Atlas Slave* (Florence, Accad.; see fig. 3 above), devised as a corner figure for the tomb of *Julius II*, was excavated from two adjacent faces of the block simultaneously.

These varied practices indicate that Michelangelo took the greatest pains to predetermine the appearance of his carvings. On at least one occasion, for the New Sacristy (Florence, S Lorenzo), he also made full-scale models for several of the figures. Only one such model, the *River God* (Florence, Accad.), has survived. Pressure to finish the decoration of the chapel may have forced him to act uncharacteristically in this instance since, during this period, he was also assisted by contemporaries including Raffaello da Montelupo and Niccolò Tribolo, who were contracted to carve figures under his direction. This episode in Michelangelo's career may have been unusual, but some degree of studio intervention should be assumed, especially in completed works. Finish was the responsibility of subordinates. When Sebastiano del Piombo wrote that Michelangelo's assistant Pietro Urbano had spoilt the *Risen Christ* (Rome, S Maria sopra Minerva) while giving it the final touches, he did not imply that it was unusual for Michelangelo to entrust the figure to an assistant, but that Urbano had done his job badly.

In spite of the evidence that Michelangelo carefully planned his work and was less unwilling to delegate than has been assumed, it is true that, even as a sculptor, he did alter plans. In parts of the *St Matthew* and the Taddei Tondo (London, RA) he deliberately allowed for the adjustment of contour, as might be expected of an experienced carver. There are indications of more radical changes elsewhere, however: in the New Sacristy, the figures of *Night* and *Day* do not fit the curve of the lid of Giuliano de' Medici's sarcophagus; the *Day* was carved from a block of different size from that of the other figures and the left arm of *Night* has been adjusted. From these indications, it has been argued that Michelangelo modified his designs as work proceeded.

A certain willingness to improvise seems to match the description of Michelangelo at work given by the 16th-century French writer Blaise de La Viginère, who vividly described the ferocity with which the artist assaulted the marble. The impression of recklessness, however, may be misleading. Blaise saw Michelangelo as an old man, working without commission. The reliability of this report has been questioned (Steinberg, 1968). It is possible that Blaise saw Michelangelo roughing out a new block. On the other hand his savage treatment of the two late sculptures of the Pietà may indicate that the Frenchman witnessed an expression of Michelangelo's dissatisfaction with himself, or, as hinted in one of the sonnets, with the limitations of his art. A contrary view, that Michelangelo was careless of finish even in his early maturity, has been proposed, based on observation of the forceful use of the chisel on the 'perilously thin skin' of the Taddei Tondo (Larson, 1991). The Tondo may not be a sound basis for generalization, however. Like the *Brutus* (Florence, Bargello) and the Rondanini *Pietà* (Milan, Castello Sforzesca), it was almost certainly worked on after Michelangelo abandoned it. In sculpture, as in painting, Michelangelo's standards of craftsmanship were high. Perhaps, as Vasari hinted, they proved too exacting to allow him to complete many works.

BIBLIOGRAPHY

B. Cellini: *Due trattati alle otto principali arti dell'oreficeria: L'altro in materia dell'arte della scultura* (Florence, 1568); Eng. trans. by C. R. Ashbee as *The Treatises of Benvenuto Cellini on Goldsmithing and Sculpture* (London, 1888/R New York, 1967)

B. de la Viginère: *Les Images ou tableaux de plate peinture* (Paris, 1579)

F. Kriegbaum: *Die Bildwerke* (Berlin, 1940)

L. Goldscheider: *A Survey of Michelangelo's Models in Wax and Clay* (London, 1962)

E. Battisti: 'I "coperchi" delle tombe medicee', *Arte in Europa: Scritti di storia dell'arte in onore di Eduardo Arslan*, ed. E. Arslan (Milan, 1967), pp. 517–30

L. Steinberg: 'Michelangelo's Florentine Pietà: The Missing Leg', *A. Bull.*, l (1968), pp. 343–59

C. Klapisch-Zuber: *Les Maîtres du marbre: Carrare, 1300–1600* (Paris, 1969)

T. Verellen: 'Cosmas and Damian in the New Sacristy', *J. Warb. & Court. Inst.*, xlii (1979), pp. 274–7

C. Avery: '"La cera sempre aspetta": Wax Sketch Models for Sculpture', *Apollo*, cxix (1984), 3–11

J. Larson: 'The Cleaning of Michelangelo's Taddei Tondo', *Burl. Mag.*, cxxxiii (1991), pp. 844–6

2. PAINTING. As a painter, Michelangelo's working procedures were traditionally methodical. Through drawings ranging from first sketches to cartoons, the process of preparation seemingly allowed little room for spontaneity. The unpainted areas of the *Entombment* (London, N.G.) are firmly contoured blanks awaiting colour. While cleaning has revealed the brilliance and, in fresco, the brio of his brushwork, his painting nevertheless was based on controlled analysis of outline and internal modelling. His method was the opposite of the improvisatory approach to image-making developed by Giorgione in Venice, and his reputation as the exemplar of Florentine *disegno* is deserved.

It is characteristic that for mural painting Michelangelo favoured *buon fresco*, a technique demanding unerring swiftness of execution. After Sebastiano del Piombo prepared the altar wall of the Sistine Chapel for oil paint,

Michelangelo had the surface demolished, reputedly declaring that oil painting was fit only for women and idlers. For Michelangelo, true fresco, like stone cutting, was manly work because it allowed no correction of errors. Comparing the arts of painting and sculpture, he wrote that he had once thought carving nobler than painting as it represented the fruit of 'greater judgement ... difficulty, obstacles and labour'.

In spite of Michelangelo's insistence on decisiveness, however, he made important alterations to many of his works at the eleventh hour. The change in style between the earlier and later parts of the Sistine Chapel Ceiling is an example of adjustment on a large scale, but he also often altered details traced from the cartoon. For some of the lunette figures of Christ's Ancestors, he worked without a full-scale drawing. As a rule, the more time he had to spend on a project, the more likely he was to develop it.

BIBLIOGRAPHY

M. Levey and others: *Michelangelo's 'Entombment of Christ': Some New Hypotheses and Some New Facts* (London, 1970)
M. Hirst and J. O'Malley: *The Sistine Chapel: Michelangelo Rediscovered* (London, 1986)
C. B. Cappel: 'Michelangelo's Cartoon for the *Crucifixion of St Peter* Reconsidered', *Master Drgs*, xv (Summer 1987), pp. 131–2
J. Beck: 'The Final Layer: L'ultima mano on Michelangelo's Sistine Ceiling', *A. Bull.*, lxx (1988), pp. 502–3
F. Hartt: '*L'ultima mano* on the Sistine Ceiling', *A. Bull.*, lxxi (1989), pp. 508–9
F. Hartt and G. Colalucci: *La Cappella Sistina*, 3 vols (Milan, 1989–90)
J. Shearman and F. Mancinelli: *Michelangelo e la Sistina: La tecnica, il restauro, il mito* (Rome, 1990)
Atti del convegno 'Michelangelo e la Sistina': Vatican City, 1991

ANTHONY HUGHES

3. ARCHITECTURE. An unusually large body of surviving architectural drawings (*Corpus*, iv) makes it possible to reconstruct Michelangelo's design process from the site plan through to drawn profiles of mouldings to be cut in metal for the stonemasons. Early in his architectural career, *c.* 1515–16, he made copies after the Codex Coner, Bernardo della Volpaia's recently completed model book of studies after ancient buildings. Characteristically, Michelangelo ignored the archaeological identifications and measurements and copied freehand, concentrating especially on lively profiles. The drawings for the rare-books room of the Biblioteca Laurenziana (*see* §I, 4(i)(c) above) show him first sketching over a ruled site-plan, then working up the revised design into a modello in pen and wash, adding a scale and explanatory annotations for his patron. Drawings of this type continued to be a feature of his practice up to the time of the S Giovanni dei Fiorentini project. From the 1520s he increasingly elaborated designs for such details as windows and doors by superimposing ideas one over the other on a single sheet (e.g. the Palazzo Farnese window drawing, *Corpus*, 589; and designs for the Porta Pia). The layered, palimpsest-like character of his finished buildings often owe much to the process of drawing itself. Instructions to the work-force would be conveyed through template profiles, full-scale drawings on walls, wooden models and, above all, by constant personal supervision.

Wooden models had long been used in Italian architectural practice to convey three-dimensional ideas to a patron more effectively than drawings, and to provide an enduring record of the design during building. Michelangelo also made 'study' models from clay, which must have helped him towards the more moulded spatial forms of his later architecture. In addition to the normal small-scale wooden models of complete designs, he liked to make full-scale models of wood to judge the effect of a solution *in situ*— as with the cornice of the Palazzo Farnese and the cornice below the drum of St Peter's. Distrusting proportional systems and preconceived rules, he was quoted as believing that the artist should 'have his compasses in his eyes and not in his hands'. For similar reasons, he tended to design each stage of a building as construction proceeded, rather than working out every detail in advance.

Michelangelo's anxiety to distance himself from workshop practice and the mechanical arts is evident in his angry response to his nephew's demeaning gift of a measuring rod when asked for the length of the Florentine braccio 'as if I were a builder or a woodworker'. However, his belief in design as an intellectual activity did not mean that he confined his contribution to initial designs and models. He was suspicious of such bureaucratic offices of works as those of the St Peter's *fabbrica* and the Florentine Opera del Duomo, and liked to gather control of the executant team and the ordering of materials into his own hands, using a small, trusted group of assistants wherever possible. Perhaps because he did not espouse the increasingly sophisticated techniques of architectural drafting, his presence was needed on site, as the débâcle of the St Peter's hemicycle vaults demonstrated. Only at the end of his life did he restrict architectural involvement to the supply of drawings. Thus, despite his role in freeing the Renaissance artist from the workshop, he remained in many ways faithful to 15th-century Florentine architectural practices.

For bibliography *see* §I, 4 above.

CAROLINE ELAM

III. *Character and personality.*

Michelangelo was below average height, wore a sparse beard and had 'horn-coloured' eyes flecked blue and yellow. Surprisingly, he loved natural scenery and was a good judge of a horse. For years, a kidney stone made urination painful for him. These details were recorded by Condivi in 1553. But the sense of intimacy they promise is false. Michelangelo's personality remains elusive. His words, as Vasari remarked, were often ambiguous: so was his behaviour. There is, for instance, no doubt of his family piety. He lost no chance to promote the status of the Buonarroti clan, even claiming kinship with the counts of Canossa. He hectored his nephew on the need to marry and maintain the family name. Yet he himself remained celibate and solitary.

His difficult character impressed people in different ways. According to anecdote, he overawed Pope Leo X. Battista Figiovanni, prior of S Lorenzo, however, declared that Job would have lost patience with him. Greed for commissions and contempt for peers led him to behave unscrupulously early in his career and he poisoned many friendships. In 1517 Jacopo Sansovino sent a memorably bitter letter, justifiably accusing him of breach of faith about the S Lorenzo façade project. Although he experienced considerable guilt concerning mismanaged transactions and more than once offered to make financial restitution for unfinished work, he remained sensitive to professional rivalry. He accepted admirers, but trained no pupil of merit. Nevertheless he was capable of great generosity, for example towards his assistant Antonio Urbino and his wife.

Michelangelo's sexual history is unknowable. Condivi claimed that he remained perfectly chaste; PIETRO ARETINO perniciously hinted at pederasty. His writings are often used illegitimately to reconstruct a secret life of the affections. Although he undoubtedly experienced a powerful erotic attraction to Cavalieri, the language of letters and poems he sent to him is highly conventional. It no more constitutes evidence of sexual involvement than the Petrarchan courtesies he addressed to VITTORIA COLONNA with whom there is no question of a physical liaison. In both cases, he was engaged in highly publicized exchanges with social superiors: a large element of refined and courtly play is to be expected.

About Michelangelo's religious life, there is no doubt. At all stages of his career Michelangelo was sensitive to climates of piety. According to Condivi, he never forgot the voice of GIROLAMO SAVONAROLA, whose sermons he heard as a youth in Florence. Especially in later years, his commitment to Christian observance deepened. Condivi recorded clandestine works of charity. In letters, poems and drawings he meditated on death and redemption. It is this grand, sombre, secretive adherent of the Catholic reform movement that probably forms the most persistent image of the artist.

BIBLIOGRAPHY
G. Spini: 'Politicità di Michelangelo', *Riv. Stor. It.*, lxxvi (1964), pp. 557–600; repr. in *Atti del convegno di studi michelangioleschi: Florence, 1964*, pp. 110–70

R. De Maio: *Michelangelo e la controriforma* (Bari, 1978)

IV. Critical reception and reputation.

1. GENERAL. The Michelangelo literature is vast, and much material was produced in the artist's lifetime. Throughout the 16th century his name was cited in a variety of documents. Already by 1527, the first biography of him was written, a short account by Paolo Giovio. In the very earliest documents he was not always represented as the intimidating giant familiar from later accounts. He appears, for example, as an unusually urbane and modest authority on Dante in a dialogue by Donato Giannotti. With the first edition of Vasari's *Vite* in 1550, however, the outlines of the Michelangelo myth were already apparent. Michelangelo was virtually the only living artist included in this edition, and he was depicted as the man sent by God to perfect the arts of painting, sculpture and architecture. Although Vasari's tone was adulatory he still portrayed Michelangelo as an artist firmly rooted in Florentine history and culture and this sense of historical placement was given greater emphasis in the second edition of 1568, in which he included other living artists, with Michelangelo as the first among equals. A great deal in Vasari's life is fabulous rather than strictly historical, as Barolski has pointed out, but the Michelangelo myth was created largely by ASCANIO CONDIVI, probably in close

consultation with Michelangelo. Condivi's biography was written to 'correct' the first version of Vasari's Life, especially the implication that the artist had behaved badly over the tomb of *Julius II*. Condivi remains a valuable source in some matters of detail, but he deliberately represented Michelangelo as a force of nature, virtually untutored, owing nothing to predecessors or contemporaries. Although his extravagant estimate found echoes, especially in the romantic biographies of the 19th and 20th centuries, Condivi's book is probably the most uncritical evaluation of Michelangelo ever offered.

During his lifetime Michelangelo's authority became very great, and he was frequently invoked by 16th-century artists. He left behind no aesthetic teaching, however, apart from a few, ambiguous remarks, either reported by his biographers or scattered among letters or poems. Attempts have been made to piece together a theory from these fragments (Clements, 1961) and to see how 16th-century terminology was modified by Michelangelo's practice and dicta (Summers, 1981), but as both writers acknowledged, although he was a profoundly reflective artist, Michelangelo held to no particular system. It is difficult, therefore, to determine to what extent certain texts reflect Michelangelo's opinions. The problem is acute in relation to the dialogues on painting recorded by Francisco de Holanda, but it also occurs with later 16th-century literature. 'Michelangelo's' explanation of the *figura serpentinata* in Giovanni Paolo Lomazzo's *Treatise on the Art of Painting* (1584), for example, may derive from some crumb of table talk, but it is set out in implausibly systematized form by Lomazzo.

Even for 16th-century Italians, Michelangelo's authority was not absolute, but varied according to the art under discussion or a writer's local patriotism. In contemporary opinion he was almost unanimously accorded pre-eminence as a sculptor, but his reputation as a painter came to be higher in central, than in northern, Italy. In Venice his abilities were questioned by Ludovico Dolce (1557) who unfavourably compared Michelangelo's narrow expertise in depicting the male nude with the greater variety displayed by Raphael and Titian. Dolce's attack was part of the dispute about the relative merits of Florentine and Venetian painting (see DISEGNO E COLORE), in which Michelangelo was cast as the chief representative of *disegno*, the model for the 'grand manner', an intellectual rather than sensuous style, totally lacking in sweetness.

In Dolce's *Dialogo* these complaints are voiced by Pietro Aretino, who had been among the first to write that Michelangelo's fresco of the *Last Judgement* was a licentious display of skill rather than a proper depiction of a holy subject. Although Aretino's comment separates form from content in a seemingly modern way, it was a malicious appeal to pious sensibilities, and the accusation became a commonplace of clerical literature. Opinion about the *Last Judgement* was never uniform, however. Engravings of the fresco were published throughout the late 16th century, and the inquisitor who interrogated Paolo Veronese remarked that there was nothing that was not 'spiritual' about the nudes of the *Last Judgement*.

Michelangelo continued to be admired throughout the following centuries. For Joshua Reynolds, the major proponent of a grand manner in the 18th century, he was a touchstone of value for the visual arts, and while Reynolds's 'classicist' view was conservative, his tone of homage anticipated a more emotional literature that represented Michelangelo as a dark, titanic, often tortured spirit. Alexandre Dumas's *Vie de Michel-Ange* initiated a series of romantic biographies of a kind still popular in the 20th century. Even scholarly works shared characteristics with the novelistic lives. The study by Grimm, in which Michelangelo is presented as the transcendent expression of Renaissance Italy, is the best-grounded historically. In a strictly scholarly sense, Grimm was superseded by Gotti, whose biography was deeply informed by Milanesi's great edition of the letters and contracts. There was dissent from this general hero worship, however. The most dramatic attack was by John Ruskin, who characterized Michelangelo's sculpture as dishonest and violently theatrical.

Romantic interpretations of Michelangelo's life should not be dismissed as vulgar sideshows. The view that his art could be understood as a form of autobiography has continued to inform many of the most ambitious scholarly accounts of the 20th century. Michelangelo's adherence to some form of Neo-Platonism, first argued by Hettner, has had several supporters. Frommel's study of Michelangelo's relationship with Tommaso de' Cavalieri convincingly relates the artist's letters and poems to the circle of Neo-Platonists he met in the household of Lorenzo the Magnificent. J. A. Symonds's *The Life of Michelangelo Buonarroti* was significant as it acknowledged a homosexual Michelangelo. Since then a significant strand of the literature has been psychoanalytic in character: examples include the intelligent popular introduction by Hibbard and the unconvincing clinical study by Liebert. Psychoanalysis also informs the writings of Steinberg. Among the legacies of the 19th-century tradition are the iconological interpretations offered by Panofsky, Tolnay and Hartt that have dominated mid-20th-century Michelangelo studies. Although these were inspired by a genuine desire to explain Michelangelo's imagery historically in 16th-century terms, their claims are often unconvincing. Many such iconological readings now seem fantastic in detail, but they still contain valuable information and comment. Panofsky's interpretation of the presentation drawings is notably persuasive, and the huge monograph of CHARLES ERICH DE TOLNAY, despite its old-fashioned emphasis on the influence of Neo-Platonism, remains the most sustained attempt this century to deal with the total range of Michelangelo's work apart from architecture. The subsequent trend, however, has been towards more cautious, sociologically orientated interpretations, continuations of the scholarly literature that has been devoted to the discovery and editing of sources and to solving particular problems. During the 20th century this genre was best represented by Barocchi, Elam, Frey, Hirst, Steinmann, Wallace and Wilde.

BIBLIOGRAPHY

P. Giovio: *Michaelis Angeli Vita* (1523–7); repr. in P. Barocchi: *Scritti d'arte del cinquecento*, i (Milan and Naples, 1921); Eng. trans. by L. Murray in *Michelangelo: His Life, Work and Times* (London, 1984)

D. Giannotti: *Dialoghi di Donato Giannotti, de' giorni che Dante consumò nel cercare l'inferno e il purgatorio*, ed. D. Redig de Campos (Florence, 1939)

J. de Vasconcelos: *F. de Holanda: Vier Gespräche über die Malerei, geführt zu Rom 1538* (Vienna, 1899); Eng. trans. by C. Holroyd in *Michael Angelo Buonarroti* (London, 1903, London and New York, 2/1911)

L. Dolce: *Dialogo della pittura intitolato l'Aretino* (Venice, 1557); repr. in P. Barocchi: *Trattati d'arte del cinquecento*, i (Bari, 1960); Eng. trans. by M. W. Roskill in *Dolce's 'Aretino' and Venetian Art Theory of the Cinquecento* (New York, 1968)

G. A. Gilio da Fabriano: *Due dialoghi di M. Andrea Gilio da Fabriano* (Camerino, 1564); repr. in P. Barocchi, ed.: *Trattati d'arte nel cinquecento*, ii (Bari, 1961)

G. Paleotti: *Discorso intorno alle immagine sacre e profane* (Rome, 1582); repr. in P. Barocchi, ed.: *Trattati d'arte nel cinquecento*, ii (Bari, 1961), pp. 117–503

G. P. Lomazzo: *Idea del tempio della pittura* (Milan, 1584)

J. Reynolds: *Discourses on Art* (London, 1778); ed. R. R. Wark (San Marino, CA, 1959/*R* New Haven and London, 1975)

H. Grimm: *Leben Michelangelos* (Vienna, 1860–63)

J. Ruskin: *The Relation between Michael Angelo and Tintoret: Seventh of the Course of Lectures on Sculpture Delivered at Oxford, 1870 and 1871* (London, 1872)

A. Gotti: *Vita di Michelangelo Buonarroti con l'aiuto di nuovi documenti*, 2 vols (Florence, 1875)

A. Dumas: *Vie de Michel-Ange* (Paris, 1878)

H. Hettner: 'Michelangelo und die Sixtinische Kapelle', *Italienische Studien zur Geschichte der Renaissance* (Brunswick, 1879), pp. 247–72

J. A. Symonds: *The Life of Michelangelo Buonarroti: Based on Studies in the Archives of the Buonarroti Family at Florence*, 2 vols (London, 1893)

K. Frey: *Michelagniolo Buonarroti: Quellen und Forschungen zu seiner Geschichte und Kunst*, i (Berlin, 1907)

E. Steinmann: *Michelangelo im Spiegel seiner Zeit* (Leipzig, 1930)

E. Panofsky: 'The Neoplatonic Movement and Michelangelo', *Studies in Iconology: Humanistic Themes in the Art of the Renaissance* (New York, 1939, rev. 2/1962), pp. 171–230

R. Clements: *Michelangelo's Theory of Art* (New York, 1961)

L. Steinberg: 'The Metaphors of Love and Birth in Michelangelo's Pietàs', *Studies in Erotic Art* (New York, 1970), 231–85

C. L. Frommel: *Michelangelo und Tommaso dei Cavalieri* (Amsterdam, 1979)

H. Hibbard: *Michelangelo* (London, 1979)

J. Bury: *Two Notes on Francisco de Holanda* (London, 1981)

D. Summers: *Michelangelo and the Language of Art* (Princeton, 1981)

R. S. Liebert: *Michelangelo: A Psychoanalytic Study of his Life and Images* (New Haven and London, 1983)

J. M. Saslow: '"A Veil of Ice between my Heart and Fire": Michelangelo's Sexual Identity and Early Modern Constructs of Homosexuality', *Genders* (1988), pp. 77–90

W. E. Wallace: 'Michelangelo at Work: Bernardino Basso, Friend, Scoundrel and Capomaestro', *I Tatti Stud.*, 3 (1989), pp. 235–77

P. Barolsky: *Michelangelo's Nose: A Myth and its Maker* (University Park and London, 1990)

For further bibliography *see* the relevant sections above.

ANTHONY HUGHES

2. ARCHITECTURE. Responses to Michelangelo's architecture have always been divided between admiration for his originality and distaste at his licence. Even Vasari, whose biography of Michelangelo was the culmination of the first edition of the *Vite*, and who considered his 'grazia' the summit of art as the product of visual judgement rather than rules, was uneasy at the 'grotesque' architectural forms perpetrated by Michelangelo's more presumptuous followers. He tried to assimilate Michelangelo's eccentricities into the Vitruvian language of the orders by classifying his detail as 'composite', and others defended the 'grotesque' as legitimate artistic licence. But Michelangelo's successor at St Peter's, Pirro Ligorio, attacked his use of capricious ornament in sacred buildings as an offence against decorum, and this was the first example in a critical tradition that extended from Inigo Jones through to Francesco Milizia, and as far as Michelangelo's best 19th-century biographer, John Addington Symonds.

Michelangelo did not write an architectural treatise. Neither his drawings nor his finished buildings furnished examples that could be exported or adopted wholesale, and there is no real 'Michelangelesque' movement in architecture although his motifs soon became influential through engravings. In Italy his influence in Florence was enduring but superficial; architects who trained in Rome, such as Galeazzo Alessi, took his ornamental ideas to northern Italy, but it was in the Rome of Borromini that his spatial inventions were taken up and developed. As the 'father of the Baroque' (Wölfflin, 1964) Michelangelo was further vilified by Neo-classical critics.

A more balanced reconsideration of Michelangelo's architectural achievement came with Heinrich Wölfflin's re-evaluation of the Baroque in 1888. The pioneering monographic studies of Geymueller, Frey and Thode before World War I were followed up by Tolnay's detailed consideration of the Casa Buonarroti drawings, by Wittkower's classic article on the Biblioteca Laurenziana and by Ackerman's exemplary monograph. As Ackerman pointed out, understanding of Michelangelo's architectural ideas has not been greatly enhanced by the 20th-century predilection for 'Mannerism' as a stylistic label.

BIBLIOGRAPHY

H. Wölfflin: *Renaissance und Barock* (Munich, 1888; Eng. trans., London, 1964)
H. Thode: *Michelangelo: Kritische Untersuchungen über seine Werke: Verzeichnis der Zeichnungen, Kartons und Modelle*, 3 vols (Berlin, 1913)

For further bibliography see §I, 4 above.

CAROLINE ELAM

Michelangelo Buonarroti the younger. *See* BUONARROTI, MICHELANGELO.

Michelangelo delle Battaglie. *See* CERQUOZZI, MICHELANGELO.

Michelangelo di Campidoglio. *See* PACE DEL CAMPIDOGLIO, MICHELE.

Michelangelo di Pietro [Mencherini] (*fl* Lucca, 1489–1521). Italian painter. He painted the *St Anthony Enthroned with SS Andrew, Dominic, Francis and Bartholomew* (*c.* 1497; Lucca, S Pietro Somaldi; see Tazartes), previously attributed (by Ferretti and Kiel) to the MASTER OF THE LATHROP TONDO (*see* MASTERS, ANONYMOUS, AND MONOGRAMMISTS, §I). Michelangelo di Pietro had an active workshop in Lucca and received prestigious commissions, working in close contact with other Lucchese artists such as the painter Vincenzo Frediani and the sculptors Masseo di Bartolomeo Civitali (*d* after 1511) and Matteo Civitali. Some of the paintings previously given to the Master of the Lathrop Tondo may be the work of Michelangelo di Pietro, but his oeuvre has still to be established.

BIBLIOGRAPHY

M. Ferretti: 'Mostra del restauro, Pisa 1972', *An. Scu. Norm. Sup. Pisa*, n.s. 2, ii/2 (1972), p. 1057
H. Kiel: 'Pisa, mostra del restauro 1972', *Pantheon*, xxx/6 (1972), p. 508
M. Tazartes: 'Anagrafe lucchese, III. Michele Angelo (del fu Pietro "Mencherini"): Il Maestro del tondo Lathrop?' *Ric. Stor. A.*, 26 (1985), pp. 28–39

MAURIZIA TAZARTES

Michel d'ixnard, Pierre. *See* IXNARD, PIERRE-MICHEL D'.

Michele da Firenze [Michele di Niccolaio; Michele di Niccolò detto Scalcagna; Master of the Pellegrini Chapel] (*fl c.* 1404–43). Italian sculptor. He was an assistant in Lorenzo Ghiberti's workshop during the execution of the north door of the Baptistery in Florence (1404–7), and the influence of Ghiberti is apparent throughout his work, which largely consists of small-scale terracotta sculpture. He remained in Florence during the 1420s and probably established his own workshop, producing a vast number of small devotional reliefs in terracotta, originally polychromed and gilt, such as the *Virgin and Child with Angels beneath a Niche* (*c.* 1420; Prato, Mus. Com.). These almost certainly were executed in serial fashion for sale to private clients. Michele is credited with the terracotta tomb of *Francesco Roselli* (*c.* 1430; Arezzo, S Francesco), but by 1433–5 he had left Tuscany for the Veneto, where he has been identified with the sculptor of the Pellegrini Chapel in S Anastasia, Verona (executed in 1433–8). This is Michele's first independently documented work and is considered to be his masterpiece. In place of the customarily frescoed narrative scenes, Michele encased the chapel walls with an impressive terracotta revetment, originally polychromed, consisting of 24 individual panels depicting the *Life, Passion and Death of Christ*. Among the most notable are the *Kiss of Judas* and the *Adoration of the Magi*, the latter particularly showing an intrinsic debt in its gentle style and architectural motifs to Ghiberti's bronze panels for the north doors of the Baptistery in Florence.

By 1440–41 Michele was in Emilia, where he worked at S Maria degli Angeli di Belfiore, Ferrara. Around 1442–3 he was in Modena, where he was responsible for the terracotta *Virgin and Child* on the altar delle Statuine in the cathedral. This statuette and that of the *Virgin 'della Rondini'* (terracotta, *c.* 1442–3) in S Adriano Spilamberto, Modena (both originally polychromed), are among his latest known works. Along with a *Virgin* of *c.* 1442 (Florence, Bargello), they exhibit the continuing high quality and inventiveness of his statuary and the mature expressive forms of his late career. In the absence of an up-to-date critical catalogue of the artist, his oeuvre remains subject to revision, and the attribution to him of some pieces has been questioned.

BIBLIOGRAPHY

G. Fiocco: 'Michele da Firenze', *Dedalo*, xii (1932), pp. 542–63
E. Baglioni: 'La Porta Nord (Parri Spinelli e Michele da Firenze)', *Lorenzo Ghiberti: Materia e ragionamenti* (exh. cat., Florence, Accad. and Mus. S Marco, 1978), pp. 116–17
L. Righi: 'Una *Madonna* di Michele da Firenze nel Modenese', *Mus. Ferrar.: Boll. Annu.*, ix–x (1979–80), pp. 67–75
G. P. Marchini: *Sta. Anastasia* (Verona, 1982)
G. Bonsanti: 'Michele da Firenze', *Donatello e i suoi: Scultura fiorentina del primo rinascimento* (exh. cat., ed. A. Darr and G. Bonsanti; Florence, Forte Belvedere, 1986), pp. 198–200
F. Piccinini: 'Uno scultore quercesco–donatelliano ad Adria', *Ric. Stor. A.*, xxx (1986), pp. 99–103

Michele dai Unii [Michele da Ungaria]. *See under* PANNONIO, MICHELE.

Michele di Matteo da Bologna [da Calcina; da Fornace] (*fl* 1410–69). Italian painter. Not to be confused with the painter Michele di Matteo recorded in Bologna in 1393, nor with the fictitious Michele di Matteo Lambertini, he is first documented in 1410, when he collaborated with Francesco Lola (1393–1419) in the design of decorations to celebrate the arrival of the anti-pope Alexander V (*reg* 1409–10) in Bologna. His name appears on the register of the Quattro Arti in 1415 and various minor works by him are documented in the following years, including the decoration, in 1418, of a flag (untraced). In 1426 he executed his first important work, a polyptych (untraced) for the Compagnia dei Calzolari, Bologna. In 1428 Michele was working with Giovanni da Modena and Pietro Lianori (*fl* 1446–60), and their influence is reflected in the dry, incisive drawing style and harshness of expression in both face and gesture that can be seen, for example, in the *Death of the Virgin* and *St Bartholomew and the Emperor Constantine* (both Pesaro, Mus. Civ.), the *Coronation of the Virgin* (Pisa, Mus. N. & Civ. S Matteo) and the frescoes of the *Road to Calvary* and the *Crucifixion* in S Stefano, Bologna.

From around 1430 to 1437 Michele was in Venice, where he executed a polyptych depicting the *Virgin and Child with Saints and Scenes from the Cross* (Venice, Accad.), one of his most characteristic works, in which his earlier harshness is tempered by a more lyrical vision and a more meticulously crafted quality inspired by Michele Giambono and the Venetian followers of Gentile da Fabriano. In 1443 Michele signed a fresco (destr.) in the portico of S Matteo delle Pescherie, Bologna, and in 1447 he frescoed the tribune of the baptistery in Siena with scenes from the *Life of Christ*. Among the many surviving works by Michele in Bologna are the panels of *St Petronius* and the *Virgin and Child* (both Bologna, Mus. S Stefano). He was, however, unable to adapt to the Renaissance style that dominated the artistic scene in Emilia from the middle of the 15th century, and he continued to work in a severe, old-fashioned Late Gothic style, repeating his tested formulae for a conservative clientele.

BIBLIOGRAPHY
Bolaffi
S. Bottari: *La pittura in Emilia nella prima metà del '400* (Bologna, 1958)
L. Castelfranchi Vegas: *Il gotico internazionale in Italia* (Rome, 1966)
F. Filippini and G. Zucchini: *Miniatori e pittori a Bologna: Documenti nel secolo XV* (Rome, 1968)
R. Longhi: 'Il tramonto della pittura medievale nell'Italia del Nord', *Lavori in Valpadana dal '300 al primo '500, 1934–1964* (Florence, 1973), pp. 91–153
MARIA CRISTINA CHIUSA

Michelena, Arturo (*b* Valencia, 16 July 1863; *d* Caracas, 29 July 1898). Venezuelan painter, draughtsman and illustrator. He executed his first drawings in 1869. In 1874 he met the writer Francisco de Sales Pérez, for whom he illustrated the book *Costumbres venezolanas* (1877). In 1879 he founded a school of painting with his father, the painter Juan Antonio Michelena, at his home in Valencia. From then on he began to receive drawing and painting commissions. His vast output was academic in character and varied in subject. An excellent draughtsman, he was awarded second prize at the Exposición Nacional in Caracas in 1883. He travelled to Paris in 1885 on a government scholarship, and studied at the Académie Julian under Jean-Paul Laurens. The accolades he received in France included a medal at the Exposition Universelle in Paris (1889) for the painting *Charlotte Corday* (Caracas, Gal. A. N.). Michelena returned to Venezuela in 1889 to public acclaim, but went back to Paris in 1890 and illustrated a luxury edition of Victor Hugo's *Hernani*. In 1892 he returned definitively to Venezuela. He began the project of decorating the Miraflores Palace in Caracas in 1896 and exhibited *Miranda in La Carraca* (1896; Caracas, Gal. A. N.; *see* VENEZUELA, fig. 7) in the exhibition commemorating the 80th anniversary of the death of the liberation fighter Francisco de Miranda.

BIBLIOGRAPHY
J. Rohl: *Arturo Michelena, 1863–1898* (Caracas, 1966)
C. Goslinga: *Estudio biográfico y crítico de Arturo Michelena* (Maracaibo, 1967)
J. Calzadilla: *Arturo Michelena* (Caracas, 1973)
MARÍA ANTONIA GONZÁLEZ-ARNAL

Michelet, Raoul. *See* UBAC, RAOUL.

Micheli [Michieli], **Parrasio** (*b* ?Venice, *c.* 1516; *d* Venice, 19 May 1578). Italian painter and draughtsman. The natural son of a Venetian aristocrat, Salvador Michiel, he pursued his early training in the workshop of Titian and later in his career was associated with Paolo Veronese, who provided him with drawings for his paintings. He is known to have been in Rome before 1547. Micheli's earliest work is an altarpiece depicting the *Virgin and Child with SS Lorenzo and Ursula* (1535; Murano, S Pietro Martire), which was commissioned by Ursula Pasqualigo in memory of her deceased husband, the former Procurator Lorenzo Pasqualigo. There is also a *Venus and Cupid* (*c.* 1547; London, priv. col.) and a *Lucrezia* (*c.* 1547; London, Mond col.). In 1550 he married the daughter of a German baker. Several documented paintings have been destroyed or are untraced: the painting of *Doge Lorenzo Priuli Accompanied by Ten Senators with Personifications of Fortune and Venice* (1563), for which he received 225 ducats, was destroyed in the fire in the Doge's Palace of 1574. The work is known from a preparatory study (Berlin, Kupferstichkab.) and a contract of 22 October 1563. Five paintings known to have been in the Libreria Marciana that same year are also untraced. The large painting depicting the *Adoration of the Dead Christ* (Venice, S Giuseppe), signed and dated *parrhasio Micheli dipinse nel 1573*, includes a self-portrait. Micheli also painted portraits of Venetian noblemen (e.g. *Girolamo Zane*, Venice, Accademia; *Tommaso Contarini*, Venice, Doge's Palace) and associated with prominent men of letters including Paolo Giovio and Pietro Aretino. He corresponded with Philip II, King of Spain, and two signed paintings by Micheli are in the Prado. He left a will dated 17 April 1578 (Venice, Archv Stato).

BIBLIOGRAPHY
Thieme–Becker
D. von Hadeln: 'Parrasio Micheli', *Jb. Kön.-Preuss. Kstsamml.*, xxxiii (1912), pp. 149–72
——: 'Parrasio Michieli', *Apollo*, vii (1928), pp. 17–21
A. Venturi: *Storia*, ix/4 (1929), pp. 1047–54
EDWARD J. OLSZEWSKI

Michelin, Jean (*b* before 1616; *d* Paris, 16 March 1670). French painter. The first of two Protestant painters in Paris with this name, whose careers overlap, was active around 1650 and was mentioned by Louis-Henri de Loménie, Comte de Brienne, as a painter of *bambocciate*, which he sold at fairs, passing them off as pictures by the

Le Nain brothers. In 1933 Paul Jamot proposed the grouping together of an oeuvre (which now comprises some 20 compositions) that he centred around the *Baker's Cart* (signed and dated 1656; New York, Met.). The artist, apparently inspired by the steady, still quality of the work of the Le Nain brothers, set out to transfer this atmosphere to an urban universe, in low-life figures of street traders. The compositions, setting accessories such as staffs or hoops against emphatic vertical divisions, display a frieze of characters without having any anecdotal content. The modelling is fluid and the colouring subdued. Religious paintings, such as the *Adoration of the Shepherds* (1659; Paris, Louvre), include similar contemporary figures.

Another Jean Michelin (*b* Langres, 1629; *d* Jersey, 1 March 1696) was accepted (*reçu*) by the Académie Royale in 1660 as a history painter but was expelled in 1681 for being a Protestant. He directed a tapestry manufactory in Hannover from 1668 to 1686 under the patronage of Herzog Wilhelm von Brunswick-Lüneberg, for whom he executed a series of portraits in miniature, preserved at Herrenhausen near Hannover and in the Rijksmuseum, Amsterdam.

BIBLIOGRAPHY
P. Jamot: 'Sur les frères Le Nain, II: Essais de classement de l'oeuvre des Le Nain', *Gaz. B.-A.*, v (1922), pp. 293–308
——: 'Autour des Le Nain: Disciple inconnu: Jean Michelin', *Rev. A.* [Paris], lxiii (1933), pp. 206–18
C. Sterling: 'Un Tableau de Jean Michelin acquis par le musée du Louvre', *Bull. Mus. France*, ix (1938), pp. 151–4
'Jean Michelin', *Les Frères Le Nain* (exh. cat., ed. J. Thuillier; Paris, Grand Pal., 1978), pp. 339–47

SOPHIE BIASS-FABIANI

Michelino, Domenico di. *See* DOMENICO DI MICHELINO.

Michelino (de' Molinari) da Besozzo (*fl* 1388; *d* after 1450). Italian painter and illuminator. Milanese writers from the humanist Uberto Decembrio (1350–1427) to Giovanni Paolo Lomazzo in the 16th century described Michelino as the greatest artist of his time. He was especially praised for his skill and prodigious talent in the naturalistic portrayal of animals and birds. Records of payments made in 1388 to a 'Michelino pictore' who painted scenes from the *Life of St Augustine* in the second cloister of the Augustinian convent of S Pietro in Ciel d'Oro, Pavia, are thought to be the earliest references to the artist. He was still resident in Pavia in 1404, when the Fabbrica of Milan Cathedral decided to consult him as 'the greatest in the arts of painting and design'. The frescoes in S Pietro in Ciel d'Oro and a panel by Michelino dated 1394 that was in S Mustiola, Pavia, in the 17th century have not survived, but two of the manuscripts with illumination firmly attributed to Michelino date from his time in Pavia: St Augustine's *Commentary on the Psalms* (Rome, Vatican, Bib. Apostolica, MS. Vat. lat. 451), which was probably made for Marco Gallina, an Augustinian professor of theology at Pavia University, in 1396, and the *Funeral Eulogy and Genealogy of Giangaleazzo Visconti* (Paris, Bib. N., MS. lat. 5888), dated 1403. Similarities in the style of illuminated initials and in the scale and layout of the foliate borders painted by Michelino with those of the Augustinian friar Pietro da Pavia suggest a direct relationship between the two artists at the beginning of

Michelino's career. Stylistic analogies with the work of Stefano da Verona, now known to be the son of Jean d'Arbois, painter to Philip the Bold, Duke of Burgundy from 1373 to 1375, raise the question of whether both artists may have trained with the French painter, who is thought to have been in Pavia from 1385.

Michelino is not recorded in either Pavia or Milan between 1404 and 1418, and he may have left Lombardy during the unstable years of Giovanni Maria Visconti's rule (1402–14). In 1410 he was in Venice, where he gave a recipe for ultramarine to Johannes Alcherius, who wrote of him as 'the most excellent painter among all the painters of the world'. Michelino may have moved to the city, where major artistic projects underway in S Marco and the Doge's Palace had attracted other artists from northern and central Italy, including Gentile da Fabriano and Pisanello. The damaged fresco decoration of the tombs of *Giovanni Thiene* and *Marco Thiene* in S Corona, Vicenza, is the only work attributable to Michelino that survives in the Veneto. He was, however, also responsible for some of the illumination in the *Epistles of St Jerome* (London, BL, Egerton MS. 3266), a manuscript that is likely to have been produced in Venice around 1414, the date of an additional index. One frontispiece (fol. 8r) is painted in a distinctly Venetian style, except for the marginal drawing of an archer and a deer; the other frontispiece (fol. 15r) contains the arms of the Cornaro family of Venice. The drawing of the hunt and the entire second frontispiece exemplify the fluidity of line and subtle colouring fundamental to the style of Michelino.

From 1418 all references to Michelino place him in Milan. In that year he was paid for the first of many undertakings for the cathedral when he ornamented the marble boss of the vault behind the high altar. Subsequent entries in the Fabbrica accounts are explicit about Michelino's supremacy as a master of glass, and he not only adjudicated the work of others but also designed and painted glass himself. In 1425 he was paid for 24 panels of glass for the window next to the altar dedicated to SS Quirico and Giulitta. Michelino, whose assistants included his son Leonardo da Besozzo, had been paid for the pictorial decoration of this altar in 1421. Six trefoils with half-length *Prophets* (Milan Cathedral, south transept, window 15) have been identified as from this window, and, although heavily restored, they are Michelino's only surviving documented work in glass. These figures are types readily recognizable in the attributed manuscripts.

The artist rented a house close to the Castello Visconteo in 1428, and he may have worked for the Duke of Milan: Pier Candido Decembrio in his *Life* of Filippo Maria Visconti recounted how highly the Duke valued the portrait of his brother by Michelino. The artist does not appear in the cathedral accounts between 1429, when he painted a standard, and 1439, when he painted a *Crucifix*. In 1441 he was at work on more stained glass for the cathedral, and his final documented activity was in 1445, when he painted frescoes in the palace of the Borromeo family.

Only damaged or repainted fragments survive from these documented works, and the corpus of attributions to Michelino centres on a panel, the *Mystic Marriage of St Catherine* (Siena, Pin. N.), with the signature *Michelinus fecit*. The painting combines high quality and rich colouring with a very distinctive style: the figures have simplified, curved contours, often enveloped in flowing drapery with curling folds; female faces are smooth and round with small features, while the men have large bent noses and deep-set eyes; heads tend to crane forward on long necks. A comparison with the securely datable works shows that these qualities remained characteristic of Michelino's style throughout his career; consequently there has been no consensus on the dating of other works attributed to the artist. Furthermore, his influence on his contemporaries and the ease with which such idiosyncratic features could be adopted have led to an expanded body of attributions, few of which are universally accepted. One of the undisputed works, although placed by different scholars at dates varying from the first to the fourth decade of the 15th century, is a prayerbook (New York, Pierpont Morgan Lib., MS. M. 944), which best demonstrates the sophistication of design and delicacy of handling that distinguishes Michelino from his followers. The manuscript contains 47 prayers for Church feasts from both the Temporal and Sanctoral, mostly arranged according to the calendar. Originally the opening of each prayer was faced by a full-page miniature, and both miniature and text were surrounded by matching borders with flowering tendrils springing from golden roots and entwined around golden supports. Most of the flowers are identifiable, and the borders appear to be a stylized evocation of contemporary

Michelino da Besozzo: *St Martin Dividing his Cloak*; miniature from a prayerbook, first half of the 15th century (New York, Pierpont Morgan Library, MS. M. 944, fol. 80*v*)

botanical illustrations. The coherence of the decorative scheme often extends to the gold background of the miniature, which is patterned with the same flower depicted in the border. All the prayer openings with borders and 22 of the full-page miniatures survive. The subtle combinations of pastel and saturated shades, burnished gold and silver and the decoration with gold paint give these pages a sumptuous and scintillating appearance resembling that of contemporary enamelled goldsmiths' work.

The precise and naturalistic treatment of St Martin's horse (fol. 80*v*; see fig.) and St Luke's ox (fol. 75*v*) in the Pierpont Morgan Library prayerbook and the portrait busts of the Visconti genealogy give some indication of Michelino's accomplishment in two of the areas for which he was praised. Otherwise the surviving works do little to reflect the wide range in subject-matter as well as in technique that the early sources indicate were produced during the artist's long and highly successful career. Nothing survives, for example, that is remotely comparable to the lewd genre scene of four peasants described by Lomazzo. It was presumably the combination of the rich variety of his invention with a polished and distinctive style that accounts for Michelino's renown and influence.

BIBLIOGRAPHY

P. Toesca: *La pittura e la miniatura nella Lombardia dai più antichi monumenti alla metà del quattrocento* (Milan, 1912/R Turin, 1966), pp. 185–93

G. Biscaro: 'Note di storia dell'arte e della cultura a Milano dai Libri Mastri Borromeo (1427–78)', *Archv Stor. Lombardo*, 5th ser., i (1914), pp. 71–108

O. Pächt: 'Early Italian Nature Studies and Early Calendar Illustration', *J. Warb. & Court. Inst.*, xiii (1950), pp. 13–47

R. Schilling: 'Ein Gebetbuch des Michelino da Besozzo', *Münchn. Jb. Bild. Kst*, n. s. 1, viii (1957), pp. 65–80

Arte lombarda dai Visconti agli Sforza (exh. cat., ed. R. Longhi; Milan, Pal. Reale, 1959), pp. 52–8

S. Matalon: *Michelino da Besozzo e 'l'ouvraige de Lombardie'*, Maestri Colore, 219 (Milan, 1966)

D. Sellin: *Michelino da Besozzo* (diss. University Park, PA State U., 1968; microfilm, Ann Arbor, 1969)

C. Eisler: *The Prayer Book of Michelino da Besozzo* (New York, 1981) [pls]

Dix Siècles d'enluminure italienne (exh. cat., ed. Y. Zatuska and others; Paris, Bib. N., 1984), pp. 107–8

C. Pirana: *Le vetrate del duomo di Milano*, Corp. Vitrearum Med. Aevi (Milan, 1986), pp. 97–118

G. Algeri: 'L'attività di Michelino da Besozzo in Veneto', *A. Crist.*, 718 (1987), pp. 17–32

M. Dachs: 'Neue Überlegungen zum sogennanten Studienblatt des Michelino da Besozzo in der Graphischen Sammlung Albertina in Wien', *Mitt. Ksthist. Inst. Florenz*, xxxv (1991), pp. 1–20

——: 'Zur künstlerischen Herkunft Michelinos da Besozzo', *Wien. Jb. Kstgesch.* (in preparation)

KAY SUTTON

Michelozzo di Bartolomeo (*b* Florence, 1396; *d* Florence, 7 Oct 1472). Italian sculptor and architect. He was both an extremely talented sculptor and one of the pioneers of Renaissance architecture. He was extensively employed by the Medici family, especially Cosimo de' Medici, becoming in effect his personal architect. His success can be attributed to an enthusiasm for innovation and a willingness to tailor his designs to his clients' wishes. Characteristic of his work is the variety of styles, sometimes with medieval and Renaissance elements placed together in the same design.

1. Life and career. 2. Work. 3. Critical reception and posthumous reputation.

1. LIFE AND CAREER.

(i) 1420–40. Michelozzo was the son of Bartolomeo di Gherardo Borgognone, a tailor of French origin but a Florentine citizen for 20 years, who lived in the Via Larga. Michelozzo must have trained as a workshop apprentice, because in 1410 he is recorded in the registers of the Fiorinaio (coinmakers' guild) as an engraver working for the Florentine mint. His apprenticeship in metalwork would have qualified him to assist Lorenzo Ghiberti on the north doors of the Baptistery of Florence Cathedral (completed *c.* 1419). In 1420 he became a member of the Arte dei Maestri di Pietra e Legname (stonemasons' and carpenters' guild), and in the following year his employment with Ghiberti became a genuine collaboration when he was called on for the second casting of the statue of *St Matthew* destined for the tabernacle of the Arte del Cambio (money-changers' guild) in Orsanmichele. As a direct employee of the Calimala (cloth finishers' guild), he participated in the initial work on the final set of Baptistery doors, the *Gates of Paradise* (1424).

In 1424–5, possibly after a visit to Venice, Michelozzo entered into partnership with DONATELLO and opened a workshop, principally to carry out private commissions. Michelozzo's role was both that of working artist and administrator. The need to work extensively in marble, which in Florence was supplied exclusively through the Opera del Duomo, encouraged them to open a second workshop in Pisa, nearer to the Carrara quarries and the port. The workshop received important commissions from both private and public patrons. Some works were executed by Donatello alone, such as the bronze *Feast of Herod* panel (1423–5) on the font of the Siena Baptistery and the *Prophets* on the exterior of the Campanile (1416–35), Siena, but several were genuine collaborations, notably the tomb monuments of *Cardinal Baldassare Coscia* (the anti-pope John XXIII; 1424–8; Florence Cathedral, Baptistery), *Cardinal Rinaldo Brancaccio* (1426–8; Naples, S Angelo a Nilo; see fig. 1) and of *Bartolomeo Aragazzi* (1427–38; dismantled after 1616; fragments in Montepulciano Cathedral and London, V&A), and the pulpit of the Sacro Cingolo (1433–8; exterior of Prato Cathedral). The workshop was well run, although there were financial irregularities, and in 1428 Michelozzo ran into money difficulties, as he was to do several times subsequently.

Michelozzo's first documented construction project was in 1430 when, together with Brunelleschi, Donatello and other Florentine artists, he was involved in the plans to excavate dykes in order to divert the River Serchio and flood the besieged city of Lucca. In 1432 he was employed as a military engineer at Montepulciano. During this period he became increasingly close to the Medici family. In 1430 he travelled with Averardo, Cosimo de' Medici's cousin, to Venice, Padua and Verona, where he executed 'a small work' as a gift for an influential friend of the Medici. He took the opportunity of asking Averardo to intercede with the Florence mint to have his post left open until the following year.

Michelozzo eventually returned to Florence and was placed in charge of the mint in 1435; his transformation

1. Michelozzo di Bartolomeo: tomb of *Cardinal Rinaldo Brancaccio*, marble and bronze, h. 9.1 m, 1426–8 (Naples, S Angelo a Nilo)

of the Medici Villa at Cafaggiolo, which was then owned by Averardo, may date from this period. He was also by then in contact with Cosimo de' Medici, who had been a consul of the Arte del Cambio when the statue of *St Matthew* was commissioned, and who was the official responsible for the Coscia tomb. According to Vasari, Michelozzo accompanied Cosimo in his brief exile in Venice (1433–4) and built a library, financed by Cosimo, for the monastery of S Giorgio Maggiore (destr.). Three major buildings from this period are linked with the patronage of Cosimo and have been attributed to Michelozzo: the monastery at Bosco ai Frati in the Mugello (perhaps 1420s), the nearby villa of Trebbio, which was already complete and inhabited by 1427, and the monastery of S Marco, Florence (begun *c.* 1436).

In 1437 Michelozzo returned to Montepulciano to complete the *Aragazzi* tomb; the project involved litigation, and he was not paid until at least 1469. In Montepulciano he supplied a design, his first documented work as an architect, to the *priori*, the governors of the town, for the façade of the Palazzo Comunale (1440), which was built in travertine stone and supervised by a Florentine mason. Michelozzo was probably also responsible for the restructuring of the interior, which included the main staircase, courtyard and loggias, and some upper rooms. Meanwhile, perhaps from 1437, and certainly from 1439, he recommenced work (having been involved from 1425) on the casting of panels for the east doors of the Florence Baptistery, perhaps also contributing to their design: until at least 1443 he is referred to as 'sculptor of the doors of S Giovanni'.

(ii) 1441–72. During the 1440s Michelozzo's architectural career was at its peak. From 1441 he probably supervised the construction of Brunelleschi's S Lorenzo for Cosimo de' Medici (he appears in the accounts of 1444 and 1454), and he undoubtedly designed the Palazzo Medici (from 1444; for illustration see PALAZZO) as Vasari claims. At around the same time Michelozzo probably also designed Cosimo's villa at Careggi and was involved in the reconstruction of the monastic buildings at Santa Croce, which were partly financed by Cosimo. In 1444 work began on the tribune of SS Annunziata (*see* FLORENCE, §IV, 3); designed and initially supervised by Michelozzo, it was financed by Ludovico II Gonzaga, 2nd Marquis of Mantua. Work was interrupted when the Servite Order took possession of the monastery (1447), although it was they who initiated the reconstruction of the monastery, still under Michelozzo's control. The elaborate monastery tabernacle (1448), to house the miraculous painting of the *Annunciation*, was paid for by Cosimo's son Piero de' Medici, who also paid for a tabernacle (1447) in S Miniato al Monte that is probably also the work of Michelozzo. In 1445 Michelozzo married Francesca Galigari and purchased first a vineyard and then a house near San Donnino a Brozzi, west of Florence. He joined the Compagnia de' Magi (Company of Magi), whose members included some of the highest officials of the Florentine government, for which he organized a grand celebration (1446).

After 1444 Michelozzo established himself with the Opera del Duomo as a supervisor of bronze fixings such as lamps, gratings and bells, as well as other articles of liturgical furniture. In 1446 the Opera del Duomo commissioned Michelozzo, Luca della Robbia and Maso di Bartolommeo to make bronze doors for the north sacristy in the cathedral, but the project was beset with problems and was eventually completed by Luca alone. The problems partly resulted from Michelozzo's many other commitments, especially his appointment as Master of the Cathedral Works after the death of Brunelleschi in 1446. The appointment represented the official recognition of Michelozzo as Florence's leading architect and principally involved the construction of Brunelleschi's project for the cathedral lantern. He designed its component parts and decoration, as well as the complex machinery required to hoist the sections of marble to a height of almost 100 m. As head of the cathedral works, he also supervised the

defences of the Florentine Republic, in this case the castle of Castellina in Chianti, and also such hydraulic engineering projects as the lake at Castiglione della Pescaia (1447–8) and the fisheries at Mantignano (1460). He was particularly talented in this type of specialized work: in both Venice and Florence he is said to have eliminated the damaging effects of water penetration in buildings. In Florence this concerned the replacement of three disintegrating columns in the Palazzo Vecchio courtyard; this ultimately led to the transformation and extension of the building (from 1457), although this was mostly carried out by his successors.

Various other works dating between 1445 and 1455 have been attributed to Michelozzo, but with no documentary foundation, although it is possible that he was involved with S Girolamo at Volterra, S Girolamo at Fiesole, the monastery at S Miniato (*see* FLORENCE, §IV, 7), the Palazzo dello Strozzino (1458–65), Florence, and the Medici villa at Fiesole (*c.* 1466). During the 1450s, however, his career gradually declined. He was increasingly involved in litigation relating to the payment of securities or to disputes on site, as at SS Annunziata in 1455. He also became less active as a designer: only a few payments are recorded for his 'design' for the hospital of S Paolo (1455), Florence, and he was not closely involved in the building of the Ceppo Hospital at Pistoia, for which he provided designs (1451). He appears instead to have concentrated on the cathedral, but his contract with the cathedral authorities was not renewed from 1460. In the following year, possibly after a visit to Milan, where he is said by Vasari to have left designs for the Medici Bank (1454–9), he accepted a post offered by the city of Ragusa (now Dubrovnik) to supervise the strengthening of the city walls.

Among Michelozzo's other projects was an unspecified commission (begun 1464) from the powerful Venetian Giustiniani family on the island of Chios in the Aegean, but it was abandoned, and his payments were withheld. In 1464, after repeated requests, his son Niccolò joined him on Chios and, although not in the best of health, Michelozzo wrote to Matthias Corvinus, King of Hungary, offering to provide him with a hydraulic machine for his copper mines. Michelozzo and his son set out to return to Florence in 1467, stopping at Crete to visit the ruins at Knossos, but their ship was blockaded in Ancona and did not reach Florence until 1469. After an illness in 1470, he was appointed to the commission supervising the completion of the cathedral choir in the following year. He was buried two years later at S Marco, Florence.

2. WORK.

(i) Sculpture. Michelozzo's contribution to Ghiberti's first Baptistery doors remains unclear. Attempts have been made to recognize Michelozzo's influence in the simple architectural backgrounds and especially in their distinctive early Renaissance details, but their design should instead be associated with Ghiberti himself, who also worked as an architect during this period. The culmination of Michelozzo's technical development as a metalworker came with the casting of the *St Matthew*, Ghiberti's initial casting having proved defective. The hybrid style of this monumental statue, with its classical and Gothic elements, has

much in common with Michelozzo's subsequent work, which reveals a strong tendency to emulate the Antique, as is particularly noticeable in the three great funerary monuments executed in partnership with Donatello.

The *Coscia* monument (1424), being wall-mounted and surmounted by a draped canopy, is derived from such Venetian prototypes as that of *Tomaso Mocenigo* (1423; Venice, SS Giovanni e Paolo) by the Florentine Piero di Niccolò Lamberti. Michelozzo's monument, which is inserted between two of the Baptistery's interior columns, has a high base decorated with garlands and putti heads, upon which stand three theological Virtues in shell niches and framed by pilasters. The sarcophagus above is supported by corbels and bears a commemorative inscription on a scroll, held open by two putti. Above this, lying on an *all'antica* bier supported by lions, is the gilt-bronze figure of the cardinal with a singularly youthful face similar to Donatello's *St Louis* (1423; Florence, Mus. Opera Santa Croce), and above this in turn is a bust of the *Virgin and Child* set against a lunette filled by a large shell, and finally a marble drape apparently hanging by a ring from the architrave of the Baptistery's lower storey. Although it is not clear what Michelozzo's particular contribution to the work may have been, it is likely that he was at least involved in the general design and that he was responsible for some of the carving. Usually attributed to him is the bust of the *Virgin and Child*, which with its flowing composition and formal simplification is reminiscent of Ghiberti.

The *Brancaccio* tomb (1426–8; see fig. 1) in S Angelo a Nilo, Naples, by contrast, is an example of the floor-standing baldacchino type, based on Angevin tombs such as that of *Ladislas, King of Naples* (after 1414; Naples, S Giovanni a Carbonara) as well as Roman examples, such as the tomb of *Philippe d'Alençon*. These models, however, are reinterpreted in an early Renaissance architectural vocabulary usually attributed to Michelozzo, but which is comparable with other works of the period, for example Donatello's *St Louis* tabernacle (*c.* 1423; Florence, Orsanmichele). The sarcophagus, surmounted by a canopy supported by composite columns, is carried by marble caryatids—a favourite motif in Neapolitan tombs, for example Tino di Camaino's monument of *Catherine of Austria* (after 1323; Naples, S Lorenzo Maggiore)—which are probably the work of Michelozzo. Their identities are still uncertain, being either Christian Virtues or Classical Fates, although they appear to derive from Roman reliefs of religious processions but with an added movement that appears to capture an instant in the funeral ceremony. The simplification of the angular figures recalls both classical prototypes, especially their idealized heads, and the work of other 14th-century artists such as Giovanni Pisano.

The dismembered *Aragazzi* monument at Montepulciano (1427) is almost exclusively the work of Michelozzo and would have been still more classicizing and archaeological in spirit. The two reliefs that decorated the sarcophagus (still in the church, now Montepulciano Cathedral) are closely based on Roman processional reliefs. More dynamic are two reliefs of angels (London, V&A) once flanking a full-length male figure, perhaps the risen Christ in Montepulciano Cathedral. The antiquarianism can be related to the cultural background of the patron, Bartolomeo Aragazzi (whose effigy by Michelozzo is also

in the Cathedral), who, as secretary and then chancellor to Pope Martin V, was a pioneering researcher of Classical texts. The *Aragazzi* monument anticipates Bernardo Rossellino's *Bruni* monument (1444; Florence, Santa Croce) and Desiderio da Settignano's *Marsuppini* monument (*c.* 1453; Florence, Santa Croce) in associating sculptural antiquarianism with the humanist avant-garde. Although the reliefs of the Prato pulpit (1428) were largely the work of Donatello, the architectural elements, especially the elaborate bronze supporting capital, were possibly Michelozzo's and are characteristic of his creative and fanciful approach to *all'antica* design. There is little evidence that he contributed to the design of Ghiberti's *Gates of Paradise* (completed 1452; Florence Cathedral, Baptistery) although he has been connected with the panels of *Isaac* and *Jacob*. His silver statuette of *St John the Baptist* (1452; Florence, Mus. Opera Duomo), however, is a masterpiece of metalwork.

(ii) Architecture.

(a) Early work. Michelozzo's earliest buildings reveal that he was capable of operating in a wide range of styles. What they have in common is an emphasis on form and volume, a sparing articulation and a willingness to mix stylistic elements. The façade of the Palazzo Comunale at Montepulciano (1440) is so closely based on the late medieval Palazzo Vecchio in Florence that, although it is arranged into a symmetrical composition, it can be considered as a quotation.

The monastery of S Francesco at Bosco ai Frati (1420s) rises from the ruins of a hermitage and, although somewhat marred by the insistent use of the Medici *palle* (their coat of arms) as a decorative motif, it was restructured without the loss of its sober medieval austerity. The dormitory was enlarged, loggias were built over the garden, and the church was lengthened and splendidly vaulted. Work on the Trebbio villa (1420s), also for the Medici, involved alterations to a medieval tower-fortress of a compact and regular shape, strategically positioned high above the Mugello valley north of Florence. The medieval appearance of the villa, with its castellations, is difficult to reconcile with the spirit of humanist architecture but is appropriate for the country residence of a family with social aspirations. The Cafaggiolo villa (1420s), not far from Trebbio, has all the qualities of a palazzo, with a courtyard and loggias, fortified walls and moat. The use of plaster on the exterior is characteristic of Michelozzo, as are the simple volumetric elements of the design, especially the dominant central tower, a feature typical of fortresses that gives dignity to the villa. The irregularly arranged windows with their dark frames contrast with the light walls and lend the building a medieval character, and architectural elements such as the cornices of the doors (similar to those of the later Noviciate at Santa Croce) and the triangular corbels are certainly of medieval form. More unusual, however, is the sophisticated combination of volume with surrounding space and garden, which is no longer an enclosed medieval *hortus* but a synthesis of utility and ornament.

The monastery of S Marco (*c.* 1436), Florence, develops on a larger scale the ideas initiated at Bosco ai Frati.

Cosimo de' Medici's motives for financing the rebuilding, rather than hoarding his money like other merchants and bankers, would have been faithful to the moral stance of Dominican theologians as well as to Ciceronian ethics. Early writers attributed an initial design for the new monastery to Brunelleschi, who then entrusted the project to Michelozzo because he had too much work in hand. Michelozzo's design did not greatly change the original building. In the church he added a vaulted choir to the existing presbytery and framed it with fluted Corinthian pilasters, applied to piers. The body of the church was subdivided according to Dominican tradition into three areas, for the monks, for laymen and for women, and Michelozzo added the gabled bell-tower. The basic layout of the adjoining monastery, which Vasari judged 'the most comfortable and beautiful … in all Italy', was retained, with the pilgrims' guest wing along the front aligned with the unadorned façade of the church (replaced 1780). The cloister at the side of the church was rebuilt in Renaissance style, with stone Ionic columns and slightly flattened arches. Around the courtyard on the upper floor are the simple monks' cells, many of which were frescoed by Fra Angelico.

The main innovation of the monastery complex is the library (see fig. 2), the first purpose-built example in the Renaissance, which occupies the upper floor of a wing facing on to a second cloister to the north. The library has three aisles, a layout derived from 14th-century dormitories—as, for example, at S Maria Novella—but here they are divided by slender Ionic columns with a central barrel vault and groin vaults at either side. The windows are small and situated at the reader's eye-level. In this library

2. Michelozzo di Bartolomeo: library of the monastery of S Marco, Florence, begun *c*. 1436

were kept the precious Greek and Latin manuscripts acquired in 1437 by Cosimo de' Medici from the heirs of the humanist Niccolò Niccoli as well as texts recommended by Tommaso Parentucelli (later Pope Nicholas V).

(b) Mature work. The Medici chapel at Santa Croce, Florence (1440s), is a simple design that became a model for many other buildings. The body of the chapel has two square bays with groin vaults supported on corbels, and an altar space at the end, framed by pilasters, which is flanked by service areas as in Brunelleschi's Old Sacristy for S Lorenzo. The tall vaulted corridor nearby that links the medieval church with new monastic buildings is lit by three elegant tripartite arched windows, of a basically medieval type but reinterpreted in Renaissance style. The monastic buildings at Santa Croce, which incorporate Brunelleschi's Pazzi Chapel (perhaps under construction at the same time), have a similar layout to those at S Marco, with spacious barrel- or groin-vaulted stairways, and sleeping wings divided into small cells with white walls and simple stone cornices. At S Lorenzo it has been suggested that alterations made by Michelozzo (after Cosimo's return in 1434) to Brunelleschi's design can be seen in the transept ends, the dome, and even the nave colonnades.

Michelozzo's design for the Palazzo Medici (now Palazzo Medici–Riccardi; 1444; see fig. 3), Florence, may have been inspired by Brunelleschi's grandiose design, which had been rejected, perhaps because it was considered incompatible with Cosimo de' Medici's political and cultural image. Michelozzo's design, however, with its relatively regular plan organized around a central colonnaded courtyard, its rear garden flanked by loggias, and with its three-storey façades crowned by massive cornices, became a model for early Renaissance architecture. The graduated stone facing, from the rusticated basement to the smooth masonry of the second floor, and the round-headed mullioned windows can be traced to 14th-century palaces, for example the Palazzo Vecchio and Palazzo Davanzati. The Corinthian cornice, however, is derived from Roman examples, and the rustication may have been thought evocative of such ancient monuments as the Etruscan walls at Fiesole. The interior of the palace was splendidly decorated, especially the chapel with the fresco cycle by Benozzo Gozzoli and its elaborately carved wooden fittings and coffered ceilings, which perhaps follow Michelozzo's designs.

Unlike Trebbio and Cafaggiolo, the Careggi villa, about three miles from Florence, was not a fortified stronghold, despite its external castellations, but a suburban residence with courtyards and open loggias overlooking a garden. Its curious plan is due to the irregular shape of the site and to its being a remodelling of an earlier structure. Careggi marks the revival of the classical ideal of villa life. The Medici villa (*c*. 1460) at Fiesole is also attributed to Michelozzo, although its construction was supervised by Antonio Manetti Ciaccheri (1405–60). The design, a simple block with a loggia overlooking a terraced garden, reflects a new interest in the villa as a place of rest and culture as described by Cicero and Pliny.

3. Michelozzo di Bartolomeo: courtyard of the Palazzo Medici (new Palazzo Medici–Riccardi), Florence, begun 1444

The most extraordinary and fascinating of Michelozzo's architectural projects was the tribune of SS Annunziata, Florence. Its unprecedented circular plan with nine radiating chapels served as a presbytery, choir and funerary chapel (see fig. 4). From the start of work (1444) the building was criticized by Brunelleschi and other architects, who suggested it was an unsuitable attachment to a basilican church. The design of the tribune is apparently derived from the Temple of Minerva Medica in Rome and would be one of the earliest, as well as one of the most far-reaching, instances of this sort of revivalism in the 15th century. Michelozzo's transformation of the rest of the church under the new administration of the Servites (1447) involved the conversion of the side aisles into chapels and the construction of a new sacristy. Other work at SS Annunziata included the rebuilding of the large cloister and the building of a forecourt, the Chiostro dei Voti, the neighbouring oratory of S Sebastiano dei Pucci, and the creation of the elaborately carved marble tabernacle (1448) supported by four columns, two Corinthian and two Composite, to house the miraculous painting of the *Annunciation*. The tabernacle was executed by Pagno di Lapo (Portigiani) and Maso di Bartolommeo, two former colleagues from the workshop who also worked at S Lorenzo.

The Ceppo Hospital (1451) at Pistoia and the hospital of S Paolo (1455), with their spacious courtyards and columns carrying arches without intermediate mouldings, were both only routine work for Michelozzo. In each case the front loggia dates from the late 15th century, and it is therefore unclear whether the design, which is based on Brunelleschi's Ospedale degli Innocenti in Florence, may be attributed to Michelozzo.

3. CRITICAL RECEPTION AND POSTHUMOUS REPUTATION. Michelozzo was almost totally ignored by 15th-century treatise and chronicle writers, although he was mentioned by Benedetto Dei, who described him as an 'architect and sculptor of all things', while Filarete included him with other sculptors who turned to architecture, such as Pagno di Lapo and Bernardo Rossellino. The first catalogue of Michelozzo's work (1516–20) was by Antonio Billi, who incorrectly referred to him as Michelozzo Michelozzi. This was Vasari's primary source in the first edition of his *Vite* (Florence, 1550), although in the second edition he attempted to distinguish Michelozzo's personality as a sculptor from that of his 'master' Donatello, emphasizing Michelozzo's administrative role in the partnership and in particular his work as an architect. For the first time the Palazzo Medici, the modernization of Palazzo Vecchio and the fortifications outside Florence were added to the list of attributions. Vasari's account forms the basis of those by Borghini, Scamozzi and the comprehensive guide of Bocchi. The view that Michelozzo's design for Palazzo Medici was a mere fall-back to replace the destroyed project of Brunelleschi became

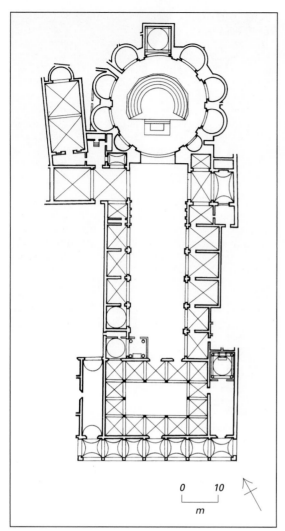

4. Michelozzo di Bartolomeo: plan of SS Annunziata, Florence, begun 1444

independent artist, especially in studies dating from between the two world wars, attempts began to be made to characterize his style more precisely (notably in works of particular importance, such as the SS Annunziata tribune), recognizing both his classical and gothicizing designs, such as the church at Bosco ai Frati, and his apparent ability to adapt his style in accordance with his various patrons. Despite a number of excellent studies, Michelozzo regained his due recognition as one of the great sculptors of the Renaissance only with Janson's thesis (1942). Subsequent studies have reaffirmed this view, and his formative influence has been recognized, particularly in the evolution of the Renaissance tomb monument.

BIBLIOGRAPHY

EARLY SOURCES

A. Filarete: *Trattato di architettura* (1451–64); ed. A. M. Finoli and L. Grassi (Milan, 1973), p. 171

B. Dei: *Descrizione de Firenze* (1472); ed. G. C. Romby, *Descrizioni e rappresentazioni della città di Firenze nel XV secolo* (Florence, 1976), p. 72

A. Billi: *Il libro di Antonio Billi* (MS.; *c.* 1516–20; Florence, Bib. N. Cent.); ed. C. von Fabriczy (Florence, 1891), p. 27

G. Vasari: *Vite* (Florence, 1550, rev. 2/1568); ed. G. Milanesi (1878–85), ii, pp. 431–51

R. Borghini: *Il riposo di Raffaello Borghini, in cui della pittura, e della scultura si favella* (Florence, 1584); ed. M. Rosci (Milan, 1967), p. 322

F. Bocchi: *Le bellezze della città di Fiorenza* (Florence, 1591); ed. G. Cinelli (Florence, 1677), p. 87

V. Scamozzi: *L'idea della architettura universale* (Venice, 1615), p. 29

F. Baldinucci: *Notizie* (Florence, 1681–1728); ed. F. Rinalli (1845–7), i, p. 406

F. L. del Migliore: *Firenze città nobilissima* (Florence, 1684), p. 199

GENERAL WORKS

F. Milizia: *Le vite de' più celebri architetti d'ogni tempo* (Rome, 1768), pp. 169–70; rev. as *Memorie degli architetti antichi e moderni* (Bassano, 4/1785), i, pp. 127–9

A. Rau and M. Rastrelli: *Serie degli uomini più illustri nella pittura, scultura, e architettura . . .* (Florence, 1769–76), xiii, p. 50

A. C. Quatremère de Quincy: *Histoire de la vie et des ouvrages des plus célèbres architectes du XIe siècle jusqu'à la fin du XVIIIe*, i (Paris, 1830), p. 72

F. Wolff: *Michelozzo di Bartolomeo: Ein Beitrag zur Geschichte der Architektur und Plastik im Quattrocento* (Strasbourg, 1900)

C. von Fabriczy: 'Michelozzo di Bartolomeo', *Jb. Kön.-Preuss. Kstsamml.*, xxv (1904), pp. 34–110

O. Morisani: *Michelozzo architetto* (Turin, 1951) [full bibliog.]

L. Gori Montanelli: *Brunelleschi e Michelozzo* (Florence, 1957)

H. McNeal Caplow: *Michelozzo*, 2 vols (New York, 1977)

H. Saalman: 'Documenti inediti sulla cappella della SS Annunziata', *Scritti di storia dell'arte in onore di U. Procacci* (Milan, 1977), pp. 225–7

M. Ferrara and F. Quinterio: *Michelozzo di Bartolomeo* (Florence, 1984)

J. Beck: 'New Notices for Michelozzo', *Renaissance Studies in Honour of Craig Hugh Smith* (Florence, 1985), ii, pp. 23–36

SCULPTURE

H. W. Janson: *The Sculpted Works of Michelozzo di Bartolomeo* (diss., Cambridge, MA, Harvard U., 1942)

——: *The Sculpture of Donatello*, 2 vols (Princeton, 1957)

O. Morisani: 'Il monumento Brancacci nell'ambiente napoletano del quattrocento', *Atti dell'VIII convegno internazionale di studi sul rinascimento: Donatello e il suo tempo: Firenze, 1968*, pp. 207–13

F. Gurrieri: *Donatello e Michelozzo nel pulpito di Prato* (Florence, 1970)

F. Finiello Zervas: *Systems of Design and Proportion used by Ghiberti, Donatello and Michelozzo in their Large-scale Sculptural Ensembles between 1412–1434* (Baltimore, 1973)

H. McNeal Caplow: 'Sculptors' Partnerships in Michelozzo's Florence', *Stud. Ren.*, xxi (1974), pp. 145–75

R. W. Lightbown: *Donatello and Michelozzo: An Artistic Partnership and its Patrons in the Early Renaissance*, 2 vols (London, 1980)

A. Natali: *L'umanesimo di Michelozzo* (Florence, 1980)

ARCHITECTURE

H. Folnesics: 'Der Anteil Michelozzos an der Mailander Renaissancearchitektur', *Repert. Kstwiss.*, xl (1917), pp. 129–37

particularly popular (del Migliore), and the number of erroneous attributions increased. Milizia was more critically objective, praising some of the formal solutions of Palazzo Medici but condemning the strongly decorative trends of the Annunziata tabernacle.

Perhaps the first attempt to define the architectural personality of Michelozzo was that of Rau and Rastrelli, who saw Michelozzo as an imitator of Brunelleschi but one who strove 'to abandon . . . the barbarous German style', a view underlying the writings of Quatremère de Quincy and others. The reappraisal of Michelozzo's career, based on documentary material, began with Milanesi and culminated with Fabriczy (1904) and the first monographs on Michelozzo by Wolff and Folnesics. At the same time critical assessment and typological comparison became an increasingly important aspect of the study of Michelozzo, and his work began to be seen as having had a formative influence on building in Florence from 1440 to 1460. Once Michelozzo had been elevated to the rank of an

H. Saalman: 'The Palazzo Comunale in Montepulciano: An Unknown Work by Michelozzo', *Z. Kstgesch.*, xxviii (1965), pp. 1–46

——: 'Michelozzo Studies: I. Michelozzo at Santa Croce', *Burl. Mag.*, cviii (1966), pp. 242–50

——: 'Michelozzo Studies: The Florentine Mint', *Festschrift Ulrich Middeldorf* (Berlin, 1968), i, pp. 140–42

P. Roselli: *Coro e cupola della SS Annunziata a Firenze* (Pisa, 1971)

H. McNeal Caplow: 'Michelozzo at Ragusa: New Documents and Revaluations', *J. Soc. Archit. Hist.*, xxxi/2 (1972), pp. 108–19

M. Gori Sassoli: 'Michelozzo e l'architettura di villa del primo rinascimento', *Stor. A.*, xxiii (1975), pp. 5–51

E. Casalini: 'Brunelleschi e Michelozzo all'Annunziata', *Le due cupole: Firenze, 1977*, pp. 29–63

R. A. Goldthwaite and W. Rearick: 'Michelozzo and the Ospedale di San Paolo in Florence', *Mitt. Ksthist. Inst. Florenz*, xxi (1977), pp. 221–306

H. Teubner: 'Das Langhaus der SS Annunziata in Florenz: Studien zu Michelozzo und Giuliano da Sangallo', *Mitt. Ksthist. Inst. Florenz*, xxii (1978), pp. 27–60

——: 'San Marco: Umbauten vor 1500 ein Beitrag zum Werk des Michelozzo', *Mitt. Ksthist. Inst. Florenz*, xxiii (1979), pp. 239–72

B. L. Brown: *The Tribuna of SS Annunziata in Florence* (diss., New York U., 1980)

FRANCESCO QUINTERIO

Michelsen, Hans (*b* Hegstad, Melhus, *bapt* 30 Aug 1789; *d* Christiania [now Oslo], 20 June 1859). Norwegian sculptor. He joined the army in 1810 but in 1815 obtained a discharge and moved to Stockholm to pursue an artistic career. There he studied at the Konstakademi from 1815 to 1819 under Erik Gustav Göthe and in 1820 moved to Rome, where he worked with the Danish sculptor Bertel Thorvaldsen. In Rome he made copies of antique sculptures, including a marble *Head of Bacchus* (1820–26; Oslo, N.G.) copied from a work in the Museo Capitolino. This Classical influence was reinforced by Thorvaldsen's Neoclassicism. After leaving Rome in 1826 he spent a while in Christiania before moving to Stockholm again, where he worked as an assistant to Göthe and Johan Niklas Byström.

In 1833 Michelsen began work on statues of the 12 *Apostles* for the church at Trondheim, which were finished by 1840. Widely acknowledged as his finest work, the *Apostles* have a monumentality and grandeur associated with Renaissance sculpture. The year of their completion Michelsen became a member of the Kunstakademi in Christiania and at the same time was given the title of Royal Sculptor. He settled in Christiania in 1842 and spent the rest of his life based there. Among his other public works are four statues for Oscarshall Castle, executed in 1849, and statues of *St Sunniva* and *St Olav* for the Catholic church in Christiania. Michelsen also produced portrait busts, including that of *Peder Kolbjørnsen* (*c.* 1850; Oslo, N.G.). Though a competent sculptor, Michelsen never achieved any great originality in his work, which remained largely under the influence of his various teachers and the sculpture of the past.

NBL
BIBLIOGRAPHY
J. H. Langaard, ed.: *Norsk og fremmed skulptur i Nasjonal Galleriet* [Norwegian and foreign sculpture in the National Gallery] (Oslo, 1937), pp. 5–6

Michelucci, Giovanni (*b* Pistoia, 2 Jan 1891; *d* Florence, 1991). Italian architect and writer. He graduated from the Scuola Superiore di Architettura (1911) and then studied until 1914 at the Accademia di Belle Arti (both in Florence). His first work was a series of three villas near Pistoia (1924–5), whose unadorned walls and delicate surface articulations recall Josef Hoffmann's work. In 1920 he moved to Rome, where he taught interior design in Roberto Papini's Scuola d'Arte in Via Monteverde. In 1928 he accepted the offer of a professorship at the Scuola Superiore di Architettura in Florence. From these years date his first contacts with the Rationalist group MIAR, whose influence is visible in the project for a villa (1931) in Rome for the musician Alfredo Casella. Michelucci's first major work was S Maria Novella Railway Station (1933–5; with N. Baroni, P. N. Berardi, S. Guarnieri, L. Lusanna and I. Gamberini), Florence, one of the outstanding monuments of modern Italian architecture. Situated next to S Maria Novella, it used traditional materials such as *pietra forte* and kept an understated profile. Through its great glazed entrance hall, open at both ends, it related both visually and spatially to the surrounding urban fabric. The interior furnishings are also in rich materials with careful detailing (two murals by Ottone Rosai survive). By comparison subsequent projects up to 1939, including the Istituto di Mineralogia (1932–5) in the Città Universitaria, Rome, the Palazzo del Governo (1936) in Arezzo and the addition to the Villa Contini Bonaccosi (1939) at Forte dei Marmi, were increasingly in the predominant classicizing *Novecento* manner with practically no Rationalist elements.

After World War II Michelucci's work can be divided into two periods. Up to the early 1960s this focused on a sophisticated exploration of traditional building types. Two outstanding examples are a church at Collina da Pontelungo (1953–4), Pistoia, a derivation from the vernacular in brick and stone with long, tiled mono-pitched roofs, and the Casa Ventura (1956–7) in Via Guicciardini, Florence, which was based on the typical medieval residence with shops on the ground floor. The façade was of wood, stone, glass and concrete, creating a complex pattern of advancing and receding elements. The Cassa di Risparmio (1961), Florence, displayed a similar sensitivity for materials; the plan is based on an internal street, in which the regularly vaulted structure contrasts with the intricate overlaying of side-balconies projecting at different angles. These works also reflect an approach to urban design based on the slow processes of stratified change found in Italy's smaller urban centres.

The Osteria del Gambero (1961) marked the beginning of a more personal and flamboyant phase in Michelucci's work, characterized by bold and irregular geometries. This is best exemplified in S Giovanni Battista (1964) in Campi Bisenzio near Florence, dedicated to the memory of the workers who lost their lives working on the Autostrada del Sole. Michelucci conceived it as a piece of environmental sculpture, with a path (unrealized) winding up the roof to a viewing platform. The sweeping profile of the roof established a strong visual link with both the motorway and the Tuscan hills further off, while the branching concrete supports inside create an almost maze-like atmosphere. Similar spatial disjunctions can be seen in his Brutalist Post Office (1964–7), Via Verdi, Florence; the plasticity of the façade, with aggressively cantilevered floors jutting out at different angles, engages the street in an active, even challenging way. Throughout his long career, Michelucci worked in a variety of styles, from the modernism of his earliest works to the neo-Expressionism of his late phase. While his buildings tended to be conservative in terms of spatial organization and construction, they all display a high level of craftsmanship and a unique concern for context. Michelucci was also a prolific writer. In 1945 he founded *La nuova città*, a journal concerned with the synthesis of architecture and urban design. The journal came out irregularly during the 1950s. He produced several unrealized urban schemes for Florence and took an active part in discussions over the city's future. He held university chairs in Florence until 1948, and in 1948–9 he directed the Istituto di Architettura Tecnica in Bologna. He won the Feltrinelli Prize for Architecture in 1958 and the San Luca International Prize for Architecture in 1963.

WRITINGS

with A. Ardigo and F. Borsi: *Il quartiere di Santa Croce nel futuro di Firenze* (Rome, 1968)
with F. Borsi and others: *Michelucci: Il linguaggio dell'architettura* (Rome, 1979)
La felicità dell'architettura (Pistoia, 1981)

BIBLIOGRAPHY

E. Detti: 'Giovanni Michelucci', *Comunità*, 23 (1954), pp. 38–42
F. Borsi, ed.: *Giovanni Michelucci* (Florence, 1966)
L. Lugli: *Giovanni Michelucci: Il pensiero e le opere* (Florence, 1966)
G. K. Koenig: *L'architettura in Toscana, 1931–1968* (Turin, 1968)
M. Cerasi: *Michelucci* (Rome, n.d.) [?1969]
P. Portoghesi: 'Tavola rotonda sull'opera di G. Michelucci', *Ist. Elem. Archit. & Rilievo Mnmt.* [Genova]: *Quad.*, 2 (1969), pp. 9–18
Giovanni Michelucci (exh. cat., London, RIBA, Heinz Gal., 1978)
M. Tafuri: *Storia dell'architettura italiana, 1944–1985* (Turin, 1986), pp. 39–42

LIBERO ANDREOTTI

Michetti, Francesco Paolo (*b* Tocco da Casauria, nr Sulmona, 2 Oct 1851; *d* Francavilla al Mare, nr Pescara, 5 March 1929). Italian painter. He was one of the foremost artists of the later 19th century to paint the Abruzzo region. He depicted its people, animals and local events and festivals in a style that was painterly, emotionally charged and often highly fantastic.

1. BEFORE 1880. In 1864, after the death of his father, Crispino, who was a music teacher and composer, he moved from Tocco da Casauria to Chieti, where he was taught the rudiments of painting by the fresco painter Francesco Paolo Marchiani. In 1868, having obtained a small grant to help him pursue his studies, he left Chieti for Naples where, with the assistance of Edoardo Dalbono, he was admitted to full-time study at the Accademia di Belle Arti e Liceo Artistico. From the outset his teacher Domenico Morelli noted his marked independence of expression and natural talent for painting. With this in mind, in 1869 the Director of the Accademia, convinced that studying in a real life situation would be of far greater benefit to Michetti than would a full-time academic course, authorized the provincial administration in Chieti to allow him to return to his native region of Abruzzo, while still paying him a grant. On his return home *c.* 1870, he found in Abruzzo a source of emotional and aesthetic inspiration and began to depict children at play and young peasants, as well as dogs, chickens and sheep, in small, lively paintings, vibrant with light and bursting with sparkling, luminous colour. These early works, with their emphasis on nature and animals, tend to be influenced by Filippo

Palizzi's paintings, rather than by Morelli's. Michetti introduced a gentle, personal aspect to the truthfulness of the scenes that he painted. His bold brushstrokes can be seen in *Girl with Chicken* (1873; Naples, Mus. N. S Martino), where the thick areas of colour glitter with flashes of light. Many of his works produced during these years were acquired by the collector Paolo Rotondo and subsequently entered the collections of the Museo Nazionale di San Martino in Naples. Rotondo was among the first admirers of Michetti's art, having met him through Morelli. Michetti signed a contract with the Neapolitan art dealer Gerald Reitlinger for the promotion of his paintings in France, which helped to increase his popularity there.

In 1871 he travelled to Paris, where he was invited to show at the Salons of 1872 and 1875. Between 1872 and 1874 he was a member of the so-called Scuola di Resina, a group of painters in Naples that included Giuseppe De Nittis, Marco di Gregorio (1829–76) and Federico Rossano (1835–1912), and whose aim was to bring Italian art into the mainstream of European art. A determining factor in the development of Michetti's art was his meeting in 1874 with Mariano José Bernardo Fortuny y Marsal, who influenced his use both of colour and of tone. From 1877 he almost exclusively used the medium of pastel, which permitted gentler effects of light and colour. One of his most successful pastel works is a *Self-portrait Aged 26* (1877; Naples, Banco di Napoli, on loan to Naples, Capodimonte). In this work he has used controlled tones of great lightness and elegance to integrate perfectly the psychological interpretation of the face with the formal representation. In other paintings, however, his use of Fortuny's methods gave rise to harsh criticism. For example in *Corpus Domini*, exhibited in 1877 at the Prima Esposizione Nazionale di Belle Arti in Naples, the realistic spirit has been transformed into an imaginative, folkloric motif executed as a composition of jumbled figures, teeming with brushstrokes and vibrant with colour and light. It represents the first of a series of paintings that celebrate the Abruzzo region. However, the painting was offensive to those who saw in it an affectedly graceful style and a facile disregard for pictorial substance and perspective. In allowing the definition of form to be broken down into layers of colour, he was, on the contrary, confirming his bias towards his earlier paintings of country idylls and was merely emphasizing their fantastic elements. *Corpus Domini* provoked still more debate with regard to its unusual terracotta frame, painted dark grey and designed by Michetti himself, who from 1872 had been producing small, unusual decorative sculptures in clay.

2. 1880 AND AFTER. In 1880, at the Esposizione Nazionale di Belle Arti in Turin, Michetti received much public acclaim and shared with Giacomo Favretto the prizes for genre painting. The following year, at the Esposizione Nazionale di Belle Arti in Milan, he exhibited 34 studies in pastel and tempera. These works sold well and they were admired by the public, both for their speed of execution and for their contrived innovations in the relationship of the sheet of paper to the frame and the glass. Critics, however, began to be intolerant of Michetti's mannerisms. In 1883 he was granted permission by the Commune of Francavilla al Mare to purchase the old

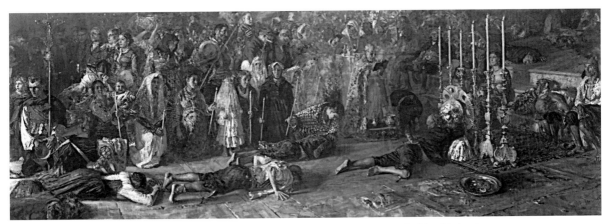

Francesco Paolo Michetti: *The Vow*, oil on canvas, 2.5×7.0 m, begun 1880 (Rome, Galleria Nazionale d'Arte Moderna)

Franciscan convent of S Maria del Gesù where he established both his home and his studio. For the next 20 years the convent became a meeting-place for the many exponents of the culture of the Abruzzo region. Among them was Gabriele D'Annunzio, who in 1883 had celebrated Michetti in *Ricordi francavillesi* (1883) and with whom he enjoyed a long friendship. They shared a taste for the wild and pastoral Abruzzo region, which demanded to be painted in vibrant colours applied with passion, and where extraordinary events were favoured and recorded with a sensitivity ranging far beyond the threshold of normal human experience. Michetti's gracious charm is partially suppressed in his large painting *The Vow* (2.5×7.0 m; Rome, G.N.A. Mod.; see fig.), which was begun in 1880 but was shown as unfinished at the Esposizione Nazionale di Belle Arti in Rome in 1883. The unpolished and relaxed pictorial style draws its inspiration from the feast day of St Pantaleon at Migliónico in Basilicata and seems to accentuate the crude and dramatic aspects of a popular superstitious ritual. His dusty figures, expanded to the extent of appearing transparent, are squeezed into ill-defined spaces and have an unsettling effect generated by their uncompromising intensity. *The Vow* has always been treated as part of the genre of social realism, as also practised by Teofilo Patini and Achille D'Orsi. It is, however, more than a mere nonconformist portrayal of the poverty of the working classes: the painting's mood is sombre and its situation tragic, devoid of any relief or redemption, and this arouses in the viewer a sense of uneasiness and revulsion.

Michetti's most productive years were between 1884 and 1896, when he painted about 30 large works at the convent. During this period he began to utilize the medium of photography which, as a truthful record taken from life, was to stimulate the development of new working methods. Unlike many professional photographers working at the turn of the century, he did not exploit the picturesque possibilities of the photograph. Instead he often produced exact photodocumentations that would be used with great accuracy as guidelines for his paintings. In 1895, at the height of his career, he painted *Daughter of Iorio* (Pescara, Pal. Gov.), from which D'Annunzio drew inspiration for his tragedy performed in 1904, and for

which Michetti was both set and costume designer. During the 1880s and 1890s he took part in numerous international exhibitions and painted the events and the rituals of his native Abruzzo. In 1899, at the third Biennale in Venice, he exhibited about 200 studies, encompassing two decades of his career, which were eventually sold to the German businessman Ernst Seeger and exhibited at the Grosse Deutsche Kunstausstellung in Berlin in 1912 and in Vienna. His final large tempera paintings, *The Cripples* and *The Snakes* (both 1900), were hastily prepared for the Exposition Universelle in Paris in 1900 and received a somewhat lukewarm response, although he was awarded a gold medal. After this show, he decided not to exhibit any more and to abandon painting. He sold his studio and lived the rest of his life as a recluse, although he was elected a senator in 1909. Michetti's style of painting, which earlier in his career had been the subject of exaggerated enthusiasm, was later rejected outright by critics for its overly illustrative nature and for its exuberant and superficial tendency to indulge in detailed description.

BIBLIOGRAPHY
G. D'Annunzio: 'Ricordi francavillesi', *Fanfulla Domenica* (7 Jan 1883)
——: 'Il *Voto*: Quadro di F. P. Michetti', *Fanfulla Domenica* (14 Jan 1883)
U. Ojetti: 'Artisti contemporanei: F. P. Michetti', *Emporium*, cxcii (1910), pp. 402–28
T. Sillani: *Francesco Paolo Michetti* (Milan and Rome, 1932)
M. Miraglia: *Francesco Paolo Michetti fotografo* (Turin, 1975)
Francesco Paolo Michetti (exh. cat., ed. Fondazione Michetti; Francavilla al Mare, Pal. Sirena, 1979)
F. Di Tizio: *Francesco Paolo Michetti nel cinquantenario della morte* (Pescara, 1980)
A. Dragon: 'Un "solachianiello" mancato: Francesco Paolo Michetti', *Ottocento*, xvi (Milan, 1987)

SILVIA LUCCHESI

Michetti, Niccolò [Nicola, Nicolò; Miketti, Nikola] (*b* Rome, between 1672 and 1681; *d* Rome, Jan 1759). Italian architect. He assisted Carlo Fontana on the rebuilding of SS Apostoli (1708–12), Rome, and succeeded him in 1714 on the extension of the Ospizio di S Michele. He later worked on schemes for the papal authorities. In 1718 Peter I summoned him to Russia, where he designed and supervised the construction of the Yekaterinental (now Kadriorg) Palace (1718–23) at Tallinn in a restrained Italian Baroque style, with a magnificent central salon. He completed three pavilions at Peterhof (1719) to the plans of Alexandre-Jacques-Baptiste Leblond after the latter's death, and he redesigned the Strel'na Palace (1720–23; rebuilt) as an Italian villa that composed well with its formal park. He was also a skilled landscape gardener and designer of fountains. His projects in St Petersburg included the Peter's Garden School (1721) with a Baroque chapel. He designed a lighthouse at Kronshtadt (1721–2; unexecuted; model in St Petersburg, Cent. Naval Mus.) in the form of a bell-tower with open stages topped by a spire. Michetti returned to Rome in 1723, where he rebuilt the Palazzo Colonna from 1731; only the two end pavilions remain to his design. From 1733 until his death he served as architect of the Camera Apostolica and the Theatine Order.

BIBLIOGRAPHY

I. Grabar': 'Arkhitektory-inostrantsy pri Petre Velikom' [Foreign architects under Peter the Great], *Staryye gody* (July–Sept 1911), pp. 132–50

E. Lo Gatto: *Gli artisti italiani in Russia*, 2 vols (Rome, 1934–5)

M. Lumiste: *Kadriorgskiy dvorets* [The Kadriorg Palace] (Tallinn, 1976)

V. G. Dolbin: 'Po zamyslu Miketti' [To Michetti's design], *Stroitel'stvo & Arkhit. Leningrada*, vii (1979), pp. 34–5

Arkhitekturnaya grafika Rossii: Pervaya polovina XVIII veka: Sobraniye Ermitazha [Architectural drawings of Russia: first half of the 18th century: the Hermitage collection], Leningrad, Hermitage cat.; intro. A. N. Voronikhina (Leningrad, 1981)

N. A. YEVSINA

Michiel, Marcantonio (*b* Venice, *c.* 1484; *d* Venice, 9 May 1552). Italian writer and collector. He was an important Venetian dilettante and connoisseur whose surviving writings constitute a valuable source of information on 16th-century art patronage in the Veneto. He received his education from the renowned scholar Giovanni Battista Egnazio (1473/8–1553), Canon of S Marina, whose own active interest in the arts and literature no doubt had a formative influence on him. In his youth Michiel travelled to Dalmatia and Corfu; in 1514 he visited Florence and in 1516 Bergamo, of which he wrote a Latin description, his only work published in his lifetime. In 1518 he travelled to Rome, where he stayed for two years.

Michiel's diary, which he kept from 1511, reveals his increasing interest in art and architecture, no doubt stimulated by his experience of the papal court, where he came into contact with Baldassare Peruzzi and possibly Sebastiano del Piombo and Raphael. Michiel also explored the ancient ruins of Rome and Naples. While in Rome he maintained contact with his Venetian friends, to whom he wrote about current affairs and major events in the city's art life, such as Raphael's death, the decoration of the Vatican Loggie, the display of seven of Raphael's tapestries and the praise received by Sebastiano del Piombo's *Raising of Lazarus* (1519; London, N.G.; *see* SEBASTIANO DEL PIOMBO, fig. 3) when it was displayed in the Vatican in December 1519.

Soon after his return to Venice, Michiel began assembling concise notes describing civic buildings, churches and their contents and, most importantly, private collections located in the Veneto; now arranged geographically, the largest sections are devoted to Padua and Venice. These notes (Venice, Bib. N. Marciana, Ital. XI.67 (7351)), which were compiled intermittently between 1521 and 1543, were discovered in 1800 by Jacopo Morelli (1745–1819) and were known as the *Anonimo Morelliano* until

the identification of their author by Daniele Francesconi (*d* 1835). Michiel used a variety of sources: written, oral and personal visits. His description of Milan was taken directly from Cesare Cesariano's *Di Lucio Vitruvio Pollione de Architectura Libri Dece* (Como, 1521), and he frequently cited the authority of Hieronimo Campagnola (*d* 1522). While undertaking his research, Michiel also consulted personal friends, such as the Paduan sculptor Andrea Riccio, whose opinion he quoted regarding the authorship of various Paduan fresco cycles, and the Neapolitan humanist Pietro Summonte, who sent him letters describing both ancient and modern works of art in Naples. Michiel also corresponded with Pietro Aretino, Guido Celere and possibly knew the sculptor Giovanni Maria Mosca Padovano. The notes, which were probably made for Michiel's own interest rather than with a view to publication, provide a first-hand insight into the richness and diversity of private collections in the Veneto, to which, as a patrician and collector, he had access; many were owned by his acquaintances. His information must, however, be used with caution, for the succinct accounts are by no means exhaustive; nor was he wholly reliable with regard to attribution or the identification of religious iconography, and gaps remain in the text where he was unable to discover the identity of certain artists. In Padua he visited Niccolò Leonico Tomeo (1456–1531), Pietro Bembo and Marco di Mantova Benavides, and in Venice he viewed some major collections, including those of Cardinal Domenico Grimani (1521), Gabriele Vendramin (1530) and Andrea Odoni (1532). Michiel's notes attest to connoisseurs' admiration for landscapes, portraits, antiquities and early Netherlandish paintings and to one of the earliest recorded instances of an attributional problem: the debate as to whether a painting owned by Antonio Pasqualino, identified as Antonello da Messina's *St Jerome in his Study* (*c.* 1474–6; London, N.G.), was an Italian or Flemish work (*see* ANTONELLO DA MESSINA, fig. 1). The notes also contain the earliest existing description of Mantegna's frescoes (1454–7; partly destr. 1844; remnants *in situ*) in the Ovetari Chapel (Padua, Eremitani) and are an important source for studies of Giorgione; though there is no evidence that they were acquainted, Michiel owned at least one work by Giorgione. The works of art acquired and commissioned by Michiel were probably kept in his family palazzo at S Marina, where he had a *studiolo*. Although not described in his notes, at least some of its contents can be determined from an undated inventory (Venice, Bib. Correr, MS PD C 1267 [8]). It included marble sculptures, paintings (mostly portraits), reliefs, drawings and small bronze statuettes of *all'antica* subjects similar to those produced by Riccio. Also itemized is the marble statuette of a running *Mercury* (London, V&A) that Michiel commissioned from Antonio Minello in 1527, with a bronze horoscope set in the base.

Although Michiel's writings on artistic matters are significant, most of his work was devoted to current affairs and politics. He regarded himself primarily as a historian and prepared notes for studies of Venetian history and Pisan/Venetian relations. In February 1527 he married Maffea Soranzo (*d* 1576), a member of a powerful family, and after several attempts to secure public office he was elected to the Venetian senate on 28 September 1527, but his political ambitions were never fully realized.

UNPUBLISHED SOURCES

Venice, Bib. Correr, MS. Cicogna 2848 [diary, 1511–20]

WRITINGS

Agri et Urbis Bergomatis descriptio anno 1516 (Bergamo, 1516); *R* in F. Bellafina: *De origine et temporibus Urbis Bergomi* (Venice, 1532)

Venice, Bib. N. Marciana, Ital. XI 67 (7351), pub. as *Notizia d'opere di disegno nella prima metà del secolo XVI* (MS.; 1521–43), ed. J. Morelli (Bassano, 1800, rev. Bologna, 1884); *Notizie d'opere di disegno* (MS.; *c.* 1520–40), ed. G. Frizzoni (Bologna, 1884); Eng. trans. by P. Mussi, ed. G. C. Williamson, as *The Anonimo* (London, 1903/*R* New York, 1969); *Der Anonimo Morelliano*, Quellenschr. Kstgesch. & Ksttech., ed. T. Frimmel (Vienna, 1896)

BIBLIOGRAPHY

E. A. Cicogna: 'Intorno la vita e le opere di Marcantonio Michiel Patrizio veneto della prima metà del secolo XVI', *Mem. Ist. Ven. Sci., Lett. & A.*, ix (1861), pp. 359–425

C. von Fabriczy: 'Summonte's Brief an Marcantonio Michiel', *Repert. Kstwiss.*, xxx (1907), pp. 143–68

F. Nicolini: *L'arte napoletana del rinascimento e la lettera di Pietro Summonte a Marcantonio Michiel* (Naples, 1925)

W. Hartner: 'The Mercury Horoscope of Marcantonio Michiel of Venice', *Vistas in Astronomy*, ed. A. Beer, i (London and New York, 1955), pp. 83–138; *R* in *Oriens-Occidens* (Hildesheim, 1968), pp. 440–95

J. Fletcher: 'Marcantonio Michiel's Collection', *J. Warb. & Court. Inst.*, xxxvi (1973), pp. 382–5

J. Eade: 'Marcantonio Michiel's Mercury Statue: Astronomical or Astro-logical?', *J. Warb. & Court. Inst.*, xliv (1981), pp. 207–9

J. Fletcher: 'Marcantonio Michiel: His Friends and Collection', *Burl. Mag.*, cxxiii, no. 941 (1981), pp. 453–67

L. Campbell: 'Notes on Netherlandish Pictures in the Veneto in the Fifteenth and Sixteenth Centuries', *Burl. Mag.*, cxxiii, no. 941 (1981), pp. 467–75

J. Fletcher: 'Marcantonio Michiel, "che ha veduto assai"', *Burl. Mag.*, cxxiii, no. 941 (1981), pp. 602–8

L. Olivato: 'Con il Serlio tra i "dilettanti di architettura" veneziani della prima metà del '500: Il ruolo di Marcantonio Michiel', *Les Traités d'architecture de la Renaissance. Actes du colloque: Tours, 1981*, pp. 247–54

Collezioni di antichità a Venezia nei secoli della Repubblica (exh. cat., ed. M. Zorzi; Venice, Bib. N. Marciana, 1988), pp. 41–50

HELEN GEDDES

Michiel, Master. *See* SITTOW, MICHEL.

Michieli, Andrea. *See* VICENTINO, ANDREA.

Michikaze. *See* ONO NO MICHIKAZE.

Michizane. *See* SUGAWARA NO MICHIZANE.

Michurin, Ivan (Fyodorovich) (*b* 1700; *d* 1763). Russian architect. He studied with Niccolò Michetti in St Petersburg (1720–23) and also in the Netherlands (1723–9), then worked in St Petersburg and, from 1731, in Moscow. While preferring a restrained version of northern European Baroque, he sometimes introduced forms from ancient Russian architecture, inspired by his work in remodelling a number of monasteries and restoring the roof of the cathedral of the Resurrection, New Jerusalem Monastery, and the Nicholas Tower of the Kremlin in Moscow following the fire of 1737. From 1734 to 1739 he directed the general plan for Moscow and proposed the adoption of a regular street plan. His churches in Moscow include St Paraskeva Pyatnitsa (1739–44) and SS Peter and Paul (1740–44), the tiered bell-towers of both being given expressive silhouettes with groups of columns and pilasters and projecting entablatures. He also collaborated with Dmitry Vasil'yevich Ukhtomsky on the bell-tower (1741–67) at the monastery of the Trinity and St Sergius, Zagorsk (now Sergiyev Posad), and designed the Trinity Church on the Arbat (completed 1741) and the gate-house church of the Chrysostom Monastery (1742; destr.). In Kiev, Michurin built the church of St Andrew (1747–53) and the Mariya Palace (1745–52) to designs by Bartolomeo Francesco Rastrelli. He probably designed the monumental five-domed cathedral of the Assumption (1749–58) at the Svensky Monastery in Bryansk, where Baroque decoration is placed next to a traditional Russian columnar portal, surmounted by a *kokoshnik* (ogee gable). His assistants and pupils played a notable role in Russian architecture in the mid-18th century.

BIBLIOGRAPHY

I. Ye. Grabar': 'Moskovskaya arkhitektura 30–40kh godov XVIII v.' [Moscow architecture of the 1730s and 1740s], *Istoriya russkogo iskusstva* [History of Russian art], v (Moscow, 1960), pp. 151–73

Yu. S. Aseyev and others, eds: *Pamyatniki gradostroitel'stva i arkhitektury Ukrainskoy SSR* [Monuments of town planning and architecture in the Ukrainian SSR], i (Kiev, 1983), pp. 16, 89

N. A. YEVSINA

Micrography. Minute writing arranged in geometric shapes or drawn as outlines of objects, animals or humans. Hebrew micrography is one of the most characteristic of Jewish art forms.

The earliest Hebrew micrographic texts date possibly from the late 9th century AD and the 10th and were written in Tiberias in Palestine (now in Israel) and in Egypt, where the *masorah*, the concordance-like notes that appeared in the margins of Bible codices, was at times written into figural shapes, a form known as internal micrography. Masoretic notes and occasionally psalms or dedications might also be combined with painted ornament to compose full-page finispieces (external micrography). Examples include the Moshe Ben-Asher Codex of the Prophets (dated AD 895–6; Cairo, Karaite Synagogue), the Leningrad Codex (a Bible, St Petersburg, Rus. N. Lib., MS. B.19ª) and a Pentateuch (New York, priv. col., see Avrin, pl. 13) from the early 11th century by the same scribe, Samuel ben Jacob. In Egypt *ketubbot* (marriage contracts; *see* KETUBBAH) were decorated micrographically from the 12th century.

Jewish micrography flourished in western Europe and the Yemen from the 13th to the 15th century. Sephardi Bibles are characterized by Islamic-influenced interlace and vegetal carpet pages (*see* JEWISH ART, §V, 1) and geometric and architectural frames, and very occasionally with painted designs at the beginning and end of the codex and between the individual books. Psalms frequently provided the external micrographic text, but internal micrography, which at times depicted stylized animal forms, continued to be used only for masoretic notes. One scribe from 14th-century Barcelona specialized in full-page frontispieces and marginal decoration in Bibles, prayerbooks and *haggadot*. He is known to have accomplished micrographic illustrations for a Bible (Jerusalem, Jew. N. & U. Lib., Nahum MS., heb. 8° 5147), a machzor (*see* MACHZOR)—the Catalan Machzor (Jerusalem, Jew. N. & U. Lib., heb. 8° 6527; see fig.)—and the liturgical

Micrography of psalms in the shape of a griffin within a frame, page size 195×155 mm; from the Catalan Machzor (festival prayerbook), 14th century (Jerusalem, Jewish National and University Library, heb. 8° 6527, fol. 14*r*)

poetry (*piyyutim*) in a Haggadah (Manchester, U. Lib., MS. heb. 6).

In Ashkenazi Bibles, figured *masorah* was often concentrated in the initial-word panels, which occupied a third of the page at the openings of the books of the Bible. Full-page illustrations and designs were rare. Marginal illustrations were related to the text on the same page more commonly than in the Sephardi Bibles. German micrographers drew on the Romanesque repertory of grotesques for their animals (*see* BIBLE, §II and fig. 11). Typical Ashkenazi micrographed Bibles are found in the Bibliothèque Nationale, Paris (MS. héb. 5 and 8–10), and the Staatsbibliothek zu Berlin Preussischer Kulturbesitz, Berlin (MS. Or. fol. 1212; MSS Or. fols 1–4, 5–7). Few medieval micrographers signed their work; most were anonymous, but a few of these can be recognized in several books by their style of drawing.

Following the introduction of printing, when fewer manuscript Bibles were made, scribes in Italy in the early 17th century began to decorate *ketubbot* with micrography (e.g. London, BL, Or. MS. 6706; Modena, 1557). The most popular texts were the Song of Solomon and the books of Esther and Ruth, along with other biblical passages appropriate to weddings. In Europe from the 18th century micrographic pictures portraying biblical or symbolic subjects related to holidays or prayers were written on parchment and paper and were intended to be hung in homes. Small books of benedictions for special occasions were also commissioned from scribes. In the 18th century micrographic portraits of royalty began to appear; in the 19th century rabbis, authors and leading Zionists were popular subjects, as were holy sites in Jerusalem. By that time the art had spread back to the Near East and to the USA, and many micrographic illustrations were reproduced by lithography. In the late 20th century Jewish scribes and calligraphers continued to practise the art, introducing new subjects and finding creative applications of this ancient art form.

BIBLIOGRAPHY
T. Metzger: 'La Masora ornementale et le décor calligraphique dans les manuscrits hébreux espagnols au moyen âge', *La Paléographie hébraïque médiévale* (Paris, 1974), pp. 87–116
L. Avrin: *Micrography as Art* (Jerusalem and Paris, 1981)
'Hebrew Micrographers Then and Now', *Callig. Idea Exch.*, iv/4 (1987), pp. 40–50
T. Metzger: 'Josue ben Abraham ibn Gaon et la *masora* du MS. Iluminado 72 de la Biblioteca Nacional de Lisbonne', *Cod. MSS*, xv/5 (1990), pp. 1–27

LEILA AVRIN

Micronesia, Federated States of. Group of four volcanic island complexes—Yap, Chuuk (Truk), Pohnpei (Ponape) and Kosrae (Kusaie)—and 460 small, widely scattered coral islets, with a total land area of 700 sq. km, spread over *c.* 2170 million sq. km of the western Pacific Ocean. With Palau (Belau) they comprise the Caroline Islands. The islands were subject to successive periods of Spanish, German and Japanese colonial rule until World War II, after which the USA administered them as part of the Trust Territory of the Pacific Islands (TTPI). In 1979 the Federated States of Micronesia Constitution was adopted, binding the states of Yap, Chuuk, Pohnpei and Kosrae into one political entity. In 1986 they became a fully self-governing, sovereign nation. The total population in mid-1990 was estimated at 108,480. The capital is Kolonia on Pohnpei. The art of this area has received only limited attention from scholars (see bibliography). Important collections are held by museums in Europe (e.g. London, BM; Hamburg, Mus. Vlkerknd.; Berlin, Mus. Vlkerknd.) and the USA (e.g. Washington, DC, N. Mus. Nat. Hist.; Honolulu, HI, Bishop Mus.; Salem, MA, Peabody Mus.; New York, Met.).

The islands are small and generally poor in such resources as timber, stone, clay and fibre, although the high basaltic islands are better endowed than the low coral atolls. Local communities were small and widely dispersed. The first people to inhabit the islands came in outrigger canoes from the Fiji–New Hebrides area of Melanesia before 1500 BC. They settled in the Chuuk–Pohnpei–Kosrae area and later in the atolls west of Chuuk and on Yap. The subsequent development of art forms, especially in canoe design, architecture, personal ornament, containers, tattoo, loom-weaving and plaitwork, displays both common features and considerable diversity owing to the local isolation of communities. Functional need and simplicity of form dominated the production of material culture. However, the geometric patterns in tattoo, woven materials, plaited mats and on wood artefacts reflected a rich system of meaning and value. Whether crafted for everyday needs or for esoteric communication with the

Micronesian woven sash, banana fibre, wool, shell and glass beads, l. 1.67 m, w. 0.09 m, from Pohnpei, *c.* 1830 (Salem, MA, Peabody Museum of Salem)

spirit world, art was produced by highly respected specialists.

The art of Yap stands between the Indonesian-influenced art of Palau and the Mariana Islands and the Micronesian art of the atolls to the east. The impact of the former is evident in the stone 'money' of Yap. This consisted of huge, flat-sided limestone discs quarried and shaped in Palau and rafted to Yap where they were publicly exhibited as evidence of wealth. It is also evident in its stone images, its solidly built men's houses (*faluw*) with sennit-lashed timbers and in its undecorated clay pottery. With the eastern atolls, Yap shared traditions of tattoo, with complex geometric patterning, and of canoe design, characterized by the use of a single outrigger, an asymmetrical hull and a pandanus-leaf lateen sail. In weaving, the backstrap loom was used, with dyed warp and weft yarns of banana and hibiscus fibre being employed to make loincloths and wraparound skirts.

The north and west atolls of Chuuk State (Namonuito, Puluwat etc) had trading relations with atolls in Yap State and shared much of the latter's marine-orientated art production. Chuuk itself had closer ties with the southeast Mortlock atolls. Chuuk art featured the use of stylized sea-bird and fish motifs in the decoration of wooden bowls and of canoe bow and stern pieces (e.g. Washington, DC, N. Mus. Nat. Hist.). Shoulder-length ear pendants, bracelets, belts and girdles, incorporating discs and beads carved from marine and coconut shells, were used to decorate the body. Of less importance were loom weaving, tattoo and meeting-house design. The large wooden human-faced masks used in ceremonial dances by Satawan (Mortlock) islanders (e.g. Honolulu, HI, Bishop Mus.) provide the sole example of Micronesian mask art. This art form was probably brought from western Melanesia by drifting canoe voyagers.

In the high islands of Pohnpei and Kosrae outstanding work was achieved in architecture, tattoo and loom weaving. The ruins of stone ceremonial centres with walled structures of uncut columnar basalt fed by extensive canal systems are to be found at Nan Madol on the east coast of Pohnpei and at Lelu on Kosrae. These are the seats of the ancient dynasties ruling the islands. Complex tattoo and weaving arts were practised up to the early 1900s. A woman's hips, waist and thighs were tattooed with intricate geometric motifs and patterns, similar in form and meaning to those carved and painted on ceremonial dance paddles. Outrigger paddle canoes were also similarly decorated. Sashes, 50–150 mm wide, were woven from very fine banana fibre (see fig.). The Pohnpeian-Kosraen technology combined knotted-in warp striping, brocading and beading with pieces cut from marine shell.

Late 20th-century art forms have incorporated new materials, colours, techniques and subject-matter. Men carve and paint model canoes, doll-like figures and miniature masks, while women weave and plait belts, skirts, mats, baskets, fans, hats and necklaces, all of these being produced for the tourist trade.

BIBLIOGRAPHY

EWA: 'Micronesian Cultures'

G. Thilenius, ed.: *Ethnographie: Mikronesien*, 13 vols (Hamburg, 1914–16), II/B/i–xii of *Ergebnisse der Südsee-Expedition, 1908–1910* ed. G. Thilenius (Hamburg, 1914–16)

J. Hornell: *The Canoes of Polynesia, Fiji, and Micronesia* (1936), i of *Canoes of Oceania* by A. C. Haddon and J. Hornell, Bishop Mus. Special Pubn, xxvii (Honolulu, 1936), pp. 374–412

S. H. Reisenberg and A. H. Gayton: 'Caroline Island Belt Weaving', *SW J. Anthropol.*, viii/3 (1952), pp. 342–75

F. M. LeBar: *The Material Culture of Truk*, Yale U., Pubns Anthropol., lviii (New Haven, 1964)

W. H. Alkire: *An Introduction to the Peoples and Cultures of Micronesia* (Menlo Park, CA, 1977)

P. W. Steager: 'Where Does Art Begin in Puluwat?', *Exploring the Visual Art of Oceania: Australia, Melanesia, Micronesia and Polynesia*, ed. S. M. Mead (Honolulu, 1979), pp. 342–53

The Art of the Pacific Islands (exh. cat. by P. Gathercole, A. L. Kaeppler and D. Newton, Washington, DC, N.G.A., 1979), pp. 266–71

L. Hanson and F. A. Hanson: *The Art of Oceania: A Bibliography*, Ref. Pubns A. Hist. (Boston, MA, 1984)

The Art of Micronesia (exh. cat. by J. Feldman and D. Rubinstein, Honolulu, U. Hawaii A.G., 1986)

W. N. Morgan: *Prehistoric Architecture in Micronesia* (Austin, TX, 1988/*R* London, 1989)

LEONARD MASON

Micronesia. Conventional geographic and cultural division of the South Pacific Ocean comprising *c.* 2500 islands with a total land area of *c.* 2874 sq. km scattered over *c.* 13 million sq. km of the western Pacific Ocean. It has a population of *c.* 0.4 million. Culturally, Micronesia is especially famous for its rich traditions of communal architecture and canoe-building. For discussion of these and other Micronesian arts *see under* PACIFIC ISLANDS; *see also* FEDERATED STATES OF MICRONESIA; KIRIBATI; MARIANA ISLANDS; MARSHALL ISLANDS; NAURU; and PALAU.

Micus, Eduard. *See under* SYN.

Midas City. *See under* PHRYGIAN.

Middeldorf, Ulrich (*b* 23 June 1901; *d* 19 Feb 1983). American art historian of German birth. He studied at the University of Munich with Heinrich Wölfflin and A. L. Mayer, and in Berlin, where, under Adolph Gold-schmidt, he wrote a thesis (unpublished) entitled *Die thüringisch-sächsische Skulptur von 1250 bis 1350*. He then joined the Kunsthistorisches Institut in Florence, first as a Fellow, and then, from 1926, as Keeper of the photographic library. In 1935, on Bernard Berenson's recommendation, he was appointed Assistant Professor of art history at the University of Chicago, where he remained until 1953, becoming Professor and Chairman of his department. He continued his studies in Italian sculpture, which was based primarily on the study of the actual works, and he also initiated a number of important purchases for the Art Institute of Chicago. From 1953 until his retirement in 1968 he was Director of the Kunsthistorisches Institut in Florence, which he built up into one of the foremost institutions in Europe for the study of art history. His generosity towards other scholars became legendary.

WRITINGS

Raphael's Drawings (New York, 1945)
Sculptures from the Samuel H. Kress Collection: European Schools, XIV–XIX Century (London, 1976)
Raccolta di scritti, 3 vols (Florence, 1979–81)

BIBLIOGRAPHY

A. Kosegarten and P. Tiegler, eds: *Festschrift Ulrich Middeldorf*, 2 vols (Berlin, 1968)
H. Keutner: 'Ulrich Middeldorf, 23. Juni 1901–19. Februar 1983', *Mitt. Ksthist. Inst. Florenz*, xvii (1983), pp. 257–60
J. Pope-Hennessy: 'Professor Ulrich Middeldorf', *Apollo*, cxvii (1983), p. 520

□

Middelthun, Julius Olavus (*b* Kongsberg, 3 July 1820; *d* Christiania [now Oslo], 5 May 1886). Norwegian sculptor. He worked first as an apprentice goldsmith in Christiania, and then studied under Herman Wilhelm Bissen from 1840 to 1851 at the Kunstakademi in Copenhagen. Here he adopted a conservative, late classical style, inspired by the art and literature of Denmark's golden age. He lived in Rome between 1851 and 1860 and became familiar with the works of Classical and Renaissance masters. This experience increased his self-doubt, and he later became harshly self-critical. A font reflecting his admiration for Berthel Thorvaldsen is Middelthun's only great work from this period (plaster, 1859; marble, 1865; Oslo, Trefoldig-hetskirken). He returned to Norway in 1860 and executed a series of busts, which established him as Norway's leading portrait sculptor. His bust of the poet *Johan Sebastian Welhaven* (plaster, 1861; Oslo, Ubib.; marble, 1865; Oslo, N.G.), one of the most important examples of Norwegian portrait sculpture, is herm-like in form and, with its sense of classical balance and harmony, embodies the poet's ideals. Middelthun's later head-and-shoulders bust of the composer *Halfdan Kjerulf* in contemporary dress (bronze, 1871–4), in the Kjerulfs plass, Oslo, reveals a greater attention to form and detail. Middelthun worked very slowly; his bronze statue of the historian *Anton*

Martin Schweigaard (1870–83, U. Oslo) is regarded as his greatest work, but it is also the only one of his larger sculptures that he managed to complete. Middelthun taught at Christiania's Kongelige Tegneskole from 1869 to 1886. He was made a knight of the Order of St Olav in 1883.

BIBLIOGRAPHY

NKL, ii, pp. 926–8 [with comprehensive bibliog.]
H. Gran: *Billedhuggeren Julius Middelthun og hans samtid* [The sculptor Julius Middelthun and his contemporaries] (Oslo, 1946)
O. Thue: *Norsk skulptur 1814–1870*, *Norges kunsthistorie*, iv (Oslo, 1981), pp. 293–340

GLENNY ALFSEN

Middle Niger cultures. Group of geographically and historically related cultures known through a number of chance finds and limited archaeological research in present-day Mali, West Africa.

1. Introduction. 2. Art forms. 3. Dating. 4. Interpretation. 5. Conclusion.

1. INTRODUCTION. The Middle Niger stretches *c.* 450 km from San in the south to Timbuktu in the north. The area of the Middle Niger, however, is many times vaster, since the low-lying terrain forms an extensive inundation zone, the Inland Niger Delta, which is flooded by the Niger and its major tributaries and distributaries for several months of the year. North of Lake Debo, this zone is characterized by the presence of numerous large lakes. Throughout the inundation zone, thousands of island-like habitation mounds (often referred to as *tell*s after their better-known counterparts in the Near East) testify to the successful permanent settlement of the floodplain throughout much of the West African Iron Age (*c.* 500 BC–1000 AD). There is, as yet, no evidence to suggest that permanent settlement in the Inland Delta occurred prior to the introduction of iron to West Africa *c.* 500 BC. North of Lake Debo, in the Lakes Region, elaborate funerary mounds, or tumuli, are also characteristic of the archaeological landscape. Since the beginning of the colonial era in Mali (1892), thousands of terracotta sculptures and copper-alloy figurines have been recovered from the *tell*s and tumuli of the Middle Niger, clandestinely in all but a small number of cases (see fig. 1). Although many of these pieces have entered private collections before ever becoming publicly documented, the existing corpus of photographic documentation clearly indicates the astonishing variety of forms, subjects and styles from the region. The terracottas especially have been widely illustrated (see bibliography for references). There are also a number of examples in public collections. The works illustrated here are those in the Musée National du Mali, Bamako. While perhaps not the most aesthetically pleasing, they are among the very few works to have been recovered through proper archaeological research and not to have been looted. Much has been written about the terracotta art of the Middle Niger Cultures. Unfortunately, however, most of the literature is speculative and based on very little hard information. This entry re-examines the present state of knowledge and suggests what further research is required if understanding of this remarkable art tradition is to be increased.

2. ART FORMS. The terracotta statuettes have received much more attention than the 'bronzes' (analyses to determine the alloy involved have not yet been undertaken), so discussion here focuses on them. The first attempt at systematic description of the Middle Niger terracottas was made by Evrard, and many elements of her analysis appear to have been incorporated and expanded by de Grunne. The majority of the documented statuettes are between 100 and 250 mm high and represent a male or female, sometimes both together, in various sitting, kneeling or semi-reclining attitudes (see fig. 1). The treatment of the head is highly stylized, with a narrow, elongated cranium and a flattened, out-jutting jaw. Protruding lips modelled perpendicular to the facial plane reinforce the prognathic effect. The eyes bulge beyond the plane of the face, usually with a horizontal median ridge. They may be outlined with concentric ridges or radiating lines. The body is generally more crudely treated. The figures are often naked except for an apron and may wear a variety of accoutrements: neck torques, pendants or beads, bracelets, anklets, daggers, quivers, scarification on the face or body, coiled or writhing snakes, hats or helmets (see fig. 2). Some also have clay pastilles, possibly representing buboes or some other sign of disease.

2. Middle Niger statuette, terracotta, h. 255 mm (excluding base), from Jenne-jeno, Mali (Bamako, Musée National du Mali)

A much smaller group of statuettes represent bearded equestrian figures, in embroidered shorts and capes, bearing daggers and quivers, and riding disproportionately small horses. Some of these figures are extremely well executed and show so many formal similarities that de Grunne attributed them to related workshops (1980, p. 51). Equestrian figures in a very different style, purportedly from the Guimbala area of the Lakes Region, have also appeared on the market. Statuettes representing semi-humans and animals (especially snakes, fish and lizards or crocodiles) are more crudely modelled, as are humans and animals represented in appliqué. Of the former, many are headless. Snakes (or undulating lines) running 'longitudinally' down small spherical pots are a common, presumably ritual motif.

3. DATING. Understanding this impressive variability in the statuettes is the key to understanding the art itself and the social context of its production. Unfortunately, virtually nothing is known of the vast majority of terracottas, since they have been removed clandestinely from the archaeological context and therefore cannot provide information about the various factors accounting for their diversity. The possibility of geographical variation within the area is real, but this cannot be addressed in the absence of provenance information for individual statuettes. The small number of statuettes with published find-spots allows little more to be done at present than to indicate the minimum area of statuette production.

Variation through time is also a possibility, particularly in view of the archaeological evidence for major changes in other aspects of material culture throughout the first and second millennia AD (McIntosh and McIntosh, 1988). Again, the lack of independent archaeological evidence on chronology is a major obstacle. Collectors have attempted to overcome this problem with thermoluminescence (TL) dating. De Grunne (1987) reported on 240 TL dates available for Inland Delta statuettes, which range from the 8th to the 18th centuries AD. There are two major reasons

1. Middle Niger statuette, terracotta, h. 220 mm, from Jenne-jeno, Mali (Bamako, Musée National du Mali)

why discussions of Middle Niger terracotta chronology based on TL dating should be regarded sceptically. The first is that the physics of thermoluminescence are such that local conditions, including water content of soil, duration of burial and the context of deposition, as well as levels of radon and other types of radiation, affect the amount of thermoluminescence present in a fired object (Aitken). When known and evaluated, these can be taken into account in determining a TL date. Since local conditions are unknown in the case of every statuette that has been TL dated so far, there is a dramatic increase in the possible error in the results. The 240 TL dates available are calculated with a 15% error, but even this is perhaps not sufficiently conservative. Discussions of the TL chronology for statuettes rarely acknowledge the degree of uncertainty and, in some cases, proceed as if the error value itself were irrelevant. This attitude is the second reason for scepticism: the frequent claim in the literature that the flourishing of the Middle Niger statuette tradition dates to the 14th and 15th centuries comes from uncritical interpretation of the TL dates. In truth, knowing nothing of their context, it is not possible to know how they were used, when or by whom.

4. INTERPRETATION.

(i) Ethnography. De Grunne seized upon the ethnographic record in the Inland Delta and elsewhere as a primary means of providing a context for these pieces. Using as a starting-point interviews with a few elderly informants from different villages, de Grunne wove their responses to his interpreter's questions about the meaning and use of the statuettes into an elaborate hypothesis relating gesture and body pose to a 'widespread and profound religious tradition'. He argued that the statuettes represent portraits of deified ancestors, nobles and village founders. By assuming the posture of the terracotta, one could worship the historical individual, and, by performing blood sacrifices involving eight animal species but especially humans, one could interpret the wishes of the ancestor. As 'proof of the importance, proliferation and persistence of this cult in the Inland Niger Delta', de Grunne offered the fact that 'contemporary people who may be the descendants of those who made the terracotta statuary still remember some of these ritual gestures' (de Grunne, 1987, p. 231). It is unclear what de Grunne meant by the 'persistence' of the cult, since none of his informants had ever seen a terracotta in use; they recalled only 19th-century family traditions concerning their use. Several suspect assumptions, both methodological and theoretical, are involved here. Methodologically, there is the assumption that ethnographic fieldwork is a relatively straightforward matter of asking informants questions and recording their responses. The possibility of subtle prompting of informants by the interpreter to elicit desired information (such as specific gestures or postures) is not discussed. De Grunne reported that his informants 'spontaneously' assumed the attitudes of prayer they could remember. Nor is the issue discussed of how conflicting information from different informants was assessed. Instead, authority was conferred on one particularly useful informant, and there is no explanation offered for preferring his responses over those of other informants.

The theoretical underpinnings of this approach are equally disheartening. It is hardly possible, as this interpretation requires, that the linkage of symbol and belief had persisted unchanged over many centuries, unaffected by the penetration of Islam. Although de Grunne forcefully argued against the possibility of internally generated stylistic change over time (1987, p. 96), the style and iconography of the statuettes cannot have been immune to the currents of change in the Middle Niger. Likewise, de Grunne argued against any regional variation in meaning (1987, pp. 19, 231). However, the Middle Niger is an ethnic mosaic in which different groups use dress, language, traditions and other symbols to maintain social distance between themselves. It would have been peculiar if all the groups in the area had subscribed through many centuries to a common meaning and use for the statuettes.

(ii) Archaeology. Such questions relate to the larger issue of uniformitarian assumptions underlying the use of ethnography to interpret the past. To assume that we can never know of beliefs, behaviours or aesthetics that have not persisted to the present severely limits what we can hope to know about the past. This approach would make a mockery of recent trends in art history and in archaeology that view a society's use of technology, material culture, symbols and traditions as dynamic sources of information about individual and group behaviour. The premise of the alternative approach to the ancient Middle Niger cultures presented here is the need for a grounding in social and economic context provided by recovery of this art from controlled, scientific excavations. This allows an attempt to view the terracottas, bronze miniatures or any other preserved aspect of material culture as the remains of past action on multiple aspects of the world as socially constructed by the community that produced and used them. What are the stratigraphic patterns in variation of statuette use at different slices in time? How do style and associations with other artefacts change through time, and how does that change correlate with changes in other elements in the archaeological record? Such an approach assumes change through time, in style, iconographic repertory and context of use, to be the main focus of interest. It also acknowledges that archaeologically detectable changes may be internally generated, reflecting shifting strategies of social mediation in the societies that produced them. This view of the statuettes and appropriate ways of understanding them is diametrically opposed to the ethnographic approach outlined above, which is driven by the assumption that cultures remain static until change is introduced by external agencies.

Programmes of archaeological research since 1970 in the Inland Delta have provided insights into the contexts and chronology of the terracottas. In 1972 Barth reported finding terracotta statuettes in funerary urns at Togguere Doupwil (Barth, 1976 and 1977). Much more substantial work was done at this site in 1974 and 1975 by Bedaux (1978, p. 94), although no more statuettes were found, despite the excavation of numerous funerary urns. At the *tell* of Jenne-jeno, excavations in 1977 and 1981 by McIntosh and McIntosh recovered more than 30 whole and fragmentary terracottas and figures in clay appliqué from archaeological deposits that were firmly radiocarbon dated to the period AD 900–1400. Documented contexts for these terracottas at Jenne-jeno include deliberate burial in house floors in association with utilitarian and ritual ceramics; deliberate placement in wall niches; association with (but not in) funerary urns; and secondary deposition in rubbish tips. Within this final phase of occupation at Jenne-jeno, at least four distinct statuette styles are represented, three of them in the same level (a probable rubbish tip) in one excavation unit.

The fact that all the statuettes thus far documented from wall-niche or floor contexts were in kneeling postures, with hands either on knees or shoulders, is interesting. Future investigations should attempt blood-residue analysis on the statuette surface and chemical analyses of clay surfaces on which the statuettes rested to evaluate de Grunne's claim that they were recipients of blood sacrifices. Through detailed archaeological work it should also be possible to ascertain, for example, whether the frequency of broken statuary (specifically, with the head knocked off) rises significantly at sites where conversion to Islam is documented. If, on the other hand, deliberate burial of statuette bodies accompanied by broken heads (as found at Jenne-jeno) is widely distributed through time in the Inland Delta, then alternative explanations must be sought, such as the ritual 'killing' of statuettes. It may also be possible to identify statuette production and ritual use by particular sub-groups of Inland Delta society. The association of one statuette at Jenne-jeno with sandstone slabs, ceramic vessels with serpent motifs, and a pile of iron rods, in deposits that contained a great deal of iron slag, suggests a context related to blacksmithing.

An additional advantage of this kind of analysis is that it fits into a broader interpretative perspective concerned with understanding the emergence of larger-scale, more complexly organized societies during the West African Iron Age. The archaeological record at Jenne-jeno has revealed that the initial village, established c. 250 BC, grew rapidly to an urban settlement of over 40 ha by AD 500. Such an increase in settlement scale would have been accompanied by changes in social organization. Small-scale societies are organized by gender, age and such kin categories as family, clan or lineage. During the long, slow coalescence of the city, a far larger population becomes increasingly subdivided into new classes of loyalties or 'corporations'. Corporations may be characterized by ethnic or dialect affiliation, subsistence or artisan specialization, residence in particular quarters or adherence to different cults. As the process picks up pace, one has ever more daily encounters with persons of increasing social distance. Emerging urbanism brings unprecedented ambiguities of belonging. Those ambiguities have to be resolved if conflict is to remain at manageable levels. It has proved useful to view several classes of material culture, including terracotta art, as having an active role as 'corporate insignia', material symbols manipulated by different corporate groups as codes to identity in a context of increasingly plural belonging.

From this proposition certain expectations can be tested against the archaeological record. In the absence of centralized authority or of unifying ideology, burgeoning urbanism may create a multi-voiced corporate discourse reflected in material symbols. Change in one class of symbols should correlate with change in others, although certain artefacts may wax and wane in effectiveness as insignia of belonging. Some, such as dress, hairstyles, scarification and linguistic variation, will probably always be lost to the archaeologist.

5. CONCLUSION. Archaeologists have been accustomed to thinking of all West African societies in the last millennium BC and early first millennium AD as small-scale, simply organized and relatively isolated except for some low-level exchange with near neighbours. However, the great diversity of style and context of discovery in Nok terracotta sculptures of Nigeria, as well as the technical expertise of Nok smiths, suggests that some specialization, some stable heterogeneity characterized this society from c. 5th century BC to the 2nd century AD (Shaw; see also NOK). Did the terracottas serve here also as corporate insignia, as vehicles for the symbolic arbitration of identity in a newly emergent complex society? Even less is known of the dating and provenance of the corpora of highly varied terracottas to have come from the 700 or so *tell*s in the southern floodplain of Lake Chad (Lebeuf). Is it possible that the explosion in art production and diversity, at least in the durable medium of terracotta, reflects similar processes of increasingly complex social organization? Or does the art explosion perhaps suggest ancient corridors of contact? Contact need not have been exclusively commercial, as in the documented Soninke and later Dyula 'diaspora' (S. K. McIntosh, 1981). Art-historical and archaeological research can be formulated to ask whether, over the centuries, contact took the form of the spread and maintenance of relations between associations of blacksmiths, griots, leatherworkers, sorcerers and warriors across West Africa (McNaughton, 1991 and 1992). Perhaps the terracotta art of the Middle Niger cultures holds clues to the social and institutional reasons for the formal and conceptual similarities of much West African art of later periods.

BIBLIOGRAPHY

H. K. Barth: 'Zum Alter der Grab- und Siedlungshügel im Binnendelta des Niger, Mali', *Paideuma*, xx (1976), pp. 231–5

——: 'L'Age de la civilisation des tumulus et des anciens habitats du Delta intérieur du Niger (Mali)', *Notes Afr.*, clv (1977), pp. 57–61

J. Evrard: *Archéologie ouest-africaine: Les Figurines en terre cuite du Mali— Description morphologique et essai de typologie*, 3 vols (diss., Leuven, U. Catholique, 1977)

R. M. A. Bedaux and others: 'Recherches archéologiques dans le delta intérieur du Niger', *Palaeohistoria*, xx (1978), pp. 91–220

R. J. McIntosh and S. K. McIntosh: 'Terracotta Statuettes from Mali', *Afr. A.*, xii/2 (1979), pp. 51–3, 91

B. de Grunne: *Terres cuites anciennes de l'ouest africain*, Publications historiques et art archéologiques de la Université Catholique de Louvain, 22 (Leuven, 1980)

J.-P. Lebeuf: 'Afrique: La Statuaire en céramique', *Encyclopaedia Universalis* (Paris, 1980), pp. 98–101

S. K. McIntosh and R. J. McIntosh: *Prehistoric Investigations at Jenne*, Cambridge Monographs in African Archaeology, 2 (Cambridge, 1980)

——: 'Empire of Mali: Evidence from Jenne-Jeno', *J. Afr. Hist.*, xxii/1 (1981), pp. 1–22

S. K. McIntosh: 'A Reconsideration of Wangara/Palolus, Island of Gold', *J. Afr. Hist.*, xxii/2 (1981), pp. 145–58

T. Shaw: 'The Nok Sculptures of Nigeria', *Sci. Amer.*, ccxliv (1981), pp. 154–66

Ancient Treasures in Terra Cotta (exh. cat., New York, Afr.-Amer. Inst., 1981)

La Statuaire en terre cuite (exh. cat., Munich, Gal. Biedermann, 1982)

P. Fontes and others: 'Analyse chimique des céramiques médiévales du delta intérieur du Niger par la méthode Pixe', *Archéologie africaine et sciences de la nature appliquées à l'archéologie: 1er symposium international: Bordeaux, 1983*, pp. 271–84

Le Poterie ancienne du Mali: Quelques Remarques préliminaires (exh. cat. by B. de Grunne, Munich, Gal. Afr. Kst, 1983)

F. H. Nesmith jr: 'The Jenne Bronze Question', *Afr. A.*, xvii/3 (1984), pp. 64–9, 90–91

M. J. Aitken: *Thermoluminescence Dating* (New York, 1985)

R. J. McIntosh and S. K. McIntosh: 'Dilettantism and Plunder: Dimensions of the Illicit Traffic in Ancient Malian Art', *Mus.: Rev. Trimest.*, xxxviii/1 (1986), pp. 49–57

B. de Grunne: *Divine Gestures and Earthly Gods: A Study of the Ancient Terracotta Statuary from the Inland Niger Delta in Mali* (diss., New Haven, CT, Yale U., 1987)

R. J. McIntosh and S. K. McIntosh: 'From *siècles obscurs* to Revolutionary Centuries on the Middle Niger', *World Archaeol.*, xx/1 (1988), pp. 141–65

R. McIntosh: 'Middle Niger Terracottas before the Symplegades Gateway', *Afr. A.*, xxii/2 (1989), pp. 74–83, 103–4

B. Bernardi and B. de Grunne: *Terra d'Africa, terra d'archeologia: La grande scultura in terracotta del Mali Djenne VIII–XVI sec.* (Florence, 1990) [It. and Fr. text]

R. Lehuard: 'Les Terres cuites de Djenne au C.C.F. de Rome', *A. Afrique Noire*, 75 (1990), pp. 11–13

R. J. McIntosh and S. K. McIntosh: 'Reconnaissances archéologiques le long du Moyen-Niger', *Recherches archéologiques au Mali: Prospections et inventaire des fouilles et études analytiques en zone lacustre*, ed. M. Raimbault and K. Sanogo (Paris, 1991), pp. 99–120

P. McNaughton: 'Is there History in Horizontal Masks?', *Afr. A.*, xxiv (1991), pp. 40–53, 88–90

——: 'From Mande komo to Jukun Akuma: Approaching the Difficult Question of History', *Afr. A.*, xxv (1992), pp. 76–85, 99–100

Vallées du Niger (exh. cat., Paris, Réunion Musées N., 1993)

RODERICK J. MCINTOSH, SUSAN KEECH MCINTOSH

Middleton, John (*b* Norwich, 9 Jan 1827; *d* Norwich, 11 Nov 1856). English painter and etcher. His father, John Middleton (*d* 1848), was a painter and decorator and his mother, Ann (*d* 1830), was an amateur flower painter. Middleton's artistic development had reached full maturity when he was 20 years old. On a sketching tour to Kent in 1847 he produced watercolours which, in their free use of wash, show a marked improvement on his work of the previous year. His teacher Henry Bright accompanied him on this trip. Their watercolours were remarkably similar at this time, and it is evident that Middleton's rapid development influenced the work of his own teacher.

In 1847 Middleton moved to London and exhibited at the Royal Academy for the first time. When his father died he returned to Norwich to continue the family business. Middleton's development during the 1850s is difficult to follow because few of his watercolours can be dated to these years, but in essence his work appears to have become more heavily finished. The over-elaborate concern for detail in his oils is reminiscent of the work of his first teacher, John Berney Ladbrooke (1803–79). He exhibited many oils in London between 1847 and 1855, and in Norwich. Middleton was also a skilful etcher and a keen amateur photographer. In 1852 he published a set of nine etchings, which reproduce some of his most successful compositions, such as *Gunton Park* (1849; Norwich, Castle Mus.). These often transform the oil versions with considerable subtlety of line. His last sketching tour was to Scotland in 1853. He died aged 29 of consumption.

BIBLIOGRAPHY
W. F. Dickes: *The Norwich School of Painting* (Norwich, 1905)
F. W. Hawcroft: 'John Middleton: A Sketch of his Life and Work', *The Saturday Book*, xvi (London, 1956), pp. 37–41
A. W. Moore: *The Norwich School of Artists* (Norwich, 1985), pp. 132, 142–5

For further bibliography see NORWICH, §2.

ANDREW W. MOORE

Midjawmidjaw, Jimmy (*b* Croker Island, N. Territory, 1897; *d c.* 1985). Australian Aboriginal painter. His language group was Kunwinjku, and he belonged to the clan Mirarr. During his life he occasionally moved between living on Croker Island and at Oenpelli on the mainland. He was well known for his broad ceremonial experience. His first bark paintings were made for the anthropologists Ron Berndt and Catherine Berndt when they visited Oenpelli in 1947 and in 1949–50. He produced a number of paintings of ceremonial and sorcery themes for them, as well as a sculpted clay figure. He was living at Croker Island with Yirawala when the French anthropologist Karel Kupka collected their work in 1963. Midjawmidjaw's early paintings, such as *Warramurrungunjdji, the Fertility Mother* (*c.* 1963; Canberra, N.G.), show a strong affinity with rock painting techniques in the bold and rough textured application of paint in solid blocks of colour. While living at the Oenpelli mission he began producing works for sale there in the 1960s. The production of art and craft had become a major community occupation by then. Midjawmidjaw's common subjects were images of the animal species and spirit figures celebrated in ceremonies of the region. He occasionally employed the characteristic body designs of these ceremonies to infill his figures. For example Ron Berndt collected the *Mythic Kangaroo Nadulmi* (1948; Perth, U. W. Australia, Anthropol. Res. Mus.), in which the body design *kunmed*, a pattern consisting of rings of coloured dots, was used to decorate an image of the antilopine kangaroo as celebrated in the Wubarr ceremony.

BIBLIOGRAPHY
K. Kupka: *Peintres Aborigines d'Australie* (Paris, 1972), pp. xxxvii–cxi
R. M. Berndt, C. H.Berndt and J. E. Stanton: *Australian Aboriginal Art: A Visual Perspective* (Sydney, 1982), p. 151

LUKE TAYLOR

Miel, Jan (*b* Beveren-Waes, nr Antwerp, 1599; *d* Turin, April 1664). Flemish painter, active in Italy. Miel must have arrived in Rome in the early 1630s; he immediately came under the influence of Pieter van Laer (il Bamboccio) and the BAMBOCCIANTI. His earliest paintings of *bambocciate* (low-life scenes) are the *Bowls Players* (1633; Paris, Louvre) and its companion piece *The Cobbler* (Besançon, Mus. B.-A. & Archéol.). Shortly after his arrival in Rome, Miel joined the Schildersbent, a confraternity of Netherlandish artists, and was given the nickname 'Bieco' ('threatening look'). His presence in Rome is documented from 1636 to 1658, when he moved to Turin and entered the service of Charles-Emanuel II, Duke of Savoy. Other early paintings that can be attributed to the 1630s include *Halt at the Inn* (Marseille, Mus. B.-A.) and *Hunters' Rest* (Warsaw, N. Mus.). Both are reworkings, in their subject-matter and composition, of contemporary paintings by van Laer, such as his *Hunters Resting* (Florence, Uffizi) and *Halt at the Inn* (Paris, Louvre). Miel is known to have made direct copies of paintings by van Laer, which he bequeathed to Agostino Franzone in his will.

During the 1640s and 1650s Miel, together with Michelangelo Cerquozzi, widened the scope of *bambocciate* compositions, paying less attention to the landscape setting and instead emphasizing the anecdotal aspects of town and country life, as for example in *Peasants Dancing* and the *Morra Players* (both Madrid, Prado), and in *Return from the Vintage* and *Arrival of the Travellers* (both priv. col., see Trezzani, figs 4.12–4.13). These paintings reveal both the merits and the limitations of Miel's self-confident, spirited but occasionally superficial narrative vein; they were used repeatedly as models by the Bamboccianti in the second half of the century and by the genre painters active in Rome during the early 18th century.

Miel's most original contributions to genre painting, however, are his carnival scenes, among them the *Carnival* (1653; Madrid, Prado) and the *Carnival in the Piazza Colonna* (Hartford, CT, Wadsworth Atheneum; see fig.). The large size (890×1760 mm) and horizontal format of the latter, commissioned by Marchese Antonio Raggi in the late 1640s, allowed Miel to incorporate around the central theme of carnival celebrations a wide variety of scenes: actors from the *commedia dell'arte*, pedlars, musicians and a fortune-teller. Some groups of figures, for instance the beggars playing morra at the lower right, appear in other works by Miel, such as the *Tooth-puller* (ex-A. Caraceni priv. col., Rome, see Trezzani, fig. 4.22).

In 1648 Miel became the first northern Italianate artist to be admitted to the Accademia di S Luca. Around 1650 he began to paint fewer *bambocciate* and to concentrate on large-scale religious paintings for Roman churches. These include the scenes from the *Life of St Anthony of Padua* in S Lorenzo in Lucina, the scenes from the *Life of St Lambert* in S Maria dell'Anima, and *St Cyril Baptizing the Sultan of Iconium* in S Martino ai Monti. In addition to church decoration, Miel also painted small canvases with religious subjects for private patrons, such as the *Adoration of the Shepherds* and the *Adoration of the Magi* (both Rome, Pal. Barberini) and *St Roch Distributing Alms to the Poor* (Toronto, A.G. Ont.). He also collaborated with other artists, providing figures for the *vedute* (view paintings) of Viviano Codazzi and Alessandro Salucci and the landscapes of Gaspard Dughet and Angeluccio (see Trezzani, figs 4.38–4.40), and he worked with Andrea Sacchi on *Urban VIII Visiting the Gesù* (1641; Rome, Pal. Barberini).

Miel had already been to Turin before 1654, when he painted a *Virgin and Saints* for Chieri Cathedral (*in situ*). Following his permanent move there in 1658 he decorated the royal hunting-lodge at Venaria with large-scale hunting scenes (parts of which are now lost). His last genre subject was the *Encampment* (1659; Rojo Villanova priv. col.). In Piedmont he was increasingly active as a painter of history subjects, such as *Dido and Aeneas Hunting* (Cambrai, Mus. Mun.), which shows a strengthening of the classical inflection already present in the religious paintings of the 1650s. Having shifted his energies almost exclusively to history painting, Miel studied and copied paintings by Raphael and the Carracci, just as, at the start of his career, he had copied the works of van Laer.

Miel was also a competent engraver. He designed the frontispiece for Padre Daniello Bartoli's *La povertà contenta* (Rome, 1650) and did the illustrations for *De bello belgico* (Rome, 1647) by Famiano Strada.

BIBLIOGRAPHY

Hollstein: *Dut. & Flem.*

G. B. Passeri: *Vite* (1679); ed. J. Hess (1934), pp. 220–24

F. Baldinucci: *Notizie* (1681–1728); ed. F. Ranalli (1845–7), v, pp. 110–16

A. Busiri Vici: 'Carnevalate popolari romane di Jan Miel', *Stud. Romani*, vi (1958), pp. 39–50

——: 'Opere di Jan Miel alla corte sabauda', *Boll. Soc. Piemont. Archeol. & B.A.*, xii–xiii (1958–9), pp. 3–27, 94–118

Jan Miel: *Carnival in the Piazza Colonna*, oil on canvas, 0.89×1.76 m, *c.* 1645 (Hartford, CT, Wadsworth Atheneum)

T. Kren: *Jan Miel (1599–1664): A Flemish Painter in Rome* (diss., New Haven, CT, Yale U., 1979)

L. Trezzani: 'Jan Miel', *I Bamboccianti: Pittori della vita quotidiana a Roma nel seicento*, eds G. Briganti, L. Trezzani and L. Laureati (Rome, 1983; Eng. trans., 1983), pp. 91–131

Masters of Seventeenth-century Dutch Genre Painting (exh. cat. by P. Sutton and others, Philadelphia, PA, Mus. A.; London, RA; Berlin, Gemäldegal.; 1984)

LUDOVICA TREZZANI

Mielich [Muelich], **Hans** (*b* Munich, 1516; *d* Munich, 10 March 1573). German painter and illuminator. He was a leading painter in Munich of religious compositions, manuscript illuminations and portraits. He studied with his father, Wolfgang Mielich, a Munich municipal painter, who appears in the Munich tax records from 1509 onwards, but the years 1536–9, spent with Albrecht Altdorfer in Regensburg, were decisive for Hans Mielich's approach to colour. In 1536 he illuminated the title-page to the *Freiheitenbuch* of the city of Regensburg (Regensburg, Stadtmus.). In 1541 Mielich travelled to Rome on a commission from Duke William IV of Bavaria. He stayed there until 1543, when he became a master in Munich. From 1545 onwards Duke Albert V of Bavaria helped him obtain commissions, and in 1558 Mielich became leader of the Munich painters' guild. He consistently signed his works with the monogram HM (=M in H).

In an early religious work, the *Crucifixion* (1536; Hannover, Niedersächs. Landesmus.), Mielich adhered to the traditions of Bavarian Late Gothic painting. *St Jerome* (1536; Regensburg, Stadtmus., on loan from Munich, Bayer. Staatsgemäldesammlungen) shows a feeling for nature and an ability to reflect atmosphere fostered by the encounter with Altdorfer. *Mount Calvary* (1539; Madrid, Real Acad. S Fernando) is the most ambitious work of his pre-Italian period, with numerous figures, a geometric basis to the composition and total control over aerial

Hans Mielich: *Albert V of Bavaria* and his wife *Anne of Austria*, oil on canvas, each canvas 2.09×1.11 m, 1556 (Vienna, Kunsthistorisches Museum)

perspective. The experience of Italy completely changed Mielich's style of religious painting. Naked, mobile and foreshortened figures filled the pictorial surface and supplanted space. The fragmented *Mocking of Christ* and *Entombment* (1543; Solna, nr Stockholm) from a passion-altar were followed by the Ligsalz Epitaph, a funerary painting with two wings containing the *Conversion of Saul*, *Christ Triumphant* and *St Martin and the Beggar* (all Munich Cathedral). In 1554 he produced an epitaph for the Bavarian Chancellor, Leonhard von Eck (Munich, Bayer. Nmus.), the upper section copied from Michelangelo's *Last Judgement* and the lower a virtuoso representation of a sacred space in Renaissance style. In 1572, with studio assistance, Mielich completed the retable for the high altar of the Kirche Unserer Lieben Frau, Ingolstadt, as part of the Counter-Reformation revitalization of ecclesiastical art. This altar, rich in pictures, sought to forge links with the age of Dürer, but without abandoning the more recent Italian-influenced gains in depicting space and figures. Its preparatory drawings (Dresden, Kupferstichkab.; Göttingen, Kstsamml. U.; Stuttgart, Staatsgal.) are superior to the oil paintings in their fluidity of movement.

Mielich's much-admired miniatures include the *Kleinodieninventar Herzog Albrechts V.* (1546–55; individual sheets, Munich, Bayer. Nmus.) and the *Kleinodienbuch seiner Gemahlin Anna von Oesterreich* (1552–5; Munich, Bayer. Staatsbib.), documenting with finesse the goldsmith's works in the ducal collection. He also illuminated the *Motetten des Cyprian de Rore* (1557–9) and the *Busspsalmen des Orlando di Lasso* (1560–61; both Munich, Bayer. Staatsbib.), in which the initial letters and borders, the genre-like illustrations, the architecture and landscape, the portraits (including two self-portraits) and fluent scroll-work inspired by Dutch originals reveal Mielich as an artist of rich imagination and great ability. As a woodcutter he is known for *Emperor Charles V's Military Camp before Ingolstadt* (1546).

As a portrait painter Mielich learnt from Barthel Beham, whom he surpassed in pictorial qualities, and to a lesser extent from Hans Schöpfer I, whom he far exceeded in acuity of vision and creative power. Mielich was the favourite painter of the Munich middle class for over three decades. Up to 1541 he liked including atmospheric landscape prospects in his portraits. Notable portraits include *Hans Ligsalz and his Wife* (1540; Munich, Alte Pin.); *Peter Fröschl* (c. 1540; Washington, DC, N.G.A.); *Portrait of a Man* (1543; Raleigh, NC Mus. A.); pendant portraits of *Pankraz von Freyburg* (1545; Karlsruhe, Staatl. Ksthalle) and his wife *Maria Kitscher* (1545, Cleveland, OH, Mus. A.); *William IV of Bavaria on his Deathbed* (1550; Munich, Bayer. Nmus.); *Herr Tucher* (1551; Nuremberg, Ger. Nmus.) and *Frau Tucher* (1551; Germany, priv. col.); and *Herr Ligsalz* (1559; Hamburg, Ksthalle). His best-known full-length portraits are those of *Albert V of Bavaria* and his wife *Anne of Austria* (1556; both Vienna, Ksthist. Mus.; see fig.) and his finest that of *Duke Ladislaus zu Haag with a Panther* (1557; Vaduz, Samml. Liechtenstein). Mielich's works after mid-century reveal increasingly Mannerist characteristics.

BIBLIOGRAPHY

Thieme–Becker

B. H. Röttger: *Der Maler Hans Muelich* (Munich, 1925)

O. Hartig: 'Die Kunsttätigkeit in München unter Wilhelm IV und Albrecht V (1520–1579)', *Münchn. Jb. Bild. Kst*, n. s. x (1933), pp. 147–246

L. Schütz: *Hans Mielichs Illustrationen zu den Busspsalmen des Orlando di Lasso* (diss., U. Munich, 1966)

K. Löcher: 'Studien zur oberdeutschen Bildnismalerei des 16. Jahrhunderts', *Jb. Staatl. Kstsamml. Baden-Württemberg*, iv (1967), pp. 66–76

G. van Osten and H. Vey: *Painting and Sculpture in Germany and the Netherlands, 1500–1600*, Pelican Hist. A. (Harmondsworth, 1969), pp. 213–14

H. Geissler: 'Der Hochaltar im Münster zu Ingolstadt und Hans Mielichs Entwürfe', *Ingolstadt die Herzogstadt. Die Universitätsstadt. Die Festung*, ed. T. Müller and W. Reissmüller, ii (Ingolstadt, 1974), pp. 145–78

H. G. Gmelin: 'Ein frühes Gemälde der Kreuzigung Christi von Hans Mielich', *Niederdt. Beitr. Kstgesch.*, xvi (1977), pp. 32–44

S. Hofmann: 'Der Hochaltar zur Schönen Unserer Lieben Frau in Ingolstadt', *A. Bavar.*, 10 (1978), pp. 1–18

J. Rapp: 'Das Ligsalz-Epitaph des Münchner Renaissancemalers Hans Mielich', *Anz. Ger. Nmus.* (1987), pp. 161–93

——: 'Kreuzigung und Höllenfahrt Christi: Zwei Gemälde von Hans Mielich in der National Gallery of Art, Washington', *Anz. Ger. Nmus.* (1990), pp. 65–96

KURT LÖCHER

Mielżyński, Seweryn Józef Stanisław (*b* Posen [now Poznań], 11 Nov 1804; *d* Miłosław, nr Poznań, 17 Dec 1872). Polish statesman, collector, designer and painter. He completed his education in natural sciences and military architecture in Geneva. In 1823 he studied painting with Jean Léonard Lugardon (1801–84) and was active in the Polish national uprising in 1830. From 1831 to 1842 he lived in Geneva and Paris and travelled to England, Scotland, Italy and Saxony. In 1842 he took control of the family estate at Miłosław, turning it into a cultural and artistic centre. He painted and drew landscapes, portraits and religious scenes and redesigned the palace, church and bell-tower in Miłosław. He also designed the landscape garden and hunting-lodge in Miłosław and the mausoleum of General Dąbrowski in Winnogóra. In 1871 he presented to the Poznań Society of Friends of Sciences his collection of archaeological artefacts (Poznań, Archaeol. Mus.), medals, coins, paintings and 5000 engravings (most now Poznań, N. Mus.) and his library, which had been housed in a gallery designed by him in 1870. In 1871 he also compiled a catalogue of the paintings in his collection, which included 31 Polish and 170 European works, for example a *Sacra conversazione* by Palma Vecchio, an *Entombment* by Giovanni Lodi, an *Adoration of the Magi* by Joos van Cleve (i), *Landscape with a Windmill* by Pieter Molyn and *Fishing Port* by Jan van Goyen (all Poznań, N. Mus.). From 1874 the collection was situated in the Society of Friends of Sciences House in Poznań, and in 1922 the paintings were given to the Muzeum Wielkopolskie, now the Muzeum Narodowe w Poznaniu (National Museum) in Poznań.

BIBLIOGRAPHY

PSB

Seweryn Mielżyński i jego kolekcja: Zbiory Poznańskiego Towarzystwa Przyjaciół Nauk w Muzeum Narodowym w Poznaniu [Seweryn Mielżyński and his collection: the collection of the Society of Friends of Sciences in the National Museum, Poznań] (exh. cat. by H. M. Warkoczewska, Poznań, N. Mus., 1982), pp. 25–31

KONSTANTY KALINOWSKI

Mierevelt [Miereveld], **Michiel (Jansz.) van** (*b* Delft, 1 May 1567; *d* Delft, 27 June 1641). Dutch painter. The son of a Delft goldsmith, he received his first training as a painter under Willem Willemsz. and Augustus, two otherwise unknown masters. In 1581 he continued his training with Anthonie Blocklandt in Utrecht, where he remained for two years. He then returned to Delft where, as early as 1589, he became an officer of the Guild of St Luke.

At first van Mierevelt worked in the style of Blocklandt, as in the *Judgement of Paris* (1588; Stockholm, Nmus.), but he soon turned to portraiture, in which he was influenced by his fellow-townsman Jacob Willemsz. Delff the elder. Van Mander praised van Mierevelt as a portrait painter, but very little work from his early period is known. He worked steadily from about 1607, the date of his portrait of *Prince Maurits of Orange Nassau* (Delft, Stadhuis). The same year he became official painter to the stadholder court and began to produce many portraits of members of the House of Orange Nassau. He was the most popular portrait painter with the leading citizens of Delft and soon also received commissions from other noble families of the Dutch Republic as well as from foreign diplomats based in The Hague. He was one of the relatively few Dutch portrait painters in the first half of the 17th century whose patrons were not limited to his own place of residence. Among his foreign sitters were the English ambassador *Sir Dudley Carleton* (later 1st Viscount Dorchester; 1620; Montacute House, Somerset, NT; see fig.) and *Edward Cecil, Viscount Wimbledon* (1631; London, N.P.G.). Van Mierevelt's portraits are characterized by a rather dry, linear style that, without flattery, accurately portrays his sitters' features.

During this, his most prolific period, van Mierevelt must have had a large workshop with many pupils, including his own sons, Pieter van Mierevelt (1596–1623) and Jan van Mierevelt (1604–33). His assistants painted the subordinate motifs in his portraits and also made replicas in various formats. Such copies could be made on demand, but replica portraits of the most popular sitters

were also kept in stock. Van Mierevelt often had copies made of his portraits of private citizens for circulation within the family, a practice not unknown in 17th-century Holland but especially common with van Mierevelt (e.g. the portraits of *Paulus van Beresteyn* and *Volckera Knobbert* and those of *Maerten Ruychaver* and *Aletta van der Laen*; all Amsterdam, Rijksmus.).

Van Mierevelt influenced many other Dutch portrait painters, including Jan van Ravesteyn, and his works were widely known through the prints engraved after them by WILLEM DELFF, who became his son-in-law in 1618. On van Mierevelt's death his workshop was transferred to his grandson Jacob Willemsz. Delff the younger. Although many later copies after his works have been mistaken for originals, during his lifetime van Mierevelt painted at least a thousand portraits with the help of his assistants, of which several hundred are extant. The number of works executed entirely by his own hand is far lower. During his later years he was gradually driven from his position as court painter to the Prince of Orange by the rising popularity of the more modish Gerrit van Honthorst.

BIBLIOGRAPHY
K. van Mander: *Schilder-boeck* ([1603]–1604), fols 281–2
H. Havard: *L'Art et les artistes hollandais*, i (Paris, 1879), pp. 11–82
——: *Michiel van Mierevelt et son gendre* (Paris, 1894)
A. Bredius: 'Michiel Jansz. van Mierevelt, een naleezing', *Oud-Holland*, xxvi (1908), pp. 1–17
J. M. Montias: *Artists and Artisans in Delft: A Socio-economic Study of the Seventeenth Century* (Princeton, 1982)
Dawn of the Golden Age: Northern Netherlandish Art, 1580–1620 (exh. cat., Amsterdam, Rijksmus., 1993–4), pp. 310–11, 592–4
RUDOLF E. O. EKKART

Mieris, van. Dutch family of artists. The earlier generation includes three brothers, Frans (Bastiaensz.) van Mieris (*c.* 1576–before 1625), Dirck (Bastiaensz.) van Mieris (*d* 1638) and Jan (Bastiaensz.) van Mieris (*c.* 1586–1650), all of whom were gold- and silversmiths in Leiden, as was Frans's son, Willem (Fransz.) van Mieris (*c.* 1600–1656). The most important artist of the family was Jan's son, the painter (1) Frans van Mieris (i), who had two sons who also became painters: the eldest Jan [Johannes] van Mieris (1660–90), and the fourth child, the more famous (2) Willem van Mieris. Both were apprenticed to their father. Only a few works are known by Jan, who died in Rome aged 30; those that survive (e.g. *Self-portrait of the Artist in his Studio*, 1688; Hamburg, Ksthalle) show that he was a talented painter whose style resembles that of his father's later work. (3) Frans van Mieris (ii), grandson of (1) Frans van Mieris (i) and son of (2) Willem van Mieris, also became a good painter, who left behind an extensive oeuvre.

BIBLIOGRAPHY
O. Naumann: *Frans van Mieris the Elder (1635–1681)*, 2 vols (Doornspijk, 1981)
E. J. Sluijter: 'Een Zelfportret en "de schilder in zijn atelier": Het aanzien van Jan van Mieris', *Leids Ksthist. Jb.*, vi (1987), pp. 287–307
Leidse fijnschilders: Van Gerrit Dou tot Frans van Mieris de jonge, 1630–1760 (exh. cat., ed. E. J. Sluijter, M. Enklaar and P. Nieuwenhuizen; Leiden, Stedel. Mus. Lakenhal, 1988)
De Hollandse fijnschilders: Van Gerard Dou tot Adriaen van der Werff (exh. cat. by P. Hecht, Amsterdam, Rijksmus., 1989)

(1) Frans van Mieris (i) (*b* Leiden, 16 April 1635; *d* Leiden, 12 March 1681). Painter and draughtsman. Along with Gerrit Dou, he was the most important artist among

Michiel van Mierevelt: *Sir Dudley Carleton*, oil on panel, 635×502 mm, 1620 (Montacute House, Somerset, NT)

the LEIDEN 'FINE' PAINTERS, famous for his small-scale genre scenes, which were painted with exceptional refinement. The prices paid for his work during his lifetime were among the highest for Dutch paintings in the 17th century.

1. LIFE AND WORK. Frans (i) seemed destined to follow in the family tradition of gold- and silversmith work when he was apprenticed at the age of 12 to his cousin and guardian, Willem (Fransz.) van Mieris. However, by 1651 (assuming he was the 'Frans' who was paid that year for making a painting of *St Eloy* for the guild of gold- and silversmiths), he had already begun to paint. According to Houbraken, he received his training as a draughtsman and painter first from Abraham Toorenvliet (*c.* 1620–92), a drawing-master and glass-engraver, then from the Leiden 'Fine' painter Gerrit Dou, then from the portrait and history painter Abraham van den Tempel and finally from Dou again. In all, this probably lasted from *c.* 1649 to *c.* 1654. Van Mieris adopted Dou's meticulous manner and never used the broader technique that he must have learnt from van den Tempel. He entered the Leiden Guild of St Luke in 1658 but was apparently active as an independent painter for several years before then, since his earliest dated works are from 1657 and a considerable number of paintings, mostly signed, were presumably made before that (see Naumann, 1981, nos 1–19). He followed Dou closely in his earliest known works, probably painted before the mid-1650s. Works such as the *Elderly Couple Sitting down to a Simple Meal, Seen through an Arched Window* (Florence, Uffizi) and the *Pen Grinder by an Arched Window* (Dresden, Gemäldegal. Alte Meister) are distinguished from those of his master by the placement of the figures further back in the window space and especially by the more powerful use of light, with its lively reflections cast over all surfaces. The slightly later *Inn Scene with Two Peasants and a Maid* (*c.* 1655–6; Leiden, Stedel. Mus. Lakenhal), with its warm light dancing over the surfaces and reflected in bright colours, departs even further from Dou's concentrated chiaroscuro. This stylistic development was probably prompted by the early paintings of Gabriel Metsu and perhaps also by the work of an Italianate painter such as Jan Baptist Weenix. The choice of subject (also a departure from Dou's practice) reveals the influence of Adriaen van Ostade, and the spatial structure of the scene that of Quiringh van Brekelenkam, an older Leiden artist.

In 1657–9 van Mieris produced some of the best paintings of his career, including the *Doctor's Visit* (1657; Vienna, Ksthist. Mus.), the *Lute-player with a Young Woman Playing the Virginal* (1658; Schwerin, Staatl. Mus.), the *Inn Scene with an Officer and Maid* (1658; The Hague, Mauritshuis) and the *Man Offering Oysters to a Young Woman* (1659; St Petersburg, Hermitage). Stylistically they are a continuation of his previous work, but technically they are suddenly of exceptionally high standard. In them he strove to make his brushstrokes invisible, unlike Dou whose brushstrokes can always be distinguished on close scrutiny. Van Mieris's extremely subtle and lively handling of light prevented his paintings from becoming stiff in character. Whereas Dou's interiors are largely shrouded in darkness, van Mieris's are filled with light, which defines

1. Frans van Mieris (i): *Cloth Shop*, oil on panel, 545×427 mm, 1660 (Vienna, Kunsthistorisches Museum)

everything precisely. Van Mieris often employed a rigidly geometrical layout, with emphatic horizontal and vertical lines that clearly outline the spatial structure. He expanded significantly the range of subjects commonly depicted by Leiden artists: his prosperous and sophisticated figures move in elegant surroundings (usually in an amorous context) and are strongly reminiscent of those by Gerard ter Borch (ii). Thematically and stylistically, van Mieris's paintings of the late 1650s and early 1660s soon influenced other masters, as is obvious from the work of Metsu, Jan Steen, Jacob Ochtervelt, Johannes Vermeer and Eglon van der Neer. The immediacy of this effect and the fact that his *Cloth Shop* (1660; Vienna, Ksthist. Mus.; see fig. 1) sold almost at once to Archduke Leopold Wilhelm for an unusually high price of 2000 guilders (Sandrart) shows the high esteem in which his work of this period was held.

During the first half of the 1660s van Mieris maintained this high level of achievement in, for example, *Teasing the Pet* (1660; see fig. 2), *Offering Oysters* (1662) and *Boy Blowing Bubbles* (1663; *see* ICONOGRAPHY AND ICONOLOGY, fig. 9; all The Hague, Mauritshuis). He occasionally repeated Dou's niche motif and sometimes recalled it in the arched top of the panel. In the late 1660s his colours became darker and the figures more stylized, as in *Young Woman at her Toilet* (1667; Dresden, Gemäldegal. Alte Meister) and *Sleeping Courtesan* (1669; Florence, Uffizi). This trend continued in the 1670s, the enamel-like smoothness and the harsh, restless reflections of the light becoming, seemingly, an end in themselves, and the figures more stereotyped (e.g. the *Family Concert*, 1675; Florence,

2. Frans van Mieris (i): *Teasing the Pet*, oil on panel, 275×200 mm, 1660 (The Hague, Koninklijk Kabinet van Schilderijen 'Mauritshuis')

Uffizi; the *Young Woman at her Toilet*, 1678; Paris, Louvre; and the *Young Woman Writing a Letter*, 1680; Amsterdam, Rijksmus.). Unlike most other Dutch genre painters, he left a substantial number of drawings, mostly highly detailed works in black chalk, probably intended as independent works of art, such as the *Seated Old Woman* (London, BM), the *Sick Woman* (Vienna, Albertina) and the *Cavalier Playing the Lute* (Haarlem, Teylers Mus.).

2. Critical reception and posthumous reputation. Van Mieris's paintings had a strong influence on younger artists, anticipating the late 17th-century development of a precious, more stylized form. It is remarkable how often during his lifetime and shortly afterwards his subjects were copied or slightly modified by others, including his sons Jan and Willem. Apart from his sons, the only other artist known to have been apprenticed to him is Karel de Moor, who, with Willem, probably contributed to some of his later works. The *Holy Family* (1681; priv. col., see Naumann, 1981, ii, pl. 121), signed and dated the year of Frans's death, is thought to be largely by Willem.

The extent to which van Mieris was highly respected during his life is also clear from the praise he received from contemporary writers, such as Cornelis de Bie, Joachim von Sandrart and Roger de Piles (the last two esteeming him more highly than Dou). All three emphasized the exorbitant prices paid for his paintings, which were much sought-after not only by wealthy citizens in

Leiden, such as the famous physician François de la Boe Sylvius (1614–73), but also by foreign collectors. Archduke Leopold Wilhelm invited him to work at his court in Vienna on a substantial allowance, but van Mieris declined. In 1669 Cosimo III de' Medici, Grand Duke of Tuscany, visited his studio, after which two self-portraits and three genre paintings were acquired by the Florentine court. His *Family Concert* fetched the then unheard-of price of 2500 guilders. The correspondence of Giovacchino Guasconi, who was Cosimo's agent in the Netherlands, documents van Mieris's contact with the Florentine court and supports Houbraken's anecdotes about the artist's heavy drinking. The letters also reveal that van Mieris was inept with money, which would explain why, despite the prices paid for his paintings, he never achieved great prosperity. Although van Mieris has always been recognized as one of the leading Dutch genre painters of the 17th century, the exceptional standing of his work during the late 17th century and the 18th fell off in the late 19th century. However, during the last decades of the 20th century there was an increased interest in his paintings; special attention has been paid to the iconological interpretation of his works, which often show amorous situations of a slightly erotic nature.

BIBLIOGRAPHY

C. de Bie: *Het gulden cabinet* (1661), p. 404

J. von Sandrart: *Teutsche Academie* (1675–9); ed. A. R. Peltzer (1925), p. 196

R. de Piles: *Abrégé de la vie des peintres avec des reflections sur leurs ouvrages* (Paris, 1699), pp. 441–2

A. Houbraken: *De groote schouburgh* (1718–21), iii, pp. 1–12

O. Naumann: 'Frans van Mieris as a Draughtsman', *Master Drgs*, xvi (1978), pp. 3–34

Masters of Seventeenth-century Dutch Genre Painting (exh. cat., ed. P. Sutton; Philadelphia, PA, Mus. A.; Berlin, Gemäldegal.; London, RA; 1984), pp. xvi, xli–ii, 256–60; pls 57–9

See also family bibliography above.

(2) Willem van Mieris (*b* Leiden, 2 June 1662; *d* Leiden, 26 Jan 1747). Painter and draughtsman, son of (1) Frans van Mieris (i). He trained with his father and probably contributed to several of his later works. It is almost certain, for example, that he finished his father's signed painting of the *Holy Family* (1681; priv. col., see Naumann, 1981, ii, pl. 121). The earliest examples signed and dated by Willem himself are from 1682, after which there is a large oeuvre of dated works up to the 1730s, when he became partly blind. In 1693 he joined the Leiden Guild of St Luke, for which he served as headman several times and once as dean. Around 1694, with the painters Jacob Toorenvliet (*c.* 1635–1719) and Karel de Moor, he founded a drawing academy in Leiden, which he and de Moor directed until 1736.

Willem's earliest work followed the technique and subject-matter of his father's late paintings, with the same enamel-like smoothness, harsh reflections of light, emphatic display of virtuosity in the rendering of detail and stereotyped figures. From the beginning, however, he concentrated more than his father had on history painting, including religious scenes, subjects from Classical and Renaissance literature and pastoral themes, for instance *Satyrs and Nymphs* (1682; Utrecht, Cent. Mus.), *Joseph and Potiphar's Wife* (1685; Hannover, Niedersächs. Landesmus.), *Bacchus and Ariadne* (1704; Dresden, Gemäldegal. Alte Meister) and *Rinaldo and Armida* (1709; The Hague, Mauritshuis). In so doing, he applied the aesthetic ideals and rules of decorum of classical, late 17th-century art theory, in combination with the technique of the LEIDEN 'FINE' PAINTERS. Most of these compositions are peopled with small figures, usually nude women, and set in palatial surroundings or in an idealized landscape. The poses of the figures are often taken from prints of Classical sculpture in the pattern-books of François Perrier and Jan de Bisschop (i) and the work of the popular ivory-carver and sculptor Frans de Bossuit.

The majority of Willem van Mieris's oeuvre, however, consists of genre scenes, including almost all the subjects and motifs developed by previous generations of Leiden 'Fine' painters, several of the earlier ones depicting elegant young women or musicians and drinkers, directly recalling paintings by his father, as in the *Young Woman with an Aging Lover* (1683; Vienna, Ksthist. Mus.), the *Young Woman Setting Free a Little Bird* (1687; Hamburg, Ksthalle) and the *Drinking Violin-player with a Maidservant Pouring Wine* (1699; Dresden, Gemäldegal. Alte Meister). After the turn of the century he specialized in shops and kitchens seen through arched windows, usually with a painted low relief underneath (after Francesco Du Quesnoy or de Bossuit). These settings include saleswomen or maidservants, often counterbalanced by a man, and surrounded by a lavish display of groceries, vegetables, fish or game, such as the *Kitchen Maid and Fishmonger* (1713; London, N.G.; see fig.) and the *Woman with Boy in a Grocery Shop* (1717; The Hague, Mauritshuis). In form,

these follow the niche pictures by Gerrit Dou (e.g. the *Poultry Shop*, London, N.G.), but in character they are completely different, with cool colours, rather evenly spread light, highly stylized figures and a profusion of objects and minutely rendered details. From the 1720s van Mieris's figures became more stereotyped and wooden, and he repeated the same compositional schemes, as in the *Young Woman and Man in a Poultry Shop* (1733; Amsterdam, Rijksmus.). His technical virtuosity continued unimpaired until the end of the decade and thereafter declined.

Van Mieris was a good portraitist and also painted a number of landscapes in the style of Johannes Glauber and Jan Griffier. He was a competent draughtsman, too, as can be seen from the many surviving drawings, which include figure and compositional studies in black chalk, carefully worked-out preparatory drawings and copies of his own paintings in pencil and/or black chalk and exceptionally detailed and colourful drawings in gouache. The highly finished drawings were undoubtedly intended as independent works of art. He also made four clay models for a set of garden vases with low reliefs showing mythological scenes symbolizing the Four Seasons (Windsor Castle, Berks, Royal Col.); these are the only surviving examples of low reliefs cast after his clay models.

Van Mieris's principal pupils were his son (3) Frans van Mieris (ii) and Hieronymus van der Mij (1678–1761), a Leiden painter of portraits, genre scenes and historical subjects. Many prominent collectors took an interest in his work, and his paintings sold for high prices. Among his most important patrons were Petronella Oortmans-De la Court (1624–1707), her much younger nephew Pieter de la Court van der Voort (1664–1739), who was an immensely wealthy cloth magnate in Leiden, and his nephew Cornelis Backer (1693–1775). Pieter de la Court van der Voort not only commissioned free compositions but also ordered copies of works by Frans van Mieris the elder and other Leiden 'Fine' painters and asked Willem to complete or add figures to paintings by other artists in his collection. During his lifetime many of his paintings were bought by Christoph August von Wackerbarth for the Dresden gallery of August the Strong, Elector of Saxony and King of Poland. In the 18th century most important German and French collectors acquired examples of his paintings.

BIBLIOGRAPHY
J. C. Weyerman: *De levens-beschrijvingen der Nederlandse konstschilders en konst-schilderessen*, 4 vols (The Hague, 1729–69), iii, pp. 387–92
J. van Gool: *De nieuwe schouburgh der Nederlandse kunstschilders en schilderessen*, 2 vols (The Hague, 1750–51), i, pp. 191–203
C. W. Fock: 'Willem van Mieris als ontwerper en boetseerder van tuinvazen' [Willem van Mieris as designer and modeller of garden vases], *Oud-Holland*, lxxxvii (1973), pp. 27–48
R. E. O. Ekkart: *Leids kunstlegaat: Kunst en historie rondom 'Ars Aemula Naturae'* [Leiden's art inheritance: art and history concerning the 'Ars Aemula Naturae'] (Leiden, 1974), pp. 10–14
C. W. Fock: 'Willem van Mieris en zijn mecenas Pieter de la Court van der Voort', *Leids Ksthist. Jb.*, ii (1984), pp. 261–82
E. Elen-Clifford Kocq van Bruegel: 'Tekeningen van Willem van Mieris in relatie tot zijn schilderijen', *Leids Ksthist. Jb.*, iv (1985), pp. 147–64

See also family bibliography above.

(3) Frans van Mieris (ii) (*b* Leiden, 24 Dec 1689; *d* Leiden, 22 Oct 1763). Painter and writer, grandson of (1) Frans van Mieris and son and pupil of (2) Willem van

Willem van Mieris: *Kitchen Maid and Fishmonger*, oil on panel, 495×410 mm, 1713 (London, National Gallery)

Mieris. His oeuvre comprises portraits, several small history paintings and many genre scenes (e.g. the *Grocer's Shop Seen through an Arched Window*, 1715; Amsterdam, Rijksmus.), which stylistically and thematically are similar to his father's work. His most important picture, the *Three Generations* (1742; Leiden, Stedel. Mus. Lakenhal; *see* LEIDEN, fig. 2), shows himself standing alongside his father, Willem, and holding in one hand a portrait of his famous grandfather, Frans, while pointing with the other to Houbraken's *De groote schouburgh*, which lies open at an engraved portrait of the latter. In this way he demonstrated, with obvious pride, that he was from a distinguished family of painters, who for three generations had occupied a central position among Leiden artists. In addition to being a painter, he was well known for his historical and numismatic writings.

WRITINGS

Beschrijving der bisschoppelijke munten en zegelen van Utrecht in 't bijzonder [Description of episcopal coins and seals of Utrecht in particular] (Leiden, 1726)
Groot charterboek der graven van Holland, van Zeeland en Heeren van Vriesland, 4 vols (Leiden, 1753)

ERIC J. SLUIJTER

Mies van der Rohe, Ludwig (*b* Aachen, 27 March 1886; *d* Chicago, IL, 17 Aug 1969). German architect, furniture designer and teacher, active also in the USA. With Frank Lloyd Wright, Walter Gropius and Le Corbusier, he was a leading figure in the development of modern architecture. His reputation rests not only on his buildings and projects but also on his rationally based method of architectural education.

1. Education and early work, before 1919. 2. Europe, 1919–38. 3. USA, 1938–69.

1. EDUCATION AND EARLY WORK, BEFORE 1919. He was born Ludwig Mies but later adopted his mother's name, van der Rohe. The son of a master stone mason, Mies van der Rohe had no formal architectural education. He attended the Domschule in Aachen until 1900 and then the local trade school (1900–02) while working on building sites for his father, from whom he acquired a respect for the nature of building materials. The town's many fine medieval buildings stimulated a youthful interest in architecture, and their characteristically clear and honest construction exerted a lasting influence upon his creative work. Two years as a draughtsman and designer for a firm specializing in stucco decoration followed, before he left for Berlin in 1905. Wishing to improve his knowledge of construction in wood, he became an apprentice to Bruno Paul. He received an independent commission to build a house for Dr Riehl, a philosopher, who first sent him for three months to Italy, where he visited Vicenza, Florence and Rome. The Riehl House (completed 1907), Neubabelsberg, Berlin, is ostensibly a single-storey house, traditional to the vicinity, with a steeply pitched roof, which sweeps smoothly over dormer windows. The placing of the house on a steeply sloping site is remarkable: a tetrastyle verandah at one end of the house rises from a retaining wall at entrance level. The house brought him to the attention of Peter Behrens, in whose office he then worked (1908–12), and towards the end of his time there he

supervised Behrens's robust neo-classical German Embassy in St Petersburg (1911–12). He saw and was impressed by the work of Frank Lloyd Wright when it was exhibited in Berlin (1910).

Mies van der Rohe established his own office in Berlin in 1912, and for the next two years or so his work showed the influence of Karl Friedrich Schinkel, whose sparse Neo-classic manner he had seen reflected in Behrens's prestigious non-industrial commissions alongside the new rationalism of his industrial buildings and products. An invitation to design a house and art gallery (1912; unexecuted) for Hélène Kröller-Müller at The Hague led Mies van der Rohe to the Netherlands, where he saw the work of H. P. Berlage with its clarity of structure and honest use of materials. He built three houses in the Berlin area before World War I began and from 1915 to 1918 served in the Engineers Corps of the German Army.

2. EUROPE, 1919–38. In the first half of the 1920s the newly established Weimar Republic offered few opportunities for building in Germany, but progressive developments in the arts were beginning to find a hospitable European centre in Berlin. Mies van der Rohe participated fully in these activities. He directed the architectural division of the Novembergruppe (1921–5), helped to finance and wrote for the magazine *G* (*Gestaltung*) and prepared a remarkable series of projects in which he explored the architectural possibilities of the new building materials. Studies for glass skyscrapers (1919–21; *see* ARCHITECTURAL DRAWING, fig. 9), in which multi-faceted glass skins enclosed open skeletal structures, were followed by an equally prophetic seven-storey concrete office building (1922) in which the cantilevered structure is the dominant exterior element, with the windows recessed in continuous horizontal bands. Two projects for country houses followed in 1923–4, one in brick, one in concrete. In them he developed the concept of decellurization of interior space as initiated by Frank Lloyd Wright.

Many other projects were designed during this period, all to remain unbuilt. The Karl Liebknecht and Rosa Luxemburg Monument to the November Revolution (1926; destr.) in the cemetery at Friederichsfelde in Berlin was a vigorously three-dimensional symbolic wall, composed of recessed and raised overlapping rectilinear blocks of brickwork and carrying a five-pointed star and standard. He designed and built the Wolf House (1926; destr.) at Guben, a finely crafted flat-roofed brick house, and municipal housing in the Afrikanischestrasse (1926–7) in Wedding, Berlin, three- and four-storey buildings with balconies on the south side. The decade closed, however, with two notable achievements. In 1927, as First Vice President of the DEUTSCHER WERKBUND, Mies van der Rohe directed one of the most successful of the inter-World War initiatives, the Weissenhofsiedlung exhibition in Stuttgart. He invited the foremost European architects to participate, among them Walter Gropius, Le Corbusier, Behrens, Max Taut and Bruno Taut. Twenty permanent residential buildings were built around his own four-storey steel-framed apartments. They provide a remarkable exhibition of comparative individual interpretations of the new architecture. It was not, however, until 1929 that the ideas of the earlier experimental period were finally realized

1. Ludwig Mies van der Rohe: German (or Barcelona) Pavilion for the Exposición Internacional, Montjuïc, Barcelona, 1929 (destr.; reconstructed 1986)

in one of the most important buildings of the Modern Movement, the German (or Barcelona) Pavilion (destr.; reconstructed 1986), Montjuïc, Barcelona (see fig. 1). It was a last-minute addition to the German section of the Exposición Internacional in Barcelona in 1929 for which Mies van der Rohe and Lilly Reich (with whom he collaborated on exhibition projects) had been given overall design responsibility by the government in 1928. Here Mies van der Rohe used the open (decellurized) plan as an architectural analogy of the social and political openness to which the new German republic aspired. Space-defining elements were dissociated from the structural columns, planning was free and open, merging interior and exterior spaces: unbroken podium and roof planes were held apart by a regular grid of slender cruciform steel columns, giving a clear field for spatial design, using opaque, translucent and transparent walls freely disposed between the columns. These ideas were crucial to all his subsequent work. The rich materials of the space-defining walls, the reflecting pools—in one of which stands a sculpture by Georg Kolbe—and the furniture that he designed specifically for the pavilion (the well-known Barcelona chair, stools and table), all added to the architectonic qualities in a building of great poetic beauty. The Tugendhat House (1928–30; badly damaged by war but now refurbished; see CZECH REPUBLIC, fig. 6), Brno, Czech Republic, interprets the ideas of the German Pavilion in a domestic context. These two buildings and the furniture that he designed for them established him as an architect and furniture designer of international stature. In 1930, at the recommendation of Walter Gropius, Mies van der Rohe was appointed Director of the Bauhaus, but by 1932, under political pressure from the Nazi party, he moved the school from Dessau to a disused factory in Steglitz, Berlin, where he ran it privately for one further session. Following further Nazi interference he closed the school in 1933, with the full support of his colleagues.

3. USA, 1938–69. In 1938 Mies van der Rohe settled in Chicago and took up an appointment as Director of the Architecture Department of Armour Institute, which in 1940 became the College of Architecture, Planning and Design at Illinois Institute of Technology. He also re-established his architectural practice and for the next 20 years he divided his time between it and his teaching duties. His work in both capacities reflected a philosophy of architecture, based upon Thomas Aquinas's proposition that reason is the first principle of all human work. It led him to question open speculation and personal expression as the main bases for creative architecture and to follow certain general principles that he learnt from the buildings of the great architectural epochs of the past: namely that architecture is derived from, and eventually becomes an expression of, the significant forces that combine to determine the ethos of an epoch or a civilization; that architecture's physical realization is accomplished through the use of clear construction, elevated to a higher plane through an understanding of the art of building—Baukunst; that a language of architecture gradually evolves during the epoch in response to the epoch's particular needs and means, guided by a grammar based upon the principle of structure—the morphological and organic relationship of things that permeates the whole building fabric, illuminating each part as necessary and inevitable. At Illinois Institute of Technology (IIT) he set up a curriculum based on these principles and the belief that 'The function of education is to lead us from irresponsible opinion to truly responsible judgement; and since a

2. Ludwig Mies van der Rohe (with Pace Associates): Crown Hall (College of Architecture), Illinois Institute of Technology, Chicago, Illinois, 1950–56

building is a work and not a notion, a method of work, a way of doing should be the essence of architectural education' (Carter, 1964, p. 141).

The North American technological environment facilitated the realization of these architectural ideas. During the first ten years or so in the USA, the development of his characteristically clear, highly influential concept of architecture was made possible by the Armour Foundation and IIT as clients: first a master-plan for the campus (1940–41), and successively the Research Buildings for Minerals and Metals (1942–3) and for Engineering (1944–6), both for the Armour Research Foundation; the Alumni Memorial Hall (1945–6); and Perlstein Hall (Metallurgy and Chemical Engineering) and Wishnick Hall (Chemistry), both 1945–6, for IIT. All these were executed in association with Holabird & Root, except the last, which was undertaken in association with Friedman, Alschuler and Sincere. In parallel with these buildings he designed and built a country retreat (1945–50) for Dr Edith Farnsworth on the Fox River at Plano, IL. Many other buildings on the IIT campus followed throughout the period of his tenure of the Directorship of the School of Architecture, including the Students' Commons Building (1952–3; with Friedman, Alschuler and Sincere) and Crown Hall (1950–56; with Pace Associates; see fig. 2). His first high-rise buildings resulted from a meeting in the mid-1940s with Herbert S. Greenwald, an active young developer with particular interests in the field of urban renewal. Promontory Apartments (1946–9; with Pace Associates and Holsman, Holsman, Klekamp and Taylor), 5530 South Shore Drive, Chicago, was the first of many buildings to result from an association that continued for more than a decade until Greenwald's untimely death in an air crash. Many multi-storey urban high-rise buildings were designed by Mies van der Rohe in the following 20 years, which by virtue of their precise, almost Platonic images found worldwide emulation and placed him in the forefront of 20th-century urban design. The list of high-rise structures includes several of the best-known and most widely discussed buildings of the mid-century: 860 Lake Shore Drive Apartments (1948–51; collaboration with same

practices), Chicago; the Seagram Building (1954–8; with Philip Johnson, and Kahn & Jacobs; and with Phyllis Lambert representing the client), Park Avenue, New York; Pavilion and Colonnade Apartments (1958–60), Colonnade Park, Newark, NJ; and later the Toronto-Dominion Centre (1963–9) for which Mies van der Rohe was consultant architect to John B. Parkin Associates and Bregman and Hamann.

These buildings show clearly Mies van der Rohe's development and refinement of a structural aesthetic based on an open flexible plan. In contrast to many of his contemporaries, Mies van der Rohe profoundly questioned the concept 'form follows function' because he recognized that functional requirements often change. He believed that building solutions should allow for an optimum degree of flexibility in order to accommodate economically the frequent need to revise the arrangement of living and working spaces. Thus, within a concept of overall size and complexity of function taken in generalized terms, he chose to develop and work within three trabeated building types: the low-rise skeleton frame building, the high-rise skeleton frame building, and the single-storey clear-span building. In all these types those functions not requiring daylight, such as lecture theatres and law courtrooms, and the fixed core accommodating lifts, stairs, toilets and service ducts, are located within the interior spaces of the plan, leaving the peripheral areas available for the flexible arrangement of classrooms, workshops, laboratories, offices, flats or exhibition spaces as the particular building's function required. The development of the low-rise building type is apparent in the numerous campus buildings at IIT (1939–58), or between the clear formal disciplines of the early examples such as the IIT Metallurgical and Chemical Engineering Building (1945–6; with Holabird and Root) and the later spatial and structural sophistication of such buildings as the Bacardi Administration Building (1957–61) in Mexico City or the School of Social Service Administration (1962–5) for the University of Chicago.

Refinement of the high-rise building type moved from the reinforced concrete structural frame with brick and glass infill at Promontory Apartments, to the fireproofed steel structural frame enclosed by a skin of black-painted steel mullions, column and floor fascia plates with clear glass at the 26-storey 860 Lake Shore Drive Apartments (*see* UNITED STATES OF AMERICA, fig. 10), through to the prestigious Seagram Building with its skin of bronze mullions, floor fascia plates, glazing frames and louvres, with tinted glass and marble. The former visually expressed both columns and floors externally, the latter expressed the floor lines and the corner and ground-floor columns. For the 30- and 42-storey buildings of the Chicago Federal Centre (1959–63; with Schmidt, Garden and Erickson, C. F. Murphy Associates and and A. Epstein and Sons Inc.) the skin follows the Seagram Building's solution but comprises black-painted steel components with aluminium glazing frames and louvres, with tinted glass. There are also subtle differences in proportions between bay sizes and the positioning of projecting mullions to express scale in terms of an overall category of use or to take account of the building's magnitude.

Following a number of unrealized projects, the first built example of Mies van der Rohe's single-storey clear-span building was the Farnsworth House, Plano, IL (see fig. 3)—one of the best-known houses of the 20th century. The house, which is raised above the ground against the Fox River's spring flooding, comprises a classically proportioned and finely crafted white steel structure with rectangular floor and roof planes cantilevering beyond externally positioned 'I' section columns—the space between being subdivided into interior and exterior living areas. In the interior area (enclosed by large sheets of plate-glass and paved with Roman Travertine marble), living, sleeping and kitchen spaces are subtly defined around a free-standing wood-panelled core housing bathrooms and services. The exterior area, also paved with Travertine, forms a protected terrace, and this is connected by a flight of steps to a lower open floating terrace and similar steps to the ground. There is no suggestion of a contrived formal relationship between the house and its natural surroundings, and the building's occurrence in the landscape would seem almost fortuitous were it not for the harmony achieved between it and the terrain. Its independence of, and at the same time interdependence with, its surroundings creates a convincing and moving image in a technological era and is prophetic of the handling of the relationships of buildings to context in many future projects. As a microcosm of the mature work of Mies van der Rohe the Farnsworth House has all the elements of the developed clear-span single-storey building type as exemplified by the larger Crown Hall (College of Architecture) at IIT and the new Nationalgalerie (1962–8), Tiergarten, Berlin. The former has a rectangular steel roof structure carried by external steel plate girder portal frames; the latter has a square steel roof structure supported in a cantilevered manner by eight peripherally located steel cruciform columns.

In many of Mies van der Rohe's buildings his introduction of externally projecting steel, aluminium or bronze 'I'-shaped mullions at the module reference points causes the visible elements of the building's fireproofed structure and its glass infill to become architecturally fused—a modern interpretation of the Greek, Roman and Gothic principle of manifest structural order. As in classical buildings, the design is honed to greater perfection in each successive building by subtle improvements in proportion and detailing rather than by radical changes in overall expression. This also resulted in buildings with an immediately recognizable Miesian look.   The majority of Mies van der Rohe's buildings were designed for centrally located urban sites, including the campus of IIT and his best-known housing development for Greenwald, the Lafayette Park urban renewal scheme in central Detroit. The master-plan of the latter was made between 1955 and 1956 in collaboration with his ex-Bauhaus colleague and then Director of City and Regional Planning Department at IIT, Ludwig Hilberseimer, and the landscape architect Alfred Caldwell. Mies van der Rohe designed the low-rise town houses and Pavilion Apartments for Lafayette Park in 1958 and the high-rise Lafayette Towers flats in 1963. The Toronto-Dominion Centre is another of the traffic-free schemes in which it is notable that the attention to scale in descending order through structure, plan module and components of construction extends also to those elements that confront the pedestrian: paving, steps, benches etc. The common recognizable factor in all Mies van der Rohe's urban design is the ability to handle the space between buildings and the integration of space with landscaping. No one can walk between the high and low buildings of Lafayette Park, or between the buildings at IIT, without being conscious of the spatial definition achieved without formal enclosure. Mies van der Rohe's

3. Ludwig Mies van der Rohe: Farnsworth House, Plano, Illinois, 1945–50

projected Mansion House Square (1967), London, which brought a new office building and existing historical structures together through the introduction of a public landscaped square, was rejected by the British planning authorities.

Because Mies van der Rohe developed his concept of architecture in a logical manner from one building to another, his work as a whole is endowed with a unity of purpose and expression. Regardless of magnitude or function the works belong together as a coherent group and speak with a single architectural language. This consanguinity is due to a number of factors: structural systems have been selected in accordance with the overall requirements of the building's functions, and their components are revealed, either actually or symbolically: non-load-bearing external skins and interior space-defining divisions are articulated separately from stressed members, leaving no doubt as to what is structural and what is not; materials, whether natural or industrially produced, are used in such a way as to acknowledge the nature of each; visible modules represent subdivisions of the structural bays in relation to function and provide a tool for internal planning and a practical inducement to flexibility in use; careful and thorough detailing exemplifies to the user the visual refinement called for in the further division of space; subtle proportions result from visual judgements, not systems; provisions are made for expressive response to changing conditions of light and weather. In Mies van der Rohe's hands the critical interaction between building function, construction and structure, which is at the heart of architecture, frequently touched true poetic expression.

Few architects practising after World War II have remained completely untouched by Mies van der Rohe's influence—even if only in terms of a heightened concern for detailing; and the fact that he worked within traditional architectural principles facilitated acceptance of his ideas in countries with diverse social and economic backgrounds. He believed architecture to be a historical process, and that in consequence architects should recognize relationships between the significant facts of their own epoch and the ideas that are capable of guiding these facts in a direction beneficial to society in general. In his own work he tried to reach a practical synthesis of this ideal with the disciplines set by the principle of structure: he tried to evolve a truly contemporary language for architecture, a language that comes from the past yet is open to the future.

Mies van der Rohe was awarded the Gold Medal of the Royal Institute of British Architects (1959), that of the American Institute of Architects (1960) and the United States Presidential Medal of Freedom (1963).

BIBLIOGRAPHY

P. C. Johnson: *Mies van der Rohe* (New York, 1947)
L. Hilberseimer: *Mies van der Rohe* (Chicago, 1956)
P. Blake: *Mies van der Rohe: Architecture and Structure* (New York, 1960)
P. Carter: 'Mies Interviewed', *20th C.* (Spring 1964), pp. 138–43
L. Hilberseimer: *Contemporary Architecture, its Roots and Trends* (Chicago, 1964)
W. Blaser: *Mies van der Rohe: The Art of Structure* (London, 1965)
L. Glaeser: *Ludwig Mies van der Rohe: Drawings in the Collection of the Museum of Modern Art* (New York, 1969)
P. Carter: *Mies van der Rohe at Work* (New York and London, 1974)
A. Swenson and P.-C. Chang: *Architectural Education at IIT* (Chicago, 1980)
D. Spaeth: *Mies van der Rohe* (London, 1985)
W. Blaser: *Mies van der Rohe: Less Is More* (New York and Zurich, 1986)
A. Drexler, ed.: *The Mies van der Rohe Archive: Part 1, 1910–1937* (New York and Zurich, 1986)
F. Schulze: *Mies van der Rohe: A Critical Biography* (London, 1986)
J. Zukowsky, ed.: *Mies Reconsidered: His Career, Legacy and Disciples* (New York, 1986)
E. S. Hochman, ed.: *Architects of Fortune: Mies van der Rohe and the Third Reich* (New York, 1989)
F. Schulze, ed.: *Mies van der Rohe: Critical Essays* (New York, 1989)
PETER CARTER

Mieza. *See under* LEUKADIA.

Mi Fu [Mi Fei]. *See* MI, (1).

Migéon, Pierre, II (*b* Paris, 1701; *d* Paris, 5 Sept 1758). French cabinetmaker. He was the son of the cabinetmaker Pierre Migéon I (*b c.* 1670). He started work in 1726, as his day-book (Paris, Bib. N.), originally attributed to his father, indicates. As much a dealer as a craftsman, Migéon sold a large number of luxury objects to a cosmopolitan clientele, and subcontracted extensively to colleagues. He carried out many commissions for the Garde Meuble de la Couronne, both directly and through the cabinetmakers Antoine-Robert Gaudreaus and Gilles Joubert. He worked in the Louis XV style using geometric veneering, some floral marquetry and lacquer, enhanced by beautiful bronze mounts. His most important works include desks (e.g. Paris, Louvre; Stockholm, Kun. Husgerådskam.), commodes (*see* FRANCE, fig. 57), corner-cupboards (e.g. Munich, Residenzmus.; Basle, Haus Kirschgtn) and *secrétaires en pente* (e.g. Washington, DC, N.G.A.). After his death, his son Pierre Migéon III (1733–75) and later his son's widow continued to use his stamp until 1785.

BIBLIOGRAPHY

F. de Salverte: *Les Ebénistes du XVIIIème siècle, leurs oeuvres et leurs marques* (Paris, 1923, rev. 5/1962)
J. Viaux: *Bibliographie du meuble (Mobilier civil français)*, 2 vols (Paris, 1966–88)
JEAN-DOMINIQUE AUGARDE, JEAN NÉRÉE RONFORT

Migge, Leberecht (*b* Danzig [now Gdańsk, Poland], 20 March 1881; *d* 30 May 1935). German landscape architect and writer. After a horticultural apprenticeship and training in Hamburg he joined the landscape-gardening firm of Jakob Ochs in 1902. He rose quickly from technician to principal designer. In 1913 he left to become self-employed. Migge had joined the Deutscher Werkbund in 1912 and through designing a number of public parks in Germany he began to develop his theories about the role and function of landscape gardening. He wrote extensively on the subject, and in such books as *Jedermann Selbstversorger* (1918) and *Die Gartenkultur des 20. Jahrhunderts* (1920) he explained his ideas about the socialization of urban green space, of transforming the city into an autonomous entity without exploiting the surrounding countryside. From 1920 he put his theories into practice first with his Sonnenhof project at the artists' colony at Worpswede, and then through his involvement with the housing reform movement. During the 1920s and early 1930s he designed the landscaping for many of the Modern Movement housing estates of the Weimar Republic. He worked with such architects as Otto Haesler (1880–1962), at Georgsgarten, Celle (from 1926), Bruno Taut and Martin Wagner at Britz, Neukölln, Berlin (from 1925), and Waldsiedlung Zehlendorf (from 1926), Berlin; with Ernst May he shaped the housing and landscape policies of Frankfurt am Main. A fierce critic of his profession and motivated by radical political beliefs, Migge fused garden-city ideas with those of the modernists of the 1920s in an attempt to create a socially responsible and engaged landscape architecture.

BIBLIOGRAPHY
N. Huse: *Neues Bauen 1918 bis 1933: Moderne Architektur in der Weimarer Republik* (Munich, 1975)
L. Burckhardt, ed.: *Werkbund: Germania Austria Svizzera* (Venice, 1977); Eng. trans. as *The Werkbund: Studies in the History and Ideology of the Deutscher Werkbund, 1907–1933* (London, 1980), pp. 66–71
Leberecht Migge, 1881–1935, Gartenkultur des 20. Jahrhunderts, ed. Fachbereich Stadt- und Landschaftsplanung der Gesamthochschule Kassel (Worpswede, 1981)

CLAUDIA BÖLLING

Migliara, Giovanni (*b* Alessandria, 5 Oct 1785; *d* Milan, 18 April 1837). Italian painter and teacher. He began his career as a scene painter with Gaspare Galiari (1761–1823) in Milan, working at the Teatro Carcano in 1804 and at La Scala from 1805 to 1809. Owing to illness, after 1810 he turned to small-scale works in watercolour or oil using various supports, including silk and ivory. At this date Milanese painting was dominated by Andrea Appiani and Luigi Sabatelli, both leading Neo-classical artists. However, Migliara remained aloof from this dominant movement and instead drew on medieval and historical subjects with Romantic undertones. His precise, jewel-like technique and choice of subject-matter found favour with aristocratic patrons in Milan. His figures are generally stilted and burdened by their costumes, though the crowd in *Sacking of Minister Prina's House* (1814; Milan, Gal. A. Mod.) is depicted with unusual fluency. In 1822 Migliara was appointed Professor of Perspective at the Accademia di Belle Arti, Milan, and in 1833 he was nominated painter to the court of Charles-Albert, King of Sardinia (*reg* 1831–49). More typical of his historical scenes is *Entrance to the Castle of Plessis de la Tour* (Turin, Gal. Civ. A. Mod.), which was exhibited at the Brera in 1833. He also produced many topographically precise pictures of church interiors in which he combined his training as a scene painter with his knowledge of intaglio techniques. In such pen-and-wash studies as *Church and Gothic Tomb* (1831; Turin, Gal. Civ. A. Mod.) he displayed a greater sensitivity to light and tone than in his oil paintings (e.g. *Vestibule of a Convent*, 1833; Alessandria, Pin. Civ.). He particularly excelled as a painter of small medieval church interiors, as did several of his pupils, including his daughter Teodolinda Migliara (1816–66), Frederico Moja (1802–85), Pompeo Calvi (1806–84), Luigi Bisi (1814–86) and Angelo Inganni (1806–80).

Comanducci
BIBLIOGRAPHY
L. Ozzola: 'Cronachetta Artistica: Civico Museo e Pinacoteca in Alessandria', *Emporium*, xxxiv/203 (1911), pp. 397–8
R. Ghezzi: *Giovanni Migliara* (Alessandria, 1935)

LUCINDA LUBBOCK

Migliaro, Vincenzo (*b* Naples, 8 Oct 1858; *d* Naples, 16 March 1938). Italian painter. He studied with the sculptor Stanislao Lista (1824–1908) and then at the Istituto di Belle Arti in Naples under Federico Maldarelli (1826–93), Raffaele Postiglione (1818–97) and Domenico Morelli. In 1877 he won second prize in a national painting competition and in 1884 exhibited, to great acclaim, his view of a Neapolitan square, *Piazza Francese* (priv. col., see Schettini, p. 33), at the Esposizione Nazionale in Turin. He then spent some time in Paris and Venice. Work shown in Naples in 1886 and 1888 was noticed by Francesco Netti, who admired two opposing tendencies in Migliaro's style: a spontaneous approach with strict regard for effects of light and atmosphere, and a roughness and imprecision resulting in distortion and a lack of realism.

Migliaro took his subjects from contemporary life and preferred urban genre scenes, frequently basing his paintings on themes encountered in lithographs, engravings and photography. His work was not motivated by social concerns, as was that of Michele Cammarano and Teofilo Patini, nor was he tempted by historical subjects, as in the case of Mariano Fortuny y Marsal. Working in Naples, he tried to record the old buildings and the poorer inhabitants of the city in a fresh, unconventional manner. Despite his genuine sympathy for the misery of life in the back streets, however, he tended to depict such areas as picturesque and exotic. In 1887 he was commissioned by the Ministry of Education to carry out a series of paintings recording quarters of Naples that were about to disappear in the implementation of the Slum Clearance Law of 1885. Migliaro was explicitly chosen for his proven capacity to observe minute detail, in contrast to the manner of the Impressionists. His scenes of Naples include *Vico Forno*, *Vico Grotte* (both 1887), *Santa Lucia*, *Strada Pennino* (both 1888), *Strettoia degli orefici* ('Goldsmiths lane'), a second version of *Piazza Francese* (both 1889), *A Street near the Port* (1893) and *Vico Cannucce* (1901; all Naples, Mus. N. S Martino).

In the early years of the 20th century Migliaro's colouring grew bolder and less controlled, and his use of abrupt cropping and other techniques suggested by instant photography became repetitive. In addition to paintings he produced engravings and etchings and made lithographs for posters (Treviso, Mus. Civ. Bailo; see 1988 exh. cat.). He was also active as an illustrator of such literary texts as the short stories and sonnets of Salvatore di Giacomo (for example, *Minuetto Settecento* and *A San Francisco*), and he provided sculptures for the Neapolitan Caffè Gambrinus (destr.). During the last years of his life he served as the Head of Painting at the Accademia in Naples.

BIBLIOGRAPHY
V. Pica: 'Artisti contemporanei: Vincenzo Migliaro', *Emporium*, xliii (1916), pp. 163–83
Migliaro (exh. cat. by V. Ciardo, Venice, Biennale, 1940)
A. Schettini: *Vincenzo Migliaro* (Naples, [1950])
M. A. Pavone: *Napoli scomparsa nei dipinti di fine ottocento* (Rome, 1987) [principally about Migliaro]
I manifesti Mele (exh. cat., ed. M. Picone Petrusa; Treviso, Mus. Civ. Bailo, 1988)

MARIANTONIETTA PICONE PETRUSA

Migliore, Ferdinando Leopoldo del (*fl* Florence, 1664–97). Italian historian. He was from a distinguished Florentine family and was educated for an ecclesiastical career but became a historian whose archival research undertaken for his few publications and extensive unpublished manuscripts was of particular importance. Although sparsely documented, his role as a historian has been defined by E. L. Goldberg. He was the rival in Florence of Giovanni Cinelli (1625–1706) and Filippo Baldinucci. His published works are *Senatori fiorentini* (1665), which is a list, and the detailed guide *Firenze città nobilissima illustrata* (1684), in which his central theme is the celebration of Florence and its great achievements arising from the collective nobility of the Florentine soul.

UNPUBLISHED SOURCES

Florence, Bib. N. Cent., MSS Magliabechi, ix 66 [MS. of G. Cinelli: *Toscana Letterata* (1670s and after)]

Florence, Bib. N. Cent., MSS Magliabechi [extensive col. MSS of F. L. del Migliore, incl. *Gabella dei contratti*, xxvi 147 (1697)]

Florence, Bib. N. Cent., MS. II iv 218 [MS. of F. L. del Migliore: *Reflessioni e aggiunte alle 'Vite de'pittori' di Giorgio Vasari aretino*]

WRITINGS

Senatori fiorentini (Florence, 1665)

Firenze città nobilissima illustrata (Florence, 1684)

BIBLIOGRAPHY

J. Schlosser Magnino: *La letteratura artistica* (Florence, 1967), pp. 545, 587

P. Barocchi: 'Le Postille di del Migliore alle *Vite* vasariane', *Il Vasari storiografo e artista. Atti del congresso internazionale del IV centenario della morte: Florence, 1974*, pp. 439–47

E. L. Goldberg: *After Vasari: History, Art, and Patronage in Late Medici Florence* (Princeton, 1988)

MILES L. CHAPPELL

Migliorisi, Ricardo (*b* Asunción, 6 Jan 1948). Paraguayan painter. He studied in the studio of the painter Cira Moscarda but was basically self-taught and gained his formative experience in various Latin-American countries working as a designer of theatre costumes and scenery. His early work, biting and irreverent in style, and with psychedelic and Pop art elements, created a considerable stir in Paraguay's artistic community. Much of this work was in the form of drawings and paintings, but he also devised environments, happenings, audio-visual experiences and montages (see Escobar, 1984, pp. 172, 194). His subject-matter comprised unrealistic hybrid characters, animals and objects from classical mythology, popular Latin-American subjects, kitsch opera, circus and cabaret, television and gossip columns, portrayed in a style linked to Latin-American Magic Realism and to expressionist caricature. Humour, eroticism and the absurd animate his work, giving it a flavour of hallucination and nightmare.

BIBLIOGRAPHY

O. Blinder and others: *Arte actual del Paraguay* (Asunción, 1983), pp. 47, 48, 49, 162, 173, 174, 192

T. Escobar: *Una interpretación de las artes visuales en el Paraguay*, ii (Asunción, 1984)

T. Escobar: *Migliorisi, los retratos del sueño* (Asunción, 1986)

TICIO ESCOBAR

Mignard. French family of painters. (1) Nicolas Mignard was a successful painter of religious subjects, decorative schemes and portraits, first in Avignon and then in Paris; his work, which at first displayed Mannerist tendencies, came, after a stay in Italy, to reflect the influence of the Bolognese painters. His more distinguished brother (2) Pierre Mignard, similarly influenced by training in Italy, became the most outstanding portrait painter of his generation; his career was to some extent hampered by

the opposition of the Académie Royale de Peinture et de Sculpture in Paris and Charles Le Brun, and reached its high point when he succeeded the latter as Premier Peintre du Roi.

BIBLIOGRAPHY

A. Félibien: *Entretiens* (1685–8; rev. 1725)

A. P. F. Robert-Dumesnil: *Le Peintre-graveur français* (1835–71), i (Paris, 1835), pp. 99–109

(1) Nicolas Mignard [Mignard d'Avignon] (*bapt* Troyes, 7 Feb 1606; *d* Paris, 20 March 1668). According to Félibien, he first studied painting with some local master at Troyes and then travelled to Fontainebleau, in order to study and copy the Mannerist decorations in the château. The influence of these works is certainly visible in, for example, the *Devotion of Marcus Curtius* (*c.* 1630; Avignon, Mus. Calvet), in which the principal figure is closely derived from a composition by Luca Penni, engraved by Jean Mignon. Mignard was first recorded in Provence in 1633, when he painted an *Assumption of the Virgin* (Avignon, Notre-Dame-des-Doms) for the convent of the Dames de Ste Praxède; this work shows the light colours of Simon Vouet, together with a distinctive realism that Mignard later abandoned. In 1635 he travelled to Rome in the train of Alphonse-Louis du Plessis, Cardinal Archbishop of Lyon (brother of Cardinal Richelieu), who probably lodged him in the Palazzo Farnese. The only work dating from his two-year stay in Rome is a small *Crucifixion* on copper (?1636; Troyes, Mus. B.-A.), but the influence of paintings by the Bolognese masters proved to be enduring. Mignard's *Assumption of the Virgin* of 1643 (Tarascon, Ste Marthe) is a direct transcription of Annibale Carracci's celebrated work of 1600–01 in S Maria del Popolo in Rome. Moreover, in 1637 Mignard produced nine etchings after the Carracci decorations in the Palazzo Farnese in Rome.

After his return to Avignon in 1636 Mignard continued, with increasing success, to produce altarpieces, often of large size, for churches and religious houses in that city and the surrounding region. He also undertook (*c.* 1655–9) an extensive decorative scheme for a bedroom in the Hôtel de Tonduti-Lescarène (overdoors of the *Four Seasons* and three mythological elements in Avignon, Mus. Calvet). His *Apollo and Daphne* (1656–9; Avignon, Mus. Calvet) shows the influence of the classicism of Charles Le Brun. Around 1657 he painted a portrait of *Molière as Caesar in 'La Mort de Pompée'* (Paris, Mus. Comédie-Fr.). In 1660 the French court visited Avignon and Mignard was commissioned to paint numerous portraits of courtiers, including one of *Cardinal Mazarin* (untraced). Louis XIV summoned him to Paris, where he continued to practise as a portrait painter; the King sat to him several times (see 1979 exh. cat., pp. 106–7). He rose steadily through the ranks of the Académie Royale: he was received (*reçu*) in 1663 but was excused a *morceau de réception*, became Professor and Assistant Rector in 1664, and Rector in 1666. His success was assisted by his support for Charles Le Brun against his own brother (2) Pierre Mignard, with whom he remained on poor terms. In 1666 Mignard was commissioned to decorate the Petit Appartement Bas du Roi in the Tuileries in Paris; of this work, which presented *Louis XIV as Apollo* and which was based on the earlier series for the Hôtel de Tonduti-Lescarène, there remains only one canvas, *Apollo Giving King Midas Ass's Ears* (Lille, Mus. B.-A.).

BIBLIOGRAPHY
A. Marcel: 'Mignard d'Avignon, peintre et graveur (1606–1668)', *Mém. Acad. Vaucluse*, xxxi (1931), pp. 1–109
Catalogue du centenaire desseins: Fonds Nicolas Mignard (exh. cat., Paris, Paul Prouté SA, 1978)
La Peinture en Provence au XVIIe siècle (exh. cat., ed. H. Wytenhove; Marseille, Mus. B.-A., 1978)
Mignard d'Avignon (1606–1668) (exh. cat. by A. Schnapper, Avignon, Pal. Papes & Mus., 1979)
A. Schnapper: 'Après l'Exposition Nicolas Mignard', *Rev. A.*, lii (1981), pp. 29–36

(2) Pierre Mignard I [Mignard le Romain] (*b* Troyes, 17 Nov 1612; *d* Paris, 30 May 1695). Brother of (1) Nicolas Mignard.

1. TRAINING IN FRANCE AND EARLY YEARS IN ROME, TO 1657. Pierre Mignard studied first under Jean Boucher in Bourges, then copied the 16th-century decorations at the château of Fontainebleau by Rosso Fiorentino, Francesco Primaticcio and other artists. He later went to Paris, where in 1633 he entered the studio of Simon Vouet, the most prominent representative of the Italian Baroque style in France. There he formed a lasting friendship with the painter and, later, writer Charles-Alphonse Dufresnoy. Towards the end of 1635 Mignard left Paris for Rome, staying in Italy until October 1657. Monville, his first biographer, recorded several portraits painted in Italy, as well as some large religious compositions, including a *St Charles Giving Communion to the Dying* (1677; untraced). Only two portraits are known to survive, those of the Ambassador of Malta to the Holy See: *Commandeur Des Vieux* (1653; Valetta, N. Mus.) and a man presumed to be *Senator Marco Peruta* (Prague, N.G., Šternberk Pal.), which was painted during Mignard's stay in Venice in 1654. Both portraits already show the quality that was to make Mignard one of the outstanding portrait painters of his time: the ability to catch a vivid and natural likeness, in contrast to the stern stiffness of earlier 17th-century French portraiture.

In 1655 Mignard returned to Rome from Venice via Bologna and Florence. He was called to the Vatican to paint the portrait of the newly elected *Pope Alexander VII* (untraced; engraving by van Schuppen, 1661, in Paris, Bib. N.), and collaborated with other artists under the supervision of Nicolas Poussin on the copying of the famous decorations by Agostino Carracci and Annibale Carracci in the Palazzo Farnese, made for Alphonse-Louis du Plessis, brother of Cardinal Richelieu (exh. Paris, Louvre, late 18th century; untraced). The influence of the art of the Carracci, uniting the Roman emphasis on drawing with Venetian colourism, persisted in Mignard's religious and historical paintings throughout his career. He was also influenced by such painters of the contemporary Roman School as Pietro da Cortona and Andrea Sacchi, but was mainly attracted by the soft and graceful style of the Bolognese master Francesco Albani, whom he knew and whose works to some degree inspired his famous paintings of the Madonna (e.g. *Madonna with the Grapes*, c. 1656; Paris, Louvre). The latter were known by the punning title of 'Mignardes' because of their sweet beauty, and have

often been attributed to such Italian painters as Sassoferrato.

2. MATURITY IN PARIS, 1657–c. 1680. When Mignard left Rome for France in 1657 he was a member of the Accademia di S Luca and had a certain reputation as a portrait painter and a degree of prosperity. During a brief stay in Avignon he met up with his brother Nicolas and became acquainted with the dramatist Molière, of whom he went on to paint several portraits, now known only from engravings and descriptions. In 1658 he went to Fontainebleau to paint the first of his ten portraits of Louis XIV, the originals of which are impossible to identify among the profusion of copies. With the exception of a short visit to Avignon in 1664, Mignard remained in Paris, where he soon became the most fashionable and prolific portrait painter of his time. The calm pride and self-assurance that mark the faces of his paintings, so typical of 17th-century portraiture, exemplify his ability to render the austere majesty of the court of Louis XIV. Unfortunately, few of his large allegorical portraits survive or are preserved in engravings. For the most part Mignard's abilities as a portrait painter must be judged by works from late in his career (*see* §3 below). An exception is the portrait of a *Lady with her Son* (late 1660s; Dole, Mus. Mun.), an example of a genre—women with their children—in which he excelled. His skill in rendering embroidered materials, lace and flowers, together with a rich palette of strong blue, gold, red and black, make his portraits among the most elegant and festive of the 17th century. Although Mignard was considered a 'Rubéniste'

1. Pierre Mignard: *Louise-Renée de Keroualle, Duchess of Portsmouth*, oil on canvas, 1181×937 mm, 1682 (London, National Portrait Gallery)

by many of his contemporaries, he remained true to the facture of the Bolognese school: the strongly coloured, smooth surfaces, the opaque whiteness of the flesh tones and the detailed ornamentation of his portraits are also typical of his historical compositions throughout his career.

In spite of his success as a portrait painter, Mignard longed to paint large historical compositions, and his greatest wish was to show the knowledge of fresco technique that he had acquired in Italy: in 1662 he was commissioned by the Queen Mother, Anne of Austria, to paint the cupola of the church of the Val-de-Grâce in Paris (completed 1666). The theme of the decoration is the celebration of the birth of her son, Louis XIV. With some 200 figures representing the French royal family surrounded by the celestial court of apostles, prophets, saints and angels hovering among the clouds, it is among the most ambitious Baroque decorative ensemble in Paris. Other Parisian decorative works of this period by Mignard included those in the house of the banker Barthélemy Hervart (c. 1606–76) executed in 1665 and frescoes (1669) in the baptismal chapel of St Eustache: neither scheme survives.

3. THE WORKS OF OLD AGE, AFTER c. 1680. In his later years, when he was famous and wealthy, Mignard was able to dedicate more of his time to large historical and religious compositions: *Christ Carrying the Cross* (1684; Paris, Louvre); *Neptune Offering the Sea Empire to*

2. Pierre Mignard: *Marquise de Seignelay as Thetis with her Two Sons*, oil on canvas, 1.94×1.55 m, 1691 (London, National Gallery)

the King (1684; Compiègne, Château) and the *Family of Darius before Alexander* (1689; St Petersburg, Hermitage) all show the influence of his years in Rome. Mignard's long-term rivalry with the Premier Peintre du Roi, Charles Le Brun, also a pupil of Vouet, had kept him away from major royal decorative commissions such as those at the château of Versailles. However, with the death of Le Brun's protector, Jean-Baptiste Colbert, in 1683, the Premier Peintre's power was diminished, and Mignard began to enjoy royal patronage: he executed the much admired ceiling decorations of the gallery of the château of Saint-Cloud in 1677/8 (destr. 1870; engraved by Jean-Baptiste de Poilly) and in 1685 the ceiling of the Petite Galerie at Versailles (destr.; engraved by Girard Audran). Tapestries executed after the decorations at Saint-Cloud (Pau, Mus. N. Château) give some idea of Mignard's talent as a secular decorator.

A number of Mignard's finest portraits date from the last phase of his career. They include signed and dated canvases of *Louise-Renée de Keroualle, Duchess of Ports-mouth* (1682; London, N.P.G.; see fig. 1), mistress of Charles II of England, with an African girl offering her the gifts of the maritime Empire in a large shell, and of the wife of the Minister of Marine, the *Marquise de Seignelay as Thetis with her Two Sons* (1691; London, N.G.; see fig. 2), depicted against a background of the sea and a volcano. This was also the period of Mignard's large and decorative group portraits, the *Grand Dauphin and his Family* (1687–8; Versailles, Château) and the drawing of the exiled English king *James II with his Family* (1694–5; Paris, Louvre).

The death of Le Brun in 1690 led to Mignard's appointment as Premier Peintre, and, despite the fact that he had previously refused to join the Académie Royale, remaining loyal to the Académie de St Luc, he succeeded to Le Brun's posts of professor, treasurer, rector and director. His *Self-portrait* (?1690; Paris, Louvre), presented by his daughter to the Académie Royale in 1686, shows him with the works he considered his most important: the oil sketch for the cupola of the Val-de-Grâce and a project for a triumphal column for the Place Royale (now Place des Vosges), Paris (unexecuted; drawing in *Self-portrait*). This portrait was, perhaps, his retort to the portrait of *Charles Le Brun* by Nicolas de Largillierre (1696; Paris, Louvre), which showed Le Brun among some of his famous works.

Although Mignard was nearly 80 in 1690, in the last few years of life he experienced a renewed burst of activity. He not only painted the portraits already mentioned, but also made designs (Paris, Louvre) for the decoration of the church of Les Invalides, Paris, painted two ceilings for the Petit Appartement du Roi at Versailles (fragments Fontainebleau, Château; Lille, Mus. B.-A., and elsewhere), and painted a series of religious pictures including *Christ and the Woman of Samaria* (1690; Paris, Louvre) and *St Cecilia* (1691; Paris, Louvre). His last work was his *Self-portrait with St Luke Painting the Virgin* (1695; Troyes, Mus. B.-A. & Archéol.), an unusual subject in 17th-century French art, but one clearly designed to express his pride in his achievement. The Musée du Louvre, Paris, has a collection of over 300 of his drawings.

BIBLIOGRAPHY
S. P. de Monville: *La Vie de Mignard, Premier Peintre du Roy* (Paris, 1730)
E. Lebrun-Dalbanne: 'Etude sur Pierre Mignard', *Mém. Soc. Acad. Agric., Sci., A. & B.-Lett. Dépt. Aube* (1866), pp. 367–438
Mignard et Girardon (exh. cat., Troyes, Mus. B.-A. & Archéol., 1955)
J. Wilhelm: 'Quelques portraits peints par Pierre Mignard', *Rev. Louvre*, xii/4 (1962), pp. 165–74
J.-C. Boyer: 'Un Chef-d'oeuvre retrouvé de Pierre Mignard (1612–1695): *Pan et Syrinx*', *Rev. Louvre*, xxx/3 (1980), pp. 152–6
——: 'L'Inventaire après décès de l'atelier de Pierre Mignard', *Bull. Soc. Hist. A. Fr.* (1980), pp. 137–65
G. de Lastic: 'Contribution à l'oeuvre de Pierre Mignard portraitiste', *Bull. Soc. Hist. A. Fr.* (1980), pp. 167–76
L. Nikolenko: *Pierre Mignard: The Portrait Painter of the Grand Siècle* (Munich, 1983)
Le Voeu d'Anne d'Autriche: Trésors d'art sacré à l'ombre du Val-de-Grâce (exh. cat. by Jacques Charles, Paris, Val-de-Grâce, 1988)
Le Peintre, le roi, le héros: 'L'Andromède' de Pierre Mignard (exh. cat. by J.-C. Boyer, Paris, Louvre, 1990)
R. W. Berger: 'Pierre Mignard at Saint-Cloud', *Gaz. B.-A.*, n. s. 5, cxxi (1993), pp. 1–58
J.-C. Boyer: *Pierre Mignard (1612–1695): Avec un catalogue raisonné de l'oeuvre* (in preparation)
                                              LADA NIKOLENKO

Mignon, Jean (*fl* 1535–55). French painter and etcher. His work as a decorative painter at the château of Fontainebleau between 1538 and 1544 is recorded in the *Comptes des bâtiments du roi*, but no work by him in this medium has been identified. He signed two etchings, of which one was an ornamental cartouche dated 1544. On stylistic criteria Herbet attributed 27 engravings to him and Zerner 60.

Mignon made a few engravings after Andrea del Sarto, for example *Charity* (Zerner, no. 6; the only picture in Francis I's collection of which an engraving was made by the Fontainebleau etchers), and after Francesco Primaticcio, but he worked almost exclusively after drawings by Luca Penni; these depicted religious and mythological subjects, often tinged with eroticism, elegant and somewhat cold in style. In the background he introduced poetic landscapes of his own invention. His manner, at first rather crude as in *Naked Men Fighting* (z 33), developed in his later work into a learned complexity, as in *Saint John Preaching in the Desert* (z 55), or in the *Metamorphosis of Actaeon* (z 60), which was highly esteemed by his contemporaries, as many copies attest.

BIBLIOGRAPHY
F. Herbet: *Les Graveurs de l'Ecole de Fontainebleau*, iv of *Les Eaux-fortes nommées ou marquées* (Paris, 1901), pp. 41–50
H. Zerner: *Ecole de Fontainebleau: Gravures* (Paris, 1969) [z]
L'Ecole de Fontainebleau (exh. cat., Paris, Grand Pal., 1972–3), pp. 314–21
H. Zerner: *Italian Artists of the Sixteenth Century*, 33 [XVI/ii] of *The Illustrated Bartsch*, ed. W. Strauss (New York, 1979), pp. 366–7
G. Albricci: 'Luca Penni e i suoi incisori: Raccolta delle stampe A. Bertarelli', *Rass. Stud. & Not.*, x (1982), pp. 86–166
                                              MARIANNE GRIVEL

Mignon, Léon (*b* Liège, 9 April 1847; *d* Schaerbeek, Brussels, 30 Sept 1898). Belgian sculptor. He studied under the sculptor Prosper Drion (1822–1906) at the Académie in Liège from 1857 to 1871. He was a particular admirer of the anecdotal sculpture of Léopold Harzé (1831–93). His vocation as a sculptor of animal subjects began in Rome, where he studied on a grant from 1872 to 1876. He exhibited in Ghent (1874) and on several occasions in Paris (where he lived from 1876 to 1882) at the Salon des Artistes Français. He achieved prominence

Léon Mignon: *Hubert Bellis*, bronze, h. 475 mm, *c.* 1894 (Brussels, Musée d'Art Moderne)

at the Exposition Universelle of 1878 in Paris with his *Bulls Fighting in the Roman Countryside* (Brussels, Mus. A. Mod.). In 1880–81 he shared a studio with the Belgian sculptor Paul De Vigne, whom he had met in Rome. Mignon's *Bull Tamer* (Liège, Parc Avroy) took the gold medal at the Salon of 1880. In 1882 he settled in Brussels and in 1888 produced the *Labours of Hercules* reliefs for the stairway of the palace of Charles de Lorraine (now part of the Bibliothèque Royale Albert Ier). He sculpted several historical figures for the provincial law courts and a *Philosopher* (1892) for the Université de Liège. As a sculptor of animal subjects, Mignon occupies a leading place in Belgian Realist art. He also modelled busts of Belgian personalities as well as a statuette of the Belgian painter *Hubert Bellis* (see fig.), figurines of workers, soldiers from the Belgian regiments (*c.* 1889) and an equestrian statue of *Leopold II* (1886; Brussels, Mus. A. Mod.). His works are preserved in the Musée de l'Art Wallon, Liège, and the Musée d'Art Moderne, Brussels. He was completing a frieze for the Hôtel Somzée in Brussels when he died unexpectedly.

BIBLIOGRAPHY
BNB
J. du Jardin: *L'Art flammand*, vi (Brussels, 1900)
Léon Mignon: Exposition rétrospective (exh. cat., Liège, 1905)
A. Micha: *Inauguration du monument Léon Mignon, 21 juillet 1906: Discours* (Liège, n.d.)
La Sculpture belge au 19ème siècle, ii (exh. cat., Brussels, Gén. de Banque, 1990), pp. 504–8
                                      JACQUES VAN LENNEP

Migration period. Term used to describe a period spanning the decline and fall of the Roman Empire and the foundation of the medieval Christian kingdoms of Europe between the 5th and 8th centuries AD. The arts of the European Migration period are varied, reflecting the styles, techniques and beliefs of the many different peoples involved, yet there are so many common features that it is possible to speak of Migration period art as a unified concept. From the surviving evidence, it is mainly a metalworkers' art, carried out in a highly skilled manner by able craftsmen; the stone sculpture and architecture of the Classical civilizations were copied, though with a different approach. There must also have been much richly decorated organic material, but the survival of wood, leather and textiles is only fragmentary.

1. Historical background. 2. Artistic influences. 3. Peoples. 4. Styles. 5. Techniques.

1. HISTORICAL BACKGROUND. Although the period of migrations is sometimes regarded as a disruption following the stable conditions of the Roman Empire, the constant movement of tribes and peoples was in fact the common pattern of prehistoric Europe; the Roman imposition of frontiers created barriers that were eventually penetrated by the sheer pressure of population movements. In the first few centuries AD there were two main currents of migration. The Goths, peoples from Scandinavia and the Baltic area, moved south-eastwards to settle in the lands north of the Black Sea. There was also a strong east to west movement, originating in Asia and bringing the Huns into eastern Europe; this caused the peoples whom they displaced to put pressure on the eastern frontiers of the Roman Empire. Such movements can be traced artistically. The broadly abstract, though symbolic, decorative art of northern Europe came into contact with the representational style of the Classical world. Specialist craftsmen became aware of the mass-production methods of the Roman Empire. The Goths adopted the Iranian jewellery techniques of their neighbours in the south Russian steppes. With the many further migrations that were set off by the chain of events, the decorated possessions of the restless tribes reflected these general themes as well as the influence of the existing local styles.

The political situation in the 5th century was that of a series of tribes on the move, putting pressure on the frontiers of Rome. During the next century, the old western Empire was occupied by the migrating peoples from the north and the east. They can be broadly grouped into the west and east Germans. The west Germans were the Franks, Alemans, Saxons, Frisians and Thuringians; the east Germans were the Goths, Vandals, Burgundians, Lombards and Gepids. Further to the east were the Huns and Slavs, with subsequent incursions by Avars and Magyars. In Scandinavia the stable Germanic population remained in artistic contact with Continental developments, and both contributed to and drew from them. The decorated possessions associated with these various groups all represent the art of the Migration period.

2. ARTISTIC INFLUENCES. An important characteristic of Germanic art was its ability to absorb and transform new influences. The various territories occupied by the migrating tribes had their own styles and techniques; these were drawn upon and fused into something quite new.

Germanic art as practised in the Scandinavian and Baltic homelands consisted mainly of the abstract, geometric decoration of artefacts, including pottery, together with some simple human and animal outline figures of symbolic purpose. The stimulus of new contacts brought about rapid stylistic developments, which showed the constantly inventive and adaptable nature of Germanic art.

There were already strong links with the art of the Empire. The border tribes were familiar with Roman art through trade and gifts; Roman goods were widely distributed beyond the frontiers, and much native metalwork imitates Roman forms and patterns. Roman art was itself beginning to reflect the more abstract and stylized approach of the many non-Latin peoples settled within the frontiers as auxiliary soldiers or federated tribes. This abstract, expressionistic quality had originated in the Empire's eastern provinces, where religious cults inspired a symbolic rather than naturalistic art. The major religion from the east was Christianity; the earliest Christian art drew on the existing traditions of Hellenistic art, but by the 5th century new iconography and symbolism were being developed. Much of this representational art was reproduced during the Migration period, after the conversion of the Germanic tribes.

Another form of oriental influence was the use of an increasing range of colour and surface patterning, seen mainly in jewellery, where many techniques were adopted from the metalworkers of south Russian and ultimately Iranian tradition. These were then taken back to north and west Europe by the Gothic tribes and became some of the most distinctive features of Migration period art. An element of this can also be traced in architecture, where different coloured stonework and non-functional shallow-carved decoration are employed alongside the surviving Classical tradition.

The evidence for the arts of the period is extremely uneven and incomplete. Almost all the finds come from cemeteries, but the nature of decorated items chosen to accompany the dead may not necessarily reflect daily life. Metalwork survives best in the ground, and so the styles and techniques of dress-fittings, jewels and weapons are the best-known aspects of Migration period art. Glass and pottery also survive well, organic materials much less so. It is the cemetery evidence that shows the differences both between the various Germanic peoples and between the native populations. There are also some individual high status burials with fine grave goods. Carved stone memorials show attempts to copy the format of the Classical world. Architectural evidence, where it exists, again reveals strong Classical influence, though tempered with a new approach to decoration, while village plans and excavated houses show the continuity of the north European building tradition.

3. PEOPLES. Despite the general unity of style, there is some variety in the evidence for the different areas and peoples, with contrasting cemetery contents and other material remains. Of the west Germans, the Franks (see MEROVINGIAN ART) occupied Roman Gaul and were to overcome and absorb their immediate neighbours. These included the Alemans, a confederation of several Germanic tribes who had migrated from the upper Rhine

Valley to Switzerland and eastern France by the end of the 5th century AD. As mounted warriors, their characteristic grave goods included horse gear and a long-sword with decorated gold-leaf pommel; typical brooches had a semi-circular head and uniform-sized foot decorated with animal ornament and interlace, while other metalwork showed the influence of late Roman techniques. Their pottery was incised with geometric patterns.

Another people who were to become subject to the Franks were the Burgundians, originally of eastern Germanic origin from the Baltic area, who settled in the Rhône Valley and the Savoy region and were already highly Romanized when they were conquered by the Franks in 532 and absorbed into the Merovingian kingdom. They were originally related to the Goths and Vandals but quickly adapted to the influence of the Empire (although described adversely by Sidonius Appollinaris as being constantly drunk and perfuming their hair with rancid butter). Their jewellery is clearly influenced by Roman art but also has some eastern features as part of the common Gothic heritage. One characteristic element is the use of damascening, a metal inlay technique of Syrian origin, which can be seen on a range of silver buckles. The abundant cemetery finds have other distinctive elements, including gilded shield bosses, cicada-shaped brooches in cloisonné inlay, brooches in the form of a bird of prey with hooked beak, gold and cloisonné buckles of late Roman type, silver brooches with bird heads at the feet and silver filigree earrings. Openwork belt buckles with figural designs show the direct influence of Mediterranean Early Christian art. Interlace ornament is also common from the late 6th century; its rather unstructured nature suggests that it did not originate among the Burgundians, but it became a very characteristic feature of their art. Other Germanic neighbours of the Franks from the east bank of the River Rhine were the Thuringians, who were also gradually absorbed into the Merovingian empire; they remained pagan, however, and were therefore resistant to the current of Christian art, which was influencing other Germanic peoples. The Bavarians, also from east of the Rhine, joined in the Lombard invasion of Italy; their art shows the more direct contacts with Mediterranean ornament. They were eventually brought into the Frankish kingdom in the 8th century.

The art of those peoples living beyond the boundaries of the old Empire shows a purer Germanic style, with fewer attempts to copy Late Antique or Early Christian art, and the emphasis almost entirely on surface ornament. In north Europe the Frisians, who occupied the coastal plain of the Netherlands and were to be absorbed by the Franks in the 8th century, were great maritime traders. Their prosperity is attested by a number of merchants' hoards and by their settlements of regularly planned villages with sunken-floor huts (*Grubenhäuser*) or three-aisled houses. Their distinctive artefact was a bronze key, with openwork head decorated by a cross or by animal motifs. Frisian textiles were famous, but none has survived. The Frisians may have taken part, together with the Angles, Saxons and Jutes, in the settlement of England (*see* ANGLO-SAXON ART, §I); decoration on the earliest Anglo-Saxon pottery suggests many Continental links. In Scandinavia, the main source of impetus of many of the

Germanic artistic phases, art remained pagan until the 11th century and went through an elaborate sequence of development based entirely on animal forms (*see* VIKING ART, §II, 1(i)).

The Goths moved west from the Black Sea area in two main waves. The Visigoths (*see* VISIGOTHIC ART) occupied southern France and Spain, where they adapted the sculpture and architecture of the Empire. Similarly the Ostrogoths (*see* OSTROGOTHIC ART) combined Byzantine art and architecture with Germanic decorative techniques. Further south, the Vandals, originally from Scandinavia, had moved from Spain to north Africa, where they entirely adopted the modes of the Roman Empire; their kingdom was, however, reconquered by the Byzantines in AD 534.

From eastern Europe the Lombards, a Germanic tribe who had occupied Hungary in the 6th century, moved on to Italy in AD 568. Their 7th-century cemeteries show that they retained a distinctively Germanic style of ornament; they did not develop Italian monumental art in the manner of the Ostrogoths (*see* LOMBARD ART). Their neighbours in Hungary, the Gepids, originally from the Baltic, combined Lombardic and Frankish art forms. Their most characteristic ornament was an eagle-headed buckle; other typical jewellery included ornamental buckles of gold or silver decorated with garnets, belt-purses and ornamented hairpins combining late Roman geometric patterns with Germanic animal art. Excavations have provided evidence of richly carved woodwork, including beds, chairs, candlesticks, plates and shields. There are also documentary accounts of wooden palaces and halls.

The Gepids and Lombards had close relationships with the Avars, an Asiatic nomadic tribe with whom they were alternately allied or at war. The Avars had moved west into Hungary, where they established a powerful kingdom from the middle of the 6th century. Their art combined imported luxury Byzantine objects, such as dress, coins and silverware, with more Asiatic features of bone plates for saddles and quivers carved with floral patterns or mythical scenes. The distinctive Avar belt mountings show a fusion of these elements, with an Asiatic rather than a Germanic adaptation of later Roman art. The other non-Germanic peoples in the east were the earlier invaders, the Huns, who by the 5th century had been driven back to Hungary; their surviving artistic remains include great bronze cauldrons decorated with semicircular ornament, cicada brooches, which were adopted by some of the Germanic tribes, and round bronze mirrors.

Eastern Europe remained subject to migrations long after the Germanic kingdoms of the West had stabilized. The Slavs, who began to settle there from the 6th century, were influenced both by Avar art and by the pervasive Germanic ornament present in the area. Their own animal style retained some elements of Scythian art. Evidence comes mainly from princely burials and cremation cemeteries, but the 9th-century timber church at Zalavár (Hungary) suggests a strong wooden architectural tradition. Finally, the Magyars were a people of possibly Finnish origin who came to Hungary in the 10th century; they inherited the modified Asiatic styles of the area.

4. STYLES. Although the various peoples of the Migration period came from different backgrounds and were

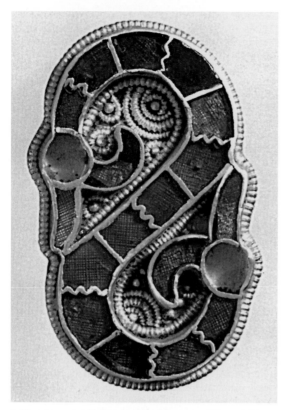

1. Migration period fibula, gold cloisonné garnet and filigree, l. 55 mm, from the Alemanic cemetery, Deisslingen, Germany, late 6th century AD (Stuttgart, Württembergischer Kunstverein)

are there, but they are unrecognizably rearranged in some allusive symbolism. This is known as Style I, after the classification formulated by the Swedish archaeologist Bernhard Salin. It developed during the 5th century in Scandinavia and flourished all over northern Europe in the areas of Germanic settlement, on brooches, bracteates, pendants, buckles, mounts and every type of metalwork, in bronze, silver and gold.

This was gradually replaced by the second main phase, Style II (see fig. 2), in which the animal body became more coherent, sinuous and interlacing; it is sometimes difficult to distinguish such an animal from the quite separate feature of interlace, another ornamental device learnt by the Germanic tribes from their contacts with Classical art. Style II was in existence by the first half of the 6th century and probably originated in the wide Frankish territories as a result of the influence of the linear patterning of interlace on the mosaic-like creatures of Style I. Style II animals were certainly not thought to be incompatible with Christianity since they were used in contexts such as gravestones and church carvings, as well as on the clothing and jewellery of Christian kings. The style flourished throughout the 7th century and continued into the 8th, being gradually superseded by the more representational art of the Mediterranean world, which had been adopted by the tribes settling there; aspects of interlacing animals were, however, firmly rooted in Christian art and were still employed in illuminated manuscripts in the 9th and 10th centuries. In pagan Scandinavia alone a pure animal style continued during the pagan Viking age.

Interlace patterns were also characteristic of the period. The simple two-strand interlace, which had been used on Roman mosaics and stone sculpture, was adopted and

influenced by the art of the various areas in which they settled, the dominating impression of their art is its uniformity. The main reasons for this are the attempts of a more primitive people to copy the arts of the Roman Empire that they had inherited, combined with the assimilative vigour of Germanic art. The resulting conflict between abstract and representational art can be traced through the animal ornament that is the hallmark of the period.

The use of an ornamentally distorted animal form is seen in almost every aspect of Migration period art. There is some chronological development, with different geographical manifestations; the styles appear in both pagan and Christian contexts. The origin of the sequence of animal art lies in the attempts by the various Germanic peoples on the fringes of the Empire to copy the animals of later Classical art, which were used on Roman metalwork and other products; military equipment, personal jewellery, bowls and glassware were decorated with dolphins, lions, griffins and sea-horses (see fig. 1). There was also some influence from the exclusively animal art of the Scythian and Sarmatian tribes of the steppes of south Russia; the Goths in this area adopted the birds of prey and animal combat scenes, as well as their elaborate metalworking techniques. These elements were gradually combined into a form of ornament in which the body of an animal is depicted in a fragmented way; all the parts

2. Migration period sandstone gravestone depicting a mounted warrior with Style II ornament below, h. 770 mm, from Hornhausen, Germany, 7th century AD (Halle, Landesmuseum für Vorgeschichte)

transformed through the Germanic innate talent for abstract art and the metalworkers' skills into a richly varied form of ornament. No surfaces were left undecorated, with the versatile nature of interlace making it appropriate as a space-filler. This again was to remain a feature of Christian art, particularly in the British Isles.

Figural ornament was less successfully treated, although the representational scenes of Roman and Early Christian art were widely adopted. Horse and rider scenes were used on metalwork, as openwork discs and helmet plaques, and on stone-carving (see fig. 2). Other plaques showed griffins, animal groups and biblical themes, particularly that of *Daniel in the Lions' Den* (see fig. 3). Other creatures treated more recognizably than the distorted Styles I and II were the predatory bird, with hooked beak and prominent claw, which was widespread as a brooch, and the mouche or cicada, used as a brooch or plaque; these may both have reached north-west Europe from the art of the steppe nomads.

5. TECHNIQUES. The great contribution of the Migration period to medieval art was the range of techniques employed by the jewellers and metalworkers, whose products form the most substantial surviving material remains of the period. Like the animal ornament, these were borrowed from the older Roman and Asiatic cultures but developed to new levels of excellence. The Roman technique of chip-carving (*Kerbschnitt*), which gives bronzework a multi-faceted, glittering surface, helped to inspire Style I animals, whose fragmented nature was partly a product of this technique. The use of coloured inlays in jewellery had been learnt by the Goths in south Russia from the jewellery of the Sarmatians, made under Iranian influence. Brightly coloured hardstones (most commonly red garnets), gems, glass and enamels were set in gold frames or cloisons on a base of gold foil. This cloisonné jewellery was adopted over the entire area of the Germanic settlements, from Visigothic Spain to the British Isles; it was again to survive in fully Christian contexts, such as crosses and church treasures, as well as being used to depict Style II animals.

Filigree, a delicate wire made of drops of gold or silver and probably adopted from late Roman art, was further developed by the Germanic craftsmen to a high standard and used extensively in jewellery. Other techniques included niello (a black paste inlay on silver), engraving, chasing and punching to decorate surfaces. Metalwork was also textured by repoussé, granulation and soldering. Smiths were as skilled and prized in society as the gold jewellers; the damascening of sword blades both strengthened and individually decorated these important weapons. Textiles, wood and bone would also have been highly coloured and patterned.

For barbarian peoples, personal, portable, ornamented possessions were status symbols and signs of power. They were worn and admired in daily life and accompanied their owners after death. It was an exuberant art of display, brilliantly assimilating the styles and techniques of the older civilizations while creating something entirely new. It was in the Migration period that the foundations of medieval art were laid, through the innovative skills of the Germanic peoples drawing on the principles of Classical

3. Migration period bronze belt buckle depicting *Daniel in the Lions' Den*, l. 45 mm, from Burgundy, France, 7th century AD (Dijon, Musée Archéologique)

art and the methods of Oriental goldsmiths: these were to fuse together to develop into a fully Christian art.

BIBLIOGRAPHY
B. Salin: *Die altgermanische Thierornamentik* (Stockholm, 1904)
N. Åberg: *The Occident and the Orient in the Art of the Seventh Century*, 3 vols (Stockholm, 1943–7)
E. Salin: *La Civilisation mérovingienne*, 4 vols (Paris, 1949–59)
W. Holmqvist: *Germanic Art during the First Millennium AD* (Stockholm, 1955)
D. Talbot Rice, ed.: *The Dark Ages* (London, 1965)
H. Busch and B. Lohse, eds: *Pre-Romanesque Art* (London, 1966)
M. Backes and R. Dölling: *Art of the Dark Ages* (New York, 1969)
J. Hubert, J. Porcher and W. F. Volbach: *Europe in the Dark Ages* (London, 1969)
P. Anker: *The Art of Scandinavia*, i (London, 1970)
I. Bona: *The Dawn of the Dark Ages* (Budapest, 1976)
G. Haseloff: *Die germanische Ornamentik der Völkerwanderungszeit* (Berlin, 1981)
M. Durliat: *Des Barbares à l'an mil* (Paris, 1985)

CAROLA HICKS

Mihailov, Nikola (*b* Shumen, 30 Jan 1876; *d* Hamburg, 30 May 1960). Bulgarian painter and teacher, active in Germany. He studied in Bulgaria under Professor Murkvichka and in 1895–7 at private art schools in Athens and Munich. He returned temporarily to Bulgaria in 1897 to take part in the second national exhibition of the Society for Supporting Art in Bulgaria. In 1899 he graduated in painting from the Akademie der Bildenden Künste, Munich. While enrolled at the Académie Julian in Paris, he developed a liking for portrait painting, which later became his favoured means of expression. In London he continued his interest in portraiture by copying in the galleries and studying the painting of the Old Masters. In 1900 he founded a private art school in Munich and for the next several years taught evening classes in art at the National Academy of Arts in Sofia. Some of his most accomplished paintings are portraits of famous Bulgarian writers, several of whom were his friends (e.g. *P. U. Todorov*, 1908; the poet *Pencho Slaveikov*, 1909; *Ivan Vazov*, 1909; all Sofia, N.A.G.). From 1911 he lived and worked in Berlin and Hamburg, although he travelled extensively in the USA, Argentina, Brazil, Italy and England and painted a number of portraits of well-known people and aristocrats (e.g. *Baroness Lanken*, 1927, and *King Karl of Sweden*, 1930; both priv. cols). His portraits of women are notable for their gracious and melancholic air and their balance between physical beauty and spiritual harmony, a combination sought out in a specific type of model. He was also interested in detailed renderings of interiors and accessories of clothing, as in *Ida Mugler, Wife of the Artist* (1905–7; Sofia, N.A.G.).

BIBLIOGRAPHY

A. Protich: 'Nikola Mihailov as Portrait-painter', *Khudozhnik*, 2 (1905–6)
L. Marinski: *Bulgarian Painting*, Sofia, N.A.G. cat. (Sofia, 1971), p. 99

JULIANA NEDEVA-WEGENER

Mihintale [Mihintalē; also Pali: Chetyapabbata, Chetiyagiri; Sinhal.: Segiriya, all three meaning 'mountain of stupas']. Mountain range in the north-central dry zone of Sri Lanka, 8 km east of Anuradhapura, where Mahinda, the head of the Buddhist mission from north India to Sri Lanka in the year 246 BC, is said to have arrived. The site appears to have flourished from the 3rd century BC to the 12th century AD, after which it was more or less deserted. It was 'rediscovered' in the 19th century and has become one of the main centres of Buddhist pilgrimage in Sri Lanka.

Mihintale has 62 known caves, probably once monastic dwellings, some with Brahmi inscriptions (75 inscriptions are published in Paranavitana, 1970). Important examples of early architecture include the remains of stupas and structures identified as a relic-house, an assembly hall, refectories and a hospital. The main stupas, among the earliest on the island, are the Kantaka Chetiya, Mihindu Chetiya, Sila Chetiya, Ambastala Chetiya and the Indikatuseya. A later residential monastery, the Hadayunha Pirivena, was built by a general of Kasyapa IV (*reg* AD 898–914) in the 10th century AD. Metal, stone and terracotta sculpture were found at Mihintale (Anuradhapura, Archaeol. Mus.), and the remains of wall paintings, probably of the 8th century AD, survive in the relic chamber of one unnamed stupa to the east of the Kantaka Chetiya.

BIBLIOGRAPHY

C. W. Nicholas: 'Historical Topography of Ancient and Medieval Ceylon', *J. Ceylon Branch Royal Asiat. Soc.*, n. s., vi (1963) [special issue]
S. Paranavitana: *Inscriptions of Ceylon*, i (Colombo, 1970)
——: *Art of the Ancient Sinhalese* (Colombo, 1971)
——: *Glimpses of Ceylon's Past* (Colombo, 1972)
S. Bandaranayake: *Sinhalese Monastic Architecture* (Leiden, 1974)

H. T. BASNAYAKE

Mihrab [miḥrāb]. Niche, usually concave, in the qibla (Mecca-orientated) wall of a mosque. The mihrab is commonly believed to be a prayer niche that indicates the direction of prayer, but as Muslims pray towards the Ka'ba in Mecca, which stands beyond the wall in which the mihrab lies, not towards the mihrab itself, its origins must lie elsewhere. Philologists maintain that the Arabic word *miḥrāb* either derives from the Ethiopic *mekuerāb* ('naos' or 'sanctuary') or is related etymologically to the Arabic word *ḥarba*, a lance symbolizing authority in ancient Arabia. The word *miḥrāb* occurs only five times in the Koran, where it means 'chamber' or 'fine structure'. In early Arabic secular literature its meanings included the part of a palace in which a ruler sits, a niche for an image, or a colonnaded platform.

Historical sources suggest that the earliest mosques at Fustat (Old Cairo) and Damascus had a feature referred to as a mihrab, but, instead of niches, these appear to have

1. Silver dirham of the caliph 'Abd al-Malik, diam. 30 mm, AD 695–6/AH 75 (New York, American Numismatic Society)

been columned bays that fulfilled functions later associated with the MAQṢŪRA, which, as well as being the place from which the imam led prayers, was also used for the conduct of official business and the dispensation of justice. The *miḥrāb mujawwaf*, the semicircular recessed niche that became ubiquitous in mosque architecture (*see* MOSQUE), first appeared in the Prophet's mosque in Medina when it was rebuilt by the caliph al-Walid I (*reg* 705–15). Scholars have long debated the origins of the form and purpose of the mihrab: some traced it to the Buddhist cult niche, others to the apse of a Christian church, while still others related it to the royal throne recess in an audience hall. At the mosque of MEDINA it identified the spot where the Prophet had planted his lance (*'anaza*) when leading prayers to indicate and define the prayer space (*suṭra*). Niches—whether empty like the mihrab or filled with a statue—were ubiquitous elements of the Late Antique decorative vocabulary that the renovators of the mosque used elsewhere in the building. The rapid acceptance of the new form throughout the lands of Islam represents a genuine innovation in mosque architecture. Beyond Medina, the semicircular mihrab apparently defined the limits of the prayer space for the imam when he led communal prayer.

As well as its practical function, from the outset the semicircular mihrab may also have had a symbolic meaning, for a rare silver coin minted in AH 75 (AD 695–6)—ten years before the semicircular mihrab was introduced into the mosque—depicts a beribboned lance within an arch supported by a pair of spiral columns (see fig. 1). G. C. Miles identified the lance as the Prophet's *'anaza* and compared the coin to a series of Greek imperial coins that depicted images sheltered by ciboria. The earliest Islamic coins minted in Syria had flagrantly imitated Byzantine models; the group to which this particular silver coin belonged adapted and translated earlier models into Islamic terms; later Islamic coins would abandon foreign models for the purely epigraphic content that characterized all Islamic coinage during the following millennium. Although designs such as that depicting a lance in a niche were quickly abandoned, worshippers may have continued to associate the empty semicircular niche in the mosque with the memory and veneration of the Prophet. The multiple mihrab ensembles (e.g. Cairo, Mashhad of Sayyida Ruqayya, 1133) erected under the patronage of the Fatimid dynasty in Egypt (*reg* 969–1171) have been interpreted as commemorating other members of the Prophet's family. The semicircular mihrab was widely but not universally accepted. In some regions of North Africa, for example, the sect of Ibadi Kharijites preferred a rectangular niche; this became the norm among the peoples of the western Sudan converted to Islam under their aegis.

About a dozen small Umayyad mosques in Syria preserve some architectural indication that a semicircular mihrab once existed in them, but the earliest complete example to survive is believed to be a monolithic marble mihrab in Baghdad (see fig. 2). A shallow niche with a shell hood resting on a pair of engaged spiral columns, it was found in the Khassaki Mosque (1659) in east Baghdad, but the material and style suggest that the mihrab was carved in northern Syria in the 8th century before being brought to Baghdad, perhaps for use in the mosque that the Abbasid caliph al-Mansur (*reg* 754–75) constructed

2. Mihrab cut from a single piece of marble, 2.06×1.00 m, probably from northern Syria, ?8th century AD (Baghdad, Baghdad Museum)

there. Another early example is the mihrab in the mosque at Kairouan in Tunisia, datable to the mid-9th century. It consists of a deep niche (h. 4.5 m; w. 2 m) formed by a horseshoe arch resting on two red marble columns with fine Byzantine vine-leaf capitals. The niche is lined with 28 carved white marble panels arranged in four registers separated by bands inscribed with Koranic verses. The hood is formed of curved wooden planks painted with a continuous vine scroll. The band separating the walls of the mihrab from the hood, as well as the outer face of the mihrab arch and the rectangular surface surrounding it, are inlaid with monochrome and polychrome lustre tiles arranged in a diaper pattern. The individual elements of the mihrab ensemble were probably imported to Kairouan from the east and assembled on the spot.

The use of the horseshoe arch for the mihrab surround became standard practice in the Islamic West. The mihrab of the Great Mosque of Córdoba (965; *see* ISLAMIC ART, fig. 45 and CÓRDOBA, fig. 2) is undoubtedly the most sumptuous example. The mihrab surround occupies the entire width of the central bay of the mosque and consists of a broad horseshoe arch supported by small black marble colonnettes set within a rectangular panelled frame. Apart from the spandrels, which are carved stucco, the arch and the rectangular framing panels are decorated with glass mosaics with vegetal and epigraphic motifs. The niche itself is an unusually deep octagonal chamber over 3 m in diameter, covered with a stucco shell dome contained within the thickness of the qibla wall. The seven walls of the mihrab are decorated with blind trilobed arches supported on paired columns, carved stucco panels and inscription bands. Although no other extant mihrab in Spain or western North Africa is as elaborate, the Córdoban example became the model for mihrabs throughout the region: for example, mosques at Tlemcen in Algeria, Tinmal in Morocco and Saragossa in Spain all have a deep, roomlike mihrab within a rectangular surround.

A flat white marble mihrab (1.30×0.83 m) in the cave beneath the Dome of the Rock in Jerusalem has long been ascribed to the founder of the building, the Umayyad caliph 'Abd al-Malik (*reg* 685–705), but on stylistic and palaeographic grounds it is now dated to the late 9th century or early 10th. Moreover, the cave itself is first mentioned as a place of prayer in the early 10th century. Flat—not concave—mihrabs apparently became popular in Egypt under the Tulunid (*reg* 868–905) and Fatimid dynasties, for a variety of both stationary examples in carved stucco and portable examples in carved wood is known. Some scholars have suggested that portable wooden mihrabs were used to define the *sutra* for individual worshippers, while others have suggested that many mihrab-shaped objects of stone and ceramic were actually tombstones (*see* STELE, §5). Stone mihrabs were also erected on the Haram al-Sharif in Jerusalem to honour biblical prophets.

The movable wooden mihrab from the mausoleum of Sayyida Ruqayya in Cairo (Cairo, Mus. Islam. A.) is, however, concave. Measuring over 2 m high, it is considered one of the finest examples of late Fatimid woodcarving and joinery and was presented to the shrine by the wife of the caliph al-Amir (*reg* 1101–30). Its finished back indicates that it was not inserted into a wall, like the earlier wooden mihrab made for the Azhar Mosque in Cairo, but meant to be brought out on special occasions (see also ISLAMIC ART, §VII, 1(i)(b)).

Carved stucco mihrabs enjoyed a spectacular development and popularity when the Saljuq dynasty (reg 1038–1194) ruled in Iran. They typically consist of a series of nested niches, and the most accomplished examples are extremely complex, multi-levelled compositions, often deeply undercut, exhibiting a wide variety of geometric, vegetal and epigraphic motifs. The earliest Iranian stucco mihrabs, such as that in the 10th-century congregational mosque of Na'in, indicate the close technical relationship with earlier Iraqi stuccowork. The greatest Iranian examples, such as the ones in the Gunbad-i Alaviyyan at Hamadan (12th century), the Masjid-i Haydariyya (?1220) at Qazvin, the shrine of Pir-i Bakran (1303–12) at Linjan near Isfahan (see ISLAMIC ART, fig. 77), and in the winter prayer-hall (1310) of the Friday Mosque at Isfahan, show that the production of fine stucco mihrabs continued well into the 14th century.

The interest in exploiting the sculptural possibilities that stucco allowed also manifested itself in moulded lustre tile mihrabs, and tile ensembles, of the late Saljuq period, for the same craftsmen often worked in both media. Two of the most famous examples are the mihrab dated AH 612 (1215) by the master potters Muhammad ibn Abu Tahir (see ABU TAHIR, (1)) and ABU ZAYD in the shrine at Mashhad and the mihrab dated AH 623 (1226) from the Maydan Mosque in Kashan (Berlin, Mus. Islam. Kst). During the period of Ilkhanid rule (1256–1353), lustre mihrabs were made for many major and minor shrines, for example at Najaf in Iraq (in situ) and Natanz in central Iran (London, V&A, 71–1885).

Not all lustre tiles depicting niches were intended to be inserted vertically in a wall as mihrabs. Many now identified as mihrabs were made to cover the top of a cenotaph, for example sets of three tiles forming a blind arched panel in Lisbon (Mus. Gulbenkian, 1562) and New York (Met., 09.87). They reflect a tradition of tombstones with mihrab designs that can be documented as early as the first decades of the 9th century at Mosul in Iraq and the later 9th century in Egypt.

Ceramic tile was also cut and assembled to produce multicoloured mihrabs of tile mosaic. A mid-14th-century example (New York, Met., 39.20) measures over 3 m high and uses five colours (white, black, light blue, dark blue and ochre), angular and cursive scripts and a wide variety of arabesque and border patterns. The technique became especially popular under the Timurid (reg 1370–1506) and Safavid (reg 1501–1732) dynasties. A cheaper means to the same end promoted the development of cuerda seca tiles in mihrab surrounds made in Anatolia in the early 15th century under the Ottoman dynasty, such as those of the Green Mosque and Tomb in Bursa. Cuerda seca tiles gave way in the 16th century to magnificent underglaze-painted tile ensembles produced at Iznik. These not only lined the mihrab niche itself but also surrounded it with huge displays of tile, which provided a climax to the interior decoration. In the finest examples, such as the mihrabs of the mosques of Sokollu Mehmed Pasha or Rüstem Pasha

in Istanbul, the splendour of the multicoloured tile surrounds contrasts sharply with the stark plainness of the mihrab or the mihrab hood.

The first mihrabs of the period of Sultanate rule in India (1206–1555) were made of stone, intricately carved with geometric, vegetal and epigraphic motifs. They combined ideas current in contemporary Iranian stucco or ceramic examples with local stonecutting practices. Later monuments erected under the Mughal dynasty (reg 1526–1858) use pietra dura inlay techniques in a similar free interpretation of Timurid tile mosaic by local masons.

The wide variety of materials, niche forms and decorative motifs used on mihrabs throughout the lands of Islam can often obscure the persistent scale of all mihrabs since the invention of the form. The difference between the smallest and largest mihrabs is not commensurate with the difference between the smallest and largest mosques; the constant scale indicates that the mihrab was always measured in human terms. Other persistent features include the use of columns on either side of the niche and a shell hood, both features already present in the Khassaki mihrab of the 8th century. One of the most common motifs of mihrab design is a mosque lamp hanging by a chain from the niche hood. The first known example is a mihrab painted on the interior of a tomb (1067–8) at Kharraqan in Iran, and the device later appears on Egyptian tombstones and Iranian lustre tiles of the 12th and 13th centuries. It became a cliché on so-called 'prayer-rugs'. Although popularly associated with the 'Light Verse' of the Koran (xxiv.36), which likens God to a lamp shining in a niche, this verse is rarely, if ever, found decorating mihrabs, probably because the association rests on a misunderstanding of the Koranic text, which states that the lighted wick is in a mishkāt—a reference to a wickholder, not a niche.

For further illustration see ISLAMIC ART, figs 30 and 75.

Enc. Islam/2

BIBLIOGRAPHY

G. C. Miles: 'Miḥrāb and 'Anazah: A Study in Islamic Iconography', Archaeologia Orientalia in Memoriam Ernst Herzfeld (Locust Valley, 1952), pp. 156–71
R. B. Serjeant: 'Miḥrāb', Bull. SOAS, xxii (1959), pp. 439–53
G. Fehévári: 'Tombstone or Mihrab? A Speculation', Islamic Art in the Metropolitan Museum of Art, ed. R. Ettinghausen (New York, 1972), pp. 241–54
O. Grabar: The Formation of Islamic Art (New Haven and London, 1973, rev. 1987)
L. A. Popadopoulo: 'Le Miḥrāb dans l'architecture et la religion musulmanes', Actes du colloque international tenu à Paris en Mai, 1980
E. Baer: 'The Mihrab in the Cave of the Dome of the Rock', Muqarnas, iii (1985), pp. 8–19
E. Whelan: 'The Origins of the Miḥrāb Mujawwaf: A Reinterpretation', Int. J. Mid. E. Stud., xviii (1986), pp. 205–23
N. N. N. Khoury: 'The Mihrab Image: Commemorative Themes in Medieval Islamic Architecture', Muqarnas, ix (1992), pp. 11–28

JONATHAN M. BLOOM

Mihr 'Ali [Mihr 'Alī] (fl c. 1795–1830). Persian painter. He produced at least ten full-size oil paintings of the Qajar monarch Fath 'Ali Shah (reg 1797–1834). One of the earliest (1797–8; Calcutta, Victoria Mem. Hall), a portrait of him kneeling on a carpet, was probably sent as a present to the amirs of Sind in 1800. Two fine portraits (1803–4 and 1804–5) were painted for the Hall of the Marble Throne in the Gulistan Palace, Tehran, and a third, of the

King enthroned (undated; Versailles, Château), was sent to Napoleon. These early portraits show Fath 'Ali Shah with a squat neck and round face, but Mihr 'Ali's drawings improved in the first decade of the 19th century and later portraits show the King with more flattering proportions. These later paintings include portraits of the King standing (1809–10; St Petersburg, Hermitage), kneeling and holding a mace (1813–14; St Petersburg, Hermitage), and a third with the date obliterated (London, B. W. Robinson priv. col.). Mihr 'Ali's finest portrait, and perhaps the finest Persian oil painting in existence (1812–13; Tehran, Nigaristan Mus., ex-Amery col.; see ISLAMIC ART, fig. 243), is an impressive full-length portrait of the King wearing a magnificent robe of gold brocade and a huge crown and holding a jewelled staff of majesty surrounded by Solomon's hoopoes.

Mihr 'Ali may also have painted women at the court, for several unsigned paintings of women (Tehran, Nigaristan Mus.) are stylistically similar to his portraits of Fath 'Ali Shah. Other works that can be attributed to Mihr 'Ali include a large canvas depicting the King hunting with his sons, which now hangs on the ceiling of the ballroom in the official residence of the President of India (New Delhi, Rashtrapati Bhavan), and several paintings on glass (Tehran, Ethnog. Mus.; see ISLAMIC ART, §VIII, 6). Sir William Ouseley, who visited Isfahan in July 1811, saw in the Fattehabad Palace there a series of life-size portraits signed by Mihr 'Ali depicting the ancient kings of Persia. He also signed a varnished ('lacquered') book cover with a rose and nightingale (1803; Dublin, Chester Beatty Lib., Mugh. 31; see ISLAMIC ART, §VIII, 10). His last dated work is a small watercolour study of a man's head (1829) executed as a model for his pupil Abu'l-Hasan Ghaffari (see GHAFFARI, (2)).

BIBLIOGRAPHY
S. Y. Amiranashvili: *Iranskaya stankovaya zhivopis'* [Iranian painting] (Tbilisi, 1940)
B. W. Robinson: 'The Court Painters of Fath 'Ali Shah', *Eretz- Israel*, vii (1964), pp. 94–105
S. J. Falk: *Qajar Paintings* (London, 1972)
B. W. Robinson: 'Persian Painting in the Qajar Period', *Highlights of Persian Art*, ed. R. Ettinghausen and E. Yarshater (Boulder, 1979), pp. 331–62
——: 'Persian Royal Portraiture and the Qajars', *Qajar Iran*, ed. E. Bosworth and C. Hillenbrand (Edinburgh, 1983), pp. 291–310
M. A. Karimzada Tabrizi: *Aḥvāl u āthār-i naqqāshān-i qadīm-i īrān* [The lives and art of old painters of Iran] (London, 1985), no. 1297
B. W. Robinson: 'Persian Painting under the Zand and Qājār Dynasties', *From Nadir Shah to the Islamic Republic*, vii of *The Cambridge History of Iran* (Cambridge, 1991), pp. 870–90

☐

Mihu de la Crişul Alb (*fl* second half of the 14th century AD). Romanian painter. The only works attributed to him are in the narthex of Rîmet monastery church near Alba, in Transylvania province, Romania. One of the jambs of the archway connecting the narthex with the naos of the church shows a full-length *St Gregory the Great* accompanied by an inscription referring to Mihul, his patron Bishop Ghelasion and the date 1377. Other images include *St Basil the Great* on the jamb opposite, *SS Anthony the Great and Andronicus* on the intrados of the arch and a partially preserved *Deësis* above the arch. On the partitioning wall either side of the archway are *SS Nicholas and Procopius*, and *SS John Chrysostomos and Nestor*. In general the paintings reflect the influence of Palaiologan art, but they also contain certain Late Gothic elements found in the Catholic artistic environment of Transylvania. The figures are drawn with firm, expressive lines, while the volume of their bodies is rendered by subtle shading in ochres and browns with white highlights. They are shown in static, fully frontal or three-quarter poses, wearing a variety of fine vestments in ochres, greens, blues and reds. The restoration of these paintings was completed in 1990.

BIBLIOGRAPHY
V. Drăguţ: 'Zugravul Mihu şi epoca sa' [The painter Mihu and his epoch], *SCIA*, Ser. II, i (1968)
L. Tugearu: 'Biserica mănăstirii Rîmet' [The Rîmet monastery church], *Repertoriul picturii murale medievale din România (sec. XIV–1450)* [The repertory of medieval mural painting in Romania (14th century–1450)] (1985), V/i of *Pagini de veche artă românească* [Pages of ancient Romanian art] (Bucharest, 1970–), pp. 149–73

TEREZA-IRENE SINIGALIA

Miidera. *See* ONJŌJI.

Mijae. *See* NAM KU-MAN.

Mijares, José (Maria) (*b* Havana, 23 June 1922). Cuban painter, active in the USA. He was a graduate of the Academia de San Alejandro in Havana (1938–45), where he taught from 1960 to 1961. He fled from Cuba in 1968 and settled in Miami, FL, where his studio became a focal point of cultural life for other exiled Cuban intellectuals. He was already a principal artist in Cuba, and his work was seen in expatriate circles as a continuity of the Cuban vision, particularly during the 1970s. In his paintings Constructivism and biomorphic Surrealism are fused with baroque elements derived from colonial Caribbean design in a mixture of influences that also preoccupied many other Cuban artists between 1940 and 1970, including Amelia Peláez del Casal, Cundo Bermúdez, Mario Carreño, René Portocarrero and Jorge Camacho. Mijares's 'organic abstractions' of the 1970s and 1980s are reminiscent of similar work by Wifredo Lam and Yves Tanguy, and he retained his fascination of the 1950s for geometric forms and dependency on line to represent form, as in *High Priestesses of Illusion* (1971; New York, Cintas Found.). The intense blues and greens of the paintings that he called *vitrales* allude to colonial stained-glass windows. He participated in the biennials at São Paulo in 1953, and Venice in 1956, as well as in numerous group exhibitions in Latin America, Europe and Japan.

BIBLIOGRAPHY
F. Baeza and others: *Mijares* (Miami, 1971)
Outside Cuba/Fuera de Cuba (exh. cat. by I. Fuentes-Perez, G. Cruz-Taura and R. Pau-Llosa, New Brunswick, NJ, Rutgers U., Zimmerli A. Mus.; New York, Mus. Contemp. Hisp. A.; Oxford, OH, Miami U., A. Mus.; and elsewhere; 1987–9), pp. 156–61

RICARDO PAU-LLOSA

Mijn [Myn], van der. Dutch family of painters, active also in England. (1) Heroman van der Mijn was a portrait and still-life painter of some distinction, although his work shows little originality. His sister Agatha van der Mijn (*fl* early 18th century) painted similar subjects and accompanied her brother to England shortly after 1721. Six of Heroman's children became painters: his daughter Cornelia van der Mijn (*b* 1710) and his sons Gerard van der

Mijn (*b* 1706), Andreas van der Mijn (*b* ?1714), (2) Frans van der Mijn, (3) George van der Mijn and Robert van der Mijn (*b* 1724), of whom only Frans and George established important reputations. Frans became an accomplished and fashionable portrait painter in Amsterdam and London; George excelled both his father and brother in originality and may be regarded as one of the best Dutch portrait painters of the 18th century.

(1) Heroman [Herman] **van der Mijn** (*b* Amsterdam, *c.* 1684; *d* London, Nov 1741). He was a pupil of Ernst Stuven (1660–1712). After his marriage in 1706, he lived in Amsterdam, then in Antwerp (1712–13) and finally in Düsseldorf, where he worked for the Elector Palatine, John William. In 1716, after the Elector's death, van der Mijn returned to Antwerp and thence went to London. His surviving early paintings are mainly flower still-lifes (e.g. Munich, Alte Pin.); from his period in Antwerp there are some undistinguished history pieces. After 1721 he concentrated on portrait painting. His portrait of *James Brydges, 1st Duke of Chandos* (London, N.P.G.) dates from his early days in England and, in common with his other portraits, shows the influence of Godfrey Kneller. Like Kneller, van der Mijn worked for the English court. This association was severed temporarily when one of his paintings was refused in 1727/8 but, happily for the artist's stricken finances, restored upon the arrival of Prince William IV of Orange Nassau. He went with the Prince and Princess to the Netherlands, and he was working at the palace of Het Loo in 1736. A portrait of *William IV* (Groningen, Groninger Mus.) bears the date 1737. Apparently he soon fell out of favour with his patron and returned to London, where he died.

RUDOLF E. O. EKKART

(2) Frans van der Mijn (*b* Antwerp, *c.* 1719; *d* London, 20 Aug 1793). Son of (1) Heroman van der Mijn. Frans was taught by his father for whom he probably worked as an assistant. His *Portrait Group* (1744; Amsterdam, Rijksmus.) has the polished appearance of his father's work but is less contrived. In style it shows an affinity with the work of Cornelius van Troost, but van der Mijn also painted rather voluptuous female figures (e.g. *Portrait of a Young Lady Dressed in Blue*; sold London, Sotheby's, 17 Nov 1982, lot 99), which has similarities to the work of earlier artists such as Gerrit van Honthorst and Dirck van Baburen.

After establishing himself as a portrait painter in Amsterdam (1742–9), Frans travelled to England (*c.* 1750) where he received many commissions. He exhibited at the Free Society until 1772, and there is some evidence that he painted in both Cambridge and Norwich. A few paintings survive that reflect the strong individuality of his work in the 1750s and 1760s, seen for example in his portraits of *Sir Thomas Robinson* (175(?); Hon. Lady Carey priv. col., see Staring, 1968, p. 200) and *Robert Leveridge* (exh. 1761; London, Garrick Club). By the 1770s his style had weakened, as in *Lady Wray with her Son* (1773; sold London, Christie's, 14 July 1930, lot 57), which lacks the compositional drama of those earlier portraits. Excessive drinking restricted Frans van der Mijn's work in later years, and he died a poor man.

HUGH BELSEY

(3) George van der Mijn (*b* London, *c.* 1726–7; *bur* 15 Dec 1763). Son of (1) Heroman van der Mijn. Like his elder brother (2) Frans, he studied with his father, after whose death he became a pupil of Frans. He moved to Amsterdam with Frans and remained there until his death. Little survives of George van der Mijn's early work. His excellent portraits of *Cornelis Ploos van Amstel* and *Elisabeth Troost* (The Hague, Mauritshuis) may be early and may date from 1748, as was once thought, or could have been painted as late as 1758. The majority of his 15 or so remaining paintings date from 1757–63. Besides individual portraits, he produced some of the best examples of the Dutch conversation piece of the 18th century, including two group portraits, both from 1763: the *Hasselaer Family* (Amsterdam, Rijksmus.) and the *Van Sypesteyn Children* (Loosdrecht, Kasteel-Mus. Sypesteyn). He also made a number of miniatures, pastels and drawings. In 1761, the year of his marriage, he painted the ceiling of an Amsterdam patrician's house.

BIBLIOGRAPHY
A. Staring: *De Hollanders thuis: Gezelschapsstukken uit drie eeuwen* [The Dutch at home: conversation pieces from three centuries] (The Hague, 1956), pp. 35, 136–7
——: 'De Van der Mijns in Engeland', *Ned. Ksthist. Jb.*, xvii (1966), pp. 201–45; xix (1968), pp. 171–203

Mijnnesten, Jan van den. *See* MASTERS, ANONYMOUS, AND MONOGRAMMISTS, §III: MASTER IAM OF ZWOLLE.

Mijtens [Meytens; Mytens]. Dutch family of painters of Flemish origin. The earliest known artist of this family was Aert Mijtens (*b* Brussels, 1541; *d* Rome, 1602), a history and portrait painter who worked in Naples and Rome. His brother Martin Mijtens, a saddle- and coach-maker, fled to the northern Netherlands and had two sons who also became painters: (1) Daniel Mijtens I, who was prominent in England for a period as a portrait painter in the Stuart court, and Isaac Mijtens (*b c.* 1602; *bur* The Hague, 22 Aug 1666), a portrait painter in The Hague. (2) Jan Mijtens was a nephew of these brothers and father of the portrait painter Daniel Mijtens II (*b* The Hague, 7 Aug 1644; *bur* The Hague, 23 Sept 1688). (3) Martin Mijtens I, himself a son of Isaac, moved to Sweden where he worked as a portrait painter in Stockholm, while his son (4) Martin van Meytens II later became a portrait painter at the imperial court in Vienna. Several other minor members of the Mijtens family established reputations as painters.

(1) Daniel [Daniël] **Mijtens I** (*b* Delft, *c.* 1590; *d* The Hague, *c.* 1647). He undertook his training either in The Hague, where he lived from an early age, with Jan Anthonisz. van Ravesteyn, or in his native town of Delft, with Michiel van Miereveld. In 1610 he joined the guild of painters in The Hague; two years later he married Gratia Cletcher, sister of the goldsmith Thomas Cletcher the elder. No work survives from this early period.

By August 1618 Daniel was working in London, where he painted the portraits of *Thomas Howard, 2nd Earl of Arundel* (*see* LONDON, fig. 16) and his wife, *Aletheia Talbot, Countess of Arundel*. These paintings have been identified as the two unsigned full-scale portraits (London, N.P.G., on loan to Arundel Castle) showing in the background the sculpture gallery and the family portrait gallery of Arundel House in London. Mijtens can already be seen combining stylistic elements from his Delft–Hague background with certain formal aspects of the Elizabethan and Jacobean tradition of English court portraiture. His preference for full-length portraits, for instance, reflects this English tradition. In his later work Mijtens gradually arranged his compositions with more ease, a skill he first developed under the influence of Paul van Somer, who also worked at the English court from 1616 to 1621.

Within only a few years after his arrival in England, Mijtens had won the approval of both King James I and his son Charles, Prince of Wales. In 1624 James granted him an annuity, which was increased by Charles I in 1625. For most of the 1620s and in the early 1630s Mijtens was the leading court artist, as is evident from the numerous payments he received for portraits of the King or people connected with the court and for the many copies he made after the work of other artists. During these years Mijtens twice crossed to Holland, once in 1626 and once in 1630.

Mijtens's development as a painter can be traced in his series of portraits of *Charles I*, most of which survive in more than one version. The three earliest images, painted while he was still Prince of Wales (*c.* 1621, Parham House, W. Sussex, Mrs P. A. Tritton priv. col., see 1972 exh. cat., no. 18; 1623, British Royal Col.; and 1624, Ottawa, N.G.), are rather stiff in style, a quality completely resolved in the images painted between 1627 and 1633. In a number of cases replicas were made, suggesting the existence of a workshop and assistants. The portrait of *Charles I* of 1631 with the monogram *CJ* (Chatsworth, Derbys) shows that among the artists working in Mijtens's circle was Cornelis Jonson van Ceulen; it closely follows the original portrait painted and signed by Mijtens himself in 1629 (New York, Met.). The stylistic contrast between the early and late work painted in England is also evident in a comparison between the two portraits of *James Hamilton, 3rd Marquess and 1st Duke of Hamilton*: the rather stiff portrait from 1624 (London, Tate) shows the artist's skill in the detailed rendering of the sitter's face and costume, while the impressive portrait of 1629 (Edinburgh, N.P.G.; see fig.), with its sophisticated silver-grey tonality and lucid arrangement of accessories, may be regarded as one of Mijtens's finest works.

Although there are a few smaller paintings from the English years, the bulk of the work from this period consists of life-size portraits showing the sitter at full length. These large paintings were the products of a new phase in the development of formal portraiture in England. Mijtens's achievements, however, seem to have had little lasting effect on other artists: in 1632 Anthony van Dyck arrived in London and soon became the city's most influential painter. Between 1632 and 1634 Mijtens executed a few more commissions, but by then his position was clearly overshadowed by the success of the Flemish master, who originally adopted some of the concepts developed by his Dutch colleague.

After the death of his first wife, Mijtens married the miniature painter Susanna Droeshout in 1628; in 1634 he returned to The Hague, where he became active not only as a painter but also as an art dealer, and his clients included the 2nd Earl of Arundel, whose portrait he had

Daniel Mijtens I: *James Hamilton, 3rd Marquess and 1st Duke of Hamilton*, oil on canvas, 2.06×1.29 m, 1629 (Edinburgh, National Portrait Gallery)

painted in England. Only four paintings survive from the artist's last 14 years, all bust-length portraits of excellent quality. They include the portraits of his first wife's nephew, the goldsmith *Thomas Cletcher the Younger* and his wife *Anna Hoeufft* (both 1643; The Hague, Gemeentemus.). These late paintings reveal clearly Mijtens's qualities as a portrait painter, despite being on a smaller scale and thus lacking the grandeur of his best English work. There is no documentary evidence of any pupils Mijtens may have had, but it seems that his nephew and later son-in-law Jan Mijtens may have been apprenticed to him for a while.

BIBLIOGRAPHY
Thieme–Becker; Wurzbach
O. ter Kuile: 'Daniel Mijtens: "His Majesty's Picture-Drawer"', *Ned. Ksthist. Jb.*, xx (1969), pp. 1–106
The Age of Charles I: Painting in England, 1620–1649 (exh. cat. by O. Millar, London, Tate, 1972), pp. 12–13, 24–8
B. Haak: *The Golden Age: Dutch Painters of the Seventeenth Century* (New York, 1984), pp. 218–19

(2) **Jan Mijtens** (*b* The Hague, *c.* 1614; *d* The Hague, *bur* 24 Dec 1670). Nephew of (1) Daniel Mijtens I. He was the son of Daniel's elder brother David, a saddlemaker in The Hague. Jan may have learnt to paint from his uncle Isaac Mijtens. After 1634 he may have trained

with his uncle Daniel, who had by then returned to The Hague; Jan married Daniel's daughter Anna in 1642. In 1639 he had been admitted to The Hague's guild of painters, of which he became a governor in 1656. In the latter year he helped to found the painters' society De Pictura; from 1667–8 he was a governor of this society and from 1669–70 its dean.

Throughout his life Jan Mijtens worked as a portrait painter in The Hague. He received commissions from prominent citizens, members of the nobility and high-placed government officials as well as from the stadholder's circle, from families such as the Dohnas and the van Brederodes. He seems to have worked chiefly for those loyal to the Orange Nassau family and to have been considerably less popular with the opposing political factions. Jan's oeuvre consists of an extensive series of portraits, the earliest from 1638, the year he entered the painters' guild, and the latest from 1668. His work divides into two main groups: life-size three-quarter-length and half-length portraits of individuals, and family groups painted on a smaller scale. Although his paintings are reminiscent of the later work of Anthony van Dyck, Jan Mijtens cannot be considered an immediate follower of the master, especially since technically he adhered to the Dutch tradition of portrait painting. The colourful and elegant manner in which he presented his sitters shows, however, that he worked in the same spirit as van Dyck. Typical is the *Lady Playing a Lute* (1648; Dublin, N.G.), painted in the elegant international style also used by Peter Lely and others.

The paintings surviving from Jan Mijtens's early years are mainly group portraits, which are always set in a landscape and usually show the figures at considerably less than life-size. Remarkably often they include deceased members of the sitter's family, who in some cases are given a space of their own, in others incorporated into the main group. The figures in the earliest group portraits, for instance the portrait of an *Unknown Family* (1638; Versailles, Château), are stiffly arranged, but Mijtens soon developed a talent for composing groups, as in *Pieter Stalpaert van der Wiele and his Family* (1645; The Hague, Gemeentemus.). One of his best-known compositions shows the *Marriage of Friedrich Wilhelm, Elector of Brandenburg, and Louise Henriette of Orange Nassau* (1647; Rennes, Mus. B.-A. & Archéol.), a work rather over-crowded with figures and not one of his most successful. It was followed by numerous commissions from the courts in The Hague and Berlin, resulting in, for example, the group portrait of *Elector Friedrich Wilhelm and his Family* (1667; Berlin, Jagdschloss Grunewald).

Among the surviving works of Jan Mijtens's later years are some individual portraits, good examples being the young *Wolphaert van Brederode* (*c.* 1663; The Hague, Mauritshuis) and *Admiral Cornelis Tromp* (see fig.) and his wife *Margaretha van Raephorst* (both 1668; Amsterdam, Rijksmus.). Of greater importance are the few dozen group portraits, such as The Hague burgomaster *Willem van der Does and his Family* (1650; Antwerp, Mus. Mayer van den Bergh), the councillor *Willem van den Kerckhoven and his Family* (1652; The Hague, Gemeentemus.), the English court dignitary in exile *Sir Charles Cotterell and his Family* (1658; Fredericton, Beaverbrook A.G.) and the

Jan Mijtens: *Admiral Cornelis Tromp*, oil on canvas, 1.34×1.05 m, 1668 (Amsterdam, Rijksmuseum)

Unknown Family (1661; Dublin, N.G.). These later family portraits are, on the whole, larger than the early ones and show Mijtens's sense of arrangement, elegance and colour at its best. Besides his group portraits with pastoral elements, Mijtens painted a number of purely Arcadian scenes, which can be regarded as 'portraits historiés', for example the undated *Granida and Daiphilo* (Amsterdam, Rijksmus.).

BIBLIOGRAPHY

Thieme–Becker; Wurzbach

W. Martin: *De Hollandsche schilderkunst in de zeventiende eeuw*, 2 vols (Amsterdam, 1935–6), ii, pp. 161–2

A. McNeil Kettering: *The Dutch Arcadia: Pastoral Art and its Audience in the Golden Age* (Montclair, 1983)

B. Haak: *The Golden Age: Dutch Painting in the Seventeenth Century* (New York, 1984), pp. 334–5

RUDOLF EKKART

(3) Martin Mijtens [Meytens] **I** (*b* The Hague, 1 June 1648; *d* Stockholm, *bur* 6 Aug 1736). Nephew of (1) Daniel Mijtens I. In 1677 he moved to Sweden, where he became one of the most important portrait painters of this period. He painted the nobility, gentry and priesthood but not royalty, the position of court painter being held by David Klöcker Ehrenstrahl. Martin Mijtens's portraits combined the sumptuousness of Ehrenstrahl with a Dutch-inspired individualism, which gives his pictures both a formal and an informal character. He was influenced by Italian, French, Dutch and Flemish portraiture, especially that of Anthony van Dyck.

One of Martin's first Swedish portraits is that of *Margareta von Emersen* (1677; Västmanland, Fullerö Manor House). The lady, rotund, compact and seemingly humorous, is elegantly dressed and coiffured and is sitting in an ornate armchair in a clearly aristocratic milieu. She was the widow of the mining entrepreneur Gerard de Besche. The artist's ability to depict personality can also be seen in two portraits of high-ranking state officials, *Count Nils Gyldenstolpe* (Uppland, Leufsta Slott) and the *Marquis Knut Kurck*. The Count is shown sitting in a long gown, his hands firmly planted on the arms of his chair. His face is broad and reassured, accentuated by his rather flat, wide wig. He gives an impression of authority along with harmonious well-being and good humour. The portrait of the Marquis was commissioned shortly after he became a widower, and he is rendered as a mourner, in a long, black gown and with a beard (not seen in other portraits of him). His posture and countenance are dejected, his lean, pale face directed slightly upwards. This picture was clearly meant to convey sorrow, and it is a very sensitive portrayal, even if somewhat theatrical.

A portrait of *Admiral Erik Siöblad* (Södermanland, Wibyholm Castle) shows him dressed theatrically as a Roman soldier, leaning casually on a large cannon; in the background are his battleships, with sails bulging and flags fluttering in the wind. From this scene of naval triumph, the Admiral looks on the spectator quite amiably, almost as if to say, 'War is fun, come and join me', evidence of the artist's ability to combine pomp and a certain informality of expression.

Several of Mijtens's female portraits are noteworthy, one of the finest being that of *Katarina Charlotta Oxenstierna* (Uppland, Krusenberg Slott): a splendidly dressed young lady picks a flower in an aristocratic park landscape, cheeks blooming, brocades and jewellery sparkling. In

contrast is the straightforward portrait of the octogenarian industrialist *Gerdt Störning* (1690): old, rather ugly, plainly dressed and implying a strikingly firm, perhaps bitter personality.

Martin Mijtens's most famous portrait is that of the Uppsala professor *Olof Rudbeck* (1696; Uppsala U. Kstsaml.; see fig.). Here Mijtens was clearly inspired by one of the most formidable personalities of contemporary Sweden. The venerable scholar is seated in his library, clad in a long, black gown with a loosely knit piece of lace under his chin; he wears no fashionable wig, his natural hair falling in long, grey locks. He gestures towards a table with implements indicating his various specialities, and in the background are bookshelves laden with volumes of his own writings. Framing part of the scene is a bulging drapery arrangement in red, contrasting with the black figure of Rudbeck. His countenance is sensitively modelled and coloured and completely dominated by his sparkling eyes, his expression one of extreme vigour and wittiness.

Martin Mijtens seems to have been forgotten very quickly after his death, and it was not until the 1840s that there was renewed interest in him. His wide scope of portrait types is noteworthy, as is the adaptation of his style to modern standards during his extremely long career, beginning with his heavily dressed models of the 1670s and ending with an early Rococo portrait of his daughter *Johanna Mijtens* (*c.* 1720).

BIBLIOGRAPHY

SKL; Thieme–Becker

B. von Maimborg: *Martin Mijtens* (Stockholm, 1960)

TORBJÖRN FULTON

(4) Martin van Meytens II (*b* Stockholm, 24 June 1695; *d* Vienna, 23 March 1770). Son of (3) Martin Mijtens I. After training with his father, he started his career by painting small enamel pictures in London (1714), Paris (1717) and Vienna (1721). He was in Italy between 1723 and 1729 and was especially successful with his small portraits in Florence, Milan and Turin. After visiting his family and working for a short time in Sweden, he settled in Vienna *c.* 1730; he was appointed court painter in 1732.

Van Meytens worked predominantly as a portrait painter, depicting members of the imperial family and the upper nobility in Austria, Hungary, Moravia and Bohemia. Some of these are large group portraits in splendid palatial interiors or in the open air, such as the *Family of Graf Nikolaus Pálffy* (Vienna, Belvedere) and *Joseph of France and his Family* (Stockholm, Nmus.). Most, however, are individual full-length, life-size portraits, in which a commanding pose and rich clothing play a special role, and the grand settings include such Baroque trappings as undulating draperies. The many versions of the portrait of *Empress Maria Theresa* (e.g. Vienna, Belvedere)—as a young woman, as Queen of Hungary, as sovereign with the insignia of monarchy, in her widow's weeds, as an old woman etc—and the portraits of *Graf Dénes Báuffy* (Budapest, Mus. F.A.) and the jeweller *Johann Michael Grosser* (Stockholm, Nmus.) fall into this category. Van Meytens also portrayed famous scholars, writers and artists of the day, in a series of subtly characterized, three-quarter-length and head-and-shoulders paintings (e.g. *Franz Christoph Scheyb*, Vienna, Schloss Schönbrunn). In self-portraits he also showed his convincing powers of observation and

Martin Mijtens I: *Olof Rudbeck*, oil on canvas, 0.99×1.28 m, 1696 (Uppsala, Universitet Konstsamling)

employed harmonious, warm colouring; these works present him at the various stages of his career, as a young man wearing a romantic costume (Florence, Uffizi) and in court garb with his medals of honour and awards (e.g. Budapest, Mus. F.A.; Stockholm, Nmus.). Engravings based on many of his works were made in Germany and Austria by several contemporaries, including Johann Esaias Nilson, Andreas Schmutzer (*b* 1658), Johann Schmutzer (1700–40) and Johann Gottfried Haid (i).

Van Meytens also played a leading role in the art life of Vienna; not only was he Director of the Kunstakademie from 1759, but he was also in charge of a large studio and organized important artistic projects. For instance, he oversaw the commissioning of a series of history paintings for the imperial castles representing important events and ceremonies at court, such as the *Empress Awarding the Order of Maria Theresa and Stephen* (Vienna, Schloss Schönbrunn). These pictures were executed between 1764 and 1768 by the foremost Viennese history painters, including Vinzenz Fischer, Franz Sigrist and Johann Greipel (1720–98). Van Meytens enjoyed royal favour into his old age and was generally held in high esteem. He was considered extremely cultured, spoke many languages, played music and showed a close interest in physics and mineralogy. He was lauded by von Hagedorn as the 'van Dyck of the present day'.

For illustration of work *see* VIENNA, fig. 9.

BIBLIOGRAPHY
Thieme–Becker
C. L. von Hagedorn: *Lettre à un amateur de la peinture* (Dresden, 1755)
B. Lisholm: *Martin van Meytens d. y.* (Malmö, 1974)
E. Baum: *Katalog des Österreichischen Barockmuseums im unteren Belvedere in Wien*, 2 vols (Vienna and Munich, 1980)

KLÁRA GARAS

Mikeshin, Mikhail (Osipovich) (*b* Maksimovka, Smolensk province, 21 Feb 1836; *d* St Petersburg, 31 Jan 1896). Russian sculptor, painter and draughtsman. He studied with an icon painter and then at the Academy of Arts in St Petersburg (1852–8) under the battle painter Bogdan Pavlovich Villeval'de (1818–1903). Mikeshin was awarded gold medals for the paintings *Battle near Basgedikler* and *Duke Tilly in Magdeburg in 1631* (sketches, St Petersburg, Rus. Mus.). In 1859 Mikeshin won the competition for a design for a monument for the millennium of Russia, erected in Novgorod (bronze, 1859–62; *in situ*). The monument—one of the best known in the Russian tradition—is in the shape of a bell bearing a standing angel with a cross and a kneeling female figure representing Russia. Around the edge of the bell are two rows of leading figures from national history, the upper row cast in the round and the lower one in relief. The other important monument by Mikeshin is that to the *Empress Catherine II* in Ostrovsky Square in St Petersburg (bronze, 1862–73; *in situ*), which consists of a pedestal with the figure of the Empress surrounded by the figures of her principal associates.

Mikeshin also worked on the equestrian monument to Bogdan Khmel'nitsky in Bogdan Khmel'nitsky Square, Kiev (bronze and granite, 1870–88). At the same time he made many pen drawings, including illustrations to the works of Aleksandr Pushkin and Nikolay Gogol', and

designs for further monuments. Although lacking any special sculptural training, Mikeshin profited, in his sculptural commissions, from working with professional sculptors. Compositional inadequacies were thus corrected, while his tendency towards theatrical and picturesque forms found full expression.

BIBLIOGRAPHY
A. Savinov: *Mikeshin* (Moscow, 1971)
S. N. Semanov, ed.: *Pamyatnik 'Tysacheletiyu Rossii' fotoal'bom* [Monument to the 'Millennium of Russia'] (Moscow, 1974)
V. G. Smirnov: *Rossiya v bronze: Pamyatnik Tysyacheletiyu Rossii i yego geroyi* [Russia in bronze: a monument to the millennium of Russia and its heroes] (Novgrad, 1993)

SERGEY ANDROSSOV

Miketti, Nikola. *See* MICHETTI, NICCOLÒ.

Mikhaylov, Andrey (Alekseyevich) (*b* St Petersburg, 8 Aug 1773; *d* St Petersburg, 1849). Russian architect. He assisted in the construction of the Kazan' Cathedral (1801–11) in St Petersburg under Andrey Voronikhin, which marked a major phase in Russian 19th-century architecture, the assertion of the Russian Empire style. Mikhaylov, however, was more conservative: his plan for the Russian Academy on the 1st Line, Vasil'yevsky Island, St Petersburg (1802–4), for example, resembled an 18th-century palace with a central mass and wings along the line of the street (built by Vasily Stasov, 1811–14; rebuilt by Christian Meyer, 1840s). A similar approach was used in the Mariya (now Dostoyevsky) Hospital on Dostoyevsky Street in Moscow (1803–5). He designed the church of St Catherine (1811–23) on Congress Line (S'yezdovskaya liniya), Vasil'yevsky Island, in the form of a Greek cross, but its single dome placed on a drum and its portico (removed by Andrey Bolotov when the bell-tower was erected in 1863) recalled the Kazan' Cathedral. In putting into effect Karl Rossi's plan for developing the area around Mikhail Square in St Petersburg (1824–6), Mikhaylov built the Ordnance House on Sadovaya Street with a staircase inspired by the Mineral Cabinet in the Stroganov Palace (1791; by Voronikhin). The suite of Neo-classical state rooms (1822–5) in the Bobrinsky House on Galernaya Street, St Petersburg, and his success in a competition for the building of the Bol'shoy Theatre in Moscow (1821; design used in its final version by Osip Bove) brought Mikhaylov fame. The façade of the Korsakov Palace on Vladimir Prospect (1826–8) has an attic storey rather than a triangular pediment, marking the change from Neo-classicism to eclecticism, which was later developed by such architects as Aleksandr Bryullov and Konstantin Ton, Mikhaylov's former students at the St Petersburg Academy of Arts, where he was a professor from 1814 to 1830.

BIBLIOGRAPHY
L. A. Medersky: *Zhizn' i tvorchestvo arkhitektora Andreya Mikhaylova (1773–1849)* [The life and work of the architect Andrey Mikhaylov (1773–1849)] (diss., U. Leningrad, 1962)

SERGEY KUZNETSOV

Miki, Tomio (*b* Tokyo, 18 Dec 1937; *d* Kyoto, 15 Feb 1978). Japanese sculptor. After finishing junior high school, he entered a barbers' school in Tokyo. As an artist he was self-taught. From 1957 until 1963 he exhibited at the Yomiuri Independent Exhibitions. His works from this period have a strong anti-art element and are composed of such things as lorry tyres or smashed beer and whisky bottles. During this time he was also active in the avant-garde group Neo-Dadaism Organizers, although he was not actually a member. In 1963 he held a one-man show at the Naika Art Gallery, Tokyo, in which he exhibited a sculpture of an ear made from aluminium alloy. After this he continued to use the human ear as his motif, creating a sculpture of a giant ear taller than a human being and a relief composed of a collection of dozens of small ears. In 1964 he received a prize at the sixth Gendai Nihon Bijutsu Ten (Contemporary Art Exhibition of Japan). In 1967 he received a prize for *Pink Ear 12* (polyester resin, h. 2.7 m, 1967; Tokyo, Dentsū Corp.) at the ninth Nihon Kokusai Bijutsu Ten (International Art Exhibition of Japan) at the Tokyo Metropolitan Art Museum. In the same year, he was also a prizewinner at the fifth Jeune Biennale de Paris. In 1968 his work was shown at the Venice Biennale. In 1979 his work *Ear* (aluminium alloy, h. 1.69 m, 1965; Tokyo, N. Mus. Mod. A.) was exhibited at a show entitled *Gendai sekai bijutsu ten: Higashi to nishi no taiwa* ('Contemporary art from around the world: the dialogue between East and West'), sponsored by the National Museum of Modern Art in Tokyo. In 1971 he lived in the USA for a year at the invitation of the Rockefeller Foundation. Around this time he tried to move away from creating sculptures of ears. In 1977 a one-man exhibition entitled *Ringoen yori haru no kokoro* ('The heart of spring from an apple garden') was shown at the Green Collections in Tokyo.

BIBLIOGRAPHY
Miki Tomio (exh. cat., essay M. Ono; Fukuoka, A. Mus., 1981)
1960 Nendai—Gendai bijutsu no tenkanki [The 1960s—a decade of change in contemporary Japanese art] (exh. cat., essay T. Miki; Tokyo, N. Mus. Mod. A., 1981)

YASUYOSHI SAITO

Miknās. *See* MEKNÈS.

Mikon (*fl* earlier 5th century BC). Greek painter and sculptor. He came from Athens and although none of his work survives, paintings by Mikon and his great contemporary POLYGNOTOS OF THASOS decorated several buildings erected at the instigation of the Athenian general Kimon (*c.* 512–449 BC). An *Amazonomachy* depicting the battle between the Amazons and the Athenians, led by Theseus, which hung in the Stoa Poikile (Painted Stoa) was certainly by Mikon, and some ancient authors also ascribed to him the most famous painting in that building, depicting the *Battle of Marathon*, although it was generally attributed to PANAINOS. Pausanias (*Guide to Greece* I.xvii.2–4) saw three or four paintings in the Sanctuary of Theseus, built on the south side of the Agora after Kimon had brought Theseus' bones back from Skyros (474/3 BC): an *Amazonomachy*, a *Centauromachy*, *Theseus Recovering the Ring of Minos from the Sea* and perhaps *Theseus in the Underworld with Peirithoos*. It is possible that Mikon painted all the pictures in the sanctuary. Finally, a picture of the *Argonauts* by Mikon decorated the Sanctuary of the Dioskouroi. In it, the artist's greatest efforts were said to have been expended on the figures of Akastos and his horses. Ancient critics claimed that Mikon erroneously gave his horses lashes on their lower lids, although the mistake was sometimes attributed to Apelles or Polygnotos. An innovation associated with Mikon and Polygnotos seems to be reflected in some Attic Red-figure vases from *c.* 460 BC, which departed from a single ground line. Mikon once painted the helmet and an eye of a soldier called Butes, with the rest of the figure obscured (so that 'Faster than Butes' became a proverb for a task easily accomplished), and the motif of figures partially concealed behind hills was also taken up by Attic Red-figure vase painters. Pliny (*Natural History* XXXIV.xix.88) included Mikon in his list of bronze sculptors and said that his statues were much admired. Pausanias (VI.vi.1) saw one at Olympia, which represented the pankratiast Kallias of Athens (victor in 472 BC), and its base has been found.

BIBLIOGRAPHY
J. Overbeck: *Die antiken Schriftquellen zur Geschichte der bildenden Künste bei den Griechen* (Leipzig, 1868/R Hildesheim, 1959), nos 1054, 1058, 1070–71, 1080–93
J. P. Barron: 'New Light on Old Walls: The Murals of the Theseion', *J. Hell. Stud.*, xcii (1972), pp. 20–45

C. HOBEY-HAMSHER

Mikre Vigla. *See under* NAXOS, §1.

Milà, Alfonso. *See under* CORREA & MILÀ.

Milagro–Quevedo. Pre-Columbian culture that developed in the Guayas River basin of coastal Ecuador during the period *c.* AD 700–1500. Its populous chiefdoms flourished through the sophisticated cultivation of the seasonally flooded riverine wetlands. The most prominent cultural features on this lowland landscape are large elevated earthen platforms known as *tolas*, which were used for both habitation and burial purposes. Excavation of these mounds has yielded most of the surviving material upon which knowledge of Milagro–Quevedo artistic production is based. Milagro–Quevedo artisans employed a variety of exotic raw materials, often imported from far afield. These include marine shells from the Pacific coast of Ecuador, copper from northern Peru and gold, which probably originated in eastern Ecuador. Metalworking techniques such as hammering and repoussé were used to fashion elaborate nose rings, earrings, necklaces and pendants in copper and gold-and-copper alloys. The most sophisticated jewellery was embellished with filigree work. Perhaps the best-known copper objects are the large ceremonial axes and their smaller moulded counterparts. Hundreds of such axes were deposited in burial caches, having previously figured as non-utilitarian status items in long-distance trade (*see* SOUTH AMERICA, PRE-COLUMBIAN, §VIII, 5). By comparison pottery production was more rustic, the most notable items being large funerary urns and tripod bowls popularly known as 'witches' cauldrons'. These bear repetitive appliqué motifs featuring snakes, frogs and human figures. The production of high-quality textiles is inferred from a handful of surviving fragments and there is also a small corpus of free-standing zoomorphic and human figurines sculpted in stone.

For discussion of Pre-Columbian Ecuador *see also* SOUTH AMERICA, PRE-COLUMBIAN, §II.

BIBLIOGRAPHY
M. H. Saville: *Antiquities of Manabí*, 2 vols (New York, 1907–10)
E. Estrada: *Prehistoria de Manabí*, Museo Victor Emilio Estrada, iv (Guayaquil, 1957)

——: *Arqueología del Manabí Central*, Museo Victor Emilio Estrada, vii (Guayaquil, 1962)

B. J. Meggers: *Ecuador* (London, 1965)

M. I. Silva: *Pescadores y agricultores de la costa central del Ecuador: Un modelo socio-economico de asentamientos precolombinos* (MA thesis, Urbana, U. IL, 1984)

A. M. Mester: *The Pearl Divers of Los Frailes: Archaeological and Ethno-historical Explorations of Sumptuary Good Trade and Cosmology in the North and Central Andes* (diss., Urbana, U. IL, 1990; microfilm, Ann Arbor, 1990)

C. McEwan: 'Sillas de Poder', *5000 años de ocupación—Parque Nacional Machalilla*, ed. P. Norton (Quito, 1992)

MARIA ISABEL SILVA, with COLIN MCEWAN

Milan [It. Milano; Lat. Mediolanum]. Italian city and capital of Lombardy, with a population of *c.* 1.5 million. A Celtic settlement that became a Roman colony in 89 BC, it served as the capital of the Western Empire from AD 280 to 402 and also became a prominent Early Christian centre under Archbishop Ambrose (*reg* AD 374–97). By the mid-11th century it had developed into one of the early Italian communes and from 1257 to 1499 was ruled by a succession of powerful families: the Torriani, the Visconti and the Sforzas. Between 1499 and 1859 Milan fell to the invading powers of France, Spain and Austria. Much of the city centre was destroyed in World War II.

BIBLIOGRAPHY

A. Bosisio: *Storia di Milano* (Milan, 1958)

P. Mezzanotte and G. C. Bascapè: *Milano nell'arte e nella storia* (Milan, 1968)

G. Bologna: *Milano nei libri e nei documenti del suo archivio storico* (Milan, 1980)

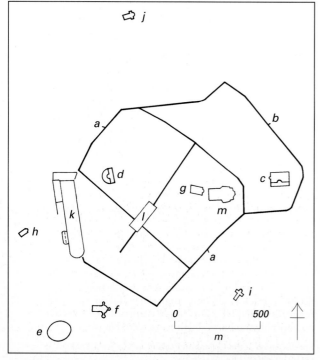

1. Milan, plan, late 4th century AD: (a) circuit wall of 49 BC; (b) late 3rd-century AD extension of wall; (c) Baths of Hercules; (d) theatre; (e) amphitheatre; (f) S Lorenzo; (g) S Tecla; (h) S Ambrogio; (i) Basilica Apostolorum; (j) S Simpliciano; (k) circus; (l) forum; (m) Basilica Vetus

M. Mirabella Roberti, A. Vincenti and G. M. Tabarelli: *Milano città fortificata* (Rome, 1983)

I. History and urban development. II. Art life and organization. III. Centre of production. IV. Buildings.

I. History and urban development.

1. Before 1162. 2. 1162–1499. 3. 1500–1714. 4. After 1714.

1. BEFORE 1162. The name Mediolanum is of Celtic origin, indicating a central place or point of convergence, and it reflects the town's location on a plain at the junction of early trade routes by land and water, including the route from the Alps to the north. The first permanent settlement was established by the Gauls, who crossed into Italy in 388 BC and recognized its favourable geographical position. Owing to the local importance of pig farming, a tradition arose that the name was derived from a sow with hair on her back only (Lat. *medio-lanum*, 'half-woolly'); the animal appears on oil lamps (e.g. 4th century AD; Milan, Civ. Mus. Archeol.).

The town was conquered by the Romans in 222 BC and granted the status of a Latin colony in 89 BC. The earliest evidence for the settlement's appearance dates from after this time, when a *castrum* (*c.* 9 ha) was built on the site. After 49 BC this was enclosed by a circuit wall in stone and brick (see fig. 1a), which was extended by the emperor Maximian (*reg* AD 286–305) around an area of 15 ha (1b). The wall was equipped with a pair of 24-sided towers, one of which survives to its full height of 16.6 m. The gates arranged along the wall reflected the radial street plan, which was to determine the city's development. Other remains from the 1st to the 3rd century AD include the Baths of Hercules (1c), a theatre (1d), an amphitheatre (1e) and 16 large columns that were later reused for the external portico of the basilica of S Lorenzo (1f; *see* §IV, 3 below).

From AD 280 to AD 402 Milan was the capital of the Western Empire. A new period of building activity began with the appointment of Ambrose as archbishop in 374. Although the city had its own churches by then, including possibly the basilica of S Tecla (1g; destr. 1455; *see* §IV, 4 below), Ambrose founded the basilica of S Ambrogio (1h; *see* IV, 2(i) below), the cruciform Basilica Apostolorum (1i; 380–85; now S Nazaro) and probably the basilica of S Lorenzo. Another late 4th-century church is the basilica of S Simpliciano (1j; *see* §IV, 5 below). The Roman walls were partially dismantled during the barbarian invasions of the 5th and 6th centuries, and in 538 the city was half destroyed by the Ostrogoths. Following a brief period of Byzantine rule (553–69), the city fell to the Lombards, who in turn were eventually overthrown by Charlemagne in 774.

In the 9th century the city began to acquire greater autonomy, particularly under Archbishop Ansperto da Biasono (*reg* 868–81). The affirmation of episcopal authority reached its culmination with Archbishop Ariberto d'Antimiano (*reg* 1018–45), who united the citizens against Emperor Conrad II (*reg* 1024–39). A symbol of this union was the so-called 'Caroccio'—an ox-drawn war cart bearing the cross and the standard of the city. Between the 9th and 10th centuries the organization of the city underwent a change: communities gathered around the houses of the most powerful citizens, who exercised patronage and charity to the poor. Merchants and bankers resided in the city centre, artisans in the suburbs, and the area in between was occupied by convents, hospitals and charitable institutions. More churches were also built in this period, including S Vincenzo in Prato (9th century) and the basilica of S Maria Maggiore (9th century; destr. late 14th century or 15th; *see* §IV, 1(i) below). In the late 11th century S Eustorgio was rebuilt (destr. 1162; reconstructed 1190–1220) on the site of the former church begun in the 4th century and in which were preserved the relics of the Magi.

The invasion of northern Italy by Frederick I in 1158 led to the construction of new defensive walls by a certain Master Guglielmo or Guintellino, comprising an external ditch and an earth embankment. Openings were inserted corresponding to the lines of the roads coming from the old inner walls, thus emphasizing the city's ancient radial plan.

BIBLIOGRAPHY

M. Mirabella Roberti: *Milano romana e paleocristiana* (Milan, 1972/*R* 1984)
R. Krautheimer: *Three Christian Capitals: Topography and Politics* (London, 1983)
C. Bertelli, ed.: *Milano: Una capitale da Ambrogio ai Carolingi* (1987), i of *Il millennio ambrosiano*, 3 vols (Milan, 1987) [with extensive bibliog.]

ALESSANDRA ANSELMI

2. 1162–1499. On 1 March 1162 the Milanese were forced to capitulate to Frederick I after a 7-month siege, during which canals were dug around the walls. The walls, towers and palaces of the beautiful medieval city were completely demolished: only the churches were left standing. The inhabitants were forced to evacuate the city and lived in four districts of poor housing built outside the city walls (Nosedo, Vigentino, Siro alla Vepra and Lambrate). Five years later, however, in defiance of the imperial decree that prohibited their return to the city, the Milanese began to reconstruct it with the help of the Paduan Commune. They started with the walls, which surrounded the city in an elliptical route that followed the ring of canals, the Navigli, roughly corresponding to the present inner ring road. Six fortified gateways with double arches and lateral towers were inserted in the walls, of which only a tiny section survives in Via Francesco Sforza. These gates connected with the main streets of the six districts: traces remain of the medieval Porta Nuova (the arches in Via Manzoni), Porta Romana (low reliefs now in Milan, Castello Sforzesco) and Porta Ticinese (rest. 1861–5). Of the numerous individual arches (*pusterle*) inserted at intervals along the walls, only the Pusterla di S Ambrogio (rebuilt 1939) remains. The walls enclosed 240 ha, making Milan the largest Italian city of the time.

2. Milan, Castello Sforzesco, from 1358

After the defeat of Frederick at the Battle of Legnano (1176) the Milanese Commune reverted to a life characterized by opposition between the aristocracy, who belonged to the Motta party, and the emerging mercantile and artisan classes, who formed a political organization called the Credenza di S Ambrogio. The continuing disputes gradually pushed the city towards a form of monarchical government. The first skirmishes at the Signoria occurred when Martino della Torre (*d* 1263) was elected Anziano Perpetuo del Popolo di Milano (1257), which effectively sanctioned the rule of the Torriani. In 1277 the Guelph Torriano party was defeated by the aristocratic pro-Ghibelline party headed by Archbishop Ottone Visconti (*d* 1295) after a bloody battle at Desio, near Milan. The VISCONTI quickly pacified the city's factions and consolidated their rule. Ottone appointed his great-nephew Matteo I (*reg* 1310–22) as Captain of the People. Despite resistance from the Torriani (1302–11) and disputes with the imperial authorities, the dominion of the Visconti family became absolute. Under Galeazzo I (*reg* 1322–8), Azzo (*reg* 1328–39), Galeazzo II (*reg* 1354–78) and Bernabò (*reg* 1354–85) numerous other cities became subject to Visconti Milan, which thus became the capital of a state.

The political and economic expansion that took place in the 13th and 14th centuries naturally led to a surge of building and urban development. The city conquered by the Visconti had numerous ecclesiastical buildings, many of which were Early Christian basilicas rebuilt in the Romanesque style, for example S Lorenzo, S Nazaro Maggiore (rebuilt 1075; altered), S Celso (rebuilt 996 and 11th century; altered) and S Ambrogio. The canal system was expanded with the extension to Milan of the Naviglio Grande (1257), which stretched for 50 km and brought the waters of the River Ticino to Milan. From 1269 the Naviglio Grande was completely navigable. The canals had a defensive function as well as allowing the transport of goods and food and providing running water for the workshops of dyers, tanners, smiths, millers and papermakers. More canals were dug in the 14th century, for example the Redefossi, Vettabbia, Ticinello and Naviglio Pavese.

The Visconti were associated with a series of building projects that testified to their power and largesse. Bernabò Visconti reinforced the Porta Romana and the Porta Nuova (1358), while Gian Galeazzo Visconti (*reg* 1378–1402) fortified the Rocca di Porta Giovia (1358–68), thus founding the Castello di Porta Giovia (later Castello Sforzesco; see fig. 2), which he made his official seat. His withdrawal from the Palazzo di Corte Ducale was symbolic of his increasing detachment from the people. A practical reason for the move was the construction of a new cathedral (begun 1306; see §IV, 1(i)(a) below), which was to occupy part of the palace's site. Gian Galeazzo was created Duke of Milan in 1395. His death in 1402 not only meant that work on the cathedral was halted, but had important repercussions throughout the state of Milan. Under Gian Galeazzo the city's dominion had extended to nearly all of northern Italy and the area beyond the Apennines, including Pisa, Perugia and Siena. Following his death, the republics of Florence and Venice now formed a coalition against Milan and reduced its territories

3. Milan, S Maria delle Grazie, interior of the choir, by Donato Bramante, from 1492

to Lombardy. Giovanni Maria (*reg* 1402–12) and Filippo Maria (*reg* 1412–47) were forced to defend themselves against repeated attacks by the two republics and the Papal State.

Filippo Maria employed as condottiere Francesco Attendolo (known as Francesco Sforza I; see SFORZA, (1)), who married the Duke's daughter, Bianca Maria (see SFORZA, (3)). When Filippo Maria died without a male heir, the Milanese proclaimed the Golden Ambrosian Republic, inspired by the city states. The new yet rather anachronistic system failed to consolidate power or to prevent the desertion of the Lombard cities. Venice in particular began to threaten Milan, and the 24 heads of the republic turned for help to Francesco Sforza, who made an agreement first with the Milanese, and then with Venice; he successfully besieged Milan (1450) and claimed the duchy. He presided over a period of prosperity and renewal, aided by the peace that was confirmed with the Treaties of Lodi (1454). Francesco encouraged the city's flourishing production of tapestries, goldwork, armour and precious silks. While Milanese merchants exploited new trade routes, the city became the market for the surrounding plain's agricultural produce.

In 1455 the cylindrical towers of the Castello Sforzesco were begun (see fig. 2), and in 1456 Francesco commissioned the Ospedale Maggiore (now university; see FILARETE and fig. 2): its construction dragged on for centuries. Francesco also initiated the paving of the main streets.

Francesco's son Galeazzo Maria (*reg* 1466–76) inherited a flourishing city that played host to humanists and scholars, such as Luca Pacioli. When Galeazzo Maria was assassinated, his son Gian Galeazzo (*reg* 1476–94) was too young to rule, and so his uncle Ludovico Sforza ('il Moro') gradually took control. Under Ludovico and his wife, Beatrice d'Este, the city flourished. Ludovico surrounded himself with the finest artists, in emulation of Lorenzo de' Medici: he brought Leonardo da Vinci to Milan, and Bramante designed S Maria presso S Satiro (from 1478; *see* BRAMANTE, §I, 2(ii)(a), and fig. 1), S Maria delle Grazie (from 1492; see fig. 3) and parts of the S Ambrogio monastic complex. Ludovico also added a lantern (1470–1500) to the cathedral, commissioned the Lazzaretto (1488–1513) and ordered the excavation of the Naviglio della Martesana from the River Adda to Milan. Among other works, GIOVANNI DI DOMENICO BATTAGGIO designed S Maria della Passione (begun before 1486) in a style heavily influenced by that of Bramante.

Louis XII of France asserted his claim to Milan in alliance with the Aragonese rulers of Naples, Venice and the Pope. In 1499 Ludovico was forced to abandon the city and was captured by the French.

BIBLIOGRAPHY

B. Corio: *Patria historia* (Milan, 1503)

F. Cognasso: 'Note e documenti sulla formazione dello stato visconteo', *Boll. Soc. Pavese Stor. Patria*, xxiii (1923), pp. 23–169

C. Santoro: *Gli offici del comune di Milano e del dominio visconteo-sforzesco, 1216–1515* (Milan, 1968)

L. Cerioni: *La diplomazia sforzesca nella seconda metà del quattrocento*, 2 vols (Rome, 1970)

Popolo e stato in Italia nell'età di Federico Barbarossa: Alessandria e la Lega Lombarda (Turin, 1970)

N. Raponi: *Lo stato di Milano nell'età sforzesca* (Milan, 1971)

G. Martini: 'La battaglia di Legnano: Realtà e mito', *Nuova Antol.*, cxi (1976), pp. 357–71

M. Bellonci, G. A. dell'Acqua and C. Perogalli: *I Visconti a Milano* (Milan, 1977)

G. Lopez: *Gli Sforza a Milano* (Milan, 1978)

P. Zerbi: *Tra Milano e Cluny: Momenti di vita e cultura ecclesiastica nel XII secolo* (Rome, 1978)

La città nell'età di Ludovico il Moro: Atti del convegno su Leonardo a Milano, 1482–1982: Milano, 1983

Ludovico il Moro: La sua città e la sua corte, 1480–1499 (exh. cat., Milan, Archv Stato, 1983)

3. 1500–1714. Louis XII of France initially gained the trust of the Milanese by restoring the Senate, an assembly of noble citizens elected by the French crown. He also reduced taxation by instituting protectionist measures in favour of some categories of craftsmen. The numerous wars fought by the French monarch, however, led to an increase in taxation and a decrease in his popularity. The church of S Maurizio Maggiore (rest.) at the Monasterio Maggiore was erected from 1503, possibly to a design by Giovanni Giacomo Dolcebuono, while the pro-French condottiere GIAN GIACOMO TRIVULZIO commissioned Bramantino to build a large family funerary chapel (*c.* 1512) in front of the church of S Nazaro Maggiore. Between 1508 and 1509 the French governor, Charles d'Amboise II, commissioned the sanctuary of S Maria alla Fontana (rest.); Leonardo da Vinci was possibly involved in the project.

The creation of the Holy League, which aimed to expel the French from the Italian peninsula, resulted in Louis's defeat at Ravenna in 1513 and the restoration of the Sforzas. Massimiliano Sforza (*reg* 1512–15), however, was beaten by Francis I of France at the Battle of Marignano (1515). During the second period of French rule, Milan was involved in the dispute between France and Habsburg Spain and Austria. Francis allowed the existing citizens' council to continue to function, but he ruled through greedy and unpopular governors. In 1521 the Spanish troops of Emperor Charles V reclaimed Milan for the Habsburgs. Charles established Francesco Sforza II (*d* 1535) as Governor of Milan and took direct possession of the city on the latter's death.

CRISTOFORO LOMBARDO worked on a number of buildings: he participated in the construction of S Maria presso S Celso from 1530; he rebuilt the Palazzo Stampa di Soncino (from 1534), which culminated in a tower decorated with the heraldic devices of Charles V; and he designed the lantern (1550–51) of S Maria della Passione. DOMENICO DI GIOVANNI GIUNTI was architect to the Spanish governor, Ferrante Gonzaga (*reg* 1546–55), for whom he executed a number of commissions, including the transformation of the suburban Villa Gonzaga (now Villa Simonetta; 1547–52; see fig. 4). The new city fortifications (mostly destr.), often known as the Spanish bastions, were commissioned by Ferrante Gonzaga in 1548 and largely completed before 1560. The nine-pointed bastions closely followed the outline of the Visconti ditches, with gateways aligned with the existing gates. Built from spolia, the ramparts had irregular, battered walls and a rough surface. The gates had two pilasters covered by a pitched roof and were flanked by toll-houses. In the city, Galeazzo Alessi designed a number of churches and the influential Palazzo Marino (begun 1558; *see* ALESSI, GALEAZZO and fig. 3).

Spanish rule was recognized by the other great powers in the treaty of Cateau-Cambrésis (1559). Milan declined from the capital of an independent duchy to a provincial capital within an empire. The Spanish governor made his headquarters in the Palazzo Ducale. A little administrative autonomy was granted to the 60 noble members of the citizens' council, but in general the city suffered from the political and economic rigidity of Spanish rule. There was a considerable decline in building activity and few notable building projects, although from 1560 a programme of modernization was carried out in the medieval city centre. The Piazza dei Mercanti was enriched with a series of monumental palazzi containing public offices, the Palazzo dei Giureconsulti (1561; for illustration *see* SEREGNI, VINCENZO) and the Tribunale di Provvisione.

Spanish misgovernment was counteracted by the strength of the Church, particularly under Archbishop Carlo Borromeo (*reg* 1563–84). He was extremely active during the Council of Trent (1545–65), the decrees of which he rigorously applied. He wished to make Milan a stronghold of the Catholic Counter-Reformation and tried to prevent Protestant infiltration. His charitable works included the foundation of institutions to educate clergymen and, indirectly, the lay rulers: the Seminario Arcivescovile (from 1565), Collegio Elvetico and Collegio dei Nobili. He took strict control of the conduct of the clergy, sponsoring new religious orders such as the Theatines, Barnabites and Oblates of St Ambrose, and suppressing those that he deemed corrupt (e.g. the Humiliati; suppressed 1571). Several times he was involved in direct clashes with the Spanish authorities and Philip II of Spain concerning public order and the arrival in Milan of the Spanish Inquisition, which was strongly supported by Philip and equally opposed by Carlo.

Carlo's moral and political jurisdiction was sustained by his cousin, Archbishop Federico Borromeo (*reg* 1595–1631), who continued Carlo's reforming work through such cultural activities as the foundation of the Biblioteca Ambrosiana (built 1607–9) and Accademia Ambrosiana. Federico's charitable work was focused on helping the population during the terrible plague of 1630. The age of the Borromei left its mark on the city in the form of the numerous buildings erected by the two archbishops. In the old centre they continued the work on the cathedral and built the Canonica (designed 1565; built 1572; see fig. 5) at the Palazzo Arcivescovile, S Fedele (from 1569) and S Sebastiano (from 1577), all by Pellegrino Tibaldi (*see* TIBALDI, (1) and fig. 2), as well as S Raffaele (from 1575); MARTINO BASSI worked on a number of churches in the city. The archbishops also completed the remodelling of the Piazza dei Giureconsulti. Francesco Maria Ricchini enlarged the Ospedale Maggiore with a new courtyard (1625–49) and designed such churches as S Giuseppe (1607–30; *see* RICCHINI, FRANCESCO MARIA, fig. 1) and numerous palazzi (e.g. Palazzo Annoni, from 1631). The archbishops built various schools, including

the Collegio di Brera (from 1591) and the Collegio degli Svizzeri (from 1608). Stations of the Cross (columns supporting a cross or the statue of a saint) were erected in the piazzas and the streets to commemorate the makeshift altars set up during the plague of 1576.

Many churches and monasteries built (e.g. S Alessandro, 1601) or rebuilt (e.g. S Antonio Abate, from 1582) during this period determined the city's character in the 17th century. By contrast, civic building activity was limited by economic difficulties to a few notable works: the Palazzo del Capitano di Giustizia, or delle Carceri Nuove (*c.* 1570–after 1624, by Pietro Antonio Barca), the great arch of the Porta Romana (1598), and the completion of the fortification of the former Castello Sforzesco with the construction of a series of angle bastions. The plague of 1630 halved the former population of *c.* 130,000. Numbers began to grow substantially only after 1650, and building activity slowly increased, mostly along the roads that ran from the new gates in the Spanish bastions into the old city. Carlo Buzzi imitated the lines of the Palazzo dei Giureconsulti and the Tribunale di Provvisione in the Palazzo delle Scuole Palatine (1644–5) opposite them. A substantial fringe of houses, palaces and monasteries was built, which backed on to orchards and gardens irrigated by numerous ditches, especially to the south-east. The nobility favoured the streets around Porta Romana and

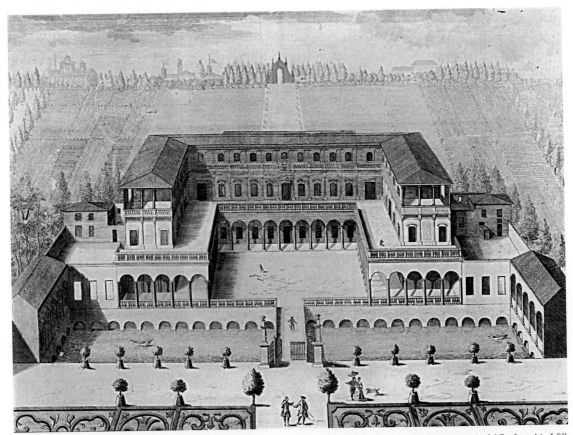

4. Milan, Villa Gonzaga (now Villa Simonetta) by Domenico di Giovanni Giunti, 1547–52; engraving by Marc'Antonio dal Re from his *Ville di Delizia o siano Palagi Camparecci nello stato di Milano* (Milan, 1726) (London, Victoria and Albert Museum)

5. Milan, Canonica of the Palazzo Arcivescovile, by Pellegrino Tibaldi, 1572

Porta Ticinese, while the areas of Porta Comacina and Borgo degli Ortolani remained more consistently working-class. The aristocracy later moved to the shady, quiet areas around Porta Nuova and Porta Orientale.

In 1706, during the War of the Spanish Succession (1701–14), Milan came under Austrian dominion when Eugene, Prince of Savoy, occupied the city. Habsburg possession of the city was ratified in the Treaty of Rastadt (1714).

BIBLIOGRAPHY

C. Torre: *Il ritratto di Milano* (Milan, 1674, rev. 2/1714)
L. Beltrami: *Relazione di Don Ferrante Gonzaga, Governante di Milano, inviata all'imperatore Carlo V, nel 1552 in difesa della progettata cinta dei bastioni* (Milan, 1897)
C. Baroni: *Documenti per la storia dell'architettura a Milano nel rinascimento e nel barocco*, 2 vols (Florence and Rome, 1940–68)
A. Ballo and B. Caizzi: *Milano nell'età spagnola* (Rome, 1960)
C. Bascape: *Vita e opere di Carlo, Arcivescovo di Milano, Cardinale di Santa Prassede* (Milan, 1965)
F. Chabod: *Lo stato e la vita religiosa a Milano all'epoca di Carlo V* (Turin, 1971)
——: *Storia di Milano all'epoca di Carlo V* (Turin, 1971)
H. Jedin: *Carlo Borromeo* (Rome, 1971)
U. Petronio: *Il senato di Milano: Istituzioni giuridiche ed esercizio del potere nel ducato di Milano da Carlo V a Giuseppe II* (Milan, 1972)
L. Ferrario: *La guerra e la peste nella Milano dei Promessi Sposi: Documenti inediti tratti dagli Archivi spagnoli* (Madrid, 1975)
A. Buratti: *La città rituale: La città e lo stato di Milano nell'età dei Borromeo* (Milan, 1982)
A. de Maddalena: *Dalla città al borgo: Avvio di una metamorfosi economica e sociale nella Lombardia spagnola* (Milan, 1982)
D. Sella: *L'economia lombarda durante la dominazione spagnola* (Bologna, 1982)

4. AFTER 1714. Milan remained under Austrian control until the unification of Italy (1859), apart from the brief period of Franco-Savoyard rule (1733–6) and the Napoleonic occupation (1796–1814). The appearance of the city changed considerably in the 18th century, although urban development was confined to the undeveloped areas within the Spanish bastions. The buildings and land of the suppressed religious houses were adapted (see below). In the early 18th century Baroque-influenced Roman and Milanese architects built a few private palaces and public buildings, such as the cemetery complex of the Rotonda della Besana (from 1713), designed by Attilio Arrigoni (*fl* 1695–1725). During the Wars of Succession—Spanish (1701–14), Polish (1733–8) and Austrian (1740–48)—Giovanni Ruggieri built some influential urban palaces in Milan, for example the Palazzo Cusani (from 1715; for discussion and illustration *see* RUGGIERI, GIOVANNI). Other important architects of the period were Carlo Giuseppe Merlo, Benedetto Innocente Alfieri and Francesco Croce (1696–1780).

A new golden age began for Milan in the second half of the 18th century, chiefly owing to the important reforms effected by Empress Maria-Theresa and her son, Emperor Joseph II (*reg* 1765–90). With the collaboration of a group of civil servants and the absolute support of the city's aristocracy, the Austrian monarchs launched a series of new policies, including a modern system of taxation based on the new land register, and the systems of leasing and indirect taxation were reformed. Among significant ecclesiastical reforms were state control of Church benefices and the abolition of religious tribunals, censorship and the Inquisition. Monasteries and churches considered superfluous were suppressed; of the 300 in the city in 1768, almost half were closed in the following 20 years. The Austrians also promoted politics and culture: the historic collection *Rerum italicarum scriptores* (Milan, 1723–38) by Lodovico Antonio Muratori (1672–1750) was published, the Scuole Palatine was reorganized, and the observatory (1763), the Biblioteca di Brera (1770) and the Accademia di Brera (1776) were founded.

When Giuseppe Piermarini became royal architect in 1769 he straightened the road from Porta Romana and razed the medieval gate. Other streets were made to align with elegant Neo-classical buildings, as on the Corsia del Giardino (now Via Manzoni) and the Corsia dei Servi (now Corso Vittorio Emanuele II and Via Montenapoleone), and new piazzas (e.g. Piazza Fontana) were created. Within the city centre, he replaced S Maria alla Scala with the Teatro alla Scala (1776–8; for discussion and illustration *see* PIERMARINI, GIUSEPPE). He also radically remodelled the Palazzo Ducale (1770–78) and the Palazzo di Brera (1779) and in 1780 completed the grandiose suburban Villa di Monza, the summer home of the Austrian archdukes. Piermarini's strong personality influenced

6. Milan, Arco della Pace, by Luigi Cagnola, from 1807

other architects of the time, among them Simone Cantoni and Leopoldo Pollack.

Joseph II continued his mother's reforms, but the suppression of the Milanese senate (1787) and above all the French Revolution from 1789 provoked strong anti-Habsburg sentiments. When Napoleon entered the city in 1796, the Milanese welcomed him enthusiastically. He declared Milan the capital of the Cisalpine Republic, which initiated three years of political euphoria. In 1799 the Austrians reconquered the city, but Napoleon returned after his victory at the Battle of Marengo (1800). In 1805 he crowned himself King of Italy in Milan Cathedral.

Under the French, some areas of the city were considerably changed through new building programmes, most notably the reorganization, designed in 1801 by GIOVANNI ANTONIO ANTOLINI, of the area around the Castello Sforzesco, where a vast forum, the Foro Bonaparte, was to be built. This remained unrealized, but the area was transformed nonetheless by the creation of the esplanade of the Piazza d'Armi and the construction of the Arena (1805–13) by LUIGI CANONICA. Grandiose Neo-classical arches or porches, such as the 'Atrium' of Porta Marengo (1801–14) at Porta Ticinese and the Arco della Pace (from 1807; see fig. 6), both designed by LUIGI CAGNOLA, were erected near the gates. Giuseppe Pistocchi designed numerous unexecuted monuments for the city (for discussion and illustration *see* PISTOCCHI, GIUSEPPE). S Francesco Grande was demolished and replaced in 1807 by the S Ambrogio (now Veliti) barracks as part of the continuing suppression of religious orders under Napoleon.

In 1814 Milan was returned to Austrian rule to become merely another provincial city. The reserve and authoritarianism of the Austrians provoked hostility, and the opposition movement and the first conspiracies were quashed in 1821 and 1824.

The city's growing population led to much building activity, both in undeveloped areas within the Spanish walls and in the Corpi Santi, the extramural working-class areas that had grown up along the main roads. GIACOMO MORAGLIA designed various buildings in the city, including the Palazzo Melzi d'Eril (1841–6). The widening, straightening and paving of many streets, and the introduction of gas street-lighting from 1845, altered the city's appearance. The diffusion of the political theory of Giuseppe Mazzini (1805–72) stirred up anti-Austrian feelings even among the poor and made possible the Five Days of Milan popular uprising (1848), which led to the temporary expulsion of the Austrians. In 1849 Field Marshal Joseph Radetzky (1766–1858) reimposed order through a strict, repressive regime. Meanwhile, in the settlements along the edges of the Spanish walls, the first railway stations were built (1840–58), and work on the Central Station began in 1857.

In 1859 Milan requested annexation to Piedmont and in 1861 it became part of the unified Italy. Milan was the economic capital of the new state, and publishing houses were set up and newspapers founded. The first mayor, A. Beretta, established the town hall in the Palazzo Marino and transformed the old centre by implementing Giuseppe Mengoni's plan to reorganize the area around the Piazza del Duomo, building the Galleria Vittorio Emanuele II (from 1863; for discussion and illustration *see* MENGONI,

7. Milan, Central Station, by Ulisse Stacchini, completed 1931

GIUSEPPE) and creating the Solferino district. In 1881 the city hosted the Esposizione Nazionale. Rail links were expanded with the opening of the St Gotthard tunnel (1882).

Between 1884 and 1888 the first large-scale urban planning schemes were drawn up to modernize Milan by architects such as Luca Beltrami and Camillo Boito. Among proposals in the *Piano Beruto* (1884) were the creation of a street linking the castle and the cathedral (now Via Dante), the covering of the Navigli and considerable development north-west of the city with the creation of elegant quarters around the Parco del Sempione. While new districts were being planned, for example around the former Lazzaretto (destr. 1880), and such large public schemes as Carlo Maciachini's Cimitero Monumentale (from 1863) were being laid out, the first heavy industries began to be established in the suburbs (Pirelli, Treves and Carlo Erba). The resulting growth in population and the creation of a working class led to demands for workers' rights that were frequently suppressed by force. The discontent provoked by this repression later resulted in the assassination of King Umberto I (*reg* 1878–1900) in Monza, near Milan.

From 1900 to 1914 Milan's industries, including Alfa Romeo, Breda, Marelli and Falck, grew towards Sesto S Giovanni and Bovisa. In 1912 an urban plan by Cesare Saldini (1848–1922) was approved that laid out the long rectangle from Viale Lombardia to Viale Omero in the east, moved the railways to the outer ring of the city and

included Ulisse Stacchini's scheme for the new Central Station (completed 1931; see fig. 7). In 1914 the socialist Emilio Caldara became mayor and instituted a vast development programme, including the construction of cheap housing. Nonetheless, after World War I, political, social and economic difficulties encouraged the development of the Fascist party, which initiated a series of cultural and urban projects: between 1921 and 1924 the Catholic University and the State University were founded, and an urban plan was approved in 1926. This project, the work of the architects Piero Portaluppi (1888–1976) and Marco Semenza, considered for the first time the entire city and 11 surrounding municipalities. Its principal aim was to divert traffic from the centre by creating a network of peripheral streets. It also aimed to modernize the centre, where brutal demolition was carried out to create new piazzas (e.g. Diaz, S Babila, degli Affari and della Repubblica) and main roads (Corso Matteotti, Via Turati). Important new buildings of the period include Giuseppe De Finetti's Casa della Meridiana (1924–5) and Marcello Piacentini's Palazzo di Giustizia (1932–40), while in the suburbs the S Siro Stadium (1926; altered 1950), Idroscalo (1928), Forlanini (or Linate) Airport (1935–6; enlarged 1958–63, 1984), the new Ospedale Maggiore (1938) at Niguarda and much cheap housing were built.

Development was drastically curtailed by World War II. In 1943 Allied bombing destroyed much of the old centre, and a quarter of the city's buildings were damaged, including S Maria delle Grazie, S Ambrogio and the Teatro alla Scala. From 1945 the city confronted the huge problems of reconstruction, and various revisions of the urban plan were proposed that focused on the creation of a commercial zone between the Central Station and Porta Garibaldi and on demolition within the old centre to open up streets and piazzas of questionable aesthetic value (e.g. Via Larga, Piazza Missori). Huge areas of cheap housing were created on the outskirts: the Q.T.8 (begun 1947), near S Siro, for example, is noted for its severity and functionality. Most of the country's publishing houses were based in Milan, and the city's cultural prestige was regained with the reconstruction of the Teatro alla Scala (1945–6) and the founding of the Piccolo Teatro (1947). The first high-rise buildings also appeared, including the Pirelli Building (1955–9) by Gio Ponti (for illustration *see* PONTI, GIO) and the Galfa Building (1959) by Melchiorre Bega.

The post-war boom ended in the late 1960s, and it was not until the early 1980s that the city began to recover, mostly owing to increased activity in the advertising, fashion and computing industries. In the late 20th century the city shared the common metropolitan problems of traffic congestion and pollution. Local government reversed its policies and focused on the conservation of the historic centre, simultaneously trying to meet the demands of the modern city by expanding the underground transport system and moving factories and tertiary industry to autonomous industrial zones on the outskirts of the city.

See also ITALY, §II, 6.

BIBLIOGRAPHY

S. Latuada: *Descrizione di Milano* (Milan, 1737)
G. Bianconi: *Nuova guida di Milano* (Milan, 1782)
G. Mongeri: *Descrizione del nuovo cimitero monumentale di Milano* (Milan, 1870)
D. Bazzoni: *Progetto di ampliamento della città di Milano* (Milan, 1880)
C. Beruto: *Progetto di piano regolatore della città di Milano* (Milan, 1885)
L. Beltrami: *Indagini e documenti riguardanti la torre principale del Castello di Milano ricostruita in memoria di Umberto I* (Milan, 1905)
A. Pavia and G. Masera: *Piano generale regolatore edilizio e di ampliamento della città di Milano* (Milan, 1912)
F. Valsecchi: *L'assolutismo illuminato in Austria e in Lombardia*, 2 vols (Bologna, 1934–6)
P. Torriano: *Architetture di Giovanni Muzio* (Milan and Geneva, 1936)
L. Grassi: 'Razionalismo settecentesco e architettura neoclassica milanese', *Scritti in onore di Cesare chiodi* (Milan, 1937)
M. Roberti: *Milano capitale napoleonica: La formazione di uno stato moderno, 1796–1814*, 3 vols (Milan, 1946–7)
P. Bottoni: *Il Q.T.8.: Ottava Triennale di Milano* (Milan, 1947)
F. Reggiori: *Milano, 1800–1943: Itinerario urbanistico-edilizio* (Milan, 1947)
B. Zanei: *L'opera di rinnovamento della Lombardia austriaca durante il governo del conte Carlo Firmian* (Trieste, 1948)
R. Aloi: *Nuove architetture a Milano* (Milan, 1959)
G. Treccani degli Alfieri: *L'età della riforme, 1706–1796* (1959), xii of *Storia di Milano* (Milan, 1953–)
M. L. Gatti Perer: *Carlo Giuseppe Merlo architetto* (Milan, 1966)
L. Grassi: *Province del barocco e del rococo: Proposta di un lessico bibliografico d'architetti in Lombardia* (Milan, 1966)
G. Mezzanotte: *Architettura neoclassica in Lombardia* (Naples, 1966)
——: *Il centro antico di Milano: Sviluppo e declino delle città settecentesche* (Milan, 1970)
G. Galli: 'Il movimento operaio milanese alla fine dell'ottocento', *Città Milano* (1971), no. 6
Lo sviluppo edilizio di Milano nei secoli XVIII e XIX (Milan, 1971)
D. Franchi and R. Chiumeo: *Urbanistica a Milano in regime fascista* (Florence, 1972)
G. Galli: 'Il movimento operaio milanese agli inizi del novecento', *Città Milano* (1972), nos 1–2
L. L. Secchi: *1778–1978: Il Teatro alla Scala: Architettura, tradizione e società* (Milan, 1977)
La trasformazione sociale e geografica milanese degli anni '50 (Milan, 1977)
L. Patetti and M. D. Bardeschi: *L'idea di magnificenza civile: Architettura a Milano, 1770–1848* (Milan, 1978)
G. Bonvini and A. Scalpelli: *Milano fra guerra e dopoguerra* (Bari, 1979)
A. Ferrari: *Le porte di Milano* (Milan, 1980)
F. Alberoni, ed.: *La società industriale metropolitana e i problemi dell'area milanese* (Milan, 1981)
G. Giani: *La stazione centrale di Milano: Mostra del cinquantenario* (Milan, 1981)
L. Carossi and R. Pozzi: *1930–1942: La città dimostrativa del razionalismo europeo* (Milan, 1982)
G. Mezzanotte: *L'architetto della Scala nell'età neoclassica* (Milan, 1982)
M. Prizzon and L. Fiori: *La Torre Velasca: Disegno e progetto della Torre Velasca* (Milan, 1982)
C. Pirovano: *Piermarini e il suo tempo* (Milan, 1983)
A. Burg: *Novecento milanese: I novecentisti e il rinnovamento dell'architettura a Milano, fra il 1920 e il 1940* (Milan, 1991)
F. Dal Co and S. Polano, eds: '20th Century Architecture and Urbanism: Milano', *A + U* (Dec 1991), pp. 4–280
C. Mozzarelli: *Milano fin de siècle e il caso Bugatti Valsecchi: Memorie e progetto per la metropoli italiana* (Milan, 1991)

MARCO CARMINATI

II. Art life and organization.

1. Before 1278. 2. 1278–1499. 3. 1500–1714. 4. After 1714.

1. BEFORE 1278. Between the late Roman Empire and the age of Communes, most important works of art in Milan were made to commissions by the archbishops. Among the various saints represented on the mosaics in the 4th-century votive chapel of S Vittore in Ciel d'Oro (in S Ambrogio) is St Ambrose, who was the first to play a leading role in the city's civic and artistic life. He probably inspired the construction in Milan of three of the most important Early Christian basilicas: S Ambrogio, S Nazaro and S Simpliciano (*see* §IV, 2 and 5 below and EARLY CHRISTIAN AND BYZANTINE ART, §II, 2(i)). They were built after the construction, begun by 355, of S Tecla, which was later destroyed and replaced by the cathedral (begun in 1386), and of the Basilica Palatina, later renamed S Lorenzo (*see* §IV, 3 below). This church preserves two important apse mosaics in the side chapel of S Aquilino (see fig. 8).

The Lombard invasion of 568 destroyed the historical milieu in which Late Antique art still flourished but fostered the production of small examples of goldsmiths' work, notably those preserved in the treasury of Monza Cathedral. Around the time when Charlemagne conquered the Lombard kingdom (774), the classicism of the Carolingian *renovatio* spread in northern Italy. The highest artistic achievements around this time include the magnificent frescoes in S Maria Foris Portas, near Castelseprio, which date from the 7th or 8th century (for illustration *see* CASTELSEPRIO) and the Golden Altar (*c.* 835) of S Ambrogio, Milan, which was commissioned by Archbishop Angilbert II (*reg* 824–59) and signed by Vuolvinius the Smith (*see* CAROLINGIAN ART, §V and fig. 11). In the last quarter of the 10th century another archbishop, probably Gotfredus (*reg* 975–80), commissioned the reliefs on the ciborium above the altar of S Ambrogio. The style of these sculptures is related to that of such ivories as the SITULA (Milan, Tesoro Duomo), inscribed with the name of *Gotofredo*, and the plaque (983; Milan, Castello Sforzesco)

8. Milan, S Lorenzo, *Christ with the Apostles*, apse mosaic in the chapel of S Aquilino, late 4th century AD or early 5th

with a representation of Otto II, Theophanu and their infant son adoring Christ enthroned.

The beginning of the 11th century is marked by the cycle of frescoes in the basilica of S Vincenzo at Galliano (near Cantù, Como), datable soon after 1007 and commissioned by Ariberto d'Antimiano, Archbishop of Milan (*reg* 1018–44). The painters probably followed Byzantine iconographic models, and the style of the frescoes, while based on the Western tradition, recalls Constantinopolitan paintings. Archbishop Arnolfo III (*reg* 1093–7) is thought to have ordered the rebuilding of several churches including the Benedictine monastery and S Calocero in Civate (nr Lecco) and S Pietro al Monte and S Benedetto, on a hill near the town. The iconographic programme of the frescoes in these churches emphasizes the passage of mankind from earthly slavery (e.g. the *Ten Plagues of Egypt*; S Calocero) to the Heavenly Jerusalem (e.g. the frescoes in S Pietro, which include *Christ in the Heavenly Jerusalem* and the *Four Rivers of Paradise*).

Only a few fragments of 12th-century frescoes survive in the city's churches, mainly votive images showing saints or the Virgin and Child. From the same period there are, however, numerous Milanese manuscripts with illuminated initials and delicate racemes in the shape of intertwined spirals, probably based on French models. The majestic Trivulzio Candlestick (Milan Cathedral) is a French masterpiece produced *c.* 1210, probably from the circle of Nicholas of Verdun, and it represents the same decorative type as the manuscripts. It is possible to identify the activities of important painters only from the 13th century, including the Master of the de Cottis grave, who

frescoed the tomb of *Guglielmo de Cottis* (*d* 1267; Milan, S Ambrogio). A number of works may be attributed to the Master of Angera, named after the fresco cycle in the castle at Angera; these depict the victory of Archbishop Ottone Visconti over his rivals, the Torriani family, at the Battle of Desio (1277). In many ways the paintings, which were probably produced immediately after the battle, put an end to the series of commissions by Milanese archbishops; the city's princes, beginning with the Visconti, took over as leading patrons.

BIBLIOGRAPHY
P. Toesca: *La pittura e la miniatura nella Lombardia: Dai più antichi monumenti alla metà del quattrocento* (Milan, 1912, rev. 1966)
C. Bertelli, ed.: *Città del vescovo dai Carolingi al Barbarossa* (Milan, 1988)
For further bibliography *see* §I, 1 above.

GIOVANNI VALAGUSSA

2. 1278–1499.

(i) *Artistic organization.* Milanese artists, like members of other professions, were organized into corporations, of which the oldest surviving statutes date from the 14th century. The three types of corporation that artists could join were the *paratici, università* and *scuole*. The differences among these organizations are not entirely clear, particularly as the terms are often used interchangeably in corporation documents. It would appear that *scuole* were fraternal organizations devoid of any legal status; they were similar to religious confraternities, but created for workers in a particular trade or craft. The *scuola* aspiring to the status of *università* was required to draw up, or revise, its statutes and submit them for approval to the

Ufficio di Provvisione, whence they would be passed to the duke for final confirmation. The corporation would then become a legally recognized *università*, entitled to the duke's protection; in addition to privileges, recognition brought with it certain obligations, mostly financial, to the State. The *paratico* differed from the *università* chiefly in that its privileges were greater and its civic obligations correspondingly heavier.

Of the artists' corporations, perhaps the oldest is the goldsmiths', which was established as a *scuola* as early as 1311 and had its statutes formulated in 1343; by the end of the century at least, it had requested and received official confirmation as a *paratico*. Other artists' organizations were less ambitious, or perhaps less willing to shoulder the financial burden imposed on the *paratici*. The painters and woodworkers first formed *scuole*, then (reluctantly at that) *università*, but did not choose to advance further. These bodies were intended to regulate the activities of their members and so ensure a high standard of craftsmanship. It should be noted that in Milan, unlike Florence, for example, there was no legal limit on the number of corporations that might exist, and so no *arti* operated under the control of larger and more important organizations. Neither did the Milanese corporations have significant political power or influence: the rules of commerce were fixed by the Ufficio di Provvisione, technically an organ of the Commune but actually subservient to the State.

The painters' *arte* was probably founded towards the end of the 14th century, although there is no documentary information regarding its establishment. The earliest reference to its activity is a notarial act from 1438 concerning the election of officials for the Scuola di S Luca. In 1481 the painters drew up statutes and—under pressure from the duke—requested recognition as a *università*. This was presumably granted (in later documents the organization is always referred to as a *università*), although no record of the event or the statutes, said to consist of 29 articles, has survived. It is clear, however, that the corporation was governed by an annually elected prior and a board of 12 syndics, who were appointed for life. These officers were assisted by a *canepario* (a kind of treasurer), a notary and a messenger. Members, all qualified masters, were obliged to pay annual dues, inscribe their names in the *matricola* and doubtless to inform the prior if they decided to take an apprentice (in all the surviving artisans' statutes, the number of apprentices that any single master could employ is strictly limited). The prior was empowered to settle disputes among members or between a member and his client, and fine any member who contravened the corporation's statutes.

The sculptors had no universal professional organization, although stonecutters employed by the cathedral workshop were members of the Scuola dei Quattro Coronati. Major figure sculptors, however, whether they worked at the cathedral or not, did not belong, perhaps because the demand for sculpture was limited, other than for the most important projects, and the number of independent figure sculptors active at any one time was correspondingly small.

JANICE SHELL

(ii) Stylistic development and patronage. In the 14th century the Gothic style was introduced by such artists as GIO-VANNI DI BALDUCCIO, who apparently arrived in Milan in 1334 and whose most important works include the shrine of St Peter Martyr (signed and dated 1339) in the Dominican church of S Eustorgio (*see* GOTHIC, §III, 1(iv)(c) and fig. 40). Giotto, who painted frescoes (*c.* 1335; destr.) in Azzo Visconti's palace, was Azzo's other main artistic import, and this discernment was continued by succeeding members of the Visconti family, including Bernabò Visconti and Galeazzo II Visconti, whose commissions included work by the Gothic sculptor Bonino da Campione. In the late 14th century Gian Galeazzo Visconti (see fig. 9) presided over an influx of artists employed to work on the cathedral (*see* §IV, 1(ii) below), not only Italians, including Giovannino de Grassi (*see* GRASSI, DE, (1)), but also such foreigners as Lasse of Hungary (*fl* 1391) and Hans Fernach (*fl* 1387–94). In the 15th century sculpture at the cathedral was dominated by Italians, including Matteo Raverti and Giovanni Antonio Amadeo, who were active at the beginning and end of the century respectively, and whose work demonstrates how Milanese sculptors turned from Gothic to Renaissance forms.

A similar development also occurred in the work of Milanese painters in this period. The Late Gothic style is exemplified by wall paintings of ball games and other activities (first half of the 15th century; Milan, Pal.

9. Giovannino de Grassi (attrib.): *King David Blessing* and *Gian Galeazzo Visconti*, 247×175 mm; miniature from the Visconti Hours, before 1395 (Florence, Bib. N. Cent., MS. Banco Rari 397, fol. 115)

Borromeo). As the century progressed, however, the new Renaissance style was encouraged by various patrons, including the Florentine Pigello Portinari (*d* 1468), the representative of the Medici Bank in Milan. Between 1462 and 1466 he built the Portinari Chapel in S Eustorgio, which is decorated with remarkable frescoes of the *Life of St Peter Martyr* (late 1460s; *see* FOPPA, VINCENZO, §1 and fig. 1). Portinari also helped finance the building of S Pietro in Gessate (1447–75). Its other patrons included Ambrogio Grifi (*d* 1493), whose burial chapel contains a fresco cycle depicting the *Life of St Ambrose* (1490–93) by Bernardino Butinone and Bernardo Zenale, and the coloured marble tomb of *Ambrogio Grifi* by BENEDETTO BRIOSCO. The Sforza family were particularly important patrons. Their commissions included the decoration of the Castello Sforzesco by such artists as Bonifacio Bembo (*see* BEMBO, (1)) and Stefano de Fedeli (*fl* 1472–81), including frescoes in the ducal chapel (1473). As well as his architectural projects (*see* §I, 2 above), Bramante produced a number of decorative designs, including a coloured terracotta frieze of putti and male busts (executed by Agostino Fonduli in 1483) for the baptistery of S Maria presso S Satiro and the wall painting of the *Argus* (*c.* 1490–93) in the Cortile della Rocchetta of the Castello Sforzesco.

Apart from Bramante, the most significant artist in Milan during the late 15th century was Leonardo da Vinci, who by 1483 had arrived at the court of Ludovico Sforza (*see* LEONARDO DA VINCI, §I, 2). He was involved in designing various spectacles, such as the *Festa del paradiso*, staged as a wedding celebration in 1490, and was also able to pursue his diverse intellectual interests. Despite the range of his activities, Leonardo executed a number of important paintings in Milan, most notably the fresco of the *Last Supper* (*c.* 1495–*c.* 1497) in the refectory of S Maria delle Grazie. He also designed a bronze equestrian monument to *Francesco Sforza* (unexecuted). The clay model (untraced) that he displayed in 1494 seems to have been one of the many casualties of the French conquest of Milan in 1499, and Leonardo himself left the city in December of that year.

BIBLIOGRAPHY
L. Beltrami: *Il castello di Milano sotto il dominio dei Visconti e degli Sforza* (Milan, 1894)
F. Malaguzzi-Valeri: *Milano*, i–ii (Bergamo, 1906)
——: *Bramante e Leonardo* (1915), ii of *La corte di Ludovico il Moro* (Milan, 1913–23)
C. Ponzoni: *Le chiese di Milano* (Milan, 1930)
R. Cipriani, G. A. Dell'Acqua and F. Russoli: *La cappella Portinari in Sant'Eustorgio a Milano* (Milan, 1963)
G. Lise: *Santa Maria presso San Satiro* (Milan, 1974)
E. Brivio and A. Majo: *Il duomo di Milano nella storia e nell'arte* (Milan, 1977)
E. Brivio: *La scultura del duomo di Milano: La fede narrata nel marmo di Candoglia* (Milan, 1982)
M. T. Fiorio, ed.: *Le chiese di Milano* (Milan, 1985)
G. Lopez, A. S. Tosini and L. M. Rossi: *Il Castello Sforzesco di Milano* (Milan, 1986)
P. C. Marani, R. Cecchi and G. Mulazzani: *Il Cenacolo e Santa Maria delle Grazie* (Milan, 1986)

3. 1500–1714. In the opening years of the 16th century the brilliant Renaissance culture of the Sforza court remained important. Vincenzo Foppa, dominant in the reign of Ludovico Sforza, was succeeded by Ambrogio Bergognone. With the arrival of the French, Bramantino served the Francophile general Gian Giacomo Trivulzio, for whom he made cartoons for 12 tapestries of *The Months* (1501–8; Milan, Castello Sforzesco), woven in Vigevano; in 1525 Bramantino became official architect and painter to Francesco Maria Sforza, who also patronized Giovanni Girolamo Savoldo. Leonardo da Vinci was again in Milan from 1508 to 1513, where he completed the *Virgin of the Rocks* (London, N.G.) and served the French and Trivulzio. Leonardo's writings stimulated an interest in art theory, which later found expression in the writings of Giovanni Paolo Lomazzo and Gregorio Comanini. The most distinguished of Leonardo's heirs were Giovanni Antonio Boltraffio, Andrea Solario, Cesare de Sesto and Bernardo Luini. The large family workshop headed by Luini, together with that of the Piedmontese artist Guadenzio Ferrari, dominated Milanese painting in the mid-16th century.

Under Spanish rule artists from outside Milan were favoured. Charles V gave a house in Milan to LEONE LEONI, where the sculptor created what was perhaps the first private art gallery in Milan. Leoni executed several imperial commissions in Milan, and his monument to *Gian Giacomo de' Medici* (completed 1563; Milan Cathedral) brought an awareness of Michelangelo's classicism to the city. The Spanish governor of Milan, Alfonso d'Avalos (1502–46), commissioned from Titian the *Marques del Vasto Addressing his Soldiers* (Madrid, Prado), which Titian himself brought to Milan in 1541; Titian was also commissioned (1540) by the Confraternità della Santa Corona to paint the *Christ Crowned with Thorns* (1540–42; Paris, Louvre) for a chapel in the church of S Maria delle Grazie, Milan. Other Venetian works in Milan were Jacopo Tintoretto's *Christ among the Doctors* (Milan, Mus. Duomo) and canvases by Paris Bordone and Moretto in S Maria presso S Celso.

Carlo Borromeo and his cousin Federico Borromeo (*see* BORROMEO, (1) and (2)) left a deep imprint on the cultural and artistic history of the city. Carlo Borromeo brought Pellegrino Tibaldi with him from Rome in 1565, and with him the influence of Michelangelo. His patronage, informed by his belief in the didactic purpose of art, encouraged the production of clear and direct religious narratives, drawn from the Bible or lives of the saints. Scenes from the *Life of Christ* (1578–82) were painted for the charterhouse at Garegnano by the Bergamese Simone Peterzano, while the Cremonese brothers Antonio Campi and Vincenzo Campi, who directed a large family studio, were active in the church of S Paolo Converso (1586–9). Caravaggio was apprenticed to Peterzano in 1584. In the 1580s the Procaccini family moved from Bologna to Milan, and Camillo Procaccini became a leading painter of straightforward religious illustrations. Camillo was the protégé of Pirro Visconti, a distinguished collector, and produced cabinet pictures and drawings for private collectors. The cathedral workshop remained a powerful patron. The high altar was designed by Tibaldi, the organ shutters (for which a competition was held in 1590) painted by Giuseppe Meda (*d* 1599), Ambrogio Figino and Camillo Procaccini, and the marble enclosure around the presbytery decorated with carvings by Francesco Brambilla the younger.

Federico Borromeo settled in Milan in 1601, where he became official overseer of ecclesiastical art. In this period the most distinguished Lombard painters, who included Daniele Crespi, Cerano and Morazzone, worked in Milan. Cerano, Giulio Cesare Procaccini, Morazzone and others were commissioned to produce two cycles of pictures (Milan, Mus. Duomo) of the *Life and Miracles of St Carlo Borromeo* (see fig. 10) to be hung on the piers of the cathedral, which were intended both to celebrate Carlo Borromeo as the perfect embodiment of Counter-Reformation sanctity and, through an intense realism, to invite the participation of the faithful in the episodes represented.

Federico had a deep interest in art and culture as instruments for upholding the faith. In 1607 he founded the Biblioteca Ambrosiana and in 1618 the Pinacoteca Ambrosiana, where he displayed works by Italian Renaissance artists, landscapes and still-lifes by Flemish artists such as Jan Breughel the elder and Paul Bril, and copies of celebrated Roman frescoes. The influence of the Scuola di S Luca had diminished from the mid-16th century, and in 1613 Federico decided to set up an Accademia del Disegno attached to the Biblioteca Ambrosiana, for which he solicited the advice of the collector Girolamo Borsieri (1588–1629) and of Ludovico Carracci. He wished that its members should dedicate themselves to the creation of a

religious art responsive to the tenets of Tridentine theology. It was to be directed by three masters—a painter, a sculptor and an architect—and their activity, and that of the 24 scholars, was to be strictly limited to instruction and study. Emphasis was placed on making copies of assigned works and producing original inventions developed from selected themes, on the study of the nude in the approved 'classical' manner and on the execution of prints, as that medium was of fundamental importance for the diffusion of sacred images.

The plague of 1629–30 and the political decline of the city had a dampening effect on artistic activity. Yet Cesare Monti, who became Archbishop in 1631, was a passionate collector, who created the Archbishop's Gallery of 16th- and 17th-century paintings of the Lombard–Venetian school, now divided between the Brera and the Palazzo Arcivescovile, Milan. It seems that Borromeo's academy was disbanded during the plague. Although it was decided to reopen it in 1667, it was not inaugurated until 1668, owing to a dispute between the followers of the painter Antonio Busca and those of the sculptor Dionigi Bussola. The academicians immediately set about not only making copies, as before, but also furnishing decorations for the Ambrosiana itself, the most important of which was a series of four large canvases illustrating scenes from the

10. Daniele Crespi: *St Carlo Borromeo Erecting the Crosses at the Gate to Milan*, tempera on canvas, 4.75×6.00 m, 1602–3 (Milan, Museo del Duomo)

Life of Federico Borromeo. Yet conflicts within the organization hampered progress, and by the end of the century the Accademia Ambrosiana had lost much of its prestige. At that time a rival institution, the Accademia di S Luca, was founded, about which little is known.

New elements were introduced into Milanese painting by the presence of Sebastiano Ricci, who frescoed the *Souls of the Blessed Ascending to Heaven* (1694–5) in S Bernardino alle Ossa, and by the arrival of works by Salvator Rosa, including *St Paul the Hermit* (1662; Milan, Brera) for the Milanese church of S Maria della Vittoria. The last generation of 17th-century Milanese painters, among them Filippo Abbiati (1640–1715), Stefano Maria Legnani (1660–1715) and Andrea Lanzani, lightened the dark and gloomy atmosphere of late 17th-century Lombard painting, introducing lighter colours and a more original iconography that anticipates the Rococo.

BIBLIOGRAPHY
A. Santagostino: *L'immortalità del pennello, ovvero catalogo delle pitture insigni che stanno esposte al pubblico nella città di Milano* (Milan, 1671); ed. M. Bona Castellotti (Milan, 1980)
C. Torre: *Ritratto di Milano* (Milan, 1714)
G. Mongeri: *L'arte in Milano* (Milan, 1872)
A. Paredi, G. A. dell' Acqua and L. Vitali: *L'Ambrosiana* (Milan, 1968)
M. Valsecchi: *Gli arazzi dei 'Mesi' del Bramantino* (Milan, 1968)
Il seicento lombardo, 3 vols (exh. cat., Milan, Pal. Reale, 1973)
Omaggio a Tiziano: La cultura artistica milanese nell' età di Carlo V (exh. cat. by B. W. Meijer, Milan, Pal. Reale, 1977)
A. Paredi: *Storia dell'Ambrosiana* (Milan, 1981)
La Ca' Granda: Cinque secoli di storia e d'arte dell'Ospedale Maggiore di Milano (exh. cat. by G. Testori and others, Milan, Pal. Reale, 1981)
M. Bona Castellotti: *La pittura lombarda del seicento* (Milan, 1985)
J. Shell: *Painters in Milan, 1490–1530* (diss., New York U., 1986)
I Piazza da Lodi: Una tradizione di pittori del cinquecento (Milan, 1989)
Il settecento lombardo (exh. cat., ed. R. Bossaglia and V. Terraroli; Milan, Pal. Reale, 1991)
G. A. Dell' Acqua: *La maniera nella pittura lombarda dal 1550 al 1630* (Milan, n.d.)

MARCO CARMINATI, JANICE SHELL

4. AFTER 1714. The end of Spanish rule brought a period of artistic revival to the city. In the first half of the century Milanese artists tended to follow in the footsteps of Abbiati, Lanzani and Legnani (*see* §3 above). More innovative painters came from outside Milan, including the Genoese Alessandro Magnasco and the Venetian Giambattista Tiepolo (*see* TIEPOLO, (1)). Tiepolo spent several extended periods in Milan, during which he executed various frescoes, for example the *Chariot of the Sun* (1740; *see* ITALY, fig. 40) on the great vaulted ceiling of the Palazzo Clerici. The indifference of Milanese painters to this magnificent Baroque work may be due to the presence of Alessandro Verri (1741–1816), Pietro Verri (1728–97), Cesare Beccaria (1738–94) and Giuseppe Parini (1729–99), who made the city one of the most influential centres of the Enlightenment and laid the basis for Neoclassicism. The Accademia di Belle Arti, which was established in 1770 and transferred in 1773 to the Palazzo dei Gesuiti in Brera, made a decisive contribution to the spread of Neo-classicism. It brought together the painter and engraver GIULIANO TRABALLESI, the engraver Domenico Aspari (1745–1831), the architect, decorator and teacher Giocondo Albertolli (*see* ALBERTOLLI, (1)) and the furniture-maker Giuseppe Maggiolini, who together contributed to the development of Lombard Neoclassicism.

In 1795 the entry of Napoleon's troops into Milan forced many artists compromised by collaboration with the Austrian rulers to leave the city, including Piermarini. The interior decoration of Piermarini's Palazzo Reale continued under the leadership of the Milanese painter ANDREA APPIANI, who became the official painter of the French Emperor. He produced some important celebratory fresco cycles in the Palazzo Reale, such as the *Apotheosis of the Emperor Napoleon* (1808; now Tremezzo, Villa Carlotta; see fig. 11), and the 35 episodes illustrating the *Feats of Napoleon* (1807; destr.). The most important event for the city's art life during the Napoleonic occupation was the creation of the Pinacoteca di Brera next to the Accademia. Originally endowed with works confiscated in the Veneto, the Marches and Emilia, the museum was further enriched under the administration of GIUSEPPE BOSSI and Appiani. It opened in 1809 in rooms obtained through the demolition of S Maria di Brera, and by 1812 it had 800 paintings, which were listed in the *Inventario Napoleonico*, a catalogue that was updated until 1842.

During the years of the Austrian restoration (1815–59) the city became the cultural centre of the liberal, Romantic movements that fostered the Italian Risorgimento. A notable exponent of this culture was FRANCESCO HAYEZ, who painted several pictures in the sentimental manner that became the trademark of Lombard historical Romanticism. Other fine landscape painters, for example GIOVANNI MIGLIARA, Angelo Inganni (1806–80) and Giuseppe Bisi (1787–1869), painted scenes showing 19th-century Milan. Hayez and Luigi Sabatelli taught at the Accademia; Domenico Induno and Gerolamo Induno (*see* INDUNO) were among their students. The city gained new civic museums in the castle, and some private art collections were opened to the public. Outstanding among the latter was that of GIAN GIACOMO POLDI PEZZOLI, who left to the city his house in Via Manzoni with an extraordinary collection of paintings dating from the Renaissance to the 18th century, porcelain, armour and other objects. Cesare Tallone taught at the Accademia.

In the field of painting the GLI SCAPIGLIATI movement came to prominence, supported by such artists as Federico Faruffini, Daniele Ranzoni, LUIGI CONCONI, GIUSEPPE GRANDI and TRANQUILLO CREMONA. Working alongside these artists was Mosè Bianchi, who produced popular, sentimental paintings. Gli Scapigliati continued to influence such artists as Giovanni Segantini, GAETANO PREVIATI and Medardo Rosso, who were linked with the Divisionist movement, and at this time the Famiglia Artistica, an exhibiting group, was active in the city.

Milan was still an avant-garde city at the beginning of the 20th century, when the founders of the Futurist movement gathered there (*see* FUTURISM). Filippo Tommaso Marinetti was the guiding spirit, while UMBERTO BOCCIONI, LUIGI RUSSOLO and CARLO CARRÀ were among the most sensitive interpreters of Futurism. The first Futurist exhibition, the *Mostra d'arte libera*, was held in 1911 in the former Ricordi factory. Meanwhile, the city acquired numerous palazzi in the *Stile Liberty*; the elegant interior decoration, including wrought-ironwork, was often entrusted to ALESSANDRO MAZZUCOTELLI, who ran the Scuola d'Arte Decorativa di Monze from 1922. Other

11. Andrea Appiani: *Apotheosis of the Emperor Napoleon*, detached fresco (1808) from the Palazzo Reale, Milan (Tremezzo, Villa Carlotta)

major movements in 20th-century Italian painting also found expression in Milan. The NOVECENTO ITALIANO developed around the Galleria Pesaro, with Achille Funi, Mario Sironi, Adolfo Wildt and Piero Marussig among its most vigorous exponents. The Chiaristi and CORRENTE groups also formed and attracted such artists as Aligi Sassú, Renato Birolli, Giuseppe Migneco (*b* 1908), Bruno Cassinari, Ennio Morlotti and Ernesto Treccani (*b* 1920). The first Italian abstract painters gathered around the Galleria Il Milione, for example Osvaldo Licini and Antonio Corpora.

In the late 20th century Milan was one of the most important centres of contemporary art in Italy; it welcomed the main post-war avant-garde movements—the Fronte Nuovo delle Arti, Neo-cubist Realism and the Movimento Arte Concreta, as well as *Spazialismo* and *Arte nucleare*, both inspired by the work of Lucio Fontana, the conceptual art of PIERO MANZONI and the Pop art of Valerio Adami and Emilio Tadini. Sculpture has flourished with the influence of GIACOMO MANZÙ and MARINO MARINI and the civic works of the Cascella brothers, ARNALDO POMODORO, Giuseppe Spagnolo and Igor Mitora.

BIBLIOGRAPHY

S. Pagani: *La pittura lombarda della Scapigliatura* (Milan, 1955)

A. Ottino della Chiesa: *L'età neoclassica in Lombardia* (Como, 1959)

L. Marchetti: *La galleria di Milano* (Milan, 1967)

F. Bellonzi and T. Fiori: *Archivi del divisionismo*, 2 vols (Milan, 1968)

E. Piceni and M. Monteverdi: *Pittura lombarda dell'ottocento* (Milan, 1969)

Andrea Appiani: Pittore di Napoleone (exh. cat., ed. M. Precerutti Garberi; Milan, Gal. A. Mod., 1969)

A. M. Brizio and others: *Mostra dei maestri di Brera, 1776–1859* (Milan, 1975)

Inventario Napoleonico (R Milan, 1976)

A. Scotti: *Brera, 1776–1815: Nascita e sviluppo di una istituzione culturale milanese* (Florence, 1979)

G. Anziani and L. Caramel: *Scultura moderna in Lombardia* (Milan, 1981)

Hayez (exh. cat., ed. M. T. Gozzoli and F. Mazzocca; Milan, Pal. Reale and Brera; 1983)

Divisionismo italiano (Milan, 1990)

Il settecento lombardo (exh. cat., ed. R. Bossaglia and V. Terraroli; Milan, Pal. Reale, 1991)

MARCO CARMINATI

III. Centre of production.

1. ROCK CRYSTAL. In the course of the 16th century Milan became the most important centre in Europe for the production of vases and plaques of rock crystal, a material that was readily available near the St Gotthard Pass. Whole families of artisans specialized in this craft and from the mid-16th century were patronized by the most important courts of Europe.

Production consisted mostly of engraved plaques decorated with complex religious or mythological scenes, plant motifs and portraits, used to embellish furniture and vases. Carved and engraved vases, however, made not only of rock crystal but also of pietre dure formed the most important production of these craftsmen, who could create bizarre designs inspired by the natural form of the rock crystal. The most frequent forms were those of fantastic animals, birds, fish and ships. Ewers and goblets could also be adorned with whimsical handles in the shape of monsters and lids decorated with bird heads or lions (e.g. ewer, *c.* 1570–80; Munich, Residenzmus.). These splendid ornamental vases were often further embellished with elaborate enamelled gold mounts.

In most instances it remains difficult to identify the production of individual workshops; despite the large number of surviving vases, there is little documentation. The stylistic criteria adopted by Kris in 1929 are still the fundamental point of departure, although some of these have been called into question by recent archival work.

The workshop of the Saracchi brothers (Giovanni Ambrogio, *b* 1540; Simone, *b* 1547; Stefano, *b* 1550; Michele; Raffaello) produced many objects (*see* ROCK CRYSTAL, fig. 1), but is particularly associated with vessels in the form of a ship. A ewer decorated with engraved scenes from the life of Moses (Munich, Residenzmus.) was made for Albert V, Duke of Bavaria, and was still in his possession in 1579. Another, made by the same family in Florence, was probably created for the marriage of Ferdinand I de' Medici and Christine of Lorraine in 1589. This also has scenes of the life of Moses, with additional images of knights and a figure of Neptune on the lid. It has splendid enamelled gold mounts, with handles in the form of *termini*, and a carved, enamelled border set with cameos.

Ambrogio and Stefano Caroni (*d* 1611) moved from Milan to Florence in 1572, followed in 1575 by Giorgio Gafurri and his sons Cristofano and Bernardino (*d* 1606), who had been invited by the Medici to set up specialized workshops for the Florentine court; these artisans produced many important vases, which are documented in the Medici inventories of the second half of the 16th century (*see* FLORENCE, §III, 2(i)). Another important family of carvers originally from Milan, the MISERONI, are also well documented, particularly for their activities in Prague.

The sculptor ANNIBALE FONTANA produced vases decorated with complex mythological scenes and carved plant motifs and crystal plaques with allegories of the seasons for a small chest (Madrid, Pal. Real). His two panels with figures of Jove and Juno recall the decoration of a jug from the Saracchi workshop, carved with allegories

of the elements (Florence, Pitti). Another Milanese craftsman active in the late 16th century and the early 17th, Giovan Battista Metellino, is known to have produced various works, among which is an interesting form of vase consisting of a dolphin with a carved shell resting against its head. Two such vases can be seen, in Florence at the Museo degli Argenti and in Dresden at the Grünes Gewölbe.

The production of Milanese craftsmen, while largely linked to commissions from Italian and European courts, also included some interesting pieces made for the local clergy, for example the Castiglioni monstrance with pearl and enamelled gold mounts (Milan, Tesoro Duomo). The execution of these works continued into the 17th century; in 1614, for example, Cerano produced the design for an urn in crystal and silver for S Carlo.

BIBLIOGRAPHY
DBI: 'Caroni'
E. Kris: *Meister und Meisterwerke der Steinschneidekunst in der italienische Renaissance*, 2 vols (Vienna, 1929/*R* 1979)
G. Weinholz: 'Zu Bergkristallarbeiten von Giovanni Battista Metellino', *Jb. Staatl. Kstsamml. Dresden* (1967), pp. 131–8
B. Heinzel-Wied: 'Studi sull'arte della scultura in pietre dure durante il rinascimento: I fratelli Sarachi', *Ant. Viva*, 6 (1973), pp. 37–58
R. Distelberger: 'Die Sarachi Werkstatt und Annibale Fontana', *Jb. Ksthist. Samml. Wien*, lxxi (1975), pp. 150–78
——: 'Die Steinschneidewerkstaetten der Miseroni in Mailand und Prag', *Jb. Ksthist. Samml. Wien*, lxxiv (1978), pp. 79–152
A. M. Massinelli and F. Tuena: *Treasures of the Medici* (London, 1992)

ANNA MARIA MASSINELLI

2. MAIOLICA. Although maiolica had been made in Milan from the 15th century, production reached its apogee when high-quality wares were made during the 18th century. Among the many workshops in production during the 18th century were those of Giuseppe Confalonieri (*fl* 1775–83), Pasquale Rubati (*fl* 1756–1796) and Felice Clerici (1745–88). Decoration, in both high-fired colours and enamels, included chinoiseries inspired by or imitating East-Asian porcelain, figures after the characters painted by Jacques Callot, flowers and characters from the *commedia dell'arte*. Sometimes the decorative motifs were worked in relief or were reserved in panels, imitative of contemporary French porcelain. The elegance of the wares and the high-quality enamelling, enriched with touches of gold, are distinctive features of Milanese maiolica.

BIBLIOGRAPHY
C. Baroni: *Le maioliche di Milano* (Milan, 1940)
Maioliche di Lodi, Milano e Pavia (exh. cat., Milan, Mus. Poldi Pezzoli, 1964)
G. Maggi: 'Maioliche di Lodi, Milano e Pavia', *Ant. Viva*, iv (1965), pp. 68–80

LUCIANA ARBACE

IV. Buildings.

1. Cathedral. 2. S Ambrogio. 3. S Lorenzo. 4. S Tecla. 5. S Simpliciano.

1. CATHEDRAL.

(i) Architecture. (ii) Sculpture. (iii) Treasury. (iv) Cathedral works.

(i) Architecture.

(a) Before c. 1400. Construction probably began on 23 May 1385, on the site of the ancient basilica of S Maria Maggiore, by order of Archbishop Antonio da Saluzzo, a cousin of Gian Galeazzo Visconti. At that time there were still two basilicas in the city: the 4th-century S Tecla and

S Maria Maggiore, which dated from the Carolingian period. Both were in a very precarious state, and after a few attempts at restoration it was decided to build a new cathedral. This was to have five aisles, as at S Maria Maggiore, but somewhat wider. The new building was orientated and, following usual practice, construction began at the east end, so that the Holy Sacrament could be placed in one of the two sacristies for the immediate consecration of the church. S Maria Maggiore was enclosed within the new perimeter and remained in use for some time; it was gradually demolished as the new construction progressed.

The work was carried out by an administrative body called the Superstantia, which had formerly been in charge of S Maria Maggiore. Following the discovery (1965–73) of brick walls under the present marble facing of the north sacristy and part of the apse, it was determined that the new building was originally designed to be built in brick, in keeping with the Lombard Gothic tradition. According to a tradition only partly confirmed by documents, as early as 1387 Gian Galeazzo Visconti ordered that the brickwork be replaced with marble, as part of his plan to transform Milan into one of the main artistic centres of Europe. On 23 October 1387 he assigned the marble quarrying rights for the cathedral to the quarries of Candoglia. Probably for economic reasons, or perhaps to avoid breaking with tradition, it was decided to retain those parts of the original project that had already been built and face them with marble. The adoption of the new material introduced various technical problems that were new to Lombard building practice although they were common in the construction of the great cathedrals of the Empire. For example, equipment was required for transporting and lifting blocks of marble to heights formerly unknown in Milanese building; furthermore, many different skills had to be coordinated at every level, from the ironworkers who designed and made the clips to hold the marble slabs together to the carpenters who built the new scaffolding.

In 1387 Visconti created a new, more complex administrative structure, the Fabbrica del Duomo (*see* §(iv) below). Simone da Orsenigo (*fl* 1387–95), who had formerly worked in the Superstantia, was appointed chief engineer of the Fabbrica at double his former salary. Under the direction of this body the new work began on 7 May 1387, as Simone da Orsenigo himself (mentioned in another source as a notary) witnessed in a document (untraced). In order to help resolve the technical problems that resulted from the adoption of marble Visconti also called in foreign architects, mostly those working on other Gothic cathedrals, as consultants. These men worked alongside the local masters and often came into conflict with them. This phase of works was marked by controversies over the planning and building of the cathedral; documents mention disputes with Simone da Orsenigo (perhaps as early as 1389) and these must have been acrimonious, for he left the project in 1391. In the meantime a low-relief portrait was mounted above the marble facing, which by then covered the external walls of the apse, under the large central window. It was a common practice in many Gothic cathedrals to commemorate the architect in a place of honour within the building

he had designed, but while such a figure was usually represented in a long working coat and with a square, a compass and a ruler, the figure in the Milanese effigy holds a pen, the emblem of a notary. If Simone da Orsenigo was indeed both a notary and an architect, he was certainly the subject of the portrait. As an architect he would have created at least the basic plan for the later structure, an achievement that would have warranted such recognition.

Already in 1389 Simone da Orsenigo was replaced by the Frenchman Nicolas de Bonaventure, who was called to direct the building of first elevations and who designed the apse windows (1390). In 1391 Hans von Freiburg (*fl* 1390–91), the next engineer of the Fabbrica, was asked to make a report on the works that had been carried out; in the same year Heinrich von Gmünd (of the Parler family)—who must have proposed the insertion of small chapels between the aisles—set out his observations on the new building in 11 points, which were discussed (1 May 1392) in a meeting of historic importance for the definition of the architectural scheme. Meanwhile, on 12 July 1391 the Italian architect and painter Giovannino de Grassi was appointed engineer of the Fabbrica and produced a wide range of works including the design of the pier capitals (see below and fig. 12). Towards the end of the 14th century work began on the Camposanto, which, like other Italian examples (e.g. Pisa), was meant to contain the tombs of principal figures associated with the cathedral. It was designed as a large porticoed cloister, adjacent to the cathedral apse, but building was soon interrupted and never resumed; it became the chapter house as well as the site of the workshop. By 1400 the cathedral's piers had been largely completed, and the question of vaulting had to be addressed. Jean Mignot (*d* 1410), a master from

12. Milan Cathedral, interior of nave looking east, begun 1385

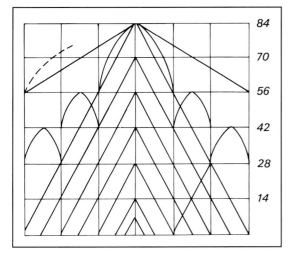

84

70

56

42

28

14

13. Milan Cathedral, cross-section designed by Gabriele Stornaloco, 1391

Paris, was asked for an assessment of the construction and he reported that a number of errors had been made. Further experts were invited, including Bernardo da Venezia (*fl* 1391–1428) and Bartolino da Novara, who proposed the building of a chapel in the retrochoir.

The construction of the cathedral disrupted the urban fabric and led to the destruction of some ancient buildings. For example, the first section to be built, the north sacristy, was erected on one of Milan's most sacred sites, the area of the baptistery of S Stefano alle Fonti. Similarly, the cathedral façade was later built on the baptistery of S Giovanni alle Fonti. The regular articulation of space in the cathedral was also related to the earlier structures. This is evident in the apse and the twin sacristies, which were part of the original plan and which must have been built during the first stage of construction. Each sacristy is built in the *ad quadratum* system and on a module of 16 braccia (9.5 m), based on the measurements of the earlier church. This module determines the width of each of the four aisles (9.5 m); the nave is twice as wide (19 m). The architect would have used this module to determine the dimensions of various elements of the structure, and these resulting dimensions can undoubtedly also be linked with symbolic meanings. For example, the most significant numbers in the 'Heavenly Jerusalem'—72 and 144—correspond to the length of the choir and the maximum width of the cathedral measured in braccia. Similarly, the number of weeks in the liturgical calendar matches that of the 52 piers, which are arranged in the *ad quadratum* system and bounded by the position of the two ancient baptisteries. At the same time some aspects of the complex design may have originated in the freemasonries, institutions that brought together such leading master builders as Simone da Orsenigo; members of these groups shared not only technical expertise but also a particular symbolism inspired by the builder's trade.

The overall plan (in the form of a Latin cross with a nave and four aisles) is based on the *ad quadratum* system and initially the cross-section was designed on the same principle. This was, however, changed to the *ad triangulum*

system, with the cross-section based on an equilateral triangle. The various problems stemming from this change were resolved in 1391 by Gabriele Stornaloco (see fig. 13), a mathematician who had been working on the cathedral of Piacenza (for further discussion *see* MASON (i), §IV, 3(iii)).

The cathedral's exterior is notable for its high plinth, which is unusual in the Gothic tradition (see fig. 14). It is closer to the Lombard Romanesque both in its height (7 m), which reduces the ascending effect of the structure, and in the relatively slight projection of the exterior buttresses, which are uniform in section. Their regular spacing matches that of the internal piers (also of uniform section). An impression of accentuated vertical thrust is created by the eight shafts of the piers, but this is interrupted by the tall capitals (6 m high; see fig. 12 above). The latter—designed by Giovannino de Grassi in the form of sculptured tabernacles—seem to form a line of separation, above which the vaults appear to be detached; the effect is not at all Gothic. The responds above the capitals are identically profiled to the pier shafts below. Higher still, at the springing of the vaults, the imposts are held together by chains, as was often done in Romanesque churches to reinforce the whole structure. A similar function is served by the second set of vaults, superimposed above the first. This must have been designed from the start with a view to the present, unusual terraced roof, realized in the 19th century. The aisle windows span only one third of the distance between the external buttresses and as such they are a good deal narrower than in most Gothic churches (although the three rose windows of the apse are larger than others of the period). Nevertheless,

14. Milan Cathedral, view from the south-east, begun 1385

as in contemporary cathedrals, the stained glass was conceived as one of the main decorative features, alongside the statuary and ornamental carvings.

BIBLIOGRAPHY

Il Duomo di Milano: Dizionario storico, artistico e religioso (Milan, 1986)
G. B. Sannazzaro: 'Duomo di Milano', *Dizionario della Chiesa Ambrosiana*, ii (Milan, 1988), pp. 1080–87
G. B. Sannazzaro and G. Sironi: 'Per Simone da Orsenigo ingegnere e notaio', *A. Crist.*, lxxvii (1989), p. 403
G. B. Sannazzaro: 'La cattedrale', *Stor. Milano* (in preparation)

(b) After c. *1400.* Until the fall of the Visconti (1447) construction works in the cathedral were directed by Filippino degli Organi (*fl* 1400–50), under whom the vaults in the apse area were completed and the transept arms built. The old basilica of S Maria Maggiore was partly enclosed when work began on the main vessel beyond the crossing. Intensive architectural activity was resumed under Francesco Sforza (*reg* 1450–66). Parts of the Palazzo Ducale and the remains of S Giovanni alle Fonti and S Tecla were demolished in order to make space for the new cathedral and the square, and in 1456 a red marble column was placed to mark the position planned for the new façade of the cathedral. (The façade of S Maria Maggiore was reassembled and erected there in 1489 as a temporary measure.)

Around 1470 Guiniforte Solari began to solve the problem of the lantern (or *tiburio*). The original plan must already have determined that it was to be positioned above the crossing of the nave and transept, and its central role in the cathedral's iconographic programme must also have been established. Evidence survives to indicate that the lantern was to symbolize God Enthroned, surrounded by four spires representing the Evangelists. In order to reinforce further the four large pointed arches already erected to support the lantern, Solari added four round arches without vertical members—a structural system that was also being experimented with in the same period at Clairvaux Abbey and in the Certosa di Pavia (also designed by Solari). Thus the complicated structural problems posed by the lantern led to the most important architectural debate of the 15th century. The Austrian Hans Niesenberger was engaged as engineer of the Fabbrica in 1483 but dismissed after only three years; he was the last specialist from northern Europe to be employed in this capacity. Luca Fancelli, Leonardo and Bramante were consulted in 1487, while Pietro da Gorgonzola (*fl* 1488–90) and Giovanni Majer were asked the following year. The debate over the lantern continued in 1490 with the appointment of Francesco di Giorgio Martini, Simone da Sirtori (*fl* 1490–1503) and GIOVANNI ANTONIO AMADEO; Amadeo completed the structure together with Giovanni Giacomo Dolcebuono. The lantern was finished on 25 September 1500 and shows a stylistic consistency and continuity with the rest of the building. Between 1507 and 1516 Amadeo built the first of the four large spires above the piers supporting the lantern; the last was not finished until the 19th century. Meanwhile, the problem of the portals at the ends of the transepts was under consideration from 1503, and in 1535 CRISTOFORO LOMBARDO worked out the final design. Two years later Vicenzo Seregni presented his overall design for the cathedral, with its façade flanked by two tall campanili at the corners.

The first Gothic phase of the cathedral's architecture ended in 1565, when Archbishop Carlo Borromeo came to Milan and introduced a period of classical, or 'Roman', design, aiming to turn the cathedral into a model Counter-Reformation church. In 1567 he appointed PELLEGRINO TIBALDI, who planned a grandiose classical façade and rearranged the interior to conform to the new liturgical practices. Tibaldi planned and built the new presbytery, installed the great tabernacle above the main altar to emphasize the Eucharistic rite against the negations of the Protestants, built the new canons' choir and completed the great organs. Two majestic pulpits were built against the nave piers that supported the lantern; the baptistery was placed in the centre while along the side walls Tibaldi planned a series of altars that permitted more frequent celebration of Mass.

The classical style was continued under Archbishop Federico Borromeo, after whose death (1631) the Gothic tradition again took hold. This is reflected in the history of the façade, the most controversial issue of the century. It was begun in the early 1600s to Tibaldi's design, and a few changes were made to the upper storey following suggestions by Francesco Maria Ricchini. In 1645 Carlo Buzzi proposed a new, Gothic design but retained Tibaldi's portals; other designs were later put forward by leading 17th- and 18th-century architects, including Carlo Giuseppe Merlo, Filippo Juvarra and Luigi Vanvitelli.

Meanwhile, the old façade was demolished in 1682 following the completion of the westernmost bays. Throughout the 17th century one of the most important projects inside the cathedral was the construction of the chapel of the Madonna dell'Albero, designed by Ricchini and others; the chapel directly opposite, dedicated to S Giovanni Buono, was finished in the 18th century. The main spire was erected (1767–70) by Francesco Croce (1696–1780), after the static problems involved were debated by various experts including the mathematicians Ruggero Boscovich and Francesco De Regis.

Following orders given by Napoleon in 1805 the façade was rapidly completed by Carlo Amati and Giuseppe Zanoia (1752–1817), largely following Buzzi's design. Work continued throughout the 19th century on the cathedral's final details, including the flying buttresses and the roof with its terraces and spires. A major international competition was held in 1886–8 for the design of a new façade; the winner was GIUSEPPE BRENTANO, but his design was never realized. The upper part of the façade was restored in 1935, and other works of restoration and maintenance were continued throughout the 20th century, including two particularly important projects (completed 1986): the restoration of the lantern piers and the refurbishment of the presbytery.

BIBLIOGRAPHY

C. L. V. Meeks: *Italian Architecture, 1750–1914* (New Haven and London, 1966), pp. 106, 230–37
Il Duomo di Milano: Dizionario storico, artistico e religioso (Milan, 1986)
G. B. Sannazzaro: 'La cattedrale', *Stor. Milano* (in preparation)

(ii) Sculpture. The earliest sculptures in the cathedral, including the sarcophagus of *Ariberto* and four pairs of *Apostles* (1185–7; for illustration *see* CAMPIONESI), were taken from S Maria Maggiore. The first works carved for the new cathedral date from the 14th century and include

the corbels of the base and the first *Giants* on the exterior and the sacristy portals (1393) by Giacomo da Campione and Hans Fernach (*fl* 1387–94) inside. These works are characterized by an agitated style and were executed by Italian and foreign sculptors including Lasse of Hungary (*fl* 1391), GIOVANNINO DE GRASSI, Pietro di Francia (*fl* 1393) and Annex Marchestens (*fl* 1390; *d* 1404). Other sculptors recorded in this period include Bernardo da Venezia (*fl* 1391–1428), who carved a *Virgin* (1392; Milan, Mus. Duomo); his son Nicolò da Venezia (*fl* 1399–1403); Jacobello dalle Masegne and Pierpaolo dalle Masegne, who were employed for a three-month trial period; and Giorgio Solari, who carved a statue of *St George* (1403–4; *in situ*) for the Carelli spire.

In the first half of the 15th century a greater proportion of Italian sculptors were working on the project, and their style was more subdued. Among them were Filippino degli Organi (*fl c.* 1400–50), Isacco da Imbonate (*fl* 1419), Alberto da Campione and Antonio Briosco (*fl* 1414–57); Jacopino da Tradate carved a statue of *Pope Martin V* (1421; Milan, Mus. Duomo); Paolino da Montorfano (*fl* 1402–30) worked on the large central window, while he and MATTEO RAVERTI also worked on the *Giants*. Sculptural activity in the second half of the 15th century was centred around Giovanni Antonio Amadeo; works produced at this time, for example the statues (inside the lantern) of *Prophets* and *Sibyls* (by the Master of S Paolo Eremita and sculptors from the circle of Cristoforo Mantegazza and Antonio Mantegazza) still exhibit Gothic elements.

This period was followed by a more classicizing one represented by such sculptors as Benedetto Briosco, Cristoforo Solari and AGOSTINO BUSTI, who introduced Leonardesque elements into their work. Great altarpieces and expressive statues were carved by Angelo Marini and MARCO D'AGRATE (e.g. the latter's *St Bartholomew*, 1562, in the south transept). At about the same time CRISTOFORO LOMBARDO and Francesco Brambilla the younger carried out the sculptural decoration of the chapel of the Madonna dell'Albero, and LEONE LEONI carved the monument to *Gian Giacomo de' Medici* (1560–63; *in situ*). From 1565 Brambilla, Pietro Antonio Daverio (*fl* 1588–1622), Marcantonio Prestinari (*d* 1621) and Gian Pietro Lasagna (*fl* 1611–58) were among those who contributed to the 'classical' transformation ordered by Carlo Borromeo. As part of this campaign GASPARE VISMARA carved low reliefs above the portals, to designs by Cerano Procaccini and Giulio Cesare Procaccini.

In 1621, following the bequest of Guido Mazenta, Federico Borromeo founded an important school of sculpture as part of the Accademia Ambrosiana. The teachers were *protostatuari* (chief sculptors of the Fabbrica) and over the centuries included GIAN ANDREA BIFFI, Gaspare Vismara, DIONIGI BUSSOLA, Carlo Simonetta (*d* 1693), Giuseppe Rusnati (*c.* 1650–1713), Carlo Francesco Mellone (*fl* 1695–1726), ELIA VINCENZO BUZZI, Carlo Maria Giudici (1723–84) and Grazioso Rusca (1757–1829).

Throughout the 19th century sculpture was subject to the control of the Accademia di Brera. The sculptures for the façade were completed by Pompeo Marchesi, CAMILLO PACETTI and Gaetano Monti of Ravenna, while Odoardo

Tabacchi, Giuseppe Grandi and Enrico Butti (1847–1932) continued the sculptural decoration of walls, capitals and spires. In 1906 Lodovico Pogliaghi (1857–1950) completed a pair of bronze doors with scenes from the *Life of the Virgin* for the central portal of the façade. From 1935 Filippo Tallone, Fausto Melotti, Eros Pellini and Tino Bartoletti worked on other sculptural decoration of the cathedral, while from 1937 to 1965 four more pairs of bronze doors were made for the other portals of the façade by Arrigo Minerbi (1881–1960), Giannino Castiglioni (1884–1971), Franco Lombardi (1891–1942) and Luciano Minguzzi. After World War II a number of statues in the cathedral were replaced with copies, and the originals were removed to the Museo del Duomo.

BIBLIOGRAPHY

U. Nebbia: *La scultura del Duomo di Milano* (Milan, 1909)
R. Bossaglia: 'Scultura', *Il Duomo di Milano*, ii (Milan, 1973), pp. 67–176
R. Bossaglia and M. Cinotti: *Il Tesoro e il Museo del duomo*, Milan Cathedral cat., ii (Milan, 1978)
——: 'Scultura', *Il Duomo di Milano: Dizionario storico, artistico e religioso* (Milan, 1986), pp. 536–43
G. B. Sannazzaro and G. Sironi: 'Per il tiburio del Duomo di Milano nuovi documenti', *A. Crist.*, lxxvii (1989), pp. 242–3
F. Tasso: 'I *Giganti* e le vicende della prima scultura del Duomo di Milano', *A. Lombarda*, 92–3 (1990), pp. 55–62

(iii) Treasury. Most of the cathedral's treasure is held in special exhibition rooms in the so-called Scurolo di S Carlo, an octagonal chapel designed by Francesco Maria Ricchini in 1606; objects still used in services are kept in the chapter sacristy. Some of the objects listed in the earliest inventories (15th century), many of which came from other churches, are still in the treasury. These include several ivory diptychs, for example the five-part diptych (late 5th century), the *Passion* diptych (early 9th century; *see* OTTONIAN ART, §VI) and the Greek diptych (late 10th–early 11th century), as well as the situla of Archbishop Gotfredus (*reg* 975–80; *see* SITULA), the cover of the Aribert Evangeliary (late 10th century–early 11th; MS. Inv. 1431) and the painting of the *Virgin of the Idea* (*c.* 1419), which has been attributed to Michelino da Besozzo. The Trivulzio candlestick (*c.* 1210) in the chapel of the Madonna dell'Albero was altered in 1561 (*see also* NICHOLAS OF VERDUN, §2(iii)). The inventory compiled for Carlo Borromeo in 1565 documents other surviving pieces, including the pax (early 1560s) of Pius IV, which has been attributed to Leone Leoni. In 1610, the year of Carlo's canonization, the Università degli Orefici donated the silver statue of *St Carlo Borromeo* designed by Gian Andrea Biffi. This stands on the high altar with a statue of *St Ambrose*, which was made by several artists, including Dionigi Bussola, and was donated in 1698. Of the documented tapestries, all that remain are the *Passion* (Brussels; *c.* 1540), which was possibly based on a cartoon by Michiel Coxcie, and three *Scenes from the Life of Moses* (1555–62) from the workshop of NICOLAS KARCHER. Among the numerous vestments, the frontals embroidered by Ludovica Antonia Pellegrini have been preserved; she also executed the standard of the Rosary, commissioned between 1584 and 1587. Many precious objects were offered to the scurolo during the 17th century (e.g. the Farnese and Airoldi chalices) and the 18th (e.g. the Cross of Maria-Theresa of Austria). Gifts in the 19th century included the Taverna credence table (1835), designed by Abbondio

Sangiorgio (1798–1879), and other objects have been donated in the 20th century. Precious articles from the Milanese churches of S Nazaro (including a silver casket of c. 382) and S Celso (e.g. the Cross of Clairvaux, Venice; last quarter of the 13th century) have been deposited on permanent loan in the treasury.

BIBLIOGRAPHY

R. Bossaglia and M. Cinotti: *Il Tesoro e il Museo del duomo*, Milan Cathedral cat. (Milan, 1978)

G. B. Sannazzaro: 'Tesoro', *Il Duomo di Milano: Dizionario storico, artistico e religioso* (Milan, 1986), pp. 601–10

N. Forti Grazzini: 'Arazzi', *Dizionario della chiesa Ambrosiana*, i (Milan, 1987), pp. 199–201

(iv) Cathedral works. An administrative council known as the Fabbrica del Duomo was set up to supervise the construction and decoration of the cathedral. The Superstantia that had administered the repair and conservation of the basilica of S Maria Maggiore was entrusted with the construction of the new cathedral, and the ancient basilica was gradually demolished as the new structure took shape. The substitution of marble for brick as the principal building material (*see* §(i)(a) above) brought technical and structural problems previously unknown to the Lombard building tradition, and consequently a broader and more complex administrative structure was required to coordinate the new works at every level and deal with the technical and administrative complications. The Fabbrica del Duomo was founded by Giangaleazzo Visconti on 16 October 1387. The fact that it replaced the Superstantia is confirmed by the appointment of the Master of the Works, Simone da Orsenigo, as chief engineer at double his former salary. It is probable that he was responsible for the initial design, in which he would have set out the basic plan.

The original document establishing the Fabbrica detailed its duties, working standards, management and technical–administrative structure in a system that has survived into the 20th century, albeit with inevitable modernizations. This document, therefore, forms the historical and legal basis of the Fabbrica, together with the ducal decrees regarding the quarries at Candoglia, which were assigned for the use of the cathedral on 24 October 1387 and became its property on 21 August 1473. In the 20th century the offices of the Fabbrica were still housed in the so-called Camposanto palace next to the cathedral apse. This building, begun in the late 14th century or the early 15th, was originally intended for a cemetery and constructed in the form of a large porticoed cloister with groin vaults on round piers, resembling the Camposanto in Pisa. It includes the main workshop with stores of materials, the *cassine* (artisans' shops), the chapter house (1404), formerly decorated with paintings (destr.) by such masters as Bernardino Luini, Ambrogio Bergognone, Cesare Cesariano (1513) and CERANO, and also the architects' living-quarters and studio. The nearby oratory of the Fabbrica (S Maria Annunziata, 'Relogus') was first built (1467) by Guiniforte Solari, demolished by order of Carlo Borromeo, and later rebuilt (1695) by Giovanni Battista Quadrio (1659–1723/7) with a small cupola (1743) by Franceso Croce (1696–1780) and a relief of the *Annunciation* by Pellegrino Tibaldi over the altar. The Late Gothic palace was destroyed in the 19th century as part of the scheme (included in the Napoleonic Regulatory Plan of 1807) to enable the cathedral to be seen as a whole and give access to the area around the apse. The building was reconstructed in Neo-classical form (1841–6) by Pietro Pestagalli (1776–1853), the architect of the Fabbrica; it includes the oratory, while the cathedral workshops are now located under the cathedral itself.

BIBLIOGRAPHY

Annali della fabbrica del Duomo di Milano dall'origine fino al presente: Pubblicati a cura della sua amministrazione, 9 vols (Milan, 1877–85)

E. Cattaneo and others: 'Il Duomo cuore e simbolo di Milano: IV centenario della dedicazione (1577–1977)', *Archivio Ambrosiano*, xxxii (Milan, 1977), pp. 15–155

Il Duomo di Milano: Dizionario storico, artistico e religioso (Milan, 1986)

GIOVANNI BATTISTA SANNAZZARO

2. S AMBROGIO.

(i) Architecture. The church is a foremost representative of Lombard Romanesque architecture, with an early example of rib vaulting in Italy. It served as the model for a large number of Italian churches, even in such distant regions as Apulia. The *basilica martyrum*, the predecessor of the present church, had probably been started when St Ambrose (c. 339–97) was appointed bishop in 374. Ambrose was buried in the church alongside the relics of SS Gervase and Protasius. This building had an aisled nave with a columnar arcade and an apse; its dimensions were those of the present church excluding the presbytery and choir. A Benedictine monastery was founded in 784, but problems of co-existence were created by Charlemagne's decree of 791 that the building should be served by its own canons. An atrium may have been added by Abbot Anspert (*reg* 869–81).

The present basilica (l. 78.9 m) is of brick with ashlar detailing and is fronted by a rectangular atrium (see fig. 15), with groin vaults supported on composite piers. A two-storey narthex with staggered arches leads to the façade of the church. The nave and aisles end in apses, with a deeper central apse, and two square bell-towers, the so-called monks' tower on the south and the canons' tower on the north. The exterior decoration (partly concealed by later structures) consists of eaves, arches and pilaster strips round the apse, and the octagonal lantern over the fourth bay has two superposed galleries of small columnar arcades decorated by intersecting arches and saw-toothed friezes. The monks' tower is unarticulated, but the canons' tower has six storeys, with hanging arches and Lombard bands. Inside, the rectangular, barrel-vaulted presbytery preceding the apse is raised above a crypt. The broad two-storey nave (h. 16.1 m) has three (originally four) double bays, with alternating compound piers and a low gallery. The main vault has broad ribs and the aisles have domed groin vaults.

The building history is controversial. It was postulated that the east end was enlarged in the late 9th century, when the first apse was demolished and the present apse built further east, with the presbytery, followed by the side apses. The monks' tower is said also to have been built at this time. In a campaign between 1018 and 1050 the piers replaced the nave columns; the aisles and galleries were vaulted and a wood roof built over the main vessel; and the crypt and present atrium were built. This was followed

15. Milan, S Ambrogio, atrium and façade, late 11th century

by the lantern in 1098 and the nave vaults, which some scholars are now inclined to date to the 12th century (*see* ROMANESQUE, §II, 3). The rivalry between monks and canons led to the construction of the canons' tower between 1128 and 1144. In 1196 the fourth bay of the nave collapsed beneath the weight of the lantern, and both were rebuilt with reinforcing arches, the vault with a Gothic profile (destr.).

Off the north side of the church is the Canonica courtyard, left unfinished by Donato Bramante in 1499 (rest.), and Bramante also designed a monastic complex (built later 16th century) for S Ambrogio (*see* BRAMANTE, DONATO, §I, 2(ii)(b)). The side chapels were built in the 16th century, and in the first half of the 17th there was a general reorganization, particularly around the lantern. The crypt was rebuilt in the 18th century. Lengthy restoration work in the mid-19th century returned the building to its supposed appearance before the collapse of 1196, and further restorations were undertaken in the 20th century, especially after severe damage in World War II required the rebuilding of the apse, lantern and north aisle.

EWA

BIBLIOGRAPHY

F. de Dartein: *Etude sur l'architecture lombarde et sur les origines de l'architecture romano-byzantine*, 2 vols (Paris, 1865/*R* 1963)
A. K. Porter: *Lombard Architecture*, 3 vols (New Haven, 1917)
P. Toesca: *Storia dell'arte italiana*, i–ii (Turin, 1927)
E. Arslan: 'L'architettura dalla conquista longobarda al 1000', *Stor. Milano*, ii (1954), pp. 501–608
——: 'L'architettura romanica milanese', *Stor. Milano*, iii (1954), pp. 397–521
K. J. Conant: *Carolingian and Romanesque Architecture, 800–1200*, Pelican Hist. A. (Harmondsworth, 1959, rev. 2/1978)
E. Cattaneo and F. Reggiori: *La basilica di Sant' Ambrogio* (Milan, 1966)
A. M. Romanini: *Milano: S Ambrogio* (Bologna, 1966)
S. Chierici: *La Lombardia* (1978), i of *Italia Romanica* (Milan, 1978–)

LIA DI GIACOMO

(ii) Sculpture. The earliest sculpture is the interlace, foliate and animal relief on the west doors, which dates from the 8th- and 9th-century alterations. Dates for the Romanesque sculpture largely depend on comparisons with other dated monuments. Architectural sculpture is limited to the capitals of the atrium and nave and seems like an overlay to the Early Christian structure.

The rectangular pilaster capitals are carved with animal combat scenes and heraldic images of eagles, lions, horses and human figures in low relief, closely resembling the capitals at S Savino, Piacenza (1096), and S Eufemia, Piacenza (*c.* 1106). Many of the motifs must have been inspired by Near Eastern textiles, and some derive from Early Christian compositions. They are combined without any apparent programme, with alternating northern interlace and classicizing acanthus friezes on the archivolts and cornices. All the carving is shallow and angular, with flat-bodied figures conforming to the geometric shapes that they adorn. These are common features of the late 11th-century *corrente comasca* (de Francovich 1935), and particularly close to capitals in the narthex, interior and crypt of S Sigismondo, Rivolta d'Adda.

Non-architectural sculpture includes decoration on the ciborium over the high altar and the pulpit. The ciborium, supported by antique porphyry columns, has stucco figures dated to the early 11th century: together with those at S Pietro al Monte, Civate, they belong to a school of stucco-carvers that shared a stylistic vocabulary with the Ottonian group of ivory-carvers in Milan. Beneath the ciborium is the remarkable Golden Altar (*c.* 835; *see* CAROLINGIAN ART, §V). The pulpit of *c.* 1130 was crushed when the lantern fell in 1196; its fragments were reassembled in the 13th century and set over an Early Christian sarcophagus (see fig. 16). On the rear is a banquet scene and on the front an animal frieze, both carved in higher relief than the capitals. An eagle and a human figure, probably symbols of the Evangelists John and Matthew, are placed under the lectern. The capitals, bearing a mixture of animal, foliate and heraldic motifs, support decorative archivolts with bands of low-relief interlace, acanthus *rinceaux* and geometric patterns. The spandrels of the arches are filled with animals and single figures, of which the crouching atlas figure set on the corner with his feet turned in is particularly impressive. His stocky proportions and the summary rendering of his drapery folds are close to the figure style on the pulpit of S Giulio on Lago d'Orta and are typical of the second generation of Lombard sculptors in Pavia.

16. Milan, S Ambrogio, pulpit, *c.* 1130; reassembled 13th century

BIBLIOGRAPHY

G. de Francovich: 'La corrente comasca nella scultura romanica europea', *Riv. Reale Ist. Archeol. & Stor. A.*, v (1935), pp. 267–305; vi (1937), pp. 45–129

——: 'Arte carolingia e ottoniana in Lombardia', *Röm. Jb. Kstgesch.*, vi (1942–4), pp. 113–252

E. Arslan: 'La scultura romanica', *Stor. Milano*, iii (1954), pp. 523–600

G. H. Crichton: *Romanesque Sculpture in Italy* (London, 1954)

A. Peroni: 'La plastica in stucco nel S Ambrogio di Milano', *Arte ottoniana e romanica in Lombardia. Kolloquium über spätantike und frühmittelalterliche Skulptur: Mainz, 1972*, pp. 59–119

CHRISTINE VERZAR

3. S LORENZO. The Early Christian church of S Lorenzo, remodelled in the 12th and 16th centuries, was stripped during the 1930s to expose the surviving original fabric. The date of its foundation is disputed, whether in the later 4th or early 5th century, and its original dedication is unknown.

The basic plan of the church is a quatrefoil of so-called double-shell design. The central space (23.8 m square; originally possibly 27.5 m high) has four L-shaped stone piers at the corners connected by four wide double-storey exedrae, each with two superimposed colonnades. Ambulatories and galleries envelop the core and are lit by the wide windows. Four towers are structurally integrated with the corner piers and the outer walls. This configuration suggests that the central square may originally have been covered by a groin vault, although some scholars have argued for other solutions. The walls of brick-faced concrete were covered in the interior by splendid decoration (marble revetment and mosaic, carved wood and marble sculpture, and stucco friezes). Much of this was destroyed by fires in 1071 and 1124.

The atrium to the west and the two chapels of SS Ippolito and Aquilino, which adjoin the east and south lobes of the tetraconch respectively, also form part of the original complex (see fig.17). The atrium's external portico comprises 16 2nd-century Corinthian columns, perhaps from a 2nd-century pagan temple. The chapels are both octagonal, but, whereas that of S Ippolito has four internal rectangular niches, the larger chapel of S Aquilino has alternating rectangular and semicircular niches, with a window above each. S Aquilino is covered by the original domical vault and is connected to the main church by a double-apsed vestibule. Its interior was decorated with marble revetment and mosaics, some of which survive and have been stylistically dated to the late 4th century or the early 5th. That in the conch of the south-west niche depicts *Christ with Apostles* (see fig. 8 above). A fragmentary scene in the conch of the south-east niche is generally identified as the *Ascension of Elijah*, although some believe that it represents Christ-Helios. The mosaic remains on the vestibule walls show Old Testament patriarchs and saints.

Although S Lorenzo may distantly recall the double-shell design of Constantine the Great's 'Golden Octagon' at Antioch (*see* ANTIOCH (i), §3), most double-shell churches built between the late 4th century and the 7th were tetraconchs. They are found throughout the Christian East, for example at Perushtitsa (early 6th century) in Bulgaria, Apamea, Bosra, Aleppo and Rusafa in Syria (all *c.* 500), and at Zvart'nots (642–61) in Armenia. S Lorenzo is one of only two examples in Italy. The reconstruction of the dome of S Lorenzo in the Romanesque style after the fire of 1124 is known from an anonymous drawing (probably mid-16th century; Milan, Castello Sforzesco, Scuola B. 56). It apparently surpassed in size and complexity other contemporary *tiburii*, such as that of S Ambrogio (*see* §2 above).

During the Renaissance the architecture of S Lorenzo was much admired. FILARETE praised it explicitly in his *Trattato d'architettura* (1465), and its influence on Donato Bramante appears clearly in his earliest projects for St Peter's, Rome. The Romanesque dome collapsed in 1573 and Martino Bassi transformed the central square into an octagon in order to support the present domical vault (for illustration *see* BASSI, MARTINO). In its lower reaches the exterior of this vault is masked by an eight-sided drum pierced by windows, supporting a dome.

BIBLIOGRAPHY

A. Calderini: *La zona monumentale di S Lorenzo in Milano* (Milan, 1934)
A. Calderini, G. Chierici and C. Cecchelli: *La Basilica di S Lorenzo Maggiore in Milano* (Milan, 1951)
A. Rovetta: 'Le fonti monumentali milanesi delle chiese a pianta centrale del Trattato d'Architettura del Filarete', *A. Lombarda*, lx (1981), pp. 24–32
G. A. dell'Acqua, ed.: *La Basilica di San Lorenzo in Milano* (Milan, 1985)
R. Cecchi: 'La Basilica di S Lorenzo Maggiore: Quale modello per l'architettura bramantesca?', *A. Lombarda*, lxxviii (1986), pp. 72–80
C. Bertelli, ed.: *Milano: Una capitale da Ambrogio ai carolingi* (1987), i of *Il millennio ambrosiano*, 3 vols (Milan, 1987), pp. 60–65, 162–77

DALE KINNEY

4. S TECLA. Former cathedral built by AD 386. St Ambrose (*c.* 339–97) referred to it as 'Basilica major/nova' (Letter lxxvi). The remains of the cathedral and the baptistery of S Giovanni alle Fonti were discovered under the modern Piazza del Duomo by de Capitani d'Arzago in 1943 and further excavated by Mirabella Roberti in 1960–62. During the Middle Ages it was dedicated to S Tecla.

In plan and size the excavated structure is similar to the basilica of S Giovanni in Laterano (*see* ROME, §V, 15(ii)), being a basilica (*c.* 80×45 m) with small, square rooms at the north-east and south-east corners, projecting from the outer lateral aisles (*see* EARLY CHRISTIAN AND BYZANTINE ART, fig. 14). A raised pathway (*solea*) in the nave led to the *bema*, which continued to the springing of the apse. The precise construction of the transverse aisle remains unclear; it may have had tripartite transepts, which in the 5th and 6th centuries were to be frequently used in the Aegean region, for example at Epidauros (*c.* 400). The church was destroyed in the 5th century and rebuilt with a narrower apse to the east of the original one. It was further remodelled in the 11th century when a crypt was installed, the presbyterium was made higher, the columns were repositioned and the walls of the transverse aisle were dismantled. The church was demolished in 1461 to make way for the construction of the present cathedral. All that remains of the internal decoration are fragments of the *opus sectile* floor. There are several medieval tombs in the vicinity of the basilica, some with sculptural decoration.

The octagonal baptistery of S Giovanni alle Fonti (*c.* 19 m from corner to corner; destr. 1394) stood to the east of the church. In an epigram (Sylloge of Lorsch; Rome, Vatican, Bib. Apostolica) St Ambrose alluded to

17. Milan, S Lorenzo, view from the south-east showing the chapels of S Aquilino (left) and S Ippolito (right), after *c.* 370s; reconstructed after 1124 and after 1573

the number symbolism of its form, by which the number eight symbolizes resurrection and salvation. Inside, the domed central space was surrounded by alternating round and rectangular niches flanked by columns. In the centre was an octagonal font (*c.* 7 m from corner to corner), with steps leading down from all sides, except the east. The baptistery floor was covered with black and white marble slabs set in a geometric pattern. Fragments indicate that the walls and dome were decorated with marble revetment and mosaic respectively.

See also BAPTISTERY.

BIBLIOGRAPHY

St Ambrose: *Letters* [*c.* 386]; ed. M. Zelzer in *Sanctis Ambrosi Opera* (1982), lxxxii of *Corpus scriptorum ecclesiasticorum latinorum* (Vienna, 1866–), x/3, p. 108
F. J. Dölger: *Zur Symbolik des altchristlichen Taufhauses* (1934), iv of *Antike und Christentum*, 6 vols (Münster, 1930–76), pp. 153–87
A. de Capitani d'Arzago: *La 'chiesa maggiore' di Milano: Santa Tecla* (Milan, 1952)
G. Traversi: *Architettura paleocristiana milanese* (Milan, 1964), pp. 47–61, 119–25
G. Bovini: *Antichità cristiane di Milano* (Bologna, 1970), pp. 76–120
M. Mirabella Roberti and A. Paredi: *Il battistero ambrosiano di S Giovanni alle Fonti* (Milan, 1974)
B. M. Apollonj Ghetti: 'Le cattedrali di Milano ed i relativi battisteri: Nota sulla basilica di S Lorenzo Maggiore', *Riv. Archaeol. Crist.*, lxiii (1987), pp. 23–84

5. S SIMPLICIANO. Late 4th-century basilican church extensively remodelled in the 12th century. A series of architectural surveys undertaken by Edoardo Arslan from 1944 established that the original structure, which may be identified with the 'basilica virginum' that was dedicated to all virgin saints by Bishop Simplicianus (*d* 401), survives substantially intact. The cross plan of the basilica (*c.* 63×21 m), with its long eastern apse (destr. 12th century), was probably derived from Constantine the Great's church of the Holy Apostles (*see* ISTANBUL, §III, 9(i)); it is probable that this plan was first used in Milan for the Basilica Apostolorum (380–85), which was founded by St Ambrose (*c.* 339–97) and is incorporated within the Romanesque S Nazaro. A narthex and low side chambers originally enveloped the structure on three sides. The brick walls are pierced by two rows of windows and articulated on the exterior by a double order of blind arcades. These features are similar to those of the north basilica of the double cathedral at Trier (*see* TRIER, §3(i)). To the north-east of S Simpliciano is a small martyrium of uncertain date.

The 12th-century remodelling of the church included the construction of a tower, a new façade and apse, the division of the nave into three aisles, the vaulting of the transept and the erection of a cupola over the crossing. The apse is decorated with a fresco of the *Coronation of the Virgin* (1515) by Ambrogio Bergognone and inlaid wooden choir-stalls (1588). The two cloisters date from the 15th and 16th centuries.

BIBLIOGRAPHY
G. Traversi: *Architettura paleocristiana milanese* (Milan, 1964), pp. 111–17
S. Levis: 'The Latin Iconography of the Single-naved Cruciform Basilica Apostolorum in Milan', *A. Bull.*, li (1969), pp. 205–19
J. Schmitz: *Gottesdienst im altchristlichen Mailand* (Cologne and Bonn, 1975), pp. 263–72

FRANZ RICKERT

Milan, Dukes of. *See under* SFORZA.

Milan, Pierre (*fl* 1545–57). French medallist and engraver. He is first recorded in 1545 and was working as an assistant to the medallist Marc Béchot (*c.* 1520–57) in 1547. His prints are unsigned and were for a long time attributed to RENÉ BOYVIN, who was his pupil in 1549–50. He has been identified with the copper-plate engraver Pierre de La Cuffle, who is mentioned by Karel van Mander I. He was often in debt and was several times obliged to pledge his plates to his creditors, who included François Clouet. He remained in close contact with Boyvin, who in 1553 finished two plates begun by Milan. They worked together on the inventory drawn up on the death of Luca Penni in 1557. Zerner attributed seven engravings to him, including *Dance of the Dryads* (see Zerner, no. 1) after Rosso Fiorentino, *Jupiter and Callisto* (Z 4) after Francesco Primaticcio and *Clelia Escaping from the Camp of Porsena* (Z 6) after Giulio Romano. Perhaps the most interesting of the works attributed to him is the print of the *Nymph of Fontainebleau* (Z 7; *see* FONTAINE-BLEAU SCHOOL, fig. 1), the only part of the decorative ensemble of the Galerie François I at the château of Fontainebleau to be engraved by the Parisian printmakers of the time. It contributed to the spread of the theme of Diana in French 16th-century engraving. It seems likely that some engravings attributed to Boyvin are by Milan.

BIBLIOGRAPHY
Y. Metman: 'Un Graveur inconnu de l'école de Fontainebleau: Pierre Milan', *Bib. Humanisme & Renaissance*, i (1941), pp. 202–14
H. Zerner: *Ecole de Fontainebleau: Gravures* (Paris, 1969) [z]
L'Ecole de Fontainebleau (exh. cat., Paris, Grand Pal., 1972), pp. 322–6

MARIANNE GRIVEL

Milanesi, Gaetano (*b* Siena, 9 Sept 1813; *d* Florence, 11 March 1895). Italian art historian and palaeographer. He trained as a lawyer, but his studies in literature and history led him to spend a great deal of his time in the Biblioteca Comunale at Siena. There he became extraordinarily proficient in deciphering early Italian handwriting. He concentrated on documents relating to the history of art

and began transcribing those he was to publish throughout his life.

In 1845 Milanesi founded the Società di Amatori delle Belle Arti with his brother Carlo Milanesi (1816–67), the Dominican father Vincenzo Marchese and Carlo Pini. Their new edition of Giorgio Vasari's *Vite dei pittori* appeared between 1846 and 1870 and immediately transformed the study of the Italian Renaissance from being largely speculative to being rooted in solid foundations of documented fact. The principles of the edition arose partly from the abundance of documentation that Milanesi possessed and partly from the conviction that Vasari, however entertaining and illuminating, was fundamentally unreliable as an historian. Milanesi's faith in 19th-century empiricism may occasionally have caused Vasari's text to become secondary to the commentary, but the result was a documentary history of Italian art in the Renaissance of unique importance.

The first of Milanesi's collections of transcribed documents appeared in 1854 as *Documenti per la storia dell'arte senese* and comprised more than 700 documents drawn particularly from the Archivio dell'Opera de Duomo at Orvieto. Further collections followed, all relating to the art of Siena and Florence, and providing the basis for all subsequent work on the Tuscan Renaissance. Milanesi's public career, however, was modest. He moved from Siena to Florence in 1856 to be 'accademico residente' in the Accademia della Crusca and in 1858 was appointed Deputy Director of the Archivio di Stato in Florence. His edition of Michelangelo's letters, published in 1875 on the quatercentenary of the artist's birth, is particularly notable. He continued collecting documents and revising his earlier work, and a new edition of Vasari was published between 1878 and 1885. It differed in method rather than in scope from the first, and included all Vasari's writings, corrected numerous errors, doubled the critical apparatus and incorporated many more genealogical trees.

In 1883 Milanesi became Arciconsolo of the Accademia della Crusca and he ended his career as Soprintendente degli Archivi Toscani (1889–91). His generosity towards other scholars was exemplary. His astonishing capacity for work and his meticulous attention to detail enabled him to lay the foundation of modern Italian art history.

WRITINGS
Le Vite de' più eccellenti pittori, scultori e architetti, di Giorgio Vasari, 14 vols (Florence, 1846–70)
Documenti per la storia dell'arte senese, 3 vols (Siena, 1854–6)
Le lettere di Michelangelo Buonarroti (Florence, 1875)
Sulla storia dell'arte toscana: Scritti vari (Siena, 1878/*R* Soest, 1973)
Le opere di Giorgio Vasari, 9 vols (Florence, 1878–85)
Nuovi documenti per la storia dell'arte senese (Siena, 1898/*R* Soest, 1970)
Nuovi documenti per la storia dell'arte toscana dal XII al XV secolo (Florence, 1901/*R* Soest, 1973)

BIBLIOGRAPHY
E. Ridolfi: 'Gaetano Milanesi', *Nuova Antol.*, 3rd ser., lvii (1895), pp. 359–66

□

Milan Hours. *See* TURIN-MILAN HOURS.

Milani, Aureliano (*b* Bologna, 1675; *d* Bologna, 1749). Italian painter, draughtsman and engraver. He was distantly related to the Carracci family and zealous to revive their style for his generation of Bolognese artists. As a

Aureliano Milani: *Christ Carrying the Cross*, engraving, 0.76×1.47 m, 1725 (London, British Museum)

young artist, trained briefly by his uncle Giulio Cesare Milani and then by Lorenzo Pasinelli and Cesare Gennari (1637–88), he undertook a long and diligent study of the celebrated fresco cycles by the Carracci in the Palazzo Magnani and the Palazzo Fava in Bologna. He was given free access to the Fava palace, and financial assistance, by Count Alessandro Fava. Milani also made copies, in both drawing and painting, of major pictures by the Carracci in Bologna and emulated the vigorous rhythmic articulation of musculature and contour that they used to convey the powerful energy of the male figure in movement.

Initially Milani's reputation was established in Bologna with altarpieces such as the *Martyrdom of St Stephen* (*c.* 1715; destr., see Roli, 1977, fig. 206b) for the important church of S Maria della Purificazione, and the altarpiece of *St Jerome*, commissioned by the Ghislieri family, for the church of S Maria della Vita (*in situ*). His *Resurrection* (Bologna, Pal. Arcivescovile) of this period is an impressive paraphrase of Annibale Carracci's *Resurrection* (Paris, Louvre); it has a plastic vigour and weight equalled only in the works of Giuseppe Maria Crespi among Milani's Bolognese contemporaries. At this time Zanotti noted (p. 162) two impressive history paintings (untraced) that Milani had done for Francesco Farnese, Duke of Parma, and also wrote of a large drawing, a *Christ Carrying the Cross* (Paris, Louvre) with many figures, that the artist had given to Senator Paolo Magnani. Milani later rendered this composition in an engraving of exceptional size (see fig.).

During these years in Bologna, Milani became responsible for a large family, of nine children. Assistance of various kinds was given by the influential General Ferdinando Marsigli, who attempted to ensure a favourable reception for Milani in Rome; he advised him to send a large drawing, the *Fall of Simon Magus* (untraced), to the Bolognese pope, Clement XI, and equipped him with a letter of introduction to the Secretary of State, Cardinal Fabrizio Paolucci. Milani settled in Rome in 1718, and Paolucci awarded him his first Roman commission, a fresco of the *Martyrdom of St Pancras* (Albano Cathedral),

and in 1722 gave him a commission for six altarpieces for his titular church of SS Giovanni e Paolo. Milani remained one of the more active painters in Rome, painting altarpieces and frescoes, among them a *Beheading of St John the Baptist* (1732) in the church of S Bartolomeo dei Bergamaschi and frescoes (1732) in the apse and triumphal arch of S Maria Maddalena. His most impressive Roman work was the fresco cycle of scenes from the *Labours of Hercules* (1732–3) in the vault of the Galleria degli Specchi in the Palazzo Doria-Pamphili. In these works, where powerful and muscular nudes enrich a sumptuous *quadratura* setting, Milani revived the energy of Annibale Carracci's decoration of the Galleria Farnese in Rome. His return to the style of the Carracci is also evident in his drawings, which were highly praised by both Zanotti and Crespi.

As a kind of antidote to his official commissions, Milani painted genre scenes, also inspired by the work of the Carracci. For Paolo Magnani, by this time Bolognese ambassador to Rome, he painted *The Mission* (Merano, Molinari Prodelli priv. col., see Roli, 1977, fig. 353b) and its pendant, *Market Scene in a Roman Square* (Pesaro, Mus. Civ.); in these works he unexpectedly revealed an intriguing fancy for the picturesque character of contemporary Italian life and a surprisingly fine ability in landscape painting.

BIBLIOGRAPHY

G. P. Zanotti: *Storia dell' Accademia Clementina di Bologna* (Bologna, 1739), ii, pp. 159–67

L. Crespi: *Vite de' pittori bolognesi non descritte nella Felsina pittrice* (Rome, 1769), pp. 146–50

R. Roli: 'Per l'attività romana di Aureliano Milani', *A. Ant. & Mod.*, vii/27 (1964), pp. 341–8

Italy in the Eighteenth Century: Rococo to Romanticism (exh. cat., ed. J. Moxon and J. J. Rishel; Chicago, IL, A. Inst.; Minneapolis, MN, Inst. A.; Toledo, OH, Mus. A.; 1970), pp. 138–9 [article on Aureliano by D. Miller]

D. Miller: '*Israelites Worshipping the Golden Calf* by Aureliano Milani', *Burl. Mag.*, cxvi (1974), pp. 332–4 [with bibliog.]

R. Roli: *Pittura bolognese, 1650–1800: Dal Cignani ai Gandolfi* (Bologna, 1977), pp. 57–8

L'arte del settecento emiliano: La pittura dell' Accademia Clementina (exh. cat., Bologna, Pal. Podestà, 1979), pp. 48–52

DWIGHT C. MILLER

Milano, Giovanni da. *See* GIOVANNI DA MILANO.

Milde, Carl [Karl] **Julius** (*b* Hamburg, 16 Feb 1803; *d* Lübeck, 19 Nov 1875). German painter, draughtsman, stained-glass designer, illustrator and restorer. In Hamburg he studied drawing with Gerdt Hardorff the elder (1769–1864) and painting with Christopher Suhr (1771–1842) and Siegfried Bendixen (1786–1864). His admiration for early German art was inspired during a sketching trip through Schleswig-Holstein in June 1823 with Erwin Speckter. Drawings from this period include a copy of Hans Memling's altarpiece in Lübeck Cathedral. Following a sojourn in Dresden in 1824, Milde and Speckter travelled to Munich in the summer of 1825 where they studied history painting at the Akademie. In 1826 they lived briefly in Rome; and Milde again worked in Rome from 1830 to 1832 where he was in contact with the Lukasbrüder. Their preference for an outline style reinforced Milde's own primitivizing linear manner derived from his study of Northern Renaissance art. Milde's few extant paintings are mostly portraits from the 1830s, although history paintings, genre scenes, marine views and landscapes have also been attributed to him. Milde completed both bust-length oil portraits and family groups set in domestic interiors, which provide a detailed record of middle-class life in Hamburg at this time. In watercolours such as *Pastor Rautenberg and his Family* (1833) or *Professor Classen and his Family* (1840; both Hamburg, Ksthalle) the sitters are posed around tables, drinking tea or coffee in the typically Biedermeier hybrid of portrait and genre painting. Milde's pictures are usually characterized by diagonal viewpoints and asymmetrical compositions, often sharply cropped. In the portraits this evokes an air of intimacy and informality. Milde's most famous painting, now known only through a lithograph, was a commissioned group portrait of the *Hamburg Senate* (Hamburg, Mus. Hamburg. Gesch.) from the late 1830s. In 1838 Milde moved to Lübeck where he remained until his death. During this period he completed many stained-glass commissions, culminating in the *Last Judgement* window (1865–70) in the west portal of Cologne Cathedral. Milde was also active in fighting for the conservation of early German architecture and art in Schleswig-Holstein, contributing much time to the restoration of the Marienkirche in Lübeck. He illustrated the *Denkmäler bildender Kunst in Lübeck* (2 vols, Lübeck, 1843–7) and several surgical textbooks on muscular and anatomical systems. He was also an amateur naturalist and amassed extensive collections of plants, insects, butterflies and animal skeletons, which he catalogued and donated to the Naturhistorisches Museum in Lübeck.

BIBLIOGRAPHY

ADB; Thieme–Becker

A. Lichtwark: *Das Bildnis in Hamburg*, ii (Hamburg, 1898), pp. 155–6

——: 'Carl Milde als Naturforscher', *Jb. Ges. Hamburg. Kstfreunde*, xi (1905), p. 37

W. L. von Lütgendorff: *C. J. Milde* (Lübeck, 1908)

G. Pauli: *Die Hamburger Meister der guten alten Zeit* (Munich, 1925)

E. M. Krafft and C. W. Schümann, eds: *Katalog der Meister des 19. Jahrhunderts in der Hamburger Kunsthalle* (Hamburg, 1969)

M. Bernhard, ed.: *Deutsche Romantik-Handzeichnungen,* i (Munich, 1973), pp. 855–76

MARSHA L. MORTON

Mildenhall Treasure. Hoard consisting of 24 items of Roman silverware (London, BM), mainly from the 4th century AD, found in 1942 by a ploughman working near Mildenhall, Suffolk. The outstanding object, now known as the Mildenhall Great Dish or the Oceanus dish (diam. 605 mm; *see* METAL, colour pl. I, fig. 2), is a shallow circular platter decorated over its whole surface with Bacchic scenes in low relief; it constitutes one of the greatest masterpieces of the Roman silversmith's art. The central motif is the head of a sea god with seaweed and dolphins in his hair and beard; surrounding it is a narrow frieze of sea nymphs riding on mythological marine creatures. The principal, outer zone of decoration depicts a Bacchic revel presided over by Bacchus himself (*see* ROME, ANCIENT, fig. 108). Several satyrs and maenads with Pan and Silenus dance and play flutes, pipes and tambourines, while Hercules, the loser in a drinking contest with Bacchus, the god of wine, is kept from drunken collapse only by the support of two companions. The entire decoration thus incorporates the sea thiasus and the land thiasus of Bacchus. As on other silverwork of the period, the figures lack the perfect proportions of their late Hellenistic and early Imperial predecessors, but the vivid, spirited rendering of movement and atmosphere compensates for their occasional awkwardness.

A pair of small platters (diam. 188 and 185 mm) in the treasure are clearly by the same artist. They depict respectively Pan and a maenad, and a satyr and maenad surrounded by animals and objects symbolic of the cult of Bacchus. The theme is repeated in the decoration of four bowls with broad horizontal rims, as well as on a deep, domed lid added in the 4th century AD to a flanged bowl, which is the earliest piece in the hoard, a Gallo-Roman product of the 3rd century AD. Another platter almost as large as the Great Dish is much more simply decorated with floral and geometric patterns inlaid in niello. Most of the bowls and dishes are bordered with a row of raised bosses, typical of 4th-century AD table silver. A deep, fluted bowl with drop handles has chased foliate ornament and a central geometric figure delineated in broad, shallow grooves. The predominantly pagan iconography is modified only by the presence of Christian inscriptions on three of the eight spoons in the hoard. Such combinations of pagan and Christian elements are common on 4th-century AD material.

The relief decoration was executed in a chasing technique that involved virtually carving the surface of the metal. Fine detail was rendered in delicately incised lines and tiny punched dots; perspective was suggested to some extent by slight variations in the height of the relief and by leaving the most distant elements in incised line only. The techniques are typical of those used on ornate display silver of the 4th century AD and exemplify the impressive level of skill attained by late-Roman silversmiths.

BIBLIOGRAPHY

J. W. Brailsford: *The Mildenhall Treasure: A Handbook* (London, 1947, 2/1955)

K. S. Painter: 'The Mildenhall Treasure: A Reconsideration', *BMQ.*, xxxvii (1973), pp. 154–80

——: *The Mildenhall Treasure* (London, 1977)

CATHERINE JOHNS

Mildert, Hans van (*b* Köningsberg, Prussia [now Kaliningrad, Russia], *bapt* 17 Jan 1588; *d* Antwerp, 21 Sept 1638). Flemish sculptor. He was the son of the Antwerp painter Antoon van Mildert (*d* 1597), who had established himself in Köningsberg. After his father's death he returned to Antwerp, where in 1610 he became a free master in the Guild of St Luke. The monumental alabaster chimney-piece that he made in 1618 for the Marriage Chamber of Antwerp Town Hall is in the Mannerist style of Cornelis Floris and was possibly based on a drawing by him. From about this time van Mildert also began to work in the Baroque style of his friend Peter Paul Rubens, to whose design he constructed a black and white marble altar (1618) for Notre-Dame de la Chapelle, Brussels. This structure (now St Joost ten Noode, nr Brussels) was the first stone altar in the form of a portico in the Netherlands. Van Mildert also executed the famous arcaded screen wall at Rubens's house in Antwerp. Despite the Baroque nature of this architectural work, his figure sculpture continued to follow the undynamic forms of the Renaissance style. His statue of *St Gummarus* for the Baroque altar erected in 1620 in the church of that name at Lier is heavy in its proportions, unrealistic in detail and static in pose. Late works such as his *St Simon* (marble, 1638) in St Rombout, Mechelen, are, however, livelier and more realistic.

BIBLIOGRAPHY

BNB; Thieme–Becker

I. Leyssens: 'Hans van Mildert 158?–1638', *Gent. Bijdr. Kstgesch.*, vii (1941), pp. 73–136

M. Casteels: *De Antwerpse beeldhouwer Hans van Mildert (1588–1638), vriend en medewerker van Rubens* [The Antwerp sculptor Hans van Mildert, friend and collaborator of Rubens] (diss. Brussels, Acad. Royale Sci., Lett., & B.-A. Belgique, 1974)

La Sculpture au siècle de Rubens (exh. cat., Brussels, Mus. A. Anc., 1977), pp. 246–50

IRIS KOCKELBERGH

Mildorfer, Josef Ignaz (*b* Innsbruck, 13 Oct 1719; *d* Vienna, 8 Dec 1775). Austrian painter. After training under his father, Michael Ignaz Mildorfer (1690–1747), in Innsbruck, from 1738 he worked as an assistant to Paul Troger in Vienna. In 1741 he won a prize at the Akademie der Kunst for a life drawing, and in 1742 another for an oil painting of *Cain Killing his Brother Abel* (Innsbruck, Tirol. Landesmus.). His major early works included frescoes (1743) in the dome of the Wallfahrtskirche zu Unseren Lieben Frau in Hafnerberg, altarpieces of the *Pietà* (1742; Telfs, Heimatmuseum), the *Assumption of the Virgin* (1743–4; abbey of Novacella, nr Bressanone) and the *Last Judgement* (1748; Wilten, Stiftsgal.) and a series of smaller panels depicting battle scenes (1742; Salzburg, Barockmus.). In 1745 he was elected a member of the Vienna Akademie, and in 1751 he became professor of painting there; at the same time he was appointed court painter to Duchess Emmanuela of Savoy. He was commissioned to decorate the Menagerie Pavilion at Schönbrunn in 1752 and in 1753 to execute a fresco in the dome of the Kapuzinergruft depicting the *Vision of the Prophet Ezekiel*. His most important altar painting of this period

was the *Departure of the Apostles Peter and Paul* (*c.* 1760; Vienna, Ulrichskirche).

After 1760 Mildorfer mainly worked in Moravia and Hungary, notably at Esterházy Palace in Fertőd, where he painted frescoes in the chapel (1764). His works develop the expressiveness of Troger's style, showing figures with elongated proportions and accentuated movements; the method of painting is freer, occasionally verging on the visionary.

BIBLIOGRAPHY

H. Schwarz: 'Regesten zum Leben und Werk des Malers Joseph Ignaz Mildorfer', *Kirchenkunst*, vii (1935), pp. 89–91

E. Eccel: 'Josef Ignaz Mildorfer und das Hochaltarblatt von Neustift bei Brixen', *Cult. Atesina*, xvii (1963), pp. 21–48

E. Payer: *Der Maler Josef Ignaz Mildorfer, 1719–1775* (diss., U. Innsbruck, 1968)

K. Rossacher: 'Der Tiroler Barockmaler Josef Ignaz Mildorfer in neuer Sicht', *Alte & Mod. Kst*, xvii/123 (1972), pp. 16–23

K. Garas: 'Unbekannte Fresken von Josef Ignaz Mildorfer', *Mitt. Österreich. Gal.*, xxiv–xxv (1980–81), pp. 93–131

JOHANN KRONBICHLER

Miles, Philip John (*b* 1773; *d* 24 March 1845). English merchant, politician and collector. The son of Philip Miles (1732–1823), a successful Jamaica merchant who settled at Bristol, Miles was elected MP for Bristol in 1820. His Italianate house, Leigh Court near Bristol, was built in 1814 by Thomas Hopper expressly to house the outstanding picture collection he had acquired from his friend Richard Hart Davis, MP for Bristol. The latter, who was rumoured to have spent over £100,000 on pictures, had bought such expensive masterpieces as Domenichino's *St John the Evangelist* (Glyndebourne, E. Sussex, Sir George Christie priv. col.), for which Miles is said to have paid £12,000, and the Altieri paintings by Claude Lorrain (Anglesey Abbey, Cambs, NT). The collection was unusually well balanced and offered a very complete summary of contemporary conventional taste; Waagen (1838) wrote that it 'would have done the highest honour to the palace of the greatest monarch in Europe'. There were such early Italian pictures as Raphael's predella panel *The Way to Calvary* (London, N.G.), and a major group of Bolognese works; pictures by Murillo and Rubens; Michiel Sweerts's *Plague* (ex-Cook col., Richmond, Surrey), then attributed to Poussin; Dughet's *Calling of Abraham* (London, N.G.), formerly in the Colonna collection, Rome; as well as notable English pictures including Hogarth's *Shrimp Girl* (London, N.G.). Young's catalogue of the collection was published in 1822. The collection was largely dispersed at Christie's (28 June 1884): a number of works then bought in were sold at Christie's, 13 May 1899.

Philip Miles's grandson, George Francis ('Frank') Miles (*b* 22 April 1852; *d* 15 July 1891) was a minor painter who specialized in portraits of women.

BIBLIOGRAPHY

J. Young: *A Catalogue of the Pictures at Leigh Court, near Bristol; the Seat of Philip John Miles, Esq. M.P.* (London, 1822)

G. F. Waagen: *Works of Art and Artists in England*, iii (London, 1838), p. 134

——: *Treasures of Art in Great Britain*, iii (London, 1854), pp. 178–86

FRANCIS RUSSELL

Mileševa [Milešovo]. Monastery and church of the Ascension, near Prijepolje, Serbia. It was built by Vladislav I of Serbia (*reg* 1233–42) in 1234–5 and decorated with magnificent frescoes. Sava (*c.* 1175–1235), the first arch-bishop of the independent Serbian Church and the greatest Serbian saint, was buried here; his relics were burnt by the Turks in 1594. Stephen Tvrtko I (*d* 1391) was crowned King of Serbia and Bosnia at Mileševa in 1377, after which it became one of the centres of Orthodoxy in Bosnia and was briefly a metropolitan see. The church was burnt several times, and much of the existing structure dates from the 1860s.

The church comprises an aisleless, barrel-vaulted and domed nave typical of other Raška mountain churches such as those at STUDENICA and Sopoćani (*see* SOPOĆANI, HOLY TRINITY MONASTERY). This formula was somewhat modified by its construction over a much earlier church, with the result that the prothesis and diaconicon abut on to the earlier apse wall; the bay in front of the apse is missing, and the transepts are irregular in plan. The two-storey, domed exonarthex, which contained the body of St Sava, was built several years after the nave. Certain features of the church's sculptural decoration such as the corbel-table friezes and pilaster-strips are of south Italian derivation.

In contrast to the crude architecture of Mileševa, the frescoes decorating the nave, narthex and exonarthex are among the significant paintings of the 13th century. They have been attributed to three distinct groups of painters: two groups were mosaicists, imitating the effect of tessera in the gold and blue background; and one, working in the nave, was probably Greek, judging by the resemblance to Early Byzantine mosaics in Thessaloniki. Representations of the *Eucharist*, the *Deposition* and the *Mission of the Apostles* decorate the walls of the dome's cubic drum, disturbing the natural iconographic order. This caused most of the compositions to follow from the right to the left. The *Evangelical Cycle* runs continuously throughout the nave and exonarthex. The transepts are occupied by the *Forty Martyrs*, *Apostles* and an assembly of saints, modelled in contrasting tones of red, ochre and green, including those most respected in Serbia such as SS Stephen and Nicholas. In the narthex special prominence was given to portraits of the Nemanjić family, arranged in a kind of horizontal family tree: Stephen Nemanja as the monk Simeon, St Sava and Stephen Prvovenčani (*reg* 1217–27). All these figures are imbued with a humanity and classical elegance that could only have come from a metropolitan school of painting. The only set of frescoes of lesser distinction are those of the monumental *Last Judgement* in the exonarthex.

BIBLIOGRAPHY

N. L. Okunev: 'Mileševo: Pamyatnik serbskogo iskusstva XIII v.' [Mile-ševa: a monument of 13th-century Serbian art], *Byzantinoslavica*, vii (1937–8), pp. 34–5, 41–96

S. Radojčić: *Mileševa* (Belgrade, 1963)

V. J. Djurić: *Vizantijske freske u Jugoslaviji* [Byzantine frescoes in Yugoslavia] (Belgrade, 1974; Ger. trans., Belgrade, 1976), pp. 250–51

D. Bošković and M. Čanak-Medić: 'Neka pitanja najstarijeg razdoblja Mileševe' [Concerning the earliest period at Mileševa], *Saopštenja*, xv (1983), pp. 7–23 [Fr. summary]

V. J. Djurić, ed.: *Colloque scientifique international. Mileševa dans l'histoire du peuple serbe: Belgrade, 1987*

SRDJAN DJURIĆ

Miletos. Site on the west coast of Turkey, near the mouth of the River Meander (now Bügük Menderes). The city flourished under the Greeks and the Romans from the 5th century BC to the 3rd century AD. A large Byzantine church was built there in the 6th century. Miletos was once a port but is now 9 km from the sea. German archaeologists have been excavating there since the late 19th century. Milesian architecture played a significant role in the development of ancient Greek architecture in general. It comprised three phases of varying importance.

1. MYCENAEAN TO ARCHAIC PERIOD (16TH CENTURY BC–EARLY 5TH). Little is known of the first settlement, established near the Theatre Bay in the late 16th century BC, except that it consisted of largish but fairly simple dwellings. Towards the end of the 13th century BC it was fortified with a strong wall, mud-brick on stone foundations, 4.3 m high and reinforced by bastions; it enclosed an oval area measuring *c.* 400×200 m. Nonetheless, the town was destroyed *c.* 1200 BC, though not totally abandoned. During the Ionian migration (11th–10th century BC) a new settlement was established and by the 8th–7th century BC this occupied *c.* 70–80 ha, stretching from Kalabaktepe in the south to the area that was later the North Agora. The southern area of the town was based on an irregular network of alleys, but the northern part near the Port of the Lions was rebuilt in the second half of the 6th century BC with a regular street plan similar to that of the later city. Few dwellings have been uncovered; consequently no standard pattern emerges. Nearly all have courtyards, while several doubled as workplaces. Some of the few shrines from this phase (Apollo Delphinios, Dionysus) were simple courtyards, which contained a total of at least 12 largish altars, adorned with corner palmettes. Others were fairly small temples (Athena, temple on the Kalabaktepe). The principal Milesian temple, however, was that of Apollo Didymaios about 15 km away at DIDYMA, although its relation to the city proper at this early period remains unclear.

2. CLASSICAL TO HELLENISTIC PERIOD (EARLY 5TH CENTURY BC–LATE 1ST). In 494 BC Miletos was destroyed by the Persians and its population dispersed; it was resettled after the end of the Persian wars (480/79 BC) and was soon being rebuilt on a larger scale. One of the first projects was surely the reconstruction of the city walls. The first stretches were erected on earlier foundations and sometimes had mud-brick superstructures. The southern section (late 2nd–early 1st century BC) was of markedly superior design and execution, with sawtooth curtain walling and numerous towers and sallyports. The planning of the new town is attributed to HIPPODAMOS of Miletos. Its various districts were laid out on a grid pattern, with minor differences in orientation. The intention from the outset was to move the town centre to the area by the Port of the Lions, and, following the Hellenistic reconstruction of the old sanctuaries, the South (official) Agora, the North Agora (the centre of commerce) and the most important public buildings were indeed built there: the prytaneion probably in the 4th century BC, the bouleuterion *c.* 175–*c.*150 BC and the gymnasium *c.* 150 BC. (For a plan of the South Agora *see* GREECE, ANCIENT, fig. 11.)

A large Ionic Temple of Athena was erected *c.* 479–*c.* 450 BC, though perhaps never quite completed. It stands on a high platform, unusual for Ionia, and has an equally unusual plan (possibly pseudodipteral, i.e. without the inner row of columns). Only modest reconstructions of sanctuaries have been found from the 5th and 4th centuries BC (Apollo Delphinios, Dionysus); from the turn of the 4th century BC, however, large-scale temple building resumed, beginning with a new Temple of Apollo at Didyma. Two particularly large temples at Miletos itself were that of Dionysus (early 3rd century BC), which was unusual in combining Ionic columns with antae, and that of Demeter (late 3rd century BC), an Ionic prostyle building in a prominent position on the northern tip of the peninsula. Both were cleared away or built over in Christian times. Similarly, the remains of a large Doric building lying under the Great Basilica (6th century AD) consist only of foundations and a few architectural elements, so that its original form is uncertain. More remains of the public buildings in the area adjoining the Sacred Way. Most notable is the bouleuterion (*c.* 170 BC; *see* GREECE, ANCIENT, fig. 28), a rectangular council chamber (34.84×24.28 m) with a slightly more than semicircular auditorium. Pilasters divided its inside walls into panels, some equipped with windows. Outside, the building was adorned with engaged Doric half-columns and pilasters at each corner, on a ledge well above ground. The columns' echinuses bore egg-and-dart mouldings, an Ionic feature symptomatic of the tendency to combine the orders at this period. The court in front of the chamber was lined on three sides by Doric colonnades, incorporating a Corinthian gateway with extremely elaborate column capitals opposite the chamber's entrance. At the court's centre was an altar for the cult of the Roman emperors, also with Corinthian columns. To the east is a gymnasium (*c.* 197–*c.*159 BC), with a Doric peristyle court fronted by an Ionic porch. While grey marble from local quarries on the Gulf of Latmos was the main material used for sacred and public buildings, mud-brick was widely used for houses, so that little is known of their plans.

3. ROMAN IMPERIAL PERIOD (1ST–4TH CENTURIES AD). Because Ephesos was the residence of the proconsul of Asia, Miletos was less politically and economically important at this time. Nonetheless, after regaining its autonomy in *c.* 39 BC it undertook a substantial civic building programme and maintained high building standards even until the 4th century AD. Around AD 100–150 the central area of the town was raised, the processional way linking Miletos to Didyma was extended, and an aqueduct several kilometres long was constructed. Three bath–palaestra complexes were built—Capito (*c.* AD 47–*c.* 54), Faustina (AD 161–80; *see* ROME, ANCIENT, fig. 45) and Humeïtepe (late 1st to early 2nd century AD)—as well as the great nymphaeum (late 1st century AD) and the ceremonial gateway leading into the South Agora (*c.* AD 125; Berlin, Pergamonmus.). Although it had a Hellenistic predecessor, the theatre's remains (see fig.) are almost entirely Roman, and its auditorium is of typically Roman form, being semicircular rather than over semicircular and largely free-standing on an arched substructure rather than completely recessed into a hillside. It has a

Miletos, aerial view of the theatre (1st–2nd centuries AD), showing the North Agora in the background

frontage of 140 m, and it accommodated around 15,000 spectators in three tiers, each with twenty rows of seats. The lowest tier is composed of five wedges, divided by stairways, the middle one of ten and the highest of twenty. The 'royal box' in the middle of the first tier is marked by four reused columns, of which two survive. Inscriptions designate other reserved seats and also record a labour dispute that arose during the theatre's construction. Building took place in two phases: phase 1 during the reign of Nero (AD 54–68) and phase 2 around the mid-2nd century AD, when the two-storey stage building (l. 40 m) received a third level, and the *scaenae frons* was rebuilt. Several important commemorative monuments and two heroa were also erected, while the latest extant structures from this era are a large complex behind the nymphaeum with a monumental arched gateway (early 3rd century AD) and a small shrine to Serapis (mid- to late 3rd century AD).

BIBLIOGRAPHY
T. Wiegand, ed.: *Milet: Ergebnisse der Ausgrabungen und Untersuchungen seit dem Jahre 1899* (Berlin, 1906–)
G. Kleiner: *Alt-Milet* (Wiesbaden, 1966)
——: *Die Ruinen von Milet* (Berlin, 1968)
A. Mallwitz and W. Schiering: 'Der alte Athena-Tempel von Milet', *Istanbul. Mitt.*, xviii (1968), pp. 87–160
A. Mallwitz: 'Gestalt und Geschichte des jüngeren Athenatempels von Milet', *Istanbul. Mitt.*, xxv (1975), pp. 67–90
W. Müller-Wiener, ed.: *Milet, 1899–1980: Ergebnisse, Probleme und Perspektiven einer Ausgrabung* (Tübingen, 1986)
W. Müller-Wiener: 'Milet, 1976–1986', *Ant. Welt*, xix/4 (1988), pp. 31–42
WOLFGANG MÜLLER-WIENER

Milev, Ivan (*b* Kazanlŭk, 19 Feb 1897; *d* Sofia, 25 Jan 1927). Bulgarian painter, stage designer, printmaker and stained-glass designer. At the time of his graduation in 1925 from the National Academy of Arts, Sofia, he had already had three successful solo exhibitions in which his interest in decorative paintings of ethnic themes was already apparent. He continued to work in a rather avant-garde style, painting Bulgarian folk themes that avoided the excesses of academic realism and ethnographic detail. He worked in a wide variety of media, executing figure compositions, portraits and landscapes that depict the romance and fantasy of Bulgarian folklore and mythology, as in *St Elijah* (distemper and ink, 1923; Sofia, priv. col.), a *Rebec-player* (watercolour, 1924; Sofia, N.A.G.) and *Shepherds* (India ink, 1926; Sofia, N.A.G.). He also painted frescoes and designed stained glass. In 1926, after returning from Italy and Austria, he held a further exhibition in Sofia and worked as senior scene-painter at the National Theatre (Naroden Teatâr Ivan Vazov) in Sofia, a position he held until his death in 1927. His unique set designs were influenced by the work of Egon Schiele and Viennese *Jugendstil*; among the most original are those for the performances of the Ballets Russes and for Shakespeare's *A Midsummer Night's Dream* (1927; Sofia, Ivan Vazov N. Theat.). His best-known paintings include *Our Mothers Always Wear Black*, *Sun's Wedding* and *Peasant Madonna* (all 1926; Sofia, N.A.G.). He was also a prominent member of the NATIONAL ART SOCIETY OF BULGARIA. Although his career was short, he set standards for Bulgarian painting in the 20th century.

BIBLIOGRAPHY
E. Peteva-Fillova: *Ivan Milev* (Sofia, 1940)
A. Stamenov: *Ivan Milev* (Sofia, 1958)
V. Dinova-Rousseva: *Ivan Milev in the Bulgarian Theatre* (Sofia, 1970)
G. Shapkarov, L. Vlakhova and K. Tanchev: *Ivan Milev, 1897–1927: Po sluchay 90 godishninata ot rozhdenyeto mu* [Ivan Milev, 1897–1927: on the occasion of the 90th anniversary of his birth] (Sofia, 1987)
JULIANA NEDEVA-WEGENER

Milhomme, François-Dominique-Aimé (*b* Valenciennes, 20 Aug 1758; *d* Paris, 24 May 1823). French sculptor. He was trained in the Valenciennes studio of the local sculptor Pierre-Joseph Gillet (1734–1810) and later became the pupil in Paris of André-Jean Lebrun (1737–1811) and Christophe-Gabriel Allegrain. In the 1790s, during the French Revolution, he executed decorative sculpture and also produced models for the goldsmith Robert Joseph Auguste or his son Henry Auguste. In 1801, at the age of 43, he won the Prix de Rome with the bas-relief *Caius Gracchus Leaving his Wife Licinia to Dispute in the Forum with the Consul Opimius* (plaster; ex-Mus. B.-A., Valenciennes; untraced). He shared the prize with Joseph-Charles Marin. His herm bust of *Andromache Mourning Hector* (tinted plaster, 1800; Paris, Louvre) reveals a delicate Neo-classical sensibility that was developed during his years at the Académie de France in Rome after 1802 to 1809. During this period he produced his finest works, including a statue of *Psyche Abandoned by Cupid* (marble, 1806; Compiègne, Château), in which a form derived from antique sculpture was given a recognizably modern sentiment, and a colossal seated statue of *General Lazare Hoche* (marble, 1808; Versailles, Château) based on the Ludovisi *Mars* (Rome, Mus. N. Romano), in which the heroic nudity of the original is perhaps a little incongruous for an official monument. On his return to Paris in 1809 he exhibited numerous portrait busts, both contemporary and historical, such as those of the actor *François-Joseph Talma* (exh. Salon 1812; untraced) and of *Henry IV* (plaster, exh. Salon 1814; untraced). He also executed a small number of full-length statues, including an unusual one of *Jean-Baptiste Colbert* (marble, 1820;

Versailles, Château). He made models for several monuments that were not executed. Among those large-scale works that were carried out is the impressive figure of *Sorrow* (marble, 1816) for the tomb of *Pierre Gareau* in Père Lachaise Cemetery, Paris.

BIBLIOGRAPHY
Lami
Nouvelles Acquisitions du Département des Sculptures (1980–1983), Paris, Louvre cat. (Paris, 1984), pp. 72–3
La Sculpture française au XIXe siècle (exh. cat., ed. A. Pingeot; Paris, Grand Pal., 1986)
GÉRARD HUBERT

Milián, Raúl (*b* Havana, 1914; *d* Havana, 1984). Cuban painter. He was a member of the Grupo de los Once, which introduced Abstract Expressionism into Cuba without great success, although he is difficult to categorize in any one school. He had no formal training and worked entirely in small formats with ink and watercolour, producing haunting images of flowers (e.g. *Sunflower*, 1961; Havana, Mus. N. B.A.) and figures as well as purely abstract work (e.g. *Abstraction*, 1959; Havana, Mus. N. Cuba). His dark palette enabled him to have a subtle control of colour and transparency. His first solo exhibition in Havana was not until 1953. A silver medallist at the third São Paulo Biennial, Milián has works in the Museo Nacional de Bellas Artes, Havana; Museum of Modern Art, New York; and Milwaukee Art Museum.

BIBLIOGRAPHY
Enciclopedia de Cuba (Madrid, 1975), vii, pp. 200–02
RICARDO PAU-LLOSA

Milioti. Russian family of painters.

(1) Nikolay (Dmitriyevich) Milioti (*b* Moscow, 29 Jan 1874; *d* Paris, 26 Dec 1962). The styles of both Nikolay and his brother (2) Vasily Milioti were formed under the influence of Mikhail Vrubel' and the writings of the second generation of Russian Symbolist poets, Andrey Bely and Aleksandr Blok. A friendly critic writing in 1906 praised Nikolay Milioti's 'hovering pale veils', while Vladimir Stasov, the champion of Realism in Russian art, attacked the 'bacilli' and 'bacteria' (of corruption, presumably) that he perceived in Nikolay Milioti's works. Both comments may have been applied to one of his most frequently reproduced paintings, *Angel of Sorrow* (*c*. 1906–7; untraced, see Gray, 1986, pl. 44). This decorative panel painting has obvious affinities, in both subject-matter and style, with the painting by Vrubel' of the *Demon* (1890; Moscow, Tret'yakov Gal.). In each painting the central figure is a spiritual being, but in Milioti's it is a two-dimensional, wraith-like apparition rather than a fully three-dimensional, muscular presence. However, the construction in separate coloured facets derives from the treatment of the landscape in the painting by Vrubel', and presumably it was this faceting that elicited Stasov's unfavourable comments.

Both Milioti brothers contributed to the 1907 Blue Rose exhibition in Moscow, organized by Pavel Kuznetsov. Nikolay Milioti subsequently exhibited with the second World of Art (Mir Iskusstva) Society from 1910. Works from this period include *Pastoral* (1905; Moscow, Tret'yakov Gal.) and *Self-portrait* (1912; Moscow, Tret'yakov Gal.); other works are in the Russian Museum,

St Petersburg. After the October Revolution Nikolay emigrated to France.

(2) Vasily (Dmitriyevich) Milioti (*b* Moscow, 18 Feb 1875; *d* Moscow, 5 March 1943). Painter and writer, brother of (1) Nikolay Milioti. Like his elder brother, Vasily Milioti was one of the younger generation of Symbolist artists resident in Moscow that emerged under the influence of the paintings of Mikhail Vrubel' and Victor Borisov-Musatov. In the mosaic-like patterning of *Legend* (1905; untraced, see Gray, 1986, pl. 47), the resemblance to the work of Vrubel' is striking. He also used similar imagery to his brother, for example in *Legend*, in which a wraith-like female face appears out of a dense backdrop of foliage. To contemporary critics, however, Vasily Milioti seemed more closely allied to Victor Borisov-Musatov, who shared his desire to create decorative ensembles. His crayon drawing *Morning* (1906; London, priv. col., see Bowlt, 1973, pl. between pp. 176 and 177) is entirely made up of curved lines, recalling aspects of the style of both Borisov-Musatov and of Paul Gauguin in his Tahitian period.

By the time of the first GOLDEN FLEECE exhibition in Moscow (1908) a change had occurred in his work. In the paintings shown at that exhibition, according to Gray, 'his curling, twisted line pursued a pulsing organic rhythm in a freer form'. In *Poet* (1907–8; untraced, see Gray, 1962, pl. 49), rich hues of blue with gold and pink enhance the oriental appearance of the figures. Milioti was a major contributor of graphic designs to the journal *Vesy* ('Scales') from 1904 to 1909. He also contributed costume designs for Vsevolod Meyerhold's production of Ibsen's *Hedda Gabler* in St Petersburg in 1907. He was art correspondent for the journal *Zolotoye runo* ('Golden Fleece') from October 1906 to 1909. After the revolution of 1905, he took little part in official art life, but he continued to write in the same Symbolist manner, showing his work only to a narrow circle of family and friends.

BIBLIOGRAPHY
C. Gray: *The Great Experiment: Russian Art 1863–1922* (London, 1962, rev. by M. Burleigh-Motley, enlarged, 1986)
J. Bowlt: 'Russian Symbolism and the "Blue Rose" Movement', *Slav. & E. Eur. Rev.*, li/123 (1973), pp. 161–81
——: 'The Blue Rose: Russian Symbolism in Art', *Burl. Mag.*, cxviii (1976), pp. 566–74
M. Kiselyov: 'Poeticheskiy mir Vasiliya Milioti' [The poetic world of Vasily Milioti], *Iskusstvo*, v (1978), pp. 44–51

MARIAN BURLEIGH-MOTLEY

Military architecture and fortification. Buildings associated with warfare—usually defensive warfare—and political control.

See also CASTLE.

I. Introduction II. Ancient. III. Western. IV. Islamic world. V. Indian subcontinent. VI. Central Asia. VII. East Asia. VIII. South-east Asia. IX. Africa. X. Pre-Columbian Americas.

I. Introduction.

Military architecture has existed for millennia, ever since men have needed to compete for territory. It follows and tries to anticipate developments in tactics and weaponry, but historically it has also reflected current political organization and social structures. Prehistoric communal strongholds had additional economic and ritual functions; city walls were a defensive response to siegecraft; forts and camps were built for tactical advance and to consolidate military achievement; and in the medieval period the castle symbolized both local control and defensive capability. From the deployment of gunpowder artillery in the late 14th century until the mid-19th century, the design of fortifications responded to the use of ever more powerful artillery and the limitations imposed on an army dependent on horse transport. With the introduction of rifled artillery and motor-driven armoured vehicles, designs again underwent fundamental changes, until military architecture as such was rendered obsolete by the deployment after World War II of guided missiles that could overfly and destroy the most powerful fortifications. Although military architecture is inherently functional and utilitarian, its aesthetic and symbolic aspects are equally significant.

BIBLIOGRAPHY
C. Bisset: *The Theory and Construction of Fortification* (London, 1751)
S. Toy: *A History of Fortification from 3000 BC to AD 1700* (London, 1955)
J. Boudet: *The Ancient Art of Warfare*, 2 vols (London, 1966)
Q. Hughes: *Military Architecture* (London, 1974)
R. A. Brown: *The Architecture of Castles* (London, 1984)
R. Muir: *Castles and Strongholds* (London, 1990)

1. Glossary. 2. Symbolism.

1. GLOSSARY. An unusually extensive and specialist vocabulary has developed in the field: a glossary has therefore been supplied to guide the reader through the technical terms used in the literature of military architecture and fortification. Cross-references within this subsection are indicated in the form 'See *Outwork*'; cross-references to other articles in the dictionary are in the usual form '*See* DONJON'.

Advanced work. See *Outwork*.

Alcazaba. See *Qaṣaba*.

Amṣār [Arab.]. Garrison town.

Arg [*arq*; Pers.]. Citadel. See also *Kuhandiz*.

Bailey. Enclosure containing a castle's residential buildings. See also *Motte*.

Barbette. Raised terrace from which mounted heavy guns may fire over the parapet.

Barbican. Projecting defensive position to protect a town or castle gate, or placed at the head of a fixed bridge or drawbridge.

Bāshūra [Arab.]. Bent entrance.

Bastejas. Raised gun platforms; the term is usually applied to north European fortifications in the early 16th century.

Bastion. Projecting tower at the angle of two walls in a fortification. For developments from the mid-15th century *see* BASTION.

Batter. Backward slope of the surface of a wall; inward inclination from the vertical; to slope inward.

Bergfried [Ger.]. Tall, slim watch-tower, rarely residential.

Berm. Ledge; space on top of the scarp wall to prevent loose earth falling in the ditch or moat; continuous bank of earth against a masonry wall.

Brattice [brattish, bretasche, bretesse, brettice; Fr. *bretèche*]. Timber tower or projecting gallery on a castle wall; fixed wooden tower used in siege operations.

Broch. Dry-built roundhouse, common particularly in Scotland during the Late Iron Age (*c.* 75 BC–2nd century AD).

Burj [*burdj*; Arab.]. Tower; the term is used in Islamic architecture, especially in India, and may be applied generally to any tower from lofty edifices to watch-towers and signal-towers.

Cantonment. Corners of a fortification strengthened with projecting, often rusticated, pilasters; temporary quarters of troops; in India, formerly, a permanent military town.

Caponier. Sheltered passage across a ditch leading to the outworks; horseshoe-shaped blockhouse.

Casemate. Chamber (later vaulted) built within the rampart walls; may be used as a magazine, barracks or gun position with embrasures.

Cavalier. Raised gun platform.

Chemin-de-ronde [Fr.]. Continuous wall-walk behind a parapet, providing communications and access to all points along the wall.

Cheval-de-frise [pl. *chevaux-de-frise*; Fr.: 'horse of Friesland']. Spiky defensive structure of wood or stone; may be set in open ground to deter cavalry or on top of a barrier to prevent climbing.

Citadel [It. *cittadella*, diminutive of *città*: 'city']. Fortress in or near a city.

Counterscarp. Outer sloping wall of the ditch or the area between the parapet and the glacis.

Crenel [crenelle]. Open space between merlons on a parapet, forming the characteristic notching of a battlement (crenellation). See also *Embrasure*.

Curtain. Main wall of a defensive work or the part of a rampart between two bastions; a protective barrier in general. *See* CURTAIN WALL (i).

Demi-lune. Outwork with a crescent-shaped gorge. See also *Ravelin*.

Ditch. Linear excavation, either wet (moat) or dry, intended as an obstacle to attackers or a sheltered line of communications for defenders.

Donjon [keep]. Main tower of a castle; the ultimate refuge and the lord's residence. *See* DONJON.

Embrasure. Opening in a wall or between two merlons on a parapet, through which weapons are fired; sometimes wider at the rear to increase the arc of fire.

Enceinte. Area enclosed within a defended place's main line of ramparts, but excluding its outworks.

Enfilade. Fire that rakes a line or position from end to end.

Escalade. Scaling of walls by attackers using ladders.

Face. Exposed outer surface, particularly a bastion's wall between its salient angle and flank.

Fasil [Arab.]. Intervallum.

Fausse-braye [Fr.]. Low outer wall sometimes used in the 16th and 17th centuries to protect the main curtain wall.

Flank. Side or wing of an army; a body of soldiers on the extreme right or left of a formation; area of a defensive work that provides flanking fire to support another section of the defences; part of a bastion between its face and the curtain wall.

Fort. Structure designed primarily for defence, as distinct from a CASTLE, which also provides living accommodation; small fortress.

Fortification rasante [Fr.]. Low-level fortification.

Fortress. Important fortified complex, often designed to surround and protect an entire city.

Gala'a. See QAL'A.

Garillum. Earth and timber barrier or palisade.

Gila. See QAL'A.

Glacis. Long, gentle descent from the ramparts to open countryside, kept clear to provide no cover for attacking troops.

Gorge. Rear face of a defensive work.

Hornwork. Outwork with angular points (or horns), comprising two half-bastions (demi-bastions) joined by a bastion or section of curtain wall.

Kal'a. See QAL'A.

Kasba. See *Qaṣaba*.

Kasr. See *Qaṣr*.

Keep. See *Donjon*.

Khandaq [*khandak*; Pers. & Arab.]. Ditch, trench or moat.

Kuhandiz [Pers.]. Citadel. See also *Arg*.

Machicolation. Provision of openings between corbels on a curtain wall or gateway, through which burning pitch, quicklime and missiles might be dropped on attackers; a projecting gallery incorporating such openings. *See* MACHICOLATION.

Martello tower. Small circular or oval tower, often just two storeys high (the lower for provisions, the upper for troops), with a gun mounted on the flat roof; substantial numbers were erected in southern England, Ireland, Jersey and elsewhere during the Napoleonic Wars.

Merlon [It. *merlone*: 'battlement']. The solid, tooth-like, raised portion of a crenellated parapet, set between embrasures or crenels.

Migdol. Watch-tower or citadel in ancient Israel and Palestine; ancient Egyptian fortress-temple.

Motte. Steep, artificial earthern mound forming the base of a castle's stronghold, typically employed during the 11th and 12th centuries in association with a bailey.

Nuraghe [*noraghe*; Sardinian: 'heap of stones with internal cavity']. Prehistoric round tower, typically comprising a central tower surrounded by a fortified wall with bastions and ramparts. *See* NURAGHE.

Orillion. Protective, curved construction attached to the angle between the face and flank of a bastion.

Outwork [*advanced work*]. Defensive work located beyond the glacis, but close enough to receive protection from the main fortification; designed to compel an enemy to start a siege from a distance.

Parapet. Breastwork designed to cover troops from observation and fire.

Pentagonal fort. Five-sided fortified work, providing improved lines of fire around the perimeter.

Pentagonal beaked tower. Bastion of Byzantine origin in the form of an irregular pentagon projecting from the curtain wall; developed for defensive fire artillery by Italian engineers *c.* 1500.

Postern [sallyport]. Tunnel providing access to a ditch or outside fortified work; may be intended as a means of escape, for sorties in a siege or as a shortcut during peace.

Qal'a [*gala'a, gila, kal'a*; Arab.]. Citadel or fortress built on a hill or set across the city walls.

Qaṣaba [Arab.; Eng. kasba; Sp. *alcazaba*]. Garrison fortress.

Qaṣr [*kasr*; Arab.]. Palace, castle or mansion.

Rampart. Protective embankment or mound raised inside the curtain wall.

Ravelin [demi-lune]. Outwork with two faces and a gorge, set beyond the ditch in front of the curtain wall.

Redan. Triangular outwork; may be arranged together in the form of a serrated edge.

Redoubt. Small work in a bastion or ravelin, or located beyond the glacis but within defensive fire.

Reduit. Inner fortified retreat for the garrison.

Réduit modèle [Fr.]. Semicircular coastal defence tower built in France during the Napoleonic Wars.

Revetment. The facing of a wall with temporary materials (e.g. sandbags), stone or brick to strengthen the rampart; the retaining wall in a ditch.

Ribāṭ [Arab.]. Fortified monastery.

Ring-fort. Defended refuge of the Iron Age or later, enclosed within earthen ramparts; outer circle of detached fortified works arranged around a late 19th-century entrenched camp or fortress.

Ring-work. Concentric earthwork defences.

Rocca [It.]. Fort, often located as a citadel on the highest point of an urban area.

Salient angle. Outward point of a bastion or any projecting work.

Sallyport. See *Postern.*

Scarp. Inner wall of a ditch or the wall in front of the rampart.

Sconce. Small earthwork.

Shahristān [Pers.]. Walled settlement.

Shiro, -jō [Jap.]. Castle.

Star fort. Fort with earthworks, bastions etc arranged in the shape of a star.

Talus [tallus]. Sloping wall, wider at its base. See also *Batter.*

Tenaille [tenail]. Small, low-lying work, positioned between bastions in the ditch, to provide extra cover for the curtain wall.

Tenshu [*tenshukaku*; Jap.]. Donjon.

Tetrapyrgion [Gr.]. Byzantine fort with square corner towers.

Tour modèle. Square coastal tower built in France during the Napoleonic Wars.

Trace. Ground-plan of a fortification.

Trunnion. Either of a pair of side projections, on which, typically, a big gun is pivoted to move in a vertical plane.

Vallum. Rampart, generally raised using earth excavated from a broad, flat-bottomed, outer ditch and typically used by the Romans to surround their camps; system also used as a boundary or defensive line, for example along Hadrian's Wall, England.

Yamajiro [Jap.]. Mountain fort.

          ☐

2. SYMBOLISM. Being 'military architecture' does not make fortification solely utilitarian; it requires that it be much more. The message of power, dignity and awe constitutes the metaphysics of fortification. Vitruvius (*On Architecture* X) remarked on the symbolism of war expressed in architecture: just as the dangers of defeat could be represented by architectural devices, so a feeling of strength could be imparted to deter an attacker. Protection without resort to force, achieved by deterrence alone, was always important but of greatly varying significance; and it did not exhaust the psychological component. By showing how fortification partook of motives common to other art forms, this section seeks to draw together themes inherent in subsequent sections and to consider the meaning beyond the physical possessed by fortification.

(i) Introduction. (ii) Aesthetics and metaphysics. (iii) Inherent symbolism. (iv) Explicit symbolism.

(i) Introduction. Enclosures expressed the taboos of early societies by marking out the sacred precinct: banks flanking Neolithic long barrows, the ring-ditches of causewayed camps, such places of ceremonious assembly as the temple temenos of ancient Greece and the sculpture-clad gateways of Egyptian and Mesopotamian sanctuaries, all defended

by force of spiritual exclusiveness. Even the domestic verge was defined by the ditch and fence. Subsequently notions of defended space, security and power became materialized and endowed with physical capability to resist intrusion, but the element of taboo remained: the Forbidden City of Beijing was also a stronghold, Stonehenge and the Temple of Amun at Karnak never were.

This duality is less paradoxical than modern analysis would suggest. Such elaborate Roman city gates as the Porta Nigra at Trier or the Balkerne Gate, Colchester (Essex), outshone those of their castra, being toll-points, jurisdictional transitions and expressions of corporate identity as well as defences. In the Middle Ages, the supreme era of defensive symbolism, walls denoted the chartered borough and demarcated its franchise, as also did the crenellated walls of ecclesiastical precincts. The elongated, devious entrance-ways of an acropolis or hill-fort have affinities with the circuitous carriage-drives of 18th-century mansions. They are as ambivalent as the threatening machicolated parapets, murder holes and redoubled barriers of a medieval gateway. All possess elements of psychological and physical defence.

This is equally true of fortifications in the starkest reinforced concrete. The 'pill-boxes' of World War II and the Admiralty Fort (Citadel) on Horse Guards Parade in London have their own charisma, even if no more than the inherent symbolism of shape or sheer size. Twentieth-century fortification could display a very clear symbolism, especially when ideology was strong. The German gun-emplacements of the Atlantic Wall have a chunky, Cubist elegance, while flak towers at Berlin and Vienna had more than a touch of romantic medievalism. Shell-shaped, multi-storey, air-raid shelters, like ballistic missiles on the launching-pad, have a futuristic nostalgia transcending the utilitarian Nissen hut or Anderson shelter.

(ii) Aesthetics and metaphysics. Narrowly military interpretations of fortification are now recognized to be insufficient: cultural, social, aesthetic and psychological factors all belong. Such phrases as 'show of force', 'deterrence', 'civic pride', 'psychological and functional' (not a true antithesis) and 'Baroque character' in different ways acknowledge the importance of symbolism. The message conveyed to the modern observer is, however, generally presumed to be that intended by the builder, which is certainly more true of the general effects of 'inherent symbolism' than it is of the very complex field of 'explicit symbolism', lying as it does in the interpretation of specific architectural features, the precise meaning of which has often become obscure.

Fortress design sprang from aesthetic as well as military factors. Simple technical determinism will not do: although the replacement of square towers by round in later 12th-century Europe was once attributed to fear of mining, both forms were almost equally vulnerable, and the uneven stair-risers ('Norman trip stairs'), thought to display obsessive cunning, perhaps owe more to poor workmanship. While it cannot be doubted that 1st- and 2nd-century AD Roman turrets resembling sentry-boxes gave way for defensive reasons to outwardly projecting solid bastions provided with turn-tables for *ballistae* (e.g. Burgh Castle, Suffolk; *c.* AD 275), any single explanation must be used

with great caution. The use of structurally inefficient horseshoe arches in Islamic fortification and the imitation of the late Roman and Byzantine castrum in the Arabian caravanserai require cultural explanations, of which symbolism is most important. The varied forms of battlements, so essential to fortification as to be its most universal symbol, defy any common military purpose. From the earliest multivallate Iron Age hill-fort and Mediterranean acropolis down to the seemingly puritan functionalism of 19th-century artillery fortresses (e.g. the defences of Portsmouth; Western Heights complex, Dover; both 1860s) symbolism continues to unite fortification with art because the personal or social motives of communities and of patrons transcend calculating fears. The resultant architecture is militant rather than military, demonstrative as much as defensive.

Current perceptions are derived from the 19th-century tendency to think in categories. The militarism of 19th-century Europe made every gentleman a potential officer. Individual military initiative had succumbed to state monopoly, so that private fortifications (i.e. the castle) seemed anti-social, if romantic, and the 'public works' of, for example, the Roman Empire were more acceptable. Fortification became a military science, and defence works expressed state power, defending frontiers and belonging to the sphere of the professional soldier. Centrally governed societies such as the Roman and Byzantine provided the best models, with their linear or continuous defences. However, the approach clashed with the medieval castle and its corporate version in town walls. Seemingly perversely, the castle was 'domestic' as well as 'military', more 'private' than 'public'. Symbolism, moreover, was not admitted to have a legitimate function in fortifications, and this particularly affected the study of the medieval period, when castellated symbolism was both essential and all-pervasive.

(iii) Inherent symbolism. Symbolism inherent in fortification can be the victim of an individual's subjective vision and inability to distinguish between modern perceptions and those of the past. If a building is impressive to modern eyes, it would have been still more so to its contemporaries. This may suffice to assess the inherent symbolism of general visual impact, but it is inadequate to explain the explicit symbolism of particular features, the significance of which lies more within its own context than in the common human domain. The power, mass and logical clarity of the Elizabethan trace of Berwick-upon-Tweed (Northumb.; 1558–65) was intended to affirm possession of a much-contested frontier outpost and to deter the Scots. It was a chief function of fortification to advertise an accomplished permanence, whether personal, dynastic or collective, and to attempt, as at CHÂTEAU-GAILLARD (1190s), to make it good. The 'rock' and 'high tower' of the psalmist's metaphor (e.g. Psalms 31:3) is a pure distillation of the essence of security; and such synonyms for fortress as the Italian *rocca* or the French *puy* show the same imagery. To contemporaries, especially the rural majority, the large, logically laid-out stone legionary forts, town walls and sacred precincts were the more impressive by contrast with the rural environment of wattle, timber and thatch. Most fortifications in their prime, moreover,

1. Château of Mehun-sur-Yèvre depicted in the *Temptation of Christ* by the Limbourg brothers; miniature from the Très Riches Heures, *c.* 1411/13–16 (Chantilly, Musée Condé, Château de Chantilly, MS. 65, fol. 161*v*)

were even more 'powerful' than now. Maiden Castle (Dorset) no longer possesses its stone revetments, palisading or timber-works of the 1st century AD, but its awesome extent, relief and complexity still effectively proclaim the determination and authority of the first builders. In the Roman attack in AD 44 the legionary field *ballistae* outranged native slingers: Roman traditions of victory over 'barbarians' morally disarmed the symbolism of the 'great dun'.

Wherever a masonry style or other device can suggest antiquity a strong appeal was made. Nostalgic allusion is significant but elusive. Sparse evidence helps a little. Styles evidently passed quickly out of date. Nevertheless those majestic later 14th-century machicolated towers, Guy's and Caesar's, at Warwick Castle (Warwicks) recall the glamour and chivalry of the Hundred Years' War (1337–1453). The composition is too dramatic to be mere prosaic flanking of the curtain wall. Moats and lakes gave superb scenic effects, which medieval castellated architecture greatly exploited, as at Broughton (Oxon; early 14th century), Shirburn (Oxon; *c.* 1380) and Bodiam (E. Sussex; 1385–90). In France numerous dramatic wall-heads with superimposed levels, conical roofs, pinnacles and lofty chimneys can still be seen, for example at Pierrefonds (Oise; 1390s), built by Louis, Duc d'Orléans, and at Vèz (Oise; 1390–1410). Remote from the grim realities of war,

they convey seigneurial panache and chivalric romanticism. The symbols are enhanced by the Limbourg brothers' miniatures for the Très Riches Heures of Jean, Duc de Berry (Chantilly, Mus. Condé, MS. 65). A comparison of the extant remains with the exquisitely detailed miniatures of castle-palaces of, for example, Mehun-sur-Yèvre (fol. 161*v*; see fig. 1), Poitiers (fol. 7*v*) and Lusignan (fol. 3*v*) clearly shows that patrons wished to convey an idealized version of reality, wholly transformed into the pure symbolism to which actuality aspired. Perhaps the clearest expression of the quality sought occurs in Henry III's instruction to the Constable of Dover Castle in 1247 to show off the rebuilt castle to a distinguished continental visitor 'in eloquent style, so that he may see the magnificence (*nobilitas*) of the castle and perceive no defects in it' (London, PRO, Close Rolls of. . .Henry III, 1247–51, p. 8).

(iv) Explicit symbolism. Explicit symbolism, often apparently obscure, resides in detailed features, almost always defensive in origin and use, that have been deliberately sublimated in varying degrees into symbols. Interpolated elements must be distinguished: for instance, the rusticated jambs and classical pediment of the grand entrance of an 18th-century artillery fort (e.g. the Porte de Strasbourg, Neuf-Brisach; 1708) deliberately introduce a note of culture, taste and refinement among the emphatic brutality of revetted ditches, casemates and mathematically murderous gunpower. Such adornments are extraneous to the structure. Many later castles such as Hylton (Durham) and Lumley (Northumb.) are similarly ornamented with heraldic devices or simple emblems, of which variants representing lions were placed by the Percy family at Warkworth and Alnwick (both Northumb.), by the Venetians as the lion of St Mark, and on the Lion Gate at ancient Mycenae. Pepper-pot watch-turrets or sentry-boxes, perched on the acute angle of a bastion (as at Edinburgh Castle; see fig. 2), and the heavy roll-mouldings marking the junction of sloping talus and vertical curtain qualify as integral features because they arise from structural as well as aesthetic needs. The geometrical rigour of the vast layout, composed of large-scale units, required (as did the defence) these explicit but quaintly incongruous hints of humanity. In 17th-century England, which was parsimonious, parliamentarian and also insular, great artillery forts so expressive of state power were far fewer than in the France of Louis XIV and Sébastien Leprestre de Vauban. Britain spent money chiefly on ephemeral warships and on accompanying dockyards and port facilities. The theme is more evident in conquered Scotland (Fort George and Fort Augustus, both near Inverness, Highland; see fig. 14b below) and overseas, particularly in India. In the 19th century military logic often did away with such ambivalent features, substituting cheaper and cruder brick for stone.

Such great public works have affinities beyond the Middle Ages, although Edward I's castles in Wales, six of which have walled towns appended, symbolized and perpetuated the conquest (*see* CAERNARFON CASTLE). In the Greek and Roman worlds city walls marked corporate status and identity, and revolt was punished by razing them. At Jerusalem only the Temple substructure and fragments of Herod's palace survived the razing of AD 132. The same dual significance attached to the great Byzantine

2. Pepper-pot watch-turrets on the angled bastions of Edinburgh Castle, *c.* 1735

frontier fortification schemes of Justinian I (*reg* AD 527–65) and the Komnenian dynasty, but for fully explicit symbolism, latent in specific architectural features, medieval Europe affords the clearest examples.

Of cardinal significance was the lordship symbol of the donjon, be it an earthwork motte once crowned by a timber tower or a free-standing 'great tower'. In the 19th century, military preoccupations caused scholars to label 'keep' what was simply a tall, fire-resistant stone house with a first-floor hall, and to miss the powerful symbolism it retained throughout its long history (*see* CASTLE, §1). Evidence from 13th-century northern France shows that mural towers (including miniaturized ones) and archery loops for crossbows were strongly emotive symbols of the lordly status with which fortification in a feudal society was so intimately linked.

Into the 16th century and beyond, emphatic gate-houses were deliberate statements, occurring suitably modulated in castellated manor houses, episcopal palaces and precincts and in urban enceintes. The portcullis and drawbridge were clear symbols. City seals show crenellated gates and walls. In manuscript illustrations, such as those in the Douce Apocalypse (*c.* 1270–75; Oxford, Bodleian Lib., MS. Douce 180, p. 58), they were used to denote the Heavenly Jerusalem. Henry VIII's coastal gun-castles of the 1540s preserve the power of the medieval imagery of fortification, where symbols of castellation remain despite their incomplete adaptation to artillery. The best and least altered exemplars of this are the miniature and grimly pretty granite forts of Falmouth Haven and St Mawes (see fig. 14a below) and Pendennis (all Cornwall). Their nearby

Elizabethan successors show a very different spirit, their symbolism reticent and inherent.

In France the castle image survived, replete with the explicit symbolism of the genre, scarcely modified by the Renaissance, in Francis I's Chambord (Loir-et-Cher) and in the entire château tradition. Even classicism failed to destroy what Romanticism was soon to revive, as may be seen in England at Waddesdon Manor (Bucks) and in many German castles. The grim Aragonese artillery castle of Salses (Roussillon; 1496) and the angle-bastioned forts of the Venetian empire, such as those at Herakleion (mid-16th century) and Nicosia (1565–70) had long since abandoned nostalgia. Crenellation survived beyond the 18th century in Mughal India and in parts of the Islamic world; and in Europe battlements remained long after the wall-walk had become a mere parapet-gutter. Whether in the attributes of the Roman *praefectus castrorum* or in the tombs of the Tudor nobility, crenellation in a wide variety of form, scale and position outlasted all other explicit symbols of fortification. Only the inherent symbolism lasted longer.

Symbols in fortification are both aesthetic and materialistic, and their relative strength is different in each case. When a fortification gives only token acknowledgement to current improvements in warlike technique, especially when the builders' resources allowed and his responsibilities might seem to have demanded radical adaptation to resist them, danger has been ignored and symbolic means have taken over the task. Fortifications where this is complete are not to be dismissed as 'sham'. In them the spiritual message has triumphed over the materialistic.

BIBLIOGRAPHY
H. F. Thuillier: *The Principles of Land Defence* (London, 1902)
A. Tuulse: *Borgar i västerlandet* [Castles of the western world] (Stockholm, 1952; Eng. trans., London, 1958)
P. A. Faulkner: 'Domestic Planning from the Twelfth to the Fourteenth Century', *Archaeol. J.*, cxv (1958), pp. 150–83
S. Cruden: *The Scottish Castle* (London, 1960)
P. A. Faulkner: 'Castle-planning in the Fourteenth Century', *Archaeol. J.*, cxx (1963), pp. 213–35
L. R. Shelby: *John Rogers: Tudor Military Engineer* (Oxford, 1967)
P. Contamine: *Guerre, état et société à la fin du moyen âge, 1337–1494* (Paris, 1972)
K. Mallory and A. Ottar: *Architecture of Aggression: Military Architecture of Two World Wars* (London, 1973)
C. L. H. Coulson: 'Castellation in the County of Champagne in the Thirteenth Century', *Château Gaillard: Etudes de castellologie médiévale*, ix–x: *Actes des colloques internationaux: Basle and Durham, 1978 and 1980*, pp. 347–64
——: 'Structural Symbolism in Medieval Castle Architecture', *J. Brit. Archaeol. Assoc.*, cxxxii (1979), pp. 73–90
A. W. Lawrence: *Greek Aims in Fortification* (Oxford, 1979)
J. Mesqui and C. Ribéra-Pervillé: 'Les Châteaux de Louis d'Orléans et leurs architectes, 1391–1407', *Bull. Mnmtl*, cxxxviii (1980), pp. 293–345
B. Morley: 'Aspects of Fourteenth Century Castle Design', *Collectanea Historica: Essays in Memory of Stuart Rigold*, ed. A. Detsicas (Maidstone, 1981), pp. 104–13
C. L. H. Coulson: 'Hierarchism in Conventual Crenellation: An Essay in the Sociology and Metaphysics of Medieval Fortification', *Med. Archaeol.*, xxvi (1982), pp. 69–100
J. Coad: *Historic Architecture of the Royal Navy* (London, 1983)
M. W. Thompson: *The Decline of the Castle* (Cambridge, 1987)
C. L. H. Coulson: 'Some Analysis of the Castle of Bodiam, East Sussex', *Medieval Knighthood*, iv (Woodbridge, 1992), pp. 51–107
——: 'Battlements and the Bourgeoisie: Municipal Status and the Apparatus of Urban Defence in Later-Medieval England', *Medieval Knighthood*, iv (in preparation)

C. L. H. COULSON

II. Ancient.

1. Prehistoric Europe. 2. Ancient Near East. 3. Egypt. 4. Greece. 5. Rome.

1. PREHISTORIC EUROPE. The development of fortified enclosure settlements in Europe began during the Neolithic period, for which there is evidence of the enclosure of habitation sites with ditches and/or timber palisades. Such enclosing features later developed into genuine fortifications, their strength reflecting not only the need to protect a settlement and its contents, but also a desire to display power and wealth as a sign of rank at a time of emerging social differentiation.

The fortified Greek sites of the 5th–4th millennia BC are among the earliest in Europe. They include SESKLO and DIMINI, where earlier, unfortified, settlements were enclosed by substantial stone walls in the 4th millennium BC. At about the same time, the site of Habaşeşti in Romania was defended by cutting off the promontory on which it was sited by means of two substantial ditches. By the end of the 4th millennium BC, fortified settlements were widespread across south-eastern, central and western Europe, extending from Polyanitsa in Bulgaria to Hambleton Hill in Dorset, England. At Crickley Hill in Gloucestershire, England, a series of banks and ditches was eventually replaced by a strong wall with massive gates: a find of 400 flint arrowheads embedded in the bank near the entrance, and evidence of burning, underlined the necessity of such defences.

During the 3rd millennium BC, the defences of many sites became more complex: at LOS MILLARES in Spain, for example, the massively built walls were partly constructed in the dry-stone technique, but included areas where stonework was bonded with a mixture of limestone and clay. These walls were embellished with semicircular bastions similar to those at the Greek island sites of Kastri, near Chalandriani on SYROS in the Cyclades and LERNA in the Peloponnese. VILLANOVA DE SÃO PEDRO in Portugal had three concentric lines of defences; at Zambujal, also in Portugal, a similar series of three massively built concentric stone walls included complex bastion structures that guarded such weak spots as the gates. These sites were large, enclosing a considerable number of structures; smaller sites of the same period—for example Homolka in the Czech Republic where the timber palisades enclosed only a hectare—may have fulfilled a very different function in society.

The early part of the second millennium BC was marked in eastern Europe by the development of a number of fortified sites. Some of these had inner fortified enclosures, which have often been paralleled with Greek acropoleis. One example is Spišský Štvrtok in Slovakia which, like similar contemporary sites, has yielded concentrations of sophisticated metalworking debris. In western Europe, this combination of inner enclosure and fortification did not occur until the 1st millennium BC. From the middle of the 2nd millennium BC, an extraordinary series of defensive towers was developed in Corsica and Sardinia. More properly described as tower-houses, the structures are called nuraghi, and in plan are not unlike the much later Scottish brochs (see below). Entered by a passage, the towers had passages and rooms built within the thickness of the walls, which is up to 8 m thick. Some were later augmented with further towers and surrounding walls with integral towers, as at the site of Su Nuraxi near BARUMINI, Sardinia. There were up to 7000 such towers on Sardinia alone.

Between the second half of the 2nd millennium BC and the middle of the 1st millennium BC, there was a considerable increase in the number of settlements that were either built as fortified sites or were fortified at a later date, a development that eventually affected most of Europe. In Poland and eastern Germany, where the bronze-using Lausitz culture emerged, there was a wide range of fortification types. Hilltop sites were enclosed by ramparts of timber-laced or timber box-framed construction, often with complex entrance systems—a combination of timber and stone that was used throughout Europe during the 1st millennium BC. Lakeside and island settlements, such as BISKUPIN in Poland, were built with massive timber-framed ramparts and defended gateways, and were surrounded by bands of pointed stakes to deter waterborne attacks. At Senftenberg in Germany, access to the main gate was impeded by enclosing the entrance passage, while at Crickley Hill the same end was achieved by the addition of an outer hornwork.

During the Iron Age (c. 750 BC–c. 50 BC), the bow was largely superseded as a weapon of battle, and as a result there was little use of bastions in the 1st millennium BC. An imitation of a Mediterranean wall type constructed at the HEUNEBURG, Germany, in the 6th century BC, incorporated bastions set too close together to be functionally useful; clearly an attempt to impress as well as to defend, the fashion was not copied elsewhere. However, guard chambers and entrance passages that could be closed at both ends with gates were very much in evidence, and the piles of slingstones found at strategic points along the walls of such forts as MAIDEN CASTLE in Dorset, England, show that the defences were sometimes necessary. Areas of Europe in closer contact with Italy and Greece developed similar fortifications: at Ullastret in Spain, occupied between c. 600 BC–c. 200 BC, the 6th-century towers were later linked with a curtain wall of massive dry-stone blocks, and a circular tower replaced with a trapezoidal bastion. Walls with bastions and other embellishments were also built in southern France at such sites as Cayla de Mailhac, Enserune and Entremont. Further north, large defended sites such as Manching in Germany, Mont Beuvray in France and Stradonice, Závist and Staré Hradisko in the Czech Republic represent the first true towns of non-Mediterranean Europe. The walls of Závist enclosed a total area of 170 ha and were massively built of stone and timber, with inturned entrances. In many cases the timber framework was held together with iron nails—a construction technique labelled *murus gallicus* by the Romans.

In some parts of Europe, including Spain, Scotland and Ireland, hill-forts and other defended sites were equipped with an outer defence comprising a band either of sharp timber spikes as at Kaimes in Scotland or of sharp, closely set stones, as at DUN AENGUS and Ballykinvarga in Ireland. It is clear that these bands, known as *chevaux-de-frise* after the medieval defence system that was intended to counteract challenges on horseback, could have effectively delayed attackers on foot, rendering them vulnerable to assault from the walls. The stone forts of Ireland and the brochs of Scotland, with chambers, passages and stairways built into the thickness of their stone walls, clearly represent individual or family responses to times of stress, and are very similar to the earlier nuraghi. Whether in the form of central sites such as Maiden Castle, or of individual fortified dwellings, such as the broch at MOUSA in Scotland, defended settlements were clearly considered necessary, though in many parts of Europe the vast majority of the population must have lived without such security.

See also PREHISTORIC EUROPE, §§V, 3(i) and VI, 2(i).

BIBLIOGRAPHY
C. Tsountas: *Oi proistorikoi akropoleis Dhiminiou kai Seklo* [The prehistoric acropoleis of Dimini and Seklo] (Athens, 1908)
R. E. M. Wheeler: *Maiden Castle* (London, 1943)
Inventory of Shetland, Royal Commission on the Ancient Monuments of Scotland (Edinburgh, 1946), pp. 48–55 [description of the broch at Mousa]
J. L. Caskey: 'Excavations at Lerna, 1952–3 (1954; 1955; 1956; 1957)', *Hesperia*, xxiii (1954), pp. 3–30; xxiv (1955), pp. 25–49; xxv (1956), pp. 147–73; xxvi (1957), pp. 142–62; xxvii (1958), pp. 125–44
G. Lilliu: *I Nuraghi: Torri preistorische di Sardegna* (Cagliari, 1962)
Z. Rajewski: *Biskupin: Osiedle obronne wspólnot pierwotnych sprzed 2500 lat* [Biskupin: defensive settlement of primitive communities of 2500 years ago] (Warsaw, 1970)
P. Harbison: 'Wooden and Stone Chevaux-de-frise in Central and Western Europe', *Proc. Prehist. Soc.*, xxxvii/1 (1971), pp. 195–225
J. Jesson and D. Hill: *The Iron Age and its Hill-forts* (Southampton, 1971)
H. N. Savory: 'The Cultural Sequence at Vila Nova de S. Pedro: A Study of the Section Cut Through the Innermost Rampart of the Chalcolithic Castro in 1959', *Madrid. Mitt.*, xiii (1972), pp. 23–7
J. Collis: *Defended Sites of the Late La Tène*, Brit. Archaeol. Rep., Suppl. Ser. 2 (Oxford, 1975)
W. Kimmig: *Die Heuneburg an der Oberen Donau* (Tübingen, 1978)
J. M. Coles and A. F. Harding: *The Bronze Age in Europe* (London, 1979)
J. Collis: 'A Theoretical Study of Hill-forts', *Hill-fort Studies: Papers Presented to Dr. A. H. A. Hogg*, ed. G. Guilbert (Leicester, 1981), pp. 66–76
B. W. Cunliffe: *Danebury: Anatomy of an Iron Age Hillfort* (London, 1983)
SARA CHAMPION

2. ANCIENT NEAR EAST. The earliest fortified structures of the Near East are Neolithic. A circular stone tower (h. 8.5 m; diam. 10 m) belonging to the phase known as Pre-Pottery Neolithic A (8th millennium BC) was excavated at JERICO. It was solid with an internal staircase and associated with a wall 3 m thick and a ditch cut into bedrock. In Anatolia (now Turkey), at HACILAR, level II (6th millennium BC), buildings covering some 2000 sq. m were enclosed within a mud-brick wall up to 3 m thick with small towers and three gates. The enclosure wall of a similar period at TELL ES-SAWWAN (Iraq) formed a fairly regular quadrilateral; it was more than 1 m thick and was preceded by a ditch. From these enclosure systems the more elaborate regional fortifications of later periods probably developed.

(i) Mesopotamia. Until recently it was believed that no elaborate urban fortifications existed in Mesopotamia (now Iraq) before the 3rd millennium BC. However at HABUBA KABIRA in northern Syria—a city probably founded in the Uruk period (second half of the 4th millennium BC) under southern Mesopotamian influence—excavations revealed a double city wall with regularly spaced towers. This suggests that similar defensive systems probably existed in southern Mesopotamia at least during the 4th millennium BC.

Typical urban fortifications of the Early Dynastic period (c. 2900–c.2340 BC) consisted of double enclosures and thick mud-brick walls with buttresses or turrets on the outer face. At URUK the enclosure wall (length c. 9.5 km) was built of plano-convex bricks, which have an upper convex face characteristic of the period. The inner wall had a slight batter and was reinforced by semicircular and quadrangular buttresses. The outer wall was probably about 3 m thick but is badly preserved. According to an inscription of the 2nd millennium BC, the builder of these fortifications was the legendary hero Gilgamesh, who was probably king of Uruk c. 2600 BC. The partly excavated Early Dynastic wall at Tell Agrab, in the DIYALA REGION, was 5.5 m thick with semicircular buttresses every 15 m. Double walls were also used for important buildings such as the Temple Oval at Khafajeh, also in the Diyala region, which had an oval outer wall c. 1.5 m thick and an inner wall c. 3.5 m thick separated on three sides by a corridor 3–8 m wide.

The earliest evidence for fortification walls with casemates (inner rooms) appears in the sacred enclosure (temenos) areas of the Third Dynasty of Ur (2112–2004 BC) at Ur (see UR, fig. 1) and Uruk. It is probable that town walls followed the same pattern. A small terracotta relief from Larsa (first half of the 2nd millennium BC; Paris, Louvre) depicts a goddess above fortifications with buttresses, towers, a parapet with crenellations and a huge arched gateway. Around 1700 BC some cities in Babylonia were surrounded by mud *levées* c. 50 m thick at the base, which were continuously renewed until the 1st millennium BC. These structures were studied during excavations at Tell ed-Der and SIPPAR (Gasche and Paepe, 1980); it seems that their primary function was to protect the inner cities from flooding, but at times they may also have been used as military defences.

Elaborate fortifications were built by Assyrian and Babylonian kings during the 1st millennium BC. The best example is at KHORSABAD, where the rectangular city was surrounded by a city wall straddled by a citadel on which the palaces and temples were built. The wall was of mud-brick on stone foundations, with stepped crenellations of stone. It was strengthened by projecting platforms every 27 m, and the outer face was battered to a height of 3 m or more. Long fortification walls were built at least twice to protect Babylonia against invasion. The wall built by Shu-Sin, King of Ur (*reg* 2037–2029 BC), against the Amorites has not been located, but that built by Nebuchadnezzar II (*reg* 604–562 BC) and referred to by Xenophon as the 'Median Wall' stretched for 50 km between the Tigris and Euphrates rivers. A length has probably been located north of Sippar; it is at least 6 m wide and consists of an earth core faced with baked bricks (some of them inscribed) set in a bitumen mortar (Gasche and others, 1987).

(ii) Anatolia. The best-preserved example of military architecture of the 2nd millennium BC is to be found at the Hittite capital Boğazköy. Both the city and the citadel were fortified, generally with casemate walls with an overall thickness of 7.8 m for the earlier phase (before c. 1400 BC) and 4.25 m for the later phase (c. 1400–c.1200 BC). Towers projected from the exterior wall at fairly regular intervals,

and a lower outer wall also had towers. The lower part of the walls was of stone, and traces suggest that the upper part consisted of a wooden framework and mud-bricks, topped by crenellation. The walls stood at the top of a steep slope, which was natural in some places but elsewhere was formed by artificial earth ramparts with a stone-paved glacis. Some natural rock outcrops were incorporated into the fortifications by daring feats of engineering, including a bridge across a gorge. The artificial embankment was pierced beneath the walls in nine places by posterns (*see* ANATOLIA, ANCIENT, §II, 2 and fig. 6), which were tunnels (l. *c.* 50–70 m) with corbelled vaults built of large stone blocks (Cyclopean masonry). There were probably eight city gates, four of which had doorways with parabolic arches flanked by towers and decorated with sculptures (for illustrations *see* BOĞAZKÖY and ANATOLIA, ANCIENT, fig. 7).

Another impressive fortification is the city gate of the Phrygian capital at GORDION (8th century BC). It is 9 m wide and 23 m deep with a sloping floor, and its battered limestone walls were covered by a layer of whitewashed stucco. It survives to a height of 9 m and supports the later Persian gate (5th–4th century BC). The walls (2.5–4 m thick) were faced with masonry over a rubble core. In eastern Anatolia, between the 9th and 7th centuries BC the Urartians (*see* URARTIAN, §2) built a series of strategically placed fortresses and citadels to guard the mountain passes and routes through their kingdom against Assyrian attack. The fine ashlar walls followed the natural contours and were strengthened with corner bastions and square buttresses. A bronze model (London, BM) and a rock relief from ADILCEVAZ (Ankara, Mus. Anatol. Civiliz.) show walls and towers with stepped crenellations, arched doorways and up to four upper storeys with rectangular windows. The upper part of the walls was probably of brick, and the projecting parapets may have been wooden structures built out on beams.

(iii) Syria–Palestine. Three main phases (Early and Middle Bronze Ages and Israelite kingdoms) are distinguishable in Palestine, and the same general distinctions are also valid for Syria. The Early Bronze Age fortifications of Syria–Palestine (3rd millennium BC) were composed of massive, straight walls (8–10 m thick), built of mud-brick, stone or mud-brick on a stone base, with towers at regular intervals (e.g. at BYBLOS, MEGIDDO and AI). They enclosed large settlements, so the enceintes may have been several kilometres long. The presence of numerous gates and posterns seems to have been a feature of Early Bronze Age fortifications.

Middle Bronze Age fortifications (first half of the 2nd millennium BC) generally enclosed smaller settlements, and there were usually only one or two main gates as, for example, at TELL ATCHANA (Turkey), EBLA (Syria) and Megiddo and Gezer (Israel). The walls were thinner (2–3 m) and often curvilinear. Towers appear only at Gezer, but there are frequent breaks in wall alignments, forming salients. The slopes outside the walls were consolidated by a revetment of beaten earth or calcareous material so as to form a glacis. Another type of Middle Bronze Age defence consisted of earth *levées c.* 50 m wide at the base and 15 m high (e.g. probably at HAZOR, Israel).

Although much the same development is to be found throughout Syria and Palestine, the fortifications of UGARIT, a city of the Canaanites (*see* CANAANITE) on the north Syrian coast (second half of the 2nd millennium BC), are remarkable in that they show features similar to those of contemporaneous Hittite sites (e.g. Boğazköy). A form of fortified watch-tower (*migdol*) found in some sites was adopted in temple design (e.g. at SHECHEM; *see* SYRIA-PALESTINE, fig. 6), a type seen also in Egypt (*see* §3 below). In the late 2nd and early 1st millennia BC casemate walls were frequently used (see fig. 3a). Elaborate gates, such as those at Megiddo, Hazor and Gezer (see fig. 3b), have towers and four partition walls on either side of a central passage, dividing them into successive compartments for additional security (*see also* ISRAELITE). This type of gate has been attributed to King Solomon (*reg c.* 961–922 BC). Assyrian reliefs of the 9th to the 7th century BC (e.g. London, BM) depict many Syrian and Palestinian towns. Sennacherib's reliefs of the siege of Lachish in southern Palestine (701 BC; London, BM) show double parallel walls with salient towers. The inner wall was higher than the outer, and both walls stood at the top of a glacis.

(iv) Ancient Iran. Much of the evidence for fortifications from ancient Iran is pictorial. Some seal impressions from Susa (late 4th millennium BC; e.g. Paris, Louvre) show a

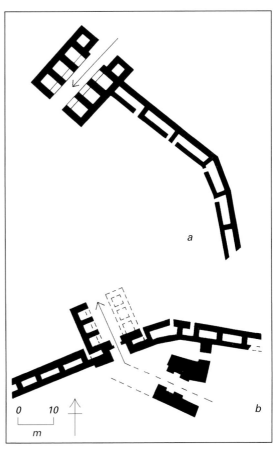

3. Fortifications in Syria–Palestine, 10th century BC: (a) plan of Hazor; (b) plan of Gezer

temple surrounded by flat-topped, niched walls. The fortifications of CHOGHA ZANBIL (13th century BC) were strengthened by numerous double buttresses, and the gates were flanked by massive bastions of solid brickwork. Assyrian reliefs depict walled citadels with crennellated parapets and unwalled lower cities (e.g. London, BM). Contemporary excavated sites such as Hasanlu and Godin Tepe have straight stretches of wall between square towers and quadrangular buttresses. In Sasanian times (c. 224 BC–AD 651) many sites (e.g. Takht-i Sulayman) were surrounded by circular fortifications with semicircular buttresses or towers at regular intervals. The Sasanian hilltop palace at Qal'a-i Dukhtar, near FIRUZABAD, is, however, surrounded by a casemate wall that follows the contours of the hill.

See also MESOPOTAMIA, §II; ANATOLIA, ANCIENT, §II; SYRIA-PALESTINE, §§I, 2(iv) and (v), and II; JEWISH ART, §II, 2(i); and IRAN, ANCIENT, §II.

BIBLIOGRAPHY

R. Naumann: *Architektur Kleinasiens von ihren Anfängen bis zum Ende der hethitischen Zeit* (Tübingen, 1955, rev. 2/1971), pp. 236–335

Y. Yadin: *The Art of Warfare in Biblical Lands in the Light of Archaeological Discovery* (London, 1963)

R. Opificius: 'Befestigungen des Zweistromlandes im Beginn des zweiten Jahrtausends', *Baghdad. Mitt.*, iii (1964), pp. 78–90

P. Parr: 'The Origin of the Rampart Fortifications of Middle Bronze Age in Palestine and Syria', *Z. Dt. Palästina-Ver.*, lxxxiv (1968), pp. 18–45

N. Lapp: 'Casemate Walls in Palestine', *Bull. Amer. Sch. Orient. Res.*, ccxxiii (1970), pp. 25–42

H. Gasche and R. Paepe: 'The Surrounding Wall of Abu Habbah (Sippar) in Relation to that of Tell ed-Der and to the Regional Fluviatile System', *Sounding at Abu Habbah (Sippar)* (1980), iii of *Tell ed-Der*, ed. L. De Meyer (Leuven, 1971–), pp. 37–52

A. Gunter: 'Representations of Urartian and Western Iranian Fortress Architecture in the Assyrian Relief', *Iran*, xx (1982), pp. 103–12

G. R. H. Wright: *Ancient Building in South Syria and Palestine*, 2 vols, Handbuch der Orientalistik (Leiden, 1985), pp. 172–215

H. Gasche and others: 'Habl as-Sahr, 1983–85: Nebuchadnezzar II's Cross-country Wall North of Sippar', *N. Akkad Proj. Rep.*, i (1987), pp. 3–46

ÖNHAN TUNCA

3. EGYPT. Since the ancient Egyptians' concepts of religion and war were closely intertwined, the clear modern distinction between military and religious architecture cannot be generally applied. Their temples—symbolic bastions of harmony amid chaos—were often decorated with battle reliefs and invariably surrounded by thick, fortified enclosure walls. The mortuary temple of Ramesses III (c. 1160 BC; *see* THEBES (i), §VII), for example, had two gateways, the surviving one of which is in the form of a fortified Syrian watch-tower (*migdol*; *see* §2(iii) above). In the same way the frequently elegant and symmetrical designs of Egyptian fortresses incorporate many monumental features of temples as well as practical defensive measures.

The first pictorial evidence for fortifications in ancient Egypt takes the form of schematic depictions of circular and rectangular fortified towns (usually shown in the process of being stormed by the king's armies), which appear as elements in the scenes of warfare on ceremonial palettes and maceheads of the late Predynastic and Protodynastic periods (c. 3000 BC; *see* PALETTE (i); for illustration *see* NARMER). The earliest surviving archaeological remains of Egyptian fortifications are the roughly circular walls of the early cities of Hierakonpolis and el-Kab, both

in Middle Egypt. The el-Kab Protodynastic fortifications comprised an inner and outer wall (2.4 m and 2.7 m thick respectively) separated by a gap of 5 m. At Hierakonpolis the Protodynastic walls surrounding the town and temple were replaced in the Old Kingdom (c. 2575–c. 2150 BC) by a rectangular enclosure wall. However, Egyptian towns were apparently fortified only at times of political instability, such as the Early Dynastic phase and the three so-called Intermediate Periods.

Military fortresses and garrisons, as opposed to fortified civilian communities, were crucial to the defence of Egypt's frontiers. The natural barriers of the Eastern and Western deserts, the Sinai Peninsula and the Mediterranean Sea helped to keep foreign armies at bay for most of the Dynastic period, but from the earliest times these topographical defences were backed up by strings of fortresses along the borders with Nubia, western Asia and the Libyan desert. In the reign of Ammenemes I (reg c. 1938–c. 1908 BC) a row of forts, known as the Walls of the Prince (Egyp. *inbw hka*), were established across the north-eastern Delta in order to protect Egypt against invasion along the coastal road from the Levant. The same border was later protected by a number of fortresses set up by Ramesses II (reg c. 1279–c. 1213 BC). The traditional location of the border with Nubia (around modern Aswan) was marked by a walled town strategically placed on the island of Elephantine, in the region of the 1st Nile cataract (a rocky, unnavigable stretch of the river). The land route at Elephantine, by which river-borne trade goods were conveyed for 7.4 km along the bank, was fortified for the whole of its length by a large mud-brick wall built mainly in the 12th Dynasty (c. 1938–c. 1756 BC).

During the Middle Kingdom (c. 2008–c. 1630 BC) the area of Lower Nubia from the 1st to the 3rd cataract, which had been peacefully exploited by Egyptian mineral prospectors during the Old Kingdom, became part of the Egyptian empire. A group of at least 17 fortresses was built, mainly between the reigns of Sesostris I and Sesostris III (c. 1918–c. 1818 BC), apparently serving both practical and symbolic purposes. On the one hand, they were intended to control and protect the king's monopoly on the valuable trade route from the lands to the south. On the other, their large scale—apparently disproportionate to the task—must have served as physical propaganda in an increasingly militaristic age. The designs of these fortresses, stretching from Aswan to Dongola, incorporate many ingenious architectural devices that would be more readily associated with medieval architecture. Eleven of the fortresses—south to north: Semna South, Kumma, Semna (*see* EGYPT, ANCIENT, fig. 32), Uronarti (*see* EGYPT, ANCIENT, fig. 33), Shalfak (see fig. 4), Askut, Mirgissa, Dabenarti, Dorginarti, Kor and Buhen (*see* EGYPT, ANCIENT, fig. 34)—were constructed in the area of the 2nd cataract where the Nile Valley is at its narrowest. Although they share many common architectural features (such as bastions, walls, ditches, internal grid plans and walled stairways connecting with the Nile), their various shapes and sizes were each designed to conform to differing local topographical and strategic requirements. The Semna fort, for instance, was L-shaped because of the configuration of the rocky outcrop on which it stood.

By far the largest and most complex forts were those at Buhen and Mirgissa, which were rectangular and evidently intended to act as depots for trade goods. The Buhen fort incorporated the most comprehensive range of defensive architectural components, such as berms, loopholes, counterscarps and bastions. The outer wall at Buhen—over 700 m long and 4 m thick—was strengthened by 32 semicircular, projecting platforms and surrounded by a ditch that followed the outline of the wall, allowing archers to fire on attackers through loopholes. The western wall was heavily fortified against attack from the desert, with five towers and a huge gateway known as the Barbican, which developed over the years into a tower (47×30 m) with baffle entrances, wooden doors and a drawbridge running on rollers.

In the New Kingdom (c. 1540–c. 1075 BC) the Nubian fortresses were substantially rebuilt and elaborated, but the role of the fortifications appears to have become much more symbolic. Temples began to be built outside the fortress walls, and new towns were established with relatively perfunctory defences. Essential fortresses and garrisons continued to be built on the western and eastern borders of the Delta, but the economic resources of the pharaohs in the New Kingdom and Late Period (c. 750–332 BC) were increasingly transferred from fortresses to temples.

For more detailed discussion of Egyptian military architecture (particularly the Middle Kingdom fortresses in Nubia) *see* EGYPT, ANCIENT, §VIII, 3, and NUBIA, §II.

BIBLIOGRAPHY
W. S. Smith: *The Art and Architecture of Ancient Egypt*, Pelican Hist. A. (Harmondsworth, 1958, rev. 2/1981), pp. 173–6, 446
D. Dunham and J. M. A. Janssen: *Second Cataract Forts*, 2 vols (Boston, MA, 1961–7)
Y. Yadin: *The Art of Warfare in Biblical Lands in the Light of Archaeological Discovery* (London, 1963)
A. W. Lawrence: 'Ancient Egyptian Fortifications', *J. Egyp. Archaeol.*, li (1965), pp. 69–94
A. Badawy: *The First Intermediate Period, the Middle Kingdom and the Second Intermediate Period* (1966), ii of *A History of Egyptian Architecture* (Giza, Berkeley and Los Angeles, 1954–68)
J. Vercoutter: *Mirgissa*, 2 vols (Paris, 1970–75)
W. Y. Adams: *Nubia: Corridor to Africa* (Princeton, 1977, rev. 2/1984), pp. 175–92
W. B. Emery and others: *The Fortress of Buhen*, 2 vols (London, 1977–9)
I. Shaw: *Egyptian Warfare and Weapons* (Princes Risborough, 1991)

IAN M. E. SHAW

4. GREECE. The citadels, gateways and wall-circuits of Bronze Age Greece and Cyprus depended for their strength not on planning but on size and adaptation to the terrain. Greek fortifications were normally defensive, aimed at providing lasting protection against current siege techniques, without being inordinately expensive. Mud-brick walls could be erected quickly and cheaply and are found in all periods; for hilltop circuits, however, stone, obtainable on the spot, was usually more convenient. Stone also needed less maintenance, and from later Classical times it was increasingly preferred. Massive rubble construction, although as effective under siege as closely fitted masonry, was generally confined to fieldworks and temporary forts. For large Hellenistic city circuits, where walls and gates were designed for visual impressiveness as

4. Ancient Egyptian fortress of Shalfak, 2nd cataract area of Nubia, c. 1860 BC; reconstruction

well as functional efficiency, coursed masonry was normally used, being easier to assemble than irregular or polygonal blocks.

(i) Late 10th century–c. 490 BC. (ii) c. 490 –2nd century BC.

(i) Late 10th century–c. 490 BC. In the first centuries after the fall of the Mycenaeans, Greek communities usually had neither resources nor technical skills for large-scale building and, like their predecessors, faced no threat of direct assault with siege engines. Steep-sided promontories walled across the neck, as at ZAGORA on Andros (late 9th century–c. 700 BC), or small hilltop circuits, as at Melie near Güzelçamı on Samsun Dağı (before 700 BC) or Emborio on Chios (c. 700–c. 600 BC), provided adequate sanctuary against attack by neighbours or pirates. These primitive defences are perhaps mirrored in the Homeric account of the Greek wall at Troy (*Iliad* VII.436–41; XII). Early walls were usually rubble or mud-brick on a rubble base. Clay mortar might be used to bind the larger facing-stones together; between the faces was a core of unworked stones and loose earth. The walls were high enough to discourage escalade and had some sort of parapet along the outer edge to protect the defenders from spears, arrows and sling-bullets. The Geometric period walls of Old Smyrna (Bayraklı Tepe) are the most imposing such structures yet discovered (for illustration *see* SMYRNA, 1).

During the 7th century BC, the wealthier Eastern Greek cities increasingly attracted the attention of covetous neighbours, especially the Lydian kings, who were by then mastering siegecraft techniques learnt from the Near East. Old Smyrna, despite a great increase in area, was content with higher and thicker mud-brick walls enclosing the original peninsula; thus c. 600 BC Alyattes of Lydia (*reg c.* 610–560 BC) stormed the walls from the top of a great siege-mound. Yet Greek coastal cities, if provided with adequate fortifications connecting citadel and harbour, could obtain provisions by sea: during the 7th and 6th centuries BC, for instance, the Lydians were unable to take Miletos by land or to blockade it by sea and had to offer special terms. Many other Eastern Greek cities, however, accepted Lydian overlordship without struggle, and their walls, often hastily built, or rebuilt after the Achaemenid conquest of Lydia in 546 BC, were easily overcome by the mounds of the Persian general Harpagus.

Nevertheless, the advantages of both strong walls and a strong fleet, especially for island cities, were by then clear. Herodotus recounted that between *c*. 550 and 490 BC circuits linking citadel, city and harbour were built on many Greek islands, including Samos (III.liv–lvi), Thasos (VI.xxviii, xlvi–xlvii), Karystos and Eretria in Euboia (VI.xcix–ci); at Samos lower-lying sectors of wall were even protected by a rock-cut ditch. Mainland cities were evidently slower to enlarge their circuits; in 490–480 BC Athens had only an enlarged acropolis circuit, which Thucydides (I.xciii) described as being 'extended in all directions' after 479 BC. Significant for the history of Greek military architecture were such Eastern Greek strongholds as Buruncuk in Aeolis (later 6th century BC), which was probably the residence of a Persian vassal; its solidly built two-storey towers may represent Persian rather than Greek defensive theory, although the style of masonry is purely Greek.

Greek colonies overseas, for example in the Black Sea and the western Mediterranean, although not threatened by Lydian or Persian siegecraft, frequently faced hostility from dispossessed native peoples. Thus they too began, quite early, to build city (rather than acropolis) circuits, as in Sicily at Leontinoi (now Lentini) and Akragas (now Agrigento; 7th century BC–early 6th). Megara Hyblaea, in Sicily, and Poseidonia (*see* PAESTUM), on mainland Italy, even occupied completely open sites, with neither acropolis nor natural defences, surviving simply by the strength of their walls.

(ii) c. 490–2nd century BC. When in 494 BC the Persians stormed Miletos, Eastern Greeks had had considerable experience of Persian siegecraft involving mounds, as at Old Smyrna and at OLD PAPHOS, Cyprus (499–498 BC); mines, as at Miletos; and rams, probably included among Herodotus' 'every known device' at Miletos (VI.xviii). The fall of Eretria and Karystos (490 BC) and of Athens (480 BC) showed the mainland Greeks also that complete and easily defensible city circuits were more important than an acropolis. Yet walls of modest height and thickness might still resist escalade, provided the curtains were

enfiladed where necessary by flanking towers, and natural defensive features were used wherever possible. The Themistoklean walls of Athens were hastily built (479–478 BC) to provide a barrier 'of defensible height'. For Peiraeus, however, Themistokles planned a much more substantial rampart, but construction reached only half the intended height.

The Long Walls built by the Athenians from Megara to its port at Nisaia (461–460 BC), and the Athenian Long Walls (*c*. 457–456 BC and 440 BC), which converted Athens and Peiraeus to a single great fortress, were among the first examples of the so-called 'great circuits' that were to become common in large cities for some 150 years. Other examples included those at Thasos (*c*. 475–440 BC) and 5th-century BC Mantinea (the latter again mud-brick on a stone socle). The circuit of Eleusis was extended by Pericles, and many circuits mentioned by Thucydides during the Peloponnesian War were built earlier, such as those at Plataia (II.lxxv–lxxvi) and Amphipolis (V.ii–iii, vi–viii, x–xi). In these new systems two-storey towers became more common, especially in the exposed sectors. Some already had a hollow ground storey, for both storage and shelter for defending troops; occasionally (e.g. Megara, perhaps Athens) clay for mud-bricks was dug just outside the wall-line, the trench remaining as an additional defensive barrier.

Siege engines (rams and protective sheds) appeared in Greek warfare only in the Athenian siege of Samos (440 BC), but they were not very successful; and throughout the Peloponnesian War sieges usually ended in blockade (e.g. at Plataia, Mytilene, Melos and Syracuse). Moreover, defenders had begun to adopt a more active policy, making sallies in force against enemy works; the Athenians, for instance, built both border and coastal forts (Oinoe, Panakton, Sounion) and forts in enemy territory (e.g. at Pylos), as did the Spartans at Dekeleia in Attica.

Older Greek cities contributed little to the revolution in siegecraft during this period. 'Great circuits' continued to be built (Corinth–Lechaion system, early 4th century BC; Megalopolis and MESSENE after 371 BC). Even the Dionysian circuit of Syracuse and the Mausollan walls of Halikarnassos followed similar lines. Yet in Sicily the Carthaginian assaults on Selinus and Himera in 409 BC, and on Akragas in 406 BC, heralded a revolution in both fortifications and defensive siegecraft. Already at Akragas

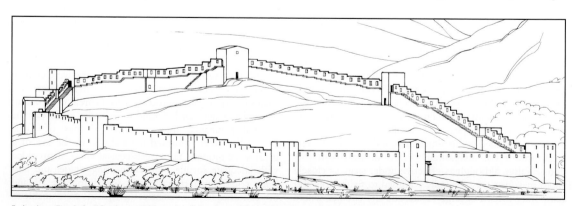

5. Ancient Greek fortification at Kydna, view from the east, late 4th century BC; reconstruction

6. Euryalus Fort, Syracuse, Sicily, *c.* 270 BC and 214–212 BC

and Himera the defenders were making determined sallies against the Carthaginian siegeworks; in new systems greater provision for such sallies was made by greatly increasing the number of posterns, both in city circuits (Mantinea, 360s BC) and in border forts (Attic Eleutherai, second half of the 4th century BC). Towers with ground-storey chambers also became more common in the 4th century BC and later (see fig. 5), sometimes with posterns in the side wall of the chamber, as at Mantinea; and the approach of enemy engines might be further hindered by a moat or ditch (Mantinea; Athens, after 338 BC). The Persians added a ditch to the defences of Halikarnassos, against Alexander's attack; and 'great circuits' of the late 4th century BC clung more determinedly to high ground (Stratos, Kalydon).

The most influential development, however, for both attack and defence, was the development of early non-torsion catapults at Syracuse (398–397 BC) and of torsion weapons, a generation later, probably by the engineers of Philip II, King of Macedonia. When mounted in the attackers' huge, specially constructed siege-towers (*hele-poleis*), originally developed by the Carthaginians and Dionysios I (*reg* 405–367 BC), advanced torsion artillery allowed the attackers to demolish protective screen walls and even damage towers with stone-throwers (*lithoboloi, petroboloi*) and to cripple effective defence by volleys of

bolts from arrow-shooters (*oxybeleis*); rams and siege-sheds could then be brought against the rampart. Before long, however, artillery was being used defensively as well as offensively, with smaller arrow-shooters mounted on the curtains and various sizes of arrow-shooters and stone-throwers in the towers. While the engines of Philip II and Alexander the Great swept everything before them, De-metrios I Poliorketes (*reg* 336–283 BC) failed in 305–304 BC to capture Rhodes, despite his awe-inspiring siege-train.

Although separated by fewer than 75 years, the walls of Messene and Herakleia under Latmos belong to different worlds. The curtains at Herakleia are significantly higher; the Messenian crenellations are replaced by a high screen wall with shuttered windows; and the towers have two roofed chambers above the curtains (instead of a single chamber with an open platform above), thicker walls and some apertures clearly designed as artillery-ports. Even more intricate, though fragmentary, are the walls built at Rhodes after Demetrios' attack. One extremely thick curtain is built entirely of squared blocks, as recommended by Hellenistic theorists. Preserved elsewhere are: the ground-chamber of a huge artillery tower, standing for-ward from the curtain on a short spur wall; and another curtain, apparently with ground-level artillery emplace-ments, protected by an outwork (*proteichisma*) and perhaps also by a ditch. Similarly projecting towers are found at

Hellenistic Samos. Moreover, Philo of Byzantium (*c.* late 3rd century BC; *see* §III, 4 below) mentioned the elaborate design (presumably for installing artillery) of the curtains at Rhodes, Archimedes made similar provision at Syracuse (212 BC), and 'galleries' survive in curtains at Perge and Side (*c.* 200 BC).

Artillery, still virtually unknown in the mid-4th century BC, developed dramatically *c.* 335–*c.* 270 BC, with additional later Hellenistic and Roman improvements. The primary aim of Hellenistic defensive strategy was to destroy or disable enemy artillery and rams at a distance from the walls, either by defensive fire from walls and outworks or by trapping them in ditches. Hellenistic artillery towers sometimes exceeded 20 m in height (Perge, Sillyon and Isaura), with outworks and forward artillery emplacements of increasing complexity (North Gate, Selinus; Euryalus Fort, Syracuse, *c.* 270 BC and 214–212 BC; see fig. 6). On level ground each curtain might be covered by a nearby tower and postern (southern crosswall, Miletos, after 100 BC) and perhaps strengthened by outworks and ditches. Intricate defences such as these largely nullified earlier progress in siegecraft, so that sieges were again likely to end in blockade. Significantly, Philip V, King of Macedonia (*reg* 221–179 BC), despite his many successes in siegecraft elsewhere, did not even attempt direct assault on Pergamon.

Nevertheless, by the end of the 3rd century BC and the beginning of the 2nd, Hellenistic theories of fortification and siegecraft had taken root far beyond the Hellenistic heartland of the eastern Mediterranean. The walls of Ai-Khanum (Afghanistan) and Vani in Colchis (Georgia), although in each case built in local style and technique, are completely Hellenistic in overall design. The gate of Vani was defended by a battery of artillery; a magazine incorporated in the thickness of the curtain yielded many stone balls of the type familiar from Pergamon, Rhodes and Goritsa in Thessaly. Hannibal's assault on Saguntum in Spain (219 BC), like those of the Romans at Syracuse (*c.* 214–212 BC), and later in Greece itself, followed a classic Hellenistic pattern (Livy: XXI.vii–viii, xi–xii). Even the Land Walls of Constantinople, laid out in the first half of the 5th century AD, are still textbook illustrations of Hellenistic theory and practice, complete with main rampart and towers, lower outer wall and large ditch (*see* §III, 1 below).

See also CYCLADIC, §II; HELLADIC, §II; CYPRUS, especially §II, 2(ii) and (iv); GREECE, ANCIENT, especially §§II, 2(iii) and III, 2; and EARLY CHRISTIAN AND BYZANTINE ART, §II, 3(i)(a).

BIBLIOGRAPHY

R. L. Scranton: *Greek Walls* (Cambridge, MA, 1941)
F. G. Maier: *Griechische Mauerbauinschriften*, 2 vols (Heidelberg, 1959–61)
E. W. Marsden: *Greek Artillery*, 2 vols (Oxford, 1969–71)
F. E. Winter: *Greek Fortifications* (Toronto and London, 1971)
A. Wokalek: *Griechische Stadtbefestigungen* (Bonn, 1973)
Y. Garlan: *Recherches de poliorcétique grecque* (Athens, 1974)
A. W. Lawrence: *Greek Aims in Fortification* (Oxford, 1979)
Actes du colloque international: La Fortification dans l'histoire du monde grecque: Valbonne, 1982
J.-P. Adam: *L'Architecture militaire grecque* (Paris, 1982)
J. Ober: 'Early Artillery Towers: Messenia, Boiotia, Attica, Megarid', *Amer. J. Archaeol.*, xci (1987), pp. 570–604
——: 'Les Fortifications grecques de Mycènes à Alexandre', *Doss. Archéol.*, 172 (June 1992)
——: 'Towards a Typology of Greek Artillery Towers: The First and Second Generation, *c.* 375–275 BC', *Fortifications Antiquae*, ed. S. van de Maele and J. M. Fossey, McGill U. Monographs Class. Archaeol. & Hist., xii (Amsterdam, 1992), pp. 147–69
——: 'A la découverte des forteresses grecques', *Doss. Archéol.*, 179 (Feb 1993)

F. E. WINTER

5. ROME. The art of fortification among the Romans began with the need to defend temporary camps set up by armies on the march, and it developed in response to changing circumstances. Alterations in shapes and plans were purely tactical and invariably the result of greater defensive needs, but the change of building material from timber and turf to stone also reflected the Romans' policy of establishing permanence. In the later Empire more naturally defensive sites were used, and walls, towers and gates were modified to accommodate developments in strategic planning and artillery.

(i) Before AD 235. (ii) The late Empire.

(i) Before AD 235. The archetypal Roman marching camp or Castra was developed to a standard plan that facilitated both the tactical deployment of troops and the maintenance of discipline. These marching camps were not designed to withstand a serious attack, since the Romans preferred to fight in the open, and it has been suggested that their importance was as much psychological as functional. Only later did the Romans show more concern over the siting of forts, utilizing naturally defensive positions as the Greeks had done.

The type of camp described by Polybius (*c.* 200–after 180 BC) in the mid-2nd century BC (*Histories* VI.xxvii–xlii), which could hold two legions and auxiliary forces, was to endure for centuries, as is made clear by descriptions some 300 years later in *De munitionibus castrorum*, a technical treatise attributed to Hyginus. From at least the 1st century BC temporary camps and, later, permanent establishments assumed a standard rectangular shape with rounded corners, the so-called 'playing-card' plan. There were four gateways, one in each side, with the main one facing the potential enemy; inside there were two main roads at right angles to each other, forming a junction near the centre of the fort. The two side gates were known as the *porta principalis sinistra* and the *porta principalis dextra*. The main road, the *via praetoria*, ran from the main gate (*porta praetoria*) to the headquarters complex (*principia*) and parade-ground in the centre of the fort, behind the *via principalis*, which ran across the fort from one side gate to the other. Access to the rear gate (*porta decumana*) was from the perimeter track (*via sagularis*) between the buildings and the defences. In larger camps, such as those described by Polybius and Hyginus, a second crossroad (*via quintana*) ran between the *via principalis* and the *porta praetoria*, dividing the camp into three equal parts. However, the *via principalis* normally divided the camp into two unequal parts, the *retentura* being two-thirds of the space behind the road and the *praetentura* the third in front. In the *praetentura* were the houses of the tribunes (senior officers); the *retentura* was occupied by barracks, various ancillary buildings, horse-lines and, in or near the *principia*, the PRAETORIUM (commander's quarters). Barrack accommodation in the early camps was provided in leather tents; timber buildings appeared later in semi-permanent camps.

The fortifications consisted of a ditch (*fossa*) and an earth rampart (*agger*). The ditch would be V-shaped, usually of the type known as *fastigata*, with a slot at the bottom designed as an ankle-breaker; the rampart would be reinforced with a turf facing, the top flattened and fronted by a wooden palisade. In front of the four entrances to the camp, oblique breaks in the ditch and rampart were intended to prevent a rush of the entrance and to expose the unshielded flank of an attacker. Marching camps, often occupied for a single night, could be built in a few hours, as at LAMBAESIS in North Africa, where a camp was built as a spectacle for Hadrian in AD 128. Slightly more permanent camps were built for sieges, with much more elaborate fortifications: at Numantia in Spain (133 BC) and Masada in Judaea (AD 70) the siege-camps had stone fortifications and wall-footings, although scarcity of timber was also a factor. The siege-works of 52 BC at Alesia (now Alise-Sainte-Reine, France), described by Julius Caesar (*Gallic War* VII.lxix–lxxiv), included a double line of ramparts, multiple ditches and towers. As the Roman world expanded, troops were regularly quartered in semi-permanent camps, which were essentially the old marching camps with firmer fortifications.

After the Empire was consolidated and the frontiers rationalized by Augustus at the end of the 1st century BC, more permanent forts were built, although there were no longer any serious rivals in the art of siegecraft. Legionary camps were placed at strategic sites, usually to form part of a frontier line, but they were still regarded as bases from which to engage the enemy rather than as strongholds. A typical legionary fortress, designed to hold some 6000 men, would measure *c.* 500×400 m and contain several ancillary buildings as well as barracks, usually all built of timber. These included the *principia*, *praetorium*, officers' quarters, hospital, storehouses, stables, a small training amphitheatre, baths, armoury and often a prison. Fortifications of the legionary camp varied according to the degree of local hostility anticipated, but they could be substantial, with up to three ditches, the outermost being of a type known as Punic, with a vertical outer slope to trap an enemy attracted by the shallow inner slope. Other devices included thorn hedges or concealed metal spikes (*lilia*). A flat berm separated the ditches from the ramparts, usually not more than 50 m wide, to keep the ditches within firing range. Ramparts were often up to 2.5 m high with a palisade on top; their earthen fill made them impregnable against battering-rams. They were frequently built on a corduroy of logs, laid at a right angle to the wall-line and reinforced on the inside by timbers placed at strategic points such as towers, gates and corners, especially if they carried artillery. Some, however, consisted of a wooden framework (box rampart) filled with earth, though these too were sometimes faced with clay or turf to protect them against fire. Square towers flanked the gateways, with interval towers on the walls, flush with the outer façade.

From the mid-1st century AD the timber and turf forts along the Rhine frontier began to be replaced by stone-walled forts, and by the time of Trajan (early 2nd century AD) many new forts were built entirely of stone, a material that required less maintenance and symbolized permanence. The transition was slow, however; some gateways remained in timber, and early stone fortifications, *c.* 1 m thick, still fronted an earthen rampart, the top of which formed a walkway behind a stone parapet. Although the demise of the earthen rampart was some way off, in some sites on the Rhine–Danube frontier it was replaced with a series of stone piers against and buttressing the walls and supporting a timber walkway above. This created more space within the fort and allowed the ground floors of gateway towers to be used as guard-chambers. The internal buildings were still generally of timber, although sometimes on stone foundations. The use of stone also depended on time and local availability: the legionary camp of *c.* AD 84 at Inchtuthil (Tayside, Scotland) had plain stone walls with a ditch and rampart. There is evidence that the site was only partially built and then dismantled, which has led to suggestions that a standard plan, if not prefabrication, may have been involved. A classic example of the characteristic 'playing-card' plan built in stone was the base of the 16th Legion at Novaesium (now Neuss) on the lower Rhine in Germany. An embellishment here is the monumental projecting gateway, also seen at the fortress in York, England, which reflects civilian rather than military types of gate and was perhaps the precursor of the eventual full external projection of all towers.

In the eastern provinces Roman military encampments sometimes took over earlier strongpoints, but troops were usually billeted in the larger cities and cantonments within the cities gradually evolved into specific military areas, as at Dura Europos (*see* DURA EUROPOS, §2) in east Syria. Evidence from north Syria, however, indicates that in the 1st century AD the Romans were also building the standard western type of fort. By the time of the Empire most urban settlements were walled. Not necessarily substantial, the walls were more a matter of civic pride (*see* §I, 2 above) and often incorporated monumental gateways.

The mid-1st-century AD push into Germany between the rivers Rhine and Danube resulted in the construction of a line of watch- or signal-towers and forts, for example at Kesselstadt. Trajan's use of auxiliaries on the frontiers, keeping his legions farther back, led to the building of smaller forts, often square but with rounded corners and an internal rampart, as at Benningen on the Rhine frontier. Hadrian abandoned the expansionist policy of his predecessor and consolidated the frontiers with spectacular linear arrangements based on small unit garrisons at the frontiers and larger fortresses in the rear, as in the Fossatum Africae in North Africa, a long ditch with forts behind it, and HADRIAN'S WALL in Britain. The latter ran for 118 km, was 2.5 m thick and 4.5 m high to the rampart walkway, with the parapet and merlons adding nearly 2 m more, and there was a series of ditches on both sides. Every 0.5 km there was a stone turret recessed into the line of the wall, and every 1.5 km a gate and small, fortified mile-castle (*c.* 21×17 m); larger forts were also built, most of which were behind the wall. They were still of the 'playing-card' shape, with towers at the four gateways and corners and an earth rampart inside the stone walls. The later, more northerly, Antonine Wall was almost entirely of turf and timber; it was not conceived as a replacement for Hadrian's Wall and was eventually abandoned.

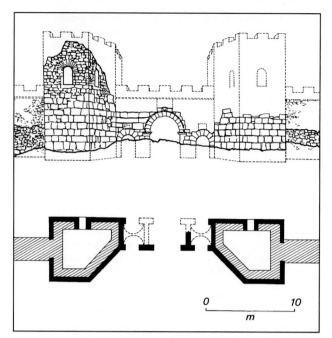

7. Roman fortification at Gheria el-Garbia, Libya, showing cutaway gate-towers, AD 198

In the unsettled conditions of the later 2nd century AD, fortress design was often severely tested. Timber was increasingly replaced by stone, walls became thicker and their foundations heavier as earthen ramparts were less widely employed. Projecting gateway towers and interval towers became more common, although the tactical value of towers projecting from rounded corners was limited. The number of ditches was also increased, except in the east where ditches were rare. Smaller outposts were increasingly used in frontier areas, such as the fort at Tisavar in North Africa, which measured only 40×30 m. It had one gateway but no other towers, and the corners were rounded. An important space-saving innovation here was the construction of the barracks around and against the walls, the roofs of which also served as a parapet.

With the accession of the Severan dynasty in AD 193 there was an unprecedented amount of fortification building, with sites more often utilizing natural defences. Interval towers projected, but rarely more than 2 m; and as square gate-towers revealed a blind spot they were quickly modified to a 'cutaway' form (see fig. 7) and later rounded. Both types were built at Gheria el-Garbia (Libya), and rounded gate-towers were built at, for example, Verulamium in England (see ST ALBANS, §1(i)) in the late 2nd century AD. There were few new forts in the East, but some smaller ones developed from earlier watchtowers; these were square with projecting corner towers, forerunners of the Byzantine *tetrapyrgia* (see §III, 1 and fig. 9 below), as at Qaṣr al-Hallabat (Jordan).

(ii) The late Empire. The uncertainties following the end of the Severan dynasty in AD 235 ushered in the period of late Roman fortifications, with a policy of defence in depth. With the legions pulled back from the frontiers,

the old-style forts were required to stall the enemy until help arrived from the rear. Under Aurelian (*reg* AD 270–75), Rome itself was provided with a new wall that was 18 km long (*see* ROME, ANCIENT, §II, 2(i)(g) and fig. 35). It was built largely of concrete and brick, although it incorporated many existing buildings; it had 30 interval towers, nearly all rectangular or square, and rounded gateway towers, all projecting more than 3 m. Other new forts began to use rounded interval towers, either horseshoe-shaped or nearly circular, and with nearly circular corner towers.

The 3rd-century AD Saxon Shore forts on the southeast coast of Britain, built for defence against raiders from north-west Europe, developed from a plan based on the 'playing-card' pattern, such as that at Regulbium (now Reculver, Kent), to a later version with square or semicircular externally projecting towers (e.g. Portchester, Hants; see fig. 8); most had thick masonry walls. Regional variations predominated in the late 3rd century and early 4th; the 'playing-card' shape, for example, was still preserved in new forts along Hadrian's Wall. Rounded corners and internally projecting towers gradually disappeared elsewhere, however, and existing fortifications of this type were often modified with splayed, fan-shaped towers added to the rounded corners, as at Visegrád (Hungary; early 4th century), and interval towers were now provided with external projections. Rounded towers became standard in the late 3rd century, often projecting up to 6.5 m. Owing to the unsettled conditions, old city walls were strengthened and new ones built, out of necessity rather than pride, and often with reused materials, but incorporating the latest military developments, such as projecting rounded towers (e.g. Senlis, France; late 3rd century).

In the East, small square forts with massive square corner towers and barracks set against the walls, as at Han Aneybe (Syria; late 4th century AD), continued to predominate; but in larger forts an innovation seems to have been the U-shaped tower, often projecting more than 9 m. A good example of this type is the legionary fortress at Lejjun (Jordan; late 3rd century or early 4th), the small size of which (242×190 m) reflected the reduced size of the Roman legion; its square corners have large fan-shaped projecting towers and its interval towers are U-shaped. Examples of U-shaped towers also existed in the West, mostly in Lower Moesia (e.g. Iatrus on the Danube, 293–319), where the shape of the fortress accommodates the naturally defensive topography. Circular towers straddling the walls occurred in the middle Rhine region in the early 4th century, and polygonal towers also appeared, mostly in Britain, as at York; although they also occur at Diocletian's palace at Spalato (now Split), Dalmatia, Croatia, they may have been built as much for artistic purposes as military.

Although tower shapes were to some extent regional and were originally conceived as surveillance points, an increasing concern over defensibility strengthened their nature and usage. For the newer and heavier artillery the large U-shaped towers were ideal, combined with a widened outer berm and a single, wide, flat-bottomed ditch. Enemy siege capabilities were still slight, except in the East, where a number of Roman forts were successfully reduced by the Sasanians.

8. Roman Saxon Shore fort at Portchester, Hampshire, 3rd century AD

Roman fortification design remained basically uniform, although the increasing divergence from the marching-camp plan was a reflection of differing problems on different frontiers, resulting from a centralized strategic concern. The works of Valentinian I (*reg* AD 364–75) were the last manifestations of Roman fortifications in the West. He reintroduced the aggressive attitude of pre-emptive strikes into enemy territory, establishing surveillance posts and strongholds on high ground, and reoccupying abandoned forts. Walls were heightened, splayed fan-shaped towers were added to corners and gates were walled up. In the East some new watch-towers were built, although the continuation of a central government and a more coherent enemy necessitated a greater manpower more thinly deployed than in the previous century.

BIBLIOGRAPHY

I. A. Richmond: 'Trajan's Army on Trajan's Column', *Pap. Brit. Sch. Rome*, xii (1935), pp. 1–40
H. von Petrikovits: *Die Innenbauten römischer Legionslager während der Principätszeit* (Opladen, 1975)
G. Webster: *The Roman Imperial Army* (London, 1975/R 1979)
E. N. Luttwak: *The Grand Strategy of the Roman Empire* (Baltimore, 1976)
A. Johnson: *Roman Forts of the 1st and 2nd centuries AD in Britain and the German Provinces* (London, 1983)
S. Johnson: *Late Roman Fortifications* (London, 1983)
J. Lander: *Roman Stone Fortifications: Variation and Change from the First Century A.D. to the Fourth*, Brit. Archaeol. Rep., Int. Ser., 206 (Oxford, 1984)

J. M. C. BOWSHER

III. Western.

The Greco-Roman tradition of masonry walls and towers remained strong in the Near East and survived the collapse of the Roman Empire in the West during the 5th century AD. In both areas, however, as well as in eastern Europe, other forms and materials were also employed. Most medieval fortifications developed existing ideas, the most significant new building type to develop being the castle (*see* CASTLE, §I), which emerged in north-western Europe, more particularly in France and England, from the 10th century. Essentially the fortified residence of a feudal lord, the castle was closely related to the structure of the society that produced it, and it was distinct in both form and function from the Byzantine citadel and residential tower (*see* EARLY CHRISTIAN AND BYZANTINE ART, §II, 3(i)(a), (ii)(a) and (iii)(a)); the castle appeared in the Crusader kingdoms in fully developed form only after 1200 (*see* JERUSALEM, LATIN KINGDOM OF).

Radical changes were needed only with the adoption of fire artillery from the late 14th century, which resulted in the invention of the BASTION in Italy in the mid-15th century. From then until the 19th century and the introduction of rifled artillery, fortifications became increasingly complex variations on the bastion and its derivations.

1. Medieval, *c.* AD 500–*c.* 1450. 2. Age of gunpowder, *c.* 1450–*c.* 1870. 3. Age of technology, after *c.* 1850/70. 4. Designers and theoreticians.

1. MEDIEVAL, *c.* AD 500–*c.* 1450. Medieval fortifications were built for defence and to withstand siege, and until the end of the period they were generally plain and unadorned (*see* §I, 2 above). The design of defences depended on the materials available, and although almost every surviving fortification is of stone, timber was common throughout the period, especially over much of eastern Europe and the Russian plain, where there was no suitable building stone. The great *cherta* (border) barriers, chains of wooden watch-towers linked by palisades, were built across southern Russia as late as the 16th and 17th

centuries and were comparable in scope with the Great Wall of China. Even in regions with good stone, a combination of materials was employed. In the West there are numerous examples of what are normally classed as 'earthwork' fortifications, the massive banks of which were held up by buried timber structures, in some cases revetting the scarp of the defence, in others affording a framework supporting the bulk of the defensive structure. On rocky ground a site would usually be chosen for its natural defences, although most peoples could not emulate the headquarters of the Strathclyde Britons at Alcluit (now the Castle Rock of Dumbarton, Strathclyde); but where natural escarpments were lacking, piled stone walling was used, either simply laid to form a vertical face or bound together by a buried timber framework.

Despite their different histories, both the Byzantine empire and the Latin West descended from the Greco-Roman tradition; and the two cultures, together with that of Islam, met from the late 11th century in the Levant as a result of the Crusades. This section will, therefore, analyse the art of fortification of both Christian East and West from the early Middle Ages to the development of gunpowder artillery. For a discussion of fortifications in the Islamic world, *see* §IV, 2 and 3 below.

(i) Before *c.* 1100. (ii) *c.* 1100–*c.* 1300. (iii) After *c.* 1300.

(i) Before c. *1100.* Throughout the early Middle Ages in the West, Roman remains and Roman methods (*see* §II, 5 above) were used in attempts, notably by Alfred the Great (*reg* AD 871–99) and Henry the Fowler, Duke of Saxony (*reg* AD 919–36), to keep invading peoples in check. The principal guide for future fortification, however, was in the Eastern empire: the great Land Wall of Constantinople (*see* EARLY CHRISTIAN AND BYZANTINE ART, fig. 29), built against possible barbarian attack by Emperor Theodosios II (*reg* 408–50) in 411–13 (modified after 447 and repeatedly until the 15th century). A classic example of concentric planning, the double line of walls and towers was designed for simultaneous defence from both lines: unlike general concentric fortification, where command of the main line of walls and towers was sufficient to permit shooting down to the head of the counterscarp, here the towers of the two lines alternate, so that those of the outer line stand in front of sections of the inner curtain wall. As the latter are comparatively short, an assailant was confronted by an alarming series of towers wherever he approached. The towers themselves are usually square, heavily vaulted and pierced for catapults. There are a few semicircular examples, and on the original, inner line, close to the Sea of Marmara, there are a number of octagonal towers.

Although Byzantine fortification towers are usually square, this is not militarily the strongest form, and it represents a wide divergence between theory and practice. Such Greek writers as Philo of Byzantium (*see* §4 below) had advocated the pentagonal beaked tower, presenting two flanks perpendicular to the curtain wall and two forming the beak, which resembles in plan the pentagonal bastion later developed against artillery (*see* §2(ii) below). Not many pentagonal towers were built, however, although 6th-century AD examples survive at Antioch (now Antakya, Turkey), and even the beaked towers of the

citadel (mid-7th century) of Ancyra (now Ankara, Turkey) were thoroughly irregular in plan.

In the Eastern empire the architecture of both the empire and its pupils—neighbours or enemies—was developing uninterruptedly along reasonably traditional lines, but in what had been the Western empire local rulers and proprietors were dealing as best they could with the later stages of the Migration period. Roman remains and examples could help in the defence of towns, but the numerous private estates, based on villas founded by earlier invaders, had also to be contracted and strengthened. Between the 9th and 11th centuries the villas gradually developed into private castles. Perimeters were tightened, ramparts reinforced and a new, important defensive element was introduced: the motte. Up to this point earthwork defences, however complex their timber support, formed lines of ditch and vallum (ramparts) around the defended area, but as the latter contracted they became close defences around the residence of the proprietor. They mostly formed simple loops—ring-works—around the earthwork, often with a very small central pit within the powerful ring. It is possible that the motte, typical of France and her neighbours, was produced by the continued contraction and strengthening of this type of earthwork, but in the motte the central pit was replaced by a truncated cone with a level summit.

The earliest identifiable motte seems to be the ploughed-out French example at Vinchy (Nord), dated to AD 979. Easy to erect in a short time without skilled labour, mottes were particularly suited to the needs of the Norman conquerors of England in 1066; and mottes and ring-works are especially clustered in frontier areas such as the Marches of Wales and the Rhineland. They were topped by a form of timber structure, a *garillum*: post-hole evidence from such sites as Abinger (Surrey, England) and Der Husterknupp (Rhineland) indicates that this consisted of a double range of stakes, planked or wattled to make timber walls and enclosing a mass of loose stones and earth to form the bulk of the fortification and carry its wall-walk; the front row of stakes, more regular in sequence, is generally reconstructed to a man's height or more above the inner row and topped by a line of battlements like those on a stone fortification. Owing to the close relation between stone and timber buildings the direction of influence can probably never be determined.

The central mass of earth and stones in the motte could support a DONJON or keep of a variety of forms: Abinger had room for no more than a rectangular tower within the palisade, but the many mottes with flat tops wider than that of Abinger could have carried a far more substantial building. Such timber castles as the 12th-century donjon at Durham, England, were often later rebuilt in stone, as was Der Husterknupp. A wall could replace the *garillum* around the rim of the scarp, or the face of the motte could be revetted, as at South Mimms (Herts) where the motte, thrown up round the tower, was revetted in timber. The most formidable example of a revetted motte is perhaps that at Pontefract Castle (N. Yorks), where the 13th-century masonry revetment envelops the earlier Norman motte.

The *Consuetudines et justicie* (*PL*, cxlix (1853), 1329) associated with William the Conqueror of England gives some idea of the state of castle building in mid-11th-century northern France. It laid down conditions for the depth of ditches and the appearance of palisades, but did not particularly refer to mottes or masonry castles. The express prohibition on castle building in Normandy was probably the outcome of William's attempt to reduce the number of unauthorized castles that were built during his long minority; similar situations confronted his great-grandson, Henry II of England, after the feeble reign of Stephen (*reg* 1135–54), and across the North Sea, when King Valdemar III (*reg* 1340–75) and his daughter Margaret I (*reg* 1387–1412) rebuilt the Danish kingdom in the late 14th century. Rulers in this situation were understandably harsh in their view of castles. William the Conqueror himself at least began two very complex stone donjons at Colchester (Essex) and the Tower of London (*see* LONDON, §V, 4). In England, however, he and his sons were obliged to control their vassals more lightly, and the castles of the invading Normans rose in great numbers, although many were little more than mottes. The *Consuetudines* does, however, demonstrate that the important function of the castle was to control the surrounding country.

(ii) c. 1100–c. 1300. The great event of the late 11th century was the First Crusade of 1095–9, which brought much of the north European aristocracy into contact with the Byzantine empire and its neighbours. There was, however, very little cross-fertilization between East and West. At this stage the less advanced Franks did not try to impose their ideas on the more competent masons of the Holy Land, but followed their advice. The essentially residential lordly castle did not exist in the East before the Crusades: there, fortifications were in the Byzantine tradition of public works, forts, great towers and fortified settlements (*see* EARLY CHRISTIAN AND BYZANTINE ART, §II, 3). A number of square towers suitable for habitation by Western nobles were built, but in simplified form and generally only two storeys in height. More important strongholds include a number of *tetrapyrgia*, the standard type of small Byzantine fort with a single square tower at each corner, as at Gibelet (see fig. 9). These were frequently given some extra features: a big donjon at one corner or in the middle, and towers projecting to flank the entry.

These designs were not brought back to Europe, even though many who returned from the First Crusade, or had seen the wonders of the Holy Land as pilgrims or mercenaries, were aware of developments in the East. This scientific knowledge had little or no acceptance in the West, where designs could be copied from surviving examples of late Roman military architecture, and it was to reappear there only well after the return of the early crusaders. The principal step in the west European advance towards scientific fortification involved the use of stretches of straight curtain wall (*see* CURTAIN WALL (i)) enfiladed by projecting towers (at first square, as were the few scattered mural towers of earlier periods), which seems to have been undertaken at the earliest in the 1160s in England at Windsor and DOVER CASTLE, under the instructions of Henry II, a king who had never been on a crusade.

In the East, the crucial date of 1187 marked the shattering victory of Salah al-Din (*reg* 1169–93) over the crusaders at Hattin, Palestine. Although before then most Frankish castles were generally of the unenterprising type described above, some 12th-century fortresses were more complicated: the huge mass of Kerak-in-Moab (now Kirhareseth, Jordan; begun 1142), which the victorious Muslims had to starve out; and Saône (Byz. Sigon; now Sahyun, Syria; 1120s), built on a rocky spur between two precipitous gorges, where there had been a Byzantine fortress probably since the 10th century, with a deep series of successive defences on the sole approachable side.

9. Byzantine *tetrapyrgion* or fort at Gibelet, Byblos (now Djebail, Lebanon), late 12th century

10. Beaumaris Castle, Anglesey, North Wales, from 1295

These were replaced by a line of towers (one a donjon) along a terrible artificial ditch. Most significant of all, since it anticipated later practice, was BELVOIR CASTLE (now Kôkhov ha-Yardēn, Israel), built by the Knights Hospitaller after 1168: this is a development of the *tetrapyrgion*, with the double enceinte of the later castles of the crusaders. Non-feudal fortifications built by the crusaders included fortified religious houses and the refuge tower at the new town of Magna Mahumeria (now al-Bria), built in 1115.

After the Third Crusade (1189–92), neither side could look back on success or forward with confidence; accordingly the 13th century was the period of the great castles, and the feudal castle of Western type was introduced to the Holy Land by the crusaders. A number of Christian proprietors passed their estates to the military orders, who became the most important builders: the principal castles are KRAK DES CHEVALIERS and Margat (now Marqab, Syria), built by the Knights Hospitaller, and Tortosa (now Tarṭus, Syria) and Château Pèlerin (Israel) of the Knights Templar, together with their Chastel Blanc (now Safita, Syria) and Montfort (Israel), built by the Teutonic Knights. Most of these were already in existence (for example, the Krak des Chevaliers was based on an 11th-century Arab fortress), and their later form was due to additions and alterations by the Knights. Attempts to assign one style or another to each order (e.g. round towers to the Knights Hospitaller and square towers to the Knights Templar) are accordingly useless. In any case, there is enormous variation between one castle and another.

The influence of systems adopted in the crusader castles on fortification in the West was significant in only a few respects, the most important of which were the huge size of the castles and their frequent use of concentric defences. The first acted as a stimulus to castle builders, particularly

royalty; the second inspired some founders of castles in late 13th-century England, most particularly Edward I, who had been briefly on a crusade and who fitted out the Tower of London and the lake-castle of Leeds (Kent) as concentric fortresses, as well as building several more to support his conquest of North Wales (*see* JAMES OF ST GEORGE); examples include Rhuddlan (1277–*c.* 1282), Aberystwyth (1277–89), Harlech (1283–95) and Beaumaris (from 1295; see fig. 10). Other Eastern elements, which appeared earlier, are the common type of arrow slits opening below the battlements.

(iii) After c. 1300. The development of medieval castles and other fortifications in Europe and the Near East displays considerable regional variation. Thus, from the outbreak of the Scottish wars at the beginning of the 14th century, English castles fall into two distinct groups, north and south of the River Humber, the former based on square towers of relatively poor flanking. In France the Midi had its own story of development, while the mountain-castles of the Holy Roman Empire have a characteristic broken plan and central *Bergfried* (keep), tall and narrow, with little accommodation outside its donjon. The castles of Armenian Cilicia, bordering on the Latin Kingdom of Jerusalem, have an appearance all their own, with round towers rising irregularly from rocky summits (e.g. Sis and Yilan in Turkey; both 12th century); even Ireland has, among its many square towers, one tall and narrow type peculiar to the country (e.g. Cahir, Kilkenny; 1142; rebuilt mid-15th century).

From the 14th century developments were concerned with the introduction of gunpowder, although the power of the new weapon, particularly in offence, should not be overemphasized. By the later 14th century, however, guns were a legitimate element in a nation's armaments, and in the same period it became common practice to pierce walls and towers with primitive loopholes for the generally small ordnance of the day.

The impact of fire-artillery on medieval fortification produced three other phased changes. Plans were altered to give scope to the guns of the defence, and there was increased protection against the artillery of a besieger. These two stages tended to be simultaneous, or at least confused, as the power of the artillery in defence and attack increased. English examples seldom reached beyond the first phase: the science of defence, once led by English practitioners, was by then very decadent (*see* §2(iv) below). At this time England had none of the massive castles and works to be found in other parts of Europe: in France, Ham (Somme; 15th century) and the great 'last baronial castle' of Bonaguil (Lot-et-Garonne; enlarged 1482–1530); in Scotland Ravenscraig (Fife; 1460s; destr. 1651) and Craignethan (Strathclyde; 1530s; dismantled 1570s), built very robustly to stand up to artillery; and in Italy the great and splendid series of late medieval castles or *rocce*.

The final change brought about by the appearance of fire-artillery occurred after the end of the Middle Ages, when artillery had become formidable, and a new system of *fortification rasante*, with the low defences hidden behind outer counterscarps, had to be organized, developing into a series of huge bastioned defences.

BIBLIOGRAPHY

E.-E. Viollet-le-Duc: *Essai sur l'architecture militaire au moyen-âge* (Paris, 1854; Eng. trans., Oxford, 1860)

G. Köhler: *Die Entwicklung des Kriegswesens und der Kriegführung in der Ritterzeit von Mitte des 11. Jahrhunderts bis zu den Hussiten-Kriegen,* 3 vols (Breslau, 1886–90)

D. Macgibbon and T. Ross: *The Castellated and Domestic Architecture of Scotland from the Twelfth to the Eighteenth Century,* 2 vols (Edinburgh, 1887)

C. H. Haskins: *Norman Institutions* (New York, 1918/*R* 1960)

G. de Jerphanion, S J: 'La Citadelle byzantine d'Angora', *Mél. U. St-Joseph,* xiii/1 (1928), pp. 144–219

P. Deschamps: *Les Châteaux des croisés en Terre Sainte,* 3 vols (Paris, 1934–73)

H. G. Leask: *Irish Castles and Castellated Houses* (Dundalk, 1944)

K. Andrews: *Castles of the Morea* (Princeton, 1953/*R* 1978)

B. Hope-Taylor: 'The Norman Motte at Abinger, Surrey, and its Wooden Castle', *Recent Archaeological Excavations in Britain,* ed. R. L. S. Bruce-Mitford (London, 1956), pp. 223–50

P. Heliot: 'Les Châteaux-forts en France du Xe au XIIe siècle à la lumière de travaux récents', *J. Sav.* (1965), pp. 483–514

A. Bon: *La Morée franque* (Paris, 1969)

B. Davison: 'Early Earthwork Castles: A New Model', *Château Gaillard: Etudes de castellologie médiévale,* iii (1969), pp. 37–47

M. Benvenisti: *The Crusaders in the Holy Land* (Jerusalem, 1970)

M. Rouche: 'Vinchy: Le Plus Ancien Château à motte', *Mélanges d'archéologie et d'histoire médiévales en l'honneur du Doyen Michel de Boüard* (Geneva, 1982), pp. 365–9

C. Foss and D. Winfield: *Byzantine Fortifications: An Introduction* (Pretoria, 1986)

L. Alcock: *Economy, Society and Warfare among the Britons and Saxons* (Cardiff, 1987)

R. W. Edwards: *The Fortifications of Armenian Cilicia* (Washington, DC, 1987)

L. Alcock: *Bede, Eddius and the Forts of the North Britons* (Jarrow, 1988)

R. A. Higham: 'Timber Castles: A Reassessment', *Fortress,* i (1989), pp. 50–60

D. Pringle: 'Crusader Castles: The First Generation', *Fortress,* i (1989), pp. 14–25

J. R. Kenyon: *Medieval Fortifications,* The Archaeology of Medieval Britain (London and Leicester, 1990)

R. Higham and P. Barker: *Timber Castles* (London, 1992)

H. Kennedy: *Crusader Castles* (Cambridge, 1994)

For further bibliography *see* CASTLE, §I; JERUSALEM, LATIN KINGDOM OF; EARLY CHRISTIAN AND BYZANTINE ART, §II, 3(i)(a); and entries under individual castles.

D. J. CATHCART KING, with JOHN R. KENYON

2. AGE OF GUNPOWDER, *c.* 1450–*c.* 1870. The development and distribution of effective gunpowder artillery from the second half of the 15th century initiated a revolution in military architecture, the key component and most important and long-lasting product of which was the BASTION. In combination with the squat earthwork ramparts and deep ditches that replaced the towers and curtain walls of the Middle Ages, the bastion not only changed the face of Europe's castles and cities but also exercised a profound influence on the conduct of warfare among all technically advanced powers. It spread from Italy and western Europe to the south and east Mediterranean, where bastion fortifications were built against the Turkish advance by the Venetians in the mid-16th century at, for example, Candia (now Herakleion), Crete, and Nicosia in Cyprus.

(i) Introduction of the bastion. (ii) Italy. (iii) France. (iv) Britain and northern Europe. (v) European influence abroad. (vi) North America, 1775–1865.

(i) Introduction of the bastion. In its simplest form the bastion was little more than a solid platform projecting from a fortress or town wall. Guns mounted on its sides or flanks swept the walls with defensive fire. From the forward faces, artillery protected only by a parapet could beat the approaches and engage enemy siege batteries. The angle or Italian bastion, as it was later defined, consisted of two angled faces, joined by shorter flanks to the curtain, the angle between the faces being determined by the need to keep all parts of the defensive enceinte exposed to flanking fire. Bastions thus formed a mutually defensive system. Although round or square platforms could give the same combination of gun positions, the angled shapes that were to give the characteristic star-shaped patterns of most 16th- to 19th-century fortifications (see fig. 13 below) were the only plan forms capable of eliminating the blind spots in the defensive fire plan.

Initially, however, the architectural response to the challenge of artillery took a wide variety of forms. Essentially passive measures included the thickening of walls to form reinforced earth ramparts, the massive scarping or battering of their bases and the stripping of the elaborate and easily damaged battlements that had provided the picturesque broken silhouette of medieval castles. Many medieval fortifications were modified to accommodate defensive artillery: old towers were cut down to wall-level, filled with earth and converted into makeshift gun platforms; Angers Castle (1589) is the classic example (*see* ANGERS, §2(iv)). During the late 15th century and early 16th many new towers were designed with lower, squatter proportions than the medieval towers they superseded, as, for example, the Tours de Navarre et d'Orval (1519–21) at Langres, which were described and illustrated by Viollet-le-Duc. In this respect they can be seen as a transitional step towards the fully developed platform bastions of the mid-16th century. Elsewhere the new artillery fortifications went high: the semicircular gun-towers built by Francis II, Duke of Brittany (*reg* 1458–88), at Fougères in 1480 provided no fewer than five tiers of internal casemates, an open gun-gallery and a seventh level raised above it. This was a strikingly vertical solution to the problem of accommodating a concentration of defensive artillery, examples of which were reproduced throughout northern Europe. Until well into the 16th century, English, Spanish, French, German and eastern European fortress builders—as well as a number of Italians—concentrated on the round (or semicircular) gun-tower (*see* §(iv) below) rather than the squat, angled shapes that gave rise to the Italian bastion proper.

(ii) Italy. Circular works also dominated the best-known design drawings from the transitional period in Italy. The Sienese FRANCESCO DI GIORGIO MARTINI, once believed to have invented the angle bastion, illustrated a number of bastion-shaped works in his *Trattato dell'architettura ingegneria ed arte militare* (*see* §4 below) and incorporated these features in some of the works he built for the Duchy of Urbino. Nearly all his designs and buildings, however, employ round towers. Leonardo da Vinci's well-known design (Milan, Bib. Ambrosiana, Codex Atlanticus, fols 41*v*, 48*r*) for the Appiani, lords of Piombino, shows an entire fortress planned on concentric circular lines. Albrecht Dürer's scheme for Regensburg, illustrated in *Etliche Vnderricht, zu Befestigung der Stett, Schlosz vnd Flecken* (Nuremberg, *c.* 1527), again used semicircular works. These and other features are all demonstrated very

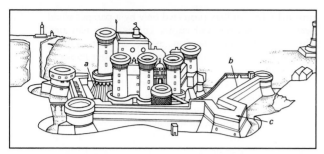

11. Castelnuovo, Naples; reconstruction drawing based on a view of 1540 by Francisco de Holanda: (a) artillery platform and scarping around the landward face of the castle, 1451–3; (b) outer enceinte with circular gun-towers raised slightly above rampart levels, 1503–19 (destr.); (c) triangular bastion built to replace a round tower, 1536 (destr.)

clearly in the 15th- and 16th-century schemes for the modernization of the fortifications of the Castelnuovo in Naples (see fig. 11 and NAPLES, §IV, 4).

By the end of the 15th century, however, a number of Italian architects had mastered the essentials of angle

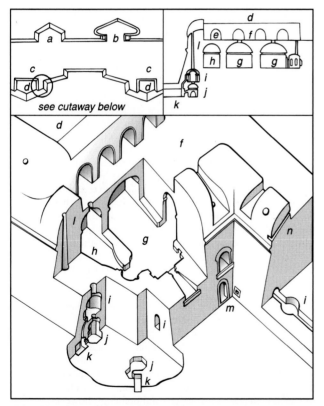

12. Bastion at Porta Ardeatina, Rome, by Antonio da Sangallo the younger, from 1537: plan of single bastions and Sangallo's double bastion (top left), section through the Ardeatine bastion (top right) and cutaway axonometric drawing showing a corner of the bastion (bottom): (a) early 16th-century bastion with straight flanks; (b) later 16th-century bastion with *orecchioni*; (c) double bastion with cavaliers; (d) cavaliers, raised gun platforms; (e) bomb-proof shelters; (f) open gun platforms; (g) casemates; (h) magazine; (i) countermine gallery; (j) well-shaft; (k) countermine shaft; (l) ventilation flue; (m) sallyport; (n) angled embrasure

bastion design in projects that employed the new works systematically on a variety of sites. Poggio Imperiale (1495–1513), designed by Giuliano da Sangallo and Antonio da Sangallo the elder, provides a good example of its use on a defended circuit that runs for *c.* 1.5 km around the crest of a hill above Poggibonsi. Many of the bastions built on this extensive site employed an obtuse angle between the faces, which gave the most spacious internal gun positions and the best outward angles of fire. For the coastal fortress of Nettuno (1501–3) the same architects employed very short flanks, protected by curved projections known as orillions by the French and English and as *orecchioni* ('big ears') by the Italians. This is a much smaller project than Poggio Imperiale, and the four corner bastions are more acutely angled, providing relatively confined platforms and internal spaces. Here, too, the fortress retains much the same vertical proportions as the typical medieval castle. The pronounced scarping of the lower walls is a contemporary feature, but the curved salients and the vestigial machicolated brackets (used here as decoration) reflect an earlier tradition. On the confined riverside site, where Giuliano da Sangallo built the Florentine fortress of Pisa (1509–12; destr.), a triangular plan had to be used, with correspondingly even smaller internal spaces. The logic of all-round flanking cover and well-proportioned bastions led inevitably to polygons of five or more sides for isolated fortresses. This was finally achieved in the classic pentagonal design of Antonio da Sangallo the younger and his team of collaborators for the Fortezza da Basso (1533–6) on a flat site astride the northern wall of Florence.

While working on the Fortezza da Basso, Sangallo's team prepared a scheme for the refortification of Rome. Although only fragments of it were completed, the section built from 1537 near the Porta Ardeatina (see fig. 12) was the most advanced bastion design of the period. By doubling the number of flanks, employing two tiers of guns on each flank and locating cavaliers or elevated gun positions where they too could contribute flanking fire, Antonio provided positions from which up to 24 guns could sweep the ground in front of each curtain. The double bastion also contained elaborate underground works devised to detect and frustrate enemy mining activity, to protect the network of countermine galleries from underground incursions and to light and ventilate the system. These complex and sophisticated internal arrangements are invisible from outside. Like most contemporary military buildings, the double bastion at the Porta Ardeatina is characterized by severely functional plain brickwork surfaces and the gently curved protective shapes of the parapets and gun embrasures.

Even such a consummate technician as Antonio da Sangallo the younger was sometimes willing to embellish his fortresses when suitably protected sections presented themselves. Over one of the side entrances to the Rocca Paolina at Perugia he installed the architectural framework and sculptures of the salvaged Etruscan Porta Marzio. For the masonry of the gate-house in the city face of the Fortezza da Basso, Sangallo employed a diamond-and-ball low-relief pattern (variously interpreted as cannon balls, or the pawnbrokers' balls that had been adopted by the Medici into their coat of arms). This was, however, a rare example of decoration applied to a large area of 16th-century fortification. Fortifications were usually enlivened only by the classical architectural settings for the gates, occasional coats of arms, dressed stone quoins at the junctions of brick faces and flanks, frames for sallyports or gun embrasures, and a moulded string course at the join of the battered lower section of ramparts and the vertical element.

Although stone or brickwork was favoured for permanent works, the bastioned system of fortification lent itself very well to semi-permanent rammed earthwork construction, which could be assembled around a reinforcing framework of timber and faced with turf, giving a structure that was capable of absorbing heavy punishment from enemy gunfire as well as blending into the landscape. Indeed, bastioned fortifications would often have been difficult to see from any distance. Francesco di Giorgio Martini anticipated events with great prescience when he emphasized the importance of the ditch, describing it as 'the principal member of any fortress that is not on a steep and high mountain. . . . A fortress without a ditch is like an animal without one of its limbs.' By the end of the 16th century the best fortifications were set in deep ditches, with the parapets of their bastions and ramparts just visible over the glacis. Except for a few elevated artillery and observation platforms, the bastioned system presented a low profile to enemy gunners. Compared with the picturesque silhouette of medieval castles or city walls, it was almost invisible.

BIBLIOGRAPHY

C. Promis: *Dell'arte dell'ingegnere e dell'artiglierie in Italia dalla sua origine sino al principio del XVI secolo: Memorie storiche* (Turin, 1841)
E.-E. Viollet-le-Duc: *Dictionnaire raisonné de l'architecture française du XIe au XVe siècle* (Paris, 1854–68), i, pp. 327–452
C. Promis: *Biografie di ingegneri militari italiani dal secolo XIV alla metà del XVIII* (Turin, 1874)
H. de La Croix: 'Military Architecture and the Radial City Plan in Sixteenth Century Italy', *A. Bull.*, xlii (1960), pp. 263–90
——: 'The Literature of Fortification in Renaissance Italy', *Technol. & Cult.*, vi (1963), pp. 30–50
J. R. Hale: 'The Early Development of the Bastion: An Italian Chronology, c. 1450–c. 1534', *Europe in the Late Middle Ages*, ed. J. R. Hale, J. R. L. Highfield and B. Smalley (London, 1965), pp. 466–94
——: 'The End of Florentine Liberty: The Fortezza da Basso', *Florentine Studies*, ed. N. Rubinstein (London, 1970), pp. 501–32
H. de La Croix: *Military Consideration in City Planning: Fortifications* (New York, 1972)
S. Pepper: 'The Meaning of the Renaissance Fortress', *Archit. Assoc. Q.*, v (1973), pp. 22–7
J. R. Hale: *Renaissance Fortification: Art or Engineering?* (London, 1977)
S. von Moos: *Turm und Bollwerk: Beiträge zu einer politischen Ikonographie der italienischen Renaissance-Architektur* (Zurich, 1978)
C. Duffy: *Siege Warfare: The Fortress in the Early Modern World, 1494–1660* (London, 1979)
S. Pepper and N. Adams: *Firearms and Fortifications: Military Architecture and Siege Warfare in Sixteenth Century Siena* (Chicago and London, 1986)
G. M. Porbellini: *The Fortress of Nicosia: Prototype of European Renaissance Military Architecture* (Nicosia, 1994)

SIMON PEPPER

(iii) France. The development of military architecture in post-medieval France was strongly affected by French interest in order and standardization. As early as the reign of Charles VII (*reg* 1422–61) the brothers Jean Bureau (*fl* 1425–63) and Gaspard Bureau (*fl* 1442–69) were commissioned to reform French artillery so that it could fire mass-produced cast-iron shot. This, with the casting of

trunnions and the improvement in firepower, enabled the French to reconquer Normandy in 1450, expel the English from most of France and invade Italy in 1494. By the second half of the 17th century French ordnance had been standardized, and c. 1764 Jean-Baptiste Vaquelte de Gribeauval (1715–89) introduced a classification system that was soon adopted by the other great powers.

Under the Duc de Sully there was the growth of an efficient corps of military engineers and heavy state expenditure on building and converting fortresses. In 1600 Jean Errard de Bar-le-Duc (1554–1610) published at royal command the first important French book on bastion fortifications, to be followed by a flood of publications as the use of the Italian system became widespread (*see* §4 below). Blaise de Pagan (1604–65) realized the importance of elaborate, protective outworks in front of the bastions. Guns began to be moved out of casemates, which had proved to be death-traps filled with choking smoke. The guns were placed on a solid terreplein, sometimes firing through embrasures.

SÉBASTIEN LEPRESTRE DE VAUBAN, who was influenced by Pagan, brought together and rationalized the ideas of his predecessors, producing three practical solutions, called by his followers 'systems', for defending towns with bastions. The First System (see fig. 13) adapted the Italian method to include a ravelin and tenaille covering the vulnerable curtain between the bastions. In the Second System, realizing that if the bastion fell the town would

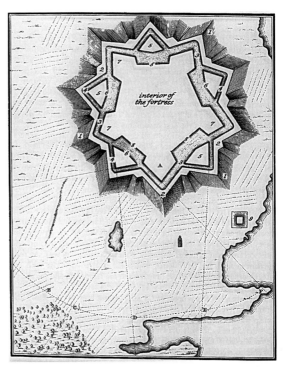

13. French plan showing parts of a fortress: (1) glacis; (2) covered way; (3) main ditch; (4) ditches of the ravelins; (5) ravelins or demi-lunes; (6) throats of the ravelins; (7) bastions; (8) curtain walls; (9) redoubt; from Sébastien Leprestre de Vauban: *Mémoire pour servier d'instruction dans la conduite des sièges et dans la défense des places* (Leiden, 1740)

also fall, he detached the bastion, surrounding it with a ditch. The Third System was a more complex and expensive version of the Second, and he used it only once, at Neuf-Brisach (1698–1706). Where the site was flat and open he designed fortresses in the form of regular figures, like pentagons, but usually he had to modify the shape to suit the irregularity of the terrain. The Citadel at Lille (begun 1668), a regular five-sided fort designed according to Vauban's First System, was surrounded by a broad ditch in which lay ravelins built according to his Third System. Beyond them a further ditch was dug and seven lunettes built as protective outworks: successive rings of radiating defences, which were joined at two points to the strong walls of the town. Many of Vauban's fortresses still stand; particularly good examples are found at Neuf-Brisach, Besançon (after 1674), Blaye (1681), Briançon (1692), Le Quesnoy (1676–98), Mont-Dauphin (1692), Mont-Louis (1681) and Rocroi (1691). Owing to Vauban's reputation, later engineers found it impossible to promote any totally new system. The only safe course was to make well-organized amendments. Thus the basic bastion systems were retained in France up to the end of the Franco-Prussian War in 1871. Whereas previously Italians had been much sought after by the other powers and invited to design fortifications abroad, such as those at Würzburg attributed to Antonio Petrini (*see* WÜRZBURG, fig. 1), in the late 17th century and the 18th the name of Vauban was held in great respect, and French engineers were much in demand and their ideas copied.

French engineers always produced excellent drawings, a demonstration of the pride they took in their work; these usually showed—in different colours—the fortification that was projected, that which had been completed in masonry and that which was already constructed in earthwork. They also used new techniques to represent the topography of the ground. Guillaume-Henri Dufour (1787–1875) was one of the first to develop and use a system of contour lines drawn through all the points represented on the surface that were of equal height above sea-level. Previously the terrain had been indicated by shading and hatching on the hills, occasionally introducing spot heights, but from about 1811 Dufour's staff began to draw contours on many of their plans. Gaspard Monge introduced the 'Geometric Cut', where a line drawn on a plan is marked off in heights so that a profile could be drawn along that section. Finally, cast shadows, used on drawings since the early 18th century to give a three-dimensional appearance to the fortifications, were arranged so that the light appears to come from the top left-hand corner of the drawing, casting shadows towards the bottom right of the sheet, but, until the full introduction of geometrical sciagraphy, this was not always consistent.

With the land frontiers to secure, coastal defence had to play a secondary, but nonetheless important, role, particularly in view of the strength of the British navy. Vauban also developed the best basic solution to a coastal fort: a semicircle of guns firing through embrasures out to sea, with its landward side covered and secured by a defensible tower. A well-preserved example is Fort Lupin, built in 1683 on the coast of Brittany. This design became almost standardized. During the Napoleonic Wars (1793–1815) the French also developed square *tours modèles* and

semicircular *réduits modèles*, two standard types of coastal defence works. The towers were available in five sizes to suit all demands. The designs, the French counterpart of the British Martello tower (*see* §(iv) below), were approved in 1811. In 1846 new model square towers were designed, not dissimilar to the earlier ones. Despite the introduction of rifled artillery firing explosive shells, these masonry towers continued in use until the 1870s, protected with earth mounds.

After the Franco-Prussian War of 1870–71 General Raymond Séré de Rivières (1815–95) was charged with the task of fortifying the new frontier. Mainly in the area from Verdun to the Swiss border, he reconstructed some of the older fortresses and built new polygonal forts, their guns firing forward rather than from flanking bastions and somewhat similar to those being built in Germany and Britain (*see* §(iv)(a) and (d) below). The ditches were protected by caponiers (see fig. 16 below) placed at the salient corners of the forts.

For bibliography *see* §(iv) below.

(iv) Britain and northern Europe.

(a) Britain. Before 1538, when Henry VIII hurriedly fortified the south coast of England with a series of coastal defence forts against the threat of invasion, castles in Britain were not characterized by any remarkable changes in the techniques of fortification. By the 16th century, however, the gunpowder cannon had changed everything. Required to defend the coast against bombardment by enemy ships, Henry's forts were designed in a series of geometric curves with batteries of cannon firing from casemates through gunports and through embrasures in curved parapets designed to deflect enemy shot, the guns stacked on levels like the concentric castles, tier upon tier. The inspiration for these forts is uncertain. There was a widespread and varied continental tradition of rounded gun-towers, both high and low. The ideas for these possibly came from *bastejas*, the large, round gun-platforms of northern Europe (see fig. 23 below), for the German military engineer Stefan von Haschenperg was employed on the work, or, more likely, from Italian coastal defence forts in such areas as the Adriatic. Each of the British forts is different in plan, usually in the form of a symmetrical geometric figure that combined aesthetic appeal with functional demands, reminiscent of the interwoven patterns found in the intricate decoration familiar to the court of Henry VIII. From 1538 the forts were built at great speed, with good examples at Deal and Walmer (Kent), Portland (Dorset), and Pendennis and St Mawes (both Cornwall; see fig. 14a), the money for their construction being made available through the dissolution of the monasteries.

Still fearful of invasion, in the last years of the century Elizabeth I continued to strengthen the realm with extensive fortifications, using the bastion system at Carisbrooke Castle (Isle of Wight) by Federico Genebelli (*fl* 1585–1602), Pendennis Castle, Elizabeth Castle (Jersey) and Castle Cornet (Guernsey) by Paul Ive (*d* 1604). Most of the new works were for coastal defence, and Ive was one of the first military architects to produce forts designed with bastions on the landfront to hold off an infantry attack and with a tenaille trace to provide maximum gun platforms facing out to sea to ward off broadsides from attacking ships. To the north, England faced the possibility of a land attack by the Scots, so at Berwick-upon-Tweed (Northumb.) Richard Lee surrounded the vulnerable parts of the town with broad bastions and ramparts in the latest Italian style (1558), making Berwick a fortified town that could match those on the Continent.

The Civil War (1641–9) caused many earthwork forts, sconces and redoubts to be built hurriedly, as attackers and besieged dug in to defend themselves against sorties and assault. The works were mostly modelled on Dutch practice (*see* §(v)(b) below), for many of the soldiers had fought in the Netherlands. Charles I began to encircle Oxford with a large-scale double envelope of bastions and *fausse-braye* (destr.) in the Dutch style, while Parliamentarian London was ringed by nine bastion forts, thirteen redoubts, some star-shaped, and hornworks (all destr.), also Dutch in style. At the restoration of the monarchy in 1660 a Dutch engineer, Sir Bernard de Gomme (1620–85), built the Citadel at Plymouth (Devon) and strengthened Fort Tilbury (Essex) and the defences of Portsmouth (Hants).

In the 18th century, although most of England was at peace, there were wars in Scotland and Ireland and, from time to time, threats of invasion. Thus a number of classical bastioned forts, somewhat in the French manner of Vauban, were built, most notably Fort Cumberland (1786), outside Portsmouth, and Fort George (1747–69), near Inverness (Highland; see fig. 14b). The latter, beautifully preserved, perfected Ive's solution at Castle Cornet to a land and sea attack. During the Napoleonic Wars Britain was forced to strengthen the defences in her overseas possessions and take steps against a French invasion. The main architectural deterrent was the Martello tower, a thick-walled, round or oval structure named from a similar tower (at Cape Mortella) on the coast of Corsica, which withstood a British naval bombardment in 1783. A gun designed to cover a vulnerable stretch of coast was mounted on the roof. The Martello tower was a strengthened version of the earlier watch-towers, many of which had been built on the Channel Islands, and, from the early 19th century, the British began to construct them there, along the south and east coasts, on the west coast of Ireland and in many places abroad (*see* §(v)(e) below). In Britain some were supported by batteries and by larger circular forts or redoubts, as at Harwich (Essex), Dymchurch (Kent) and Eastbourne (E. Sussex; 1804–12).

By the mid-19th century Arthur Wellesley, 1st Duke of Wellington, was again warning of the dangers of a French invasion, prompted by the fear of attack by steam-driven propeller warships. Influenced by Russian coastal defence forts encountered during the Crimean War (1854–6), Britain began a further programme of fort construction to protect her naval stations. Following continental practice, the bastion was abandoned and polygonal forts were built with guns firing out across the countryside, and, around Milford Haven (Wales), Cork (Ireland), Portsmouth, Plymouth and Chatham (Kent), the forts were designed in a ring to be mutually supportive. New coastal batteries were installed, armed with heavy muzzle-loading guns in casemates, their muzzles protected by armour plating.

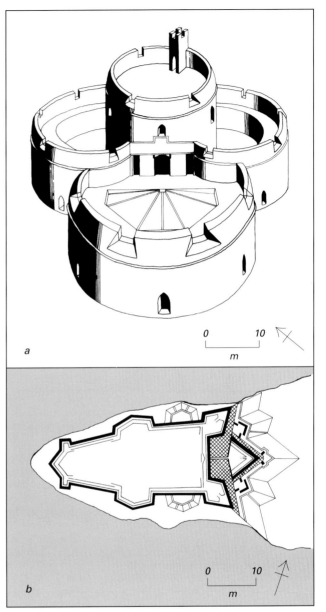

14. British fortifications: (a) St Mawes Castle, Cornwall, England, built by Henry VIII, 1540; (b) Fort George, near Inverness, Highland, Scotland, showing bastions facing land and a tenaille trace facing sea, 1747–69

Some iron-armoured forts were built in the sea (e.g. Horse Sand Fort in the Solent; *c*. 1870). The design of fortifications was continuously modified as the techniques of attack and defence changed, particularly after the experiences in siege and coast warfare during the American Civil War (1861–5).

(b) The Netherlands. The pressure of the Wars of Independence against the Spanish from 1568 to 1648 led to the rapid development of military architecture in the northern and southern Netherlands, as both sides felt the need to construct elaborate water defences; since most of

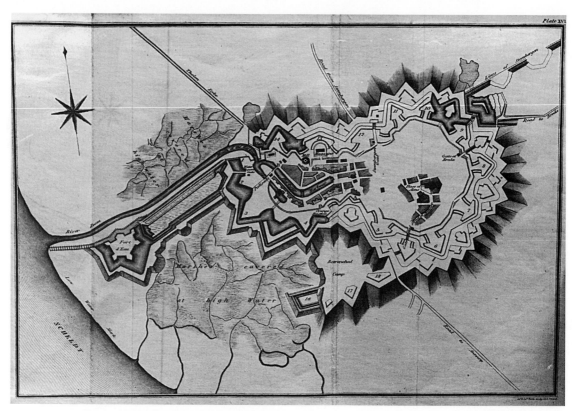

15. Dutch fortifications: plan of Bergen-op-Zoom, the Netherlands, designed by Menno van Coehoorn, completed 1700; from John T. Jones: *Journals of the Sieges Carried on by the Army of the Duke of Wellington in Spain . . .* (London, 1827), iii, pl. XVI

the country lay close to sea-level. With little stone available, the ramparts were built of earth, which was resistant to artillery bombardment. The Dutch tended to widen their fortifications by adding ditches and outworks, and they invented an elaborate form of the latter, known as the hornwork. The Flemish school, which was based at Antwerp, came under strong Italian influence, and Francesco Paciotto built the fine pentagonal bastioned citadel for the Spanish army there in 1567.

In the wars with France towards the end of the 17th century, the theories of the Dutch engineer Baron MENNO VAN COEHOORN were most important, differing from those of Vauban in that van Coehoorn sacrificed everything to surprise and the use of heavy artillery bombardment. Of van Coehoorn's finest fortified town, Bergen-op-Zoom, completed in 1700 (see fig. 15), few defences remain. One of the best-preserved and regularly fortified towns in the Netherlands is Naarden, its defences reconstructed in 1673 based on van Coehoorn's New Dutch System of successive defensive rings (*see* §4 below). After the Battle of Waterloo in 1815, many of the fortified towns in northern France and Belgium were in a sorry state, and the British and Dutch governments undertook a £5 million project for the reconstruction of these barrier fortresses under the direction of the Duke of Wellington. In 1846, after Belgium had become independent, a new enceinte was begun around Antwerp, which consisted, starting at the citadel, of two girdles of defence—a continuous

fortified line (completed 1859; destr.) and a ring of detached forts (completed 1868) that protected the town with the largest fortification system in the world. A third outer girdle of forts was built between 1908 and 1914, and both Liège and Namur were defended by rings of detached forts. By that time this was standard practice for the defence of important towns throughout Europe. Another defensive system that the Dutch worked on from 1815 until the outbreak of World War II was the New Dutch Waterline, relying for their security on large areas of inundation, together with powerful forts around Utrecht, in particular Fort Rhijnauwen, begun in 1868.

(c) Scandinavia. From 1618 Denmark began to fortify Copenhagen in the Dutch style, surrounding the citadel with a continuous enceinte of bastions and curtain walls, built mainly in the 1680s, that made it one of the strongest cities in Europe. When besieging a fort, Swedish generals usually depended on little more than a heavy bombardment, displaying none of the niceties of Vauban's ordered sieges. In the late 17th century fortress building was pushed ahead at a furious pace as the Swedes pressed against the Danes and across the Baltic. Erik Dahlbergh, the most important Swedish engineer, fortified more than 50 places, including the great fortress of Göteborg, from 1687, and he was one of the earliest engineers to revive a dependence on strong, round towers at the centre of his fortifications.

(d) Germany and central Europe. The power of Prussia stretched from the Baltic to the borders of Galicia. In the north the Prussians built powerful fortified towns, extending the medieval and Renaissance defences into a new complexity at Königsberg (now Kaliningrad), Danzig (now Gdańsk), Thorn (now Toruń), Posen (now Poznań), Stettin (now Szczecin), and south-west of the River Oder a line of fortified towns was built to block the approaches to Germany across the lowlands of Silesia. Glogau (now Głogów), Breslau (now Wrocław), Schweidnitz (now Swidnica), Silberberg (now Srebrna Góra), Glatz (now Kłodzko), Neisse (now Nysa) and Koźle were all put into a state of defence.

There were two great periods of Prussian fortification. The Old Prussian System was dominated by the work of Gerhard Cornelius von Walrave (1692–1773), a Dutchman who initially absorbed the system of Vauban. His work was characterized essentially by the reintroduction of the tenaille trace (*see* §(iii) above). In front of the main tenaille line he placed forts in a continuous pattern, acting like ravelins, or individually sited on dangerous lines of approach. For example, at Schweidnitz he bound the inner enceinte with a ring of tenaille forts linked by a continuous trenchwork; further out he placed detached forts.

The New Prussian System, which dominated work in Silesia after the mid-19th century, exploited a number of older devices modified to suit the striking power of new, more powerful guns. The polygonal fort, as opposed to the bastion fort, had been advocated by Francesco di Giorgio Martini, Giacomo Castriotto and Girolamo Maggi (*d* 1572; *see* §4 below), and it was revived by the French engineer Marc-René, Marquis de Montalembert (1714–1800), who found it difficult to get his ideas accepted by his colleagues. The Prussians used the polygonal fort after 1827 at Posen and Toruń, and soon it became standard. Caponiers, illustrated by both Francesco di Giorgio and Albrecht Dürer, were reintroduced in a modified, stronger form by Montalembert (see fig. 16) and adopted in Prussia, where, housing massed guns of much greater power, they became active, aggressive elements within the defensive enceinte of forts. The third feature was the reuse of keeps, strong places of last resort containing barracks—the descendants of the medieval donjon. These were reintroduced into Poland at Toruń in 1824.

BIBLIOGRAPHY

S. Leprestre de Vauban: *Mémoire pour servier d'instruction dans la conduite des sièges et dans la défense des places* (Leiden, 1740); Eng. trans. as *A Manual of Siegecraft and Fortification* (Ann Arbor, 1978)
A. F. Lendy: *Treatise on Fortification* (London, 1862)
E. M. Lloyd: *Vauban, Montalembert, Carnot: Engineer Studies* (London, 1887)
M. Parent and J. Verroust: *Vauban* (Paris, 1971, rev. 1982)
S. Sutcliffe: *Martello Towers* (Newton Abbot, 1972)
P. Rocolle: *2000 Ans de fortification française*, 2 vols (Paris, 1972–3)
C. Duffy: *Fire and Stone: The Science of Fortress Warfare, 1660–1860* (Newton Abbot, 1975)
——: *Siege Warfare: The Fortress in the Early Modern World, 1494–1660* (London and Henley-on-Thames, 1979)
Q. Hughes: 'A Project for the Defence of Paris', *Fort*, xii (1984), pp. 25–66
C. Duffy: *The Fortress in the Age of Vauban and Frederick the Great, 1660–1789* (London, 1985)
A. Saunders: *Fortress Britain: Artillery Fortification in the British Isles and Ireland* (Liphook, 1989)

QUENTIN HUGHES

(v) European influence abroad. By the end of the 15th century some western European nations were exploring the wider world for conquest, trade and the spreading of Christianity by force or conversion. As Venice dominated the Mediterranean, a flanking sea route had to be found to open up trade with the East. The five principal colonizing nations were the Roman Catholic Portuguese, Spanish and French and the Protestant Dutch and British. The principal tools of conquest were the newly developed heavy, smooth-bore cannon firing broadsides from strongly built sailing-ships, a lethal combination that assured European world domination for the next three or four centuries. The Europeans further secured their power by building several thousand forts throughout their colonies. Since dominion was founded on mastery of the seas, the forts frequently were placed on the coasts, up navigable rivers or at lagoon mouths.

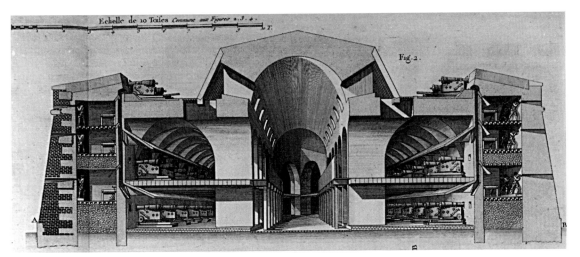

16. Multi-gun caponier, designed by Marc-René, Marquis de Montalembert, 1776; from his *La Fortification perpendiculaire* (Paris, 1776–94), ii, p. 144

The design of overseas forts followed those in Europe. Many had a trading role, with warehouses included within the fortifications. Often they also had a Christian religious role and contained a church. The Europeans found themselves among peoples of different races and religions: the forts had to resist attack not only by those local inhabitants, usually poorly armed, but also by well-armed Europeans of other nations.

(a) Portuguese. (b) Dutch. (c) Spanish. (d) French. (e) British.

(a) Portuguese. The empire founded by the Portuguese after *c.* 1500 stretched from Brazil in the west to China in the east at its greatest extent; centred on the Indian Ocean, its overseas capital and seat of the Viceroys was at Goa in western India. Forts were built throughout the territory, including East Africa, where important examples are Fort Jesus in Mombasa, Kenya, and Fort St Sebastian in Mozambique. A characteristic of such forts is their flexible and adaptable design approach; ardently devoted to their religion, the Portuguese named each bastion after a saint.

Fort St Sebastian (see fig. 17) is a typical Portuguese overseas fort. Founded in 1559, it was primarily intended as a staging-post between Portugal and Goa, but the high mortality from malaria restricted that function; nevertheless it remained the key Portuguese fort on the East African coast. Its design follows the usual lines of artillery fortification, with low, inward-sloping bastions and ramparts *c.* 6 m high, and it has an internal area of *c.* 2 ha. It occupies the head of a peninsula with the town of Mozambique (Moçambique) on the landward side, and its irregular form was designed to follow the terrain of the rocky peninsula: the four bastions are of unusual shape, three having very short flanks and the fourth enlarged to a hexagon. One of the landward-facing bastions has an inset flank. Three of the ramparts slope inwards to form obtuse angles at their centres. There are low outworks on two of the seaward sides, ringed by rough coral rock. While the design of this fort departed in some respects

from the regular geometry of model artillery fortifications, its clever adaptation to local physical features increased its strength without departing from the general principles laid down for European military architecture. It successfully withstood three sieges (1607, 1608 and 1670), two of them by the Dutch.

BIBLIOGRAPHY
J. Ribeiro: *Fatalidade histórica da ilha de Ceilão* (Lisbon, 1836; Eng. trans., Colombo, 1909/*R* 1948)
C. R. Boxer and D. de Azevedo: *Fort Jesus and the Portuguese in Mombasa, 1593–1729* (London, 1960)
C. R. Boxer: *The Portuguese Seaborne Empire, 1415–1825* (London, 1969)
J. S. Kirkman: *Fort Jesus: A Portuguese Fortress on the East African Coast* (Oxford, 1974)

(b) Dutch. Following the Portuguese to the Indian Ocean *c.* 1600, the Dutch engaged them in a long and bitter war, a continuation overseas of their Eighty Years' War for freedom from the rule of Spain. Although their attacks on East Africa failed, the Dutch won, among other territories, the coastal areas of Ceylon (now Sri Lanka). In 1652 they expelled the Portuguese from their last holding in Ceylon, the square fort at Jaffna in the north. Over the next 50 years the Dutch rebuilt almost all the Portuguese fortifications in Ceylon in a more advanced style, often with reduced internal areas; of more than 30 stone-faced forts constructed there, about half remain. A typical feature of these forts is a more rigid and regular design approach than the Portuguese, and the republican Dutch named their bastions after Dutch provinces.

The Dutch fort at Jaffna (see fig. 18), which covers 5.7 ha, was a regular pentagonal citadel (i.e. with no civilian population) designed to overawe the adjoining town and guard against attack from Madras by the British East India Company. The fort has five bastions and ramparts (h. *c.* 6 m), a surrounding wet-ditch and access to the lagoon by water-gate. There is a complicated entry to the

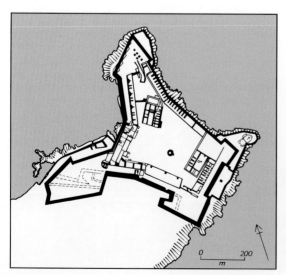

17. Portuguese overseas fort design: Fort St Sebastian, Mozambique, founded 1559

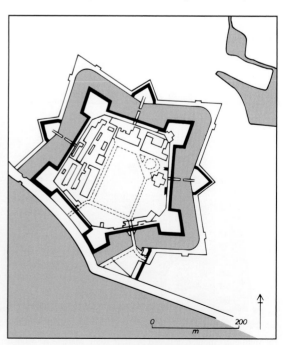

18. Dutch overseas fort design: Fort Jaffna, Sri Lanka, *c.* 1700

south, with, beyond the ditch, the customary covered way, three triangular ravelins for guns and musketry and an external glacis. The fort's design is a classic solution that does not depart from the designs of those being constructed everywhere in Europe in the 17th and 18th centuries. The Dutch, however, originally included a warehouse in the plan because of their interest in trade. Both the Dutch and the Portuguese continued to build overseas forts along the patterns of those erected in their homelands until *c.* 1850.

BIBLIOGRAPHY

R. Knox: *An Historical Relation of the Island Ceylon, in the East-Indies* (London, 1681); *R* as *An Account of the Captivity of Capt. Robert Knox in the Island of Ceylon, 1660–80* (London, 1818/*R* Colombo, 1908)

C. Schweitzer: *Journal- und Tage-buch seiner sechs-jährigen ost-indianischen Reise angefangen . . . 1675, und vollendet 1682* (Tübingen, 1688); ed. C. E. Fayle (London, 1929)

C. Fryke: *C. Frikens ost-indianische Räysen und krieges-Dienste* (Ulm, 1692); ed. C. E. Fayle (London, 1929)

P. M. Bingham and others: *History of the Public Works Department, Ceylon, 1796 to 1913*, 3 vols (Colombo, 1921–3)

R. G. Antonisz: *The Dutch in Ceylon*, 2 vols (Colombo, 1929)

C. R. Boxer: *The Dutch Seaborne Empire, 1600–1800* (London, 1965)

R. L. Brohier: *Links between Sri Lanka and the Netherlands* (Colombo, 1978)

C. R. Boxer: *Jan Compagnie in Peace and War, 1602–1799* (Hong Kong, 1979)

L. Blussé and J. de Moor: *Nederlanders overzee* (Franeker, 1983)

W. A. Nelson: *The Dutch Forts of Sri Lanka* (Edinburgh, 1984)

R. K. de Silva: *Early Prints of Ceylon, 1800–1900* (London, 1985)

W. A. NELSON

(c) Spanish. Faced by natives poorly armed by Western standards, Spain had no great need to fortify strongly many of her colonial towns in the Americas, but when the need arose to extract the wealth from those colonies, the situation was different. As her fleets were threatened by predatory attacks, from the 1560s Spain instituted a strategy of armed convoys and strongly fortified bases that for a century and a half protected her ships wintering in the Caribbean. Cartagena (Colombia), Havana (Cuba), and San Juan (Puerto Rico) received coastal and bastioned forts and defences modelled on contemporary European practice. Fort Moro, one of those covering Havana, was thought to be invincible until 1762, when it was captured by an amphibious British force. Along the south-eastern Atlantic seaboard, Spanish outposts and garrisons had to be protected by forts against both an aggressive native population and the pressure from other European colonists. Thus, strategically placed forts were built, often of such temporary materials as timber and earth, to maintain land claims and limit the expansion of others. Most forts were square in plan, with a bastion at each corner and with the entrance protected by a triangular ravelin. Some, like the Castillo de San Marcos (1572–1756) at San Agustín de la Florida (now ST AUGUSTINE), designed to express the symbol of power at the most northerly outpost of the Spanish empire, were stoutly constructed of stone and faced with stucco. The Castillo de San Marcos had a large, square courtyard, and its four corner bastions were surrounded by a broad moat in which stood the ravelin. The entrance passed through it and over a drawbridge into the fort. Elsewhere *presidios* (garrison towns), sometimes octagonal in plan and surrounded by bastions and a ditch, were built next to missions to protect and control large areas of territory.

(d) French. The French were also strongly committed to the colonization of North America, their forces moving up the St Lawrence River in 1541 and, close to Spanish colonies, along the southern Atlantic seaboard in the 1560s. Fort Caroline (1564) in Florida is typical of French work, a triangular fort with acutely pointed bastions and a ditch, part of its walls built in masonry but with one side consisting of posts and walls made of timber, a material readily available in that area.

In the north, the French sought to control the waterways and in the 18th century built a string of forts, such as Fort Niagara (1718–26) and Fort Vaudreuil (now Ticonderoga; 1755), both in New York. The former had an irregular trace, being well sited on a peninsula so that it faced a siege on one side only, protected by two demi-bastions and a central ravelin, flanked by two large redoubts. Hampered by local conditions and a shortage of resources, the French reduced the science of fortification to essentials, producing effective square forts with corner bastions, which were often simple loopholed stockades. Partly owing to a shortage of manpower, they developed strongly fortified regional centres at Montreal and Quebec. In 1721 Jean François du Verger de Verville (*c.* 1680–1729) began the great fortress of Louisbourg on Ile Royale (now Cape Breton, Nova Scotia), controlling the entrance to the Gulf of St Lawrence and the St Lawrence River. It consisted of a town laid out on a grid plan along a peninsula, the neck of which was closed off by two large bastions and two half-bastions. One of the full bastions was, in fact, a miniature citadel, formed into a self-contained work intended to hold out if other parts fell. In 1745 Louisbourg was captured by the British, handed back under the Treaty of Aix-la-Chapelle (1748) and finally recaptured ten years later, signalling the collapse of French power in America.

Always using European models, France also fortified her colonial possessions in India before they too were captured by the British, and Ile-de-France (now Mauritius), lying on the route to India, was fortified by the French East India Company early in the 18th century. Ships that preyed on British merchantmen were protected in the harbour of Port Louis by coastal forts guarding the entrance and by extensive lines of advanced fortification consisting of broad bastions, ravelins, tenailles and square forts intended to hold off an encircling enemy force. After the British took Fort Louis in 1810, they strengthened the coastal defences, building new coastal forts.

(e) British. Early British settlers in North America were militarily unorganized and had little knowledge of fortification. They built stockades of timber and strangely formed pseudo-bastioned forts, such as Fort Raleigh (1585) on Roanoke Island in North Carolina, consisting of a diamond superimposed on a square, with one corner of the diamond converted into a rudimentary heart-shaped bastion and another point cut short to form the entrance. From these primitive beginnings Britain was eventually to spend more of her expertise and resources in defending her colonies than she did in safeguarding her home islands. The Spanish forts in Florida were acquired in 1736, and by 1759 work began on such full pentagonal forts as Fort Pitt, PA, by Harry Gordon (*d* 1787) and Fort Ontario, NY, by Thomas Sowers. Following the capture of the

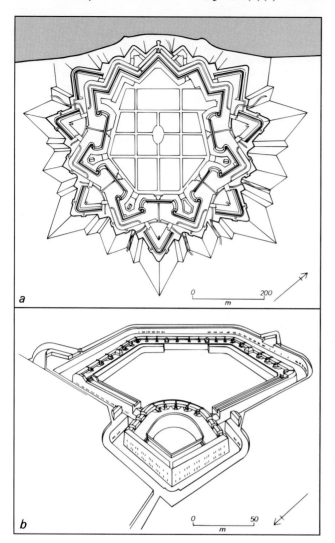

19. British overseas fort design: (a) Fort George, Vido Island, Corfu, begun 1824; (b) Fort William, Calcutta, India, rebuilt 1757

Some of the strongest British naval bases were built in the Mediterranean. Gibraltar was captured in 1704, and the Spanish fortifications protecting the town were, over the years, modified and extended with a series of galleries and casemates cut into the sheer north face of the Rock so that guns could fire on the flat isthmus joining it to Spain. Menorca was held by the British, off and on, from 1708 until handed to Spain in 1802. The British extended Fort San Felipe (destr. 1807), adding a series of powerful outworks in the form of redoubts, the outer walls of their ditches being defended by continuous counterscarp galleries dug into the rock-face: an idea copied from the Dutch. Thirteen round towers, forerunners of the Martello towers, were built between 1798 and 1802 to defend the coast. On Corfu, a vast array of Italian fortifications was taken over after the Napoleonic Wars, and the British vacillated between maintaining what had been inherited and destroying fortifications to concentrate on three key points—the citadel, Fort Neuf and Vido Island. In 1824 they began to build in secret a revolutionary fort (destr.) on Vido Island that abandoned the bastions, replacing them with broad artillery fronts. The geometric plan form of the resulting structure, Fort George (see fig. 19a), which was based on an irregular pentagon, its obtuse faces packed with guns firing out to sea, was to become the standard shape for detached forts throughout the world, superseding the bastioned fort. In addition, it had a detached keep at the back, also mounting heavy guns, and the ditch was protected by galleries cut into both the scarp and the counterscarp walls.

When Britain took over Malta from the French in 1800, she inherited one of the strongest fortresses in the world, built by the Knights Hospitaller, to which further fortifications were added (see MALTA, §III, 1). In the 1860s heavy guns were brought in and new self-defensible coastal forts constructed. Fort S Leonardo is a fine example, consisting of an irregular pentagon, broadly copying Fort George on Corfu, but mounting heavy, rifled, muzzle-loading guns on the faces towards the sea and having a strong diamond-shaped keep at the rear, separated by its own ditch. In 1873 the Victoria Lines, a string of forts and entrenchments, was built across the island to hold off an attack on the dockyard. Malta eventually became Britain's most powerful naval base.

In India, the British East India Company began to rebuild its main fortress at Calcutta in 1757 to the design of Captain John Brohier, modelled on French engineering work, for a large fully bastioned fortress with a tenaille front facing the river (see fig. 19b). At Madras, Brohier, with Colonel Patrick Ross (?1740–1804), began a complete reconstruction of Fort St George between 1755 and 1783, laying out a trace in the form of a large semi-octagon, its back facing the sea, and using the expedients of bastions against a land attack and a tenaille front for the defence of the coast.

To defend the long supply lines to India, at first round the Cape of Good Hope and later through the Suez Canal and the Red Sea, fortified bases and staging posts had to be secured. Thus St Helena (1658), Freetown (Sierra Leone; much later), Ascension Island (*c.* 1830), South Africa (where the first Martello towers were built in 1796), Mauritius, its defences captured from the French, and

French strongholds in the north, a number of strong citadels were designed and built to defend and hold down the territory. At Quebec City in 1767 Gordon designed an irregular seven-sided polygon with broad bastions standing high above the St Lawrence River and forming the end of the fortified front line of the city. This was built in a modified form after 1818. The Citadel at Halifax, Nova Scotia (begun 1828; see §(vi) below), is an interesting rectangular form, its long sides protected by four half-bastions, its ends by recessed tenailles, its centres and curtains by ravelins. In Upper Canada, Fort Henry (1832–6) at Kingston (Ontario) formed the citadel of a group of innovative projects, a pentagonal design with its main front consisting of three broad faces mounting numerous guns, its rear defended by two half-bastions and the entrance curtain covered by a spur, resembling a ravelin or advanced battery pushed well forward with long straight sides joining it to the fort.

Ceylon, captured from the Dutch, were all fortified. In the second half of the 18th century the British realized that it was necessary to have a naval base further east in order to protect the Bay of Bengal and the passage to China. The bases chosen were Penang (now in Malaysia; 1786), Batavia (now Jakarta, Indonesia; 1811) and finally Singapore (after 1824); the last was built up mainly after 1863 with a series of coastal defence forts to become the most powerful naval base in the Far East.

BIBLIOGRAPHY

A. C. Manucy: *The Building of Castillo de San Marcos* (Washington, DC, 1961)

Q. Hughes: *Military Architecture* (London, 1974, rev. Liphook, 1991)

J. J. Greenough: *The Halifax Citadel, 1825–60: A Narrative and Structural History*, Canadian Historic Sites: Occasional Papers in Archaeology, 17 (Ottawa, 1977)

W. B. Robinson: *American Forts: Architectural Form and Function* (Urbana, IL, 1977)

C. Duffy: *Siege Warfare: The Fortress in the Early Modern World, 1494–1660* (London and Henley-on-Thames, 1979)

P. K. Yeoh: 'Fortress Singapore', *Fort*, vii (1979), pp. 12–51

Q. Hughes: *Britain in the Mediterranean and the Defence of her Naval Stations* (Liverpool, 1981)

A. Charbonneau, Y. Desloges and M. Lafrance: *Québec: The Fortified City: From the 17th to the 19th Century* (Ottawa, 1982)

Q. Hughes: 'Defending the All Pink Route to India', *Bull. Inst. Int. Châteaux Hist.*, xli (1983), pp. 46–56

C. Duffy: *The Fortress in the Age of Vauban and Frederick the Great, 1660–1789* (London, 1985)

QUENTIN HUGHES

(vi) North America, 1775–1865. Following the American revolutionary war (1775–83), the art of fortification in North America developed in two directions: in Canada the Royal Military Engineers continued to employ principles of defence formulated in England, while in the USA engineers followed the French school of fortification (*see also* §(v)(d) and (e) above). This the Americans continued until the Civil War (1861–5), when Renaissance systems were rendered ineffective by rifled cannons. After that, new designs were heavily influenced by experience on the field of battle.

At first, when fortifying various points of Canada's frontiers, engineers continued to employ bastioned fortifications. Both the Citadel (1820–32) at Quebec City and a new work on Ile-aux-Noir (projected in 1790) exemplify this tendency, the latter designed while Gother Mann (1747–1830) was in command of the Royal Engineers. For economic reasons as well as military effectiveness, however, engineers soon began building polygonal forts and redoubts, as well as Martello towers, which were simpler in form than bastioned works and required less material and work. While polygonal works generally had the same profile as a bastioned enceinte, they were usually simple in plan; but they were occasionally designed with a series of salient and re-entrant angles, the latter represented by the Citadel at Halifax, Nova Scotia, begun in 1828 (*see also* §(v)(e) above). Each particular trace took account of the terrain and potential modes of attack. Ravelins or advanced batteries usually protected the most exposed curtains, and counterscarp galleries often defended the ditches. In at least one instance, at Fort Henry (1832–6), Ontario, this type of polygonal work was reinforced by Martello towers. A line of Martello towers was included in the defences of both Quebec City and Kingston against

possible American aggression. Closely related to the Martello tower was the type of fort consisting of a large blockhouse (essentially a keep or donjon) surrounded by earth ramparts and a ditch with an economical *chevaux-de-frise*—seen, for example, at Fort Wellington (1812; rebuilt 1837), Prescott, Ontario.

The USA, meanwhile, had undertaken the fortification of its extensive coastline. Partially executed by French engineers who had remained after the American Revolution, the first forts were largely temporary structures, consisting of blockhouses and batteries, as at Fort Nelson (1794, by John Jacob Ulrich Rivardi), VA. In several instances, however, including Fort McHenry (from 1798, by Jean Foncin; see fig. 20), Baltimore, MD, these were bastioned works, laid out according to formal theory. Early in the 19th century the American government hired a French engineer, Simon Bernard (1779–1839), to develop a coordinated system of coastal fortifications to protect vital harbours. Developing unique plans for each fort, Bernard employed massive bastioned fronts revetted with masonry as a defence against land attack, and multiple tiers of artillery to concentrate fire on enemy shipping. Fort Adams, RI, built from 1824, was a fort of this kind, but where sites were well fortified by nature, notably Fort Macon, NC, dating from 1826, Bernard constructed polygonal works with deep ditches and vaulted counterfire rooms.

In the mid-19th century the latest developments in France were adopted in the USA in fronts with detached scarps, designs that were thought to strengthen forts against a *coup de main* by allowing destruction of the scarp without seriously weakening the enceinte (as at Fort Clinch, FL, built in 1851 by Joseph G. Totten, the army's chief engineer from 1838 to 1864). At the same time, the walls, arches and vaults of these structures displayed advanced techniques of masonry construction. During the Civil War, however, all these masonry and earth fortifications were soon found to be ineffective against new, powerful rifled cannons. After an experimental period,

20. Fort McHenry, Baltimore, Maryland, by Jean Foncin, from 1798

massive works of concrete protected by earthworks were built at strategic points along the Atlantic coast, sometimes within or adjacent to earlier works. They contained both large rifled cannons and rapid-firing artillery, and they remained in use until after World War II, when aircraft finally made such fortifications obsolete.

While fortification of the coast was under way in the 19th century, forts were built along the inland frontier as a defence against attacks by the Indians. Although some military establishments had walls or stockades, more often than not the inland frontier fort was simply an open complex of buildings, formally organized as at Fort Leavenworth, KS. These, like the coastal forts, were products of functionalism and a clear sense of geometric order, although occasionally non-essential ornament did appear. Although most Canadian and American forts have been destroyed, some have survived as museums.

BIBLIOGRAPHY

W. F. D. Jervois: *Report on the Defense of Canada and the British Naval Stations in the Atlantic* (London, 1864)

W. B. Robinson: *American Forts: Architectural Form and Function* (Urbana, IL, 1977)

——: 'Maritime Frontier Engineering: The Defense of New Orleans', *Louisiana Hist.*, xviii (1977), pp. 5–62

WILLARD B. ROBINSON

3. AGE OF TECHNOLOGY, AFTER *c.* 1850/70. In the mid-19th century the most significant technical change to affect the fortress engineer was the development of rifled artillery, which was a far more accurate and destructive form of fire than hitherto, and thus the traditional forms of fortress architecture had to alter. Instead of seeking to terrify the enemy with a show of force in the form of bastions, redans, cavaliers and similar constructions, the engineer now had to conceal his fort against artillery fire and provide it with guns capable of defeating attack. Unfortunately for the engineers, the development of artillery was to outpace the construction of fortification by a considerable ratio.

The New Prussian System, which came into being in the 1850s (*see* §III, 2(iv)(d) above), relied on a series of massive caponiers linked by a bastioned line of rampart and ditch. The caponier in this case was not a simple structure reaching into the ditch to give covering fire, but a massive, self-sufficient building, horseshoe-shaped to enclose a courtyard, with three or four tiers of casemates for artillery and musketry. The roof of the caponier was covered with 3 m of earth to absorb artillery fire, and the structure could accommodate up to 1000 troops for its defence and that of the adjacent ramparts.

The American Civil War (1861–5) demonstrated that combined earthen and masonry defence works could withstand artillery fire far better than masonry alone, for a shell bursting against masonry did damage that could not easily be repaired and the shattered stone became a shower of secondary missiles. The Franco-Prussian War of 1870–71 and the Russo-Turkish War of 1877–8 reinforced this lesson, and when the French and Germans began to refortify their new frontiers in the 1870s they developed a new style of defensive work, typified by Fort Gambetta at Metz, a pentagonal fort with small towers or caponiers at the forward angles and ample overhead protection. Most of the magazine and store accommodation was buried, and the gorge (the rear face of the fort) was protected by a large, caponier-like structure that also functioned as a redoubt of last resort.

An entirely separate aspect of fortification began to rise in the 1860s with the development of the iron-clad ship. An armoured warship with heavy guns was needed to defeat the iron-clad ship, but such guns were also a threat to land fortifications. Powerful defensive works therefore had to be built to protect naval bases and commercial harbours. The first forts of the 1860s were usually granite structures with wrought-iron armour-plate shields protecting the individual guns, as at Bovisand Fort, Plymouth (Devon; see fig. 21), although where the fort had to be sited in a position where it could be approached closely by enemy ships, as at Fort Cunningham, Bermuda, it was thought advisable to make the whole fort exterior from armour-plate. As the gun became capable of greater range, the coastal defence works could be sited further inland, and the 'disappearing carriage' was developed: the gun emplacement was a reinforced concrete pit, blending with the surrounding terrain. With the realization by the turn of the century that naval gunfire, directed from a ship moving on the surface of the sea, was inherently too inaccurate to hit the gun even if it was visible, the disappearing carriage was replaced by fixed 'barbette' mountings, which were quicker to operate and presented a microscopic target when seen from a ship.

The land-fort assimilated some features from coastal defence and naval practice, notably the use of armour-plate and the adoption of the armoured turret. The design of land-forts reached its apogee in the late 19th century, notably in those by Henri de Brialmont (1821–1903), a Belgian military engineer, whose forts consisted of a triangular or square area with a central, underground, reinforced-concrete redoubt surmounted by armoured gun turrets. Around the redoubt was a rifle parapet, and outside this parapet were smaller turrets carrying searchlights and machine-guns. The ground fell away from the redoubt to meet the floor of the ditch, which was liberally strewn with barbed wire and obstacles, and the vertical

21. Bovisand Fort, Plymouth, Devon, 1860s

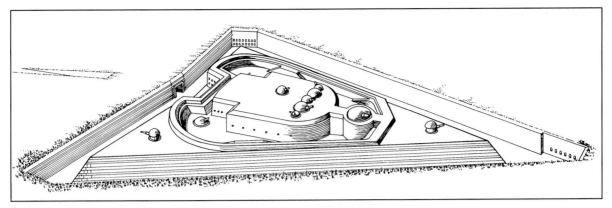

22. Liège fort, Belgium, by Henri de Brialmont, 1888–92; reconstruction

outer wall of the ditch contained loopholed 'counterscarp galleries' from which rifles and machine-guns could pour fire into the ditch. Forts of this type were built in rings around such cities as Antwerp, Liège (see fig. 22), Namur and Bucharest, and they were to be found on most of the European land frontiers by the early 20th century.

The defects of the Brialmont type of fort were that the amount of protection (some 3.5 m of concrete overlaid with 4 m of earth) and the defensive power (21-cm guns) had been dictated by the maximum size of offensive artillery that could be taken into the field by a team of horses. With the constant improvement of artillery and the arrival of mechanical traction, the rules were changed. In 1914, at the beginning of World War I, the German army was able to overcome the ring of defensive forts surrounding Liège in under three days. As a result of this and of the fall of several other European fortresses, the concept of fortification as a viable defence suffered, although it was restored to some degree by the successful resistance to shelling of many of the French forts surrounding Verdun.

After 1918 the French government decided that the only form of defence against any future German threat would be to reproduce the 1914–18 trench lines in more permanent form, and they drew up plans for a line of buried fortifications stretching from Switzerland to the North Sea. This 'Maginot Line' (named after André Maginot, the Minister of War from 1929) was not completed, owing to political and technical difficulties; the Belgian border and the Ardennes were left unprotected. Those parts that were built were the epitome of modern defensive thinking, with armoured gun turrets and thick concrete defences, and were able to accommodate a totally self-contained garrison under the ground. In 1940, however, the German army entered France through the unprotected area of the border. In so doing the Germans had to assault the Belgian fort of Eben Emael, which had been built to command the bridges over the Albert Canal and River Maas. It was a wedge-shaped structure, the sides formed by the canal and river and the fort rising clifflike above them. It was considered impregnable, and it probably was to any known form of attack, but it was overcome by glider troops who landed on its top in darkness and attacked the turrets with explosive shaped charges that pierced the armour and immobilized the guns. Once more, technology had overcome conventional forms of defence.

Coastal defences managed to remain viable throughout World War II and continued to do so until the end of the 20th century in several countries, although some major nations abandoned coastal defence as being impractical in the face of intercontinental ballistic missiles. In the latter part of the 20th century the arts of the fortress engineer remained in demand, although less for pure defence than for protecting either methods of offence ('hardened' missile silos) or the population at large in deep underground shelters capable of withstanding nuclear blast.

BIBLIOGRAPHY
A. F. Lendy: *Treatise on Fortification* (London, 1862)
C. Orde-Browne: *Armour and its Attack by Artillery* (London, 1887)
E. R. Kenyon: *Notes on Land and Coast Fortification* (London, 1894)
H. de Brialmont: *La Défense des côtes* (Brussels, 1896)
G. S. Clarke: *Fortification: Its Past Achievements, Recent Developments and Future Prospects* (London, 1897, 2/1907)
L. Claudel: *La Ligne Maginot* (Lausanne, 1974)
P. Gamelin: *Le Mur atlantique* (Brussels, 1974)
I. V. Hogg: *History of Fortification* (London, 1981)

IAN V. HOGG

4. DESIGNERS AND THEORETICIANS. From earliest times men have thought how to defend themselves and attack others. Some have written their ideas down, as part of treatises on the design of buildings or as manuals of fortification often combined with a study of artillery and military tactics. The first fully illustrated treatises on fortification appeared in Italy in the 15th century.

BIBLIOGRAPHY
M. J. D. Cockle: *A Bibliography of Military Books up to 1642* (London, 1900, 2/1957)
J. R. Hale: *Renaissance Fortification: Art or Engineering?* (London, 1977)

(i) Classical theorists. (ii) Medieval and Renaissance, *c.* 1480–*c.* 1650. (iii) After *c.* 1650.

(i) *Classical theorists.* The surviving treatise of Aeneas Tacitus, *c.* 355 BC, describes the defence of fortified positions, and 3rd-century BC developments in the Greek world were discussed by Ctesibius (*fl* 270 BC; edited by Heron of Alexandria *c.* AD 62), Philo of Byzantium and Biton. Later refinements were described by Aegistratus (used by Athenaeus Mechanicus, ?1st century BC, and Vitruvius). Offensive and defensive siegecraft were discussed by Philo, in the *Poliorketika* of APOLLODOROS OF

DAMASCUS (1st century AD), and by the Byzantine excerptors.

The works of two important Roman writers have survived: Vitruvius (late 1st century BC), who in Book X of *On Architecture* discusses the fortification and layout of towns and the construction of artillery (*see* VITRUVIUS, §2); and Flavius Vegetius Renatus, writing possibly *c.* AD 390, who described methods of attacking and defending a fortress and who influenced both Byzantine and Western medieval theory.

BIBLIOGRAPHY

Aeneas Tacitus: Treatise on fortification (*c.* 355 BC); ed. and Eng. trans., Illinois Greek Club, Loeb Class. Lib. (London and New York, 1923)

Biton: *Kataskeuai polemikon organon kai katapaltikon* [Construction of war engines and artillery] (3rd or 2nd century BC); ed. and Eng. trans. E. W. Marsden, *Technical Treatises* (1971), ii of *Greek Artillery* (Oxford, 1969–71)

Philo of Byzantium: *Belopoiika* [On war-catapults] (late 3rd century BC); ed. and Eng. trans. E. W. Marsden, *Technical Treatises* (1971), ii of *Greek Artillery* (Oxford, 1969–71)

——: *Mechanike syntaxis* [Mechanical system], vii and viii (late 3rd century BC); ed. and Eng. trans. Y. Garlan, *Recherches de poliorcétique grecque* (Athens, 1974); Eng. trans. A. W. Lawrence, *Greek Aims in Fortification* (Oxford, 1979), pp. 69–107

Asklepiodotos: Treatise on fortification (1st century BC); ed. and Eng. trans., Illinois Greek Club, Loeb Class. Lib. (London and New York, 1923)

Athenaeus Mechanicus: *Peri mechanematon* [On war engines] (?1st century BC); ed. C. Wescher, *Poliorcétique des Grecs* (Paris, 1867)

Vitruvius: *De architectura libri decem* (*c.* 17 BC); ed. and Eng. trans. F. Granger, Loeb Class. Lib. (London and New York, 1934)

Onasander: Treatise on fortification (*c.* AD 45); ed. and Eng. trans., Illinois Greek Club, Loeb Class. Lib. (London and New York, 1923)

Heron of Alexandria: *Belopoiika* [On war-catapults] (*c.* AD 62); ed. and trans. E. W. Marsden, *Technical Treatises* (1971), ii of *Greek Artillery* (Oxford, 1969–71)

Apollodoros of Damascus: *Poliorketika* [Engines of war] (1st century AD); ed. C. Wescher, *Poliorcétique des Grecs* (Paris, 1867)

Flavius Vegetius Renatus: *Epitoma rei militaris* (*c.* ?AD 390); Eng. trans. (London, 1767)

(ii) Medieval and Renaissance, c. 1480–c. 1650. One of the first writers to realize the implications of the gunpowder-firing cannon was CHRISTINE DE PIZAN, whose *Livre des faitz d'armes et de chevalerie*, written early in the 15th century for the king of France, described the nature of war. From the end of the 14th century there had been a new interest in the art of war and fortification as such writers as Konrad Keyser described and illustrated the growth of new technology (*c.* 1405; Göttingen, Niedersächs. Staats-& Ubib., Codex phil. 63), depicting elaborate machines with armoured cars, multi-gun chariots, mobile bridges and paddle-boats (*Bellifortis*). Most of the earlier writers were theorists and humanists rather than practising soldiers or engineers, but MARIANO TACCOLA, who showed a drawing of explosive mines in *De machinis* (1449; e.g. Paris, Bib. N., MS. Lat. 7239), was a military engineer from Siena. Many of his drawings depict medieval counterweight artillery developed with new ingenuity. The illustrations in *De re militari* (1460) by Roberto Valturio (1405–75) borrow much from Taccola; Valturio showed little awareness of the importance of the new cannon but developed medieval methods of attack and defence and, using the symbolism of terror, disguised his military machines as dragons and other fierce beasts. LEON BATTISTA ALBERTI was no military man, but his *De re aedificatoria* (1485) contains useful advice on designing and defending fortified cities, emphasizing the need for deep broad ditches and

walls laid out 'so that whoever offers to approach between the towers, is exposed to be taken in flank and slain'. He believed victory would be gained 'more by the art and skill of the architects, than by the conduct and fortunes of the generals'.

The introduction of effective field guns into siege warfare at the end of the 15th century marked the rapidly changing nature of war. Many engineers grappled with the problem of deflecting shot and minimizing the impact of the gunpowder-firing cannon. The treatise of Francesco di Giorgio Martini (*see* FRANCESCO DI GIORGIO MARTINI, §1), written in the 1480s and 1490s, is the first major work on the art of fortification in the modern world: he believed that the strength of a fortress depended on its plan rather than on the thickness and height of its walls. In his drawings he proposed numerous solutions for defending a fortress, suggesting broad ditches with *capanatti* or armoured pill-boxes in them, large drum-towers as gun platforms, and forts designed like stars with a zigzag trace or with embryonic pentagonal bastions. Most of the ideas that were developed by later military architects were indicated in his treatise. Sketches by Leonardo da Vinci (Milan, Bib. Ambrosiana, Cod. Atlanticus; Paris, Bib. Inst. France, MS. A–M) show his involvement in military architecture when, in 1502, Cesare Borgia made him his engineer-general (*see* LEONARDO DA VINCI, §II, 4). Leonardo tried to minimize damage from projectiles by making his exposed surfaces elliptical, having asked himself the question, 'why a ball hitting a wall obliquely does not go through as when it hits at right angles'. His designs for square and circular forts, to be built tier within tier and often protected by outworks in the form of ravelins, were to contain many guns in rooms or casemates with elaborate air-ventilation systems to extract the foul smoke.

Various methods were adopted to try to counter the attacker's new, more powerful guns. One was to lower the defences into broad and deep dry ditches so that less of their walls showed, and to convert their high towers into low, strong gun platforms. Another was to move the defender's guns, as Leonardo had suggested, into casemates, their muzzles firing through embrasures. Both these solutions are illustrated in the *Etliche Vnderricht, zu Befestigung der Stett, Schlosz vnd Flecken* (*c.* 1527) by Albrecht Dürer (*see* DÜRER, (1)), one of the first printed books on the subject (see fig. 23). Printing, in particular the use of the printed woodcut illustration, was to revolutionize the transmission of ideas. In the 16th century far more books on fortification were published than on civil and ecclesiastical architecture, and the printed illustration was to convey a wealth of information that would have taken pages of text to describe.

It was the printed and fully illustrated book that really spread the fashion for the bastion fortress in the mid-16th century. Such authors as Girolamo Maggi (*d* 1572) and Giacomo Castriotto were able to convey with perspective sketches the intricate way in which several levels of guns could be installed in the flank of a bastion. This and other useful information soon found its way to many sympathetic readers all over Europe and in the distant European colonies needing rapidly to rebuild their castles and forts in the most up-to-date manner. *I quattro primi libri di architettura* (1554) by PIETRO CATANEO and the treatise

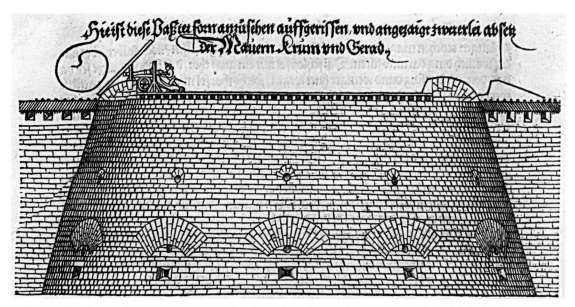

23. *Basteja* with embrasures for cannon in casemates and on the roof; woodcut by Albrecht Dürer from his *Etliche Vnderricht, zu Befestigung der Stett, Schlosz vnd Flecken* (Nuremberg, *c.* 1527) (London, British Library)

of 1615 (see fig. 24) by Vincenzo Scamozzi (*see* SCAMOZZI, (2)) are two of the few to include both civil and military architecture, because, by the mid-16th century, architectural writings were being forced to become more specialized.

After *c.* 1550, books devoted exclusively to military architecture by Italian writers, starting with Giovanni Battista Zanchi, followed each other in rapid succession. They usually began with a study of geometry and continued with a description of the bastion. For example, Giacomo Lanteri (*d c.* 1560) wrote in 1557: 'Defence should be relative to the power of artillery defending it. Thus, the artillery in the flanks should not only cover the curtain from flank to flank, but also the front of the bastions opposite.' In addition to those already mentioned, Francesco Ferretti, Carlo Theti (*d* 1589), Antonio Lupicini (*d* 1598), Girolamo Ruscelli (1538–1604), Girolamo Cataneo and GIOVANNI BATTISTA BELLUZZI all published well-illustrated treatises, mainly in the Republic of Venice, some of which ran into several editions. The *Delle fortificationi* (1570) by GALASSO ALGHISI used metal engravings rather than woodcuts, allowing him to show the setting out of a fort in fine line, with portions that he wanted to emphasize drawn in a bold line. *Delle architettura militare* (1599) by Francesco de Marchi (1504–76) is copiously illustrated with fine metal-engraved plates that show almost every conceivable solution to a fortification problem. More importantly, taking full advantage of the fine lines obtainable on plates, de Marchi drew in the possible lines of fire from all the gun positions; in woodblock the lines would have run together, obliterating the layout of the fort.

Other European writers included DANIEL SPECKLE, in whose book (1589) all aspects of illustration came together: the bird's-eye view showing the complete layout

of a fort, the sunlight and shadows, the precision of metal-plate engraving and—something new—the depiction of a scene from more than one viewpoint. The view from above, which clarifies the disposition of the parts of a fortress, is supplemented by a view at ground-level showing the fortified town as it would appear to an approaching soldier. In one plate Speckle was able to depict the exact lines of fire of the bombarding cannon and the sapping, bombardment and assault upon a broken bastion. In another he showed the positions for defending guns and intricate details of involved mechanical devices.

Many fine engravers produced detached plates depicting most of the fortified towns of Europe, which were often extremely accurate and were sometimes taken directly from the architect's original drawings. ANTOINE LAFRÉRY

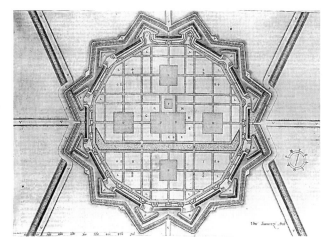

24. Plan of ideal city surrounded by bastions; from Vincenzo Scamozzi: *L'idea dell'architettura universale, ecc.*, i (Venice, 1615) (London, British Library)

did this with the plans (*c.* 1566; Cortona, Laparelli–Pitt. Col.) by Francesco Laparelli (1521–70) for the new city of Valletta, Malta. Probably best known is the large collection of bold engravings, showing fortified towns viewed from the air, that was published by Georgius Braun and Franz Hogenberg (*see* HOGENBERG, (2)), the numerous copper-plate engravings of Matthäus Merian the elder (*see* MERIAN, (1)) and the fine town plans of Nicolas de Fer (1646–1720).

Some of the architectural writers who followed owed much to these prolific engravers, especially Jean Errard de Bar-le-Duc (1554–1610), who depicted fortified towns realistically sited in a rocky landscape, with cliffs and ravines explained by shading and hatching. Both Samuel Marolois (1572–1627) and Pietro Paolo Floriani (1584–1638) show field entrenchments, obstacles and barriers, features that would be difficult to explain in an unillustrated text. On one sheet Floriani was able to show six solutions to the problem of providing a small fort in a landscape, a type used during the English Civil War, and, in a splendid aerial view, he showed all the stages in an attack upon a bastion and the various retrenchments constructed by its defenders. Floriani, a well-known practitioner who built extensive fortifications on Malta, is said to have been the first to employ a double covered way, thus pushing his outer defence of the ditch well forward, and also to have invented the tenaille, which was later accepted by Sébastien Leprestre de Vauban. Thus ideas were transmitted from country to country and from generation to generation.

Many of the books produced in England were translations of Italian or Dutch texts, some plagiarized without giving credit, such as Robert Corneweyle's *The Maner of Fortification* (1559; London, BM, Add. MS. 28,030), which is taken straight from Zanchi. *The Practice of Fortification* (1589) by Paul Ive (*d* 1604) describes the Italian system of bastions.

BIBLIOGRAPHY

Christine de Pisan: *Livre des faitz d'armes et de chevalerie* (MS.; early 15th century); Eng. trans. T. Caxton (London, 1489/*R* 1932)
M. Taccola: *De machinis* (MS; 1449); ed. G. Scaglia, 2 vols (Wiesbaden and New York, 1971)
R. Valturio: *Elenchus et index rerum militarium (De re militari)* (MS.; 1460) (Venice, 1472)
Francesco di Giorgio Martini: *Trattato dell'architettura, ingegneria ed arte militare* (MS.; *c.* 1482–92); ed. C. Maltese (Milan, 1967)
L. B. Alberti: *De re aedificatoria* (Florence, 1485); ed. J. Rykwert as *Alberti's Ten Books on Architecture* (New York, 1966)
A. Dürer: *Etliche Vnderricht, zu Befestigung der Stett, Schlosz vnd Flecken* (Nuremberg, *c.* 1527)
N. Tartaglia: *Sul modo di fortificare le città rispetto la forma* (Venice, 1536); Eng. trans. as *Three Books of Colloquies concerning the Arte of Shooting in Great and Small Pieces of Artillerie . . .* (London, 1588)
——: *Nova scientia* (Venice, 1537)
——: *Quesiti et inventioni diverse de N. Tartaglia Bresciano* (Venice, 1546)
P. Cataneo: *I quattro primi libri di architettura* (Venice, 1554)
G. B. Zanchi: *Del modo di fortificar le città* (Venice, 1554)
G. Lanteri: *Due dialoghi . . . del modo di disegnare le piante delle fortezze, ecc.* (Venice, 1557)
R. Corneweyle: *The Maner of Fortification of Cities, Townes, Castelles and Other Places* (MS.; 1559) (London, 1972)
G. Maggi and G. Castriotto: *Della fortificazione delle città*, iii (Venice, 1564)
F. Ferretti: *Della osservanza militare . . .* (Venice, 1568)
G. Ruscelli: *Precetti della militia moderna, tanto per mare quanto per terra . . .* (Venice, 1568)
C. Theti: *Discorsi sulle fortificationi* (Rome, 1569)
G. Alghisi: *Delle fortificationi*, x (Venice, 1570)
G. Braun and F. Hogenberg: *Civitates orbis terrarum*, 6 vols (Cologne, 1572–1618)

A. Lupicini: *Architettura militare con altri avvertimenti appartenenti alla guerra* (Florence, 1582)
G. Cataneo: *Opera nuova di fortificare, offendere et difendere . . .* (Brescia, 1584)
P. Ive: *The Practice of Fortification, in All Sorts of Situations . . .* (London, 1589/*R* 1972)
D. Speckle: *Architectura von Vestungen* (Strasbourg, 1589)
G. B. Belici [Belluzzi]: *Nuova inventione di fabricare fortezze di varie forme* (Venice, 1598)
F. de Marchi: *Delle architettura militare* (Brescia, 1599)
J. Errard de Bar-le-Duc: *La Fortification réducte en art et démonstrée . . .* (Paris, 1600)
G. Lanteri: *Delle offese et difese delle città et fortezza di G. Lanteri . . . con due discorsi d'architettura militare d'A. Lupicini*, 5 vols (Venice, 1601)
V. Scamozzi: *L'idea dell'architettura universale, ecc.*, 6 vols (Venice, 1615)
S. Marolois: *Fortification ov architecture militaire, tant offensive que deffensive . . .* (Amsterdam, 1628)
P. P. Floriani: *Difesa et offesa delle piazze* (Macerata, 1630)
W. Dilich: *Peribologia* (Frankfurt am Main, 1640)
M. Merian the elder: *Topographia Germaniae*, 16 vols (Frankfurt am Main, 1642–54); ed. L. H. Wüthrich (Kassel and Basle, 1959–65)
N. de Fer: *Les Forces de l'Europe ou description des principales villes avec leur fortifications, etc.*, 2 vols (Paris, 1690–95)

(iii) After c. 1650. By the end of the 17th century the layout of fortresses, with all their elaborate outworks, was becoming so complicated as to make a descriptive book without illustrations a useless undertaking. The introduction of subtle curves, the interlocking of parts and the three-dimensional aspects of the structure had taken on a Baroque character. The drawings of Baron Menno van Coehoorn (see below) show well this development, and the question as to which branch of architecture inspired the other is insoluble. Although the profession had divided, military and civil attitudes were interwoven, and both required a complete mastery of spherical geometry. When the decoration was important and formed part of the military architecture that was being described, then an illustration was indispensable. No words could convey the complexity of ornament and the distribution of the Baroque components in the city gates depicted by Wilhelm Dilich (1571/2–1655) in *Peribologia* (1640). His sliced isometric section through the ramparts of a fortified work is so clear that it became standard practice to depict ramparts in that way.

By the 17th century French writers and practising engineers had been forced to master the bastion system and, with a well-organized central state system and a carefully planned educational policy, they were able largely to wrest the leadership of military engineering from the Italians. Around 1706 SÉBASTIEN LEPRESTRE DE VAUBAN, France's pre-eminent military engineer, wrote *Traité de l'attaque . . . des places* as a secret document not intended for publication. In it he applied systematic thought to the best method of attack, advocating ricochet fire to dismount the defenders' guns on their ramparts, an ordered attack to a strict timetable and the use of regular zigzags running between parallel trenches in an approach to the front he proposed to assault (*see also* §2(iii) and fig. 13 above). His formidable Dutch opponent, Baron MENNO VAN COEHOORN, published three systems of fortifications known as the New Dutch System in 1685. They had complex bastions, their orillions or ears built of hollow counterforts consisting of several membranes to absorb gunfire, in front of which lay broad wet ditches (*see also* §2(iv)(b) and fig. 15 above). His books influenced British engineers, who probably took from them the counterscarp gallery, a device dug into the far side of the ditch in order to defend it with muskets.

Under Vauban's overwhelming influence the French adhered to his bastion trace when other countries had largely abandoned it. Louis de Cormontaigne (1692–1752), one of his disciples, devised an intricate geometrical development of Vauban's bastion trace known as 'The Modern Front', which he used in 1728 at Fort Moselle and Fort Bellscroix at Metz. Henri-Jean-Baptiste de Bousmard (1765–1807) curved the faces of his bastions into eight broken lines, in an attempt to save them from ricochet fire, and pushed out further into the countryside with more and more elaborate outworks to hold an enemy at arm's length. François-Charles-Louis, Marquis de Chasseloup-Laubat (1754–1833), who fortified Alessandria (Piedmont) after 1805 (destr. 1814), proposed several systems that were mainly a combination of those by Bousmard and Marc-René, Marquis de Montalembert (1714–1800). To improve the bastion system he placed ravelins, with their keeps, outside the main ditch and beyond the sloping glacis. He was followed by Gaspard Noizet and Pierre-Marie-Théodore Choumara (1787–1870), who proposed two main principles: to isolate the line of his parapets from the general trace of the bastions and the scarp wall, and to provide an inner glacis to shield that wall. He also proposed many flanks in his bastions, rising tier upon tier. The Swiss general Guillaume Dufour (1787–1875) used what was called the Modern System and protected his guns in the ravelins by building in front a high, shock-absorbing bonnet and, behind, a detached reduit for further cover.

The other important development in military architecture was the revival of the tower or keep as strongpoint and place of last resort. In 1776, Maurice, Count de Saxe, working in the French army, proposed to encircle a fortress with mutually supporting towers spaced 4500 m apart. The detached tower had already been constructed by General D'Arcon in a group of detached lunettes, and the ideas came together in the work on polygonal fortification by Montalembert (1777). His proposals, which included multi-storey towers with many guns in casemates and in powerful caponiers that were almost detached forts in themselves, projecting from a straight line of defence, eventually replaced the bastion system and formed the basis of the New Prussian System (*see also* §2(iv)(d) and fig. 16 above).

Lazare-Nicolas Marguerite, Comte Carnot (1753–1823), proposed to base the defence on the aggressive use of sorties and vertical fire from mortars. He also invented the Carnot Wall, defended by musketry fire and placed to prevent debris from the ramparts falling under bombardment into the ditch—a device influential throughout Europe.

The other strand of military thinking—an elaborate and rapid use of field fortifications to suit tactical situations, as opposed to the provision of permanent concrete underground forts, expensive in both time and money—was represented during the Crimean War by General Count Franz Edouard Ivanovich Todleben (1818–84), whose epic defence of Sevastopol (1854–5) was aided by a ceaseless improvisation using earthwork defences and

redoubts. Todleben corresponded with Henri de Brialmont (1821–1903) and visited England in 1864 to examine and comment upon British proposals for the defence of the dockyards at Portsmouth and Plymouth (see fig. 21 above). These were designed by engineers under the influence of Sir William Jervois (1821–97), who had previously devised detached forts for Malta and Canada. After his appointment in 1859 as secretary to the Royal Commission on defences of the United Kingdom, he was largely responsible for the construction of the forts around the naval dockyards.

The increasing complexity of the vast 20th-century systems of fortification, such as the Maginot Line (*see* §3 above) and the Atlantic Wall, demanded a collaborative effort by military engineers rather than the work of individuals.

BIBLIOGRAPHY

Baron Menno van Coehoorn: *Nieuwe vestingbouw . . . van de Fransche royale seshoek . . .* [New building of fortifications . . . of the French royal hexagon . . .] (Leeuwarden, 1702; Eng. trans., London, 1705)

S. Leprestre de Vauban: *Traité de l'attaque et de la défense des places*, 2 vols (The Hague, 1737–42/*R* Paris, 1828–9)

L. de Cormontaigne: *L'Architecture militaire, ou l'art de fortifier*, 3 vols (The Hague, 1741)

Marc-René, Marquis de Montalembert: *La Fortification perpendiculaire: ou, essai sur plusieurs manières de fortifier*, 11 vols (Paris, 1776–94)

——: *La Fortification polygonale . . .* (Paris, 1777)

H.-J.-B. de Bousmard: *Essai général de fortification, et d'attaque, et défense des places . . .*, 3 vols (Berlin, 1797)

Lazare-Nicolas Marguerite, Comte Carnot: *De la Défence des places fortes . . . Mémoire sur la fortification primitive, etc* (Paris, 1810)

François-Charles-Louis, Marquis de Chasseloup-Laubat: *Essais sur quelques parties de l'artil. et de la fortification* (Milan, 1811)

P.-M.-T. Choumara: *Mémoire sur la fortification* (Paris, 1827, 2/1847)

François-Joseph Noizet: *Principes de fortification* (Paris, 1859)

For further bibliography *see* §2(ii)–(iv) above.

QUENTIN HUGHES

IV. Islamic world.

Internal security within the lands of the caliphate during the early Islamic period meant that there was little need for military architecture. Political fragmentation and increasing insecurity after *c.* AD 900 led to the walling of cities and the construction of fortresses. These fortifications became increasingly sophisticated in later centuries as architects responded to the use of gunpowder artillery.

1. Before *c.* AD 900. 2. *c.* AD 900–1250. 3. After *c.* 1250.

1. BEFORE *c.* AD 900. Early Muslims had little knowledge of or use for fortifications. Like most nomads, their primary means of defence was rapid retreat into the desert, a strategy used during the conquest of Iraq, where such garrison towns (Arab. *amṣār*) as BASRA and KUFA were built without walls but next to the open desert on the south bank of the Euphrates (Kufa was given ramparts and a moat in the 8th century AD). Even after the Muslims had occupied the walled cities of the Byzantine and Sasanian empires (*see* §II, 2 and 5 above) they continued to disregard fortifications, often allowing walls to deteriorate and turning citadels into little villages with shrines for local saints or prophets (e.g. Aleppo).

Two types of early Islamic building show some of the forms and functions of forts or fortified palaces. The desert structures associated with the Umayyad dynasty of Syria (*reg* AD 661–750), such as QASR KHARANA and the square enclosures at QASR AL-HAYR EAST, are a hybrid of the villa rustica and the castrum, two Roman building types common in Syria and Palestine (*see* ISLAMIC ART, §II, 3(iii)). These Umayyad buildings usually had a fortified exterior with a single projecting entrance flanked by two semicircular towers and similar, though smaller, towers arranged at regular intervals along the four walls. The entrances are of the straight-through type; only the gate at the palace at UKHAYDIR (*c.* 775) in Iraq contains a portcullis. The fortified appearance of these buildings has led them to be called fortress (Arab. *qaṣr*), but they copy only the external forms of their Roman prototypes, not their interior articulation and defensive functions, since most of their towers were solid.

The other fortified building type was the frontier *ribāṭ*, which combined the functions of a fortress with those of a monastery; the most celebrated example is the one built at Sousse (Tunisia) in the late 8th century AD. It is a fortified square building with a central courtyard surrounded by a portico and chambers arranged on two storeys. Much of the southern side is occupied on the second storey by a mosque with a peculiar domed tower. In form the *ribāṭ* bears some resemblance to the Umayyad desert palaces, but it is better designed, possibly because it was meant to fulfil specific defensive and devotional needs (*see* ISLAMIC ART, §II, 4(iii)). Similar but simpler and smaller (*c.* 25 m to a side) structures of mud-brick remain at Darzin, a town between Kirman and Bam in south-east Iran; these fortresses have been dated to the 8th and 9th centuries on the basis of structural analogies to the *ribāṭ* at Sousse and other buildings of the early Islamic period.

The first fortified city in Islam was the Round City built by the Abbasid caliph al-Mansur (*reg* AD 754–75) at BAGHDAD (*see* ISLAMIC ART, fig. 20). Begun in 762, the city continued the tradition of the circular cities of Sasanian Iran and Mesopotamia but added some new defensive features. The circumference, which measured some 8 km, was surrounded from the exterior to the interior by a moat (Arab. *khandaq*), an outer wall, an intervallum (*faṣīl*) and a doubled inner wall with another intervallum. The mud-brick walls were pierced by four gates midway between the cardinal points and fortified by towers at regular intervals. The exterior gates had bent entrances (*bāshūra*), a remarkable feature that had also existed in ancient Egypt. Despite the obvious military advantage of forcing the intruder to make repeated turns, thereby exposing his weaker side, neither the circular plan nor the bent entrance had any immediate impact on later Islamic fortification. Few other cities in the Islamic lands were fortified in this period except in Spain, where fortifications closely followed Byzantine models. The Alcazaba (*al-qaṣaba*: 'fortress') of Mérida (835), for example, measures about 130 m to a side. The walls (2.7 m thick) have towers at the corners and along the sides. The original gate on the north led into a forecourt and then into a small rectangular enclosure.

2. *c.* AD 900–*c.* 1250. In this period political fragmentation and insecurity, as well as the crusader threat, led to the development of fortification in several regions of the Islamic lands.

(i) Central Islamic lands. Several fortified cities were built by the FATIMID dynasty (*reg* AD 909–1171) in North Africa and Egypt. MAHDIA, their first capital in Tunisia, was on a rocky peninsula, protected by a wall and a massive gate, both of which were often rebuilt. Cairo, the Fatimid capital in Egypt, was founded in 969 to the north of the unwalled city of Fustat as a rectangular enclosure with seven gates of baked brick in a mud-brick wall (*see* CAIRO, §I, 1). The walls were expanded and rebuilt between 1087 and 1092 by the vizier Badr al-Jamali; 316 m of the northern curtain wall, including the Bab al-Nasr ('Gate of victory'; *see* CAIRO, fig. 3) and the Bab al-Futuh ('Gate of conquest'), and a section to the east of the Bab Zuwayla remain intact. These works are among the greatest achievements of medieval fortification and testify to the survival of a vigorous school of stone architecture in northern Syria, whence the architects of these fortifications came. The three gates are of the straight-through type with flanking towers, square in the Bab al-Futuh and semicircular in the Bab al-Nasr and Bab Zuwayla, and contain neither portcullis nor machicolation, making them closer to Roman gates than to the more advanced gates of the post-crusader period. The three Cairene gates are quite similar in size and proportions: approximately 23–25.7 m wide (from tower to tower) and about 21–23.7 m high (from the original ground-level). The curtain wall between the northern gates is protected by several towers and the Great Salient, which wraps around the northern minaret of the mosque of al-Hakim. The curtain wall and the gates are connected and defended by a long vaulted passage pierced by numerous loopholes, allowing the defenders to move from tower to tower under cover. A *chemin-de-ronde* with crenellated parapets on the upper level provided a secondary zone of defence.

During the 12th century the Crusades and interdynastic wars among Muslim princes strengthened the earlier trend of rulers establishing themselves in urban citadels and outposts. Citadels and fortresses were rebuilt and enlarged, utilizing the latest innovations in military architecture, and whole cities were enclosed within solid masonry walls pierced by fortified gates. The fortifications built by the Ayyubid dynasty (*reg* 1169–1260) at ALEPPO and Damascus are among the most impressive and best preserved. The bent entrance was perfected and applied to all defensive gates in city walls and citadels. The medieval bent-axis gate (e.g. Bab Antakiya at Aleppo) differs from earlier rudimentary examples in having two towers instead of one, of which the right one is usually pierced by a door that leads into a hall with another door at right angles to the first. This bent axis impeded the progress of attackers and exposed them to the missiles of the defenders. The innovation was considered so effective that it was even added to Roman gates with triple openings (e.g. Bab Sharqi at Damascus), by closing two of the gates and adding a bent-axis tunnel to one of the smaller ones. The combination of the bent entrance with machicolation, another innovation of the period, added immeasurably to the strength of the fortifications.

Citadels in this period served as both military barracks and administrative and royal centres, and hence they were carefully furbished and defended. The citadels of Aleppo and Damascus occupy vastly different terrains and thus represent two essentially different types of fortress. The Aleppo citadel (see fig. 25), a truncated conical tell, soars some 40 m above street-level and some 60 m above the deep moat encircling it. Its glacis was once paved with smooth limestone ashlars that, combined with the 48-degree incline, made it extremely difficult to scale. The lower courses of the glacis are reinforced by cut column shafts, a technique that became standard in later military architecture. The walls of the citadel rise above the glacis to a height of 12–13 m and are reinforced at regular intervals by rectangular towers of different periods. These towers are not especially large or powerful, but did not have to be, since the citadel enjoyed excellent natural defences. In contrast, the citadel of DAMASCUS sits on level ground but makes up for its lack of natural defence by tall crenellated curtains and 12 massive towers. Its masonry is rusticated in typical Ayyubid fashion, with smooth edges and a rough central projection intended to resist the impact of stones hurled by mangonels. A moat originally surrounded the citadel and was regularly filled from the nearby Barada River.

Towers in this period attained gigantic proportions, for they were intended both for defence and for the permanent housing of a large number of troops in spacious chambers with easy and safe access to other towers and the ramparts of the enceinte. The north-east tower of the Damascus citadel (24×20×25 m) consists of three vaulted floors topped by a double-height balcony, with a *chemin-de-ronde* and a crenellated parapet. More than 50 embrasures and arrow slits could have been increased in times of siege by the construction of temporary wooden roughwallings. Still, this tower should not be considered a donjon in the Western medieval sense of the word because of its insufficient isolation from the other defences of the citadel and its inappropriateness as a residence for the sultan. Similar stonework and towers may been seen in the Cairo citadel, also an Ayyubid foundation. Its western and northern parts, which are naturally defended by the Muqattam spur on which they stand, have insignificant towers, but its level southern and eastern sides are protected by truly massive towers. These are slightly battered and built of large rusticated stones. Some, like Burj al-Turfa, a square 30 m per side rising to a height of almost 20 m, are almost independent fortresses, with large vaulted rooms on two or three levels, numerous machicolations and a top part with two tiers of defence.

The numerous fortresses erected or rebuilt in this period do not differ much from urban citadels, except perhaps in terms of their strategic siting. The fortress of Shayzar (11th century) in central Syria straddles a long, narrow and steep promontory; its eastern front descends sharply into the Asi (Orontes) River and its western front faces the Ghab Valley. Naturally defended on its long sides, the fortress was made virtually impregnable by two enormous towers; the northern served as an entrance block and the southern may be termed a donjon. It is distinguished from the other towers in the citadel by its greater size and height and by having embrasures on all its fronts. Furthermore, its only entrance, located some 5 m above ground-level, has no stairs leading up to it; instead, a removable wooden ladder would have provided access. This tower would have been the last resort for the defenders of the fortress.

25. Citadel, Aleppo, Syria, ramp and entrance block, 13th–16th century

The walls of Diyarbakır on the upper Tigris River have a roughly elliptical trace (1700×1300 m) and are built of masonry rubble between basalt ashlar facings (h. 8–12 m; w. 3–5 m). They have square, round and polygonal towers and gates at the four cardinal points. The walls, supposedly the longest medieval city wall in existence (5.5 km), are decorated with inscription plaques recording repeated repairs from the 10th to the 19th century and figural representations, such as eagles, emblems of the Artuqid dynasty (*reg* 1098–1232). As in Egypt, city gates became increasingly elaborate. For example, the Baghdad Gate at RAQQA in northern Syria, long attributed to the 8th century but probably of the 12th, has elaborate decoration in brick. The Talisman Gate (1221; destr. 1917), the only element of the fortifications of Baghdad to have survived until modern times, was surmounted by a depiction of a seated monarch, presumably the Abbasid caliph al-Nasir (*reg* 1180–1225), holding two dragons by their tongues (*see* ISLAMIC ART, fig. 78). In Anatolia the Saljuq dynasty of Rum (*reg* 1077–1307) drew upon the traditions of Byzantine fortification, as in the walls of such towns as Alanya, Antalya, Kayseri, Bayburt and Ankara, which date to the first half of the 13th century.

(ii) Western Islamic lands. The cities and fortresses of north-west Africa and Spain underwent major development between the late 11th century and the 13th, attributable in part to the successes of the Almoravid (*reg* 1056–1147) and Almohad (*reg* 1130–1269) dynasties. Rubble and ashlar masonry was gradually introduced into the predominantly mud-brick and rammed-earth walls, and such new forms as round towers and barbicans were brought in from Christian Spain. Typical Almohad enceintes, such as those at FEZ, RABAT and MARRAKESH, consisted of curtains and irregular rectilinear towers, surmounted by a *chemin-de-ronde*, with pyramidal crenellated parapets. Both curtains and towers were made of rammed earth, to which brick was often added; cut stone was reserved for the gates to cities and fortresses (Arab. *qaṣaba*). These gates are the most impressive part of the enceinte, often covering mediocre military effectiveness with grandiose designs and splendid decoration. Most

26. Udayas Gate, Rabat, Morocco, after 1191

gates have bent entrances but differ from those in the central Islamic lands by having one tower instead of two and a central instead of a side entry, changes that enhanced visual impact at the expense of military strength. Perhaps the finest of the Almohad gates is the Udayas Gate in Rabat (see fig. 26), built after 1191 as a royal entrance to the palace. Resting above a flight of steps and flanked by projecting salients, the richly carved horseshoe arch in ochre masonry displays a studied balance between elegance and power, the like of which is unknown in the Middle East. The gate leads to a succession of three vaulted chambers, the last two of which contain doors in their side walls leading to the fortress.

(iii) Eastern Islamic lands. The typical city in Iran and western Central Asia (see §VI, 1 below) continued the pre-Islamic tradition of a walled settlement (Pers. *shahristān*) with a separate citadel (*arg*, *kuhandiz*) and suburbs (*bīrūn*). The mud-brick walls often had a round or square trace with gates in the centre of each side and projecting towers. Indications of these early enclosures have been found at Bukhara and Merv. The new walls, built in the 11th century to protect the cities from depredations by nomads, often enclosed the suburbs and had gates with iron fittings. The Khatir Gate at Yazd (1040–41), for example, was decorated with inscriptions naming the patrons, Signs of the Zodiac and an image of an elephant carrying a howdah. The walls at Isfahan, built by the local ruler 'Ala al-Dawla Muhammad in 1037, are said to have measured more than 15,000 paces in circumference, not including extensions around several suburbs, and had 12 gates. The population was heavily taxed to finance the new fortifications. The fortress at Baku on the Caspian Sea was extensively rebuilt

by the sharvanshar Manuchihr II (*reg* 1120–49), and the enormous multi-storey bastion known as the Maiden's Tower probably dates from this period.

BIBLIOGRAPHY

Enc. Islam/2: 'Bāb' [Gate]; 'Burdj' [Tower]
H. Basset and H. Terrasse: 'Sanctuaires et forteresses almohades', *Hespéris*, iv (1924), pp. 9–91, 181–203; v (1925), pp. 311–76; vi (1926), pp. 102–270; vii (1927), pp. 117–71, 287–345; also as *Sanctuaires et forteresses almohades* (Paris, 1932)
J. Sauvaget: 'La Citadelle de Damas', *Syria*, xi (1930), pp. 59–90, 216–41
D. J. King: 'The Defences of the Citadel of Damascus', *Archaeologia*, xciv (1951), pp. 57–96
K. A. C. Creswell: 'Fortifications in Islam before AD 1250', *Proc. Brit. Acad.* (1952), pp. 89–125
——: *The Muslim Architecture of Egypt*, 2 vols (Oxford, 1952–9)
G. Marçais: *L'Architecture musulmane d'occident* (Paris, 1954)
E. Herzfeld: *Matériaux pour un corpus inscriptionum Arabicarum*, ii: *Syrie du Nord: Inscriptions et monuments d'Alep*, 2 vols (Cairo, 1954–6)
J. Warren: 'The Date of the Baghdād Gate at Raqqa', *A. & Archaeol. Res. Pap.*, xiii (1978), pp. 22–3
A. Rihawi: *Qal'at Dimashq* [The citadel of Damascus] (Damascus, 1979)
M. Shokoohy: 'Monuments of the Early Caliphate at Dārzīn in the Kirmān Region (Iran)', *J. Royal Asiat. Soc. GB & Ireland* (1980), pp. 3–20
K. A. C. Creswell: *A Short Account of Early Muslim Architecture*, 2nd edn rev. and enlarged by J. W. Allan (Aldershot, 1989)
S. S. Blair: *The Monumental Inscriptions from Early Islamic Iran and Transoxiana* (Leiden, 1992), pp. 111–17

YASSER TABBAA

3. AFTER *c*. 1250. Revolutionary changes in the techniques of siege warfare after the mid-14th century, in particular the development of gunpowder artillery and the explosive mine, were paralleled by changes in the design of fortification. Developments in both siege technology and fortification show marked regional differences dictated by varying rates of technological change and local political and social factors.

(i) Western Islamic lands. (ii) Anatolia and the Balkans. (iii) Central Islamic lands. (iv) Eastern Islamic lands.

(i) Western Islamic lands. The Marinids (*reg* 1196–1465) initiated an extensive programme of fortification after the mid-13th century at such sites as Fez, Salé and Chella (near Rabat) in Morocco and Mansura (near Tlemcen) in Algeria (see ISLAMIC ART, §II, 6(iv)(b)). The ramparts of their capital at New Fez (Fās al-jadīd; 1276) typify defensive works of the period. The two curtains are separated by an intervallum of a dozen metres, a formula already used by Andalusian builders at Córdoba and Seville in the Almohad period. The walls (7×1.2–2 m) are marked by rectangular towers and emphasize elevation rather than width. Gates such as the Bab Agdal on the western face have a simple portal flanked by two angled towers in the outer wall and a more substantial inner gate with a double bent passage leading into the enceinte.

Late Islamic defensive works on the Iberian peninsula survive at Granada, Málaga, Gibraltar and Antequera. Although the walls and gates of Granada have largely disappeared, those of the Alhambra, the palace citadel of the Nasrid kings, are substantially intact (see GRANADA, §III, 1 and fig. 3). Built of durable masonry, they follow the edge of the plateau overlooking the town and have square and rectangular towers. On the north above the valley of the Darro where attack was improbable, the tower interiors are arranged into sumptuous apartments. On the south, four gates occupying salients give access to the interior. The principal gateway, known as the Justicia

Gate (1348), has a triple bend and opens on to the lateral face of a tower. The western end contains the fortress (Alcazaba; Arab. *al-qaṣaba*) with a double enceinte and projecting towers, among which the great Vela Tower functioned as a donjon. Hispano-Moresque architecture followed the traditions of Christian fortification in constructing great rectangular donjons, but instead of occupying a central position, as in French castles, these form part of the defences of the enceinte, generally within an angle. In addition to the Vela Tower at the Alhambra, examples include the towers called 'del Homenaje' at Málaga and Antequera. The most powerful donjon of Andalusia is the Calahorra (1342–4; 20×17.5 m) at Gibraltar, which forms a salient at the north-east angle of the fortress and the old Muslim town. The interior has a massive base surmounted by chambers covered with a variety of domes and vaults.

Fortifications of the traditional type continued to be built in the Maghrib during the 14th and 15th centuries, but military works adapted to the use of artillery and capable of resisting bombardment also appeared. The Bastiun of Taza in eastern Morocco, built by the Saʿdian sultan Ahmad al-Mansur (*reg* 1578–1603) as a defence against attack by the Turks of Algiers, is traditional in form. A massive block (26×26×20 m) of brick and stone masonry astride the town's south-east gate, it is flanked by two towers. The impact of new military technologies is apparent in the gunports opening in three of its sides. Similarly traditional in form are the two forts built by al-Mansur in 1582 overlooking Old Fez (Fās al-bālī), the Northern and Southern towers (Arab. *burj*). Nonetheless, they too are provided with gunports, and contemporary texts refer to them as *bastiūn* (from It. *bastion*). The rather traditional enceinte and triple-walled citadel of MEKNÈS was erected by Ismaʿil (*reg* 1672–1727), who also built isolated kasbas, fortified posts used to secure his hold over the restless Berber tribes of the Middle Atlas and protect the principal roads of the empire. Typically found in open country, they have regular perimeters, masonry walls marked by square or rectangular salients and gateways of the straight or bent-axis type. Examples include Adekhsan on the northern slopes of the Atlas, Agouti in the Middle Atlas, and Tadla and Hamidouch on the western plains.

Ismaʿil and his successor Muhammad III (*reg* 1757–90) also carried on an active programme of coastal fortification to repel attack by the Christians. Ismaʿil, for example, renovated the Spanish walls of Mehdia, a fortress at the mouth of the Sebou River, and Muhammad III was responsible for the defences of Casablanca, Rabat, Larache and Tangier. The most celebrated is the Kasba of the Udaya (Oudaia), commanding the mouth of the Bou Regreg River at Rabat. Said to have been constructed by a Christian renegade, the fortress resembles the works of the Spaniards at Oran and those of the Portuguese at Safi and Mazagan.

The Algerian littoral came under Ottoman control in the middle of the 16th century. At Algiers the Turks enclosed the town with walls of the traditional type, preceded by a ditch and having nine gates. Flanked by bastions, the Turkish gateways were, with the exception of that linking the city with the interior of the kasba, of simple straight-axis plan, in contrast to the bent entrances

common in Morocco. The battered walls of the city and fortress (h. 12 m; w. 1.6–2.5 m) are occasionally marked by rectangular salients. A wall-walk extends along the top of the wall, the parapet of which was protected with crenellations and embrasures for cannon- and rifle-fire. In contrast to the enceinte, the forts that protect the approaches to Algiers hardly recall medieval Muslim tradition. Three principal forts, dating to the second half of the 16th century—Fort de l'Etoile, Fort d'Eluj Ali and the Fort l'Empereur—were the work of Sicilian renegades and are laid out along European lines.

Turkish Tunisia was intimately connected with Europe, and European military architecture had a strong impact. As in Morocco, those fortresses designed to resist Christian assault are distinct from those that countered the attacks of the indigenous tribes. The ramparts of Kairouan, rebuilt in the early 18th century, are an example of the latter type, and their brick walls and gates have a strikingly medieval aspect. Protected by semicircular salients, the wall-walks also have a parapet of rounded merlons, a silhouette already known in the 9th century. Although older in date, the Burj al-Kabir at Mahdia (1595) is nonetheless more up-to-date in character: the battered stone ramparts of the fortress are provided with artillery embrasures. Likewise, the enceintes of such coastal towns as Hammamet and Tunis, rebuilt in the 18th and 19th centuries, closely follow European military architecture.

(ii) Anatolia and the Balkans. Military architecture in Anatolia from the mid-13th century to the 14th drew on local traditions of fortification under Byzantine and Saljuq rule. High, thin and crenellated walls were protected by moats and forewalls, articulated by irregularly spaced quadrangular or circular towers and entered through bent entrances, as for example at the fortresses of Kütahya and Karaman (both rest. 14th century) and the citadel of Bursa (destr.), reconstructed by the Ottomans after they took the city in 1326.

The adoption of artillery and fire-arms by the Ottomans in the first years of the 15th century initially had little impact on the character of Turkish military architecture. The great Ottoman military works on the Bosporus made no special provision for defence against fire-arms, although guns were mounted in both Anadolu Hisar ('Anatolian fortress') and Rumeli Hisar ('European fortress'). Anadolu Hisar, the earlier of these works, was begun in 1395 by Bayezid I (*reg* 1389–1402) on the eastern shore of the Bosporus *c.* 7 km north of the Golden Horn, at a point where the waterway is at its narrowest. The fortress was enlarged and strengthened in 1452 by Mehmed II (*reg* 1444–81 with interruption) to cut communication between Constantinople (now Istanbul) and the Black Sea. A small fortress, it consisted of a roughly square keep with square and circular turrets spaced irregularly along the curtain. The walls of rubble masonry (h. 8; w. 2.3 m) have wall-walks and crenellated parapets. Mehmed added an irregular outer ward of similar construction, originally bordering the shore, with three great circular turrets along the north. Thirteen gunports in its west (sea) face facilitated the interdiction of shipping through the Bosporus.

Rumeli Hisar (see fig. 27), built by Mehmed in 1452 on the site of earlier Byzantine works opposite Anadolu Hisar,

27. Rumeli Hisar, Istanbul, 1452

was similar in concept but considerably larger in scale. Also known as Boğazkesen ('Cutter of the Bosporus'), it stretches some 250 m north–south and 125 m east–west on steep slopes extending down to the water. Laid out in the form of an irregular triangle, it is dominated by three great towers at the north-west and south-west angles and at the mid-point of the eastern wall along the shore. The rubble walls (h. 10–13 m; w. 3–5 m) are more powerful than those at Anadolu Hisar and are crowned by crenellated parapets and wall-walks. Round and polygonal towers are spaced irregularly along all sides of the curtain, which is penetrated by three gateways (north, east and west) defended by machicolation and heavy, double-leaved doors. A barbican provided with gunports precedes the main gateway on the water's edge, and guns were also set up in the adjacent eastern tower.

After the conquest of Constantinople in 1453, Mehmed repaired the Theodosian land-walls of Istanbul and erected (*c.* 1458) a powerful citadel in the vicinity of the Golden Gate. The walls (h. 16 m; w. 6 m) of Yediküle ('Castle of seven towers') retain their medieval form and are ill-adapted to withstand artillery siege. Despite the Turkish use of artillery in the conquest, no provision for defence by fire-arms was incorporated into the planning of the fortress, which is of medieval character throughout, with walls and towers of great height and loopholes and battlements suitable for defence by medieval weapons only. Nonetheless, Yediküle is a powerful fortress, and, with its star-shaped plan, round towers (h. 30 m) projecting well out from the points to command not only the outer faces of the adjacent curtain but also those opposite, and redans at the re-entry angles, Mehmed's fort shows a remarkable advance in the provision made for enfilading fire along curtain walls. In this respect, Yediküle can be seen as a prototype of the fort developed in Italy in the early 16th century (*see* §III, 2(ii) above).

Mehmed also renovated the fortress of Anadolu Kavak (the castle of Hieron) on the Asian side of the Bosporus *c.* 24 km north of Istanbul, and had a pair of fortresses built flanking the Dardanelles (now Çanakkale Boğazı) at the narrowest point of their southern reaches. These fortresses, Kale-i Sultaniyye ('Sultan's castle'; later Kale-i Çanak or Çanakkale; 1459 or 1464) on the Asian shore and Kilid al-Bahr ('Lock to the sea') on the European, were similar to the Istanbul fortresses, although they were substantially reworked in later times (1511, 1658–60, late 18th century–early 19th). In addition, new forts built *c.* 1660 at the Aegean mouth of the Dardanelles—Sedd al-Bahr on the European and Kumkale on the Asiatic shores—also underwent extensive renovation in the 18th and 19th centuries to accommodate modern artillery. Kale-i Sultaniyye is a typical example: roughly rectangular in plan with rubble walls (h. 9 m; w. 5 m) topped by wall-walks and crenellated parapets, it has great circular or polygonal towers at the four corners and additional towers in the east (land) and south walls to enhance the effectiveness of enfilading fire. A great semicircular tower with double-bent axis on the north curtain provides access to the bailey, where a massive rectangular keep (Turk. *ahmedek*; 30×44×20 m) stands at the eastern end. The three-storey interior has numerous firing chambers with gun embrasures piercing the walls. According to contemporary historians, the fortress was armed by Mehmed with 'stone-shooting cannon and crossbows'. In the course of later rebuildings, however, ample provision was made for an extensive artillery complement, which was effective in sinking the British battleship *Queen Elizabeth* during the Battle of Gallipoli in 1915.

Powerful and heavily armed Ottoman fortresses were also built or renovated on the Austrian and Persian frontiers, on the coasts of the Greek mainland and islands and along the northern shore of the Black Sea. Fortresses facing the Habsburgs and Venetians had to accommodate the technological advances of European armies. In the Peloponnese, several Ottoman fortresses built in the 16th and 17th centuries to repel Venetian attack (e.g. New Navarino, Negroponte) show how the Ottomans responded to the European military revolution. New Navarino (1573), built to protect the western shore of the Peloponnese, consists of a large irregular enclosure on sloping ground descending to the water's edge, where two large square bastions with vaulted gun casements cover the entrance to Navarino Bay. On the high ground to the south, a hexagonal citadel with six angle-bastions dominates the surrounding terrain. With an elaborate trace describing a snowflake pattern, the citadel has broad gun platforms and numerous, well-built artillery embrasures. It is clearly designed in conformity with contemporary Italian planning notions, although its walls are too thin to withstand concentrated artillery fire. In contrast, the fortresses on the Persian frontier, where artillery was less extensively employed, are far more traditional. The fortress of Ahlat (1568) on Lake Van, for example, consists of a roughly rectangular enceinte sloping down to the shore of the lake. High, thin stone walls with hollow round towers are poorly adapted to artillery siege. The square citadel located midway along the southern curtain is entered through a powerful bent entrance (late 17th century) flanked by a pair of round towers.

The Ottomans also built or renovated many isolated fortresses in Anatolia and the Balkans to subjugate and pacify local peoples and enforce the payment of tribute.

Because the native populations were ill-armed, such isolated fortresses did not need to withstand prolonged siege or artillery attack. The fortress of Kelepha (*c.* 1650) in the Peloponnese, for example, is a large rectangular enclosure with simple, straight entrances in the east and west curtains and large, projecting angle bastions reinforcing the four corners. Although its trace recalls European fortification of a somewhat earlier date (such as the 16th-century Venetian citadel of La Canea (Chania) on Crete, which was conquered by the Turks in 1645), its masonry walls topped by narrow wall-walks and crenellated small-arms parapets have none of the massive terrepleining found in contemporary European fortification, nor is the fortress preceded by ditch, outworks or glacis. Kelepha's primary function was to enforce the pacification of the unruly Greek tribes and enforce the payment of tribute on the border of interior Mani. A similar conservatism can be seen in the Kurdish fortress of Hoşap Kale (1649), south of Lake Van on the road to Hakkari. Built on a high crag, it is enclosed by a high, thin wall with irregularly spaced round towers along the wall. A powerful round tower in the eastern curtain with bent passage serves as a gateway.

In the 18th and 19th centuries Ottoman fortifications came increasingly into line with European practice and were frequently designed by European military advisers such as the French Baron de Tott who repaired the Dardanelles forts at the end of the 18th century, the British colonel Fenwick Williams who modernized the fortresses of Kars, Erzurum and Trebizond during the Crimean War (1853–6), and the German military mission which assisted in the redesign of the Bosporus and Dardanelles forts in the 1880s and the construction of fortifications around Erzurum in the years before 1914.

(iii) Central Islamic lands. The victory of the Mamluks (*reg* 1250–1517) over the Ayyubids and the last of the crusader states brought an end to the system of Arab and Frankish feudalism in the Levant and replaced it with centralized military and political administration. Most of the isolated fortress strongholds of the feudal regimes lost their importance and were systematically destroyed by Baybars (*reg* 1260–77) and Qala'un (*reg* 1280–90), although some of the great interior fortresses such as Hisn al-Akrad (*see* KRAK DES CHEVALIERS), al-Marqab (Margat) and Harim retained significance as military garrisons and as administrative centres and were repaired and modified. The Mamluks also renovated the defences of key Syrian and Egyptian cities. Attempts were likewise made to defend coastal towns against the depredations of the Christian fleets operating out of Cyprus and elsewhere. Byblos was refortified, Tyre was moved some 3 km inland and the old port fortified with a series of powerful towers, and ALEXANDRIA was protected by fortifications, including those erected by Qa'itbay (*reg* 1468–96) at the harbour mouth. With the growth of the Ottoman threat, Qa'itbay and his successors reinforced the defences of the northern frontier in Syria.

Military architecture of the early Mamluk period continued the splendid tradition of late Ayyubid fortification. This work is seen to advantage in the guard-towers on the shore at Al-Mina, the port of Tripoli in Lebanon. The two-storey Burj al-Siba' ('Lion's tower'), the best-preserved of the original seven, is built of powerful rusticated ashlars with column shafts used as headers, the façades and portal on the west being enriched by delicate relief ornament and polychrome stonework. The powerful walls (20.5×28.5 m) are pierced by numerous firing ports and arrow slits. Consoles suggest the existence of brattices over the portals and some of the other openings. Of imposing appearance, fine proportions and a pleasing sense of ornament, the Burj al-Siba' was probably built under Barquq (*reg* 1382–99) and given its final form by Qa'itbay *c.* 1477.

Mamluk fortification can be seen on a grander scale at ALEPPO. Its enceinte was restored after being dismantled by the Mongols. Built of great blocks of carefully dressed stone with column shafts used as headers, the walls are again pierced by archery openings and defended by loopholed brattices on stone consoles. Topped by a crenellated parapet and wall-walk, the high curtains have square salients and several gates. Some of the Mamluk gates are flanked by pairs of towers, and the passage is perpendicular to the face of the curtain; others, such as the 15th-century Bab Qinnasrin, open in the side of a tower parallel to the curtain and make an angle into the city. The Ayyubid citadel (Arab. *qal'a*) was likewise restored after the Mongol devastations. With the shifting of the eastern trace to the Khandaq al-Rum after 1428, the citadel became an isolated strong point within the city, the seat of the governor and garrison. In the 15th century two advanced towers were constructed on the talus of the citadel to protect exposed points, and these towers were rebuilt under the last Mamluks, along with the barbican before the entrance, to accommodate guns. The southeast tower, the largest and most attractive of the advanced towers, was built of finely drafted stone in 1505 by Qansuh al-Ghawri (*reg* 1501–16) on a large, sloping foundation. Square in plan, it has rounded corners and corner brattices to lessen the effect of artillery fire. Two round openings (possibly of Ottoman date) below the inscription on the main façade are gunports.

The Mamluks also renovated the citadel of CAIRO, especially in the late 15th century and early 16th. Seen to best advantage along the eastern end of the north curtain and in the region of the Burj al-Sahra, these Mamluk restorations are characterized by great thickness (4.95 m) and must have been built in response to the threat of artillery siege; they can be attributed to Janbalat (*reg* 1500–01) or Tuman Bay I (*reg* 1501), whose reigns coincided with the growth of the Ottoman menace. That such precautions were insufficient is clear from the Ottoman victories over the Mamluks at Marj Dabik and before the walls of Cairo in 1516–17.

Military architecture in Syria and Egypt after the Ottoman conquest continues many features of the Mamluk tradition. Thus when Süleyman II (*reg* 1520–66) rebuilt the Mamluk walls, gates and citadel of JERUSALEM between 1537 and 1541, he did little to accommodate the possibility of an artillery siege. The thin high curtain crowned with wall-walk and crenellated parapet has rectangular towers, generally open at the back and pierced by arrow slits (later transformed into cannon ports) in front, and is preceded on the north and west by a moat. The gates are bent in

28. Damascus Gate, Jerusalem, 16th century

axis, the Damascus Gate being flanked by towers and having a small brattice on consoles above the portal (see fig. 28). The citadel located astride the western wall is defended on the east by a moat crossed by a drawbridge giving access to a barbican. Beyond, one enters the main gate of the fortress, a double-bent entrance debouching on a rectangular upper terrace enclosed by curtains with wall-walks and crenellated parapets. Four great square towers (one, the Tower of David, perhaps of Roman date), crowned by crenellations and defended by brattices/machicolation on brackets and arrow slits, reinforce the curtain. A lower terrace on the west has an enormous stone glacis in front.

Contemporary Ottoman military works in the citadel of Cairo are far more innovative. The well-preserved Burj Muqattam on the south-west, for example, is a powerful round tower with stone walls 7 m thick. Built of smooth blocks in contrast to the rusticated Mamluk masonry, it has interior vaults constructed of brick, a material used nowhere else in the citadel. The entrance from the wall-walk leads to the third of its four floors; stairways through the thickness of the walls provide passage from floor to floor. Artillery chambers with rectangular gunports surmounted by secondary openings providing ventilation and light are built within the massive walls of the three upper storeys. Although the lower half is slightly battered, the upper part rises vertically to a brattice projecting boldly beyond its upper edge.

Iraq was the scene of a prolonged struggle between the Sunni Ottomans and the Shi'ite Safavids of Iran, and powerful fortresses were maintained at BAGHDAD, Mosul, Basra and elsewhere. Baghdad repeatedly changed hands in the course of the 16th and 17th centuries, and its walls were subjected to destructive sieges and rebuilt several times (1638, 1642, 1657, 1682, 1780) before being torn down in the 1880s. Constructed of brick, the roughly rectangular enceinte was built on the foundations of earlier walls and had 45 towers on the river side and 118 towers along the land walls, which were preceded by a ditch. The towers, 60 cubits high and 10–12 cubits thick, were pierced

by gunports with brass cannon planted on the larger towers. The citadel lay astride the north curtain. Three gates opened on the land sides, and a fourth gate on the west opened to the bridge of boats across the River Tigris. The defences of Baghdad, despite their medieval character and appearance, were nonetheless sufficient to resist the two sieges by the Afsharid ruler Nadir Shah (*reg* 1736–47) in 1737 and 1743. Sections of the north-east curtain and the Bab al-Wastani, a 13th-century gate, still stand.

In the Arabian peninsula, considerable military construction was carried out in the late 18th century and the 19th as a result of the rise to power of the Saudi dynasty (*reg* 1746–). The fortifications and city walls of such towns as Medina, Yanbu', Riyadh, Ha'il and Al-Hufuf date from this period. Intended as defence against mounted warriors, the fortresses, though late in date, have a form and appearance appropriate to a period preceding artillery sieges. With high, relatively thin curtains of mud-brick (or occasionally stone or coral as at Medina or Jiddah), they have corner bastions and towers at irregular intervals and were sometimes, as at Riyadh, preceded by a ditch. Walls and towers often have brattices and are crowned by wall-walks, crenellated parapets and loopholes. Typical examples include the Qasr Masmak, the old citadel of Riyadh, the walls of Sudus and the Qasr 'Abid and Qasr Ibrahim at Al-Hufuf. In the Yemen and Oman, castle strongholds and fortified residences for the imams are found at San'a, Nizwa, Bahla, Sohar and elsewhere.

(iv) Eastern Islamic lands. Military architecture in Iran and western Central Asia remained highly conservative even into the 19th century. Although fire-arms were introduced by the Aqqoyunlu in the 15th century, they were always used by Iranian military formations on a modest scale. Massive artillery fortifications were rarely necessary to counter lightly armed siege forces or tribal skirmishers. Numerous fortified strongholds and walled residences of local *khān*s and chiefs were built throughout the Iranian countryside and along commercial routes, and frontier fortresses were erected in the eastern and western borderlands, but the character of later Iranian fortification is best attested by city walls. Although many of these have been demolished since the late 19th century to make way for urban expansion, enough remains to suggest their essential character.

Although few fortifications remain intact and unmodified from the period of Timurid (*reg* 1370–1506) or Safavid (*reg* 1501–1732) rule, a good impression of this type of fortification can be gleaned from such sites as the abandoned walled city of BAM east of Kirman on the road to Sistan and India. Already fortified in the 10th century, Bam consists of a walled circumvallated town (Pers. *shahristān*) and a raised citadel (*arg*) along the northern walls. The present curtain (probably 18th century) follows the irregular trace of the earlier walls and is preceded by a ditch. Constructed of mud-brick and rammed earth, the walls are provided with alternating round and square towers and rise to an elevation of at least 10 m. They are characterized by a slight batter and are crowned by a crenellated parapet, wall-walk and downward-sloping loopholes for small arms. The citadel, located at the top of a hill rising some 45 m above the surrounding plain, commands the lower town and is entered through a barbican of fired brick with wall-walk, crenellation and gun slits, preceding the main gateway of the fortress.

Similar fortifications existed until the early 20th century to defend several Iranian cities. The walls of Tehran (*see* TEHRAN, §1), for example, were erected during the reign of the Safavid ruler Tahmasp I (*reg* 1524–76) and were rebuilt and strengthened in 1759 by the Zand ruler Muhammad Karim Khan (*reg* 1750–79) and again in 1796 by the Qajar ruler Agha Muhammad (*reg* 1779–97). The walls formed an irregular hexagon, with the citadel, site of the Gulistan Palace, on the north. As at Bam, they were preceded by a ditch, and the high thin curtains had round towers. A wall-walk around the parapet was protected by merlons and pierced by loopholes. The six gates to the city were of fired brick and flanked by massive round towers with decorative brickwork to enrich their façades. New walls were built by German military advisers in the 1870s at the order of Nasir al-Din (*reg* 1848–96). Modelled on those of Paris, they gave the appearance, with their triangular bastions, of being true artillery fortifications, but with their weak ornamental gateways they were of little defensive utility and were torn down in 1937 by the Pahlavi ruler Riza Shah (*reg* 1925–41). Although the walls of Shiraz, Kirman and Tabriz were demolished in the early part of the 20th century, their citadels remain intact. The citadel of SHIRAZ, one of the finest, was built in 1767–8 as a fortress and luxury residence by Muhammad Karim Khan. Measuring *c.* 80 m square with a single gate and four great corner towers, it was built of fired brick and is located within the *shahristān* walls in the northern part of the city. Its walls, some 13 m in elevation, are pierced by loopholes and preceded by a ditch. Typically a broad open maidan (an open space in or near a town, sometimes used as a parade-ground) stands before the gate.

Some of the most remarkable examples of Iranian fortification survive in the east Iranian borderlands, Afghanistan and western Central Asia, where remains were found (until the end of the 19th century) at Tashkent and SAMARKAND and still survive in part at BUKHARA. Such features as the irregular organic traces preceded by ditches, brick construction, flanking towers, simple gateways and crenellated parapets recall the fortifications of western and central Iranian cities. Walls around other eastern Iranian cities were laid out with a regular geometric trace, and the gateways in each of the four sides of the curtain gave access to pairs of cross-axial thoroughfares, which formed the backbone of the street grid. This arrangement is of Indian or perhaps Chinese origin, and outstanding examples are found at KHIVA in the Khwarazm delta of Uzbekistan and at HERAT and Kandahar in Afghanistan. Dating to the latter part of the 18th century, Khiva is roughly rectangular in plan with battered walls of mud-brick and rammed earth preceded by a ditch. Round towers are set at irregular intervals along the trace, and five simple gates of fired brick, flanked by towers, give access to the interior. The citadel and the residence of the *khān*s of Khiva lay on the western wall of the city. Making no provision for an artillery defence, the walls, while extremely thick at the base, are quite thin at the parapet and are crenellated in places with merlons and pierced by loopholes.

The far more extensive walls of Herat, dating at least to the 15th century, were a more elaborate and powerfully constructed example of the same arrangement. With a roughly square trace pierced by four gates, the fortifications of Herat are notable for their extent and the scale on which the work was carried out. The citadel is situated on a raised mound in the northern quarter of the city and still serves as a military area. Typically, the curtains emphasized elevation, as they were intended to protect against light arms. In the late 19th century some attempt was made under British supervision to adapt portions of the *shahristān* wall to an artillery defence with bastions and artillery embrasures. In the face of European armies traditional Iranian military architecture proved to be of little utility.

BIBLIOGRAPHY

WESTERN ISLAMIC LANDS

G. Marçais: *L'Architecture musulmane d'occident* (Paris, 1954)

A. Lézine: *Mahdiya: Recherches d'archéologie islamique* (Paris, 1965), pp. 17–62

A. Hutt: *Islamic Architecture: North Africa* (London, 1977)

L. Prussin: *Hatumere: Islamic Design in West Africa* (Berkeley, 1985)

ANATOLIA AND THE BALKANS

S. Toy: 'The Castles of the Bosporus', *Archaeologia*, lxxx (1930), pp. 215–28

H. Högg: *Türkenburgen an Bosporus und Hellespond: Ein Bild frühosmanischen Wehrbaus bis zum Ausgang des 15. Jahrhunderts* (Dresden, 1932)

A. Gabriel: *Châteaux turcs du Bosphore* (Paris, 1943)

S. Toy: 'The Castle of Yedi Couli or the Seven Towers, Constantinople', *J. Brit. Archaeol. Assoc.*, 3rd ser., xiv (1951), pp. 27–44 and pls xii–xxi

K. Andrews: *Castles of the Morea* (Princeton, 1953)

S. Lloyd and D. S. Rice: *Alanya (Ala'iyya)* (London, 1958)

W. Müller-Wiener: *Bildlexikon zur Topographie Istanbuls* (Tübingen, 1977), pp. 335–41

C. Foss: *Survey of Medieval Castles of Anatolia I: Kütahya*, British Institute of Archaeology at Ankara, 7 (Oxford, 1985)

CENTRAL ISLAMIC LANDS

J. L. Burckhardt: *Travels in Arabia* (London, 1829), pp. 8–9, 323–6, 419–20

P. Cassanova: *Histoire et description de la citadelle du Caire* (Paris, 1894)

M. van Berchem and E. Fatio: *Voyage en Syrie*, i (Paris, 1914)

J. Sauvaget: 'Sur les défenses de la marine de Tripoli', *Matériaux pour un corpus inscriptionum arabicarum: Syrie du Nord*, i, ed. M. van Berchem and E. Fatio (Cairo, 1914)

M. van Berchem: *Matériaux pour un corpus inscriptionum arabicarum: Syrie du Sud: Jerusalem ville*, i (Cairo, 1920)

H. StJ. Philby: *The Heart of Arabia* (New York, 1923), i, pp. 67–76

K. A. C. Creswell: 'Archaeological Researches at the Citadel of Cairo', *Bull. Inst. Fr. Archéol. Orient.*, xxiii (1924), pp. 89–167

E. Rutter: *The Holy Cities of Arabia*, ii (New York, 1928), pp. 208–9

J. Sauvaget: *Alep: Essai sur le développement d'une grande ville syrienne des origines au milieu du XIXe siècle* (Paris, 1941)

S. al-Daywahjī: 'Suwar al-Mawṣil' [The walls of Mosul], *Sumer*, iii (1947), pp. 117–28

——: 'Qal'at al-Mawṣil fī mukhtalif al-'uṣūr' [The citadel of Mosul at different periods], *Sumer*, x (1954), pp. 94–111

E. Herzfeld: *Matériaux pour un corpus inscriptionum arabicarum*, ii: *Syrie du Nord: Inscriptions et monuments d'Alep*, 2 vols (Cairo, 1954–6)

EASTERN ISLAMIC LANDS

G. N. Curzon: *Persia and the Persian Question*, 2 vols (London, 1894)

A. Hamilton: *Afghanistan* (New York, 1906)

O. Olufsen: *The Emir of Bokhara and his Country* (Copenhagen, 1911)

A. Lézine: 'Herat: Notes de voyage', *Bull. Etud. Orient.*, xviii (1963–4), pp. 127–45

B. Fabritsky and I. Shmeliov: *Khiva* (Leningrad, 1973)

M. H. Shah: 'Riwan and Jul (Two Fortresses in Sistan)', *Afghanistan Q.*, xxxiii (1980), pp. 27–33

M. Klinkott: *Islamische Baukunst in Afghanische-Sistan* (Berlin, 1982)

HOWARD CRANE

V. Indian subcontinent.

From Kashmir in the north to Coromandel in the south India is studded with imposing fortresses. Their origins are usually lost in antiquity; most of India's forts were transformed after the Muslim invasion of the 12th century, and although some retain early work, the nature of the indigenous legacy is revealed primarily in ancient India's great literature—religious, epic and professional. The earliest treatises (*shastras*) on architecture date from well into the second half of the Christian era, but they were compiled from material found in venerable religious and secular works. Foremost are the Vedas and the great epics, the *Rāmāyaṇa* and the *Mahābhārata*, but much has been gleaned from the *Jātaka* legends woven about the life of Buddha. Of the theorists, primacy goes to the Mauryan chancellor Kautilya whose treatise on statecraft was probably written for the emperor Chandragupta of the Maurya dynasty (*reg c.* 321–297 BC). Kautilya classified forts according to the character of the site, a system also followed in the *Mānasāra*, a south Indian treatise of *c.* 6th century AD. They were preferably perched on precipitous outcrops of rock with a town at their base, or isolated by forest, desert or water. Often strategy overruled tactics and a fort had to be built in the open plain. In this case, water was introduced to a moat by tapping or damming the nearest river and the land beyond was laid waste to form a field open to the fire of the defenders. Beyond their natural advantages—or artificial devices—the strength of all ancient forts depended on the ramparts and the materials used in them—mud, stone, timber etc—sometimes made further categories.

Where necessary, and in metropolitan forts in particular, the ramparts were formed from the impacted mud dug from the ditches. Kautilya called for three ditches, spiked and filled variously with sand, mud and constantly flowing water alive with crocodiles. The ramparts were to be planted with poisonous bushes and crowned by several ring walls of brick, graded in height and twice as high as they were broad. There were to be square towers and roofed walks wide enough to accommodate patrols in both directions. Gates, between twin towers and large enough for elephants, were to be preceded by a drawbridge spanning the moats, and assailants were to be thwarted by a wide range of obstacles including tortuous deflections of the path. Apart from their fundamental grasp of all the advantages of naturally defensible sites, it is clear from Kautilya that the ancient Indians were familiar with the basic methods of augmenting them: walls covered by flanking fire from regularly spaced towers, defence in depth provided by moats and concentric rings of walls with advanced outworks controlling the approach.

Among the most important early remains are the walls and bastions of RAJGIR, in part of cyclopean masonry, and the great battered walls of fired brick revealed by excavations at KAUSAMBI and other places in the Gangetic basin. In general, these remains do not contradict the vivid depictions in bas-reliefs at SANCHI (*see* INDIAN SUBCONTINENT, fig. 23) and other Buddhist monastic centres. The reliefs indicate some crenellation and embrasures for marksmen. The projection of the gate-towers' top storey may have provided for the dropping of stones and boiling oil on to assailants, though there appears to be no conclusive evidence, textual or archaeological, for machicolation in ancient India. Engines for sending missiles from the ramparts were known even to the Ayodhya of the *Rāmāyaṇa*. Most often mentioned are catapults capable of hurling boulders and crossbows capable of shooting several arrows at once. References to *agni curna* (a compound of saltpetre, sulphur and charcoal) in late treatises have led to claims for the early Indian invention of gunpowder. The probability that the references were interpolated after the advent of the Muslims has not been discounted, and no conclusive evidence exists for any of this in India until the 14th century.

Examples of the fortress types enumerated in the canonical literature can be found throughout India. The most familiar category is an isolated acropolis protecting a settlement in the plain. Outstanding examples are GWALIOR (see fig. 29), JODHPUR, CHITTAURGARH, DAULATABAD and GINGEE, but there are many others. Forest forts, a category depleted by the destruction of the forests, are well represented by Kalanjar and Ranthanbor, keys to the control of Bundelkhand and Rajasthan. JAISALMER, founded in the late 12th century and much expanded in the 14th and 15th centuries on the profits won from control of trade routes across the Thar, is the supreme example of a desert fort. Jodhpur, too, draws its strategic advantage as much from the desert as from its formidable crag. Rivers and lakes play a crucial role in the defence of many forts that fit into other categories—Orccha, UDAIPUR and Amer for instance. The most prominent surviving water forts, such as Vijayadurga on the west coast or VELLORE in the south, were built for Hindu rulers but took their present form well after the advent of the Muslims, colonial powers and gunpowder. VIJAYANAGARA, whose boulder-strewn site has the advantages of a wilderness, is an outstanding example of those great metropolitan forts founded for Hindu rulers. Hardly less significant are the Vijayanagaran emperor's provincial outposts, like GINGEE, or those adapted as seats by his rivals for power in the Deccan, the Bahaminis and their successors—especially Gulbarga, Bidar and Bijapur. Other

29. Fortifications at Chittaurgarh, begun before 600 AD

outstanding examples are Mandu, a hill and forest fort, and Gaur, where river and marsh played a crucial role.

The use of artillery in Europe from the 14th century fundamentally changed the nature of fortification there. The height and thickness of walls had formerly been crucial, but it was gradually realized that they had to be brought low and sunk into ditches to present a minimal target and to give their cannon command of the level of approach. Instead of missiles hurled forward from a great height, saturation coverage by cross-fire was essential. With steady improvement in the range and accuracy of fire-arms, bastions covering one another had to be pushed further out. Thickness was greatly increased by massive battering, but the curved forms effective against sapping were replaced by angular ones to deflect shot. There is no conclusive evidence for any of these features in India before the 14th century.

Apart from the sophistications introduced with the advent of artillery, fortifications built in India after the Muslim invasion also reflect earlier developments in the West—notably in the Holy Land of the crusaders. The great rectangular keep (familiar in France and England) provided a last resort against external assault or internal treachery. After the 11th century, it was sometimes isolated within concentric rings of ramparts; but in the late Middle Ages the trend was to transform it into a massive towered structure integrated with the main line of defence. Parallel ranges of walls were tiered for maximum coverage in depth. Not to hinder marksmen manning the parapets, the machicolations were grouped behind hoods projecting at regular intervals rather than continuously around the curtain. Though the potential of angular forms was to be realized by the colonial powers in India, these developments are well represented by the metropolitan forts of the emperor Akbar (reg 1556–1605). Pronounced aesthetic sensibility was brought to bear on the design even of the utilitarian elements, achieving a compromise between oppressive power and festive display that is most admirable at AGRA.

The isolation of a citadel from a more expansive outwork was common in Inida. This applied the motte-and-bailey principle of the crusaders, but beyond that is the venerable practice of establishing a settlement under the protection of a naturally defensible eminence, as at Daulatabad. Indeed it is the rare exception to this in India, where recourse was to a wholly manmade stronghold, such as at GULBARGA or in the concentric system centred on the Arquila at BIJAPUR, that follows from familiarity with crusader practice. At Daulatabad, furthermore, the extraordinary projecting triple gate of the most powerful double-walled, double-moated second circuit, added by the Muslims, has semi-segmental outer walls like the donjon of Château-Gaillard in France. The isolation of a citadel from a more expansive outwork was also common in India. This applied the crusader motte-and-bailey principle.

Just as India's early forts followed the ideals set out in the technical literature, so the star-shaped plan introduced at Daman in the 16th century by the Portuguese sprang from the ideal Vitruvian city of the Italian Renaissance. The French military engineer SÉBASTIEN LEPRESTRE DE VAUBAN perfected the principles of defence underlying this type in the 17th century. They were then applied by the British to MADRAS and CALCUTTA during the rebuilding that followed the Seven Years' War. Regular polygonal geometry and salient triangular bastions with recessed flanks at each angle maximized all-round cover and minimized the vulnerability of the curtain wall. Defence in depth was assured by interposing ditches and earthworks between the main bastions and lower, outlying salients beyond which lay the gently sloping field of fire. These fields became the open maidans of the greatest post-imperial cities of India.

See also INDIAN SUBCONTINENT, §III, 3 and 7.

BIBLIOGRAPHY

R. Shamasastry: *Kautiliya's Arthashastra* (Mysore, 1929)
A. K. Coomaraswamy: 'Early Indian Architecture I: Cities and City-gates, etc., II: Bodhigharas', *E. A.*, ii (1930), pp. 209–35
——: 'Early Indian Architecture III: Palaces', *E. A.*, iii (1931), pp. 181–217
P. K. Acharya: *The Manasara Series* (London, 1946)
S. Toy: *Strongholds of India* (London, 1957)
——: *Fortified Cities of India* (London, 1965)
A. P. Singh: *Forts and Fortifications in India (with Special Reference to Central India)* (Delhi, 1993)

CHRISTOPHER TADGELL

VI. Central Asia.

1. WESTERN. From earliest times most settlements in western Central Asia were surrounded by ramparts, some enclosing only the city proper, others enclosing suburbs and surrounding villages. Fortified oval or polygonal settlements of proto-urban type came into existence in southern Turkmenistan in the late 3rd millennium BC and early 2nd. At the end of the 2nd millennium BC and beginning of the 1st, large settlements with a rectangular plan and a separate citadel were built in Turkmenistan and Bactria. Large walled cities were founded when most of western Central Asia was under Achaemenid rule (6th-4th century BC). Cities such as MERV, Afrasiab (*see* SAMARKAND, §1(i)) and YAR KURGAN were usually rectangular or circular in shape. Fortified cities founded after the conquest of western Central Asia by Alexander the Great in the 4th century BC, like earlier ones, exploited the terrain and usually had a citadel within the fortified section. For example, the site of AI KHANUM in Afghanistan had a massive mud-brick wall (w. 6–8 m) and rectangular monolithic towers placed at 30-m intervals, and the fortified walls of Afrasiab (3rd–2nd century BC) had an internal gallery and frequent pilasters with embrasures for shooting.

From the 1st century BC to the 3rd century AD urban settlements became more numerous, and existing cities increased in area and became more densely built, although the fortified walls of most cities covered a smaller area (17–30 ha). In the 4th and 5th centuries AD, during the crisis of urban civilization, small fortified settlements (up to 1 ha) appeared in all regions (*see* CENTRAL ASIA, §I, 2(i)(c)), and in the 5th and 6th centuries earlier fortified settlements were transformed into the citadels of the new towns (e.g. PENDZHIKENT). Cities typically had a threefold structure, comprising the fortified citadel dominating the city proper and the suburbs. The mud-brick walls normally had a round or square trace with gates in the centre of each side and projecting towers. These practices continued after the Islamic conquests in the late 7th century and early 8th. Some cities, such as 10th-century CHACH, were protected by a series of walls, the upkeep of which was a heavy burden on the citizens. Isolated structures in the countryside were also fortified, such as RIBAT-I MALIK, a caravanserai on the route between Bukhara and Samarkand, where impressive mud-brick walls were faced with baked brick.

Remarkable medieval fortifications survived until the late 19th century at TASHKENT and Samarkand, and they still survive in part at BUKHARA. Following irregular traces preceded by ditches, the walls were built of mud-brick with towers flanking simple gateways and had crenellated parapets. The mud-brick and pisé fortifications at KHIVA (late 18th century) follow the medieval type, with battered walls of rectangular plan preceded by a ditch and set irregularly with round towers. Five simple gates of baked brick give access to the interior. Along the western wall stands the citadel where the *khān*s of Khiva resided. The walls, while extremely thick at the base, are quite thin at the parapet, making them unsuitable for defence against artillery.

For more information and bibliography *see* CENTRAL ASIA, §I, 2(iii).

□

2. EASTERN. Forts, watch-towers and fortified walls developed at strategic sites on the SILK ROUTE, which connected China with India and the West, from the Han period (206 BC–AD 220) to the beginning of the Ming dynasty (1368–1644). Most of these structures, which acted as defences against the nomadic Huns to the north and Tibetans to the south, are in ruins, the result primarily of wind erosion. Yet what does remain discloses the general characteristics of these fortified structures.

A chain of watch-towers and connecting walls survives for at least an 80-km stretch near Dunhuang, Gansu Province. Begun as early as the Han period, these frontier border-walls and towers were built of brick and rammed earth. The towers are as much as 6 m square at the base, rising to around 9 m. A number of small garrisons has also been found at various strategic locations along the Silk Route. One is the Tang-period fort at Endere, which was occupied by both Chinese (early 8th century AD) and Tibetan forces (late 8th century). The walls were built of sun-dried brick, possibly faced with stucco. Eroded tower-like structures also survive. Within the fort are underground chambers with fireplaces. At Miran there are surviving remains of a fort built as an irregular rectangle, about 27×60 m. From the approximate centre of each wall projects a massive bastion. The construction is of rammed earth, strengthened at intervals by tamarisk brushwood. Probably of Tibetan construction, the fort was built between the late 8th century and the mid-9th.

Numerous ruins are found along the western area of the Silk Route, in the vicinity of Kashgar and within the Tarim River basin, regions open to attacks from nomads across the Tian shan range. Near Kashgar are two small ruined forts, built of sun-dried brick. Parts of the surviving walls show rows of loopholes. One of the forts has two towers on its eastern side.

Karakhoto, a fortified town at the north-eastern limit of the Silk Route (now in southern Inner Mongolia), was possibly the 'city of Exzina' visited by Marco Polo. Its rammed earth walls (about 9 m high) enclose a space of 424×347 m. The stamped clay walls are reinforced by a timber framework. The gates of the eastern and western walls are protected by massive rectangular outworks. The walls have circular bastions at the corners (some capped by Tibetan-style stupas) and rectangular ones along the sides. These fortifications are the best-preserved examples in eastern Central Asia from the 13th century or earlier. The Ming-dynasty fort of JIAYUGUAN, east of Dunhuang, marks the starting-point of the Silk Route in China. Its brick walls, 10.5 m high, have a circumference of over 300 m. Its walls and gate-houses have been heavily renovated and restored.

See also CENTRAL ASIA, §II, 2(ii)(a).

BIBLIOGRAPHY
M. A. Stein: *Ruins of Desert Cathay*, 3 vols (New York and London, 1912)
——: *Serindia*, 4 vols (Oxford, 1921/*R* Delhi, 1981)
——: *Innermost Asia*, 4 vols (Oxford, 1928)
M. A. Stein, ed.: *On Ancient Central Asian Tracks*, intro. J. Mirsky (London, 1933, New York, 2/1964)

WALTER SMITH

VII. East Asia.

1. TIBET. Tibetan records indicate the existence of numerous royal palaces (Tib. *mkhar*). According to *juan* 196 of the *Jiu Tang shu* ('Former standard history of the Tang'), compiled in the Later Jin period (AD 936–46), there were also guard-towers every 100 *li* (576 m) over the whole of the realm. The palaces of the Yarlung dynasty (7th–9th century AD) were fortified citadels, built on the peaks of hills and mountains, for example the Yumbu Lakhar (Tib. yum bu bla mkhar) in the Yarlung Valley, central Tibet. This has undergone many reconstructions and restorations but retains some of the characteristics of the original foundations, such as the technique of construction using roughly squared stones bound with clay mortar. In terms of plan and volume it also shows marked affinities with the forts occupied by Tibetans in Central Asia, such as MIRAN and Mazar Tagh, north of Khotan (now in Xinjiang Uygur Autonomous Region), including the typical asymmetry of the building units or modules, of different heights and with irregular openings, that follow the contours of the land.

The regions of Ladakh, Spiti, Kunavar, Lahul and Zanskar (now in India, but classified in art-historical terms as western Tibet) had been conquered by the Tibetans in the 7th and 8th centuries AD, and the Tibetan taste in architecture continued from the 10th century to the 15th. None of the fortified palaces of this period has survived intact, but documentary sources as well as the great number of ruins prove that there was a vast amount of building activity. At Shey, which may have been the first capital of Ladakh, the royal castle stood on the summit of the hill on the slopes of which the settlement lay. A similar separation can be seen in the castle of the capital of the western Tibetan kingdom of Guge, Tsaparang, which contained a great assembly hall (*c.* 400 sq. m). In the traditional regions of Ü and Tsang in central Tibet, given the constant destruction and reconstruction, a continuation of the models of the monarchic age must be assumed. The ruins of castles and citadels of the 10th century to the mid-11th show that they were placed on heights apart from the settlements, and that they displayed characteristic dissonance in the assembly of various modules of different sizes. The most important temple complexes of the period were often built in valleys not far from such fortified centres.

From the 13th century to the mid-14th, when the Sakyapa school of Tibetan Buddhism controlled Tibet with the support of the Yuan dynasty (1279–1368), there was a great surge in construction of fortified palaces, or *dzong* (Tib. *rdzong*), belonging to local lords. The *dzong* of GYANTSE, erected on a height by a local prince in the 14th century on the ruins of an ancient castle, does not have a real façade like its prototypes; it is composed of a series of multi-functional modules, organically assembled with stepped buttresses and connecting walls. The whole complex is nine storeys high. The outer walls contain only a few small openings.

Following the decline of Sakyapa rule, for a century (mid-14th century to mid-15th) the Phagmodupa sect, whose base was in Ü, managed to unify most of Tibet and tried to renew the splendours of the monarchic age. Subdividing the territory into districts dependent on a *dzong*, they stimulated the reconstruction and restoration of existing fortresses and the building of new ones. There was a progressively more homogeneous fusion of different architectural elements. This can be seen in the *dzong* at Shigatse, capital of Tsang and seat of the prefects of Rinpung, which was drastically modified in the first decades of the 17th century. It may have been the model for the Potala Palace in LHASA.

From the 15th century onwards the architecture of central Tibet became the standard. In western Tibet, large multi-functional religious complexes presenting the characteristics of fortified citadels were built on slopes and peaks. For palaces too, central Tibet was a constant point of reference. For example, the palace in Leh, the Lechen Pelkar (gle chen dpal mkhar), has similarities with the *dzong* of Shigatse. Founded by Senge Namgyel (seng ge rnam rgyal; *reg* 1590–1635), it has the canonical number of nine storeys, a façade with many overhanging projections and windows that correlate with the contours of the land. Harmonious and unified, it lies on the slope and crest of a hill. With the assumption of political power of the Gelugpa school of Tibetan Buddhism from the 16th century, the styles and structures of aristocratic and monastic architecture became more synchronized, culminating in the construction of the Potala Palace (from 1645) on the site of an ancient royal castle (*see* TIBET, fig. 5). Typical of eastern Tibet, especially the Gyarong region (now part of China's northern Sichuan Province), is the isolated stone tower standing on a square base with buttresses at eight points, producing a singular star-like plan (e.g. the Bakalo Tower at Chala). Some dwellings are built in the powerful Tibetan 'fortress' style (e.g. at Ngaba in Gyarong).

See also TIBET, §II.

BIBLIOGRAPHY
R. A. Stein: 'L'Habitat, le monde et le corps humain en Extrême Orient et en Haute Asie', *J. Asiat.*, ccxlv/1 (1957), pp. 37–74
E. Haarh: *The Yar-luṅ Dynasty* (Copenhagen, 1969)
P. Denwood: 'Forts and Castles: An Aspect of Tibetan Architecture', *Shambhala Occas. Pap. Inst. Tib. Stud.*, i (1971), pp. 7–17
——: 'Introduction to Tibetan Architecture', *Tibet News Rev.*, i/2 (1980), pp. 3–12
G. Toffin, L. Barre and C. Jest: *L'Homme et la maison en Himalaya* (Paris, 1981)
Dimore umane, santuari divini: Origini, sviluppo e diffusione dell'architettura tibetana/Demeures des hommes, sanctuaires des dieux: Sources, développement et rayonnement de l'architecture tibetaine (exh. cat., ed. P. M. Vergara and G. Béguin; Rome, La Sapienza; Paris, Mus. Guimet, 1987)

PAOLA MORTARI VERGARA CAFFARELLI

2. CHINA. Cities in ancient China were enclosed by walls. In Chinese, from ancient to modern times the walled city has been denoted by the word *cheng*. The character consists of two components, the radical for 'earth' and the symbol for 'piling up'. At the end of the Neolithic period (*c.* 6500–*c.* 1600 BC) Chinese cities and villages were surrounded by earth-piled walls, as is visible at the LONGSHAN (*c.* 3000–*c.* 1700 BC) site of Chengziyai in Shandong Province. Later, walled cities proper were constructed. Notably, the city identified as the second Shang (*c.* 1600–*c.* 1050 BC) capital of Ao, near present-day ZHENGZHOU in Henan Province, was surrounded by a series of very thick and high walls built with rammed earth (*hangtu*).

For the Zhou period (*c.* 1050–256 BC), the Confucian classic the *Zhou li* ('Rites of Zhou') provides a description, if an idealized one, of the bureaucratic and social system. The *Kaogong ji* ('Record of trades'), one of the six volumes of the *Zhou li*, gives details of the ideal plan of the capital city: important features are the square layout, the grid pattern of the streets and, as regards fortification, the surrounding wall with three gates on each of its four sides. Since there is no archaeological evidence that such a regular type of city existed before the Han period (206 BC–AD 220), it is difficult to ascertain whether the description in the *Kaogong ji* represents a Confucian utopia or a realistic plan for construction. The model of the double city wall had certainly been established by the Eastern Zhou period (771–256 BC): the philosopher Guanzi (*d* 645 BC) made a distinction between the palace or inner wall (*guo*) and the city or outer wall (*cheng*).

During the Eastern Zhou, particularly the Warring States period (403–221 BC), cities were important as military centres where troops were quartered. From the Eastern Zhou there is more precise literary evidence about fortification as, for example, in the 20 chapters from the last part of the *Mozi* (a philosophical work named after its author), ranging from the 'Bei chengmen' ('Defence of wall gates') to 'Zashou' ('Several kinds of defence'). Mozi (*fl c.* late 5th century BC) described the middle class of walled city of the later Zhou. His basic principles of fortification are to set watch-towers at standard intervals along the wall, to build double gates in the wall, to attach bastions outside the wall and to construct a moat with a drawbridge. He also investigated techniques of defending a walled city, such as *yangqian* (raising up earth to hold the wall) and *yifu* (soldiers scaling the wall).

The importance of rammed-earth wall-building technology is evident in the building of the GREAT WALL OF CHINA by the first emperor of the Qin dynasty (221–206 BC), Qin Shi Huangdi (*reg* 221–210 BC). Created by joining together existing defensive walls, the original Great Wall extended east from present-day Gansu Province to

30. City walls, Xi'an, China, Ming period, 1368–1644

the coast and functioned as a defence against the northern Xiongnu people. Successive dynasties rebuilt the Great Wall along different routes.

In the Tang (AD 618–907), Song (960–1279) and Ming (1368–1644) periods systematic and detailed manuals of fortification appeared. The *Wujing zongyao* (1044; 'Collection of important military techniques'), produced by Zeng Gongliang and others under imperial orders, provides a comprehensive survey of the long tradition of Chinese military technology. It documents such features as *mamian* ('horse faces'), fortified buildings outside the city wall, and also newly developed defence methods such as use of the cannon. From the 14th century outer walls were sometimes faced with brick (see fig. 30).

See also CHINA, §II, 3.

BIBLIOGRAPHY
N. Steinhardt: *Chinese Imperial City Planning* (Honolulu, 1990)

TAN TANAKA

3. KOREA. Korean fortifications were made by taking advantage of natural terrain. This feature is most pronounced in border fortifications but is also evident both in the walled town fortresses constructed to defend provincial towns, which encompass part of the mountain behind the town, and in the mountain fortresses constructed to provide a place of safety in times of invasion. Mountain fortresses, which might have a circumference of up to 9 km, were not inhabited in peacetime. However, once war broke out, local residents took refuge in the fortress, which was provided with wells, grain stores, buildings and other facilities.

In early times earthen and wooden ramparts were set up; stone was widely used for fortifications in later periods. The survival intact of the walls of Samnyŏn mountain fortress in North Ch'ungch'ŏng Province 1500 years after their original construction is credited to the building method employed. Flat stones akin to those used in a hypocaust were carefully piled up, creating a structure that is difficult to destroy.

The first recorded fortification in Korea was Wanggŏmsŏng, a walled town fortress built (on the site of modern P'yŏngyang) in 194 BC as the capital of the early kingdom of Wiman Chosŏn. In the Three Kingdoms period (57 BC–AD 668) Koguryŏ, Silla and Paekche each built mountain fortresses, walled capitals and border fortifications. Samnyŏn mountain fortress, built in AD 470 by the king of Silla, has kept most of its original form. It is about 1.7 km in circumference, and the walls, built almost vertically, are 10–15 m high and 10 m wide. Four gates and ten half-moon-shaped outer protective fortifications remain.

Seoul itself, the capital since 1394, was first surrounded by a wall a year later. Four city gates remain. Mountain fortresses built at strategic points to the north (Bukhan) and south (Namhan) of Seoul served as further defences of the capital. They were equipped with gates, some made of naturally shaped rock or stone, known as *ammun*, with stone military platforms (*changdae*), wells, offices and even temples. The fortress walls have generally survived well. The fortified area of the town of Suwŏn dates to 1794–6. It is 5.5 km in circumference and has four large gates, four naturally shaped stone gateways, two floodgates and two military platforms on stone stands. Suwŏn is recognized as the best equipped among Korean fortifications.

BIBLIOGRAPHY
Sin Hŏn: *Minbo chipsŏl* [Compilation of national fortresses] (n.p., 1867)
A. D. Clark and D. N. Clark: *Seoul: Past and Present* (Seoul, 1969), pp. 35–70
Kim Kyu-song, ed.: *Mangi yoram haeje* [Commentary on 'Essentials of the perusal of 10,000 decisions'] (Seoul, 1971)
E. B. Adams: *Through Gates of Seoul*, 2 vols (Seoul, 1974), i, pp. 255–68; ii, pp. 135–45, pls 5–34
Hwansong songyok uigye (Suwŏn, 1977)

SON YOUNG SIK

4. JAPAN. Fortified settlements were common in Japan in prehistoric and protohistoric times. From the 12th century manor houses were fortified with palisades and towers. Hilltop forts near by were used in time of war. Military architecture attained its supreme expression during the 'age of castles' (1576–1639), when nearly 100 castles (Jap. *shiro, -jō*) were built, including AZUCHI CASTLE (the first built) and Himeji (the best preserved; *see* HIMEJI, §2). Many of them were constructed on a monumental scale and displayed highly sophisticated building techniques derived in part from the multi-storey Buddhist pagoda. The castle with its dominant keep (*tenshu*) was not only an expression of military power but also a palatial residence for rulers and a centre of civil administration and patronage. Castle towns (*jōkamachi*) were established around the castles. The castles were demolished for political reasons by the Tokugawa government after 1615 and by the Meiji government after 1868; only 12 *tenshu* survive.

For further information and bibliography *see* JAPAN, §III, 4(ii)(c).

VIII. South-east Asia.

Apart from the great capital cities of the powerful kingdoms that flourished in the region, little remains of the enclosures of most pre-colonial citadels and fortified settlements in South-east Asia or the buildings within them, because these were generally made of wood or bamboo and have therefore long since perished. The plan of such citadels and fortified sites can, however, sometimes be ascertained from a study of the earthworks and moats that often surround them.

1. PRE-COLONIAL. At Nghi Ve, near Bac Ninh, in northern Vietnam, a chambered tomb dating from the Eastern Han (AD 25–220) or Six Dynasties (222–589) period, during most of which the Red, Ma and Ca river valleys were under Chinese domination, was found to contain a clay model of a fort of Chinese inspiration. It has high walls surrounding a square court and small gates providing the only opening on all four sides; watch-towers mark the four corners. At Co Loa, 15 km from Hanoi, the fortified capital of the semi-legendary king An Duong (3rd century BC), only fragments of the walls survive. Two irregular circular walls of rammed earth on huge stone blocks, the outer wall *c.* 8 km in circumference, surrounded a square walled citadel. Within was the royal city, its regular plan of Chinese derivation. In Champa, an Indianized kingdom that existed from the late 2nd century AD for more than 1500 years in the plains on the eastern seaboard of central Vietnam, the remains of about 15 fortified citadels, some of which may date from the 5th century, have been identified in the area between Mt Deo Ngang in the north and Phan Ri in the south (*see* CHAMPA, §II, 2). The city of Angkor Thom in northern Cambodia, built by the Khmer rulers of Angkor between 1181 and *c.* 1220 (*see* ANGKOR, §2(v)), provides an outstanding example of the defensive aspects of pre-colonial South-east Asian formal architecture. Surrounding the centre of the city, which contained the state temple (the Bayon) and the king's palace, were thick stone walls and a wide moat crossed by five causeways leading to five monumental gateways (*see* ANGKOR, fig. 4). In northern Thailand there are only fragmentary remains of fortified cities, and these have been little investigated by archaeologists. At CHIANG MAI, 697 km north of Bangkok, are remnants of city walls, gates and forts, some of which may date back to the foundation of the city in the 1290s by King Mangrai as capital of the northern Thai kingdom of Lanna. The most modern of the fortifications date from the 18th century. Of 17th-century date are the remnants of the fort of Thung Setthi, at Nakhon Chum, near Kamphaeng Phet (358 km north of Bangkok). The angular bastions of its corners are of European inspiration. In Vietnam impressive fortified walls were built in 1631 at Dong Hoi, 166 km north of Hue, just north of the 17th parallel, by the Nguyen rulers in order to block entry to their lands from the north by their rivals in Hanoi, the Trinh. The walls of Dong Hoi were about 6 m high and 18 km long and were marked every few metres by pavilions containing artillery. Dong Hoi was almost completely destroyed in the 1964–75 period of the Vietnam War.

Angkor Thom, the capital of an inland agrarian kingdom in Cambodia, and the citadels built by the Chams, the Thais and the Vietnamese, may be contrasted with MALACCA, on the south-west coast of Malaysia, which grew up during the 15th century as a trade centre and capital of a powerful Muslim state on the narrow straits between Peninsular Malaysia and Sumatra. The fort was located on a hill (later to be named St Paul's Hill by the Dutch) that was made defensible by the construction of a surrounding wall within which was the sultan's palace and other official buildings. Beyond the ramparts were markets and the settlements of Malacca's cosmopolitan population of traders. The Portuguese, who captured Malacca in 1511, strengthened the walls and ramparts and thereby created the fortress known as A Famosa, which was one of the most impregnable strongholds in Portuguese Asia, but left the layout of the surrounding town largely unchanged. The Dutch, who took the city in 1641, added bastions with platforms for cannon. Most of the fort was destroyed by the British in 1807, and of the five gateways erected by the Portuguese only one survives, the Santiago Gate, at the foot of St Paul's Hill. Its central archway is flanked by engaged columns and towers. In contrast, the Arakanese city of Mrauk U (Mrohaung; Burm. Myohaung) in west-central Burma, the capital of the ARAKAN kingdom from the 13th century, remained, despite its overseas trade contacts, free of European architectural forms. The palace at the centre of the city was surrounded by three stone walls. The outer city was partially encompassed by stone walls and by lakes and canals, which also performed a defensive role.

The Batak village of Pematang Purba in northern Sumatra provides an example of a vernacular defensive structure outside the urban context. The area surrounding the small hill on which the village stands was formerly planted with poisonous trees, and access to the village was through tunnels known only to the residents. The first building within the village compound is the gate-house (*balai buttu*), the headquarters of the village guards. It is 7 m high and stands on a base of logs laid horizontally.

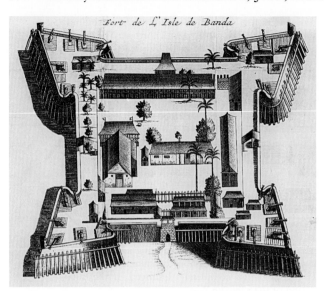

31. Fort Hollandia, Lontor, Banda Islands, Indonesia, early 17th century; engraving from B. Leonardo y Argensola: *Histoire de la conquête des iles Moluques par les Espagnols, par les Portugais & par les Hollandais...* (Amsterdam, 1706), iii, p. 115

The upper structure is 6 m square and capped with a thatched hipped roof.

2. COLONIAL. In the Philippines the imposition of Spanish colonial rule necessitated the building of numerous fortified structures. The settlement established in 1565 on the island of Cebu by Miguel Lopez de Legazpi, first Spanish governor of the Philippines (1564–72), included Fort San Pedro. A triangular structure, 432 m in circumference, its corners were fortified by bulwarks. In 1571 Legazpi occupied Manila and replaced the Islamic fort and settlement with a city modelled after the ideas of the Italian theorist Leon Battista Alberti. The city is an irregular pentagon, with the fort forming a narrow triangle at the north-west end. The city walls of stone and brick, punctuated by bastions and gates, were built between 1590 and 1593. Numerous other forts were built in the Spanish Philippines during the 17th century, often at the instigation of the religious orders, such as Nuestra Señora del Pilar de Zaragoza at Zamboanga, south-east Mindanao, built by Governor Cerezo de Salamanca in 1635 in response to appeals from the Jesuits, and the several forts constructed for the Augustinian Recollects on the island of Palawan.

Several forts were built in Indonesia by the Dutch and English. In the 17th century the Dutch United East India Company (VOC) built forts at various strategic points in the spice islands and elsewhere in eastern Indonesia, some of them on the site of 16th-century Portuguese forts (e.g. Fort Hollandia, Lontor, Banda Islands (see fig. 31); Fort Victoria, Ambon; Fort Belgica, Bandanaira; Benteng Toloko, Ternate). Duurstede Fort was built on the island of Saparua in 1691 by Governor-General Nicolas van Saghen. It resembles in general form and conception the plan for an ideal fortified city by the German writer on architecture Josef Furttenbach. The fort of Ujung Pandang (formerly

Makassar) in South Sulawesi (Celebes) was begun *c.* 1545 by the rulers of the Gowa kingdom. The structure was modified by the Dutch, who captured the city in 1667. They added polygonal bastions at the corners and centre of the western wall, thereby causing the plan to approximate to those of polygonal forts then being developed in Europe. Fort Marlborough in Bengkulu (Bencoolen), on the south-western coast of Sumatra, was built by the British East India Company between 1709 and 1714. In 1824 it was ceded to the Dutch, who maintained it until Indonesian independence in 1945. Restored by the Indonesian government between 1977 and 1984, it now functions as an army base and contains a small museum.

Many impressive citadels were built in Vietnam in imitation of French models in the late 18th century and the 19th, such as Phien An (*c.* 1792; *see* VIETNAM, §II, 3), now part of Ho Chi Minh City, and HUE (1802–16). Both Phien An and Hue are thought to be modelled on the works of the French engineer and architect Sébastien Leprestre de Vauban, for example his fortress of 1698 at Neuf-Brisach (Alsace). At Hue the massive fortification walls, 2.8 km long, with their seven bastions, are entirely European in form and construction. The gates, however, are surmounted by wood and brick watch-towers that are completely Chinese in conception.

In the late 19th century and the early 20th several forts were built in Sarawak, East Malaysia, by successive rulers of the Brooke family, the so-called White Rajas. Among these relatively simple structures are Fort Margherita (1879) in the capital, Kuching, now the Police Museum; Fort Sylvia (1880); a wooden fort at Kapit on the Rajang River in south-west Sarawak; and Fort Hose (1901) at Marudi, north-east Sarawak, which has ironwood tiles and a fine collection of brass cannon.

BIBLIOGRAPHY

H. Gourdon: *L'Art de l'Annam* (Paris, 1933)
L. Bezacier: *L'Art du Viêtnam* (Paris, 1955)
M. Morini: *Atlante di storia dell'urbanistica* (Milan, 1963)
T. G. McGee: *The Southeast Asian City* (New York, 1967)
Sumet Jumsai: *Seen: Architectural Forms of Northern Siam and Old Siamese Fortifications* (Bangkok, 1970)
Aung Thaw: *Historical Sites in Burma* (Rangoon, 1972/R 1978)
H. de La Croix: *Military Considerations in City Planning: Fortifications* (New York, 1972)
G. T. Sergeant and R. Saleh: *Batak Simalungun and Batak Mandailing* (1973), iii of *Traditional Buildings of Indonesia* (Bandung, 1973)
C. A. du Marchie Sarvaas: *Dynamics of Indonesian History* (Amsterdam, 1978)
P. Benteng: *Ujung Pandang, Sulawesi Selatan; Marlborough, Bengkulu; Duurstede, Maluku* (Jakarta, 1986)
W. Klassen: *Architecture in the Philippines* (Cebu City, 1986)
S. Vlatseas: *A History of Malaysian Architecture* (Singapore, 1990)
R. M. Zaragoza: *Old Manila* (Singapore, 1990)

WALTER SMITH

IX. Africa.

In Africa, fortifications result from the need to protect life, food and water supplies and any accumulated wealth. For many centuries pre-colonial Africa experienced mass population movements and the formation and dissolution of great and powerful states. In these conditions of uncertainty, defence was essential for continuing existence, although the ability of small-scale near-subsistence communities to devote time and manpower to the construction of defensive structures was strictly limited. Instead, the response to aggression might be flight to remote areas and the construction of ingenious, rather than massive, defensive structures. Among the most interesting of these are the cactus mazes of the Nigerian Plateau area. These consist of long cactus tunnels often beginning nearly a mile from the village. Too narrow for horsemen to turn in, the tunnels had blind alleys and passages returning on themselves to confuse hostile forces. Breaking through the hedge when ambushed was no mean feat, even with axes, as the cactus exudes a caustic white juice when cut that can burn the skin and cause blindness.

In pre-colonial Africa, the most common form of village defence was a live hedge and palisade, sometimes combined with a ditch. In such cases as the Hehe of central Tanzania, the palisade was reinforced with wooden watch-towers at entrance gates. Concentrically arranged walls or fences may also have been common, even in small settlements. Kia Gimen on the River Lubudi in Zaïre was defended on the river side by a single wall 1 m wide and 3 m high. Towards the plains, however, seven concentric enclosures joined the ends of the river wall, and within each was a spike-lined ditch and a narrow path. Access was along the path and through a series of staggered gates, so enemies could be dealt with effectively before they reached the city. A natural defence was often afforded by the terrain: DOGON villages in Mali clinging to the rocky Bandiagara escarpment were inaccessible to the cavalry of marauding communities (Gardi, 1973; Guidoni, 1975). In such areas as Burkina Faso and the East African highlands underground houses were built as 'bolt holes' at times of attack (Denyer, 1978).

Arab travellers and European explorers described large fortified settlements throughout the Sahel and the savannah zones of West Africa. These cities occupied strategic positions on the trans-Saharan trading routes and became centres of commerce, with some developing into capitals of extensive empires. Djenné and TIMBUKTU in the western part of the Sudan region of sub-Saharan North Africa and Kanem at the heart of the Kanem–Bornu empire centred on Lake Chad are examples of such fortified medieval cities. In addition, the seven related city states of Hausaland—Hausa Bakwai—occupied the central part of the West African Sudan, between the empires of the east and west. Each city, itself highly fortified, was surrounded by a galaxy of walled satellite towns. In 1904 Lugard estimated that there were 40 walled towns within a 50 km radius of Kano, and 170 in the whole of what was then the province of Kano. In the mid-19th century Barth described the defensive structures of Kano as consisting of a mud wall 9 m to 12 m high and c. 16 km in circumference. The wall had 13 gates and was surmounted by a battlement. In places it had two moats and an encircling road on the outer face. Although in a ruinous condition, the walls of Kano and of another Hausa city, Zaria, are still evident, and it is not difficult to imagine the magnitude of this remarkable pre-industrial earth-moving enterprise (Moughtin, 1985). Other Nigerian peoples such as the Borgu, Bussa, Nupe, Yoruba and Bini also built large-scale fortifications. In Yorubaland, for example, Gboho had three defensive walls, while Ilesha and IFE had two each.

An interesting variation in fortification is seen in Mandinka town walls of the 19th century. Described as zigzag

in plan or as comprising a succession of round or square towers joined by short lengths of wall, their shapes gave maximum advantage to the defenders. With the introduction of fire-arms into Africa, further changes in design ensued. Yoruba town walls, for example, became more slender, allowing the formation of effective gun holes, while in Hausaland the 'looped parapet' was developed. European commercial interest in Africa brought further developments as European-style forts were built. In the late 16th century the Portuguese built a fort at Accra, Ghana, and another, Fort Jesus, in Mombasa, Kenya. Colonial annexation was often reinforced by the construction of such fortifications as, for example, the fort at Kumasi, Ghana, built by the British in the last few years of the 19th century.

For Islamic fortifications in Africa see §IV, 2(ii) and 3(i) above.

BIBLIOGRAPHY
R. Gardi: *Indigenous African Architecture* (New York, 1973)
E. Guidoni: *Architettura primitiva* (Milan, 1975; Eng. trans. by R. E. Wolf, New York, 1978; also trans. London, 1979)
S. Denyer: *African Traditional Architecture* (London, 1978)
Des architectures de terre (exh. cat. by J. Dethier, Paris, Pompidou, 1981); Eng. trans. by R. Eaton as *Down to Earth, Mud Architecture: An Old Idea, A New Future* (London, 1982)
J. C. Moughton: *Hausa Architecture* (London, 1985)

J. C. MOUGHTIN

X. Pre-Columbian Americas.

Warfare was the normal condition of life in the Pre-Columbian Americas, as much for tribal peoples with only light, portable buildings as for the urbanized civilizations engaged in monumental construction. Throughout North America and Mesoamerica the military architecture of these cultures consisted primarily of timber palisades and masonry defensive walls. In South America there was a more varied situation that included castle-like structures as well as defensive walls. Because the technology of warfare in the Pre-Columbian Americas did not include heavy missiles, the purely military demands on structures were not great, and therefore defensive walls were not very different from precinct walls built for ceremonial purposes.

1. NORTH AMERICA. Palisades of vertical timbers—built as defence works around permanent or semi-permanent settlements, and equipped with ramparts—are known from the accounts of early explorers and from archaeological excavations throughout north-eastern North America, in particular among the Iroquois and Huron nations. The ceremonial centres built in eastern North America, mostly from c. AD 500 to c. 1500, often incorporated perimeter constructions in timber and earth that appear defensive. Several were enclosed within earthworks topped by timber palisades and protected by outer moats, either dry or wet. Some had timber bastions at regular intervals; others had perimeters defined by earthworks or moats with large openings and may have served to set the area apart as a sacred place rather than to defend it militarily. In at least one case—Irene, GA—a timber palisade had been placed around the top of a major platform within a ceremonial centre, a position suggesting precinct enclosure more than defensive measure. The plans of palisades and earthworks include circles, squares, rectangles and other figures that

are not in themselves defensive. It seems most probable that the enclosures erected around ceremonial centres were precinct walls with defensive capabilities, and that site geometry reflects sacredness, while details such as bastions were literally militaristic.

2. MESOAMERICA. Similar considerations apply to Mesoamerica. A number of well-known sites have perimeter wall systems, and, as in eastern North America, these are ceremonial centres. The most famous is probably the Late Post-Classic (c. 1200–1521) Maya centre of TULUM, enclosed within a rectangular masonry wall on the land side and located on the only stretch of shore where stone cliffs rise out of the sea, 12 m at the highest point (see fig. 32). The walls were 4 m to 6 m high, with battered surfaces. Their thickness (3–6 m) suggests a defensive purpose, but their height was inadequate in this regard. The issue is further complicated by the presence of numerous ancient residential remains outside the wall, suggesting that the site may have been just the central precinct of the settlement. Of course this does not disqualify it as a refuge in time of war, or as a defensive mechanism. The great Ciudadela compound at TEOTI-HUACÁN, although primarily a precinct, could also have been used for a defensive redoubt. On the other hand, it is well known that certain important ceremonial centres were contained within very substantial precinct walls that were certainly not defensive. The prime example is the 15th-century Aztec ceremonial centre of Tenochtitlán (see MEXICO CITY, §I). The temple precinct was an area c. 396 m sq., reported in early sources (Sahagún) as enclosed within a masonry wall called the 'serpent wall' and

entered through three or four gateways at the cardinal directions. The descriptions in these historical documents make it clear that the wall was essentially a precinct *boundary*. However, it was probably also in some sense a fortress protecting the area within or, at the very least, emphasizing the special character and significance of the precinct that it contained. Cempoala, the Totonac capital in the north Gulf Coast region at the time of the Spanish conquest, has a ceremonial centre enclosed by walls, topped with a step-fret motif that greatly resembles battlements. These may be the walls that were so burnished that the Spaniards mistook them for silver. If so, they would have been surfaced with plaster, and though defensive in appearance, would essentially have been precinct walls.

Nevertheless, Mesoamerican archaeologists can cite three periods during which there was an increase in warfare, manifested, among other evidence, by an increase in the number of hilltop settlements, presumably for their defensive positions. The first period was at the end of the Late Pre-Classic (c. 300 BC–c. AD 250) and the beginning of the Early Classic (c. AD 250–c. 600) periods. In the Central Highlands during this time the number of hilltop settlements increased as the conflict between Teotihuacán and its southern Basin of Mexico rival, CUICUILCO, grew; and massive stone retaining walls were built at the south-eastern corner of Lake Texcoco. A colonial site was established at Gualupita las Dalias to the east, in north-western Puebla, on a hilltop with deep ravines on three sides, look-out structures and an easily guarded entrance. In the Maya region the dry moat and parapet surrounding

32. Perimeter wall, Tulum, Late Post-Classic period, c. 1200–1521

the site of Becán, Campeche, was built during the Late Pre-Classic or Early Classic period and allowed to deteriorate during the Late Classic period (c. AD 600–c. 900) when some of the most impressive buildings at the site were built. If Becán was initially built as a fortification the need for defence must have declined, although other evidence suggests an increase in Maya warfare during the Classic period. A similar but much longer moat and parapet partially surround TIKAL, one of the largest sites in the southern Maya lowlands. Although this would appear to be essentially a fortification, it is so long and so easily scaled that it would seem impossible to defend it successfully. These features may be territorial markers, defensive in form only, and not truly intended as protection against attack.

Evidence for increasing warfare in the Late Classic period in both the Central Highlands and in the Maya region is prominent in mural painting (see MESOAMERICA, PRE-COLUMBIAN, §V) and, again, in an increase in the number of hilltop sites. As the power of Teotihuacán waned, rival city states asserted or reasserted themselves. Cities such as CACAXTLA and XOCHICALCO are located on hilltop promontories commanding wide views of the surrounding countryside. Similarly, with the breakup and sometimes even abandonment of many lowland Maya cities, hilltop highland Maya cities in Chiapas and Guatemala became more prominent.

The Post-Classic period (c. AD 900–1521) was a time of empire building, and for the Late Post-Classic there is much more concrete evidence of real defensive structures throughout Mesoamerica. At LA QUEMADA, a settlement (possibly Toltec) on the northern fringes of Mesoamerica, a fortress was built with crudely constructed walls of rough stone, presumably as a defence against incursion from northern barbarian tribes. Aztec attempts at conquest to the west and north-west of the Basin of Mexico met with stiff resistance from the Tarascan kingdom. The Matlazinca–Aztec city of Teotenago in the Toluca Valley, immediately west of the Basin, sat on a hilltop with wide views in all directions, and eventually both the Aztecs and the Tarascans established lines of forts along their mutual border on the western edge of the Toluca Valley and south into Guerrero.

In the Southern Highlands periodic warfare between the Mixtec and Zapotec peoples, and later their resistance to Aztec conquest, resulted in numerous fortified cities and towns. Real defensive constructions are found in the Valley of Oaxaca, at MITLA and YAGUL. In the cliffs above these two sites there are rough stone walls closing off access paths between cliffs and outcrops. They do not enclose any significant structures and appear to be hilltop fortresses or refuges. The walls themselves are crude constructions of rough stone. The Mixtec fortress of Tepexi el Viejo in southern Puebla sat at 1700 m above sea-level on a hill with deep ravines on three sides. A series of massive plastered walls, 3–5 m high, surrounded the town and prevented erosion. Two gates were constructed so as to cause the attacker to expose his right, unshielded side. The Zapotec fortress of Guiengola in the southern Tehuantepec Peninsula was apparently a specialized military town that never held a large population. It sat on the eastern flanks and ridges of a mountain with easy access

on only one path and stairway. Its defence comprised 40 km of massive double walls 1.5 m thick and 3 m high, enclosing the town structures and including two natural wells and numerous water-catchment holes.

In the Maya region the Late Post-Classic Maya city of MAYAPÁN (13th–16th century) in northern Yucatán is surrounded by a thick stone wall about 2 m high that encloses an area of more than 4 sq. km and contains more than 2000 residential buildings. This would appear to be a true walled city, although again, despite its thickness, the wall is too low to have provided effective defence. The Late Post-Classic centres of Mixco Viejo and IXIMCHÉ in the highlands of Guatemala were sited in similar defensive locations and equipped with substantial walls, but these enclosed ceremonial centres and thus were more than just fortresses.

See also MESOAMERICA, PRE-COLUMBIAN, §IV, 1(ii)(b).

3. SOUTH AMERICA. In the Andean region the most famous ancient fortress is SACSAHUAMAN, above Cuzco. It is renowned for its zigzag walls, like terrace facings, that incorporate truly gigantic individual stones. The structure above these walls was a combination of temple, palace and fortress, where the ruling Inca performed ceremonial rituals. Although generally referred to as a fortress the function of Sacsahuaman remains unclear. It may be another instance of a defensive architectural form used for essentially non-militaristic purposes that had both religious and governmental aspects. The case of Paramonga, near the Pacific coast north of Lima, is more complex. It was located at or near the southern edge of the area controlled by the Chimú empire during the Middle Horizon (c. AD 600–c. 1000). Three levels of high defensive walls with corner salients and bastions surround a natural hilltop supporting the central sanctuary. As a defensive mechanism this structure far exceeds the demands of warfare with slings, spear-throwers and javelins. It may have been built as a temple but was used as a fortress in defence against the Inca expansion and was taken only after a prolonged siege. The Chimú capital of CHAN CHAN was developed in the form of a series of rectangular enclosures known as *ciudadelas*. These are known to have been the palaces of Chimú kings, not fortresses. However, their architectural form and layout are strongly defensive in character, with high, blank outer walls and narrow, tortuous circulation systems that would frustrate an invading enemy and could be effectively defended by a small force.

BIBLIOGRAPHY

B. de Sahagún: *Historia general de las cosas de Nueva España* (MS., untraced, 1569; copy, *Florentine codex*, Florence, Bib. Medicea-Laurenziana, MS. Palat. 218–20, n.d.); facs. as *Códice florentino: El manuscrito 218–20 de la Colección palatina de la Biblioteca medicea laurenziana*, 3 vols (Mexico City and Florence, 1979); ed. C. M. de Bustamante (Mexico City, 1829–30); Eng. trans. ed. C. E. Dibble and A. J. O. Anderson as *Florentine Codex: General History of the Things of New Spain*, 13 vols (Santa Fe, NM, 1950–69)

B. Díaz del Castillo: *Historia verdadera de la conquista de la Nueva España* (Madrid, 1576); Eng. trans., abridged J. M. Cohen, as *The Conquest of New Spain* (London, 1963)

I. Marquina: *Arquitectura prehispanica* (Mexico City, 1950, 2/1964/R 1981)

J. E. Hardoy: *Ciudades precolombinas* (Buenos Aires, 1964); Eng. trans. by J. Thorne as *Pre-Columbian Cities* (New York, 1973)

M. D. Coe: *The Maya* (London and New York, 1966, rev. 4/1987)

E. P. Lanning: *Peru Before the Incas* (Englewood Cliffs, 1967)

J. F. Hayes: *Wilderness Mission: The Story of Sainte-Marie-Among-the Hurons* (Toronto, 1969)

M. P. Weaver: *The Aztecs, Maya and their Predecessors: Archaeology of Mesoamerica* (New York, 1972, rev. 2/1981)

W. R. Coe: *Tikal: A Handbook of the Ancient Maya Ruins* (Philadelphia, 1976)

W. N. Morgan: *Prehistoric Architecture in the Eastern United States* (Cambridge, 1980)

E. Pasztory: *Aztec Art* (New York, 1983)

E. V. Pacheco: 'Consideraciones generales sobre las fortificaciones militares en Tulum, Quintana Roo, México', *Estud. Cult. Maya*, xv (1984), pp. 176–85

H. STANLEY LOTEN

Milizia, Francesco (*b* Oria, Apulia, 1725; *d* Rome, March 1798). Italian writer. He studied in Naples, Rome and Padua and in 1761 he settled in Rome. There he began the publication of an influential series of theoretical works, beginning with a biographical encyclopedia of architects (1768). Ferdinand IV, King of Naples (*reg* 1759–1825), appointed him superintendent of the Farnese buildings in the Papal States, but he soon resigned this post (1780) to resume his literary career. He was friendly with José Nicolás de Azara and the painter Anton Raphael Mengs, whose art he promoted. Although Milizia advocated 'great masses, great forms and great tracts' in architecture, he adopted in his works a stance that was strongly opposed to the Baroque, regarding the 16th century as an age of correctness in comparison to the 17th, which he saw as an age of corruption. He criticized St Peter's, Rome, for being divided into too many parts and denounced Michelangelo's *Moses* as 'a horrible watchdog dressed like a stoker, badly placed and useless'. Francesco Borromini's followers were categorized as 'a delirious sect', while of Guarino Guarini he wrote, 'whoever likes his architecture, much good may it do him, but he would be a nitwit'.

Although Milizia's theories of art are not free from inconsistencies—he himself admitted that he was 'a heterogeneous compound of contradictions'—his general approach was influenced by the rationalism of Carlo Lodoli and Marc-Antoine Laugier. Milizia denounced excessive ornamentation in buildings, which he considered led to the '*bizzaria*', destroying order and the forms dictated by Nature; nevertheless his insistence on 'soft transitions' and the avoidance of abrupt contrasts reveals the subliminal persistence of Baroque influence on his views. The functionalism that underlies Milizia's theories is clearly evident in the essay on architecture that precedes his biographical dictionary, where he enunciated principles on which perfect architecture should be based. These include symmetry and unity, combined with variety. All features should appear to be necessary and performing a specific function; hence 'everything which is done just for the purpose of decoration is vicious'. The architectural orders, however, he regarded as structural rather than ornamental, although he maintained that the authority of ancient design should not be cited to impede the pursuit of reason. Milizia's attacks helped to provoke a rejection of Baroque that persisted for a century until appreciation was rekindled by such scholars as Cornelius Gurlitt. Although Milizia implied that the legacy of Antiquity was exhausted, his writings did much to promote the rise of Neo-classicism.

WRITINGS

Le vite de' più celebri architetti. . .precedute da uno saggio sopra l'architettura (Rome, 1768)

Del teatro (Rome, 1771)

Dell'arte di vedere nelle belle arti di disegno secondo i principi di Sulzer e di Mengs (Venice, 1781)

Memorie degli architetti antichi e moderni (Parma, 1781)

Principj di architettura civile (Finale, 1781)

Roma: Delle belle arti del disegno (Bassano, 1787)

Dizionario delle belle arti del disegno (Bassano, 1797)

BIBLIOGRAPHY

G. Antolini: *Osservazioni ed aggiunte ai principi di architettura civile di Francesco Milizia proposte agli studiosi ed amatori di architettura* (Milan, 1817)

E. Kauffmann: *Architecture in the Age of Reason* (Cambridge, MA, 1955)

P. Zampetti: 'Francesco Milizia: Uomo e critico d'arte', *Sensibilità e razionalità nel settecento* (Florence, 1967)

I. Prozzillo: *Francesco Milizia teorico e storico d'architettura* (Naples, 1971)

J. Rykwert: *On Adam's House in Paradise* (New York, 1972)

Mill, industrial. Type of factory and warehouse building chiefly associated with the British Industrial Revolution from the early 18th century to the late 19th. The first and most impressive industrial mills were textile factories, massive, largely unadorned structures in Lancashire and West Yorkshire. The term 'mill' is also applied to works for sawing timber, paper-making, pressing olive oil or grinding corn and other foods; such mills may be small workshops, concrete towers, single-storey sheds or even ornate city-centre buildings such as the Molino Stucky, an eight-storey Gothic Revival flour mill and store begun in 1883 and extended by Ernest Wullekopf in 1897, which dominates the skyline of the Giudecca in Venice; it ceased production in 1954.

The layout and form of the industrial mill was pioneered in the silk mills built in the foothills of the Italian Alps, where, by the 13th century, strands of silk were twisted or 'thrown' in mills operated by water-wheels. Examples survive at Lake Como, where the silk industry became established *c.* 1510. The Italian form of throwing mill was introduced to England in the early 18th century: in 1702 Thomas Cotchett (1685–1739) completed a three-storey silk-spinning mill (destr.) in Derby; a larger, more successful works (destr. 1910) was erected close by in 1718–21 by Thomas Lombe (1685–1739). These mills, probably the first factories of the Industrial Revolution, established a form and aesthetic that was to survive well into the 20th century: a solid, unornamented building housing a complex range of machinery driven from a single power source and accommodated within bays of standardized area, and with as much natural lighting as possible through regular rows of rectangular windows.

Early cotton mills, as shown by surviving examples built in the 1770s and 1780s for Richard Arkwright (1732–92) in Cromford, Derbys, were of essentially traditional construction with wooden columns, beams and floors; Joseph Wright of Derby painted several interior scenes and landscapes featuring these mills (e.g. *Arkwright's Mill by Moonlight, c.* 1782–3; priv. col., see *Wright of Derby*, exh. cat. by J. Egerton, London, Tate, 1990, no. 127). The need for strength to carry the weight and vibration of machinery, and for a structure that could resist fire, promoted the use of iron, an innovation fully exploited in the flax mill at Shrewsbury, Salop, built in 1796–7 with a full iron frame.

This mill, by Marshall, Benyon and Bage, was also one of the earliest to be powered entirely by steam rather than by water.

The agglomeration of stark, brick structures developed from 1797 by the Rochdale Canal in Manchester epitomized the gaunt industrial landscape of lowland Lancashire, shocking to Victorian socialists but later celebrated in the paintings of L. S. Lowry (e.g. *Industrial Landscape*, 1955; London, Tate). Not all mills were utilitarian in their materials or their architectural expression. Stone was used with great virtuosity for the woollen mills of Gloucestershire and the West Riding of Yorkshire, while the most prestigious firms often adopted Italianate, Gothic or even Egyptian styles. Stanley Mill (1812–13) in Stroud, Glos, combined a lavish iron frame with formal elevations of rusticated stonework, rubbed bricks and Venetian windows. Some of the cotton mills of Bolton, Lancs, dating from the first decade of the 20th century, had watertowers in an Elizabethan or Byzantine Revival style and engine houses lined with decorative tilework.

The textile mill reached its apogee in the American cotton towns of New England. The first American mills with spinning machinery date from *c.* 1790. During the 1820s Lowell, MA, developed as the cotton capital of the USA, with its massive brick factories surmounted by belltowers and powered from a network of canals. Washington Mills (1886–7), by engineers Lockwood-Greene Company, in Lawrence, MA (begun 1846 as Bay State Mills), survives as probably the largest mill complex in the world. These mills were built with wooden beams and iron columns (as a gesture towards fireproofing) and were powered primarily by water-turbine. With heavier machinery single-storey construction became more widely adopted, first for weaving and some other processes from the mid-19th century, and for complete factories from *c.* 1900. Iron columns were supplanted by steel or concrete framing, and water power by electricity.

BIBLIOGRAPHY

J. Nasmith: *Recent Cotton Mill Construction and Engineering* (Manchester, 1890, rev. by F. Nasmith, 3/1909)

J. Coolidge: *Mill and Mansion: A Study of Architecture and Society in Lowell, Massachusetts, 1820–1865* (New York, 1942)

A. W. Skempton and H. R. Johnson: 'The First Iron Frames', *Archit. Rev.* [London], cxxxi (1962), pp. 175–86

S. D. Chapman: *The Early Factory Masters* (Newton Abbot, 1967)

J. Tann: *The Development of the Factory* (London, 1970)

E. Jones: *Industrial Architecture in Britain, 1750–1939* (London, 1985)

J. H. Longworth: *The Cotton Mills of Bolton, 1780–1985* (Bolton, 1987)

C. Giles and I. H. Goodall: *Yorkshire Textile Mills, 1770–1930* (London, 1992)

MICHAEL STRATTON

Millais, Sir John Everett (*b* Southampton, 8 June 1829; *d* London, 13 Aug 1896). English painter.

1. Life and work. 2. Working methods and technique. 3. Patrons, dealers and engravers.

1. LIFE AND WORK.

(i) Early career, before 1863. Millais showed a prodigious natural facility for drawing, and his parents groomed him from an early age to become an artist. His father was a man of independent means from an old Jersey family. He spent his childhood in Southampton (where his mother's family were prosperous saddlers), Jersey and Dinan in Brittany, before going to London in 1838. After a brief period at Henry Sass's private art school, he was accepted into the Royal Academy Schools in 1840, its youngest-ever student. He won a silver medal there in 1843 for his drawing from the Antique, made his début at the Royal

1. John Everett Millais: *Christ in the Carpenter's Shop*, oil on canvas, 0.86×1.40 m, 1849–50 (London, Tate Gallery)

Academy exhibition in 1846 with the accomplished though conventional history painting *Pizarro Seizing the Inca of Peru* (London, V&A) and won a gold medal in 1847 for the *Tribe of Benjamin Seizing the Daughters of Shiloh* (priv. col., sale cat., London, Sotheby's, 21 Nov 1973, lot 44), a composition with struggling nudes in the manner of William Etty.

At the Academy Schools Millais became friendly with his fellow student William Holman Hunt and was influenced by his radical views about the state of British art. The Academy was still under the intellectual sway of Sir Joshua Reynolds, its revered first president. Reynolds's *Discourses* encouraged young British artists to follow in the Renaissance tradition, worship Raphael and adhere to the basic principle of idealization, i.e. the notion that art should improve upon Nature. Hunt and Millais reacted against this view and resolved that their paintings would show people and things precisely as they were; abjuring all showy brushwork, they would make their art the mirror of reality. Taking heart from the natural observation they saw in art from before the time of Raphael and the High Renaissance, they and a small group of colleagues of a similar persuasion, including Dante Gabriel Rossetti, decided to call themselves the Pre-Raphaelite Brotherhood (PRB; *see* PRE-RAPHAELITISM). The excited discussion that led to the formation of the PRB took place at Millais's house, 83 Gower Street, in September 1848.

Millais's first major Pre-Raphaelite composition, *Isabella* (Liverpool, Walker A.G.), from Keats's poem *Isabella, or the Pot of Basil* (for illustration *see* PRE-RAPHAELITISM), was exhibited at the Royal Academy in 1849. It shows the use of portraiture as an antidote to idealization, the stiffness of pose intended to recall medieval art, the minute, all-over detailing and the high colour key that characterize early Pre-Raphaelitism. In the following year his *Christ in the Carpenter's Shop* (London, Tate; see fig. 1), with its ungainly Christ, emaciated Virgin and Joseph with dirty fingernails, was offered as a realistic corrective to traditional images of the Holy Family and received as a piece of wilful blasphemy. From 1852, however, when he exhibited *Ophelia* (London, Tate) and *A Huguenot* (Makins priv. col.), he enjoyed increasing public and critical acclaim, leading to his election as ARA in 1853. With its pathetic subject of star-crossed lovers caught up in a historical conflict, *A Huguenot* was especially popular. In 1856 it became Millais's first work to be published as a print, and he painted several versions of it, as well as such variations on the same basic theme as the *Black Brunswicker* (1859–60; Port Sunlight, Lady Lever A.G.).

Millais spent the summer of 1853 on holiday in Scotland with Ruskin, the critic and champion of Pre-Raphaelitism, and Ruskin's wife Effie, who had modelled for the *Order of Release* (1852–3; London, Tate). He began his portrait of *John Ruskin* (1853–4; priv. col.; *see* RUSKIN, JOHN, fig.1) at Brig o' Turk, where he and Effie fell in love. Their marriage on 3 July 1855 provoked scandal, and soon afterwards they settled in Perth, near Effie's parents. Later that year Millais painted *Autumn Leaves* (Manchester, C.A.G.; see fig. 2), an experiment in suppressing narrative content in the interests of mood and aesthetic effect. Hitherto, his major works had related stories, with heroes and heroines depicted in settings full of clues to what had

happened and what was to come. *Autumn Leaves*, which simply shows a group of girls building a bonfire of dead leaves at sunset, evokes a universal theme, the transience of life, rather than any specific narrative. The girls' gestures and expressions are strangely solemn, as if they are engaged in some sacrament. Because the scene is set at twilight, the painting is less tightly detailed than Millais's earlier Pre-Raphaelite work, and the slight blurring of details enhances an overall dreaminess. Millais produced several other pictures in a similar vein, notably *A Dream of the Past: Sir Isumbras at the Ford* (1856-7; Port Sunlight, Lady Lever A.G.) and the *Vale of Rest* (1858-9; London, Tate). The former was attacked by Ruskin, and both pictures proved difficult to sell. Subsequently Millais reverted to more accessible and easily likeable subject-matter.

Though primarily a painter, Millais was a leading figure in the boom in wood-engraved book and magazine illustration that took place in the 1850s and 1860s (*see* BOOK ILLUSTRATION, §IV). His first important commission was for designs for Edward Moxon's edition of Tennyson (1857), illustrated by the Pre-Raphaelites and others. From 1859 he contributed regularly to the magazine *Once a Week* and from 1860 illustrated a series of Anthony Trollope's novels: *Framley Parsonage* (published in the *Cornhill Magazine*, 1860–61), *Orley Farm* (published in parts, 1861–2) and *The Small House at Allington* (*Cornhill Magazine*, 1862–4). His career as an illustrator reached its climax with the celebrated *Parables of Our Lord*, which appeared first in *Good Words* in 1863, then as a separate

2. John Everett Millais: *Autumn Leaves*, oil on canvas, 1041×736 mm, 1855 (Manchester, City Art Gallery)

volume in 1864. After that date his output in this field declined rapidly. No doubt he became more conscious of the inferior professional status of illustrative work with his election as an RA in 1863.

2. Later career, 1863–96. The most important new development in Millais's art in the early 1860s was the painting of sweet, simple pictures of pretty children. Living in London from 1861 in a comfortable home in Cromwell Place, he was by now very much the Victorian family man and doting father, and his models were often his own offspring. Eventually he was to use his grandchildren too. His first major work in this vein was *My First Sermon* (London, Guildhall), exhibited in 1863. It shows his daughter Effie sitting attentively in a pew. The diploma picture he submitted to the Academy in 1868 was also a child subject, *Souvenir of Velázquez* (London, RA), and his 1886 picture of his grandson Willie James as *Bubbles* (London, A. & F. Pears Ltd) became famous as an advertisement for Pears's soap (*see* EPHEMERA, PRINTED, fig. 3). The childhood theme was a mainstay of his later career; his serious historical compositions, which he continued to paint, though less frequently, tended to feature children too: for example the *Boyhood of Raleigh* (1869–70; London, Tate) and the *Princes in the Tower* (1878; Egham, U. London, Royal Holloway & Bedford New Coll.).

By the end of the 1860s Millais had developed a painterly technique and a taste for the Old Masters that ran quite contrary to the Pre-Raphaelite principles of his youth. His later style pays homage to Velázquez, to Hals and, above all, to 18th-century English portraiture. With the 1868 pendants *Stella* (Manchester, C.A.G.) and *Vanessa* (Liverpool, Walker A.G.), he began a line in paintings of attractive young women in 18th-century fancy dress, which helped to fuel an 18th-century revival that affected art, architecture and fashion alike. His triple portrait *Hearts are Trumps* (1872; London, Tate) is a variation on a theme provided by Reynolds's portrait of the *Ladies Waldegrave* (1781; Edinburgh, N.G.), and the picture of a little girl in a mob-cap entitled *Cherry Ripe* (1879; priv. col., see Millais, 1899, ii, p. 119) alludes to that artist's portrait of *Penelope Boothby* (priv. col., on loan to Oxford, Ashmolean). Reynolds became Millais's touchstone, especially when it came to the depiction of children. The *Discourses* urged the modern artist to make quotations and borrowings from the art of the past, so in painting 'souvenirs' of Reynolds's works Millais was in fact following that advice.

From about 1870 Millais built up an impressive portrait practice, imparting a strong sense of character to his sitters by accentuating texture and colour, particularly in the treatment of complexions; like Velázquez and Hals he achieved a concentration on pose and facial expression by using featureless backgrounds. He painted many of the most prominent figures of the age: *Thomas Carlyle* in 1877, *William Ewart Gladstone* in 1879, *Benjamin Disraeli* in 1881, *Archibald Philip Primrose, 5th Earl of Rosebery* in 1886 and *Sir Arthur Sullivan* in 1888 (all London, N.P.G.), along with *Lillie Langtry* (1878; St Helier, Jersey Museums Service), *Alfred Tennyson* (1881; Port Sunlight, Lady Lever A.G.) and *Henry Irving* (1883; London, Garrick Club). There was also a steady flow of commissions to paint

society ladies and the children of the rich in a style that recalled the aristocratic elegance of the 18th century. Prices varied, but for a three-quarter- or full-length portrait he would typically charge £1000.

Millais usually spent his holidays in Scotland, staying with his wife's parents in Perth and further up the River Tay, in and around Birnam and Dunkeld, where he enjoyed shooting and fishing. Beginning in 1870 with the view of a windswept backwater entitled *Chill October* (priv. col., on loan to Perth, Tayside, Mus. & A.G.), he expressed his taste for the scenery along the Tay in a series of large autumn and winter landscapes that are remarkably unpicturesque in both content and composition. The unrelieved marshland of *Murthly Moss* (1887; priv. col., see Millais, 1899, ii, p. 201) and the impenetrable undergrowth of *Dew-drenched Furze* (1890; priv. col., see Millais, 1899, ii, p. 295) are characteristic of the raw natural material, bleak and moody, that he delighted in treating. Free from the self-conscious traditionalism that marks much of Millais's later work, the landscapes possess a grandeur and a sense of mystery that he seldom achieved with other types of subject-matter.

Millais was created a baronet in 1885—the first painter to be so honoured—and elected PRA in the last year of his life.

2. WORKING METHODS AND TECHNIQUE. Millais seems to have had little difficulty with the precision of touch and detail that was demanded by the early Pre-Raphaelite manner. Indeed, it was his obvious technical brilliance, though applied to a style of which many disapproved, that ensured that the work of the PRB was at least noticed. Like Holman Hunt, Millais worked with small brushes, occasionally floating translucent colours over a wet white ground to achieve a high degree of luminosity. This was a painstaking process, especially when practised out of doors (for the greatest possible truth to nature), as with the background to *Ophelia*. Millais grew gradually impatient with the rigours of Pre-Raphaelitism, however, and in the later 1850s experimented with a technique that was softer and less time-consuming, notably in *Autumn Leaves*. By the end of the 1860s this continuing tendency had prompted, and been reinforced by, a conversion to the painterly virtuosity of the Old Masters, and works such as the *Souvenir of Velázquez* show a bravura taken almost to the point of exaggeration. His pure landscapes and some of his landscape backgrounds he continued to paint outdoors from nature, but they were far less elaborate than the landscape elements in his Pre-Raphaelite works, relying more on general effect than on the observation of minutiae.

3. PATRONS, DEALERS AND ENGRAVERS. In his early career Millais enjoyed the patronage of sympathetic individuals with whom he was on close terms. He understood their particular tastes and could cater to them. In 1851 he painted the *Return of the Dove to the Ark* (Oxford, Ashmolean) to suit his High Church friend THOMAS COMBE, and the portrait of Ruskin that he painted in 1853–4 reflects an enthusiasm for the critic's ideas that was fired by personal contact. As he became better known and more sought after on the open market, Millais was

taken up by the important London art dealers Gambart in the 1850s and Agnew's from the 1860s, and it was through them that his work reached leading collectors such as B. G. Windus, William Graham, Samuel Mendel (1810/11–84) and Albert Grant. The dealers inevitably encouraged him (perhaps to the detriment of his art) to repeat his most popular compositions in thinly disguised variations and to aim for a broad common ground of taste. He did this so successfully that he became the wealthiest and most celebrated artist of his time, living in splendour in an imposing mansion at 2 Palace Gate, London, from 1878 until his death. By 1885 he is reported to have been earning £30,000 a year.

His main forum was always the Royal Academy exhibition, but he also contributed to the new exhibitions that sprang up in competition in the 1870s, particularly those at the Grosvenor Gallery. The reviewers noticed Millais from the beginning of his exhibiting career, recognized him as the coming man in the later 1850s and 1860s, and from the 1870s afforded him more attention than any other artist. His popularity among the public was spread by means of prints after his paintings, usually mezzotints by such leading engravers as Thomas Oldham Barlow and Samuel Cousins. Indeed he could generally expect his publishers (most commonly Henry Graves or Agnew's) to pay as much for the copyright of a suitable picture as for the picture itself. His child subjects were especially in demand, and the most successful of all the prints made from his works was the chromolithograph of *Cherry Ripe* published in the *Graphic* magazine in 1880, which sold 600,000 copies.

BIBLIOGRAPHY

W. Armstrong: 'Sir John Millais, RA: His Life and Work', *A. J.* [London] (1885) [Christmas number]
M. H. Spielmann: *Millais and his Works* (London, 1898)
A. L. Baldry: *Sir John Everett Millais: His Art and Influence* (London, 1899)
J. G. Millais: *The Life and Letters of Sir John Everett Millais*, 2 vols (London, 1899)
M. Lutyens: *Millais and the Ruskins* (London, 1967)
Millais: PRB, PRA (exh. cat. by M. Bennett; London, RA; Liverpool, Walker A.G.; 1967)
M. Bennett: 'Footnotes to the Millais Exhibition', *Liverpool Bull.*, xii (1967), pp. 32–59
E. Morris: 'The Subject of Millais's *Christ in the House of his Parents*', *J. Warb. & Court. Inst.*, xxxiii (1970), pp. 343–5
M. Lutyens, ed.: 'Letters from Sir John Everett Millais and William Holman Hunt in the Henry E. Huntington Library', *Walpole Soc.*, xliv (1974), pp. 1–93
M. Warner: 'John Everett Millais and the Society of Arts', *J. Royal Soc. A.*, cxxiv (1976), pp. 754–7
M. Mason: 'The Way We Look Now', *A. Hist.*, i (1978), pp. 309–40 [Millais's illustrations to Trollope]
M. Warner: 'Notes on Millais's Use of Subjects from the Opera, 1851–4', *Pre-Raphaelite Rev.*, ii (1978), pp. 73–6
G. Millais: *Sir John Everett Millais* (London, 1979)
The Drawings of John Everett Millais (exh. cat. by M. Warner, ACGB, 1979)
N. J. Hall: *Trollope and his Illustrators* (London, 1980)
M. Warner: 'John Everett Millais: Drawings from 7 to 18 Years', *Six Children Draw* (exh. cat., ed. S. Paine; U. London, Inst. Educ., 1981), pp. 9–22, 93–4
L. Oakley: 'The Evolution of Sir John Everett Millais's *Portia*', *Met. Mus. J.*, xvi (1982), pp. 181–94
M. Lutyens and M. Warner, eds: *Rainy Days at Brig o' Turk: The Highland Sketchbooks of John Everett Millais, 1853* (Westerham, 1983)
J. Treuherz: 'The Cat and the Cradle', *J. Warb. & Court. Inst.*, xlvi (1983), pp. 240–42 [on Millais's *A Flood* of 1870]
M. Warner: 'John Everett Millais's *Autumn Leaves*: "A Picture Full of Beauty and without Subject"', *Pre-Raphaelite Papers*, ed. L. Parris (London, 1984)
——: *The Professional Career of John Everett Millais to 1863, with a Catalogue of Works to the Same Date* (diss., U. London, 1985)
For a full bibliography up to 1965 see W. E. Fredeman: *Pre-Raphaelitism: A Bibliocritical Study* (Cambridge, MA, 1965), pp. 138–44, 289–95.

For further bibliography *see* PRE-RAPHAELITISM.

MALCOLM WARNER

Millan, Carlos B(arjas) (*b* São Paulo, 29 Aug 1927; *d* 5 Dec 1964). Brazilian architect. He graduated from the School of Architecture at Mackenzie University, São Paulo, in 1951 and in the same year won the student prize at the first Biennale in São Paulo. His early work showed the influence of Marcel Breuer's and Walter Gropius's work in New England; like almost all his generation of architects in Brazil, he was also influenced by Rino Levi and Oswaldo Arthur Bratke. This phase of his work culminated in the O. Fujiwara house (1954), which shows a complete mastery of construction techniques in stone and wood, while also revealing the limitations of the craftsmanship available to him. His preoccupation with the social and economic development of Brazil led him then to change direction: by rationalizing construction methods and using prefabricated components, he sought a compromise between technological development and the unskilled labour that is abundant in Brazilian cities. An important work of this more mature phase is the R. Millan house (1960), Rua Alberto Faria, São Paulo, which received an honourable mention in the 6th Biennale in São Paulo and is often studied by students for its regular structure, exposed prefabricated concrete elements and a central two-storey hall integrating internal and external spaces. Of the same period are some single-storey blocks of flats on pilotis, such as the N. Oliveira house (1960) and his own house (designed 1963; unexecuted), both in São Paulo. Other important works include his designs for the Faculty of Philosophy, Letters and Human Sciences (1961–2) at the University of São Paulo, the church of N S Aparecida (1962) at São Caetano do Sul, São Paulo, and the prize-winning competition entry for the 4th Zone Air Barracks (1963) at São Paulo. He taught at the Mackenzie University from 1957 and the University of São Paulo from 1958.

BIBLIOGRAPHY

'Sede Social do Jockey Club de São Paulo', *Acrópole*, 259 (1960), pp. 159–65
'Carlos Millan', *Acrópole*, 317 (1965), pp. 21–44; 332 (1966), pp. 19-42 [special feature]

PAULO J. V. BRUNA

Millán, Pedro (*fl* Seville, 1487; *d* before 1526). Spanish sculptor and wood-carver. He was trained by Nufro Sánchez, one of the artists responsible for the choir-stalls in Seville Cathedral. Millán is documented as working on the high altar retable of Seville Cathedral in 1507–8, where two scenes depicting the *Meeting of Joachim and Anna at the Golden Gate* and the *Birth of the Virgin* can be attributed to him. The only earliest known work in wood attributed to him is the statue of *St Agnes* on the portal of S Inés, Seville. Although he was a good wood-carver, Millán is better known for his work in polychrome terracotta. The signed archivolt prophets on the baptism portal of the west façade of Seville Cathedral show that he was influenced by Lorenzo Mercadante de Bretaña, who had earlier worked there. Other works by Millán in polychrome terracotta, made for the chapel of S Laureano in Seville Cathedral, are a *Man of Sorrows* (Seville, Mus. B.-A.) from El Garrobo (Huelva), a *Lamentation* group (St Petersburg, Hermitage) from Aracena Abbey near Seville and a *Deposition* (Seville, Mus. B.-A.). Also in Seville Cathedral are a signed terracotta statue of the *Virgen del Pilar* in the chapel of Our Lady and a *St James the Greater* (1506). In 1504 Millán made a tondo in maiolica depicting *SS Cosmas and Damian* for the portal of S Paula, Seville, which also incorporated work imported from the della Robbia workshop in Florence. He also made *Christ at the Column* (Seville, Mus. B.-A.) for S Inés, Seville, and a *St Michael* from the convent of S Florentina de Ecija (London, V&A).

Millán's style is eclectic and characterized by a 'lyric realism'. It has been suggested that he may have been of Netherlandish origin but, although his style is firmly rooted in the traditions of Netherlandish Gothic, other characteristics are Spanish, such as the three-dimensional rather than linear treatment of forms and the gentle physiognomies; it is therefore more likely that he was influenced by Seville.

BIBLIOGRAPHY
A. Durán Sanpere and A. Ainaud de Lasarte: *Escultura gótica*, A. Hisp., v (Madrid, 1956)
T. Müller: *Sculpture in the Netherlands, Germany, France and Spain, 1400–1500*, Pelican Hist. A. (Harmondsworth, 1966)
F. Pérez-Embid: *Pedro Millán y los orígenes de la escultura en Sevilla* (Madrid, 1972)
M. F. Morón de Castro: 'Análisis histórico-estilístico', *El retablo mayor de la catedral de Sevilla* (Seville, 1981), pp. 121–72
——: 'La "Lamentación" del imaginero Pedro Millán en el Museo del Ermitage', *Revista Laboratorio de arte* (Seville, 1994)

M. FERNANDA MORÓN DE CASTRO

Millares, Manolo [Manuel] (*b* Las Palmas de Gran Canaria, 17 Feb 1926; *d* Madrid, 14 Aug 1972). Spanish painter. From 1948 he was influenced by Surrealism, which had been a major force in the Canary Islands since the 1930s. Following the example of Paul Klee and Joan Miró, in 1949 he began to make paintings that employed abstract motifs such as circles, spirals, squares, rhomboids and triangles as symbols, basing his language on the indigenous art of the Canary Islands; these were known by 1952 as *pictografías canarias*. He remained in Las Palmas until his move to Madrid in 1955, enthusiastically supporting new trends in art and poetry and founding and directing *Los arqueros del arte contemporáneo*, a series of monographs on contemporary artists. Millares's reputation was already established by the time he arrived in Madrid, and in 1957 he was a founder-member there of the El Paso group. He was particularly active within the group and exhibited his work internationally.

Millares began producing his most characteristic work *c.* 1955, using such materials as sewn sackcloth in such works as *Composition 9* (whiting and lampblack on burlap and string, 1957; New York, MOMA). He worked primarily in black and white, his initial preference for black gradually giving way to white after 1969. His use of sackcloth was inspired by the clothes used to shroud the mummies of the original inhabitants of the Canary Islands.

What could be seen in the picture, gradually gaining in volume, was a human body, shattered and tortured, a contradictory testimony to the power of life. Millares frequently made use of waste material, including old shoes and clothing that seemed to have come his way by chance, but he formalized such elements and presented them with sombre drama and existential anguish. From 1958 his treatment of the body gradually became more overt, for example in *Painting 150* (1961; London, Tate), in which he represented a pre-human form that he called 'homunculus' in sackcloth on a larger scale and with an increased emphasis on its volume.

BIBLIOGRAPHY
J. Ayllón: *Millares* (Madrid, 1952)
J. M. Moreno Galván: *Manolo Millares* (Barcelona, 1970)
Millares: Manuel Millares 1926–1972 (exh. cat., Madrid, Mus. A. Contemp., 1975)
J.-A. França: *Millares* (Barcelona, 1977)

JOSÉ CORREDOR-MATHEOS

Miller, Alfred Jacob (*b* Baltimore, MD, 10 Jan 1810; *d* Baltimore, 1874). American painter. From 1831–2 he studied with the portrait painter Thomas Sully in Philadelphia, PA. In 1832 he went to France, where he studied in Paris at the Ecole des Beaux-Arts. He also visited Rome before returning to Baltimore, to open a portrait studio in 1834. Three years later Miller moved to New Orleans, LA, and was engaged by Captain William Drummond Stewart to accompany an expedition to the Rocky Mountains. The journey brought Miller into close contact with the Native Americans, whose hunting and social customs he depicted in 200 watercolour sketches, and with the Far West fur trappers at their annual trading gatherings. He was one of the first artists to leave a detailed visual account of the life of the American mountain men (*see* WILD WEST AND FRONTIER ART). Miller's Rocky Mountain paintings are among the most romantic images of the American West ever created. His works are often panoramic and dramatic, yet he was equally adept at depicting charming, intimate scenes. His free, vigorous painting style brings to life both the Native American and the rugged pioneer. Such paintings as the *Lost Greenhorn* (1837; Cody, WY, Buffalo Bill Hist. Cent.; watercolour version, Baltimore, MD, Walters A.G.; sepia wash version, Omaha, NE, Joslyn A. Mus.) and the *Trapper's Bride* (Omaha, NE, Joslyn A. Mus.) convey the drama, danger and picturesque qualities of the American West of his day.

Following the expedition Miller returned to New Orleans and then to Baltimore, where he resumed his career as a portrait painter. In 1840 he travelled to Scotland to execute a series of paintings based on his Western sketches for Captain Stewart's hunting lodge in Perthshire. By 1842 he had returned to Baltimore and his portrait studio. A collection of 200 of Miller's watercolours (1859–60) is in the Walters Art Gallery, Baltimore.

BIBLIOGRAPHY
W. H. Hunter: *The Paintings of Alfred Jacob Miller* (Baltimore, 1930)
A Descriptive Catalogue of a Collection of Watercolour Drawings by Alfred Jacob Miller in the Public Archives of Canada (Ottawa, 1951)
M. C. Ross: *The West of Alfred Jacob Miller* (Norman, OK, 1951/R Baltimore, 1968)
M. Bell: *Braves and Buffalo* (Toronto, 1973)
W. R. Johnston: 'Alfred Jacob Miller: Would-be Illustrator', *Walters A.G. Bull.*, xxx/3 (1977), pp. 2–3

Pictures from an Expedition: Early Views of the American West (exh. cat. by M. A. Sandweiss, New Haven, CT, Yale, Cent. Amer. A., 1979)
Alfred Jacob Miller: Artist on the Oregon Trail (exh. cat., ed. R. Tyler; Baltimore, Walters A.G.; Fort Worth, TX, Amon Carter Mus.; 1981–2) [incl. cat. rais. by K. D. Reynolds and W. R. Johnston]

LESLIE HEINER

Miller, Dorothy C(anning) (*b* Hopedale, MA, 6 Feb 1904). American museum official, writer and art consultant. She studied at Smith College, Northampton, MA, and New York University before she began her long association with MOMA, New York. She served the museum as assistant to the director in 1934; as associate curator of painting and sculpture, 1935–43; curator of painting and sculpture, 1943–7; curator of the museum collections, 1947–67; and as senior curator of painting and sculpture, 1967–9. Miller also edited many of the MOMA exhibition catalogues, writing biographical entries and selecting illustrations. Her interests ranged across all modern American art but concentrated on younger painters and sculptors through influential group exhibitions such as *The New American Painting* (1958), which through its European tour confirmed Abstract Expressionism as a major 20th-century movement, and *16 Americans* (1959), at which artists such as Jasper Johns and Frank Stella gained their first substantial exposure.

Miller always maintained an active civic life, holding positions with the Mark Rothko Foundation, the Gottlieb Foundation, the Port Authority of New York and New Jersey, and the Art Committee of Chase Manhattan Bank. After her retirement she continued to serve as an art adviser and consultant to many corporations and private collectors.

WRITINGS
ed.: *Charles Sheeler* (exh. cat., New York, MOMA, 1939)
The New American Painting (exh. cat., New York, MOMA, 1958)

DAVID M. SOKOL

Miller, Godfrey (Clive) (*b* Wellington, New Zealand, 20 Aug 1893; *d* Sydney, 10 May 1964). Australian painter. After completing his architectural studies in Wellington in 1917, he met the Dunedin painter A. H. O'Keefe and determined to be an artist. He was able to do this with the assistance of a private income. He travelled to China, Japan and the Philippines and in 1919–20 moved to Warrandyte, on the outskirts of Melbourne, where he began painting. He studied intermittently in London from 1929, with some attendance at the Slade School of Fine Art, and travelled extensively through Europe and the Middle East until the beginning of World War II, when he returned to Australia and lived in Sydney.

Miller's arrival in Sydney marked a development in his work from conventional landscapes and some Cubist-style experiments towards a mosaic-like picture surface, which became characteristic for the remainder of his career. His paintings of still-lifes (e.g. *Still-life with Musical Instruments*, 1950–60; Melbourne, N.G. Victoria), landscapes and the human form, broken down into tiny geometric divisions, reflected not so much a regional version of Post-Impressionism as a mystical philosophy derived from the artist's early interests in the ancient cultures of the Middle East and Asia. The resolution between unity and fragmentation in his paintings was to Miller a counterpart to the forces of continuity in the universe.

In 1948 Miller began to teach at the National Art School in Sydney. His first exhibition, in Sydney in 1957, followed by a retrospective at the National Gallery of Victoria two years later, established his reputation as a modern Australian painter of distinction, unconventional but legendary in his impact upon the generation of artists who came directly in contact with him. In 1961 the Tate Gallery purchased his *Triptych with Figures* (*c.* 1944–50) from the exhibition *Recent Australian Painting* at the Whitechapel Art Gallery in London.

BIBLIOGRAPHY
Godfrey Miller (exh. cat., Melbourne, N.G. Victoria, 1959)
Recent Australian Painting (exh. cat., London, Whitechapel A.G., 1961)
J. Henshaw, ed.: *Godfrey Miller* (Sydney, 1965)

BARRY PEARCE

Miller, John Douglas (*b* Hadley, nr London, 1860; *d* 1903). English engraver. He produced mainly portraits, after such painters as Joshua Reynolds, George Richmond, Luke Fildes and Frank Dicksee, but he also engraved such figure compositions as Leighton's *Invocation* (1889; C. Gridley priv. col.), published in January 1893 by Arthur Tooth & Sons. Douglas's style is particularly soft, more like that of 18th-century pure mezzotints than that of the mixed mezzotints, which had become so popular in the mid-19th century. Ten examples of his work were exhibited at the Royal Academy between 1882 and 1893.

BIBLIOGRAPHY
Engen

ANTHONY DYSON

Miller, John Harmsworth. *See under* COLQUHOUN AND MILLER.

Miller, Kenneth Hayes (*b* Oneida, NY, 11 March 1876; *d* 1 Jan 1952). American painter and teacher. He studied with Kenyon Cox and William Merritt Chase before travelling to Europe in 1899. In the same year he also joined the staff of the New York School of Art. In 1911 he moved to the Art Students League, where he taught intermittently until 1951. As leader of the 14th Street school of urban genre painting, Miller was one of the most influential teachers of American artists since Robert Henri; his students included Isabel Bishop, Edward Hopper, George Bellows, Reginald Marsh and George Tooker (*b* 1920). His early work consists of romantic depictions of nude or semi-nude figures inhabiting dreamlike landscapes (e.g. *The River*, 1919; Chicago, IL, A. Inst.), evocative of the work of his close friend Albert Pinkham Ryder.

For a period in 1919 Miller worked in the style of Auguste Renoir, but he soon became more interested in Renaissance composition and techniques, including the use of underpainting and glazes. From the early 1920s he began to concentrate on painting contemporary themes with allusions to Renaissance compositions, for example *Ice Skaters, after the 'Conversion of St Paul' by Signorelli* (1942; ex-William Benton priv. col., see Rothschild, fig. 92). In 1923 he acquired a studio on 14th Street, New York, near Union Square, in the heart of a shopping district. His greatest subject was the sociology of women shoppers, seen in such works as the *Shoppers in Passing* (1926; Washington, DC, Phillips Col.), and the consumer culture of bargain hunters at S. Klein's department store. In their classical poses and formalized compositions, Miller's shoppers become ovoid and columnar forms in cloche hats and chokers, a study of geometricized volumes in space trying to inhabit a single shallow picture plane. Although his work was immensely popular during his own lifetime, he was all but forgotten during the 1950s and 1960s; it was not until the 1970s that Miller's work was greeted with renewed critical acclaim.

BIBLIOGRAPHY
L. Goodrich: *Kenneth Hayes Miller* (New York, 1930)
L. Rothschild: *To Keep Art Alive: The Effort of Kenneth Hayes Miller, American Painter (1876–1952)* (Philadelphia, 1974)
L. Alloway: 'Art', *The Nation*, 210 (1979), pp. 412–13
M. H. Young: 'The Fourteenth Street School', *Apollo*, n.s. 1, cxiii/229 (1981), pp. 164–71

M. SUE KENDALL

Miller, Lee [Elizabeth; Lady Penrose] (*b* Poughkeepsie, NY, 23 April 1907; *d* Chiddingly, E. Sussex, 21 July 1977). American photographer. She studied art briefly in Paris, before studying painting, theatrical design and lighting at the Art Students League in New York (1927–8). From 1927 she worked as a model, photographer and writer for *Vogue*. Between 1929 and 1932 she lived with Man Ray in Paris and collaborated on photographs; together they developed the solarization process, seen in Miller's portrait of a woman, *Paris* (1930; *see* PHOTOGRAPHY, fig. 5). She was a friend of Picasso and the community of Surrealists in Paris and in 1947 married Roland Penrose. From 1929 to 1934 she ran her own photographic studios in New York and then Paris, where her elegant portraits became widely sought after. After working as an independent photographer in the Middle East (1937–9), she became a member of the London War Correspondents Corps and worked for British *Vogue*. From 1944 to 1945 Miller was a war correspondent for the magazine in France, Germany, Romania and on the Russian Front. Her early war photographs were the inspiration for the book *Grim Glory*, intended to heighten American awareness of the war; photographs such as *Revenge on Culture* (1940; *see* Penrose, 1985, p. 107) demonstrate her affinity with Surrealist imagery. After World War II she worked as a freelance photographer.

PHOTOGRAPHIC PUBLICATIONS
Contributions to *Vogue*

BIBLIOGRAPHY
E. Carter, ed.: *Grim Glory: Pictures of Britain under Fire*, preface E. R. Murrow (New York, 1940)
K. M. Palmer: *Wrens in Camera* (London, 1945)
N. Hall-Duncan: *The History of Fashion Photography* (New York, 1979)
A. Penrose: *The Lives of Lee Miller* (New York, 1985)
A. Penrose, ed.: *Lee Miller's War* (London, 1992)

MARY CHRISTIAN

Miller, Sanderson (*b* Radway, Warwicks, *bapt* 9 Aug 1716; *d* London, 23 April 1780). English architect and landscape designer. He was an amateur architect who fostered his career with the aim of turning professional should the financial need arise. Miller's architectural work was very much part of a busy social life and the day-to-day demands of running his own estate at Radway Grange,

Edgehill (Warwicks). His earliest work was the construction of Radway's terrace (1739) to give a view of the neighbouring Civil War battlefield, where newly planted clumps represented the combatants' positions. The thatched cottage (1743–4) that he built on the brow of Edgehill was calculated to give the appearance of a blasted stone fortress appropriated to domestic use. It was followed by the widely celebrated Edgehill Castle Tower (1745–7), modelled on one at Warwick Castle, the highest room of which was resplendently embellished with heraldic decoration, stained glass and Gothick plasterwork. A ruined arch was added (1749–50), completing an ensemble that presented a powerful skyline at Edgehill's summit. In contrast to the bold simplicity of these buildings, Miller's improvements of the same period to Radway Grange were more delicate, and his drawing for Radway's canted-bay windows (1746) reveal him to have been a competent draughtsman and original designer in Gothick by this time. Both Radway and Farnborough (from 1745), Warwicks, were original landscape designs that depended on the surrounding scenery to heighten their impact. At Radway the landscape was dominated by the brooding, Gothick mass on the skyline; Farnborough was given a bold, ascending terrace punctuated by classical buildings. Miller's experience of creative and practical land management also involved him in more conventional landscape designs, and at Wroxton Abbey (from 1744), Oxon, Hagley Hall (from 1748), Hereford & Worcs, and Honington Hall (1749), Warwicks, a succession of Gothick, classical or chinoiserie buildings and waterworks were linked by winding walks.

Miller's success at Edgehill brought requests for sham castle ruins at Hagley Hall (1748; *see* GARDEN, fig. 52), and Wimpole Hall (designed 1749–50, built 1772), Cambs. They reveal his growing sophistication and sense of authenticity in design, although Radway's bay windows were repeated in essence in the new front for Adlestrop Park (designed 1750), Glos, and at Arbury Hall (1751–2), Warwicks. Miller's Gothick interiors displayed greater variety, although often the medieval atmosphere was achieved largely by lightly applied ornament rather than archaeological correctness. Arbury Hall's dressing-room was carried out in conjunction with its owner, Sir Roger Newdigate (1719–1806), and the rooms at Belhus (1752–7), Essex, involved yet another owner–amateur, Thomas Barrett Lennard (afterwards 17th Lord Dacre); but Durham Castle's dining-room (1751–2) and All Souls Old Library (1751) at Oxford are by Miller alone. His Gothick schemes were to reach their peak in the airy and spectacular Great Hall at Lacock Abbey (1753–6; *see* ENGLAND, fig. 7), Wilts, for which he provided full designs, even supplying large-scale details for the workmen. Other Gothick projects included garden buildings at Enville (1750–55), Staffs, and Wroxton Abbey (1750–60).

Miller's classical work was less adventurous. Hagley Hall (1754–60) was a complex committee job involving John Chute and Thomas Prowse (1708–67) as well as Miller (who supervised the building work). Warwick's Shire Hall (1752–8) involved Prowse once again, but here Miller's own wishes took precedence. Generally he collaborated happily with other self-taught builders and architects, for he was also involved with Lancelot Brown and Henry Keene at the start of their careers. His own activities were checked by intermittent attacks of insanity in later years, and he built little after 1760. Accurate assessment of Miller's contribution to and influence upon the Early Gothic Revival is difficult: few buildings and fewer drawings survive. Certainly he was highly regarded in his day, even by Horace Walpole; in 1755 Miller was hailed by William Pitt the elder as 'the true, great master of Gothick'.

Colvin

BIBLIOGRAPHY

L. Dickins and M. Stanton: *An Eighteenth-century Correspondence* (London, 1910)
A. C. Wood and W. Hawkes: 'Sanderson Miller of Radway and his Work at Wroxton', *Cake & Cockhorse*, iv (1969), pp. 79–110
W. Hawkes: 'The Gothic Architectural Work of Sanderson Miller', *A Gothick Symposium*, intro. J. Mordaunt Crook (London, 1983)

H. W. HAWKES

Milles, Carl (Wilhelm Emil) (*b* Lagga, nr Uppsala, 23 June 1875; *d* Lidingö, nr Stockholm, 19 Sept 1955). Swedish sculptor, teacher and medallist. Having attended the Kungliga Tekniska Högskola in Stockholm (1895–7), he then visited Paris where he remained until 1904 and attended, among others, the Académie Colarossi. During this period he was deeply influenced by Impressionism and by Rodin's sculptures. From 1904 to 1906 he lived in Munich, where he was influenced by the language of form of Adolf von Hildebrand. Having returned to Sweden in 1908, he was appointed Professor at the Konsthögskola, Stockholm (1920–31). In 1931 he moved to the USA and taught (1931–45) at the Cranbrook Academy of Art, Bloomfield Hills, MI. In 1945 he became an American citizen. Milles became a much-esteemed sculptor and carried out numerous official commissions in Swedish cities, including *Europa and the Bull* (1926) in Halmstad, south of Göteborg, the Poseidon Fountain (1927–30) in Göteborg and *Orpheus* (1936) in Stockholm. Works in the USA include the Delaware Monument (1938) in Wilmington, DE, the *Meeting of the Waters* (1940) in St Louis, MO, and the Resurrection Fountain (1950–52) in Falls Church, VA, near Washington, DC. The large villa and studio that he and his wife, Olga, had acquired in 1909 later became a museum, Carl Millesgården, Lidingö, near Stockholm. Here the development of his works, from the early, slightly eclectic pieces to the later, exuberant and occasionally burlesque examples, can be appreciated in the open air. Milles also achieved success as a medallist.

BIBLIOGRAPHY

H. Cornell: *Carl Milles och hans verk* [Carl Milles and his work] (Stockholm, 1963)
U. Abel: *Carl Milles: Form, idé, medaljkonst* [Carl Milles: form, idea, medal art] (Stockholm, 1980)
E. Lidén: *Between Water and Heaven: Carl Milles's Search for American Commissions* (Stockholm, 1986)

JACQUELINE STARE

Millet, Aimé (*b* Paris, 28 Sept 1819; *d* Paris, 14 Jan 1891). French sculptor. Son of a miniature painter, he studied at the Petite Ecole (Ecole Gratuite de Dessin) and the Ecole des Beaux Arts, Paris, where he was a student of David d'Angers. He moved in Romantic circles both during and after his student years and became a close friend of the poet Gérard de Nerval. Belated success came in 1857 when his statue of *Ariadne* (marble version, New York, Met.) won a first-class medal at the Salon. Millet gained a reputation for colossal statuary with his *Vercingetorix*,

erected in 1865 on the site of the Battle of Alesia, Alise-Sainte-Reine, Côte d'Or. Commissioned by Napoleon III, it was executed in beaten copper over an iron frame with technical assistance from Eugène-Emmanuel Viollet-Le-Duc, who later designed the structure of the statue of *Liberty*, New York Harbor. The immense group crowning the Paris Opéra, *Apollo between Dance and Music* (1869–70), was entrusted to Millet on the strength of his experience in producing *Vercingetorix*, although it was later decided that the group should be conventionally cast in bronze. Millet also executed several deeply felt tomb effigies, including the retrospective memorial to *Alphonse Baudin* (bronze, 1872; Paris, Montmartre Cemetery), a Republican representative shot during Napoleon III's coup in 1851.

Lami

BIBLIOGRAPHY

H. Dumesnil: *Aimé Millet: Souvenirs intimes* (Paris, 1891)

PHILIP WARD-JACKSON

Millet, Eugène-Louis (*b* Paris, 21 May 1819; *d* Cannes, 24 Feb 1879). French architect and restorer. He entered the Ecole des Beaux-Arts, Paris, in 1837 and studied under Henri Labrouste. In 1847 he was appointed assistant architect to Viollet-le-Duc in the Commission des Monuments Historiques, and the following year he became architect for diocesan buildings in Troyes (Aube) and Châlons-sur-Marne (Marne). In 1849 he was promoted within the Commission des Monuments Historiques, and thereafter he carried out major restoration work on numerous medieval churches, including St Pierre, Souvigny (Allier), the former abbey church at St Benoît-sur-Loire (Loiret) and Notre-Dame at Paray-le-Monial (Saône-Loire). In 1855 Millet was appointed architect in charge of the château of Saint-Germain-en-Laye, near Paris. On the death of Jean-Baptiste-Antoine Lassus in 1857 he took over the rebuilding of the cathedral at Moulins (Allier), where a Gothic Revival nave was grafted on to a 15th-century choir. In 1863 Millet was appointed Professor of Building at the Ecole des Beaux-Arts, but he resigned two years later. In 1874 he took over the restoration of Reims Cathedral from Viollet-le-Duc, and the same year he succeeded his former teacher Henri Labrouste as Inspector-General of Diocesan Buildings.

Although he is best known as a restoring architect working for the state, Millet also developed a private practice, designing houses, hospitals and churches. These included the Hospice de Greffühle (1869) at Levallois-Perret and a new church at Maisons-sur-Seine (both Hauts-de-Seine). His career was in many ways typical of the period in which he lived, which was characterized by debates and conflicts between the supporters of the Gothic Revival and the supporters of Neo-classicism. However, although he belonged to the group of architects surrounding Viollet-le-Duc, Millet's conception of Gothic was archaeological, rational and rather cold, in contrast to that of the more instinctive and poetic Lassus. He nevertheless earned a reputation for precision and meticulous workmanship. Many highly detailed drawings for his buildings survive, notably those for Moulins and Saint-Germain-en-Laye.

BIBLIOGRAPHY

Encyclopédie de l'architecture, 2nd. ser. (Paris, 1879)
Rev. Archit. & Trav. Pub., xxxvi (Paris, 1879), p. 38
J.-M. Leniaud: *J. B. Lassus, ou le temps retrouvé des cathédrales* (Paris, 1980)
Viollet-le-Duc (exh. cat., Paris, Grand Pal., 1980)
F. Loyer: *Le Siècle de l'industrie, 1789–1914* (Geneva, 1983)
D. Colmont: *Eugène-Louis Millet (1819–1879) et la construction de la nef de la cathédrale de Moulins, 1857–1879* (MA thesis, U. Rennes, 1986)

DOMINIQUE COLMONT

Millet, Francisque [Jean-François] (*b* Antwerp, *bapt* 27 April 1642; *d* Paris, *bur* 23 June 1679). French painter. The little that is known about his life is derived from the chapter on Flemish, German and Dutch painting in Le Comte's work (1699). His oeuvre remains ill-defined, in part because he seems never to have signed his paintings and in part because after his death (by poisoning) both his son Jean Millet (*c.* 1666–1723) and later his grandson Joseph Millet (*c.* 1688–1777) took the name Francisque and continued to paint landscapes in his style. The firmest point of reference for attributions to Millet is a series of 28 engravings after his works (see Davies) made by one

Théodore, possibly a pupil. They are all landscapes, some with religious, mythological or heroic genre subjects, and have been identified with a number of surviving paintings that can therefore be given to Millet on this evidence.

Millet was the son of an ivory-carver from Dijon and a Flemish mother. In 1659 he went to Paris in the company of his master Laureys Franck (*fl* 1622–62), whose daughter he married shortly afterwards. With the exception of journeys to Holland, Flanders and England, he spent the rest of his short life in Paris. He was approved (*agréé*) by the Académie Royale de Peinture et de Sculpture in 1673, exhibiting two pictures (untraced) at that year's Salon. He never became a full member of the Académie Royale. According to Le Comte, he began his career making copies after modern and Old Master paintings for the collector Everard Jabach: the inventory drawn up after Jabach's death in 1695 contains references to 57 paintings by Millet, both copies and original works. Among the copies, works after Nicolas Poussin explain that artist's lasting influence on Millet. Copies after the Carracci family, Guido Reni, Titian and Giulio Romano are also mentioned, indicating

Francisque Millet: *Italian Landscape with Bathers*, oil on canvas, 1.07×1.19 m, *c.* 1670 (Munich, Alte Pinakothek)

a solid grounding in the Italian artistic tradition, while references to Millet's original paintings include a *Still-life with Birds*, a *Sea Port*, a *Murder in a Cave* (probably a mythological scene), a *St John the Baptist* and a *Judgement of Paris* (all untraced). Le Comte also mentioned a number of important commissions: four paintings (datable to 1666–8) for the Cabinet de la Reine at the Palais des Tuileries, Paris; others for the Président de Bercy; and 26 scenes from Ovid's *Metamorphoses* to decorate the gallery of an unnamed private client (all untraced). Those surviving paintings that can be identified as Millet's work from Théodore's engravings fall into two broad categories of artistic inspiration. In the *Storm* (London, N.G.) or *Italian Landscape with Bathers* (*c.* 1670; Munich, Alte Pin., see fig.) he created scenes of which details seem to have been observed from life. The action, sometimes obscure, takes place in the foreground, but the greatest weight is given to the landscape itself. Despite some similarities to the work of Gaspard Dughet, particularly in the use of thick impasto, this realistic strand in Millet's art is Flemish in derivation. Works such as the *Daughters of Cecrops* (versions, Brussels, Mus. A. Anc.; Petworth House, W. Sussex, NT), on the other hand, are clearly inspired by the classicizing landscapes of Poussin. The *Finding of Moses* (Berlin, Bodemus.) is, moreover, closely related to the art of such followers of Poussin as Nicolas Colombel. The absence of any external evidence to establish a chronology for Millet's paintings means, however, that it is impossible to trace the evolution of his style. He appears to have been relatively prolific, as is suggested by the fact that several of his works are known in more than one version (e.g. *Landscape with a Flock of Sheep*, Hamburg, Ksthalle; Moscow, Pushkin Mus. F.A.; Paris, Petit Pal.). Numerous drawings have been attributed to him; among the few that relate to a known painting is that for *Mountainous Landscape with Five Figures* (drawing, Rouen, Mus. B-A.; version of painting, Southampton, C.A.G.).

BIBLIOGRAPHY

F. Le Comte: *Cabinet des singularitez d'architecture, peinture, sculpture et gravure*, ii (Paris, 1699), pp. 329–32
M. Davies: 'A Note on Francisque Millet', *Bull. Soc. Poussin*, ii (1948), pp. 12–26
M. Roethlisberger: 'Quelques Nouveaux Indices sur Francisque', *Gaz. B.-A.*, 6th ser., lxxvi (1970), pp. 317–24
La Peinture française du XVIIe siècle dans les collections américaines (exh. cat. by P. Rosenberg, Paris, Grand Pal.; New York, Met.; Chicago, A. Inst.; 1982), pp. 290–91, 365
C. Wright: *French Painting of the Seventeenth Century* (London, 1985), pp. 231–2
Masterpieces of Reality: French 17th-century Painting (exh. cat. by C. Wright, Leicester, Mus. & A.G., 1985–6), pp. 123–4

THIERRY BAJOU

Millet, Gabriel (*b* St Louis, Senegal, 1867; *d* Paris, 8 May 1953). French art and architectural historian. His main interest was in Byzantine art of the medieval period, and he was one of the first Western European scholars to take a serious interest in the art of the Palaiologan period (1261–1453). Most of his original research was based on field work undertaken between 1890 and 1914 in Trebizond, Greece and Serbia. This resulted in the publication (1916) of two major works, one relating medieval paintings in Greece to liturgical sources and the other an attempt to develop a classification of regional schools and chronology

in Byzantine architecture. Although some of the methodology is now outdated, these pioneering works are still of value, as are his study of the monastery of Dafni and his albums of illustrative material on the Byzantine monuments at Mystras and Mt Athos. Another major contribution to Byzantine studies was the large photographic library he assembled at the Ecole des Hautes Etudes in Paris. His interests led him to the art and architecture of other regions influenced by Constantinople, especially in the Balkans and the Slavic countries. His study of medieval Serbian churches is still fundamental, and he edited an important collection of papers on the impact of Byzantine art on the Slavs. Millet's work in this field was of particular interest to art historians in the countries of south-eastern Europe who were seeking the roots of their national artistic traditions.

WRITINGS

Le Monastère de Dafni (Paris, 1899)
Monuments byzantins de Mistra (Paris, 1910)
L'Ecole grecque dans l'architecture byzantine (Paris, 1916)
Recherches sur l'iconographie de l'Evangile aux XIVe, XVe et XVIe siècles (Paris, 1916)
L'Ancien Art serbe: Les Eglises (Paris, 1919)
Monuments de l'Athos (Paris, 1927)
ed.: *L'Art byzantin chez les Slaves* (Paris, 1930–32)

BIBLIOGRAPHY

A. Grabar: Obituary, *Byzantion*, xxii (1952), pp. 519–25

SEBASTIAN WORMELL

Millet, Jean-François (*b* Gruchy, nr Gréville, 4 Oct 1814; *d* Barbizon, 20 Jan 1875). French painter, draughtsman and etcher. He is famous primarily as a painter of peasants. Although associated with the BARBIZON SCHOOL, he concentrated on figure painting rather than landscape except during his final years. His scenes of rural society, which nostalgically evoke a lost golden age, are classical in composition but are saturated with Realist detail (*see* REALISM). Millet's art, rooted in the Normandy of his childhood as well as in Barbizon, is also indebted to the Bible and past masters. His fluctuating critical fortunes reflect the shifting social and aesthetic lenses through which his epic representations of peasants have been viewed.

1. Life and work. 2. Working methods and technique.

1. LIFE AND WORK. Born into a prosperous peasant family from Normandy, Millet received a solid general education and developed what became a lifelong interest in literature. After studying with a local portrait painter, Bon Du Mouchel (1807–46), he continued his professional training in Cherbourg with Lucien-Théophile Langlois (1803–45), a pupil of Antoine-Jean Gros. The talented young artist received a stipend from the city of Cherbourg and went to Paris where he entered the atelier of the history painter Paul Delaroche. Frustrated and unhappy there, Millet competed unsuccessfully for the Prix de Rome in 1839 and left the Ecole des Beaux-Arts. One of the two portraits that he submitted to the Salon of 1840 was accepted. In 1840 Millet moved back to Cherbourg and set himself up as a portrait painter, returning the following year to Paris.

1. Jean-François Millet: *The Gleaners*, oil on canvas, 853×1110 mm, 1857 (Paris, Musée d'Orsay)

Millet's early years (*c.* 1841–8) were dominated by portraiture, which represented the most lucrative (and often the only) means for a 19th-century artist to earn a living, especially in the provinces. Such early portraits as his *Self-portrait* (*c.* 1840–41) and the touching effigy of his first wife, *Pauline-Virginie Ono* (1841; both Boston, MA, Mus. F.A.), are characterized by strongly contrasted lighting, dense, smooth brushwork, rigorous simplicity and directness of gaze. The beautiful black conté crayon study of his second wife, *Catherine Lemaire* (*c.* 1848–9; Boston, MA, Mus. F.A.), with its sensitive crayon strokes and monumentality, heralds a new phase in Millet's artistic evolution, which coincided with his move to Barbizon in 1849. After 1845 Millet painted few portraits, although he continued to make portrait drawings. During the 1840s Millet struggled to survive financially in Paris, lost his first wife in 1844 and failed to achieve critical recognition. In addition to portraits, he produced pastoral subjects and nudes during the 1840s. Around 1848 Millet became acquainted with several of the Barbizon artists, notably Théodore Rousseau who became a close friend. Through an arrangement with Alfred Sensier (1815–77), Millet was able to guarantee his family's livelihood.

Millet's epic naturalist style, which surfaced in the peasant scenes he painted after he settled in Barbizon, coincided with the Revolution of 1848 and his escape from the city. From 1849 Millet specialized in rural genre subjects, which melded together current social preoccupations and artistic traditions. In the aftermath of the Revolution these subjects took on socio-political connotations. Rural depopulation and the move to the cities made the peasant a controversial subject. At the Salon of 1850–51, Millet attracted the attention of both conservative and liberal critics with *The Sower* (1850; Boston, MA, Mus. F.A.; *see* PRINTS, fig. 2). The powerful, striding peasant, exhibited in the same year as Gustave Courbet's controversial *Stonebreakers* (destr.) and *Burial at Ornans* (Paris, Mus. d'Orsay), imbued the common man with a sort of epic grandeur. Millet's *Sower* represents the endless cycle of planting and harvesting and physical toil with dignity and compassion. To conservative critics, there was something distinctly disquieting about this hulking, monumental peasant with his forceful gesture and coarse, unidealized features. To progressive critics, however, the art of Millet and Courbet signalled change and the coming of age of the common man as a subject worthy of artistic representation. Yet, ironically, Millet himself was a pessimist who held little hope for reform. In fact, his paintings of peasants often portray archaic farming methods in nostalgic colours and sometimes allude to biblical passages, as in *Harvesters Resting (Ruth and Boaz)* (1850–53; Boston, MA, Mus. F.A.). Millet made numerous preparatory studies for this painting, which he considered his masterpiece and which won him his first official recognition at the Salon of 1853. In this monumental, classicizing harvest scene, Millet paid homage to his heroes, Michelangelo and Nicolas Poussin. The critic Paul de Saint-Victor (1825–81) perceptively described Millet's *Harvesters* as 'a Homeric idyll translated into the local dialect' (*Le Pays*, 13 Aug 1853).

2. Jean-François Millet: *The Angelus*, oil on canvas, 555×660 mm, 1857–9 (Paris, Musée d'Orsay)

In 1857 Millet exhibited *The Gleaners* (Paris, Mus. d'Orsay; see fig. 1) at the Salon. This grandiose canvas represents the summation of Millet's epic naturalism. Three poor peasant women occupy the foreground of the composition, painfully stooping to gather what the harvesters have left behind as they were entitled to by the commune of Chailly. In the background Millet painted with chalky luminosity the flat, fruitful expanse of fields with the harvest taking place. The painting was attacked by conservative critics, such as Saint-Victor, who characterized the gleaners as 'the Three Fates of pauperdom' (*La Presse*, 1857). The three impoverished women, like the figure in *The Sower*, raised the spectre of social insurrection and belied government claims about the eradication of poverty. However, Millet's painting was defended by leftist critics for its truth and honesty. The Realist critic Jules-Antoine Castagnary noted the beauty and simplicity of the composition despite the misery of the women and evoked Homer and Virgil. The monumental, sculptural figures, with their repetitive gestures, are in fact reminiscent of the Parthenon frieze, and the painting itself, despite its apparent naturalism, is composed with

mathematical precision. *The Gleaners*, like Millet's other canvases, both reflects and transfigures the realities of rural life by filtering them through the lenses of memory and past art.

The Angelus (1857–9; Paris, Mus. d'Orsay; see fig. 2), which was commissioned by Boston artist Thomas Gold Appleton (1812–84), exemplifies Millet's fluctuating critical reputation. Its widespread vulgarization and unusually specific subject-matter verging on the mawkish have made it Millet's most popular painting. A young farmer and his wife, silhouetted against the evening sky, pause as the angelus tolls, the woman bowed in prayer, the man awkwardly turning his hat in his hands. In 1889 the painting was the object of a sensational bidding war between the Louvre and an American consortium that bought it for the unprecedented sum of 580,650 francs. Billed as the most famous painting in the world, *The Angelus* was triumphantly toured around the USA. In 1890 Hippolyte-Alfred Chauchard acquired the painting for 800,000 francs, and it entered the Louvre in 1909. However, by that date Millet had fallen out of fashion and the painting became a subject of derision. *The Angelus*, with its rigid gender differentiation, later became a veritable obsession for the Surrealist artist Salvador Dalí.

During the 1860s Millet continued to exhibit peasant subjects, most often single figures. Successful and financially secure, he enjoyed a growing reputation, enhanced by the retrospective of his work held at the Exposition Universelle of 1867 in Paris. In 1868 he was awarded the Légion d'honneur. From 1865 Millet turned frequently to pastels and devoted himself increasingly to landscape painting although he never abandoned the human figure. In particular, he completed the monumental series the *Four Seasons* (1868–74; Paris, Mus. d'Orsay), commissioned by Frédéric Hartmann (*d* 1881) for 25,000 francs. These landscapes, with their loose, painterly brushwork and glowing colour, form the connecting link between the Barbizon school and Impressionism. In 1870 Millet exhibited at the Salon for the last time. At a public sale held in 1872 his works fetched high prices. In 1874 Millet was commissioned to paint murals illustrating the life of St Geneviève for the Panthéon, Paris, which he was unable to carry out. One of his last completed works is the horrifying but hauntingly beautiful *Bird Hunters* (1874; Philadelphia, PA, Mus. A.), which represents an apocalyptic nocturnal vision recollected from his childhood—an elemental drama of light and dark, of life and death. Severely ill, Millet married his second wife, Catherine, in a religious ceremony on 3 January 1875 and died on 20 January. He was buried at Barbizon next to Rousseau.

2. WORKING METHODS AND TECHNIQUE. Millet was an exceptional draughtsman whose drawings have perhaps withstood the test of time better than his paintings. His varied graphic oeuvre ranges from rapid preparatory studies (most often in black crayon) to carefully finished pastels, which he sold to collectors for high prices during the last decade of his career. Drawings, which enabled Millet to perfect his compositions, were the building blocks for his paintings. Millet worked in the traditional manner, sometimes producing numerous preparatory studies for a single painting. In particular, he was a master of light and dark, as such nocturnal scenes as *Twilight* (black conté crayon and pastel on paper, *c.* 1859–63; Boston, MA, Mus. F.A.) attest. Millet's drawings, in their predilection for the expressive effects of black and white, foreshadow those of Georges Seurat and Odilon Redon.

Technically it is Millet's pastels, many of which were commissioned by the collector Emile Gavet (1830–1904), that are the most innovative. Although he had worked in pastel as early as the mid-1840s, Millet turned to the medium with increasing regularity after 1865 and developed an original technique in which he literally drew in pure colour. Beginning with a light chalk sketch, he applied the darks, then rubbed in the pastels to create the substructure and finally built up the surface with mosaic-like strokes of colour. He soon lightened his technique and experimented with different coloured papers, which he allowed to show through in the finished composition. Millet's pastels, in their marriage of line and colour, point forward to Impressionism and Edgar Degas. With typical modesty, Millet referred to his pastels simply as *dessins*.

Although printmaking was never a central activity for Millet, he created in the 1850s and 1860s a series of etchings that often reproduced motifs from his paintings. Millet, like other artists of his generation, was part of the general revival of printmaking in the mid-19th century. He probably began etching about 1855, although Melot (1978) has suggested that he may have begun earlier. Alfred Sensier urged Millet to create a series of etchings from his own designs for commercial publication in the hopes of expanding the market for his art. Millet's etchings, such as *Woman Churning Butter* (1855–6; Delteil, no. 10), illustrate his technical skill with the etching needle although they are generally less forceful than his preparatory drawings. In some instances, however, Millet's etchings anticipate his paintings as in the case of *The Gleaners. Woman Carding Wool* (1855–6; D 15) is one of the most monumental images that Millet created in the etching medium.

Millet's work illustrates the complexity of the Realist enterprise at mid-century. His art is a dialogue between past and present—radical in its humanitarian social creed but traditional in technique and classicizing in composition. Millet's rural subjects are drawn from contemporary social reality but interpreted in a highly personal manner. His art influenced Impressionist and Post-Impressionist painters, notably Camille Pissarro and Vincent van Gogh, who idolized Millet and copied a number of his compositions. Even if the peasant no longer strikes the same sympathetic chords for the 20th-century viewer, one cannot help but be moved by the humble majesty of Millet's ageless figures who fill the gap between earth and sky. The retrospective exhibitions held in Paris and London (1975–6) and Boston, MA (1984), provided comprehensive overviews of Millet's varied oeuvre.

BIBLIOGRAPHY

E. Wheelwright: 'Personal Recollections of Jean-François Millet', *Atlantic Mthly*, 38 (Sept 1876), pp. 257–76
A. Sensier and P. Mantz: *La Vie et l'oeuvre de Jean-François Millet* (Paris, 1881) [primary source]
J. Cartwright: 'The Pastels and Drawings of Millet', *Portfolio* [London], xxi (1890), pp. 191–7, 208–12
——: *Jean-François Millet: His Life and Letters* (London, 1896)
A. Thompson: *Millet and the Barbizon School* (London, 1903)
L. Bénédite: *Les Dessins de J.-F. Millet* (Paris, 1906; Eng. trans., London and Philadelphia, 1906)
L. Delteil: *J.-F. Millet, Th. Rousseau, Jules Dupré, J. Barthold Jongkind* (1906), i of *Le Peintre-graveur illustré* (Paris, 1906–30/*R* 1969) [D]
E. Moreau-Nélaton: *Millet raconté par lui-même*, 3 vols (Paris, 1921)
S. Dalí: 'Interprétation paranoïaco-critique de l'image obsédante de Millet', *Minotaure*, i (1933), pp. 65–7
R. Herbert: 'Millet Revisited', *Burl. Mag.*, civ (1962), pp. 294–305, 377–86
Barbizon Revisited (exh. cat. by R. Herbert, Boston, Mus. F. A., 1962)
S. Dalí: *Le Mythe tragique de l'Angélus de Millet* (Paris, 1963)
R. Herbert: 'Millet Reconsidered', *Mus. Stud.* [A. Inst. Chicago], i (1966), pp. 29–65
——: 'City vs. Country: The Rural Image in French Painting from Millet to Gauguin', *Artforum*, viii/6 (1970), pp. 44–55
L. Lepoittevin: *Jean-François Millet*, 2 vols (Paris, 1971–3)
T. J. Clark: *The Absolute Bourgeois: Artists and Politics in France, 1848–1851* (London, 1973)
R. Herbert: 'Les Faux Millet', *Rev. A.*, 21 (1973), pp. 56–65
R. Bacou: *Millet dessins* (Paris, 1975); Eng. trans. as *Millet: One Hundred Drawings* (London and New York, 1975)
J.-J. Lévêque: *L'Univers de Millet* (Paris, 1975) [drawings; good plates]
Millet et le thème du paysan dans la peinture française au 19e siècle (exh. cat., Cherbourg, Mus. Henry, 1975)
Jean-François Millet (exh. cat. by R. Herbert, Paris, Grand Pal.; London, Hayward Gal.; 1975–6) [best gen. disc. of Millet's work; full bibliog.]
A. Fermigier: *Jean-François Millet* (Geneva, 1977) [good plates]
M. Melot: *L'Oeuvre gravé de Boudin, Corot, Daubigny, Dupré, Jongkind, Millet, Théodore Rousseau* (Paris, 1978)

Jean-François Millet (exh. cat. by A. R. Murphy, Boston, Mus. F.A., 1984) [catalogues extensive Millet holdings of the Museum of Fine Arts, Boston; previously unpubd letters]

K. Powell: 'Jean-François Millet's *Death and the Woodcutter*', *Artsmag*, 61 (1986), pp. 53–9

B. Laughton: 'J.-F. Millet in the Allier and the Auvergne', *Burl. Mag.*, cxxx (1988), pp. 345–51

——: *The Drawings of Daumier and Millet* (New Haven and London, 1991)

B. Laughton and L. Scalisi: 'Millet's *Wood Sawyers* and *La République* Rediscovered', *Burl. Mag.*, cxxxiv (1992), pp. 12–19

HEATHER McPHERSON

Millich, Nicolaas (*b* Antwerp, *c.* 1630; *d* Stockholm, after 1687). Flemish sculptor and architect. He was enrolled as a master sculptor in the Guild of St Luke in Antwerp in 1657–9. In 1664–5 he established himself in Amsterdam where, according to Nicodemus Tessin (i), he became a 'pupil' (more correctly, an assistant) of Rombout Verhulst, who was then engaged on sculptural works for the town hall (now the Koninklijk Paleis). In 1669 Millich travelled to Stockholm, where he was appointed sculptor to the Swedish court. There he began a series of sculptures of the *Nine Muses* for the decoration of the staircase of Drottningholm Slott. He had finished four by the time he returned to Antwerp in 1676. In Antwerp he designed the elegant Baroque spire of St Paul's church, for which he also made the sculptured terms on the corners of the octagonal drum. He also carved two more muses for Drottningholm. He completed the series after his return to Sweden in 1683. Other sculptures by Millich are still extant in Swedish collections. Millich's work exemplifies the Flemish High Baroque, which had taken shape in Antwerp and which was further developed in the workshops of Artus Quellinus I and Verhulst in Amsterdam.

BIBLIOGRAPHY

M. Van Notten: *Rombaut Verhulst sculpteur* (The Hague, 1908), pp. 92–3

O. Sirén: *Nicodemus Tessin D.Y. Studieresor* [Nicodemus Tessin the younger's study trip] (Stockholm, 1914), pp. 42, 71, 79, 245

K. Steneberg: 'Le Blon, Quellinus, Millich and the Swedish Court "Parnassus"', *Queen Christina of Sweden: Documents and Studies*, Analecta Reginiensia, i (Stockholm, 1966), pp. 346–53

F. Baudouin: 'De toren van de Sint-Carolus-Borromeuskerk te Antwerpen', *Acad. Anlct.: Kl. S. Kst.*, xciv/3 (1983), pp. 43–5

FRANS BAUDOUIN

Millin de Grandmaison, Aubin-Louis (*b* Paris, 19 July 1759; *d* Paris, 14 Aug 1818). French antiquarian and art historian. Destined for an ecclesiastical life, he abandoned this to become a scholar, becoming a specialist in Classical and medieval history. He found his vocation as an art historian during the French Revolution, when he carried out an inventory of historical monuments, particularly churches and monasteries, that were in the course of being vandalized. This project led to his imprisonment in 1793. Released after the fall of Robespierre in 1794, he was appointed Keeper of the Department of Antiquities at the Bibliothèque Nationale in Paris, where he also taught the history of art. During the period of the Empire he visited the south of France and in 1811–12 undertook a study journey to Italy, in particular to Rome and Naples.

Millin contributed substantially to the appreciation of the architectural heritage of the French Middle Ages. His publication *Antiquités nationales* (1790), plentifully illustrated with engraved plates, describes the châteaux and churches worthy of note, although his commentary stresses their significance for the history of France rather than the history of art. The same kind of scholarly approach, that of the antiquary, characterizes his studies of Greek vases and of modern medals; however, his *Dictionnaire des beaux-arts* (1806) can be considered as the most complete work of that type that had yet appeared. It contains an ample bibliography, making considerable use of German and Italian writings on aesthetics. Millin was also a great mediator between French culture and that of the rest of Europe, especially Germany; he also translated James Dallaway's *Anecdotes of the Arts in England* (London, 1800) as *Les Beaux-arts en Angleterre* (Paris, 1807). His famous publication, the *Magazin encyclopédique* contains abundant information on the artistic life, archaeology, art history and scholarship of his time.

WRITINGS

ed.: *Mag. Enc.* (1795–1816)

Antiquités nationales (Paris, 1790)

Dictionnaire des beaux-arts (Paris, 1806)

Voyage dans les départements du Midi de la France, 5 vols and atlas (Paris, 1807–11)

Voyage en Savoie, en Piémont, à Nice et à Gênes, 2 vols (Paris, 1816)

Voyage dans le Milanais, à Plaisance, Parme, Modène, Mantoue, Crémone et dans plusieurs autres villes de l'ancienne Lombardie, 2 vols (Paris, 1817)

ed.: *Annales encyclopédiques* (1817–18)

BIBLIOGRAPHY

Michaud

B.-J. Dacier: *Notice nécrologique sur Millin* (Paris, 1821)

F. Arquié-Bruley: 'Au Cabinet des estampes, dessins exécutés en Italie de 1811 à 1813, pour Aubin-Louis Millin', *Rev. Bib. N.* (Spring 1975), pp. 24–43

PASCAL GRIENER

Millington, Edward (*d* London, 1703). English art dealer. He began as a book auctioneer in London, but from 1689 he also held sales of works of art, consisting principally of Old Master paintings, drawings and prints. His auctions, conducted under the ascending bid system and using printed catalogues and previews, took place at tea- and coffee-houses in London on winter afternoons, and at the fashionable spa town of Tunbridge Wells on summer mornings. On 22 January 1692 he opened the earliest specialized art auction room documented in England, the Vendu in Charles Street, Covent Garden, London.

BIBLIOGRAPHY

For a collection of Millington's catalogues, see *1689–92*, i of *The Art Sales Catalogues* (London, BL, 1402.g.1).

An Elegy upon the Lamented Death of Edward Millington, the Famous Auctioneer (London, 1703)

F. Lugt: *Ventes* (1938–64)

I. Bignamini: 'The Auction House', *The Accompaniment to Patronage: A Study of the Origins, Rise and Development of an Institutional System for the Arts in Britain, 1692–1768* (diss., U. London, 1988)

ILARIA BIGNAMINI

Mills, J(ohn) Saxon (*b* Ashton-under-Lyne [now in Greater Manchester], 1863; *d* Oxhey, Herts, 27 Nov 1929). English writer. He was originally a school master, but at about the age of 30 his family connections in newspaper publishing and his successful contributions to many publications encouraged him to become a full-time journalist. He spent several years on the editorial staff of various newspapers and contributed regularly to the daily, weekly and monthly press.

In 1914 Mills collaborated with Hubert von Herkomer on *The Old Wood Carver: A Tale of the Fourteenth Century Retold* (London, [1914]), a book version of one of Herkomer's experimental films, which was illustrated with 52 stills from the film. Subsequently Mills was chosen to write a biography of Herkomer and was given full access to the painter's private papers and those of his family; the book remains the standard text on the artist.

WRITINGS

The Life and Letters of Sir Hubert von Herkomer C.V.O., R.A.: A Study in Struggle and Success (London, 1923)

BIBLIOGRAPHY

Obituary, *The Times* (28 and 30 Nov 1929)
Who Was Who, iii: *1929–1940* (London, 1941)

PHILIP MCEVANSONEYA

Mills, Peter (*b* East Dean, Sussex, *bapt* 12 Feb 1598; *d* London, *bur* 25 Aug 1670). English architect. The son of a country tailor, Mills was apprenticed to a London bricklayer and became a prominent member of that trade. In 1643 he was appointed Bricklayer to the City of London, and in 1649–50 he was Master of the Tylers and Bricklayers Company. After the Great Fire of 1666, he was one of the four surveyors appointed by the city to supervise the rebuilding of London, the others being Wren, May and Pratt. In conjunction with Hooke and John Oliver (*c.* 1616–1701) he made a detailed survey of the destroyed areas and directed the staking out of the new and widened streets. He was the author of a scheme for replanning the city that has not survived and of which nothing is known, except that it was considered inferior to the one made by Hooke. Mills was also involved in rebuilding the property of St Bartholomew's Hospital, London, of which he was a governor, and it was in the church of St Bartholomew-the-Less that he was buried.

Mills was one of the leading surveyors and architects in 17th-century London. In 1667 the Gresham Trustees would have employed him to rebuild the Royal Exchange but for 'the great burthen of businesse lying upon him for this city att this time', which led them to appoint Edward Jerman (*d* 1668) as 'the most able knowne artist (besides him) that the city now hath'. The earliest evidence of Mills's employment as a surveyor or architect is in 1638, when he was involved on behalf of the churchwardens of the parish of St Michael-le-Querne, London, in negotiations with Inigo Jones (acting on behalf of the Privy Council) over the rebuilding of their church, which was prominently situated at the end of Cheapside. It is apparent from this case that Mills and Jones did not see eye to eye in architectural matters, and Mills's executed works show that he was in fact a leading exponent of that style of mannerist classicism characteristic of the city as opposed to the court. An outstanding example of this style is Thorpe Hall, near Peterborough, the country house that Mills designed for the Cromwellian Chief Justice, Oliver St John, in 1654–6. There the exterior, in its grouping of the windows and its treatment of the roof, shows the influence of the illustrations of Genoese palaces published by Rubens in *Palazzi di Genova* (1622). Inside, the exaggeration of such features as the lugged architraves in the panelling (now at Leeds Castle, nr Maidstone, Kent) was characteristic of Artisan Mannerism, of which Mills

was a master. Wisbech Castle (Cambs, *c.* 1658; destr. 1815) built by John Thurloe, Cromwell's Secretary of State, is another country house in the same style that can confidently be attributed to Mills. Tyttenhanger (Herts) is a brick house that he may well have designed.

In London no building attributable to Mills survives, but he was responsible for a number of houses there, including a row in Great Queen Street, Lincoln's Inn Fields (*c.* 1640), which was the Artisan Mannerist equivalent of a street by Inigo Jones. Despite his association with prominent parliamentarians, Mills designed the triumphal arches for Charles II's coronation procession through London in association with 'another person, who desir'd to have his name conceal'd', probably Sir Balthazar Gerbier (J. Ogilby: *Relation of His Majesty's Entertainment*, 1661). In 1661–3 he remodelled the central block of Cobham Hall, Kent, for Charles Stuart, Duke of Richmond and Lennox, in a manner that shows that by then he had largely assimilated the new domestic style associated with architects such as May and Pratt.

BIBLIOGRAPHY

Colvin

T. F. Reddaway: *The Rebuilding of London after the Great Fire* (London, 1940)

O. Hill and J. Cornforth: *English Country Houses: Caroline* (London, 1966), pp. 102–10

HOWARD COLVIN

Mills, Robert (*b* Charleston, SC, 12 Aug 1781; *d* Washington, DC, 3 March 1855). American architect, engineer, cartographer and writer. He claimed to be the first native-born American to have completed 'a regular course of study of Architecture in his own country' and believed this training distinguished him both from 18th-century dilettantes and from contemporary competitors who came to architecture from the building trades. His work is indicative of an informed interest in new building types, materials and techniques and a recognition of the symbolic importance of style. He viewed his profession as a public trust and concentrated on the design of civic buildings and monuments. An influential architect, he promoted both fireproof construction and rational classicism, which later became hallmarks of American federal architecture. His efforts did much to define the nature of American architectural practice in the 19th century.

1. Training and early work, to 1820. 2. Work in South Carolina and Washington, DC, after 1820.

1. TRAINING AND EARLY WORK, TO 1820. Mills studied English and European pattern books and learnt the rudiments of draughting and structure. In 1800 he moved to Washington, DC, and entered the office of James Hoban, who was then directing construction of the President's House (designed 1792). During his two years with Hoban, he met President Thomas Jefferson, who furthered his education by commissioning drawings, by directing his reading and by prompting a tour (in 1803) of the Eastern seaboard, perhaps the first programmatic architectural tour ever made in the USA. Jefferson then recommended Mills to Benjamin Henry Latrobe, with whom he remained as a pupil and assistant until 1808. Under Latrobe's direction he participated in a broad range of architectural and engineering projects: the Chesapeake

and Delaware Canal (1803–5); fireproof offices (1805) for the US Treasury in Washington, DC; a lighthouse (1805–7) intended for the mouth of the Mississippi river; the Roman Catholic Cathedral (1805–6), Baltimore, MD; the Bank of Philadelphia (1807–8); and a number of private residences in Philadelphia. This extended apprenticeship shaped Mills's career: his subsequent use of the form of Neo-classicism then practised by John Soane in England, his penchant for masonry vaulting and hydraulic cement and his interest in acoustics, transportation and public waterworks can all be traced back to Latrobe's influence.

The earliest signed drawings by Mills are those for the South Carolina College competition of 1802. He shared the prize with another competitor, Hugh Smith (1782–1826), but Mills's proposal was not executed. The whole of the principal façade in his drawing is retardataire, a bilaterally symmetrical composition with a projecting, octagonal central block surmounted by a cupola and flanked by wings terminating in projecting pavilions. This elevation reflected the influence of Hoban and of the designs to be found in 18th-century pattern books. The rear façade was, however, altogether different: the base of its wings consisted of an arcade, which gave access to all public rooms at ground- (or entry) level. Although commonplace in Oxford and Cambridge in England, such an arcade was without precedent in American academic architecture; in 1774 Jefferson had suggested an arcaded quadrangle for the College of William and Mary in Williamsburg, VA, and it is probable that Mills's proposal, which foreshadowed his tendency to look beyond local tradition, was an adaptation of Jefferson's plan. Also through Jefferson's assistance Mills learnt of dome construction, based upon laminated wooden ribs, as advocated by Philibert de l'Orme. He used this method to fabricate a saucer dome with a diameter of 30 m for the circular Congregational Church (1804; destr.) for Charleston. This was the first of his five round or octagonal churches, which he based upon the Pantheon, Rome, on the round churches illustrated in James Gibbs's *Book of Architecture* (1728) and on Latrobe's theory of acoustics; as avant-garde auditoria they established his reputation in the USA.

Mills continued to work in Philadelphia for Latrobe until 1808 when his design for the Mount Holly Prison (now Historic Burlington County Prison Museum), NJ, was accepted; this marked the beginning of his independent practice. Its five-bay façade is unified by blind arches, sombre ashlar construction and a strongly projecting string course; except for a heraldic low relief of crossed keys and chains above the central entry, the elevation is wholly without ornament. Public and communal rooms were confined to the rectangular central block; wings containing solitary cells extended from either end to enclose an exercise court. This was Mills's earliest fireproof building; its plan recalls Latrobe's Virginia Penitentiary (1797) in Richmond, and Latrobe, in turn, admitted having drawn upon Jefferson's study of the work of Pierre Gabriel Bugniet in Lyon, France. Mills also cited the writings of John Howard, a prominent English advocate of penal reform. Mount Holly Prison exemplified both the scope of Mills's knowledge and his penchant for institutional planning.

Mills married in 1808 and established himself in Philadelphia. He was active in the Society of Artists, applied unsuccessfully for admission to the American Philosophical Society and obtained commissions for houses: Franklin Row (1809–10; destr.) and Benjamin Chew House (1810); churches: Sansom Street Baptist Church (1811–12) and Octagon Unitarian Church (1812–13; destr.); and public buildings: fireproof office wings (destr.) for the State House (1809–12), Washington Hall (1814; destr.), and a Toll House and exterior finish for the Upper Ferry Bridge (1813; destr.).

During this period Mills largely rejected the forms associated with the Georgian period and Robert Adam (i) in particular and perpetuated by the Carpenters' Company of Philadelphia, adopting instead the spare geometry of John Soane, the robust simplicity of the Doric order and the aesthetic freedom promoted by rational Neo-classicists. The coffered niche with its screen of columns that formed the focal point of the façade of Washington Hall was without precedent in the USA and was based upon the Hôtel Guimard (1772) in Paris. His Upper Ferry Toll House, which took the form of a peripteral temple, was probably derived from a design by Gibbs for a garden pavilion (*Book of Architecture*, pl. LXXII) at Hackwood, Hants, England, for Charles Paulet, 3rd Duke of Bolton. This form of temple, despite its pedigree, had rarely been built in the USA.

The most notably idiosyncratic early building by Mills is the Monumental Church (1812–17; see fig. 1), Richmond, VA. His fifth centrally planned church, it is built on an octagonal plan and supports a saucer dome after de l'Orme and, since it is a memorial to victims of a theatre fire, the principal feature of its façade is a 'Monumental Porch' housing a cinerary urn. For this porch Mills used the primitive Delian Doric order, distyle *in antis*, with fluting restricted to the uppermost and lower drums of the shaft; ornament is restricted to recessed panels, projecting string courses and lachrymatories in the frieze. A lack of funds precluded the execution of acroteria and a steeple. Richmond's Monumental Church, as built, reflected Mills's growing interest in the juxtaposition of unadorned masses. Latrobe had also wanted this commission, and Mills's victory marked his coming of age as a professional, signifying the beginning of his reputation as a designer of public monuments.

Mills's next major work was the Washington Monument (1813–42), Baltimore, the first large American monument to be built in honour of George Washington. Its Delian Doric column rises 50 m above a cubical base, and it is surmounted by a 5-m statue (by Enrico Causici) that presents Washington as Cincinnatus resigning his commission at Annapolis. The column is hollow and contains a spiral staircase leading to an observation platform upon the abacus; despite Mills's disclaimers, it takes its place in a series of commemorative columns, such as those to Trajan and Hadrian in Rome, Christopher Wren's monument in London to the Great Fire, the Nelson Columns in Edinburgh (1805) and Dublin (1808; destr.) and the Colonne Vendôme (1806; destr.) in Paris. Mills's plans included an elaborate iconographic scheme, but financial constraints prompted modifications that resulted in an

1. Robert Mills: Monumental Church, Richmond, Virginia, 1812–17

unadorned shaft, one often cited as a milestone in the development of the Greek Revival in the USA.

Between 1815 and 1819 Mills lived and worked primarily in Baltimore, directing construction of the Washington Monument. A significant percentage of his time was then focused upon engineering projects: he served as President of the Baltimore Water Company (1816–19), proposed flood controls for Jones Falls (Baltimore, 1816–20) and built numerous hot-air furnaces for heating homes, churches and factories. He also drew up proposals for a canal (1816) at Richmond and for powder magazines (1817) at Baltimore. Attempting to supplement his income, he invested in rental housing, a quarry and, disastrously, in the speculative construction of row houses. In Baltimore he built churches, offices and houses, and his first notable Egyptian Revival design, the monument to Aquilla Randall (1817), North Point. His elevation for the Randall Monument depicts a truncated obelisk rising from a cubical plinth, crowned by a tripod supporting an orb. The tripod and bas-relief ornament were not executed, but later he used an identical programme for the monument to *Jonathan Maxcy* (1824–7) at the campus of the University of South Carolina, Columbia, which was his first complex Egyptian Revival monument to be executed. The depression of 1819 brought construction to a standstill in Baltimore, and Mills moved to South Carolina to accept the newly created position of Acting Commissioner of the Board of Public Works.

2. WORK IN SOUTH CAROLINA AND WASHINGTON, DC, AFTER 1820. During his years in South Carolina (1820–29) Mills participated in an ambitious, state-supported programme of internal improvements. These included the development of canals, the design or supervision of sixteen courthouses, three jails and two hospitals, the fireproof County Record building (1822–7), Charleston, a complex of powder magazines (1824–6; destr.) in Charleston and various private commissions. These were for churches: Bethesda Presbyterian Church (1821–3), Camden; St Peter's Catholic church (1824), Columbia; and for homes: Ainsley Hall House (1823), Columbia. In December 1823 the state's legislature became alarmed by mounting construction costs and Mills's position as Superintendent of Public Buildings was abolished. For the next seven years he continued to work for the state on a building-by-building basis, supplementing his income through publications. In 1826, for example, he published his *Atlas of the State of South Carolina, 1825* and a massive companion volume, the *Statistics of South Carolina*. He also published articles and pamphlets on railways and canals and prepared a manuscript concerning his design for a rotary engine. As early as 1822 he had begun to seek work outside South Carolina, for his situation there was always financially precarious. His buildings in South Carolina are notable as a group for the extensive use made of fireproof masonry vaulting and the frequent appearances of Palladian raised basements, the tripartite window that reflected the influence of Latrobe,

2. Robert Mills: design for the Washington Monument, built 1848–84; from a view of Washington, DC, showing projected improvements, by B. F. Smith jr, 1852 (Washington, DC, Library of Congress)

and giant Doric columns and elevations articulated by means of massing and planar adjustment. The Insane Asylum (1822–7), Columbia, exemplifies his best work of this period: at 18,000 sq. m, it was the largest building in the state. A five-storey central block contained the asylum's public and communal rooms; this block was flanked by curving dormitory wings, four storeys high, which framed the grounds. The plan reflected English theories of psychiatric care, and its progressive provisions covered heating, ventilation, a roof-garden and the securing of its patients. The cost of construction was more than treble the original estimates and, although this is attributable to Mills's insistence upon fireproof construction, it damaged his local reputation.

In 1830, seeking federal employment, Mills moved to Washington, DC, where he remained until his death. Engaged briefly as a clerk in the Land Office, he soon found more meaningful work, directing alterations and restorations at the White House, the Executive Office buildings and the Capitol. At the Capitol he remodelled the House of Representatives, raising the floor and improving its acoustics, and he also improved the entire water supply and heating system. Through such comparatively mundane tasks he established himself in the city. As a result, his design for a marine hospital was accepted and erected (1831–4) by the federal government in Charleston; it served as a prototype for a series of hospitals, all characterized by galleries for patients and cross-ventilated wards. Four granite, fireproof custom houses were also built to his specifications (Middletown and New London, CT, and New Bedford and Newburyport, MA, 1834–5); each is on a square plan and has a Doric portico,

unfluted pilasters at the corners, a plain frieze and decorative detailing restricted to variations in the hammered surface of the stone. They show his response to the Greek Revival and to the Boston Granite style.

In 1836 Mills's design for a fireproof federal treasury in Washington, DC, was adopted. Although never completed as designed, it is arguably the most significant Greek Revival office building in the USA. Its 15th Street façade is screened by a 150-m-long colonnade based upon the Ionic of the Erechtheum; its ground-plan consists of barrel-vaulted corridors flanked by groin-vaulted offices, a repetitive module reflecting the work of Jean-Nicolas-Louis Durand. As Architect of the Federal Buildings, Mills also began construction (1836) of the US Patent Office, which had been designed by William Parker Elliot in collaboration with Ithiel Town and Alexander Jackson Davis. The south wing is thought to be largely Mills's own; here Delos-type columns and vaulted corridors and offices recall his earlier work. The same interior plan is repeated in his final notable federal building, the Old Post Office (1839–42), but, unlike anything he had done before, it draws upon the Renaissance palazzo for its elevation: a rusticated basement, a *piano nobile* articulated through the use of Corinthian pilasters and an attic storey. The eclecticism that marked his maturity was further demonstrated by a Norman Revival jail (1839–41; destr.) and a proposal in the same revival style for the Smithsonian Institution (1847–9), both Washington, DC. Although Mills did not obtain the latter commission, he did supervise construction of James Renwick's Gothic Revival building for the Smithsonian.

In 1845 Mills's plan for the Washington Monument (Washington, DC, designed 1833, executed 1848–84) was adopted. It anticipated an obelisk 200 m high, rising from a circular Doric temple 80 m in diameter (see fig. 2). The temple-base (not executed) was to have served as a Pantheon for founders of the republic; Mills prescribed for it a complex iconography of low relief, paintings and sculpture. The concept was derived from a proposal (1791) for a memorial to the destruction of the Bastille by Jacques Molinos and Jacques-Guillaume Legrand, to which Mills had access in Jefferson's library. A shortage of funds thwarted full realization of Mills's plan; nonetheless, it is one of the tallest masonry structures in the world (555 feet, or *c.* 170 m) and among the most famous public monuments in the USA.

As a public servant Mills was vulnerable to the vicissitudes of political life, and in 1842 Congress abolished his office. He continued to work on specific commissions as he had in South Carolina, but in 1851 a controversy arose concerning the vaulting at the Patent Office and plans for the extension of the US Capitol. Thomas Ustick Walter, Mills's most effective critic, was appointed the Capitol's architect and given responsibility for the Patent Office. Mills was forced from federal service, although his influence was important: the profile of the Capitol dome by Walter is similar to one Mills had proposed; Walter's extension of the building is similar to Mills's earlier plan; and Mills's maligned vaults still stand at the Treasury and Patent Offices. Like his buildings and monuments, Mills's commitments to usefulness, public service and the symbolic import of design were a lasting and constructive influence upon architecture in the USA.

WRITINGS

Atlas of the State of South Carolina, 1825 (Charleston, 1826)
Statistics of South Carolina (Charleston, 1826)
B. Glenn, ed.: *Some Letters of Robert Mills, Engineer and Architect* (Columbia, 1938)
H. Cohen, ed.: 'The Journal of Robert Mills, 1828–1830', *SC Hist. & Geneal. Mag.*, lii (1951), pp. 133–9, 218–24; liii (1952), pp. 31–6, 90–100

BIBLIOGRAPHY

Macmillan Enc. Architects
H. M. P. Gallagher: *Robert Mills* (New York, 1935)
R. L. Alexander: 'Baltimore Row Houses of the Nineteenth Century', *Amer. Stud.*, xvi (1975), pp. 65–76
J. M. Bryan and J. M. Johnson: 'Robert Mills's Sources for the South Carolina Lunatic Asylum, 1822', *J. S. Carolina Medic. Assoc.*, lxxv/6 (1979), pp. 264–8
G. Waddell: 'Robert Mills's Fireproof Building', *SC Hist. Mag.*, lxxx/2 (1979), pp. 105–35
G. Waddell and R. W. Liscombe: *Robert Mills's Courthouses & Jails* (Easley, SC, 1981)
E. F. Zimmer and P. J. Scott: 'Alexander Parris, Benjamin Henry Latrobe, and the John Wickham House in Richmond, Virginia', *J. Soc. Archit. Hist.*, xli (1982), pp. 202–11
J. M. Bryan: 'Robert Mills, Benjamin Henry Latrobe, Thomas Jefferson and the South Carolina Penitentiary Project, 1806–1808', *J. SC Hist. Soc.*, lxxxv (1984), pp. 1–21
——: *Robert Mills*, Master Builders (Washington, DC, 1985)
R. W. Liscombe: *The Church Architecture of Robert Mills* (Easley, SC, 1985)

JOHN MORRILL BRYAN

Milltown, 1st Earl of. *See* LEESON, JOSEPH.

Milly, Baron de. *See* PERRAULT, (1).

Milne, David B(rown) (*b* nr Paisley, Ont., 8 Jan 1882; *d* Bancroft, Ont., 26 Dec 1953). Canadian painter and printmaker. He studied at the Art Students League in New York (1903–5), supporting himself as a commercial artist. His voracious appetite for the avant-garde led him to examine all that was available in New York, particularly the French modernists at Alfred Stieglitz's 291 Gallery. His strong and personal style incorporated aspects of the work of the American and French Impressionists, Whistler, Cézanne, Maurice Prendergast and the Fauves. Milne exhibited his works in watercolour societies in New York and Philadelphia from 1909 to 1916. He was one of two Canadians represented in the Armory Show (1913) and he won a silver medal at the Panama-Pacific International Exposition (1915, San Francisco). The chief work of his New York period is *Billboard* (1912; Ottawa, N.G.).

Milne moved to rural Boston Corners, NY, in 1916. Working with a more limited palette and looser, fluid brushwork, he began to depict the same landscape subjects in oil and watercolour under varying climatic conditions. In early 1918 Milne enlisted in the Canadian army and successfully applied for a position as a war artist, working in Britain, France and Belgium. There followed a complete change in his style and approach to painting. His 107 watercolours produced for the Canadian War Records (Ottawa, N.G.) are rendered in dry nervous lines of four to five vivid colours on stark white paper.

At the same time Milne began to analyse his work in writing. He returned to Boston Corners in late 1919, where he augmented his aesthetic theory with an intensive reading programme that included Clive Bell, Roger Fry, Ruskin and Thoreau. This dichotomy between formal modernist analysis and a Victorian philosophical response to nature has made it difficult to categorize Milne. While he imposed rigid aesthetic principles and strove for apparent spontaneity and simplicity of execution, he always wanted to convey the emotional feeling of pure painting through the imagery of the natural world. To consolidate his analytical methodology, Milne copied Thoreau's experience at Walden Pond, by living alone and recording his experiences in an isolated cabin on Alander Mountain (near Boston Corners) during the winter of 1920–21. During the following years he began to work in series, repeating the same subject in different media. After drybrush watercolours such as *Across the Lake* (Ottawa, N.G.) he employed an unusual method of multiple-plate colour drypoints.

In 1929 Milne returned to Canada and lived in various parts of Ontario. His best-known work, *Painting Place* (1930; Ottawa, N.G.), made in Weston, is the culmination of his style of the 1920s. At Palgrave he developed his palette through his colour prints (e.g. *Prospect Shaft*; 1931; Ottawa, N.G.) and refined his draughtsmanship and compositions in his oil paintings (e.g. *Barns*; 1930; priv. col., on loan to Edmonton, Alta, A.G.). By the end of the 1930s Milne returned to watercolours, which dominated the remainder of his career. His use of rich washes, wet-on-wet brushwork and sparkling points of colour established him as the pre-eminent Canadian watercolourist. His modernist philosophy as much as his internationalist sentiments kept him separate from Canada's nationalist art movements such as the Group of Seven. He never received widespread public attention during his lifetime; however, he did attract critical and financial support from a small but influential circle of admirers, which included Vincent Massey.

See also CANADA, §III, 2, and fig. 5.

WRITINGS
'Feeling in Painting', *Here & Now*, i/2 (1948), pp. 57–8
'David Milne: His Journals and Letters of 1920 and 1921, a Document of Survival', ed. D. Milne jr and N. Johnson, *Artscanada*, xxx/3 (1973), pp. 15–55

BIBLIOGRAPHY
Reflections in a Quiet Pool: The Prints of David Milne (exh. cat. by R. L. Tovell, Ottawa, N.G., 1980)
David Milne: The New York Years 1903–1916 (exh. cat. by J. O'Brian, Edmonton, Alta, A.G., 1981)
David Milne (exh. cat., ed. I. M. Thom; Vancouver, A.G.; Kleinburg, Ont., McMichael Can. A. Col.; 1991)

ROSEMARIE L. TOVELL

Milner, John (*b* London, 17 Oct 1752; *d* Wolverhampton, 19 April 1826). English priest, historian and writer. He was appointed priest at Winchester in 1779, where he commissioned John Carter to build the Roman Catholic church of St Birinus (1792; later St Peter; largely rebuilt 1926). Although the shell survives, the liturgical furnishings, sculpture, stained glass and paintings, the iconography of which Milner described in his *History of Winchester* (1798), are lost. Milner himself advised on the decoration of the chapel of the Benedictine nuns at Winchester (1794; destr.) and later those at Sedgley Park School (1800–01; destr.), Staffs, and at Oscott College (1820; now Maryvale House), Old Oscott Hill, Birmingham. It was not only as a church decorator but also as an architectural polemicist that Milner anticipated A. W. N. Pugin. His *Dissertation on the Modern Style of Altering Antient Cathedrals, Exemplified in the Cathedral of Salisbury* (1798) attacked James Wyatt, who had destructively rearranged and altered Salisbury Cathedral in 1789–92. In contrast, Milner's feeling for the Gothic was part morphological and archaeological, part Catholic Romantic. His essay on 'The Rise and Progress of Pointed Architecture' was the first work thus to describe the Gothic; first published in his *History of Winchester*, it was later published separately (1800). His entry on 'Gothic Architecture' for Abraham Rees's *Cyclopaedia* (1810) was an abridgement of his *Treatise on the Ecclesiastical Architecture of England during the Middle Ages* (1811). His defence of the rights of the clergy among English Catholics earned him appointment in 1803 as bishop in the Midlands.

WRITINGS
Dissertation on the Modern Style of Altering Antient Cathedrals, Exemplified in the Cathedral of Salisbury (London, 1798, 2/1811)
The History, Civil and Ecclesiastical, and Survey of the Antiquities of Winchester, 2 vols (Winchester, 1798–1801); 3rd edn (Winchester, 1839) [with suppl. and memoir of the author by F. C. Husenbeth]
Observations on the Means Necessary for the Further Illustrating of Gothic Architecture of the Middle Ages (London, 1800)
'Gothic Architecture', *Cyclopaedia*, ed. A. Rees (London, 1810)
A Treatise on the Ecclesiastical Architecture of England during the Middle Ages (London, 1811)

BIBLIOGRAPHY
DNB
F. C. Husenbeth: *The Life of John Milner DD* (Dublin, 1862)

RODERICK O'DONNELL

Milos. *See* MELOS.

Milow, Keith (*b* London, 29 Dec 1945). English sculptor, painter and printmaker. As a student at Camberwell School of Art, London, from 1962 to 1967 and at the Royal College of Art from 1967 to 1968, he produced representational paintings of modern architectural imagery. These were followed in 1970 by a series of wall hangings made of resin, crayon and fibreglass titled *Improved Reductions*, for example *1 2 3 4 5 6 . . . B* (1970; London, Tate), in which his painted copy of a sculpture by Anthony Caro was cut into strips and then reassembled into a parabolic shape. Elements of paintings and sculpture were also combined in his *Infinity Drawings* (e.g. *Infinity Drawing (ID/16B/75)*, 1975; Brit. Council Col.), in which he used a plasterer's comb to score surfaces painted with aquatec gel mixed with oxidized copper powder. Here the equation of fragmented patterns suggestive of mathematical symbols involves the spectator in games of mental transference.

In the mid-1970s Milow began a series of more than 100 *Crosses between Painting and Sculpture*: Latin crosses, often cast in concrete in emulation of the surfaces of modern buildings, such as *114th Cross* (concrete, resin and fibreglass, 1979; London, Nigel Greenwood Gal.). Inspired by Minimalism, conceptual art and the work of Jasper Johns, Milow intended no religious or symbolic overtones but in 1979 again chose an image redolent with associations, Edwin Lutyens's Whitehall Cenotaph (1919–20), as the source for aggressively sculptural objects hung in pairs from opposite walls, such as *Iron Cenotaph* (iron powder, resin, fibreglass and wood, 1979; London, Nigel Greenwood Gal.). After settling in New York in the early 1980s, Milow experimented briefly with a form of expressionist painting characterized by perspectival illusion before returning to reliefs made of plywood covered in sheets of lead, such as *Man Made Art* (1986; London, Nigel Greenwood Gal.), reminiscent of architectural forms such as castles, prisons and modern Brutalist architecture.

BIBLIOGRAPHY
A. Seymour: 'Choice States: Keith Milow in Conversation', *Studio Int.*, clxxiii/942 (1972), pp. 112–15
A. Lewis: 'Keith Milow at Nigel Greenwood', *Artscribe*, 12 (1978), p. 58
British Art Now (exh. cat. by D. Waldman, New York, Guggenheim, 1980)

ADRIAN LEWIS

Milpurrurru, George (*b* Milingimbi, Northern Territory, 1938). Australian Aboriginal painter. He was a member of the Gurrumba Gurrumba clan of the Ganalbingu language group, who occupy the region of the Arafura swamp in Central Arnhem Land. Milpurrurru began his working life as a stockman. He was taught to paint *c.* 1960 by his father, Ngulmarrmar (*c.* 1911–*c.* 1977), a well-known bark painter. Milpurrurru first gained a reputation as a leading Aboriginal artist when he lived in the early 1970s at Maningrida, from where he moved to Ramingining, close to his clan lands. He painted themes from his Ganalpuyngu country, in particular ones associated with the magpie goose and the life of the swamplands (e.g. *Wurrurrung: Fishing Net*, 1985; Perth, A.G. W. Australia). Although his paintings are derived in style and subject-matter from those of his father, he was an innovative artist and his painting style developed considerably as he matured. He was a featured artist at the Sydney Biennale of 1980, and his first one-man exhibition was in 1985 at the Aboriginal Art Centre in Sydney. His paintings are well represented in the major state art galleries in Australia and in collections elsewhere in the world, including the British Museum in London and the Kluge Collection, a private collection in Virginia, USA. His sister Dorothy Djukulul (*b* 1942) was one of the leading women artists in Central Arnhem Land.

WRITINGS
'Bark Painting: A Personal View', *Windows on the Dreaming: Aboriginal Paintings in the Australian National Gallery*, ed. W. Caruana (Canberra, 1989), pp. 18–22

BIBLIOGRAPHY
The Inspired Dream (exh. cat., ed. M. West; Brisbane, Queensland A.G., 1988), pp. 56–9, 93

HOWARD MORPHY

Milroy, Lisa (*b* Vancouver, 13 Jan 1959). Anglo-Canadian painter. After a period as a student at the Université de Paris-Sorbonne (1977–8), she settled in London and studied art at St Martin's School of Art (1978–9) and Goldsmith's College, University of London (1979–82). At the latter her teachers included Michael Craig-Martin and Tony Carter. Her first solo exhibition, in 1984, was of small still-life paintings depicting common objects, either singly or in sets. These were technically remarkable works drawing on the painterly language of Manet and the Post-Impressionists. Her subsequent series of paintings of objects in groups (rows, clusters, layers or grids) borrowed the language of hardware catalogues, shop display windows and formal arrangements in art and photography, while yet creating autonomous visual statements. Sometimes her arrangement of objects was influenced by their functional identity, so that, for example, stamps become islands for the eyes to travel between or wheels speed forward at an unstoppable visual pace (e.g. *Tyres*, 1987; London, Saatchi Col.). Later works continued to emphasize the arrangement of objects in relation to the picture plane, and in such works as *Plates* (1992; London, Nicola Jacobs and Tony Schlesinger priv. col.), in which four blocks of plates are presented in rows of four, six, three and five against a plain mid-grey background, an element of time was also introduced by giving the view of each block from a different height. Other works from the 1990s include landscapes, cityscapes and crowds. *Crowd* (1992; e.g. London, Nicola Jacobs and Tony Schlesinger priv. col.) demonstrates the artist's continued interest in the technical aspect of the painting process, with strokes, dabs, dashes, dots, planes of colour and other painterly marks layering the surface.

BIBLIOGRAPHY
Lisa Milroy (exh. cat., Glasgow, Third Eye Cent.; Southampton, C.A.G.; 1989)
Lisa Milroy (exh. cat., Berne, Ksthalle, 1990)
Lisa Milroy (exh. cat., London, Waddington Gals; Velbert, Städt. Museen, Schloss Hardenberg; 1993)
Tokyo Story (exh. cat., Tokyo, Shokonagai Gal., 1994) [solo exh.]

Milton, John (*b* 19 July 1759; *d* London, 11 Feb 1805). English medallist, die-sinker and gem-engraver. It is not known where Milton was first trained, but he is most likely initially to have studied seal-engraving. His earliest known works, a medal for the Society of Industry, a seal and an engraved gem, date from 1785. From 1787 to 1797 he was employed at the Royal Mint where he received training in die-engraving. He is thought to have executed a number of dies designed by Lewis Pingo as well as executing his own designs. Besides official work, Milton, encouraged by Pingo, developed a thriving private business. He was forced to leave the Mint, following the discovery that he had supplied dies of foreign coin to counterfeiters, but his career does not appear to have suffered unduly, and he continued working until 1804. Medals such as those for the Society for the Improvement of Naval Architecture of 1791 or the Bath and West of England Society (1802) display his skill as an engraver, although his compositions can appear stilted. He also executed dies for coins and tokens, including the celebrated Anglesey pattern penny of 1786 bearing a druid's head (which was not adopted) and the 1788 and 1792 Barbados pennies, as well as a number of passes and tickets. He exhibited at the Royal Academy, London, from 1785 to 1802.

BIBLIOGRAPHY
DNB; Forrer; Thieme–Becker
T. Stainton: 'John Milton, Medallist, 1759–1809', *Brit. Numi. J.*, liii (1983), pp. 133–59

PHILIP ATTWOOD

Milunović, Milo (*b* Cetinje, 6 Aug 1897; *d* Belgrade, 11 Feb 1967). Montenegrin painter. He studied painting with Alberto Giacometti in Florence. The influence of Giotto and the Italian Quattrocento is perceptible in his work. After World War I he spent some time in Paris, where he broke with his Impressionist practice under the influence of Cézanne and Cubism. He painted his most successful works between 1926 and 1932, for example *Still-life with Violin* (1930; Belgrade, N. Mus.). These works were characterized by a rationalistic approach, both to composition and space. Anti-illusionistic devices were used in the representation of space. The composition was rigid; it focused on primary visual elements and was built geometrically.

Later on, particularly on his return to Montenegro after World War II, Milunović began to depict more often the coastline and everything that is associated with the sea. The horizontal line of the sea, smoothed by intersecting verticals and dynamized by diagonals, formed a mosaic of tonal colour.

BIBLIOGRAPHY
M. B. Protić: *Milo Milunović* (Belgrade, 1959)
Milo Milunović (exh. cat., text A. Čelebonović; Belgrade, Cult. Cent. Gal., 1967)

JURE MIKUŽ

Milvus, F. *See* KYTE, FRANCIS.

Milyutin, Nikolay (Aleksandrovich) (*b* St Petersburg, 21 Dec 1889; *d* Moscow, 1942). Russian politician, patron, urban planner and theorist. He was the son of a St Petersburg fishmonger who lacked the means to give him a full-time higher education. Working as a carpenter, he entered part-time architectural classes in the Volnyyi (open) Polytechnic, St Petersburg, where in 1908 he joined the Russian Social Democratic Party. By the February Revolution of 1917 he had been elected to the Petrograd Workers Soviet and commanded a Red Guard platoon; and in the October Revolution he took part in the storming of the Winter Palace. In the post-Revolutionary years he was a close colleague of Lenin, occupying a series of high-ranking positions, including commissariats for various aspects of labour affairs, People's Commissar for Social Welfare (1922–4) and from 1924 to 1929 People's Commissar of Finance for the Russian Republic (Rus. Narkomfin). Throughout the 1920s he was also a member of the Bolshevik Party Central Committee.

The support of a political figure at Milyutin's level was an extraordinary bonus to the Constructivist architecture group OSA, as seen in his involvement with Moisey Ginzburg on the finest Modernist housing scheme of the Soviet avant-garde, the Narkomfin complex in Moscow (1928–30; for illustration see GINZBURG, MOISEY). There is no record of how the relationship between Milyutin and Ginzburg began, but it was close, genuine and creative. Extensive rethinking of housing types conducted by Ginzburg and the Constructivist group produced wholly new concepts of 'minimal' family flats supported by communal facilities, as a 'transitional' form that was halfway towards the fully socialized communal housing advocated by ideological extremists. Sketches are extant in his short book Sotsgorod (1930), in which Milyutin depicts these units assembled into a four- to five-storey building according to Le Corbusier's stylistic principles, but it is not clear how these sketches relate to the Narkomfin complex. Also in Milyutin's hand are the design, equipping, colour scheme and all details of the penthouse flat on top of the Narkomfin building where he lived until his death.

Milyutin is best known, however, for his role in resolving the debate arising from the massive new towns programme (1929–30) undertaken as part of the Soviet first Five-Year Plan. In the so-called 'urbanist–disurbanist' debate about the continuing relevance of the conventional town, the extreme position of linear decentralization was adopted by the Constructivists, but their rational, technical and social arguments were too radical. Taking elements of the linear model, however, Milyutin produced a simple and practical system of parallel zoning of residential, recreational and production belts, which combined healthy living environments with efficient journeys to work and servicing of the industrial plants. He thus effectively resolved the theoretical arguments by providing a practical formula appropriate to current Soviet circumstances. Notable applications of his model were in Stalingrad (now Volgograd) and Magnitogorsk. The planning concept was explained and illustrated with housing ideas largely derived from Constructivist work in Sotsgorod.

From 1930 Milyutin's power began to decline. That year he was appointed chairman of the Central Administration of Soviet Cooperatives (Tsentrosoyuz) and chairman of the research section for Housing and Socialist Settlement in the Communist Academy, where Ginzburg and his colleagues were employed to continue their design research. However, the realignments (1932) attending the enforcement of Socialist Realist principles throughout architecture and the handing over of planning issues to technical cadres soon led to the abandonment of significant investigations.

Milyutin's involvement with the avant-garde radicals of the mid-1920s led, under Stalin's repressions, to his removal from senior appointments. However, as Deputy Commissar for Education of the Russian Republic in mid-1931, he was in an ideal position to soften the Communist Party's policy of aesthetic dictatorship, which in 1932 abolished all the independent architectural groups formed in the 1920s and defined Soviet Modernism as 'a bourgeois deviation'. In this mediating role he became editor (1931–3) of Sovetskaya arkhitektura, the official journal of the newly formed Union of Soviet Architects. He used the journal as the platform for an ideologically 'correct' aesthetic programme in a series of lengthy position-defining papers, but in 1933 he was moved to a job in the film production industry. Here he brought many young architects into a massive building programme, while he himself enrolled in 1935 for a formal architectural qualification at the Moscow Architectural Institute. He graduated in 1940 with a design of obligatory historicism and pretension, being then employed in a sinecure in the Palace of Soviets construction office. Subsequent commentators seeking to rehabilitate Milyutin have described his writings on planning and architectural theory as important, innovative contributions. Certainly Sotsgorod established his place in the history of modern urban planning, but it is basically a sensible synthesis of ideas that others had already circulated. His writings in Sovetskaya arkhitektura, which are strongly coloured by the political situation, hardly do justice to his concern for improving the lives of ordinary individuals.

WRITINGS

Sotsgorod: Problema stroitel'stva sotsialisticheskikh gorodov [Sotsgorod: the problem of building socialist cities] (Moscow and Leningrad, 1930; Eng. trans. with intro. by A. Sprague, Cambridge, MA, and London, 1974)
Regular contributions to Sov. Arkhit. (1933)

BIBLIOGRAPHY

G. G. Collins: 'Linear Planning throughout the World', J. Soc. Archit. Hist., xviii/3 (1959), pp. 74–93
A. Senkevitch: Soviet Architecture, 1917–32: A Bibliographical Guide to Source Material (Charlottesville, 1972)
'Nikolay Aleksandrovich Milyutin', Mastera sovetskoy arkhitektury ob arkhitekture [Masters of Soviet architecture on architecture], ed. M. G. Barkhin (Moscow, 1975), pp. 80–104
P. Baum and V. Rabinovich: 'Narkom Milyutin o sotsgorodakh i genplan Moskvy' [People's Commissar Milyutin on the socialist town and general plan of Moscow], Stroitel'stvo & Arkhit. Moskvy, iii (1990), pp. 8–10

CATHERINE COOKE

Mimesis. Imitation or realistic representation (see ILLUSIONISM, REALISM and XENOPHON).

□

Mina, al-. Site at the mouth of the Orontes in northern Syria. The town functioned as a port and appears to have been both one of the earliest and the most important of the trading posts established by the Greeks in the eastern Mediterranean in the 8th century BC. Excavated by Sir Leonard Woolley in 1936–7, al-Mina yielded the earliest Greek material to have been found in the Near East. Other sites, such as Tyre, were found later to have even earlier pottery, but al-Mina retains its pre-eminence in the region in terms of the quantity of Greek material recovered.

Woolley identified ten levels at the site, calling the earliest X and the latest I. Some areas had been washed away by the river, but at least part of the earliest levels remains. Levels X to VIII date from *c.* mid-9th century BC to *c.* 700 BC. The buildings were made of mud-brick on stone foundations; it appears that Level VIII reused walls from Levels X and IX and that the site was restored in Level VII. There seems to have been a native settlement at the site initially, with Green material appearing some time into the 8th century BC. Other wares at the site include Cypriot, Phoenician and North Palestinian, and the population was probably mixed. Most of the Greek material in this phase was pottery, the earliest being pendent semicircle skyphoi—cups bearing semicircles drawn with a compass—which are most likely to have originated in Euboia. Among other late 8th-century Greek Geometric pottery from this first phase at al-Mina are further types of skyphoi and straight-sided cups from Euboia, kotylai from Corinth and a few fragments of East Greek, probably Rhodian, wares. If there were Greeks in al-Mina at this time, they must have been a small body of traders.

The site was briefly abandoned *c.* 700 BC, but a new town, with the same building style as the first phase, was later set up on the ruins of the old. This phase comprised Woolley's Levels VI and V and lasted until *c.* 600 BC. In this phase Greek pottery at the site increased in quantity and appears to have been the dominant element. The evidence indicates a shift from a major Euboian element in the earlier phases to predominantly East Greek and Corinthian wares, the latter perhaps not brought directly by Corinthian traders. The East Greeks were clearly very active traders during this phase.

There is less evidence after *c.* 600 BC for continued settlement of the site, and not until the last quarter of the 6th century BC did trade with Greece pick up again. The rise of Babylonian power seems to have been responsible for the change in fortunes at al-Mina, which did not fully recover until the Persians dominated the area from 539 BC. In the second half of the 6th century BC al-Mina was thus rebuilt again (Level IV) and later in the century was trading once more, apparently as a totally Greek venture, probably still run by East Greeks. The plan and layout of Level IV was very different from what had preceded it, with large warehouses built to store the trade goods.

Al-Mina continued to flourish as a trading centre until the very end of the 4th century BC. There were further changes to its plan and the layout of its buildings as a result of destruction by fire, until the building of the city of Seleucia in 301 BC, just to the north, led to al-Mina's permanent decline.

BIBLIOGRAPHY
C. L. Woolley: 'Excavations at Al Mina, Sueidia', *J. Hell. Stud.*, lviii (1938), pp. 1–30, 133–70
J. Boardman: *The Greeks Overseas* (London, 1973, rev. 1980)

LOUISE SCHOFIELD

Minard, Louis-François-Martial (*b* Ghent, 7 June 1801; *d* Ghent, 5 Aug 1875). Belgian architect and collector. The son of a French immigrant, he trained in architecture at the Academie voor Schone Kunsten in Ghent under the direction of Louis Joseph Adrien Roelandt and between 1817 and 1835 obtained several prizes but competed without success for the Prix de Rome at Amsterdam in 1827. Appointed a professor at the academy of The Hague

in 1829, he returned to Ghent after the Belgian Revolution (1830) and there became a most successful and wealthy architect–builder and was elected a town councillor. Minard's architectural works, mostly in eastern Flanders, include the building or restoration of churches, for example at Melle (1837–9), Adegem (1842–4), Burst (1852–5), Ertvelde (1854) and Wetteren (1865), private houses in Ghent, country houses and châteaux (Olsene (1854), Deurle (destr.), Vosselare (destr.), Nazareth-Scheldevelde, Lovendegem, Melle, Lochristi, Wetteren (destr.), Wondelgem, Drongen, Erpe), school and industrial buildings and funeral monuments. His first works, such as the Hôtel Godefroy (1826) and the Gebroeders Van Eyck, named after the Van Eyck brothers in Ghent, were in the Neoclassical style, but after 1830 he was involved in the development of historicist architecture, with the Gothic Revival style, designs in the German-inspired *Rundbogenstil* and pioneering designs in the Renaissance Revival mode.

Minard's own house (1838) in Ghent, Grote Huidevettershoek, could be considered as the quintessence of his work. Behind its Neo-classical façade it contains a Gothic Revival staircase and gallery and rooms with elaborate detailing in Byzantine, Renaissance and Baroque Revival styles. It originally housed Minard's impressive collection of antiquities from the guilds of Ghent and a large collection of furniture, metalwork, ironwork, ceramics and glass from the medieval period to the 18th century. Minard amassed the collection from 1835, and it was one of the richest in the country. It was dispersed in 1883, and part of the collection is now in the Oudheidkundig Museum van de Bijloke in Ghent. Adjoining the house, he built at his own expense the theatre that still carries his name and within which he planned the staging of Flemish plays in order to help preserve the Flemish language.

BIBLIOGRAPHY
BNB
I. S. van Doosselaere: *Le Musée Minard-van Hoorebeke à Gand; Notice biographique et descriptive* (Ghent, 1865)
D. V. S.: 'Louis-Francies-Martial Minard', *Vl. Sch.*, xxi (1875), p. 163
L. Minard-van Hoorebeke: *Description des méreaux et autres objets anciens des gildes et corps de métiers, églises etc*, 2 vols (Ghent, 1877–9)
H. van Duyse: *Catalogue des objets d'art et antiquités composant la magnifique collection de feu Monsieur L. Minard, architecte à Gand* (Ghent, 1883)
J. van Cleven: 'Tussen burgerlijke romantiek en grootstedelijke realiteit', *Gent en architectuur*, ed. N. Poulain (Bruges, 1985), pp. 91–107

JEAN VAN CLEVEN

Minardi, Tommaso (*b* Faenza, 4 Dec 1787; *d* Rome, 12 Jan 1871). Italian painter, draughtsman, teacher and theorist. He studied drawing with the engraver Giuseppe Zauli (1763–1822) who imbued Minardi with his enthusiasm for 15th-century Italian art and introduced him to his large collection of engravings after the work of Flemish artists such as Adriaen van Ostade. However, Minardi was strongly influenced by the Neo-classical painter Felice Giani, who ran a large workshop in Faenza, and whose frescoes of mythological scenes (1804–5) at the Palazzo Milzetti he saw being painted. In 1803 he went to Rome on an annual stipend provided by Count Virgilio Cavina of Faenza (1731–1808), and he received (1803–8) additional financial assistance from the Congregazione di S Gregorio. He was given the use of Giani's studio and through him met Vincenzo Camuccini who, with Canova, dominated the artistic establishment in Rome at that time.

Tommaso Minardi: *Self-portrait*, oil on canvas, 1813 (Florence, Galleria degli Uffizi)

Although Minardi learnt the precepts of Neo-classicism from Camuccini, he did not share his interest in heroic art. His first works done in Rome show his interest in the theme of master and acolyte. In *Socrates and Alcibiades* (1807; Faenza, Pin. Com.), for example, he has included himself among a group of elderly philosophers and young students who are placed on either side of a portrait bust of Zauli. He sent this drawing to his patrons, the Congregazione di S Gregorio, no doubt to reassure them of his aptitude and moral correctness. *Supper at Emmaus* (c. 1807; Faenza, Pin. Com.) was another painting destined for the same patrons. The confined pictorial space, with a single source of light entering through a small window, and the casual poses of the figures are reminiscent of Flemish art and of the works of the northern Caravaggisti, familiar to the artist through engravings. From 1808 to 1813 he had an *alunnato* from the Accademia di Belle Arti in Bologna and sent back the painting *Diogenes* (1813; Bologna, Pin. N.), which is unusual both in its bold design and large size (1340×987 mm).

In his *Self-portrait* (see fig.), convincingly dated to 1813 (Piperno, pp. 175–6), Minardi created a crystalline, austere atmosphere. Light entering from two windows reveals a humble interior and a sombre occupant. Minardi's early contact with the Nazarenes, who were in Rome from 1810, served to increase his preference for the aesthetic and spiritual qualities of early 15th-century art. In 1812 he received a commission from the Milanese printmaker and writer Giuseppe Longhi to execute a detailed drawing (Rome, Vatican, Bib. Apostolica) of Michelangelo's *Last Judgement* (1535–41; Rome, Vatican, Sistine Chapel). This project was to occupy him for 13 years but was never published. His close study of Michelangelo's work, for which he produced over 40 related drawings (Rome, G.N.A. Mod.), also became an excuse for self-doubt as a painter. He wrote in his unpublished autobiography that 'from then I lived in a state of complete isolation and squalor'. On account of this 'inability' to paint, in 1817 he refused a commission from Camillo Massimo to decorate his casino, Villa Massimo Lancelotti, and the work was given instead to several Nazarene painters, much to Minardi's regret.

In 1818 Canova proposed Minardi as Director of the Accademia di Belle Arti in Perugia, a post that he held from 1819 to 1821. In 1821, on the strength of his merits as a draughtsman, students at the Accademia di S Luca in Rome put his name forward for the directorship. Even though he was endorsed by both Canova and Pope Pius VII, this was insufficient to sway members of the Accademia in his favour. He was, however, created Professor of Drawing there in 1822, a position he held until 1858. From this time his drawing technique became increasingly linear, and his subjects almost entirely religious, except for several themes derived from Dante. The *Angel of the Apocalypse* (1824; Faenza, Pin. Com.) is a perfect expression of the ideals of Purismo and recalls John Flaxman's style as does the sombre *Soul of the Shepherd's Baby* (c. 1825; Forlì, Bib. Com. Saffi).

At the Accademia Minardi opposed the formal and rational theories propounded by academic artists and, together with Friedrich Overbeck, he dominated religious art in Rome until about 1850. A decisive influence on both of these men was the presence of Ingres in Rome from 1834 to 1841 as Director of the Académie de France. In 1834 Minardi gave a controversial lecture ('Delle qualità essenziali della pittura italiana . . .') at the Accademia in which he questioned the basis of academic painting. He rejected the need to make a slavish study of ancient sculpture and the works of Raphael, although he recognized the latter's 'divine' quality. Geniuses, he felt, were always the cause of decadence in art. Instead, he placed greater emphasis on the spiritual perception of nature as opposed to the replication of real things; for him, a return to the essentials of Giotto's art was desirable. The leading exponent of Purismo in Rome, he contributed to the manifesto *Del purismo nelle arti*, which he, Overbeck, Pietro Tenerani and Antonio Bianchini co-signed in 1843. Among his religious paintings of this period is the *Virgin of the Rosary* (1840; Rome, G.N.A. Mod.), which is strongly reminiscent of Perugino's work. By the 1840s his pupils were carrying out his designs, and many of his later works (e.g. *Missions of the Apostles*, 1864; Rome, Pal. Quirinale) are monotonous and sterile in composition. This decline in powers indicates that, although he had an enormous influence on painters of religious subjects, he was unable to sustain his own theories in practice. Among his many followers were Constantino Brumidi, Antonio Ciseri, Francesco Coghetti and Guglielmo De Sanctis, who wrote Minardi's biography.

UNPUBLISHED SOURCES

Forlì, Bib. Com. Saffi, MS. 288CR 194 [autobiog.]

BIBLIOGRAPHY
G. De Sanctis: *Tommaso Minardi e il suo tempo* (Rome, 1900)
E. Ovidi: *Tommaso Minardi e la sua scuola* (Rome, 1902)
I. Faldi: 'Il purismo e T. Minardi', *Commentari*, I (1950), pp. 238–46
A. M. Corbo: 'T. Minardi e la scuola romana di S Luca', *Commentari*, 1–2 (1969), pp. 131–41
L. Piperno: 'Disegni giovanili di T. Minardi', *Quad. Neoclass.*, iv (1978), pp. 173–210
L'età neoclassica a Faenza, 1780–1820 (exh. cat., ed. A. Ottani; Faenza, Pal. Milzetti, 1979)
J. C. Taylor: *Nineteenth-century Theories of Art*, CA Stud. Hist. A., xxiv (Berkeley, 1987)

Minaret. Tower attached to a mosque from which the muezzin gives the call to prayer (Arab. *adhān*). The English term 'minaret' derives (via French) from the Turkish *minare*, which itself derives from the Arabic *manāra*, 'a place or thing that gives light' (cf. Heb. *menorah*). Medieval Arabic had other terms for the tower attached to the mosque: *manār*, *mi'dhana* and *ṣawma'a*. Eventually all these terms became synonymous, but it seems that at first they had limited geographical currency or referred to different functional types.

With the possible exception of the dome, the minaret is the most distinctive external feature of Islamic architecture, giving a characteristic 'Islamic' aspect to the Taj Mahal and to the skylines of Cairo and Istanbul (*see* ISLAMIC ART, §II). Minarets vary in form and materials of construction, from the square towers of North Africa and Spain, through the multi-storey stone spires of Egypt, the pencil-thin stone shafts of Ottoman Turkey and the cylindrical brick towers of Iran, to the monumental combinations of flanged octagonal and cylindrical shafts erected in medieval Afghanistan and India. While the minaret is a common feature of Islamic religious architecture, it is, however, neither necessary nor ubiquitous: some regions of the Islamic world, for example East Africa, Kashmir and Bengal, eschewed minarets at certain times.

1. Early history. 2. Regional developments.

1. EARLY HISTORY. The earliest mosques did not have a specific place for the call to prayer. According to Muslim tradition, the Prophet Muhammad deliberated about the most appropriate way to call the faithful to prayer. Some of his Companions suggested using fire as the Magians did, a gong or bell as did the Christians, or a horn as did the Jews, but eventually one of them dreamed of summoning people with the human voice. The Prophet approved of the idea and commanded Bilal, an Ethiopian freed man, to call the faithful to prayer. Thus was the *adhān* invented and the role of muezzin (Arab. *mu'adhdhan*) created. During the Prophet's lifetime, and certainly under his immediate successors, the Orthodox caliphs (*reg* 632–61), the call to prayer was given from a high or public place, often the doorway or roof of a mosque, an elevated neighbouring structure or the city wall.

Most historians have dated the introduction of the minaret to the middle of the 7th century, yet no example of a tower built specifically for the call to prayer can be produced from this early date. Lighthouses (Arab. *manār*) may have been built along navigable rivers, coasts and caravan routes, but they had no religious function and

apparently continued pre-Islamic practice. Manar Mujida, the isolated tower between Ukhaydir and Kufa in Iraq, is an early example of this type. Literary sources suggest that some, but by no means all, mosques were given small aedicules on their roofs to shelter the muezzins from the elements: officially termed *mi'dhana* ('place of the *adhān*'), these small structures were popularly likened to the cells to which Christian hermits withdrew and were therefore also called *ṣawma'a* ('monk's cell'). Reached either by a movable ladder or by a flight of steps, these structures, which have been compared to sentry-boxes, were the forerunners of the 'staircase minaret' found in various remote areas of the Muslim world. The earliest extant staircase minaret is at the Great Mosque of Bosra, Syria (*see* BOSRA, §2), where a fragmentary inscription dated AH 102 (720–21) refers to the construction of a *mi'dhana* that can be identified with a narrow external flight of steps leading to the mosque's roof. An inscription taken from Ashkelon and dated AH 155 (774; Istanbul, Mus. Turk. & Islam. A.) records the construction of a *mi'dhana*, apparently referring to another 'staircase minaret'. More recent staircase minarets have been found in Upper Egypt, East Africa, Anatolia and along the Persian Gulf.

Mosques built under the Umayyad caliphs (*reg* 661–750) do not generally have towers, although the Great Mosque of Damascus (*see* DAMASCUS, §3) incorporated two of the four towers that stood at the corners of the ancient temple enclosure on the site. However, when the caliph al-Walid

1. Helicoidal minaret, Great Mosque of the caliph al-Mutawakkil, Samarra', Iraq, 848–52

rebuilt the Mosque of the Prophet in Medina, a tall slender tower, termed *manāra*, was erected at each of its four corners. The purpose of these towers is not clear but can be related to the special status of the mosque, which had been the Prophet's house and was his burial place. The Abbasid caliphs (*reg* 749–1258) initially continued Umayyad practice, building their mosques without towers, but in the late 8th century four towers were added to the Masjid al-Haram (the mosque surrounding the Ka'ba) in Mecca, during the reconstruction they had ordered.

From early in the 9th century a single massive tower began to be built in or beyond the middle of the outer wall opposite the mihrab in mosques throughout the Islamic world. The oldest extant examples can be found as far apart as Kairouan in Tunisia, Damascus in Syria and SIRAF, a medieval trading port on the Persian Gulf. At Kairouan the massive three-storey tower should be dated to the rebuilding of the mosque in 836, not, as previously thought, to a century earlier. Its square form derives not from Syrian belfries, for its battered lower storey has no precedent there, but from a Roman lighthouse that once stood near by on the coast at Salakta (anc. Sullecthum). The unnecessarily massive construction testifies to the builder's unfamiliarity with erecting towers. The most impressive Abbasid minaret is attached to the Great Mosque built by the caliph al-Mutawakkil between 848 and 852 at SAMARRA' (see fig. 1), the 9th-century Abbasid capital north of Baghdad. The helicoidal brick tower, 50 m high, rests on a base 33 m square and is said to have been modelled on Mesopotamian ziggurats. No ziggurats of this form survived into the Muslim era, and ziggurats were associated with idol worship and would have been inappropriate models for an Islamic religious building. It is far

more likely that Abbasid architects chose this form as a secure means of raising the tower to a height proportional to the immense size of the mosque. While nothing prevented the use of these towers for the call to prayer, the monumentality of the form suggests that they were raised primarily for symbolic purposes. Indeed, in the mosque that Ahmad ibn Tulun, governor of Egypt from 868 to 884, built at Fustat (*see* CAIRO, §III, 2), he copied the Samarra' minaret, but the muezzins are known to have given the call to prayer from a two-storey fountain house in the middle of the courtyard of the mosque.

Shi'ites were strongly opposed to giving the call to prayer from such elevated places, citing a tradition of the caliph 'Ali (*reg* 656–61), whom they revered second only to Muhammad himself, that it should be given from a place no higher than the roof of the mosque. When the Shi'ite Fatimid dynasty built the mosque of MAHDIA in Tunisia at the beginning of the 10th century and the mosque of al-Hakim in Cairo (*see* CAIRO, §III, 4) a century later, they replaced the tower minaret with a monumental portal, from which the call to prayer seems to have been given. However, during the 11th century, the popularity of the tower became so widespread that even Fatimid patrons eventually allowed tower minarets to be added to their mosques.

2. REGIONAL DEVELOPMENTS. The real formal development of the minaret occurred during the 10th, 11th and 12th centuries and culminated in some of the largest and most impressive minarets ever built. The earliest extant minarets in Spain date from the 10th century, although they probably followed 9th-century models. Pride of place must go to the minaret now encased in the bell-tower of Córdoba Cathedral, which was built by the Umayyad caliph 'Abd al-Rahman III in 951–2. Originally it measured 8.5 m square and 47 m high. Two independent spiral staircases ascended the structure, which was decorated with carved panels and surmounted by a small aedicule topped by silver and gold finials. The same ruler introduced the square-shaft minaret to Morocco when, in 955 and 956, he commissioned new minarets for the two congregational mosques of Fez, apparently as a symbol of the efforts he had made to counter Fatimid advances in the region. While the Fez minarets were quite plain on the exterior, the 11th-century minaret at the QAL'AT BANI HAMMAD in Algeria was decorated with shallow vertical panels, cusped arches and ceramic tiles, clearly showing its Andalusian origins.

Neither the political instability of the 11th century nor the conservatism of the Almoravid dynasty (*reg* 1056–1147) was conducive to the building of minarets in Spain and North Africa. The Almoravids did not destroy extant minarets but preferred to have the call to prayer given from the doorways of mosques. Under their successors, the Almohad dynasty (1130–1269), the square-shaft minaret of the Córdoban type was developed to a scale never before seen in the Islamic west. Three great minarets dating from the end of the 12th century, the Kutubiyya in Marrakesh (see fig. 2), the Giralda in Seville (*see* BRICK, fig. 13) and the Tour Hassan in Rabat, stood nearly 70 m high, five times their width, and were adorned with increasingly sophisticated cusped arch and lozenge net

2. Kutubiyya minaret, Marrakesh, Morocco, late 12th century

decoration arranged in rectangular panels. Not only did the square Almohad minarets become the archetype for later, usually more modest, minarets in North Africa, but ironically they also decisively influenced the developing form of the Spanish Christian bell-tower, as numerous *mudéjar* churches in Castile and Aragon show.

The few minarets that were built in Syria during the 9th and 10th centuries were square stone towers, varying in height and decoration. A medieval Arabic source states that the minaret added to the Great Mosque of Damascus was entirely decorated with mosaic; the minarets (destr.) at Homs were quite plain. Towards the end of the 11th century, however, there was a brilliant rebirth of stone architecture in Syria, exemplified by such monuments as the minarets of the Great Mosques of Aleppo and Ma'arrat an-Nu'man, with their intricate mouldings and delicate inscriptions on the traditional square shaft. In Egypt no minarets were built during the first century of Fatimid rule (from 969), but a series of 11th-century tapered cylindrical brick minarets on square bases in Upper Egypt testifies to a lively vernacular style closely related to examples, now lost, in the Hijaz (western Arabia). An inventive tradition of building stone and brick minarets began with the return of Sunni rule to Egypt in 1173. It continued in an unbroken sequence under the Ayyubid dynasty (*reg* 1173–1250) and their Mamluk successors, there and in Syria, and only ended with the Ottoman conquest of 1517. Mamluk minarets are generally divided into three storeys separated by intricately constructed cornices made up of projecting tiers of squinch-like cells (*muqarnas*) and supporting balconies for the muezzin. The contrasting square, cylindrical and octagonal stages are decorated with an increasing variety of complex geometric and epigraphic motifs. Whereas early minarets were sited with reference to the internal plan of the mosque, Mamluk minarets were placed to dominate urban vistas most effectively. Minarets were now added to a wide variety of religious monuments, including madrasas, *khānaqāh*s (Sufi hospices and meeting-houses) and tombs (*see* ISLAMIC ART, §II, 6(iii)(a)).

In the eastern Islamic lands of the 11th century there began a brilliant series of brick minarets loosely identified with the Saljuq dynasty (*reg* 1038–1194). Over 60 towers dating from before the Mongol conquests of 1256–8 still stand in Iran, western Central Asia and Afghanistan, either attached to mosques or free-standing. While few 10th-century minarets are known, the 11th-century explosion is of such formal and decorative self-assurance that earlier experiments must be assumed. Generally these cylindrical towers have an internal spiral stairway leading to the gallery that is supported by a deep *muqarnas* cornice. The exterior is usually covered with broad bands of geometric brick decoration, often separated by guard bands and inscriptions. Sometimes the towers are on low plinths, the shafts have lobes and flanges or are decorated with blind arcading. Far less expensive than building an entire mosque, yet gratifyingly visible, these towers could be added as acts of piety to existing structures, often built in mud-brick, much as baked-brick domes and iwans were also added to existing mud-brick mosques at this time (*see* ISLAMIC ART, §II, 5(i)(b)).

The loss of the mosques to which they were attached means that some towers now appear as free-standing

3. Khusrawgird minaret, Ziyar, Iran, 11th–12th centuries

structures. Others were conceived as such, either to guide caravans across the desert (Khusrawgird, Ziyar; see fig. 3) or simply to signify the presence of Islam. The most impressive of this latter type is the minaret of Jam (*see* ISLAMIC ART, fig. 32), once Firuzkuh, the capital of the Ghurid dynasty. Situated in a remote Afghan valley, this enormous three-tiered brick structure was built by the Ghurid ruler Ghiyath al-Din Muhammad (*reg* 1163–1203). It is *c.* 65 m tall and decorated with a variety of brick and stucco geometric ornament and inscriptions in kufic, including all of chapter xix of the Koran. The Qutb Minar (72.5 m tall; *see* DELHI, fig. 2), begun in 1199 as the minaret of the Quwwat al-Islam Mosque in Delhi and the first great Muslim construction in India, was probably partly inspired by the minaret at Jam and erected to symbolize the Muslim conquest of India. Although one of the Khalji sultans attempted to build a minaret twice its height a century later, the project failed to be realized. No other minarets in India rivalled the height and bulk of the Qutb Minar. Subsequent developments under the Mughals and other Muslim dynasties were closely tied to Iranian precedents.

In earlier times minarets had been deemed appropriate only to mosques, but by the 12th century, in the eastern

Islamic world as in Egypt, they were commonly added to other religious structures that contained places of worship, particularly madrasas. Multiple minarets were also introduced and developed in this period; they were often placed in pairs on either side of a portal or the iwan arch in the main façade of a courtyard, an idea that was quickly carried from Iran west to Anatolia and east to India. Double minarets flanking a portal became standard in Iran under the Ilkhanid dynasty (*reg* 1256–1353) and their successors in the 14th century and remained so under the Timurids (*reg* 1370–1506) and Safavids (*reg* 1507–1732). Indeed, the single minaret, as at NATANZ (restored 1325), became the exception rather than the rule. The mosque at the Mongol capital, SULTANIYYA, had four minarets, two flanking the main portal and two at the corners of the principal façade; the mausoleum of Sultan Uljaytu (*see* ISLAMIC ART, fig. 48) in the same city was crowned by eight minarets, surpassing the seven that by then adorned the expanded Masjid al-Haram in Mecca.

In Anatolia the earliest surviving Ottoman minarets, such as that of the Green Mosque at Iznik (1378–91), followed the model developed under the Saljuqs in the 12th and 13th centuries: a slender cylindrical brick shaft, often decorated with glazed tiles, supports a circular balcony by means of several tiers of *muqarnas*. The shaft continues above the balcony where it is capped by a conical roof. Many of the earliest Ottoman mosques surviving in Bursa did not originally have minarets, although they were eventually added. The Üç Şerefeli ('Three Balcony') Mosque in Edirne (1438–47) was apparently the first Ottoman mosque to have had not only several minarets but also several balconies on a single minaret. Each of its four stone minarets has a different form of shaft; that at the north-west corner has three balconies and rises to a height of 67 m. The varied shafts of early Ottoman architecture gave way to plain or modestly faceted cylindrical types, and only the mosques built by sultans were entitled to have more than one minaret. The Süleymaniye mosque in Istanbul (1550–56; *see* ISLAMIC ART, fig. 63) has a minaret at each corner of the courtyard: the taller pair are 76 m high and have three balconies each. At the Selimiye Mosque in Edirne (completed 1574–5), four identical minarets frame the dome: each is over 70 m tall and has three balconies. This development culminated in the mosque of Sultan Ahmed in Istanbul ('Blue Mosque'; 1609–17), where six minarets, a pair with two balconies and four with three balconies, frame the mosque and courtyard.

It is recorded that teams of muezzins gave the call to prayer antiphonally from two or more balconies of minarets; however, the increasing height and multiplication of minarets in Ottoman times cannot be explained solely by piety. On the one hand they framed the mosque in space; on the other, they were used in profusion as a symbol of Islam triumphant. The Ottoman 'candle-snuffer' minaret became a familiar sight as Ottoman domination extended into Syria, Egypt, North Africa, Greece and the Balkans. Nevertheless the traditional square minaret continued to hold its own in North Africa as did a hybrid octagonal type.

Beyond the traditional North African and south-west Asian lands of Islam, minarets have a varied history. In West Africa, for example, the battered mud tower over the mihrab of traditional mosques shows some formal similarities to Almohad experiments in minaret placement, while along the East African coast the traditional staircase minaret was most common in medieval times. In China minarets are not common; the tapering cylindrical shaft of the minaret at Canton is unique. In Java, apart from the brick tower at Kudus, which is identified as a 16th-century minaret, although it shows many formal and functional similarities to pre-Islamic gate-houses, the earliest minarets postdate the earliest mosques and follow either Dutch or Arabian tower traditions. In many peripheral regions of the Islamic world a minaret tradition did not develop because such structures were frowned upon by local religious authorities.

Since the invention of the loudspeaker, the minaret has become functionally obsolete. Nevertheless architects and builders continue to consider it the most significant symbol of Islamic architecture. Whereas a dome can be used for a variety of purposes in Islamic and non-Islamic architecture and thereby assume a variety of meanings, the slender tower crowned by a balcony is a perennial and now universal sign of Islam.

BIBLIOGRAPHY

Enc. Islam/2: 'Manāra'
K. A. C. Creswell: *Early Muslim Architecture*, 2 vols (Oxford, 1940–69)
——: *The Muslim Architecture of Egypt*, 2 vols (Oxford, 1952–60)
J. Sourdel-Thomine: 'Deux Minarets d'époque seljoukide en Afghanistan', *Syria*, xxx (1953), pp. 105–36
A. Lézine: *Architecture de l'Ifriqiya: Recherches sur les monuments Aghlabides* (Paris, 1966), pp. 39–52
A. B. M. Husain: *The Manara in Indo-Muslim Architecture* (Dacca, 1970)
F. Hernández Giménez: *El Alminar de 'Abd al-Rahmān III en la mezquita mayor de Córdoba: Genesis y repercusiones* (Granada, 1975)
J. M. Bloom: 'Five Fatimid Minarets in Upper Egypt', *J. Soc. Archit. Hist.*, xliii (1984), pp. 162–7
B. O'Kane: 'Salğūq Minarets: Some New Data', *An. Islamol.*, xx (1984), pp. 85–102
D. Behrens-Abouseif: *The Minarets of Cairo* (Cairo, 1985)
J. Bloom: *Minaret: Symbol of Islam* (Oxford, 1989); review by B. O'Kane in *Orient. A.*, xxxviii (1992), pp. 106–13
——: 'Mosque Towers and Church Towers in Early Medieval Spain', *Künstlerische Austausch/Artistic Interchange: Akten des XXVIII. Internationalen Kongresses für Kunstgeschichte: Berlin, 1992*, pp. 361–71
R. Hillenbrand: *Islamic Architecture: Form, Function and Meaning* (Edinburgh, 1994), pp. 129–72

JONATHAN M. BLOOM

Minaux, André (*b* Paris, 5 Sept 1923). French painter and printmaker. He studied under Maurice Brianchon at the Ecole National Supérieure des Arts Décoratifs in Paris (1941–5). From 1944 he exhibited at the Salon d'Automne, Salon des Indépendants and Salon de Mai and had his first one-man show at the Galerie des Impressions d'Art in Paris in 1946. In 1949 he participated in the second Homme-Témoin group exhibition at the Galerie Claude and the same year won the Prix de la Critique. The social realism of Homme-Témoin was in tune with Minaux's own work, in which he pared away detail and employed thickly painted, expressive brushstrokes in subdued colours to depict everyday scenes, as in *Seated Woman* (*c.* 1949; see Chevalier, pl. 4). In the same style were a number of townscapes, such as *Landscape of Toury Ferrotes* (1950; Paris, Pompidou), and such still-lifes as *Armchair in an Interior* (1951; London, Tate). He also made lithographs to illustrate books, for example Jules Amédée

Barbey d'Aurevilly's *L'Ensorcelée* (1955), Jules Renard's *Les Philippe* (1958) and Blaise Cendrars's *La Grande Route*. In 1960 Minaux exhibited the large work *The Wedding* (1957–60; see Besson, pl. 1) at the Maison de la Pensée Française in Paris. Covering an area of 20 sq. m, the painting depicted an interior scene with figures gathered in celebration, which was compared by contemporaries to Gustave Courbet's *Burial at Ornans* (1849–50; Paris, Mus. d'Orsay). From the 1960s his colours brightened yet his work became more serene, although the subject-matter remained the same. In the 1970s he concentrated on the theme of women in interiors in a series of coloured etchings, where the forms were flattened and abstracted, as in *Denise* (1976–7; see exh. cat., p. 17). Also in the 1970s he made etchings of still-lifes mainly depicting elements taken from the artist's studio, as in *Two Palettes* (1976–7; see exh. cat., p. 4).

BIBLIOGRAPHY

D. Chevalier: *André Minaux* (Paris, 1951)
G. Besson: *André Minaux* (Paris, 1960)
Minaux graveur (exh. cat. by P. Mazars, Paris, Gal. Sagot-Le Garrec, 1978)

ALBERTO CERNUSCHI

Minbar [Arab.; Turk. *minber*]. Pulpit in a mosque, often made of wood or stone. The largest, indeed sometimes the only piece of furniture in a mosque, the minbar derived from the judge's seat in pre-Islamic Arabia. The first minbar in Islam (*c.* AD 628–31) is reported to have been the wooden chair with two steps ordered for the mosque of Medina by the prophet Muhammad; from it he preached and led prayers. After Muhammad's death in 632 it became customary for a new caliph to receive homage while seated on this minbar. The Umayyad caliph Mu'awiya (*reg* 661–80) raised the Prophet's minbar on a six-stepped platform in 670. As a sign of legitimate authority, minbars were used by the Umayyad caliphs (*reg* 661–750) and their governors as pulpits from which to make important announcements as well as for delivering the Friday sermon. It became customary for the name of the reigning sovereign to be mentioned in the sermon (Arab. *khutba*), and this became one of the two most important public signs of political power, the other being the inclusion of the ruler's name on the coinage. Eventually, a minbar (rarely, more than one) was installed in every mosque in which Friday prayers were performed, and the minbar came to be used principally for the Friday sermon. Minbars may also be found in the prayer-halls of some important madrasas and at other places where religious orations are made, such as several of the pilgrimage sites around Mecca. Minbars are almost always placed against the qibla (Mecca-facing) wall of a prayer-hall, to the right of the mihrab.

Muhammad's minbar, with its many added steps, became the principal model for later examples. Minbars with nine steps, modelled on the two steps and the seat of Muhammad's minbar plus the six steps added by Mu'awiya, are known to have been made as early as 786, although no particular number of steps was favoured universally. In its most developed form, the minbar is a triangular structure, its hypotenuse formed by a narrow flight of steps. The steps lead to a platform at the top; both steps and platform

are enclosed by railings, and the platform is often surmounted by a cupola. In some cases the entrance at the bottom of the steps is framed as a doorway, usually closed by a door of two leaves. The major fields for decoration are the minbar's large triangular sides, but in the finest examples all parts were elaborately decorated. In common with Muhammad's minbar, later examples were normally made of wood, often richly carved and sometimes painted and gilded as well, although specimens made of stone or brick are known. The earliest minbars were portable, being brought out into the mosque when needed, and from an early date some minbars were mounted on wheels to facilitate their positioning. The widespread early practice of storing the minbar when it was not in use has survived only in East Africa and the Maghrib (western North Africa), where a recess was often built in the qibla wall to accommodate it. Maghribi minbars were often mounted on rollers or wheels. Stationary minbars may contain cupboards at the back, beneath the platform, for storage of such items as books used in the mosque.

The earliest extant minbar is the one in the Great Mosque of Kairouan, Tunisia (*c.* 860, restored *c.* 1050), which is made of teak and has 11 steps. It was imported in whole or in part from Iraq by the Aghlabid governor Abu Ibrahim Ahmad (*reg* 856–63), who also ordered the decoration of the mosque's mihrab. The sides and even the risers of the steps of the Kairouan minbar are covered with scores of wooden panels carved with geometric, architectonic and foliate designs in a style apparently continuing that of Umayyad wood-carving in Syria (*see* ISLAMIC ART, §VII, 1(i)(a) and (iii)). Other minbars preserved in Algiers, Nédroma, Constantine, Fez, Marrakesh and Taza and made in the western Islamic lands between the 10th century and the 15th form a rich source for the study of Islamic woodwork, its style and its regional variations. The earliest and most important minbar in this series was ordered by the Spanish Umayyad caliph al-Hakam II (*reg* 961–76) for the Great Mosque of Córdoba; inlaid with ivory and precious woods, it was greatly admired in its day but is no longer extant. Some memory of it may be preserved in another minbar made in Córdoba *c.* 1125–30 and also inlaid with wood and ivory (see fig.). The decoration on the sides is executed in a distinctive technique, in which small cubes of wood and ivory are formed into strapwork bands around octograms and other geometric forms finely carved with arabesque ornament in high relief. The risers are covered with architectonic designs in marquetry. Originally placed in the Almoravid mosque in Marrakesh, it was transferred by the Almohads to the Kutubiyya Mosque there as a symbol of their assumption of power (now Marrakesh, Badi' Pal. Mus.).

The best-known minbars were made in Egypt and Syria between the late 11th century and the 15th under the patronage of the Fatimid, Zangid, Ayyubid and Mamluk dynasties. The earliest of this series is the wooden minbar made for the Mashhad al-Husayn at Ascalon (1091) on the order of the Fatimid vizier Badr al-Jamali; it was later transferred to the Haram al-Khalil Mosque, Hebron. The sides are decorated with tongue-and-groove panelling in a hexagonal strapwork pattern and framed with inscription bands in kufic script. In 1169 the Zangid ruler Nur al-Din (*reg* 1146–74) ordered a splendid minbar made in Aleppo

Minbar, wood and ivory, 3.86×3.46×0.89 m, from the Kutubiyya Mosque, Marrakesh, *c.* 1125–30 (Marrakesh, Badi' Palace Museum)

for the Aqsa Mosque in Jerusalem, then in the hands of the Crusaders. The Ayyubid sultan Salah al-Din installed the minbar in its intended place in 1187 after his conquest of the city. The minbar, which was destroyed by arson in 1969, was perhaps the finest example of the prolific Syrian school of wood-carving (*see* ISLAMIC ART, §VII, 1(i)(b) and 2(ii)), and was signed by no fewer than four artisans. Elegant inscriptions in cursive script framed the balustrades, which were composed of turned wood grilles in a complex geometric frame. The sides were decorated with octograms and the extensions of their sides traced in a net of joinery; the polygonal interstices were filled with minutely detailed arabesques. The portal and the platform were crowned with gilded *muqarnas.*

Minbars made under the patronage of the Mamluk dynasty (*reg* 1260–1517) continue the same form, but many of those made in Cairo are inlaid with ivory or bone, ebony and mother-of-pearl. Among the many outstanding examples are those in the mosque of al-Salih Tala'i' (1300) and the mosque of al-Mu'ayyad Shaykh (1415–20). In these minbars the geometry of multipointed stars and the radial extensions of their sides are developed, with the enclosed polygons filled with carved arabesques. Above the *muqarnas* canopy over the platform, bulging domes like those crowning Mamluk minarets were raised. A minbar of this type in the name of the Mamluk sultan Qa'itbay (*reg* 1468–96), is exhibited in the Victoria and Albert Museum, London. Stone minbars were also made

in Cairo, including a rather plain one in the madrasa of Sultan Hasan (*c.* 1360), which, however, has heavily ornamented bronze doors, and a heavily carved one ordered by Qa'itbay in 1483 for the funerary *khānaqāh* of the Mamluk sultan Faraj. Both imitate the form of wooden minbars.

In Iran heavily carved wooden minbars of the 11th and 12th centuries made considerable use of the BEVELLED STYLE, in which vegetal forms are continuously modelled, with no distinction between subject and ground. This type of carving is also characteristic of Anatolian and Mesopotamian minbars of the same date. More unusual is a group of 15th-century Iranian minbars decorated with tile mosaic, such as the one of the Masjid-i Maydan, Kashan (1468), in which star geometries are variously realized. In contrast to those of Egypt and Syria, Iranian minbars do not have domes over their platforms. Turkish minbars of the 13th to the 15th centuries are generally similar to Syrian minbars in form and motifs; they usually show great relief and inventiveness in their carved woodwork but lack *muqarnas* cresting. Under the Ottoman dynasty (*reg* 1281–1924), stone became more popular as a medium for minbars; the form of the wooden minbar was retained, but its decoration was often simplified or reduced in area. The dome over the platform developed into a distinctive, high polygonal cone, like the roofs of Ottoman minarets. The finest examples, such as the stone minbar in the Selimiye Mosque in Edirne (*c.* 1570), use arcading and broad expanses of pierced geometric design to open up the body of the minbar. Late Ottoman minbars, such as the one in the Dolmabahçe Mosque in Istanbul, follow the trend of architecture of the period in their eclectic borrowings from the European Baroque. The form of the minbar is more variable in the Indian subcontinent. No old wooden minbars appear to have been preserved, and stone is the preferred medium, as in the Jami' Mosque at Fatehpur Sikri (late 16th century).

BIBLIOGRAPHY

Enc. Islam./2: "Ādj' [Ivory], 'Minbar'

C. H. Becker: 'Die Kanzel im Kultus des alten Islam', *Orientalische Studien Theodor Nöldecke gewidemet* (Giessen, 1906), pp. 331–51

M. van Berchem: *Matériaux pour un corpus inscriptionum arabicorum,* ii/2 (Cairo, 1927), pp. 393–402

H. Basset and H. Terrasse: *Sanctuaires et forteresses almohades* (Paris, 1932)

K. A. C. Creswell: *Early Muslim Architecture,* ii (Oxford, 1940), pp. 314–19

J. Sauvaget: 'Sur le minbar de la Kutubīya de Marrakech', *Hespéris,* xxxvi (1949), pp. 313–19

J. Schacht: 'An Unknown Type of Minbar and its Historical Significance', *A. Orient.,* ii (1957), pp. 150–73

S. L. Mostafa: *Kloster und Mausoleum des Faraq b. Barquq* (Glückstadt, 1968), pp. 16–17, 121, 130–31

G. S. Karnouk: 'Form and Ornament of the Cairene Baḥrī Minbar', *An. Islam.,* xvii (1981), pp. 113–39

B. O'Kane: 'The Tiled Minbars of Iran', *An. Islam.,* xxii (1986), pp. 133–53

Al-Andalus: The Art of Islamic Spain (exh. cat., ed. J. D. Dodds; Granada, Alhambra; New York, Met.; 1992), pp. 249–51, 362–7

Minchō. *See* CHŌDENSU MINCHŌ.

Mincu, Ion (*b* Focşani, 20 Dec 1852; *d* Bucharest, 6 Dec 1912). Romanian architect and teacher. He studied engineering at the School of Bridges and Roads, Bucharest, graduating in 1875, and then studied architecture at the

Académie des Beaux-Arts, Paris, between 1877 and 1884, in the studio of Julien Azais Gaudet. From 1884 he established himself in independent practice in Bucharest, where he formed a group of disciples and influenced such architects as Petre Antonescu, Nicolae Ghika-Budeşti and Cristofi Cerchez through his attempts to revive various formal and ornamental elements of Romanian vernacular architecture. He was the first to articulate the 'neo-Romanian' style in such works as the Lahovary Building (1886; now the Dr I. Cantacuzino Hospital), Bucharest, which uses the traditional Romanian elements of the verandah and lancet arch. However, the clearest expression of Mincu's neo-Romanian style is the restaurant Bufetul (c. 1890; now Doina Restaurant), Bucharest, based on plans (1889; unexecuted) for a Romanian Restaurant–Pavilion at the Exposition Universelle in Paris (1889). He achieved here a picturesque effect with asymmetrical composition resulting from variations in height and roof pitch, which are balanced by rich decoration in the upper areas only. The focal element is a watch-tower, which is placed on the left of the main façade and combines vernacular decorative elements in traditional materials of brick, wood, coloured ceramics and tiles. Although the component elements are easily identified as having historical models, Mincu's interpretation and integration of them is original. He was a founder-member (1891) and later President (1895) of the Society of Romanian Architects. Between 1896 and 1908 he was a professor at the High School (later Academy) of Architecture, Bucharest.

BIBLIOGRAPHY
M. Caffé: *Arhitectul Ion Mincu* [The architect Ion Mincu] (Bucharest, 1960, 2/1970)
M. Lupu: *Şcoli naţionale în arhitectură* [National schools in architecture] (Bucharest, 1977), pp. 135–44

CODRUŢA CRUCEANU

Minden, Master Bertram von. *See* BERTRAM, MASTER.

Minderhout, Hendrik van (*b* Rotterdam, 1632; *d* Antwerp, 22 July 1696). Dutch painter, active in the southern Netherlands. For unknown reasons, he was known as the 'Green Knight of Rotterdam'. In 1644 he married Margareta van den Broecke, and in 1652 he went to Bruges, where in 1663 he entered the Guild of St Luke; the marine painting that he submitted to the Guild to become a member used to be displayed in the Salle d'Académie as a companion piece to the picture submitted by Rubens on his entry to the Guild. In 1672 van Minderhout moved to Antwerp, where he was admitted to the Guild the same year and where, in return for exemption from all obligations as a guild member, he presented a large canvas representing an Eastern seaport. In 1673 he married his second wife, Anna-Victoria Claus. They had five children, including two sons, Antoon van Minderhout (*b* 26 Sept 1675; *d* 22 Dec 1705) and Willem August van Minderhout (*b* 28 Aug 1680; *d* 31 June 1752), who also became painters. Hendrik van Minderhout painted mostly sea and harbour views, in the tradition of Jan Baptist Weenix and Johannes Lingelbach. His subjects included the port of Antwerp, as well as imaginary views of Mediterranean harbours (e.g. Dunkirk, Mus. B.-A.) and oriental seaports (e.g. Antwerp, Kon. Mus. S. Kst.). The wide variety of works bearing the signature of Hendrik van Minderhout suggests that two artists of the same name may have been active at the same time.

BIBLIOGRAPHY
NKL; Thieme–Becker
F. Donnet: *Het jonstich versaem der Rederijkkamer de Olijftak sedert 1480* [The noble company of the Chamber of Rhetoric of the 'Olive Branch' from 1480] (Antwerp, 1907), pp. 385–6
W. Bernt: *Die niederländischen Maler des 17. Jahrhunderts* (Munich, 1948–62), ii, no. 536
'Hendrick van Minderhout (1632–1696)', *Duits Q.*, v (1964), pp. 10–16

TRUDY VAN ZADELHOFF

Mindlin, Henrique E(phim) (*b* São Paulo, 1 Feb 1911; *d* Rio de Janeiro, 6 July 1971). Brazilian architect, writer and teacher. He was the son of Russian immigrants and grew up in an artistic environment. He graduated in 1932 as an engineer–architect from the Mackenzie School of Engineering, São Paulo, and went into practice in São Paulo, carrying out some Modernist work. In 1942 he moved to Rio de Janeiro, where he came into contact with the architects who had been influenced by Le Corbusier, including Lúcio Costa, Oscar Niemeyer, Alfonso Eduardo Reidy and Jorge Moreira; like them, Mindlin became involved with the development of a Brazilian version of Le Corbusier's rationalist Modernism. His first project in Rio was a prizewinning design for the new Ministry of Foreign Affairs (1942; unexecuted) at Itamaraty; thereafter he won several prizes, becoming well known for his participation in competitions and exhibitions. In 1943–4 he studied architecture and construction projects in the USA. He then embarked on a prolific career, designing houses, blocks of flats, offices, industrial buildings, hotels and shops. His domestic work was highly creative, often using butterfly roofs, sunscreens and naturally finished wall planes, and his commercial work incorporated the latest technology, for example the Avenida Central Building (1956), Rio, which was the first steel-framed skyscraper in Brazil. From 1955 to 1966 he also worked in partnership with Giancarlo Palanti (1906–77), producing buildings such as the headquarters of the Bank of London & South America (1957), São Paulo, with a curtain-wall construction, and undertaking the urban development of the Tróia Peninsula, Setúbal, Portugal, where he also had an office (1965–7). In his later work he developed the use of exposed concrete in the Brutalist style, for example the Guanabara State Bank Headquarters (1963), Rio de Janeiro, and for the IBM Factory (1969), São Paulo, he used a space frame structure. Mindlin was also an important writer and critic, contributing numerous articles to journals such as *Acrópole* and producing an important record of early Brazilian Modernism in his book (1956); he was also a spokesman for modern Brazilian architecture at international congresses. He was Professor at the Faculty of Architecture, Federal University of Rio de Janeiro (1968–71), and he also taught in the USA and England.

WRITINGS
Modern Architecture in Brazil (Amsterdam and Rio de Janeiro, 1956)

BIBLIOGRAPHY
H. R. Hitchcock: *Latin American Architecture since 1945* (New York, 1955)
C. B. Yoshida: *Henrique Ephim Mindlin* (São Paulo, 1973)
Y. Bruand: *Arquitetura contemporânea no Brazil* (São Paolo, 1981)

CARLOS A. C. LEMOS

Minello (de' Bardi). Italian family of masons and sculptors. (1) Giovanni Minello was active in Padua for almost 60 years, notably at Il Santo, where he was assisted by his son (2) Antonio Minello. Their work ensured the continuing influence of the Lombardo family into the early 16th century.

(1) Giovanni (d'Antonio) Minello (de' Bardi) (*b* Padua, *c.* 1440; *d* Padua, 1528). Mason and sculptor. Although his talent was mediocre, he was one of the principal figures in Paduan sculpture after Donatello, primarily as a contractor and specialist in decorative work. Described in 1467 as 'magister', he was head of a workshop three years later. That he had enough capital to run his own shop by 1470 indicates he was born before 1450 and perhaps as early as 1440. Pietro Lombardo was in Padua from 1463 to 1468 and employed Giovanni Minello then (Rigoni); he and not Bartolomeo Bellano must be considered Minello's master. This theory is further supported by the many features of Lombardo's style present in Giovanni Minello's work, especially the tomb of *Cristoforo da Recanati* (1483–9; destr.; fragment in Padua, Mus. Civ.), in which he followed the Tuscan format established in Padua by Lombardo's tomb for *Antonio Roselli* (1464–7; Padua, Il Santo). Giovanni Minello's presentation drawing of this tomb survives in the Museo Civico, Padua.

Giovanni Minello's earliest known commission (1471) was for decorative work in the Leoni Chapel of S Bernardino (destr.). His association with Il Santo, for which most of his work was done thereafter, began in 1482 when he was commissioned to ornament the choir-screen around the sides of the high altar with statues, candelabra, a marble revetment of pilasters and a frieze of seraphim heads. In 1490 he also contracted to make the marble for Bellano's bronze reliefs for the choir. This complex was dismantled in the 17th century, and the architectural members are all that survive of Giovanni Minello's work. They, like the fragment of the *Recanati* tomb, show his style to be dry, hard and linear, lacking in animation or corporeality.

Fabriczy attributed several terracottas to Giovanni Minello; Moschetti and Planiscig added more. Carpi, however, disproved some of these attributions on documentary evidence, and none can be securely given to Minello. These forceful, if sometimes crude, terracottas find no echo in Giovanni Minello's works in stone, and it is more reasonable to reject them than try, as earlier scholars did, to reconcile two opposing styles. It is very doubtful that Giovanni Minello was a major figure in Paduan terracotta sculpture.

In 1500 Giovanni Minello was named *protomaestro* of the project to rework the funerary chapel of S Antonio in Il Santo. He has been called the designer of the complex, but this honour more likely belongs to Tullio Lombardo. In 1501 Giovanni Minello and his son (2) Antonio Minello were commissioned to carve a relief of the *Miracle of the Ass* (unexecuted). Over the next 20 years Giovanni Minello, often assisted by Antonio, continued to work on the chapel, carving figures in the friezes, small reliefs of prophets, modillions, steps, rosettes and other details, together with three holy water stoups and a well for the cloister. He was released from his duties as *protomaestro* in 1521, but continued to work: in 1522 he recarved an inscription his son had bungled. In 1527 he set up his own epitaph.

The tomb of *Giovanni Calfurnio* (1512), now in the Novitiates' cloister of Il Santo, speaks for Giovanni Minello's meagre gifts as a figural sculptor: he always signed himself as a *tagiapietra* (stone mason). Although he was previously considered a prime exponent of 'post-Donatellian naturalism' (Planiscig) in Padua, his importance lies in the lower level of codifying a classical decorative language at Il Santo and in running the largest workshop in Padua, where such artists as Giovanni Maria Mosca Padovano and Giovanni Rubino were trained.

BIBLIOGRAPHY

Thieme–Becker

C. von Fabriczy: 'Giovanni Minello: Ein Paduaner Bildner vom Ausgang des Quattrocento', *Jb. Kön.-Preuss. Kstsamml.*, xxviii (1907), pp. 53–89

L. Planiscig: *Der venezianische Bildhauer der Renaissance* (Vienna, 1921), pp. 155–70

P. Carpi: 'Nuove notizie e documenti intorno a Giovanni Minello e all'arte del suo tempo', *Boll. Mus. Civ. Padova*, n. s., vi (1930), pp. 40–91

E. Rigoni: 'Giovanni Minello e la cappella dell'Arca di S Antonio', *Atti & Mem. Accad. Patavina Sci., Lett. & A.*, xlv (1953–4), pp. 90–96; also in *L'arte rinascimentale in Padova: Studi e documenti*, Med. & Uman., ix (Padua, 1970), pp. 259–64

——: 'Notizie riguardanti Bartolomeo Bellano e altri scultori padovani', *L'arte rinascimentale in Padova: Studi e documenti*, Med. & Uman., ix (Padua, 1970), pp. 123–39

A. Sartori: *Documenti per la storia dell'arte a Padova* (Vincenza, 1976), pp. 148–59

Dopo Mantegna (exh. cat., Milan, 1976), no. 87, p. 128

S. Wilk: 'La decorazione cinquecentesca della cappella dell'Arca di S Antonio', *Le sculture del Santo di Padova*, ed. G. Lorenzoni (Padua, 1984), pp. 115–17, 123–4

(2) Antonio (di Giovanni) Minello (de' Bardi) (*b* Padua, *c.* 1465; *d* Venice, ?1529). Italian sculptor, son of (1) Giovanni Minello. He worked in a stolid, classicizing style influenced by the Lombardo family of sculptors and architects. Antonio is first recorded working as an assistant to his father on 10 April 1483. They worked together on the choir-screen of Il Santo in Padua and, after 1500, on the chapel of S Antonio in the basilica. During 1510–11 he carved 15 half-length *Prophets* on the portal of S Petronio, Bologna, together with Antonio da Ostiglia. On his return to Padua, Minello completed the statue of *St Justina* in the leftmost niche above the entrance to the chapel of S Antonio in 1512 and in 1517 delivered the *Investiture of St Anthony*, the first relief on the left in the chapel. From 1523 to 1529 he worked on the relief of the *Miracle of the Parrasio Boy*, which was finished by Jacopo Sansovino in 1536. Schulz also attributed to him the tombs of *Nicolo Orsini*, *Leonardo da Prato* and *Dionigi Naldi* (1513–15; Venice, SS Giovanni e Paolo). In the early 1520s Minello moved to Venice, where, in 1524, he purchased the contents of the workshop of Lorenzo Bregno. He completed a *Virgin* (Montagnana Cathedral) begun by Bregno and also took over Bregno's commission for statues of saints on the Trevisan altar (Venice, S Maria Mater Domini). In 1527 Minello executed a statuette of *Mercury* (London, V&A) for Marcantonio Michiel. A head of *Hercules* (untraced), recorded by Michiel as in Andrea Odoni's collection, is probably depicted on the right in Odoni's portrait by Lorenzo Lotto (London, Hampton Court, Royal Col.). Minello was last documented in January 1529 and presumably he died that year.

BIBLIOGRAPHY

E. Rigoni: 'Giovanni Minello e la cappella dell'Arca di S Antonio', *Atti & Mem. Accad. Patavina Sci., Lett. & A.*, xlv (1953–4), pp. 90–96; also in *L'arte rinascimentale in Padova: Studi e documenti, med. & uman.*, ix (Padua, 1970), pp. 259–64

A. Sartori: *Documenti per la storia dell'arte a Padova* (Vicenza, 1976), pp. 150–51, 156–63

J. Eade: 'Marcantonio Michiel's *Mercury* Statue: Astronomical or Astrological?', *J. Warb. & Court. Inst.*, lxiv (1981), pp. 207–9

S. Wilk: 'La decorazione cinquecentesca della cappella dell'Arca di S Antonio', *Le sculture del Santo di Padova*, ed. G. Lorenzoni (Padua, 1984), pp. 128–9, 137–9, 161–2

A. Schulz: 'Four New Works by Antonio Minello', *Mitt. Ksthist. Inst. Florenz*, xxi (1987), pp. 291–325 [with full bibliog.]

THOMAS MARTIN

Minet el Beida. *See under* UGARIT.

Minfeng. *See* NIYA.

Mingachevir. Group of archaeological sites at the town of the same name, 60 km east of Ganja, Azerbaijan. The sites range in date from the Late Neolithic period and Bronze Age (3rd millennium BC) to the 17th century AD. Systematic excavations have been conducted there since 1946, and many silver and gold articles (Baku, State Hist. & Archit. Mus.), such as chased, granulated and filigree earrings, clasps, necklaces, pendants, pins, bracelets and goblets, have been found in Bronze Age and Early Iron Age burial grounds. Characteristic of objects dating to the period from the 4th century BC to AD 400 are vessels in the shape of ducks, a dove, a cow and a goat, and jugs with animal-shaped handles. Particularly noteworthy is a red clay rhyton in the form of a deer's head (1st century BC; Baku, State Hist. & Archit. Mus.). A group of Christian churches (6th–9th centuries) date to the period of the ancient Caucasian country of Albania. One of the churches contains traces of wall painting, and a carved stone capital with two peacocks and an Albanian inscription has been discovered.

BIBLIOGRAPHY

G. M. Aslanov, R. M. Vaidov and G. I. Ione: *Drevniy Mingachevir* [Ancient Mingachevir] (Baku, 1959)

R. M. Vaidov: *Mingachevir v III–VIII vv* [Mingachevir in the 3rd–8th centuries] (Baku, 1961)

G. M. Aslanov, T. I. Golubkina and Sh. G. Sadykhzade: *Katalog zolotykh i serebryanykh predmetov iz arkheologicheskikh raskopok Azerbaydzhana* [A catalogue of gold and silver objects from the archaeological excavations in Azerbaijan] (Baku, 1966)

V. YA. PETRUKHIN

Ming dynasty. Chinese dynasty dating to 1368–1644, founded by a Chinese peasant–monk, Zhu Yuanzhang, who became the Hongwu emperor (*reg* 1368–98). The first Ming capital was at Nanjing. In 1421 the Yongle emperor (*reg* 1403–24) established a northern capital at Beijing, which by 1421 had become the official capital.

The early Ming period was prosperous and experienced a renewal of Chinese culture and national consciousness, which under the Mongol YUAN DYNASTY (1279–1368) had been submerged. Ming emperors promoted such works as the *Yongle dadian* (1408), an encyclopedic compendium of Chinese learning. The early period was marked by great building projects, including the Forbidden City and the rebuilding of the Great Wall in north China, military expansion and maritime expeditions.

Under the Xuande emperor (*reg* 1426–35) a regular system of court patronage of the arts developed. Painters tended to divide into three groups: court artists included Shi Rui (*fl* 1426–35) and Shang Xi (*fl* 1430–40); the academic ZHE SCHOOL (in Zhejiang), founded by Dai Jin, was much influenced by Southern Song silk scroll paintings; and the literati WU SCHOOL (named after the town that is modern Suzhou), in which Shen Zhou was prominent, was influenced by such Yuan masters as Ni Zan (*see also* CHINA, §V, 3(iv(a)). There were also individualists, some of whom, such as Wu Bin, merged both Song and Yuan influences (*see also* CHINA, §IV, 2(vi)(c)). The influential Dong Qichang asserted that divergences of style were a symptom of decline and postulated NORTHERN SCHOOL and SOUTHERN SCHOOL traditions, emphasizing that literati painters should follow the Southern school excusively.

In ceramics, blue-and-white wares were refined in technique and decoration, and overglaze enamels were applied to porcelain for the first time, in some instances combined with underglaze blue to create *doucai* ('fitted colours') and *wucai* ('five colours'). The cool blue and turquoise *fahua* glazes previously used for tiles and architectural ceramics were applied to large wine jars and vases. Whitewares known as *blanc de Chine* were produced at Dehua in Fujian Province, and unglazed stonewares, intended for use by scholars, at Yixing in Jiangsu Province. The kilns at JINGDEZHEN supplied not only the court but also the export market in West Asia, Japan and South-east Asia (*see also* CHINA, §VII, 3(vi)(a) and (c)). The shapes and decoration of Ming cloisonné and lacquer suggest an interaction with porcelain. The art of Chinese cloisonné first became developed in the Ming period (*see* CHINA, §XIII, 6), and lacquer reached its height in artistic and technical development at this time (*see* CHINA, §IX). The creation of gardens also bcame important during the Ming (*see* GARDEN, §VI, 1).

The active, early imperial patronage of the arts gradually lessened; palace orders became huge and wasteful. In the long reigns of the Jiajing (1522–66) and Wanli (1573–1620) emperors, power was gradually lost to corrupt, eunuch officials and large landowners. Tax increases fuelled urban and peasant uprisings but were insufficient to meet financial crises. The emperors were too distracted to respond to the rise in the north-east of the Manchus, who in 1644 supplanted them and founded the QING DYNASTY (1644–1911).

For discussion of Ming imperial tombs *see* CHINA, §II, 6(ii).

BIBLIOGRAPHY

W. T. De Bary, ed.: *Self and Society in Ming Thought* (New York, 1970)

E. L. Farmer: *Early Ming Government* (Cambridge, MA, 1976)

J. Cahill: *Parting at the Shore, Chinese Painting of the Early and Middle Ming Dynasty, 1368–1580* (New York, 1978)

C. O. Hucker: *The Ming Dynasty: Its Origins and Evolving Institutions*, Michigan Papers in Chinese Studies, 34 (Ann Arbor, 1978)

D. Lion-Goldschmidt: *Ming Porcelain* (London, 1978)

J. Spence: *The Memory Palace of Matteo Ricci* (London, 1985)

From Innovation to Conformity: Chinese Lacquer from the 13th to 16th Centuries (exh. cat. by R. Krahl and B. Morgan (London, 1989)

A. Paludan: *The Ming Tombs* (Hong Kong, Oxford and New York, 1991)

CAROL MICHAELSON

Mingei. 'People's crafts', a term coined by MUNEYOSHI YANAGI, the founder of the Japanese folk crafts movement. Formed against a background of growing cultural nationalism and colonial expansion in Asia, especially Korea, this concept and the movement associated with it attained wide influence in the mid-20th century (*see also* JAPAN, §XV).

1. EARLY YEARS. The *mingei undō* ('folk craft movement') grew out of the early association of Yanagi and the Japanese potters SHŌJI HAMADA, KENKICHI TOMIMOTO, KANJIRŌ KAWAI and the Englishman BERNARD LEACH. In 1926 the four Japanese announced a plan to establish a museum for folk crafts, heralding the discovery of a 'new realm of beauty' in the ordinary utensils of daily living—robust, wholesome, traditional handicrafts made by anonymous artisans for the common people. Yanagi called these objects *mingei*, explaining the term as an abbreviation of *minshūteki kōgei* ('people's crafts'), and gave the English translation as 'folk crafts'. The proclaimed objectives of the group were not only to assemble and document a collection of old folk crafts but to encourage the production of new *mingei*. This necessitated a survey of surviving folk craft centres, guidance to craftsmen and assistance in the marketing of authentic products, as well as a campaign to educate the public through publications, lectures and exhibitions.

In his youth Yanagi had been an ardent admirer of Western arts and cosmopolitan ideas. The imprint of Western thought, notably the mysticism and populism of WILLIAM BLAKE and the social commitment of JOHN RUSKIN and WILLIAM MORRIS, was to be seen in the movement's early direction. However, in the years preceding 1926 Yanagi had been preoccupied with Korean crafts, especially the ceramics of the Chosŏn period (1392–1910). In their effortless beauty, Yanagi saw the hand of the 'unknown craftsman'—a man of selfless humility and piety, faithful to tradition and at one with nature—an image that became central to Yanagi's *mingei* theory. He emphasized dependence on *tariki* ('power of another'), meaning the redeeming power of Buddha, but also implying the cumulative wisdom of generations and the blessings of the natural environment and the community. Having identified beauty with utility, he directed his emotional appeals for involvement not only to the makers of crafts, but to users as well, whose role he perceived to be creative, as in the tradition of the tea ceremony. Yanagi's writings and the enthusiasm of the group escalated into a crusade and a movement as others rallied to the cause.

The scholars Hakkyō [Noritaka] Asakawa (1884–1964) and his brother Takumi (1890–1937) contributed their expertise to the assemblage of superb Korean ceramics for the collection. Others who joined the movement were Toyotarō Tanaka (1899–1981), psychiatrist and art critic Ryūzaburō Shikiba (1898–1965), and literary critic and craft historian Bunshō Jugaku (1900–92), who was to contribute studies of the art and history of papermaking. Shōya Yoshida (1898–1972) and Kichinosuke Tonomura (1898–1993) became energetic leaders in their localities, Tottori and Okayama prefectures. More visible were the artist–craftsmen (besides the above-mentioned): KEISUKE SERIZAWA, master dyer; weaver Yoshitaka Yanagi (*b* 1911); woodworker Tatsuaki Kuroda (1904–82); woodblock print artist SHIKŌ MUNAKATA; potters Michitada Funaki (1900–63) and Tōtarō Sakuma (1900–76). Joining later were potters Tatsuzō Shimaoka (*b* 1919), Kenji Funaki (*b* 1927) and Kōichi Takita (*b* 1927) and papermaker Eishirō Abe (1902–84) among others.

Japan at the time was undergoing industrialization, which threatened to hasten the demise of many traditional handicrafts. On the other hand, studio craftsmen of Kyoto and Tokyo, having distanced themselves from the exposition mentality of the Meiji period (1868–1912), strove to combine technical virtuosity with refinement, as they aspired to status as artists and sought acceptance of artistic crafts in the prestigious government exhibitions. Yanagi questioned the superiority of such 'aristocratic' precious wares. He believed *mingei* to be the best of crafts because of their honesty, health and fidelity to function.

The movement developed two strands: preservation (or revitalization) of rural handicrafts; and a search for a new aesthetic in modern crafts. Yanagi's theories pertained mainly to the condition of the rural craftsman, but the movement's dynamic was largely in the interest stimulated among *kojin sakka* ('individual artists'), who came to be known as *mingei sakka* ('folk craft artists'; a seemingly contradictory term, applied as well to the craftsmen–founders of the movement). Priority was accorded to individual, modern studio craftsmen, on the principle that they would play leading roles in regional crafts. The Kamigamo Mingei Kyōdan, a small experimental crafts commune established under the founding group's sponsorship in Kyoto in 1927 and intended to emulate the craft guilds of medieval Europe, was composed of such members. The experiment collapsed within two years while Yanagi was a visiting lecturer at Harvard. In 1928 the Kokugakai, an independent association of painters, sculptors and printmakers, initiated a crafts section, largely through the efforts of Tomimoto. Despite vicissitudes, the Kokugakai crafts section became the forum for the *mingeiha* ('folk crafts school') of artist–craftsmen. It was the first group to challenge the newly established crafts section of the government-sponsored Teiten (Exhibition of the Imperial Fine Arts Academy), whose emphasis on technical polish and art-for-show was anathema to the *mingei* movement.

On a different level was the populist crafts movement involving rural folk craft centres, stimulated by frequent visits by Yanagi, Hamada and Kawai, who also encouraged recruitment of local patrons and entrepreneurs into the *mingei* fold. Establishment of the Takumi craft shops in Tottori (1932) and Tokyo (1933) and creation of the Nihon Mingei Kyōkai (Japan Folk Craft Society) in 1934 furthered the nationwide effort. Also in that year the first large-scale exhibition of folk kiln products (9000 items from 43 kilns) was arranged by Takumi and held at Matsuzakaya Department Store (Tokyo). Stencil dyeing, weaving, birch-bark crafts, grass matting and bamboo furniture were also promoted through workshops and exhibitions directed by Serizawa, Kawai and others.

2. MINGEIKAN COLLECTION. Construction of the Nihon Mingeikan (Japan Flk A. Mus.) at Komaba, Tokyo, was completed in 1936 with the financial assistance of

Magosaburō Ōhara (1880–1943), and Yanagi became its first director. The collection was assembled in the course of numerous forays into the countryside and abroad by the movement's leaders, most often Yanagi, Hamada and Kawai, which continued after the museum's opening. Their collecting was in roughly four categories: arts and crafts of pre-industrial Japan, formerly overlooked by art historians because of their plebeian or utilitarian nature; crafts of Korea and Okinawa, not necessarily folk crafts (certain of these, e.g. Korean white porcelains and most of the Okinawan textiles, were strictly for the nobility) but seen as neglected because of their minority status (Korea was under Japanese rule at the time); folk art of other regions of the world; and contemporary crafts of followers of the movement (mostly work of the *mingei*-school artist–craftsmen, but also examples of new work produced at folk craft centres). The three-volume *Mingei zukan*, with the English title *A Harvest of Folk Crafts*, was published in 1960–61 as a selective catalogue of the collection with emphasis on the first two categories. The more comprehensive five-volume *Mingei Taikan: Sōetsu Yanagi Collection* was published in 1981–2.

The journal *Kōgei* (1931–51), the voice of the movement, has been considered a landmark publication not only for its beautifully handcrafted design and its substantive content, but for maintaining a balanced and staunch democratic viewpoint through traumatic times. Surveys and research on *mingei* were pursued throughout World War II, but the promised comprehensive national study by Yanagi, the work of 20 years, was lost to fire near the end of the war. A short version, *Teshigoto no Nihon* ('Japan, land of handicrafts') was published in 1948.

3. POST-WAR PERIOD. The movement's democratic nature, pre-war ties between its members and the West, attention from the Occupation authorities and a general sense of renewal aided the early revival of *mingei* activities after the war. Chapters of the Mingei Kyōkai formed in most prefectures; a dozen regional museums were independently organized, and branch museums of the Nihon Mingeikan were established in Naha (Okinawa Prefect.) and at the Expo '70 site (Osaka). There were setbacks, such as the 1953 defection of Chūichi Miyake (1900–82) and a number of his sympathizers, who left the Kyōkai to form the Nihon Mingei Kyōdan in Osaka. The move was prompted by a feeling among some rural artisans that the 'unknown craftsman' principle was threatened by the prominence of *mingei* artists and their intrusions in the craft communities. Miyake's group built museums in Osaka and Koishiwara (Fukuoka Prefect.) and limited exhibitions strictly to anonymous work. Despite concern over the movement's goals, however, the popular appeal of *mingei* grew, accentuated by the rapid rise of the artists Munakata, Hamada, Serizawa and Kawai, and produced a *mingei* boom that reached its height in the 1960s. Successful ceramic centres such as Mashiko (Tochigi Prefect.), where Hamada made his home, and Onta (Ōita Prefect.), an exemplary folk kiln publicized by Leach's visit in 1954, became tourist attractions. *Mingei* shops and department store '*mingei* corners' proliferated, and the influence of *mingei* reached abroad in publications and exhibitions, as well as through wares bought by foreign visitors.

Such success, together with the high cost of hand labour in an industrial society, made it difficult to maintain the original character and quality of local crafts. Increasingly, wares of standardized appearance and dubious quality pervaded the market. Thus to most Japanese, *mingei* came to mean a style of modern commercial product, while the works of '*mingei* artists' became luxury goods, and the true folk crafts of old Japan became *komingei* ('old *mingei*').

4. LEGACY. The most significant consequence of the *mingei* movement was the new awareness of the creative role of the common people. The Mingeikan collection was itself a momentous achievement, testimony to the aesthetic values espoused by Yanagi and to his rare insight and superb eye. It has served to 'prove by example', in Yanagi's words, the excellence of crafts not previously honoured and to broaden the vistas of Japan's cultural heritage.

The term *mingei* also clings to a school of artist–craftsmen, whose achievements (not to be considered folk art) may be of more lasting importance than the extended life of rural handicrafts associated with *mingei*. Worth noting is that the leading *mingei* school artists benefited from their involvement with local crafts (a notable instance of this was the blending of Okinawan influences in the creations of Hamada, Kawai and Serizawa, adding new dimensions to Japanese art). The styles of these artists are varied; at their best, they have in common a fusion of folk tradition with a personal vision that is distinctly contemporary. A number of artists associated with the *mingei* school have been designated *jūyō mukei bunkazai* (Important Intangible Cultural Asset) by the Japanese government: Shōji Hamada (trailed glazes), Keisuke Serizawa (stencil dyeing), Tatsuaki Kuroda (woodwork) and Eishirō Abe (*ganpi* paper). Kenkichi Tomimoto, an early *mingei* leader, left the movement, feeling his aspirations as an artist to be at variance with *mingei* precepts. Much honoured in the art world, he was designated *jūyō mukei bunkazai* for his achievement in enamelled porcelain.

Writing in 1948 of the movement's achievements, Yanagi commented that *mingei* had no equivalent in the West and that 'folk crafts' was not an adequate translation. He described the movement as one of 'faith', and his search for a workable formula for the continuation of *mingei* production was inextricably tied to his religious beliefs. Yanagi's idealized view of the common people, in harmony with his Buddhist world view, gave the movement a mystique that was a great part of its appeal and contributed to its momentum. Ultimately, however, it became apparent that there was an inherent contradiction between an aggressive modern movement and Yanagi's vision of an innocent, unselfconscious craftsman giving birth to folk crafts. After Yanagi's death in 1961, Hamada took over the direction of the Mingeikan, to be succeeded after his death in 1978 by Yanagi's son Munemichi [Sōri] (*b* 1915).

BIBLIOGRAPHY

Kōgei [Crafts], Nihon Mingei Kyōkai; 120 vols (Tokyo, 1931–51)

Gekkan mingei [Mingei monthly], Nihon Mingei Kyōkai (Tokyo, 1939–42)

Mingei, Nihon Mingei Kyōkai (Tokyo, 1942–88; discontinued Jan 1945–June 1946, July 1948–Dec 1954)

I. Kumakura: *Mingei no hakken* [The discovery of *mingei*], Nihon bunka [Japanese culture], x (Tokyo, 1978)

B. Moeran: *Lost Innocence: Folk Craft Potters of Onta, Japan* (Berkeley, 1984)
E. Frolet: *Yanagi Soetsu ou les éléments d'une renaissance artistique au Japon* (Paris, 1986)
Mingei: Masterpieces of Japanese Folkcraft (exh. cat., Tokyo, Japan Flk A. Mus., 1991)

VICTOR AND TAKAKO HAUGE

Minguzzi, Luciano (*b* Bologna, 24 May 1911). Italian sculptor. He trained as a sculptor with his father, also a sculptor, and completed his education at the Accademia di Belle Arti in Bologna, exhibiting for the first time in 1943. His early works were influenced by the archaism of Arturo Martini, but during the 1940s and the 1950s he evolved his own style in which suggestions of ancient sculptural models, both Etruscan and Asian, combined rather originally with an awareness of contemporary developments, particularly those of Picasso and Marino Marini. His style was dry and vigorous, characterized by a narrative sense at times visionary, at times verging on the grotesque. Among the most important works of this period are the *Dog among the Sticks, No. 1* (bronze, 1949; New York, MOMA) and the *Contortionists* and *Acrobats* of 1952–3 (e.g. *Acrobat on the Trapeze*, 1952; Rome, G.N.A. Mod.). In 1950 he won the main prize for sculpture at the Venice Biennale.

A new direction in Minguzzi's work was indicated by *Shadows in the Wood* (1957; Rome, G.N.A. Mod.). While the use of primitive forms and naturalistic references was retained, the sculpture showed a new degree of imagination. The work that followed included cage-like structures with a spiky fragility, reminiscent of the sculpture of Alberto Giacometti and Lynn Chadwick. In the 1960s he began to use such components as metal piping and doors around fragile human forms to suggest torture or gas chambers, and he also experimented with wood, stone and terracotta. However, his greatest achievements remained those in bronze: for example he showed great technical skill in the fifth door of Milan Cathedral with its 14 bronze panels. The door was produced after he won a competition in 1950, and it was inaugurated in 1965. The *Good and Bad* bronze door for St Peter's in Rome (1978) and the *Monument to the Carabiniere* (1983) in Piazza Diaz in Milan, an enormous symbolic statue with a powerful visual impact, were among the most celebrated of his later works.

BIBLIOGRAPHY
C. Gnudi: 'Luciano Minguzzi', *Boll. Gal. Milione* (Feb 1955)
Luciano Minguzzi (exh. cat. by M. Valsecchi, Bologna, Gal. A. Mod., 1975)

ANTONELLO NEGRI

Minhagim books. In Jewish tradition a *minhag* (pl. *minhagim*) is defined as a well-established religious practice or usage, which, though unsupported by Written Law, assumes the force of a binding regulation. However, while the prescriptions of the Written Law are universally accepted by all Jews, a *minhag* may vary from one community to another. Books recording such variations developed from the Middle Ages (the earliest known work dates to *c.* 8th century AD) and are generally referred to as *minhagim* books. A vast literature of this genre was created especially among Ashkenazi Jews, while the Sephardim and Jews of Islamic lands dedicated lesser efforts to recording their particular customs. Illustrated editions of *minhagim* books flourished among Ashkenazi Jews in Europe especially in the 17th and 18th centuries, printed by Hebrew presses in Italy, Germany, Holland and Bohemia. The most popular editions were generally compiled in Yiddish and thus were accessible to a wide readership, including women and children. These editions were often accompanied by a series of small woodcuts illustrating Jewish holidays, religious observances, ceremonies in the life cycle (circumcisions, weddings, funerals), the Signs of the Zodiac and Labours of the Months.

The earliest illustrated edition of a *minhagim* book, employing the Yiddish version compiled by Simeon Levi Gunzburg, was published by Giovanni di Gara in Venice, 1593. Executed by an anonymous folk artist, the woodcuts in this pioneering edition served as models for many future editions (printed chiefly in Amsterdam, Prague, Hamburg and Frankfurt), often replicating the originals without any significant change. Moreover, the popular *minhagim* woodcuts were used to illustrate books with other texts (e.g. Passover Haggadot and 'Grace after Meals'), and even inspired the illustrations in a non-Jewish work by the Dutch Calvinist Johannes Leusden (*Philologus Hebraeo-Mixtus*; Utrecht, 1663). The transplanted woodcuts must, therefore, be studied with caution and cannot testify categorically to the customs prevalent in the place and time of a given published work. At the same time, and despite their naivety, they contain considerable information on the social life of Ashkenazi Jews, including their customs and popular beliefs, the interiors of home and synagogue, male and female costumes, and ceremonial objects shown being used in context.

It should be noted that some contemporary books on Judaism and Jewish life written by Christian Hebraists and theologians such as Johannes Buxtorf (1564–1629) and Johann Christoph Bodenschatz (1717–1797) contain parallel episodes of Jewish ceremonies. The relationship between the illustrations in these books and those of the *minhagim* books is yet to be studied.

BIBLIOGRAPHY
A. Rubens: *A Jewish Iconography* (London, 1954, rev. 1981)
A. M. Habermann: 'The Jewish Art of the Printed Book', *Jewish Art: An Illustrated History*, ed. C. Roth (Greenwich, CN, 1971), pp. 163–74
I. Ta-Shema, I. Klein and C. Roth: 'Minhagim Books', *Enc. Jud.*, xii (Jerusalem, 1972), cols 26–31
M. Epstein: 'Simon Levi Ginzburg's Illustrated Customal (Minhagim Book) of Venice, 1593, and its Travels', *Proceedings of the Fifth World Congress of Jewish Studies*, iv (Jerusalem, 1973), pp. 197–218
C. Shmeruk: 'Ha-iyyurim min ha-minhagim be-Yiddish, Veneziah 1593' [Illustrations in the Yiddish Book of Customs, Venice 1593], *Stud. Bibliog. & Bklore*, xv (Cincinnati, 1984), pp. 31–52 [in Hebr.]
——: *Ha-iyyurim le-sifrei Yiddish ba-me'ot ha-16-ha-17* [Illustrations in Yiddish books of the sixteenth and seventeenth centuries] (Jerusalem, 1986) [in Hebr. with Eng. summary]
N. Feuchtwanger-Sarig: 'An Illustrated *Minhagim* Book Printed in Amsterdam', *Bibliotheca Rosenthaliana: Treasures of Jewish Booklore*, ed. A. K. Offenberg and others (Amsterdam, 1994), pp. 36–7

SHALOM SABAR

Miniato, Giovanni [Nanni]. *See under* FORA, DEL.

Miniature. Term applied both to paintings in manuscripts (*see* §I below) and to the related form of independent, small paintings, particularly portraits, that developed in the 16th century (*see* §II below). It derives from the Latin *minium*, the red lead employed to emphasize initial letters in a text, and thus originally referred to rubrication; since the 16th century, however, the term has been applied more widely to encompass the small-scale painted illustrations in manuscripts, the result of a mistaken etymology, which associated the word with 'minute'. In the medieval period a manuscript miniature was referred to as *historia*, and contemporaries called portrait miniatures 'limnings' (from illumination) or 'pictures in little'.

I. Manuscript. II. Portrait and related forms.

I. Manuscript.

In its strict sense the term miniature when applied to manuscripts is restricted to paintings in gouache, often combined with gold, but it is sometimes more loosely and less accurately used to refer to illustrations in other techniques such as grisaille and line drawing. The format of such miniatures varies: they may be framed or unframed, full-page, half-page or smaller, independent of the text or set above or within it; they may be a single image or form part of a cycle; multiple, successive scenes may also be shown by dividing the space into bands or compartments. Horizontal registers, for instance, are characteristic of frontispieces in Carolingian Gospel books and Bibles from Tours (e.g. *see* BIBLE, fig. 3). Smaller divisions into squares, rectangles or medallions are found from the Romanesque period (e.g. *see* ROMANESQUE, fig. 60) and with increasing frequency in Gothic manuscripts. Miniatures in the latter are sometimes laid out like stained-glass windows; this is strikingly evident in the 13th-century *Bibles moralisées* (*see* BIBLE, fig. 8). Alternatively, the miniature space might be divided by the use of architectural frames (e.g. *see* GOTHIC, fig. 72). The iconography of a miniature is often extended by combining it with such other decorative elements as initials (*see* INITIAL, MANUSCRIPT), borders (*see* BORDER, MANUSCRIPT) and small BAS-DE-PAGE scenes at the foot of the page (see fig. 1). More unusually the format may reflect the didactic purpose of a miniature, taking the form of a table (e.g. *see* CANON TABLE) or a diagram, intended to summarize a text or act as an aide-mémoire.

The function of a miniature was not limited to the aesthetic: for instance by marking the beginnings of chapters and other textual divisions, the hierarchical structure of the text was clarified, the book made easier to handle and the importance of its contents emphasized and impressed on the reader's mind. Particularly effective examples of this are the carpet pages marking the major divisions of Insular Gospel books (*see* INSULAR ART, fig. 3).

The content of a miniature might reflect the whole of a text (e.g. an AUTHOR PORTRAIT, the figure shown writing or reading), the circumstances of its origin (e.g. a consecrative or a dedication miniature; *see* CAROLINGIAN ART, fig. 8) or be more directly related to the meaning of the text. Scientific treatises call for didactic illustration (e.g. *see* HERBAL, fig. 1; MEDICAL ILLUSTRATED BOOKS, §1), but literary texts (among others) were accorded narrative interpretation (*see* ROMANCE, MANUSCRIPT), as were such religious texts as the APOCALYPSE, which by the 13th century contained cycles of *c.* 80 scenes, and SAINTS'

1. Miniature of the *Birth of St John the Baptist*, 135×110 mm; with *bas-de-page* scene of the *Baptism*, 42×110 mm; from the Turin–Milan Hours, from Bruges, *c.* 1440–45 (Turin, Museo Civico d'Arte Antica, MS. 47, fol. 93*v*)

LIVES. Indirect illustration was based on various associations: the illustration of the Office of the Virgin in a Book of Hours with scenes from the Life of the Virgin reflected not the content but the use of the book; in liturgical manuscripts a scene depicting part of the liturgy was sometimes used (for illustration *see* SERVICE BOOK; *see also* ROMANESQUE, fig. 56); philosophical and theological texts were illustrated by personification and allegory (*see* ALLEGORY, figs 2 and 3). Certain types of book, religious and secular (e.g. the PSALTER, the BOOK OF HOURS and Classical authors such as TERENCE), had a more or less standard iconographic repertory.

The relation of a miniature to the text it accompanied changed over its history. Most early medieval miniature cycles were placed before the beginning of a text or interspersed within it, more or less at random. Later miniatures were more closely related to the text, often placed within the column of text at the appropriate place in the narrative or with accompanying inscriptions. By the 15th century the position of the viewer in relation to the text had also changed and the division between the viewer and the miniature space blurred. This was achieved by various means: figures were made to overlap the miniature frames, as if stepping into the foreground, a technique adopted in Netherlandish work of *c.* 1400; in the late 15th century artists such as Simon Marmion introduced enlarged, half-length figures into the foreground of his miniatures, thereby diminishing their narrative content and creating a more immediate presence; in this period the artists of the GHENT-BRUGES SCHOOL used naturalistic details in the margins of their miniatures to give a *trompe l'oeil* effect (*see* BORDER, MANUSCRIPT, fig. 3); similar illusionistic effects were created in humanistic Italian manuscripts, using naturalistic architectural details to frame the miniature.

BIBLIOGRAPHY

J. Dominguez Bordona: *La miniatura española*, 2 vols (Florence, 1929)
J. Porcher: *L'Enluminure française* (Paris, 1958)
M. Rickert: *La miniatura inglese*, 2 vols (Milan, 1959–61)
D. Diringer: *The Illuminated Book: Its History and Production* (London, 1967)
L. M. J. Delaissé: *A Century of Dutch Manuscript Illumination* (Berkeley and Los Angeles, 1968)
A. Goldschmidt: *German Illumination* (London, 1970)
L. Donati: *Bibliografia della miniatura*, 2 vols, Biblioteca di bibliografia italiana, lxix (Florence, 1972)
D. M. Robb: *The Art of the Illuminated Manuscript* (Cranbury, NJ, 1972)
M. Smeyers: *La Miniature*, Typologie des sources du moyen-âge occidental, viii (Turnhout, 1974) [app.: *Mise à jour*, 1985]
F. Brunello: *De arti illuminandi e altri trattati sulle technica della miniature medievale* (Vicenza, 1975)
O. Mazal: *Buchkunst der Gotik*, Buchkunst im Wandel der Zeiten, i–ii (Graz, 1975–8)
J. Backhouse: *The Illuminated Manuscript: The Craft of the Scribe* (London, 1979)
E. G. Grimme: *Die Geschichte der abendländischen Buchmalerei*, DuMont Dokumente (Cologne, 1980)
W. Csapodi-Gardonyi: *Europäische Buchmalerei* (Leipzig and Weimar, 1982)
R. Calkins: *Illuminated Books in the Middle Ages* (New York, 1983)
Renaissance Painting in Manuscripts: Treasures from the British Library (exh. cat., ed. T. Kren; London, BL; Malibu, CA, Getty Mus.; New York, Pierpont Morgan Lib.; 1983–4)
O. Pächt: *Buchmalerei des Mittelalters* (Munich, 1984; Eng. trans., New York, 1986)
C. De Hamel: *A History of Illuminated Manuscripts* (Oxford, 1986, rev. 1994)
G. Dogaer: *Flemish Miniature Painting in the 15th and 16th Centuries* (Amsterdam, 1987)

M. SMEYERS

II. Portrait and related forms.

In Europe the independent miniature or 'limning' evolved from the illuminated manuscript *c.* 1520. Since then the main occupation of the miniature painter has been to provide small portraits, a genre that enjoyed widespread popularity in the Western world for nearly four centuries, although the technique of the miniaturist was also still applied to themes derived from history, myth, genre or landscape. Miniature portraits appealed to a fundamental desire for likenesses in little. Like jewels, they displayed delicacy of execution and could be carried or worn, and they were able to convey a more intimate interpretation of character than the more formal and public presentation proper to a large-scale oil painting. Most portrait miniatures were painted in watercolour and gouache, at first on vellum and later on ivory. In the 17th century developments in the craft of enamelling led to its use as another medium for the portrait miniature. Enamel miniatures have a history and style so nearly akin to that of the watercolour miniature that they require inclusion in a

general survey. There is a cognate type of small portrait in oil, usually on a metal support, the study of which belongs to that of large-scale portraiture in oil.

1. *c.* 1520–*c.* 1620: from Clouet to Hilliard. 2. *c.* 1620–*c.* 1730: from the Coopers to Boit. 3. *c.* 1730–*c.* 1770: from Massé to Høyer. 4. *c.* 1770–*c.* 1820: from Hall to Isabey. 5. After *c.* 1820.

1. *c.* 1520–*c.* 1620: FROM CLOUET TO HILLIARD. The emergence of the miniature as a separate branch of portraiture can be traced to the illuminated manuscript *Les Commentaires de la guerre gallique* (3 vols: London, BM; Paris, Bib. N.; Chantilly, Mus. Condé), produced *c.* 1518–20 for Francis I to commemorate his victory over the Swiss at Marignano in 1515. Among the illuminations are head-and-shoulders portraits of the seven commanders who supported the King, the 'Preux de Marignan', shown three-quarter-face in circles *c.* 50 mm in diameter (vol. 2; Paris, Bib. N.). These are executed on the vellum, against a blue background, with an illuminator's technique; they are portrait miniatures in every sense except that they are not separated from the manuscript page. The evidence of the drawings (Chantilly, Mus. Condé) from which the portraits were derived shows that these limnings are by the court painter Jean Clouet.

The crucial event of detaching the miniature portrait from the manuscript occurred *c.* 1526. In that year Francis I's sister Marguerite, Duchesse d'Alençon, gave Henry VIII two lockets (untraced) whose lids opened to reveal

2. Hans Holbein (ii): *Jane Small* (formerly known as *Jane Pemberton*), watercolour on vellum, diam. 52 mm, *c.* 1536 (London, Victoria and Albert Museum)

in one case the portrait of Francis I, and in the other a double portrait of his two sons, the Dauphin François and Henri, Duc d'Orléans, then hostages after the Battle of Pavia (1525). These were evidently miniatures as we now understand the term and may well have been by Jean Clouet. At almost exactly the same time, Lucas Horenbout painted several portrait miniatures of Henry VIII aged 35 (e.g. Cambridge, Fitzwilliam). It is not possible to say which event preceded the other. Horenbout, however, pursued the art of portrait miniature painting with more assiduity than Jean Clouet, and, according to Karel van Mander I, he taught the technique of limning to Hans Holbein (ii), who painted a number of miniatures of unsurpassed quality during his second visit to England from 1532. These include such masterpieces as the round *Anne of Cleves* (London, V&A) and *Jane Small* (see fig. 2). Both Jean Clouet and Lucas Horenbout came from the Netherlands, where the portrait miniature was not cultivated. An exception is provided by Simon Bening, of whom there are two versions of a *Self-portrait at the Age of 75* (1558; London, V&A; New York, Met.). Bening's daughter Levina Teerlinc worked as a limner for Elizabeth I and her entourage, but her oeuvre has yet to be established.

Although France had been the birthplace of the art, there was only a sporadic production of portrait miniatures in that country during the next two centuries. François Clouet, the son of Jean Clouet, painted a few miniatures of considerable finesse, such as the oval portraits of *Charles IX* and *Catherine de' Medici* in a contemporary jewelled locket (Vienna, Ksthist. Mus.). But he had so little indigenous following in this field that Nicholas Hilliard was in great demand for small portraits when he visited France from 1576 to 1578, shortly after François Clouet's death.

Hilliard was the representative figure in, and virtually the second founder of, a strong English tradition in this art, following an unproductive interregnum after the deaths of Holbein in 1543 and Horenbout in 1544. In the reign of Elizabeth I (1558–1603), Hilliard developed a type of miniature portraiture that appealed to a wide range of sitters, and he established a peculiarly English type of vision, dependent on clear lighting and elegant line, which embodies the creative urge and lyricism of the Elizabethan resurgence.

Hilliard's career played a decisive role in naturalizing the genre in England. The breadth of patronage accorded to him and the scope of his practice gave this specialized art a standing of its own. He adopted the oval shape favoured by Mannerist taste—his first known use of the format is in an early portrait of *Elizabeth I* (1572; London, N.P.G.). As well as employing the bust portrait, he also introduced the miniature full-length, as in the intensely poetic *Young Man Leaning against a Tree among Roses* (*c.* 1588; London, V&A; see fig. 3), and portraits with emblematic features, such as that of a *Man Clasping a Hand from a Cloud* (1588; London, V&A). In his treatise *The Arte of Limninge*, written *c.* 1600, Hilliard combined technical advice on miniature painting with an emphasis on the gentility of the pursuit and extolled its achievements above those of large-scale portraiture.

3. Nicholas Hilliard: *Young Man Leaning against a Tree among Roses*, watercolour on vellum, oval, 136×73 mm *c.* 1588 (London, Victoria and Albert Museum)

Over the 17th century England possessed the most patronized and the most continuously active group of portrait miniature painters in Europe. Hilliard was succeeded by his pupils Isaac Oliver and Laurence Hilliard, his son. Oliver had a busy practice as a portrait miniaturist, developing a style more dependent than Hilliard's on late 16th-century European portraiture on the scale of life, as in his rectangular full-length miniature of *Richard Sackville, 3rd Earl of Dorset* (1616; London, V&A). He also painted miniature compositions with historical and religious subjects. His most ambitious *Entombment* (Angers, Mus. B.-A.) was finished by his son Peter Oliver, but thereafter historical miniature painting in England was virtually confined to the making of small, limned copies of Old Master paintings in important collections.

The tradition of limned history paintings was, however, stronger in Italy and especially in the German territories. Giulio Clovio was described by Vasari as the 'Michelangelo in little'. Although much of his limned work forms a part

4. Daniel Fröschl: *Adam and Eve*, gouache on parchment, 238×176 mm, 1604 (Vienna, Graphische Sammlung Albertina)

rendering of character was more searching than that of his British contemporaries, whether they painted in oils or smaller compass. He became one of the most renowned miniature artists in Europe in the 17th century, with a great reputation in France, the Netherlands and Italy: one of his many miniatures of *Oliver Cromwell* was sent to Queen Christina of Sweden with Latin verses by John Milton. Samuel's brother Alexander played an important role in disseminating the art of the miniature in Europe. These representative figures were joined by miniaturists from a diversity of backgrounds: Richard Gibson, a page and a dwarf; Thomas Flatman, a poet and a lawyer; Nicholas Dixon, who succeeded Samuel Cooper as limner to Charles II; and Peter Cross, the son of a merchant draper. These artists adapted the styles of van Dyck and Sir Peter Lely to the portrayal in little of a substantial section of the elegant world.

Although the history of miniature painting in mainland Europe in the 17th century does not display the unbroken tradition and continuity of talent found in England, it provides many instances of intermittent activity. So far as any judgement can be formed in the context of a little-studied topic, it would seem that this branch of art was most popular at Northern and Protestant courts. The weighty political and marital links between the leading families encouraged the employment of the same artists in more than one centre, sometimes painters who were not specialists in limning alone. The career of Alexander Cooper provides a good example of the peripatetic nature of the miniaturist's profession in these circumstances. He was invited to the exiled court of Frederick V of Bohemia in The Hague *c.* 1630 and worked there for Elizabeth of Bohemia and the Palatinate family. Then in 1647 he was recruited by Queen Christina in her drive to encourage the arts in Sweden. Among his works is the bold portrait of the Queen's favourite *Count Magnus Gabriel De la Gardie* (Stockholm, Nmus.). While in her employ he occasionally left Stockholm to visit England, and in 1656 he was invited to Copenhagen to paint Frederick III and his family (e.g. Copenhagen, Rosenborg Slot).

In Germany a diligent though unnamed artist working at the courts of Brunswick-Lüneburg and Brandenburg had painted *c.* 1595 a large series of miniatures of members of those princely houses. Some 50 of these are in the British Royal Collection (Windsor Castle, Berks, Royal Col.), having been arranged by Caroline of Ansbach (1683–1737), wife of George II, in the Queen's Closet at Kensington Palace, London. Friedrich Brentel portrayed *Duke George of Brunswick-Lüneburg* (1630; Windsor Castle, Berks, Royal Col.) and was also patronized by Margrave William of Baden-Baden (*d* 1677). In addition to portraits he painted subject miniatures, such as the *Mortals' Vain Fight against Time and Death* (untraced; see Schidlof, 1964, no. 167), and described his technique for painting miniatures in watercolour on vellum in a manuscript of 1642 called *Mahler und Illuminir Büchlein* (Göttingen, Universitätsbib.). Brentel was followed in Baden-Baden by Thomas Le Febure (*c.* 1630–1720), who had been born in Brussels and also worked for the Margrave Frederick V of Baden-Durlach (*reg* 1659–77) and Frederick I, Duke of Saxe-Gotha (1646–91). The Frenchman Jean Michelin worked in Hannover from 1668 to 1686, painting members

of such manuscripts as the Farnese Hours (*c.* 1537–46; New York, Pierpont Morgan Lib.), he also painted a number of independent miniature subject pictures including *Crucifixion with Mary Magdalene* (Florence, Uffizi), as well as portraits, among them that of *Eleanora di Toledo* (*c.* 1551–3; Welbeck Abbey, Notts). Joris Hoefnagel and his son Jacob Hoefnagel (1575–*c.* 1630) produced subject miniatures at the court of Rudolf II. Joris's *Allegory of the Brevity of Life* (1591; Lille, Mus. B.-A.) is an example. Daniel Fröschl was appointed miniature painter to Rudolf II in Prague in 1601. His portrait of the Emperor (London, priv. col.) was in Charles I's collection, and he also painted a notable miniature of *Adam and Eve* (Vienna, Albertina; see fig. 4).

2. *c.* 1620–*c.* 1730: FROM THE COOPERS TO BOIT. In England, Nicholas Hilliard and Isaac Oliver were followed by Peter Oliver and John Hoskins. In the work of the latter, who turned from painting in oils to miniatures such as the portrait of *Katherine Howard, Lady d'Aubigny* (*c.* 1640; London, V&A), the achievement of the most accomplished portrait painter of the period, Anthony van Dyck, was assimilated into the tradition of English miniature painting. Edward Norgate continued to emphasize the suitability of limning as a pursuit for the gentleman in his manuscript treatise *Miniatura or the Art of Limning*. The dominant figures of the next generation, Samuel Cooper and Alexander Cooper, were the nephews and wards of John Hoskins. Samuel Cooper mastered a way of translating the methods of oil painting into those appropriate to the miniature painter's technique. His

of the ducal house in Roman attire (e.g. Hannover, Fürstenhaus Herrenhausen-Mus.).

Queen Christina invited Pierre Signac (*c.* 1624–*c.* 1684) to Sweden from France in 1647. He practised in Stockholm, initially as an enamel painter (e.g. *Queen Christina in White*; Stockholm, Nmus.) but learnt the technique of painting on vellum from Alexander Cooper, producing such pieces as *Queen Ulrica Eleanora in a Yellow Dress* (1682; Stockholm, Nmus.). He thereby laid the foundations of a national school in Sweden in both media and was followed in the next generation by Elias Brenner (1647–1717), Charles Boit and the brothers David Richter (1664–1741) and Christian Richter (1678–1732), the latter working mainly in England.

In Denmark, Alexander Cooper had been preceded by Jacob van Doort, an artist of Dutch origin who may have been trained in England and who worked for Christian IV. He was followed by Paul Prieur (?1620–after 1683), a Frenchman who had been trained in enamel painting in Geneva, Louis Goullon (*d* 1680) from Paris, and Georg Saleman (*d* 1729), who had been born in Reval (Tallinn). The cosmopolitan nature of the miniaturist's life is further illustrated by the career of Perpète Evrard (1662–1727), who was born in the Netherlands, worked in Madrid and Vienna and died in The Hague.

In the main, limning in France does not present a connected history in the 17th century. While Michelin, Goullon and Signac worked abroad, Louis Du Guernier, a founder-member of the Académie Royale, was one of the few to pursue watercolour limning in France as a career. The enamellist Jean Petitot, also an exception to the nomadic habits of the majority, worked in England for the court of Charles I from 1637, producing fine portraits such as that of *Mary, Duchess of Richmond* (Stockholm, Nmus.). Leaving England on the outbreak of the Civil War in 1642, he stayed in Paris for over 40 years, not returning to his native Switzerland until the revocation of the Edict of Nantes in 1685. He perfected the technique of the portrait miniature on enamel, and he maintained a meticulous standard of excellence to the end of his long career. His brother-in-law Jacques Bordier (1616–84) was his life-long assistant and is credited with painting the costumes in the enamels. Petitot's prolific output includes many portraits of Louis XIV and of courtiers and mistresses (e.g. *Louise de La Vallière*, 1670; Geneva, Mus. A. & Hist.; see fig. 5). Although he usually took contemporary portraits as a model, Petitot varied his representations of the King by procuring sittings from the life. His small and exquisite works were prized as gifts and were frequently set into snuff-boxes or mounted into other costly jewellery. He was followed as an enamellist by his son, Jean Petitot the younger (1653–1702), and emulated by Henry Toutin (1614–83).

Many miniature painters who came into prominence in the 17th and 18th centuries were born or trained in Switzerland, which was in the forefront in promoting the craft of enamelling, especially through the achievements of Petitot and Prieur. Joseph Werner, who was born in Berne, became a miniaturist of great accomplishment in watercolour on vellum. He studied in Rome and worked in Augsburg and Vienna. He visited Paris in 1662–6/7 but was disappointed in his ambition to become miniature

5. Jean Petitot: *Louise de La Vallière*, enamel on copper, 28×24 mm, 1670 (Geneva, Musée d'Art et d'Histoire)

painter to Louis XIV and returned to Geneva for the last phase of a distinguished career. Among his most remarkable works is *Self-portrait before an Easel* (1662; London, V&A).

By the end of the 17th century the flow of native-born talent that had sustained the continuity of the English school of miniaturists had come temporarily to a halt. Susan Penelope Rosse (*c.* 1652–1700), a daughter of Richard Gibson, continued to work in a style she had learnt from Samuel Cooper. In a longer life span Peter Cross carried the late 17th-century method of pointillé stippling into the 18th century. The demand was unabated, but a change in taste brought a preference for the enamel miniature over the watercolour miniature. Foreign artists filled the gap, among them Charles Boit and Christian Richter, who brought from Sweden a style implanted there by Alexander Cooper and Pierre Signac. Richter, working in watercolour on vellum, was mainly a copyist of existing oil portraits. Among his most charming works is the oval triple portrait of *Isabella, Elizabeth and Anna Lawson* (priv. col., see Schidlof, 1964, no. 988). Boit had a more adventurous life. He visited Paris as a student in 1682 and arrived in England in 1687 in the wake of his fellow-countryman Michael Dahl. By 1700 he was in Vienna, working for Emperor Leopold I, for whom he painted a large family portrait in enamel (Vienna, Ksthist. Mus.; see fig. 6). In 1714 he fled debts incurred in England in connection with a very large and never completed enamel commemorating the Battle of Blenheim and settled in Paris as a protégé of Philippe II, Duc d'Orléans. Christian Friedrich Zincke from Dresden went to England in 1704 or 1706, became a pupil of Boit and succeeded him as the acknowledged leader in the field of miniature portraiture in enamels (e.g. London, V&A; Oxford, Ashmolean). His success and that of his followers, such as André Rouquet,

6. Charles Boit: *Emperor Leopold I and his Family*, enamel on copper, 385×476 mm, *c.* 1700 (Vienna, Kunsthistorisches Museum)

who was born in Geneva and died in Paris, emphasize the extent to which enamels had replaced miniatures on vellum in contemporary estimation.

Meanwhile, around 1700 a technical innovation was introduced that eventually revolutionized miniature painting and created the possibility of remarkable international achievements in the last quarter of the 18th century. The Venetian artist Rosalba Carriera, noticing the lacquered decoration on snuff-boxes made for the popular market, developed the idea of painting miniatures in watercolour on an ivory ground. Since she was an accomplished pastellist she was able to imbue the new material with breadth of touch and a light range of colours, as in the *Girl with Dove*, her diploma piece for the Accademia di S Luca (Rome; Accad. N.S. Luca). Her considerable following ensured that the new method became widely known, both to those who visited her in Venice and on her journey to Paris (1720–21). One of the earliest artists in any country to follow Carriera in her use of ivory as a support was the Englishman Bernard Lens III. His vision was naive and his drawing uncertain, but he laid the foundations of a later rebirth of the national school. The progress of the new technique was, however, a gradual one, and in

many centres the enamel retained its popularity for a considerable time.

In France in the early 18th century, when the patronage of the office of *Menus Plaisirs du Roi* became of increasing importance, portrait miniatures played a less significant role than subject miniatures: commissions for luxurious gifts of diplomatic significance abounded, especially for snuff-boxes decorated with subjects, or sometimes portraits, in miniature. Karl Gustav Klingstedt (1657–1734), who had been born in Riga and served first in the Swedish and then in the French army, came to specialize in small figurative compositions of an erotic nature, such as the grisaille miniature *Blackmail* (priv. col., see Schidlof, 1964, no. 649). Known in France as 'Clinchelet', he was called by Guillaume, Cardinal Dubois, 'le Raphael des tabatières'. Jacques-Antoine Arlaud, born in Geneva, also enjoyed great success in France, where he became miniature painter to Philippe II, Duc d'Orléans. He created a sensation when he visited London in 1721 by selling for £600 a limning of *Leda and the Swan* (untraced), after either Michelangelo or Correggio, to James Brydges, 1st Duke of Chandos.

3. *c.* 1730–*c.* 1770: FROM MASSÉ TO HØYER. After the death of Boit in 1727 and the return to Geneva of

Arlaud in 1729, the biggest reputation as portrait miniaturist in France was enjoyed by Jean-Baptiste Massé. Knowledge of his work, hitherto scanty, was advanced by the emergence at the end of the 1980s of ten miniatures, one of *Louis XV*, the others of the artist's family (sold Geneva, Sotheby's, 16 Nov 1989 (lots 8–12) and 15 Nov 1990 (lots 3–7); illustrated in colour in sale cats). In his long life Massé influenced two artists of entirely different generations and origins. The Geneva-born Jean-Etienne Liotard was apprenticed to him in 1723, and Cornelius Høyer, a Dane, was his pupil from 1764 to 1766. Klingstedt was followed as a subject painter by Jacques Charlier (1720–90), who painted miniature versions of François Boucher's compositions (e.g. London, Wallace), and by the Flemish-trained artist Louis-Nicolas van Blarenberghe and his son Henri-Joseph van Blarenberghe (1741–1826), who painted genre scenes and landscapes with many figures for the decoration of snuff-boxes (a large and representative collection at Waddesdon Manor, Bucks, NT). Hubert Drouais also deserved his contemporary reputation if the miniatures of *Voltaire* and the *Marquise du Châtelet* in the Wallace Collection, London, are attributed to him correctly.

In England the resurgence of a native school of miniature painting can be sensed in the work of Zincke's follower Gervase Spencer (*d* 1763), who started to work in watercolour on ivory as well as in enamel. He was the forerunner of a number of artists who worked on a modest scale and with a reticent approach to the interpretation of character. Among the more successful were Nathaniel Hone (i), who also worked on the scale of life, Luke Sullivan (1701–71) and Samuel Cotes (1734–1818). In the mid-18th century many European centres continued to rely on migrant artists for their miniatures: the Swiss Liotard, who was a pastellist, oil painter and draughtsman as well as an enamel painter, had a particularly varied and colourful career. After training with Massé in Paris he worked in Italy, where he was patronized by the English diplomat William Ponsonby (1704–93), later 2nd Earl of Bessborough, who took him to Constantinople. He stayed there for five years, grew a long beard and adopted Turkish dress, as he depicted in an oval miniature *Self-portrait* (1748; Versoix, priv. col., see Schidlof, 1964, no. 752). On his return he worked in Vienna, Venice, Darmstadt, Geneva, Paris, the Netherlands and England, often depicting his sitters in oriental dress and settings.

A number of new national schools date their rise from the middle of the 18th century. Daniel Nikolaus Chodowiecki moved as a young man from his birthplace, Danzig (now Gdansk, Poland), to Berlin. There, as the employee of a firm making small decorated fancy goods, he taught himself how to paint miniatures. He was extensively employed by Frederick the Great, but his clientele ranged far beyond the confines of the Prussian court. In his miniature portraits, his book illustrations and his drawings, he gave a comprehensive portrayal of the life and manners of the German bourgeoisie. Høyer, who was Massé's pupil 40 years after Liotard and painted his portrait (see Colding, no. 49, fig. 26), brought a new distinction to Danish miniature painting. He visited Rome and Stockholm and painted Catherine II, Empress of Russia. The influence upon him of Rosalba Carriera is exemplified by his *Roman*

Hunter Returning from the Hunt (exh. Berlin, Charlottenburg, 1769; Copenhagen, Stat. Mus. Kst).

4. *c.* 1770–*c.* 1820: FROM HALL TO ISABEY. In the second half of the 18th century Heinrich Füger led the revival of miniature painting in Austria, forming an independent style that shows evidence of an English influence, as in his oval portrait on ivory of *Countess Thun* (Cleveland, OH, Mus. A.). A similar style is also apparent in the work of his pupils Karl Agricola (1779–1852) and Moritz Michael Daffinger.

The most considerable achievements in the later 18th century, however, originated in France, where the potentialities of painting on ivory were first fully realized. The outstanding master of this phase was Peter Adolf Hall. He was born in Sweden and was first trained in Stockholm by the pastellist Gustaf Lundberg. In 1766 he went to Paris, where he soon built up the reputation of being the foremost miniaturist of his time. He exhibited a group of miniatures at the Salon of 1769, including that of the *Dauphin Louis*, son of Louis XV (priv. col., see Schidlof, 1964, no. 508), which was perceived by critics to be quite different from the customary run of such works. He developed the possibilities of the genre and medium to the full, painting in gouache on luminous sheets of thin ivory and conveying by the breadth of his brushwork and the harmony of his colour the bravura of the mature Rococo style, for instance the fine *Portrait of the Artist's Family* (London, Wallace). A slighter interpretation of the same taste is to be found in the miniatures attributed to Jean-Honoré Fragonard, the authorship of which is disputed between him and his wife Marie-Anne Gérard (1745–1823), who exhibited miniatures at the Paris Salon from 1779 to 1782.

Among Hall's most successful contemporaries was Niclas Lafrensen (Lavreince), who worked in Stockholm and Paris. He had a notable gift for painting in miniature intimate scenes from domestic life or of a lightly erotic nature, such as the *Sultan's Bath* (Paris, Louvre; see fig. 7). These became widely known through engravings made after them by Robert de Launay and Jean-François Janinet. Other contemporaries much in demand for miniature portraits were Antoine Vestier, who also painted portraits in oils, and Louis-Marie Sicardi (1746–1825), both of whom worked for Louis XVI, and the enamel painter Jacques Thouron (1740–1839). They were followed by a gifted group of artists, who had been born in the region of Nancy and trained by the painters attracted to the court of the exiled king of Poland, Stanislav I, Duke of Lorraine. The earliest to achieve prominence was François Dumont (1751–1831), who adapted to suit the new Neo-classical principles the style that he had learnt in the days of Louis XVI. His finest miniatures are painted on rectangular sheets of ivory of a relatively large size and are imbued with great charm, as in the case of his portrait of *Queen Marie-Antoinette Seated in a Park with Two of her Children* (Paris, Louvre). Jacques Deranton (1756–1832), also from Nancy, worked in a similar manner. The fame of these two artists was overtaken in the early years of the 19th century by that of Jean-Baptiste Augustin and of Jean-Baptiste Isabey. Augustin responded to the more severe taste of the Republican and Empire periods by abandoning

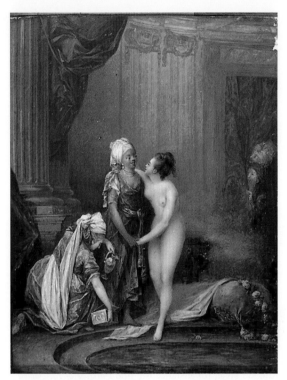

7. Niclas Lafrensen: *Sultan's Bath*, gouache on ivory, 164×126 mm, 1774 (Paris, Musée du Louvre)

his earlier *ancien régime* flamboyance, as exemplified by such works as the circular three-quarter-length *Portrait of ?Mme de Boufflers Reclining on a Sofa* (1791; priv. col., see Schidlof, 1964, no. 45), with their reminiscences of the work in oils of Elisabeth Vigée-Lebrun. Such later miniatures as the rectangular, half-length portrait of the cornet player *Frédéric Duvernois* (1817; Meilen, priv. col., see Schidlof, 1964, no. 48) share stylistic characteristics with the Neo-classical portraits in oils of François Gérard and Jean-Auguste-Dominique Ingres. An early and impressive work by Isabey is the rectangular half-length portrait of a *Hunter in a Blue Coat* (1796; priv. col., see Schidlof, 1964, no. 603). In his later work he adopted the device of stretching paper over metal as a base for miniatures, thereby giving himself scope for the luminous fluency of the Romantic portraits, including that of *Princess Bagration in a White Muslin Dress* (1820; Paris, Louvre), which succeeded the solemnity of his numerous images of Napoleon.

The influence of Hall and his French followers was paramount in Europe at the end of the 18th century. It can be traced in the work of the well-travelled Domenico Bossi (1765–1853), who was born in Trieste and worked in Hamburg, Munich, Paris, Vienna, Stockholm and St Petersburg. The patronage of Catherine the Great attracted many miniature painters to Russia. The most gifted native-born miniaturist was Augustin Ritt (1769–99), who returned from Revolutionary France in 1792. He painted numerous portraits of members of the court in St Petersburg, among them that of the *Empress Maria Feodorovna* (Paris, Louvre).

In England miniature painting took a different course, though there too the art flourished in the second half of the 18th century. The first considerable master to emerge was Jeremiah Meyer. He was the son of a portrait painter at the court of Württemberg and was taken to England in 1749, where he was taught the technique of enamel painting by the elderly Zincke. His main practice was in watercolour miniature painting on ivory, and his eminence was recognized by his election as a founder-member of the Royal Academy in 1768. His style is characterized by its cross-hatches and transparent modelling, and this linear approach, quite distinct from the broad impasto of the French artists, was followed by Meyer's successors. Richard Cosway gave the surface of the ivory full scope by restricting his drawing to the essentials required for rendering the features (e.g. London, Wallace and V&A); his miniatures represent the nearest approach on a small scale to the fluent calligraphy of Thomas Gainsborough. Cosway enjoyed conspicuous social success as a prominent and none too scrupulous member of the circle of George, Prince of Wales (later George IV). Whereas Richard Crosse (1742–1810) used a greenish tinge for his flesh tones, Ozias Humphry introduced a depth of tone that recalls the Venetian qualities of Sir Joshua Reynolds's portraits. The detailed finish achieved by John Smart (1743–1811) in such works as his oval *Self-portrait* (1797; London, V&A) on ivory recalls the fused colours of the enamellists. In the early years of the 19th century George Engleheart abandoned the colourful elegance of his early oval miniature portraits in favour of a sombre approach to dress and character, and a use of rectangular sheets of ivory. An example is *Mrs Boulton* (1812; London, V&A).

The careers of these artists coincided with a remarkable increase in the demand for miniature portraits. Engleheart's ledgers show that he painted an average of 124 miniatures a year over 30 years—in one year alone he painted 288. Scores of lesser miniaturists worked to meet the requirements for portraiture in little, which came from many sections of society. Among minor artists who have an individual style may be mentioned Samuel Shelley (1750 or 1756–1808), Andrew Plimer (1763–1837), William Wood (1769–1810), George Chinnery, who also painted in oils, and Anne Mee (?1774–1851). The American school, typified by Charles Willson Peale and Edward Greene Malbone, centred around Philadelphia and other eastern coastal cities and derived its style from the example of England rather than from the Continent.

5. AFTER *c.* 1820. In France in the 19th century, Isabey continued to dominate miniature painting into the 1830s. His abilities showed no decline in his 70th year, and most of his younger contemporaries were his pupils or followers. Among the more notable was Leon Larue, called 'Mansion' (1785–1834 or after), a pupil whose *Letters on the Art of Miniature Painting* were first published in English in 1822, then in French in 1823, and in German in 1824. Mme Aimée-Zoë Lizinka de Mirbel (1796–1849), miniature painter to Louis XVIII, Charles X and Louis-Philippe, was the artist chosen by Honoré de Balzac to represent miniature painting in *La Comédie humaine*, his sequence of novels devoted to life in France in the 1830s and 1840s.

A change of technique in 19th-century English miniatures was inaugurated by Andrew Robertson, who rebelled against the sketch-like, linear characteristics of the school of Cosway and set out to emulate the depth of oil painting. He painted on large rectangular sheets of ivory, as in *Sir Francis Leggatt Chantrey with his Bust of George IV* (1831; Windsor Castle, Berks, Royal Col.), an ambitious choice of subject, demonstrating that the miniature was becoming a small picture for public display rather than an intimate personal possession. Robertson's pupil William Charles Ross was the last artist to make an original contribution to the English tradition of miniature painting, in such works as *Prince Ernst and Prince Edward of Leiningen with Queen Victoria's Macaw and her Dog 'Islay'* (1839; Windsor Castle, Berks, Royal Col.; see fig. 8).

The rise of photography in the 1840s and 1850s had a profound effect on the vogue for the portrait miniature. The *carte-de-visite* replaced the hand-painted image in satisfying the desire for the likeness in little. In 1837 over 200 miniatures were shown in the annual exhibition of the Royal Academy, London; in 1870 there were barely more than 30. A similar decline in patronage occurred in all centres where the miniature had once been a cherished form of portraiture. Later exponents of the art had to depend on the loyalty of those who, like Queen Victoria, retained their faith in its special qualities as a type of portraiture that preserves privacy while interpreting personality.

Foskett

BIBLIOGRAPHY

E. Lemberger: *Die Bildnis-Miniatur in Deutschland von 1550 bis 1850* (Munich, 1909)

L. R. Schidlof: *Die Bildnis-Miniatur in Frankreich* (Vienna and Leipzig, 1911)

E. Lemberger: *Die Bildnis-Miniatur in Scandinavien*, 2 vols (Berlin, 1912)

P. Lespinasse: *La Miniature en France au XVIIIe siècle* (Paris and Brussels, 1929)

G. Reynolds: *The English Miniature* (London, 1952, rev. Cambridge, 1988)

T. H. Colding: *Aspects of Miniature Painting* (Copenhagen, 1953) [the origins of the portrait miniature and developments in technique]

L. R. Schidlof: *The Miniature in Europe*, 4 vols (Graz, 1964) [comprehensive illustrated lexicon]

G. Cavalli-Björkman: *Svenskt miniatyrmåleri* (Stockholm, 1981)

J. Murdoch, ed.: *The English Miniature* (London and New Haven, 1981)

D. T. Johnson: *American Portrait Miniatures* (New York, 1990)

T. H. Colding: *Miniature og emaillemaleri i Danmark, 1606–1850* (Copenhagen, 1991)

GRAHAM REYNOLDS

Minimalism. Term used in the 20th century, in particular from the 1960s, to describe a style characterized by an impersonal austerity, plain geometric configurations and industrially processed materials. It was first used by David Burlyuk in the catalogue introduction for an exhibition of John Graham's paintings at the Dudensing Gallery in New York in 1929. Burlyuk wrote: 'Minimalism derives its name from the minimum of operating means. Minimalist painting is purely realistic—the subject being the painting itself.' The term gained currency in the 1960s. Accounts and explanations of Minimalism varied considerably, as did the range of work to which it was related. This included the monochrome paintings of Yves Klein, Robert Rauschenberg, Ad Reinhardt, Frank Stella and Brice Marden, and even aspects of Pop art and Post-painterly Abstraction. Typically the precedents cited were Marcel Duchamp's ready-mades, the Suprematist compositions of Kazimir Malevich and Barnett Newman's Abstract Expressionist paintings. The rational grid paintings of Agnes Martin were also mentioned in connection with such Minimalist artists as Sol LeWitt.

After the work of such critics as Clement Greenberg and Michael Fried, analyses of Minimalism tended to focus exclusively on the three-dimensional work of such American artists as Carl André, Dan Flavin, Donald Judd, LeWitt, Robert Morris and Tony Smith, although Smith himself never fully subscribed to Minimalism. These artists never worked or exhibited together as a self-defined group, yet their art shared certain features: geometric forms and use of industrial materials or such modern technology as the fluorescent electric lights that appeared in Flavin's works. Minimalists also often created simple modular and serial arrangements of forms that are examples of SYSTEMS ART. LeWitt's serial works included wall drawings as well as sculptures.

Judd and Morris were the principal artists to write about Minimalism. Judd's most significant contribution to this field was the article 'Specific Objects' (1965). Judd's article began by announcing the birth of a new type of three-dimensional work that could not be classified in terms of either painting or sculpture and, in effect, superseded both traditions. Judd's concept became retrospectively identified with his own boxes and stark geometric reliefs of the period (*see* ABSTRACT ART, fig. 3). Originally, however, he explained his idea with reference to the work of a heterogeneous selection of artists, including Lee Bontecou, John Chamberlain, Klein, Yayoi Kusama (*b* 1929), Claes Oldenburg, Richard Smith, Frank Stella and

8. William Charles Ross: *Prince Ernst and Prince Edward of Leiningen with Queen Victoria's Macaw and her Dog 'Islay'*, watercolour on ivory, 190×146 mm, 1839 (Windsor Castle, Berks, Royal Collection)

Minimalist sculpture by Carl André: *Equivalent VIII*, firebricks, 2292×127×686 m, 1966 (London, Tate Gallery)

H. C. Westermann (1922–81). The article was also copiously illustrated with works by such artists as Richard Artschwager, Flavin, Jasper Johns, Phillip King, Morris, Rauschenberg, Stella, and with one of Judd's own pieces. Judd distinguished the new work by means of its compositional 'wholeness', which, unlike previous art, was not 'made part by part, by addition'. He was later to focus the critical implications of this distinction with a dismissive reference (1969) to the 'Cubist fragmentation' of Anthony Caro's work. For Judd, his own work achieved its formal integrity principally by adapting into a third dimension the 'singleness' that he observed in the compositions of such painters as Barnett Newman, Jackson Pollock, Mark Rothko and Clyfford Still.

Morris's influential 'Notes on Sculpture' appeared a year after Judd's article. In it he established the criteria by which his own recent work could be evaluated. Like Judd, he repudiated an aesthetic based on Cubist principles. 'The sensuous object, resplendent with compressed internal relations, has had to be rejected' (*Artforum*, v/2 (Oct 1966), p. 23). In its place Morris proposed a more compact, 'unitary' art form. He was especially drawn to simple, regular and irregular polyhedrons. Influenced by theories in psychology and phenomenology, Morris argued that these configurations established in the mind of the beholder 'strong gestalt sensation', whereby form and shape could be grasped intuitively. Judd and Morris both attempted to reduce the importance of aesthetic judgement in modernist criticism by connecting the question of the specificity of the medium to generic value. Nevertheless,

a distinction between the categories of art and non-art was maintained with Judd's claim that 'A work needs only to be interesting'.

For Greenberg and Fried, Minimalist work was united by the threat it posed to their modernist aesthetic. The modernist response to Minimalism was outlined in Greenberg's 'Recentness of Sculpture' and Fried's 'Art and Objecthood' (both 1967). Both critics were troubled by claims for Minimalism as a new art form, and were also concerned at the Minimalist elimination of complex compositional relations and subtle nuances of form, which they believed to be essential qualities of modernist sculpture. The critical resistance that Minimalism met in its initial stages persisted, and censure arose not only from modernist critics but also from the tabloid press. This was particularly evident in the abuse that was given to André's sculpture made from building bricks, *Equivalent VIII* (1966; London, Tate; see fig.), upon the occasion of its exhibition at the Tate Gallery in London in 1976.

From the 1960s the Minimalists' work remained remarkably consistent, continuing its geometric and serial forms (e.g. LeWitt's *Cube Structures Based on Five Modules*, 600×800×700 mm, 1971–4; Edinburgh, N.G. Mod. A.). Conceptual art inherited many of the concerns as well as the contradictions of Minimalist discourse. Attempts were made by Joseph Kosuth, among others, to resolve its complex views on the relationship between aesthetic judgement and the art object. Minimalism's sense of 'theatricality' stimulated much subsequent work in the fields of installation and performance art, where it helped facilitate a critical engagement with the spectator's perception of space and time. The concept of 'theatricality' was first used in connection with Minimalism by Michael Fried to characterize the absence of 'presentness' in the spatial and temporal experience of the art work. While Fried was critical of this situation, his analysis led, by default, to a reassessment of Minimalism from an anti-humanist perspective.

BIBLIOGRAPHY

D. Judd: 'Specific Objects', *A. Yb.*, 8 (1965), pp. 74–82
R. Morris: 'Notes on Sculpture', *Artforum*, iv/6 (Feb 1966), pp. 42–4; v/2 (Oct 1966), pp. 20–23; v/10 (June 1967), pp. 23–9
M. Fried: 'Art and Objecthood', *Artforum*, v/10 (June 1967), pp. 12–23
C. Greenberg: 'Recentness of Sculpture', *American Sculpture of the Sixties* (exh. cat., Los Angeles, CA, Co. Mus. A., 1967) [intro.]
G. Battcock, ed.: *Minimal Art: A Critical Anthology* (New York, 1968) [incl. ess. by Morris, Greenberg and Fried cited above]
C. Harrison: 'Expression and Exhaustion in the Sixties', *Artscribe*, 56 (Feb–March 1986), pp. 44–9; 57 (April–May 1986), pp. 32–5
T. de Duve: 'The Monochrome and the Blank Canvas', *Reconstructing Modernism: Art in New York, Paris and Montreal, 1945–1964*, ed. S. Guilbaut (Cambridge, MA, and London, 1990), pp. 244–310
C. Harrison: *Essays on Art and Language* (Oxford and Cambridge, 1991) [esp. pp. 37–47]

CHRISTOPHER WANT

Minio, Tiziano (*b* Padua, *c.* 1511–12; *d* Padua, 1552). Italian stuccoist and sculptor. He probably trained as a founder under his father, Guido Minio (*fl* 1511–16), called Lizzaro, and later alternated this trade with his work as a sculptor. His first documented activity is as a stuccoist in 1533, employed on the vault of the chapel of St Anthony in Il Santo, Padua, under the architect Giovanni Maria Falconetto and alongside two members of Jacopo Sansovino's circle, Silvio Cosini and Danese Cattaneo. In 1535–6 Minio executed his first independent work, the stucco altar (now Padua, Mus. Civ.) for the confraternity of S Rocco in Padua. Large and ungainly, this altar has the crude vigour often associated with provincial workmanship; its female saints show, nonetheless, the influence of Sansovino's style, while the deployment of the sculptures in general is indebted to arrangements at Sansovino's Loggetta, Venice.

Minio began working for Sansovino in 1536 at Venice, where he made stucco decorations for the atrium of S Marco and helped cast Sansovino's first bronze reliefs for the choir. Minio was clearly valued by Sansovino for his skill as a stuccoist and founder, while receiving from Sansovino a new formal language for his own work. This influence can be seen in all of Minio's subsequent figural designs, especially in the plasterwork of the Odeo Cornaro, built in Padua for Alvise Cornaro, and in the bronze reliefs for the baptismal font in S Marco.

The stucco decorations of the Odeo Cornaro (1539–43) furnish the best index of Minio's abilities in this field. As Wolters has shown, they combine direct quotations from Sansovino's bronze reliefs in S Marco with reflections of the work of Donatello and of Giulio Romano's Palazzo del Tè, Mantua. The transformation from Minio's earlier altar for S Rocco is almost beyond recognition. During these years he also became a member of Alvise Cornaro's household, thus gaining access to one of the Veneto's most notable artistic and intellectual circles. Cornaro advanced his career on several occasions, most notably when he stood surety for Minio's execution of a bronze

cover for S Marco's baptismal font. The contract for this work, drawn up in 1545, was also signed by Desiderio da Firenze, a protégé of Pietro Bembo. Sansovino seems to have exercised an editorial authority over this project, but the bulk of the design reflects Minio's idiom as found in the Odeo's stucco panels. Desiderio's role may have been confined to decorative frames; these frames were lost by the 19th century. The main panels consist of four scenes from the *Life of St John the Baptist* and the four *Evangelists*. The narrative panels are peopled with the same types as are found in the Odeo, along with stylistic allusions to Lorenzo Ghiberti and Donatello. Recent cleaning has shown them to be outstanding examples of Venetian bronze-casting of the period and a testimonial to Minio's skill in low relief. Vasari implied that Minio was to have executed a statue of *St John the Baptist* for the baptistery, but this was pre-empted by the sculptor's death.

Minio contributed stucco decorations for the performance of Pietro Aretino's *La Talenta*, mounted by Giorgio Vasari in Venice in 1542. Vasari also stated that Minio carved 'alcune figurette', by which he probably meant the minor figural elements on Sansovino's Loggetta. In 1543 Minio and Cattaneo contracted to furnish a series of bronze gates for the entrance arcade of the chapel of St Anthony in Il Santo, Padua; but although some portions were cast, the whole was left unfinished at Minio's death. His extant late works include the Contarini arms (1541) and the figure of *Justice* (1552) on the façade of the Palazzo del Podestà (now Palazzo Municipale), Padua, which once again are indebted to the influence of Sansovino.

Minio's early death and the ephemeral nature of many of his creations pose problems for an exact estimation of his abilities as a sculptor. In addition, the promiscuous attribution of small bronzes to him by Planiscig has severely distorted the picture; few, if any, of these small bronzes can be by him. By concentrating on his documented pieces, it can be seen that Minio was an artist of high decorative ability, capable of translating Sansovino's style into the media of stucco and bronze. His position in Padua made him central to the dissemination of the master's style there, and his association with Agostino Zoppo (*fl* 1555–9) and, indirectly, with his own nephew TIZIANO ASPETTI fostered the continuation of that style into the latter part of the 16th century.

BIBLIOGRAPHY

G. Vasari: *Vite* (1550, rev. 2/1568); ed. G. Milanesi (1878–85), vii, pp. 515–16
B. Scardeone: *De antiquitate urbis Patavii* (Padua, 1560), pp. 376–7
A. Venturi: *Storia* (1901–40), X/iii, pp. 36–57
L. Planiscig: *Venezianische Bildhauer der Renaissance* (Vienna, 1921), pp. 389–408
G. Fiocco: 'La prima opera di Tiziano Minio', *Dedalo*, xi/1 (1931), pp. 600–10
W. Wolters: 'Tiziano Minio als Stukator in Odeo Cornaro zu Padua', *Pantheon*, xxi (1963), pp. 20–28, 222–30
P. Sambin: 'I testamenti di Alvise Cornaro', *Italia Med. & Uman.*, ix (1966), pp. 295–385
E. Rigoni: 'Notizie sulla vita e la famiglia dello scultore Tiziano Aspetti detto Minio', *L'arte rinascimentale in Padova* (Padua, 1970), pp. 201–15 [fundamental source material]
C. Fillarin, ed.: *Documenti per la storia dell'arte a Padova* (Vicenza, 1976), pp. 164–5
Alvise Cornaro e il suo tempo (exh. cat., ed. L. Puppi; Padua, Loggia Cornaro; Odeo Cornaro; Pal. Ragione; 1980)

BRUCE BOUCHER

Minka [Jap.: 'folk houses']. Japanese architectural term designating town houses (*machiya*) and farmhouses (*nōka*). Fishermen's houses (*gyoka*), residences of low-ranking samurai and storehouses (*kura*) are also often grouped with *minka*. Design differs according to regional tradition, weather and function. Most *minka* feature an area with an earthen floor (*doma*), used particularly for cooking, and raised-floor rooms with mats (*tatami* or *mushiro*) for other activities and for sleeping. Virtually all extant *minka* date from the Edo period (1600–1868) or later, although written sources and picture scrolls give a fairly clear representation of *minka* before the 17th century. The rapid pace of modernization since the 19th century in both cities and rural areas has greatly reduced the number of *minka*. Some older examples have been designated as Important Cultural Properties and thus preserved *in situ*, while other *minka* have been reconstructed at open-air museums or gardens, such as the Nihon Minkaen in Kawasaki, Kanagawa Prefecture; the Nihon Minka Hakubutsukan, Toyonaka, Osaka; the Shikoku Minka Hakubutsukan, Takamatsu, Kagawa Prefecture; and the Hyakumangoku Bunkaen Edo Mura, Kanazawa, Ishikawa Prefecture.

See also JAPAN, §III, 4(ii)(b).

BIBLIOGRAPHY

T. Itoh: *Minka* (Tokyo, 1970)

Minne, George (*b* Ghent, 30 Aug 1866; *d* Laethem-Saint-Martin, 18 Feb 1941). Belgian sculptor, draughtsman and illustrator. He studied at the Académie Royale des Beaux-Arts in Ghent (1879–86) and worked in Ghent (until 1895) and Brussels (1895–9) before settling in Laethem-Saint-Martin, a village near Ghent. His first works were delicate sculptures and sparse drawings of grieving and injured figures. The emotional power of these works was recognized by many Symbolist poets including Maurice Maeterlinck, Charles Van Lerberghe and Grégoire Le Roy, who saw in them an expression of their own pessimistic view of life. He illustrated several of their collections of poetry (e.g. Grégoire Le Roy: *Mon Coeur pleure d'autrefois* (Paris, 1889); Maurice Maeterlinck: *Serres chaudes* (Paris, 1889)). From 1890 he was involved with the progressive element among the artists and authors of Brussels. He exhibited for the first time that year under the auspices of the avant-garde society Les XX in Brussels, and two years later he participated in the Salon de la Rose+Croix in Paris. His principal supporter was Emile Verhaeren.

In 1895 Minne went to study for a year at the Académie Royale des Beaux-Arts in Brussels, where he had a studio. He lived first in the city, later in the suburbs. During this period he developed his familiar statue of a kneeling boy, sunk in reverie, for example *Kneeling Youth* (polished plaster, 1898; Laethem-Saint-Martin, priv. col., see Haesaerts, p. 106). He subjected this figure to an increasing simplification of line; it became a prototype of Art Nouveau elegance, in which the *fin-de-siècle* preoccupation with youth and narcissism was also expressed.

Thanks to influential personages such as Henry Van de Velde and Julius Meier-Graefe, Minne was introduced in the international Art Nouveau centres of Paris, Germany and, in particular, Vienna. He took part in many exhibitions, such as the Secession exhibitions in Berlin and Vienna and the Biennales in Venice. In Vienna his work attracted the attention of artists such as Gustav Klimt, Egon Schiele and Oskar Kokoschka. Although Minne's art remained limited in terms of theme and form, many artists acknowledged the spiritual power of his simple works. Minne himself took Auguste Rodin's work as his point of departure but did not venture to compete with Rodin's powerfully plastic expressivity. He preferred smaller-scale works and sought some kinship with medieval art. In this sphere he achieved a formal language suggestive of primitivism as well as daring exaggerations that point to Expressionism and were continued in a more explicit fashion in the work of Ernst Barlach, Käthe Kollwitz and Wilhelm Lehmbruck.

Minne modelled his sculptures in clay and had them cast in plaster. After this they were worked out in bronze, stone or wood, mostly on order from abroad. He received his most important commission from the German collector Karl Ernst Osthaus, who called on Henry Van de Velde for the construction and furnishing of the Folkwang Museum in Hagen. In addition to various other sculptures, Minne produced his principal work for the entrance hall of the Folkwang Museum: the *Fountain of Kneeling Figures*, in which he repeated the figure of the kneeling boy around a circular basin. He showed designs for this fountain from 1899 in a succession of exhibitions. The only surviving model in plaster is in the Museum voor Schone Kunsten, Ghent (see Haesaerts, p. 94); the final version in marble (1905) is in the Folkwang Museum, Essen.

At the time that Minne was executing these commissions, he had a small studio in Laethem-Saint-Martin. Here he was the central figure in a colony of artists including Gustave Van de Woestijne, Valerius De Saedeleer and Albert Servaes, who were in search of a common goal of spiritual renewal. He himself produced no new work of significance. During World War I he fled with his extensive family to Wales, where he spent the subsequent four years making drawings on the themes of *Mother and Child* (e.g. *Mother and Child*, charcoal, 1920; Ghent, Mus. S. Kst.) and the Christ figure (e.g. the *Eucharist Christ*, charcoal on wood, 1922; Brussels, Mus. A. Mod.); an important body of these is in the Museum voor Schone Kunsten, Ghent. When he returned to Belgium after the war, he made drawings of mothers and children as well as nudes and different objects which drew on his earlier work. In contrast to Minne's expressive works from before 1900, this later work, which brought him considerable fame in his own country, is more decorative.

BIBLIOGRAPHY

J. Meier-Graefe: 'George Minne', *Ver Sacrum* (1900), pp. 27–46

K. van de Woestijne: *Kunst en geest in Vlaanderen* [Art and spirit in Flanders] (Bussum, 1911), pp. 220–36

M. Maeterlinck and others: 'George Minne', *La Nervie*, 8 (1923), pp. 205–15

K. van de Woestijne: *De Schroeflijn I: Opstellen over plastische kunst* [The spiral I: essays on fine art] (Brussels, 1928), pp. 39–57

L. van Puyvelde: *George Minne* (Brussels, 1930)

P. Haesaerts: *Laethem-Saint-Martin: Le Village élu de l'art flamand* (Brussels, 1963)

George Minne en de kunst rond 1900 (exh. cat., Ghent, Mus. S. Kst., 1982)

ROBERT HOOZEE

Minneapolis. North American city in the state of Minnesota. It is the economic and cultural centre of the upper Midwest and, with 2 million inhabitants, the largest city in a metropolitan area that includes St Paul (the State capital), Edina and Orona. European settlement dates from the establishment of Fort Snelling (1820–22) at the confluence of the Mississippi and Minnesota rivers. After 1848 growth focused on the Falls of St Anthony, eight miles upstream, which formed the upper barrier to navigation on the Mississippi and provided a cheap, unlimited source of industrial power. Thus assured of effective economic control over the vast forests and agricultural lands of the upper Midwest, Minneapolis grew to become the world's largest timber- and flour-milling centre. While retaining its important agricultural base, the metropolitan economy has diversified into finance, commerce and high technology.

Minneapolis experienced phenomenal growth in the 1880s, and a number of structures were built in the Romanesque Revival style of H. H. Richardson, of which the Masonic Temple (1889; by Louis L. Long and Fred Kees) is the best remaining. The concurrent development of a city-wide system of parks transformed Minneapolis. The Chicago-based landscape architect H. W. S. Cleveland first designed a parks system in 1883 (unexecuted), but a civic committee chaired by William Watts Folwell eventually proposed in 1891 the famed 'Grand Rounds' system, which overlays a continuous, naturalistic pattern on to the city's street grid, interconnecting six large lakes, Minnehaha Creek and the Mississippi over 55 miles of parkways. After 1900 civic improvement was dominated by the construction of individual buildings, the most significant of which were the residential works of William Gray Purcell and George Grant Elmslie (see PURCELL & ELMSLIE), including Purcell's own house (1913) at 2328 Lake Place, in characteristic Prairie school style. Major regional works included the Minnesota State Capitol (1893–1903) in St Paul by CASS GILBERT, with its dome modelled on that of St Peter's in Rome.

Between 1918 and the early 1950s residential development in south-west Minneapolis, adjacent Edina and suburban St Paul was characterized in middle-class areas by frame or stucco houses in a variety of traditional styles and in higher-income enclaves by very sophisticated Period houses. Most important within both groups are the residences built by Edwin H. Lundie (1886–1972), whose work was characterized by a highly personal style and

Minneapolis Institute of Arts, by McKim, Mead & White, 1912–14

elegant detail. After 1955 attention shifted back to large-scale transformation of the city centre. Replanning between 1958 and 1970 was symbolized by the creation of the Nicollet Mall (1958–67), an early pedestrian mall by Lawrence Halprin. Major new buildings of the period included the high-rise IDS (Investors Diversified Services) Center (1968–73) by Philip Johnson and John Burgee (*b* 1933) in association with Edward F. Baker Associates, the Federal Reserve Bank (1968–72) by Gunnar Birkerts (*b* 1925) and the Orchestra Hall (1973–5) by Hardy Holzman Pfeiffer. Notable buildings from the 1980s include the WCCO-TV Building (1980–83) by Hardy Holzman Pfeiffer, the Lincoln Center (1984–7) by Kohn Pedersen Fox and the Winton Guest House (1983–4) in suburban Orona by Frank O. Gehry. The Lincoln Center is a restrained Post-modernist tower in grey granite, while the Winton Guest House is an extraordinary visual assemblage, conceived by Gehry as a large outdoor sculpture.

The artistic life of the city is dominated by the Walker Art Center (founded 1879) and the Minneapolis Institute of Arts (founded 1883). The comprehensive collection of the Institute is housed in a complex (see fig.) originally designed in a classical style by McKim, Mead & White in 1912–14, which was extensively enlarged in 1972–4 by Kenzō Tange. The Walker focuses principally on contemporary art, which is housed in a gallery originally designed in 1969 by Edward Larrabee Barnes, although it shares its site with the Tyrone Guthrie Theater, designed in 1962–3 by Ralph Rapson (*b* 1914). Other important visual arts institutions near by include the Minnesota Museum of Art in St Paul and the Northwest Architectural Archives at the University of Minnesota at Minneapolis; the latter's collection of over 250,000 items includes the papers and drawings of Purcell & Elmslie, Edwin H. Lundie, HARVEY ELLIS and the American Terra Cotta Company.

BIBLIOGRAPHY
E. Bennett: *Plan of Minneapolis* (Minneapolis, 1917)
T. Wirth: *Minneapolis Park System, 1883–1944* (Minneapolis, 1946)
D. Gebhard: 'Purcell and Elmslie Architects', *Prairie Sch. Rev.*, ii/1 (1965), pp. 5–24
D. Torbert: *Significant Architecture in the History of Minneapolis* (Minneapolis, 1969)
D. Gebhard and T. Martinson: *A Guide to the Architecture of Minnesota* (Minneapolis, 1977), pp. 24–79

TOM MARTINSON

Minnebroer, Frans. *See* CRABBE, FRANS.

Minniti [Menniti; Minnitti], **Mario** (*b* Syracuse, 8 Dec 1577; *d* 22 Nov 1640). Italian painter. With Alonzo Rodriguez he represents the most direct Sicilian response to the new art of Caravaggio, with whom he became acquainted, during a lengthy stay in Rome, between the 1590s and the first years of the 17th century. He had returned to Sicily by 1606 and in 1610 extended hospitality to Caravaggio in Syracuse, where he directed a workshop. He worked principally in Messina, where he stayed many times, and it seems likely that he also visited Malta (Susinno). There are no dated works before 1624, yet a group of paintings united by their closeness to Caravaggio's late style may precede this date. The group, mainly executed in Messina, includes the *Beheading of St John the Baptist* (Messina, Mus. Reg.), the *Road to Calvary* and the *Flagellation* (both Milazzo, Fond. Lucifero). The last two

may have formed part of a series inspired by the scenes from the *Passion* that had been commissioned in Messina from Caravaggio by Nicolò di Giacomo, of which only the *Road to Calvary* (untraced) was ever completed.

Documented works by Minniti from 1624 to 1625 include the *Miracle of St Clare* (1624; Syracuse, Pal. Bellomo), *St Benedict Arranging his own Burial* (1625; Syracuse, S Benedetto) and the *Ecce homo* (1625; Mdina, Cathedral Mus.), a copy of an untraced painting by Caravaggio. The composition of the first two works reflects the influence of Filippo di Benedetto Paladini (*fl* Sicily, 1601–14), while the drawing and colour reveal a response to Orazio Gentileschi and Carlo Saraceni. Echoes of Minniti's debt to Roman art persist in the *Raising of the Widow's Son* (Messina, Mus. Reg.), in which traces of the influence of Rodriguez and of the Neapolitan Caravaggisti are also present, suggesting that the artist may have visited Naples, possibly between 1634 and 1637. His late works, among which is the *Allegorical Scene* (1639; Catania, Mus. Civ. Castello Ursino), move towards a more classical grandeur.

BIBLIOGRAPHY
F. Susinno: *Le vite dei pittori messinesi* (MS.; 1724); ed. V. Martinelli (Florence, 1960), pp. 110, 116–21
S. L. Agnello: 'Mario Minniti e Antonio Maddiona nelle *Vite* di Francesco Susinno', *Archv Stor. Siracus.*, x (1964), pp. 75–92
A. Moir: *The Italian Followers of Caravaggio* (Cambridge, MA, 1967), i, pp. 185–9; ii, p. 87
F. Campagna Cicala: 'Intorno all'attività di Caravaggio in Sicilia: Due momenti del caravaggismo siciliano, Mario Minniti e Alonzo Rodriguez', *Caravaggio in Sicilia: Il suo tempo, il suo influsso* (exh. cat., Syracuse, Pal. Bellomo, 1984), pp. 101–44, 174–9

LUIGI HYERACE

Mino. Centre of ceramics production in Japan, near the cities of Tajimi and Toki, Gifu Prefecture. Mino is one of the oldest pottery centres in Japan and is most renowned for its production of tea-ceremony utensils (*see* JAPAN, §XIV, 3), which are widely held as the highest achievement of the Japanese potter's art. Mino produced Sue ware (*see* JAPAN, §VIII, 2(ii)(a)) from the 7th century AD, but in the 12th century, under the influence of the SANAGE kilns to the south-west, potters began to produce large numbers of small bowls, narrow-mouthed jars (*tsubo*), wide-mouthed jars (*kame*) and kitchen mortars (*suribachi*) in a new-style tunnel kiln (*anagama*; *see* JAPAN, §VIII, 1(v)) with a flame-dividing pillar. About 250 such kilns have been found, and among these a small number produced four-handled jars and ewers inspired by Chinese ceramics of the Southern Song period (1127–1279).

In the mid-15th century advanced glaze technology spread to Mino from nearby SETO, and Mino potters began to make ash-glazed and iron-glazed functional wares almost identical to those being produced in Seto (*see* JAPAN, §VIII, 3(i)(c)). At the beginning of the 16th century a new kiln, the *ōgama*, was introduced. This was built above ground and loaded from the side, and was designed to create a partial downdraught, making for a more efficient and even firing. During the 16th century Mino potters continued working in the staple iron and ash glazes, but by the third quarter of the 16th century, under the influence of the *wabi* tea ceremony then emerging in Sakai (Osaka Prefect.) and Kyoto, they began to experiment with new shapes and glazes, resulting in the styles known as Yellow

Seto (*Kiseto*), Black Seto (*Setoguro*) and Shino (*see* JAPAN, fig. 145). The glaze of Yellow Seto, probably the oldest of the three, combined the old Seto ash glaze with clay in an attempt to produce celadon; a devitrified yellow surface resulted instead. Black Seto made use of the traditional Seto iron glaze, but the sudden withdrawal of the product (mostly teabowls) from the kiln at peak temperature made the surface turn a stony black. Shino ware seems to have resulted from the search for a transparent glaze to cover underglaze painting, but the use of a glaze of almost pure feldspar resulted in its distinctive snowy texture.

From about 1600 the technology of the multi-chambered climbing kiln (*noborigama*) was introduced from KARATSU to the Mino kiln at Motoyashiki. This kiln, together with several others in the district, produced Oribe wares (*see* JAPAN, fig. 145), characterized by unusual shapes, a broad variety of underglaze iron designs, and asymmetrical copper-green glaze accents. Oribe wares declined in the second quarter of the 17th century, but Mino potters continued to produce utilitarian ash-glazed wares, including imitations of Ofuke ware, a transparent glazed ceremonial ware made under official auspices in Seto. Again following the lead of Seto, Mino also began to make underglaze blue decorated porcelain from the beginning of the 19th century.

BIBLIOGRAPHY

S. Narasaki: *Seto, Mino* (1976), ix of *Nihon tōji zenshū* [Complete collection of Japanese ceramics], ed. M. Satō and others (Tokyo, 1975–7)

M. Momoi: 'Edo jidai no Mino gama' [Mino kilns in the Edo period], *Nihon yakimono shūsei* [Survey of Japanese pottery], ed. M. Tadanari, N. Shōichi and H. Seizō, iii (Tokyo, 1981), pp. 132–5

S. Taguchi: 'Mino no chūsei gama' [Medieval kilns in Mino], *Nihon yakimono shūsei* [Survey of Japanese pottery], ed. M. Tadanari, N. Shōichi and H. Seizō, iii (Tokyo, 1981), pp. 118–21

Shino and Oribe Kiln Sites (exh. cat., ed. R. Faulkner and O. Impey; Oxford, Ashmolean, 1981)

RICHARD L. WILSON

Minoan. Civilization that flourished during the Greek Bronze Age (*c.* 3500/3000–*c.* 1050 BC) on the Aegean island of CRETE. The term was coined by ARTHUR EVANS and derived from Minos, legendary king of Knossos. The rediscovery of the Cretan Bronze Age civilization was pioneered by Evans's excavations of the great Minoan palace at KNOSSOS beginning in the year 1900. Although chance finds had been made before, these excavations were the first that systematically recovered remains from the Minoan past. Others soon followed, revealing three further palaces at PHAISTOS, MALLIA and KATO ZAKROS, as well as towns, country houses and sanctuaries throughout the island (see fig. 1). The chronological system devised by Evans remains in use, with modifications (*see* §I, 4 below). There was much cross-fertilization between the Minoan civilization and the Bronze Age cultures of mainland Greece (*see* HELLADIC) and the CYCLADIC islands. By the middle of the 17th century BC the influence of Minoan Crete on these two cultures was especially strong. One vital factor that led to Crete's dominant position in the Aegean was the foundation, in the Middle Minoan (MM) IB period, of the Minoan palaces and the subsequent development of a palace-based administration, the system for which the Minoans are, in fact, best known. Each palace controlled its immediate area, perhaps independently at first, though eventually under the overall control of Knossos. At about the time of the foundation of the palaces writing first appeared in Crete: the unknown Minoan language was first written in the Hieroglyphic script, which was replaced by Linear A. Linear B, an early form of Greek, began to be used when it is thought that Knossos fell under Mycenaean control (*c.* 1425–*c.* 1360 BC).

GENERAL BIBLIOGRAPHY

A. J. Evans: *The Palace of Minos at Knossos*, 4 vols and index (London, 1921–36, 2/1964)

J. D. S. Pendlebury: *The Archaeology of Crete* (London, 1939/*R* New York, 1963)

H. J. Kantor: *The Aegean and the Orient in the Second Millennium BC* (Bloomington, IN, 1947)

C. Zervos: *L'Art de la Crète néolithique et minoenne* (Paris, 1956)

S. Marinatos and M. Hirmer: *Crete and Mycenae* (London, 1960)

R. W. Hutchinson: *Prehistoric Crete* (Harmondsworth, 1962)

W. S. Smith: *Interconnections in the Ancient Near East* (New Haven, 1965)

R. A. Higgins: *Minoan and Mycenaean Art* (London, 1967)

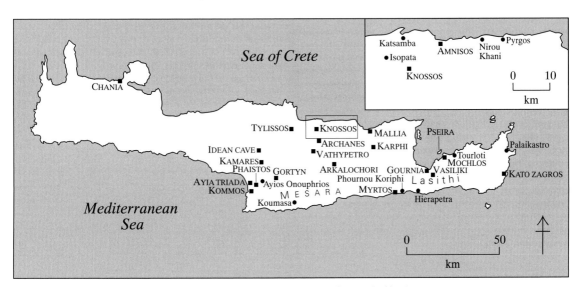

1. Map of Minoan sites in Crete; those with separate entries in this dictionary are distinguished by CROSS-REFERENCE TYPE

S. Alexiou: *Minoan Civilization* (Herakleion, 1969)

K. Branigan: *The Foundations of Palatial Crete* (London, 1969)

R. F. Willetts: *Everyday Life in Ancient Crete* (London, 1969)

S. Hood: *The Minoans* (London, 1971)

C. Renfrew: *The Emergence of Civilization* (London, 1972)

C. Davaras: *Guide to Cretan Antiquities* (Park Ridge, NJ, 1976)

S. Hood: *The Arts in Prehistoric Greece*, Pelican Hist. A. (Harmondsworth, 1978)

P. Darcque and J.-C. Poursat, eds: *L'Iconographie minoenne: Actes de la Table Ronde d'Athènes 21–22 avril 1983*, Bull. Corr. Hell., suppl. xi (1985)

G. Walberg: *Tradition and Innovation: Essays in Minoan Art* (Mainz, 1986)

J. W. Myers, E. E. Myers and G. Cadogan, eds: *The Aerial Atlas of Ancient Crete* (Berkeley, Los Angeles and Oxford, 1992)

I. Introduction. II. Architecture. III. Pottery. IV. Wall paintings and reliefs. V. Sculpture. VI. Ivory and bone. VII. Faience. VIII. Seals. IX. Metalwork. X. Stone vases. XI. Forgeries. XII. Museums.

I. *Introduction.*

1. Geography and climate. 2. Trade. 3. Religion and iconography. 4. Chronological overview.

1. GEOGRAPHY AND CLIMATE. The prosperity of the Minoan civilization and its importance in the eastern Mediterranean resulted, at least in part, from the position and natural resources of Crete itself. Some 250 km long and varying in width from *c.* 13 to *c.* 60 km, Crete is the largest and most southerly of the Aegean islands. It is situated almost midway between mainland Greece, Asia Minor and Africa. Further east are Egypt, Cyprus and Syria, and beyond these were the older civilizations of Mesopotamia.

While overseas contacts were always important, Crete was itself both large enough and sufficiently rich in natural resources to develop an independent and unique culture. The island has hot, dry summers with substantial rainfall in winter. Its mountainous spine shelters fertile coastal plains and inland plateaux, and the Minoan farmers grew grain, grapes and olives as well as rearing sheep, goats, pigs and some cattle. Sheep, which thrive in the mountainous terrain, were important not only for food but also for wool, and records on a series of clay tablets inscribed in the Linear B syllabary show that in Late Minoan times the palace at Knossos was an important centre of textile production. Building materials were also readily available: Crete is essentially composed of limestone, which formed the basis of most Minoan structures, while sporadic outcrops of gypsum provided the smooth slabs for covering walls and floors (*see* §II below). Other, rarer stones were used for special architectural purposes, such as schist for paving and breccia or marble for decorative column bases, while vases were produced from various native stones, notably serpentine, though some were made from imported materials (*see* §X below). Timber was more plentiful in antiquity than it is today, and timber-frame construction was common in Minoan buildings, a factor that increased their elasticity and made them more resistant to earthquakes. The characteristic downward taper of Minoan columns may be derived from the shape of inverted tree trunks.

J. LESLEY FITTON

2. TRADE. Long before the beginning of Minoan civilization, the inhabitants of Crete had to import certain raw materials. Initially the most important was obsidian, imported before 5000 BC from the Cyclades, especially the island of Melos. With the introduction of metalworking, Cretan dependence on raw materials from abroad increased. Reserves of copper were very limited, and Crete had virtually no supplies of gold or silver. Lead isotope analyses have revealed that soon after 3000 BC Crete began to acquire silver and lead from the Cyclades and Attica. Substantial quantities of Attic copper were also imported, and smaller quantities came perhaps from Turkey. The acquisition of these raw materials was inevitably accompanied by a smaller-scale trade in manufactured products, such as pottery and figurines. The transport of these various commodities was facilitated by the construction of larger ships, itself made possible by the new carpenters' tools manufactured from imported metals. Exactly what the people of Crete were able to offer in exchange for these imports is still not known. The few Cretan jewellery pieces, seals or metal weapons found outside Crete must have been exported with other, probably perishable goods such as foodstuffs, timber and cloth. Equally uncertain are the nature and extent of Cretan contacts with the eastern Mediterranean before *c.* 2000 BC, but the use of hippopotamus ivory for Cretan seals, the occasional use of tin bronze (tin alloyed with copper) and the importation of a few Egyptian stone vases suggest at least minor trading links with that region.

In the Middle Minoan period, around the time of the construction of the first Minoan palaces (for Minoan chronology *see* §4 below), trading contacts with the eastern Mediterranean apparently increased. Egyptian scarabs (amulets), ivory, Syrian daggers and cylinder seals were all imported in small quantities, along with greater numbers of Egyptian stone vases. The widespread adoption of tin bronze required a regular supply of tin, and the inhabitants of Crete and the Aegean in general probably obtained this via the Levant from somewhere further east. Middle Minoan painted Kamares pottery (*see* §III, 3(ii) below) and a few elegant Minoan bronze daggers have been found in Cyprus, Syria and Egypt, and there may have been other perishable exports such as perfumes, oils and textiles. During this period, increasing amounts of Kamares ware occur both at Cycladic sites and on the Greek mainland (*see* CYCLADIC, §III, 2; HELLADIC, §III, 3). The Cretans still depended on Cycladic and Attic supplies of silver and lead, and most of the copper used in Cretan bronze production apparently still came from Attica. Trade with both the Aegean and the Near East was thus becoming increasingly important, though there is still little evidence that the authorities in the newly built palaces exercised any direct control over it.

In the 17th century BC, however, this situation may have changed. Minoan pottery and stone vases were exported in far greater quantities, and local imitations appear in large numbers. The abrupt rise in the quantity of exported goods was accompanied by the introduction to the Cyclades of Minoan writing and weighing systems, along with internal architectural features of Minoan derivation and Minoan religious artefacts and wall paintings (*see* CYCLADIC, §§II and VI). This does not necessarily imply Minoan political or commercial control over the rest of the Aegean but possibly indicates that groups of

Minoans settled on several Cycladic islands (e.g. at Ayia Irini on KEA) and were active in local commerce. The role of the Minoan palace authorities in this is unclear, though they seem to have been increasingly involved in Minoan trade with the eastern Mediterranean. A few imported Egyptian artefacts of this period bear the cartouches of Egyptian pharaohs, suggesting that diplomatic exchanges of gifts between rulers took place, a common practice in the Near East. In Egypt itself, early 18th Dynasty (*c.* 1540–*c.* 1292 BC) paintings depict people called 'Keftiu' bringing tribute, or gifts, to the pharaoh. The Keftiu are almost certainly Cretans, and some of the goods they carry seem to be Minoan products.

The importance of Minoan trading connections was not simply commercial. During the 3rd millennium BC, it was the acquisition of raw metals from other parts of the Aegean that enabled the Cretans to develop many specialist crafts and technologies. At the same time, trading contacts opened up Crete to the important cultural and artistic influence of the Cyclades. In Middle Minoan times the direction of influence was perhaps reversed, and by the 17th century BC Minoan craftsmen may have been as much in demand as their products. Cretan domination of Aegean trade prompted the widespread adoption of Minoan weights and measures, writing and accounting, so creating a commercial lingua franca for the region. At the same time, increasing Minoan contacts with the great civilizations of the Near East, particularly Egypt, probably had an impact on social and political conditions on Crete itself.

BIBLIOGRAPHY

R. Hagg and N. Marinatos, eds: *The Minoan Thalassocracy: Myth and Reality. Proceedings of the Third International Symposium at the Swedish Institute, Athens 1982*

N. Gale and Z. Stos-Gale: 'Bronze Age Copper Sources in the Mediterranean: A New Approach', *Science*, ccxvi (1982), pp. 11–19

KEITH BRANIGAN

3. RELIGION AND ICONOGRAPHY. The study of Minoan religion and iconography (the two are intrinsically linked) was begun by Sir Arthur Evans, excavator of the palace of Knossos, in a seminal article published in 1901. Working from an iconography derived mostly from seal-stones, he concluded that the prehistoric Cretan cult was one of 'primitive' aniconic worship. His analysis was succeeded by the work of the Swedish scholar Martin Nilsson, whose *Minoan–Mycenaean Religion and its Survival in Greek Religion* (1927), while suffering from the bias evident in its title—the assumption that earlier religious beliefs can be extrapolated from later ones—still remains a basic textbook on prehistoric Aegean cult. Axel Persson's *Religion of Greece in Prehistoric Times* (1942), another essential study, possesses the same flaw. Studies produced since the mid-20th century, aided by material brought to light by 50 years of additional excavation, have tended to concentrate more on archaeological evidence and less on unsubstantiated interpretation, as Minoan religion has come to be seen as a coherent, autonomous system of belief and practice rather than merely as a precursor to Classical Greek cult.

Minoan iconography and religion are so closely related that it is impossible to discuss one without reference to the other. Certain general themes recur throughout the range of depictions on wall paintings, seals, stone-carvings and in the decoration of such materials as faience, ivory and hardstones: the idea of death and regeneration and the use of nature imagery to express this concept; scenes of a fertility goddess and a warrior-hunter god, who appear in both wild landscapes and in association with architecture, either alone, with attributes or with worshippers; and various types of hunting, procession, dancing, rites-of-passage, offering and pure landscape scenes.

Minoan cult practices and rituals were carried out in the palaces and in houses (*see* §II, 3 below), at peak sanctuaries and in caves. Obvious scenes of cult activity are depicted on seals and rings, stone vases, wall paintings and decorative objects. Cult equipment (known from actual archaeological remains as well as depictions) included libation tables and altars with incurved sides (as were painted on either side of the throne at Knossos), offering tables, sacrificial tables and libation vessels (rhyta), sometimes in the shape of animal heads. Priests, priestesses or deities might hold a double axe, which was not a weapon or instrument of sacrifice but a cult symbol, the meaning of which is unclear; it marked a sacred place or might be set up between horns of consecration, symbolic bulls' horns that are one of the more ubiquitous symbols in Minoan religion. Priests might hold a stone mace (apparently associated with sacrificial rites); other cult equipment included kernoi and tubular snake stands. Male and female votive figurines, most often with one hand to the head in devotional salute, are also common; many have been found in peak sanctuaries, where they were offered to the deity (*see* §4(ii) below). In the Post-Palatial period, terracotta sculpture was part of the cult equipment found in shrines (see below).

Whether the Minoans worshipped a single female fertility goddess under different aspects or several deities is still debated. The female goddess is most frequently depicted as the Mistress of Animals, accompanied by animals arranged heraldically—lions, griffins, birds, fish, even monkeys. Lions and griffins are her most common familiars, the griffin a composite monster whose iconography originated in the Near East, combining the features of lion and eagle, appropriate for a guardian animal (*see* §IV, 2(v) below). Griffins appear with male gods as well, but they only flank goddesses.

Where surroundings are depicted, the goddess is almost always shown in a natural, outdoor setting, often on a mountaintop. A bird-goddess occurs occasionally, perhaps the result of a merging of the goddess and her attribute in the way Egyptian deities were normally portrayed. Other variants of the Mistress of the Animals involve the goddess accompanied by dolphins, as on seals from Palaikastro and Knossos (Herakleion, Archaeol. Mus.), perhaps indicating her marine connections as the birds and quadrupeds signify her air and earth associations (*see also* CYCLADIC, §VI, 2). The two faience statuettes of the goddess found in the Temple Repositories at Knossos (MM III; see fig. 21 below) depict her, as do virtually all other images, dressed in a long flounced skirt and open bodice curved around her breasts, this time with snakes wound round her arms and torso or held in her hands. Arthur Evans and Martin Nilsson after him associated the snake with a domestic house cult, serving as guardian of the palace; its association with death and rejuvenation and with cyclical fertility must also be noted, however. (For discussion of wall paintings on the theme of the Minoan nature cult and the goddess, *see* §IV, 2(ii) below.)

The goddess is also shown attended by human figures, most frequently female. It has been argued (Marinatos, 1993) that these adorant priestesses included in their duties of pouring libations, taking part in processions, dancing, bringing offerings of flowers or jewellery or taking part in sacrifices the function of impersonating the goddess in actual epiphany rites. The priestess who probably sat on the throne at Knossos would have been flanked by wall paintings of griffins, lilies and palm trees (a sacred tree) with, at her feet, depictions of Minoan altars with incurved sides. Priestesses and other females are often depicted wearing the so-called 'sacral knot', a bowlike arrangement of the hair at the back (*see* §4(iii) and fig. 17 below).

Despite the predominance of women in Minoan iconography, Bronze Age Cretans also worshipped a male god, a Master of the Animals or a hunter, usually shown with lions, sometimes with bulls. He is dressed in a typical Minoan loincloth or codpiece with belt. As the goddess figure is almost always shown in her role as a nature goddess, protectress of wild things and natural places and symbol of natural cycles, so the male god may have been associated with urban centres (although he also appears in natural landscapes): a seal impression from Chania, the so-called Master Impression (Herakleion, Archaeol. Mus.), depicts the god (some would say king) standing protectively atop the architecture of a town. Male priests are distinguished by long Syrian-type robes or, in some ceremonial scenes such as a harvest procession (as on the Harvester Vase from Ayia Triada, LM I), by a type of cuirass, and by their particular hairstyle, sometimes a beard, and accoutrements: stone mace or curved axe, occasionally with a bow or pair of lances. Their role appears to have been the carrying out of sacrifices and their association with hunting and the harvest.

In addition to (and in combination with) scenes of deities, apparently secular scenes were also created, most frequently in wall paintings, though some scholars have asserted that these should also be seen as though having at least an ideological purpose. Examples include painted relief scenes of bull-leaping (the bull was a potent symbol of power and virility, and its horns were associated with cult; *see* §IV, 2(iv) and fig. 16 below); swimming dolphins, as reconstructed on the walls of the so-called Queen's Megaron at Knossos; monkeys in a flowery landscape (e.g. the *Saffron Gatherer* fresco from Knossos, showing blue monkeys in a garden gathering crocuses (Herakleion, Archael. Mus.; *see* §4(ii) below; dolphins and monkeys also appear in association with the goddess); and scenes of procession and court ritual (some of these in miniature paintings; *see* §IV, 2(vi) and (iii) below). Landscapes and scenes of nature were also extremely popular, the sacred lily and crocus being the most common flowers (*see* §IV, 2(i) and fig. 15 below). Landscape scenes have been seen by some scholars as religious in nature by virtue of their suggestion of fertility and natural cycles of death and rebirth; on the other hand, the sensitive and pleasure-loving Minoans must also have appreciated them for their beauty alone.

Symbols of warfare and military prowess include the boars'-tusk helmet and the figure-of-eight shield, depicted, for example, on the walls of the Grand Staircase at Knossos (for discussion of martial arts themes in wall paintings *see* §IV, 2(vii) below). Scenes of ritual combat (e.g. the Boxer Rhyton from Ayia Triada (see fig. 28 below) and the scene of the *Boxing Boys* at Akrotiri (*see* CYCLADIC, fig. 12)) and puberty initiation rites (e.g. the apparently unconnected but thematically related scenes of young women and a bloody shrine on the walls of the adyton in Xeste 3 at Akrotiri must also be ritual in nature (*see* CYCLADIC, §VI, 1(i); for discussion of adyta *see* §II, 3 below).

In the Post-Palatial period on Crete, town shrines became the place where ritual was carried out after the destruction and abandonment of the palaces. Using the example of Gournia, these were accessible from the street and usually had one room with a bench against the far wall; there might also be a niche and/or an additional platform. At Gournia were found tubular terracotta stands decorated with horns of consecration and snakes, small clay figures of birds and a clay female figurine perhaps representing the goddess (see fig. 19 below for a terracotta statuette of a goddess from Gazi, LM IIIA:2). In the LM III Shrine of the Double Axes at Knossos a number of items were found *in situ* on the bench: a female votive figurine with arms folded on her chest, horns of consecration, a small steatite double axe and other female votive figurines, some with birds and one with raised arms, which may have represented the goddess. Paintings on Post-Palatial larnakes (clay coffins) frequently incorporated plant and animal motifs derived from earlier ritual art and sometimes show actual scenes of sacrifice (for illustration *see* AYIA TRIADA; *see also* §4(iii) below).

See also §V below and CYCLADIC, §§I, 3 and VI.

BIBLIOGRAPHY

A. J. Evans: 'The Mycenaean Tree and Pillar Cult', *J. Hell. Stud.*, xxi (1901), pp. 99–204

M. P. Nilsson: *The Minoan–Mycenaean Religion and its Survival in Greek Religion* (Lund, 1927, rev. 1950)

A. W. Persson: *The Religion of Greece in Prehistoric Times* (Berkeley, 1942)

C. R. Long: *The Ayia Triada Sarcophagus: A Study of Late Minoan and Mycenaean Funerary Practices and Beliefs*, Stud. Medit. Archaeol., xli (Göteborg, 1974)

P. Warren: *The Aegean Civilizations: From Ancient Crete to Mycenae* (Oxford, 1975, 2/1989)

Sanctuaries and Cults in the Aegean Bronze Age. Proceedings of the First International Symposium at the Swedish Institute at Athens: Athens, 1980

Minoan Society. Proceedings of the Cambridge Colloquium: Cambridge, 1981

R. Hagg: 'Epiphany in Minoan Ritual', *BICS*, xxx (1983), pp. 184–5

N. Marinatos: *Art and Religion in Thera* (Athens, 1984)

The Function of the Minoan Palaces. Proceedings of the Fourth International Symposium at the Swedish Institute at Athens: Athens, 1984

G. Gesell: *Town, Palace, and House Cult in Minoan Crete*, Stud. Medit. Archaeol., lxvii (Göteborg, 1985)

C. Renfrew: *The Archaeology of Cult: The Sanctuary at Philakopi* (London, 1985)

N. Marinatos: *Minoan Sacrificial Ritual: Cult Practice and Symbolism* (Stockholm, 1986)

B. Rutkowski: *The Cult Places in the Aegean* (New Haven and London, 1986)

Early Greek Cult Practice. Proceedings of the Fifth International Symposium at the Swedish Institute at Athens: Athens, 1986

Thanatos: Les Coutîmes funéraires en Egée à l'âge du bronze. Actes du colloque de Liège: Liège, 1986

L. Morgan: *The Miniature Wall Paintings from Thera: A Study in Aegean Culture and Iconography* (Cambridge, 1988)

Celebrations of Death and Divinity in the Bronze Age. Proceedings of the Sixth International Symposium at the Swedish Institute at Athens: Athens, 1988

P. Warren: *Minoan Religion or Ritual Action* (Göteborg, 1989)

A. A. D. Peatfield: 'Minoan Peak Sanctuaries: History and Society', *Opuscula Athen.*, xviii (1990), pp. 117–31

N. Marinatos: *Minoan Religion: Ritual, Image and Symbol* (Columbia, SC, 1993)

O. Dickinson: *The Aegean Bronze Age*, Cambridge World Archaeology (Cambridge, 1994)

4. CHRONOLOGICAL OVERVIEW. Following ARTHUR EVANS, most archaeologists divide the Minoan Bronze Age into three periods: Early, Middle and Late Minoan (EM, MM, LM). These are themselves subdivided on the basis of changing pottery styles and are broadly parallel to those adopted for the contemporary cultures of mainland Greece and the Cyclades (*see* HELLADIC, §I, 4 and CYCLADIC, §I, 4). Although the chronological periods (see fig. 2a) are separated into discrete units, there was some overlap from one phase to the next: the inhabitants of one site might retain older pottery types for many years while another site changed to new styles. This 'regionalism' was particularly common during the Neolithic and EM periods and at the end of LM.

Approximate absolute dates for these chronological periods are derived from radiocarbon analysis and from links with Egypt and the Near East, where relatively secure dates are based on historical dynastic sequences (*see* EGYPT, ANCIENT, fig. 2, and ANCIENT NEAR EAST, fig. 2). Nevertheless, the field of Aegean Bronze Age chronology has been the subject of considerable scholarly controversy since the 1980s. Many archaeologists believe that dates should be higher by a century. This argument is based largely on new radiocarbon dates suggesting that the eruption of the volcanic island of THERA took place *c.* 1625 BC instead of *c.* 1525 BC, making the beginning of the Late Bronze Age approximately 100 years earlier, with concomitant effects on succeeding periods (see fig. 2b). However, not all archaeologists are convinced of the efficacy of the new scientific dating methods for the periods in question, not least because the higher chronology tends to weaken proven links with ancient Egypt. The dating system in figure 2a is the traditional chronology, although individual scholars may vary the details.

Another chronological system, preferred particularly among Italian and Greek archaeologists, is one based on developments in architecture rather than pottery: Pre-Palatial period (EM–MM IA); Proto-Palatial period (MM IB–MM III); Neo-Palatial period (MM III/LM IA–LM IB); Post-Palatial period (LM II–LM IIIC). Other systems, usually devised for a single site or period, have not been widely accepted. Even the Palatial system has lost support, because it does not permit divisions small enough to deal with brief phases. The tripartite pottery system is thus generally the most successful framework for Minoan history and art.

BIBLIOGRAPHY

P. M. Warren and V. Hankey: *Aegean Bronze Age Chronology* (Bristol, 1989)

D. A. Hardy and A. C. Renfrew, eds: *Chronology*, iii of *Thera and the Aegean World III* (London, 1990)

P. M. Warren: 'The Minoan Civilisation of Crete and the Volcano of Thera', *J. Anc. Chron. Forum*, iv (1990–91), pp. 29–39 [n. 22 with previous bibliog.]

Late Neolithic		*c.* 4500-*c.* 3800 BC
Final Neolithic		*c.* 3800-*c.* 3500/3000 BC
Early Minoan (EM)		*c.* 3500/3000-*c.* 2050 BC
	EM I	*c.* 3500/3000-*c.* 2900/2600 BC
	EM II	*c.* 2900/2600-*c.* 2200 BC
	EM III	*c.* 2200-*c.* 2050 BC
Middle Minoan (MM)		*c.* 2050-*c.* 1600 BC
	MM IA	*c.* 2050-*c.* 1900 BC
	MM IB	*c.* 1900-*c.* 1800 BC
	MM II	*c.* 1800-*c.* 1675 BC
	MM IIIA	*c.* 1675-*c.* 1635 BC
	MM IIIB	*c.* 1635-*c.* 1600 BC
Late Minoan (LM)		*c.* 1600-*c.* 1050 BC
(a)	LM IA	*c.* 1600-*c.* 1480 BC
	LM IB	*c.* 1480-*c.* 1425 BC
	LM II	*c.* 1425-*c.* 1390 BC
	LM IIIA:1	*c.* 1390-*c.* 1360 BC
	LM IIIA:2	*c.* 1360-*c.* 1335 BC
	LM IIIB	*c.* 1335-*c.* 1190 BC
	LM IIIC	*c.* 1190-*c.* 1050 BC
(b)	LM IA	*c.* 1700-*c.* 1610 BC
	LM IB	*c.* 1610-*c.* 1475 BC
	LM II	*c.* 1475-*c.* 1440 BC
	LM IIIA:1	*c.* 1440-*c.* 1375 BC
	LM IIIA:2	*c.* 1375-*c.* 1325 BC
	LM IIIB	*c.* 1325-*c.* 1180 BC
	LM IIIC	*c.* 1180-*c.* 1050 BC
Sub-Minoan		*c.* 1050-*c.* 1000 BC

2. Chronological chart showing the major Minoan periods with their subdivisions: (a) traditional chronology; (b) alternative chronology of the Late Minoan period

S. Manning: *The Absolute Chronology of the Aegean Early Bronze Age* (Sheffield, 1995)

C. D. FORTENBERRY

(i) Early Minoan. (ii) Middle Minoan. (iii) Late Minoan.

(i) Early Minoan. The Minoan culture originated in the Final Neolithic period, a transitional phase between the Stone Age and Early Minoan (EM). Many of its distinguishing features had already appeared by this time, and EM I was a continuation of their development more than an innovative new phase. By EM I, the inhabitants of Crete were already living in large houses of stone or mud-brick on stone foundations, burying their dead in circular tombs (*see* §II, 5 below) and other communal graves and making distinctive pottery that prefigured the styles generally associated with Early Minoan. Certain artistic features, such as the use of pattern-burnished pottery, suggest Anatolian cultural influences. Even so, EM buildings were uniquely Cretan, with few close parallels discovered elsewhere (*see* §II below). Houses were of rubble, stone or

mud-brick on stone foundations, their walls already reinforced with the half-timbering characteristic of Minoan architecture throughout the Bronze Age. Good examples of EM houses have been found in eastern Crete (e.g. VASILIKI and at Phournou Koriphi near MYRTOS). Those at Phournou Koriphi cluster on an easily defensible hill, the rooms packed tightly together. No defensive wall has been found, but the house walls themselves may have formed a protective circuit. Roofs were flat, providing additional living space. Some walls were plastered and painted red or brown, but floors were of beaten earth. The community probably consisted of only a few households but was largely self-sufficient, with its own storerooms, working areas and shrine.

EM tombs varied considerably in form, suggesting that the island received settlers from different areas. Burials were usually multiple, sometimes containing several hundred bodies. The simplest burials, common in eastern Crete, consisted of rock shelters. These were simple depressions or overhangs at the side of a cliff, sometimes improved by hollowing out the bluff or by adding a wall or two for extra protection. Built tombs in eastern Crete were usually rectangular and above ground, though they were often set against a cliff to make use of the natural rock on one or more sides. Usually called house tombs, good examples were found at MOCHLOS and at GOURNIA. House tombs may have been intended to imitate natural caves, since these were often used for burial, especially in northern and western Crete. In the south the tombs were circular. Known as THOLOS TOMBS, they constitute the most monumental of EM structures. The earliest examples were built in the Final Neolithic period (e.g. at Lebena), but the type persisted into the Late Bronze Age. They had stone walls and a single doorway, but no complete example survives. Their roofs may have been flat or may have taken the form of a corbelled dome. The tombs were probably used as cult centres, since they incorporated several secondary rooms in which offerings were placed, as also occurred in the main burial chamber. Additional objects were often placed around the tombs and in small courtyards near their entrances. The EM offerings include tools and weapons, especially bronze or copper daggers, animal figurines, stone vases and implements, seals, jewellery and many types of pottery. Some of the pottery was made in unusual shapes, such as birds or animals, suggesting special productions for ceremonies associated with the dead.

Besides architecture, little monumental art survives from the EM period; assessment of Minoan tastes and styles must derive primarily from small, portable objects, chiefly from tombs. These indicate a diversity of styles and approaches, yet are recognizably Minoan. Almost all surviving EM sculpture is miniature (see §V below). The only exception is a stylized monolithic stone figure, 675 mm high, from Samba Pediados (Herakleion, Archaeol. Mus.), consisting of a smooth pillar with a featureless oval head—an anthropomorphic shape closely resembling contemporary Cycladic figurines (see CYCLADIC, §IV, 1). Smaller marble images of Cycladic type have been found at several sites, especially Koumasa (now in Herakleion, Archaeol. Mus.). Carved from flat pieces of marble, with simplified features and a slim, schematized

body, most depict nude female figures with arms folded. As in Cycladic figurines, the sexual attributes are not prominent.

Simple clay figurines were also made, most of them of animals, especially quadrupeds. Many are hollow so that they could serve as containers, and they provide some of the wittiest and most imaginative examples of EM art. Jugs were fashioned into birds by adding wings and eyes to vessels with beaklike spouts (see fig. 8b below), and shapes imitated by other vases include bulls and gourds. Hollow female figures may well represent deities. A fine example from Phournou Koriphi near Myrtos (Ayios Nikolaos, Archaeol. Mus.) holds a jug, and one from Koumasa (Herakleion, Archaeol. Mus.) handles snakes. These may be divine attributes, though they may also reflect ritual practices. Other hollow female figurines (Herakleion, Archaeol. Mus.) have pierced breasts for pouring liquid (for illustration see MOCHLOS).

Among the most plentiful EM artefacts are pottery vases, and their decoration, in red, white or dark paint, is crucial to establishing the evolution of EM artistic styles (see §III, 3 below). Stone vases were also produced at this time, some of them highly expressive (see §X below). Examples occur throughout Crete, the finest coming from the east of the island. Two chlorite schist pyxides (boxes with lids) from Mochlos and KATO ZAKROS (Herakleion, Archaeol. Mus.) have handles in the form of reclining dogs on their lids (see fig. 3). Many of the vases were made from naturally patterned stones such as banded marble or mottled serpentinite, which could both suggest and enhance the carved designs. The range of shapes of stone vases was almost as varied as that of pottery containers.

Engraved seals (see §VIII below) survive from EM II, though the tradition is assumed to have had its origins in EM I. These were used to stamp images into clay or wax (as in Egypt), rather than for rolling (as was the custom in Mesopotamia). They were often shaped like chess pawns, though cones, discs, cubes and even animal forms were occasionally engraved as seals. The materials from

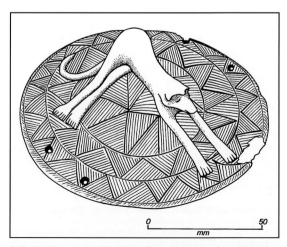

3. Early Minoan pyxis lid with handle in the shape of a reclining dog, chlorite schist, from Mochlos, EM II (Herakleion, Archaeological Museum)

which they were carved also varied but tended to be fairly soft, suitable for working with stone or bronze tools. Ivory, bone, serpentinite and probably wood were the most common. Designs, which survive as impressions as well as on the seals themselves, include geometric, floral or animal motifs and household objects. All are highly stylized, though the quality of engraving varies from accomplished to crude.

Jewellery was often placed in tombs with the dead and was clearly popular, because many types survive. Beads were made of different materials, including faience and hardstones (amethyst, cornelian and rock crystal). Pendants were of stone and other materials. Bronze pins and rings may have been used in the hair. The most attractive jewellery was made of sheets of gold with embossed designs (*see* §IX, 1(i) below). The finest examples come from Mochlos (Ayios Nikolaos, Archaeol. Mus., and Herakleion, Archaeol. Mus.) and date from EM II. Some were cut into wide strips for use as diadems or for attaching to leather clothing or headdresses. Others were shaped into flowers, leaves, beads or other objects. Large diadems have dot-repoussé decorations depicting animals, geometric designs and, on one particularly striking band, a pair of human eyes (EM II; Herakleion, Archaeol. Mus.). Since the jewellery has parallels in north-west Anatolia, it may have been made by travelling craftsmen. If so, this would explain the rapid spread of new styles and techniques to distant areas. Alternatively, the jewellery may have been brought by immigrants or obtained through trade in either the objects themselves or the craftsmen who made them, or as gifts or spoils or dowry items. It is likely that several of these factors operated at the same time.

By the end of EM III, Crete enjoyed a unified artistic culture, easily distinguishable from those of its neighbours. Good communications enabled ideas to spread quickly, and foreign influences were soon incorporated into the local Minoan styles.

(ii) Middle Minoan. During the Middle Minoan (MM) period Crete achieved an ever widening sphere of both artistic and economic influence; by the end of the period it dominated the Aegean. Whether the Minoanizing settlements of the Cyclades and nearby areas were true colonies or independent towns that adopted Minoan culture as a sign of sophistication (the so-called 'Versailles effect') is a matter of controversy. But it is clear that Crete was the most advanced civilization of the Aegean; its impact was felt from Greece to Asia Minor, from Thrace to the Nile Valley.

Much of this influence seems to have derived from a new political and social organization on Crete, first evidenced by the building of the Old Palaces in MM IB. The scope of the building operations during MM I suggests a tradition of monumental architecture, though the builders eliminated almost all trace of earlier structures. Large MM palaces stood at KNOSSOS, PHAISTOS, MALLIA, CHANIA and probably several other sites. They must have functioned as political, artistic, social, religious, commercial and economic centres. The palatial rulers seem to have organized production in the surrounding countryside, creating a period of prosperity, leisure and cultural sophistication during which the arts flourished.

MM architecture developed the EM skills and techniques, with stone, timber and mud-brick still the principal building materials. Roofs were always flat, and houses often had over a dozen rooms on different levels. Palaces were constructed around a central courtyard on a north–south axis; houses in outlying villages often had courts also. The main features of later Minoan domestic architecture were already well developed.

Tombs from the MM period also continued with established practices; in fact, many EM tombs were still in use. New developments affected details rather than basic forms. Among the few significant developments was the increasing use of burial jars and larnakes as receptacles for the dead. A larnax was a large, rectangular or oval chest or tub, usually with a lid. The earliest examples come from a burial cave at Pyrgos, in north-central Crete, and date from the EM period. Jars and larnakes were initially placed in tombs alongside more conventional burials, but by the end of MM times some cemeteries consisted of hundreds of jars buried in the soil (e.g. at Pacheia Ammos and Sphoungaras in eastern Crete). Offerings were placed in the jar or in its pit or in open areas within the cemetery. The sides of jars and larnakes provided ample scope for painted decoration, but this was not fully exploited until LM times.

The earliest Minoan wall paintings have not survived, but the tradition was fully developed by the end of the MM period (*see* §IV below). One of the earliest extant examples (Herakleion, Archaeol. Mus.) shows blue monkeys in a garden and includes the fragmentary figure often called the 'Saffron Gatherer', which was reconstructed as a boy, although it is now known to depict a monkey. The painting's white flowers on a red ground closely resemble those on contemporary painted vases. In the wall paintings the colours were applied to lime plaster, though opinion is divided on the question of whether or not the technique was true fresco (i.e. painted while the plaster was wet); mixing lime into the paint may have achieved a similar effect.

Painted pottery also flourished, especially after the introduction of the potter's wheel in MM IB (*see* §III, 4 below). Its high point is represented by the style called Kamares ware (see figs 8f and 10 below), which used floral and geometric patterns in white, red and orange on a dark ground. This was plentiful during MM IB-II, especially at the palaces of Knossos, Mallia and Phaistos and in their vicinities. Complex schemes of interlocking curves were used to create an effect known as torsion, which draws the eye around a vase by giving an impression of balanced motion.

Sculpture continued to be made primarily in miniature, and terracotta figurines were produced in large numbers (*see* §V below). They seem most often to have been used as offerings, and some 'peak sanctuaries' have yielded hundreds of examples. These sanctuaries were religious focal points placed on high hills (see fig. 7 below). They were the recipients of some of the most interesting art objects of the time, especially figurines. Many are of simplified human figures, the males usually dressed in the typical abbreviated costume of codpiece and belt or loincloth, with a dagger at the waist; they often clasp the chest or forehead in gestures of worship or devotion.

Female figures wear long, wide skirts with short-sleeved jackets, the low bodices of which often leave the breasts exposed. Coiffures or hats are occasionally large and ornamental. Animals, especially quadrupeds, continued to be popular.

Faience figurines were also produced (*see* §VII, 2 below). This material, which probably entered Crete from Egypt originally, was made by fusing a mixture of fine sand with fluxes and copper salts in a kiln. The best selection of faience objects comes from the Temple Repositories at Knossos and dates from MM III. Besides two well-known female figures probably representing priestesses or snake-goddesses (see fig. 21 below), faience pieces from the Temple Repositories include cups and vases, a miniature female costume and flat plaques depicting animals. Also from Knossos are small representations of Minoan houses (*see* §II, 4 below) once set into a gaming-board or some other perishable object (all Herakleion, Archaeol. Mus.). Their naturalistic style seems likely to have been a Knossian innovation, which spread to other centres gradually, over a period of many years.

New techniques, especially the introduction of the mechanical cutting wheel used with abrasives, enabled seals to be cut from harder stones (*see* §VIII below). Quartzes, such as agate, chalcedony, jasper, cornelian, amethyst and crystal, were not only more durable than the substances used in EM times but also permitted crisper and more finely detailed engraving. Seals were made in several shapes, but three-sided prisms and discs with flat or rounded faces were the most common. Designs included geometric motifs, inanimate objects, human or animal figures and hieroglyphic signs. A series of seals depicting ships, some under full sail, began to be produced in MM I; the best-known large group of motifs occurs on clay sealings for jugs and other containers from Phaistos and dates from MM II (Herakleion, Archaeol. Mus.). The commonest scheme has geometric designs in a circular format, often with three or more elements radiating out from the centre. Hieroglyphic signs were first used in MM I or slightly earlier. They seem to represent an early form of the Minoan writing system that would develop by the close of the MM period into the fully formed syllabary called Linear A.

Jewellery and metalwork were also produced with greater technological sophistication during MM times (*see* §IX below). A good example is a gold pendant from a tomb at Mallia (Herakleion, Archaeol. Mus.; see fig. 24 below) depicting two heraldic bees or wasps with outspread wings. The insects' bodies were cast in one piece, but some details were added in granulation, a difficult technique by which tiny gold balls were fused on to a backing without the use of solder. Several types of bronze objects, including the earliest European swords, also provide evidence of greater skill in production. Metalware vases were probably more common than the small number of surviving examples suggests. One of the finest is a silver kantharos from Gournia (Herakleion, Archaeol. Mus.), with a fluted rim and a carinated body (see fig. 4). A hoard of gold and silver vases from el-Tod in Egypt (Paris, Louvre) may include Minoan imports, since several bowls are decorated with typically Minoan spirals, and a fragment of a clay cast or mould for a similar spiral-decorated bowl

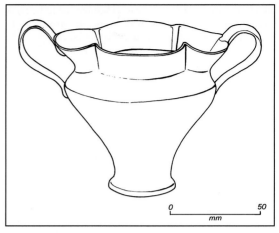

4. Middle Minoan silver kantharos with fluted rim, from Gournia, MM IB–II (Herakleion, Archaeological Museum)

has been found at Mallia. Such vessels were probably produced in copper and bronze as well.

Objects were made from many other materials. Those that survive include stone vessels, which continued to be highly regarded (*see* §X below). Ivory, bone and other hard substances were fashioned into useful and attractive objects, from spindle whorls and weights to pendants and pins (*see* §VI below). Casts from excavations at Mallia provide evidence for complex and attractive basketwork, with weaves rivalling the intricate patterns of Kamares ware. Textiles, rugs, leatherwork, carved wood, furniture, plasterwork and many other perishable objects must also have been produced in this rich and multi-skilled culture.

(iii) Late Minoan. The first stage of the Late Minoan (LM) period is defined by the spread of a new pottery style using glossy dark-brown to black paint on pale clay (see fig. 11 below). At about the same time Minoan art became more naturalistic, and new building programmes were begun at many centres. Knossos was rebuilt after its destruction by earthquake during or around the end of MM III. The town around the palace had become a prosperous metropolis, and like many smaller sites, it expanded during early LM I. Crete was a densely inhabited island, its population distributed among isolated farmhouses, comfortable villas with clusters of dependent buildings, small villages, large towns and palaces. Palaces of this period have been excavated at Kato Zakros, Mallia, Phaistos and Knossos. Other monumental LM I complexes, probably also palaces, have been found at ARCHANES, KOMMOS, Chania and elsewhere, but have not yet been fully excavated. Knossos continued to be the largest and most influential centre.

By LM I, the Knossian palace was almost fully developed. Set around a north–south courtyard, it housed both the palace bureaucracy and the ruling dynasty. It provided workshops for artists and craftsmen, basement storage areas, kitchens, archives, religious shrines and private areas, including royal apartments and dining-rooms. This extensive complex exhibited a uniquely Minoan plan (*see* KNOSSOS, fig. 2), at once informal and highly complex, with labyrinthine corridors linking its various elements. Minoan architecture is also characterized by other typical features:

much of Cretan life must have taken place out of doors, and buildings were opened up with porticos, windows and courts. Most houses had at least one court, though some are so small that they are designated as light wells. Lustral basins, sunken rectangular chambers lined with stone, may have been used for sacred libations or (less likely) simply as baths. Pier-and-door partition walls, consisting of several doors separated by narrow jambs, allowed rooms to be completely opened up or partly or wholly closed. (On the functions of lustral basins and pier-and-door partition walls *see also* §II, 3 below). Columns were thicker at the top than at the bottom, like inverted tree trunks, and had spreading capitals with convex profiles. By LM I masons had become so skilled that they routinely used large square blocks, even in the walls of outlying buildings.

Controversy still surrounds the history of Knossos in the later part of the LM period. The palace was remodelled in LM II, following damage or partial destruction—perhaps by invaders from the mainland—at the end of LM IB, and it continued to be important into LM IIIA:1. It was destroyed by fire at the beginning of LM IIIA:2, and some scholars believe this marked the end of the palace-based administration. Others contend that a series of clay tablets inscribed in the Linear B syllabary date from after this destruction. Since the tablets represent the records of a palatial economy, this would imply that Knossos continued as a major centre into LM IIIA:2 or LM IIIB. Events in Crete as a whole are easier to assess. Most sites were destroyed, no doubt in the same way as Knossos, at the end of LM IB. The next phase, LM II, was much less prosperous, but by LM IIIA:1 the economy had recovered. With many new influences from the Greek mainland, the island continued to prosper until the end of the Bronze Age.

During LM I, most burials continued in the Middle Minoan tradition. Tholos tombs remained in use at sites such as Kamilari in the south, and house tombs and rock shelters were still used in the east. Pithos cemeteries also became popular in some communities. A new type of tomb, the chamber tomb, first came into widespread use in LM II, perhaps as a result of Mycenaean influence. It consisted of a long passageway (dromos) leading to an underground chamber blocked by a doorway. Many of these tombs, notably the 'warrior graves' of Knossos and its vicinity, contained swords and other weapons as well as rich burial goods in many materials. By LM IIIA:2 the chamber tomb had become the most common form of Cretan burial.

Late Minoan buildings were more often decorated with wall paintings than they had been (*see* §IV below). One of the finest, from the House of the Frescoes at Knossos, depicts monkeys and birds surrounded by rocks, flowers and streams (see fig. 15 below); another, from AYIA TRIADA, features cats and birds in a similar style (both in Herakleion, Archaeol. Mus.). Details are more stylized than in MM III: some of the floral motifs (for example the 'papyrus' designs, which borrow some details from lilies) have mixed characteristics of different species, and rocks have colourful textured designs as though sawn and polished. All elements are two-dimensional, and overlapping is avoided where possible, so the compositions lack depth. Curves, particularly sinuous ones, were preferred to straight lines, producing an impression of subtle,

harmonious movement. During LM I, artists began exploring a larger range of subjects. From a fine house at AMNISOS come a series of wall paintings depicting lilies against rectilinear backgrounds (Herakleion, Archaeol. Mus.). Several paintings from Knossos show human figures, including an elaborate miniature of spectators at some important event (Herakleion, Archaeol. Mus.). Sites outside Crete provide even richer examples of Minoan painting, including a seascape with flying fish from Phylakopi on Melos (Athens, N. Archaeol. Mus.), beautiful lilies from Rhodes and elsewhere, and a series of figural scenes and landscapes from Akrotiri on Thera (Athens, N. Archaeol. Mus.).

In Crete itself, the finest painting was that done on plaster relief, the only extant monumental sculpture from LM I. Large scenes of bulls and acrobats (Herakleion, Archaeol. Mus.) adorned the west and north entrances of the palace of Knossos, and it is possible that reliefs were considered more appropriate than frescoes for important rooms. A room in the civic shrine at PSEIRA, destroyed in LM IB, provides a date for the introduction of painted reliefs. Its decoration includes figures of seated women in elaborate costumes, perhaps goddesses or participants in a ceremony. One of the best-known relief figures, the so-called *Priest-King* fresco or *Lily Prince* from Knossos, is an incorrect restoration combining the upper torso of a male figure (see fig. 5), possibly a boxer or god, with fragments from other reliefs.

LM miniature sculpture achieved a naturalism that would not be equalled for the next millennium (*see* §V below). Among the finest examples are the stone vessels carved with reliefs of human figures or animals (*see* §X below). A series from Ayia Triada includes a conical rhyton (a vessel with a tiny hole in the bottom for pouring liquid) decorated with scenes of boxing and bull-leaping (the Boxer Rhyton; see fig. 28 below), a cup with two youths standing in solemn poses with sword and staff (the Chieftain Cup) and a globular rhyton (the Harvester Vase) showing rows of singing men in a procession, possibly accompanying the planting or harvesting of crops. A rhyton from Kato Zakros depicts a shrine in a rural landscape with goats (see fig. 7a below). Small fragments of gold found on it suggest an attempt to copy repoussé, the technique by which thin metal sheets are pressed from behind to create raised designs (all the above vases LM I; Herakleion, Archaeol. Mus.). It is likely that both of the fine repoussé gold cups from a tomb at Vapheio on the Greek mainland (probably LM IB; Athens, N. Archaeol. Mus.; see fig. 25 below) were made in Crete. They are ornamented with vigorous scenes of the capturing of wild bulls in a landscape of trees and shrubs (*see also* §IX, 1(ii) below).

Bronze-casting in the lost-wax process, already in use by MM times, became increasingly popular (*see* §IX, 2 below). Most are single figures, generally men or women in attitudes of adoration, or small herd animals suitable as offerings to deities. Some of the finest LM I metalwork was discovered outside Crete, because Cretan finds are often fragmentary, and the practice of placing costly objects in graves began to decrease at the start of the LM period. The shaft graves at MYCENAE produced especially rich examples of LM I metalwork: a silver bull's-head rhyton, vessels of silver, gold and bronze, and numerous swords and

5. Late Minoan painted relief fresco, known as the *Priest-King* fresco or the *Lily Prince*, palace of Knossos, LM IB (Herakleion, Archaeological Museum); the work is actually incorrectly restored from several frescoes and includes an upper torso facing left and a headdress from a woman or sphinx

other weapons (Athens, N. Archaeol. Mus.). The most elaborate weapons had blades inlaid with hunting scenes (*see* MYCENAE, fig. 3), river landscapes, animals or plants. Although the emphasis on hunting and military skills seems foreign to Minoan Crete, the iconography, style and technique of the inlaid blades leave no doubt that they were made by Cretans.

Other forms of art during LM I made use of a wide variety of materials, many imported. Ostrich eggs were cut into attractive vessels with added fittings for mouth and neck. Ivory (*see* §VI below) was carved into figures and other objects, and stone vessels include a fine bull's head from Knossos (*see* KNOSSOS, fig. 4) and a rhyton carved from a single quartz crystal from Kato Zakros (both Herakleion, Archaeol. Mus.). Gem-cutting became a major art, and miniature designs were executed in a variety of styles, ranging from abstract symbols to naturalistic masterpieces. The best renderings of animals and humans in action have a distinctive fluidity of movement. There are suggestions from scant remains in tombs of a tradition of fine carpentry and furniture-making, and paintings show that textiles and rich embroidery were also produced. LM I was almost certainly the highpoint of Minoan artistic skill and productivity. Minoan art later became more stylized, a tendency most evident on the painted pottery and cut gems, which survive in significant quantity, though it applies equally to other fields. Carefully observed depictions of the natural world declined, and human activity, symbolism and geometric designs became more important.

In wall paintings after the LM IB destructions, landscapes were often schematized or eliminated, and figures became larger in relation to the whole picture. Good examples of later landscapes come from a large building, the so-called Caravanserai, south of the palace at Knossos. This had a room decorated with a frieze of partridges and at least one hoopoe (LM II or slightly later; Herakleion, Archaeol. Mus.). The animals were shown in a stylized setting, with artificial-looking rocks. The Throne Room at Knossos, of about the same date, has a stone throne attended by formal heraldic paintings of wingless griffins against undulating coloured bands, with only a few plants to suggest a landscape or garden. A scene of a male and two female acrobats leaping over a bull, from the Court of the Stone Spout at Knossos, is slightly later (LM II or slightly later; Herakleion, Archaeol. Mus.; see fig. 16 below). The style of this painting is far removed from the painstaking naturalism of LM I: the setting is not indicated, and the anatomical features are more or less eliminated, so that were it not for the convention of painting men reddish-brown and women white, even the sexes of the performers would be uncertain. The figures appear to float in suspended animation: the bull's four hooves are raised in the 'flying gallop', and none of the acrobats' feet touches the ground-line. One acrobat grasps the animal's horns, while the second does a handstand on its back and the third is painted behind it with hands upraised.

Hierarchical considerations also caused figures to be shown on different scales. The *Camp Stool* fresco (Herakleion, Archaeol. Mus), from an upper room in the north-west corner of the palace at Knossos, included two large female figures probably presiding over a religious ceremony. One, usually called *La Parisienne* (see fig. 17 below), has a sacral knot at her back and thus may be a goddess or priestess. Her curvilinear contours and ringlets of dark hair modulate the severely two-dimensional style of the painting, in which an enlarged frontal eye is combined with a face in profile.

Floors as well as walls were decorated with paintings. Marine scenes adorned a floor at Ayia Triada, and a panel of dolphins and fish from Knossos (Herakleion, Archaeol. Mus.) may have occupied a similar position. The creatures, which are shown from the side and never overlap, were painted in scattered groups, resulting in compositions with no central focus. One of the finest paintings from LM IIIA occurs on a plastered stone larnax from Ayia Triada (Herakleion, Archaeol. Mus.). On the front is a procession of men bringing gifts to a male figure standing before a building or tomb, while two women and a man playing a lyre perform a ceremony involving the pouring of liquid between two pillars surmounted by double axes (for illustration *see* AYIA TRIADA). A similar ritual scene was represented on the back. Here, a sacrificial bull lies trussed up on a table, while a woman acts out a ceremony before an altar. A procession of several figures arrives from the left, and to the right stands a shrine topped by horns of consecration and a palm tree. The end panels depict figures in chariots. Although many details in the paintings are ambiguous, they clearly involve religious ceremonies, and services associated with the dead would naturally be suitable for a sarcophagus. The style of the paintings, which are dominated by human figures and give little indication of setting, is related to that of the *Bull-leapers* discussed above and other paintings from LM IIIA.

By the end of LM IIIB, artistic styles had become freer and more abstract. Pottery was often decorated with repetitive standardized patterns, many of them simple, and careful work, such as a long series of detailed octopus designs on various vessels, was exceptional. The process of stylization and simplification continued, leading to rigorously schematic compositions. The last stage of the Minoan Bronze Age, LM IIIC, is represented predominantly by small portable objects, often produced for export. Even the finest designs, for example some highly schematic octopus paintings on stirrup jars (see fig. 11f below) and other pottery shapes, reveal an artistic culture in decline. Yet new ideas were still being tried. Painters had long used the large spaces offered by larnakes, whose funerary function invited religious symbolism. Several individual styles can be distinguished, including that of a group based somewhere in eastern Crete, which painted horse-drawn chariots, cattle and other animals in a simple, lively manner close to caricature. Among the best work of LM IIIA–B are a group of larnakes from Armenoi near Rethymnon (Rethymnon, Archaeol. Mus.). They depict simplified, vigorous scenes of hunters, armed with spears and axes and accompanied by dogs, pursuing wild cattle and wild goats (agrimi). They suggest that the Minoan artistic tradition survived until the end of the Bronze Age, ultimately influencing the art of Classical Greece (480–323 BC).

BIBLIOGRAPHY

A. Evans: *The Palace of Minos at Knossos* (London, 1921–35)
L. Pernier: *Il palazzo minoico di Festòs* (Rome, 1935)
J. D. S. Pendlebury: *The Archaeology of Crete* (London, 1939)
L. Pernier and L. Banti: *Il palazzo minoico di Festòs II* (Rome, 1951)
R. W. Hutchinson: *Prehistoric Crete* (Baltimore, MD, 1962)
K. Branigan: *The Foundations of Palatial Crete* (London, 1970)
——: *The Tombs of Mesara* (London, 1970)
M. S. F. Hood: *The Minoans* (London, New York and Washington, DC, 1971)
N. Platon: *Zakros* (New York, 1971)
D. Levi: *Festòs e la civiltà minoica* (Rome, 1976)
M. S. F. Hood: *The Arts in Prehistoric Europe* (London and New York, 1978)
P. P. Betancourt: *The History of Minoan Pottery* (Princeton, NJ, 1985)

PHILIP BETANCOURT

II. Architecture.

Unknown until the beginning of the 20th century and still not completely understood, the type of architecture characteristic of Bronze Age Crete appeared without external precedent and developed into an elegant, sophisticated and lively art form, uninterrupted by foreign invasion and largely uninfluenced by architectural practices in contemporary societies elsewhere. Buildings were designed with a confidence, deft artistry and supreme functionality that may explain why Minoan architectural styles did not

survive the collapse of the society for which they were created.

1. Introduction. 2. Structure and materials. 3. Palaces and shrines. 4. Towns, houses and villas. 5. Tombs.

1. INTRODUCTION. Although there is clear evidence for development in architectural styles and techniques throughout the history of Minoan building, the similarity of function, structure and plan in regard to specific types of building, whatever their date, is striking. Structures may be divided conveniently into palaces (the traditional term for what was probably a combination of cult centre, 'royal' residence and administrative centre), large mansions or 'villas', smaller houses and the towns in which they stood, and tomb structures.

Evidence for Minoan architecture comes primarily from excavated sites across Crete, although in no case do the remains extend above ground-floor level; some information about the layout and function of upper rooms can be gleaned from surviving foundations and supporting structures and from the study of objects and construction debris that fell from upper floors when the buildings were destroyed. Additional information is provided by a group of faience plaques (Herakleion, Archaeol. Mus.) from Knossos depicting the façades of town houses (see §4 below), and representations of architecture on seals, stone vases, in wall paintings and in the form of terracotta house models.

The best surviving and most completely excavated remains from the period before the appearance of the first palaces on Crete are at VASILIKI and at Phournou Koriphi, MYRTOS, both dated to Early Minoan (EM) II and both possessing elements of planning, function and construction that are also present in the later palaces. At Vasiliki the stone and mud-brick walls, still with traces of red-painted plaster, preserve gaps that once held timbers to strengthen them, and the buildings fronted on to a paved, west-facing courtyard—all features found in Middle Minoan (MM) and Late Minoan (LM) architecture. At Phournou Koriphi a large, single-building complex of some 90 rooms with connecting passages was planned round a central open space probably used as a communal court; well-defined functional areas were used as storage magazines, kitchens, work and living rooms, and there was even a domestic shrine.

The first Minoan palaces—that is, a large, multi-roomed building arranged on four sides of a rectangular court and orientated more or less north–south, with a second court on the west side of the complex (e.g. *see* KNOSSOS, fig. 2)—were built in MM IB, and their destruction, probably by earthquake, took place in MM III—a period of some 200 years, sometimes called the Proto-Palatial period. The palaces were rebuilt, restored and expanded almost immediately and functioned as the religious, administrative and economic centres of Crete until they, along with the island's villas and towns, were destroyed or severely damaged in LM IB, perhaps by Mycenaean invaders from mainland Greece. Knossos continued to function, possibly as a base of Mycenaean control of the island, until LM IIIA: 1, when some scholars believe it too was effectively destroyed (*see* KNOSSOS, §1); others assert that there is evidence for continued prosperity at Knossos after LM

IIIA: 1 (*see* §I, 4(iii) above). Some monumental architecture continued to be constructed afterwards, in the Post-Palatial period, but for the most part buildings were smaller and simpler.

2. STRUCTURE AND MATERIALS. Minoan walls were not originally built on deep foundations, even tall structures being bedded on earth or a few layers of small stones; not until the Neo-Palatial period (MM III–LM IB) were foundations laid of limestone blocks in deep, wide trenches. Walls were made of rubble mixed with mud mortar on the ground-floor and basement rooms, while upper storeys and most interior walls were of mud-brick; interior walls were often plastered and painted or faced with finer stone (see fig. 6), or they might be built of dressed stone where exposed to rain. Important external façades were often built of fine stone masonry. In the Proto-Palatial period orthostates commonly formed the lowest course of large buildings, whereas in later structures courses of rectangular blocks were used from ground-level, laid on a stepped plinth. Blocks were joined with mud mortar, and there is evidence at Knossos for wooden clamps. Limestone was the most commonly used stone, though gypsum, a soft, calcinous stone, was favoured at Knossos, as was sandstone at Mallia and Kato Zakros and alabaster (a fine form of gypsum; *see* ALABASTER, §2(i)) at Phaistos and Ayia Triada. Pillars (usually of stone) and columns (wood) were used as supporting members and, in the case of the former, sometimes as the focus of cult activity.

Timbers set into the walls were probably intended to lend strength, and they may have contributed some flexibility as protection from earthquakes; wood was also used for door and window frames, ceilings (the basis for the floor above) and columns. These characteristically tapered downwards, so that they were smaller in diameter at the bottom than at the top; they might be either round or oval in section. They were set directly on the paving, without a base, and the capital, to judge from wall paintings at Knossos, consisted of a rounded element surmounted by a square block, similar to the Classical Greek echinus and abacus (*see* ORDERS, ARCHITECTURAL, fig. 1(xi–xii)). Roofs were uniformly flat and were probably constructed of reeds and straw mixed with clay laid on a timber framework.

Stairways were simple in construction but often monumental and dramatic in effect, as, for example, the Grand Staircase leading into the palace from the West Court at Phaistos and that in the palace at Knossos, off the Central Court in the east wing. Both are marvels of Minoan architectural skill, the Knossos stairway for its five surviving graceful stone flights flanked by columns, from which landings led off to various rooms and passages (*see* STAIRCASE, fig. 1); that at Phaistos could also have been used for seating when festivals were held in the West Court.

An elaborate and sophisticated system of water supply and drainage is known largely from Knossos, though cisterns exist at Kato Zakros and Phaistos. Running water was supplied through a system of terracotta pipes that ran

6. Phaistos, Second Palace, north residential quarter showing gypsum-faced wall, LM IA

beneath the floors at Knossos and Zakros, each section narrower at one end to fit tightly into the next. At Knossos, rainwater was drained from light wells and from the Central Court by means of a cement-lined underground channel; this system also served the toilet in the east wing of the palace. At the East Bastion the drain used to handle rainwater can be seen running alongside the stairs, entering a small settling pool where mud and debris would collect.

While most ordinary houses were surely planned and built by craftsmen–builders or by the occupants themselves, it has been suggested that the second palace at Phaistos and the palace at Kato Zakros were designed by a single architect, and the unity exhibited in their plans supports the idea. Rebuilding of the Mallia and Knossos palaces and perhaps the design of the large country villas may also have been in the hands of a specialist, although the word 'architect' is probably anachronistic. It seems clear also that a standardized system of measurement was used to lay out the palaces, though J. W. Graham's proposal of a Minoan 'foot' of 30.36 cm is not borne out in every case.

3. PALACES AND SHRINES. The first palaces (MM IB–III) exhibit essentially the same architecture as the later ones (MM III–LM IB and IIIA 1). Remains of the Proto-Palatial period survive at Mallia, both in the structure of the later palace and in Quartier Mu (MM II), where a group of large buildings with staircases, storerooms, plastered walls and benches and a so-called 'lustral basin' is associated with a series of workshops; at various spots in the north and west of the existing palace at Knossos; at Chania; and at Kato Zakros, though it is not clear that these signify an actual palace. A unique MM II building at Ayia Photeia is not a palace, but it does display a large Central Court surrounded by rooms. Evidence for these first palaces is most clearly visible at PHAISTOS, however, where the destruction debris of the Middle Minoan palace was covered with cement and used as a foundation for the later structures. As a result, much survives of the original building: the paved West Court and part of the west façade of the old palace, an entrance corridor possibly leading to a Central Court with columned portico, shrine rooms, storage magazines and substantial stone walls that must once have supported upper storeys.

The plan and details of the later palaces—KNOSSOS, MALLIA, PHAISTOS and KATO ZAKROS, the last probably an entirely new foundation of MM IIIB—are, of course, much better understood. (Palatial complexes probably also existed at Kommos, Archanes, Chania and elsewhere.) The term 'palace' was coined by Sir ARTHUR EVANS to describe his discovery at Knossos and continues to be used for the sake of convenience. It appears, however, that in addition to functioning as the residence of a ruling family and as the economic and administrative centre for the region that it controlled, the Minoan palace served— perhaps primarily—as a cult centre, with religious activity carried out in many separate shrines and ritual rooms within the complex. The overall design of the four palaces appears to have served ritual purposes, an interpretation supported by the iconography of the wall paintings from Knossos (see §IV below) and their positions within the palace (see Marinatos). The central courts were flanked by

7. Minoan peak sanctuary: (a) carved on a stone rhyton from Kato Zakros, MM IIIB–LM IA; (b) reconstruction drawing of the sanctuary depicted

shrines and ceremonial complexes, and the west courts at Knossos, Mallia and Phaistos were probably used as ceremonial areas, perhaps in part in connection with a harvest festival procession such as that depicted on the Harvester Vase from Ayia Triada (MM III–LM I; Herakleion, Archaeol. Mus.). Raised stone walkways led to underground granaries (*kouloures*) sunk into these courts. The west façades of the palaces were constructed in a series of setbacks, probably an indication of the placement of windows in the upper floors; appearance of a priestess or other personage at these windows may have been part of the ceremony. Judging from the large number of religious objects found in the area, the west wing of each palace was specifically devoted to ritual, though rooms identified as shrines of one sort or another occur throughout the palaces.

The so-called 'lustral basin', a sunken, rectangular room reached from floor-level usually by means of an L-shaped staircase, has been seen as either a cult room or bathroom or both; but the artefacts associated with these rooms— offering tables, small cups and jugs, double axes—and the wall paintings featuring religious iconography clearly indicate their ritual function. Indeed, they have been more correctly termed adyta, a word used for the inner shrine in a Classical Greek temple. These lustral basins are very often associated with uniquely Minoan rooms the walls of which are formed of a series of pier-and-door (*polythyron*) partitions, a screenlike system of open bays for double doors, separated by wooden piers. These are found in what are commonly called the residential quarters of palaces, and they have been assumed to act as light and air regulators (*see* KNOSSOS, §2(i)). It is more likely, however, that these rooms with their walls of identical doors served as passageways to the adyta behind them, the architecture being manipulated to produce dramatic contrasts of light and dark. The Minoan palace also certainly housed people, probably a ruling family and surely religious functionaries, two groups that may or may not have been the same. The residential quarters were probably on the upper floors, however, the architecture of which must remain speculative.

Shrines have also been identified in the palace 'pillar crypts', where stone pillars often bear carved signs (called 'masons' marks' but accepted as magico-religious symbols of some sort); in dining complexes with benches round the walls; in the so-called balustrade shrines, such as that in the House of the Chancel Screen at Knossos; and in the Knossos Throne Room complex itself. Depictions of architecture on such objects as the stone rhyton from Kato Zakros (see fig. 7), a model from Petsofas and a fragmentary rhyton from Knossos have been used to reconstruct shrine buildings in peak sanctuaries in mountainous areas of Crete, though it has been suggested that these may reveal only a symbolic formula for the depiction of this type of structure. The buildings shown are axial in plan, built of coursed masonry with tripartite façades having a large central niche and two flanking smaller niches; details include ceremonial flag poles, altars and horns of consecration.

4. TOWNS, HOUSES AND VILLAS. Surviving Minoan towns date almost exclusively from the Neo-Palatial period, though remnants of earlier settlement can be found here and there. Roads and town houses are known in the areas surrounding the palaces at Phaistos, Mallia, Kato Zakros and Knossos, and more or less well-preserved towns exist at Ayia Triada, Palaikastro, GOURNIA, Mochlos and PSEIRA. Palaikastro is notable for its wide main street lined with fine town houses built in ashlar masonry. The other towns are less elegant settlements, with winding, sometimes stepped streets and smaller houses of mud-brick and rubble masonry, though at Gournia the small

'palace' at the top of the ridge had alabaster façades facing the paved West Court and the south-facing Town Court. The construction techniques and materials of town houses are well observed in the Town Mosaic (Herakleion, Archaeol. Mus.), a set of polychrome faience plaques from Knossos that were originally part of a larger picture inlaid into a box or frame. These provide striking information about the external appearance of Minoan houses, showing two- or three-storey house façades with flat roofs, wooden window frames and doors, and timbers running the length of the walls, sometimes shown as horizontal lines, elsewhere as circles representing the ends of beams. A three-dimensional terracotta model of a similar building (Herakleion, Archaeol. Mus.) was found at the Minoan cemetery at Archanes.

Large rural mansions, often called villas, are unique to the Neo-Palatial period and probably extended the functions of the palaces into the countryside. Their architecture imitates, on a smaller scale, that of the palaces, with a *polythyron* arrangement of room openings, light wells, storerooms, shrine rooms, paved courtyards with raised walkways (though no central courts), drains, plastered and painted walls, pillar crypts, ashlar masonry and offset façades for windows. The finest of these villas are at Nirou Khani, TYLISSOS, VATHYPETRO, Pyrgos (MYRTOS) and AYIA TRIADA (the last sometimes also referred to as a palace).

Architecture after the destruction of the palaces continued monumental in places, as is evident in the large LM IIIA:1 Building P at Kommos, comprising a row of rooms that have been interpreted as ship sheds, and the stoa-like structure at Ayia Triada (LM IIIA). The country villas were not rebuilt, however, and towns and houses of the Post-Palatial era are simpler: the site of Kephali Chondrou (founded LM IIIA) resembles Gournia in its narrow, paved streets and rubble masonry house walls. Later still, in LM IIIC, settlements at sites difficult of access, such as KARPHI and Vrokastro, were clearly established for protection from marauders, and the very simple, purely functional construction of small houses and streets reflects the uncertainty of the times.

5. TOMBS. Minoan Crete has produced a wide variety of tomb types, always for communal burial. The Early Minoan circular stone tombs of the MESARA plain had inclining walls with a corbelled stone or timber-frame roof. Rectangular rooms attached to these tholoi functioned as ossuaries, storerooms for grave goods and ritual areas associated with funerary cult. Other EM tomb types include rock-cut tombs, cave burials and cemeteries of rectangular stone 'house tombs', such as that at MOCHLOS. The construction of these house tombs resembles that of actual houses, and some were given similar architectural features: internal pillars, corridors, on rare occasions an upper storey and plastered walls.

The Chrysolakkos tomb at MALLIA, dating to the Proto-Palatial period, is a large, rectangular structure (*c.* 30×38 m) with numerous internal rooms joined by corridors, built of finely dressed stone with a first course of orthostates. It was long assumed to be a royal burial place, but it probably functioned as a ritual complex for burial ceremonies, rather than as an actual tomb.

Evidence for Late Minoan tombs is surprisingly scarce. Tombs established in early periods continued in use, and a mainland type, the chamber tomb, reached by a passageway carved into the slope of a hill, appeared around the palace at Knossos in LM II. The Temple Tomb at Knossos (*see* KNOSSOS, §2(ii)) is a very fine and elaborate version of the house tomb, though it is equally likely that, as with the Chrysolakkos tomb, this structure functioned primarily as a locus for funerary cult rather than actual burial.

See also §I, 4 above.

BIBLIOGRAPHY
J. W. Graham: *The Palaces of Crete* (Princeton, 1962/*R* 1988)
J. W. Shaw: *Minoan Architecture: Materials and Techniques* (Rome, 1971)
P. Warren: *The Aegean Civilizations: From Ancient Crete to Mycenae* (Oxford, 1975, rev. 1989)
G. Cadogan: *Palaces of Minoan Crete* (London and New York, 1976, rev. 1980)
J. C. McEnroe: *Minoan House and Town Arrangement* (PhD diss., U. Toronto, 1979)
D. Preziosi: *Minoan Architectural Design: Formation and Signification* (Berlin, 1983)
R. Hagg and N. Marinatos, eds: *The Function of the Minoan Palaces: Proceedings of the Fourth International Symposium at the Swedish Institute in Athens: Athens, 1984*
R. Hagg, ed.: *The Function of the Minoan Villa: Proceedings of the Eighth International Symposium at the Swedish Institute in Athens: Athens, 1992*
N. Marinatos: *Minoan Religion: Ritual, Image and Symbol* (Columbia, SC, 1993)
O. Dickinson: *The Aegean Bronze Age*, Cambridge World Archaeology (Cambridge, 1994)

For additional bibliography on individual sites, *see* site entries.

C. D. FORTENBERRY

III. Pottery.

Minoan pottery styles, particularly in the Early Minoan (EM) period, developed slowly, but occasionally the transformations were sufficiently dynamic and deep-seated to allow the study of individual workshops and craftsmen. Indeed, many Minoan vases were unique creations that arguably may be described as high art.

1. Materials and techniques. 2. Final Neolithic. 3. Early Minoan. 4. Middle Minoan. 5. Late Minoan.

1. MATERIALS AND TECHNIQUES. By the Neolithic period European and Asian craftsmen understood that clays moistened with water became plastic enough to form objects or containers, which hardened if heated. By the time the craft reached Crete during the Early Neolithic period, the basic techniques were well developed. Tempering, the addition of crushed stone or some other aplastic material, which prevented breakage by reducing shrinkage during drying and firing, was routine. Rubbing the surface before firing, a process called burnishing, was used to create a smoother surface that was more resistant to liquids and soiling. Decoration included the addition of knobs or strips of clay, scratched or pecked motifs, and designs painted on in a contrasting colour of clay (slip). Even the burnishing could create a design of sorts. Most Cretan slips were coloured by iron oxides, red if fired in the presence of oxygen and grey or black if fired in unventilated kilns. Most Neolithic vases were relatively simple utilitarian containers. Open-mouthed bowls and jars predominated, with cursory geometric ornament limited mainly to incised lines and dots. At the end of the

Neolithic period, however, several stylistic changes occurred, and though their causes and sequences are disputed, they heralded the emergence of the Minoan civilization, a time of outstanding artistic achievement in many media; among these artistic products ceramic vases occupied an important position.

2. FINAL NEOLITHIC. The transitional Final Neolithic period was a time of profound change in the development of Minoan pottery, during which several new styles were introduced. How much these styles overlapped with the earlier and later phases is not really known. Crete was evidently inhabited by small groups of agriculturalists, some of whom were very conservative in their pottery styles, so that it is not always clear how soon a new feature was adopted throughout the island.

Final Neolithic pottery was dark-surfaced, with most pieces fired brown to black. Shapes included open jars and bowls, cups, bottles or jars with closed mouths, small rounded pyxides (boxes) with cylindrical lids, and several other vases. Horns and lugs were common, placed either

8. Early and Middle Minoan pottery: (a) chalice, Pyrgos ware with burnished horizontal, vertical and diagonal lines, h. 280 mm, from Pyrgos Cave, EM I; (b) bird-shaped jug, h. 172 mm, from Koumasa, EM II; (c) jug, Koumasa ware, h. 73 mm, from the type site, EM II; (d) jug, h. 165 mm, from Mochlos, EM III; (e) narrow-necked jar decorated with quadruple spiral motif, h. 460 mm, from Phaistos, MM II; (f) jug, Kamares ware, h. 267 mm, from Phaistos, MM II (all Herakleion, Archaeological Museum)

on rims or on shoulders. Usually the surface was burnished by rubbing it with a tool such as a smooth pebble or a wooden burnisher; on the pottery known as Pyrgos ware, burnishing was used to produce linear decoration. Other decorative systems included pricking or incising geometric designs before firing, scoring the surface with the sharp ends of a bundle of reeds or with a comblike instrument (Scored ware) and painting simple lines in red ochre directly on to the clay. Some of these characteristics are also found in the pottery of north-western Asia Minor (Anatolia), but its relationship to Final Neolithic Cretan pottery is unclear. Since Anatolian tomb types and other cultural features did not occur in Crete, it is possible the ceramic products represent technological diffusion rather than a movement of population.

3. EARLY MINOAN. EM pottery was more diverse than that of either earlier or later periods. It could be red, buff or grey, coarse or fine, with decorative methods that included incising, stamping, painting in several styles, and modelling to create three-dimensional images. Perhaps because of experimentation, some pieces were fanciful, while others were so unusual in shape that their function is unknown.

(i) Early Minoan I. Several new pottery styles were introduced in EM I, of which the most important was Ayios Onouphrios I ware, named after a site near Phaistos. Small pyxides and askoi (closed vases with a small opening at one upper corner) became characteristic Minoan pottery shapes, and askoi were already being made in the shape of animals. At the same time improvements in kiln design and construction enabled potters to control their results more consistently. Evenly coloured, grey or buff pottery could be achieved at will.

In addition to new styles, Pyrgos ware and Scored ware persisted in EM I. The parallel scratches on Scored ware were much the same as in Final Neolithic times, though they were applied to new shapes such as spouted jugs. EM I Pyrgos ware, however, was considerably more advanced than its predecessor. It was most common in north-central Crete, where it was used for bowls, cups and a few closed shapes. Its most striking product was the footed chalice, a cup on a high base (see fig. 8a). The decoration often consisted of simple horizontal or vertical burnished lines, but some better specimens combined several different burnished patterns, of which the most common were solid areas, zigzags, crosshatching and parallel lines.

Painting began in earnest in EM I. Ayios Onouphrios I ware had parallel or crosshatched red lines long enough to sweep around the curvature of the buff clay vessel. The style, particularly common in central Crete, was used on a range of new shapes, especially spouted jugs with rounded bottoms designed to be suspended rather than set on a flat surface. Well finished and skilfully painted, the pottery was probably regarded as the best ware of its time. Its only counterpart was Lebena ware. Most common in southern Crete, it employed the same geometric linear patterns as Ayios Onouphrios I ware, applied in white paint on a solid red slip.

(ii) Early Minoan II. Many new towns were founded in Crete during EM II, and the island probably supported a much larger population. Pottery styles changed appreciably. Existing shapes improved, with jugs that sat on small feet (fig. 8b) or rested on flat bases, an advance on the rounded bottoms of EM I. New shapes, such as teapots and small goblets, reflected changes in tastes or customs.

Two varieties of linear-painted pottery spread throughout Crete in EM IIA: Koumasa ware, decorated with dark paint, and Ayios Onouphrios II ware, ornamented with red paint. In both cases the decoration consisted of well-painted crosshatched triangles and other simple geometric designs (fig. 8c), usually on the upper shoulder of closed shapes such as jugs and jars and on the interiors or exteriors of bowls and cups. The style differed from Ayios Onouphrios I ware in its tighter control, with patterns that seem more stilted, more restricted and less related to the rounded form of the vessel (see fig. 9). The contemporary Fine Grey ware was finer textured than earlier grey pottery, fired to a uniform tint all the way through the wall. A geometric decoration was usually incised before firing; especially popular were herringbones and other simple linear designs.

During the second half of EM II, painted and incised vases became less popular. Most vases were plain, but an elaborate ware named after a site in eastern Crete spread to a few sites in the central and western districts: Vasiliki ware was entirely covered with a coat of slip mottled during firing to achieve a brilliant variegated effect. It was the first Minoan pottery to be decorated in more than one colour: the mottling varied from browns to yellowish browns to reds to black. The unusual slip effects were used on a long series of shapes, some of them bizarre, with exaggerated forms such as teapots with long spouts,

9. Early Minoan jug, Ayios Onouphrios II ware, h. 215 mm, EM II (Herakleion, Archaeological Museum)

jugs with tall beaked spouts or tiny goblets sometimes with unnecessary handles or spouts. The technique used to achieve the mottling is not completely understood, but it clearly involved exposing selected parts of a vessel to oxidation and reduction at the end of the firing cycle, perhaps after it had been removed from the kiln.

(iii) Early Minoan III. Painted pottery regained its popularity in EM III, and Vasiliki ware ceased to be made. Painted ornament had first re-emerged in the form of a few white lines on the red to dark surface of EM IIB Vasiliki ware, but it soon commanded almost the entire fine ware production. Called White-on-dark ware, the new pottery had crisp geometric motifs in off-white paint applied to an even, dark coat of slip. New designs included spirals, quirks, elaborate circles and fancy diagonal bands (see fig. 8d above). Such was the popularity of this ware in EM III–MM IA that on some sites it accounts for more than 90% of the fine pottery of this date. Although White-on-dark ware was used throughout Crete, its most dynamic production centres were north-eastern sites. The ware has been found at MALLIA, GOURNIA, PSEIRA, VASILIKI, Palaikastro and MOCHLOS. Its repertory of spirals, complex circle motifs and other curvilinear designs suggests that White-on-dark ware was probably the main forerunner of Kamares ware, the finest ceramic achievement of the Middle Minoan period.

4. MIDDLE MINOAN. During the Middle Minoan (MM) period Cretan pottery followed the fortunes of a series of palatial centres. In MM IB, new palaces were built at Knossos and Phaistos, probably expanding on pre-existing structures levelled to make way for the new establishments. The pottery of these two centres was dynamic and innovative, influencing production throughout the island, while that from the palace at Mallia was also of a high quality. Most other pottery centres produced humbler ware, imitating the shapes and a few of the less complex designs used in the palatial workshops.

(i) Middle Minoan I. MM IA pottery was still made entirely by hand; it is chiefly distinguished by the use of red paint alongside the off-white of earlier times. As in EM III, the white and red designs were applied to a contrasting solid dark slip. Almost all were abstract and linear, exhibiting great variety and far more elaboration than in EM III: spirals, circle designs, quirk bands, dot bands, straight or diagonal lines and a few cursory foliate designs were regularly used. These gradually increased in complexity, and often several were used on the same vessel. Shapes included jars and jugs of several types, as well as bowls and cups. Often the jugs had only a small upturned spout, much shorter than in the Early Bronze Age. The small stemmed goblet (or egg-cup) was particularly common in central Crete; in the region of PHAISTOS it almost died out at the end of the period, but in the north-central area it persisted much longer. Handmade carinated cups, tall conical cups without handles (tumblers) and cylindrical cups with one vertical handle were all typical of the period. Plain wares also acquired forms that distinguished them from their EM ancestors. The conical cup, a small handle-less bowl or cup, was the most common unpainted shape, while pithoi for large-scale storage, tripod pots for cooking,

small lamps and the first bathtubs were among the other characteristic products.

Although a few tentative wheelmade saucers are known from MM IA, the introduction of the potter's wheel marks the transition to MM IB, an innovation that led to developments that continued over several centuries. The clay discs from several Minoan potters' wheels survive: they are always thick and heavy to enhance the wheel's centrifugal force, with the upper surface smoothed from use and the underside having a socket at the centre for attachment to a vertical axle. The wheels were probably mounted close to the ground and were turned by assistants, as shown in contemporary Egyptian wall paintings.

The potter's wheel was evidently not introduced to all workshops at once. Many MM IB pots were still handmade, even including fine cups, and numerous pieces can barely be distinguished from their MM IA predecessors. New shapes included a thin, well-made carinated cup with a cylindrical upper half, a conical lower part and a thin, metallic-looking handle, bowls and cups with crinkled or undulating rims and wheelmade bridge-spouted jars with two horizontal handles for lifting. Handmade vessels, both plain and painted, continued the styles of MM IA: tumblers, jars, jugs, tripod cooking pots, bowls of many types, amphorae, pithoi and bathtubs. Eggcups were common in the north. Thousands of conical cups were produced, either plain or with just a band or with a trace of decoration, and for the next 600 years they would be a ubiquitous feature of Minoan houses.

As early as the Neolithic period, Cretan potters had experimented with roughening the surface of a vase, a texture that became popular at the beginning of the Middle Bronze Age, giving rise to Barbotine ware. It was mostly produced in the MESARA near Phaistos, but examples were also made around KNOSSOS and Mallia, and pieces occur sporadically throughout the island. Several types existed, the clay worked up to form irregular ridges, or with knobs, bumps or rough bands applied to the surface. This relief decoration often formed spirals, triangles or other typical Minoan motifs and was usually combined with painted designs. After reaching its high point in MM IB, the ware remained popular into MM IIA but then declined, only a few examples being produced in the later stages of the MM period.

(ii) Middle Minoan II. Following the dramatic rise of the palace workshops in MM II, the contrast between village and palace productions increased. Especially at the palaces of Knossos, Phaistos and Mallia, potters began turning out a sequence of sophisticated ceramic designs superior in both shape and ornament to anything produced in the provinces. The technology of the potter's wheel permitted the production of extremely delicate walls, sometimes literally as thin as eggshells. Handles, spouts and other details were often copied from metalware. New ornaments were invented, especially by stylizing the curvilinear tendrils and leaves of plants (see fig. 8e). With an increased use of orange and crimson paints to supplement the white and red of MM I, Cretan pottery reached new artistic heights.

Plain and less expansively decorated vases were also made at the palaces as well as in village workshops. The conical cup remained the most common open shape. Other cups had carinated, straight-sided or S-shaped profiles, as in MM I. Jugs with small raised spouts, jars of various kinds, especially with bridged spouts, amphorae with two opposed handles extending from rim to shoulder, and most other MM I shapes continued. As before, it was not unusual for a potter, even in a remote village, to invent unique details of shape or decoration. Among the new shapes was the rhyton, a closed vessel with two openings, one at the top for filling and one at the base so that liquid could stream out. Its use, whether in ritual or in daily life, is often debated. Some rhyta took the form of animal heads, especially bulls', while askoi were occasionally shaped like complete animals, as they had been in earlier times.

The main palatial pottery of MM II was Kamares ware, often regarded as a highpoint in Minoan art. Its clay was first covered with the same dark slip used in MM I, and a rich assortment of ornaments in several colours was added. Small vases were almost always wheelmade, though the hand methods of earlier times were retained, principally for larger vessels. Floral motifs, especially curvilinear, were prolific, though geometric designs and a few carefully selected figural devices were also used. Since the decoration usually comprised several well-proportioned designs and two or three different colours, the effect was richly ornamental. Kamares ware adopted sophisticated decorative principles: each motif, whether figural, floral or geometric, was reduced to a simple two-dimensional form. Overlapping of colours was employed to enrich the ornamentation, as when red dots were placed on a white line, but not to create an illusion of depth. Most motifs incorporated curves, so were well suited to rounded forms. They were arranged on the vessels in various compositional schemes, often with two or more opposed diagonals twisting around the vase (see fig. 8f). This device, known as torsion, was a major Minoan artistic innovation, designed to produce a sense of suspended movement from the balancing of opposed compositional forces. First

attested on seals and pottery, it became a feature of the finest Minoan art in other media for several centuries. A bridge-spouted jar from Knossos (Herakleion, Archaeol. Mus.; see fig. 10) illustrates the exuberant qualities of the ware. Petals and tendrils flow and whirl around small circles of linked diamonds, creating a brilliant 'skin' of painted decoration on the vase's surface, and handles and spout are an integral part of the overall ornament.

(iii) Middle Minoan III. In many ways, MM III was a transitional period: its earliest pottery essentially represented a continuation of MM II types. During a later phase, best called MM IIIB, the pottery advanced along several fronts, until it had left its Middle Bronze Age style well behind and was anticipating LM I.

The potting and the pyrotechnology changed substantially. By MM IIIB, most ceramic products were thicker-walled than their MM II counterparts, and their clay was grittier. The paint often flaked badly. Clay fabrics in central Crete tended to be less dense than in MM II, indicating a lower firing temperature or a shorter time in the kiln or possibly comprising a different mixture of raw materials. The shapes developed as well: cups were larger, closed vessels were taller and more slender, and rounded vases such as bridge-spouted jars and piriform jars were often given a constricted lower body. A few shapes, such as the carinated cups, were no longer made.

The decoration of MM III vases is so different from that of MM II that it is sometimes termed Post-Kamares. Orange and red paint were used more sparingly, and compositions were greatly simplified, as were the decorative motifs themselves, leading to the gradual elimination of most types of rosettes, petals and other elaborate floral designs. In contrast, spirals, especially large retorted ones, became more common. At the same time, an important class of vase began to be decorated in a more naturalistic style, perhaps related to the beginning of wall painting in the palaces. Its most characteristic motifs are lilies, crocus blossoms and palms, combined with elaborate spirals set in series with areas of solid white.

A new ceramic technology also appeared. Its products were harder and glossier and soon supplanted the earlier MM dark-surfaced vases. The earliest specimens belonged to a class of vases decorated with ripple designs and wavy bands. The most common pottery of the new group, known as Tortoiseshell Ripple ware, occurs throughout Crete. Closely spaced vertical lines were burnished before firing to create a rippled effect in the ornament as the burnishing compressed and polished the surface. When spirals and floral decorations were added in the new technique, the Middle Bronze Age was over.

5. LATE MINOAN. The construction of the new palaces at the beginning of the Late Bronze Age stimulated dramatic developments in many artistic media, but especially in pottery, given its widespread use at all levels of Minoan society. The role of the new palaces as patrons of the arts cannot be overemphasized.

(i) Late Minoan I. The earliest Late Minoan (LM) vases were only slightly more advanced in style than those of MM IIIB, but there was an essential difference: spirals and floral designs were painted in dark-firing slip on the pale ground of the vase, not in white on the dark slip. Using the dense, burnished fabric of Ripple ware, which was

10. Middle Minoan bridge-spouted jar, Kamares ware, h. 235 mm, from Knossos, MM II (Herakleion, Archaeological Museum)

11. Late Minoan pottery: (a) conical rhyton, h. 325 mm, from Gournia, Room C58, LM IB; (b) ovoid rhyton, Marine style, h. *c.* 240 mm, from Palaikastro, LM IB; (c) bridge-spouted jar, Special Palatial tradition, Floral style, h. 165 mm, from Knossos, LM IB; (d) 'Ephyraean' goblet, h. 150 mm, from the Temple Tomb, Knossos, LM II; (e) jar, Palace style, h. 850 mm, from Knossos, LM II–IIIA:1 (all Herakleion, Archaeological Museum); (f) stirrup jar, Close style, h. 105 mm, from a tomb at Tourloti, LM IIIC (Philadelphia, PA, University of Pennsylvania, University Museum of Archaeology and Anthropology)

painted with a wide range of motifs, the LM I potters gave their ceramics a wholly new appearance. By LM IA the new styles were being diffused throughout Crete, and by LM IB Minoan ceramic products were so uniform that sometimes only clay analysis can distinguish the products of widely separated areas. Except for the Special Palatial tradition, a small but highly influential palatial production, many of the LM IB styles were so widely spread that they constituted a common ceramic tradition.

Pottery shapes developed considerably during LM I. The handleless conical cup continued to be the most common plain shape among the finer pieces, while straight-sided, semi-globular and bell-shaped cups, all with handles, were the most numerous of the painted cups. The latter were usually well made, with even walls and well-shaped ribbon handles. Among the closed shapes, the jug was still predominant. Many varieties occur: globular, squat or pear-shaped bodies, flat or rising spouts or no spout at all,

12. Late Minoan jar, h. 760 mm, from Pseira, LM IA (or ?B) (Herakleion, Archaeological Museum)

the period: bulls' heads in front view alternate with double axes, with leafy branches placed vertically between them. Bulls were important sacrificial animals in Minoan religion, and the axe, probably used to slaughter them, had become a religious symbol. Axes also adorn the jar's rim, while elaborate ivy leaves and typical LM IA spirals decorate the lower body.

The LM IB vases of the Special Palatial tradition excelled even the finest LM IA works in the inventiveness of their shapes and the vividness of their marine and floral decoration. The Marine style, the most attractive aspect of the tradition, used argonauts, octopuses, starfish, coral, shells and other such details in a lively evocation of underwater life (see fig. 11b). The best-known example is a flask by the so-called Marine Style Master (Herakleion, Archaeol. Mus.; see fig. 13), which was found at Palaikastro in eastern Crete, though its style and fabric suggest that it was almost certainly exported from Knossos. Each side bears an octopus in front view, with fierce eyes and writhing tentacles. Small sea creatures and plants act as filling motifs. A feeling of suspended motion, especially appropriate for a subject floating beneath the Aegean, is projected by the diagonal curved lines and the sinuous tentacles and seaweed.

A Floral style and an Abstract and Geometric style also formed part of the Special Palatial tradition. In the first, flowers, especially imaginary hybrids based on papyrus plants, palms or lilies, were painted exuberantly (see fig. 11c). In the second, new kinds of spirals and foliate bands were invented; and in addition to geometric devices, abstract motifs from the natural world (e.g. double axes)

mouths that range from constricted to wide. By the end of the period the most common closed form, used for small decorated jars and amphorae as well as for jugs, had a pear-shaped body with a small neck. Its widest diameter was at the shoulder, where the main decoration was placed. Rarer shapes included the rhyton, the most notable specimens being of conical (see fig. 11a), ostrich-egg or bull's-head form. Sometimes made in moulds, bull-shaped askoi and bull's-head rhyta were now much more naturalistic.

Decorative schemes continued the principles of the Middle Bronze Age, with two-dimensional floral motifs, especially ivy leaves, flowers, rosettes, grasses and branches, accompanying spirals and other geometric designs. The development of a few individual motifs can be traced in detail. The LM IA spiral, for example, often had a large dot as its centre surrounded by tiny white dots, but by the end of LM IB this type had been abandoned and was usually replaced by a quickly made whorl, drawn from the inside out. Similarly, the foliate band developed from a fairly naturalistic representation of a branch with leaves on both sides to an abstract design composed of two rows of dots or crescents with a line between them. In general, LM IA vases were more carefully painted than those of LM IB.

A large jar from Pseira (Herakleion, Archaeol. Mus.; see fig. 12) illustrates the LM IA decoration at its most elaborate. The motifs in its largest frieze are unusual for

13. Late Minoan lentoid flask, Special Palatial tradition, Marine style, h. 270 mm, from Palaikastro, LM IB (Herakleion, Archaeological Museum)

were used. Since many of the shapes were also new to pottery, the tradition seems very innovative, but in fact it depended on a wide range of immediate sources, especially metalware and monumental painting. A late variation of the tradition, known as the Alternating style, used individual motifs in strict alternation around the vase in an empty field.

Also during LM I, the pithos, a large storage jar that had gradually developed during the Early to Middle Bronze Ages, reached a peak of size and splendour. In EM times pithoi had been plain jars, perhaps a metre high, but during LM I they became much more elaborate and increased in height to almost 2 m. The most common of several shapes of giant pithoi had a heavy rim and rather wide mouth, a slightly swelling shoulder and straight walls that contracted a little towards the base. Decoration usually consisted of raised bands indented with finger impressions and known as ropework, though some workshops added circular medallions or other simple plastic designs (*see* KNOSSOS, fig. 3). Each pithos had several handles, designed to receive a hoisting rope. However, the giant pithoi are chiefly remarkable for their manufacture and firing. They were built by hand, by the addition of successive slabs of clay to build up the walls, probably while the vessels were rotated on a turntable. Firing a pithos of great size demanded a kiln of sophisticated design because breakage would occur if the temperature were not uniform. Taken together, the giant pithoi and the eggshell-thin Kamares ware productions indicate the astonishing versatility of Minoan potters in forming techniques, kiln design and general pyrotechnology.

(ii) Late Minoan II. This stage of the Late Bronze Age, which was probably of short duration, followed a time of widespread destructions in Crete, and many of the burnt towns were either not rebuilt or experienced a loss of population. Several new influences entered the local ceramic traditions. Most of the new shapes, which included the squat alabastron and the krater (a deep bowl with two opposed horizontal handles), had already occurred on the Greek mainland, so the influences were probably Mycenaean (*see* HELLADIC, §III, 4). Among other Mycenaean shapes adopted by the Minoans, the 'Ephyraean' goblet (also called the 'Ephyraean' kylix) is noteworthy (see fig. 11d above): the vessel consisted of a conical bowl on top of a stemmed base, but it possessed a smooth, unbroken curve from rim to base and had opposed vertical handles extending from rim to body.

Mycenaean Greece and Minoan Crete had been in contact for many centuries, but before LM II most of the ideas in pottery-making had gone from the island to the mainland. The change in direction of influence was sudden and fundamental: besides the Mycenaean shapes, the Minoans adopted several mainland ornamental motifs and something of the Mycenaean pyrotechnology. Many scholars see the destructions in Crete at the end of LM IB as inflicted by invading Mycenaeans.

Yet despite the fact that LM II pottery absorbed new influences, especially Mycenaean, it was still firmly in the Minoan tradition. For instance, not all LM II vase shapes came from Mycenaean Greece. Many, such as the conical cup, semi-globular cup, jug, bridge-spouted jug and jar,

piriform jar, alabastron, rhyton and most of the storage vessels, were simple developments of LM I shapes. Unpainted pottery, especially conical cups, remained in vogue.

The ornament on painted LM II vases was more abstract than that on LM IB specimens. 'Ephyraean' goblets often had only a single element on each side of the body, set cleanly on the pale Minoan clay. Other vases, especially cups and conical bowls, usually bore a single frieze, with only a few painted bands on their lower bodies. The Marine style persisted but without much of its former energy. Octopuses were more attenuated and often more symmetrical. Florals were stylized, as if the artists were copying designs rather than nature. Open space became more of a force in compositional design.

The most exciting development of LM II was the Palace style. Although it originated exclusively from Knossos, it profoundly influenced ceramics throughout Crete. The style basically represented a movement towards the grandiose. Vases, particularly large ones, were decorated with expansive and often elaborate and symmetrical compositions, featuring floral and geometric motifs and occasionally unusual elements such as marine ornaments or even a warrior's helmet. Many of the style's ornamental elements were borrowed from the Special Palatial tradition, especially the Alternating style, of LM IB. A major difference is that motifs used previously as small filling ornaments were now enlarged and employed as the main focus of a vessel. In addition, they were occasionally abstracted and used in a more formal, symmetrical way. The style continued into LM IIIA, with many of the best examples dating from late in the tradition (fig. 11e).

(iii) Late Minoan III. This period has been divided into three phases, the first having two parts. Although these phases closely follow the chronology of Mycenaean Greece, Minoan sequences are not as easily unravelled, because each contains more variations than those of Late Helladic III.

LM IIIA vase painting continued the stylization and abstraction of LM II, which led to a series of motifs whose natural origins were not readily visible. But technology was greatly improved. Except at a few centres, such as Knossos, LM II fabrics were softer than those of LM IB, though the potting was always expertly done. By LM IIIA the firing could achieve a dense, firm fabric, and it continued to improve during LM IIIB. LM IIIA ornament was more abstract than that of LM II, and bands of repeated designs became the standard for semi-globular cups and bowls and for many closed shapes. The direction faced by individual motifs often alternated between bands, creating a zigzag, flowing movement. A few of the finest LM IIIA vases depict stylized landscapes in which birds and floral motifs, including some very elaborate plant designs, were used to create lush scenes probably related to the more naturalistic Nilotic scenes of LM I, known from monumental paintings, inlaid metal daggers and a few other art objects.

The shapes of LM IIIA vases developed naturally from those of LM II. The plain conical cup was still used, but its popularity was already declining. It may have been replaced

14. Late Minoan krater, restored h. 345 mm, from Knossos, LM IIIC (Herakleion, Archaeological Museum)

by the unpainted kylix and by an increasingly large output of painted cups. The kylix was taller than it had been in LM II, with a more conical bowl. The one-handled cup was quite different from the earlier varieties; all the LM I–II types had coalesced into a hemispherical shape with a tiny ledge rim, which died out at the end of LM IIIA:1 in favour of a nearly straight rim. A new type of stemmed goblet with one handle (usually called a champagne cup) appeared at the beginning of LM IIIA:2. Kraters, bowls, jugs, amphorae and jars continued to be produced, and storage pithoi had become smaller and plainer. Stirrup jars, now an important transport vessel, were made in many sizes, both painted and plain.

During LM IIIB the repertory of shapes was more standardized. Conical cups had almost vanished. Kylikes, cups and bowls, both painted and plain, were used for drinking. The occurrence of large numbers of amphorae and kraters, and dippers with long handles, suggests that the Classical Greek practice of mixing water with wine was already well established. All of the LM IIIA:2 shapes continued to be used.

Motifs became still more abstract, and those in decorative friezes were usually more widely spaced; alternating the direction in which they faced became rare. LM IIIB designs thus lacked the flowing character of the earlier bands and seemed more monotonous. Most of the designs were also greatly simplified, continuing the tendency that had begun much earlier and in some cases descending to absurdity, such as replacing the octopus and its many sinuous tentacles with a single wavy line. Usually several variants of a motif coexisted, so that, for example, more complete octopuses were painted at the same time as vestigial ones.

Human or animal figures had occasionally appeared on Minoan pottery since the Early Bronze Age, but only at the end of LM IIIA did they become common. A new fashion in figural work appeared on kraters (see fig. 14) and a few other large shapes. Probably inspired by a contemporary Mycenaean tradition, the usually symmetrical compositions are less lively.

During LM IIIC, Minoan vase painting effectively ended; the Sub-Minoan period that followed was as much a transition to the next phase as a continuation of existing practices. Simplification of the existing motifs continued, while the disappearance of many of the designs left an impoverished and overly repeated repertory. At the same time, potting and firing declined in quality at many centres, so that vases were softer and more likely to flake. An Open style of decoration (also called Plain style), which left most of the vessel unpainted except for a simple design such as irregular concentric triangles or semicircles or a wavy line and bands, coexisted with a Close style characterized by elaborate ornament and fine hatching over the whole surface. Close-style vases, especially small stirrup jars with symmetrical octopuses whose tentacles were more ornament than animal (see fig. 11f above), exhibit the last really vigorous Bronze Age painting in Crete, and with a revival of expert potting and firing they became popular for some time, a number being exported to several regions, including Rhodes. Thereafter, Cretan pottery went into decline until it was revived by the influence of Attic Protogeometric.

BIBLIOGRAPHY

A. J. Evans: *The Palace of Minos at Knossos*, 4 vols and index (London, 1921–36, 2/1964)
A. Furness: 'The Neolithic Pottery of Knossos', *Annu. Brit. Sch. Athens*, 48 (1953), pp. 94–134
C. Zervos: *L'Art de la Crète néolithique et minoenne* (Paris, 1956)
M. R. Popham: *The Last Days of the Palace at Knossos: Complete Vases of the Late Minoan IIIB Period* (Lund, 1964)
——: *The Destruction of the Palace at Knossos: Pottery of the Late Minoan IIIA Period* (Göteborg, 1970)
D. Levi: *Festòs e la civiltà minoica*, i (Rome, 1976)
G. Walberg: *Kamares* (Uppsala, 1976)
L. Vagnetti and P. Belli: 'Characters and Problems of the Final Neolithic in Crete', *Stud. Micenei & Egeo-Anatol.*, xix (1978), pp. 125–63
G. Walberg: *The Kamares Style: Overall Effects* (Uppsala, 1978)
P. Betancourt and others: *Vasilike Ware: An Early Bronze Age Pottery Style in Crete* (Göteborg, 1979)
A. Kanta: *The Late Minoan III Period in Crete* (Göteborg, 1980)
B. J. Kemp and R. S. Merillees: *Minoan Pottery in Second Millennium Egypt* (Mainz am Rhein, 1980)
G. Walberg: *Provincial Middle Minoan Pottery* (Mainz am Rhein, 1983)
P. Betancourt, ed.: *East Cretan White-on-dark Ware* (Philadelphia, 1984)
P. Betancourt: *The History of Minoan Pottery* (Princeton, 1985)
W. D. Niemeier: *Die Palaststilkeramik von Knossos* (Berlin, 1985)

PHILIP BETANCOURT

IV. Wall paintings and reliefs.

The largest number of extant Minoan wall paintings and reliefs comes from the palace at KNOSSOS, the main administrative and religious centre on Crete. Wall paintings adorned the rich town houses around the palace and important villas on Crete, but surprisingly little has been found in the other Cretan palaces. Poorer houses in Knossos, provincial towns and the country had no pictorial paintings, only striped bands or spiral friezes.

The earliest pictorial wall paintings date from Middle Minoan (MM) IIIA, walls having previously been painted monochrome white or red or with simple bands or patterns. While it is difficult to date Minoan painting precisely—paintings remain on walls long after their execution, so that the destruction or abandonment of a building provides only a *terminus ad quem*, and the contexts themselves are often not secure—the paintings fall roughly into two periods: MM IIIA to Late Minoan (LM) IB throughout the island, and LM II to LM IIIA at Knossos and AYIA TRIADA. Some themes (griffins, bulls) continued in both periods; others disappeared in the later period (nature), while new ones emerged (processions, libation, chariots, soldiers, shields).

When excavated, Minoan paintings are found in small fragments, fallen from the walls and usually thrown with collapsed floors from upper storeys to basements. In time, paints flake, plaster is pulverized, and many of the fragments are irretrievable. In the early years of Minoan archaeology, at the beginning of the 20th century, the fragments were over-zealously restored, and much of what is on exhibition in the Herakleion Archaeological Museum on Crete is modern reconstruction into which the original fragments have been fitted. Only the Theran paintings permit full-scale restoration, owing to their excellent state of preservation (*see* CYCLADIC, §VI, and THERA, §1). Otherwise, reconstructions are today more likely to occur on paper.

1. Materials and techniques. 2. Subject-matter.

1. MATERIALS AND TECHNIQUES. Dispute surrounds the issue of whether the technique of Minoan wall painting was true *buon fresco* or *fresco secco* (*see* WALL PAINTING, §1). The uncertainty may arise because a mixed technique was employed, guidelines and background washes being applied to the wet plaster, details to dry plaster. The term 'fresco' is traditionally used in naming (e.g. miniature frescoes, *Procession* fresco), but the term 'wall painting' is more neutral.

Lime plaster was applied to the walls on to a backing plaster of mud, and the borders and overall design were planned while it was wet. Taut string was pressed into the plaster to mark the border bands; these string lines were also used for alignment of features, such as architecture or complex patterns on garments. Dividers or compasses were used for rosettes. A monochrome wash was applied to the wall, reserving spaces for the figures. At the same time the border bands were coloured. Preliminary sketches were then made in red or yellow. In painting, each colour was applied separately and the details—hair, eyes, outlines, dress patterns—applied last. Finally the surface was polished.

The colours used were red (haematite) and yellow ochre, from natural iron oxides; black, from carbonaceous shale; white, from calcined lime; and blue, from a manufactured frit coloured by copper–calcium silicate imported from Egypt or from the mineral glaucophane (these were expensive, so blue was used sparingly outside Knossos). Green was made by mixing yellow and blue. Opaque or water-diluted paint was applied mainly with the brush, though sponges were occasionally used to dab it on to the wall. White impasto was sometimes applied in dots. In the earlier paintings, backgrounds may be white or red or a combination of both. Later, blue and yellow were favoured at Knossos and Ayia Triada. Sometimes the background was divided into wavy vertical or horizontal zones of colour.

Some MM IIIA–LM IB paintings were executed in relief, either built up in a single layer (low relief) or with added layers of plaster supported by wooden pegs (high relief, used especially for anatomy). Flat and relief techniques can appear together in a single painting (e.g. *Jewel* fresco from Knossos, now destr.). Occasionally the in cavetto technique (reverse of relief) was employed, especially for floors: areas of plaster were cut out and filled with thick paint or another layer of painted plaster.

Paintings usually decorated the upper storeys of buildings, though at Knossos large-scale processional figures were painted along the ground-floor corridors. Paintings either covered the whole wall, were applied to panels or formed a broad frieze with a wide dado or a continuous narrow frieze set at eye-level or above the lintel. Border bands defined the upper and lower limits of the painting. Dados often imitate variegated gypsum veneer, others imitate wood. Ceilings painted with spirals and rosette filling motifs were favoured at Knossos. Some floors were painted red, while others were stone-flagged with red-painted stucco in the interstices; a few had in cavetto patterns, and one from a Knossos town house (Royal Road) imitates an animal skin. Floor paintings from Knossos and Ayia Triada feature dolphins and small fish in seascapes.

Some representational conventions are similar to those of Egyptian painting (*see* EGYPT, ANCIENT, §IV, 2), but Minoan painting is freer, more rhythmic and less hierarchic. Men are painted red, women white. Figures are shown with heads in profile, and their bodies are defined in outline, sometimes with black lines indicating leg muscles (e.g. *Toreador* frescoes). In the Miniature frescoes, the crowds are drawn in a lively shorthand technique, without detail. In landscape scenes, rocks descend as well as rise, like stalactites and stalagmites, and the rockwork is variegated, like the interiors of cut stone. Plants are painted from observation and imagination, sometimes resulting in artistic hybridization.

2. SUBJECT-MATTER. Minoan wall painting is characterized by a vivid sense of life and an empathy with the natural world. Plants and animals abound, a reflection of the world of the nature goddess, who herself appears life-size in paintings from town and country houses. In the palace of Knossos, a wider variety of subjects was depicted but still within a defined range: processions, cult scenes, bull-sports, festivals, protective griffins. Life expressed through the paintings is without war, old age or daily labour. It is an idealized world filled with joyful observation of the natural environment and youthful celebration through ritual.

(i) The natural world. (ii) Nature cult and the female figure. (iii) Miniatures. (iv) Bull-sports. (v) Griffins. (vi) Processions and palatial cult scenes. (vii) Martial themes. (viii) Programmes.

(i) The natural world. The earliest Minoan paintings (MM IIIA) consist of spirals, bands, foliate bands, lattice, chequers and imitation stone and woodwork. During the same period, the first representational paintings, from town houses by the Royal Road at Knossos, draw their inspiration from the rich plant life of Crete, depicting reeds, myrtle, grass, lilies or vetch.

After MM IIIA until LM IB nature scenes predominate in the houses and country villas. Plants are the most popular subject, with examples (sometimes difficult to identify

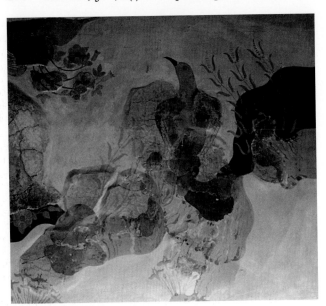

15. Wall painting depicting a frieze of birds and monkeys (detail), from the House of the Frescoes, Knossos, LM IA (Herakleion, Archaeological Museum); partly reconstructed

owing to artistic hybridization) from the Knossos town houses (Royal Road, Hogarth's houses, Savakis's Bothros, Unexplored Mansion), nearby AMNISOS, ARCHANES, a villa at TYLISSOS and the palaces of Knossos and PHAISTOS. The most commonly depicted are white (madonna) lilies, a flower shown by the iconography of seals and later Aegean wall paintings to have been a cult plant and an offering to the deity. Paintings of white and red lilies also came from the Cycladic islands of Thera and MELOS (see CYCLADIC, §VI) and the Minoan settlement of Ialysos on Rhodes. At Amnisos, two panels of white lilies and one of iris and reeds were found in a room with a painted offering table. Here nature is cultivated: the iris and reeds rise from a built, stepped base, and the lilies stand against an architectonic background. The offering table shows that the room was a shrine.

Animals and birds in a landscape are the subject of paintings in some of the Knossos town houses. From the South-east House, a fragment shows mice among sedges; lilies and rocks were associated. A bird ('swallow'), reeds, pebbles and a water-pool came from the South House. At the Caravanserai, a building assumed to have been used to accommodate visitors, a narrow frieze of partridges ran along the top of a wall of one of the rooms. The partridges stand on a rocky terrain, delineated by wavy lines and interspersed with variegated rocks. Tall, leafy plants stand between the birds, and the background is part white, part blue. On a bush or small tree sits a hoopoe. The landscape is stylized but evocative and the birds stately and still.

A magnificent frieze of birds and monkeys was found in the House of the Frescoes (see fig. 15). The frieze ran continuously around three walls. The background is part red, part white. Veined rocks in blue, red and yellow rise sinuously into the picture leaving reserved areas for the animal action and the rich plant life of spring or early

summer: rock rose, vetch, crocus, honeysuckle, myrtle, mallow, ivy, dwarf iris, lily. Waterfalls gush down past grey rocks, and a stream meanders through the painting, reeds and papyrus following its course. Doves, painted blue with pink dots circling their necks, fly with outstretched wings or perch on rocks. The monkeys, blue with distinctive facial markings, scramble among the rocks and plants, apparently looking for birds' eggs in the summarily depicted nests. One holds an egg to its mouth. Monkeys may have been imported to Crete as exotic park animals from East Africa via Egypt. Fragments of an associated painting show two wild Cretan goats (agrimi), an olive tree, crocuses and undulating bands.

The *Saffron Gatherer* fresco was found north-west of the Central Court at the palace of Knossos (area of the Early Keep). The frieze had at least two blue monkeys in a rocky landscape with crocuses. The head of the best-preserved monkey is missing from the fragments, and when the painting was discovered the convention of a blue figure was misunderstood, so it was reconstructed as a boy (it remains in this form; Herakleion, Archaeol. Mus.). It is now known that blue is the conventional colour for the depiction of monkeys, and the figure has been reconstructed correctly on paper. The background is red. White crocuses appear as large single heads with prominent stamens growing from the tips of rocks that rise from the bottom of the painting and fall from the top, framing the monkey in the central field of the picture. The monkey strides forward, bending at the waist to place crocuses into pots resting on the rocks. Instead of being represented as a creature roaming in a natural landscape, as seen in the House of the Frescoes, the monkey is anthropomorphized in a mythic role associated with the crocus. This role is further developed in the paintings from Thera; for example, in the *Saffron* (or *Crocus*) *Gatherers* fresco the flowers are collected by young girls and offered by a blue monkey to a seated nature goddess.

(ii) Nature cult and the female figure. A goddess of nature among plants is the most prevalent theme of wall paintings in Minoan villas. Most of the figures are fragmentary, their identification circumstantial. In a town house at Palaikastro a woman's arm in relief was found associated with a crocus fragment. Other fragmentary female figures represented with plants occurred in villas at Prasa and Epano Zakros and at the palace of Knossos. A miniature fragment with birds and reeds from a house at Katsamba, the harbour town of Knossos, has been identified as belonging to the girdle or skirt of a goddess. Relief paintings of seated women from the offshore island of PSEIRA presumably belong to the same cycle of goddess figures, while at the villa of Nirou Chani a painting of a sacral knot (a feature of priestly robes, cf. the figure of *La Parisienne* from Knossos; see §(vi) below) may have been a symbol of the goddess. Garlands, found in a painting in a house at Knossos, may have been sacred emblems of the Minoan gods or goddesses and perhaps symbolize those worn in ritual dances and processions. They were found in association with fragments of female figures (skirts), a built structure and landscape.

The only unequivocal cult scenes from Crete in which female figures are set within a true landscape are the related paintings covering three walls of Room 14 at the villa (or summer palace) of Ayia Triada. On one wall was a nature scene with wild cats stalking birds and with two running deer, set in a rocky landscape with ivy, myrtle, papyrus and other plants (cf. the elements of the landscape miniature frieze from Thera; see CYCLADIC, §VI, 1(ii)). On another, a female figure kneels among crocuses and lilies, the two main plants of the Minoan cult. On a narrower wall between these two stood the goddess (or priestess) in a flounced skirt, with a built shrine behind her. Here the two main themes of wall paintings in Minoan houses—the natural world and a female priestess or deity associated with plants—come together, the cult scene providing evidence of their religious function.

In the palace of Knossos, large-scale female figures occur in a number of fragmentary compositions. Women wearing richly decorated textiles have been termed the *Ladies in Blue* and the *Ladies in Red*. Their open bodices expose their breasts, and they are adorned with multiple necklaces. One fragment shows a hand fingering a necklace, recalling the *Jewel* fresco relief, in which a male hand places a necklace on a female, perhaps in a robing ceremony. A fragment of a woman found near the Queen's Megaron was dubbed the *Dancing Lady*, from her flowing locks and outstretched arm; she has since been interpreted as holding out a staff in a reverential gesture.

(iii) Miniatures. In Minoan art, miniature painting is the term applied to narrow painted friezes that ran along the tops of walls and depicted small-scale figures in public festivals. These are action pictures, with a large number of figures accommodated in a small space. They are known from the palace of Knossos and a villa at Tylissos, as well as from the islands of Thera and KEA (see CYCLADIC, §VI, 1(ii), 2 and 3).

The miniature friezes at Knossos came from a small room off the north-west side of the Central Court and probably ran around three of the walls. (A spiral-relief ceiling came from the same area and would have completed the decoration of the room, which was no doubt a shrine.) Two friezes have been reconstructed from the extant fragments. In the *Shrine* frieze, spectators are crowded into areas around a central tripartite shrine. Next to it are seated women in flounced skirts, engaged in lively conversation, painted against a white background. To the sides, more women stand on stepped platforms with pillars. Crowds of male spectators appear above and below. Only their heads are visible, painted against a red background in shorthand strokes of black, with white dots for eyes and necklaces. The tripartite shrine has columns supporting the roofs, on which are rows of horns of consecration. Both are features of Minoan architecture, the latter being imitation bulls' horns of stone or stucco, used to designate an area as sacred. An actual tripartite shrine existed on the west side of the Central Court and would have been visible from the room with the miniatures. Presumably the spectators are watching an event taking place in the Central Court, conceivably the bull-sports. In the *Sacred Grove and Dance* frieze, crowds of male and female spectators watch a dance in an outdoor area with pathways and olive trees. Some men in loincloths stand in lines; those at the top (i.e. back) wave their arms. A ritual dance is performed by

women in flounced skirts moving from left to right, arms held high. The location has been identified as either the West Court or the Theatral Area at Knossos.

Two fragments found in the North-west Fresco Heap show women in architectural frames—one of windows, one a balustrade—that should be related to the main scenes. Other fragments on a slightly larger scale and by a different hand were found in the Thirteenth Magazine. They show a miniature shrine, male spectators and the head of a bull, suggesting a bull-leaping scene.

Several fragments from the palace have miniature designs (bird, griffin, sphinx, bucranium, flutes), as do some from houses near Knossos (plant designs from Knossos town, Prasa, Katsamba), but these probably represent clothing patterns belonging to large-scale figures. A miniature frieze decorated a room of a villa at Tylissos. The extant fragments show a building, a tree, and men and women moving from right to left. The men, in loincloths, carry poles with large pots slung over them. The women may have been dancing, as at Knossos. One fragment shows male spectators facing to the right. The condition is fragmentary, but enough remains to suggest an outdoor festival similar to those shown in the miniatures of Knossos and the islands.

(iv) Bull-sports. The theme of bull-leaping has a long history in the Aegean; it appears on other media (seals, ivory, metal, clay and in miniature painting on a crystal plaque) as well as in Mycenaean painting (see HELLADIC, §IV, 2(ii)). In Minoan painting the theme reflects an important event of ritual competition, which took place in the palatial court(s) at Knossos. Depictions of bulls and bull-sports were thus restricted to Knossos, where they were extremely popular. The earliest depictions in relief date from MM IIIB–LM IA. The animals' heavy bodies and the bull-leapers' sinuous musculature were ideal for relief modelling. A scene in relief of a charging bull, fragments of bull-leapers, an olive tree, myrtle and rocks were found in the North Entrance area at Knossos; a bull above a dado was found *in situ* at the West Entrance, and there were also earlier versions. Thus two of the main entrances, from the Royal Road and the West Court, greeted the visitor to the palace with an image of a bull. From the Central Court, the antechamber to the Throne Room was also decorated with a bull, found *in situ* above a stone bench. Other fragments of bulls were found in the House of the Sacrificed Oxen (relief, flung from the south-east angle of the palace), the North-west Treasury (bull and tree) and the Royal Road, while the theme of bull-leaping is reflected in fragments from the Residential Quarters (bull with plant, associated with miniature female bull-leapers) and in the Thirteenth Magazine (miniature, associated with a shrine and spectators). In high reliefs associated with a presumed Great East Hall, fragments of boxers, (?)wrestlers and acrobats were found along with relief fragments of bulls.

The best-known depictions of the sport are the series of *Toreador* frescoes from the Court of the Stone Spout. Fragments of five panels were found, one of which has been restored (see fig. 16). Each had three figures, male and female, wearing the same loincloths but distinguished by colour. One holds the bull's horns, one vaults over the

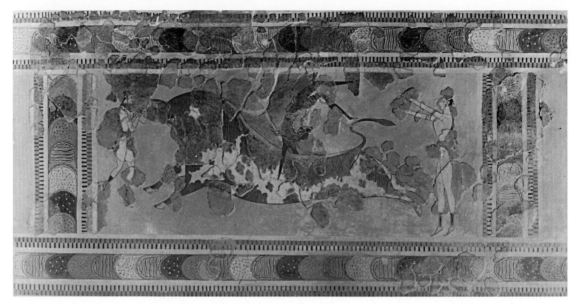

16. *Bull-leapers*, from the *Toreador* frescoes, Court of the Stone Spout, palace of Knossos, late LM II or early LM III (Herakleion, Archaeological Museum)

back and one stands at the back either waiting to catch the leaper or having landed after vaulting (three participants or three stages in the sport). The bulls have dappled hide and facial-hair markings. Backgrounds are blue or yellow (indicating a later date, probably LM II), and the friezes are bordered by imitation variegated stone, like rows of cut pebbles, simulating stone dados. Unusually (since Minoan paintings generally show an ideal world) a bull-leaping accident is shown in a fragment from the same area.

(v) Griffins. Griffins—mythical creatures, half lion, half bird, which frequently had a guardian role in Aegean iconography—were a common theme at Knossos. A relief fresco shows griffins tied to a pillar, an abbreviation for a shrine. The Throne Room at Knossos was painted with heraldic griffins in a setting of papyrus and palm against a wavy (riverine) background, resting on an imitation marble dado above a row of stone benches. On the north wall, the seated griffins appear to have flanked the throne, as though guarding its occupant, who, based on comparison with scenes of heraldic griffins on seals, may have been a priestess, perhaps enacting an epiphany of the goddess. On the west wall, griffins faced the door to the 'inner shrine'. The theme recurs in the Mycenaean throne-room at PYLOS (*see* HELLADIC, §IV, 2(iii)).

(vi) Processions and palatial cult scenes. Leading along the corridor from the West Entrance into the palace of Knossos was the *Procession* fresco. It was still standing on the walls at the time of the final destruction of the palace and was painted by Cretan artists during the Mycenaean occupation (LM II–IIIA). A row of feet was found *in situ*. The procession of life-size figures, mainly male, walks towards the interior of the palace, bearing offerings. At the front of the reconstructed section is a female figure, the priestess or epiphany of the goddess, in front of whom more men walk backwards in reverence. The procession

continued from the long corridor up the main staircase to the upper storey. Only one figure, the *Cupbearer*, is well preserved. Fallen from the west wall of the South Propylaion, he wears a patterned Mycenaean kilt and jewellery and carries a funnel-shaped vessel used for libations. Here the figures may have been painted in registers, as in contemporary Egyptian painting. Hundreds of figures must have been painted on the walls of the long corridor and the South Propylaion at the end of it. A comparable procession, surviving only in fragments haphazardly thrown out, has been attributed to the Grand Staircase on the east side of the palace (Cameron, 1978).

From the passageway on the south side of the palace came the *Priest-King* or *Lily Prince* relief fresco. The painting survives in three pieces: a torso wearing a lily necklace (see fig. 5 above), a leg and a feathered crown of lilies. The pieces have been variously interpreted as male (from the anatomy) or female (from the colour), as a priest-king leading a griffin, a parading bull-leaper leading a bull prior to the games, a boxer or a god holding a staff. The pieces are reconstructed in the Herakleion Museum as a single figure facing left and wearing a feathered crown; but in a subsequent reconstruction (Niemeier, 1987, p. 95), one figure stands to the right holding a staff (torso), flanked by a male votary (leg), with either a priestess or a sphinx wearing the lily crown.

The only paintings on Crete outside Knossos at this time (*c.* 1400 BC) also depict processions. These come from a shrine within the late (LM IIIA) settlement at Ayia Triada. All are cult scenes. In one, a woman leads deer to an altar. A fragment of a man in a long robe may have belonged to the same composition. Rosettes form a lower frame to the picture. In another, a line of dancing women approaches a sanctuary. These paintings were associated with what is known as the Marine Floor.

Fragments of another painting found just outside the village may have decorated a tomb. On a blue background with rosette border is depicted a procession of male and female figures carrying vessels or playing musical instruments (the man at the front of the procession plays a lyre). Remarkably similar scenes were painted on the sides of a sarcophagus found in a tomb near by (LM IIIA; Herakleion, Archaeol. Mus.). On one of the long sides (for illustration *see* AYIA TRIADA), women carrying similar vessels pour libations between two pillars, and behind them a man plays a lyre, while three other men approach a tomb or shrine bearing funerary offerings (two calves and a boat). Receiving the offerings before the tomb is a figure presumably representing the deceased. On the other long side, a procession of women approaches a shrine, a bull has been trussed up for sacrifice and a man plays the double flute. Other scenes pertaining to the funerary cult were painted on the short sides: women ride chariots, one drawn by horses, the other by griffins. The pictures are bordered by rosettes, as in the wall paintings, and the same painter seems to have been at work.

A cult scene from Knossos, known as the *Camp Stool* fresco, fell from an upper-storey hall on the north-west side of the palace. The figures are arranged in two, perhaps four, registers divided by horizontal bands, with a background of blue and yellow vertical divisions. Seated on folding stools are male figures in long robes. They face one another, exchanging a cup (Mycenaean kylix) or chalice. A female figure, known by her curls, retroussé nose and red lips as *La Parisienne* (see fig. 17), wears a sacral knot at her shoulder suggesting that she is a goddess or priestess.

The so-called *Palanquin* fresco, depicting a male figure seated in a structure (previously thought to be a sedan chair but now interpreted as a shrine), has been associated with pieces of a *Chariot* fresco found near by (Cameron, *Archäol. Anz.*, 1967). The latter show a man standing in a dual chariot led by horses and followed by a bull, presumably intended for sacrifice. Chariots became a common theme of Mycenaean art.

(vii) Martial themes. Fragments of a painting known as the *Captain of the Blacks* were found near the House of the Frescoes. On an alternating blue and yellow background, a male (red) figure wearing a kilt and a horned cap and carrying two spears leads foreign soldiers, black-skinned and also in kilt and cap. This is the only instance of a martial theme in Cretan painting, but life-size paintings of oxhide figure-of-eight shields, restored in the Hall of the Colonnades adjacent to the Grand Staircase, symbolically reflect the militaristic emphasis of much Mycenaean art and recur in mainland palaces.

(viii) Programmes. According to Cameron (1984, 'The "Palatial" Thematic System. . .' and in preparation), a thematic thread, or programme, ran through all the wall paintings of the palace at Knossos. The paintings were thought by him to represent different stages of a major annual religious festival in celebration of the Minoan goddess: procession and offerings escorting a goddess-impersonator into the palace (*Procession* fresco), libations (*Camp Stool*) and adornment (*Jewel* fresco), epiphany of the goddess through a priestess (*Sacred Dance*), gathering of the people for the spectacle (*Triparte Shrine, Ladies in Blue*), ritual games (bull-sports), seating of the goddess-impersonator in the cult room (Throne Room). Although the surviving paintings are of differing dates, the supposition is that a thematic unity was retained on the walls of the palace at any one time. The fragmentary nature of the surviving material has made wall painting programmes difficult to reconstruct, but the spectacular discoveries on Thera since the late 1960s have provided many new insights into the religious themes of Aegean wall painting.

17. *La Parisienne*, fragment of a priestess, from the *Camp Stool* fresco, palace of Knossos, LM IIIA:2 (Herakleion, Archaeological Museum)

BIBLIOGRAPHY

GENERAL

N. Heaton: 'Minoan Lime Plaster and Fresco Painting', *RIBA J.*, xviii (1911), pp. 697–710

P. Duell and R. J. Gettens: 'A Review of the Problem of Aegean Wall Painting', *Tech. Stud.* (1942), pp. 179–223

H. A. Groenwegen-Frankfort: *Arrest and Movement* (London, 1951)

W. Schierung: 'Steine und Malerei in der minoischen Kunst', *Jb. Dt. Archäol. Inst.*, lxxv (1960), pp. 17–36

——: 'Die Naturanschauung in der altkretischen Kunst', *Ant. Kst*, ix (1965), pp. 3–12

W. S. Smith: *Interconnections in the Ancient Near East* (New Haven and London, 1965)

M. A. S. Cameron: 'New Restorations of Minoan Frescoes from Knossos', *Bull. Inst. Class. Stud. U. London*, xvii (1970), pp. 163–6

——: 'On Theoretical Principles in Aegean Bronze Age Mural Restoration', *Temple University Aegean Symposium*, i (1976), pp. 20–41

B. Kaiser: *Untersuchungen zum minoischen Relief* (Bonn, 1976)

E. S. Hirsch: *Painted Decoration of the Floors of Bronze Age Structures on Crete and the Greek Mainland*, Stud. Medit. Archaeol., lii (Göteborg, 1977)

J. Schafer: 'Zur kunstgeschichtlichen Interpretation altägäischer Wandmalerei', *Jb. Dt. Archäol. Inst.*, xcii (1977), pp. 1–23

M. A. S. Cameron: 'Theoretical Interrelations among Theran, Cretan and Mainland Frescoes', *Thera and the Aegean World*, ed. C. Doumas, i (London, 1978), pp. 579–92

S. Hood: *The Arts in Prehistoric Greece*, Pelican Hist. A. (Harmondsworth, 1978), pp. 48–77

E. S. Hirsch: 'Another Look at Minoan and Mycenaean Interrelationships in Floor Decoration', *Amer. J. Archaeol.*, lxxxiv (1980), pp. 453–62

J. Coulomb: 'Les Boxeurs minoens', *Bull. Corr. Hell.*, cv (1981), pp. 27–40

S. Peterson: *Wall Paintings in the Aegean Bronze Age: The Procession Frescoes* (diss., Minneapolis, U. MN, 1981)

S. A. Immerwahr: 'The People in the Frescoes', *Minoan Society: Proceedings of the Cambridge Colloquium: Cambridge, 1981*

R. Hägg: 'Iconographical Programs in Minoan Palaces and Villas', *L'Iconographie minoenne: Actes de la Table Ronde Athènes*, ed. P. Darque and J. C. Poursat, *Bull. Corr. Hell.*, suppl. xi (1985), pp. 209–17

S. A. Immerwahr: 'A Possible Influence of Egyptian Art in the Creation of Minoan Wall Painting', *L'Iconographie minoenne: Actes de la Table Ronde Athènes*, ed. P. Darque and J. C. Poursat, *Bull. Corr. Hell.*, suppl. xi (1985), pp. 41–50

——: *Aegean Painting in the Bronze Age* (Pennsylvania and London, 1990)

M. A. S. Cameron: *Minoan Frescoes*, ed. L. Morgan, *Annu. Brit. Sch. Athens*, suppl. vol. (in preparation)

L. Morgan, ed.: *Aegean Wall Painting: A Tribute to Mark Cameron* (in preparation)

KNOSSOS

T. Fyfe: 'Painted Plaster Decoration at Knossos with Special Reference to the Architectural Schemes', *RIBA J.*, x (1902–3), pp. 107–31

N. Heaton: 'The Mural Paintings of Knossos: An Investigation into the Method of their Production', *J. Royal Soc. A.*, lviii (1910), pp. 206–12

H. Reusch: 'Zum Wandschmuck des Thronsaales in Knossos', *Minoica: Festschrift Johannes Sundwall*, ed. E. Grumach (Berlin, 1958), pp. 334–58

M. A. S. Cameron: 'An Addition to "La Parisienne"', *Kritika Chron.* (1964), pp. 38–53

——: 'Notes on Some New Joins and Additions to Well-known Frescoes from Knossos', *Europa: Studien zur Geschichte und Epigraphik der frühen Aegaeis* (Berlin, 1967), pp. 45–74

——: 'Unpublished Fresco Fragments of a Chariot Composition from Knossos', *Archäol. Anz.*, iii (1967), pp. 330–44

M. A. S. Cameron and S. Hood: *Catalogue of Plates in Sir Arthur Evans' Knossos Fresco Atlas* (London, 1967)

M. A. S. Cameron: 'Unpublished Paintings from the "House of Frescoes" at Knossos', *Annu. Brit. Sch. Athens*, lxiii (1968), pp. 1–31

——: '"The Lady in Red": A Complementary Figure to the "Ladies in Blue"', *Archaeology*, xxiv (1971), pp. 35–43

——: 'Savakis's Bothros: A Minor Sounding at Knossos', *Annu. Brit. Sch. Athens*, lxxi (1976), pp. 1–13

C. W. Hawke-Smith: 'The Knossos Frescoes: A Revised Chronology', *Annu. Brit. Sch. Athens*, lxxi (1976), pp. 65–76

M. A. S. Cameron and R. E. Jones: 'Scientific Analyses of Minoan Fresco Samples from Knossos', *Annu. Brit. Sch. Athens*, lxxii (1977), pp. 121–84

J. Coulomb: 'Le Prince aux lis de Knossos reconsideré', *Bull. Corr. Hell.*, ciii (1979), pp. 29–50

C. Boulotis: 'Nochmals zum Prozessionsfresko von Knossos: Palast und Darbringung von Prestige-Objekten', *The Function of the Minoan Palaces: Proceedings of the Fourth International Symposium at the Swedish Institute in Athens: Athens, 10–16 June 1984*, pp. 145–56

M. A. S. Cameron: 'The Frescoes', *The Minoan Unexplored Mansion at Knossos*, ed. M. R. Popham (Oxford, 1984), pp. 127–50

——: 'The "Palatial" Thematic System in the Knossos Murals: Last Notes on Knossos Frescoes', *The Function of the Minoan Palaces: Proceedings of the Fourth International Symposium at the Swedish Institute in Athens: Athens, 10–16 June 1984*, pp. 321–8 [résumé by N. Marinatos]

E. Davis: 'The Knossos Miniature Frescoes and the Function of the Central Courts', *The Function of the Minoan Palaces: Proceedings of the Fourth International Symposium at the Swedish Institute in Athens: Athens, 10–16 June 1984*, pp. 157–61

W.-D. Niemeier: 'On the Function of the "Throne Room" in the Palace at Knossos', *The Function of the Minoan Palaces: Proceedings of the Fourth International Symposium at the Swedish Institute in Athens: Athens, 10–16 June 1984*, pp. 163–8

P. M. Warren: 'The Fresco of the Garlands from Knossos', *L'Iconographie minoenne: Actes de la Table Ronde Athènes*, ed. P. Darque and J. C. Poursat, *Bull. Corr. Hell.*, suppl. xi (Paris, 1985), pp. 41–50

R. B. Koehl: 'The Reconstruction of a Marine Style Floor from the Palace at Knossos', *Amer. J. Archaeol.*, xc (1986), pp. 406–17

W.-D. Niemeier: 'The "Priest King" Fresco from Knossos: A New Reconstruction and Interpretation', *Problems in Greek Prehistory: Papers Presented at the Centenary Conference of the British School of Archaeology at Athens: Athens, April 1986*, pp. 235–44

——: 'Zur Deutung des "Thronraumes" im Palast von Knossos', *Mitt. Dt. Archäol. Inst.: Athen. Abt.*, ci (1986), pp. 63–95

——: 'Das Stuckrelief des "Prinzen mit der Federkrone" aus Knossos und minoische Götterdarstellungen', *Mitt. Dt. Archäol. Inst.: Athen. Abt.*, cii (1987), pp. 65–98

ELSEWHERE

M. C. Shaw: 'The Miniature Frescoes of Tylissos Reconsidered', *Archäol. Anz.*, lxxxvii (1972), pp. 171–88

C. R. Long: *The Ayia Triadha Sarcophagus: A Study of Late Minoan and Mycenaean Funerary Practices and Beliefs*, Stud. Medit. Archaeol., xli (Göteborg, 1974)

M. A. S. Cameron and R. E. Jones: 'A Note on the Identification of Fresco Material from the British Campaigns at Palaikastro, 1902–1906', *Annu. Brit. Sch. Athens*, lxi (1976), pp. 15–19

M. C. Shaw: 'A Minoan Fresco from Katsamba', *Amer. J. Archaeol.*, lxxxii (1978), pp. 27–34

LYVIA MORGAN

V. Sculpture.

Figures of humans and animals were made throughout the Minoan period in a variety of materials, including stone, clay, terracotta and metal (discussed in this subsection), as well as ivory and faience (treated in separate subsections; see §§VI, 2 and VII, 2 below). Most sculptures were relatively small, and many served as votive offerings, the human figurines representing worshippers, the animals perhaps sacrificial victims. Some female figurines have been identified as goddesses, and these may have had larger counterparts in wood (the bronze locks of hair found by Sir Arthur Evans at Knossos may have belonged to such works). Large-scale relief frescoes, in which the figures are built up in plaster, were certainly made by the Minoans (see §IV above), but unlike the contemporary Egyptians (see EGYPT, ANCIENT, §IX), they apparently did not produce large stone sculptures or reliefs. This difference may partly be explained by Crete's shortage of suitable stone, or it may simply be that the Minoans preferred small-scale works. Given their skill at stone-carving, as is demonstrated by stone rhyta (ritual vessels) in the shape of animals' heads and by relief scenes on stone vases (see §X below), it seems certain that they would have been capable of working on a larger scale. What Minoan figurines lack in monumentality, however, is more than compensated for by their inventiveness, carefully observed detail and imaginative design.

1. NEOLITHIC AND EARLY MINOAN. The earliest Cretan figurines date from the Neolithic period, when both male and female figures were made in stone or clay. They include obese female figurines, usually seated, belonging to a type found throughout the Aegean area at this time and sometimes identified as fertility goddesses. Early Minoan (EM) figurines are much more common and come from both settlements and cemeteries. They are

profoundly influenced by the distinctive white-marble folded-arm figurines produced in large numbers in the Cyclades (*see* CYCLADIC, §IV, 1) in the Early Cycladic II period. Cycladic figurines were imported into Crete, and Cycladic types were extensively imitated in local marble, as well as in such other materials as ivory, bone and steatite. In Crete, as in the Cyclades, they comprise both schematic and naturalistic types. Typical Cretan schematic forms include peg-shaped examples with a rounded head, separated by a grooved neck from a long, roughly cylindrical body, and others with squat, rounded bodies. Limbs and facial features are only occasionally indicated, though the latter are carefully depicted on the otherwise completely schematic figures of the Ayios Onouphrios group (Herakleion Archaeol. Mus.).

Naturalistic folded-arm figurines are also found on Crete, and a typically Cretan variant, known as the Koumasa type, evolved. These thin and angular figures with broad shoulders and short legs may have been carved by Cycladic craftsmen resident on Crete. Unusual forms also occur, including a pair of steatite figurines sharing a single base, from Teke near Knossos (Herakleion, Archaeol. Mus.). The bone figurines from the Lasithi Plain represent another Cretan variety. Their legs are separated and their arms folded with the left below the right (contrary to normal Cycladic practice), while their faces have a sharp ridge down the middle and carved features. In late EM and early MM times more naturalistic stone figurines were produced, which increasingly broke away from Cycladic conventions.

2. MIDDLE MINOAN I AND II. During MM I and II, peak sanctuaries flourished on Crete. Among the main cult practices associated with them was the dedication of human and animal figurines, which seem usually to have been thrown into sacred fires. The ashes containing the offerings were swept up and preserved in fissures in the rocks. Most of these figurines were of clay, though some were of bronze. Terracotta figures representing worshippers are rarely over 200 mm high. The women characteristically have bell-shaped skirts, short-sleeved tops that either leave the breasts bare or have very low necklines, and various elaborate hairstyles, tall headdresses or hats. While some are rather roughly made with pinched, birdlike faces, others have finely modelled facial features and detailing of clothing and coiffure. The male figures often wear a loincloth and dagger and have the arms raised in gestures of worship: sometimes both hands rest on the chest, sometimes one hand is raised to the forehead. Both male and female terracotta figures were painted. Earlier examples often have red or brown decoration on a light ground, in a manner no doubt influenced by EM pottery, while some MM figures are covered with a dark, lustrous wash and decorated in red and white, again like contemporary vases. The terracotta animals were also mostly small. Domestic animals predominate, especially bulls, oxen, sheep and goats. Wild animals are rare but include weasels and wild goats. These figurines may have been substitutes for real sacrifices, perhaps dedicated with prayers for the protection of livestock. Similarly, while the human figurines were probably left by worshippers as a substitute for continual presence at the shrine, the pieces

representing parts of bodies and single limbs that also occur were no doubt left with prayers for the healing of specific afflictions.

3. MIDDLE MINOAN III AND LATE MINOAN. From MM III more elaborate groups and models were included among terracottas. One, from a tholos tomb at Kamilari, near Phaistos, apparently depicts worshippers bringing offerings to two pairs of seated deities, while another shows four figures dancing, and a third depicts a woman kneading dough (all Herakleion, Archaeol. Mus.). While these scenes may all have religious significance, a fine model of a two-storey house from ARCHANES seems purely secular (Herakleion, Archaeol. Mus.).

Most of the finest bronze figurines date from LM I. Elsewhere in the Aegean, bronze figures were rare before the Iron Age, so their production was a specifically Minoan accomplishment. Again, most are small, usually under 250 mm high, and most seem to have been made as votive offerings, since several come from peak sanctuaries and even more from sacred caves. Both male and female human figures have been found, the males usually given the same typical Minoan costumes as their terracotta counterparts and the females attired in long, flounced skirts and open-fronted jackets. They are generally shown in attitudes of prayer. Many animal figures, including horses, deer, goats, bulls and oxen, were also dedicated. One particularly fine LM I bronze group (London, BM) shows an acrobat leaping over the back of a bull (see fig. 18). He is attached to the bull's head by his long, trailing hair and so caught in arrested motion. His forearms and his lower legs may have been lost during casting.

Minoan bronzes were cast solid using the lost-wax method, in which a wax model is enclosed in a clay mould and then heated. The melted wax runs out of the mould, to be replaced by molten metal. The surfaces of Minoan figurines are rough and bubbly, and almost no finishing work seems to have been carried out once the bronze was removed from the mould. Poor casting technique and the

18. Late Minoan sculptural group of an acrobat leaping over the back of a bull, bronze, h. 111 mm, from ?Rethymnon, LM I (London, British Museum)

19. Late Minoan statuette of a goddess, terracotta, h. 525 mm, from the sanctuary of Gazi, LM IIIA:2 (Herakleion, Archaeological Museum)

animal figurines produced in Crete towards the end of the Bronze Age (probably from *c.* 1200 BC). The heads and legs were handmade, and the animals had painted decoration similar to that on contemporary vases. This style was widely imitated elsewhere in Greece, persisting beyond Minoan times.

BIBLIOGRAPHY
A. J. Evans: 'On a Minoan Bronze Group of a Galloping Bull and Acrobatic Figure from Crete', *J. Hell. Stud.*, lxi (1921), pp. 247–59
C. Zervos: *L'Art de la Crète néolithique et minoenne* (Paris, 1956)
S. Alexiou: 'E Minoike thea meth'upsomenon cheiron' [The Minoan Goddess with Raised Arms], *Kritika Chron.*, xii (1958), pp. 179–299
R. A. Higgins: *Greek Terracottas* (London, 1967)
——: *Minoan and Mycenaean Art* (London, 1967)
P. J. Ucko: *Anthropomorphic Figurines* (Richmond, VA, 1968)
K. Branigan: 'Cycladic Figurines and their Derivatives in Crete', *Annu. Brit. Sch. Athens*, lxvi (1971), pp. 57–78
M. S. F. Hood: *The Arts in Prehistoric Greece*, Pelican Hist. A. (Harmondsworth, 1978)
C. Verlinden: *Les Statuettes anthropomorphes crétoises en bronze et en plomb, du IIIe millénaire au VIIe siècle av. J-C* (Providence, RI, 1984)
B. Rutkowski: *The Cult Places of the Aegean* (New Haven, 1986)
J. LESLEY FITTON

VI. Ivory and bone.

Ivory was imported to Crete from the east (Africa, Egypt and possibly the Levant) to be carved by craftsmen using the same techniques as were developed for the handling of bone, wood and soft stone. As an import it had luxury status, and its exploitation was prompted by the existence of an élite, who put it to both secular and ritual use. Although the shapes of some products, such as pyxides and some seals, were derived from the physical nature of the material, the majority show a considerable independence of object type and decorative scheme. Unless otherwise indicated, all finds are in Herakleion, Archaeological Museum.

1. INTRODUCTION. By Early Minoan (EM) II ivory was employed for figurines and other luxury items such as amulets, seals, handles and pommels (found in graves in the Mesara and at Mochlos). Hippopotamus-tusk ivory was much used at this early stage, elephant tusk far less so; boar's tusk and antler also appear. By Middle Minoan (MM) I, decorative inlays were being produced at Gournia(Ayios Nikolaos, Archaeol. Mus.), thus establishing the third of the three main types of ivory work: figurines, personal ornaments and seals, and inlays. From MM I to MM IIIA the craft was thinly represented, although an ivory seal was found in the Sealmaker's House in Mallia's Quartier Mu (MM II-III), and inlays, bangles and statuettes found at the Chrysolakkos burial complex near Mallia and at Mallia itself show that the tripartite repertory was maintained. This eclipse may be an illusion, because the range and quality of pieces made from MM IIIB to Late Minoan (LM) IB reveal a craftsmanship that must have been founded on skills developed earlier. The considerable increase in the use of elephant ivory may have facilitated this advance. The luxury status of ivory was now even more evident: vessels, combs and other ornaments, statuettes (mostly human) and much inlay work (for gaming-boards) exhibit features that go beyond the purely ritual or functional, such as delicate carving, the use of paints, metal foils and stones to enhance appearance, and skilful

nature of the metal may partly account for this surface, but leaving it in that state was clearly deliberate. Lead figurines also survive, and there may have been others in precious metals. Certainly gold was sometimes combined with ivory in the most precious of all extant Minoan sculptures (*see* §VI below).

An impressive series of terracotta figurines has been found on the Cycladic island of KEA (Kea, Archaeol. Col.; *see* CYCLADIC, §I, 4(iii)). Their size and elaboration have led to their interpretation as goddesses and perhaps as cult statues, though it is possible that they are simply representations of worshippers. The figures are Cretan in style and dress but far larger than anything yet known from Crete, many of them originally standing 1.5 m high or more. They may therefore shed some light on the possible nature of large-scale Minoan statues in wood.

Fairly large (*c.* 500–800 mm high) terracotta figurines with wheelmade skirts were produced in Crete during the LM period, and these too have been identified as goddesses. Angular and somewhat ungainly, with upraised arms, they often wear diadems bearing a variety of motifs, such as birds and poppyheads (see fig. 19). The earliest may date from as early as the first half of the 15th century BC, but they continued to be made into Sub-Minoan times. The potter's wheel was also used to make the bodies of certain joinery with pegs, mortice-and-tenon joints and guide-marks. There were LM IB production centres at Knossos (House of the Ivories, Royal Road) and Kato Zakros (South Wing, Room xlviii).

The destructions throughout Crete at the end of LM IB seriously disrupted the craft, with uncertain effects in the long term. By LM IIIA a new iconographic approach had emerged, as can be seen in the heavy encrustation and inlaying of wooden furniture with such motifs as warrior heads and shields. In addition, new types of ivory object such as mirror-handles were being produced, but statu-ettes, pyxides and the sorts of decorative inlay previously made for gaming-boards probably ceased production. The more repetitive, sometimes heavier-handed spirit now evident suggests an external influence, possibly Mycenaean (*see* HELLADIC, §VI, 2), or even production outside the island. Following the collapse of the palace-based admin-istrations (*see* §I, 4(iii) above), the craft became impover-ished, largely confined to pins and small pieces of jewellery. The relatively ordinary items found at Praisos—bone comb and pommel, ivory rosette plaque and handles (LM IIIC or later)—thus acquire a disproportionate prominence. Pro-duction continued haltingly into the Early Iron Age.

Much is known about the manufacturing techniques of ivory, the House of the Ivories at Knossos proving especially fruitful. Ivory could be worked from its raw state to include the finest carved details with bronze tools, in particular saws, drills, chisels, points and blades. Abra-sives were used in the final stages of shaping and polishing, and paints and gilt were often applied to the finished article. Sections of carved ivory were assembled with great precision.

2. FIGURINES. The figurines produced during EM II–MM IA show two influences: a schematic form derived from the folded-arm figurines of the Cyclades (*see* CY-CLADIC, §IV, 1) and a naturalistic form first evident on seals based on animal shapes. By MM IB–II the formerly predominant schematic strand had fallen into disuse, but the naturalistic strand had evolved into composite human figures, of which the arm found at Chrysolakkos is a representative part. Production reached its zenith in MM III–LM IB, and about 20 such figures from this time have been recovered, mostly at Knossos, in the Ivory Deposit (MM III) and the House of the Ivories (LM IB). Inspired by athletic events, possibly of a ritual nature, these figures manifest close attention to detail, such as veins on hands. The figurines were often too large to be carved in one piece and had to be joined in sections. Metal was some-times added to depict locks of hair, though the chrysele-phantine series (e.g. Oxford, Ashmolean; Toronto, Royal Ont. Mus.) may not be authentic (*see* §XI below); however, the discovery in 1986–7, in an LM IB context at Palaikastro, of the ivory head, torso, forearms, legs and feet of a young man or god, with fragments of gold on and around the figure (Siteia, Archaeol. Mus.), may rehabilitate some of these, because it demonstrates that the Minoans did pro-duce chryselephantine artefacts. After LM IB production declined or even ceased. The range of ivory pieces in the round from MM IB onwards also included what are thought to have been gaming-pieces—a gold-covered lion's head and a bull's leg from Phaistos (MM IB–II) and cones from

Knossos (MM II–III)—and a duck- (or boat-) shaped pyxis from Zapher Papoura cemetery, Knossos (LM IIIA:1).

3. PERSONAL ORNAMENT AND SEALS. Exploiting the ease with which ivory can be carved, much of the output after MM IIIA was elaborate. Pyxides were either carved in low relief, as on a piece from Katsamba with a bull-hunting scene (?LM IB, but found in an LM IIIA context) and one from Archanes, featuring a lion's head (LM IIIA), or incised, as on a specimen from Ayia Triada depicting worship at a shrine (LM I). What seem to have been box lids, made of bone, could be plain (e.g. from Knossos; LM IIIB or before; Knossos, Stratig. Mus.) or incised (e.g.

20. Ivory low-relief plaque with a bird alighting in rocky terrain, h. 70 mm, from Palaikastro, LM IB (Herakleion, Archaeological Museum)

from Phaistos; LM IIIA). In LM IB combs were sometimes plain (one with a wavy back was found in the House of the Ivories at Knossos), but there were also more elaborate pieces with decoration in more than one register (e.g. from Palaikastro with low-relief crocodiles). This decorated type was still being produced in LM IIIB: examples from LM IIIA, both ribbed and with crocodile motifs, were discovered at Archanes. Other decorations included sphinxes and chevrons. A Mycenaean influence may be detected in these later pieces and in mirror-handles, dating mainly from LM IIIA, decorated with palms and rosettes that were partly incised (from Phaistos) or with animals or sphinxes in relief (from Archanes and Zapher Papoura respectively).

These sculpted pieces can be related to the elaborate relief plaques. Some, dating from LM I, are carved in a naturalistic style, for example a depiction of a griffin seizing the leg of a bull on a plaque from Knossos and others, from Palaikastro, on which are depicted a bird alighting (see fig. 20), lilies and sacred emblems. By LM IIIA iconography had changed, with stiffer, more heraldic compositions, but the carving is generally good. Again, a Mycenaean influence seems detectable, as in the relief plaque featuring a goat and a lion found at Archanes.

Ivory and bone provided a variety of handles for tools and weapons found in settlements and tombs of all periods. Ivory jewellery consisted of simple beads and bangles (roughly MM I–LM I) and a range of hairpins, both straight and crook-headed (similar to those in bronze and silver) or even terminating in carved figures, such as the LM IB hairpin from Nirou Chani. Ivory or bone seals and rings were made almost exclusively during EM–MM I, examples being found in the Mesara and at Mochlos and Archanes, and almost ceased production during MM II–III (rare examples were found at Knossos and Mallia). Seal shapes include cylinders, pyramids and animals (birds, lions, apes), with simpler forms such as rings and conoids also occurring in bone or boar's tusk: they are similar to their stone equivalents (see §VIII below).

4. INLAY. Small pieces of ivory were always much used as inlays, presumably for wooden furniture, to create a marquetry pattern of component parts, which might be plain or simply moulded or grooved. EM and MM squares and strips found at Gournia (Ayios Nikolaos, Archaeol. Mus.) may be early examples of inlays, but various shapes are recorded from MM I–II at Mallia, though the material used was sometimes bone or shell. The fullest, most elaborate range dates from MM III to LM I. The Royal Gaming-board from Knossos has inlaid bars and curved strips, plain plaques and plaques decorated with daisies and argonauts (MM IIIB). There were also plain items, many made from hippopotamus ivory, such as the squares, strips and D-plaques found in the House of the Ivories (LM IB; Knossos, Stratig. Mus.). By the middle of the 2nd millennium BC high-quality articles were made combining ivory with faience, rock crystal, silver or gold foils and blue paste. In LM III more elaborate compositions appeared in the Mycenaean style, including the so-called 'footstools' from Archanes with ivory-inlaid shields and warrior heads and the box lids from Zapher Papoura, inlaid with shields or lilies. To this category and period belong the chariot and (?)horse-harness enlivened with ivory details that is described in a Knossian Linear B tablet.

BIBLIOGRAPHY

R. C. Bosanquet: 'Excavations at Praesos, I', *Annu. Brit. Sch. Athens*, viii (1901–2), pp. 231–70
L. Savignoni: 'Scavi e scoperta nella necropoli di Phaestos', *Mnmt. Ant.: Lincei*, xiv (1904), pp. 501–667
A. J. Evans: 'The Prehistoric Tombs of Knossos', *Archaeologia* [Soc. Antiqua. London], n. s. 1, ix/2 (1906), pp. 391–562
——: *The Palace of Minos*, 4 vols and index (London, 1921–36, 2/1964)
R. C. Bosanquet and R. M. Dawkins: *The Unpublished Objects from the Palaikastro Excavations (1902–6)*, Brit. Sch. Athens, Suppl. Paper, i (London, 1923)
S. Xanthoudídes: *The Vaulted Tombs of Mesará* (London, 1924)
P. Demargne: 'Fouilles exécutées à Mallia: Exploration des nécropoles (1921–33): Objets d'os et d'ivoire', *Etud. Crét.*, vii (1945), pp. 57–9
M. S. F. Hood and P. de Jong: 'Late Minoan Warrior Graves from Agios Ioannis and the New Hospital Site at Knossos', *Annu. Brit. Sch. Athens*, xlvii (1952), pp. 243–77
D. Levi: 'La campagna di scavi a Festos nel 1953', *Annu. Scu. Archeol. Atene & Miss. It. Oriente*, xxx–xxxii (1952–4), pp. 389–469
P. Demargne and H. G. de Santerre: 'Fouilles exécutées à Mallia: Exploration des maisons et quartiers d'habitation (1921–48), i: divers', *Etud. Crét.*, ix (1953), pp. 18–21
J. Chadwick, ed.: *Documents in Mycenaean Greek* (Cambridge, 1956, rev. 1973), pp. 365–6
C. Zervos: *L'Art de la Crète néolithique et minoenne* (Paris, 1956)
M. R. Popham and others: 'Excavations at Palaikastro, VI', *Annu. Brit. Sch. Athens*, lx (1965), pp. 248–315
S. Alexiou: *Husterominoikoi taphoi limenos Knosou (Katsamba)* [Late Minoan tombs from the harbour of Knossos (Katsamba)] (Athens, 1967)
I. A. Sakellarakis: 'Elaphantosta ek ton Arkhanon' [Ivories from Archanes], *Atti e memorie del I. congresso internazionale di Micenologia: Rome, 27 Sept–3 Oct 1967*, i, pp. 245–61 [incl. It. summary, pp. 257–61]
——: 'Minoan Cemeteries at Archanes', *Archaeology*, xx/4 (1967), pp. 276–81
N. Platon: *Iraklion: Die Siegel der Vorpalastzeit* (Berlin, 1969)
O. Pelon: 'Fouilles exécutées à Mallia: Exploration des maisons et quartiers d'habitation (1963–66), iii, *Etud. Crét.*, xvi (1970), pp. 67–8
K. Branigan: 'Cycladic Figurines and their Derivatives in Crete', *Annu. Brit. Sch. Athens*, lxvi (1971), pp. 57–78
I. A. Sakellarakis: 'Anaskaphe Archanon hupo Ioannou A. Sakellarakou' [Excavations at Archanes by Ioannis A. Sakellarakis], *Praktika Athen. Archaiol. Etaireias* (1972), pp. 310–53
K. Davaras: 'Gournia', *Archaiol. Deltion*, xxviii/2b (1973), pp. 588–9
J. P. Michaud: 'Chronique des fouilles en 1972', *Bull. Corr. Hell.*, xcvii (1973), pp. 253–412
B. Detournay: 'Petits objets', *Etud. Crét.*, xx (1975)
A. Dessenne: 'Mallia Steinschneidewerkstätten', *Iraklion Archäologisches Museum, 2: Die Siegel der Altpalastzeit*, ed. N. Platon, I. Pini and G. Salies (Berlin, 1977), pp. 109–270
F. Halbherr, E. Stefani and L. Banti: 'Hagia Triada nel periodo Tardo Palaziale', *Annu. Scu. Archeol. Atene & Miss. It. Oriente*, xxxix (1977)
S. Hood: *The Arts in Prehistoric Greece*, Pelican Hist. A. (Harmondsworth, 1978)
O. H. Krzyszkowska: 'Wealth and Prosperity in Pre-palatial Crete', *Minoan Society: Proceedings of the Cambridge Colloquium: Cambridge, 1981*, pp. 163–70
D. Evely: 'The Other Finds of Stone, Clay, Ivory, Faience, Lead etc.', *The Minoan Unexplored Mansion at Knossos*, ed. M. R. Popham, Brit. Sch. Athens, Suppl. Paper 17 (Oxford, 1984), pp. 223–59
O. H. Krzyszkowska: 'Ivory in the Aegean Bronze Age: Elephant Tusk or Hippopotamus Ivory?', *Annu. Brit. Sch. Athens*, lxxxiii (1988), pp. 209–34
——: 'Early Cretan Seals: New Evidence for the Use of Bone, Ivory and Boar's Tusk', *Corpus der minoischen und mykenischen Siegel*, iii (Berlin, 1989), pp. 111–26

VII. Faience.

Few forms of Minoan faience are unique to the material, as comparison with objects made from stone, ivory and bone indicate: the Minoans, despite developing their own skills in modelling and polychromy, did not create a repertory stemming solely from faience's physical properties. That is not to say that they regarded it merely as a cheaper substitute for some other material, however: the emphasis was always on luxury and ritual products for palatial use. Unless otherwise noted, all objects are in Herakleion, Archaeological Museum.

1. INTRODUCTION. The basic techniques of faience production were probably introduced to Crete from Mesopotamia (and possibly Egypt) by Early Minoan (EM) II. Early examples were simple in form and execution: beads and a bowl have been found in funerary contexts in the Mesara and Mochlos. From EM III to Middle Minoan (MM) II there was a modest expansion in production: seals were moulded and carved, imitating those made of stone (*see* §VIII below). Pieces were manufactured as individual works, such as a vase and the arm of a statuette from Knossos, and inlays, destined as parts of composite items such as furniture. An interest developed in combining faience with other materials as a luxury craft, and it became part of the common artistic expression that developed in the palaces. All later products may be traced back to this time.

From MM III to Late Minoan (LM) I output was considerable, with a varied repertory remarkable for its technical and aesthetic qualities. Polychromy was achieved by ensuring the presence of various metals and elements (mainly copper, iron, manganese and calcium) in the silicate base. Natural subjects were accurately portrayed. The Temple Repositories at Knossos yielded many representative examples, including vessels, human figurines, moulded plaques and components of complex inlaid work (MM IIIB). During this period faience products were distributed throughout the island, reaching Tylissos, Phaistos, Ayia Triada and Pyrgos, and a production centre was established in the palace at Kato Zakros. During the brief Mycenaean presence at Knossos (LM II–IIIA:1) there was a dramatic decline in the quantity and range of most types of object as glass began to replace the faience. This trend was maintained throughout LM IIIA:2–IIC, when little beyond beads, pendants and seals was produced. It is as if the LM IB destructions throughout Crete halted the craft's development; its failure to recover may have derived from social or economic factors.

Little of the craft's techniques is known: work areas are limited to the South Wing of the palace at Kato Zakros and, presumably, in the Knossos area. But what may be stone and clay moulds are reported from the Knossos region (three at least), Palaikastro, Choumeriakos and Gournia (clay). Modern investigation has concentrated on compositional analysis and on definition of the material (*see also* FAIENCE (i)).

2. FIGURINES. Whether depicting deities or worshippers, faience figurines are relatively independent of comparable items in other substances: their closest match is in the ivory pieces (*see* §VI, 2 above). The three so-called snake-goddesses from the Temple Repositories at Knossos, among the best-known images of Minoan sculpture, demonstrate the skilled modelling, the range of available polychromy and the delicacy of detail characteristic of this

21. Faience figurine of a snake-goddess, deity or worshipper, h. 295 mm, from the Temple Repositories, Knossos, MM IIIB (Herakleion, Archaeological Museum)

group. The two best-preserved examples hold snakes and wear unusual headgear: one a crown surmounted by an animal, perhaps a leopard (see fig. 21), the other a tall hat entwined with a snake. Their traditional flounced skirts and open bodices are painted in bright colours, contrasting with their white flesh.

The same naturalism is displayed in animal-head rhyta, such as the LM IB bull's and cat's heads and the marine shells, such as the LM IB argonaut, all from Kato Zakros, and the LM I triton from Pyrgos. No less accurate are the renditions of other vessel shapes, adapted from their stone, ceramic and metal counterparts. These include the MM IIIB blossom bowl and ewer from Knossos and the baskets, chalices, flask, bowl and ewer from the Temple Repositories at the same site. The cup, bowl and offering table from Kato Zakros (LM IB) and the peculiar 'sheep bells' from the Knossos harbour of Poros (MM–LM) are of commensurate quality.

3. PERSONAL ORNAMENT AND SEALS. Jewellery was the faience group kept longest in production and the most widely dispersed among the population. Beads were very common, often recalling their stone and even their metal

counterparts. Those of EM–MM IA were relatively simple variants on cylinders and spheres, in rare cases ribbed; blue predominated, but green, yellow, red, white and grey–black are known. During MM IB–IIIA more elaborate forms were made, with fluted patterns and subdued polychromy (from Mochlos, from the Mesara tholoi and from the Vat Room and the Mavrospilio tombs at Knossos). Numbers increased during MM III–LM I, and lentoids were among the few additions to the range of shapes (e.g. from the Temple Repositories and the Temple Tomb at Knossos and from Sphoungaras and Pyrgos). Thereafter, glass began to be used as well, and the range of colours and shapes gradually diminished. Pendants (effectively miniature figurative pieces strung as beads) were rarer but existed at all periods: an example featuring a lily and papyrus was found in the Temple Repositories (MM IIIB), and others with figure-of-eight shields came from tombs in the Knossos area (LM IIIB). Seals were limited almost exclusively to EM–MM III, corresponding closely in their types and motifs to the more numerous ivory and stone equivalents.

4. INLAY. Inlay plaques (destined for furniture or luxury items) constitute the third group for which faience was much exploited. The most elaborate portray sensitively modelled naturalistic scenes (such as a cow and calf and a goat and kids from the Temple Repositories; MM IIIB) or highly complex representations of town (and siege?) life (such as the Town Mosaic at Knossos; MM II–III; see §II, 4 above). Both these elaborate forms find echoes in fresco work, especially at THERA (Late Cycladic I, corresponding to LM IA in Crete; see also CYCLADIC, §VI, 1), and in contemporary seal iconography. During MM III–LM I most tend to divide into naturalistic forms and geometric shapes. The first encompass floral (lily, fruit, buds) and marine (shells of many sorts, fish, rocks and seaweed) subjects that are well represented in ivory, metal and stone and that have provided the names for the two main ceramic styles of LM I (see §§III, 5 (i) and VI, 4 above, and §X, 3 below). In the geometric class (e.g. rectangles, triangles, crescents), the Minoan interest in combining materials found expression. From Knossos three gaming-boards and a chest have been identified, together with less obvious pieces (MM III–LM I) of faience, ivory or bone and rock crystal, decorated with gold and silver foil, and a blue paste (possibly the 'kyanos' mentioned in Linear B tablets). Comparable work has been found at Tylissos, Phaistos and Ayia Triada. As inlays, the pieces may bear guidemarks scratched on the reverse.

BIBLIOGRAPHY

A. J. Evans: 'The Prehistoric Tombs of Knossos', *Archaeologia* [London Soc. Antiqua.], lix (1905), pp. 449, 461–2, fig. 81b
H. B. Hawes: *Gournia, Vasiliki and Other Prehistoric Sites on the Isthmus of Hierapetra* (Philadelphia, 1908), p. 35, figs 13–14
E. H. Hall: *Sphoungaras* (Philadelphia, 1912), p. 12
R. B. Seager: *Explorations in the Island of Mochlos* (Boston, 1912)
A. J. Evans: *The Palace of Minos*, 4 vols and index (London, 1921–36, 2/1964)
J. Hazzidakis: *Tylissos* (Paris, 1921), fig. 33
R. D. Bosanquet and R. M. Dawkins: *The Unpublished Objects from the Palaikastro Excavations (1902–06)*, Brit. Sch. Athens, Suppl. Paper, i (London, 1923), p. 150, fig. 134
S. Xanthoudídes: *The Vaulted Tombs of Mesará* (London, 1924)
J. D. S. Pendlebury: *Archaeology of Crete* (London, 1939/R New York, 1963), p. 140
S. Hood, G. Huxley and N. Sandars: 'A Minoan Cemetery on Upper Gypsades', *Annu. Brit. Sch. Athens*, liii–liv (1958–9), pp. 194–262
I. A. Sakellarakis: 'Minoan Cemeteries at Archanes', *Archaeology* [New York], xx/4 (1967), pp. 276–81
I. A. Sakellarakis and V. E. G. Kenna: *Iraklion Sammlung Metaxas* (1969), iv of *Corpus der minoischen und mykenischen Siegel* (Berlin, 1969)
N. Platon: *Zakros* (New York, 1971), p. 142
I. A. Sakellarakis: 'A Mycenaean Grave Circle at Crete', *Athens An. Archaeol.*, v (1972), pp. 399–419
H. Hughes-Brock: 'The Beads, Loomweights, etc.', *Knossos: The Sanctuary of Demeter*, ed. N. Coldstream (Oxford, 1973), pp. 114–23, fig. 26
M. R. Popham: 'Sellopoulo Tombs 3 and 4: Two Late Minoan Graves near Knossos', *Annu. Brit. Sch. Athens*, lxix (1974), pls 33–41, pp. 195–257
G. Cadogan: 'Pyrgos, Crete 1970–77', *Archaeol. Rep.: Council Soc. Promotion Hell. Stud. & Managing Ctte Brit. Sch. Archaeol. Athens*, xxiv (1977–8), pp. 70–84, fig. 26
S. Hood: *The Arts in Prehistoric Greece*, Pelican Hist. A. (Harmondsworth, 1978)
K. P. Foster: *Aegean Faience of the Bronze Age* (New Haven, 1979) [fullest and best-illustrated account]
A. Kacmarczyk and K. P. Foster: 'X-ray Fluorescence Analyses of Some Minoan Faience', *Archaeometry*, xxiv/2 (1982), pp. 143–57
A. Kacmarczyk and R. E. M. Hedges: *Ancient Egyptian Faience* (Warminster, 1983)
M. S. Tite: 'Characterisation of Early Vitreous Materials', *Archaeometry*, xxix/1 (1987), pp. 21–34

D. EVELY

VIII. Seals.

Crete's long and continuous tradition of glyptic art is assumed to have had its beginnings in Early Minoan (EM) I under the stimulus of contemporary Anatolian and Egyptian cultures (see ANCIENT NEAR EAST, §II, 1(ii); EGYPT, ANCIENT, §XVI, 15). The few seals datable to this period are close in style to the more rudimentary forms of EM II. Designs on EM II stamp seals are simple: random linear scratches, hatching, angle-filled crosses and S-scrolls. Carved from bone, ivory and soft stone, early shapes range from simple conical to more complex forms, such as pear-shaped seals with double animal-head handles, or they are ring-shaped with bezels. In the period of development that followed, while a few parallels can be found with the richer repertory of Early Helladic (EH) II seals (see HELLADIC, §X), some basic compositional differences are noticeable. Minoan glyptic art evolved its own characteristics independently. As well as symmetrical and static designs, some compositions show a sense of rotation within the confines of the seal face, while others ignore the perimeter and allow all-over patterns notionally to overflow into the surrounding space.

By the end of EM III and the beginning of Middle Minoan (MM) I, there were several centres of seal-carving. A distinctive group of bone or ivory seals, mainly conoids or cylinders engraved at both ends, is associated with the Mesara area of southern Crete, though examples are known from other parts of the island. On the principal face stylized lions with hatched manes pad in an endless procession round the edge, while the secondary face often carries an abstract pattern such as linked scrolls. Another related group is characterized by complex theriomorphic forms (crouching lion, seated monkey, dove sheltering young) with simple crosshatching or meander patterns on the bases. A further group, which made use of soft stone as well as ivory, comprises seals of simple form (disc, cylinder, dome and animal shape) with designs such as leaves, rosettes and animals disposed within a border line.

The occasional occurrence of hieroglyphs may be due to influence from a school of seal-carving in north-central Crete that was totally different in character. This school produced crudely cut, three-sided stone prisms, with motifs including men, goats and other quadrupeds, animal heads, birds, fish, scorpions, insects, vases, ships, ornamental designs, and on later examples recognizable hieroglyphs. Broken and unfinished seals of this group were excavated together with lapidaries' tools from a workshop at Mallia.

Early seals, whether of ivory or soft stone such as steatite and serpentine, were carved by means of a hand graver with copper blade or obsidian point, or by a slow hand-held drill. A revolution in technique came in MM II with the introduction of fast-turning rotary tools: the fixed bow-powered lathe with solid and tubular drills and cutting wheels. This allowed harder stones such as quartz, jasper, chalcedony, agate and carnelian to be cut and new styles of engraving and seal shapes to emerge. Typical of this period are prisms with three or more elliptical or rectangular faces, various animal types, the disc seal with convex faces, the 'flattened cylinder' (rectangular, with curved faces) and the stemmed signet, which apparently derived from a metal prototype; contemporary sealings suggest that metal seals were in use at this period. Many of the prism seals are exquisitely engraved with hieroglyphic signs often combined with ornamental devices reminiscent of the patterns painted on Kamares-style pottery (see §III, 4(ii) above). On other seals, single motifs resembling hieroglyphs appear rather as decorative elements, though perhaps with a talismanic function.

From the First Palace at Phaistos (MM IB–II) comes an important deposit of clay sealings bearing impressions of seals in use at the end of MM II, including heirlooms such as an ivory seal of the lion procession group, as well as more recent types. The majority appear to have been soft stone or wooden seals with round faces engraved predominantly with ornamental motifs but also with animal figures. The latest sealings include impressions of metal rings with oval bezels and more naturalistic representations and impressions of hardstone seals—discs, perhaps of rock crystal, with architectonic devices and stemmed signets with motifs in the hieroglyphic style. The impression of a seated owl on one of the sealings may have come from a seal engraved by the same craftsman as produced a signet in the Ashmolean Museum (see fig. 22). Apart from a single nodule with impressions of two simple characters from one face of a three-sided prism, the Phaistos sealings include no examples with hieroglyphic inscriptions.

In contrast, further north at Knossos, sealings from the Hieroglyphic Deposit (Herakleion, Archaeol. Mus.), dating from roughly the same period, are dominated by impressions from hardstone prisms engraved with hieroglyphic signs. However, as at Phaistos, stemmed signets with hieroglyphic-style motifs are also represented, as well as more naturalistic scenes such as a rocky seascape with a clearly identifiable dolphin fish (*Coryphaena hippurus*) attacking a cephalopod (Herakleion, Archaeol. Mus.). Three designs of human heads in profile, stylized but with such individual features as to suggest somewhat unsuccessful attempts at portraiture, are also remarkable (Athens, N. Archaeol. Mus. and Herakleion, Archaeol. Mus.).

22. Green jasper signet with owl, preserved h. 9 mm, diam. 11 mm, MM II (Oxford, Ashmolean Museum)

Sealings from the MM IIIB–LM IA Temple Repositories at Knossos also include types represented earlier at Phaistos. In some compositions simple figurative motifs, instead of occurring singly, are grouped formally to produce a pattern perfectly suited to the circular face of the seal—four cockle shells around a central point, for example, or two whorl shells arranged head-to-tail. Other designs display a greater naturalism both in the delicacy of the modelling and in the composition: of these the most delightful fragment depicts a suckling fawn. Human figures are also portrayed in violent action: an acrobat somersaults over the back of a bull, a pugilist strides menacingly with muscles tensed, and divine personages pace beside attendant lions.

By the end of the Middle Minoan period, while engraved motifs showed increasing diversity in subject and technique, seal shapes became more limited, dictated perhaps by the use of the bow lathe. The majority of stone seals were lentoids (a form evolved from the old discoid), amygdaloids (a new form) and the occasional 'flattened cylinder', all biconvex forms on which the rotating drill and cutting wheel could be used to most effect. These, along with the oval-bezelled gold signet ring, continued to be the main shapes of Late Minoan (LM) seals. Some engravers had used the basic cuts of their tools unsoftened to produce the patterns characteristic of the Phaistos sealings, the architectonic designs and stylized animal

23. Gold ring with female ?worshippers, from Isopata royal tomb, 16×22.5 mm, LM IB–II (Herakleion, Archaeological Museum)

motifs; others had experimented further with secondary engraving to produce subtler modelling for the more naturalistic representations. Both techniques found their exponents at the beginning of the Late Bronze Age. The so-called 'Talismanic' group, which originated in MM III but seems in certain respects descendent from the early three-sided prisms, is characterized by the economic but effective technique of applying only the basic cuts of drills and wheel with little or no further working. Its repertory is dominated by a limited range of stylized motifs, including some that do not appear in other contemporary groups: vases of various shapes combined with vegetation, marine creatures (fish, cephalopods, crabs), animals, birds, bucrania, papyrus plants, ships, double axes, enigmatic heart shapes and 'bundles', rosettes and panelled ornamentation. Another group related in style is characterized by schematic animal motifs rendered with strong linear cuts.

Working in the east of the island and inspired by the same local traditions as produced the 'Talismanic' group was the Zakros Master, whose bold, deeply modelled compositions transform old subjects into new fantasies. Among his favourite themes are bird-women, minotaurs and other monsters, and animal masks. At other centres, engravers, influenced by the ideas of fresco painters, were producing cult scenes and animal and bird studies in a fluid, naturalistic style, exploring the modelling not only of anatomical details but of subjects in motion and contortion. Contemporary with the fine art of the palace craftsmen working in hardstone or on gold rings (see fig. 23) there was also a 'Popular' group with moderately naturalistic animals and human figures on lentoids of humble serpentine.

While Minoan glyptic art strongly influenced that of the mainland at the beginning of the Late Bronze Age, the trend was reversed from LM II, with Mycenaean political domination of the island. Fine seals were still produced for a while, including typical Minoan subjects such as studies of waterfowl, but gradually naturalism gave way to more conventional styles, and iconography became more restricted. The finest Minoan and Mycenaean glyptic art was associated with palace bureaucracy, and although

when worn on the wrist or as pendants seals might double as jewellery or amulets, their prime function was for official identification and security. With the destruction in LM IIIA of the palace at Knossos and the collapse of the central bureaucracy on Crete, the manufacture of seals rapidly declined.

BIBLIOGRAPHY

N. Platon: *Die Siegel der Vorpalastzeit* (1969), i of *Iraklion Archäologisches Museum*, Corpus der minoischen und mykenischen Siegel, ii (Berlin, 1964–)

J. Boardman: *Greek Gems and Finger Rings* (London, 1970)

I. Pini: *Die Siegelabdrücke von Phästos* (1970), v of *Iraklion Archäologisches Museum*, Corpus der minoischen und mykenischen Siegel, ii (Berlin, 1964–)

N. Platon, I. Pini and G. Salies: *Die Siegel der Altpalastzeit* (1977), ii of *Iraklion Archäologisches Museum*, Corpus der minoischen und mykenischen Siegel, ii (Berlin, 1964–)

S. Hood: *The Arts in Prehistoric Greece*, Pelican Hist. A. (Harmondsworth, 1978), pp. 209–32

P. Yule: *Early Cretan Seals: A Study of Chronology*, Marburger Studien zur Vor- und Frügeschichte, iv (Mainz, 1980)

N. Platon and I. Pini: *Die Siegel der Nachpalastzeit* (1984), iii of *Iraklion Archäologisches Museum*, Corpus der minoischen und mykenischen Siegel, ii (Berlin, 1964–)

——: *Die Siegel der Nachpalastzeit* (1985), iv of *Iraklion Archäologisches Museum*, Corpus der minoischen und mykenischen Siegel, ii (Berlin, 1964–)

The Erlenmeyer Collection of Cretan Seals, text J. Betts (sale cat., London, Christie's, 5 June 1989)

J. G. Younger: *A Bibliography for Aegean Glyptic in the Bronze Age*, Corpus der minoischen und mykenischen Siegel, suppl. iv (Berlin, 1991)

MARGARET A. V. GILL

IX. Metalwork.

1. GOLD AND SILVER. Gold and silver were first used in Crete soon after the beginning of the Early Minoan (EM) period. Gold was always more common than silver, and considerable quantities of gold jewellery have been found in EM tombs at Mochlos and in the Mesara. The few surviving EM precious-metal vessels and weapons were made of silver, though in later periods Minoan craftsmen used both gold and silver for such items. Unless otherwise noted, all objects are in Herakleion, Archaeological Museum.

(i) Jewellery.

(a) Early Minoan. The basic materials used for EM jewellery (besides beads made of hardstones) were sheet-gold, gold foil and gold wire, from which craftsmen fashioned diadems, headbands and hairpins, beads, pendants and ornamental chains, armlets, bracelets and finger-rings, and decorative clothing ornaments. Items of silver jewellery were, by contrast, much rarer (e.g. a pendant from a burial cave near Amnisos, north of Knossos, ?EM III). Diadems were made from sheet-gold beaten and cut to shape, then decorated, mostly with geometric patterns, in dot repoussé (pointillé). Occasionally the designs include human or animal motifs, as on a diadem with a pair of eyes or another with two pairs of dogs (both EM II). A third example (also EM II), with scenes of wild goats, had upright 'antennae' of sheet-gold attached to its upper edge.

Separately made hairpins, of sheet-gold and wire, were sometimes attached to the edges of diadems. These took the form of flowers and leaves (e.g. from Mochlos), as did pendants, which were suspended from delicate loop-in-loop gold chains. Some pendants and beads incorporated gold with other materials, such as bronze and rock crystal. Bracelets were made of gold foil covering some other, perishable material (e.g. wood or leather) and were decorated with embossed patterns. Clothing ornaments, also of sheet-gold, were made in the form of stars, strips, discs and bosses; they had small holes at their edges by which they were sewn on to clothing.

(b) Middle Minoan. Little Middle Minoan (MM) jewellery survives, probably because few tombs of the period escaped wholesale looting. The early part of the period is represented chiefly by a few pieces from the much-robbed collective burials of the Mesara Plain. For the later part, the mortuary complex at Mallia known as Chrysolakkos ('gold hole'), which was also severely looted, has yielded a few outstanding pieces, but the bulk of the surviving material comes from the so-called Aigina Treasure (MM III; London, BM). Although these items may well have been made on Aigina, where they were found, they are probably the work of Cretan craftsmen.

Silver was still scarce or unfashionable, but during the MM period the quality of Cretan goldwork improved considerably, especially with the development of new techniques, including filigree, granulation, repoussé and cloisonné inlay. The earliest known use of filigree, in which the surface is decorated with designs of fine gold wire, is found on small gold beads (MM I) adorned with decorative spirals from tombs in the Mesara. Granulation, a more advanced technique that involved the careful manufacture, sorting and soldering of hundreds of tiny grains of gold on to an object's surface, was used on beads shaped like animals, such as a frog or crouching lion (both from Koumasa in the Mesara, MM I).

Arguably the finest extant piece of MM jewellery is the well-known gold pendant from Mallia (MM II; see fig. 24), which combines, with great virtuosity, several new MM goldworking techniques. Two bees or wasps are posed heraldically over the granulated centre of what is thought to be a honeycomb or flower (?daisy). Discs, which were formerly inlaid, hang from the centre where the bees' abdomens meet and from the embossed outline of each of two wings, and the whole is topped by a tiny filigree sphere with a loose gold bead inside and by a loop from which the pendant was suspended. Another pendant of slightly later date but of simpler workmanship is part of the Aigina Treasure and depicts a Minoan nature-god standing in a field of lotuses (MM III; London, BM). In each hand he holds a water-bird, both of which rest on what seem to be composite bows. From the base-line and the bows hang five discs, similar to those attached to the bee pendant. Although the influence of Egyptian art is strong, this is a genuine Minoan creation.

A handsome hairpin in the form of a flower-head, a development of the EM prototypes from Mochlos, was also found at Mallia (MM II). Other articles of MM jewellery include hoop-shaped earrings and finger-rings with circular or oval bezels.

(c) Late Minoan. There was no break in the development of jewellery between the MM and Late Minoan (LM)

periods. Evidence for LM I jewellery is scarce but shows that technical standards were maintained. The Temple Tomb at Knossos has yielded a fine set of beads in gold and hardstones, notable among which is a naturalistically rendered pendant in the form of a reclining calf. Tomb 5 at Ayia Triada is the source of two exquisite sets of beads, one representing bulls' heads, the other crouching lions (LM I). Hoop earrings continued to be made, some of which were combined with a granulated cone-shaped pendant, a new form known as the mulberry earring. Also appearing for the first time in LM I were mass-produced relief-beads, which characterized the subsequent phase of jewellery production during the Mycenaean occupation and its aftermath (LM II–IIIB). Although Cretan in origin, these beads became so much a part of the mainland repertory that they, like enamelled rings, are generally considered Mycenaean (*see* HELLADIC, §VIII, 2). Not as common in the Mycenaean world were the gold signet rings made in Minoan palace workshops and eventually buried with their royal owners. Also popular in Crete during this phase was an enlarged version of the mulberry earring, up to *c.* 35 mm long.

During LM IIIC there was something of a revival in jewellery-making on Crete. New decorative motifs, based on undulating lines of filigree and granulation, occurred on works made in the eastern part of the island, especially ring-bezels, but the new style terminated *c.* 1150/1050 BC with the demise of the Minoan-Mycenaean world.

BIBLIOGRAPHY
R. Higgins: *Greek and Roman Jewellery* (London, 1960, rev. 2/1980), pp. 53–85
S. Hood: *The Arts of Prehistoric Greece*, Pelican Hist. A. (Harmondsworth, 1978), pp. 187–207
O. Sargnon: *Les Bijoux préhelléniques* (Paris, 1987)

KEITH BRANIGAN, REYNOLD HIGGINS

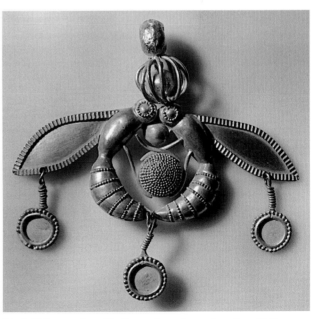

24. Gold bee pendant, 51×47 mm, from the royal tomb at Mallia, MM II (Herakleion, Archaeological Museum)

25. Gold cup with scene of bull-hunting, h. 79 mm, from Vapheio, MM IIIB–LM IB (Athens, National Archaeological Museum)

(ii) Vessels and weapons. While silver was rarely used for jewellery during the EM period, it was employed for at least two cups and two daggers, all clearly intended to bring prestige to their owners. A few silver drinking cups also survive from the MM period, for example a kantharos with fluted rim, found at Gournia (see fig. 4 above). By LM times Cretan craftsmen were producing fine gold and silver vessels, and the two gold cups with scenes of bull-hunting from Vapheio in mainland Greece (MM IIIB–LM IB; Athens, N. Archaeol. Mus.; see fig. 25) were probably made either on Crete or by expatriate Cretan craftsmen.

Fine gold repoussé and openwork were used from MM times to decorate the hilts and pommels of ceremonial swords and daggers. This practice continued in LM, when gold-leaf was also used to embellish stone vases.

BIBLIOGRAPHY

S. Hood: *The Arts of Prehistoric Greece*, Pelican Hist. A. (Harmondsworth, 1978), pp. 153–70, 173–86

P. Betancourt, ed.: *Gold in the Aegean Bronze Age: Proceedings of the Temple University Aegean Symposium, 8: Philadelphia, 1983*

2. BRONZE. Minoan bronzeworking evolved in three stages. The earliest metal objects from Crete date from EM times and were of copper rather than bronze. Initially, some of the copper was probably extracted locally, but later the island increasingly depended on imported copper from the Cyclades and Attica (*see* CYCLADIC, §VII, 2, and HELLADIC, §VII, 2). It may have been from the Cyclades that the Minoan workshops learnt how to make the arsenical bronze that many produced during EM II. This was, of course, a dangerous alloy to make and use because of the arsenical fumes given off during smelting, so, as access was opened up to tin supplies, probably from the Near East, the Cretans adopted tin bronze for tools and weapons. Copper or very low-tin bronze remained in use for jewellery, toilet implements and other delicate or ornamental items.

Most EM bronzework was devoted to the manufacture of weapons. Short, leaf-shaped daggers and long, narrow ones were the commonest items, though these were perhaps all-purpose knives rather than weapons. Carpenters' tools included various chisels, saws and awls, as well as the first axe-adzes and double axes. Toilet implements such as razors, tweezers and cosmetic scrapers also occur. Only a few other items of copper or arsenical bronze were made at this time; they include bangles, rings, pins and fish-hooks.

In MM times bronzesmiths developed their skills to produce impressive weapons, notably long-swords and spearheads. The swords, up to *c.* 800 mm long, cannot have been used in combat since they are very weakly hafted. They were, however, given gold-embellished hilts and elaborate pommels and presumably served a ceremonial function. New techniques include lost-wax casting and even an early form of 'Sheffield plating' used to silver plate the bronze heads of the rivets in some newly introduced broad, flat daggers.

Abundant supplies of copper and tin were clearly available in LM times, judging by both the quantity of material that survives and the ambitious way in which it was used. Massive cauldrons and huge two-man saws such as those from Tylissos point to a greatly increased scale of production, as does the stack of 'oxhide-type' copper ingots found at Ayia Triada. Numerous weapons, tools and bronze vessels (see fig. 26) occur in LM tombs and settlements and as many as three houses in the small town of Gournia provide evidence of bronzeworking. There must have been hundreds of bronzesmiths in Late Bronze Age Crete, though probably few were specialist craftsmen.

For bronze sculpture *see* §V and fig. 18 above.

BIBLIOGRAPHY

K. Branigan: *Aegean Metalwork of the Early and Middle Bronze Age* (Oxford, 1974)

H. Matthäus: *Die Bronzegefässe der kretisch-mykenischen Kultur* (Munich, 1980)

KEITH BRANIGAN

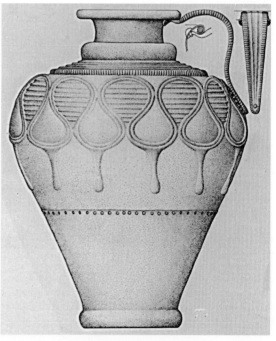

26. Bronze ewer, h. 345 mm, from the North-west Treasury at Knossos, LM I (Herakleion, Archaeological Museum)

X. Stone vases.

The manufacture of stone vessels in Crete began during Early Minoan (EM) II, at a time when other crafts such as seal-carving and metalwork underwent their first substantial development (*see* §§VIII and IX above). These beginnings, joining the long-established pottery industry, mark the onset of specialization of labour, which contributed to the increasingly complex economic and social organization of Cretan villages. The growth of the craft industries was given further impetus in Middle Minoan (MM) IB by the building of the first palaces. Stone vase-making pursued an increasingly brilliant course until the major destruction of the Minoan civilization in Late Minoan (LM) IB.

1. EARLY MINOAN. The first vessels, similar to those being produced in the Cyclades (*see* CYCLADIC, §V), were bowls and pyxides in chlorite or steatite, hollowed out with small chisels and usually featuring on the outside incised decoration or relief spirals related to the applied-wire decoration on metal jewellery. These softish green stones were perhaps first chosen because of their similarity in colour to copper-bearing rocks. During EM II a wider range of Cretan rocks was being selected, including banded marbles and limestones, polychrome breccias, calcites, wavy-veined tufa and mottled serpentines. In addition, two new manufacturing techniques were being used: the extraction of the interior of the vase with drills made from hollow reeds, and the undercutting of the shoulder inside with small transverse bits of different sizes, mounted on a cylindrical piece of wood or bone or perhaps on the reed. Extracted cylindrical cores are found as waste material on many Minoan settlement sites. The range of shapes expanded, and external decoration came to include small inlays of red or white material.

Most EM stone vessels come from tombs (e.g. on Mochlos and in the Mesara), indicating that, as in ancient Egypt, their function was largely funerary. The tombs were in use for families or clans over hundreds of years, so many stone vessels cannot be closely placed within the period EM II–MM II. But there is enough evidence to show that most of the rocks and the most complex shapes, such as the 'teapot', were already in use during EM II.

2. MIDDLE MINOAN I AND II. Alongside the use of many small shapes for tomb offerings a new development occurred at the beginning of the MM period, prompted by increased urbanization and, soon afterwards, by the establishment of the first palaces. This was the manufacture for household use of larger vases, chiefly various forms of bowl, in blue–black mottled serpentine, a Cretan rock employed for about half of all known Minoan stone vases. The increased size of vessels required more advanced techniques of hollowing out the interior. Quite regular horizontal striations around interior walls of vessels show that large, transversely mounted bits, probably of obsidian or quartz, were employed in MM II. By this time, too, hard and beautiful stones had begun to be imported: *rosso antico*, the deep pink, fine-grained marble from southern Mani in the Peloponnese, and white-spotted black obsidian from Gyali in the Dodecanese.

27. Stone vase in the shape of a dolium shell, white-spotted black obsidian, h. 285 mm, from Ayia Triada, LM IB (Herakleion, Archaeological Museum)

3. MIDDLE MINOAN III AND LATE MINOAN. The highest attainments of the vase lapidaries came during MM III and LM I, evidenced by the variety and sizes of the shapes produced, the technical skills mastered and the range of attractive and hard rocks used. As well as bowls and bucket-shaped jars, shapes included amphorae, chalices, large ewers and other jugs, jars with bridge-spouts, lamps, offering tables, rhytons (for pouring ritual libations) in conical, inverted-pear, bull's- and lion's-head forms, and shell imitations (see fig. 27). The height of the largest vessels is over 500 mm. A major technical advance was provided by the lathe, its use proved by two unfinished jars from the palace at Mallia (Herakleion, Archaeol. Mus.) and from Akrotiri on the Cycladic island of Thera. A hollow cylinder, probably of copper or bronze, would have been fitted to project from another cylinder, solid, heavy and probably wooden. The cutting would have been achieved by the combination of the lathe's weight, abrasive powder (emery from Naxos in the Cyclades or sand) and water as the lathe was rotated down on to the vessel. The diameter of the circular cutting on the Akrotiri jar is *c*. 300 mm.

Much technical skill was also shown in surface decoration, which included precisely parallel horizontal flutings and grooves, ribbing and mouldings, as well as the carving of startlingly naturalistic scenes in relief, with human figures, bulls, birds, flowers, marine creatures and sanctuaries. The most outstanding relief vases are the Boxer Rhyton (see fig. 28), the Chieftain Cup, the Harvester Vase from AYIA TRIADA and the Peak Sanctuary Rhyton

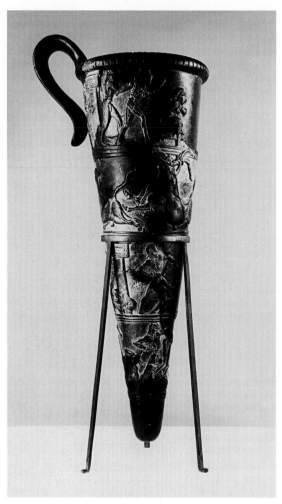

28. Boxer Rhyton, conical serpentine vase, h. 465 mm, from Ayia Triada, LM IB (Herakleion, Archaeological Museum)

many of the finest vessels coming from shrine treasuries; domestic usage in houses and palaces, chiefly vessels of Cretan serpentine; and use as burial gifts, though these were now on a much reduced scale. In addition, vases were exported to Minoan settlements abroad and to other sites in the Aegean. Many of the finer pieces may have been presents or gift exchanges with local rulers, designed to encourage trade.

After the Cretan destructions in LM IB, large vessels (alabastrons and amphorae) were produced at Knossos in a new, soft stone: gypsum. The rulers at this time may have been Mycenaean Greeks, and a new lapidary technique, involving the use of a cutting compass to engrave elaborate spiral decoration, is paralleled in architectural stonework on the Greek mainland.

BIBLIOGRAPHY

R. B. Seager: *Explorations in the Island of Mochlos* (Boston and New York, 1912) [fine colour illus. of EM pieces]
S. Xanthoudides: *The Vaulted Tombs of Mesará* (Liverpool, 1924)
C. Zervos: *L'Art de la Crète néolithique et minoenne* (Paris, 1956)
S. Marinatos and M. Hirmer: *Crete and Mycenae* (London, 1960) [excellent pls of vessels with scenes in relief]
P. M. Warren: 'Minoan Stone Vases as Evidence of Minoan Foreign Connexions in the Aegean Late Bronze Age', *Proc. Prehist. Soc.*, xxxiii (1967), pp. 37–56
——: *Minoan Stone Vases* (Cambridge, 1969)
N. Platon: *Zakros: The Discovery of a Lost Palace of Ancient Crete* (New York, 1971) [excellent pls]
P. M. Warren: 'The Unfinished Red Marble Jar at Akrotiri, Thera', *Thera and the Aegean World*, ed. C. Doumas, i (London, 1978), pp. 555–68 [manufacture of stone vases]
C. Baurain and P. Darcque: 'Un Triton en pierre à Malia', *Bull. Corr. Hell.*, cvii (1983), pp. 3–73
P. Darcque: 'Crète. L'Art des sculptures de coquillages: Un Triton en pierre trouvé à Malia', *Archaeologia*, 211 (1986), pp. 30–38
P. M. Warren: 'Stone Vessels in Minoan Crete', *Minoan and Greek Civilization from the Mitsotakis Collection* (exh. cat., ed. L. Marangou; Athens, Mus. Cyclad. & Anc. Gr. A., 1992), pp. 151–5
R. D. G. Evely: 'Minoan Crafts: Tools and Techniques. An Introduction', *Stud. Medit. Archaeol.*, xcii/1 (1993), pp. 172–94 [manuf. of stone vases]

P. M. WARREN

from Kato Zakros (MM III–LM I; Herakleion, Archaeol. Mus.; *see also* §I, 3(iii) above; for illustration of detail of the Zakros vase see fig. 7a above). Gold leaf was sometimes applied over these scenes, in imitation of gold vessels such as the famous cups from Vapheio (see fig. 25 above). Vases were often made in separate parts, cleverly joined by bronze wires through holes. These technical skills were also used to adapt imported Egyptian vessels to Minoan taste, by the addition of new parts or gold sheeting. Some shapes were common to pottery, metal, faience and stone.

As well as rather soft Cretan serpentine, a brilliant range of local and imported hardstones (up to 7 on Moh's scale) was used, comprising Cretan gabbro and diorite; *lapis Lacedaemonius* and *rosso antico* from the Peloponnese; Gyali obsidian and a jet-black obsidian, very possibly Anatolian; Egyptian alabaster (calcite); large rock crystals, probably from Egypt; Cycladic or local white marble; and fine polychrome and creamy-white limestones, both similar to marble.

The functions of stone vases also became more diverse during MM III–LM I and included use in religious rituals,

XI. Forgeries.

Forgeries of Minoan artefacts were first produced in the early 20th century, in quite large numbers. By then enough genuine objects had been discovered to provide forgers with models, but often too few to enable scholars to detect flaws in concept or execution. Such stylistic analysis remains the chief means of detection, though scientific techniques are increasingly used to identify materials and methods of production. Opportunities for mischief have dwindled accordingly, and all objects discussed here belong to this earlier phase. A collection of forgeries is maintained at the Herakleion Archaeological Museum.

Among the most famous supposed forgeries is a group of six ivory figurines, of which five are chryselephantine: a toreador (Toronto, Royal Ont. Mus.); three goddesses (Boston, MA, Mus. F.A.; Baltimore, MD, Walters A.G.) and two boy gods (one in Oxford, Ashmolean; the other untraced). They are linked by stylistic details such as facial expressions, the rendition of hair and tiara headdresses, the use of gold pins for nipples and the openwork treatment of bodices, and it is these details that have led to their condemnation. Though their poses, no doubt intentionally, recall those of the faience figurines from the

Temple Repositories at Knossos (*see* §VII and fig. 21 above), their heads resemble 20th-century works and feature details not seen in other Minoan work, for example the sunken eye-sockets on the Boston goddess and an Archaic-period (*c.* 700–480 BC) smile on the Baltimore one. The use of gold foil, as well as aspects of the costume so portrayed, arouses suspicion, though less so since the 1986–7 discovery at Palaikastro in a Late Minoan (LM) IB context of an ivory and serpentine statuette with fragments of gold on and around it (Siteia, Archaeol. Mus.; *see* §VI, 2 above). Four stone figurines also appear to be forged: a marble goddess (Cambridge, Fitzwilliam), a limestone snake-goddess, a goddess of limestone, and another female figure of 'steatite', reputedly from Tylissos (the last three untraced). The first three resemble each other and the ivories in several respects, though the fourth is somewhat different. The grounds for doubting their authenticity are their modern facial features, their suspect poses (hands on breasts or on hips), details of dress (e.g. an unusual cap on the Tylissos figure) and an unusual finishing technique (painted 'fresco' on the Tylissos figure). Traces left on the figure in the Fitzwilliam indicate the anachronistic use of a steel gouge.

Although iconographical analysis is vital, the dangers of dismissing a work simply because it is unique are illustrated by a gold ring from Archanes (?LM I; Herakleion, Archaeol. Mus.) that is now authenticated but was previously suspected because it employs known motifs in a novel fashion. The most spectacular rehabilitation was undergone by the gold Ring of Minos reputedly from Knossos (?LM I; untraced). Certain details in its depiction of rocks, a shoreline and trees, once regarded as clear evidence of forgery, have been shown to be paralleled by the Master Impression of Chania (?LM IB; Chania, Archaeol. Mus.). Other rings and seals, however, remain condemned, including the notorious San Giorgi group, which comprises numerous stone specimens (chiefly of cornelian and agate) and a few of glass, produced by one or two craftsmen. They are rejected partly because of general characteristics such as oddities of shape and an over-high polish, but more specifically because of unconvincing compositions and idiosyncratic motifs (e.g. lions with 'dotted' foreheads; camel-like profiles and branching horns or antlers for deer and goats). Other individual stone and ivory or bone seals have been dismissed on technical as well as stylistic grounds. Forgeries of valuable objects also include a series of relief vessels in steatite. Clumsier attempts to deceive are exemplified by a male head with spectacularly un-Minoan features and improbably executed in antler. Perhaps surprisingly, pottery fakes either do not exist or have not been commented upon by scholars.

BIBLIOGRAPHY

L. D. Caskey: 'A Chryselephantine Statuette of the Cretan Snake Goddess', *Amer. J. Archaeol.*, xix (1915), pp. 237–49
E. J. Forsdyke: 'A Stag-Horn Head from Crete', *J. Hell. Stud.*, xl (1920), pp. 174–9
A. J. Evans: *The Palace of Minos*, i, iii, iv/1 and 2 (London, 1921, 1930, 1935, 2/1964)
A. J. B. Wace: *A Cretan Statuette in the Fitzwilliam Museum* (Cambridge, 1927)
S. Casson: *The Technique of Early Greek Sculpture* (Oxford, 1933)
D. K. Hill: 'Two Unknown Minoan Statuettes', *Amer. J. Archaeol.*, xliv (1942), pp. 254–60
J. A. Sakellarakis: 'Minoan Cemeteries at Archanes', *Archaeology*, xx (1967), pp. 276–81
J. A. Sakellarakis and V. E. G. Kenna: *Iraklion, Sammlung Metaxas* (1969), iv of *Corpus der minoischen und mykenischen Siegel* (Berlin, 1969)
J. H. Betts: 'Some Early Forgeries: The San Giorgi Group', *Corpus der minoischen und mykenischen Siegel*, i (Berlin, 1981), pp. 17–35
E. Hallager: *The Master Impression*, Stud. Medit. Archaeol., lxix (Göteborg, 1985)
I. Pini: 'Zum "Ring of Minos"', *Eilapine, In Honour of Prof. N. Platon*, i (Herakleion, 1987), pp. 441–55
P. M. Warren: 'The Ring of Minos', *Eilapine, In Honour of Prof. N. Platon*, i (Herakleion, 1987), pp. 485–500
O. H. Krzyszkowska: 'Early Cretan Seals: New Evidence for the Use of Bone, Ivory and Boar's Tusk', *Corpus der minoischen und mykenischen Siegel*, iii (Berlin, 1989), pp. 111–26
H. Sackett and S. MacGillivray: 'Boyhood of a God', *Archaeology*, xlii/5 (1989), pp. 26–31

D. EVELY

XII. Museums.

The Archaeological Museum in Herakleion, Crete, contains 15 galleries devoted to exhibits drawn from its enormous collection of Minoan antiquities, which provides a representative record of all aspects of Cretan Bronze Age culture throughout the island. Objects of the Early Minoan (EM) period include pottery, goldwork, copper daggers, stone vases and figurines from settlements, caves and tombs at various sites in central and eastern Crete. Among the most interesting of the objects in the EM gallery are a number of ivory and steatite seals from the round tombs in the Mesara and a terracotta model of a four-wheeled cart from near Palaikastro that, dating from the transition from Early to Middle Minoan (MM), provides the earliest evidence for wheeled vehicles in the Aegean.

MM I–II are represented by finds from the early palaces at Knossos, Mallia and Phaistos and from contemporary settlement, cemetery and sanctuary sites on the island. Notable among these is the range of cult and votive objects from the 'peak sanctuaries' of central and eastern Crete and the Town Mosaic from Knossos—a series of small faience plaques representing the façades of two- or three-storey houses that provide a vivid glimpse of contemporary Minoan architecure (*see* §II, 4 above). Material on display from Phaistos includes examples of clay objects inscribed in the early Cretan hieroglyphic and protolinear scripts, and the enigmatic Phaistos disc (*see* PHAISTOS, fig. 2), which dates from LM I.

MM III and Late Minoan (LM) I are represented by a rich diversity of material from the later palaces at Knossos, Phaistos and Mallia and from the palace at Kato Zakros. From the final phase of the palace of Knossos (LM I–IIIA:1) comes the series of clay tablets written in the Linear B syllabic script, which provides evidence of the presence of Greek-speakers at Knossos at this time. The museum also contains a wide range of objects of clay, bronze, stone, ivory, gold and other materials from Cretan cemeteries, villas, caves and other sites, dating from MM III to Sub-Minoan times. There are separate galleries devoted to exhibits of LM III painted terracotta sarcophagi and to restorations of the colourful frescoes (including some relief frescoes) from Neo-Palatial palaces and villas.

Smaller museums at Ayios Nikolaos and Hierapetra, in the eastern part of Crete, and Chania and Rethymnon, in the west of the island, contain EM, MM and LM material from various sites in their localities, including the important LM site of Kastelli at Chania, where excavations have been taking place since the late 1960s.

The Ashmolean Museum, Oxford, contains one of the most representative collections of Minoan antiquities outside Crete, the greater part of which derives from the excavations of Sir ARTHUR EVANS, who was Keeper of the Museum from 1884 to 1907. Stratified ceramic material from Evans's excavations at Knossos, together with material from subsequent excavations at the site, is housed at the Stratigraphical Museum, Knossos. The University Museum, University of Pennsylvania, in Philadelphia, also possesses a good collection of Minoan material from excavations carried out at sites in eastern Crete in the early years of the 20th century. Other, smaller collections of Minoan antiquities can be found in a number of European and North American museums.

The most important private collection of Minoan objects is that assembled under special permit by the late Dr Giamalakis, which is displayed in its own gallery in the Herakleion Archaeological Museum. The Mitsotakis Collection (Chania, Archaeol. Mus.) is believed to include a large number of objects from tombs near Odigitrias Monasterion in southern Crete (see 1992 exh. cat.). Particularly numerous among long-standing private collections are those consisting of Minoan sealstones. Among the largest and most important of these are the Metaxas Collection (Herakleion, Archaeol. Mus.), the Seager Collection (New York, Met., and Philadelphia, U. PA, Mus.) and the Evans Collection (Oxford, Ashmolean).

An international exhibition of Minoan antiquities travelled to Herakleion, Rome and Athens in 1984–5 to mark 100 years of Italian excavation in Crete. Exhibitions have recently also been mounted in Duisburg (1990) and at the Allard Pierson Museum in Amsterdam (1992–3).

BIBLIOGRAPHY

F. Matz, H. Biesantz and I. Pini, eds.: *Corpus der minoischen und mykenischen Siegel*, i–xiii (Berlin, 1964–)

S. Alexiou: *A Guide to the Archaeological Museum of Heraclion*, intro. N. Platon, Eng. trans. by D. French and E. French (Athens, 1968)

P. Betancourt: *Minoan Objects Excavated from Vasilike, Pseira, Sphoungaras, Priniatikos, Pyrgos, and Other Sites* (1983), i of *The Cretan Collection in the University Museum, University of Pennsylvania*, University Museum Monograph, xlvii (Philadelphia, 1983)

Creta antica: Cento anni di archaeologia italiana, 1884–1984 (exh. cat., Herakleion, Rome, Athens, 1984–5)

A. Kofou: *Crete: All the Museums and Archaeological Sites* (Athens, 1989)

Kreta: Das Erwachen Europas (exh. cat., Duisburg, 1990)

Minoan and Greek Civilization from the Mitsotakis Collection (exh. cat., ed. L. Marangou, Athens, Mus. Cyclad. & Anc. Gr. A., 1992)

Kreta, Bakermat van Europa [Crete, cradle of Europe] (exh. cat., Amsterdam, Allard Pierson Mus., 1992–3)

SUSAN SHERRATT

Mino da Fiesole [Mino di Giovanni] (*b* Papiano, nr Poppi in Casentino, 1429; *d* Florence, 1484). Italian sculptor. He worked in both Florence and Rome and apparently established large workshops in both cities, producing many important tombs, altars and tabernacles; he was also one of the first Renaissance sculptors in Florence to carve portrait busts, and his revival of this antique form gave expression to the humanism of Medicean Florence. The majority of his Florentine works are dated or datable, but there is little solid evidence for the dating of his Roman projects, and consequently there is some confusion over his chronology. Because of his familiarity with two distinct sculptural traditions he became a transmitter of ideas between Rome and Florence.

1. LIFE AND WORK.

(i) Training and early career. Mino's first documented work, the portrait bust of *Piero de' Medici* (1453; Florence, Bargello; *see* BUST, fig. 2), is also the first securely dated portrait bust of the Renaissance. The head is derived from antique Roman busts, but the carving of the patterned tunic and the inclusion of the shoulders and part of the torso are 15th-century innovations. Although nothing is known about his training, the importance of this early commission suggests that Mino may have trained in the workshop of one of the major artists working for Piero de' Medici during the 1450s. Vasari's description of Mino as a hapless student of Desiderio da Settignano can be refuted on stylistic and chronological grounds, since the two sculptors were probably born within a year of each other. However, an association with Michelozzo di Bartolommeo might account for the attention of Piero de' Medici (Carrara, 1956); there are also reflections of Michelozzo in Mino's later works.

During the 1450s Mino produced a steady stream of portrait busts that benefited from his study of antique busts in Rome; the inscription on the marble bust of *Niccolò Strozzi* (Berlin, Skulpgal.; see fig. 1) records that it was carved in Rome in 1454. The almost brutal naturalism of the portrait, the alert expression of the subject, with the head set at an angle to the torso, and the elegant surface finish of both flesh and cloth are sophisticated solutions to the problem of bust portraiture, not the work of a tentative beginner. It is generally assumed that Mino's next bust, of *Astorgio Manfredi II* (1455; Washington, DC, N.G.A.), was made in Naples; Mino used the pattern of the sitter's chain-mail armour to frame and accentuate the face, which exaggerates the lifelike qualities of the features.

1. Mino da Fiesole: *Niccolò Strozzi*, marble, h. 490 mm, 1454 (Berlin, Skulpturengalerie mit Frühchristlich–Byzantinischer Sammlung)

These early busts show a remarkably sensitive appreciation of the dual nature of portraits as both a record of individual features and a commemoration of the sitters' status. Mino's insistence on a sense of movement and on an almost palpable link between viewer and bust is present in all his portraits.

Mino was again in Rome in the early 1460s: a single payment was made to him for work on Pius II's Benediction Loggia (destr.) on 5 July 1463. It would seem probable that he was already in Rome working on an important commission from Cardinal Guillaume d'Estouteville for the ciborium for the high altar of S Maria Maggiore (destr.; fragments in apse and sacristy), originally inscribed with the date 1461. The attribution and dating of this work are of critical importance in establishing a coherent chronology for Mino. The ciborium has also been attributed to MINO DEL REAME, but it is difficult to make a firm association. If the design and some of the carving are the work of Mino da Fiesole, with the participation of his workshop, the dating of the monument becomes even more significant. A date of c. 1461–3 would make the ciborium Mino's first large-scale project; thus his first relief-carving would have been done in Rome, and his style defined by his experiences there. The apparent disparity between the ciborium reliefs and his later Florentine reliefs may reflect a deliberate adjustment of his Roman style to Florentine taste. The innovative design is based in part on Arnolfo di Cambio's 13th-century prototypes but incorporates details taken from Michelozzo. This skilful synthesis of Early Christian elements with 13th-century and contemporary Florentine forms to satisfy the new demands of function and scale is also apparent in his other sacrament tabernacles and carved altarpieces. The reliefs for the d'Estouteville altar of *St Jerome* (destr.; fragments, Rome, Pal. Venezia), also for S Maria Maggiore, were probably made around the same time. These two projects may have necessitated the establishment of a large workshop that could have continued to function after Mino returned to Florence in 1464.

(ii) Mature work. On 28 July 1464 Mino was inscribed in the Arte della Pietra in Florence, and he began to accept commissions from Florentines in the Medici circle. In 1464 Diotisalvi Neroni commissioned a marble altar in half relief with the *Virgin and Child with SS Leonard and Lawrence* (Florence, Badia Fiorentina) for his family chapel in S Lorenzo, and he also had Mino carve his portrait (1464; Paris, Louvre). The altar was not completed in the four months stipulated in the contract, since in 1466, when Neroni was exiled from Florence, the marble was still in Mino's possession; it was only in 1470 that he sold the completed altar to the Badia, Florence. Within a Brunelleschian architectural frame, appropriate for the altar's intended setting, the saints' figures are shown frontally; the stylized linearity of the drapery, the inconsistencies of scale between the figures and the shifts in relief depth reflect the influence of Isaia da Pisa and other sculptors active in Rome, while the format and style are based on Early Christian ivories.

Some time before Bishop Leonardo Salutati's death in 1466, Mino carved his portrait and probably began plans for the marble decoration of his funerary chapel in Fiesole

Cathedral, comprising a tomb into which the Bishop's portrait bust was set and an elaborate marble altarpiece with the Virgin and SS Leonard and Martin in half relief and, in front of them, in much higher relief, the Holy Children and St Martin's beggar. The tomb of *Bernardo Giugni* (d 1466; Florence, Badia Fiorentina), which includes a powerful profile portrait of the deceased, and a Sacrament tabernacle (1467–71; Volterra Cathedral) share a marked interest in the articulation of the architectural structure and a tendency to abstract the human form through the use of repetition and pattern, particularly in the tabernacle, where identical pairs of angels support symbols of the Passion on all four sides.

In 1469 Mino began work on the tomb of *Count Hugo of Tuscany* (d 1001; Florence, Badia Fiorentina), probably completing at that time the recumbent effigy on the bier and the high-relief personification of *Charity*. In this work Mino's style of figural relief-carving achieved a high level of linear abstraction; the tomb's size and solidity seems far removed from the decorative emphasis of Mino's model, Desiderio da Settignano's *Marsuppini* tomb (Florence, Santa Croce). The marble tondo of the *Virgin and Child* (c. 1470; Florence, Bargello; see fig. 2) was designed to be set above the doorway of the Badia. It is in an elaborate frame that, together with the minute costume details, helps to emphasize the surface of the relief, while the linear pattern formed by the drapery defines the radius of the circle. Seen from below, the direction of the glances and the angles of the haloes intensify the projection of the forms into space, creating a strong sense of three-dimensionality; the work is also skilfully undercut to compensate

2. Mino da Fiesole: *Virgin and Child*, marble, diam. *c.* 900 mm, *c.* 1470 (Florence, Museo Nazionale del Bargello)

for the steep angle at which it was intended to be viewed. Mino discarded the popular 15th-century image of the embracing Mother and Child in favour of a frontal, almost iconic presentation. In 1473 Mino contributed two reliefs, the *Feast of Herod* and the *Beheading of St John the Baptist*, to the circular marble interior pulpit in Prato Cathedral, the overall design of which has been attributed to Mino and to Antonio Rossellino, among others.

It is assumed that between 1474 and 1480 Mino was working chiefly in Rome. He probably went there specifically to work on the tomb of *Paul II* (d 1471; destr.; fragments, Rome, Grotte Vaticane), a commission that he shared with GIOVANNI DALMATA. Cardinal Marco Barbo, the Pope's nephew, employed both sculptors in order to complete the tomb quickly, perhaps in time for the Holy Year of 1475; Vasari wrote that it was finished in two years. It was the largest 15th-century tomb in Rome, and responsibility for the reliefs was divided equally between the two sculptors and their workshops. The overall design, which emphasizes the architectural frame, may have been Mino's work. Mino and his assistants carved reliefs of the *Fall of Man*, *Faith*, *Charity*, *St John*, *St Luke* and the large lunette of the *Last Judgement*. Mino's style is more delicate and stereotyped than Giovanni's. Mino worked on a series of important tombs in Rome, sometimes collaborating with Andrea Bregno, as on that of *Cristoforo della Rovere* (Rome, S Maria del Popolo). In the monuments to *Cardinal Forteguerri* (d 1473; Rome, S Cecilia) and to *Cardinal Giacomo Ammanati-Piccolomini* (d 1479; Rome, S Agostino, cloister), Mino refined ideas he had previously developed for the papal tomb and that of *Count Hugo*.

In 1480 Mino returned to Florence and resumed work on *Count Hugo*'s tomb (finished 1481); the elaborately carved, classicizing lunette decorated with palmettes and egg-and-dart moulding framing a tondo of the *Virgin and Child*, and the base, with its elegantly lettered inscription, probably date from this time. His final project was the large marble reliquary altar for S Ambrogio, Florence (1481; *in situ*), which, in form and iconography, combines altar and tabernacle. Within a fanciful architectural framework crowned with a pediment with a relief of *God the Father in Glory*, the main scene, with the *Christ Child and Saints*, is in high relief, while the low-relief predella scene is set at a strongly raking angle. This was the second time that Mino had worked in association with Cosimo Rosselli, who painted the chapel frescoes (the first occasion was in the Salutati Chapel in Fiesole Cathedral; see Padoa Rizzo, 1977). Mino was buried in the entrance of S Ambrogio.

2. WORKING METHODS AND TECHNIQUE. When designing his major monuments, Mino must have used drawings that could later be modified as required. This practice may have been necessitated by his dependence on a large workshop from the time he was engaged on the d'Estouteville projects in the 1460s. The broad, linear quality of these reliefs reflects Mino's attempt to create a standardized, legible pattern for his assistants to follow. The likelihood that drawings remained in the workshop and were reused is suggested by comparing the angels on the Volterra tabernacle with those on a small tabernacle (Florence, Bargello, inv. no. 264) that is obviously a workshop production. Mino frequently adapted designs

from one type of monument for use in another context. It is probable that he designed his compositions in two dimensions and not with three-dimensional models.

The number of signed works in Rome that are apparently not autograph may be accounted for by Mino's practice of supplying drawings for his assistants in Rome, leaving the carving and the control of the shop to an assistant in his absence. The relationship between Mino da Fiesole and Mino del Reame can probably be explained by this workshop system. He presumably had another shop in Florence organized in a similar fashion.

BIBLIOGRAPHY

EARLY SOURCES

F. Albertini: *Opusculum de mirabilibus novae urbis Romae* (Rome, 1510), ed. A. Schmarsow (Heilbronn, 1886), pp. 16–17

G. Vasari: *Vite* (1550, rev. 2/1568); ed. G. Milanesi (1878–85), vol. iii, pp. 115–27

GENERAL

Thieme–Becker

A. Venturi: *Storia* (1901–40/*R* 1967), vol. vi, pp. 634–7

F. Burger: *Geschichte des florentinischen Grabmals von den ältesten Zeiten bis Michelangelo* (Strasbourg, 1904)

G. Davies: *Renascence: The Sculptured Tombs of the Fifteenth Century in Rome* (London, 1910)

R. Mather: 'Documents Mostly New Relating to Florentine Painters and Sculptors of the Fifteenth Century', *A. Bull.*, xxx (1948), pp. 20–66 (60–64)

J. Pope-Hennessy: *Italian Renaissance Sculpture* (London, 1963, rev. Oxford, 3/1985)

C. Seymour jr: *Sculpture in Italy, 1400–1500*, Pelican Hist. A. (Harmondsworth, 1966)

I. Lavin: 'On the Sources and Meaning of the Renaissance Portrait Bust', *A. Q.* [Detroit], xxxiii (1970), pp. 207–26

Palazzo Venezia: Paolo II e le fabbriche di S Marco (exh. cat., ed. M. L. Casanova Uccella; Rome, Pal. Venezia, 1980), pp. 33–6

Italian Renaissance Sculpture in the Time of Donatello (exh. cat., ed. A. Darr; Detroit, MI, Inst. A., 1985), pp. 185–9

MONOGRAPHS

D. Angeli: *Mino da Fiesole* (Florence, 1905)

H. Lange: *Mino da Fiesole: Ein Beitrag zur Geschichte der florentinischen und römischen Plastik des Quattrocentos* (Greifswald, 1928)

J. Rusconi: *Mino da Fiesole* (Rome, 1931)

M. Cionini Visani: *Mino da Fiesole*, I Maestri della Scultura (Milan, 1962)

G. C. Sciolla: *La scultura di Mino da Fiesole* (Turin, 1970); review by A. Markham Schulz in *A. Bull.*, liv (1972), pp. 208–9

SPECIALIST STUDIES

L. Courajod: 'Un Bas-relief de Mino da Fiesole', *Mus. Archeol.*, ii (1877), pp. 47–69

H. von Tschudi: 'Ein Madonnenrelief von Mino da Fiesole', *Jb. Kön.-Preuss. Kstsamml.*, vii (1886), pp. 122–8

D. Gnoli: 'Le opere di Mino da Fiesole in Roma', *Archv Stor. A.*, ii (1889), pp. 455–67; iii (1890), pp. 89–106, 175–86, 258–71, 424–40

G. Poggi: 'Mino da Fiesole e la Badia Fiorentina', *Riv. A.*, i (1903), pp. 98–103

C. Fabriczy: 'Alcuni documenti su Mino da Fiesole', *Riv. A.*, ii (1904), pp. 40–45

C. Ricci: 'Il tabernacolo e gli angeli di Mino da Fiesole in Volterra', *Riv. A.*, ii (1904), pp. 260–67

C. Fabriczy: 'Portate al catasto di Mino da Fiesole', *Riv. A.*, iii (1905), pp. 265–7

U. Dorini: 'La casa di Mino e i disegni murali di essa recentemente scoperti', *Riv. A.*, iv (1906), pp. 49–55

D. Cavalleni: 'Il tabernacolo del Corpo di Nostro Signor Gesù Cristo di Maestro Mino da Fiesole, scultore di pietra', *A. Crist.*, iv/1 (1916), pp. 6–13

J. Alazard: 'Mino da Fiesole à Rome', *Gaz. B.-A.*, 4th ser., xiv (1918), pp. 75–86

G. Biasiotto: 'Di alcune opere scultorie conservate in S Maria Maggiore di Roma', *Rass. A.*, xviii (1918), pp. 42–57 (52–6)

W. R. Valentiner: 'A Portrait Bust of Alfonso I of Naples', *A. Q.* [Detroit], i (1938), pp. 61–88 (76–88)

E. Marrucchi: 'Dove nacque Mino da Fiesole', *Riv. A.*, xxi (1939), pp. 324–6

W. R. Valentiner: 'Mino da Fiesole', *A. Q.* [Detroit], vii (1944), pp. 151–80; also in W. R. Valentiner: *Studies in Italian Renaissance Sculpture* (London, 1950), pp. 70–96

J. Phillips: 'The Case of the Seven Madonnas', *Bull. Met.*, iv/1 (1945), pp. 18–28

L. Carrara: 'Nota sulla formazione di Mino da Fiesole', *Crit. A.*, iii (1956), pp. 76–83

G. Corti and F. Hartt: 'New Documents concerning Donatello, Luca and Andrea della Robbia, Desiderio, Mino, Uccello, Pollaiuolo, Filippo Lippi, Baldovinetti and Others', *A. Bull.*, xliv (1962), pp. 155–67 (166–7)

M. Pepe: 'Sul soggiorno napoletano di Mino da Fiesole', *Napoli Nob.*, v (1966), pp. 116–20

G. C. Sciolla: 'L'ultima attività di Mino da Fiesole', *Crit. A.*, xciv (1968), pp. 35–44

F. Negri Arnoldi: 'Il monumento sepolcrale del Card. Niccolò Forteguerri in Santa Cecilia a Roma e il suo cenotafio nella cattedrale di Pistoia', *Egemonia fiorentina ed automonie locali nella Toscana nord-occidentale del primo rinascimento: Vita, arte, cultura: Pistoia, 1975*, pp. 211–33

A. Padoa Rizzo: 'La cappella Salutati nel duomo di Fiesole e l'attività giovanile di Cosimo Rosselli', *Ant. Viva*, xvi (1977), pp. 3–12

E. Carli: *Il pulpito interno della cattedrale di Prato* (Prato, 1981)

G. Zander: 'Considerazioni su un tipo di ciborio in uso a Roma nel rinascimento', *Boll. A.*, 4th ser., lxix (1984), pp. 99–106

SHELLEY E. ZURAW

Mino del Pelicciaio, Giacomo di. *See* GIACOMO DI MINO DEL PELLICCIAIO.

Mino del Reame [Mino del Regno] (*fl* Rome, *c.* 1460–80). Name given by Vasari to an Italian sculptor who worked in Rome during the second half of the 15th century. The name, which means 'from the Kingdom [of Naples]', suggests that Mino was from Naples. No documentation except for Vasari's *Vita* has been discovered to support the existence of this artist. The confusion between Mino del Reame and MINO DA FIESOLE was already evident in Vasari's writings and resurfaced in the early 20th century (Fraschetti, Angeli). The majority of works at present attributed to the Neapolitan sculptor have traditional associations—some as early as the 16th century—with the Florentine Mino.

The name Mino del Reame first appeared in Vasari's description of a competition between the sculptor and Paolo Romano to make a statue for Pius II, which would imply that Mino was already working in Rome in the early 1460s. In fact, two of the sculptures that Vasari stated were the work of Mino del Reame are documented works by Paolo Romano: the marble statues of *St Peter* and *St Paul* for the stairs leading to Old St Peter's, Rome (both Rome, St Peter's; see Rubinstein). Reliefs of two angels decorating the portal of S Giacomo degli Spagnuoli, Rome, one signed OPUS PAULI, the other OPUS MINI (the signature used by Mino da Fiesole), are cited as examples of the rivalry between the two sculptors. Vasari's suggestion that Mino del Reame was also active in Naples has led critics to associate the sculptor with Jacopo della Pila (*fl* Naples, 1472–1502), whose works resemble those attributed to Mino del Reame in Rome (Causa). However, the affinities in their carving styles do not necessarily confirm the identification, especially since Mino da Fiesole produced reliefs with similar qualities.

Vasari attributed the tomb of *Paul II* (*d* 1471; destr., frags in Rome, St Peter's) to Mino del Reame in that artist's biography; however, in his *Vita* of Mino da Fiesole, he contradicted himself and correctly said it was the work of the latter. Despite Vasari's confusion, however, he clearly identified them as two different sculptors.

Vasari's account suggests that Mino del Reame arrived in Rome *c.* 1460 and was active there in the 1460s and 1470s, years in which Mino da Fiesole is also presumed to have been working in the same city. Some scholars have interpreted the identical signatures and the stylistic similarities as evidence to deny the existence of Mino del Reame altogether (Langton Douglas). Others assume that Mino del Reame was a separate personality (Pope-Hennessy). By removing from Mino da Fiesole's canon of works those sculptures that seem inimical to his Florentine manner, and assigning them to Mino del Reame, a limited oeuvre has been established. Some of these works—the angel relief, a sacrament tabernacle (Rome, S Maria in Trastevere) and the marble ciborium of Cardinal d'Estouteville for S Maria Maggiore, Rome (destr.; frags *in situ* and Cleveland, OH, Mus. A.)—are signed OPUS MINI, but none is mentioned by Vasari. The most elaborate project in the group, the ciborium, is properly to be attributed to Mino da Fiesole. The flat, decorative carving technique and abstracted, simplified forms can be linked to his documented works (Caglioti).

A series of smaller works have also been attributed to Mino del Reame, including a *Crucifixion* relief (Rome, S Balbina), the monument of *Antonio Rido* (Rome, S Francesca Romana) and *St John the Baptist* (Rome, S Giovanni dei Fiorentini). It has been assumed that he either returned to Naples or died in Rome in the 1480s. The stylistic cohesion of the works attributed to Mino derives more from their resemblance to Mino da Fiesole's designs than from any internal unity.

BIBLIOGRAPHY

Thieme–Becker

F. Albertini: *Opusculum de mirabilibus novae urbis Romae* (Rome, 1510); ed. A. Schmarsow (Heilbronn, 1886), pp. 16–17

G. Vasari: *Vite* (1550, rev. 2/1568); ed. G. Milanesi (1878–85), ii, pp. 647–55; iii, pp. 115–27

S. Fraschetti: 'Una disfida artistica a Roma nel quattrocento', *Emporium*, xiv (1901), pp. 101–16

A. Venturi: *Storia* (1901–40), vi, pp. 658–71

D. Angeli: 'I due Mino', *Nuova Antol.*, n. s. 4., lxiii (1904), pp. 423–35

S. A. Callisen: 'A Bust of a Prelate in the Metropolitan Museum, New York', *A. Bull.*, xviii (1936), pp. 401–6

U. Middeldorf: [review of A. Grisebach: *Römische Porträtbüsten der Gegenreformation* (Leipzig, 1936)], *A. Bull.*, xx (1938), pp. 111–17

Italian Gothic and Early Renaissance Sculpture (exh. cat. by W. R. Valentiner, Detroit, MI, Inst. A., 1938), no. 100

W. R. Valentiner: 'Mino da Fiesole', *A. Q.* [Detroit], vii (1944), pp. 151–80; also in W. R. Valentiner: *Studies in Italian Renaissance Sculpture* (London, 1950), pp. 70–96

R. Langton Douglas: 'Mino del Reame', *Burl. Mag.*, lxxxvii (1945), pp. 217–24

——: *Burl. Mag.*, lxxxviii (1946), p. 23 [letter]

R. Causa: 'Contributi all conoscenza della scultura dell '400 a Napoli', *Scultura lignea nella Campania* (exh. cat., ed. F. Bologna and R. Causa; Naples, Pal. Reale, 1950), pp. 105–21 (116–21)

S. Nodelman: *Mino del Reame* (diss., New Haven, CT, Yale U., 1959)

H. Leppien: *Die neapolitanische Skulptur des späteren Quattrocento*, 2 vols (diss., Tübingen, Eberhard-Karls-U., 1960), pp. 132–43

J. Pope-Hennessy: *Italian Renaissance Sculpture* (London, 1963, rev. 3/Oxford, 1985) pp. 287–8, 321–2

A. Riccoboni: 'Nuovi apporti all'arte di Mino del Regno a Roma', *L'Urbe*, xxix/1 (1966), pp. 16–23

V. Golzio and G. Zander: *L'arte in Roma nel secolo XV*, Storia di Roma, xxviii (Bologna, 1968), pp. 323–5, 429–30, 479

R. Rubinstein: 'Pius II's Piazza S Pietro and St. Andrew's Head', *Enea Silvio Piccolomini, Papa Pio II; Atti del convegno per il quinto centenario della morte e altri scritti: Siena, 1968*, pp. 221–44 (230–35)

Italian Renaissance Sculpture in the Time of Donatello (exh. cat., ed. A. Darr; Detroit, MI, Inst. A., 1985), pp. 190–92

F. Caglioti: 'Per il recupero della giovinezza romana di Mino da Fiesole: Il 'ciborio' della neve', *Prospettiva* [Florence], 49 (1987), pp. 15–32

For further bibliography *see* MINO DA FIESOLE.

Minoru Kawabata. *See* KAWABATA, MINORU.

Minorca. *See under* BALEARIC ISLANDS.

Minorites. *See* FRANCISCAN ORDER.

Minotaurgruppen [Swed.: 'Minotaur group']. Swedish Surrealist group, founded in Malmö in 1943 and dissolved in the same year. Its members were C. O. Hultén, Endre Nemes, Max Walter Svanberg, Carl O. Svensson and the Latvian-born Adja Yunkers (*b* 1900). The name was probably inspired by that of the French Surrealist review *Minotaure* (1933–9) and also by the role that myth, particularly that of the minotaur, had assumed in Surrealist art. The group had one exhibition, at the Radhus in Malmö, showing work that was typically Surrealist, with grotesque metamorphoses of creatures and disconcerting juxtapositions of objects, as in Svanberg's *Melancholy Emotion* (gouache, 1943; priv. col., see Pierre, p. 27).

BIBLIOGRAPHY

C. O. Hultén: *Arbeten, 1938–1968* (exh. cat. by C. Dotremont and others, Lund, Ksthall, 1968)

J. Pierre: *Max Walter Svanberg et le règne feminin* (Paris, 1975)

Minsk [Belarus' Miensk]. Capital of Belarus', situated at the confluence of the Niamiha (Nemiga) and Svislač (Svisloch') rivers. It is the political, economic, scientific and cultural centre of the Republic (independent from 1991). It grew up in the 11th century as a fortress of the Połack (Polotsk) Principality, and from 1104 it was the centre of the Minsk Principality. It became part of the Grand Duchy of Lithuania in the first half of the 14th century, and from 1793 it was part of the Russian empire and later the Soviet Union. The historic architectural monuments and complexes of Minsk, which was devastated during World War II, are preserved only in small areas. Among these are Baroque monasteries, including the Bernardine monastery and convent, both from the 17th century, and the former church of the Bernardines, SS Peter and Paul (1642; rebuilt 18th and 19th centuries). From the mid-19th century to the early 20th building in Minsk was dominated by eclecticism, the pseudo-Russian style and Gothic Revival style (e.g. church of SS Simeon and Helen, 1908–10; original plan by B. Marconi and T. Poyazdersky, built by G. Yu. Gay and S. Z. Svitnitsky).

In the 1930s there was extensive urban development: buildings were erected that are landmarks of Soviet architecture, including the Government Building of the Belarusian SSR (1929–34; see fig.), now occupied by the Council of Ministers of the Republic of Belarus', and the main building of the Belarusian Academy of Sciences (1934–9), both by Iosif Langbard and both built in the severe, monumental neo-classical style typical of Stalinist architecture. In the course of the post-war reconstruction and development, city building was given a new, powerful impulse in the creation of the Lenin (now Independence), Central, Victory and Yakub Kolas squares, connected to each other by Lenin (now Frantishek Skarin) Prospect, and of Pryvahzalnaja (Privokzal'naya; Station) Square. After 1968 the city centre developed along the River Svislač, and new housing areas sprang up. Modern Minsk is a city of broad horizons, combining expressive public

Minsk, Government Building of the Belarusian SSR, by Iosif Langbard, 1929–34

buildings and complexes with vast housing estates and parks, and with numerous monumental decorative sculptures, including works by Zair Azgur, Andrej Bembel' (1905–86) and Anatoly Aleksandrovich Anikiejčyk (Anikeychik; 1932–89). The Art Museum of Belarus' in Minsk has one of the greatest collections of Belarusian art from the medieval to modern periods, including icons, sculpture, paintings and graphic works. It also houses an important collection of Russian art of the 19th century to the early 20th. The group RAMB (Revolutionary Organization of Belarusian Artists) was founded in the 1920s.

BIBLIOGRAPHY

E. M. Zagorul'sky: *Starazhytny Minsk* [Old Minsk] (Minsk, 1963)

Minsk: Entsyklapedychny davednik [Minsk: encyclopedic reference book] (Minsk, 1983)

T. Charnyawskaya and A. Pyatrosava: *Pomniki arkhitektury Minska XVII–pachatku XX stagoddzyaw* [Architectural monuments of Minsk from the 17th to early 20th centuries] (Minsk, 1984)

G. Picarda: *Miensk: A Historical Guide* (London, 1993)

L. N. DROBOV

Minton, (Francis) John (*b* Cambridge, 25 Dec 1917; *d* London, 20 Jan 1957). English painter and illustrator. He attended St John's Wood School of Art from 1935 to 1938. A celebrity of London's bohemia and a key figure of NEO-ROMANTICISM in the 1940s, he lived and worked with most of the younger generation Neo-Romantics including Michael Ayrton (1921–76), Robert Colquhoun, Robert MacBryde and Keith Vaughan. Invalided out of the army in 1943, he devoted himself to art, producing work for seven one-man shows between 1945 and 1956.

Minton's eclectic style combined elements of French and British Neo-Romanticism. His main theme, partly homoerotic, was the young male figure in emotionally charged settings. Five phases in his work have been identified, ranging from landscapes reminiscent of those of Samuel Palmer, for example *Recollections of Wales* (1944; Brit. Council; for illustration *see* NEO-ROMANTICISM), to scenes of urban decay, such as *Rotherhithe from Wapping* (1946; Southampton, C.A.G.). In the post-war years he was attracted to exotic places in search of new subjects.

Although Minton was dedicated to painting, his reputation depended largely on his skill as an illustrator, for example the Corsican illustrations for *Time Was Away* by Alan Ross (London, 1948). He taught at Camberwell School of Art (1943–6), Central School of Art and Crafts (1946–8) and at the Royal College of Art until 1957, devoting the last part of his life to theatre design. A product of his age, Minton was charismatic, charming and generous but also melancholic and self-destructive. His illustrative style had become the fashionable norm of the period, but as a figurative painter the arrival of abstraction increased feelings of self-doubt, compounding personal problems, which led to his suicide.

BIBLIOGRAPHY

John Minton, 1917–1957: Paintings, Drawings, Illustrations and Stage Designs (exh. cat., intro. J. Rothenstein; Reading, Mus. & A.G.; Sheffield, Graves A.G.; 1974)

A Paradise Lost: The Neo-Romantic Imagination in Britain, 1935–55 (exh. cat., ed. D. Mellor; London, Barbican A.G., 1987)

M. Yorke: *The Spirit of the Place: Nine Neo-Romantic Artists and their Times* (London, 1988), pp. 168–95, *passim*

F. Spalding: *Dance till the Stars Come Down: A Biography of John Minton* (London, 1991)

John Minton, 1917–1957: A Selective Retrospective (exh. cat., London, Royal Coll. A.; Bath, Victoria A.G.: Llandudno, Oriel Mostyn; Newtown, Oriel 31; 1994)

VIRGINIA BUTTON

Minton Ceramic Factory. English ceramics factory in Stoke-on-Trent, Staffs. Thomas Minton (1766–1836), who had worked at the Caughley porcelain factory and was the reputed originator of the 'Willow' pattern, established his own company in 1796 with partners William Pownall and Joseph Poulson in Stoke-on-Trent. Production started with blue-printed earthenwares. By 1798 cream-coloured earthenware and bone china were produced, and by 1810 the range included stoneware, painted earthenwares and bone china. Production, dominated by tableware, included ornaments, figures and such unusual items as asparagus trays. Decoration was printed, enamelled and gilded, and designs included landscapes, Imari palettes, chinoiseries and floral patterns. In 1817 Minton's sons Thomas Webb Minton (1791–1870) and Herbert Minton (1793–1858) joined the firm, and in 1823 Herbert Minton became joint partner. Hard-paste porcelain was introduced in 1821, and figure production was expanded; the porcelain factories of Derby, Meissen and Sèvres provided the main sources of inspiration. Artists who moved from Derby to Minton included Joseph Bancroft (1796–1860), George Cocker (1794–1868) and the painter Samuel Bourne (*c*. 1789–1865), who was the chief designer (*c*. 1828–63). After Thomas Minton's death, Herbert Minton took John Boyle (*d* 1845) into partnership (1836–42) and then in 1845 Michael Daintry Hollins and his nephew Colin Minton Campbell. Herbert Minton introduced new ranges including encaustic and printed tiles and parian porcelain during the 1840s.

Léon Arnoux (1816–1902) was art director from 1849, and he encouraged such French artists as the designer and sculptor Albert-Ernest Carrier-Belleuse and Pierre-Emile Jeannest (1813–57) to come to Stoke-on-Trent. Arnoux led the revival of Renaissance styles and in 1849 developed the use of earthenware with thick coloured glazes, which he called 'majolica' and which he introduced at the Great Exhibition of 1851 in London. Colin Minton Campbell took control of the factory in 1858 following Herbert Minton's death. The acid-gold process was developed at Minton in 1863. In 1870 Marc-Louis-Emanuel Solon (1835–1913) introduced the *pâte-sur-pâte* decorative technique from Sèvres to the factory. Wares were often decorated at the South Kensington Art Pottery Studio, which was set up in London by Minton in 1871. The International Exhibitions strengthened Minton's reputation, and this was consolidated by Queen Victoria's patronage, especially of their parian porcelain. In the 20th century Secessionist ware and Art Deco styles were produced. Later output was dominated by richly decorated bone-china tableware and commemorative items. In 1968 Minton became a member of the Royal Doulton Tableware Group (for further illustration *see* TILE, fig. 5).

BIBLIOGRAPHY

G. A. Godden: *Illustrated Encyclopaedia of British Pottery and Porcelain* (London, 1966)

——: *Minton Pottery and Porcelain of the First Period, 1793–1850* (London, 1968)

Minton, 1798–1910 (exh. cat. by A. Aslin and P. Atterbury, London, V&A, 1976)

K. SOMERVELL

Minujín, Marta (*b* Buenos Aires, 30 Jan 1943). Argentine performance artist and sculptor. After completing her studies in Buenos Aires at the Escuela Nacional de Bellas Artes Manuel Belgrano, the Escuela Nacional Prilidiano Pueyrredón and the Escuela Nacional Ernesto de la Cárcova, she moved in 1960 to Paris on a scholarship from the Fondo Nacional de las Artes. There she became involved with the presentation of happenings at the Galerie Raymond Cordier and in the Impasse Roussin. On her return to Argentina in 1964 she continued this activity in Buenos Aires and Montevideo and became associated with Argentine Pop artists; later that year she was awarded first prize by the Instituto Torcuato Di Tella in Buenos Aires for a series of strangely shaped and violently coloured hanging cushions. She presented two further installations at the same venue in 1965, one involving audience participation (with members of the public receiving blows or confronting unusual situations) and the other including live animals. In 1966 she collaborated with Allan Kaprow in New York and Wolf Vostell in Berlin on a project involving the mass-media forms of cinema, photography, television, radio, telephone and telegrams.

Minujín settled in New York in 1967 on being awarded a Guggenheim scholarship. There she created a *Menu–Phone*, which produced different sensory effects in the spectator according to the number dialled and which led on to other works combining modern technology and audience participation over the next four years. As a brief respite from these activities she exhibited erotic paintings and drawings in 1973 before returning to complex projects such as *Communicating with the Earth* (1976; Buenos Aires, Cent. A. & Comunic.), which sought to establish a communication network among Latin American artists. From the late 1970s she also created objects such as the *Cheese Venus* (1981; Buenos Aires, Knoll Argentina), a replica of the Venus de Milo made of iron covered with pieces of cheese, as a way of provoking reflection on the value of monuments and of permitting festive participation in a visual and gastronomic spectacle. These were followed by a series of replicas of Classical Greek sculptures, sometimes fragmented or with displaced elements presented to the spectator as a dynamic image.

BIBLIOGRAPHY

J. Glusberg: *Del Pop-art a la Nueva Imagen* (Buenos Aires, 1985), pp. 321–56

NELLY PERAZZO

Minusca, Gabriel del Barco y. *See* BARCO Y MINUSCA, GABRIEL DEL.

Min Yŏng-hwan (*b* Seoul, 1861; *d* Seoul, 1905). Korean calligrapher and painter. Born into the Min household, a distinguished and influential family during the period of King Kojong (*reg* 1864–1907), he held a number of high-ranking government posts, reaching the position of Grand Chamberlain in 1905. However, he strongly opposed the Protection Treaty concluded with force by Japan in that year and committed suicide. As well as being an accomplished calligrapher, he excelled in painting bamboos and orchids in Chinese ink, but few of his works survive.

BIBLIOGRAPHY

Kim Yong-yun, ed.: *Hanguk sŏhwa inmyŏng saso* [Biographical dictionary of Korean painters and calligraphers] (Seoul, 1959)

Min Yŏng-ik [*ho* Wŏnchŏng, Ch'ŏnsimchukche] (*b* Seoul, 1860; *d* Shanghai, 1914). Korean calligrapher and painter. He was active at the end of the Chosŏn period (1392–1910) and was a nephew of Queen Myŏngsŏng, a member of the Min clan and wife of King Kojong (*reg* 1864–1907); under the Queen's protection he played a central role among the conservatives from the age of 19 but abandoned politics to take up painting and calligraphy. In 1895, when the Queen was assassinated by the Japanese, he fled to Shanghai in China, where he spent his days as a calligrapher and painter, earning fame for his ink-orchids and ink-bamboo. Basing himself on the painting style of KIM CHŎNG-HŬI, he achieved a level of excellence in his work characterized by strong, sharp brushstrokes. Idiosyncratic features in his paintings of orchids were the blunt tips and right-angled bend in the middle of the orchid leaves. Such paintings were highly regarded, even in the calligraphy and painting world of Shanghai. Fine examples of his work are two ink paintings, *Orchids* and *Orchids with Bare Roots* (both Seoul, Ho-am A. Mus.), and *Bamboo* (ink painting; Seoul, N. Mus.). The calligrapher and painter Kim Yong-jin was among those influenced by his style.

BIBLIOGRAPHY

Kim Ch'ŏng-kang: *Min Yŏng-ik-ŭi yesul kwa saeng'ae* [Min Yŏng-ik's art and life] (Seoul, 1980)

HONG SŎN-P'YO

Mio, Giovanni de. *See* DEMIO, GIOVANNI.

Mio, Vangjush (*b* Korçë, 5 March 1891; *d* Korçë, 29 Dec 1957). Albanian painter. He studied painting at the Art School in Bucharest (1915–19) and at the Istituto Statale d'Arte in Rome (1920–24). The realist landscapes he painted as a student, such as *Dusk* (1919; Tiranë, A.G.), are permeated by a romantic spirit. He painted in various cities in Romania and Italy, then returned to Albania, where he travelled widely, basing himself in Korçë, teaching drawing at the local Lyceum.

Mio's personal style was established in the period between his two one-man exhibitions (1928 in Tiranë and 1933 in Korçë), where he exhibited a great variety of local landscapes and still-lifes. New features of his style became apparent in paintings such as *Lake Ohrid* (1929; Tiranë, A.G.) and *Boats at Pogradec* (1929; Tiranë, A.G.). Here he abandoned dusks and sombre colours and replaced them with blue sky, clear air and shining sun, in depictions of any season. He was noted for his ability to make a poetic, peaceful landscape from the most ordinary place, using a soft, smooth brush. He depicted clear atmospheres that always permit an uninterrupted view towards a distant horizon. Mio's full maturity as a painter became apparent at his one-man exhibition of 1945 in Tiranë and his first retrospective in Tiranë in 1957. In paintings such as *Autumn in Drenovë* (1934; Tiranë, A.G.), *Tiranë* (1939; Tiranë, A.G.) and *Street in Korçë* (1940; Tiranë, A.G.) his realistic depiction is created in fresh Impressionist colours and is direct and forceful. Known as the most powerful and poetic Albanian landscape painter, Mio was at his best as a realist with his pre-war landscapes. He left *c.* 400 paintings and *c.* 500 drawings (in pencil, ink and charcoal). His house in Korçë was turned into a museum and contains many of his paintings.

UNPUBLISHED SOURCES
Tiranë, A. G. [MSS]

BIBLIOGRAPHY
Artet figurative Shqiptare [Albanian figurative art] (Tiranë, 1978), pls 16–26
Ekspozita e Piktorit të Popullit Vangjush Mio [Exhibition of the Painter of the People, Vangjush Mio] (exh. cat., Tiranë, A.G., 1983)

GJERGJ FRASHËRI

Mique, Richard (*b* Nancy, 18 Sept 1728; *d* Paris, 9 July 1794). French architect, designer and engineer. He was a son of Simon Mique (*d* 1763), an architect and builder related to the Mieg family from Alsace. He studied in Paris under Jacques-François Blondel, and on his return to Lorraine he was appointed Architecte-Ingénieur to Stanislav Leszczyński, Grand Duke of Lorraine and former King of Poland, for whom Simon Mique had rebuilt a wing at the château of Lunéville. Richard Mique's schemes in Nancy include the Porte St Stanislas and the Porte Ste Catherine (1761), built as Doric triumphal arches in the style of Blondel. On the death of Emmanuel Héré (1763) he was appointed Directeur Général des Bâtiments.

On the death of Stanislav I in 1766 and the reversion of Lorraine to France, Mique was called to Versailles by Maria Leszczyńska, daughter of Stanislav and queen of Louis XV, to design a convent and school for the Ursulines (now the Lycée Hoche). The layout comprises a courtyard flanked by visiting-rooms (*parloirs*) and a chapel on the far side, behind which the convent is sited around three courtyards. The chapel at the centre of the convent is a masterpiece of 18th-century religious architecture. Mique originally intended it to take the form of a basilica but ended with a centralized plan, inspired by Andrea Palladio's Villa Rotonda, Vicenza, with a dome flanked by two half domes. This Palladian influence, softened by the 18th-century spirit, is also evident at his chapel (1779–84) at Saint-Denis, Paris, built for Mme Louise de France, a daughter of Louis XV, with the same centralized plan, a dome, and a façade inspired by Greek temples.

From 1770 Mique worked as official architect to Marie-Antoinette, wife of Louis XVI, for whom he redesigned the rooms in the Queen's Apartments at the château of Versailles in a decorative style of extreme elegance determined by the Queen herself, and produced landscaped gardens incorporating subtly designed structures. The Neo-classical spirit can also be found in his peripteral rotunda, Temple de l'Amour (1778), the Théâtre de la Reine (1779–80) and the Salon du Rocher (1781) at the Petit Trianon (*see* VERSAILLES, §4); the Méridienne (1781), the Cabinet Doré (1783) and the Salon des Nobles (1785) at Versailles; and the Escalier d'Honneur (1785) and the chapels (1788) at the château of Saint-Cloud (destr. 1872). In his architecture Mique favoured the Ionic order, façades with a pediment and low reliefs and friezes in the *style antique*; in his interior decoration he associated the vocabulary of Classical architecture with sphinxes and Pompeian caryatids, flowers, arabesques and fantastical motifs, pearls or decorative trimmings. For Mme Adelaïde de France and Mme Victoire de France, daughters of Louis XV, Mique designed interiors in this style for the bathroom (1780) at Versailles and at Bellevue (1775–82), and he also redesigned their gardens (1779) at Montreuil, the Hermitage in Versailles (1782; destr.) and Bellevue (1778–82) in an *anglo-chinois* style that he had developed for Marie-Antoinette at the Trianon in 1774. Mique was a landscape designer of some note, and from 1783 to 1785, with technical advice from Hubert Robert, he worked on the Hameau at the Trianon, a group of cottages by an artificial lake where the Queen and her ladies played at being villagers. He built another hamlet for the Mesdames de France at Bellevue (destr.).

The progress of Mique's career was rapid: he was made a chevalier of the Order of St Michael in 1763, worked as principal architect to Marie-Antoinette from 1770, was appointed Intendant Général des Bâtiments du Roi from 1776 and Directeur of the Académie Royale d'Architecture, Paris, in 1782. In 1773, however, he was accused by an individual masquerading as his half-brother, and subsequently by the latter's daughter, of misappropriating his rights of succession, and the '*affaire* Mique' became the subject of a series of lawsuits up to the Revolution (1789–95). Mique was arrested in 1794, and his property was confiscated. He was executed, together with his son Simon Mique, in 1794. The absence of any documentation and the destruction of the châteaux of Saint-Cloud and Bellevue help to explain Mique's relative neglect, but what remains of his work is strong evidence of his abilities, and he is perhaps one of the most underrated French Neo-classical designers of the 18th century.

BIBLIOGRAPHY
Macmillan Enc. Architects
H. Clouzot: *Des Tuileries à Saint-Cloud: L'Art décoratif du second empire* (Paris, 1925)
P. Biver: *Histoire du château de Bellevue* (Paris, 1933)
P. Mieg: *Histoire généalogique de la famille Mieg* (Mulhouse, 1934)
L. Hautecoeur: *Architecture classique* (1943–57)
P. Verlet: *Le Mobilier royal français: Meubles de la couronne conservés en France* (Paris, 1945)
M. Müntz de Raïssac: 'Quatre vases en porphyre de la collection Richard Mique', *Rev. Louvre*, v (1990)
——: 'Les Appartements de Marie-Antoinette à Versailles', *18th C. Life* (1993)

MURIEL MÜNTZ DE RAÎSSAC

Mir (i Trinxet), Joaquim [Joaquin] (*b* Barcelona, 6 Jan 1873; *d* Barcelona, 27 April 1940). Spanish Catalan painter. A pupil of Lluis Graner (1863–1929), he also studied at the Escola de Belles Arts (Llotja) of Barcelona (1894–5). Mir was a member of la Colla del Safrà, a group of young artists who painted the fields in the countryside outside Barcelona. The *Cathedral of the Poor* (1898; priv. col., see Jardí, pl. 25, pp. 36–7) is among his most important works of this period: it is a realistic group portrait of beggars near Antoni Gaudí's Temple de la Sagrada Familia during its construction in Barcelona. In 1899 Mir settled with Santiago Rusiñol in Mallorca, where he knew the Belgian symbolist painter William Degouve de Nuncques. However, preferring to live alone, he went to the area around the Torrent de Pareis, a canyon in the north of the island; there he painted a number of extraordinary works, for example the large-scale *Enchanted Cove* (1.55×2 m; Montserrat, Mus. Abadia), in which the forms merged into evanescent stains of colour. His one-man exhibition in 1901 at the Sala Parés in Barcelona met with public incomprehension, but he was praised by critics as the new great painter of the Catalan landscape. An accident and psychiatric illness ended his Mallorcan period (1904), and he was interned in the psychiatric institute of Reus (1905–6). During his convalescence, which he spent near Tarragona, Mir produced his most creative work, representing the light and colour of the landscape in a bold, almost abstract way, for example *Landscape* (José Miarnau priv. col., see 1971 exh. cat., cover pl.). He won a first-class medal at the fifth Exposició Internacional in Barcelona (1907) and showed 90 works in a one-man exhibition at the Faianç Català gallery in Barcelona in 1909. He also participated in several group exhibitions in Madrid, Paris, Pittsburgh, Washington, DC, Philadelphia and elsewhere, and won the medal of honour of the Exposición Nacional de Bellas Artes of Madrid in 1930. In later years he continued to exhibit internationally, for example in Oslo, Venice, Amsterdam, Buenos Aires and London, but his painting became more conventional. This later work did not, however, diminish his achievement from the beginning of the century to the 1920s, not only as an exceptionally creative force in Catalan art but also as one of the most undervalued European Post-Impressionists.

BIBLIOGRAPHY

J. Pla: *El pintor Joaquin Mir* (Barcelona, 1944)
Joaquin Mir (1873–1940): Exposición antológica (exh. cat.; Madrid, Dir. Gen. B.A., 1971)
Exposición Joaquin Mir (exh. cat., text by M. T. Camps Miró and others; Barcelona, Mus. A. Mod., 1972)
E. Jardí: *J. Mir* (Barcelona, 1975)
F. Fontbona: *Mir* (Barcelona, 1983)

FRANCESC FONTBONA DE VALLESCAR

Mirabello di Salincorno. *See* CAVALORI, MIRABELLO.

Mirador. Site of Pre-Columbian MAYA city in the lowland forests of northern Petén, Guatemala. It flourished *c.* 150 BC–*c.* AD 150, but parts were also used in later periods. Survey and excavation work indicates that its centre measured *c.* 16 sq. km, making it the largest known concentration of Maya civic and religious structures. Its acropoleis were surmounted by immense platforms, plazas and other buildings. Such monumental structures were commonly constructed of cut-stone block masonry, plastered over and ornamented with stucco masks of Maya gods. According to Ray T. Matheny and others, Mirador provides evidence that such Pre-Classic Maya cities were the focus of early states that rivalled later, Classic period (*c.* AD 250–*c.* 900) Maya civilization. The creation of a city as immense as Mirador would certainly have required strong and complex social controls to produce the architects and artisans and to mobilize the necessary workforce and supplies.

The Tigre Complex, about half the size of the ceremonial centre at Maya TIKAL, includes the truncated Tigre Pyramid (h. 53 m, base 150×145 m). As is common at Mirador, it was surmounted by three temples, with the Tigre Temple, decorated with stucco masks, at the centre of the group. The pyramid faced a plaza surrounded on three sides by lower platforms supporting various structures, some of which also had stucco-mask decoration. Pottery found in the excavation of the Tigre Complex indicates that it was built in the 2nd and 1st centuries BC and abandoned *c.* AD 150. The Monos Complex, 42 m high and covering *c.* 28,000 sq. m, also includes a pyramid, plaza and other constructions. Its lower structures date to the Middle Pre-Classic period (*c.* 1000–*c.* 300 BC) and the upper structures to the Late Pre-Classic period (*c.* 300 BC–*c.* AD 250).

A wide central stairway leads from the huge Central Plaza to the Central Acropolis, *c.* 330×100 m. At the top of the stairway is an altar platform of 12 stone slabs set in sockets. The stones are about the size of stelae but lack surface carving, and they may have been painted instead. A stone altar, for example, was covered with red paint. The Central Plaza and Central Acropolis make up a sacred precinct, entered through a low wall of mortared limestone blocks, where a partially carved stele was found. This precinct was used from *c.* 440 BC to the Early Classic period (*c.* AD 250–*c.* 600). One Late Pre-Classic period structure was probably an élite residence. Its stucco-covered walls of carefully cut stone were found in good condition, and remains of painted wall decoration and sculpture included a room with bright red and yellow bands on the threshold.

The Danta Complex, to the east of the Central Plaza, is the highest in Mirador, because it was constructed on a hill. Covering approximately 150,000 sq. m, it includes two great pyramids on a single platform, with a plaza between them. The base measurement of the larger Danta Pyramid is 300×250 m, but it is only one of many structures in the complex. The complex is approached by a raised causeway, one of several in and around the site that allowed access during seasonal flooding.

BIBLIOGRAPHY

B. H. Dahlin: 'A Colossus in Guatemala', *Archaeology*, xxxvii/5 (1984), pp. 18–25
R. T. Matheny: 'Early States in the Maya Lowlands during the Late Classic Period', *City States of the Maya*, ed. E. P. Benson (Denver, 1986), pp. 1–44
——: 'El Mirador', *N. Geog.*, clxxii (1987), pp. 316–39
W. K. Howell and D. R. Evans Copeland: *Excavations at El Mirador, Peten, Gautemala: The Danta and Monos Complexes*, Pap. New World Archaeol. Found., lx, lxi (Provo, UT, 1989)
R. D. Hansen: *Excavations in the Tigre Complex, El Mirador, Peten, Guatemala*, Pap. New World Archaeol. Found., lxii (Provo, UT, 1990)

ELIZABETH P. BENSON

Miradori, Luigi [il Genovesino] (*b* Genoa, *c.* 1600–10; *d* ?Cremona, 1656–7). Italian painter. He is documented in Genoa in 1630 and 1631 and himself declared his Genoese origins in inscriptions on several paintings. In 1632 he was in Piacenza, where he seems to have lived for several years. His first dated picture, the *Holy Family* (1639; Piacenza, Mus. Civ.), was probably painted there. A group of works that predate this painting suggest that the sources of his early style united aspects of the art of Lombard painters (particularly Morazzone and Francesco Cairo) with Emilian and, above all, Genoese sources. The four *Legends of Samson* (Milan, priv. col., see 1973 exh. cat., figs 196, 197, cat. nos 175–6), which probably date from the artist's early years, and the *Pagan Sacrifice* (Parma, G.N.) are all strongly influenced by Bernardo Strozzi,

Gioacchino Assereto and Domenico Fiasella, whereas the *Martyrdom of a Saint* (ex-Borg de Balzan priv. col., Florence) is indebted to Andrea Ansaldo. The animals in the foreground of the Piacenza *Holy Family* recall the art of Sinibaldo Scorza. Throughout his career Miradori's art is distinguished by his naturalistic rendering of detail and a subtle use of spotlit effects, which suggest an awareness of Caravaggesque painting. Indebted to this tradition is his youthful *St Sebastian Tended by St Irene* (Cremona, Cavalcabo priv. col., see 1973 exh. cat., fig. 192), although this is also reminiscent of Tanzio da Varallo, and his *Lute Player* (Genoa, Gal. Pal. Rosso; see fig.), which has in the past been attributed to Orazio Gentileschi.

It has been suggested (see 1951 exh. cat.) that Miradori visited Rome before moving to Cremona, where he is first recorded in 1641. The first dated Cremonese work is the *Immaculate Conception* (1640; Castelleone, parish church). In 1642 he painted the *Birth of St Charles* and the *Death of St Charles* (Cremona, Mus. Berenziano), also the *Martyrdom of St Paul* (Cremona, Mus. Civ. Ala Ponzone), painted for S Lorenzo in Cremona, which bears an inscription that acknowledges the artist's dependence on a prototype by Guercino for its composition. For the same church at about that time Miradori executed the *Birth of the Virgin* (Cremona, Mus. Civ. Ala Ponzone) and the *Martyrdom of the Blessed Bernard* (Soresina, parish church). The latter is close to aspects of Spanish art, in particular to that of Zurbarán, and it may be significant that one of

Miradori's Cremonese patrons was Don Alvaro de Quiñones, the Spanish governor and castellan of the city, who sent some of the artist's works to Spain.

The *Martyrdom of St Lawrence* and the *Massacre of the Innocents* (both 1643; Piacenza, priv. col.), which are rich in detail and lively incident, reveal Miradori's gift for narrative. This is again apparent in the paintings that decorate the altar of St Roch in Cremona Cathedral; these include three large canvases representing the *Procession with the Statue of St Roch*, *St Roch Visiting the Plague-stricken* and *St Roch and the Animals* and six small scenes of the *Life and Miracles of St Roch*. A surprisingly strong anecdotal streak is apparent in these works, particularly in the small scenes, which are filled with small spirited figures often set in attractive landscapes. In this they are comparable to the Lombard works of Carlo Ceresa and Giovanni Giacomo Barbello (1590–1656), but above all they reveal a familiarity with contemporary Genoese painting, especially that of Giovanni Benedetto Castiglione.

Miradori tended to humanize religious imagery and to insert scenes of everyday life into his religious pictures, a characteristic that suggests a familiarity with the work of the Dutch Italianates and supports the thesis of a visit to Rome. His *Miracle of the Loaves and Fishes* (1647; Cremona, Pal. Com.) incorporates a striking foreground depiction of beggars and of the poor. On the extreme right of the picture, set among other figures, is Miradori's self-portrait, which corresponds perfectly with Biffi's vivid image: 'He would march around the city with a red cap on his head, moustache in the Spanish manner and little goatee beard.' This naturalistic treatment of religious subject-matter, which also characterizes the *Miracle of the Host* (Soresina, S Maria del Cingaro), points to the continuing influence of Caravaggesque painting.

In the late 1640s and early 1650s Miradori executed works for Milan and other Lombard towns, and he received many commissions for Cremona and its surroundings. Among these are the *St Jerome* (1646; Treviglio, S Martino) and the *Virgin and Child with Saints* (1646; Castello Cabiaglio, nr Varese, parish church). In 1648 he executed the *Virgin Appearing to St John of Damascene* (Cremona, S Maria Maddalena) and in 1651 the *Virgin Appearing to the Blessed Felice da Cantalice* (Compiègne, Château). The genre-like *Rest on the Flight into Egypt* (1651; Cremona, S Imerio), with its spacious landscape setting with Classical ruins, indicates the artist's awareness of the *vedute* of Viviano Codazzi. Various 17th-century inventories suggest that Miradori also painted landscapes, although few are known; the *Idealized View of Genoa*, signed and dated 1648 (ex-Apolloni priv. col., Rome), is close in style to contemporary Roman landscape painting, while the foreground figures again recall the Dutch Italianates.

Dated paintings survive from the artist's last years. In 1652 he executed the *Virgin of the Rosary* (Casalbuttano, parish church) and the *Martyrdom and the Triumph of St Ursula* (Cremona, S Marcellina). The *Last Supper* (Soresina, parish church) dates from 1653 and the *St Nicholas, Bishop of Myra, Praying for Genoa* (Milan, Brera) from 1654. Miradori was also celebrated as a portrait painter, and his gifts are confirmed by rare surviving works including the portraits of an *Olivetan Monk of the Pueroni*

Luigi Miradori: *Lute Player*, oil on canvas, 1.38×1.00 m (Genoa, Galleria di Palazzo Rosso)

Family (New York, Hisp. Soc. America), which is close in style to Zurbarán, of *Gian Giacomo Teodoro Trivulzio* (ex-Keinberger Anderson Gal., New York, see Gregori, 1954, fig. 13a) and the *Portrait of a Girl* (ex-Chaucer A.G., London).

BIBLIOGRAPHY

Thieme–Becker [with bibliog. to 1930]

G. Biffi: *Memorie per servire alla storia degli artisti cremonesi* (Cremona [18th century]); ed. L. Bandera (Cremona, 1989)

Caravaggio e dei caravaggeschi (exh. cat. by R. Longhi, Milan, Pal. Reale, 1951), pp. 61–2

M. Gregori: 'Alcuni aspetti del Genovesino', *Paragone*, v/59 (1954), pp. 7–29 [fundamental study]

Il seicento lombardo, 3 vols (exh. cat., ed. G. A. dell' Acqua; Milan, Pal. Reale, 1973), i, pp. 67–9

M. Tanzi: 'Un ritratto del Genovesino', *Ric. Stor. A.*, xxxiii (1987), pp. 87–90

F. Arisi: 'Dipinti "piacentini" del Genovesino', *Strenna Piacent.* (1989), pp. 43–63

M. Tanzi: 'Genovesino a Castelponzone', *Ric. Stor. A.*, xxxviii (1989), pp. 91–5

M. Gregori: 'La presenza del Genovesino', *La pittura a Cremona dal romanico al settecento* (Milan, 1990), pp. 60–63, 292–5

FRANCESCO FRANGI

Mir Afzal. *See* AFZAL.

Mirailhet [Miralhet; Miralheti], **Jean** [Johes] (*fl* ?1400; *d* by 8 Oct 1457). French painter. He is documented from 1418 in Nice and Marseille and was cited as a citizen of the latter in 1432. He may perhaps be identified with the Jean Mirailhet who was enrolled at the head of the statutes of painters and glaziers of Montpellier on 13 May 1400, for he is designated on several occasions as a painter from Montpellier. He is last mentioned in a receipt of 18 July 1444.

Jean Mirailhet was commissioned to paint altarpieces depicting the *Annunciation and SS Anthony and Catherine* (1432) for a chapel in the church of La Major, Marseille, the *Virgin and Child with SS John the Baptist and Honoré and Seven Praying Figures* (1440) from a merchant of Toulon and *St Catherine with SS Agatha and Lucy* (1443) for the chapel of the Crucifix in St Jacques-de-la-Corrigerie, Marseille; all these are untraced. In 1437 the Confrérie des Tisserands of Aix ordered from him a banner that was to include depictions of the Trinity, the symbols of the guild (shuttles) and the arms of King René I of Naples (Duke d'Anjou).

Mirailhet's only surviving work is the large polyptych (2.60×2.19 m; Nice, Chapel of the Pénitents Noirs) from the chapel of the Confrérie de la Miséricorde in Ste Réparate, Nice: the right panel with *SS Sebastian and Gregory* is signed HOC PINXIT JOH[ANN]ES MIRALHETI. Generally dated *c.* 1425, it has been heavily restored. The influence of Catalan art in the arrangement of the frame, the treatment of the gold and the stiffness of the figures in the polyptych are also seen in contemporary works by other Provençal painters: a slightly later *Calvary with Saints and Donors* (Aix-en-Provence, Mus. Arbaud) and a *Virgin and Child with Six Angels* by Jacobus Cairolus of Brignoles (*fl* 1436–54), signed and dated 1436 (Philadelphia, PA, Fleischer A. Mem.).

BIBLIOGRAPHY

G. Brès: *Questioni d'arte regionale: Studio critico: Altre notizie inedite sui pittori nicesi* (Nice, 1911), pp. 44–54

L. H. Labande: 'Les Peintres niçois des XVe et XVIe siècles', *Gaz. B.-A.*, liv (1912), pp. 279–97

Abbé H. Requin: 'Les Primitifs niçois chez les notaires d'Aix', *Nice Hist.* (1912), pp. 105–16

Catalogue de l'exposition rétrospective d'art régional (exh. cat., ed. J. Levrot; Nice, Mus. B.-A., 1912), pp. 66–8

L. H. Labande: *Les Primitifs français: Peintres et peintres-verriers de la Provence occidentale* (Marseille, 1932), p. 133

C. Sterling: *La Peinture française: Les Peintres du moyen âge* (Paris, 1942), p. 27; XIVe siècle suppl. A, p. 10

Primitifs de Nice et des écoles voisines (exh. cat., ed. J. Thirion; Nice, Mus. Masséna, 1960), p. 13

DOMINIQUE THIÉBAUT

Mirak [Mīrak Naqqāsh; Amīr Rūḥallāh] (*fl* Herat, *c.* 1468–1507). Persian calligrapher, illuminator and illustrator. The chroniclers Mirza Muhammad Haydar Dughlat and Dust Muhammad refer to Mirak as the teacher of the painter BIHZAD, who was also brought up by Mirak, according to the author Qazi Ahmad. Mirak rose to become director of the library of the Timurid sultan Husayn Bayqara (*reg* 1470–1506; *see* TIMURID, §II(8)) and attended the Sultan closely, on journeys and at court. According to Haydar Dughlat, Mirak worked in the open air and was known for his athletic abilities. Paintings attributed to him include four illustrations (one a double frontispiece) from a copy of Nizami's *Khamsa* ('Five poems'; 1494–5; London, BL, Or. MS. 6810) to which Mirak's name has been added in the margins by later hands. He was probably responsible for the four contemporary paintings in a copy of 'Attar's *Mantiq al-ṭayr* ('Conference of the birds'; New York, Met., 67.210.1–67; *see* ISLAMIC ART, fig. 121) and may have planned the compositions for the other four not finished until the early 17th century. Mirak's figures are stiffer and more archaic in comparison to Bihzad's work. The Timurid historian Khwandamir related that Mirak designed most of the inscriptions in the buildings of Herat and died during the occupation of Khurasan by Muhammad Shaybani (*reg* 1500–10).

BIBLIOGRAPHY

Ghiyāth al-Dīn Khwāndamīr: *Ḥabīb al-siyar* [Beloved of careers] (1523–4); ed. J. Huma'i, iv (Tehran, Iran. Solar 1333/1954), p. 349; Eng. trans., ed. W. M. Thackston in *A Century of Princes: Sources on Timurid History and Art* (Cambridge, MA, 1989), pp. 101–236 (225)

Mīrzā Muḥammad Ḥaydar Dughlāt: *Tārīkh-i Rashīdī* [Rashidian history] (1541–7); extract ed. M. Shafi' as 'Iqtibās az *Tārīkh-i Rashīdī*', *Orient. Coll. Mag.*, x/3 (1934), pp. 150–72 (167); Eng. trans., abridged, ed. W. M. Thackston in *A Century of Princes: Sources on Timurid History and Art* (Cambridge, MA, 1989), pp. 357–62 (362)

Dūst Muḥammad: *Preface to the Bahram Mirza Album* (1544); Eng. trans., ed. W. M. Thackston in *A Century of Princes: Sources on Timurid History and Art* (Cambridge, MA, 1989), pp. 335–50 (347)

Qāẓī Aḥmad ibn Mīr Munshī: *Gulistān-i hunar* [Rose-garden of art] (*c.* 1606); Eng. trans. by V. Minorsky as *Calligraphers and Painters* (Washington, DC, 1959), p. 180

I. S. Stchoukine: *Les Peintures des manuscrits tîmurîdes* (Paris, 1954), pp. 20–21, 78–81, 131–2

M. L. Swietochowski: 'The Language of the Birds: The Fifteenth-century Miniatures', *Bull. Met.*, xxv (May 1967), pp. 317–38

A. S. Melikian-Chirvani: 'Khwāje Mīrak Naqqāsh', *J. Asiat.*, cclxxvi (1988), pp. 97–146

S. J. VERNOIT

Mir 'Ali Husayni Haravi [Mīr 'Alī Ḥusaynī Haravī] (*b* Herat, *c.* 1476; *d* Bukhara, 1543). Persian calligrapher. Mir 'Ali worked in Herat and Mashhad under the Timurids and continued working in Herat after the Safavid conquest in 1506. When the Uzbeks occupied the city in 1529 he was taken to Bukhara, where he remained until his death.

A master of *nasta'līq* (a rhythmic curvilinear script), Mir 'Ali designed architectural inscriptions and penned manuscripts and calligraphic specimens (Pers. *qit'a*) in which Persian quatrains are written on the diagonal. He used a thick line, often omitting diacritical marks and never adding the stroke to distinguish the letter *gāf* from *kāf*. During Mir 'Ali's lifetime his calligraphy was popular but not universally admired. The Ottoman chronicler Mustafa 'Ali commented with astonishment that in his day (late 16th century) a specimen of Mir 'Ali's calligraphy could command up to five or six thousand akçes, while a first-rate specimen by SULTAN 'ALI MASHHADI brought no more than four or five thousand. Nonetheless Mir 'Ali's calligraphy, if lacking some of the discipline and formality of Sultan 'Ali's hand, became the model of *nasta'līq* (*see* ISLAMIC ART, §III, 2(iv)(b)) and was eagerly collected, particularly by the Mughal emperors of India. Albums created for Jahangir (*reg* 1605–27) and Shah Jahan (*reg* 1628–58), such as the Kevorkian Album (New York, Met.; Washington, DC, Freer) and the Berlin Album (Berlin, Staatsbib. Preuss. Kultbes., Orientabt.), contain many examples of Mir 'Ali's calligraphy brilliantly illuminated by the artisans of the Mughal workshops. According to Mustafa 'Ali, Mir 'Ali permitted his pupils to put his signature on their works, and this may account for the large number of calligraphic specimens attributed to him.

BIBLIOGRAPHY

Enc. Iran.: "'Alī Heravī"
Muṣṭafā 'Ali: *Manāqib-i hunarvarān* [Virtues of artists] (1587); ed. I. M. Kemal (Istanbul, 1926), pp. 44ff
Qāẓī Ahmad ibn Mīr Munshī: *Gulistān-i hunar* [Rose-garden of art] (*c*. 1606); Eng. trans. by V. Minorsky as *Calligraphers and Painters* (Washington, DC, 1959), pp. 126–31
The Grand Mogul (exh. cat. by M. C. Beach, Williamstown, MA, Clark A. Inst.; Baltimore, MD, Walters A.G.; Boston, MA, Mus. F.A.; New York, Asia House Gals; 1978–9), pp. 43, 46, 51, 55–8
M. Bayani: *Aḥvāl va āthār-i khūshnivīsān* [Biographies and works of calligraphers], 2nd edn in 4 vols (Tehran, Iran. Solar 1363/1984–5), pp. 493–516
A. Schimmel: 'The Calligraphy and Poetry of the Kevorkian Album', *The Emperors' Album*, ed. S. C. Welch and others (New York, 1987), pp. 32–6

WHEELER M. THACKSTON

Mir 'Ali Shir. *See* 'ALISHIR NAVA'I.

Mir 'Ali Tabrizi [Mīr 'Alī ibn Ḥasan al-Tabrīzī al-Sulṭānī] (*fl c.* 1340–*c.* 1420). Persian calligrapher. He is acknowledged as the inventor of *nasta'līq*, a fluid, rhythmic and curvilinear script, but his life and identity are shrouded in confusion. In a treatise by the Timurid calligrapher SULTAN 'ALI MASHHADI, Mir 'Ali is mentioned as a contemporary of the poet Khwaju Khujandi (*d* 1400), an older contemporary of the poet Hafiz (1325–90). Two calligraphers named Mir 'Ali Tabrizi were active in the late 14th century: Mir 'Ali ibn Ilyas, who worked for the last Jalayirid ruler of Baghdad, Ahmad ibn Uways (*reg* 1382–1410), and Mir 'Ali ibn Hasan al-Sultani, described by his most famous student JA'FAR Baysunghuri as the 'inventor of the archetype', namely *nasta'līq* script. The only surviving example of Mir 'Ali's hand is an incomplete manuscript (Washington, DC, Freer) of Nizami's *Khusraw and Shirin* copied at Tabriz (*see* ISLAMIC ART, fig. 99). The date of the manuscript is lost, but the style of its fine paintings, which are contemporary with the text, suggests it was copied between

1405 and 1415, near the end of Mir 'Ali's life. His students, such as Ja'far, made *nasta'līq* the predominant vehicle for copying poetry in the 15th century.

BIBLIOGRAPHY
P. P. Soucek: 'The Arts of Calligraphy', *The Arts of the Book in Central Asia, 14th–16th Centuries*, ed. B. Gray (London and Paris, 1979), pp. 18–24
From Concept to Context: Approaches to Asian and Islamic Calligraphy (exh. cat. by S. Fu, G. D. Lowry and A. Yonemura, Washington, DC, Freer, 1986), pp. 128–9; no. 45

SHEILA R. CANBY

Miran. Site of Buddhist monastic complexes and Tibetan fort in south-eastern Xinjiang Uygur Autonomous Region, China. The earliest Buddhist complexes in eastern Central Asia, containing paintings of the 3rd–4th century AD, were discovered by Aurel Stein in 1906–7. Altogether Stein identified 16 buildings, some in a fragmentary state. Among them were two clay-brick stupas, which he called M. III and M. V. M. III consisted of a cella, the ground-plan of which was square externally and circular internally. In the centre stood a stupa on a circular base, probably of several storeys, with an ambulatory passageway round it. The interior of the cella was lit by three windows facing south, east and north; the entrance faced west. The walls of the ambulatory were covered with painted friezes ranged one above the other. The lower part of the wall was painted with lunette friezes separated from the paintings above by a dark, patterned band. The friezes in the north-east and south-east consisted of six lunettes. In the arch of each was depicted a human, winged creature whose soft round face with large eyes was turned to the left in three-quarter profile; apart from a thick tress on the top of the head and a wavy lock in front of the ear the hair was shorn (e.g. New Delhi, N. Mus.; see Yaldiz, pl. XXXII). The main paintings in the north-east and south-east sections—pictures of Buddhist legends—had become detached. One showed a standing Buddha with a nimbus in three-quarter profile. Based on a comparison with the style of GANDHARA, the great curly, flowing knot of hair, wide-open eyes and moustache would suggest that this was an early Buddha type (New Delhi, N. Mus.; see Yaldiz, pl. XXXIII).

The stupa–temple M. V, architecturally very similar to M. III, consisted of a round cella with a stupa in the centre, but in this case there were no windows and the entrance faced north. The external ground-plan was square, with an additional corridor; the pictures on its walls were in a better state of preservation and richer in content than those in M. III. The lower sections again consisted of lunettes depicting winged human creatures and figures bearing garlands. The upper frieze included a small, naked figure in combat with a griffin (see Stein, i, pl. 133), another subject borrowed from the art of Gandhara. To the left of the entrance on the south-eastern section of the circular ambulatory, friezes included figures bearing garlands, separated by a border from scenes from the popular Vishvantara legend, one of many stories of the past lives of the Buddha (e.g. New Delhi, N. Mus.; see Yaldiz, pls 105–107). The style of the wall paintings was very simple.

The more recent complex that Stein called M. I, a Tibetan fort, is of historical interest. More than 1000 documents in the Tibetan language were found here, some dated, which suggest that the complex was used by Tibetans as a military station between AD 775 and 860. Its strategic importance is incontrovertible, as the small oasis could be relatively easily reached from Lhasa and formed a point of entry into eastern Central Asia. Among finds here were items of lacquered armour (*see* CENTRAL ASIA, §II, 5(i) and (ix)).

See also CENTRAL ASIA, §II, 3(ii)(a), 4(i) and (ii)(a).

BIBLIOGRAPHY

M. A.-M. Boyer: 'Inscriptions de Miran', *J. Asiat.*, xvii (May–June 1911), pp. 413–30
M. A. Stein: *Serindia: Detailed Report of Explorations in Central Asia and Westernmost China*, 5 vols (Oxford, 1921/*R* New Delhi, 1981)
F. H. Andrews: *Catalogue of Wall Paintings from Ancient Shrines in Central Asia and Sistan, Recovered by Sir Aurel Stein* (Delhi, 1933)
H. G. Franz: *Von Gandhara bis Pagan* (Graz, 1979)
M. Yaldiz: *Archäologie und Kunstgeschichte Chinesisch-Zentralasiens (Xinjiang)* (1987), iii/2 of *Handbuch der Orientalistik*, ed. B. Spuler and others (Leiden, 1978–)
C. Paula: *Miran and the Paintings from Shrines M. III and M. V* (diss., U. London, 1992)

M. YALDIZ

Miranda, Fernando (*fl* 1811–54). Spanish illustrator and painter. He devoted himself mainly to magazine illustration and contributed to numerous journals, such as *Semanario pintoresco español*, *Periodico ilustrado*, *Siglo pintoresco*, *La Semana* and *Ilustración española*. Miranda also illustrated many general books on Spanish topics, including *Historia de la marina real española* (Madrid, 1854) by José March y Labores, *El panorama español*, *Historia de El Escorial*, *Estado mayor del Ejército*, *Galería regia* and *El pavellón español*. Among the novels he illustrated were editions of Cervantes: *Historia de los trabajos de Persiles y Sigismunda* and *Galatea* (both Madrid, 1805); other works include *El curato mandamiento* and *Memorias de un hechicero*. He sometimes used the signature *F. Miranda*, which has led to the confusion of his work with that of the engraver Francisco Miranda.

BIBLIOGRAPHY

M. Ossorio y Bernard: *Galería biográfica de artistas españoles del siglo XIX* (Madrid, 1868, 2/1883–4/*R* Barcelona, 1975)
E. Paez Rios: *Répertorio*, ii (1981), pp. 226–7

BLANCA GARCÍA VEGA

Miranda, Juan Carreño de. *See* CARREÑO DE MIRANDA, JUAN.

Miranda, Juan García de. *See* GARCÍA DE MIRANDA, JUAN.

Miricenis [Miricenys, Miricinus, Miriginus, Mirycinis], **Petrus.** *See* HEYDEN, PIETER VAN DER.

Miriliano, Giovanni. *See* MARIGLIANO, GIOVANNI.

Mir 'Imad [Mīr 'Imād; 'Imād al-Ḥasanī] (*b* ?1554; *d* Isfahan, 1615). Persian calligrapher. He studied calligraphy with Mulla Muhammad Tabrizi and then travelled extensively, visiting Anatolia, the Hijaz and Khurasan, where he served Farhad Khan Qaramanlu, commander-in-chief of the Safavid shah 'Abbas I. After Farhad Khan's death in 1598, Mir 'Imad moved to Qazvin and the following year settled in Isfahan, where he became one of the most famous masters of *nasta'līq* script at the court of 'Abbas

(*see* ISLAMIC ART, §III, 2(iv)(b)). Mir 'Imad vied for the monarch's favour with the calligrapher 'Ali Riza, who is said to have arranged his rival's assassination; he was buried in the mosque of Maqsud Beg. Mir 'Imad continued the tradition of MIR 'ALI HUSAYNI HARAVI and penned many books, epistles and single folios with Persian quatrains written on the diagonal. Specimens of his work are included in the Leningrad Album (St Petersburg, Acad. Sci., Inst. Orient. Stud., E/14) and other albums in Tehran (Royal Lib.), Paris (Bib. N.) and Istanbul (U. Lib.).

BIBLIOGRAPHY

Qāżī Aḥmad ibn Mīr Munshī: *Gulistān-i hunar* [Rose-garden of art] (*c.* 1606); Eng. trans. by V. Minorsky as *Calligraphers and Painters* (Washington, DC, 1959), pp. 167–8
A. A. Ivanov, T. B. Grek and O. F. Akimushkin: *Album indiiskikh i persidskikh miniatur XVI–XVIII vv.* [Album of Indian and Persian miniatures, 16th–18th century] (Moscow, 1962), pls 6, 104–11
M. Bayani: *Aḥvāl va āthār-i khushnivīsān* [Biographies and works of calligraphers], 2nd edn in 4 vols (Tehran, Iran. Solar 1363/1984–5), pp. 518–38

Mir Iskusstva. *See* WORLD OF ART.

Mirko (Basaldella) (*b* Udine, 28 Sept 1910; *d* Cambridge, MA, 24 Nov 1969). Italian sculptor. In the late 1920s he studied at the Accademia di Belle Arti in Florence, and in the early 1930s he became a pupil of Arturo Martini at the Istituto Superiore per le Industrie Artistiche in Monza. He moved in 1934 to Rome, where he became a follower of the Scuola Romana and worked closely with Corrado Cagli, whose sister he married in 1938.

In 1936 Mirko held his first one-man exhibition in the Galleria della Cometa in Rome. The works of this period show his interest in the Antique and the prehistoric, as in the *Chimera* (1935; Rome, priv. col., see Crispolti, 1974, pp. 32–3). This interest led him to try to reconcile ancestral forms drawn from ancient civilizations with the aims of the avant-garde movements of the 20th century and in particular with Cubism and Surrealism. In December 1939 he took part in the second exhibition organized by the Corrente group in the Galleria Grande in Milan. His works, including a vast collection of graphics, display his use of a variety of materials and techniques, as in the three gates at the Cancello delle Fosse Ardeatine in Rome (1949–51) and the *Totem* series of 1955–66 (now Rome, priv. col.). From 1957 Mirko lived principally in Cambridge, MA, where he was Director of the Design Workshop at Harvard University. His brother, Afro Basaldella, was a painter.

BIBLIOGRAPHY

Sculture di Mirko (exh. cat. by C. Scarfoglio, Rome, Gal. Cometa, 1936)
E. Crispolti: *Le sculture di Mirko* (Bologna, 1974)

SAVERIO SIMI DE BURGIS

Mir Muhammad Yusuf. *See* MUHAMMAD YUSUF.

Mir Musavvir [Mīr Muṣavvir] (*b* Termez or Badakhshan, late 15th century; *fl* Tabriz, *c.* 1510–48; *d* India, *c.* 1555). Persian illustrator and painter. According to the contemporary chronicler Dust Muhammad, Mir Musavvir and AQA MIRAK were two matchless sayyids in service to the Safavid royal library who did wall paintings for the palace of Prince Sam Mirza and illustrations for royal manuscripts of Firdawsi's *Shāhnāma* ('Book of kings') and Nizami's

Khamsa ('Five poems'). *Manuchihr Enthroned* (fol. 60*v*) from the monumental copy (dispersed; ex-Houghton priv. col.) of the *Shāhnāma* made for Tahmasp (*reg* 1524–76) is signed on a courtier's turban, and a verse couplet written in the iwan in *Nushirwan and the Owls* (fol. 15*v*) in a magnificent copy (London, BL, Or. MS. 2265) of the *Khamsa*, made for the Shah between 1539 and 1543, says that it was penned by Mir Musavvir in 1539–40. A portrait of the steward Sarkhan Beg (London, BM, 1930–11–12–02) is also inscribed as the work of Mir Musavvir.

Based on these attributions or signatures, Dickson and Welch have reconstructed his biography. Having contributed one painting (fol. 59*r*) to a manuscript (St Petersburg, Saltykov–Shchedrin Pub. Lib., Dorn 441) of 'Arifi's *Gūy ū chawgān* ('Ball and bandy') copied at Tabriz in 1524–5, and one (fol. 321*v*) to a copy (New York, Met., 13.228.7) of the *Khamsa* transcribed in the same year at Herat, the artist turned his energies to the great *Shāhnāma*. Dickson and Welch attribute eight of its paintings to him, including the *Nightmare of Zahhak* (fol. 28*v*), the most complex composition in the manuscript. In *Ardashir and the Slave Girl Gulnar* (fol. 516*v*), the only dated painting in the manuscript (1527–8), the artist's loving attention to detail—the rope dangling from the wall, the flowering trees against the night sky and the shoes neatly positioned beside the bed—combines with his wonderfully modulated palette and convincing portrayal of figures to produce an intensely sweet and lyrical work. Dickson and Welch surmise that the artist then succeeded SULTAN-MUHAMMAD as director of the *Shāhnāma* project, supervising and correcting the work of others. According to the Safavid chronicler Qazi Ahmad, when the Mughal emperor Humayun was in exile at the Safavid court in 1544 he offered 1000 tumans in exchange for Mir Musavvir. The offer tempted the artist's son, MIR SAYYID 'ALI, to leave for India, and his father followed in 1548 (*see also* INDIAN SUBCONTINENT, §V, 4(i)(a)).

BIBLIOGRAPHY

Dūst Muḥammad: Preface to the Bahram Mirza Album (1544); Eng. trans., ed. W. M. Thackston in *A Century of Princes: Sources on Timurid History and Art* (Cambridge, MA, 1989), pp. 348–9

Qāżī Aḥmad ibn Mīr Munshī: *Gulistān-i hunar* [Rose-garden of art] (*c.* 1606); Eng. trans. by V. Minorsky as *Calligraphers and Painters* (Washington, DC, 1959), p. 185

M. B. Dickson and S. C. Welch: *The Houghton Shāhnāmeh* (Cambridge, MA, 1981), pp. 87–94 [many pls]

SHEILA R. CANBY

Miró, Joan (*b* Barcelona, 20 April 1893; *d* Palma de Mallorca, 25 Dec 1983). Spanish painter, sculptor, printmaker and decorative artist. He was never closely aligned with any movement and was too retiring in his manner to be the object of a personality cult, like his compatriot Picasso, but the formal and technical innovations that he sustained over a very long career guaranteed his influence on 20th-century art. A pre-eminent figure in the history of abstraction and an important example to several generations of artists around the world, he remained profoundly attached to the specific circumstances and environment that shaped his art in his early years. An acute balance of sophistication and innocence and a deeply rooted conviction about the relationship between art and nature lie behind all his work and account in good measure

for the wide appeal that his art has continued to exercise across many of the usual barriers of style.

1. Life and work. 2. Influence and posthumous reputation.

1. LIFE AND WORK.

(i) Childhood and work, to 1919. (ii) Paris, 1920–39. (iii) Paintings, 1939–*c.* 1950. (iv) Experiments with printmaking, ceramics, sculpture and painting in the 1940s and 1950s. (v) After 1960.

(i) Childhood and work, to 1919. Miró came from a family of craftsmen. His father Miquel, the son of a blacksmith, was a goldsmith from the vicinity of Tarragona in southern Catalonia; his mother, Dolors Ferrà, was the daughter of a carpenter from Mallorca. He initially obeyed his family's wishes that he follow a business career by studying at the Escuela de Comercio in Barcelona from 1907 to 1910, but in 1911 an attack of typhus, coupled with nervous depression, enabled him to abandon the course. He recuperated in his parents' country house at Montroig, south of Tarragona, a peaceful place to which he often returned in later life and in which his artistic vocation and devotion to nature were confirmed. Plants, insects, simple forms of life; the stars, sun, moon and sea, especially the Mediterranean; the cultivated countryside itself, together with elements of rural existence, all later found their way into his work.

In 1907 Miró began his artistic training in Barcelona at the Escuela de Artes y Oficios de la Lonja, where Picasso had studied 12 years earlier; his teachers were Modest Urgell (1839–1919) and Josep Pascó (1855–1910). In 1912 he entered the escuela de arte run by the great teacher Francesc Galí (1880–1965), and there met the potter Josep Llorens ARTIGAS, with whom he formed a lifelong friendship. Galí noticed that Miró had an aptitude for colour but difficulty in delineating shapes, and therefore blindfolded him so that he would acquaint himself with the forms by touching them before drawing them or modelling them in clay. Miró's first paintings date from this period, for example *The Peasant* (1914; Paris, Gal. Maeght, see 1981 exh. cat., p. 49). In 1915 Miró left the Escuela Galí and began attending drawing classes at the Círculo Artístico de Sant Lluc, where Artigas was again a fellow student and where he met Joan Prats (1891–1970), who became another great friend. In 1918 Miró became one of the first members of the Grupo Courbet, an association of artists founded by Artigas with other students from Sant Lluc.

Between 1915 and 1918 Miró briefly painted in a manner that he himself described as Fauve, using strong, bright colours. His tendencies, however, to geometry, broad brushwork and a clarity of construction distanced his work from the earlier movement. During this period he painted figures, as in his portrait of *V. Nubiela* (1917; Essen, Mus. Flkwang), as well as landscapes and views of villages in the province of Tarragona, for example *The Road from En Güell* (1917; New York, MOMA). 1918 was a decisive year: Miró held his first one-man show in the Barcelona gallery run by Lluís Dalmau, a key figure in the Catalan avant-garde, who in 1912 had dared to exhibit the Paris Cubist painters. It was vital to Miró's development that Barcelona was then a very lively cultural centre that attracted foreign artists seeking refuge from World War I.

Miró remained faithful to the brilliance of colour of his early work, but under the influence of Paul Cézanne and

1. Joan Miró: *Vegetable Garden with Donkey*, oil on canvas, 640×700 mm, 1918 (Stockholm, Moderna Museum)

Cubism he continued to emphasize the underlying construction of his pictures. In his works of 1918 to 1922 he introduced a meticulousness and precision of drawing, not out of an interest in illusionism or in a slavish adherence to perceived reality but as a means of concentrating attention on particular details. This new tendency is especially evident in paintings such as *Vegetable Garden with Donkey* (1918; Stockholm, Mod. Mus.; see fig. 1) and *Montroig, the Church and the Village* (1919; Spain, priv. col., see 1986 exh. cat. by R. S. Lubar and others, no. 16). The self-portrait sometimes known as *Young Man in Red Shirt* (1919; Paris, Mus. Picasso) and subsequent works, such as *Standing Nude* (1921; Chicago, IL, Alsdorf Found.), display a stylization and flatness, which can perhaps be traced to the Romanesque paintings that had greatly impressed him in the Museu d'Art de Catalunya in Barcelona. The general sense is of containment, as opposed to the almost uncontrolled colour and violence of the previous period.

(ii) Paris, 1920–39. The failure of Miró's exhibition of 1918 caused him to reconsider his methods, particularly after his move to Paris in 1920 after a trial visit there in 1919. He worked initially in Pablo Gargallo's workshop at 45 Rue Blomet. In 1921, thanks to Lluís Dalmau, he held his first exhibition in Paris at the Galerie La Licorne but failed to make any sales. Following the exhibition and in many succeeding summers, he returned to his refuge in Montroig. There, after a period of reflection, he began work on *The Farm* (1921–2; Washington, DC, N.G.A.), his best-known painting of the period, with which he seemed to return to the simple things that he found around him in the Tarragona countryside. The apparent ingenuousness of detail and innocence exuded by objects and organic forms alike masks only partly the growing sophistication of Miró's conscious and carefully elaborated visual language. None of the dealers to whom he showed the painting was interested in buying it, but he later sold it to Ernest Hemingway, with whom he had struck up a friendship at a gymnasium where they both boxed.

In 1923 there were signs of another change. The *Tilled Field* (1923–4; New York, MOMA) is representative of this period, which follows on from *The Farm* in its mixture of recognizable natural forms with more or less invented shapes; colour is now treated with less restraint, freed from the demands of realism. The stylized realism of his previous portraits is still in evidence in the treatment of the woman and cat in the *Farmer's Wife* (1922–3; priv. col., see 1986 exh. cat. by R. S. Lubar and others, no. 22), but the main direction of his work, already evident in *Vegetable Garden with Donkey*, was towards an explosion of form verging on abstraction. This development culminated in *Harlequin's Carnival* (1924–5; Buffalo, NY, Albright–Knox A.G.), which can be regarded as Miró's first characteristic image, in which the space is populated by fantastic shapes, suggestive of living organisms, no matter how tenuously figurative they at first appear. Miró here established the limits of abstraction, to which he would remain faithful until *c.* 1960, characterized by an urge to retain at least vestigial references to perceived reality.

However resistant Miró felt to being part of wider artistic movements, he was influenced during the 1920s by the spirit of both Dada rebellion and SURREALISM. André Breton himself remarked that 'Miró is the most surrealist of us all', in spite of the fact that Miró never officially joined the group. In Paris in 1925 Jacques Viot's Galerie Pierre held not only a one-man show of Miró's work but also an exhibition of Surrealist painting, which included Miró along with Picasso and Paul Klee.

Miró's most abstract early paintings were virtually monochromatic canvases produced between 1925 and 1927, often dominated by a blue background, as in *Painting* (1925; New York, Guggenheim). These were to prove a powerful influence on the later development of abstract art, particularly in the USA, where the succeeding generations associated with Abstract Expressionism and colour field painting both owed much to his example. In works such as *This Is the Colour of My Dreams* (1925; priv. col., see 1986 exh. cat. by R. S. Lubar and others, no. 42), in which the title is inscribed next to a pool of blue paint, he used writing to change the significance of apparently abstract shapes, creating a kind of concrete poetry that recalled similar methods used in the previous decade by Guillaume Apollinaire and by Dadaists such as Francis Picabia.

Head of a Smoker (1925; Chicago, IL, Mr & Mrs M. G. Neumann priv. col., see 1986 exh. cat. by R. S. Lubar and others, no. 41) features the undulating biomorphic shapes that Miró was to favour in his subsequent work. In 1928, after a trip to the Netherlands, he produced a series of *Dutch Interiors* such as *Dutch Interior I* (1928; New York, MOMA), based on postcard reproductions of Old Master paintings. In these a greater curvilinear freedom was introduced to the sharp definition of shapes that had characterized earlier works such as *The Farm*. He reinterpreted other works by earlier artists in a series of *Imaginary Portraits* such as *Portrait of Mrs Mills in 1750 (after Constable)* (1929; New York, MOMA). During this period he also incorporated collage elements into paintings such as *Spanish Dancer* (1928; New York, Acquavella Gals, see 1986 exh. cat. by R. S. Lubar and others, no. 59) as a means of enriching the surface; a group of these was exhibited in 1928 at the Galerie Georges Bernheim, Paris.

Miró's marriage in Palma de Mallorca on 12 October 1929 to Pilar Juncosa, a cousin on his mother's side, followed by their move to Paris, provided him with the stability and concentration that he always needed for his work. Paradoxically this domestic tranquillity initiated a period of extreme rebelliousness in his art. Between 1929 and 1931 he sought to break all conventions including, on occasion, the very notion of painting itself; he even spoke of 'the murder of painting'. He began to produce reliefs such as the wood and metal *Construction* (1930; New York, MOMA) and sculptural assemblages such as *Sculpture-object* (1931; Amsterdam, Stedel. Mus.), and he intensified his use of collage by incorporating unusual materials. His spirit of experimentation was especially evident in *Drawing-collage* (1933; New York, MOMA) and other similarly titled works made at Montroig in summer 1933, in which he combined humour with compositional freedom, and a series of collage paintings initiated in 1933, such as *Painting-collage* (1934; Philadelphia, PA, Mus. A.), in which he relied both on intuition and on a meticulous and rational examination of form.

From 1934 to 1936 Miró produced a series of *Wild Paintings*, such as *Rope and People I* (1935; New York, MOMA), which manifested a violence that had heretofore generally been kept under control. Aggression, sexuality and drama here took a deformed and grotesque human form which was emphasized by strange and unexpected materials and surfaces; in some cases paint was mixed with sand and applied to cardboard, while in others he scrawled graffiti on masonite or over paper prepared with tar.

A particularly important painting from this period, marked by a shocking conjunction of intense imagery and shrill colour, is *Still-life with an Old Shoe* (24 Jan–29 May 1937; New York, MOMA), painted at the beginning of the Spanish Civil War. The political tensions of the period are likewise reflected in *The Reaper*, also known as *Catalan Peasant in Revolt* (1937; lost, see Dupin, 1962, p. 329), which he painted for the Spanish pavilion of the Exposition Internationale des Arts et Techniques dans la Vie Moderne in Paris in 1937 but which disappeared when the pavilion was dismantled. The rage against injustice that it embodied was categorically expressed also in the poster that he designed for the Republican cause, *Help Spain* (1937; see Corredor-Matheos, 1981, pl. 2), in which the slogan 'Aidez l'Espagne' was emblazoned over the image of a figure with outstretched arm and clenched fist.

(iii) Paintings, 1939–c. 1950. In 1939 Miró settled in Varengeville, a small village in Normandy, where he sought refuge from the conflict in Spain and in Europe at large. There he produced a series of pictures named after the town, for example *A Drop of Dew Falling from the Wing of a Bird Awakening Rosalie Asleep in the Shadow of a Cobweb* (Dec 1939; Iowa City, U. IA Mus. A.), in which he made recourse to memories of his childhood and of the countryside of Montroig. In such works he expressed

a poetic wonder at the universe in a solitary communion with objects and living things, by means of imagery of almost childlike innocence: skies filled with stars, birds and schematic female figures all engaged in a sacred dance. These are among the high points of Miró's art and of his vision of the world.

On his return to Spain, Miró spent some years in quiet retirement because of his opposition to the Franco regime. Nevertheless his art continued to evolve. During 1940–41, in Palma de Mallorca and in Montroig, he painted a series entitled *Constellations*. These pictures, such as the *Beautiful Bird Revealing the Unknown to a Pair of Lovers* (1941; New York, MOMA; see fig. 2), represent the culmination of the abstract tendencies of his early work. The first major retrospective exhibition of his work, held in 1941 at the Museum of Modern Art, New York, was of great importance in gaining him wider international recognition; the exhibition catalogue was the first major study of his work.

During 1942 and 1943 Miró developed elements from the *Constellations* in an intense burst of experimental activity. He worked almost exclusively on paper in a variety of media including oil, gouache, watercolour, pastel, coloured pencils, Indian ink, pencil and even blackberry jam. Works from this period, such as the watercolour *Woman, Bird, Star* (1942; Lucerne, Gal. Rosengart, see 1986 exh. cat. by R. S. Lubar and others, no. 125), are marked by great spontaneity and elegance.

The success of Miró's New York retrospective and of his 1945 exhibition at the Pierre Matisse Gallery, also in

2. Joan Miró: *Beautiful Bird Revealing the Unknown to a Pair of Lovers*, gouache and oil on paper, 460×380mm, 1941 (New York, Museum of Modern Art)

New York, led to a commission for a mural measuring 3×10 m for the Gourmet Restaurant, Terrace Hilton Hotel, Cincinnati (1947; Cincinnati, OH, Thomas Emery's Sons, see Dupin, 1962, p. 404). In 1946 he exhibited for the first time in the Galerie Maeght in Paris, with which he thereafter maintained a close relationship.

The fullness of Miró's art emerged in the 1940s. *Bullfight* (1945; Paris, Pompidou) is typical of this period in its graphic style and rounded forms, by which colour masses are contrasted with line drawing. *Women at Sunrise* (17 June 1946; Kansas City, MO, Nelson–Atkins Mus. A.) relies on a similar combination of drawing and coloured shapes on a neutrally coloured background. One of the major works of this period is *The Red Sun Gnaws at the Spider* (2 April 1948; New York, Stephen Hahn, see 1986 exh. cat. by R. S. Lubar and others, no. 135), in which the characters are almost completely abstract, and two of the shapes appear surrounded by a halo, the whole set against a uniform green background.

In general Miró established a dialogue between two or more figures. Occasionally he linked the separate elements with a line, as he had done in the *Constellations*, for example in *Dragonfly with Red Pinions in Pursuit of a Snake Gliding in a Spiral towards a Comet-star* (1951; Barcelona, Fund. Miró), although the festive atmosphere of the earlier series is now less in evidence. In other works such as *The Little Blonde in the Amusement Park* (1950; Berlin, Neue N.G.), colour is the decisive factor in defining the principal shapes. It could be said that a certain coarseness creeps into the joy and gaiety of the early 1940s, although one can still enjoy the play of pure colour in such witty works as *Mural Painting for Joaquím Gomis* (oil on fibro-cement, 1948; Barcelona, J. Gomis priv. col., see Dupin, 1962, p. 555).

(iv) Experiments with printmaking, ceramics, sculpture and painting in the 1940s and 1950s. Having thus completed the elements of his artistic vocabulary and self-contained world of imagery, Miró nevertheless sought new challenges by introducing further techniques in a continued defiance of accepted conventions. He returned to printmaking and in 1944 completed a series of 50 black-and-white lithographs entitled *Barcelona* (see fig. 3), which he had begun in 1939: aggressive images full of monstrous, threatening characters, a private denunciation of war.

Miró also began at this time to work with ceramics in collaboration with his friend Josep Llorens Artigas. Having produced his first vase in 1941 (Paris, Pompidou), from 1944 to 1946 he decorated irregularly shaped fragments of pots, which had been broken during the firing process.

3. Joan Miró: *Barcelona Series XLVII*, transfer lithograph, 255×330 mm, 1944 (New York, Museum of Modern Art)

Typical of these were the *Plaques* completed in 1945–6 (see Corredor-Matheos and Pierre, 1974, nos 13–45). Miró again worked with Artigas from 1953 to 1956, this time on a series collectively known as *Lands of Great Fire*: cups, plates and extremely varied shapes, in which Miró, with Artigas's technical assistance, explored the sculptural possibilities of clay. The French title, *Terres de grand feu*, made punning reference not only to the firing process and to the medium (*terre cuite*, Fr.: terra cotta) but also to the prevalence of natural shapes in works such as *Monument* (1956; Hamburg, Mus. Kst Gew.). Architectural forms also feature in large-scale works such as *Portico* (h. 3.6 m, 1956; New York, Guggenheim).

Prior to 1950 Miró had exhibited a series of sculpture-objects in Paris, but it was only after his involvement with ceramics that he began to produce sculptures on a larger scale. In 1954 he carried out a series of seven *Projects for a Monument* (Barcelona, Fund. Miró), in which he combined bronze, stone, wood and cement with more unusual materials such as porcelain, leather and even a telephone bell.

Between 1949 and 1950 in Barcelona, Miró produced 55 paintings and approximately 150 drawings, sculptures, objects and prints reflecting two distinct and contrasting approaches: on the one hand carefully wrought and reflective, on the other extremely spontaneous. He continued in the 1950s to develop the methods he had used in the previous decade, but in works such as *Personage on Cloudy Background* (1953; Paris, Gal. Maeght) he began to favour a less precise line, as if to dissociate the figures from the more abstract signs that came progressively to dominate his painting. His activities as a printmaker, which had heretofore been limited to etchings and lithographs printed in black, from 1948 included a wider range of media such as colour lithographs, colour etchings, drypoints, woodcuts and later carborundum prints; on occasion he added hand-coloured elements, as in the *Parchment* series (1953), in which he superimposed bold designs in bright watercolour on to etchings printed in black on irregularly shaped sheets.

(v) After 1960. Miró's work underwent a profound change in 1960, when he began to use black both to outline shapes and to fill them in. His later work is dramatic, even tragic, with colour often suppressed or counteracted by the weight accorded to black, as in *Woman and Bird* (1964; Saint-Paul-de-Vence, Fond. Maeght). His faith in abstraction was expressed during this period with particular eloquence in large canvases such as *Blue II* (1961; Paris, Pompidou), in which broad strokes of colour are set against sensuously painted backgrounds, as in his paintings of the mid-1920s; the simplicity of gesture and boldness of scale and handling make these among his most impressive and influential later works.

In his last years, before old age began to limit his apparently irrepressible vitality, Miró continued to experiment with different techniques. He collaborated with Joan Gardy Artigas (*b* 1938) on ceramics, with Josep Royo (*b* 1945) on tapestries and with the Barcelona theatre group Claca on the presentation of a play, *Mori el Merma*, inspired by Alfred Jarry's *Ubu roi* (1896). He worked prolifically during his later years as a printmaker, notably

4. Joan Miró: *Lunar Bird*, bronze, h. 2.34 m, 1966 (Philadelphia, PA, Fairmount Park Art Association, on loan to Philadelphia, PA, Museum of Art)

in a series of highly inventive *livres d'artiste* printed in a variety of techniques, such as *A toute épreuve* (1958, with 77 woodcuts accompanying poetry by Paul Eluard), *Ubu roi* (1966, with 13 colour lithographs illustrating Jarry's text) and *Journal d'un graveur* (1964, 15 drypoints and one colour etching published in 1975 in three volumes). Many of the books that he illustrated were of poetry by writers whom he knew personally, such as Jacques Prévert, Michel Leiris, André Breton, Tristan Tzara, René Crevel, René Char, Robert Desnos, Jacques Dupin and Georges Ribemont-Dessaignes. Miró also produced a large number of posters, often for his own exhibitions but also in response to political causes, at a time of strong popular pressure against the declining Franco dictatorship, for example *Amnesty International* (1976, see Corredor-Matheos, 1981, pl. 93).

Miró's experiments with ceramics were succeeded from 1960 to 1963 by a group of sculptures, some very large, for the gardens of the Fondation Maeght at Saint-Paul-de-Vence, and by ceramic murals on which he collaborated with Josep Llorens Artigas, beginning with *The Sun* and *The Moon* (both 1958; Paris, UNESCO), for which he was awarded the Guggenheim Foundation's Grand Prize. These were followed by a number of commissioned ceramic murals such as those for Harvard University

(1960), the Guggenheim Museum in New York (*Alicia*, 1966), Barcelona Airport (1970) and the Kunsthaus Zürich (1971). His use of cement and ceramic fragments recalled techniques used in the Parque Güell (Barcelona) and other architectural works by Gaudí, a cultural hero in Catalonia.

From 1966 Miró worked intensely on sculptures based principally on small objects, often *objets trouvés*, which he joined in surprising ways. Stones, branches and other objects discovered on his walks along the beach at Montroig, as well as manufactured items, were wedded in a spirit that still owed something to Surrealism but that also revealed his need for contact with nature and simple things, as also in bronzes such as *Lunar Bird* (1966; Philadelphia, PA, Mus. A.; see fig. 4). An element of fun remains, particularly in brightly painted bronze sculptures cast from juxtaposed objects, such as *Seated Woman and Child* (1350×600×350 mm, 1967; Barcelona, Fund. Miró), in which an ordinary chair acts as a stand-in for a figure. Miró's final work, completed posthumously, was the monumental sculpture *Woman and Bird*, which was installed in gardens on the former site of the Barcelona abattoir.

2. INFLUENCE AND POSTHUMOUS REPUTATION. The large retrospectives devoted to Miró in his old age in towns such as New York (1972), London (1972), Saint-Paul-de-Vence (1973) and Paris (1974) were a good indication of the international acclaim that had grown steadily over the previous half-century; further major retrospectives took place posthumously. Political changes in his native country led in 1978 to the first full exhibition of his painting and graphic work, at the Museo Español de Arte Contemporáneo in Madrid. The Fundació Joan Miró was inaugurated in Barcelona in 1975 in a building designed by his friend Josep Lluís Sert, housing a large number of paintings, drawings, sculptures and prints donated by the artist. In 1992, in accordance with the wishes expressed by the artist, the Fundació Pilar i Joan Miró was inaugurated in Palma de Mallorca; it has its headquarters in the studios of Son Abrines i Son Boter, where he used to work but in a new building designed by the architect Rafael Moneo. In 1993, the year of the hundredth anniversary of his birth, several exhibitions were held, among which the most prominent were those held in the Fundació Pilar i Joan Miró, Barcelona, the Museum of Modern Art, New York, the Centro de la Reina Sofia, Madrid, and the Galerie Lelong, Paris.

WRITINGS

'Je travaille comme un jardinier', *XXe Siècle*, i/1 (15 Feb 1959) (Barcelona, 1964)
Selected Writings and Interviews, ed. M. Rowell (Boston, 1986)

BIBLIOGRAPHY

MONOGRAPHS

J. E. Cirlot: *Joan Miró* (Barcelona, 1949)
C. Greenberg: *Joan Miró* (New York, 1949)
F. Elgar: *Miró* (Paris, 1954)
J. Prévert and G. Ribemont-Dessaignes: *Joan Miró* (Paris, 1956)
S. Hunter: *Joan Miró: L'Oeuvre gravé* (Paris, 1958)
J. Dupin: *Joan Miró: La Vie et l'oeuvre* (Paris, 1961; Eng. trans., London, 1962)
G. Weelen: *Miró*, 2 vols (Paris, 1961)
S. Gasch: *Joan Miró* (Barcelona, 1963)
J. Lassaigne: *Miró* (Lausanne, 1963)
Y. Bonnefoy: *Miró* (New York, 1967)
J. Dupin: *Miró* (Milan, 1967)

C. Greenberg: *Miró* (New York, 1969)
R. Penrose: *Miró* (London, 1970)
M. Tapié: *Joan Miró* (Paris, 1970)
M. Rowell: *Miró* (New York, 1971)
F. Català-Roca and J. Prats: *Miró escultor* (Barcelona, 1972) [with text by J. Dupin]
M. Leiris and F. Mourlot: *Joan Miró: Lithographs* (New York and Barcelona, 1972)
A. Jouffroy and J. Teixidor: *Miró sculptures* (Paris, 1973, rev. 1980)
J. Corredor-Matheos and J. Pierre: *Céramiques de Miró et Artigas* (Paris, 1974)
M. Leiris and R. Quenau: *Joan Miró litógrafo II* (Barcelona, 1975)
G. Picon: *Carnets catalans*, 2 vols (Paris, 1976)
A. Cirici: *Miró-mirall* (Barcelona, 1977)
G. Raillard: *Joan Miró: Ceci est la couleur de mes rêves* (Paris, 1977)
A. Cirici-Pellicer: *Miró et son temps* (Paris, 1978)
P. Gimferrer: *Miró: Colpir sense nafrar* (Barcelona, 1978)
J. Corredor-Matheos: *Miró's Posters* (New Jersey, 1980)
J. Dupin: *Miró graveur I: 1928–1960* (Paris, 1984)
G. Weelen: *Miró* (Paris, 1984)
P. A. Serra: *Miró and Mallorca* (New York, 1986)

EXHIBITION CATALOGUES

Joan Miró (exh. cat. by J. J. Sweeney, New York, MOMA, 1941)
Constellations (exh. cat. by A. Breton, Paris, Gal. Berggruen, 1959)
Joan Miró (exh. cat. by J. T. Soby, New York, MOMA, 1959)
Miró: Magnetic Fields (exh. cat. by R. Krauss and M. Rowell, New York, Guggenheim, 1972)
Joan Miró (exh. cat. by J. Leymarie and J. Dupin, Paris, Grand Pal., 1974)
Miró: L'Oeuvre graphique (exh. cat. by M. Benhoura, Paris, Mus. A. Mod. Ville Paris, 1974)
Dessins de Miró (exh. cat. by P. Georgel, Paris, Pompidou, 1978)
Miró: Selected Paintings (exh. cat. by C. W. Millard and J. Freeman, Washington, DC, Hirshhorn, 1980)
Miró Milano: Pittura, scultura, ceramica, disegni, sobreteixims, grafica (exh. cat., ed. M. Abate and D. Pertocoli; Milan, Comune di Milano, 1981)
W. Schmalenbach: *Joan Miró* (Berlin, 1982)
Miró in America (exh. cat. by B. Rose, Houston, TX, Mus. F.A., 1982)
Joan Miró (exh. cat. by R. S. Lubar and others, Zurich, Ksthaus; Düsseldorf, Städt. Ksthalle; New York, Guggenheim, 1986)
Miró escultor (exh. cat. by G. Moure, Madrid, Cent. Reina Sofía, 1986)
Miró in Montreal (exh. cat. by J. Dupin, R. Penrose and others, Montreal, Mus. F.A., 1986)
Joan Miró: A Retrospective (exh. cat. by R. S. Lubar, J. Dupin, W. Schmalenbach and T. M. Messer, New York, Guggenheim, 1987)
The Captured Imagination: Drawings from the Fundació Joan Miró (exh. cat., Philadelphia, PA, Mus. A., 1987)
G. Raillard: *Miró: Les Chefs-d'oeuvre* (Paris, 1989)
R. M. Malet: *Joan Miró* (Barcelona, 1992)
J. Dupin: *Miró* (Paris, 1993)

JOSE CORREDOR-MATHEOS

Mirou, Antoine [Anthonie] (*b* ?Antwerp, *c.* 1570; *d* ?Antwerp, 1661 or after). Flemish painter and draughtsman. Around 1580, various painters of his name were registered as members of the Antwerp Guild of St Luke. His Protestant family, like many others from Flanders and Brabant, took refuge from religious persecution in Frankenthal, under the protection of the Elector Palatine and staunch Calvinist, Frederick III. Mirou's father, the apothecary Hendrik Mirou, is documented repeatedly in Frankenthal from 1586. On 8 May 1602 Antoine married Suzanna van Coninxloo there, and he is frequently mentioned in the local archives until 1620, when he presumably returned to Antwerp. He is counted among the most distinguished of the landscape artists often referred to as the FRANKENTHAL SCHOOL, the best known of whom is Gillis van Coninxloo. Van Coninxloo had a strong influence on Mirou's style, either through direct contact or, more probably, via the work of another Frankenthal artist, Pieter Schoubroeck.

Mirou painted both forest landscapes, mainly before 1614 (e.g. *Forest with the Temptation of Christ*, 1607; Munich, Alte Pin.; and *The Hunters*, 1611; Prague, N.G., Šternbeck Pal.), and village scenes, executed mainly after 1614. His wooded landscapes, which conform to the traditional three-colour scheme (brown foreground, green middle ground, blue background), show van Coninxloo's influence in their composition and in the use of certain details, such as rock fortresses, waterfalls, high bridges and hunting motifs. His village scenes, which characteristically portray a road flanked by rustic dwellings and bounded by wooded hills in the background, are enlivened by countless figures. Such works follow the manner of Schoubroeck's *Village Landscape* (Copenhagen, Stat. Mus. Kst) but are also reminiscent of scenes by Jan Breughel I in the predominant use of green and blue, the thin application of paint and the accuracy of detail.

A series of drawn views of Schwalbach (*c.* 1615), in which Mirou clearly delighted in the picturesque aspects of the scenes but refrained from introducing any fantastic elements, reveal his genuine interest in topography. Matthäus Merian (i) made prints of 26 of these drawings and published them in 1620 as *Novae quaedem ac paganae regiunculae circa acidulas Swalbacenses delineatae per Antonium Mirulem in aes vero incisae per Mathae Merianem* (Hollstein, xiv, nos 1–26). The etcher Hendrik van der Borcht the elder (1583–1660) also made prints after drawings by Mirou published in commemoration of the entry of the Elector Frederick V and his wife into Frankenthal on 4 June 1613 (Hollstein, iii, nos 3–24). The last known work by Mirou is a painting dated 1661 (Parma, Pin. Stuard).

BIBLIOGRAPHY

Hollstein: *Dut. & Flem.*; Thieme–Becker

E. Plietzsch: *Die Frankenthaler Maler: Ein Beitrag zur Entwicklungsgeschichte der niederländischen Landschaftsmalerei* (Leipzig, 1910/*R* Soest, 1972), pp. 99–116

Y. Thiéry: *Les Peintres flamands de paysage au XVIIe siècle* (Paris and Brussels, 1953), p. 224

HANS DEVISSCHER

Mirror. Type of reflecting surface, usually of silvered glass, metal or highly polished stone.

I. Ancient world. II. East Asia. III. Indian subcontinent. IV. Islamic lands. V. Pre-Columbian Americas. VI. Western world.

I. Ancient world.

1. NEAR EAST AND EGYPT. The earliest objects interpreted as mirrors are circular discs made of highly polished obsidian. These discs (Ankara, Mus. Anatol. Civiliz.), measuring about 90 mm in diameter, come from the Neolithic settlement of Çatal Hüyük in Anatolia (Turkey) and date to *c.* 6000–5900 BC. A class of metal objects usually described as mirrors was first produced in the late 4th millennium BC. The objects are small copper discs with edges turned down to permit a comfortable grip, convex discs or round or oval discs with short or long handles. Their manufacture continued in the 3rd millennium in regions of Mesopotamia (Iraq) and northwest Iran.

During the 2nd and 1st millennia BC mirrors made from bronze were common throughout the Near East. Two types are known: the handle mirror and the tanged mirror

(see fig. 1a). The latter probably resulted from the need to hold larger and heavier bronze discs. The disc and tang were cast in one piece, and the straight-sided or tapered tang was inserted into a wood, bone or ivory handle. Extant isolated ivory handles of the 8th and 7th centuries BC are in the shape of a column, a single nude female posed frontally or two or four females standing back to back. Representations in art (e.g. on ivories and reliefs) show mirrors held by goddesses and royal and upper-class women; the mirrors consist of circular discs and handles that are either plain or have foliate designs.

A type of socketed mirror developed during the 7th or 6th century BC, perhaps in Anatolia. It is composed of three parts: a biconvex disc, a metal piece or clamp that is secured to the disc by rivets and a columnar handle that is slipped into a cavity at the bottom of the clamp. These mirrors have engraved linear decorations along the outer border of both sides of the disc.

During the Predynastic period (before 3000 BC) in Egypt, smoothly polished pieces of stone may have been wetted and used for reflection. Mirrors of the Early Dynastic period, Old Kingdom and First Intermediate Period (*c.* 2925–*c.* 2008 BC) were made of copper and generally cast and hammered. Discs were circular, pear-shaped or elliptical, and their reflective surfaces measured from 65 mm to 240 mm. The short tang, made thick for strength, was secured to the disc from each side.

Bronze mirrors of the Middle Kingdom and Second Intermediate Period (*c.* 2008–*c.* 1540 BC) were cast, hammered and annealed. Silver mirrors are known from at least the Middle Kingdom (e.g. Cairo, Egyp. Mus.). Handles were made of wood, ivory, steatite or faience and were commonly composed of two pieces (finial and shaft) joined together by a peg either wedged or cemented inside them. Handles were plain or shaped like a club, column, papyrus or a lotus bud. Mirrors often had the same type of papyrus-shaped handles as those seen on divine standards, surmounted by falcons, uraei or heads of the goddess Hathor. In one outstanding example from the 19th century BC (Cairo, Egyp. Mus.) a gold, double-faced head of Hathor with cow's ears decorates a papyrus-shaped obsidian handle that is attached to a thick silver mirror disc.

During the New Kingdom (*c.* 1540–*c.* 1075 BC) mirrors of extraordinary beauty were crafted. Bronze discs retained the same forms as in earlier periods. The handles are mainly of the lotus or Hathor types but some are shaped in the image of the god Bes, a bearded, dwarf-like figure, or are in the form of naked females (e.g. New York, Brooklyn Mus.; see fig. 2). In the Late Period (*c.* 750–332 BC) gilded silver mirror-handles were sometimes shaped into four figures of goddesses encircling the shaft of a papyrus column.

2. GREECE AND ROME. Hand mirrors have been found at Mycenaean sites of about 1400 BC but do not reappear in Greece until *c.* 700 BC, when they are also attested in visual and written records. Of the three distinct types of metal mirror—hand mirror, stand mirror and box mirror—the earliest and most common was the hand-held mirror with a single handle. When not in use it could lie flat or be hung by a hole in its handle. The disc, made of

copper or bronze, is generally circular. The handle, which was cast in one piece with the disc or made of wood or bone into which a tanged disc could be inserted, is oblong, columnar or some specific cut-out shape. The reverse of later mirror-discs are elaborately engraved with mythological subjects, while the outer borders are ornamented with vegetal, figural or patterned motifs.

The stand mirror has a reflecting disc on a support, the end of which is enlarged so that the object can stand alone. In addition to various columnar and plant shapes forming the support, human figures in the round, known as caryatids, are used (1b). The number of pieces joined to form the caryatid mirror varies from two units, the disc and the figure-base, to as many as fifteen. Female caryatids used as supports on mirrors may be either nude or semi-nude girls standing on an animal or simple round base or

women garbed in chiton (tunics) or peplos (outer robes). Male caryatids (Atlantids), either nude or wrapped in a large cloak, are also employed as supports.

By the late 5th century BC the box mirror had been invented (1c). This is a small, round disc of polished bronze without a handle, protected by a rimmed cover that fits over it. The lid may also be hinged to flip away, like a modern powder-compact. Lids are often decorated with relief or repoussé representations that range from profile heads and mythological scenes to the erotic and even pornographic. Decorated box mirrors continued to be produced in Roman times.

In Etruria bronze mirrors with engraved decoration are known from the end of the 6th century BC (1d; *see also* ETRUSCAN, §VI). The Etruscan mirror is shaped as a circular or pear-shaped convex reflecting disc with a peg

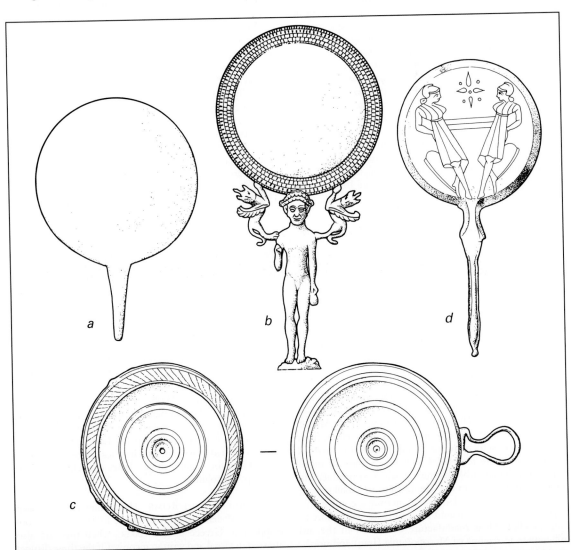

1. Mirrors: (a) tanged mirror, bronze, diam. 133 mm, from ancient Iran, 4th century BC (London, British Museum); (b) caryatid stand mirror, bronze, h. 338 mm, diam. 162 mm, 550–525 BC (New York, Metropolitan Museum of Art); (c) box mirror and cover, bronze, diam. 118 mm, *c.* 400 BC (Boston, MA, Museum of Fine Arts); (d) Etruscan mirror with engraving of the Dioscuri, bronze, h. 238 mm, diam. 120 mm, 6th century BC (Bologna, Museo Civico Archeologico)

framed with a border of openwork or relief in silver gilt. In the 1st century AD silver hand mirrors (e.g. Naples, Mus. N. S. Martino; see fig. 3) were widely used and commonly consist of a disc in a frame of decorated moulding with concentric circles on the reverse; a long handle is attached by arms to the disc. Metal mirrors of the 2nd to 4th centuries AD consist of plain discs, sometimes decorated with concentric circles, with either a loop or a grip handle fixed to the back. Glass mirrors were produced during the Roman period by blowing and then cutting up large glass bubbles, sections of which were backed with a dark resin or a metallic substance to create a reflective surface. Glass mirrors were generally surrounded by plaster or set in a wooden frame.

BIBLIOGRAPHY

W. F. Petrie: *Objects of Daily Use* (London, 1927)
D. E. Strong: *Greek and Roman Gold and Silver Plate* (Ithaca, 1966)
D. Rebuffat-Emmanuel: *Le Miroir étrusque: D'après la collection du Cabinet des Médailles*, 2 vols (Rome, 1973)
G. Zahlhaas: *Römische Reliefspiegel*, Munich, Prähist. Staatssamml. cat., xvii (Munich, 1975)
C. Husson: *L'Offrande du miroir dans les temples égyptiens de l'époque gréco-romaine* (Lyon, 1977)
C. Lilyquist: *Ancient Egyptian Mirrors from the Earliest Times through the Middle Kingdom* (Munich, 1979)
R. Adam: *Recherches sur les miroirs prénestins* (Paris, 1980)
L. O. K. Congdon: *Caryatid Mirrors of Ancient Greece* (Mainz, 1981)

2. Mirror with a handle in the shape of a nude female, bronze, h. 222 mm, from Egypt, *c.* 1570–1350 BC (New York, The Brooklyn Museum)

or tang to be inserted into a handle of wood or bone. The concave reverse side is engraved with a rich variety of subjects, including the cycle of a woman's life, native histories and imported Greek myths. Inscriptions often name characters in the scenes represented. Around the outer borders of the disc are ivy, vine or wave-pattern ornaments. After 480 BC mirrors decorated with reliefs were introduced: the disc is cast solid, and the reliefs are flat and resemble drawings. The preferred themes are the exploits of Herakles (e.g. 5th-century BC mirror from Atri; London, BM) and romances of Greek mythology.

A type of Roman mirror that came into fashion in the 1st century BC has a baluster handle, often decorated with relief on one side; it combines the forms of the Greek box mirror and the Etruscan hand mirror. A small group of wall mirrors may belong to the same period. These consist of a bronze or bronze-alloy disc, backed with wood and

3. Mirror with baluster handle, silver, diam. 210 mm, from the House of the Menander, Pompeii, 1st century AD (Naples, Museo Nazionale di San Martino)

P. Albenda: 'Mirrors in the Ancient Near East', *Source*, iv/2–3 (1985), pp. 2–9

R. S. Bianchi: 'Reflections of the Sky's Eyes', *Source*, iv/2–3 (1985), pp. 10–18

L. O. K. Congdon: 'Greek Mirrors', *Source*, iv/2–3 (1985), pp. 19–25

N. T. de Grummond: 'The Etruscan Mirror', *Source*, iv/2–3 (1985), pp. 26–33

K. R. Nemet-Nejat: 'A Mirror Belonging to the Lady-of-Uruk', *The Tablet and the Scroll: Near Eastern Studies in Honour of William Withallo* (Bethesda, MD, 1993), pp. 163–9

PAULINE ALBENDA

II. East Asia.

East Asian mirrors are characteristically round, although a few are square. Usually they are made of cast metal, mostly bronze but occasionally iron, with a smoothly polished, reflecting surface on one side and decoration on the back; some mortuary items were in earthenware. They were held by a fabric cord passed through a loop located at the centre of the decorated back. The origin of this type of mirror is unclear. While most were used for cosmetic purposes, mirrors were also believed to have the power to avert evil, probably reflected in the practice of the Dian tribe in Yunnan Province, China, of wearing mirrors on belts and also that of burying mirrors with the dead.

1. China. 2. Korea. 3. Japan.

1. CHINA. The height of artistic achievement and production for the early Chinese mirror occurred from the 6th to 1st centuries BC, that is during the later part of the Eastern Zhou (771–256 BC) and early part of the Han (206 BC–AD 220) periods.

(i) Shang to Qin periods (c. 1600–206 BC). The history of the Chinese mirror goes back to the beginning of the second millennium BC, as illustrated by two examples found among Qijia cultural remains in western China. One of these from Guinan, Qinghai Province, is decorated with a seven-point star design on its back (see Li Xueqin, fig. 110). The distinguishing feature of the Qijia mirrors and the handful of decorated examples from subsequent Shang burials at Anyang (see *Yinxu Fu Hao mu*, pl. 68:4–5, fig. 65) is their geometric designs, which are unrelated to the complex zoomorphic ornaments of other contemporary bronzes. Mirrors are extremely rare as compared with the large numbers of bronze ritual vessels and weapons of the period. Known examples from the Western Zhou (*c.* 1050–771 BC) and early Eastern Zhou periods are also few.

Of the later Eastern Zhou mirrors of known provenance, most are from burials of the state of Chu in the vicinity of Changsha in Hunan Province. They range from early examples decorated with an overall ground pattern of relief curls to later ones with complex floral, animal and abstract motifs superimposed over the ground ornaments on their backs. The motifs include smooth T-shapes arranged radially around the centre, forming a large, pointed, star-like pattern. This appears to have been widely popular, for examples have been found throughout China. (Chu silks bearing similar motifs have been found as far afield as Central Asia.) The T motif is sometimes accompanied by leaf-shaped and floral elements, with many possible variations, the best of which is illustrated by a large mirror (Cambridge, MA, Sackler Mus.) unrivalled in

elegance and workmanship. The main animal ornaments used in Chu mirror decoration include various dragons, birds and other creatures in sets of three or four (e.g. Stockholm, Östasiat. Mus.) or in convoluted, interlacing configurations (see Watson, pl. 98), stylistically connected to motifs common on Chu painted lacquers, silks and embroideries of the 4th and 3rd centuries BC (*see* CHINA, §§IX, 2 and XII, 2(i). These mirrors were once regarded as northern types on account of their different ground and secondary ornaments (see Karlgren, 1941, and Watson, chap. 5). However, not only is this geographical distinction unsupported by later archaeological evidence, but it also seems unconvincing on stylistic grounds. For, in addition to the birds or dragons that are typical Chu ornamental motifs, the rhombic and interlocking geometric ground patterns on many of the mirrors were also probably modelled after similar ones on Chu embroidered silks and textiles.

Purely descriptive motifs also occur on Chu mirrors, albeit rarely. One mirror, excavated from a late 3rd-century BC tomb in Hubei Province, shows an armed hunter stalking a rearing feline creature (see *Yunmeng Shuihudi Qin mu*, pl. 4). Equally rare are mirrors decorated with painted rather than cast or inlaid pictorial motifs. An unusually well-preserved example of this type (Cambridge, MA, Fogg; 1943.52.156) shows landscape and horse-and-rider scenes that closely parallel those on contemporary Chu lacquered objects.

The few mirrors of the Eastern Zhou period found in burials outside Hunan, particularly outside Chu territory, are clearly distinguishable from southern examples by their ornament. Decorations on mirrors from the north parallel closely contemporary ornamental styles on bronze ritual vessels, rather than artefacts in other media. Motifs include relief interlace dragons and animal-masks (e.g. London, BM; 1934.6-12.1), as well as abstract or pictorial patterns often lavishly inlaid with a variety of materials ranging from turquoise, malachite, jade and glass to copper, gold and silver (e.g. Tokyo, Hosokawa col.). The decorative scheme on northern mirrors lacks the distinction between superimposed motif and ground pattern characteristic of many southern designs.

The north-eastern region of Liaoning and neighbouring provinces yields yet another unusual type of Eastern Zhou mirror. Examples unearthed in Liaoning have geometric patterns (see *Kaogu* (1986), 2, p. 165, figs 2–3), some of which seem comparable to early Shang geometric mirrors. However, these mirrors carry not one but two or three loops on the back, arranged in a straight row away from the centre. This type of mirror spread to Korea during the last centuries BC (*see* §2 below).

(ii) Han to Ming periods (206 BC–AD 1644). Representative mirrors of the Han period (206 BC–AD 220) are set apart from their Eastern Zhou predecessors by a distinct change in the vocabulary of ornament. Inscriptions, representing dedicatory or laudatory poems or expressions of goodwill, were introduced as part of the decorative scheme. Symbols used in the layout of a board for a popular late Zhou and Han game were incorporated in the decorative schema of *guiju* ('square rule') or TLV mirrors (see fig. 4). The late Zhou scalloped dragons and

4. Mirror with a *guiju* ('square rule') or TLV design, encircled by a poem, bronze, diam. 160 mm, from China, 1st century AD (London, British Museum)

birds that originally filled the spaces on the board were replaced by Daoist and cosmological figures and symbols (e.g. Summit, NJ, Paul Singer priv. col., see Watson, pl. 99a; London, BM, 1954.2-20.3).

Han mirrors are also often distinguished from Eastern Zhou ones by greater size, thickness and weight. The modest central loop of the earlier mirrors was replaced by a large pierced dome. While most early Han mirrors retain the flat, linear form of late Zhou design, later Han examples, especially those with Daoist figural and animal ornaments, are characterized by robust high relief.

Such mirrors continued to be made at the beginning of the Six Dynasties period (AD 222–89), with Buddhist motifs sometimes replacing Daoist deities and elements. The peak of production of Buddhist and Daoist mirrors occurred in the 3rd century AD. The main centre of production was at Shaoxing in Zhejiang Province. Zhejiang masters who emigrated from China became the teachers of Korean and Japanese craftsmen (*see* §§2 and 3 below) in the 5th and 6th centuries. Cast-iron mirrors often overlaid with thick gold sheets cut into scalloped scroll patterns, which had first appeared in the late Han period, also gained in popularity; this was perhaps because bronze supplies had been depleted by the increased manufacture of weapons for use in the continual warfare of the Six Dynasties period.

Peace and unification under the Sui (AD 581–618) and Tang (AD 618–907) dynasties brought a resurgence in mirror production. New scalloped and pointed floral-shaped mirrors were introduced, together with new ornamental techniques using shell, mother-of-pearl and sheet gold and silver repoussé (e.g. Cambridge, MA, Fogg, 1943.52.168). Decorations range from the traditional, such as the dragon and Buddhist, Daoist and floral motifs, to the exotic, such as the lion-and-grapevine motif, reflecting

the influx of Central and West Asian cultures at the height of the Tang period.

In the Song (AD 960–1279) to Ming (1368–1644) periods two distinctive cultural trends, archaistic revival and the dominance of painting, are reflected in mirror design. New archaistic mirrors were cast from moulds taken from ancient Han models. Landscape and bird-and-flower compositions in current painting styles were also used in mirror decoration. Mirrors became more unconventional in shape—representing peaches, bells or censers, or rectangular, or floral—and some had handles (see *Kaogu yu wenwu* (1985), 4, pl. 4). The mirror was now produced as an ordinary consumer commodity, as illustrated by the many examples that are undecorated apart from a shop mark or manufacturer's seal cast on the back (see *Kaogu yu wenwu* (1985), 4, pp. 96–103). From the mid-Ming period the glass mirror began to replace the bronze mirror as the common cosmetic accessory.

See also CHINA, §VI, 3(iv)(b), (v), (vi) and (vii).

BIBLIOGRAPHY
B. Karlgren: 'Huai and Han', *Östasiat. Mus. [Stockholm]: Bull.*, xiii (1941), pp. 1–125
S. Cammann: 'The Lion and Grape Patterns on Chinese Bronze Mirrors', *Artibus Asiae*, xvi/4 (1953), pp. 265–91
Shaanxi sheng chutu tong jing [Bronze mirrors from Shaanxi Province] (Beijing, 1959)
A. Bulling: *The Decoration of Mirrors of the Han Period* (Ascona, 1960)
Hunan chutu tong jing tulu [An illustrated catalogue of bronze mirrors from Hunan] (Beijing, 1960)
W. Watson: *Ancient Chinese Bronzes* (London, 1962)
B. Karlgren: 'Some Pre-Han Mirrors', *Bull. Mus. Far E. Ant.*, xxxv (1963), pp. 161–9
N. Thompson: 'The Evolution of the Tang Lion and Grape-vine Mirror', *Artibus Asiae*, xxix/1 (1968), pp. 25–54
C. C. Riely: *Chinese Art from the Cloud Wampler and other Collections in the Everson Museum* (New York, 1969)
T. Higuchi: *Kokyo* [Ancient mirrors] (Tokyo, 1979)
Yinxu Fu Hao mu [The Tomb of Fu Hao at Yinxu] (Beijing, 1980, rev. 1984), pl. 68:4–5, fig. 65
Yunmeng Shuihudi Qin mu [Qin tombs at Shuihudi, Yunmeng] (Beijing, 1981)
Li Xueqin: *Dong Zhou yu Qin dai wenming*, Eng. trans. by K. C. Chang as *Eastern Zhou and Qin Civilizations* (New Haven and London, 1985)
'Song dai tong jing jian lun' [A brief discussion of Song dynasty bronze mirrors], *Kaogu yu wenwu* (1985), 4, pp. 96–103
Zhang Xiying: 'Shilun Dongbei diqu Xian Qin tongjing' [On the pre-Qin mirrors of the North-East], *Kaogu* (1986), 2, p. 165
Wang Shilun, ed.: *Zhejiang chutu tong jing* [Bronze mirrors from Zhejiang] (Beijing, 1987)
Wong Yanchung: 'Bronze Mirror Art of the Han Dynasty', *Orientations*, 12 (1988), pp. 42–53   □

2. KOREA. The art of the bronze mirror in Korea was influenced by two major stylistic traditions: in the 1st millennium BC by the early Bronze Age cultures in the north (i.e. Liaoning Province in present-day China and its vicinity), and from the Han period (206 BC–AD 220) by the Chinese mirror tradition.

Mirrors dating from *c.* 700–200 BC found on the Korean peninsula are related to those found in Liaoning Province in their characteristic multiple off-centre loops and linear geometric designs (see 1984 exh. cat., pl. 15). With the establishment of the Chinese commandery at Nangnang (Chin. Lelang), near modern P'yŏngyang, in 108 BC, Chinese art began to exert a strong influence on Korean art. Han Daoist mirrors have been found at Nangnang (*A Pictorial Encyclopedia of the Oriental Arts: Korea*, no. 14);

during the later part of the Three Kingdoms period (57 BC–AD 668) TLV and Daoist mirrors from Shaoxing were both imported and manufactured in Korea. These were highly prized: an example modelled after Chinese prototypes was found in the tomb of King Munyŏng (*reg* AD 501–23) of Paekche outside Kongju in South Ch'ungch'ŏng Province. It was through Korea that Shaoxing mirrors were introduced to Japan at this time (*see* §3 below).

China played a key role in the unification of Korea under Silla in the 7th century, and the elegant designs of Tang (AD 618–907) and later Song (960–1279) mirrors, notably those with lobed edges, dragons and other pictorial designs (*A Pictorial Encyclopedia of the Oriental Arts: Korea*, no. 90) may be seen in Korean mirror art of that period.

See also KOREA, §VII, 1(i)(b).

BIBLIOGRAPHY

A Pictorial Encyclopedia of the Oriental Arts: Korea (New York, 1969)
5000 Years of Korean Arts (Tokyo, 1976)
Treasures from Korea (exh. cat., ed. R. Whitfield; London, BM, 1984)
M. Riotto: *The Bronze Age in Korea*, Italian School of East Asian Studies, Occasional Papers, 1 (Kyoto, 1989)

JENNY F. SO

3. JAPAN. Bronze mirrors (*kagami*) are among the earliest examples of casting of art objects in Japan and, like much else in that country, have their origins in China, where production of Daoist and Buddhist mirrors, principally at Shaoxing, was at its height in the 3rd century AD (*see* §1 above). Usually circular but sometimes with four or eight shallow cusps, the earliest-known mirrors in Japan, believed to have been made no later than the 7th century BC, have been found in dolmens and are either Chinese imports via Korea or Japanese copies, sometimes with deviation in decoration, such as those with small bells around the edge. Mirrors of the Nara period (AD 710–94) are hard to distinguish in appearance or technique from those of the Chinese Tang period (AD 618–907), but from the Heian period (AD 794–1185) the Japanese gradually ceased to copy Chinese designs.

Mirror-casters had considerable prestige, manifest in their use of honorary titles, such as those given to swordsmiths, for example Mutsu no Kami (Lord of Mutsu). An eight-cusped mirror, the Yata no Kagami, forms, with a sword and necklace, the imperial regalia of Japan. These early mirrors had a central pierced boss, often formed as a tortoise—in Chinese mythology a divinely constituted creature that, besides being a longevity symbol, was believed to assist an elephant in supporting the universe. A woven-silk tasselled cord was attached to the boss. Both these items were dispensed with when mirrors with flat, rectangular handles, usually bound with rattan, were introduced in the 17th century. Mirrors of the Kamakura (1185–1333) and Muromachi (1333–1568) periods were often decorated with floral scrolls and ducks or geese, birds with butterflies, sparrows and maples or chrysanthemums, autumn plants and other subjects drawn from nature.

From the late 16th century an individual from a craft guild such as the *kagami-shi* (mirror-makers) could be elected to the title of Tenka-Ichi (First under Heaven).

This designation can be found on some 19th-century mirrors, although by then it was no longer a sign of quality. Towards the end of the 17th century mirrors became larger to reflect the increased size of ladies' hair arrangement (*mage*). The faces of these bronze mirrors were highly polished and usually coated with an amalgam of mercury or tin. A decline in bronze mirror-casting started in the late 18th century, when carefully finished mould-cast mirrors were gradually superseded by mass-produced types, often copied from existing mirrors by pressing the latter into wet sand. Repeated sand-casting soon caused a loss of sharpness and quality.

Designs were often formed from such longevity symbols as cranes, pine trees and water-tortoises with water-weed tails, known as *minogame*. Such mirrors were considered suitable as wedding gifts, and their designs sometimes included family badges (*mon*) or large Chinese characters in a flowing calligraphic style known as *sōsho* (cursive or grass script). When not in use on a stand, mirrors were wrapped in a cloth and kept in fitted wood boxes usually decorated in gold lacquer on a black ground with scrolling Chinese vines (*karakusa*) and family badges; the interiors were coated in red lacquer or *nashiji* (sprinkled gold pearskin ground). The advent of mass-produced glass mirrors in the 19th century meant the end of the traditional bronze types, many of which were exported as curios, while some suffered the indignity of forming the circular bottoms of large bronze vases.

See also JAPAN, §XII.

BIBLIOGRAPHY

R. T. Paine and A. Soper: *The Art and Architecture of Japan*, Pelican Hist. A. (Harmondsworth, 1955/*R* 3/1981), pp. 279–80, pl. 175
T. Higuchi: *Kokyo* [Ancient mirrors] (Tokyo, 1979)
'Money, Mirrors and Clocks', *Japanese Art: Masterpieces in the British Museum*, ed. L. Smith, V. Harris and T. Clark (London, 1990), pp. 134–45

WILLIAM TILLEY

III. Indian subcontinent.

Mirrors are thought to have come to the Indian subcontinent through its trade with the Roman Empire. Bronze mirrors dating from the 2nd century AD were discovered in archaeological sites at Taxila and Brahmipuri. Onward trade through India, where mirrors developed as precious works of art as early as the 7th century AD, was instrumental in diffusing West Asian and Indian mirrors in East Asia: Chinese references attest to the sale from India of mirrors with transparent surfaces encrusted in precious stones at this date, and in the 12th century the Chinese Zhao Rugua in his *Zhufanji* ('Record of foreign nations') mentions their place of manufacture as the Coromandel coast, in southwest India, a major source of gems.

During the MUGHAL period (1526–1858) mirrors reached a height of design and elaboration reflecting the splendour of the rulers, who were sometimes portrayed holding a hand mirror of European design, as in a portrait of *Jahangir* (*reg* 1605–27) *as Prince Salim* (London, V&A). Trade and ambassadorial exchanges brought gifts to India, and mirrors were particularly in demand. They were also imported from Europe (*see* VI, 2 below) and the Islamic world (*see* §IV below). According to the records of the East India Co., mirrors were mainly used by the nobility and were given as presents to the 'Princes of the East Indies', who particularly favoured 'large ones which would be acceptable by the king who affects not value but rarity'. Sir Thomas Roe (*d* 1644), English ambassador to the Mughal court, mentioned seven Venetian mirrors presented to Jahangir, and Fransisco Pelsaert, a Dutch merchant, recorded in his letters that '10 to 20 gilt mirrors, costing 8–10 guilders each, but no large ones, with ebony frames' should be sent for sale in Agra. De Laet of the Dutch East India Co. gave an account of the imperial treasury at Agra, mentioning several precious mirrors.

Jade studded with precious stones was commonly used for the manufacture of Indian mirror-frames, although opaque green glass was often substituted. The imitation jade was extremely convincing and often mistaken for the real stone. Mirrors were normally rectangular in shape; their backs were inset with gold wires in arabesque designs indented with hollows for precious stones (see fig. 5). Similar settings were also created around the border of the frame on the front of the mirror; the looking plate, which was sometimes made of rock crystal, was fixed to the unpolished jade backing with mastic or beeswax. Gold, ebony and cedar were also used as frames; in the late 18th century ivory mirrors inlaid with lac were produced as part of a general fashion for ivory furniture, and silver mirrors, often decorated with filigree work, were widely used in the 19th century.

Mirrors were also used in interior decoration: Bernier, describing the Khas Mahal in Delhi, referred to its decoration consisting of magnificent mirrors. Manucci, a Venetian physician, reported that Shah Jahan (*reg* 1628–58) had a large hall decorated with mirrors built in Delhi; on the ceiling of the hall, between each mirror, were strips of gold studded with jewels. He also described the palanquin of Shah Jahan's daughter, which was covered with cloth of gold embroidered with precious stones and small mirrors, and the ladies of the harem wearing rings set with mirrors on their right thumbs. Every palace had a gallery of mirrors, or 'Shish Mahal', where small mirrors were set into the wall in a trellis pattern that created an attractive effect in candlelight.

In many folk traditions of the subcontinent, mirrors are often used as symbols in local customs: for example, a bride is supposed to look at her husband for the first time through her mirrored ring. Embroidery using small mirrors to form mosaic patterns on garments is a speciality of Gujarat and Rajasthan, originating in the use of mirrors on clothes or horse trappings to deflect the evil eye.

BIBLIOGRAPHY

M. G. Dikshit: *History of Indian Glass* (Bombay, 1969)
India and Italy, Archaeological Survey of India (Rome, 1974)
J. Jain: *Folk Art and Culture of Gujarat* (Ahmadabad, 1980)
M. Latif: *Mughal Jewels* (Brussels, 1982)
An Age of Splendour: Islamic Art in India (Bombay, 1983)
S. C. Welch: *India, Art and Culture, 1300–1900* (New York, 1985)
Aditi: The Living Arts of India (Washington, DC, 1985)
Mughal Silver Magnificence (Brussels, 1987)

NADA CHALDECOTT

IV. Islamic lands.

In early Islamic times, the mirror (Arab. *mir'āt*; Pers. *ā'ina*; Turk. *ayna*) apparently followed late Roman and Byzantine models, taking the form of polished discs of cast bronze

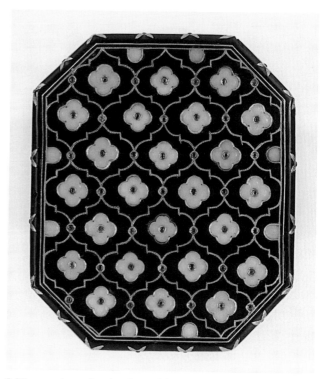

5. Mirror, rock crystal set in a frame of dark green jade inlaid with gold, white jade and rubies, 131×112 mm, from India, Mughal period, mid-17th century (London, Victoria and Albert Museum)

or copper, sometimes with straight handles. Few examples of artistic interest confidently ascribed to early Islamic times have been excavated or are in museum collections, although it is assumed that metal mirrors were in use throughout the Islamic world in early medieval times. In addition to their use for personal inspection, mirrors were used for divination. A mirror-back carved in relief with addorsed birds with crossing tails (diam. 104 mm; Athens, Benaki Mus.) has been attributed on stylistic grounds to 11th-century Iran.

By the 12th century AD a second type of mirror, the back decorated in relief and having a pierced boss in the centre for a cord or thong, was used widely under the Saljuqs (*reg* 1038–1194) and their successor dynasties in Iran, Anatolia and Syria. Patterned after Chinese cast-bronze examples (*see* §II, 1 above), they vary in size (70 mm to 140 mm in diameter), and many examples are thought to have been made in the province of Khurasan. The backs of these mirrors are often decorated with arabesques, zodiacal motifs or confronting or addorsed harpies, lions, griffins or dragons. Several examples (e.g. London, V&A, 928–1886) carry inscriptions in Arabic, usually expressing good wishes to the owner. Some disc-shaped mirrors from Saljuq times or earlier were made with straight handles and often cast in one piece. A mirror made from a circular slab of steel with an attached straight handle (Istanbul, Topkapı Pal. Mus.) is attributed to the first half of the 13th century and was made in Iran or Anatolia. The back is decorated in low relief with a mounted hunter depicted in a style identical to that of the

6. Mirror, steel inlaid with gold and silver, diam. 240 mm, from Egypt or Syria, *c.* 1300 (Istanbul, Topkapı Palace Museum)

celebrated enamelled pottery of the early 13th century (*see* ISLAMIC ART, §V, 3(iii)).

After *c.* 1250 polished metal mirrors were decorated with a wide variety of precious materials; surviving examples from Egypt, Iran, the Ottoman empire and India, all with handles, show the exploration of various shapes in addition to the traditional disc, and incorporate jade, gold, ivory and precious stones. A magnificent inlaid steel mirror (see fig. 6) made for a Mamluk vizier by the master Muhammad (possibly identified as MUHAMMAD IBN AL-ZAYN) is decorated with inscriptions and signs of the zodiac. An ivory example (1543–4; Istanbul, Topkapı Pal. Mus.; *see* ISLAMIC ART, fig. 238) made by the master Ghani for the Ottoman sultan Süleyman is one of the most beautiful of later mirrors: its shape, in the form of a complex decorative pendant, is typical of the repertory of shapes found in the 16th and 17th centuries.

Glass mirrors with mercury reflectors were imported from Venice (*see* §VI, 1 and 2 below) as early as the 16th century and soon became popular in the Islamic world. By the mid-17th century mirrors were used in Iran for architectural decoration in place of traditional ceramic tiles (*see* ISLAMIC ART, §II, 9(v)). In the 18th century European mirrors using the new process pioneered at the Saint-Gobain glassworks in France accompanied the fashion for European architecture in Ottoman Turkey, and large mirrors became as common a feature in the palaces of Ottoman notables as they were in the great houses of Europe.

BIBLIOGRAPHY

Enc. Iran.: 'Ā'ina-kārī [Mirror-work]; *Enc. Islam/2*: 'Mir'āt' [Mirror]
J. W. Allan: *Persian Metal Technology* (London, 1979)

——: *Nishapur: Metalwork of the Early Islamic Period* (New York, 1982), pp. 33–7
A. S. Melikian-Chirvani: *Islamic Metalwork from the Iranian World, 8th–18th Centuries*, London, V&A cat. (London, 1982), p. 131

WALTER B. DENNY

V. Pre-Columbian Americas.

Mirrors played an important role in trade and ritual in many cultures of Pre-Columbian America, particularly in Mesoamerica. Pyrite and haematite mirrors have been found at sites from Panama (e.g. SITIO CONTE) in the Intermediate area of Pre-Columbian South America (*see* SOUTH AMERICA, PRE-COLUMBIAN, §II, 1) to the Hohokam culture of south-west USA (e.g. SNAKETOWN), where their presence in association with other items indicates Late Classic–Early Post-Classic period (*c.* AD 600–*c.* 1200) influence from Mesoamerica. Polished jet mirrors are known from ancient Andean cultures (e.g. Caballo Muerto and Los Reyes, both in Peru), as well as metal mirrors for ritual fire-making, the use of which by the Inca was described by the early 17th-century Spanish writer Garcilaso de la Vega el Inca; tribes on the North American Plains carved horse effigies on polished stone mirrors (*see* NATIVE NORTH AMERICAN ART, §III, 5).

The role of mirrors in trade has been especially well documented in Mesoamerica, so much so that the manufacture and exchange of polished pyrite mirrors is regarded as one of the diagnostic traits of Mesoamerican culture (*see* MESOAMERICA, PRE-COLUMBIAN, §I). In the Early and Middle Pre-Classic periods (*c.* 2000–*c.* 300 BC) artisans at San José Mogote in the Oaxaca Valley exploited local deposits of magnetite and ilmenite to make small flat mirrors, some only the size of a thumb-nail (*see* MESO-AMERICA, PRE-COLUMBIAN, §II, 2(i)); contemporary figurines show that they were worn around the neck. From Oaxaca they were traded north-east and north-west as far as the Olmec sites of SAN LORENZO TENOCHTITLÁN and LA VENTA in the Gulf Coast region and CHALCATZINGO in Morelos.

Near the start of the Middle Pre-Classic period, after *c.* 900 BC, as San Lorenzo Tenochtitlán declined and La Venta began to grow more prosperous, the import of flat mirrors from Oaxaca ceased, and larger, concave mirrors were made locally. For example, a concave haematite mirror was found at the intersection of a cross-shaped design of 20 jade and serpentine celts over one of the mosaic pavements at La Venta (Mexico City, Mus. N. Antropol.). Concave magnetite and ilmenite mirrors, with holes at the edge for hanging around the neck (as demonstrated on Olmec figurines), were also found in other offerings. It is believed that such items would have belonged only to the élite.

In the Classic period (*c.* AD 250–*c.* 900) mirrors of both pyrite and polished obsidian were produced in large numbers at TEOTIHUACÁN in the Basin of Mexico and at Lowland Maya sites. Teotihuacán controlled the sources of obsidian in the Central Highlands and exported its products widely. The Maya had to import pyrite and haematite to make mirrors of these materials. Obsidian and slate mirrors were also found in the roughly contemporary shaft-tomb offerings of west Mexico in Jalisco,

Colima and Nayarit (*see* WEST MEXICAN ART, PRE-COLUM-
BIAN); pyrite mirrors were among offerings in burials at
Highland Maya KAMINALJUYÚ, where there is extensive
evidence of Teotihuacano influence (*see* MAYA, §2).

Classic period mirrors were usually round (although a
few square examples are also known), from *c.* 75 to
c. 300 mm in diameter and *c.* 5 mm thick. Obsidian mirrors
were normally of one piece; pyrite mirrors comprised
several closely set, highly polished plates, although some
smaller examples are of a single piece. Inlays of haematite,
jade, shell and other materials were sometimes added and
the plates backed with slate or sandstone—usually a single
piece but sometimes multiple edge-joined pieces. A hole
was made near the edge or in the centre for suspension.
The back edge was usually bevelled and painted red or
blue-grey. Backs were sometimes elaborately carved, stuccoed and painted. The backs of pyrite and haematite
mirrors from TAJÍN, for example, were carved in the
distinctive central Gulf Coast style (*see* MESOAMERICA,
PRE-COLUMBIAN, §§V, 3(i) and VIII).

Post-Classic period (*c.* AD 900–1521) mirrors were similar. Aztec mirrors were set into carved wooden frames,
sometimes gilded (see fig. 7), or hung on loops of cord. A
greenstone relief of a goddess from the Templo Mayor,
Tenochtitlán (*see* MEXICO CITY, §I), has a framed disc on
its chest that may represent a mirror (Mexico City, Mus.
N. Antropol.). Sixteenth-century Spanish accounts describe the Aztec use of mirrors in divination, and indeed,
the god Tezcatlipoca (a creator deity) had a left foot, torn
off in battle with the earth monster, transformed into a
smoking mirror, the Náhuatl meaning of his name. Pyrite
mirrors have also been found at Late Post-Classic Apat-
zingán in Michoacán, West Mexico.

BIBLIOGRAPHY
W. Bray: *Everyday Life of the Aztecs* (London, 1968)
M. P. Weaver: *The Aztecs, Maya and their Predecessors: Archaeology of
    Mesoamerica* (New York, 1972, rev. 2/1981, 3/1993)
G. F. Ekholm: 'The Archaeological Significance of Mirrors in the New
    World', *Atti del congresso internazionale degli Americanisti*, xl/1 (1973),
    pp. 133–5
J. D. Jennings, ed.: *Ancient Native Americans* (San Francisco, 1978)
J. Soustelle: *Les Olmèques* (Paris, 1979); Eng. trans. by H. R. Lane as *The
    Olmecs: The Oldest Civilization in Mexico* (Norman, 1985)
E. Pasztory: *Aztec Art* (New York, 1983)
D. C. Grove: *Chalcatzingo: Excavations on the Olmec Frontier* (London,
    1984)
R. W. Keating, ed.: *Peruvian Prehistory: An Overview of Pre-Inca and Inca
    Society* (Cambridge, 1988)

DAVID M. JONES

VI. Western world.

1. Before 1600. 2. 1600–1800. 3. After 1800.

1. BEFORE 1600. Medieval reflective surfaces fall into
three main categories—polished metal, rock crystal and
blown glass. Medieval mirrors were small, often circular,
and highly prized, their ownership limited to a privileged
group. The types of mirror in use included those for the
pocket or purse, the dressing-case or the girdle. They were
usually boxed, cased or fitted into leather covers or
protected by carved ivory frames with swivelling covers
decorated with poetic allegories and scenes from religious
or secular life (e.g. mirror with carved ivory case depicting
a jousting scene, 14th century; Paris, Mus. Cluny; see
fig. 8). Less valuable frames were made in plain or carved

7. Aztec mirror, obsidian in a carved and gilded wooden frame, diam. 260 mm,
c. 1350–1521 (New York, American Museum of Natural History)

wood, often painted and polished. Gold and silver frames
encrusted with gemstones were reserved for royalty and
courtiers.

Medieval and Renaissance inventories often mention
'steel' mirrors, but the use of this word to describe metal
mirrors of this date is confusing. It may refer to polished
metallic rocks, for example iron, pyrite and obsidian. Metal
mirrors in the Middle Ages were also made of an alloy of
rose copper and tin mixed with red tartar, white arsenic
and nitre that produced a hard and resistant surface; once
polished like glass, it only needed wiping with deer- or
goatskin to maintain its reflective qualities. Polished metal
mirrors provided an adequate reflection but, because of
their thickness and weight, were less portable than glass
mirrors. Rock crystal was also highly prized for mirrors.
Despite inherent flaws in the crystal, once foil- or metal-
backed, it provided a better reflection than metal.

In the 15th and 16th centuries there were advances in
the production of glass suitable for mirrors, and different
forms of mirror—wall-mounted, hand-held and standing—
appeared. Jan van Eyck's double portrait of *Giovanni
Arnolfini and Giovanna Cenami* (1434; London, N.G.; for
detail *see* BELGIUM, fig. 27, and for entire picture *see* EYCK,
VAN, (2), fig. 3) shows a wall-mounted mirror of deep
convex form, clearly reflecting the contents of the room.
This convex mirror, backed with a metallic coating, was
probably made from a blown bubble of glass that was cut
during the annealing process. Italian, especially Venetian,
mirrormaking was predominant from the Renaissance
period (*see* ITALY, §VIII and VENICE, §III, 3). Between
1450 and 1460 Murano glassmakers developed a colourless
glass that was named '*cristallo*'. Specialist mirrormakers in
Venice polished the glass and added a thin coating of tin

8. Mirror with a carved ivory case depicting a jousting scene, diam. 100 mm, from France, 14th century (Paris, Musée de Cluny)

or mercury. Italian Renaissance wall-mounted mirrors continued to be small and were enclosed in carved wood, gilded or painted tabernacle and cassetta frames. The design of frames for wall-mounted mirrors was influenced by the prevailing architectural styles, and in many cases they differ little from frames made for paintings. Tabernacle frames containing rectangular or circular mirror plates were often fitted with a sliding shutter to protect the glass.

In the 15th and 16th centuries in northern Europe carved ivory and boxwood mirror-frames, the latter often incorporated into double-sided carved combs fitted with sliding shutters, were widely popular. Pocket mirrors were usually of the folding type, the mirror protected by a hinged cover lined with fabric and enclosed in a shagreen or, in rare examples, an enamel case. The hand-held toilet mirror developed into the standing dressing mirror with the addition of a circular foot, as depicted on the *Lady and the Unicorn* tapestry (15th century; Paris, Mus. Cluny). When the Mannerist style spread to northern Europe from Italy, mirror-frame makers began to use more extravagant forms of frame in precious metals, bronze, enamels and plain, carved, gilded and painted wood. The inventory (1547) of Henry VIII, King of England, for example, shows that he possessed a number of 'glasses' in wooden frames painted or covered with rich coloured velvets embroidered with pearls, knots of silk, gold and jewels.

2. 1600–1800.

(i) Manufacture. Throughout the 17th century the difficulty and expense of making flat glass that was suitable for mirrors confined their ownership to an exclusive minority. Kings and queens considered mirrors suitable gifts to be exchanged with other heads of state. The risks involved in the processes of grinding, silvering and transportation heightened the rarity of mirrors. Mirror-glass produced by the two main flat-glass processes, 'board' and 'crown' glassmaking (*see* GLASS, §II, 1), required grinding and polishing to achieve smooth surfaces: one unblemished enough to receive a backing of hammered tin, the other to give an undistorted image. Dr Martin Lister (1638–1711), in *A Journey to Paris in the Year 1698* (London, 1699), described the grinding process thus: '. . . they grind the course glass with sand stone, the very same they pave the Streets in Paris. . .'. The plate was then secured to a stone base and fixed in place by plaster of Paris. Strong bows of yew-wood were secured by one end to the ceiling of the workshop and by the other, under tension, to a polishing pad drenched in tripoli or rottenstone and tempered with water.

Bevelling or 'diamond cutting' is a feature often found on 17th- and 18th-century mirror-plates: the edge of the plate was ground and polished at an angle, often barely discernible. Early 18th-century English mirror-plates often have bevelled border-glasses following the shape of the top of the frame. To turn a sheet of ground and polished glass into a mirror it had to be backed to make it reflect, a process known as silvering or foiling. Polished plates were laid on sheets of hammered tin, which were soaked in mercury. The plate was then turned and spread with sheets of paper to exclude dust. The mercury was drained off, and the plate was left to dry.

Throughout the 17th century Venice and the island of Murano exported mirror-glass to many European countries, as well as to Islamic lands and the Indian subcontinent. This near monopoly later dwindled as the secrets of glassmaking were spread through Europe by emigrant Venetian glassworkers. By the late 17th century and the early 18th most European countries had their own mirror-glass-making industry, particularly England (*see* ENGLAND, §VIII, 2 and 3) and France (*see* FRANCE, §VIII, 2). George Villiers, 2nd Duke of Buckingham (1628–87), collected glassmaking patents and created a near monopoly of mirror-glass-making in England. The most celebrated of his enterprises was the Vauxhall Glass Works, London, founded in 1663. The term 'Vauxhall Glass' is often used to describe any soft-coloured, shallow-bevelled, late 17th- or early 18th-century mirror-plate, but there is no definitive method of ascribing mirror-plates to any particular glassworks. In 1664 the Worshipful Company of Glass-Sellers and Looking-Glass Makers was incorporated. In the same year importation into England of 'Rough glass plates or wrought into looking-glasses' was prohibited.

The production of mirror-glass in France was accelerated by the patronage of Louis XIV and the invention in 1687 of cast plate-glass by Bernard Perrot (*d* 1709). The majority of plate-glass used in England until 1776 was imported from Saint Gobain in Picardy, where it was made by the casting process. Production of cast plate-glass for mirrors was begun in England in 1776 by the British Cast Plate Glass Company at Ravenhead, St Helens, Lancs, under the control of Jean-Baptiste-François Graux de la Bruyère (*b* 1739), from Saint Gobain.

9. Mirror with painted, gilded and lacquered chinoiserie decoration, 387×838×241 mm, c. 1750 (London, Victoria and Albert Museum)

(ii) Form and decoration. The majority of mirror-frames made in Europe during the 17th and 18th centuries were made from wood or used wood as a base. Most European framemakers were slavish in their devotion to fashion. Various forms of decoration were used, for example carving, inlaying with other woods or metals, gilding, lacquering and painting. Carved wooden frames were made from soft, easily worked timber; the lime tree, or European linden, was ideal for this purpose (e.g. carved frame by Grinling Gibbons, 1680; London, V&A). Box-wood and other close-grained timbers were suitable for sharply delineated carving. Pine and deal frames were gilded or painted. Natural polished timbers were used by themselves or with contrasting woods for inlaid work. Other fashionable woods for frames included walnut, mahogany, satinwood and rosewood.

During the 17th century craftsmen in Germany produced highly decorative frames for mirrors that employed many different materials: the gold- and silversmiths of Augsburg, for example, produced delicately worked frames

in precious metals, while the framemakers of Dresden were famed for their work with amber; ivory was employed in Munich. Cut and shaped glass was used by framemakers in Bohemia and Venice. Silver frames were particularly popular for toilet mirrors (e.g. of 1658–76; Copenhagen, Rosenborg Slot) and for mirrors forming part of a triad set—a luxurious set of furniture also incorporating silvered candlestands and a table. Needlework mirror-frames were produced during the late 17th century in England by gentlewomen from freehand and published designs in works such as Edward Topsell's *The History of Four-footed Beasts and Serpents, whereunto is now added The Theatre of Insects* (London, 1658) and P. Stent's *Booke of Flowers, Fruits, Beasts, Birds and Flies* (1661).

From the end of the 17th century larger, better quality mirrors were manufactured. Pier-glasses that filled the space between windows were made of two or more plates abutted together with bevelled border-glasses. Rooms were panelled with large plates of mirror-glass (*see* CABINET (i), §4(ii)), the most elaborate example being the Galerie des Glaces at the château of Versailles. Wider and taller mirrors that matched console-tables and were used as overmantels in the early and mid-18th century incorporated many plates of differing shapes and sizes surrounding a large plate, with the joins covered by areas of carved, painted or gilded wood in many ingenious designs (e.g. mirror with painted, gilded and lacquered chinoiserie decoration, *c.* 1750; London, V&A; see fig. 9). Mirrors and pier-glasses were designed by both cabinetmakers, for example Thomas Chippendale (i), and architects, for example Nicolas Pineau (for illustration *see* PINEAU, NICOLAS) and Robert Adam (e.g. of 1769; New York, Met.), often as an integral part of an interior decorative scheme. Painted panels and *verre églomisé* glass were also used as decoration on mirrors in the 18th century, as well as engraved and etched glass.

3. AFTER 1800. There are three major technical developments that are responsible for the modern mirror. The first in 1835 was the invention by Justus von Leibeg of a process of backing glass with silver instead of mercury. The second, in 1860, was the development by Hans Siemens of a regenerative furnace; the Wanne, or tank furnace, was first created for the founding of steel and allowed the raw materials to be fed in a continuous process, and glass flowed constantly from it. The third was in 1959 when Alistair Pilkington conceived the process of manufacturing float glass, which enabled a continuous ribbon of glass to be run from the furnace along the surface of a bath of molten tin. The ribbon was then held at a high temperature for sufficient time for any irregularities to melt out and both surfaces to become flat; this meant that there was no need for grinding and polishing the surface. Modern technology has enabled glass to be silvered by spraying. First the glass is flooded with cerium oxide to remove any dust and grease, then treated with stanous chloride to provide a key. The glass is sprayed with silver nitrate and an ammonia-based solution; the ammonia reacts with the silver nitrate to form a nitrate solution, leaving the silver particles to precipitate out of the solution and on to the glass. Technical advances in the production of mirror glass have enabled 20th-century

architects and designers to use large mirrors on exteriors and in interiors to achieve perspective and create the impression of greater size. Mirrors can be used unframed, held fast by hidden clips or mirror-headed screws. Frames can be made from almost any material, ranging from stone and steel to plastic and perspex. With continuing interest in 'antiques', modern technology has been employed in reproducing antique mirrors and mirror frames from plastic injection mouldings; compressed air is used to fix mitred corners with steel wedges.

BIBLIOGRAPHY

R. Edwards: *Dictionary of English Furniture* (London, 1964)
H. Schiffer: *The Mirror Book* (Exton, 1983)
S. Rocke: *Mirrors* (Tübingen, 1985)
G. Child: *World Mirrors, 1650–1900* (London, 1990)

GRAHAM CHILD

Mirror cabinet. *See* CABINET (i), §4(ii).

Mir Sayyid Ahmad [Mīr Sayyid Aḥmad al-Ḥusaynī al-Mashhadī] (*b* Mashhad; *fl* 1550–74; *d* Mazandaran, 1578). Persian calligrapher. He belonged to a family of Husayni sayyids, or descendants of the Prophet, and his father was a chandler. He was trained in calligraphy at Herat by MIR 'ALI HUSAYNI HARAVI. When Mir 'Ali was taken to Bukhara by the Uzbeks in 1529, Mir Sayyid Ahmad followed his master and was employed in the workshop of 'Abd al-'Aziz Khan, Shaybanid ruler of Bukhara. After the Khan's death in 1550, Mir Sayyid Ahmad returned to Iran. For some years he served the Safavid shah Tahmasp (*reg* 1524–76) before retiring to Mashhad, where he taught calligraphy. When Tahmasp revoked his pension, Mir Sayyid Ahmad lived in penury until Mir Murad Khan, governor of Mazandaran province, visited Mashhad in 1557 and invited the calligrapher to his court. After Mir Murad Khan's death, Mir Sayyid Ahmad returned again to Mashhad. He was in charge of assembling the Amir Ghayb Beg Album (Istanbul, Topkapı Pal. Lib., H. 2161), a splendid album of painting and calligraphy completed in 1564–5. In the introduction Mir Sayyid Ahmad gives a short history of Persian painting and calligraphy, and the album contains numerous specimens of his calligraphy, which exhibits the fluid elegance and exaggerated differentiation between thin vertical and thick horizontal strokes typical of Mir 'Ali's *nasta'līq* script. In 1576 the Safavid shah Isma'il II (*reg* 1576–8) invited Mir Sayyid Ahmad to the court at Qazvin. After the Shah's death, Mir Sayyid Ahmad returned to Mazandaran, where he died. His students included Qazi Ahmad, the author of *Gulistān-i hunar* ('Rose-garden of art'), one of the major sources of information on 16th-century calligraphers and painters.

WRITINGS

Preface to the Amir Ghayb Beg Album (Istanbul, Topkapı Pal. Lib., H. 2161); Eng. trans., ed. W. M. Thackston in *A Century of Princes: Sources on Timurid History and Art* (Cambridge, MA, 1989), pp. 353–6

BIBLIOGRAPHY

Qāżī Aḥmad ibn Mīr Munshī: *Gulistān-i hunar* [Rose-garden of art] (*c.* 1606); Eng. trans. by V. Minorsky as *Calligraphers and Painters* (Washington, DC, 1959), pp. 138–41
M. Bayani: *Aḥvāl va āthār-i khūshnivīsān* [Biographies and works of calligraphers], 2nd edn in 4 vols (Tehran, Iran. Solar 1363/1984–5), pp. 44–54

WHEELER M. THACKSTON

Mir Sayyid 'Ali [Mīr Sayyid 'Alī-i Tabrīzī] (*b* Tabriz, *c.* 1510; *d* Mecca, after 1572). Persian painter, active also in India. He was the son of the Safavid-period painter Mir Musavvir. Though Qazi Ahmad, writing in the late 16th century, deemed him more clever in art than his father, Mir Sayyid 'Ali reveals paternal influence in his meticulous rendering of ornamental patterns and details. As he was a junior artist at the time of the royal *Shāhnāma* of *c.* 1525–35 (dispersed, see Dickson and Welch), his contribution to this was limited. Only two miniatures (fols 135*v* and 568*r*; priv. col. and New York, Met., respectively; see 1979–80 exh. cat., nos 20 and 33) are attributed to him, and possibly passages in other works by Sultan Muhammad and Aqa Mirak. By the time of the illustration of the *Khamsa* ('Five poems') of Nizami of 1539–42 (London, BL, Or. MS. 2265), Mir Sayyid 'Ali was a first-rank Safavid court artist, painting four (or possibly five) miniatures, three (or possibly four) of which were subsequently removed from the manuscript (Cambridge, MA, Sackler Mus., 1958.75 and 1958.76; Edinburgh, Royal Mus. Scotland, 1896-70; and possibly Washington, DC, Sackler Gal., 586.0221). The painting *Nomadic Encampment* (Cambridge, MA, Sackler Mus., 1958.75; *see* ISLAMIC ART, fig. 9) typifies his mature work at the Safavid court. Presumably illustrating the meeting of the fathers of Layla and Majnun, who confer in a large tent in the foreground, the scene contains detailed renderings of textiles and carpets—and even a minute hennaed arabesque on a washerwoman's hand. Tents overlapping tents, hillocks and animals imply spatial recession but do not alleviate the two-dimensionality of the picture. Moreover, the urgent emotional content of the episode is lost; the figures barely interact or even look directly at each other. The *School Scene* (Washington, DC, Sackler Gal., 586.0221) may represent Mir Sayyid 'Ali's fifth illustration to the *Khamsa*. A drawing of a *Seated Youth* in the same collection (586.0291), signed by the artist, may be a self-portrait.

Mir Sayyid 'Ali was one of the first Safavid artists to emigrate to India at the invitation of the Mughal emperor in exile, Humayun (*reg* 1530–40; 1555–6). After an interim period of five years in Kabul (1549–54), Mir Sayyid 'Ali settled in Delhi, where he gave painting lessons to Prince Akbar. After Humayun's death in 1556, Mir Sayyid 'Ali kept his important position in the Mughal atelier, holding the directorship of the vast *Hamzanāma* project from 1562 or later to 1572, when he left for Mecca where he died.

Two portraits are attributed to Mir Sayyid 'Ali working for his Mughal patrons, Humayun and Akbar. The first, a *Young Scribe* (San Diego, CA, Mus. A. Binney Col., 1486:57), depicts a youth kneeling in a landscape and bears an inscription reading 'Mir Sayyid 'Ali, who is the rarity of the realm of Humayun Shah, painted this'. Datable *c.* 1550–55 or later, the painting conforms largely to Mir Sayyid 'Ali's Safavid style with its attention to detail, the flat treatment of forms and the abstracted expression of the sitter. The greater realism of the sitter's facial expression in *Mir Musavvir Presenting a Petition* (Paris, Louvre, 3.6191,b), attributed to Mir Sayyid 'Ali, suggests a response to Akbar's taste for naturalism.

As director of the *Hamzanāma* (dispersed), Mir Sayyid 'Ali oversaw numerous artists illustrating the adventures of Amir Hamza, the uncle of the Prophet. According to contemporary accounts, the complete work consisted of 14 volumes with 100 illustrations each. In the first seven years of the project, Mir Sayyid 'Ali saw to completion only four volumes (the others were supervised by 'ABD AL-SAMAD). While none of the early illustrations has been attributed to Mir Sayyid 'Ali himself, the complex, overlapping compositions, multitude of vignettes and abundant detail of some of them (e.g. Richmond, Surrey, Keir priv. col., V.3) suggest his influence if not his hand. Mir Sayyid 'Ali introduced the rigorous depiction of objective reality to Mughal painting but left his followers to develop the naturalism characteristic of the Mughal school.

See also ISLAMIC ART, §III, 4(vi)(a) and INDIAN SUBCONTINENT, §V, 4(i)(a).

BIBLIOGRAPHY
Qazi Ahmad: *Gulistān-i hunar* [Rose-garden of artifice] (MS.; 1596–1606); Eng. trans. by V. Minorsky as *Calligraphers and Painters* (Washington, DC, 1959)
P. Chandra: *The Tūtī-Nāma Manuscript of the Cleveland Museum of Art and the Origins of Mughal Painting* (Graz, 1976)
Wonders of the Age (exh. cat. by S. C. Welch, London, BL; Washington, DC, N.G.A.; Cambridge, MA, Fogg; 1979–80)
M. B. Dickson and S. C. Welch: *The Houghton Shahnameh* (Cambridge, MA, 1981), pp. 178–91
The Imperial Image: Paintings for the Mughal Court (exh. cat. by M. C. Beach, Washington, DC, Freer, 1981)
G. D. Lowry and M. C. Beach: *An Annotated Checklist of the Vever Collection* (Washington, DC, 1988), pp. 300–01, no. 350; pp. 340–41, no. 412
A Jeweler's Eye: Islamic Arts of the Book from the Vever Collection (exh. cat. by G. Lowry, Washington, DC, Sackler Gal., 1988), p. 182, no. 59; p. 192, no. 64
A. Welch: 'The Worldly Vision of Mir Sayyid 'Ali', *Persian Masters: Five Centuries of Painting*, ed. S. R. Canby (Bombay, 1990)
SHEILA R. CANBY

Mirza 'Ali [Mīrzā 'Alī ibn Sultān-Muḥammad] (*b* ?Tabriz, *c.* 1510; *d* before 1576). Persian illustrator. According to the Safavid chronicler Qazi Ahmad, during the lifetime of the famous painter SULTAN-MUHAMMAD, his son Mirza 'Ali worked in the library of the Safavid ruler Tahmasp I and had no match in figural and decorative painting and in portraiture. The Ottoman historian Mustafa 'Ali placed Mirza 'Ali at the head of the list of designers and called him a celebrated master and painter. Two paintings in the magnificent copy (London, BL, Or. MS. 2265, fols 48*v* and 77*v*) of Nizami's *Khamsa* ('Five poems') made for Tahmasp in 1539–43 are ascribed to Mirza 'Ali. Their realism, logical arrangement of space and psychological insight led Dickson and Welch to attribute other works to the artist and trace a long career, stretching into the 1570s. They suggested that in the 1530s and 1540s Mirza 'Ali worked on the major manuscripts produced for the Safavid court, contributing six paintings to the monumental copy (ex-Houghton priv. col., fols 18*v*, 295*r*, 339*r*, 402*r*, 638*r* and 731*r*) of Firdawsi's *Shāhnāma* ('Book of kings') made for Tahmasp and two paintings added to a small copy (London, BL, Add. MS. 25900, fols 241*v* and 250*v*) of the *Khamsa*. Other works assigned to Mirza 'Ali include a double frontispiece with a hunting scene, his most ambitious painting, in a copy (1549; St Petersburg, Rus. N. Lib., Dorn 434) of Jami's *Silsilat al-Dhahab* ('Chain of gold'), and the idealized *Seated Princess with a Spray of Flowers* (Cambridge, MA, Sackler Mus., 1958.60), one of

the finest single figures in Safavid art. His best work of the 1540s shows his intellectual brilliance, penetrating eye and concern for landscape. Later works, such as the six paintings that Welch assigns to him in the splendid copy (1556–65; Washington, DC, Freer, 46.12, fols 10*r*, 38*v*, 52*r*, 153*v*, 191*v*, 221*v*) of Jami's *Haft Awrang* ('Seven thrones') and a double-page *Rest during a Hunt* (New York, Met., 12.223.1, and Boston, MA, Mus. F.A., 14.624), show the artist's increasing spirituality and mannerism.

BIBLIOGRAPHY
Muṣṭafā 'Alī: *Manāqib-i hunarvarān* [Virtues of artists] (1587) (Istanbul, 1926), p. 64
Qāzī Aḥmad ibn Mīr Munshī: *Gulistān-i hunar* [Rose-garden of art] (*c.* 1606); Eng. trans. by V. Minorsky as *Calligraphers and Painters* (Washington, DC, 1959), p. 186
M. B. Dickson and S. C. Welch: *The Houghton Shahnameh* (Cambridge, MA, 1981), pp. 129–53, pls 6, 169, 176, 191, 243, 258; col. pls 15–17
SHEILA S. BLAIR

Mirza Baba [Mīrzā Bābā] (*fl c.* 1795–*c.* 1830). Persian painter. Reportedly a native of Isfahan, he was employed by the Qajar family at Astarabad, as indicated by a signed drawing of a dragon and phoenix (1788–9; ex-Pozzi priv. col.). After Agha Muhammad (*reg* 1779–97) ascended the throne, Mirza Baba worked at the Qajar court in Tehran in a wide variety of materials, techniques and scales. His oil portrait (1789–90; Tehran, Nigaristan Mus.) of the Sasanian king Hurmuzd IV (*reg* AD 579–90) probably belonged to a series of historical portraits, for Mirza Baba painted a second series a decade later. One of the two surviving paintings from the later series (Tehran, A. H. Ibtihaj priv. col.) shows the Saljuq ruler Malikshah (*reg* 1072–92) with his two ministers. Other early works by Mirza Baba include a still-life with pomegranates, watermelon and flowers (?1793–4; Tehran, Nigaristan Mus.) and an arched panel showing *Shirin Visiting Farhad as He Carves Mt Bisitun* (1793–4; priv. col., see *Treasures of Islam*, no. 184). Many of these early oil paintings follow the style set by MUHAMMAD SADIQ (*see* ISLAMIC ART, §VIII, 11(i)).

Under Fath 'Ali Shah (*reg* 1797–1834) Mirza Baba was entrusted with important commissions designed to spread the glory of the monarchy. In 1798–9 he painted a superb life-size portrait of the ruler (London, Commonwealth Relations Trust), which Lord Wellesley presented to the East India Company in 1806. Mirza Baba also worked on the magnificent manuscript (Windsor Castle, Royal Lib., MS A/4) of the ruler's *Divān* (collected poetry) written under the pen-name Khaqan; the Shah's ambassador presented it to the Prince Regent, later George IV, in 1812. In addition to its splendid varnished covers and gold marginal illumination, Mirza Baba contributed two miniature portraits, one of the royal poet and another of his uncle and predecessor. The artist's signature on the portraits includes the title *naqqāsh bāshī* ('painter laureate'), the first use of this title (*see* ISLAMIC ART, §III, 4(vi)(b) and fig. 130). A varnished casket (1803–4; Tehran, Archaeol. Mus.) is decorated with a beautiful design of birds perched in flowering bushes. An enamelled snuff-box (1809–10; Tehran, Bank Markazi, Crown Jewels Col.) has a fine depiction of an old man and two women on its lid. Although Sir William Ouseley, who was in Tehran in 1811–12, mentioned a Mirza Baba condemned to death for financial misdeeds, such signed works as a painted enamel tray (1826–7; Tehran, Bank Markazi, Crown Jewels Col.) show that this reference was to another figure of the same name.

BIBLIOGRAPHY

B. W. Robinson: 'The Court Painters of Fatḥ 'Alī Shāh', *Eretz-Israel*, vii (1964), pp. 94–105

——: 'Qājār Painted Enamels', *Painting from Islamic Lands*, ed. R. Pinder-Wilson (Oxford, 1969), pp. 187–204

S. J. Falk: *Qajar Paintings: Persian Oil Paintings of the 18th and 19th Centuries* (London, 1972)

B. W. Robinson: 'Persian Painting in the Qajar Period', *Highlights of Persian Art*, ed. R. Ettinghausen and E. Yarshater (Boulder, 1979), pp. 331–62

M. A. Karimzada Tabrizi: *Aḥvāl u āthār-i naqqāshān-i qadīm-i īrān* [The lives and art of old painters of Iran] (London, 1985), no. 1315

Treasures of Islam (exh. cat., ed. T. Falk; Geneva, Mus. A. & Hist., 1985)

B. W. Robinson: 'Qajar Lacquer', *Muqarnas*, vi (1990), pp. 131–46

Mīr Zayn al-ʿĀbidīn Tabrīzī. *See* ZAYN AL-ʿABIDIN.

Mirzoyam. *See* ZHAMBYL.

Mis-en-page. Compositional distribution of motifs on a page.

Misericord [Lat. *misericordia*: 'act of mercy']. Hinged choir-stall seat, which, when tipped up, gives support to the clergy, who according to the Rules of St Benedict (6th century) were required to stand during the Divine Offices, consisting of the seven Canonical Hours. The term is first mentioned in the 11th-century *Constitutiones* of Hirsau Abbey, Germany (chapter xxix), when they were confined to the upper rows of the stalls and used by the old and weak monks only, who had previously been allowed crutches. The use of misericords is restricted to western Europe. Their undersides are usually carved, and the earliest surviving examples date from the 13th century (e.g. Exeter Cathedral, *c.* 1230–60).

In contrast to other church art, the subject-matter of misericords is predominantly secular, illustrating the humorous side of life, proverbs, games, fables, professions and a vast repertory of grotesques, animals and plants. Scenes based on the scriptures are few (e.g. Amiens Cathedral, 1508–19). However, the apparently humorous scenes often have moral implications (see fig.), inspired by sermons, and the animals are frequently derived from bestiaries, which ascribed moral meanings to them.

In the 13th century the motifs were simple, and the foliage was of trefoil or cinquefoil pattern, which gradually changed to a naturalistic type in the 14th century (e.g. Wells Cathedral, *c.* 1330–40). The style and iconography of the motifs developed parallel to contemporary stone-carvings and manuscript illuminations, and by the beginning of the 14th century they were closely related to the marginal drolleries in manuscripts. English misericords were at their height in the 14th and 15th centuries, whereas their climax in France was in the 15th and 16th centuries. By the 17th century the motifs had in general been reduced to a repetitive, decorative pattern of foliage and flowers, following the Council of Trent (1563), which forbade secular subjects in churches and led to the destruction of misericords in Roman Catholic countries such as Italy and southern Germany. In England medieval choir stalls (e.g. Canterbury Cathedral) were destroyed during the Cromwellian period (mid-17th century).

In England, and rarely in other countries, misericords have subsidiary carvings emanating from either side of the seat ledge, called supporters. (English misericords have a greater narrative content than those of other countries.)

Misericord showing a winged devil eavesdropping on two women (centre), a demon recording the women's chatter (left supporter) and a centaur-like figure with a club and shield (right supporter), *c.* 1365, Chapel of the Royal Foundation of St Katharine, Stepney, London

This allowed the narrative to be expanded, telling a detailed story with many small figures, rather than one large, representational one. They are noted for their originality and local interest, as in the *Labours of the Months* in Worcester Cathedral and Ripple Church, Hereford & Worcs, or the story of the local saint Werbugh in Chester Cathedral.

Surviving misericords in Belgium and the Netherlands date mainly from 1430 to 1550. Proverbs are frequently depicted, as are scenes of drunkenness and the *Battle for the Breeches* (e.g. Hoogstraten, St Katharina; 1546). Netherlandish influence affected the style and iconography of the misericords in northern France, and the style of the Italian Renaissance is prevalent in the stalls originally from Gaillon Castle (1508–12; Saint-Denis Abbey; Paris, Mus. Cluny; priv. cols). In Spain, Barcelona Cathedral has a complete set of misericords (1394–9), and the carvings of the stalls in Seville Cathedral (1464–78) and León Cathedral (1467/8–81) are outstanding in their vitality and individuality. Many German medieval stalls are now without misericords, but those from Cologne Cathedral (1308–11) represent the most elegant style in the 14th century, influenced by Parisian work; those from Ulm Minster (1469–74) illustrate the supreme carving of the 15th century. Most choir-stalls in Switzerland date from the 17th and 18th centuries, and the misericord carvings are of little variety. Earlier examples of interest are in Lausanne Cathedral (*c.* 1260), St Etienne, Moudon (1501–2), and St Laurentius, Estavayer-le-Lac (1522–6).

Only a small number of carvers are recorded, for example Jörg Syrlin (i) (*see* SYRLIN, (1)), who was responsible for the Ulm choir-stalls. If not made by the master carver himself, the misericords were carved under his direction, with more than one carver working on the larger sets. Similarities in style and iconography between different sets of misericords point to the movement of carvers and the use of common models, as demonstrated by the connection between the misericords of Lincoln Cathedral, Chester Cathedral and Nantwich parish church, Ches. At the end of the 15th century and the beginning of the 16th especially, Netherlandish carvers worked abroad (e.g. Windsor Castle, St George; Westminster Abbey, London; Rouen Cathedral). Rodrigo Alemán worked on several choir-stalls in Spain. The dissemination of patterns in the 14th century and much of the 15th was through sketchbooks and manuscripts, whereas prints were available from the second half of the 15th century. Thus, engravings by Albrecht Dürer were used in Westminster Abbey, and a print by the Master b ⋉ ℊ (German) was used both in Ripon, N. Yorks, and in Baden-Baden.

BIBLIOGRAPHY
H. Reiners: *Die rheinischen Chorgestühle der Frühgotik*, Stud. Dt. Kstgesch., cxiii (Strasbourg, 1909)
F. Bond: *Misericords* (1910), i of *Wood Carvings in English Churches*, (Oxford, 1910)
F. Neugass: *Mittelalterliches Chorgestühl in Deutschland*, Stud. Dt. Kstgesch., ccxlix (Strasbourg, 1927)
R. Busch: *Deutsches Chorgestühl in sechs Jahrhunderten* (Hildesheim, 1929)
G. Druce: 'Misericords: Their Form and Decoration', *J. Brit. Archaeol. Assoc.*, n. s., xxxvi (1931), pp. 244–64
W. Loose: *Die Chorgestühle des Mittelalters* (Heidelberg, 1931)
J. Purvis: 'The Use of Continental Woodcuts and Prints by the Ripon School of Woodcarvers', *Archaeologia*, lxxxv (1936), pp. 107–28
P. Ganz and T. Seeger: *Das Chorgestühl in der Schweiz* (Frauenfeld, 1946)
G. L. Remnant: *A Catalogue of Misericords in Great Britain*, intro. M. D. Anderson (Oxford, 1969)
J. Verspaandonk: *Misericorde-reeks*, 7 vols (Amsterdam, 1972–94)
J. K. Steppe: *Wereld van Vroomheid en Satire* (Kasterlee, 1973)
C. Grössinger: 'English Misericords of the Thirteenth and Fourteenth Centuries and their Relationship to Manuscript Illuminations', *J. Warb. & Court.-Inst.*, xxxviii (1975), pp. 97–108
D. Kraus and H. Kraus: *The Gothic Choirstalls of Spain* (London, 1986)
——: *Le Monde caché des miséricordes* (Paris, 1986)
U. Bergmann: *Das Chorgestühl des Kölner Domes*, 2 vols (Neuss, 1987)
C. Tracy: *English Gothic Choir-stalls, 1200–1400* (Woodbridge, 1987)
——: *English Gothic Choir-stalls, 1400–1540* (Woodbridge, 1990)

CHRISTA GRÖSSINGER

Miseroni. Italian family of craftsmen. The Miseroni workshop in Milan specialized in the carving of rock crystal and hardstones and gained international recognition in the mid-16th century. Imperial patronage from the Habsburgs prompted the re-establishment in 1588 of the workshop in Prague, where it flourished until 1684.

Ambrogio Matteo Miseroni was a goldsmith in Milan, and his two sons, Gasparo (*b* Milan, 1518; *d* before 24 April 1573) and Girolamo (*b* Milan, 1522; *d* after 25 May 1584), inherited the workshop. Morigia recorded that they were pupils of the famous gem-engravers Jacopo da Trezzo I and Benedetto Poligino, but this is unlikely because they belonged to the same generation as Trezzo. Gasparo and Girolamo lived in the family home in Milan and ran the workshop together. They worked as goldsmiths and as pietre dure carvers in Milan; membership of the same guild allowed both activities. They excelled at the carving of vases, ewers and bowls in rock crystal and pietre dure, and documents show that they collaborated on the production of particular pieces.

There are no secure references that identify particular works as being solely by the hand of Girolamo. He must have been a sculptor of high quality, judging by the importance of such commissions as a crystal vase with gold trimmings (untraced), completed in 1550 for the convent of S Maria di Monte Oliveto in Rome, for which the high price of 800 scudi was paid. Girolamo is mentioned for the last time in a document of 25 May 1584 in Milan: in that year he went to Spain, where he worked with Jacopo da Trezzo I at the court of Philip II.

The work of Gasparo Miseroni has been reconstructed, first by Fock, in a study limited to the vases made for the Medici court, and then in an extensive essay by Distelberger (1983). Gasparo's patrons included Ferdinand I, Holy Roman Emperor, and Paul IV, for whom he made a rock crystal bowl in 1557. Between 1552 and 1562 Eleonora de Toledo bought many rock crystal vases and jewels from Gasparo, and in 1562 she commissioned an agate cameo with the portrait of Philip II of Spain and his children. From the 1550s Gasparo had close relations with the Medici court, and in 1560 and 1564 he went to Florence to deliver in person two rock crystal objects to Cosimo I.

Several pieces from the Medici collection (Florence, Pitti) have been identified as Gasparo's work. These include a bloodstone cup in the long, sinuous shape of a fantastic animal, which Vasari mentioned admiringly in the *Vite*. He made a similar cup of lapis lazuli for Catherine de' Medici, for whom he also created a crystal goblet (both Florence, Pitti), which was later fitted with a cover bearing the initials of Henry II of France and Diane of Poitiers.

These rock crystal vases are characterized by a sober elegance of form and extraordinary refinement in their rich engraved decoration. Gasparo received commissions for similar vases (Vienna, Ksthist. Mus.) from Maximilian II, Holy Roman Emperor, especially in the 1560s. In 1573 the Florentine Court again received from Gasparo and Girolamo a group of lapis lazuli vases and other works, but the document recording their delivery, dated 24 April 1573, mentions Gasparo as already dead.

Girolamo's sons transplanted the Miseroni workshop to Prague. Ottavio (*b* Milan, 1567; *d* Prague, 16 July 1624), who was trained in his father's workshop, was in Prague after 22 January 1588, at the invitation of Emperor Rudolf II, with a monthly salary of 15 florins. He remained there and founded an active and highly skilled stone-carving workshop, where he was assisted by his brothers Giovanni Ambrogio Miseroni and Alessandro Miseroni.

In the vases made in the 1590s Ottavio, while inspired by the work of Gasparo and Girolamo, already revealed the characteristics of his own style, which sought to avoid sharp edges and to model the forms with soft lines; to this period belong the jade goblet in the form of a shell (Stuttgart, Württemberg. Landesmus.) and the nephrite goblet with a large mask (Vienna, Ksthist. Mus.; *see also* HARDSTONES, colour pl. II, fig. 1). Ottavio's skill was so refined that he could model such difficult materials as hardstones as if they were soft wax. His style reached its maturity in 1608 with the great bloodstone bowl (Paris, Louvre) created to celebrate 20 years of work for the Emperor and his own elevation to noble rank. The gold decorations and mountings of Ottavio's carved vases, many with sculptural motifs, were often executed by the

Flemish goldsmith Hans Vermeyen (*d c.* 1606). Products of this collaboration include the enamelled mounting of a translucent chalcedony goblet (*c.* 1600; Vienna, Ksthist. Mus.) and the gold Bacchus surmounting a bloodstone goblet (1605; Vienna, Ksthist. Mus.; see fig.).

Ottavio was also active as a cameo carver, which probably earned him the admiration of Rudolf II. His first securely attributed work in this medium is a cameo with the Emperor's portrait (1590 or after; Vienna, Ksthist. Mus.), in which Ottavio was clearly inspired by the style of Jacopo da Trezzo I. Shortly afterwards he made a cameo of the Virgin, with a rich mounting by Vermeyen (*c.* 1600; Vienna, Ksthist. Mus.), which shows the evolution of his technique towards a delicate refinement of modelling and exploitation of the chromatic qualities of the stone. In the same years Ottavio perfected a technique in pietre dure (*see* GEM-ENGRAVING, §I, 10) in which small mosaic reliefs or sculptures in the round are made up of different stones, worked separately and then assembled. Ottavio's works in this medium include an oval with the Magdalene in bas-relief (*c.* 1610) and a second Magdalene carved in the round and signed (both Vienna, Ksthist. Mus.).

After the death of Rudolf II in 1612, Ottavio's vases became more static in form, characterized by fine polishing and sharp edges in the inner cavities (e.g. shell-shaped goblet in smoked quartz; Vienna, Ksthist. Mus.). He made large bowls less frequently; the Emperor Matthias probably had little interest in them and left them unmounted. Following Ottavio's death, his son Dionisio (*d* Prague, 29 June 1661) continued the workshop with great success. He served Ferdinand III, Holy Roman Emperor, as official hardstone carver and keeper of the royal treasures. His son Ferdinand Eusebius also held these titles, and it was only with his death in 1684 that the workshop closed.

BIBLIOGRAPHY

G. Vasari: *Vite* (1550, rev. 2/1568); ed. G. Milanesi, v (1882), p. 389
Morigia: *La nobilità di Milano* (Milan, 1595), p. 291
E. Kris: *Meister und Meisterwerke der Steinschneidekunst in der italienischen Renaissance*, 2 vols (Vienna, 1929)
C. W. Fock: 'Vases en lapis-lazuli des collections médicéennes du seizième siècle', *Münchn. Jb. Bild. Kst* (1967), pp. 119–54
R. Distelberger: 'Beobachtungen zu den Steinschneiderwerkstätten der Miseroni in Mailand und Prag', *Jb. Ksthist. Samml. Wien*, lxxiv (1978), pp. 79–152
——: 'Dionysio und Ferdinando Eusebio Miseroni', *Jb. Ksthist. Samml. Wien*, lxxv (1979), pp. 109–88
——: 'Nuove ricerche sulla biografia dei fratelli Gasparo e Girolamo Miseroni', *Firenze e la Toscana dei Medici nell'Europa del'500: Florence, 1983*, iii, pp. 877–84
Prag um 1600: Kunst und Kultur am Hofe Kaiser Rudolfs II, 2 vols (exh. cat., Vienna, Ksthist. Mus., 1988)

ANNAMARIA GIUSTI

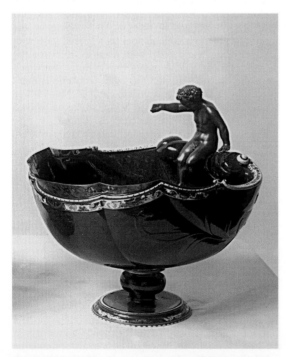

Ottavio Miseroni: bloodstone goblet, with gold figure of Bacchus and enamelled base by Hans Vermeyen, h. 193 mm, 1605 (Vienna, Kunsthistorisches Museum)

Miskin [Miskīn; Miskīna] (*fl c.* 1580–1604). Indian miniature painter, son of MAHESH. One of the finest painters at the court of the Mughal emperor Akbar (*reg* 1556–1605), he combined in his work the elegant rhythms of Persian painting with new European conventions for rendering volume and depth. The *Āyin-i Akbarī*, a contemporary account of Akbar's administration, lists both Mahesh and Miskin among Akbar's outstanding painters.

Miskin's talent allowed him to rise rapidly from apprentice to master in the 1580s. He is named in inscriptions as a colourist, a position usually held by a younger or trainee artist, in two manuscripts commissioned by Akbar early in that decade, the *Dārābnāma* ('History of Darab'; *c.* 1580; London, BL, Or. MS. 4615) and the *Razmnāma* ('Book of war'; 1582–6; Jaipur, Maharaja Sawai Man Singh II Mus., MS. AG. 1683-1850), a Persian translation of the Hindu epic the *Mahābhārata*. However, in the *Tārīkh-i Khāndān-i Tīmūriyya* ('History of the house of Timur'; *c.* 1584; Patna, Khuda Bakhsh Lib.) and *Rāmāyaṇa* (*c.* 1588–92; Jaipur, Maharaja Sawai Man Singh II Mus., MS. AG. 1851-2026), Hinduism's second great epic, Miskin is named in the more prestigious position of designer. Miskin played a major role in the illustration of such manuscripts as the *Akbarnāma* ('History of Akbar'; *c.* 1590; London, V&A, MS. IS. 2-1896). Inscriptions name him as the designer of 17 paintings, indicating that his career by this time had eclipsed that of his father, who is named as colourist on one of the miniatures (no. 99/117).

Strong diagonals organize many of Miskin's compositions in the *Akbarnāma*, but rarely contribute to significant pictorial depth. Although most works are complicated in design, they remain quite flat, with the action focused in the middleground and a view of the distance obscured by clusters of trees or buildings. Miskin generally scattered relatively small and numerous figures across his compositions, but occasionally isolated the protagonists in an open central space, grouping secondary characters along fences, tents or ridges. The arrangement of the figures—and particularly the angles of their outthrust arms—often contributes to the mood of a scene effecting the tumult of battle (e.g. no. 88/117), the bustle of construction (e.g. nos 45–6/117) or the concerted effort of a siege (e.g. nos 66–7, 72, 74/117). Miskin's portraits of Akbar in two of the illustrations (29, 55/117) display rich surface modelling and the artist's customary square jaw and sloping nose.

A series of paintings in de luxe manuscripts produced for Akbar in the mid-1590s were apparently painted by Miskin unassisted and provide the clearest picture of his mature style. The most celebrated, an illustration in the *Bahāristān* ('Spring garden') of Jami (1595; Oxford, Bodleian Lib., MS. Elliot 254; see fig.), depicts a cuckold discovering his wife's unfaithfulness. Miskin conveys the ire and dismay of the situation with such stock gestures as the husband's rigidly extended arm and one woman's upraised finger. The female conspirators, united by their common pose and placement along a band of dull green, attempt to restrain the angry husband, while a young man persuaded to take the wife's place in her tent peeps through the door. The figures' slender proportions are delineated by their drapery, whose strong modelling betrays an obvious origin in European prints. Persian influence is manifest in the grotesques hidden within the nodules of the billowing rocks. Set within the nocturnal landscape are auxiliary scenes of a herdsman, master and pupil and the surreptitious lovers. Miskin includes in the yellow-streaked landscape a trio of frolicking horses, one of his trademark motifs, and an assortment of dozing animals.

Rivalled as an animal painter only by the younger artist Mansur, Miskin was responsible for a spectacular double-page hunting scene in the *Akbarnāma* (nos 55–6/117) as well as two representations of the animal kingdom in the

Miskin: *Husband Attempting to Beat a Youth for Substituting for his Wife while She Meets her Lover*, opaque watercolour and gold on paper, 239×134 mm; from Jami: *Bahāristān* ('Spring garden'), 1595 (Oxford, Bodleian Library, MS. Elliot 254, fol. 42*r*)

Anvār-i Suhaylī ('Lights of Canopus'; 1596–7; Varanasi, Banaras Hindu U., Bharat Kala Bhavan, MS. 9069/1–27, fols 48 and 71). In the latter works Miskin's extraordinarily fluid draughtsmanship produced a host of creatures with rhythmically arched backs and necks, making them more lively than naturalistic. The narrow dark corona around these elegant contours thrusts each beast to the surface, virtually precluding any semblance of pictorial depth. Narrowed or even crossed eyes impart an unmistakable mischievousness to the animals, whose human expressions are in keeping with their role as examples of worldly behaviour.

Three paintings in a second *Akbarnāma* (1596–7; two are in London, BL, Or. MS. 12988, and one in Baltimore, MD, Walters A.G., W.684B; alternatively dated *c.* 1604) display the major features of Miskin's figure style, which changed little over two decades. Miskin added extensive contour modelling to an essentially linear conception of form. He favoured three-quarter faces with finely rendered, intense expressions, but also employed profile views set at owlish angles on rounded shoulders. In his most successful works, colour is muted or even eliminated altogether, as in the many animal scenes in the uncoloured *nīm qalam* style at the end of the 1590s, including, for example, *Buffaloes in Combat* (New York, Met., 1983.258).

BIBLIOGRAPHY
W. Staude: 'Muskine', *Rev. A. Asiat.*, v (1928), pp. 169–82
D. Barrett and B. Gray: *Painting of India* (Lausanne, 1963); R as *Indian Painting* (New York, 1978)
Rai Krishnadasa: 'A Fable Book for Akbar', *Times of India Annu.* (1966), pp. 31–40
S. C. Welch: *Imperial Mughal Painting* (New York, 1978)
The Grand Mogul: Imperial Painting in India, 1600–1660 (exh. cat. by M. C. Beach, Williamstown, MA, Clark A. Inst.; Baltimore, MD, Walters A.G.; Boston, MA, Mus. F.A.; New York, Asia Soc. Gals; 1978–9)
The Imperial Image: Paintings for the Mughal Court (exh. cat. by M. C. Beach, Washington, DC, Freer, 1981)
N. Titley: *Persian Miniature Painting and its Influence on the Art of Turkey and India* (Austin, TX, 1983)
G. Sen: *Paintings from the Akbarnama* (Varanasi, 1984)
P. Vaughan: 'Miskin', *Master Artists of the Imperial Mughal Court*, ed. P. Pal (Bombay, 1991), pp. 17–38

JOHN SEYLLER

Miskina. *See* MASKANA.

Mi Son [Mī-sọn]. Important Shaivite site in Champa, situated rather inaccessibly in a circular plain surrounded by mountains, 40 km to the south-east of Da Nang in central Vietnam. Inscriptions found at the site indicate that it flourished from the 4th and 5th centuries AD until the 12th century, although no buildings remain from the first three centuries of this period. The monuments of Mi Son are irregularly sited from south to north on either side of a winding river, and in the early 20th century archaeologists classified them into nine groups, according to their location and not their chronology, as follows: A (13 monuments), A' (4 monuments), B (14 monuments), C (7 monuments), D (6 monuments), E (9 monuments), F (3 monuments), G (5 monuments) and H (4 monuments). They have been protected and gradually cleared and restored since the Vietnam War (1954–75), during which they suffered greatly.

Groups E and F date from the 7th and 8th century and groups A, A', B, C and D from the 10th century. Group D also includes buildings earlier than those in groups B and C. The small groups G and H date from the 12th century and show signs of the decadence that resulted from the removal of the capital southwards to Binh Dinh (*c.* AD 1000) and from conflicts with the Khmer empire of Angkor in the 12th and early 13th centuries. The 7th- and 8th-century sculptures, especially on the monuments in group E, reveal certain similarities with pre-Angkor Khmer art, and some of them, such as the pedestal of Mi Son E1 (*see* CHAMPA, §III, 1), are among the highest achievements of Cham art. The 10th-century buildings in the style of Mi Son A1, consisting of various sanctuaries and their adjacent halls, are characteristic of Cham architecture (*see* CHAMPA, §II, 1(iv) and fig. 4). Their restrained decoration shows the influence of Indonesian art of the period.

For illustrations *see* CHAMPA, figs 7 and 8.

BIBLIOGRAPHY
L. Finot: 'Deux nouvelles inscriptions de Bhadravarman I roi de Champa', *Bull. Ecole Fr. Extrême-Orient*, ii (1902), pp. 185–91
——: 'Les Inscriptions de Mi-son', *Bull. Ecole Fr. Extrême-Orient*, iv (1904), pp. 897–977
H. Parmentier: 'Les Monuments du cirque de Mi-son', *Bull. Ecole Fr. Extrême-Orient*, iv (1904), pp. 805–96
——: *Inventaire descriptif des monuments cams de l'Annam*, Pubns Ecole Fr. Extrême-Orient (Paris, 1918)
P. Stern: *L'Art du Champa (ancien Annam) et son évolution* (Toulouse, 1942)

EMMANUEL GUILLON

Miss, Mary (*b* New York, 27 May 1944). American sculptor, draughtsman, film maker and environmental artist. As a child she was taken by her father on many visits to early forts, Indian sites and abandoned mines. In Stuttgart with her family she saw the remains of demolished buildings as well as medieval towns and castle ruins, which left a strong impression. She studied at the University of California, Santa Barbara (BA 1966), and at the Rhine Art School of Sculpture, Maryland Art Institute, Baltimore (MFA 1968). On a summer sculpture course at Colorado College, Colorado Springs (1963), she became aware of the work of John Cage, Robert Rauschenberg and Robert Morris and of ideas initiated by contemporary Minimalist sculptors and land artists. Her early landscape works dealt primarily with the measurement of distances in relation to a specific location in a temporal work: for example, *Untitled* (wood, 12×6 ft [3.66×1.83 m] sections at 50 ft [15.25 m] intervals, 1973; New York, Battery Park landfill), intended to relate the visual with the physicality of the objects and landscape. Miss first exhibited in 1970 at the Whitney Annual and exhibited regularly from 1972. Later works draw on the architecture, landscape design, gardens and history of worldwide cultures. Her films include *Cut-off*, focusing on the interaction of landscape, viewer and set. Photographs taken during walking treks in various parts of the world inform her practice.

WRITINGS
'On a Redefinition of Public Sculpture', *Perspecta*, 21 (1984), pp. 52–70

BIBLIOGRAPHY
Mary Miss: Projects, 1966–1987 (exh. cat. by D. Cromption and V. Wilson, essay by Joseph Giovannini; London, Archit. Assoc. 1987) [incl. pubd conversation between Miss and A. Boyarsky]

□

Missal. Book containing prayers, benedictions, invocations, readings and instructions used in the ritual of the Roman Catholic Mass. The basic service of the Mass contained in the *Ordo missae* (Ordinary of the Mass) consists of the Mass of the Catechumens, the Offertory, prefaces for the common masses and for high feast days, the Canon of the Mass, in which the bread and wine of the Eucharist are consecrated, and the Order of Holy Communion. Three additional sections provide the devotions required for special occasions. The Temporal (or Proper of Time) contains the feasts that occur on Sundays and are based on the events of the life of Christ. The Sanctoral (or Proper of Saints) contains prayers, lessons and recitations appropriate for the feast days of special saints occurring on set dates. By the end of the Middle Ages the sequence of feasts in both sections followed the order of the liturgical year, usually beginning with the first Sunday in Advent (the Sunday closest to 30 November). A third section, the Common of Saints, contains prayers, recitations and lessons for saints or groups of saints for whom there are no special commemorative rites or fixed feast days. The Missal might also contain special votive Masses, such as the Mass of the Dead, and a variety of other benedictions, hymns and special prayers.

1. MANUSCRIPT. The Missal evolved from the Sacramentary, a compilation of only those elements that the celebrant recited for high or solemn Mass. As the liturgy of the Mass became more complicated and additional elements were added to the book, including musical notations for chants (*see* CHOIR-BOOK), lessons and other formulae for low mass, various specialized types of service books were developed (*see* SERVICE BOOK). The first Missal with these accretions appeared in the 10th century.

The decoration of the Sacramentary remained fairly restricted in the early Middle Ages. The most important part of the book was the Canon of the Mass, preceded by prefaces, yet in such an early manuscript as the 7th-century Bobbio Missal (Paris, Bib. N., MS. lat. 13246) the opening of the preface, *Vere dignum*, received only a slightly larger initial than the rest of the text, and the *Te igitur* opening the Canon received a six-line initial with typical patterned Merovingian decoration. The earliest example of an appropriate opening to the Canon occurs in the mid-7th-century Gellone Sacramentary (Paris, Bib. N., MS. lat. 10248), in which the Crucified Christ is placed against the letter T, symbolizing the essential nature of the sacrificial rite celebrated in this part of the Mass.

A Sacramentary produced for Archbishop Drogo of Metz (845–55; Paris, Bib. N., MS. lat. 9428) revealed the full decorative potential of these texts for the Mass. Architectural frames in a shape combining an altar table with a Classical temple façade surround the prefaces,

2. Lytlington Missal, *Crucifixion with Scenes from the Passion*, 1383–4 (London, Westminster Abbey, MS. 37, vol. ii, fol. 157*v*)

1. Missal (the Drogo Sacramentary), historiated initial T, 845–55 (Paris, Bibliothèque Nationale, MS. lat. 9428, fol. 15*v*)

which follow a mounting decorative sequence, from a full-page historiated V that cuts through the text of the *Vere dignum*, to a Seraph set against the text of the *Sanctus*, and to a monumental historiated T set within the *Te igitur* (see fig. 1). The medallions within the letter contain appropriate representations of Old Testament prefigurations of the Crucifixion: the sacrifices of Abel, Melchisedec and Abraham. This folio faces the continuation of the text ('. . . clementissime . . .') in smaller decorative capitals, then follows a page in Roman square capitals before the rest of the text reverts to the uncial script. Later Mass books did not follow this dramatic decorative progression. Instead a formula of monogrammatic fusion of the VD was used to open the Preface, and the Te for the Canon was treated similarly, as in a Franco-Saxon Sacramentary of the later 9th century (Vienna, Österreich. Nbib., Cod. 958). The Drogo Sacramentary also introduced historiated initials at the beginning of the masses of the Temporal. Particularly large initials were reserved for major feasts, such as a *Nativity* for the Christmas Mass, an *Adoration of the Magi* for Epiphany and the *Three Marys at the Tomb* for Easter.

When the Missal, with its additional texts containing other parts of the Mass, supplanted the Sacramentary after the 11th century, the tradition of illustrating the major feasts was continued in those Missals that received luxurious decoration. In these books, where the Temporal and Sanctoral were separated, miniatures introducing the masses for saints' days usually showed their martyrdom. The sequence still followed that of the liturgical year, and the Canon was usually introduced by a miniature of the *Crucifixion*.

Since the text for Easter Mass occurred roughly halfway through the book, from the 11th century it became customary to place the Canon of the Mass after the Mass for Holy Saturday and just before that of Easter. This tradition remained virtually constant for the rest of the Middle Ages, and it became usual to depict the *Crucifixion* or a *Celebration of the Mass* in a historiated T or a large, full-page miniature of the *Crucifixion* facing the opening of the Canon. An elaborate *Crucifixion* framed with small vignettes of *Passion* scenes appears in this position in the Missal of Abbot Nicholas Lytlington (1383–4; London, Westminster Abbey, MS. 37; see fig. 2).

2. PRINTED. Owing to their heavy use, Missals were frequently produced on early printing presses after *c.* 1470. An early edition, for example, was printed in Basle after 1472, perhaps using a type fount of even earlier date. During the 1480s and 1490s hundreds of editions were published for the usage of numerous dioceses. One of the most magnificent was a Missal for the Use of Langres published by Jean du Pré (*fl* 1483–1519) in Paris in 1491. It contains 12 woodcuts and metalcuts, the first of which, depicting the *Mass of St Gregory* on the opening page with the text for Advent, was printed in green and surrounded by border metalcuts in red. Several Missals were published by Erhard Ratdolt (1447–1527/8) in Augsburg from 1491, using large type and decorative woodcut initials; they also contain large woodcuts of the *Virgin and Child* and, in a Missal of 1494, a large woodcut of the *Crucifixion* prefacing the Canon.

BIBLIOGRAPHY

V. Leroquais: *Les Sacramentaires et les missels manuscrits des bibliothèques publiques de France*, 4 vols (Paris, 1924)

K. Gamber: *Sakramentartypen: Versuch einer Gruppierung der Handschriften und Fragmente bis zur Jahrtausendsende* (Beuron, 1958)

Liturgical Manuscripts for the Mass and Divine Office. (exh. cat. by J. Plummer, New York, Pierpont Morgan Lib., 1964), pp. 9–13, 23–7

A. Hughes: *Medieval Manuscripts for Mass and Office: A Guide to their Organization and Terminology* (Toronto, 1982), pp. 81–98, 124–59

R. Calkins: *Illuminated Books of the Middle Ages* (Ithaca, NY, and London, 1983), pp. 161–93

O. Pächt: *Buchmalerei des Mittelalters* (Munich, 1984; Eng. trans., New York, 1986)

ROBERT G. CALKINS

Mission Revival. *See under* COLONIAL REVIVAL.

Mistra [Mistras]. *See* MYSTRAS.

Mistruzzi, Aurelio (*b* Villaorba di Basiliano, 7 Feb 1880; *d* Rome, 25 Dec 1960). Italian sculptor, medallist and die-engraver. As a traditionalist, he declared that great art could be created only as the result of outside commissions; this philosophy is demonstrated by such work as his sculpture on the façade of the Palazzo Communale in Udine and in his many funerary and war monuments, fountains and portrait busts. His strong attachment to the Church resulted in numerous works, including low reliefs

for the abbey of Montecassino and the *Nerazzini Pietà* (Montepulciano). From 1910 he also worked as a medallist, producing 330 medals. In 1920 he was appointed die-engraver to the Holy See and in 1930 supervised production of a new series of papal medals depicting ancient symbols of the Church. Notable among his coins is the first series (1929; for illustrations see Orsini, pp. 56–59) for Pope Pius XI (*reg* 1922–39). Mistruzzi was a traditional, academic artist; his art is not innovative or even very original, but it is confident, balanced and technically superb.

BIBLIOGRAPHY

A. Patrignani: 'Un decennio di attività medaglistica di Aurelio Mistruzzi', *Numismatica*, xiv (1948), pp. 30–38

M. Valeriano: *Arte della medaglia in Italia* (Rome, 1972), pp. 215–20

O. Orsini: 'Aurelio Mistruzzi, graveur du Saint-Siège', *Bull. Club Fr. Médaille*, lviii (1978), pp. 54–63

STEPHEN K. SCHER

Misu (i). *See* YI IN-NO.

Misu (ii). *See* HŎ MOK.

Mitannian. Predominantly HURRIAN people, possibly ruled by a small Indo-European aristocracy, who set up a kingdom, Mitanni, in northern Mesopotamia that flourished during the 15th and 14th centuries BC. The precise location of the capital city, Washshukkanni, is unknown; it was somewhere in the Mitannian heartland, in the region of the Upper Khabur River. In their heyday, during the reign of Saushtatar (*fl c.* 1450 BC), the Mitannians' kingdom extended from the foothills of the Zagros Mountains to the shores of the Mediterranean, and their vassals included the kings of Assyria, Aleppo, Alalakh (TELL ATCHANA), Mukish and Kizzuwadna (east Cilicia).

The Mitannians, clad in scale-armour, skilled in horse breeding and masters of chariot warfare, opposed the advance of Egyptian forces into northern Syria. About 1395 BC, however, a treaty between King Artatama of Mitanni and Tuthmosis IV of Egypt put an end to hostilities, and the peace was cemented by marriages between Mitannian princesses and successive pharaohs. A series of letters found at EL-AMARNA includes a number of tablets (written in the Hurrian language using cuneiform script) sent from Artatama and his successor Shuttarna to the Egyptian kings Amenophis III and Akhenaten. These letters profess eternal friendship, list the treasures sent as the princesses' dowries and ask for 'much gold' as the bride price. The lists of treasures are imperfectly understood, but they supplement the scant archaeological evidence about Mitannian civilization.

Crafts and industries at the Mitannian court included ivory-carving, the manufacture of glass and glazes, and the working of bronze and iron. The palaces at Alalakh and NUZI (now Yorgan Tepe) were decorated with wall paintings. Mitannian cylinder seals (see fig.) bear designs combining Babylonian, Egyptian and even Aegean motifs, as well as other elements that may be Hurrian. The last independent king of Mitanni, Tushratta, was driven from his capital by the Hittites (*c.* 1360 BC), and his successor became a Hittite vassal. In about 1270 BC the kingdom of Mitanni, by then known as Hanigalbat, was finally incorporated into the Assyrian empire by Shalmaneser I (*reg* 1273–1244 BC).

Mitannian cylinders, drawings of seal impressions on tablets found both at Nuzi (Iraq) and at Tell Brak (Syria), inscribed 'Shaushtatar, son of Parsatatar, King of Mitanni', h. 29 mm, *c.* 1450 BC

BIBLIOGRAPHY

R. F. S. Starr: *Nuzi: Report on the Excavations*, 2 vols (Cambridge, MA, 1937–9)

A. Moortgat: *The Art of Ancient Mesopotamia* (London, 1969)

M. S. Drower: 'Syria, *c.* 1550–1400 BC', *History of the Middle East and the Aegean Region, c. 1800–1380 BC*, ed. I. E. S. Edwards and others (Cambridge, 3/1973), II/i of *Cambridge Anc. Hist.*, pp. 417–525

D. Collon: *First Impressions: Cylinder Seals in the Ancient Near East* (London, 1987)

G. Wilhelm: *The Hurrians* (Warminster, 1989)

M. S. DROWER

Mitchell, Joan (*b* Chicago, 12 Feb 1926; *d* Paris, 30 Oct 1992). American painter. She studied at Smith College in Northampton, MA, from 1942 to 1944, and then at the Art Institute of Chicago (1944–9) and at Columbia University in New York (1950). From 1950 to 1955, when she had a studio on St Mark's Place, in the heart of Greenwich Village in New York, she was part of a close-knit community of abstract painters and was profoundly influenced by Abstract Expressionism, especially by the work of Willem de Kooning, Arshile Gorky and Franz Kline. However much she was affected by their work, however, her aim was less to express emotional states than to convey her experience of landscape, as in *City Landscape* (1955; Chicago, IL, A. Inst.).

Mitchell left New York for France in 1955, living first in Paris and later outside the city at Vétheuil. She continued to paint without regard to changing fashions, producing large pictures that shimmer with vibrant skeins and drips of paint, creating a vivid web of colour against a pale, neutral background. Often alluding to her sources in landscape through her use of suggestive titles, as in *Mont St Hilaire* (1957; Palm Beach, FL, Lannan Found.), she displayed a devotion to nature suggesting an affinity with the earlier work of artists such as Cézanne and Kandinsky, but expressed in wholly contemporary terms.

BIBLIOGRAPHY

M. Tucker: *Joan Mitchell* (New York, 1974)

J. Bernstock: *Joan Mitchell* (New York, 1988)

PATTI STUCKLER

Mitchell, (Arthur George) Sydney (*b* Headswood, nr Larbert, Central, 1856; *d* Gullane, Lothian, 1930). Scottish architect. The only son of Sir Arthur Mitchell, he trained in Edinburgh in the office of Rowand Anderson and in 1883 set up his own practice, which became large and was concerned equally with designs for churches, public buildings and country houses. He was official architect to the General Board of Lunacy in Scotland, the Royal Infirmary, Edinburgh, and the Commercial Bank of Scotland. Much of his work was based on his knowledge of historical sources. Well Court (1885–6), Dean Village, Edinburgh, a quadrangle with flats, a detached community hall and a resident factor's house, derives from the Earl's Palace, Kirkwall, Orkney, and Scottish 17th-century architecture. Craighouse, Edinburgh, an immense château built in the French Renaissance style as a private hospital in 1889–94 for the Royal Edinburgh Asylum, is situated on the north slope of Craiglockhart Hill, and its picturesque composition splendidly exploits the natural contours of the slope. His addition to Ramsay Gardens (1893–4), Castle Hill, Edinburgh, a hall of residence and block of flats, is a mixture of the Scottish Baronial and English traditional cottage styles and also exploits the profile of Edinburgh Castle and its Esplanade. Mitchell's most attractive church is the Chalmer's Memorial (1904), Cockenzie, Lothian, a small Arts and Crafts building with a saddleback tower surmounted by a Swiss-inspired spirelet. Designs for the grand houses of his important friends and clients included a scheme for Barnbougle Castle (1889; unexecuted), Lothian, in the style of Linlithgow Palace, Lothian, for the Prime Minister, the Earl of Rosebery (1847–1928). Mitchell was not an innovator. He ended his prosperous life in a house he designed himself at Gullane, Lothian. The Pleasance (1902; now Muirfield Gate) is harled and tile hung and is protected from the sea breezes behind its own miniature gatehouse. The Edwardian interiors, known from contemporary photographs, reflected his well-off bachelor existence. His partner George Wilson (1844–1912) appears to have acted as his office administrator and coordinator.

BIBLIOGRAPHY

Bldr's J. & Archit. Rec., viii (1898), pp. 115–18

A. Eddington: *Edinburgh and the Lothians* (Edinburgh, 1904)

CATHERINE H. CRUFT

Mitchell/Giurgola. American architectural partnership formed in Philadelphia in 1958 by Ehrman B(urkman) Mitchell jr (*b* Harrisburg, PA, 25 Jan 1924) and Romaldo [Aldo] Giurgola (*b* Rome, 2 Sept 1920). Mitchell studied architecture at the University of Pennsylvania, Philadelphia, and Giurgola at the University of Rome and Columbia University, New York. Mitchell is known primarily for his work in the American Institute of Architects, of which he was elected President in 1979. Giurgola was the dominant designer in the firm, and his work could be categorized as modified Brutalism with influences from Louis Kahn, Alvar Aalto and, to a limited extent, from James Stirling. Together with Jaimini Mehta, Giurgola published a large-format collection of Kahn's drawings in *Louis I. Kahn* (Boulder, CO, 1975). The 'new monumentality' of Kahn, together with the innovative natural lighting and spatial effects of both Kahn and Aalto, can be seen in Mitchell/Giurgola's St Bede's Abbey (1973), Peru, IL, in Tredyffrin Public Library (1976), Strafford, PA, and in Feinberg Library (1977), State University College, Plattsburg, NY. Stirling's influence on Giurgola's use of form and materials is particularly apparent in the American College (1972), Bryn Mawr, PA. Giurgola captured the spirit of Kahn, Aalto and Stirling while developing a language of place. His concept of urban place, for example, is found in the United Way Headquarters Building (1971), Philadelphia, a glass box surrounded by sun screens, which looks rather like a cardboard architectural model with horizontal cut-outs; this building spawned a whole series of projects using screens of various types. Industrial commissions led to Giurgola's appointment as designer of the Volvo Headquarters (1984), Gothenburg, Sweden. Among his most important works is the new Parliament House of Australia, Canberra, won in international competition in 1980 (completed 1988; with Richard Thorp); Giurgola's design, with free-standing screen façades and large, outward-curving ramped walls, incorporates a monumental axiality that responds to the axes of Walter Burley Griffin's urban plan of 1912 (for further discussion and illustration *see* CANBERRA). Giurgola, who was Professor of Architecture at Columbia University, was awarded the Gold Medal of both the American Institute of Architects (1981) and the Royal Australian Institute of Architects (1988).

WRITINGS

Mitchell/Giurgola, Architects (New York, 1983)

BIBLIOGRAPHY

H. Beck, ed.: *Parliament House, Canberra: A Building for the Nation* (Sydney, 1988)

LAWRENCE WODEHOUSE

Mitelli. Italian family of artists.

(1) Agostino (Stanzani) Mitelli (*b* Battidizzo, 16 March 1609; *d* Madrid, 14 Aug 1660). Painter. He and his collaborator ANGELO MICHELE COLONNA are renowned as pre-eminent exponents of *quadratura*, the painting of illusionistic architectural perspectives. They learnt this art from Girolamo Curti, who had made a speciality of it in Bologna. The two artists created a range of ceiling enframements and decorative ensembles that were architecturally the most unified and rational of their time. This achievement, recognized as the 'Bolognese style', was widely applauded and imitated until the advent of Neo-classicism, when it was criticized for excesses and violations of architectural probity.

Early in his collaboration with Colonna and Curti, Mitelli revealed a superior talent for design and decoration, and he more frequently took the role of *quadraturista*, leaving that of *figurista* to Colonna. Colonna and Mitelli's major frescoes include the Sala Grande, Palazzo Spada, Rome (1635–6), the Jupiter reception room, Palazzo Pitti, Florence (1639–41), and the Grande Salone at the Palazzo d'Este, Sassuolo, near Modena (1646–7). Mitelli returned to the last of these palaces in 1650 to assist in, if not to initiate, the decoration of the Galleria with frescoes by Jean Boulanger and his Bolognese assistants. The partners also worked in the chapel of the Rosary, S Domenico, Bologna (1654–6), and the Palazzo Balbi, Genoa (1655). In 1657–8 Philip IV of Spain summoned them to Madrid, where their introduction of the art of fresco was to influence the development of Spanish decorative painting. However, their *Pandora* ceiling (*c.* 1659) for the Hall of Mirrors in the Alcázar is destroyed, and all that remains of their Spanish work is Mitelli's modello (*c.* 1659) for the ceiling of a loggia in the Casón de Buen Retiro, Madrid.

Mitelli executed many perspective view paintings (all untraced) and three ornamental prints. He also left a large number of *quadratura* drawings (most in Berlin, Kstbib. & Mus.), which possess all the elegance and refinement of his frescoes. Followers and imitators carried his style into the 18th century, and it has been claimed that he influenced Bolognese architects and stuccoists.

(2) Giuseppe Maria Mitelli (*b* Bologna, ?1634; *d* Bologna, 4 Feb 1718). Etcher, painter and sculptor, son of (1) Agostino Mitelli. He studied with several prominent Bolognese painters and in 1658 accompanied his father to Spain, petitioning the officials there after Agostino's death for his back wages. He owes his reputation, however, to over 500 etched prints of contemporary manners and morals. His most renowned series of etchings is *L'arti per via* (Bologna, 1660; B. 117–57), loosely based on drawings by Annibale Carracci (untraced) celebrating the vendors and artisans of Bologna. A series of etchings after motifs by Agostino Mitelli, *Disegni e abbozzi di Agostino Mitelli* (B. 164–87), are important in validating his father's draughtsmanship. Altogether his large print oeuvre, illustrating ceremonies and pageants, warfare, folklore, trades and religious paintings, provides a rich cultural source for contemporary Bolognese life, but as a fairly rare 17th-century Italian political and social satirist he remains relatively unknown outside his own country.

Giuseppe Maria was among the 40 founders of the Accademia Clementina in Bologna (1710) and one of its early directors. He also worked in terracotta, though his only documented sculpture is a *Self-portrait* (Bologna, Accad. B.A. & Liceo A.). His son Agostino Mitelli (*bapt* Bologna, 1 May 1671; *d* 1696) was also, for the span of his brief career, an etcher: 6 small figural etchings (1684) after Stefano della Bella, a series of 12 grotesque masks (1688), a plan of Bologna (1692) and a small drawing of his family's country house are his only known works.

UNPUBLISHED SOURCES

Bologna, Bib. Com. Archiginnasio, MS. B. 3375 ['*Vita e opere di Agostino Mitelli*' by G. Mitelli]; MS. B. 148, n.1 ['*Cronica con molte notizie pittoresche ricavata dalla originale scritta dal Padre Giovanni Mitelli*']

BIBLIOGRAPHY

C. C. Malvasia: *Felsina pittrice* (1678); ed. M. Brascaglia (1971), pp. 352–72

G. B. Passeri: *Vite* (1679); ed. J. Hess (1934), pp. 269–72

C. C. Malvasia: *Le pitture di Bologna* (1686); ed. A. Emiliani (Bologna, 1969)

A. Arfelli: 'Per la bibliografia di Agostino e Giuseppe Maria Mitelli', *A. Ant. & Mod.*, 3 (1958), pp. 295–301

E. Feinblatt: 'A "Boceto" by Colonna–Mitelli in the Prado', *Burl. Mag.*, cvii (1965), pp. 149–57

Agostino Mitelli Drawings (exh. cat. by E. Feinblatt, Los Angeles, CA, Co. Mus. A., 1965)

A. M. Matteucci: 'Contributo alla storia dell'architettura tardo-barocca bolognese', *Atti & Mem. Stor. Pat. Romagna* (1972), pp. 226, 227, 230, 231–2, 233

R. Roli: *Pittura bolognese, 1650–1800* (Bologna, 1977), pp. 3, 4, 17, 21, 34, 39, 40, 43, 70, 73–5, 205, 206, 211 [Agostino]; 181, 183, 205–8 [Giuseppe Maria]

F. Varignana, ed.: *Le collezioni d'arte della Cassa di Risparmio in Bologna: Le incisioni. I. Giuseppe Maria Mitelli* (Bologna, 1978), pp. 455–63 [comprehensive analytical bibliog., incl. data on the younger Agostino Mitelli]

J. T. Spike, ed.: *Italian Masters of the 17th Century*, 42 [XIX/ii] of *The Illustrated Bartsch*, ed. W. Strauss (New York, 1978–81) [B.]

M. Pirondini, ed.: *Ducale Palazzo di Sassuolo* (Genoa, 1982), pp. 55–7, 97

E. Feinblatt: 'Observations on Some Colonna–Mitelli Drawings', *Master Drgs*, xxi (1983), pp. 167–72

E. FEINBLATT

Mithinari (*b* 1929; *d* 1976). Australian Aboriginal painter and sculptor. He was a member of the Galpu clan of the Yolngu-speaking people of north-east Arnhem Land, Northern Territory, and he lived most of his adult life at Yirrkala. With Wandjuk Marika and Larrtjinga (*b* 1932), he was one of a group of young men of the Dhuwa moiety whose principal teacher was Mawalan Marika. Mithinari soon gained a reputation as an outstanding painter, and in the 1950s and 1960s his paintings were acquired by major collectors, including Louis Allen, Dorothy Bennett, Jim Davidson, Karel Kupka, Ed Ruhe and Stuart Scougall. He was one of the artists who contributed to the panels in Yirrkala Church, painted in 1962–3. Towards the end of his life he became a reclusive figure who lived and worked under a palm-leaf shade on the beach at Yirrkala. His early paintings, with their detailed structure and complex composition, show Marika's influence strongly. He later developed his own style, characterized by the dynamism of his compositions and by the way in which the figurative images were integrated within the background designs. He worked rapidly, and his output was prodigious. An example of his work is the *Great Snake Legend* (*c.* 1962; Canberra, N.G.). He also produced wooden sculptures, such as a figure of a *Darwin Policeman* (1964; Perth, U. W. Australia, Berndt Mus. Anthropol.). His paintings are represented in all the major Australian collections.

BIBLIOGRAPHY

A. Wells: *This is their Dreaming* (St Lucia, 1971), p. 34

H. Groger-Wurm: *Eastern Arnhem Land*, i of *Australian Aboriginal Bark Paintings and their Mythological Interpretations* (Canberra, 1973), p. 22

W. Caruana, ed.: *Windows on the Dreaming: Aboriginal Paintings at the Australian National Gallery* (Canberra, 1989), pp. 118–21

HOWARD MORPHY

Mithradatkirt. *See* NISA.

Mitilíni. *See* LESBOS.

Mitla. Site of a Pre-Columbian ZAPOTEC and MIXTEC city in the eastern arm of the Valley of Oaxaca, Mexico. Much confusion about Mitla has resulted from what Fray Francisco de Burgoa wrote about it some 150 years after the Spanish Conquest. Burgoa was deceived by the biased account he received from its colonial rulers, who recalled the name of only one Pre-Columbian ruler—a Mixtec. Excavations have revealed that Mitla was a small Zapotec town around AD 400. Mixtec rule began *c.* AD 1000, when the city became a royal burial centre, but even then most of the population was still probably Zapotec.

Mitla (Nahuatl: 'Arrow place', a corruption of 'Miquitla', 'Death place', which was a rough translation of Zapotec 'Lyobaa', 'Inside-tomb') comprises groups of surviving palaces and platforms that are a late part of the ancient community, most of which lies under the modern town. The area has been inhabited at least since *c.* 9000 BC, and the town was settled *c.* 1000 BC. The palaces for which it is known were probably built during the 14th century AD, when Mixtec rulers dominated the Valley of Oaxaca and many Zapotecs had migrated east to the Isthmus of Tehuantepec. Unlike the religious buildings of Zapotec MONTE ALBÁN, Mitla's palaces are secular constructions. The excavated site of Santo Domingo de Oaxaca, north of the Valley of Oaxaca, provides the best antecedent for 'Mixtec-style' palace construction, and several nearby sites in the valley, including YAGUL, have similar palaces. Other examples of stone mosaic decorations using geometric motifs occur at TAJÍN near the Gulf Coast and at UXMAL in the northern Maya lowlands, both several centuries earlier than Mitla. Those at Tajín cover far larger proportions of the façades, and those at Uxmal also include non-geometric reliefs.

The relief panels at Mitla are smaller but incorporate a wider variety of motifs. The basic design appears to form a highly stylized, angular serpent's body and nostril, fragmented and reassembled in dozens of variations, some curvilinear, some even more angular than the original (see fig.). Visual variety was thus achieved within closely controlled symbolism. In Zapotec and Mixtec beliefs serpents stand for clouds, rain, lightning and fertility.

Similar discipline and elaboration occur in the designs of the palaces (Church Group, Column Group and Arroyo

Mitla, north room of the Palace of Columns with stone mosaic geometric designs, probably 14th century AD

Group). Three or four sides of each large square patio are enclosed by low, extremely wide, but shallow buildings, often leaving the corners open. In a region of earthquakes, the construction has proved technically sound. Thick walls of poured adobe have only a veneer of stone or plaster. One building has three low, nearly square doorways with lintels of enormous stone blocks. Flat masonry roofs were supported by wooden beams or by monolithic stone columns. Rainwater was channelled into underground drains. In the highest part of the sloping palace area, the buildings were placed almost upon bedrock; buildings lower down the slope were raised on modest platforms. One palace group has two grand cruciform tombs, decorated with geometric serpent motifs carved on large stones. Similar, smaller, tombs have been found elsewhere in and near modern Mitla.

The mosaic decorations on the outside walls of palaces were made with thousands of small, roughly triangular stones, whose points were pressed into the adobe walls and whose flat faces were cut to join perfectly. The stones were embedded at different depths to make the designs stand out in relief. Interior walls of some smaller chambers have such decoration on their entire upper halves, but ostentation was avoided because such narrow rooms were each lit by only a single, low doorway in one long wall. Some façades have circular holes beside their doors that formerly held tenoned heads. One such head was still in place as late as 1900 but has since disappeared. It depicted a near life-size, crudely carved human face, in startling contrast to the perfection of nearby mosaic patterns. Similar, but smaller, heads were found beside the doors of tombs 12, 29 and 30 at Yagul, and some examples in Oaxaca museums represent serpent heads.

Only tiny fragments remain of most Mitla wall paintings. Those on the front of the northernmost palace of the Church Group are in the same style as the Mixtec codices but executed in shades of red rather than multicoloured (see MESOAMERICA, PRE-COLUMBIAN, §V). They were drawn by Eduard Seler in the late 19th century, and some sections have since crumbled away, but even at the time of their discovery they were never complete enough to 'read' as a historical codex.

The religious architecture of late Mitla is represented west and south of the palace groups by two other, less well preserved groups of structures. The Adobe Group (c. AD 900–1521) forms a plaza within two low platforms and a pyramid. The Southern Group (begun c. AD 100, later enlarged) has four pyramids around a plaza, and smaller complexes (now destroyed) joined to it on the north and south.

Because of frequent looting and despite excavation, few known objects have a reliable Mitla provenance.

BIBLIOGRAPHY

E. Mühlenpfordt: *Los palacios de los zapotecos en Mitla* (Mexico City, 1851); ed. J. A. Ortega y Medina and J. Monjarás Ruiz (Mexico City, 1984) [important drgs]

E. Seler: *Wandmalereien von Mitla: Eine mexicanische Bilderschrift in Fresko, nach eigenen, an Ort und Stelle aufgenommen Zeichnungen herausgegeben und erläutert* (Berlin, 1895); Eng. trans. as 'The Wall Paintings of Mitla: A Mexican Picture Writing in Fresco', *Bureau Amer. Ethnol. Bull.*, xxviii (1904), pp. 247–324

W. Holmes: *Archaeological Studies among the Ancient Cities of Mexico*, ii (Chicago, 1897)

M. Saville: *The Cruciform Structures of Mitla and Vicinity* (New York, 1909)

C. Rickards: *The Ruins of Mexico* (London, 1910)

A. Caso and D. Rubín de la Borbolla: *Exploraciones en Mitla, 1934–1935* (Mexico City, 1936)

A. Caso and I. Bernal: *Urnas de Oaxaca* (Mexico City, 1952)

I. Bernal: 'The Mixtecs in the Archaeology of the Valley of Oaxaca', *Ancient Oaxaca: Discoveries in Mexican Archaeology and History*, ed. J. Paddock (Stanford, 1966), pp. 345–66 [many illus.]

H. Hartung: 'Notes on the Oaxaca *tablero*', *Bol. Estud. Oaxaqueños*, 27 (1970) [whole issue]

——: 'El tablero de Oaxaca: Notas sobre un elemento arquitectónico precolombino', *Cuad. Arquit. Mesoamer.*, ii (1984), pp. 66–74

N. Robles: 'Problemática urbana de la zona de monumentos de Mitla', *Cuad. Arquit. Mesoamer.*, vii (1986), pp. 17–26

JOHN PADDOCK

Mitre. *See under* VESTMENTS, ECCLESIASTICAL, §1(iii).

Mitsakis, Nikolaos [Nikos] (*b* Pyrgos, Peloponnese, 1899; *d* Athens, 25 Apr 1941). Greek architect. He studied at the School of Architecture, National Technical University of Athens (1917–21), where he later became assistant (1931–3) to the Professor of Architectural Design, Ernest Hébrard (1866–1933). In 1926 he joined the Department of Technical Works, Ministry of Education. He became Director (1930) of the Ministry's Design Department, in which position he was able to assume a leading role in Greek architecture, mainly through the Programme of New School Buildings. He was significantly influenced by DIMITRIS PIKIONIS, as seen in his school building (1928) in Tinos, where vernacular elements appear alongside Byzantine Revival ones. His most representative and important works, however, are his surprisingly mature Modernist school buildings, whose morphological and functional elements became the trademark of Modernist schools in Greece. One of the most important was the building (1932) on Koletti Street, Athens, skilfully placed on a small, irregular site. Other projects include the Church of the Virgin (with Kyriakos F. Panagiotakos, 1931; unexecuted), Tinos, the first application of Modernism to ecclesiastical architecture in Greece, and the Civil Servants Share Fund building (1938; unexecuted), Athens, the first instance of a curtain-wall design and free planning in modern Greek architecture.

BIBLIOGRAPHY

A. Giacumakatos: 'Nikos Mitsakis and the Renewal of Greek Architecture', *Archit. Des.*, lvi/12 (1986), pp. 41–5

A. Panoussakis: 'N. Mitsakis (1899–1941): A First Approach to his Work', *Archit. Themata*, xx (1986), pp. 28–33

ALEXANDER KOUTAMANIS

Mitsuhiro. *See* KARASUMARU MITSUHIRO.

Mitsumochi. *See* TOSA, (2).

Mitsunobu (i). *See* TOSA, (1).

Mitsunobu (ii). *See* KANŌ, (7).

Mitsuoki (i). *See* TOSA, (3).

Mitsuoki (ii). *See* TAKAHASHI DŌHACHI.

Mitsuyori. *See* KANŌ, (8).

Miturich, Pyotr (Vasil'yevich) (*b* St Petersburg, 12 Sept 1887; *d* Moscow, 27 Oct 1956). Russian painter, graphic artist and designer. He studied at the Kiev School of Art (1906–9) and in St Petersburg, at the Academy of Arts (1909–16). While serving in the army (1916–21) he may have received some education in military engineering.

Between 1918 and 1922 he made a series of abstract painted reliefs and constructions, using paper, cardboard and wood. He called these works 'Spatial Graphics', 'Spatial Posters' and 'Spatial Paintings'. Influenced by Cubism and Futurism and current experiments of the Russian avant-garde, these pieces showed a painterly concern with relationships of line, plane and volume in both real and illusory space. Miturich subsequently destroyed all of these structures, except for *Spatial Graphics No. 46* of 1921 and the graphic alphabet of small cubes of 1919 (both Moscow, artist's family priv. col., see Lodder, pls 1.43 and 1.46).

Miturich taught drawing in the Graphics Faculty of the Vkhutemas (Higher Artistic and Technical Workshops) from 1923 to 1930, returning thereafter to a more figurative style of drawing. He exhibited with the moderate Four Arts Society of Artists from 1925 to 1929. At the same time his investigations into the energy-saving potential of wavelike motion (*kolebatel'noye dvizheniye*) aligned him with the organic trend in Russian Constructivism. He used this principle in his designs for a flying apparatus without a motor (*The Flyer*, 1922; see Lodder, pl. 7.16) and for various vehicles, called undulators (*vol'noviki*), designed for travelling through the air, through water (a fish-shaped boat, 1931) and on land (*The Caterpillar*, 1933); he even drew up the organization of an entire city based on this idea (all designs, Moscow, artist's family priv. col., see Lodder, pls 7.17–7.22).

WRITINGS

'Chuvstvo mira' [A feeling for the world], *Tvorchestvo*, iv (1976), pp. 14–17

BIBLIOGRAPHY

N. N. Rozanova, ed.: *P. V. Miturich: Al'bom* (Moscow, 1972)

C. Lodder: *Russian Constructivism* (New Haven, 1983), chaps 1, 7

Pyotr Miturich, 1887–1956 (exh. cat., Moscow, Pushkin Mus. F.A., 1988)

M. Sokolov: 'V gibkom zerkale prirody': O suerkhzadache iskusstva Pyotra Mituricha' [In the adaptable mirror of nature: on the ultimate aim of the art of Pyotr Miturich], *Iskusstvo*, 1989, pp. 21–5

CHRISTINA LODDER

Miville, Jakob Christophe (*b* Basle, 18 Nov 1786; *d* Basle, 29 June 1836). Swiss painter and printmaker. He was trained in landscape painting *c*. 1800 in the studio of Peter Birmann in Basle. In 1802 he went to Berne to work under the painter and etcher Johann Kaspar Huber (1752–1827). He was in Rome from 1805, where he was particularly influenced by the classical landscapes of Joseph Anton Koch. His earliest works there have ordered, largely imaginative compositions, as in *Italian Landscape near Rome* (1805–6; Basle, Kstmus.). He went to Moscow in 1809, having been promised patronage that never materialized. However, he remained in Russia until 1814, painting landscape studies for himself as he was unable to obtain commissions. Many of these works were subsequently lost. He left Russia and travelled extensively, returning in 1816 to Basle where he painted the dynamic *Landscape View* (*c*. 1816; Zurich, Ksthaus). A visit to the Bernese Alps in 1822 inspired one of his few aquatints, *Peasant Festival on the Balisalp* (*c*. 1823; e.g. Berne, Kstmus.). He travelled to Paris in 1826 and then returned to Basle to teach at the Sonntagsschule der Gemeinnützigen Gesellschaft. He also painted sensitive portraits, the finest of which are probably of his daughters *Elisa Miville-Baumann* and *Rosa Miville-Krug* (both *c.* 1824–5; Basle, Kstmus.). His most original works are to be found in his private sketchbooks (examples in Zurich, Ksthaus). These drawings amply demonstrate his powers of observation and his sometimes adventurous manner in depicting landscape. Through his teaching, he was instrumental in forming the Basle school of landscape painting, which flourished in the first half of the 19th century.

See also SWITZERLAND, §III.

BIBLIOGRAPHY
H. Lanz: *Der Basler Maler Jakob Christophe Miville, 1786–1836* (Lörrach, 1954)
J. Gantner and A. Reinle: *Kunstgeschichte der Schweiz*, iv (Frauenfeld, 1962), pp. 143–7

WILLIAM HAUPTMAN

Mi xian [Mi hsien]. County in Henan Province, China, south of the city of Zhongzhou. Near the village of Dahuting in Mi xian two large tombs, apparently of court officials, dating from the later part of the Han period (206 BC–AD 220), were discovered in 1960. The naturalistic decorations with lively genre details on the walls of the tombs are extraordinary in the corpus of Han-period art.

Tomb 1 is built of large stone blocks jacketed by layers of large bricks. Tomb 2 is primarily of brick, with some doors and other architectural members in stone. The tombs had been robbed of all artefacts. In layout, both have a large, vaulted central chamber, with smaller rooms accessible through stone doors on four sides. The detailed engravings depicting daily life on the walls of Tomb 1 reveal that the layout imitates that of a large house, with a parlour in front (south-west) leading through a short corridor to the central chamber; a coffin chamber in the rear (north-west), beside the ladies' chamber (north-east); a kitchen to the side (east) and courtyard, granary and stables in front (south-east). The floor plan of Tomb 2 is similar. Judging from paintings of finely dressed women, acrobats and feasting in Tomb 2, the central chamber appears to have been reserved for entertainment.

In Tomb 1 doors, pilasters, lintels and the borders of the wall engravings are richly decorated with cloud scrolls and a variety of animals and spirits intended to bless and protect the tomb occupants. The decorations are devoted exclusively to everyday scenes. Figures are somewhat larger than half life-size and, unusually for this period, cover several stones. They are engraved on fine-grained, polished limestone with a thin line remarkably sensitive to nuances in weight, bulk, movement and texture. In Tomb 2 the vaulted chamber was plastered and painted: the figures of women are similar in scale to the figures in Tomb 1. Unlike other Han artists, the painter of this tomb eschewed thick outlines and relied instead on colour and tone areas to define contours and masses. Such features as the shifting weight of a woman's coiffure or the diaphanous quality of her skirt were convincingly rendered using transparent washes and subtle changes in contour.

The subject-matter of the scenes matches the function of each room, usually in such a way as to make clear the wealth of the tomb occupant. Genre scenes are common, showing such moments as a toddler waving a feather or a steward collecting horse droppings. Kitchen and carriage technology are documented in detail. There are no official

scenes or classical subjects. In these respects, the Dahuting depictions differ from those at Han monuments associated with provincial officials, such as at YI'NAN or at the Wu family shrines in Jiaxiang County, Shandong Province. They resemble more closely three late Han tombs at a nearby site called Houshiguo, a group of tombs affiliated with the court eunuch Cao Teng (*fl* mid-2nd century AD) in Bo xian (Bo County), Anhui Province, and the so-called Zhu Wei shrine in Jinxiang, Shandong Province, and offer a rare glimpse into the life of court élites as opposed to that of provincial officials.

BIBLIOGRAPHY
An Jinhuai and Wang Yugang: 'Mi xian Dahuting Han dai huaxiangshi mu he bihua mu' [A Han-period stone tomb with pictorial decoration and a tomb with wall paintings from Dahuting in Mi County], *Wenwu* (1972), no. 10, pp. 49–50
J. Fontein and Wu Tung: *Han and Tang Murals* (Boston, 1976), pp. 50–53
Li Can: 'Bo xian Cao Cao zongzu muzang' [The tombs of Cao Cao's clan in Bo County], *Wenwu* (1978), no. 8, pp. 32–45
Sun Zuoyun: 'Henan Mi xian Dahuting Dong Han huaxiangshi mu diaoxiang kaoshi' [An investigation of the engravings in the decorated eastern Han tomb at Dahuting, Mi County, Henan], *Kaifeng Shiyuan Xuebao* (1978), no. 3, pp. 59–77
M. J. Powers: *Art and Political Expression in Early China* (New Haven, 1991), chaps 10 and 11

MARTIN J. POWERS

Mixtec. Term commonly used for a people and an aesthetic tradition that flourished during the Late Post-Classic period (*c.* AD 1200–1521) in the Southern Highlands of Mesoamerica, in the western portion of what is now the state of Oaxaca, Mexico (*see also* MESOAMERICA, PRE-COLUMBIAN, §I). The term is derived from the Nahuatl name *Mixteca*, meaning 'person of Mixtlan ("cloud place")', designating speakers of the dominant indigenous language of the region. In the Colonial period the region became known as the Mixteca, being subdivided into three areas: Alta (eastern), Baja (north-western) and de la Costa (Pacific coastal region). The Mixtecs referred to themselves as Ñuu Dzavui ('people of the rain deity'). The striking and sophisticated art style that flourished in the Mixteca is one of the most impressive achievements of indigenous America.

1. CULTURAL CONTEXT. In late Pre-Columbian times Mixtec speakers were organized into a series of essentially autonomous city states. This political fragmentation was probably related, at least in part, to the mountainous, broken topography of much of their territory. Often in conflict, they were also frequently confederated by dynastic alliances. By the time of the Spanish Conquest most Mixtec city states had been conquered by the AZTEC Triple Alliance (Tenochtitlán–Tetzcoco–Tiacopan; *see* MESOAMERICA, PRE-COLUMBIAN, §II, 4(ii)) and were regularly paying tribute to it. Mixtec speakers shared most basic culture patterns with their neighbours, particularly those speaking languages of the same Otomanguean family: Cuicatec, Ichcatec, Chocho-Popoloca, Mazatec, Chinantec, Trique and Amuzgo; and the term 'Tetlamixteca' has been proposed for this group of culturally and linguistically related peoples. The Mixtecs were often either in conflict with or allied to the ZAPOTECS, who spoke another Otomanguean language, to the south-east of them. Probably at some time in the 13th century AD the Mixtecs

took advantage of a dynastic marital union between Yanhuitlan, a prominent Mixteca Alta city state, and Zaachila (Teozapotlan), the major Zapotec power in the Valley of Oaxaca, and began to settle in the valley. They established their principal centre at Coyolapan (modern Cuilapa) and steadily increased in population and political influence until they dominated much of the valley. In the later 15th century close interaction with their Aztec conquerors had significant repercussions and further intensified the cultural similarity between Central Highland and Southern Highland peoples.

Archaeological evidence shows that during the Classic period (c. AD 250–c. 900) Mixteca Alta peoples largely participated in Zapotec MONTE ALBÁN culture, centred in the Valley of Oaxaca. In the Mixteca Baja, a closely related but somewhat divergent tradition flourished, known as 'Ñuiñe'. The stylistic canons of these Classic-period traditions, although distinct, anticipated many aspects of Post-Classic Mixtec culture. The explanation for this Classic–Post-Classic stylistic break is intimately bound up with the question of the origin and early development of a broader stylistic and iconographic tradition called MIXTECA-PUEBLA, in which the Mixteca region was the centre of a major substyle. The precise time and place of origin still pose a major problem in Mesoamerican archaeology, but, with regional variation, Mixteca–Puebla styles dominated much of Mesoamerican aesthetic culture in the Late Post-Classic period. The style was characterized by a highly structured and consistent iconography, with an extensive array of standardized symbols and a rich pantheonic imagery that featured, with typical diagnostic insignia, most of the deities of Post-Classic Mesoamerica. Polychrome ceramics and painted codices, depicting ritual, divinatory, historical and genealogical information, were particularly important. Many elements inherited from earlier stylistic traditions, including those of TEOTIHUACÁN, Monte Albán, TAJÍN, XOCHICALCO and CACAXTLA, were restructured in a bold, striking new aesthetic synthesis.

2. ARTISTIC TRADITIONS. The Mixteca has yielded some of the most exquisite examples of the arts and crafts of Pre-Columbian Mesoamerica. It was a major centre for the production of fine polychrome pottery closely related to Cholulteca ware, another major polychrome ceramic tradition centred in Puebla, to the north. Both ceramic traditions include a category called *tipo códice*, featuring symbols and anthropomorphic and zoomorphic figures in the same style as those of the Mixteca–Puebla style codices (*see* MESOAMERICA, PRE-COLUMBIAN, §VI). A characteristic form, rare elsewhere in Mesoamerica, is the collared, globular vessel with tripod supports, often decorated with *tipo códice* imagery.

The Mixtecs' ornamental metallurgy, in gold, copper and silver, also typifies their craftsmanship. Examples have been found throughout the Mixteca region, but the greatest number were found in three tombs in the Valley of Oaxaca: Tomb 7 at Monte Albán (found by Alfonso Caso in 1932; now Oaxaca, Mus. Reg.) and tombs 1 and 2 at Zaachila (found by Roberto Gallegos in 1962; now Mexico City, Mus. N. Antropol.). (The Zaachila tombs also yielded many elaborately decorated polychrome pottery vessels,

many decorated with *tipo códice* motifs.) Most of the superb gold ornaments in these tombs, including pectorals, necklaces and rings, were produced by the lost-wax process of casting, but other techniques included hammering, gilding, filigree and soldering.

Wood-carving was another major art of the Mixteca. The best-known examples are horizontal slit gongs (Nahuatl *teponaztli*s) and spear-throwers (Nahuatl *atlatl*s). As with *tipo códice* pottery, the motifs on some *teponaztli*s and *atlatl*s include symbols and images similar to those in the codices. Some *atlatl*s are intricately carved and were originally covered with gold leaf. Three particularly outstanding examples in Florence (Mus. Archeol.) and Rome (Mus. N. Preist. & Etnog.) were apparently part of the loot of the Spanish Conquest. A closely related art was bone-carving, also featuring codex motifs and symbols. Tomb 7 at Monte Albán and tombs 1 and 2 at Zaachila yielded numerous examples, mainly of carved jaguar bones. Mixtec sculpture in stone was mostly small scale; monumental three-dimensional sculpture, a major achievement of contemporaneous Aztec art, was rare. However, the art of turquoise mosaic, although not confined to the Mixteca, was particularly well-developed there; more surviving specimens, mainly masks and shields, came from the Mixteca than from any other Mesoamerican region, and some Mesoamerican mosaics in European collections may also have originated there. Other Mixtec lapidary crafts included making nose bars, ear plugs, labrets, necklaces and other ornaments of jade, rock crystal, amethyst and obsidian.

More painted histories and dynastic genealogies derive from the Mixteca than from any other region of Mesoamerica (see fig.). Some Post-Conquest examples are annotated in Mixtec, and most are ascribable to Mixtec-speaking communities. Certain features are characteristic of Mixtec works, for example the consistent use of interlaced A/O year signs, 'chevron strip' war symbols, stepped-fret (*greca*) toponymic signs and the assignment of calendric names, in addition to pictographic 'nicknames', to almost all personages portrayed, both historical and supernatural. In format, the 'meander history'—the sequence of reading of the pictographic images that constitute the narrative, arranged in a meander or boustrophedon pattern indicated by red guidelines—appears to be virtually confined to the group. In basic structure Mixtec writing was similar to the Aztec system of the late Pre-Columbian Central Highlands—essentially pictographic and symbolic but with some employment of the principle of phonetic transfer ('rebus') in personal name and place signs. The Borgia Group of Late Post-Classic ritual and divinatory pictorial codices has been ascribed by some to the Mixtecs. Other scholars ascribe part of the group to the Mixtecs and other parts to painters in Puebla–Tlaxcala, or the Gulf Coast. Whatever the case, stylistically and iconographically the Borgia Group codices overlap with those of indisputable Mixtec affiliation, and both types can be clearly differentiated from the contemporaneous Aztec pictorial style in the Central Highlands (*see* MESOAMERICA, PRE-COLUMBIAN, §VI).

No important examples of Mixtec wall painting, one of the major Mesoamerican aesthetic achievements, have been discovered. However, the palaces of MITLA, an

Mixtec representation of the conquest of the Island of the Red and White Loincloth by the great Mixtec conqueror 8 Deer 'Jaguar Claw', accompanied by two other lords, paint on animal skin coated with lime plaster, *c.* 185×245 mm; detail from the Codex Zouche-Nuttall screenfold, *c.* 0.18×11.41 m, possibly from Teozacoalco, Oaxaca, ?15th/16th centuries (London, Museum of Mankind)

important Zapotec sacred centre in the Valley of Oaxaca, have remnants of wall paintings in a style and iconography similar to the Mixtec codices, probably owing to the close cultural, political and dynastic ties that linked Zapotec and Mixtec speakers.

The superb aesthetic quality of many archaeological pieces from the Mixteca has led some scholars to visualize the region as the pre-eminent Late Post-Classic centre for fine craftsmanship, actively exporting both products and master artisans. This argument has been used to promote a kind of 'pan-Mixtec' interpretation of Late Post-Classic Mesoamerican art, as a means of explaining the widespread diffusion of the Mixteca–Puebla style. Nevertheless, other closely related styles were developed by a number of Mesoamerican peoples, including Post-Classic Zapotec speakers of the Valley of Oaxaca and various groups occupying territories to the north-east of the Mixteca, such as the Chocho-Popoloca, Ichcatec, Cuicatec and Chinantec. The widespread distribution of Cholulteca polychrome ceramics and the altar paintings of Tizatlán show that Nahua speakers of southern Puebla and Tlaxcala, and possibly of the central Gulf Coast, were active users of the Mixteca–Puebla style and may also have been involved in its genesis and diffusion. Although the Mixtecs moved into the Valley of Oaxaca by conquest and dynastic alliance, there is no evidence of long-range movements on their part; by contrast, Nahua speakers migrated at least as far south and east as Panama.

To what extent Mixtec fine craft items, particularly polychrome pottery and gold ornaments, were exported by trade to other regions of Late Post-Classic Mesoamerica is unclear. Few pieces in indubitable Mixtec style have been found outside the Mixteca or the immediately adjoining territories. Aztec pictorial tribute rolls, which include most of the provinces located in the Mixteca, display no ceramics or gold ornaments. Even so, while the artistic achievements of other provinces of the Late Post-Classic Aztec empire should not be underestimated, the accomplishments of the Mixtec artists and craftsmen remain truly impressive.

BIBLIOGRAPHY

E. Seler: *Wandmalereien von Mitla: Eine mexicanische Bilderschrift in Fresko, nach eigenen, an Ort und Stelle aufgenommen Zeichnungen herausgegeben und erläutert* (Berlin, 1895); Eng. trans. as 'The Wall Paintings of Mitla: A Mexican Picture Writing in Fresco', *Bureau Amer. Ethnol. Bull.*, xxviii (Washington, DC, 1904), pp. 247–324

H. B. Nicholson: 'The Mixteca–Puebla Concept in Mesoamerican Archaeology', *Men and Cultures: Selected Papers from the Fifth International Congress of Anthropological and Ethnological Sciences: Philadelphia, 1956*, pp. 612–17

——: 'The Use of the Term "Mixtec" in Mesoamerican Archaeology', *Amer. Ant.*, xxvi (1961), pp. 431–3

A. Caso: 'Lapidary Work, Goldwork and Copperwork from Oaxaca', *Hb. Mid. Amer. Ind.*, iii (1965), pp. 896–930

I. Bernal: 'The Mixtecs in the Archaeology of the Valley of Oaxaca', *Ancient Oaxaca: Discoveries in Mexican Archaeology and History*, ed. J. Paddock (Stanford, 1966), pp. 345–66

A. Caso: 'The Lords of Yanhuitlán', *Ancient Oaxaca: Discoveries in Mexican Archaeology and History*, ed. J. Paddock (Stanford, 1966), pp. 313–35

J. Paddock: 'Oaxaca in Ancient Mesoamerica', ibid., pp. 367–85

D. Robertson: 'The Mixtec Religious Manuscripts', ibid., pp. 298–312

R. Spores: *The Mixtec Kings and their People* (Norman, 1967)

A. Caso: *El tesoro de Monte Albán* (Mexico City, 1969)

M. E. Smith: *Picture Writing from Ancient Southern Mexico: Mixtec Place Signs and Maps* (Norman, 1973)

J. R. Ramsey: 'An Examination of Mixtec Iconography', *Aspects of the Mixteca–Puebla Style and Mixtec and Central Mexican Culture in Southern Mesoamerica: 41st International Congress of Americanists: Mexico City, 1974*, pp. 33–42

——: *An Analysis of Mixtec Minor Art, with a Catalogue* (Ann Arbor, 1975)

H. B. Nicholson: 'The Mixteca–Puebla Concept Revisited', *The Art and Iconography of Late Post-Classic Central Mexico: A Conference at Dumbarton Oaks: 1977*, pp. 227–54

A. Caso: *Reyes y reinos de la Mixteca*, 2 vols (Mexico City, 1977–9)

R. Gallegos Ruíz: *El Señor 9 Flor en Zaachila* (Mexico, 1978)

N. Troike: 'Fundamental Changes in the Interpretation of the Mixtec Codices', *Amer. Ant.*, xliii (1978), pp. 553–68

J. Paddock: 'Mixtec Impact on the Postclassic Valley of Oaxaca', *The Cloud People: Divergent Evolution of the Zapotec and Mixtec Civilizations*, ed. K. V. Flannery and J. Marcus (New York, 1983), pp. 272–77

R. Spores: *The Mixtecs in Ancient and Colonial Times* (Norman, 1984), pp. 3–96

M. Jansen: 'Mixtec Pictography: Conventions and Contents', *Supplement to the Handbook of Middle American Indians*, ed. V. R. Bricker, v, *Epigraphy* (Austin, 1992), pp. 20–33

Mixteca–Puebla. Stylistic and iconographic tradition in Mesoamerica during the Post-Classic period (*c.* 900–1521).

1. INTRODUCTION. The term was coined in 1938 by the American archaeologist George Vaillant for what he variously defined as a 'culture', 'civilization' or 'culture complex' that developed after the Teotihuacán collapse in the region of the modern Mexican state of Puebla and the western portion of Oaxaca, an area known as the Mixteca (from the predominant indigenous language of the region). He hypothesized that Mixteca–Puebla diffused into the Basin of Mexico during what he termed the 'Chichimec' period, providing 'the source and inspiration of Aztec civilization'. He believed that aspects of the complex spread widely throughout Mesoamerica during its final major era, the Post-Classic, which he suggested should be labelled the 'Mixteca–Puebla period'.

Although Vaillant never defined his concept with precision, he clearly had in mind a distinctive artistic style and its concomitant iconography, particularly exemplified by the members of the 'Codex Borgia group' of ritual and divinatory screenfolds (see fig.; *see also* MESOAMERICA, PRE-COLUMBIAN, §VI), as well as the Post-Classic polychrome ceramics, called both 'Cholulteca' and 'Mixtec', emanating from southern Puebla and western Oaxaca. Outstanding stylistic characteristics include an emphasis on symbolic use of colour and anthropomorphic and zoomorphic imagery that exaggerates prominent features in a fashion akin to that of modern caricature. The extensive repertory of standardized Mixteca–Puebla symbols includes solar and lunar discs; Venus or bright star symbols; stylized stellar 'eyes'; celestial and terrestrial bands; frequent death imagery, including skulls and skeletons, often with double-outlined bones; the stepped fret design; and distinctive stylized symbols for precious stones, the elements and natural phenomena. Particularly important is the 'water and fire' (Nahuatl *atl tlachinolli*) symbol for war. The 20 day-signs of the 260-day divinatory cycle (*tonalpohualli*) were in use throughout Mesoamerica, but there are specific variations that appear for the first time in Mixteca–Puebla. Zoomorphic images are also distinctive, featuring serpents—including fantastic versions, both feathered (*quetzalcoatl*) and sectioned and snouted (*xiuhcoatl*)—as well as crocodiles and other saurians, jaguars and pumas, deer, canines, rabbits, bats, spiders and fish. Characteristic ornithological representations include eagles and other raptorial birds, vultures, quetzals and owls. Although the anthropomorphic deities often share insignia, they are typically quite individualized and identifiable.

Archaeological research undertaken since World War II has necessitated some reformulation of Vaillant's original Mixteca–Puebla concept, but it continues to be used

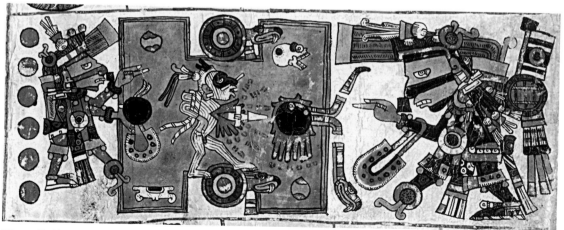

Mixteca–Puebla: upper register detail (95×260 mm) from the Codex Borgia, animal skin coated with lime plaster, each page *c.* 270×265 mm, possibly from southern Puebla, probably 14th or 15th century AD (Rome, Vatican, Biblioteca Apostolica, MS. Borg. Mess. 1, recto p. 21)

as an interpretative tool in reconstructions of the history of Pre-Columbian Mesoamerican cultures. Some authors have employed the briefer, linguistic term 'Mixtec' instead of Mixteca–Puebla, but Vaillant's longer, hyphenated geographical designation for this tradition is to be preferred. There is abundant evidence that Mixteca–Puebla stylistic canons cut across linguistic boundaries in Post-Classic Mesoamerica, and it is likely that, along with speakers of Mixtec and other related Otomanguean languages, the Nahua-speaking inhabitants of the Central Highlands actively participated in its development and diffusion.

2. ORIGINS AND DEVELOPMENT. Archaeological evidence as to the dating of the Mixteca–Puebla tradition is somewhat ambiguous, and leading scholars have often differed sharply in their opinions. The proposed date of the earliest appearance of polychrome ceramics bearing characteristic Mixteca–Puebla motifs ranges from as early as AD 700 to as late as 1350. Most scholars assign the earliest indubitable Mixteca–Puebla presence to some time during the Early Post-Classic period (c. 900–c. 1200). Since the tradition was manifested in its most typical and intense form in southern Puebla, western Oaxaca and the Gulf Coast (Veracruz), it is assumed initially to have crystallized there. Opinions also differ sharply as to whether the first or the second region had priority in the earliest stage in its development; the Gulf Coast has rarely been considered in this connection. However, archaeological knowledge of the very late Classic and Post-Classic periods of the Gulf Coast is slight; therefore this strategically situated region may have played a more significant role in the Mixteca–Puebla genesis than was previously thought.

Whatever its derivation, it is clear that Mixteca–Puebla constituted a significant new synthesis, restructuring various aesthetic and iconographic traditions that had preceded it in Mesoamerica. Its most immediate ancestors appear to have been the very late Classic traditions of Xochicalco, Cacaxtla and Cholulteca I in the Central Highlands, Tajín on the Gulf Coast and Monte Albán IV in the Southern Highlands. Terminal Classic (c. AD 800–c. 900) lowland Maya styles probably also played a role, especially in view of the importance of polychromy in some of its ceramic wares. Teotihuacán, the dominant Central Highlands civilization of the Classic period (c. AD 250–c. 900), may have been a more remote source. Some iconographic continuities from Teotihuacán are obvious: feathered serpents, speech scrolls, goggled and fanged anthropomorphic images and female deities wearing serpentine helmet masks.

3. REGIONAL VARIANTS. Various regional expressions of the overall Mixteca–Puebla stylistic and iconographic tradition have been recognized. The 'Mixteca–Puebla heartland' can be divided into a north-western zone ('Cholulteca'), centred on Cholula, Puebla, and a south-eastern zone (MIXTEC in the narrower sense), centred on the Mixteca Alta region and the Valley of Oaxaca. The hallmark of the south-eastern zone is a distinctive ceramic form, the tripod, necked globular jar, often decorated with so-called '*tipo códice*' motifs, including

gods, feathers, bird-heads and flowers, that closely resemble those of the ritual/divinatory and historical screenfolds. The north-western zone is particularly characterized by tall, cylindrical vases, often decorated with skulls and crossed-bone designs. Other forms common to both zones and frequently ornamented with *tipo códice* devices are shallow plates (often with zoomorphic and/or aviform tripod supports) and pedestal vessels (*see* MESOAMERICA, PRE-COLUMBIAN, fig. 32).

Broadly defined, the Early Post-Classic Toltec style, centred on the archaeological site of Tula, in the state of Hidalgo (and its offshoot at Chichén Itzá, Yucatán), could also be considered as a peripheral sub-style of early Mixteca–Puebla. Its successor, the Aztec style, which flourished in the Central Highlands during the Late Post-Classic period, has also been regarded by some as a major Mixteca–Puebla substyle. During the same period, the Huastec culture of northern and southern Tamaulipas featured a distinctive variant of Mixteca–Puebla. Various archaeological phases of Post-Classic West Mexico exhibit Mixteca–Puebla elements, primarily in the ceramics, especially at the sites of Cojumatlan, Tizapan el Alto, Amapa, Peñitas, Chametla, Culiacan and Guasave.

The Mixteca–Puebla style is also evident in eastern Mesoamerica during the Late Post-Classic period. In striking manifestations it blends with the indigenous lowland Maya aesthetic and iconographic tradition at Tulum, Tancah and Xelha on the east coast of Yucatán (state of Quintana Roo) and Santa Rita (in Belize). A variant of Mixteca–Puebla also appears to have prevailed in Post-Classic highland Guatemala, especially exemplified by wall paintings at IXIMCHÉ (Tecpán Cuauhtemallán), the Cakchiquel Maya capital at the time of the Spanish Conquest. There are some manifestations of the tradition throughout the Mesoamerican south-eastern salient, extending through El Salvador and Pacific Nicaragua into north-western Costa Rica, especially exemplified by certain motifs decorating ceramic vessels belonging to the type known as 'Vallejo polychrome'. In view of its extensive geographical distribution and in spite of its putatively broad temporal range, Mixteca–Puebla fits to some extent the definition of a 'horizon style' (i.e. a style that encompasses a wide spread of sites), which can be explained by the wide-ranging Post-Classic commercial networks and the religious pilgrimage patterns.

BIBLIOGRAPHY

G. C. Vaillant: 'A Correlation of Archaeological and Historical Sequences in the Valley of Mexico', *Amer. Anthropologist*, xl/4 (1938), pp. 535–73
——: *Aztecs of Mexico: Origin, Rise and Fall of the Aztec Nation* (New York, 1941)
E. Noguera: *La cerámica arqueológica de Cholula* (Mexico, 1954)
H. B. Nicholson: 'The Mixteca–Puebla Concept in Mesoamerican Archaeology', *Men and Cultures: Selected Papers from the Fifth International Congress of Anthropological and Ethnological Sciences: Philadelphia, 1956*, pp. 612–17
——: 'The Use of the Term "Mixtec" in Mesoamerican Archaeology', *Amer. Ant.*, xxvi/3 (1961), pp. 431–3
J. Paddock, ed.: *Ancient Oaxaca* (Stanford, 1966)
D. Robertson: 'The Tulum Murals: The International Style of the Late Post-Classic', *Verhandlungen des XXXVIII internationalen Amerikanistenkongresses: Stuttgart and Munich, 1968*, ii, pp. 77–88
R. Carmack and L. Larmer: 'Quichean Art: A Mixteca–Puebla Variant', *Katunob*, vii/3 (1969), pp. 12–35

N. Castillo Tejero: 'La llamada "Cerámica Policroma Mixteca" no es un producto Mixteco', *Proyecto Puebla-Tlaxcala, Comunicaciones* (Mexico City, 1974), xi, pp. 7–10

C. W. Meighan: 'Prehistory of West Mexico', *Science*, 184 (1974), pp. 1254–61

H. B. Nicholson: 'The Mixteca–Puebla Concept Revisited', *The Art and Iconography of Late Post-Classic Central Mexico: A Conference: Dumbarton Oaks, 1977*, pp. 227–54

H. Von Winning: 'Rituals Depicted on Polychrome Ceramics from Nayarit', *Pre-Columbian Art History: Selected Readings*, ed. A. Cordy-Collins and J. Stern (Palo Alto, 1977), pp. 121–34

M. Lind: 'Cholula Polychrome in Mesoamerica', *U. Missouri-Columbia Mus. Anthropol., 1977–78 Annu. Rep.*, ed. L. Feldman (Columbia, 1978), pp. 63–7

F. Müller: *La alfarería de Cholula* (Mexico City, 1978)

D. Schávelzon: *El complejo arqueológico Mixteca-Puebla: Notas para una redefinición cultural* (Mexico City, 1980)

M. E. Smith and C. M. Heath-Smith: 'Waves of Influence in Postclassic Mesoamerica? A Critique of the Mixteca–Puebla Concept', *Anthropology*, iv/2 (1980), pp. 15–50

A. G. Miller: *On the Edge of the Sea: Mural Painting at Tancah-Tulum, Quintana Roo* (Washington, DC, 1982)

D. Stone, ed.: *Aspects of the Mixteca–Puebla Style and Mixtec and Central Mexican Culture in Southern Mesoamerica: Papers from a Symposium Organized by Doris Stone* (New Orleans, 1982)

H. B. Nicholson and E. Quiñones Keber, eds: *Mixteca–Puebla: Discoveries and Research in Mesoamerican Art and Archaeology* (Culver City, 1994)

H. B. NICHOLSON

Miyagawa, Jun (Atsushi) (*b* Tokyo, 13 March 1933; *d* Tokyo, 21 Oct 1977). Japanese critic. He graduated from the Art History Department of Tokyo University in 1955 and began to write on fine art. Miyagawa established a reputation in 1963 with his essay *Anfuorumeru Igo* ('Post-informel'). During the early 1960s he wrote prolifically on the state of the fine arts. Although Japanese painting had previously been strongly influenced by international *Art informel*, Miyagawa's work appeared at a time when numerous 'anti-art' movements were being developed, challenging the very concept of art. Miyagawa pointed out a fundamental contradiction in these movements, for although many of the works produced could be called contemporary (*gendai*) in terms of their formal characteristics, they were still part of a deeper-rooted modern (*kindai*) tradition in terms of their values and thematic content. He also adopted elements of French critical thought of the 1960s, particularly in his account of Pop art. From the mid-1960s he turned his attention away from fine art and concentrated on poetry, having already produced, however, some of the most notable achievement in Japanese post-war art criticism.

WRITINGS
Miyagawa Jun chosakushū [Collected works of Jun Miyagawa], 3 vols (Tokyo, 1980–81)

SHIGEO CHIBA

Miyagawa Chōshun [Chōzaemon; Shunkyōkudō] (*b* Miyagawa, Owari Prov. [now Aichi Prefect.], 1682; *d* Edo [now Tokyo], 1752). Japanese painter. He went to Edo from his native Owari to study the traditional painting styles of the Kanō and Tosa schools but quickly came under the influence of *ukiyoe* ('pictures of the floating world') artists HISHIKAWA MORONOBU and Kaigetsudō Ando (*see* KAIGETSUDŌ, (1); *see also* JAPAN, §VI, 4(iv)(b)). Unlike other followers of Moronobu, Chōshun was exclusively a painter; he never designed single-sheet woodblock prints or book illustrations. He is primarily known as a painter of *bijin* ('beautiful women'), whom he depicted with a fine brushwork technique and a rich, dark palette. His representative painting in the *bijin* genre is *Yūjo monkōzu* ('Courtesan smelling incense'; see fig.). He also painted several genre paintings (*fūzokuga*; *see* JAPAN, §VI, 4(iv)(a)), including *Fūzoku zukan* ('Picture scroll of manners and customs'; Tokyo, N. Mus.) and *Edo fūzoku zukan* ('Picture scroll of manners and customs in Edo'; London, BM).

Miyagawa Chōshun: *Courtesan Smelling Incense*, hanging scroll, colours on silk, 876×367 mm (Tokyo, National Museum)

Chōshun founded the Miyagawa school of *ukiyoe ni-kuhitsuga* (polychrome painting), but his teaching style was quite different from that of the Kaigetsudō masters, who also specialized in *nikuhitsuga*. Chōshun gave his students great freedom in terms of composition, technique and subject-matter. He attracted many capable followers, including Chōki, Isshō (1689–1779) and Chōsui. The Miyagawa school prospered until 1749, when Chōshun and his students were embroiled in a dispute with painters of the Kanō school over the restoration of the painting at the Tokugawa mausoleum in Nikkō, for which Chōshun was exiled from Edo for two years.

BIBLIOGRAPHY

Kodansha Enc. Japan

TADASHI KOBAYASHI

Miyamoto Musashi Niten (*b* Harima, Hyōgo Prefecture, 1584; *d* Kumamoto Prefecture, 1645). Japanese painter and swordmaster. Niten is the artist's name (*gō*) of Miyamoto Musashi, a samurai renowned for his swordsmanship and particularly noted for developing a two-handed fighting style. As a young man, he took part in the power struggles that marked the Momoyama (1568–1600) and early Edo (1600–1868) periods. After fighting on the losing side in the decisive battle of Sekigahara (1600), Niten became a masterless samurai (*rōnin*) and wandered around Japan, fighting in major battles and reputedly winning over 60 duels before the age of 30. In the late 1630s he took the post of sword instructor in the service of the powerful Hosokawa clan and settled in Kumamoto on the island of Kyushu. In 1645 he wrote *Gorin no sho* ('A book of five rings'), an influential treatise on strategy in war and single combat. It is thought that most of Niten's 25 or so extant paintings, which are undated and seldom even signed, were executed during this late period of stability.

When and how Niten acquired his skill as a wielder of the brush rather than the sword is uncertain. He may have been self-taught or may have studied with the KANŌ painter Yano Yoshishige (*fl* 17th century), who also served the Hosokawa clan. One theory, that Niten studied with the samurai painter KAIHŌ YŪSHŌ, is based on similarities in their use of the *gempitsu* (abbreviated brushstroke) technique, in which forms are executed swiftly with a limited number of sweeping strokes, and on the indebtedness of both artists to the vigorous and expressive brushwork of the Chinese painter LIANG KAI. Certainly, Niten was familiar with Yūshō's style, whether or not direct tutelage was involved.

Niten's subjects, generally executed in monochrome ink, are roughly divided between explicitly Zen themes, such as *Hotei Watching a Cockfight* (hanging scroll, ink on paper; Fukuoka, A. Mus.), and studies of birds, such as *Screens of Waterfowl* (pair of six-panel folding screens, ink and gold dust on paper; Tokyo, Eisei Bunko) and his most famous painting, *Shrike on a Withered Branch* (hanging scroll, ink on paper; Osaka, Izumi Met. Kubosō Mem. A. Gal.), all painted *c.* 1630 to 1645.

The inclusion of a pair of fighting cocks in Niten's painting of Hotei is not part of the standard iconography for that popular subject of Zen painting. It may derive from a prototype by Kaihō Yūshō or by Liang Kai. The beady-eyed intensity with which this Hotei watches the cockfight, however, is Niten's own.

In *Shrike on a Withered Branch* the shrike perches on a long, bare, thorny branch and waits quietly for the caterpillar that is unsuspectingly inching its way towards its death by impalement on the shrike's cruel, sharply hooked beak. The two long strokes of the brush that Niten used to depict the branch have always been compared to the slashing sword strokes for which he was so famous; and his energetic, bold brushwork has in general been described as a visual expression of the martial spirit of the samurai.

Niten was an eccentric individual of single-minded intensity, and his prowess as a swordsman was the stuff of legends. In the *kabuki* plays of the Edo period, in popular literature and even in the films of today, he epitomizes the samurai ideal. His intensity, which can also be seen in his painting, makes him one of the most original ink painters of the early Edo period.

WRITINGS

Gorin no sho (1645); Eng. trans. by V. Harris as *A Book of Five Rings* (New York, 1974)

BIBLIOGRAPHY

E. Yoshikawa: *Miyamoto Musashi* (Tokyo, 1935–9); Eng. trans. by C. S. Terry as *Musashi* (New York, 1981)

S. Addiss and G. C. Hurst III: *Samurai Painters* (Tokyo, 1983)

JOAN H. O'MARA

Miyawaki, Mayumi (*b* Nagoya, 14 May 1936). Japanese architect. He inherited a great skill in drawing from his father, Kazuo Miyawaki, and his mother, both of whom were artists, and he studied first at Tokyo National University of Fine Arts and Music (BA, 1959); he then specialized in urban design at the University of Tokyo (Master of Technology, 1961). In the late 1960s and early 1970s he conducted scholarly studies of historic Japanese villages. In 1966 he began his career with the design of a house called Chalet Moby Dick, Yamanashi, which incorporated characteristics of both Shinto and Buddhist architecture on the outside, with a cavelike interior. In 1971 he formed the avant-garde group ARCHITEXT with four other architects, but no common design philosophy was promoted.

Miyawaki's designs in the 1970s were governed by his idea of 'primary architecture', characterized by the manipulation of cubic form, an emphasis on bright colours, interesting windows and skylights, and the creation of warm interiors. His use of the concrete box reflected his defensive attitude towards the disturbing influence of the external urban environment. Examples include the series of Akita Sogo Bank branches (Morioka and Sendai, 1970; Futsatsui, 1971; Honjō, 1973) and many 'box' houses such as Blue Box (1971), Tokyo, Green Box (Nos 1 and 2, 1972), Kanagawa Prefecture, Yoshimi Box (1979), Yokohama, and Matsukawa Box houses (1971 and 1978), Tokyo, for which he received the Architectural Institute of Japan prize (1980). His work in the 1980s increasingly combined elements of traditional Japanese architectural form with those of modern living spaces.

BIBLIOGRAPHY
I. Kurita, ed.: *Miyawaki Mayumi, Gendai Nihon kenchikuka zenshū* [Complete collection of modern Japanese architects], xxiv (Tokyo, 1973)
Japan Architect, 292 (1981) [whole issue]

TOSHIAKI NAGAYA

Mi Youren [Mi-jen]. *See* MI, (2).

Mizraḥ [Heb.: 'east']. Term used among Ashkenazi (west and east European) Jews to designate a decorated plaque hung on the eastern wall of homes to indicate the direction of prayer. The custom of praying while facing east—towards Jerusalem and the Temple Mount—is based on the biblical account of the prayers of Solomon and Daniel (1 Kings viii.38, 44, 48; Daniel vi.10–11). *Mizraḥ* plaques are known from about the 18th century and are executed in different techniques and various media such as paper (*see* PAPERCUT), wood or metal. They were made chiefly by students in traditional Jewish schools devoted to the study of the Talmud, rabbinic laws based on Bible interpretation.

A typical *mizraḥ* consists of appropriate quotations and pictures. Most often, the word *mizraḥ* is written in large square letters in the centre. As an acronym, *mizraḥ* gives rise to a phrase that is sometimes included: 'From this side [i.e. east] the spirit of life'. Also common is the verse 'From the rising [*mi-mizraḥ*] of the sun unto the going down of the same the Lord's name is to be praised' (Psalm 113.3). Such quotes were accompanied by characteristic Jewish representations, including the Temple and its implements, holy places, biblical episodes and heroes (especially Moses and Aaron), rampant lions and other symbolic animals. These motifs were at times exquisitely cut from paper or parchment and placed against a coloured background (see fig.). In other cases, the plaques were mass-produced as colour lithographs.

A votive tablet known as the *shivviti*, after the first word in the verse that is centrally inscribed on it, 'I have set [*shivviti*] the Lord before me' (Psalm 16.8), is related to the *mizraḥ*. The most prominent motif on these tablets is the seven-branched candlestick or *menorah*. Intended mainly for synagogue use and common also among the communities under Islamic rule, they serve the same basic function as the *mizraḥ*, though primarily for devotional purposes rather than orientation.

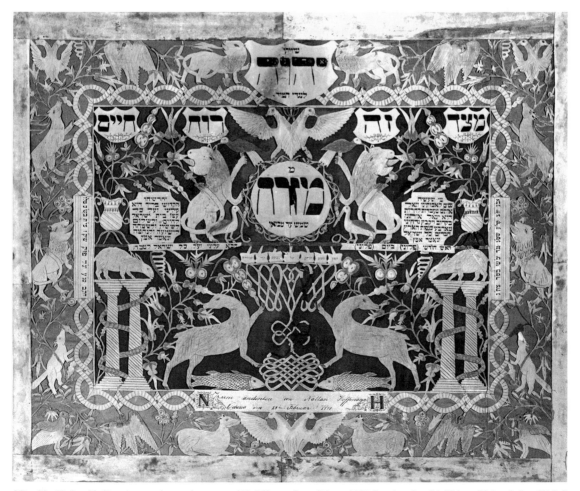

Mizraḥ by Nathan Hoffman, watercolour and papercut, 610×762 mm, from Odessa, 1890 (Los Angeles, CA, Hebrew Union College Skirball Museum)

BIBLIOGRAPHY

Enc. Jud.: 'Mizrah'; 'Shivviti'

J. Ooleželová: '*Mizraḥs* from the Collections of the State Jewish Museum in Prague', *Jud. Boh.*, xi (1975), pp. 14–28

A. M. Greenwald: 'The *Mizraḥ*: Compass of the Heart', *Hadassah Mag.*, lxi/2 (1979), pp. 12–13

B. Yaniv: 'Migzeret ha-mizrah' [The *mizraḥ* papercut], *Jerusalem Stud. Jew. Flklore*, iii (1982), pp. 105–11 [Eng. summary pp. xii–xiii]

G. Frankel: *Migzarot neyar: Omanut yehudit amamit* [Papercuts: Jewish folk art] (Givataim, 1983)

A. M. Greenwald: 'The Masonic *Mizraḥ* and Lamp: Jewish Ritual Art as a Reflection of Cultural Assimilation', *J. Jew. A.*, x (1984), pp. 87–101

S. Sabar and others: *Mizraḥ: Compass for the Heart* (exh. cat., New York, Hebrew Un. Coll., Jew. Inst. Relig., 1985)

SHALOM SABAR

Mizuno, Seiichi (*b* Kobe, 24 March 1905; *d* Kyoto, 25 May 1971). Japanese sinologist and archaeologist. He graduated in Oriental History from the Imperial University in Kyoto (now Kyoto National University) in 1928 and went on to study Chinese archaeology in the Tōa Kōkogakkai (Archaeological Society of the Far East) in Beijing (1929–31). During the years up to 1945 he carried out extensive and detailed research in northern China as a member of the Tōhō Bunka Gakuin (Academy of Oriental Culture) of Kyoto and was the co-author of several publications. From 1948 to 1968 Mizuno was a research member of the Jinbun Kagaku Kenkyūjo (Research Institute of Social Science) at Kyoto University. During 1948–57 he published his research on China and also conducted archaeological excavations in Japan. After a visit to China in 1959 he went to Afghanistan and Pakistan to supervise the excavation of Buddhist sites (1959–67). As his many publications testify, Mizuno's archaeological achievements brought him in contact with Chinese ceramics, early painting, bronze vessels and mirrors and jade, but his main interest was the history and iconography of the Buddhist sculpture of north Chinese cave-temple sites, such as LONGMEN and YUNGANG. The subsequent publications of his painstaking research in pre-war China contain a vast amount of invaluable material.

WRITINGS

Un-ko: Seireki goseiki ni okeru Chūgoku hokubo bukkyō kutsuin no kōkogakuteki chōsa hōkoku/Yun-kang: The Buddhist Cave-Temples of the Fifth Century AD in North China, 16 vols (Kyoto, 1952–6)

Kōkogaku jiten [Archaeological dictionary] (Tokyo, 1959)

Hōryūji (Tokyo, 1965), Eng. trans. by R. L. Gage as *Asuka Buddhist Art: Hōryūji*

Chūgoku no bukkyō bijutsu [The Buddhist art of China] (Tokyo, 1968)

BIBLIOGRAPHY

J. Edward Kidder, Jr: 'Seiichi Mizuno, 1905–1971', *Artibus Asiae*, xxxv (1973), pp. 163–4

BENT NIELSEN

Mleiha. *See under* ARABIA, PRE-ISLAMIC, §§II–IV.

Mlkʻe, Gospels of Queen. *See* GOSPELS OF QUEEN MLKʻE.

Mnesikles (*fl* 430s BC). Greek architect. He designed the Propylaia, the monumental gateway to the Athenian Acropolis (*see* ATHENS, §II, 1(i)). Begun in 437 BC but never finished, probably due to the outbreak of the Peloponnesian War (431 BC), this building may have undergone several changes in design while under construction. Mnesikles showed great originality in adapting it to a restricted area on different levels. The Propylaia departs from the largely conventional character of earlier Greek architecture in giving an illusion of symmetry, housing a multiplicity of activities under abutting roofs, accommodating different ground levels and using darker stone not only for highlighting but also to create an optical illusion. The basic design, with a central structure (the gatehouse proper, consisting of porches to east and west separated by a wall with five openings) framed by projecting wings, inspired several buildings in the Athenian Agora, and probably also the *skene* (stage building) with projecting wings that became standard for Greek theatres. Though the Propylaia remained unfinished, the quality of its workmanship is exceptional. This must be attributed to Mnesikles' dual role as designer and master builder.

BIBLIOGRAPHY

R. Bohn: *Die Propylaeen der Acropolis zu Athen* (Berlin, 1882)

W. B. Dinsmoor: *The Architecture of Greece and Rome* (London, 1902, rev. 2/1950 as *The Architecture of Ancient Greece*), pp. 199–205

J. A. Bundgaard: *Mnesicles* (Copenhagen, 1957)

C. Tiberi: *Mnesicle l'architetto dei Propilei* (Rome, 1964)

ANASTASIA N. DINSMOOR

Moab. *See under* EDOM AND MOAB.

Moalla, el- [Arab. al-Muʻallah]. Ancient Egyptian site, 22 km south of modern Luxor (Egypt). Tentatively identified as ancient Hefat, it is best known for the painted decoration in the tomb of Ankhtifi, nomarch of the 2nd and 3rd Upper Egyptian nomes during the First Intermediate Period (*c.* 2150–*c.* 2008 BC). Biographical inscriptions in the decorated sepulchre record political instability and famine, and Ankhtifi's efforts to relieve the resultant misery. The quality of these provincial paintings is typically low, but they nevertheless display a new and original spirit of creativity, being accomplished without preliminary sketching on a surface of stucco and Nile mud (for further discussion of provincial art, *see* EGYPT, ANCIENT, §XVII). The depictions include scenes of daily life, such as cooking, butchery, fishing (see fig.), transport of the harvest and storage of grain, spinning and woodworking. There are also representations of the troops whom Ankhtifi led into battle against the 4th and 5th Upper Egyptian nomes, scenes of hunting (including the spearing of a hippopotamus), dancing and, most importantly, the presentation of offerings.

The tomb of Sebekhotpe, probably a predecessor in the office of nomarch and an ancestor of Ankhtifi, preserves painted scenes of the deceased and his consort seated before the offering table and representations of the hunting of wild cattle and desert game. The tomb-stele of Sebekaa (London, BM, 1372), dating to the First Intermediate Period, is notable for an unconventional depiction of a man stretched out on a bier or bed, with a second person (probably a woman) lying on top of him in what is presumably to be construed as sexual intercourse.

BIBLIOGRAPHY

LÄ: 'Hefat'

A General Introductory Guide to the Egyptian Collections in the British Museum (London, 1930), fig. 87

J. Vandier: *Moʻalla: La Tombe d'Ankhtifi et la tombe de Sébekhotep*, Bibliothèque d'Etude, xxviii (Cairo, 1950)

El-Moalla, tomb of Ankhtifi, wall painting of a fishing scene, *c.* 2100 BC

C. Desroches Noblecourt: 'Concubines du mort et mères de famille au moyen empire', *Bull. Inst. Fr. Archéol. Orient.*, liii (1953), pp. 23–4; figs 9, 10
D. Wildung: *Sesostris und Amenemhet* (Munich, 1984), pp. 28–32

KAROLA ZIBELIUS-CHEN

Mobile. Form of kinetic sculpture, incorporating an element or elements set in motion by natural external forces. The term, which is also sometimes used more loosely to describe sculptural works with the capacity for motorized or hand-driven mechanical movement, was first used by Marcel Duchamp in 1932 to describe works by Alexander Calder (*see* CALDER, (3)). The notable feature of Calder's sculptures, which were suspended by threads, was that their movement was caused solely by atmospheric forces, such as wind and warm air currents. Movement was not, therefore, merely suggested by the treatment, as in traditional sculpture, but took place directly and unpredictably in the object. Because the kinetic sequences of the mobile could not be fixed or programmed, predictability and repeatability were eliminated.

The main inspiration behind the development of the mobile was Duchamp, whose ready-made *Bicycle Wheel* (1913; untraced; editioned replica 1964; Cologne, Mus. Ludwig; *see* DUCHAMP, MARCEL, fig. 2) gave rise to many innovations in KINETIC ART. It consisted of a stool and a movable bicycle wheel rim, both of which came from a department store and were subjected to almost no artistic modification. What mattered to Duchamp was the different meaning given to the objects by their unfamiliar montage, their new context and the ability of the wheel to move. The development of the mobile was taken further by Aleksandr Rodchenko with his *Oval Hanging Construction No. 12* (*c.* 1920; Moscow, Tret'yakov Gal.), one of the first suspended structures in 20th-century sculpture. Consisting of a single sheet of plywood cut into concentric rings, the two-dimensional surface is made to appear like a three-dimensional structure by rotation. The circular trajectories of the parts appear spherical and weightless, suggesting the movement of electrons circling the nucleus of an atom. At about the same time the Dadaists, and especially Man Ray, were contributing to the development of the mobile. Man Ray's *Obstruction* (1920; see A. Schwarz: *Man Ray: The Rigour of Imagination*, New York, 1977, p. 149), for example, was built up from a pyramid of coat-hangers, each with two more hangers suspended from its ends. Man Ray continued this system in arithmetic progression until almost the whole room was obstructed. Because of its regular structure the pyramid had an even but changeable equilibrium; if only one hanger was set in motion, the whole pyramid oscillated with it. Alberto Giacometti's Surrealist sculpture *Suspended Ball* (iron and plaster, 1930–31; Zurich, Ksthaus.; *see* SURREALISM, fig. 2) can also be considered a mobile in that it has a sphere suspended above a crescent within a metal frame. Giacometti's achievement was to enlarge the mobile concept decisively, so that formal innovation could be reconciled with the Surrealist interest in subconscious associations. If Rodchenko was primarily interested in rational, technical innovation, the Surrealists' enthusiasm

Mobile by Alexander Calder: *125*, painted steel plate, 1957 (New York, John F. Kennedy International Airport)

was aroused mainly by the possibilities of unconscious, playful expression opened up by the mobile.

In the early 1930s Calder, who was trained as an engineer, systematically set about developing the hanging sculpture into an art form in its own right. Through his association with José de Creeft, whom he had met in Paris in the 1920s, and through his study of wire sculpture and contemporary tin-plate toys, Calder evolved his own artistic standpoint. *Calderberry Bush* (steel rod, wood and sheet aluminium, 2.25×0.84×1.21 m, 1932; New York, Whitney) is regarded as his first standing mobile. Made up of a tetrahedron serving as the base and a balancing bar with a weight and a mobile hanging from its ends, it forms a balanced system. By using the principle of the lever of unequal length it has the configuration of an unstable equilibrium, so that any shock or touch produces a movement of the balancing bar. If a movement is imparted to the structure at any point, all the other motions change direction at the same time. About 1933 Calder produced the first mobiles hanging freely in space, including his *Ebony Mobile* (priv. col., see 1983 exh. cat., p. 86), which combines elements from various formal tendencies; for example, the use of suspension recalls Man Ray's *Obstruction*, while the shapes of the suspended elements themselves have links to the paintings of Arp and Miró. The sculpture makes visible a combination of forms moving between geometry and the sphere of biomorphic forms. In Calder's later mobiles the range of hanging elements

broadened to include spheres, bars, spirals, spindles, propellers and stars. Calder also produced large-scale mobiles for assembly halls, staircases, airports (e.g. *125*, 1957; see fig.) and urban sites, such as his *Spiral* (1958) in front of the UNESCO building in Paris.

Apart from Calder, the artist who worked most notably with mobiles was Bruno Munari. In 1933 he began producing his *Useless Machines* series, which, suspended by silk threads, were also set in motion by air movement and performed spherical rotations. In the late 1940s Lynn Chadwick began producing mobiles based on animal forms, and in the 1950s Kenneth Martin introduced additional aleatoric elements, such as a continual alternation from standstill to motion, which made the kinetic sequences considerably more complicated. In the 1950s and 1960s Jean Tinguely concentrated on using motors to animate his sculptures, and artists connected with the Groupe de Recherche d'Art Visuel, such as Julio Le Parc, Yvaral (Jean-Pierre Vasarely; *b* 1934) and Joël Stein (*b* 1926), also experimented with the mobile in the 1960s. The work of George Rickey in the same period confronted the viewer with quasi-scientific constructions, using high-grade steel and embodying universal joints (e.g. *Summer III*, stainless steel, 3.96×0.84 m, 1962–3; Washington, DC, Hirshhorn). Although Rickey's hanging sculptures were restricted in their possible movements, they demonstrated the continuing interest in the enigmatic and incalculable aspects of the mobile.

BIBLIOGRAPHY

J.-P. Sartre: 'Les Mobiles de Calder', *Calder* (exh. cat., Paris, Louis Carré, 1946), pp. 9–19

P. G. Brugière: 'L'Objet mobile de Calder', *Cah. A.*, xxix (1954), pp. 221–8

G. Rickey: 'The Morphology of Movement', *A.J.* [New York], xii/4 (1963), pp. 220–31

P. Wember: *Bewegte Bereiche der Kunst* (Krefeld, 1963)

F. Popper: *Origins and Development of Kinetic Art* (London, 1968)

——: *Die kinetische Kunst: Licht und Bewegung, Umweltkunst und Aktion* (Cologne, 1975)

J. Lipman: *Calder's Universe* (New York, 1976)

Calder: Mostra retrospettiva (exh. cat. by G. Carandente, Turin, Pal. a Vela, 1983)

GERHARD GRAULICH

Mocenigo. Italian family of statesmen, patrons and collectors. Six members of the family occupied the office of Doge of Venice. The first of these was Tommaso Mocenigo (*b* 1343; *d* 3 April 1423), whose rule was characterized by continued peace and the promotion of commercial prosperity through maritime trade. His marble tomb (*c.* 1425) by Pietro di Niccolò Lamberti and Giovanni di Martino da Fiesole (*fl c.* 1425–60) is in the church of SS Giovanni e Paolo and typifies an emerging Renaissance style in Venetian monumental sculpture and tomb architecture. Its unresolved amalgamation of Late Gothic and early Renaissance devices is augmented by a relief depicting *Prudence* and two figures representing *Faith* and *Charity*, almost certainly derived from Donatello. The tombs of two other Mocenigo doges are also in SS Giovanni e Paolo. The marble tomb of Tommaso's nephew *Pietro Mocenigo* (*b* 1406; *d* 23 Feb 1476) was executed *c.* 1476–81 by Pietro Lombardo and is considered the earliest example of the artist's mature style. Iconographically, its decorative elements emphasize Pietro's career as a naval commander prior to his election as Doge. The tomb of his brother *Giovanni Mocenigo* (*b* 1408; *d* 4 Nov 1485), executed by Tullio Lombardo *c.* 1500–10, exhibits an increasingly sympathetic assimilation of antique prototypes and is perhaps the best known of the three Renaissance *Mocenigo* tombs in the church. Giovanni is also the subject of two important portraits, both generally attributed to Gentile Bellini: the votive picture of *Doge Giovanni Mocenigo before the Virgin and Child* (late 15th century; London, N.G.) and the profile portrait of *Doge Giovanni Mocenigo* (late 15th century; Venice, Correr).

The Mocenigo family owned numerous palaces and properties along the Grand Canal in the parish of S Samuele, of which the oldest was the 'Casa Vecchia'. During the 16th century sites contiguous to it were acquired and their existing structures largely demolished to construct three new palaces, thereby creating an imposing sequence of four family edifices along the Grand Canal. The grandest of the new palaces, the 'Casa Nuova' (completed *c.* 1579), has been attributed to Palladio, who had clearly designed a residence for this pyramidal site by *c.* 1570, but some exterior elements suggest that the author was a follower of Palladio, perhaps Mauro Bergamasco. The 'Casa Nuova' and the 'Casa Vecchia' were connected by two palazzetti of lower elevation, whose canal façades were subsequently painted with scenes of Roman subjects by Giuseppe Albardi (see Bassi, fig. 136).

The 'Casa Nuova' was probably built for, and possibly even by, Doge Alvise I Mocenigo (*b* 1507; *d* 4 June 1577),

whose portrait was executed by Tintoretto (*c.* 1570–75; Venice, Accad.) and by an anonymous Venetian master (*c.* 1575; Venice, Correr). Alvise is thought to have been highly influential in determining the Giudecca as the site for Palladio's new votive church, Il Redentore (begun 1576; see PALLADIO, ANDREA, fig. 7), and was prominently portrayed with a possible model for the Redentore in an anonymous painting (?mid-1570s; ex-A. di Robilant priv. col., see Timofiewitsch, fig. xvii). He also initiated the enlargement of the Palazzo Mocenigo at S Stae, although most work there dates from *c.* 1590 to 1600; its structure recalls the architectural ideas of Sebastiano Serlio. Alvise also began the reconstruction of the family's 15th-century palazzetto on the Giudecca, later rebuilt by an unidentified architect who had closely studied the works of Palladio. Leonardo Mocenigo (?1522–75), who may have been the brother of Alvise, was among Palladio's most important Venetian patrons, employing him from 1558 in the construction of his new residence in the S Sofia district of Padua. He also commissioned Palladio *c.* 1561–2 to design a large country villa (incomplete) at Marocco (Treviso), for which three sketches (*c.* 1561–2; Venice, Archv Stato), plans and façade elevations (Palladio: *I quattri libri*) survive, and a villa on the River Brenta, for which there are two pen-and-ink sketches (*c.* 1570; London, RIBA); it remains unclear, however, whether any portion of this structure was ever executed.

Patronage by the family during the subsequent century included Francesco Contini's renovation (1623–5) of the 'Casa Vecchia', and Sebastiano Ricci was commissioned to execute nine canvases depicting the *Pagan Divinities* (1698–1700; Berlin, Gemäldegal.) for the 'Casa Nuova'. During the 18th century Doge Alvise IV Mocenigo (*b* 1701; *d* 31 Dec 1778) probably commissioned Tiepolo to execute *Aurora Dispersing the Clouds of Night*, also known as the *Triumph of Truth* (*c.* 1755–60; Boston, MA, Mus. F.A.). *Ceremonies at the Installation of the Doge*, a cycle of 12 pictures representing scenes from Alvise IV's inauguration (*c.* 1763–70; 11 now in Paris, Louvre; the other in Brussels, Mus. A. Anc.) by Francesco Guardi, was also probably commissioned by Alvise himself or a member of his immediate family. These may have been executed after drawings (*c.* 1763) by Canaletto and are closely related to the engravings (*c.* 1766; Venice, Correr) executed after those drawings by Giambattista Brustolon. During the 19th century much of the family's collection of art, furnishings and antiquities was dispersed by auction; the remainder was either lost or removed from Venice during World War II.

BIBLIOGRAPHY

A. Palladio: *I quattri libri dell'architettura* (Venice, 1570)

P. Zampetti: 'Il Palazzo Mocenigo', *A. Ven.*, viii (1954), pp. 330–33

W. Timofiewitsch: *La chiesa del Redentore. Corpus Palladianum*, iii (Vicenza, 1969)

O. Logan: *Culture and Society in Venice, 1470–1790: The Renaissance and its Heritage* (London, 1972), pp. 148–219, 314–15

I. Chiappini di Sorio: 'Affreschi settecenteschi veneziani: Palazzo Mocenigo', *Not. Pal. Albani*, iii (1974), pp. 66–78

G. Goldner: 'The Tomb of Tommaso Mocenigo and the Date of Donatello's *Zuccone* and of the Coscia Tomb', *Gaz. B.-A.*, lxxxiii (1974), pp. 187–92

E. Bassi: *Palazzi di Venezia* (Venice, 1976, 2/1978)

A. Foscari: 'L'invenzione di Palladio per un "sito piramidale" in Venezia', *A. Ven.*, xxxiii (1979), pp. 136–41

L. Puppi: 'Palladio e Leonardo Mocenigo: Un palazzo a Padova, una villa "per un . . . sito sopra la Brenta", e una questione di metodo', *Klassizimus: Epoche und Probleme: Festschrift für Erik Forssman zum 70. Geburtstag*, ed. J. M. zur Capellen and G. Oberreuter-Kronabel (Hildesheim, 1987), pp. 337–62

Mocetto [Moceto; Mozeto; Mozzetto], **Girolamo** (*b* Murano, *c.* 1470; *d* ?Venice, after 21 Aug 1531). Italian engraver, painter and designer of stained glass. He was born into a family of glass painters, and, although there is no documentary evidence that he worked outside Venice, his early paintings and engravings show the influence of Domenico Morone and of Mantegna and his circle, which would suggest that Mocetto's training may not have been exclusively Venetian. His artistic evolution is most clearly seen in a comparison of early works still close to Morone, such as a series of three engravings of the *Battle between Israel and the Amalekites* (see Hind, nos 719–20) or the painting of the *Battle* (Pavia, Pin. Malaspina), to works of a few years later, such as the two small paintings of the *Massacre of the Innocents* (London, N.G.; see fig.) and the engravings of *Pagan Sacrifices* (H 726–7), the *Metamorphosis of Amymone* (H 728) and the *Calumny of Apelles* (H. 727), all datable to *c.* 1500. In the later works, whole passages or motifs are copied or adapted from drawings and engravings by Mantegna. Mocetto may have had direct contact with the court of Mantua (the *Metamorphosis of Amymone* is an allegory of the city of Mantua); two engravings dating from the first years of the 16th century, *St John the Baptist* (H 724) and *Judith with the Head of Holofernes* (H 725), both bear a close resemblance to the contemporary work of Giulio Campagnola, who was in Mantua in 1499.

From *c.* 1500 Mocetto began to study the work of other artists from Venice and the Veneto. In his engraving of *Bacchus* (H 726), the pose of the god is derived from a soldier in Giovanni Bellini's *Resurrection* (Berlin, Gemäldegal.), while Bellini's *Assumption of the Virgin* (Murano, S Pietro Martine) inspired Mocetto's mediocre engraving of the same subject (H 717). Mocetto's several engravings of the *Virgin and Child Enthroned* (H 730–32) are derived from prototypes by Bartolomeo Montagna, Cima da Conegliano and possibly also Bellini. Mocetto's paintings of the *Virgin between Joachim and Anne* (*c.* 1500–10; Amsterdam, Rijksdienst Beeld. Kst., on dep. Maastricht, Bonnefantemus.) and *Virgin and Child* (*c.* 1500–10; Vicenza, Mus. Civ. A. & Stor.) mark the high point of his interest in Cima and Montagna. His engraving of the *Baptism of Christ* (*c.* 1515; H 729) is a pastiche of Cima's *Baptism of Christ* (Venice, S Giovanni in Brágora) and Bellini's painting of the same subject (Vicenza, S Corona). In this engraving, atmospheric effects are obtained by means of dense cross-hatching, a characteristic device of his.

One of Mocetto's most successful works was the lower band of stained-glass panels (*c.* 1515) for a window in SS Giovanni e Paolo, Venice. The figures of *St Theodore*, *SS John and Paul* and *St George and the Princess* are shown in a continuous landscape setting that runs behind the stone divisions of the Gothic window; this contrasts with the upper part of the window, in which the four saints are conceived in isolation. Within the contours of the forms delineated by the leading, Mocetto modelled the figures and created subtle chiaroscuro effects by using a technique of fine cross-hatching similar to that used in his drawings and engravings. The fresco cycle formerly on the façade of a house at Acqua Morta, Verona (*c.* 1517; four fragments in Verona, Castelvecchio), is probably correctly attributed to Mocetto and his workshop.

Only a few works can be ascribed to the last phase of the artist's career. They include panels of *St Helen* (Milan, Castello Sforzesco) and *St Catherine* (Padua, Mus. Civ.), both of which are inspired by Cima and Bellini. A drawing of *Children Playing with Masks* (Paris, Louvre) is executed in a somewhat academic style and reverts to the antiquarian taste of Mocetto's early work but is free of any trace of Mantegna's style.

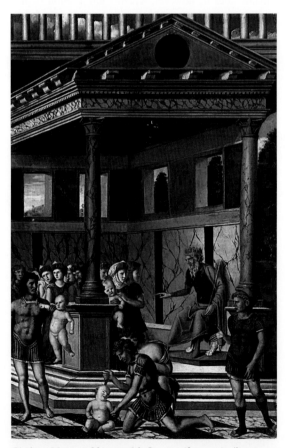

Girolamo Mocetto: *Massacre of the Innocents* (fragment), oil on canvas (?transferred from panel), 679×445 mm, *c.* 1500 (London, National Gallery)

BIBLIOGRAPHY

E. Galichon: 'Girolamo Mocetto, peintre et graveur vénitien', *Gaz. B.-A.*, ii (1859), pp. 321–36

P. Nanin: *Disegni di varie dipinture a fresco che sono in Verona* (Verona, 1864)

C. Von Fabriczy: 'Über Heimat und Namen G. Mocettos und Bonifazios von Verona', *Repert. Kstwiss.*, xii (1889), p. 15

G. Ludwig: 'Archivalische Beiträge zur Geschichte der venezianischen Malerei', *Jb. Kön.-Preuss. Kstsamml.*, xxiv (1903), pp. 44–57

J. Guibert: 'Notes sur une *Resurrection* du Musée Royal de Berlin: Giovanni Bellini et le graveur Mocetto', *Gaz. B.-A.*, xxxiv (1905), pp. 380–83

A. Venturi: 'Appunti sul Museo Civico di Verona', *Madonna Verona*, i/1 (1907), pp. 49–50

E. Waldmann: 'Zu Mocetto', *Mhft. Kstwiss.*, i (1908), pp. 193–5

B. Baron: 'Girolamo Mocetto: Painter-engraver', *Madonna Verona*, iii/1 (1909), pp. 61–6

G. Fiocco: 'Il primo dipinto di Girolamo Mocetto', *Madonna Verona*, viii/2–3 (1914), pp. 81–4

A. M. Hind: *Early Italian Engravings*, v (London, 1948) [H]

L. Puppi: 'Di Benedetto Montagna, del Mocetto e di altri problemi', *A. Ant. & Mod.*, 11 (1960), pp. 281–90

——: 'Schedule per la storia della pittura veronese tra la fine del '400 e l'inizio del '500', *A. Ant. & Mod.*, 28 (1964), pp. 416–27

Early Italian Drawings from the National Gallery of Art (exh. cat., ed. K. Oberhuber, J. Levenson and J. Sheehan; Washington, DC, N.G.A,, 1973), pp. 382–9

L. Zecchin: 'I Mozetto, vetrai muranesi del quattrocento', *Riv. Staz. Spermntl Vetro* (1978), pp. 111–15

S. Romano: 'La vetrata dei SS Giovanni e Paolo: Esercizi di attribuzione', *A. Ven.*, xxxvi (1982), pp. 41–51

La grande vetrata di S Giovanni e Paolo (exh. cat., Venice, Ala Napoleonica, 1982)

S. Romano: *Girolamo Mocetto* (Modena, 1985) [with full bibliog.]

SERENA ROMANO

Moche [Mochica]. Pre-Columbian culture and art style that evolved on the north coast of Peru approximately a thousand years before the beginning of the INCA empire. It is also the name given to the site of the Pre-Columbian city that existed in the Moche Valley, near present-day Trujillo. The Moche had no writing system, yet they produced a vivid artistic record of their activities and their environment. The realism and subject-matter of Moche art make it one of the most appealing of all Pre-Columbian styles. (For general discussion of the Pre-Columbian art of the region *see* SOUTH AMERICA, PRE-COLUMBIAN, §III.)

1. Introduction. 2. Art and architecture.

1. INTRODUCTION. The Moche lived in one of the world's driest deserts. Human life in the area is confined to the river valleys that cut across this desert, draining rainfall from the Andes back into the Pacific Ocean.

The Moche style began *c.* AD 100, and by *c.* AD 500 it was dominant in all of the valleys from Lambayeque to Nepeña, a distance of more than 250 km north–south. Moche settlements are found in nearly all parts of these valleys, from the sea to the point where the flood-plain narrows as it enters the canyons leading up into the mountains. This is generally a distance of *c.* 50 km east–west. Isolated occurrences of Moche material or Moche stylistic features have been found beyond these boundaries, indicating some degree of contact with the surrounding areas.

Moche subsistence was based primarily on agriculture, supplemented extensively by maritime resources. To a lesser degree, hunting of land mammals, birds and land snails added to the diet. The domesticated llama and alpaca were the primary source of meat and wool, and llamas also served as beasts of burden. The Muscovy duck and guinea-pig were domesticated and used for food.

Metal-casting techniques, the alloying of metals and the widespread use of copper and silver appear to have been added by Moche craftsmen to an already highly developed goldworking technology that was known to earlier artists (*see* SOUTH AMERICA, PRE-COLUMBIAN, §VIII, 5). Similarly, Moche potters added the use of moulds to an extensive list of techniques for producing fine ceramic objects. Loom weaving of cotton and wool fibres was practised, and a great variety of techniques was utilized to produce elaborate textiles.

The Moche people built temples, palaces and platform mounds of rectangular sun-dried mud-bricks—a construction material well-suited to the arid climate of the northern Peruvian coast. Some of their structures were plastered and painted with colourful designs.

Moche graves were usually rectangular pits in which the bodies were placed in an extended position. Sometimes the pits were lined with mud-bricks or stone and roofed with large cane beams. Many elaborately furnished graves have been found, and the marked differentiation in the quality and quantity of grave goods indicates a highly developed social class system and a complex division of labour. These aspects of society are also demonstrated by the way people and activities are depicted by the Moche artists.

Moche artistic expression is amazingly varied. Men, women, animals, plants, anthropomorphized demons and deities are shown engaged in a wide range of activities, including hunting, fishing, combat, punishment, sexual acts and elaborate ceremonies. Architectural details of temples, pyramids and houses are all depicted in Moche art, as are features of clothing and adornment. The representations, both painted and modelled, are detailed and quite realistic. Some of the ceramic bottles are actually portraits of specific individuals. Much of the art appears to tell a story and to give tantalizing glimpses into the daily life, ceremonies and mythology of the people who created it.

Moche culture flourished for more than six centuries. During this time Moche art changed gradually but clearly maintained its characteristic themes and manner of representation. Then, *c.* AD 750, Moche art began to disappear from the north coast. The circumstances under which this took place are not well understood, although it has been suggested that its end was brought about by an invasion of HUARI people from the southern mountain regions of Peru. Archaeological research has demonstrated that the end of the Moche kingdom is contemporary with the introduction of the Huari style on the north coast, but there is no conclusive evidence to show that the two events are causally related.

It is only with the arrival of Europeans in the early 16th century that we have any written accounts of the native people who lived on the north coast of Peru. Since the earlier cultures had no writing system, their story must be reconstructed entirely on the basis of archaeological research. This involves the painstaking excavation of what remains of their palaces, temples and tombs, as well as their domestic architecture and refuse deposits. Archaeological research in this area is particularly instructive, however, because the arid climate has preserved perishable material such as plant remains, basketry and textiles, which are absent from archaeological sites in most other areas of the world. The remarkably complete archaeological record makes possible a detailed reconstruction of the ancient culture—a reconstruction that is greatly enhanced by the wealth of information contained in Moche art.

BIBLIOGRAPHY
R. Larco Hoyle: *Los Mochicas* (Lima, 1938–9)
C. Evans: 'Finding the Tomb of the Warrior-god', *N. Geog.*, xci (1947), pp. 453–82
G. Kutscher: *Chimú: Eine altindianische Hochkultur* (Berlin, 1950)
——: 'Iconographic Studies as an Aid in the Reconstruction in Early Chimú Civilization', *Trans. NY Acad. Sci.*, n. s., xii/6 (1950), pp. 194–203
E. Benson: *The Mochica: A Culture of Peru* (New York, 1972)
C. B. Donnan: *Moche Art and Iconography* (Los Angeles, 1976)
——: *Moche Art of Peru* (Los Angeles, 1978)
W. Alva: 'Discovering the New World's Richest Unlooted Tomb', *N. Geog.*, clxxiv (1988), pp. 510–49 [Sipán]
C. B. Donnan: 'Unraveling the Mystery of the Warrior-Priest', *N. Geog.*, clxxiv (1988), pp. 550–55 [Sipán]
W. Alva: 'The Moche of Ancient Peru: New Tomb of Royal Splendor', *N. Geog.*, clxxvii (1990), pp. 2–15 [Sipán]
C. B. Donnan: 'Masterworks of Art Reveal a Remarkable Pre-Inca World', *N. Geog.*, clxxvii (1990), pp. 16–33
W. Alva and C. B. Donnan: *Royal Tombs of Sipán* (Los Angeles, 1993)

CHRISTOPHER B. DONNAN

2. ART AND ARCHITECTURE.

(i) Pyramids. (ii) Pottery and other arts.

(i) Pyramids. The most prominent structures at Moche itself and at other Moche sites are truncated pyramids, the highest of which reaches 40 m. The first monumental truncated adobe pyramids of the north coast were probably erected during the first few centuries AD by the late GALLINAZO people. The tradition was then adopted and developed by the emerging Moche state, whose regional centres boasted impressive pyramids symbolizing their social, political and religious pre-eminence. The function of the Moche pyramids is a matter of long-standing controversy. From the time of the Spanish Conquest, pyramids and other ancient, major artificial constructions in the Andean area have been called *huacas*, signifying something sacred.

(a) Huaca del Sol and Huaca de la Luna. The most spectacular monuments are the Huaca del Sol (Pyramid of the Sun) and the Huaca de la Luna (Pyramid of the Moon) at Moche, which dominated the capital. It should be clearly noted, however, that these names are modern impositions and by no means reflect the monuments' original designations or purposes.

The cross-shaped Huaca del Sol (see fig. 1) is a spectacular landmark measuring *c.* 350 m long and *c.* 40 m high,

1. Moche, Huaca del Sol (Pyramid of the Sun), *c.* AD 100–*c.* 550

with an estimated volume of 2,000,000 cu. m. The pyramid was constructed of adobe bricks and fill, with little use of mortar or other binders. A 90 m-long, 6 m-wide ramp on the north side gave access to the summit. The main body of the pyramid consisted of a basal platform, built as a series of steps measuring 3 m high by 2 m wide and surmounted by a 23 m-high superstructure. The profile of the best-preserved south-eastern portion of the pyramid thus resembles a huge staircase, a form that may have served to minimize buttressing problems. It has been estimated that there were at least eight construction stages, which probably began late in Moche Phase 1 (*c.* AD 1–*c.* 200) or early in Phase 2 (*c.* AD 200–*c.* 300) and lasted until Phase 4 (*c.* AD 450–*c.* 550), consuming over 143 million adobe bricks. Such a large-scale use of brick indicates power over an immense labour force. The contemporary Huaca de la Luna, at the west base of the conical peak of Cerro Blanco, was also built in at least four stages, using over 50 million bricks and eventually attaining overall dimensions of *c.* 95×*c.* 85 m and a height of some 25 m.

Nearly all Moche pyramids were constructed using a simple system originally developed by the Gallinazo builders in which high, thick walls were juxtaposed to form parallel, vertical planes. This horizontal and vertical separation from the ordinary world was combined with restricted access to underline the power and sacredness of the pyramid, and it has been commented upon by Bishop Martínez de Compañón at the end of the 18th century and by many others since. During his pioneering excavation of 1903 at the Huaca del Sol, Max Uhle noted that many of the constituent bricks of excavated walls bore on their upper surface a simple mark made with fingers or stamps while the bricks were still wet. From such marks, Uhle suggested that allotments of bricks had been contributed by various communities or clans. In 1930, Alfred L. Kroeber reached a similar conclusion, noting that the simplicity of the construction technique and a certain 'slovenliness' in the execution implied the use of unskilled mass labour under a system of labour tax, where individual communities were responsible for building their own segments. These conclusions were elaborated in 1975 by Charles Hastings and Michael E. Moseley, who showed that bricks taken from sampled vertical segments were nearly always uniform in size, soil quality, colour and, where applicable, identification marks. At the Huaca del Sol, such marks appear on one-fifth to over one-half of sampled bricks in individual segments, including 93 distinct marks confined to construction stages IV–VIII of Moche Phases 2–4 (*c.* AD 200–*c.* 550). Data from the Huaca de la Luna show similar conclusions. The appearance of brick marking seems to follow the initial wave of Mochica territorial expansion, which may have broadened the area from which the workforce was drawn and facilitated the accounting of tribute labour. The variability of construction and brick quality found in the Moche pyramids was effectively masked by layers of plaster applied over the exterior surfaces, which, typically, were then painted.

(b) Huaca Fortaleza. Pyramid form and construction technique underwent a significant transformation during the transition from Moche Phase 4 (*c.* AD 450–*c.* 550) to

Phase 5 (*c.* AD 550–*c.* 650), as seen at the Huaca Fortaleza, the ceremonial centre of PAMPA GRANDE, the Moche capital during Phase 5. In contrast to the incremental growth of the solid adobe structures at the Huaca del Sol and the Huaca de la Luna over perhaps 400 years, the Fortaleza pyramid, boasting the impressive dimensions of 270×180×38 m, was built in two distinct stages, possibly within a single generation. An estimated 80–85% of the pyramid's volume (estimated at 1,500,000 cu. m.) was built using an innovative 'chamber and fill' technique, the interior largely comprising several hundred square adobe-and-mortar walled chambers measuring from 1 to 5 m sq. and 15–20 m high, containing sand and other locally available loose fill. The resultant lattice of filled chambers was buttressed by thick exterior adobe walls built in standardized, vertical segments *c.* 2 m wide and *c.* 1 m thick. This technique was cost-effective in that it rapidly achieved height and volume while reducing the number of bricks needed and maximizing the use of readily available filling material. Organizationally, however, it required greater on-site coordination than did the traditional approach. As bricks of differing dimensions were used for the chamber walls, they were probably pooled together and then laid by workers (not necessarily their makers).

Access to the 10 m-high first terrace was provided by an impressive 290 m-long walled ramp with three 'checkpoints' (interior cross walls at intervals along the ramp, each providing only restricted passage between them). Traffic then passed through a two-tiered platform at the west end and reached the middle terrace, over 5 m high, before making the final steep climb to the summit. This platform had a back wall and a solid roof supported by three rows of wooden columns; many were set in square, sand-filled adobe sockets, some of which contained sacrificed llamas. Although the top of the main body of the pyramid has been badly eroded, some preserved superstructures were excavated, providing a glimpse of the site's former splendour. The entire summit was probably walled in with the northern front reinforced by a boulder embankment. Inside, a major portion was occupied by an extensive court with a roof supported by wooden columns.

A complex of well-built, spacious rooms, with indirect access through baffled entries formally arranged at the higher, south end of the main body, is indicative of the function of the Huaca Fortaleza. The ceremonial significance of this complex is indicated not only by its elevated location and carefully planned construction but also by a mural showing a row of identical seated feline creatures, by a number of under-floor offerings and by the nature of artefacts found on the floor. One such offering placed in the ramp contained a llama skeleton and child remains covered with shell pendants, turquoise and sodalite beads, and a necklace and beads of *Spondylus* (colourful tropical thorny oyster). Floor artefacts included a stone macehead, copper tweezers, quartz crystals, ceramic drum frames and fine black ceramic bowls, as well as food remains (llama bones and small shells) and jars that probably contained drinks. Such data point both to ceremonial and residential functions for the summit, though it is uncertain whether

the privileged élite resided there permanently. Uhle, however, believed a religious function was obvious from the pyramidal form alone.

(c) Decoration. The polychrome murals that decorated the plastered façades of Moche pyramids expressed the socio-political and religious dogma of the ruling élite. The best-known preserved example comes from Pañamarca in the Nepeña Valley, near the southern end of the Moche domain. This masterful mural, depicting an elaborately costumed standing figure holding a goblet, an anthropomorphic bat, a feline figure and bound human prisoners, is believed to represent an elaborate ritual involving the offering of human sacrificial blood. Although the plaster has often been eroded away or covered over, most Moche pyramids no doubt originally had colourful, striking murals, as attested by recent excavations at the Huaca de la Luna and the Huaca El Brujo (Chicoma Valley).

Until recently, the Huaca de la Luna retained a few Moche paintings and what may be Moche–Huari murals. The best-known is a Moche fresco depicting a battle between men and anthropomorphic weapons, which is thought to relate to a widespread ancient Pre-Columbian American myth popularly called the 'revolt of objects'. Another mural, probably painted shortly after the Moche abandonment of the site (*c.* AD 550–*c.* 600), shows a full-face anthropomorphic figure holding in either hand a staff with stylized animal-headed terminals. In contrast to the curvilinear Moche style, this mural was executed with rectilinear lines reminiscent of contemporary Central Andean textiles. It was subsequently overpainted with a chequer-work design, each square bearing a stylized motif possibly representing a crab. This, in turn, was painted over with a pattern of squares in which an anthropomorphic standing figure alternated with motifs of a composite snake, a bird and a humanoid head.

(d) Function and interpretation. Whatever other significance they had, Moche pyramids certainly had a funerary function. Many Spanish colonists, sometimes together with local Indian leaders, formed commercial mining companies systematically to loot hidden treasures (grave goods) buried in the pyramids. In 1602, for example, the Moche River was diverted against the Huaca del Sol, washing away over two thirds of the pyramid and exposing an immense treasure. One looted burial attributed to the Huaca de la Luna yielded various gilt masks, among other material, and may have been a royal burial. Although there is no indication that any Moche pyramid was originally built to house specific burials, evidence from looting and modern excavation makes it clear that they did serve as important burial sites while in use. Not all the burials can be dismissed as dedicatory in nature. Another recent interpretation, based on considerable food remains found on top of the Huaca del Sol and in the domestic structures at its base, is that it was the civic centre where ruler and ruled interacted regularly. By the same token, Topic (1982) regards the inaccessible throne room on top of the Huaca de la Luna as a sacrosanct precinct and royal residence. The possibility that the food refuse at the Huaca del Sol represents occasional ceremonial feasts and offerings cannot be discounted, but with so much of the pyramid

already washed away, resolution of this debate remains difficult. It is interesting that an immediately post-Moche, Huari-affiliated population utilized the Huaca del Sol rather than the Huaca de la Luna for burial and ceremonial purposes.

BIBLIOGRAPHY

M. Uhle: 'Die Ruinen von Moche', *J. Soc. Américanistes*, x (1913), pp. 95–117
A. L. Kroeber: *Archaeological Explorations in Peru, Part II: The Northern Coast*, Anthropological Series, Field Museum of Natural History, ii (Chicago, 1930)
R. P. Schaedel: 'Major Ceremonial and Population Centers in Northern Peru', *Civilizations of Ancient America: Selected Papers of the 29th International Congress of Americanists* (Chicago, 1951), pp. 232–43
D. Bonavia: *Ricchata quellccani: Pinturas murales prehispánicas* (Lima, 1974); Eng. trans. by P. J. Lyon as *Mural Painting in Ancient Peru* (Bloomington, 1985)
C. M. Hastings and M. E. Moseley: 'The Adobes of Huaca del Sol and Huaca de la Luna', *Amer. Ant.*, xl (1975), pp. 196–203
C. B. Donnan: *Moche Art and Iconography* (Los Angeles, 1976)
D. Menzel: *The Archaeology of Ancient Peru and the Work of Max Uhle* (Berkeley, 1977)
C. B. Donnan and C. J. Mackey: *Ancient Burial Patterns in the Moche Valley, Peru* (Austin, 1978)
I. Shimada: 'Economy of a Prehistoric Urban Context: Commodity and Labor Flow at Moche V Pampa Grande, Peru', *Amer. Ant.*, xliii (1978), pp. 569–92
T. L. Topic: 'The Early Intermediate Period and its Legacy', *Chan Chan: Andean Desert City*, ed. M. E. Moseley and K. C. Day (Albuquerque, 1982), pp. 255–84
J. Haas: 'Excavations on Huaca Grande: An Initial View of the Elite of Pampa Grande, Peru', *J. Field Archaeol.*, xii (1985), pp. 391–409
I. Shimada and R. Cavallato: 'Monumental Adobe Architecture of the late Prehispanic Northern North Coast of Peru', *J. Soc. Américanistes*, lxxi (1986), pp. 41–78
I. Shimada: *Pampa Grande and the Mochica Culture* (Austin, 1994)
S. Uceda and E. Mujica: *Moche: Propuestas y Perspectivas* (Lima, 1994)

IZUMI SHIMADA

(ii) Pottery and other arts. Moche artistic expression is manifested most dramatically in its ceramics. Pots were both moulded (see fig. 2) and hand-modelled, in high and low relief. Decorations were modelled, stamped, carved and painted on flat surfaces—in red-brown or black-brown lines on a cream or beige slip, or in cream or beige lines on a red-brown slip—creating an enormous variation in appearance. Effigy vessels were common, revealing more about myth and ritual than in any other Andean culture. Also frequent were hollow and solid mould-made figurines, most depicting human beings; these were generally made from a rougher clay and were rarely painted.

Among the many forms produced by Moche potters, stirrup-spout jars were especially frequent; *floreros* (large flat-bottomed dishes with flaring sides) and 'poppers' (flattened spheroid 'dippers' with a restricted opening and a straight handle) were of secondary importance. Vessels were well made, of a reddish-brown paste with quartz sand temper, thin walled (3–4 mm) and usually well controlled in firing. As most pots were mould made, this allowed for the production of multiple copies of popular forms. The most common form for the stirrup-spout jar was a sphere, with a flattened base. The stirrup was attached to the top of the sphere, and the body was painted. Bichrome decoration was most common, with red-brown paint on a white or cream slip the most frequent combination. Black was occasionally added for detail. Archaeologists have arranged Moche ceramics into five stylistic phases, through which painted designs became

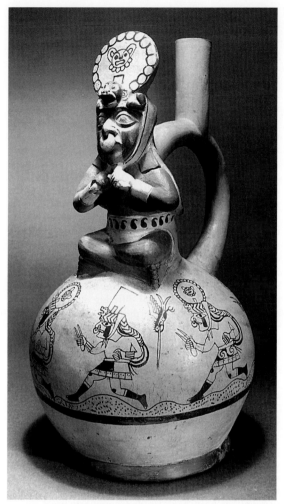

2. Moche ceramic bottle with fine-line drawings of runners and a modelled figure wearing the characteristic headdress of runners, 270×197 mm, *c.* AD 200 (Chicago, IL, Art Institute of Chicago)

more complicated, with more characters engaged in more elaborate activities and less of the vessel surface left empty. The more complex modelled forms were also mould-made and painted, and the exigencies of the two-part mould were the only limit to the fantastic variety of shapes produced. Modelled jars also became more elaborate through time but were rare in Phase 5.

The remarkable range of themes depicted in Moche ceramic art has long excited comment. Themes range from the everyday to the mythological and are both anecdotal and iconographic, revealing much about Mochica daily activity (see fig. 3). Many simple, modelled stirrup-spout jars represent local animals and plants: llamas, felines, owls, sea-birds, potatoes and gourds are frequently modelled, while a wider range of land and marine life is painted on vessel walls. Many of these naturalistic representations convey warmth and humour, for example three frogs sitting on top of each other. Humans are represented even more frequently. The famous portrait-head jars, especially typical of Phases 3 and 4, present proud,

3. Moche fine-line designs on pottery (redrawn), showing (top) deer-hunters and (bottom) musicians

commanding faces clearly modelled from life. Facial painting, ear spools and turbans or headdresses embellish the portraits. A wider range of individuals is shown in vessels on which entire human figures are modelled. Individuals are presented in a variety of costumes and headdresses, carrying tools, weapons or other paraphernalia that give clues to the individual's occupation or position in life. Warriors are often shown on one knee with shield and club at the ready; regal figures, seated cross-legged, display elaborate headdresses and large ear spools. Physical deformities are a favourite theme, with blindness, cleft palates and hunchbacks clearly displayed.

More complex vessels combine modelling with elaborate fine-line painting. Humans, anthropomorphic figures and most animals are shown in profile, with their actions wrapped around the vessel. Some scenes are divided into sections by horizontal lines, vertical lines or both, but within individual sections there is little concern with perspective. There must have been strict canons for many of the fine-line scenes, as they are repeated without variation over dozens of vessels. The warrior reappears in this context, often kneeling atop a base on which other warriors are painted. More elaborate military scenes also show naked prisoners, sometimes lashed to frames or with arms bound, tormented by vultures or cats. Deer hunting is another common theme, painted and modelled on pottery and also worked in gold and hardstones on ear spools. The deer is usually shown pierced by a spear, often with a net in the background. More complete scenes

include hunters and dogs. Women are relatively rare in Moche art. They are, however, frequent on the so-called 'erotic' pots, which comprise a small but interesting part of the ceramic repertory, are sometimes seen as mothers, weavers or exemplars of various infirmities and are usually in simple dress. They are never featured on portrait-head jars. Of special interest are representations of supernatural creatures, with combinations of human and non-human attributes, wearing fantastic costumes, headdresses and masks. They occur singly or as participants in complex scenes and must have been important in Moche myth.

Earlier interpretations of Moche art, by Larco Hoyle and Elizabeth Benson in particular, stress the realistic nature of the representations in clay and other media. Mochica potters, it was argued, depicted the world they saw around them, and the images they produced could be used as text for reconstructing their daily lives. The more recent interpretive trend is to emphasize the predominance of mythological and shamanic themes, especially in some of the complex scenes painted in fine lines on stirrup-spout jars in Phases 3 to 5. Christopher Donnan pointed out that certain scenes are repeated many times, with all of the details faithfully copied. The 'presentation scene', for example, shows an anthropomorphic masked being with a rayed headdress, larger than the other characters and obviously of higher status. Offerings are presented to him by smaller, but still elaborately dressed, beings. On the periphery of this central action, bound captives are sacrificed by humans and by feline-faced beings, and their blood is collected in cups. The most detailed representations of the scene contain still more characters, animals and objects. Specific characters or activities are frequently segregated out from the scene and featured by themselves. Donnan inferred that viewers were familiar with the scene and knew the actors and their roles in it. The meaning of the complete scene could be evoked by the visual representation of only part of it, by a single character or by a symbol.

The shamanic theme is also expressed in several ways. Healers are shown conducting curing sessions, and sometimes unsuccessful healers are staked out to be eaten by birds. Skeletons play musical instruments, dance and engage in sexual activity with women. Shamans are depicted with clenched fists with the middle knuckle raised, the five fingers sometimes transformed into five mountain peaks that shelter human or animal figures. The San Pedro cactus (*Trichocereus pachanoi*), source of a powerful hallucinogenic brew, is frequently represented. Another theme depicts the ritual chewing of coca leaves, including careful representations of the bag containing the leaves and of the gourd and stick for the lime used with the leaves. Sometimes only the chewers are depicted, but their dress clearly identifies them as participants in the coca ritual. The principal deity of the Mochica, depicted on both pottery and plastered walls (see below), was Chavin-derived. His distinctive features included feline canines and a belt with snake-head appendages, and sometimes figure-of-eight ears and lidded eyes.

The art style served as a unifying mechanism for the Moche kingdom, which in Phase 3 began to expand its political control over several adjacent coastal valleys. The repertory of images was large, but the uniformity with which they were executed assured iconographic standards throughout the entire territory. Though the more elaborate modelled and painted Moche vessels are most common in the Moche and Chicama valleys, the kingdom's heartland, they have also been found in peripheral valleys. For example, the 'presentation scene' is depicted on a wall at Pañamarca, near the southern limit of Mochica expansion, demonstrating the spread of Moche ideology. The prestige of the Moche art style is demonstrated by its spread well to the north and south of the kingdom's territory, but it was rare for sierra peoples to import Moche ceramics. Nevertheless, Moche style influenced some motifs and themes in the Recuay style of the Callejon de Huayla.

BIBLIOGRAPHY
R. Larco Hoyle: *Los Mochicas* (Lima, 1938–9)
G. Kutscher: *Nordperuanische Keramik* (Berlin, 1954)
C. B. Donnan: 'Moche Ceramic Technology', *Ñawpa Pacha*, iii (1965), pp. 115–38
E. Benson: *The Mochica: A Culture of Peru* (New York, 1972)
C. B. Donnan: *Moche Art and Iconography* (Los Angeles, 1976)
——: *Moche Art of Peru* (Los Angeles, 1978)

THERESA LANGE TOPIC

Mochi, Francesco (*b* Montevarchi, 29 July 1580; *d* Rome, 6 Feb 1654). Italian sculptor. The son of Lorenzo Mochi, not of Orazio Mochi as was previously believed, he studied in Florence with Santi di Tito. Around 1600 he went to Rome to continue his training with the Venetian sculptor Camillo Mariani, whom he may have assisted on his masterpiece, the eight colossal statues of saints for S

Bernardo alle Terme (e.g. *St Catherine of Alexandria*, *c.* 1600). At this time Mochi attracted the attention of Duke Mario Farnese (*d* 1619), who secured for him his first independent commission, the large marble *Annunciation* group for Orvieto Cathedral (*c.* 1603–9; Orvieto, Mus. Opera Duomo). Originally placed on opposite sides of the high altar, the two free-standing figures of the *Virgin* and the *Angel Gabriel* electrify the broad space between them by their complementary gestures and powerful emotions. The treatment of the Annunciation as an unfolding drama broke decisively with earlier sculptural traditions, which focused on self-contained, individual figures. Rudolf Wittkower has likened its vitality to a 'fanfare raising sculpture from its sleep'. Often considered the first truly Baroque sculpture of the 17th century, Mochi's innovations compare to those of the early Roman Baroque painters Caravaggio and Annibale Carracci.

After returning to Rome in 1610, Mochi assisted Mariani and, a year later, stepped in to complete several commissions for S Maria Maggiore that had been left unfinished at Mariani's death. Around this time he also worked on a commission from the Barberini family: *St Martha* (*c.* 1610–17), for their family chapel in S Andrea della Valle, Rome. In 1612 Ranuccio I Farnese, the reigning Duke of Parma, called him to Piacenza to execute two monumental bronze equestrian statues (1612–29; Piacenza, Piazza Cavalli) for the central piazza, one of the Duke himself and the other of his late father, *Alessandro Farnese* (for illustration *see* PIACENZA). The Farnese had recently put down an uprising in Piacenza, and Mochi seems to have designed the statues to make an explicit political statement. The statue of *Ranuccio Farnese*, executed first, is linked in style and type to earlier Renaissance models that depicted the rider as peacemaker and statesman, for example Giambologna's *Cosimo de' Medici I* (1587–93; Florence, Piazza della Signoria). However, in the statue of *Alessandro Farnese*, Mochi broke entirely new ground to create the first dynamic equestrian monument of the Baroque. In an unprecedented manner, he used the device of a billowing cloak to unify the rider with the bulk of the horse and to create the illusion of warlike energy. The two statues presented Piacenza with a clear choice between obeisance to an enlightened prince, Ranuccio, or a return to the repressive tactics of an earlier time. Gestures of the riders and the inward tilt of the horses' heads unify the monumental bronzes across the piazza and assert the dynastic continuity of the Farnese. During the casting, Mochi quarrelled with the founder and took over the job himself; other than Domenici Guidi, he was the only major Roman sculptor with the expertise to cast his own work.

When Mochi returned to Rome in 1629, he had in hand several commissions from the Barberini family. He first executed the marble *St John the Baptist* (1629; Dresden, Hofkirche) for the Barberini Chapel in S Andrea della Valle. This was intended as a companion figure to the earlier *St Martha*, but for unknown reasons it was never installed. Shortly thereafter he received a commission for what is probably his best-known work, the giant marble statue of *St Veronica* (1629–39; Rome, St Peter's; see fig.). At the request of Pope Urban VIII (Maffeo Barberini), Gianlorenzo Bernini had begun a massive reconstruction

Francesco Mochi: *St Veronica*, marble, h. 5 m, 1629–39 (Rome, St Peter's)

of the crossing of St Peter's in 1626. His design called for great niches in the crossing piers to be filled with monumental saints carved by Rome's leading sculptors: Bernini, Mochi, François Du Quesnoy and Andrea Bolgi. Bernini provided models for three of the statues but gave Mochi free reign with the *Veronica*. Influenced by Hellenistic sculpture and Santi di Tito's fresco of the *Madness of Nebuchadnezzar* (1562–4; Rome, Vatican, Cortile Belvedere), Mochi conceived his figure in strongly emotional terms. The saint, in agony, holds the sudarium in trembling outstretched hands. Spiralling, thin, drapery folds create an illusion of motion, as though the figure is rushing forth from the niche. Contemporary critics were not pleased; they attacked the statue for its awkward pose and the wild drapery folds, which undermine its stability. Compared to the heroic calm of the figures designed by Bernini, especially the statue he carved of *St Longinus* (1629–38), the *Veronica* is frenzied, jarring and inconsistent with the majestic tone of the crossing. Mochi's very personal vision was here out of place.

Having ranked among Rome's best sculptors in the early 1630s, Mochi was soon overshadowed by Bernini and Alessandro Algardi. During the last twenty years of his career Mochi had only five significant commissions, and two of these were withdrawn and awarded to Bernini and Algardi. Either unable or unwilling to adapt to the new artistic climate in Rome, his works of the 1640s and

1650s display an even more pronounced agitation than the *Veronica*. His *St Thaddeus* (1631–44) for Orvieto Cathedral (*in situ*) is gaunt, elongated and spiritually intense. It is the only late work by Mochi that was actually accepted on completion. The marble group of the *Baptism* (*c.* 1634–50; Rome, Pal. Braschi) and his *SS Peter and Paul* (1638–52; Rome, Porta del Popolo) were both rejected by their patrons and subsequently installed in locations other than those for which they had been intended. These late 'expressionistic' works have generated more discussion than any other aspect of Mochi's career. One interpretation suggests that they are reversions to Florentine Mannerism, while another compares them to a trend in painting of the late 1630s and 1640s that emphasized an internalization of emotion and a dematerialization of form. Disappointed and frustrated by his situation, Mochi increasingly gained a reputation for being bitter and difficult to work with. A false report of his death in 1646 may indicate that he suffered from some lingering illness that may also have hampered his work.

BIBLIOGRAPHY
V. Martinelli: 'Contributi alla scultura del 600: Francesco Mochi a Piacenza', *Commentari*, ii (1951), pp. 224–35; iii (1952), pp. 35–43
R. Wittkower: *Art and Architecture in Italy, 1600–1750*, Pelican Hist. A. (Harmondsworth, 1958, 3/1973/R 1986), pp. 130–32
E. Borea: *Francesco Mochi*, I maestri della scultura, xxxxiii (Milan, 1966)
I. Lavin: 'Duquesnoy's *Nano di Crèqui* and Two Busts by Francesco Mochi', *A. Bull.*, lii (1970), pp. 132–49
G. Pantaleoni: *Il barocco del Mochi nei cavalli farnesiani* (Piacenza, 1975)
C. del Bravo and M. Bertoni: *Francesco Mochi* (Montevarchi, 1981) [sculptural details photographed by Bertoni]
M. Gregori and others: *Francesco Mochi, 1580–1654* (Florence, 1981) [best general source]
Francesco Mochi, 1580–1654, 2 vols (exh. cat., Montevarchi, Mus. A. Sacra, 1981); review by J. Montagu, *Burl. Mag.*, cxxv/964 (1983), pp. 432–3
J. Montagu: 'A Model by Francesco Mochi for the *Saint Veronica*', *Burl. Mag.*, cxxiv (1982), pp. 430–36
I bronzi di Piacenza rilievi e figure di Francesco Mochi dei monumenti equestri farnesiani (exh. cat., ed. P. C. Lavagetto; Bologna, Mus. Civ. Archeol., 1986)
I. Wardropper: 'A New Attribution to Francesco Mochi', *Mus. Stud.*, xvii (1991), pp. 102–19

Mochi, Orazio (*b* Florence, 1571; *d* Florence, 20 March 1625). Italian sculptor. He was long thought to have been the father of Francesco Mochi. This misconception lingers, even in many modern publications, and is doubtless due to the fact that he did indeed have a sculptor son called Francesco Mochi (1603–49), but—like his brother Stefano Mochi—he was a minor figure, and his work is virtually unknown. Mochi trained in the early 1590s with the Mannerist sculptor Giovanni Battista Caccini and later in that decade collaborated with him in Pisa on a set of bronze doors for the Porta Regia of the cathedral. Mochi's contribution included the large bronze panel of the *Incarnation of the Virgin* (*c.* 1598–9) and portions of the decorative frieze. After 1604 he worked in Florence, modelling small decorative sculptures in the grand-ducal workshop, the Opificio delle Pietre Dure. His best-known pieces are the exquisite inlaid stone relief of *Grand Duke Cosimo II de' Medici Praying* (*c.* 1610; Florence, Pitti) and the small witty bronze of *Saccomazzone Players* (*c.* 1621; Paris, J. Petit-Hory priv. col., see Brook, pp. 433–4), which the sculptor Romolo Ferrucci (*c.* 1550–1621) later enlarged to life-size for the Boboli Gardens. Mochi's works typically blend hints of Baroque naturalism with a Mannerist precocity that well suited the tastes of his patron. Like many of his contemporaries, he worked in a style that hovered between the late Mannerism of his teacher Caccini and the early Baroque brio of Francesco Mochi.

BIBLIOGRAPHY

A. Brook: *Il seicento fiorentino: Arte a Firenze da Ferdinando I a Cosimo III* (Florence, 1986), i, pp. 433–4; iii, pp. 128–9

BRIAN C. BARNES, LAURIE G. WINTERS

Mochlos. Tiny island off the north coast of Crete on the eastern edge of the Gulf of Mirabello. The island was almost certainly joined to the mainland by a narrow isthmus during Minoan times, when it was the site of an important settlement. The island was explored by the American archaeologist Richard Seager in 1908, but his discoveries have never been fully published. The settlement was apparently occupied from the Early to the Late Minoan period (for discussion of absolute dates *see* MINOAN, §I, 4), but most of the information available concerns the Early Minoan (EM) and Middle Minoan (MM) tombs that Seager excavated (see fig.). Some of these were simple pit graves or burials in clefts in the rock, but at least 20 were built tombs. Some were large and impressively constructed, with different types of stone apparently selected for different parts of the tomb structure. These variations in type of tombs may reflect differences of

Mochlos, anthropomorphic jug, EM III (Herakleion, Archaeological Museum)

social status among their occupants, particularly since the grave goods from the larger built tombs are more numerous and of better quality than those from the other burials.

Some of the finest gold jewellery of EM Crete came from the chamber tombs of Mochlos, including gold diadems with pendant ribbons and flowers, which must have been prestigious items to own (*see* MINOAN, §IX, 1(i)). Alongside them was a smaller quantity of bronze objects, mostly daggers but also toilet implements, as well as carved sealstones and a superb series of miniature vases made from a variety of coloured stones. Among the latter is a chlorite pyxis, the handle of its lid beautifully carved in the form of a sleeping dog (EM II; Herakleion, Archaeol. Mus.; *see* MINOAN, fig. 3). Certain objects from these tombs suggest that Mochlos was an important trading centre even in the Early Bronze Age. Metals used include Cycladic silver and lead, and probably imported copper too; some of the sealstones may be of ivory from the eastern Mediterranean. Connections with the East are also hinted at by the Egyptian shapes of some of the stone vases, and particularly by the discovery of a silver cylinder seal of Near Eastern type (EM II; Herakleion, Archaeol. Mus.). Mochlos may have been one of the most important settlements in pre-palatial Crete, and its location and the protected beaches on either side of its isthmus must have played a part in this. From the limited evidence available, however, its importance seems to have declined with the establishment of the palace-based civilization around MM IB.

BIBLIOGRAPHY

R. B. Seager: *Explorations on the Island of Mochlos* (Boston and New York, 1912)

C. Davaras: 'Early Minoan Jewellery from Mochlos', *Annu. Brit. Sch. Athens*, lxx (1975), pp. 101–14

J. Soles: *The Prepalatial Cemeteries at Mochlos and Gournia* (Princeton, 1990)

K. Branigan: 'Mochlos: An Early Aegean "Gateway Community"?', *Aegeum*, vii (1991), pp. 97–106

J. S. Soles: 'Mochlos', *The Aerial Atlas of Ancient Crete*, ed. J. W. Myers, E. E. Myers and G. Cadogan (Berkeley, 1992), pp. 184–91

KEITH BRANIGAN

Mock, Johann Samuel (*b* Saxony, *c.* 1687; *d* Warsaw, 4 Aug 1737). German painter, draughtsman and theatrical designer, active in Poland. Educated in the international artistic milieu of Dresden, he demonstrated decidedly French features in his work. He was employed at the court of the Saxon Electors, supplying cartoons for the manufacture of tapestries in Dresden and producing paintings, usually in gouache, depicting ceremonial occasions in the city and at court, for example the *Solemn Entrance* (1710; untraced) and the *Arrival of King Augustus III in Warsaw, 25 November 1734* (Dresden, Schloss Moritzburg). In *c.* 1723 he settled in Warsaw, where from at least 1724 he painted scenery for the royal theatre, exhibiting a developed decorative sense and a versatile facility. In 1731 he became court painter to Augustus II, King of Poland, and in 1735 'first painter' to Augustus III. A citizen of Old Warsaw from 1732, converted to Roman Catholicism, he amassed a considerable fortune from business schemes.

In Warsaw, as in Dresden, Mock painted scenes of major court ceremonies, designed architectural and decorative projects for such occasions and executed decorative symbolic scenes, such as allegories of the nations, including

Asia, Africa and America (1731; untraced). He also produced richly coloured harem fantasies in a Rococo *turquerie* genre (four, Warsaw, N. Mus.). Highly prolific and versatile, Mock also drew designs of townscapes and portraits for engraving, such as *The Palace and Halls of Marymont in Warsaw*, and painted altarpieces and portraits. Among his assistants and pupils were Johann-Benedikt Hofmann II (*d* 1777) and Łukasz Smuglewicz (1709–80).

BIBLIOGRAPHY

PSB

ANDRZEJ RYSZKIEWICZ

Mocker, Josef (*b* Citoliby, nr Louny, 22 Nov 1835; *d* Prague, 15 Jan 1899). Bohemian architect and conservator. After graduating from the Czech Technical University, Prague, he went to Vienna, where he studied at the Akademie der Bildenden Künste with Eduard Van der Nüll and August Siccard von Siccardsburg. Later he became a pupil of Friedrich von Schmidt and devoted himself to the study of Gothic art. Schmidt employed Mocker from 1864 to 1869 as a supervisor of his projects, and the two also collaborated from 1863 on the reconstruction and completion of the Stephansdom in Vienna. In 1869 Schmidt sent Mocker to Děčín in northern Bohemia, where he worked for the aristocratic Thun family until 1872. He also designed schools in the area, for example at Litoměřice and Mladá Boleslav, and a railway station in Lovosice.

A turning-point in Mocker's life came in 1873 with his appointment as master builder for the completion of the cathedral of St Vitus, Prague. This campaign, of great national significance, had been taken up from 1861 by Josef Ondřej Kranner (1801–71). Mocker added a completely new west façade with its towers and spires in a Late Gothic style. The completion of the building is an outstanding testament to 19th-century Gothic Revival architecture and embodied ideas about restoration that were highly influential for the treatment of medieval buildings. Mocker was responsible for numerous such restoration projects, for example in the church of St Henry and the church of St Peter (both 1875–9), both in Prague. His work on the Old Town Bridge Tower (1874–8), the Jindřišská Belfry (1886) and the Powder Gate (1882–9) in Prague was particularly sensitive. He was also responsible for much restoration outside Prague. Among such works are the cathedral of St Barbara (1884–1905), Kutná Hora, and the church of St Mary (1886), Pisek. In addition to working on religious buildings Mocker did impressive work on the castles of Křivoklát (from 1882), Karlstejn (1887–94) and Konopiště (1894). He also designed such Gothic Revival buildings as the church of St Ludmilla (1888–93) in Vinohrady and the church of St Procopius in Žižkov in eastern Prague.

Mocker is comparable to Eugène-Emmanuel Viollet-le-Duc both in the number and variety of buildings on which he worked. He was a considerable scholar of medieval architecture, especially in Bohemia, and in his writings he emphasized the importance of thorough initial investigation of primary sources before beginning restoration work. He always sought the purity of the essential medieval composition and advocated the necessity of reconstructing and completing old buildings in that style.

However, he was prone to a certain stylization and to inaccuracies caused by lack of time and money, and his research and study of the relevant material were not always comprehensive; indeed he approached medieval architecture very much from the standpoint of his own time.

BIBLIOGRAPHY
Z. Wirth: 'Sté výročí narození architekta Josefa Mockera' [The 100th anniversary of the birth of the architect Josef Mocker], *Umění*, ix (1935), pp. 185–8
P. Toman: *Slovník českých výtvarných umělců* [Dictionary of Czech artists] (Prague, 1947)
Y. Janková: 'Josef Mocker', *Archit. ČSR*, xliv/5 (1985), p. 228

YVONNE JANKOVÁ

Modanino, Paganino. *See* MAZZONI, GUIDO.

Model, architectural. *See* ARCHITECTURAL MODEL.

Model, artist's. Person subjecting his or her body to an artist's observation. A tradition of working from living models, begun in Classical times, was revived in Europe in the Renaissance and was an important feature of academic practice until the 20th century.

1. Classical and medieval. 2. 15th century. 3. 16th century. 4. 17th century. 5. 18th century. 6. 19th century. 7. 20th century.

1. CLASSICAL AND MEDIEVAL. The model, in the academic sense, was from its inception until the 19th century synonymous with the male figure. The earliest recorded reference to artists' models comes from Pliny the elder, who states that 'nude statues holding a spear' were 'modelled after young men in the gymnasium'. But earlier than this, Greek sculptors had drawn on empirical observation and imitation of the nude male, using the individual as the basis for the construction of an aesthetic ideal. Polykleitos, for example, whose system of proportions for the human figure was embodied in a treatise (the *Canon*) and a statue (the *Doryphoros*, late 5th century BC; copy, Naples, Mus. Archeol. N.), based his work exclusively on the male nude. There was, by way of contrast, no attempt to quantify the beauty of the female form. The female model was regarded, as the earliest references indicate, in a highly subjective manner. Commonly assumed to be the artist's mistress, she was regarded as a physical embodiment of his muse. Pliny, for example, relates how Apelles, painting *Aphrodite Rising from the Sea* (destr.), used as the model his mistress Campaspe, who had been presented to him by Alexander the Great. Pliny's story of Zeuxis choosing five individuals from among the women of Croton from whom to synthesize an idealized representation of the goddess Helena was to prove highly influential for later artistic theory.

Byzantine and medieval artists relied largely on a schematic approach to the human figure. The division of the body into a number of ready-made units and the use of model-books, containing sheets of figures deemed suitable for copying, made the individual human model superfluous. As late as *c.* 1390 Cennino Cennini conceived of the model largely as a figure to be copied from other artists. Yet *Il libro dell'arte* shows that he did perceive the need to confront nature, singling out the enormous contribution towards naturalism of Giotto's insistent observation 'from nature, of living people'. For Cennini the male figure continued to be the sole measure of human form. He deliberately omitted any discussion of women because, as he stated, 'there is not one of them perfectly proportioned'.

2. 15TH CENTURY. The tradition of spontaneous sketching from the living model has its roots in the practice of artists in and around Florence in the mid-15th century. Examples can be found from Domenico Veneziano (e.g. studies of two male nudes; Florence, Uffizi), Pisanello's drawings (mostly Paris, Louvre, Codex Villardi) and from the workshop of Botticelli (e.g. three studies of a male nude; Lille, Mus. B.-A.). Such drawings, which were all made from the male figure, coincide roughly with the publication of Alberti's theoretical findings on the human figure in *De pictura* (1435). Alberti expounded a system of human proportions based closely on measurements that he had taken personally from a selection of living models (he quotes as a precedent the practice of Zeuxis). Also in *De statua* (1440s) Alberti investigated the three-dimensionality of the human figure through Classical statuary; this line of inquiry was followed by Antonio Pollaiuolo, the first artist known to represent on one sheet the living model seen from the front, side and back (drawing, Paris, Louvre). The increasing availability in the 15th century of more versatile drawing materials, such as chalk and paper, made sketching of the posed model a readier option for artists, explored notably in the drawings of Luca Signorelli (e.g. *Nude Man Seen from Behind*; Bayonne, Mus. Bonnat; see fig. 1). The new materials enabled the artist to invest his subject with greater subtlety of tone and vigour of movement.

3. 16TH CENTURY. By the early 16th century the depiction of the posed male model was common in central Italy. The relation between sketch and finished composition was, however, often oblique. Preliminary compositional drawings, as one can determine from the practice of Raphael, were made using clothed studio assistants, or *garzoni*. These served for both male and female figures (a practice also apparent in the drawings of his master, Perugino). Detailed studies of the naked model were made only when details of the final composition had been evolved; for example Raphael's drawing of a naked youth in two poses (Vienna, Albertina) for the *Battle of Ostia* (*c.* 1515–17; Rome, Vatican, Stanza dell'Incendio). Despite the demise of the medieval 'model-book' tradition, artists continued to borrow poses made from each other in addition to working directly from the model. In this respect the most important source was undoubtedly Michelangelo's drawing of *Bathers* (destr. 17th century; copy by Bastiano da Sangallo, Norfolk, Holkham Hall) for the *Battle of Cascina* (*c.* 1515; destr.), described by Benvenuto Cellini as a 'drawing academy for the whole world'.

Throughout the Renaissance the male model remained the pre-eminent embodiment of physical beauty. While there is an early reference to a female model in an account-book of Lorenzo Lotto, Michelangelo, the greatest exponent of figure drawing, drew exclusively from the male and then, stated Vasari, only from the most beautiful specimens. Raphael, on the other hand, although he wished to draw the naked female model, admitted with reference

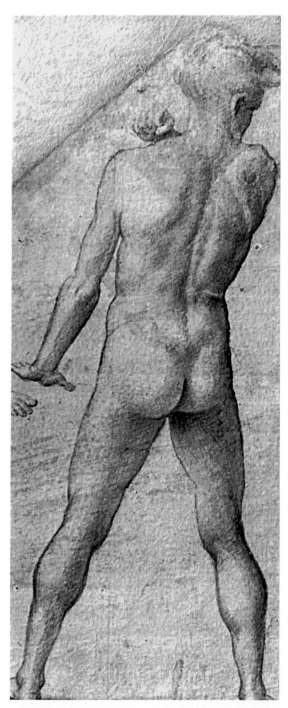

1. Artist's model drawn by Luca Signorelli: *Nude Man Seen from Behind*, black chalk heightened with ink on paper, 370×120 mm (Bayonne, Musée Bonnat)

to his *Galatea* (*c.* 1512; Rome, Villa Farnesina) that 'being deprived of beautiful women I make do with a certain idea which comes into my head'. Nonetheless drawings of the female model by Raphael do exist, for example *Girl Holding a Mirror* (*c.* 1517–18; Paris, Louvre), and slightly later Rosso Fiorentino drew a *Recumbent Nude Female Asleep* (*c.* 1530–40; London, BM). Far more informal than their male counterparts, these sketches may perhaps be the results of private study.

By the mid-16th century the all-pervasive influence of Classical statuary on the study of the model was tempered increasingly by the attention of artists to the actual mechanics of the human body through the study of anatomy. Foremost among these artist–anatomists were Leonardo da Vinci and Albrecht Dürer. Their work had profound implications for the study of the model. For Leonardo, knowledge of the way in which the body moved and functioned superseded the Platonic idea of the figure as a static object designed to impart aesthetic pleasure. Dürer went even further in some ways than Leonardo. For in basing his measurements of the body on a variety of human types, young and old, and of both sexes, he implicitly inaugurated the erosion of the ideal as an acceptable mean. Henceforth artists were free to draw their models from a far wider spectrum of humanity. Nor was there the automatic assumption that spiritual perfection need be reflected in physical perfection.

The other important development in the 16th century was the incorporation, for the first time, of the living model into a regulated academic system. Among the earliest 'academies' was that established in the Vatican in 1531 by Baccio Bandinelli, whose name is associated with the earliest examples (e.g. *Standing Male Nude in Profile*; London, BM) of the ACADEMY FIGURE; that is, a finished drawing of the model not intended for direct use in pictorial composition but purely as an instructive exercise in drawing. Studies such as these were the foundations on which future academic drawing was based. Although study of the model within the academy remained fitful during the 16th century, attempts to promote teaching of life drawing were made by Giorgio Vasari in Florence and by Federico Zuccaro in Rome. In the most important academy to emerge during the late 16th century, that established in the workshop of the Carracci *c.* 1585, the study of the cast and of the *écorché* figure was encouraged, but the main focus of attention was the informal, communal study of the living model—without, it should be noted, the restraints of an externally imposed hierarchy. Life drawings by the Carracci were engraved as early as 1608, for example in Odoardo Fialetti's primer *Il vero modo* (Venice, 1608). These prints were disseminated, as paradigms, across 17th-century Europe.

4. 17TH CENTURY. During the 17th century continual attempts were made to regulate the practice of drawing from the model. In 1596 the Accademia di S Luca in Rome sought a monopoly on the model by attempting to ban students from drawing the model in private. The same measure was tried by the Académie Royale in Paris in 1655, but again to little effect. Extensive study from the model continued in the studio and in small, privately sponsored academies. Although the study of the female model was still absent from public academies such as those of Rome and Paris, private academies, for example Venice and Stockholm, being free from the dictates of professional bodies, introduced the practice.

While classical notions of the role of the model in official academies hardened, notably in the absolutist Académie Royale established by the French government, strongly anti-academic attitudes towards the model also emerged. As early as the 1590s Caravaggio had deliberately spurned the ideal and selected models not for their physical beauty but for their potential to express emotion. As a result his version of *St Matthew and the Angel* (1602; ex-Berlin, Kaiser-Friedrich Mus., destr. 1945) was rejected by the episcopal authorities because St Matthew resembled too literally the dirty peasant whom Caravaggio had used as his model.

The growing awareness of the model as an individual and not a mere cipher for the artist's aims also emerged in the 17th century in the use of the model as a genre subject in its own right. In the previous century Vasari in his *Vite* had included a number of anecdotes about artists' relations with their models (including the notorious episode of Filippo Lippi's seduction of a novice in a convent while she posed for the Virgin). Henceforth artists began to depict themselves with their female models. Among the earliest such pictures are Rembrandt's *Self-portrait with a Model* (*c.* 1648; Glasgow, A.G. & Mus.) and Vermeer's *Allegory of Painting* (*c.* 1666–7; Vienna, Ksthist. Mus., see fig. 2). Rembrandt made intimate nude studies of his own wife, as did Rubens in his 1638 portrayal of *Hélène Fourment* (Vienna, Ksthist. Mus.). Such works implicitly sanctioned the notion that the relationship between male artist and female model was inevitably personal as well as professional.

5. 18TH CENTURY. Two distinct developments in the use of the model occurred during the 18th century. First, the number of academies where the living model could be studied expanded rapidly, especially after 1750. In 1720 there were only four public academies, in the modern sense of the word: in Paris, Rome, Bologna and Florence. By 1789 there were well over 100, although some—Madrid and Edinburgh, for example—did not allow the study of the living model, students being confined to copying casts of antique statues. Pevsner has noted how this growth coincided with the spread of Neo-classicism in Europe, with its attendant emphasis on the centrality of the human figure to artistic theory and practice. A prominent feature of the Neo-classical academy was its promotion of study of the living model in direct relation to the Antique. In most public academies, notably the Royal Academy of Arts in London, students had to prove their ability to draw from the cast before they were allowed to study the living model. Even then the living model was viewed in direct reference to the cast, set in attitudes reminiscent of recognizable Classical statues and posed under artificial light. Aside from London, where the female model was studied in subscription academies from at least the 1720s and in public from 1769, the life school continued to be the exclusive province of the male model.

Secondly, the teaching studio, or atelier, was established in France. The honour of inaugurating it was claimed by Joseph-Marie Vien, who kept a permanent 'stable' of models in his own studio for use by his pupils. The practice was continued in turn by Vien's pupil Jacques-Louis David and, in the 19th century, by David's own pupils, such as

2. Artist and model painted by Johannes Vermeer: *Allegory of Painting*, oil on canvas, 1.2×1.0 m, *c*. 1666–7 (Vienna, Kunsthistorisches Museum)

Antoine-Jean Gros and Ingres. The establishment of the atelier meant that artists could work in oils, under the close supervision of a practising artist, relating their studies of the model directly towards specific historical compositions. In France, by the early 19th century, finished oil studies of the model had reached a very high technical standard in the hands of such artists as Gericault and Isidore-Alexandre Pils. By comparison, the efforts of their English contemporary William Etty, who produced innumerable studies of both the male and female model, were not harnessed to any native tradition and lacked both discipline and direction.

6. 19TH CENTURY. In the 19th century the artist's model became associated, at least in the public mind, with the female rather than the male figure. There were a number of reasons for this. First, with the rise of the atelier artists were freer to study the model in their own studios. Secondly, by the end of the century the female model was in most places available for study in the academy. Thirdly, and most importantly, the social distinctions that had hitherto divided artist and model were broken down, and modelling to an artist became regarded as a means of climbing the social ladder. From the 1850s the Pre-Raphaelites, in a deliberate conflation of art and life, invested their female models with a mystique quite disproportionate to the mundane reality of the profession. This romantic vision of the model was later echoed in literature, most notably in George Du Maurier's novel *Trilby* (1894).

From the late 18th century artists had begun to depict the theme of the artist and his female model historically: Angelica Kauffman's *Zeuxis with the Women of Crotona* (*c.* 1778; Providence, RI, Annmary Brown Mem.), David's *Apelles and Campaspe* (1813; Lille, Mus. B.-A.). From the 1820s artists, most notably in France, began to produce narrative paintings, often based on Vasari, depicting Old Masters at work with models: Paul Delaroche's *Filippo Lippi Falling in Love with his Model* (Dijon, Mus. Magnin), for example, or Alexandre-Evariste Fragonard's *Raphael Adjusting the Pose of his Model for the Virgin and Child* (1820; Grasse, Mus. Fragonard; see fig. 3). By the mid-19th century, artists in England, notably William Powell Frith with his *Sleeping Model* (*c.* 1853; London, RA), began to conceive of the model as a subject for contemporary genre painting. The unfortunate, but inevitable, consequence was that this type of picture became increasingly voyeuristic, as for example Frank Hyde's pair the *Artist's Studio* and the *Eton Boy* (*c.* 1885; priv. col., sold London, Sothebys, 15 June 1988). In France a more pragmatic view of the model emerged: in 1854 Gustave Courbet included her as the central focus of his large autobiographical painting the *Artist's Studio* (Paris, Louvre), and later in the century the *Models* of Georges Seurat (small version, 1888; Munich, Alte Pin., on loan) are directly depicted in the studio. Degas's work, showing models in more casual domestic surroundings, in turn prompted anti-academic studies of the model by English artists, notably Walter Sickert and Philip Wilson Steer.

From the mid-19th century a number of artists, including Delacroix, Bonnard and Degas, worked from photographs of the model as well as directly from the life. The American artist Thomas Eakins was notably innovative, collaborating in 1884 with the photographer Eadweard Muybridge on photographs of the model that did much to further the understanding of movement in the human figure. Eakins was also outspoken during the 1880s in his championship of the study of the living nude model: he resigned his post at the Pennsylvania Academy of the Fine Arts in 1886 owing to official opposition to the model. His stance is encapsulated in his manifesto-like painting *William Rush Carving his Allegorical Figure of the Schuylkill River* (1877; Philadelphia, PA, Mus. F.A.).

3. Artist and model painted by Alexandre Evariste Fragonard: *Raphael Adjusting the Pose of his Model for the Virgin and Child*, oil on canvas, 1820 (Grasse, Musée Fragonard)

7. 20TH CENTURY. The role of the professional artist's model in the 20th century was inevitably, especially in mid-century, negated by the dominance of self-referential and non-representational art. A fascination with stylized forms, whether taken from primitive art or from the imagination, pushed the model to a peripheral position. By the late 1940s the very existence of the life class within the academy had become threatened with extinction, as Quentin Crisp whimsically observed in his memoirs of life as a model, *The Naked Civil Servant* (London, 1977). The study of the model continued to hold its place in the curriculum at certain art schools, in England notably at the Slade School of Art in London, where, under the guidance of William Coldstream, a more objective approach to the model was fostered, finding expression in the work of such artists as Euan Uglow. By the 1950s more radical uses were being made of the model, for instance the French artist Yves Klein's practice of painting the body of the female model (before an audience), which was then pressed against the canvas. At the same time artists as diverse as Picasso (the *Artist and Model*; Paris, Pompidou), David Hockney (*Model with Unfinished Self-portrait* (1977)), Philip Pearlstein and Lucian Freud continued to find inspiration through study of the model.

BIBLIOGRAPHY

Pliny the Elder: *Natural History*
N. Pevsner: *Academies of Art, Past and Present* (Cambridge, 1940)
F. Borzello: *The Artist's Model* (London, 1982)
A. W. A. Boschloo and others, eds: 'Academies of Art between Renaissance and Romanticism', *Leids Ksthist. Jb.*, v–vi (1986–7)
F. Borel: *The Seduction of Venus: Artists and Models* (Geneva, 1990)
The Artist's Model: Its Role in British Art from Lely to Etty (exh. cat. by I. Bignamini and M. Postle, U. Nottingham A.G.; London, Kenwood House; 1991)

MARTIN POSTLE

Model, Lisette [née Seybert, Elise Felice Amélie] (*b* Vienna, 10 Nov 1906; *d* New York, 30 March 1983). American photographer of Austrian birth. A school-friend of Gertrude Schœnberg, she studied music first with her father Arnold Schœnberg, before continuing her studies in Paris. She was a self-taught photographer and tried to find ways of working in photography, training as a technician in a photographic laboratory. In 1938 she settled in New York. Two years later the photographer Ralph Steiner (1899–1986) published her series of photographs, *Promenade des Anglais*, which she had taken in Nice in 1937. The series was characteristic of her work in revealing her obvious love of people, seen for example in *Promenade des Anglais* (1937; see Abbott, p. 22), which depicts a rotund woman in a large sunhat, sitting precariously on a bench. The photographers Alexey Brodovitch (1898–1971) and Beaumont Newhall (*b* 1908) were impressed by her work.

After 1941 Model worked as a freelance photographer for the magazines *PM* and *Harper's Bazaar*, and later for *Look* and *Ladies Home Journal*. She exhibited several times in the Museum of Modern Art, including in the *Family of Man* exhibition, organized by Steichen in 1955. Her photographic report on delinquent black children (1942) attracted much attention, as did her report for *Paris Match*, 'Pourquoi la France a été vaincue' (1941). Among Model's favourite themes were shop-window reflections, jazz and legs, captured in *Fifth Avenue* (1950s; see Abbott, p. 38). In the 1950s she taught photography at the New York School for Social Research. She won a Guggenheim Scholarship in 1966, and from 1974 to 1975 she taught at the San Francisco Institute and the University of California.

PHOTOGRAPHIC PUBLICATIONS

Lisette Model: Portfolio (Washington, DC, 1976)
Lisette Model, preface B. Abbott (New York, 1979)

BIBLIOGRAPHY

The Family of Man (exh. cat., ed. E. Steichen; New York, MOMA, 1955)
Camera, lvi/12 (1977) [issue devoted to Model]
Lisette Model (exh. cat., Essen, Mus. Flkwang, 1982)

REINHOLD MISSELBECK

Model book. *See under* PATTERN BOOK.

Modello [It.: 'model']. Term used to refer to the comparatively highly finished drawings or three-dimensional models made by an artist before executing the final work. The drawn modelli were most frequently created for paintings but were also employed for sculptures, architectural projects and decorative artworks. Three-dimensional modelli were used almost exclusively for sculptures. Historically, the treatment of the term is complex and varied. The earliest editions (1612, 1623 and 1691) of the dictionaries compiled by the Tuscan Accademia della Crusca invoke its derivation from the Latin *modulus* or *typus*: 'a model, type or example for emulation or imitation'. Modelli fulfilled various functions: within the workshop or studio they enabled an artist to delegate some or most of the final execution to assistants, while outside this they might be presented to a patron to win or confirm a commission. In sculpture the modello was preceded by less finished versions called either models, *bozzetti* or maquettes, and these earlier stages are also discussed here. For the other preliminary stages in painting *see* CARTOON; DRAWING, §II; OIL SKETCH; and PRESENTATION DRAWING.

I. Drawn. II. Sculpted.

I. Drawn.

As generally used in the context of draughtsmanship, modello designates a drawing on paper or parchment that demonstrates clearly and in detail the appearance of a composition, figure or motif prior to its execution in another medium. Besides the cognates for 'model', the following less precise terms are used as equivalents in the literature on non-Italian drawings: 'design' (Eng.); '*étude*' (Fr.); '*Entwurf*' or '*Werkzeichnung*' (Ger.); and '*diseño*', or '*estudio*' (Sp.). Such demonstration drawings are usually relatively highly finished and smaller in scale than the final work. Practices in preparing modelli, however, varied greatly. The use of the term in Italian primary sources from the early 14th century to the late 18th century poses substantial problems of interpretation. These sources do, however, establish that such drawings served both a creative, practical function within the artist's workshop or studio and a contractual function between artist and patron. In the latter sense the terms presentation drawing and contract drawing are sometimes used to denote a modello.

A reconstruction of the modello as a drawing type remains problematic for two reasons. First, from the earliest use of the term modello in 14th-century documents the word designated both a preliminary drawing on paper and, more frequently, a preliminary three-dimensional model. The two meanings were, however, closely allied within the Tuscan tradition of design. For example, an important element of 15th- and 16th-century design practice consisted of drawing after sculptural models representing the human figure (modelli), usually fashioned of wax or clay. These drawings after models allowed the artist to study foreshortening, chiaroscuro, disposition of draperies and counterpoints of pose. In his introduction to the *Vite*, Vasari included this practice in a sequence of steps leading to the execution of a composition, modelli (models) being the only step that was not a type of drawing: 1) *schizzi* (sketches); 2) *disegni* (drawings); 3) *modelli* (models); and 4) *cartoni* (cartoons). Second, the term modello was understood and used in its broadest meaning: an object serving as an example, model or type for work to be carried out. In this general sense, a drawing, a three-dimensional representation, or even a painting, could serve as a preliminary model. Pozzo (1693–1700), for example, referred to the production of a preliminary, painted model (*modello colorito*) before the painting of a full-scale fresco. In Book III of *De pictura* (1435), Alberti recommended the use of modelli drawn on paper, scaled with parallels (e.g. squared proportionally), as a necessary step in designing a figural composition. Yet Vasari, in his introduction to the *Vite*, a seminal text for the formation of a theory and vocabulary of *disegno* (drawing and design), did not give the term modello as denoting a drawing. He used the term '*disegni*' to refer to the carefully rendered compositional drawings that we would designate today as modelli. Other sources follow Vasari in this respect, including Gilio (1564), Borghini (1584), Armenini (1586–7) and Baldinucci (1681), who also did not use the term modello as designating a drawing. This evidence suggests that drawings functioning as modelli, as demonstrations of works to be carried out, whether done for use in the design process or for use by the patron, were not recognized as a specific, formal drawing type. Thus, the creative, practical and contractual functions of the drawings that are generally called modelli appear ambiguous only if an overly restrictive system of classification is used.

From the 1420s artists in Italy prepared compositions in an increasingly systematic fashion by drawing on paper, rather than directly on the final working surface as in medieval practice, and by following distinct steps. The modello thus began to play a significant role, particularly in the central Italian tradition of design. As defined by this tradition, and as adopted by non-Italian artists well into the period of the Beaux-Arts ACADEMY in the 19th century, the modello was a form of summary, rather than an exploratory drawing type: after developing a design in a sequence of rapid figural or compositional sketches, as well as in more elaborate studies after the live model, the artist or his assistants attempted to synthesize this research in a carefully rendered, small-scale drawing—the modello. Although surviving modelli from the 15th to the 19th century exemplify a rich diversity of drawing media and techniques, they are usually characterized by a precise, often emphatic disposition of both outline and CHIARO-SCURO and incorporate a reference to the size of the final work in the form of squaring grids, measurements or ruled scales. During the 15th century linear drawing media predominated: METALPOINT on prepared paper, as well as pen and ink. In the 16th and 17th centuries artists favoured more painterly techniques: black or red chalk, sometimes with STUMPING to obtain even transitions of tone; as well as ink, wash, GOUACHE, or, more rarely, watercolour, applied with a brush. From the late 18th century GRAPHITE was also commonly employed.

The modello often served as the final drawing from which the design was enlarged to its full scale on the working surface and subsequently executed. To facilitate this enlargement, the modello was usually overlaid with a grid of squares proportional to a grid of squares constructed on the working surface. Such a grid is visible on the head and body of the Virgin in Masaccio's fresco of the *Trinity* (c. 1425–7; Florence, S Maria Novella). It suggests that Masaccio transferred the design directly on to the fresco surface from a smaller-scale drawing, a modello, of the Virgin. Although the drawing no longer survives, this fresco is recognized as the earliest extant application of the method. The earliest surviving example of such a modello is Paolo Uccello's coloured drawing (Florence, Uffizi, 31 F) for the fresco commemorating Sir John Hawkwood (1436; Florence Cathedral). Uccello's

1. Modello by Raphael for the *Entombment*, pen and brown ink with red and black chalk, pricked, 288×298 mm, c. 1506–7 (Florence, Galleria degli Uffizi)

modello is in metalpoint on green prepared paper, with purple wash and highlights in white gouache. It is indented with a grid of squares, and the few incised lines on the fresco surface itself—notably the vertical centering line—correspond to this grid.

From shortly before the mid-15th century the modello more frequently preceded the elaboration of a cartoon, or full-scale drawing on paper, and often both were squared proportionally. An unusually complete sequence of preliminary drawings by Raphael survives for the *Entombment* (1507; Rome, Gal. Borghese), for the Baglione Chapel in S Francesco, Perugia. Raphael's large modello (Florence, Uffizi, 538 E; see fig. 1), precisely drawn and crosshatched in pen and brown ink over an UNDERDRAWING in black chalk, exhibits two squaring grids: one in red chalk under the drawing, another in pen and brown ink on top of it. The grid in red chalk helped the artist to correlate the differing scales of the figural and compositional studies that preceded the modello, while that in pen and brown ink served as a more accurate reference in enlarging the scale of the modello to that of the cartoon. From the late 15th century, with the increased use of the oil medium, which permitted a more direct manner of painting, artists often omitted full-scale cartoons. In such cases the modello, squared for proportional enlargement, served to transfer the design directly on to the final working surface.

The presence of squaring in countless compositional drawings readily identifies them as modelli fulfilling a design function in the workshop or studio. Italian examples include drawings by Pontormo (c. 1525–8; e.g. Oxford, Christ Church Pict. Gal., 1336) for the *Lamentation* in S Felicità, Florence, by Giorgio Vasari (c. 1558–62; Paris, Louvre, 2175) for the ceiling of the Sala di Papa Leone X in the Palazzo Vecchio, Florence, and by Pietro Testa (c. 1645–6; Darmstadt, Hess. Landesmus., AE 1447) for the *Vision of St Angelo Carmelitano* in S Martino ai Monti, Rome. Like many central European artists of his generation, Joseph Heintz (i) followed Italian practice in his modello (*c.* 1596–1600; Vaduz, Samml. Liechtenstein) for a *Sacra Conversazione with SS Catherine and Barbara*. The handling of the media—pen and brown ink with brush and grey wash over traces of black chalk and white heightening—is intended to emphasize chiaroscuro and clarity of outline. Progressive draughtsmen working in Spain at this time also derived much of their practice from Italy. Two modelli by Vicente Carducho prepared between 1626 and 1632 for a cycle of paintings originally for the charterhouse of Paular, the *Death of the Venerable Odo of Novara* (Madrid, Rodriguez Moñino col.) and the *Apparition of the Virgin to a Carthusian* (Madrid, Bib. N., B. 27) have extensive descriptions of their unusual iconography written in the hand of the artist. Drawn in pen and brown ink with brush and brown wash over black chalk, and heightened with white on grey-green paper, these highly finished drawings are squared, and the squares along the borders of the composition bear consecutive numbers. The compositions of the final paintings (Burgos, Charterhouse of Miraflores; Madrid, Prado) differ from those in the two modelli in only minor details. Examples from the French academic tradition in the 17th century include Nicolas Poussin's squared modello (London, BM, Sloane 5237–147; see fig. 2), for a *Bacchanalian Revel before a Term of Pan* (*c.* 1637–9; London, N.G.), which is among his rare surviving drawings squared for transfer to the

canvas; Charles Le Brun's monumental modello of the *Death of Darius* (*c.* 1667; Paris, Louvre, 27 657), for a cycle of scenes from the life of Alexander the Great, which was never realized; and Pierre Mignard I's *Parnassus* (Béziers, Mus. B.-A.) for a painting in the Galerie d'Apollon (1677–8) in the château of Saint-Cloud (destr. 1870). Raphael frequently prepared his narrative compositions by drawing all the figures nude, a practice followed by François-André Vincent in one of his squared modelli (Montpellier, Mus. Atger, 288) for the painting of *Zeuxis Choosing his Model* (1789; Paris, Louvre). In 19th-century France the squared modelli by Jean-Auguste-Dominique Ingres and his contemporaries conclude this tradition. Carefully drawn in ink, watercolour and graphite, one of Ingres's early modelli (Montauban, priv. col.) for the *Dream of Ossian* (1813; Montauban, Mus. Ingres) evokes the orderly progression of design first fully documented in Raphael's mature projects, such as the Borghese *Entombment*.

Detailed modelli were indispensible when the execution of the composition was to be done by an artist other than the designer. In 1502–3 Raphael drew the highly finished, squared modello of the *Departure of Aeneas Silvius Piccolomini to the Council of Basle* (Florence, Uffizi, 520 E) for Bernardino Pinturicchio to fresco in the Piccolomini Library of Siena Cathedral. Drawn in an almost painterly technique with pen and brown ink, brush and brown washes, and white heightening over black chalk, Raphael's large modello also includes detailed, autograph notes

2. Modello by Nicolas Poussin for the *Bacchanalian Revel before a Term of Pan*, 234×341 mm, *c.* 1635 (London, British Museum)

regarding the iconography of the scene. The division of labour in the designing and painting of the Piccolomini programme is documented in the contract (1502) and in Vasari's biographies of both artists. For complex sculptural and architectural projects, designers, or professional draughtsmen hired specifically for this purpose, often drafted carefully rendered modelli in addition to fashioning three-dimensional models, also termed modelli (*see* §II below). Examples of drawn modelli for sculpture include tomb designs attributed to Andrea Sansovino and Agostino Busti (London, V&A, 8621, 2260, 2315). Examples of drawn architecture modelli are the façade designs for S Lorenzo, Florence, by Giuliano da Sangallo (Florence, Uffizi, 276 A, 278 A, 281 A) and possibly by Michelangelo (Florence, Casa Buonarroti, 45 A). A detailed modello often further enabled the delegation of the execution of a project, particularly in the decorative arts. Inscriptions on Cristoforo Sorte's modello (London, V&A, E.509–1937) for the ceiling of the Sala del Senato in the Doge's Palace, Venice, confirm the craftsmen's commitment to follow Sorte's designs. The long inscription on the bottom of the architect Juan Gómez de Mora's modello (1614; Madrid, Bib. N., B 365) for the main retable in the church of the monastery of Our Lady, Guadalupe, indicates that it served a contractual purpose: 'His Majesty therefore commands that nothing herein be altered without his personal sanction'. Elaborately rendered in pen and ink with brush and washes over black chalk, the drawing itself is referred to in the inscription as the '*traça* (design)'. The style of ornamentation for the framing members, as well as the various materials to be employed for the carving, are specified; Vicente Carducho and Eugenio Cajés are named as the painters of the altarpiece panel. Three vigorously drawn, squared modelli by Peter Paul Rubens survive for the marble sculptures for the central portal of the Jesuit church of St Carolus Borromeus in Antwerp (1615–18): a CARTOUCHE supported by cherubs (London, BM, Oo.9–28; see fig. 3) crowns an arch, while pendant angels blowing trumpets occupy spandrels (New York, Pierpont Morgan Lib., I.233 and 1957.I). The sculptor of Rubens's designs was most likely Hans van Mildert, who is repeatedly mentioned in the account-books of St Carolus Borromeus; members of the de Nole family may also have worked on the commission—Jean (*d* 1624), Robert (*d* 1636) and Andris (1598–1639). Among the modelli by Sir James Thornhill for the decoration of James Bateman's house in London, that for the stained-glass windows (1719; Providence, RI Sch. Des., Mus. A.) bears the name of the patron, whose approval was essential, and also that of the painter, Francis Price (*fl* 1734–7?; *d* 1753), who was to execute the work along with specific instructions. A nearly contemporary modello (Berlin, Kstbib., 825) attributed to Pierre Legros (ii) for a tomb of a member of the French royal family provides scales, measurements and iconographic notes in both Italian and French for accurate communication. Edward Burne-Jones's squared modello for a tile design portrays the *Marriage at Cana* in green chalk over graphite (1886; Birmingham, Mus. & A.G.). The instruction he inscribed on the modello, 'all to be richly covered with grass & flowers', was for the ceramicist who would paint the tile.

3. Modello by Peter Paul Rubens for marble sculpture on the Jesuit church of St Carolus Borromeus, Antwerp, 1615–18 (London, British Museum)

A division of labour between design and execution was typical of printmaking. Modelli drawn for this purpose are full scale and show the indented outlines left by the stylus used to transfer the image to the plate, with the composition usually in reverse. Dirck Barendsz.'s highly finished modello of *Mankind Awaiting the Last Judgement* (London, V&A, Dyce 442) was engraved by Jan Sadeler (i). Rubens's *Adoration of the Magi* (New York, Pierpont Morgan Lib., I.230) is among a number of extant modelli for the engraved illustrations of the *Breviarium Romanum* (1614; Antwerp), published by Balthasar Moretus. Rubens delegated much of the drawing for reproductive engraving; the modello for the *Flight into Egypt* (London, BM, Gg.2–234), based on his painting (1614; Kassel, Schloss Wilhelmshöhe, Gemäldegal. Alte Meister), was drawn and used expressly for the engraving by Marinus Robyn van der Goes. The basic drawing in black chalk was done by a pupil; Rubens reworked the drawing with chalk, as well as grey washes.

The drawing of a modello was laborious and required a skill for synthesis rather than invention. Although Raphael produced his own modelli early in his career (e.g. Florence, Uffizi, 538 E), after *c.* 1515 he often delegated this task to his workshop assistants (e.g. Paris, Louvre, 3884; Oxford, Ashmolean, P II 574; Windsor Castle, Royal Lib., RL 12739; London, BM, 1900–6-11–2). At times Michelangelo may also have entrusted to assistants the drafting of elaborately constructed and rendered modelli for his

4. Modello for the frieze of a palace vestibule, pen and watercolour over black chalk, 215×387 mm, central Italian (?Roman), early 17th century (Oxford, Christ Church Picture Gallery)

sculptural and architectural projects (e.g. Paris, Louvre, 837, 838; Florence, Casa Buonarroti, 45 A).

Although they were not often used strictly as contractual drawings, modelli enabled the patron to approve, criticize or reject an artist's design. Hans Holbein the younger's modello (Basle, Kstmus., 1662.31) for the group portrait of the *Family of Sir Thomas More* (*c*. 1527–8; destr.) offers unusual documentation in this respect. Drawn with precise outlines in pen and black ink over black chalk, the large Basle modello also bears inscriptions and sketchily drawn suggestions for changes in the details of the composition. These were added in brown ink, apparently in Holbein's own hand (the sitters' names and ages are a later insertion). For instance, next to the kneeling figure of More's wife a note states '*Dise soll sitze[n]*' ('she must sit'), and a small ape climbing her skirt is sketched. The autograph modifications to the Basle modello are reflected in a copy of Holbein's painting by Rowland Lockey (*c*. 1530; Nostell Priory, W. Yorks). The modello was sent by the More family to Desiderius Erasmus, and his two letters of acknowledgement discuss the drawing in great detail.

A book of architectural designs by Nanni di Baccio Bigi (New York, Pierpont Morgan Lib., MA 1346 [32]), Michelangelo's rival, includes plans drawn in pen and brown ink for two storeys of a house. The descriptive inscriptions explicitly designate the plans as 'modelli'. The plans are signed and approved by the two men who had apparently commissioned the house. Similarly, the modello signed by Eugenio Cajés for the decoration of a vault (1621; Madrid, Archv Hist. N.) also bears the signature of the patron and his notes on the subject-matter of the scenes to be painted. A modello by Jacob Jordaens for an unidentified architectural project (*c*. 1630–35; Amsterdam, Rijksmus., A. 1926) offers alternative designs for the pediment: one plainly curved with a sphinx; one scrolled

with a *putto*. Such motifs were left to the patron's choice. Finally, a detailed list of modifications dictated by the patron appears on the *verso* of Marco Benefial's modello (Berlin, Kupferstichkab., KdZ 15845) for an altarpiece portraying the *Assumption of the Virgin with SS Terentius and Mustiola* in Pesaro Cathedral.

Modelli were crucial in the commissioning of works of art, for an attractively finished drawing could help procure a commission from a private patron or a public competition. In his life of Antonio del Pollaiuolo (1568), Vasari mentioned his design and model (*disegno e modello*) for an equestrian statue of Francesco Sforza, Duke of Milan. He noted that there were two versions of the design: these have been identified with two highly finished drawings in pen and ink with brush and wash over black chalk (New York, Met., Robert Lehman Col.; Munich, Staatl. Graph. Samml., 1908:168). Detailed inscriptions, written in a semi-literate style, on a 17th-century central Italian (?Roman) design for the frieze of a palace vestibule (Oxford, Christ Church, 0958; see fig. 4) make explicit the artist's eagerness to please his patron: 'This is the idea for the entrance hall of the castle, but other [sketches] have been made. Your Excellency, choose which you like best . . . By taking the trouble, here we will duplicate your plinths in a beautiful manner . . .'. Some of Giulio Romano's modelli for lavishly ornamented tableware exhibit autograph inscriptions with the names of his Mantuan patrons (London, V&A, E.5129–1910, E.5131–1910). Vasari's account of the competition held in 1564 for the decoration of the Scuola Grande di S Rocco, Venice, is also significant. While Giuseppe Salviati, Federico Zuccaro and Paolo Veronese prepared the standard demonstration drawings, Jacopo Tintoretto won over the judges by producing the completed painting as his demonstration piece. Tintoretto's justification was that 'designs (disegni) and models (modelli) should be such that they do not deceive'.

BIBLIOGRAPHY

EARLY SOURCES

L. B. Alberti: *De pictura* (MS. 1435); ed. C. Grayson, Biblioteca degli scrittori d'Italia degli editori Laterza (Rome and Bari, 1975), pp. 102–3; Eng. trans. by C. Grayson (London, 1972)

G. Vasari: *Vite* (1550, rev. 2/1568); ed. G. Milanesi (1878–85), iii, p. 525; vi/2, pp. 592–4

——: *Vite* (1550, rev. 2/1568); ed. R. Bettarini, annotated by P. Barocchi (Florence, 1966–87), i, pp. 117–24; iii, pp. 507, 572–3; iv, p. 159

G. A. Gilio: *Due dialoghi: Degli errori e degli abusi de' pittori circa l'istoria* (Camerino, 1564)

R. Borghini: *Il riposo* (Florence, 1584), pp. 138–49

G. B. Armenini: *De' veri precetti della pittura, libri tre* (Ravenna, 1586–7/R New York, 1971), pp. 89–99; Eng. trans. by E. Olszewski (New York, 1977)

Vocabolario degli accademici della Crusca (Florence, 1612; rev. 5/1910), x, pp. 398–400

F. Baldinucci: *Vocabolario toscano dell'arte del disegno* (Florence, 1681/R Florence, 1975), pp. 99–100

A. Pozzo: 'Breve instruttione per dipingere a fresco', *Perspectiva pictorum et architectorum* (Rome, 1693–1700, rev. 1717), ii, §§5–6

GENERAL

N. Tommaseo: *Dizionario della lingua italiana* (Turin, 1915), v, pp. 314–15

E. Borsook: *The Mural Painters of Tuscany* (London, 1960, rev. Oxford, 2/1980), pp. xlvi, 59–63, 77–9

S. Battaglia: *Grande dizionario della lingua italiana* (Turin, 1978), x, pp. 644–8

M. Hollingsworth: 'The Architect in Fifteenth-century Florence', *A. Hist.*, vii (1984), pp. 385–410

DRAWINGS

J. Meder: *Die Handzeichnung* (Vienna, 1919); Eng. trans. and rev. by W. Ames as *The Mastery of Drawing*, 2 vols (New York, 1978), i, pp. 236–57, 286–8, 528 ('contract drawing'), 529 ('modello')

H. Tietze and E. Tietze-Conrat: *The Drawings of the Venetian Painters in the 15th and 16th Centuries*, i (New York, 1944), pp. 12–17

B. Degenhart and A. Schmitt: *Corpus der italienischen Zeichnungen, 1300–1450: Teil I. Süd- und Mittelitalien* (Berlin, 1968), I/i, pp. xiii–li [esp. pp.xxi (note 41), xxii–xl]; I/ii, pp. 383–6 (no. 302), p. 516 [the role of modelli in early It. drg practice; Paolo Uccello's Uffizi modello; doc. regarding Alesso Baldovinetti's modelli]

E. Berckenhagen: *Die französischen Zeichnungen der Kunstbibliothek Berlin: Kritischer Katalog*, W. Berlin, Kstbib. & Mus. (Berlin, 1970), pp. 156–7 (no. 825)

J. Harris: *A Catalogue of British Drawings for Architecture, Decoration, Sculpture and Landscape Gardening, 1550–1900, in American Collections* (Upper Saddle River, NJ, 1971), pp. 232–61

C. Monbeig Goguel: *Vasari et son temps: Inventaire général des dessins italiens. I. Maîtres toscans nés après 1500, morts avant 1600*, Paris, Louvre, Cab. Dessins cat. (Paris, 1972), pp. 162–4 (no. 211)

J. Byam-Shaw: *Drawings by Old Masters at Christ Church, Oxford*, i (Oxford, 1976), pp. 65, 165–6 (nos 119, 594)

D. Angulo and A. Pérez Sánchez: *A Corpus of Spanish Drawings: Madrid, 1600–1650* ii (London, 1977), pp. 27, 34, 50 (nos 107, 156, 274)

P. Dreyer: *Kupferstichkabinett Berlin: Italienische Zeichnungen* (Stuttgart and Zurich, 1979), pp. 34–8

J. Leymarie, G. Monnier and B. Rose: *Drawing: History of an Art* (Geneva and New York, 1979), pp. 102–3

P. Ward-Jackson: *Victoria and Albert Museum Catalogues: Italian Drawings. Volume One: 14th–16th Century*, (London, 1979), pp. 30–32, 78–9, 146–8, 153–4 (nos 28, 159–60, 311–12, 321)

M. Roland Michel: *Die französische Zeichnung im 18. Jahrhundert* (Munich, 1987), pp. 129–36

EXHIBITION CATALOGUES

Ingres (exh. cat. by M. Serullaz and others, Paris, Petit Pal., 1967–8), p. 94 (no. 62)

Drawing: Technique and Purpose (exh. cat. by S. Lambert, London, V&A, 1981)

Drawings by Raphael from the Royal Library, the Ashmolean Museum, the British Museum, Chatsworth and other English Collections (exh. cat. by

J. A. Gere and N. Turner, London, BM, 1983), pp. 239–40, 242 (nos 191–2, 194)

Reading Drawings: An Introduction to Looking at Drawings (exh. cat. by S. Lambert, New York, Drg Cent., 1984)

Hans Holbein d. J.: Zeichnungen aus dem Kupferstichkabinett der Öffentlichen Kunstsammlung Basel (exh. cat. by C. Müller, Basle, Öff. Kstamml., 1988), pp. 208–12 (no. 65)

Michelangelo Architect: The Façade of San Lorenzo and the Drum and Dome of St Peter's (exh. cat. by H. Millon and C. Smyth, Washington, DC, N.G.A., 1988), pp. 3–31, 79–83

Pietro Testa, 1612–1650: Prints and Drawings (exh. cat. by E. Cropper, Philadelphia, PA, Mus. A., 1988), pp. 193–7 (no. 90)

Prag um 1600: Kunst und Kultur am Hofe Kaiser Rudolf II (exh. cat., Vienna, Ksthist. Mus., 1988), p. 154 (no. 619)

Dessins français du XVIIe siècle dans les collections publiques françaises (exh. cat., Paris, Louvre, 1993), pp. 174–5 (no. 84)

MONOGRAPHS

W. Friedlaender and A. Blunt, eds: *The Drawings of Nicolas Poussin* (London, 1953), v, p. 27 (no. 198)

J. Held: *Rubens: Selected Drawings, with an Introduction and a Critical Catalogue*, 2 vols (Oxford, 1959, rev. 2/1986), i, pp. 16–41, 100, 117–19 (nos 77, 125–7)

K. Oberhuber: *Raphaels Zeichnungen: Abt. IX. Entwürfe zu Werken Raphaels und seiner Schule im Vatikan 1511/12 bis 1520* (Berlin, 1972), pp. 20–24, 139–40, 162–4, 166–7, 174 (nos 452, 457, 459b, 469)

R. A. d'Hulst: *Jordaens Drawings*, i (Brussels, 1974), pp. 209–10 (no. A 114)

F. Ames-Lewis: *The Draftsman Raphael* (New Haven and London, 1986), pp. 1–11, 39–59, 73–100, 126–36

M. Hirst: *Michelangelo and his Drawings* (New Haven and London, 1988), pp. 79–90; review by C. Bambach Cappel in *A. Bull.*, lxxii (1990), pp. 493–8; see also M. Hirst in *A. Bull.*, lxxiv (1992), p. 172 and C. Bambach Cappel in *A. Bull.*, lxxiv (1992), pp. 172–3

M. Gareau: *Charles Le Brun: Premier Peintre du roi Louis XIV* (Paris, 1992), pp. 122–3

SPECIALIST STUDIES

A. Grote: *Das Dombau-amt in Florenz, 1285–1370: Studien zur Geschichte der Opera di Santa Reparata* (Munich, 1960), pp. 113–19 [doc. mentioning modelli]

K. Oberhuber: 'Vorzeichnungen zu Raffaels Transfiguration', *Jb. Berlin. Mus.*, iv (1962), pp. 116–49

L. Shelby: 'The Role of the Master Mason in Mediaeval English Building', *Speculum*, xxxix/3 (1964), pp. 387–403

J. Shearman: 'Raphael's Unexecuted Projects for the Stanze', *Walter Friedlaender zum 90. Geburtstag* (Berlin, 1965), pp. 158–80

M. Fitzsimmons: 'Purpose and Quality in Architectural Drawings', *Drawing*, iv/3 (1982), pp. 55–9

F. Toker: 'Gothic Architecture by Remote Control: An Illustrated Building Contract of 1340', *A. Bull.*, lxvii (1985), pp. 67–95

W. Wallace: 'Two Presentation Drawings for Michelangelo's Medici Chapel', *Master Drgs*, xxv (1987), pp. 242–60

B. Barnes: 'A Lost *Modello* for Michelangelo's *Last Judgment*', *Master Drgs*, xxvi (1988), pp. 239–48

CARMEN BAMBACH CAPPEL

II. Sculpted.

The laborious techniques involved in sculpture, in particular when hewing large images out of stone or wood, and the difficulty of visualizing anything in three dimensions has led to the widespread use among sculptors of models in easily worked and cheap materials, on a small scale or at full size, before setting to work on the final block of material. It is, however, far from certain when the practice of making such models began; the relatively simple forms and straightforward poses of Egyptian (*see* EGYPT, ANCIENT, §VII, 1) or Archaic Greek statues may be visualized without great difficulty and were probably achieved by drawing the desired outlines from different viewpoints on the faces of a block. Similar, small-scale figures were modelled in clay or carved out of wood as votive offerings in these civilizations and might have served as reference models, but there is no evidence of the deliberate use of preliminary modelli. It is thought that artists generally carved directly into the block, a technique revived in the 20th century, as being more truly 'sculptural' and somehow metaphysically superior to copying from a modello.

Wittkower convincingly attributes the introduction of modelli, probably worked in clay, to Athens in the 5th century BC, when much more lifelike figures and poses were being introduced and when the sheer size of the programmes of three-dimensional architectural sculpture would have required the simultaneous participation of many craftsmen in the labour of blocking-out and carving (see GREECE, ANCIENT, §IV, 1(iv)(b)). Sculptures such as those from the Parthenon in Athens (London, BM) cannot have been carved directly, for their poses and drapery patterns are far too complex; the uniform style and finish also strongly suggests that the many sculptors involved must have had modelli from which to work. The drill, the tool necessary for transferring the measurements taken from a working modello into the uncarved block, was much in use by this time. The idea of using modelli may have been the catalyst that led to the emergence of Classical from Archaic sculpture. Modelling in clay (plastica) was held in high esteem but differentiated as an art from carving (sculptura) and casting (fusoria) in antiquity, as codified by Pliny the elder in the 1st century AD.

Descriptions of technique are rare until the Renaissance, and even later, for craftsmen may have been barely literate, and some details may also have constituted trade secrets, for example among masons. Secondly, it was not until the High Renaissance, around 1500, that the processes of creation, including an artist's sketchy preparations, whether on paper or in wax or clay, became of general interest. The emergence of interest in the history of art that came with the writings c. 1550 of Vasari had as a concomitant factor a new regard for the artist as a creator, not just as an artisan, and this in turn promoted a concern for all his creations, be they preliminary ideas or finished works. At this time Neo-Platonic philosophy also revived the belief that things on Earth were imperfect renderings of heavenly 'ideas', and the act of creation by an artist was likened to that of God in the Book of Genesis. Indeed, the creation of Adam out of a handful of earth had clear analogies with the making of copies of human figures in the same basic material by a sculptor. By Vasari's time there was even emerging an aesthetic preference for modelli over their finished counterparts, at least as regards painting. It was yet more applicable to sculpture, where the labour of carving (or casting) involved hours of tedious work, as well as delegation to juniors, whose necessary intervention might tend to stultify the artist's initial spontaneity, achieved in such ductile materials as wax or clay.

The principal materials used for making modelli—beeswax and clay—are easily available; softwood may also be carved into a modello, as was the practice among Late Gothic German silversmiths and bronze-founders. Beeswax, sometimes mixed with tallow for extra malleability, has the advantages of ductility and cleanliness in use (see WAX, §II, 1(i)). It is slow to harden and so permits change over a longer period: 'Wax always waits' was an adage of the Florentine studios, quoted by Ridolfo Sirigatti (fl 1594–1601) in his observations on sculpture techniques in Raffaele Borghini's Il riposo (Florence, 1584).

The disadvantages of wax are that it is extremely fragile and is prone to melt and thus sag with undue heating. It may also be re-melted and reused, which may explain why more wax modelli have not survived. To preserve the form of a wax modello, it is necessary to take piece-moulds from it, so that a cast in plaster, bronze or another inert and durable material may be made. Some Renaissance bronze statuettes, apparently solid and with unfinished and waxy surfaces, are such 'relict' casts. They also have an iron-wire armature embedded in the bronze; this was necessary to support the original wax figure if it had limbs projecting from the body or was undercut in other ways. Several such examples exist and are believed to come from the workshops of Donatello (e.g. the David with the Head of Goliath, Berlin, Bodemus.), Antonio del Pollaiuolo (e.g. David, c. 1470; Paris, Louvre) and Francesco di Giorgio Martini (e.g. David, c. 1470; Naples, Capodimonte).

Clay is also ductile but is messy to use and hardens quite quickly, unless it is kept under damp rags; also, its surface does not take quite as fine detail as does wax. It does, however, have the advantage over wax that by drying in the sun or firing in a kiln, it becomes hard and, as terracotta (see TERRACOTTA, §I), virtually indestructible. Its use did not therefore necessitate the extra labour of casting to preserve one's efforts. It is probably on account of this durability that the earliest surviving sketch modelli are made in terracotta; dating from the later years of the Florentine Renaissance, they are virtually intact. In at least one case, that of Andrea del Verrocchio's modello (c. 1477; London, V&A) for the monument to Cardinal Forteguerri, preservation, initially at least, may be due to the terracotta having been physically attached to a legal contract for the erection of the monument in Pistoia Cathedral (in situ), but also because it was the evidence on which Verrocchio won the competition to execute the commission. Several modelli survive from this period, and their aesthetic appeal may have played a part in their preservation. Examples include Antonio Rossellino's modello for the Virgin with the Laughing Child and Benedetto da Maiano's series of plaques with Franciscan scenes for the pulpit of Santa Croce, Florence (all London, V&A).

By the end of the 15th century such modelli were generally regarded as collectable objects: a modello for Jacopo Sansovino's St James the Greater in Florence Cathedral was presented to Bindo Altoviti; now lost, this must have resembled that of his St Paul in terracotta (Paris, Mus. Jacquemart-André). Another modello, a tableau of the Deposition (1510; London, V&A), with figures in wax and real textiles and a wooden cross and ladders, was created by Sansovino as a modello for the painter Perugino and survived because it was presented after use to Giovanni de' Gaddi, as a work of art in its own right. Sansovino also created modelli for the painter Andrea del Sarto; the use of these is evident in the latter's grisaille frescoes of statuary in the Chiostro dello Scalzo, Florence. A modello of the Virgin and Child (c. 1515; Budapest, Mus. F.A.) is probably Sansovino's entry in a competition for a commission for the Mercato Nuovo, Florence.

Michelangelo is famed for his preparatory pen-and-ink or chalk drawings for sculpture, but relatively few of his three-dimensional modelli survive. This was not because of a lack of interest among collectors—indeed the sculptor

5. Modello by Giambologna for *Florence Triumphant over Pisa*, red wax on wire armature, h. 222 mm, 1565 (London, Victoria and Albert Museum); (right) radiograph of the modello

gave one to Leone Leoni for making a portrait of him—but because he deliberately destroyed his creations from time to time, fearing that other, less gifted artists might steal his ideas without acknowledgement. A wax modello (1516; London, V&A) for the *Young Slave* from the tomb of *Pope Julius II* (Rome, St Peter's) is one of the survivors that is generally accepted to be autograph, but Michelangelo's authority and international fame were such that younger artists studied his work by making modelli from them, and this causes great confusion, even to specialists.

After the High Renaissance the making (and occasional preservation) of modelli became common practice, and Vasari in his *Vite* and Cellini in his *Tratatti* set out clearly the successive stages: first thoughts (*pensieri*) were committed to paper and then (or sometimes omitting the drawing stage) to wax or clay modelli on a very small scale,

usually with a wire armature. X-ray radiographs of Giambologna's wax modelli in the Victoria and Albert Museum, London, show that in one instance the armature is simply a bent nail hammered into an off-cut of wood, while in another it is a more elaborate structure with knitted wire to give bulk to a torso and to prevent the warm wax from slipping down the straighter wire axis of the figure (see fig. 5). Similar armatures have been used ever since and are evident in, for example, the wax modelli of horses and ballerinas made by Degas in connection with his paintings. Some 20th-century sculptors (e.g. Giacometti) have raised the minimalist, linear concept of such an armature to the status of a finished sculpture.

After the initial sketch had been approved by the sculptor, and possibly also by his patron, he would 'flesh out' the composition in a clay modello 300–450 mm in height. The torso could be hollowed out, to withstand the eventual firing, and some parts cut off with wires, for separate piece-moulding; studies of heads and hands in greater detail might be made separately. From such a modello (e.g. Giambologna's *Florence Triumphant over Pisa*, terracotta, h. 380 mm; London, V&A) assistants could create a yet larger, final modello, the size of the final sculpture (e.g. Giambologna's *Florence Triumphant over Pisa*, whitewashed clay; Florence, Pal. Vecchio). The term 'modello' was used specifically to describe this type of modello, which was built up round a wooden armature in a mixture of clay and plaster. Too big to be fired in a kiln, it could only be dried in the sun or by the heat of stoves and would thus be more friable than terracotta and prone to fall apart if exposed to rain. Few of these inconveniently large and relatively immovable modelli have survived, although that for Giambologna's *Rape of a Sabine* (h. 4.10 m) is in the Accademia, Florence. From this modello, stone-carvers would transfer the measurements into the raw block of marble by drilling into it at various depths and from various fixed points. They would then carve down to just short of the bottoms of these holes,

6. Modello by Gianlorenzo Bernini of an angel for the Ponte Sant'Angelo, Rome, terracotta, h. 298 mm, *c.* 1667–8 (Cambridge, MA, Fogg Art Museum)

leaving enough scope for the sculptor or his foreman to adjust the eventual surfaces exactly as he wished and then to finish the work in every detail.

Bernini did not leave any wax modelli and seems to have worked from sketches on paper directly into clay modelli some 300 mm high: a good number of these, showing various designs for many of his commissions, survive, for example those of the angels for the balustrades of Ponte Sant'Angelo, Rome (1667–8; Cambridge, MA, Fogg, see fig. 6; Fort Worth, TX, Kimbell A. Mus.; St Petersburg, Hermitage; Rome, Pal. Venezia). His modelli were avidly collected, and some may have been produced to satisfy the demands of collectors, not just as preliminary sketches.

These techniques remained standard until the 19th century; a variation was introduced, however, by such Neo-classical sculptors as Canova and Thorvaldsen and their French contemporaries. Among them it became usual to produce a plaster cast of the initial clay modello and to work with it, rather than with the clay modello fired into terracotta. This cast is known as the 'original plaster' (Fr. *plâtre originale*), thus distinguishing it from copies of the final sculpture cast in plaster. Many of Canova's and Lorenzo Bartolini's original plasters are easily recognized by the large number of metal points attached to their surfaces, for use in the process of transferring measurements to the marble block. During the same period it became common for an artist to preserve all his original plasters, not only to enable the making of several versions in marble at later dates but also as a record of his artistic achievement: these plasters, points and all, often provided the mainstay for posthumous museums of the sculptors' work (e.g. the Gipsoteca Canoviana, Possagno, and the Thorvaldsens Museum, Copenhagen). Similarly, original modelli often survived due to their being part of the 'studio effects' inherited by or sold on to another artist. In England in the late 18th century such artists as Richard Cosway, Joseph Nollekens and Thomas Lawrence all owned modelli believed to be by Michelangelo (although in fact they were more often by Giambologna) as exemplars of High Renaissance compositions. Nollekens even created a series of small modelli of mythological figure compositions, in imitation of Italian practice, most of which are now in the Victoria and Albert Museum, London.

From the Renaissance, but particularly during the 18th century in France and England, elaborate modelli for façades or tombs were often produced with wax or clay figurines and reliefs mounted on a wooden architectural carcass: these were used, together with scale drawings, to demonstrate a commission to a patron. Examples include Louis-François Roubiliac's models (London, V&A) for the monuments to *John Montagu, 2nd Duke of Montagu* (1749; Warkton, Notts, St Edmund) and *John Campbell, 2nd Duke of Argyll* (1745; London, Westminster Abbey).

In the 19th century, with the proliferation of bronze-casting, it was usual to preserve the original wax modello in bronze, and often to label it as such. Several of Anthoine-Louis Barye's meticulously detailed wax modelli of animals survive (Paris, Louvre), as well as those by other figurative sculptors. Some of the most aesthetically exciting modelli are those made by Degas in connection with his paintings, for they show immense verve in rendering form and movement spontaneously and were probably executed from life: wire armatures were bent into shape and then red wax was rapidly applied (e.g. Washington, DC, N.G.A.; Cambridge, Fitzwilliam; see fig. 7). His executors destroyed many modelli that had, in their view, deteriorated too far, but saw to it that the remainder were preserved for posterity by authorizing a limited edition in bronze (e.g. *Young Dancer of Fourteen*, Paris, Mus. d'Orsay).

During the 20th century the admiration for spontaneity and the quest for originality that was initiated by Rodin has elevated what would once have been dismissed as working modelli to the status of works of art, leading them to be regarded as satisfactory in themselves, however incomplete their conception. The very lack of completion is seen as a challenge to the spectator, who is thereby encouraged mentally to complete them for himself in whatever way he chooses.

BIBLIOGRAPHY

A. E. Brinckmann: *Barock-Bozzetti* (Frankfurt am Main, 1923)
L. Réau: 'Les Maquettes des sculpteurs français du XVIIIe siècle', *Bull. Soc. Hist. A. Français* (1936), pp. 7–28
I. Lavin: 'Bozzetti and Modelli', *Stil und Überlieferung in der Kunst des Abendlandes. Akten des 21. internationalen Kongresses für Kunstgeschichte: Bonn, 1964* (Berlin, 1967), pp. 93–104, pl. III
R. Wittkower: *Sculpture: Processes and Principles* (London, 1977)
C. Avery: 'Terracotta: The Fingerprints of the Sculptor', *Fingerprints of the Artist: European Terra-cotta Sculpture from the Arthur M. Sackler Collection* (exh. cat., ed. L. Katz; Washington, DC, N.G.A.; New York, Met.; Cambridge, MA, Fogg; 1981), pp. 16–25 [repr. in Avery, 1988]
——: 'La cera sempre aspetta: Wax Sketch Models for Sculpture', *Apollo*, cxix (1984), pp. 166–76 [repr. in Avery, 1988]
M. Baker: 'Roubiliac's Models and Eighteenth-century English Sculptors' Working Practices', *Entwurf und Ausführung in der europäischen Barockplastik* (Munich, 1986), pp. 59–84
C. Avery: *Studies in European Sculpture*, ii (London, 1988)
M. Baker: 'Roubiliac's Argyll Monument and the Interpretation of Eighteenth-century Sculptors' Designs', *Burl. Mag.*, cxxxiv (1992), pp. 785–97

CHARLES AVERY

Modello, Pietro Paolo del. *See* BALDINI, PIETRO PAOLO.

Modena [anc. Mutina]. Italian city in Emilia-Romagna, situated in the Po Valley at the crossroads of the Via Emilia and the road leading north to the Brenner Pass. It is rich in both Neolithic and Bronze Age remains, and it was an Etruscan settlement from the 4th century BC. In 218 BC Modena became a fortified centre and then a Roman colony, assuming importance with the building of the Via Emilia after 187 BC. It was praised by Cicero as 'the most splendid and strongest colony of the Roman people'. From the Lombard period only scarce finds and the epitaph of Gundeberga (AD 570) in the cathedral survive.

Under Bishop Leodoino (*reg* 872–92) Modena again began to prosper; and in 1099 this was marked by the construction of the new cathedral (*see* §1 below) with the support of Contessa Matilda of Canossa. Under Bishop Eriberto (*reg c.* 1054–94) the city state was established. The bishop and the new commune supported the papal party in the Investiture Dispute, for which the cathedral, the bishop's palace and the main square functioned as a symbol and focal point.

7. Modello by Edgar Degas for *Dancer, Arabesque over the Right Leg, Left Arm in Front*, red wax and wire, h. 206 mm, *c.* 1882–95 (Cambridge, Fitzwilliam Museum)

The third important period in Modena's history occurred under the Este family of Ferrara, who gained control of the city in 1288. It became a flourishing cultural centre during the 15th, 16th and 17th centuries. The Este established their seat there in 1598, and the ducal palace was rebuilt in the mid-17th century by BARTOLOMEO AVANZINI. They built up one of the richest libraries in Europe with 600,000 books and 15,000 manuscripts, including the celebrated BIBLE OF BORSO D'ESTE (Modena, Bib. Estense, MS. V.G. 12–13, lat. 422–3), and commissioned painters from Venice (e.g. Veronese and Jacopo Tintoretto), Emilia (e.g. Correggio, Parmigianino and Dosso Dossi) and Spain (Diego Velázquez; *see* ESTE (i)). The topography of the city was altered during this period, although the disposition of the main Roman and some of the medieval streets is still apparent in parts of the city centre. Since World War II Modena has become an important commercial and gastronomic centre, and it is known especially for its car and shoe design factories.

CHRISTINE VERZAR

1. CATHEDRAL. The cathedral is dedicated to St Geminianus, Bishop of Modena in the 4th century and patron saint of the city. The present church was founded in 1099 on the site of an earlier and smaller cathedral that lay on a more northerly axis. This had a nave and four aisles, with articulated supports and brick walling dating to the second half of the 11th century, but it soon fell into ruin.

A contemporary account, the *Relatio translationis corporis Sancti Geminiani* (see 1984 exh. cat.), gives some information on the first building phase of the Romanesque cathedral (1099–1106). On the outside of the building three inscriptions bear the dates of foundation and consecration, as well as the names of the architect LANFRANCO and the sculptor Wiligelmo. On 9 June 1099 the first stone was laid, with the old cathedral still partially standing. Building probably began simultaneously from both ends: the junction of the two building processes can clearly be seen in an arch on the south side of the cathedral (penultimate bay before the apse), which, because of an error in the calculations, is narrower than the rest. The relics of St Geminianus are said to have been translated on 30 May 1106, when the choir and crypt of the new church must already have been completed. On 12 July 1184 the cathedral was consecrated by Pope Lucius III (*reg* 1181–5).

The appearance of Lanfranco's building has been modified over the centuries. The Campionesi masters carried out a series of works from the later 12th century to the early 14th, including the rose window on the façade (which involved lowering the arch of the porch beneath) and the two lateral façade portals. They were also responsible for the present appearance of the Porta Regia on the south side of the cathedral and the Ghirlandina bell-tower on the north. In the interior, they erected the great rood screen and pulpit (*see* §(ii)(a) below) and made alterations around the presbytery, creating a false transept. Towards the middle of the 15th century, rib vaults replaced the original wooden roof of the nave and aisles. In 1984, on the eighth centenary of its consecration, the cathedral façade was restored.

(i) Architecture. Despite the alterations, Modena Cathedral has essentially retained its late 11th-century appearance. The façade is divided into three parts by two square-sectioned buttresses crowned by octagonal pinnacles with pyramidal spires, restored in 1936. Halfway up, the façade is crossed by a row of small galleries, the arches of which are grouped into threes within broad containing arches, supported by tall half-columns. These galleries, the most characteristic motif of Lanfranco's work, continue all round the sides and apses of the building. The façade is completed by the rose window and the three portals, the central one of which has a two-storey porch on columns.

The south side of the church, on the Piazza Grande, has two portals, the Porta dei Principi and the magnificent Porta Regia. The upper part of the south transept 'façade' rests on the last three arches on the side of the church. The main apse is higher than the two side ones, resulting in differences in the level of the galleries. The north side, with the Porta della Pescheria, adjoins a narrow street and is thus difficult to see. The lower five storeys of the Ghirlandina bell-tower are square in section; the upper portion is octagonal, topped by a spire.

The exterior of the building is faced in stone, but the interior is of brick. The church is basilican, with a nave and two aisles with apses and a presbytery raised over the crypt (see fig. 1; for ground-plan, *see* ROMANESQUE, fig. 10). The main arcade has alternating clustered piers and marble columns, each of the main nave bays corresponding to two aisle bays. The 15th-century vaults are divided by large pointed transverse arches, but the main vessel may originally have had diaphragm arches supporting the wooden roof. In the nave is a false gallery with no floor, formed of a series of three-light windows within containing arches. The presbytery is spatially independent

1. Modena Cathedral, interior looking east, begun 1099

of the rest of the church and constitutes a non-projecting transept. The church has an internal length of 63.1 m and a height of 20.8 m.

There was close collaboration between architect and sculptor. Wiligelmo may have been responsible for the façade, but the modular and rhythmic design of the apse exteriors represents the acme of Lanfranco's architecture. In the interior Lanfranco was responsible for combining the alternating system with a wooden roof, but the Gothic vaulting has imposed a vertical aspect on the church that the architect never intended.

Lanfranco was clearly familiar with Lombard buildings. The gallery motif with groups of small tripartite arches implies a development of the Lombard decorative motif of small hanging arches; and Modena Cathedral represents the end of a stylistic process already prefigured in Lombardy, beginning with S Maria Maggiore at Lomello (first half of the 11th century; *see* ROMANESQUE, fig. 9), where the church is divided into bays but has a truss roof, less complex in form than Lanfranco's original roof. Modena Cathedral soon became a model for numerous churches in Emilia, the Po Valley and the Veneto in general, for instance Ferrara Cathedral and S Zeno Maggiore, Verona.

For bibliography, *see* §(ii) below.

LIA DI GIACOMO

(ii) Sculpture. The sculptural decoration of the cathedral forms an integral part of its architecture, and two main phases can be discerned. The first, *c.* 1099–1110, is associated with the sculptor WILIGELMO, while the second, related to the final building campaign leading up to the

consecration of 1184 and continuing into the 13th century, was the work of the CAMPIONESI masters; it included the remodelling of the main façade.

(a) First phase. The west façade sculpture comprises four reliefs depicting scenes from Genesis, two flanking the main portal and two above the lateral doors; a dedication plaque bearing Wiligelmo's signature, held by figures representing *Enoch* and *Elijah*, and two reliefs of torch-bearing putti (see fig. 2; all set into the masonry flanking the portal above the Genesis reliefs); and the main portal, which has figures of twelve *Prophets* on the inner face of the jambs and a classicizing inhabited scroll, supported by atlantes, on the outer face, the lintel and the archivolt (there is no tympanum). All these sculptures have been attributed to Wiligelmo himself, while the fragments of the four *Evangelist Symbols* surmounting the rose window are by another master in his workshop. The two-storey porch, supported by reused Roman column-bearing lions, was probably added by the Campionesi in the later 12th century.

According to Quintavalle (1964–5), the Genesis reliefs and the other façade sculptures by Wiligelmo and his workshop were originally intended for a different location and for use as church furnishings: the Genesis scenes may have formed the parapet of the original screen, which was replaced by the present one c. 1160–70, while the *Evangelist* fragments may derive from a pulpit and the signed dedication plaque and the putti reliefs from the sides of an altar or sarcophagus for the patron saint. Other scholars have rejected this hypothesis, however, insisting that the figures and reliefs were intended for the façade from the beginning.

The Porta dei Principi on the south flank of the nave, facing the large public square and the bishop's palace, is the earliest known example of a two-storey porch portal, a distinct north Italian architectural form that has been

2. Modena Cathedral, façade relief by Wiligelmo of a torch-bearing putto, marble, h. *c.* 1 m, *c.* 1099–1110

shown to allude symbolically to themes of judgement; it served as a backdrop for the bishop in his capacity as civic judge and leader in the emergent city state. The lintel bears six scenes from the *Legend of St Geminianus*, the patron saint who travelled to Constantinople in the 4th century to exorcize the emperor's daughter. The door-frame repeats the inhabited scroll of the west portal, but it is carved in a slightly different style; on its inner face the figures of the *Twelve Apostles* appear, placed under arches, like the twelve *Prophets* on the west façade portal. On the north side of the nave is the Porta Pescheria, again two-storey, facing the old fish-market and the Via Emilia, from where travellers and pilgrims arrived. Its archivolt bears an Arthurian cycle, identified by the names of the protagonists, in which horsemen ride towards a castle to liberate Queen Guinevere. The lintel shows scenes from animal fables, and the jambs bear inhabited scrolls supported by atlantes on the outer face and the *Labours of the Months* on the inner face.

Although the figure style of these two portals is slightly different from that of the main façade portal, the sculptures have been associated with the nucleus of Wiligelmo's workshop: they all follow a similar decorative repertory and relationship to the architectural frame. Thematically, all three portals form a coherent and complementary symbolic programme. The Genesis scenes, which start with the *Creation* and continue to the *Rescue of Noah's Ark from the Flood*, have been related to sermons by the local bishop, associated with the Investiture Dispute and the emergent independence of Modena, and also to liturgical drama. The Old Testament prophets on the jambs of the main façade portal have a typological counterpart in the similarly arranged Apostles of the Porta dei Principi. The lintels of the two lateral portals are complementary, one relating the patron saint's mission and the other the rescue of the lady in the castle by a heroic knight; the focus on the rescue of women has also been thought to refer symbolically to the patroness, Matilda of Canossa. The depiction of fables, *Labours of the Months* and inhabited scrolls all help to weave together such daily concerns as work, pilgrimage, crusade, the liturgy and the Christian year. All the portals bear elaborate inscriptions identifying single figures and biblical, liturgical and popular texts, many of didactic character.

The blind arcading articulating the exterior walls of the cathedral bears capitals carved by Wiligelmo with foliage, animals, hybrids and human figures. The capitals of the interior are largely foliate. A relief of *Truth Extracting the Tongue of Fraud* and *Jacob Fighting the Angel* is set in the south wall of the nave; its form and that of the large metopes bearing single acrobatic figures and a siren (Modena, Mus. Lapidario), originally intended to crown the nave walls, have been thought to have Burgundian connections. They all show stylistic similarities to the works of Wiligelmo.

(b) Second phase. The main sculptural work of the later 12th century was the rood screen with its attached pulpit. It spans the entire width of the nave and forms a balustrade supported by column-bearing lions and atlantes in front of the raised choir and crypt (see fig. 3). The narrative reliefs of the parapet bear five *Passion* scenes (*Christ*

3. Modena Cathedral, pulpit and rood screen attributed to Anselmo da Campione, marble, c. 1160–70

Washing the Feet of the Disciples, the *Last Supper*, *Christ before Herod*, the *Flagellation* and *Christ Carrying the Cross*), while the capitals show the *Sacrifice of Isaac, Samson and the Lion* and the *Martyrdom of St Lawrence*, all of which relate typologically to the Passion. The theme of the *Passion*, with the *Last Supper* as the central focus, stresses its symbolic link to the sacrament of communion received by the lay congregation at the balustrade. Although the work is unsigned, documents refer to the construction of this *pulpitum* between 1160 and 1170, which allows a probable assignation to Anselmo da Campione. The Ghirlandina bell-tower seems to have been built at the same time and by *c.* 1169–70 probably was completed, with its single sculptures in the upper registers carved by Enrico and the mason Alberto. The Porta Regia (1209–31), most probably built by Enrico and Anselmo, is much larger than the 12th-century portals and closer in form to the porch portals of Benedetto Antelami at Parma Cathedral and Borgo San Donnino (Fidenza).

Stylistic links with Provence for these sculptures were first suggested by Porter and Hamann, and the connection is still stressed by many. The figure style and some of the subjects chosen show very close correlations. The *Passion* cycle is close to the one on the Crucifixion portal at Saint-Gilles-du-Gard and to Notre-Dames-des-Pommiers, Beaucaire, and a single capital at Modena of the *Three Marys at the Tomb* is related to a relief at Beaucaire. The sculptures show a development towards monumentality and naturalism. The carving is stiff and uses jagged lines, and the faces are elongated with sulky mouths, typical of the late school of Nicholaus and the so-called Scuola di

Piacenza; but the figural and narrative style of Wiligelmo is also still strongly felt in these scenes.

BIBLIOGRAPHY

G. Bertoni: *Atlante storico-paleografico del duomo di Modena* (Modena, 1909)
A. K. Porter: *Lombard Architecture*, i, iii (New Haven, 1915–17)
G. Bertoni: *Atlante storico-artistico del duomo di Modena* (Modena, 1921)
R. Hamann: *Deutsche und französische Plastik im Mittelalter*, i (Marburg, 1923)
A. K. Porter: *Romanesque Sculpture of the Pilgrimage Roads* (Boston, 1923/*R* New York, 1966)
R. S. Loomis: 'The Date, Source and Subject of the Arthurian Sculpture at Modena', *Memorial Studies in Memory of Gertrude Schoepperle Loomis* (New York, 1927), pp. 209–28
P. Toesca: *Il medioevo* (1927), i of *Storia dell'arte italiana* (Turin, 1927–50/*R* 1965)
L. Olschki: 'La cattedrale di Modena e il suo rilievo arturiano', *Archv Romanicum*, xix (1935), pp. 145–82
R. S. Loomis: 'Geoffrey of Monmouth and the Modena Archivolt: A Question of Precedence', *Speculum*, xiii (1938), pp. 221–31
G. de Francovich: 'Wiligelmo da Modena e gli inizi della scultura romanica europea', *Riv. Reale Ist. Archeol. & Stor. A.*, vii (1940), pp. 225–94
——: *Benedetto Antelami*, 2 vols (Milan and Florence, 1952)
R. Salvini: *Wiligelmo e le origini della scultura romanica* (Milan, 1956)
K. J. Conant: *Carolingian and Romanesque Architecture, 800–1200*, Pelican Hist. A. (Harmondsworth, 1959, rev. 2/1978)
J. Stiennon and R. Lejeune: 'La Légende arthurienne dans la cathédrale de Modena', *Cah. Civilis. Méd.*, iv (1963), pp. 281–96
A. C. Quintavalle: *La cattedrale di Modena: Problemi di romanico emiliano*, 2 vols (Modena, 1964–5)
R. Salvini: *Il duomo di Modena e il romanico nel modenese* (Modena, 1966)
A. C. Quintavalle: *Romanico padano, civiltà d'occidente* (Florence, 1967)
——: *Wiligelmo e la sua scuola* (Florence, 1967)
E. Fernie: 'Notes on the Sculpture of Modena Cathedral', *A. Lombarda*, xiv/2 (1969), pp. 88–93
F. Gandolfo: 'Problemi della cattedrale di Modena', *Commentari*, xxii (1972), pp. 124–55
Atti del convegno internazionale degli studi. Romanico padano, romanico europeo: Parma, 1977

F. Gandolfo: 'Il protiro lombardo: Una ipotesi di formazione', *Stor. A.*,
xxxiv (1978), pp. 211–23
A. C. Quintavalle and others: *Romanico, mediopadano: Strada, città, ecclesia*
(Parma, 1983) [cat. of exh. held in 1977]
R. Salvini: *Il duomo di Modena* (Modena, 1983)
*Lanfranco e Wiligelmo. Il duomo di Modena: Quando le cattedrali erano
bianche* (exh. cat., Modena, 1984), 3 vols [contains full bibliog.; vol. i
incl. the *Relatio translationis corporis sancti Geminiani*, ed. S. Lomartire,
pp. 757–8]
*Atti del convegno internazionale degli studi. Wiligelmo e Lanfranco nell'Europa
romanica: Modena, 1985*
A. Peroni: *Il duomo di Modena: Atlante grafico* (Modena, 1988) [pls]

For further bibliography *see* MATILDA OF CANOSSA, ROMANESQUE, §III,
1(vi)(c) and WILIGELMO.

CHRISTINE VERZAR

Modena, Barnaba da. *See* BARNABA DA MODENA.

Modena, Giovanni da. *See* GIOVANNI DA MODENA.

Modena, Nicoletto da. *See* NICOLETTO DA MODENA.

Modena, Tomaso da. *See* TOMASO DA MODENA.

Moderne Kunstkring [Dut.: 'Modern art circle']. Group
of Dutch artists founded in November 1910 on the
initiative of Conrad Kikkert (1882–1965), a Dutch painter
and critic, who had moved to Paris in the same year. The
objective was to convey to the Netherlands the latest
developments in painting in Paris. Its members included
a large number of Dutch painters who either had connections with Paris or lived there. Kikkert financed the
venture. The first exhibition was held between 6 October
and 5 November 1911 at the Stedelijk Museum, Amsterdam. It was a great success, attracting 6000 visitors. Of
the 166 works shown, half came from abroad. As 'father
of Cubism', Paul Cézanne was well represented by 28
works from the Hoogendijk collection; also exhibited
were 19 works by Auguste Herbin, 7 by Pablo Picasso and
6 by Georges Braque. The Paris-based painter Lodewijk
Schelfhout (1881–1943), one of the first Dutch artists to
paint in a Cubist style, submitted 12 works; other Dutch
artists, such as Jan Sluyters, Kees van Dongen and Piet
Mondrian, were mainly influenced by Fauvism. Mondrian
showed the triptych *Evolution* (1910–11) and *Red Mill*
(1910), in which, in addition to a vivid use of colour, he
first divided the surface in a schematic manner; after
December 1911, when he went to Paris at Kikkert's
insistence, he came under the influence of Cubism.

The second Moderne Kunstkring exhibition was held
between 6 October and 7 November 1912 at the Stedelijk
Museum, Amsterdam, and attracted 8000 visitors. It
marked the beginning of abstract art in the Netherlands.
Cubism still dominated, represented in the work of Alex-
ander Archipenko, Braque, Albert Gleizes, Herbin, Fer-
nand Léger, Jean Metzinger and Picasso. Mondrian's first
Cubist work, the *Blossoming Apple Tree* (1912; The Hague,
Gemeentemus.), was a notable exhibit; with Petrus Alma
he was one of the few Dutch artists to emulate Picasso's
Analytical Cubism. Kikkert, Henri Le Fauconnier and
Schelfhout worked more according to the principles of
Gleizes and Metzinger. Jacob Bendien's first abstract
paintings were also shown at this exhibition.

After 1912 the Moderne Kunstkring was no longer the
only place outside the French Salon des Indépendants

where Paris-based Dutch artists, such as Alma, Mondrian,
Otto van Rees and Schelfhout, exhibited. In 1912 they
exhibited at the *Sonderbund* exhibition in Cologne. During
that year the general interest moved towards developments
in German painting. In 1913 the third Moderne Kunstkring
exhibition was held, which included 18 works by Franz
Marc and 14 by Vasily Kandinsky. Earlier that year Le
Fauconnier and Kikkert had broken away from the Cubism
of Picasso and Braque, finding it too theoretical. As a
result, these painters were no longer represented: Le
Fauconnier, on the other hand, exhibited 27 paintings and
was honoured as leader of the Cubists; Schelfhout, who
was represented with 16 paintings, displayed a moderate
form of Cubism still based on recognizable forms of
representation. Mondrian exhibited 6 paintings, *Tableaux
I* to *VI*, a series of abstractions of trees and plants, which
revealed Picasso's influence. Jacoba Heemskerck van
Beest's work was similarly influenced by Picasso.

In 1913 Kikkert was instrumental in expelling Sluyters
(who had already resigned from the governing committee
at the end of 1912) and Leo Gestel from the society
because they were also members of the Hollandse Kun-
stenaarskring, which promoted Impressionism. Chairman
Jan Toorop was given the ineffectual, but impressive-
sounding, role of Honorary President. As a result of these
problems Mondrian withdrew from the committee. In
1914, at the outbreak of World War I, Alma, Kikkert,
Mondrian and Schelfhout returned to the Netherlands and
the Moderne Kunstkring lost its bridging function to
artistic life in Paris.

BIBLIOGRAPHY
A. Venema: 'De stormachtige beginjaren van de Moderne Kunstkring,
1910–1915' [The stormy early years of the Moderne Kunstkring, 1910–
1915], *Tableau*, i/2 (1978–9), pp. 34–43, 48
G. Imanse: 'Het ontstaan van de abstracte kunst in Nederland *c.* 1900–
1918 en het artistieke klimaat in die periode' [The beginning of abstract
art in the Netherlands *c.* 1900–1918 and the artistic climate of this
period], *Van Gogh bis Cobra: Holländische Malerei, 1880–1950* (exh.
cat. by G. Imanse and others, Stuttgart, Württemberg. Kstver.; Utrecht,
Cent. Mus.; Bonn, Rhein. Landesmus.; 1980–81), pp. 93–135 [also pubd
in Dut.]

JOHN STEEN

Modernism. Term applied to the invention and the
effective pursuit of artistic strategies that seek not just
close but essential connections to the powerful forces of
social MODERNITY. The responses of modernists to
modernity range from triumphal celebration to agonized
condemnation and differ in mode from direct picturing of
the impacts of modernization to extreme renovations of
purely artistic assumptions and practice. Such strategies—
pursued by artists working individually or, often, in groups,
as well as by critics, historians and theorists—occur in all
of the arts, although in distinctive forms and across varying
historical trajectories. They have been strongest in painting, design and the MODERN MOVEMENT in architecture,
highly significant in literature and in music, but quite
muted in the crafts. They have echoes in aspects of
commercial and popular culture. Despite being intermittent in their occurrence and unsystematic in nature, these
strategies have been most effective in Europe and its
colonies from the mid-19th century and in the USA from
the early 20th, moving from the margins to the centre of

visual cultures, from reactive radicality to institutionalized normality.

Some early usages of the term 'modernism' occur in the context of the recurrent battle between the new and the old. In 1737 Jonathan Swift complained to Alexander Pope about 'the corruption of English by those Scribblers, who send us over their trash in Prose and Verse, with abominable curtailings and quaint modernisms' (*Published Works*, 1757, ix: 218b). Yet such disputes were usually local ones, occurring within broader frameworks of cultural continuity, except at periods of epochal change. During the 19th century in Europe, however, modernizing forces became hegemonic, and by the mid-20th century modernity had become the norm in many parts of the world, its effects being felt everywhere.

Within this fast-changing context, certain moments in the history of the visual arts stand out as definitively modernist. The play of modernizing forces in Paris in the 1850s and 1860s was manifest in Courbet's critical realism, Manet's induction of the aesthetics of popular spectacle into high art, and the poetics and art criticism of CHARLES BAUDELAIRE. 'By *modernité*', Baudelaire wrote in 1863, 'I mean the ephemeral, the fugitive, the contingent, the half of art whose other half is the eternal and the immutable'. These artists and writers recognized that to make significant, potentially timeless art, it was necessary to begin from the transitory, ever-changing present. This reversed the historical teachings of the academies. Towards the end of the 19th century the term 'modernist' was adopted to identify ART NOUVEAU tendencies in many European countries. A related usage appeared in the claims of SECESSION artists in Germany and elsewhere.

In the years after 1900 Paris was the centre of an explosion of artistic innovations, by Fauvist and Cubist artists, which inspired radical experimentation by Futurists in Italy, Suprematists and Constructivists in Russia, Dadaists in Germany and many others. Subsequent tendencies, such as Surrealism, explored the social and psychological impacts of modernization even more deeply. In general, these artists passed from drastic transformations of tradition to fundamental interrogations of art itself. Such extreme reflexivity, emphasizing negative criticism of the conventional and pursued by these artists usually working in groups, constitutes the avant-garde within modernism.

At the same time developments in modern art were fashioned into influential historical narratives in such exhibitions as *Manet and the Post-Impressionists* (London, 1910), opened by the critic ROGER FRY, and new markets for modernist art were created by the ARMORY SHOW (New York, 1913) and others. Those involved in these developments usually identified each movement or grouping by its name and referred to 'the new art' or, increasingly after 1920, 'modern art' as the generic term for what was emerging as a broad tendency. Meanwhile, product designers made the term 'modernist' fashionable for their ART DECO elegances, but defenders of tradition during the first half of the 20th century saw 'modernistic' art as indicative of political excess, diseased social values and the insanity of those who made it.

As a name for the mainstream tendency in 20th-century abstract art 'modernism' came into widespread usage only in the 1960s. It was applied to the Abstract Expressionists and to contemporary hard-edge painting, colour field painting and abstract sculpture, most influentially by the American critic CLEMENT GREENBERG. Its lineage was traced back to Manet as the initiator of a sequence of formal innovations, particularly those that lessened illusionism in painting and mimeticism in sculpture. Reflecting the economic and cultural ascendency of the USA and the enormous power of the New York art market, this viewpoint became orthodox internationally. It was, however, subject to subversion by Pop and Minimalist artists and to devastating criticism by conceptual, political and feminist artists and commentators. By the early 1970s it was displaced as a paradigm for most artists, although it persists in many museums, galleries and educational systems.

What were the practices of modernist artists? A typical strategy was to provoke the shock of the new, to reveal the present as replete with blindingly self-evident value and, at the same instant, to consign the recent past to anachronism. Another was to imagine the future as within reach, and still another was to reclaim the distant and even ancient past as a generalized precedent, a repository of essential values that transcended the style-bound historicisms of the 19th century. Typical modes were these: picturing the environments, artefacts, styles and attitudes of everyday life in the modern world; inventing forms, compositional formats and systems of visual signage that parallel those of the forces of modernization; insisting on art's autonomy—its obligation to secure a space for unbridled creativity, for pure possibility; promoting abstraction as an inevitable historical unfolding; highlighting the separateness of the arts or mixing them in startling ways; constantly disturbing fixed relationships between artists and works of art and between works and viewers. The basic impulse of modernism within modernity is the drive to create previously unimagined objects and new ways of seeing them.

In the late 20th century, however, the limitations of modernism, its wasteful exclusions, became increasingly evident. Aspects of the cultures of non-European peoples were often incorporated into modernist experimentality as estranging devices and signals of 'primitive' otherness. This occurred throughout the vanguard movements in Europe around 1900, but from a post-colonial perspective it can be seen as a legacy of imperialism. While the agenda for world art seemed to be set by mainstream Ecole de Paris art movements, and then, after World War II, by developments in American art, artistic practice in the cultural and economic colonies is not necessarily a matter of dependent provincialism. Local artists adopt, adapt and often transform elements that circulate throughout a system of exchange, which is itself becoming increasingly international. Regional, local, even national, modernisms have occurred all over the world since the 1920s, each with their own distinctive concerns and values. Feminist art historians draw attention to the exclusion of significant work by women artists from the canon of modernist masterpieces, to the social restrictions that prevented these artists from entering many of the spaces so vital to modern life, and to the persistence in early modernism of women seen as aesthetic objects (*see* WOMEN AND ART HISTORY).

Similarly, modernist art constantly pirated popular and commercial visual cultures, while still insisting on an essential critical distance from the everyday life of modernity. No longer a source of strength, this contradictory pattern of incorporation and exclusion has contributed to modernism's decline.

While modernism no longer inspires artists, its heroic history and its accumulation of masterworks have became standard fare within educated taste as it consumes the visual arts with ever-increasing enthusiasm. Modern Masters, fine designers, great geniuses, modest decorators: a diverse and conflict-free aesthetic has spread outwards from the centres of artistic innovation to become an international modernist culture among the upper and middle classes in most countries with a European heritage.

Post-modern artists and theorists (*see* POST-MODERN-ISM) tend to reject modernism as a historical narrative binding on current practice, while at the same time rehearsing some of its strategies and quoting instances of early modernist art as allusions within their circulating of imagery from, potentially, anywhere and any time. Post-modernism is, however, obsessed with modernity; and the issue of whether human societies have moved into a post-modern phase remains open. Another modernist moment in art cannot, therefore, be ruled out.

BIBLIOGRAPHY

C. Baudelaire: *Le Peintre de la vie moderne* (Paris, 1863; Eng. trans. by J. Mayne, London, 1964)
C. Greenberg: 'Modernist Painting', *A. & Lit.*, 4 (Spring 1965), pp. 193–201; also in *Modern Art and Modernism: A Critical Anthology*, ed. F. Frascina and C. Harrison (London, 1982)
H. H. Arnason: *A History of Modern Art* (New York, 1969)
M. Bradbury and T. McFarlane: *Modernism, 1890–1930* (Harmondsworth, 1976)
R. Hughes: *The Shock of the New* (London, 1980, rev. 2/1991)
E. Lunn: *Marxism and Modernism* (Berkeley, 1982)
B. H. D. Buchloh, S. Guilbaut and D. Solkin, eds: *Modernism and Modernity* (Halifax, NS, 1983)
T. J. Clark: *The Painting of Modern Life: Paris in the Art of Manet and his Followers* (Princeton, 1984)
M. Calinescu: *The Five Faces of Modernity* (Durham, NC, 1987)
D. J. Singal: 'Modernist Culture in America', *Amer. Q.*, xxxix/1 (Spring 1987) [special issue]
G. Pollock: *Vision and Difference: Feminism, Femininity and Histories of Art* (London, 1988)

Modernisme. *See* ART NOUVEAU.

Modernity. Term applied to the cultural condition in which the seemingly absolute necessity of innovation becomes a primary fact of life, work and thought. Modernity appeared first in Europe in the 16th century and became dominant in the mid-19th century, with enormous consequences for colonized non-European countries and for residual cultural formations within Europe. It has been described as the first truly 'world' culture, universalizing in its ambitions and impact. Modernity is more than merely the state of being modern or the opposition between old and new. This article discusses the nature of modernity and its relation to art.

1. THE NATURE OF MODERNITY. The ecology of pre-modern societies was largely agricultural, based on using renewable resources in restorable conditions, but modern societies in pursuit of greater productivity, profits and the spread of 'well-being' are built around machine processing of unrenewable resources. Constant technological progress is required to keep ahead of accelerating consumption, as is the flexibility to switch from exhausted resources to new ones. Incessant change becomes central to cultural experience. The agenda for change is, however, concentrated in the hands of relatively few, is partial in scope and largely arbitrary in its effects. Thus its forms are felt as ambiguous and conflicted. Modernity is the accumulating impact of these forces of modernization on individuals, societies and environments.

New ideas and modes of expression have occurred in many societies throughout human history, even in civilizations that changed as slowly as did that of ancient Egypt. Also frequent is the sense of being modern—that is, being up to date, 'of today', or, less strongly, part of the present or recent past. Modernity, however, is much more active, engaged and widespread than these occasional and circumstantial occurrences. It is what happens to both everyday and exceptional experience when large sections of a society are undergoing modernization. It is an unfolding of active processes, of changes in all spheres, away from accepted traditions, customary conventions and current practices towards imaginary, often utopian, futures. It is experienced as a constant encounter with the new as a set of challenges and thus demands a reorientation of our sense of self around the presumption that change is the inevitable result of the functioning of forces outside of ourselves, is largely unpredictable and yet may be influenced, to some degree, by individual belief and action. Modernity provokes a preoccupation in us with its definition, occurrence and significance. Modernity is living in, and with, perpetual flux.

In *The Communist Manifesto* of 1848, Karl Marx and Friedrich Engels wrote:

> Constant revolutionizing of production, uninterrupted disturbance of all social conditions, everlasting uncertainty and agitation distinguish the bourgeois epoch from all earlier ones. All fixed, fast-frozen relations, with their train of ancient and venerable prejudices and opinions, are swept away, all newly formed ones become antiquated before they can ossify. All that is solid melts into air, all that is holy is profaned, and man is at last compelled to face with sober senses, his real conditions of life, and his relations with his kind. (*Selected Works*, p. 38)

These changes had been resisted from the beginning of the Industrial Revolution. The poet Oliver Goldsmith, in his essay *Visit to Elysium* of 1773, was rudely confronted by Luddite reality: 'I should certainly have fallen beneath the hands of this company of men, who gloried in the title of Modernicides' (*Miscellaneous Works*, London, 1837, I.213).

While many of these ideas were nascent in the RENAISSANCE (leading some to label it the Early Modern period), it was during the 19th century in Europe that modernizing forces came to dominate material life: the capitalist system of economic exchange became nearly global; industrialists used new technologies and rationalized management to introduce mass production; faster means of transportation and communication spread everywhere; millions of people migrated between nations and into cities; governmental and corporate surveillance became increasingly pervasive and was strongly resisted by organized and revolutionary political movements; everyday life was secularized, traditional values were cast as mere nostalgia, and popular culture was shaped into spectacles infused with desires for commodities. Overt ideological struggle is thus characteristic of modernity (*see also* IDEOLOGY). At stake is the direction of modernity itself. Typically, attempts are made by some to recruit modernity's victims as willing subjects and by others to encourage them to radical resistance. Both sides, however, share an assumption about the inevitability of a modernized future, while rejecting continuity from the past and viewing its persisting forms as anachronistic survivals. They aim to reduce actual global diversity of outlook by insisting on the necessity of unifying, integrative conceptual frameworks, by promoting abstract organizational forms over individual choice. They oppose the inherited hierarchies and also the autonomous differentiality of tradition-based communities—especially those beyond the major European cities—with claims that rationality, materialism and pragmatism are essentially universal. In general, the rhetoric of disruption disguises modernity's fundamental sleight-of-hand: its eventual absorption of tradition, otherness and its own novelty into its expansionary self.

The ideology of modernity is evident in its narratives of universal liberation, a number of which compete and combine. They all presume European leadership and include the revolutionary overthrow of aristocratic, theocratic order to establish the democratic nation state, the promise of progressively increasing wealth for all offered by the political economy of capitalism, and the hope for the realization of rationality in the minds and actions of men held out by Enlightenment philosophy, above all by Kant and Hegel. MARXISM, a widely influential ideology during the period of modernity's hegemony, was a critique of these narratives accompanied by its own narrative of the revolutionary destruction of the bourgeois state, the establishment of a socialist state and, eventually, the communism of pure liberation. A less systematic critique of modernity was offered by such philosophers as FRIEDRICH NIETZSCHE and MARTIN HEIDEGGER and by such political philosophies as anarchism.

2. MODERNITY AND THE ARTS. These ideologies and materialities have profoundly shaped art and literature. They surfaced first in the QUARREL OF THE ANCIENTS AND MODERNS in 17th-century France and England in particular. During the following 150 years, the applied empiricism of the *Encyclopédie* project (1751–72) of Denis Diderot and the ROMANTICISM of many writers and artists mapped out, respectively, a science and an aesthetic increasingly independent of classical precedent. By 1848 THÉOPHILE GAUTIER could assert: 'It goes without saying that we accept civilization as it is, with its railways, steamboats, English scientific research, central heating, factory chimneys and all its technical equipment, which have been considered impervious to the picturesque' (*Souvenir*, p. 203). Others were less sanguine—thus the cry from CHARLES BAUDELAIRE in 'Le Cygne': 'Old Paris is gone (the form of the city . . . changes much faster, alas! than the mortal heart)' (Baudelaire, p. 209). Such grief for a past visibly disappearing, shot through with anxiety about whether it is possible to keep up with the necessity

of novelty, recoil from the present while being embroiled in a searching for the future within it—this dialectical ambivalence is a typically modern mix.

Seeing the Paris of the Second Empire as a key site of modernity, WALTER BENJAMIN traced its definitive figures: the city itself obliterating the countryside except as memory and place of leisure; the volatile crowd against whom individuality was now measured (especially that of the *flâneur*, a new model for the artist); the dislocations of the experience of time and space; the dominance of the world by its 'phantasmagorias', its fanciful, fantastic, engrossing yet misleading projections of itself through advertising and political ideologies. In the years after 1900 mass-produced visual imagery proliferated throughout city spaces and in the burgeoning variety of communicative media. International, national, regional and local cultures defined themselves increasingly in terms of identificatory visual images, as did political parties, urban subcultures and even small, occasional, groupings of people. Advertising, entertainment, propaganda and fashion were the primary vehicles for an imagery of modernity that celebrated the MASS PRODUCTION process and then its products. Modern design symbolized the age of mass consumption. Images of factories and workers, cities and crowds, products and consumers appeared regularly in the incessant circulation of signs of the new. Modernist art claimed a definitive closeness to the essential spirit of modernity (*see* MODERNISM). In its avant-garde forms, it also insisted on the necessity of art's autonomy, its pure experimentality. It is also arguable, however, that the various realist tendencies in art since the late 18th century, further inspired by the example of Gustave Courbet in the mid-19th century, express the experience of modernity even more directly, if more critically, often picturing its forces at work on individuals seen as part of a social fabric.

Since the late 1960s modernity has been radically reinterpreted. The forces of modernization have been blamed for creating alienating, repressive societies that are increasingly divided between rich and poor, for accelerating the inequities between nations and for wide-scale environmental destruction. Nation states based on such universal systems as socialism, communism and many forms of capitalism are rapidly losing the consent of their citizens, which in turn is leading to greater repression or the creation of hybrid forms of power-sharing. Theorists of post-modernity argue that the master narratives that have sustained consent in modernizing societies—ideals of progress, democracy, humanism, modernity itself—have become illegitimate and that the dream of universal rationality that inspired the Enlightenment has ended. Post-modernists call for a new era of anything-goes, open-ended possibility. Yet in practice, old beliefs, especially theocratic ones, are revived, often fanatically, and new cynicisms flourish beside naive hopes for particular, local changes. This has led, in the late 20th century, to a revisionary reading of the period of modernity as not necessarily closed but rather as a many-sided phenomenon, marked by the ruins of its earlier phases, but still profoundly formative of the present. This situation seems destined to generate textures of experience even more complex than those encompassed by such generic terms as modernity and post-modernity, however expansively they may be defined.

BIBLIOGRAPHY

K. Marx and F. Engels: 'The Communist Manifesto' (1848), *Selected Works* (Moscow, 1970)

C. Baudelaire: 'Le Cygne' (1859); Eng. trans. by F. Scarfe in *Baudelaire: Selected Verse* (Harmondsworth, 1961), p. 209

T. Gautier: *Souvenir de théâtre, d'art et de critique* (Paris, 1883)

W. Benjamin: *Charles Baudelaire: Ein Lyriker Dichter im Zeitalter des Hochkapitalismus* (Frankfurt am Main, 1938; Eng. trans., London, 1973)

M. Weber: *Wirtschaft und Gesellschaft* (Tübingen, 1956)

M. Foucault: *Les Mots et les choses* (Paris, 1966); Eng. trans. as *The Order of Things* (New York, 1971)

G. Simmel: *Sociology* (Glencoe, IL, 1969)

M. Heidegger: *The Question Concerning Technology and Other Essays* (New York, 1977)

W. Benjamin: 'Passagen-Werk', *Gesammelte Schriften*, ed. R. Tiedemann, v (Frankfurt am Main, 1983)

M. Berman: *All that Is Solid Melts into Air* (New York, 1983)

S. Kern: *The Culture of Time and Space, 1880–1918* (London, 1983)

J. Baudrillard: 'Modernité', *Encyclopedia universalis*, xii (Paris, 1985)

S. Buck-Morss: *The Dialectics of Seeing: Walter Benjamin and the Arcades Project* (Cambridge, MA, 1990)

A. Giddens: *The Consequences of Modernity* (Stanford, 1990)

J. Habermas: *Der philosophische Diskurs der Moderne*, Eng. trans. by F. G. Lawrence (Cambridge, MA, 1990)

B. Latour: *Nous n'avons jamais été modernes: Essais d'anthropologie symétrique* (Paris, 1991; Eng. trans. by C. Porter, Cambridge, MA, 1993)

T. Smith: *Making the Modern: Industry, Art and Design in America* (Chicago, 1993)

TERRY SMITH

Modern Movement. Term applied to the architecture of simple geometrical forms and plain undecorated surfaces, free of historical styles, that developed mainly in Europe in the late 19th century and the early 20th prior to World War II. The origin of the term is especially associated with Nikolaus Pevsner, whose book *Pioneers of the Modern Movement* (1936) traced the sources of the movement from William Morris to Walter Gropius. Pevsner capitalized the words and asserted that the Modern Movement had resulted in 'the recognized accepted style of our age'. After 1932 the term INTERNATIONAL STYLE was widely used synonymously with Modern Movement to describe such work of this period, which is also encompassed within the more popular global term Modernism.

See also RATIONALISM (ii) and FUNCTIONALISM.

1. Origins, 1860–c. 1907. 2. Deutscher Werkbund and the aesthetics of Functionalism, c. 1907–16. 3. De Stijl to Der Ring, 1917–25. 4. Towards an international style, 1926–32.

1. ORIGINS, 1860–c. 1907. The European Modern Movement embraced not only radical changes in the formal and stylistic characteristics of buildings but also a sense of social involvement. Both had their origins in Britain in the Arts and Crafts Movement, which itself had grown out of a reaction against the overblown forms and uncontrolled decoration of machine-made objects of the mid-19th century. William Morris, for example, sought to combine social amelioration with better design: the handcrafted products of the company he set up were believed to convey socio-cultural as well as professional satisfaction to the craftsmen who made them, while their unpretentious, traditional forms also looked forward to the aesthetic values of the Modern Movement. Architects associated with the Arts and Crafts Movement, including Philip

Webb and A. H. Mackmurdo, favoured extended plain surfaces in buildings: Mackmurdo designed Brooklyn (c. 1886) at Enfield, London, a remarkable, early flat-roofed house with unadorned walls and horizontal windows to the upper floor. Elegant, uncomplicated interiors and undecorated surfaces also characterize such houses as the Orchard (1899–1900), Chorleywood, Herts, by C. F. A. Voysey, a member of the Arts and Crafts Exhibition Society (founded 1888) and perhaps the most important figure of the English domestic revival; externally his houses were often simply and boldly modelled, with uninterrupted surfaces (e.g. Perrycroft, 1893, near Malvern, Worcs). These innovative British developments prompted the German Government to second the architect Hermann Muthesius to the German Embassy in London from 1896 to 1903 to study and report on British architecture and design.

New attitudes to volumetric form also began to appear in the 1890s, especially in the work of Victor Horta in Belgium (e.g. Maison Tassel, 1892–3; *see* HORTA, VICTOR, fig. 1) and that of Héctor Guimard in France. Their approach was inspired by the freedoms implicit in the two-dimensional origins of Art Nouveau, a movement that began in opposition to *fin-de-siècle* eclecticism and accentuated the use of the curved line for decorative features. Art Nouveau detailing was combined with unadorned stone masses and extensive glazed areas in the Glasgow School of Art (begun 1896; *see* MACKINTOSH, CHARLES RENNIE, fig. 1); the work of Mackintosh, who was influenced by Voysey, was rejected by the Arts and Crafts Movement in Britain but proved to be influential in Europe.

The new freedom of form also found expression in Vienna, for example in Josef Maria Olbrich's Secession Building (1897–8; *see* AUSTRIA, fig. 9); in Turin, in Raimondo D'Aronco's exuberant *Stile Liberty* buildings for the Esposizione Internazionale d'Arte Decorativa Moderna (1902); and in Barcelona, where Gaudí set whole buildings on the move (e.g. Casa Milà, 1906–10; *see* GAUDÍ, ANTONI, fig. 1). Other overt uses of uninhibited, non-historical forms included Olbrich's remarkable Hochzeitsturm (1905–8), Darmstadt (for illustration *see* OLBRICH, JOSEF MARIA), and the two white, marble-clad examples of Secession *Gesamtkunstwerk*: Wagner's Postsparkasse (1903), Vienna, its banking hall lit by a great glazed roof (*see* WAGNER, OTTO, fig. 2), and Hoffmann's Palais Stoclet (1905–11), Brussels (*see* HOFFMANN, JOSEF, fig. 2). Also in the Viennese circle after his return from Chicago in 1896 was Adolf Loos, who published an influential diatribe in opposition to the *Gesamtkunstwerk* ethic in his 'Ornament und Verbrechen' (*Cah. Aujourd'hui*, June 1913). His Goldman & Salatsch Building (Looshaus; 1910; *see* LOOS, ADOLF, fig. 1) and his early houses in Vienna, with openings set irregularly in plain rendered wall surfaces (e.g. Steiner House, 1910, and Scheu House, 1912–13), are among the important early images of the Modern Movement.

Structural rationalism, another fundamental component of Modernism, was newly evident in H. P. Berlage's Beursgebouw (1896–1903), Amsterdam (for illustration *see* EXCHANGE), built on the strictest principles of Viollet-le-Duc and with an exposed steel roof structure. The first decisive move towards an overt structural rationalist expression, however, was seen in the work of the Perret brothers in France, whose exposed reinforced-concrete frame-and-panel construction produced some of the earliest astylar façades of the Modern Movement (e.g. eight-storey block of flats at 25 Rue Franklin, Paris, 1903–5; *see* PARIS, fig. 11). Also designed for concrete construction, the buildings of Garnier's projected *Cité industrielle* (exhibited 1904; for illustration *see* GARNIER, TONY) assumed elemental cubic forms. In the USA an uncompromising interpretation of framed structure was expressed in the upper floors of Sullivan's Schlesinger & Mayer Store, Chicago (1899; now Carson Pirie Scott Store; *see* SULLIVAN, LOUIS, fig. 2; *see also* CHICAGO SCHOOL). At the same time a unique planar horizontality was purveyed by Frank Lloyd Wright (who had studied with Sullivan) in his proposals for the Prairie House, for example in the Ward Willits House (1902) in Highland Park, IL (*see* UNITED STATES OF AMERICA, fig. 8 and WRIGHT, (1), fig. 1; *see also* PRAIRIE SCHOOL). The planning, simple massing, unadorned surfaces and environmental control of Wright's Larkin Building (1903–6; destr. 1950), Buffalo, NY, in particular, were prophetic of burgeoning Modernism.

2. DEUTSCHER WERKBUND AND THE AESTHETICS OF FUNCTIONALISM, *c.* 1907–16. One of the most important events in the development of the Modern Movement was the foundation (1907) in Munich of the DEUTSCHER WERKBUND with the aim of bringing together industrialists, artists and craftsmen with a common interest in 'ennobling' German products. Its foundation was stimulated by Muthesius's return to Germany in 1903 and his appointment to the Handelsministerium with a brief to improve the country's system of education in the applied arts. The schools were then still largely dedicated to hand crafts, although the influential political theorist Friedrich Naumann put forward a German idealist case for a sophisticated machine aesthetic aimed at improving the quality as well as the economic accessibility of German goods. The Deutscher Werkbund had an initial membership of 13 artist-designers, including Hoffmann, Olbrich and Peter Behrens, and 10 industrial groups, including the Werkstätten für Handwerkskunst, as well as private firms. Its acceptance of industrialization and the machine led to such radical new industrial buildings as those designed between 1907 and 1919 for the Allgemeine Elektrizitäts-Gesellschaft (AEG) by Behrens (see fig. 1; *see also* BEHRENS, PETER, fig. 1) and the Fagus Factory (1911–13) on the Leine at Alfeld, by Walter Gropius and Adolf Meyer; these are among the best-known images of the early Modern Movement. Poelzig's Milch Chemical Factory at Luban (for illustration *see* POELZIG, HANS) and his five-storey shop and office building at Breslau (now Wrocław, Poland; both 1911–12) were equally uncompromising stylistically, although more dynamic in form: taken in combination with the undoubted symbolism of Behrens's Turbinenfabrik, they represent the beginnings of architectural Expressionism.

1. Modern Movement building by Peter Behrens: AEG Turbinenfabrik, Moabit, Berlin, 1909

The few years immediately before World War I were critical in determining aesthetic trends, with formal developments in the Modern Movement influenced by both Cubism and Futurism from about 1912. Cubist painting from 1908 had shown that everyday objects could be dissolved and re-synthesized as geometric or transparent superimposed compositions, and this aesthetic was well suited to express the nascent forms arising from the new building technology (*see* CUBISM, §II). More literal interpretations such as CZECH CUBISM, however, produced little more than the eccentric façades designed by such architects as Josef Chochol (*see* PRAGUE, fig. 6) and Josef Gočár. A more dynamic urban utopia was depicted by the Italian Futurists, whose stylized, industrial monumentalism was in touch with faster transport systems and engineering virtuosity (*see* FUTURISM, §2). The architect-prophets of Futurism were Antonio Sant'Elia and Mario Chiattone, both of whom showed their work at the first Nuove Tendenze exhibition in Milan in 1914 (for illustration *see* SANT'ELIA, ANTONIO).

A rift between the supporters of machine aesthetics and those of hand crafts emerged at the Werkbund conference and exhibition (1914) at Cologne, at which Muthesius, who proposed a form of standardization related to machine production, confronted the Expressionist lobby headed by Henry Van de Velde, the Belgian head of the Kunstgewerbeschule at Weimar, who was supported by Gropius and Bruno Taut. The Expressionist group favoured artistic independence and freedom to create forms that would be realized through the building crafts. Among notable buildings erected for the exhibition, a model factory by Gropius and Meyer was a further development along the lines of the Fagus Factory, though showing additional influences from Frank Lloyd Wright; while Van de Velde's model theatre (*see* VAN DE VELDE, HENRY, fig. 2) and Bruno Taut's Glashaus (for illustration *see* TAUT, (1)) were important early precedents in the development of Expressionism (*see* EXPRESSIONISM, §2). The growing Werkbund controversy was set aside with the onset of war, and when Van de Velde left Germany he recommended that Gropius should succeed him as head of the Weimar Kunstgewerbeschule. Although few buildings of importance to the Modern Movement were built during World War I, in 1914–15 Le Corbusier proposed the elemental 'Dom-Ino' slab-and-column system (unexecuted) for building houses; around this time Jan Wils and Robert van't Hoff were producing a simplified architecture in the Netherlands (e.g. van't Hoff's buildings at Huis ter Heide, near Utrecht), and in the USA Irving Gill, who had worked for Sullivan, was building white, astylar houses in Los Angeles of which the Dodge House (1914–16), Hollywood, is the best-known example (for illustration *see* GILL, IRVING).

3. DE STIJL TO DER RING, 1917–25. A major contribution to the forms of the emerging Modern Movement was made by the abstracted, rectilinear geometry espoused by the De Stijl group (founded Leiden, 1917), which was able to flourish during the war because of the neutrality of

2. Modern Movement building by Gerrit Rietveld: Schröder House, Utrecht, 1924

the Netherlands. Much influenced by Cubism and Neoplasticism, De Stijl was formally antithetical to the contemporary Expressionist and sometimes eccentric AMSTERDAM SCHOOL, and it attracted such designers as El Lissitzky, who had worked with Kazimir Malevich, and Gerrit Rietveld, a furniture-designer turned architect. Rietveld's Schröder House (1924; see fig. 2), Utrecht, has been held to demonstrate better than any other building the meaning of 20th-century architecture (see Sharp, p. 74). In Rotterdam a technologically orientated group DE OPBOUW was formed (1920); members included J. J. P. Oud, Mart Stam and J. A. Brinkman, and it had a notable impact on public housing in the city in the 1920s (*see* OUD, J. J. P.).

In Germany the radical ARBEITSRAT FÜR KUNST and the NOVEMBERGRUPPE were both founded towards the end of 1918, the former by Bruno Taut on socialist-idealist lines and the latter declaring for innovation and new forms. Most of the architectural avant-garde, including Gropius, Otto Bartning, Hugo Häring, Hans Scharoun, Bruno Taut and Max Taut, were members of both groups, and some of them also joined Bruno Taut's Gläserne Kette, a correspondence group formed in 1919 to keep radical design ideals alive during the ensuing period of economic instability. In Weimar, the seat of the new German government, Gropius was courted by both the Kunstgewerbeschule and the Hochschule für Bildende Kunst, and in 1919 he merged them to form the Staatliches Bauhaus (*see* BAUHAUS), which became highly influential in the development of the Modern Movement.

The radical lobby of the immediate post-war period championed the formal freedoms of Expressionism—seen especially in Mendelsohn's Einstein Tower (1920–24),

Potsdam (*see* MENDELSOHN, ERICH, fig. 1)—and the hand-craft ideal as opposed to the industrialization of the building process, which they associated with capitalism. Poelzig was elected president of the reassembled Werkbund at Stuttgart in 1919, and for a brief period Expressionism gained ground even in the Bauhaus itself. This trend was, however, reversed, partly under the influence of De Stijl (Theo van Doesberg was a visiting lecturer at the Bauhaus in 1923) and Russian Constructivism. The Werkbund dissociated itself from the hand-craft organizations, and by 1923 Gropius stood at the head of a school '…devoted to Machine-Age architecture' (see Banham, p. 12). This was also the year in which the Werkbund met at Weimar, in which Gropius spoke of the new technology as part and parcel of a functional architecture, and in which Le Corbusier exhibited his Citrohan designs of 1920–22 at the *Haus am Horn* exhibition (1923) at the Bauhaus. These were published in the *Bauhausbuch* under the prophetic general title *Internationale Architektur* (Munich, 1925).

Another radical group, DER RING, was founded in Berlin in 1923–4 to encourage the advancement of the international movement in architecture and to support *Neues Bauen*, a term widely used in Germany (*Nieuwe Bouwen* in the Netherlands) after 1920, initially to stress the role of technology in determining form but eventually applied generally to a rational modern architecture constructed with the new building techniques. Der Ring extended its membership in 1926 to include architects from all shades of the design spectrum, from the dynamism of Expressionism to the more rigorous rectilinear geometry inspired by Neue Sachlichkeit (a name first used in 1925 to categorize an anti-Expressionist movement in painting) and notions of Functionalism: Poelzig, Mendelsohn and Ludwig Mies van der Rohe, as well as most of the members of the Novembergruppe and the Gläserne Kette (disbanded in 1920), were then united in a single, more broadly based movement.

Notable supporters of the Modern Movement in France included, in addition to Le Corbusier, Henri Sauvage, who completed the Futurist-inspired eight-storey block of flats in the Rue des Amiraux, Paris, in 1927. In 1925 the Exposition Internationale des Arts Décoratifs et Industriels Modernes was held in Paris, which, although mainly associated with the origins of Art Deco, also included important buildings associated with the Modern Movement, such as the Soviet Pavilion by Konstantin Mel'nikov and, in particular, Le Corbusier's influential Pavillon de l'Esprit Nouveau (both destr.). The latter was named after the journal *L'Esprit nouveau*, which in January 1921 published the principal manifesto of PURISM. The philosophy of the Purist movement, initiated originally in painting by Le Corbusier and Amédée Ozenfant as a reaction to Cubism, embraced an admiration for the beauty and purity of machine aesthetics; it characterized many of Le Corbusier's buildings of the late 1920s and early 1930s, among them some of the best-known works of the Modern Movement (*see* §4 below).

4. TOWARDS AN INTERNATIONAL STYLE, 1926–32. In 1925 the Bauhaus was relocated at Dessau, at first in temporary accommodation. The concept of *Neues Bauen*

seemed wholly appropriate to its new range of buildings there, designed by Gropius (with Meyer), which were completed the following year (*see* GERMANY, fig. 12). There were also signs of increasing international patronage for the Modern Movement in two renowned houses, one in the USA and one in Britain: the Lovell Beach House (1922–5), Newport Beach, CA, by the immigrant Austrian architect RUDOLPH SCHINDLER, and the unpretentious house New Ways (1923–5), Northampton, designed by Behrens for the Bassett-Lowke family.

The highest point in the development of the Modern Movement to date was, however, represented in the Weissenhofsiedlung (1927), a collaborative permanent exhibition of mixed housing mounted by the Deutscher Werkbund at Weissenhof, a suburb of Stuttgart, to demonstrate the potential of *Neues Bauen*. The exhibition, held under the direction of Mies van der Rohe, who had been elected vice-president of the Werkbund in 1926, combined work of both the older and younger generations of the progressive Werkbund membership and other invited Europeans. Almost all the original 21 separate buildings survive, and the surprisingly consistent result—all the buildings have plain walls, asymmetrical openings and flat roofs, and almost all are rectilinear in shape—more than justified the Werkbund's aim to produce a model for social housing using new technologies and free of historical references (for further discussion and illustration *see* DEUTSCHER WERKBUND). The influence of the Weissenhofsiedlung was immediate and worldwide. The socio-political importance of housing in the late 1920s and early 1930s was vital to the development of the Modern Movement and, even in less élitist circumstances than the Werkbund exhibition, it continued to produce memorable results, for example the Grossiedlung (1931), Siemensstadt, near Berlin, designed for the German electrical firm Siemens by several members of Der Ring, including such architects of widely dissimilar approaches as Gropius, Scharoun and Häring.

The international status of the Modern Movement implicit in the participation at Weissenhof of such architects as Le Corbusier, Mart Stam, J. J. P. Oud and Victor Bourgeois, in addition to the German members of the Werkbund, seemed to be confirmed with the foundation of CIAM (Congrès Internationaux d'Architecture Moderne) in Switzerland in 1928 at the instigation of Hélène de Mandrot, Sigfried Giedion and Le Corbusier. In Germany the broadening aesthetic base of the movement ranged from the sweeping dynamism of Mendelsohn's Schocken department store (1928; destr. 1960; *see* MENDELSOHN, ERICH, fig. 2) in Stuttgart and Chemnitz (1928) and Scharoun's block of flats (see fig. 3) at the second Werkbund exhibition, *Wohnung und Werkraum*, held at Breslau (now Wrocław, Poland) in 1929, to the interlocking rectilinear volumes and rich planar surfaces of the German Pavilion at the Exposición Internacional, Barcelona (1929; *see* MIES VAN DER ROHE, LUDWIG, fig. 1), which has become one of the icons of the Modern Movement.

Important developments also took place elsewhere in Europe. In the Netherlands the ARCHITECTENGROEP DE 8 was founded (1927) in Amsterdam with aims similar to those of the earlier *De Opbouw*, expressed in such buildings as the Zonnestraal Sanatorium (1926–8), Hilversum (for illustration *see* BIJVOET & DUIKER), and the Van Nelle Tobacco Factory (1925–31), Rotterdam (for illustration *see* BRINKMAN, (2)). In Italy the rationalist GRUPPO 7 was founded in 1926, ultimately leading to the formation of a country-wide movement (*see* RATIONALISM (ii)), the principles of which were expressed particularly in the Novocomum block of flats (1927–8), Como (for illustration *see* TERRAGNI, GIUSEPPE). In France, Le Corbusier's Villa Stein-de Monzie (1926–7), Garches, Paris (*see* LE CORBUSIER, fig. 2) and Villa Savoye (1929–31), Poissy, near Versailles (*see* VILLA, fig. 10), were the ultimate achievements of his Purist phase that did much to establish the image of the Modern Movement.

In spite of the economic depression of the 1930s, the new forms also influenced such architects as Fernando García Mercadal and Rafael Bergamín (1891–1970) in Spain, Thomas Tait, Maxwell Fry, Amyas Connell and Joseph Emberton in Britain, Paul Artaria, Hans Schmidt and Rudolf Steiger in Switzerland, Josef Kranz, Jan Visek (1890–1966) and Bohuslav Fuchs in Czechoslovakia, Bohdan Lachert, Józef Szanajca and other members of the Praesens group in Poland, Gunnar Asplund in Sweden and Alvar Aalto in Finland. Even before 1930 the aesthetics of the movement, as well as the populist principles of its early exponents, were carried further afield by immigrant architects or those returning home from training in Europe: Richard Neutra in the USA, Alberto Prebisch and Antonio Ubaldo Vilar in Argentina, Gregori Warchavchik, Lúcio Costa and Rino Levi in Brazil, and Jose Villagrán García and Luis Barragán in Mexico are a few well-known examples. The buildings of the European Modern Movement dominated the exhibition of architecture (1932) at MOMA, New York, described and illustrated in the accompanying book by Henry-Russell Hitchcock and Philip Johnson, *The International Style: Architecture since 1922* (New York, 1932), which led to the widespread adoption of the term International Style to describe the work of these architects as well as later developments.

BIBLIOGRAPHY
H. Muthesius: *Stilarchitektur und Baukunst* (Berlin, 1902)
N. Pevsner: *Pioneers of the Modern Movement* (London, 1936, rev. New York, 2/1949); rev. as *Pioneers of Modern Design from William Morris to Walter Gropius* (London, 1960)
S. Giedion: *Space, Time and Architecture* (Cambridge, MA, 1941)
——: *A Decade of New Architecture* (Zurich, 1951)
B. Zevi: *Poetica dell'architettura neoplastica* (Milan, 1953)
H. Eckstein: *50 Jahre Deutscher Werkbund* (Frankfurt am Main, 1958)
H.-R. Hitchcock: *Architecture: Nineteenth and Twentieth Centuries*, Pelican Hist. A. (Harmondsworth, 1958, rev. 2/1963)
P. R. Banham: *Theory and Design in the First Machine Age* (London, 1960)
L. Benevolo: *Storia dell'architettura moderna*, 2 vols (Milan, 1960)
P. Collins: *Changing Ideals in Modern Architecture* (London, 1965)
H. Sting: *Der Kubismus und seine Einwirkung auf die Wegbereiter der modernen Architektur* (Aachen, 1965)
D. Sharp: *Modern Architecture and Expressionism* (London, 1966)
B. Miller Lane: *Architecture and Politics in Germany, 1918–1945* (Cambridge, MA, 1968)
H. Wingler: *The Bauhaus: Weimar, Dessau, Berlin and Chicago* (Cambridge, MA, 1969)
R. Macleod: *Style and Society: Architectural Ideology in Britain 1835–1914* (London, 1971)
N. Pevsner: 'Secession', *Archit. Rev.* [London], clix/887 (1971), pp. 73–4
C. Jencks: *Modern Movements in Architecture* (London, 1973, rev. 2/1985)
W. Pehnt: *Expressionist Architecture* (London, 1973)

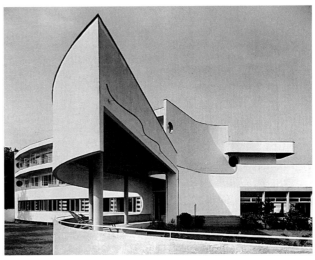

3. Modern Movement building by Hans Scharoun: hostel and flats at the *Wohnung und Werkraum* Werkbund exhibition, Breslau (now Wrocław), 1929

N. Powell: *The Sacred Spring: The Arts in Vienna, 1898–1918* (New York, 1974)
C. Benton, ed.: *Documents: A Collection of Source Material on the Modern Movement* (Milton Keynes, 1975)
C. Benton and T. Benton, eds: *A Source Book on the History of Architecture and Design 1890–1939* (Milton Keynes, 1975)
T. Benton, S. Muthesius and B. Wilkins: *Europe, 1900–14* (Milton Keynes, 1975)
J. L. Marfany: *Aspectes del modernisme* (Barcelona, 1975)
M. Tafuri and F. Dal Co: *Architettura contemporanea*, 2 vols (Milan, 1976; Eng. trans., New York, 1979) [esp. vol. i]
J. Campbell: *The German Werkbund: The Politics of Reform in the Applied Arts* (Princeton, 1978) [with bibliog.]
G. Gresleri: *L'Esprit nouveau* (Milan, 1979)
K. Frampton: *Modern Architecture: A Critical History* (London, 1980) [esp. pt 2, chaps 1–19, and bibliog.]
W. J. R. Curtis: *Modern Architecture since 1900* (Oxford, 1982, rev. 2/1987) [esp. pt 1–2]
I. B. Whyte: *Bruno Taut and the Architecture of Activism* (Cambridge, 1982)
R. Pommer and C. F. Otto: *Weissenhof 1927 and the Modern Movement in Architecture* (Chicago, 1991)
D. Sharp: *Twentieth-century Architecture: A Visual History* (London, 1991)

JOHN MUSGROVE

Moderno [Mondella, Galeazzo] (*b* Verona, 1467; *d* Verona, 1528). Italian plaquette designer and gem-engraver. A coherent group of 12 plaquette designs (from some 45 currently credited to this master; Washington, DC, N.G.A.; Vienna, Ksthist. Mus.) are signed with initials or contractions of MODERNUS FECIT or OPUS MODERNI: both the signed and attributed groups establish a claim for the recognition of their author as the most accomplished designer of plaquettes in Italy in the Renaissance. References to the art of the western Veneto in the early work and to that of Venice in later examples make it virtually certain that Moderno was Galeazzo Mondella of Verona. The plaquettes display an intimate awareness of preceding and contemporary Veronese art, with special loyalties to Andrea Mantegna, the Falconetto family, Francesco Bonsignori and Liberale da Verona. Galeazzo's brother Girolamo Mondella (1464–1512) was a painter and an intimate of the Este court at Ferrara. Moderno's earliest works (from about 1485) reflect both Ferrarese painting and a disposition towards the humanist themes favoured by the court. Ferrara also gave him the opportunity to see Bolognese art; in his early years he may have known Emilian art mainly from drawings. The same was true of Lombard art: he knew of Vincenzo Foppa in Brescia (which was then Venetian), but of art in Milan and Pavia perhaps only through Foppa's involvement there.

Within the Veneto, Moderno was attracted to Bartolomeo Montagna and his pupil Cima, as well as to the Vivarini family, Antonello da Messina, the Bellini family, and Carlo Crivelli in Venice. His main inspiration came from Mantegna, above all during Mantegna's period in Mantua, where Moderno may have had access to his studio. It is striking that his work has virtually no parallels with the art of Padua.

Moderno appears to have chosen his pseudonym as early as 1487 at Mantua, where he evidently worked as a medallist; thereafter he must have frequented the Mantuan court regularly. Within the Verona–Ferrara–Mantua area he seems to have been almost as peripatetic as a contemporary engraver, Nicoletto da Modena (*fl* 1480–1507), whom he may well have known: many of Nicoletto's prints reflect Moderno's plaquettes, and they are often the sources of later copies by Giovanni Antonio da Brescia (*fl* 1490). From about 1500 Moderno's work suggests he had first-hand experience of the expressive terracotta sculpture groups that were characteristic of Modena and Bologna. Contacts at Mantua may have introduced him to the greatest patron of his late years, Cardinal Domenico Grimani of Venice: through this connection he seems to have developed a considerable Venetian clientele and perhaps turned more to gem-engraving.

Moderno's work moves from a tentative provincial eclecticism based mostly on Mantegna to a confident and authoritative Roman Renaissance classicism based on Raphael and the Antique, often interpreted in forms similar to those of Tullio Lombardo and Antonio Lombardo in Venice and Ferrara. He may not have travelled far from the Veneto during the discernible years of his working life (1485–1515), although it is likely that Cardinal Grimani helped him to visit Rome in the latter part of that period, perhaps during the invasions of the Veneto (1509–16). There seem to be no new designs by Moderno after about 1512, the year he became head of the Mondella family workshop. Moderno may have turned from art to civic affairs after the restoration of his family to the council of nobles in Verona in 1517, or he may have travelled to France, as Vasari supposed; there are no records of his whereabouts from 1517 until 1527, when he is documented in Verona. After his death, the family shop was inherited by his son Giambattista Mondella (1506–*c*. 1572), who was also a metalworker. Moderno's designs continued to be reissued for some time, as well as augmented, adapted and further developed. Their inclusion in fine castings on Paduan utensils around 1530 and later (perhaps by Desiderio da Firenze) suggests that a few of his most popular matrices may have been transferred to Padua. His plaquettes were widely admired and conspicuously influential in the Veneto, Emilia and Lombardy; farther afield, his designs were sketched by Albrecht Dürer and Hans Holbein (ii) and incorporated into French Renaissance sculpture; one of the best, *Zeus Hurling a Thunderbolt at Phaeton* (Windsor Castle, Berks, Royal Col.), provided Michelangelo with the model of a figure for his *Last Judgement* in the Sistine Chapel (Rome, Vatican; *see* ROME, fig. 43).

BIBLIOGRAPHY

G. Vasari: *Vite* (1550, rev. 2/1568); ed. G. Milanesi (1878–85), v, pp. 375–6

L. Rognini: 'Galeazzo e Girolamo Mondella, artisti del rinascimento veronese', *Atti Mem. Accad. Agric., Sci. & Lett. Verona*, ser. 6, xxv (1975), pp. 95–119

D. Lewis: 'The Medallic Oeuvre of "Moderno": His Development at Mantua in the Circle of "Antico"', *Italian Medals*, ed. J. G. Pollard, 'Studies in the History of Art', xxi (Washington, DC, 1987), pp. 77–97

——: 'The Plaquettes of "Moderno" and his Followers', *Italian Plaquettes*, ed. A. Luchs, 'Studies in the History of Art', xxii (Washington, DC, 1989), pp. 105–41

DOUGLAS LEWIS

Modersohn-Becker [née Becker], **Paula** (*b* Dresden, 8 Feb 1876; *d* Worpswede, 20 Nov 1907). German painter. She trained in Bremen in 1892 and subsequently studied in London. From 1894 to 1896 she took a teacher's training course at her family's insistence but then with their permission attended the Berlin Malerinnenschule, from 1896 to 1898. In 1897 she met members of the artists' colony in Worpswede, near Bremen, and in the autumn of 1898 she moved there, believing that in this unsophisticated farming village she could more easily achieve her artistic objective of simplicity (*see* WORPSWEDE COLONY). Her teacher was Fritz Mackensen, but her friendship with the painter Otto Modersohn (1865–1943) was more important to her artistic development. She soon, however, came to feel that further progress depended on fresh experience. On 31 December 1899 she left for Paris, where she attended the Académie Cola Rossi. In Paris she first saw paintings by Cézanne, which confirmed her own artistic aims.

In summer 1900, Paula Becker returned to Worpswede, where her circle of friends included the sculptor Clara Rilke-Westhoff (1878–1954), the writers Rainer Maria Rilke and Carl Hauptmann, the *Jugendstil* artist Heinrich Vogeler, and later the sculptor Bernhard Hoetger. In May 1901 she married Otto Modersohn, and a year of close collaboration followed. Gradually she began to question Modersohn's predominantly emotive view of nature, favouring instead a clear, straightforward structure. In landscape paintings she stressed formal principles by depicting treetrunks and the horizon in strictly vertical and horizontal terms. Images were likewise treated as interlocking surfaces of colour. She spent brief periods in Paris in spring 1903 and again in 1905. She visited museums, studying ancient Faiyum mummy portraits, Gothic sculptures, Rembrandt and the Impressionists. She also looked at more contemporary work, such as that of the Nabis, especially Maurice Denis and Pierre Bonnard. But the most significant influences were Cézanne, Gauguin and van Gogh.

Modersohn-Becker's consistent, and almost totally unrecognized, pursuit of simplification and abstraction left her isolated on her return to Worpswede. In February 1906 she again set off for Paris, wanting to break away for good from the colony. It was at this time that she produced her most striking works: semi-nude or nude self-portraits and mother and child images. In her many self-portraits she radically simplified the formal structure of the face.

Paula Modersohn-Becker: *Naked Woman Breast-feeding her Child,* oil on canvas, 1.13×0.74 m, 1907 (Berlin, Neue Nationalgalerie)

She showed her body as a symbol of animal vitality, a life-giving vessel, less an individual character than an image of femininity itself. In *Naked Woman Breast-feeding her Child* (Berlin, Neue N.G.; see fig.) she rejected the genre's sentimental tradition in order to convey the experience of giving new life while already sensing one's own death. A naked woman, like an archaic matriarchal goddess, is kneeling breast-feeding her child: light falls on the child, while her face is in shadow. The setting, with oranges and plants, enhances the impression of ritual activity. It is clear that the example of Cézanne and Gauguin helped her to achieve the simplification of form seen in her last works.

In summer 1906 Otto Modersohn joined his wife in Paris. By spring of the following year she was expecting a baby, and the couple returned to Worpswede. She died of an embolism three weeks after their daughter's birth.

WRITINGS

G. Busch and L. von Reinken, eds: *Paula Modersohn-Becker in Briefen und Tagebüchern* (Frankfurt am Main, 1979)

BIBLIOGRAPHY

G. Pauli: *Paula Modersohn-Becker* (Leipzig, 1919)

R. Hetsch, ed.: *Paula Modersohn-Becker: Ein Buch der Freundschaft* (Berlin, 1932)

C. Murken-Altrogge: *Paula Modersohn-Becker: Leben und Werk* (Cologne, 1980)

G. Busch: *Paula Modersohn-Becker: Malerin, Zeichnerin* (Frankfurt am Main, 1981)

L. von Reinken: *Paula Modersohn-Becker* (Hamburg, 1983)

HANS GERHARD HANNESEN

Modhera. Temple site in northern Gujarat, India. Settlements existed at Modhera as early as the 2nd century AD, as finds of Kshatrapa coins indicate. The major monument is the great Surya Temple, ascribed to Bhima I (*reg c.* 1023–62) of the SOLANKI dynasty because of its grand scale, elaboration of detail and an inscription on the shrine interior bearing a date equivalent to 1026–7. This date corresponds with the retreat of Mahmud of Ghazna (*reg* 998–1030) following his occupation of the area, and the lavish scale of the temple may have been a statement of the Solanki dynasty's regained supremacy.

Facing east, the temple complex consists of a large bathing tank, a detached dance pavilion—an open, pillared structure faced by a fragmentary gateway (Skt *toraṇa*)—and the temple proper, comprising an audience hall and a shrine joined by a buffer wall. The inner sanctum is surrounded by a circumambulatory passage. Breaks in the sanctum's floor reveal a lower chamber, usually interpreted as a treasury but possibly a repository for sacred objects associated with the temple's consecration. The roofs of all the buildings have collapsed, perhaps as the result of an earthquake in the early 19th century. In its elevation and sculpted detail the temple exemplifies the mature phase of the Maru-Gurjara style (Dhaky, 1975). The dance pavilion and gateway were probably built *c.* 50 years later than the temple proper: differences in the sculptural styles and proportional adjustments necessitated by the space available between the tank and the temple indicate that they were not part of the original conception.

Twelve images of Surya, probably meant to indicate the *aditya*s (aspects of Surya identified with the 12 months of the year), are placed along the interior walls of the audience hall and shrine. The exterior wall facets of the audience hall are carved with 12 images of goddesses alternating with guardians of the directions (*lokapāla*s), while on the shrine guardians alternate with the 12 *aditya*s. The goddesses can be tentatively identified with the *dvādaśagaurī*s ('Twelve Gauris'), aspects of the supreme goddess, whose iconography is described in the *Aparājitapṛcchā* ('Enquiry to the Unconquered One'), a 12th-century Sanskrit text from Gujarat. While their precise role in the pantheon surrounding Surya is unclear, they can perhaps be seen here as female analogues (*śakti*s) of the *aditya*s.

See also INDIAN SUBCONTINENT, §§III, 5(i)(c) and IV, 7(iii)(a).

BIBLIOGRAPHY

J. Burgess and H. Cousens: *The Architectural Antiquities of Northern Gujarat, More Especially the Districts Included in the Baroda State,* Archaeol. Surv. W. India, New Imp. Ser., xxxii (1903), pp. 71–81

S. Bharucha: 'The Sun Temple at Modhera', *Marg,* v/1 (1951), pp. 50–56

M. A. Dhaky: 'Date of the Dancing Hall of the Sun Temple, Modhera', *J. Bombay Branch Royal Asiat. Soc.,* xxxviii (1963–4), pp. 211–22

L. P. Pandey: *Sun-worship in Ancient India* (Delhi, 1972)

M. A. Dhaky: 'The Genesis and Development of Māru-Gurjara Temple Architecture', *Studies in Indian Temple Architecture,* ed. P. Chandra (New Delhi, 1975)

W. Lobo: *The Sun-temple at Modhera* (Munich, 1982)

WALTER SMITH

Modigliani, Amedeo (*b* Livorno, 12 July 1884; *d* Paris, 24 Jan 1920). Italian painter, draughtsman and sculptor. While he is acknowledged to be one of the major artists of his generation, he was not as experimental and daring as his contemporaries. The direction of Picasso's work, for instance, changed radically between 1906 and 1909 as a result of the influence of Cézanne and other styles of art (notably African), but Modigliani's assimilation of these sources had no such far-reaching consequences. Given Modigliani's limited subject-matter in painting and sculpture, he achieved an extraordinary range of psychological interpretations of the human face, maintaining his individuality through his distinctive elongations of face or form.

1. Training and early work, to 1909. 2. Sculpture, 1909–14. 3. Final years, 1914–20.

1. TRAINING AND EARLY WORK, TO 1909. Modigliani was the youngest of four children of Flaminio Modigliani and Eugenia Garsin, who were both of Jewish descent. Never physically very strong, Modigliani was severely ill three times during his youth. In 1897, when he was 13, his mother wrote that he already saw himself as a painter. On 1 August 1898 he began to study in Livorno with the painter Guglielmo Micheli (1886–1926), a late representative of the Macchiaioli school of Italian *plein-air* painting.

Modigliani's studies in Livorno were often interrupted by illness. In late 1900 or early 1901 he contracted pleurisy, which left him with a tubercular lung. When his health improved, he toured Italy with his mother. His visits to Naples, Capri, Amalfi, Rome, Florence and Venice exposed him to many of Italy's most important works of art. During his travels Modigliani corresponded with his friend Oscar Ghiglia; the five surviving letters (see Mann, pp. 19–22) provide a rare and invaluable first-hand account of the young artists' idealism and aspirations. In May 1902 he enrolled at the Accademia di Belle Arti in Florence. The following year he moved to Venice, where he continued his academic studies for three more years. The only surviving work from this period is the pastel portrait of *Fabio Mauroner* (*c.* 1905; Milan, Gal. Naviglio).

In January 1906 Modigliani arrived in Paris, where, during the next few years, he absorbed a number of influences as he experimented and struggled to find a personal style. He settled in Montmartre, where he joined in artists' gatherings at Le Bateau-Lavoir and other studios, and enrolled at the Académie Colarossi. In autumn 1907 he met Dr Paul Alexandre, who became his first patron and a close friend until 1914. During this time the young doctor acquired about 25 paintings and numerous drawings.

The watercolour *Head of a Woman Wearing a Hat* (1907; Boston, MA, William Young, see Hall, pl. 6), with its linear outlines and flat planes of colour, is clearly related to the work of Toulouse-Lautrec. Modigliani also admired Fauvism and Picasso's Blue Period canvases. The tonality and subject-matter of *Head of Girl* (1908) is closely related to Picasso's Blue Period portraits, as is *The Jewess* (1908; priv. col., see Mann, p. 47), exhibited in Paris at the Salon des Indépandants (1908) along with four other paintings and a drawing. However, he seemed somewhat in awe, if not a little jealous, of Picasso's prodigious talent. The elegant pose of the model in *The Horsewoman* (1909; Mr

and Mrs Alexander Lewyt priv. col., see Hall, pl. 7) superficially resembles the fashionable society portraits of Giovanni Boldini and Sargent, in which he was also interested, but it lacks the slick bravura of their brushwork.

Cézanne's late portraits were the single most important influence on Modigliani's development. In *Portrait of Pedro* (1909; priv. col., see Hall, pl. 1) the deep-blue background, the blue-black colour of the jacket and the rich earth colours of the face are a paraphrase of Cézanne's modelling: structure and volume are defined by the accretion of tightly knit sequences of colour patches. After 1909 Modigliani's work ceased to reflect so blatantly that of another artist.

2. SCULPTURE, 1909–14. As early as 1902 Modigliani had produced his first three-dimensional work (untraced) at Pietrasanta, near Carrara, and thereafter declared to friends and family that he was a sculptor. Some time during the first six months of 1909 he moved to a new studio in Montparnasse, 14 Cité Falquière. Dr Alexandre introduced him to Constantin Brancusi, a meeting that stimulated Modigliani's sculptural ambitions. Brancusi's early stone carvings, such as the *Head of a Girl* (1907; untraced, see F. Back: *Constantin Brancusi: Metamorphosen plastischer Form*, Cologne, 1987), with its smooth face, elongated nose and small mouth, certainly influenced the style of Modigliani's series of thin stone heads executed between 1909 and 1914 (e.g. *c.* 1911; New York, Guggenheim). But even more important was the moral example of Brancusi, who retained his individuality and remained fiercely independent of current movements of the avant-garde in Paris. Modigliani, dedicated to working directly in stone, followed Brancusi's dictum, 'Direct carving is the true path towards sculpture'.

Owing to ill-health Modigliani produced relatively few sculptures, one of the greatest disappointments of his life. His early sculptures in wood (1907–8) are untraced. From 1909 he produced carvings in stone, of which there are 25 examples generally accepted to be by him: 23 heads, a standing figure (1912; priv. col., see Mann, p. 75) and a caryatid (*c.* 1913; New York, MOMA). While it is impossible to establish an accurate chronology of these works, it is generally agreed that Modigliani concentrated on sculpture and related drawings between 1909 and 1914. It was during this period that he began subtly to assimilate non-European sculptural traditions, African art being the most influential.

Modigliani had met Picasso before 1909 and must have been aware of his interest in African, Greek, Khmer and Egyptian art; he may have seen works in Picasso's collection. Modigliani's friendship with Jacques Lipchitz and Brancusi was another link with African art. His thin, elongated stone heads, such as *The Head* (*c.* 1911; London, Tate; see fig. 1), have usually been associated with Baule masks from the Ivory Coast. Other styles may also have been sources of inspiration, for example the masks of the Fang and Yaure peoples (of Gabon and the Ivory Coast respectively). Other sources have also been suggested, including Archaic Greek kore and Khmer and Egyptian sculpture. But just as Modigliani in his paintings consciously maintained his independence from the work of

1. Amedeo Modigliani: *The Head*, stone, h. 635 mm, *c.* 1911 (London, Tate Gallery)

Picasso and the avant-garde, so in his sculpture he was careful not to fall prey to mere imitation.

The stone heads were conceived as a series, as was his unexecuted group of caryatids. Seven were exhibited at the Salon d'Automne (1912) as *Têtes, ensemble décoratif.*

Lipchitz saw some of the sculptures arranged 'like tubes of an organ, to produce the special music he wanted'. Epstein recalled that at night Modigliani 'would place candles on the top of each one and the effect was that of a primitive temple'.

Both as painter and as sculptor Modigliani concentrated on making portraits. Though he abandoned sculpture in late 1913 or early 1914 to return to painting, the years he had devoted to sculpture influenced the style of his portraits of 1914–20. The most striking example is *Lola de Valence* (1915; New York, Adelaide Milton de Groot priv. col.), which is more a re-creation in two dimensions of his stone heads than it is a representative portrait.

3. FINAL YEARS, 1914–20. In 1914 Modigliani met Paul Guillaume, who became his dealer for the next two years, and he began a stormy two-year relationship with Beatrice Hastings, the subject of several portraits (e.g. 1915; Toronto, A.G. Ont.), most of them lifeless. Between 1914 and 1916 he executed studies of his lovers, friends and colleagues, which are among the finest portraits in early 20th-century art. His work was intensely autobiographical by comparison with most painters of his generation and provides the most striking evidence of his numerous contacts with the artistic and literary avant-garde in Paris. His subjects included *Diego Rivera* (1914; priv. col., see Hall, pl. 16), *Pablo Picasso* (1915; New York, Perls Galleries), *Juan Gris* (1915; New York, Met.), *Jacques Lipchitz* (1916; Chicago, IL, A. Inst.), *Henri Laurens* (1915; priv. col., see Mann, p. 100), *Moïse Kisling* (pencil, 1915; priv. col., see Mann, p. 102), *Max Jacob* (1916; Düsseldorf, Kstsamml. Nordrhein-Westfalen), *Jean Cocteau* (1916; New York, Pearlman Found. Inc., see Hall, pl. 22), *Paul Guillaume* (1916; Milan, Gal. A. Mod.) and *Leopold Zborowski* (1918; priv. col., see Hall, pl. 35). In contrast to the tentative, experimental manner of the pre-war paintings, Modigliani's uniquely personal style and vision attain maturity in these works.

The painter Chaïm Soutine was the subject of one of Modigliani's most penetrating character studies of the period, *Chaïm Soutine Seated at a Table* (*c.* 1916–17; Washington, DC, N.G.A.; see fig. 2). While some of his portraits are either impersonal—the eyes are often left blank—or almost caricatures of the sitter, this painting is a devastatingly honest, penetrating interpretation of the subject's psychological state of mind. Apart from the characteristically long neck, Modigliani avoided the highly stylized facial features found in many of his portraits, which tend to distance the viewer from the model. This is one of the most naturalistic of all Modigliani's portraits. The eyes, one slightly higher than the other, brilliantly portray Soutine's sense of despair and hopelessness, attitudes with which Modigliani could readily identify.

In 1916 Leopold Zborowski became Modigliani's dealer and began to support him with regular payments. The following year Modigliani met Jeanne Hébuterne, with whom he lived until his death (their daughter, Jeanne Modigliani, was born in 1919). His many portraits and half-length studies of her (e.g. 1918; priv. col., see Mann, p. 170) define his late, highly mannered style, in which the elongation of the neck is increasingly exaggerated. In the

2. Amedeo Modigliani: *Chaïm Soutine Seated at a Table*, oil on canvas, 917×597 mm, *c.* 1916–17 (Washington, DC, National Gallery of Art, Chester Dale Collection)

BIBLIOGRAPHY

A. Basler: *Modigliani* (Paris, 1931)
R. Goldwater: *Primitivism in Modern Painting* (New York, 1938, 2/1967), pp. 125–30
J. Lipchitz: *Amedeo Modigliani* (New York, 1952)
A. Ceroni: *Amedeo Modigliani: Peintre* (Milan, 1958) [ambitious attempt at a cat. rais. of the ptgs; useful ref.]
J. Modigliani: *Modigliani senza leggenda* (Florence, 1958); Eng. trans. as *Modigliani: Man and Myth* (London, 1959)
F. Russoli: *Modigliani* (London, 1959)
Modigliani (exh. cat. by J. Russell, London, ACGB, 1963)
A. Ceroni: *Amedeo Modigliani: Dessins et sculptures* (Milan, 1965)
A. Werner: *Modigliani the Sculptor* (London, 1965)
P. Sichel: *Modigliani* (London, 1967)
N. Ponente: *Modigliani* (London, 1969)
W. Fifield: *Modigliani: The Biography* (London, 1978)
D. Hall: *Modigliani* (London, 1979, rev. 1984) [excellent colour pls]
C. Mann: *Modigliani* (London, 1980)
Amedeo Modigliani (exh. cat., Paris, Mus. A. Mod. Ville Paris, 1981)
J. Modigliani: *Jeanne Modigliani racconta Modigliani* (Livorno, 1984) [important letts and docs; extensive bibliog.]
Modigliani, dipinti e disegni, incontri italiani (exh. cat. by O. Patani, Verona, Gal. Scuodo, 1984) [good source mat.]
A. G. Wilkinson: 'Paris and London: Modigliani, Lipchitz, Epstein and Gaudier-Brzeska', *'Primitivism' in 20th-century Art: Affinity of the Tribal and the Modern*, ii (exh. cat., ed. W. S. Rubin; New York, MOMA, 1984), pp. 417–50 [on the stone carvings of 1909–14]
The Unknown Modigliani: Drawings from the Collection of Paul Alexandre (exh. cat. by N. Alexandre, London, RA, 1994)

ALAN G. WILKINSON

Modillion. One of a series of brackets supporting the corona under a Corinthian cornice, often in the form of scrolls but sometimes appearing as plain blocks (*see* ORDERS, ARCHITECTURAL, fig. 1xxix). In the Doric order the modillion was replaced by the MUTULE.

Modotti, Tina [Assunta Adelaide Luigia] (*b* Udine, Italy, 16 Aug 1896; *d* Mexico City, 6 Jan 1942). Italian photographer, active in Mexico. She emigrated to the USA in 1918 and met Edward Weston in 1921, moving with him to Mexico City in 1923. There he taught her photography. Modotti's early platinum prints were close-up photographs of still-lifes such as wine glasses, folds of fabric or flowers, as in *Calla Lilies* (*c.* 1927; see Constantine, p. 98). She also made prints of finely composed architectural spaces. By 1927, when she joined the Communist Party, she was starting to incorporate more overt social content in her work. She also gave up making expensive and time-consuming platinum prints in favour of silver gelatin prints.

Modotti photographed political events, for example *Diego Rivera Addressing a Meeting of the International Red Aid, Mexico* (*c.* 1928; see Constantine, p. 117), as well as bullfights and the circus; she focused on the proud faces and hands of mothers, children, artisans and labourers. She was, however, deported from Mexico for her political activities in 1929. During the next decade she dedicated herself to revolutionary and anti-fascist activities in Russia and Spain and took few photographs. In 1939 she returned to Mexico City. Although Modotti photographed from 1923–32, her work is relatively scarce. There is a large collection at MOMA, New York.

BIBLIOGRAPHY

M. Constantine: *Tina Modotti: A Fragile Life* (New York, 1975, rev. 1983, 2/1993)

best of these portraits Modigliani sympathetically captures the warmth and affection of his lover.

In December 1917 Modigliani exhibited his great series of reclining nudes at the Galerie Berthe Weill, Paris; the exhibition was closed by the police on the grounds of obscenity. Yet these works continue the great tradition of the nude exemplified in the work of Giorgione, Titian, Goya and Manet. For example, the pose of *Reclining Nude with Blue Cushion* (1917; Milan, G. Mattioli priv. col.) appears to have been directly inspired by Giorgione's *Sleeping Venus* (Dresden, Gemäldegal. Alte Meister). The eroticism and unabashed sensuality of Modigliani's nudes are heightened by the models' portrayal as individual women. Their expressions seem inviting, yet there is a sense of intrusion into their private world. In 1918, when Modigliani's health began to deteriorate, he went with Jeanne to the south of France. Somewhat recovered, he returned to Paris the following year. His last works include portraits of his friend *Lunia Czechowska* (1919; priv. col., see Mann, p. 189), of *Jeanne Hébuterne* (1919; priv. col., see Mann, p. 201) and a *Self-portrait* (1919; priv. col., see Mann, p. 197). Modigliani died of tubercular meningitis, aggravated by drugs and alcohol, in a Paris hospital, and he was buried at Père-Lachaise cemetery.

A. Conger: 'Tina Modotti and Edward Weston: A Re-evaluation of their Photography', *EW: 100, Centennial Essays in Honor of Edward Weston* (Carmel, 1986), pp. 62–79

A. Stark: 'The Letters from Tina Modotti to Edward Weston', *The Archive*, 22 (1986), pp. 3–81

C. Barckhausen: *Auf den Spuren von Tina Modotti* (Cologne, 1988)

M. Hooks: *Tina Modotti: Photographer and Revolutionary* (London, 1993)

AMY RULE

Moesman, Johannes (Hendrikus) (*b* Utrecht, 6 Jan 1909; *d* Tull en 't Waal, 3 Feb 1988). Dutch painter and draughtsman. He had drawing lessons with Jos Hoevenaar (1840–1926), Theo van der Laar (1861–1939) and Willem van Leusden from 1919 to 1929. He was self-taught as a painter. Between 1923 and 1925 he trained at the School voor Grafische Vakken in Utrecht. From 1925 until 1968 he worked as a lithographer for N. V. Nederlandse Spoorwegen. He produced his first surreal drawings, inspired by the January issue of the magazine *Variétés*, in 1929. As a result of his contact with Pyke Koch he joined the society De Onafhankelijken (The Independents) in Amsterdam where the first exhibition of Surrealist work was held in 1931. In 1933 his painting *Afternoon* (1932; Utrecht, Cent. Mus.) was removed from an exhibition in the Stedelijk Museum, Amsterdam, on the grounds of alleged obscenity. In 1934 another painting, *The Arrivals* (1933; see de Vries, p. 17), was removed for similar reasons. Moesman subsequently left the society for lack of support. In 1961 Her de Vries brought his work to the attention of André Breton's circle in Paris, and thereafter it was shown at various international Surrealist exhibitions.

BIBLIOGRAPHY

H. de Vries and others: *Moesman* (Utrecht, 1971)

F. Keers and J. Steen: *Moesman* (Zwolle, 1994)

JOHN STEEN

Moeyaert, Claes [Nicolaes] **(Cornelisz.)** (*b* Durgerdam, nr Amsterdam, 1591; *bur* Amsterdam, 26 Aug 1655). Dutch painter, etcher and draughtsman. He was the son of an aristocratic Catholic Amsterdam merchant and moved to the city with his family in 1605. He was the most prolific of the history painters now called the PRE-REMBRANDTISTS, whose representations of biblical and mythological narratives, as well as of more recent secular history, give particular emphasis to dramatic and psychological effects. After working initially as a draughtsman and etcher, Moeyaert soon made his name as a painter. Landscapes with animals feature prominently in both his etchings and his paintings. At first he followed the lead of Adam Elsheimer, then of fellow Pre-Rembrandtists Pieter Lastman and Jan and Jacob Pynas, eventually, in the mid-1630s, coming under the influence of Rembrandt himself.

1. LIFE AND WORK.

(i) Paintings. About 100 of Moeyaert's paintings are preserved, and there are documentary references to at least 200 more. What are considered his earliest surviving paintings are undated pictures of the *Dismissal of Hagar* (Düsseldorf, priv. col.; see Tümpel, fig. 96) and *Elisha and the Shunamite Woman* (Moscow, Pushkin Mus. F. A.), both of which date from before 1624. Small, decorative

figures reminiscent of Elsheimer's move across a sketched-out landscape, and in places the painting is crude. There is already a marked emphasis on animated gestures, but the repertory of motifs is limited, and individual landscape elements have been borrowed directly from compositions by Jacob Pynas.

From 1624 onwards dated paintings occur at regular intervals, enabling a chronology to be established with some degree of certainty. The essentials of his style appear in the earliest dated examples: figures of powerful volume, using varied gestures, and clear, warm light, which suffuses the landscape and strongly models the figures, as in the *Allegory of Spring* (1624; Nuremberg, Ger. Nmus.). In some cases the horizon is so far distant that the figures are silhouetted against the sky, as in *Jacob Being Shown Joseph's Bloodstained Coat* (1624; Warsaw, N. Mus.).

Around 1629 Moeyaert's compositions and individual forms became calmer and simpler under the influence of Jan Pynas. This is evident in *Christ and the Captain from Capernaum* (1629; Herentals, St Waldetrudiskerk). Then, until *c.* 1636, he showed a preference for subjects with fewer figures (e.g. the *Good Samaritan Paying the Innkeeper*, *c.* 1635; ex-art market, Rome; see Tümpel, fig. 136); because of this, a compact, almost square format replaced the broad oblong. The change is evident in *Hippocrates and Democritus in Abdera* (*c.* 1636; Nijmegen, Radbout-Sticht.). However, the economy of movement and the unrelenting emphasis on the vertical often made the paintings appear monotonous, and up to *c.* 1633, the impression is one of outright rigidity. From this period dates the commission to portray one of the highest-ranking clerics in Amsterdam, *Sibrandus Sixtius* (1631; versions, Haarlem, Bisschopp. Mus.; Amsterdam, Begijnhof).

The new liveliness of style that is noticeable in the works of the mid-1630s can be directly attributed to the influence of Rembrandt. Moeyaert's colours became more intense and luminous, and he used them to greater narrative effect, while at the same time his repertory of motifs grew richer and his figures more animated. In 1638 he collaborated with the poets Samuel Coster and Jan Vechter on the triumphal arches erected in Amsterdam to receive Marie de' Medici; there are nine surviving preparatory drawings (all St Petersburg, Hermitage) for associated *tableaux vivants*. In the same year he painted a *Descent from the Cross* (Zwolle, Onze-Lieve-Vrouwekerk), and in 1640 he was commissioned to do a group portrait of the *Regents and Regentesses of the Old People's Home* (Amsterdam, Hist. Mus.). Between 1639 and 1641 he was also closely involved with the Amsterdam Theatre. In these and other paintings of the end of the decade he achieved a more complex and exciting structuring of space, as in the *Flight of Cloelia from Porsenna's Camp* (1640; St Petersburg, Hermitage).

In the 1640s Moeyaert returned to Lastman's example, adopting a number of his themes and quoting copiously from his basic compositions and individual motifs, as in *Joseph Selling Corn in Egypt* (1644; ex-art market, Stockholm; see Tümpel, fig. 154) and *Paul and Barnabas in Lystra* (1645; Imbshausen, Schloss). In 1643 he completed two monumental paintings commissioned four years earlier by Christian IV of Denmark: the *Burial of the Last Pagan King of Denmark* (Bålsta, Skoklosters Slott) and the *Baptism of the First Christian King of Denmark* (Hamburg,

Claes Moeyaert: *Finding of Moses*, oil on canvas, 495×645 mm, 1649 (St Petersburg, Hermitage Museum)

priv. col.; see Tümpel, fig. 23). In Moeyaert's latest work there was yet another change: space receded and the figures became larger but at the same time coarser (e.g. the *Finding of Moses*, 1649; St Petersburg, Hermitage; see fig.). Between 1647 and 1652 he painted numerous portraits of Catholic dignitaries and, *c.* 1650, three altarpieces for the chapel of the Begijnenhof (two in Amsterdam, Johannes-en-Ursulakerk). His last two dated paintings, both of 1653, are the *Stoning of Stephen* (ex-art market, Vienna, see Tümpel, fig. 169) and the *Raising of Lazarus* (Warsaw, N. Mus.).

(ii) Drawings and etchings. A large number of Moeyaert's drawings in pen and chalk have been preserved, as well as many copies; research has yet to identify the originals. Perhaps the earliest drawing, albeit one where the signature and date have been tampered with, is the *View of a Garden behind a House* (?1615; Berlin, Kupferstichkab.), which he used for the *Allegory of Spring*. His later drawings are more generous in scope, both in their details and in the composition as a whole. The strong chiaroscuro contrast that was present around 1624 later gave way to an airy brightness. Right up to his latest drawings (e.g. the preparatory study for the *Raising of Lazarus*, untraced; see Tümpel, fig. 66), he produced drawings that were fully

worked out as finished pictures; these too used strong chiaroscuro effects. His draughtsmanship was generally skilful but not innovative.

About 20–30 etchings by Moeyaert are known, mostly from before 1624 and depicting history subjects in landscape settings, although some are pure landscapes, such as the *Shepherd with Cattle* (1638; see de Groot, no. 89). He may also have made the 18 etchings of sea battles and foreign lands that illustrate David Pietersz. de Vries's *Verscheyden voyagiens in de vier deelen des wereldsronde* ('Various voyages in the four parts of the globe'; Hoorn, 1655).

2. POSTHUMOUS REPUTATION. Moeyaert, like the other Pre-Rembrandtists, always sought out challenging subjects, which he strove to represent in a lively and dramatic way. However, his narrative style was generally dry and occasionally obscure, as when his failure to distinguish compositionally between the principal and secondary characters makes interpretation of the event difficult. In other cases confusion is produced by a surfeit of figures. However, as his career progressed, his handling became freer and looser and his colouring softer and more unified. He was an influential figure for the next generation of landscape painters, and his pupils included the leading

Italianate landscape painters Nicolaes Berchem and Jan Baptist Weenix, as well as Jacob van der Does (1623–73), who painted landscapes with cattle, and Salomon Koninck, the history painter. As early as 1618 he was praised in Theodore Rodenburgh's poem 'Opsomming van de beroemdste Amsterdamse kunstenaars' ('Summary of the most famous Amsterdam artists').

BIBLIOGRAPHY
Hollstein: *Dut. & Flem.*; Thieme–Becker
P. J. J. van Thiel: 'Moeyaert and Bredero: A Curious Case of Dutch Theatre, as Depicted in Art', *Simiolus*, vi (1972–3), pp. 29–49
A. Tümpel: 'Claes Cornelisz. Moeyaert', *Oud-Holland*, lxxxviii (1974), pp. 1–163, 245–90
The Pre-Rembrandtists (exh. cat., ed. A. Tümpel; Sacramento, CA, Crocker A. Mus., 1974), pp. 79–113
I. de Groot: *Landscape Etchings by the Dutch Masters of the Seventeenth Century* (London, 1979), no. 89
Dutch Landscape: The Early Years (exh. cat. by C. Brown, London, N.G., 1986), pp. 193–5
ASTRID TÜMPEL

Mogensen, Børge (Vestergaard) (*b* Ålborg, 13 April 1914; *d* Gentofte, 5 Oct 1972). Danish designer. After finishing his apprenticeship as a cabinetmaker in 1934, he studied in Copenhagen at the Kunsthåndværkerskole (1936–8) and the furniture school of the Kunstakademi (1938–41) under Kaare Klint, who exerted a great influence on his approach to furniture-making. As head of the furniture design studio (1942–50) of the Fællesforeningen for Danmarks Brugsforeninger (Danish Cooperative Wholesale Society), Mogensen designed several lines that broke new ground for Danish industrial furniture production. As the range was intended for an average family, the furniture needed to be simple, practical, durable and cheap. In 1950 Mogensen established his own design studio. In the mid-1950s he developed the 'Boligens Byggeskabe' (Residential Cupboard Units) system and the unit furniture series 'Oresund' (Sound) in collaboration with Grethe Meyer (*b* 1918). The dimensions were based on extensive research and analysis, and the unit systems therefore continued Klint's functional experiments.

Traditional cabinetmaking formed the basis for Mogensen's work, and he designed furniture for several of the best Danish firms. In the late 20th century many of his robust and uncomplicated pieces were still in production. Mogensen tried to arrive at coherent and simple forms, often taking as his starting point familiar types that had proved their practical value and durability over centuries. His furniture is sustained by broad, international tradition; for instance, he received inspiration from English Windsor chairs and American Shaker furniture. His preferred material was oak, often combined with leather or woollen upholstery. Together with the weaver Lis Ahlmann (1894–1979) he designed furniture fabrics for the textile company C. Olesen A/S, for whom he began to work as artistic consultant in 1953. Mogensen also designed fittings and furnishings for various interior design projects, including the Danske Kunstindustrimuseum in Copenhagen (1954–62).

See also DENMARK, fig. 17.

BIBLIOGRAPHY
A. Karlsen: *Furniture Designed by Børge Mogensen* (Copenhagen, 1968)
LENE OLESEN

Moghul [Mogul]. *See* MUGHAL.

Mohedano (de la Gutiéra), Antonio (*b* Lucena, nr Córdoba, 1561; *d* Antequera, nr Málaga, 1626). Spanish painter. He was trained to paint in Córdoba around 1580, where the most important master was the painter Pablo de Céspedes. He also took part in literary activities of the humanist circle in the city. From 1590 he worked in Lucena, and in 1599 he was in Seville. Towards 1610 he settled in Antequera, where he was active until his death.

In the few works that can be attributed to Mohedano the draughtsmanship is firm and decisive, and his solemn and statuesque figures are usually precisely outlined and in ecstatic poses. His compositions are often based on strict symmetrical axes. His brushwork is firm, and it is evident that he worked slowly and deliberately. His minute observation of reality led him to include much naturalistic detail in his paintings. He particularly liked to represent domestic objects such as clothes and drapery, folds of which he rendered with great care: in his treatment of drapery he may be considered a precursor of Zurbarán. There is documentary evidence that he was considered an able painter of still-lifes with flowers and fruit and of landscapes, but no example in these genres survives. He is also known to have been an excellent fresco painter, but his works in this medium have mostly been lost: neither the paintings he executed for Córdoba Cathedral nor those for the church of S Francisco in Seville have survived. However, in the vault of the chancel of S Mateo, Lucena, there are frescoes of cherubs with sprays of flowers (*c.* 1600).

Mohedano's earliest known painting on canvas is the *Annunciation* in the upper part of the altarpiece in the former Jesuit church in Seville (now the University Church), painted between 1604 and 1605, in which the artist's style is fully mature. The *Holy Family* (*c.* 1605; Seville, Mus. B.A.) has a strongly geometrical composition into which the figures are rigidly integrated. The structural severity of the work is tempered by the somewhat sentimentally expressive faces. A group of works in the Museo Municipal, Antequera, includes a *Virgin and Child with the Guardian Angel*, a *Virgin of Silence* (an intimate domestic scene derived from a composition by Lavinia Fontana), a *St Lucy* and an *Assumption of the Virgin* (both frontal, severely geometric presentations), while a *Virgin of La Antigua* derives from the 14th-century fresco in the chapel of La Antigua in Seville Cathedral. Mohedano also painted a large altarpiece depicting the *Transfiguration* for the church of S Sebastian in Antequera. The open-armed figure of Christ forms the central axis of the characteristically symmetrical composition, with the figures of the prophets on one side corresponding to those of the apostles on the other.

BIBLIOGRAPHY
J. M. Fernández: 'El pintor Antonio Mohedano de la Gutiéra', *Archv Esp. A.*, xxi (1948), pp. 113–19
R. González Zubieta: *Vida y obra del artista andalúz Antonio Mohedano de la Gutiéra* (Córdoba, 1981)
E. Valdivieso and J. M. Serrera: *Pintura sevillana del primer tercio del siglo XVI* (Madrid, 1985)
A. E. Pérez Sánchez: *Pintura barroca en España (1600–1750)* (Madrid, 1992), p. 173
ENRIQUE VALDIVIESO

Mohenjo-daro. Site of an ancient city on the west bank of the Indus River, about 90 km south-west of Shikarpur, Sind, Pakistan. It was a settlement of the Mature or Urban Phase of the Indus or Harappan civilization (*c.* 2550–2000 BC) and covers an area of some 100 ha. Mohenjo-daro (Sindhi: 'mound of the dead men') is the modern place name; the ancient name of the city is not known. It was first visited by an archaeologist in 1911–12 (see Bhandarkar), but its significance was not recognized until the 1920s. Excavations by R. D. Banerji for the Archaeological Survey of India in 1921–2 around the *c.* 2nd–4th-century AD Buddhist stupa on the western mound, the so-called 'Citadel', uncovered stamp seals similar to those found at HARAPPA 644 km to the north-east (Marshall, p. 10). These finds led to the full excavation of Mohenjo-daro, initially under John Marshall, then under Ernest Mackay, between 1922 and 1931. A season of excavation by George F. Dales for the Pennsylvania State University Museum of Art (now University Park, PA State U., Palmer Mus. A.) in 1964 produced the most authoritative book on Indus pottery (Dales and Kenoyer). From 1979 to 1987 Michael Jansen of the Rheinisch-Westfälische Technische Hochschule, Aachen, studied the architecture and mapping of the site. In the late 20th century the massive conservation problems that the site faced owing to the high modern water-table and the salinity of the soil were being addressed by UNESCO and the Government of Pakistan.

Because Mohenjo-daro was built of fired brick and excavated so extensively, much of the ancient city is still visible, including houses and shops with stairways to upper floors. The high, small, western mound has many impressive buildings, including the Great Bath (*see* INDIAN SUBCONTINENT, fig. 22) and an adjacent structure that is often interpreted, albeit without conclusive evidence, as a warehouse or state granary. The Lower Town, an extensive set of rolling mounds to the east, is the area where the bulk of the population lived and worked. This section of the site (some 1000×600 m) is laid out on a grid plan and contains the best examples of Harappan fired-brick architecture, including a drainage system connecting houses to a system of public sanitation. Curiously no temple or palace buildings have been identified at Mohenjo-daro or any other Harappan sites. The size of the population at Mohenjo-daro is unknown, but the most frequent estimates suggest a range of 20,000–30,000 at any given moment.

Major finds among several pieces of sculpture include a steatite statuette of the so-called 'Priest–King' and a slender dancing girl in bronze (*see* INDIAN SUBCONTINENT, figs 130 and 137). The stamp seals are generally of very high quality. Harappan long barrel beads are among the best of their kind in the ancient world, for the Harappan artisan was a skilled beadmaker who had mastered the art of drilling, etching and of producing cornelian and faience. Metalworkers had mastered working with copper, bronze, tin, lead, antimony, electrum, gold and silver.

See also INDIAN SUBCONTINENT, §§II, 1(i); III, 2(ii); IV, 2; and VII, 10(i).

BIBLIOGRAPHY
D. R. Bhandarkar: 'Excavation', *Archaeol. Surv. India, Prog. Rep., W. Circ.* (1911–12), pp. 4–5

J. Marshall, ed.: *Mohenjo-daro and the Indus Civilization*, 3 vols (London, 1931/*R* Delhi, 1973)
E. J. H. Mackay: *Further Excavations at Mohenjo-daro*, 2 vols (Delhi, 1937–8)
G. F. Dales: 'New Investigations at Mohenjo-daro', *Archaeology*, xviii (1965), pp. 145–50
Master Plan: Preservation of Moenjo-daro, Pakistan Department of Archaeology and UNESCO (Karachi, 1972)
Moenjo Daro: New Life for the City of the Dead, Pakistan Department of Archaeology and UNESCO (Karachi, 1974)
M. Jansen and G. Urban, eds: *Reports on Field Work Carried Out at Mohenjo-daro, Pakistan by the Ismeo-Aachen University Mission: Interim Reports* (Aachen and Rome, 1983–), i, *1982–83* (1983); ii, *1983–84* (1987); iii, *1983–86*, ed. M. Jansen and M. Tosi (1988)
G. F. Dales and J. M. Kenoyer: *Excavations at Mohenjo Daro, Pakistan: The Pottery* (Philadelphia, 1986)
M. Jansen, M. Mulloy and G. Urban, eds: *Forgotten Cities on the Indus: Early Civilization in Pakistan from the 8th to the 2nd Millennium B.C.* (Mainz, 1991)

GREGORY L. POSSEHL

Moholy [née Schultz], **Lucia** (*b* Prague, 18 Jan 1894; *d* Zurich-Zollikerberg, 17 May 1989). British photographer, writer and teacher of Bohemian birth. She took up photography in Germany in 1922, assisting her husband, LÁSZLÓ MOHOLY-NAGY, with his theoretical formulations and photographic experiments. At the Bauhaus (1923–8), her stark analytical records of products, buildings and people epitomized Neue Sachlichkeit (e.g. *Georg Muche*, 1927; San Francisco, CA, MOMA). Many were reproduced in Bauhaus books, which she sub-edited. She trained as a professional photographer in Weimar (1923–4) and Leipzig (1925–6), before practising and teaching in Berlin (1928–33) and London (1934–9). Her book, *A Hundred Years of Photography, 1839–1939* (Harmondsworth, 1939), and leadership in international microfilming schemes by the Association of Special Libraries and Information Bureaux (Aslib) and UNESCO (1942–59) highlighted her concern with the social consequences of new techniques.

BIBLIOGRAPHY
W. Gropius: *Bauhausbauten Dessau*, Bauhausbücher 12 (Munich, 1930/*R* 1974) [contains many illus. by Moholy]
R. Sachsse: *Lucia Moholy* (Düsseldorf, 1985)

Moholy-Nagy [Weisz], **László** (*b* Bácsborsod, Mohol Puszta, Hungary, 20 July 1895; *d* Chicago, 24 Nov 1946). American painter, sculptor, photographer, designer, film maker, theorist and teacher, of Hungarian birth. Moholy-Nagy's importance in the 20th century is based as much on his theories as on his practical work. His ideologies related to the relationship between space, time and light and the interaction of man with these forces. His great achievement was that he applied his mystical outlook to highly practical enterprises and always recognized the purpose behind his creativity.

1. Life and work. 2. Working methods and technique.

1. LIFE AND WORK.

(i) Formative years in Hungary, 1895–1919. Moholy-Nagy's ambition developed when he exchanged village life for the city of Szeged after his father left his family. Academically outstanding, Moholy-Nagy read law for a year at Budapest University before joining the artillery in World War I. Influential praise for his war sketches converted his aspiration from literature to art. His expressionist style, social conscience and investigation of light

paralleled trends in the Hungarian avant-garde, from THE EIGHT (iii) to Lajos Kassák's messianic MA GROUP. His meditations included the reflection, 'Space, Time, Material—are they One with Light?'. He absorbed the Cubist and Futurist influences of the Activist painters of MA—Béla Uitz, József Nemes Lampérth and Sándor Bortnyik, as well as Rembrandt and Vincent van Gogh whom they greatly admired. The Budapest Communist revolution (March–July 1919), in which Uitz and others participated, disappointed Moholy-Nagy with its prevarications over social and cultural transformation. He remained detached from party politics in counter-revolutionary Szeged. Moholy-Nagy looked forward to what he later termed 'the dawn of a new life' (see *Malerei, Photographie, Film*, 1925), and he achieved a nationally unparalleled, reductionist perception with *Build! Build!* ('*Epíts!*') (1919; Hungary, ex-artist's col., see Moholy-Nagy, *R* 1961, p. 71), a drawing that codified feasible, elementary procedures with his current interest, linear construction.

(ii) Vienna and Berlin, 1919–23. Moholy-Nagy followed MA refugees to Vienna in November 1919, but six weeks of its enervating gentility drove him to industrial Berlin. Converging, radical ideologies from eastern and western Europe over the following three years made Berlin a centre of intellectual ferment; Dadaism had common sympathies with Dutch De Stijl and Russian revolutionary abstraction. A new consciousness of time and concern with objective, universal values and laws predominated. At the heart of events, Moholy-Nagy responded selectively in his art and writing. He signed joint manifestos, became Berlin representative of the *MA* journal and, with Kassák, published *Buch neuer Künstler* (1922), a pictorial survey of correlations in recent art, architecture, technology and music. He dated the progress of his art from this period.

The year 1922 was particularly significant: Moholy-Nagy's work was toured nationally by the major Berlin gallery, the Sturm-Galerie; he was appointed by Walter Gropius to his Bauhaus school of design; and he resolved his proposition of a definitive production hypothesis, which had advocated interdisciplinary cooperation in a new, objective programme of fundamental research to enhance human life. The artist would re-evaluate media as springs of unfamiliar, rather than reproduced experience, to stretch the individual through the unified, biological functioning of his eager senses.

In 1921, after assimilating Dadaist influences, Moholy-Nagy began a systematic investigation of the interrelationship of space, time, mass and light. Using theoretically neutral, geometric forms, he made sculpture in materials that emphasized light play and painted motifs of transparent, overlapping colours, sometimes repeated and distorted; he thought of these in terms of kinetic light performances, where different coloured lights would be projected with each other, with the effect of overlapping. Interrelating components, including linkages, became his space–time devices. The production hypothesis opened up coherent experiments with other media such as theatre and film, although he began with photograms: images produced directly on light-sensitive paper in the darkroom, without a camera or negative, by covering part of the surface with objects or shapes and then exposing it to light. Similar methods were being used at that time by MAN RAY and CHRISTIAN SCHAD.

Moholy-Nagy shared Raoul Hausmann's Dadaist 'optophonetic construct' of 1922, a theory of the relationships between perception, preconception and the fundamental unity of light and sound; Viking Eggeling's abstract film experiments also related to his own concepts. His interest in Russian non-imitative construction and conception of forms as energy channels brought accusations of plagiarism from the purist Constructivists, El Lissitzky and Naum Gabo.

(iii) Bauhaus: Weimar and Dessau, 1923–8. In spring 1923, Moholy-Nagy took over as head of the Bauhaus preliminary course and metal workshop from Johannes Itten, whose anti-rational, individualistic position had threatened Gropius's industrial policy. With Gropius's support, he turned emphasis away from the predominant Expressionism, causing some enmity, and changed the direction from subjective to practical, objective experiment. He retained Itten's accent on materials and visual contrasts in the compulsory, six-month preliminary course but turned to detached, heuristic experiment with properties of space, volume, weight, strength, structure, facture, texture, construction, equilibrium and motive inference. His half of the course approached general, elementary values, while his colleague Josef Albers steered his part towards the ensuing specialist workshop training. Moholy-Nagy geared the metal workshop to industrial mass production by changing the priority from elaborate, precious metalwork to simple, practical, geometric designs for electrical household appliances, including light fittings. Schwintzer & Gräff of Berlin, for instance, manufactured 53 Bauhaus lamp designs. Students proceeded from training in a chosen area, such as silversmithing, to an experimental section.

Moholy-Nagy's ebullient open-mindedness proved ideal for putting into effect Gropius's call of summer 1923 for a new unity between art and technology. Within a year, Moholy-Nagy had replaced Vasily Kandinsky as Gropius's closest, most valued associate. Between 1925 and 1930, they co-edited 14 Bauhaus books on facets of modern art and design by leading exponents, including Kasimir Malevich, Piet Mondrian and Theo van Doesburg. Moholy-Nagy wrote two: *Malerei, Photographie, Film* and *Von Material zu Architektur*. These expanded on the implications of the production hypothesis for assessing cultural progressions: the first, in media, from painting to modern challenging, kinetic light; the second, from bygone static mass to contemporary transparency and motion, as proclaimed in his Bauhaus lectures. He contributed to Oskar Schlemmer's book on theatre (Bauhausbücher 4), demanding clarification and intensification of expressive properties through technology before reintroducing actors. His graphic design, including most of these books, introduced the new, asymmetrical typography to the Bauhaus.

Unofficial photographic experiments conducted with his wife Lucia (who assisted with much of his work) became very influential. In 1926 he qualified his theory by emphasizing the agile, perceptive qualities of the mind, as opposed to its practical functioning, as the constant, progressive source. As a humanist artist–engineer, he differed from the Russian Productivists, including Vladimir Tatlin, who rejected 'pure art' in favour of utilitarian or 'production art'. His view of the Bauhaus as balanced, productive education ultimately antagonized the head of the new architecture department, Hannes Meyer, whose overt Communism undermined the apolitical policy and encouraged student demands for utilitarian, vocational training. Consequently, Moholy-Nagy left in spring 1928 with Gropius and others.

(iv) Commercial practice in Berlin, Amsterdam and London, 1929–37. Moholy-Nagy set up a freelance design office in Berlin and subsequently received commissions for magazine layouts, exhibition designs and, notably, Berlin theatre sets, including *Tales of Hoffman* (Kroll Opera) and the *Merchant of Berlin* (Piscator Theatre), both in 1929.

In 1929 he designed his *Light Prop* (1.51×0.7 m including base; Cambridge, MA, Harvard U., Busch-Reisinger Mus.; replicas, 1970; Berlin, Bauhaus-Archv; Eindhoven, Van Abbemus.), a mobile sculpture designed for 'the purpose of experimenting with painting with light' (see Passuth). He had envisaged the object as early as 1922 but finally realized it for the Deutscher Werkbund exhibition in Paris, constructing it of plastics, wood and metal. He

1. László Moholy-Nagy: *Light Prop* from the film *Light Play: Black and White and Grey*, photograph, 375×275 mm, *c.* 1930 (New York, Museum of Modern Art)

also used it as the subject for his film, *Light Play: Black and White and Grey* (*c.* 1930; see fig. 1), in which he again explored the interaction of space, time and light. In summer 1933 he filmed the Greek cruise of the Congrès Internationaux d'Architecture Moderne.

By December, Moholy-Nagy had moved to Amsterdam to become art director of a new periodical, *International Textiles*, which resulted in unprecedented commercial dissemination of the new typography, or *typophoto*, in which typographic material and photography were correlated for what he claimed to be 'the most exact rendering of communication' and used to highlight the cloth industry. He experimented for finer colour reproduction but with limited success. Early in 1935, he designed important corporate exhibition stands in Utrecht and Brussels for the Dutch artificial silk industry.

Moholy-Nagy was obliged by professional and political anxieties to join Gropius in London from May 1935 to July 1937. Although unaccustomed to English conservative insularism, he prospered, helped by a few associates conversant with the Bauhaus. He became design consultant to Simpson Ltd, a new menswear store in Piccadilly, where his unfamiliar, Constructivist vocabulary attracted public interest. Among his freelance undertakings were his first commercial films including a documentary, *Lobsters* (1936), and brief special effects for Alexander Korda's film *Things to Come* (1936), based on the novel by H. G. Wells. He produced three photographic series depicting class-life for books about London streetmarkets, Eton College and Oxford University from 1936 to 1938. A fourth stemmed from a lecture visit to Hull (1937). Isokon Furniture Company, London Underground and Imperial Airways commissioned publicity material.

In London Moholy-Nagy was a member of an avant-garde artistic circle that included Barbara Hepworth, Ben Nicholson, Henry Moore, John Piper, John Grierson (1898–1972) and Herbert Read. It was at this time that he began to produce 'space modulators', which were made of flat or curved panels of transparent Rhodoid plastic, the designs of which interrelated with their own, metamorphosed light projections.

(vii) Chicago: New Bauhaus, 1937 and after. On Gropius's recommendation, the American Association of Arts and Industries appointed Moholy-Nagy to direct their New Bauhaus in Chicago, opening in October 1937. A year later, the Association withdrew support. He and his faithful staff struggled to relaunch the School of Design in February 1939, which was renamed Institute of Design in spring 1944 and upgraded to university status. Unfortunately Moholy-Nagy died of leukaemia as the financial prospects of the Institute were improving, aided by the return of servicemen on government grants.

Moholy-Nagy had adhered to the German Bauhaus framework as consolidated by his production hypothesis but accepted that intervening modern design, art movements, film, aeroplanes, radio, television, communications, transportation and distribution had absorbed earlier lessons on artistic and technological unity. Consequently, goals could be extended further beyond physical, labour-saving devices into psychological and psycho-physical considerations, regulated by scientific findings, technological processes (e.g. lamination, new plastics, functional streamlining, complete die-stamping and electronics), economics and social changes. He had extended the original Bauhaus concept of integration under architecture towards 'seeing everything in relationship', or *Vision in Motion*, as he entitled his final book. His target was the designer of functionalist objects, as much as the artist.

The school reached the wider community through children's classes, summer schools and exhibitions. During World War II Moholy-Nagy joined the municipal camouflage committee while the school trained camouflage personnel and occupational therapists for the disabled and handicapped, including the blind. Metal shortages led the furniture manufacturer, Seng, to purchase rights to wooden springs developed by the school. Student projects ranged from plywood seating to jet-propelled and solar-powered cars. Moholy-Nagy's most well-known commercial design was the Parker '*51*' fountain pen (1941). His personal interests, such as tubular structures, plastics, the atomic bomb and even leukaemia, emerged as abstract subject-matter for his paintings and sculptures.

2. WORKING METHODS AND TECHNIQUE. Moholy-Nagy's German and American teaching included theory that he based on Raoul France's (1874–1943) seven biotechnical, or functional, plant forms. For instance, Moholy-Nagy had used the spiral from 1921, but his preferred circle and strip also invoked Malevich's Suprematist primary forms. His upright grids reflected awareness of De Stijl, his diagonal arrangements of Suprematism and van Doesburg's counter-compositions. Ultimately, his experience of compound curvatures in tubular furniture influenced his American painting and sculpture, including his hand-moulded Perspex (Plexiglas) space modulators.

Moholy-Nagy continued to paint with brush and canvas but also started to use impersonal industrial techniques for standardized machine precision, such as the air-brush and spray-gun, with new synthetic materials such as Trolitan, Galalith, Cellon and aluminium, deriving titles for the works from their abbreviated names. For instance, the series *Em 1* (Chicago, priv. col., see Herzogenrath, 1974, p. 31), *Em 2* and *Em 3* (both New York, MOMA; see fig. 2) or '*Telephone Pictures*' (vitreous enamel on steel, all 1922) presented one configuration in three sizes (940×600 mm, 470×300 mm and 235×150 mm, respectively), ordered, as if by telephone, from a vitreous enamel (Ger. Emaille) factory, to impartially examine colour and scale reciprocity.

Photography, Moholy-Nagy's first productive test-case, exemplified his continuous, synthesizing procedure with disparate strains of imagery and media. Thus, the rich, abstracted chiaroscuro of the photogram could inform realistic camera photography and film in their precise, uncompensated rendition of appearances, employing, for instance, unusual or microscopic views. He fused realistic photography and abstraction to achieve *typophoto* and analogical 'photoplastics' (photomontages) after 1923, which, with photographic series, schematically evoked film. In 1925, he used X-ray photography and, in 1926, predicted electro-magnetic astronomy. His condensed film, *Light Play: Black and White and Grey*, made from

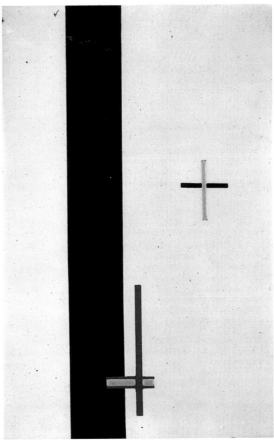

2. László Moholy-Nagy: *Telephone Picture: Em 2*, vitreous enamel on steel, 470×300 mm, 1922 (New York, Museum of Modern Art)

the *Light Prop*, directly inspired an oil painting on Formica, *CHF Space Modulator* (1.54×0.6 m, 1942; Hattula Moholy-Nagy priv. col., see Moholy-Nagy, 1947, p. 172). He frequently employed assistants for his work, and between 1930 and 1945 the Hungarian artist György Kepes (*b* 1906) realized commercial designs and taught for him.

WRITINGS

with L. Kassák, ed.: *Buch neuer Künstler* (Vienna, 1922/*R* 1977)
'Produktion—Reproduktion', *De Stijl*, v/7 (1922), pp. 98–100; Eng. trans. in *Studio Int.*, cxc (July–Aug 1975), p. 17
'Richtlinien für eine synthetische Zeitschrift', *Pásmo*, i/7–8 (1924), p. 5
'Das Bauhaus in Dessau', *Qualität*, iv/5–6 (1925), pp. 81–8
with F. Molnár and O. Schlemmer: *Die Bühne im Bauhaus*, Bauhausbücher 4 (Munich, 1925/*R* 1965; Eng. trans., Middletown, CT, 1961)
Malerei, Photographie, Film, Bauhausbücher 8 (Munich, 1925; 2/1927/*R* 1967; Eng. trans., London, 1969)
'Geradlinigkeit des Geistes—Umwege der Technik', *Bauhaus*, 1 (1926), p. 5; Eng. trans. in Kostelanetz (1970)
'Die Photographie in der Reklame', *Phot. Korr.*, lxiii/9 (1927), pp. 257–60
'Fotografie ist Lichtgestaltung', *Bauhaus*, ii/1 (1928), pp. 2–9; Eng. trans. in Haus (1980), pp. 47–50
Von Material zu Architektur, Bauhausbücher 14 (Munich, 1929/*R* Mainz, 1968); Eng. trans. of 1st edition by D. M. Hoffman as *The New Vision: From Material to Architecture* (New York, 1930); rev. 4 as *The New Vision and Abstract of an Artist* (New York, 1947/*R* 1961)
'Lichtrequisit einer elektrischen Bühne', *Die Form*, v (1930), pp. 297–9; Eng. trans. in Passuth, pp. 310–11
'An Open Letter to the Film Industry and to All who Are Interested in the Evolution of the Good Film', *Sight and Sound*, iii/10 (1934), pp. 56–7

'Education in Various Arts and Media for the Designer', *National Society for the Study of Education: The Fortieth Yearbook* (1941), pp. 652–7

'Better than Before', *Technol. Rev.*, xliv/1 (1943), pp. 21–52

'Space-time and the Photographer', *Amer. Annu. Phot.: 1943* (1942), pp. 7–14

'New Education—Organic Approach', *A. & Indust.*, xl/237 (1946), pp. 66–77

Vision in Motion (Chicago, 1947)

BIBLIOGRAPHY

P. Mátyás: *Moholy-Nagy szám* (Vienna, 1921)

F. Roh, ed.: *L. Moholy-Nagy: 60 fótos*, Fototek 1 (Berlin, 1930)

H. Read: 'A New Humanism', *Archit. Rev.*, lxxviii (Oct 1935), pp. 150–51

M. Benedetta: *The Streetmarkets of London* (London, 1936/R 1972)

F. Kalivoda, ed.: *Telehor*, i (1936) [issue dedicated to Moholy-Nagy]

B. Fergusson: *Eton Portrait* (London, 1937/rev. 1949 as *Portrait of Eton*)

J. Betjeman: *An Oxford University Chest* (London, 1938/R 1970)

S. Moholy-Nagy: *Moholy-Nagy: Experiment in Totality* (New York, 1950/rev. 1969)

R. Kostelanetz, ed.: *Moholy-Nagy* (New York, 1970)

P. Laszlo: 'The Young Years of Moholy-Nagy', *New Hung. Rev.*, xiii/46 (1972), pp. 62–72

L. Moholy: *Marginalien zu Moholy-Nagy* (Krefeld, 1972)

W. Herzogenrath, T. Osterwold and H. Weitemeier: *László Moholy-Nagy* (Stuttgart, 1974)

A. Haus: *Moholy-Nagy: Fotos und Fotogramme* (Munich, 1978; Eng. trans., London, 1980)

I. Jánósi: *László Moholy-Nagy: His Early Life in Hungary, 1895–1919* (MA thesis, U. Bloomington, IN, 1979)

I. C. Lusk: *Montagen ins Blaue: László Moholy-Nagy: Fotomontagen und -collagen, 1922–43* (Giessen, 1980)

L. Moholy-Nagy (exh. cat. by K. Passuth and T. A. Senter, London, ICA; Leicester, Mus. & A.G.; Edinburgh, N.G. Mod. A.; U. Newcastle upon Tyne, Hatton Gal.; 1980)

T. A. Senter: 'Moholy-Nagy's English Photography', *Burl. Mag.*, xxiii (1981), pp. 659–71 [contains photographic series on Hull]

K. Passuth: *Moholy-Nagy* (London, 1985)

T. Suhre: *Moholy-Nagy: A New Vision for Chicago* (Springfield, 1990)

László Moholy-Nagy (exh. cat. by C. David, G. Randolino, A. Nakov and V. Loers, Valencia, IVAM Cent. Julio Gonzalez; Kassel, Mus. Fridericianum; Marseille, Mus. Cantini; 1991) [well illustrated]

TERENCE A. SENTER

Mohr, Christian (*b* Andernach, 15 April 1823; *d* Cologne, 13 Sept 1888). German sculptor, writer, designer, collector, dealer and furniture-restorer. From 1846 to 1871 he made gothicizing sculptures for Cologne Cathedral: for example figures of evangelists, martyrs and angels and figured reliefs (limestone; south transept, portals and buttresses). He also produced sculpture in period styles for castles, public buildings and private houses, for example 36 limestone statues of German emperors (1882–7; Aachen, Rathaus). The balanced form of his blocklike standing figures shows the influence of classical sculpture, and their generally pensive expression may be traced to the influence of the Lukasbrüder (*see* NAZARENES). With the help of costumes, Mohr adapted sculpted figures to the style of architecture, but in general his work after 1860 is characterized by massiveness, broad surfaces and an expression of pathos.

Mohr's later work suggests an admiration for Michelangelo and for the monumental sculpture of Mohr's contemporaries Ernst Rietschel and Johannes Schilling. The sculptures Mohr made between 1882 and 1885, however, have the effect of reliefs and a continuous, linear internal design. Mohr's few portrait sculptures, for example the marble busts of *Friedrich von Schmidt* (1868) and *Johann Jakob vom Rath* (1870; both Cologne, Stadtmus.), are in the tradition of the Berlin school of Christian Daniel

Rauch. Mohr also designed decorative but functional items for the bourgeois interior, for example a bowl of gilded silver (1877; Cologne, Stadtmus.). In the last years of his life Mohr assembled his ideas about history and art in several books on Cologne.

WRITINGS

Köln in seiner Glanzzeit (Cologne, 1885)

Die Kirchen von Köln (Berlin, 1889)

BIBLIOGRAPHY

E. Trier and W. Weyres, eds: *Plastik*, iv of *Kunst des 19. Jahrhunderts im Rheinland* (Düsseldorf, 1980)

C. Weinstock: 'Der plastische Bildschmuck an der Fassade des Aachener Rathauses 1864–1901', *Aachen. Kstbl.*, xlix (1980–81), pp. 51–230

WALTER GEIS

Möhring, Bruno (*b* Königsberg [now Kaliningrad, Russia], 11 Dec 1863; *d* Berlin, 26 March 1929). German architect and urban planner. He studied architecture at the Technische Hochschule in Charlottenburg, Berlin, and spent most of his working life in Berlin. He and Alfred Grenander (1863–1931) were Berlin's prime exponents of the Art Nouveau style. This was mainly expressed in the bridges and railway stations of Berlin's elevated tram system, for example Möhring's station at Bülowstrasse (1902). His individual artistic designs of iron constructions, in particular bridges, were the result of his attempts to express fully the structural forces at work. In the field of exhibition design he was also very prominent, being involved with the German exhibits at the international exhibitions in Paris (1900), St Louis (1904, where he was in charge of the whole German section), Brussels (1910) and San Francisco (1915). In Berlin he was a member of the Werkring, a group of artists promoting modern housing and living, and from 1899 he was co-editor of the magazine *Berliner Architekturwelt*. Through his involvement with the Werkring he became interested in urban planning and the design of housing estates, including Oberhausen (1909) and Grundhof (1918), near Liebenwerder. His greatest success was a prize-winning entry for the urban planning competition (1908–10) for greater Berlin, in conjunction with the economist Rudolf Eberstadt (1856–1922) and the traffic engineer Richard Petersen (*b* 1865). Influenced by Camillo Sitte and Raymond Unwin, the plan proposed radial green wedges and a strict division between the inner city, a monumental complex of government and administrative buildings, and the suburbs, which were envisaged as picturesque satellite towns on garden-city lines. The scheme eventually executed, however, was by Hermann Jansen (*b* 1869).

BIBLIOGRAPHY

Thieme–Becker; Wasmuth

J. Posener: *Berlin auf dem Wege zu einer neuen Architektur: Das Zeitalter Wilhelms II*, Studien zur Kunst des 19. Jahrhunderts, xl (Munich, 1979)

Moilliet, Louis (René) (*b* Berne, 6 Oct 1880; *d* Vevey, 24 Aug 1962). Swiss painter. While at school in Berne he met the young Klee, who was to become a close friend. In 1898 he began work as a decorative painter in Berne and in 1900 studied drawing under the German sculptor Ferdinand Huttenlocher (*b* 1859). From 1901 to 1903 he was at the artists' colony of Worpswede in northern Germany, working with Fritz Mackensen, and during this time also studied under the German painter Hans Olde

(1855–1917) in Weimar. In 1904 he studied at the Akademie in Stuttgart under Leopold Kalckreuth before travelling to Paris with Klee and Hand Bloesch in 1905. From 1907 to 1909 he travelled widely, visiting Rome, Tunisia, Corsica and France and in 1909 first met August Macke. He spent the winter of 1910–11 with Klee in Munich and in 1911 became acquainted with Kandinsky and Franz Marc. He took part in the first Herbstsalon in Berlin in 1913, and many of his works of this period were inspired by circus and cabaret life, as in *In the Variété* (1913; Berne, Kstmus.). In 1914 he accompanied Klee and Macke on their famous trip to Tunisia. After the mid-1910s watercolour became his dominant medium and remained so thereafter.

After spending World War I in Switzerland, Moilliet was in North Africa from 1920 to 1921, visiting Tunisia, Algeria and Morocco. The watercolours derived from his travels, such as *Tunis, Kasbah* (1920; Berne, Kstmus.), showed the influence of Macke and combined a Cubist structure with Orphist colour. From 1926 to 1934 he was again travelling, visiting the Balearic Islands, Tunisia, Brittany and, from 1930 to 1934, Spain. His watercolours had by then become more abstract, incorporating large flat areas of colour, as in *View of Sitges* (1932; priv. col., see 1973 exh. cat., pl. 113). From 1934 to 1936 he worked on designs for the stained-glass windows of Lukaskirche in Lucerne. After 1936 he produced no new works, instead reworking earlier ones. In 1939 he used the *sgraffito* technique to decorate the outer wall of the Abdankungshalle of the Schlosshaldenfriedhofes in Berne. He designed the windows for the Zwinglikirche in Winterthur from 1940 to 1945 and those of the Kapelle des Burgerspitals in Berne from 1948 to 1959.

BIBLIOGRAPHY
Louis Moilliet (exh. cat. by J.-C. Ammann, Berne, Ksthalle, 1963)
Louis Moilliet 1880–1962 (exh. cat. by H. Wagner, Berne, Kstmus., 1973)

□

Moillon, Louise (*b* Paris, 1610; *d* Paris, 1696). French painter. She was the daughter of the Protestant Nicolas Moillon (1555–1619), a painter of portraits and landscapes, picture-dealer and member of the Académie de St Luc. She grew up in the St-Germain-des-Prés district of Paris, which, from the beginning of the 17th century, was a centre for painters from the southern Netherlands seeking refuge from religious persecution. Flemish influences appear in her still-life work, a specialization in which she followed her stepfather, François Garnier (*c.* 1600–58).

Moillon worked from childhood on studies of fruit such as the characteristic *Basket of Peaches and Grapes* (1631; Karlsruhe, Staatl. Ksthalle). A basket of perfect, luminous fruit is set at eye-level on a table-top, apparently sloping towards the viewer, and against an indeterminate background. Meticulous care is taken with the depiction of the textures of the basket, the grapes and leaves. *Trompe l'oeil* elements, such as the drops of dew and the leaf overhanging the edge of the table, and the colouring, which juxtaposes warm and cool tones, all owe something to Flemish precedent, but the elegance of the composition is uniquely French. Sometimes one or more female figures stand behind table-tops laden with baskets of fruit and vegetables, as in the *Fruit and Vegetable Seller* (sometimes

known as the *Mistress and Servant*; 1630; Paris, Louvre; *see* FRANCE, fig. 19), in which the emphasis on the transaction between the seller and her customer and the wealth of fruit displayed suggests a celebration of bourgeois comfort rather than the rustic simplicity found in the work of contemporaries such as René Nourrisson (*c.* 1610–50). With Jacques Linard she was the first French artist to combine successfully the female form with still-life elements, although the human figures never dominate their compositions.

Moillon enjoyed a notable reputation. Georges de Scudéry drew hyperbolic analogies between Moillon, Linard and Pierre Boucle and Michelangelo, Raphael and Titian. After her marriage in 1640 to the Calvinist Etienne Girardot, a dealer in wood, her output seems to have steadily decreased, possibly because of domestic duties and the birth of her children. After the Revocation of the Edict of Nantes in 1685, she and her family suffered religious persecution. There are no recorded works after this date, though paintings by her continue to be rediscovered.

Several of her seven brothers and sisters were also artists, most notably Isaac Moillon (1614–73) who, unlike Louise, became a member of the Académie Royale.

BIBLIOGRAPHY
C. Sterling: *La Nature morte de l'antiquité à nos jours* (Paris, 1952), pp. 69–70, 101–3
J. Wilhelm: 'Louise Moillon', *Oeil*, 21 (1956), pp. 6–13
M. Faré: *La Nature morte en France: Son histoire et son évolution du XVIIe au XXe siècle*, 2 vols (Geneva, 1962), pp. 41–3, 98–100
LESLEY STEVENSON

Moine, Antonin-Marie (*b* Saint-Etienne, 30 June 1796; *d* Paris, 18 March 1849). French sculptor and painter. He was a pupil of Pierre Révoil in Lyon, then of Anne-Louis Girodet and Antoine-Jean Gros at the Ecole des Beaux Arts in Paris from 1817, initially studying painting. He showed an early interest in the sculpture of the French Renaissance, and many of his works have a linear grace that owes much to the school of Fontainebleau and the sculpture of Cellini.

Moine only exhibited sculptures at the Salon from 1831 to 1836, beginning with the intensely Romantic relief *Fall of a Horseman* (plaster; Tours, Mus. B.-A.), which recalls the fantastic paintings of Louis Boulanger. In 1833 he exhibited an important state commission, the charmingly homely bust of *Queen Marie-Amélie* (marble; Paris, Mus. Carnavalet), and in 1836 two magnificent plaster models of female personifications of *The Church* and *Faith* (Paris, Petit Pal.), intended to decorate the holywater stoops of the church of La Madeleine, Paris. However, a number of his more original works were rejected by the increasingly conservative Salon jury in 1835 and 1836, and despite further state commissions, such as the sensitively carved neo-Renaissance chimney-piece in the Salles des Conférences of the Chambre des Deputés, Palais Bourbon, Paris (1839; *in situ*), he was obliged to earn his living by modelling statuettes for commercial reproduction. In addition to these works, which were either portraits of famous contemporaries such as the singer *Mme Malibran* or fantasy pieces such as *Woman with a Falcon*, he also painted landscapes, of which the gouache *Waterfall among*

Rocks (Colmar, Mus. Unterlinden) is an example. From 1843 to 1848 he showed pastels at the Salon.

He took his own life in a fit of depression, hoping 'thus to obtain a pension for his widow'.

BIBLIOGRAPHY
A. Le Bail: *Antonin Moine*, Ecole Louvre (Paris, 1977)
I. L.-J. Lemaistre: *La Sculpture française au XIXe siècle* (exh. cat., ed. Réunion des musées nationaux; Paris, Grand Pal., 1986), pp. 204–6, 324

ISABELLE LEMAISTRE

Moiré. Term for a pattern with a watery or ripple appearance, usually applied to a TEXTILE.

Moissac, St Pierre. Former Benedictine abbey in Tarn-et-Garonne, south-western France. The abbey church that legend ascribed to Clovis was in fact founded towards 628–48, but only the foundations of an early church survive under a successively rebuilt complex of buildings, some of which were destroyed during the 19th century. The present church was built on the substructure of one consecrated in 1063 by Durandus of Bredon (*d* 1072), the recently appointed Bishop of Toulouse who had been made Abbot of Moissac when the monastery became a Cluniac possession in 1047. The 11th-century church was flanked to the north by a cloister under the abbacy of Ansquitil (1085–1115), then rebuilt during the course of the 12th century in a style characteristic of south-western France, that is with a single-cell nave of two large square bays vaulted with domes on pendentives and a choir with radiating chapels. The domes were replaced by Abbot Bertrand de Montaigu (1260–95) with quadripartite rib vaults, and the choir was rebuilt by Peter and Anthony de Caraman (1449–1501). Important sculpture remains in the cloister, in the western tower and in the porch on its south side.

1. CLOISTER. The cloister is dated 1100 by an inscription (*see* CHRISTIANITY, fig. 10). The four arcades are composed of alternating twin and single columns with square piers at the corners and at the centre of each side. The original arcades were replaced by Gothic arches and enclosed by other claustral buildings after being damaged during a siege in 1212. A fountain house, last mentioned in 1645, once stood in the north-west corner. Pier reliefs and capitals have, however, survived from what is the earliest known sculptural programme in a medieval cloister.

The central piers of the east and west arcades each carry a large marble plaque (*c.* 1.6×0.7 m) on the side facing into the galleries. That on the west pier bears the dated inscription ANNO INCARNATIONE ETERNI PRINCIPIS MILLESIMO CENTESIMO FACTUM EST CLAUSTRUM ISTUD TEMPORE DOMINI ANSQUITIL ABBATIS AMEN, while the one on the east pier is carved with the image of the first Cluniac abbot, Durandus, in episcopal regalia and carrying a pastoral staff (see fig. 1). He is represented full length between shafts carrying an arch inscribed SANCTUS DURANDUS EPISCOPUS TOLOSANUS ET ABBAS MOYSIACO. The sides of the corner piers facing the gallery are also decorated with large marble reliefs (*c.* 1.6×0.5 m), presumably taken from one side and the bottom of sarcophagi.

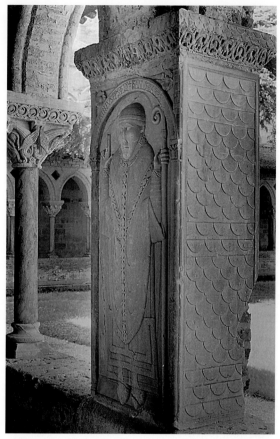

1. Moissac, St Pierre, cloister pier with relief representing *Abbot Durandus*, marble, 1100

They are carved with representations of eight Apostles (Peter and Paul, Andrew and Philip, James and John, Matthew and Bartholomew). Another, narrower relief representing Simon is now set on the garden side of the pier with the dated inscription. It may have belonged to a pier from the fountain house, but until the 19th century it was located at the porch entrance.

The tall, narrow pier reliefs are characterized by a consistent format. A single, full-length figure is represented frontally under a narrow arch supported by slender columns. All but Durandus are portrayed with heads in slight three-quarter profile, with one leg bent and feet splayed. The firm, simplified contours of the figures crowd the enclosing frame and define stylized postures, which are outlined by schematized togas with broad borders. Drapery is articulated by rhythmically spaced 'comma' folds of the type used on the relief plaques at St Sernin, Toulouse, by the marble carvers associated with BERNARDUS GELDUINUS, whose name is inscribed on the altar table consecrated there in 1096. A number of impost blocks in the Moissac cloister, also carved in marble, are decorated with angels carrying medallions in the manner of the edge of the altar table at St Sernin; the motif reappears at Saint-Caprais d'Agen.

The columns are decorated by 76 capitals with imposts carved by related artists, here working in limestone. The tapered profiles of the capitals accommodated biomorphic motifs as well as figure groups, and the narrative scenes are frequently explained by background inscriptions. The original sequence of capitals may have been disturbed in the 13th-century rebuilding. In keeping with a setting consecrated to Durandus's memory and to the communal life of daily prayer, the capitals refer to biblical episodes and the lives of saints recommending perseverance in the face of adversity (e.g. *Cain Slaying Abel*, the *Sacrifice of Isaac*, *David Slaying Goliath*, *Daniel in the Lions' Den*, the *Temptation of Christ*, *Peter and Paul Delivered from Prison* and the *Apotheosis of Martyrs*) with the promise of salvation (e.g. an Infancy cycle, *Miracles of Christ*, the *Beatitudes*, the *Vision of St John*, the *Victory of the Angels*, the *Sign of the Cross* and the *Heavenly Jerusalem*).

Short figures with large heads are either applied frontally or in three-quarter profile in narrative compositions readily grasped from one side or another. The drapery treatment is regular and schematic and in general appears to have been inspired by that of the large marble relief figures, but the ornament points to origins in the early workshop of St Sernin, Toulouse. The carver of the historiated capitals in one arcade has been identified as the author of the first group of capitals from the cloister of La Daurade, Toulouse. Carving in a related style appeared soon after at other Benedictine abbeys in the Quercy and Albigeois such as Saint-Michel de Lescure and Saint-Maffre near Bruniquel. Sculpture from the ruined church of Saint-Rustice is also related in style.

2. TOWER PORCH PORTAL. Soon after the cloister was finished, a tower porch was built to the west of Durandus's church. Both the porch and upper storey were vaulted with ribs of rectangular section springing from handsome capitals. Another layer of masonry was applied to this structure, embracing part of the nave and the deep recess framing the portal that opens on the south towards the River Tarn. Steps around the three inner sides of the porch have been discovered leading down to the original pavement, which is almost a metre lower than believed. The tower porch is comparable to those of Limousin churches (e.g. Saint-Martial), but the recessed portal surmounted by a tympanum, possibly intended for the west façade, is evidently the earliest of its kind. Furthermore, the reliefs that decorate the walls flanking the portal are close in style to the tympanum and were obviously intended for the setting and belong to the same iconographic programme. Although the sculpture has been dated early because Aymeric de Peyrac, a 14th-century chronicler, ascribed the porch to the abbacy of Ansquitil (*d* 1115), it has generally been dated at least a decade later because a commemorative statue of his successor, Roger (*d* 1131), appears on the rampart above the porch.

The giant tympanum, over 6 m wide, represents a theophanic vision, the iconographic source of which has been disputed. Christ, enthroned and wearing a crown, is surrounded by the four living creatures and the twenty-four Elders described in Revelation 4; they carry cups and musical instruments as in Revelation 5 (see fig. 2). The

2. Moissac, St Pierre, south portal, tympanum and lintel, *c.* 1125

closed and open scrolls of the flanking seraphim (Isaiah 6), who hold phylacteries, seem to reflect medieval commentaries in which the apocalyptic vision stresses the future promise of salvation rather than the end of time. The central group is remarkable for its dynamic effect: the proportions and poses contribute to the sense of movement both away from and towards Christ. This figure is four times larger than those of the Elders, who wear similar costumes and have agitated poses. They are arranged in three horizontal zones divided by clouds, one under Christ's feet and two in the spandrels of the lunette.

The meaning of the vision is amplified by the figures on the jambs and trumeau (for illustration, *see* COLUMN STATUE) as well as by the relief panels on the walls flanking the portal. The interlacing lions on the trumeau are flanked by contrasting images: Jeremiah faces Isaiah on the jamb to Christ's left, where the scroll of the Cherub is closed, and St Paul faces St Peter to Christ's right, where the scroll of the Seraph is open. The wall reliefs show the *Parable of Lazarus* on the left wall and the *Incarnation* on the right. On the upper frieze of the left wall, the leper Lazarus starving at the rich man's door appears with Moses and Abraham, who offer salvation; the narrative continues in the two blind arches below with the rich man's death and vivid references to his torments in the form of monstrous embodiments of avarice and lust. In contrast, the narrative on the right wall begins at the bottom with the *Annunciation* and *Visitation* and continues above with the *Adoration of the Magi*, which, like the rich man's death, spans two arches; the cycle concludes across the upper frieze with the *Flight into Egypt* and *Presentation in the Temple*.

Although the sculptures have been ascribed to two phases in the history of a single workshop, their style is fairly homogeneous. The figures are elongated or short, depending on their setting and relative scale. Heads are angular and oblong, drapery is broadly articulated by patterns of regular ridges and overlapping folds, and the ornate hems fall in zigzag patterns. The same style appears, presumably later, at Souillac and Beaulieu-sur-Dordogne. The porch type was repeated at those churches and at other sites in the Limousin and the Dordogne as well as in the Cantal (*see* ROMANESQUE, §III, 1(ii)(g)).

BIBLIOGRAPHY

E. Rupin: *L'Abbaye et les cloîtres de Moissac* (Paris, 1897)
E. Mâle: *L'Art religieux du XIIe siècle en France: Etude sur les origines de l'iconographie du moyen âge* (Paris, 1922)
M. Schapiro: 'The Romanesque Sculpture of Moissac', *A. Bull.*, xiii (1931), pp. 249–350, 464–531; repr. in *Romanesque Art: Selected Papers* (New York, 1977) and as book (New York, 1985)
Moissac et l'Occident au XIe siècle: Actes du colloque international de Moissac: Moissac, 1963
N. Mezoughi: 'Le Tympan de Moissac: Etudes d'iconographie', *Cah. Saint-Michel de Cuxa*, ix (1977), pp. 171–200

THOMAS W. LYMAN

Moitte. French family of artists. Its most prominent members were (1) Pierre-Etienne Moitte, a late 18th-century engraver who worked after many contemporary artists, and his eldest son, (2) Jean-Guillaume Moitte, a sculptor and draughtsman in the Neo-classical style. Five of Pierre-Etienne's other children became artists. François-Auguste Moitte (1748–90), Rose-Angélique Moitte and Elisabeth-Mélanie Moitte were engravers; Alexandre Moitte (1750–1828) became a painter, and Jean-Baptiste-Philibert Moitte (1754–1808) was an architect.

(1) Pierre-Etienne Moitte (*b* Paris, 1 Jan 1722; *d* Paris, 4 Sept 1780). Engraver. He studied in Paris with Jacques-Firmin Beauvarlet and Pierre-François Beaumont (1719–?69). He was accepted (*agréé*) in 1771 by the Académie Royale de Peinture et de Sculpture and subsequently signed his prints 'Graveur du Roi'. Between *c.* 1747 and 1754 he was one of the principal engravers commissioned to work for the *Cabinet de S.E.M. Le Comte de Brühl*, a collection published in Dresden in 1754 and consisting of 50 plates after selected paintings from the celebrated collection owned by Heinrich von Brühl. In addition to the *Mystic Marriage of St Catherine* after Correggio and three history subjects after Jean-Baptiste Corneille, Moitte contributed 11 masterly pieces after Dutch and Flemish paintings, including the *Dutch Merchant* and the *Flemish Cook* after Gerrit Dou; the *Broken Egg*, after Frans van Mieris the elder; the *Judgement of Paris* after Rubens; four landscapes after Jacob van Ruisdael and Guillam Dubois (*c.* 1610–80); and *Travellers' Rest* and *Horses at the Watering Trough* after Philips Wouwerman. Moitte enjoyed a successful career in Paris by reproducing works after 18th-century French painters such as Nicolas Lancret, François Boucher and Pierre-Antoine Baudouin. Above all, he popularized sentimental genre paintings by Greuze, producing such prints as the *Wrathful Mother*, *Repentance* and the *Idle Woman*. Like most reproductive printmakers of the period, Moitte also engraved designs for book illustrations; thus he provided 17 plates after drawings by Jean-Baptiste Oudry for the four-volume folio edition of Jean de La Fontaine's *Fables* published between 1755 and 1759.

BIBLIOGRAPHY

Portalis–Beraldi; Thieme–Becker
V. Atwater: *A Catalogue and Analysis of Eighteenth-century French Prints after Netherlandish Baroque Paintings* (diss., Seattle, U. WA, 1988)

VIVIAN ATWATER

(2) Jean-Guillaume Moitte (*b* Paris, 11 Nov 1746; *d* Paris, 2 May 1810). Sculptor and draughtsman, son of (1) Pierre-Etienne Moitte. He first trained in Jean-Baptiste Pigalle's studio, and later in that of Jean-Baptiste Lemoyne (ii). In 1768 he won the Prix de Rome for sculpture and stayed in Rome from October 1771 to May 1773, before making a slow start to his career, chiefly with drawing. In particular, he drew for Robert-Joseph Auguste designs for silver- and goldsmith's work. In 1783 Moitte was finally accepted (*agréé*) by the Académie Royale de Peinture et de Sculpture and obtained commissions for several statues and low reliefs (1784; *in situ*) for the Hotel de Salm (now Palais de la Légion d'Honneur). Moitte was involved (1786–8) in the decoration of the *barrières* (toll-houses) in Paris, constructed by Claude-Nicolas Ledoux; however, his only royal commission was for a statue of *Jean-Dominique Cassini* (Paris, Mus. Observatoire), one of the more successful works in a series of 'great men'. The plaster was exhibited at the Salon of 1789; its pose was apparently inspired by that of Jacques-Louis David's *Brutus*, exhibited at the same Salon.

In 1792–3 he sculpted a new pediment for the Panthéon, depicting the *Motherland Bestowing Crowns on Virtue and on Genius* (destr.). In 1795 he won the competition for a monument to *Jean-Jacques Rousseau* (unexecuted; sketch model, Paris, Carnavalet). He executed a monument (1805) to *Général Louis Desaix* for the chapel of the hospice of Grand-Saint-Bernard and then the bronze relief for the column of the *Grande Armée* near Boulogne-sur-Mer. He continued to draw profusely, with a nervous, incisive line. Though still not very well known, he was one of France's most committed and talented exponents of Neo-classical sculpture.

Lami

BIBLIOGRAPHY

G. Hubert: 'Early Neo-classical Sculpture in France and Italy', *The Age of Neo-classicism* (exh. cat., London, V&A, 1972), pp. lxxvi–lxxxii
G. Bresc-Bautier: *Sculpture française: XVIIIe siècle* (Paris, 1980), no. 56
G. Gramaccini: *Jean-Guillaume Moitte: Leben und Werk*, 2 vols (Berlin, 1993)

PHILIPPE DUREY

Moje, Klaus (*b* Hamburg, 1936). German glass artist active in Australia. He was initially apprenticed as a glass grinder and cutter in the family glass workshop and then went on to study at the Staatliche Glasfachschule, Rheinbach, and at Hadamar, Germany. In 1960 he established a joint studio in Hamburg with his first wife, Isgard Moje-Wohlgemuth (*b* 1941). After 1974 he was closely associated with the Pilchuck School founded in Seattle, USA, by his colleague and friend, the American glass artist, Dale Chihuly (*b* 1941). In 1980 Moje went to the Canberra School of Art, Australia, where he established the Glass Workshop of which he was head from 1983.

Moje's work continues the tradition of Roman intricate mosaic vessels of the 1st century AD. It reveals a fastidious approach to technique and can be considered as parallel, albeit on a reduced scale, to such critical mainstream movements of the modern period as colour field painting, optical art and minimalism. Indeed, there are potent elements of each of these styles in Moje's vessels and free-standing forms, which are based, almost without exception, on dynamic fields of regular pattern rendered with a pure and resonant palette. Moje's adaptation of the ancient process of developing mosaic patterns with tiny slices of multi-coloured glass 'canes' reached new heights in his most recent work, which interposes fine expanses of softly opalescent, herringbone patterns with tilting slabs of swirling, marbled colour. In Australia, Moje has been an unstinting advocate of the development of exacting kiln techniques that include fusing, casting and *pâte de verre* (*see* GLASS, §II, 1(i)). At the same time, he has been particularly successful in his efforts to foster a heightened sense of professionalism among both his students and Australian artists at large, and this campaign has led to the consolidation of a new direction in Australian studio glass based upon crisply formalized mosaic forms and vessels executed in resplendent polychrome. His work is represented in numerous public and private collections throughout the world.

GEOFFREY R. EDWARDS

Mokuan Reien [Yu'an] (*fl* after 1323; *d* China, 1345). Japanese painter. His career spans the later Kamakura period (1185–1333) and early Muromachi period (1333–1568). He was one of the first Japanese painters to master the new *suiboku* (ink-wash) style then being introduced from China along with Zen (Chin. Chan) Buddhism (*see* JAPAN, §VI, 4(iii)). Mokuan's birthdate is unknown, but by 1323 he had taken priestly vows at a Zen monastery in Kamakura. He went to China in 1326–8 for further Zen training and spent the remainder of his life there, studying at several Chan monasteries. There he saw many examples of ink painting from the contemporary Yuan period (1279–1368) and the preceding Song period (AD 960–1279), including works by the Chan priest–painter MUQI.

Mokuan was not a professional painter; to judge from his few surviving works, he practised ink painting, depicting mostly Zen figural subjects, as one aspect of Zen discipline. When he visited the Liutong si (Hangzhou, Zhejiang Province), founded by Muqi, legend has it that he was greeted as the reincarnation of Muqi and presented with one of his seals. For Mokuan to be accorded such a high honour may be taken as an indication that his style was well formed by then and that his facility with monochrome ink and wash was such that even the Chinese were impressed. Distinctive features of Mokuan's style are the contrasts between light and dark ink accents and the varied types of brush movement.

Among the paintings most securely attributable to Mokuan are two depicting the carefree wanderer Hotei (Chin. Budai): a hanging scroll in ink on paper (Kyoto, Sumitomo Col.; *see* JAPAN, fig. 91) and a second version (Atami, MOA Mus. A.). There are also several versions of the *Byakue Kannon* ('White-robed Kannon'; e.g. hanging scroll, ink on paper; Washington, DC, Freer) and *Shisuizu* (the 'Four Sleepers'; hanging scroll, ink on paper; Tokyo, Maeda Ikutokukai Found. Lib.), depicting the eccentrics Hanshan (Jap. Kanzan) and Shide (Jap. Jitoky) flanking the Abbot Fenggan and his pet tiger, all blissfully sleeping in a gentle parody of traditional Buddhist triads in which Buddhas are attended by subordinate deities. These paintings all bear inscriptions by Chinese Chan priests and were painted in China, where Mokuan died in 1345, apparently just before he intended to return to Japan. After his death Japanese priests who visited China brought works by him back to Japan, where they had a tremendous impact on the development of *suiboku* painting. Long held to be a Chinese artist, even in Japanese accounts, Mokuan and the monk painter KAŌ SŌNEN are regarded as the two foremost Japanese pioneers of a major current of Japanese painting.

BIBLIOGRAPHY

Y. Shimizu: *Problems of Mokuan Reien (?1323–1345)* (diss., Princeton, U., NJ, 1974)
I. Tanaka: *Kao, Mokuan, Minchō* (1974), v of *Suiboku bijutsu taikei* [Compendium of the art of ink painting] (Tokyo, 1977–8)

JOAN H. O'MARA

Mokuan Shōtō [Muan Xingtao; Wu] (*b* Quanzhou Prefecture, Fujian Province, 1611; *d* Nagasaki, 1684). Chinese monk, calligrapher, painter and poet. He was the second abbot of MANPUKUJI and a prominent early patriarch of Ōbaku Zen Buddhism in Japan. Together with INGEN RYŪKI (Yinyuan Longqi) and SOKUHI NYOITSU (Jifei Ruyi), he became known as one of the Three Brushes of Ōbaku (Ōbaku no Sanpitsu), noted master Zen calligraphers (*see also* JAPAN, VII, 2(iv)(c)). Mokuan was ordained at the age of 18 (19 by Chinese reckoning) and studied under the eminent Chinese monks Miyun Yuanwu (1566–1642) and Feiyin Tongrong (1593–1661) before training at Wanfu si on Mt Huangbo (Fujian Province) under

1. Mokuan Shōtō: *So shi sei rai i* ('What is the meaning of the Patriarch's coming from the west?'), hanging scroll, ink on paper, 1305×400 mm, 1655–84 (St Louis, MO, Art Museum)

Ingen. Mokuan received *dharma* transmission from Ingen in 1650 and went on to serve as abbot of the monasteries Taiping si on Mt Lianshi and Huiming si on Mt Xiang in south-eastern China. In 1655, at Ingen's behest, Mokuan emigrated to Nagasaki, where he took over as abbot of the monastery Fukusaiji and served as Ingen's senior disciple in Japan. Sokuhi Nyoitsu and Mokuan gained renown as the 'Two Gates to the Nectar [of liberation]' (Jap. *nikanromon*), a euphemism implying mastery of the Buddha's teachings. In 1660, Ingen summoned Mokuan to the capital region to assist in the founding of a major monastery, Manpukuji (now in Uji, Kyoto Prefecture). Mokuan became abbot following Ingen's retirement in 1664. During his 16-year tenure, Mokuan received substantial financial support and recognition from the government, oversaw the construction of major monastic halls and played a prominent role in the spread of Ōbaku Zen in metropolitan Japan. In 1670, Mokuan was granted the purple robe (a privilege reserved for monks of the highest rank, typically abbots of major public monasteries) and founded the monastery Zuishōji in Edo (now Tokyo). Mokuan retired to Fukusaiji in 1680, where he remained until his death. His body was enshrined in the Manjuin memorial chapel on the grounds of Manpukuji. Mokuan's religious lineage grew to dominate the Ōbaku Zen school well into the 19th century.

A prolific writer and calligrapher, Mokuan is best known for his pithy Chinese Buddhist verses brushed in large characters. His work, which features dynamic forms comprised of a minimal number of thick, rounded strokes, is thought to be reminiscent of the spontaneous and original style of the late Ming-period (1368–1644) calligrapher FU SHAN. The raw power of Mokuan's hand is evident in the semi-cursive composition *So shi sei rai i* (Chin. *Zu shi xi lai yi*; 'What is the meaning of the Patriarch's coming from the west?'; after 1655; hanging scroll, ink on paper; St Louis, MO, A. Mus.; see fig. 1). Numerous compositions by Mokuan survive as titles and colophons on paintings. He is also noted for his ink paintings, which commonly feature literati subjects but also comprise Buddhist themes. His best-known composition combines both in a triptych of Hotei (Chin. Budai; a figure from Zen mythology), traditionally identified as an incarnation of Miroku (Skt Maitreya; the Future Buddha) and later in Japan regarded as one of the Seven Gods of Good Fortune, flanked by narcissus and orchid: *Hotei, keiran, suizen* (Chin. *Budai, huilan, shuixian*; 'Hotei, orchid, narcissus'; 1664; set of three hanging scrolls, ink on paper; Uji, Manpukuji; see fig. 2).

Mokuan's circle of literary acquaintances in China included Zhang Qianfu (*fl* 17th century), son of the late Ming-period painter and calligrapher ZHANG RUITU, who was much appreciated in Japan during his lifetime. Calligraphy and paintings by Zhang Ruitu and noted WU SCHOOL masters were transmitted by Ingen, Mokuan and other Ōbaku monks to Japan, where they were also treasured by pioneers in the Japanese tradition of literati painting and calligraphy.

BIBLIOGRAPHY

K. Chang: 'Chang Jui-t'u (1570–1641), Master Painter-calligrapher of the Late Ming, Parts I–III', *N. Pal. Mus. Bull.*, xvi (1981); Pt I, pp. 1–20; Pt II, pp. 1–17; Pt III, pp. 1–13

2. Mokuan Shōtō: *Hotei, keiran, suizen* ('Hotei, orchid, narcissus'), central scroll (inscription by Ingen Ryūki) depicting Hotei from the set of three hanging scrolls, ink on paper, each 1145×390 mm, 1664 (Uji, Manpukuji)

M. Otsuki: 'Mokuan no kaiga shumi ni tsuite' [On Mokuan's paintings], *Ōbaku bunka*, lxvii (1983), pp. 353–5
Masters of Japanese Calligraphy: 8th–19th Century (exh. cat. by Y. Shimizu and J. M. Rosenfield, New York, Japan House Gal., 1984), pp. 118–19, 160–67
M. Otsuki, S. Katō and Y. Hayashi, eds: *Ōbaku bunka jinmei jiten* [Biographical dictionary of Obaku culture] (Kyoto, 1988)

ELIZABETH HORTON SHARF

Mokugo. *See* ASAI CHŪ.

Mokujiki. *See* MYŌMAN MOKUJIKI.

Mol, Pieter Laurens (*b* Breda, 26 Oct 1946). Dutch photographer and conceptual artist. He first trained as a carpenter before studying at the academy in Breda (1963–5). From 1970 to 1980 he specialized in photographs of volatile and ephemeral materials such as smoke or shadow, which he referred to as 'photo-sculptures'. Like other conceptual artists in the late 1960s, he used photography to create personal worlds and to visualize ideas rather than to record reality. The photograph *Untitled* (1979; see 1983 exh. cat., p. 159) shows a man crouching on a table that he is sawing in half; on either side of him are a telescope and a microscope. Inherent in the image are attitudes to death, suicide and existence, and the relationship between art and science. Language has been important for Mol in all the media in which he has worked, and his works are often titled in English. In 1985 he produced a series of works on the theme of *waan* (delusion), slightly altering this word and placing it in different visual and verbal contexts to evoke a broad range of possible meanings, associations and emotions.

BIBLIOGRAPHY
Pieter Laurens Mol (exh. cat. by A. Petersen, Amsterdam, Stedel. Mus., 1977) [incl. interview in Dut. and Eng.]
Contemporary Art from the Netherlands (exh. cat. by A. von Graevenitz, Chicago, IL, Mus. Contemp. A., 1982)
Kunst mit Photographie (exh. cat. by R. H. Krauss, M. Schmalriede and M. Schwarz, W. Berlin, N.G., 1983)

HRIPSIMÉ VISSER

Mol, Pieter van (*bapt* Antwerp, 17 Nov 1599; *d* Paris, 8 April 1650). Flemish painter. Once mistakenly considered a pupil of Rubens, he was actually an apprentice in 1611 with the little-known painter Siger van der Graeve and was received as master of the Antwerp Guild of St Luke in 1622. André Félibien first suggested that Artus Wolffordt, a minor follower of Peter Paul Rubens, may also have been van Mol's master. Some of van Mol's early paintings such as the *Deposition* (Reims, Mus. St Denis) are stylistically close to Artus Wolffordt's oeuvre.

Van Mol left Antwerp for Paris in 1631. In 1635 he decorated the chapel of Jacques d'Estampes at St Joseph-des-Carmes. This ensemble was unique in Paris at the time, owing to the richness of van Mol's colours and the flamboyance of the decorative scheme. It consists of a *Transfiguration* in the vault and ten scenes painted on the walls below: four glorifying St James the Greater, three St Dominic and three St Louis. Two preparatory studies connected with the decoration (Paris, Louvre) are the only known drawings by van Mol. In 1642 he was appointed Painter to Queen Anne of Austria. The following year the Flemish Confraternity in Paris commissioned from him a large altarpiece of the *Adoration of the Shepherds* for the abbey church of St Germain des Prés (368×272 mm, 1643; Marseille, Mus. B.-A.), which is representative of his Parisian works. The increased feeling for volume, which also characterizes such paintings as the *Deposition* (Paris, Louvre) or *St Francis* (Florence, Pitti), is enhanced by greater compositional clarity. Van Mol's brushwork remains bold and slightly heavy-handed, but the colour scheme has been simplified, with less emphasis on the carmine reds of the earlier works.

Van Mol also painted numerous portraits (known through engravings) and some genre scenes (known from 17th-century inventories). He was a founder-member of the Académie Royale de Peinture et de Sculpture in Paris in 1648. His son Robert van Mol (*d c.* 1680) became a painter and engraver.

BIBLIOGRAPHY

A. Félibien: *Entretiens* (1666–8); rev. (1725)

L. Dimier: 'Un Chef d'oeuvre d'art flamand à Paris avant 1650', *Rev. A.*, xxviii (1926), pp. 149–55

M. L. Hairs: *Dans le sillage de Rubens: Les Peintres d'histoire anversois au XVIIème siècle* (Liège, 1977), pp. 227–9

Le Siècle de Rubens dans les collections publiques françaises (exh. cat., ed. J. Foucart and J. Lacambre; Paris, Grand Pal., 1977–8), pp. 127–32

BARBERINE BESNARD

Mola (i). Term for a colourful appliqué blouse worn by Kuna Indian women on the mainland and San Blas Islands of Panama and in the Darien region of north-western Colombia. *Mola* is the Kuna word for cloth, but it also applies to the woman's blouse and the front and back panels from which it is made. *Mola* blouses first appeared in the second half of the 19th century. Although made from European trade cloth, they were an indigenous development and their complex patterns relate to earlier body paint designs.

Mola panels are hand-stitched, using cutwork and appliqué techniques. Two or more layers of different-coloured fabric are used. Each layer is cut to the shape of the design and stitched to the layer beneath, so that motifs may be outlined in a number of colours. Embroidery is sometimes added to the top layer. The stitching is extremely fine, and no fabric is wasted. The front and back panels of a blouse are usually similar, but never the same. Design subjects include mythological patterns, birds, animals, plants, people and scenes from daily life. Advertisements, magazines, political posters and biblical themes often provide inspiration. The finished front and back panels are made up with a yoke and sleeves of plain or printed fabric (see fig.).

Mola blouse, cotton, Kuna Indian, from Panama, 1922 (Oxford, Oxford University, Pitt Rivers Museum)

The *mola* blouse is worn with a printed cotton skirt, a red and yellow printed headscarf, a gold nose-ring and other jewellery of gold, beads, coins, seeds and shells. Nearly all Kuna women continue to wear this costume proudly as a symbol of their identity. However, while women have traditionally made *mola*s for their own use, they have also responded to the demands of tourism by selling blouses and panels to visitors. Thus, the *mola* has become a significant part of the Kuna economy, and standards of workmanship remain high.

BIBLIOGRAPHY

A. Parker and A. Neal: *Molas: Folk Art of the Kuna Indian* (Barre, MA, 1977)

M. L. Salvador: *Yer Dailege! Kuna Women's Art* (Albuquerque, 1978)

H. Puls: *Textiles of the Kuna Indians of Panama* (Princes Risborough, 1988)

LINDA MOWAT

Mola [Moli; Molo] **(ii).** Italian family of artists.

(1) Gasparo Mola (*b* Coldre, nr Milan, *c.* 1580; *d* Rome, 24 Jan 1640). Sculptor, goldsmith and medallist. He first worked in Milan as a goldsmith; his earliest extant work is an engraved silver crucifix, signed and dated 1592 (Church of Tavernerio, nr Como). He next became an assistant gunsmith in Florence, where he is known to have produced a series of crucifix figures after a model by Giambologna. In 1597 Mola succeeded Michele Mazzafiri as a die-cutter at the Florentine Mint; he was commissioned *c.* 1600 to make two of the bronze reliefs for the door of Pisa Cathedral. Soon afterwards he moved to Turin, to work for Charles Emmanuel I, Duke of Savoy, as a medallist and also as purchasing agent for antiquities. Between 1609 and 1611 Mola returned to Florence to work as a die-cutter, remaining on the court payroll until 1625, although his medals show that he worked for Ferdinando Gonzaga, 6th Duke of Mantua, from *c.* 1613. He left Florence for good in 1623, to become Master of the Mint in Rome in 1625; he remained in that office until his death. Mola was a metalworker of superlative skill. For the Medici court he made a parade helmet and shield (1608–9; Florence, Bargello), long attributed to Benvenuto Cellini; a panel relief with a view of the *Piazza della Signoria* in hardstones and gold (Florence, Pitti); and a jewel casket in cut steel (London, V&A). A gold equestrian statue (untraced) of *Louis XIII, King of France* is documented as a work by Mola; it was commissioned in 1611 and finished in 1623. In Rome, Mola made a spectacular silver-gilt dish for the Boncompagni family (see Bulgari, pl. 13), to commemorate the reform of the calendar in 1583 by Pope Gregory XIII. Medals by Mola were both cast in bronze and struck in various metals, his style being that of the Italy of his time, dominated by the work of Leone Leoni at Milan. A small group of wax models for medals and coins by Mola has survived (London, BM). Alessandro Algardi made in the late 1630s a portrait bust in terracotta of Mola, taken from life (St Petersburg, Hermitage). This bust is the source for the painted portrait of *Mola* by an unknown artist in the Accademia di S Luca, Rome.

BIBLIOGRAPHY

Forrer; Thieme–Becker

A. Bertolotti: 'Giacomo Antonio Moro, Gaspero Mola e Gaspero Morone-Mola: Incisori nella zecca di Roma', *Archv Stor. Lombardo*, iv (1877), pp. 295–335

G. F. Hill: 'Notes on Italian Medals, XXVI', *Burl. Mag.*, xxxi (1917), pp. 211–17

E. Martinori: *An. Zecca Roma*, 14 (Rome, 1917), pp. 56, 70–78, 86

A. Magnaguti: *Le medaglie mantovane* (Mantua, 1921), pp. 58, 101, nos 70, 165–8

C. Bulgari: *Argentieri, gemmari e orafi d'Italia*, ii (Rome, 1959), p. 160

Z. Giunta di Roccagiovine: 'Gasparo Mola: Un artista troppe volte dimenticato', *Ant. Viva*, i (1963), pp. 57–63

A. Magnaguti: *Le medaglie dei Gonzaga*, ix of *Ex nummis historia* (Rome, 1965), pp. 51–3, nos 57–8, 69, 75, 78–9

H. M. von Erffa: 'Das Programm des Westportals des Pisaner Domes', *Mitt. Ksthist. Inst. Florenz*, xii (1965–6), p. 60, pl. II

A. Baudi di Vesme: *Schede Vesme: L'arte in Piemonte*, ii (Turin, 1966), p. 704

R. W. Lightbown: 'A Medici Casket', *V&A Mus. Bull.*, iii (1967), pp. 81–9

C. W. Fock: 'Goldsmiths at the Court of Cosimo II de' Medici', *Burl. Mag.*, cxiv (1972), pp. 15–16

J. F. Hayward: *Virtuoso Goldsmiths and the Triumph of Mannerism, 1540–1620* (London, 1976), pp. 157–8, 321

J. Montagu: *Alessandro Algardi* (New Haven and London, 1985), pp. 175, 177, 439

J. G. Pollard: *Medaglie italiane del rinascimento/Italian Renaissance Medals* (Florence, 1985), pp. 852–76 [bilingual text]

(2) Gasparo Morone Mola (*b* ?Milan; *d* Rome, 1669). Medallist and die-cutter, nephew of (1) Gasparo Mola. He was probably Milanese, a pupil of his uncle, from whom he inherited a quantity of dies for coins and medals. He is recorded as being active in Mantua from 1627, producing coins and medals for Vincenzo II Gonzaga, 7th Duke of Mantua, and Carlo I Gonzaga, 8th Duke of Mantua; his medals for Carlo I are dated 1628 and 1629. The regent Maria Gonzaga, Dowager Duchess of Mantua (*d* 1660), recommended Morone Mola to Pope Innocent X, probably in 1637, and in 1640 he was appointed Incisore dei Ferri della Zecca e Medagliere in Rome, a post he held until his death.

In Rome he worked principally for Innocent X, producing coins and medals. None of the coins is signed, but there are 23 signed medals, both in large bronze castings and struck in various metals. The series of struck medals for Innocent X includes two of the annual issues, for 1649 and 1650/51, with reverse types designed by Alessandro Algardi. Many of Morone Mola's medals depict major architectural schemes commissioned by the Pope, including the work of Bernini. These include the reverse (1657) of the medal struck to commemorate the foundation of the new piazza in front of St Peter's, to the design of Bernini.

Thieme–Becker   BIBLIOGRAPHY

C. F. Hill: 'Notes on Italian Medals, XXVI', *Burl. Mag.*, xxxi (1917), pp. 211–17, pl. k

E. Martinori: *An. Zecca Roma*, 15 (Rome, 1919), pp. 13, 22, 29, 32, 35–38, 67, 70–75, 85, 89

A. Magnaguti: *Le medaglie dei Gonzaga*, ix of *Ex nummis historia* (Rome, 1965), pp. 53–4; p. 108, nos 80–82; pp. 109–10, nos 85–92

F. Bartolotti: *La medaglia annuale dei romani pontefici* (Rimini, 1967), p. 70, no. E 666, no. 2

Roma Resurgens: Papal Medals from the Age of the Baroque (exh. cat., ed. N. T. Whitman and J. L. Varriano; South Hadley, MA, Mount Holyoke Coll. A. Mus., 1981), pp. 98–101, nos 80–82; p. 103, no. 84 [medals of the piazza of St Peter's]

J. Montagu: *Alessandro Algardi* (New Haven and London, 1985), pp. 92–3, nos. A.217, A.218

J. G. POLLARD

Mola (iii). Italian family of artists. They originated from the Swiss canton of Ticino, but the family moved to Rome when (1) Giovanni Battista Mola became architect to the Camera Apostolica. His brother Giacomo Mola (*b* Coldrerio, Ticino; *fl* Rome, 1615–42), also an architect, erected his own memorial (1615) in S Maria in Aracoeli, Rome, and in 1624 remodelled the 16th-century Cappella Albertini at S Francesco a Ripa, Rome, for Marchese Baldassare Paluzzi Albertoni. He assisted Giovanni Battista on the hospital wings (*c.* 1636) of S Giovanni in Laterano and the chapel of the men's hospital, dedicated to SS Andrea and Barolomeo, as well as in the decoration of the sacristy (1640s) at S Maria del Pianto, Rome. The most important member of the family, however, was Giovanni Battista Mola's eldest son (2) Pier Francesco Mola, a painter who received several important commissions in Rome.

(1) Giovanni Battista Mola (*b* Coldrerio, Ticino, 1585; *d* Rome, 23 Jan 1665). Architect, stuccoist and writer. He was one of the many building craftsmen who left the canton of Ticino for Rome in the late 15th and early 16th centuries. Mola was still living in Coldrerio in 1612, but by 1616 he had been appointed architect to the Camera Apostolica in Rome, a post he held until 1634. In 1630, in the service of the Papal Curia, Mola worked on the enlargement of the fortress of St Urbano (destr.) near Castelfranco. The exterior of this simple, functional building is known from a signed drawing by Mola. The dominant central portion was accentuated by a projection articulated by an order of Tuscan pilasters and an entablature with triglyphs; the interruption of the entablature by a statue niche in the middle bay betrays the continuing influence of late Mannerism within an early Baroque overall structure. A mingling of Mannerist features with early Baroque classicism is also found in the Cappella della SS Icone (1626) in Spoleto Cathedral and in the two hospital wings (*c.* 1636) of S Giovanni in Laterano in Rome that Mola built with his brother Giacomo Mola. His stucco ornamentation in S Eligio dei Ferrari and in the sacristy of S Maria del Pianto in Rome, dating from the 1640s, are also characterized by old-fashioned features.

At about this time Mola, with the patronage of the Pamphili family, took part in one of the most important competitions of the period, that for the building of S Agnese in Piazza Navona, Rome. His plan (Oxford, Ashmolean) provides for a longitudinally extended, oval domed space with four semicircular apses to be erected on the rounded end of the piazza. The spatial design of the interior is a simplified derivative of Francesco Borromini's S Carlino (1638–41), Rome, but the façade, which does not aim at a scenographic effect, is again a stylistically backward-looking structure with its rectilinear central projection. Mola's work displays solid craftsmanship and technical skill. His main importance, however, lies in his guidebook *Roma l'anno 1663*, not only a detailed source for his own work and that of his son Piero Francesco Mola but also containing valuable references to architectural practice in early 17th-century Rome.

UNPUBLISHED SOURCES

New York, Met. [sketchbook]

Oxford, Ashmolean [plan for S Agnese, 1640s]

Rome, Accad. N. S Luca [drawings]

Rome, Archv Cent. [drawings]

WRITINGS

K. Noehles, ed.: *Roma l'anno 1663* (Berlin, 1966)

BIBLIOGRAPHY

N. Pio: *Vite* (1724); ed. C. Enggass and R. Enggass (1977)
K. Noehles: 'L'architetto G. B. Mola e la sua guida romana del 1663', *A. Lombarda*, xi/2 (1966), pp. 192–6
G. Eimer: *La fabbrica di S Agnese in Navona*, 2 vols (Stockholm and Innsbruck, 1970)

BIRGITTA RINGBECK

(2) Pier Francesco Mola (*b* Coldrerio, nr Lugano, *bapt* 9 Feb 1612; *d* Rome, 13 May 1666). Painter and draughtsman, son of (1) Giovanni Battista Mola. His most characteristic works are small, intensely romantic scenes from mythology, the Bible, and from works by the poet Torquato Tasso, set in landscapes inspired by Venetian art. Yet he also received important public commissions for frescoes and altarpieces, and in his mature work he achieved an impressive synthesis of 17th-century Roman *gran maniera* painting with the stronger chiaroscuro and richer palette of the 16th-century Venetian style. He was a prolific and versatile draughtsman, who drew for pleasure as well as in preparation for commissions; he was also a witty caricaturist, who mocked himself and his friends as much as more typical targets, such as clerics and art patrons.

1. EARLY WORKS AND TRAVELS IN NORTHERN ITALY, BEFORE 1647. He moved with the family to Rome in 1616 and, except for two periods of absence while training, remained there in the family residence near Palazzo Mattei di Giove all his life. His earliest recorded works are pen and chalk figure sketches that he added to several architectural drawings in a sketchbook by his father (New York, Met.). Several sheets are dated 1631, including a sheet of ink and chalk studies entitled *Standing Man, Flying Angels, and a Design for a Decorative Panel* (fol. 45), which are entirely by him. These drawings show that, before any known contact with Venetian and Bolognese painting, apart from what he could see in Rome, he already displayed greater interest in chiaroscuro than in form. The pen and chalk strokes, in his typically fluid line, are buttressed with characteristic passages of parallel hatching in a mix of pen and chalk softened with wash.

During the years 1633–40 and 1641–7 Mola was in northern Italy, finishing his training and launching his career, but his movements are too poorly documented to allow any detailed account of his stylistic development. A signed and dated portrait drawing of his friend *Pietro Testa* (Montpellier, Mus. Fabre) records his presence in Lucca in 1637. He was in Rome for Easter 1641 and by August 1641 had returned to Coldrerio, where he began his first recorded commission, for frescoes in the Cappella Nuova of the Madonna del Carmelo, which show *St Sebastian* and *St Roch, God the Father Blessing*, the *Madonna of the Rosary Enthroned with Members of the Confraternity* and the *Madonna of the Rosary Saving Souls from Purgatory*. These frescoes show that Mola was a slow starter. The composition of the lateral fresco, the *Madonna of the Rosary Saving Souls from Purgatory*, is borrowed from Cerano's *Mass of St Gregory for Souls in Purgatory* in S Vittore, Varese (Genty, 1968), suggesting that Mola lacked confidence in creating a multi-figured, dramatic composition. In the facing fresco, the *Madonna of the Rosary Enthroned with*

Members of the Confraternity, though it is less obviously derivative, the poses of the Virgin and Child are based on Titian's Pesaro *Madonna* (Venice, S Maria Gloriosa dei Frari). His evident familiarity with these works shows that by 1641 he must have travelled widely in northern Italy. He may have been in Venice in 1644. Francesco Albani, in a letter of 1658, says that Mola studied with him in Bologna for two years, and G. B. Passeri, Mola's biographer and personal acquaintance, wrote that Mola studied with Albani during his second visit to northern Italy. Perhaps the difficulties he had experienced with the Coldrerio frescoes encouraged him to seek out a master experienced in fresco, which would account for him joining Albani's studio after 1642, rather than in 1633 when he first travelled north.

A number of small cabinet paintings by Mola, in which the landscape dominates the figures, probably date from before 1647, when Mola finally established himself in Rome. None of them can be traced to a Roman 17th-century collection, and the landscape settings are strongly Venetian, their idyllic mood suggesting Albani's influence. Among them are three paintings of the *Rest on the Flight to Egypt* (New York, Met.; Milan, priv. col; see Cocke, 1972, pl. 26), the *Landscape with St Bruno in Ecstasy* (London, Mahon col.; see Cocke, 1972, pl. 98) and the pendants of the *Prophet Elisha and the Rich Woman of Shunhem* and the *Prophet Elijah and the Widow of Zarephath* (Sarasota, FL, Ringling Mus. A.).

2. PUBLIC COMMISSIONS AND MATURE WORKS IN ROME, 1647–57. In 1647 Mola established himself in Rome, his style by this time reflecting his deep knowledge of the work of Titian, the Bassano family, Guercino and Albani, artists he had particularly admired in northern Italy. The commissions he received in Rome for frescoes and altarpieces demanded the creation of a grander style, and his first documented work there, the *Image of St Dominic Carried to Soriano by the Virgin, St Catherine and St Mary Magdalene* (Rome, SS Domenico e Sisto), was a deliberate attempt to fuse key elements of Roman 17th-century painting and northern Italian art of the 16th and 17th centuries, a programme that he pursued for the remainder of his career. A pen, ink and wash compositional study (Haarlem, Teylers Mus.) shows the direct impact of Albani's style, but the monumentality of the figures and the rich, dark colours reveal a different artistic temperament and are deeply indebted to Guercino. The wine red, dark green, deep blue and chocolate brown accented with white are a palette reminiscent of Titian and the Bassano family, yet with the addition of the complex violet greys of Guercino. The realism of some passages, such as the monk's veined hands and hollow cheeks, reveals a straightforward naturalism more typical of northern Italy than of Rome.

As a fresco painter Mola was still tentative and uncertain, as is demonstrated by the ceiling fresco *Bacchus and Ariadne* (*c.* 1650; Rome, Pal. Costaguti; see Cocke, 1972, pl. 40). Later in the 1650s his Roman fresco commissions reveal his growing admiration for the most monumental works of the Roman High Renaissance by Raphael and Michelangelo. This development is apparent in *St Peter Baptizing in Prison* and the *Conversion of St Paul* (Rome,

1. Pier Francesco Mola: *Joseph Greeting his Brethren*, brush and brown wash, pen and brown ink over red and black chalk, 321×442 mm, *c.* 1656 (London, British Museum); preparatory drawing for fresco in the gallery of Alexander VII, Palazzo del Quirinale, Rome

Gesù, Ravenna Chapel), yet these works were less assured in their treatment of space than the large *Joseph Greeting his Brethren* (1656–7; Rome, Pal. Quirinale) and should be dated earlier than it, perhaps to 1649 when Francesco Ravenna, the patron who commissioned them, became a consul of the city. The Quirinale fresco, Mola's most important Roman commission, fills one end of Alexander VII's gallery, and 10 drawings (examples, London, BM; see fig. 1; Düsseldorf, Kstmus.) attest to the care with which he prepared it. The staging of the drama, with Joseph standing on the left, arms outstretched to greet his 12 brothers (several of whom have dropped to their knees to express their chagrin and astonishment), recalls that of Raphael's tapestry cartoon *Christ's Charge to St Peter* (London, V&A). The grouping is less planar than Raphael's, however, and the eye is led back in stages through majestic architecture to a typically lush landscape. The main figures have the heroic proportions of Michelangelo's Sistine Chapel *ignudi*, while the cleverly arranged cloak of Joseph, framing his arms and giving bulk to his slight proportions, shows that Mola understood Bernini's use of similar devices to impart drama to his figure sculpture.

Mola's private commissions of this period gradually attained a new Roman grandeur. The splendid *Barbary Pirate*, his only signed and dated picture (1650; Paris, Louvre), is a romantic, three-quarter-length figure in exotic eastern dress. The works, whose presence in Roman private collections formed during his lifetime suggests a date in the Roman period (e.g. the *Expulsion of Hagar and Ishmael* and *Rebecca and Eliezer*, both Rome, Gal. Colonna; *Bacchus*, Rome, Gal. Spada; and the *Dream of Endymion*, Rome, Pal. Conserv., Braccio Nuova), are large canvases in which the figures dominate. A group of cabinet pictures, with figures between the small scale of the early works (1632–46) and the heroic scale of his later paintings, may belong to a transitional phase, as Mola adjusted the scale of his private commissions to the grandeur of his public style. These evocative and poetic works include the *Mercury and Argus* (Oberlin Coll., OH, Allen Mem. A. Mus.), *Erminia Guarding Her Flocks* and its pendant, the lyrical *Erminia and Vafrino Tending the Wounded Tancred* (early 1650s; Paris, Louvre; see fig. 2).

3. LATE WORKS, 1658 AND AFTER. In 1658 Mola prepared and began a fresco of mythological scenes for the ceiling of the Stanza dell'Aria in Prince Camillo Pamphili's summer palace at Valentino. A number of surviving drawings (e.g. Berlin, Kupferstichkab.; Chatsworth, Derbys; Florence, Uffizi; Madrid, Real Acad. S Fernando) record his ambitious and attractive scheme. Unfortunately he became involved in a dispute with the Pamphili that resulted in a lengthy lawsuit (1659–64), and

2. Pier Francesco Mola: *Erminia and Vafrino Tending the Wounded Tancred*, oil on canvas, 720×970 mm, early 1650s (Paris, Musée du Louvre)

his partially finished work was destroyed and replaced with one by Mattia Preti in 1661. Despite this setback he continued to attract important patrons, among them Pope Alexander VII and the Colonna family. Pascoli records his contacts with Queen Christina of Sweden, and two pictures, the *Death of Archimedes* (Rome, priv. col.; see Cocke, 1972, pl. 90), one of a group of pictures of philosophers, and the *Head of Medusa* (untraced), were in her collection.

Mola's late works, such as the impressive *Vision of St Bruno* (1662–3; Malibu, CA, Getty Mus.; see Cocke, 1972, pl. 136) painted for Prince Agostino Chigi (ii), nephew of Alexander VII, became increasingly dramatic and powerful. Mola explored this subject first in a series of exceptionally beautiful drawings (Darmstadt, Hess. Landesmus.; St Petersburg, Hermitage; Frankfurt am Main, Städel. Kstinst. & Stadt. Gal.) and in the painting produced his finest resolution of Venetian colouring and Roman grandeur. The saint, reclining in the lower left corner in a flowing white robe, looks up and gestures towards two cherubim who hover in the upper right against a brilliant sky. The saint is shaded by two trees, their crossed trunks and their branches reaching up beyond the top of the canvas. A panoramic landscape fills the right side of the picture. The composition is indebted to Andrea Sacchi's *Vision of St Romuald* (1631; Rome, Pin. Vaticana); the

strong tonal contrasts of the landscape are reminiscent of Guercino, while the mountain ranges and azure blue tones suggest the influence of Titian. In his drawings, for example *Erminia and Vafrino Tending the Wounded Tancred* (Düsseldorf, Kstmus.), his use of curved pen lines enlivened with patches of brown ink wash suggests Guercino's style, but Mola usually mixed pen and chalk, especially red chalk, to achieve a variety of tonal effects.

Mola became principal of the Accademia di S Luca, Rome, in 1662, but resigned a year later owing to ill-health. Passeri confirms that his health was affected by the lawsuit with the Pamphili and says that studio assistants worked on some of his later commissions. Several of Mola's caricatures suggest a melancholy discontent; in a drawing inscribed 'Adio speranze' (London, BM), an artist sits brooding beside his palette and brushes, which lie scattered on the ground. An upturned cornucopia, a symbol of abundance, pours forth onions. Mola was only 54 when he died.

BIBLIOGRAPHY

G. Baglione: *Vite* (1642); ed. V. Mariani (1935), p. 361
M. Boschini: *La carta del navegar pitoresco* (Venice, 1660)
G. B. Passeri: *Vite* (1679); ed. J. Hess (1934), pp. 367–72
F. Baldinucci: *Notizie* (1681–1728); ed. F. Ranalli (1845–7)
N. Pio: 'Vita di P. F. Mola', MS. Vatican Capponiano 257 (1724); also in
   L. Ozzola: 'L'arte alla corte di Alessandro VII', *Archv. Soc. Romana Stor. Patria* (1908), pp. 51–3

L. Pascoli: *Vite* (1730–36), i, pp. 122–9

H. Voss: 'Di Pierfrancesco Mola, pittore ed incisore Comasco', *Riv. Archeol. Prov. & Ant. Dioc. Como* (1910), pp. 59–61, 117–209

V. Golzio: *Documenti artistici sul seicento nell'archivio Chigi* (Rome, 1939)

L. Montalto: 'Gli affreschi di Palazzo Pamphili in Valmontone', *Commentari*, vi/4 (1955), pp. 267–302

F. Haskell: *Patrons and Painters: A Study in the Relations and Society in the Age of the Baroque* (London, 1963, rev. New Haven, 1980)

A. B. Sutherland: 'Pier Francesco Mola: His Visits to North Italy and his Residence in Rome', *Burl. Mag.*, cvi/736 (1964), pp. 363–8

E. Arslan: 'Disegni del Mola a Stoccolma', *Essays on the History of Art Presented to Rudolf Wittkower* (London, 1967), pp. 197–9

R. W. Lee: 'Mola and Tasso', *Studies in Renaissance Baroque Art Presented to Sir Anthony Blunt* (London, 1967), pp. 136–41

Drawings from the New York Collections, II: The Seventeenth Century in Italy (exh. cat. by J. Bean and F. Stampfle, New York, Met. and Pierpont Morgan Lib., 1967)

R. Cocke: 'Mola's Designs for the Stanza dell'Aria at Valmontone', *Burl. Mag.*, cx/784 (1968), pp. 558–65

J. Genty: *Pier Francesco Mola in Patria* (Bellinzona, 1968)

S. Rudolph: 'Contributi per Pier Francesco Mola', *A. Illus.*, xi/15–6 (1969), pp. 10–25

R. Cocke: *Pier Francesco Mola* (Oxford, 1972)

E. Schleier: 'Pier Francesco Mola a S Maria della Quercia', *Ant. Viva*, xvi/6 (1977), pp. 12–22

J. Genty: *Pier Francesco Mola pittore* (Lugano, 1979)

Pier Francesco Mola, 1612–1666 (exh. cat., Lugano, Mus. Cant. A.; Rome, Mus. Capitolino; 1989–90) [with bibliog. and illustrations]; review by A. Sutherland Harris in *Master Drgs*, xxx/2 (1992), pp. 216–23

ANN SUTHERLAND HARRIS

Molanus [Vermeulen; van der Meulen], **Johannes** [Jan] (*b* Lille, 1533; *d* Leuven, 18 Sept 1585). South Netherlandish theologian and writer. He became professor of theology and rector of the university at Leuven in 1578 and, one year later, first president of the royal college. In 1573, as dean of the faculty of theology, he was the inspiration and first signatory of the letter from this faculty to Philip II of Spain, which sought to have the Duque de Alba recalled from the Netherlands. Molanus was also dean in 1576 when the faculty concluded that the Pacification of Ghent, which united all the provinces of the northern and southern Netherlands against the Spanish, was not inconsistent with the Catholic religion.

Molanus achieved fame chiefly through his publications, which included a number of hagiographic works and religious histories. In his *De picturis et imaginibus sacris liber unus* (1570) he was the first writer to dwell on the implications of the Council of Trent (1545–63) for the visual arts; the resolutions agreed at the closing session of the Council called for no false doctrines to be represented, and thus the avoidance of voluptuousness and 'tempting charm'. In addition, bishops were to ensure that such 'unorthodox images' as representations of new miracles were not depicted in churches until approved by higher authority. The outburst of iconoclasm in the Netherlands in 1566 had made the debate about images shockingly real; Molanus took the opportunity to explain orthodox teaching about the worship of saints' images. He reacted sharply against Erasmus's humanism and, above all, against the *Byenkorf der H. Roomsche Kercke* ('Beehive of the Holy Roman Catholic Church') by the Dutch Calvinist Marnix van Sint-Aldegonde (1540–98). Following the example of the Church's Index of prohibited books, Molanus catalogued specific pictorial subjects as dangerous and consequently forbidden. In his detailed discussions, he used historical and archaeological criteria to decide how biblical stories should be depicted, stressing attention to textual accuracy. He rejected the depiction of nudity and went as far as to object to the Christ Child's nakedness in traditional nativity scenes. Subjects that contained false dogmas or that depicted heresies or heretical subjects were dangerous. Molanus was nevertheless surprisingly tolerant about the Apocrypha, taking the position that everything that the Church had traditionally regarded as acceptable in literature should be equally acceptable in painting. Consequently he thus taught that everything that served to encourage the mass of the people to worship would be tolerated. The exhaustive discussion of the images once employed for holy figures, saints and their attributes, and of the meaning and origin of these depictions, make this text one of the first works of Christian iconography, one that remains an important reference work for both art historians and archaeologists.

WRITINGS

De picturis et imaginibus sacris liber unus (1570); rev. as *Historia sanctarum imaginum* (Leuven, 1594); ed. J. N. Paquot (Leiden, 1722)

BNB; NBW

D. Freedberg: 'Johannes Molanus on Provocative Paintings', *J. Warb. & Court. Inst.*, xxiv (1971), pp. 229–45

——: 'Art and Iconoclasm, 1525–1580', *Kunst voor de Beeldenstorm* [Art before the iconoclasm] (exh. cat., ed. J. P. Filedt Kok; Amsterdam, Rijksmus., 1986), pp. 69–84

C. Eire: *War against the Idols: The Reformation of Worship from Erasmus to Calvin* (Cambridge, 1989)

JOHAN DECAVELE

Molder, Jan de [Jean] (*fl c.* 1513–18). Netherlandish wood-carver. He is known only for the production of two carved altarpieces for the abbey of Averbode. The first, destined for the altar of the Holy Sacrament and commissioned in 1513, has been positively identified with the altarpiece bearing the Antwerp mark of quality and the arms of the abbey of Averbode now in the Musée de Cluny, Paris. The carved scenes of the *Meeting of Abraham and Melchisedek*, the *Mass of St Gregory* and the *Last Supper* are identical with those specified in the Averbode contract; the painted shutters, which were to represent other scenes relating to the Holy Sacrament, are now lost. The contract also shows that Jan de Molder was the brother-in-law of the reigning prior of Averbode, Adriaen. This first altarpiece is a transitional work. The beginnings of Antwerp Mannerism may be seen in the elaborate arched frame and the crowded compositions, but the compact and animated figure types, unaffected gestures and angular drapery folds are more characteristic of late 15th-century carving. The second altarpiece (untraced) was a more expensive work, commissioned for the altar of All Saints, inspected and approved by the wardens of the Antwerp Guild of St Luke and delivered in 1518.

BIBLIOGRAPHY

J. Lavalleye: 'Le Retable d'Averbode conservé au Musée de Cluny à Paris', *Rev. A.*, xxviii (1926), pp. 141–8

P. Lefèvre: 'Textes concernant l'histoire artistique de l'abbaye d'Averbode', *Rev. Belg. Archéol. & Hist. A.*, Belge Tijdschr. Oudhdknde & Kstgesch., v (1935), pp. 52–3

R. Szmydki: 'Jan de Molder, peintre et sculpteur d'Anvers au XVIe siècle', *Jb.: Kon. Mus. S. Kst.* (1986), pp. 31–58

KIM W. WOODS

1. Map of Moldova; those sites with separate entries in this dictionary are distinguished by CROSS-REFERENCE TYPE

Moldova [Moldavia, Bessarabia; formerly Moldavian Soviet Socialist Republic, Soviet Moldavia]. Country in southeastern Europe bordered by the Ukraine to the north, east and south and by Romania to the west (see fig. 1). It is a gently rolling plain covering 33,700 sq. km with the River Dnestr on the east and the Prut River on the western frontier. The capital is CHIŞINĂU (formerly Kishinyov), and the population numbers *c.* 4 million, most of whom speak Romanian, from 1939 written in Cyrillic script.

In the 9th century AD the territory of present-day Moldova was part of Kievan Rus'. In the 14th century, however, it was settled by the Vlachs, and in 1359 the independent principality of Moldavia was established, consisting of the area of Moldova and land west of the Prut that is now in Romania. In the 13th and 14th centuries frequent Tatar-Mongol raids led to the collapse of the Old Russian culture. From the early 16th century the principality was a vassal of the Ottoman empire, but the territory east of the Prut (Bessarabia) was annexed by Russia in 1812. In 1918 Romania seized most of Bessarabia. A narrow strip of land east of the Dnestr, however, remained in Russian hands and became the Moldavian Autonomous SSR. In 1940 Russia recovered Bessarabia and transformed it into the Moldavian SSR; it was briefly reoccupied (1941–4) by German and Romanian forces. In 1991 the country gained its independence and became known as Moldova.

This article covers the art produced in Moldova from the 9th century AD. For a discussion of earlier art in the region *see* MIGRATION PERIOD and PREHISTORIC EUROPE. The art of western Moldavia is covered in the article on ROMANIA.

1. Architecture. 2. Painting, graphic arts and sculpture. 3. Decorative arts.

1. ARCHITECTURE. In the 9th century AD, when the territory of Moldova was part of Kievan Rus', Slavonic influence became established, and by the 10th century towns began to be surrounded by fortifications made of earth and timber and of stone and timber. In the 15th century, particularly under Stephen III (*reg* 1457–1504), towns comprising fortresses with surrounding settlements expanded, and market squares took shape. In the 16th century fortified castles were built at Stary Orkhey, Soroki and Bendery. A local tradition of Orthodox church architecture developed: the basic form is that of a triconch with a single nave and an extended narthex, as at the church of the Dormition at Kapriany Monastery (mid-16th century). Some stone churches, for example at Orgeyev and Kaushany, have a semidome within the thick walls of the apse. A unique system known as 'Moldavian vaults' was devised, with two tiers of arches supporting the drum of the cupola, as in the church (1774) of the Rud' Monastery. Outstanding examples of 16th- and 17th-century architecture include the cave monasteries in Sakharna and Zhabka and the church near the village of Butucheny. Exterior decoration often comprises ornamental blind arcading and carved designs on portals. Wooden churches of the 18th century usually had a rectangular or octagonal plan, with a hipped roof.

After the annexation of Bessarabia by Russia in 1812, Russian influence became apparent. Towns expanded rapidly, with buildings mainly in Neo-classical style, such as the cathedral of the Nativity (1835; by Avraam Mel'nikov), the triumphal arch in Chişinău (1840; by I. Zaushkevich), the column commemorating the *Battle of Kaluga* (1845; by F. K. Boffo) and numerous large private houses set in their own grounds. Features of Neo-classicism are also evident in several churches and monastery complexes, for example at Tyganeshty (1846) and Gyrzhavka (1848).

In the second half of the 19th century and the early 20th eclecticism became dominant in architecture. The most important local architect of the period was A. I. Bernardatsi (1831–1907), whose buildings include the local government building and girls' school in Chişinău. In Romanian-occupied Bessarabia (1918–40) many private houses were built in Art Nouveau and Constructivist styles, while in the Moldavian Autonomous SSR public buildings and multi-storey blocks of flats were constructed in neo-classical style, with occasional Constructivist influence. Among the most important buildings of the period are the Theatre Square complex (1936) in the centre of Tiraspol', the capital of the Moldavian ASSR, with the theatre building by G. M. Gotgelf, the Pedagogical Institute by M. E. Petrov and the Higher Agricultural School by D. P. Kovalenko.

After World War II cities were rebuilt and modernized, and their layout changed as main thoroughfares were constructed and new industrial enterprises, social and cultural institutions and schools were erected. In the 1940s and early 1950s buildings were decorated with motifs from vernacular architecture, using ceramics and stone-carving. From 1955 residential districts were erected on the outskirts of cities, and standardized buildings of limestone blocks and reinforced-concrete slabs were constructed. In the 1960s architecture became more picturesque, with balconies and loggias and the use of more colourful materials.

2. PAINTING, GRAPHIC ARTS AND SCULPTURE. The wall paintings on the exterior of 16th- and 17th-century churches in the principality of Moldavia are notable for the expressiveness of their imagery, often displaying the features of the local ethnic type, and for their harmonious colour schemes in a range of sombre tones (e.g. at the monastery church at Voroneţ, 1488; now in Romania). The church of the Dormition in Kaushany features a high standard of interior wall painting (18th century), combining late Byzantine and Balkan traditions with motifs from folk art. In the icons of the 17th century to the early 19th, Balkan and Old Russian traditions combine with techniques from folk art; the chiaroscuro modelling of faces is often contrasted with flat treatment of clothing, as in the *Christ Pantokrator* (17th century), the *Virgin Hodegetria* (17th century) and the *Virgin and Child Enthroned* (1813; by Ioan Yavorsky; all in Chişinău, Mus. F.A.). Several highly decorated manuscripts, such as the Psalter of 1470 and the Gospels of 1534 (both St Petersburg, Rus. N. Lib.), date to the 15th–17th centuries; their decoration includes geometric motifs in blues, reds and browns, with the background in gold. Manuscript miniatures reached a peak in the 17th century in the so-called Krimkovich school. In the 18th century engravings from M. Strel'bitsky's early printed books became widely known.

The early 19th century was marked by a rapid growth of secular elements in art, particularly portraiture. The portrait of the *Vornik Bran* by Johann Kraus (1851; Chişinău, Mus. F.A.) and the work of the early 19th-century portraitist Ion Balomir display features similar to the Russian *parsuna* style of portraiture, overcoming the stiffness and conventionality of the treatment of the human figure in icons. The professional training of artists was furthered in the 1890s when N. Zubkov, who had trained at the St Petersburg Academy of Arts, set up the City Drawing School in Chişinău. In the early 20th century Vladimir Okushko (1862–1919) reorganized the Drawing School into the College of Art. In paintings such as *Ploughing* (1896; Chişinău, Mus. F.A.) he reproduced typical scenes of Moldovan nature and peasants at work. In 1903 a society of art lovers was set up in Chişinău; it held regular exhibitions involving both local artists and major figures from St Petersburg and Moscow. Members of the society took part in exhibitions organized by the South Russian Society of Artists and also arranged several exhibitions of work by the Russian Wanderers group (Peredvizhniki). Artists working in Chişinău in the late 19th century and early 20th include Yevgeniya Maleshevskaya (1868–1940), who taught Il'ya Repin, the sculptor Aleksandr Plamadyala (1888–1940), August Bal'yer (1881–1962), who painted both portraits and still-lifes, and Sh. G. Kogan (1880–1940), who was known particularly for his etchings.

In the 1920s and 1930s painting in the Moldavian ASSR developed along the lines of the ASSOCIATION OF ARTISTS OF REVOLUTIONARY RUSSIA (AKhRR), and Aleksandr Foynitsky (1886–1957) created a series of paintings and graphic work embodying scenes of the socialist transformation of the republic. The graphic artist Yevgeny Merega (1910–79) illustrated the first editions of books in the Moldovan language and designed political posters. The reunification of Bessarabia and the Moldavian ASSR in 1940 and the formation of the Moldavian SSR opened up new prospects for the development of a national artistic culture. A museum of art, an artists' union and an architects' union were established in Chişinău, and the College of Art was reorganized. The USSR's entry into World War II prevented further developments, however, and more than a third of all artists went to the front. Moldovan artists nonetheless produced several paintings and sculptures reflecting the people's struggle against Fascism, for example *Moldavian Partisans* (1942) by Moisey Gamburd (1903–54) and *Hostages* (1944) by Aleksey Vasil'yev (1907–75). The most important work on the war is the dramatic *Moldavia on Fire* (1943) cycle of sculptures by Lazar' Dubinovsky (1910–82). Boris Nesvedov (1903–63), who saw action, produced numerous drawings from life and prints of the events of the war.

After the war, despite pressure to produce works of SOCIALIST REALISM, several important paintings were executed that reflect the diversity of the artists' outlook, as in the *Anti-Illiteracy Campaign* (1947) by Gamburd, portraits by Konstantin Kitayka (1914–62), such as *P. Vershigora* (1949), and landscapes by Aleksey Vasil'yev, such as *Evening at Leusheny* (1960; all Chişinău, Mus. F.A.). In the late 1950s and early 1960s increased creative freedom and a higher level of skill led to greater individuality among Moldovan painters. Whereas paintings such as '*La Zhok*' *(Invitation to the Dance)* (1956) by Valentina Rusu-Ciobanu (*b* 1920), *Tatarbunari Uprising* (1957) by Mikhail Greku (*b* 1916) and the early work of Igor' Viyeru (1923–88) are closely related in approach, by the 1970s and 1980s each of these artists was creating individual work.

Among the most important paintings of the 1960s–80s is Greku's triptych *Story of a Life* (1967; Moscow, Tret'yakov Gal.), in which he allegorically allies his own destiny with that of his native land. In the 1980s the development of a metaphorical language led to the creation of paintings that are closely linked to Abstract Expressionism, and in many canvases of this period this language is enriched by the traditions of folk art. In the 1970s and 1980s Rusu-Ciobanu departed from her former tonal drawing and chiaroscuro treatment of space, turning to a more severe and expressive manner. In her portrait of the *Actor D. Fusu in Armour* (1976; Chişinău, Mus. F.A.; see fig. 2) and in portraits of the writers *A. Lupan* and *G. Viyeru*, the sharpness of the drawing and the contrasts of local colour bring out the individuality of the sitter. These same qualities enhance the expressive nature of her thematic paintings, such as *Moon Walk* and *Children and Sport*.

Lyricism predominates in Igor' Viyeru's scenes of modern Moldovan village life. Sometimes he used symbolism and allegory, as in *Song of the Land*, but more often he depicted the peasant and his work realistically, with great warmth and artistic power, as in *July Night*. Other painters active in Moldova in the 1960s–80s include Mikhail Burya (*b* 1924), Ivan Zhumaty (*b* 1909), Sergey

2. Valentina Rusu-Ciobanu: *Actor D. Fusu in Armour*, acrylic on canvas, 900×740 mm, 1976 (Chişinău, Museum of Fine Art)

conveying the inner world of the subject and to making more subtle use of the characteristics of the material.

Graphic art developed in the post-war years both in book illustration, which coincided with the expansion of book publishing in the republic, and as separate prints and drawings for exhibition. Il'ya Bogdesko (*b* 1923) introduced a new and original approach in his illustrations for Moldovan classics by I. Kryange and for the folk ballads *Mioritsa* and *Kodryan*, using folkloric motifs and the script of ancient manuscripts. His illustrations for the work of Erasmus (1981) and Jonathan Swift (1985) unite the language of the grotesque with clear and subtle literary images. Georgy Vrabiye (*b* 1939) used the language of contemporary graphic art in his illustrations for the works of M. Eminesku and I. Kryange. The illustrations executed in the 1970s and 1980s by B. Brynzey (*b* 1930), I. Kyrmu (*b* 1932) and A. Usov (*b* 1938) are notable for their originality and fresh reading of literature.

Artists producing independent examples of graphic art worked in varying genres, using a variety of techniques. Leonid Grigorashchenko (*b* 1924), who produced several major series in the 1960s–80s dedicated to key events in the Moldovan people's history, worked in watercolour. The etchings of Viktor Ivanov (*b* 1910) continued the tradition of Bessarabian graphic art of the 1920s–30s. Other notable works of graphic art were produced in the 1960s–80s by Emil Kildesku (*b* 1937) and A. Kolybnyak (*b* 1943), among others. The overall trend in graphic art in post-war Moldova was towards increasing freedom of self-expression, heightened use of metaphor and the use of complex modern techniques and materials.

Kuchuk (*b* 1940) and Eleonora Romanescu (*b* 1926). Common features of their work are a lyrical and poetic attitude, special attention to rural life and landscape, and the inclusion of elements of traditional Moldovan folk art.

The sculpture of the post-war period reached creative maturity earlier than painting. Sculptural portraits, such as Lazar' Dubinovsky's *Head of a Moldavian Girl* (1947), and genre compositions were highly developed, although such compositions as Dubinovsky's *Wine-growers* (1949) and *Harvest Dance* (1948) by Klavdiya Kobizeva (*b* 1905) showed a literary, naturalistic and dry approach, to conform with the demands imposed by official art organizations. Monumental sculpture began to develop from the mid-1950s. Dubinovsky's monument *To the Heroic Komsomol* in Chişinău (1957) successfully combines the allegorical presentation of a girl holding a torch with the realism of the relief figures around the base of the stele. The *P. Tkachenko* monument (1960) in Bendery by Naum Eppelbaum (*b* 1929) and Brungil'da Eppelbaum-Marchenko (*b* 1928) expresses the revolutionary's single-mindedness, courage and human simplicity. In the monumental sculpture of the 1970s and 1980s artists paid particular attention to the organization of space within the ensemble, as in *Liberation* (1970) in Chişinău by Dubinovsky and Eppelbaum and *Khotin Uprising* (1974) by Yury Kanashin (*b* 1939). In the smaller compositions of the 1970s–80s sculptors made more active use of space, as in Eppelbaum's *Flame of the Revolution, Peace March* by I. D. Kitman (*b* 1936) and *Harvest Festival* by Eppelbaum-Marchenko. In portraiture greater attention was paid to

3. DECORATIVE ARTS. In the 19th century industrial output gradually killed traditional crafts. By the early 20th century crafts such as metalwork and decorative leatherwork had died out, and carpet-making, which had been the pride of folk art, ceramics and national costumes had been considerably impoverished. After the October Revolution of 1917, however, state workshops were established to continue the traditions of popular carpet-making, ceramics, wood-carving, basketwork and other crafts. Specially trained artists worked alongside traditional craftsmen, creating templates for mass production. Thus, major carpet factories operated in Chişinău, Orgeyev, Chadyr-Lunga, Chimishliya and elsewhere. In 1948 a special section was created within the Moldavian Artists' Union for artists making carpets and ceramics. From the outset the group's activity was geared towards exhibitions rather than production. Exhibitions of the 1950s–60s included displays of ceramics by Sergey Chokolov (1892–1977), V. E. Nechayeva (1909–77) and I. N. Postolaki (1906–76) and carpets by Chokolov and V. K. Polyakova. Their work aimed to absorb folk traditions in these crafts and to rework them for mass production. In the late 1960s, however, and particularly in the 1970s and 1980s, decorative artists changed direction, no longer striving to imitate folk art or to create purely utilitarian artefacts. In the work of Yelena Rotaru (*b* 1936) and others, Moldovan carpets are turned into figurative or decorative tapestries that draw from folk tradition only the general principles of colouring and imagery. Ceramicists, including N. N. Sazhina (*b* 1938) and E. L. Greku (*b* 1918), and

glassmakers such as M. I. Graty (*b* 1939) moved away from utilitarianism and produced independent creative work unrelated to industrial design. Decorative ceramics and glass, tapestries and wooden artefacts were designed for the interiors of public buildings and private homes.

In the 1960s–80s stage design became a separate field in Moldovan art. In the immediate post-war years stage designers had seen their work as no more than a setting for a performance, but in the 1970s and 1980s they began to use their designs as a representational commentary on the imagery of the performance. The most interesting approaches to stage design were those of A. V. Shubin (1913–80), K. I. Lodzeysky (1913–78) and B. Ye. Sokolov (*b* 1916).

BIBLIOGRAPHY

L. S. Berg: *Bessarabiya: Strana, lyudi, khozyaystvo* [Bessarabia: the land, the people, the economy] (Petrograd, 1918)
M. Ya. Livshits and L. I. Chezza: *Izobrazitel'noye iskusstvo Moldavii* [The fine art of Moldavia] (Kishinyov, 1958)
A. I. Zakharov: *Narodnaya arkhitektura Moldavii* [Moldavian vernacular architecture] (Moscow, 1960)
A. M. Zevina and K. D. Rodnin: *Izobrazitel'noye iskusstvo Moldavii* [The fine art of Moldavia] (Kishinyov, 1965)
Istoriya Moldavii [A history of Moldavia], 2 vols (Kishinyov, 1968)
M. Ya. Livshits: *Dekor v arkhitekture Moldavii* [Decoration in Moldavian architecture] (Kishinyov, 1971)
Arkhitektura sovetskoy Moldavii [The architecture of Soviet Moldavia] (Moscow, 1973)
Iskusstvo Moldavii, 1924–1974: Bibliograficheskiy sbornik [Moldavian art, 1924–1974: a bibliography] (Kishinyov, 1975)
Khudozhniki moldavskoy knigi [Moldavian book illustrators] (Kishinyov, 1977)
I. S. Grosul, ed.: *Moldavane* [The Moldavians] (Kishinyov, 1977)
M. Ya. Livshits: *Dekorativno-prikladnoye iskusstvo moldavskoy SSR* [The decorative and applied art of the Moldavian SSR] (Moscow, 1979)
L. A. Toma: *Portret v moldavskoy zhivopisi* [The portrait in Moldavian painting] (Kishinyov, 1983)
Ya. N. Taras: *Pamyatniki arkhitektury Moldavii XIV–XX vv.* [Moldavian architectural monuments of the 14th–20th centuries] (Kishinyov, 1986)

M. YA. LIVSHITS

Molenaer, Jan Miense (*b* Haarlem, *c.* 1610; *d* Haarlem, *bur* 19 Sept 1668). Dutch painter and draughtsman. The surprisingly large oeuvre of this remarkably versatile genre painter displays an inventive symbolism, wit and humour, which identify him as the true forerunner of Jan Steen.

1. LIFE. He was the son of Jan Mienssen Molenaer and Grietgen Adriaens. The year of his birth is suggested by a notarized document of 21 November 1637 giving his age as about 27. His brother Bartholomeus Molenaer (*d* 1650) also painted, specializing in rustic peasant interiors in the manner of Adriaen van Ostade. Later in his career Jan Miense Molenaer occasionally collaborated with his nephew Klaes Molenaer (1630–76), a landscape painter and the son of another brother, Claes Jansz. Molenaer. On 1 June 1636 Molenaer married the genre painter JUDITH LEYSTER in Heemstede, near Haarlem; only two of their five children, Helena and Constantijn, survived childhood. Also in 1636, following the court's confiscation of his property to pay debts, Molenaer and Leyster moved to Amsterdam, and a year later he was commissioned to paint an elaborate wedding portrait for the van Loon family, the *Wedding of Willem van Loon and Anna Ruychaver* (1637; Amsterdam, Mus. van Loon). His financial situation appears to have improved during his Amsterdam years, thanks in part to an inheritance received by

Leyster in 1639. It was during this period that the painter Jan Lievens briefly lived with Molenaer (1644). After 12 years in Amsterdam, Molenaer purchased a house in Heemstede and moved there in October 1648. He acquired two more houses in 1655, one on the Voetboogstraat in Amsterdam (occupied for only six months), the other in Haarlem on the Lombardsteech; his remaining years were spent in the Haarlem/Heemstede area. Despite his house speculation, the painter regularly appeared in court for non-payment of debts; settlement often involved either full or partial payment in paintings. Molenaer was also arraigned on charges of fighting and using abusive language. A posthumous inventory of his possessions conducted on 10 October 1668 lists a large collection of 16th- and 17th-century paintings.

2. WORKS. Colourful genre paintings, genre-like group portraits and history paintings characterize the first half of Molenaer's career. The earliest works (*c.* 1628–30) reveal a strong affinity to paintings by Frans Hals from the 1620s. Examples such as *Children Playing with a Cat* (Dunkirk, Mus. B.-A.) and the *Breakfast Scene* (1629; Worms, Ksthaus Heylshof) suggest that Hals was Molenaer's teacher. As did Hals, he often depicted exuberant children and merrymakers in large half-length format. Paintings from this period have often been misattributed to Hals and Leyster, although Molenaer's brushwork tends to be more descriptive and his figures more substantial. An impulse to compress interior space often accompanies awkward neck and shoulder areas of his figures.

During the 1630s and into the 1640s Molenaer painted an enormous range of subjects, in which the boundaries between genre, portraiture and history are often unclear; examples include *Pastoral Scene* (1632; Paris, Louvre), the *Denial of St Peter* (1636; Budapest, Mus. F.A.), *Scene from Bredero's 'Lucelle'* (1639; Amsterdam, Ned. Theat. Inst.) and *The Duet* (*c.* 1630; Seattle, WA, A. Mus.). His imagery also reveals a unique combination of symbolism and allegory, description and humour, as in the *Artist in his Studio* (1631; Berlin, Bodemus.), the *Woman of the World* (1633; Toledo, OH, Mus. A.), *Boys with Dwarfs* (1646; Eindhoven, Stedel. van Abbemus.) and *The Dentist* (Brunswick, Herzog Anton Ulrich-Mus.). Molenaer's creative use of traditional themes, particularly the Virtues and Vices, has attracted the attention of iconographers and cultural historians. The riotous, often violent, actions of peasants often signal a warning to the upper classes found within the same compositions, as in the *Allegory of Marital Fidelity* (1633; Richmond, VA, Mus. F.A.). Molenaer's pictorial treatment varied greatly, depending on the subject represented: a coarse, painterly application and tonalist palette is usually reserved for peasant imagery (e.g. the *Five Senses*, 1637; The Hague, Mauritshuis); by contrast, representations of the upper classes involve a more controlled and polished treatment, with the use of brilliant local colours (e.g. *Family Making Music*, 1635–6; The Hague, Rijksdienst Beeld. Kst, on dep. Haarlem, Frans Halsmus.).

As Molenaer's debt to Frans Hals lessened, other stylistic influences ranging from Dirck Hals and Thomas de Keyser to the little-known Haarlem painter Isack Elyas (*fl* 1626) can be isolated. From the 1640s Molenaer

Jan Miense Molenaer: *Peasants Carousing*, oil on canvas, 1.12×1.30 m, 1662 (Boston, MA, Museum of Fine Arts)

specialized exclusively in low-life genre, his repeated variations of merry companies, peasant weddings, games and village scenes revealing the influence of Adriaen van Ostade. The compositions are crowded, the scale smaller and the colours muted; a script signature replaces the block lettering seen in earlier signatures and monograms; and the paintings are rarely dated. This dramatic change in Molenaer's art prompted many early commentators to conclude that his oeuvre was the work of two painters. The masterpiece of the second half of his career, the signed and dated *Peasants Carousing* (1662; Boston, MA, Mus. F.A.; see fig.), displays the lively humour, vivid description and ambitious composition that place it on a level with the best of his earlier works. Although Molenaer painted a number of exceptional works during the 1650s and 1660s, the overall quality of his paintings is poor. Scores of mediocre works have been misattributed to him, many of these by Jan Jansz. Molenaer (*d* 1685), whose figures are easily recognized by their heavy white highlights and pinched features.

Molenaer's graphic oeuvre consists of a handful of drawings of village scenes executed in the 1650s (e.g.

Peasants on their Way to a Fair; Haarlem, Teylers Mus.). A few prints have also been attributed to him.

BIBLIOGRAPHY

Hollstein: *Dut. & Flem.*; *NKL*; Thieme–Becker

T. Schrevelius: *Harlemias of de eerste stichting der stad Haarlem* [Harlemias, or the first founding of the city of Haarlem] (Haarlem, 1648), p. 384

W. Bode and A. Bredius: 'Der Haarlemer Maler Johannes Molenaer in Amsterdam', *Jb. Kön.-Preuss. Kstsamml.*, xi (1890), pp. 65–78

A. Bredius: 'Jan Miense Molenaer: Nieuwe gegevens omtrent zijn leven en zijn werk', *Oud-Holland*, xxvi (1908), pp. 41–2

P. J. J. van Thiel: 'Marriage Symbolism in a Musical Party by Jan Miense Molenaer', *Simiolus*, ii (1967–8), pp. 91–9

I. H. van Eeghen: 'De groepsportretten in de familie van Loon', *Amstelodamum*, lx (1973), pp. 121–7

Tot lering en vermaak [Towards learning and leisure] (exh. cat., ed. E. de Jongh; Amsterdam, Rijksmus., 1976), pp. 176–85

C. E. Bruyn-Berg: 'Bredero's *Lucelle*, Jan Miense Molenaer ca. 1610–1668', *Jversl. Ver. Rembrandt* (1978), pp. 25–8

Die Sprache der Bilder: Realität und Bedeutung in der niederländischen Malerei des 17. Jahrhunderts (exh. cat., ed. L. Dittrich; Brunswick, Herzog Anton Ulrich-Mus., 1978), pp. 106–15

C. Brown: *Scenes of Everyday Life: Dutch Genre Painting of the Seventeenth Century* (London, 1984), p. 228

B. Haak: *The Golden Age: Dutch Painters of the Seventeenth Century* (London, 1984), pp. 72, 235–6

Masters of Seventeenth-century Dutch Genre Painting (exh. cat., ed. P. Sutton; Philadelphia, PA, Mus. A.; Berlin, Gemäldegal.; London, RA; 1984), xxxiv and pp. 260–65

P. Hecht: 'The Debate on Symbol and Meaning in Dutch Seventeenth-century Art: An Appeal to Common Sense', *Simiolus*, xvi (1986), pp. 173–87

N. Salomon: 'Political Iconography in a Painting by Jan Miense Molenaer', *Mercury*, iv (1986), pp. 23–38

Portretten van echt en trouw: Huwelijk en gezin in der Nederlandse kunst van de zeventiende eeuw [Portraits of spousage and loyalty: marriage and family in Dutch art of the seventeenth century] (exh. cat., ed. E. de Jongh; Haarlem, Frans Halsmus., 1986), pp. 689, 215–17, 280–84

DENNIS P. WELLER

Moles, Pedro Pascual (*b* Valencia, 1741; *d* Barcelona, 1797). Spanish engraver. He was a pupil of José Vergara, José Camarón y Boronat and Vicente Galcerán (*d* 1788) in Valencia, and in 1759 he moved to Barcelona to study with Francisco Tramulles (1717–71). Moles was appointed a supernumerary member of the Real Academia de Bellas Artes de S Fernando, Madrid, for his participation in the *Mascara Real* (1764), a publication commemorating the accession of the Bourbon king Charles III in 1759. In 1766 the Junta de Comercio de Barcelona awarded him a scholarship to study in Paris under Nicolas-Gabriel Dupuis and Charles-Nicolas Cochin II. In 1770 Moles became an *académico de mérito* of the Real Academia de S Fernando for his engraving of *St Gregory the Great Refusing the Papal Tiara*, after Louis Michel van Loo. In 1774 he executed an engraving after François Boucher's *Crocodile Hunt* (1739; Amiens, Mus. Picardie). On his return to Barcelona in 1775, Moles was appointed Director of the recently created Escuela Gratuita de Dibujo y Grabado, a post he held until his death.

Ceán Bermúdez
BIBLIOGRAPHY
Baron de Alcahali: *Diccionario biográfico de artistas valencianos* (Valencia, 1897)
V. Genoves Amoros: 'Repertori dels gravats de Pere Pasqual Moles', *Bol. Soc. Castell. Cult.*, xiv/2 (1933), p. 97
J. Ainaud Lasarte: *Grabado*, A. Hisp., xviii (Madrid, 1958)
P. Bohigas: *El libro español* (Barcelona, 1962)
A. Gallego: *Historia del grabado en España* (Madrid, 1979)
E. Páez: *Repertorio de grabados españoles en la Biblioteca Nacional* (Madrid, 1981–5)
A. Tomás and M. S. Silvestre: *Estampas y planchas de la Real Academia en el Museo de Bellas Artes de Valencia* (Valencia, 1982)
J. Carrete, F. Checa and V. Bozal: *El grabado en España: Siglos XV al XVIII*, Summa A., xxxi (Madrid, 1987)

BLANCA GARCÍA VEGA

Molière, Marinus Jan Granpré. *See* GRANPRÉ MOLIÈRE, MARINUS JAN.

Molin, Johan Peter (*b* Göteborg, 17 March 1814; *d* Stockholm, 27 July 1873). Swedish sculptor. He undertook his principal training in 1843–5 with the sculptor Hermann Wilhelm Bissen and the medallist Christen Christensen (1806–45) in Copenhagen. After this he went to Rome, where he remained until his return to Sweden in 1853. There he became a teacher at the Konstakademi, court sculptor and sculptor of statues. By that time he had had significant success with, among others, his sleeping *Bacchante* (Stockholm, Nmus., on loan to Ulriksdal, nr Stockholm, Orangerie Mus.), and he executed a series of commissions, for example the statue of *Oscar I* (1851–4; Göteborg, Stora Börssalen). During his last two decades

Molin produced numerous portrait medals, busts and tomb monuments, but above all three central works in Stockholm: the *Knife Fighters* (outside Nmus.), the statue of *Charles XII* and 'Molin's Fountain' in Kungsträdgården.

In the *Knife Fighters* Molin interpreted a subject from the Viking era with dynamic realism: two young men bound together by a cord around their waists, fighting with knives. It attracted international attention when exhibited at the Paris Salon of 1859 and, cast in bronze, in Berlin and at the London World Exhibition of 1862. The forceful bronze statue of *Charles XII* (unveiled, 1868) is one of Stockholm's most important royal monuments. The fountain was executed for the Scandinavian Art and Industry Exhibition in 1866, remodelled and placed in bronze on its present location in 1873. There, around a twisted column, Molin represented the mythical water spirit, the *Nixie* (Swed. Näcken), along with other characters from Nordic folklore and mythology, with a fluid richness of form characteristic of Bernini. Sculptural plasticity has been exchanged for looser, painterly modelling with splintered contours. In such works Molin distanced himself from the Neo-classical tradition in which he was educated and adopted the late 19th-century organic, decorative sculptural style. There are numerous works by Molin in Swedish museums, and some of his sketches and notebooks are to be found in Lund (Kstmus., Arkv Dek. Kst).

BIBLIOGRAPHY
E. Högestätt: 'Molins fontän', [Molin's fountain], *Tidskr. Kstvet.*, xxix (1952), pp. 9–43
B. Wennberg: *French and Scandinavian Sculpture in the Nineteenth Century: A Study of Trends and Innovations* (Stockholm and Atlantic Highlands, NJ, 1978)

PONTUS GRATE

Molina, Francisco Daniel (*b* Vich, Barcelona, 1815; *d* Barcelona, 1867). Spanish architect. He was one of the principal exponents of Neo-classicism. He first studied under José Casademunt Torrens (1804–68) in the Escuela de la Lonja in Barcelona, together with José Oriol Mestres (1804–68), Miguel Garriga and Elías Rogent. He later trained in the Real Academia de Bellas Artes de S Fernando, Madrid, graduating in 1843. One of Molina's most notable works was the Teatro Principal (1845), which was to rival the Gran Teatro del Liceo (1847), both in Barcelona. The surviving curved façade is dominated by three large arches containing the openings on to the main level. An octagonal vestibule leads on the left to the semicircular auditorium (now cinema), while on the right is the circular café (now exhibition room). Molina was also one of the first architects to cultivate the neo-Gothic style, as in his Fuente de la Plaza del Rey, Barcelona (1853). He frequently collaborated with sculptors when he constructed monuments of importance, such as the Column of Admiral Garcerán Marquet (1850) with Damian Campeny y Estrany and the Fuente del Genio Catalán (1856) with Fausto Baratta (1832–1904), both of which were Neo-classical in design. Molina's best work was in the field of urban planning. From 1855 he was the municipal architect for Barcelona, took part in the competition held by the City Council for the plans to extend the city (1859) and obtained the second prize. He was responsible for the plans for the urban development of

Sabadell (1864) and created many beautiful squares. His masterpiece was the Plaza Real (1848–60). It is rectangular in plan and completely surrounded with ranges of buildings. The most notable elements are opposite, and on either side of, the single entrance route. A ground floor portico of ashlar semicircular arches supports the upper storeys. These are articulated with Corinthian pilasters, which have balconies between them.

BIBLIOGRAPHY

J. A. Gaya Nuño: *Arte del siglo XIX*, A. Hisp., xix (Madrid, 1966)

J. Bassegoda: *Los maestros de obras de Barcelona* (Barcelona, 1972)

P. Navascués and others: *Del neoclasicismo al modernismo* (Madrid, 1979)

ALBERTO VILLAR MOVELLÁN

Molina, Gonzalo Argote de. *See* ARGOTE DE MOLINA, GONZALO.

Molinari, Antonio (*b* Venice, 21 Jan 1655; *d* Venice, 3 Feb 1704). Italian painter and draughtsman. He was the son of the painter Giovanni Molinari (1633–87) and studied in Venice with Antonio Zanchi. His style had its origins in the naturalism and tenebrism of Neapolitan painting, introduced to Venice in the mid-17th century. Although his work always retained some traces of this naturalism, the typically violent subject-matter and intensity of the Neapolitan style were considerably tempered by the addition of classicizing elements and of rich, glowing colours. By the 1680s Molinari had developed his characteristic manner of depicting figures in poses of extreme torsion and vigorous movement, arranged in graceful compositions. His subject-matter included episodes from the Old and New Testaments, antiquity and Classical mythology. His classical idiom was most pronounced in his large canvases painted for churches, such as the *Feeding of the Five Thousand* (1690; Venice, S Pantalon) and the *Death of Uzzah* (*c*. 1695; Murano, S Maria degli Angeli). In the *Death of Uzzah* a long procession moves diagonally across the canvas through an arcadian landscape, and the figures are arranged in patterns of overlapping triangles and planes of alternating light and dark.

Many of Molinari's drawings survive, a large number in Düsseldorf (Kstmus.). His preliminary studies for known paintings, laid out in free and flowing ink and chalk lines with wash and hatching to indicate tone, show great speed and fluency in the conception of compositional schemes. Molinari has been called an artist of transition, but he was never a direct precursor of Venetian 18th-century styles. His voluminous, firmly modelled forms and his rich, deep colours remained rooted in the Baroque. He had few followers, but his pupil Giovanni Battista Piazzetta carried some elements of his style into the next century.

BIBLIOGRAPHY

A. M. Pappalardo: 'Il pittore veneziano Antonio Molinari', *Atti Reale Ist. Veneto Sci., Lett. & A.*, cxii (1953–4), pp. 439–61

L. Moretti: 'Antonio Molinari rivisitato', *A. Veneta*, xxxiii (1979), pp. 59–69

R. Green: 'Molinari Drawings in Düsseldorf', *Master Drgs.*, xxii (1984), pp. 194–205

RICHARD C. GREEN

Molinari, Guido (*b* Montreal, 12 Oct 1933). Canadian painter and theorist. He attended evening classes from 1948 to 1951 at the Ecole des Beaux-Arts, Montreal, before studying briefly under the Canadian painters Marian Scott (*b* 1906) and Gordon Webber (1909–65) at the Montreal Museum of Fine Arts School of Art from 1951. From 1955 to 1957 he ran Galerie l'Actuelle in Montreal, which was devoted exclusively to showing abstract art. Molinari's rigorous pursuit for over 30 years of the essence of painterly structure had a major influence on art in Quebec, substantially developing the terms of its particular modernist character.

In an essay written in 1955 Molinari projected the radical drive of modern painting from Cézanne, through Mondrian and Jackson Pollock, to a new pictorial space that he called 'colour–light'. In his art of the 1950s, consisting mostly of works on paper, he sought to reconcile the gestures of intuitive expression with the demand for objective pictorial structure. His first one-man exhibition of paintings in 1956 was of works such as *Black Angle* (oil on canvas, 1.52×1.83 m, 1956; Ottawa, N.G.; *see* CANADA, fig. 6), in each of which he balanced black and white rectilinear forms in an economical arrangement so that neither colour read as figure or ground. Through the 1960s, in paintings such as *Black* (1962; Toronto, A.G. Ont.), he used a formal structure of hard-edge columns of colour in rational rhythmic sequences, treating painting both as an objective, formal system and as the subjective content of the spectator's perceptions; his intention was that space be created by the spectator in the process of looking at the picture. From the end of the 1960s to the mid-1970s Molinari worked with a variety of geometric structures, often concentrating on the aggressive effect of juxtapositions of colour, as in the enormous triptych *Dyad Brown–Blue, Dyad Orange–Green, Dyad Green–Red* (2.9×6.9 m, exh. 1969; Ottawa, N.G.). His later paintings, notably his *Quantifier* series of 17 paintings executed in 1978–9 (exh. Montreal, Mus. A. Contemp., 1979), consist of wide bands of saturated colour sometimes so closely related in tone that they can be differentiated only under close scrutiny.

WRITINGS

P. Théberge, ed.: *Ecrits sur l'art (1954–1975)* (Ottawa, 1976)

BIBLIOGRAPHY

Guido Molinari (exh. cat. by P. Theberge, Ottawa, N.G., 1976)

Guido Molinari: Works on Paper (exh. cat. by D. Burnett, Kingston, Ont., Queen's U., Agnes Etherington A. Cent., 1981)

DAVID BURNETT

Molinari, Leonardo de'. *See* LEONARDO DA BESOZZO.

Molinier, Emile (*b* Nantes, 26 April 1857; *d* Paris, 5 May 1906). French art historian, museum curator and dealer. Under the influence of his brother Auguste Molinier (1851–1904), a great medievalist scholar, he trained at the Ecole des Chartes (1875–8) in Paris and then worked for a year in the Cabinet des Estampes at the Bibliothèque Nationale, before joining the Département des Objets d'art at the Louvre in 1879. He became a curator noted for his erudition, energy and perspicacity. On leaving the Ecole des Chartes, he at first edited medieval texts but soon turned to the history of the decorative arts and, without abandoning his study of the Middle Ages, developed a passion for the Italian Renaissance, publishing such works as *Les Plaquettes* (Paris, 1886), a pioneer study of the art form, which has remained indispensable. At the same time he compiled many catalogues of works of art, in the Louvre and other collections, including the Tesoro di S Marco in Venice (*Le Trésor de la basilique de St Marc à Venise*, Venice, 1888) and the Wallace Collection in London (*La Collection Wallace (objets d'art) à Hertford House*, Paris, 1903–4). After his brilliant overview of the history of enamelwork (*L'Emaillerie*, Paris, 1891), he wrote the first four volumes of the vast *Histoire générale des arts appliqués*, which included the first study of Byzantine ivories. The organization of a retrospective exhibition of French art for the Exposition Universelle in 1900 was the crowning achievement of his administrative career at the Louvre. Apparently disappointed not to receive the promotion he had hoped for, he left the museum to devote himself to art-dealing and writing, but he died suddenly, worn out by overwork.

WRITINGS

Donation du Baron Charles Davillier (Paris, 1885) [cat. of col. in Paris, Louvre]
Les Plaquettes (Paris, 1886)
Les Ivoires (1896); *Les Meubles du Moyen Age et de la Renaissance* (1897); *Le Mobilier du XVIIe et du XVIIIe siècle* (n.d.); *L'Orfèvrerie du Ve au XVe siècle* (1902), 4 vols of *Histoire générale des arts appliqués à l'industrie, du Ve à la fin du XVIIIe siècle* (Paris, 1896–1911)

BIBLIOGRAPHY

A. Thomas: 'Discours prononcé à ses obsèques', *Bibl. Ecole Chartes*, lxvii (1906), pp. 329–32
Catalogue des objets d'art et de haute curiosité du Moyen Age, de la Renaissance et autres composant la succession de feu E. Molinier (Paris, 1906)
Catalogue général des livres imprimés de la Bibliothèque nationale, cxvi (Paris, 1932), col. 929–38

BERTRAND JESTAZ

Molinos, Jacques (*b* Lyon, 4 June 1743; *d* Paris, 19 Feb 1831). French architect. He studied at the Académie Royale d'Architecture, Paris, under Jacques-François Blondel. His early work included the château of Puisieux (1780–85), near Villers-Cotterêts, which he built for the Marquis de Vasan, but his most important projects were realized in partnership with JACQUES-GUILLAUME LEGRAND. Together they built a glass and timber dome (1781; destr.) to cover the courtyard of Nicolas Le Camus de Mézières's Halle au Blé, Paris, supporting it on light trusses, and later the Halle aux Draps (1786; destr. 1855), using the same type of construction, which had first been proposed by Philibert de L'Orme during the 16th century. They also built their own house (1789) at 6, Rue Saint-Florentin, and the Hôtel Marbeuf in the Faubourg Saint-Honoré, which is famous for its refined, polychrome decoration in the manner of the Antique. In 1789–90 Molinos and Legrand erected the Théâtre Feydeau (destr.), for performances of Italian opera. It had a semicircular façade, reflecting the shape of the auditorium, pierced on the ground floor by three arched openings framing entrances articulated by Doric columns; the piers of the first-floor arcade were faced with caryatids, a striking manifestation of Neo-classicism that subsequently influenced Friedrich Gilly's design (*c*. 1798; unexecuted) for the Schauspielhaus in Berlin. Molinos and Legrand also designed the Hôtel de Ville (1792), Auteuil, in the form of an ancient temple, and their lecture hall for chemical, botanical and anatomical demonstrations in the Jardin des Plantes, Paris, was inspired by small Hellenistic temples. Molinos's other civic works included the Fontaine Valhubert, the Marché Saint-Honoré (1809) and the Halle au Vieux Linge (1808–11)

in the Enclos du Temple, all in Paris. In 1817 Molinos became municipal architect for the city of Paris and designed decorations for city festivals. He also built the Barrière de Rochechouart (1826) and the Marché Popincourt (1829–31), both in Paris.

BIBLIOGRAPHY

L. Hautecoeur: *Architecture classique*, iv–vi (Paris, 1952–5)
L. Moncet: 'Une Fête révolutionnaire à Auteuil', *Notre XVTème* (1964), p. 3
A. Braham: *The Architecture of the French Enlightenment* (London, 1980, 2/1989)

GÉRARD ROUSSET-CHARNY

Molisson, de. *See* MONTLUÇON, DE.

Molitor, Bernard (*b* Betzdorf, nr Luxembourg, *c*. 1730; *d* Fontainebleau, 17 Nov 1833). German cabinetmaker, active in France. He served his apprenticeship in Germany. He and his brother Michel Molitor (1734–1810) arrived in Paris at the beginning of the 1770s, and by 1787 Bernard had become a master *ébéniste*. Few pieces bearing his stamp exist, most attributions being made on stylistic grounds (e.g. toilet-table; London, Wallace). Two of his known, stamped, pieces (secrétaire à abattant and commode, *c*. 1788–92; sold Paris, Crédit Municipal, 26 Nov 1970) make a group with two similar, unmarked desks (London, V&A; Moscow, Pushkin Mus. F.A.). All four are in beautifully figured mahogany veneer with delicate ormolu mounts featuring *rinceaux*, palmettes and angle columns with ormolu ivy spiralled round them. From 1788 he received commissions from the court. The furniture he made for 'Mesdames Tantes', the aunts of Louis XVI, for the château at Bellevue (1789; Paris, Louvre) makes use of small-scale ormolu eagles, griffins and thunderbolts, anticipating the Empire style. In 1790 Marie-Antoinette commissioned a pair of ebony secrétaire-cabinets, decorated with black and gold Chinese lacquer (Paris, Louvre), and Molitor continued to produce work for the imperial family and court until 1815. Some other pieces use panels of Oriental lacquer (e.g. secrétaire à abattant and matching bookcase, 1814–16; London, Buckingham Pal., Royal Col.). The lack of marked pieces may indicate that Molitor had a close trade relationship with one of the *marchands-merciers*, the most likely being Dominique Daguerre, who ordered furniture from him for the château of Saint-Cloud in 1788.

BIBLIOGRAPHY

P. Kjellberg: *Le Mobilier français du XVIIIe siècle*, ii (Paris, 1980)
U. Leben: *Molitor: Ebéniste from the Ancien Régime to the Bourbon Restoration* (London, 1992)

BRUCE TATTERSALL

Mölk [Mölck; Mölckh], **Josef Adam**, Ritter von (*b* ?South Germany, *c*. 1710; *d* Vienna, 18 Feb 1794). Austrian painter and building contractor. He was the son of a painter from Blumenegg in Swabia, Mathias Mölk (*d* 1731), who had lived in Vienna since 1700, although there is no record of his son's birth there. Nikolowski suggested that he was born in South Germany when his parents were visiting their families. Mölk received his first commission in Bavaria in 1730. In 1738 he married in Rottenburg am Neckar and is documented as having been a ducal cabinet painter there. He married again in the Tyrol in 1742, where he lived until 1764. In 1744 he was ennobled by Maria-Theresa.

In 1755 Mölk became the imperial court painter in the Tyrol. One of his most important commissions in this region was for the frescoes in the parish church in Schlanders (1758–9; nave, scenes from the *Life of the Virgin*; dome, *Esther and Ahasuerus*). In 1760 he painted frescoes (overpainted *c*. 1818–20 by Josef Schöpf; destr. 1945) for the church of the Servite Order, Innsbruck, which led to further commissions for the Order, such as the frescoes and altarpieces of scenes from the *Life of the Virgin* (1773) in the church of Maria Langegg, Lower Austria. Mölk's organizational talents, his quick working methods and his large workshop enabled him to obtain nearly all the important commissions in Styria, such as the frescoes in the Servite church of Frohnleiten (1764) and the convent of Rein (1766). From 1780 he worked in Lower Austria.

In confronting the problems of illusionistic decoration on ceilings of irregular shape, Mölk was influenced first by Andrea Pozzo and later by Matthäus Günther and Cosmas Damian Asam. Mölk borrowed freely from these artists' *quadratura* schemes, while he disguised his weakness at representing figures by painting fewer of them. His style remained virtually unchanged through nearly 40 years of activity.

Egg (1970) proposed that Mölk also worked as a building contractor, removing Gothic elements from the building he was decorating. Although Egg provided no documentary evidence for this, Kraft (p. 286) cited a petition in which Mölk mentions work on both the architecture and the decoration of a parish church.

BIBLIOGRAPHY
Thieme–Becker
J. Kraft: 'Zur Lebensgeschichte des Malers Josef Adam Mölk', *Z. Ferdinandeums Tirol & Voralberg*, n. s. 3, lix (1915), pp. 277–93
F. Nikolowski: *Josef Adam Mölk und seine Werke in Tirol* (diss., Innsbruck, Leopold-Franzens U., 1950)
W. Pannold: *J. A. Mölk und sein Werk in der Steiermark* (diss., Innsbruck, Leopold-Franzens U., 1960)
E. Egg: *Kunst in Tirol: Baukunst und Plastik* (Munich, 1970), p. 210
——: *Kunst in Tirol: Malerei und Kunsthandwerk* (Munich, 1972), pp. 218–19
G. Brucher: 'Die Barocke Deckenmalerei in der Steiermark', *Jb. Ksthist. Inst. Graz*, viii (1973), pp. 87–96

THOMAS KARL

Molkenboer, Theo(dorus Henricus Antonius Adolf) (*b* Leeuwarden, 23 Feb 1871; *d* Lugano, 1 Dec 1920). Dutch painter, draughtsman, designer and writer. He received his first artistic training at the Rijksnormaalschool voor Tekenonderwijs in Amsterdam (1889–91) and in the studio of the architect P. J. H. Cuypers in 1891. Under the influence of the work of his uncle Antoon Derkinderen he decided to exchange his architectural training for painting at the Rijksakademie in Amsterdam (1891–2). During this time he became friendly with Gerrit Willem Dijsselhof and C. A. Lion Cachet, with whom he shared a great interest in Symbolism.

In 1895 Molkenboer exhibited his first portraits, which form the most important body of his work and which assured him of a steady stream of commissions. Their realism is strongly inspired by that of Jan van Scorel and the Flemish Old Masters; the portrait of *W. B. G. Molkenboer* (1896; Netherlands, priv. col., see Viola) is one of the many examples of this. His portraits of the

Artist's Mother by the Linen Cupboard (1895; Assen, Prov. Mus. Drenthe) and of various famous contemporaries such as *Eduard Brom* (1897; untraced, see Viola) are also well known. Molkenboer's work in the field of applied arts is also of importance. Between 1901 and 1904 he was Artistic Director of a delftware factory, Holland, in Utrecht. Furthermore, between 1901 and 1905 he wrote reviews and essays in the magazine *Van onze tijd* ('Of our time') and was active as a designer of books. His brother Antoon (1872–1960) was also an artist and was particularly active as a designer of such objects as posters, stamps, costumes and glasses.

WRITINGS
Christelijke kunst (Amsterdam, 1909)
De Nederlandsche nationale kleederdrachten [Dutch national costumes] (Amsterdam, 1917)

BIBLIOGRAPHY
Scheen
M. Viola: 'Theo Molkenboer, portretschilder', *Elsevier's Geïllus. Mdschr.*, xxvi (1903), pp. 355–66
E. Braches: *Het boek als Nieuwe Kunst* (Utrecht, 1973)
Antoon Molkenboer, ontwerpen voor muziek en toneel, 1895–1917 [Antoon Molkenboer, designs for music and stage, 1895–1917] (exh. cat., ed. E. Muller and M. Kyrova; The Hague, Gemeentemus., 1983)

G. JANSEN

Moll. Austrian family of sculptors. Nikolaus Moll (*b* Blumenegg, nr Bludenz, Vorarlberg, 5 March 1676; *d* Innsbruck, 20 April 1754) probably studied with Balthasar Permoser during the latter's stay in Salzburg. Moll is documented as being in Innsbruck from 1709. His early work, such as the façade figures (1716) of the collegiate church in Wilten, Innsbruck, is somewhat coarse. His most important work was the pulpit (1724) in the St Jakobskirche, Innsbruck (*in situ*). His strength lay in his richly imaginative use of decoration and his ability to combine sculptural and ornamental elements. Moll had a tendency to produce individual figures with exaggerated pathos, as in the four life-size *Statthalter* statues in the Landhaus Sitzungssaal, Innsbruck (*in situ*). His sons were also artists, the most notable son being (1) Balthasar Ferdinand Moll. His eldest son, Johann Nikolaus Moll von Blumenegg (*b* Innsbruck, 1 April 1709; *d* Vienna, 2 Oct 1743), was trained in Innsbruck (1729) in the style of Georg Raphael Donner; from 1730 he was in Vienna. His chief work was *Austria Mourning* on the sarcophagus of the Emperor Charles VI (1742; Vienna, Capuchin church). A third son, Anton Cassian Moll (*b* Innsbruck, 12 Aug 1722; *d* Vienna, 6 Dec 1757), was a medallist in Vienna from 1741.

BIBLIOGRAPHY
Thieme–Becker
A. Ilg: 'Die Bildhauer Moll', *Ber. & Mitt. Altert.-Ver. Wien*, xxv (1889), pp. 129–43
A. Schuschnigg: *Die Barockbildhauerfamilie Moll* (diss., U. Innsbruck, 1928)
E. Braun, ed.: *Katalog des österreichischen Barockmuseums in unteren Belvedere in Wien*, ii (Vienna, 1980), pp. 439–53

A. GERHARDT

(1) Balthasar Ferdinand Moll (*b* Innsbruck, 4 Jan 1717; *d* Vienna, 3 March 1785). He probably first trained in his father's studio in Innsbruck. There is documentary evidence that in 1738 he was in Vienna, where he took part unsuccessfully in the annual competition at the Akademie der Bildenden Künste. The first works known to be by him date from 1739 and 1740 and strongly reflect the influence of Georg Raphael Donner. There is no documentary evidence that Moll spent a period in Donner's studio in Pressburg (now Bratislava), but it is possible that he worked there until 1739. His first major project in Vienna, where he settled permanently at this time, was the figurative section of the pulpit of the Servite church, which he completed in 1739 (*in situ*). In 1745 he won the gold medal in the Akademie competition. More significant recognition, however, did not come until 1751, when the Empress Maria-Theresa commissioned from him a sarcophagus for her mother, the Empress Elisabeth-Christine (Vienna, Capuchin church). He followed this work with a series of state tombs for the Habsburg family, also intended for the Capuchin church in Vienna. These included one of the most grandiose and important Rococo monuments in Austria, the double sarcophagus for *Francis I of Lorraine and Maria-Theresa* (1753–4; *in situ*). The Empress also commissioned the elaborate monument to *Field-Marshal Leopold, Graf Daun* for the Georgskapelle of the Augustinian church (marble, *in situ*). Moll subsequently produced other works for the court and the nobility, for example a statue of *Maria-Theresa* (destr. 1873) for Klagenfurt, commissioned by the Diet of Carinthia in 1765.

Most of Moll's work was in metal, his favourite material for casting being tin, although he sometimes also used bronze and lead; works made from wood and marble were less common. His earlier work was generally traditional and within the confines of the ornate, courtly style of the period. Rococo elements occur principally in Moll's liberal use of rocaille ornamentation and in his fragmented, restless surface, but his basic forms and concepts were essentially still late Baroque. By this stage there is little evidence of Donner's influence other than in the rather bland, smooth lines of Moll's idealized allegorical figures. As a professor of sculpture at the Akademie (1751–9), Moll did much to continue the tradition of metal-casting in Vienna, and he influenced the younger generation of sculptors, including Franz Xaver Messerschmidt and Johann Georg Dorfmeister (1736–86).

In the changed artistic climate of Vienna after the early 1770s, Moll's sculpture became more classical in approach. His willingness to adapt is apparent in some of his surviving works from this period, for example the two bronze busts of *Francis I of Lorraine* (Vienna, Ksthist. Mus. and Belvedere) and the monument to *Dr Gerard van Swieten* (1772; Vienna, Augustinian church; destr. except for bust). He also tried to incorporate classicism into the figures of the Triumphal Gate in Innsbruck (stone, *in situ*), returning to Donner's style. The attribution to Moll of another work of this transitional period, the marble statue of *Francis I of Lorraine* (Vienna, Belvedere), now appears to be doubtful. Despite these changes in Moll's style, influential artistic circles in Vienna failed to appreciate his work at this time, and he received fewer and fewer commissions. After the death of Maria Theresa he also lost his position at court. His last major public commission was for the equestrian statue of *Joseph II* (gilded lead, 1777–8; Laxenburg, Altes Schloss). With its schematic, harsh modelling and austere approach, this is a typical product of the *Zopfstil*. Also from this period is the equestrian monument to *Francis of Lorraine* (lead, 1781; Vienna, Burggtn). Moll offered this

work, which he apparently undertook without a commission, to Emperor Joseph II, but it was refused, and it was only in 1800 that Moll's heirs were able to sell the monument to the Viennese court.

BIBLIOGRAPHY

U. König: *Balthasar Ferdinand Moll* (diss., U. Vienna, 1976)

C. Diemer: 'Balthasar Ferdinand Moll und Georg Raphael Donner: Die Portraitreliefs im österreichischen Barockmuseum und ihre Vorbilder', *Mitt. Österreich. Gal.*, xxi (1977), pp. 67–113

M. Pötzl-Malikova: 'Das Grabmal Gerard van Swietens in der Augustinerkirche in Wien', *Alte & Mod. Kst*, xxix (1984), pp. 25–8

——: 'Die Kanzel der Servitenkirche in Wien und die Bozzetti der theologischen Tugenden von B. F. Moll im Kunstgewerbemuseum in Köln', *Österreich. Z. Dkmlpf.*, xli (1987)

MARIA PÖTZL-MALIKOVA

Moll, Carl (*b* Vienna, 23 April 1861; *d* Vienna, 12 April 1945). Austrian painter. He studied (1880–81) at the Akademie der Bildenden Künste in Vienna but had to abandon his course because of ill-health. Subsequently he studied privately with the Austrian painter Emil Jakob Schindler (1842–92), and in 1895 he married Schindler's widow and became the stepfather of her daughter, later Alma Mahler. From 1888 he exhibited in the Künstlerhaus in Vienna but did not become a member until 1892. In 1897 he joined the Vienna Secession. He became one of its leading organizers, working on the magazine *Ver sacrum* and taking responsibility for most of the exhibitions of foreign artists, including the French Impressionist exhibition of 1903. In 1900–01 he was president of the Secession, leaving it along with the Klimt group in 1905. In 1908–9 he took part in the Vienna Kunstschau, and until 1912 he was an adviser at the Galerie Miethke in Vienna. He was active in helping the young painters Oskar Kokoschka, Anton Kolig and Franz Wiegele. In 1930 he published a monograph on Schindler.

Moll was one of the Vienna Secession painters who saw the pointillist techniques of the French Impressionists as a revelation. The painterly application of colour was connected to the structural elements of contemporary decorative painting, so that his paintings have a charming mixture of pointillist style and a strict organization of the surface of the painting, as in *Twilight* (1900; Vienna, Belvedere). Along with landscapes and subjects drawn from nature he painted numerous interiors, such as *Interior of the Artist's House* (1903; Vienna, Belvedere), depicting his own Vienna home, built and decorated by Josef Hoffmann. In his prints he mainly depicted the outskirts of Vienna, as in the colour woodcut *Winter* (*c.* 1903; Vienna, Hist. Mus.).

WRITINGS

Emil Jakob Schindler, 1842–1892: Eine Bildnisstudie (Vienna, 1930)

BIBLIOGRAPHY

M. Fritz: *Der Wiener Maler Carl Moll* (diss., Innsbruck, Leopold-Franzens U., 1962)

H. Dichand, ed.: *Carl Moll: Seine Freunde, sein Leben, sein Werk* (Salzburg, 1985)

R. Maegle: *Die Schaffensperiode Carl Molls von 1911 bis 1945* (Vienna, 1989)

EDWIN LACHNIT

Moll, Oskar (*b* Brieg, Germany [now Brzeg, Poland], 21 July 1875; *d* Berlin, 19 Aug 1947). German painter and collector. After studying natural science, briefly, he took private drawing and painting lessons from Lovis Corinth and others (1897) in Berlin. From 1898 to 1906 he travelled widely, and in 1907 he moved to Paris. Through contact with the German painter Hans Purrmann and the group of artists centred around the Café du Dôme, he participated in the formation of the Académie Matisse. From then on his rather solid impressionistic style, for example *Côte d'Azur* (Trier, Städt. Mus.), remained the basis of his work, with only brief experiments with Cubism. After his return to Berlin, he acquired a fine collection of modern French art. By 1914 he had the largest collection of works by Matisse in Germany; it was eventually sold in Berlin.

In 1918 Moll was appointed professor at the academy in Breslau (now Wrocław), where in 1925 he became director. His appointments of the former Bauhaus masters Oskar Schlemmer and Georg Muche, as well as Johannes Molzahn (1892–1965) and Alexander Kanoldt (1881–1939), made it one of the foremost modern institutions in Germany until it was closed by the government in 1932. He accepted an appointment at the Staatliche Kunstakademie, Düsseldorf, from which he was dismissed by the Nazis in 1933. In 1935 he was prohibited from exhibiting his work. In 1946 he returned to Berlin, where he retained his basic style, applying bold colours in landscapes and still-lifes, for example *Winter Window with Oranges and Glass Bowl* (watercolour, 1946; Dortmund, Mus. Ostwall). Most of his works were destroyed during the war, in particular during a bombing raid on Berlin in 1943.

BIBLIOGRAPHY

H. Braune, ed.: *Oskar Moll mit einer Selbstbiographie* (Leipzig, 1921)
Poelzig—Endell—Moll und die Breslauer Kunstakademie, 1911–1932 (exh. cat., E. Berlin, Akad Kst. DDR, 1965)
Oskar Moll: Gedächtnisausstellung zum 20. Todestag (exh. cat., Duisburg, Lehmbruck-Mus., 1967)
S. Salzmann and D. Salzmann: *Oskar Moll: Leben und Werk* (Munich, 1975) [contains bibliog. and cat. of works]

PETER W. GUENTHER

Möller, Anton, I (*b* Königsberg, 1563–5; *d* Danzig [Gdańsk], 1611). German painter, draughtsman and woodcutter. The son of a surgeon to Duke Albert I of Prussia, he served his apprenticeship in Königsberg from 1578 to 1585, mainly studying prints by Dürer. By 1587 Möller was in Danzig; a year later he obtained his first large commission, to portray the bench of lay judges (Gdańsk, Artus Court). A pen drawing of a *Country Fair* (1587; Berlin, Kupferstichkab.) is reminiscent in draughtsmanship of the Nuremberg Little Masters and in composition and shading of Pieter Bruegel the elder and Hans Bol. Between 1588 and 1590 Möller must have visited Italy (Venice at least) and the Netherlands. Returning, he became the best regarded painter in Danzig and its environs, mingling old German touches and Italian influences (Tintoretto) in his work. A large canvas of the *Last Judgement* (1601–2; Gdańsk, Artus Court) untypically shows Mannerist influence: Möller's works, with their genre elements, tend otherwise to a fresh realism rare among German contemporaries. Ceiling pictures (1602–3) in the town hall at Toruń, painted with the help of assistants, are accompanied by a large lunette of the *Parable of the Tribute Money*, with an impressive town view inspired by the Venetian *vedute* of Joseph Heintz (i); another lunette of *Church Building* transcends the perspectival scenes of Hans Vredeman de Vries, who had previously worked in Danzig, peopling the architecture with rich detail of masons at work. A large panel showing the *Works of Mercy* (1607; Gdańsk, St Mary) adopts the Tree of Jesse—Faith replacing Jesse—with medallion scenes in the branches. The high altarpiece at St Catherine (started 1609), with a view of Danzig, was completed by Izaak van den Blocke.

There are—or were—superb portraits by Möller, for instance the richly clad daughter of a Danzig patrician (1598; ex-Gdańsk, Stadtmus.). His drawings often blend old German and Dutch ideas. In an excellent pen drawing of a chapel interior (*c.* 1595; Berlin, Kupferstichkab.) an old patrician, seeming to foreshadow one of Rembrandt's patriarchs, sits in an armchair before a Gothic winged altar, listening to a small choir singing from large music sheets. A robust pen-and-ink satire on monkhood (Stuttgart, Staatsgal.) and such woodcuts as *Death and Woman* illustrate the marked genre element in Möller's art.

BIBLIOGRAPHY

W. Gyssling: *Anton Möller und seine Schule* (Strasbourg, 1917)
W. Drost: *Danziger Malerei vom Mittelalter bis zum Ende des Barock* (Berlin, Leipzig, 1938), pp. 117–21
Zeichnung in Deutschland: Deutsche Zeichner, 1540–1640, ii (exh. cat. by H. Geissler, Stuttgart, Staatsgal., 1979–80), pp. 15–18, 159–61

HANS GEORG GMELIN

Møller, C(hristian) F(rederik) (*b* Skanderborg, Jutland, 31 Oct 1898). Danish architect. He was apprenticed as a bricklayer and at the same time attended the Technical School in Århus, before being admitted to the School of Architecture in Copenhagen in 1920. He won a number of competitions in partnership with various fellow students, including those for the Gentofte Kommunes Borgerhjem (1928), a community centre, and the block of flats called Hans Tausens Gård (1929) on Struenseegade, Copenhagen, with Carl Neye. Møller's early work was inspired by Kay Fisker, in whose office he worked and with whom he went into partnership in 1929. Fisker's housing blocks had transformed Danish domestic architecture; their subdued classical idiom, open yards with gardens and use of domestic building materials were a great improvement on standard housing. Although Møller belonged to the functionalist generation, he continued Fisker's use of materials and always preferred to work in brick and wood rather than concrete and steel.

Møller's first important work, Århus University, became a lifelong project. With Povl Stegmann and Kay Fisker he won the competition for it in 1931. His partnership with Fisker continued for the first few years of the project, but after 1943 Møller worked alone. The buildings comprising Århus University were freely arranged by function. The undulating terrain was landscaped by Carl Theodor Sørensen, and much importance was attached to the interplay between architecture and nature. Handmade bricks and matching yellow tiles were produced for the building, making the roofs look lighter and creating a delicate play of colour. Møller himself explained the influence of German modernism on the design for the competition project: he used greatly simplified shapes, and even the gutters were built in so as not to break the lines. The donation of materials supplemented the minimal construction budget and gave a specifically Danish character:

clinkers from Hasle, oak parquet flooring, pine furniture and plain doors without mouldings, then fairly unusual. Some of the buildings, including the professorial residences (1933), student hostels (1934) and the Natural History Museum (1937–8), were finished before World War II; most of the classrooms were built during the war, as were the main building with the great hall, Solgården (a courtyard) and the State Library with its book tower. Møller managed to maintain the University's unity in terms of both form and materials during the extensions and alterations that took place after the 1930s.

Møller moved to Århus when work on the University began, and his subsequent activity was based in Jutland. He was a promoter of the School of Architecture in Århus, where he became professor and Principal (1965–9). In addition to Århus Municipal Hospital, planned at the same time as the University, Møller designed hospitals in Kolding, Vejle and Fredericia. He also built the 4th of May College (1949) on Fuglsangsalle, Århus, Møllevang Church (1959) and Århus Kunstmuseum (1966). In a large oeuvre dominated by undemonstrative brick buildings, Møller often combined light and dark bricks to obtain warm tones and a highly-textured effect on the large wall surfaces. The long lines, simple shapes and traditional building materials evoke vernacular Jutland architecture. In a logical continuation of the work of such architects as Fisker, Povl Baumann and Ivar Bentsen, Møller's break with tradition was not violent, and his style was not strained.

WRITINGS
Århus Universitets bygninger [The Århus University buildings] (Århus, 1978)

BIBLIOGRAPHY
A. G. Jørgensen: 'Om Århus Universitet', *Arkitekten* [Copenhagen], li, 11–12 (1949), pp. 185–208

WIVAN MUNK-JØRGENSEN

Møller, Erik (*b* Århus, 7 Nov 1909). Danish architect. He first worked with Arne Jacobsen in the early 1930s and adopted Jacobsen's preference for clean-cut shapes and thorough planning. In 1936, with Flemming Lassen (*b* 1902), he won the competition for a new public library in Nyborg (1938–40). With his own houses in Århus (1940) and Copenhagen (1944), the library is among the earliest and best examples of Danish architecture that reflect the transition from international modernism to a national vernacular style. The library, in two main blocks, is surrounded by a moat and built of brick and tile, in the proportions of traditional Danish buildings. Jacobsen and Møller won the competition for a new town hall in Århus in 1937. The interiors were elegant and influenced by Gunnar Asplund's work. After returning to Copenhagen, Møller built the Advent Church (1942–4) in the same sober brick as the Nyborg library. Among his later projects were the Milestedet housing development (1956–60), the Industriens Hus office block (1978–80) and the housing development at Wilders Plads (1978), all in Copenhagen. It is, however, as a fastidious restorer that Møller achieved greatest recognition: for example the renovation of historic streets in Pistolstræde (1971) and Rosengade (1976–8), the conversion of Niels Eigtved's warehouse into premises for the Danish Ministry of Foreign Affairs (1982) and of Gammel Dok (Old Dock) into an architecture centre (1986; all in Copenhagen).

BIBLIOGRAPHY
S. E. Rasmussen: *Nordische Baukunst* (Berlin, 1940), pp. 146–9
'Town Hall at Århus', *Archit. Rev.* [London], c (1946), pp. 48–50
'Church of the Advent, Copenhagen', *Archit. Rev.* [London], ciii (1948), pp. 236–40
'Recent Building in Denmark', *Archit. Rev.* [London], civ (1948), pp. 229–38
'Bebyggelse ved Rosengade i København' [Development at Rosengade, Copenhagen], *Arkitektur DK*, xxi–xxii (1978), pp. 173–80
'Boligbebyggelse på Wilders Plads, København' [Housing development on Wilders Plads, Copenhagen], *Arkitektur DK*, xxiii–xxiv (1979), pp. 144–9
'Restaurering af Skindergade 8, København' [Restoration of a building in Skindergade, Copenhagen], *Arkitektur DK*, xxiii–xxiv (1979), pp. 140–43
'Industriens Hus i København' [House of Industry in Copenhagen], *Arkitektur DK*, xxv–xxvi (1981), pp. 4–10
'De gamle huse i Amagergade, København' [The old houses in Amagergade, Copenhagen], *Arkitektur DK*, xxvii–xxviii (1983), pp. 46–8
'Linderangskjemmet, psykiatrisk plejehjem i Helsingør' [Linderang nursing home, Helsingør], *Arkitektur DK*, xxvii–xxviii (1983), pp. 86–91
'Udenrigsministeriet restauering af fredede byginger' [Restoration of the Ministry of Foreign Affairs], *Arkitektur DK*, xxvii–xxviii (1983), pp. 30–38

NILS-OLE LUND

Moller, Georg (*b* Diepholz, nr Hannover, 21 Jan 1784; *d* Darmstadt, 13 March 1852). German architect, urban planner and writer. He started his architectural training in the early years of the 19th century in Hannover. From 1802 until 1807 he studied in Karlsruhe under Friedrich Weinbrenner, whose Neo-classical theories he pursued throughout his career. On completion of his studies, Moller spent three years in Italy investigating the architecture and mixing with German artists and writers in Rome. On his return to Germany in 1810 he was appointed Court Architect by Ludwig I, Grand Duke of Hesse-Darmstadt (*reg* 1806–30). His greatest achievement was the remodelling of the capital, Darmstadt, into a modern, Neo-classical city (*see* DARMSTADT, §1). Moller's predecessor, Johann Heinrich Müller (1746–1830), had earlier begun to lay out parts of the city on a grid plan. Working within this framework, Moller continued much of the original scheme but modified the formal pattern and linked the new town with the old parts of the city in a picturesque manner. In this work he was clearly indebted to Weinbrenner's planning of Karlsruhe.

In his architecture, Moller was a pure Neo-classicist. One of his first public commissions was the Hoftheater (1818–20; destr. and reconstructed) in Darmstadt; he also designed the theatre in Mainz (1833) and remodelled the ducal palace in Wiesbaden (1836–7). His principal ecclesiastical buildings were the unfinished Catholic Ludwigskirche (1822–6; destr. 1944; reconstructed; *see* DARMSTADT, fig. 2), which was built as a large rotunda, with 28 free-standing Corinthian columns inside, below the dome, and the Neo-classical basilica of St Georg (1825–30) in Bensheim, Hesse. Moller designed numerous private houses and mansions. In addition to Grand Duke Ludwig I, his aristocratic patrons included the Landgrave Friedrich VI Joseph of Hesse-Homburg (1769–1829), for whom he designed the picturesque Gothic House (1823–4) in Homburg and remodelled the 17th-century palace of Homburg (1825–41). He was also a distinguished engineer, and several constructional techniques were named after him, such as a particular type of bonding used for barrel vaults.

A notable example of his engineering work is his viaduct (1841) across the Göhltal, near Aachen. He was also active in the emerging conservation movement, for which Hesse-Darmstadt passed the first law in 1818; in his restoration of Mainz Cathedral (1827) he designed a spectacular iron crossing dome (destr. 1870).

Moller was undoubtedly most influential, however, through his architectural scholarship and writing. His *Denkmäler der deutschen Baukunst* (begun in 1815) was the first in a series of costly illustrated books of northern architecture. It traced the development of German architecture from Romanesque to the mature Gothic of the 14th century, and its accurate measured drawings and accompanying text, which advocated the use of comparative evidence in the process of dating, were widely acclaimed, particularly in England, where a translation was published in 1824. Together with Thomas Rickmann, Moller was regarded as the most respectable architectural scholar of the first quarter of the 19th century. In 1835 he was among the first elected honorary members of the Institute of British Architects. His *Denkmäler* and many individual studies of medieval buildings gave great impetus to the Gothic Revival movement. In 1814 he and Sulpiz Boisserée discovered the medieval drawings of Cologne Cathedral, which were later used in its reconstruction and completion. He also supplied the engravings of the cathedral for Boisserée's description (pubd 1823–31). Despite his involvement in the resurrection of Gothic architecture, however, he regarded its use for contemporary buildings, other than for restoration, as wholly inappropriate. For him, Gothic architecture was rooted only in the Middle Ages, unlike classical architecture, which he considered had a permanent validity.

WRITINGS

Denkmäler der deutschen Baukunst, 3 vols (Darmstadt, 1815–51; Eng. trans. 1824, rev. 1836)
Bemerkungen über die aufgefundenen Originalzeichnungen des Domes zu Köln (Darmstadt, 1818)
with F. Heger: *Entwürfe ausgeführter und zur Ausführung bestimmter Gebäude* (Darmstadt, 1825–6)
Beiträge zu der Lehre von den Constructionen (Darmstadt, 1832–44)

BIBLIOGRAPHY

Macmillan Enc. Architects; Thieme–Becker; Wasmuth
G. Haupt: *Die Bau- und Kunstdenkmäler der Stadt Darmstadt*, 2 vols (Darmstadt, 1952–4)
M. Fröhlich and H. G. Sperlich: *Georg Moller: Baumeister der Romantik* (Darmstadt, 1959)
Darmstadt in der Zeit des Klassizismus und der Romantik (exh. cat., ed. B. Krimmel; Darmstadt, Ausstellhallen Mathildenhöhe, 1979)

CLAUDIA BÖLLING

Mollet. French family of artists. Jacques Mollet (*fl* to 1595) was employed by Charles de Lorraine, Duc d'Aumale, at ANET, Eure-et-Loire, where he worked in collaboration with the architect Etienne Dupérac and made the first *parterre de broderie* in France (after 1582). His son Claude Mollet (i) (*c.* 1564–*c.* 1649) trained under him at Anet, afterwards becoming 'premier jardinier de France'. The sites at which Claude Mollet worked include Fontainebleau, Saint-Germain-en-Laye, Monceau-en-Brie and, most notably, the Tuileries in Paris. His assistants included, in turn, Pierre Le Nôtre and Jean Le Nôtre, grandfather and father respectively of André Le Nôtre, who became the greatest garden designer of the 17th century. Claude

Mollet, whose *Théâtre des plans et jardinages* was posthumously published in Paris in 1652, had a number of his elaborate parterre designs illustrated in Olivier de Serres's *Théâtre d'agriculture et mesnage des champs* (Paris, 1600); these had been laid out with help from his sons, all of whom appear to have become gardeners and designers. They include Pierre Mollet (*d* 1659), Noël Mollet, Claude Mollet (ii) (*d* 1664), Charles Mollet (*fl* 1660–93) and (1) André Mollet, who enjoyed an international reputation. Charles's son (2) Armand-Claude Mollet was a successful architect of town houses in Paris in the early 18th century; his works include the Hôtel d'Evreux and its gardens (1718), now the Palais de l'Elysée. His son André-Armand Mollet (1708–47) also practised as an architect.

BIBLIOGRAPHY

S. Karling: 'The Importance of André Mollet and his Family for the Development of the French Formal Garden', *The French Formal Garden*, ed. F. H. Hazlehurst and E. B. MacDougall (Washington, DC, 1974), pp. 3–25
G. Jellicoe, P. Goode and M. Lancaster: *The Oxford Companion to Gardens* (Oxford, 1986)
K. Woodbridge: *Princely Gardens: The Origins and Development of the French Formal Style* (London, 1986)

(1) André Mollet (*d c.* 1665). Landscape designer. Trained by his father, Claude Mollet (i), he travelled *c.* 1630 to England, where Charles I and Queen Henrietta Maria employed him to make improvements to the gardens at Wimbledon House (destr.), London. In 1633–5 he was in the Netherlands, designing new gardens for the old palace at Buren and for Honselaarsdijk (destr.), near The Hague, and Nieuburck, near Rijswijk, for Frederick Henry, Prince of Orange (1584–1687). Soon after his return to France in 1635 he succeeded his father as Désignateur de Plants et Jardins du Roy at the Tuileries. He undertook further work at Wimbledon House in 1642 and four years later was engaged by Queen Christina of Sweden, although he did not travel to Stockholm until 1648; there he made the first fashionable French-style garden in the country with his King's Garden at the Royal Palace. He may also have taken responsibility for the gardens of the Queen's palace at Uppsala and during his stay was employed by various members of the Swedish nobility. Leaving one of his sons in charge of the Swedish royal gardens, André returned to France in 1653. By 1661 he was once again employed by the English court, working as Charles II's chief gardener at St James's Park, London.

André Mollet's treatise, *Le Jardin de plaisir* (1651), was also published in Swedish and German editions, thereby further spreading the principles and practices of French formal garden design. In it he stressed the desired visual harmony between a garden, its buildings and the main house; this, he argued, could be realized only by considering the garden as part of the overall architectural programme. This strong architectonic sense became an important tenet of André Le Nôtre when undertaking his own layouts later in the 17th century.

WRITINGS

Le Jardin de plaisir (Stockholm, 1651)

BIBLIOGRAPHY

S. Karling: *Trädgårdskonstens historia i Sverige* [History of garden art in Sweden] (Stockholm, 1931)

F. HAMILTON HAZLEHURST

(2) Armand-Claude Mollet (*b c.* 1670; *d* Paris, 23 Jan 1742). Architect, nephew of (1) André Mollet. The son of Charles Mollet, the Maître des Jardins of the Louvre from 1668, he succeeded his father in this position in 1692. He was also appointed Contrôleur des Bâtiments du Roi (1698) and was made a first-class member of the Académie Royale d'Architecture in 1718. In 1732 he received the prestigious Cordon de Saint-Michel. Mollet's designs were unanimously praised by contemporaries for the manner in which they suited the needs of his individual patrons and, particularly, for the convenient arrangement of the rooms. He was one of the first architects in France to place the dining-rooms close to the kitchens and to include bathrooms near the bedrooms.

In all Mollet's designs his patrons' comfort and manner of living was a major concern. This is certainly true of his first major work, the Hôtel d'Humières (1715; destr. 1906), Paris. The ground-plan of this building was simple and symmetrical, consisting of a *cour d'honneur* with a lower court to the left, bordered by stables on one side and kitchens on the other. The *corps de logis* was a two-storey structure with end pavilions, crowned by a mansard roof. The *avant-corps* of the garden façade featured three round-headed windows on the ground floor and three rectangular windows above, while the court façade displayed an Ionic portico surmounted by pilasters and crowned by a pediment.

Mollet's best-known work was the Hôtel d'Evreux (1718; now the Palais de l'Elysée), Paris. This building was originally designed for Louis-Henri de La Tour d'Auvergne, Comte d'Evreux, and since 1849 it has been occupied by the presidents of France. Formerly the Hôtel de Pompadour, it was used as a residence by Napoleon and his wife Josephine after the Battle of Waterloo (1815). The Hôtel was approached from the street by a *porte-cochère* that led into a large open court. To the left was a kitchen court and to the right another smaller court in front of a sizeable stable, reflecting the Comte d'Evreux's position as a cavalry officer. The ground-floor plan of the *corps de logis* consisted of a central entrance vestibule on the court side with a salon overlooking the garden behind it. To the right of the vestibule on the court was a Grande Salle, used by the count when meeting his business associates. The patron also requested an intimate apartment for himself, located between the kitchen court and a small flower garden. The *corps de logis* of the Hôtel d'Evreux was similar in style to the Hôtel d'Humières, being a two-storey structure surmounted by a mansard roof. The court façade has a Tuscan portico with Corinthian pilasters above, crowned by a pediment. Instead of the tightly spaced windows of the Hôtel d'Humières, however, Mollet here employed wider wall massings decorated with busts on scroll consoles. The *avant-corps* of the garden façade has three round-headed windows framed by an order of Tuscan pilasters on the ground floor, repeated above with engaged columns. This façade originally looked over a large and beautiful garden, which contemporaries compared to Tivoli and Monceau.

Mollet also designed the Château de Stains (1714), near Saint-Denis, for M Toussaint Bellanger, Treasurer of Sceau; it was noted for the provision of bathrooms in the *corps de logis* and an elaborate garden incorporated into a pentagonal plan. Mollet is also attributed with the Galerie Neuve (1719; now the rear wing of the Bibliothèque Nationale) of the Hôtel de Nevers, Paris; alterations to the Hôtel de Conti (1719), Paris, for the Duc du Maine; the gallery (1720) of the Hôtel de Bullion, Paris; the enlargement (1720) of the Hôtel de la Rochefoucauld, Paris; outbuildings (1720) of the Château de Roissy; and houses on the Rue d'Anjou, Rue de La Ville-l'Evêque and Rue de Bourbon (1739–41), all in Paris. His son, André-Armand Mollet, continued the family tradition by becoming a member of the Académie Royale d'Architecture.

BIBLIOGRAPHY

Mariette
A. Lance: *Dictionnaire des architectes français*, ii (Paris, 1872)
L. Hautecoeur: *Architecture classique* (1943–57)
G. Pillement: *Paris inconnu* (Paris, 1965)
——: *Paris disparu* (Paris, 1966)
M. Gallet: *Paris: Domestic Architecture of the Eighteenth Century* (London, 1972)
W. G. Kalnein and M. Levey: *Art and Architecture of the Eighteenth Century in France*, Pelican Hist. A. (Harmondsworth, 1972)

KATHLEEN RUSSO

Molli, Benedetto (*b* Rome, 16 March 1597; *d* Rome, 1 Oct 1657). Italian architect. At the age of 20 he became a lay brother with the Society of Jesus. He had presumably received his professional training before this, but it was not until 1626 that he became a mason and architect. In Perugia he directed the construction of the theological college (1627–30) and supervised the planning of the Jesuit villa in Panicale. In 1630 he designed the Jesuit college in Montepulciano and from 1631 onwards (in collaboration with Paolo Maruscelli) the unexecuted plans for the Collegium Germanicum in Rome.

In 1633 Molli moved to Poland where, in 1635, he designed the collegiate church of Ołyka (now in Ukraine). He also supervised and designed Jesuit projects at Ostróg (1634–54), Łuck (1646)—both now in Ukraine—and Kraków (1651). Of particular note was his design (unrealized) for a spacious Jesuit college alongside SS Peter and Paul, Kraków. The drawings for this project are in the collection of the Collegium Germanicum, Rome, with a series of Molli's idealistic and theoretical designs, all similar in nature. He certainly deserves respect as an architectural draughtsman. His preferred method of representation was that developed by Baldassare Peruzzi (but seldom used by his contemporaries): by showing buildings as rising from ground-plans in parallel projection, Molli was able to illustrate both plan and elevation simultaneously. In Umbria, and even more so in Poland, he designed functional, rigorously structured college buildings and churches inspired by the ecclesiastical architecture of Jacopo Vignola's successors.

BIBLIOGRAPHY

J. Vallery Radot: *Le Recueil de plans d'édifices de la Compagnie de Jésus conservé à la Bibliothèque Nationale de Paris* (Rome, 1960)
A. Miłobędzki: *Architektura polska XVII wieku*, 2 vols (Warsaw, 1980), i, pp. 282, 331; ii, p. 464
R. Bösel and J. Garms: 'Die Plansammlung des Collegium Germanicum-Hungaricum', *Röm. Hist. Mitt.*, xxiii (1981), pp. 338, 361–3; xxv (1983), pp. 254–6
R. Bösel: *Die Baudenkmäler der römischen und der neapolitanischen Ordensprovinz* (1985), i of *Jesuitenarchitektur in Italien, 1540–1773* (Vienna, 1985–)

RICHARD BÖSEL

Mollino, Carlo (*b* Turin, 6 May 1905; *d* Turin, 27 Aug 1973). Italian architect, designer and writer. He was the son of the engineer Eugenio Mollino (1873–1953), and he studied at the faculty of architecture of the Politecnico, Turin, graduating in 1931. Among early influences were the 'second Futurism' of the post-war period and a close friendship with the painter and scholar Italo Cremona (*b* 1905). At the beginning of his career Mollino collaborated with his father but also worked independently, producing such notable designs as the headquarters of the Confederazione degli Agricoltori (1933–4), Cuneo, and particularly the headquarters of the Società Ippica Torinese (1935–9; destr.) in Turin. In the latter Mollino interpreted the doctrines of Neo-plasticism and Rationalism with great freedom, adapting spatial, material and technical ideas with complete originality. His first experiments in furnishings also date from this period, including promotional stands, residential rooms and individual items of furniture (*see* ITALY, fig. 73). His large range of prototype furnishings (1944–6) for the Minola House was made by the firm of Apelli and Varesio.

Mollino had an enduring interest in mountain architecture, and his responsiveness to natural surroundings is evident in his cable railway station and small hotel (1946–7) at Lago Nero (Salice d'Ulzio) and the cable railway station (1950–53) of the Fürggen (Cervima). His two principal late works, both in Turin, are most notable, however, for their use of structural innovations for specific functional ends. The Camera di Commercio (1968–73), with Alberto Galardi (*b* 1930) and Carlo Graffi (*b* 1925), recalls the concept of *tensistruttura*, introduced by the engineer Guido Fiorini (*b* 1891) at the time of 'second Futurism'. Large roof-level corbels support a perimetric line of steel beams, obviating the need for internal columns. His reconstruction (1965–73; with others) of Benedetto Innocente Alfieri's Teatro Regio (1738; destr. 1936) consists of a wholly modern interior behind the 18th-century façade. The entrance hall is surmounted by a network of aerial gangways resting on arches arranged at several levels, and the auditorium itself, conceived as a large red shell, is memorable for the profusion of transparent stalactite-like forms. Mollino also experimented with aeroplane design and wrote an important essay on photography.

WRITINGS

with F. Vadacchino: *Architettura, arte e tecnica* (Turin, 1947)
Messaggio della camera oscura (Turin, 1949)

BIBLIOGRAPHY

G. Brino: *Carlo Mollino: Architettura come autobiografia: Architettura, mobili, ambientazioni, 1928–1973* (Milan, 1985)
M. Besset: *L'Etrange Univers de l'architecte Carlo Mollino* (Paris, 1989)
P. Zermani: *Carlo Mollino, 1905–1973* (Milan, 1989)

ROBERTO GABETTI

Molnár, Farkas [Wolfgang] (*b* Pécs, 21 June 1897; *d* Budapest, 12 Jan 1945). Hungarian architect and lithographer. He studied in Budapest at the Fine Arts College and the Hungarian Palatine Joseph Technical University but before completing his degree departed for Germany, where he studied (1921–5) at the Bauhaus, Weimar. During his course he produced a portfolio of lithographs, and his house design entitled 'Der rote Würfel' featured in the Bauhaus exhibition of 1923. His U-Theater design appeared in a collaborative book on theatre design published by the Bauhaus in 1925. He worked in the office of Walter Gropius, who influenced his work until the end of the 1930s. In 1925 he returned to Budapest; he resumed his studies and graduated in 1928. In the same year he was appointed Hungarian delegate to CIAM and led the Hungarian affiliated group from 1928 to 1938.

Molnár designed mainly villas and residential blocks in Budapest, which reflect the stripped functionalism of his instructors at the Bauhaus. His buildings were usually constructed of brick with reinforced-concrete infill. His earliest villa is Napraforgó Street 17 (1931), Budapest, designed with Pál Ligeti (1885–1941). A single-storey family house, its form is a closed prism with flat wall surfaces and unframed windows. The small bedroom balcony projects minimally from the façade. The villa at Lejtö Street 2a (1932), Budapest, with a conservatory and a large balustraded upper terrace, won first prize at the Esposizione Triennale (1933), Milan. The Heidegger House (1933) at Balatonakarattyá is a reduced version of the 'Rote Würfel' design. The larger house (1936), Pasaréti Street 7, Budapest, is more expressive, with contrasting windows and loggias arranged in a chequered pattern. Molnár's last work, the Hungarian Holy Land Church (1940–49), Heinrich István Street 3–5, Budapest, is his only church building and was unfinished at his death. An oval concrete-shell cupola (unexecuted) was to cover a central space surrounded by 16 chapels, most of which were built. Molnár was one of the secretaries of the short-lived CIAM-Ost, which was founded in 1937 to organize the Modernist architects of eastern Europe.

WRITINGS

with L. Moholy-Nagy and O. Schlemmer: *Die Bühne im Bauhaus*, Bauhausbücher, 4 (Munich, 1925/*R* 1965; Eng. trans., Middletown, CT, 1961)

PRINTS

with H. Stefan: *Italia* (Weimar, 1922) [12 lithographs]

BIBLIOGRAPHY

Molnár Farkas munkái, 1923–1933 [Farkas Molnár's work], intro. by L. Moholy-Nagy (Budapest, [1933])
E. Gábor: *A CIAM magyar csoportja, 1928–1938* [The Hungarian CIAM group, 1928–1938] (Budapest, 1972)
O. Mezei: *Molnár Farkas* (Budapest, 1987)

ESZTER GÁBOR

Molotov. *See* PERM'.

Molteni, Giuseppe (*b* Affori, 1799; *d* Milan, 11 Jan 1867). Italian painter, restorer and museum director. The son of an impoverished innkeeper, from the age of 10 he was supported by a Milanese family called Brocca, who financed his education at the painting school in the Brera, Milan. There he studied with Giuseppe Longhi to become a painter of sentimental genre-pieces and fashionable portraits. After graduating he was employed as a restorer by the Abbate Massinelli, a priest from Bergamo, who had acquired a collection of pictures (later bought by Edward Solly) from churches and religious institutions in Lombardy. Molteni then studied at Bologna with Giuseppe Guizzardi (1779–1861), a well-known restorer, and returned to Milan in the 1820s. Elected a member of the Accademia di Brera in 1839, he became Consigliero Ordinario in 1851 and was given a studio there. This was frequented by such museum directors as Sir Charles Lock Eastlake (i), such dealers as Otto Mündler and such private collectors as Sir Austen Henry Layard and Gian Giacomo Poldi Pezzoli, who took their new acquisitions to Molteni for restoration. From the 1850s Molteni was closely associated with Giovanni Morelli and Mündler, and their friendship, as revealed in Molteni's letters to Morelli, testifies to the close alliance between conservation and the developing science of connoisseurship (Anderson). From 1861 until his death Molteni was director of the Brera, an office that also involved responsibility for restoration.

The last of the gifted artist-restorers of the 19th century, Molteni was also a talented academic painter, who sometimes repainted the Old Masters brought to him for restoration rather too freely, especially when working for his private clients or for Eastlake (who preferred to have his new acquisitions restored in Italy before taking them to England). Molteni's most famous public restorations were of Raphael's *Marriage of the Virgin* (Milan, Brera) and the fresco cycle by Bernardo Zenale and Bernardino Butinone (Milan, S Pietro in Gessate), while his work for private collectors is exemplified in his restorations of Lorenzo Lotto's *Double Portrait of the Brothers Della Torre* and Pisanello's *Virgin and Child Enthroned with SS George and Anthony Abbot* (both London, N.G.).

WRITINGS

'Relazione intorno alle operazioni fatte al quadro di Raffaello rappresentante lo Sposalizio di Maria Vergine' [MS.; Milan, Archv Vecchio]; ed. C. Bertelli and others in *Lo Sposalizio della Vergine di Raffaello* (Treviglio, 1983), pp. 76–80

BIBLIOGRAPHY

A. Caimi: 'Commemorazione del cav. Giuseppe Molteni, Conservatore delle RR. Gallerie, letta nell'adunanza finale del consiglio accademico dell'anno mdccclxvii dal Professore segretario Antonio Caimi', *Atti della Reale Accademia di Belle Arti di Milano* (1867), pp. 5–22
[?Giovanni Morelli]: Obituary, *Allgemeine Zeitung* (1 April 1867)
C. Gould: 'Eastlake and Molteni: The Ethics of Restoration', *Burl. Mag.*, cxvi (1974), pp. 530–34
A. Mottola Molfino: *Gian Giacomo Poldi-Pezzoli 1882–1879* (Milan, 1979), pp. 11–14, 68–70
A. Conti: 'Vicende e cultura del restauro', *Stor. A.*, x (1981), pp. 39–111
M. Natale: *Museo Poldi Pezzoli: Dipinti* (Milan, 1982)
J. Anderson: 'Morelli and Layard', *Austen Henry Layard tra l'oriente e Venezia: Venice, 1983*, pp. 109–37
J. Dunkerton, A. Roy and A. Smith: 'The Unmasking of Tura's *Allegorical Figure*: A Painting and its Concealed Image', *N.G. Tech. Bull.*, xi (1987), pp. 5–35
G. Morelli: *Della pittura italiana, studi storico-critici: Le gallerie Borghese e Doria-Pamphili in Roma*, ed. J. Anderson (Milan, 1991), pp. 529–38

JAYNIE ANDERSON

Moltke, Adam Gottlob, Count (*b* Walkendorf, Mecklenburg, 10 or 11 Nov 1710; *d* Bregentved, 25 Sept 1792). Danish statesman and collector. A prominent figure at the court of Frederick V, he was the head of the government until the King's death in 1766. His wealth derived from his service at court and his close contact with the King, whom he advised on artistic as well as political matters. His own collection of paintings was in many ways complementary to the royal gallery at Christiansborg (established 1762–4); it consisted mainly of 17th-century Dutch and Flemish works, including *Head and Shoulders of a Dominican Friar* by Rubens and Meindert Hobbema's *Road with Tall Trees through a Village* (both now Copenhagen, Stat. Mus. Kst). Moltke helped develop Frederiksstaden, a part of Copenhagen that included the new royal palace of Amalienborg, and had his own quarters in one of the four Amalienborg mansions, designed by the architect Niels Eigtved, with interior decoration by Boucher, Jean-Baptiste Oudry and Joseph-Marie Vien. It housed Moltke's collection in the great hall and in a summer-house in the gardens. In 1804, after the collection had been moved to the Thottske Mansion at No. 15 Bredgade in Copenhagen, it was opened to the public; for many years it was the only place in Copenhagen where the work of Old Masters could easily be seen. In 1932 the collection was sold at auction at Winkel & Magnussen's.

BIBLIOGRAPHY

T. H. Colding: 'Kongen og Kunsten', *Dan. Ksthist.*, 3 (1972)
B. Jørnaes: 'Jardins Volière og Harsdorffs Kolonnade—La Volière de Nicolas Henri Jardin et la Colonnade Harsdorff', *Amalienborg*, ed. V. S. Møller (1973)
M. Stein: 'Den franske kunst i Moltkes Palæ—l'art français au Palais Moltke', *Amalienborg*, ed. V. S. Møller (1973)
H. Raabyemagle: 'Moltkes Palæ at Amalienborg. Forsøg paa en rekonstruktion af Byggeriets "dagbog"' [Attempt at a reconstruction of the 'diary' of building activities], *Architectura: Arkithist. Aaskr.*, 1983

GRETHE KUSK

Moluccas islands [Maluku]. *See under* INDONESIA.

Molvig, Jon (*b* Newcastle, NSW, 27 May 1923; *d* Brisbane, 15 May 1970). Australian painter. He studied at the East Sydney Technical College (1947–9) under the Commonwealth Reconstruction Training Scheme and in 1955 moved to Brisbane. He developed a strong, linear drawing style and found a subject-matter that suited his expressive verve and his sardonic nature. The work produced between 1955 and 1959 was expressionistic and emotional in subject, for example *Lovers* (oil and wax on hardboard, 2.1×1.1 m, 1955; Austin, U. TX, Huntington A.G.). The *Eden Industrial* paintings (1960–63; e.g. 1961, Brisbane, Queensland A.G.) show the new, mechanized Eden, based on Molvig's experience of Newcastle.

A second period began in 1964 with the *Pale Nudes* series, but it was cut short by illness in 1967. The most schematic and abstract pictures of Molvig's career, the *Tree of Man* series (1968–9; e.g. 1968, Canberra, N.G.), followed. A trip to central Australia in 1958 alerted him to the vitality of Aboriginal art. Molvig's *Pale Nudes* use the abbreviated gesture of the mythic figures of Arnhem Land, and the *Tree of Man* series, while acknowledging American hard-edge painting, also refers to an Aboriginal motif known as the 'tree of life' and to the informal layering and placement of Aboriginal cave painting. He won a number of prizes, including the Archibald prize for his portrait of *Charles Blackman* (1966; Adelaide, A.G. S. Australia).

BIBLIOGRAPHY

B. Smith: *Australian Painting, 1788–1960* (Melbourne, 1962, rev. 1971), pp. 305, 332
R. Hughes: *The Art of Australia* (Ringwood, 1966), pp. 213–18, 246
B. Churcher: *Molvig: The Lost Antipodean* (Ringwood, 1984)

BETTY CHURCHER

Molyn [Molijn], **Pieter (de)** (*b* London, *bapt* 6 April 1595; *d* Haarlem, *bur* 23 March 1661). Dutch painter, draughtsman and etcher of English birth and Flemish descent. His father, Pieter de Molijn, came from Ghent and his mother, Lynken van den Bossche, from Brussels. It is not known why they went to England, perhaps for employment rather than to avoid religious persecution. Pieter the younger apparently remained proud of his birthplace throughout his life, as can be inferred from his designation as 'The Londoner' in archival documents.

The earliest evidence of Molyn's presence in the Netherlands is his entry at the age of 21 into the Guild of St Luke in Haarlem in 1616, although no dated works by him before 1625 are known. Having apparently settled permanently in Haarlem, on 26 May 1624 he published his intention to marry Mayken Gerards, who also lived there. In the same year he became a member of the Dutch Reformed Church. Seven children were born to the couple between 1625 and 1639, not all of whom reached maturity. Molyn was also a member of the Haarlem Civic Guards in 1624, 1627 and 1630. Throughout the 1630s and 1640s he held the office of Dean and Commissioner in the Guild of St Luke. In 1637–8 he was the guild's alms collector. At his death he was buried in St Bavo's in Haarlem.

1. PAINTINGS. Molyn's painted oeuvre can be divided into three distinct periods. During his early years, from 1625 to 1631, he employed an enormous variety of styles and subject-matter, including dune landscapes, travelling people and wagons, cavalry battles, ambushes, winter scenes, cottages among trees and conversing and reposing peasants. His figures are typically shown with long noses and masklike faces (e.g. *Nocturnal Street Scene*, 1625; Brussels, Mus. A. Anc.). His compositions range from the multi-figured *Prince Maurice and Prince Frederick Henry Going to the Chase* ('The Stadholder is Going to the Chase') (1625; Dublin, N.G.) to the simplified arrangement found in his 'Sandy Road' (Dune Landscape with Trees and a Wagon) (1626; Brunswick, Herzog Anton Ulrich-Mus.), in which Molyn employed the dynamic diagonal composition that was to become his hallmark. The small 'Sandy Road' panel also represents an early stage of the style known by historians as the 'tonal phase' of 17th-century Dutch painting, in which simple vistas of the countryside are characterized by a broad painterly manner and a restricted palette of greys, greens, browns, dull yellows and blues. These early paintings are characterized by a dramatic play of light and dark, at times using a spotlight effect to establish the focus of the picture.

Molyn's paintings from 1632 to 1647 have simpler compositions, with fewer figures, firmly integrated within the landscape. His foliage becomes denser, but overall his compositions are more spacious and expansive. Solemnity

Pieter Molyn: *Peasants Returning Home*, oil on canvas, 760×935 mm, 1647 (Haarlem, Frans Halsmuseum)

of mood and strong atmospheric effects permeate some of these paintings, and the light is more evenly diffused on the picture surface, with strong patches of local colour. Although Molyn's dated paintings of the 1630s are scarce, his output from the 1640s is prodigious. The high point of his career is the *Peasants Returning Home* (1647; Haarlem, Frans Halsmus.; see fig.), in which the monumentality of the composition may owe something to the influence of the young Jacob van Ruisdael. Yet the directness of expression, the forceful depiction of figures and the magnificent foliage are Molyn's own. In these years Molyn's compositional schemes also reflect the possible interchange of ideas with Salomon van Ruysdael and Jan van Goyen, although he did not prescribe to their full tonality.

During these middle years Molyn was busy as a teacher of Gerard ter Borch (ii) and may also have had other students. He collaborated with ter Borch, Frans Hals and possibly with Pieter de Grebber, Jacob de Wet, Jacob Pynas and Nicolaes Berchem. Molyn painted landscape backgrounds for their figure compositions, while in some instances they added figures to his landscapes. In his late years, from 1648, Molyn produced numerous variations on previous compositions, refining their established stylistic and iconographic patterns. He shows more imagination in the elaboration and arrangement of his designs (e.g. *River Valley*, 1659; Berlin, Gemäldegal.), possibly under the influence of the work of Hercules Segers. The thick impasto of the foreground may have been inspired by Rembrandt's example (Stechow).

2. PRINTS AND DRAWINGS. In 1625, the year of Molyn's first dated landscape painting, he also produced a series of four etchings depicting rustic and military figures set in landscapes with dilapidated huts in the manner of Abraham Bloemaert. These prints, Molyn's only firmly established work in the medium, are remarkable for his exploitation of the expressive possibilities of the blank sky, which is contrasted with the undulating patterns of the foreground. He also explores in them the same diagonal composition used a year later in the Brunswick painting. This format, with a high foreground on one side and a distinct panoramic view on the other, was taken over by generations of later Dutch landscape painters.

Molyn was a prolific landscape draughtsman, particularly in his later years. His earliest drawings, in pen and ink (e.g. two dated 1626; Brussels, Mus. A. Anc.), are similar to the graphic style of his etchings and have been compared to the landscape drawings of Jan II van de Velde (i), Hendrick Goltzius and Jacques II de Gheyn. Most of his drawings, however, are executed in black chalk with grey wash. They are almost invariably signed, and most are dated, the majority in the 1650s.

3. CRITICAL RECEPTION AND POSTHUMOUS REPUTATION. Molyn's work encompassed elements of both fantasy and reality. He was a transitional figure in the history of Dutch landscape painting whose oeuvre formed a bridge between the manneristic devices of the previous century and the new naturalism of the 17th century. He integrated both extremes in his art in an imaginative and individualistic manner. One of his contributions is the

sensitive and keenly observed way in which he depicted the contemporary rural life of the Netherlands and its inhabitants. Although his figures are rather weakly drawn throughout his career, they are an important and integral part of his compositions.

Molyn was appreciated as an outstanding artist in his own lifetime by Samuel Ampzing and Theodor Schrevelius. Although Houbraken later devoted only a short paragraph to Molyn, his name found its way into the influential 18th-century dictionaries. In the 19th century Adam Bartsch established the artist as a fine printmaker, while van der Willigen uncovered archival evidence of his life and art. Only since the mid-1960s, however, has Molyn come to be recognized as one of the leading figures of early 17th-century Dutch landscape art along with Esaias van de Velde (i) and Jan van Goyen.

BIBLIOGRAPHY
Hollstein: *Dut. & Flem.*; Thieme–Becker
S. Ampzing: *Beschryvinge der stad Haarlem in Holland* [Description of the city of Haarlem in Holland] (Haarlem, 1628), p. 372
T. Schrevelius: *Harlemum* (Haarlem, 1647), p. 294
A. Houbraken: *De groote schouburgh* (1718–21), i, p. 25; ii, pp. 95, 343; iii, p. 183
A. von Bartsch: *Le Peintre-graveur* (1803–21), iv, pp. 7–12
A. van der Willigen: *Les Artistes de Haarlem* (Haarlem, 1870/R Nieuwkoop, 1970), pp. 18, 19, 21, 225–7
O. Granberg: 'Pieter de Molyn und seine Kunst', *Z. Bild. Kst*, xix (1884), pp. 369–77
R. Grosse: *Die holländische Landschaftskunst, 1600–1650* (Stuttgart, 1925), pp. 55–63
W. Stechow: *Dutch Landscape Painting of the Seventeenth Century* (London, 1966/R 1981), pp. 23–8
W. Strauss, ed.: *The Illustrated Bartsch*, v (New York, 1979), pp. 10–13
Dutch Landscape: The Early Years, Haarlem and Amsterdam, 1590–1650 (exh. cat. by C. Brown, London, N.G., 1986), pp. 151–4
E. J. Allen: *The Life and Art of Pieter Molyn* (diss., U. MD, 1987)
Masters of 17th-century Dutch Landscape Painting (exh. cat. by Peter C. Sutton, Amsterdam, Rijksmus.; Boston, MA, Mus. F.A.; Philadelphia, Mus. A.; 1987), pp. 374–6
A. M. Kettering: *Drawings from the Ter Borch Estate in the Rijksmuseum* (The Hague, 1988), V/i, pp. 86–91, 118–29; V/ii, pp. 772–3
H.-U. Beck: *Künstler um Jan van Goyen: Maler und Zeichner* (Doornspijk, 1991), pp. 273–91
                                                    EVA J. ALLEN

Mölzlagl, Simon. *See* JUNG, MORIZ.

Momoyama period. Period in Japanese history, 1568–1600. The key figures who effected major military and political changes in this period were three brilliant generals, ODA NOBUNAGA, TOYOTOMI HIDEYOSHI and Tokugawa Ieyasu (1543–1616). They brought to a climax the Sengoku ('country at war') period, which began after the Ōnin War (1467–77) and ended with the establishment of the Tokugawa shogunate in 1603 (*see* EDO PERIOD). During the Momoyama period, Japanese artistic values were thoroughly revolutionized by the development of patronage to an important degree. In cultural terms, the subdued, reflective style of the monochrome ink paintings predominant in the MUROMACHI PERIOD (1333–1568) were unsuited to the new warrior barons, who required majestic images to match their ambitions for power. Strikingly innovative art forms first became evident in AZUCHI CASTLE, built by Nobunaga in 1576; they matured in the sumptuous cultural displays of Hideyoshi in his castles of

Osaka (*see* OSAKA, §I), Jūraku and Momoyama and ended with the destruction of Osaka Castle in 1615, though the Momoyama style in architecture persisted into the 1630s (*see* JAPAN, §III, 4(ii)(c)).

The fortified castle was the symbol of the age. For generations the Japanese countryside, divided into dozens of small feudatories, each claimed and protected by a feudal warlord, had been dotted with small wooden fortresses. In 1542, the Portuguese introduced firearms into Japan. The Japanese lost no time in reproducing them, and in 1576 Nobunaga used them to win a decisive victory over a stunned enemy. These new weapons put extra demands on defensive structures, which drastically altered the style and scale of castle building. Azuchi Castle, magnificent both inside and out, inaugurated a new age in architecture, when buildings symbolized military and political power. The artist who embellished the interior was Kanō Eitoku (*see* KANŌ, (5)), whose bold new forms, introducing abstract pictorial elements, transformed Japanese painting style. A flurry of castle building in the Momoyama period required the talents of many other notable artists, who used a range of new subject-matter to cover the vast expanses of the castle interiors.

Christian missionaries first arrived in Japan in 1549, when, ironically, the country was at its moment of greatest turmoil. The correspondence they sent back to Europe provides vivid insights into the conditions, events and people they encountered. For a time they were openly received by Nobunaga, but in 1587 Hideyoshi issued an edict curtailing Christian missionary activities and in 1639, following bitter persecutions, the shogunate banned the religion from Japanese soil.

As European painting was shifting from the classical Renaissance style to the richly expressive Baroque, so Japanese painters were abandoning the monochrome in favour of large-scale images. However, the classical restraint found in Nō theatre (*see* JAPAN, §XIII, 1) and in garden designs in Zen monasteries was carried forward in the *wabi* ('quiet simplicity') tea-ceremony style of SEN NO RIKYŪ, tea master to Nobunaga and, later, to Hideyoshi (*see* JAPAN, §XIV). The tastes of Rikyū and Hideyoshi differed totally: Hideyoshi preferred the tea ceremony to be ostentatious and flamboyant (*bassara*), performed before large audiences and using tea vessels of solid gold; Rikyū prepared the tea in a modest hut before one or two guests. These two extremes are vivid symbols of an era poised between the medieval and the early modern world.

BIBLIOGRAPHY

M. Cooper, ed.: *They Came to Japan: An Anthology of European Reports on Japan: 1543–1640* (Berkeley, CA, 1965)
Y. Okamoto: *Namban bijutsu*, Nihon no bijutsu [Arts of Japan], xix (Tokyo, 1965); Eng. trans. by R. K. Jones as *The Namban Art of Japan*, Heibonsha Surv. Jap. A., xix (New York and Tokyo, 1972)
Y. Yamane: *Momoyama no fūzokuga*, Nihon no bijutsu [Arts of Japan], xvii (Tokyo, 1967); Eng. trans. by J. M. Shields as *Momoyama Genre Painting*, Heibonsha Surv. Jap. A., xvii (New York and Tokyo, 1973)
M. Hinago: 'Shiro', *Nihon No Bijutsu*, liv (Nov 1970) [whole issue]; Eng. trans. by W. H. Coaldrake as *Japanese Castles* (Tokyo, 1986)
T. Takeda: *Kanō Eitoku* (Tokyo, 1977)
G. Ellison, ed.: *Warlords, Artists, Commoners: Japan in the Sixteenth Century* (Honolulu, 1981)

BONNIE ABIKO

Momper, de. Flemish family of artists and dealers. Jan de Momper I (*fl* 1512–16) was a painter in Bruges; his son Josse de Momper I (1516–59) was known as an artist and dealer who moved from Bruges to Antwerp, where his son Bartolomeus de Momper (1535–after 1597) inherited both occupations, as well as being an engraver. Bartholomeus's sons (1) Josse de Momper II and Jan de Momper II were both landscape painters, but Josse the younger, an engraver and draughtsman as well, was the outstanding artist of the family. His art, which was popular and influential in his own time, belongs to the transitional period between late 16th-century Mannerism and the tendency towards greater realism that developed in the early 17th century. Although two of Josse the younger's sons, Gaspard de Momper (*fl* 1627) and Philips de Momper I (*fl* 1622–34), were painters, little is known of their work, except that Philips was a staffage painter who executed the figures in some of his father's paintings; he also spent some years in Rome, where he had travelled with Jan Breughel the younger. Jan de Momper the younger's son (2) Frans de Momper was, like his uncle, a landscape painter and draughtsman; he worked for 20 years in the Dutch Republic, and his style reflects that of the younger generation of Dutch artists in its monochrome colouring, while owing much to his uncle's influence in the preference for wide vistas. Frans's brother, Philips de Momper II (*fl* 1622; *d* 1675), was also a painter.

Thieme–Becker

BIBLIOGRAPHY

A. Laes: 'Paysages de Josse et Frans de Momper', *Mus. Royaux B.-A. Belgique: Bull.*, i (1952), pp. 57–67

(1) Josse [Joos] **de Momper II** (*b* Antwerp, 1564; *d* Antwerp, 5 Feb 1635). Painter and draughtsman. He received his first training from his father, and as early as 1581 he was registered as a master in the Antwerp Guild of St Luke by his father—who was at the time the dean of the Guild. In Antwerp on 4 September 1590 Josse married Elisabeth Gobyn, by whom he had ten children, including Gaspard and Philips. In 1611 Josse became dean of the Guild, and the following year he evidently went to Brussels with Sebastiaen Vrancx on guild business. It has long been maintained that de Momper had gone to Italy in the 1580s, since Lodewijk Toeput, who was then active in Venice, was mentioned as his teacher in an inventory of 1624. That this hypothetical trip to Italy actually took place was proved in 1985 when the frescoes in the church of S Vitale in Rome, previously attributed to Paul Bril, were given to Josse de Momper the younger (see Gerzsi).

Over 500 paintings have been attributed to de Momper, but only a few are signed and only one is dated, the *Mountain Landscape* (1623; Neer-Heylissem, Comte d'Oultremont priv. col.). De Momper painted two kinds of landscape: panoramic or 'fantastic world landscapes' in the tradition of Joachim Patinir and those in the manner of Jan Breughel the elder, in which the forms are already much more realistic. The panoramic landscapes follow the conventional colour scheme of late Mannerist landscape painting, with tones of brown used for foreground, green for the middle ground and blue for the background. Yet the separate narrative scenes within the compositions are already very individual and strikingly decorative. The artist's painting technique is characterized by rapid, flowing brushstrokes that sharply define the contours of the foreground; also typical are tiny dots of impasto colour used to create the aerial perspective in the background and the modelling of the middle ground. This is particularly noticeable in his panoramic landscapes with a high viewpoint, such as the *Wide River Landscape with a Boar Hunt* (Amsterdam, Rijksmus.), the *Mountain Landscape with a Company of Riders* (Madrid, Prado), the *Mountain Landscape with a Water-mill* (Dresden, Gemäldegal. Alte Meister; see fig.) and the *Mountain Landscape with Dancing Figures* (U. Rochester, NY, Mem. A.G.).

The *Mountain Landscape with Bridges* (Cologne, Wallraf-Richartz-Mus.) represents the other type of mountain landscape: the viewpoint is lower, and the foreground is flat and bordered by steep rocks, like stage scenery for the figures. However, the figures are always—unlike those in Breughel's images—without narrative meaning. Josse de Momper's landscapes are usually conventionally framed on the sides with groups of trees or rocks; the real development takes place in the importance given to the centre of the composition. Here he explored the potential of the flat Dutch landscape by varying the viewpoint, which gradually sinks, culminating in the so-called grotto landscapes (e.g. *Landscape with a Grotto and Painter*, Bonn, Rhein. Landesmus.; *Waterfall in a Cave*, U. Manchester, Whitworth A.G.), in which the picture seems to flow out from a figure placed almost at eye-level with the viewer.

Alongside the numerous mountain landscapes, which earnt the painter the nickname 'pictor montium' on his portrait in van Dyck's *Iconolography* (*c.* 1632–44), Josse also painted other types of paintings. In his town and village landscapes, the houses and people, previously mere accessories in the mountain landscapes, became the main focus of the pictures, as in the *Washing Place in Flanders* (Madrid, Prado), with its wandering perspective disappearing into a broad bluish distance, and in *Autumn* (Brunswick, Herzog Anton Ulrich-Mus.). The houses in the middle ground of the latter almost close off the composition. This convention is most common in the so-called winter landscapes (e.g. *Winter Landscape with a Village and Antwerp Cathedral*, Germany, priv. col.), in which the village scene spreads over the middle of the whole picture. There are countless variations of these landscapes by de Momper, who is generally seen as the inventor of the genre landscape. He is also well known for his cycles of *Seasons*, the best of which is in Brunswick (Herzog Anton Ulrich-Mus.). These landscapes alternate between high and low viewpoints, referring back to the compositions of the panoramic landscapes. However, in terms of technique, execution and the amount of detail, they are already close to 17th-century realistic landscape painting. There is also a small group of drawings attributed to him, for example *Rider Crossing the Mountains* (1598; U. London, Courtauld Inst. Gals); these follow the development of his landscape paintings.

Josse de Momper II: *Mountain Landscape with a Water-mill*, oil on panel, 530×715 mm (Dresden, Gemäldegalerie Alte Meister)

Josse de Momper's pictures were already greatly valued during his lifetime; they were first mentioned in inventories *c.* 1608. He was also praised by van Mander as early as 1604. His mountain landscapes were included in contemporary cabinet pictures by Frans Francken the younger, Jan Breughel the elder, Willem van Haecht etc. Some of these artists—for instance Francken and Breughel—as well as Sebastiaen Vrancx, Jan Breughel the younger and Hendrik van Balen painted figures in Momper's mountain landscapes. However, the extent of their collaborative work has not been examined in detail.

BIBLIOGRAPHY

K. Zoeg von Manteuffel: 'Die Ausstellung Joos de Momper in der Kunsthall Chemnitz', *Z. Bild. Kst*, lxi (1927–8)
J. A. Graf von Raczyncki: *Die flämische Landschaftsmalerei vor Rubens* (Frankfurt am Main, 1937), pp. 66–76
O. Koester: 'Joos de Momper the Younger: Prolegomena to the Study of his Paintings', *A.: Period. F.A.*, ii (1966), pp. 5–70
W. Stechow: *Dutch Landscape Painting in the Seventeenth Century* (London, 1966), pp. 131–2, 134, 142
H. Gerson: '*Everzwijnjacht*, Joos de Momper (1564–1634)' [*Boarhunt* by Joos de Momper (1564–1634)], *Openb. Ksthez.* (1968)
T. Gerzsi: 'Joos de Momper und die Bruegel-Tradition', *Netherlandish Mannerism* (Stockholm, 1985), pp. 155–64
K. Ertz: *Josse de Momper der Jüngere (1564–1634): Die Gemälde mit kritischen Oeuvre-Katalog* (Freren, 1986)

IRENE HABERLAND

(2) Frans de Momper (*b* Antwerp, 17 Oct 1603; *d* Antwerp, 1660). Painter and draughtsman, nephew of (1) Josse de Momper II. In 1629 he became a master in the Antwerp Guild of St Luke. He left Antwerp for the northern Netherlands, working initially at The Hague; by 1647 he was in Haarlem and the following year Amsterdam, where he married in 1649. In 1650 Frans returned to Antwerp, where he painted numerous monochrome landscapes in the manner of Jan van Goyen. Paintings such as the *Valley with Mountains* (*c.* 1640–50; Philadelphia, PA, Mus. A.) prefigure the imaginative landscapes of Hercules Segers. The impression of vast panoramic spaces in Frans's work is adopted from his uncle's art. Frans executed a number of variations on the theme of a river landscape with boats and village (e.g. pen-and-ink drawing, Edinburgh, N.G.). In the late painting *Landscape with a Château Encircled by Doves* (Bordeaux, Mus. B.-A.), the low horizon and light-filled sky are adopted from the new Dutch school of tonal landscape painting, while the delicacy of the figures, feathery trees and buildings are features of the Italo-Flemish tradition exemplified by his uncle. Similar qualities of refinement and luminosity characterize the *Winter Landscape* (*c.* 1650; Prague, N.G., Šternberk Pal.), a favourite theme. The stylistic blend in these paintings builds on the success of Paul Bril and Jan Breughel the elder, both active in Italy at the end of the 16th century and in the first quarter of the 17th.

BIBLIOGRAPHY

Y. Thiery: *Les Peintres flamands de paysage au XVIIème siècle*, ii (Brussels, 1987), pp. 57–63
Masters of the 17th-century Dutch Landscape Painting (exh. cat. by P. C. Sutton, Amsterdam, Rijksmus.; Boston, MA, Mus. F.A.; Philadelphia, PA, Mus. A.; 1987), pp. 376–8, pl. 41
L'Or et l'ombre (exh. cat. by O. Le Bihan, Bordeaux, Mus. B.-A, 1990), pp. 201–3, 414

LOUISE S. MILNE

Mon. *See under* HERALDRY, §IV.

Monaco, Principauté de. Small sovereign principality on the Mediterranean coast in the south-east corner of France, with a population of about 30,000. It was first settled by the Phoenicians, but its name, Monoichos (Gr.: 'isolated habitation'), was derived from its association with the Greek legend of Hercules. It was ceded to Genoa in 1191 by the Holy Roman Emperor Henry VI (*reg* 1190–97) but in 1297 was taken by the Genoese François Grimaldi, whose family ruled it until 1731. In that year the French Goyon-Matignon family succeeded to the principality by marriage but adopted the Grimaldi name. It has been allied to France throughout its history, except from 1524 to 1641 when it was under Spanish protection. It was officially annexed to France during the period of the French Revolution and the First Empire (1789–1814), and in 1860 the towns of Menton and Roquebrune in the principality became part of France. During World War II it was occupied by the Italians and then the Germans. Present-day Monaco consists of four parts: the town of Monaco (nicknamed 'La Roche'), La Condamine, Monte Carlo and Fontvieille, the last a newer district. Monaco town, occupying the heights of the headland of a peninsula, is the oldest part and includes the Palais Grimaldi, which grew out of the early 13th-century Genoese fortress. Home of the monarchs, it was enlarged over successive periods, especially during the reigns of Honoré II (*reg* 1604–62) and Louis I (*reg* 1662–1701), when additions were made in the style of the Italian Renaissance. Inside is a huge staircase of Carrara marble, comparable to that at the château of Fontainebleau, and frescoes by such artists as Orazio de' Ferrari and Luca Cambiaso, as well as some attributed to Annibale Carracci. The palace contains a notable art collection, largely of portraits of earlier monarchs and royalty by such artists as Nicolas de Largillierre, Pierre Mignard I, Hyacinthe Rigaud and Carle Vanloo. During the reign of Charles III (*reg* 1856–89) the cathedral in Monaco town was built by Charles Lenormand (*b* 1835) in the Romanesque Revival style. Dedicated to St Nicholas, it was consecrated in 1868, and it contains a retable (1500) by Louis Bréa, depicting *St Nicholas Surrounded by SS Stephen, Lawrence, Michael and Mary Magdalene*. A sumptuous casino and theatre in Monte Carlo designed by CHARLES GARNIER was opened in 1879 to replace the plainer building of 1861. Various paintings and sculptures were commissioned to decorate the building, among them *Music* by Sarah Bernhardt (1845–1923) and *Dance* by Gustave Doré, both located in the Salle des Fêtes. From 1922 to 1929 the theatre was the winter base for Serge Diaghilev's Ballets Russes.

BIBLIOGRAPHY

L.-H. Labande: *Histoire de la principauté de Monaco* (Monaco and Paris, 1934)
C. Y.-M. Kerboul: *La Principauté de Monaco* (Rennes, 1982)

□

Monaco, Lorenzo. *See* LORENZO MONACO.

Monaco, Pietro (*b* Belluno, 22 Sept 1707; *d* Venice, 9 June 1772). Italian printmaker. He lived in Venice from 1732 and specialized in engravings and etchings after Venetian painters. In 1743 he published the *Raccolta di cinquanta cinque storie sacre*. He also engraved a number of portraits of procurators (e.g. his portrait of *Zaccaria Canal*; Venice, Fond. Querini-Stampalia), painters and patriarchs, as well as views of Rome and seven Tuscan landscapes after Giuseppe Zocchi, which were included in the collection of prints entitled *Vedute delle ville e d'altri luoghi della Toscana* (Florence, 1744). It included prints after works by Giambattista Tiepolo, Gaspare Diziani and Sebastiano Ricci, executed in an extremely refined style, with subtle chiaroscuro effects. In 1750 Monaco was appointed to supervise the restoration work on the mosaics of the basilica of S Marco. He produced a more complete version of his *Raccolta* in 1763, with the new title *Raccolta di centododici stampe di pittura della storia sacra* and published by Guglielmo Zerletti. He engraved 21 plates for the *Tabulae anatomicae*, illustrated by Giuseppe Maria Lancisi and published by Bartolomeo Locatelli in 1769. His followers were his son, Giacomo Monaco, and Antonio Sandi, a native of Belluno.

BIBLIOGRAPHY

G. Moschini: *Dell'incisione in Venezia* (Venice, 1924), pp. 157–8
L. Alpago Novello: 'Gli incisori bellunesi', *Atti Reale Ist. Ven. Sci., Lett. & A.*, xcix (1939–40), pp. 524–57
A. Alpago Novello: 'Giunte alle schede delle opere degli incisori bellunesi di Luigi Alpago Novello', *Marco Ricci e gli incisori bellunesi del '700 e '800*, ed. B. Passamani (Venice, 1968), p. 171
Da Carlevarijs ai Tiepolo: Incisori veneti e friulani del settecento (exh. cat., ed. D. Succi; Gorizia, Mus. Prov. Pal. Attems; Venice, Correr; 1983), pp. 256–9

DARIO SUCCI

Monaldi, Carlo (*b* Rome, 1683; *d* Rome, 1760). Italian sculptor. He became a member of both the Congregazione dei Virtuosi del Pantheon (1720) and the Accademia di S Luca (4 June 1730), having previously been a member of the Compagnia dei Falegnami (Company of Carpenters). From very early on in his career, Monaldi enjoyed a privileged relationship with Portuguese patrons. His signed sculpture of *St Francis of Assisi* (1720; Rome, St Peter's) was carried out at the expense of the Franciscan José Maria de Fonseca e Evora (1690–*c.* 1760), the Portuguese plenipotentiary minister to the Holy See. For the series of statues of founders of the various religious orders placed in niches along the central nave and in the transepts of St Peter's, Rome, Monaldi sculpted *St Gaetano da Thiene* (signed and dated 1730). On the election of the Corsini Pope Clement XII, Portuguese patrons made almost exclusive use of artists involved in the grand papal projects. Monaldi sent a number of sculptures to Portugal, including *St Teresa*, *St Sebastian*, *St Vincent*, *St Elias* and *St Philip Neri* (all 1731–2; Mafra, Pal. N. and Basilica). For the portal of the basilica in Mafra he sculpted a *Virgin and Child with St Anthony*. With Benedetto Luti, Monaldi was also active in Rome as a teacher at the Portuguese Academy, founded in 1720. In 1736 his *Plenty* and *Magnificence* were added to the funerary monument to *Clement XII* (Rome, S Giovanni in Laterano, Corsini Chapel). The last work by the artist consists of six elegant reliefs with *Scenes from the Lives of the Apostles* (1743–4; Rome, S Marco), executed as part of the embellishment of the nave in the restored basilica.

BIBLIOGRAPHY

F. Titi: *Descrizione delle pitture, sculture e architetture esposte al pubblico in Roma* (Rome, 1763), pp. 21, 181, 219, 363

R. Enggass: *Early Eighteenth-century Sculpture in Rome* (University Park, PA, 1976), pp. 183–8
——: 'A Relief by Monaldi', *Paragone*, xxxii (1981), pp. 44–6
A. Nava Cellini: *La scultura del settecento* (Turin, 1982), pp. 36–7
Roma lusitana—Lisbona romana (exh. cat. by S. V. Rocca, G. Borghini and P. Ferraris, Rome, S Michele a Ripa, 1990)

DONATELLA GERMANÒ SIRACUSA

Monaldi, Jakub [Giacomo] (*b* Rome, 1734; *d* Warsaw, 1798). Italian sculptor, active in Poland. He studied sculpture at the Accademia di S Luca in Rome. In 1768 he was invited to Poland by King Stanislav II Poniatowski to be court sculptor in Warsaw, together with André Le Brun (1737–1811). Here Monaldi copied antique sculptures and made mythological and historical figures, for example *Chronos with a Clock* (1784; Warsaw, Royal Castle) and *Kasimir the Great* (1793–5; Warsaw, Łazienki Pal.). Together with Franciszek Pinck (1733–98), Monaldi made the figures of the *Four Evangelists* (1784) on the façade of the church of St Anne in Warsaw. He also sculpted tombs for *Archbishop Antoni Kazimierz Ostrowski* (1780; Skierniewice), for the *Bishop of Poznań* and for the Crown Chancellor Andrzej Stanisław Młodziejowski (before 1784; Słubice). In his mature work, Monaldi gradually evolved from a style characteristic of late Baroque to one showing elements of Neo-classicism.

BIBLIOGRAPHY

PSB; Thieme–Becker
T. Mańkowski: *Rzeźby zbioru Stanisława Augusta* [The collection of sculptures of Stanislas Augustus] (Kraków, 1948)
D. Kaczmarzyk: 'Rzeźby nagrobne Jakuba Monaldiego' [Sepulchral sculptures of Jakub Monaldi], *Biul. Hist. Sztuki*, xiv (1952), pp. 72–83

JERZY KOWALCZYK

Monaldi, Paolo (*fl* Rome, *c.* 1750–1800). Italian painter. Luigi Lanzi described him as a pupil and minor follower of Andrea Locatelli. He painted mainly *bambocciate*, setting his low-life figures in an arcadian atmosphere without, however, subordinating them to the landscape, as did Locatelli in the paintings for which he was best known. Monaldi's canvases depict scenes of simple country life (games, dances and drinking sessions) in settings that are characterized by ruined, thatched buildings. More realistic in approach is his signed and dated portrait of the *Horse Aquilino* (1752; Rome, Pal. Braschi), painted for Prince Camillo Rospigliosi, who was passionately fond of horses and commissioned Monaldi and Giovanni Reder (*b* 1639) to paint those in his stables. Monaldi's religious oeuvre is limited to two small pendants, the *Betrayal* and the *Agony in the Garden* (both 1758; ex-Hazlitt Gal., London), and a painting on copper of the *Blessed Giacinta Marescotti* (Rome, Gal. Barberini). The holy figures in these possess the evanescent sweetness that often characterizes 18th-century religious sentiment, for example in the work of Sebastiano Conca and Francesco Trevisani.

In 1767 Monaldi helped Paolo Anesi in the decoration of the Villa Chigi on Via Salaria, Rome, where he painted, in certain first-floor rooms and in the smoking-room, a series of idyllic scenes (Milan, Alemagna priv. col., see Busiri Vici, figs 128b–160). In the 1770s he probably participated in another such decorative venture in the 18th-century apartments of the Palazzo Barberini, where the *bambocciate* on the doors have been attributed to him.

An engraving by Sebastiano Bombelli, taken from a lost painting, suggests that Monaldi was still active in 1779.

BIBLIOGRAPHY

Thieme–Becker

L. Lanzi: *Storia pittorica della Italia* (Bassano, 1795–6, rev. 4/1818), ii, p. 271

Il settecento a Roma (exh. cat., ed. S. De Luca; Rome, Pal. Espos., 1959), figs 387–8

A. Busiri Vici: *Trittico paesistico romano del '700: Paolo Anesi, Paolo Monaldi, Alessio de Marchis* (Rome, 1975)

'*Capture of Christ, Agony in the Garden*: Two Canvases by Paolo Monaldi', *Burl. Mag.*, cxviii/879 (1976) [advertisement suppl.], pls 25–6

G. Magnanimi: 'The Eighteenth-century Apartments in the Palazzo Barberini', *Apollo* (1984), pp. 258–9

SOPHIE ANNE GAY

Monamy, Peter (*b* London, 12 Jan 1681; *d* London, 1 Feb 1749). English painter. It seems likely that his family origins and name were French. The Painter-Stainers' Company records that he was apprenticed as a house painter to William Clarke from 1696, but by 1710 he had become a marine artist, filling the gap in the market left by the death of Willem van de Velde the younger in 1707. Most of his subsequent career was devoted to careful imitations of van de Velde's style (and, in some cases, of particular pictures), by which, according to Vertue, 'he distinguished himself and came into reputation'. He maintained his links with the Painter-Stainers, of which he had been made a freeman in 1703, and in 1726 he was admitted to the guild on presentation of a sea-piece (destr. World War II).

Monamy had few English rivals in his chosen field, although in his early years he must have competed for patronage with Isaac Sailmaker (1633–1721) and later with Samuel Scott. Among his employers were the Byng family (a group of his paintings, sold to the Whitbreads, remains at Southill Park, Beds) and Thomas Walker, a commissioner of Customs and a keen picture collector who was portrayed by Hogarth discussing a sea-piece with Monamy (*Monamy Showing a Picture to Mr Walker*, *c.* 1730–32; Knowsley Hall, Lancs). He decorated supper-boxes at Vauxhall Gardens; the *East Indiaman* (*c.* 1740; London, N. Mar. Mus.) may be a fragment of one of these decorations. Although Monamy did much to develop English taste for marine painting, later exploited by Charles Brooking, Nicholas Pocock and others, he himself did not prosper notably; Vertue observed that his 'moderate prices kept him but in indifferent circumstances to his end'.

BIBLIOGRAPHY

G. Vertue: 'Notebooks', *Walpole Soc.*, 6 vols (1929–52)

D. Cordingly: *Marine Painting in England, 1700–1900* (London, 1974)

Peter Monamy, 1681–1749: Marine Artist (exh. cat., ed. C. Harrison-Wallace; Chichester, Pallant House Gal., 1983)

STEPHEN DEUCHAR

Monari [Monarico], **Cristofano**. *See* MUNARI, CRISTOFORO.

Monasterboice. Site of an Irish monastery, Co. Louth, celebrated in the annals in the 10th and 11th centuries as a seat of learning. A round bell-tower, two small ruined churches and three sculptured crosses remain. Two of the crosses, the 'West cross' and 'Muiredach's cross', belong to the group of so-called 'scripture crosses'. With their well-articulated designs, bold figure style and rich display of Christian iconography—over 40 subjects are depicted—they are among the outstanding sculptures of early medieval Europe.

Muiredach's cross (*see* INSULAR ART, fig. 5) is named from an inscription at the base of the shaft (west face) asking for prayers for Muiredach who caused the cross to be made. The deaths of abbots with this name are recorded at Monasterboice in 844 and 923, the latter generally assumed to belong to the patron of the cross. Cut from hard quartzy sandstone, the monument is 5.4 m high and survives in almost perfect condition. It consists of three standard elements: a truncated pyramidal base, a main shaft and ring, and a small cap in the form of an oratory or house shrine with gable finials and a shingled roof. The Redemption constitutes the underlying theme of the iconographic programme, with the *Crucifixion* depicted at the centre of the west face. Prominent subjects from the Passion include *Christ Mocked as King of the Jews*, the *Flagellation* and *Pilate Washing his Hands*. St Paul and St Anthony carved on the capstone extend the eucharistic theme. A *Last Judgement* is located in the centre of the east face, and Old Testament subjects depicted on the shaft below include a number of typological themes. The sides of the cross are meticulously decorated with frets, serpents, bosses, vine scrolls, interlace and entangled figures, while the badly weathered base bears enigmatic carvings of animals, monsters and a horseman.

The 'West cross' (h. *c.* 7 m) is similar in style, though less well preserved, and may also date from the early 10th century. It is formed of four pieces of sandstone, the shaft and ringed head being made of separate elements. The west face bears a *Crucifixion*, placed above a series of badly worn *Passion* subjects. The east side is dominated by an image of 'Christus Militans', below which are a series of Old Testament typologies, including a fine carving of the *Three Hebrews in the Fiery Furnace*. Many panels on the cross have not been identified with certainty.

On both crosses figures are carved in bold relief (up to 60 mm deep on Muiredach's cross), and they are distinguished by their rounded heads, curly hair and long moustaches. The origin of this style and the source of the iconography, with its emphasis on symbolism and doctrine rather than narrative, remain obscure. Some scholars have suggested Early Christian prototypes, while others have stressed the possibility of Carolingian models.

BIBLIOGRAPHY

R. A. S. Macalister: *Monasterboice, Co. Louth* (Dundalk, 1946)

F. Henry: *Irish High Crosses* (Dublin, 1964), pp. 30–32

——: *Irish Art during the Viking Invasions (800–1020 AD)* (London, 1967), pls 76–89, 106–7, 111

H. M. Roe: *Monasterboice and its Monuments* (Dundalk, 1981)

P. Harbison: *The High Crosses of Ireland* (Bonn, 1992)

ROGER STALLEY

Monasterio, Luis Ortiz. *See* ORTIZ MONASTERIO, LUIS.

Monasterios, Rafael (*b* Barquisimeto, 22 Nov 1884; *d* Barquisimeto, 2 Nov 1961). Venezuelan painter. He studied under Antonio Herrera Toro at the Academia de Bellas Artes, Caracas (1903–10). Monasterios travelled to Barcelona, Spain, in 1911 to further his studies and entered the Escuela de Artes y Oficios La Lonja. With the outbreak of World War I (1914), he returned to Venezuela and lived in Barquisimeto. Three years later he moved to Caracas and dedicated himself to teaching drawing and painting and to mural painting. In 1919 he met the Russian painter Nicolas Ferdinandov, with whom he travelled around the island of Margarita. On returning to Caracas he held an exhibition with Armando Reverón at the Escuela de Música y Declamación de la Academia de Bellas Artes, in which he showed works executed in Margarita. Between 1930 and 1955 he alternated his painting with teaching in Caracas, Maracaibo and Barquisimeto. A landscape painter, Monasterios was concerned with capturing the light and colour of various Venezuelan regions (e.g. *Caricuao Turret*, 1930; Caracas, Gal. A. N.). In 1941 he was awarded the Premio Nacional de Pintura. Although he was not an original member of the Círculo de Bellas Artes, his resolutely innovative character drew him towards the intellectual and artistic group, and while with them he executed some outstanding work.

BIBLIOGRAPHY
A. Boulton: *La obra de Rafael Monasterios* (Caracas, 1969)
P. Erminy and J. Calzadilla: *El paisaje como tema en la pintura venezolana* (Caracas, 1975)
R. Esteva-Grillet: *Rafael Monasterios, un artista de su tiempo* (Caracas, 1988)

YASMINY PÉREZ SILVA

Monastery. Group of buildings within which individuals are able to pursue their lives of prayer and self-denial with the moral support afforded by being with like-minded fellows. Although secluded religious communities are found in cultures throughout the world, this article discusses the development of the two principal traditions, Christian and Buddhist.

I. Christian. II. Buddhist.

I. Christian.

1. Monastic planning. 2. Monastic buildings.

1. MONASTIC PLANNING. The earliest Christian monasteries, in Egypt and Palestine, were hardly more than gatherings of separately housed hermits who sought little from each other beyond the knowledge that they were among brethren whose aims were identical with their own. It was perhaps inevitable that the Edict of Milan of AD 313, by which the Church was given official standing within the Roman Empire, should lead to major changes and the beginnings of an organized format for the monastic life, devised *c.* 320 by St Pachomius and later by St Basil (*d* 379).

Western monasticism owes the basis of its medieval development to a Rule compiled *c.* 529 from a variety of sources by St Benedict of Nursia (*d c.* 553), the abbot of MONTECASSINO in southern Italy. In this the essential corporateness of the monastic life was stressed, along with the strong duty of obedience to the head of the community that became one of the most cohesive factors in Benedictine monasticism. The life of a monk following the Rule of St Benedict was closely directed in every aspect, and from this it also followed that the architectural framework of Western monasticism tended to be strongly standardized. A plan type that had certainly been developed in its essentials by the earlier part of the 8th century was taken

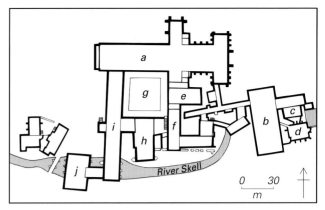

1. Fountains Abbey, North Yorkshire, founded 1132, plan: (a) church; (b) infirmary; (c) chapel; (d) kitchen; (e) chapter house; (f) dormitory undercroft; (g) cloister; (h) refectory; (i) lay brothers' range and cellarium; (j) lay brothers' infirmary

up throughout almost the whole of western Europe as the ideal setting for a religious community. Successive reform movements modified elements of the way of life, but the arrangement of buildings continued to follow the same pattern with surprisingly little change for some 700 years (see fig. 1), during which time monasticism was seen as one of the most valid pursuits of religious perfection in the Western Church. Beyond this, moreover, this basic layout was perceived to be so ideally suited to the religious life as a whole that it was also accepted by the orders of regular canons. It was only the more specialized requirements of such as the hermit monks of the Carthusian Order and of the mendicant friars that led to any significant adaptation, although even for them the Benedictine plan provided a basis for their planning needs. Monasticism remained a force of varying degrees of vitality after the Protestant Reformation, especially as a tool of the Counter-Reformation and in countries of divided religious loyalties, but from the 16th century its architectural setting was never again to be so standardized. This article concentrates on the development of monastic planning, particularly in western Europe, until the end of the Middle Ages.

See also CHRISTIANITY, §IV; CHAPTER HOUSE; CLOISTER; and SCRIPTORIUM.

(i) Early monastic planning in the Eastern Church. (ii) Early monasteries in the West. (iii) The Benedictine plan. (iv) Cistercian perfection of the Benedictine plan. (v) Variants within the standard Benedictine plan. (vi) The Carthusian plan. (vii) Mendicant planning.

(i) Early monastic planning in the Eastern Church. It was an essential concomitant of the austere ethos of early monasticism that a formal architectural setting should be consciously rejected; the earliest communities chose to live in caves, to construct simple hovels of readily accessible and easily worked materials, or to adapt existing structures for their needs. Purpose-built complexes, with buildings to house the diverse functions, probably began to evolve only in the late 4th century as an inevitable corollary of the increased institutional and imperial importance of the monasteries following the Edict of Milan of 313. Early monasteries were as much agricultural enterprises as houses of prayer, for the monks had to be

economically self-sufficient. Most monasteries were sited on the edge of a village, with access to the surrounding fields. It was only towards the end of the early Byzantine period (*c.* 800), when urban populations decreased, that monasteries were established within city walls, a trend particularly evident in Constantinople. As early as the mid-5th century, however, there were already well-established regional plan types. The sources of these types are insufficiently understood, but both secular church architecture and military planning provided major inspiration; it is also possible that earlier religious architecture, such as that of the Essene community at Qumram, was an influence.

Among the most significant early evidence is that provided by Syria, where the Islamic incursions of the 7th century left many sites abandoned and without subsequent modification. Qasr al-Benât (*c.* 425) has a modular plan in which the constituent elements of refectory, dormitory, hostels and ancillary buildings, set to the north of the church, are separate units linked by porticos. This type was to continue little modified into the next century, sometimes with enveloping corridors and porches giving a degree of homogeneity to the layout. A tendency to develop an enclosed and inward-looking quadrangular plan is to be seen in north and east Syria. At the vast pilgrimage complex of QAL'AT SIM'ĀN (*c.* 480) the various structures of the monks and pilgrims are grouped in ranges around three sides of a courtyard on the south side of the great church's eastern limb. In quadrangular planning of this type there are some analogies with forms developed in south Syria, where Umm is-Surab (489) is an example of a plan type that has a tightly defined two-storey quadrangular block against the north side of the church, with a rectangular colonnaded atrium at its core. An alternative, but probably slightly later, development in south Syria was to group the main conventual buildings around the axial approach to the church, where they might form a forecourt, as at Id Dêr. This arrangement must have been inspired by the great atria that preceded several of the basilicas built under imperial patronage.

Another area of likely importance for early monastic architecture was North Africa, and in Upper Egypt there is a somewhat similar variety of plan types to those in Syria. Elsewhere in North Africa conventual structures might be ranged along the flanks of the church, as appears to have been the case at the pilgrimage church at Tebessa (Algeria; *c.* 400). The monastic enclosure there is defined by a massively strong, rectangular enclosing wall with towers and ramparts resembling contemporary Roman military works. Such a wall was also to become a characteristic feature of Middle Byzantine monastic planning over an extended period.

Perhaps as early as the 5th century at DAFNI (Greece) there was a heavily fortified rectangular enclosure, with the monastic church at its centre, but there the monastic buildings were ranged around the perimeter wall, looking inwards, rather than set against the church. It was probably the policies of Justinian I (*reg* 527–65) that most actively fostered the development of this type. A combination of concern for the defence of the provinces with insistence on stricter regulation of the monastic life resulted in buildings such as the defensible monastery complex of *c.* 540 on Mt Sinai (*see* SINAI, §2), which aimed to provide

a physical and spiritual bulwark for Palestine. Variants on this type were to be erected throughout the empire in purely monastic form and were for long to remain the norm across the Byzantine world. The 10th-century Great Lavra on MT ATHOS (Greece), for example, is essentially built to the same formula. The ancillary buildings and workshops were usually constructed immediately against the enclosing walls, while the monastic cells were in turn built against them (as at Hosios Meletios, Attica) or were themselves placed directly against the walls. In larger communities the cells might be ranged in as many as four storeys with connecting loggias, reflecting Late Antique house and barrack types that had remained current in Syria. The more important communal buildings, and in particular the refectory, were generally placed facing the entrance of the church.

For further information *see* EARLY CHRISTIAN AND BYZANTINE ART, §II, 2.

(ii) Early monasteries in the West. Understanding of the early development of monastic architecture in western Europe is clouded through the inadequacy of the available evidence. The first monastic leader of real stature was St Martin of Tours (*c.* 316–97), around whose dwelling a monastery is known to have developed. In this the monks are said to have occupied cells set along the perimeter walls, centred on a two-storey building that had the rooms of the leaders set below a refectory. It cannot be assumed, however, that developments in monastic life were necessarily immediately reflected in architecture. St Benedict himself does not appear to have envisaged any particular arrangement of buildings, despite his profound concern for communal discipline. Nevertheless, the main functions for which building types eventually emerged are anticipated in his Rule, and the general adherence to the Rule was to be of the utmost importance in the eventual development of a standardized approach to monastic planning in the West (*see* §(iii) below).

Most early monastic sites in the West, like those in the East, usually consisted of irregular groupings of cells around one or more oratories. In Ireland and the western parts of the British Isles there are indications of ramparts defining extensive monastic precincts in the 6th century, as at Clonmacnois (*see* CLONMACNOIS MONASTERY, §1) and IONA, the sub-rectangular forms of which may indicate some Roman or Near Eastern influence. Other sites, like the 7th-century complex at Nendrum (Co. Down), appear to have been established within existing defences or behind promontory fortifications, which may have been the gifts of local rulers. With many of these sites, as is well illustrated at Tintagel (Cornwall), it is difficult to distinguish between secular and monastic settlement, since the architectural forms adopted by both were broadly similar. For communities established on virgin sites the Celtic tradition appears to have preferred a circular or oval precinct similar to those of civilian settlements, intended as much to give a sense of enclosure against the forces of evil in the world as to provide a defensive barrier. At first these contained a more or less random distribution of huts, oratories and communal buildings of roughly rounded form, probably initially built of wood in many cases, albeit soon to be replaced in more permanent materials.

A clearer picture began to emerge in the 7th century. At Whitby (N. Yorks), which has been taken to be the Streonaeshalch founded by St Hilda (614–80) in 657, remains have been found of a number of rectangular cells within what appears to be a curved enclosure wall. The relative regularity of both their form and interrelationship provides important information for what appears to have been one of the major Saxon foundations. Of rather greater evidential value, on account of the care with which they have been excavated, are the remains at Benedict Biscop's twin Northumbrian foundations of MONKWEAR-MOUTH ABBEY and Jarrow Abbey. At the former, founded in 674, traces of a rectilinear arrangement of structures have been traced to the south of the church. These include a covered walkway running southwards, which had a slated roof, plastered and painted masonry walls and glazed windows. At Jarrow, where the church was consecrated in 681, a pair of subdivided halls, also with slated roofs and glazed windows, ran parallel to the church. It has been reasonably postulated that one was a refectory and the other contained a private room and a communal hall.

In such layouts the beginnings of a more formalized approach to monastic planning are clearly evident, although the total enclosure of a cloister area as the setting for the monastic life appears not yet to have been regarded as essential. A closer approach to enclosure may have been achieved a little earlier in Normandy, however, at the foundation (c. 654) of JUMIÈGES ABBEY by St Philibert (d 684). A description of it in the *Vita Sancti Filiberti* refers to a defensive rectangle within which was a cruciform church with an arcaded enclosure of some form, and one of the constituent buildings is known to have been of two storeys with a dormitory above a buttery and refectory. It cannot be determined with any certainty, however, when or where the fully enclosed cloister, with conventual buildings around three sides of an open square and the fourth side formed by the church, was first achieved. Several other areas may also have made some contribution to its achievement. The first buildings at LORSCH ABBEY (Hesse; c. 760) were ranged around three sides of a square, with a wall across the fourth and what appear to have been covered walks around all four sides. Yet there the basis of the layout was a Roman villa, and it is uncertain how far the plan of the monastery was consciously chosen or whether it was largely imposed by retention of the existing buildings. There is more certainty with Abbot Ansegis's foundation of Fontanella (at Saint-Wandrille in Normandy) between 822 and 833. According to a description in the *Gesta abbatum Fontanellensium* the church was on the south, the camera on the north and the refectory and cellar faced the dormitory across the other two sides. By the time that Fontanella was under construction, however, the whole monastic movement was being given a firmer sense of direction as part of the Carolingian renewal, and in this the development of a more systematic approach to planning was to be of fundamental importance.

(iii) The Benedictine plan. It was at least partly through the efforts of St Benedict of Aniane that the Benedictine Rule came to be established as the basis for western European monasticism (*see* BENEDICTINE ORDER), and the synod he assembled at Aachen in 817 probably did as much to foster the development of a universally accepted plan type as to encourage the acceptance of a common way of life. The fullest expression of the architectural ideals represented by the synod is the idealized plan preserved at St Gall (*see* ST GALL ABBEY, §2), which it has been suggested was drawn up c. 820 by Abbot Heito of Reichenau and sent for guidance to Abbot Gozbert of St Gall (816–37). In several respects this plan shows what was to be the standard layout for monastic houses in the West during the remainder of the Middle Ages.

The nucleus of the St Gall plan is the grouping of the principal buildings for the choir monks around a fully enclosed cloister (*see* CLOISTER), with the great church on its north side. On the opposite side of the cloister is the refectory, with the cellar for storing provisions on the west side, and a free-standing kitchen building set in the corner between the two. Across the east side of the cloister, continuing the projection of the transept, is the calefactory (warming house), above which is the dormitory. To the south of the dormitory range are further free-standing blocks containing the bathhouse and the latrine. The compelling good sense of this arrangement made it one of the most widely repeated of all architectural formulae. The only significant subsequent addition was the chapter house (*see* CHAPTER HOUSE, §1), the daily meeting room, which came to be prominently placed in the east range. Among the merits of the plan were that it allowed the church to dominate the complex without blocking the light from the other buildings, the storage areas in the cellar were placed so as to be readily accessible from the more public parts of the precinct, and buildings whose functions carried a risk of fire were carefully isolated. Most important of all, the monks were fully insulated from the inevitable disturbances associated with the functioning of what had become a highly complex institution, and the only access to their cloister other than through the church was by a narrow parlour in the west range.

The buildings that housed the many other functions of a major monastery as envisaged in the St Gall plan were carefully allocated to interrelated groupings, although in this respect actual monasteries seldom approached such a systematic gridlike disposition. On an eastward extension of the church's axis were interlinked but self-contained complexes around small courtyards for the infirmary and novitiate; their position and plan reflected the fact that these housed the groups requiring the greatest seclusion. North of the church were to be the residence of the head of the community (already it was envisaged that the abbot's role might no longer allow him to be fully integrated with the community), a guesthouse and a school. On the opposite side of the church, beyond the cloister, were to be some of the necessary ancillary buildings and workshops. West of the church, flanking the main approach by which the laity were permitted access, were those buildings that called for the closest contact with the outside world: accommodation for animals and servants, and perhaps also some further hostels for visitors of less exalted station.

The St Gall plan probably represents the idealization of an arrangement that had already evolved to an advanced stage, and the layout of Fontanella, for example, in which the main nucleus appears to have closely paralleled that of St Gall, must have been nearly contemporary with it. Nevertheless, only from the 10th century is there sufficient evidence that the plan was beginning to be widely adopted. In England it was probably the reforms of St Dunstan that resulted in the regular claustral arrangements first known at GLASTONBURY ABBEY, where he became abbot *c*. 940, and then at Christ Church, Canterbury, where he became archbishop in 959. The fullest early development of the plan, however, is best seen in Burgundy, at Cluny Abbey (*see* CLUNIAC ORDER, §III), the spearhead of monastic reform in the 10th and 11th centuries.

Reconstruction of the monastic buildings at Cluny II (see fig. 2) followed the consecration of Abbot Mayeul's new church in 981, and Abbot Odilo (994–1049) was probably responsible for most of the work. The best evidence for its plan is a description contained in the *Disciplina Farvensis*, although the interpretation of this account is fraught with difficulty since the buildings had to be repeatedly modified to meet expanding needs, particularly in the 11th century, when there was large-scale rebuilding. The main buildings were related to each other essentially as on the St Gall plan. The refectory was placed on the south side of the cloister, the cellar on the west and the dormitory at first-floor level on the east. At Cluny, however, additional provision had to be made for a chapter house in the east range, from which, rather unusually, a Lady chapel projected eastwards. This range was thus more compartmented at Cluny than its idealized counterpart at St Gall, and further complications arose from the alignment of the range to the east of the church transept, which apparently led to an irregular plan for the cloister itself.

To accommodate the large number of novices attracted by the prestige of Cluny, a second cloister seems to have been provided to the south of the refectory. The position of the novitiate itself in relation to this second cloister was

2. Cluny Abbey, Burgundy, bird's-eye view from the south-east; reconstruction of monastery as in 1157, showing second and third abbey churches

probably changed on a number of occasions, but novices and choir monks shared the same latrine block, which projected at 90° to the monks' dormitory. The infirmary at Cluny II, although separated from the novitiate, was still placed to the east of the main complex, as in the St Gall plan. It was set on a diagonal alignment, and a small subsidiary cloister was probably formed by connecting corridors running between the infirmary and east range.

At Cluny II, Odilo also had to provide accommodation for the *conversi* or lay brethren, who were at this time beginning to emerge as a distinct group with responsibility for much of the physical labour of the community, leaving the choir monks free to spend a growing proportion of their time in church. As might be expected, this accommodation was placed to the west of the main complex, allowing less restricted intercourse with the outside world. A narrow courtyard was defined by an extended range, which crossed the main approach to the abbey church and housed both the lay brethren and several of the functions for which they were responsible. Guest halls and hospices for the various degrees of pilgrims and visitors to the abbey were also provided within this courtyard.

(iv) Cistercian perfection of the Benedictine plan. With their strict emphasis on totally enclosed self-sufficiency and on a uniformly exact adherence to the Rule of St Benedict, the Cistercians brought the most stringently logical and systematic approach to monastic planning (*see* CISTERCIAN ORDER). In colonizing a new site, preferably on virgin land, the first buildings, which might be of timber, were commonly erected by an advance party of lay brethren pending the construction of more permanent structures. The choice of site for the permanent structures was closely conditioned by the water supply and necessities of drainage (see fig. 1 above), and there might be no compunction in abandoning true orientation, as at RIEVAULX ABBEY (N. Yorks), where the configuration of the terrain made it essential.

The development of one of the Order's major sites is well illustrated at CLAIRVAUX ABBEY (Champagne; see fig. 3), the third daughter of the mother house of CÎTEAUX ABBEY (Burgundy), which was founded in 1115 by St Bernard (*d* 1153), the Order's greatest apologist. A particular interest of the site at Clairvaux is that it included the original settlement occupied by St Bernard and his companions between 1115 and *c*. 1135. The core of the permanent conventual complex was probably laid out to the east of this first monastery during Bernard's lifetime, and it may therefore represent what he saw as the ideal disposition. The new church was consecrated in 1145, and it is likely that at least some of the monastic buildings were occupied soon after, although many of them were later rebuilt.

On the east side of the cloister itself (rebuilt by Abbot Jean II, 1286–91), immediately next to the church transept, there was a small library cell accessible from the cloister, with a sacristy entered from the church to its east. In some houses, as at Clairvaux's daughter house of FOUNTAINS ABBEY (N. Yorks), the sacristy had a treasury directly above it. Next to the sacristy was the chapter house, the main business and meeting room of the monks, where a chapter of Benedict's Rule was read after the Morrow

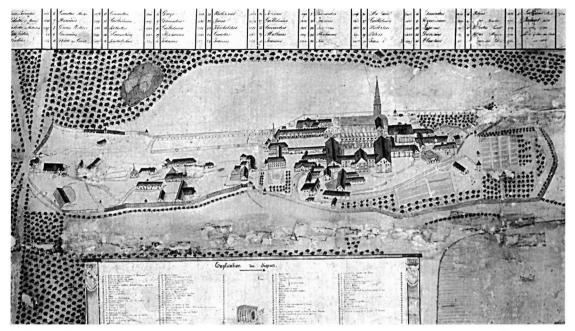

3. Clairvaux Abbey, Champagne, founded 1115; drawing by Dom Milley, 1708 (Troyes, Bibliothèque Municipale)

Mass. At Clairvaux the square chamber was covered by nine bays of vaulting and was contained entirely within the range. Elsewhere, as originally at Fontenay Abbey (Burgundy), it might project beyond the main body of the range, and in Britain it became common for this structure to be considerably elongated on an eastward axis and to be higher than would have been possible if fully contained within the range. In some cases there appears to have been a narrow, lower part at the west end, forming a vestibule that permitted communication between dormitory and church on the floor above, with the rest rising to the considerably greater height considered appropriate for what was regarded as the second most important of the structures around the cloister.

South of the chapter house was the inner parlour, where necessary conversation was allowed and where the daily tasks of the monks might be allotted to them by the prior. The parlour also commonly provided access to the area beyond the cloister, although there could be a separate slype (passage) for this purpose, as at Kirkstall Abbey (W. Yorks). Adjacent to the parlour at Clairvaux was the stair that gave daytime access between the cloister and dormitory; the stair for services at night led directly from the dormitory into the south transept of the church. The customary Cistercian position for the day stair was at the south-east corner of the cloister, but in a number of houses (e.g. Fontenay) it was within the south rather than the east range. To give sufficient length for the size of dormitory necessary in many Cistercian houses, the east range usually projected well beyond the cloister; at Clairvaux the lower stage of the east range beyond the day stair was the monks' hall, but it had originally been used as the novitiate, as at many other houses. The dormitory itself, running the length of the east range at first-floor level, was invariably one of the largest spaces within the abbey after the church

but was seldom given any great architectural character (*see* §2 (i) below). It was also one of the few interiors that were generally left open to the rafters rather than vaulted, although a magnificent exception may be seen at the 12th-century barrel-vaulted dormitory hall of Senanque Abbey (Vaucluse; see fig. 9 below). Privacy for the individual monks would have been provided simply by curtains around the beds, later usually replaced by fixed partitions. The latrine block, astride the drain, extended to the east of the range at Clairvaux, and would have been entered directly from the dormitory. The precise relationship between dormitory and latrine varied according to the line of the drain.

The south range was dominated by the refectory, which in most Western monasteries ran parallel to the cloister walk. Clairvaux, however, may have been the first example of what was to become a common Cistercian arrangement, in which the refectory was set on a north–south axis at 90° to the cloister walk, allowing extra length and thus housing more brethren (*see* §2(ii)(a) below). At Clairvaux it was vaulted in three aisles of five bays and had a pulpit for the meal-time readings in the middle of its west wall. The kitchen stood to its west, within the body of the range and close to the line of the main drain. The vogue for elaborate free-standing kitchens seen in the houses of some of the less austere orders, and typified by that at FONTEVRAULT ABBEY (Anjou), was rarely followed by the Cistercians. East of the refectory, and again within the body of the range, was the warming house, the one place in the abbey where the monks were allowed to warm themselves in cold weather. It was also here that they had their heads shaved. At some abbeys, such as Fountains, the warming house had a muniment room directly above it, presumably because here dampness was less of a threat to the precious documents that established the community's claim to its estates; at other houses this upper level might be a wardrobe.

Directly in front of the entrance to the refectory was the lavatory or washing place, where the monks ritually cleansed themselves before eating and where the *mandatum* or weekly washing of feet took place in Cistercian houses. The Cistercians placed particular symbolic importance on the lavatory, and the building housing it was often given considerable emphasis, as in the hexagonal structures at POBLET ABBEY and Santes Creus Abbey (Catalonia); but the Order was certainly not alone in giving a prominent setting to the ritual washing before meals, as may be seen from the superb basin provided about 1180 for the Cluniac monks of Much Wenlock Abbey (Salop).

The west side of the cloister in a Cistercian house was the province of the lay brethren. To insulate the cloister itself from the inevitable noises associated with their work, this range at Clairvaux was separated from the cloister by a narrow lane. This arrangement was repeated at many other houses, although sometimes later suppressed when the recruitment of the *conversi* declined; a good example of a lane may be seen at Byland Abbey (N. Yorks). By 1708 the west range at Clairvaux, which partly survives, was described simply as the cellar and granary, and the main complex for the lay brethren was situated further to the south. This, however, may represent a later modification, since the *conversi* were usually housed within the main west range, with their refectory adjacent to the cellar and their dormitory above the two. Nevertheless, the vast numbers of lay brethren attracted to Cistercian houses at the height of the Order's popularity meant that many abbeys had to provide extended housing for them soon

4. Fontenay Abbey, Burgundy, dormitory and cloister, *c.* 1150

after the completion of the original buildings, as at Melrose Abbey (Borders) and perhaps at Clairvaux. In the orders that did not have lay brethren, the upper floor of the west range, above the cellar, was often chosen for the residence of the head of the house. This was the case at the Cluniac priory of Castle Acre (Norfolk); indeed, at Cluny itself this was eventually the position of the abbatial lodging. For orders other than the Cistercians, the west range usually also contained an outer parlour, which provided a second means of access to the cloister and within which the monks might have some contact with the laity. A parlour is also occasionally found in this position in Cistercian houses, as at Roche Abbey (S. Yorks).

The infirmary, novitiate and abbot's residence at Clairvaux were, as was common, placed south-east of the main nucleus of buildings. The infirmary, rebuilt along with the cloister by Abbot Jean II, was connected to the east claustral range by a second cloister, which had a scriptorium on its north side (although this was more usually in the north walk of the great cloister). The infirmary itself is shown as having an unbuttressed T-shaped plan. The principal chapel linked with the infirmary was a 12th-century cruciform structure built by the counts of Flanders at the north end of the main hall. The novitiate, apparently ranged around the sides of yet another small cloister, was to the north-east of the infirmary, while the abbot's residence lay to the south-east. The Cistercian system of visitation of daughter abbeys by the mother house's abbot may have been the reason for some houses providing themselves with two abbatial residences, as at Kirkstall, where a second house was later constructed between the abbot's own residence and the infirmary.

North of the church was the monks' cemetery, which could be reached either directly from the main door of the north transept or by a path from the infirmary cloister. West of the church was a courtyard flanked by all the necessary ancillary buildings of a great self-supporting religious institution, and the abbot's residence was also later placed in this area. This indicates the more outward-looking attitudes that inevitably developed once the Order's initial fervour had passed, another indicator of which is the increasing provision of guest accommodation. As early as the third quarter of the 12th century two substantial guest houses were built in the outer court at Fountains, for example, close to the quarters of the lay brethren, and these were extended and modified several times.

Many Cistercian foundations have preserved something of their original appearance of extreme simplicity, but this is particularly well seen in the east range and cloister of Clairvaux's second daughter house of FONTENAY ABBEY, where construction of the whole complex was started *c.* 1139 under the patronage of Bishop Everard of Norwich. Although the buildings had to be sufficient to accommodate the numbers of professed monks, the range was simply designed as an extended block beneath a continuous unbroken roof. No one part was emphasized, except that at the lower level the chapter house and adjoining sacristy originally projected to the same line as the adjacent eastern chapels of the church's transept, whereas the rest of the range was the same width as the main body of the transept. The internal structure of the range is indicated by the way in which the buttresses rise only far enough to abut the stone vaults of the ground floor, leaving the lighter, open timber roof of the dormitory above unbuttressed. Otherwise the walls are devoid of articulation. Within the cloister itself the surrounding vaulted walks open on to the central garth through an unbroken succession of round-arched openings, most of which contain paired sub-arches (see fig. 4). The walls of the church and dormitory rise above the roofs of the cloister walks, the only differentiation between them being the wider spacing of the nave windows as dictated by its bay system.

(v) Variants within the standard Benedictine plan. The general arrangement of buildings around the main cloister as exemplified by Clairvaux was to be employed at the great majority of religious houses in the West. Nevertheless, considerable variations were acceptable when required by the limitations of the site or other considerations. The exigencies of providing fresh water and drainage probably led to the greatest number of deviations from the standard plan. Most commonly this simply meant placing the monastic buildings to the north of the church, as in the Cistercian abbeys of Maulbronn (Baden-Württemberg; *see* MAULBRONN ABBEY) or Melrose. Perhaps the most graphic illustration of the importance of the water supply to a monastery is the drawing (*c.* 1167) of the Benedictine cathedral priory of Canterbury in the Eadwine Psalter (Cambridge, Trinity Coll., MS. R.17.1), which depicts in some detail the network of pipes and drains connecting the principal buildings, ponds and water tower. Canterbury was one of those houses where the conventual buildings were placed north of the church. Elsewhere even more drastic departures from convention were required, as at two other English cathedral priories, Worcester and Durham (see fig. 5), where the riverside sites of the two cathedrals required the monks' dormitory to be placed on the west side of the cloister.

The particular combination of functions at the English cathedral priories tended to encourage other planning anomalies, including the need to provide substantial independent lodgings for both the bishop and the prior. The prior, as acting head of the community, usually had his house well within the main precinct, often placed east of the cloister. At Norwich (Norfolk) and Durham it projected directly from the east range, but at Christ Church, Canterbury, it wrapped around the west end of the infirmary, which was north-east of the church. At Ely (Cambs) the prior had an extensive residence on the south side of the cloister, in which position it was linked to the refectory by the kitchen, perhaps to maintain the appearance of communal co-existence with his flock, although he also had his own kitchen at one end of the great hall. Linked to this kitchen was yet another hall, in which he entertained the more important visitors to the house. By virtue of his office within a land-holding corporation, the prior was also an important member of the feudal hierarchy of the nation, with duties of hospitality to his peers and with an inevitable need to spend part of his time outside the monastery. The bishop, however, despite being the nominal superior of the community, was hardly a member of it at all and necessarily had far closer contact with the outside world. In a monastic cathedral the residence for a

5. Durham Cathedral, dormitory and cloister, 1398–1404

bishop and his household, which would be only one of several such official residences, was thus frequently west of the precinct, as was the case at Ely and Canterbury. At Durham the configuration of the land meant that the magnificent castle of its prince bishop was to the north of the main enclosure, and the spreading episcopal residence at Norwich was similarly on that side of the cathedral, although contained within the precinct.

It was also in a cathedral monastery, that of Worcester, that the English taste for circular or polygonal chapter houses apparently first appeared (see fig. 6), although this taste soon spread both to other religious houses and to secular cathedrals. It is possible that the emphasis given to chapter houses in cathedral monasteries, of which this development was one aspect, was an attempt to emphasize the distinct corporate identity of the priory within the larger cathedral organization. At both Winchester (Hants) and Canterbury, for example, although the chapter houses were rectangular, they were so high that the dormitory could not extend to meet the transept of the church and thus had no direct communication with it.

Eccentricities of planning at other houses might be a consequence of the site's physical difficulties or of the necessity for adapting an existing plan. A striking illustration of the former category is MONT-SAINT-MICHEL ABBEY (Normandy), where provision of the necessary conventual buildings around the church on the apex of the island rock site was progressively made in the form of a ring of buildings raised above massive substructures. The dormitory was built immediately flanking the north side of the nave, the cloister and refectory were placed a little further east on top of a magnificently lofty range

6. Worcester Cathedral, chapter house, c. 1150

known appropriately as the Merveille, and the abbot's lodging was wrapped round the southern side of the choir, beyond the staircase that winds round the rock to its summit. Similar expedients had to be resorted to at other rock-top sites dedicated to St Michael, such as Sagra di San Michele, near Turin.

In the second category of irregularities, those stemming from later adaptations, the example of 11th- and 12th-century Cluny may be cited. Around 1088, when St Hugh (*d* 1109) began to build the massive church of Cluny III (see fig. 2 above) to the north of Cluny II, many of the existing monastic buildings were either enlarged or replaced. At the same time the cloister was extended towards the new church through the earlier one, although parts of the east end and Galilee of the earlier structure were retained in a way that apparently constricted the north end of the enlarged garth. Such inconsistencies well demonstrate that however much a standardized plan might be regarded as the ideal in laying out a new monastery, it might nevertheless be accepted that circumstances could impose significant deviations.

In the smaller houses and cells of many of the orders, a more flexible approach to planning must often have been necessary from the start; this is probably most true of the AUGUSTINIAN CANONS. Although their larger establishments usually conformed closely to the established patterns of monastic planning, some of the lesser foundations were attached to existing parish churches and, particularly in poorer countries, an unorthodox arrangement of the conventual buildings might be forced upon the canons. At Pittenweem (Fife), for example, an irregular quadrangle of structures of notably domestic appearance was eventually constructed a short distance to the south of the pre-existing parish church.

Other orders had constitutions that called for more specialized planning. This is particularly true of the Carthusians and the mendicants (*see* §(vi) and (vii) below). For the double orders, such as the Gilbertines and the BRIGITTINE ORDER, the chief difficulty was to house both the principal community of the nuns and the monks or canons who ministered to their spiritual needs. At Sempringham (Lincs), the first home of the Gilbertine Order, the church was divided longitudinally by a solid wall; the larger, northern portion was used by the canons. At another house of the Order at Watton (N. Humberside), the associated conventual buildings were set out as two separate groups, each with its own cloister. In both groups a church or chapel was placed on the south, the chapter house and dormitory on the east and the refectory on the north. The canons' cloister had a cellar and prior's lodging to its west, and the nuns' cloister had accommodation for the lay sisters and for guests in this position. The only physical connection between the two parts was a corridor, although the main church, which was attached to the nuns' cloister, was longitudinally subdivided by a wall, as at Sempringham. In their one English house of Syon (London), the Brigittines also seem to have had completely separated accommodation for the nuns and the religious men, with a single church set between the two, in which the nuns had the use of galleries at an upper level (*see also* VADSTENA ABBEY).

On occasions another type of double foundation might develop when one group of clergy serving a church was supplemented by another, usually with the initial intention that the newcomers, representing more advanced ideas, should oust an earlier community that had come to be considered degenerate or outmoded. This was the case at the great church of S Ambrogio in Milan (*see* MILAN, §IV, 2(i)): in the late 8th century monks were introduced to a church where there was already a community of canons, who themselves chose to adopt a regular life and continued to co-exist with the monks. The canons had their conventual buildings round a cloister to the south of the church and the monks had theirs to the north.

(vi) The Carthusian plan. The synthesis of the eremetic and the coenobitic ways of life, as represented by the discipline of the CARTHUSIAN ORDER (founded 1084), called for particularly specialized planning. Although the life was organized around the Rule of St Benedict, each monk passed the greater part of his day in the solitude of his own cell. Only on Sundays and chapter feast days were most of the offices recited within the church, meetings held in the chapter house and meals taken together in the refectory. On other days nothing but the celebration of mass and the recitation of certain of the offices took the monk away from his cell. Individual cells were, therefore, a prominent feature of the layout, with less emphasis on the communal buildings.

Once developed, the Carthusian plan was probably even less subject to change than the standard Benedictine plan. Despite differences of architectural veneer, there is a striking similarity between Mount Grace Priory (N. Yorks), founded in 1398 by Thomas Holland, Duke of Surrey (*d* 1400), and the house at Villefranche-de-Rouergue in south-west France, founded by a local merchant in 1451.

At both, the most prominent element of the plan is the great cloister, a spacious area also used as the community's burial ground and surrounded by covered walks. Leading directly off these walks were the individual dwelling cells of the monks, each set within its own walled garden. The cells at Villefranche are gone, but at Mount Grace they had two storeys, with a lobby, living-room and combined bedroom and oratory on the ground floor; the upper floor was apparently a workroom. Pentice walks led to a latrine at the bottom of each garden, and along the wall against the cloister walk. At the centre of the cloister was a conduit house, which is portrayed in a 15th-century drawing (London, Charterhouse) of the London Charterhouse as a handsome pavilion.

The communal buildings of church, chapter house and refectory, together with the cell of the annually elected prior, were grouped around a smaller cloister, set between the great cloister and the outer courtyard. Although the main buildings might be handsomely detailed, as at Villefranche, they were seldom of any great size: at Mount Grace (see fig. 7) the church was originally a simple rectangle, barely distinguishable from the other buildings. An exception to such simplicity might be when a ruling family took a particular interest in the foundation, as at the Certosa di Pavia (see PAVIA, §2(i)), founded by Giangaleazzo Visconti, Duke of Milan, in 1390, where the church was on an unwontedly monumental scale and the Duke had a palace between the outer court and little cloister. As with the Cistercian Order, the churches of the Carthusians were divided into two parts to provide separate accommodation for the monks and the *conversi*. On

occasion the distinction between the two parts might be emphasized by passing an extension of one of the cloister walks between them, as at Buxheim Abbey (Swabia).

The Carthusian outer court, like that of other orders, was partly surrounded by ancillary buildings such as barns, stables and brew- and bakehouses; eventually guest houses were also found in this position, despite the Order's original distaste for any form of lay involvement. The living-quarters of the *conversi* would also be in this area, since they were responsible for all physical labour and maintained necessary contacts with strangers and laymen. The lay brethren also cared for the sick and aged monks, but, since they were looked after within their own cells, there was no requirement for a separate infirmary building in a charterhouse.

(vii) Mendicant planning. The founders of the two principal mendicant orders, St Francis (see FRANCISCAN ORDER, §I) and St Dominic (see DOMINICAN ORDER, §I), had little interest in any architectural framework for their activities; indeed, for the former this would have been directly contrary to his pursuit of poverty. As the orders became more institutionalized in response to their rapid growth, however, it was inevitable that they should come to need an organized architectural setting. Mendicant planning never became as standardized as that for the coenobitic orders, partly on account of the limitations of the urban sites that were their preferred choice and because the way of life was less rigidly disciplined than that of the more enclosed monks or canons. Nevertheless, it was the Benedictine plan, with its central cloister, which provided the natural starting-point for the architectural layout of friaries, although there was little hesitation in departing from it in many respects.

The more public nature of a friary, with its encouragement of lay access to the church and, to a lesser extent, to some of its conventual buildings, fostered an arrangement increasingly at variance with that of the Benedictine plan. In some countries there was also an early tendency to give each member of the house an individual cell rather than an allotted space in a common dormitory, while there was no need for a palatial abbot's residence, although eventually the warden or guardian of the house was often more expansively accommodated. Because of the emphasis on preaching to the local laity, the church was usually placed so that it could be entered from the street, with access to the conventual buildings lying beyond it either around or through the church. In England, access through the church was commonly provided by a walkway surmounted by a bell-tower, set between the friars' choir and the preaching nave, as at the Franciscan church of King's Lynn (Norfolk).

The cloister, around which several of the main rooms were often set at first-floor level, might be separated from the church by a lane or yard. This separation was sometimes due to the irregularities and piecemeal development of the site, as was probably the case in the Norwich Dominican house, but might be simply through choice. In the friaries of the British Isles the walks around the cloister were sometimes incorporated within the body of the range rather than being lean-to corridors, as at the Franciscan houses of Walsingham (Norfolk) or Askeaton (Co. Limerick). The placing of the constituent buildings in relation

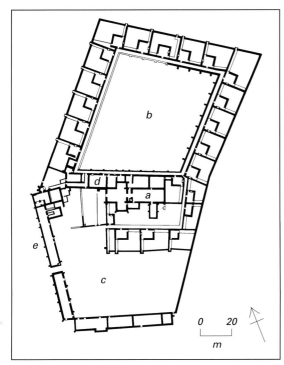

7. Carthusian plan at Mount Grace Priory, North Yorkshire, founded 1398, plan: (a) church; (b) cloister, surrounded by monks' cells; (c) outer court; (d) prior's cell; (e) guest house

8. Dominican Friary, Norwich, cloister, 15th century

to the cloister shows considerable variety. Both the London Franciscans and the Norwich Dominicans, for example, chose to place their refectory on the west side of their cloister, although their chapter house was more conventionally set in the east range (see fig. 8).

The progressive growth on periodically enlarged sites meant that at many establishments more than one cloister was eventually needed. The second cloister of the London Franciscans was probably associated with the infirmary and guardian's lodging, but the uses of outer cloisters were never standardized. The tremendous expansion of many Italian houses resulted in an even larger number of cloisters at the major establishments, and the Dominicans of Florence, at S Maria Novella, eventually had ranges extending around seven cloisters. It was also in Italy that the lay-following attracted by the mendicants was perhaps most graphically illustrated in the architectural benefactions to their houses. At the Florentine Franciscan friary of Santa Croce (see FLORENCE, §IV, 4) the exquisite chapter house (1442–6), which was built by Filippo Brunelleschi, served additionally as a chapel for the Pazzi family; since refectories and infirmaries might also be the resort of the laity, they too were natural objects of beneficence.

BIBLIOGRAPHY

EARLY SOURCES

Benedict of Nursia: *The Rule of St Benedict* [*c.* 530]; Eng. trans., ed. T. Fry, as *RB 1980: The Rule of St Benedict in Latin and English with Notes* (Collegeville, MN, 1981)

Vita Sancti Filiberti abbatis Gemeticensis [*c.* 700]; ed. L. d'Achery and J. Mabillon in *Acta SS Ordinis S Benedicti* (Paris, 1969), pp. 819ff

Gesta Ansigi abbatis Fontanellensis coenobii [9th century]; ed. G. H. Pertz in *Monumenta Germaniae historiae scriptores*, ii (Hannover, 1829), pp. 299–301

Farfa Customary [1043]; *Consuetudines Farvensis* (1900), i of *Consuetudines monasticae*, ed. B. Albers, 5 vols (Stuttgart, 1900–12), pp. 137–9

Descriptio positionis seu monasterii Clarae-Velensis [12th century]; ed. M. H. d'Arbois de Jubainville in *Etudes sur l'état intérieur des abbayes cisterciennes et principalement de Clairvaux au XIIe et au XIIIe siècle* (Paris, 1858), pp. 329–34

EARLY MONASTICISM

A. Vööbus: *History of Asceticism in the Syrian Orient*, 2 vols (Leuven, 1958–60)

A. J. Festugière: *Les Moines d'Orient*, 4 vols (Paris, 1959–65)

O. Meinardus: *Monks and Monasteries of the Egyptian Deserts* (Cairo, 1962)

Le Millénaire du Mont Athos, 963–1963, 2 vols (Chevetogne, 1963–4)

R. Cramp: 'Excavations at the Saxon Monastic Sites of Wearmouth and Jarrow', *Med. Archaeol.*, xiii (1969), pp. 21–65

C. Thomas: *The Early Christian Archaeology of North Britain* (London, 1971)

W. Horn and E. Born: *The Plan of St Gall: A Study of the Architecture and Economy of, and Life in, a Paradigmatic Carolingian Monastery*, 3 vols (Berkeley, Los Angeles and London, 1979)

GENERAL

D. MacGibbon and T. Ross: *The Ecclesiastical Architecture of Scotland*, 3 vols (Edinburgh, 1896–7)

A. H. Thompson: *English Monasteries* (Cambridge, 1923)

M. R. James: *Abbeys* (London, 1926)

D. Knowles: *The Monastic Orders in England* (Cambridge, 1940, 2/1963)

——: *The Religious Orders in England*, 3 vols (Cambridge, 1948–59)

D. Knowles and J. K. St Joseph: *Monastic Sites from the Air* (Cambridge, 1952)

D. Knowles and R. N. Hadcock: *Medieval Religious Houses: England and Wales* (London, 1953, 2/1971)

H. G. Leask: *Irish Churches and Monastic Buildings*, 3 vols (Dundalk, 1955–60)

I. B. Cowan and D. E. Easson: *Medieval Religious Houses: Scotland* (London, 1957, 2/1976)

R. Gilyard-Beer: *Abbeys: An Introduction to the Religious Houses of England and Wales* (London, 1958)

S. H. Cruden: *Scottish Abbeys* (Edinburgh, 1960)

W. Braunfels: *Abendländische Klosterbaukunst*, 2 vols (Cologne, 1969); Eng. trans. as *Monasteries of Western Europe: The Architecture of the Orders* (London, 1972/R Princeton, 1980)

P. Meyvaert: 'The Medieval Monastic Claustrum', *Gesta*, xii (1973), pp. 53–9

E. Fernie: *The Architecture of the Anglo-Saxons* (London, 1983)

MONASTIC ORDERS

R. Willis: 'The Architectural History of the Cathedral and Monastery at Worcester: The Monastic Buildings', *Archaeol. J.*, xx (1863), pp. 254–72, 301–18

W. H. St J. Hope: 'Fountains Abbey, Yorkshire', *Yorks Archaeol. J.*, xv (1900), pp. 269–402

——: 'The Gilbertine Priory of Watton, in the East Riding of Yorkshire', *Archaeol. J.*, lviii (1901), pp. 1–34

H. V. Le Bas, W. Brown and W. H. St J. Hope: 'Mount Grace Priory', *Yorks Archaeol. J.*, xviii (1905), pp. 241–309

W. H. St J. Hope and J. Bilson: *Architectural Description of Kirkstall Abbey*, Thoresby Society Publications, xvi (1907)

L. Bégule: *L'Abbaye de Fontenay et l'architecture cistercienne* (Lyon, 1912, rev. Paris, 4/1966)

C.-H. Besnard: *Mont-Saint-Michel* (Paris, 1912)

A. R. Martin: *Franciscan Architecture in England* (Manchester, 1937)

R. Graham and H. Braun: 'Excavations on the Site of Sempringham Priory', *J. Brit. Archaeol. Assoc.*, n. s. 2, v (1940), pp. 73–101

J. Laurent: *Diocèse de Langres et Dijon*, Abbayes et prieurés de l'ancienne France (Paris, 1941), pp. 308–44

M. Aubert: *L'Architecture cistercienne en France*, 2 vols (Paris, 1943, 2/1947)

K. J. Conant: *Cluny: Les Eglises et la maison du chef d'ordre* (Cambridge, MA, and Mâcon, 1968)

M.-A. Dimier: *L'Art cistercien: Hors de France*, Nuit Temps (La Pierre-qui-vire, 1971)

M. Melot: *L'Abbaye de Fontevrault* (Paris, 1971)

P. Fergusson: *Architecture of Solitude: Cistercian Abbeys in Twelfth Century England* (Princeton, 1984)

RICHARD FAWCETT

2. MONASTIC BUILDINGS.

(i) Dormitory. (ii) Refectory.

(i) Dormitory. The room where the monks, nuns or lay brothers slept was also known in the British Isles as the dorter. The earliest documentary evidence dates from the 6th century; the building type still exists, although modern requirements for privacy and individual study have rendered it rare in monasteries. The term dormitory itself did not come into general use until the Carolingian period, when it was commonly used in imperial decrees. Previously the dormitory was more frequently referred to as a house (*domus*) or cell (*cella*) for quiet or sleeping. Once standardized, it was located at the second level of the east range of the cloister, unless site restrictions forced an alternative layout, as at Mont-Saint-Michel Abbey (Normandy) and Durham (*see* §1(v) above). A stairway (night stair) normally led down from the dormitory into the transept of the church to facilitate access for night services; a second stairway (day stair) connecting the dormitory with the cloister was usually found in the centre of the room, as at Eberbach Abbey (Rheingau, Hesse), or towards its south end, as at Fountains Abbey (N. Yorks).

The use of individual cells by the earliest, eremitical monks continued during the Middle Ages for several orders, including Augustinian canons, friars and Carthusians, and it is the general practice today. The existence of a communal sleeping room is documented by the 6th century in the Rule of St Benedict (*see* §1 above), which states in chapter 22, 'If it be possible, let them all sleep in one place; but if their numbers do not allow of this, let them sleep by tens or twenties, with seniors to supervise them.' The idea and use of the dormitory depend upon the application of an ordered communal life, as reflected in the St Gall plan (*c.* 820; *see* ST GALL ABBEY, §2), even if not consistently followed until later.

Other early documentary evidence of a common dormitory, in the *Vita Sancti Filiberti* (*see* §1(ii) above), describes what would be the largest dormitory known (88.4×15.2 m), at Jumièges Abbey, founded *c.* 654. The St Gall plan, which gives the earliest surviving visual evidence of a dormitory, makes provision for 77 beds. Extant

9. Dormitory of Senanque Abbey, Vaucluse, late 12th century

structures remain from the 12th century and later at, for example, Fontenay (Burgundy; *c.* 1139), Le Thoronet (Var; late 12th century), Santes Creus (Catalonia; 1191), Forde (Dorset; 13th century), Eberbach (*c.* 1275–1345) and Bebenhausen (Baden-Württemberg; 1513–16). Many ruined or fragmentary dormitories survive, for instance the lay brothers' dormitory of the late 12th century and early 13th at Fountains.

The dormitory was one of the first and most important of the claustral buildings to be erected, and it was often the largest; dimensions vary from about 9–12 m wide to 23–85 m long. It was generally constructed of stone for durability and for a sense of permanence, and it was usually built over a ground floor or undercroft (the sub-dorter). Stone vaulting was unusual until the late 12th century, but even then a timber roof, such as the 16th-century example at Fontenay, or a flat ceiling remained common. In Mediterranean areas timber roofs on stone diaphragm arches occur (e.g. the abbeys of Santes Creus and Poblet in Catalonia). Barrel-vaulted examples, as at Le Thoronet and Senanque (Vaucluse; late 12th century; see fig. 9), maintained undivided space. In groin- or rib-vaulted dormitories a row or rows of supports produced aisles: two at Le Val (Seine-et-Oise; *c.* 1220), three at Eberbach, and a rare case of four at Chaalis (Oise; 13th century).

Sleeping in one room was fundamental to communal life, and the few architectural details reflect the unitary goal. A row of windows, usually one at each bed, allowed the monks to read after the midday meal, as specified in chapter 48 of the Rule of St Benedict. Occasionally there were larger windows above the reading windows (e.g. Le Val and Poblet). The articulation of roof and vault supports was generally minimized, and walls were probably white-washed and painted with false masonry jointing but otherwise left plain.

Furniture may have included cupboards to store a change of clothing, writing-desks and lamps, and chairs, especially in the later Middle Ages when time was devoted more to study than to manual work. There may have been low partitions between the beds, partly to serve as headboards when the monks read during the rest period. Fireplaces were occasionally added, but they were discouraged or banned until the 17th century.

In the later Middle Ages, increasing interest in study and privacy led to full-height partitions, which were developed into enclosed rooms with doors: the earliest evidence dates from the 12th century, and the practice was unsuccessfully banned in 1335 by the Cistercian pope Benedict XII. These were effectively individual cells (as at Bebenhausen, 1513–16, and Durham, 1398–1404), formerly the privilege only of the abbot, prior or sub-prior. The abbot often occupied a separate dwelling, although this was Benedictine practice rather than Cistercian until the later Middle Ages.

The undercroft was always vaulted upon piers or columns in order to support the room above; at Fountains Abbey there were two aisles in the monks' sub-dorter and three in the lay brothers'. The undercroft helped to keep the dormitory warmer, cleaner and free from damp. At times the monks' sub-dorter served as the warming room, or calefactory (as in the St Gall plan), and perhaps as the common room or day room for work. The lay brothers' sub-dorter served as their refectory and the monastery cellar.

LM

BIBLIOGRAPHY

W. Horn: 'On the Origins of the Medieval Cloister', *Gesta*, xii (1973), pp. 13–52
L. Shelby: 'Monastic Patrons and their Architects: A Case Study of the Contract for the Monks' Dormitory at Durham', *Gesta*, xv (1976), pp. 91–6
L. J. Lekai: *The Cistercians: Ideals and Reality* (Kent, OH, 1977)
W. Horn and E. Born: *The Plan of St Gall: A Study of the Architecture and Economy of, and Life in, a Paradigmatic Carolingian Monastery*, 3 vols (Berkeley, Los Angeles and London, 1979)
G. Binding and M. Untermann: *Kleine Kunstgeschichte der mittelalterlichen Ordensbaukunst in Deutschland* (Darmstadt, 1985)
N. Bauer: 'Monasticism after Dark: From Dormitory to Cell', *Amer. Benedictine Rev.*, xxxviii (1987), pp. 95–114

VIRGINIA JANSEN

(ii) Refectory. As a communal activity, the taking of sustenance was accorded a spiritual significance in monastic life, in which parallels were drawn with the Last Supper and its symbolism of the communion between Christ and his disciples. Thus the refectory, the main dining-hall of a monastery, which was necessarily one of the largest buildings in the complex, was also one of the most important. In the systematically organized hierarchy of structures that emerged in Western monasticism it was seen as ranking third after the church and chapter house.

(a) Architecture. In the Eastern Church there was considerable variety in the form of the refectory, although it always occupied a prominent place within the monastery, often being placed directly facing the church. It was usually planned as an elongated rectangle, perhaps like a secular basilica, with an apse to create axial emphasis, as at Hosios Meletios (Attica; 11th century). Within it there might be either a table running the length of the room or individual tables set in nichelike enclosures along the walls, as at the Great Lavra on Mt Athos (*see* MT ATHOS, fig. 2). Like the other major monastic buildings, it was often vaulted in stone.

The importance accorded to the refectory in the West is also apparent from an early date. St Philibert's Jumièges

Abbey (Normandy) of *c.* 654 included a refectory, and at Benedict Biscop's late 7th-century foundation at Jarrow (Tyne & Wear) one of the two large halls has been identified as such. With the emergence of a relatively standardized Benedictine plan from the 9th century onwards, the refectory was generally placed on the opposite side of the cloister from the church and usually occupied the greater part of the south claustral range. For most orders it was a large, open hall set parallel to the church, as shown on the St Gall plan (*c.* 820; *see* ST GALL, §2). Internally there were two main points of emphasis: the dais, on which the abbot's table was set, and the elevated pulpit, often partly constructed within the wall thickness, from which readings were made to the brethren during meals.

The refectory might be set either on the same level as the cloister or, as in many secular halls, raised above a vaulted undercroft and reached by stairs at one end. An elevated position had the practical advantages of being above any likely dampness and of allowing larger windows unobstructed by the roofs of the cloister walk. There may also, however, have been a symbolic significance in the raised refectory, with its potential for allusion to the Last Supper in the Upper Room. Many refectories are known to have been decorated with a depiction of that event (*see* MT ATHOS, fig. 3). From the mid-12th century, probably starting with Clairvaux Abbey (Champagne), many Cistercian houses chose to realign the refectory through 90°, thus setting it at right angles to the axis of the church. This was perhaps chiefly to allow greater flexibility of size, but it has been suggested that, in an order that emphasized strict adherence to the enclosure ordained by the Rule, it

10. Refectory of Noirlac Abbey, Berry, early 13th century

also allowed the kitchen to be incorporated within the range so that it could be visited without leaving the cloister in the course of the Sunday procession around the buildings. In areas where important interiors were vaulted, the refectory was usually so constructed, with one or more ranks of supporting piers, as at the early 13th-century Noirlac Abbey (Berry; see fig. 10; *see also* MAULBRONN ABBEY, fig. 1).

The refectory probably never lost its central significance in the monastic life, but a number of developments did tend to qualify this importance. First was the less strict adherence to the vegetarian diet required by the Rule that had emerged by the early 13th century. Although meat-eating was still forbidden in the refectory, it was sometimes allowed in the infirmary or with the abbot in his own residence. Meat-eating by the healthy within the infirmary was formally condoned by the papacy only in 1316; but by then there was a well-established tradition at many houses that meat might be consumed in a second dining-hall set close to the infirmary, known as the misericord or *deportus*. Since as many as half the community could be allowed this richer diet at any one time, the importance of the refectory itself was inevitably reduced.

Towards the end of the Middle Ages, when recruitment declined, at some houses the community was divided into a series of separate households grouped around the principal office holders, between which the main buildings were subdivided. Something approaching this may have happened at Lindisfarne (Northumbria), where the refectory was absorbed into the prior's lodging and the cloister abandoned.

See also §1 above.

BIBLIOGRAPHY
C. Gilbert: 'Last Suppers and their Refectories', *The Pursuit of Holiness in Late Medieval and Renaissance Religion*, ed. C. Trinkhaus and H. A. Oberman (Leiden, 1974), pp. 371–402
P. Fergusson: 'The Twelfth Century Refectories at Rievaulx and Byland Abbeys', *Cistercian Art and Architecture in the British Isles*, ed. C. Norton and D. Park (Cambridge, 1986), pp. 160–80
——: 'The Refectory at Easby Abbey: Form and Iconography', *A. Bull.*, lxxi (1989), pp. 334–51

RICHARD FAWCETT

(*b*) *Decoration.* The importance of the refectory in the life of the community was initially indicated through its architectural scale rather than its decoration. This was intended so that there should be no distraction from prayer and meditation at meals, as extracts from the order's Rule, the martyrology or the Bible were read to the assembled monks and friars. The strictest observance of this practice was evident among the Cistercians (e.g. late 1230s; Heilsbronn Abbey), but less austere orders permitted some decoration. At Cluny II, for example, the refectory was enlarged (*c.* 1075–86; destr.) and decorated with a wall painting of the *Last Judgement*, while the east end of the refectory at Worcester Cathedral has a carved *Christ in Majesty* and *Symbols of the Evangelists* (*c.* 1220–30). The decoration by JUAN OLIVER in the refectory of Pamplona Cathedral included scenes from the *Passion* and the *Resurrection* (1330; now Pamplona, Mus. Navarra; *see* GOTHIC, fig. 81).

Allusions to the Last Supper influenced both the layout of the refectory (*see* §(a) above) and provided the commonest theme for its decoration. The iconography of the

11. Taddeo Gaddi: *Tree of Life, Lives of Saints and Last Supper* (*c.* 1360; detail), fresco, refectory, Santa Croce, Florence

Last Supper teaches the religious at table and the origin of the Eucharist. It also recalls the warning of evil in the betrayal of Judas and provides visual reminders of St Paul's instructions not to eat and drink with devils at the table and to examine one's conscience before partaking of the table of the Lord (1 Corinthians 10:21, 11.28). Similar exhortations that appear in the *Life of Jesus Christ Our Redeemer* by Ludolf of Saxony (*d* 1378), a German Carthusian, have sometimes been cited as contributing to the iconography of refectories, notably the idea that the monastic life may be seen as a type of entombment. A subject of particular significance in Franciscan refectories was St Bonaventure's *Lignum vitae* (*see* FRANCISCAN ORDER, §II), which was sometimes illustrated alongside the *Last Supper* and other subjects, for example in Taddeo Gaddi's frescoes (*c.* 1360; see fig. 11) in the former refectory of Santa Croce, Florence. The varying iconographic traditions of monastic, mendicant and military orders is illustrated by the wall paintings of former Grand Masters of the Teutonic Order that Master Peter executed in 1402 for the Winter Refectory of Malbork Castle.

Throughout the 15th century the decoration of refectories followed current stylistic trends, as is demonstrated by the *Last Supper* that formed part of a cycle, with the *Crucifixion*, *Entombment* and *Resurrection* (1447) in S Apollonia, Florence (*see* CASTAGNO, ANDREA DEL, §1(ii)). An interesting development of the late 15th century involves the integration of the painted *Last Supper* into the architecture of the refectory, giving the impression that the scene is taking place within the building, with a view outside into the monastery garden in the cloister. An early example is Domenico Ghirlandaio's *Last Supper* (1480) in the refectory of the monastery of the Ognissanti, Florence (*see* GHIRLANDAIO, (1), §I, 2(i)(a)). In Leonardo's *Last Supper* (begun *c.* 1495) in the refectory of S Maria delle Grazie, Milan, the architecture of the painting becomes an extension of the room and is constructed in accelerated perspective, while the figures appear to change their poses according to the viewer's position (*see* LEONARDO DA VINCI, §§I, 2 and II, 1(ii)).

Such sophisticated technical displays, however, lay far beyond the simplicity and modesty usually deemed appropriate for the decoration of refectories. The decorative programme, including an *Annunciation*, a *Nativity* and a *Last Supper* (*c.* 1514), executed by Franciabigio for the convent of S Giovanni della Calza, Florence, contains nothing exhilarating or novel to draw attention to itself and away from the creation of a meditative atmosphere. In some monastic houses the earlier ideals were maintained, but later in the 16th century there is evidence of a growing acceptance of the introduction of secular iconography into the traditional themes.

The most renowned example of this trend is the *Last Supper* (1573; Venice, Accad.) commissioned from Veronese for SS Giovanni e Paolo, Venice (*see* VERONESE, PAOLO, §I, 3 and fig. 4). It was not the lavishness of the work that led to an investigation by the Inquisition, but the inclusion of inappropriate, trivial details, such as the presence of a dog. In the event all that was necessary to secure its acceptance was a title change to the *Feast in the House of Levi*. This established a precedent for the more relaxed and ornate styles that characterized Baroque refectory decoration.

BIBLIOGRAPHY
G. Bossi: *Del 'Cenacolo' di Leonardo da Vinci* (Milan, 1810)
S. J. Freedberg: *Painting of the High Renaissance in Rome and Florence*, 2 vols (Cambridge, MA, 1961)
L. Vertova: *I cenacoli fiorentini* (Turin, 1965)
The Great Age of Fresco: Giotto to Pontormo (exh. cat., New York, Met., 1968)
M. Meiss, ed.: *The Great Age of Fresco: Discoveries, Recoveries, and Survivals* (New York, 1970)

JOHN N. LUPIA

II. Buddhist.

The development of the Buddhist monastery is inextricably linked to that of the Buddhist order of ordained monks and nuns, known as the *saṅgha*. Together with the Buddha and the *dharma* (Skt: doctrine, or law, preached by the Buddha), the *saṅgha* is one of the Three Jewels of Buddhism in which the faithful take refuge in order to find deliverance from the cycle of rebirth (*see* BUDDHISM, §I). The monastic order is the central institution of Buddhism; indeed, its importance is such that Buddhism is only considered established in a region when the order has been fixed there and a native of the area ordained. Conversely, the destruction of the monasteries in a region leads directly to the extinction of Buddhist doctrine there, as occurred in northern India with the Muslim invasion of the late 12th century. Because of this close relationship between the *saṅgha* and the establishment of Buddhism, the diffusion of Buddhist doctrine and the spread of Buddhist monasticism occurred simultaneously, the initial adoption of other essential Buddhist monuments—such as stupas (*see* STUPA), image halls or temples—being part of the same movement. It should be noted that a great number of Buddhist religious compounds commonly referred to as temples are in fact monastic complexes comprising a functional area, containing monks' cells, kitchens, a refectory and sometimes a library, and a consecrated area centred around the stupa or the main image hall.

1. INTRODUCTION. The *saṅgha* was originally a peripatetic order, with community life limited to the three or four months of the rainy season when the roads became impassable. The early monasteries that welcomed the monks during their retreat were thus little more than agglomerations of huts on land provided by pious laymen. Gradually, as more monks remained in the monastery all year round to administer the buildings, better-organized, permanent institutions developed. The plan of the Buddhist monastery has undergone a number of changes since the first establishments were founded in northern India during the Buddha's lifetime (*c.* 6th–5th century BC), but certain building types recur in every region. Among the essential elements are the monks' living-quarters and a hall or gathering area, ideally large enough to accommodate the entire monastic community, where important ceremonies are held. The role played by the monastery in the preservation and transmission of the doctrine also calls for libraries where scriptures can be stored and studied. As Buddhist scholarship developed, some monasteries became known for certain specialities, such as translating scriptures (Dacien si, Xi'an, Shaanxi Province, China), storing scriptures (Haeinsa, Korea), medicine (Chakpori, Tibet) or printing (Nartang, Tibet), while others served as schools for the local lay community.

The Buddhist monk is essentially a mendicant; as such, he relies on the generosity of the lay community for subsistence and renounces all possessions save those expressly permitted, such as alms bowl and robes. When fully ordained, he lives by a strict disciplinary code that covers such matters as celibacy, food and dress and regulates his daily life. It should be noted that there is traditionally no distinction between priest and monk within the *saṅgha*. The monk's goals are to strive for his own enlightenment and to preserve the doctrine for others to follow. The nature of his contact with the laity varies from region to region; it may be limited to his daily round of begging for food or include preaching and teaching, but with the exception of funerals he will almost never officiate in services. Only in some sects, as in Japan, has the monk taken on a more priestly role. In Burma, Laos and Thailand, where Theravada Buddhism is the religion of the majority of the population, the strict boundaries between layman and monk are blurred by the custom of many men becoming monks for a short period during their lifetime. A monk may choose at any time to withdraw from the order and, as long as he has committed no offence, may later be reordained. In Burma, this has led to a particularly close relationship between the *sangha* and the lay community, and virtually every village there supports a monastery through alms.

2. REGIONAL VARIATIONS.

(i) South and South-east Asia. The centuries following the Buddha's death witnessed a remarkable expansion of monasticism throughout northern India, beginning in the middle Gangetic plain, where the Buddha had journeyed and had ordained the first monks (*bhiksu*) and nuns (*bhiksuni*). The movement spread west to GANDHARA and south to Orissa and the Deccan. One of the most important figures in this early diffusion of Buddhism was the Mauryan ruler Ashoka (*reg c.* 269–232 BC) who, in a series of rock and pillar inscriptions, tells of his conversion to Buddhism and his zeal in sending missionaries to regions beyond the limits of his empire. His son, Mahinda, is credited with the successful conversion of the Sri Lankan ruler Devanampiya Tissa (*reg c.* 250–210 BC).

Little remains of the thousands of monasteries in ancient India known from textual references and archaeological evidence. The Chinese monk Xuanzang, who travelled widely in India between AD 630 and 644 at a time when Buddhism had already begun to decline there, recorded the existence of some 4500 monasteries housing a total of 250,000 monks and nuns. Excavations suggest that such large monastic complexes as those at SANCHI, Bodhgaya (*see* BODHGAYA AND GAYA), KUSHINAGARA and Taxila (*see* TAXILA, §2(ii)) included stupas, temples, residential buildings (*vihāras*), consisting of cells around a courtyard, and even colleges. Each centre, however, seems to have developed in a rather haphazard manner with buildings added according to need. At NALANDA, one of the greatest centres of Buddhist scholarship, there is evidence of successive reconstruction on the same site from the 6th century AD to the 12th.

From the mid-3rd century BC a special type of monastery developed in the mountains of western India. This was the rock-cut cave monastery, which lasted until the mid-7th century AD and is represented by such sites as BHAJA, AJANTA, KARLE and NASIK. At each site, large congregational halls (*caityas*) containing rock-cut stupas and residential chambers (*vihāras*) were dug directly into the cliff face. In its basic form, a *vihāra* was composed of a square central hall edged with rows of between two and seven small cells, each containing a stone bed (see fig. 12). This layout appears to imitate that of the earliest monasteries (no longer extant), which were built of wood and thatch.

In Burma, Thailand and Laos (*see* BURMA, §II, 1(ii)(b) and (iii); THAILAND, §II, 1(iv), (v) and (vi)(a); and LAOS, §II, 1), the monastic complex usually comprises, in addition to the monks' living-quarters, a stupa, an ordination hall, one or more assembly halls and a library in which the

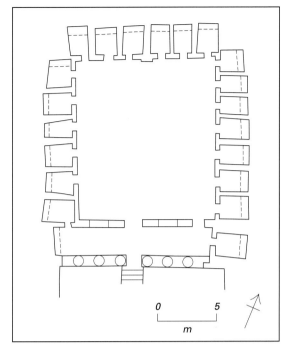

12. Plan of a rock-cut *vihāra*, Cave III, Nasik, India, showing monks' cells surrounding a central chamber, early 2nd century AD

sacred texts are stored. Libraries are often built on high bases or over water to protect the texts from termites.

(ii) Himalayan region and Tibet. The introduction of Buddhism into Nepal from eastern India appears to have occurred at an early date and is traditionally attributed to Ashoka. Under the influence of Hinduism, however, Nepalese monasticism was considerably laicized as monks abandoned celibacy and formed communities of hereditary castes, divided into scholars and teachers (*vajracarya*) and lower-ranking monks (*sakya-bhiksu*). The basic Buddhist monastery of the Kathmandu Valley consists of a square inner courtyard surrounded on all four sides by buildings of two or more storeys, a plan reminiscent of that of early Indian monasteries. Opposite the entrance hall stands the main sanctuary; the monks' cells, library and service rooms would originally have been located in the buildings on the other two sides of the courtyard. In the late 20th century the monasteries are inhabited by married monks and their families; new buildings and courtyards are added to the complex as the community grows. The Chhusya Bahal (1649) and the Musya Bahal (1663) in Kathmandu are among the oldest of the 400 surviving Buddhist monasteries in the valley (*see* NEPAL, §III).

In Tibet, where Buddhism was introduced in two waves in the 7th century and late 10th, the faith developed into a particular form of Tantrism, or Vajrayana, also known as Lamaism. Tantrism is a road to spiritual realization that makes use of complex symbology, ritual and magic. One of its central elements is the *mandala* (Skt), a symbolic representation of the cosmos depicting Mt Meru as the hub of the universe surrounded by continents, countries, seas, planets and constellations. Certain early monasteries, such as SAMYE (founded *c.* AD 770 and probably Tibet's first monastery), are considered to be three-dimensional representations of a *maṇḍala*. In the very centre of the monastery, symbolizing Mt Meru, stands the main temple. Around it, at the four cardinal points, chortens (the Tibetan stupa) represent the continents and seas. The whole complex is surrounded by a high wall representing the outer limit of the *maṇḍala*. While few monasteries are such clear replicas of *maṇḍala*s, certain recurring architectural features are derived from these diagrams, including the positioning of temple entrances on the south side of the building and altars on the north. Within the complex, secular constructions are generally placed in the south and sacred ones in the north.

The reforms of Tibetan Buddhism carried out in the 11th century and early 14th led to the emergence of several schools, each of which founded its own monasteries. The largest was the monastic city of Drepung (Lhasa) in which some 10,000 monks still lived in 1951. Middle-sized monasteries house between 50 and 200 monks and include a temple for the main divinity (Tib. *lhakhang*), an assembly hall (*dukhang*), a temple for the protective deities (*gonkhang*), a library, the abbot's quarters (always on an upper floor), a kitchen, living-quarters for the monks and a courtyard for the performance of the masked dances that form an important part of the annual ritual cycle (*see* TIBET, §II).

Tibetan Buddhism is well established in other regions of the Himalayas, notably in Ladakh and Zanskar, Sikkim, Bhutan and the Mustang and Dolpo regions of Nepal. A characteristic architectural feature of these regions is the frequent use of wood, in comparison to Tibet, where stone is the most abundant material. Two types of monastery have developed in Bhutan. The first, perhaps the older, is often termed the 'cluster' type and consists of a nucleus of one or two temples surrounded by buildings including living-quarters (e.g. Phajoding in Thimphu Valley and Tharpaling in Bhumthang Valley). The second type is the fortified monastery (*dzong*), with a tall central tower housing the temples and the assembly hall; the earliest example of this type is the Simthoka Dzong, built in 1617. Such fortresses frequently function as regional administrative centres as well as housing the monastic community (*see* BHUTAN, §II).

Lamaist Buddhism was also adopted in Mongolia (*see* MONGOLIA, §I, 5) and gained a foothold in northern China, where it influenced architecture in Beijing (e.g. the Lama Temple) and Chengde.

(iii) Central and East Asia. During the first centuries AD, Buddhist pilgrims and monks following the Silk Route brought the faith to the Central Asian oases of present-day Tajikistan, Kyrgyzstan and the Xinjiang Uygur Autonomous Region of China, finally reaching China proper around the beginning of the Eastern Han period (AD 25–220). Under imperial patronage Buddhism flourished there from the 4th century, reaching its heyday during the Sui (581–618) and Tang (618–907) periods. From China Buddhism spread to the Korean states of Paekche and Koguryŏ (4th century) and Silla (6th century), and from there to Japan (6th century).

The layout of the East Asian monastery is based on the repetition of courtyards of varying sizes and importance enclosed by walls or corridors. This plan is easily adapted to differing terrains as well as to the needs of different sects. In general, the administrative buildings and living-quarters of the monks are set behind or at the side of the main temples. They tend to be much simpler in style and decoration than the latter and are rarely more than a single storey in height. Main worship halls may rise to two or three storeys. In mountain monasteries, small hermitages for the monks are frequently built on the slopes above and at some distance from the main temple. Zen (Chin. Chan; Kor. Sŏn) monasteries, where meditation is of great importance, tend in particular to be built in secluded settings (*see* JAPAN, §III, 3(ii) and 4(i)).

See also BUDDHISM, §III.

BIBLIOGRAPHY
J. Prip-Møller: *Chinese Buddhist Monasteries: Their Plan and its Function as a Setting for Buddhist Monastic Life* (Copenhagen and London, 1937/*R* Delhi, 1985)
D. C. Twitchett: 'Monastic Estates in T'ang China', *Asia Major*, v (1956), pp. 123–46
D. Snellgrove: *Buddhist Himalaya* (Oxford, 1957)
D. C. Twitchett: 'The Monasteries and China's Economy in Mediaeval Times', *Bull. SOAS*, xix (1957), pp. 526–49
R. J. Miller: *Monasteries and Culture Change in Inner Mongolia* (Wiesbaden, 1959)
K. Ch'en: *Buddhism in China* (Princeton, 1972)
V. Dehejia: *Early Buddhist Rock Temples* (London, 1972)
H.-D. Evers: *Monks, Priests and Peasants: A Study of Buddhism and Social Structure in Central Ceylon* (Leiden, 1972)
E. M. Mendelson: *Sangha and State in Burma* (Ithaca, NY, 1975)
H. Bechert and R. Gombrich: *The World of Buddhism: Buddhist Monks and Nuns in Society and Culture* (London, 1984)

HELEN LOVEDAY

Monastir. *See* BITOLJ.

Moncalvo, il [Caccia, Guglielmo] (*b* ?Montabone, Asti, 1568; *d* Moncalvo, 13 Nov 1625). Italian painter and draughtsman. His first known works are an *Annunciation* (1585; Guarene, church of the Annunciata) and a *Virgin and Child with Saints* (1585; Guarene, S Michele). His early style was derived from late 16th-century painting in Piedmont, which was influenced by the followers of Gaudenzio Ferrari and from which Moncalvo developed a restrained naturalism. An interest in colour, which is not yet handled with complete assurance, dominates the pictures at Guarene, yet in the years *c.* 1590–93 he was increasingly influenced by Ferrari. He was well established by 1590 and obtained a series of commissions: *c.* 1590 he frescoed *Angels* in the chapel of the Presentation of the Virgin in the Temple at the sacromonte at Crea and in 1593 executed the *Crucifixion with Saints* (Calliano, parish church). There followed, also in 1593, frescoes of scenes from the *Life of Christ*, among which was a *Flight into Egypt* for S Michele, Candia Lomellina, and the decoration of the chapel of the Natività della Vergine for the sacromonte at Crea, commissioned by Vincenzo I Gonzaga, 4th Duke of Mantua. Moncalvo's *Franciscan Allegory* (1593; Moncalvo, S Francesco), which is derived from an engraving of 1584 by Agostino Carracci, displays a response to a wider range of artistic sources than hitherto. His interest in the naturalism of the Carracci is also suggested by his *Virgin and Child with Saints and Donors*

(1595; Grana, Asti, parish church), and it is possible that he visited Bologna between 1594 and 1595. The expression of emotion became more subtle and assured in works from these years.

The next documented works are the *Virgin and Child between SS Victor and Francis* and the *Virgin of the Rosary* (both 1602; Cioccaro, parish church), and in these Moncalvo created an individual version of Late Mannerist naturalism. He was in Turin from 1605, where he created a number of works for the now vanished Palazzo del Viboccone. His most important project from this period was his collaboration, between 1606 and 1608, with the Roman Federico Zuccari in the decoration of the Grande Galleria (destr.) planned by Charles-Emanuel I, Duke of Savoy, to link the Palazzo Madama with the new Palazzo Ducale in Turin. Moncalvo's art was enriched by this experience, and a new interest in narrative simplicity is evident in works that can be dated to this period, such as the ceiling frescoes of mythological scenes in the Casa Tizzoni, Vercelli; the *Birth of St John the Baptist* (Casal Cermelli, oratory of S Giovanni); the *Virgin of the Rosary* (1606; Pontestura, parish church); the lunettes depicting scenes from the *Life of St Nicholas Tolentino* (?1607; Casale Monferrato, Mus. Civ.); and the *St Francis before the Crucified Christ* (1608; Villanova d'Asti, S Pietro).

Moncalvo's skill was manifest in a long series of works that repeated, without re-elaborating, successful themes and compositions such as the *Virgin of the Rosary* (see pls in Natale); an example of this, painted between 1611 and 1615, is in S Domenico, Chieri (Turin). After 1613 he completed the frescoed decoration of the chapel of S Carlo Borromeo in S Marco, Novara, and that of the choir of S Domenico, Chieri (1615–16).

At the end of 1617 Moncalvo went to Milan, where he received payment for work on the frescoed decoration of the dome of S Vittore al Corpo in 1617 and 1618. He also worked at Monza, where he painted a *Beheading of St John the Baptist* in the cathedral, and at Pavia, where he painted a *St Anne* (1618; Pavia, S Maria del Carmine), an altarpiece of the *Martyrdom of St Lucy* and frescoes in the chapel of S Lucia (before 1619; Pavia, S Michele). In Milan he painted an *Adoration of the Magi* (before 1619) in S Alessandro and frescoes in the chapel of S Bruno in S Pietro in Gessate, with his pupil, Daniele Crespi, who is documented as working with him in 1619.

After his return to Piedmont *c.* 1620 Moncalvo painted a *Deposition* (before 1621) for S Gaudenzio, Novara, and several altarpieces for churches in Turin; these include the *Martyrdom of St Maurice* for the church of the Cappuccini, the *Adoration of the Magi* for the brotherhood of the Mercanti and the *Ecstasy of St Teresa* (1625) for S Teresa. He painted these himself, although in these years his daughter, Orsola Maddalena Caccia (1596–1676), played an increasingly important role as his assistant.

BIBLIOGRAPHY

DBI

A. Baudi di Vesme: *L'arte in Piemonte dal XVI al XVIII secolo*, i (Turin, 1963), pp. 216–23

G. Romano: *Casalesi del cinquecento: L'avvento del Manierismo in una città padana* (Turin, 1970), pp. 75–101

——: 'Sei disegni del Moncalvo alla Biblioteca Reale di Torino', *Scritti di storia dell'arte in onore di Federico Zeri* (Milan, 1984), ii, pp. 535–44

V. Natale: 'Per un repertorio alessandrino', *Pio V e Santa Croce di Bosco: Aspetti di una committenza papale*, ed. C. Spantigati and G. Ieni (Alessandria, 1985), pp. 437–41

M. Gregori and E. Schleier, eds: *La pittura in Italia: Il seicento*, ii (Milan, 1989), p. 659 [with earlier bibliog.]

RICCARDO PASSONI

Moncunill (i Perellada), Lluís (*b* Sant Vincenç de Falç, Manresa, 25 Feb 1868; *d* Terrassa, 15 April 1931). Spanish Catalan architect. His professional work in Terrassa coincided with the industrial expansion and growth of the town. The plastic quality of the arches in his Almacén Farnés (1905) anticipates his masterpiece, the Masía Freixa (1907–10) in Terrassa, where he achieved a perfect correlation between construction and expression, comparable to the effect obtained in the cornice of the Casa Battló (1904–6) and the façade of the Casa Milà (1906–10), both by Gaudí. In the Fábrica Aymerich (1907–8), Amat y Jover, Terrassa—now the Museo de la Ciència i de la Tècnica de Catalunya—he experimented satisfactorily with undulating roof-forms. His importance within Catalan Art Nouveau lies in the originality with which he adapted Gaudí's inclined shapes and elliptical forms, producing expressive structures, stripped of all ornament.

BIBLIOGRAPHY

M. Freixa: 'Lluis Moncunill constructor de la civdad industrial', *Estud. Pro A.*, v (1976), pp. 6–20

JORDI OLIVERAS

Mond. English family of businessmen and collectors of German origin.

(1) Ludwig Mond (*b* Kassel, 7 March 1839; *d* London, 11 Dec 1909). He was educated in Kassel and studied under Hermann Kolbe in Marburg and Robert Wilhelm Bunsen in Heidelberg (1855–6). He began his career in industry in 1859 and was in England from 1862 to 1864 and from 1867 until his death, acquiring British nationality in 1880. He made his fortune from chemical factories, in particular the Brunner, Mond & Co. factory at Winnington, near Northwich, which became one of the largest producers of alkalis in the world. He also set up the Mond Nickel Co. in Canada and at Clydach, near Swansea. He was elected an FRS in 1891. Mond had a great interest in art and in 1884 appointed the art historian JEAN PAUL RICHTER to buy paintings for him, of a quality suitable for a public gallery and from all schools of Italian art, although the result was a collection especially strong in early Italian art. The collection included works by Giovanni Bellini, Sandro Botticelli, Vincenzo Catena, Correggio, Carlo Crivelli, Dosso Dossi, Fra Bartolommeo, Francesco Guardi, Leonardo da Vinci, Alessandro Longhi, Mantegna, Raphael and Titian, as well as Lucas Cranach (i) and Rubens. Works that Mond did not wish to keep were donated to public galleries: the National Gallery, London, and galleries in Germany benefited from such gifts. On his death the greater part of Mond's collection was bequeathed to the National Gallery, London, together with money to house it, although the transfer did not occur until his wife's death (1924). The bequest included Botticelli's *Four Scenes from the Early Life of St Zenobius* and *Three Miracles of St Zenobius*, the *Crucified Christ with the Virgin Mary, Saints and Angels* (*c.* 1502) by Raphael and a late work, *Madonna and Child*, by Titian. Mond also bequeathed £20,000 to the Akademie der Bildenden Künste, Munich, for the training of art students.

BIBLIOGRAPHY

DNB

J. P. Richter: *The Mond Collection: An Appreciation*, 2 vols (London, 1910)
L. M. Richter: *Recollections of Dr Ludwig Mond* (London, 1910)

(2) Alfred Moritz Mond, 1st Baron Melchett (*b* Farnworth, Lancs, 23 Oct 1868; *d* London, 27 Dec 1930). Politician, businessman and collector, son of (1) Ludwig Mond. This one-time Minister of Food and Chairman of Imperial Chemical Industries formed one of the last collections of ancient Greek and Roman sculptures in Great Britain, in the lingering tradition of the GRAND TOUR. His sculptures, which included a nucleus from the Hope collection, were carefully displayed at Melchett Court near Romsey in Hampshire, where they were catalogued by Eugénie Strong in 1928 with photographs by Bernard Ashmole. The prize statue, the Hope *Hygieia*, was sold to William Randolph Hearst in 1936, and the entire collection was finally dispersed in 1951.

BIBLIOGRAPHY

E. Strong: *Catalogue of the Greek and Roman Antiquities in the Possession of Lord Melchett* (Oxford, 1928)

G. B. WAYWELL

Mondella, Galeazzo. *See* MODERNO.

Mondo, Domenico (*b* Capodrise, nr Caserta, 1723; *d* Naples, 10 Jan 1806). Italian painter and draughtsman. There is little documentary evidence concerning his life. His training was dependent on the late style of Solimena, which Mondo applied to a re-evaluation of Mattia Preti's tenebrism and Baroque solidity. However, already in his early work Mondo achieved a pictorial style very close to the compositional freedom of Giordano. Mondo's early works include the canvases (e.g. *St Jerome*, signed and dated 1747) in S Andrea at Capodrise (Spinosa, 1970, p. 86, no. 13) as well as *Coriolanus* (early 1740s; Naples, Corradini priv. col., see 1979–80 exh. cat., no. 130), which refers to the work of both Solimena and Giordano.

During the 1760s and 1770s Mondo developed small-format compositions, generally with secular subjects. These were characterized by a more spontaneous vision of reality and were thus closer to the rocailles and capriccios fashionable at that time. Notable among these canvases is *Mercury Appearing to Dido* (Naples, Perrone Capano priv. col.), which is one of the masterpieces of late 18th-century Neapolitan art on account of its Rococo preciosity and chromatic refinement. The same stylistic trend can be identified in the eight altarpieces on canvas painted for the church of the Annunziata at Marcianise and dating from the mid-1770s. From these paintings it can be seen that, even in the production of sacred works, commissioned by an ecclesiastical patron with a conservative taste that was linked to the triumphant and devotional figurative models popular at court, Mondo provides a pastoral and Arcadian interpretation of the religious subject, using the free pictorialism of his secular work. Another example can be found in the altarpiece for the church of the Immacolata at Capodrise, representing the *Madonna of the Rosary with Dominican Saints* (*c*. 1775).

From the mid-1770s and throughout the following decade Mondo adopted the classical style of the late Rococo. He achieved this by experimenting with particular aspects of Roman classicism, which he had already assimilated in the four paintings (*c*. 1770; e.g. *St Peter Baptizing St Aspren*) for S Aspreno ai Crociferi in Naples. While remaining outside the academic artistic environment of the Bourbon court at least until 1789, he worked at the royal palace of Caserta (*see* CASERTA, PALAZZO REALE) on the frescoes of *Classical Heroes* (1781) for the overdoors of the Sala delle Dame and the famous *Apotheosis of the Bourbon Arms* (1787) for the Salone degli Alabardieri. These works are a reinterpretation of the tradition of Solimena, in which the iconography and pictorial scheme are solemn and still far from a rational and Neo-classical illustration of sentiments and facts.

Mondo did not continue for long as a defender of the Neapolitan tradition when faced with new aesthetic demands. In 1789 he won the competition for the directorship of the Accademia del Disegno, together with the prominent German painter Johann Heinrich Wilhelm Tischbein, and he remained as co-director until 1799, after which he was sole director until 1805. During this time he was active as a teacher and artistic coordinator, fully in tune with Neo-classical and academic currents. Mondo's work during this period and up to his death is practically unknown, although it is reasonable to suppose a continuation of his graphic work, an area in which the artist had always flourished. Mondo's drawings are perhaps more interesting than his paintings and were executed in pen, watercolour and white lead. His frenetic draughtsmanship and flowery style render his drawings very close to a *bozzetto*, sketch or even a painting. After his death Neapolitan graphic art regressed to a concern with outline and to a non-pictorial form of draughtsmanship.

BIBLIOGRAPHY

P. Orlandi: *Abecedario pittorico* (Florence, 1788), col. 1402
P. Napoli Signorelli: *Vicende della cultura delle due Sicilie* (Naples, 1811), p. 87
C. T. Dalbono: *Storia della pittura in Napoli e in Sicilia dalla fine del 1600 a noi* (Naples, 1859), pp. 109–10
M. Volpi: 'Domenico Mondo pittore "Letterato"', *Paragone*, cxix (1959), pp. 51–63
N. Spinosa: 'Domenico Mondo e il rococò napoletano', *Napoli Nob.*, 3rd ser., vi (1967), pp. 191–203
——: 'Pittori napoletani del secondo settecento: Jacopo Cestaro', *Napoli Nob.*, 3rd ser., ix (1970), pp. 73–87
——: 'La pittura napoletana da Carlo a Ferdinando IV di Borbone', *Stor. Napoli*, viii (Naples, 1971), pp. 486, 498–501, 537–8
Civiltà del '700 a Napoli, 1734–1799, 2 vols (exh. cat. by R. Causa and others, Naples, Capodimonte; Naples, Pal. Reale; Naples, Villa Pignatelli; and elsewhere; 1979–80), i, pp. 135–47, 258–63, 362–7, 392–5; ii, p. 441
N. Spinosa: *Pittura napoletana del settecento dal rococò al classicismo* (Naples, 1986), pp. 16, 45, 61, 77–84, 164, 444–5
A. Spinosa: 'Mondo, Domenico', *La pittura in Italia: Il settecento*, ed. G. Briganti, ii (Milan, 1990), p. 800

RAFFAELLA BENTIVOGLIO-RAVASIO

Mondrian [Mondriaan], **Piet(er Cornelis)** (*b* Amersfoort, 7 March 1872; *d* New York, 1 Feb 1944). Dutch painter, theorist and draughtsman. His work marks the transition at the start of the 20th century from the Hague school and Symbolism to Neo-Impressionism and Cubism. His key position within the international avant-garde is determined by works produced after 1920. He set out his theory in the periodical of DE STIJL, in a series of articles that were summarized in a separate booklet published in Paris in 1920 under the title *Le Néo-plasticisme* (*see* NEO-PLASTICISM) by Léonce Rosenberg. The essence of Mondrian's ideas is that painting, composed of the most fundamental aspects of line and colour, must set an example to the other arts for achieving a society in which art as such has no place but belongs instead to the total realization of 'beauty'. The representation of the universal, dynamic pulse of life, also expressed in modern jazz and the metropolis, was Mondrian's point of departure. Even in his lifetime he was regarded as the founder of the most modern art. His artistic integrity caused him to be honoured as a classical master by artists who were aligned with entirely different styles, as well as by musicians and architects. He was able to make a living from the sale of his works in the Netherlands, Germany, Switzerland, England and the USA.

I. Life and work. II. Working methods and technique.

I. Life and work.

1. Early life and experimentation with avant-garde styles, to *c*. 1917. 2. Involvement with De Stijl, *c*. 1917–*c*. 1924. 3. Later career, after *c*. 1924.

1. EARLY LIFE AND EXPERIMENTATION WITH AVANT-GARDE STYLES, TO *c*. 1917. Mondrian grew up in a milieu that was engaged with artistic and spiritual activities. His father, Pieter Cornelis Mondriaan (1839–1921), had been brought up in aristocratic circles in The Hague. Through his drawings of historical figures, he played an active part in Amersfoort in the political movement that attempted to emancipate Protestant groups and that opposed the prevailing liberalism. Mondrian's brother Willem Frederik Mondriaan (1874–1944) emigrated in the 1890s to South Africa, where he played an important part in cultural life and also painted. Louis Cornelis Mondriaan (1877–1942), Mondrian's younger brother, was involved with the emancipation movement in education and also moved in Amsterdam's artistic circles in the early 20th century.

Mondrian acquired the rudiments of drawing very early from the retired Amsterdam drawing teacher J. B. van Ueberfeldt (1807–94), who had settled near Winterswijk, to which Mondrian's family also moved. Mondrian was taught by using reproductions of 19th-century works in art journals. Frits Mondriaan (1853–1932), Mondrian's uncle, active in The Hague, was his example for a career as a painter. Mondrian became qualified to give drawing lessons in lower schools in 1889 and in middle schools in 1892. From 1892 to 1894 he was registered as a pupil at the Rijksakademie van Beeldende Kunsten in Amsterdam; from 1895 to 1897 he attended evening classes in drawing. He competed unsuccessfully for the Prix de Rome in 1898 and 1901. Having joined the Kunstliefde group in Utrecht in 1892, with whom he regularly exhibited, mostly still-lifes, in 1897 he became a member of the St Luke's and Arti et Amicitiae groups in Amsterdam. He earned his living partly through such varied work as book illustrating (1894), painting tiles, decorating a ceiling in an Amsterdam canal house, making portraits and copies of paintings in the Rijksmuseum, designing panels for a pulpit and giving drawing lessons.

Mondrian's work of the 1890s shows that he studied the three current styles: the Hague school, the Amsterdam Impressionists and Symbolism. Landscapes of the fields and rivers south of Amsterdam—at Duivendrecht, Watergraafsmeer and 'T Gein—were favourite subjects, together with boats on the Amsterdam canals. All the qualities that Mondrian developed in the first decade of the 20th century are evident in the works made in Winterswijk, or the 'Winterswijk group' (1898–1901). His work was distinctive in colour as well as composition, using garish orange and purple expressively. Unlike the artists of the Hague school, Mondrian eschewed the possibility of distant panoramas and an exaggerated suggestion of space. Frontality and a very high horizon were by this time recognizable features of his drawings, pastels, watercolours and oil sketches. Mondrian's inclination towards Symbolism is shown in his portraits of girls, while his still-lifes indicate a knowledge of Neo-Platonism. He also was interested in modern theatre (e.g. by August Strindberg) and music. From 1898 to 1904 he produced many watercolours, which were eagerly bought. During a stay of about a year in Noord-Brabant (1904–5), he also began to concentrate on the theme of windmills, a recurring motif up to 1912 (e.g. *Mill at Evening*, *c*. 1905; The Hague, Gemeentemus.).

In 1905 a large exhibition of Vincent van Gogh's work at the Stedelijk Museum in Amsterdam had a lasting influence on many artists, ending the domination of the Hague school and transforming the character of Symbolism and Neo-Impressionism. Through the use of varied colours Mondrian sought new forms of expression in landscapes conceived in 1906–7, near Saasveld. He took up again the theme of evening and nocturnal landscapes, already a subject in the 'Winterswijk group', producing compositions, loaded with symbolism, divided into three parts: air, trees and their reflections in water. Details were kept to a minimum, thus emphasizing the main contours. The natural cycle of 'growth, flowering and passing away' was also the basis for the 'flower series' of drawings, watercolours, pastels and paintings, which from 1906 made up a large part of the artist's work. From 1906 Mondrian was also intensely involved with THEOSOPHY and ANTHROPOSOPHY, which convinced him that painting could be the expression of both the spiritual essence and the natural exterior. Neo-Impressionist tendencies, given a symbolic significance, predominated after Mondrian stayed in 1908 on the island of Walcheren at the artists' colony led by Jan Toorop in and around Domburg. From 1908 to 1916 Mondrian stayed annually on the island in Domburg and its surroundings, where the strong vertical and horizontal lines in the landscape, such as church spires and sea views, defined the composition of much of his boldly painted work.

In 1909 Mondrian exhibited works of the previous decade at the Stedelijk Museum in Amsterdam together with his friends the painters Cornelis Spoor (1867–1928) and Jan Sluijters. This exhibition, Mondrian's first retrospective, was probably intended to show that his artistic development necessarily had to continue on the same lines. As a result, he was regarded as one of the most important representatives of the avant-garde. One year later the St Luke's group in Amsterdam exhibited works by the 'Luminists', the name given to the Dutch Neo-Impressionists. The art scene in Amsterdam underwent a fundamental change in 1909–10, particularly as a result of the opening of a new wing at the Rijksmuseum, the so-called Drucker building, which included works by such artists as van Gogh, Paul Cézanne and Edouard Vuillard. The Dutch public's acquaintance with such works considerably strengthened the younger generation's aspirations. Critics who opposed the nationalism of the Hague school called for a movement of *Nieuwe Beelding* (New Plastic Image) in all the visual arts. The leader of the progressives was the critic Conrad Kickert (1882–1965), who lived in Paris and organized the MODERNE KUNSTKRING, which Mondrian joined. The group's first exhibition, at the Stedelijk Museum in Amsterdam in 1911, displayed, among other things, the change from Luminism to Cubism that had occurred in the second half of 1910 in the work of many Dutch artists active in Paris. Works by Picasso and Braque were also on view: the first Cubist pictures to be publicly exhibited in Holland. The works that Mondrian exhibited at the show apparently reflect these developments to some extent (e.g. the *Evolution* triptych, *Large*

Dune Landscape and the *Mill at Domburg (The Red Mill)* (all conceived second half of 1910; all The Hague, Gemeentemus.). Critics emphasized the general switch to Cubism to explain the 'geometric' divisions of the surfaces of Mondrian's works and the large, smooth areas of colour. The compositions, determined by larger and smaller triangular elements arranged all over the canvas, are monumental, either emphatically vertical or horizontal. Mondrian's first move towards Cubism is particularly well illustrated by comparing the Luminist and Cubist versions of the *Church at Domburg* (see fig. 1) and *Church at Zoutelande* (1910–11; Pittsburgh, PA, Carnegie).

Kickert convinced Mondrian that he should settle in Paris. He moved in early 1912, initially living in Kickert's studio in Avenue du Maine. Subsequently he rented a studio in the complex on the Rue du Départ, which was also occupied by Lodewijk Schelfhout (1881–1943) and Diego Rivera, whom Mondrian befriended. The latest developments in art were discussed at the artists' cafés La Coupole and Café du Dôme, as well as at soirées, such as those given weekly by Kickert in 1912 and 1913. There Mondrian met, for example, Fernand Léger, with whom he formed a lasting friendship, and Georges Braque. Mondrian continued to move between Paris and the Netherlands, however, where he spent some of 1912, 1913 and 1914, mostly in Domburg. He exhibited work in Paris at the Salon des Indépendants, in Amsterdam and at the artists' colony in Domburg. Dutch Cubists including Mondrian exhibited at the major retrospectives of contemporary art at Cologne (*Sonderbund*, 1912) and Berlin (*Erster Deutscher Herbstsalon*, 1913). Moderne Kunstkring continued to form the link between developments in Amsterdam and Paris in 1912 and 1913. Kickert organized a 'Salle Hollandaise' at the Salon des Indépendants in 1913. However, after Parisian Cubism passed its zenith in 1913, Kickert also turned away from it, and Moderne Kunstkring declined.

Mondrian's involvement with Cubism is characteristic of his highly personal approach to various artistic tendencies of the 20th century. The Cubists' rejection of natural forms and their concept of painting as an autonomous discipline with its own order are fundamental characteristics of Mondrian's work between 1911 and 1915. In the series of paintings and drawings of Parisian façades, he adopted a particular autonomy of expression and distance from naturalism. From 1912 he ceased giving individual titles to his works, using instead the general designation 'composition'. The purpose of this was to allow the observer to experience the work as the expression of a 'higher sentiment', for example 'magnificence' or 'monumentality'. Mondrian's treatment of the subject 'starlit night over the sea' represents his definitive departure from Cubism: for example in *Composition No. 10* (see fig. 2) from the 'Pier and Ocean' series, by adopting an 'overall' pattern of horizontal and vertical 'lines' he achieved an expression characterized in the art criticism of the day as 'a sacred voice'. The experience of the painting as an image regardless of its naturalistic basis makes plain how he had progressed towards a completely autonomous kind of painting.

The outbreak of World War I in August 1914 forced Mondrian to remain in the Netherlands. After a short stay

1. Piet Mondrian: *Church at Domburg*, oil on canvas, 1114×750 mm, 1910–11 (The Hague, Haags Gemeentemuseum)

2. Piet Mondrian: *Composition No. 10*, oil on canvas, 850×1080 mm, 1915 (Otterlo, Rijksmuseum Kröller-Müller)

in Domburg in 1914 and 1915 he settled in Laren, south of Amsterdam, a base for many intellectuals. He lived there briefly with the composer J. van Domselaer, whom he had known in Paris, who composed *Proeven van Stijlkunst* (completed 1915) as a result of conversations with Mondrian. He also met Bart van der Leck, Theo van Doesburg (1915) and the Christosophist Dr M. H. J. Schoenmaekers, whose latest study, *Het nieuwe Wereld-beeld*, had just appeared. Many of the book's ideas found points of contact with the aesthetic attitudes Mondrian himself had been developing since *c.* 1908.

2. INVOLVEMENT WITH DE STIJL, *c.* 1917–*c.* 1924. In 1917 van Doesburg founded the periodical *De Stijl: Maandblad voor nieuwe kunst, wetenschap en kultuur*, in which between 1917 and 1920 Mondrian published 'De nieuwe beelding in de schilderkunst' and 'Abstract en reele schilderkunst', an autobiographical account of his own development as a painter, with the apposite subtitle 'during a walk from the countryside to the town'. He explained in detail that the painting of the future must be the expression of universal cosmic order. In painting, these regularities could best be 'represented' by dynamically related line and colour. The painter's only but necessary means for achieving this are line, restored to its two fundamental aspects,

namely the horizontal and the vertical, and colour. Only the primary colours—red, blue and yellow—filled in with white and black were required in order to express universal light.

Mondrian did not intend his writings to be a formula for the art of the future, considering writing about art and making paintings to be two separate disciplines. For Mondrian the creative process was essentially determined by the cosmic principle of intuition, which defined all life. Writing about art served to make Mondrian more aware of the reality of the evolution that was expressed through making paintings: the writing concerns the works, without explaining them. The best illustration of this is Mondrian's work itself: not one single piece made while he was publishing his ideas in *De Stijl* is entirely in line with them. All the work from 1916 to 1920 is distinguished by an 'experimental' character. A specific concept was often expressed in several versions. The group of 'grid-paintings', where the composition is based on a regular division of the picture surface, usually into eight by eight fields or double that, explored the visual expression of vertical and horizontal lines without colour. Another series explored the expression of areas of colour without any lines. In these ways the paintings tested such elementary characteristics as symmetry or asymmetry.

After his return to Paris in 1919, it was clear to Mondrian that avant-garde art had been transformed since 1914. The artists grouped around *De Stijl* and *Nieuwe Beelding* were quite unknown in Paris. His activities in the first two years after his return were therefore directed towards finding a place for *Nieuwe Beelding* ideas in the Parisian art climate: for example the publication of *Le Néo-plasticisme* in 1920.

Although Mondrian's financial situation was very difficult in the first years in Paris—he often contemplated giving up painting—his works and ideas were well received not only there but also in Germany. His articles were published in French avant-garde journals, while a collection of his essays was published in 1925 by the Bauhaus press. On his 50th birthday in 1922 some friends organized a retrospective of his work at the Stedelijk Museum in Amsterdam. Two years later (1924) the Rotterdam Kunststichting put on a show of his work of the previous decade. His status as an internationally recognized artist was then generally accepted.

Mondrian's works of the two years following his return to Paris show a remarkable development. In a series of paintings exhibited at Léonce Rosenberg's Galerie de L'Effort Moderne, Mondrian abandoned the regular division of the painting surface into the 'grid paintings'. The composition was defined by several areas in the same colour—red, blue, yellow or white—placed asymmetrically in relation to each other, which strengthened the dynamic balance of the juxtaposition. The inclination to limit compositional elements increased in subsequent years. Two points of departure can be discerned in the composition of most of his later works: either one dominant colour (usually red) forms the axis around which areas in another colour (blue or yellow) are grouped, or there is one grey or white area in the centre of the composition around which small areas in the three primary colours are then grouped, often at the edge of the canvas. The size relationships of the different shapes play an essential part.

3. LATER CAREER, AFTER *c.* 1924. Van Doesburg's development of Elementarism, in which the diagonal was given a principal role from 1925, caused a definitive break between *De Stijl* and Mondrian. The last three short articles that Mondrian published for the periodical (1923 and 1924) showed that he was as militant as ever. He exhibited his work regularly in the Netherlands and Paris and in Germany, where his reputation increased considerably, thus significantly enlarging his opportunities for sales. An exhibition of the Société Anonyme, Inc. in 1926 displayed his works in the USA for the first time. He had his only one-man show in Paris in February 1928 at the Galerie Jeanne-Bucher, with drawings by fellow Dutchman Nikolas Eekman (*b* 1889).

During this period El Lissitzky created several opportunities for Mondrian: in Dresden he organized a one-man show for him in 1925 at the Galerie Kuhl und Kühn and incorporated his work in the 'Room for Constructive Art' at the Internationale Kunstausstellung of 1926. In Hannover in the 'Abstrakt Kabinett' (1927) at the Provinzialmuseum (now Niedersächsisches Landesmuseum) he placed two works by Mondrian on permanent show. In 1926 Mondrian was commissioned to design colour schemes for a small library in the house in Dresden of the collector I. Bienert. Though the three colour schemes were not realized, they are the only surviving examples of his *Nieuwe Beelding* ideas for colours in interiors (Dresden, Kupferstichkab.). He had given these ideas partial shape in his own studio in Rue du Départ, where the walls, painted white and light grey, were covered by red, yellow or blue cardboard squares in various changing arrangements, creating an impression of lightness, space and convenience. He had his studio photographed in 1926 to illustrate the article on *Nieuwe Beelding* and architecture that he published in that year in the new avant-garde periodical *I 10*.

Van Doesburg's introduction of the diagonal into the composition was probably the stimulus for a number of works by Mondrian that once again emphasize *Nieuwe Beelding*'s horizontal and vertical compositions: in particular the diamond-shaped paintings, of which *c.* ten were executed in 1925–33. Several colours dominate in the first. Subsequently the colour was limited to one, often only a small area, and there are three without any colour at all, just gradations of grey and white. This group was completed by *Composition with Yellow Lines* (see fig. 3), the first piece in which the lines, all four of different thicknesses, are in one colour only without the use of black. The development in this special group is also reflected in other works, with colour restricted in many paintings, usually to no more than two areas.

In late 1929 Michel Seuphor (*b* 1901) founded CERCLE ET CARRÉ in Paris, together with Joaquín Torres García. Mondrian published an important article as a statement for the movement in the first issue of the journal of the same name. Through Seuphor's activities Mondrian came to be in the centre of the group. Mondrian had already made three small models of set designs (1926; destr., see

3. Piet Mondrian: *Composition with Yellow Lines*, oil on canvas, 1933 (The Hague, Haags Gemeentemuseum)

Henkels, 1976, pp. 54, 56, 59) for Seuphor's play *L'Ephé-mère est éternel*, while in 1928 he produced a *tableau-poème* illustrating Seuphor's poem *Textuel* (for illustration see Henkels, 1976, p. 78).

Abstraction–Création was formed in 1931 as successor to Cercle et Carré, and Mondrian published a number of articles in its journal *Abstraction, création, art non-figuratif*. He began to write a book (unpublished) in which he claimed that the principles of *Nieuwe Beelding* could also be applied to social relationships (see Holtzman and James, eds, 1986, pp. 244–77). His work had a great influence on CIAM architects, who on several occasions sent messages of support to him from their annual meetings. A number of notable changes became evident in his work of the early 1930s. In many of them the composition is determined from the middle of the surface in a horizontal as well as a vertical direction. Colour often remains limited to one area. Several parallel lines, horizontal and vertical, some-times close to each other, sometimes further apart, sur-round a number of areas, such that the domination of one or two areas is enhanced and the dynamic relations become visibly more complex. There are often two areas in the same colour next to each other, which produce a field of tension with many smaller and larger grey or white areas.

Mondrian's reputation as 'the most modern' artist gained increasing strength among artists and collectors in the USA. Many of them visited him in his studio and bought and displayed his works. Harry Holtzman (1912–87) was among the artists who decided to see him personally in his studio (1934), resulting in a lasting friendship. At the same time there were friendly contacts with Ben Nicholson and Winifred Nicholson. One of Mondrian's best articles, 'Plastic Art and Pure Plastic Art', his first in English, appeared in *Circle: International Survey of Constructive Art* in 1937 through their mediation. Although Mondrian's market position was improving at the start of the 1930s, not least through Swiss architects' and collectors' interest in his work, the economic depres-sion did not pass him by. On the occasion of his 60th birthday a number of his friends arranged to buy *Compo-sition with Yellow Lines* and donate it to the Haags Gemeentemuseum in The Hague. The writings on Mon-drian's work published by his fellow artist Jacob Bendien in the first half of the 1930s are among the best on *Nieuwe Beelding* to be produced in Mondrian's lifetime. After recovering from a serious illness in 1935 Mondrian had to find a new studio because of the imminent demolition of the complex on Rue du Départ. He moved to a new studio at 278 Boulevard Raspail in March 1936. Although his recent work was exhibited at group shows in Oxford and London (*Abstract and Concrete*), the first time his devel-opment was shown to an American audience was at the exhibition *Cubism and Abstract Art* (1936) at MOMA, New York, which was helped by many loans from Dutch collections.

Mondrian's search for a new concept in the relationship of coloured areas and lines proceeded in the new studio. He was very well acquainted with developments in Nazi Germany, where his work was regarded as *entartete Kunst*. After the Munich Agreement of 1938, he was convinced his life and work were in serious danger as the conflict intensified. In anticipation of moving later to the USA, he

travelled with Winifred Nicholson to seek temporary shelter in London, where English friends had found a studio for him at 60 Parkhill Road. During the two years spent there, he completed various unfinished works brought from Paris. With the help of friends he began to translate various articles into English and started writing 'Art Shows the Evil of Nazi and Soviet Oppression' (see 1980–81 exh. cat., pp. 29–33). At this time he probably conceived the idea of a series of works whose titles would pay tribute to the cities where he had received hospitality (e.g. *Trafalgar Square*, 1939–43; New York, MOMA). The occupation of the Netherlands and the subsequent fall of Paris in 1940 prompted him to take up Holtzman's offer to go to the USA. Soon after German bombs landed near his studio, he left, arriving in New York on 3 October 1940, where he soon took a studio found for him by Holtzman at 353 East 56th Street. Mondrian's reputation had preceded him. For years before his arrival some of his compositions could be seen on permanent show at A. E. Gallatin's Museum of Living Art in New York. The artists associated with American Abstract Artists saw Mondrian as one of the most important founders of abstract art. He encountered once more many friends from the Netherlands, Paris and London. Two impulses seem to have influenced his visual creations to an impor-tant degree—the city of New York as the ultimate mani-festation of culture, 'the furthest from nature', and his acquaintance with the latest developments in jazz, where rhythm and counter-rhythm were displacing melody.

In his first year in New York Mondrian completed many works he had conceived in Paris and London. These show signs of the search for a new relationship between coloured areas and lines. In completing these works, he further emphasized the dynamic rhythm between the coloured areas in such a way that they attained an increasingly autonomous function within the composition. In his last completed work, *Broadway Boogie Woogie* (see fig. 4), within the horizontal and vertical lines the force towards more autonomy in the separate coloured areas becomes even stronger. This is the essential character of the unfinished last composition, *Victory Boogie Woogie* (1942–4; New York, priv. col., see Ottolenghi, 1974, pl. lxiv). In his last years in New York Mondrian achieved a great evolution in his work, and interest in his writings increased enormously. The journalist and artist Charmion von Wiegand (*d* 1984), who regularly visited him over a long period, assisted him in translating his articles, old and new, into English. In January to February 1942 a retro-spective exhibition was held at the Valentine Gallery. A year later Mondrian showed his latest compositions there, including *Broadway Boogie Woogie*, together with sculptures by the Brazilian Surrealist sculptor Maria Martins (1900–84). At the end of 1942 the museum curator James Johnson Sweeney had the idea of organizing a large retrospective exhibition at MOMA. Delayed by the artist's death, an exhibition was eventually held in 1945. As a tribute to Mondrian, his executor, Holtzman, opened his studio at 15 East 59th Street after his death for a few weeks for interested people and friends. Holtzman and Fritz Glarner photographed this studio in black-and-white and colour.

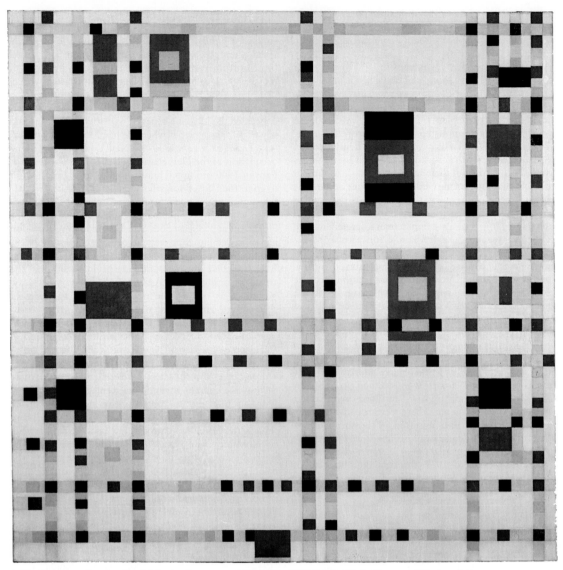

4. Piet Mondrian: *Broadway Boogie Woogie*, oil on canvas, 1.27×1.27 m, 1942–3 (New York, Museum of Modern Art)

Mondrian himself remained modest about the contribution he had made to his intended goal of achieving the union of art and life. In a letter to von Wiegand he expressed it thus: 'Shopping, I passed yesterday Second Avenue and saw the moon so nice in the still blue sky. *All* was in that. But all was also *mixed up*. So I felt again that men must come to be conscious of so much.'

II. Working methods and technique.

In his work in the late 19th and early 20th centuries, Mondrian showed himself to be an accomplished practitioner of *plein-air* painting, producing small oil sketches, as well as watercolours, often large-scale, pastels and drawings. Although the oil sketches frequently did not result in finished works, he did produce some monumental paintings, for example those conceived near Saasveld in 1906–7. Such work often developed themes through many

versions (e.g. the *Windmills*) or specific subjects studied from several viewpoints.

Piet Mondrian's work developed a strong expressive quality, particularly from 1908 to 1916, through his free handling of paint and the use of as many unmixed colours as possible, unconnected with each other; these were techniques adopted by such other artists as Jan Toorop and van Gogh (in his later work). His practice of sketching continued after he came under the influence of Cubism: for example, drawings in the pages of a small sketchbook show how Mondrian analysed visually the buildings in the surroundings of his studio after he moved to Paris (New York, Guggenheim; New York, Sidney Jarvis Gal.; The Hague, Gemeentemus.). A single viewpoint is fixed in the first sketch for the eventual composition of the painting in contrast to the Cubists' use of multiple viewpoints. However, in accordance with the Cubists, he restricted his use of colour in such works as those on the 'trees' theme (1912–13).

With Mondrian's final departure from Cubism, his paintings abandoned their dependence on naturalistic references. The primary colours and black and grey were employed in highly disciplined geometric arrangements that displayed total autonomy from external visual reality. The edges of the canvas were essential to the definition of the composition. Mondrian often used a recessed strip of wood along all four sides of the canvas as a 'frame' in order to make the canvas visually even more separate from the wall, which was also emphasized by tilting the canvas. He first tried this in *Composition with Grey Lines* (1918; The Hague, Gemeentemus.). The complex process by which he composed his works is illustrated by his use of coloured tape in the production of works after his move to New York. After setting down the basic principles of the composition, the use of tape enabled him to refine the details of the dynamic relationship between the work's various coloured areas. Mondrian endlessly moved the pieces of tape in relation to each other until exactly the right dynamic was found. His preoccupation with the development of composition is exemplified by his decoration of the walls of his studio with coloured shapes. These certainly performed a function in the work process, their arrangement changing soon after one group of paintings was completed and a new group was conceived. Indeed, visitors were struck by the relationship between the studio and the works within it.

UNPUBLISHED SOURCES

London, Tate [correspondence with Hepworth and Ben Nicholson]

The Hague, Gemeentemus. [correspondence with S. B. Slijper and Winifred Nicholson]

The Hague, Rijksbureau Ksthist. Doc. [correspondence with van Doesburg]

New Haven, CT, Yale U., Beinecke Lib. [manuscripts]

Paris, Fond. Custodia, Inst. Néer. [correspondence with Oud]

WRITINGS

Le Néo-plasticisme (Paris, 1920)

Neue Gestaltung, Bauhausbücher 5 (Munich, 1925/R 1974)

H. Holtzman, ed.: *Plastic Art and Pure Plastic Art, 1937, and other Essays, 1941–1943* (New York, 1945)

Two Mondrian Sketchbooks, 1912–1914 (Amsterdam, 1969) [facsimile with Eng. trans. by R. P. Walsh]

H. Holtzman, ed.: *Tutti gli scritti* (Milan, 1975)

H. Henkels, ed.: *Piet Mondrian, gedurende een wandeling van buiten naar de stad: Dialoog en trialoog over de Nieuwe Beelding* [Piet Mondrian, during a walk from the countryside to the town: dialogue and trialogue on the New Painting] (The Hague, 1986)

H. Holtzman and M. S. James, eds: *Piet Mondrian: The New Art—The New Life: The Collected Writings of Piet Mondrian* (Boston, 1986)

BIBLIOGRAPHY

GENERAL

J. Bendien: *Nieuwe richtingen in de schilderkunst: Het neo-plasticisme* [New directions in painting: Neo-Plasticism] (Amsterdam, 1935), pp. 21–45

C. L. Raggianti: *Mondrian e l'arte del XX secolo* (Milan, 1962)

C. Blok: *Piet Mondriaan: Een catalogus van zijn werk in Nederlands Openbaar bezit* (Amsterdam, 1967) [with extensive bibliog.]

H. Henkels, ed.: *Michel Seuphor* (Antwerp, 1976)

K. S. Champa: *Mondrian Studies* (Chicago, 1985)

H. Henkels, ed.: *From Figuration to Abstraction* (Tokyo, The Hague and London, 1988) [incl. articles by and interviews with Mondrian]

H. Henkels: *Mondrian Acquisitions, 1979–1988* (The Hague, 1988)

——: *Mondrian in the Sidney Janis Family Collections* (The Hague, 1988)

J. Milner: *Mondrian* (London, 1992)

T. Messer, ed.: *Two Roads to Abstraction: Mondrian and Kandinsky* (Barcelona, in preparation)

CATALOGUES RAISONNÉS

M. Seuphor: *Piet Mondrian: Life and Work* (New York and Amsterdam, 1956)

M. G. Ottolenghi: *L'opera completa di Mondrian* (Milan, 1974)

J. Joosten and R. Welsh: *Piet Mondrian: A catalogue raisonné* (in preparation)

EXHIBITION CATALOGUES

Piet Mondrian (exh. cat. by M. Seuphor and others, Amsterdam, Stedel. Mus., 1946)

Piet Mondrian (exh. cat. by L. J. F. Wijsenbeek and M. Seuphor, The Hague, Gemeentemus., 1955)

Piet Mondrian, 1872–1944 (exh. cat. by R. P. Welsh, Toronto, A.G., 1966)

Mondrian (exh. cat. by M. Seuphor, Paris, Mus. Orangerie, 1969)

Piet Mondrian: Centennial Exhibition (exh. cat. by L. J. F. Wijsenbeek and others, New York, Guggenheim, 1971)

Piet Mondrian, 1872–1944 (exh. cat. by L. J. F. Wijsenbeek, Berne, Kstmus., 1972)

Mondrian: The Diamond Compositions (exh. cat. by E. A. Carmean jr, Washington, DC, N.G.A., 1979)

Mondrian and Neo-Plasticism in America (exh. cat. by N. J. Troy, New Haven, CT, Yale U. A.G., 1979) [incl. correspondence with Katharine S. Dreier]

Mondrian: Drawings, Watercolours, New York Paintings (exh. cat. by H. Henkels and others, Stuttgart, Staatsgal.; The Hague, Gemeentemus.; Baltimore, Mus. A.; 1980–81) [Ger., Dut. and Eng.]

SPECIALIST STUDIES

M. S. James: 'Mondrian and the Dutch Symbolists', *A. J.*, xxiii/2 (1963–4), pp. 103–11

M. Shapiro: 'Mondrian: Order and Randomness in Abstract Painting', *Selected Papers: Modern Art, 19th and 20th Century* (New York, 1978), pp. 233–61

N. J. Troy: 'Mondrian's Designs for the Salon de Madame B. à Dresden', *A. Bull.*, lxii/4 (Dec 1980), pp. 640–47

Y. A. Bois: 'Mondrian et la théorie de l'architecture', *Rev. A.* [Paris], 53 (1981), pp. 39–52

H. Henkels: 'Must Architecture Be Inferior to Painting? Mondrian's Challenge to Architecture', *De Stijl—Neo-Plasticism in Architecture* (Delft, 1983), pp. 162–75

Y. A. Bois: 'New York City I, 1942 de Piet Mondrian', *Cah. Mus. N. A. Mod.*, 15 (1985), pp. 60–85

H. Henkels: *La Vibration des couleurs: Mondrian, Sluyters, Gestel* (Winterswijk, 1985)

C. Boekraad: 'Mondrian maquette: Nieuw onderzoek naar het atelier aan de Rue du Départ', *Archis*, 5 (1988), pp. 28–37

H. Henkels, ed.: *'T is alles een grote eenheid, Bert': De vriendschap tussen A. van den Briel en Mondrian* (Haarlem, 1988)

E. Hoek: 'Mondrian in Disneyland', *A. America*, li (Feb 1989), pp. 136–43

C. de Mooy and M. Trappeniers: *Mondrian: Een jaar in Brabant, 1904–1905* (Zwolle, 1990)

D. Shapiro: *Mondrian's Flowers* (New York, 1991)

H. HENKELS

Mone [Monet], **Jean** [Jan; Jehan] (*b* Metz, *c.* 1485–90; *d* ?Mechelen, ?1549). Sculptor from Lorraine, active in the southern Netherlands. In 1512 and 1513 he executed four stone statues for the portal of the cathedral of Aix-en-Provence (destr. 1794). The classicizing pilasters sculpted by Jean Guiramand (*d* 1557) for the walnut doors of the cathedral were a significant early influence, exemplifying the Renaissance forms that Mone was to develop in the Netherlands. In 1516, probably after a stay in Italy, he worked in Barcelona, from 1517 to 1519 as assistant to Bartolomé Ordóñez in the decoration of the choir of the cathedral of S Eulalia. This collaboration was a decisive influence on Mone's style. In 1521 he was in Antwerp, where Albrecht Dürer drew a portrait of him.

In 1522 Mone was appointed sculptor to the Holy Roman Emperor Charles V; from then on his career flourished under the patronage of the Emperor and his court. Between 1522 and 1526 Mone executed some important works for the Celestine church at Heverlee, the foundation of Charles V's former tutor Guillaume de Cröy, Seigneur de Chièvres. The alabaster and parcel gilt tomb that Mone made for him and his wife is destroyed, but engravings and descriptions bear witness to several stylistic and iconographical innovations. An even more advanced funerary monument, that to the Seigneur de Chièvres's nephew *Cardinal Guillaume de Cröy*, was erected in the same church in 1525–8; its attribution to Mone is supported by historical evidence as well as stylistic analysis. It is an alabaster wall monument in the Italian style, a prototype being Andrea Sansovino's monument to *Cardinal Ascanio Sforza* (Rome, S Maria del Popolo), and its structure, themes, ornamentation and treatment were new to the Netherlands. Among the themes depicted are the *Last Judgement*, the *Evangelists* (inspired by the engravings of Agostino dei Musi after Giulio Romano) and *Our Lady of Toledo*, as well as a figure of the Cardinal reading and an allegorical frieze depicting his misfortunes. The ornamentation is purely Renaissance and includes some fine panels of grotesques; the entire work is executed in a flowing, sensitive style, graceful in the free-standing sculpture and extremely delicate in the *schiacciato* reliefs. The monument, which was damaged during the French Revolution (1789–95), is now in the Capuchin church at Enghien in Belgium. From 1524 onwards Mone bore the title of Artiste de l'Empereur and lived in Mechelen, where he had been invited by Margaret of Austria. The town helped him to buy a house and gave him a pension until 1549.

After his work at Heverlee, Mone took on the decoration of the château of Hoogstraten and revised the plans for the Brugse Vrije chimney-piece (Bruges, Vrije Mus.). By 1533 he had become Maître-artiste de l'Empereur, signing himself thus on his best-preserved work, the alabaster altar at Notre-Dame-de-Hal (see fig.). Although the structure of this monument is less satisfactory, its technique and style are excellent and fully imbued with a 15th-century Italian tradition, as is the ornamentation. In the tondi of the *Seven Sacraments* the influence of Ordóñez is clear, although Mone was more classical. His draperies have a remarkable fluidity. The figures of the *Evangelists* and of the *Fathers of the Western Church*, which stand in the recesses, are reminiscent of those in the monument to *Cardinal Guillaume de Croy*. In 1536 the executors of the will of Philip the Fair of Burgundy (1478–1506) commissioned from Mone an altarpiece for the chapel in the palace at Brussels: it was completed in 1537 but replaced in 1541 by a 'richer' work and has been identified as the altarpiece of the *Passion* now in Brussels Cathedral. If the alabaster reliefs in an architectural setting of precious marbles are in fact by Mone, they indicate a development towards a more pictorial space, with *schiacciato* backgrounds.

Mone probably executed the tomb of *Antoine de Lalaing* (*d* 1540) and his wife *Isabeau de Culembourg* (*d* 1555) in the church of St Catherine at Hoogstraten, as well as that of *Maximilien de Hornes* (*d* 1542) in St Rémy at Braine-le-Château. Their attribution to Mone, first suggested by Destrée (1908), is further supported by publication of the contract for the tomb of *Guillaume de Cröy, Seigneur de Chièvres* (Valvekens). The recumbent figures in these three

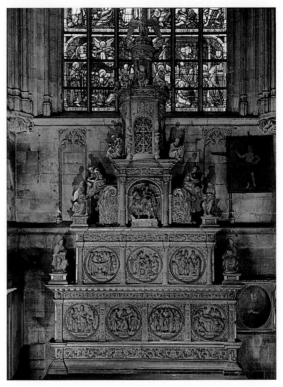

Jean Mone: altar, alabaster, 1533 (Notre-Dame-de-Hal)

monuments are in traditional attitudes, but their costumes, the fabrics of which are embroidered with grotesque motifs, and the secondary figures, notably the childlike putti, are indications of a new approach. Mone was among the first Italianizing artists in the Netherlands; he was also one of the most famous, and his works reveal sensitivity and a perfect understanding and assimilation of the forms introduced during the Renaissance.

BIBLIOGRAPHY
BNB
A. Sanderus: *Chorographie sacra Brabantiae* (1662), between pp. 142 and 143
J. Destrée: 'Jean Mone', *Bull. Mus. Royaux A. Déc. & Indust.*, n. s. 1, (1908), pp. 46–7, 63–4
E. Hensler: 'Die Grabdenkmäler von Jean Mone', *Belgische Kunstdenk-mäler*, ed. P. Clemen, ii (Munich, 1923), pp. 91–112
D. Roggen: 'Jehan Mone: Artiste de l'empereur', *Gent. Bijdr. Kstgesch. & Oudhdknd.*, xiv (1953), pp. 207–47
P. Valvekens: 'Nieuwe gegevens over Jan Mone', *Jb. Gesch. Oudhdknd. Kring Leuven & Omgev.*, xxiii (1983), pp. 3–69

LYDIE HADERMANN-MISGUICH

Monegro, Juan Bautista de (*b* Toledo, *c.* 1541; *d* Toledo, 16 Feb 1621). Spanish sculptor and architect. He was the half-brother of the painter Luis de Carvajal. Monegro began his career as a sculptor in wood and stone in Toledo in 1567, subsequently designing altarpieces. His first known work is the statue of *St Leocadia* (1575; Toledo, Mus. Santa Cruz), followed by a *St Julian* at the Puente de S Martín, Toledo. In 1577 he carved wooden figures of *Virtues* and *Prophets* for the principal retable of S Domingo el Antiguo, to designs by EL GRECO. He also executed the three altarpieces there, correcting the proportions and details of the painter's scheme. In 1579 Monegro designed and sculpted the retable of the convent of S Clara, with a crucifix and paintings of the donors. His most important works as a sculptor were created for the monastery of the Escorial (*see* ESCORIAL, §3). There he carved in granite the six gigantic *Kings of Judah* (h. *c.* 5 m; 1580–84) on the façade of the basilica, the enormous *St Lawrence* in white stone (h. *c.* 4.2 m; 1582–3) on the main façade and the *Evangelists* in marble in the main cloister (1589–93). Other important sculptural works attributed to Monegro or his studio include the bust of *Gianello Turriano* (Toledo, Mus. Santa Cruz), the funeral monuments of *Pedro Soto Cameno* (Toledo, S Pedro Mártir) and *Francisco de Eraso and Mariana de Peralta with St Francis* for Mohernando Church (now in Sigüenza, Mus. Dioc.). The last is an imitation of his documented monument of the *Condes de Barajas* (1587; destr.), erected in Barajas, near Madrid. His sculpture reflects the introduction of the style of Pompeo Leoni into Toledo, with its Escorial-type classicism. Nevertheless, Monegro did not completely break with the Toledan style epitomized in the early Mannerist tradition of Alonso Berruguete, since the heroic, serene quality of his figures is modified, especially in his early and late works, by their complex, mannered poses and voluminous robes.

A similar evolution can be noted in Monegro's style of retable design. His complicated structures of the 1570s gave way to simpler compositions, such as the main retable (1591) in the church of the Concepción Francisca in Toledo, the retable (1603; destr.) of S María de Ocaña, Madrid, and that (1605) of the Meneses Chapel in S Isabel de los Reyes, Toledo, as well as the main retable (1607) of S Pedro Mártir, Toledo. The influence of Juan de Herrera's retable in the Escorial is evident in this movement towards strictly classical structures. There is originality in Monegro's new type of funeral monument, which lacks statuary and which is reduced to a simple model of a casket with a pyramid inside a niche, for example *Fernando Niño de Guevara* (1612) in the Hieronymite church of S Pablo, Toledo.

Monegro came to architecture later, when he was appointed Master of the Works at the Alcázar in Toledo (1591) and at Toledo Cathedral (1606). His commissions soon multiplied, beginning with S Antonio de Padua (1594) and the Capilla Ovalle (1597) of S Vicente Mártir, both in Toledo. In Madrid he designed the church of La Merced (1598; destr.), a work of pure classicism in the new manner of ESTILO DESORNAMENTADO established by Herrera and Nicolas Vergara (ii). His design for a portal (1605) at S Juan de los Reyes, Toledo, to be built on the lines of a triumphal arch, reverts to the Gothic style of the 15th-century building. His final works return to a greater ornateness and spatial complexity. They include the portals of S Pedro Mártir and the Sagrario (1608) of Toledo Cathedral, where he followed retable designs by El Greco, the hermitage (1611) of the Virgen de la Estrella, Toledo, with the first known example of a *camarín*, and the completion of the chapel of the Virgen del Sagrario in Toledo Cathedral (1608–21)—a work in which wall decoration using hard stones with polychrome effect occurs for the first time.

Monegro was a highly cultured man: an antiquarian and inventor, he also contributed to contemporary artistic debates. Although his apprenticeship had been based on the Toledan tradition of the mid-16th century, he was able to adapt to the new artistic influences entering Spain without, however, definitively renouncing the use of decoration—the chief characteristic of late Spanish Mannerism and exemplified at the Escorial.

BIBLIOGRAPHY

V. García Rey: 'Juan Bautista Monegro, escultor y arquitecto: Datos relativos a su vida y sus obras', *Bol. Soc. Esp. Excurs.*, xxxix (1931), pp. 109–25, 183–9; xl (1932), pp. 22–38, 236–44; xli (1932), pp. 129–45; xli (1933), pp. 140–52, 204–24; xlii (1934), pp. 202–33; xliii (1935), pp. 211–37; xliv (1935), pp. 53–72, 214–36

B. G. Proske: *Pompeo Leoni: Work in Marble and Alabaster in Relation to Spanish Sculpture* (New York, 1956)

J. M. de Azcárate: *Escultura del siglo XVI*, A. Hisp., xiii (Madrid, 1958)

F. Marías: *La arquitectura del renacimiento en Toledo, 1541–1631*, 4 vols (Toledo, 1983–6)

FERNANDO MARÍAS

Monemvasia [anc. Minoa]. Site of a Greek city on the east coast of the Peloponnese, *c.* 32 km north of Cape Malea, built on a precipitous promontory 1.6 km long and 200 m high (see fig. 1), which is joined to the mainland by a strip of land and formerly a bridge (destr. 19th century).

1. HISTORY. The city was founded around the time of the Slav invasions of the 6th century AD by the inhabitants of Sparta, who emigrated there with their bishop. The privileges and institutions enjoyed by Monemvasia (Gr.: 'only entrance') gave the city a semi-autonomous status, and its port, used for both military and commercial purposes, was an important link connecting Constantinople (now Istanbul) with Sicily and Italy. Little is known of the period from the 6th to the 11th centuries, but during the 12th, 13th and 14th centuries, despite a brief Frankish occupation, Monemvasia grew into one of the most prosperous cities and ports of the Byzantine empire. 'Malmsey' wine originated from this area. A series of imperial documents offered the city and its ecclesiastical

1. Monemvasia, view from the west

see exceptional privileges; safeguarding these was a primary concern for many centuries. After the fall of Byzantine Morea or Peloponnese to the Turks in 1460, the city declined; it came under the control of Pope Pius II from 1460 to 1462 and of Venice from 1462 to 1540, when it fell to the Turks. Venice recaptured it in 1690. In 1715 it surrendered to the Turks and was liberated in 1821 by the Greeks.

Several icons of various periods have been preserved, among them the large and important *Crucifixion* (Athens, Byz. Mus.), dating from the last third of the 14th century and possibly painted in Mystras, from the Metropolitan church (*see* §2(ii) below). A 15th-century embroidery, an *epitaphios*, belonging to the Monemvasiot Nikolaos Eudaimonoiannis, the imperial ambassador to central Europe, is preserved in the Victoria and Albert Museum, London.

2. URBAN DEVELOPMENT. Monemvasia is in two parts, both fortified: the upper city on the sloping plateau on the cliff top and the lower city, hidden from the mainland on the south-east side of the rock. Both are characterized by the continuity of building methods that date to Late Antiquity, and some details of the houses are peculiar to Monemvasia.

(i) Upper city. Formerly exclusive to the aristocracy, the upper city occupies an area 600×300 m, running from east to west. There are two fortified ascents into it, one from the lower city and the other from the north, protected by a typical 6th-century rectangular fort with corner towers, built at the highest point of the rock where it also defended the bridge. The north entrance has been sealed by the 'Mura Rossa', the wall built by the Turks after an unsuccessful attempt by the Knights of St John (Knights Hospitaller) to capture the city in 1564.

2. Monemvasia, church of the Hodegetria (now Hagia Sophia), 12th century

The upper city may have been built to a grid plan, following Roman tradition, which is also suggested by the extensive use of vaults. Although the layout is no longer clear, there were probably two main streets running the length of the site. The only known square or open space is the area inside the main gate to the lower town; this has altered in size and shape over the centuries. The upper city does not seem to have been very densely built, and the houses, which may have had gardens, formed clusters rather than lining the streets. Important mansions of two storeys, sometimes fortified, were the dominant buildings. Not far from the fort a 'palace' survived until the end of the first Venetian period. The large number of surviving cisterns indicate that there was no need for a public water supply or baths. Existing buildings were extensively modified by the Turks, who did not allow Greeks to live in the upper city. All but one of the churches and monasteries have disappeared, and the surviving church of the Hodegetria (now Hagia Sophia; see below) was converted to a mosque. Smaller houses were built, but they were more densely clustered; and public cisterns were created out of the ruins of other buildings. When the Turkish population left in 1690 the upper city was abandoned; during the second Venetian period some houses were repaired and used by the garrison and officials, and, when the Turks returned, they used a very few houses, which were abandoned after 1821. The upper city gradually fell into ruin, with the exception of Hagia Sophia.

Hagia Sophia (formerly the Hodegetria; see fig. 2) was possibly attached to a monastery. Built in the 12th century, it is different from all the other churches, being a domed octagon church constructed in a combination of sandstone and limestone, with extreme delicacy in its tracings. Stylistically it is similar to the katholikon at Dafni. Shortly after the completion of Hagia Sophia, a two-aisled gallery was added on the south side. The marble sculpture is technically accomplished and features a wide variety of patterns, some of a classicizing nature. Birds and animals decorate the lintels of doors and windows; the figure of a female dancer that embellishes one window has been identified as Salome. Similarities have been noted between these sculptures and the work at Hosios Meletios (completed before 1100) on Mt Hymettos. Some wall paintings in Constantinopolitan style survive. The most important is in the prothesis and shows scenes from the *Life of St Nicholas*, whose relics were transported to Bari via Monemvasia in 1087.

(ii) Lower city. All business activities were concentrated in the lower city. A main street, the Agora, still follows the line of the medieval commercial street through the middle, but the commercial area probably extended to other parts and down to the sea-gate, where there was a small port or pier. The original street layout may have been a grid, but it has undergone many changes, and former streets are sometimes discovered incorporated in houses. The main (possibly only) square was in the centre of the town in front of the Metropolitan church (see below). At least one monastery (?10th century; destr.) and a large number of small churches were built, of which 27 survive or can be traced despite subsequent rebuildings; they mostly date from the first centuries of the city's existence. A cistern

with marble columns, known as Katechoumena, also survives and may have originally belonged to the monastery. Shops and workshops were small and vaulted, with dwellings above them. No traces of non-residential buildings of the Byzantine period survive, except for the ruin of a building considered by local tradition to have been the palace of Andronikos II (*reg* 1282–1328). Constructions concerned with the function of the port were probably distributed at various points on the rock and the mainland.

During the 14th century the city expanded to the foot of the cliff, and walls were restored in the 1430s. With the collapse of the Byzantine empire and the Turkish invasion of the Morea, Monemvasia lost much of its territory and commercial markets, and it shrank. During the first Turkish period (1540–1690) the lower city was inhabited by both Greeks and Turks; there was extensive rebuilding of houses and the city walls. In the second Venetian period (1690–1715) most of the churches and almost all the houses were rebuilt. During the second half of the 19th century and the early 20th two large squares were created, properties were joined together, a number of houses were rebuilt and some areas of the city abandoned.

Despite the continuous cycle of decay and rebuilding, construction methods in Monemvasia have remained more or less unchanged for centuries. Houses in the lower city are usually three-storey with cisterns and vaulted cellars in the ground floor, domestic quarters on the two upper storeys and wooden roofs. Rain-water collected from the roofs supplies the cisterns by way of open, almost horizontal gutters and built-in vertical clay ducts, a system apparently unique to Monemvasia. Terraces have been extensively used. Since 1966 several buildings have been restored by H. A. Kalligas and A. G. Kalligas.

The Metropolitan church (founded 6th–7th century; rebuilt 11th century) is a large basilica dedicated to Christos Elkomenos, with dependent buildings. It was originally built with three aisles and a wooden roof; in the 11th century the windows were transformed into Middle Byzantine double windows, and the iconostasis was remodelled at the same time. In the 16th century the church was vaulted. A dome, narthex and carved wooden iconostasis were added in the second Venetian period. Almost all the other churches in the city were simple vaulted buildings with walls of rough limestone and vaults, doors and windows of hewn sandstone. Although wall paintings have not survived in the Metropolitan church they are preserved in several others, for example Hagios Nikolaos (10th century) near the Agora; figures of saints (13th century) in Hagios Andreas; the *Birth of the Virgin* and other figures (15th century) in the church of the Forty Martyrs.

BIBLIOGRAPHY

R. Traquair: 'Laconia: i. The Mediaeval Fortresses', *Annu. Brit. Sch. Athens*, xii (1905–6), pp. 270–74

W. Miller: 'Monemvasia during the Frankish Period', *Essays on the Latin Orient* (Cambridge, 1921)

K. Andrews: *Castles of the Morea* (Princeton, 1953)

P. Witteck: 'The Castle of Violets: From Greek Monemvasia to Turkish Menekshe', *Bull. SOAS*, xx (1957), pp. 601–13

H. A. Kalligas: 'The Church of Haghia Sophia at Monemvasia: Its Date and Dedication', *Deltion Christ. Archaiol. Etaireias*, ix (1977–9), pp. 217–21

——: 'I ekklisiastiki architektoniki sti Monemvasia kata ti B Enetokratia kai to katholiko parekklisi tis Agias Annas' [The ecclesiastical architecture of Monemvasia during the second Venetian period and the Catholic chapel of Hagia Anna], *Ekklisies stin Ellada meta tin Alosi, 1453–1850* [Churches in Greece after the fall, 1453–1850] (Athens, 1979), pp. 245–56

A. G. Kalligas and H. A. Kalligas: *Monemvasia* (Athens, 1986)

H. A. Kalligas: *Byzantine Monemvasia: The Sources* (Monemvasia, 1990)

——: *Engkomio pros to froorio ton ion: I Monemvasia ton 17o aiona opos tin idhe o Evliya Tselebi* [Encomium on the castle of violets: Monemvasia in the 17th century as seen by Evliya Çelebi] (in preparation)

——: *Evayi idhrimata ke latiniki naï sti Monemvasia yiro sto 1700* [Charitable institutions and Latin churches in Monemvasia, c. 1700] (in preparation)

H. A. KALLIGAS

Moneo (Vellés), (José) Rafael (*b* Tudela, Navarre, 9 May 1937). Spanish architect, teacher and theorist. His architectural studies at the Escuela Técnica Superior de Architectura in Madrid were complemented by an apprenticeship under Francisco Javier Sáenz de Oíza and Jørn Utzon and a place at the Accademia di Spagna in Rome. In his early career Moneo was connected with the Nueva Forma group and influenced by Expressionist and organic architecture, for example in his project (1961) for the Centro de Restauraciones, Madrid (in collaboration with Fernando Higueras), or the Fábrica Diestre (1964–7), Saragossa, more like Alvar Aalto's work in its alignments. The Edificio Urumea (1968), San Sebastian, however, is an early example of the contextual integration that became one of the overriding concerns of Moneo's later architecture. The Edificio Bankinter (1972–7), Madrid, with its explicit rejection of the Functionalism of the new office tower-blocks on the Paseo de la Castellana, its dialogue with an earlier urban architecture and its eclectic references and complex geometry, opened a new phase in Moneo's work, and the style was reaffirmed in the Ayuntamiento (1973–81) in Longroño. The Museo Nacional de Arte Romano (1980–85) in Mérida owes its conceptual message and formal motif to an evocation of Roman architecture; it is superimposed on the site's still existing archaeological remains (*see* MUSEUM, §II). In 1991 Moneo won the competition to design a new museum of modern art in Stockholm and the Lido Cinema Palace in Venice; other recent works included: the Pilar and Joán Foundation (1987–93) in Palma de Mallorca, Spain; the Davis Museum (1989–93) at Wellesley College, MA, and the Diagonal Block (1986–93) in Barcelona. He was also active as a teacher in Barcelona and Madrid, at the Cooper Union in New York and as dean of the Graduate School of Design at Harvard.

BIBLIOGRAPHY

J. Quetglas: 'La hermandad postrafaelista', *El Croquis*, xx (1985), pp. 12–15

R. Moneo: 'La soledad de los edificios', *A + U*, ccxxvii (Aug 1989), pp. 32–40 [text in Eng. and Jap.]

J. Quetglas: 'The Dance and the Procession', *El Croquis*, lxiv (1994), pp. 27–45

W. Curtis: 'Pieces of City, Memories of Ruins', *El Croquis*, lxiv (1994), pp. 47–66

JORDI OLIVERAS

Moner, Muntaner. *See* MUNTANER.

Monet, (Oscar-)Claude (*b* Paris, 14 Nov 1840; *d* Giverny, 6 Dec 1926). French painter. He was the leader of the Impressionist movement in France; indeed the movement's name, IMPRESSIONISM, is derived from his *Impression, Sunrise* (1873; Paris, Mus. Marmottan). Throughout his long career, and especially in his series from the 1890s onwards, he explored the constantly changing quality of light and colour in different atmospheric conditions and at various times of the day.

1. Life and work. 2. Working methods and technique.

1. LIFE AND WORK.

(i) The 1850s and 1860s. (ii) The 1870s and 1880s. (iii) The 1890s and after.

(i) The 1850s and 1860s. Although born in Paris, Monet grew up on the Normandy coast in Le Havre, where his father was a wholesale grocer serving the maritime industry. His mother died in 1857, whereupon his aunt, Marie-Jeanne Lecadre, supported his efforts to become an artist and encouraged him during his early career. By *c.* 1856 Monet had attained a local reputation as a caricaturist, attracting the interest of the landscape painter Eugène Boudin, who succeeded in turning Monet's attention to *plein-air* painting. After a year of military service in Algeria in 1861–2 he was released due to illness. In the autumn of 1862 he obtained his father's permission to study art in Paris, where he entered the atelier of the academician Charles Gleyre, studying with him intermittently until *c.* 1864. Of greater consequence for Monet's development was the friendship and informal tutelage of the Dutch landscape painter Johann Barthold Jongkind, whom Monet met in 1862. The combined teaching of Boudin and Jongkind proved formative for Monet's future direction as a landscape painter.

Two landscapes, deriving from his first year of active production in 1864 and worked up on a large scale, earned him, on his first attempt, admission to the Salon of 1865: the *Seine Estuary at Honfleur* (1865; Pasadena, CA, Norton Simon Mus., see Wildenstein, no. 51) and *Pointe de la Hève at Low Tide* (1865; Fort Worth, TX, Kimbell A. Mus., W 52). Monet's work appeared again at the Salon in 1866 and 1868, but, having been rejected in the intervening year and with further rejections in 1869 and 1870, he did not submit works thereafter except once, in 1880.

During the second half of the 1860s Monet became the key figure among a group of colleagues whom he had first met at Gleyre's atelier: FRÉDÉRIC BAZILLE, Auguste Renoir and Alfred Sisley. They occasionally made painting trips to Fontainebleau Forest, where in 1865 Monet began a daring project, his *Déjeuner sur l'herbe*, attempting to bring the freshness of outdoor painting to a canvas of life-size figures gathered at a picnic in the forest setting. The painting was intended to make his mark in dramatic fashion at the Salon of 1866, but, working in his Paris studio, he failed to complete the monumental (*c.* 4.5×6.0 m) canvas in time and was forced to send two other, less challenging, works, both of which were accepted: *Camille* (1866; Bremen, Ksthalle, W 65) and the *Pavé de Chailly* (*c.* 1865; Switzerland, priv. col., W 19). The canvas was rolled up and put aside and later partly ruined by moisture; two fragments of the final painting (both Paris, Mus. d'Orsay, W 63a–b) and a large (1.30×1.81 m) final sketch (Moscow, Pushkin Mus. F.A., W 62) are all that remain of this ambitious project.

In his next major painting, *Women in the Garden* (1866–7; Paris, Mus. d'Orsay, W 67; *see* DRESS, fig. 51), Monet sought to approach a contemporary subject on a large but more manageable scale (2.56×2.08 m), a canvas that would be executed from start to finish out of doors. Despite his efforts he failed to complete the work at the site, not finishing it until the following winter. Consistent with the shift from *plein-air* to studio, the finished painting demonstrates a flattened, decorative treatment of figures and space, aided by the introduction of delicately coloured blue shadows in a system of close-valued hue relationships that deviate from the traditional form-defining technique of chiaroscuro. It was probably such innovations that resulted in his first rejection when he submitted the painting to the Salon of 1867.

In addition to his professional setback at the Salon, Monet suffered grave personal problems during that year. His mistress, Camille Doncieux, whom he had met about 1865, was pregnant; his father, who disapproved of the relationship, refused to help financially, and Monet, all but penniless, was forced to leave Camille in Paris, while he accepted the shelter offered to him alone by his family in Le Havre. In July, as the birth approached, he suffered a partial loss of sight, preventing him temporarily from working out of doors and clearly a sign of his anxious state. But it was also a period of restless probing and experimentation in his art. Following the completion of *Women in the Garden* early in 1867, he pursued his interest in contemporary subject-matter, painting three views of Paris from the east balcony of the Louvre (e.g. *St Germain-l'Auxerrois*; Berlin, Neue N.G.; W 84) in which he further explored the nature of Realism as embodied in *plein-air* painting. In Normandy, despite the temporary problem with his sight, his work ranged from the powerful artifice of his *Terrace at Sainte-Adresse* (New York, Met., W 95; *see* IMPRESSIONISM, colour pl. VI, fig. 2), inspired in part by the style of Japanese prints, to the open, atmospheric naturalism of the *Beach at Sainte-Adresse* (Chicago, IL, A. Inst., W 92).

Aided by his first patron, Louis-Joachim Gaudibert of Le Havre, Monet was able to resume his life with Camille and his infant son Jean in 1868; *The Luncheon* (1868; Frankfurt am Main, Städel. Kunstinst. & Städt. Gal., W 132) depicts mother and child at table in their rented house near Etretat in Normandy. Camille also appears in the foreground of *The River* (1868; Chicago, IL, A. Inst., W 110), a work that offers a major statement of Monet's attempt to integrate *plein-air* investigation and stylistic experiment in the last years of the decade (*see also* OIL PAINTING, colour pl. III).

In 1869 Monet worked alongside Renoir at La Grenouillère, a popular boating and bathing spot on the Seine near Paris. Both artists were aiming once again towards the Salon, at which they hoped (as had Monet in 1865 with *Déjeuner sur l'herbe*) to make an impact with a large-scale depiction of a contemporary subject. Neither artist succeeded in producing such a painting, Monet ruefully referring to the 'bad sketches' with which he had to be content (letter to Bazille, 25 Sept). These sketches, however, became the hallmark of a new style of painting. In such works as Monet's version of *La Grenouillère* (London, N.G., W 135; *see* fig. 1) the traditional academic sketch

1. Claude Monet: *La Grenouillère*, oil on canvas, 730×920 mm, 1869 (London, National Gallery)

was in effect reinvented and converted into the Impressionist *tableau*. The fragmented, varied brushwork of this painting suggests the ephemeral character of the subject and reveals the means by which the illusion of the scene was created.

(ii) The 1870s and 1880s. Monet and Camille were married on 28 June 1870. During that summer the Franco-Prussian War broke out, and Monet fled with his young family to London in the autumn, in order to avoid conscription. There he renewed ties with Camille Pissarro, with whom he had painted in the Paris suburbs during 1869, and was introduced to Paul Durand-Ruel, who became his first dealer soon thereafter. During a stay of approximately nine months he painted numerous views of the Thames (e.g. the *Thames below Westminster*, London, N.G., W 166), *Hyde Park* (Providence, RI Sch. Des., Mus. A., W 164) and *Green Park* (Philadelphia, PA, Mus. A., W 165). Having spent the summer of 1871 in Holland, where he painted several splendid pictures in the style of *La Grenouillère*, he returned to a war-torn France further depleted by the bloody civil war over the Paris Commune. Late that year he settled at Argenteuil, a growing industrial town and boating centre on the Seine to the west of Paris, which was to be his home until 1878.

From 1872 to 1876 Argenteuil became the hub of Impressionist painting. Renoir, Sisley, Pissarro, Edouard Manet and Gustave Caillebotte were each drawn there in turn by the magnetic presence of Monet, whose paintings of the Seine, the interior of the town and the garden settings of his house placed their powerful stamp on the movement's evolution. During the first two years at Argenteuil, Monet profited from the support of Durand-Ruel, who began to purchase the paintings of Monet and his friends. When declining fortunes led Durand-Ruel to suspend his purchases towards the end of 1873, the painters revived the idea of holding an independent exhibition that they had first considered in the mid-1860s. Monet was one of the leading figures in the formation of the Société Anonyme des Artistes Peintres, Sculpteurs, Graveurs etc, which held its first exhibition in April 1874 at the recently vacated galleries of the photographer Nadar on the Boulevard des Capucines in the centre of Paris. Monet's views of Paris painted from the premises late in 1873 include the *Boulevard des Capucines* (Moscow, Pushkin Mus. F.A., W 292), which was shown at the exhibition at Nadar's. One of Monet's exhibited pictures, *Impression, Sunrise* (1873; Paris, Mus. Marmottan, W 263; *see* IMPRESSIONISM, fig. 1), a sketchy view of the harbour at Le Havre under morning fog, became the occasion for the naming of the group because of its title: they emerged from the exhibition dubbed by the critics the Impressionists. Although *Impression, Sunrise* was not typical of Monet's work at the time, it seems fitting that it played the role it did, for Monet was clearly the most powerful figure among the landscape and *plein-air* painters who dominated the group. His views of the Seine, such as the two versions of the *Bridge at Argenteuil* (1874; Paris, Mus. d'Orsay; Washington, DC, N.G.A.; w 311–12), have come to epitomize the Impressionist effort in the popular imagination just as they influenced his friends.

By 1876 Monet had begun to look for new subject-matter outside Argenteuil. Seeking new patrons and collectors, he accepted the commission of Ernest Hoschedé in 1876 to produce four decorative paintings for the grand salon of the Château de Rottembourg, Hoschedé's country home at Montgeron: *Turkeys* (Paris, Mus. d'Orsay, w 416), *The Hunt* (France, priv. col., w 433), *Corner of the Garden at Montgeron* and *Pond at Montgeron* (both St Petersburg, Hermitage, w 418, 420). In January 1877, turning his attention to Paris, he took up a subject that had attracted Manet and Caillebotte in the immediately preceding years; he obtained permission to paint at St-Lazare Station (at the Paris end of the line from Argenteuil), where he produced more than a dozen views of the station and its surroundings (see fig. 2), several of which

appeared at the Third Impressionist Exhibition in the spring, for example *Le Pont de l'Europe, Gare St-Lazare* (Paris, Mus. Marmottan, w 442; *see also* OIL PAINTING, colour pl. IV).

In 1878 the fortunes of Monet and the Impressionists declined sharply. An auction sale of Jean-Baptiste Faure's collection of Impressionist paintings brought low prices, as did the forced sale of Hoschedé's pictures following his declaration of bankruptcy the previous year. In the autumn Monet and Camille, along with Jean and their infant son, Michel, born in March, set up a joint household with the Hoschedés at Vétheuil on the Seine, about 65 km from Paris. Camille died in September 1879, and, as Ernest Hoschedé soon began to spend most of his time in Paris attempting to renew his fortunes, Monet was left as the head of a household including Ernest Hoschedé's wife Alice (his unacknowledged lover) and eight children. Harassed by a combination of personal loss and commitments and acutely beset by financial worries, Monet separated himself from his Impressionist colleagues, his work appearing at the fourth group show in 1879 only through the intercession of Caillebotte. In 1880 Monet followed the course taken by Renoir, Paul Cézanne and Sisley and approached the Salon once more in the hope of reaping financial benefits; one of his two submissions

2. Claude Monet: *Gare St-Lazare*, oil on canvas, 755×1040 mm, 1877 (Paris, Musée d'Orsay)

was accepted, a large view of ice floes on the Seine, *Floating Ice* (Shelburne, VT, Mus., W 568).

Following three years at Vétheuil and a short stay in Poissy, Monet, Alice Hoschedé and the children moved to a rented house in Giverny in 1883, achieving, despite the irregularity of their arrangement, a degree of domestic stability that he had never known before. Giverny was to be his home for the rest of his life; he was able to purchase the house in 1890, and in 1892 Alice became his second wife, following the death of Ernest the preceding year.

Even before settling at Giverny, Monet had begun a pattern of activity that he pursued throughout the 1880s. During the decade he made several painting trips to the Normandy coast, working at Fécamp in 1881, at Pourville and Varengeville in 1882 and at Etretat in 1883 and 1885. In 1886 he spent part of the autumn at Belle-Ile, off the south coast of Brittany, and in 1889 worked during the winter in the Creuse Valley of central France. Between these journeys, in which he engaged with rugged and dramatic scenery in the most changeable of weathers, he visited the Mediterranean, where he was challenged by the clear light and intense colour of the south at Bordighera on the French–Italian border in 1884 and at Antibes and Juan-les-Pins in 1888. These trips were designed to sharpen his sensibilities as a painter and to enlarge the range and appeal of his paintings for prospective buyers. At other times he concentrated on the landscape around Giverny and, during the second half of the 1880s, executed a number of outdoor paintings for which the Monet and Hoschedé children posed, for example *Woman with a Parasol, Turned to the Left* (1886; Paris, Mus. d'Orsay, W 1077).

(iii) The 1890s and after.

(a) The series paintings. At the beginning of the 1890s Monet began to elaborate and refine a process that he had begun during his journeys of the 1880s, when he had sought to develop extended groups of canvases devoted to specific sites under differing conditions of light and weather. On a given day, moving with the light and changing position as the weather shifted, he would work on perhaps as many as eight canvases, devoting an hour or less to each one (as he indicated, in an early instance, in a letter to Alice Hoschedé, 7 April 1882). By the end of the decade, working in the Creuse Valley, the programme of the series was all but fully elaborated.

The development of the series was Monet's great effort of the 1890s: they were a factor in all of his exhibitions during the decade. In 1891 *The Grainstacks* appeared at Durand-Ruel's gallery in Paris; in 1892, also at Durand-Ruel's, he presented his first exhibition devoted exclusively to a single series, the *Poplars on the Epte*. Later that year and again in 1893 he worked in Rouen; 20 of the 50 paintings shown at Durand-Ruel's in 1894 depicted the façade of Rouen Cathedral seen under varying conditions of light, weather and atmosphere (e.g. *Rouen Cathedral, the Façade in Sunlight*; Williamstown, MA, Clark A. Inst., W 1358; see fig. 3). There followed in 1895 a limited series done in Norway and, in 1896–7, a reprise of subjects painted earlier in the 1880s at Pourville and Varengeville and a major series of *Mornings on the Seine* (e.g. *Early Morning on the Seine, Morning Mists*; Raleigh, NC Mus. A.,

3. Claude Monet: *Rouen Cathedral, the Façade in Sunlight*, oil on canvas, 1.06×0.73 m, 1894 (Williamstown, MA, Sterling and Francine Clark Art Institute)

W 1474), representing the dawn hours on the river at Giverny. Both groups were shown in a major exhibition at the Galerie Georges Petit, Paris, in 1898. Three trips to London (where his son Michel was studying) from 1899 to 1901 yielded an extended series of *Views of the Thames*, including *Charing Cross Bridge and Westminster* (1902; Baltimore, MD, Mus. A., W 1532), the *Houses of Parliament, Stormy Sky* (1904; Lille, Mus. B.-A., W 1605) and *Waterloo Bridge, London* (1903; Pittsburgh, PA, Carnegie Mus. A., W 1588). After three years of reworking in Giverny they were exhibited at Durand-Ruel's gallery in 1904. A last journey was undertaken with Alice in 1908 to Venice, although the resulting pictures were not exhibited until 1912, a year after Alice's death, at the Galerie Bernheim-Jeune.

At Giverny, during the 1890s, Monet began to develop a large flower-garden in front of his house; in 1893 he acquired another parcel of land, just across the road and single-track railway that fronted the property, which included a small pond and a stream. He built an arched bridge, based on Japanese designs, across one end of the pond and received permission to control the flow of water entering from the stream, thus creating a receptive environment for the introduction of exotic species of waterlily. He enlarged the pond in 1901 and 1910. The house and water gardens became his dominant subjects for the rest of his life; they were designed mainly to fulfil his dream

4. Claude Monet: *Japanese Bridge and the Waterlily Pool—Giverny* (*Le Bassin et nymphéas*), oil on canvas, 892×934 mm, 1899 (Philadelphia, PA, Museum of Art)

that painting out of doors should be equivalent to working in a studio. He set up easels around the pond to enable him to work from different vantage-points and devoted himself to a continuous series of waterlily paintings from the late 1890s to 1910.

In 1900 Monet exhibited his first group of pictures of the garden, devoted primarily to the Japanese bridge (e.g. the *Japanese Bridge and the Waterlily Pool—Giverny* (*Le Bassin et nymphéas*), 1899; Philadelphia, PA, Mus. A.; see fig. 4). From 1903 to 1908 he concentrated on the enlarged pond with its floating pads and blossoms set in orderly clusters against the reflections of trees and sky within its depths. The results were seen in the largest and most unified series to date, a suite of 48 canvases known as *Waterlilies, a Series of Waterscapes* shown at Durand-Ruel's gallery in May 1909 and subsequently dispersed.

(b) The waterlilies decoration. During the 1890s Monet had begun to plan a decorative cycle of paintings devoted to the water garden and apparently made some first attempts in that direction. But it was only after a period of 15 years or so, after the final enlargement of the pond in 1910 and the death of Alice, that the plan was renewed. In 1914, encouraged by his close friend the politician Georges Clemenceau to overcome the weariness and depression that had persisted since Alice's death and the shock of his son Jean's death in February, Monet made plans to construct a new, large studio in which he could carry out the project on a grand scale. He persisted despite suffering increasingly from cataracts, which necessitated three operations on his right eye in 1923 and continual, variably successful, experiments with corrective lenses thereafter. Most of the work was done c. 1916–21, following completion of the studio, in which he installed his

large canvases on moving easels to approximate the oval shape of the scheme he envisaged, a continuous band of paintings of the pond that would entirely surround the viewer.

In 1918 Monet announced plans to donate the decoration to the State, and in 1920 it was decided that the Government would build a pavilion in the grounds of the Hôtel Biron (now the Musée Rodin) in order to provide a permanent installation. Within a year the site was changed: in April 1921 a new announcement specified the Orangerie, at the far end of the Tuileries Gardens from the Musée du Louvre, as the intended home for the murals. The two oval rooms, situated at ground-level on the south side of the building, were designed by the architect Camille Lefèvre. On 16 May 1927, five months after Monet's death, the decoration was opened to the public for the first time. Here the changeable, fragile natural environment of Giverny, created and nurtured by Monet over a period of almost 50 years, is given its synoptic form in paint. The Musée Claude Monet, his house and gardens at Giverny, was refurbished and opened to the public in 1981.

2. WORKING METHODS AND TECHNIQUE. During the 1860s Monet was primarily interested in furthering the Realists' concerns with the contemporary in subject and the verifiable in nature by assuming *plein-air* painting as a fundamental principle of his art. He sought to combine his Realist investigation with an inquiry into the possibilities of creating a new style of painting, following the lead that Manet had offered early in the decade. In the paintings produced at La Grenouillère in 1869 he found a way to resolve the often contradictory claims of nature and style, establishing a provocative tension between appearances and painterly invention that proved sufficient basis for the developed Impressionist manner of the 1870s and thereafter.

During the 1870s Monet's touch became softer, his strokes smaller and more varied. His palette tended towards a pastel range, with a play of warm and cool colours; at times he also employed a muted scale of greys—for example in response to dull weather (*Bridge at Argenteuil, Grey Weather*, 1874; Washington, DC, N.G.A., w 316)—or a harsh staccato of reds and greens, as in many sunlit garden pictures of the mid-decade at Argenteuil (e.g. *Gladioli*, 1876; Detroit, MI, Inst. A., w 414). By the mid-1870s he had all but eliminated black from his palette and reduced the role of earth tones as he sought to restrict value contrasts and effects of modelled form. These experiments with colour were played off against and within a traditional spatial framework, essentially perspectival in nature (e.g. *Gare St-Lazare*, 1877; Paris, Mus. d'Orsay, w 438).

At the beginning of the 1880s there was an identifiable change in Monet's choice of subjects, palette and approach to space. Notably in his paintings of the Normandy and Brittany coasts, for example the *Coastguard's Cottage, Varengeville* (1882; Rotterdam, Boymans–van Beuningen, w 732), he coaxed the large forms of cliffs and sea into cursive formulations—arabesques and broad, arching shapes—that served as decorative fields for an ever more refined, minutely particular application of coloured strokes. He became increasingly interested in harmonious distributions of warm and cool hues—varieties of pink, orange and mauve along with blues and greens (e.g. *Villas at Bordighera*, 1884; Santa Barbara, CA, Mus. A., w 856)—and in an overall organization based on the contrast of complementary colours, for example in *Field of Poppies* (1890; Northampton, MA, Smith Coll. Mus. A., w 1251), with its red meadow set before a row of green trees. His greatest challenge was the Mediterranean, at Bordighera in 1884 and Antibes in 1888, where he translated the brilliance of Mediterranean light into paintings such as the *Gardener's House, Antibes* (1888; Cleveland, OH, Mus. A., w 1165), which he feared would be sure to arouse the ire of 'the enemies of blue and pink' (letter to Durand-Ruel).

In the series of the 1890s and later he sought to convey the unifying effects of atmosphere (the *ambiance* and the *enveloppe*) and tended increasingly to reduce the identity of local colour in favour of decorative, chromatic harmonies, geared in part to natural effects but ultimately determined by the matching of canvas to canvas within the ensemble.

Early in his career, from about the mid-1860s, Monet began to work on canvases primed with a light-toned ground, most frequently a warm grey or light tan. He used a pure white priming only occasionally in the 1870s and then more frequently during the 1880s; after 1890, for the major series, he turned to white grounds almost exclusively. His method of building up his paintings was fairly consistent throughout his career, despite a gradual move towards a more complex microstructure and heavier texture after 1880 and in many of the series, most notably *The Grainstacks* and *Rouen Cathedral*. He would first lay down a preliminary *ébauche* (underpainting) in polychrome—the colours muted but matched to the basic tonalities of the subject, the strokes ranging from broad and contour-defining to a variety of quickly applied filler strokes for the main masses. From that base he would move (whether in a single day or over a period of days or even months) towards ever greater refinement, differentiation and definition of line, texture and palette, his colours becoming more complex and intense as he proceeded. The final product often provided a record of this process, as areas of the toned ground remained untouched to the end, as broad strokes from the early stages of the *ébauche* stayed visible alongside more elaborated applications, or as the texture of the brushwork from early stages made its presence felt in the final working, perhaps interrupting or affecting the adhesion of the later strokes and resulting in an unpremeditated chromatic and textural complexity of the finished painting.

Beginning in the 1880s, then more persistently and programmatically in the series after 1890, Monet brought more than one canvas to the site, the different canvases geared to differing conditions of light and weather; as the light changed he would put one canvas aside and pick up another, repeating the process when necessary. Perhaps the most deliberate use of this procedure was at Rouen in 1892–3 and in London in the years around 1900, when he painted from protected vantage-points, in the latter case from his window balcony at the Savoy Hotel, where he had perhaps as many as 100 canvases from which to choose. In later years he recalled that he would work on a single canvas 20 to 30 times. He did not, however, relinquish work in the studio. Although in interviews he insisted upon the primacy and even exclusivity of his activity outdoors, his letters to Durand-Ruel from the beginning of the 1880s clearly reveal his regular practice of reviewing and reworking his paintings once he returned from the site; the series, in particular, were completed and exhibited only after an often prolonged process, during which he continued to revise his canvases, comparing them with one another, seeking a unity of the ensemble of paintings before releasing them for exhibition.

Monet's drawings, notably the pencil drawings contained in eight sketchbooks at the Musée Marmottan, Paris, rarely played any part in the execution of individual paintings but were rather a means of quickly noting down subjects and motifs. He also made a small number of drawings from his paintings between 1880 and 1892 for publication in magazines such as *Vie Moderne* (e.g. *View of Rouen*, 1883, Williamstown, MA, Clark A. Inst.; after the painting of c. 1872, priv. col., W 217; see *Gaz. B.-A.*, n.s. 2, xxvii (1883), p. 344).

During his career Monet had no students, although an international colony of painters had gathered at Giverny by the late 1880s, including Lilla Cabot Perry and Theodore Earl Butler (*b* 1876). Closest to him, perhaps, was the American painter Theodore Robinson, who left a diary in which he described his contacts with Monet in the 1890s (MS., New York, Frick).

Monet's chief dealer throughout his career was the firm of Durand-Ruel. Although Paul Durand-Ruel's initial support in the early 1870s was soon halted due to financial difficulties, he resumed regular purchases of Monet's paintings in 1881, permitting Monet to begin his extended painting trips of the 1880s. Other dealers to whom Monet turned, usually against the wishes of Durand-Ruel, were Georges Petit, beginning in 1879, and, from 1887, Boussod Valadon, through their branch manager in Paris, Theo van Gogh. Thanks to their efforts and to Durand-Ruel's successful dealings in the USA from 1886, to which Monet was opposed, his prices rose impressively, permitting him to purchase the house at Giverny in 1890. From that time on his financial position was secured.

BIBLIOGRAPHY

EARLY SOURCES

E. Taboureux: 'Claude Monet', *Vie Mod.*, ii (1880), pp. 380–82
Le Peintre Claude Monet (exh. cat. by T. Duret, Paris, Salons *Vie Mod.*, 1880)
W. G. C. Byvanck: 'Une Impression', *Un Hollandais à Paris en 1891* (Paris, 1892; Eng. trans. in Stuckey, 1985)
M. Guillemot: 'Claude Monet', *Rev. Ill.*, xiii (15 March 1898; Eng. trans. in Stuckey, 1985)
F. Thiébault-Sisson: 'Claude Monet, les années d'épreuve', *Le Temps* (26 Nov 1900; Eng. trans. in Stuckey, 1985)
G. Grappe: *Claude Monet* (Paris, [1909])
M. Pays: 'Une Visite à Claude Monet dans son ermitage de Giverny', *Excelsior*, (26 Jan 1921)
G. Geffroy: *Claude Monet: Sa Vie, son temps, son oeuvre* (Paris, 1922, 2/1924)
M. Elder: *A Giverny, chez Claude Monet* (Paris, 1924)
L. Gillet: *Trois variations sur Claude Monet* (Paris, 1927)
L. C. Perry: 'Reminiscences of Claude Monet from 1889 to 1909', *Amer. Mag. A.*, xviii (1927), pp. 119–25
R. Régamey: 'La Formation de Claude Monet', *Gaz. B.-A.*, n.s. 5, xv (1927), pp. 65–84
Duc de Trévise: 'Le Pèlerinage à Giverny', *Rev. A. Anc. & Mod.*, li (1927), pp. 42–50, 121–34 (Eng. trans. in Stuckey, 1985)

MONOGRAPHS, EXHIBITION CATALOGUES AND CATALOGUES RAISONNÉS

M. de Fels: *La Vie de Claude Monet* (Paris, 1929)
Claude Monet (exh. cat. by D. Cooper and J. Richardson, ACGB, 1957)
Claude Monet (exh. cat., ed. W. Seitz; St Louis, MO, A. Mus., 1957)
J. P. Hoschedé: *Claude Monet, ce mal connu* (Geneva, 1960)
Claude Monet: Seasons and Moments (exh. cat. by W. C. Seitz, New York, MOMA (1960)
W. C. Seitz: *Claude Monet* (New York, 1960)
D. Wildenstein: *Claude Monet: Biographie et catalogue raisonné*, 5 vols (Lausanne, 1974–91) [complete cat. of ptgs and lett.] [W]
Paintings by Monet (exh. cat., ed. G. Seiberling; Chicago, A. Inst., 1975)
Monet Unveiled: A New Look at Boston's Paintings (exh. cat. by E. H. Jones, A. Murphy and L. H. Giese, Boston, Mus. F.A., 1977, 2/1987)
J. Isaacson: *Claude Monet: Observation and Reflection* (Oxford, 1978)
Monet's Years at Giverny: Beyond Impressionism (exh. cat., New York, Met., 1978)
Hommage à Claude Monet (exh. cat. by H. Adhémar, A. Distel and S. Gache, Paris, Grand Pal., 1980)
Claude Monet au temps de Giverny (exh. cat., Paris, Cent. Cult. Marais, 1983; Eng. trans., 1983)
R. Gordon and A. Forge: *Monet* (New York, 1983) [extensively illus. with good colour pls]
J. Rewald and F. Weitzenhoffer, eds: *Aspects of Monet: A Symposium on the Artist's Life and Times* (New York, 1984)
C. F. Stuckey, ed.: *Monet: A Retrospective* (New York, 1985) [with Eng. trans. of primary source materials and interviews with Monet]
J. House: *Monet: Nature into Art* (New Haven, 1986) [detailed study of working methods; numerous, excellent illus.]
Monet in Holland (exh. cat., preface R. de Leeuw; Amsterdam, Rijksmus. van Gogh, 1986)
Monet in London (exh. cat., ed. G. Seiberling; Atlanta, GA, High. Mus. A., 1988)
Monet in the '90s (exh. cat. by P. Hayes, Boston, Mus. F.A.; Chicago, A. Inst.; London, RA; 1990)
V. Spate: *Claude Monet: Life and Work* (New York, 1992)
——: *The Colour of Time: Claude Monet* (London, 1992)

SPECIALIST STUDIES

G. Clemenceau: *Claude Monet: Les Nymphéas* (Paris, 1928)
S. Gwynn: *Claude Monet and his Garden* (London, 1934) [early photographs]
G. H. Hamilton: *Claude Monet's Paintings of Rouen Cathedral* (London, 1960, Williamstown, MA, 2/1969)
I. Sapego: *Claude Monet* (Leningrad, 1969) [ptgs in St Petersburg and Moscow]
J. Isaacson: *Monet: Le Déjeuner sur l'herbe* (London, 1972)
J. Elderfield: 'Monet's Series', *A. Int.*, xviii (1974), pp. 28, 45–6
C. Joyes: *Monet at Giverny* (London, 1975, 2/1985)
S. Z. Levine: 'Monet's Pairs', *A. Mag.*, xlix (1975), pp. 72–5
——: *Monet and his Critics* (New York, 1976)
G. Seiberling: *Monet's Series* (New York, 1981)
P. H. Tucker: *Monet at Argenteuil* (New Haven, 1982)
R. R. Bernier: 'The Subject and Painting: Monet's "Language of the Sketch"', *A Hist.*, xii (Sept 1989), pp. 297–321
J. Pissarro: *Monet's Cathedrals: Rouen, 1892–1894* (New York, 1990)
R. Herbert: *Monet on the Normandy Coast: Tourism and Painting, 1867–1886* (New Haven and London, 1994)

For further bibliography see IMPRESSIONISM.

JOEL ISAACSON

Monfort y Asensi, Manuel (*b* Valencia, 1736; *d* Valencia, 1806). Spanish engraver. He was trained in the workshop of his father, Benito Monfort (1716–85), a printer, and he became a founder-member of the Valencian Academia de S Bárbara (1753), promoting engraving in that city. In 1762 he was made an Académico de Mérito at the Real Academia de S Fernando, Madrid, and in 1765 was appointed director of engraving at the Real Academia de S Carlos, Valencia, which was founded officially in 1768. He took up residence in Madrid, where he became the director of the Imprenta Real, from 1784, and in 1788 presented the 'Plan de grabadores del Rey', which led to the creation of the Real Calcografía in 1789. He was responsible for the illustration of important publications of the period, including the Spanish translation of the Roman historian Sallust's work (*La Conjuración de Catilina y la Guerra de Yugurta*, Madrid, 1772) and an edition (1777) of *Don Quixote*.

BIBLIOGRAPHY

Baron Alcahalí: *Diccionario biográfico de artistas valencianos* (Valencia, 1897), p. 28

J. Gil y Calpe: 'Noticia biográfica de Don Manuel Monfort y Asensi, primer Director de Grabado de la Real Academia de Bellas Artes de S Carlos', *Archv A. Valenc.*, xx (1934), p. 88

Marques de Lozoya: *Historia del arte hispánico*, v (Barcelona, 1949), pp. 59–110

P. Bohigas: *El libro español* (Barcelona, 1962), p. 263

E. Paez Rios: *Repertorio* (1981–3)

A. Tomás and M. Silvestre: *Estampas y planchas de la Real Academia en el Museo de Bellas Artes de Valencia* (Valencia, 1982)

J. Carrete, F. Checa and V. Bozal: *El grabado en España (siglos XV al XVIII)*, Summa A., xxxi (Madrid, 1987)

BLANCA GARCÍA VEGA

Monfreid, (Georges-)Daniel de (*b* Paris, 14 March 1856; *d* Corneilla-de-Conflent, Pyrénées-Orientales, 26 Nov 1929). French painter, wood-engraver and stained-glass designer. He enrolled in Paris at the Académie Julian in 1874 and the Académie Colarossi in 1882, attending the latter until World War I in order to work from live models. In 1880 he unsuccessfully submitted a landscape to the Salon in Paris; consequently he did no serious painting for several years. Having built his own boat, he went sailing in the western Mediterranean (1882–5). During the voyage he wrote seafaring tales that appeared in *Le Yacht* (1883–5) accompanied by his own illustrations. After returning to Paris, in 1887 he met Gauguin, with whom he became close friends. That year he painted his first finished canvases, views of Catalonia and the Languedoc, inspired by Neo-Impressionism (e.g. *Church at Angoustrine*, 1887; Paris, Mus. d'Orsay). At this time he also painted portraits of his first wife and of his friends. In 1894 he completed some interior designs with his friend Barbin in Algeria and in Tunisia (Hammam Lif, Casino), and in 1896 he designed some stained-glass windows. His only sculpture, *Calvary* (Vernet-les-Bains, Parish Church), was made in 1897. Monfreid exhibited at the Salon des Indépendants (1893–7) and at the Galerie Durand-Ruel (1899, 1901). After 1900 he painted fewer landscapes, preferring instead to concentrate on individual and group portraits and still-lifes, in which he often incorporated a motif from one of Gauguin's paintings. After visits to Algeria and Ethiopia in 1922–3, he again painted landscapes, where he emphasized the intensity of light and the contrasts of colour in the foliage. He was also a wood-engraver, illustrating the new edition of Victor Ségalen's *Des Immémoriaux* (Paris, 1921) and Gauguin's *Noa-Noa* (Berlin, 1926–8). In Gauguin's honour he painted *Hommage* (1925; Perpignan, Mus. Rigaud), in which he depicted his wife, his sister-in-law and himself surrounding Gauguin.

BIBLIOGRAPHY

R. Puig: *Paul Gauguin, G.-D. de Monfreid et leurs amis* (Perpignan, 1958)

Georges-Daniel de Monfreid (1856–1929) (exh. cat. by R. Cogniat, Paris, Gal. Spiess, 1976)

R. Le Passat and others: *Conflent*, 165 (1990) [issue ded. Monfreid]

AUDE PESSEY-LUX

Monge, Gaspard, Comte de Péluse (*b* Beaune, Côte-d'Or, 9 May 1746; *d* Paris, 28 July 1818). French mathematician, scientist and writer. He was a pupil first at the Collège de l'Oratoire in Beaune and then at the Collège de la Trinité (1762–4) in Lyon. At the beginning of 1765 he took up a position as a draughtsman and technician at the prestigious Ecole Royale du Génie at Mézières, preparing plans for fortifications and making architectural models. There, in response to the practical problems of designing fortifications, he formulated an efficient graphical procedure from which his descriptive geometry developed (*see* MILITARY ARCHITECTURE AND FORTIFICATION, §III, 2(iii)). He soon began teaching both mathematics and experimental physics, and in 1775 he received the official title of Royal Professor of Mathematics and Physics. From 1780 he was obliged to visit Paris regularly following his election to the Académie des Sciences as Adjoint Géomètre, and in 1784 he relinquished his post at Mézières completely. During this period he devoted much of his time to experimental chemistry, assisting Antoine Laurent de Lavoisier (1743–94). In the wake of the dissolution of the royal academies, the Revolutionary Convention appointed Monge in 1794 to a commission responsible for setting up a school to train engineers for the revolutionary army. Monge was an instructor in the resulting Ecole Centrale des Travaux Publics (from September 1795 called the Ecole Polytechnique). The new descriptive geometry taught by Monge was subsequently of great importance to Jean-Nicolas-Louis Durand, who in 1824 erected an obelisk to the memory of Monge, Etienne-Louis Boullée and Julien-David Leroy. In 1796 Monge was appointed to a committee of six to select the works of art that the looting French army would bring back to Paris. This marked the beginning of a political life that deprived him increasingly of time for teaching and that brought him into close contact with Napoleon I.

WRITINGS

Géométrie descriptive (Paris, 1799) [lectures]

Feuilles d'analyse appliquée à la géométrie (Paris, 1801)

Application de l'algèbre à la géométrie (Paris, 1805)

BIBLIOGRAPHY

F. Arago: *Gaspard Monge* (Paris, 1853, rev. 1965)

R. Taton: *L'Oeuvre scientifique de Gaspard Monge* (Paris, 1951)

P.-V. Aubry: *Monge, le savant ami de Napoléon, 1746–1818* (Paris, 1954)

RICHARD JOHN

Mongolia. Mongolia is a cultural area that stretches from the Hinggan Mountains of China in the east to eastern Central Asia and the Altai (Altay) Mountains in the west (see fig. 1). It is bounded by the Siberian taiga in the north and the Great Wall of China in the south. Mongolia is now politically divided. Most of the territory is included in Mongolia, an independent state from 1992 that had strong links to the former Soviet Union and was previously known as the Mongolian People's Republic and before that as Outer Mongolia. The southern and eastern portions of the region, known as Inner Mongolia, form the Inner Mongolia Autonomous Region (Chin. Nei Mongol Zizhiqu) of the People's Republic of China. A much smaller area to the north, around Lake Baikal, is populated by Buryat Mongols and forms the Republic of Buryatia.

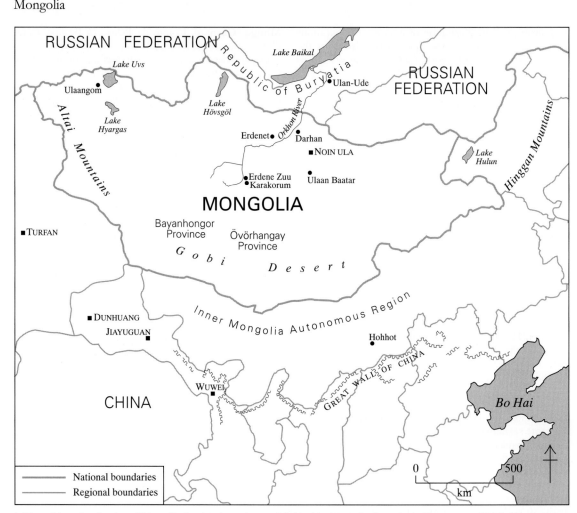

1. Map of the cultural region of Mongolia showing the main areas inhabited by Mongols; those sites with separate entries in this dictionary are distinguished by Cross-reference type

I. Introduction. II. Iconography and subject-matter. III. Architecture. IV. Other arts. V. Patronage. VI. Historiography. VII. Archaeology. VIII. Museums. IX. Exhibitions.

I. Introduction.

1. Geography, climate and ethnic groups. 2. History. 3. Settlement patterns and modern urban structure. 4. Trade. 5. Religion.

1. GEOGRAPHY, CLIMATE AND ETHNIC GROUPS. Most of Mongolia is a plateau between 1000 and 2000 m above sea-level. Its huge expanse of rolling steppe includes a variety of environments, ranging from well-watered grasslands in the east to the semi-desert of the Gobi and the mountain pastures of the Altai. Positioned in the centre of the Eurasian land-mass, Mongolia experiences an extreme variation of climate, ranging from a savage −40°C in the winter to 40°C in the hot summers.

Most Mongols speak mutually intelligible dialects of the same language, which belongs to the Mongol–Turkic group. There is little cultural variation between the different Mongolian ethnic groups. About three-quarters of the two million inhabitants of Mongolia are of the Khalkha ethnic group; 120,000 are Kazakh (a Turkish group); most of the remainder are from such Mongolian groups as the Buryat. In Inner Mongolia, the majority of the population is not Mongolian, but Chinese, most of whom migrated into the region from the 1950s. In 1984 they made up 83% of the Inner Mongolian population of 20 million, although they are mostly confined to the urban and agricultural population. The three million Mongols constitute only about a seventh of the region's population but, thinly dispersed throughout the countryside, still inhabit much of Inner Mongolia's steppe. Ethnic groups include the Oirat and Ordos Mongols in the west and in the east the Chahar, Uzemchin, Barga and Buryat. Mongols also live in the Chinese provinces of Liaoning, Jilin, Qinghai, Heilongjiang and Xinjiang.

Although many Mongols practise agriculture or live in cities, almost all of Mongolia is populated by people who still move their felt tents with their herds of animals. Today this migration involves a smaller yearly cycle than in the past, and people do not usually travel more than around 150 km from their local government settlement. At these centres there are government buildings, a school, a post office and some permanent dwellings (*see also* §3 below).

2. HISTORY. From as early as 1000 BC the grasslands of Mongolia were the home of a succession of nomadic pastoralist peoples. Renowned for their skills of riding and archery, nomadic warriors frequently invaded the agricultural states on their borders and founded by conquest many of the dynasties that ruled northern China, including the Liao (AD 907–1125), Jin (1115–1234) and Yuan (1279–1368). The first recorded steppe empire was that of the Xiongnu, from the 3rd century BC. The Han dynasty (206 BC–AD 220) felt so threatened by the nomads that the GREAT WALL OF CHINA was built as a defensive measure. Part of the Xiongnu migrated west and probably attacked first Germanic tribes and later the Roman Empire in Europe, where they became known as the Huns. A succession of other peoples formed confederations and empires that ruled the steppes until the 13th century, when a hitherto obscure tribe called the Mongols, under their leader Temujin (*reg* 1206–27), conquered the other nomads of the region and founded the Mongolian nation. Temujin adopted the title Genghis Khan (Mong. Chinggis Khan) and embarked on an unparalleled series of military conquests; by the time of his death he ruled Central Asia, Persia and northern China. The successors to his throne continued the Mongol advance, conquering Russia and southern China.

By the mid-13th century the Mongols ruled the largest empire in history, stretching from Hungary in the west to Korea in the east. Such a huge territory could not be efficiently ruled from Mongolia, and soon segments of the empire became independent. Kublai Khan—Genghis Khan's grandson—founded the Yuan dynasty (1279–1368) in China and accelerated the fragmentation of the Mongol empire by moving the capital from Karakorum in Mongolia to Beijing in China. The Yuan unified China by conquest, a unity that it has retained to the present day. The rest of the empire was divided into three states—the Chagadai Khanate stretched from the Altai to the Oxus, to the west of this lay the Il-Khanate of Persia, and the Russian steppe became the home of the Khanate of the Golden Horde, which ruled Russia until the end of the 15th century. Mongolia itself reverted to a nation of nomadic pastoralists and never again achieved the unity and strength it had possessed under Genghis Khan. In the 17th century the Mongols came under the rule of the increasingly powerful Manchus, who conquered the Ming dynasty (1368–1644) and took control of China as the Qing dynasty (1644–1911). By this time Mongolia had a social structure that resembled that of a feudal state: the aristocracy inherited fiefs of pasture land and administrative positions; the commoners owed fealty to their lord and were tied to his areas of grazing land. The Buddhist church became increasingly rich and powerful.

The Manchu emperors of China divided Mongolia into Inner Mongolia, which was close enough to be administered directly, and Outer Mongolia, which was ruled through the governor in the capital city of Urga (now Ulaan Baatar). When the Qing dynasty fell, Outer Mongolia took the opportunity to become independent of the new Republic of China. In 1921 a revolution brought a Soviet-style Communist government to power and Outer Mongolia became the Mongolian People's Republic. Despite a period of theoretical independence as a Japanese puppet state, Inner Mongolia was unable to become independent of China and since 1949 has been an autonomous region of the People's Republic of China. In the late 1980s the Mongolian People's Republic began a series of political reforms, as did other Soviet-style states, which resulted in democratic government. In 1992 the name of the country was changed to Mongolia.

DAVID SNEATH

3. SETTLEMENT PATTERNS AND MODERN URBAN STRUCTURE. The early nomadic tribes of Mongolia lived in *khürees*, or circles (an idea probably derived from earlier steppe nomad tribes, mentioned from 800 BC onwards), in the centre of which stood the elder's hooded cart (*gerlug*) surrounded by an encampment of *gers*, or tents, that provided a form of defence. The khans adopted this circular design from the start of the Mongol empire, but instead of the *gerlug* they built a palace (*bukh ord*) and monastic compound in the centre and surrounded the whole camp with a fortified wall or fence. The choice of site was governed by the principles of geomancy and by geographical and climatic considerations. Later settlements were established on the same sites because they were in prime positions with good access to water and other necessities. Most nomadic settlements moved countless times; for example, Nomyn Ih *khüree* (now Ulaan Baatar) had 21 different locations before becoming established on its present site in the 18th century. The traditional *khüree* design greatly influenced the system of urban planning in Mongolia and was the basic format until the 20th century. Under Russian domination most monastic towns were razed to the ground and new Soviet-style towns built.

Each of the 18 provinces (*aimags*) of Mongolia has its own capital city. Every province is subdivided into sections (*sum*), each of which has its own administrative centre, more akin to a village than a town. The three main cities in Mongolia in the late 20th century were the capital, Ulaan Baatar, the industrial centre of Darhan and the copper-mining town of Erdenet. A city's government and administration offices are situated in a central square dedicated to a national hero (*baatar*). Surrounding this is a geometric system of roads that subdivides the city into districts. High-rise concrete apartment blocks provide living accommodation, but the majority of the population still prefers to live in *gers* or wooden shacks in the suburbs.

ZARA FLEMING

4. TRADE. Trade was extremely important for such pastoralists as the Mongols, who gained the agricultural and urban produce they needed by exchanging their animal products. Since ancient times products such as silk, iron, tea and grain were bought from the sedentary populations to the south of Mongolia. Chinese dynasties usually attempted to control the trade that took place along China's northern borders so as to increase their influence on the steppes, and nomadic rulers in many centuries went to war in order to gain better prices for their products and other advantages in this trade. The Xiongnu raided the territory of the Han dynasty in the 2nd century BC and

wrung the right to trade at the frontier. The Xionbei also adopted this strategy in the 2nd century AD to increase the benefits and subsidies of trade, and Esen Khan of the Oirad Mongols did this to the Ming in the 15th century.

Lying just to the north of the eastern end of the Silk Route, Mongolia was strongly influenced by commerce (*see* SILK ROUTE, §2). From time to time the rulers of the nomadic pastoralists of the steppes moved to control the lucrative trade routes through Central Asia. The forests of Siberia to the north and Manchuria to the east were rich in furs and other valuable produce, such as silver and hardstones, and trade routes for these products lay across Mongolia. Despite these influences, Mongols traditionally did not specialize in trade. During the Qing period Chinese traders operated throughout the region, engaging in trade on terms that drove both common people and the administration of Mongolia into progressively deeper debt. When Outer Mongolia declared its independence in 1911 after the fall of the Manchu, one of the goals of the state was to break free from the debts it owed to Chinese merchants. Outer Mongolia favoured Russian merchants, and its successor, the Mongolian People's Republic, traded almost entirely with Soviet enterprises. In the early 1990s the newly democratic Mongolia sought to increase its international trade.

5. RELIGION. In the time of Genghis Khan (*reg* 1206–27), the Mongols worshipped a pantheon of deities and lesser spirits ruled over by Mönkh Khŏkh Tenger (Mong.: 'Eternal blue heaven'). Spirits of fire, rivers, lakes, forests and mountains were venerated, as were guardian ancestor spirits residing in small felt idols. The principal religious specialists were shamans who could communicate with these spirits through trances (*see also* SHAMANISM). Some of these ancient beliefs and practices still exist in some form, although there are few Mongolian shamans today.

Soon after the establishment of the Mongol empire in the 13th century, some Mongol rulers, including Kublai Khan, turned to Buddhism (*see* BUDDHISM, §II, 7) but most of their subjects retained their traditional religion. This situation lasted until the 16th century when Altan Khan (1507–82) made an alliance with Tibetan Buddhists of the Gelugpa sect and in 1577 gave their leader the title Dalai Lama. Altan Khan's conversion led to the gradual spread of Buddhism in Mongolia, while the Dalai Lama and his sect gained predominance in Tibet with Mongol support. Altan Khan made Buddhism the official religion, suppressing the old beliefs. As Tibetan Buddhism spread, shamans were persecuted and the felt idols burnt. Under Manchu rule lamaist institutions became enormously rich and powerful. Such monasteries as Erdene Zuu, Amarbayasgalant, Tugeemel Amarjuulagch in Khobdo (now Hovd), Ih Zuu in Hohhot, Inner Mongolia, and the Gandantegchinling Monastery in Ulaan Baatar supported artists who produced Buddhist art in the Tibetan style, as well as scholars.

The revolutionary government that took control of Outer Mongolia in 1921 considered the Buddhist church corrupt and exploitative. Monastery wealth was confiscated, and most of the monks were forced to do other work. The Buddhist clergy in Inner Mongolia was similarly suppressed after the Chinese Communist Party took control of the region and during the Cultural Revolution (1966–76). By the late 20th century, however, Buddhism was tolerated by governments in both Inner and Outer Mongolia and experienced something of a revival.

BIBLIOGRAPHY

EWA: 'Mongolian Art'
O. Lattimore: *Studies in Frontier History: Collected Papers 1928–1958* (London, 1962)
E. D. Phillips: *The Royal Hordes: Nomad Peoples of the Steppes* (London, 1965)
W. Heissig: *A Lost Civilization: The Mongols Rediscovered* (London, 1966)
C. R. Bawden: *The Modern History of Mongolia* (London, 1968)
W. Heissig: *The Religions of Mongolia* (London, 1970)
M. Rossabi: *China and Inner Asia (From 1368 to the Present Day)* (London, 1975)
J. K. Fairbank, ed.: *The Cambridge History of China*, x (Cambridge, 1978)
G. Tucci and W. Heissig: *Die Religionen Tibets und der Mongolei* (Stuttgart, 1970); Eng. trans. as *The Religions of Mongolia* (London, 1980)
M. Sanjdorj: *Manchu Chinese Colonial Rule in Northern Mongolia* (London, 1980)
N. Tsultem: *The Eminent Mongolian Sculptor, G. Zanabazar* (Ulaan Baatar, 1982) [text in Rus., Eng., Fr., Sp.]
D. Morgan: *The Mongols* (Oxford, 1986)
A. J. K. Sanders: *Mongolia: Politics, Economics and Society* (London, 1987)
N. Tsultem: *Mongolian Architecture* (Ulaan Baatar, 1988)
T. J. Barfield: *The Peribus Frontier: Nomadic Empires and China* (Cambridge, MA, 1989)
M. C. Goldstein and C. M. Beall: *The Changing World of Mongolia's Nomads* (Berkeley, 1994)

DAVID SNEATH

II. Iconography and subject-matter.

The iconography and subject-matter of Mongolian art can be divided into two categories: the naturalistic and animal motifs used in secular painting and the sacred iconography used in religious painting and sculpture. The subject-matter of secular art reflects the shamanistic beliefs and nomadic lifestyle of the Mongolians and includes clouds, waves, botanical patterns and depictions of the animals on which their livelihood depends. The deep symbolism used in their religious art is derived from the vast Indo-Tibetan Buddhist pantheon comprising Buddhas, *bodhisattvas*, protectors of the religion (Skt *dharmapalas*) and tutelary deities (*istadevas*) and is supplemented by various indigenous Mongolian deities and historic personages.

A fundamental characteristic of Mongolian religious art is its fidelity to precise iconographic and iconometric rules. Although paintings and sculptures can be viewed in terms of aestheticism and artistic merit, for Mongolians they have a purely sacred function. The Buddhist practitioner uses religious art as a visual aid for meditation in order to bring about an altered state of consciousness. The meditational technique of visualization used in Vajrayana Buddhism is not to be confused with worship of an external deity; it is a process of identification with the inspiration or energy that the deity represents, until the devotee becomes one with the essence of that deity. Iconography is a codified system of portraying individual deities, and iconometry is a codified system governing the proportions for each class of deity. The former includes the attributes, colours, number of heads and limbs, gestures and postures of each deity. The latter prescribes the mathematical proportions to which the artist must adhere when constructing the images belonging to the different categories

Mongolians remained faithful to the Gelugpa tradition. Considerable prominence was therefore given to Tsong Khapa (1357–1419), the founder of the Gelugpas, to the Dalai Lamas, the Panchen Lamas and to the important Gelugpa deities. These include the *bodhisattva*s Avalokiteshvara, Manjushri, Vajrapani and Tara, the Tantric deities Kalachakra, Guhyasamaja, Samvara and Vajrayogini, and the protective *dharmāpala*s Yama, Mahakala, Sri Devi, Vaishravana, Pehar and Sertrap. White Mahakala was especially chosen by the 13th Dalai Lama to be the main protective deity of Mongolia. Among didactic paintings, popular themes include the Wheel of Life, stories of the life of Shakyamuni, the historical Buddha, the Gelugpa lineage tree, the Four Amicable Friends (*tumbashi*), the Long Life portrait (*tserendung*) and symbolic offerings (see fig. 2). The Mongolian Vajrayana Buddhist pantheon differs slightly from the Tibetan as it includes several local shamanistic deities, among them the equestrian figures of Sulde Tngri, Dyaicn Tngri and Gesar Khan, and the deity Begtse. The latter tried to prevent the 3rd Dalai Lama's journey to Mongolia in 1575 but was defeated and converted to Buddhism. Many shamanistic gods were replaced by wrathful Buddhist deities, the suffix *tngri* ('eternal') being added so that the Mongolians would more readily accept them. There are also representations of important Mongolian historical figures, such as the various incarnations of the Khalka Jetzundamba, the Jankya Hutukthu and other important lamas.

Stylistically, the main influence on Mongolian religious painting was undoubtedly Tibetan art (*see also* §IV, 9(i) below), but China was also a source of cultural inspiration. In Mongolian art the basic aesthetic principles of symmetry, order and harmony prevail, with the emphasis always on the central figure. Iconographic rules restrict artistic expression, but certain Mongolian characteristics are apparent in the fluidity of costume drapery and the vitality expressed in the depiction of animals and naturalistic elements. Today, with the renaissance of Buddhism in Mongolia, the iconographic tradition is being revived and further expanded with the discovery of new texts.

BIBLIOGRAPHY
W. Heissig: *The Religions of Mongolia* (London, 1970)
N. Tsultem: *The Eminent Mongolian Sculptor, G. Zanabazar* (Ulaan Baatar, 1982) [text in Rus., Eng., Fr., Sp.]
——: *Mongol Zurag* (Ulaan Baatar, 1986)
L. Chandra: *Buddhist Iconography*, 2 vols (New Delhi, 1987)
N. Tsultem: *Mongolian Sculpture* (Ulaan Baatar, 1989) [text in Rus., Eng., Fr., Sp.]
Wisdom and Compassion: The Sacred Art of Tibet (exh. cat. by M. M. Rhie and R. A. F. Thurman; San Francisco, CA, Asian A. Mus.; New York, IBM Gal. Sci. & A.; London, RA; 1991–2)

III. Architecture.

The development and basic principles of the traditional architecture of the Mongols were determined by the nomadic way of life, which made it necessary to evolve a mobile structure that was light and easy to dismantle: the round, dome-shaped tent, or *ger* (*see also* §VI below and TENT, §II, 2). The size and decoration of the *ger* depended on whether it served as an ordinary dwelling, a religious edifice or a khan's residence. *Ger* encampments were arranged in a circle and became the basic format of urban

2. Symbolic offerings *tangka*, colours on linen, 1.25×0.82 m, 18th century (Prague, National Gallery)

of the pantheon; for this Mongolians observed the ten-palm linear measurement known as *Dashatala* (Skt: 'consisting of 10 divisions').

For knowledge of the correct iconography and iconometry, artists referred to the Indian Buddhist *sūtra*s and *tantra*s, and in particular to three texts that were later incorporated into the Mongolian Buddhist canon: the *Citralakasana*, the *Pratimalaksana* and the *Kālacakra* (Skt: 'wheel of time'). They also relied on the existing artwork and sketchbooks of Tibetan masters and on the Tibetan oral tradition. By the 18th century, textbooks had been written by the Mongolian scholars Ishbaljir (1704–88), Lama Agvanhaidub (1779–1839) and Agvaan Balden (1797–1840). In 1811 two xylographic handbooks depicting the main Tantric deities (Mongol. *Burhans*)—*Collection of 300 Burhans* and *500 Burhans*—were published in Urga (now Ulaan Baatar). But perhaps the greatest inspiration was provided by the prolific work of the lama Zanabazar (1635–1723). He not only founded the Mongolian school of Buddhist art but also left outstanding examples of sculpture and painting (*see* §IV, 13(i) below).

Although it was the Sakyapas who initially introduced Buddhism into Mongolia, from the 16th century the planning until the 20th century (*see* §I, 3 above). However, archaeological evidence suggests that there were also fixed settlements before the 1st century AD. The earliest known buildings are those constructed as burial sepulchres, for instance several quadrangular barrows (4th–1st centuries BC) discovered in the provinces of Bayanhongor, Övörhangay and Dornod. During the first millennium AD this part of Asia was ruled by various nomadic and semi-nomadic tribes: in chronological order, the Xiongnu, Turks, Uygurs and Khitan (Qidan). When supreme power passed from one tribe to another, their administrative and cultural capital also moved or was destroyed in warfare. From the surviving ruins it is known that their capitals were strongly fortified palace compounds. The Uygur khan's 8th-century palace at Ordu-Balik was one such complex, where the fortifications were further strengthened by a moated surround.

At the beginning of the 13th century, Genghis Khan (*reg* 1206–27) united the various warring tribes and forged the powerful Mongol empire. The centre of his operations was a vast tented city situated at an important junction of caravan routes in the Orkhon Valley. Under his son Ogedei (*reg* 1228–41) this became the renowned capital Karakorum. According to archaeologists, it was constructed on an artificial hill composed of alternate layers of sand and clay. The city itself was surrounded by a thick

earth wall, several km long, with four entrance gates. Within the city walls lay Ogedei's palace, which the friar Willem van Rubruck described as being like a church, with a central nave and two aisles supported by symmetrical rows of pillars. Outside the palace compound were administrative buildings and trading areas. Karakorum was further expanded under Mengu Khan (*reg* 1251–9). Van Rubruck reports on the Khan's toleration of various religions and the building of two mosques, a church and 12 Buddhist temples—including an impressive five-tiered construction with pitched, tiled roofs—within the compound. The majority of buildings at Karakorum seem to have been inspired by contemporary Chinese architecture, but it should be taken into account that the city was built with the participation of architects and artisans from the Middle East and Europe and therefore most probably had a *mélange* of styles. The city thrived for 300 years until the collapse of the empire.

When Kublai Khan (*reg* 1260–94) became the first emperor of the Yuan dynasty (1279–1368) in China, he had already constructed Kaiping (later known as Shangdu and immortalized as Xanadu by Coleridge) as a rival capital to Karakorum. This was a Chinese imperial city in all but name. Based on Chinese principles of GEOMANCY, it formed a near perfect square with each side facing one of the four points of the compass. A total of eight Buddhist

3. Erdene Zuu Monastery, Mongolia, 1586

monasteries was constructed at the four main and mid-cardinal points. It was built almost entirely by Chinese artists and craftsmen, as was his next great capital of Dadu (the site of modern Beijing; *see also* CHINA, §II, 2(vii)), but he also patronized Newari artists from Nepal introduced to him by the Tibetan lama Phagspa.

The spread of Buddhism in the 16th century resulted in many monasteries being built throughout the country. The best known of these is Erdene Zuu (1586; see fig. 3), which originally had 100 temples (only three survive). It was designed in the form of a square-plan cosmic diagram (Skt *maṇḍala*) encircled by 108 stupas evenly spaced along the wall. The stupa, which originated in India as a Buddhist reliquary (*see* STUPA, §1), is known in Mongolia as *suburgan*. The styles of the various temples at Erdene Zuu are a combination of Chinese and Tibetan classical architecture, a fusion that became the standard format for monastery design. Tiled pagoda roofs with ornate animal decoration (e.g. Amarbayasgalant Monastery, 1737) were Chinese in inspiration, whereas the single-storey buildings with flat roofs and simple Buddhist adornment (e.g. the main temple at Erdene Zuu) were Tibetan in origin. The development of a more national style of architecture is only apparent in the square marquee or round, *ger*-style temple. The latter followed the original *ger* design, but more permanent materials were used in construction; the foundations were made of stone, the felt was replaced with wood, and more substantial crossbeams were used to support the roof poles. Under the communist regime of the 1930s most monasteries were destroyed, although those in Ulaan Baatar survived. A typical example of a *ger* monastery is Tashichoiling, and the marquee style can be seen in the temples of Dashchoelling and Kongachoiling. The temple of Megzid Janraiseg at Ganden Thekchen Ling Monastery was erected as a monument to independence in 1912; this is a typical example of a fusion of styles, with a Tibetan two-storey base topped by a marquee-style temple.

Before the revolution (1921) Mongolia was dependent on China and Tibet for any additional architectural inspiration. The modern municipal and domestic architecture of Ulaan Baatar and other cities in the post-revolution era was designed by Soviet and European architects, for example the State Printing House (1920s) by the German Karel Maher. B. Chimid, a member of a Mongol-Soviet group of architects, is known for the buildings of the Central Council of the Trade Unions, the Drama Theatre and the Ulaanbaatar Hotel (1961) in Ulaan Baatar. After 1990 more Mongolian characteristics were incorporated. Monastic architecture also underwent a revival; although buildings retained their traditional *ger* or Sino-Tibetan exterior, the interior decoration was much more Mongolian in design with typical Mongolian scenery (often depicting *ger*s).

BIBLIOGRAPHY
W. Heissig: *A Lost Civilization: The Mongols Rediscovered* (London, 1966)
P. Brent: *The Mongol Empire* (London, 1976)
E. Alexander: 'Un Monastère lamaïque du XVIe siècle en Mongolie', *Etud. Mongol. & Sibér.*, x (1979), pp. 7–32
N. Tsultem: *Mongolian Architecture* (Ulaan Baatar, 1988)
P. Jackson and D. Morgan: *The Mission of Friar William of Rubruck: His Journeys to the Court of the Great Khan Mongke, 1253–1255* (Cambridge, 1990)
ZARA FLEMING

IV. Other arts.

1. Arms and armour. 2. Books. 3. Dress. 4. Embroidery. 5. Jewellery. 6. Leatherwork. 7. Metalwork. 8. Musical instruments. 9. Painting. 10. Rock art. 11. Seals. 12. Scripts. 13. Sculpture. 14. Woodwork.

1. ARMS AND ARMOUR. Practically no weapons or pieces of armour survive from the time of the 13th-century Mongolian empire. However, illustrations from that period, such as those in the Japanese *Mongol Invasion Scroll* and Rashid al-Din's *World History* (see Talbot Rice) show Mongols wearing helmets and coats of iron or leather lamellar armour reaching to the elbow and knee. Similar armour was also made for horses. Lamellar armour, which was widely used in Central Asia from ancient times, was made from narrow metal or lacquered leather plates bound together to form horizontal rows from which suits were made (*see also* CENTRAL ASIA, §II, 5(i) and ISLAMIC ART, fig. 114).

The distinctive weapon of Mongolia until modern times was the recurve composite bow. Mongolian bows with leather cases and quivers are kept in the State Central Museum, Ulaan Baatar (see 1989 exh. cat., pls 152–9). The cases and quivers are beautifully decorated with stitching, metal studding and small plaques, using cloud and ram's-horn motifs among others. One quiver has a tiger-striped decoration produced by working ridges into the dyed leather. The Inner Mongolian Museum, Hohhot, also has an excellent Mongolian bow, case and quiver, and a quiver of the same type is on display in Britain at the Museum of Archaeology and Anthropology, Cambridge University. Stone thumb rings that were used to draw the powerful composite bows have survived better than the bows themselves and were often made of hardstones (Hohhot, Inner Mongol. Mus.).

BIBLIOGRAPHY
H. R. Robinson: *Oriental Armour* (London, 1967)
Shinshu Nihon Emakimono Zenshu [Japanese Mongol invasion scroll], x (Tokyo, 1975)
D. Talbot Rice: *The Illustrations to 'the World History of Rashid-al-Din'*, ed. B. Gray (Edinburgh, 1976)
S. R. Turnbull: *The Mongols*, Men at Arms (London, 1980)
Die Mongolen, 2 vols (exh. cat., ed. W. Heissig and C. C. Müller; Munich, Haus Kst, 1989)
DAVID SNEATH

2. BOOKS. Even if ancestors of the Mongols used a script and possessed books, the actual Mongolian script—and thus Mongolian book art—originated in 1206. The oldest extant blockprint is dated 1312. Paper was imported mostly from China, later from Russia; local paper-making followed the Chinese example (*see* CHINA, §XIII, 18). Writing was carried out with calamus and brush, and a birch-fibre fragment from the 16th/17th century indicates that other materials were occasionally used as well. The Mongols were familiar with printing plates of cast bronze or embossed or chiselled copper, and earlier they used carved stone. Printing, however, was mostly done xylographically, i.e. by means of a wooden relief plate.

Book formats conform to Indian or Chinese custom. Of Chinese origin are the 'folding book' and the 'double-leaf book': in both cases the writing was horizontal as well as vertical. Most books, however, conform to the format of the Indian palm-leaf manuscript (Skt *pustaka*), i.e. written horizontally and roughly three times as long as wide. These books are not bound but are often protected by two wooden, sometimes carved, covers and are stored wrapped in scarves. There are oversized editions as well as minute pocket versions. Mongol notebooks generally consist of four small wooden boards, bound together along the longer side and covered with a layer of wax and soot, which the writer could inscribe with a calamus. The writing can be wiped out simply by rubbing. The exteriors of the first and last board are decorated with paintings. These booklets were also used by children as exercise books.

Painting was an important means of decorating books. Buddhist texts were illuminated with representations of deities or holy symbols in keeping with Buddhist iconography (*see also* §II above). This also applied to texts in which illustration was an essential means of expression: astrological and medical treatises, divination manuals or edifying tales such as stories relating the Descent to Hell. In the latter case a migrant narrator would back up his oral recitation with such illustrations, some of which covered an entire page.

Other methods of decoration with purely ornamental purposes are found almost exclusively in Buddhist canonical texts. The simplest consisted of using coloured ink. There are also many books with leaves hardened and covered with black varnish to allow the use of gold- or silver-coloured ink (ink mixed with gold or silver). Rarer (being more complicated) methods include writing with the 'nine jewels': inks mixed with powdered gold, silver, coral, pearls, turquoise, lapis lazuli, mother of pearl, copper or brass; embroidery of books (and also script) with colourful silk thread; and production of books with leaves of solid silver plates, the relief of the embossed or engraved script being gilded.

BIBLIOGRAPHY

G. Kara: *Knigi mongol'skikh kochevnikov* [Books of the Mongol nomads] (Moscow, 1972)

Č. Šügder: *Mongolcuudyn nom chevledeg arga* (Ulaan Baatar, 1976)

G. Kara: 'Blockdrücke und Handschriften', *Die Mongolen* (exh. cat., ed. W. Heissig and C. C. Müller; Munich, Haus Kst, 1989), ii, pp. 250–52

DOMINIQUE M. DUMAS

3. DRESS. The product of a climate of extremes and an economy of nomadic herding and hunting, the basic Mongolian garment has probably changed little since the 13th century. It consists of a wide, calf-length tunic (*deel*) with very long sleeves, fastening down the right side and usually sashed, over loose trousers and leather knee-boots. The shawl-type neck opening was replaced by a tight stand-up collar under Manchu influence (17th–18th century). A sleeveless waistcoat may be worn over the tunic (see fig. 4). In extreme cold an overcoat of skins is sometimes worn, with the hair outward. The tunic is of sheepskin or other animal skins in winter, worn hair inward, with the outer side dressed almost white or entirely covered with bright silk. The material in summer is silk, wadded cotton or skins. Textiles were entirely imported, from China and latterly Russia, until the 20th century. The part played by textiles (and consequently by colour) in dress tended to increase with proximity to China along a north-west–south-east axis. Women's costume differs

4. Dress of Khalkha Mongol man, silk decorated with velvet, brocade and gold edging, *c.* 1900 (Ulaan Baatar, Central Museum)

from men's chiefly in detail and ornamentation. Facings and borders of varicoloured braid appear in all groups (e.g. exh. cat., i, pl. 94), embroidery very locally (Uzemchin and Altai Uriankhai groups). The waistcoat is often long, reaching to the hem of the tunic.

This basic model varies between different Mongol groups, particularly in the details of women's dress. The shoulder of the sleeves of the Khalkha Mongol tunic is padded and raised (exh. cat., pl. 89). A broad, pleated, white collar and a centre-front opening to the bodice of the tunic—rather than on the right—distinguish the dress of the western (Oirat) Mongols (exh. cat., i, pl. 93). The tunics of Buryat (northern Mongol) and Oirat women have a dropped waist seam instead of falling from the shoulders (exh. cat., i, pl. 90). Headgear for both sexes is elaborate and varied; basic in winter is a fur-lined bonnet, or cap with flaps over ears and nape. Until recently women wore a headdress of silver and hardstones beneath the hat, and sheathed long hair in cases of silk or silver. Men's ornaments are knife, flint and steel, hanging from the sash (*see also* §7 below).

The dress of noblemen was heavily influenced by Manchu court dress from the 17th century (exh. cat., i, pl. 73). In the 20th century Communist regimes encouraged standardization of dress on the model of the simple sashed tunic, so that ethnic variations virtually disappeared. Shamans and Buddhist clergy wore ritual costume. Wrestlers have a specific ornamented costume of cutaway jacket, or bolero, and briefs (exh. cat., ii, p. 209). The baggy trousers of the past are still seen in Inner Mongolia.

See also §§4 and 5 below.

BIBLIOGRAPHY
H. H. Hansen: *Mongol Costumes* (Copenhagen, 1950, rev. London, 2/1994)
M. Boyer: *Mongolian Jewellery* (Copenhagen, 1952)
Ü. Yadamsüren: *National Costumes of the MPR* (Ulaan Baatar, 1967)
Die Mongolen, 2 vols (exh. cat., ed. W. Heissig and C. C. Müller; Munich, Haus Kst, 1989)

4. EMBROIDERY. Embroidery on felt is structural; on textiles or dressed leather it is purely ornamental. Felt made of sheep's wool (*see also* FELT, §2(i)) is a basic material of the Mongol nomads, who did not practise weaving. Felt can be strengthened and stiffened by quilting, which covers the whole surface with close ornamental designs; the thread is hand-twisted from undyed camel's wool. Strengthening is essential for rugs, floor felts and the door flap of the tent (*see* TENT, §II, 2), but the tent felts are not quilted. Finer quilting is used on felt socks. Although Chinese design elements appear occasionally, patterns found on felt are native to Central Asia; some designs still in use (all-over geometric lattice patterns, combined with borders of curling forms) appear on Xiongnu felts of the 1st century AD from NOIN ULA (see Rudenko, fig. 49).

Fine embroidery on textiles or chamois leather decorates accessories—pouches for the snuff bottle or for tobacco, protective covers for drinking bowls—but rarely appears on garments. The thread is coloured Chinese silk, and Chinese influence is apparent in both technique and ornamentation; much use is made of shading in parallel rows of chain stitch or Peking stitch, but satin stitch, unable to withstand the wear inherent in nomadic life, is not found. The importance of embroidery tends to increase with proximity to China; in some Inner Mongolian areas it decorates even cloth boots or the tent doorway (Uzemchin group). Embroidered goods were frequently imported from China; these are often hard to distinguish from Mongol work. In western Mongol areas, influence from the neighbouring Turkic peoples appears in the occasional use of coarse Bokhara stitch (Altai Uriankhai group) and in embroidered hangings inside the tent. Here

the white collars of the women and head-scarves worn by both sexes are embroidered with toothed borders.

Ornamental knotting and braiding are developed to a high degree; although these were usually executed by hand, some simple forms of apparatus were in use up to the turn of the century. Varicoloured silk braid appliqué on dress and on the leather of boots gives the impression of an embroidered surface. Fine braids are essential to the appliqué technique used in Buddhist *tangkas*; a coloured braid border surrounds each cut-out piece. The Museum of Fine Art, Ulaan Baatar, has a good collection of these *tangkas*, including a 19th-century *tangka*, in silk and gold brocade with pearls and coral beads, of the Urga school, representing the tutelary deity (*yidam*) Kuṅrig i Nam-par sNaṅ-urdzad in Vajra posture (see 1989 exh. cat., i, pl. 215). The technique has remained in use under the present political regimes for commemorative banners.

BIBLIOGRAPHY
S. I. Rudenko: *Die Kultur der Hsiung-nu* (Bonn, 1969)
K. Chabros: 'Quilted Ornamentation on Mongol Felts', *Cent. Asiat. J.*, xxxii (1988), pp. 34–60
——: 'Mongolische abgesteppte Filze', *Die Mongolen* (exh. cat., W. Heissig and C. C. Müller; Munich, Haus Kst, 1989), ii, pp. 182–3 [wrongly attributed to S. Synkiewicz]
——: 'Der Gebrauch der Applikationstechnik bei der Thanka-Herstellung', *Die Mongolen* (exh. cat., ed. W. Hessig and C. C. Müller; Munich, Haus Kst, 1989), ii, pp. 184–6
K. Chabros and L. Batčuluun: 'Mongol Examples of Proto-weaving', *Cent. Asiat. J.*, xxxvii (1993), pp. 20–32

KRYSTYNA CHABROS

5. JEWELLERY. In the last 50 years Mongolians have neither produced nor worn their traditional jewellery, and it is for the most part only to be found in museums. Silver, coral (red, white and, more rarely, black), turquoise, pearls, amber and various precious gemstones and hardstones were used (*see also* CORAL, fig. 3). Jewellery made of solid gold was extremely rare; more frequent was gold-plated silver. Beating, engraving, chasing and damascening were the most popular techniques.

Western Mongols wore simple jewellery, of which metal (silver) was the most dominant component and in which Central Asian influences were manifest. Coral and stones were used to a greater extent further along the north-west–south-east axis. Southern Mongols often enamelled silver ornaments, apparently in imitation of Chinese cloisonné work. Especially favoured were ornamental interlace pieces, in particular the endless knot, the swastika and the spiral- or meander-shaped ram's horn motif. Numerous Buddhist and Chinese motifs were introduced (*see also* §II above). The main items of everyday hair adornment worn by girls and women were a curved comb and hair clasps worn at the nape of the neck and at the end of the plait. Men's personal adornment consisted primarily of a belt outfit made up of eating implements and fire lighters (*see also* §7 below). Both sexes wore rings and earrings, set mostly with red coral or turquoise.

The married woman's festive jewellery, the most lavish of Mongolian jewellery, consisted of an unchanging set of basic elements: plait clasps—cloth cases appliquéd with brocade, quilted or embroidered, with a variety of lavish ornamental mounts—that held the bride's two plaits; two pieces of jewellery (*süikh*) with the symbolic significance of a wedding ring, which hung either side of the face and were connected across the chest by one or more chains; slide pendants, fastened to the dress at hip height and made of silver disks, to which were attached brightly coloured silk scarves or silver chains ending in miniature versions of everyday objects and lucky charms; and the talismanic chest decoration, probably influenced in form and symbolism by Buddhism, and composed of one or more small amulet boxes attached to necklaces or brocade ribbons.

The headdress of the Khalkha Mongol woman consisted of a cap worked with thick filigree and usually set with coral and turquoise, with small chains hanging down at the temples. Six to eight matching clasps held the hair in place after it was shaped into two broad, horn-like wings (see 1989 exh. cat., i, pl. 86). Favoured by the southern Mongols (Chahar, Uzemchin) was a headband set with silver fittings and/or a thick network of pearls, with chains that formed a fringe across the forehead and dangled down the temples (see 1989 exh. cat., i, pl. 94a). The Zabaikal Buryat women wore a wreath set with large balls of coral, stone and amber.

BIBLIOGRAPHY

M. Boyer: *Mongol Jewellery*, Nationalmuseets skrifter, Etnografisk roekke, 5 (Copenhagen, 1952)

K. Uray-Köhalmi: 'Grob und Feinschmiedearbeiten', *Die Mongolen* (exh. cat., ed. W. Heissig and C. C. Müller; Munich, Haus Kst, 1989), ii, pp. 187–91

DOMINIQUE M. DUMAS

6. LEATHERWORK. The use of crafted leather objects is among the oldest traditions of the Mongols, who supported themselves by animal husbandry. Leather made from horse or cattle hide, tanned with salt water and/or sour milk and depilated, was decorated with wet-stamped motifs (e.g. on small leather flasks and cases) or with colourful (green, purple, blue) vine scroll or interlaced motifs in appliquéd leather on a brown or black background on the traditional boots, shabracks, saddles, bow cases and quivers. The latter two objects might also be decorated with fittings of silver or silver-damascened iron. Bridles and the leather boleros of wrestlers (see 1989 exh. cat., p. 209) had only metal fittings (*see also* §7 below). To produce the appliquéd and stamped leather motifs, wooden blocks, iron and bone awls, stamps and small knives were used.

BIBLIOGRAPHY

V. Ronge: 'Handwerkertum bei den Mongolen: Filz, Leder, Holz und ihre Verarbeitung', *Die Mongolen* (exh. cat., ed. W. Heissig and C. C. Müller; Munich, Haus Kst, 1989), ii, pp. 173–81

S. Szynkiewicz: 'Sport und Spiele', *Die Mongolen* (exh. cat., ed. W. Heissig and C. C. Müller; Munich, Haus Kst, 1989), ii, pp. 205–15

CATHERINE URAY-KÖHALMI

7. METALWORK. Mongolian metalware consists of three main categories: personal implements and weapons, domestic utensils and religious artefacts. The bronzeworking Karasuk culture (*c.* 1200–800 BC), centred in the Minusinsk Basin in southern Siberia, influenced Mongolia in its late stage, before Mongolia became part of the nomadic Xiongnu empire in *c.* 200 BC. The royal tombs at NOIN ULA in northern Mongolia yielded gold, bronze and silver belt plaques, buckles, horse trappings, bronze cauldrons, knives (Ulaan Baatar, Mus. F.A.) and mirrors and gold jewellery (Ulaan Baatar, Fund Precious Metals & Depository).

Embossed work is the main form of surviving decoration, notably on a silver plaque depicting a yak on a mountain among trees (diam. 135 mm; St Petersburg, Hermitage; Lubo-Lesnichenko, p. 52). Chinese and western Central Asian influences are strong, with elements of late ANIMAL STYLE. The Xiongnu had a cult of the sword, and such a weapon remained important. In their imperial expansion during the 13th century, the Mongols first used a straight sword, then adopted a curved scimitar (a sabre was still favoured by officers leading the revolution in the 20th century). A heavy knife, part of a man's personal equipment until recent times, was either carried separately in a sheath or combined as an eating set with chopsticks in a case. Along with a steel flint on a leather tinder pouch and metal toilet implements, the set—more or less decorative in the use of silver fittings and mounts according to wealth and social status—was suspended by belt rings from the sash. A lighter knife was carried by women and Buddhist monks. Bridles and saddles were decorated with silver boss mounts and sheet silver shapes, cut out around birch-bark stencils, overlaid by hammering then decorated by blueing. This method was also used to decorate quivers. Silver was especially valued for its purity by Outer Mongolians.

The motifs used in Mongolian metalware after the 16th century are largely Buddhist and include the Eight Auspicious Symbols, especially the lotus and the endless knot (*see also* §II above). Also popular are some Chinese motifs: the long-life (*shou*) and double happiness characters, the key, swastika and *ruyi* motifs, the bat and horns, and the dragon with a jewel. The mixture of styles and decoration of Mongolian metalware reflects the variety of influences current after the establishment of the Mongolian empire by Genghis Khan (*reg* 1206–27) and his successors.

Captured craftsmen from many parts of Eurasia, including Persia and China, were taken to the Mongol courts and capital at Karakorum, shared among the rulers and aristocracy and often given preferential treatment. According to Willem von Rubruck (*c.* 1210–*c.* 1270), in 1253 William Buchier, a Parisian goldsmith captured in Hungary, was making exotic metalware such as a silver wine fountain at the court of Mengu Khan (*reg* 1251–9) at Karakorum (Rachewiltz, 1971). Chinese metalworkers adapted Chinese designs to suit the tastes of their new Mongol overlords. These craftsmen stimulated craft development among such Mongolian tribal groups as the Khalkha and the Derbets, with some becoming famous for specializations: the Dariganga for silver chasing and the Dalai Choinkhor for its blacksmiths. Techniques of carving in steel and deep undercutting in silver and copper developed that are still practised in Mongolia.

After Tibetan Buddhism became established *c.* 1550–1600 Mongolian craftsmen combined Indian principles and Tibetan and Nepalese practice with their own aesthetic in the manufacture of religious figures and apparatus—bells, thunderbolts, lamps—and such utensils as teapots and cauldrons. A notable exemplar of the monastic artist tradition in Mongolia was Zanabazar (1635–1723), the first Khutuktu, or supreme religious authority, and a pre-eminent metal-sculptor. In the 1680s he made numerous large, hollow-cast, gold figures of Buddhist deities with details chased in traditional Mongolian patterns on the

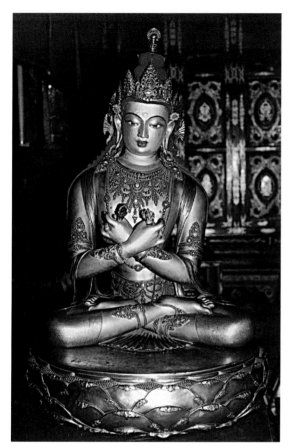

5. Zanabazar: *Vajradhara*, hollow-cast gilt, 1680s (Ulaan Baatar, Ganden Thekchen Ling Monastery)

ornaments and clothing (see fig. 5; see also §13(i) below). Zanabazar's monastic pupils (mostly anonymous) followed his principles, producing some fine images, including large silver figures with a polished finish and insets of hardstones (Ulaan Baatar, Mus. Relig.; Erdeni Zuu, Monastery Mus.), as well as temple ornaments, ritual apparatus and utensils, using gold inlay in steel, a technique valued more highly than silverwork. The increasing demand for figures and ritual apparatus and the importation of cheap Chinese products led to a decline in quality from the late 18th century, with some exceptions; Dawadorj of Urga, *c.* 1900, used a method of sand-casting according to Zanabazar's written instructions to make 600 bells with differing tones. In 1940 the Mongolian People's Republic decreed that all artistic work should have a political message, but such products as copper teabowls, plaques and jewellery often still incorporate Buddhist and animal motifs.

See also ORDOS.

BIBLIOGRAPHY
K. Jettmar: *Art of the Steppes* (New York, 1967)
I. de Rachewiltz: *Papal Envoys to the Great Khans* (London, 1971)
N. Tsultem: *The Eminent Mongolian Sculptor, G. Zanabazar* (Ulaan Baatar, 1982) [text in Rus., Eng., Fr., Sp.]
——: *Mongolian Arts and Crafts* (Ulaan Baatar, 1987) [text in Rus., Eng., Fr., Sp.]
E. I. Lubo-Lesnichenko: 'The Huns, Third Century B.C. to Sixth Century A.D.', *Nomads of Eurasia* (Seattle and London, 1989)
N. Tsultem: *Mongolian Sculpture* (Ulaan Baatar, 1989) [text in Rus., Eng., Fr., Sp.]
Die Mongolen, 2 vols (exh. cat., ed. W. Heissig and C. C. Müller; Munich, Haus Kst, 1989)

KEN TEAGUE

8. MUSICAL INSTRUMENTS. Mongolian musical instruments may be classified as religious or secular. Buddhist wind, percussion and stringed instruments spread throughout Mongolia with the renewed dissemination of Tibetan Buddhism in the second half of the 16th century. Its failure to eradicate completely the indigenous religion of SHAMANISM is clear from the collection in recent years of several shaman round frame drums (*khets*) with single skins. On a Bayad example collected in western Mongolia the wooden grip is carved in the shape of a female figure thought to contain the spirit of an ancestral shaman (Ulaangom, Mus.). A Buryat drum collected from Hentiy Province, northern Mongolia, has drawings of a hawk, sun and moon on the skin (Ulaan Baatar, Acad. Sci.).

There are two categories of secular instruments: wind and stringed. The latter are decorated using a combination of strong, bright colours and intricate carving techniques. A half-tube zither (*yataga*) collected from the Chahar Mongols of Inner Mongolia in 1938–9 is elaborately carved with Buddhist motifs and symbolic figures from Mongolian folk mythology (Stockholm, Etnog. Mus., H.29). The tradition of carving animal heads as decoration goes back at least to the 16th century, when the *shanagan khuur* ('ladle fiddle') had ornamental representations of a dragon or sea monster's head on its top. Western Mongolian groups carve the heads of different animals and birds on top of the two-stringed plucked lute (*tobshuur*) used to accompany epics.

The two-stringed spike fiddle, so called because of the handle that passes through the trapezoidal skin or wooden sound-box and bears the strings, is sometimes decorated at the top with a horse's head. This is characteristic of the Khalkha Mongols, who call the instrument the horse-head fiddle (*morin khuur*), and the Chahar Mongols of Inner Mongolia, who refer to it as the *khil khuur*. The horse's head is important in Mongolian folk, shamanist and Buddhist religious traditions. The Museum of Fine Arts, Ulaan Baatar, has on display an instrument crowned with three green horses' heads (Tsultem, 1987, nos 110–11). Other groups, including the Oirat Mongols in the west, use such symbols as the sun and the moon, peacock feathers, and the Chandman' wish-granting jewel of Buddhist mythology, or leave them undecorated. The four-stringed spike fiddle (*dörvön chihtei khuur*, 'fiddle with four ears') is similarly carved with a variety of symbols, including real and mythological animals.

Secular instruments made throughout the 20th century continued to be decorated with ancient Mongol and Buddhist symbols. A tradition in eastern Mongolia is to carve a second head, the half-crocodile/half-bee of Mongolian folklore, below the horse's head, either immediately above the emergence of the strings or spewing the strings out of its gaping mouth, such as the Chahar *khil khuur* in the Nationalmuseum, Copenhagen (Haslund-Christiansen Col., no. 18/39, R. 833) (Tsultem, 1987). The neck and the skin or wooden sound-board of the *khuur* are often ornamented with folk and Buddhist symbols such as the hammer design (*alkhan khee*; e.g. London, Horniman Mus. & Lib. and Paris, Mus. Homme, M.H.67.101.7) symbolizing protection against external spiritual or physical enemies and internal chaos. In common with the endless knot (*ölzii utas*) sometimes placed at the centre of the sound-board, it also symbolizes the strength and infinite nature of all things. Patterns used on the *morin khuur* neck include the khan's bracelet (*khan buguivch*), representing alliance, trust and lasting friendship (see Purev), spiral patterns, plant designs and Buddhist symbols (U. Cambridge, Mus. Archaeol. & Anthropol., Lindgren Col.). Natural phenomena such as waves, fire, clouds and, rarely, trees and animals may be painted on the sound-board (e.g. Paris, Mus. Homme, M.H.57.61.3). More recently, decoration on the *khuur* has also included the *soyombo*, the first letter of a new script designed by the 17th-century Mongolian Buddhist leader and sculptor, Zanabazar (1635–1723), and since 1924 the symbol of the independent Mongolian nation (*see also* §12 below).

BIBLIOGRAPHY

E. Emsheimer: 'Preliminary Remarks on Mongolian Music and Instruments', *The Music of the Mongols, 1: Eastern Mongolia: Reports from the Scientific Expedition to the Northwestern Provinces of China under the Leadership of Dr Sven Hedin* (Stockholm, 1943)

N. Tsultem: *Mongolian Arts and Crafts* (Ulaan Baatar, 1987) [text in Rus., Eng., Fr., Sp.]

R. Purev: 'Khee, Ugalznii utga, aguulga' [The essence and meaning of decoration and ornamentation], *Mongol Maikhan asar khiikh arga zui* [The method of making Mongolian cloth and field tents] (Ulaan Baatar, 1988), pp. 15–16

CAROLE PEGG

9. PAINTING.

(i) Religious. After the Tibetan form of Tantric Buddhism (*see* BUDDHISM, §III, 6) was established in Mongolia in the 16th century, the religious paintings of the Mongols became deceptively similar to the sacred art of Tibet. Like Tibetan painting, this is a visionary art serving the sole purpose of illustrating the holy legends and the detailed descriptions of Buddhas and meditation deities found in the scriptures (see fig. 6). The iconography follows a fixed scheme, the images of deities being drawn according to unchanging rules (*see also* §11 above). However, there is sufficient scope for free treatment of backgrounds and scenes. This system was developed in India, only reaching Mongolia via Tibet in the 17th century, by which time the individual artistic styles had been consolidated in Tibet. To this extent an analysis of Mongolian religious painting can only be undertaken in comparison with Tibetan painting, which deals with the same subject-matter. Only the stylistic differences in proportion, expression and detail justify discussion of an independent Mongolian Buddhist style of painting.

The religious painting of the Mongols is not more than two centuries old. As the Central Tibetan Mensar style of the 17th century, which later developed into the Üri style, was favoured especially by the reformed Gelugpa school, this school exerted the greatest influence on the Mongols through intensive cultural contacts (*see also* §I, 5 above). The influence should be seen as reciprocal, above all in the artistic sphere, since many Mongols travelled to central Tibet to study. Thus it cannot be ruled out that many

6. Zanabazar: *White Tara* (*Sitatara*), colours on linen, 17th century (Ulaan Baatar, Fine Arts Museum)

central Tibetan sculptures were produced with the collaboration of Mongolian artists or that Tibetan artists worked in Mongolia. A rigorous stylistic division is impossible.

Nevertheless, in considering Mongolian scroll paintings (Tib. *tangka*) a number of differences from Tibetan paintings on the same subjects can be noted. In the 19th-century *tangka* entitled *Caturmukha Mahākāla* ('Four-faced Mahakala') by an unknown artist of the Urga school of painting, the Mongolian execution—as compared to the delicate, fine brushwork of the Üri style in a Tibetan scroll painting (e.g. Baader, fig. 1)—has a graphic, linear appearance with flat areas of colour. The treatment of the lotus throne, in particular, seems too ornate. The faces of the angry deities in Mongolian works are longer, and their eyes are more demonic and terrible than the serene gaze of the protective gods painted in the Tibetan style. A 20th-century *tangka* on a black ground with contour painting, a work by the painter Zam 'jan entitled *White Mahakala* (Ulaan Baatar, Mus. F.A., 2581–451; see 1989 exh. cat., no. 225), exemplifies the poster-like, statuesque style of the Mongols in contrast to the openness and dynamism of the east Tibetan Mensar style (Baader, fig. 3).

Whereas the Chinese landscape painting of the Mongol Yuan period (1279–1368) stylistically influenced the east Tibetan Karma Gartri school of painting with its strong three-dimensionality, inclusion of landscape and emphatically transcendental, visionary aspect, it had no effect on the late religious painting of the Mongols. This is explained by the time factor: the Mongols adapted Tibetan Buddhism at a time when monastic institutions in Tibet had degenerated into political power centres at the expense of the inner, meditative activity of the clergy. Thus Tibetan Buddhist paintings of the 19th and 20th centuries have a more material, poster-like quality than the great works of earlier epochs. In the Buddhist art of the Mongols the equivalent of this shortcoming is over-ornateness.

See also TIBET, §IV.

BIBLIOGRAPHY
Die Mongolen, 2 vols (exh. cat., ed. W. Heissig and C. C. Müller; Munich, Haus Kst, 1989)
J. Baader: 'Schoettle Ostasiatika', *Die Weltkunst*, lix/9 (1989)
A. Loseries-Leick: 'Die lamaistische Malerei der Mongolen', *Die Weltkunst*, lix/9 (1989)
ANDREA LOSERIES-LEICK

(ii) Secular. The secular art of Mongolia has deep roots in the ancient traditions of the steppes (*see* §10 below). After Genghis Khan (*reg* 1206–27) and his successors unified Asia, Mongolia became a channel of new artistic expression, and artists assimilated and adapted various styles to suit their own traditions. Artists and craftsmen from all over the world began working at the imperial court; for instance, Willem van Rubruck remarks on the Parisian goldsmith responsible for creating a tree-shaped fountain for Mengu Khan (*reg* 1251–9). The European tradition of portrait painting became a popular way of glorifying the khans.

Although the predominant inspiration for religious art came from Tibet, with their awareness of other artistic traditions the Mongols evolved a narrative folk style of painting known as *Mongol Zurag* ('traditional folk art'), which dates back to the 12th or 13th century. This style of painting, inspired by the heroic epics of the past and by scenes from everyday life, was characterized by an absence of shadows, lack of perspective and great attention to detail. The term *Mongol Zurag* applies mainly to secular paintings from the 18th century onwards when the style became more prolific. The Mongols also excelled in the meticulous hand-painting of playing cards (e.g. the games of *khözör* and *üichüür*; see Tsultem, 1986, pp. 139–40).

At the beginning of the 20th century Buddhism declined, and a new national liberation movement and artistic style emerged in Urga (now Ulaan Baatar). The art of the time, inspired by Soviet Socialist Realism, began to reflect the Mongolians' struggle for freedom and independence. Political posters were introduced. Yet despite artists' preference for expressing the social issues of the day, they did not neglect their earlier traditional style. Whole series of paintings depicted such important festivities as the *Tsam* (religious festivals marked by the performance of mystery plays) and *Naidam* ('manly sports'; a summer fair featuring horse-riding, wrestling and archery) or everyday activities of nomadic life. A well-known example is *One Day of Mongolia*—two canvases depicting household and nomadic activities in the summer and in the winter—by Balduugin Sharav (1869–1920). This is typical of the Urga school, with its narrative composition, its freedom from iconographical restrictions, its uncomplicated approach and yet its wealth of detail. Sharav was also known for portraits in a photorealist style (e.g. the *8th Jebzundamba*; Ulaan Baatar, Pal. Mus.). The paintings and drawings (e.g.

7. Lodai: *Spring*, ink drawing on paper, 315×255 mm, 1938 (Copenhagen, Nationalmuseum)

Spring; see fig. 7) made in 1938 in Inner Mongolia by the lama Lodai (who came from Outer Mongolia) continue the traditional narrative folk style (*Mongol Zurag*) in the depiction of scenes from everyday life. Also introduced at this time were landscapes accurately depicting towns and monasteries from a bird's-eye viewpoint (e.g. Jugda's *Urga*; Ulaan Baatar, Pal. Mus.). In the late 20th century, with the new wave of freedom sweeping the country, exposure to artistic styles and ideas from all over the world was evident in the paintings of Yadamsuren (e.g. the *Old Storyteller*; Ulaan Baatar, F.A. Mus.), Sengetsohip (e.g. the *Black Camel*; Ulaan Baatar, F.A. Mus.), Dawahuu, Dunkharjab, Hurel Baatar, Arvis and Bold.

BIBLIOGRAPHY
N. Tsultem: *Mongol Zurag* (Ulaan Baatar, 1986)
——: *Mongolian Arts and Crafts* (Ulaan Baatar, 1987) [text in Rus., Eng., Fr., Sp.]
Die Mongolen, 2 vols (exh. cat., ed. W. Heissig and C. C. Müller; Munich, Haus Kst, 1989)
P. Jackson and D. Morgan: *The Mission of Friar William of Rubruck: His Journeys to the Court of the Great Khan Mongke, 1253–1255* (Cambridge, 1990)
ZARA FLEMING

10. ROCK ART. The rock art of Mongolia has been the subject of research by both Russian and Mongol scholars. The oldest examples are prehistoric, but rock art continued practically to modern times. Despite uncertainties regarding the dating of the earliest figures and atypical figures, Mongolian petroglyphs are perfectly ambiented in the major currents of the rock art of Central Asia (*see also* SCYTHIAN AND SARMATIAN ART, §3). The representations, often grouped on rock walls besides rivers, identify gathering places, religious sites and such secular sites as springs.

This was an art of nomad shepherds and hunters, executed with simple tools mostly by hammering.

Prehistoric caves discovered at Khojt-Cenkherijn-aguj were decorated with animals painted in ochre that probably date from the Palaeolithic age. From the Neolithic period (6th–5th millennia BC) there are groups of carvings on walls in the open air, such as those at Chandaman. In the Chalcolithic age (4th millennium BC), ibex and stylized bovids were carved at sites identified as open-air sanctuaries, such as Chuluut, which continued to be used in various successive periods. Characteristic representations from the Bronze Age (3rd–2nd millennia BC) include, in addition to animals, scenes of hunting with the bow and figures with harnessed chariots (Cagaan-gol, Khovd-somon, Chuluut etc) that are part of a system of such representations extending from the Pamir Range to China through Kazakhstan, Kyrgyzstan and the Tuva. The anthropomorphic figures of archers from this period often have a mushroom-shaped coiffure and a bundle of weapons at their sides.

During the late Bronze Age and early Iron Age (c. 800–c. 200 BC), Mongolian rock art ventured into representation of zoomorphic motifs already known in other media, particularly on the carved stelae known as stag-stones that were erected close to burial tumuli. In hunting scenes, such as at Chuluut, stylized stags with long muzzles and flamboyant antlers are found alongside large cats and wild boar. The most recent research has revealed that this late Bronze Age art is associated with the Karasuk culture (c. 1200–800 BC), which extended throughout southern Siberia. The ANIMAL STYLE, which subsequently became characteristic of the Saka period in Central Asia, is thought to be a direct descendant of Karasuk art. The rock-carvings depict objects that are generally found in the tombs of Karasuk culture: decorated knives and bronze axes in particular.

During the Xiongnu (Hun) period, animal and human figures were accompanied by a certain number of stylized signs (Turk: *tamga*s; 'signs of identification') and with figures influenced by Chinese art of the Han period (206 BC–AD 220), such as the 'princess of Khanyn-khad' transported in a chariot escorted by horsemen. In the Old Turkic period (c. AD 400–c. 800), the characteristic type of representation is a galloping rider carrying a long lance decorated with a flag, reminiscent of the Chinese horsemen of Tang-period (AD 618–907) art.

BIBLIOGRAPHY

EWA: 'Turkic art', cols 446–8
E. A. Novgorodova: *Alte Kunst der Mongolei* (Leipzig, 1980)
——: *Mir petroglifov Mongolii* [The world of Mongolian petroglyphs] (Moscow, 1984) [Eng. sum.]
——: *Drevnyaya Mongoliya* [Ancient Mongolia] (Moscow, 1989)
HENRI-PAUL FRANCFORT

11. SEALS. The first evidence of the use of seals in Mongolia dates from the nomadic empire of the Uygurs (7th–9th centuries AD), whose sophisticated culture was strongly influenced by contact with the early Christian and Islamic civilizations. The Uygurs developed their own alphabet, derived from the Syriac letters of the Nestorians, which was then used as the standard script on bronze seals. The use of the Ugyur script continued beyond the height of their influence in Mongolia, after AD 840. With the rise of the Mongol empire in the 13th century, the use of seals became commonplace. Personal seals were used instead of a signature on letters and to mark private property. Nearly all Mongol men carried an iron or bronze seal suspended from the belt. Official seals and ciphers were copied from those used in China during the Han period (206 BC–AD 220; *see also* CHINA, §XIII, 22(ii)). The use of red ink (made from oxide of mercury or cinnabar) served as a mark of distinction, whereas ordinary citizens used black from lampblack.

The imperial seals of the khans were made of gold, jade or silver and measured 100–150 mm sq. The scripts used were Chinese, Sogdian and Phakpa. The latter, introduced in 1269, was devised for the Mongols by the Tibetan lama of the same name. Seals were used on all official documents, and Marco Polo mentions the vermilion seal being stamped on money to authenticate the currency. The seal of Genghis Khan (*reg* 1206–27), designed by his Uygur scribe, Tatatungo, read: '*God in his heaven; on earth the Great Khan, the Power of God, the Ruler of Mankind*'. In the Biblioteca Apostolica Vaticana, Vatican, Rome, is a copy of Güyük Khan's officially sealed letter to Pope Innocent IV, dated 1246 (see Marshall, 1993, p. 154). The original was brought from Mongolia by the Franciscan monk John of Plano Carpini. The seal reads, '*By the strength of Eternal Heaven, Order of the Universal Ruler of the Empire of the Great Mongols*'. This letter, written in Persian and Uygur, sealed with a Mongol seal of Chinese style cut by Csomas, a Russian sealcutter, and sent by the hand of an Italian monk to the Pope, is an example of the cosmopolitan character of the Mongol empire, which served as a bridge between East and West.

Seals and ciphers continue to be used in Mongolia up to the present day. The traditional type after the collapse of the Mongolian empire in 1370 was of iron, with a pierced and chased brass handle, and was round or square in shape. The seal itself was engraved in Phakpa or Sogdian script with the family name, often with the addition of a Buddhist emblem.

See also §12 below.

BIBLIOGRAPHY

T. F. Carter: *The Invention of Printing in China and its Spread Westwards* (New York, 1925, rev. 2/1955)
P. Brent: *The Mongol Empire* (London, 1976)
Die Mongolen, 2 vols (exh. cat., ed. W. Heissig and C. C. Müller; Munich, Haus Kst, 1989)
R. Marshall: *Storm from the East* (London, 1993)
ZARA FLEMING

12. SCRIPTS. The Mongolian script system—also known as Uygur-Mongolian—was adopted in 1204 from the Uygurs of Eastern Central Asia. It has its origins in a variant of Aramaic script used by the Sogdians and was the most important Mongolian script in common usage well into the 20th century. Local developments also took place. The west Mongolian 'clear' script, devised in 1648 by the High Lama of Jungaria, Jaya Pandita (*b* 1599), made considerable gains in clarity through the addition of supplementary diacritical marks. The north Mongolian (Buryat) Vagindra script was created in 1905 by Lama Agvaandorz on the basis of 'clear' script. In both cases the direction of writing is from top to bottom and from right to left.

Other less common types of script possess a special artistic significance. Their principal application was as seal scripts; otherwise, they were esoteric or simply decorative. The Phakpa script, created in 1269 by the Tibetan lama Phakpa (1235–80), was based on Tibetan script and used primarily as a seal script. The Soyombo script was invented in 1686 by the spiritual leader of northern Mongolia, the first Jebcundamba Khutukhtu, Ondür Gegen or Zanabazar (1635–1723), as a secret-code script. The emblem on the Mongolian flag represents the initial character of the Soyombo alphabet. The horizontal Phakpa script is also believed to have been devised by Zanabazar; it first appeared in print in 1729 and represents a syllabic horizontal form of Phakpa script. There are also decorative variations of Uygur-Mongolian that consist primarily of shaping words into geometric forms, circles or symbols of good luck.

BIBLIOGRAPHY

M. Weiers: 'Die Entwicklung der mongolischen Schriften', *Stud. Gen.*, xx/8 (1967), pp. 470–79
C. Šagdarsuren: *Mongol üseg züj* (Ulaan Baatar, 1981)

DOMINIQUE M. DUMAS

13. SCULPTURE.

(i) Religious. The art of Mongolian castings and sculpture developed in the 17th century, about a hundred years earlier than painting. As a religious art the works represent not an individual image of some deity, but the abstract tenets of Buddhism expressed through the human body as a means of making the contemplative scholastic philosophy more accessible. The artist is not permitted any changes, since the slightest deviation from the canonical rules in regard to pose, attributes, clothing etc would be an infringement of the essence and meaning of the teaching and its symbols.

The first creative genius of Mongolian sculpture was the lama–scholar Zanabazar (1635–1723), who according to his biographers made many statues of deities cast in gold, among them Vajradhara, a series of Dhyana Buddhas, 21 images of the goddess Tara, and others. One of his greatest works is a large casting in gilt bronze of *Green Tara* (770×450 mm; Ulaan Baatar, Pal. Mus.; see Tsultem, 1982, figs 45–8), which unlike other images of Tara has the appearance of a lovely, round-faced, Mongolian girl. His *Vajradhara* statue (see fig. 5 above), the chief holy relic of the Ganden Thekchen Ling Monastery at Ulaan Baatar, shows in its adornments the skilful use made of traditional Mongolian designs representing the thoughts of the nomad cattle-breeders and the benevolent symbolism of their aspirations.

Zanabazar's artistic approach greatly influenced the development of the 18th-century Urga school of Mongolian art. However, later examples of this school, for instance an *Amitabha Buddha* (Ulaan Baatar, Mus. F.A., 1845-735; 1989 exh. cat., no. 202) cast in the 19th century and a 20th-century bronze of the goddess *Penden Lhamo* (Ulaan Baatar, Mus. F.A., 7010-2386; 1989 exh. cat., no. 207), lack harmony in features and body proportions.

BIBLIOGRAPHY

N. Tsultem: *The Eminent Mongolian Sculptor, G. Zanabazar* (Ulaan Baatar, 1982) [text in Rus., Eng., Fr., Sp.]
Die Mongolen, 2 vols (exh. cat., ed. W. Heissig and C. C. Müller; Munich, Haus Kst, 1989)

(ii) Secular. During the second half of the 2nd millennium BC, which was a period of highly developed bronze-smelting, appeared the style associated with the late Bronze Age Karasuk culture (*c.* 1200–800 BC). The style can be seen in the sculpted heads of wild animals with long ears, huge eyes and giant horns on bronze knives, axes, daggers and other objects. From the 1st millennium BC date the monumental deer or stag-stones in the ANIMAL STYLE. During the 6th century AD various kinds of human images (known from the Russian as *baba*: 'old woman') were sculpted. Runic inscriptions were carved on stones, and monumental stone portraits were produced. In the 13th century Iranian art was very influential, and Chinese portraits were popular.

BIBLIOGRAPHY

EWA: 'Turkic art', cols 443–6
N.-O. Tsultem: *Iskusstvo Mongolii s drevneyshikh vremyon do nachala XX beka* [Art of Mongolia from the earliest times till the 20th century] (Moscow, 1984)
N. Tsultem: *Mongolian Arts and Crafts* (Ulaan Baatar, 1987) [text in Rus., Eng., Fr., Sp.]
Die Mongolen, 2 vols (exh. cat., ed. W. Heissig and C. C. Müller; Munich, Haus Kst, 1989)

ANDREA LOSERIES-LEICK

14. WOODWORK. In the nomadic herding economy, wooden and leather utensils largely took the place of pottery and metalware, being light, unbreakable and requiring no specialist skills or equipment to make. Forests grow chiefly in the extreme north of the Mongol areas, and wood often had to be transported long distances. Wooden domestic utensils are either roughly hollowed out (e.g. ladles, bowls, troughs and massive tea mortars made from a section of trunk) or constructed of sections hooped with metal, as is typical for milking pails. They are rarely decorated, except for the handles of ladles, which may end in an ornamental curl or an animal's head. In northern forest areas vessels may be of birch bark. Birch root is turned and polished to make drinking bowls set in silver casings. This is craftsman's work; many of the bowls were Chinese imports until recently.

The furnishings of the tent (*see also* TENT, §II, 2), originally hide bags and undecorated wooden chests held together only by camel-hide thongs, came to include chests and beds with painted ornamentation, often of Chinese make, from the late 19th century. The multicoloured designs are typically stencilled on to a red or orange ground. In those areas beyond the reach of Chinese wares, wooden manufactures from monastery workshops were sold to herdsmen. Furniture intended for the monasteries themselves was elaborately decorated by painting, gilding and a form of applied relief (*jümber*). The framework of the felt tent is entirely of wood, fixed with thongs. It was undecorated except in the case of the carved and brightly painted wood of princely or wealthy tents, but painted decoration is now more common, particularly on the wooden door. Doors came into use in the 19th century, replacing a felt flap.

Elaborate carving is uncommon, but may appear on two particular objects, the scraper used to dry the sweat from a racehorse and the ritual ladle for pouring libations of milk. Handles may end in a carved horse's head (see fig. 8), and horses and other livestock, traditional geometric designs and auspicious symbols (usually of Buddhist

8. Wooden ritual ladle for milk libations, larch-wood (Ulaan Baatar, Central Museum)

origin, including the 12 animals of the calendar cycle) decorate the flat surfaces. Chessmen and other game pieces and certain musical instruments sometimes exhibit fine work. The wooden blocks used to produce block prints were the work of monk–craftsmen.

See also §8 above.

BIBLIOGRAPHY

N. V. Kocheshkov: *Dekorativnoye iskusstvo mongolyazychnykh narodov (XIX–serediny XX veka)* [The decorative art of the Mongol-speaking nations (19th–mid-20th century)] (Moscow, 1979)

T. Disan: 'Töv xalxyn modon edleliin xee ugalzny töröl züilees' [On varieties of ornamentation on wood in Central Khalka], *Stud. Ethnog.*, ix/1–11 (Ulaan Baatar, 1985), pp. 64–71

V. Ronge: 'Handwerkertum bei den Mongolen: Filz, Leder, Holz und ihre Verarbeitung', *Die Mongolen* (exh. cat., ed. W. Heissig and C. C. Müller; Munich, Haus Kst, 1989), ii, pp. 173–81

R. H. Sheeks: 'Tea Bowls of the Himalayan and Mongolian Peoples', *A. Asia*, xxii/2 (1992), pp. 72–9

KRYSTYNA CHABROS

V. Patronage.

Archaeological finds show that the rulers of the steppes valued art objects, particularly silver and gold, from ancient times. Apart from such evidence there is little information about those who sponsored the arts in Mongolia before the time of Genghis Khan (*reg* 1206–27). It seems certain, however, that shamans supported some specialist art forms. Their elaborate costumes, headdress, drums and other religious items were carefully made and decorated, largely with stylized animal designs. Although Genghis Khan was probably not a major patron of the arts, his policy towards subject populations, by which craftsmen were not usually killed, but instead co-opted into the Mongol forces, provided his successors with personnel for artistic as well as military and engineering projects, such as the architectural diversity that occurred in the capital of Karakorum under Ogdai Khan (*reg* 1229–41). The most famous Chinggisid patron of the arts was probably Kublai Khan (*reg* 1260–94), first emperor of the Yuan dynasty (1279–1368). Like other Mongol rulers, he seems to have enjoyed pictures of horses and such hawking birds as the gerfalcon, both traditional status symbols of the steppe. This tendency of the Yuan dynasty encouraged the development of the Chinese depiction of horses.

The introduction of Buddhism by Altan Khan (1507–82) marked a new chapter in the history of Mongolian Art. Monasteries were founded all over Mongolia in the 17th century. The communities of monks practised a wide range of arts, most of them modelled on Tibetan forms. Representations of the Buddha and other holy figures of Tibetan Buddhism were widely produced in monasteries in the form of statues and paintings, and ecclesiastical architecture developed along Tibetan lines (*see also* §§III and IV, 9(i) and 13(i) above). The Buddhist church was supported by the aristocracy, by contributions from commoners and to a certain extent by the Manchu Qing dynasty (1644–1911), which ruled the region from 1691. The nobles of this period, like their Manchu counterparts, valued snuff-bottles, decorated knives and other beautifully crafted traditional items, which were made in large numbers at this time. After the revolution, art was sponsored almost entirely by the government, but later private companies supported some artistic activity.

BIBLIOGRAPHY

Yu. Bayan: *Ubur mongolan tuukhiin nairuulal* [An account of the history of Inner Mongolia] (Shanghai, 1962)

C. R. Bawden: *The Modern History of Mongolia* (London, 1968)

S. Jagchid and P. Hyer: *Mongolia's Culture and Society* (Boulder, 1979)

DAVID SNEATH

VI. Historiography.

Owing to the nomadic lifestyle of Mongolia's inhabitants until modern times, only a few elements of their art and architecture met the appreciation of literate observers, who were invariably foreigners. Among these the nomadic tent, or *ger*, known in the west as yurt, has been the object of greatest interest (*see also* TENT, §II, 2). Chapter 110 of the *Shiji* ('Records of the historian') by the Chinese historian Sima Qian (*c.* 145–90 BC) mentions the mobile dwellings of the first historical nomadic people of Mongolia, the Xiongnu. Later Chinese sources, including the *Wei shu* (6th century AD), referred to some nomadic people of Mongolia as High Carts (Chin. *gaoche*), an ethnonym that has been explained as a phonetic rendering for Kirgiz but also indicates the typical nomadic mobile cart-house. Moreover, the 7th-century AD *Bei shi* ('History of the northern dynasties') states that Khitan (Qidan) tribes who inhabited Mongolia used ox-carts on which they carried straw-covered huts.

The earliest references in Western literature to tents and to the practice of carrying them on carts can be found in the description of the nomadic Scythians (culturally related to the Xiongnu) by Hesiod (*Catalogue of Women*, 39) and Herodotus (IV. 46). The first accounts of the Mongol tent date back to the period of the Mongol empire. The 13th-century Venetian Marco Polo (Yule and Cordier, i, p. 244) and, later, such religious envoys as Willem van Rubruck (*c*. 1210–*c*. 1270; Jackson and Morgan, pp. 72–8) and John of Plano Carpini (*d* 1252; Dawson, p. 8) have left more detailed descriptions of trellis tents of average size, to be assembled on the spot, and of larger ones that were carried on huge carts, pulled by as many as 22 oxen. Rubruck also speaks of what appear to be lamaist temples in Karakorum (the capital of the Mongol empire) and of 'idols', 'all most beautifully inlaid with gold'. Various crafts were appreciated by the Mongols, and at the court of Mengu Khan (*reg* 1251–9), whom Rubruck visited, there were several foreign artists, including a Russian expert in building dwellings and a Parisian goldsmith. The fullest later description of Turco-Mongol tents and palaces is possibly that contained in the report (see Andrews) of Ruy Gonzalez de Clavijo (*d* 1412), Castilian ambassador to Timur (*see also* TIMURID, §II, 1).

Middle Eastern sources include Marvazi's mention of the Turks' 'tents and yurtas' (Minorski, 1942, p. 29), the *Persian Geography* by Hudud al-'Alam (Minorski, 1970, p. 99) for the year AD 982, and the famed Arab traveller Ibn Battuta who, in his *Travels* (see Gibb), speaks of wagons carrying not only tents but also mosques and shops. The most important Chinese works on the early Mongols are the *Meng Da beilu* ('Detailed record of the Mongol Tatars'; 1221) by Zhao Hong and the *Hei Da shilüe* ('Brief survey of the Black Tatars'; 1237) by Peng Daya and Su Ting (see Olbricht and Pinks). The first simply mentions felt tents, whereas the second gives a fuller description.

In the 20th century animal-style bronzes, mainly knives, daggers, belt-buckles and horse and cart fittings, were studied intensively (see, for instance, Salmony and Jettmar). The ancient petroglyphs and stone statuary of the early Turk period (AD 552–744; *see also* §IV, 10 and 13(ii) above) discovered in Mongolia by Soviet and Mongol archaeologists were also investigated (see Novgorodova).

BIBLIOGRAPHY

H. Yule and H. Cordier: *Ye Book of Ser Marco Polo, ye Venetian, Concerning ye Kingdoms of ye East*, 2 vols (London, 1874, rev. 3/1903/*R* 1926)
A. Salmony: *Sino-Siberian Art in the Collection of C. T. Loo* (Paris, 1933)
N. Egami: 'Kyōdo no jūkyo' [Dwellings of the Xiongnu], *Shigaku Zasshi*, ix (1935), pp. 109–11
V. Minorski: *Sharaf al-Zamān Tāhir Marvazī on China, the Turks and India (c. 1120)* (London, 1942)
C. Dawson, ed.: *The Mongol Mission: Narratives and Letters of the Franciscan Missionaries in Mongolia and China in the Thirteenth and Fourteenth Centuries* (London and New York, 1955)
H. A. R. Gibb: *The Travels of Ibn Baṭṭūṭa: A.D. 1325–1354*, 3 vols (Cambridge, 1958–71)
K. Jettmar: *Art of the Steppes* (New York, 1967)
V. Minorski: *Hudūd al-'Alam: The Regions of the World, A Persian Geography, 327 A.H.–982 A.D.* (London, 1970)
P. A. Andrews: 'The Tents of Timur: An Examination of Reports on the Quriltay at Samarqand, 1404', *Arts of the Eurasian Steppelands*, ed. P. Denwood (London, 1978), pp. 143–87
S. Jagchid and P. Hyer: *Mongolia's Culture and Society* (Boulder, 1979)
P. Olbricht and E. Pinks: *Meng-Ta Pei-Lu und Hei-Ta Shih-lüeh: Chinesische Gesandtenberichte über die frühen Mongolen 1221 und 1237* (Wiesbaden, 1980)
E. A. Novgorodova: *Drevnyaya Mongoliya* [Ancient Mongolia] (Moscow, 1989)
P. Jackson and D. Morgan: *The Mission of Friar William of Rubruck: His Journeys to the Court of the Great Khan Mongke, 1253–1255* (Cambridge, 1990)

VII. Archaeology.

European travellers and scientists started to investigate the prehistory of Mongolia in the second half of the 19th century. The first archaeological expeditions were conducted by the Finnish scholars Johan Reinhold Aspelin (1842–1915) in 1887 and 1889 and by Axel Olai Heikel (1851–1924) in 1890. In 1889 the Russian scholar Nikolay Mikhaylovich Yadrintsev (1842–94) discovered the famous Orkhon inscriptions (dated AD 716, 731 and 735) in Old Turkic script. The Russian Academy of Sciences then organized a larger expedition, headed by the eminent Turcologist Wilhelm Radloff (1837–1918) in 1891.

In the 1920s the American Central Asiatic expeditions, headed by Roy Chapman Andrews (1884–1960), investigated different aspects of natural history. The archaeologist of the expedition, N. C. Nelson (active 1925–8), brought to light several findings related to the Mongolian Neolithic period. The Sino–Swedish expedition headed by SVEN HEDIN investigated 327 sites in Inner Mongolia; its archaeologist, Folke Bergman (1902–46), unearthed mainly Palaeolithic artefacts (see Maringer). The most important work, however, was carried out by Soviet archaeologists. Two expeditions were sent to Mongolia in 1924 and 1925, headed by P. K. Kozlov (1863–1935), following the accidental discovery of bronze pieces in 1912. This expedition discovered NOIN ULA, a large burial complex of the Xiongnu period (end of 1st millennium BC), which, together with the Pazyryk complex found by Sergey Ivanovich Rudenko in the Altai Mountains, laid the foundations of scientific archaeology in Mongolia. In 1948–9 a joint Soviet–Mongol archaeological expedition began to excavate ancient cities, in particular Karakorum.

Mongol archaeologists played a more active role from the 1950s, in particular Ser-Odjav, Dorjsuren and Perlee. Ser-Odjav wrote a first survey of the Mongolian Neolithic period; in 1957 he discovered a monument complex erected in honour of the early Turk dignitary Tonyuquq (*fl* early 8th century AD), and published extensively on the culture of the early Turks (6th–8th centuries BC). Perlee investigated such ancient cities as Zuun-kherem and in the 1960s excavated several Xiongnu burials. In the early 1950s Dorjsuren conducted research on the Neolithic; later, he concentrated on the culture and history of the northern Xiongnu (3rd–1st century BC). Most archaeological research was conducted with scholars from other socialist countries, and joint expeditions were organized with Hungary (1957), Czechoslovakia (1958–9) and the Soviet Union. Especially important for the Palaeolithic and Neolithic periods is the work of the Soviet archaeologist Aleksey Pavlovich Okladnikov, who pioneered the study of petroglyphs, later continued by Eleonora A. Novgorodova. With the establishment of the Mongol Academy of Sciences in the 1960s, archaeological research was promoted on a large scale. The joint Soviet–Mongol expeditions from 1969 greatly broadened this field.

BIBLIOGRAPHY

J. Maringer: *Contribution to the Prehistory of Mongolia* (Stockholm, 1950)

E. A. Novgorodova: *Alte Kunst der Mongolei* (Leipzig, 1980)

——: *Drevnyaya Mongoliya* [Ancient Mongolia] (Moscow, 1989)

A. Derevyanko and Sh. Natsagdorj, eds: *Arkheologicheskiye, etnograficheskiye i antropologicheskiye issledovaniya v Mongolii* [Archaeological, ethnographical and anthropological research in Mongolia] (Novosibirsk, 1990)

NICOLA DI COSMO

VIII. Museums.

Four museums in Ulaan Baatar, Mongolia, conserve local art. The State Central Museum contains primarily ethnographic and archaeological collections. The Museum of Fine Arts is distinguished above all by its enormous holdings of traditional and contemporary paintings and sculptures. Two former temple complexes, the Museum of Religion (formerly also known as the Anti-Religious Museum) and the Palace Museum, preserve exclusively Buddhist cult objects, pictures (*tangka*s) and sculptures. The same holds for the oldest temple complex of north Mongolia, Erdeni Zuu (1586), near Karakorum, which has also been converted into a museum. There are also provincial museums whose contents have yet to be thoroughly catalogued. The Central Library in Ulaan Baatar preserves illuminated and other books of special artistic merit.

In the Inner Mongolian Museum in Hohhot, capital of the Inner Mongolia Autonomous Region of China, the archaeological holdings (e.g. Ordos bronzes) are most worthy of note. In the Republic of Buryatia, large collections of Buddhist art are preserved at Ulan-Ude in the Museum of Buryat History and Oriental Art. Ethnographica and folk art are in the Ethnographic Museum, Ulan-Ude.

Few European museums contain Mongolian art and artefacts except for those in the former Soviet Union. The Kalmuck Autonomous Republic and the above-mentioned Republic of Buryatia formed part of the Russian Federation of Socialist Soviet Republics; for many years the Soviet Union held a monopoly on archaeological and geographical research in the Mongolian People's Republic (now independent Mongolia) and appropriated many of the country's artistic treasures. Three museums in St Petersburg are foremost among European collections: the State Hermitage Museum, the Museum of the History of Religion, and the State Museum of Ethnography. The State Museum of Oriental Art in Moscow also owns many Mongolian artworks. A very large collection, comparable to those in St Petersburg, is held by the Etnografiska Museum, Stockholm, with the finds of the Sino–Swedish expedition under the leadership of SVEN HEDIN.

Other European collections mainly present ethnographica and folk art. The most important collection is in the Nationalmuseum, Copenhagen, for the most part acquired by H. Haslund-Christensen in 1937–9 in the Mongolian People's Republic. Mongolian art collections are found in Helsinki at the National Museum of Finland, at the Museum für Völkerkunde, Leipzig, the Museum für Völkerkunde, Berlin, and in Paris at the Musée de l'Homme (mainly Buryat objects). The large collection of Tibetan Buddhist art acquired by the German Hans Leder in the 19th century in Inner Mongolia is dispersed in ethnographic museums throughout Europe (Vienna, Prague, Budapest, Leipzig, Stuttgart, Heidelberg, Hamburg). Mongolian books are preserved in the libraries of Copenhagen, Leiden, Berlin and Paris, among others. In the USA the best collections are in the Peabody Museum of Salem, MA, and the Smithsonian Institution, Washington, DC.

BIBLIOGRAPHY

W. Hartwig: 'Ethnographica der Chalcha und Burjaten (Mongolische Volksrepublik)', *Jb. Mus. Vlkerknd. Leipzig*, xxii (Berlin, 1966), pp. 112–88

N. Tsultem: *The Eminent Mongolian Sculptor, G. Zanabazar* (Ulaan Baatar, 1982) [text in Rus., Eng., Fr., Sp.]

——: *Development of the Mongolian National Style Painting 'Mongol Zurag' in Brief* (Ulaan Baatar, 1986) [text in Rus., Eng., Fr., Sp.]

H. Halen: *Mirrors of the Void: Buddhist Art in the National Museum of Finland* (Helsinki, 1987)

N. Tsultem: *Mongolian Arts and Crafts* (Ulaan Baatar, 1987) [text in Rus., Eng., Fr., Sp.]

Övör mongyol-ün teüke-zin durasyaltu iüil [Historical relics of Inner Mongolia] (Hohhot, 1987)

Övör mongyol-ün ündüsüten-ü dursyaltu iüil [National relics of Inner Mongolia] (Beijing, 1987)

N. Tsultem: *Mongolian Sculpture* (Ulaan Baatar, 1989) [text in Rus., Eng., Fr., Sp.]

IX. Exhibitions.

The political situation in Mongol areas under the influence of the Soviet Union and the People's Republic of China meant that, in general, it was not until the mid-1980s that either the media or museums in the West concerned themselves with Mongolian themes. There were, however, three small, earlier exhibitions: in 1967 in Leipzig, in 1979 at the Horniman Museum, London, and in 1983 at the Musée de l'Homme in Paris. In 1983–4 an exhibition of Inner Mongolian relics with a primarily archaeological content was shown in Japan. Particularly worth mentioning is the Mongolia exhibition that was held in Germany in 1989. Over 250 objects from the Mongolian People's Republic were displayed: costumes, jewellery, saddles, musical instruments and other artistically rendered utilitarian objects and shamans' instruments and Buddhist art, including *tangka*s, bronzes and dance masks (see 1989 exh. cat.). In 1994–5 an exhibition of over 200 objects was organized by Adam Kessler in collaboration with the People's Republic of China and the Inner Mongolian Autonomous Region at the Natural History Museum of Los Angeles County, Los Angeles, CA, the American Museum of Natural History, New York, Tennessee State Museum, Nashville, TN, and the Royal British Columbia Museum, Victoria, BC.

BIBLIOGRAPHY

Mongolei-Ausstellung im Museum für Völkerkunde (exh. cat., Leipzig, Mus. Vlkerknd., 1967)

Mongolia: Land of the Five Animals (exh. cat., London, Horniman Mus., 1979)

Mongolie–Mongolie (exh. cat., Paris, Mus. Homme, 1983)

Inner Mongolian Nomadic Nation's Relics (exh. cat., Tokyo; Osaka; Kyoto; Naoya; 1983–4)

Övör mongyol-ün teüke-zin durasyaltu iüil [Historical relics of Inner Mongolia] (Hohhot, 1987)

Die Mongolen, 2 vols (exh. cat., ed. W. Heissig and C. C. Müller; Munich, Haus Kst, 1989)

V. N. Basilov, ed.: *Nomads of Eurasia* (Seattle and London, 1989)

DOMINIQUE M. DUMAS

Monier. *See* Mosnier.

Monigetti, Ippolit (Antonovich) (*b* Moscow, 1819; *d* St Petersburg, 1878). Russian architect. He studied at the Stroganov School in Moscow (1829–34) and at the Academy of Arts in St Petersburg (1835–9) under Aleksandr Bryullov. He continued his studies abroad, in Italy, Greece, Turkey and Egypt (1839–46). In 1847 he was made an academician for his designs for monuments in Greece and Italy. Between 1848 and 1880 he was court architect at Tsarskoye Selo (now Pushkin), where he designed some 30 buildings that made use of a wide range of forms and styles. Monigetti's buildings in St Petersburg are mainly in the Baroque or early Neo-classical style. His striving for a picturesque and silhouetted quality characteristic of Romanticism entailed a broad use of attic storeys and corner towers, as in the Zherebtsov House (1854–6), the Vorontsov House (1856) and the Stroganov House (1857; all St Petersburg). In the opulent interior of the Yusupov House (1857–9), the Gold Drawing-room in the Winter Palace, St Petersburg, and the ceremonial staircase of the Catherine Palace, Tsarskoye Selo (both 1850s), he made extensive use of Baroque and other Western styles. In his later work of the 1860s and 1870s, such as the imperial residence at Livadiya in the Crimea, the interior of the Anichkov Palace in St Petersburg, the churches in Vevey (Switzerland) and Pargolovo (nr St Petersburg) and the Baryatinski Palace, signs of growing historicism are visible in the overabundance of forms and the archaeological exactness with which elements of the various prototypes have been reconstructed. The same characteristics are found in the most famous of his buildings, the Polytechnical Museum (1877), Moscow, one of the first major public buildings in Russia to be designed with national architectural forms.

BIBLIOGRAPHY

V. N. Listov: *Ippolit Monigetti* (Leningrad, 1976)

YE. I. KIRICHENKO

Moñino, José. *See* Floridablanca, Conde de.

Monkwearmouth Abbey. Former Benedictine monastery dedicated to St Peter, in Tyne & Wear, northern England. The monastery at Monkwearmouth, one of the most illustrious in early Anglo-Saxon England, was founded by Benedict Biscop in AD 674. Its history from the later 8th century onwards is obscure; by the late 9th century some of its estates (including the site of the monastery) had come under the control of the Community of St Cuthbert, and the church thereafter became solely parochial. Some time after the Norman Conquest (1066) it became a small priory dependent on Durham, reverting to parochial status at the Reformation.

The essential feature of this sequence—considerable initial importance followed by protracted decline—is fundamental to understanding Monkwearmouth's architectural history, as it has resulted in the virtually intact preservation of the west end of the early monastery's principal church, St Peter's (see fig.), the best-preserved example in England of a monumental façade from an early Anglo-Saxon church of the first rank. The remains reveal

Monkwearmouth, St Peter, view from south-west, late 7th century to 11th

an exceptionally complex structural history spanning the first four centuries of the church's existence.

The latest phase is the top three stages of the tower, which are built up from the gable of an earlier two-storey porch. The total height is *c*. 18 m. The form of the belfry openings, probably dating from the mid- to late 11th century, may reflect the influence of the destroyed early 11th-century west tower of the Anglo-Saxon cathedral at Durham. These parts are built of regularly coursed, squared ashlar, contrasting markedly with the earlier work below, all of which uses much smaller, less regularly coursed limestone rubble with large angle quoins of sandstone, ashlar being restricted to the openings.

The two-storey porch is itself an addition to the west wall of the nave, which it abuts from ground-level upwards. It has a complex structural sequence of its own. The ground-floor barrel vault is evidently a later (perhaps 11th-century) insertion, overlying the plaster face of the walls behind and blocking a small first-floor door in the north wall, which must previously have opened into the upper chamber when its floor level was lower. The arched ground-floor openings are probably part of the original design. The present doorway into the church, with its long vertical jambs, pseudo-imposts and radial voussoirs, is so similar to the lateral arches of the porch that it must be contemporary. The blocked head of the original west door remains above its successor.

The lateral arches of the porch are now open, but are rebated for doors that originally opened into a pair of *porticus*, the southern of which has been excavated. The positions of the blocked door in the north wall and the window in the south wall of the porch's first floor show that this was erected before the flanking *porticus*, with their lean-to roofs, were demolished; very likely the *porticus* and both stages of the porch are all contemporary. The string course between the two storeys on its western face does not continue round on to the north and south sides, so presumably it formerly ran on across the flanking *porticus*.

The original context of the porch, as the central element of a wide western façade, was thus very different from its present one. Much of its effect must have derived from the monumental sculpture with which it was decorated. Traces of a large standing figure (not certainly original) survive in the gable. Below, the string course between the ground and first floors was decorated with a panelled animal frieze. Finally, the western opening itself is flanked by pairs of elaborately moulded lathe-turned baluster-shafts (conceivably themselves later insertions); the lower jambs are lined by slabs decorated with pairs of intertwined serpentine beasts with tails ending in fish-like splays. Their head and beak types are most closely paralleled in Insular manuscripts of the late 7th century and the early 8th, the absence of sculptural analogies perhaps indicating that they are also early in the history of Northumbrian sculpture.

The porch has been identified with the 'porch of entry' (*porticus ingressus*) documented as existing before 686, when Abbot Eosterwine was buried in it. This may not, however, necessarily refer to a porch at the west end. Another possibility is that the long corridor-like structure found in excavation running northwards towards the church (presumably from monastic buildings to the south) might itself have been described as a *porticus ingressus*, or might at least imply the former existence of such an entrance where it would have joined on to the church.

Shortly after the monastery was founded, in 675 or 676, Gaulish masons were procured to build a stone church. Enough was finished within a year for Masses to be celebrated, and it must have been complete by *c.* 678, when Biscop set off for Rome to acquire furnishings for it. It had an eastern '*porticus* of St Peter' (probably the chancel), a sacristy (*sacrarium*) south of the sanctuary and 'upper chambers' (*caenacula*). The simple design of the nave west wall, with its tall, narrow, plain doorway and pair of upper windows, in complete contrast to the elaborate decoration of the porch, is very probably part of this first church. Further, the dimensions of the present nave (20 m long, 5.5 m wide and 10 m high internally) may perpetuate those of the original one, the long, narrow and tall proportions being typical of early Northumbrian churches. The plain architecture was doubtless relieved by the iconographically sophisticated series of panel paintings with which Biscop decorated it: Gospel scenes on the north, Apocalyptic ones on the south. Panels of the Virgin and the Apostles stretched across the central part of the church, perhaps as the decoration of a screen.

The church's architectural context would be clearer if more archaeological investigation had taken place in Gaul, whence Benedict obtained the masons and glaziers. The probable proportions of the nave are similar to the excavated early 7th-century church of Ste Gertrude in Nivelles, Belgium, while the porch may have been comparable with structures such as the tower porch documented at the late 5th-century basilica of St Martin at Tours.

BIBLIOGRAPHY

Bede: *Lives of the Abbots of Wearmouth and Jarrow*, Eng. trans. in D. Farmer: *The Age of Bede* (Harmondsworth, 1983), pp. 185–208
H. M. Taylor and J. Taylor: *Anglo-Saxon Architecture* (Cambridge, 1965–78), i, pp. 432–46
R. J. Cramp: 'Monkwearmouth Church', *Archaeol. J.*, cxxxiii (1976), pp. 230–37

ERIC CAMBRIDGE

Monneret de Villard, Ugo (*b* Milan, 16 Jan 1881; *d* Rome, 4 Nov 1954). Italian archaeologist, art historian and epigrapher. Descended from a French noble family from Burgundy that had moved to Piedmont at the time of the French Revolution, he trained as an architect and then taught medieval architecture at the Politecnico in Milan. His early writings (to 1920) were devoted mainly to the art and architecture of Italy, especially Lombardy; his interests then turned to the Christian and Islamic Orient. In 1923 he published a work on the sculpture at Ahnas (*see* HERAKLEOPOLIS MAGNA), in which he showed how Coptic art developed out of Hellenistic and Egyptian traditions. This was followed in 1930 by a monograph on the Islamic necropolis at ASWAN, and archaeological research in Nubia led him to explain the political and cultural significance of that region in the medieval period. In 1934 he moved to Rome and, after the Italian invasion of Ethiopia in 1935–6, he familiarized himself with Ethiopian art and took part in an expedition to AKSUM and excavations at Addis Ababa. He also worked on a comprehensive exposition of the Mesopotamian Church, which emphasized the importance of Babylonian and Iranian traditions, particularly Manichaean and Sasanian art. In the last two decades of his life he collected material for a series of publications on Islamic art in Italy. The first, on an inlaid ivory casket in the Cappella Palatina of Palermo, was followed by a book about its painted ceiling. Although he taught Christian archaeology at the University of Rome (1943–4), other attempts to support his work by teaching were frustrated, and his work received few acknowledgments until 1950, when he was awarded the national prize of the Accademia Nazionale dei Lincei. In addition to his series on the Islamic monuments of Italy, work that remained unfinished at his death included a study of the textile industry of Iraq and an introduction to Islamic archaeology.

WRITINGS

La scultura ad Ahnâs: Note sull'origine dell'arte copta (Milan, 1923)
La necropoli musulmana di Aswân (Cairo, 1930)
La Nubia medioevale, 4 vols (Cairo, 1935–57)
La cassetta incrostata della Cappella Palatina di Palermo (Rome, 1938)
Le chiese della Mesopotamia (Rome, 1940)
Le pitture musulmane al soffitto della Cappella Palatina in Palermo (Rome, 1950)
'Tessuti e ricami mesopotamici ai tempi degli 'Abbāsidi e dei Selğūqidi', *Atti & Mem. Accad. N. Lincei, Atti Cl. Sci. Morali*, ser. 8, vii/4 (1955), pp. 183–234
Introduzione allo studio dell'archeologia islamica: Le origini ed il periodo omayyade (Rome and Venice, 1966/R 1968)

BIBLIOGRAPHY

G. Levi Della Vida: Obituary, *Riv. Stud. Orient.*, xxx (1955), pp. 172–88 [with bibliog.]
E. Kühnel: Obituary, *A. Orient.*, ii (1957), pp. 627–33 [includes bibliog. compiled by G. Levi Della Vida, with additions]

S. J. VERNOIT

Monnickes, Hendrik. *See* MUNNICHHOEVEN, HENDRIK.

Monnier, Henry (Bonaventure) (*b* Paris, 7 June 1799; *d* Paris, 3 June 1877). French painter, draughtsman, printmaker, writer and actor. He is best known for his satire of the mid-19th-century Parisian bourgeoisie, epitomized in the character of Joseph Prudhomme. Monnier worked as a supernumerary and then as a copy clerk in the bookkeeping department of the Département de la Justice. (He would later satirize office life in his work.) In 1817 he enrolled briefly in the studio of Anne-Louis Girodet de Roussy-Trioson, he then moved to the studio of Baron Antoine-Jean Gros, where he remained for two years before he was expelled. Known as a prankster, he impersonated various character types in improvised scenes. These and subsequent performances as a mimic and monologist in studios and salons became the basis of his first published work, *Scènes populaires dessinées à la plume* (1830), which he both wrote and illustrated and which was reprinted 12 times in various editions during his life. The same themes extended throughout Monnier's activities as a caricaturist, writer and actor.

Monnier turned from studying painting to lithography, and contributed to the popular comic albums of Parisian types and manners in the periods 1826–30 and 1840–47. The earlier period includes the series *Moeurs parisiennes* (1826), *Six Quartiers de Paris* and *Moeurs administratives* (both 1828) on bureaucratic hierarchies. Monnier also illustrated many of the quasi-satirical codes and manuals of behaviour. He drew the frontispiece for the first volume of *La Silhouette*, one of the two caricature journals published in 1830. Monnier illustrated volumes of the series *Physiologies Aubert*, which analysed the Parisian population by manner and milieu. His most notable contribution, *Physiologie du bourgeois* (1841), identified boredom as a predominant feature of bourgeois life. In 1854 he published *Les Bourgeois de Paris*.

Monnier drew series of petit-bourgeois neighbourhoods, trades, shops and theatres. For *Les Français peints par eux-mêmes* (1840–42) he contributed more than 100 illustrations on a range of physiognomic types, costumes and interiors. The series *Les Industriels: Métiers et professions en France* (1842), illustrated by Monnier with text by Emile de La Bedollière, is a taxonomy of the 'most populous classes'. Other collections of types appear in his *Cris de Paris* (1845–6) and *Code civil illustré* (1846–7).

Monnier's popular character, Joseph Prudhomme, appeared in several plays cast in such bourgeois professions as office manager, stockbroker, theatre manager and newspaper editor. He represented the quintessential bourgeoisie with his respect for institutions and conventions and was typified by his banal and sententious attitudes and statements. Honoré Daumier adopted Monnier's Prudhomme and represented him in more than 60 caricatures.

Monnier's text *Les Bas-fonds de la société* (1862) documents lower-class types, and it was intended to raise social conscience. The theme of boredom, apparent in his earlier descriptions of middle-class life, is picked up again in his series of watercolours *Les Diseurs de riens* (1866–74; Paris, Bib.N.). Monnier's detailed characterizations, particularly of the bourgeoisie, also influenced his friend and sometime collaborator Honoré de Balzac. Monnier had illustrated parts of Balzac's *Comédie humaine* (1842–8), and Balzac compared him in 1830 to Nicholas-Toussaint Charlet,

William Hogarth and Jacques Callot; in 1832 he wrote that 'Monnier is the personification of irony'. Gustave Flaubert's characterization of bourgeois mediocrity in his unfinished and posthumously published *Bouvard et Pécuchet* and *Dictionnaire des idées reçues* may have influenced by Monnier.

BIBLIOGRAPHY

T. Gautier: 'Henry Monnier', *Portraits contemporains* (Paris, 1874), pp. 33-7

Champfleury: *Henry Monnier, sa vie, son oeuvre* (Paris, 1879)

A. Daudet: 'Henry Monnier', *Trente Ans de Paris* (Paris, 1888), pp. 221-8

A. Marie: *L'Art et la vie romantiques: Henry Monnier (1799–1877)* (Paris, 1931)

E. Melcher: *The Life and Times of Henry Monnier* (Cambridge, MA, 1950)

J. Wechsler: *A Human Comedy: Physiognomy and Caricature in 19th Century Paris* (London and Chicago, 1982)

JUDITH WECHSLER

Monnot, Pierre-Etienne (*b* Orchamps-Vennes, Franche-Comté [now Doubs], 9 Aug 1657; *d* Rome, 24 Aug 1733). French sculptor, active in Italy. His father, a wood-carver, moved with his family to Besançon when Monnot was still a child. Monnot was taught to carve by his father, and at the age of 19 he moved to Dijon, where he was apprenticed to the sculptor Jean Dubois. Although he spent the years *c.* 1677–87 in Paris, he seems not to have had any connection with the Académie Royale de Peinture et de Sculpture, and his professional career was passed almost entirely outside France. His earliest dated work is a group of five small marble reliefs (1688) for the Hôtel de Ville at Poligny, Jura (*in situ*).

Around 1687 Monnot moved to Rome where, shortly after his arrival, he was commissioned by the Académie de France to make a copy (untraced) of a statue of *Julius Caesar* in the Palazzo Capitolino. Within three or four years he received the first of a series of commissions for the Landgrave Karl von Hesse-Kassel: the sculptural programme of the Marmorbad at Kassel, an ambitious project that was to occupy him intermittently for the rest of his life. For this domed, free-standing, square pavilion, surrounded on all sides by a barrel-vaulted gallery, he executed twelve life-size marble groups with mythological subjects and eight large marble reliefs depicting aquatic scenes from Ovid's *Metamorphoses*, as well as eight smaller reliefs in the triangular panels of the dome, representing the seasons and the elements (all *in situ*). The first groups, *Bacchus Offering Grapes to a Faun* and *Leda and the Swan*, are signed and dated 1692.

From this time Monnot never lacked commissions. In 1695–9 he carved two large marble reliefs, the *Adoration of the Shepherds* and the *Flight into Egypt* (both *in situ*), for the Capocaccia Chapel, opposite Gianlorenzo Bernini's Cornaro Chapel, in S Maria della Vittoria, Rome. Both compositions are crowded with over life-size figures animated by deeply channelled, twisted drapery folds characteristic of the High Baroque but with some of the restraint of the Late Baroque. His monumental tomb of *Innocent XI* (marble and bronze, completed 1701; Rome, St Peter's) is more classicizing, having been executed after designs by Carlo Maratti. Further important commissions followed. Clement XI chose him for the two most important of the twelve colossal statues of apostles for the giant niches designed by Borromini in the nave of S

Giovanni in Laterano, *St Peter* (see fig.) and *St Paul* (both marble, 1708–13; *in situ*). Both statues are highly successful, and the *St Peter* is Monnot's masterpiece. Influenced by the work of François Duquesnoy, he abandoned the nervous rhythms created by the convoluted drapery favoured by the late followers of Bernini, substituting broad, sweeping, curvilinear shapes. He suppressed detailing in order to emphasize the major motifs. There are residual Gothic echoes in the chevron folds and prominent cascades of drapery, but the whole has an integrated effect that combines vigour and power with dignity and restraint.

Perhaps as a result of having seen Monnot's animated funerary bust of *Cardinal Savio Millini* (marble, *c.* 1699–1701; Rome, S Maria del Popolo), the visiting Englishman John Cecil, 5th Earl of Exeter, ordered from him a funerary monument for himself and his wife (marble, erected 1704; Stamford, St Martin): the combination of styles, with realistic effigies in the flowing robes typical of the followers of Bernini lying side by side on top of the sarcophagus, each propped on one elbow in the Etruscan manner, was to enjoy widespread popularity in England in the 18th century. Among other works for Exeter (for illustration *see* CECIL, (3)), Monnot produced his marble group *Andromeda and the Sea Monster* (1700; New York, Met.).

From 1712 to 1728 Monnot made several visits to Kassel to work, assisted by his son Alessandro (*d* 1727), on the Marmorbad. Some of the reliefs were carved there, although most of the statue groups were done in Rome. The later reliefs, particularly the allegorical figures for the dome (seen floating in air, as if against the sky), have a lighter, more playful air than Monnot's previous work. Monnot returned to Rome in 1728, and there he completed the two last pieces for Kassel, *Flora and Zephyr* and *Minerva as Protector of the Arts*.

BIBLIOGRAPHY

F. Titi: *Nuovo studio di pittura, scoltura . . . di Roma* (Rome, 1721)
L. Pascoli: *Vite* (1730–36), ii, pp. 487–98
A. Caston: *Le Sculpteur français Pierre-Etienne Monnot* (Besançon, 1888)
A. Holtmeyer and others: *Die Bau- und Kunstdenkmäler im Regierungsbezirk Cassel*, vi (Kassel, 1923), pp. 340–50, pls 221–9
P. Francastel: 'Le Marmorbad de Cassel et les Lazienski de Varsovie', *Gaz. B.-A.*, n. s. 5, ix (1933), pp. 138–56
H. Honour: 'English Patrons and Italian Sculptors in the First Half of the Eighteenth Century', *Connoisseur*, cxli (1958), pp. 220–26
R. Wittkower: *Art and Architecture in Italy, 1600–1750*, Pelican Hist. A. (Harmondsworth, 1958, rev. 1973), pp. 366, 433, 436, 440, 442, 453, 466, 468
M. Whinney: *Sculpture in Britain, 1530–1830*, Pelican Hist. A. (Harmondsworth, 1964, rev. 1988), pp. 70, 120, 126, 253, 254, 256, 261
F. Souchal: *Les Slodtz* (Paris, 1967), pp. 146–7, 205, 226, 231, 233, 253, 302, 304
R. Enggass: *Early Eighteenth-century Sculpture in Rome* (University Park, PA, 1976), i, pp. 21–5, 46–8, 53, 59, 77–8, 111; ii, figs 20–39
——: 'Un Problème du baroque romain tardif: Projets de sculptures par des artistes non sculpteurs', *Rev. A.*, xxxi (1976), pp. 21–32
O. Raggio: 'Sculpture in the Grand Manner: Two Groups by Anguier and Monnot', *Apollo*, cvi (1977), pp. 364–75
R. Enggass: 'Settecento Sculpture in St Peter's: An Encyclopedia of Styles', *Apollo*, cxiii (1981), pp. 74–81

ROBERT ENGGASS

Monnoyer, Jean-Baptiste [Baptiste] (*b* Lille, 12 Jan 1636; *d* London, 20 Feb 1699). French painter. At an early age he studied history painting in Antwerp but had arrived in Paris by 1650, when he worked on the decoration of the Hôtel Lambert. He collaborated with Charles Le Brun on decorations for the royal châteaux of Marly (Yvelines) and Meudon (Seine-et-Oise) and the Grand Trianon at Versailles. He was presented to the Académie Royale in 1663 and received (*reçu*) in 1665. His *morceau de réception* was the painting now known as *Flowers, Fruit and Objets d'Art* (Montpellier, Mus. Fabre; see fig.). Originally entitled *a Sphinx on a Pedestal, a Clock, a Carpet, a Globe, Two Vases of Flowers*, it displays objects associated with the artist's trade with a high degree of verisimilitude. Monnoyer sent four still-lifes of flowers to his first Salon in 1673, and it was with this genre that he quickly became associated. He rose to prominence in the Académie and was created Conseiller in 1679.

Monnoyer's first marriage was to the sister of the history painter Pierre Mosnier; his second, to Marie Pétré in 1667, was celebrated in a remarkable double portrait of the *Artist and his Wife* (Paris, priv. col., see Faré, 1962, ii, fig. 228). She presents him with a basket of flowers as he paints; turning to the viewer, pointing towards her, he indicates that not only his new wife but also the fresh blooms serve as his muse. The woman and the flowers are given a fresh, spontaneous treatment quite lacking in Monnoyer's later decorative flower paintings, as if he had worked from nature; but in reality his compositions were built up from a series of drawings, with total disregard for the seasons. Monnoyer's flower paintings took the intimate French still-life and turned it into an elegant large-scale genre. Contemporaries considered the works so lifelike that they lacked nothing but the perfume, and Louis XIV

Pierre-Etienne Monnot: *St Peter*, marble, 1708–13 (Rome, S Giovanni in Laterano)

Jean-Baptiste Monnoyer: *Flowers, Fruit and Objets d'Art*, oil on canvas, 1.46×1.90 m, 1665 (Montpellier, Musée Fabre)

owned about 60 of them; now they seem slightly stiff and too stylized.

Monnoyer was employed at the Gobelins from 1666, often collaborating with his son-in-law Jean-Baptiste Belin on decorative schemes, providing floral borders for tapestries such as the *Crossing of the Rhine* (1682–3). He also worked at Beauvais on cartoons for the *Grotesques* of Jean Bérain I. Besides Le Brun, Monnoyer collaborated with artists such as René-Antoine Houasse and Hyacinthe Rigaud on decorative work for many royal houses. He worked under Philippe de Champaigne on the decoration of the Queen's apartment at the château of Vincennes (Seine), painting garlands of flowers on the ceilings.

The *procès-verbaux* of the Académie record that Baptiste, as he was generally known, asked for leave of absence to visit England for three or four months in 1690. He travelled in a team of painters, headed by Charles de La Fosse, at the invitation of Ralph Montagu, later 1st Duke of Montagu, and returned to London in 1692, decorating a number of rooms and the stairway in Montagu House (destr.). He also worked at Burlington House for Charles Howard, 3rd Earl of Carlisle, and at Kensington Palace for Charles Beauclerk, 1st Duke of St Albans (1670–1726). Remaining in England, he continued his practice of collaborating with other artists and provided ornate flowers for Godfrey Kneller's portraits. His oeuvre became

well known through engravings, and, because so few of his works were signed, paintings and decorative works by imitators are often attributed to him.

Baptiste's son Antoine Monnoyer (*b* 1672) joined him in working at Burlington House, Kensington Palace and Hampton Court. He was received (*reçu*) by the Académie Royale in 1703, presenting a *morceau de réception* of *Fruit and Flowers*, and in 1709 travelled to Rome.

BIBLIOGRAPHY

C. Sterling: *La Nature morte de l'antiquité à nos jours* (Paris, 1952); Eng. trans. as *Still-life Painting from Antiquity to the Twentieth Century* (New York, 1968, rev. 2/1981)

M. Faré: *La Nature morte en France, son histoire et son évolution du XVIIe siècle au XXe siècle* (Geneva, 1962)

S. H. Pavière: *A Dictionary of Flower, Fruit and Still-life Painters*, 4 vols (Leigh-on-Sea, 1962–4)

M. Faré: *Le Grand Siècle de la nature morte en France* (Fribourg, 1974)

LESLEY STEVENSON

Monochrome. Term applied to a work of art predominantly of a single colour or tone (for which *see* GRISAILLE), or to a type of painting originally associated with the practice of 20th-century avant-garde artists in Russia. The paintings and writings of KAZIMIR MALEVICH and ALEKSANDR RODCHENKO were responsible for the two principal interpretations of monochrome painting: the transcendental and the materialist. Malevich's *White Square on White* (1918; New York, MOMA), generally regarded as the source for 20th-century monochrome painting, was produced in the context of his programme of SUPREMA-TISM. A fascination with the asceticism of monochromatic painting and its mystical or occult associations can be found in extreme form in the work of Yves Klein and of Anish Kapoor (*b* 1954). Rodchenko's *Colour Pure Red, Colour Pure Yellow, Colour Pure Blue* (1921; Moscow, priv. col.) established the antithetical position for the monochrome as the radical materialist analysis of painting. Materialist theories value the monochrome as pure paint-ing, because it reduces the art form to its theoretical limit of a single colour uniformly dispersed on a ground. Although such work convinced Rodchenko that painting's terminus had been reached, varieties of this analytical or formal approach have remained influential and vital to ABSTRACT ART and are illustrated, for example, by the monochromatic works of Lucio Fontana, Ad Reinhardt, Ellsworth Kelly, Gerhard Richter, Robert Ryman, Frank Stella, Gottfried Honegger and Brice Marden.

Artists concerned with criticizing rather than with affirming the value of painting in art have, paradoxically, also employed the monochrome. In such cases the mon-ochrome functions polemically as metonym, substituting one type of painting for all painting or art in general. Examples of this strategy include the white and black monochromes of the early 1950s by Robert Rauschenberg and the achromes of Piero Manzoni; both artists aimed to reinvigorate the nihilism associated with earlier anti-art movements such as Dada. In the work of Olivier Mosset (*b* 1944), Niele Toroni (*b* 1937) and Terry Atkinson (*b* 1939) the monochrome signifies a radical political negativity; for Claude Rutault (*b* 1941) it represented an ironical expression of the historical impasse of painting itself.

BIBLIOGRAPHY
K. Malevich: *The Non-objective World* (Chicago, 1959)
Fundamental Painting (exh. cat., Amsterdam, Stedel. Mus., 1975)
Radical Painting (exh. cat. by T. Krens, Williamstown, MA, Williams Coll. Mus. A., 1984)
La Couleur seule: L'Expérience du monochrome (exh. cat. by M. Besset and others, Lyon, Mus. St Pierre A. Contemp., 1988)
For further bibliography *see* biographies of individual artists.
MICHAEL CORRIS

Monogrammists. *See* MASTERS, ANONYMOUS, AND MONOGRAMMISTS, §III.

Monoha [Jap.: 'object school']. Term applied to tenden-cies in the works of the Japanese artists Nobuo Sekine (*b* 1942), Katsurō Yoshida (*b* 1943), Susumu Koshimizu (*b* 1944), Katsuhiko Narita (1944–92), Shingo Honda (*b* 1944), Kishio Suga (*b* 1944) and the Korean Lee U-fan (*b* 1936) after 1968 and particularly from 1972 to 1974. The term began to be used informally to denote the fact that they took as their material natural objects, including trees, stones and earth, and manmade objects such as beams, girders, concrete, paper and glass. However, the emphasis in the works of the *Monoha* artists was not on the objects themselves, as with some Minimalist works and the Arte Povera, but on the relationship between object and object or between objects and the spaces they occupy (e.g. Suga's *Situation of Eternity*, 1970; Kyoto, N. Mus. Mod. A.). This demonstrated a new artistic approach,

unlike that of conventional sculpture or environmental art, that took as its aim the shaping of space itself. In this it had affinities with Concrete art. The central concern in *Monoha* works, however, was not a purely formal interest in creating some new kind of shape but an attempt to reconsider fundamental questions concerning humanity's involvement with the world of matter. It was thus a characteristically Japanese tendency, whatever its similari-ties with some European and American movements.

BIBLIOGRAPHY
S. Chiba: '*Monoha*', *Gendaibijutsu-itsudatsu-shi, 1945–1985* [A history of deviant art, 1945–1985] (Tokyo, 1986)
Monoha to postomonoha [*Monoha* and post-*Monoha*] (exh. cat., Tokyo, Seibu Mus. A., 1987)
SHIGEO CHIBA

Monomachos. *See* MACEDONIAN DYNASTY, (4).

Monópoli, Reginaldo Piramo da. *See* PIRAMO DA MON-ÓPOLI, REGINALDO.

Monopteros. Unwalled building of ancient Greek origin with peripteral (outer) columns. Most examples were circular in plan, with conical or domed roofs, and these resembled the round buildings known as tholoi (*see* THOLOS; as distinct from tholos tomb). A few, however, had rectangular plans. Monopteroi were often dedicated to gods or deified mortals, notably Hercules, but some served merely as pavilions in markets while others housed tombs.

1. GREECE AND ROME. The first Sikyonian Treasury at Delphi (mid-6th century BC) may have been an early rectangular example. It probably had a peristyle of 4×5 Doric columns, with triglyphs over only the columns separated by elongated metopes. An early 3rd-century BC monopteros near Alexandria, supposedly built in honour of the deified Queen Arsinoe (*reg c.* 276–270 BC), wife of Ptolemy II (*reg c.* 283–246 BC), was also rectangular, with a 4×5 column peristyle; the building no longer survives. At Knidos, on the south-east coast of Asia Minor, there is a round monopteros (diam. *c.* 17.3 m) dedicated to Aph-rodite Euploia. It had 18 columns, probably Corinthian, and four steps at the front, and it may have replaced a structure of the 3rd or 2nd century BC which had housed the famous *Aphrodite* by Praxiteles. This monopteros was copied in the 2nd century AD for Hadrian's Villa at Tivoli, while a similar building (diam. 7.48 m) on the Athenian Acropolis was dedicated to Rome and Augustus. It was centred on the east front of the Parthenon, and the easternmost intercolumniation of its peristyle of nine Ionic columns was specially widened. Other monopteroi of similar date (1st century AD) include: the Mausoleum of the Julii at Glanum (St Remy), raised on a high, arched platform, with ten Corinthian columns supporting a con-ical roof; the Mausoleum at Aquileia, in North Italy, with six Corinthian columns on a raised platform and a steep conical roof; and the monument of Babbius in Corinth, restored with eight columns.

The concrete foundations (diam 6.9 m) are all that remain of the 2nd-century AD monopteros in the Sanctuary of Poseidon at Isthmia, dedicated to Palaimon, son of Ino, who was deified after drowning. It was, however, depicted on coins and apparently had a peristyle with 11 Corinthian columns on a square platform supporting a domed roof. The easternmost intercolumniation was again widened, and the structure housed not only a statue of *Palaimon on a Dolphin* but also an underground chamber, the supposed tomb of the boy, though actually a settling basin belonging to the older stadium (6th–5th centuries BC). This was beneath the centre of the building, with a passage connecting it to the outside. Athletes were taken there in the dark and oaths administered, with threats of dire retribution for perjury (Pausanias, II.ii.1). A slightly later round building (mid-2nd century AD) in the Athenian Agora (see fig.) with a peristyle of eight, probably Corinthian, columns (diam. *c.* 7.17 m) and a domed roof was possibly dedicated to Aphrodite. Two small monopteroi (diam. *c.* 3.6 m), of similar date, each with eight Corinthian columns bearing a conical roof, formed part of the Nymphaion of Herodes Atticus at Olympia. By contrast, a large, 16-columned monopteros (diam. *c.* 18 m; 2nd century AD) stood in the market at Puteoli. The market at Djemila housed a hexagonal pavilion, about 4 m wide with six columns. Finally, another circular monopteros (diam. 9 m; 2nd or 3rd century AD), with an eight-columned peristyle, stood in the market at Hippo Regius. The function of these market monopteroi was to provide shade.

Monopteroi were also depicted in paintings and on terracotta lamps. A lamp from Athens (Athens, Agora Mus., 751) of the 3rd century AD shows a monopteros

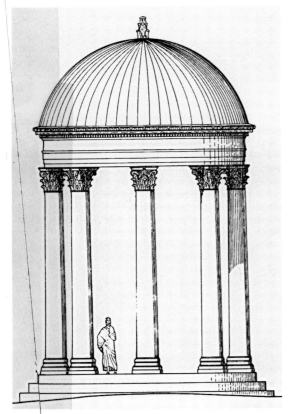

Monopteros of the Agora, Athens, mid-2nd century AD; reconstruction

with a domed roof and probably six columns, containing a statue, possibly of Aphrodite.

BIBLIOGRAPHY

W. Binder: *Der Roma-Augustus Monopteros auf der Akropolis in Athen und sein typologischer Ort* (Karlsruhe, 1969)

W. B. Dinsmoor jr: 'The Monopteros in the Athenian Agora', *Hesperia*, xliii (1974), pp. 412–27

WILLIAM B. DINSMOOR JR,
ANASTASIA N. DINSMOOR

2. LATER HISTORY. The monopteros, as a building type, suffered an eclipse in Late Antiquity and the early medieval period. A Gothic version of it emerged in the market crosses built in town centres, such as Bishop Storey's Cross (1501), Chichester, where heavy piers replace the Classical orders and rib vaults replace the dome. Some authorities have seen a prefiguration of the renewed use of the Classical monopteros in the two-colonnaded rotundas that intrude into the chapel of the Holy Shroud (SS Sindone) at Turin Cathedral (1657–74), by GUARINO GUARINI, though it is doubtful whether the term may be legitimately applied to a feature that is not in itself a free-standing structure. In the Avila Chapel (1680) of S Maria in Trastevere, Rome, Antonio Gherardi contrived a flight of four angels at the summit of the dome who hold up a monopteros that fits in the internal space of the lantern.

The monopteros finally moved out of doors again in the 18th century, when it gained popularity as a garden feature. Johann Lukas von Hildebrandt's Nepomukkapelle (1717) in the park at Göllersdorf, Austria, since it is square and embraces an altar, may perhaps be classified as a baldacchino, but less ambiguity attends the purely secular monopteros in the garden of the Petit Trianon, Versailles, erected to the designs of Richard Mique in 1778 and known as the Temple de l'Amour. A fully fluted Corinthian order supports an elaborate entablature and shallow dome. The monopteros became a common feature of the English landscape garden. Well-known examples include the Temple of Aeolus (1760) by William Chambers at the Royal Botanic Gardens, Kew. In the 19th century the monopteros was a preferred form for bandstands, and many examples of the type survive in British municipal parks. □

Monory, Jacques (*b* Paris, 25 June 1934). French painter, printmaker, photographer and film maker. He studied at the Ecole des Arts Appliqués, Paris, from 1951 to 1955 and worked as a model maker. His first paintings, exhibited in Paris in 1955 and 1959 and influenced both by *Art informel* and by Surrealist fantasy, were almost all destroyed by him in 1962 as a gesture of rejection of the aesthetics of the Ecole de Paris. In its place he adopted a representational style based on photographic reproduction, rendering his images tonally in shades of Rembrandt blue, as in *For All that We See or Seem is a Dream within a Dream* (1967; Marseille, Mus. Cantini). He allied himself with the renewal of figurative art inspired by modern life then taking place in Europe in response to Pop art; Eduardo Arroyo, the painter Peter Klasen (*b* 1935) and the French painter Bernard Rancillac (*b* 1931) were among the artists with whom he was closely associated in influential group exhibitions of the time, and with whom he was associated as part of a wave of 'new figuration'.

Monory often worked in series devoted to themes of fantasy and violence, as in the *Velvet Jungle* series of 1969–71 (e.g. *Velvet Jungle No. 10/2*, 1971; Amsterdam, Stedel. Mus.), the *N.Y.* paintings of 1971 (e.g. *N.Y. No. 8*, 1971; Rotterdam, Boymans–van Beuningen) and the *Frozen Operas* of 1974–5 (e.g. *Frozen Opera No. 2*, 1974; Liège, Mus. B.-A.). The *Murders* series of 1968, in which Monory represented the artist alternately as victim and as murderer, incorporated mirrors as a means of implicating the viewer in the acts of violence, as in *Murder No. 20/1* (1968; Paris, Pompidou). Cinematic techniques such as close-ups, freeze-frames and juxtaposed images present an incomplete scenario for a mysterious crime; the sense of unreality created by the use of monochrome is literally shattered by the reflection in the mirror of the room in which the painting is displayed. Monory's habit of repeating a shocking image, first as a hand-painted replica of a photograph and in later works as a surface printed photomechanically on sensitized canvas, was increasingly controversial because of its apparent elimination of the traditional role of the artist's hand. In 1976 he introduced a colour scheme of cyan blue, yellow and magenta in emulation of the tri-chromatic process used in modern printing, but left as zones of separate colour rather than as superimposed layers. Like Andy Warhol and other American Pop artists, Monory thus remained faithful to the metaphors and techniques of mass production central to all his mature work.

BIBLIOGRAPHY

Monory (exh. cat. by A. Jouffroy, Paris, Cent. N.A. Contemp., 1974)
J.-C. Bailly: *Monory* (Paris, 1979)
J.-F. Lyotard: *L'Assassinat de l'expérience par la peinture: Monory* (Talence, 1984)
Monory: Toxique (exh. cat., Paris, Mus. A. Mod. Ville Paris, 1984) [brief texts by artist]

ELISABETH LEBOVICI

Monosiet, Pierre (*b* Port-au-Prince, 21 April 1922; *d* Port-au-Prince, Dec 1983). Haitian painter and museum director. He began his career as an artist in 1949 by joining the Centre d'Art in Port-au-Prince, remaining there for 23 years, having studied under the Haitian painters Maurice Borno (1917–55), Lucien Price (1915–63) and George Remponneau (*b* 1916). His preferred medium was watercolour. His first one-man exhibition took place at the Centre d'Art in 1952. Noticed as a young man of talent, he was awarded a three-month scholarship that enabled him to visit museums in American cities in 1952. On his return he was made assistant to the American watercolourist Dewitt Peters (1901–66), who ran the Centre d'Art. In 1961 he resigned in order to spend a year in Germany, where he informed himself about all aspects of museum management. The next few years were difficult ones. He went to the Virgin Islands and worked at a variety of jobs unrelated to museum work, all the while studying on his own about conservation and preservation of art and the functioning of museums. On Peters's death Monosiet was called back as consultant for the planning of the Musée d'Art Haïtien in Port-au-Prince, of which he was appointed the first Director in 1972, a post he held until his death. He was always deeply committed to the work of Haitian naive artists, rather than to that of the modernists who found more favour with the Haitian public; the recognition accorded to these artists abroad confirmed his own choices and his conviction that naive painting had its own recognizable and distinct tradition.

BIBLIOGRAPHY

E. I. Christensen: *The Art of Haïti* (New York, 1975)
Haitian Art: The Legend and Legacy of the Naïve Tradition (exh. cat. by L. G. Hoffman, Davenport, IA, Mun. A.G., 1985)

DOLORES M. YONKER

Monotype. Type of print and the process in which a drawing or painting executed on a flat, unworked printing plate or other surface is transferred through pressure to a sheet of paper. As most of the image is transferred in the printing process, only one strong impression can be taken, hence the term monotype (unique, single impression). Residual ink on the printing surface occasionally permits the printing of fainter second or third impressions; these are called ghosts or cognates. A monotype is distinct from a monoprint, which is a uniquely inked and printed impression from a traditional print matrix.

1. Materials and techniques. 2. History.

1. MATERIALS AND TECHNIQUES. The often experimental genesis and comparative technical ease of monotype have combined to render very broad parameters for the process. Monotype is, in effect, the simplest printmaking process (a printed transfer of an image), but, combined with its inherent uniqueness, it has fallen between strict definitions of painting, drawing and printmaking. The classical monotype requires only a copper plate, ink, a printing press and paper. The artist may manipulate the ink on the plate with brushes, sticks, rags or fingers to create an image. Traditionally the image can be created either subtractively, from a film of ink previously laid on the plate (dark-field manner), or positively, with direct linear or tonal application of the ink on a clean plate (light-field manner). The printing of the image on to a sheet of paper is accomplished either in a traditional etching press or by manual application of pressure with a spoon or the hand itself. The primary technical variant is the trace monotype, which involves drawing with a stylus on the verso of a sheet of paper that has been laid on an inked surface; the local application of the 'printing' process transfers ink to the underside (recto) of the sheet being drawn upon.

Further variations on the monotype process are presumably without limit. The image-making media may include watercolour, chalk, crayon, pastel, oil pigment, printing ink or graphite (pencil), to name only the most common. These media may be drawn or painted upon surfaces as varied as metal printing plates, glass, perspex, cardboard or wood. The essential quality of the printing surface for a strict monotype is that it has no image already fixed on it by etching, lithography, collage or any other traditional printmaking process.

The monotype typically has relied for its appeal on the combination of the freedom and spontaneity of drawing and the interaction of pigment and paper under pressure. The transfer process usually softens hard edges in the drawn image, rendering areas more painterly and textured in the resulting impression. The extraordinary variety of media used in producing monotypes also renders an inclusive definition of their appearance difficult. One characteristic feature usually present on a monotype is the mark embossed in the paper by the edges of the printing plate; the rather 'flattened' appearance of a work which otherwise resembles a drawing is often another indication of a monotype process.

Monotypes have been utilized by artists as foundations for further elaboration with drawing or painting media over the printed impression (or the fainter cognate or ghost impressions), notably employed by Edgar Degas. The printing plate itself, which usually retains a shadow (ghost) of the original drawing, can also serve as the basis for another application of pigment and be printed again. This process may be repeated a number of times, producing an evolving series of individual, yet closely related monotype impressions. Another recent variation similarly consists of repeated applications of pigment on the printing plate, but on each occasion printing on to the same sheet of paper, thereby building up a single, multilayered monotype image.

BIBLIOGRAPHY
H. von Herkomer: *Etching and Mezzotint Engraving* (London, 1892), pp. 104–7
E. Ertz: 'Monotyping', *The Studio*, xvii (1902), pp. 172–7
H. Rasmusen: *Printmaking with Monotype* (Philadelphia, 1960)
J. Ross, C. Romano and T. Ross: *The Complete Printmaker* (New York and London, 1972; rev. New York, 1990), pp. 245–58
N. Laliberté and A. Mogelon: *The Art of Monoprint: History and Modern Techniques* (New York, 1974)
J. Ayres: *Monotype* (New York, 1991)

2. HISTORY.

(i) Introduction. The monotype does not present a direct historical development due to its elusive status as neither a true drawing nor a traditionally defined multiple (print) and to its sporadic and experimental use by artists. The impossiblity of duplication has thwarted its widespread use; it is a private medium, more akin to an artist's studio drawings. Indeed, the technique was not described in printmaking manuals until comparatively recently. Artists usually discovered monotype themselves or learnt of it through verbal tradition. While it has been employed most often by artists engaged in traditional printmaking, it has also been utilized by those who have not, particularly contemporary painters. The first published description of the method appeared in Adam von Bartsch's 1821 catalogue of Giovanni Benedetto Castiglione's prints, in which he accurately surmised the monotype process, yet left it unnamed. In 1875 an eyewitness account of the making of a monotype by Henri Guérard (1846–97) was published in the journal *Paris à l'eau-forte* (28 Nov 1875, pp. 92–3). The first published use of the word itself occurred in notices for exhibitions by Albion Harris Bicknell (1837–1915) and Charles Alvah Walker (1848–1920) in 1881 in Boston and New York and in an 1891 article by Sylvester R. Koehler (1837–1900).

(ii) Early examples. Historically, the monotype derives from the selective wiping of the surface of an etched or engraved printing plate so as to leave a tone of ink on the printed impression. Although manipulated surface tone was occasionally employed by earlier printmakers (including Albrecht Dürer), the first consistent use of such variant inkings on an intaglio plate was by Rembrandt. He explored such effects from the mid-1640s, for instance printing his *Entombment* (c. 1654; B. 86) in a range from cleanly wiped impressions (brightly lit) to ones that display a tenebrous ink tone almost completely covering the printed surface. Rembrandt may have been influenced by the experiments in tonal colour printing by Hercules Segers.

The earliest pure monotypes have usually been considered the group of c. 24 prints executed from the 1640s to 1660 by Giovanni Benedetto Castiglione (see fig. 1), who concurrently explored the effects of printed tone in his etchings, perhaps inspired by Rembrandt's example. Several monotypes (see Hollstein: *Dut. & Flem.*, xxiii, pp. 154–7, nos 13–17, *Leids. Ksthist. Jb.* and Royalton-Kisch) by the Flemish artist Anthonis Sallaert, which may predate Castiglione's efforts, do not explore the chiaroscuro effects possible in the monotype medium. (A distinction must be made between a fully developed monotype and a counterproof, a technique historically used by artists to transfer and reverse their drawn compositions. While technically monotype impressions, counterproofs are usually considered part of the artist's working process and not finished works in themselves.) Works resembling monotypes by Cornelis Bega, Jan Breughel I

1. Monotype by Giovanni Benedetto Castiglione: *God Creating Adam*, black ink, 302×205 mm, c. 1645 (Chicago, IL, Art Institute of Chicago)

and others are found from the 16th and 17th centuries but are difficult to recognize as considered explorations of the medium. Isolated monotypes have been associated with unknown followers of Castiglione, and a group has been attributed to the French marine painter Adrien Manglard.

For over two centuries after Castiglione's last known monotype in 1660, no artist of note except William Blake is known to have explored the medium. Blake produced 12 monotypes (*c.* 1795; Bindman, nos 324–36) evolving from his continuing experiments with printmaking techniques, including the development of a relief-etching method and sophisticated colour-printing techniques. He seems to have used thick cardboard as a surface for his drawings in a tempera medium, and to have printed the same outline drawing in as many as three impressions. He then re-inked the board and overprinted these impressions to add more colours, often finishing the details in pen and watercolour. His unorthodox methods and his position outside the mainstream of British art militated against other artists' adoption of the monotype medium from his example.

(iii) 19th century. The environment in which the monotype could develop a more solid tradition was not created until the Etching Revival of the 1860s in Europe (and slightly later in the USA) and, in particular, the revival of interest

2. Monotype by Edgar Degas: *Pauline and Virginie Conversing with Admirers,* black ink, 215×161 mm, *c.* 1880–83 (Cambridge, MA, Fogg Art Museum)

in Rembrandt's richly inked intaglio prints. The most notable example, perhaps in the entire history of monotype, is that of Edgar Degas, whose nearly 450 monotypes constitute the summit of achievement in the medium (see fig. 2). He learnt the technique in late 1875 or early 1876 from the circle of etchers who were experimenting with tonal inking of plates during the 1860s and 1870s, including Adolphe Appian, Henri Guérard and Ludovic (Napoléon) Lepic. Degas himself had tonally printed impressions of his portrait etching of *Joseph Tourny* (see 1984 exh. cat.) in the mid-1860s.

The experimental, private nature of pure monotype suited Degas's artistic character admirably, and he explored themes of the nude, brothel subjects, dimly lit interiors, the theatre and landscape in numerous series of monotypes up to the early 1890s. He frequently printed both a primary impression and a ghost impression, the latter often serving as the base for a finished pastel drawing. He referred to his monotypes only as 'drawings made with greasy ink and printed'. In several instances, he transferred monotype impressions to a lithographic stone, thereby pioneering a multiple printmaking technique that preserved much of the monotype's painterly quality. Other French artists who worked in pure monotype during the late 19th century were Camille Pissarro, Henri de Toulouse-Lautrec and Paul Gauguin. In 1894 Gauguin was printing monotypes in watercolour, and five years later he pioneered the trace-monotype technique during his second Tahitian sojourn.

Practitioners in Great Britain during the 19th century included George Chinnery, James Nasmyth (1808–90) and Hubert von Herkomer; the latter also developed a technique *c.* 1890 to produce electrotyped intaglio plates from monotype-inked plates to enable their multiple reproduction, which he dubbed 'spongotypes' or 'Herkotypes'. His process was an adaptation of the galvanograph, which had been used from mid-century to reproduce viscous ink drawings; examples by Joseph Sampson and August Schleich (1814–65) are known. The Italian painters Pompeo Mariani (1857–1927) and Giorgio Belloni (1861–1944) produced monotypes at the turn of the century, as did the Germans Arthur Langhammer (1854–1901), Karl Kappstein (1869–1933) and Andreas Rögels (1870–1917).

In the USA in the 1880s Charles Alvah Walker, Albion Harris Bicknell, William Merritt Chase and Otto Bacher (1856–1909) fostered the growth of a very active monotype tradition, which included the formation of a 'Monotype Club' in New York. Bacher imparted the technique to Frank Duveneck and his students in Venice in 1880; it is surmised that Rex Whistler's exposure to the monotype technique in Venice influenced the tonal printing of his own etchings. From 1891 Maurice Prendergast produced *c.* 200 monotypes, most printed in colour. Other monotype artists around the turn of the century included Karl Friedrich Wilhelm Mielatz (1864–1919), Peter Moran (1841–1914), Ernest Haskell (1876–1925) and Rufus Sheldon.

(iv) 20th century. The European artists who, after the turn of the century, utilized the monotype in their work included Pablo Picasso, Henri Matisse, Georges Rouault, Paul Klee, Jacques Villon and Oskar Schlemmer. In mid-century Jean Dubuffet made hundreds of monotypes,

revelling in the chance exploration of textures that they provided. Marc Chagall produced over 300 works in the 1960s and 1970s; Joan Miró also used the medium at the same time. The Scottish painter and printmaker Robert Colquhoun also worked in monotype (*see* PRINTS, colour pl. VIII). In the USA artists in New York centred around Robert Henri actively worked in monotype. They included John Sloan, George Luks, Everett Shinn and William J. Glackens. Other major practitioners in the early 20th century included Abraham Walkowitz, Paul Dougherty (1877–1947), Eugene Higgins (1874–1958) and Albert Edward Sterner (1863–1946). From the 1950s Milton Avery and Mark Tobey produced large numbers of monotypes.

Many of the American artists who have worked in monotype since the 1960s have credited the exhibition of Degas's monotypes in 1968 at the Fogg Art Museum, Harvard University, Cambridge, MA, as a major inspiration. Since that time many painters (and numerous art students) have explored the technique. Its quality of improvisation and a reaction against the strict limits of edition printing combined to create a solid tradition for monotype in late 20th-century art. Practitioners in this period include Adolph Gottlieb, Michael Mazur (*b* 1935), Richard Diebenkorn, Robert Motherwell, Sam Francis, Matt Phillips (*b* 1927), Mary Frank (*b* 1933), Jasper Johns, Charles Arnoldi (*b* 1946), Judy Rifka, Jim Dine, Robert Cumming, Yvonne Jacquette (*b* 1934) and Eric Fischl, to name only a few. Dry media, such as pastel and graphite, began to be utilized in monotypes. Many artists have produced multilayered impressions. Ever larger formats have been explored, some works extending to *c.* 2 m in dimension. Late 20th-century European artists who worked in monotype include Per Kirkeby, John Walker, Sean Scully, Therese Oulton (*b* 1953), Francesco Clemente, Naum Gabo, John Hoyland and Mick Moon (*b* 1937).

BIBLIOGRAPHY

Hollstein: *Dut. & Flem.*

A. von Bartsch: *Catalogue raisonné de toutes les estampes. . .de Rembrandt* (Vienna, 1797) [B.]

R. Lesclide, ed.: *Paris à l'eau-forte* (Paris, 1875)

S. R. Koehler: 'Das Monotyp', *Chron. Vervielfält. Kst*, iv (1891), pp. 17–20

F. Weitenkampf: *American Graphic Arts* (New York, 1912), pp. 133–6

Degas Monotypes (exh. cat. by E. P. Janis, Cambridge, MA, Fogg, 1968)

Paul Gauguin: Monotypes (exh. cat. by R. S. Field, Philadelphia, PA, Mus. A., 1973)

L'Estampe impressioniste (exh. cat. by M. Melot, Paris, Bib. N., 1974)

D. Bindman: *The Complete Graphic Works of William Blake* (London, 1978)

C. Langdale: *The Monotypes of Maurice Prendergast* (New York, 1979)

The Painterly Print: Monotypes from the 17th to the 20th Century (exh. cat. by S. W. Reed and others, New York, Met., 1980) [major bibliog.]

P. Bellini: *Italian Masters of the Seventeenth Century, Commentary* (1982), 46 [XXI/ii] of *The Illustrated Bartsch*, ed. W. Strauss (New York, 1978–), pp. 91–112, nos 117–40 [Castiglione]

Leids. Ksthist. Jb., ii (1983), pp. 243–60

Edgar Degas: The Painter as Printmaker (exh. cat. by S. W. Reed and B. S. Shapiro and others, Boston, MA, Mus. F.A., 1984), no. 5

A. Griffiths: 'Monotypes', *Prt Q.*, v (1988), pp. 55–60

M. Royalton-Kisch: 'A Monotype by Sallaert', *Prt Q.*, v (1988), pp. 60–61

F. Carey: 'The Monotype in Britain', *Tamarind Pap.*, xiv (1991–2), pp. 14–20

DAVID P. BECKER

Monreale Cathedral. Cathedral in Sicily that contains the largest surviving ensemble of mosaic decoration in Italy.

1. Introduction. 2. Architecture. 3. Mosaics. 4. Sculpture.

1. INTRODUCTION. It was formerly a Benedictine monastery. The foundation of the monastic house of S Maria Nuova by King William II of Sicily (*see* HAUTEVILLE, (2)) marked the climax of Norman ecclesiastical and artistic patronage on the island. The site chosen was on a hill overlooking Palermo. By a papal bull of 1174 (which refers to the monastery being under construction) the foundation was exempted from episcopal jurisdiction and made subject only to the papacy, which effectively delegated its involvement to the King as Apostolic Legate. In 1176 one hundred Cluniac monks, under the first abbot, Theobald (*reg* 1176–8), came at William's invitation from the abbey of Santa Trinità at Cava dei Tirreni near Salerno. In the same year William endowed the abbey with extensive properties, including a large area in west-central Sicily, and exempted it from royal taxation. In 1183 Pope Lucius III (*reg* 1181–5) constituted it as a metropolitan see with an abbot-archbishop; the name Monreale was used here for the first time.

Monreale was intended as a royal mausoleum and as a counterweight to the independence of Palermo Cathedral, then being rebuilt by Archbishop Gualtiero Offamilio (*reg* 1169–90). It is now known chiefly for the mosaic decoration of its church; but the cultural diversity of Norman rule in Sicily is exemplified by the contrast between the Byzantine mosaics and the sculpture of the cloister capitals, which is predominantly Romanesque. William II, who died in 1189, was the last ruler to be buried here; intended as the 'Saint-Denis of the Hautevilles', Monreale did not maintain its position after the downfall of the dynasty.

BIBLIOGRAPHY

L. T. White jr: *Latin Monasticism in Norman Sicily* (Cambridge, MA, 1938), pp. 132–45   □

2. ARCHITECTURE. The cathedral measures 102×40 m. At the west end two squat, square towers project beyond the aisle walls and flank a portico, built in 1770. The exterior of the east end is covered in polychrome decoration of inlaid stone, creating an elaborate pattern of intersecting arcades and roundels (see fig. 1). Inside, the nave appears unusually wide, with large pointed arcades supported by antique columns and capitals opening on to the aisles. The crossing with its massive, wall-like piers is almost square, and it is surmounted by a lantern pierced by large windows. The slightly projecting transepts lead to deep apsidal chapels. The dominating feature of the building is the main apse, framed by the receding sequence of arches in the chancel. The apses and presbyteries are spanned by pointed barrel vaults; other parts are covered by a timber roof. The large expanses of wall surface seem to have been designed with the mosaic decoration in mind.

BIBLIOGRAPHY

W. Krönig: *Il duomo di Monreale e l'architettura normanna in Sicilia* (Palermo, 1965)

3. MOSAICS. The scheme of mosaics begins in the nave with the *Creation* and subsequent Old Testament scenes,

1. Monreale Cathedral, exterior of the south and main apses, late 12th century

progresses to the *Life of Christ* in the crossing, transepts and nave aisles, and culminates in the apse with a hieratic array consisting of *Christ Pantokrator* with his heavenly court. The programme imitates many features of the mosaic decoration of the Cappella Palatina in Palermo, but it is more expansive; and in the absence of a cupola, the main apse and presbytery form the sole theological centre. Although the style of the mosaics is Byzantine, almost all the inscriptions are in Latin, not Greek, and the disposition of the scenes in unbroken friezes is contrary to Byzantine practice. At Monreale the walls are covered with images: the surfaces not containing the main scenes— piers, soffits and spandrels—bear prophets, saints and angels.

The mosaics of the original western entrance portico were destroyed in 1770, but it is known that they consisted of scenes from the *Life of the Virgin* and the *Infancy of Christ*. The nave bears Old Testament scenes in two tiers from the *Creation* to *Jacob Wrestling with the Angel* (see fig. 2). The cycle is similar to that in the nave of the Cappella Palatina, but some composite scenes have been expanded into separate episodes. The placing of Old Testament scenes in the nave had Italian rather than Byzantine origins. On the west wall the cycle is interrupted to include three scenes from the lives of the south Italian bishop-martyrs Castrensis, Cassius and Castus. The relics of St Castrensis had been given to William II in 1177.

The New Testament scenes form the largest surviving monumental New Testament cycle in either East or West.

No attempt is made to place the scenes usually considered most important in the most prominent positions. The *Infancy* scenes, from the *Annunciation to Zacharias* to the *Baptism*, are arranged in a double tier around the walls of the crossing. Miracle scenes fill the nave aisles. Each transept arm contains a triple tier of Christological scenes: from the *Temptations* to the *Judgement of Pilate* in the south, and in the north the continuation of the Passion with *Resurrection* scenes, ending at *Pentecost*. The iconography is predominantly Byzantine, but it appears not to be dependent on the Cappella Palatina, where many of the scenes are absent. Whereas the layout of the nave mosaics is essentially a refinement of that of the Palermo cycle— for instance in making sure that the scenes are not cut off by the arcade—in the crossing and transepts the disposition of scenes was much more experimental.

The main apse of Monreale (see ROMANESQUE, fig. 71) is a variation on that of Cefalù Cathedral. The image of Christ Pantokrator fills the conch with an all-embracing gesture. Below, the Virgin sits enthroned with the Christ Child on her knees, flanked by archangels and Apostles, with a row of saints below. Both rows continue from the apse on to the presbytery walls: but whereas the Apostles turn towards the centre, the saints below are shown in strict frontality. The choice of saints, which includes the earliest surviving representation of St Thomas Becket, canonized in 1173, seems to reflect William II's ecclesiastical policy. The side apses and chapels contain scenes from the lives of St Peter (south) and St Paul (north). Each sits enthroned in the conch of his respective apse.

2. Monreale Cathedral, mosaics depicting *Genesis* scenes on the northern nave arcade and scenes from the *Ministry of Christ* in the aisle, *c.* 1180–90

Where the Cappella Palatina had a unified sequence of scenes from their lives (in the nave aisles), at Monreale they have been separated.

Two royal images are found in the crossing. Above the royal throne on the north-east pier is a mosaic of *Christ Crowning William II*, the inspiration for which is to be found in the mosaic panel of Roger II being crowned by Christ in the church of the Martorana in Palermo, which itself depends on the coronation rituals and portraits of Byzantine emperors. On the opposite pier William is shown offering the church of Monreale to its patron, the Virgin.

Despite some discernible differences of style between the mosaics in different parts of the building, for instance in modelling techniques, the mosaics generally display a homogeneous vocabulary of faces, gestures, draperies and ornamental motifs. Entire walls are treated as unified formal units. Overall there is little evidence of stylistic change or development, nor are there conspicuous gaps or overlaps in the iconographic programme. It is likely that the mosaics were executed in a single campaign, and that they were substantially complete by the time of William II's death in 1189.

The most instructive way to look at the style of Monreale is in relation to that of the same scenes in the Cappella Palatina. For all their rhythmical agitation, the figures at Monreale are not more dramatically expressive. Drapery folds are more intricate and form swirling patterns, in which the parts of the body (hips, knees and calves) are isolated at the centre of spiral movements. Seams perform zigzags, contours ripple. Despite the strong contrasts between shadows and highlights, few deep colours are used. Individual elements are subordinated to a larger complex of forms: figures are joined in groups that form a common contour, or are inscribed within settings whose contours echo those of the characters. This style is not foreshadowed in the Cappella Palatina, and there is little well-preserved Byzantine mosaic decoration of this period outside Sicily; but the evidence of wall paintings in Serbia, Russia and Cyprus shows parallel developments and suggests that the style of Monreale was the outcome of renewed contact with Byzantine art.

The clear iconographic relationship between the Cappella Palatina and Monreale, considered together with their stylistic differences, raises questions about the transmission of compositional prototypes and the working practices of the artists involved. Demus and Kitzinger have distinguished iconographic prototypes from stylistic models, conceiving of the former being brought to life in terms of the latter. The use of 'motif' or 'pattern' books is evident in the adoption of substantially similar figure types to portray characters in similar poses in a variety of scenes.

Monreale marks the climax and the end of artistic production under the Normans in Sicily. The art forms patronized by royalty, and probably executed by Greek artists, lacked local roots and did not survive the fall of the Hauteville dynasty. For western Europe, Monreale must always have been a conspicuous artistic achievement, although its influence is difficult to measure against other sources of Byzantine art.

3. Monreale Cathedral, general view of the cloister, showing the fountain house, *c.* 1172–89

BIBLIOGRAPHY
O. Demus: *The Mosaics of Norman Sicily* (London, 1950), pp. 112–77, 195–365, 418–42
E. Kitzinger: *The Mosaics of Monreale* (Palermo, 1960)
O. Demus: *Byzantine Art and the West* (London, 1970), pp. 121–61
E. Borsook: *Messages in Mosaic: The Royal Programmes of Norman Sicily (1130–87)* (Oxford, 1990), pp. 51–79

MARTIN KAUFFMANN

4. SCULPTURE. The square cloister quadrangle on the south side of the cathedral is flanked on all sides by covered walks, which open on to the garth through pointed arcades carried on 100 double columns, each pair topped by a double capital, with quadruple columns at the corners. In the south-west corner is an open fountain house with a broad circular basin (see fig. 3). The bases, columns and capitals are made of white marble, but each alternate pair has shafts inlaid with gold, red and black glass mosaic in various patterns (chevron, scrolls, fluting, spirals etc; see fig. 4); the shafts of the quadrilobe piers at the corners are carved with low-relief vine tendrils, inhabited scrolls, etc. The double capitals are uniform. Each has a heavy abacus and impost block, both usually carved from the same block of marble as the capital so that their function is more decorative than structural. Many of the capitals have the inverted bell shape of the Corinthian order, but each face is treated as a separate field for sculptural decoration. Despite their slightly elongated proportions, the dominating effect is classical, an impression heightened by the deep, three-dimensional carving. The voussoirs of the arcades are of alternating black tufa and sandstone forming decorative patterns. The intrados of each arch overhangs its supporting abacus, making a very awkward junction, a feature that has prompted some scholars to suggest that the cloister is not in its original state and to propose various reconstructions. There are other examples of oversailing in Norman Sicily and southern Italy, however (e.g. the cloister of SS Trinità, Palermo), and there is no evidence that the cloister has ever been rearranged, nor is there anything to suggest that it was not built at the same time as the cathedral itself (c. 1172–89).

Each capital has an individual design, and most are carved with decorative motifs: fantastic animals, monsters and foliate forms (acanthus leaves, flowers, vine tendrils etc), although human figures also appear, often as caryatids. There are few historiated capitals; out of a total of 110 carved elements, including the fountain house and the corner columns, only 16 are historiated, and these are scattered at random among the others, none occurring on the south side, for example, thus blending into the general decorative effect. The variety of designs does not affect the overall impression of uniformity, however, which suggests that one master was in charge of the work, although several teams of sculptors must have collaborated simultaneously on carving the capitals in order to complete the cloister in a short time. Sculptors from Lombardy, and further afield in the Latin world, Greeks from Sicily and the Italian mainland, and Sicilian Arabs all seem to have worked there, and one of them signed his name (EGO ROMANUS FILIUS CONSTANTINUS MARMORARIUS) in the north cloister walk, but nothing else is known of him. Although they came from different regions, many of the sculptors drew on similar sources: for example, both the Greeks and Arabs employed motifs and iconography from Early Christian models. Others used ivories (e.g. Byzantine 'rosette' caskets such as that in Palermo Cathedral Treasury), silver or silver-gilt reliefs, glass and steatite, as visual models, and achieved distinctive results. In spite of the disparity of their origins and sources, however, the sculptors maintained an aesthetic harmony, and the work is generally of high quality.

The capitals fall into several main groups. Some of them are related to sculpture in Campania (e.g. pulpits in the cathedrals of Salerno and Sessa Aurunca) and are based on Corinthian and Composite forms, often decorated with human figures and monsters; a few examples have wind-blown acanthus leaves. Other classicizing groups include one associated with the capital carved by Romanus, which shows a faithful adaptation of antique models, use of the drill and a more linear execution; another classicizing group, in which the drill is also employed, is characterized by flatter relief, accentuating the linear quality of the carving, and the use of the human figure as an important decorative element. One large group has plainer designs, showing a stronger architectural sense, with the decorative elements subordinated to the structural. Another series of capitals bears such motifs as the calf-bearer and putti harvesting grapes derived from antique and Early Christian art. A larger group of capitals, related to local traditions under both Islamic and provincial Byzantine influence, bears symmetrical and stylized designs in low relief, with

4. Monreale Cathedral, detail of cloister, c. 1172–89

paired or confronted birds, lions, fantastic beasts and acanthus leaves, but no figures.

One of the most interesting aspects of the cloister carvings is their lack of a coherent iconographic programme. The selection of subjects on the historiated capitals seems to have been chosen arbitrarily from the Old and New Testaments. They include the stories of the *Fall*, *Cain and Abel*, *Joseph*, *Noah* and *Samson*; the story of *St John the Baptist*, the *Infancy of Christ*, the *Parable of Dives and Lazarus*, the *Three Marys at the Tomb*, the *Harrowing of Hell* and *Pentecost*. Several episodes (particularly the *Noah* scenes) are closely related to the mosaics in the cathedral, in both iconography and style, but others (e.g. the *Nativity of Christ* and the *Harrowing of Hell*) are quite different. Some scenes show the influence of Early Gothic sculpture in the Ile de France, particularly Chartres Cathedral (e.g. *Pentecost* and the *Flight into Egypt* on the south-west quadrilobed capital). Other themes represented are *Quo vadis*, the *Legend of the True Cross*, the *Triumph of Church over Synagogue* and the *Labours of the Months*. The last in particular shows a dependence on Lombardy (e.g. S Zeno Maggiore, Verona), in iconography if not in style. In one capital William II is depicted presenting the church of Monreale to Christ and his Mother in a composition usually associated with the *Adoration of the Magi*, an unusual use of a traditional religious form to express a contemporary event. The *Legend of the True Cross*, which, unusually, appears on the same capital as the *Triumph of the Church*, is an appropriate subject for a crusading context; William II took the Cross and the Third Crusade was being assembled at Messina at the time when the cloister was being completed.

BIBLIOGRAPHY
C. Sheppard: 'The Iconography of the Cloister of Monreale', *A. Bull.*, xxxi (1949), pp. 159–69
—: 'A Stylistic Analysis of the Cloister of Monreale', *A. Bull.*, xxxiv (1952), pp. 35–41
J. Déer: *The Dynastic Porphyry Tombs of the Norman Period in Sicily* (Cambridge, MA, 1959)
R. Salvini: *The Cloister of Monreale and Romanesque Sculpture in Sicily* (Palermo, 1962); review by C. Sheppard in *Speculum*, xl (1965), pp. 368–71
D. Glass: 'The Romanesque in Campania and Sicily: A Problem of Method', *A. Bull.*, lvi/3 (1974), pp. 315–24
CARL D. SHEPPARD

Monrealese, il. *See* NOVELLI, PIETRO.

Monro, Dr Thomas (*b* London, 29 June 1759; *d* Clayhill, Herts, 14 Feb 1833). English patron and collector. He was the son of Dr John Monro, principal physician to the Bethlem ('Bedlam') Hospital for the insane in London, and a keen art collector. Following his training at St Bartholomew's Hospital, London, in 1787 he was appointed assistant to his father, and in 1792 he became Bethlem's principal physician, following his father's death. As such, in 1811–12, he was consulted on the treatment for King George III's bouts of insanity. In 1793 Monro moved to 8 Adelphi Terrace, London, where he remained until 1820. He also had country houses at Fetcham, near Leatherhead, Surrey, from 1795 to 1805, and at Bushey, Herts, from 1807 to 1820. In 1820 he left London permanently to live at Bushey.

Monro was a voracious collector of prints and watercolours, a pioneer in his concentration on the work of contemporary British landscape watercolour painters, including Gainsborough, Thomas Hearne, John Laporte (1761–1839), Joseph Farington (whose *Diaries* are a source of information on Monro's activities), J. M. W. TURNER and THOMAS GIRTIN. He also owned Gainsborough's camera obscura and its landscapes painted on glass for projection (London, V&A). From 1794 to 1797 Monro treated John Robert Cozens for mental illness, in the course of which he gained temporary possession of Cozens's Italian sketches (*see* COZENS, (2)). During these three years he encouraged the young Turner and Girtin to spend one evening a week at his 'academy' at Adelphi Terrace where, in return for supper, they were to copy Cozens's outline drawings. These copies they coloured in grey and blue wash; Girtin drew the outlines and Turner added the washes. Other artists, probably including Paul Sandby Munn (1773–1845) and Louis Francia, also made copies after sketches by Cozens, Thomas Hearne and John Henderson (1764–1834), an amateur artist and Monro's neighbour. (Several hundred of these 'Monro School' drawings are now in the Tate Gallery, London.) From *c*.1800 John Sell Cotman, John and Cornelius Varley, William Henry Hunt and John Linnell (ii) were also associated with the Monro circle, making drawings at Fetcham and Bushey as well as at Adelphi Terrace.

Monro's own landscape style was heavily influenced by the loosely drawn late landscapes of Gainsborough rather than by the more naturalistic watercolour style of younger artists such as Turner or Girtin. He drew idealized rural scenes with frothy trees and picturesque tumbledown cottages, using thick sticks of Indian ink on dampened white, blue, grey or pink paper. He sometimes added figures cut out in white paper; these he stuck on to a drawing and then washed to tone them in with the rest. Monro's importance lies in his patronage of a young and vigorous school of British landscape artists, rather than in the merits of his own style. His collection was sold at Christie's, 26–30 June 1833.

UNPUBLISHED SOURCES
England, F. Jefferiss priv. col. [diary, 1811–33]
BIBLIOGRAPHY
M. Hardie: *Water Colour Painting in Britain*, i: *The Eighteenth Century* (London, 1966)
Dr Thomas Monro (1759–1833) and the Monro Academy (exh. cat., ed. F. Jefferiss, London, V&A, 1976)
J. Farington: *Diaries 1793–1831*, ed. K. Garlick, A. Macintyre and K. Cave, 16 vols (New Haven, 1978–84)
A. Wilton: 'The Monro School Question: Some Answers', *Turner Stud.*, iv/2 (1984), pp. 8–23
Thomas Girtin (exh. cat., ed. S. Morris, New Haven, CT, Yale Cent. Brit. A., 1986), pp. 12–14
SUSAN MORRIS

Monro Turner, Helen. *See* TURNER, HELEN MONRO.

Mons [Flem. Bergen]. Capital city of the province of Hainault in southern Belgium, noted for its production of gold and silver. The greatest flowering of gold- and silversmithing in Mons took place in the 17th century and particularly the 18th, when the voluminous production of high-quality domestic silver was comparable to that of the most important centres of the Netherlands. A castle tower was used as the hallmark, stipulated as early as the end of the 13th century and recorded in the statutes of the guild, dated 20 May 1406. Two pewter engraved plates (Mons, Mus. Jean Lescarts) survive for the period 1467–1551, with makers' names and marks.

See BELGIUM, §IX, 1(ii).

BIBLIOGRAPHY
L. Tondreau and others: *L'Orfèvrerie en Hainaut* (Tielt and Antwerp, 1985)
Les Grands Orfèvres du Hainaut (exh. cat. by R. Stilmant, Brussels, Banque-Lambert, 1988)
LEO DE REN

Monsanto, Antonio Edmundo (*b* Caracas, 10 Sept 1890; *d* Caracas, 16 April 1948). Venezuelan painter and art historian. He studied at the Academia de Bellas Artes, Caracas (1904–9) under Emilio Mauri (1855–1908) and Antonio Herrera Toro. In 1912 with Leoncio Martínez, Manuel Cabré and other artists, he co-founded the anti-academic group Círculo de Bellas Artes in Caracas. Between 1916 and 1919 he came into contact with the traveller-artists Samys Mützner, Nicolas Ferdinandov and Emilio Boggio; Mützner in particular offered helpful advice. In 1920, when Monsanto had established himself as a painter through his technical skill and clarity of concept (e.g. *Seascape*, 1920; Caracas, Gal. A.N.), he began to feel dissatisfied with his work and to call himself a 'former painter'. He retired from painting, failing to develop work that had shown much promise, and between 1921 and 1928 he dedicated himself to enhancing his knowledge of art history. He also undertook the restoration of works of art, thereby maintaining his connection with painting. In 1936 he was appointed Director of the Academia de Bellas Artes, Caracas, in that same year renamed the Escuela de Artes Plásticas y Aplicadas, and from then on he dedicated himself completely to teaching, which is where his most important contribution lay.

BIBLIOGRAPHY
L. A. López Méndez: *Círculo de Bellas Artes* (Caracas, 1969)
F. Paz-Castillo: *Entre pintores y escritores* (Caracas, 1970)
P. Erminy and J. Calzadilla: *El paisaje como tema en la pintura venezolana* (Caracas, 1975)
YASMINY PÉREZ SILVA

Monsiau [Monsiaux], Nicolas-André (*b* Paris, 1754 or 1755; *d* Paris, 31 May 1837). French painter and illustrator. He was the pupil of Jean-François-Pierre Peyron in Paris and, thanks to a sponsor, the Marquis de Couberon,

Nicolas-André Monsiau: *Death of Agis*, oil on canvas, 1789 (Paris, Musée du Petit Palais)

followed his master to Rome in 1776. He stayed four years and made the acquaintance of Jacques-Louis David and Pierre Henri de Valenciennes. On his return to Paris he exhibited at the Salons de la Correspondance of 1781 and 1782. Monsiau was approved (*agréé*) as an associate of the Académie Royale on 30 June 1787 for *Alexander Taming Bucephalus* (untraced) and was received (*reçu*) only on 3 October 1789, after a previous application had been refused; his *morceau de réception* was the *Death of Agis* (Paris, Petit Pal.; see fig.). Affected by the hangings in 1792 and 1793 of his two protectors and by the slump in commissions brought about by the Revolution, he turned to book illustration for editions of Ovid, Jean-Jacques Rousseau, Laurence Sterne, Jacques Delille and Salomon Gessner.

Monsiau was a regular exhibitor at the Salon until 1833, and his subject-matter ranged from ancient history to historical genre. In 1804 he was awarded a Prix d'Encouragement for the *Gaul Sabinus and his Wife Eponina Discovered in an Underground Cave* (Autun, Mus. Rolin). His historical subjects include *Molière Reading 'Tartuffe' to Ninon de Lenclos* (1802; Paris, Mus. Comédie-Fr.) and *Poussin Seeing Cardinal Massimi to the Door* (exh. Paris Salon, 1806; untraced), a scene illustrating the great artist's frugality and suspicion of wealth. The *Lion of Florence* (1801; Paris, Louvre) depicts a sublime example of maternal devotion: in the 18th century a lion that had escaped from the menagerie of the Grand Duke of Florence seized a child in its mouth, whereupon the mother prostrated herself and cried out until the lion released the infant. Monsiau gave the mother a near-hysterical posture, and both critics and public greatly admired this unusual subject. In his historical genre scenes Monsiau demonstrated a high degree of novelty not usually present in his history paintings.

Monsiau was favoured with an important Napoleonic commission, the *Comitia at Lyon, 26 January 1802* (exh. Paris Salon, 1808; Versailles, Château), which documents the final session of the meeting of 452 Deputies of the Cisalpine Republic, when the constitution of the new Italian Republic was read out and Napoleon was proclaimed president. During the Bourbon restoration a bout of ill-health gave a moralizing dimension to one of Monsiau's most successful paintings, the *Devotion of Monseigneur de Belzunce* (1819; Paris, Louvre). Suffering from renal colic, Monsiau was told he needed an operation; he had already started the picture and decided to finish it before having treatment, stating 'if this delay . . . proves to be the cause of my death, my last work will at least be a tribute to virtue' (sale cat., pp. 6–7). The subject concerns the plague in Marseille in 1720, when the bishop of the city, Monseigneur de Belzunce, administered extreme unction to the dying. Monsiau thus combined the two highly topical themes of a heroic deed and the past practices of the newly restored Roman Catholic Church. While an overall sense of didactic sentimentality prevails, the picture was nevertheless bought by Louis XVIII. Monsiau's approach here was not innovative; his style was illustrative and looked back to Jean Jouvenet and Gabriel-François Doyen. He relied on the pyramidal formula with repoussoir figures in the foreground and did not favour

the frieze-like compositions of Neo-classicism. The modelling is smooth, the finish precise, and mauve-grey tones predominate. Monsiau's last years were difficult. He was ill and lost his only son at the age of 22 in 1820. He suffered increasing dementia and died in a highly agitated state.

BIBLIOGRAPHY
'Notice sur la vie et les ouvrages de M. Monsiau', *Catalogue des tableaux, études, dessins, gravures . . . dépendant de la succession de M. Monsiau* (sale cat., Paris, 30–31 Aug 1837), pp. 3–7
French Painting, 1774–1830: The Age of Revolution (exh. cat., Paris, Grand Pal.; Detroit, Inst. A.; New York, Met.; 1974–5)
J. Foucart, ed.: *Musée du Louvre: Nouvelles acquisitions du Département des Peintures, 1983–1986* (Paris, 1987), pp. 129–31

SIMON LEE

Monsignori, Francesco. *See* BONSIGNORI, FRANCESCO.

Mons Regalus. *See* KRAK DE MONREAL.

Mont, Hans [Mente, Giovan de; Monte, Johann de] (*b* Ghent, *c.* 1545; *d* after 1582). Flemish sculptor and architect, active in Austria, Bohemia and Germany. In 1572 he collaborated with Giambologna, and in 1575, on Giambologna's recommendation, he entered the service of Emperor Maximilian II in Vienna. He worked in the Neugebäude, near Vienna, on wall and ceiling decorations and, according to van Mander, executed giant stucco figures. For Emperor Rudolf II's entry into Vienna (1576), he designed a large triumphal arch on the Bauernmarkt and modelled several sculptures. When Rudolf II moved his court to Prague later in 1576, Mont followed him, although his name does not appear in the inventory of the imperial Kunstkammer. In 1617 Philipp Hainhofer saw 'six statues in "marmo" and "di brunzo" on pediments by Giovan di Mente and Giovan Bologna' in the Kunstkammer, Dresden. Having lost an eye playing tennis, at the latest by early 1580, Mont apparently had to abandon sculpture. In May 1580 he was working as a master builder in Ulm, where he was employed on the city's fortifications. In 1582 he was dismissed because of deficiencies in his work.

None of Mont's documented works survives, although two drawings, attributed to him by old inscriptions, reveal stylistic similarities with works by Bartholomäus Spranger. Scholars have attributed to Mont a bronze group of *Venus and Adonis* (Stockholm, Nmus.; ex-Prague Castle, 1621). Closely resembling this in style are two statuettes of the *Callipygian Venus* (Oxford, Ashmolean; Brunswick, Herzog Anton Ulrich-Mus.) and an alabaster statuette of *Venus and Mars* (Prague, N.G., Šternberk Pal.). Mont is attributed with the outstanding stucco decorations of Bučovice Castle, Moravia, the large figures of which closely resemble the Stockholm *Venus and Adonis* group.

BIBLIOGRAPHY
K. van Mander: *Schilder-boeck* ([1603]–1604)
Disegni fiamminghi e olandesi (exh. cat., ed. E. K. J. Reznicek; Florence, Uffizi, 1964), no. 36
L. O. Larsson: 'Hans Mont van Gent', *Ksthist. Tidskr.*, xxxvi (1967), pp. 1–12 [with complete bibliog.]
——: 'Bildhauerkunst und Plastik am Hofe Kaiser Rudolfs II', *Leids Ksthist. Jb.*, i (1982), pp. 211–35
H. Lietzmann: *Das Neugebäude in Wien* (Munich, 1987), pp. 151ff

LARS OLOF LARRSON

Montage [Fr.: 'mounting']. Assemblage that results from the overlapping or joining of various materials, images or objects to form a new single picture (*see* COLLAGE, PHOTOMONTAGE and HEARTFIELD, JOHN).

□

Montagna [Cincani]. Italian family of artists. (1) Bartolomeo Montagna was the leading painter in Vicenza during the last quarter of the 15th century and the first quarter of the 16th. His son (2) Benedetto Montagna, who continued his father's style of painting, is more significant for his engravings, some of which are based on his father's work, often combined with German influences.

(1) Bartolomeo Montagna (*b* Orzinuovi, nr Brescia, or Biron, nr Vicenza, *c*. 1450; *d* Vicenza, 11 Oct 1523). Painter and draughtsman.

1. LIFE AND WORK.

(i) Early work, to c. 1485. Montagna is first documented in 1459 in Vicenza as a minor and, still a minor, in 1467. In 1469 he is recorded as a resident of Venice. In 1474 he was living in Vicenza where, in 1476 and 1478, he was commissioned to paint altarpieces (now lost). He has variously been considered a pupil of Andrea Mantegna (Vasari), Giovanni Bellini, Antonello da Messina, Alvise Vivarini, Domenico Morone and Vittore Carpaccio. While none of these artists, except Carpaccio, was irrelevant to Montagna's stylistic formation, scholars agree that Giovanni Bellini was the primary influence on his art. He may have worked in Bellini's shop around 1470. Several of Montagna's paintings of the *Virgin and Child* in which the influence of Antonello da Messina is especially marked

1. Bartolomeo Montagna: *Virgin and Child with SS Monica and Mary Magdalene*, tempera on canvas, 1.69×1.21 m, mid-1480s (Vicenza, Museo Civico d'Arte e Storia)

(e.g. two in Belluno, Mus. Civ.; London, N.G., see Davies, no. 802) are likely to be close in date to Antonello's sojourn in Venice (1475–6); they are therefore best considered Montagna's earliest extant works (Gilbert, 1967) rather than as an unexplained parenthesis around 1485 between two Bellinesque phases (Puppi, 1962). These early paintings appear to be followed by others in which the geometrically rounded forms derived from Antonello become more slender and sharper-edged. Their figures are imbued with a deeply felt, individual humanity, sometimes austere and minatory, sometimes tender. Among them are some larger-scale works, for example the *Virgin and Child Enthroned with SS Nicholas and Lucy* (Philadelphia, PA, Mus. A.) and a *Virgin and Child Enthroned with SS Ansanus, Anthony Abbot, Francis and Jerome* (often but wrongly attributed to Carpaccio; Vicenza, Mus. Civ. A. & Stor.). This group also includes a fresco fragment depicting the *Virgin and Child* (London, N.G.), the modern frame of which is inscribed, 'Painted 1481 in the choir of the church of Magrè near Schio-Vicenza'. The date seems plausible on stylistic grounds, and the work thus provides a chronological point of reference for the rest of the group. In 1482, again in Venice, Montagna undertook to paint canvases of the *Flood* and the *Creation* for the Scuola di S Marco; the former was completed in 1485–6 by Benedetto Diana, and both were subsequently destroyed by fire.

(ii) Maturity, c. 1485–1509. Having returned to Vicenza, Montagna supplied designs (after 1484) for the intarsie of the choir-stalls (*in situ*) of the Santuario di Monte Berico, executed by the intarsiatore of note Pierantonio da Lendinara (*c*. 1430–97). In 1486 he made an agreement with Giovanni di Magrè about a *Virgin and Child with Saints*, which could be (but more likely is not) that in the parish church of S Giovanni Ilarione.

Montagna's mature style is ushered in by two superb altarpieces for S Bartolomeo, Vicenza, the *Virgin and Child with SS Monica and Mary Magdalene* (see fig. 1) and the monumental high altarpiece of the *Virgin and Child Enthroned with Four Saints and Musician Angels* (both Vicenza, Mus. Civ. A. & Stor.), both of which are datable to the mid-1480s. The former sets its trenchantly characterized protagonists outdoors in a landscape whose pitted, fossil-embossed limestone, entwined roots and seething grass combine Bellinesque observation with an element of fantasy reminiscent of Francesco Squarcione's school. The air is clear, the light cool. The latter painting is a *plein-air* variant of Bellini's great Venetian altarpieces, with figures arranged in a spacious vaulted porch brimming with morning light. Here the landscape bespeaks the beauty of the everyday while fantasy finds play in the architecture of the Virgin's tall throne. Colour again is cool, dominated by sky blue, silver and cream. Besides Bellini, further sources of influence for this work may be Ercole de' Roberti (as Puppi suggests) and Benedetto Diana, whose *Virgin and Child Enthroned with Two Saints and Donors* (1486; Venice, Ca' d'Oro) similarly exploits architectural oddity, a high ratio of void to mass, and subtle, silvery tonality. Montagna's style in these altarpieces is, however, very much his own, with invention and control in perfect balance. In his small *Virgin and Child Enthroned with SS*

2. Bartolomeo Montagna: *St Jerome* and *St Paul*, oil on panel, wings from an altarpiece, each panel 1.12×0.50 m, *c.* 1490s (Milan, Museo Poldi Pezzoli)

Sebastian and Roch (1487; Bergamo, Gal. Accad. Carrara) the sophisticated interplay of colour and light depends still further on the variegated colouring of the marble in the architecture, a device he increasingly exploited thereafter. An inscription on the back of this painting states that he painted it in September 1487 for Gerolamo Roberto Bresciano; it is thus Montagna's first extant securely dated painting.

In 1488 and again in 1492 Bartolomeo was in Padua. A notation made by one of the Certosa di Pavia's monks between 1634 and 1637 states that in 1490 he painted an altarpiece depicting the *Virgin and Child Enthroned with SS John the Baptist and Jerome* (Pavia, Mus. Certosa) for the Certosa. Between 1496 and 1500 he was paid for an altarpiece for S Michele, Vicenza; it is dated 1499 and depicts the *Virgin and Child Enthroned with Four Saints and Musician Angels* (Milan, Brera). He is also documented as receiving payment between 1499 and 1504 for a *Virgin and Child Enthroned with Eight Saints* (destroyed) for Vicenza Cathedral. Dated paintings of this period include a *Virgin and Child Enthroned with SS James and John the*

Evangelist (1499; Glasgow, A.G. & Mus.), a *Nativity* (1500; Orgiano, parish church), a frescoed *Pietà* (5 Apr 1500; Vicenza, Santuario di Monte Berico), a *Christ Blessing* (1502; Turin, Gal. Sabauda) and three paintings of the *Virgin and Child* (all 1503; ex-Lugano, Donati priv. col.; Modena, Gal. & Mus. Estense; Paris, de Noailles priv. col.).

During the 1490s and into the next decade Montagna held aloof from from the general mellowing of Venetian art. He cultivated complications of cutting edge and angular junction, prismatic drapery, bizarrely decorative architecture, and quarried landscapes that memorably blend the domestic and the fantastic. These ever more anachronistic features, though, are combined with increasingly ample figures and, from the mid-1490s, often with darkened tonalities that, however, entail no atmospheric softening or indistinctness. Paradoxical though this style became, it produced impressive paintings: *St Jerome* and *St Paul* (*c.* 1490; Milan, Mus. Poldi Pezzoli; see fig. 2), *St Peter* (early 1490s; Venice, Accad.), the twilit *Virgin and Child Enthroned with SS Francis and John the Baptist* (later

1490s; Venice, Fond. Cini), the Monte Berico *Pietà*, the ruined but splendidly spacious and monumental frescoes of scenes from the *Life of St Biagio* (1504–6; Verona, SS Nazaro e Celso) and the majestic *Virgin and Child Enthroned with Four Saints and Musician Angels* (1499; Milan, Brera). This last represents a summit of achievement not only within Montagna's art but among High Renaissance altarpieces in northern Italy. The imposing figures are integrated with monumental architecture in a colour scheme of extraordinary intricacy that is given coherence by the slightly lowered tonality. The composition balances massive solids against deep, light-filled space, and complexity of detail against overall symmetry.

(iii) Late works, 1509–23. Montagna is documented in Vicenza again in 1509. The last 15 years of his career are often considered a period of decline (Borenius; Puppi, 1962), although Gilbert (1956) persuasively argued against so simple a view. In these years Montagna was less often able to resolve with complete success the contradictions implicit in his mature style, but the successes remain works of great individual distinction. He was working against increasing odds: his own advancing years; a move to Padua (1509–14), probably enforced by the ravages of war in Vicenza; and the rapid ascendancy of a style and taste very unlike his own, that promulgated by Giorgione and Titian. His adjustments to this last factor included lusher landscapes, more rotund figures, warm tonalities and, sometimes, fiery sunset skies. He ingeniously fused these elements with the complex geometric architecture and coloured marbles of his earlier works in paintings that, at their best, achieve a new, more romantic and poetic quality.

Outstanding examples are the fresco of the *Exhumation of St Anthony* (1512; Padua, Scuola S Antonio), in which eventful landscape, eccentric architecture, tumultuous crowds and striking portraits vie for the viewer's attention; and the crepuscular and nostalgic *Virgin and Child Enthroned with Four Saints* (c. 1514; Padua, S Maria in Vanzo). Having returned to Vicenza by 1517, when he was paid for work by his son (2) Benedetto Montagna, he was commissioned in 1520 to paint an altarpiece depicting the *Nativity* for the Scuola di S Giuseppe, Cologna Veneta, which was executed in 1522. In 1523 he made his last will.

2. CRITICAL RECEPTION AND POSTHUMOUS REPUTATION. Despite the number of dated works, no chronology of Montagna's oeuvre yet published can be considered definitive. He was clearly responsive to stimuli from diverse sources. Scholars disagree as to when these responses occurred, and hence in their dating of many individual paintings. For example the severely damaged *Virgin and Child* (London, N.G., see Davies, no. 1098), is dated by Puppi 1504–6, by Berenson c. 1489 and by Borenius as early as the 1470s.

Montagna's art was overwhelmingly influential for his contemporaries in Vicenza, but far less so elsewhere. Among Venetian painters, Cima da Conegliano and Vittore Carpaccio apparently consulted his art early in their careers; it had more lasting importance for Benedetto Diana and for contemporary artists active in Padua and Verona. Among Vicentines, Montagna's example determined the styles of his son Benedetto and Giovanni

Battista Speranza and, with Perugino, that of Francesco Verla (*fl* 1490–1520). It was also highly significant for Giovanni Buonconsiglio. Montagna is chiefly important, however, for his own idiosyncratic achievement. Unsurpassed, even in a generation of virtuosos, at using colour to evoke varying intensities and qualities of light, he also devised colouristic counterpoints, fascinating in their own right. Masterly and often daring in his compositions, he was also a fine draughtsman, as several surviving drawings attest (e.g. the *Drunkenness of Noah*; New York, Pierpoint Morgan Lib.; the *Risen Christ*; Paris, Louvre; and the two related *Heads* of the Virgin; Windsor Castle, Royal Lib., and Oxford, Christ Church; see 1983 exh. cat.). His formal skills were used to expressive ends. He had a deep feeling for landscape and for the human figure, face and posture as expressive agents. In many of his works all these elements combine to produce compelling realizations of a personal vision of life: sombre, truthful and compassionate.

BIBLIOGRAPHY
G. Vasari: *Vite* (1550, rev. 2/1568); ed. G. Milanesi (1878–85), iii, pp. 649–50; 672–4; vii, p. 526
C. Ridolfi: *Meraviglie* (1648); ed. D. von Hadeln, i (1914), pp. 109–11
M. Boschini: *I gioielli pittoreschi* (Vicenza, 1676)
A. Magrini: *Elogio di Bartolomeo Montagna* (Venice, 1863)
J. A. Crowe and G. B. Cavalcaselle: *A History of Painting in North Italy*, 3 vols (London, 1871); ed. T. Borenius, ii (London, 1912), pp. 121–8 [important especially for Borenius's notes]
T. Borenius: *The Painters of Vicenza: 1480–1550* (London, 1909)
A. Venturi: *Storia*, VII/iv (1915), pp. 436–500
B. Berenson: *Venetian Painting in America* (New York, 1916), pp. 173–85, 189–94
G. G. Zorzi: *Contributo alla storia dell'arte vicentina* (Venice, 1916)
M. Davies: *The Earlier Italian Schools*, London, N.G. cat. (London, 1951, rev. 1961/R 1986)
F. Barbieri: *Il Montagna al Museo di Vicenza* (Vicenza, 1954)
E. Arslan: *Vicenza: Le chiese* (Rome, 1956)
C. Gilbert: 'Alvise e compagni', *Scritti di storia dell'arte in onore di Lionello Venturi* (Rome, 1956), pp. 277–308
B. Berenson: *Venetian School* (1957)
L. Puppi: *Bartolomeo Montagna* (Vicenza, 1962) [standard mod. monograph]
G. Mantese: *Memorie storiche della chiesa vicentina*, III/ii (Vicenza, 1964)
C. Gilbert: [review of L. Puppi, *Bartolomeo Montagna* (Vicenza, 1962)], *A. Bull.*, xlix (1967), pp. 184–9
L. Puppi: 'Un integrazione al catalogo e al regesto di Bartolomeo Montagna', *Ant. Viva*, xiv/3 (1975), pp. 23–9
P. Humfrey: 'Cima da Conegliano at San Bartolomeo in Vicenza', *A. Ven.*, xxxi (1977), pp. 176–81
F. Barbieri: *I pittori di Vicenza, 1480–1521* (Vicenza, 1981), pp. 16–31
Drawing in the Italian Renaissance Workshop (exh. cat. by F. Ames-Lewis and J. Wright; Nottingham, A.G.; London, V&A; 1983), pp. 76–7, 168–9, 318–21
M. Lucco: 'La pittura del secondo quattrocento nel Veneto occidentale', *La pittura in Italia: Il quattrocento*, ed. F. Zeri (Milan, 1986), i, pp. 152–6; ii, p. 712 [incl. concise biog. of Montagna]
M. Tanzi: 'Vincenza', *La pittura nel Veneto: Il quattrocento*, ed. M. Lucco (Milan, 1990), ii, pp. 606–21, p. 760 [incl. concise biog. of Montagna by M. Lucco]

(2) Benedetto Montagna (*b* Vicenza, *c.* 1480; *d* Vicenza, 1556–8). Engraver and painter, son of (1) Bartolomeo Montagna. His approximate date of birth is derived from the fact that he was given power of attorney in 1504. In 1517 his father received payment for work (untraced) done by Benedetto in the Palazzo del Podestà, Vicenza, and in 1522 Benedetto was paid for frescoes (destr.) in S Agostino, Padua. After this date altarpieces by Benedetto are documented at intervals until 1541. As a painter he is of merely local significance. His style is based on his father's, with some admixture from contemporaries such as Moretto, Pordenone and Domenico Campagnola. He is more important, however, as an engraver. His earliest engravings are usually dated *c.* 1500 but could be somewhat earlier. They often seem to be based directly on drawings, or in one case a painting, by his father and reflect the austere beauty of these. Almost from the beginning, however, he embellished his father's style with motifs and technical borrowings from the prints of Albrecht Dürer, five of which he is known to have copied between *c.* 1500 and 1505. The unlikely amalgamation of Bartolomeo with Dürer is startlingly exemplified in *St Jerome* (B. 14). Around 1505 Benedetto was apparently in contact with Girolamo Mocetto, a contact that benefited both artists; thereafter Benedetto's technique and artistic orientation were strongly affected by the example of Giulio Campagnola. As a result, his latest engravings recall Giorgione in character, not least in regard to their subject-matter. They include seven illustrations of Ovid and other mythological, arcadian and genre scenes. Benedetto was the most prolific engraver of his generation in northern Italy and influenced others such as Girolamo Mocetto and Nicoletto da Modena (*fl* before 1500–12). 52 engravings are unmistakably his, 47 of them signed or monogrammed.

BIBLIOGRAPHY

A. von Bartsch: *Le Peintre-graveur* (1803–21), xiii, pp. 332–52 [B.]
T. Borenius: *The Painters of Vicenza: 1480–1550* (London, 1909), pp. 115–25
F. Carrington: 'Benedetto Montagna and the *Metamorphoses* of Ovid', *Prt Colr Q.*, xxviii (1941), pp. 206–32
A. M. Hind: *Early Italian Engravings: A Critical Catalogue with Complete Reproduction of all the Prints Described* (London, 1948), v, pp. 173–88; vii, pls 736–69
. Puppi: 'Appunti su Benedetto Montagna pittore', *A. Ven.*, xii (1958), pp. 53–62
arly Italian Engravings from the National Gallery of Art (exh. cat., ed. J. A. Levenson, K. Oberhuber and J. L. Sheehan; Washington, DC, N.G.A., 1973), pp. 307–32 [entries by J. L. Sheehan]
M.. Zucker: *Early Italian Masters* (1980), 25 [XIII/ii] of *The Illustrated artsch*, ed. W. Strauss (New York, 1978–), pp. 198–230; *Commentary* (984), pp. 385–432

FRANCIS L. RICHARDSON

Montagnana, Jacopo da. *See* JACOPO DA MONTAGNANA.

Montagne, Matthieu de. *See* PLATTENBERG, MATTHIEU VAN

Montagu. English and Scottish family of diplomats, politicians, patrons and collectors. For the dukes of Montagu of the second creation *see under* BRUDENELL.

(1) Ralph, 1st Duke of Montagu (*b* London, ?1638; *d* 9 March 1709). The younger son of the reclusive Edward, 2nd Baron Montagu (1616–84), he became heir to Boughton House, Northants, in 1665 on the death of his elder brother. In 1669 he was appointed Charles II's ambassador to the French court; while there he formed 'Ideas in his own Mind, both of Buildings and Gardening'. In 1671 he purchased, for £14,000, the Mastership of the Royal Wardrobe, which entitled him to apartments at Whitehall, London. In 1673 he married the widowed Lady Elizabeth Wriothesley, who brought him an additional £6000 a year. Two years later he commissioned from Robert Hooke a new house in Bloomsbury, London, which was built 'after the French pavilion way'. It was decorated by Antonio Verrio, who had returned from Paris with Montagu in 1674 in order to design cartoons for the Mortlake Tapestry Factory, which Montagu had acquired that year.

Montagu spent several years in exile in France from 1683 as a result of his implication in the Rye House Plot, a failed conspiracy by Whig extremists and republicans to murder Charles II; meanwhile, his Bloomsbury residence, Montagu House, was leased to William Cavendish, 4th Earl (and later 1st Duke) of Devonshire. After its partial destruction by fire early in 1686, it was rebuilt by an architect named Pouget brought over from France. This second Montagu House (destr. 1850) was decorated by Charles de La Fosse from 1689: the staircase walls carried landscapes showing the story of *Diana Surprised by Actaeon*, and the ceiling was painted with *Phaeton Asking Apollo for his Chariot in the Presence of the Seasons and the Gods*. The scheme is recorded in a watercolour of 1845 by George Scharf (London, BM). La Fosse was assisted by Jacques Parmentier, Jacques Rousseau and Jean-Baptiste Monnoyer. When La Fosse returned to Paris to decorate the Dôme des Invalides, they were joined by Louis Chéron, who also worked at Montagu House, Ditton, near Windsor (another inheritance of Montagu's), and at Boughton House, which Montagu had extended to include state apartments in a new 'Frenchified' north wing (possibly also designed by Pouget). The *Marriage of Hercules and Hebe* on the ceiling of Boughton's Great Hall shows Chéron's debt to the French academic tradition and in particular to the work of Charles Le Brun. Many of the Huguenot craftsmen Montagu patronized also worked for King William III, including Daniel Marot I; five decorative panels for Boughton were painted to his designs (London, V&A). Although Montagu's second marriage, to the widow of Christopher Monck, 2nd Duke of Albemarle, in 1692, was even more lucrative than his first, many of these craftsmen had not been paid in full at his death.

In addition to his patronage, Montagu also collected works by earlier artists, including 37 sketches of eminent contemporaries by Anthony van Dyck (Duke of Buccleuch priv. col.) for the *Iconographiae* (1641); these were acquired at Peter Lely's studio sale in 1682. The precise content of much of Montagu's collection is hard to determine, as it became mingled with that of Anne Douglas Scott, Countess of Buccleuch (1651–1732), another collector of the period, when their respective great-grandchildren Elizabeth Montagu and Henry Scott, 3rd Duke of Buccleuch (1746–1812), married in 1767. Both collections are now scattered between Boughton House, Drumlanrig Castle (Dumfries & Galloway) and Bowhill (Borders). In 1755 Montagu House, Bloomsbury, became the first home of the British Museum.

BIBLIOGRAPHY

DNB
The Court in Mourning, Being the Life and Worthy Actions of Ralph, Duke of Montague (London, 1709)
A. Boyer: *History of the Life and Reign of Queen Anne* (London, 1722)
J. Hayward, ed.: *The Letters of Saint Evremond* (London, 1930)
E. Croft-Murray: *Decorative Painting in England, 1537–1837*, 2 vols (Feltham, 1962–70), i, pp. 53, 66, 239, 244–5, 247–8; ii, pp. 13, 319
J. Cornforth: 'Boughton House, Northamptonshire', *Country Life*, cxlviii (3 Sept 1970), pp. 564–8; (10 Sept 1970), pp. 624–8; (17 Sept 1970), pp. 684–7; cxlix (25 Feb 1970), pp. 420–23; (4 March 1970), pp. 476–80, 536–9

G. Jackson-Stops: 'Daniel Marot and the 1st Duke of Montagu', *Ned. Ksthist. Jb.*, xxxi (1981), pp. 244–62

T. Murdoch: 'Boughton House, Northamptonshire', *Antiques*, cxxix (1986), pp. 1242–55

T. Murdoch, ed.: *Boughton House: The English Versailles* (London, 1992)

TESSA MURDOCH

(2) Charles Montagu, 4th Earl and 1st Duke of Manchester (*b* ?1660; *d* 20 Jan 1722). Distant cousin of (1) Ralph Montagu. He was educated at Trinity College, Cambridge, and abroad, and succeeded to the earldom of Manchester in 1682. A prominent supporter of the Revolution of 1688, in 1697 he became ambassador to Venice, in 1698 a member of the Privy Council, in 1699 ambassador extraordinary at Paris, and in 1701 secretary of state for the North.

In 1707 Manchester was again posted to Venice, where he commissioned Luca Carlevaris to paint the *Reception of the Fourth Earl of Manchester as Ambassador at Venice* (1707; Birmingham, Mus. & A.G.; for illustration *see* CARLEVARIS, LUCA). At the same time he commissioned John Vanbrugh to prepare a set of designs for the reconstruction of his country house, Kimbolton, Cambs, in a style that Vanbrugh described as having 'something of the Castle Air'. In a detailed correspondence, Vanbrugh reported on its battlementing, adding that 'if the Painter yr Ldship brings over be a good one, he may find work enough'. The painters in question, returning to England with Manchester in 1708, were Giovanni Antonio Pellegrini and Marco Ricci—a remarkable act of perceptive patronage. Their first paintings for Manchester were probably for the stairwell of his London house in Arlington Street (untraced). Pellegrini's paintings for Kimbolton (completed 1713) were a *Triumph of Caesar* for the stairwell, and a *Transfiguration* and *Four Evangelists* in the chapel. He also painted an easel portrait of the family; another portrait of Manchester is a kit-cat by Godfrey Kneller (*c.* 1703–10; London, N.P.G.). In 1719 Alessandro Galilei added a portico to Kimbolton (*see* GALILEI, ALESSANDRO, fig. 1). In the same year Manchester was made a duke by George I.

Manchester's importance in the history of English taste is twofold. On the one hand he was willing for Vanbrugh to give Kimbolton 'medieval' accoutrements, in order for it to make what the architect described as a 'very Noble and Masculine Shew'; on the other hand he commissioned interior paintings from Pellegrini of exceptional lightness and fluency. In both, Manchester led rather than followed the artistic appetites of his age.

UNPUBLISHED SOURCES
Huntingdon, Rec. Office [Kimbolton MSS]

BIBLIOGRAPHY
Duke of Manchester: *Court and Society from Elizabeth to Anne*, 2 vols (London, 1864)

W. Nisser: 'Lord Manchester's Reception at Venice', *Burl. Mag.*, lxx (1937), pp. 30–34

F. J. B. Watson: 'English Villas and Venetian Decorators', *RIBA J.* (1954), pp. 171–7

E. Croft-Murray: 'Giovanni Antonio Pellegrini at Kimbolton', *Apollo*, lxx (1959), pp. 119–24

——: *Decorative Painting in England, 1537–1837* (Feltham, 1970), ii, pp. 13–15, 253, 255, 264

CHARLES SAUMAREZ SMITH

(3) Walter Francis Montagu-Douglas-Scott, 5th Duke of Buccleuch [7th Duke of Queensberry] (*b* Dalkeith, 25 Nov 1806; *d* Selkirk, 16 April 1884). He succeeded to the dukedom in 1819 and inherited a fine collection of paintings that included family portraits by van Dyck, Reynolds and Gainsborough, the *Virgin of the Yarnwinder* (after 1506; Duke of Buccleuch priv. col.) by Leonardo (*see* LEONARDO DA VINCI, §II, 1(iii)), an *Old Woman Reading* (1655; Duke of Buccleuch priv. col.) by Rembrandt, and *Peasants with Cattle by a Stream in a Woody Landscape* (*c.* 1615–22; London, N.G.) by Rubens.

Walter Francis Montagu-Douglas-Scott pursued a political career after graduating from Cambridge in 1827 but also maintained an interest in the arts: among his major acquisitions were *Landscape with the Judgement of Paris* (1633) by Claude and *London: Whitehall and the Privy Garden Looking North* (*c.* 1751) by Canaletto, both of which remain in family ownership. He bought further landscapes, predominantly of the Dutch school, that hung at Dalkeith Palace, near Edinburgh, and were seen by Gustav Friedrich Waagen in 1854; Waagen was more impressed, however, with the Duke's collections at Montagu House, Portman Square, London (destr. World War II), of antique sculpture and medieval antiquities; part of the latter had been displayed at the Medieval Exhibition at the Royal Society of Arts, London, in 1850.

In addition to these artefacts the Duke purchased furniture, porcelain, books, prints and etchings. He also assembled a collection of portrait miniatures by Hans Holbein the younger, Nicholas Hilliard and Samuel Cooper, among other well-known artists. As a patron, he encouraged Scottish sculptors, supporting John Steell in his early career.

BIBLIOGRAPHY
G. F. Waagen: *Treasures of Art in Great Britain*, 4 vols (London 185 7/*R* 1970), i, pp. 37, 415; iii, pp. 312–14; iv, pp. 435–7

W. T. Whitley: *Art in England, 1800–1820* (Cambridge, 1928)

F. Herrmann: *The English as Collectors* (London, 1972), p. 65

R. WINDSOR LISCOMBE

Montaiglon, Anatole de Courde, Comte de (*b* Paris 28 Nov 1824; *d* Tours, 1 Sept 1895). French writer. After attending the Ecole des Chartes in Paris (1847–50) he joined the staff of the Louvre (1852) to work on the catalogue of medieval and Renaissance sculpture. In 1856 he was appointed supernumerary at the Bibliothèque de l'Arsenal, where he remained for four years before moving to the Bibliothèque Sainte-Geneviève as deputy librarian. In 1864 he became secretary of the Ecole des Chartes and four years later was appointed to the chair of bibliography there. His first book was on the connoisseur Pierre-Jean Mariette: *Abcedario de P.-J. Mariette* (1851). Most of his subsequent books were devoted to early art and literature in France and a few, for example *Michel-Ange et les statues de la famille de Médicis à l'église Saint Jean de Florence* (Paris, 1877), to the art of other countries. He was a regular contributor to the *Gazette des beaux-arts*, *L'Artiste* and *Moniteur des arts*, and from 1849 wrote poetry mostly inspired by the work of great artists. The *Gazette des beaux-arts* published some of his sonnets in 1852. From 1851 to 1866 he edited the *Archives de l'art français* and, on its foundation in 1870, was appointed President of the Société de l'Histoire de l'Art Français.

WRITINGS

Abcedario de P.-J. Mariette (Paris, 1851)

Mémoires pour servir à l'histoire de l'Académie royale de peinture depuis 1648 jusqu'en 1664 (Paris, 1853)

Catalogue raisonné de l'oeuvre de Claude Mellan d'Abbeville (Abbeville, 1858)

Correspondance des directeurs de l'Académie de France à Rome (Paris, 1887–9)

BIBLIOGRAPHY

La Grande Encyclopédie (Paris, 1887–1902)

J. Guiffrey: *Anatole de Courde de Montaiglon, 1824–1895: Notice biographique* (Paris, 1897)

Montalambert, Charles Forbes René de (*b* London, 15 April 1810; *d* Paris, 13 March 1870). French writer. His early childhood was spent in England, but from 1826 to 1828 he was educated at the Collège Sainte-Barbe in Paris. The conversion of his Scottish mother from Protestantism to Catholicism in 1822 deeply affected him, and he grew up an ardent, liberal Catholic; indeed it is as a religious reformer that he is most famous. In 1833 he began a campaign to preserve the Catholic art of France, and he wrote much in this cause. His earliest piece, 'Du vandalisme en France', appeared in *Revue de deux mondes* on 1 March 1833. Written as a letter to Victor Hugo, it attacked the current destruction of France's medieval religious buildings. 'De l'état actuel de l'art religieux en France', which appeared as an introduction to A. Boblet's *Monuments de l'histoire de Sainte Elisabeth* (Paris, 1837), continued the attack. He claimed that 'the beautiful is only the splendour of truth' and that of all religious art, that which arose out of Catholicism was the greatest. He lamented the fact that, while revering the Louvre and Versailles, France largely ignored its 150 cathedrals. He was appointed to the Comité Historique des Arts et Monuments in 1838 and was later made a member of the Commission des Monuments Historiques.

WRITINGS

Oeuvres, 9 vols (Paris, 1860–68) [writings on art and lit., vi: *Mélanges d'art et littérature*]

Dieu et liberté (Paris, 1970) [sel. extracts from his work with a useful intro. by A. Trannoy]

BIBLIOGRAPHY

A. Trannoy: *Montalambert* (Paris, 1947)

G. Grente: *Dictionnaire des lettres françaises*, 7 vols (Paris, 1964–72)

Montalbani, Ovidio (*b* Bologna, Nov 1601; *d* Bologna, 20 Sept 1671). Italian scholar. He was a typical exponent of 17th-century erudition, and his scholarly activity was characterized by a tenacious defence of traditional knowledge. At the university of Bologna he taught, successively, logic, medicine, mathematics and moral philosophy; and he published profusely on natural science, medicine, pharmacology, astrology and antiquarian studies. In the field of art history he is notable only for a catalogue of Bolognese artists, especially painters, which formed an appendix to the *Minervalia Bonon., Civium Anademata* (1641), a work that he published under the pseudonym of G. A. Bumaldo. The catalogue consists of 24 small pages, listing the artists in chronological order: for each one Montalbani gives brief biographical information, notes on the artist's principal works accessible to the public, and a few bibliographical indications. A veiled polemic against Vasari runs through this work, which was later cited by Malvasia. Despite its brevity it represents the first serious contribution to Bolognese artistic literature.

WRITINGS

G. A. Bumaldo [O. Montalbani]: *Minervalia Bonon., Civium Anademata, seu Bibliotheca Bononiensis: Cui accessit antiquorum pictorum, et sculptorum bononiensium brevis catalogus* (Bologna, 1641)

BIBLIOGRAPHY

G. Fantuzzi: *Notizie degli scrittori bolognesi*, VI/viii (Bologna, 1781–90), pp. 57–64

G. Perini: 'La storiografia artistica a Bologna e il collezionismo privato', *An. Scu. Norm. Sup. Pisa*, 3rd ser., xi/1 (1981), pp. 181–243

GIUSEPPE OLMI

Illustration Acknowledgements

We are grateful to those listed below for permission to reproduce copyright illustrative material and to those contributors who supplied photographs or helped us to obtain them. The word 'Photo:' precedes the names of large commercial or archival sources who have provided us with photographs, as well as the names of individual photographers (where known). It has generally not been used before the names of owners of works of art, such as museums and civic bodies. Every effort has been made to contact copyright holders and to credit them appropriately; we apologize to anyone who may have been omitted from the acknowledgements or cited incorrectly. Any error brought to our attention will be corrected in subsequent editions. Where illustrations have been taken from books, publication details are provided in the acknowledgements below.

Line drawings, maps, plans, chronological tables and family trees commissioned by the *Dictionary of Art* are not included in the list below. All of the maps in the dictionary were produced by Oxford Illustrators Ltd, who were also responsible for some of the line drawings. Most of the line drawings and plans, however, were drawn by one of the following artists: Diane Fortenberry, Lorraine Hodghton, Chris Miners, Amanda Patton, Mike Pringle, Jo Richards, Miranda Schofield, John Tiernan, John Wilson and Philip Winton. The chronological tables and family trees were prepared initially by Kate Boatfield and finalized by John Johnson.

Metabolism Photo: British Architectural Library, RIBA, London

Metal *1* © British Non-Ferrous Metals Research Association, London; *2* Photo: Dr P.T. Craddock; *6–7* Photo: Georg Jensen Silversmiths Ltd, Copenhagen; *8* Photo: John Hillelson Agency Ltd; *10* Photo: Robert Wilkins, Institute of Archaeology, Oxford; *13–14* Trustees of the British Museum, London

Metalcut Bibliothèque Nationale de France, Paris

Metalpoint Photo: Giraudon, Paris

Metapontion Archivo Museo Archeologico Nazionale, Metaponto

Meteora Benaki Museum, Athens/Photo: Nikolas Tombazis

Methodism Photo: RCHME/© Crown Copyright

Metro station Marianne Ström

Metsu, Gabriel *1–2* Rijksmuseum, Amsterdam

Metsys: (1) Quinten Metsys *1* Koninklijk Museum voor Schone Kunsten, Antwerp; *2* Photo: © RMN, Paris; *3* Royal Collection, Windsor Castle/© Her Majesty Queen Elizabeth II; *4* Trustees of the National Gallery, London

Metsys: (2) Jan Massys *1* Kunsthistorisches Museum, Vienna; *2* Hamburger Kunsthalle, Hamburg

Metsys: (3) Cornelis Massys Staatliche Museen zu Berlin, Preussischer Kulturbesitz/Kupferstichkabinett, Berlin/Photo: Jörg P. Anders

Metzinger, Jean Musée National d'Art Moderne, Paris/© ADAGP, Paris, and DACS, London, 1996

Meulen, Adam Frans van der *1* Photo: Bridgeman Art Library, London; *2* Photo: © RMN, Paris

Meunier, Constantin Photo: © ACL Brussels

Mewar Photo: Michael D. Willis

Mexico *2* Photo: Prof. Constantino Reyes Valerio; *3* Photo: Arnold Nelson/OmniQuests; *4, 8* South American Pictures, Woodbridge, Suffolk/Photo: Tony Morrison; *5* Photo: Pedro Cuevas; *6, 9* Photo: Anthony Shelton, Brighton; *7* © Julius Shulman, Hon. AIA, Los Angeles, CA; *10* Instituto Nacional de Bellas Artes, Mexico City; *11* Museum of Modern Art, New York (Gift of Allan Roos, MD, and B. Mathieu Roos); *12* Archer M. Huntington Art Gallery, University of Texas at Austin, TX (Gift of Mrs Eleanor Freed)/Photo: George Holmes; *13* Photo: Michel Zabé, Mexico City; *14* Photo: Leonore Cortina de Pintado; *15* Los Angeles County Museum of Art, Los Angeles, CA (William Randolph Hearst Collection); *16* Photo: Carlotta Mapelli Mozzi

Mexico City *2* Photo: Elizabeth Baquedano, Mexico City; *3* Photo: C. Chanfón-Olmos; *4* Photo: Instituto Nacional de Bellas Artes, Mexico City (March 1968); *5* Photo: Armando Salas-Portugal

Meynier, Charles Photo: © RMN, Paris

Mezzotint *1* Christie's Images, London; *2* Tate Gallery, London

Mi: (1) Mi Fu National Palace Museum, Taipei

Miami Photo: Robert Harding Picture Library, London

Michałowski, Piotr National Museum, Kraków

Michel, Georges Musée des Beaux-Arts, Lille

Michelangelo *1, 4–5, 8, 10–11* Photo: Archivi Alinari, Florence; *2* Photo: Lauros-Giraudon, Paris; *3* Photo: Giraudon, Paris; *6* Photo: Alinari-Giraudon, Paris; *7* Photo: Archivi Alinari, Florence/Reproduced with permission of Phaidon Press Ltd; *9* Trustees of the British Museum, London; *12* Architectural Association, London

Michelino da Besozzo Pierpont Morgan Library, New York

Michelozzo di Bartolomeo *1–3* Photo: Archivi Alinari, Florence

Michetti, Francesco Paolo Photo: Alessandro Vasari, Rome

Micrography Jewish National and University Library, Jerusalem

Micronesia Peabody Essex Museum Collection, Salem, MA/Photo: Mark Sexton

Middle Niger cultures *1–2* Musée National du Mali, Bamako

Miel, Jan Wadsworth Atheneum, Hartford, CT

Mielich, Hans Kunsthistorisches Museum, Vienna

Mierevelt, Michiel van National Portrait Gallery, London

Mieris, van: (1) Frans van Mieris (i) *1* Kunsthistorisches Museum, Vienna; *2* Mauritshuis, The Hague

Mieris: (2) Willem van Mieris Trustees of the National Gallery, London

Mies van der Rohe, Ludwig *1* Photo: Mies van der Rohe Archive, Museum of Modern Art, New York; *2* Chicago Historical Society, Chicago, IL (neg. no. 18506/L3); *3* Hedrich-Blessing, Chicago, IL

Mignard: (2) Pierre Mignard I *1* National Portrait Gallery, London; *2* Trustees of the National Gallery, London

Mignon, Léon Photo: © ACL Brussels

Migration period *1* Württembergisches Landesmuseum, Stuttgart; *2* Landesmuseum für Vorgeschichte, Halle; *3* Musée Archéologique, Dijon

Mihrab *1* American Numismatic Society, New York; *2* Department of Antiquities and Heritage, Baghdad

Mijtens: (1) Daniel Mijtens I Scottish National Portrait Gallery, Edinburgh

Mijtens: (2) Jan Mijtens Rijksmuseum, Amsterdam

Mijtens: (3) Martin Mijtens I Uppsala University, Uppsala

Milan *2, 5–7, 11–12, 15* Photo: Archivi Alinari, Florence; *3* Photo: Anthony Kersting, London; *4* Board of Trustees of the Victoria and Albert Museum, London; *8, 10* Photo: Scala, Florence; *9* Biblioteca Nazionale Centrale, Florence; *17* Photo: Dale Kinney

Milani, Aureliano Trustees of the British Museum, London

Miletos Photo: Wolfgang Müller-Wiener

Military architecture and fortification *1* Photo: Giraudon, Paris; *2* Photo: © Historic Scotland; *6* CNRS, Institut de Recherche sur l'Architecture Antique, Paris/Photo: J.P. Adam; *8* Country Life Picture Library, London/Photo: Henson; *9* Photo: Anthony Kersting, London; *10* Aerofilms of Borehamwood; *13* Library of Congress, Washington, DC; *15* Photo: Quentin Hughes; *16* Bibliothèque Nationale de France, Paris; *20* Fort McHenry National Park Service, Baltimore, MD; *23* Photo: Ian V. Hogg; *23* Trustees of the British Museum, London; *24* British Library, London (no. 50.f.13); *25* Photo: Yasser Tabbaa; *26* Ancient Art and Architecture Collection, London/Photo: B. Norman; *27* Photo: Prof. Howard Crane; *28* Photo: Ancient Art and Architecture Collection, London; *29* Photo: Christopher Tadgell; *30* Photo: Nancy Shatzman Steinhardt; *31* Photo: John Villiers; *32* Photo: George F. Andrews

Millais, John Everett *1* Tate Gallery, London; *2* Manchester City Art Galleries

Millet, Francisque Bayerische Staatsgemäldesammlungen, Munich

Millet, Jean-François *1* Photo: Bridgeman Art Library, London; *2* Photo: © RMN, Paris

Mills, Robert *1* Virginia State Library and Archives, Richmond, VA; *2* Library of Congress, Washington, DC

Minardi, Tommaso Photo: Scala, Florence

Minaret *1* Ashmolean Museum, Oxford; *2* Robert Harding Picture Library/Photo: Michael Short; *3* Photo: Dr Warwick Ball

Minbar Metropolitan Museum of Art, New York

Miniature *1* Museo Civico d'Arte Antica, Turin; *2* Board of Trustees of the Victoria and Albert Museum, London/Photo: Bridgeman Art Library, London; *3* Board of Trustees of the Victoria and Albert Museum, London; *4* Graphische Sammlung Albertina, Vienna; *5* Musée d'Art et d'Histoire de la Ville de Genève, Geneva; *6* Kunsthistorisches Museum, Vienna; *7* Photo: © RMN, Paris; *8* Royal Collection, Windsor Castle/© Her Majesty Queen Elizabeth II

Minimalism © Carl André/DACS, London, and VAGA, New York, 1996

Minneapolis Minneapolis Institute of Arts, Minneapolis, MN

Minoan *5, 9–10, 13–14, 16–17, 23, 28* Herakleion Museum (Archaeological Receipts Fund); *6* Photo: Diane Fortenberry; *12, 20–21, 24* Photo: Hirmer Fotoarchiv, Munich; *15* Ancient Art and Architecture Collection, London/Photo: M. and J. Lynch; *18* Trustees of the British Museum, London; *22* Ashmolean Museum, Oxford; *25* National Archaeological Museum, Athens (Archaeological Receipts Fund); *26* British Library, London (no. X.0415/55(2)); *27* Photo: P.M. Warren

Mino da Fiesole *1* Staatliche Museen zu Berlin, Preussischer Kulturbesitz/Skulpturensammlung, Berlin/Photo: Jörg P. Anders, 1989; *2* Photo: Conway Library, Courtauld Institute of Art, London

Minsk Photo: NOVOSTI Photo Library, London

Miró, Joan *1* © ADAGP, Paris, and DACS, London, 1996; *2* Museum of Modern Art, New York (Acquired through the Lillie P. Bliss Bequest)/© ADAGP, Paris, and DACS, London, 1996; *3* Museum of Modern Art, New York/© ADAGP, Paris, and DACS, London, 1996; *4* Philadelphia Museum of Art, Philadelphia, PA (Fairmount Park Art Association: on loan to the Philadelphia Museum of Art)

Mirror *2* Brooklyn Museum, Brooklyn NY (Charles Edwin Wilbour Fund; no. 37.635E); *3* © Pedicini snc; *4* Trustees of the British Museum, London; *5, 9* Board of Trustees of the Victoria and Albert Museum, London; *6* Topkapı Palace Museum, Istanbul; *7* Department of Library Services, National Museum of Natural History, Washington, DC; *8* Photo: © RMN, Paris

Misericord Photo: RCHME/© Crown Copyright

Miseroni Kunsthistorisches Museum, Vienna

Miskin Bodleian Library, Oxford (MS. Elliot 254, fol. 42r)

Missal *1* Bibliothèque Nationale de France, Paris; *2* Dean and Chapter of Westminster, London

Mitannian Photo: Diana Stein, Oxford

Mitla Photo: Henri Stierlin, Geneva

Mixtec Trustees of the British Museum, London

Mixteca–Puebla Biblioteca Apostolica Vaticana, Rome

Miyagawa Chōshun National Museum, Tokyo

Mizrah Skirball Museum, Hebrew Union College, Los Angeles, CA/ Photo: Marvin Rand

Moalla, el- John Ruffle, Durham

Mobile Collection Port Authority of New York and New Jersey at John F. Kennedy International Airport/© DACS, 1996

Mocetto, Girolamo Trustees of the National Gallery, London

Moche *1* Photo: Henri Stierlin, Geneva; *2* Photo: Art Institute of Chicago, Chicago, IL (Buckingham Fund, 1955.2291)/© 1996. All rights reserved; *3* Christopher B. Donnan/Drawing by Donna McClelland

Mochi, Francesco Vatican Museums, Vatican City, Rome

Mochlos Photo: Hirmer Fotoarchiv, Munich

Model, artist's *1* Musée Bonnat, Bayonne; *2* Kunsthistorisches Museum, Vienna; *3* Musée Fragonard, Grasse/Photo: Jacques Mayer, Grasse

Modello *1* Photo: Scala, Florence; *2–3* Trustees of the British Museum, London; *4* Governing Body, Christ Church, Oxford; *5* Board of Trustees of the Victoria and Albert Museum, London; *6* Harvard University Art Museums, Cambridge, MA (Alpheus Hyatt and Friends of the Fogg Art Museum Funds); *7* Syndics of the Fitzwilliam Museum, Cambridge

Modena *1* Photo: Archivi Alinari, Florence; *2–3* Photo: Vincenzo Negro Fotografo, Modena

Modern Movement *1* Photo: Bildarchiv Foto Marburg; *2* Photo: Jan Derwig, Architectuur Fotografie, Amsterdam/Schroder; *3* Staatliche Museen zu Berlin, Preussischer Kulturbesitz

Modersohn-Becker, Paula Staatliche Museen zu Berlin, Preussischer Kulturbesitz

Modigliani, Amedeo *1* Tate Gallery, London; *2* National Gallery of Art, Washington, DC (Chester Dale Collection)

Moeyaert, Claes Hermitage Museum, St Petersburg

Moholy-Nagy, László *1* Museum of Modern Art, New York/© DACS, 1996; *2* Museum of Modern Art, New York (Gift of Philip Johnson in memory of Sibyl Moholy-Nagy)/© DACS, 1996

Moissac, St Pierre *1* Photo: Thomas W. Lyman; *2* Photo: James Austin, Cambridge

Mokuan Shōtō *1* St Louis Art Museum, St Louis, MO (Purchase: W.K. Bixby Oriental Art Purchase Fund); *2* Obakusan Manpukuji Bunkaden, Kyoto

Mola (i) Pitt Rivers Museum, Oxford

Mola (iii): (2) Pier Francesco Mola *1* Trustees of the British Museum, London; *2* Photo: © RMN, Paris

Moldova *2* Museum of Fine Arts, Chisinău

Molenaer, Jan Miense Museum of Fine Arts, Boston, MA (James Fund)

Molyn, Pieter Frans Halsmuseum, Haarlem/Photo: Tom Haartsen

Momper, de: (1) Josse de Momper II Staatliche Kunstsammlungen Dresden

Monastery *2* © Yale University Press (from K. J. Conant: *Carolingian and Romanesque Architecture*, 1959, pl. viiib)/British Library, London (no. X421/8427); *3* Bibliothèque Municipale, Troyes; *4* Photo: Zodiaque, St-Léger-Vauban; *5–6* Photo: Anthony Kersting, London; *8* Norwich City Council, Norwich; *9* Photo: James Austin, Cambridge; *10* Photo: Arch. Phot. Paris/© DACS, 1996; *11* Photo: Scala, Florence

Mondrian, Piet *1, 3* Haags Gemeentemuseum, The Hague/© DACS, 1996; *2* Kröller-Müller Museum, Otterlo; *4* Museum of Modern Art, New York (Given anonymously)

Mone, Jean Photo: © ACL Brussels

Monemvasia *1–2* Photo: H.A. Kalligas

Monet, Claude *1* Trustees of the National Gallery, London; *2* Photo: © RMN, Paris; *3* © Sterling and Francine Clark Institute, Williamstown, MA; *4* Philadelphia Museum of Art, Philadelphia, PA (Mr and Mrs Carroll S. Tyson Collection)

Mongolia *2* National Gallery, Prague (Collection of Oriental Art, Zbraslav Castle); *3, 5* Photo: Merilyn Thorold; *4, 8* Staatliches Museum für Völkerkunde, Munich/Mongolian Embassy, Troisdorf-Sieglar; *6* State Publishing House, Ulaan Baatar/Photo: Merilyn Thorold; *7* Department of Ethnography, Nationalmuseum, Copenhagen

Monkwearmouth Abbey Photo: R.J. Cramp

Monnot, Pierre-Etienne Photo: Archivi Alinari, Florence

Monnoyer, Jean-Baptiste Musée Fabre, Montpellier

Monopteros American School of Classical Studies at Athens: Agora Excavations

Monotype *1* Art Institute of Chicago, Chicago, IL/Photo: © 1996. All rights reserved; *2* Fogg Art Museum, Harvard University Art Museums, Cambridge, MA (Bequest of Paul J. and Meta Sachs)

Monreale Cathedral *1* Photo: Anthony Kersting, London; *2* Photo: Luisa Guaragna Artini; *3–4* Photo: Archivi Alinari, Florence

Monsiau, Nicolas-André Musée Carnavalet, Paris/© Musées de la Ville de Paris/© DACS, 1996

Montagna: (1) Bartolomeo Montagna *1* Museo Civico d'Arte e Storia, Vicenza; *2* Photo: Archivi Alinari, Florence